The Message: Catholic/Ecumenical Edition is a
contemporary rendering of the Bible from the
original languages and the New Vulgate,
crafted to present its tone, rhythm, events,
and ideas in everyday language.

THE MESSAGE®

CATHOLIC/ECUMENICAL EDITION
THE BIBLE IN CONTEMPORARY LANGUAGE

Translated by Eugene H. Peterson
Additional translation by William Griffin

acta
PUBLICATIONS

THE MESSAGE: Catholic/Ecumenical Edition—The Bible in Contemporary Language
Copyright © 2013 by Eugene H. Peterson. All rights reserved.

THE MESSAGE: CATHOLIC/ECUMENICAL EDITION is licensed to and published by ACTA Publications, 4848 N. Clark Street, Chicago, IL 60640, (800) 397-2282, www.actapublications.com.

Published in association with the literary agency of Alive Communications, Inc., 7680 Goddard St., Suite 200, Colorado Springs, CO 80920, www.alivecom.com.

ISBN: 978-0-87946-495-0 (hardcover)
ISBN: 978-0-87946-494-3 (paperback)

Library of Congress Number: 2013935755

Printed in Canada

Year: 25 24 23 22 21 20 19 18 17 16 15 14 13

Printing: 15 14 13 12 11 10 9 8 7 6 5 4 3 2 First

CONTENTS

NEW TESTAMENT

THE CATHOLIC/
ECUMENICAL EDITION

The first edition of *The Message*, limited to the New Testament, was published in 1993. The reception was so positive and comments were so affirming that a decision to include the Old Testament resulted in the publication of the full-Bible version of *The Message* in 2002.

However, almost immediately, Catholic friends, priests, religious and laity, both men and women, began asking me why I hadn't translated the "complete" Bible, by which they meant the inclusion of the "Deuterocanonical" writings, books written in the years between the Testaments. Finally, these additional writings, termed "Apocrypha" by Protestants but recognized by Catholics and people of many other church traditions as part of the divinely inspired Scriptures, are now included in this new Catholic/Ecumenical Edition.

I was not in a position to translate these additional writings myself, but was able to find someone who is eminently qualified to do so. William Griffin is not only an excellent writer and translator who understands exactly what I have tried to do in *The Message* but also a friend and colleague of many years whom I could trust to carry on my work into this new edition. Bill is a lifelong Catholic with a history of working ecumenically and is especially aware of and sensitive to the various Christian traditions. Included in this edition are:

- TOBIT
- JUDITH
- ESTHER
- I MACCABEES
- II MACCABEES
- WISDOM
- SIRACH
- BARUCH
- DANIEL

These writings are placed in the Bible in the places most Roman Catholics are used to finding them, and Bill Griffin has written the introduction to each of them, including the additional chapters of Daniel that he added to my translation. I am responsible for all the other translations and introductions in the book and have reviewed and approved all of Bill's writings.

I am immensely grateful to my many Catholic friends and colleagues for their encouragement to "complete" *The Message*. I hope that it will lead to increased ecumenical use and dialogue. I prayerfully anticipate a fresh audience as together we cultivate the fullness of our salvation.

— Eugene H. Peterson

THE ADDITIONAL WRITINGS

I first met Eugene Peterson in the 1980s at a meeting of Christian writers and translators. He was, at the time, pastor of Christ Our King Presbyterian Church in Bel Air, Maryland. He had that quiet magisterial look one associates with an Old Testament prophet. No wonder. He had a master's degree in Semitic languages from Johns Hopkins.

In the 1990s, at another meeting of the same group, Eugene read a couple of psalms he'd recently translated from the Hebrew. We expected cool, smooth psalmody; instead, what we heard was rugged verse; closer to the original Hebrew, as he said. We were stunned; it was as if we heard a wailing shofar summoning us back to the Hebrew flock. Which was funny because he'd translated them into contemporary language, more American than English.

At these meetings, we all talked endlessly about Bible translation theory. There were two general approaches. The first, more literal translation, was favored by professional biblical scholars; it enabled them to maintain the integrity of their texts and dictated the wording of their translations. The second, more literary or paraphrasal translation, was favored by professional translators like Eugene Peterson and me; we wanted to express the meaning of the text not always found in the wording of literal translation. One would think that both approaches would have much in common; they do, but they don't know how to admit it. The scholars want to be faithful to the original words; we translators want to be faithful to the original meaning. They call for mastery of the biblical languages; we call for mastery of the English language. We both want to get it right.

When Eugene published his complete paraphrasal masterpiece, *The Message: The Bible in Contemporary Language,* in 2002, it quickly turned into a phenomenal success. As the tenth anniversary approached, the publisher thought it was time to introduce a Catholic/Ecumenical edition; that would mean adding to the Protestant Bible the additional writings familiar to Catholics, Anglicans, Orthodox, and others, variously known as Intertestamentals or Apocrypha or Deuterocanonicals. I expressed interest; the publisher asked for a sample. I translated the Book of Tobit (about 10,000 words). Apparently, I made the cut. Several years and a total of some 130,000 words later, this new edition of *The Message* has seen the light of day.

For my primary text, I could have used the Hebrew or, where necessary, the Greek manuscripts; but I didn't. As I've already indicated, they seem to me to be the exclusive possession of the biblical scholars. Instead, I chose the Latin Vulgate—not the one put together by Jerome in the fourth century but the revised and expanded edition called *Nova Vulgata* (New Vulgate) published in 1998.

Pope John Paul II wrote a brief preface to that translation in which he declared and proclaimed that the *Nova Vulgata* may be used as the authentic text when translating into English, especially in the Sacred Liturgy. And so that's what I used.

I've done a dozen paraphrasal translations from the Latin of Augustine of Hippo, Thomas à Kempis, Nicolas of Cusa. Thomas More and Desiderius Erasmus are in the works. I also write and speak Latin; the latter was improved immensely at the University of Kentucky. And for half a year I ran a program on the Internet named *Verbum Diurnum* ("Latin Word for the Day"). Unlike most other Latinists today, I consider Latin not a dead language but a language that's very much alive.

My translation of these additional writings has been reviewed by three notable Catholic writers, religious educators, and scholars. Alice Camille is the award-winning author of the monthly column on the Scriptures for *U.S. Catholic* magazine and author of *Invitation to the Old Testament*. Rev. John Pawlikowski, OSM, is director of the Catholic-Jewish Studies Program at the Catholic Theological Union and former editor of *New Theology Review*. Rev. Thomas Santa, CSSR, former publisher of Liguori Publications in St. Louis and director of the Redemptorist Renewal Center in Tucson, Arizona, is current pastor of St. Michael's Catholic Church in Chicago.

Back to the additional writings themselves. They come in a variety of formats. There are novels, histories, prayers, wisdom collections, and more than a few writings that were derived no doubt from presentations during Jewish festivals. The target audience was the Jews who were exiled against their will all over the Middle Eastern and European world, most of them in servitude or worse, but some in governmental positions. The authors of these works had one purpose, to restore dignity to the exiles and fill the gaps in their Jewish history and practice.

Eugene Peterson shouldn't be blamed for what I wrote, although I'd rejoice if my work were mistaken for his. My contributions are clearly marked by the introductions to the individual books I translated, which are followed by my initials (WG). In the Book of Daniel, the additional writings are inserted into Eugene's text, and in the Book of Esther, where the additional writings are so intertwined in the text that new passages by a different translator would be difficult to insert artfully, the publisher has chosen to present my version in its entirety.

The overall theme of the additional writings, if it can be contained in one sentence, would be something like this: *No matter where, no matter what, keep the faith.* It's a perennial theme, as valid now as then.

—WILLIAM GRIFFIN

TO THE READER

If there is anything distinctive about *The Message*, perhaps it is because the text is shaped by the hand of a working pastor. For most of my adult life I have been given a primary responsibility for getting the message of the Bible into the lives of the men and women with whom I worked. I did it from pulpit and lectern, in home Bible studies and at mountain retreats, through conversations in hospitals and nursing homes, over coffee in kitchens and while strolling on an ocean beach. *The Message* grew from the soil of forty years of pastoral work.

As I worked at this task, this Word of God, which forms and trans-forms human lives, did form and transform human lives. Planted in the soil of my congregation and community the seed words of the Bible ger-minated and grew and matured. When it came time to do the work that is now *The Message*, I often felt that I was walking through an orchard at harvest time, plucking fully formed apples and peaches and plums from laden branches. There's hardly a page in the Bible I did not see lived in some way or other by the men and women, saints and sinners, to whom I was pastor—and then verified in my nation and culture.

I didn't start out as a pastor. I began my vocational life as a teacher and for several years taught the biblical languages of Hebrew and Greek in a theological seminary. I expected to live the rest of my life as a professor and scholar, teaching and writing and studying. But then my life took a sudden vocational turn to pastoring in a congregation.

I was now plunged into quite a different world. The first noticeable difference was that nobody seemed to care much about the Bible, which so recently people had been paying me to teach them. Many of the people I worked with now knew virtually nothing about it, had never read it, and weren't interested in learning. Many others had spent years reading it but for them it had gone flat through familiarity, reduced to clichés. Bored, they dropped it. And there weren't many people in between. Very few were interested in what I considered my primary work, getting the words of the Bible into their heads and hearts, getting the message lived. They found newspapers and magazines, videos and pulp fiction more to their taste.

Meanwhile I had taken on as my life work the responsibility of get-ting these very people to listen, really listen, to the message in this book. I knew I had my work cut out for me.

I lived in two language worlds, the world of the Bible and the world of Today. I had always assumed they were the same world. But these people didn't see it that way. So out of necessity I became a "translator" (although I wouldn't have called it that then), daily standing on the border between two worlds, getting the language of the Bible that God uses to create and save us, heal and bless us, judge and rule over us, into the language of Today that we use to gossip and tell stories, give directions and do business, sing songs and talk to our children.

And all the time those old biblical languages, those powerful and vivid Hebrew and Greek originals, kept working their way underground in my speech, giving energy and sharpness to words and phrases, expanding the imagination of the people with whom I was working to hear the language of the Bible in the language of Today and the language of Today in the language of the Bible.

I did that for thirty years in one congregation. And then one day (it was April 30, 1990) I got a letter from an editor asking me to work on a new version of the Bible along the lines of what I had been doing as a pastor. I agreed. The next ten years was harvest time. *The Message* is the result.

The Message is a reading Bible. It is not intended to replace the excellent study Bibles that are available. My intent here (as it was earlier in my congregation and community) is simply to get people reading it who don't know that the Bible is read-able at all, at least by them, and to get people who long ago lost interest in the Bible to read it again. But I haven't tried to make it easy—there is much in the Bible that is hard to understand. So at some point along the way, soon or late, it will be important to get a standard study Bible to facilitate further study. Meanwhile, read in order to live, praying as you read, "God, let it be with me just as you say."

— EUGENE H. PETERSON

THE MESSAGE

Reading is the first thing, just reading the Bible. As we read we enter a new world of words and find ourselves in on a conversation in which God has the first and last words. We soon realize that we are included in the conversation. We didn't expect this. But this is precisely what generation after generation of Bible readers do find: The Bible is not only written about us but to us. In these pages we become insiders to a conversation in which God uses words to form and bless us, to teach and guide us, to forgive and save us.

We aren't used to this. We are used to reading books that explain things, or tell us what to do, or inspire or entertain us. But this is different. This is a world of revelation: God revealing to people just like us—men and women created in God's image—how God works and what is going on in this world in which we find ourselves. At the same time that God reveals all this, God draws us in by invitation and command to participate in God's working life. We gradually (or suddenly) realize that we are insiders in the most significant action of our time as God establishes his grand rule of love and justice on this earth (as it is in heaven). "Revelation" means that we are reading something we couldn't have guessed or figured out on our own. Revelation is what makes the Bible unique.

And so just reading this Bible, *The Message*, and listening to what we read, is the first thing. There will be time enough for study later on. But first, it is important simply to read, leisurely and thoughtfully. We need to get a feel for the way these stories and songs, these prayers and conversations, these sermons and visions, invite us into this large, large world in which the invisible God is behind and involved in everything visible and illuminates what it means to live here—really live, not just get across the street. As we read, and the longer we read, we begin to "get it"—we are in conversation with God. We find ourselves listening and answering in matters that most concern us: who we are, where we came from, where we are going, what makes us tick, the texture of the world and the communities we live in, and—most of all—the incredible love of God among us, doing for us what we cannot do for ourselves.

Through reading the Bible, we see that there is far more to the world, more to us, more to what we see and more to what we don't see—more to everything!—than we had ever dreamed, and that this "more" has to do with God.

This is new for many of us, a different sort of book—a book that reads us even as we read it. We are used to picking up and reading books for what we can get out of them: information we can use, inspiration to energize us, instructions on how to do something or other, entertainment to while away a rainy day, wisdom that will guide us into living better. These things can and do take place when reading the Bible, but the Bible is given to us in the first place simply to invite us to make ourselves at home in the world of God, God's word and world, and become familiar with the way God speaks and the ways in which we answer him with our lives.

⚜

Our reading turns up some surprises. The biggest surprise for many is how accessible this book is to those who simply open it up and read it. Virtually anyone can read this Bible with understanding. The reason that new translations are made every couple of generations or so is to keep the language of the Bible current with the common speech we use, the very language in which it was first written. We don't have to be smart or well-educated to understand it, for it is written in the words and sentences we hear in the marketplace, on school playgrounds, and around the dinner table. Because the Bible is so famous and revered, many assume that we need experts to explain and interpret it for us—and, of course, there are some things that need to be explained. But the first men and women who listened to these words now written in our Bibles were ordinary, everyday, working-class people. One of the greatest of the early translators of the Bible into English, William Tyndale, said that he was translating so that "the boy that driveth the plough" would be able to read the Scriptures.

One well-educated African man, who later became one of the most influential Bible teachers in our history (Augustine), was greatly offended when he first read the Bible. Instead of a book cultivated and polished in the literary style he admired so much, he found it full of homespun, earthy stories of plain, unimportant people. He read it in a Latin translation full of slang and jargon. He took one look at what he considered the "unspiritual" quality of so many of its characters and the everydayness of Jesus, and contemptuously abandoned it. It was years before he realized that God had not taken the form of a sophisticated intellectual to teach us about highbrow heavenly culture so we could appreciate the finer things of God. When he saw that God entered our lives as a Jewish servant in order to save us from our sins, he started reading the Book gratefully and believingly.

Some are also surprised that Bible reading does not introduce us to a "nicer" world. This biblical world is decidedly not an ideal world, the kind we see advertised in travel posters. Suffering and injustice and ugliness are not purged from the world in which God works and loves and saves. Nothing is glossed over. God works patiently and deeply, but often in hidden ways, in the mess of our humanity and history. Ours is not a neat and tidy world in which we are assured that we can get everything under our control. This takes considerable getting used to—there is mystery everywhere. The Bible does not give us a predictable cause-effect world in which we can plan our careers and secure our futures.

It is not a dream world in which everything works out according to our adolescent expectations — there is pain and poverty and abuse at which we cry out in indignation, "You can't let this happen!" For most of us it takes years and years and years to exchange our dream world for this real world of grace and mercy, sacrifice and love, freedom and joy — the God-saved world.

Yet another surprise is that the Bible does not flatter us. It is not trying to sell us anything that promises to make life easier. It doesn't offer secrets to what we often think of as prosperity or pleasure or high adventure. The reality that comes into focus as we read the Bible has to do with what God is doing in a saving love that includes us and everything we do. This is quite different from what our sin-stunted and culture-cluttered minds imagined. But our Bible reading does not give us access to a mail-order catalog of idols from which we can pick and choose to satisfy our fantasies. The Bible begins with God speaking creation and us into being. It continues with God entering into personalized and complex relationships with us, helping and blessing us, teaching and training us, correcting and disciplining us, loving and saving us. This is not an escape from reality but a plunge into more reality — a sacrificial but altogether better life all the way.

God doesn't force any of this on us: God's word is personal address, inviting, commanding, challenging, rebuking, judging, comforting, directing — but not forcing. Not coercing. We are given space and freedom to answer, to enter the conversation. For more than anything else the Bible invites our participation in the work and language of God.

As we read, we find that there is a connection between the Word Read and the Word Lived. Everything in this book is live-able. Many of us find that the most important question we ask as we read is not "What does it mean?" but "How can I live it?" So we read personally, not impersonally. We read in order to live our true selves, not just get information that we can use to raise our standard of living. Bible reading is a means of listening to and obeying God, not gathering religious data by which we can be our own gods.

You are going to hear stories in this Book that will take you out of your preoccupation with yourself and into the spacious freedom in which God is working the world's salvation. You are going to come across words and sentences that stab you awake to a beauty and hope that will connect you with your real life.

Be sure to answer.

EUGENE H. PETERSON is a pastor, scholar, writer, and poet. After teaching at a seminary and then giving nearly thirty years to church ministry in the Baltimore area, he created *The Message* — a vibrant Bible paraphrase that connects with today's readers like no other.

It took Peterson a full ten years to complete. He worked from the original Greek and Hebrew texts to guarantee authenticity. At the same time, his ear was always tuned to the cadence and energy of contemporary English.

Eugene and his wife, Jan, now live in his native Montana. They are the parents of three and the grandparents of six.

TRANSLATION CONSULTANTS

Peterson's work has been thoroughly reviewed by the following team of recognized Old and New Testament scholars, who ensured that it is accurate as well as faithful to the original languages.

OLD TESTAMENT TEAM

Robert L. Hubbard Jr., *North Park Theological Seminary* (chair)
Richard E. Averbeck, *Trinity Evangelical Divinity School*
Bryan E. Beyer, *Columbia Bible College*
Lamar E. Cooper Sr., *The Criswell College*
Peter E. Enns, *Westminster Theological Seminary*
Duane A. Garrett, *Gordon-Conwell Theological Seminary*
Donald R. Glenn, *Dallas Theological Seminary*
Paul R. House, *Trinity Episcopal School for Ministry*
V. Philips Long, *Regent College*
Tremper Longman III, *Westmont College*
John N. Oswalt, *Wesley Biblical Seminary*
Richard L. Pratt Jr., *Reformed Theological Seminary*
John H. Walton, *Moody Bible Institute*
Prescott H. Williams Jr., *Austin Presbyterian Theological Seminary*
Marvin R. Wilson, *Gordon College*

NEW TESTAMENT TEAM

William W. Klein, *Denver Seminary* (chair)
Darrell L. Bock, *Dallas Theological Seminary*
Donald A. Hagner, *Fuller Theological Seminary*
Moisés Silva, *Gordon-Conwell Theological Seminary*
Rodney A. Whitacre, *Trinity Episcopal School for Ministry*

The Old Testament

THE BOOKS OF MOSES

An enormous authority and dignity have, through the centuries, developed around the first five books of the Bible, commonly known as The Books of Moses. Over the course of many centuries, they account for a truly astonishing amount of reading and writing, study and prayer, teaching and preaching.

God is the primary concern of these books. That accounts for the authority and the dignity. But it is not only God; we get included. That accounts for the widespread and intense human interest. We want to know what's going on. We want to know how we fit into things. We don't want to miss out.

The Books of Moses are made up mostly of stories and signposts. The stories show us God working with and speaking to men and women in a rich variety of circumstances. God is presented to us not in ideas and arguments but in events and actions that involve each of us personally. The signposts provide immediate and practical directions to guide us into behavior that is appropriate to our humanity and honoring to God.

The simplicity of the storytelling and signposting in these books makes what is written here as accessible to children as to adults. But the simplicity (as in so many simple things) is also profound, inviting us into a lifetime of growing participation in God's saving ways with us.

An image of human growth suggests a reason for the powerful pull of these stories and signposts on so many millions of men, women, and children to live as *God's* people. The sketch shows the five books as five stages of growth in which God creates first a cosmos and then a people for his glory.

Genesis is Conception. After establishing the basic elements by which God will do his work of creation and salvation and judgment in the midst of human sin and rebellion (chapters 1–11), God conceives a People to whom he will reveal himself as a God of salvation and through them, over time, to everyone on earth. God begins small, with one man: Abraham. The embryonic People of God grow in the womb. Gradually details and then more details become evident as the embryo takes shape: Sarah, Isaac, Rebekah, Jacob and Esau, Rachel, Joseph and his brothers. The pregnancy develops. Life is obviously developing in that womb but there is also much that is not clear and visible. The background history is vague, the surrounding nations and customs veiled in a kind of mist. But the presence of life, God-conceived life, is kicking and robust.

Exodus is Birth and Infancy. The gestation of the People of God lasts a long time, but finally the birth pangs start. Egyptian slavery gives the first intimations of the contractions to come. When Moses arrives on the scene to preside over the birth itself, ten fierce plagues on Egypt accompany the contractions that bring the travail to completion: at the Red Sea the waters break, the People of God tumble out of the womb onto dry ground, and their life as a free People of God begins. Moses leads them crawling and toddling to Sinai. They are fed. God reveals himself to them at the mountain. They begin to get a sense of their Parent. They learn the language of freedom and salvation—a word here, a word there, the Ten Words (commandments) as a beginning, their basic vocabulary. The signposts begin to go up: do this; don't do that. But the largest part of their infant life is God, the living God. As they explore the deep and wide world of God, worship becomes their dominant and most important activity. An enormous amount of attention is given to training them in worship, building the structures for worship, mastering the procedures. They are learning how to give their full attention in obedience and adoration to God.

Leviticus is Schooling. As infancy develops into childhood, formal schooling takes place. There's a lot to know; they need some structure and arrangement to keep things straight: reading, writing, arithmetic. But for the People of God the basic curriculum has to do with God and their relationship with God. Leviticus is the *McGuffey's Reader* of the People of God. It is an almost totally audiovisual book, giving a picture and ritual in the sacrifices and feasts for the pivotal ways in which God's people keep alert and observant to the ways their relationship with God goes awry (sin) and the ways they are restored to forgiveness and innocence (salvation). Everyday life consists of endless and concrete detail, much of it having to do with our behavior before God and with one another, and so, of course, Leviticus necessarily consists also of endless detail.

Numbers is Adolescence. The years of adolescence are critical to understanding who we are. We are advanced enough physically to be able, for the most part, to take care of ourselves. We are developed enough mentally, with some obvious limitations, to think for ourselves. We discover that we are not simply extensions of our parents; and we are not just mirror images of our culture. But who are we? Especially, who are we as a People of God? The People of God in Numbers are new at these emerging independent operations of behaving and thinking and so inevitably make a lot of mistakes. Rebellion is one of the more conspicuous mistakes. They test out their unique identity by rejecting the continuities with parents and culture. It's the easiest and cheapest way to "be myself" as we like to say. But it turns out that there isn't much to the "self" that is thus asserted. Maturity requires the integration, not the amputation, of what we have received through our conception and birth, our infancy and schooling. The People of God have an extraordinarily long adolescence in the wilderness—nearly forty years of it.

Deuteronomy is Adulthood. The mature life is a complex operation. Growing up is a long process. And growing up in God takes the longest time. During their forty years spent in the wilderness, the People of God developed from that full-term embryo brought to birth on the far shore of the Red Sea, are carried and led, nourished and protected under Moses to the place of God's Revelation at Sinai, taught and trained, disciplined and blessed. Now they are ready to live as free and obedient men and women in the new land, the Promised Land. They are ready for adulthood, ready to be as grown up inwardly as they are outwardly. They are ready to live as a free people, formed by God, as a holy people, transformed by God. They still have a long way to go (as do we all), but all the conditions for maturity are there. The book of Deuteronomy gathers up that entire process of becoming a People of God and turns it into a sermon and a song and a blessing. The strongest and key word in Deuteronomy is *love*. Love is the most characteristic and comprehensive act of the human being. We are most ourselves when we love; we are most the People of God when we love. But love is not an abstract word defined out of a dictionary. In order to love maturely we have to live and absorb and enter into this world of salvation and freedom, find ourselves in the stories, become familiar with and follow the signposts, learn the life of worship, and realize our unique identity as the People of God who love.

The Books of Moses are foundational to the books that follow in our Bibles. A foundation, though, is not a complete building but the anticipation of one. An elaborate moral infrastructure is provided here for what is yet to come. Each book that follows, in one way or another, picks up and develops some aspect of the messianic salvation involved in becoming the People of God, but it is always on this foundation. This foundation of stories and signposts has proved over and over to be solid and enduring.

A note on translating the name of God. In the original Hebrew text of the Old Testament, the generic name for divinity used by both Israel and its neighbors is translated God (or god). But the unique and distinctively personal name for God that was revealed to Moses at the burning bush (Exodus 3:13-14) I have translated as "GOD." The Jewish community early on substituted "LORD" for the unique name out of reverence (our lips are not worthy to speak The Name) and caution (lest we inadvertently blaspheme by saying God's name "in vain"). Most Christian translators continue that practice.

GENESIS

First, God. God is the subject of life. God is foundational for living. If we don't have a sense of the primacy of God, we will never get it right, get life right, get *our* lives right. Not God at the margins; not God as an option; not God on the weekends. God at center and circumference; God first and last; God, God, God.

Genesis gets us off on the right foot. Genesis pulls us into a sense of reality that is God-shaped and God-filled. It gives us a vocabulary for speaking accurately and comprehensively about our lives, where we come from and where we are going, what we think and what we do, the people we live with and how to get along with them, the troubles we find ourselves in and the blessings that keep arriving.

Genesis uses words to make a foundation that is solid and true. Everything we think and do and feel is material in a building operation in which we are engaged all our life long. There is immense significance in everything that we do. Our speech and our actions and our prayers are all, every detail of them, involved in this vast building operation comprehensively known as the Kingdom of God. But we don't build the foundation. The foundation is given. The foundation is firmly in place.

Jesus concluded his most famous teaching by telling us that there are two ways to go about our lives—we can build on sand or we can build on rock. No matter how wonderfully we build, if we build on sand it will all fall to pieces like a house of cards. We build on what is already there, on the rock. Genesis is a verbal witness to that rock: God's creative acts, God's intervening and gracious judgments, God's call to a life of faith, God's making covenant with us.

But Genesis presents none of this to us as an abstract, bloodless "truth" or "principle." We are given a succession of stories with named people, people who loved and quarreled, believed and doubted, had children and married, experienced sin and grace. If we pay attention, we find that we ourselves are living variations on these very stories: Adam and Eve, Cain and Abel, Noah and his sons, Abraham and Sarah, Isaac and Rebekah, Jacob and Rachel, Joseph and his brothers. The stories show clearly that we are never outsiders or spectators to anything in "heaven and earth." God doesn't work impersonally from space; he works with us where we are, as he finds us. No matter what we do, whether good or bad, we continue to be part of everything that God is doing. Nobody can drop out—there's no place to drop out to. So we may as well get started and take our place in the story—at the beginning.

GENESIS

HEAVEN AND EARTH

1-2 First this: God created the Heavens and Earth—all you see, all you don't see. Earth was a soup of nothingness, a bottomless emptiness, an inky blackness. God's Spirit brooded like a bird above the watery abyss.

3-5 God spoke: "Light!"
  And light appeared.
God saw that light was good
  and separated light from dark.
God named the light Day,
  he named the dark Night.
It was evening, it was morning—
Day One.

6-8 God spoke: "Sky! In the middle of the waters;
  separate water from water!"
God made sky.
He separated the water under sky
  from the water above sky.
And there it was:
  he named sky the Heavens;
It was evening, it was morning—
Day Two.

9-10 God spoke: "Separate!
  Water-beneath-Heaven, gather into one place;
Land, appear!"
  And there it was.
God named the land Earth.
  He named the pooled water Ocean.
God saw that it was good.

11-13 God spoke: "Earth, green up! Grow all varieties
  of seed-bearing plants,
Every sort of fruit-bearing tree."
  And there it was.
Earth produced green seed-bearing plants,
  all varieties,
And fruit-bearing trees of all sorts.
  God saw that it was good.
It was evening, it was morning—
Day Three.

14-15 God spoke: "Lights! Come out!
  Shine in Heaven's sky!
Separate Day from Night.

Mark seasons and days and years,
Lights in Heaven's sky to give light to Earth."
And there it was.

16-19   God made two big lights, the larger
to take charge of Day,
The smaller to be in charge of Night;
and he made the stars.
God placed them in the heavenly sky
to light up Earth
And oversee Day and Night,
to separate light and dark.
God saw that it was good.
It was evening, it was morning—
Day Four.

20-23   God spoke: "Swarm, Ocean, with fish and all sea life!
Birds, fly through the sky over Earth!"
God created the huge whales,
all the swarm of life in the waters,
And every kind and species of flying birds.
God saw that it was good.
God blessed them: "Prosper! Reproduce! Fill Ocean!
Birds, reproduce on Earth!"
It was evening, it was morning—
Day Five.

24-25   God spoke: "Earth, generate life! Every sort and kind:
cattle and reptiles and wild animals—all kinds."
And there it was:
wild animals of every kind,
Cattle of all kinds, every sort of reptile and bug.
God saw that it was good.

26-28   God spoke: "Let us make human beings in our image, make them
reflecting our nature
So they can be responsible for the fish in the sea,
the birds in the air, the cattle,
And, yes, Earth itself,
and every animal that moves on the face of Earth."
God created human beings;
he created them godlike,
Reflecting God's nature.
He created them male and female.
God blessed them:
"Prosper! Reproduce! Fill Earth! Take charge!
Be responsible for fish in the sea and birds in the air,
for every living thing that moves on the face of Earth."

29-30   Then God said, "I've given you
every sort of seed-bearing plant on Earth

And every kind of fruit-bearing tree,
    given them to you for food.
To all animals and all birds,
    everything that moves and breathes,
I give whatever grows out of the ground for food."
    And there it was.

31 God looked over everything he had made;
    it was so good, so very good!
It was evening, it was morning—
Day Six.

1 Heaven and Earth were finished,
    down to the last detail.

2-4 By the seventh day
    God had finished his work.
On the seventh day
    he rested from all his work.
God blessed the seventh day.
    He made it a Holy Day
Because on that day he rested from his work,
    all the creating God had done.

This is the story of how it all started,
    of Heaven and Earth when they were created.

ADAM AND EVE

5-7 At the time GOD made Earth and Heaven, before any grasses or shrubs had sprouted from the ground—GOD hadn't yet sent rain on Earth, nor was there anyone around to work the ground (the whole Earth was watered by underground springs)—GOD formed Man out of dirt from the ground and blew into his nostrils the breath of life. The Man came alive—a living soul!

8-9 Then GOD planted a garden in Eden, in the east. He put the Man he had just made in it. GOD made all kinds of trees grow from the ground, trees beautiful to look at and good to eat. The Tree-of-Life was in the middle of the garden, also the Tree-of-Knowledge-of-Good-and-Evil.

10-14 A river flows out of Eden to water the garden and from there divides into four rivers. The first is named Pishon; it flows through Havilah where there is gold. The gold of this land is good. The land is also known for a sweet-scented resin and the onyx stone. The second river is named Gihon; it flows through the land of Cush. The third river is named Hiddekel and flows east of Assyria. The fourth river is the Euphrates.

15 GOD took the Man and set him down in the Garden of Eden to work the ground and keep it in order.

16-17 GOD commanded the Man, "You can eat from any tree in the garden, except from the Tree-of-Knowledge-of-Good-and-Evil. Don't eat from it. The moment you eat from that tree, you're dead."

18-20 GOD said, "It's not good for the Man to be alone; I'll make him a helper, a companion." So GOD formed from the dirt of the ground all the animals of the field and all the birds of the air. He brought them to the Man to see what he would name them. Whatever the Man called each living creature, that was its name. The Man named the cattle, named the birds of the air, named the wild animals; but he didn't find a suitable companion.

21-22 GOD put the Man into a deep sleep. As he slept he removed one of his ribs and replaced it with flesh. GOD then used the rib that he had taken from the Man to make Woman and presented her to the Man.

23-25 The Man said,
"Finally! Bone of my bone,
 flesh of my flesh!
Name her Woman
 for she was made from Man."
Therefore a man leaves his father and mother and embraces his wife. They become one flesh.
The two of them, the Man and his Wife, were naked, but they felt no shame.

1 The serpent was clever, more clever than any wild animal GOD had made. He spoke to the Woman: "Do I understand that God told you not to eat from any tree in the garden?"

2-3 The Woman said to the serpent, "Not at all. We can eat from the trees in the garden. It's only about the tree in the middle of the garden that God said, 'Don't eat from it; don't even touch it or you'll die.'"

4-5 The serpent told the Woman, "You won't die. God knows that the moment you eat from that tree, you'll see what's really going on. You'll be just like God, knowing everything, ranging all the way from good to evil."

6 When the Woman saw that the tree looked like good eating and realized what she would get out of it — she'd know everything! — she took and ate the fruit and then gave some to her husband, and he ate.

7 Immediately the two of them did "see what's really going on"— saw themselves naked! They sewed fig leaves together as makeshift clothes for themselves.

8 When they heard the sound of GOD strolling in the garden in the evening breeze, the Man and his Wife hid in the trees of the garden, hid from GOD.

9 GOD called to the Man: "Where are you?"

10 He said, "I heard you in the garden and I was afraid because I was naked. And I hid."

11 GOD said, "Who told you you were naked? Did you eat from that tree I told you not to eat from?"

12 The Man said, "The Woman you gave me as a companion, she gave me fruit from the tree, and, yes, I ate it."
GOD said to the Woman, "What is this that you've done?"

13 "The serpent seduced me," she said, "and I ate."

14-15 GOD told the serpent:
"Because you've done this, you're cursed,
 cursed beyond all cattle and wild animals,
Cursed to slink on your belly
 and eat dirt all your life.

I'm declaring war between you and the Woman,
    between your offspring and hers.
He'll wound your head,
    you'll wound his heel."

16   He told the Woman:
"I'll multiply your pains in childbirth;
    you'll give birth to your babies in pain.
You'll want to please your husband,
    but he'll lord it over you."

17-19   He told the Man:
"Because you listened to your wife
    and ate from the tree
That I commanded you not to eat from,
    'Don't eat from this tree,'
The very ground is cursed because of you;
    getting food from the ground
Will be as painful as having babies is for your wife;
    you'll be working in pain all your life long.
The ground will sprout thorns and weeds,
    you'll get your food the hard way,
Planting and tilling and harvesting,
    sweating in the fields from dawn to dusk,
Until you return to that ground yourself, dead and buried;
    you started out as dirt, you'll end up dirt."

20   The Man, known as Adam, named his wife Eve because she was the mother of all the living.

21   GOD made leather clothing for Adam and his wife and dressed them.

22   GOD said, "The Man has become like one of us, capable of knowing everything, ranging from good to evil. What if he now should reach out and take fruit from the Tree-of-Life and eat, and live forever? Never—this cannot happen!"

23-24   So GOD expelled them from the Garden of Eden and sent them to work the ground, the same dirt out of which they'd been made. He threw them out of the garden and stationed angel-cherubim and a revolving sword of fire east of it, guarding the path to the Tree-of-Life.

1   4 Adam slept with Eve his wife. She conceived and had Cain. She said, "I've gotten a man, with GOD's help!"

2   Then she had another baby, Abel. Abel was a herdsman and Cain a farmer.

3-5   Time passed. Cain brought an offering to GOD from the produce of his farm. Abel also brought an offering, but from the firstborn animals of his herd, choice cuts of meat. GOD liked Abel and his offering, but Cain and his offering didn't get his approval. Cain lost his temper and went into a sulk.

6-7   GOD spoke to Cain: "Why this tantrum? Why the sulking? If you do well, won't you be accepted? And if you don't do well, sin is lying in wait for you, ready to pounce; it's out to get you, you've got to master it."

8 Cain had words with his brother. They were out in the field; Cain came at Abel his brother and killed him.

9 GOD said to Cain, "Where is Abel your brother?"

He said, "How should I know? Am I his babysitter?"

10-12 GOD said, "What have you done! The voice of your brother's blood is calling to me from the ground. From now on you'll get nothing but curses from this ground; you'll be driven from this ground that has opened its arms to receive the blood of your murdered brother. You'll farm this ground, but it will no longer give you its best. You'll be a homeless wanderer on Earth."

13-14 Cain said to GOD, "My punishment is too much. I can't take it! You've thrown me off the land and I can never again face you. I'm a homeless wanderer on Earth and whoever finds me will kill me."

15 GOD told him, "No. Anyone who kills Cain will pay for it seven times over." GOD put a mark on Cain to protect him so that no one who met him would kill him.

16 Cain left the presence of GOD and lived in No-Man's-Land, east of Eden.

17-18 Cain slept with his wife. She conceived and had Enoch. He then built a city and named it after his son, Enoch.

Enoch had Irad,

Irad had Mehujael,

Mehujael had Methushael,

Methushael had Lamech.

19-22 Lamech married two wives, Adah and Zillah. Adah gave birth to Jabal, the ancestor of all who live in tents and herd cattle. His brother's name was Jubal, the ancestor of all who play the lyre and flute. Zillah gave birth to Tubal-Cain, who worked at the forge making bronze and iron tools. Tubal-Cain's sister was Naamah.

23-24 Lamech said to his wives,

Adah and Zillah, listen to me;

you wives of Lamech, hear me out:

I killed a man for wounding me,

a young man who attacked me.

If Cain is avenged seven times,

for Lamech it's seventy-seven!

25-26 Adam slept with his wife again. She had a son whom she named Seth. She said, "God has given me another child in place of Abel whom Cain killed." And then Seth had a son whom he named Enosh.

That's when men and women began praying and worshiping in the name of GOD.

THE FAMILY TREE OF THE HUMAN RACE

1-2 This is the family tree of the human race: When God created the human race, he made it godlike, with a nature akin to God. He created both male and female and blessed them, the whole human race.

3-5 When Adam was 130 years old, he had a son who was just like him, his very spirit and image, and named him Seth. After the birth of Seth, Adam lived another 800 years, having more sons and daughters. Adam lived a total of 930 years. And he died.

6-8 When Seth was 105 years old, he had Enosh. After Seth had Enosh, he lived another 807 years, having more sons and daughters. Seth lived a total of 912 years. And he died.

9-11 When Enosh was ninety years old, he had Kenan. After he had Kenan, he lived another 815 years, having more sons and daughters. Enosh lived a total of 905 years. And he died.

12-14 When Kenan was seventy years old, he had Mahalalel. After he had Mahalalel, he lived another 840 years, having more sons and daughters. Kenan lived a total of 910 years. And he died.

15-17 When Mahalalel was sixty-five years old, he had Jared. After he had Jared, he lived another 830 years, having more sons and daughters. Mahalalel lived a total of 895 years. And he died.

18-20 When Jared was 162 years old, he had Enoch. After he had Enoch, he lived another 800 years, having more sons and daughters. Jared lived a total of 962 years. And he died.

21-23 When Enoch was sixty-five years old, he had Methuselah. Enoch walked steadily with God. After he had Methuselah, he lived another 300 years, having more sons and daughters. Enoch lived a total of 365 years.

24 Enoch walked steadily with God. And then one day he was simply gone: God took him.

25-27 When Methuselah was 187 years old, he had Lamech. After he had Lamech, he lived another 782 years. Methuselah lived a total of 969 years. And he died.

28-31 When Lamech was 182 years old, he had a son. He named him Noah, saying, "This one will give us a break from the hard work of farming the ground that GOD cursed." After Lamech had Noah, he lived another 595 years, having more sons and daughters. Lamech lived a total of 777 years. And he died.

32 When Noah was 500 years old, he had Shem, Ham, and Japheth.

GIANTS IN THE LAND

1-2 When the human race began to increase, with more and more daughters being born, the sons of God noticed that the daughters of men were beautiful. They looked them over and picked out wives for themselves.

3 Then GOD said, "I'm not going to breathe life into men and women endlessly. Eventually they're going to die; from now on they can expect a life span of 120 years."

4 This was back in the days (and also later) when there were giants in the land. The giants came from the union of the sons of God and the daughters of men. These were the mighty men of ancient lore, the famous ones.

NOAH AND HIS SONS

5-7 GOD saw that human evil was out of control. People thought evil, imagined evil — evil, evil, evil from morning to night. GOD was sorry that he had made the human race in the first place; it broke his heart. GOD said, "I'll get rid of my ruined creation, make a clean sweep: people, animals, snakes and bugs, birds — the works. I'm sorry I made them."

8 But Noah was different. GOD liked what he saw in Noah.

9-10 This is the story of Noah: Noah was a good man, a man of integrity in his community. Noah walked with God. Noah had three sons: Shem, Ham, and Japheth.

11-12   As far as God was concerned, the Earth had become a sewer; there was violence everywhere. God took one look and saw how bad it was, everyone corrupt and corrupting—life itself corrupt to the core.

13   God said to Noah, "It's all over. It's the end of the human race. The violence is everywhere; I'm making a clean sweep.

14-16   "Build yourself a ship from teakwood. Make rooms in it. Coat it with pitch inside and out. Make it 450 feet long, seventy-five feet wide, and forty-five feet high. Build a roof for it and put in a window eighteen inches from the top; put in a door on the side of the ship; and make three decks, lower, middle, and upper.

17   "I'm going to bring a flood on the Earth that will destroy everything alive under Heaven. Total destruction.

18-21   "But I'm going to establish a covenant with you: You'll board the ship, and your sons, your wife and your sons' wives will come on board with you. You are also to take two of each living creature, a male and a female, on board the ship, to preserve their lives with you: two of every species of bird, mammal, and reptile—two of everything so as to preserve their lives along with yours. Also get all the food you'll need and store it up for you and them."

22   Noah did everything God commanded him to do.

1   **7** Next GOD said to Noah, "Now board the ship, you and all your family—out of everyone in this generation, you're the righteous one.

2-4   "Take on board with you seven pairs of every clean animal, a male and a female; one pair of every unclean animal, a male and a female; and seven pairs of every kind of bird, a male and a female, to insure their survival on Earth. In just seven days I will dump rain on Earth for forty days and forty nights. I'll make a clean sweep of everything that I've made."

5   Noah did everything GOD commanded him.

6-10   Noah was 600 years old when the floodwaters covered the Earth. Noah and his wife and sons and their wives boarded the ship to escape the flood. Clean and unclean animals, birds, and all the crawling creatures came in pairs to Noah and to the ship, male and female, just as God had commanded Noah. In seven days the floodwaters came.

11-12   It was the six-hundredth year of Noah's life, in the second month, on the seventeenth day of the month that it happened: all the underground springs erupted and all the windows of Heaven were thrown open. Rain poured for forty days and forty nights.

13-16   That's the day Noah and his sons Shem, Ham, and Japheth, accompanied by his wife and his sons' wives, boarded the ship. And with them every kind of wild and domestic animal, right down to all the kinds of creatures that crawl and all kinds of birds and anything that flies. They came to Noah and to the ship in pairs—everything and anything that had the breath of life in it, male and female of every creature came just as God had commanded Noah. Then GOD shut the door behind him.

17-23   The flood continued forty days and the waters rose and lifted the ship high over the Earth. The waters kept rising, the flood deepened on the Earth, the ship floated on the surface. The flood got worse until all the highest mountains were covered—the high-water mark reached twenty feet above the crest of the mountains. Everything died. Anything that moved—dead. Birds, farm animals, wild animals, the entire teeming exuberance of life — dead. And all people — dead. Every living, breathing creature that lived on dry land died; he wiped out the whole works — people and animals, crawling creatures and flying birds, every last one of them, gone. Only Noah and his company on the ship lived.

24 The floodwaters took over for 150 days.

1-3 8 Then God turned his attention to Noah and all the wild animals and farm animals with him on the ship. God caused the wind to blow and the floodwaters began to go down. The underground springs were shut off, the windows of Heaven closed and the rain quit. Inch by inch the water lowered. After 150 days the worst was over.

4-6 On the seventeenth day of the seventh month, the ship landed on the Ararat mountain range. The water kept going down until the tenth month. On the first day of the tenth month the tops of the mountains came into view. After forty days Noah opened the window that he had built into the ship.

7-9 He sent out a raven; it flew back and forth waiting for the floodwaters to dry up. Then he sent a dove to check on the flood conditions, but it couldn't even find a place to perch — water still covered the Earth. Noah reached out and caught it, brought it back into the ship.

10-11 He waited seven more days and sent out the dove again. It came back in the evening with a freshly picked olive leaf in its beak. Noah knew that the flood was about finished.

12 He waited another seven days and sent the dove out a third time. This time it didn't come back.

13-14 In the six-hundred-first year of Noah's life, on the first day of the first month, the flood had dried up. Noah opened the hatch of the ship and saw dry ground. By the twenty-seventh day of the second month, the Earth was completely dry.

15-17 God spoke to Noah: "Leave the ship, you and your wife and your sons and your sons' wives. And take all the animals with you, the whole menagerie of birds and mammals and crawling creatures, all that brimming prodigality of life, so they can reproduce and flourish on the Earth."

18-19 Noah disembarked with his sons and wife and his sons' wives. Then all the animals, crawling creatures, birds — every creature on the face of the Earth — left the ship family by family.

20-21 Noah built an altar to GOD. He selected clean animals and birds from every species and offered them as burnt offerings on the altar. GOD smelled the sweet fragrance and thought to himself, "I'll never again curse the ground because of people. I know they have this bent toward evil from an early age, but I'll never again kill off everything living as I've just done.

22 For as long as Earth lasts,
     planting and harvest, cold and heat,
Summer and winter, day and night
     will never stop."

1-4 9 God blessed Noah and his sons: He said, "Prosper! Reproduce! Fill the Earth! Every living creature — birds, animals, fish — will fall under your spell and be afraid of you. You're responsible for them. All living creatures are yours for food; just as I gave you the plants, now I give you everything else. Except for meat with its lifeblood still in it — don't eat that.

5   "But your own lifeblood I will avenge; I will avenge it against both animals and other humans.

6-7

    Whoever sheds human blood,
        by humans let his blood be shed,
    Because God made humans in his image
        reflecting God's very nature.
    You're here to bear fruit, reproduce,
        lavish life on the Earth, live bountifully!"

8-11   Then God spoke to Noah and his sons: "I'm setting up my covenant with you including your children who will come after you, along with everything alive around you — birds, farm animals, wild animals — that came out of the ship with you. I'm setting up my covenant with you that never again will everything living be destroyed by floodwaters; no, never again will a flood destroy the Earth."

12-16   God continued, "This is the sign of the covenant I am making between me and you and everything living around you and everyone living after you. I'm putting my rainbow in the clouds, a sign of the covenant between me and the Earth. From now on, when I form a cloud over the Earth and the rainbow appears in the cloud, I'll remember my covenant between me and you and everything living, that never again will floodwaters destroy all life. When the rainbow appears in the cloud, I'll see it and remember the eternal covenant between God and everything living, every last living creature on Earth."

17   And God said, "This is the sign of the covenant that I've set up between me and everything living on the Earth."

18-19   The sons of Noah who came out of the ship were Shem, Ham, and Japheth. Ham was the father of Canaan. These are the three sons of Noah; from these three the whole Earth was populated.

20-23   Noah, a farmer, was the first to plant a vineyard. He drank from its wine, got drunk and passed out, naked in his tent. Ham, the father of Canaan, saw that his father was naked and told his two brothers who were outside the tent. Shem and Japheth took a cloak, held it between them from their shoulders, walked backward and covered their father's nakedness, keeping their faces turned away so they did not see their father's exposed body.

24-27   When Noah woke up with his hangover, he learned what his youngest son had done. He said,

    Cursed be Canaan! A slave of slaves,
        a slave to his brothers!
    Blessed be GOD, the God of Shem,
        but Canaan shall be his slave.
    God prosper Japheth,
        living spaciously in the tents of Shem.
    But Canaan shall be his slave.

28-29   Noah lived another 350 years following the flood. He lived a total of 950 years. And he died.

THE FAMILY TREE OF NOAH'S SONS

1 10 This is the family tree of the sons of Noah: Shem, Ham, and Japheth. After the flood, they themselves had sons.

2 The sons of Japheth: Gomer, Magog, Madai, Javan, Tubal, Meshech, Tiras.

3 The sons of Gomer: Ashkenaz, Riphath, Togarmah.

4-5 The sons of Javan: Elishah, Tarshish, Kittim, Rodanim. The seafaring peoples developed from these, each in its own place by family, each with its own language.

6 The sons of Ham: Cush, Egypt, Put, Canaan.

7 The sons of Cush: Seba, Havilah, Sabtah, Raamah, Sabteca. The sons of Raamah: Sheba, Dedan.

8-12 Cush also had Nimrod. He was the first great warrior on Earth. He was a great hunter before GOD. There was a saying, "Like Nimrod, a great hunter before GOD." His kingdom got its start with Babel; then Erech, Akkad, and Calneh in the country of Shinar. From there he went up to Asshur and built Nineveh, Rehoboth Ir, Calah, and Resen between Nineveh and the great city Calah.

13-14 Egypt was ancestor to the Ludim, the Anamim, the Lehabim, the Naphtuhim, the Pathrusim, the Casluhim (the origin of the Philistines), and the Kaphtorim.

15-19 Canaan had Sidon his firstborn, Heth, the Jebusites, the Amorites, the Girgashites, the Hivites, the Arkites, the Sinites, the Arvadites, the Zemarites, and the Hamathites. Later the Canaanites spread out, going from Sidon toward Gerar, as far south as Gaza, and then east all the way over to Sodom, Gomorrah, Admah, Zeboiim, and on to Lasha.

20 These are the descendants of Ham by family, language, country, and nation.

21 Shem, the older brother of Japheth, also had sons. Shem was ancestor to all the children of Eber.

22 The sons of Shem: Elam, Asshur, Arphaxad, Lud, and Aram.

23 The sons of Aram: Uz, Hul, Gether, Meshech.

24-25 Arphaxad had Shelah and Shelah had Eber. Eber had two sons, Peleg (so named because in his days the human race divided) and Joktan.

26-30 Joktan had Almodad, Sheleph, Hazarmaveth, Jerah, Hadoram, Uzal, Diklah, Obal, Abimael, Sheba, Ophir, Havilah, and Jobab—all sons of Joktan. Their land goes from Mesha toward Sephar as far as the mountain ranges in the east.

31 These are the descendants of Shem by family, language, country, and nation.

32 This is the family tree of the sons of Noah as they developed into nations. From them nations developed all across the Earth after the flood.

"GOD TURNED THEIR LANGUAGE INTO 'BABBLE'"

1-2 11 At one time, the whole Earth spoke the same language. It so happened that as they moved out of the east, they came upon a plain in the land of Shinar and settled down.

3 They said to one another, "Come, let's make bricks and fire them well." They used brick for stone and tar for mortar.

4 Then they said, "Come, let's build ourselves a city and a tower that reaches Heaven. Let's make ourselves famous so we won't be scattered here and there across the Earth."

5 God came down to look over the city and the tower those people had built.

6-9 God took one look and said, "One people, one language; why, this is only a first step. No telling what they'll come up with next—they'll stop at nothing! Come, we'll go down and garble their speech so they won't understand each other." Then God scattered them from there all over the world. And they had to quit building the city. That's how it came to be called Babel, because there God turned their language into "babble." From there God scattered them all over the world.

10-11 This is the story of Shem. When Shem was 100 years old, he had Arphaxad. It was two years after the flood. After he had Arphaxad, he lived 500 more years and had other sons and daughters.

12-13 When Arphaxad was thirty-five years old, he had Shelah. After Arphaxad had Shelah, he lived 403 more years and had other sons and daughters.

14-15 When Shelah was thirty years old, he had Eber. After Shelah had Eber, he lived 403 more years and had other sons and daughters.

16-17 When Eber was thirty-four years old, he had Peleg. After Eber had Peleg, he lived 430 more years and had other sons and daughters.

18-19 When Peleg was thirty years old, he had Reu. After he had Reu, he lived 209 more years and had other sons and daughters.

20-21 When Reu was thirty-two years old, he had Serug. After Reu had Serug, he lived 207 more years and had other sons and daughters.

22-23 When Serug was thirty years old, he had Nahor. After Serug had Nahor, he lived 200 more years and had other sons and daughters.

24-25 When Nahor was twenty-nine years old, he had Terah. After Nahor had Terah, he lived 119 more years and had other sons and daughters.

26 When Terah was seventy years old, he had Abram, Nahor, and Haran.

The Family Tree of Terah

27-28 This is the story of Terah. Terah had Abram, Nahor, and Haran.

Haran had Lot. Haran died before his father, Terah, in the country of his family, Ur of the Chaldees.

29 Abram and Nahor each got married. Abram's wife was Sarai; Nahor's wife was Milcah, the daughter of his brother Haran. Haran had two daughters, Milcah and Iscah.

30 Sarai was barren; she had no children.

31 Terah took his son Abram, his grandson Lot (Haran's son), and Sarai his daughter-in-law (his son Abram's wife) and set out with them from Ur of the Chaldees for the land of Canaan. But when they got as far as Haran, they settled down there.

32 Terah lived 205 years. He died in Haran.

Abram and Sarai

1 **12** God told Abram: "Leave your country, your family, and your father's home for a land that I will show you.

2-3 I'll make you a great nation
    and bless you.

I'll make you famous;
  you'll be a blessing.
I'll bless those who bless you;
  those who curse you I'll curse.
All the families of the Earth
  will be blessed through you."

4-6 So Abram left just as GOD said, and Lot left with him. Abram was seventy-five years old when he left Haran. Abram took his wife Sarai and his nephew Lot with him, along with all the possessions and people they had gotten in Haran, and set out for the land of Canaan and arrived safe and sound.

Abram passed through the country as far as Shechem and the Oak of Moreh. At that time the Canaanites occupied the land.

7 GOD appeared to Abram and said, "I will give this land to your children." Abram built an altar at the place GOD had appeared to him.

8 He moved on from there to the hill country east of Bethel and pitched his tent between Bethel to the west and Ai to the east. He built an altar there and prayed to GOD.

9 Abram kept moving, steadily making his way south, to the Negev.

10-13 Then a famine came to the land. Abram went down to Egypt to live; it was a hard famine. As he drew near to Egypt, he said to his wife, Sarai, "Look. We both know that you're a beautiful woman. When the Egyptians see you they're going to say, 'Aha! That's his wife!' and kill me. But they'll let you live. Do me a favor: tell them you're my sister. Because of you, they'll welcome me and let me live."

14-15 When Abram arrived in Egypt, the Egyptians took one look and saw that his wife was stunningly beautiful. Pharaoh's princes raved over her to Pharaoh. She was taken to live with Pharaoh.

16-17 Because of her, Abram got along very well: he accumulated sheep and cattle, male and female donkeys, men and women servants, and camels. But GOD hit Pharaoh hard because of Abram's wife Sarai; everybody in the palace got seriously sick.

18-19 Pharaoh called for Abram, "What's this that you've done to me? Why didn't you tell me that she's your wife? Why did you say, 'She's my sister' so that I'd take her as my wife? Here's your wife back—take her and get out!"

20 Pharaoh ordered his men to get Abram out of the country. They sent him and his wife and everything he owned on their way.

1-2 **13** So Abram left Egypt and went back to the Negev, he and his wife and everything he owned, and Lot still with him. By now Abram was very rich, loaded with cattle and silver and gold.

3-4 He moved on from the Negev, camping along the way, to Bethel, the place he had first set up his tent between Bethel and Ai and built his first altar. Abram prayed there to GOD.

5-7 Lot, who was traveling with Abram, was also rich in sheep and cattle and tents. But the land couldn't support both of them; they had too many possessions. They couldn't both live there—quarrels broke out between Abram's shepherds and Lot's shepherds. The Canaanites and Perizzites were also living on the land at the time.

8-9 Abram said to Lot, "Let's not have fighting between us, between your shepherds and my shepherds. After all, we're family. Look around. Isn't there plenty of land out there? Let's separate. If you go left, I'll go right; if you go right, I'll go left."

10-11 Lot looked. He saw the whole plain of the Jordan spread out, well watered (this was before GOD destroyed Sodom and Gomorrah), like GOD's garden, like Egypt, and stretching all the way to Zoar. Lot took the whole plain of the Jordan. Lot set out to the east.

11-12 That's how they came to part company, uncle and nephew. Abram settled in Canaan; Lot settled in the cities of the plain and pitched his tent near Sodom.

13 The people of Sodom were evil — flagrant sinners against GOD.

14-17 After Lot separated from him, GOD said to Abram, "Open your eyes, look around. Look north, south, east, and west. Everything you see, the whole land spread out before you, I will give to you and your children forever. I'll make your descendants like dust — counting your descendants will be as impossible as counting the dust of the Earth. So — on your feet, get moving! Walk through the country, its length and breadth; I'm giving it all to you."

18 Abram moved his tent. He went and settled by the Oaks of Mamre in Hebron. There he built an altar to GOD.

1-2 **14** Then this: Amraphel king of Shinar, Arioch king of Ellasar, Kedorlaomer king of Elam, and Tidal king of Goiim went off to war to fight Bera king of Sodom, Birsha king of Gomorrah, Shinab king of Admah, Shemeber king of Zeboiim, and the king of Bela, that is, Zoar.

3-4 This second group of kings, the attacked, came together at the Valley of Siddim, that is, the Salt Sea. They had been under the thumb of Kedorlaomer for twelve years. In the thirteenth year, they revolted.

5-7 In the fourteenth year, Kedorlaomer and the kings allied with him set out and defeated the Rephaim in Ashteroth Karnaim, the Zuzim in Ham, the Emim in Shaveh Kiriathaim, and the Horites in their hill country of Seir as far as El Paran on the far edge of the desert. On their way back they stopped at En Mishpat, that is, Kadesh, and conquered the whole region of the Amalekites as well as that of the Amorites who lived in Hazazon Tamar.

8-9 That's when the king of Sodom marched out with the king of Gomorrah, the king of Admah, the king of Zeboiim, and the king of Bela, that is, Zoar. They drew up in battle formation against their enemies in the Valley of Siddim — against Kedorlaomer king of Elam, Tidal king of Goiim, Amraphel king of Shinar, and Arioch king of Ellasar, four kings against five.

10-12 The Valley of Siddim was full of tar pits. When the kings of Sodom and Gomorrah fled, they fell into the tar pits, but the rest escaped into the mountains. The four kings captured all the possessions of Sodom and Gomorrah, all their food and equipment, and went on their way. They captured Lot, Abram's nephew who was living in Sodom at the time, taking everything he owned with them.

13-16 A fugitive came and reported to Abram the Hebrew. Abram was living at the Oaks of Mamre the Amorite, brother of Eshcol and Aner. They were allies of Abram. When Abram heard that his nephew had been taken prisoner, he lined up his servants, all of them born in his household—there were 318 of them—and chased after the captors all the way to Dan. Abram and his men split into small groups and attacked by night. They chased them as far as Hobah, just north of Damascus. They recovered all the plunder along with nephew Lot and his possessions, including the women and the people.

17-20 After Abram returned from defeating Kedorlaomer and his allied kings, the king of Sodom came out to greet him in the Valley of Shaveh, the King's Valley. Melchizedek, king of Salem, brought out bread and wine—he was priest of The High God—and blessed him:

> Blessed be Abram by The High God,
>   Creator of Heaven and Earth.
> And blessed be The High God,
>   who handed your enemies over to you.

Abram gave him a tenth of all the recovered plunder.

21 The king of Sodom said to Abram, "Give me back the people but keep all the plunder for yourself."

22-24 But Abram told the king of Sodom, "I swear to GOD, The High God, Creator of Heaven and Earth, this solemn oath, that I'll take nothing from you, not so much as a thread or a shoestring. I'm not going to have you go around saying, 'I made Abram rich.' Nothing for me other than what the young men ate and the share of the men who went with me, Aner, Eshcol, and Mamre; they're to get their share of the plunder."

1 **15** After all these things, this word of GOD came to Abram in a vision: "Don't be afraid, Abram. I'm your shield. Your reward will be grand!"

2-3 Abram said, "GOD, Master, what use are your gifts as long as I'm childless and Eliezer of Damascus is going to inherit everything?" Abram continued, "See, you've given me no children, and now a mere house servant is going to get it all."

4 Then GOD's Message came: "Don't worry, he won't be your heir; a son from your body will be your heir."

5 Then he took him outside and said, "Look at the sky. Count the stars. Can you do it? Count your descendants! You're going to have a big family, Abram!"

6 And he believed! Believed GOD! God declared him "Set-Right-with-God."

7 GOD continued, "I'm the same GOD who brought you from Ur of the Chaldees and gave you this land to own."

8 Abram said, "Master GOD, how am I to know this, that it will all be mine?"

9 GOD said, "Bring me a heifer, a goat, and a ram, each three years old, and a dove and a young pigeon."

10-12 He brought all these animals to him, split them down the middle, and laid the halves opposite each other. But he didn't split the birds. Vultures swooped down on the carcasses, but Abram scared them off. As the sun went down a deep sleep overcame Abram and then a sense of dread, dark and heavy.

13-16 GOD said to Abram, "Know this: your descendants will live as outsiders in a land not theirs; they'll be enslaved and beaten down for 400 years. Then I'll punish their slave masters; your offspring will march out of there loaded with plunder. But not you; you'll have a long and full life and die a good and peaceful death. Not until the fourth generation will your descendants return here; sin is still a thriving business among the Amorites."

17-21 When the sun was down and it was dark, a smoking firepot and a flaming torch moved between the split carcasses. That's when GOD made a covenant with Abram: "I'm giving this land to your children, from the Nile River in Egypt to the River Euphrates in Assyria — the country of the Kenites, Kenizzites, Kadmonites, Hittites, Perizzites, Rephaim, Amorites, Canaanites, Girgashites, and Jebusites."

1-2 **16** Sarai, Abram's wife, hadn't yet produced a child.
She had an Egyptian maid named Hagar. Sarai said to Abram, "GOD has not seen fit to let me have a child. Sleep with my maid. Maybe I can get a family from her." Abram agreed to do what Sarai said.

3-4 So Sarai, Abram's wife, took her Egyptian maid Hagar and gave her to her husband Abram as a wife. Abram had been living ten years in Canaan when this took place. He slept with Hagar and she got pregnant. When Hagar learned she was pregnant, she looked down on her mistress.

5 Sarai told Abram, "It's all your fault that I'm suffering this abuse. I put my maid in bed with you and the minute she knows she's pregnant, she treats me like I'm nothing. May GOD decide which of us is right."

6 "You decide," said Abram. "Your maid is your business."
Sarai was abusive to Hagar and Hagar ran away.

7-8 An angel of GOD found her beside a spring in the desert; it was the spring on the road to Shur. He said, "Hagar, maid of Sarai, what are you doing here?"
She said, "I'm running away from Sarai my mistress."

9-12 The angel of GOD said, "Go back to your mistress. Put up with her abuse." He continued, "I'm going to give you a big family, children past counting.

From this pregnancy, you'll get a son: Name him Ishmael;
 for GOD heard you, GOD answered you.
He'll be a bucking bronco of a man,
 a real fighter, fighting and being fought,
Always stirring up trouble,
 always at odds with his family."

13 She answered GOD by name, praying to the God who spoke to her, "You're the God who sees me!
"Yes! He saw me; and then I saw him!"

14 That's how that desert spring got named "God-Alive-Sees-Me Spring." That spring is still there, between Kadesh and Bered.

15-16 Hagar gave Abram a son. Abram named him Ishmael. Abram was eighty-six years old when Hagar gave him his son, Ishmael.

17 When Abram was ninety-nine years old, GOD showed up and said to him, "I am The Strong God, live entirely before me, live to the hilt! I'll make a covenant between us and I'll give you a huge family."

Overwhelmed, Abram fell flat on his face.

Then God said to him, "This is my covenant with you: You'll be the father of many nations. Your name will no longer be Abram, but Abraham, meaning that 'I'm making you the father of many nations.' I'll make you a father of fathers — I'll make nations from you, kings will issue from you. I'm establishing my covenant between me and you, a covenant that includes your descendants, a covenant that goes on and on and on, a covenant that commits me to be your God and the God of your descendants. And I'm giving you and your descendants this land where you're now just camping, this whole country of Canaan, to own forever. And I'll be their God."

God continued to Abraham, "And you: You will honor my covenant, you and your descendants, generation after generation. This is the covenant that you are to honor, the covenant that pulls in all your descendants: Circumcise every male. Circumcise by cutting off the foreskin of the penis; it will be the sign of the covenant between us. Every male baby will be circumcised when he is eight days old, generation after generation — this includes house-born slaves and slaves bought from outsiders who are not blood kin. Make sure you circumcise both your own children and anyone brought in from the outside. That way my covenant will be cut into your body, a permanent mark of my permanent covenant. An uncircumcised male, one who has not had the foreskin of his penis cut off, will be cut off from his people — he has broken my covenant."

God continued speaking to Abraham, "And Sarai your wife: Don't call her Sarai any longer; call her Sarah. I'll bless her — yes! I'll give you a son by her! Oh, how I'll bless her! Nations will come from her; kings of nations will come from her."

Abraham fell flat on his face. And then he laughed, thinking, "Can a hundred-year-old man father a son? And can Sarah, at ninety years, have a baby?"

Recovering, Abraham said to God, "Oh, keep Ishmael alive and well before you!"

But God said, "That's not what I mean. Your wife, Sarah, will have a baby, a son. Name him Isaac (Laughter). I'll establish my covenant with him and his descendants, a covenant that lasts forever.

"And Ishmael? Yes, I heard your prayer for him. I'll also bless him; I'll make sure he has plenty of children — a huge family. He'll father twelve princes; I'll make him a great nation. But I'll establish my covenant with Isaac whom Sarah will give you about this time next year."

God finished speaking with Abraham and left.

Then Abraham took his son Ishmael and all his servants, whether houseborn or purchased — every male in his household — and circumcised them, cutting off their foreskins that very day, just as God had told him.

Abraham was ninety-nine years old when he was circumcised. His son Ishmael was thirteen years old when he was circumcised. Abraham and Ishmael were circumcised the same day together with all the servants of his household, those born there and those purchased from outsiders — all were circumcised with him.

※

¹⁻² 18 GOD appeared to Abraham at the Oaks of Mamre while he was sitting at the entrance of his tent. It was the hottest part of the day. He looked up and saw three men standing. He ran from his tent to greet them and bowed before them.

³⁻⁵ He said, "Master, if it please you, stop for a while with your servant. I'll get some water so you can wash your feet. Rest under this tree. I'll get some food to refresh you on your way, since your travels have brought you across my path."

They said, "Certainly. Go ahead."

⁶ Abraham hurried into the tent to Sarah. He said, "Hurry. Get three cups of our best flour; knead it and make bread."

⁷⁻⁸ Then Abraham ran to the cattle pen and picked out a nice plump calf and gave it to the servant who lost no time getting it ready. Then he got curds and milk, brought them with the calf that had been roasted, set the meal before the men, and stood there under the tree while they ate.

⁹ The men said to him, "Where is Sarah your wife?"

He said, "In the tent."

¹⁰ One of them said, "I'm coming back about this time next year. When I arrive, your wife Sarah will have a son." Sarah was listening at the tent opening, just behind the man.

¹¹⁻¹² Abraham and Sarah were old by this time, very old. Sarah was far past the age for having babies. Sarah laughed within herself, "An old woman like me? Get pregnant? With this old man of a husband?"

¹³⁻¹⁴ GOD said to Abraham, "Why did Sarah laugh saying, 'Me? Have a baby? An old woman like me?' Is anything too hard for GOD? I'll be back about this time next year and Sarah will have a baby."

¹⁵ Sarah lied. She said, "I didn't laugh," because she was afraid.

But he said, "Yes you did; you laughed."

※

¹⁶ When the men got up to leave, they set off for Sodom. Abraham walked with them to say good-bye.

¹⁷⁻¹⁹ Then GOD said, "Shall I keep back from Abraham what I'm about to do? Abraham is going to become a large and strong nation; all the nations of the world are going to find themselves blessed through him. Yes, I've settled on him as the one to train his children and future family to observe GOD's way of life, live kindly and generously and fairly, so that GOD can complete in Abraham what he promised him."

²⁰⁻²¹ GOD continued, "The cries of the victims in Sodom and Gomorrah are deafening; the sin of those cities is immense. I'm going down to see for myself, see if what they're doing is as bad as it sounds. Then I'll know."

²² The men set out for Sodom, but Abraham stood in GOD's path, blocking his way.

²³⁻²⁵ Abraham confronted him, "Are you serious? Are you planning on getting rid of the good people right along with the bad? What if there are fifty decent people left in the city; will you lump the good with the bad and get rid of the lot? Wouldn't you spare the city for the sake of those fifty innocents? I can't believe you'd do that, kill off the good and the bad alike

as if there were no difference between them. Doesn't the Judge of all the Earth judge with justice?"

26 GOD said, "If I find fifty decent people in the city of Sodom, I'll spare the place just for them."

27-28 Abraham came back, "Do I, a mere mortal made from a handful of dirt, dare open my mouth again to my Master? What if the fifty fall short by five — would you destroy the city because of those missing five?"

He said, "I won't destroy it if there are forty-five."

29 Abraham spoke up again, "What if you only find forty?"

"Neither will I destroy it if for forty."

30 He said, "Master, don't be irritated with me, but what if only thirty are found?"

"No, I won't do it if I find thirty."

31 He pushed on, "I know I'm trying your patience, Master, but how about for twenty?"

"I won't destroy it for twenty."

32 He wouldn't quit, "Don't get angry, Master — this is the last time. What if you only come up with ten?"

"For the sake of only ten, I won't destroy the city."

33 When GOD finished talking with Abraham, he left. And Abraham went home.

1-2 **19** The two angels arrived at Sodom in the evening. Lot was sitting at the city gate. He saw them and got up to welcome them, bowing before them and said, "Please, my friends, come to my house and stay the night. Wash up. You can rise early and be on your way refreshed."

They said, "No, we'll sleep in the street."

3 But he insisted, wouldn't take no for an answer; and they relented and went home with him. Lot fixed a hot meal for them and they ate.

4-5 Before they went to bed men from all over the city of Sodom, young and old, descended on the house from all sides and boxed them in. They yelled to Lot, "Where are the men who are staying with you for the night? Bring them out so we can have our sport with them!"

6-8 Lot went out, barring the door behind him, and said, "Brothers, please, don't be vile! Look, I have two daughters, virgins; let me bring them out; you can take your pleasure with them, but don't touch these men — they're my guests."

9 They said, "Get lost! You drop in from nowhere and now you're going to tell us how to run our lives. We'll treat you worse than them!" And they charged past Lot to break down the door.

10-11 But the two men reached out and pulled Lot inside the house, locking the door. Then they struck blind the men who were trying to break down the door, both leaders and followers, leaving them groping in the dark.

12-13 The two men said to Lot, "Do you have any other family here? Sons, daughters — anybody in the city? Get them out of here, and now! We're going to destroy this place. The outcries of victims here to GOD are deafening; we've been sent to blast this place into oblivion."

14 Lot went out and warned the fiancés of his daughters, "Evacuate this place; GOD is about to destroy this city!" But his daughters' would-be husbands treated it as a joke.

15 At break of day, the angels pushed Lot to get going, "Hurry. Get your

wife and two daughters out of here before it's too late and you're caught in the punishment of the city."

16-17 Lot was dragging his feet. The men grabbed Lot's arm, and the arms of his wife and daughters—GOD was so merciful to them!—and dragged them to safety outside the city. When they had them outside, Lot was told, "Now run for your life! Don't look back! Don't stop anywhere on the plain—run for the hills or you'll be swept away."

18-20 But Lot protested, "No, masters, you can't mean it! I know that you've taken a liking to me and have done me an immense favor in saving my life, but I can't run for the mountains—who knows what terrible thing might happen to me in the mountains and leave me for dead. Look over there—that town is close enough to get to. It's a small town, hardly anything to it. Let me escape there and save my life—it's a mere wide place in the road."

21-22 "All right, Lot. If you insist. I'll let you have your way. And I won't stamp out the town you've spotted. But hurry up. Run for it! I can't do anything until you get there." That's why the town was called Zoar, that is, Smalltown.

23 The sun was high in the sky when Lot arrived at Zoar.

24-25 Then GOD rained brimstone and fire down on Sodom and Gomorrah—a river of lava from GOD out of the sky!—and destroyed these cities and the entire plain and everyone who lived in the cities and everything that grew from the ground.

26 But Lot's wife looked back and turned into a pillar of salt.

27-28 Abraham got up early the next morning and went to the place he had so recently stood with GOD. He looked out over Sodom and Gomorrah, surveying the whole plain. All he could see was smoke belching from the Earth, like smoke from a furnace.

29 And that's the story: When God destroyed the Cities of the Plain, he was mindful of Abraham and first got Lot out of there before he blasted those cities off the face of the Earth.

30 Lot left Zoar and went into the mountains to live with his two daughters; he was afraid to stay in Zoar. He lived in a cave with his daughters.

31-32 One day the older daughter said to the younger, "Our father is getting old and there's not a man left in the country by whom we can get pregnant. Let's get our father drunk with wine and lie with him. We'll get children through our father—it's our only chance to keep our family alive."

33-35 They got their father drunk with wine that very night. The older daughter went and lay with him. He was oblivious, knowing nothing of what she did. The next morning the older said to the younger, "Last night I slept with my father. Tonight, it's your turn. We'll get him drunk again and then you sleep with him. We'll both get a child through our father and keep our family alive." So that night they got their father drunk again and the younger went in and slept with him. Again he was oblivious, knowing nothing of what she did.

36-38 Both daughters became pregnant by their father, Lot. The older daughter had a son and named him Moab, the ancestor of the present-day Moabites. The younger daughter had a son and named him Ben-Ammi, the ancestor of the present-day Ammonites.

20 ¹⁻² Abraham traveled from there south to the Negev and settled down between Kadesh and Shur. While he was camping in Gerar, Abraham said of his wife Sarah, "She's my sister."

²⁻³ So Abimelech, king of Gerar, sent for Sarah and took her. But God came to Abimelech in a dream that night and told him, "You're as good as dead — that woman you took, she's a married woman."

⁴⁻⁵ Now Abimelech had not yet slept with her, hadn't so much as touched her. He said, "Master, would you kill an innocent man? Didn't he tell me, 'She's my sister'? And didn't she herself say, 'He's my brother'? I had no idea I was doing anything wrong when I did this."

⁶⁻⁷ God said to him in the dream, "Yes, I know your intentions were pure, that's why I kept you from sinning against me; I was the one who kept you from going to bed with her. So now give the man's wife back to him. He's a prophet and will pray for you — pray for your life. If you don't give her back, know that it's certain death both for you and everyone in your family."

⁸⁻⁹ Abimelech was up first thing in the morning. He called all his house servants together and told them the whole story. They were shocked. Then Abimelech called in Abraham and said, "What have you done to us? What have I ever done to you that you would bring on me and my kingdom this huge offense? What you've done to me ought never to have been done."

¹⁰ Abimelech went on to Abraham, "Whatever were you thinking of when you did this thing?"

¹¹⁻¹³ Abraham said, "I just assumed that there was no fear of God in this place and that they'd kill me to get my wife. Besides, the truth is that she is my half sister; she's my father's daughter but not my mother's. When God sent me out as a wanderer from my father's home, I told her, 'Do me a favor; wherever we go, tell people that I'm your brother.'"

¹⁴⁻¹⁵ Then Abimelech gave Sarah back to Abraham, and along with her sent sheep and cattle and servants, both male and female. He said, "My land is open to you; live wherever you wish."

¹⁶ And to Sarah he said, "I've given your brother a thousand pieces of silver — that clears you of even a shadow of suspicion before the eyes of the world. You're vindicated."

¹⁷⁻¹⁸ Then Abraham prayed to God and God healed Abimelech, his wife and his maidservants, and they started having babies again. For GOD had shut down every womb in Abimelech's household on account of Sarah, Abraham's wife.

21 ¹⁻⁴ GOD visited Sarah exactly as he said he would; GOD did to Sarah what he promised: Sarah became pregnant and gave Abraham a son in his old age, and at the very time God had set. Abraham named him Isaac. When his son was eight days old, Abraham circumcised him just as God had commanded.

⁵⁻⁶ Abraham was a hundred years old when his son Isaac was born.
Sarah said,

> God has blessed me with laughter
> and all who get the news will laugh with me!

7 She also said,

> Whoever would have suggested to Abraham
> that Sarah would one day nurse a baby!
> Yet here I am! I've given the old man a son!

8 The baby grew and was weaned. Abraham threw a big party on the day Isaac was weaned.

9-10 One day Sarah saw the son that Hagar the Egyptian had borne to Abraham, poking fun at her son Isaac. She told Abraham, "Get rid of this slave woman and her son. No child of this slave is going to share inheritance with my son Isaac!"

11-13 The matter gave great pain to Abraham — after all, Ishmael was his son. But God spoke to Abraham, "Don't feel badly about the boy and your maid. Do whatever Sarah tells you. Your descendants will come through Isaac. Regarding your maid's son, be assured that I'll also develop a great nation from him — he's your son, too."

14-16 Abraham got up early the next morning, got some food together and a canteen of water for Hagar, put them on her back and sent her away with the child. She wandered off into the desert of Beersheba. When the water was gone, she left the child under a shrub and went off, fifty yards or so. She said, "I can't watch my son die." As she sat, she broke into sobs.

17-18 Meanwhile, God heard the boy crying. The angel of God called from Heaven to Hagar, "What's wrong, Hagar? Don't be afraid. God has heard the boy and knows the fix he's in. Up now; go get the boy. Hold him tight. I'm going to make of him a great nation."

19 Just then God opened her eyes. She looked. She saw a well of water. She went to it and filled her canteen and gave the boy a long, cool drink.

20-21 God was on the boy's side as he grew up. He lived out in the desert and became a skilled archer. He lived in the Paran wilderness. And his mother got him a wife from Egypt.

22-23 At about that same time, Abimelech and the captain of his troops, Phicol, spoke to Abraham: "No matter what you do, God is on your side. So swear to me that you won't do anything underhanded to me or any of my family. For as long as you live here, swear that you'll treat me and my land as well as I've treated you."

24 Abraham said, "I swear it."

25-26 At the same time, Abraham confronted Abimelech over the matter of a well of water that Abimelech's servants had taken. Abimelech said, "I have no idea who did this; you never told me about it; this is the first I've heard of it."

27-28 So the two of them made a covenant. Abraham took sheep and cattle and gave them to Abimelech. Abraham set aside seven sheep from his flock.

29 Abimelech said, "What does this mean? These seven sheep you've set aside."

30 Abraham said, "It means that when you accept these seven sheep, you take it as proof that I dug this well, that it's my well."

31-32 That's how the place got named Beersheba (the Oath-Well), because the two of them swore a covenant oath there. After they had made the covenant at Beersheba, Abimelech and his commander, Phicol, left and went back to Philistine territory.

33-34   Abraham planted a tamarisk tree in Beersheba and worshiped GOD there, praying to the Eternal God. Abraham lived in Philistine country for a long time.

1   **22** After all this, God tested Abraham. God said, "Abraham!"
          "Yes?" answered Abraham. "I'm listening."

2   He said, "Take your dear son Isaac whom you love and go to the land of Moriah. Sacrifice him there as a burnt offering on one of the mountains that I'll point out to you."

3-5   Abraham got up early in the morning and saddled his donkey. He took two of his young servants and his son Isaac. He had split wood for the burnt offering. He set out for the place God had directed him. On the third day he looked up and saw the place in the distance. Abraham told his two young servants, "Stay here with the donkey. The boy and I are going over there to worship; then we'll come back to you."

6   Abraham took the wood for the burnt offering and gave it to Isaac his son to carry. He carried the flint and the knife. The two of them went off together.

7   Isaac said to Abraham his father, "Father?"
          "Yes, my son."
          "We have flint and wood, but where's the sheep for the burnt offering?"

8   Abraham said, "Son, God will see to it that there's a sheep for the burnt offering." And they kept on walking together.

9-10   They arrived at the place to which God had directed him. Abraham built an altar. He laid out the wood. Then he tied up Isaac and laid him on the wood. Abraham reached out and took the knife to kill his son.

11   Just then an angel of GOD called to him out of Heaven, "Abraham! Abraham!"
          "Yes, I'm listening."

12   "Don't lay a hand on that boy! Don't touch him! Now I know how fearlessly you fear God; you didn't hesitate to place your son, your dear son, on the altar for me."

13   Abraham looked up. He saw a ram caught by its horns in the thicket. Abraham took the ram and sacrificed it as a burnt offering instead of his son.

14   Abraham named that place GOD-Yireh (GOD-Sees-to-It). That's where we get the saying, "On the mountain of GOD, he sees to it."

15-18   The angel of GOD spoke from Heaven a second time to Abraham: "I swear — GOD's sure word! — because you have gone through with this, and have not refused to give me your son, your dear, dear son, I'll bless you — oh, how I'll bless you! And I'll make sure that your children flourish — like stars in the sky! like sand on the beaches! And your descendants will defeat their enemies. All nations on Earth will find themselves blessed through your descendants because you obeyed me."

19   Then Abraham went back to his young servants. They got things together and returned to Beersheba. Abraham settled down in Beersheba.

20-23   After all this, Abraham got the news: "Your brother Nahor is a father! Milcah has given him children: Uz, his firstborn, his brother Buz, Kemuel

45

(he was the father of Aram), Kesed, Hazo, Pildash, Jidlaph, and Bethuel." (Bethuel was the father of Rebekah.) Milcah gave these eight sons to Nahor, Abraham's brother.

24 His concubine, Reumah, gave him four more children: Tebah, Gaham, Tahash, and Maacah.

1-2 **23** Sarah lived 127 years. Sarah died in Kiriath Arba, present-day Hebron, in the land of Canaan. Abraham mourned for Sarah and wept.

3-4 Then Abraham got up from mourning his dead wife and spoke to the Hittites: "I know I'm only an outsider here among you, but sell me a burial plot so that I can bury my dead decently."

5-6 The Hittites responded, "Why, you're no mere outsider here with us, you're a prince of God! Bury your dead wife in the best of our burial sites. None of us will refuse you a place for burial."

7-9 Then Abraham got up, bowed respectfully to the people of the land, the Hittites, and said, "If you're serious about helping me give my wife a proper burial, intercede for me with Ephron son of Zohar. Ask him to sell me the cave of Machpelah that he owns, the one at the end of his land. Ask him to sell it to me at its full price for a burial plot, with you as witnesses."

10-11 Ephron was part of the local Hittite community. Then Ephron the Hittite spoke up, answering Abraham with all the Hittites who were part of the town council listening: "Oh no, my master! I couldn't do that. The field is yours—a gift. I'll give it and the cave to you. With my people as witnesses, I give it to you. Bury your deceased wife."

12-13 Abraham bowed respectfully before the assembled council and answered Ephron: "Please allow me—I want to pay the price of the land; take my money so that I can go ahead and bury my wife."

14-15 Then Ephron answered Abraham, "If you insist, master. What's four hundred silver shekels between us? Now go ahead and bury your wife."

16 Abraham accepted Ephron's offer and paid out the sum that Ephron had named before the town council of Hittites — four hundred silver shekels at the current exchange rate.

17-20 That's how Ephron's field next to Mamre — the field, its cave, and all the trees within its borders — became Abraham's property. The town council of Hittites witnessed the transaction. Abraham then proceeded to bury his wife Sarah in the cave in the field of Machpelah that is next to Mamre, present-day Hebron, in the land of Canaan. The field and its cave went from the Hittites into Abraham's possession as a burial plot.

Isaac and Rebekah

1 **24** Abraham was now an old man. God had blessed Abraham in every way.

2-4 Abraham spoke to the senior servant in his household, the one in charge of everything he had, "Put your hand under my thigh and swear by God — God of Heaven, God of Earth — that you will not get a wife for my son from among the young women of the Canaanites here, but will go to the land of my birth and get a wife for my son Isaac."

5 The servant answered, "But what if the woman refuses to leave home and come with me? Do I then take your son back to your home country?"

6-8 Abraham said, "Oh no. Never. By no means are you to take my son back there. GOD, the God of Heaven, took me from the home of my father and from the country of my birth and spoke to me in solemn promise, 'I'm giving *this* land to your descendants.' This God will send his angel ahead of you to get a wife for my son. And if the woman won't come, you are free from this oath you've sworn to me. But under no circumstances are you to take my son back there."

9 So the servant put his hand under the thigh of his master Abraham and gave his solemn oath.

10-14 The servant took ten of his master's camels and, loaded with gifts from his master, traveled to Aram Naharaim and the city of Nahor. Outside the city, he made the camels kneel at a well. It was evening, the time when the women came to draw water. He prayed, "O GOD, God of my master Abraham, make things go smoothly this day; treat my master Abraham well! As I stand here by the spring while the young women of the town come out to get water, let the girl to whom I say, 'Lower your jug and give me a drink,' and who answers, 'Drink, and let me also water your camels'—let her be the woman you have picked out for your servant Isaac. Then I'll know that you're working graciously behind the scenes for my master."

15-17 It so happened that the words were barely out of his mouth when Rebekah, the daughter of Bethuel whose mother was Milcah the wife of Nahor, Abraham's brother, came out with a water jug on her shoulder. The girl was stunningly beautiful, a pure virgin. She went down to the spring, filled her jug, and came back up. The servant ran to meet her and said, "Please, can I have a sip of water from your jug?"

18-21 She said, "Certainly, drink!" And she held the jug so that he could drink. When he had satisfied his thirst she said, "I'll get water for your camels, too, until they've drunk their fill." She promptly emptied her jug into the trough and ran back to the well to fill it, and she kept at it until she had watered all the camels.

The man watched, silent. Was this GOD's answer? Had GOD made his trip a success or not?

22-23 When the camels had finished drinking, the man brought out gifts, a gold nose ring weighing a little over a quarter of an ounce and two arm bracelets weighing about four ounces, and gave them to her. He asked her, "Tell me about your family? Whose daughter are you? Is there room in your father's house for us to stay the night?"

24-25 She said, "I'm the daughter of Bethuel the son of Milcah and Nahor. And there's plenty of room in our house for you to stay—and lots of straw and feed besides."

26-27 At this the man bowed in worship before GOD and prayed, "Blessed be GOD, God of my master Abraham: How generous and true you've been to my master; you've held nothing back. You led me right to the door of my master's brother!"

28 And the girl was off and running, telling everyone in her mother's house what had happened.

29-31 Rebekah had a brother named Laban. Laban ran outside to the man at the spring. He had seen the nose ring and the bracelets on his sister and had heard her say, "The man said this and this and this to me." So he went to the man and there he was, still standing with his camels at the spring. Laban welcomed him: "Come on in, blessed of GOD! Why are you standing out here? I've got the house ready for you; and there's also a place for your camels."

32-33   So the man went into the house. The camels were unloaded and given straw and feed. Water was brought to bathe the feet of the man and the men with him. Then Laban brought out food. But the man said, "I won't eat until I tell my story."

Laban said, "Go ahead; tell us."

34-41   The servant said, "I'm the servant of Abraham. GOD has blessed my master — he's a great man; GOD has given him sheep and cattle, silver and gold, servants and maidservants, camels and donkeys. And then to top it off, Sarah, my master's wife, gave him a son in her old age and he has passed everything on to his son. My master made me promise, 'Don't get a wife for my son from the daughters of the Canaanites in whose land I live. No, go to my father's home, back to my family, and get a wife for my son there.' I said to my master, 'But what if the woman won't come with me?' He said, 'GOD before whom I've walked faithfully will send his angel with you and he'll make things work out so that you'll bring back a wife for my son from my family, from the house of my father. Then you'll be free from the oath. If you go to my family and they won't give her to you, you will also be free from the oath.'

42-44   "Well, when I came this very day to the spring, I prayed, 'GOD, God of my master Abraham, make things turn out well in this task I've been given. I'm standing at this well. When a young woman comes here to draw water and I say to her, Please, give me a sip of water from your jug, and she says, Not only will I give you a drink, I'll also water your camels — let that woman be the wife GOD has picked out for my master's son.'

45-48   "I had barely finished offering this prayer, when Rebekah arrived, her jug on her shoulder. She went to the spring and drew water and I said, 'Please, can I have a drink?' She didn't hesitate. She held out her jug and said, 'Drink; and when you're finished I'll also water your camels.' I drank, and she watered the camels. I asked her, 'Whose daughter are you?' She said, 'The daughter of Bethuel whose parents were Nahor and Milcah.' I gave her a ring for her nose, bracelets for her arms, and bowed in worship to GOD. I praised GOD, the God of my master Abraham who had led me straight to the door of my master's family to get a wife for his son.

49   "Now, tell me what you are going to do. If you plan to respond with a generous *yes*, tell me. But if not, tell me plainly so I can figure out what to do next."

50-51   Laban and Bethuel answered, "This is totally from GOD. We have no say in the matter, either yes or no. Rebekah is yours: Take her and go; let her be the wife of your master's son, as GOD has made plain."

52-54   When Abraham's servant heard their decision, he bowed in worship before GOD. Then he brought out gifts of silver and gold and clothing and gave them to Rebekah. He also gave expensive gifts to her brother and mother. He and his men had supper and spent the night. But first thing in the morning they were up. He said, "Send me back to my master."

55   Her brother and mother said, "Let the girl stay a while, say another ten days, and then go."

56   He said, "Oh, don't make me wait! GOD has worked everything out so well — send me off to my master."

57   They said, "We'll call the girl; we'll ask her."

They called Rebekah and asked her, "Do you want to go with this man?"

58 She said, "I'm ready to go."

59-60 So they sent them off, their sister Rebekah with her nurse, and Abraham's servant with his men. And they blessed Rebekah saying,

> You're our sister — live bountifully!
> And your children, triumphantly!

61 Rebekah and her young maids mounted the camels and followed the man. The servant took Rebekah and set off for home.

62-65 Isaac was living in the Negev. He had just come back from a visit to Beer Lahai Roi. In the evening he went out into the field; while meditating he looked up and saw camels coming. When Rebekah looked up and saw Isaac, she got down from her camel and asked the servant, "Who is that man out in the field coming toward us?"

"That is my master."

She took her veil and covered herself.

66-67 After the servant told Isaac the whole story of the trip, Isaac took Rebekah into the tent of his mother Sarah. He married Rebekah and she became his wife and he loved her. So Isaac found comfort after his mother's death.

1-2 **25** Abraham married a second time; his new wife was named Keturah. She gave birth to Zimran, Jokshan, Medan, Midian, Ishbak, and Shuah.

3 Jokshan had Sheba and Dedan.

Dedan's descendants were the Asshurim, the Letushim, and the Leummim.

4 Midian had Ephah, Epher, Hanoch, Abida, and Eldaah — all from the line of Keturah.

5-6 But Abraham gave everything he possessed to Isaac. While he was still living, he gave gifts to the sons he had by his concubines, but then sent them away to the country of the east, putting a good distance between them and his son Isaac.

7-11 Abraham lived 175 years. Then he took his final breath. He died happy at a ripe old age, full of years, and was buried with his family. His sons Isaac and Ishmael buried him in the cave of Machpelah in the field of Ephron son of Zohar the Hittite, next to Mamre. It was the field that Abraham had bought from the Hittites. Abraham was buried next to his wife Sarah. After Abraham's death, God blessed his son Isaac. Isaac lived at Beer Lahai Roi.

THE FAMILY TREE OF ISHMAEL

12 This is the family tree of Ishmael son of Abraham, the son that Hagar the Egyptian, Sarah's maid, bore to Abraham.

13-16 These are the names of Ishmael's sons in the order of their births: Nebaioth, Ishmael's firstborn, Kedar, Adbeel, Mibsam, Mishma, Dumah, Massa, Hadad, Tema, Jetur, Naphish, and Kedemah — all the sons of Ishmael. Their settlements and encampments were named after them. Twelve princes with their twelve tribes.

17-18 Ishmael lived 137 years. When he breathed his last and died he was buried with his family. His children settled down all the way from Havilah near Egypt eastward to Shur in the direction of Assyria. The Ishmaelites didn't get along with any of their kin.

JACOB AND ESAU

19-20 This is the family tree of Isaac son of Abraham: Abraham had Isaac. Isaac was forty years old when he married Rebekah daughter of Bethuel the Aramean of Paddan Aram. She was the sister of Laban the Aramean.

21-23 Isaac prayed hard to GOD for his wife because she was barren. GOD answered his prayer and Rebekah became pregnant. But the children tumbled and kicked inside her so much that she said, "If this is the way it's going to be, why go on living?" She went to GOD to find out what was going on. GOD told her,

Two nations are in your womb,
  two peoples butting heads while still in your body.
One people will overpower the other,
  and the older will serve the younger.

24-26 When her time to give birth came, sure enough, there were twins in her womb. The first came out reddish, as if snugly wrapped in a hairy blanket; they named him Esau (Hairy). His brother followed, his fist clutched tight to Esau's heel; they named him Jacob (Heel). Isaac was sixty years old when they were born.

27-28 The boys grew up. Esau became an expert hunter, an outdoorsman. Jacob was a quiet man preferring life indoors among the tents. Isaac loved Esau because he loved his game, but Rebekah loved Jacob.

29-30 One day Jacob was cooking a stew. Esau came in from the field, starved. Esau said to Jacob, "Give me some of that red stew — I'm starved!" That's how he came to be called Edom (Red).

31 Jacob said, "Make me a trade: my stew for your rights as the firstborn."

32 Esau said, "I'm starving! What good is a birthright if I'm dead?"

33-34 Jacob said, "First, swear to me." And he did it. On oath Esau traded away his rights as the firstborn. Jacob gave him bread and the stew of lentils. He ate and drank, got up and left. That's how Esau shrugged off his rights as the firstborn.

1 **26** There was a famine in the land, as bad as the famine during the time of Abraham. And Isaac went down to Abimelech, king of the Philistines, in Gerar.

2-5 GOD appeared to him and said, "Don't go down to Egypt; stay where I tell you. Stay here in this land and I'll be with you and bless you. I'm giving you and your children all these lands, fulfilling the oath that I swore to your father Abraham. I'll make your descendants as many as the stars in the sky and give them all these lands. All the nations of the Earth will get a blessing for themselves through your descendants. And why? Because Abraham obeyed my summons and kept my charge — my commands, my guidelines, my teachings."

6 So Isaac stayed put in Gerar.

7 The men of the place questioned him about his wife. He said, "She's my sister." He was afraid to say "She's my wife." He was thinking, "These men might kill me to get Rebekah, she's so beautiful."

8-9 One day, after they had been there quite a long time, Abimelech, king of the Philistines, looked out his window and saw Isaac fondling his wife Rebekah. Abimelech sent for Isaac and said, "So, she's your wife. Why did you tell us 'She's my sister'?"

Isaac said, "Because I thought I might get killed by someone who wanted her."

10 Abimelech said, "But think of what you might have done to *us*! Given a little more time, one of the men might have slept with your wife; you would have been responsible for bringing guilt down on us."

11 Then Abimelech gave orders to his people: "Anyone who so much as lays a hand on this man or his wife dies."

12-15 Isaac planted crops in that land and took in a huge harvest. GOD blessed him. The man got richer and richer by the day until he was very wealthy. He accumulated flocks and herds and many, many servants, so much so that the Philistines began to envy him. They got back at him by throwing dirt and debris into all the wells that his father's servants had dug back in the days of his father Abraham, clogging up all the wells.

16 Finally, Abimelech told Isaac: "Leave. You've become far too big for us."

17-18 So Isaac left. He camped in the valley of Gerar and settled down there. Isaac dug again the wells which were dug in the days of his father Abraham but had been clogged up by the Philistines after Abraham's death. And he renamed them, using the original names his father had given them.

19-24 One day, as Isaac's servants were digging in the valley, they came on a well of spring water. The shepherds of Gerar quarreled with Isaac's shepherds, claiming, "This water is ours." So Isaac named the well Esek (Quarrel) because they quarreled over it. They dug another well and there was a difference over that one also, so he named it Sitnah (Accusation). He went on from there and dug yet another well. But there was no fighting over this one so he named it Rehoboth (Wide-Open Spaces), saying, "Now GOD has given us plenty of space to spread out in the land." From there he went up to Beersheba. That very night GOD appeared to him and said,

I am the God of Abraham your father;
    don't fear a thing because I'm with you.
I'll bless you and make your children flourish
    because of Abraham my servant.

25 Isaac built an altar there and prayed, calling on GOD by name. He pitched his tent and his servants started digging another well.

26-27 Then Abimelech came to him from Gerar with Ahuzzath his advisor and Phicol the head of his troops. Isaac asked them, "Why did you come to me? You hate me; you threw me out of your country."

28-29 They said, "We've realized that GOD is on your side. We'd like to make a deal between us—a covenant that we maintain friendly relations. We haven't bothered you in the past; we treated you kindly and let you leave us in peace. So—- GOD's blessing be with you!"

30-31 Isaac laid out a feast and they ate and drank together. Early in the morning they exchanged oaths. Then Isaac said good-bye and they parted as friends.

32-33   Later that same day, Isaac's servants came to him with news about the well they had been digging, "We've struck water!" Isaac named the well Sheba (Oath), and that's the name of the city, Beersheba (Oath-Well), to this day.

* * *

34-35   When Esau was forty years old he married Judith, daughter of Beeri the Hittite, and Basemath, daughter of Elon the Hittite. They turned out to be thorns in the sides of Isaac and Rebekah.

* * *

1   **27** When Isaac had become an old man and was nearly blind, he called his eldest son, Esau, and said, "My son."
"Yes, Father?"

2-4   "I'm an old man," he said; "I might die any day now. Do me a favor: Get your quiver of arrows and your bow and go out in the country and hunt me some game. Then fix me a hearty meal, the kind that you know I like, and bring it to me to eat so that I can give you my personal blessing before I die."

5-7   Rebekah was eavesdropping as Isaac spoke to his son Esau. As soon as Esau had gone off to the country to hunt game for his father, Rebekah spoke to her son Jacob. "I just overheard your father talking with your brother, Esau. He said, 'Bring me some game and fix me a hearty meal so that I can eat and bless you with GOD's blessing before I die.'

8-10   "Now, my son, listen to me. Do what I tell you. Go to the flock and get me two young goats. Pick the best; I'll prepare them into a hearty meal, the kind that your father loves. Then you'll take it to your father, he'll eat and bless you before he dies."

11-12   "But Mother," Jacob said, "my brother Esau is a hairy man and I have smooth skin. What happens if my father touches me? He'll think I'm playing games with him. I'll bring down a curse on myself instead of a blessing."

13   "If it comes to that," said his mother, "I'll take the curse on myself. Now, just do what I say. Go and get the goats."

14   So he went and got them and brought them to his mother and she cooked a hearty meal, the kind his father loved so much.

15-17   Rebekah took the dress-up clothes of her older son Esau and put them on her younger son Jacob. She took the goatskins and covered his hands and the smooth nape of his neck. Then she placed the hearty meal she had fixed and fresh bread she'd baked into the hands of her son Jacob.

18   He went to his father and said, "My father!"
"Yes?" he said. "Which son are you?"

19   Jacob answered his father, "I'm your firstborn son Esau. I did what you told me. Come now; sit up and eat of my game so you can give me your personal blessing."

20   Isaac said, "So soon? How did you get it so quickly?"
"Because your GOD cleared the way for me."

21   Isaac said, "Come close, son; let me touch you—are you really my son Esau?"

22-23   So Jacob moved close to his father Isaac. Isaac felt him and said, "The voice is Jacob's voice but the hands are the hands of Esau." He didn't recognize him because his hands were hairy, like his brother Esau's.

23-24 But as he was about to bless him he pressed him, "You're sure? *You* are my son Esau?"

"Yes. I am."

25 Isaac said, "Bring the food so I can eat of my son's game and give you my personal blessing." Jacob brought it to him and he ate. He also brought him wine and he drank.

26 Then Isaac said, "Come close, son, and kiss me."

27-29 He came close and kissed him and Isaac smelled the smell of his clothes. Finally, he blessed him,

> Ahhh. The smell of my son
>   is like the smell of the open country
>   blessed by GOD.
> May God give you
>   of Heaven's dew
>   and Earth's bounty of grain and wine.
> May peoples serve you
>   and nations honor you.
> You will master your brothers,
>   and your mother's sons will honor you.
> Those who curse you will be cursed,
>   those who bless you will be blessed.

30-31 And then right after Isaac had blessed Jacob and Jacob had left, Esau showed up from the hunt. He also had prepared a hearty meal. He came to his father and said, "Let my father get up and eat of his son's game, that he may give me his personal blessing."

32 His father Isaac said, "And who are you?"

"I am your son, your firstborn, Esau."

33 Isaac started to tremble, shaking violently. He said, "Then who hunted game and brought it to me? I finished the meal just now, before you walked in. And I blessed him — he's blessed for good!"

34 Esau, hearing his father's words, sobbed violently and most bitterly, and cried to his father, "My father! Can't you also bless me?"

35 "Your brother," he said, "came here falsely and took your blessing."

36 Esau said, "Not for nothing was he named Jacob, the Heel. Twice now he's tricked me: first he took my birthright and now he's taken my blessing."

He begged, "Haven't you kept back any blessing for me?"

37 Isaac answered Esau, "I've made him your master, and all his brothers his servants, and lavished grain and wine on him. I've given it all away. What's left for you, my son?"

38 "But don't you have just one blessing for me, Father? Oh, bless me my father! Bless me!" Esau sobbed inconsolably.

39-40 Isaac said to him,

> You'll live far from Earth's bounty,
>   remote from Heaven's dew.
> You'll live by your sword, hand-to-mouth,
>   and you'll serve your brother.
> But when you can't take it any more
>   you'll break loose and run free.

41   Esau seethed in anger against Jacob because of the blessing his father had given him; he brooded, "The time for mourning my father's death is close. And then I'll kill my brother Jacob."

42-45   When these words of her older son Esau were reported to Rebekah, she called her younger son Jacob and said, "Your brother Esau is plotting vengeance against you. He's going to kill you. Son, listen to me. Get out of here. Run for your life to Haran, to my brother Laban. Live with him for a while until your brother cools down, until his anger subsides and he forgets what you did to him. I'll then send for you and bring you back. Why should I lose both of you the same day?"

46   Rebekah spoke to Isaac, "I'm sick to death of these Hittite women. If Jacob also marries a native Hittite woman, why live?"

1-2   **28** So Isaac called in Jacob and blessed him. Then he ordered him, "Don't take a Caananite wife. Leave at once. Go to Paddan Aram to the family of your mother's father, Bethuel. Get a wife for yourself from the daughters of your uncle Laban.

3-4   "And may The Strong God bless you and give you many, many children, a congregation of peoples; and pass on the blessing of Abraham to you and your descendants so that you will get this land in which you live, this land God gave Abraham."

5   So Isaac sent Jacob off. He went to Paddan Aram, to Laban son of Bethuel the Aramean, the brother of Rebekah who was the mother of Jacob and Esau.

6-9   Esau learned that Isaac had blessed Jacob and sent him to Paddan Aram to get a wife there, and while blessing him commanded, "Don't marry a Canaanite woman," and that Jacob had obeyed his parents and gone to Paddan Aram. When Esau realized how deeply his father Isaac disliked the Canaanite women, he went to Ishmael and married Mahalath the sister of Nebaioth and daughter of Ishmael, Abraham's son. This was in addition to the wives he already had.

10-12   Jacob left Beersheba and went to Haran. He came to a certain place and camped for the night since the sun had set. He took one of the stones there, set it under his head and lay down to sleep. And he dreamed: A stairway was set on the ground and it reached all the way to the sky; angels of God were going up and going down on it.

13-15   Then GOD was right before him, saying, "I am GOD, the God of Abraham your father and the God of Isaac. I'm giving the ground on which you are sleeping to you and to your descendants. Your descendants will be as the dust of the Earth; they'll stretch from west to east and from north to south. All the families of the Earth will bless themselves in you and your descendants. Yes. I'll stay with you, I'll protect you wherever you go, and I'll bring you back to this very ground. I'll stick with you until I've done everything I promised you."

16-17   Jacob woke up from his sleep. He said, "GOD is in this place—truly. And I didn't even know it!" He was terrified. He whispered in awe, "Incredible. Wonderful. Holy. This is God's House. This is the Gate of Heaven."

18-19   Jacob was up first thing in the morning. He took the stone he had used for his pillow and stood it up as a memorial pillar and poured oil over it.

He christened the place Bethel (God's House). The name of the town had been Luz until then.

20-22 Jacob vowed a vow: "If God stands by me and protects me on this journey on which I'm setting out, keeps me in food and clothing, and brings me back in one piece to my father's house, *this* GOD will be my God. This stone that I have set up as a memorial pillar will mark this as a place where God lives. And everything you give me, I'll return a tenth to you."

1-3 **29** Jacob set out again on his way to the people of the east. He noticed a well out in an open field with three flocks of sheep bedded down around it. This was the common well from which the flocks were watered. The stone over the mouth of the well was huge. When all the flocks were gathered, the shepherds would roll the stone from the well and water the sheep; then they would return the stone, covering the well.

4 Jacob said, "Hello friends. Where are you from?"
They said, "We're from Haran."

5 Jacob asked, "Do you know Laban son of Nahor?"
"We do."

6 "Are things well with him?" Jacob continued.
"Very well," they said. "And here is his daughter Rachel coming with the flock."

7 Jacob said, "There's a lot of daylight still left; it isn't time to round up the sheep yet, is it? So why not water the flocks and go back to grazing?"

8 "We can't," they said. "Not until all the shepherds get here. It takes all of us to roll the stone from the well. Not until then can we water the flocks."

9-13 While Jacob was in conversation with them, Rachel came up with her father's sheep. She was the shepherd. The moment Jacob spotted Rachel, daughter of Laban his mother's brother, saw her arriving with his uncle Laban's sheep, he went and single-handedly rolled the stone from the mouth of the well and watered the sheep of his uncle Laban. Then he kissed Rachel and broke into tears. He told Rachel that he was related to her father, that he was Rebekah's son. She ran and told her father. When Laban heard the news — Jacob, his sister's son! — he ran out to meet him, embraced and kissed him and brought him home. Jacob told Laban the story of everything that had happened.

14-15 Laban said, "You're family! My flesh and blood!"
When Jacob had been with him for a month, Laban said, "Just because you're my nephew, you shouldn't work for me for nothing. Tell me what you want to be paid. What's a fair wage?"

16-18 Now Laban had two daughters; Leah was the older and Rachel the younger. Leah had nice eyes, but Rachel was stunningly beautiful. And it was Rachel that Jacob loved.
So Jacob answered, "I will work for you seven years for your younger daughter Rachel."

19 "It is far better," said Laban, "that I give her to you than marry her to some outsider. Yes. Stay here with me."

20 So Jacob worked seven years for Rachel. But it only seemed like a few days, he loved her so much.

21-24 Then Jacob said to Laban, "Give me my wife; I've completed what we agreed I'd do. I'm ready to consummate my marriage." Laban invited everyone around and threw a big feast. At evening, though, he got his daughter Leah and brought her to the marriage bed, and Jacob slept with her. (Laban gave his maid Zilpah to his daughter Leah as her maid.)

25   Morning came: There was Leah in the marriage bed!

Jacob confronted Laban, "What have you done to me? Didn't I work all this time for the hand of Rachel? Why did you cheat me?"

26-27   "We don't do it that way in our country," said Laban. "We don't marry off the younger daughter before the older. Enjoy your week of honeymoon, and then we'll give you the other one also. But it will cost you another seven years of work."

28-30   Jacob agreed. When he'd completed the honeymoon week, Laban gave him his daughter Rachel to be his wife. (Laban gave his maid Bilhah to his daughter Rachel as her maid.) Jacob then slept with her. And he loved Rachel more than Leah. He worked for Laban another seven years.

31-32   When GOD realized that Leah was unloved, he opened her womb. But Rachel was barren. Leah became pregnant and had a son. She named him Reuben (Look-It's-a-Boy!). "This is a sign," she said, "that GOD has seen my misery; and a sign that now my husband will love me."

33-35   She became pregnant again and had another son. "GOD heard," she said, "that I was unloved and so he gave me this son also." She named this one Simeon (GOD-Heard). She became pregnant yet again—another son. She said, "Now maybe my husband will connect with me—I've given him three sons!" That's why she named him Levi (Connect). She became pregnant a final time and had a fourth son. She said, "This time I'll praise GOD." So she named him Judah (Praise-GOD). Then she stopped having children.

1   **30** When Rachel realized that she wasn't having any children for Jacob, she became jealous of her sister. She told Jacob, "Give me sons or I'll die!"

2   Jacob got angry with Rachel and said, "Am I God? Am I the one who refused you babies?"

3-5   Rachel said, "Here's my maid Bilhah. Sleep with her. Let her substitute for me so I can have a child through her and build a family." So she gave him her maid Bilhah for a wife and Jacob slept with her. Bilhah became pregnant and gave Jacob a son.

6-8   Rachel said, "God took my side and vindicated me. He listened to me and gave me a son." She named him Dan (Vindication). Rachel's maid Bilhah became pregnant again and gave Jacob a second son. Rachel said, "I've been in an all-out fight with my sister—and I've won." So she named him Naphtali (Fight).

9-13   When Leah saw that she wasn't having any more children, she gave her maid Zilpah to Jacob for a wife. Zilpah had a son for Jacob. Leah said, "How fortunate!" and she named him Gad (Lucky). When Leah's maid Zilpah had a second son for Jacob, Leah said, "A happy day! The women will congratulate me in my happiness." So she named him Asher (Happy).

14   One day during the wheat harvest Reuben found some mandrakes in the field and brought them home to his mother Leah. Rachel asked Leah, "Could I please have some of your son's mandrakes?"

15   Leah said, "Wasn't it enough that you got my husband away from me?

And now you also want my son's mandrakes?"

Rachel said, "All right. I'll let him sleep with you tonight in exchange for your son's love-apples."

¹⁶⁻²¹ When Jacob came home that evening from the fields, Leah was there to meet him: "Sleep with me tonight; I've bartered my son's mandrakes for a night with you." So he slept with her that night. God listened to Leah; she became pregnant and gave Jacob a fifth son. She said, "God rewarded me for giving my maid to my husband." She named him Issachar (Bartered). Leah became pregnant yet again and gave Jacob a sixth son, saying, "God has given me a great gift. This time my husband will honor me with gifts — I've given him six sons!" She named him Zebulun (Honor). Last of all she had a daughter and named her Dinah.

²²⁻²⁴ And then God remembered Rachel. God listened to her and opened her womb. She became pregnant and had a son. She said, "God has taken away my humiliation." She named him Joseph (Add), praying, "May GOD add yet another son to me."

²⁵⁻²⁶ After Rachel had had Joseph, Jacob spoke to Laban, "Let me go back home. Give me my wives and children for whom I've served you. You know how hard I've worked for you."

²⁷⁻²⁸ Laban said, "If you please, I have learned through divine inquiry that GOD has blessed me because of you." He went on, "So name your wages. I'll pay you."

²⁹⁻³⁰ Jacob replied, "You know well what my work has meant to you and how your livestock has flourished under my care. The little you had when I arrived has increased greatly; everything I did resulted in blessings for you. Isn't it about time that I do something for my own family?"

³¹⁻³³ "So, what should I pay you?"

Jacob said, "You don't have to pay me a thing. But how about this? I will go back to pasture and care for your flocks. Go through your entire flock today and take out every speckled or spotted sheep, every dark-colored lamb, every spotted or speckled goat. They will be my wages. That way you can check on my honesty when you assess my wages. If you find any goat that's not speckled or spotted or a sheep that's not black, you will know that I stole it."

³⁴ "Fair enough," said Laban. "It's a deal."

³⁵⁻³⁶ But that very day Laban removed all the mottled and spotted billy goats and all the speckled and spotted nanny goats, every animal that had even a touch of white on it plus all the black sheep and placed them under the care of his sons. Then he put a three-day journey between himself and Jacob. Meanwhile Jacob went on tending what was left of Laban's flock.

³⁷⁻⁴² But Jacob got fresh branches from poplar, almond, and plane trees and peeled the bark, leaving white stripes on them. He stuck the peeled branches in front of the watering troughs where the flocks came to drink. When the flocks were in heat, they came to drink and mated in front of the streaked branches. Then they gave birth to young that were streaked or spotted or speckled. Jacob placed the ewes before the dark-colored animals of Laban. That way he got distinctive flocks for himself which he didn't mix with Laban's flocks. And when the sturdier animals were mating, Jacob placed branches at the troughs in view of the animals so that they mated in front of the branches. But he wouldn't set

up the branches before the feebler animals. That way the feeble animals went to Laban and the sturdy ones to Jacob.

43 The man got richer and richer, acquiring huge flocks, lots and lots of servants, not to mention camels and donkeys.

1-2 **31** Jacob learned that Laban's sons were talking behind his back: "Jacob has used our father's wealth to make himself rich at our father's expense." At the same time, Jacob noticed that Laban had changed toward him. He wasn't treating him the same.

3 That's when GOD said to Jacob, "Go back home where you were born. I'll go with you."

4-9 So Jacob sent word for Rachel and Leah to meet him out in the field where his flocks were. He said, "I notice that your father has changed toward me; he doesn't treat me the same as before. But the God of my father hasn't changed; he's still with me. You know how hard I've worked for your father. Still, your father has cheated me over and over, changing my wages time and again. But God never let him really hurt me. If he said, 'Your wages will consist of speckled animals' the whole flock would start having speckled lambs and kids. And if he said, 'From now on your wages will be streaked animals' the whole flock would have streaked ones. Over and over God used your father's livestock to reward me.

10-11 "Once, while the flocks were mating, I had a dream and saw the billy goats, all of them streaked, speckled, and mottled, mounting their mates. In the dream an angel of God called out to me, 'Jacob!'

"I said, 'Yes?'

12-13 "He said, 'Watch closely. Notice that all the goats in the flock that are mating are streaked, speckled, and mottled. I know what Laban's been doing to you. I'm the God of Bethel where you consecrated a pillar and made a vow to me. Now be on your way, get out of this place, go home to your birthplace.'"

14-16 Rachel and Leah said, "Has he treated us any better? Aren't we treated worse than outsiders? All he wanted was the money he got from selling us, and he's spent all that. Any wealth that God has seen fit to return to us from our father is justly ours and our children's. Go ahead. Do what God told you."

17-18 Jacob did it. He put his children and his wives on camels and gathered all his livestock and everything he had gotten, everything acquired in Paddan Aram, to go back home to his father Isaac in the land of Canaan.

19-21 Laban was off shearing sheep. Rachel stole her father's household gods. And Jacob had concealed his plans so well that Laban the Aramean had no idea what was going on — he was totally in the dark. Jacob got away with everything he had and was soon across the Euphrates headed for the hill country of Gilead.

22-24 Three days later, Laban got the news: "Jacob's run off." Laban rounded up his relatives and chased after him. Seven days later they caught up with him in the hill country of Gilead. That night God came to Laban the Aramean in a dream and said, "Be careful what you do to Jacob, whether good or bad."

25 When Laban reached him, Jacob's tents were pitched in the Gilead mountains; Laban pitched his tents there, too.

26-30 "What do you mean," said Laban, "by keeping me in the dark and sneaking off, hauling my daughters off like prisoners of war? Why did you run off like a thief in the night? Why didn't you tell me? Why, I would have sent you off with a great celebration — music, timbrels, flutes! But you wouldn't permit me so much as a kiss for my daughters and grandchildren. It was a stupid thing for you to do. If I had a mind to, I could destroy you right now, but the God of your father spoke to me last night, 'Be careful what you do to Jacob, whether good or bad.' I understand. You left because you were homesick. But why did you steal my household gods?"

31-32 Jacob answered Laban, "I was afraid. I thought you would take your daughters away from me by brute force. But as far as your gods are concerned, if you find that anybody here has them, that person dies. With all of us watching, look around. If you find anything here that belongs to you, take it." Jacob didn't know that Rachel had stolen the gods.

33-35 Laban went through Jacob's tent, Leah's tent, and the tents of the two maids but didn't find them. He went from Leah's tent to Rachel's. But Rachel had taken the household gods, put them inside a camel cushion, and was sitting on them. When Laban had gone through the tent, searching high and low without finding a thing, Rachel said to her father, "Don't think I'm being disrespectful, my master, that I can't stand before you, but I'm having my period." So even though he turned the place upside down in his search, he didn't find the household gods.

36-37 Now it was Jacob's turn to get angry. He lit into Laban: "So what's my crime, what wrong have I done you that you badger me like this? You've ransacked the place. Have you turned up a single thing that's yours? Let's see it — display the evidence. Our two families can be the jury and decide between us.

38-42 "In the twenty years I've worked for you, ewes and she-goats never miscarried. I never feasted on the rams from your flock. I never brought you a torn carcass killed by wild animals but that I paid for it out of my own pocket — actually, you made me pay whether it was my fault or not. I was out in all kinds of weather, from torrid heat to freezing cold, putting in many a sleepless night. For twenty years I've done this: I slaved away fourteen years for your two daughters and another six years for your flock and you changed my wages ten times. If the God of my father, the God of Abraham and the Fear of Isaac, had not stuck with me, you would have sent me off penniless. But God saw the fix I was in and how hard I had worked and last night rendered his verdict."

43-44 Laban defended himself: "The daughters are my daughters, the children are my children, the flock is my flock — everything you see is mine. But what can I do about my daughters or for the children they've had? So let's settle things between us, make a covenant — God will be the witness between us."

45 Jacob took a stone and set it upright as a pillar.

46-47 Jacob called his family around, "Get stones!" They gathered stones and heaped them up and then ate there beside the pile of stones. Laban named it in Aramaic, Yegar-sahadutha (Witness Monument); Jacob echoed the naming in Hebrew, Galeed (Witness Monument).

48-50 Laban said, "This monument of stones will be a witness, beginning now, between you and me." (That's why it is called Galeed — Witness Monument.) It is also called Mizpah (Watchtower) because Laban said, "GOD keep watch between you and me when we are out of each other's sight. If you mistreat my daughters or take other wives when there's no one around to see you, God will see you and stand witness between us."

51-53 Laban continued to Jacob, "This monument of stones and this stone pillar that I have set up is a witness, a witness that I won't cross this line to hurt you and you won't cross this line to hurt me. The God of Abraham and the God of Nahor (the God of their ancestor) will keep things straight between us."

53-55 Jacob promised, swearing by the Fear, the God of his father Isaac. Then Jacob offered a sacrifice on the mountain and worshiped, calling in all his family members to the meal. They ate and slept that night on the mountain. Laban got up early the next morning, kissed his grandchildren and his daughters, blessed them, and then set off for home.

1-2 **32** And Jacob went his way. Angels of God met him. When Jacob saw them he said, "Oh! God's Camp!" And he named the place Mahanaim (Campground).

3-5 Then Jacob sent messengers on ahead to his brother Esau in the land of Seir in Edom. He instructed them: "Tell my master Esau this, 'A message from your servant Jacob: I've been staying with Laban and couldn't get away until now. I've acquired cattle and donkeys and sheep; also men and women servants. I'm telling you all this, my master, hoping for your approval.'"

6 The messengers came back to Jacob and said, "We talked to your brother Esau and he's on his way to meet you. But he has four hundred men with him."

7-8 Jacob was scared. Very scared. Panicked, he divided his people, sheep, cattle, and camels into two camps. He thought, "If Esau comes on the first camp and attacks it, the other camp has a chance to get away."

9-12 And then Jacob prayed, "God of my father Abraham, God of my father Isaac, GOD who told me, 'Go back to your parents' homeland and I'll treat you well.' I don't deserve all the love and loyalty you've shown me. When I left here and crossed the Jordan I only had the clothes on my back, and now look at me—two camps! Save me, please, from the violence of my brother, my angry brother! I'm afraid he'll come and attack us all, me, the mothers and the children. You yourself said, 'I will treat you well; I'll make your descendants like the sands of the sea, far too many to count.'"

13-16 He slept the night there. Then he prepared a present for his brother Esau from his possessions: two hundred female goats, twenty male goats, two hundred ewes and twenty rams, thirty camels with their nursing young, forty cows and ten bulls, twenty female donkeys and ten male donkeys. He put a servant in charge of each herd and said, "Go ahead of me and keep a healthy space between each herd."

17-18 Then he instructed the first one out: "When my brother Esau comes close and asks, 'Who is your master? Where are you going? Who owns these?' —answer him like this, 'Your servant Jacob. They are a gift to my master Esau. He's on his way.'"

19-20 He gave the same instructions to the second servant and to the third—to each in turn as they set out with their herds: "Say 'Your servant Jacob is on his way behind us.'" He thought, "I will soften him up with the succession of gifts. Then when he sees me face-to-face, maybe he'll be glad to welcome me."

21 So his gifts went before him while he settled down for the night in the camp.

22-23 But during the night he got up and took his two wives, his two maid-servants, and his eleven children and crossed the ford of the Jabbok. He got them safely across the brook along with all his possessions.

24-25 But Jacob stayed behind by himself, and a man wrestled with him until daybreak. When the man saw that he couldn't get the best of Jacob as they wrestled, he deliberately threw Jacob's hip out of joint.

26 The man said, "Let me go; it's daybreak."

Jacob said, "I'm not letting you go 'til you bless me."

27 The man said, "What's your name?"

He answered, "Jacob."

28 The man said, "But no longer. Your name is no longer Jacob. From now on it's Israel (God-Wrestler); you've wrestled with God and you've come through."

29 Jacob asked, "And what's your name?"

The man said, "Why do you want to know my name?" And then, right then and there, he blessed him.

30 Jacob named the place Peniel (God's Face) because, he said, "I saw God face-to-face and lived to tell the story!"

31-32 The sun came up as he left Peniel, limping because of his hip. (This is why Israelites to this day don't eat the hip muscle; because Jacob's hip was thrown out of joint.)

1-4 **33** Jacob looked up and saw Esau coming with his four hundred men. He divided the children between Leah and Rachel and the two maidservants. He put the maidservants out in front, Leah and her children next, and Rachel and Joseph last. He led the way and, as he approached his brother, bowed seven times, honoring his brother. But Esau ran up and embraced him, held him tight and kissed him. And they both wept.

5 Then Esau looked around and saw the women and children: "And who are these with you?"

Jacob said, "The children that God saw fit to bless me with."

6-7 Then the maidservants came up with their children and bowed; then Leah and her children, also bowing; and finally, Joseph and Rachel came up and bowed to Esau.

8 Esau then asked, "And what was the meaning of all those herds that I met?"

"I was hoping that they would pave the way for my master to welcome me."

9 Esau said, "Oh, brother. I have plenty of everything—keep what is yours for yourself."

10-11 Jacob said, "Please. If you can find it in your heart to welcome me, accept these gifts. When I saw your face, it was as the face of God smiling on me. Accept the gifts I have brought for you. God has been good to me and I have more than enough." Jacob urged the gifts on him and Esau accepted.

12 Then Esau said, "Let's start out on our way; I'll take the lead."

13-14 But Jacob said, "My master can see that the children are frail. And the flocks and herds are nursing, making for slow going. If I push them too hard, even for a day, I'd lose them all. So, master, you go on ahead of your servant, while I take it easy at the pace of my flocks and children. I'll catch up with you in Seir."

15   Esau said, "Let me at least lend you some of my men."

"There's no need," said Jacob. "Your generous welcome is all I need or want."

16   So Esau set out that day and made his way back to Seir.

17   And Jacob left for Succoth. He built a shelter for himself and sheds for his livestock. That's how the place came to be called Succoth (Sheds).

18-20   And that's how it happened that Jacob arrived all in one piece in Shechem in the land of Canaan — all the way from Paddan Aram. He camped near the city. He bought the land where he pitched his tent from the sons of Hamor, the father of Shechem. He paid a hundred silver coins for it. Then he built an altar there and named it El-Elohe-Israel (Mighty Is the God of Israel).

1-4   **34** One day Dinah, the daughter Leah had given Jacob, went to visit some of the women in that country. Shechem, the son of Hamor the Hivite who was chieftain there, saw her and raped her. Then he felt a strong attraction to Dinah, Jacob's daughter, fell in love with her, and wooed her. Shechem went to his father Hamor, "Get me this girl for my wife."

5-7   Jacob heard that Shechem had raped his daughter Dinah, but his sons were out in the fields with the livestock so he didn't say anything until they got home. Hamor, Shechem's father, went to Jacob to work out marriage arrangements. Meanwhile Jacob's sons on their way back from the fields heard what had happened. They were outraged, explosive with anger. Shechem's rape of Jacob's daughter was intolerable in Israel and not to be put up with.

8-10   Hamor spoke with Jacob and his sons, "My son Shechem is head over heels in love with your daughter — give her to him as his wife. Intermarry with us. Give your daughters to us and we'll give our daughters to you. Live together with us as one family. Settle down among us and make yourselves at home. Prosper among us."

11-12   Shechem then spoke for himself, addressing Dinah's father and brothers: "Please, say yes. I'll pay anything. Set the bridal price as high as you will — the sky's the limit! Only give me this girl for my wife."

13-17   Jacob's sons answered Shechem and his father with cunning. Their sister, after all, had been raped. They said, "This is impossible. We could never give our sister to a man who was uncircumcised. Why, we'd be disgraced. The only condition on which we can talk business is if all your men become circumcised like us. Then we will freely exchange daughters in marriage and make ourselves at home among you and become one big, happy family. But if this is not an acceptable condition, we will take our sister and leave."

18   That seemed fair enough to Hamor and his son Shechem.

19   The young man was so smitten with Jacob's daughter that he proceeded to do what had been asked. He was also the most admired son in his father's family.

20-23   So Hamor and his son Shechem went to the public square and spoke to the town council: "These men like us; they are our friends. Let them settle down here and make themselves at home; there's plenty of room in the country for them. And, just think, we can even exchange our daughters in marriage. But these men will only accept our invitation to live with us and become one big family on one condition, that all our males become circumcised just as they themselves are. This is a very good deal for us — these people are very wealthy with great herds of livestock and we're going to get our hands on it. So let's do what they ask and have them settle down with us."

24 Everyone who was anyone in the city agreed with Hamor and his son, Shechem; every male was circumcised.

25-29 Three days after the circumcision, while all the men were still very sore, two of Jacob's sons, Simeon and Levi, Dinah's brothers, each with his sword in hand, walked into the city as if they owned the place and murdered every man there. They also killed Hamor and his son Shechem, rescued Dinah from Shechem's house, and left. When the rest of Jacob's sons came on the scene of slaughter, they looted the entire city in retaliation for Dinah's rape. Flocks, herds, donkeys, belongings — everything, whether in the city or the fields — they took. And then they took all the wives and children captive and ransacked their homes for anything valuable.

30 Jacob said to Simeon and Levi, "You've made my name stink to high heaven among the people here, these Canaanites and Perizzites. If they decided to gang up on us and attack, as few as we are we wouldn't stand a chance; they'd wipe me and my people right off the map."

31 They said, "Nobody is going to treat our sister like a whore and get by with it."

35

1 God spoke to Jacob: "Go back to Bethel. Stay there and build an altar to the God who revealed himself to you when you were running for your life from your brother Esau."

2-3 Jacob told his family and all those who lived with him, "Throw out all the alien gods which you have, take a good bath and put on clean clothes, we're going to Bethel. I'm going to build an altar there to the God who answered me when I was in trouble and has stuck with me everywhere I've gone since."

4-5 They turned over to Jacob all the alien gods they'd been holding on to, along with their lucky-charm earrings. Jacob buried them under the oak tree in Shechem. Then they set out. A paralyzing fear descended on all the surrounding villages so that they were unable to pursue the sons of Jacob.

6-7 Jacob and his company arrived at Luz, that is, Bethel, in the land of Canaan. He built an altar there and named it El-Bethel (God-of-Bethel) because that's where God revealed himself to him when he was running from his brother.

8 And that's when Rebekah's nurse, Deborah, died. She was buried just below Bethel under the oak tree. It was named Allon-Bacuth (Weeping-Oak).

9-10 God revealed himself once again to Jacob, after he had come back from Paddan Aram and blessed him: "Your name is Jacob (Heel); but that's your name no longer. From now on your name is Israel (God-Wrestler)."

11-12 God continued,

I am The Strong God.
    Have children! Flourish!
A nation — a whole company of nations! —
    will come from you.
Kings will come from your loins;
    the land I gave Abraham and Isaac
I now give to you,
    and pass it on to your descendants.

13   And then God was gone, ascended from the place where he had spoken with him.

14-15   Jacob set up a stone pillar on the spot where God had spoken with him. He poured a drink offering on it and anointed it with oil. Jacob dedicated the place where God had spoken with him, Bethel (God's-House).

16-17   They left Bethel. They were still quite a ways from Ephrath when Rachel went into labor — hard, hard labor. When her labor pains were at their worst, the midwife said to her, "Don't be afraid — you have another boy."

18   With her last breath, for she was now dying, she named him Ben-oni (Son-of-My-Pain), but his father named him Ben-jamin (Son-of-Good-Fortune).

19-20   Rachel died and was buried on the road to Ephrath, that is, Bethlehem. Jacob set up a pillar to mark her grave. It is still there today, "Rachel's Grave Stone."

21-22   Israel kept on his way and set up camp at Migdal Eder. While Israel was living in that region, Reuben went and slept with his father's concubine, Bilhah. And Israel heard of what he did.

22-26   There were twelve sons of Jacob.
The sons by Leah:
    Reuben, Jacob's firstborn
    Simeon
    Levi
    Judah
    Issachar
    Zebulun.
The sons by Rachel:
    Joseph
    Benjamin.
The sons by Bilhah, Rachel's maid:
    Dan
    Naphtali.
The sons by Zilpah, Leah's maid:
    Gad
    Asher.
These were Jacob's sons, born to him in Paddan Aram.

27-29   Finally, Jacob made it back home to his father Isaac at Mamre in Kiriath Arba, present-day Hebron, where Abraham and Isaac had lived. Isaac was now 180 years old. Isaac breathed his last and died — an old man full of years. He was buried with his family by his sons Esau and Jacob.

---

1   **36** This is the family tree of Esau, who is also called Edom.

2-3   Esau married women of Canaan: Adah, daughter of Elon the Hittite; Oholibamah, daughter of Anah and the granddaughter of Zibeon the Hivite; and Basemath, daughter of Ishmael and sister of Nebaioth.

4   Adah gave Esau Eliphaz;
     Basemath had Reuel;

5   Oholibamah had Jeush, Jalam, and Korah.
     These are the sons of Esau who were born to him in the land of
     Canaan.

6-8 Esau gathered up his wives, sons and daughters, and everybody in his
     household, along with all his livestock—all the animals and possessions he had
     gotten in Canaan—and moved a considerable distance away from his brother
     Jacob. The brothers had too many possessions to live together in the same place;
     the land couldn't support their combined herds of livestock. So Esau ended up
     settling in the hill country of Seir (Esau and Edom are the same).

9-10 So this is the family tree of Esau, ancestor of the people of Edom, in
     the hill country of Seir. The names of Esau's sons:
     Eliphaz, son of Esau's wife Adah;
     Reuel, son of Esau's wife Basemath.

11-12 The sons of Eliphaz: Teman, Omar, Zepho, Gatam, and Kenaz. (Eliphaz also
     had a concubine Timna, who had Amalek.) These are the grandsons of Esau's
     wife Adah.

13   And these are the sons of Reuel: Nahath, Zerah, Shammah, and
     Mizzah—grandsons of Esau's wife Basemath.

14   These are the sons of Esau's wife Oholibamah, daughter of Anah the son
     of Zibeon. She gave Esau his sons Jeush, Jalam, and Korah.

15-16 These are the chieftains in Esau's family tree. From the sons of Eliphaz,
     Esau's firstborn, came the chieftains Teman, Omar, Zepho, Kenaz, Korah,
     Gatam, and Amalek—the chieftains of Eliphaz in the land of Edom; all of
     them sons of Adah.

17   From the sons of Esau's son Reuel came the chieftains Nahath, Zerah,
     Shammah, and Mizzah. These are the chieftains of Reuel in the land of
     Edom; all these were sons of Esau's wife Basemath.

18   These are the sons of Esau's wife Oholibamah: the chieftains Jeush,
     Jalam, and Korah—chieftains born of Esau's wife Oholibamah, daughter
     of Anah.

19   These are the sons of Esau, that is, Edom, and these are their chieftains.

20-21 This is the family tree of Seir the Horite, who were native to that land:
     Lotan, Shobal, Zibeon, Anah, Dishon, Ezer, and Dishan. These are the
     chieftains of the Horites, the sons of Seir in the land of Edom.

22   The sons of Lotan were Hori and Homam; Lotan's sister was Timna.

23   The sons of Shobal were Alvan, Manahath, Ebal, Shepho, and Onam.

24   The sons of Zibeon were Aiah and Anah—this is the same Anah who
     found the hot springs in the wilderness while herding his father Zibeon's
     donkeys.

25   The children of Anah were Dishon and his daughter Oholibamah.

26   The sons of Dishon were Hemdan, Eshban, Ithran, and Keran.

27   The sons of Ezer: Bilhan, Zaavan, and Akan.

28   The sons of Dishan: Uz and Aran.

29-30 And these were the Horite chieftains: Lotan, Shobal, Zibeon, Anah,
     Dishon, Ezer, and Dishan—the Horite chieftains clan by clan in the land
     of Seir.

31-39 And these are the kings who ruled in Edom before there was a king in Israel: Bela son of Beor was the king of Edom; the name of his city was Dinhabah. When Bela died, Jobab son of Zerah from Bozrah became the next king. When Jobab died, he was followed by Hushan from the land of the Temanites. When Hushan died, he was followed by Hadad son of Bedad; he was the king who defeated the Midianites in Moab; the name of his city was Avith. When Hadad died, Samlah of Masrekah became the next king. When Samlah died, Shaul from Rehoboth-on-the-River became king. When Shaul died, he was followed by Baal-Hanan son of Acbor. When Baal-Hanan son of Acbor died, Hadad became king; the name of his city was Pau; his wife's name was Mehetabel daughter of Matred, daughter of Me-Zahab.

40-43 And these are the chieftains from the line of Esau, clan by clan, region by region: Timna, Alvah, Jetheth, Oholibamah, Elah, Pinon, Kenaz, Teman, Mibzar, Magdiel, and Iram — the chieftains of Edom as they occupied their various regions.

This accounts for the family tree of Esau, ancestor of all Edomites.

1 ## 37 Meanwhile Jacob had settled down where his father had lived, the land of Canaan.

JOSEPH AND HIS BROTHERS

2 This is the story of Jacob. The story continues with Joseph, seventeen years old at the time, helping out his brothers in herding the flocks. These were his half brothers actually, the sons of his father's wives Bilhah and Zilpah. And Joseph brought his father bad reports on them.

3-4 Israel loved Joseph more than any of his other sons because he was the child of his old age. And he made him an elaborately embroidered coat. When his brothers realized that their father loved him more than them, they grew to hate him — they wouldn't even speak to him.

5-7 Joseph had a dream. When he told it to his brothers, they hated him even more. He said, "Listen to this dream I had. We were all out in the field gathering bundles of wheat. All of a sudden my bundle stood straight up and your bundles circled around it and bowed down to mine."

8 His brothers said, "So! You're going to rule us? You're going to boss us around?" And they hated him more than ever because of his dreams and the way he talked.

9 He had another dream and told this one also to his brothers: "I dreamed another dream — the sun and moon and eleven stars bowed down to me!"

10-11 When he told it to his father and brothers, his father reprimanded him: "What's with all this dreaming? Am I and your mother and your brothers all supposed to bow down to you?" Now his brothers were really jealous; but his father brooded over the whole business.

12-13 His brothers had gone off to Shechem where they were pasturing their father's flocks. Israel said to Joseph, "Your brothers are with flocks in Shechem. Come, I want to send you to them."

Joseph said, "I'm ready."

14 He said, "Go and see how your brothers and the flocks are doing and bring me back a report." He sent him off from the valley of Hebron to Shechem.

15 A man met him as he was wandering through the fields and asked him, "What are you looking for?"

16 "I'm trying to find my brothers. Do you have any idea where they are grazing their flocks?"

17 The man said, "They've left here, but I overheard them say, 'Let's go to Dothan.'" So Joseph took off, tracked his brothers down, and found them in Dothan.

18-20 They spotted him off in the distance. By the time he got to them they had cooked up a plot to kill him. The brothers were saying, "Here comes that dreamer. Let's kill him and throw him into one of these old cisterns; we can say that a vicious animal ate him up. We'll see what his dreams amount to."

21-22 Reuben heard the brothers talking and intervened to save him, "We're not going to kill him. No murder. Go ahead and throw him in this cistern out here in the wild, but don't hurt him." Reuben planned to go back later and get him out and take him back to his father.

23-24 When Joseph reached his brothers, they ripped off the fancy coat he was wearing, grabbed him, and threw him into a cistern. The cistern was dry; there wasn't any water in it.

25-27 Then they sat down to eat their supper. Looking up, they saw a caravan of Ishmaelites on their way from Gilead, their camels loaded with spices, ointments, and perfumes to sell in Egypt. Judah said, "Brothers, what are we going to get out of killing our brother and concealing the evidence? Let's sell him to the Ishmaelites, but let's not kill him — he is, after all, our brother, our own flesh and blood." His brothers agreed.

28 By that time the Midianite traders were passing by. His brothers pulled Joseph out of the cistern and sold him for twenty pieces of silver to the Ishmaelites who took Joseph with them down to Egypt.

29-30 Later Reuben came back and went to the cistern — no Joseph! He ripped his clothes in despair. Beside himself, he went to his brothers. "The boy's gone! What am I going to do!"

31-32 They took Joseph's coat, butchered a goat, and dipped the coat in the blood. They took the fancy coat back to their father and said, "We found this. Look it over — do you think this is your son's coat?"

33 He recognized it at once. "My son's coat — a wild animal has eaten him. Joseph torn limb from limb!"

34-35 Jacob tore his clothes in grief, dressed in rough burlap, and mourned his son a long, long time. His sons and daughters tried to comfort him but he refused their comfort. "I'll go to the grave mourning my son." Oh, how his father wept for him.

36 In Egypt the Midianites sold Joseph to Potiphar, one of Pharaoh's officials, manager of his household affairs.

1-5 **38** About that time, Judah separated from his brothers and hooked up with a man in Adullam named Hirah. While there, Judah met the daughter of a Canaanite named Shua. He married her, they went to bed, she became pregnant and had a son named Er. She got pregnant again and had a son named Onan. She had still another son; she named this one Shelah. They were living at Kezib when she had him.

6-7 Judah got a wife for Er, his firstborn. Her name was Tamar. But Judah's firstborn, Er, grievously offended GOD and GOD took his life.

8-10 So Judah told Onan, "Go and sleep with your brother's widow; it's the duty of a brother-in-law to keep your brother's line alive." But Onan knew that the child wouldn't be his, so whenever he slept with his brother's widow he spilled his semen on the ground so he wouldn't produce a child for his brother. GOD was much offended by what he did and also took his life.

11 So Judah stepped in and told his daughter-in-law Tamar, "Live as a widow at home with your father until my son Shelah grows up." He was worried that Shelah would also end up dead, just like his brothers. So Tamar went to live with her father.

12 Time passed. Judah's wife, Shua's daughter, died. When the time of mourning was over, Judah with his friend Hirah of Adullam went to Timnah for the sheep shearing.

13-14 Tamar was told, "Your father-in-law has gone to Timnah to shear his sheep." She took off her widow's clothes, put on a veil to disguise herself, and sat at the entrance to Enaim which is on the road to Timnah. She realized by now that even though Shelah was grown up, she wasn't going to be married to him.

15 Judah saw her and assumed she was a prostitute since she had veiled her face. He left the road and went over to her. He said, "Let me sleep with you." He had no idea that she was his daughter-in-law.

16 She said, "What will you pay me?"

17 "I'll send you," he said, "a kid goat from the flock."

She said, "Not unless you give me a pledge until you send it."

18 "So what would you want in the way of a pledge?"

She said, "Your personal seal-and-cord and the staff you carry."

He handed them over to her and slept with her. And she got pregnant.

19 She then left and went home. She removed her veil and put her widow's clothes back on.

20-21 Judah sent the kid goat by his friend from Adullam to recover the pledge from the woman. But he couldn't find her. He asked the men of that place, "Where's the prostitute that used to sit by the road here near Enaim?"

They said, "There's never been a prostitute here."

22 He went back to Judah and said, "I couldn't find her. The men there said there never has been a prostitute there."

23 Judah said, "Let her have it then. If we keep looking, everyone will be poking fun at us. I kept my part of the bargain—I sent the kid goat but you couldn't find her."

24 Three months or so later, Judah was told, "Your daughter-in-law has been playing the whore—and now she's a pregnant whore."

Judah yelled, "Get her out here. Burn her up!"

25 As they brought her out, she sent a message to her father-in-law, "I'm pregnant by the man who owns these things. Identify them, please. Who's the owner of the seal-and-cord and the staff?"

26 Judah saw they were his. He said, "She's in the right; I'm in the wrong— I wouldn't let her marry my son Shelah." He never slept with her again.

27-30 When her time came to give birth, it turned out that there were twins in her womb. As she was giving birth, one put his hand out; the midwife tied a red thread on his hand, saying, "This one came first." But then he pulled it back and his brother came out. She said, "Oh! A breakout!" So she named him Perez (Breakout). Then his brother came out with the red thread on his hand. They named him Zerah (Bright).

39

¹ After Joseph had been taken to Egypt by the Ishmaelites, Potiphar an Egyptian, one of Pharaoh's officials and the manager of his household, bought him from them.

²⁻⁶ As it turned out, GOD was with Joseph and things went very well with him. He ended up living in the home of his Egyptian master. His master recognized that GOD was with him, saw that GOD was working for good in everything he did. He became very fond of Joseph and made him his personal aide. He put him in charge of all his personal affairs, turning everything over to him. From that moment on, GOD blessed the home of the Egyptian—all because of Joseph. The blessing of GOD spread over everything he owned, at home and in the fields, and all Potiphar had to concern himself with was eating three meals a day.

⁶⁻⁷ Joseph was a strikingly handsome man. As time went on, his master's wife became infatuated with Joseph and one day said, "Sleep with me."

⁸⁻⁹ He wouldn't do it. He said to his master's wife, "Look, with me here, my master doesn't give a second thought to anything that goes on here—he's put me in charge of everything he owns. He treats me as an equal. The only thing he hasn't turned over to me is you. You're his wife, after all! How could I violate his trust and sin against God?"

¹⁰ She pestered him day after day after day, but he stood his ground. He refused to go to bed with her.

¹¹⁻¹⁵ On one of these days he came to the house to do his work and none of the household servants happened to be there. She grabbed him by his cloak, saying, "Sleep with me!" He left his coat in her hand and ran out of the house. When she realized that he had left his coat in her hand and run outside, she called to her house servants: "Look—this Hebrew shows up and before you know it he's trying to seduce us. He tried to make love to me but I yelled as loud as I could. With all my yelling and screaming, he left his coat beside me here and ran outside."

¹⁶⁻¹⁸ She kept his coat right there until his master came home. She told him the same story. She said, "The Hebrew slave, the one you brought to us, came after me and tried to use me for his plaything. When I yelled and screamed, he left his coat with me and ran outside."

¹⁹⁻²³ When his master heard his wife's story, telling him, "These are the things your slave did to me," he was furious. Joseph's master took him and threw him into the jail where the king's prisoners were locked up. But there in jail GOD was still with Joseph: He reached out in kindness to him; he put him on good terms with the head jailer. The head jailer put Joseph in charge of all the prisoners—he ended up managing the whole operation. The head jailer gave Joseph free rein, never even checked on him, because GOD was with him; whatever he did GOD made sure it worked out for the best.

40

¹⁻⁴ As time went on, it happened that the cupbearer and the baker of the king of Egypt crossed their master, the king of Egypt. Pharaoh was furious with his two officials, the head cupbearer and the head baker, and put them in custody under the captain of the guard; it was the same jail where Joseph was held. The captain of the guard assigned Joseph to see to their needs.

4-7   After they had been in custody for a while, the king's cupbearer and baker, while being held in the jail, both had a dream on the same night, each dream having its own meaning. When Joseph arrived in the morning, he noticed that they were feeling low. So he asked them, the two officials of Pharaoh who had been thrown into jail with him, "What's wrong? Why the long faces?"

8   They said, "We dreamed dreams and there's no one to interpret them."

Joseph said, "Don't interpretations come from God? Tell me the dreams."

9-11   First the head cupbearer told his dream to Joseph: "In my dream there was a vine in front of me with three branches on it: It budded, blossomed, and the clusters ripened into grapes. I was holding Pharaoh's cup; I took the grapes, squeezed them into Pharaoh's cup, and gave the cup to Pharaoh."

12-15   Joseph said, "Here's the meaning. The three branches are three days. Within three days, Pharaoh will get you out of here and put you back to your old work—you'll be giving Pharaoh his cup just as you used to do when you were his cupbearer. Only remember me when things are going well with you again—tell Pharaoh about me and get me out of this place. I was kidnapped from the land of the Hebrews. And since I've been here, I've done nothing to deserve being put in this hole."

16-17   When the head baker saw how well Joseph's interpretation turned out, he spoke up: "My dream went like this: I saw three wicker baskets on my head; the top basket had assorted pastries from the bakery and birds were picking at them from the basket on my head."

18-19   Joseph said, "This is the interpretation: The three baskets are three days; within three days Pharaoh will take off your head, impale you on a post, and the birds will pick your bones clean."

20-22   And sure enough, on the third day it was Pharaoh's birthday and he threw a feast for all his servants. He set the head cupbearer and the head baker in places of honor in the presence of all the guests. Then he restored the head cupbearer to his cupbearing post; he handed Pharaoh his cup just as before. And then he impaled the head baker on a post, following Joseph's interpretations exactly.

23   But the head cupbearer never gave Joseph another thought; he forgot all about him.

1-4   **41** Two years passed and Pharaoh had a dream: He was standing by the Nile River. Seven cows came up out of the Nile, all shimmering with health, and grazed on the marsh grass. Then seven other cows, all skin and bones, came up out of the river after them and stood by them on the bank of the Nile. The skinny cows ate the seven healthy cows. Then Pharaoh woke up.

5-7   He went back to sleep and dreamed a second time: Seven ears of grain, full-bodied and lush, grew out of a single stalk. Then seven more ears grew up, but these were thin and dried out by the east wind. The thin ears swallowed up the full, healthy ears. Then Pharaoh woke up—another dream.

8   When morning came, he was upset. He sent for all the magicians and sages of Egypt. Pharaoh told them his dreams, but they couldn't interpret them to him.

9-13   The head cupbearer then spoke up and said to Pharaoh, "I just now remembered something—I'm sorry, I should have told you this long ago. Once when Pharaoh got angry with his servants, he locked me and the head baker in the house of the captain of the guard. We both had dreams on the same night, each dream with its own meaning. It so happened that there was a young Hebrew slave there with us; he belonged to the captain of the guard. We told him our dreams and he interpreted them for us, each dream separately. Things turned out just as he interpreted. I was returned to my position and the head baker was impaled."

¹⁴ Pharaoh at once sent for Joseph. They brought him on the run from the jail cell. He cut his hair, put on clean clothes, and came to Pharaoh.

¹⁵ "I dreamed a dream," Pharaoh told Joseph. "Nobody can interpret it. But I've heard that just by hearing a dream you can interpret it."

¹⁶ Joseph answered, "Not I, but God. God will set Pharaoh's mind at ease."

¹⁷⁻²¹ Then Pharaoh said to Joseph, "In my dream I was standing on the bank of the Nile. Seven cows, shimmering with health, came up out of the river and grazed on the marsh grass. On their heels seven more cows, all skin and bones, came up. I've never seen uglier cows anywhere in Egypt. Then the seven skinny, ugly cows ate up the first seven healthy cows. But you couldn't tell by looking—after eating them up they were just as skinny and ugly as before. Then I woke up.

²²⁻²⁴ "In my second dream I saw seven ears of grain, full-bodied and lush, growing out of a single stalk, and right behind them, seven other ears, shriveled, thin, and dried out by the east wind. And the thin ears swallowed up the full ears. I've told all this to the magicians but they can't figure it out."

²⁵⁻²⁷ Joseph said to Pharaoh, "Pharaoh's two dreams both mean the same thing. God is telling Pharaoh what he is going to do. The seven healthy cows are seven years and the seven healthy ears of grain are seven years—they're the same dream. The seven sick and ugly cows that followed them up are seven years and the seven scrawny ears of grain dried out by the east wind are the same—seven years of famine.

²⁸⁻³² "The meaning is what I said earlier: God is letting Pharaoh in on what he is going to do. Seven years of plenty are on their way throughout Egypt. But on their heels will come seven years of famine, leaving no trace of the Egyptian plenty. As the country is emptied by famine, there won't be even a scrap left of the previous plenty—the famine will be total. The fact that Pharaoh dreamed the same dream twice emphasizes God's determination to do this and do it soon.

³³⁻³⁶ "So, Pharaoh needs to look for a wise and experienced man and put him in charge of the country. Then Pharaoh needs to appoint managers throughout the country of Egypt to organize it during the years of plenty. Their job will be to collect all the food produced in the good years ahead and stockpile the grain under Pharaoh's authority, storing it in the towns for food. This grain will be held back to be used later during the seven years of famine that are coming on Egypt. This way the country won't be devastated by the famine."

³⁷ This seemed like a good idea to Pharaoh and his officials.

³⁸ Then Pharaoh said to his officials, "Isn't this the man we need? Are we going to find anyone else who has God's spirit in him like this?"

³⁹⁻⁴⁰ So Pharaoh said to Joseph, "You're the man for us. God has given you the inside story—no one is as qualified as you in experience and wisdom. From now on, you're in charge of my affairs; all my people will report to you. Only as king will I be over you."

⁴¹⁻⁴³ So Pharaoh commissioned Joseph: "I'm putting you in charge of the entire country of Egypt." Then Pharaoh removed his signet ring from his

finger and slipped it on Joseph's hand. He outfitted him in robes of the best linen and put a gold chain around his neck. He put the second-in-command chariot at his disposal, and as he rode people shouted "Bravo!"

Joseph was in charge of the entire country of Egypt.

44 Pharaoh told Joseph, "I am Pharaoh, but no one in Egypt will make a single move without your stamp of approval."

45 Then Pharaoh gave Joseph an Egyptian name, Zaphenath-Paneah (God Speaks and He Lives). He also gave him an Egyptian wife, Asenath, the daughter of Potiphera, the priest of On (Heliopolis).

And Joseph took up his duties over the land of Egypt.

46 Joseph was thirty years old when he went to work for Pharaoh the king of Egypt. As soon as Joseph left Pharaoh's presence, he began his work in Egypt.

47-49 During the next seven years of plenty the land produced bumper crops. Joseph gathered up the food of the seven good years in Egypt and stored the food in cities. In each city he stockpiled surplus from the surrounding fields. Joseph collected so much grain—it was like the sand of the ocean!—that he finally quit keeping track.

50-52 Joseph had two sons born to him before the years of famine came. Asenath, daughter of Potiphera the priest of On, was their mother. Joseph named the firstborn Manasseh (Forget), saying, "God made me forget all my hardships and my parental home." He named his second son Ephraim (Double Prosperity), saying, "God has prospered me in the land of my sorrow."

53-54 Then Egypt's seven good years came to an end and the seven years of famine arrived, just as Joseph had said. All countries experienced famine; Egypt was the only country that had bread.

55 When the famine spread throughout Egypt, the people called out in distress to Pharaoh, calling for bread. He told the Egyptians, "Go to Joseph. Do what he tells you."

56-57 As the famine got worse all over the country, Joseph opened the storehouses and sold emergency supplies to the Egyptians. The famine was very bad. Soon the whole world was coming to buy supplies from Joseph. The famine was bad all over.

1-2 ## 42

When Jacob learned that there was food in Egypt, he said to his sons, "Why do you sit around here and look at one another? I've heard that there is food in Egypt. Go down there and buy some so that we can survive and not starve to death."

3-5 Ten of Joseph's brothers went down to Egypt to get food. Jacob didn't send Joseph's brother Benjamin with them; he was afraid that something bad might happen to him. So Israel's sons joined everyone else that was going to Egypt to buy food, for Canaan, too, was hit hard by the famine.

6-7 Joseph was running the country; he was the one who gave out rations to all the people. When Joseph's brothers arrived, they treated him with honor, bowing to him. Joseph recognized them immediately, but treated them as strangers and spoke roughly to them.

He said, "Where do you come from?"

"From Canaan," they said. "We've come to buy food."

8 Joseph knew who they were, but they didn't know who he was.

9 Joseph, remembering the dreams he had dreamed of them, said, "You're spies. You've come to look for our weak spots."

10-11 "No, master," they said. "We've only come to buy food. We're all the sons of the same man; we're honest men; we'd never think of spying."

12 He said, "No. You're spies. You've come to look for our weak spots."

13 They said, "There were twelve of us brothers—sons of the same father in the country of Canaan. The youngest is with our father, and one is no more."

14-16 But Joseph said, "It's just as I said, you're spies. This is how I'll test you. As Pharaoh lives, you're not going to leave this place until your younger brother comes here. Send one of you to get your brother while the rest of you stay here in jail. We'll see if you're telling the truth or not. As Pharaoh lives, I say you're spies."

17 Then he threw them into jail for three days.

18-20 On the third day, Joseph spoke to them. "Do this and you'll live. I'm a God-fearing man. If you're as honest as you say you are, one of your brothers will stay here in jail while the rest of you take the food back to your hungry families. But you have to bring your youngest brother back to me, confirming the truth of your speech—and not one of you will die." They agreed.

21 Then they started talking among themselves. "Now we're paying for what we did to our brother—we saw how terrified he was when he was begging us for mercy. We wouldn't listen to him and now we're the ones in trouble."

22 Reuben broke in. "Didn't I tell you, 'Don't hurt the boy'? But no, you wouldn't listen. And now we're paying for his murder."

23-24 Joseph had been using an interpreter, so they didn't know that Joseph was understanding every word. Joseph turned away from them and cried. When he was able to speak again, he took Simeon and had him tied up, making a prisoner of him while they all watched.

25 Then Joseph ordered that their sacks be filled with grain, that their money be put back in each sack, and that they be given rations for the road. That was all done for them.

26 They loaded their food supplies on their donkeys and set off.

27-28 When they stopped for the night, one of them opened his sack to get food for his donkey; there at the mouth of his bag was his money. He called out to his brothers, "My money has been returned; it's right here in my bag!" They were puzzled—and frightened. "What's God doing to us?"

29-32 When they got back to their father Jacob, back in the land of Canaan, they told him everything that had happened, saying, "The man who runs the country spoke to us roughly and accused us of being spies. We told him, 'We are honest men and in no way spies. There were twelve of us brothers, sons of one father; one is gone and the youngest is with our father in Canaan.'

33-34 "But the master of the country said, 'Leave one of your brothers with me, take food for your starving families, and go. Bring your youngest brother back to me, proving that you're honest men and not spies. And then I'll give your brother back to you and you'll be free to come and go in this country.'"

35 As they were emptying their food sacks, each man came on his purse of money. On seeing their money, they and their father were upset.

36 Their father said to them, "You're taking everything I've got! Joseph's gone, Simeon's gone, and now you want to take Benjamin. If you have your way, I'll be left with nothing."

37 Reuben spoke up: "I'll put my two sons in your hands as hostages. If I don't bring Benjamin back, you can kill them. Trust me with Benjamin; I'll bring him back."

38 But Jacob refused. "My son will not go down with you. His brother is dead and he is all I have left. If something bad happens to him on the road, you'll put my gray, sorrowing head in the grave."

1-2 **43** The famine got worse. When they had eaten all the food they had brought back from Egypt, their father said, "Go back and get some more food."

3-5 But Judah said, "The man warned us most emphatically, 'You won't so much as see my face if you don't have your brother with you.' If you're ready to release our brother to go with us, we'll go down and get you food. But if you're not ready, we aren't going. What would be the use? The man told us, 'You won't so much as see my face if you don't have your brother with you.'"

6 Israel said, "Why are you making my life so difficult! Why did you ever tell the man you had another brother?"

7 They said, "The man pressed us hard, asking pointed questions about our family: 'Is your father alive? Do you have another brother?' So we answered his questions. How did we know that he'd say, 'Bring your brother here'?"

8-10 Judah pushed his father Israel. "Let the boy go; I'll take charge of him. Let us go and be on our way—if we don't get going, we're all going to starve to death—we and you and our children, too! I'll take full responsibility for his safety; it's my life on the line for his. If I don't bring him back safe and sound, I'm the guilty one; I'll take all the blame. If we had gone ahead in the first place instead of procrastinating like this, we could have been there and back twice over."

11-14 Their father Israel gave in. "If it has to be, it has to be. But do this: stuff your packs with the finest products from the land you can find and take them to the man as gifts—some balm and honey, some spices and perfumes, some pistachios and almonds. And take plenty of money—pay back double what was returned to your sacks; that might have been a mistake. Take your brother and get going. Go back to the man. And may The Strong God give you grace in that man's eyes so that he'll send back your other brother along with Benjamin. For me, nothing's left; I've lost everything."

15-16 The men took the gifts, double the money, and Benjamin. They lost no time in getting to Egypt and meeting Joseph. When Joseph saw that they had Benjamin with them, he told his house steward, "Take these men into the house and make them at home. Butcher an animal and prepare a meal; these men are going to eat with me at noon."

17-18 The steward did what Joseph had said and took them inside. But they became anxious when they were brought into Joseph's home, thinking, "It's the money; he thinks we ran off with the money on our first trip down here. And now he's got us where he wants us—he's going to turn us into slaves and confiscate our donkeys."

19-22 So they went up to Joseph's house steward and talked to him in the doorway. They said, "Listen, master. We came down here one other time to buy food. On our way home, the first night out we opened our bags and found our money at the mouth of the bag—the exact amount we'd paid. We've brought it all back and have plenty more to buy more food with. We have no idea who put the money in our bags."

23 The steward said, "Everything's in order. Don't worry. Your God and the God of your father must have given you a bonus. I was paid in full." And with that, he presented Simeon to them.

24-25 He then took them inside Joseph's house and made them comfortable—gave them water to wash their feet and saw to the feeding of their donkeys. The brothers spread out their gifts as they waited for Joseph to show up at noon—they had been told that they were to have dinner with him.

26 When Joseph got home, they presented him with the gifts they had brought and bowed respectfully before him.

27 Joseph welcomed them and said, "And your old father whom you mentioned to me, how is he? Is he still alive?"

28 They said, "Yes—your servant our father is quite well, very much alive." And they again bowed respectfully before him.

29 Then Joseph picked out his brother Benjamin, his own mother's son. He asked, "And is this your youngest brother that you told me about?" Then he said, "God be gracious to you, my son."

30-31 Deeply moved on seeing his brother and about to burst into tears, Joseph hurried out into another room and had a good cry. Then he washed his face, got a grip on himself, and said, "Let's eat."

32-34 Joseph was served at his private table, the brothers off by themselves and the Egyptians off by themselves (Egyptians won't eat at the same table with Hebrews; it's repulsive to them). The brothers were seated facing Joseph, arranged in order of their age, from the oldest to the youngest. They looked at one another wide-eyed, wondering what would happen next. When the brothers' plates were served from Joseph's table, Benjamin's plate came piled high, far more so than his brothers. And so the brothers feasted with Joseph, drinking freely.

1-2 44 Joseph ordered his house steward: "Fill the men's bags with food—all they can carry—and replace each one's money at the top of the bag. Then put my chalice, my silver chalice, in the top of the bag of the youngest, along with the money for his food." He did as Joseph ordered.

3-5 At break of day the men were sent off with their donkeys. They were barely out of the city when Joseph said to his house steward, "Run after them. When you catch up with them, say, 'Why did you pay me back evil for good? This is the chalice my master drinks from; he also uses it for divination. This is outrageous!'"

6 He caught up with them and repeated all this word for word.

7-9 They said, "What is my master talking about? We would never do anything like that! Why, the money we found in our bags earlier, we brought back all the way from Canaan—do you think we'd turn right around and steal it back from your master? If that chalice is found on any of us, he'll die; and the rest of us will be your master's slaves."

10 The steward said, "Very well then, but we won't go that far. Whoever is found with the chalice will be my slave; the rest of you can go free."

11-12 They outdid each other in putting their bags on the ground and opening them up for inspection. The steward searched their bags, going from oldest to youngest. The chalice showed up in Benjamin's bag.

13 They ripped their clothes in despair, loaded up their donkeys, and went back to the city.

14 Joseph was still at home when Judah and his brothers got back. They threw themselves down on the ground in front of him.

15 Joseph accused them: "How can you have done this? You have to know that a man in my position would have discovered this."

16 Judah as spokesman for the brothers said, "What can we say, master? What *is* there to say? How can we prove our innocence? God is behind this, exposing how bad we are. We stand guilty before you and ready to be your slaves — we're all in this together, the rest of us as guilty as the one with the chalice."

17 "I'd never do that to you," said Joseph. "Only the one involved with the chalice will be my slave. The rest of you are free to go back to your father."

18-20 Judah came forward. He said, "Please, master; can I say just one thing to you? Don't get angry. Don't think I'm presumptuous — you're the same as Pharaoh as far as I'm concerned. You, master, asked us, 'Do you have a father and a brother?' And we answered honestly, 'We have a father who is old and a younger brother who was born to him in his old age. His brother is dead and he is the only son left from that mother. And his father loves him more than anything.'

21-22 "Then you told us, 'Bring him down here so I can see him.' We told you, master, that it was impossible: 'The boy can't leave his father; if he leaves, his father will die.'

23 "And then you said, 'If your youngest brother doesn't come with you, you won't be allowed to see me.'

24-26 "When we returned to our father, we told him everything you said to us. So when our father said, 'Go back and buy some more food,' we told him flatly, 'We can't. The only way we can go back is if our youngest brother is with us. We aren't allowed to even see the man if our youngest brother doesn't come with us.'

27-29 "Your servant, my father, told us, 'You know very well that my wife gave me two sons. One turned up missing. I concluded that he'd been ripped to pieces. I've never seen him since. If you now go and take this one and something bad happens to him, you'll put my old gray, grieving head in the grave for sure.'

30-32 "And now, can't you see that if I show up before your servant, my father, without the boy, this son with whom his life is so bound up, the moment he realizes the boy is gone, he'll die on the spot. He'll die of grief and we, your servants who are standing here before you, will have killed him. And that's not all. I got my father to release the boy to show him to you by promising, 'If I don't bring him back, I'll stand condemned before you, Father, all my life.'

33-34 "So let me stay here as your slave, not this boy. Let the boy go back with his brothers. How can I go back to my father if the boy is not with me? Oh, don't make me go back and watch my father die in grief!"

1-2 **45** Joseph couldn't hold himself in any longer, keeping up a front before all his attendants. He cried out, "Leave! Clear out — everyone leave!" So there was no one with Joseph when he identified himself to his brothers. But his sobbing was so violent that the Egyptians couldn't help but hear him. The news was soon reported to Pharaoh's palace.

3 Joseph spoke to his brothers: "I am Joseph. Is my father really still alive?" But his brothers couldn't say a word. They were speechless — they couldn't believe what they were hearing and seeing.

4-8 "Come closer to me," Joseph said to his brothers. They came closer. "I am Joseph your brother whom you sold into Egypt. But don't feel badly, don't blame yourselves for selling me. God was behind it. God sent me here ahead of you to save lives. There has been a famine in the land now for two years; the famine will continue for five more years — neither plowing nor harvesting. God sent me on ahead to pave the way and make sure there was a remnant in the land, to save your lives in an amazing act of deliverance. So you see, it wasn't you who sent me here but God. He set me in place as a father to Pharaoh, put me in charge of his personal affairs, and made me ruler of all Egypt.

9-11 "Hurry back to my father. Tell him, 'Your son Joseph says: I'm master of all of Egypt. Come as fast as you can and join me here. I'll give you a place to live in Goshen where you'll be close to me — you, your children, your grandchildren, your flocks, your herds, and anything else you can think of. I'll take care of you there completely. There are still five more years of famine ahead; I'll make sure all your needs are taken care of, you and everyone connected with you — you won't want for a thing.'

12-13 "Look at me. You can see for yourselves, and my brother Benjamin can see for himself, that it's me, my own mouth, telling you all this. Tell my father all about the high position I hold in Egypt, tell him everything you've seen here, but don't take all day — hurry up and get my father down here."

14-15 Then Joseph threw himself on his brother Benjamin's neck and wept, and Benjamin wept on his neck. He then kissed all his brothers and wept over them. Only then were his brothers able to talk with him.

16 The story was reported in Pharaoh's palace: "Joseph's brothers have come." It was good news to Pharaoh and all who worked with him.

17-18 Pharaoh said to Joseph, "Tell your brothers, 'This is the plan: Load up your pack animals; go to Canaan, get your father and your families and bring them back here. I'll settle you on the best land in Egypt — you'll live off the fat of the land.'

19-20 "Also tell them this: 'Here's what I want you to do: Take wagons from Egypt to carry your little ones and your wives and load up your father and come back. Don't worry about having to leave things behind; the best in all of Egypt will be yours.'"

21-23 And they did just that, the sons of Israel. Joseph gave them the wagons that Pharaoh had promised and food for the trip. He outfitted all the brothers in brand-new clothes, but he gave Benjamin three hundred pieces of silver and several suits of clothes. He sent his father these gifts: ten donkeys loaded with Egypt's best products and another ten donkeys loaded with grain and bread, provisions for his father's journey back.

24 Then he sent his brothers off. As they left he told them, "Take it easy on the journey; try to get along with each other."

25-28 They left Egypt and went back to their father Jacob in Canaan. When they told him, "Joseph is still alive — and he's the ruler over the whole land of Egypt!" he went numb; he couldn't believe his ears. But the more they talked, telling him everything that Joseph had told them and when he saw the wagons that Joseph had sent to carry him back, the blood started to flow again — their father Jacob's spirit revived. Israel said, "I've heard enough — my son Joseph is still alive. I've got to go and see him before I die."

※

1 **46** So Israel set out on the journey with everything he owned. He arrived at Beersheba and worshiped, offering sacrifices to the God of his father Isaac.

2 God spoke to Israel in a vision that night: "Jacob! Jacob!"

"Yes?" he said. "I'm listening."

3-4 God said, "I am the God of your father. Don't be afraid of going down to Egypt. I'm going to make you a great nation there. I'll go with you down to Egypt; I'll also bring you back here. And when you die, Joseph will be with you; with his own hand he'll close your eyes."

5-7 Then Jacob left Beersheba. Israel's sons loaded their father and their little ones and their wives on the wagons Pharaoh had sent to carry him. They arrived in Egypt with the livestock and the wealth they had accumulated in Canaan. Jacob brought everyone in his family with him — sons and grandsons, daughters and granddaughters. Everyone.

8 These are the names of the Israelites, Jacob and his descendants, who went to Egypt:

Reuben, Jacob's firstborn.

9 Reuben's sons: Hanoch, Pallu, Hezron, and Carmi.

10 Simeon's sons: Jemuel, Jamin, Ohad, Jakin, Zohar, and Shaul the son of a Canaanite woman.

11 Levi's sons: Gershon, Kohath, and Merari.

12 Judah's sons: Er, Onan, Shelah, Perez, and Zerah (Er and Onan had already died in the land of Canaan). The sons of Perez were Hezron and Hamul.

13 Issachar's sons: Tola, Puah, Jashub, and Shimron.

14 Zebulun's sons: Sered, Elon, and Jahleel.

15 These are the sons that Leah bore to Jacob in Paddan Aram. There was also his daughter Dinah. Altogether, sons and daughters, they numbered thirty-three.

16 Gad's sons: Zephon, Haggi, Shuni, Ezbon, Eri, Arodi, and Areli.

17 Asher's sons: Imnah, Ishvah, Ishvi, and Beriah. Also their sister Serah, and Beriah's sons, Heber and Malkiel.

18 These are the children that Zilpah, the maid that Laban gave to his daughter Leah, bore to Jacob — sixteen of them.

19-21 The sons of Jacob's wife Rachel were Joseph and Benjamin. Joseph was the father of two sons, Manasseh and Ephraim, from his marriage to Asenath daughter of Potiphera, priest of On. They were born to him in Egypt. Benjamin's sons were Bela, Beker, Ashbel, Gera, Naaman, Ehi, Rosh, Muppim, Huppim, and Ard.

22 These are the children born to Jacob through Rachel — fourteen.

23 Dan's son: Hushim.

24 Naphtali's sons: Jahziel, Guni, Jezer, and Shillem.

25 These are the children born to Jacob through Bilhah, the maid Laban had given to his daughter Rachel — seven.

26-27 Summing up, all those who went down to Egypt with Jacob — his own children, not counting his sons' wives — numbered sixty-six. Counting in the two sons born to Joseph in Egypt, the members of Jacob's family who ended up in Egypt numbered seventy.

28-29 Jacob sent Judah on ahead to get directions to Goshen from Joseph. When they got to Goshen, Joseph gave orders for his chariot and went to Goshen to meet his father Israel. The moment Joseph saw him, he threw himself on his neck and wept. He wept a long time.

30 Israel said to Joseph, "I'm ready to die. I've looked into your face—you are indeed alive."

31-34 Joseph then spoke to his brothers and his father's family. "I'll go and tell Pharaoh, 'My brothers and my father's family, all of whom lived in Canaan, have come to me. The men are shepherds; they've always made their living by raising livestock. And they've brought their flocks and herds with them, along with everything else they own.' When Pharaoh calls you in and asks what kind of work you do, tell him, 'Your servants have always kept livestock for as long as we can remember—we and our parents also.' That way he'll let you stay apart in the area of Goshen—for Egyptians look down on anyone who is a shepherd."

1 **47** Joseph went to Pharaoh and told him, "My father and brothers with their flocks and herds and everything they own have come from Canaan. Right now they are in Goshen."

2-3 He had taken five of his brothers with him and introduced them to Pharaoh. Pharaoh asked them, "What kind of work do you do?"

3-4 "Your servants are shepherds, the same as our fathers were. We have come to this country to find a new place to live. There is no pasture for our flocks in Canaan. The famine has been very bad there. Please, would you let your servants settle in the region of Goshen?"

5-6 Pharaoh looked at Joseph. "So, your father and brothers have arrived—a reunion! Egypt welcomes them. Settle your father and brothers on the choicest land—yes, give them Goshen. And if you know any among them that are especially good at their work, put them in charge of my own livestock."

7-8 Next Joseph brought his father Jacob in and introduced him to Pharaoh. Jacob blessed Pharaoh. Pharaoh asked Jacob, "How old are you?"

9-10 Jacob answered Pharaoh, "The years of my sojourning are 130—a short and hard life and not nearly as long as my ancestors were given." Then Jacob blessed Pharaoh and left.

11-12 Joseph settled his father and brothers in Egypt, made them proud owners of choice land—it was the region of Rameses (that is, Goshen)—just as Pharaoh had ordered. Joseph took good care of them—his father and brothers and all his father's family, right down to the smallest baby. He made sure they had plenty of everything.

13-15 The time eventually came when there was no food anywhere. The famine was very bad. Egypt and Canaan alike were devastated by the famine. Joseph collected all the money that was to be found in Egypt and Canaan to pay for the distribution of food. He banked the money in Pharaoh's palace. When the money from Egypt and Canaan had run out, the Egyptians came to Joseph. "Food! Give us food! Are you going to watch us die right in front of you? The money is all gone."

16-17 Joseph said, "Bring your livestock. I'll trade you food for livestock since your money's run out." So they brought Joseph their livestock. He traded them food for their horses, sheep, cattle, and donkeys. He got them through that year in exchange for all their livestock.

18-19   When that year was over, the next year rolled around and they were back, saying, "Master, it's no secret to you that we're broke: our money's gone and we've traded you all our livestock. We've nothing left to barter with but our bodies and our farms. What use are our bodies and our land if we stand here and starve to death right in front of you? Trade us food for our bodies and our land. We'll be slaves to Pharaoh and give up our land — all we ask is seed for survival, just enough to live on and keep the farms alive."

20-21   So Joseph bought up all the farms in Egypt for Pharaoh. Every Egyptian sold his land — the famine was that bad. That's how Pharaoh ended up owning all the land and the people ended up slaves; Joseph reduced the people to slavery from one end of Egypt to the other.

22   Joseph made an exception for the priests. He didn't buy their land because they received a fixed salary from Pharaoh and were able to live off of that salary. So they didn't need to sell their land.

23-24   Joseph then announced to the people: "Here's how things stand: I've bought you and your land for Pharaoh. In exchange I'm giving you seed so you can plant the ground. When the crops are harvested, you must give a fifth to Pharaoh and keep four-fifths for yourselves, for seed for yourselves and your families — you're going to be able to feed your children!"

25   They said, "You've saved our lives! Master, we're grateful and glad to be slaves to Pharaoh."

26   Joseph decreed a land law in Egypt that is still in effect, *A Fifth Goes to Pharaoh*. Only the priests' lands were not owned by Pharaoh.

※

27-28   And so Israel settled down in Egypt in the region of Goshen. They acquired property and flourished. They became a large company of people. Jacob lived in Egypt for seventeen years. In all, he lived 147 years.

29-30   When the time came for Israel to die, he called his son Joseph and said, "Do me this favor. Put your hand under my thigh, a sign that you're loyal and true to me to the end. Don't bury me in Egypt. When I lie down with my fathers, carry me out of Egypt and bury me alongside them."

"I will," he said. "I'll do what you've asked."

31   Israel said, "Promise me." Joseph promised.

Israel bowed his head in submission and gratitude from his bed.

1-2   **48** Some time after this conversation, Joseph was told, "Your father is ill." He took his two sons, Manasseh and Ephraim, and went to Jacob. When Jacob was told, "Your son Joseph has come," he roused himself and sat up in bed.

3-7   Jacob said to Joseph, "The Strong God appeared to me at Luz in the land of Canaan and blessed me. He said, 'I'm going to make you prosperous and numerous, turn you into a congregation of tribes; and I'll turn this land over to your children coming after you as a permanent inheritance.' I'm adopting your two sons who were born to you here in Egypt before I joined you; they have equal status with Reuben and Simeon. But any children born after them are yours; they will come after their brothers in matters of inheritance. I want it this way because, as I was returning from Paddan, your mother Rachel, to my deep sorrow, died as we were on our way through Canaan when we were only a short distance from Ephrath, now called Bethlehem."

8 Just then Jacob noticed Joseph's sons and said, "Who are these?"

9-11 Joseph told his father, "They are my sons whom God gave to me in this place."

"Bring them to me," he said, "so I can bless them." Israel's eyesight was poor from old age; he was nearly blind. So Joseph brought them up close. Old Israel kissed and embraced them and then said to Joseph, "I never expected to see your face again, and now God has let me see your children as well!"

12-16 Joseph took them from Israel's knees and bowed respectfully, his face to the ground. Then Joseph took the two boys, Ephraim with his right hand setting him to Israel's left, and Manasseh with his left hand setting him to Israel's right, and stood them before him. But Israel crossed his arms and put his right hand on the head of Ephraim who was the younger and his left hand on the head of Manasseh, the firstborn. Then he blessed them:

> The God before whom walked
> my fathers Abraham and Isaac,
> The God who has been my shepherd
> all my life long to this very day,
> The Angel who delivered me from every evil,
> Bless the boys.
> May my name be echoed in their lives,
> and the names of Abraham and Isaac, my fathers,
> And may they grow
> covering the Earth with their children.

17-18 When Joseph saw that his father had placed his right hand on Ephraim's head, he thought he had made a mistake, so he took hold of his father's hand to move it from Ephraim's head to Manasseh's, saying, "That's the wrong head, Father; the other one is the firstborn; place your right hand on his head."

19-20 But his father wouldn't do it. He said, "I know, my son; but I know what I'm doing. He also will develop into a people, and he also will be great. But his younger brother will be even greater and his descendants will enrich nations." Then he blessed them both:

> Israel will use your names to give blessings:
> May God make you like Ephraim and Manasseh.

In that he made it explicit: he put Ephraim ahead of Manasseh.

21-22 Israel then said to Joseph, "I'm about to die. God be with you and give you safe passage back to the land of your fathers. As for me, I'm presenting you, as the first among your brothers, the ridge of land I took from Amorites with my sword and bow."

1 **49** Jacob called his sons and said, "Gather around. I want to tell you what you can expect in the days to come."

2 Come together, listen sons of Jacob,
> listen to Israel your father.

3-4
Reuben, you're my firstborn,
   my strength, first proof of my manhood,
   at the top in honor and at the top in power,
But like a bucket of water spilled,
   you'll be at the top no more,
Because you climbed into your father's marriage bed,
   mounting that couch, and you defiled it.

5-6
Simeon and Levi are two of a kind,
   ready to fight at the drop of a hat.
I don't want anything to do with their vendettas,
   want no part in their bitter feuds;
They kill men in fits of temper,
   slash oxen on a whim.
7
A curse on their uncontrolled anger,
   on their indiscriminate wrath.
I'll throw them out with the trash;
   I'll shred and scatter them like confetti throughout Israel.

8-12
You, Judah, your brothers will praise you:
   Your fingers on your enemies' throat,
   while your brothers honor you.
You're a lion's cub, Judah,
   home fresh from the kill, my son.
Look at him, crouched like a lion, king of beasts;
   who dares mess with him?
The scepter shall not leave Judah;
   he'll keep a firm grip on the command staff
Until the ultimate ruler comes
   and the nations obey him.
He'll tie up his donkey to the grapevine,
   his purebred prize to a sturdy branch.
He will wash his shirt in wine
   and his cloak in the blood of grapes,
His eyes will be darker than wine,
   his teeth whiter than milk.

13
Zebulun settles down on the seashore;
   he's a safe harbor for ships,
   right alongside Sidon.

14-15
Issachar is one tough donkey
   crouching between the corrals;
When he saw how good the place was,
   how pleasant the country,
He gave up his freedom
   and went to work as a slave.

16-17
Dan will handle matters of justice for his people;
   he will hold his own just fine among the tribes of Israel.
Dan is only a small snake in the grass,

a lethal serpent in ambush by the road
When he strikes a horse in the heel,
and brings its huge rider crashing down.

18   I wait in hope
for your salvation, GOD.

19   Gad will be attacked by bandits,
but he will trip them up.

20   Asher will become famous for rich foods,
candies and sweets fit for kings.

21-26   Naphtali is a deer running free
that gives birth to lovely fawns.

Joseph is a wild donkey,
a wild donkey by a spring,
spirited donkeys on a hill.
The archers with malice attacked,
shooting their hate-tipped arrows;
But he held steady under fire,
his bow firm, his arms limber,
With the backing of the Champion of Jacob,
the Shepherd, the Rock of Israel.
The God of your father—may he help you!
And may The Strong God—may he give you his blessings,
Blessings tumbling out of the skies,
blessings bursting up from the Earth—
blessings of breasts and womb.
May the blessings of your father
exceed the blessings of the ancient mountains,
surpass the delights of the eternal hills;
May they rest on the head of Joseph,
on the brow of the one consecrated among his brothers.

27   Benjamin is a ravenous wolf;
all morning he gorges on his kill,
at evening divides up what's left over.

28   All these are the tribes of Israel, the twelve tribes. And this is what their
father said to them as he blessed them, blessing each one with his own special
farewell blessing.

29-32   Then he instructed them: "I am about to be gathered to my people. Bury me
with my fathers in the cave which is in the field of Ephron the Hittite, the
cave in the field of Machpelah facing Mamre in the land of Canaan, the field
Abraham bought from Ephron the Hittite for a burial plot. Abraham and his
wife Sarah were buried there; Isaac and his wife Rebekah were buried there; I
also buried Leah there. The field and the cave were bought from the Hittites."

33   Jacob finished instructing his sons, pulled his feet into bed, breathed his last, and was gathered to his people.

1   5O Joseph threw himself on his father, wept over him, and kissed him.

2-3   Joseph then instructed the physicians in his employ to embalm his father. The physicians embalmed Israel. The embalming took forty days, the period required for embalming. There was public mourning by the Egyptians for seventy days.

4-5   When the period of mourning was completed, Joseph petitioned Pharaoh's court: "If you have reason to think kindly of me, present Pharaoh with my request: My father made me swear, saying, 'I am ready to die. Bury me in the grave plot that I prepared for myself in the land of Canaan.' Please give me leave to go up and bury my father. Then I'll come back."

6   Pharaoh said, "Certainly. Go and bury your father as he made you promise under oath."

7-9   So Joseph left to bury his father. And all the high-ranking officials from Pharaoh's court went with him, all the dignitaries of Egypt, joining Joseph's family—his brothers and his father's family. Their children and flocks and herds were left in Goshen. Chariots and horsemen accompanied them. It was a huge funeral procession.

10   Arriving at the Atad Threshing Floor just across the Jordan River, they stopped for a period of mourning, letting their grief out in loud and lengthy lament. For seven days, Joseph engaged in these funeral rites for his father.

11   When the Canaanites who lived in that area saw the grief being poured out at the Atad Threshing Floor, they said, "Look how deeply the Egyptians are mourning." That is how the site at the Jordan got the name Abel Mizraim (Egyptian Lament).

12-13   Jacob's sons continued to carry out his instructions to the letter. They took him on into Canaan and buried him in the cave in the field of Machpelah facing Mamre, the field that Abraham had bought as a burial plot from Ephron the Hittite.

14-15   After burying his father, Joseph went back to Egypt. All his brothers who had come with him to bury his father returned with him. After the funeral, Joseph's brothers talked among themselves: "What if Joseph is carrying a grudge and decides to pay us back for all the wrong we did him?"

16-17   So they sent Joseph a message, "Before his death, your father gave this command: Tell Joseph, 'Forgive your brothers' sin—all that wrongdoing. They did treat you very badly.' Will you do it? Will you forgive the sins of the servants of your father's God?"

When Joseph received their message, he wept.

18   Then the brothers went in person to him, threw themselves on the ground before him and said, "We'll be your slaves."

19-21   Joseph replied, "Don't be afraid. Do I act for God? Don't you see, you planned evil against me but God used those same plans for my good, as you see all around you right now—life for many people. Easy now, you have nothing to fear; I'll take care of you and your children." He reassured them, speaking with them heart-to-heart.

22-23 Joseph continued to live in Egypt with his father's family. Joseph lived 110 years. He lived to see Ephraim's sons into the third generation. The sons of Makir, Manasseh's son, were also recognized as Joseph's.

24 At the end, Joseph said to his brothers, "I am ready to die. God will most certainly pay you a visit and take you out of this land and back to the land he so solemnly promised to Abraham, Isaac, and Jacob."

25 Then Joseph made the sons of Israel promise under oath, "When God makes his visitation, make sure you take my bones with you as you leave here."

26 Joseph died at the age of 110 years. They embalmed him and placed him in a coffin in Egypt.

EXODUS

The human race is in trouble. We've been in trouble for a long time. Enormous energies have been and continue to be expended by many, many men and women to get us out of the trouble we are in—to clean up the world's mess. The skill, the perseverance, the intelligence, the devotion of the people who put their shoulders to the wheel to pull us out of the muck—parents and teachers, healers and counselors, rulers and politicians, writers and pastors—are impressive.

At the center and core of this work is God. The most comprehensive term for what God is doing to get us out of the mess we are in is *salvation*. Salvation is God doing for us what we can't do for ourselves. Salvation is the biggest word in the vocabulary of the people of God. The Exodus is a powerful and dramatic and true story of God working salvation. The story has generated an extraordinary progeny through the centuries as it has reproduced itself in song and poem, drama and novel, politics and social justice, repentance and conversion, worship and holy living. It continues to capture the imagination of men and women, especially men and women in trouble.

It is significant that God does not present us with salvation in the form of an abstract truth, or a precise definition or a catchy slogan, but as *story*. Exodus draws us into a story with plot and characters, which is to say, with design and personal relationships. Story is an invitation to participate, first through our imagination and then, if we will, by faith—with our total lives in response to God. This Exodus story continues to be a major means that God uses to draw men and women in trouble out of the mess of history into the kingdom of salvation.

About half the book (chapters 1–19 and 32–34) is a gripping narrative of an obscure and severely brutalized people who are saved from slavery into a life of freedom. The other half (chapters 20–31 and 35–40) is a meticulous, some think tedious, basic instruction and training in living the saved, free life. The story of salvation is not complete without both halves.

EXODUS

1-5 **1** These are the names of the Israelites who went to Egypt with Jacob, each bringing his family members:
Reuben, Simeon, Levi, and Judah,
Issachar, Zebulun, and Benjamin,
Dan and Naphtali, Gad and Asher.

Seventy persons in all generated by Jacob's seed. Joseph was already in Egypt.

6-7 Then Joseph died, and all his brothers—that whole generation. But the children of Israel kept on reproducing. They were very prolific — a population explosion in their own right— and the land was filled with them.

"A New King . . . Who Didn't Know Joseph"

8-10 A new king came to power in Egypt who didn't know Joseph. He spoke to his people in alarm, "There are way too many of these Israelites for us to handle. We've got to do something: Let's devise a plan to contain them, lest if there's a war they should join our enemies, or just walk off and leave us."

11-14 So they organized them into work-gangs and put them to hard labor under gang-foremen. They built the storage cities Pithom and Rameses for Pharaoh. But the harder the Egyptians worked them the more children the Israelites had—children everywhere! The Egyptians got so they couldn't stand the Israelites and treated them worse than ever, crushing them with slave labor. They made them miserable with hard labor—making bricks and mortar and back-breaking work in the fields. They piled on the work, crushing them under the cruel workload.

15-16 The king of Egypt had a talk with the two Hebrew midwives; one was named Shiphrah and the other Puah. He said, "When you deliver the Hebrew women, look at the sex of the baby. If it's a boy, kill him; if it's a girl, let her live."

17-18 But the midwives had far too much respect for God and didn't do what the king of Egypt ordered; they let the boy babies live. The king of Egypt called in the midwives. "Why didn't you obey my orders? You've let those babies live!"

19 The midwives answered Pharaoh, "The Hebrew women aren't like the Egyptian women; they're vigorous. Before the midwife can get there, they've already had the baby."

20-21 God was pleased with the midwives. The people continued to increase in number—a very strong people. And because the midwives honored God, God gave them families of their own.

22 So Pharaoh issued a general order to all his people: "Every boy that is born, drown him in the Nile. But let the girls live."

Moses

1-3 **2** A man from the family of Levi married a Levite woman. The woman became pregnant and had a son. She saw there was something special about him and hid him. She hid him for three months. When she couldn't hide him any longer she got a little basket-boat made of papyrus, waterproofed it with tar and pitch, and placed the child in it. Then she set it afloat in the reeds at the edge of the Nile.

4-6   The baby's older sister found herself a vantage point a little way off and watched to see what would happen to him. Pharaoh's daughter came down to the Nile to bathe; her maidens strolled on the bank. She saw the basket-boat floating in the reeds and sent her maid to get it. She opened it and saw the child—a baby crying! Her heart went out to him. She said, "This must be one of the Hebrew babies."

7   Then his sister was before her: "Do you want me to go and get a nursing mother from the Hebrews so she can nurse the baby for you?"

8   Pharaoh's daughter said, "Yes. Go." The girl went and called the child's mother.

9   Pharaoh's daughter told her, "Take this baby and nurse him for me. I'll pay you." The woman took the child and nursed him.

10   After the child was weaned, she presented him to Pharaoh's daughter who adopted him as her son. She named him Moses (Pulled-Out), saying, "I pulled him out of the water."

11-12   Time passed. Moses grew up. One day he went and saw his brothers, saw all that hard labor. Then he saw an Egyptian hit a Hebrew—one of his relatives! He looked this way and then that; when he realized there was no one in sight, he killed the Egyptian and buried him in the sand.

13   The next day he went out there again. Two Hebrew men were fighting. He spoke to the man who started it: "Why are you hitting your neighbor?"

14   The man shot back: "Who do you think you are, telling us what to do? Are you going to kill me the way you killed that Egyptian?"

Then Moses panicked: "Word's gotten out—people know about this."

15   Pharaoh heard about it and tried to kill Moses, but Moses got away to the land of Midian. He sat down by a well.

16-17   The priest of Midian had seven daughters. They came and drew water, filling the troughs and watering their father's sheep. When some shepherds came and chased the girls off, Moses came to their rescue and helped them water their sheep.

18   When they got home to their father, Reuel, he said, "That didn't take long. Why are you back so soon?"

19   "An Egyptian," they said, "rescued us from a bunch of shepherds. Why, he even drew water for us and watered the sheep."

20   He said, "So where is he? Why did you leave him behind? Invite him so he can have something to eat with us."

21-22   Moses agreed to settle down there with the man, who then gave his daughter Zipporah (Bird) to him for his wife. She had a son, and Moses named him Gershom (Sojourner), saying, "I'm a sojourner in a foreign country."

23   Many years later the king of Egypt died. The Israelites groaned under their slavery and cried out. Their cries for relief from their hard labor ascended to God:

24   God listened to their groanings.

God remembered his covenant with Abraham, with Isaac, and with Jacob.

25   God saw what was going on with Israel.

God understood.

3 Moses was shepherding the flock of Jethro, his father-in-law, the priest of Midian. He led the flock to the west end of the wilderness and came to the mountain of God, Horeb. The angel of GOD appeared to him in flames of fire blazing out of the middle of a bush. He looked. The bush was blazing away but it didn't burn up.

Moses said, "What's going on here? I can't believe this! Amazing! Why doesn't the bush burn up?"

GOD saw that he had stopped to look. God called to him from out of the bush, "Moses! Moses!"

He said, "Yes? I'm right here!"

God said, "Don't come any closer. Remove your sandals from your feet. You're standing on holy ground."

Then he said, "I am the God of your father: The God of Abraham, the God of Isaac, the God of Jacob."

Moses hid his face, afraid to look at God.

GOD said, "I've taken a good, long look at the affliction of my people in Egypt. I've heard their cries for deliverance from their slave masters; I know all about their pain. And now I have come down to help them, pry them loose from the grip of Egypt, get them out of that country and bring them to a good land with wide-open spaces, a land lush with milk and honey, the land of the Canaanite, the Hittite, the Amorite, the Perizzite, the Hivite, and the Jebusite.

"The Israelite cry for help has come to me, and I've seen for myself how cruelly they're being treated by the Egyptians. It's time for you to go back: I'm sending you to Pharaoh to bring my people, the People of Israel, out of Egypt."

Moses answered God, "But why me? What makes you think that I could ever go to Pharaoh and lead the children of Israel out of Egypt?"

"I'll be with you," God said. "And this will be the proof that I am the one who sent you: When you have brought my people out of Egypt, you will worship God right here at this very mountain."

Then Moses said to God, "Suppose I go to the People of Israel and I tell them, 'The God of your fathers sent me to you'; and they ask me, 'What is his name?' What do I tell them?"

God said to Moses, "I-AM-WHO-I-AM. Tell the People of Israel, 'I-AM sent me to you.'"

God continued with Moses: "This is what you're to say to the Israelites: 'GOD, the God of your fathers, the God of Abraham, the God of Isaac, and the God of Jacob sent me to you.' This has always been my name, and this is how I always will be known.

"Now be on your way. Gather the leaders of Israel. Tell them, 'GOD, the God of your fathers, the God of Abraham, Isaac, and Jacob, appeared to me, saying, "I've looked into what's being done to you in Egypt, and I've determined to get you out of the affliction of Egypt and take you to the land of the Canaanite, the Hittite, the Amorite, the Perizzite, the Hivite, and the Jebusite, a land brimming over with milk and honey."'

"Believe me, they will listen to you. Then you and the leaders of Israel will go to the king of Egypt and say to him: 'GOD, the God of the Hebrews, has met with us. Let us take a three-day journey into the wilderness where we will worship GOD — *our* God.'

19-22   "I know that the king of Egypt won't let you go unless forced to, so I'll intervene and hit Egypt where it hurts — oh, my miracles will send them reeling! — after which they'll be glad to send you off. I'll see to it that this people get a hearty send-off by the Egyptians — when you leave, you won't leave empty-handed! Each woman will ask her neighbor and any guests in her house for objects of silver and gold, for jewelry and extra clothes; you'll put them on your sons and daughters. Oh, you'll clean the Egyptians out!"

1   4 Moses objected, "They won't trust me. They won't listen to a word I say. They're going to say, 'GOD? Appear to him? Hardly!'"

2   So GOD said, "What's that in your hand?"

"A staff."

3   "Throw it on the ground." He threw it. It became a snake; Moses jumped back — fast!

4-5   GOD said to Moses, "Reach out and grab it by the tail." He reached out and grabbed it — and he was holding his staff again. "That's so they will trust that GOD appeared to you, the God of their fathers, the God of Abraham, the God of Isaac, and the God of Jacob."

6   GOD then said, "Put your hand inside your shirt." He slipped his hand under his shirt, then took it out. His hand had turned leprous, like snow.

7   He said, "Put your hand back under your shirt." He did it, then took it back out — as healthy as before.

8-9   "So if they don't trust you and aren't convinced by the first sign, the second sign should do it. But if it doesn't, if even after these two signs they don't trust you and listen to your message, take some water out of the Nile and pour it out on the dry land; the Nile water that you pour out will turn to blood when it hits the ground."

10   Moses raised another objection to GOD: "Master, please, I don't talk well. I've never been good with words, neither before nor after you spoke to me. I stutter and stammer."

11-12   GOD said, "And who do you think made the human mouth? And who makes some mute, some deaf, some sighted, some blind? Isn't it I, GOD? So, get going. I'll be right there with you — with your mouth! I'll be right there to teach you what to say."

13   He said, "Oh, Master, please! Send somebody else!"

14-17   GOD got angry with Moses: "Don't you have a brother, Aaron the Levite? He's good with words, I know he is. He speaks very well. In fact, at this very moment he's on his way to meet you. When he sees you he's going to be glad. You'll speak to him and tell him what to say. I'll be right there with you as you speak and with him as he speaks, teaching you step by step. He will speak to the people for you. He'll act as your mouth, but you'll decide what comes out of it. Now take this staff in your hand; you'll use it to do the signs."

18   Moses went back to Jethro his father-in-law and said, "I need to return to my relatives who are in Egypt. I want to see if they're still alive."

Jethro said, "Go. And peace be with you."

19   GOD said to Moses in Midian: "Go. Return to Egypt. All the men who wanted to kill you are dead."

20 So Moses took his wife and sons and put them on a donkey for the return trip to Egypt. He had a firm grip on the staff of God.

21-23 GOD said to Moses, "When you get back to Egypt, be prepared: All the wonders that I will do through you, you'll do before Pharaoh. But I will make him stubborn so that he will refuse to let the people go. Then you are to tell Pharaoh, 'GOD's Message: Israel is my son, my firstborn! I told you, "Free my son so that he can serve me." But you refused to free him. So now I'm going to kill *your* son, *your* firstborn.'"

24-26 On the journey back, as they camped for the night, GOD met Moses and would have killed him but Zipporah took a flint knife and cut off her son's foreskin, and touched Moses' member with it. She said, "Oh! You're a bridegroom of blood to me!" Then GOD let him go. She used the phrase "bridegroom of blood" because of the circumcision.

27-28 GOD spoke to Aaron, "Go and meet Moses in the wilderness." He went and met him at the mountain of God and kissed him. Moses told Aaron the message that GOD had sent him to speak and the wonders he had commanded him to do.

29-31 So Moses and Aaron proceeded to round up all the leaders of Israel. Aaron told them everything that GOD had told Moses and demonstrated the wonders before the people. And the people trusted and listened believingly that GOD was concerned with what was going on with the Israelites and knew all about their affliction. They bowed low and they worshiped.

MOSES AND AARON AND PHARAOH

1 **5** After that Moses and Aaron approached Pharaoh. They said, "GOD, the God of Israel, says, 'Free my people so that they can hold a festival for me in the wilderness.'"

2 Pharaoh said, "And who is GOD that I should listen to him and send Israel off? I know nothing of this so-called 'GOD' and I'm certainly not going to send Israel off."

3 They said, "The God of the Hebrews has met with us. Let us take a three-day journey into the wilderness so we can worship our GOD lest he strike us with either disease or death."

4-5 But the king of Egypt said, "Why on earth, Moses and Aaron, would you suggest the people be given a holiday? Back to work!" Pharaoh went on, "Look, I've got all these people bumming around, and now you want to reward them with time off?"

6-9 Pharaoh took immediate action. He sent down orders to the slave-drivers and their underlings: "Don't provide straw for the people for making bricks as you have been doing. Make them get their own straw. And make them produce the same number of bricks — no reduction in their daily quotas! They're getting lazy. They're going around saying, 'Give us time off so we can worship our God.' Crack down on them. That'll cure them of their whining, their god-fantasies."

10-12 The slave-drivers and their underlings went out to the people with their new instructions. "Pharaoh's orders: No more straw provided. Get your own straw wherever you can find it. And not one brick less in your daily work quota!" The people scattered all over Egypt scrabbling for straw.

13 The slave-drivers were merciless, saying, "Complete your daily quota of bricks—the same number as when you were given straw."

14 The Israelite foremen whom the slave-drivers had appointed were beaten and badgered. "Why didn't you finish your quota of bricks yesterday or the day before—and now again today?"

15-16 The Israelite foremen came to Pharaoh and cried out for relief: "Why are you treating your servants like this? Nobody gives us any straw and they tell us, 'Make bricks!' Look at us—we're being beaten. And it's not our fault."

17-18 But Pharaoh said, "Lazy! That's what you are! Lazy! That's why you whine, 'Let us go so we can worship GOD.' Well then, go—go back to work. Nobody's going to give you straw, and at the end of the day you better bring in your full quota of bricks."

19 The Israelite foremen saw that they were in a bad way, having to go back and tell their workers, "Not one brick short in your daily quota."

20-21 As they left Pharaoh, they found Moses and Aaron waiting to meet them. The foremen said to them, "May GOD see what you've done and judge you—you've made us stink before Pharaoh and his servants! You've put a weapon in his hand that's going to kill us!"

22-23 Moses went back to GOD and said, "My Master, why are you treating this people so badly? And why did you ever send me? From the moment I came to Pharaoh to speak in your name, things have only gotten worse for this people. And rescue? Does this look like rescue to you?"

1 6 GOD said to Moses, "Now you'll see what I'll do to Pharaoh: With a strong hand he'll send them out free; with a strong hand he'll drive them out of his land."

2-6 God continued speaking to Moses, reassuring him, "I am GOD. I appeared to Abraham, Isaac, and Jacob as The Strong God, but by my name GOD (I-Am-Present) I was not known to them. I also established my covenant with them to give them the land of Canaan, the country in which they lived as sojourners. But now I've heard the groanings of the Israelites whom the Egyptians continue to enslave and I've remembered my covenant. Therefore tell the Israelites:

6-8 "I am GOD. I will bring you out from under the cruel hard labor of Egypt. I will rescue you from slavery. I will redeem you, intervening with great acts of judgment. I'll take you as my own people and I'll be God to you. You'll know that I am GOD, *your* God who brings you out from under the cruel hard labor of Egypt. I'll bring you into the land that I promised to give Abraham, Isaac, and Jacob and give it to you as your own country. *I AM GOD.*"

9 But when Moses delivered this message to the Israelites, they didn't even hear him—they were that beaten down in spirit by the harsh slave conditions.

10-11 Then GOD said to Moses, "Go and speak to Pharaoh king of Egypt so that he will release the Israelites from his land."

12 Moses answered GOD, "Look—the Israelites won't even listen to me. How do you expect Pharaoh to? And besides, I stutter."

13 But GOD again laid out the facts to Moses and Aaron regarding the Israelites and Pharaoh king of Egypt, and he again commanded them to lead the Israelites out of the land of Egypt.

THE FAMILY TREE OF MOSES AND AARON

14 These are the heads of the tribes:

The sons of Reuben, Israel's firstborn: Hanoch, Pallu, Hezron, and Carmi — these are the families of Reuben.

15 The sons of Simeon: Jemuel, Jamin, Ohad, Jakin, Zohar, and Saul, the son of a Canaanite woman — these are the families of Simeon.

16 These are the names of the sons of Levi in the order of their birth: Gershon, Kohath, and Merari. Levi lived 137 years.

17 The sons of Gershon by family: Libni and Shimei.

18 The sons of Kohath: Amram, Izhar, Hebron, and Uzziel. Kohath lived to be 133.

19 The sons of Merari: Mahli and Mushi.

These are the sons of Levi in the order of their birth.

20 Amram married his aunt Jochebed and she had Aaron and Moses. Amram lived to be 137.

21 The sons of Izhar: Korah, Nepheg, and Zicri.

22 The sons of Uzziel: Mishael, Elzaphan, and Sithri.

23 Aaron married Elisheba, the daughter of Amminadab and sister of Nahshon, and she had Nadab and Abihu, Eleazar and Ithamar.

24 The sons of Korah: Assir, Elkanah, and Abiasaph. These are the families of the Korahites.

25 Aaron's son Eleazar married one of the daughters of Putiel and she had Phinehas.

These are the heads of the Levite families, family by family.

26-27 This is the Aaron and Moses whom GOD ordered: "Bring the Israelites out of the land of Egypt clan by clan." These are the men, Moses and Aaron, who told Pharaoh king of Egypt to release the Israelites from Egypt.

"I'LL MAKE YOU AS A GOD TO PHARAOH"

28 And that's how things stood when GOD next spoke to Moses in Egypt.

29 God addressed Moses, saying, "I am GOD. Tell Pharaoh king of Egypt everything I say to you."

30 And Moses answered, "Look at me. I stutter. Why would Pharaoh listen to me?"

1-5 God told Moses, "Look at me. I'll make you as a god to Pharaoh and your brother Aaron will be your prophet. You are to speak everything I command you, and your brother Aaron will tell it to Pharaoh. Then he will release the Israelites from his land. At the same time I am going to put Pharaoh's back up and follow it up by filling Egypt with signs and wonders. Pharaoh is not going to listen to you, but I will have my way against Egypt and bring out my soldiers, my people the Israelites, from Egypt by mighty acts of judgment. The Egyptians will realize that I am GOD when I step in and take the Israelites out of their country."

6-7 Moses and Aaron did exactly what GOD commanded. Moses was eighty and Aaron eighty-three when they spoke to Pharaoh.

8-9 Then GOD spoke to Moses and Aaron. He said, "When Pharaoh speaks to you and says, 'Prove yourselves. Perform a miracle,' then tell Aaron, 'Take your staff and throw it down in front of Pharaoh: It will turn into a snake.'"

10 Moses and Aaron went to Pharaoh and did what GOD commanded. Aaron threw his staff down in front of Pharaoh and his servants, and it turned into a snake.

11-12 Pharaoh called in his wise men and sorcerers. The magicians of Egypt did the same thing by their incantations: each man threw down his staff and they all turned into snakes. But then Aaron's staff swallowed their staffs.

13 Yet Pharaoh was as stubborn as ever — he wouldn't listen to them, just as GOD had said.

STRIKE ONE: BLOOD

14-18 GOD said to Moses: "Pharaoh is a stubborn man. He refuses to release the people. First thing in the morning, go and meet Pharaoh as he goes down to the river. At the shore of the Nile take the staff that turned into a snake and say to him, 'GOD, the God of the Hebrews, sent me to you with this message, "Release my people so that they can worship me in the wilderness." So far you haven't listened. This is how you'll know that I am GOD. I am going to take this staff that I'm holding and strike this Nile River water: The water will turn to blood; the fish in the Nile will die; the Nile will stink; and the Egyptians won't be able to drink the Nile water.'"

19 GOD said to Moses, "Tell Aaron, 'Take your staff and wave it over the waters of Egypt — over its rivers, its canals, its ponds, all its bodies of water — so that they turn to blood.' There'll be blood everywhere in Egypt — even in the pots and pans."

20-21 Moses and Aaron did exactly as GOD commanded them. Aaron raised his staff and hit the water in the Nile with Pharaoh and his servants watching. All the water in the Nile turned into blood. The fish in the Nile died; the Nile stank; and the Egyptians couldn't drink the Nile water. The blood was everywhere in Egypt.

22-25 But the magicians of Egypt did the same thing with their incantations. Still Pharaoh remained stubborn. He wouldn't listen to them as GOD had said. He turned on his heel and went home, never giving it a second thought. But all the Egyptians had to dig inland from the river for water because they couldn't drink the Nile water.

Seven days went by after GOD had struck the Nile.

STRIKE TWO: FROGS

1-4 **8** GOD said to Moses, "Go to Pharaoh and tell him, 'GOD's Message: Release my people so they can worship me. If you refuse to release them, I'm warning you, I'll hit the whole country with frogs. The Nile will swarm with frogs — they'll come up into your houses, into your bedrooms and into your beds, into your servants' quarters, among the people, into your ovens and pots and pans. They'll be all over you, all over everyone — frogs everywhere, on and in everything!'"

5 GOD said to Moses, "Tell Aaron, 'Wave your staff over the rivers and canals and ponds. Bring up frogs on the land of Egypt.'"

6 Aaron stretched his staff over the waters of Egypt and a mob of frogs came up and covered the country.

7 But again the magicians did the same thing using their incantations —

they also produced frogs in Egypt.

8   Pharaoh called in Moses and Aaron and said, "Pray to GOD to rid us of these frogs. I'll release the people so that they can make their sacrifices and worship GOD."

9   Moses said to Pharaoh, "Certainly. Set the time. When do you want the frogs out of here, away from your servants and people and out of your houses? You'll be rid of frogs except for those in the Nile."

10-11   "Make it tomorrow."

Moses said, "Tomorrow it is — so you'll realize that there is no God like our GOD. The frogs will be gone. You and your houses and your servants and your people, free of frogs. The only frogs left will be the ones in the Nile."

12-14   Moses and Aaron left Pharaoh, and Moses prayed to GOD about the frogs he had brought on Pharaoh. GOD responded to Moses' prayer: The frogs died off — houses, courtyards, fields, all free of frogs. They piled the frogs in heaps. The country reeked of dead frogs.

15   But when Pharaoh saw that he had some breathing room, he got stubborn again and wouldn't listen to Moses and Aaron. Just as GOD had said.

STRIKE THREE: GNATS

16   GOD said to Moses, "Tell Aaron, 'Take your staff and strike the dust. The dust will turn into gnats all over Egypt.'"

17   He did it. Aaron grabbed his staff and struck the dust of the Earth; it turned into gnats, gnats all over people and animals. All the dust of the Earth turned into gnats, gnats everywhere in Egypt.

18   The magicians tried to produce gnats with their incantations but this time they couldn't do it. There were gnats everywhere, all over people and animals.

19   The magicians said to Pharaoh, "This is God's doing." But Pharaoh was stubborn and wouldn't listen. Just as GOD had said.

STRIKE FOUR: FLIES

20-23   GOD said to Moses, "Get up early in the morning and confront Pharaoh as he goes down to the water. Tell him, 'GOD's Message: Release my people so they can worship me. If you don't release my people, I'll release swarms of flies on you, your servants, your people, and your homes. The houses of the Egyptians and even the ground under their feet will be thick with flies. But when it happens, I'll set Goshen where my people live aside as a sanctuary — no flies in Goshen. That will show you that I am GOD in this land. I'll make a sharp distinction between your people and mine. This sign will occur tomorrow.'"

24   And GOD did just that. Thick swarms of flies in Pharaoh's palace and the houses of his servants. All over Egypt, the country ruined by flies.

25   Pharaoh called in Moses and Aaron and said, "Go ahead. Sacrifice to your God — but do it here in this country."

26-27   Moses said, "That would not be wise. What we sacrifice to our GOD would give great offense to Egyptians. If we openly sacrifice what is so deeply offensive to Egyptians, they'll kill us. Let us go three days' journey into the wilderness and sacrifice to our GOD, just as he instructed us."

28   Pharaoh said, "All right. I'll release you to go and sacrifice to your GOD in the wilderness. Only don't go too far. Now pray for me."

29   Moses said, "As soon as I leave here, I will pray to GOD that tomorrow the flies will leave Pharaoh, his servants, and his people. But don't play games with us and change your mind about releasing us to sacrifice to GOD."

30-32   Moses left Pharaoh and prayed to GOD. GOD did what Moses asked. He got rid of the flies from Pharaoh and his servants and his people. There wasn't a fly left. But Pharaoh became stubborn once again and wouldn't release the people.

STRIKE FIVE: ANIMALS

1-4   **9** GOD said to Moses, "Go to Pharaoh and tell him, 'GOD, the God of the Hebrews, says: Release my people so they can worship me. If you refuse to release them and continue to hold on to them, I'm giving you fair warning: GOD will come down hard on your livestock out in the fields—horses, donkeys, camels, cattle, sheep—striking them with a severe disease. GOD will draw a sharp line between the livestock of Israel and the livestock of Egypt. Not one animal that belongs to the Israelites will die.'"

5   Then GOD set the time: "Tomorrow GOD will do this thing."

6-7   And the next day GOD did it. All the livestock of Egypt died, but not one animal of the Israelites died. Pharaoh sent men to find out what had happened and there it was: none of the livestock of the Israelites had died—not one death. But Pharaoh stayed stubborn. He wouldn't release the people.

STRIKE SIX: BOILS

8-11   GOD said to Moses and Aaron, "Take fistfuls of soot from a furnace and have Moses throw it into the air right before Pharaoh's eyes; it will become a film of fine dust all over Egypt and cause sores, an eruption of boils on people and animals throughout Egypt." So they took soot from a furnace, stood in front of Pharaoh, and threw it up into the air. It caused boils to erupt on people and animals. The magicians weren't able to compete with Moses this time because of the boils—they were covered with boils just like everyone else in Egypt.

12   GOD hardened Pharaoh in his stubbornness. He wouldn't listen, just as GOD had said to Moses.

STRIKE SEVEN: HAIL

13-19   GOD said to Moses, "Get up early in the morning and confront Pharaoh. Tell him, 'GOD, the God of the Hebrews, says: Release my people so they can worship me. This time I am going to strike you and your servants and your people with the full force of my power so you'll get it into your head that there's no one like me anywhere in all the Earth. You know that by now I could have struck you and your people with deadly disease and there would be nothing left of you, not a trace. But for one reason only I've kept you on your feet: To make you recognize my power so that my reputation spreads in all the Earth. You are still building yourself up at my people's expense. You are not letting them go. So here's what's going to happen: At this time tomorrow I'm sending a terrific hailstorm—there's never been a storm like this in Egypt from the day of its founding until now. So get your livestock under roof—everything exposed in the open fields, people and animals, will die when the hail comes down.'"

20-21   All of Pharaoh's servants who had respect for GOD's word got their workers and animals under cover as fast as they could, but those who didn't take God's word seriously left their workers and animals out in the field.

22   God said to Moses: "Stretch your hands to the skies. Signal the hail to fall all over Egypt on people and animals and crops exposed in the fields of Egypt."

23-26   Moses lifted his staff to the skies and God sent peals of thunder and hail shot through with lightning strikes. God rained hail down on the land of Egypt. The hail came, hail and lightning—a fierce hailstorm. There had been nothing like it in Egypt in its entire history. The hail hit hard all over Egypt. Everything exposed out in the fields, people and animals and crops, was smashed. Even the trees in the fields were shattered. Except for Goshen where the Israelites lived; there was no hail in Goshen.

27-28   Pharaoh summoned Moses and Aaron. He said, "I've sinned for sure this time—God is in the right and I and my people are in the wrong. Pray to God. We've had enough of God's thunder and hail. I'll let you go. The sooner you're out of here the better."

29-30   Moses said, "As soon as I'm out of the city, I'll stretch out my arms to God. The thunder will stop and the hail end so you'll know that the land is God's land. Still, I know that you and your servants have no respect for God."

31-32   (The flax and the barley were ruined, for they were just ripening, but the wheat and spelt weren't hurt—they ripen later.)

33   Moses left Pharaoh and the city and stretched out his arms to God. The thunder and hail stopped; the storm cleared.

34-35   But when Pharaoh saw that the rain and hail and thunder had stopped, he kept right on sinning, stubborn as ever, both he and his servants. Pharaoh's heart turned rock-hard. He refused to release the Israelites, as God had ordered through Moses.

STRIKE EIGHT: LOCUSTS

1-2   **10** God said to Moses: "Go to Pharaoh. I've made him stubborn, him and his servants, so that I can force him to look at these signs and so you'll be able to tell your children and grand-children how I toyed with the Egyptians, like a cat with a mouse; you'll tell them the stories of the signs that I brought down on them, so that you'll all know that I am God."

3-6   Moses and Aaron went to Pharaoh and said to him, "God, the God of the Hebrews, says, 'How long are you going to refuse to knuckle under? Release my people so that they can worship me. If you refuse to release my people, watch out; tomorrow I'm bringing locusts into your country. They'll cover every square inch of ground; no one will be able to see the ground. They'll devour everything left over from the hailstorm, even the saplings out in the fields—they'll clear-cut the trees. And they'll invade your houses, filling the houses of your servants, filling every house in Egypt. Nobody will have ever seen anything like this, from the time your ancestors first set foot on this soil until today.'"

    Then he turned on his heel and left Pharaoh.

7   Pharaoh's servants said to him, "How long are you going to let this man harass us? Let these people go and worship their God. Can't you see that Egypt is on its last legs?"

8   So Moses and Aaron were brought back to Pharaoh. He said to them,

"Go ahead then. Go worship your GOD. But just who exactly is going with you?"

9 Moses said, "We're taking young and old, sons and daughters, flocks and herds — this is our worship-celebration of GOD."

10-11 He said, "I'd sooner send you off with GOD's blessings than let you go with your children. Look, you're up to no good — it's written all over your faces. Nothing doing. Just the men are going — go ahead and worship GOD. That's what you want so badly." And they were thrown out of Pharaoh's presence.

12 GOD said to Moses: "Stretch your hand over Egypt and signal the locusts to cover the land of Egypt, devouring every blade of grass in the country, everything that the hail didn't get."

13 Moses stretched out his staff over the land of Egypt. GOD let loose an east wind. It blew that day and night. By morning the east wind had brought in the locusts.

14-15 The locusts covered the country of Egypt, settling over every square inch of Egypt; the place was thick with locusts. There never was an invasion of locusts like it in the past, and never will be again. The ground was completely covered, black with locusts. They ate everything, every blade of grass, every piece of fruit, anything that the hail didn't get. Nothing left but bare trees and bare fields — not a sign of green in the whole land of Egypt.

16-17 Pharaoh had Moses and Aaron back in no time. He said, "I've sinned against your GOD and against you. Overlook my sin one more time. Pray to your GOD to get me out of this — get death out of here!"

18-19 Moses left Pharaoh and prayed to GOD. GOD reversed the wind — a powerful west wind took the locusts and dumped them into the Red Sea. There wasn't a single locust left in the whole country of Egypt.

20 But GOD made Pharaoh stubborn as ever. He still didn't release the Israelites.

STRIKE NINE: DARKNESS

21 GOD said to Moses: "Stretch your hand to the skies. Let darkness descend on the land of Egypt — a darkness so dark you can touch it."

22-23 Moses stretched out his hand to the skies. Thick darkness descended on the land of Egypt for three days. Nobody could see anybody. For three days no one could so much as move. Except for the Israelites: they had light where they were living.

24 Pharaoh called in Moses: "Go and worship GOD. Leave your flocks and herds behind. But go ahead and take your children."

25-26 But Moses said, "You have to let us take our sacrificial animals and offerings with us so we can sacrifice them in worship to our GOD. Our livestock has to go with us with not a hoof left behind; they are part of the worship of our GOD. And we don't know just what will be needed until we get there."

27 But GOD kept Pharaoh stubborn as ever. He wouldn't agree to release them.

28 Pharaoh said to Moses: "Get out of my sight! And watch your step. I don't want to ever see you again. If I lay eyes on you again, you're dead."

29 Moses said, "Have it your way. You won't see my face again."

STRIKE TEN: DEATH

11 GOD said to Moses: "I'm going to hit Pharaoh and Egypt one final time, and then he'll let you go. When he releases you, that will be the end of Egypt for you; he won't be able to get rid of you fast enough.

"So here's what you do. Tell the people to ask, each man from his neighbor and each woman from her neighbor, for things made of silver and gold." GOD saw to it that the Egyptians liked the people. Also, Moses was greatly admired by the Egyptians, a respected public figure among both Pharaoh's servants and the people at large.

Then Moses confronted Pharaoh: "GOD's Message: 'At midnight I will go through Egypt and every firstborn child in Egypt will die, from the firstborn of Pharaoh, who sits on his throne, to the firstborn of the slave girl working at her hand mill. Also the firstborn of animals. Widespread wailing will erupt all over the country, lament such as has never been and never will be again. But against the Israelites—man, woman, or animal—there won't be so much as a dog's bark, so that you'll know that GOD makes a clear distinction between Egypt and Israel.'

"Then all these servants of yours will go to their knees, begging me to leave, 'Leave! You and all the people who follow you!' And I will most certainly leave."

Moses, seething with anger, left Pharaoh.

GOD said to Moses, "Pharaoh's not going to listen to a thing you say so that the signs of my presence and work are going to multiply in the land of Egypt."

Moses and Aaron had performed all these signs in Pharaoh's presence, but GOD turned Pharaoh more stubborn than ever—yet again he refused to release the Israelites from his land.

12 GOD said to Moses and Aaron while still in Egypt, "This month is to be the first month of the year for you. Address the whole community of Israel; tell them that on the tenth of this month each man is to take a lamb for his family, one lamb to a house. If the family is too small for a lamb, then share it with a close neighbor, depending on the number of persons involved. Be mindful of how much each person will eat. Your lamb must be a healthy male, one year old; you can select it from either the sheep or the goats. Keep it penned until the fourteenth day of this month and then slaughter it—the entire community of Israel will do this—at dusk. Then take some of the blood and smear it on the two doorposts and the lintel of the houses in which you will eat it. You are to eat the meat, roasted in the fire, that night, along with bread, made without yeast, and bitter herbs. Don't eat any of it raw or boiled in water; make sure it's roasted—the whole animal, head, legs, and innards. Don't leave any of it until morning; if there are leftovers, burn them in the fire.

"And here is how you are to eat it: Be fully dressed with your sandals on and your stick in your hand. Eat in a hurry; it's the Passover to GOD.

"I will go through the land of Egypt on this night and strike down every firstborn in the land of Egypt, whether human or animal, and bring judgment on all the gods of Egypt. I am GOD. The blood will serve as a sign on the houses where you live. When I see the blood I will pass over you—no disaster will touch you when I strike the land of Egypt.

14-16   "This will be a memorial day for you; you will celebrate it as a festival to GOD down through the generations, a fixed festival celebration to be observed always. You will eat unraised bread (matzoth) for seven days: On the first day get rid of all yeast from your houses—anyone who eats anything with yeast from the first day to the seventh day will be cut off from Israel. The first and the seventh days are set aside as holy; do no work on those days. Only what you have to do for meals; each person can do that.

17-20   "Keep the Festival of Unraised Bread! This marks the exact day I brought you out in force from the land of Egypt. Honor the day down through your generations, a fixed festival to be observed always. In the first month, beginning on the fourteenth day at evening until the twenty-first day at evening, you are to eat unraised bread. For those seven days not a trace of yeast is to be found in your houses. Anyone, whether a visitor or a native of the land, who eats anything raised shall be cut off from the community of Israel. Don't eat anything raised. Only matzoth."

21-23   Moses assembled all the elders of Israel. He said, "Select a lamb for your families and slaughter the Passover lamb. Take a bunch of hyssop and dip it in the bowl of blood and smear it on the lintel and on the two doorposts. No one is to leave the house until morning. GOD will pass through to strike Egypt down. When he sees the blood on the lintel and the two doorposts, GOD will pass over the doorway; he won't let the destroyer enter your house to strike you down with ruin.

24-27   "Keep this word. It's the law for you and your children, forever. When you enter the land which GOD will give you as he promised, keep doing this. And when your children say to you, 'Why are we doing this?' tell them: 'It's the Passover-sacrifice to GOD who passed over the homes of the Israelites in Egypt when he hit Egypt with death but rescued us.'"

The people bowed and worshiped.

28   The Israelites then went and did what GOD had commanded Moses and Aaron. They did it all.

29   At midnight GOD struck every firstborn in the land of Egypt, from the firstborn of Pharaoh, who sits on his throne, right down to the firstborn of the prisoner locked up in jail. Also the firstborn of the animals.

30   Pharaoh got up that night, he and all his servants and everyone else in Egypt—what wild wailing and lament in Egypt! There wasn't a house in which someone wasn't dead.

31-32   Pharaoh called in Moses and Aaron that very night and said, "Get out of here and be done with you—you and your Israelites! Go worship GOD on your own terms. And yes, take your sheep and cattle as you've insisted, but go. And bless me."

33   The Egyptians couldn't wait to get rid of them; they pushed them to hurry up, saying, "We're all as good as dead."

34-36   The people grabbed their bread dough before it had risen, bundled their bread bowls in their cloaks and threw them over their shoulders. The Israelites had already done what Moses had told them; they had asked the Egyptians for silver and gold things and clothing. GOD saw to it that the Egyptians liked the people and so readily gave them what they asked for. Oh yes! They picked those Egyptians clean.

37-39   The Israelites moved on from Rameses to Succoth, about 600,000 on foot, besides their dependents. There was also a crowd of riffraff tagging along, not to mention the large flocks and herds of livestock. They baked unraised cakes with the bread dough they had brought out of Egypt; it hadn't raised — they'd been rushed out of Egypt and hadn't time to fix food for the journey.

THE PASSOVER

40-42 The Israelites had lived in Egypt 430 years. At the end of the 430 years, to the very day, GOD's entire army left Egypt. GOD kept watch all night, watching over the Israelites as he brought them out of Egypt. Because GOD kept watch, all Israel for all generations will honor GOD by keeping watch this night — a watchnight.

43-47 GOD said to Moses and Aaron, "These are the rules for the Passover:
No foreigners are to eat it.
Any slave, if he's paid for and circumcised, can eat it.
No casual visitor or hired hand can eat it.
Eat it in one house — don't take the meat outside the house.
Don't break any of the bones.
The whole community of Israel is to be included in the meal.

48 "If an immigrant is staying with you and wants to keep the Passover to GOD, every male in his family must be circumcised, then he can participate in the Meal — he will then be treated as a native son. But no uncircumcised person can eat it.

49 "The same law applies both to the native and the immigrant who is staying with you."

50-51 All the Israelites did exactly as GOD commanded Moses and Aaron. That very day GOD brought the Israelites out of the land of Egypt, tribe by tribe.

1-2 **13** GOD spoke to Moses, saying, "Consecrate every firstborn to me — the first one to come from the womb among the Israelites, whether person or animal, is mine."

3 Moses said to the people, "Always remember this day. This is the day when you came out of Egypt from a house of slavery. GOD brought you out of here with a powerful hand. Don't eat any raised bread.

4-5 "You are leaving in the spring month of Abib. When GOD brings you into the land of the Canaanite, the Hittite, the Amorite, the Hivite, and the Jebusite, which he promised to your fathers to give you, a land lavish with milk and honey, you are to observe this service during this month:

6 "You are to eat unraised bread for seven days; on the seventh day there is a festival celebration to GOD.

7 "Only unraised bread is to be eaten for seven days. There is not to be a trace of anything fermented — no yeast anywhere.

8 "Tell your child on that day: 'This is because of what GOD did for me when I came out of Egypt.'

9-10   "The day of observance will be like a sign on your hand, a memorial between your eyes, and the teaching of GOD in your mouth. It was with a powerful hand that GOD brought you out of Egypt. Follow these instructions at the set time, year after year after year.

11-13   "When GOD brings you into the land of the Canaanites, as he promised you and your fathers, and turns it over to you, you are to set aside the first birth out of every womb to GOD. Every first birth from your livestock belongs to GOD. You can redeem every first birth of a donkey if you want to by substituting a lamb; if you decide not to redeem it, you must break its neck.

13-16   "Redeem every firstborn child among your sons. When the time comes and your son asks you, 'What does this mean?' you tell him, 'GOD brought us out of Egypt, out of a house of slavery, with a powerful hand. When Pharaoh stubbornly refused to let us go, GOD killed every firstborn in Egypt, the firstborn of both humans and animals. That's why I make a sacrifice for every first male birth from the womb to GOD and redeem every firstborn son.' The observance functions like a sign on your hands or a symbol on the middle of your forehead: GOD brought us out of Egypt with a powerful hand."

17   It so happened that after Pharaoh released the people, God didn't lead them by the road through the land of the Philistines, which was the shortest route, for God thought, "If the people encounter war, they'll change their minds and go back to Egypt."

18   So God led the people on the wilderness road, looping around to the Red Sea. The Israelites left Egypt in military formation.

19   Moses took the bones of Joseph with him, for Joseph had made the Israelites solemnly swear to do it, saying, "God will surely hold you accountable, so make sure you bring my bones from here with you."

20-22   They moved on from Succoth and then camped at Etham at the edge of the wilderness. GOD went ahead of them in a Pillar of Cloud during the day to guide them on the way, and at night in a Pillar of Fire to give them light; thus they could travel both day and night. The Pillar of Cloud by day and the Pillar of Fire by night never left the people.

THE STORY AND SONG OF SALVATION

1-2   **14** GOD spoke to Moses: "Tell the Israelites to turn around and make camp at Pi Hahiroth, between Migdol and the sea. Camp on the shore of the sea opposite Baal Zephon.

3-4   "Pharaoh will think, 'The Israelites are lost; they're confused. The wilderness has closed in on them.' Then I'll make Pharaoh's heart stubborn again and he'll chase after them. And I'll use Pharaoh and his army to put my Glory on display. Then the Egyptians will realize that I am GOD."

And that's what happened.

5-7   When the king of Egypt was told that the people were gone, he and his servants changed their minds. They said, "What have we done, letting Israel, our slave labor, go free?" So he had his chariots harnessed up and got his army together. He took six hundred of his best chariots, with the rest of the Egyptian chariots and their drivers coming along.

8-9   GOD made Pharaoh king of Egypt stubborn, determined to chase the Israelites as they walked out on him without even looking back. The Egyptians gave chase and caught up with them where they had made camp by the sea — all Pharaoh's horse-drawn chariots and their riders, all his foot soldiers there at Pi Hahiroth opposite Baal Zephon.

10-12   As Pharaoh approached, the Israelites looked up and saw them — Egyptians! Coming at them!

They were totally afraid. They cried out in terror to GOD. They told Moses, "Weren't the cemeteries large enough in Egypt so that you had to take us out here in the wilderness to die? What have you done to us, taking us out of Egypt? Back in Egypt didn't we tell you this would happen? Didn't we tell you, 'Leave us alone here in Egypt — we're better off as slaves in Egypt than as corpses in the wilderness.'"

13   Moses spoke to the people: "Don't be afraid. Stand firm and watch GOD do his work of salvation for you today. Take a good look at the Egyptians today for you're never going to see them again.

14   GOD will fight the battle for you.
        And you? You keep your mouths shut!"

15-16   GOD said to Moses: "Why cry out to me? Speak to the Israelites. Order them to get moving. Hold your staff high and stretch your hand out over the sea: Split the sea! The Israelites will walk through the sea on dry ground.

17-18   "Meanwhile I'll make sure the Egyptians keep up their stubborn chase — I'll use Pharaoh and his entire army, his chariots and horsemen, to put my Glory on display so that the Egyptians will realize that I am GOD."

19-20   The angel of God that had been leading the camp of Israel now shifted and got behind them. And the Pillar of Cloud that had been in front also shifted to the rear. The Cloud was now between the camp of Egypt and the camp of Israel. The Cloud enshrouded one camp in darkness and flooded the other with light. The two camps didn't come near each other all night.

21   Then Moses stretched out his hand over the sea and GOD, with a terrific east wind all night long, made the sea go back. He made the sea dry ground. The seawaters split.

22-25   The Israelites walked through the sea on dry ground with the waters a wall to the right and to the left. The Egyptians came after them in full pursuit, every horse and chariot and driver of Pharaoh racing into the middle of the sea. It was now the morning watch. GOD looked down from the Pillar of Fire and Cloud on the Egyptian army and threw them into a panic. He clogged the wheels of their chariots; they were stuck in the mud.

The Egyptians said, "Run from Israel! GOD is fighting on their side and against Egypt!"

26   GOD said to Moses, "Stretch out your hand over the sea and the waters will come back over the Egyptians, over their chariots, over their horsemen."

27-28   Moses stretched his hand out over the sea: As the day broke and the Egyptians were running, the sea returned to its place as before. GOD dumped the Egyptians in the middle of the sea. The waters returned, drowning the chariots and riders of Pharaoh's army that had chased after Israel into the sea. Not one of them survived.

29-31   But the Israelites walked right through the middle of the sea on dry ground, the waters forming a wall to the right and to the left. GOD delivered Israel that day from the oppression of the Egyptians. And Israel looked at the Egyptian dead, washed up on the shore of the sea, and realized the tremendous power that GOD brought against the Egyptians. The people were in reverent awe before GOD and trusted in GOD and his servant Moses.

˚ゞ

15 Then Moses and the Israelites sang this song to GOD, giving voice together,

> I'm singing my heart out to GOD—what a victory!
>   He pitched horse and rider into the sea.
> GOD is my strength, GOD is my song,
>   and, yes! GOD is my salvation.
> *This* is the kind of God I have
>   and I'm telling the world!
> *This* is the God of my father—
>   I'm spreading the news far and wide!
> GOD is a fighter,
>   pure GOD, through and through.
> Pharaoh's chariots and army
>   he dumped in the sea,
> The elite of his officers
>   he drowned in the Red Sea.
> Wild ocean waters poured over them;
>   they sank like a rock in the deep blue sea.
> Your strong right hand, GOD, shimmers with power;
>   your strong right hand shatters the enemy.
> In your mighty majesty
>   you smash your upstart enemies,
> You let loose your hot anger
>   and burn them to a crisp.
> At a blast from your nostrils
>   the waters piled up;
> Tumbling streams dammed up,
>   wild oceans curdled into a swamp.

9

> The enemy spoke,
>   "I'll pursue, I'll hunt them down,
> I'll divide up the plunder,
>   I'll glut myself on them;
> I'll pull out my sword,
>   my fist will send them reeling."

10-11

> You blew with all your might
>   and the sea covered them.
> They sank like a lead weight
>   in the majestic waters.
> Who compares with you
>   among gods, O GOD?
> Who compares with you in power,
>   in holy majesty,
> In awesome praises,
>   wonder-working God?

12-13
> You stretched out your right hand
>   and the Earth swallowed them up.
> But the people you redeemed,
>   you led in merciful love;
> You guided them under your protection
>   to your holy pasture.

14-18
> When people heard, they were scared;
>   Philistines writhed and trembled;
> Yes, even the head men in Edom were shaken,
>   and the big bosses in Moab.
> Everybody in Canaan
>   panicked and fell faint.
> Dread and terror
>   sent them reeling.
> Before your brandished right arm
>   they were struck dumb like a stone,
> Until your people crossed over and entered, O GOD,
>   until the people you made crossed over and entered.
> You brought them and planted them
>   on the mountain of your heritage,
> The place where you live,
>   the place you made,
> Your sanctuary, Master,
>   that you established with your own hands.
> Let GOD rule
>   forever, for eternity!

19   Yes, Pharaoh's horses and chariots and riders went into the sea and GOD turned the waters back on them; but the Israelites walked on dry land right through the middle of the sea.

20-21   Miriam the prophetess, Aaron's sister, took a tambourine, and all the women followed her with tambourines, dancing. Miriam led them in singing,

> Sing to GOD—
>   what a victory!
> He pitched horse and rider
>   into the sea!

TRAVELING THROUGH THE WILDERNESS

22-24   Moses led Israel from the Red Sea on to the Wilderness of Shur. They traveled for three days through the wilderness without finding any water. They got to Marah, but they couldn't drink the water at Marah; it was bitter. That's why they called the place Marah (Bitter). And the people complained to Moses, "So what are we supposed to drink?"

25   So Moses cried out in prayer to GOD. GOD pointed him to a stick of wood. Moses threw it into the water and the water turned sweet.

26   That's the place where GOD set up rules and procedures; that's where he started testing them.

God said, "If you listen, listen obediently to how God tells you to live in his presence, obeying his commandments and keeping all his laws, then I won't strike you with all the diseases that I inflicted on the Egyptians; I am God your healer."

27 They came to Elim where there were twelve springs of water and seventy palm trees. They set up camp there by the water.

1-3 16 On the fifteenth day of the second month after they had left Egypt, the whole company of Israel moved on from Elim to the Wilderness of Sin which is between Elim and Sinai. The whole company of Israel complained against Moses and Aaron there in the wilderness. The Israelites said, "Why didn't God let us die in comfort in Egypt where we had lamb stew and all the bread we could eat? You've brought us out into this wilderness to starve us to death, the whole company of Israel!"

4-5 God said to Moses, "I'm going to rain bread down from the skies for you. The people will go out and gather each day's ration. I'm going to test them to see if they'll live according to my Teaching or not. On the sixth day, when they prepare what they have gathered, it will turn out to be twice as much as their daily ration."

6-7 Moses and Aaron told the People of Israel, "This evening you will know that it is God who brought you out of Egypt; and in the morning you will see the Glory of God. Yes, he's listened to your complaints against him. You haven't been complaining against us, you know, but against God."

8 Moses said, "Since it will be God who gives you meat for your meal in the evening and your fill of bread in the morning, it's God who will have listened to your complaints against him. Who are we in all this? You haven't been complaining to us—you've been complaining to God!"

9 Moses instructed Aaron: "Tell the whole company of Israel: 'Come near to God. He's heard your complaints.'"

10 When Aaron gave out the instructions to the whole company of Israel, they turned to face the wilderness. And there it was: the Glory of God visible in the Cloud.

11-12 God spoke to Moses, "I've listened to the complaints of the Israelites. Now tell them: 'At dusk you will eat meat and at dawn you'll eat your fill of bread; and you'll realize that I am God, *your* God.'"

13-15 That evening quail flew in and covered the camp and in the morning there was a layer of dew all over the camp. When the layer of dew had lifted, there on the wilderness ground was a fine flaky something, fine as frost on the ground. The Israelites took one look and said to one another, *man-hu* (What is it?). They had no idea what it was.

15-16 So Moses told them, "It's the bread God has given you to eat. And these are God's instructions: 'Gather enough for each person, about two quarts per person; gather enough for everyone in your tent.'"

17-18 The People of Israel went to work and started gathering, some more, some less, but when they measured out what they had gathered, those who gathered more had no extra and those who gathered less weren't short—each person had gathered as much as was needed.

19 Moses said to them, "Don't leave any of it until morning."

20 But they didn't listen to Moses. A few of the men kept back some of it until morning. It got wormy and smelled bad. And Moses lost his temper with them.

21-22 They gathered it every morning, each person according to need. Then the sun heated up and it melted. On the sixth day they gathered twice as much bread, about four quarts per person.

Then the leaders of the company came to Moses and reported.

23-24 Moses said, "This is what GOD was talking about: Tomorrow is a day of rest, a holy Sabbath to GOD. Whatever you plan to bake, bake today; and whatever you plan to boil, boil today. Then set aside the leftovers until morning." They set aside what was left until morning, as Moses had commanded. It didn't smell bad and there were no worms in it.

25-26 Moses said, "Now eat it; this is the day, a Sabbath for GOD. You won't find any of it on the ground today. Gather it every day for six days, but the seventh day is Sabbath; there won't be any of it on the ground."

27 On the seventh day, some of the people went out to gather anyway but they didn't find anything.

28-29 GOD said to Moses, "How long are you going to disobey my commands and not follow my instructions? Don't you see that GOD has given you the Sabbath? So on the sixth day he gives you bread for *two* days. So, each of you, stay home. Don't leave home on the seventh day."

30 So the people quit working on the seventh day.

31 The Israelites named it manna (What is it?). It looked like coriander seed, whitish. And it tasted like a cracker with honey.

32 Moses said, "This is GOD's command: 'Keep a two-quart jar of it, an omer, for future generations so they can see the bread that I fed you in the wilderness after I brought you out of Egypt.'"

33 Moses told Aaron, "Take a jar and fill it with two quarts of manna. Place it before GOD, keeping it safe for future generations."

34 Aaron did what GOD commanded Moses. He set it aside before The Testimony to preserve it.

35 The Israelites ate the manna for forty years until they arrived at the land where they would settle down. They ate manna until they reached the border into Canaan.

36 According to ancient measurements, an omer is one-tenth of an ephah.

1-2 **17** Directed by GOD, the whole company of Israel moved on by stages from the Wilderness of Sin. They set camp at Rephidim. And there wasn't a drop of water for the people to drink. The people took Moses to task: "Give us water to drink." But Moses said, "Why pester me? Why are you testing GOD?"

3 But the people were thirsty for water there. They complained to Moses, "Why did you take us from Egypt and drag us out here with our children and animals to die of thirst?"

4 Moses cried out in prayer to GOD, "What can I do with these people? Any minute now they'll kill me!"

5-6 GOD said to Moses, "Go on out ahead of the people, taking with you some of the elders of Israel. Take the staff you used to strike the Nile. And go. I'm going to be present before you there on the rock at Horeb. You are to strike the rock. Water will gush out of it and the people will drink."

6-7 Moses did what he said, with the elders of Israel right there watching. He named the place Massah (Testing-Place) and Meribah (Quarreling) because of the quarreling of the Israelites and because of their testing of GOD when they said, "Is GOD here with us, or not?"

8-9   Amalek came and fought Israel at Rephidim. Moses ordered Joshua: "Select some men for us and go out and fight Amalek. Tomorrow I will take my stand on top of the hill holding God's staff."

10-13   Joshua did what Moses ordered in order to fight Amalek. And Moses, Aaron, and Hur went to the top of the hill. It turned out that whenever Moses raised his hands, Israel was winning, but whenever he lowered his hands, Amalek was winning. But Moses' hands got tired. So they got a stone and set it under him. He sat on it and Aaron and Hur held up his hands, one on each side. So his hands remained steady until the sun went down. Joshua defeated Amalek and its army in battle.

14   GOD said to Moses, "Write this up as a reminder to Joshua, to keep it before him, because I will most certainly wipe the very memory of Amalek off the face of the Earth."

15-16   Moses built an altar and named it "GOD My Banner." He said,

Salute GOD's rule!
GOD at war with Amalek
Always and forever!

1-4   **18** Jethro, priest of Midian and father-in-law to Moses, heard the report of all that God had done for Moses and Israel his people, the news that GOD had delivered Israel from Egypt. Jethro, Moses' father-in-law, had taken in Zipporah, Moses' wife who had been sent back home, and her two sons. The name of the one was Gershom (Sojourner) for he had said, "I'm a sojourner in a foreign land"; the name of the other was Eliezer (God's-Help) because "The God of my father is my help and saved me from death by Pharaoh."

5-6   Jethro, Moses' father-in-law, brought Moses his sons and his wife there in the wilderness where he was camped at the mountain of God. He had sent a message ahead to Moses: "I, your father-in-law, am coming to you with your wife and two sons."

7-8   Moses went out to welcome his father-in-law. He bowed to him and kissed him. Each asked the other how things had been with him. Then they went into the tent. Moses told his father-in-law the story of all that GOD had done to Pharaoh and Egypt in helping Israel, all the trouble they had experienced on the journey, and how GOD had delivered them.

9-11   Jethro was delighted in all the good that GOD had done for Israel in delivering them from Egyptian oppression. Jethro said, "Blessed be GOD who has delivered you from the power of Egypt and Pharaoh, who has delivered his people from the oppression of Egypt. Now I know that GOD is greater than all gods because he's done this to all those who treated Israel arrogantly."

12   Jethro, Moses' father-in-law, brought a Whole-Burnt-Offering and sacrifices to God. And Aaron, along with all the elders of Israel, came and ate the meal with Moses' father-in-law in the presence of God.

13-14   The next day Moses took his place to judge the people. People were standing before him all day long, from morning to night. When Moses' father-in-law saw all that he was doing for the people, he said, "What's going on here? Why are you doing all this, and all by yourself, letting everybody line up before you from morning to night?"

15-16 Moses said to his father-in-law, "Because the people come to me with questions about God. When something comes up, they come to me. I judge between a man and his neighbor and teach them God's laws and instructions."

17-23 Moses' father-in-law said, "This is no way to go about it. You'll burn out, and the people right along with you. This is way too much for you—you can't do this alone. Now listen to me. Let me tell you how to do this so that God will be in this with you. Be there for the people before God, but let the matters of concern be presented to God. Your job is to teach them the rules and instructions, to show them how to live, what to do. And then you need to keep a sharp eye out for competent men—men who fear God, men of integrity, men who are incorruptible—and appoint them as leaders over groups organized by the thousand, by the hundred, by fifty, and by ten. They'll be responsible for the everyday work of judging among the people. They'll bring the hard cases to you, but in the routine cases they'll be the judges. They will share your load and that will make it easier for you. If you handle the work this way, you'll have the strength to carry out whatever God commands you, and the people in their settings will flourish also."

24-27 Moses listened to the counsel of his father-in-law and did everything he said. Moses picked competent men from all Israel and set them as leaders over the people who were organized by the thousand, by the hundred, by fifty, and by ten. They took over the everyday work of judging among the people. They brought the hard cases to Moses, but in the routine cases they were the judges. Then Moses said good-bye to his father-in-law who went home to his own country.

MOUNT SINAI

1-2 **19** Three months after leaving Egypt the Israelites entered the Wilderness of Sinai. They followed the route from Rephidim, arrived at the Wilderness of Sinai, and set up camp. Israel camped there facing the mountain.

3-6 As Moses went up to meet God, GOD called down to him from the mountain: "Speak to the House of Jacob, tell the People of Israel: 'You have seen what I did to Egypt and how I carried you on eagles' wings and brought you to me. If you will listen obediently to what I say and keep my covenant, out of all peoples you'll be my special treasure. The whole Earth is mine to choose from, but you're special: a kingdom of priests, a holy nation.'

"This is what I want you to tell the People of Israel."

7 Moses came back and called the elders of Israel together and set before them all these words which GOD had commanded him.

8 The people were unanimous in their response: "Everything GOD says, we will do." Moses took the people's answer back to GOD.

9 GOD said to Moses, "Get ready. I'm about to come to you in a thick cloud so that the people can listen in and trust you completely when I speak

with you." Again Moses reported the people's answer to GOD.

10-13   GOD said to Moses, "Go to the people. For the next two days get these people ready to meet the Holy GOD. Have them scrub their clothes so that on the third day they'll be fully prepared, because on the third day GOD will come down on Mount Sinai and make his presence known to all the people. Post boundaries for the people all around, telling them, 'Warning! Don't climb the mountain. Don't even touch its edge. Whoever touches the mountain dies — a certain death. And no one is to touch that person, he's to be stoned. That's right — stoned. Or shot with arrows, shot to death. Animal or man, whichever — put to death.'

    "A long blast from the horn will signal that it's safe to climb the mountain."

14-15   Moses went down the mountain to the people and prepared them for the holy meeting. They gave their clothes a good scrubbing. Then he addressed the people: "Be ready in three days. Don't sleep with a woman."

16   On the third day at daybreak, there were loud claps of thunder, flashes of lightning, a thick cloud covering the mountain, and an ear-piercing trumpet blast. Everyone in the camp shuddered in fear.

17   Moses led the people out of the camp to meet God. They stood at attention at the base of the mountain.

18-20   Mount Sinai was all smoke because GOD had come down on it as fire. Smoke poured from it like smoke from a furnace. The whole mountain shuddered in huge spasms. The trumpet blasts grew louder and louder. Moses spoke and God answered in thunder. GOD descended to the peak of Mount Sinai. GOD called Moses up to the peak and Moses climbed up.

21-22   GOD said to Moses, "Go down. Warn the people not to break through the barricades to get a look at GOD lest many of them die. And the priests also, warn them to prepare themselves for the holy meeting, lest GOD break out against them."

23   Moses said to GOD, "But the people can't climb Mount Sinai. You've already warned us well telling us: 'Post boundaries around the mountain. Respect the holy mountain.'"

24   GOD told him, "Go down and then bring Aaron back up with you. But make sure that the priests and the people don't break through and come up to GOD, lest he break out against them."

25   So Moses went down to the people. He said to them:

1-2   **20** GOD spoke all these words:
    I am GOD, your God,
    who brought you out of the land of Egypt,
    out of a life of slavery.

3 No other gods, only me.

4-6 No carved gods of any size, shape, or form of anything whatever, whether of things that fly or walk or swim. Don't bow down to them and don't serve them because *I* am GOD, your God, and I'm a most jealous God, punishing the children for any sins their parents pass on to them to the third, and yes, even to the fourth generation of those who hate me. But I'm unswervingly loyal to the thousands who love me and keep my commandments.

7 No using the name of GOD, your God, in curses or silly banter; GOD won't put up with the irreverent use of his name.

8-11 Observe the Sabbath day, to keep it holy. Work six days and do everything you need to do. But the seventh day is a Sabbath to GOD, your God. Don't do any work—not you, nor your son, nor your daughter, nor your servant, nor your maid, nor your animals, not even the foreign guest visiting in your town. For in six days GOD made Heaven, Earth, and sea, and everything in them; he rested on the seventh day. Therefore GOD blessed the Sabbath day; he set it apart as a holy day.

12 Honor your father and mother so that you'll live a long time in the land that GOD, your God, is giving you.

13 No murder.

14 No adultery.

15 No stealing.

16 No lies about your neighbor.

17 No lusting after your neighbor's house—or wife or servant or maid or ox or donkey. Don't set your heart on anything that is your neighbor's.

18-19 All the people, experiencing the thunder and lightning, the trumpet blast and the smoking mountain, were afraid—they pulled back and stood at a distance. They said to Moses, "You speak to us and we'll listen, but don't have God speak to us or we'll die."

20 Moses spoke to the people: "Don't be afraid. God has come to test you and instill a deep and reverent awe within you so that you won't sin."

21 The people kept their distance while Moses approached the thick cloud where God was.

22-26 GOD said to Moses, "Give this Message to the People of Israel: 'You've experienced firsthand how I spoke with you from Heaven. Don't make gods of silver and gods of gold and then set them alongside me. Make me an earthen Altar. Sacrifice your Whole-Burnt-Offerings, your Peace-Offerings, your sheep, and your cattle on it. Every place where I cause my name to be honored in your worship, I'll be there myself and bless you. If you use stones to make my Altar, don't use dressed stones. If you use a chisel on the stones you'll profane the Altar. Don't use steps to climb to my Altar because that will expose your nakedness.'"

1 21 "These are the laws that you are to place before them:

2-6 "When you buy a Hebrew slave, he will serve six years. The seventh year he goes free, for nothing. If he came in single he leaves single. If he came in married he leaves with his wife. If the master gives him a wife and she gave him sons and daughters, the wife and children stay with the master and he leaves by himself. But suppose the slave should say, 'I love my master and my wife and children—I don't want my freedom,' then his master is to bring him before God and to a door or doorpost and pierce his ear with an awl, a sign that he is a slave for life.

7-11 "When a man sells his daughter to be a handmaid, she doesn't go free after six years like the men. If she doesn't please her master, her family must buy her back; her master doesn't have the right to sell her to foreigners since he broke his word to her. If he turns her over to his son, he has to treat her like a daughter. If he marries another woman, she retains all her full rights to meals, clothing, and marital relations. If he won't do any of these three things for her, she goes free, for nothing.

12-14   "If someone hits another and death results, the penalty is death. But if there was no intent to kill—if it was an accident, an 'act of God'—I'll set aside a place to which the killer can flee for refuge. But if the murder was premeditated, cunningly plotted, then drag the killer away, even if it's from my Altar, to be put to death.

15   "If someone hits father or mother, the penalty is death.

16   "If someone kidnaps a person, the penalty is death, regardless of whether the person has been sold or is still held in possession.

17   "If someone curses father or mother, the penalty is death.

18-19   "If a quarrel breaks out and one hits the other with a rock or a fist and the injured one doesn't die but is confined to bed and then later gets better and can get about on a crutch, the one who hit him is in the clear, except to pay for the loss of time and make sure of complete recovery.

20-21   "If a slave owner hits a slave, male or female, with a stick and the slave dies on the spot, the slave must be avenged. But if the slave survives a day or two, he's not to be avenged—the slave is the owner's property.

22-25   "When there's a fight and in the fight a pregnant woman is hit so that she miscarries but is not otherwise hurt, the one responsible has to pay whatever the husband demands in compensation. But if there is further damage, then you must give life for life— eye for eye, tooth for tooth, hand for hand, foot for foot, burn for burn, wound for wound, bruise for bruise.

26-27   "If a slave owner hits the eye of a slave or handmaid and ruins it, the owner must let the slave go free because of the eye. If the owner knocks out the tooth of the male or female slave, the slave must be released and go free because of the tooth.

28-32   "If an ox gores a man or a woman to death, the ox must be stoned. The meat cannot be eaten but the owner of the ox is in the clear. But if the ox has a history of goring and the owner knew it and did nothing to guard against it, then if the ox kills a man or a woman, the ox is to be stoned and the owner given the death penalty. If a ransom is agreed upon instead of death, he must pay it in full as a redemption for his life. If son or daughter is gored, the same judgment holds. If it is a slave or a handmaid the ox gores, thirty shekels of silver is to be paid to the owner and the ox stoned.

33-34   "If someone uncovers a cistern or digs a pit and leaves it open and an ox or donkey falls into it, the owner of the pit must pay whatever the animal is worth to its owner but can keep the dead animal.

35-36   "If someone's ox injures a neighbor's ox and the ox dies, they must sell the live ox and split the price; they must also split the dead animal. But if the ox had a history of goring and the owner knew it and did nothing to guard against it, the owner must pay an ox for an ox but can keep the dead animal."

1-3   **22** "If someone steals an ox or a lamb and slaughters or sells it, the thief must pay five cattle in place of the ox and four sheep in place of the lamb. If the thief is caught while breaking in and is hit hard and dies, there is no bloodguilt. But if it happens after daybreak, there is bloodguilt.

3-4   "A thief must make full restitution for what is stolen. The thief who is unable to pay is to be sold for his thieving. If caught red-handed with the stolen goods, and the ox or donkey or lamb is still alive, the thief pays double.

5 "If someone grazes livestock in a field or vineyard but lets them loose so they graze in someone else's field, restitution must be made from the best of the owner's field or vineyard.

6 "If fire breaks out and spreads to the brush so that the sheaves of grain or the standing grain or even the whole field is burned up, whoever started the fire must pay for the damages.

7-8 "If someone gives a neighbor money or things for safekeeping and they are stolen from the neighbor's house, the thief, if caught, must pay back double. If the thief is not caught, the owner must be brought before God to determine whether the owner was the one who took the neighbor's goods.

9 "In all cases of stolen goods, whether oxen, donkeys, sheep, clothing, anything in fact missing of which someone says, 'That's mine,' both parties must come before the judges. The one the judges pronounce guilty must pay double to the other.

10-13 "If someone gives a donkey or ox or lamb or any kind of animal to another for safekeeping and it dies or is injured or lost and there is no witness, an oath before GOD must be made between them to decide whether one has laid hands on the property of the other. The owner must accept this and no damages are assessed. But if it turns out it was stolen, the owner must be compensated. If it has been torn by wild beasts, the torn animal must be brought in as evidence; no damages have to be paid.

14-15 "If someone borrows an animal from a neighbor and it gets injured or dies while the owner is not present, he must pay for it. But if the owner was with it, he doesn't have to pay. If the animal was hired, the payment covers the loss.

16-17 "If a man seduces a virgin who is not engaged to be married and sleeps with her, he must pay the marriage price and marry her. If her father absolutely refuses to give her away, the man must still pay the marriage price for virgins.

18 "Don't let a sorceress live.

19 "Anyone who has sex with an animal gets the death penalty.

20 "Anyone who sacrifices to a god other than GOD alone must be put to death.

21 "Don't abuse or take advantage of strangers; you, remember, were once strangers in Egypt.

22-24 "Don't mistreat widows or orphans. If you do and they cry out to me, you can be sure I'll take them most seriously; I'll show my anger and come raging among you with the sword, and your wives will end up widows and your children orphans.

25 "If you lend money to my people, to any of the down-and-out among you, don't come down hard on them and gouge them with interest.

26-27 "If you take your neighbor's coat as security, give it back before nightfall; it may be your neighbor's only covering — what else does the person have to sleep in? And if I hear the neighbor crying out from the cold, I'll step in — I'm compassionate.

28 "Don't curse God; and don't damn your leaders.

29-30 "Don't be stingy as your wine vats fill up.

"Dedicate your firstborn sons to me. The same with your cattle and sheep — they are to stay for seven days with their mother, then give them to me.

31   "Be holy for my sake.

"Don't eat mutilated flesh you find in the fields; throw it to the dogs."

1-3   **23** "Don't pass on malicious gossip.

"Don't link up with a wicked person and give corrupt testimony. Don't go along with the crowd in doing evil and don't fudge your testimony in a case just to please the crowd. And just because someone is poor, don't show favoritism in a dispute.

4-5   "If you find your enemy's ox or donkey loose, take it back to him. If you see the donkey of someone who hates you lying helpless under its load, don't walk off and leave it. Help it up.

6   "When there is a dispute concerning your poor, don't tamper with the justice due them.

7   "Stay clear of false accusations. Don't contribute to the death of innocent and good people. I don't let the wicked off the hook.

8   "Don't take bribes. Bribes blind perfectly good eyes and twist the speech of good people.

9   "Don't take advantage of a stranger. You know what it's like to be a stranger; you were strangers in Egypt.

10-11   "Sow your land for six years and gather in its crops, but in the seventh year leave it alone and give it a rest so that your poor may eat from it. What they leave, let the wildlife have. Do the same with your vineyards and olive groves.

12   "Work for six days and rest the seventh so your ox and donkey may rest and your servant and migrant workers may have time to get their needed rest.

13   "Listen carefully to everything I tell you. Don't pay attention to other gods — don't so much as mention their names.

14   "Three times a year you are to hold a festival for me.

15   "Hold the spring Festival of Unraised Bread when you eat unraised bread for seven days at the time set for the month of Abib, as I commanded you. That was the month you came out of Egypt. No one should show up before me empty-handed.

16   "Hold the summer Festival of Harvest when you bring in the firstfruits of all your work in the fields.

"Hold the autumn Festival of Ingathering at the end of the season when you bring in the year's crops.

17   "Three times a year all your males are to appear before the Master, GOD.

18   "Don't offer the blood of a sacrifice to me with anything that has yeast in it.

"Don't leave the fat from my festival offering out overnight.

19   "Bring the choice first produce of the year to the house of your GOD.

"Don't boil a kid in its mother's milk.

20-24 "Now get yourselves ready. I'm sending my Angel ahead of you to guard you in your travels, to lead you to the place that I've prepared. Pay close attention to him. Obey him. Don't go against him. He won't put up with your rebellions because he's acting on my authority. But if you obey him and do everything I tell you, I'll be an enemy to your enemies, I'll fight those who fight you. When my Angel goes ahead of you and leads you to the land of the Amorites, the Hittites, the Perizzites, the Canaanites, the Hivites, and the Jebusites, I'll clear the country of them. So don't worship or serve their gods; don't do anything they do because I'm going to wipe them right off the face of the Earth and smash their sacred phallic pillars to bits.

25-26 "But you — you serve your God and he'll bless your food and your water. I'll get rid of the sickness among you; there won't be any miscarriages nor barren women in your land. I'll make sure you live full and complete lives.

27 "I'll send my Terror on ahead of you and throw those peoples you're approaching into a panic. All you'll see of your enemies is the backs of their necks.

28-31 "And I'll send Despair on ahead of you. It will push the Hivites, the Canaanites, and the Hittites out of your way. I won't get rid of them all at once lest the land grow up in weeds and the wild animals take over. Little by little I'll get them out of there while you have a chance to get your crops going and make the land your own. I will make your borders stretch from the Red Sea to the Mediterranean Sea and from the Wilderness to the Euphrates River. I'm turning everyone living in that land over to you; go ahead and drive them out.

32-33 "Don't make any deals with them or their gods. They are not to stay in the same country with you lest they get you to sin by worshiping their gods. Beware. That's a huge danger."

1-2 **24** He said to Moses, "Climb the mountain to God, you and Aaron, Nadab, Abihu, and seventy of the elders of Israel. They will worship from a distance; only Moses will approach God. The rest are not to come close. And the people are not to climb the mountain at all."

3 So Moses went to the people and told them everything God had said — all the rules and regulations. They all answered in unison: "Everything God said, we'll do."

4-6 Then Moses wrote it all down, everything God had said. He got up early the next morning and built an Altar at the foot of the mountain using twelve pillar-stones for the twelve tribes of Israel. Then he directed young Israelite men to offer Whole-Burnt-Offerings and sacrifice Peace-Offerings of bulls. Moses took half the blood and put it in bowls; the other half he threw against the Altar.

7 Then he took the Book of the Covenant and read it as the people listened. They said, "Everything God said, we'll do. Yes, we'll obey."

8 Moses took the rest of the blood and threw it out over the people, saying, "This is the blood of the covenant which God has made with you out of all these words I have spoken."

9-11 Then they climbed the mountain—Moses and Aaron, Nadab and Abihu, and seventy of the elders of Israel—and saw the God of Israel. He was standing on a pavement of something like sapphires—pure, clear sky-blue. He didn't hurt these pillar-leaders of the Israelites: They saw God; and they ate and drank.

12-13 GOD said to Moses, "Climb higher up the mountain and wait there for me; I'll give you tablets of stone, the teachings and commandments that I've written to instruct them." So Moses got up, accompanied by Joshua his aide. And Moses climbed up the mountain of God.

14 He told the elders of Israel, "Wait for us here until we return to you. You have Aaron and Hur with you; if there are any problems, go to them."

15-17 Then Moses climbed the mountain. The Cloud covered the mountain. The Glory of GOD settled over Mount Sinai. The Cloud covered it for six days. On the seventh day he called out of the Cloud to Moses. In the view of the Israelites below, the Glory of God looked like a raging fire at the top of the mountain.

18 Moses entered the middle of the Cloud and climbed the mountain. Moses was on the mountain forty days and forty nights.

INSTRUCTIONS ON THE MOUNTAIN: THE OFFERINGS

1-9 **25** GOD spoke to Moses: "Tell the Israelites that they are to set aside offerings for me. Receive the offerings from everyone who is willing to give. These are the offerings I want you to receive from them: gold, silver, bronze; blue, purple, and scarlet material; fine linen; goats' hair; tanned rams' skins; dolphin skins; acacia wood; lamp oil; spices for anointing oils and for fragrant incense; onyx stones and other stones for setting in the Ephod and the Breastpiece. Let them construct a Sanctuary for me so that I can live among them. You are to construct it following the plans I've given you, the design for The Dwelling and the design for all its furnishings.

THE CHEST

10-15 "First let them make a Chest using acacia wood: make it three and three-quarters feet long and two and one-quarter feet wide and deep. Cover it with a veneer of pure gold inside and out and make a molding of gold all around it. Cast four gold rings and attach them to its four feet, two rings on one side and two rings on the other. Make poles from acacia wood and cover them with a veneer of gold and insert them into the rings on the sides of the Chest for carrying the Chest. The poles are to stay in the rings; they must not be removed.

16 "Place The Testimony that I give you in the Chest.

17 "Now make a lid of pure gold for the Chest, an Atonement-Cover, three and three-quarters feet long and two and one-quarter feet wide.

18-22 "Sculpt two winged angels out of hammered gold for either end of the Atonement-Cover, one angel at one end, one angel at the other. Make them of one piece with the Atonement-Cover. Make the angels with their wings spread, hovering over the Atonement-Cover, facing one another but looking down on it. Set the Atonement-Cover as a lid over the Chest and place in the Chest The Testimony that I will give you. I will meet you there at set times and speak with you from above the Atonement-Cover and from between the angel-figures that are on it, speaking the commands that I have for the Israelites.

THE TABLE

23-28 "Next make a Table from acacia wood. Make it three feet long, one and one-half feet wide and two and one-quarter feet high. Cover it with a veneer of pure gold. Make a molding all around it of gold. Make the border a handbreadth wide all around it and a rim of gold for the border. Make four rings of gold and attach the rings to the four legs parallel to the tabletop. They will serve as holders for the poles used to carry the Table. Make the poles of acacia wood and cover them with a veneer of gold. They will be used to carry the Table.

29 "Make plates, bowls, jars, and jugs for pouring out offerings. Make them of pure gold.

30 "Always keep fresh Bread of the Presence on the Table before me.

THE LAMPSTAND

31-36 "Make a Lampstand of pure hammered gold. Make its stem and branches, cups, calyxes, and petals all of one piece. Give it six branches, three from one side and three from the other; put three cups shaped like almond blossoms, each with calyx and petals, on one branch, three on the next, and so on—the same for all six branches. On the main stem of the Lampstand, make four cups shaped like almonds, with calyx and petals, a calyx extending from under each pair of the six branches, the entire Lampstand fashioned from one piece of hammered pure gold.

37-38 "Make seven of these lamps for the Table. Arrange the lamps so they throw their light out in front. Make the candle snuffers and trays out of pure gold.

39-40 "Use a seventy-five-pound brick of pure gold to make the Lampstand and its accessories. Study the design you were given on the mountain and make everything accordingly."

THE DWELLING

1-6 **26** "Make The Dwelling itself from ten panels of tapestry woven from fine twisted linen, blue and purple and scarlet material, with an angel-cherubim design. A skilled craftsman should do it. The panels of tapestry are each to be forty-six feet long and six feet wide. Join five of the panels together, and then the other five together. Make loops of blue along the edge of the outside panel of the first set and the same on the outside panel of the second set. Make fifty loops on each panel. Then make fifty gold clasps and join the tapestries together so that The Dwelling is one whole.

7-11 "Next make tapestries of goat hair for a tent that will cover The Dwelling. Make eleven panels of these tapestries. The length of each panel will be forty-five feet long and six feet wide. Join five of the panels together, and then the other six. Fold the sixth panel double at the front of the tent. Now make fifty loops along the edge of the end panel and fifty loops along the edge of the joining panel. Make fifty clasps of bronze and connect the clasps with the loops, bringing the tent together.

12-14 "Hang half of the overlap of the tapestry panels over the rear of The Dwelling. The eighteen inches of overlap on either side will cover the sides of the tent. Finally, make a covering for the tapestries of tanned rams' skins dyed red and over that a covering of dolphin skins.

15-25 "Frame The Dwelling with planks of acacia wood, each section of frame

fifteen feet long and two and one-quarter feet wide, with two pegs for securing them. Make all the frames identical: twenty frames for the south side
with forty silver sockets to receive the two pegs from each of the twenty
frames; the same construction on the north side of The Dwelling; for the
rear of The Dwelling, which faces west, make six frames with two additional
frames for the rear corners. Both of the two corner frames need to be double
in thickness from top to bottom and fit into a single ring—eight frames
altogether with sixteen sockets of silver, two under each frame.

26-30   "Now make crossbars of acacia wood, five for the frames on one side of
The Dwelling, five for the other side, and five for the back side facing west.
The center crossbar runs from end to end halfway up the frames. Cover the
frames with a veneer of gold and make gold rings to hold the crossbars. And
cover the crossbars with a veneer of gold. Then put The Dwelling together,
following the design you were shown on the mountain.

31-35   "Make a curtain of blue, purple, and scarlet material and fine twisted
linen. Have a design of angel-cherubim woven into it by a skilled craftsman.
Fasten it with gold hooks to four posts of acacia wood covered with a veneer
of gold, set on four silver bases. After hanging the curtain from the clasps,
bring the Chest of The Testimony in behind the curtain. The curtain will
separate the Holy Place from the Holy-of-Holies. Now place the Atonement-
Cover lid on the Chest of The Testimony in the Holy-of-Holies. Place the
Table and the Lampstand outside the curtain, the Lampstand on the south
side of The Dwelling and the Table opposite it on the north side.

36-37   "Make a screen for the door of the tent. Weave it from blue, purple, and
scarlet material and fine twisted linen. Frame the weaving with five poles
of acacia wood covered with a veneer of gold and make gold hooks to
hang the weaving. Cast five bronze bases for the poles."

THE ALTAR

1-8   2️⃣7️⃣ "Make an Altar of acacia wood. Make it seven and a half feet
square and four and a half feet high. Make horns at each of the
four corners. The horns are to be of one piece with the Altar
and covered with a veneer of bronze. Make buckets for removing the ashes,
along with shovels, basins, forks, and fire pans. Make all these utensils from
bronze. Make a grate of bronze mesh and attach bronze rings at each of the
four corners. Put the grate under the ledge of the Altar at the halfway point of
the Altar. Make acacia wood poles for the Altar and cover them with a veneer
of bronze. Insert the poles through the rings on the two sides of the Altar for
carrying. Use boards to make the Altar, keeping the interior hollow.

THE COURTYARD

9-11   "Make a Courtyard for The Dwelling. The south side is to be 150 feet long.
The hangings for the Courtyard are to be woven from fine twisted linen,
with their twenty posts, twenty bronze bases, and fastening hooks and
bands of silver. The north side is to be exactly the same.

12-19   "For the west end of the Courtyard you will need seventy-five feet of
hangings with their ten posts and bases. Across the seventy-five feet at the
front, or east end, you will need twenty-two and a half feet of hangings,
with their three posts and bases on one side and the same for the other
side. At the door of the Courtyard make a screen thirty feet long woven
from blue, purple, and scarlet stuff, with fine twisted linen, embroidered

by a craftsman, and hung on its four posts and bases. All the posts around the Courtyard are to be banded with silver, with hooks of silver and bases of bronze. The Courtyard is to be 150 feet long and seventy-five feet wide. The hangings of fine twisted linen set on their bronze bases are to be seven and a half feet high. All the tools used for setting up The Holy Dwelling, including all the pegs in it and the Courtyard, are to be made of bronze.

20-21 "Now, order the Israelites to bring you pure, clear olive oil for light so that the lamps can be kept burning. In the Tent of Meeting, the area outside the curtain that veils The Testimony, Aaron and his sons will keep this light burning from evening until morning before GOD. This is to be a permanent practice down through the generations for Israelites."

THE VESTMENTS

1-5 **28** "Get your brother Aaron and his sons from among the Israelites to serve me as priests: Aaron and his sons Nadab, Abihu, Eleazar, Ithamar. Make sacred vestments for your brother Aaron to symbolize glory and beauty. Consult with the skilled craftsmen, those whom I have gifted in this work, and arrange for them to make Aaron's vestments, to set him apart as holy, to act as priest for me. These are the articles of clothing they are to make: Breastpiece, Ephod, robe, woven tunic, turban, sash. They are making holy vestments for your brother Aaron and his sons as they work as priests for me. They will need gold; blue, purple, and scarlet material; and fine linen.

THE EPHOD

6-14 "Have the Ephod made from gold; blue, purple, and scarlet material; and fine twisted linen by a skilled craftsman. Give it two shoulder pieces at two of the corners so it can be fastened. The decorated band on it is to be just like it and of one piece with it: made of gold; blue, purple, and scarlet material; and of fine twisted linen. Next take two onyx stones and engrave the names of the sons of Israel on them in the order of their birth, six names on one stone and the remaining six on the other. Engrave the names of the sons of Israel on the two stones the way a jeweler engraves a seal. Then mount the stones in settings of filigreed gold. Fasten the two stones on the shoulder pieces of the Ephod—they are memorial stones for the Israelites. Aaron will wear these names on his shoulders as a memorial before GOD. Make the settings of gold filigree. Make two chains of pure gold and braid them like cords, then attach the corded chains to the settings.

THE BREASTPIECE

15-20 "Now make a Breastpiece of Judgment, using skilled craftsmen, the same as with the Ephod. Use gold; blue, purple, and scarlet material; and fine twisted linen. Make it nine inches square and folded double. Mount four rows of precious gemstones on it.

First row: carnelian, topaz, emerald.
Second row: ruby, sapphire, crystal.
Third row: jacinth, agate, amethyst.
Fourth row: beryl, onyx, jasper.

20-21 "Set them in gold filigree. The twelve stones correspond to the names of the Israelites, with twelve names engraved, one on each, as on a seal for the twelve tribes.

22-28 "Then make braided chains of pure gold for the Breastpiece, like cords. Make two rings of gold for the Breastpiece and fasten them to the two ends. Fasten the two golden cords to the rings at the ends of the Breastpiece. Then fasten the other ends of the two cords to the two settings of filigree, attaching them to the shoulder pieces of the Ephod in front. Then make two rings of gold and fasten them to the two ends of the Breastpiece on its inside edge facing the Ephod. Then make two more rings of gold and fasten them in the front of the Ephod to the lower part of the two shoulder pieces, near the seam above the decorated band. Fasten the Breastpiece in place by running a cord of blue through its rings to the rings of the Ephod so that it rests secure on the decorated band of the Ephod and won't come loose.

29-30 "Aaron will regularly carry the names of the sons of Israel on the Breastpiece of Judgment over his heart as he enters the Sanctuary into the presence of GOD for remembrance. Place the Urim and Thummim in the Breastpiece of Judgment. They will be over Aaron's heart when he enters the presence of GOD. In this way Aaron will regularly carry the Breastpiece of Judgment into the presence of GOD.

THE ROBE

31-35 "Make the robe for the Ephod entirely of blue, with an opening for the head at the center and a hem on the edge so that it won't tear. For the edge of the skirts make pomegranates of blue, purple, and scarlet material all around and alternate them with bells of gold — gold bell and pomegranate, gold bell and pomegranate — all around the hem of the robe. Aaron has to wear it when he does his priestly work. The bells will be heard when he enters the Holy Place and comes into the presence of GOD, and again when he comes out so that he won't die.

THE TURBAN, TUNIC, UNDERWEAR

36-38 "Make a plate of pure gold. Engrave on it as on a seal: 'Holy to GOD.' Tie it with a blue cord to the front of the turban. It is to rest there on Aaron's forehead. He'll take on any guilt involved in the sacred offerings that the Israelites consecrate, no matter what they bring. It will always be on Aaron's forehead so that the offerings will be acceptable before GOD.

39-41 "Weave the tunic of fine linen. Make the turban of fine linen. The sash will be the work of an embroiderer. Make tunics, sashes, and hats for Aaron's sons to express glory and beauty. Dress your brother Aaron and his sons in them. Anoint, ordain, and consecrate them to serve me as priests.

42-43 "Make linen underwear to cover their nakedness from waist to thigh. Aaron and his sons must wear it whenever they enter the Tent of Meeting or approach the Altar to minister in the Holy Place so that they won't incur guilt and die. This is a permanent rule for Aaron and all his priest-descendants."

CONSECRATION OF PRIESTS

1-4 **29** "This is the ceremony for consecrating them as priests. Take a young bull and two rams, healthy and without defects. Using fine wheat flour but no yeast make bread and cakes mixed with oil and wafers spread with oil. Place them in a basket and carry them along with the bull and the two rams. Bring Aaron and his sons to the entrance of the Tent of Meeting and wash them with water.

5-9 "Then take the vestments and dress Aaron in the tunic, the robe of the Ephod, the Ephod, and the Breastpiece, belting the Ephod on him with the embroidered waistband. Set the turban on his head and place the sacred crown on the turban. Then take the anointing oil and pour it on his head, anointing him. Then bring his sons, put tunics on them and gird them with sashes, both Aaron and his sons, and set hats on them. Their priesthood is upheld by law and is permanent.

9-14 "This is how you will ordain Aaron and his sons: Bring the bull to the Tent of Meeting. Aaron and his sons will place their hands on the head of the bull. Then you will slaughter the bull in the presence of GOD at the entrance to the Tent of Meeting. Take some of the bull's blood and smear it on the horns of the Altar with your finger; pour the rest of the blood on the base of the Altar. Next take all the fat that covers the innards, fat from around the liver and the two kidneys, and burn it on the Altar. But the flesh of the bull, including its hide and dung, you will burn up outside the camp. It is an Absolution-Offering.

15-18 "Then take one of the rams. Have Aaron and his sons place their hands on the head of the ram. Slaughter the ram and take its blood and throw it against the Altar, all around. Cut the ram into pieces; wash its innards and legs, then gather the pieces and its head and burn the whole ram on the Altar. It is a Whole-Burnt-Offering to GOD, a pleasant fragrance, an offering by fire to GOD.

19-21 "Then take the second ram. Have Aaron and his sons place their hands on the ram's head. Slaughter the ram. Take some of its blood and rub it on Aaron's right earlobe and on the right earlobes of his sons, on the thumbs of their right hands and on the big toes of their right feet. Sprinkle the rest of the blood against all sides of the Altar. Then take some of the blood that is on the Altar, mix it with some of the anointing oil, and splash it on Aaron and his clothes and on his sons and their clothes so that Aaron and his clothes and his sons and his sons' clothes will be made holy.

22-23 "Take the fat from the ram, the fat tail, the fat that covers the innards, the long lobe of the liver, the two kidneys and the fat on them, and the right thigh: this is the ordination ram. Also take one loaf of bread, an oil cake, and a wafer from the breadbasket that is in the presence of GOD.

24-25 "Place all of these in the open hands of Aaron and his sons who will wave them before GOD, a Wave-Offering. Then take them from their hands and burn them on the Altar with the Whole-Burnt-Offering — a pleasing fragrance before GOD, a gift to GOD.

26 "Now take the breast from Aaron's ordination ram and wave it before GOD, a Wave-Offering. That will be your portion.

27-28 "Consecrate the Wave-Offering breast and the thigh that was held up. These are the parts of the ordination ram that are for Aaron and his sons. Aaron and his sons are always to get this offering from the Israelites; the Israelites are to make this offering regularly from their Peace-Offerings.

29-30 "Aaron's sacred garments are to be handed down to his descendants so they can be anointed and ordained in them. The son who succeeds him as priest is to wear them for seven days and enter the Tent of Meeting to minister in the Holy Place.

31-34   "Take the ordination ram and boil the meat in the Holy Place. At the entrance to the Tent of Meeting, Aaron and his sons will eat the boiled ram and the bread that is in the basket. Atoned by these offerings, ordained and consecrated by them, they are the only ones who are to eat them. No outsiders are to eat them; they're holy. Anything from the ordination ram or from the bread that is left over until morning you are to burn up. Don't eat it; it's holy.

35-37   "Do everything for the ordination of Aaron and his sons exactly as I've commanded you throughout the seven days. Offer a bull as an Absolution-Offering for atonement each day. Offer it on the Altar when you make atonement for it: Anoint and consecrate it. Make atonement for the Altar and consecrate it for seven days; the Altar will become soaked in holiness—anyone who so much as touches the Altar will become holy.

38-41   "This is what you are to offer on the Altar: two year-old lambs each and every day, one lamb in the morning and the second lamb at evening. With the sacrifice of the first lamb offer two quarts of fine flour with a quart of virgin olive oil, plus a quart of wine for a Drink-Offering. The sacrifice of the second lamb, the one at evening, is also to be accompanied by the same Grain-Offering and Drink-Offering of the morning sacrifice to give a pleasing fragrance, a gift to GOD.

42-46   "This is to be your regular, daily Whole-Burnt-Offering before GOD, generation after generation, sacrificed at the entrance of the Tent of Meeting. That's where I'll meet you; that's where I'll speak with you; that's where I'll meet the Israelites, at the place made holy by my Glory. I'll make the Tent of Meeting and the Altar holy. I'll make Aaron and his sons holy in order to serve me as priests. I'll move in and live with the Israelites. I'll be their God. They'll realize that I am their GOD who brought them out of the land of Egypt so that I could live with them. I am GOD, *your* God."

THE ALTAR OF INCENSE

1-5   **30** "Make an Altar for burning incense. Construct it from acacia wood, one and one-half feet square and three feet high with its horns of one piece with it. Cover it with a veneer of pure gold, its top, sides, and horns, and make a gold molding around it with two rings of gold beneath the molding. Place the rings on the two opposing sides to serve as holders for poles by which it will be carried. Make the poles of acacia wood and cover them with a veneer of gold.

6-10   "Place the Altar in front of the curtain that hides the Chest of The Testimony, in front of the Atonement-Cover that is over The Testimony where I will meet you. Aaron will burn fragrant incense on it every morning when he polishes the lamps, and again in the evening as he prepares the lamps for lighting, so that there will always be incense burning before GOD, generation after generation. But don't burn on this Altar any unholy incense or Whole-Burnt-Offering or Grain-Offering. And don't pour out Drink-Offerings on it. Once a year Aaron is to purify the Altar horns. Using the blood of the Absolution-Offering of atonement, he is to make this atonement every year down through the generations. It is most holy to GOD."

THE ATONEMENT-TAX

11-16   GOD spoke to Moses: "When you take a head count of the Israelites to keep track of them, all must pay an atonement-tax to GOD for their life at the time of being registered so that nothing bad will happen because of the registration. Everyone who gets counted is to give a half-shekel (using the standard Sanctuary shekel of a fifth of an ounce to the shekel)—a half-shekel offering to GOD. Everyone counted, age twenty and up, is to make the offering to GOD. The rich are not to pay more nor the poor less than the half-shekel offering to GOD, the atonement-tax for your lives. Take the atonement-tax money from the Israelites and put it to the maintenance of the Tent of Meeting. It will be a memorial fund for the Israelites in honor of GOD, making atonement for your lives."

THE WASHBASIN

17-21 GOD spoke to Moses: "Make a bronze Washbasin; make it with a bronze base. Place it between the Tent of Meeting and the Altar. Put water in it. Aaron and his sons will wash their hands and feet in it. When they enter the Tent of Meeting or approach the Altar to serve there or offer gift offerings to GOD, they are to wash so they will not die. They are to wash their hands and their feet so they will not die. This is the rule forever, for Aaron and his sons down through the generations."

HOLY ANOINTING OIL

22-25 GOD spoke to Moses: "Take the best spices: twelve and a half pounds of liquid myrrh; half that much, six and a quarter pounds, of fragrant cinnamon; six and a quarter pounds of fragrant cane; twelve and a half pounds of cassia—using the standard Sanctuary weight for all of them—and a gallon of olive oil. Make these into a holy anointing oil, a perfumer's skillful blend.

26-29 "Use it to anoint the Tent of Meeting, the Chest of The Testimony, the Table and all its utensils, the Lampstand and its utensils, the Altar of Incense, the Altar of Whole-Burnt-Offerings and all its utensils, and the Washbasin and its base. Consecrate them so they'll be soaked in holiness, so that anyone who so much as touches them will become holy.

30-33 "Then anoint Aaron and his sons. Consecrate them as priests to me. Tell the Israelites, 'This will be my holy anointing oil throughout your generations.' Don't pour it on ordinary men. Don't copy this mixture to use for yourselves. It's holy; keep it holy. Whoever mixes up anything like it, or puts it on an ordinary person, will be expelled."

HOLY INCENSE

34-38 GOD spoke to Moses: "Take fragrant spices—gum resin, onycha, galbanum—and add pure frankincense. Mix the spices in equal proportions to make an aromatic incense, the art of a perfumer, salted and pure—holy. Now crush some of it into powder and place some of it before The Testimony in the Tent of Meeting where I will meet with you; it will be for you the holiest of holy places. When you make this incense, you are not to copy the mixture for your own use. It's holy to GOD; keep it that way. Whoever copies it for personal use will be excommunicated."

BEZALEL AND OHOLIAB

1-5 **31** GOD spoke to Moses: "See what I've done; I've personally chosen Bezalel son of Uri, son of Hur of the tribe of Judah. I've filled him with the Spirit of God, giving him skill and know-how and expertise in every kind of craft to create designs and work in gold, silver, and bronze; to cut and set gemstones; to carve wood—he's an all-around craftsman.

6-11 "Not only that, but I've given him Oholiab, son of Ahisamach of the tribe of Dan, to work with him. And to all who have an aptitude for crafts I've given the skills to make all the things I've commanded you: the Tent of Meeting, the Chest of The Testimony and its Atonement-Cover, all the implements for the Tent, the Table and its implements, the pure Lampstand and all its implements, the Altar of Incense, the Altar of Whole-Burnt-Offering and all its implements, the Washbasin and its base, the official vestments, the holy vestments for Aaron the priest and his sons in their priestly duties, the anointing oil, and the aromatic incense for the Holy Place—they'll make everything just the way I've commanded you."

SABBATH

12-17 GOD spoke to Moses: "Tell the Israelites, 'Above all, keep my Sabbaths, the sign between me and you, generation after generation, to keep the knowledge alive that I am the GOD who makes you holy. Keep the Sabbath; it's holy to you. Whoever profanes it will most certainly be put to death. Whoever works on it will be excommunicated from the people. There are six days for work but the seventh day is Sabbath, pure rest, holy to GOD. Anyone who works on the Sabbath will most certainly be put to death. The Israelites will keep the Sabbath, observe Sabbath-keeping down through the generations, as a standing covenant. It's a fixed sign between me and the Israelites. Yes, because in six days GOD made the Heavens and the Earth and on the seventh day he stopped and took a long, deep breath.'"

18 When he finished speaking with him on Mount Sinai, he gave Moses two tablets of Testimony, slabs of stone, written with the finger of God.

"MAKE GODS FOR US"

1 **32** When the people realized that Moses was taking forever in coming down off the mountain, they rallied around Aaron and said, "Do something. Make gods for us who will lead us. That Moses, the man who got us out of Egypt—who knows what's happened to him?"

2-4 So Aaron told them, "Take off the gold rings from the ears of your wives and sons and daughters and bring them to me." They all did it; they removed the gold rings from their ears and brought them to Aaron. He took the gold from their hands and cast it in the form of a calf, shaping it with an engraving tool.

The people responded with enthusiasm: "These are your gods, O Israel, who brought you up from Egypt!"

5 Aaron, taking in the situation, built an altar before the calf.

Aaron then announced, "Tomorrow is a feast day to GOD!"

6 Early the next morning, the people got up and offered Whole-Burnt-Offerings and brought Peace-Offerings. The people sat down to eat and drink and then began to party. It turned into a wild party!

7-8 GOD spoke to Moses, "Go! Get down there! Your people whom you brought up from the land of Egypt have fallen to pieces. In no time at all they've turned away from the way I commanded them: They made a molten calf and worshiped it. They've sacrificed to it and said, 'These are the gods, O Israel, that brought you up from the land of Egypt!'"

9-10   GOD said to Moses, "I look at this people — oh! what a stubborn, hard-headed people! Let me alone now, give my anger free reign to burst into flames and incinerate them. But I'll make a great nation out of you."

11-13   Moses tried to calm his GOD down. He said, "Why, GOD, would you lose your temper with your people? Why, you brought them out of Egypt in a tremendous demonstration of power and strength. Why let the Egyptians say, 'He had it in for them — he brought them out so he could kill them in the mountains, wipe them right off the face of the Earth.' Stop your anger. Think twice about bringing evil against your people! Think of Abraham, Isaac, and Israel, your servants to whom you gave your word, telling them 'I will give you many children, as many as the stars in the sky, and I'll give this land to your children as their land forever.'"

14   And GOD did think twice. He decided not to do the evil he had threatened against his people.

15-16   Moses turned around and came down from the mountain, carrying the two tablets of The Testimony. The tablets were written on both sides, front and back. God made the tablets and God wrote the tablets — engraved them.

17   When Joshua heard the sound of the people shouting noisily, he said to Moses, "That's the sound of war in the camp!"

18   But Moses said,

> Those aren't songs of victory,
> And those aren't songs of defeat,
> I hear songs of people throwing a party.

19-20   And that's what it was. When Moses came near to the camp and saw the calf and the people dancing, his anger flared. He threw down the tablets and smashed them to pieces at the foot of the mountain. He took the calf that they had made, melted it down with fire, pulverized it to powder, then scattered it on the water and made the Israelites drink it.

21   Moses said to Aaron, "What on Earth did these people ever do to you that you involved them in this huge sin?"

22-23   Aaron said, "Master, don't be angry. You know this people and how set on evil they are. They said to me, 'Make us gods who will lead us. This Moses, the man who brought us out of Egypt, we don't know what's happened to him.'

24   "So I said, 'Who has gold?' And they took off their jewelry and gave it to me. I threw it in the fire and out came this calf."

25-26   Moses saw that the people were simply running wild — Aaron had let them run wild, disgracing themselves before their enemies. He took up a position at the entrance to the camp and said, "Whoever is on GOD's side, join me!" All the Levites stepped up.

27   He then told them, "GOD's orders, the God of Israel: 'Strap on your swords and go to work. Crisscross the camp from one end to the other: Kill brother, friend, neighbor.'"

28   The Levites carried out Moses' orders. Three thousand of the people were killed that day.

29 Moses said, "You confirmed your ordination today—and at great cost, even killing your sons and brothers! And God has blessed you."

30 The next day Moses addressed the people: "You have sinned an enormous sin! But I am going to go up to GOD; maybe I'll be able to clear you of your sin."

31-32 Moses went back to GOD and said, "This is terrible. This people has sinned—it's an enormous sin! They made gods of gold for themselves. And now, if you will only forgive their sin. . . . But if not, erase me out of the book you've written."

33-34 GOD said to Moses, "I'll only erase from my book those who sin against me. For right now, you go and lead the people to where I told you. Look, my Angel is going ahead of you. On the day, though, when I settle accounts, their sins will certainly be part of the settlement."

35 GOD sent a plague on the people because of the calf they and Aaron had made.

1-3 **33** GOD said to Moses: "Now go. Get on your way from here, you and the people you brought up from the land of Egypt. Head for the land which I promised to Abraham, Isaac, and Jacob, saying 'I will give it to your descendants.' I will send an angel ahead of you and I'll drive out the Canaanites, Amorites, Hittites, Perizzites, Hivites, and Jebusites. It's a land flowing with milk and honey. But I won't be with you in person—you're such a stubborn, hard-headed people!—lest I destroy you on the journey."

4 When the people heard this harsh verdict, they were plunged into gloom and wore long faces. No one put on jewelry.

5-6 GOD said to Moses, "Tell the Israelites, 'You're one hard-headed people. I couldn't stand being with you for even a moment—I'd destroy you. So take off all your jewelry until I figure out what to do with you.'" So the Israelites stripped themselves of their jewelry from Mount Horeb on.

7-10 Moses used to take the Tent and set it up outside the camp, some distance away. He called it the Tent of Meeting. Anyone who sought GOD would go to the Tent of Meeting outside the camp. It went like this: When Moses would go to the Tent, all the people would stand at attention; each man would take his position at the entrance to his tent with his eyes on Moses until he entered the Tent; whenever Moses entered the Tent, the Pillar of Cloud descended to the entrance to the Tent and GOD spoke with Moses. All the people would see the Pillar of Cloud at the entrance to the Tent, stand at attention, and then bow down in worship, each man at the entrance to his tent.

11 And GOD spoke with Moses face-to-face, as neighbors speak to one another. When he would return to the camp, his attendant, the young man Joshua, stayed—he didn't leave the Tent.

12-13 Moses said to GOD, "Look, you tell me, 'Lead this people,' but you don't let me know whom you're going to send with me. You tell me, 'I know you well and you are special to me.' If I am so special to you, let me in on your plans. That way, I will continue being special to you. Don't forget, this is *your* people, your responsibility."

14   GOD said, "My presence will go with you. I'll see the journey to the end."

15-16   Moses said, "If your presence doesn't take the lead here, call this trip off right now. How else will it be known that you're with me in this, with me and your people? Are you traveling with us or not? How else will we know that we're special, I and your people, among all other people on this planet Earth?"

17   GOD said to Moses: "All right. Just as you say; this also I will do, for I know you well and you are special to me. I know you by name."

18   Moses said, "Please. Let me see your Glory."

19   GOD said, "I will make my Goodness pass right in front of you; I'll call out the name, GOD, right before you. I'll treat well whomever I want to treat well and I'll be kind to whomever I want to be kind."

20   GOD continued, "But you may not see my face. No one can see me and live."

21-23   GOD said, "Look, here is a place right beside me. Put yourself on this rock. When my Glory passes by, I'll put you in the cleft of the rock and cover you with my hand until I've passed by. Then I'll take my hand away and you'll see my back. But you won't see my face."

1-3   **34** GOD spoke to Moses: "Cut out two tablets of stone just like the originals and engrave on them the words that were on the original tablets you smashed. Be ready in the morning to climb Mount Sinai and get set to meet me on top of the mountain. Not a soul is to go with you; the whole mountain must be clear of people, even animals — not even sheep or oxen can be grazing in front of the mountain."

4-7   So Moses cut two tablets of stone just like the originals. He got up early in the morning and climbed Mount Sinai as GOD had commanded him, carrying the two tablets of stone. GOD descended in the cloud and took up his position there beside him and called out the name, GOD. GOD passed in front of him and called out, "GOD, GOD, a God of mercy and grace, endlessly patient — so much love, so deeply true — loyal in love for a thousand generations, forgiving iniquity, rebellion, and sin. Still, he doesn't ignore sin. He holds sons and grandsons responsible for a father's sins to the third and even fourth generation."

8-9   At once, Moses fell to the ground and worshiped, saying, "Please, O Master, if you see anything good in me, please Master, travel with us, hard-headed as these people are. Forgive our iniquity and sin. Own us, possess us."

10-12   And GOD said, "As of right now, I'm making a covenant with you: In full sight of your people I will work wonders that have never been created in all the Earth, in any nation. Then all the people with whom you're living will see how tremendous GOD's work is, the work I'll do for you. Take careful note of all I command you today. I'm clearing your way by driving out Amorites, Canaanites, Hittites, Perizzites, Hivites, and Jebusites. Stay vigilant. Don't let down your guard lest you make covenant with the people who live in the land that you are entering and they trip you up.

13-16   "Tear down their altars, smash their phallic pillars, chop down their fertility poles. Don't worship any other god. GOD — his name is The-

Jealous-One — is a jealous God. Be careful that you don't make a covenant with the people who live in the land and take up with their sex-and-religion life, join them in meals at their altars, marry your sons to their women, women who take up with any convenient god or goddess and will get your sons to do the same thing.

17 "Don't make molten gods for yourselves.

18 "Keep the Feast of Unraised Bread. Eat only unraised bread for seven days in the month of Abib — it was in the month of Abib that you came out of Egypt.

19 "Every firstborn from the womb is mine, all the males of your herds, your firstborn oxen and sheep.

20 "Redeem your firstborn donkey with a lamb. If you don't redeem it you must break its neck.

"Redeem each of your firstborn sons.

"No one is to show up in my presence empty-handed.

21 "Work six days and rest the seventh. Stop working even during plowing and harvesting.

22 "Keep the Feast of Weeks with the first cutting of the wheat harvest, and the Feast of Ingathering at the turn of the year.

23-24 "All your men are to appear before the Master, the GOD of Israel, three times a year. You won't have to worry about your land when you appear before your GOD three times each year, for I will drive out the nations before you and give you plenty of land. Nobody's going to be hanging around plotting ways to get it from you.

25 "Don't mix the blood of my sacrifices with anything fermented.

"Don't leave leftovers from the Passover Feast until morning.

26 "Bring the finest of the firstfruits of your produce to the house of your GOD.

"Don't boil a kid in its mother's milk."

27 GOD said to Moses: "Now write down these words, for by these words I've made a covenant with you and Israel."

28 Moses was there with GOD forty days and forty nights. He didn't eat any food; he didn't drink any water. And he wrote on the tablets the words of the covenant, the Ten Words.

29-30 When Moses came down from Mount Sinai carrying the two Tablets of The Testimony, he didn't know that the skin of his face glowed because he had been speaking with GOD. Aaron and all the Israelites saw Moses, saw his radiant face, and held back, afraid to get close to him.

31-32 Moses called out to them. Aaron and the leaders in the community came back and Moses talked with them. Later all the Israelites came up to him and he passed on the commands, everything that GOD had told him on Mount Sinai.

33-35 When Moses finished speaking with them, he put a veil over his face, but when he went into the presence of GOD to speak with him, he removed the veil until he came out. When he came out and told the Israelites what he had been commanded, they would see Moses' face, its skin glowing, and then he would again put the veil on his face until he went back in to speak with GOD.

BUILDING THE PLACE OF WORSHIP

35 ¹ Moses spoke to the entire congregation of Israel, saying, "These are the things that GOD has commanded you to do: ²⁻³ "Work six days, but the seventh day will be a holy rest day, GOD's holy rest day. Anyone who works on this day must be put to death. Don't light any fires in your homes on the Sabbath day."

THE OFFERINGS

4 Moses spoke to the entire congregation of Israel, saying, "This is what GOD has commanded:

5-9 "Gather from among you an offering for GOD. Receive on GOD's behalf what everyone is willing to give as an offering: gold, silver, bronze; blue, purple, and scarlet material; fine linen; goats' hair; tanned rams' skins; dolphin skins; acacia wood; lamp oil; spices for anointing oils and for fragrant incense; onyx stones and other stones for setting in the Ephod and the Breastpiece.

10-19 "Come — all of you who have skills — come and make everything that GOD has commanded: The Dwelling with its tent and cover, its hooks, frames, crossbars, posts, and bases; the Chest with its poles, the Atonement-Cover and veiling curtain; the Table with its poles and implements and the Bread of the Presence; the Lampstand for giving light with its furnishings and lamps and the oil for lighting; the Altar of Incense with its poles, the anointing oil, the fragrant incense; the screen for the door at the entrance to The Dwelling; the Altar of Whole-Burnt-Offering with its bronze grate and poles and all its implements; the Washbasin with its base; the tapestry hangings for the Courtyard with the posts and bases, the screen for the Courtyard gate; the pegs for The Dwelling, the pegs for the Courtyard with their cords; the official vestments for ministering in the Holy Place, the sacred vestments for Aaron the priest and for his sons serving as priests."

20-26 So everyone in the community of Israel left the presence of Moses. Then they came back, every one whose heart was roused, whose spirit was freely responsive, bringing offerings to GOD for building the Tent of Meeting, furnishing it for worship and making the holy vestments. They came, both men and women, all the willing spirits among them, offering brooches, earrings, rings, necklaces — anything made of gold — offering up their gold jewelry to GOD. And anyone who had blue, purple, and scarlet fabrics; fine linen; goats' hair; tanned leather; and dolphin skins brought them. Everyone who wanted to offer up silver or bronze as a gift to GOD brought it. Everyone who had acacia wood that could be used in the work, brought it. All the women skilled at weaving brought their weavings of blue and purple and scarlet fabrics and their fine linens. And all the women who were gifted in spinning, spun the goats' hair.

27-29 The leaders brought onyx and other precious stones for setting in the Ephod and the Breastpiece. They also brought spices and olive oil for lamp oil, anointing oil, and incense. Every man and woman in Israel whose heart moved them freely to bring something for the work that GOD through Moses had commanded them to make, brought it, a voluntary offering for GOD.

BEZALEL AND OHOLIAB

30-35   Moses told the Israelites, "See, GOD has selected Bezalel son of Uri, son of Hur, of the tribe of Judah. He's filled him with the Spirit of God, with skill, ability, and know-how for making all sorts of things, to design and work in gold, silver, and bronze; to carve stones and set them; to carve wood, working in every kind of skilled craft. And he's also made him a teacher, he and Oholiab son of Ahisamach, of the tribe of Dan. He's gifted them with the know-how needed for carving, designing, weaving, and embroidering in blue, purple, and scarlet fabrics, and in fine linen. They can make anything and design anything."

1   **36** "Bezalel and Oholiab, along with everyone whom GOD has given the skill and know-how for making everything involved in the worship of the Sanctuary as commanded by GOD, are to start to work."

2-3   Moses summoned Bezalel and Oholiab along with all whom GOD had gifted with the ability to work skillfully with their hands. The men were eager to get started and engage in the work. They took from Moses all the offerings that the Israelites had brought for the work of constructing the Sanctuary. The people kept on bringing in their freewill offerings, morning after morning.

4-5   All the artisans who were at work making everything involved in constructing the Sanctuary came, one after another, to Moses, saying, "The people are bringing more than enough for doing this work that GOD has commanded us to do!"

6-7   So Moses sent out orders through the camp: "Men! Women! No more offerings for the building of the Sanctuary!"

The people were ordered to stop bringing offerings! There was plenty of material for all the work to be done. Enough and more than enough.

THE TAPESTRIES

8-13   Then all the skilled artisans on The Dwelling made ten tapestries of fine twisted linen and blue, purple, and scarlet fabric with an angel-cherubim design worked into the material. Each panel of tapestry was forty-six feet long and six feet wide. Five of the panels were joined together, and then the other five. Loops of blue were made along the edge of the outside panel of the first set, and the same on the outside panel of the second set. They made fifty loops on each panel, with the loops opposite each other. Then they made fifty gold clasps and joined the tapestries together so that The Dwelling was one whole.

14-19   Next they made tapestries of woven goat hair for a tent that would cover The Dwelling. They made eleven panels of these tapestries. The length of each panel was forty-five feet long and six feet wide. They joined five of the panels together, and then the other six, by making fifty loops along the edge of the end panel and fifty loops along the edge of the joining panel, then making fifty clasps of bronze, connecting the clasps to the loops, bringing the tent together. They finished it off by covering the tapestries with tanned rams' skins dyed red, and covered that with dolphin skins.

The Framing

20-30   They framed The Dwelling with vertical planks of acacia wood, each section of frame fifteen feet long and two and a quarter feet wide, with two pegs for securing them. They made all the frames identical: twenty frames for the south side, with forty silver sockets to receive the two tenons from each of the twenty frames; they repeated that construction on the north side of The Dwelling. For the rear of The Dwelling facing west, they made six frames, with two additional frames for the rear corners. Both of the two corner frames were double in thickness from top to bottom and fit into a single ring—eight frames altogether with sixteen sockets of silver, two under each frame.

31-34   They made crossbars of acacia wood, five for the frames on one side of The Dwelling, five for the other side, and five for the back side facing west. The center crossbar ran from end to end halfway up the frames. They covered the frames with a veneer of gold, made gold rings to hold the crossbars, and covered the crossbars with a veneer of gold.

35-36   They made the curtain of blue, purple, and scarlet material and fine twisted linen. They wove a design of angel-cherubim into it. They made four posts of acacia wood, covered them with a veneer of gold, and cast four silver bases for them.

37-38   They made a screen for the door of the tent, woven from blue, purple, and scarlet material and fine twisted linen with embroidery. They framed the weaving with five poles of acacia wood covered with a veneer of gold, and made gold hooks to hang the weaving and five bronze bases for the poles.

The Chest

1-5   **37** Bezalel made the Chest using acacia wood: He made it three and three-quarters feet long and two and a quarter feet wide and deep. He covered it inside and out with a veneer of pure gold and made a molding of gold all around it. He cast four gold rings and attached them to its four feet, two rings on one side and two rings on the other. He made poles from acacia wood, covered them with a veneer of gold, and inserted the poles for carrying the Chest into the rings on the sides.

6   Next he made a lid of pure gold for the Chest, an Atonement-Cover, three and three-quarters feet long and two and a quarter feet wide.

7-9   He sculpted two winged angel-cherubim out of hammered gold for the ends of the Atonement-Cover, one angel at one end, one angel at the other. He made them of one piece with the Atonement-Cover. The angels had outstretched wings and appeared to hover over the Atonement-Cover, facing one another but looking down on the Atonement-Cover.

The Table

10-15   He made the Table from acacia wood. He made it three feet long, one and a half feet wide and two and a quarter feet high. He covered it with a veneer of pure gold and made a molding of gold all around it. He made a border a handbreadth wide all around it and a rim of gold for the border. He cast four rings of gold for it and attached the rings to the four legs parallel to the tabletop. They will serve as holders for the poles used to carry the Table. He made the poles of acacia wood and covered them with a veneer of gold. They will be used to carry the Table.

16   Out of pure gold he made the utensils for the Table: its plates, bowls, jars, and jugs used for pouring.

THE LAMPSTAND

17-23   He made a Lampstand of pure hammered gold, making its stem and branches, cups, calyxes, and petals all of one piece. It had six branches, three from one side and three from the other; three cups shaped like almond blossoms with calyxes and petals on one branch, three on the next, and so on—the same for all six branches. On the main stem of the Lampstand, there were four cups shaped like almonds, with calyxes and petals, a calyx extending from under each pair of the six branches. The entire Lampstand with its calyxes and stems was fashioned from one piece of hammered pure gold. He made seven of these lamps with their candle snuffers, all out of pure gold.

24   He used a seventy-five-pound brick of pure gold to make the Lampstand and its accessories.

THE ALTAR OF INCENSE

25-28   He made an Altar for burning incense from acacia wood. He made it a foot and a half square and three feet high, with its horns of one piece with it. He covered it with a veneer of pure gold, its top, sides, and horns, and made a gold molding around it with two rings of gold beneath the molding. He placed the rings on the two opposing sides to serve as holders for poles by which it will be carried. He made the poles of acacia wood and covered them with a veneer of gold.

29   He also prepared with the art of a perfumer the holy anointing oil and the pure aromatic incense.

THE ALTAR OF WHOLE-BURNT-OFFERING

1-7   **38** He made the Altar of Whole-Burnt-Offering from acacia wood. He made it seven and a half feet square and four and a half feet high. He made horns at each of the four corners. The horns were made of one piece with the Altar and covered with a veneer of bronze. He made from bronze all the utensils for the Altar: the buckets for removing the ashes, shovels, basins, forks, and fire pans. He made a grate of bronze mesh under the ledge halfway up the Altar. He cast four rings at each of the four corners of the bronze grating to hold the poles. He made the poles of acacia wood and covered them with a veneer of bronze. He inserted the poles through the rings on the two sides of the Altar for carrying it. The Altar was made out of boards; it was hollow.

THE WASHBASIN

8   He made the Bronze Washbasin and its bronze stand from the mirrors of the women's work group who were assigned to serve at the entrance to the Tent of Meeting.

THE COURTYARD

9-11   And he made the Courtyard. On the south side the hangings for the Courtyard, woven from fine twisted linen, were 150 feet long, with their twenty posts and twenty bronze bases, and fastening hooks and bands of silver. The north side was exactly the same.

12-20   The west end of the Courtyard had seventy-five feet of hangings with ten posts and bases, and fastening hooks and bands of silver. Across the seventy-five feet at the front, or east end, were twenty-two and a half feet of hangings, with their three posts and bases on one side and the same for the other side. All the hangings around the Courtyard were of fine twisted linen. The bases for the posts were bronze and the fastening hooks and bands on the posts were of silver. The posts of the Courtyard were both capped and banded with silver. The screen at the door of the Courtyard was embroidered in blue, purple, and scarlet fabric with fine twisted linen. It was thirty feet long and seven and a half feet high, matching the hangings of the Courtyard. There were four posts with bases of bronze and fastening hooks of silver; they were capped and banded in silver. All the pegs for The Dwelling and the Courtyard were made of bronze.

21-23   This is an inventory of The Dwelling that housed The Testimony drawn up by order of Moses for the work of the Levites under Ithamar, son of Aaron the priest. Bezalel, the son of Uri, son of Hur, of the tribe of Judah, made everything that GOD had commanded Moses. Working with Bezalel was Oholiab, the son of Ahisamach, of the tribe of Dan, an artisan, designer, and embroiderer in blue, purple, and scarlet fabrics and fine linen.

24   Gold. The total amount of gold used in construction of the Sanctuary, all of it contributed freely, weighed out at 1,900 pounds according to the Sanctuary standard.

25-28   Silver. The silver from those in the community who were registered in the census came to 6,437 pounds according to the Sanctuary standard— that amounted to a *beka*, or half-shekel, for every registered person aged twenty and over, a total of 603,550 men. They used the three and one-quarter tons of silver to cast the bases for the Sanctuary and for the hangings, one hundred bases at sixty-four pounds each. They used the remaining thirty-seven pounds to make the connecting hooks on the posts, and the caps and bands for the posts.

29-31   Bronze. The bronze that was brought in weighed 4,522 pounds. It was used to make the door of the Tent of Meeting, the Bronze Altar with its bronze grating, all the utensils of the Altar, the bases around the Courtyard, the bases for the gate of the Courtyard, and all the pegs for The Dwelling and the Courtyard.

1   **39** Vestments. Using the blue, purple, and scarlet fabrics, they made the woven vestments for ministering in the Sanctuary. Also they made the sacred vestments for Aaron, as GOD had commanded Moses.

2-5   Ephod. They made the Ephod using gold and blue, purple, and scarlet fabrics and finely twisted linen. They hammered out gold leaf and sliced it into threads that were then worked into designs in the blue, purple, and scarlet fabric and fine linen. They made shoulder pieces fastened at the two ends. The decorated band was made of the same material — gold, blue, purple, and scarlet material, and of fine twisted linen — and of one piece with it, just as GOD had commanded Moses.

6-7   They mounted the onyx stones in a setting of filigreed gold and engraved the names of the sons of Israel on them, then fastened them on the shoulder pieces of the Ephod as memorial stones for the Israelites, just as GOD had commanded Moses.

8-10　　Breastpiece. They made a Breastpiece designed like the Ephod from gold, blue, purple, and scarlet material, and fine twisted linen. Doubled, the Breastpiece was nine inches square. They mounted four rows of precious gemstones on it.

　　First row: carnelian, topaz, emerald.

11　　Second row: ruby, sapphire, crystal.

12　　Third row: jacinth, agate, amethyst.

13-14　　Fourth row: beryl, onyx, jasper.

　　The stones were mounted in a gold filigree. The twelve stones corresponded to the names of the sons of Israel, twelve names engraved as on a seal, one for each of the twelve tribes.

15-21　　They made braided chains of pure gold for the Breastpiece, like cords. They made two settings of gold filigree and two rings of gold, put the two rings at the two ends of the Breastpiece, and fastened the two ends of the cords to the two rings at the end of the Breastpiece. Then they fastened the cords to the settings of filigree, attaching them to the shoulder pieces of the Ephod in front. Then they made two rings of gold and fastened them to the two ends of the Breastpiece on its inside edge facing the Ephod. They made two more rings of gold and fastened them in the front of the Ephod to the lower part of the two shoulder pieces, near the seam above the decorated band of the Ephod. The Breastpiece was fastened by running a cord of blue through its rings to the rings of the Ephod so that it rested secure on the decorated band of the Ephod and wouldn't come loose, just as GOD had commanded Moses.

22-26　　Robe. They made the robe for the Ephod entirely of blue. The opening of the robe at the center was like a collar, the edge hemmed so that it wouldn't tear. On the hem of the robe they made pomegranates of blue, purple, and scarlet material and fine twisted linen. They also made bells of pure gold and alternated the bells and pomegranates—a bell and a pomegranate, a bell and a pomegranate—all around the hem of the robe that was worn for ministering, just as GOD had commanded Moses.

27-29　　They also made the tunics of fine linen, the work of a weaver, for Aaron and his sons, the turban of fine linen, the linen hats, the linen underwear made of fine twisted linen, and sashes of fine twisted linen, blue, purple, and scarlet material and embroidered, just as GOD had commanded Moses.

30-31　　They made the plate, the sacred crown, of pure gold and engraved on it as on a seal: "Holy to GOD." They attached a blue cord to it and fastened it to the turban, just as GOD had commanded Moses.

32　　That completed the work of The Dwelling, the Tent of Meeting. The People of Israel did what GOD had commanded Moses. They did it all.

33-41　　They presented The Dwelling to Moses, the Tent and all its furnishings:

　　fastening hooks
　　frames
　　crossbars
　　posts
　　bases
　　tenting of tanned ram skins
　　tenting of dolphin skins
　　veil of the screen
　　Chest of The Testimony

with its poles
and Atonement-Cover
Table
with its utensils
and the Bread of the Presence
Lampstand of pure gold
and its lamps all fitted out
and all its utensils
and the oil for the light
Gold Altar
anointing oil
fragrant incense
screen for the entrance to the Tent
Bronze Altar
with its bronze grate
its poles and all its utensils
Washbasin
and its base
hangings for the Courtyard
its posts and bases
screen for the gate of the Courtyard
its cords and its pegs
utensils for ministry in The Dwelling, the Tent of Meeting
woven vestments for ministering in the Sanctuary
sacred vestments for Aaron the priest,
and his sons when serving as priests

42-43 The Israelites completed all the work, just as GOD had commanded. Moses saw that they had done all the work and done it exactly as GOD had commanded. Moses blessed them.

"MOSES FINISHED THE WORK"

1-3 **40** GOD spoke to Moses: "On the first day of the first month, set up The Dwelling, the Tent of Meeting. Place the Chest of The Testimony in it and screen the Chest with the curtain.

4 "Bring in the Table and set it, arranging its Lampstand and lamps.

5 "Place the Gold Altar of Incense before the Chest of The Testimony and hang the curtain at the door of The Dwelling.

6 "Place the Altar of Whole-Burnt-Offering at the door of The Dwelling, the Tent of Meeting.

7 "Place the Washbasin between the Tent of Meeting and the Altar and fill it with water.

8 "Set up the Courtyard on all sides and hang the curtain at the entrance to the Courtyard.

9-11 "Then take the anointing oil and anoint The Dwelling and everything in it; consecrate it and all its furnishings so that it becomes holy. Anoint the Altar of Whole-Burnt-Offering and all its utensils, consecrating the Altar so that it is completely holy. Anoint the Washbasin and its base: consecrate it.

12-15 "Finally, bring Aaron and his sons to the entrance of the Tent of Meeting and wash them with water. Dress Aaron in the sacred vestments. Anoint him. Consecrate him to serve me as priest. Bring his sons and put tunics on them. Anoint them, just as you anointed their father, to serve me as priests. Their anointing will bring them into a perpetual priesthood, down through the generations."

16 Moses did everything GOD commanded. He did it all.

17-19 On the first day of the first month of the second year, The Dwelling was set up. Moses set it up: He laid its bases, erected the frames, placed the crossbars, set the posts, spread the tent over The Dwelling, and put the covering over the tent, just as GOD had commanded Moses.

20-21 He placed The Testimony in the Chest, inserted the poles for carrying the Chest, and placed the lid, the Atonement-Cover, on it. He brought the Chest into The Dwelling and set up the curtain, screening off the Chest of The Testimony, just as GOD had commanded Moses.

22-23 He placed the Table in the Tent of Meeting on the north side of The Dwelling, outside the curtain, and arranged the Bread there before GOD, just as GOD had commanded him.

24-25 He placed the Lampstand in the Tent of Meeting opposite the Table on the south side of The Dwelling and set up the lamps before GOD, just as GOD had commanded him.

26-27 Moses placed the Gold Altar in the Tent of Meeting in front of the curtain and burned fragrant incense on it, just as GOD had commanded him.

28 He placed the screen at the entrance to The Dwelling.

29 He set the Altar of Whole-Burnt-Offering at the door of The Dwelling, the Tent of Meeting, and offered up the Whole-Burnt-Offerings and the Grain-Offerings, just as GOD had commanded Moses.

30-32 He placed the Washbasin between the Tent of Meeting and the Altar, and filled it with water for washing. Moses and Aaron and his sons washed their hands and feet there. When they entered the Tent of Meeting and when they served at the Altar, they washed, just as GOD had commanded Moses.

33 Finally, he erected the Courtyard all around The Dwelling and the Altar, and put up the screen for the Courtyard entrance.

Moses finished the work.

34-35 The Cloud covered the Tent of Meeting, and the Glory of GOD filled The Dwelling. Moses couldn't enter the Tent of Meeting because the Cloud was upon it, and the Glory of GOD filled The Dwelling.

36-38 Whenever the Cloud lifted from The Dwelling, the People of Israel set out on their travels, but if the Cloud did not lift, they wouldn't set out until it did lift. The Cloud of GOD was over The Dwelling during the day and the fire was in it at night, visible to all the Israelites in all their travels.

LEVITICUS

One of the stubbornly enduring habits of the human race is to insist on domesticating God. We are determined to tame him. We figure out ways to harness God to our projects. We try to reduce God to a size that conveniently fits our plans and ambitions and tastes.

But our Scriptures are even more stubborn in telling us that we can't do it. God cannot be fit into our plans, we must fit into his. We can't use God—God is not a tool or appliance or credit card.

"Holy" is the word that sets God apart and above our attempts to enlist him in our wish-fulfillment fantasies or our utopian schemes for making our mark in the world. Holy means that God is alive on God's terms, alive in a way that exceeds our experience and imagination. Holy refers to life burning with an intense purity that transforms everything it touches into itself.

Because the core of all living is God, and God is a holy God, we require much teaching and long training for living in response to God as he is and not as we want him to be. The book of Leviticus is a narrative pause in the story of our ancestors as they are on their way, saved out of Egypt, to settle in the land of Canaan. It is a kind of extended time-out of instruction, a detailed and meticulous preparation for living "holy" in a culture that doesn't have the faintest idea what "holy" is. The moment these people enter Canaan they will be picking their way through a lethal minefield of gods and goddesses that are designed to appeal to our god-fantasies: "Give us what we want when we want it on our own terms." What these god-fantasies in fact do is cripple or kill us. Leviticus is a start at the "much teaching and long training" that continues to be adapted and reworked in every country and culture where God is forming a saved people to live as he created them to live—holy as God is holy.

The first thing that strikes us as we read Leviticus in this light is that this holy God is actually present with us and virtually every detail of our lives is affected by the presence of this holy God; nothing in us, our relationships, or environment is left out. The second thing is that God provides a way (the sacrifices and feasts and Sabbaths) to bring everything in and about us into his holy presence, transformed in the fiery blaze of the holy. It is an awesome thing to come into his presence and we, like ancient Israel, stand in his presence at every moment (Psalm 139). Our Lord is not dwelling in a tent or house in our neighborhood. But he makes his habitation in us and among us as believers and says, "I am holy; you be holy"

(1 Peter 1:16, citing Leviticus 11:44-45; 19:2; 20:7).

Once we realize this, the seemingly endless details and instructions of Leviticus become signposts of good news to us: God cares that much about the details of our lives, willing everything in and about us into the transformation that St. Paul later commended:

> So here's what I want you to do, God helping you: Take your everyday, ordinary life—your sleeping, eating, going-to-work, and walking-around life—and place it before God as an offering. Embracing what God does for you is the best thing you can do for him. Don't become so well-adjusted to your culture that you fit into it without even thinking. Instead, fix your attention on God. You'll be changed from the inside out. Readily recognize what he wants from you, and quickly respond to it. Unlike the culture around you, always dragging you down to its level of immaturity, God brings the best out of you, develops well-formed maturity in you. (Romans 12:1-2)

LEVITICUS

WHOLE-BURNT-OFFERING

1-2 Goᴅ called Moses and spoke to him from the Tent of Meeting: "Speak to the People of Israel. Tell them, When anyone presents an offering to Goᴅ, present an animal from either the herd or the flock.

3-9 "If the offering is a Whole-Burnt-Offering from the herd, present a male without a defect at the entrance to the Tent of Meeting that it may be accepted by Goᴅ. Lay your hand on the head of the Whole-Burnt-Offering so that it may be accepted on your behalf to make atonement for you. Slaughter the bull in Goᴅ's presence. Aaron's sons, the priests, will make an offering of the blood by splashing it against all sides of the Altar that stands at the entrance to the Tent of Meeting. Next, skin the Whole-Burnt-Offering and cut it up. Aaron's sons, the priests, will prepare a fire on the Altar, carefully laying out the wood, and then arrange the body parts, including the head and the suet, on the wood prepared for the fire on the Altar. Scrub the entrails and legs clean. The priest will burn it all on the Altar: a Whole-Burnt-Offering, a Fire-Gift, a pleasing fragrance to Goᴅ.

10-13 "If the Whole-Burnt-Offering comes from the flock, whether sheep or goat, present a male without defect. Slaughter it on the north side of the Altar in Goᴅ's presence. The sons of Aaron, the priests, will throw the blood against all sides of the Altar. Cut it up and the priest will arrange the pieces, including the head and the suet, on the wood prepared for burning on the Altar. Scrub the entrails and legs clean. The priest will offer it all, burning it on the Altar: a Whole-Burnt-Offering, a Fire-Gift, a pleasing fragrance to Goᴅ.

14-17 "If a bird is presented to Goᴅ for the Whole-Burnt-Offering it can be either a dove or a pigeon. The priest will bring it to the Altar, wring off its head, and burn it on the Altar. But he will first drain the blood on the side of the Altar, remove the gizzard and its contents, and throw them on the east side of the Altar where the ashes are piled. Then rip it open by its wings but leave it in one piece and burn it on the Altar on the wood prepared for the fire: a Whole-Burnt-Offering, a Fire-Gift, a pleasing fragrance to Goᴅ."

GRAIN-OFFERING

1-3 "When you present a Grain-Offering to Goᴅ, use fine flour. Pour oil on it, put incense on it, and bring it to Aaron's sons, the priests. One of them will take a handful of the fine flour and oil, with all the incense, and burn it on the Altar for a memorial: a Fire-Gift, a pleasing fragrance to Goᴅ. The rest of the Grain-Offering is for Aaron and his sons—a most holy part of the Fire-Gifts to Goᴅ.

4 "When you present a Grain-Offering of oven-baked loaves, use fine flour, mixed with oil but no yeast. Or present wafers made without yeast and spread with oil.

5-6 "If you bring a Grain-Offering cooked on a griddle, use fine flour mixed with oil but without yeast. Crumble it and pour oil on it—it's a Grain-Offering.

7   "If you bring a Grain-Offering deep-fried in a pan, make it of fine flour with oil.

8-10   "Bring the Grain-Offering you make from these ingredients and present it to the priest. He will bring it to the Altar, break off a memorial piece from the Grain-Offering, and burn it on the Altar: a Fire-Gift, a pleasing fragrance to GOD. The rest of the Grain-Offering is for Aaron and his sons — a most holy part of the gifts to GOD.

11-13   "All the Grain-Offerings that you present to GOD must be made without yeast; you must never burn any yeast or honey as a Fire-Gift to GOD. You may offer them to GOD as an offering of firstfruits but not on the Altar as a pleasing fragrance. Season every presentation of your Grain-Offering with salt. Don't leave the salt of the covenant with your God out of your Grain-Offerings. Present all your offerings with salt.

14-16   "If you present a Grain-Offering of firstfruits to GOD, bring crushed heads of the new grain roasted. Put oil and incense on it — it's a Grain-Offering. The priest will burn some of the mixed grain and oil with all the incense as a memorial — a Fire-Gift to GOD."

THE PEACE-OFFERING

1-5   3 "If your offering is a Peace-Offering and you present an animal from the herd, either male or female, it must be an animal without any defect. Lay your hand on the head of your offering and slaughter it at the entrance of the Tent of Meeting. Aaron's sons, the priests, will throw the blood on all sides of the Altar. As a Fire-Gift to GOD from the Peace-Offering, present all the fat that covers or is connected to the entrails, the two kidneys and the fat around them at the loins, and the lobe of the liver that is removed along with the kidneys. Aaron and his sons will burn it on the Altar along with the Whole-Burnt-Offering that is on the wood prepared for the fire: a Fire-Gift, a pleasing fragrance to GOD.

6-11   "If your Peace-Offering to GOD comes from the flock, bring a male or female without defect. If you offer a lamb, offer it to GOD. Lay your hand on the head of your offering and slaughter it at the Tent of Meeting. The sons of Aaron will throw its blood on all sides of the Altar. As a Fire-Gift to GOD from the Peace-Offering, present its fat, the entire fat tail cut off close to the backbone, all the fat on and connected to the entrails, the two kidneys and the fat around them on the loins, and the lobe of the liver which is removed along with the kidneys. The priest will burn it on the Altar: a meal, a Fire-Gift to GOD.

12-16   "If the offering is a goat, bring it into the presence of GOD, lay your hand on its head, and slaughter it in front of the Tent of Meeting. Aaron's sons will throw the blood on all sides of the Altar. As a Fire-Gift to GOD present the fat that covers and is connected to the entrails, the two kidneys and the fat which is around them on the loins, and the lobe of the liver which is removed along with the kidneys. The priest will burn them on the Altar: a meal, a Fire-Gift, a pleasing fragrance.

16-17   "All the fat belongs to GOD. This is the fixed rule down through the generations, wherever you happen to live: Don't eat the fat; don't eat the blood. None of it."

THE ABSOLUTION-OFFERING

1-12   4 GOD spoke to Moses: "Tell the Israelites, When a person sins unintentionally by straying from any of GOD's commands, breaking what must not be broken, if it's the anointed priest who sins and so brings guilt on the people, he is to bring a bull without defect to GOD as an Absolution-Offering for the sin he has committed. Have him bring the bull to the entrance of the Tent of Meeting in the presence of GOD, lay his hand on the bull's head, and slaughter the bull before GOD. He is then to take some of the bull's blood, bring it into the Tent of Meeting, dip his finger in the blood, and sprinkle some of it seven times before GOD, before the curtain of the Sanctuary. He is to smear some of the blood on the horns of the Altar of Fragrant Incense before GOD which is in the Tent of Meeting. He is to pour the rest of the bull's blood out at the base of the Altar of Whole-Burnt-Offering at the entrance of the Tent of Meeting. He is to remove all the fat from the bull of the Absolution-Offering, the fat which covers and is connected to the entrails, the two kidneys and the fat that is around them at the loins, and the lobe of the liver which he takes out along with the kidneys — the same procedure as when the fat is removed from the bull of the Peace-Offering. Finally, he is to burn all this on the Altar of Burnt Offering. Everything else — the bull's hide, meat, head, legs, organs, and guts — he is to take outside the camp to a clean place where the ashes are dumped and is to burn it on a wood fire.

¹³⁻²¹ "If the whole congregation sins unintentionally by straying from one of the commandments of GOD that must not be broken, they become guilty even though no one is aware of it. When they do become aware of the sin they've committed, the congregation must bring a bull as an Absolution-Offering and present it at the Tent of Meeting. The elders of the congregation will lay their hands on the bull's head in the presence of GOD and one of them will slaughter it before GOD. The anointed priest will then bring some of the blood into the Tent of Meeting, dip his finger in the blood, and sprinkle some of it seven times before GOD in front of the curtain. He will smear some of the blood on the horns of the Altar which is before GOD in the Tent of Meeting and pour the rest of it at the base of the Altar of Whole-Burnt-Offering at the entrance of the Tent of Meeting. He will remove all the fat and burn it on the Altar. He will follow the same procedure with this bull as with the bull for the Absolution-Offering. The priest makes atonement for them and they are forgiven. They then will take the bull outside the camp and burn it just as they burned the first bull. It's the Absolution-Offering for the congregation.

²²⁻²⁶ "When a ruler sins unintentionally by straying from one of the commands of his GOD which must not be broken, he is guilty. When he becomes aware of the sin he has committed, he must bring a goat for his offering, a male without any defect, lay his hand on the head of the goat, and slaughter it in the place where they slaughter the Whole-Burnt-Offering in the presence of GOD — it's an Absolution-Offering. The priest will then take some of the blood of the Absolution-Offering with his finger, smear it on the horns of the Altar of Whole-Burnt-Offering, and pour the rest at the base of the Altar. He will burn all its fat on the Altar, the same as with the fat of the Peace-Offering.

"The priest makes atonement for him on account of his sin and he's forgiven.

²⁷⁻³¹ "When an ordinary member of the congregation sins unintentionally, straying from one of the commandments of GOD which must not be broken, he is guilty. When he is made aware of his sin, he shall bring a goat, a female without any defect, and offer it for his sin, lay his hand on the head of the Absolution-Offering, and slaughter it at the place of the Whole-Burnt-Offering. The priest will take some of its blood with his finger, smear it on

the horns of the Altar of Whole-Burnt-Offering, and pour the rest at the base of the Altar. Finally, he'll take out all the fat, the same as with the Peace-Offerings, and burn it on the Altar for a pleasing fragrance to GOD.

"In this way, the priest makes atonement for him and he's forgiven.

32-35 "If he brings a lamb for an Absolution-Offering, he shall present a female without any defect, lay his hand on the head of the Absolution-Offering, and slaughter it at the same place they slaughter the Whole-Burnt-Offering. The priest will take some of the blood of the Absolution-Offering with his finger, smear it on the horns of the Altar of Burnt-Offering, and pour the rest at the base of the Altar. He shall remove all the fat, the same as for the lamb of the Peace-Offering. Finally, the priest will burn it on the Altar on top of the gifts to GOD.

"In this way, the priest makes atonement for him on account of his sin and he's forgiven."

---

1 5 "If you sin by not stepping up and offering yourself as a witness to something you've heard or seen in cases of wrongdoing, you'll be held responsible.

2 "Or if you touch anything ritually unclean, like the carcass of an unclean animal, wild or domestic, or a dead reptile, and you weren't aware of it at the time, but you're contaminated and you're guilty;

3 "Or if you touch human uncleanness, any sort of ritually contaminating uncleanness, and you're not aware of it at the time, but later you realize it and you're guilty;

4 "Or if you impulsively swear to do something, whether good or bad — some rash oath that just pops out — and you aren't aware of what you've done at the time, but later you come to realize it and you're guilty in any of these cases;

5-6 "When you are guilty, immediately confess the sin that you've committed and bring as your penalty to GOD for the sin you have committed a female lamb or goat from the flock for an Absolution-Offering.

"In this way, the priest will make atonement for your sin.

7-10 "If you can't afford a lamb, bring as your penalty to GOD for the sin you have committed two doves or two pigeons, one for the Absolution-Offering and the other for the Whole-Burnt-Offering. Bring them to the priest who will first offer the one for the Absolution-Offering: He'll wring its neck but not sever it, splash some of the blood of the Absolution-Offering against the Altar, and squeeze the rest of it out at the base. It's an Absolution-Offering. He'll then take the second bird and offer it as a Whole-Burnt-Offering, following the procedures step-by-step.

"In this way, the priest will make atonement for your sin and you're forgiven.

11-12 "If you cannot afford the two doves or pigeons, bring two quarts of fine flour for your Absolution-Offering. Don't put oil or incense on it — - it's an Absolution-Offering. Bring it to the priest; he'll take a handful from it as a memorial and burn it on the Altar with the gifts for GOD. It's an Absolution-Offering.

13 "The priest will make atonement for you and any of these sins you've committed and you're forgiven. The rest of the offering belongs to the priest, the same as with the Grain-Offering."

COMPENSATION-OFFERING

14-16   GOD spoke to Moses: "When a person betrays his trust and unknowingly sins by straying against any of the holy things of GOD, he is to bring as his penalty to GOD a ram without any defect from the flock, the value of the ram assessed in shekels, according to the Sanctuary shekel for a Compensation-Offering. He is to make additional compensation for the sin he has committed against any holy thing by adding twenty percent to the ram and giving it to the priest.

"Thus the priest will make atonement for him with the ram of the Compensation-Offering and he's forgiven.

17-18   "If anyone sins by breaking any of the commandments of GOD which must not be broken, but without being aware of it at the time, the moment he does realize his guilt he is held responsible. He is to bring to the priest a ram without any defect, assessed at the value of the Compensation-Offering.

18-19   "Thus the priest will make atonement for him for his error that he was unaware of and he's forgiven. It is a Compensation-Offering; he was surely guilty before God."

1-6   6 GOD spoke to Moses: "When anyone sins by betraying trust with GOD by deceiving his neighbor regarding something entrusted to him, or by robbing or cheating or threatening him; or if he has found something lost and lies about it and swears falsely regarding any of these sins that people commonly commit—when he sins and is found guilty, he must return what he stole or extorted, restore what was entrusted to him, return the lost thing he found, or anything else about which he swore falsely. He must make full compensation, add twenty percent to it, and hand it over to the owner on the same day he brings his Compensation-Offering. He must present to GOD as his Compensation-Offering a ram without any defect from the flock, assessed at the value of a Compensation-Offering.

7   "Thus the priest will make atonement for him before GOD and he's forgiven of any of the things that one does that bring guilt."

FURTHER INSTRUCTIONS

8-13   GOD spoke to Moses: "Command Aaron and his sons. Tell them, These are the instructions for the Whole-Burnt-Offering. Leave the Whole-Burnt-Offering on the Altar hearth through the night until morning, with the fire kept burning on the Altar. Then dress in your linen clothes with linen underwear next to your body. Remove the ashes remaining from the Whole-Burnt-Offering and place them beside the Altar. Then change clothes and carry the ashes outside the camp to a clean place. Meanwhile keep the fire on the Altar burning; it must not go out. Replenish the wood for the fire every morning, arrange the Whole-Burnt-Offering on it, and burn the fat of the Peace-Offering on top of it all. Keep the fire burning on the Altar continuously. It must not go out.

14-18   "These are the instructions for the Grain-Offering. Aaron's sons are to present it to GOD in front of the Altar. The priest takes a handful of the fine flour of the Grain-Offering with its oil and all its incense and burns this as a memorial on the Altar, a pleasing fragrance to GOD. Aaron and his sons eat the rest of it. It is unraised bread and so eaten in a holy place — in the Courtyard of the Tent of Meeting. They must not bake it with yeast. I have designated it as their share of the gifts presented to me. It is very holy, like the Absolution-Offering and the Compensation-Offering. Any male descendant among Aaron's sons may eat it. This is a fixed rule regarding GOD's gifts, stretching down the generations. Anyone who touches these offerings must be holy."

19-23   GOD spoke to Moses: "This is the offering which Aaron and his sons each are to present to GOD on the day he is anointed: two quarts of fine flour as a regular Grain-Offering, half in the morning and half in the evening. Prepare it with oil on a griddle. Bring it well-mixed and then present it crumbled in pieces as a pleasing fragrance to GOD. Aaron's son who is anointed to succeed him offers it to GOD — this is a fixed rule. The whole thing is burned. Every Grain-Offering of a priest is burned completely; it must not be eaten."

24-30   GOD spoke to Moses: "Tell Aaron and his sons, These are the instructions for the Absolution-Offering. Slaughter the Absolution-Offering in the place where the Whole-Burnt-Offering is slaughtered before GOD — the offering is most holy. The priest in charge eats it in a holy place, the Courtyard of the Tent of Meeting. Anyone who touches any of the meat must be holy. A garment that gets blood spattered on it must be washed in a holy place. Break the clay pot in which the meat was cooked. If it was cooked in a bronze pot, scour it and rinse it with water. Any male among the priestly families may eat it; it is most holy. But any Absolution-Offering whose blood is brought into the Tent of Meeting to make atonement in the Sanctuary must not be eaten, it has to be burned."

1-6   7 "These are the instructions for the Compensation-Offering. It is most holy. Slaughter the Compensation-Offering in the same place that the Whole-Burnt-Offering is slaughtered. Splash its blood against all sides of the Altar. Offer up all the fat: the fat tail, the fat covering the entrails, the two kidneys and the fat encasing them at the loins, and the lobe of the liver that is removed with the kidneys. The priest burns them on the Altar as a gift to GOD. It is a Compensation-Offering. Any male from among the priests' families may eat it. But it must be eaten in a holy place; it is most holy.

7-10   "The Compensation-Offering is the same as the Absolution-Offering — the same rules apply to both. The offering belongs to the priest who makes atonement with it. The priest who presents a Whole-Burnt-Offering for someone gets the hide for himself. Every Grain-Offering baked in an oven or prepared in a pan or on a griddle belongs to the priest who presents it. It's his. Every Grain-Offering, whether dry or mixed with oil, belongs equally to all the sons of Aaron.

11-15 "These are the instructions for the Peace-Offering which is presented to GOD. If you bring it to offer thanksgiving, then along with the Thanksgiving-Offering present unraised loaves of bread mixed with oil, unraised wafers spread with oil, and cakes of fine flour, well-kneaded and mixed with oil. Along with the Peace-Offering of thanksgiving, present loaves of yeast bread as an offering. Bring one of each kind as an offering, a Contribution-Offering to GOD; it goes to the priest who throws the blood of the Peace-Offering. Eat the meat from the Peace-Offering of thanksgiving the same day it is offered. Don't leave any of it overnight.

16-21 "If the offering is a Votive-Offering or a Freewill-Offering, it may be eaten the same day it is sacrificed and whatever is left over on the next day may also be eaten. But any meat from the sacrifice that is left to the third day must be burned up. If any of the meat from the Peace-Offering is eaten on the third day, the person who has brought it will not be accepted. It won't benefit him a bit — it has become defiled meat. And whoever eats it must take responsibility for his iniquity. Don't eat meat that has touched anything ritually unclean; burn it up. Any other meat can be eaten by those who are ritually clean. But if you're not ritually clean and eat meat from the Peace-Offering for GOD, you will be excluded from the congregation. And if you touch anything ritually unclean, whether human or animal uncleanness or an obscene object, and go ahead and eat from a Peace-Offering for GOD, you'll be excluded from the congregation."

22-27 GOD spoke to Moses: "Speak to the People of Israel. Tell them, Don't eat any fat of cattle or sheep or goats. The fat of an animal found dead or torn by wild animals can be put to some other purpose, but you may not eat it. If you eat fat from an animal from which a gift has been presented to GOD, you'll be excluded from the congregation. And don't eat blood, whether of birds or animals, no matter where you end up living. If you eat blood you'll be excluded from the congregation."

28-34 GOD spoke to Moses: "Speak to the People of Israel. Tell them, When you present a Peace-Offering to GOD, bring some of your Peace-Offering as a special sacrifice to GOD, a gift to GOD in your own hands. Bring the fat with the breast and then wave the breast before GOD as a Wave-Offering. The priest will burn the fat on the Altar; Aaron and his sons get the breast. Give the right thigh from your Peace-Offerings as a Contribution-Offering to the priest. Give a portion of the right thigh to the son of Aaron who offers the blood and fat of the Peace-Offering as his portion. From the Peace-Offerings of Israel, I'm giving the breast of the Wave-Offering and the thigh of the Contribution-Offering to Aaron the priest and his sons. This is their fixed compensation from the People of Israel."

35-36 From the day they are presented to serve as priests to GOD, Aaron and his sons can expect to receive these allotments from the gifts of GOD. This is what GOD commanded the People of Israel to give the priests from the day of their anointing. This is the fixed rule down through the generations.

37-38 These are the instructions for the Whole-Burnt-Offering, the Grain-Offering, the Absolution-Offering, the Compensation-Offering, the

Ordination-Offering, and the Peace-Offering which GOD gave Moses at Mount Sinai on the day he commanded the People of Israel to present their offerings to GOD in the wilderness of Sinai.

THE ORDINATION OF PRIESTS

¹⁻⁴ 8 GOD spoke to Moses: He said, "Take Aaron and with him his sons, the garments, the anointing oil, the bull for the Absolution-Offering, the two rams, and the basket of unraised bread. Gather the entire congregation at the entrance of the Tent of Meeting." Moses did just as GOD commanded him and the congregation gathered at the entrance of the Tent of Meeting.

⁵ Moses addressed the congregation: "This is what GOD has commanded to be done."

⁶⁻⁹ Moses brought Aaron and his sons forward and washed them with water. He put the tunic on Aaron and tied it around him with a sash. Then he put the robe on him and placed the Ephod on him. He fastened the Ephod with a woven belt, making it snug. He put the Breastpiece on him and put the Urim and Thummim in the pouch of the Breastpiece. He placed the turban on his head with the gold plate fixed to the front of it, the holy crown, just as GOD had commanded Moses.

¹⁰⁻¹² Then Moses took the anointing oil and anointed The Dwelling and everything that was in it, consecrating them. He sprinkled some of the oil on the Altar seven times, anointing the Altar and all its utensils, the Washbasin and its stand, consecrating them. He poured some of the anointing oil on Aaron's head, anointing him and thus consecrating him.

¹³ Moses brought Aaron's sons forward and put tunics on them, belted them with sashes, and put caps on them, just as GOD had commanded Moses.

¹⁴⁻¹⁷ Moses brought out the bull for the Absolution-Offering. Aaron and his sons placed their hands on its head. Moses slaughtered the bull and purified the Altar by smearing the blood on each of the horns of the Altar with his finger. He poured out the rest of the blood at the base of the Altar. He consecrated it so atonement could be made on it. Moses took all the fat on the entrails and the lobe of liver and the two kidneys with their fat and burned it all on the Altar. The bull with its hide and meat and guts he burned outside the camp, just as GOD had commanded Moses.

¹⁸⁻²¹ Moses presented the ram for the Whole-Burnt-Offering. Aaron and his sons laid their hands on the head of the ram. Moses slaughtered it and splashed the blood against all sides of the Altar. He cut the ram up into pieces and then burned the head, the pieces, and the fat. He washed the entrails and the legs with water and then burned the whole ram on the Altar. It was a Whole-Burnt-Offering, a pleasing fragrance — a gift to GOD, just as GOD had commanded Moses.

²²⁻²⁹ Moses then presented the second ram, the ram for the Ordination-Offering. Aaron and his sons laid their hands on the ram's head. Moses slaughtered it and smeared some of its blood on the lobe of Aaron's right ear, on the thumb of his right hand, and on the big toe of his right foot. Then Aaron's sons were brought forward and Moses smeared some of the blood on the lobes of their right ears, on the thumbs of their right hands, and on the big toes of their right feet. Moses threw the remaining blood against each side of the Altar. He took the fat, the fat tail, all the fat that was on the entrails, the lobe of the liver, the two kidneys with their fat, and the right thigh. From

the basket of unraised bread that was in the presence of GOD he took one loaf of the unraised bread made with oil and one wafer. He placed these on the fat portions and the right thigh. He put all this in the hands of Aaron and his sons who waved them before GOD as a Wave-Offering. Then Moses took it all back from their hands and burned them on the Altar on top of the Whole-Burnt-Offering. These were the Ordination-Offerings, a pleasing fragrance to GOD, a gift to GOD. Then Moses took the breast and raised it up as a Wave-Offering before GOD; it was Moses' portion from the Ordination-Offering ram, just as GOD had commanded Moses.

30 Moses took some of the anointing oil and some of the blood from the Altar and sprinkled Aaron and his garments, and his sons and their garments, consecrating Aaron and his garments and his sons and their garments.

31-35 Moses spoke to Aaron and his sons: "Boil the meat at the entrance of the Tent of Meeting and eat it there with the bread from the basket of ordination, just as I commanded, saying, 'Aaron and his sons are to eat it.' Burn up the leftovers from the meat and bread. Don't leave through the entrance of the Tent of Meeting for the seven days that will complete your ordination. Your ordination will last seven days. GOD commanded what has been done this day in order to make atonement for you. Stay at the entrance of the Tent of Meeting day and night for seven days. Be sure to do what GOD requires, lest you die. This is what I have been commanded."

36 Aaron and his sons did everything that GOD had commanded by Moses.

THE PRIESTS GO TO WORK

1-2 9 On the eighth day, Moses called in Aaron and his sons and the leaders of Israel. He spoke to Aaron: "Take a bull-calf for your Absolution-Offering and a ram for your Whole-Burnt-Offering, both without defect, and offer them to GOD.

3-4 "Then tell the People of Israel, Take a male goat for an Absolution-Offering and a calf and a lamb, both yearlings without defect, for a Whole-Burnt-Offering and a bull and a ram for a Peace-Offering, to be sacrificed before GOD with a Grain-Offering mixed with oil, because GOD will appear to you today."

5-6 They brought the things that Moses had ordered to the Tent of Meeting. The whole congregation came near and stood before GOD. Moses said, "This is what GOD commanded you to do so that the Shining Glory of GOD will appear to you."

7 Moses instructed Aaron, "Approach the Altar and sacrifice your Absolution-Offering and your Whole-Burnt-Offering. Make atonement for yourself and for the people. Sacrifice the offering that is for the people and make atonement for them, just as GOD commanded."

8-11 Aaron approached the Altar and slaughtered the calf as an Absolution-Offering for himself. Aaron's sons brought the blood to him. He dipped his finger in the blood and smeared some of it on the horns of the Altar. He poured out the rest of the blood at the base of the Altar. He burned the fat, the kidneys, and the lobe of the liver from the Absolution-Offering on the Altar, just as GOD had commanded Moses. He burned the meat and the skin outside the camp.

12-14 Then he slaughtered the Whole-Burnt-Offering. Aaron's sons handed him the blood and he threw it against each side of the Altar. They handed him the pieces and the head and he burned these on the Altar. He washed the entrails and the legs and burned them on top of the Whole-Burnt-Offering on the Altar.

15-21　　　Next Aaron presented the offerings of the people. He took the male goat, the Absolution-Offering for the people, slaughtered it, and offered it as an Absolution-Offering just as he did with the first offering. He presented the Whole-Burnt-Offering following the same procedures. He presented the Grain-Offering by taking a handful of it and burning it on the Altar along with the morning Whole-Burnt-Offering. He slaughtered the bull and the ram, the people's Peace-Offerings. Aaron's sons handed him the blood and he threw it against each side of the Altar. The fat pieces from the bull and the ram—the fat tail and the fat that covers the kidney and the lobe of the liver—they laid on the breasts and Aaron burned it on the Altar. Aaron waved the breasts and the right thigh before God as a Wave-Offering, just as God commanded.

22-24　　　Aaron lifted his hands over the people and blessed them. Having completed the rituals of the Absolution-Offering, the Whole-Burnt-Offering, and the Peace-Offering, he came down from the Altar. Moses and Aaron entered the Tent of Meeting. When they came out they blessed the people and the Glory of God appeared to all the people. Fire blazed out from God and consumed the Whole-Burnt-Offering and the fat pieces on the Altar. When all the people saw it happen they cheered loudly and then fell down, bowing in reverence.

NADAB AND ABIHU

1-2　　**10** That same day Nadab and Abihu, Aaron's sons, took their censers, put hot coals and incense in them, and offered "strange" fire to God—something God had not commanded. Fire blazed out from God and consumed them—they died in God's presence.

3　　　Moses said to Aaron, "This is what God meant when he said,

To the one who comes near me,
　　I will show myself holy;
Before all the people,
　　I will show my glory."

Aaron was silent.

4-5　　　Moses called for Mishael and Elzaphan, sons of Uzziel, Aaron's uncle. He said, "Come. Carry your dead cousins outside the camp, away from the Sanctuary." They came and carried them off, outside the camp, just as Moses had directed.

6-7　　　Moses then said to Aaron and his remaining sons, Eleazar and Ithamar, "No mourning rituals for you—unkempt hair, torn clothes—or you'll also die and God will be angry with the whole congregation. Your relatives—all the People of Israel, in fact—will do the mourning over those God has destroyed by fire. And don't leave the entrance to the Tent of Meeting lest you die, because God's anointing oil is on you."

They did just as Moses said.

8-11　　　God instructed Aaron: "When you enter the Tent of Meeting, don't drink wine or strong drink, neither you nor your sons, lest you die. This is a fixed rule down through the generations. Distinguish between the holy and the common, between the ritually clean and unclean. Teach the People of Israel all the decrees that GOD has spoken to them through Moses."

12-15 Moses spoke to Aaron and his surviving sons, Eleazar and Ithamar, "Take the leftovers of the Grain-Offering from the Fire-Gifts for GOD and eat beside the Altar that which has been prepared without yeast, for it is most holy. Eat it in the Holy Place because it is your portion and the portion of your sons from the Fire-Gifts for GOD. This is what GOD commanded me. Also, you and your sons and daughters are to eat the breast of the Wave-Offering and the thigh of the Contribution-Offering in a clean place. They are provided as your portion and the portion of your children from the Peace-Offerings presented by the People of Israel. Bring the thigh of the Contribution-Offering and the breast of the Wave-Offering and the fat pieces of the Fire-Gifts and lift them up as a Wave-Offering. This will be the regular share for you and your children as ordered by GOD."

16-18 When Moses looked into the matter of the goat of the Absolution-Offering, he found that it had been burned up. He became angry with Eleazar and Ithamar, Aaron's remaining sons, and asked, "Why didn't you eat the Absolution-Offering in the Holy Place since it is most holy? The offering was given to you for taking away the guilt of the community by making atonement for them before GOD. Since its blood was not taken into the Holy Place, you should have eaten the goat in the Sanctuary as I commanded."

19 Aaron replied to Moses, "Look. They sacrificed their Absolution-Offering and Whole-Burnt-Offering before GOD today, and you see what has happened to me—I've lost two sons. Do you think GOD would have been pleased if I had gone ahead and eaten the Absolution-Offering today?"

20 When Moses heard this response, he accepted it.

FOODS

1-2 **11** GOD spoke to Moses and Aaron: "Speak to the People of Israel. Tell them, Of all the animals on Earth, these are the animals that you may eat:

3-8 "You may eat any animal that has a split hoof, divided in two, and that chews the cud, but not an animal that only chews the cud or only has a split hoof. For instance, the camel chews the cud but doesn't have a split hoof, so it's unclean. The rock badger chews the cud but doesn't have a split hoof and so it's unclean. The rabbit chews the cud but doesn't have a split hoof so is unclean. The pig has a split hoof, divided in two, but doesn't chew the cud and so is unclean. You may not eat their meat nor touch their carcasses; they are unclean to you.

9-12 "Among the creatures that live in the water of the seas and streams, you may eat any that have fins and scales. But anything that doesn't have fins and scales, whether in seas or streams, whether small creatures in the shallows or huge creatures in the deeps, you are to detest. Yes, detest them. Don't eat their meat; detest their carcasses. Anything living in the water that doesn't have fins and scales is detestable to you.

13-19 "These are the birds you are to detest. Don't eat them. They are detestable: eagle, vulture, osprey, kite, all falcons, all ravens, ostrich, nighthawk, sea gull, all hawks, owl, cormorant, ibis, water hen, pelican, Egyptian vulture, stork, all herons, hoopoe, bat.

20-23 "All flying insects that walk on all fours are detestable to you. But you can eat some of these, namely, those that have jointed legs for hopping on the ground: all locusts, katydids, crickets, and grasshoppers. But all the other flying insects that have four legs you are to detest.

24-25 "You will make yourselves ritually unclean until evening if you touch their carcasses. If you pick up one of their carcasses you must wash your clothes and you'll be unclean until evening.

26 "Every animal that has a split hoof that's not completely divided, or that doesn't chew the cud is unclean for you; if you touch the carcass of any of them you become unclean.

27-28 "Every four-footed animal that goes on its paws is unclean for you; if you touch its carcass you are unclean until evening. If you pick up its carcass you must wash your clothes and are unclean until evening. They are unclean for you.

29-38 "Among the creatures that crawl on the ground, the following are unclean for you: weasel, rat, all lizards, gecko, monitor lizard, wall lizard, skink, chameleon. Among the crawling creatures, these are unclean for you. If you touch them when they are dead, you are ritually unclean until evening. When one of them dies and falls on something, that becomes unclean no matter what it's used for, whether it's made of wood, cloth, hide, or sackcloth. Put it in the water — it's unclean until evening, and then it's clean. If one of these dead creatures falls into a clay pot, everything in the pot is unclean and you must break the pot. Any food that could be eaten but has water on it from such a pot is unclean, and any liquid that could be drunk from it is unclean. Anything that one of these carcasses falls on is unclean — an oven or cooking pot must be broken up; they're unclean and must be treated as unclean. A spring, though, or a cistern for collecting water remains clean, but if you touch one of these carcasses you're ritually unclean. If a carcass falls on any seeds that are to be planted, they remain clean. But if water has been put on the seed and a carcass falls on it, you must treat it as unclean.

39-40 "If an animal that you are permitted to eat dies, anyone who touches the carcass is ritually unclean until evening. If you eat some of the carcass you must wash your clothes and you are unclean until evening. If you pick up the carcass you must wash your clothes and are unclean until evening.

41-43 "Creatures that crawl on the ground are detestable and not to be eaten. Don't eat creatures that crawl on the ground, whether on their belly or on all fours or on many feet— they are detestable. Don't make yourselves unclean or be defiled by them, because I am your GOD.

44-45 "Make yourselves holy for I am holy. Don't make yourselves ritually unclean by any creature that crawls on the ground. I am GOD who brought you up out of the land of Egypt. Be holy because I am holy.

46-47 "These are the instructions on animals, birds, fish, and creatures that crawl on the ground. You have to distinguish between the ritually unclean and the clean, between living creatures that can be eaten and those that cannot be eaten."

CHILDBIRTH

1-5 **12** GOD spoke to Moses: "Tell the People of Israel, A woman who conceives and gives birth to a boy is ritually unclean for seven days, the same as during her menstruation. On the eighth day circumcise the boy. The mother must stay home another thirty-three days for purification from her bleeding. She may not touch anything consecrated or enter the Sanctuary until the days of her purification are complete. If she gives birth to a girl, she is unclean for fourteen days, the same as during her menstruation. She must stay home for sixty-six days for purification from her bleeding.

6-7 "When the days for her purification for either a boy or a girl are complete, she will bring a yearling lamb for a Whole-Burnt-Offering and a pigeon or dove for an Absolution-Offering to the priest at the entrance of the Tent of Meeting. He will offer it to GOD and make atonement for her. She is then clean from her flow of blood.

"These are the instructions for a woman who gives birth to either a boy or a girl.

8 "If she can't afford a lamb, she can bring two doves or two pigeons, one for the Whole-Burnt-Offering and one for the Absolution-Offering. The priest will make atonement for her and she will be clean."

INFECTIONS

1-3 13 GOD spoke to Moses and Aaron: "When someone has a swelling or a blister or a shiny spot on the skin that might signal a serious skin disease on the body, bring him to Aaron the priest or to one of his priest sons. The priest will examine the sore on the skin. If the hair in the sore has turned white and the sore appears more than skin deep, it is a serious skin disease and infectious. After the priest has examined it, he will pronounce the person unclean.

4-8 "If the shiny spot on the skin is white but appears to be only on the surface and the hair has not turned white, the priest will quarantine the person for seven days. On the seventh day the priest will examine it again; if, in his judgment, the sore is the same and has not spread, the priest will keep him in quarantine for another seven days. On the seventh day the priest will examine him a second time; if the sore has faded and hasn't spread, the priest will declare him clean — it is a harmless rash. The person can go home and wash his clothes; he is clean. But if the sore spreads after he has shown himself to the priest and been declared clean, he must come back again to the priest who will conduct another examination. If the sore has spread, the priest will pronounce him unclean — it is a serious skin disease and infectious.

9-17 "Whenever someone has a serious and infectious skin disease, you must bring him to the priest. The priest will examine him; if there is a white swelling in the skin, the hair is turning white, and there is an open sore in the swelling, it is a chronic skin disease. The priest will pronounce him unclean. But he doesn't need to quarantine him because he's already given his diagnosis of unclean. If a serious disease breaks out that covers all the skin from head to foot, wherever the priest looks, the priest will make a thorough examination; if the disease covers his entire body, he will pronounce the person with the sore clean — since it has turned all white, he is clean. But if they are open, running sores, he is unclean. The priest will examine the open sores and pronounce him unclean. The open sores are unclean; they are evidence of a serious skin disease. But if the open sores dry up and turn white, he is to come back to the priest who will reexamine him; if the sores have turned white, the priest will pronounce the person with the sores clean. He is clean.

18-23 "When a person has a boil and it heals and in place of the boil there is white swelling or a reddish-white shiny spot, the person must present himself to the priest for an examination. If it looks like it has penetrated the skin and the hair in it has turned white, the priest will pronounce him unclean. It is a serious skin disease that has broken out in the boil. But if the examination shows that there is no white hair in it and it is only skin deep and has faded, the priest will put him in quarantine for seven days. If it then spreads over the skin, the priest will diagnose him as unclean. It is infectious. But if the shiny spot has not changed and hasn't spread, it's only a scar from the boil. The priest will pronounce him clean.

²⁴⁻²⁸   "When a person has a burn on his skin and the raw flesh turns into a reddish-white or white shiny spot, the priest is to examine it. If the hair has turned white in the shiny spot and it looks like it's more than skin deep, a serious skin disease has erupted in the area of the burn. The priest will pronounce him unclean; it is a serious skin disease and infectious. But if on examination there is no white hair in the shiny spot and it doesn't look to be more than skin deep but has faded, the priest will put him in quarantine for seven days. On the seventh day the priest will reexamine him. If by then it has spread over the skin, the priest will diagnose him as unclean; it is a serious skin disease and infectious. If by that time the shiny spot has stayed the same and has not spread but has faded, it is only a swelling from the burn. The priest will pronounce him clean; it's only a scar from the burn.

²⁹⁻³⁷   "If a man or woman develops a sore on the head or chin, the priest will offer a diagnosis. If it looks as if it is under the skin and the hair in it is yellow and thin, he will pronounce the person ritually unclean. It is an itch, an infectious skin disease. But if when he examines the itch, he finds it is only skin deep and there is no black hair in it, he will put the person in quarantine for seven days. On the seventh day he will reexamine the sore; if the itch has not spread, there is no yellow hair in it, and it looks as if the itch is only skin deep, the person must shave, except for the itch; the priest will send him back to quarantine for another seven days. If the itch has not spread, and looks to be only skin deep, the priest will pronounce him clean. The person can go home and wash his clothes; he is clean. But if the itch spreads after being pronounced clean, the priest must reexamine it; if the itch has spread in the skin, he doesn't have to look any farther, for yellow hair, for instance; he is unclean. But if he sees that the itch is unchanged and black hair has begun to grow in it, the itch is healed. The person is clean and the priest will pronounce him clean.

³⁸⁻³⁹   "When a man or woman gets shiny or white shiny spots on the skin, the priest is to make an examination; if the shiny spots are dull white, it is only a rash that has broken out: The person is clean.

⁴⁰⁻⁴⁴   "When a man loses his hair and goes bald, he is clean. If he loses his hair from his forehead, he is bald and he is clean. But if he has a reddish-white sore on scalp or forehead, it means a serious skin disease is breaking out. The priest is to examine it; if the swollen sore on his scalp or forehead is reddish-white like the appearance of the sore of a serious skin disease, he has a serious skin disease and is unclean. The priest has to pronounce him unclean because of the sore on his head.

⁴⁵⁻⁴⁶   "Any person with a serious skin disease must wear torn clothes, leave his hair loose and unbrushed, cover his upper lip, and cry out, 'Unclean! Unclean!' As long as anyone has the sores, that one continues to be ritually unclean. That person must live alone; he or she must live outside the camp.

47-58 "If clothing—woolen or linen clothing, woven or knitted cloth of linen or wool, leather or leatherwork—is infected with a patch of serious fungus and if the spot in the clothing or the leather or the woven or the knitted material or anything made of leather is greenish or rusty, that is a sign of serious fungus. Show it to the priest. The priest will examine the spot and then confiscate the material for seven days. On the seventh day he will reexamine the spot. If it has spread in the garment—the woven or knitted or leather material—it is the spot of a persistent serious fungus and the material is unclean. He must burn the garment. Because of the persistent and contaminating fungus, the material must be burned. But if when the priest examines it the spot has not spread in the garment, the priest will command the owner to wash the material that has the spot, and he will confiscate it for another seven days. He'll then make another examination after it has been washed; if the spot hasn't changed in appearance, even though it hasn't spread, it is still unclean. Burn it up, whether the fungus has affected the back or the front. If, when the priest makes his examination, the spot has faded after it has been washed, he is to tear the spot from the garment. But if it reappears, it is a fresh outbreak—throw whatever has the spot in the fire. If the garment is washed and the spot has gone away, then wash it a second time; it is clean.

59 "These are the instructions regarding a spot of serious fungus in clothing of wool or linen, woven or knitted material, or any article of leather, for pronouncing them clean or unclean."

1-9 14 GOD spoke to Moses: "These are the instructions for the infected person at the time of his cleansing. First, bring him to the priest. The priest will take him outside the camp and make an examination; if the infected person has been healed of the serious skin disease, the priest will order two live, clean birds, some cedar wood, scarlet thread, and hyssop to be brought for the one to be cleansed. The priest will order him to kill one of the birds over fresh water in a clay pot. The priest will then take the live bird with the cedar wood, the scarlet thread, and the hyssop and dip them in the blood of the dead bird over fresh water and then sprinkle the person being cleansed from the serious skin disease seven times and pronounce him clean. Finally, he will release the live bird in the open field. The cleansed person, after washing his clothes, shaving off all his hair, and bathing with water, is clean. Afterwards he may again enter the camp, but he has to live outside his tent for seven days. On the seventh day, he must shave off all his hair—from his head, beard, eyebrows, all of it. He then must wash his clothes and bathe all over with water. He will be clean.

10-18 "The next day, the eighth day, he will bring two lambs without defect and a yearling ewe without defect, along with roughly six quarts of fine flour mixed with oil. The priest who pronounces him clean will place him and the materials for his offerings in the presence of GOD at the entrance to the Tent of Meeting. The priest will take one of the lambs and present it and the pint of oil as a Compensation-Offering and lift them up as a Wave-Offering before GOD. He will slaughter the lamb in the place where the Absolution-Offering and the Whole-Burnt-Offering are slaughtered, in the Holy Place, because like the Absolution-Offering, the Compensation-Offering belongs to the priest; it is most holy. The priest will now take some of the blood of the Compensation-Offering and put it on the right earlobe of the man being cleansed, on the thumb of his right hand, and on the big toe of his right foot. Following that he will take some oil and pour it into the palm of his left hand and then with the finger of his right hand sprinkle oil seven times before GOD. The priest will put some of the remaining oil on the right earlobe of the one being cleansed, on the thumb of his right hand, and on the big toe of his right foot, placing it on top of the blood of the Compensation-Offering. He will put the rest of the oil on the head of the man being cleansed and make atonement for him before GOD.

19-20   "Finally the priest will sacrifice the Absolution-Offering and make atonement for the one to be cleansed from his uncleanness, slaughter the Whole-Burnt-Offering and offer it with the Grain-Offering on the Altar. He has made atonement for him. He is clean.

21-22   "If he is poor and cannot afford these offerings, he will bring one male lamb as a Compensation-Offering to be offered as a Wave-Offering to make atonement for him, and with it a couple of quarts of fine flour mixed with oil for a Grain-Offering, a pint of oil, and two doves or pigeons which he can afford, one for an Absolution-Offering and the other for a Whole-Burnt-Offering.

23-29   "On the eighth day he will bring them to the priest at the entrance to the Tent of Meeting before the presence of GOD. The priest will take the lamb for the Compensation-Offering together with the pint of oil and wave them before GOD as a Wave-Offering. He will slaughter the lamb for the Compensation-Offering, take some of its blood and put it on the lobe of the right ear of the one to be cleansed, on the thumb of his right hand, and on the big toe of his right foot. The priest will pour some of the oil into the palm of his left hand, and with his right finger sprinkle some of the oil from his palm seven times before GOD. He will put some of the oil that is in his palm on the same places he put the blood of the Compensation-Offering, on the lobe of the right ear of the one to be cleansed, on the thumb of his right hand, and on the big toe of his right foot. The priest will take what is left of the oil in his palm and put it on the head of the one to be cleansed, making atonement for him before GOD.

30-31   "At the last, he will sacrifice the doves or pigeons which are within his means, one as an Absolution-Offering and the other as a Whole-Burnt-Offering along with the Grain-Offering. Following this procedure the priest will make atonement for the one to be cleansed before GOD."

32   These are the instructions to be followed for anyone who has a serious skin disease and cannot afford the regular offerings for his cleansing.

※

33-42   GOD spoke to Moses and Aaron: "When you enter the land of Canaan, which I'm giving to you as a possession, and I put a serious fungus in a house in the land of your possession, the householder is to go and tell the priest, 'I have some kind of fungus in my house.' The priest is to order the house vacated until he can come to examine the fungus, so that nothing in the house is declared unclean. When the priest comes and examines the house, if the fungus on the walls of the house has greenish or rusty swelling that appears to go deeper than the surface of the wall, the priest is to walk out the door and shut the house up for seven days. On the seventh day he is to come back and conduct another examination; if the fungus has spread in the walls of the house, he is to order that the stones affected by the fungus be torn out and thrown in a garbage dump outside the city. He is to make sure the entire inside of the house is scraped and the plaster that is removed be taken away to the garbage dump outside the city. Then he is to replace the stones and replaster the house.

43-47 "If the fungus breaks out again in the house after the stones have been torn out and the house has been scraped and plastered, the priest is to come and conduct an examination; if the fungus has spread, it is a malignant fungus. The house is unclean. The house has to be demolished—its stones, wood, and plaster are to be removed to the garbage dump outside the city. Anyone who enters the house while it is closed up is unclean until evening. Anyone who sleeps or eats in the house must wash his clothes.

48-53 "But if when the priest comes and conducts his examination, he finds that the fungus has not spread after the house has been replastered, the priest is to declare that the house is clean; the fungus is cured. He then is to purify the house by taking two birds, some cedar wood, scarlet thread, and hyssop. He will slaughter one bird over fresh water in a clay pot. Then he will take the cedar wood, the hyssop, the scarlet thread, and the living bird, dip them in the blood of the killed bird and the fresh water and sprinkle the house seven times, cleansing the house with the blood of the bird, the fresh water, the living bird, the cedar wood, the hyssop, and the scarlet thread. Last of all, he will let the living bird loose outside the city in the open field. He has made atonement for the house; the house is clean.

54-57 "These are the procedures to be followed for every kind of serious skin disease or itch, for mildew or fungus on clothing or in a house, and for a swelling or blister or shiny spot in order to determine when it is unclean and when it is clean. These are the procedures regarding infectious skin diseases and mildew and fungus."

BODILY DISCHARGES

1-3 **15** GOD spoke to Moses and Aaron: "Speak to the People of Israel. Tell them, When a man has a discharge from his genitals, the discharge is unclean. Whether it comes from a seepage or an obstruction he is unclean. He is unclean all the days his body has a seepage or an obstruction.

4-7 "Every bed on which he lies is ritually unclean, everything on which he sits is unclean. If someone touches his bed or sits on anything he's sat on, or touches the man with the discharge, he has to wash his clothes and bathe in water; he remains unclean until evening.

8-11 "If the man with the discharge spits on someone who is clean, that person has to wash his clothes and bathe in water; he remains unclean until evening. Every saddle on which the man with the discharge rides is unclean. Whoever touches anything that has been under him becomes unclean until evening. Anyone who carries such an object must wash his clothes and bathe with water; he remains unclean until evening. If the one with the discharge touches someone without first rinsing his hands with water, the one touched must wash his clothes and bathe with water; he remains unclean until evening.

12 "If a pottery container is touched by someone with a discharge, you must break it; a wooden article is to be rinsed in water.

13-15   "When a person with a discharge is cleansed from it, he is to count off seven days for his cleansing, wash his clothes, and bathe in running water. Then he is clean. On the eighth day he is to take two doves or two pigeons and come before GOD at the entrance of the Tent of Meeting and give them to the priest. The priest then offers one as an Absolution-Offering and one as a Whole-Burnt-Offering and makes atonement for him in the presence of GOD because of his discharge.

16-18   "When a man has an emission of semen, he must bathe his entire body in water; he remains unclean until evening. Every piece of clothing and everything made of leather which gets semen on it must be washed with water; it remains unclean until evening. When a man sleeps with a woman and has an emission of semen, both are to wash in water; they remain unclean until evening.

19-23   "When a woman has a discharge of blood, the impurity of her menstrual period lasts seven days. Anyone who touches her is unclean until evening. Everything on which she lies or sits during her period is unclean. Anyone who touches her bed or anything on which she sits must wash his clothes and bathe in water; he remains unclean until evening.

24   "If a man sleeps with her and her menstrual blood gets on him, he is unclean for seven days and every bed on which he lies becomes unclean.

25-27   "If a woman has a discharge of blood for many days, but not at the time of her monthly period, or has a discharge that continues beyond the time of her period, she is unclean the same as during the time of her period. Every bed on which she lies during the time of the discharge and everything on which she sits becomes unclean the same as in her monthly period. Anyone who touches these things becomes unclean and must wash his clothes and bathe in water; he remains unclean until evening.

28-30   "When she is cleansed from her discharge, she is to count off seven days; then she is clean. On the eighth day she is to take two doves or two pigeons and bring them to the priest at the entrance to the Tent of Meeting. The priest will offer one for an Absolution-Offering and the other for a Whole-Burnt-Offering. The priest will make atonement for her in the presence of GOD because of the discharge that made her unclean.

31   "You are responsible for keeping the People of Israel separate from that which makes them ritually unclean, lest they die in their unclean condition by defiling my Dwelling which is among them.

32-33   "These are the procedures to follow for a man with a discharge or an emission of semen that makes him unclean, and for a woman in her menstrual period—any man or woman with a discharge and also for a man who sleeps with a woman who is unclean."

THE DAY OF ATONEMENT

1-2   **16** After the death of Aaron's two sons—they died when they came before GOD with strange fire—GOD spoke to Moses: "Tell your brother Aaron not to enter into the Holy of Holies, barging inside the curtain that's before the Atonement-Cover on the Chest whenever he feels like it, lest he die, because I am present in the Cloud over the Atonement-Cover.

3-5   "This is the procedure for Aaron when he enters the Holy Place: He will bring a young bull for an Absolution-Offering and a ram for a Whole-Burnt-Offering; he will put on the holy linen tunic and the linen underwear, tie the linen sash around him, and put on the linen turban. These are the sacred vestments so he must bathe himself with water before he puts them on. Then from the Israelite community he will bring two male goats for an Absolution-Offering and a Whole-Burnt-Offering.

6-10   "Aaron will offer the bull for his own Absolution-Offering in order to make atonement for himself and his household. Then he will set the two goats before GOD at the entrance to the Tent of Meeting and cast lots over the two goats, one lot for GOD and the other lot for Azazel. He will offer the goat on which the lot to GOD falls as an Absolution-Offering. The goat on which the lot for Azazel falls will be sent out into the wilderness to Azazel to make atonement.

11-14   "Aaron will present his bull for an Absolution-Offering to make atonement for himself and his household. He will slaughter his bull for the Absolution-Offering. He will take a censer full of burning coals from the Altar before GOD and two handfuls of finely ground aromatic incense and bring them inside the curtain and put the incense on the fire before GOD; the smoke of the incense will cover the Atonement-Cover which is over The Testimony so that he doesn't die. He will take some of the bull's blood and sprinkle it with his finger on the front of the Atonement-Cover, then sprinkle the blood before the Atonement-Cover seven times.

15-17   "Next he will slaughter the goat designated as the Absolution-Offering for the people and bring the blood inside the curtain. He will repeat what he does with the bull's blood, sprinkling it on and before the Atonement-Cover. In this way he will make atonement for the Holy of Holies because of the uncleannesses of the Israelites, their acts of rebellion, and all their other sins. He will do the same thing for the Tent of Meeting which dwells among the people in the midst of their uncleanness. There is to be no one in the Tent of Meeting from the time Aaron goes in to make atonement in the Holy of Holies until he comes out, having made atonement for himself, his household, and the whole community of Israel.

18-19   "Then he will come out to the Altar that is before GOD and make atonement for it. He will take some of the bull's blood and some of the goat's blood and smear it all around the four horns of the Altar. With his finger he will sprinkle some of the blood on it seven times to purify and consecrate it from the uncleannesses of the Israelites.

20-22   "When Aaron finishes making atonement for the Holy of Holies, the Tent of Meeting, and the Altar, he will bring up the live goat, lay both hands on the live goat's head, and confess all the iniquities of the People of Israel, all their acts of rebellion, all their sins. He will put all the sins on the goat's head and send it off into the wilderness, led out by a man standing by and ready. The goat will carry all their iniquities to an empty wasteland; the man will let him loose out there in the wilderness.

23-25   "Finally, Aaron will come into the Tent of Meeting and take off the linen clothes in which he dressed to enter the Holy of Holies and leave them there. He will bathe in water in a Holy Place, put on his priestly vestments, offer the Whole-Burnt-Offering for himself and the Whole-Burnt-Offering for the people, making atonement for himself and the people, and burn the fat of the Absolution-Offering on the Altar.

26-28   "The man who takes the goat out to Azazel in the wilderness then will wash his clothes and bathe himself with water. After that he will be permitted to come back into the camp. The bull for the Absolution-Offering and the goat for the Absolution-Offering, whose blood has been taken into the Holy of Holies to make atonement, are to be taken outside the camp and burned— their hides, their meat, and their entrails. The man assigned to burn them up will then wash his clothes and bathe himself in water. Then he is free to come back into the camp.

29-31 "This is standard practice for you, a perpetual ordinance. On the tenth day of the seventh month, both the citizen and the foreigner living with you are to enter into a solemn fast and refrain from all work, because on this day atonement will be made for you, to cleanse you. In the presence of GOD you will be made clean of all your sins. It is a Sabbath of all Sabbaths. You must fast. It is a perpetual ordinance.

32 "The priest who is anointed and ordained to succeed his father is to make the atonement:

He puts on the sacred linen garments;

33 He purges the Holy of Holies by making atonement;

He purges the Tent of Meeting and the Altar by making atonement;

He makes atonement for the priests and all the congregation.

34 "This is a perpetual ordinance for you: Once a year atonement is to be made for all the sins of the People of Israel."

And Aaron did it, just as GOD commanded Moses.

HOLY LIVING: SACRIFICES AND BLOOD

1-7 17 GOD spoke to Moses: "Speak to Aaron and his sons and all the Israelites. Tell them, This is what GOD commands: Any and every man who slaughters an ox or lamb or goat inside or outside the camp instead of bringing it to the entrance of the Tent of Meeting to offer it to GOD in front of The Dwelling of GOD— that man is considered guilty of bloodshed; he has shed blood and must be cut off from his people. This is so the Israelites will bring to GOD the sacrifices that they're in the habit of sacrificing out in the open fields. They must bring them to GOD and the priest at the entrance to the Tent of Meeting and sacrifice them as Peace-Offerings to GOD. The priest will splash the blood on the Altar of GOD at the entrance to the Tent of Meeting and burn the fat as a pleasing fragrance to GOD. They must no longer offer their sacrifices to goat-demons— a kind of religious orgy. This is a perpetual decree down through the generations.

8-9 "Tell them, Any Israelite or foreigner living among them who offers a Whole-Burnt-Offering or Peace-Offering but doesn't bring it to the entrance of the Tent of Meeting to sacrifice it to GOD, that person must be cut off from his people.

10-12 "If any Israelite or foreigner living among them eats blood, I will disown that person and cut him off from his people, for the life of an animal is in the blood. I have provided the blood for you to make atonement for your lives on the Altar; it is the blood, the life, that makes atonement. That's why I tell the People of Israel, 'Don't eat blood.' The same goes for the foreigner who lives among you, 'Don't eat blood.'

13-14 "Any and every Israelite — this also goes for the foreigners — who hunts down an animal or bird that is edible, must bleed it and cover the blood with dirt, because the life of every animal is its blood — the blood is its life. That's why I tell the Israelites, 'Don't eat the blood of any animal because the life of every animal is its blood. Anyone who eats the blood must be cut off.'

15-16 "Anyone, whether native or foreigner, who eats from an animal that is found dead or mauled must wash his clothes and bathe in water; he remains unclean until evening and is then clean. If he doesn't wash or bathe his body, he'll be held responsible for his actions."

SEX

1-5 **18** GOD spoke to Moses: "Speak to the People of Israel. Tell them, I am GOD, your God. Don't live like the people of Egypt where you used to live, and don't live like the people of Canaan where I'm bringing you. Don't do what they do. Obey my laws and live by my decrees. I am your GOD. Keep my decrees and laws: The person who obeys them lives by them. I am GOD.

6 "Don't have sex with a close relative. I am GOD.

7 "Don't violate your father by having sex with your mother. She is your mother. Don't have sex with her.

8 "Don't have sex with your father's wife. That violates your father.

9 "Don't have sex with your sister, whether she's your father's daughter or your mother's, whether she was born in the same house or elsewhere.

10 "Don't have sex with your son's daughter or your daughter's daughter. That would violate your own body.

11 "Don't have sex with the daughter of your father's wife born to your father. She is your sister.

12 "Don't have sex with your father's sister; she is your aunt, closely related to your father.

13 "Don't have sex with your mother's sister; she is your aunt, closely related to your mother.

14 "Don't violate your father's brother, your uncle, by having sex with his wife. She is your aunt.

15 "Don't have sex with your daughter-in-law. She is your son's wife; don't have sex with her.

16 "Don't have sex with your brother's wife; that would violate your brother.

17 "Don't have sex with both a woman and her daughter. And don't have sex with her granddaughters either. They are her close relatives. That is wicked.

18 "Don't marry your wife's sister as a rival wife and have sex with her while your wife is living.

19 "Don't have sex with a woman during the time of her menstrual period when she is unclean.

20 "Don't have sex with your neighbor's wife and violate yourself by her.

21 "Don't give any of your children to be burned in sacrifice to the god Molech — an act of sheer blasphemy of your God. I am GOD.

22 "Don't have sex with a man as one does with a woman. That is abhorrent.

23 "Don't have sex with an animal and violate yourself by it.

"A woman must not have sex with an animal. That is perverse.

24-28 "Don't pollute yourself in any of these ways. This is how the nations became polluted, the ones that I am going to drive out of the land before you. Even the land itself became polluted and I punished it for its iniquities — the land vomited up its inhabitants. You must keep my decrees and laws—

natives and foreigners both. You must not do any of these abhorrent things. The people who lived in this land before you arrived did all these things and polluted the land. And if you pollute it, the land will vomit you up just as it vomited up the nations that preceded you.

29-30   "Those who do any of these abhorrent things will be cut off from their people. Keep to what I tell you; don't engage in any of the abhorrent acts that were practiced before you came. Don't pollute yourselves with them. I am GOD, *your* God."

"I AM GOD, YOUR GOD"

1-2   **19** GOD spoke to Moses: "Speak to the congregation of Israel. Tell them, Be holy because I, GOD, your God, am holy.

3   "Every one of you must respect his mother and father.
"Keep my Sabbaths. I am GOD, your God.

4   "Don't take up with no-god idols. Don't make gods of cast metal. I am GOD, your God.

5-8   "When you sacrifice a Peace-Offering to GOD, do it as you've been taught so it is acceptable. Eat it on the day you sacrifice it and the day following. Whatever is left until the third day is to be burned up. If it is eaten on the third day it is polluted meat and not acceptable. Whoever eats it will be held responsible because he has violated what is holy to GOD. That person will be cut off from his people.

9-10   "When you harvest your land, don't harvest right up to the edges of your field or gather the gleanings from the harvest. Don't strip your vineyard bare or go back and pick up the fallen grapes. Leave them for the poor and the foreigner. I am GOD, your God.

11   "Don't steal.
"Don't lie.
"Don't deceive anyone.

12   "Don't swear falsely using my name, violating the name of your God. I am GOD.

13   "Don't exploit your friend or rob him.
"Don't hold back the wages of a hired hand overnight.

14   "Don't curse the deaf; don't put a stumbling block in front of the blind; fear your God. I am GOD.

15   "Don't pervert justice. Don't show favoritism to either the poor or the great. Judge on the basis of what is right.

16   "Don't spread gossip and rumors.
"Don't just stand by when your neighbor's life is in danger. I am GOD.

17   "Don't secretly hate your neighbor. If you have something against him, get it out into the open; otherwise you are an accomplice in his guilt.

18   "Don't seek revenge or carry a grudge against any of your people.
"Love your neighbor as yourself. I am GOD.

19   "Keep my decrees.
"Don't mate two different kinds of animals.
"Don't plant your fields with two kinds of seed.
"Don't wear clothes woven of two kinds of material.

20-22   "If a man has sex with a slave girl who is engaged to another man but has not yet been ransomed or given her freedom, there must be an investigation. But they aren't to be put to death because she wasn't free. The man must bring a Compensation-Offering to GOD at the entrance to the Tent of Meeting, a ram of compensation. The priest will perform the ritual of atonement for him before GOD with the ram of compensation for the sin he has committed. Then he will stand forgiven of the sin he committed.

23-25 "When you enter the land and plant any kind of fruit tree, don't eat the fruit for three years; consider it inedible. By the fourth year its fruit is holy, an offering of praise to GOD. Beginning in the fifth year you can eat its fruit; you'll have richer harvests this way. I am GOD, your God.

26 "Don't eat meat with blood in it.

"Don't practice divination or sorcery.

27 "Don't cut the hair on the sides of your head or trim your beard.

28 "Don't gash your bodies on behalf of the dead.

"Don't tattoo yourselves. I am GOD.

29 "Don't violate your daughter by making her a whore—the whole country would soon become a brothel, filled with sordid sex.

30 "Keep my Sabbaths and revere my Sanctuary: I am GOD.

31 "Don't dabble in the occult or traffic with mediums; you'll pollute your souls. I am GOD, your God.

32 "Show respect to the aged; honor the presence of an elder; fear your God. I am GOD.

33-34 "When a foreigner lives with you in your land, don't take advantage of him. Treat the foreigner the same as a native. Love him like one of your own. Remember that you were once foreigners in Egypt. I am GOD, your God.

35-36 "Don't cheat when measuring length, weight, or quantity. Use honest scales and weights and measures. I am GOD, your God. I brought you out of Egypt.

37 "Keep all my decrees and all my laws. Yes, *do* them. I am GOD."

1-5 **20** GOD spoke to Moses: "Tell the Israelites, Each and every Israelite and foreigner in Israel who gives his child to the god Molech must be put to death. The community must kill him by stoning. I will resolutely reject that man and cut him off from his people. By giving his child to the god Molech he has polluted my Sanctuary and desecrated my holy name. If the people of the land look the other way as if nothing had happened when that man gives his child to the god Molech and fail to kill him, I will resolutely reject that man and his family, and him and all who join him in prostituting themselves in the rituals of the god Molech I will cut off from their people.

6 "I will resolutely reject persons who dabble in the occult or traffic with mediums, prostituting themselves in their practices. I will cut them off from their people.

7-8 "Set yourselves apart for a holy life. *Live* a holy life, because I am GOD, your God. Do what I tell you; *live* the way I tell you. I am the GOD who makes you holy.

9 "Any and every person who curses his father or mother must be put to death. By cursing his father or mother he is responsible for his own death.

10 "If a man commits adultery with another man's wife—the wife, say, of his neighbor—both the man and the woman, the adulterer and adulteress, must be put to death.

11 "If a man has sex with his father's wife, he has violated his father. Both the man and woman must be put to death; they are responsible for their own deaths.

12 "If a man has sex with his daughter-in-law, both of them must be put to death. What they have done is perverse. And they are responsible for their own deaths.

13 "If a man has sex with a man as one does with a woman, both of them have done what is abhorrent. They must be put to death; they are responsible for their own deaths.

14 "If a man marries both a woman and her mother, that's wicked. All three of them must be burned at the stake, purging the wickedness from the community.

15 "If a man has sex with an animal, he must be put to death and you must kill the animal.

16 "If a woman has sex with an animal, you must kill both the woman and the animal. They must be put to death. And they are responsible for their deaths.

17 "If a man marries his sister, the daughter of either his father or mother, and they have sex, that's a disgrace. They must be publicly cut off from their people. He has violated his sister and will be held responsible.

18 "If a man sleeps with a woman during her period and has sex with her, he has uncovered her 'fountain' and she has revealed her 'fountain'—both of them must be cut off from their people.

19 "Don't have sex with your aunt on either your mother's or father's side. That violates a close relative. Both of you are held responsible.

20 "If a man has sex with his aunt, he has dishonored his uncle. They will be held responsible and die childless.

21 "If a man marries his brother's wife, it's a defilement. He has shamed his brother. They will be childless.

22-23 "Do what I tell you, all my decrees and laws; live by them so that the land where I'm bringing you won't vomit you out. You simply must not live like the nations I'm driving out before you. They did all these things and I hated every minute of it.

24-26 "I've told you, remember, that you will possess their land that I'm giving to you as an inheritance, a land flowing with milk and honey. I am GOD, your God, who has distinguished you from the nations. So live like it: Distinguish between ritually clean and unclean animals and birds. Don't pollute yourselves with any animal or bird or crawling thing which I have marked out as unclean for you. Live holy lives before me because I, GOD, am holy. I have distinguished you from the nations to be my very own.

27 "A man or woman who is a medium or sorcerer among you must be put to death. You must kill them by stoning. They're responsible for their own deaths."

HOLY PRIESTS

1-4 21 GOD spoke to Moses: "Speak to the priests, the sons of Aaron. Tell them, A priest must not ritually contaminate himself by touching the dead, except for close relatives: mother, father, son, daughter, brother, or an unmarried sister who is dependent on him since she has no husband; for these he may make himself ritually unclean, but he must not contaminate himself with the dead who are only related to him by marriage and thus profane himself.

5-6 "Priests must not shave their heads or trim their beards or gash their bodies. They must be holy to their God and must not profane the name of their God. Because their job is to present the gifts of GOD, the food of their God, they are to be holy.

7-8 "Because a priest is holy to his God he must not marry a woman who has been a harlot or a cult prostitute or a divorced woman. Make sure he is holy because he serves the food of your God. Treat him as holy because I, GOD, who make you holy, am holy.

9 "If a priest's daughter defiles herself in prostitution, she disgraces her father. She must be burned at the stake.

10-12 "The high priest, the one among his brothers who has received the anointing oil poured on his head and been ordained to wear the priestly vestments, must not let his hair go wild and tangled nor wear ragged and torn clothes. He must not enter a room where there is a dead body. He must not ritually contaminate himself, even for his father or mother; and he must neither abandon nor desecrate the Sanctuary of his God because of the dedication of the anointing oil which is upon him. I am GOD.

13-15 "He is to marry a young virgin, not a widow, not a divorcee, not a cult prostitute—he is only to marry a virgin from his own people. He must not defile his descendants among his people because I am GOD who makes him holy."

16-23 GOD spoke to Moses: "Tell Aaron, None of your descendants, in any generation to come, who has a defect of any kind may present as an offering the food of his God. That means anyone who is blind or lame, disfigured or deformed, crippled in foot or hand, hunchbacked or dwarfed, who has anything wrong with his eyes, who has running sores or damaged testicles. No descendant of Aaron the priest who has any defect is to offer gifts to GOD; he has a defect and so must not offer the food of his God. He may eat the food of his God, both the most holy and the holy, but because of his defect he must not go near the curtain or approach the Altar. It would desecrate my Sanctuary. I am GOD who makes them holy."

24 Moses delivered this message to Aaron, his sons, and to all the People of Israel.

1-2 **22** GOD spoke to Moses: "Tell Aaron and his sons to treat the holy offerings that the Israelites consecrate to me with reverence so they won't desecrate my holy name. I am GOD.

3 "Tell them, From now on, if any of your descendants approaches in a state of ritual uncleanness the holy offerings that the Israelites consecrate to GOD, he will be cut off from my presence. I am GOD.

4-8 "Each and every one of Aaron's descendants who has an infectious skin disease or a discharge may not eat any of the holy offerings until he is clean. Also, if he touches anything defiled by a corpse, or has an emission of semen, or is contaminated by touching a crawling creature, or touches a person who is contaminated for whatever reason—a person who touches any such thing will be ritually unclean until evening and may not eat any of the holy offerings unless he has washed well with water. After the sun goes down he is clean and may go ahead and eat the holy offerings; they are his food. But he must not contaminate himself by eating anything found dead or torn by wild animals. I am GOD.

9 "The priests must observe my instructions lest they become guilty and die by treating the offerings with irreverence. I am GOD who makes them holy.

10-13 "No layperson may eat anything set apart as holy. Nor may a priest's guest or his hired hand eat anything holy. But if a priest buys a slave, the slave may eat of it; also the slaves born in his house may eat his food. If a priest's daughter marries a layperson, she may no longer eat from the holy contributions. But if the priest's daughter is widowed or divorced and without children and returns to her father's household as before, she may eat of her father's food. But no layperson may eat of it.

14 "If anyone eats from a holy offering accidentally, he must give back the holy offering to the priest and add twenty percent to it.

15-16 "The priests must not treat with irreverence the holy offerings of the Israelites that they contribute to God lest they desecrate themselves and make themselves guilty when they eat the holy offerings. I am God who makes them holy."

17-25 God spoke to Moses: "Tell Aaron and his sons and all the People of Israel, Each and every one of you, whether native born or foreigner, who presents a Whole-Burnt-Offering to God to fulfill a vow or as a Freewill-Offering, must make sure that it is a male without defect from cattle, sheep, or goats for it to be acceptable. Don't try slipping in some creature that has a defect—it won't be accepted. Whenever anyone brings an offering from cattle or sheep as a Peace-Offering to God to fulfill a vow or as a Freewill-Offering, it has to be perfect, without defect, to be acceptable. Don't try giving God an animal that is blind, crippled, mutilated, an animal with running sores, a rash, or mange. Don't place any of these on the Altar as a gift to God. You may, though, offer an ox or sheep that is deformed or stunted as a Freewill-Offering, but it is not acceptable in fulfilling a vow. Don't offer to God an animal with bruised, crushed, torn, or cut-off testicles. Don't do this in your own land but don't accept them from foreigners and present them as food for your God either. Because of deformities and defects they will not be acceptable."

26-30 God spoke to Moses: "When a calf or lamb or goat is born, it is to stay with its mother for seven days. After the eighth day, it is acceptable as an offering, a gift to God. Don't slaughter both a cow or ewe and its young on the same day. When you sacrifice a Thanksgiving-Offering to God, do it right so it will be acceptable. Eat it on the same day; don't leave any leftovers until morning. I am God.

31 "Do what I tell you; *live* what I tell you. I am God.

32-33 "Don't desecrate my holy name. I insist on being treated with holy reverence among the People of Israel. I am God who makes you holy and brought you out of Egypt to be your God. I am God."

The Feasts

1-2 **23** God spoke to Moses: "Tell the People of Israel, These are my appointed feasts, the appointed feasts of God which you are to decree as sacred assemblies.

3 "Work six days. The seventh day is a Sabbath, a day of total and complete rest, a sacred assembly. Don't do any work. Wherever you live, it is a Sabbath to God.

4 "These are the appointed feasts of God, the sacred assemblies which you are to announce at the times set for them:

5   "GOD's Passover, beginning at sundown on the fourteenth day of the first month.

6-8   "GOD's Feast of Unraised Bread, on the fifteenth day of this same month. You are to eat unraised bread for seven days. Hold a sacred assembly on the first day; don't do any regular work. Offer Fire-Gifts to GOD for seven days. On the seventh day hold a sacred assembly; don't do any regular work."

9-14   GOD spoke to Moses: "Tell the People of Israel, When you arrive at the land that I am giving you and reap its harvest, bring to the priest a sheaf of the first grain that you harvest. He will wave the sheaf before GOD for acceptance on your behalf; on the morning after Sabbath, the priest will wave it. On the same day that you wave the sheaf, offer a year-old male lamb without defect for a Whole-Burnt-Offering to GOD and with it the Grain-Offering of four quarts of fine flour mixed with oil — a Fire-Gift to GOD, a pleasing fragrance — and also a Drink-Offering of a quart of wine. Don't eat any bread or roasted or fresh grain until you have presented this offering to your God. This is a perpetual decree for all your generations to come, wherever you live.

15-21   "Count seven full weeks from the morning after the Sabbath when you brought the sheaf as a Wave-Offering, fifty days until the morning of the seventh Sabbath. Then present a new Grain-Offering to GOD. Bring from wherever you are living two loaves of bread made from four quarts of fine flour and baked with yeast as a Wave-Offering of the first ripe grain to GOD. In addition to the bread, offer seven yearling male lambs without defect, plus one bull and two rams. They will be a Whole-Burnt-Offering to GOD together with their Grain-Offerings and Drink-Offerings — offered as Fire-Gifts, a pleasing fragrance to GOD. Offer one male goat for an Absolution-Offering and two yearling lambs for a Peace-Offering. The priest will wave the two lambs before GOD as a Wave-Offering, together with the bread of the first ripe grain. They are sacred offerings to GOD for the priest. Proclaim the day as a sacred assembly. Don't do any ordinary work. It is a perpetual decree wherever you live down through your generations.

22   "When you reap the harvest of your land, don't reap the corners of your field or gather the gleanings. Leave them for the poor and the foreigners. I am GOD, *your* God."

23-25   GOD said to Moses: "Tell the People of Israel, On the first day of the seventh month, set aside a day of rest, a sacred assembly — mark it with loud blasts on the ram's horn. Don't do any ordinary work. Offer a Fire-Gift to GOD."

26-32   GOD said to Moses: "The tenth day of the seventh month is the Day of Atonement. Hold a sacred assembly, fast, and offer a Fire-Gift to GOD. Don't work on that day because it is a day of atonement to make atonement for you before your GOD. Anyone who doesn't fast on that day must be cut off from his people. I will destroy from among his people anyone who works on that day. Don't do any work that day — none. This is a perpetual decree for all the generations to come, wherever you happen to be living. It is a Sabbath of complete and total rest, a fast day. Observe your Sabbath from the evening of the ninth day of the month until the following evening."

33-36   GOD said to Moses: "Tell the People of Israel, GOD's Feast of Booths begins on the fifteenth day of the seventh month. It lasts seven days. The first day is a sacred assembly; don't do any ordinary work. Offer Fire-Gifts to GOD for seven days. On the eighth day hold a sacred assembly and offer a gift to GOD. It is a solemn convocation. Don't do any ordinary work.

37-38   "These are the appointed feasts of GOD which you will decree as sacred assemblies for presenting Fire-Gifts to GOD: the Whole-Burnt-Offerings, Grain-Offerings, sacrifices, and Drink-Offerings assigned to each day. These are in addition to offerings for GOD's Sabbaths and also in addition to other gifts connected with whatever you have vowed and all the Freewill-Offerings you give to GOD.

39-43   "So, summing up: On the fifteenth day of the seventh month, after you have brought your crops in from your fields, celebrate the Feast of GOD for seven days. The first day is a complete rest and the eighth day is a complete rest. On the first day, pick the best fruit from the best trees; take fronds of palm trees and branches of leafy trees and from willows by the brook and celebrate in the presence of your GOD for seven days — yes, for seven full days celebrate it as a festival to GOD. Every year from now on, celebrate it in the seventh month. Live in booths for seven days — every son and daughter of Israel is to move into booths so that your descendants will know that I made the People of Israel live in booths when I brought them out of the land of Egypt. I am GOD, *your* God."

44   Moses posted the calendar for the annual appointed feasts of GOD which Israel was to celebrate.

LIGHT AND BREAD

1-4   24 GOD spoke to Moses: "Order the People of Israel to bring you virgin olive oil for light so that the lamps may be kept burning continually. Aaron is in charge of keeping these lamps burning in front of the curtain that screens The Testimony in the Tent of Meeting from evening to morning continually before GOD. This is a perpetual decree down through the generations. Aaron is responsible for keeping the lamps burning continually on the Lampstand of pure gold before GOD.

5-9   "Take fine flour and bake twelve loaves of bread, using about four quarts of flour to a loaf. Arrange them in two rows of six each on the Table of pure gold before GOD. Along each row spread pure incense, marking the bread as a memorial; it is a gift to GOD. Regularly, every Sabbath, this bread is to be set before GOD, a perpetual covenantal response from Israel. The bread then goes to Aaron and his sons, who are to eat it in a Holy Place. It is their most holy share from the gifts to GOD. This is a perpetual decree."

10-12   One day the son of an Israelite mother and an Egyptian father went out among the Israelites. A fight broke out in the camp between him and an Israelite. The son of the Israelite woman blasphemed the Name of GOD and cursed. They brought him to Moses. His mother's name was Shelomith, daughter of Dibri of the tribe of Dan. They put him in custody waiting for GOD's will to be revealed to them.

13-16   Then GOD spoke to Moses: "Take the blasphemer outside the camp. Have all those who heard him place their hands on his head; then have the entire congregation stone him. Then tell the Israelites, Anyone who curses God will be held accountable; anyone who blasphemes the Name of GOD must be put to death. The entire congregation must stone him. It makes no difference whether he is a foreigner or a native, if he blasphemes the Name, he will be put to death.

17-22   "Anyone who hits and kills a fellow human must be put to death. Anyone who kills someone's animal must make it good—a life for a life. Anyone who injures his neighbor will get back the same as he gave: fracture for fracture, eye for eye, tooth for tooth. What he did to hurt that person will be done to him. Anyone who hits and kills an animal must make it good, but whoever hits and kills a fellow human will be put to death. And no double standards: the same rule goes for foreigners and natives. I am GOD, *your* God."

23   Moses then spoke to the People of Israel. They brought the blasphemer outside the camp and stoned him. The People of Israel followed the orders GOD had given Moses.

"THE LAND WILL OBSERVE A SABBATH TO GOD"

1-7   25 GOD spoke to Moses at Mount Sinai: "Speak to the People of Israel. Tell them, When you enter the land which I am going to give you, the land will observe a Sabbath to GOD. Sow your fields, prune your vineyards, and take in your harvests for six years. But the seventh year the land will take a Sabbath of complete and total rest, a Sabbath to GOD; you will not sow your fields or prune your vineyards. Don't reap what grows of itself; don't harvest the grapes of your untended vines. The land gets a year of complete and total rest. But you can eat from what the land volunteers during the Sabbath year—you and your men and women servants, your hired hands, and the foreigners who live in the country, and, of course, also your livestock and the wild animals in the land can eat from it. Whatever the land volunteers of itself can be eaten.

"THE FIFTIETH YEAR SHALL BE A JUBILEE FOR YOU"

8-12   "Count off seven Sabbaths of years—seven times seven years: Seven Sabbaths of years adds up to forty-nine years. Then sound loud blasts on the ram's horn on the tenth day of the seventh month, the Day of Atonement. Sound the ram's horn all over the land. Sanctify the fiftieth year; make it a holy year. Proclaim freedom all over the land to everyone who lives in it—a Jubilee for you: Each person will go back to his family's property and reunite with his extended family. The fiftieth year is your Jubilee year: Don't sow; don't reap what volunteers itself in the fields; don't harvest the untended vines because it's the Jubilee and a holy year for you. You're permitted to eat from whatever volunteers itself in the fields.

13   "In this year of Jubilee everyone returns home to his family property.

14-17   "If you sell or buy property from one of your countrymen, don't cheat him. Calculate the purchase price on the basis of the number of years since the Jubilee. He is obliged to set the sale price on the basis of the number of harvests remaining until the next Jubilee. The more years left, the more money; you can raise the price. But the fewer years left, the less money; decrease the price. What you are buying and selling in fact is the number of crops you're going to harvest. Don't cheat each other. Fear your God. I am GOD, your God.

18-22   "Keep my decrees and observe my laws and you will live secure in the land. The land will yield its fruit; you will have all you can eat and will live safe and secure. Do I hear you ask, 'What are we going to eat in the seventh year if we don't plant or harvest?' I assure you, I will send such a blessing in the sixth year that the land will yield enough for three years. While you plant in the eighth year, you will eat from the old crop and continue until the harvest of the ninth year comes in.

23-24   "The land cannot be sold permanently because the land is mine and you are foreigners—you're my tenants. You must provide for the right of redemption for any of the land that you own.

25-28   "If one of your brothers becomes poor and has to sell any of his land, his nearest relative is to come and buy back what his brother sold. If a man has no one to redeem it but he later prospers and earns enough for its redemption, he is to calculate the value since he sold it and refund the balance to the man to whom he sold it; he can then go back to his own land. If he doesn't get together enough money to repay him, what he sold remains in the possession of the buyer until the year of Jubilee. In the Jubilee it will be returned and he can go back and live on his land.

29-31   "If a man sells a house in a walled city, he retains the right to buy it back for a full year after the sale. At any time during that year he can redeem it. But if it is not redeemed before the full year has passed, it becomes the permanent possession of the buyer and his descendants. It is not returned in the Jubilee. However, houses in unwalled villages are treated the same as fields. They can be redeemed and have to be returned at the Jubilee.

32-34   "As to the Levitical cities, houses in the cities owned by the Levites are always subject to redemption. Levitical property is always redeemable if it is sold in a town that they hold and reverts to them in the Jubilee, because the houses in the towns of the Levites are their property among the People of Israel. The pastures belonging to their cities may not be sold; they are their permanent possession.

35-38   "If one of your brothers becomes indigent and cannot support himself, help him, the same as you would a foreigner or a guest so that he can continue to live in your neighborhood. Don't gouge him with interest charges; out of reverence for your God help your brother to continue to live with you in the neighborhood. Don't take advantage of his plight by running up big interest charges on his loans, and don't give him food for profit. I am your GOD who brought you out of Egypt to give you the land of Canaan and to be your God.

39-43   "If one of your brothers becomes indigent and has to sell himself to you, don't make him work as a slave. Treat him as a hired hand or a guest among you. He will work for you until the Jubilee, after which he and his children are set free to go back to his clan and his ancestral land. Because the People of Israel are my servants whom I brought out of Egypt, they must never be sold as slaves. Don't tyrannize them; fear your God.

44-46   "The male and female slaves which you have are to come from the surrounding nations; you are permitted to buy slaves from them. You may also buy the children of foreign workers who are living among you temporarily and from their clans which are living among you and have been born in your land. They become your property. You may will them to your children as property and make them slaves for life. But you must not tyrannize your brother Israelites.

47-53 "If a foreigner or temporary resident among you becomes rich and one of your brothers becomes poor and sells himself to the foreigner who lives among you or to a member of the foreigner's clan, he still has the right of redemption after he has sold himself. One of his relatives may buy him back. An uncle or cousin or any close relative of his extended family may redeem him. Or, if he gets the money together, he can redeem himself. What happens then is that he and his owner count out the time from the year he sold himself to the year of Jubilee; the buy-back price is set according to the wages of a hired hand for that number of years. If many years remain before the Jubilee, he must pay back a larger share of his purchase price, but if only a few years remain until the Jubilee, he is to calculate his redemption price accordingly. He is to be treated as a man hired from year to year. You must make sure that his owner does not tyrannize him.

54-55 "If he is not redeemed in any of these ways, he goes free in the year of Jubilee, he and his children, because the People of Israel are my servants, my servants whom I brought out of Egypt. I am GOD, *your* God.

1 **26** "Don't make idols for yourselves; don't set up an image or a sacred pillar for yourselves, and don't place a carved stone in your land that you can bow down to in worship. I am GOD, *your* God.

2 "Keep my Sabbaths; treat my Sanctuary with reverence. I am GOD.

"IF YOU LIVE BY MY DECREES . . ."

3-5 "If you live by my decrees and obediently keep my commandments, I will send the rains in their seasons, the ground will yield its crops and the trees of the field their fruit. You will thresh until the grape harvest and the grape harvest will continue until planting time; you'll have more than enough to eat and will live safe and secure in your land.

6-10 "I'll make the country a place of peace — you'll be able to go to sleep at night without fear; I'll get rid of the wild beasts; I'll eliminate war. You'll chase out your enemies and defeat them: Five of you will chase a hundred, and a hundred of you will chase ten thousand and do away with them. I'll give you my full attention: I'll make sure you prosper, make sure you grow in numbers, and keep my covenant with you in good working order. You'll still be eating from last year's harvest when you have to clean out the barns to make room for the new crops.

11-13 "I'll set up my residence in your neighborhood; I won't avoid or shun you; I'll stroll through your streets. I'll be your God; you'll be my people. I am GOD, your personal God who rescued you from Egypt so that you would no longer be slaves to the Egyptians. I ripped off the harness of your slavery so that you can move about freely.

"BUT IF YOU REFUSE TO OBEY ME . . ."

14-17 "But if you refuse to obey me and won't observe my commandments, despising my decrees and holding my laws in contempt by your disobedience, making a shambles of my covenant, I'll step in and pour on the trouble: debilitating disease, high fevers, blindness, your life leaking out bit by bit. You'll plant seed but your enemies will eat the crops. I'll turn my back on you and stand by while your enemies defeat you. People who hate you will govern you. You'll run scared even when there's no one chasing you.

18-20   "And if none of this works in getting your attention, I'll discipline you seven times over for your sins. I'll break your strong pride: I'll make the skies above you like a sheet of tin and the ground under you like cast iron. No matter how hard you work, nothing will come of it: No crops out of the ground, no fruit off the trees.

21-22   "If you defy me and refuse to listen, your punishment will be seven times more than your sins: I'll set wild animals on you; they'll rob you of your children, kill your cattle, and decimate your numbers until you'll think you are living in a ghost town.

23-26   "And if even this doesn't work and you refuse my discipline and continue your defiance, then it will be my turn to defy you. I, yes I, will punish you for your sins seven times over: I'll let war loose on you, avenging your breaking of the covenant; when you huddle in your cities for protection, I'll send a deadly epidemic on you and you'll be helpless before your enemies; when I cut off your bread supply, ten women will bake bread in one oven and ration it out. You'll eat, but barely—no one will get enough.

27-35   "And if this—*even this!*—doesn't work and you still won't listen, still defy me, I'll have had enough and in hot anger will defy you, punishing you for your sins seven times over: famine will be so severe that you'll end up cooking and eating your sons in stews and your daughters in barbecues; I'll smash your sex-and-religion shrines and all the paraphernalia that goes with them, and then stack your corpses and the idol-corpses in the same piles—I'll abhor you; I'll turn your cities into rubble; I'll clean out your sanctuaries; I'll hold my nose at the "pleasing aroma" of your sacrifices. I'll turn your land into a lifeless moonscape—your enemies who come in to take over will be shocked at what they see. I'll scatter you all over the world and keep after you with the point of my sword in your backs. There'll be nothing left in your land, nothing going on in your cities. With you gone and dispersed in the countries of your enemies, the land, empty of you, will finally get a break and enjoy its Sabbath years. All the time it's left there empty, the land will get rest, the Sabbaths it never got when you lived there.

36-39   "As for those among you still alive, I'll give them over to fearful timidity —even the rustle of a leaf will throw them into a panic. They'll run here and there, back and forth, as if running for their lives even though no one is after them, tripping and falling over one another in total confusion. You won't stand a chance against an enemy. You'll perish among the nations; the land of your enemies will eat you up. Any who are left will slowly rot away in the enemy lands. Rot. And all because of their sins, their sins compounded by their ancestors' sins.

"ON THE OTHER HAND, IF THEY CONFESS . . ."

40-42   "On the other hand, if they confess their sins and the sins of their ancestors, their treacherous betrayal, the defiance that set off my defiance that sent them off into enemy lands; if by some chance they soften their hard hearts and make amends for their sin, I'll remember my covenant with Jacob, I'll remember my covenant with Isaac, and, yes, I'll remember my covenant with Abraham. And I'll remember the land.

43-45   "The land will be empty of them and enjoy its Sabbaths while they're gone. They'll pay for their sins because they refused my laws and treated my decrees with contempt. But in spite of their behavior, while they are among their enemies I won't reject or abhor or destroy them completely. I won't break my covenant with them: I am GOD, their God. For their sake I will remember the covenant with their ancestors whom I, with all the nations watching, brought out of Egypt in order to be their God. I am GOD."

46 These are the decrees, laws, and instructions that GOD established between himself and the People of Israel through Moses at Mount Sinai.

VOWS, DEDICATIONS, AND REDEMPTIONS

1-8 *27* GOD spoke to Moses: He said, "Speak to the People of Israel. Tell them, If anyone wants to vow the value of a person to the service of GOD, set the value of a man between the ages of twenty and sixty at fifty shekels of silver, according to the Sanctuary shekel. For a woman the valuation is thirty shekels. If the person is between the ages of five and twenty, set the value at twenty shekels for a male and ten shekels for a female. If the person is between one month and five years, set the value at five shekels of silver for a boy and three shekels of silver for a girl. If the person is over sixty, set the value at fifteen shekels for a man and ten shekels for a woman. If anyone is too poor to pay the stated amount, he is to present the person to the priest, who will then set the value for him according to what the person making the vow can afford.

9-13 "If he vowed an animal that is acceptable as an offering to GOD, the animal is given to GOD and becomes the property of the Sanctuary. He must not exchange or substitute a good one for a bad one, or a bad one for a good one; if he should dishonestly substitute one animal for another, both the original and the substitute become property of the Sanctuary. If what he vowed is a ritually unclean animal, one that is not acceptable as an offering to GOD, the animal must be shown to the priest, who will set its value, either high or low. Whatever the priest sets will be its value. If the owner changes his mind and wants to redeem it, he must add twenty percent to its value.

14-15 "If a man dedicates his house to GOD, into the possession of the Sanctuary, the priest assesses its value, setting it either high or low. Whatever value the priest sets, that's what it is. If the man wants to buy it back, he must add twenty percent to its price and then it's his again.

16-21 "If a man dedicates to GOD part of his family land, its value is to be set according to the amount of seed that is needed for it at the rate of fifty shekels of silver to six bushels of barley seed. If he dedicates his field during the year of Jubilee, the set value stays. But if he dedicates it after the Jubilee, the priest will compute the value according to the years left until the next Jubilee, reducing the value proportionately. If the one dedicating it wants to buy it back, he must add twenty percent to its valuation, and then it's his again. But if he doesn't redeem it or sells the field to someone else, it can never be bought back. When the field is released in the Jubilee, it becomes holy to GOD, the possession of the Sanctuary, GOD's field. It goes into the hands of the priests.

22-25 "If a man dedicates to GOD a field he has bought, a field which is not part of the family land, the priest will compute its proportionate value in relation to the next year of Jubilee. The man must pay its value on the spot as something that is now holy to GOD, belonging to the Sanctuary. In the year of Jubilee it goes back to its original owner, the man from whom he bought it. The valuations will be reckoned by the Sanctuary shekel, at twenty gerahs to the shekel.

26-27 "No one is allowed to dedicate the firstborn of an animal; the firstborn, as firstborn, already belongs to GOD. No matter if it's cattle or sheep, it already belongs to GOD. If it's one of the ritually unclean animals, he can buy it back at its assessed value by adding twenty percent to it. If he doesn't redeem it, it is to be sold at its assessed value.

28 "But nothing that a man irrevocably devotes to GOD from what belongs to him, whether human or animal or family land, may be either sold or bought back. Everything devoted is holy to the highest degree; it's GOD's inalienable property.

29 "No human who has been devoted to destruction can be redeemed. He must be put to death.

30-33 "A tenth of the land's produce, whether grain from the ground or fruit from the trees, is GOD's. It is holy to GOD. If a man buys back any of the tenth he has given, he must add twenty percent to it. A tenth of the entire herd and flock, every tenth animal that passes under the shepherd's rod, is holy to GOD. He is not permitted to pick out the good from the bad or make a substitution. If he dishonestly makes a substitution, both animals, the original and the substitute, become the possession of the Sanctuary and cannot be redeemed."

34 These are the commandments that GOD gave to Moses on Mount Sinai for the People of Israel.

NUMBERS

Becoming a truly human community is a long, complex, messy business. Simply growing up as a man or woman demands all the wisdom and patience and courage that we can muster. But growing up with others, parents and siblings and neighbors, to say nothing of odd strangers and mean enemies, immensely complicates the growing up.

The book of Numbers plunges us into the mess of growing up. The pages in this section of the biblical story give us a realistic feel for what is involved in being included in the people of God, which is to say, a human community that honors God, lives out love and justice in daily affairs, learns how to deal with sin in oneself and others, and follows God's commands into a future of blessing. And all this without illusions.

Many of us fondle a romanticized spirituality in our imaginations. The "God's in his heaven/all's right with the world" sort of thing. When things don't go "right" we blame others or ourselves, muddle through as best we can, often with considerable crankiness, and wish that we had been born at a different time — "Bible times" maybe! — when living a holy life was so much easier. That's odd because the Bible, our primary text for showing us what it means to be a human being created by God and called to a life of obedient faith and sacrificial love, nowhere suggests that life is simple or even "natural." We need a lot of help.

We need organizational help. When people live together in community, jobs have to be assigned, leaders appointed, inventories kept. Counting and list-making and rosters are as much a part of being a community of God as prayer and instruction and justice. Accurate arithmetic is an aspect of becoming a people of God.

And we need relational help. The people who find themselves called and led and commanded by God find themselves in the company of men and women who sin a lot — quarrel, bicker, grumble, rebel, fornicate, steal — you name it, we do it. We need help in getting along with each other. Wise discipline is required in becoming a people of God.

It follows that counting and quarreling take up considerable space in the book of Numbers. Because they also continue to be unavoidable aspects of our becoming the people of God, this book is essential in training our imaginations to take in some of these less-than-romantic details by which we are formed into the people of God.

NUMBERS

CENSUS IN THE WILDERNESS OF SINAI

1-5 GOD spoke to Moses in the Wilderness of Sinai at the Tent of Meeting on the first day of the second month in the second year after they had left Egypt. He said, "Number the congregation of the People of Israel by clans and families, writing down the names of every male. You and Aaron are to register, company by company, every man who is twenty years and older who is able to fight in the army. Pick one man from each tribe who is head of his family to help you. These are the names of the men who will help you:

from Reuben: Elizur son of Shedeur
6 from Simeon: Shelumiel son of Zurishaddai
7 from Judah: Nahshon son of Amminadab
8 from Issachar: Nethanel son of Zuar
9 from Zebulun: Eliab son of Helon
10 from the sons of Joseph,
from Ephraim: Elishama son of Ammihud
from Manasseh: Gamaliel son of Pedahzur
11 from Benjamin: Abidan son of Gideoni
12 from Dan: Ahiezer son of Ammishaddai
13 from Asher: Pagiel son of Ocran
14 from Gad: Eliasaph son of Deuel
15 from Naphtali: Ahira son of Enan."

16 These were the men chosen from the congregation, leaders of their ancestral tribes, heads of Israel's military divisions.

17-19 Moses and Aaron took these men who had been named to help and gathered the whole congregation together on the first day of the second month. The people registered themselves in their tribes according to their ancestral families, putting down the names of those who were twenty years old and older, just as GOD commanded Moses. He numbered them in the Wilderness of Sinai.

20-21 The line of Reuben, Israel's firstborn: The men were counted off head by head, every male twenty years and older who was able to fight in the army, registered by tribes according to their ancestral families. The tribe of Reuben numbered 46,500.

22-23 The line of Simeon: The men were counted off head by head, every male twenty years and older who was able to fight in the army, registered by clans and families. The tribe of Simeon numbered 59,300.

24-25 The line of Gad: The men were counted off head by head, every male twenty years and older who was able to fight in the army, registered by clans and families. The tribe of Gad numbered 45,650.

26-27 The line of Judah: The men were counted off head by head, every male twenty years and older who was able to fight in the army, registered by clans and families. The tribe of Judah numbered 74,600.

28-29   The line of Issachar: The men were counted off head by head, every male twenty years and older who was able to fight in the army, registered by clans and families. The tribe of Issachar numbered 54,400.

30-31   The line of Zebulun: The men were counted off head by head, every male twenty years and older who was able to fight in the army, registered by clans and families. The tribe of Zebulun numbered 57,400.

32-33   The line of Joseph: From son Ephraim the men were counted off head by head, every male twenty years and older who was able to fight in the army, registered by clans and families. The tribe of Ephraim numbered 40,500.

34-35   And from son Manasseh the men were counted off head by head, every male twenty years and older who was able to fight in the army, registered by clans and families. The tribe of Manasseh numbered 32,200.

36-37   The line of Benjamin: The men were counted off head by head, every male twenty years and older who was able to fight in the army, registered by clans and families. The tribe of Benjamin numbered 35,400.

38-39   The line of Dan: The men were counted off head by head, every male twenty years and older who was able to fight in the army, registered by clans and families. The tribe of Dan numbered 62,700.

40-41   The line of Asher: The men were counted off head by head, every male twenty years and older who was able to fight in the army, registered by clans and families. The tribe of Asher numbered 41,500.

42-43   The line of Naphtali: The men were counted off head by head, every male twenty years and older who was able to fight in the army, registered by clans and families. The tribe of Naphtali numbered 53,400.

44-46   These are the numbers of those registered by Moses and Aaron, registered with the help of the leaders of Israel, twelve men, each representing his ancestral family. The sum total of the People of Israel twenty years old and over who were able to fight in the army, counted by ancestral family, was 603,550.

47-51   The Levites, however, were not counted by their ancestral family along with the others. GOD had told Moses, "The tribe of Levi is an exception: Don't register them. Don't count the tribe of Levi; don't include them in the general census of the People of Israel. Instead, appoint the Levites to be in charge of The Dwelling of The Testimony— over all its furnishings and everything connected with it. Their job is to carry The Dwelling and all its furnishings, maintain it, and camp around it. When it's time to move The Dwelling, the Levites will take it down, and when it's time to set it up, the Levites will do it. Anyone else who even goes near it will be put to death.

52-53   "The rest of the People of Israel will set up their tents in companies, every man in his own camp under its own flag. But the Levites will set up camp around The Dwelling of The Testimony so that wrath will not fall on the community of Israel. The Levites are responsible for the security of The Dwelling of The Testimony."

54   The People of Israel did everything that GOD commanded Moses. They did it all.

MARCHING ORDERS

1-2   **2** GOD spoke to Moses and Aaron. He said, "The People of Israel are to set up camp circling the Tent of Meeting and facing it. Each company is to camp under its distinctive tribal flag."

3-4   To the east toward the sunrise are the companies of the camp of Judah under its flag, led by Nahshon son of Amminadab. His troops number 74,600.

5-6   The tribe of Issachar will camp next to them, led by Nethanel son of Zuar. His troops number 54,400.

7-8   And the tribe of Zebulun is next to them, led by Eliab son of Helon. His troops number 57,400.

9   The total number of men assigned to Judah, troop by troop, is 186,400. They will lead the march.

10-11   To the south are the companies of the camp of Reuben under its flag, led by Elizur son of Shedeur. His troops number 46,500.

12-13   The tribe of Simeon will camp next to them, led by Shelumiel son of Zurishaddai. His troops number 59,300.

14-15   And the tribe of Gad is next to them, led by Eliasaph son of Deuel. His troops number 45,650.

16   The total number of men assigned to Reuben, troop by troop, is 151,450. They are second in the order of the march.

17   The Tent of Meeting with the camp of the Levites takes its place in the middle of the march. Each tribe will march in the same order in which they camped, each under its own flag.

18-19   To the west are the companies of the camp of Ephraim under its flag, led by Elishama son of Ammihud. His troops number 40,500.

20-21   The tribe of Manasseh will set up camp next to them, led by Gamaliel son of Pedahzur. His troops number 32,200.

22-23   And next to him is the camp of Benjamin, led by Abidan son of Gideoni. His troops number 35,400.

24   The total number of men assigned to the camp of Ephraim, troop by troop, is 108,100. They are third in the order of the march.

25-26   To the north are the companies of the camp of Dan under its flag, led by Ahiezer son of Ammishaddai. His troops number 62,700.

27-28   The tribe of Asher will camp next to them, led by Pagiel son of Ocran. His troops number 41,500.

29-30   And next to them is the tribe of Naphtali, led by Ahira son of Enan. His troops number 53,400.

31   The total number of men assigned to the camp of Dan number 157,600. They will set out, under their flags, last in the line of the march.

32-33   These are the People of Israel, counted according to their ancestral families. The total number in the camps, counted troop by troop, comes to 603,550. Following GOD's command to Moses, the Levites were not counted in with the rest of Israel.

34   The People of Israel did everything the way GOD commanded Moses: They camped under their respective flags; they marched by tribe with their ancestral families.

THE LEVITES

¹ **3** This is the family tree of Aaron and Moses at the time GOD spoke with Moses on Mount Sinai.

²⁻⁴ The names of the sons of Aaron: Nadab the firstborn, Abihu, Eleazar, and Ithamar—anointed priests ordained to serve as priests. But Nadab and Abihu fell dead in the presence of GOD when they offered unauthorized sacrifice to him in the Wilderness of Sinai. They left no sons, and so only Eleazar and Ithamar served as priests during the lifetime of their father, Aaron.

⁵⁻¹⁰ GOD spoke to Moses. He said, "Bring forward the tribe of Levi and present them to Aaron so they can help him. They shall work for him and the whole congregation at the Tent of Meeting by doing the work of The Dwelling. Their job is to be responsible for all the furnishings of The Dwelling, ministering to the affairs of The Dwelling as the People of Israel come to perform their duties. Turn the Levites over to Aaron and his sons; they are the ones assigned to work full time for him. Appoint Aaron and his sons to minister as priests; anyone else who tries to elbow his way in will be put to death."

¹¹⁻¹³ GOD spoke to Moses: "I have taken the Levites from among the People of Israel as a stand-in for every Israelite mother's firstborn son. The Levites belong to me. All the firstborn are mine—when I killed all the firstborn in Egypt, I consecrated for my own use every firstborn in Israel, whether human or animal. They belong to me. I am GOD."

¹⁴⁻¹⁶ GOD spoke to Moses in the Wilderness of Sinai: "Count the Levites by their ancestral families and clans. Count every male a month old and older." Moses counted them just as he was instructed by the mouth of GOD.

¹⁷ These are the names of the sons of Levi: Gershon, Kohath, and Merari.

¹⁸ These are the names of the Gershonite clans: Libni and Shimei.

¹⁹ The sons of Kohath by clan: Amram, Izhar, Hebron, and Uzziel.

²⁰ The sons of Merari by clan: Mahli and Mushi.

These are the clans of Levi, family by family.

²¹⁻²⁶ Gershon was ancestor to the clans of the Libnites and Shimeites, known as the Gershonite clans. All the males who were one month and older numbered 7,500. The Gershonite clans camped on the west, behind The Dwelling, led by Eliasaph son of Lael. At the Tent of Meeting the Gershonites were in charge of maintaining The Dwelling and its tent, its coverings, the screen at the entrance to the Tent of Meeting, the hangings of the Courtyard, the screen at the entrance to the Courtyard that surrounded The Dwelling and Altar, and the cords—in short, everything having to do with these things.

²⁷⁻³² Kohath was ancestor to the clans of the Amramites, Izharites, Hebronites, and Uzzielites. These were known as the Kohathite clans. All the males who were one month and older numbered 8,600. The Kohathites were in charge of the Sanctuary. The Kohathite clans camped on the south side of The Dwelling, led by Elizaphan son of Uzziel. They were in charge of caring for the Chest, the Table, the Lampstand, the Altars, the articles of the Sanctuary used in worship, and the screen—everything having to do with these things. Eleazar, the son of Aaron the priest, supervised the leaders of the Levites and those in charge of the Sanctuary.

33-37 Merari was ancestor to the clans of the Mahlites and the Mushites, known as the Merarite clans. The males who were one month and older numbered 6,200. They were led by Zuriel son of Abihail and camped on the north side of The Dwelling. The Merarites were in charge of the frames of The Dwelling, its crossbars, posts, bases, and all its equipment — everything having to do with these things, as well as the posts of the surrounding Courtyard with their bases, tent pegs, and cords.

38 Moses and Aaron and his sons camped to the east of The Dwelling, toward the rising sun, in front of the Tent of Meeting. They were in charge of maintaining the Sanctuary for the People of Israel and the rituals of worship. Anyone else who tried to perform these duties was to be put to death.

39 The sum total of Levites counted at GOD's command by Moses and Aaron, clan by clan, all the males one month and older, numbered 22,000.

40-41 GOD spoke to Moses: "Count all the firstborn males of the People of Israel who are one month and older. List their names. Then set apart for me the Levites — remember, I am GOD — in place of all the firstborn among the People of Israel, also the livestock of the Levites in place of their livestock. I am GOD."

42-43 So, just as GOD commanded him, Moses counted all the firstborn of the People of Israel. The total of firstborn males one month and older, listed by name, numbered 22,273.

44-48 Again GOD spoke to Moses. He said, "Take the Levites in place of all the firstborn of Israel and the livestock of the Levites in place of their livestock. The Levites are mine, I am GOD. Redeem the 273 firstborn Israelites who exceed the number of Levites by collecting five shekels for each one, using the Sanctuary shekel (the shekel weighing twenty gerahs). Give that money to Aaron and his sons for the redemption of the excess number of Israelites."

49-51 So Moses collected the redemption money from those who exceeded the number redeemed by the Levites. From the 273 firstborn Israelites he collected silver weighing 1,365 shekels according to the Sanctuary shekel. Moses turned over the redemption money to Aaron and his sons, as he was commanded by the word of GOD.

DUTIES OF THE KOHATHITES

1-3 4 GOD spoke to Moses and Aaron. He said, "Number the Kohathite line of Levites by clan and family. Count all the men from thirty to fifty years of age, all who enter the ministry to work in the Tent of Meeting.

4 "This is the assigned work of the Kohathites in the Tent of Meeting: care of the most holy things.

5-6 "When the camp is ready to set out, Aaron and his sons are to go in and take down the covering curtain and cover the Chest of The Testimony with it. Then they are to cover this with a dolphin skin, spread a solid blue cloth on top, and insert the poles.

7-8 "Then they are to spread a blue cloth on the Table of the Presence and set the Table with plates, incense dishes, bowls, and jugs for drink offerings. The bread that is always there stays on the Table. They are to cover these with a scarlet cloth, and on top of that spread the dolphin skin, and insert the poles.

9-10 "They are to use a blue cloth to cover the light-giving Lampstand and the lamps, snuffers, trays, and the oil jars that go with it. Then they are to wrap it all in a covering of dolphin skin and place it on a carrying frame.

11 "They are to spread a blue cloth over the Gold Altar and cover it with dolphin skins and place it on a carrying frame.

12 "They are to take all the articles used in ministering in the Sanctuary, wrap them in a blue cloth, cover them with dolphin skins, and place them on a carrying frame.

13-14 "They are to remove the ashes from the Altar and spread a purple cloth over it. They are to place on it all the articles used in ministering at the Altar—firepans, forks, shovels, bowls; everything used at the Altar—place them on the Altar, cover it with the dolphin skins, and insert the poles.

15 "When Aaron and his sons have finished covering the holy furnishings and all the holy articles, and the camp is ready to set out, the Kohathites are to come and do the carrying. But they must not touch the holy things or they will die. The Kohathites are in charge of carrying all the things that are in the Tent of Meeting.

16 "Eleazar son of Aaron the priest, is to be in charge of the oil for the light, the fragrant incense, the regular Grain-Offering, and the anointing oil. He is to be in charge of the entire Dwelling and everything in it, including its holy furnishings and articles."

17-20 GOD spoke to Moses and Aaron, "Don't let the tribal families of the Kohathites be destroyed from among the Levites. Protect them so they will live and not die when they come near the most holy things. To protect them, Aaron and his sons are to precede them into the Sanctuary and assign each man his task and what he is to carry. But the Kohathites themselves must not go in to look at the holy things, not even a glance at them, or they will die."

DUTIES OF THE GERSHONITES

21-23 GOD spoke to Moses: "Number the Gershonites by tribes according to their ancestral families. Count all the men from thirty to fifty years of age who enter the ministry of work in the Tent of Meeting.

24-28 "The Gershonites by family and clan will serve by carrying heavy loads: the curtains of the Sanctuary and the Tent of Meeting; the covering of the Tent and the outer covering of dolphin skins; the screens for the entrance to the Tent; the cords; and all the equipment used in its ministries. The Gershonites have the job of doing the work connected with these things. All their work of lifting and carrying and moving is to be done under the supervision of Aaron and his sons. Assign them specifically what they are to carry. This is the work of the Gershonite clans at the Tent of Meeting. Ithamar son of Aaron the priest is to supervise their work.

DUTIES OF THE MERARITES

29-30 "Number the Merarites by their ancestral families. Count all the men from thirty to fifty years of age who enter the ministry of work at the Tent of Meeting.

31-33 "This is their assigned duty as they go to work at the Tent of Meeting: to carry the frames of The Dwelling, its crossbars, posts, and bases, as well as the posts of the surrounding Courtyard with their bases, tent pegs, cords, and all the equipment related to their use. Assign to each man exactly what he is to carry. This is the ministry of the Merarite clans as they work at the Tent of Meeting under the supervision of Ithamar son of Aaron the priest."

34-37   Moses, Aaron, and the leaders of the congregation counted the Kohathites by clan and family. All the men from thirty to fifty years of age who came to serve in the work in the Tent of Meeting, counted by clans, were 2,750. This was the total from the Kohathite clans who served in the Tent of Meeting. Moses and Aaron counted them just as GOD had commanded through Moses.

38-41   The Gershonites were counted by clan and family. All the men from thirty to fifty years of age who came to serve in the work in the Tent of Meeting, counted by clan and family, were 2,630. This was the total from the Gershonite clans who served in the Tent of Meeting. Moses and Aaron counted them just as GOD had commanded.

42-45   The Merarites were counted by clan and family. All the men from thirty to fifty years of age who came to serve in the work in the Tent of Meeting, counted by clan, were 3,200. This was the total from the Merarite clans. Moses and Aaron counted them just as GOD had commanded through Moses.

46-49   So Moses and Aaron and the leaders of Israel counted all the Levites by clan and family. All the men from thirty to fifty years of age who came to do the work of serving and carrying the Tent of Meeting numbered 8,580. At GOD's command through Moses, each man was assigned his work and told what to carry.

And that's the story of their numbering, as GOD commanded Moses.

SOME CAMP RULES

1-3   **5** GOD spoke to Moses: "Command the People of Israel to ban from the camp anyone who has an infectious skin disease, anyone who has a discharge, and anyone who is ritually unclean from contact with a dead body. Ban male and female alike; send them outside the camp so that they won't defile their camp, the place I live among them."

4   The People of Israel did this, banning them from the camp. They did exactly what GOD had commanded through Moses.

5-10   GOD spoke to Moses: "Tell the People of Israel, When a man or woman commits any sin, the person has broken trust with GOD, is guilty, and must confess the sin. Full compensation plus twenty percent must be made to whoever was wronged. If the wronged person has no close relative who can receive the compensation, the compensation belongs to GOD and must be given to the priest, along with the ram by which atonement is made. All the sacred offerings that the People of Israel bring to a priest belong to the priest. Each person's sacred offerings are his own, but what one gives to the priest stays with the priest."

11-15   GOD spoke to Moses: "Tell the People of Israel, Say a man's wife goes off and has an affair, is unfaithful to him by sleeping with another man, but

her husband knows nothing about it even though she has defiled herself. And then, even though there was no witness and she wasn't caught in
the act, feelings of jealousy come over the husband and he suspects that
his wife is impure. Even if she is innocent and his jealousy and suspicions
are groundless, he is to take his wife to the priest. He must also take an
offering of two quarts of barley flour for her. He is to pour no oil on it or
mix incense with it because it is a Grain-Offering for jealousy, a Grain-
Offering for bringing the guilt out into the open.

16-22   "The priest then is to take her and have her stand in the presence of
GOD. He is to take some holy water in a pottery jar and put some dust from
the floor of The Dwelling in the water. After the priest has her stand in the
presence of GOD he is to uncover her hair and place the exposure-offering
in her hands, the Grain-Offering for jealousy, while he holds the bitter water
that delivers a curse. Then the priest will put the woman under oath and say,
'If no man has slept with you and you have not had an adulterous affair and
become impure while married to your husband, may this bitter water that
delivers a curse not harm you. But if you have had an affair while married to
your husband and have defiled yourself by sleeping with a man other than
your husband'—here the priest puts the woman under this curse—'may
GOD cause your people to curse and revile you when he makes your womb
shrivel and your belly swell. Let this water that delivers a curse enter your
body so that your belly swells and your womb shrivels.'

    "Then the woman shall say, 'Amen. Amen.'

23-28   "The priest is to write these curses on a scroll and then wash the words
off into the bitter water. He then is to give the woman the bitter water that
delivers a curse. This water will enter her body and cause acute pain. The
priest then is to take from her hands a handful of the Grain-Offering for
jealousy, wave it before GOD, and bring it to the Altar. The priest then is to
take a handful of the Grain-Offering, using it as an exposure-offering, and
burn it on the Altar; after this he is to make her drink the water. If she has
defiled herself in being unfaithful to her husband, when she drinks the water
that delivers a curse, it will enter her body and cause acute pain; her belly will
swell and her womb shrivel. She will be cursed among her people. But if she
has not defiled herself and is innocent of impurity, her name will be cleared
and she will be able to have children.

29-31   "This is the law of jealousy in a case where a woman goes off and has an
affair and defiles herself while married to her husband, or a husband is
tormented with feelings of jealousy because he suspects his wife. The
priest is to have her stand in the presence of GOD and go through this
entire procedure with her. The husband will be cleared of wrong, but the
woman will pay for her wrong."

NAZIRITE VOWS

1-4   6 GOD spoke to Moses: "Speak to the People of Israel; tell them, If any
of you, man or woman, wants to make a special Nazirite vow, consecrating yourself totally to GOD, you must not drink any wine or beer,
no intoxicating drink of any kind, not even the juice of grapes—in fact, you
must not even eat grapes or raisins. For the duration of the consecration, nothing from the grapevine—not even the seeds, not even the skin—may be eaten.

5   "Also, for the duration of the consecration you must not have your hair
cut. Your long hair will be a continuing sign of holy separation to GOD.

6-7   "Also, for the duration of the consecration to GOD, you must not go near a corpse. Even if it's the body of your father or mother, brother or sister, you must not ritually defile yourself because the sign of consecration to God is on your head.

8   "For the entire duration of your consecration you are holy to GOD.

9-12   "If someone should die suddenly in your presence, so that your consecrated head is ritually defiled, you must shave your head on the day of your purifying, that is, the seventh day. Then on the eighth day bring two doves or two pigeons to the priest at the entrance to the Tent of Meeting. The priest will offer one for the Absolution-Offering and one for the Whole-Burnt-Offering, purifying you from the ritual contamination of the corpse. You resanctify your hair on that day and reconsecrate your Nazirite consecration to GOD by bringing a yearling lamb for a Compensation-Offering. You start over; the previous days don't count because your consecration was ritually defiled.

13-17   "These are the instructions for the time set when your special consecration to GOD is up. First, you are to be brought to the entrance to the Tent of Meeting. Then you will present your offerings to GOD: a healthy yearling lamb for the Whole-Burnt-Offering, a healthy yearling ewe for an Absolution-Offering, a healthy ram for a Peace-Offering, a basket of unraised bread made of fine flour, loaves mixed with oil, and crackers spread with oil, along with your Grain-Offerings and Drink-Offerings. The priest will approach GOD and offer up your Absolution-Offering and Whole-Burnt-Offering. He will sacrifice the ram as a Peace-Offering to GOD with the basket of unraised bread, and, last of all, the Grain-Offering and Drink-Offering.

18   "At the entrance to the Tent of Meeting, shave off the hair you consecrated and put it in the fire that is burning under the Peace-Offering.

19-20   "After you have shaved the hair of your consecration, the priest will take a shoulder from the ram, boiled, and a piece of unraised bread and a cracker from the basket and place them in your hands. The priest will then wave them before GOD, a Wave-Offering. They are holy and belong to the priest, along with the breast that was waved and the thigh that was offered.

"Now you are free to drink wine.

21   "These are the instructions for Nazirites as they bring offerings to GOD in their vow of consecration, beyond their other offerings. They must carry out the vow they have vowed following the instructions for the Nazirite."

THE AARONIC BLESSING

22-23   GOD spoke to Moses: "Tell Aaron and his sons, This is how you are to bless the People of Israel. Say to them,

24   GOD bless you and keep you,
25   GOD smile on you and gift you,
26   GOD look you full in the face
       and make you prosper.
27   In so doing, they will place my name on the People of Israel —
       I will confirm it by blessing them."

OFFERINGS FOR THE DEDICATION

1   7 When Moses finished setting up The Dwelling, he anointed it and consecrated it along with all that went with it. At the same time he anointed and consecrated the Altar and its accessories.

2-3 The leaders of Israel, the heads of the ancestral tribes who had carried out the census, brought offerings. They presented before GOD six covered wagons and twelve oxen, a wagon from each pair of leaders and an ox from each leader.

4-5 GOD spoke to Moses: "Receive these so that they can be used to transport the Tent of Meeting. Give them to the Levites according to what they need for their work."

6-9 Moses took the wagons and oxen and gave them to the Levites. He gave two wagons and four oxen to the Gershonites for their work and four wagons and eight oxen to the Merarites for their work. They were all under the direction of Ithamar son of Aaron the priest. Moses didn't give any to the Kohathites because they had to carry the holy things for which they were responsible on their shoulders.

10-11 When the Altar was anointed, the leaders brought their offerings for its dedication and presented them before the Altar because GOD had instructed Moses, "Each day one leader is to present his offering for the dedication of the Altar."

12-13 On the first day, Nahshon son of Amminadab, of the tribe of Judah, brought his offering. His offering was:

a silver plate weighing three and a quarter pounds and a silver bowl weighing one and three-quarter pounds (according to the standard Sanctuary weights), each filled with fine flour mixed with oil as a Grain-Offering;

14 a gold vessel weighing four ounces, filled with incense;

15 a young bull, a ram, and a yearling lamb for a Whole-Burnt-Offering;

16 a he-goat for an Absolution-Offering;

two oxen, five rams, five he-goats, and five yearling lambs to be sacrificed as a Peace-Offering.

17 This was the offering of Nahshon son of Amminadab.

18-23 On the second day, Nethanel son of Zuar, the leader of Issachar, brought his offering. His offering was:

a silver plate weighing three and a quarter pounds and a silver bowl weighing one and three-quarter pounds (according to the standard Sanctuary weights), each filled with fine flour mixed with oil as a Grain-Offering;

a gold vessel weighing four ounces, filled with incense;

a young bull, a ram, and a yearling lamb for a Whole-Burnt-Offering;

a he-goat for an Absolution-Offering;

two oxen, five rams, five he-goats, and five yearling lambs to be sacrificed as a Peace-Offering.

This was the offering of Nethanel son of Zuar.

24-29 On the third day, Eliab son of Helon, the leader of the people of Zebulun, brought his offering. His offering was:

a silver plate weighing three and a quarter pounds and a silver bowl weighing one and three-quarter pounds (according to the standard Sanctuary weights), each filled with fine flour mixed with oil as a Grain-Offering;

a gold vessel weighing four ounces, filled with incense;

a young bull, a ram, and a yearling lamb for a Whole-Burnt-Offering;

a he-goat for an Absolution-Offering;

two oxen, five rams, five he-goats, and five yearling lambs to be sacrificed as a Peace-Offering.

This was the offering of Eliab son of Helon.

30-35   On the fourth day, Elizur son of Shedeur, the leader of the people of Reuben, brought his offering. His offering was:

a silver plate weighing three and a quarter pounds and a silver bowl weighing one and three-quarter pounds (according to the standard Sanctuary weights), each filled with fine flour mixed with oil as a Grain-Offering;

a gold vessel weighing four ounces, filled with incense;

a young bull, a ram, and a yearling lamb for a Whole-Burnt-Offering;

a he-goat for an Absolution-Offering;

two oxen, five rams, five he-goats, and five yearling lambs to be sacrificed as a Peace-Offering.

This was the offering of Elizur son of Shedeur.

36-41   On the fifth day, Shelumiel son of Zurishaddai, the leader of the people of Simeon, brought his offering. His offering was:

a silver plate weighing three and a quarter pounds and a silver bowl weighing one and three-quarter pounds (according to the standard Sanctuary weights), each filled with fine flour mixed with oil as a Grain-Offering;

a gold vessel weighing four ounces, filled with incense;

a young bull, a ram, and a yearling lamb for a Whole-Burnt-Offering;

a he-goat for an Absolution-Offering;

two oxen, five rams, five he-goats, and five yearling lambs to be sacrificed as a Peace-Offering.

This was the offering of Shelumiel son of Zurishaddai.

42-47   On the sixth day, Eliasaph son of Deuel, the leader of the people of Gad, brought his offering. His offering was:

a silver plate weighing three and a quarter pounds and a silver bowl weighing one and three-quarter pounds (according to the standard Sanctuary weights), each filled with fine flour mixed with oil as a Grain-Offering;

a gold vessel weighing four ounces, filled with incense;

a young bull, a ram, and a yearling lamb for a Whole-Burnt-Offering;

a he-goat for an Absolution-Offering;

two oxen, five rams, five he-goats, and five yearling lambs to be sacrificed as a Peace-Offering.

This was the offering of Eliasaph son of Deuel.

48-53   On the seventh day, Elishama son of Ammihud, the leader of the people of Ephraim, brought his offering. His offering was:

a silver plate weighing three and a quarter pounds and a silver bowl weighing one and three-quarter pounds (according to the standard Sanctuary weights), each filled with fine flour mixed with oil as a Grain-Offering;

a gold vessel weighing four ounces, filled with incense;

a young bull, a ram, and a yearling lamb for a Whole-Burnt-Offering;

a he-goat for an Absolution-Offering;

two oxen, five rams, five he-goats, and five yearling lambs to be sacrificed as a Peace-Offering.

This was the offering of Elishama son of Ammihud.

54-59   On the eighth day, Gamaliel son of Pedahzur, the leader of the people of Manasseh, brought his offering. His offering was:

a silver plate weighing three and a quarter pounds and a silver bowl weighing one and three-quarter pounds (according to the standard Sanctuary weights), each filled with fine flour mixed with oil as a Grain-Offering;

a gold vessel weighing four ounces, filled with incense;

a young bull, a ram, and a yearling lamb for a Whole-Burnt-Offering;

a he-goat for an Absolution-Offering;

two oxen, five rams, five he-goats, and five yearling lambs to be sacrificed as a Peace-Offering.

This was the offering of Gamaliel son of Pedahzur.

60-65   On the ninth day, Abidan son of Gideoni, the leader of the people of Benjamin, brought his offering. His offering was:

a silver plate weighing three and a quarter pounds and a silver bowl weighing one and three-quarter pounds (according to the standard Sanctuary weights), each filled with fine flour mixed with oil as a Grain-Offering;

a gold vessel weighing four ounces, filled with incense;

a young bull, a ram, and a yearling lamb for a Whole-Burnt-Offering;

a he-goat for an Absolution-Offering;

two oxen, five rams, five he-goats, and five yearling lambs to be sacrificed as a Peace-Offering.

This was the offering of Abidan son of Gideoni.

66-71   On the tenth day, Ahiezer son of Ammishaddai, the leader of the people of Dan, brought his offering. His offering was:

a silver plate weighing three and a quarter pounds and a silver bowl weighing one and three-quarter pounds (according to the standard Sanctuary weights), each filled with fine flour mixed with oil as a Grain-Offering;

a gold vessel weighing four ounces, filled with incense;

a young bull, a ram, and a yearling lamb for a Whole-Burnt-Offering;

a he-goat for an Absolution-Offering;

two oxen, five rams, five he-goats, and five yearling lambs to be sacrificed as a Peace-Offering.

This was the offering of Ahiezer son of Ammishaddai.

72-77   On the eleventh day, Pagiel son of Ocran, the leader of the people of Asher, brought his offering. His offering was:

a silver plate weighing three and a quarter pounds and a silver bowl weighing one and three-quarter pounds (according to the standard Sanctuary weights), each filled with fine flour mixed with oil as a Grain-Offering;

a gold vessel weighing four ounces, filled with incense;

a young bull, a ram, and a yearling lamb for a Whole-Burnt-Offering;

a he-goat for an Absolution-Offering;

two oxen, five rams, five he-goats, and five yearling lambs to be sacrificed as a Peace-Offering.

This was the offering of Pagiel son of Ocran.

78-83   On the twelfth day, Ahira son of Enan, the leader of the people of Naphtali, brought his offering. His offering was:

a silver plate weighing three and a quarter pounds and a silver bowl weighing one and three-quarter pounds (according to the standard Sanctuary weights), each filled with fine flour mixed with oil as a Grain-Offering;

a gold vessel weighing four ounces, filled with incense;

a young bull, a ram, and a yearling lamb for a Whole-Burnt-Offering;
a he-goat for an Absolution-Offering;
two oxen, five rams, five he-goats, and five yearling lambs to be sacrificed as a Peace-Offering.
This was the offering of Ahira son of Enan.

84 These were the dedication offerings of the leaders of Israel for the anointing of the Altar:

twelve silver plates,
twelve silver bowls,
twelve gold vessels.

85-86 Each plate weighed three and a quarter pounds and each bowl one and
three-quarter pounds. All the plates and bowls together weighed about
sixty pounds (using the official Sanctuary weight). The twelve gold vessels
filled with incense weighed four ounces each (using the official Sanctuary
weight). Altogether the gold vessels weighed about three pounds.

87 The sum total of animals used for the Whole-Burnt-Offering together
with the Grain-Offering:

twelve bulls,
twelve rams,
twelve yearling lambs.

For the Absolution-Offering:

twelve he-goats.

88 The sum total of animals used for the sacrifice of the Peace-Offering:

twenty-four bulls,
sixty rams,
sixty he-goats,
sixty yearling lambs.

These were the offerings for the dedication of the Altar after it was
anointed.

89 When Moses entered the Tent of Meeting to speak with GOD, he heard the
Voice speaking to him from between the two angel-cherubim above the
Atonement-Cover on the Chest of The Testimony. He spoke with him.

THE LIGHTS

1-2 GOD spoke to Moses: "Tell Aaron, Install the seven lamps so they
will throw light in front of the Lampstand."

3-4 Aaron did just that. He installed the lamps so they threw light in
front of the Lampstand, as GOD had instructed Moses. The Lampstand was
made of hammered gold from its stem to its petals. It was made precisely to
the design GOD had shown Moses.

PURIFYING THE LEVITES

5-7   GOD spoke to Moses: "Take the Levites from the midst of the People of Israel and purify them for doing GOD's work. This is the way you will do it: Sprinkle water of absolution on them; have them shave their entire bodies; have them scrub their clothes. Then they will have purified themselves.

8-11   "Have them take a young bull with its accompanying Grain-Offering of fine flour mixed with oil, plus a second young bull for an Absolution-Offering. Bring the Levites to the front of the Tent of Meeting and gather the entire community of Israel. Present the Levites before GOD as the People of Israel lay their hands on them. Aaron will present the Levites before GOD as a Wave-Offering from the People of Israel so that they will be ready to do GOD's work.

12-14   "Have the Levites place their hands on the heads of the bulls, selecting one for the Absolution-Offering and another for the Whole-Burnt-Offering to GOD to make atonement for the Levites. Then have the Levites stand in front of Aaron and his sons and present them as a Wave-Offering to GOD. This is the procedure for setting apart the Levites from the rest of the People of Israel; the Levites are exclusively for my use.

15-19   "After you have purified the Levites and presented them as a Wave-Offering to GOD, they can go to work in the Tent of Meeting. The Levites have been selected out of the People of Israel for my exclusive use; they function in place of every firstborn male born to an Israelite woman. Every firstborn male in Israel, animal or human, is set apart for my use. When I struck down all the firstborn of Egypt, I consecrated them for my holy uses. But now I take the Levites as stand-ins in place of every firstborn son in Israel, selected out of the People of Israel, and I have given the Levites to Aaron and his sons to do all the work involved in the Tent of Meeting on behalf of all the People of Israel and to make atonement for them so that nothing bad will happen to them when they approach the Sanctuary."

20-22   Moses, Aaron, and the entire community of the People of Israel carried out these procedures with the Levites, just as GOD had commanded Moses. The Levites purified themselves and scrubbed their clothes. Then Aaron presented them as a Wave-Offering before GOD and made atonement for them to purify them. Only then did the Levites go to work at the Tent of Meeting. Aaron and his sons supervised them following the directions GOD had given.

23-26   GOD spoke to Moses: "These are your instructions regarding the Levites: At the age of twenty-five they will join the workforce in the Tent of Meeting; at the age of fifty they must retire from the work. They can assist their brothers in the tasks in the Tent of Meeting, but they are not permitted to do the actual work themselves. These are the ground rules for the work of the Levites."

PASSOVER

1-3   9 GOD spoke to Moses in the Wilderness of Sinai in the first month of the second year after leaving Egypt: "Have the People of Israel celebrate Passover at the set time. Celebrate it on schedule, on the evening of the fourteenth day of this month, following all the rules and procedures."

4-5   Moses told the People of Israel to celebrate the Passover and they did—

in the Wilderness of Sinai at evening of the fourteenth day of the first month. The People of Israel did it all just as GOD had commanded Moses.

6-7 But some of them couldn't celebrate the Passover on the assigned day because they were ritually unclean on account of a corpse. So they presented themselves before Moses and Aaron on Passover and told Moses, "We have become ritually unclean because of a corpse, but why should we be barred from bringing GOD's offering along with other Israelites on the day set for Passover?"

8 Moses said, "Give me some time; I'll find out what GOD says in your circumstances."

9-12 GOD spoke to Moses: "Tell the People of Israel, If one or another of you is ritually unclean because of a corpse, or you happen to be off on a long trip, you may still celebrate GOD's Passover. But celebrate it on the fourteenth day of the second month at evening. Eat the lamb together with unraised bread and bitter herbs. Don't leave any of it until morning. Don't break any of its bones. Follow all the procedures.

13 "But a man who is ritually clean and is not off on a trip and still fails to celebrate the Passover must be cut off from his people because he did not present GOD's offering at the set time. That man will pay for his sin.

14 "Any foreigner living among you who wants to celebrate GOD's Passover is welcome to do it, but he must follow all the rules and procedures. The same procedures go for both foreigner and native-born."

THE CLOUD

15-16 The day The Dwelling was set up, the Cloud covered The Dwelling of the Tent of Testimony. From sunset until daybreak it was over The Dwelling. It looked like fire. It was like that all the time, the Cloud over The Dwelling and at night looking like fire.

17-23 When the Cloud lifted above the Tent, the People of Israel marched out; and when the Cloud descended the people camped. The People of Israel marched at GOD's command and they camped at his command. As long as the Cloud was over The Dwelling, they camped. Even when the Cloud hovered over The Dwelling for many days, they honored GOD's command and wouldn't march. They stayed in camp, obedient to GOD's command, as long as the Cloud was over The Dwelling, but the moment GOD issued orders they marched. If the Cloud stayed only from sunset to daybreak and then lifted at daybreak, they marched. Night or day, it made no difference—when the Cloud lifted, they marched. It made no difference whether the Cloud hovered over The Dwelling for two days or a month or a year, as long as the Cloud was there, they were there. And when the Cloud went up, they got up and marched. They camped at GOD's command and they marched at GOD's command. They lived obediently by GOD's orders as delivered by Moses.

THE TWO BUGLES

1-3 **10** GOD spoke to Moses: "Make two bugles of hammered silver. Use them to call the congregation together and give marching orders to the camps. When you blow them, the whole community will meet you at the entrance of the Tent of Meeting.

4-7 "When a bugle gives a single, short blast, that's the signal for the leaders, the heads of the clans, to assemble. When it gives a long blast, that's the signal to march. At the first blast the tribes who were camped on the east set out. At the second blast the camps on the south set out. The long blasts are the signals to march. The bugle call that gathers the assembly is different from the signal to march.

8-10   "The sons of Aaron, the priests, are in charge of blowing the bugles; it's their assigned duty down through the generations. When you go to war against an aggressor, blow a long blast on the bugle so that GOD will notice you and deliver you from your enemies. Also at times of celebration, at the appointed feasts and New Moon festivals, blow the bugles over your Whole-Burnt-Offerings and Peace-Offerings: they will keep your attention on God. I am GOD, *your* God."

THE MARCH FROM SINAI TO PARAN

11-13   In the second year, on the twentieth day of the second month, the Cloud went up from over The Dwelling of The Testimony. At that the People of Israel set out on their travels from the Wilderness of Sinai until the Cloud finally settled in the Wilderness of Paran. They began their march at the command of GOD through Moses.

14-17   The flag of the camp of Judah led the way, rank after rank under the command of Nahshon son of Amminadab. Nethanel son of Zuar commanded the forces of the tribe of Issachar, and Eliab son of Helon commanded the forces of the tribe of Zebulun. As soon as The Dwelling was taken down, the Gershonites and the Merarites set out, carrying The Dwelling.

18-21   The flag of the camp of Reuben was next with Elizur son of Shedeur in command. Shelumiel son of Zurishaddai commanded the forces of the tribe of Simeon; Eliasaph son of Deuel commanded the forces of the tribe of Gad. Then the Kohathites left, carrying the holy things. By the time they arrived The Dwelling would be set up.

22-24   The flag of the tribe of Ephraim moved out next, commanded by Elishama son of Ammihud. Gamaliel son of Pedahzur commanded the forces of the tribe of Manasseh; Abidan son of Gideoni commanded the forces of the tribe of Benjamin.

25-27   Finally, under the flag of the tribe of Dan, the rear guard of all the camps marched out with Ahiezer son of Ammishaddai in command. Pagiel son of Ocran commanded the forces of the tribe of Asher; Ahira son of Enan commanded the forces of the tribe of Naphtali.

28   These were the marching units of the People of Israel. They were on their way.

29   Moses said to his brother-in-law Hobab son of Reuel the Midianite, Moses' father-in-law, "We're marching to the place about which GOD promised, 'I'll give it to you.' Come with us; we'll treat you well. GOD has promised good things for Israel."

30   But Hobab said, "I'm not coming; I'm going back home to my own country, to my own family."

31-32   Moses countered, "Don't leave us. You know all the best places to camp in the wilderness. We need your eyes. If you come with us, we'll make sure that you share in all the good things GOD will do for us."

33-36   And so off they marched. From the Mountain of GOD they marched three days with the Chest of the Covenant of GOD in the lead to scout out a campsite. The Cloud of GOD was above them by day when they marched from the camp. With the Chest leading the way, Moses would say,

> Get up, GOD!
> Put down your enemies!
> Chase those who hate you to the hills!

And when the Chest was set down, he would say,

> Rest with us, GOD,
> Stay with the many,
> Many thousands of Israel.

CAMP TABERAH

1-3 **11** The people fell to grumbling over their hard life. GOD heard. When he heard his anger flared; then fire blazed up and burned the outer boundaries of the camp. The people cried out for help to Moses; Moses prayed to GOD and the fire died down. They named the place Taberah (Blaze) because fire from GOD had blazed up against them.

CAMP KIBROTH HATTAAVAH

4-6 The riffraff among the people had a craving and soon they had the People of Israel whining, "Why can't we have meat? We ate fish in Egypt—and got it free!—to say nothing of the cucumbers and melons, the leeks and onions and garlic. But nothing tastes good out here; all we get is manna, manna, manna."

7-9 Manna was a seedlike substance with a shiny appearance like resin. The people went around collecting it and ground it between stones or pounded it fine in a mortar. Then they boiled it in a pot and shaped it into cakes. It tasted like a delicacy cooked in olive oil. When the dew fell on the camp at night, the manna was right there with it.

10 Moses heard the whining, all those families whining in front of their tents. GOD's anger blazed up. Moses saw that things were in a bad way.

11-15 Moses said to GOD, "Why are you treating me this way? What did I ever do to you to deserve this? Did I conceive them? Was I their mother? So why dump the responsibility of this people on me? Why tell me to carry them around like a nursing mother, carry them all the way to the land you promised to their ancestors? Where am I supposed to get meat for all these people who are whining to me, 'Give us meat; we want meat.' I can't do this by myself—it's too much, all these people. If this is how you intend to treat me, do me a favor and kill me. I've seen enough; I've had enough. Let me out of here."

16-17 GOD said to Moses, "Gather together seventy men from among the leaders of Israel, men whom you know to be respected and responsible. Take them to the Tent of Meeting. I'll meet you there. I'll come down and speak with you. I'll take some of the Spirit that is on you and place it on them; they'll then be able to take some of the load of this people—you won't have to carry the whole thing alone.

18-20 "Tell the people, Consecrate yourselves. Get ready for tomorrow when you're going to eat meat. You've been whining to GOD, 'We want meat; give us meat. We had a better life in Egypt.' GOD has heard your whining and he's going to give you meat. You're going to eat meat. And it's not just for a day that you'll eat meat, and not two days, or five or ten or twenty, but for a whole month. You're going to eat meat until it's coming out your nostrils. You're going to be so sick of meat that you'll throw up at the mere mention of it. And here's why: Because you have rejected GOD who is right here among you, whining to his face, 'Oh, why did we ever have to leave Egypt?'"

21-22 Moses said, "I'm standing here surrounded by 600,000 men on foot and you say, 'I'll give them meat, meat every day for a month.' So where's it coming from? Even if all the flocks and herds were butchered, would that be enough? Even if all the fish in the sea were caught, would that be enough?"

23 GOD answered Moses, "So, do you think I can't take care of you? You'll see soon enough whether what I say happens for you or not."

24-25 So Moses went out and told the people what GOD had said. He called together seventy of the leaders and had them stand around the Tent. GOD came down in a cloud and spoke to Moses and took some of the Spirit that was on him and put it on the seventy leaders. When the Spirit rested on them they prophesied. But they didn't continue; it was a onetime event.

26 Meanwhile two men, Eldad and Medad, had stayed in the camp. They were listed as leaders but they didn't leave camp to go to the Tent. Still, the Spirit also rested on them and they prophesied in the camp.

27 A young man ran and told Moses, "Eldad and Medad are prophesying in the camp!"

28 Joshua son of Nun, who had been Moses' right-hand man since his youth, said, "Moses, master! Stop them!"

29 But Moses said, "Are you jealous for me? Would that all GOD's people were prophets. Would that GOD would put his Spirit on all of them."

30-34 Then Moses and the leaders of Israel went back to the camp. A wind set in motion by GOD swept quails in from the sea. They piled up to a depth of about three feet in the camp and as far out as a day's walk in every direction. All that day and night and into the next day the people were out gathering the quail—huge amounts of quail; even the slowest person among them gathered at least sixty bushels. They spread them out all over the camp for drying. But while they were still chewing the quail and had hardly swallowed the first bites, GOD's anger blazed out against the people. He hit them with a terrible plague. They ended up calling the place Kibroth Hattaavah (Graves-of-the-Craving). There they buried the people who craved meat.

35 From Kibroth Hattaavah they marched on to Hazeroth. They remained at Hazeroth.

CAMP HAZEROTH

1-2 **12** Miriam and Aaron talked against Moses behind his back because of his Cushite wife (he had married a Cushite woman). They said, "Is it only through Moses that GOD speaks? Doesn't he also speak through us?"

GOD overheard their talk.

3-8 Now the man Moses was a quietly humble man, more so than anyone living on Earth. GOD broke in suddenly on Moses and Aaron and Miriam saying, "Come out, you three, to the Tent of Meeting." The three went out. GOD descended in a Pillar of Cloud and stood at the entrance to the Tent.

He called Aaron and Miriam to him. When they stepped out, he said,

> Listen carefully to what I'm telling you.
>   If there is a prophet of GOD among you,
> I make myself known to him in visions,
>   I speak to him in dreams.
> But I don't do it that way with my servant Moses;
>   he has the run of my entire house;
> I speak to him intimately, in person,
>   in plain talk without riddles:
>   He ponders the very form of GOD.
> So why did you show no reverence or respect
>   in speaking against my servant, against Moses?

⁹ The anger of GOD blazed out against them. And then he left.

¹⁰ When the Cloud moved off from the Tent, oh! Miriam had turned leprous, her skin like snow. Aaron took one look at Miriam—a leper!

¹¹⁻¹² He said to Moses, "Please, my master, please don't come down so hard on us for this foolish and thoughtless sin. Please don't make her like a stillborn baby coming out of its mother's womb with half its body decomposed."

¹³ And Moses prayed to GOD:

> Please, God, heal her,
>   please heal her.

¹⁴⁻¹⁶ GOD answered Moses, "If her father had spat in her face, wouldn't she be ostracized for seven days? Quarantine her outside the camp for seven days. Then she can be readmitted to the camp." So Miriam was in quarantine outside the camp for seven days. The people didn't march on until she was readmitted. Only then did the people march from Hazeroth and set up camp in the Wilderness of Paran.

SCOUTING OUT CANAAN

¹⁻² **13** GOD spoke to Moses: "Send men to scout out the country of Canaan that I am giving to the People of Israel. Send one man from each ancestral tribe, each one a tried-and-true leader in the tribe."

³⁻¹⁵ So Moses sent them off from the Wilderness of Paran at the command of GOD. All of them were leaders in Israel, one from each tribe. These were their names:

> from Reuben: Shammua son of Zaccur
> from Simeon: Shaphat son of Hori
> from Judah: Caleb son of Jephunneh
> from Issachar: Igal son of Joseph
> from Ephraim: Hoshea son of Nun
> from Benjamin: Palti son of Raphu
> from Zebulun: Gaddiel son of Sodi
> from Manasseh (a Joseph tribe): Gaddi son of Susi
> from Dan: Ammiel son of Gemalli
> from Asher: Sethur son of Michael

from Naphtali: Nahbi son of Vophsi
from Gad: Geuel son of Maki.

16 These are the names of the men Moses sent to scout out the land. Moses gave Hoshea (Salvation) son of Nun a new name—Joshua (GOD-Saves).

17-20 When Moses sent them off to scout out Canaan, he said, "Go up through the Negev and then into the hill country. Look the land over, see what it is like. Assess the people: Are they strong or weak? Are there few or many? Observe the land: Is it pleasant or harsh? Describe the towns where they live: Are they open camps or fortified with walls? And the soil: Is it fertile or barren? Are there forests? And try to bring back a sample of the produce that grows there—this is the season for the first ripe grapes."

21-25 With that they were on their way. They scouted out the land from the Wilderness of Zin as far as Rehob toward Lebo Hamath. Their route went through the Negev Desert to the town of Hebron. Ahiman, Sheshai, and Talmai, descendants of the giant Anak, lived there. Hebron had been built seven years before Zoan in Egypt. When they arrived at the Eshcol Valley they cut off a branch with a single cluster of grapes—it took two men to carry it—slung on a pole. They also picked some pomegranates and figs. They named the place Eshcol Valley (Grape-Cluster-Valley) because of the huge cluster of grapes they had cut down there. After forty days of scouting out the land, they returned home.

26-27 They presented themselves before Moses and Aaron and the whole congregation of the People of Israel in the Wilderness of Paran at Kadesh. They reported to the whole congregation and showed them the fruit of the land. Then they told the story of their trip:

27-29 "We went to the land to which you sent us and, oh! It *does* flow with milk and honey! Just look at this fruit! The only thing is that the people who live there are fierce, their cities are huge and well fortified. Worse yet, we saw descendants of the giant Anak. Amalekites are spread out in the Negev; Hittites, Jebusites, and Amorites hold the hill country; and the Canaanites are established on the Mediterranean Sea and along the Jordan."

30 Caleb interrupted, called for silence before Moses and said, "Let's go up and take the land—now. We can do it."

31-33 But the others said, "We can't attack those people; they're way stronger than we are." They spread scary rumors among the People of Israel. They said, "We scouted out the land from one end to the other—it's a land that swallows people whole. Everybody we saw was huge. Why, we even saw the Nephilim giants (the Anak giants come from the Nephilim). Alongside them we felt like grasshoppers. And they looked down on us as if we were grasshoppers."

1-3 **14** The whole community was in an uproar, wailing all night long. All the People of Israel grumbled against Moses and Aaron. The entire community was in on it: "Why didn't we die in Egypt? Or in this wilderness? Why has GOD brought us to this country to kill us? Our wives and children are about to become plunder. Why don't we just head back to Egypt? And right now!"

4 Soon they were all saying it to one another: "Let's pick a new leader; let's head back to Egypt."

5 Moses and Aaron fell on their faces in front of the entire community, gathered in emergency session.

6-9 Joshua son of Nun and Caleb son of Jephunneh, members of the scouting party, ripped their clothes and addressed the assembled People of Israel: "The land we walked through and scouted out is a very good land — very good indeed. If GOD is pleased with us, he will lead us into that land, a land that flows, as they say, with milk and honey. And he'll give it to us. Just don't rebel against GOD! And don't be afraid of those people. Why, we'll have them for lunch! They have no protection and GOD is on our side. Don't be afraid of them!"

10-12 But, up in arms now, the entire community was talking of hurling stones at them.

Just then the bright Glory of GOD appeared at the Tent of Meeting. Every Israelite saw it. GOD said to Moses, "How long will these people treat me like dirt? How long refuse to trust me? And with all these signs I've done among them! I've had enough — I'm going to hit them with a plague and kill them. But I'll make you into a nation bigger and stronger than they ever were."

13-16 But Moses said to GOD, "The Egyptians are going to hear about this! You delivered this people from Egypt with a great show of strength, and now this? The Egyptians will tell everyone. They've already heard that you are GOD, that you are on the side of this people, that you are present among them, that they see you with their own eyes in your Cloud that hovers over them, in the Pillar of Cloud that leads them by day and the Pillar of Fire at night. If you kill this entire people in one stroke, all the nations that have heard what has been going on will say, 'Since GOD couldn't get these people into the land which he had promised to give them, he slaughtered them out in the wilderness.'

17 "Now, please, let the power of the Master expand, enlarge itself greatly, along the lines you have laid out earlier when you said,

18 GOD, slow to get angry and huge in loyal love,
    forgiving iniquity and rebellion and sin;
Still, never just whitewashing sin.
    But extending the fallout of parents' sins
to children into the third,
    even the fourth generation.

19 "Please forgive the wrongdoing of this people out of the extravagance of your loyal love just as all along, from the time they left Egypt, you have been forgiving this people."

20-23 GOD said, "I forgive them, honoring your words. But as I live and as the Glory of GOD fills the whole Earth — not a single person of those who saw my Glory, saw the miracle signs I did in Egypt and the wilderness, and who have tested me over and over and over again, turning a deaf ear to me — not one of them will set eyes on the land I so solemnly promised to their ancestors. No one who has treated me with such repeated contempt will see it.

24 "But my servant Caleb — this is a different story. He has a different spirit; he follows me passionately. I'll bring him into the land that he scouted and his children will inherit it.

25 "Since the Amalekites and Canaanites are so well established in the

valleys, for right now change course and head back into the wilderness following the route to the Red Sea."

26-30   GOD spoke to Moses and Aaron: "How long is this going to go on, all this grumbling against me by this evil-infested community? I've had my fill of complaints from these grumbling Israelites. Tell them, As I live — GOD's decree — here's what I'm going to do: Your corpses are going to litter the wilderness — every one of you twenty years and older who was counted in the census, this whole generation of grumblers and grousers. Not one of you will enter the land and make your home there, the firmly and solemnly promised land, except for Caleb son of Jephunneh and Joshua son of Nun.

31-34   "Your children, the very ones that you said would be taken for plunder, I'll bring in to enjoy the land you rejected while your corpses will be rotting in the wilderness. These children of yours will live as shepherds in the wilderness for forty years, living with the fallout of your whoring unfaithfulness until the last of your generation lies a corpse in the wilderness. You scouted out the land for forty days; your punishment will be a year for each day, a forty-year sentence to serve for your sins — a long schooling in my displeasure.

35   "I, GOD, have spoken. I will most certainly carry out these things against this entire evil-infested community which has banded together against me. In this wilderness they will come to their end. There they will die."

36-38   So it happened that the men Moses sent to scout out the land returned to circulate false rumors about the land causing the entire community to grumble against Moses— all these men died. Having spread false rumors of the land, they died in a plague, confronted by GOD. Only Joshua son of Nun and Caleb son of Jephunneh were left alive of the men who went to scout out the land.

39-40   When Moses told all of this to the People of Israel, they mourned long and hard. But early the next morning they started out for the high hill country, saying, "We're here; we're ready — let's go up and attack the land that GOD promised us. We sinned, but now we're ready."

41-43   But Moses said, "Why are you crossing GOD's command yet again? This won't work. Don't attack. GOD isn't with you in this — you'll be beaten badly by your enemies. The Amalekites and Canaanites are ready for you and they'll kill you. Because you have left off obediently following GOD, GOD is not going to be with you in this."

44-45   But they went anyway; recklessly and arrogantly they climbed to the high hill country. But the Chest of the Covenant and Moses didn't budge from the camp. The Amalekites and the Canaanites who lived in the hill country came out of the hills and attacked and beat them, a rout all the way down to Hormah.

MATTERS OF WORSHIP

1-5   **15** GOD spoke to Moses: "Speak to the People of Israel. Tell them, When you enter your homeland that I am giving to you and sacrifice a Fire-Gift to GOD, a Whole-Burnt-Offering or any sacrifice from the herd or flock for a Vow-Offering or Freewill-Offering at one of the appointed feasts, as a pleasing fragrance for GOD, the one bringing the offering shall present to GOD a Grain-Offering of two quarts of fine flour mixed with a quart of oil. With each lamb for the Whole-Burnt-Offering or other sacrifice, prepare a quart of oil and a quart of wine as a Drink-Offering.

6-7   "For a ram prepare a Grain-Offering of four quarts of fine flour mixed with one and a quarter quarts of oil and one and a quarter quarts of wine as a Drink-Offering. Present it as a pleasing fragrance to GOD.

8-10   "When you prepare a young bull as a Whole-Burnt-Offering or sacrifice for a special vow or a Peace-Offering to GOD, bring with the bull a Grain-Offering of six quarts of fine flour and two quarts of oil. Also bring two quarts of wine as a Drink-Offering. It will be a Fire-Gift, a pleasing fragrance to GOD.

11-12   "Each bull or ram, each lamb or young goat, is to be prepared in this same way. Carry out this procedure for each one, no matter how many you have to prepare.

13-16   "Every native-born Israelite is to follow this procedure when he brings a Fire-Gift as a pleasing fragrance to GOD. In future generations, when a foreigner or visitor living at length among you presents a Fire-Gift as a pleasing fragrance to GOD, the same procedures must be followed. The community has the same rules for you and the foreigner living among you. This is the regular rule for future generations. You and the foreigner are the same before GOD. The same laws and regulations apply to both you and the foreigner who lives with you."

17-21   GOD spoke to Moses: "Speak to the People of Israel. Tell them, When you enter the land into which I'm bringing you, and you eat the food of that country, set some aside as an offering for GOD. From the first batch of bread dough make a round loaf for an offering—an offering from the threshing floor. Down through the future generations make this offering to GOD from each first batch of dough.

22-26   "But if you should get off the beaten track and not keep the commands which GOD spoke to Moses, any of the things that GOD commanded you under the authority of Moses from the time that GOD first commanded you right up to this present time, and if it happened more or less by mistake, with the congregation unaware of it, then the whole congregation is to sacrifice one young bull as a Whole-Burnt-Offering, a pleasing fragrance to GOD, accompanied by its Grain-Offering and Drink-Offering as stipulated in the rules, and a he-goat as an Absolution-Offering. The priest is to atone for the entire community of the People of Israel and they will stand forgiven. The sin was not deliberate, and they offered to GOD the Fire-Gift and Absolution-Offering for their inadvertence. The whole community of Israel including the foreigners living there will be absolved, because everyone was involved in the error.

27-28   "But if it's just one person who sins by mistake, not realizing what he's doing, he is to bring a yearling she-goat as an Absolution-Offering. The priest then is to atone for the person who accidentally sinned, to make atonement before GOD so that it won't be held against him.

29   "The same standard holds for everyone who sins by mistake; the native-born Israelites and the foreigners go by the same rules.

30-31   "But the person, native or foreigner, who sins defiantly, deliberately blaspheming GOD, must be cut off from his people: He has despised GOD's word, he has violated GOD's command; that person must be kicked out of the community, ostracized, left alone in his wrongdoing."

32-35 Once, during those wilderness years of the People of Israel, a man was caught gathering wood on the Sabbath. The ones who caught him hauled him before Moses and Aaron and the entire congregation. They put him in custody until it became clear what to do with him. Then GOD spoke to Moses: "Give the man the death penalty. Yes, kill him, the whole community hurling stones at him outside the camp."

36 So the whole community took him outside the camp and threw stones at him, an execution commanded by GOD and given through Moses.

37-41 GOD spoke to Moses: "Speak to the People of Israel. Tell them that from now on they are to make tassels on the corners of their garments and to mark each corner tassel with a blue thread. When you look at these tassels you'll remember and keep all the commandments of GOD, and not get distracted by everything you feel or see that seduces you into infidelities. The tassels will signal remembrance and observance of all my commandments, to live a holy life to GOD. I am your GOD who rescued you from the land of Egypt to be your personal God. Yes, I am GOD, *your* God."

THE REBELS

1-3 16 Getting on his high horse one day, Korah son of Izhar, the son of Kohath, the son of Levi, along with a few Reubenites — Dathan and Abiram sons of Eliab, and On son of Peleth — rebelled against Moses. He had with him 250 leaders of the congregation of Israel, prominent men with positions in the Council. They came as a group and confronted Moses and Aaron, saying, "You've overstepped yourself. This entire community is holy and GOD is in their midst. So why do you act like you're running the whole show?"

4 On hearing this, Moses threw himself facedown on the ground.

5 Then he addressed Korah and his gang: "In the morning GOD will make clear who is on his side, who is holy. GOD will take his stand with the one he chooses.

6-7 "Now, Korah, here's what I want you, you and your gang, to do: Tomorrow, take censers. In the presence of GOD, put fire in them and then incense. Then we'll see who is holy, see whom GOD chooses. Sons of Levi, you've overstepped *yourselves*!"

8-11 Moses continued with Korah, "Listen well now, sons of Levi. Isn't it enough for you that the God of Israel has selected you out of the congregation of Israel to bring you near him to serve in the ministries of The Dwelling of GOD, and to stand before the congregation to minister to them? He has brought you and all your brother Levites into his inner circle, and now you're grasping for the priesthood, too. It's GOD you've ganged up against, not us. What do you have against Aaron that you're bad-mouthing him?"

12-14 Moses then ordered Dathan and Abiram, sons of Eliab, to appear, but they said, "We're not coming. Isn't it enough that you yanked us out of a land flowing with milk and honey to kill us in the wilderness? And now you keep trying to boss us around! Face it, you haven't produced: You haven't brought us into a land flowing with milk and honey, you haven't given us the promised inheritance of fields and vineyards. You'd have to poke our eyes out to keep us from seeing what's going on. Forget it, we're not coming."

15 Moses' temper blazed white-hot. He said to GOD, "Don't accept their Grain-Offering. I haven't taken so much as a single donkey from them; I haven't hurt a single hair of their heads."

16-17 Moses said to Korah, "Bring your people before GOD tomorrow. Appear there with them and Aaron. Have each man bring his censer filled with incense and present it to GOD—all 250 censers. And you and Aaron do the same, bring your censers."

18 So they all did it. They brought their censers filled with fire and incense and stood at the entrance of the Tent of Meeting. Moses and Aaron did the same.

19 It was Korah and his gang against Moses and Aaron at the entrance of the Tent of Meeting. The entire community could see the Glory of GOD.

20-21 GOD said to Moses and Aaron, "Separate yourselves from this congregation so that I can finish them off and be done with them."

22 They threw themselves on their faces and said, "O God, God of everything living, when one man sins are you going to take it out on the whole community?"

23-24 GOD spoke to Moses: "Speak to the community. Tell them, Back off from the tents of Korah, Dathan, and Abiram."

25-26 Moses got up and went to Dathan and Abiram. The leaders of Israel followed him. He then spoke to the community: "Back off from the tents of these bad men; don't touch a thing that belongs to them lest you be carried off on the flood of their sins."

27 So they all backed away from the tents of Korah, Dathan, and Abiram. Dathan and Abiram by now had come out and were standing at the entrance to their tents with their wives, children, and babies.

28-30 Moses continued to address the community: "This is how you'll know that it was GOD who sent me to do all these things and that it wasn't anything I cooked up on my own. If these men die a natural death like all the rest of us, you'll know that it wasn't GOD who sent me. But if GOD does something unprecedented—if the ground opens up and swallows the lot of them and they are pitched alive into Sheol—then you'll know that these men have been insolent with GOD."

31-33 The words were hardly out of his mouth when the Earth split open. Earth opened its mouth and in one gulp swallowed them down, the men and their families, all the human beings connected with Korah, along with everything they owned. And that was the end of them, pitched alive into Sheol. The Earth closed up over them and that was the last the community heard of them.

34 At the sound of their cries everyone around ran for dear life, shouting, "We're about to be swallowed up alive!"

35 Then GOD sent lightning. The fire cremated the 250 men who were offering the incense.

36-38 GOD spoke to Moses: "Tell Eleazar son of Aaron the priest, Gather up the censers from the smoldering cinders and scatter the coals a distance away for these censers have become holy. Take the censers of the men who have sinned and are now dead and hammer them into thin sheets for covering the Altar. They have been offered to GOD and are holy to GOD. Let them serve as a sign to Israel, evidence of what happened this day."

39-40 So Eleazar gathered all the bronze censers that belonged to those who had been burned up and had them hammered flat and used to overlay the Altar, just as GOD had instructed him by Moses. This was to serve as a sign to Israel that only descendants of Aaron were allowed to burn incense before GOD; anyone else trying it would end up like Korah and his gang.

41 Grumbling broke out the next day in the community of Israel, grumbling against Moses and Aaron: "You have killed GOD's people!"

42 But it so happened that when the community got together against Moses and Aaron, they looked over at the Tent of Meeting and there was the Cloud—the Glory of GOD for all to see.

43-45 Moses and Aaron stood at the front of the Tent of Meeting. GOD spoke to Moses: "Back away from this congregation so that I can do away with them this very minute."

They threw themselves facedown on the ground.

46 Moses said to Aaron, "Take your censer and fill it with incense, along with fire from the Altar. Get to the congregation as fast as you can: make atonement for them. Anger is pouring out from GOD—the plague has started!"

47-48 Aaron grabbed the censer, as directed by Moses, and ran into the midst of the congregation. The plague had already begun. He put burning incense into the censer and atoned for the people. He stood there between the living and the dead and stopped the plague.

49-50 Fourteen thousand seven hundred people died from the plague, not counting those who died in the affair of Korah. Aaron then went back to join Moses at the entrance to the Tent of Meeting. The plague was stopped.

AARON'S STAFF

1-5 **17** GOD spoke to Moses: "Speak to the People of Israel. Get staffs from them—twelve staffs in all, one from the leader of each of their ancestral tribes. Write each man's name on his staff. Start with Aaron; write Aaron's name on the staff of Levi and then proceed with the rest, a staff for the leader of each ancestral tribe. Now lay them out in the Tent of Meeting in front of The Testimony where I keep appointments with you. What will happen next is this: The staff of the man I choose will sprout. I'm going to put a stop to this endless grumbling by the People of Israel against you."

6-7 Moses spoke to the People of Israel. Their leaders handed over twelve staffs, one for the leader of each tribe. And Aaron's staff was one of them. Moses laid out the staffs before GOD in the Tent of Testimony.

8-9 Moses walked into the Tent of Testimony the next day and saw that Aaron's staff, the staff of the tribe of Levi, had in fact sprouted—buds, blossoms, and even ripe almonds! Moses brought out all the staffs from GOD's presence and presented them to the People of Israel. They took a good look. Each leader took the staff with his name on it.

10 GOD said to Moses, "Return Aaron's staff to the front of The Testimony. Keep it there as a sign to rebels. This will put a stop to the grumbling against me and save their lives."

11 Moses did just as GOD commanded him.

12-13 The People of Israel said to Moses, "We're as good as dead. This is our death sentence. Anyone who even gets close to The Dwelling of GOD is as good as dead. Are we all doomed?"

DUTIES IN THE TENT OF TESTIMONY

1-4 **18** GOD said to Aaron, "You and your sons, along with your father's family, are responsible for taking care of sins having to do with the Sanctuary; you and your sons are also responsible for sins involving the priesthood. So enlist your brothers of the tribe of Levi to join you and assist you and your sons in your duties in the Tent of Testimony. They will report to you as they go about their duties related to the Tent, but they must not have anything to do with the holy things of the Altar under penalty of death—both they and you will die! They are to work with you in taking care of the Tent of Meeting, whatever work is involved in the Tent. Outsiders are not allowed to help you.

5-7 "Your job is to take care of the Sanctuary and the Altar so that there will be no more outbreaks of anger on the People of Israel. I personally have picked your brothers, the Levites, from Israel as a whole. I'm giving them to you as a gift, a gift of GOD, to help with the work of the Tent of Meeting. But only you and your sons may serve as priests, working around the Altar and inside the curtain. The work of the priesthood is my exclusive gift to you; it cannot be delegated—anyone else who invades the Sanctuary will be executed."

8-10 GOD spoke to Aaron, "I am personally putting you in charge of my contributions, all the holy gifts I get from the People of Israel. I am turning them over to you and your children for your personal use. This is the standing rule. You and your sons get what's left from the offerings, whatever hasn't been totally burned up on the Altar—the leftovers from Grain-Offerings, Absolution-Offerings, and Compensation-Offerings. Eat it reverently; it is most holy; every male may eat it. Treat it as holy.

11-13 "You also get the Wave-Offerings from the People of Israel. I present them to you and your sons and daughters as a gift. This is the standing rule. Anyone in your household who is ritually clean may eat it. I also give you all the best olive oil, the best new wine, and the grain that is offered to GOD as the firstfruits of their harvest—all the firstfruits they offer to GOD are yours. Anyone in your household who is ritually clean may eat it.

14-16 "You get every Totally-Devoted gift. Every firstborn that is offered to GOD, whether animal or person, is yours. Except you don't get the firstborn itself, but its redemption price; firstborn humans and ritually clean animals are bought back and you get the redemption price. When the firstborn is a month old it must be redeemed at the redemption price of five shekels of silver, using the standard of the Sanctuary shekel, which weighs twenty gerahs.

17-19 "On the other hand, you don't redeem a firstborn ox, sheep, or goat—they are holy. Instead splash their blood on the Altar and burn their fat as a Fire-Gift, a pleasing fragrance to GOD. But you get the meat, just as you get the breast from the Wave-Offering and the right thigh. All the holy offerings that the People of Israel set aside for GOD, I'm turning over to you and your children. That's the standard rule and includes both you and your children—a Covenant-of-Salt, eternal and unchangeable before GOD."

20 GOD said to Aaron, "You won't get any inheritance in land, not so much as a small plot of ground: I am your plot of ground, I am your inheritance among the People of Israel.

21-24 "I'm giving the Levites all the tithes of Israel as their pay for the work they do in the Tent of Meeting. Starting now, the rest of the People of Israel cannot wander in and out of the Tent of Meeting; they'll be penalized for their sin and the penalty is death. It's the Levites and only the Levites who are to work in the Tent of Meeting and they are responsible for anything that goes wrong. This is the regular rule for all time. They get no inheritance among the People of Israel; instead I turn over to them the tithes that the People of Israel present as an offering to GOD. That's why I give the ruling: They are to receive no land-inheritance among the People of Israel."

25-29 GOD spoke to Moses: "Speak to the Levites. Tell them, When you get the tithe from the People of Israel, the inheritance that I have assigned to you, you must tithe that tithe and present it as an offering to GOD. Your offerings will be treated the same as other people's gifts of grain from the threshing floor or wine from the wine vat. This is your procedure for making offerings to GOD from all the tithes you get from the People of Israel: give GOD's portion from these tithes to Aaron the priest. Make sure that GOD's portion is the best and holiest of everything you get.

30-32 "Tell the Levites, When you offer the best part, the rest will be treated the same as grain from the threshing floor or wine from the wine vat that others give. You and your households are free to eat the rest of it anytime and anyplace — it's your wages for your work at the Tent of Meeting. By offering the best part, you'll avoid guilt, you won't desecrate the holy offerings of the People of Israel, and you won't die."

THE RED COW

1-4 **19** GOD spoke to Moses and Aaron: "This is the rule from the Revelation that GOD commands: Tell the People of Israel to get a red cow, a healthy specimen, ritually clean, that has never been in harness. Present it to Eleazar the priest, then take it outside the camp and butcher it while he looks on. Eleazar will take some of the blood on his finger and splash it seven times in the direction of the Tent of Meeting.

5-8 "Then under Eleazar's supervision burn the cow, the whole thing — hide, meat, blood, even its dung. The priest then will take a stick of cedar, some sprigs of hyssop, and a piece of scarlet material and throw them on the burning cow. Afterwards the priest must wash his clothes and bathe well with water. He can then come into the camp but he remains ritually unclean until evening. The man who burns the cow must also wash his clothes and bathe with water. He also is unclean until evening.

9 "Then a man who is ritually clean will gather the ashes of the cow and place them in a ritually clean place outside the camp. The congregation of Israel will keep them to use in the Water-of-Cleansing, an Absolution-Offering.

10 "The man who gathered up the ashes must scrub his clothes; he is ritually unclean until evening. This is to be a standing rule for both native-born Israelites and foreigners living among them.

11-13 "Anyone who touches a dead body is ritually unclean for seven days. He must purify himself with the Water-of-Cleansing on the third day; on the seventh day he will be clean. But if he doesn't follow the procedures for the third and seventh days, he won't be clean. Anyone who touches the dead body of anyone and doesn't get cleansed desecrates GOD's Dwelling and is to be excommunicated. For as long as the Water-of-Cleansing has not been sprinkled on him, he remains ritually unclean.

14-15 "This is the rule for someone who dies in his tent: Anyone who enters the tent or is already in the tent is ritually unclean for seven days, and every open container without a lid is unclean.

16-21 "Anyone out in the open field who touches a corpse, whether dead from violent or natural causes, or a human bone or a grave is unclean for seven days. For this unclean person, take some ashes from the burned Absolution-Offering and add some fresh water to it in a bowl. Find a ritually clean man to dip a sprig of hyssop into the water and sprinkle the tent and all its furnishings, the persons who were in the tent, the one who touched the bones of the person who was killed or died a natural death, and whoever may have touched a grave. Then he is to sprinkle the unclean person on the third and seventh days. On the seventh day he is considered cleansed. The cleansed person must then scrub his clothes and take a bath; by evening he is clean. But if an unclean person does not go through these cleansing procedures, he must be excommunicated from the community; he has desecrated the Sanctuary of GOD. The Water-of-Cleansing has not been sprinkled on him and he is ritually unclean. This is the standing rule for these cases.

"The man who sprinkles the Water-of-Cleansing has to scrub his clothes; anyone else who touched the Water-of-Cleansing is also ritually unclean until evening.

22 "Anything the ritually unclean man touches becomes unclean, and the person who touches what he touched is unclean until evening."

CAMP KADESH

20 In the first month, the entire company of the People of Israel arrived in the Wilderness of Zin. The people stayed in Kadesh.

Miriam died there, and she was buried.

2-5 There was no water there for the community, so they ganged up on Moses and Aaron. They attacked Moses: "We wish we'd died when the rest of our brothers died before GOD. Why did you haul this congregation of GOD out here into this wilderness to die, people and cattle alike? And why did you take us out of Egypt in the first place, dragging us into this miserable country? No grain, no figs, no grapevines, no pomegranates — and now not even any water!"

6 Moses and Aaron walked from the assembled congregation to the Tent of Meeting and threw themselves facedown on the ground. And they saw the Glory of GOD.

7-8 GOD spoke to Moses: "Take the staff. Assemble the community, you and your brother Aaron. Speak to that rock that's right in front of them and it will give water. You will bring water out of the rock for them; congregation and cattle will both drink."

9-10 Moses took the staff away from GOD's presence, as commanded. He and Aaron rounded up the whole congregation in front of the rock. Moses spoke: "Listen, rebels! Do we have to bring water out of this rock for you?"

11 With that Moses raised his arm and slammed his staff against the rock — once, twice. Water poured out. Congregation and cattle drank.

12 GOD said to Moses and Aaron, "Because you didn't trust me, didn't

treat me with holy reverence in front of the People of Israel, you two aren't going to lead this company into the land that I am giving them."

13   These were the Waters of Meribah (Bickering) where the People of Israel bickered with GOD, and he revealed himself as holy.

⁂

14-16   Moses sent emissaries from Kadesh to the king of Edom with this message: "A message from your brother Israel: You are familiar with all the trouble we've run into. Our ancestors went down to Egypt and lived there a long time. The Egyptians viciously abused both us and our ancestors. But when we cried out for help to GOD, he heard our cry. He sent an angel and got us out of Egypt. And now here we are at Kadesh, a town at the border of your land.

17   "Will you give us permission to cut across your land? We won't trespass through your fields or orchards and we won't drink out of your wells; we'll keep to the main road, the King's Road, straying neither right nor left until we've crossed your border."

18   The king of Edom answered, "Not on your life. If you so much as set a foot on my land, I'll kill you."

19   The People of Israel said, "Look, we'll stay on the main road. If we or our animals drink any water, we'll pay you for it. We're harmless—just a company of footsore travelers."

20-21   He answered again: "No. You may *not* come through." And Edom came out and blocked the way with a crowd of people brandishing weapons. Edom refused to let them cross through his land. So Israel had to detour around him.

CAMP HOR

22   The People of Israel, the entire company, set out from Kadesh and traveled to Mount Hor.

23-26   GOD said to Moses and Aaron at Mount Hor at the border of Edom, "It's time for Aaron to be gathered into the company of his ancestors. He will not enter the land I am giving to the People of Israel because you both rebelled against my orders at the Waters of Meribah. So take Aaron and his son Eleazar and lead them up Mount Hor. Remove Aaron's clothes from him and put them on his son Eleazar. Aaron will be gathered there; Aaron will die."

27-29   Moses obeyed GOD's command. They climbed Mount Hor as the whole congregation watched. Moses took off Aaron's clothes and put them on his son Eleazar. Aaron died on top of the mountain. Then Moses and Eleazar came down from the mountain. The whole congregation, getting the news that Aaron had died, went into thirty days of mourning for him.

HORMAH

1   **21** The Canaanite king of Arad, ruling in the Negev, heard that Israel was advancing up the road to Atharim. He attacked Israel and took prisoners of war.

2   Israel vowed a vow to GOD: "If you will give this people into our power, we'll destroy their towns and present the ruins to you as a holy destruction."

3   GOD listened to Israel's prayer and gave them the Canaanites. They destroyed both them and their towns, a holy destruction. They named the place Hormah (Holy Destruction).

THE SNAKE OF FIERY COPPER

4-5 They set out from Mount Hor along the Red Sea Road, a detour around the land of Edom. The people became irritable and cross as they traveled. They spoke out against God and Moses: "Why did you drag us out of Egypt to die in this godforsaken country? No decent food; no water—we can't stomach this stuff any longer."

6-7 So GOD sent poisonous snakes among the people; they bit them and many in Israel died. The people came to Moses and said, "We sinned when we spoke out against GOD and you. Pray to GOD; ask him to take these snakes from us."

Moses prayed for the people.

8 GOD said to Moses, "Make a snake and put it on a flagpole: Whoever is bitten and looks at it will live."

9 So Moses made a snake of fiery copper and put it on top of a flagpole. Anyone bitten by a snake who then looked at the copper snake lived.

CAMPING ON THE WAY TO MOAB

10-15 The People of Israel set out and camped at Oboth. They left Oboth and camped at Iye Abarim in the wilderness that faces Moab on the east. They went from there and pitched camp in the Zered Valley. Their next camp was alongside the Arnon River, which marks the border between Amorite country and Moab. The Book of the Wars of GOD refers to this place:

> Waheb in Suphah,
>   the canyons of Arnon;
> Along the canyon ravines
>   that lead to the village Ar
> And lean hard against
>   the border of Moab.

16-18 They went on to Beer (The Well), where GOD said to Moses, "Gather the people; I'll give them water." That's where Israel sang this song:

> Erupt, Well!
> Sing the Song of the Well,
>   the well sunk by princes,
> Dug out by the peoples' leaders
>   digging with their scepters and staffs.

19-20 From the wilderness their route went from Mattanah to Nahaliel to Bamoth (The Heights) to the valley that opens into the fields of Moab from where Pisgah (The Summit) rises and overlooks Jeshimon (Wasteland).

21-22 Israel sent emissaries to Sihon, king of the Amorites, saying, "Let us cross your land. We won't trespass into your fields or drink water in your vineyards. We'll keep to the main road, the King's Road, until we're through your land."

23-27 But Sihon wouldn't let Israel go through. Instead he got his army together and marched into the wilderness to fight Israel. At Jahaz he attacked Israel. But Israel fought hard, beat him soundly, and took possession of his land from the Arnon all the way to the Jabbok right up to the Ammonite border. They stopped there because the Ammonite border was fortified. Israel took and occupied all the Amorite cities, including Heshbon and all its surrounding villages. Heshbon was the capital city of Sihon king of the Amorites. He had attacked the former king of Moab and captured all his land as far north as the river Arnon. That is why the folk singers sing,

> Come to Heshbon to rebuild the city,
>> restore Sihon's town.

28-29
> Fire once poured out of Heshbon,
>> flames from the city of Sihon;
> Burning up Ar of Moab,
>> the natives of Arnon's heights.
> Doom, Moab!
>> The people of Chemosh, done for!
> Sons turned out as fugitives, daughters abandoned as captives
>> to the king of the Amorites, to Sihon.

30
> Oh, but we finished them off:
>> Nothing left of Heshbon as far as Dibon;
> Devastation as far off as Nophah,
>> scorched earth all the way to Medeba.

31-32 Israel moved in and lived in Amorite country. Moses sent men to scout out Jazer. They captured its villages and drove away the Amorites who lived there.

33 Then they turned north on the road to Bashan. Og king of Bashan marched out with his entire army to meet Moses in battle at Edrei.

34 GOD said to Moses, "Don't be afraid of him. I'm making a present of him to you, him and all his people and his land. Treat him the same as Sihon king of the Amorites who ruled in Heshbon."

35 So they attacked him, his sons, and all the people — there was not a single survivor. Israel took the land.

BALAAM

1 The People of Israel marched on and camped on the Plains of Moab at Jordan-Jericho.

2-3 Balak son of Zippor learned of all that Israel had done to the Amorites. The people of Moab were in a total panic because of Israel. There were so many of them! They were terrorized.

4-5 Moab spoke to the leaders of Midian: "Look, this mob is going to clean us out — a bunch of crows picking a carcass clean."

Balak son of Zippor, who was king of Moab at that time, sent emissaries to get Balaam son of Beor, who lived at Pethor on the banks of the Euphrates River, his homeland.

5-6 Balak's emissaries said, "Look. A people has come up out of Egypt, and they're all over the place! And they're pressing hard on me. Come and curse them for me — they're too much for me. Maybe then I can beat them; we'll attack and drive them out of the country. You have a reputation: Those you bless stay blessed; those you curse stay cursed."

7-8 The leaders of Moab and Midian were soon on their way, with the fee for the cursing tucked safely in their wallets. When they got to Balaam, they gave him Balak's message.

"Stay here for the night," Balaam said. "In the morning I'll deliver the answer that GOD gives me."

The Moabite nobles stayed with him.

9 Then God came to Balaam. He asked, "So who are these men here with you?"

10-11 Balaam answered, "Balak son of Zippor, king of Moab, sent them with a message: 'Look, the people that came up out of Egypt are all over the place! Come and curse them for me. Maybe then I'll be able to attack and drive them out of the country.'"

12 God said to Balaam, "Don't go with them. And don't curse the others—they are a blessed people."

13 The next morning Balaam got up and told Balak's nobles, "Go back home; GOD refuses to give me permission to go with you."

14 So the Moabite nobles left, came back to Balak, and said, "Balaam wouldn't come with us."

15-17 Balak sent another group of nobles, higher ranking and more distinguished. They came to Balaam and said, "Balak son of Zippor says, 'Please, don't refuse to come to me. I will honor and reward you lavishly—anything you tell me to do, I'll do; I'll pay anything—only come and curse this people.'"

18-19 Balaam answered Balak's servants: "Even if Balak gave me his house stuffed with silver and gold, I wouldn't be able to defy the orders of my GOD to do anything, whether big or little. But come along and stay with me tonight as the others did; I'll see what GOD will say to me this time."

20 God came to Balaam that night and said, "Since these men have come all this way to see you, go ahead and go with them. But make sure you do absolutely nothing other than what I tell you."

21-23 Balaam got up in the morning, saddled his donkey, and went off with the noblemen from Moab. As he was going, though, God's anger flared. The angel of GOD stood in the road to block his way. Balaam was riding his donkey, accompanied by his two servants. When the donkey saw the angel blocking the road and brandishing a sword, she veered off the road into the ditch. Balaam beat the donkey and got her back on the road.

24-25 But as they were going through a vineyard, with a fence on either side, the donkey again saw GOD's angel blocking the way and veered into the fence, crushing Balaam's foot against the fence. Balaam hit her again.

26-27 GOD's angel blocked the way yet again—a very narrow passage this time; there was no getting through on the right or left. Seeing the angel, Balaam's donkey sat down under him. Balaam lost his temper; he beat the donkey with his stick.

28 Then GOD gave speech to the donkey. She said to Balaam: "What have I ever done to you that you have beat me these three times?"

29 Balaam said, "Because you've been playing games with me! If I had a sword I would have killed you by now."

30 The donkey said to Balaam, "Am I not your trusty donkey on whom you've ridden for years right up until now? Have I ever done anything like this to you before? Have I?"

He said, "No."

31   Then GOD helped Balaam see what was going on: He saw GOD's angel blocking the way, brandishing a sword. Balaam fell to the ground, his face in the dirt.

32-33   GOD's angel said to him: "Why have you beaten your poor donkey these three times? I have come here to block your way because you're getting way ahead of yourself. The donkey saw me and turned away from me these three times. If she hadn't, I would have killed you by this time, but not the donkey. I would have let her off."

34   Balaam said to GOD's angel, "I have sinned. I had no idea you were standing in the road blocking my way. If you don't like what I'm doing, I'll head back."

35   But GOD's angel said to Balaam, "Go ahead and go with them. But only say what I tell you to say — absolutely no other word."

And so Balaam continued to go with Balak's nobles.

36   When Balak heard that Balaam was coming, he went out to meet him in the Moabite town that was on the banks of the Arnon, right on the boundary of his land.

37   Balak said to Balaam, "Didn't I send an urgent message for help? Why didn't you come when I called? Do you think I can't pay you enough?"

38   Balaam said to Balak, "Well, I'm here now. But I can't tell you just anything. I can speak only words that God gives me — no others."

39-40   Balaam then accompanied Balak to Kiriath Huzoth (Street-Town). Balak slaughtered cattle and sheep for sacrifices and presented them to Balaam and the nobles who were with him.

41   At daybreak Balak took Balaam up to Bamoth Baal (The Heights of Baal) so that he could get a good view of some of the people.

1   23 Balaam said, "Build me seven altars here, and then prepare seven bulls and seven rams."

2   Balak did it. Then Balaam and Balak sacrificed a bull and a ram on each of the altars.

3   Balaam instructed Balak: "Stand watch here beside your Whole-Burnt-Offering while I go off by myself. Maybe GOD will come and meet with me. Whatever he shows or tells me, I'll report to you." Then he went off by himself.

4   God did meet with Balaam. Balaam said, "I've set up seven altars and offered a bull and a ram on each altar."

5   Then GOD gave Balaam a message: "Return to Balak and give him this message."

6-10   He went back and found him stationed beside his Whole-Burnt-Offering and with him all the nobles of Moab. Then Balaam spoke his message-oracle:

Balak led me here from Aram,
    the king of Moab all the way from the eastern mountains.
"Go, curse Jacob for me;
    go, damn Israel."
How can I curse whom God has not cursed?
    How can I damn whom GOD has not damned?

> From rock pinnacles I see them,
>> from hilltops I survey them:
> Look! a people camping off by themselves,
>> thinking themselves outsiders among nations.
> But who could ever count the dust of Jacob
>> or take a census of cloud-of-dust Israel?
> I want to die like these right-living people!
>> I want an end just like theirs!

11 Balak said to Balaam, "What's this? I brought you here to curse my enemies, and all you've done is bless them."

12 Balaam answered, "Don't I have to be careful to say what GOD gives me to say?"

13 Balak said to him, "Go with me to another place from which you can only see the outskirts of their camp — you won't be able to see the whole camp. From there, curse them for my sake."

14 So he took him to Watchmen's Meadow at the top of Pisgah. He built seven altars there and offered a bull and a ram on each altar.

15 Balaam said to Balak, "Take up your station here beside your Whole-Burnt-Offering while I meet with him over there."

16 GOD met with Balaam and gave him a message. He said, "Return to Balak and give him the message."

17-24 Balaam returned and found him stationed beside his Whole-Burnt-Offering and the nobles of Moab with him. Balak said to him, "What did GOD say?" Then Balaam spoke his message-oracle:

> On your feet, Balak. Listen,
>> listen carefully son of Zippor:
> God is not man, one given to lies,
>> and not a son of man changing his mind.
> Does he speak and not do what he says?
>> Does he promise and not come through?
> I was brought here to bless;
>> and now he's blessed — how can I change that?
> He has no bone to pick with Jacob,
>> he sees nothing wrong with Israel.
> GOD is with them,
>> and they're with him, shouting praises to their King.
> God brought them out of Egypt,
>> rampaging like a wild ox.
> No magic spells can bind Jacob,
>> no incantations can hold back Israel.
> People will look at Jacob and Israel and say,
>> "What a great thing has God done!"
> Look, a people rising to its feet, stretching like a lion,
>> a king-of-the-beasts, aroused,
> Unsleeping, unresting until its hunt is over
>> and it's eaten and drunk its fill.

25 Balak said to Balaam, "Well, if you can't curse them, at least don't bless them."

26 Balaam replied to Balak, "Didn't I tell you earlier: 'All God speaks, and only what he speaks, I speak'?"

27-28 Balak said to Balaam, "Please, let me take you to another place; maybe we can find the right place in God's eyes where you'll be able to curse them for me." So Balak took Balaam to the top of Peor, with a vista over the Jeshimon (Wasteland).

29 Balaam said to Balak, "Build seven altars for me here and prepare seven bulls and seven rams for sacrifice."

30 Balak did it and presented an offering of a bull and a ram on each of the altars.

1-3 **24** By now Balaam realized that GOD wanted to bless Israel. So he didn't work in any sorcery as he had done earlier. He turned and looked out over the wilderness. As Balaam looked, he saw Israel camped tribe by tribe. The Spirit of God came on him, and he spoke his oracle-message:

3-9 Decree of Balaam son of Beor,
    yes, decree of a man with 20/20 vision;
Decree of a man who hears God speak,
    who sees what The Strong God shows him,
Who falls on his face in worship,
    who sees what's really going on.

What beautiful tents, Jacob,
    oh, your homes, Israel!
Like valleys stretching out in the distance,
    like gardens planted by rivers,
Like sweet herbs planted by the gardener GOD,
    like red cedars by pools and springs,
Their buckets will brim with water,
    their seed will spread life everywhere.
Their king will tower over Agag and his ilk,
    their kingdom surpassingly majestic.
God brought them out of Egypt,
    rampaging like a wild ox,
Gulping enemies like morsels of meat,
    crushing their bones, snapping their arrows.
Israel crouches like a lion and naps,
    king-of-the-beasts— who dares disturb him?
Whoever blesses you is blessed,
    whoever curses you is cursed.

10-11 Balak lost his temper with Balaam. He shook his fist. He said to Balaam: "I got you in here to curse my enemies and what have you done? Blessed them! Blessed them three times! Get out of here! Go home! I told you I would pay you well, but you're getting nothing. You can blame GOD."

12-15　　Balaam said to Balak, "Didn't I tell you up front when you sent your emissaries, 'Even if Balak gave me his palace stuffed with silver and gold, I couldn't do anything on my own, whether good or bad, that went against GOD's command'? I'm leaving for home and my people, but I warn you of what this people will do to your people in the days to come." Then he spoke his oracle-message:

15-19
Decree of Balaam son of Beor,
　　decree of the man with 20/20 vision,
Decree of the man who hears godly speech,
　　who knows what's going on with the High God,
Who sees what The Strong God reveals,
　　who bows in worship and sees what's real.
I see him, but not right now,
　　I perceive him, but not right here;
A star rises from Jacob
　　a scepter from Israel,
Crushing the heads of Moab,
　　the skulls of all the noisy windbags;
I see Edom sold off at auction,
　　enemy Seir marked down at the flea market,
　　while Israel walks off with the trophies.
A ruler is coming from Jacob
　　who'll destroy what's left in the city.

20　　Then Balaam spotted Amalek and delivered an oracle-message. He said,

Amalek, you're in first place among nations right now,
　　but you're going to come in last, ruined.

21-22　　He saw the Kenites and delivered his oracle-message to them:

Your home is in a nice secure place,
　　like a nest high on the face of a cliff.
Still, you Kenites will look stupid
　　when Asshur takes you prisoner.

23-24　　Balaam spoke his final oracle-message:

Doom! Who stands a chance
　　when God starts in?
Sea-Peoples, raiders from across the sea,
　　will harass Asshur and Eber,
But they'll also come to nothing,
　　just like all the rest.

25　　Balaam got up and went home. Balak also went on his way.

THE ORGY AT SHITTIM

1-3 **25** While Israel was camped at Shittim (Acacia Grove), the men began to have sex with the Moabite women. It started when the women invited the men to their sex-and-religion worship. They ate together and then worshiped their gods. Israel ended up joining in the worship of the Baal of Peor. GOD was furious, his anger blazing out against Israel.

4 GOD said to Moses, "Take all the leaders of Israel and kill them by hanging, leaving them publicly exposed in order to turn GOD's anger away from Israel."

5 Moses issued orders to the judges of Israel: "Each of you must execute the men under your jurisdiction who joined in the worship of Baal Peor."

6-9 Just then, while everyone was weeping in penitence at the entrance of the Tent of Meeting, an Israelite man, flaunting his behavior in front of Moses and the whole assembly, paraded a Midianite woman into his family tent. Phinehas son of Eleazar, the son of Aaron the priest, saw what he was doing, grabbed his spear, and followed them into the tent. With one thrust he drove the spear through the two of them, the man of Israel and the woman, right through their private parts. That stopped the plague from continuing among the People of Israel. But 24,000 had already died.

10-13 GOD spoke to Moses: "Phinehas son of Eleazar, son of Aaron the priest, has stopped my anger against the People of Israel. Because he was as zealous for my honor as I myself am, I didn't kill all the People of Israel in my zeal. So tell him that I am making a Covenant-of-Peace with him. He and his descendants are joined in a covenant of eternal priesthood, because he was zealous for his God and made atonement for the People of Israel."

14-15 The name of the man of Israel who was killed with the Midianite woman was Zimri son of Salu, the head of the Simeonite family. And the name of the Midianite woman who was killed was Cozbi daughter of Zur, a tribal chief of a Midianite family.

16-18 GOD spoke to Moses: "From here on make the Midianites your enemies. Fight them tooth and nail. They turned out to be your enemies when they seduced you in the business of Peor and that woman Cozbi, daughter of a Midianite leader, the woman who was killed at the time of the plague in the matter of Peor."

CENSUS ON THE PLAINS OF MOAB

1-2 **26** After the plague GOD said to Moses and Eleazar son of Aaron the priest, "Number the entire community of Israel by families—count every person who is twenty years and older who is able to serve in the army of Israel."

3-4 Obeying GOD's command, Moses and Eleazar the priest addressed them on the Plains of Moab at Jordan-Jericho: "Count off from age twenty and older."

4-7 The People of Israel who came out of the land of Egypt:
Reuben, Israel's firstborn. The sons of Reuben were:
    Hanoch and the Hanochite clan,
    Pallu and the Palluite clan,

Hezron and the Hezronite clan,
Carmi and the Carmite clan.
These made up the Reubenite clans. They numbered 43,730.

8 The son of Pallu: Eliab.

9-11 The sons of Eliab: Nemuel, Dathan, and Abiram. (These were the same Dathan and Abiram, community leaders from Korah's gang, who rebelled against Moses and Aaron in the Korah Rebellion against GOD. The Earth opened its jaws and swallowed them along with Korah's gang who died when the fire ate them up, all 250 of them. After all these years, they're still a warning sign. But the line of Korah did not die out.)

12-14 The sons of Simeon by clans:
Nemuel and the Nemuelite clan,
Jamin and the Jaminite clan,
Jakin and the Jakinite clan,
Zerah and the Zerahite clan,
Shaul and the Shaulite clan.
These were the clans of Simeon. They numbered 22,200 men.

15-18 The sons of Gad by clans:
Zephon and the Zephonite clan,
Haggi and the Haggite clan,
Shuni and the Shunite clan,
Ozni and the Oznite clan,
Eri and the Erite clan,
Arodi and the Arodite clan,
Areli and the Arelite clan.
These were the clans of Gad. They numbered 40,500 men.

19-22 Er and Onan were sons of Judah who died early on in Canaan. The sons of Judah by clans:
Shelah and the Shelanite clan,
Perez and the Perezite clan,
Zerah and the Zerahite clan.
The sons of Perez:
Hezron and the Hezronite clan,
Hamul and the Hamulite clan.
These were the clans of Judah. They numbered 76,500.

23-25 The sons of Issachar by clans:
Tola and the Tolaite clan,
Puah and the Puite clan,
Jashub and the Jashubite clan,
Shimron and the Shimronite clan.
These were the clans of Issachar. They numbered 64,300.

26-27 The sons of Zebulun by clans:
Sered and the Seredite clan,
Elon and the Elonite clan,
Jahleel and the Jahleelite clan.
These were the clans of Zebulun. They numbered 60,500.

28-34 The sons of Joseph by clans through Manasseh and Ephraim. Through
Manasseh:
>   Makir and the Makirite clan
>   (now Makir was the father of Gilead),
>   Gilead and the Gileadite clan.
The sons of Gilead:
>   Iezer and the Iezerite clan,
>   Helek and the Helekite clan,
>   Asriel and the Asrielite clan,
>   Shechem and the Shechemite clan,
>   Shemida and the Shemidaite clan,
>   Hepher and the Hepherite clan.
>   Zelophehad son of Hepher had no sons, only daughters.
>   Their names were Mahlah, Noah, Hoglah, Milcah, and Tirzah.
These were the clans of Manasseh. They numbered 52,700.

35-37 The sons of Ephraim by clans:
>   Shuthelah and the Shuthelahite clan,
>   Beker and the Bekerite clan,
>   Tahan and the Tahanite clan.
The sons of Shuthelah:
>   Eran and the Eranite clan.
These were the clans of Ephraim. They numbered 32,500.
These are all the sons of Joseph by their clans.

38-41 The sons of Benjamin by clans:
>   Bela and the Belaite clan,
>   Ashbel and the Ashbelite clan,
>   Ahiram and the Ahiramite clan,
>   Shupham and the Shuphamite clan,
>   Hupham and the Huphamite clan.
The sons of Bela through Ard and Naaman:
>   Ard and the Ardite clan,
>   Naaman and the Naamite clan.
These were the clans of Benjamin. They numbered 45,600.

42-43 The sons of Dan by clan:
>   Shuham and the Shuhamite clan.
These are the clans of Dan, all Shuhamite clans. They numbered 64,400.

44-47 The sons of Asher by clan:
>   Imnah and the Imnite clan,
>   Ishvi and the Ishvite clan,
>   Beriah and the Beriite clan.
The sons of Beriah:
>   Heber and the Heberite clan,
>   Malkiel and the Malkielite clan.
>   Asher also had a daughter, Serah.
These were the clans of Asher. They numbered 53,400.

48-50 The sons of Naphtali by clans:
    Jahzeel and the Jahzeelite clan,
    Guni and the Gunite clan,
    Jezer and the Jezerite clan,
    Shillem and the Shillemite clan.
These were the clans of Naphtali. They numbered 45,400.

51   The total number of the People of Israel: 601,730.

52-54 GOD spoke to Moses: "Divide up the inheritance of the land based on population. A larger group gets a larger inheritance; a smaller group gets a smaller inheritance — each gets its inheritance based on the population count.
55-56   "Make sure that the land is assigned by lot.
    "Each group's inheritance is based on population, the number of names listed in its ancestral tribe, divided among the many and the few by lot."

57-58 These are the numberings of the Levites by clan:
    Gershon and the Gershonite clan,
    Kohath and the Kohathite clan,
    Merari and the Merarite clan.
The Levite clans also included:
    the Libnite clan,
    the Hebronite clan,
    the Mahlite clan,
    the Mushite clan,
    the Korahite clan.
58-61   Kohath was the father of Amram. Amram's wife was Jochebed, a descendant of Levi, born into the Levite family during the Egyptian years. Jochebed bore Aaron, Moses, and their sister Miriam to Amram. Aaron was the father of Nadab and Abihu, Eleazar and Ithamar; however, Nadab and Abihu died when they offered unauthorized sacrifice in the presence of GOD.
62   The numbering of Levite males one month and older came to 23,000. They hadn't been counted in with the rest of the People of Israel because they didn't inherit any land.

63-65   These are the ones numbered by Moses and Eleazar the priest, the People of Israel counted in the Plains of Moab at Jordan-Jericho. Not one of them had been among those counted by Moses and Aaron the priest in the census of the People of Israel taken in the Wilderness of Sinai. For GOD had said of them, "They'll die, die in the wilderness — not one of them will be left except for Caleb son of Jephunneh, and Joshua son of Nun."

THE DAUGHTERS OF ZELOPHEHAD

1 **27** The daughters of Zelophehad showed up. Their father was the son of Hepher son of Gilead son of Makir son of Manasseh, belonging to the clans of Manasseh son of Joseph. The daughters were Mahlah, Noah, Hoglah, Milcah, and Tirzah.
2-4   They came to the entrance of the Tent of Meeting. They stood before

Moses and Eleazar the priest and before the leaders and the congregation and said, "Our father died in the wilderness. He wasn't part of Korah's rebel anti-GOD gang. He died for his own sins. And he left no sons. But why should our father's name die out from his clan just because he had no sons? So give us an inheritance among our father's relatives."

5 Moses brought their case to GOD.

6-7 GOD ruled: "Zelophehad's daughters are right. Give them land as an inheritance among their father's relatives. Give them their father's inheritance.

8-11 "Then tell the People of Israel, If a man dies and leaves no son, give his inheritance to his daughter. If he has no daughter, give it to his brothers. If he has no brothers, give it to his father's brothers. If his father had no brothers, give it to the nearest relative so that the inheritance stays in the family. This is the standard procedure for the People of Israel, as commanded by GOD through Moses."

JOSHUA

12-14 GOD said to Moses, "Climb up into the Abarim Mountains and look over at the land that I am giving to the People of Israel. When you've had a good look you'll be joined to your ancestors in the grave—yes, you also along with Aaron your brother. This goes back to the day when the congregation quarreled in the Wilderness of Zin and you didn't honor me in holy reverence before them in the matter of the waters, the Waters of Meribah (Quarreling) at Kadesh in the Wilderness of Zin."

15-17 Moses responded to GOD: "Let GOD, the God of the spirits of everyone living, set a man over this community to lead them, to show the way ahead and bring them back home so GOD's community will not be like sheep without a shepherd."

18-21 GOD said to Moses, "Take Joshua the son of Nun—the Spirit is in him!— and place your hand on him. Stand him before Eleazar the priest in front of the entire congregation and commission him with everyone watching. Pass your magisterial authority over to him so that the whole congregation of the People of Israel will listen obediently to him. He is to consult with Eleazar the priest who, using the oracle-Urim, will prayerfully advise him in the presence of GOD. He will command the People of Israel, the entire community, in all their comings and goings."

22-23 Moses followed GOD's orders. He took Joshua and stood him before Eleazar the priest in front of the entire community. He laid his hands on him and commissioned him, following the procedures GOD had given Moses.

OFFERINGS

1-8 **28** GOD spoke to Moses: "Command the People of Israel. Tell them, You're in charge of presenting my food, my Fire-Gifts of pleasing fragrance, at the set times. Tell them, This is the Fire-Gift that you are to present to GOD: two healthy yearling lambs each day as a regular Whole-Burnt-Offering. Sacrifice one lamb in the morning, the other in the evening, together with two quarts of fine flour mixed with a quart of olive oil for a Grain-Offering. This is the standard Whole-Burnt-Offering instituted at Mount Sinai as a pleasing fragrance, a Fire-Gift to GOD. The Drink-Offering that goes with it is a quart of strong beer with each lamb. Pour out the Drink-Offering before GOD in the Sanctuary. Sacrifice the second lamb in the evening with the Grain-Offering and Drink-Offering the same as in the morning — a Fire-Gift of pleasing fragrance for GOD.

※

9-10 "On the Sabbath, sacrifice two healthy yearling lambs, together with the Drink-Offering and the Grain-Offering of four quarts of fine flour mixed with oil. This is the regular Sabbath Whole-Burnt-Offering, in addition to the regular Whole-Burnt-Offering and its Drink-Offering.

※

11 "On the first of the month offer a Whole-Burnt-Offering to GOD: two young bulls, one ram, and seven male yearling lambs — all healthy.

12-14 "A Grain-Offering of six quarts of fine flour mixed with oil goes with each bull, four quarts of fine flour mixed with oil with the ram, and two quarts of fine flour mixed with oil with each lamb. This is for a Whole-Burnt-Offering, a pleasing fragrance, a Fire-Gift to GOD. Also, Drink-Offerings of two quarts of wine for each bull, one and a quarter quarts of wine for the ram, and a quart of wine for each lamb are to be poured out.

14-15 "This is the first of the month Whole-Burnt-Offering to be made throughout the year. In addition to the regular Whole-Burnt-Offering with its accompanying Drink-Offering, a he-goat is to be offered to GOD as an Absolution-Offering.

※

16-17 "GOD's Passover is to be held on the fourteenth day of the first month. On the fifteenth day of this month hold a festival.

17-22 "For seven days, eat only unraised bread: Begin the first day in holy worship; don't do any regular work that day. Bring a Fire-Gift to GOD, a Whole-Burnt-Offering: two young bulls, one ram, and seven male yearling lambs — all healthy. Prepare a Grain-Offering of six quarts of fine flour mixed with oil for each bull, four quarts for the ram, and two quarts for each lamb, plus a goat as an Absolution-Offering to atone for you.

23-24 "Sacrifice these in addition to the regular morning Whole-Burnt-Offering. Prepare the food this way for the Fire-Gift, a pleasing fragrance to GOD, every day for seven days. Prepare it in addition to the regular Whole-Burnt-Offering and Drink-Offering.

25 "Conclude the seventh day in holy worship; don't do any regular work on that day.

※

26-30 "On the Day of Firstfruits when you bring an offering of new grain to GOD on your Feast-of-Weeks, gather in holy worship and don't do any regular work. Bring a Whole-Burnt-Offering of two young bulls, one ram, and seven male yearling lambs as a pleasing fragrance to GOD. Prepare a Grain-Offering of six quarts of fine flour mixed with oil for each bull, four quarts for the ram, and two quarts for each lamb, plus a he-goat as an Absolution-Offering to atone for you.

31 "These are all over and above the daily Whole-Burnt-Offering and its Grain-Offering and the Drink-Offering. Remember, the animals must be healthy.

1-5 29 "On the first day of the seventh month, gather in holy worship and do no regular work. This is your Day-of-Trumpet-Blasts. Sacrifice a Whole-Burnt-Offering: one young bull, one ram, and seven male yearling lambs—all healthy—as a pleasing fragrance to GOD. Prepare a Grain-Offering of six quarts of fine flour mixed with oil for the bull, four quarts for the ram, and two quarts for each lamb, plus a he-goat as an Absolution-Offering to atone for you.

6 "These are all over and above the monthly and daily Whole-Burnt-Offerings with their Grain-Offerings and Drink-Offerings as prescribed, a pleasing fragrance, a Fire-Gift to GOD.

7 "On the tenth day of this seventh month, gather in holy worship, humble yourselves, and do no work.

8-11 "Bring a Whole-Burnt-Offering to GOD as a pleasing fragrance: one young bull, one ram, and seven yearling male lambs—all healthy. Prepare a Grain-Offering of six quarts of fine flour mixed with oil for the bull, four quarts for the ram, and two quarts for each of the seven lambs. Also bring a he-goat as an Absolution-Offering to atone for you in addition to the regular Whole-Burnt-Offering with its Grain-Offering and Drink-Offering.

12-16 "Gather in holy worship on the fifteenth day of the seventh month; do no regular work. Celebrate a Festival to GOD for seven days. Bring a Whole-Burnt-Offering, a Fire-Gift of pleasing fragrance to GOD: thirteen young bulls, two rams, and fourteen yearling male lambs—all healthy. Prepare a Grain-Offering of six quarts of fine flour mixed with oil for each of the bulls, four quarts for each ram, and two quarts for each of the fourteen lambs. Also bring a he-goat as an Absolution-Offering in addition to the regular Whole-Burnt-Offering with its Grain-Offering and Drink-Offering.

17-19 "On the second day: twelve young bulls, two rams, and fourteen yearling male lambs—all healthy. Prepare Grain-Offerings and Drink-Offerings to go with the bulls, rams, and lambs following the prescribed recipes. And bring a he-goat as an Absolution-Offering in addition to the regular Whole-Burnt-Offering with its Grain-Offering and Drink-Offering.

20-22 "On the third day: eleven bulls, two rams, and fourteen male yearling lambs—all healthy. Prepare Grain-Offerings and Drink-Offerings to go with the bulls, rams, and lambs following the prescribed recipes. And bring a he-goat as an Absolution-Offering in addition to the regular Whole-Burnt-Offering with its Grain-Offering and Drink-Offering.

23-25 "On the fourth day: ten bulls, two rams, and fourteen male yearling lambs—all healthy. Prepare Grain-Offerings and Drink-Offerings to go with the bulls, rams, and lambs following the prescribed recipes. And bring a he-goat as an Absolution-Offering in addition to the regular Whole-Burnt-Offering with its Grain-Offering and Drink-Offering.

26-28 "On the fifth day: nine bulls, two rams, and fourteen male yearling lambs—all healthy. Prepare Grain-Offerings and Drink-Offerings to go with the bulls, rams, and lambs following the prescribed recipes. And bring a he-goat as an Absolution-Offering in addition to the regular Whole-Burnt-Offering with its Grain-Offering and Drink-Offering.

29-31 "On the sixth day: eight bulls, two rams, and fourteen male yearling lambs—all healthy. Prepare Grain-Offerings and Drink-Offerings to go with the bulls, rams, and lambs following the prescribed recipes. And bring a he-goat as an Absolution-Offering in addition to the regular Whole-Burnt-Offering with its Grain-Offering and Drink-Offering.

32-34 "On the seventh day: seven bulls, two rams, and fourteen male yearling lambs—all healthy. Prepare Grain-Offerings and Drink-Offerings to go with the bulls, rams, and lambs following the prescribed recipes. And bring a he-goat as an Absolution-Offering in addition to the regular Whole-Burnt-Offering with its Grain-Offering and Drink-Offering.

35-38 "On the eighth day: Gather in holy worship; do no regular work. Bring a Fire-Gift of pleasing fragrance to GOD, a Whole-Burnt-Offering: one bull, one ram, and seven male yearling lambs—all healthy. Prepare Grain-Offerings and Drink-Offerings to go with the bulls, rams, and lambs following the prescribed recipes. And bring a he-goat as an Absolution-Offering in addition to the regular Whole-Burnt-Offering with its Grain-Offering and Drink-Offering.

39 "Sacrifice these to GOD as a congregation at your set feasts: your Whole-Burnt-Offerings, Grain Offerings, Drink-Offerings, and Peace-Offerings. These are all over and above your personal Vow-Offerings and Freewill-Offerings."

40 Moses instructed the People of Israel in all that GOD commanded him.

VOWS

1-2 **30** Moses spoke to the heads of the tribes of the People of Israel: "This is what GOD commands: When a man makes a vow to GOD or binds himself by an oath to do something, he must not break his word; he must do exactly what he has said.

3-5 "When a woman makes a vow to GOD and binds herself by a pledge as a young girl still living in her father's house, and her father hears of her vow or pledge but says nothing to her, then she has to make good on all her vows and pledges. But if her father holds her back when he hears of what she has done, none of her vows and pledges are valid. GOD will release her since her father held her back.

6-8 "If she marries after she makes a vow or has made some rash promise or pledge, and her husband hears of it but says nothing to her, then she has to make good on whatever she vowed or pledged. But if her husband intervenes when he hears of it, he cancels the vow or rash promise that binds her. And GOD will release her.

9 "Any vow or pledge taken by a widow or divorced woman is binding on her.

10-15 "When a woman who is living with her husband makes a vow or takes a pledge under oath and her husband hears about it but says nothing and doesn't say she can't do it, then all her vows and pledges are valid. But if her husband cancels them when he hears about them, then none of the vows and pledges that she made are binding. Her husband has canceled them and GOD will release her. Any vow and pledge that she makes that may be to her detriment can be either affirmed or annulled by her husband. But if her husband is silent and doesn't speak up day after day, he confirms her vows and pledges—she has to make good on them. By saying nothing to her when he hears of them, he binds her to them. If, however, he cancels them sometime after he hears of them, he takes her guilt on himself."

16 These are the rules that GOD gave Moses regarding conduct between a man and his wife and between a father and his young daughter who is still living at home.

THE MIDIANITE WAR

1-2 **31** GOD spoke to Moses: "Avenge the People of Israel on the Midianites. Afterward you will go to be with your dead ancestors."

3-4 Moses addressed the people: "Recruit men for a campaign against Midian, to exact GOD's vengeance on Midian, a thousand from each tribe of Israel to go to war."

5-6 A fighting force of a thousand from each tribe of Israel—twelve thousand in all—was recruited. Moses sent them off to war, a thousand from each tribe, and also Phinehas son of Eleazar, who went as priest to the army, in charge of holy vessels and the signaling bugles.

7-12 They attacked Midian, just as GOD had commanded Moses, and killed every last man. Among the fallen were Evi, Rekem, Zur, Hur, and Reba—the five kings of Midian. They also killed Balaam son of Beor with the sword. The People of Israel took the Midianite women and children captive and took all their animals and herds and goods as plunder. They burned to the ground all the towns in which Midianites lived and also their tent camps. They looted and plundered everything and everyone—stuff and people and animals. They took it all—captives and booty and plunder—back to Moses and Eleazar the priest and the company of Israel where they were camped on the Plains of Moab, at Jordan-Jericho.

13-18 Moses, Eleazar, and all the leaders of the congregation went to meet the returning army outside the camp. Moses was furious with the army officers—the commanders of thousands and commanders of hundreds—as they came back from the battlefield: "What's this! You've let these women live! They're the ones who, under Balaam's direction, seduced the People of Israel away from GOD in that mess at Peor, causing the plague that hit GOD's people. Finish your job: kill all the boys. Kill every woman who has slept with a man. The younger women who are virgins you can keep alive for yourselves.

19-20 "Now here's what you are to do: Pitch tents outside the camp. All who have killed anyone or touched a corpse must stay outside the camp for seven days. Purify yourselves and your captives on the third and seventh days. Purify every piece of clothing and every utensil—everything made of leather, goat hair, or wood."

21-24 Eleazar the priest then spoke to the soldiers who had fought in the battle: "This is the ruling from the Revelation that GOD gave Moses: Gold, silver, bronze, iron, tin, and lead—and anything else that can survive fire—must be passed through the fire; then it will be ritually purified. It must also be ritually washed in the Water-of-Cleansing. Further, whatever cannot survive fire must be put through that water. On the seventh day scrub your clothes; you will be ritually clean. Then you can return to camp."

25-27 GOD said to Moses, "I want you and Eleazar the priest and the family leaders in the community to count the captives, people and animals. Split the plunder between the soldiers who fought the battle and the rest of the congregation.

28-30 "Then tax the booty that goes to the soldiers at the rate of one life out of five hundred, whether humans, cattle, donkeys, or sheep. It's a GOD-tax taken from their half-share to be turned over to Eleazar the priest on behalf of GOD. Tax the congregation's half-share at the rate of one life out of fifty, whether persons, cattle, donkeys, sheep, goats, or other animals. Give this to the Levites who are in charge of the care of GOD's Dwelling."

31 Moses and Eleazar followed through with what GOD had commanded Moses.

32-35 The rest of the plunder taken by the army:
> 675,000 sheep
> 72,000 cattle
> 61,000 donkeys
> 32,000 women who were virgins

36-40 The half-share for those who had fought in the war:
> 337,500 sheep, with a tax of 675 for GOD
> 36,000 cattle, with a tax of 72 for GOD
> 30,500 donkeys, with a tax of 61 for GOD
> 16,000 people, with a tax of 32 for GOD

41 Moses turned the tax over to Eleazar the priest as GOD's part, following GOD's instructions to Moses.

42-46 The other half-share for the Israelite community that Moses set apart from what was given to the men who fought the war was:
> 337,500 sheep
> 36,000 cattle
> 30,500 donkeys
> 16,000 people

47 From the half-share going to the People of Israel, Moses, just as GOD had instructed him, picked one out of every fifty persons and animals and gave them to the Levites, who were in charge of maintaining GOD's Dwelling.

48-50 The military officers—commanders of thousands and commanders of hundreds—came to Moses and said, "We have counted the soldiers under our command and not a man is missing. We've brought offerings to GOD from the gold jewelry we got—armlets, bracelets, rings, earrings, ornaments—to make atonement for our lives before GOD."

51-54 Moses and Eleazar the priest received the gold from them, all that fine-crafted jewelry. In total, the gold from the commanders of thousands and hundreds that Moses and Eleazar offered as a gift to GOD weighed about six hundred pounds, all donated by the soldiers who had taken the booty. Moses and Eleazar took the gold from the commanders of thousands and hundreds and brought it to the Tent of Meeting, to serve as a reminder for the People of Israel before GOD.

TRIBES EAST OF THE JORDAN

1-4 **32** The families of Reuben and Gad had huge herds of livestock. They saw that the country of Jazer and Gilead was just the place for grazing livestock. And so they came, the families of Gad and of Reuben, and spoke to Moses and Eleazar the priest and the leaders of the congregation, saying, "Ataroth, Dibon, Jazer, Nimrah, Heshbon, Elealeh, Sebam, Nebo, and Beon — the country that GOD laid low before the community of Israel — is a country just right for livestock, and we have livestock."

5 They continued, "If you think we've done a good job so far, give us this country for our inheritance. Don't make us go across the Jordan."

6-12 Moses answered the families of Gad and Reuben: "Do you mean that you are going to leave the fighting that's ahead to your brothers while you settle down here? Why would you even think of letting the People of Israel down, demoralizing them just as they're about to move into the land GOD gave them? That's exactly what your ancestors did when I sent them from Kadesh Barnea to survey the country. They went as far as the Valley of Eshcol, took one look and quit. They completely demoralized the People of Israel from entering the land GOD had given them. And GOD got angry — oh, did he get angry! He swore: 'They'll never get to see it; none of those who came up out of Egypt who are twenty years and older will ever get to see the land that I promised to Abraham, Isaac, and Jacob. They weren't interested in following me — their hearts weren't in it. None, except for Caleb son of Jephunneh the Kenizzite, and Joshua son of Nun; they followed me — their hearts were in it.'

13 "GOD's anger smoked against Israel. He made them wander in the wilderness for forty years, until that entire generation that acted out evil in his sight had died out.

14-15 "And now here you are, just one more mob of sinners stepping up to replace your ancestors, throwing fuel on the already blazing anger of GOD against Israel. If you won't follow him, he'll do it again. He'll dump them in the desert and the disaster will be all your fault."

16-19 They came close to him and said, "All we want to do is build corrals for our livestock and towns for our families. Then we'll take up arms and take the front lines, leading the People of Israel to their place. We'll be able to leave our families behind, secure in fortified towns, safe from those who live in the land. But we won't go back home until every Israelite is in full possession of his inheritance. We won't expect any inheritance west of the Jordan; we are claiming all our inheritance east of the Jordan."

20-22 Moses said, "If you do what you say, take up arms before GOD for battle and together go across the Jordan ready, before GOD, to fight until GOD has cleaned his enemies out of the land, then when the land is secure you will have fulfilled your duty to GOD and Israel. Then this land will be yours to keep before GOD.

23-24 "But if you don't do what you say, you will be sinning against GOD; you can be sure that your sin will track you down. So, go ahead. Build towns for your families and corrals for your livestock. Do what you said you'd do."

25-27 The families of Gad and Reuben told Moses: "We will do as our master commands. Our children and wives, our flocks and herds will stay behind here in the towns of Gilead. But we, every one of us fully armed, will cross the river to fight for GOD, just as our master has said."

28-30 So Moses issued orders for them to Eleazar the priest, Joshua the son of Nun, and the heads of the ancestral tribes of the People of Israel. Moses said, "If the families of Gad and Reuben cross the Jordan River with you and before GOD, all armed and ready to fight, then after the land is secure, you may give them the land of Gilead as their inheritance. But if they don't cross over with you, they'll have to settle up with you in Canaan."

31-32 The families of Gad and Reuben responded: "We will do what GOD has said. We will cross the Jordan before GOD, ready and willing to fight. But the land we inherit will be here, to the east of the Jordan."

33 Moses gave the families of Gad, Reuben, and the half-tribe of Manasseh son of Joseph the kingdom of Sihon, king of the Amorites, and the kingdom of Og, king of Bashan — the land, its towns, and all the territories connected with them — the works.

34-36 The Gadites rebuilt Dibon, Ataroth, Aroer, Atroth Shophan, Jazer, Jogbehah, Beth Nimrah, and Beth Haran as fortified cities; they also built corrals for their animals.

37-38 The Reubenites rebuilt Heshbon, Elealeh, and Kiriathaim, also Nebo and Baal Meon and Sibmah. They renamed the cities that they rebuilt.

39-40 The family of Makir son of Manasseh went to Gilead, captured it, and drove out the Amorites who lived there. Moses then gave Gilead to the Makirites, the descendants of Manasseh. They moved in and settled there.

41 Jair, another son of Manasseh, captured some villages and named them Havvoth Jair (Jair's Tent-Camps).

42 Nobah captured Kenath and its surrounding camps. He renamed it after himself, Nobah.

CAMPSITES FROM RAMESES TO JORDAN-JERICHO

1-2 **33** These are the camping sites in the journey of the People of Israel after they left Egypt, deployed militarily under the command of Moses and Aaron. Under GOD's instruction Moses kept a log of every time they moved, camp by camp:

3-4 They marched out of Rameses the day after the Passover. It was the fifteenth day of the first month. They marched out heads high and confident. The Egyptians, busy burying their firstborn whom GOD had killed, watched them go. GOD had exposed the nonsense of their gods.

5-36 The People of Israel:
> left Rameses and camped at Succoth;
> left Succoth and camped at Etham at the edge of the wilderness;
> left Etham, circled back to Pi Hahiroth east of Baal Zephon, and camped near Migdol;
> left Pi Hahiroth and crossed through the Sea into the wilderness; three days into the Wilderness of Etham they camped at Marah;
> left Marah and came to Elim where there were twelve springs and seventy palm trees; they camped there;
> left Elim and camped by the Red Sea;
> left the Red Sea and camped in the Wilderness of Sin;
> left the Wilderness of Sin and camped at Dophkah;
> left Dophkah and camped at Alush;
> left Alush and camped at Rephidim where there was no water for the people to drink;

left Rephidim and camped in the Wilderness of Sinai;
left the Wilderness of Sinai and camped at Kibroth Hattaavah;
left Kibroth Hattaavah and camped at Hazeroth;
left Hazeroth and camped at Rithmah;
left Rithmah and camped at Rimmon Perez;
left Rimmon Perez and camped at Libnah;
left Libnah and camped at Rissah;
left Rissah and camped at Kehelathah;
left Kehelathah and camped at Mount Shepher;
left Mount Shepher and camped at Haradah;
left Haradah and camped at Makheloth;
left Makheloth and camped at Tahath;
left Tahath and camped at Terah;
left Terah and camped at Mithcah;
left Mithcah and camped at Hashmonah;
left Hashmonah and camped at Moseroth;
left Moseroth and camped at Bene Jaakan;
left Bene Jaakan and camped at Hor Haggidgad;
left Hor Haggidgad and camped at Jotbathah;
left Jotbathah and camped at Abronah;
left Abronah and camped at Ezion Geber;
left Ezion Geber and camped at Kadesh in the Wilderness of Zin.

37-39 After they left Kadesh and camped at Mount Hor at the border of Edom, Aaron the priest climbed Mount Hor at GOD's command and died there. It was the first day of the fifth month in the fortieth year after the People of Israel had left Egypt. Aaron was 123 years old when he died on Mount Hor.

40 The Canaanite king of Arad—he ruled in the Negev of Canaan—heard that the People of Israel had arrived.

41-47 They left Mount Hor and camped at Zalmonah;
left Zalmonah and camped at Punon;
left Punon and camped at Oboth;
left Oboth and camped at Iye Abarim on the border of Moab;
left Iyim and camped at Dibon Gad;
left Dibon Gad and camped at Almon Diblathaim;
left Almon Diblathaim and camped in the mountains of Abarim (Across-the-River), within sight of Nebo.

48-49 After they left the mountains of Abarim they camped on the Plains of Moab at Jordan-Jericho. On the Plains of Moab their camp stretched along the banks of the Jordan from Beth Jeshimoth to Abel Shittim (Acacia Meadow).

50-53 GOD spoke to Moses on the Plains of Moab at Jordan-Jericho: "Tell the People of Israel, When you cross the Jordan into the country of Canaan, drive out the native population before you, destroy their carved idols, destroy their cast images, level their worship-mounds so that you take over the land and make yourself at home in it; I've given it to you. It's yours.

54 "Divide up the land by lot according to the size of your clans: Large clans

will get large tracts of land, small clans will get smaller tracts of land. However the lot falls, that's it. Divide it up according to your ancestral tribes.

55-56 "But if you don't drive out the native population, everyone you let stay there will become a cinder in your eye and a splinter in your foot. They'll give you endless trouble right in your own backyards. And I'll start treating you the way I planned to treat them."

Land Inheritance

1-2 34 God spoke to Moses: "Command the People of Israel. Tell them, When you enter Canaan, these are the borders of the land you are getting as an inheritance:

3-5 "Your southern border will take in some of the Wilderness of Zin where it touches Edom. It starts in the east at the Dead Sea, curves south of Scorpion Pass and on to Zin, continues south of Kadesh Barnea, then to Hazar Addar and on to Azmon, where it takes a turn to the northwest to the Brook of Egypt and on to the Mediterranean Sea.

6 "Your western border will be the Mediterranean Sea.

7-9 "Your northern border runs on a line from the Mediterranean Sea to Mount Hor, and from Mount Hor to Lebo Hamath, connects to Zedad, continues to Ziphron, and ends at Hazar Enan. This is your northern border.

10-12 "Your eastern border runs on a line from Hazar Enan to Shepham. The border goes south from Shepham to Riblah to the east of Ain, and continues along the slopes east of the Sea of Galilee. The border then follows the Jordan River and ends at the Dead Sea.

"This is your land with its four borders."

13-15 Moses then commanded the People of Israel: "This is the land: Divide up the inheritance by lot. God has ordered it to be given to the nine and a half tribes. The tribe of Reuben, the tribe of Gad, and the half-tribe of Manasseh have already received their inheritance; the two tribes and the half-tribe got their inheritance east of Jordan-Jericho, facing the sunrise."

16-19 God spoke to Moses: "These are the men who will be in charge of distributing the inheritance of the land: Eleazar the priest and Joshua son of Nun. Assign one leader from each tribe to help them in distributing the land. Assign these:

19-28 Caleb son of Jephunneh from the tribe of Judah;

Shemuel son of Ammihud from the tribe of Simeon;

Elidad son of Kislon from the tribe of Benjamin;

Bukki son of Jogli, leader from the tribe of Dan;

Hanniel son of Ephod, leader from the tribe of Manasseh son of Joseph;

Kemuel son of Shiphtan, leader from the tribe of Ephraim son of Joseph;

Elizaphan son of Parnach, leader from the tribe of Zebulun;

Paltiel son of Azzan, leader from the tribe of Issachar;

Ahihud son of Shelomi, leader from the tribe of Asher;

Pedahel son of Ammihud, leader from the tribe of Naphtali."

29 These are the men God commanded to hand out the assignments of land-inheritance to the People of Israel in the country of Canaan.

CITIES FOR LEVITES AND ASYLUM-CITIES

¹⁻³ **35** Then GOD spoke to Moses on the Plains of Moab at Jordan-Jericho: "Command the People of Israel to give the Levites as their part of the total inheritance towns to live in. Make sure there is plenty of pasture around the towns. Then they will be well taken care of with towns to live in and pastures for their cattle, flocks, and other livestock.

⁴⁻⁵ "The pasture surrounding the Levites' towns is to extend 1,500 feet in each direction from the city wall. The outside borders of the pasture are to measure three thousand feet on each of the four sides — east, south, west, and north — with the town at the center. Each city will be supplied with pasture.

⁶⁻⁸ "Six of these towns that you give the Levites will be asylum-cities to which anyone who accidentally kills another person may flee for asylum. In addition, you will give them forty-two other towns — forty-eight towns in all, together with their pastures. The towns that you give the Levites from the common inheritance of the People of Israel are to be taken in proportion to the size of each tribe — many towns from a tribe that has many, few from a tribe that has few."

⁹⁻¹⁵ GOD spoke to Moses: "Speak to the People of Israel. Tell them, When you cross the River Jordan into the country of Canaan, designate your asylum-cities, towns to which a person who accidentally kills someone can flee for asylum. They will be places of refuge from the avenger so that the alleged murderer won't be killed until he can appear before the community in court. Provide six asylum-cities. Designate three of the towns to the east side of the Jordan, the other three in Canaan proper — asylum-cities for the People of Israel, for the foreigner, and for any occasional visitors or guests — six asylum-cities to run to for anyone who accidentally kills another.

¹⁶ "But if the killer has used an iron object, that's just plain murder; he's obviously a murderer and must be put to death.

¹⁷ "Or if he has a rock in his hand big enough to kill and the man dies, that's murder; he's a murderer and must be put to death.

¹⁸ "Or if he's carrying a wooden club heavy enough to kill and the man dies, that's murder; he's a murderer and must be put to death.

¹⁹ "In such cases the avenger has a right to kill the murderer when he meets him — he can kill him on the spot.

²⁰⁻²¹ "And if out of sheer hatred a man pushes another or from ambush throws something at him and he dies, or angrily hits him with his fist and kills him, that's murder — he must be put to death. The avenger has a right to kill him when he gets him.

²²⁻²⁷ "If, however, he impulsively pushes someone and there is no history of hard feelings, or he impetuously picks up something and throws it, or he accidentally drops a stone tool — a maul or hammer, say — and it hits and kills someone he didn't even know was there, and there's no suspicion that there was bad blood between them, the community is to judge between the killer and the avenger following these guidelines. It's the task of the community to save the killer from the hand of the avenger — the community is to return him to his asylum-city to which he fled. He must stay there until the death of the High Priest who was anointed with the holy oil. But if the murderer leaves the asylum-city to which he has fled, and the avenger finds him outside the borders of his asylum-city, the avenger has a right to kill the murderer. And he's not considered guilty of murder.

28 "So it's important that he stay in his asylum-city until the death of the High Priest. After the death of the High Priest he is free to return to his own place.

※

29 "These are the procedures for making judgments from now on, wherever you live.

30 "Anyone who kills another may be executed only on the testimony of eye-witnesses. But no one can be executed on the testimony of only one witness.

31 "Don't accept bribe money in exchange for the life of a murderer. He's guilty and deserves the death penalty. Put him to death.

32 "And don't accept bribe money for anyone who has fled to an asylum-city so as to permit him to go back and live in his own place before the death of the High Priest.

33 "Don't pollute the land in which you live. Murder pollutes the land. The land can't be cleaned up of the blood of murder except through the blood of the murderer.

34 "Don't desecrate the land in which you live. I live here, too—I, God, live in the same neighborhood with the People of Israel."

THE DAUGHTERS OF ZELOPHEHAD

1 **36** The heads of the ancestral clan of Gilead son of Makir, the son of Manasseh—they were from the clans of the descendants of Joseph—approached Moses and the leaders who were heads of the families in the People of Israel.

2-4 They said, "When God commanded my master to hand over the inheritance-lands by lot to the People of Israel, my master was also commanded by God to hand over the inheritance-land of Zelophehad our brother to his daughters. But what happens if they marry into another tribe in the People of Israel? Their inheritance-land will be taken out of our ancestral tribe and get added into the tribe into which they married. And then when the year of Jubilee comes for the People of Israel their inheritance will be lumped in with the inheritance of the tribe into which they married—their land will be removed from our ancestors' inheritance!"

5-9 Moses, at God's command, issued this order to the People of Israel: "What the tribe of the sons of Joseph says is right. This is God's command to Zelophehad's daughters: They are free to marry anyone they choose as long as they marry within their ancestral clan. The inheritance-land of the People of Israel must not get passed around from tribe to tribe. No, keep the tribal inheritance-land in the family. Every daughter who inherits land, regardless of the tribe she is in, must marry a man from within her father's tribal clan. Every Israelite is responsible for making sure the inheritance stays within the ancestral tribe. No inheritance-land may be passed from tribe to tribe; each tribe of the People of Israel must hold tight to its own land."

10-12 Zelophehad's daughters did just as God commanded Moses. Mahlah, Tirzah, Hoglah, Milcah, and Noah, Zelophehad's daughters, all married their cousins on their father's side. They married within the families of Manasseh son of Joseph and their inheritance-lands stayed in their father's family.

13 These are the commands and regulations that God commanded through the authority of Moses to the People of Israel on the Plains of Moab at Jordan-Jericho.

DEUTERONOMY

Deuteronomy is a sermon—actually a series of sermons. It is the longest sermon in the Bible and maybe the longest sermon ever. Deuteronomy presents Moses, standing on the Plains of Moab with all Israel assembled before him, preaching. It is his last sermon. When he completes it, he will leave his pulpit on the plains, climb a mountain, and die.

The setting is stirring and emotion-packed. Moses had entered the biblical story of salvation as a little baby born in Egypt under a death threat. Now, 120 years later, eyesight sharp as ever and walking with "a spring in his step," he preaches this immense sermon and dies, still brimming with words and life.

This sermon does what all sermons are intended to do: Take God's words, written and spoken in the past, take the human experience, ancestral and personal, of the listening congregation, then reproduce the words and experience as a single event right now, in this present moment. No word that God has spoken is a mere literary artifact to be studied; no human experience is dead history merely to be regretted or admired. The continuous and insistent Mosaic repetitions of "today" and "this day" throughout these sermons keep attentions taut and responsive. The complete range of human experience is brought to life and salvation by the full revelation of God: Live this! Now!

The Plains of Moab are the last stop on the forty-year journey from Egyptian slavery to Promised Land freedom. The People of Israel have experienced a lot as a congregation: deliverance, wanderings, rebellions, wars, providence, worship, guidance. The People of Israel have heard a lot from God: commandments, covenant conditions, sacrificial procedures. And now, poised at the River Jordan, ready to cross over and possess the new land, Moses, preaching his great Plains of Moab sermon, makes sure that they don't leave any of it behind, not so much as one detail of their experience or God's revelation: He puts their entire experience of salvation and providence into the present tense (chapters 1–11); he puts the entire revelation of commandment and covenant into the present tense (chapters 12–28); and then he wraps it all up in a charge and a song and a blessing to launch them into today's obedience and believing (chapters 29–34).

"Let's go."

DEUTERONOMY

¹⁻² These are the sermons Moses preached to all Israel when they were east of the Jordan River in the Arabah Wilderness, opposite Suph, in the vicinity of Paran, Tophel, Laban, Hazeroth, and Dizahab. It takes eleven days to travel from Horeb to Kadesh Barnea following the Mount Seir route.

³⁻⁴ It was on the first day of the eleventh month of the fortieth year when Moses addressed the People of Israel, telling them everything GOD had commanded him concerning them. This came after he had defeated Sihon king of the Amorites, who ruled from Heshbon, and Og king of Bashan, who ruled from Ashtaroth in Edrei. It was east of the Jordan in the land of Moab that Moses set out to explain this Revelation.

MOSES PREACHES TO ISRAEL ON THE PLAINS OF MOAB

⁵ He said:

⁶⁻⁸ Back at Horeb, GOD, our God, spoke to us: "You've stayed long enough at this mountain. On your way now. Get moving. Head for the Amorite hills, wherever people are living in the Arabah, the mountains, the foothills, the Negev, the seashore — the Canaanite country and the Lebanon all the way to the big river, the Euphrates. Look, I've given you this land. Now go in and take it. It's the land GOD promised to give your ancestors Abraham, Isaac, and Jacob and their children after them."

⁹⁻¹³ At the time I told you, "I can't do this, can't carry you all by myself. GOD, your God, has multiplied your numbers. Why, look at you — you rival the stars in the sky! And may GOD, the God-of-Your-Fathers, keep it up and multiply you another thousand times, bless you just as he promised. But how can I carry, all by myself, your troubles and burdens and quarrels? So select some wise, understanding, and seasoned men from your tribes, and I will commission them as your leaders."

¹⁴ You answered me, "Good! A good solution."

¹⁵ So I went ahead and took the top men of your tribes, wise and seasoned, and made them your leaders — leaders of thousands, of hundreds, of fifties, and of tens, officials adequate for each of your tribes.

¹⁶⁻¹⁷ At the same time I gave orders to your judges: "Listen carefully to complaints and accusations between your fellow Israelites. Judge fairly between each person and his fellow or foreigner. Don't play favorites; treat the little and the big alike; listen carefully to each. Don't be impressed by big names. This is *God's* judgment you're dealing with. Hard cases you can bring to me; I'll deal with them."

¹⁸ I issued orders to you at that time regarding everything you would have to deal with.

¹⁹⁻²¹ Then we set out from Horeb and headed for the Amorite hill country, going through that huge and frightening wilderness that you've had more than an eyeful of by now — all under the command of GOD, our God — and finally arrived at Kadesh Barnea. There I told you, "You've made it to the

Amorite hill country that GOD, our God, is giving us. Look, GOD, your God, has placed this land as a gift before you. Go ahead and take it now. GOD, the God-of-Your-Fathers, promised it to you. Don't be afraid. Don't lose heart."

22   But then you all came to me and said, "Let's send some men on ahead to scout out the land for us and bring back a report on the best route to take and the kinds of towns we can expect to find."

23-25   That seemed like a good idea to me, so I picked twelve men, one from each tribe. They set out, climbing through the hills. They came to the Eshcol Valley and looked it over. They took samples of the produce of the land and brought them back to us, saying, "It's a good land that GOD, our God, is giving us!"

26-28   But then you weren't willing to go up. You rebelled against GOD, your God's plain word. You complained in your tents: "GOD hates us. He hauled us out of Egypt in order to dump us among the Amorites — a death sentence for sure! How can we go up? We're trapped in a dead end. Our brothers took all the wind out of our sails, telling us, 'The people are bigger and stronger than we are; their cities are huge, their defenses massive — we even saw Anakite giants there!'"

29-33   I tried to relieve your fears: "Don't be terrified of them. GOD, your God, is leading the way; he's fighting for you. You saw with your own eyes what he did for you in Egypt; you saw what he did in the wilderness, how GOD, your God, carried you as a father carries his child, carried you the whole way until you arrived here. But now that you're here, you won't trust GOD, your God — this same GOD who goes ahead of you in your travels to scout out a place to pitch camp, a fire by night and a cloud by day to show you the way to go."

34-36   When GOD heard what you said, he exploded in anger. He swore, "Not a single person of this evil generation is going to get so much as a look at the good land that I promised to give to your parents. Not one — except for Caleb son of Jephunneh. He'll see it. I'll give him and his descendants the land he walked on because he was all for following GOD, heart and soul."

37-40   But I also got it. Because of you GOD's anger spilled over onto me. He said, "You aren't getting in either. Your assistant, Joshua son of Nun, will go in. Build up his courage. He's the one who will claim the inheritance for Israel. And your babies of whom you said, 'They'll be grabbed for plunder,' and all these little kids who right now don't even know right from wrong — they'll get in. I'll give it to them. Yes, they'll be the new owners. But not you. Turn around and head back into the wilderness following the route to the Red Sea."

41   You spoke up, "We've sinned against GOD. We'll go up and fight, following all the orders that GOD, our God, has commanded." You took your weapons and dressed for battle — you thought it would be so easy going into those hills!

42   But GOD told me, "Tell them, 'Don't do it; don't go up to fight — I'm not with you in this. Your enemies will waste you.'"

43-46   I told you but you wouldn't listen. You rebelled at the plain word of GOD. You threw out your chests and strutted into the hills. And those Amorites, who had lived in those hills all their lives, swarmed all over you like a hive of bees, chasing you from Seir all the way to Hormah, a stinging defeat. You came back and wept in the presence of GOD, but he didn't pay a bit of attention to you; GOD didn't give you the time of day. You stayed there in Kadesh a long time, about as long as you had stayed there earlier.

2 Then we turned around and went back into the wilderness following the route to the Red Sea, as GOD had instructed me. We worked our way in and around the hills of Seir for a long, long time.

2-6 Then GOD said, "You've been going around in circles in these hills long enough; go north. Command the people, You're about to cut through the land belonging to your relatives, the People of Esau who settled in Seir. They are terrified of you, but restrain yourselves. Don't try and start a fight. I am not giving you so much as a square inch of their land. I've already given all the hill country of Seir to Esau — he owns it all. Pay them up front for any food or water you get from them."

7 GOD, your God, has blessed you in everything you have done. He has guarded you in your travels through this immense wilderness. For forty years now, GOD, your God, has been right here with you. You haven't lacked one thing.

8 So we detoured around our brothers, the People of Esau who live in Seir, avoiding the Arabah Road that comes up from Elath and Ezion Geber; instead we used the road through the Wilderness of Moab.

9 GOD told me, "And don't try to pick a fight with the Moabites. I am not giving you any of their land. I've given ownership of Ar to the People of Lot."

10-12 The Emites (Monsters) used to live there — mobs of hulking giants, like Anakites. Along with the Anakites they were lumped in with the Rephaites (Ghosts) but in Moab they were called Emites. Horites also used to live in Seir, but the descendants of Esau took over and destroyed them, the same as Israel did in the land GOD gave them to possess.

13 GOD said, "It's time now to cross the Brook Zered." So we crossed the Brook Zered.

14-15 It took us thirty-eight years to get from Kadesh Barnea to the Brook Zered. That's how long it took for the entire generation of soldiers from the camp to die off, as GOD had sworn they would. GOD was relentless against them until the last one was gone from the camp.

16-23 When the last of these soldiers had died, GOD said to me, "This is the day you cut across the territory of Moab, at Ar. When you approach the People of Ammon, don't try and pick a fight with them because I'm not giving you any of the land of the People of Ammon for yourselves — I've already given it to the People of Lot." It is also considered to have once been the land of the Rephaites. Rephaites lived there long ago — the Ammonites called them Zamzummites (Barbarians) — huge mobs of them, giants like the Anakites. GOD destroyed them and the Ammonites moved in and took over. It was the same with the People of Esau who live in Seir — GOD got rid of the Horites who lived there earlier and they moved in and took over, as you can see. Regarding the Avvites who lived in villages as far as Gaza, the Caphtorites who came from Caphtor (Crete) wiped them out and moved in.

24-25 "On your feet now. Get started. Cross the Brook Arnon. Look: Here's Sihon the Amorite king of Heshbon and his land. I'm handing it over to you — it's all yours. Go ahead, take it. Go to war with him. Before the day is out, I'll make sure that all the people around here are thoroughly terrified. Rumors of you are going to spread like wildfire; they'll totally panic."

26-28 From the Wilderness of Kedemoth, I sent messengers to Sihon, king of Heshbon. They carried a friendly message: "Let me cross through your land on the highway. I'll stay right on the highway; I won't trespass right or left. I'll pay you for any food or water we might need. Let me walk through.

29 "The People of Esau who live in Seir and the Moabites who live in Ar did this, helping me on my way until I can cross the Jordan and enter the land that GOD, our God, is giving us."

30 But Sihon king of Heshbon wouldn't let us cross his land. GOD, your God, turned his spirit mean and his heart hard so he could hand him over to you, as you see that he has done.

31 Then GOD said to me, "Look, I've got the ball rolling — Sihon and his land are soon yours. Go ahead. Take it. It's practically yours!"

32-36 So Sihon and his entire army confronted us in battle at Jahaz. GOD handed him, his sons, and his entire army over to us and we utterly crushed them. While we were at it we captured all his towns and totally destroyed them, a holy destruction — men, women, and children. No survivors. We took the livestock and the plunder from the towns we had captured and carried them off for ourselves. From Aroer on the edge of the Brook Arnon and the town in the gorge, as far as Gilead, not a single town proved too much for us; GOD, our God, gave every last one of them to us.

37 The only land you didn't take, obeying GOD's command, was the land of the People of Ammon, the land along the Jabbok and around the cities in the hills.

1 **3** Then we turned north and took the road to Bashan. Og king of Bashan, he and all his people, came out to meet us in battle at Edrei.

2 GOD said to me, "Don't be afraid of him; I'm turning him over to you, along with his whole army and his land. Treat him the way you treated Sihon king of the Amorites who ruled from Heshbon."

3-7 So GOD, our God, also handed Og king of Bashan over to us — Og and all his people — and we utterly crushed them. Again, no survivors. At the same time we took all his cities. There wasn't one of the sixty cities that we didn't take — the whole region of Argob, Og's kingdom in Bashan. All these cities were fortress cities with high walls and barred gates. There were also numerous unwalled villages. We totally destroyed them — a holy destruction. It was the same treatment we gave to Sihon king of Heshbon, a holy destruction of every city, man, woman, and child. But all the livestock and plunder from the cities we took for ourselves.

8-10 Throughout that time we took the land from under the control of the two kings of the Amorites who ruled the country east of the Jordan, all the way from the Brook Arnon to Mount Hermon. (Sirion is the name given Hermon by the Sidonians; the Amorites call it Senir.) We took all the towns of the plateau, everything in Gilead, everything in Bashan, as far as Salecah and Edrei, the border towns of Bashan, Og's kingdom.

11 Og king of Bashan was the last remaining Rephaite. His bed, made of iron, was over thirteen feet long and six wide. You can still see it on display in Rabbah of the People of Ammon.

12 Of the land that we possessed at that time, I gave the Reubenites and the Gadites the territory north of Aroer along the Brook Arnon and half the hill country of Gilead with its towns.

13 I gave the half-tribe of Manasseh the rest of Gilead and all of Bashan, Og's kingdom — all the region of Argob, which takes in all of Bashan. This used to be known as the Land of the Rephaites.

14 Jair, a son of Manasseh, got the region of Argob to the borders of the Geshurites and Maacathites. He named the Bashan villages after himself, Havvoth Jair (Jair's Tent-Villages). They're still called that.

15 I gave Gilead to Makir.

16-17 I gave the Reubenites and Gadites the land from Gilead down to the Brook Arnon, whose middle was the boundary, and as far as the Jabbok River, the boundary line of the People of Ammon. The western boundary was the Jordan River in the Arabah all the way from the Kinnereth (the Sea of Galilee) to the Sea of the Arabah (the Salt Sea or Dead Sea) at the base of the slopes of Mount Pisgah on the east.

18-20 I commanded you at that time, "GOD, your God, has given you this land to possess. Your men, fit and armed for the fight, are to cross the river in advance of their brothers, the People of Israel. Only your wives, children, and livestock (I know you have much livestock) may go ahead and settle down in the towns I have already given you until GOD secures living space for your brothers as he has for you and they have taken possession of the country west of the Jordan that GOD, your God, is giving them. After that, each man may return to the land I've given you here."

21-22 I commanded Joshua at that time, "You've seen with your own two eyes everything GOD, your God, has done to these two kings. GOD is going to do the same thing to all the kingdoms over there across the river where you're headed. Don't be afraid of them. GOD, your God — he's fighting for you."

23-25 At that same time, I begged GOD: "GOD, my Master, you let me in on the beginnings, you let me see your greatness, you let me see your might — what god in Heaven or Earth can do anything like what you've done! Please, let me in also on the endings, let me cross the river and see the good land over the Jordan, the lush hills, the Lebanon mountains."

26-27 But GOD was still angry with me because of you. He wouldn't listen. He said, "Enough of that. Not another word from you on this. Climb to the top of Mount Pisgah and look around: look west, north, south, east. Take in the land with your own eyes. Take a good look because you're not going to cross this Jordan.

28 "Then command Joshua: Give him courage. Give him strength. Single-

handed he will lead this people across the river. Single-handed he'll cause them to inherit the land at which you can only look."

29   That's why we have stayed in this valley near Beth Peor.

1-2   **4** Now listen, Israel, listen carefully to the rules and regulations that I am teaching you to follow so that you may live and enter and take possession of the land that GOD, the God-of-Your-Fathers, is giving to you. Don't add a word to what I command you, and don't remove a word from it. Keep the commands of GOD, your God, that I am commanding you.

3-4   You saw with your own eyes what GOD did at Baal Peor, how GOD destroyed from among you every man who joined in the Baal Peor orgies. But you, the ones who held tight to GOD, your God, are alive and well, every one of you, today.

5-6   Pay attention: I'm teaching you the rules and regulations that GOD commanded me, so that you may live by them in the land you are entering to take up ownership. Keep them. Practice them. You'll become wise and understanding. When people hear and see what's going on, they'll say, "What a great nation! So wise, so understanding! We've never seen anything like it."

7-8   Yes. What other great nation has gods that are intimate with them the way GOD, our God, is with us, always ready to listen to us? And what other great nation has rules and regulations as good and fair as this Revelation that I'm setting before you today?

9   Just make sure you stay alert. Keep close watch over yourselves. Don't forget anything of what you've seen. Don't let your heart wander off. Stay vigilant as long as you live. Teach what you've seen and heard to your children and grandchildren.

10   That day when you stood before GOD, your God, at Horeb, GOD said to me, "Assemble the people in my presence to listen to my words so that they will learn to fear me in holy fear for as long as they live on the land, and then they will teach these same words to their children."

11-13   You gathered. You stood in the shadow of the mountain. The mountain was ablaze with fire, blazing high into the very heart of Heaven. You stood in deep darkness and thick clouds. GOD spoke to you out of the fire. You heard the sound of words but you saw nothing—no form, only a voice. He announced his covenant, the Ten Words, by which he commanded you to live. Then he wrote them down on two slabs of stone.

14   And GOD commanded me at that time to teach you the rules and regulations that you are to live by in the land which you are crossing over the Jordan to possess.

15-20   You saw no form on the day GOD spoke to you at Horeb from out of the fire. Remember that. Carefully guard yourselves so that you don't turn corrupt and make a form, carving a figure that looks male or female, or looks like a prowling animal or a flying bird or a slithering snake or a fish in a stream. And also carefully guard yourselves so that you don't look up into the skies and see the sun and moon and stars, all the constellations of the skies, and be seduced into worshiping and serving them. GOD set them out for everybody's benefit, everywhere. But you—GOD took you right out of the iron furnace, out of Egypt, to become the people of his inheritance—and that's what you are this very day.

21-22 But GOD was angry with me because of you and the things you said. He swore that I'd never cross the Jordan, never get to enter the good land that GOD, your God, is giving you as an inheritance. This means that I am going to die here. I'm not crossing the Jordan. But you will cross; you'll possess the good land.

23-24 So stay alert. Don't for a minute forget the covenant which GOD, your God, made with you. And don't take up with any carved images, no forms of any kind — GOD, your God, issued clear commands on that. GOD, your God, is not to be trifled with — he's a consuming fire, a jealous God.

25-28 When the time comes that you have children and grandchildren, put on years, and start taking things for granted, if you then become corrupt and make any carved images, no matter what their form, by doing what is sheer evil in GOD's eyes and provoking his anger — I can tell you right now, with Heaven and Earth as witnesses, that it will be all over for you. You'll be kicked off the land that you're about to cross over the Jordan to possess. Believe me, you'll have a very short stay there. You'll be ruined, completely ruined. GOD will scatter you far and wide; a few of you will survive here and there in the nations where GOD will drive you. There you can worship your homemade gods to your hearts' content, your wonderful gods of wood and stone that can't see or hear or eat or smell.

29-31 But even there, if you seek GOD, your God, you'll be able to find him if you're serious, looking for him with your whole heart and soul. When troubles come and all these awful things happen to you, in future days you will come back to GOD, your God, and listen obediently to what he says. GOD, your God, is above all a compassionate God. In the end he will not abandon you, he won't bring you to ruin, he won't forget the covenant with your ancestors which he swore to them.

32-33 Ask questions. Find out what has been going on all these years before you were born. From the day God created man and woman on this Earth, and from the horizon in the east to the horizon in the west — as far back as you can imagine and as far away as you can imagine — has as great a thing as this ever happened? Has anyone ever heard of such a thing? Has a people ever heard, as you did, a god speaking out of the middle of the fire and lived to tell the story?

34 Or has a god ever tried to select for himself a nation from within a nation using trials, miracles, and war, putting his strong hand in, reaching his long arm out, a spectacle awesome and staggering, the way GOD, your God, did it for you in Egypt while you stood right there and watched?

35-38 You were shown all this so that you would know that GOD is, well, God. He's the only God there is. He's it. He made it possible for you to hear his voice out of Heaven to discipline you. Down on Earth, he showed you the big fire and again you heard his words, this time out of the fire. He loved your ancestors and chose to work with their children. He personally and powerfully brought you out of Egypt in order to displace bigger and stronger and older nations with you, bringing you out and turning their land over to you as an inheritance. And now it's happening. This very day.

39-40 Know this well, then. Take it to heart right now: GOD is in Heaven above; GOD is on Earth below. He's the only God there is. Obediently live by his rules and commands which I'm giving you today so that you'll live well and your children after you — oh, you'll live a long time in the land that GOD, your God, is giving you.

41-42 Then Moses set aside three towns in the country on the east side of the Jordan to which someone who had unintentionally killed a person could flee and find refuge. If the murder was unintentional and there was no history of bad blood, the murderer could flee to one of these cities and save his life:

43 Bezer in the wilderness on the tableland for the Reubenites, Ramoth in Gilead for the Gadites, and Golan in Bashan for the Manassites.

44-49 This is the Revelation that Moses presented to the People of Israel. These are the testimonies, the rules and regulations Moses spoke to the People of Israel after their exodus from Egypt and arrival on the east side of the Jordan in the valley near Beth Peor. It was the country of Sihon king of the Amorites who ruled from Heshbon. Moses and the People of Israel fought and beat him after they left Egypt and took his land. They also took the land of Og king of Bashan. The two Amorite kings held the country on the east of the Jordan from Aroer on the bank of the Brook Arnon as far north as Mount Siyon, that is, Mount Hermon, all the Arabah plain east of the Jordan, and as far south as the Sea of the Arabah (the Dead Sea) beneath the slopes of Mount Pisgah.

MOSES TEACHES ISRAEL ON THE PLAINS OF MOAB

1 **5** Moses called all Israel together. He said to them,

Attention, Israel. Listen obediently to the rules and regulations I am delivering to your listening ears today. Learn them. Live them.

2-5 GOD, our God, made a covenant with us at Horeb. GOD didn't just make this covenant with our parents; he made it also with us, with all of us who are alive right now. GOD spoke to you personally out of the fire on the mountain. At the time I stood between GOD and you, to tell you what GOD said. You were afraid, remember, of the fire and wouldn't climb the mountain. He said:

6 I am GOD, your God,
who brought you out of the land of Egypt,
out of a house of slaves.

7 No other gods, only me.

8-10 No carved gods of any size, shape, or form of anything whatever, whether of things that fly or walk or swim. Don't bow down to them and don't serve them because *I* am God, your God, and I'm a most jealous God. I hold parents responsible for any sins they pass on to their children to the third, and yes, even to the fourth generation. But I'm lovingly loyal to the thousands who love me and keep my commandments.

11 No using the name of GOD, your God, in curses or silly banter; GOD won't put up with the irreverent use of his name.

12-15 No working on the Sabbath; keep it holy just as GOD, your God, commanded you. Work six days, doing everything you have to do, but the seventh day is a Sabbath, a Rest Day — no work: not you, your son, your daughter, your servant, your maid, your ox, your donkey (or any of your animals), and not even the foreigner visiting your town. That way your servants and maids will get the same rest as you. Don't ever forget that you were slaves in Egypt and GOD, your God, got you out of there in a powerful show of strength. That's why GOD, your God, commands you to observe the day of Sabbath rest.

16 Respect your father and mother — GOD, your God, commands it! You'll have a long life; the land that God is giving you will treat you well.

17 No murder.

18 No adultery.

19 No stealing.

20 No lies about your neighbor.

21 No coveting your neighbor's wife. And no lusting for his house, field, servant, maid, ox, or donkey either — nothing that belongs to your neighbor!

22 These are the words that GOD spoke to the whole congregation at the mountain. He spoke in a tremendous voice from the fire and cloud and dark mist. And that was it. No more words. Then he wrote them on two slabs of stone and gave them to me.

23-24 As it turned out, when you heard the Voice out of that dark cloud and saw the mountain on fire, you approached me, all the heads of your tribes and your leaders, and said,

24-26 "Our GOD has revealed to us his glory and greatness. We've heard him speak from the fire today! We've seen that God can speak to humans and they can still live. But why risk it further? This huge fire will devour us if we stay around any longer. If we hear GOD's voice anymore, we'll die for sure. Has anyone ever known of anyone who has heard the Voice of GOD the way we have and lived to tell the story?

27 "From now on, *you* go and listen to what GOD, our God, says and then tell us what GOD tells you. We'll listen and we'll do it."

28-29 GOD heard what you said to me and told me, "I've heard what the people said to you. They're right — good and true words. What I wouldn't give if they'd always feel this way, continuing to revere me and always keep all my commands; they'd have a good life forever, they and their children!

30-31 "Go ahead and tell them to go home to their tents. But you, you stay here with me so I can tell you every commandment and all the rules and regulations that you must teach them so they'll know how to live in the land that I'm giving them as their own."

32-33 So be very careful to act exactly as GOD commands you. Don't veer off to the right or the left. Walk straight down the road GOD commands so that you'll have a good life and live a long time in the land that you're about to possess.

1-2 This is the commandment, the rules and regulations, that GOD, your God, commanded me to teach you to live out in the land you're about to cross into to possess. This is so that you'll live in deep reverence before GOD lifelong, observing all his rules and regulations that I'm commanding you, you and your children and your grandchildren, living good long lives.

3 Listen obediently, Israel. Do what you're told so that you'll have a good life, a life of abundance and bounty, just as GOD promised, in a land abounding in milk and honey.

4 Attention, Israel!

God, our God! God the one and only!

5 Love God, your God, with your whole heart: love him with all that's in you, love him with all you've got!

6-9 Write these commandments that I've given you today on your hearts. Get them inside of you and then get them inside your children. Talk about them wherever you are, sitting at home or walking in the street; talk about them from the time you get up in the morning to when you fall into bed at night. Tie them on your hands and foreheads as a reminder; inscribe them on the doorposts of your homes and on your city gates.

10-12 When God, your God, ushers you into the land he promised through your ancestors Abraham, Isaac, and Jacob to give you, you're going to walk into large, bustling cities you didn't build, well-furnished houses you didn't buy, come upon wells you didn't dig, vineyards and olive orchards you didn't plant. When you take it all in and settle down, pleased and content, make sure you don't forget how you got there—God brought you out of slavery in Egypt.

13-19 Deeply respect God, your God. Serve and worship him exclusively. Back up your promises with his name only. Don't fool around with other gods, the gods of your neighbors, because God, your God, who is alive among you is a jealous God. Don't provoke him, igniting his hot anger that would burn you right off the face of the Earth. Don't push God, your God, to the wall as you did that day at Massah, the Testing-Place. Carefully keep the commands of God, your God, all the requirements and regulations he gave you. Do what is right; do what is good in God's sight so you'll live a good life and be able to march in and take this pleasant land that God so solemnly promised through your ancestors, throwing out your enemies left and right—exactly as God said.

20-24 The next time your child asks you, "What do these requirements and regulations and rules that God, our God, has commanded mean?" tell your child, "We were slaves to Pharaoh in Egypt and God powerfully intervened and got us out of that country. We stood there and watched as God delivered miracle-signs, great wonders, and evil-visitations on Egypt, on Pharaoh and his household. He pulled us out of there so he could bring us here and give us the land he so solemnly promised to our ancestors. That's why God commanded us to follow all these rules, so that we would live reverently before God, our God, as he gives us this good life, keeping us alive for a long time to come.

25 "It will be a set-right and put-together life for us if we make sure that we do this entire commandment in the Presence of God, our God, just as he commanded us to do."

1-2 7 When God, your God, brings you into the country that you are about to enter and take over, he will clear out the superpowers that were there before you: the Hittite, the Girgashite, the Amorite, the Canaanite, the Perizzite, the Hivite, and the Jebusite. Those seven nations are all bigger and stronger than you are. God, your God, will turn them over to you and you will conquer them. You must completely destroy them, offering them up as a holy destruction to God.

Don't make a treaty with them.
Don't let them off in any way.

3-4 Don't marry them: Don't give your daughters to their sons and don't take their daughters for your sons — before you know it they'd involve you in worshiping their gods, and GOD would explode in anger, putting a quick end to you.

5 Here's what you are to do:

> Tear apart their altars stone by stone,
> smash their phallic pillars,
> chop down their sex-and-religion Asherah groves,
> set fire to their carved god-images.

6 Do this because you are a people set apart as holy to GOD, your God. GOD, your God, chose you out of all the people on Earth for himself as a cherished, personal treasure.

7-10 GOD wasn't attracted to you and didn't choose you because you were big and important — the fact is, there was almost nothing to you. He did it out of sheer love, keeping the promise he made to your ancestors. GOD stepped in and mightily bought you back out of that world of slavery, freed you from the iron grip of Pharaoh king of Egypt. Know this: GOD, your God, is God indeed, a God you can depend upon. He keeps his covenant of loyal love with those who love him and observe his commandments for a thousand generations. But he also pays back those who hate him, pays them the wages of death; he isn't slow to pay them off — those who hate him, he pays right on time.

11 So keep the command and the rules and regulations that I command you today. Do them.

12-13 And this is what will happen: When you, on your part, will obey these directives, keeping and following them, GOD, on his part, will keep the covenant of loyal love that he made with your ancestors:

> He will love you,
> he will bless you,
> he will increase you.

13-15 He will bless the babies from your womb and the harvest of grain, new wine, and oil from your fields; he'll bless the calves from your herds and lambs from your flocks in the country he promised your ancestors that he'd give you. You'll be blessed beyond all other peoples: no sterility or barrenness in you or your animals. GOD will get rid of all sickness. And all the evil afflictions you experienced in Egypt he'll put not on you but on those who hate you.

16 You'll make mincemeat of all the peoples that GOD, your God, hands over to you. Don't feel sorry for them. And don't worship their gods — they'll trap you for sure.

17-19 You're going to think to yourselves, "Oh! We're outnumbered ten to one by these nations! We'll never even make a dent in them!" But I'm telling you, Don't be afraid. Remember, yes, remember in detail what GOD, your God, did to Pharaoh and all Egypt. Remember the great contests to which you were eyewitnesses: the miracle-signs, the wonders, GOD's mighty hand as he stretched out his arm and took you out of there. GOD, your God, is going to do the same thing to these people you're now so afraid of.

20 And to top it off, the Hornet. GOD will unleash the Hornet on them until every survivor-in-hiding is dead.

21-24 So don't be intimidated by them. GOD, your God, is among you — GOD majestic, GOD awesome. GOD, your God, will get rid of these nations, bit by bit. You won't be permitted to wipe them out all at once lest the wild animals take over and overwhelm you. But GOD, your God, will move them out of your way — he'll throw them into a huge panic until there's nothing left of them. He'll turn their kings over to you and you'll remove all trace of them under Heaven. Not one person will be able to stand up to you; you'll put an end to them all.

25-26 Make sure you set fire to their carved gods. Don't get greedy for the veneer of silver and gold on them and take it for yourselves — you'll get trapped by it for sure. GOD hates it; it's an abomination to GOD, your God. And don't dare bring one of these abominations home or you'll end up just like it, burned up as a holy destruction. No: It is forbidden! Hate it. Abominate it. Destroy it and preserve GOD's holiness.

1-5 8 Keep and live out the entire commandment that I'm commanding you today so that you'll live and prosper and enter and own the land that GOD promised to your ancestors. Remember every road that GOD led you on for those forty years in the wilderness, pushing you to your limits, testing you so that he would know what you were made of, whether you would keep his commandments or not. He put you through hard times. He made you go hungry. Then he fed you with manna, something neither you nor your parents knew anything about, so you would learn that men and women don't live by bread only; we live by every word that comes from GOD's mouth. Your clothes didn't wear out and your feet didn't blister those forty years. You learned deep in your heart that GOD disciplines you in the same ways a father disciplines his child.

6-9 So it's paramount that you keep the commandments of GOD, your God, walk down the roads he shows you and reverently respect him. GOD is about to bring you into a good land, a land with brooks and rivers, springs and lakes, streams out of the hills and through the valleys. It's a land of wheat and barley, of vines and figs and pomegranates, of olives, oil, and honey. It's land where you'll never go hungry — always food on the table and a roof over your head. It's a land where you'll get iron out of rocks and mine copper from the hills.

10 After a meal, satisfied, bless GOD, your God, for the good land he has given you.

11-16 Make sure you don't forget GOD, your God, by not keeping his commandments, his rules and regulations that I command you today. Make sure that when you eat and are satisfied, build pleasant houses and settle in, see your herds and flocks flourish and more and more money come in, watch your standard of living going up and up — make sure you don't become so full of yourself and your things that you forget GOD, your God,

the God who delivered you from Egyptian slavery;
the God who led you through that huge and fearsome wilderness,
those desolate, arid badlands crawling with fiery snakes and scorpions;

the God who gave you water gushing from hard rock;
the God who gave you manna to eat in the wilderness, something your
ancestors had never heard of, in order to give you a taste of the hard life,
to test you so that you would be prepared to live well in the days ahead
of you.

17-18 If you start thinking to yourselves, "I did all this. And all by myself. I'm
rich. It's all mine!"—well, think again. Remember that GOD, your God,
gave you the strength to produce all this wealth so as to confirm the covenant that he promised to your ancestors—as it is today.

19-20 If you forget, forget GOD, your God, and start taking up with other
gods, serving and worshiping them, I'm on record right now as giving you
firm warning: that will be the end of you; I mean it—destruction. You'll go
to your doom—the same as the nations GOD is destroying before you; doom
because you wouldn't obey the Voice of GOD, your God.

⁂

1-2 9 Attention, Israel!
This very day you are crossing the Jordan to enter the land and
dispossess nations that are much bigger and stronger than you are.
You're going to find huge cities with sky-high fortress-walls and gigantic
people, descendants of the Anakites—you've heard all about them; you've
heard the saying, "No one can stand up to an Anakite."

3 Today know this: GOD, your God, is crossing the river ahead of you—he's
a consuming fire. He will destroy the nations, he will put them under your
power. You will dispossess them and very quickly wipe them out, just as GOD
promised you would.

4-5 But when GOD pushes them out ahead of you, don't start thinking to
yourselves, "It's because of all the good I've done that GOD has brought
me in here to dispossess these nations." Actually it's because of all the evil
these nations have done. No, it's nothing good that you've done, no record
for decency that you've built up, that got you here; it's because of the vile
wickedness of these nations that GOD, your God, is dispossessing them
before you so that he can keep his promised word to your ancestors, to
Abraham, Isaac, and Jacob.

6-10 Know this and don't ever forget it: It's not because of any good that you've
done that GOD is giving you this good land to own. Anything but! You're stubborn as mules. Keep in mind and don't ever forget how angry you made GOD,
your God, in the wilderness. You've kicked and screamed against GOD from
the day you left Egypt until you got to this place, rebels all the way. You made
GOD angry at Horeb, made him so angry that he wanted to destroy you. When
I climbed the mountain to receive the slabs of stone, the tablets of the covenant
that GOD made with you, I stayed there on the mountain forty days and nights:
I ate no food; I drank no water. Then GOD gave me the two slabs of stone,
engraved with the finger of God. They contained word for word everything that
GOD spoke to you on the mountain out of the fire, on the day of the assembly.

11-12 It was at the end of the forty days and nights that GOD gave me the two
slabs of stone, the tablets of the covenant. GOD said to me, "Get going, and
quickly. Get down there, because your people whom you led out of Egypt
have ruined everything. In almost no time at all they have left the road that
I laid out for them and gone off and made for themselves a cast god."

13-14 GOD said, "I look at this people and all I see are hardheaded, hardhearted rebels. Get out of my way now so I can destroy them. I'm going to wipe them off the face of the map. Then I'll start over with you to make a nation far better and bigger than they could ever be."

15-17 I turned around and started down the mountain — by now the mountain was blazing with fire — carrying the two tablets of the covenant in my two arms. That's when I saw it: There you were, sinning against GOD, your God — you had made yourselves a cast god in the shape of a calf! So soon you had left the road that GOD had commanded you to walk on. I held the two stone slabs high and threw them down, smashing them to bits as you watched.

18-20 Then I prostrated myself before GOD, just as I had at the beginning of the forty days and nights. I ate no food; I drank no water. I did this because of you, all your sins, sinning against GOD, doing what is evil in GOD's eyes and making him angry. I was terrified of GOD's furious anger, his blazing anger. I was sure he would destroy you. But once again GOD listened to me. And Aaron! How furious he was with Aaron — ready to destroy him. But I prayed also for Aaron at that same time.

21 But that sin-thing that you made, that calf-god, I took and burned in the fire, pounded and ground it until it was crushed into a fine powder, then threw it into the stream that comes down the mountain.

22 And then there was Camp Taberah (Blaze), Massah (Testing-Place), and Camp Kibroth Hattaavah (Graves-of-the-Craving) — more occasions when you made GOD furious with you.

23-24 The most recent was when GOD sent you out from Kadesh Barnea, ordering you: "Go. Possess the land that I'm giving you." And what did you do? You rebelled. Rebelled against the clear orders of GOD, your God. Refused to trust him. Wouldn't obey him. You've been rebels against GOD from the first day I knew you.

25-26 When I was on my face, prostrate before GOD those forty days and nights after GOD said he would destroy you, I prayed to GOD for you, "My Master, GOD, don't destroy your people, your inheritance whom, in your immense generosity, you redeemed, using your enormous strength to get them out of Egypt.

27-28 "Remember your servants Abraham, Isaac, and Jacob; don't make too much of the stubbornness of this people, their evil and their sin, lest the Egyptians from whom you rescued them say, 'GOD couldn't do it; he got tired and wasn't able to take them to the land he promised them. He ended up hating them and dumped them in the wilderness to die.'

29 "They are your people still, your inheritance whom you powerfully and sovereignly rescued."

1-2 **10** GOD responded. He said, "Shape two slabs of stone similar to the first ones. Climb the mountain and meet me. Also make yourself a wooden chest. I will engrave the stone slabs with the words that were on the first ones, the ones you smashed. Then you will put them in the Chest."

3-5 So I made a chest out of acacia wood, shaped two slabs of stone, just like the first ones, and climbed the mountain with the two slabs in my arms. He engraved the stone slabs the same as he had the first ones, the Ten Words that he addressed to you on the mountain out of the fire on the day of the assembly. Then GOD gave them to me. I turned around and came down the mountain. I put the stone slabs in the Chest that I made and they've been there ever since, just as GOD commanded me.

⁂

6-7   The People of Israel went from the wells of the Jaakanites to Moserah. Aaron died there and was buried. His son Eleazar succeeded him as priest. From there they went to Gudgodah, and then to Jotbathah, a land of streams of water.

8-9   That's when GOD set apart the tribe of Levi to carry GOD's Covenant Chest, to be on duty in the Presence of GOD, to serve him, and to bless in his name, as they continue to do today. And that's why Levites don't have a piece of inherited land as their kinsmen do. GOD is their inheritance, as GOD, your God, promised them.

10   I stayed there on the mountain forty days and nights, just as I did the first time. And GOD listened to me, just as he did the first time: GOD decided not to destroy you.

11   GOD told me, "Now get going. Lead your people as they resume the journey to take possession of the land that I promised their ancestors that I'd give to them."

12-13   So now Israel, what do you think GOD expects from you? Just this: Live in his presence in holy reverence, follow the road he sets out for you, love him, serve GOD, your God, with everything you have in you, obey the commandments and regulations of GOD that I'm commanding you today — live a good life.

14-18   Look around you: Everything you see is GOD's — the heavens above and beyond, the Earth, and everything on it. But it was your ancestors who GOD fell in love with; he picked their children — that's *you!* — out of all the other peoples. That's where we are right now. So cut away the thick calluses from your heart and stop being so willfully hardheaded. GOD, your God, is the God of all gods, he's the Master of all masters, a God immense and powerful and awesome. He doesn't play favorites, takes no bribes, makes sure orphans and widows are treated fairly, takes loving care of foreigners by seeing that they get food and clothing.

19-21   You must treat foreigners with the same loving care —
     remember, you were once foreigners in Egypt.
Reverently respect GOD, your God, serve him, hold tight to him,
     back up your promises with the authority of his name.
He's your praise! He's your God!
He did all these tremendous, these staggering things
     that you saw with your own eyes.

22   When your ancestors entered Egypt, they numbered a mere seventy souls. And now look at you — you look more like the stars in the night skies in number. And your GOD did it.

⁂

1   **11** So love GOD, your God;
     guard well his rules and regulations;
     obey his commandments for the rest of time.

2-7   Today it's very clear that it isn't your children who are front and center here: They weren't in on what GOD did, didn't see the acts, didn't experience the discipline, didn't marvel at his greatness, the way he displayed his power in the miracle-signs and deeds that he let loose in Egypt on Pharaoh king of Egypt and all his land, the way he took care of the Egyptian army, its horses and chariots, burying them in the waters of the Red Sea as they pursued you. GOD drowned them. And you're standing here today alive. Nor was it your children who saw how GOD took care of you in the wilderness up until the time you arrived here, what he did to Dathan and Abiram, the sons of Eliab son of Reuben, how the Earth opened its jaws and swallowed them with their families — their tents, and everything around them — right out of the middle of Israel. Yes, it was you — your eyes — that saw every great thing that GOD did.

8-9   So it's you who are in charge of keeping the entire commandment that I command you today so that you'll have the strength to invade and possess the land that you are crossing the river to make your own. Your obedience will give you a long life on the soil that GOD promised to give your ancestors and their children, a land flowing with milk and honey.

10-12   The land you are entering to take up ownership isn't like Egypt, the land you left, where you had to plant your own seed and water it yourselves as in a vegetable garden. But the land you are about to cross the river and take for your own is a land of mountains and valleys; it drinks water that rains from the sky. It's a land that GOD, your God, personally tends — he's the gardener — he alone keeps his eye on it all year long.

13-15   From now on if you listen obediently to the commandments that I am commanding you today, love GOD, your God, and serve him with everything you have within you, he'll take charge of sending the rain at the right time, both autumn and spring rains, so that you'll be able to harvest your grain, your grapes, your olives. He'll make sure there's plenty of grass for your animals. You'll have plenty to eat.

16-17   But be vigilant, lest you be seduced away and end up serving and worshiping other gods and GOD erupts in anger and shuts down Heaven so there's no rain and nothing grows in the fields, and in no time at all you're starved out — not a trace of you left on the good land that GOD is giving you.

18-21   Place these words on your hearts. Get them deep inside you. Tie them on your hands and foreheads as a reminder. Teach them to your children. Talk about them wherever you are, sitting at home or walking in the street; talk about them from the time you get up in the morning until you fall into bed at night. Inscribe them on the doorposts and gates of your cities so that you'll live a long time, and your children with you, on the soil that GOD promised to give your ancestors for as long as there is a sky over the Earth.

22-25   That's right. If you diligently keep all this commandment that I command you to obey — love GOD, your God, do what he tells you, stick close to him — GOD on his part will drive out all these nations that stand in your way. Yes, he'll drive out nations much bigger and stronger than you. Every square inch on which you place your foot will be yours. Your borders will stretch from the wilderness to the mountains of Lebanon, from the Euphrates River to the Mediterranean Sea. No one will be able to stand in your way. Everywhere you go, GOD-sent fear and trembling will precede you, just as he promised.

26   I've brought you today to the crossroads of Blessing and Curse.

27   The Blessing: if you listen obediently to the commandments of GOD, your God, which I command you today.

28   The Curse: if you don't pay attention to the commandments of GOD, your God, but leave the road that I command you today, following other gods of which you know nothing.

29-30   Here's what comes next: When GOD, your God, brings you into the land you are going into to make your own, you are to give out the Blessing from Mount Gerizim and the Curse from Mount Ebal. After you cross the Jordan River, follow the road to the west through Canaanite settlements in the valley near Gilgal and the Oaks of Moreh.

31-32   You are crossing the Jordan River to invade and take the land that GOD, your God, is giving you. Be vigilant. Observe all the regulations and rules I am setting before you today.

1   **12** These are the rules and regulations that you must diligently observe for as long as you live in this country that GOD, the God-of-Your-Fathers, has given you to possess.

2-3   Ruthlessly demolish all the sacred shrines where the nations that you're driving out worship their gods—wherever you find them, on hills and mountains or in groves of green trees. Tear apart their altars. Smash their phallic pillars. Burn their sex-and-religion Asherah shrines. Break up their carved gods. Obliterate the names of those god sites.

4   Stay clear of those places—don't let what went on there contaminate the worship of GOD, your God.

5-7   Instead find the site that GOD, your God, will choose and mark it with his name as a common center for all the tribes of Israel. Assemble there. Bring to that place your Absolution-Offerings and sacrifices, your tithes and Tribute-Offerings, your Vow-Offerings, your Freewill-Offerings, and the firstborn of your herds and flocks. Feast there in the Presence of GOD, your God. Celebrate everything that you and your families have accomplished under the blessing of GOD, your God.

8-10   Don't continue doing things the way we're doing them at present, each of us doing as we wish. Until now you haven't arrived at the goal, the resting place, the inheritance that GOD, your God, is giving you. But the minute you cross the Jordan River and settle into the land GOD, your God, is enabling you to inherit, he'll give you rest from all your surrounding enemies. You'll be able to settle down and live in safety.

11-12   From then on, at the place that GOD, your God, chooses to mark with his name as the place where you can meet him, bring everything that I command you: your Absolution-Offerings and sacrifices, tithes and Tribute-Offerings, and the best of your Vow-Offerings that you vow to GOD. Celebrate there in the Presence of GOD, your God, you and your sons and daughters, your servants and maids, including the Levite living in your neighborhood because he has no place of his own in your inheritance.

13-14   Be extra careful: Don't offer your Absolution-Offerings just any place that strikes your fancy. Offer your Absolution-Offerings only in the place that GOD chooses in one of your tribal regions. There and only there are you to bring all that I command you.

15   It's permissible to slaughter your nonsacrificial animals like gazelle

and deer in your towns and eat all you want from them with the blessing of GOD, your God. Both the ritually clean and unclean may eat.

16-18 But you may not eat the blood. Pour the blood out on the ground like water. Nor may you eat there the tithe of your grain, new wine, or olive oil; nor the firstborn of your herds and flocks; nor any of the Vow-Offerings that you vow; nor your Freewill-Offerings and Tribute-Offerings. All these you must eat in the Presence of GOD, your God, in the place GOD, your God, chooses — you, your son and daughter, your servant and maid, and the Levite who lives in your neighborhood. You are to celebrate in the Presence of GOD, your God, all the things you've been able to accomplish.

19 And make sure that for as long as you live on your land you never, never neglect the Levite.

20-22 When GOD, your God, expands your territory as he promised he would do, and you say, "I'm hungry for meat," because you happen to be craving meat at the time, go ahead and eat as much meat as you want. If you're too far away from the place that GOD, your God, has marked with his name, it's all right to slaughter animals from your herds and flocks that GOD has given you, as I've commanded you. In your own towns you may eat as much of them as you want. Just as the nonsacrificial animals like the gazelle and deer are eaten, you may eat them; the ritually unclean and clean may eat them at the same table.

23-25 Only this: Absolutely no blood. Don't eat the blood. Blood is life; don't eat the life with the meat. Don't eat it; pour it out on the ground like water. Don't eat it; then you'll have a good life, you and your children after you. By all means, do the right thing in GOD's eyes.

26-27 And this: Lift high your Holy-Offerings and your Vow-Offerings and bring them to the place GOD designates. Sacrifice your Absolution-Offerings, the meat and blood, on the Altar of GOD, your God; pour out the blood of the Absolution-Offering on the Altar of GOD, your God; then you can go ahead and eat the meat.

28 Be vigilant, listen obediently to these words that I command you so that you'll have a good life, you and your children, for a long, long time, doing what is good and right in the eyes of GOD, your God.

29-31 When GOD, your God, cuts off the nations whose land you are invading, shoves them out of your way so that you displace them and settle in their land, be careful that you don't get curious about them after they've been destroyed before you. Don't get fascinated with their gods, thinking, "I wonder what it was like for them, worshiping their gods. I'd like to try that myself." Don't do this to GOD, your God. They commit every imaginable abomination with their gods. GOD hates it all with a passion. Why, they even set their children on fire as offerings to their gods!

32 Diligently do everything I command you, the way I command you: don't add to it; don't subtract from it.

1-4 **13** When a prophet or visionary gets up in your community and gives out a miracle-sign or wonder, and the miracle-sign or wonder that he gave out happens and he says, "Let's follow other gods" (these are gods you know nothing about), "let's worship them," don't pay any attention to what that prophet or visionary says. GOD, your

God, is testing you to find out if you totally love him with everything you have in you. You are to follow only GOD, your God, hold him in deep reverence, keep his commandments, listen obediently to what he says, serve him — hold on to him for dear life!

5 And that prophet or visionary must be put to death. He has urged mutiny against GOD, your God, who rescued you from Egypt, who redeemed you from a world of slavery and put you on the road on which GOD, your God, has commanded you to walk. Purge the evil from your company.

6-10 And when your brother or son or daughter, or even your dear wife or life-long friend, comes to you in secret and whispers, "Let's go and worship some other gods" (gods that you know nothing about, neither you nor your ancestors, the gods of the peoples around you near and far, from one end of the Earth to the other), don't go along with him; shut your ears. Don't feel sorry for him and don't make excuses for him. Kill him. That's right, kill him. You throw the first stone. Take action at once and swiftly with everybody in the community getting in on it at the end. Stone him with stones so that he dies. He tried to turn you traitor against GOD, your God, the one who got you out of Egypt and the world of slavery.

11 Every man, woman, and child in Israel will hear what's been done and be in awe. No one will dare to do an evil thing like this again.

12-17 When word comes in from one of your cities that GOD, your God, is giv-ing you to live in, reporting that evil men have gotten together with some of the citizens of the city and have broken away, saying, "Let's go and worship other gods" (gods you know nothing about), then you must conduct a care-ful examination. Ask questions, investigate. If it turns out that the report is true and this abomination did in fact take place in your community, you must execute the citizens of that town. Kill them, setting that city apart for holy destruction: the city and everything in it including its animals. Gather the plunder in the middle of the town square and burn it all — town and plunder together up in smoke, a holy sacrifice to GOD, your God. Leave it there, ashes and ruins. Don't build on that site again. And don't let any of the plunder devoted to holy destruction stick to your fingers. Get rid of it so that GOD may turn from anger to compassion, generously making you prosper, just as he promised your ancestors.

18 Yes. Obediently listen to GOD, your God. Keep all his commands that I am giving you today. Do the right thing in the eyes of GOD, your God.

1-2 **14** You are children of GOD, your God, so don't mutilate your bodies or shave your heads in funeral rites for the dead. You only are a people holy to GOD, your God; GOD chose you out of all the people on Earth as his cherished personal treasure.

3-8 Don't eat anything abominable. These are the animals you may eat: ox, sheep, goat, deer, gazelle, roebuck, wild goat, ibex, antelope, mountain sheep — any animal that has a cloven hoof and chews the cud. But you may not eat camels, rabbits, and rock badgers because they chew the cud but they don't have a cloven hoof — that makes them ritually unclean. And pigs: Don't eat pigs — they have a cloven hoof but don't chew the cud, which makes them ritually unclean. Don't even touch a pig's carcass.

9-10 This is what you may eat from the water: anything that has fins and scales. But if it doesn't have fins or scales, you may not eat it. It's ritually unclean.

11-18　　You may eat any ritually clean bird. These are the exceptions, so don't eat these: eagle, vulture, black vulture, kite, falcon, the buzzard family, the raven family, ostrich, nighthawk, the hawk family, little owl, great owl, white owl, pelican, osprey, cormorant, stork, the heron family, hoopoe, bat.

19-20　　Winged insects are ritually unclean; don't eat them. But ritually clean winged creatures are permitted.

21　　Because you are a people holy to GOD, your God, don't eat anything that you find dead. You can, though, give it to a foreigner in your neighborhood for a meal or sell it to a foreigner.

Don't boil a kid in its mother's milk.

22-26　　Make an offering of ten percent, a tithe, of all the produce which grows in your fields year after year. Bring this into the Presence of GOD, your God, at the place he designates for worship and there eat the tithe from your grain, wine, and oil and the firstborn from your herds and flocks. In this way you will learn to live in deep reverence before GOD, your God, as long as you live. But if the place GOD, your God, designates for worship is too far away and you can't carry your tithe that far, GOD, your God, will still bless you: exchange your tithe for money and take the money to the place GOD, your God, has chosen to be worshiped. Use the money to buy anything you want: cattle, sheep, wine, or beer—anything that looks good to you. You and your family can then feast in the Presence of GOD, your God, and have a good time.

27　　Meanwhile, don't forget to take good care of the Levites who live in your towns; they won't get any property or inheritance of their own as you will.

28-29　　At the end of every third year, gather the tithe from all your produce of that year and put it aside in storage. Keep it in reserve for the Levite who won't get any property or inheritance as you will, and for the foreigner, the orphan, and the widow who live in your neighborhood. That way they'll have plenty to eat and GOD, your God, will bless you in all your work.

1-3　　**15** At the end of every seventh year, cancel all debts. This is the procedure: Everyone who has lent money to a neighbor writes it off. You must not press your neighbor or his brother for payment: All-Debts-Are-Canceled—GOD says so. You may collect payment from foreigners, but whatever you have lent to your fellow Israelite you must write off.

4-6　　There must be no poor people among you because GOD is going to bless you lavishly in this land that GOD, your God, is giving you as an inheritance, your very own land. But only if you listen obediently to the Voice of GOD, your God, diligently observing every commandment that I command you today. Oh yes—GOD, your God, will bless you just as he promised. You will lend to many nations but won't borrow from any; you'll rule over many nations but none will rule over you.

7-9　　When you happen on someone who's in trouble or needs help among your people with whom you live in this land that GOD, your God, is giving you, don't look the other way pretending you don't see him. Don't keep a tight grip on your purse. No. Look at him, open your purse, lend whatever and as much as he needs. Don't count the cost. Don't listen to that selfish voice saying, "It's almost the seventh year, the year of All-Debts-Are-Canceled," and turn aside and leave your needy neighbor in the lurch, refusing to help him. He'll call GOD's attention to you and your blatant sin.

10-11   Give freely and spontaneously. Don't have a stingy heart. The way you handle matters like this triggers God, your God's, blessing in everything you do, all your work and ventures. There are always going to be poor and needy people among you. So I command you: Always be generous, open purse and hands, give to your neighbors in trouble, your poor and hurting neighbors.

12-15   If a Hebrew man or Hebrew woman was sold to you and has served you for six years, in the seventh year you must set him or her free, released into a free life. And when you set them free don't send them off empty-handed. Provide them with some animals, plenty of bread and wine and oil. Load them with provisions from all the blessings with which God, your God, has blessed you. Don't for a minute forget that you were once slaves in Egypt and God, your God, redeemed you from that slave world.

For that reason, this day I command you to do this.

16-17   But if your slave, because he loves you and your family and has a good life with you, says, "I don't want to leave you," then take an awl and pierce through his earlobe into the doorpost, marking him as your slave forever. Do the same with your women slaves who want to stay with you.

18   Don't consider this an unreasonable hardship, this setting your slave free. After all, he's worked six years for you at half the cost of a hired hand.

Believe me, God, your God, will bless you in everything you do.

19-23   Consecrate to God, your God, all the firstborn males in your herds and flocks. Don't use the firstborn from your herds as work animals; don't shear the firstborn from your flocks. These are for you to eat every year, you and your family, in the Presence of God, your God, at the place that God designates for worship. If the animal is defective, lame, say, or blind—anything wrong with it—don't slaughter it as a sacrifice to God, your God. Stay at home and eat it there. Both the ritually clean and unclean may eat it, the same as with a gazelle or a deer. Only you must not eat its blood. Pour the blood out on the ground like water.

1-4   **16** Observe the month of Abib by celebrating the Passover to God, your God. It was in the month of Abib that God, your God, delivered you by night from Egypt. Offer the Passover-Sacrifice to God, your God, at the place God chooses to be worshiped by establishing his name there. Don't eat yeast bread with it; for seven days eat it with unraised bread, hard-times bread, because you left Egypt in a hurry—that bread will keep the memory fresh of how you left Egypt for as long as you live. There is to be no sign of yeast anywhere for seven days. And don't let any of the meat that you sacrifice in the evening be left over until morning.

5-7   Don't sacrifice the Passover in any of the towns that God, your God, gives you other than the one God, your God, designates for worship; there and there only you will offer the Passover-Sacrifice at evening as the sun goes down, marking the time that you left Egypt. Cook and eat it at the place designated by God, your God. Then, at daybreak, turn around and go home.

8   Eat unraised bread for six days. Set aside the seventh day as a holiday; don't do any work.

9-11 Starting from the day you put the sickle to the ripe grain, count out seven weeks. Celebrate the Feast-of-Weeks to GOD, your God, by bringing your Freewill-Offering — give as generously as GOD, your God, has blessed you. Rejoice in the Presence of GOD, your God: you, your son, your daughter, your servant, your maid, the Levite who lives in your neighborhood, the foreigner, the orphan and widow among you; rejoice at the place GOD, your God, will set aside to be worshiped.

12 Don't forget that you were once a slave in Egypt. So be diligent in observing these regulations.

13-15 Observe the Feast-of-Booths for seven days when you gather the harvest from your threshing-floor and your wine-vat. Rejoice at your festival: you, your son, your daughter, your servant, your maid, the Levite, the foreigner, and the orphans and widows who live in your neighborhood. Celebrate the Feast to GOD, your God, for seven days at the place GOD designates. GOD, your God, has been blessing you in your harvest and in all your work, so make a day of it — really celebrate!

16-17 All your men must appear before GOD, your God, three times each year at the place he designates: at the Feast-of-Unraised-Bread (Passover), at the Feast-of-Weeks, and at the Feast-of-Booths. No one is to show up in the Presence of GOD empty-handed; each man must bring as much as he can manage, giving generously in response to the blessings of GOD, your God.

18-19 Appoint judges and officers, organized by tribes, in all the towns that GOD, your God, is giving you. They are to judge the people fairly and honestly. Don't twist the law. Don't play favorites. Don't take a bribe — a bribe blinds even a wise person; it undermines the intentions of the best of people.

20 The right! The right! Pursue only what's right! It's the only way you can really live and possess the land that GOD, your God, is giving you.

21-22 Don't plant fertility Asherah trees alongside the Altar of GOD, your God, that you build. Don't set up phallic sex pillars — GOD, your God, hates them.

17 And don't sacrifice to GOD, your God, an ox or sheep that is defective or has anything at all wrong with it. That's an abomination, an insult to GOD, your God.

2-5 If you find anyone within the towns that GOD, your God, is giving you doing what is wrong in GOD's eyes, breaking his covenant by going off to worship other gods, bowing down to them — the sun, say, or the moon, or any rebel sky-gods — look at the evidence and investigate carefully. If you find that it is true, that, in fact, an abomination has been committed in Israel, then you are to take the man or woman who did this evil thing outside your city gates and stone the man or the woman. Hurl stones at the person until dead.

6-7 But only on the testimony of two or three witnesses may a person be put to death. No one may be put to death on the testimony of one witness. The witnesses must throw the first stones in the execution, then the rest of the community joins in. You have to purge the evil from your community.

8-9 When matters of justice come up that are too much for you — hard cases regarding homicides, legal disputes, fights — take them up to the central place of worship that GOD, your God, has designated. Bring them to the Levitical priests and the judge who is in office at the time. Consult them and they will hand down the decision for you.

10-13 Then carry out their verdict at the place designated by GOD, your God. Do what they tell you, in exactly the way they tell you. Follow their instructions precisely: Don't leave out anything; don't add anything. Anyone who presumes to override or twist the decision handed down by the priest or judge who was acting in the Presence of GOD, your God, is as good as dead — root him out, rid Israel of the evil. Everyone will take notice and be impressed. That will put an end to presumptuous behavior.

14-17 When you enter the land that GOD, your God, is giving you and take it over and settle down, and then say, "I'm going to get me a king, a king like all the nations around me," make sure you get yourself a king whom GOD, your God, chooses. Choose your king from among your kinsmen; don't take a foreigner — only a kinsman. And make sure he doesn't build up a war machine, amassing military horses and chariots. He must not send people to Egypt to get more horses, because GOD told you, "You'll never go back there again!" And make sure he doesn't build up a harem, collecting wives who will divert him from the straight and narrow. And make sure he doesn't pile up a lot of silver and gold.

18-20 This is what must be done: When he sits down on the throne of his kingdom, the first thing he must do is make himself a copy of this Revelation on a scroll, copied under the supervision of the Levitical priests. That scroll is to remain at his side at all times; he is to study it every day so that he may learn what it means to fear his GOD, living in reverent obedience before these rules and regulations by following them. He must not become proud and arrogant, changing the commands at whim to suit himself or making up his own versions. If he reads and learns, he will have a long reign as king in Israel, he and his sons.

1-2 **18** The Levitical priests — that's the entire tribe of Levi — don't get any land-inheritance with the rest of Israel. They get the Fire-Gift-Offerings of GOD — they will live on that inheritance. But they don't get land-inheritance like the rest of their kinsmen. GOD is their inheritance.

3-5 This is what the priests get from the people from any offering of an ox or a sheep: the shoulder, the two cheeks, and the stomach. You must also give them the firstfruits of your grain, wine, and oil and the first fleece of your sheep, because GOD, your God, has chosen only them and their children out of all your tribes to be present and serve always in the name of GOD, your God.

6-8 If a Levite moves from any town in Israel — and he is quite free to move wherever he desires — and comes to the place GOD designates for worship, he may serve there in the name of GOD along with all his brother Levites who are present and serving in the Presence of GOD. And he will get an equal share to eat, even though he has money from the sale of his parents' possessions.

9-12 When you enter the land that GOD, your God, is giving you, don't take on the abominable ways of life of the nations there. Don't you dare sacrifice your son or daughter in the fire. Don't practice divination, sorcery, fortunetelling, witchery, casting spells, holding séances, or channeling with the dead. People who do these things are an abomination to GOD. It's because of just such abominable practices that GOD, your God, is driving these nations out before you.

13-14 Be completely loyal to GOD, your God. These nations that you're about to run out of the country consort with sorcerers and witches. But not you. GOD, your God, forbids it.

15-16 GOD, your God, is going to raise up a prophet for you. GOD will raise him up from among your kinsmen, a prophet like me. Listen obediently to him. This is what you asked GOD, your God, for at Horeb on the day you were all gathered at the mountain and said, "We can't hear any more from GOD, our God; we can't stand seeing any more fire. We'll die!"

17-19 And GOD said to me, "They're right; they've spoken the truth. I'll raise up for them a prophet like you from their kinsmen. I'll tell him what to say and he will pass on to them everything I command him. And anyone who won't listen to my words spoken by him, I will personally hold responsible.

20 "But any prophet who fakes it, who claims to speak in my name something I haven't commanded him to say, or speaks in the name of other gods, that prophet must die."

21-22 You may be wondering among yourselves, "How can we tell the difference, whether it was GOD who spoke or not?" Here's how: If what the prophet spoke in GOD's name doesn't happen, then obviously GOD wasn't behind it; the prophet made it up. Forget about him.

1-3 **19** When GOD, your God, throws the nations out of the country that GOD, your God, is giving you and you settle down in their cities and houses, you are to set aside three easily accessible cities in the land that GOD, your God, is giving you as your very own. Divide your land into thirds, this land that GOD, your God, is giving you to possess, and build roads to the towns so that anyone who accidentally kills another can flee there.

4-7 This is the guideline for the murderer who flees there to take refuge: He has to have killed his neighbor without premeditation and with no history of bad blood between them. For instance, a man goes with his neighbor into the woods to cut a tree; he swings the ax, the head slips off the handle and hits his neighbor, killing him. He may then flee to one of these cities and save his life. If the city is too far away, the avenger of blood racing in hot-blooded pursuit might catch him since it's such a long distance, and kill him even though he didn't deserve it. It wasn't his fault. There was no history of hatred between them. Therefore I command you: Set aside the three cities for yourselves.

8-10 When GOD, your God, enlarges your land, extending its borders as he solemnly promised your ancestors, by giving you the whole land he promised them because you are diligently living the way I'm commanding you today, namely, to love GOD, your God, and do what he tells you all your life; and when that happens, then add three more to these three cities so that there is no chance of innocent blood being spilled in your land. GOD, your God, is giving you this land as an inheritance—you don't want to pollute it with innocent blood and bring bloodguilt upon yourselves.

11-13 On the other hand, if a man with a history of hatred toward his neighbor waits in ambush, then jumps him, mauls and kills him, and then runs to one of these cities, that's a different story. The elders of his own city are to send for him and have him brought back. They are to hand him over to the avenger of blood for execution. Don't feel sorry for him. Clean out the pollution of wrongful murder from Israel so that you'll be able to live well and breathe clean air.

14 Don't move your neighbor's boundary markers, the longstanding landmarks set up by your pioneer ancestors defining their property.

15 You cannot convict anyone of a crime or sin on the word of one witness. You need two or three witnesses to make a case.

16-21 If a hostile witness stands to accuse someone of a wrong, then both parties involved in the quarrel must stand in the Presence of GOD before the priests and judges who are in office at that time. The judges must conduct a careful investigation; if the witness turns out to be a false witness and has lied against his fellow Israelite, give him the same medicine he intended for the other party. Clean the polluting evil from your company. People will hear of what you've done and be impressed; that will put a stop to this kind of evil among you. Don't feel sorry for the person: It's life for life, eye for eye, tooth for tooth, hand for hand, foot for foot.

1-4 When you go to war against your enemy and see horses and chariots and soldiers far outnumbering you, do not recoil in fear of them; GOD, your God, who brought you up out of Egypt is with you. When the battle is about to begin, let the priest come forward and speak to the troops. He'll say, "Attention, Israel. In a few minutes you're going to do battle with your enemies. Don't waver in resolve. Don't fear. Don't hesitate. Don't panic. GOD, your God, is right there with you, fighting with you against your enemies, fighting to win."

5-7 Then let the officers step up and speak to the troops: "Is there a man here who has built a new house but hasn't yet dedicated it? Let him go home right now lest he die in battle and another man dedicate it. And is there a man here who has planted a vineyard but hasn't yet enjoyed the grapes? Let him go home right now lest he die in battle and another man enjoy the grapes. Is there a man here engaged to marry who hasn't yet taken his wife? Let him go home right now lest he die in battle and another man take her."

8 The officers will then continue, "And is there a man here who is wavering in resolve and afraid? Let him go home right now so that he doesn't

infect his fellows with his timidity and cowardly spirit."

9   When the officers have finished speaking to the troops, let them appoint commanders of the troops who shall muster them by units.

10-15   When you come up against a city to attack it, call out, "Peace?" If they answer, "Yes, peace!" and open the city to you, then everyone found there will be conscripted as forced laborers and work for you. But if they don't settle for peace and insist on war, then go ahead and attack. GOD, your God, will give them to you. Kill all the men with your swords. But don't kill the women and children and animals. Everything inside the town you can take as plunder for you to use and eat — GOD, your God, gives it to you. This is the way you deal with the distant towns, the towns that don't belong to the nations at hand.

16-18   But with the towns of the people that GOD, your God, is giving you as an inheritance, it's different: don't leave anyone alive. Consign them to holy destruction: the Hittites, Amorites, Canaanites, Perizzites, Hivites, and Jebusites, obeying the command of GOD, your God. This is so there won't be any of them left to teach you to practice the abominations that they engage in with their gods and you end up sinning against GOD, your God.

19-20   When you mount an attack on a town and the siege goes on a long time, don't start cutting down the trees, swinging your axes against them. Those trees are your future food; don't cut them down. Are trees soldiers who come against you with weapons? The exception can be those trees which don't produce food; you can chop them down and use the timbers to build siege engines against the town that is resisting you until it falls.

1-8   **21** If a dead body is found on the ground, this ground that GOD, your God, has given you, lying out in the open, and no one knows who killed him, your leaders and judges are to go out and measure the distance from the body to the nearest cities. The leaders and judges of the city that is nearest the corpse will then take a heifer that has never been used for work, never had a yoke on it. The leaders will take the heifer to a valley with a stream, a valley that has never been plowed or planted, and there break the neck of the heifer. The Levitical priests will then step up. GOD has chosen them to serve him in these matters by settling legal disputes and violent crimes and by pronouncing blessings in GOD's name. Finally, all the leaders of that town that is nearest the body will wash their hands over the heifer that had its neck broken at the stream and say, "We didn't kill this man and we didn't see who did it. Purify your people Israel whom you redeemed, O GOD. Clear your people Israel from any guilt in this murder."

8-9   That will clear them from any responsibility in the murder. By following these procedures you will have absolved yourselves of any part in the murder because you will have done what is right in GOD's sight.

10-14   When you go to war against your enemies and GOD, your God, gives you victory and you take prisoners, and then you notice among the prisoners of war a good-looking woman whom you find attractive and would like to marry, this is what you do: Take her home; have her trim her hair, cut her nails, and discard the clothes she was wearing when captured. She is then to stay in your home for a full month, mourning her father and mother. Then you may go to bed with her as husband and wife. If it turns out you don't like her, you must let her go and live wherever she wishes. But you can't sell her or use her as a slave since you've humiliated her.

15-17   When a man has two wives, one loved and the other hated, and they both give him sons, but the firstborn is from the hated wife, at the time he divides the inheritance with his sons he must not treat the son of the loved wife as the firstborn, cutting out the son of the hated wife, who is the actual firstborn. No, he must acknowledge the inheritance rights of the real firstborn, the son of the hated wife, by giving him a double share of the inheritance: that son is the first proof of his virility; the rights of the firstborn belong to him.

18-20   When a man has a stubborn son, a real rebel who won't do a thing his mother and father tell him, and even though they discipline him he still won't obey, his father and mother shall forcibly bring him before the leaders at the city gate and say to the city fathers, "This son of ours is a stubborn rebel; he won't listen to a thing we say. He's a glutton and a drunk."

21   Then all the men of the town are to throw rocks at him until he's dead. You will have purged the evil pollution from among you. All Israel will hear what's happened and be in awe.

22-23   When a man has committed a capital crime, been given the death sentence, executed and hung from a tree, don't leave his dead body hanging overnight from the tree. Give him a decent burial that same day so that you don't desecrate your GOD-given land — a hanged man is an insult to God.

1-3   **22** If you see your kinsman's ox or sheep wandering off loose, don't look the other way as if you didn't see it. Return it promptly. If your fellow Israelite is not close by or you don't know whose it is, take the animal home with you and take care of it until your fellow asks about it. Then return it to him. Do the same if it's his donkey or a piece of clothing or anything else your fellow Israelite loses. Don't look the other way as if you didn't see it.

4   If you see your fellow's donkey or ox injured along the road, don't look the other way. Help him get it up and on its way.

5   A woman must not wear a man's clothing, nor a man wear women's clothing. This kind of thing is an abomination to GOD, your God.

6-7   When you come across a bird's nest alongside the road, whether in a tree or on the ground, and the mother is sitting on the young or on the eggs, don't take the mother with the young. You may take the babies, but let the mother go so that you will live a good and long life.

8   When you build a new house, make a parapet around your roof to make

it safe so that someone doesn't fall off and die and your family become responsible for the death.

9   Don't plant two kinds of seed in your vineyard. If you do, you will forfeit what you've sown, the total production of the vineyard.

10   Don't plow with an ox and a donkey yoked together.

11   Don't wear clothes of mixed fabrics, wool and linen together.

12   Make tassels on the four corners of the cloak you use to cover yourself.

13-19   If a man marries a woman, sleeps with her, and then turns on her, calling her a slut, giving her a bad name, saying, "I married this woman, but when I slept with her I discovered she wasn't a virgin," then the father and mother of the girl are to take her with the proof of her virginity to the town leaders at the gate. The father is to tell the leaders, "I gave my daughter to this man as wife and he turned on her, rejecting her. And now he has slanderously accused her, claiming that she wasn't a virgin. But look at this, here is the proof of my daughter's virginity." And then he is to spread out her bloodstained wedding garment before the leaders for their examination. The town leaders then are to take the husband, whip him, fine him a hundred pieces of silver, and give it to the father of the girl. The man gave a virgin girl of Israel a bad name. He has to keep her as his wife and can never divorce her.

20-21   But if it turns out that the accusation is true and there is no evidence of the girl's virginity, the men of the town are to take her to the door of her father's house and stone her to death. She acted disgracefully in Israel. She lived like a whore while still in her parents' home. Purge the evil from among you.

22   If a man is found sleeping with another man's wife, both must die. Purge that evil from Israel.

23-24   If a man comes upon a virgin in town, a girl who is engaged to another man, and sleeps with her, take both of them to the town gate and stone them until they die—the girl because she didn't yell out for help in the town and the man because he raped her, violating the fiancée of his neighbor. You must purge the evil from among you.

25-27   But if it was out in the country that the man found the engaged girl and grabbed and raped her, only the man is to die, the man who raped her. Don't do anything to the girl; she did nothing wrong. This is similar to the case of a man who comes across his neighbor out in the country and murders him; when the engaged girl yelled out for help, there was no one around to hear or help her.

28-29   When a man comes upon a virgin who has never been engaged and grabs and rapes her and they are found out, the man who raped her has to give her father fifty pieces of silver. He has to marry her because he took advantage of her. And he can never divorce her.

30   A man may not marry his father's ex-wife—that would violate his father's rights.

23 ¹ No eunuch is to enter the congregation of GOD.

² No bastard is to enter the congregation of GOD, even to the tenth generation, nor any of his children.

³⁻⁶ No Ammonite or Moabite is to enter the congregation of GOD, even to the tenth generation, nor any of his children, ever. Those nations didn't treat you with hospitality on your travels out of Egypt, and on top of that they also hired Balaam son of Beor from Pethor in Mesopotamia to curse you. GOD, your God, refused to listen to Balaam but turned the curse into a blessing—how GOD, your God, loves you! Don't even try to get along with them or do anything for them, ever.

⁷ But don't spurn an Edomite; he's your kin.

And don't spurn an Egyptian; you were a foreigner in his land.

⁸ Children born to Edomites and Egyptians may enter the congregation of GOD in the third generation.

⁹⁻¹¹ When you are camped out, at war with your enemies, be careful to keep yourself from anything ritually defiling. If one of your men has become ritually unclean because of a nocturnal emission, he must go outside the camp and stay there until evening when he can wash himself, returning to the camp at sunset.

¹²⁻¹⁴ Mark out an area outside the camp where you can go to relieve yourselves. Along with your weapons have a stick with you. After you relieve yourself, dig a hole with the stick and cover your excrement. GOD, your God, strolls through your camp; he's present to deliver you and give you victory over your enemies. Keep your camp holy; don't permit anything indecent or offensive in GOD's eyes.

¹⁵⁻¹⁶ Don't return a runaway slave to his master; he's come to you for refuge. Let him live wherever he wishes within the protective gates of your city. Don't take advantage of him.

¹⁷⁻¹⁸ No daughter of Israel is to become a sacred prostitute; and no son of Israel is to become a sacred prostitute. And don't bring the fee of a sacred whore or the earnings of a priest-pimp to the house of GOD, your God, to pay for any vow—they are both an abomination to GOD, your God.

¹⁹⁻²⁰ Don't charge interest to your kinsmen on any loan: not for money or food or clothing or anything else that could earn interest. You may charge foreigners interest, but you may not charge your brothers interest; that way GOD, your God, will bless all the work that you take up and the land that you are entering to possess.

²¹⁻²³ When you make a vow to GOD, your God, don't put off keeping it; GOD, your God, expects you to keep it and if you don't you're guilty. But if you don't make a vow in the first place, there's no sin. If you say you're going to do something, do it. Keep the vow you willingly vowed to GOD, your God. You promised it, so do it.

24-25   When you enter your neighbor's vineyard, you may eat all the grapes you want until you're full, but you may not put any in your bucket or bag. And when you walk through the ripe grain of your neighbor, you may pick the heads of grain, but you may not swing your sickle there.

1-4   **24** If a man marries a woman and then it happens that he no longer likes her because he has found something wrong with her, he may give her divorce papers, put them in her hand, and send her off. After she leaves, if she becomes another man's wife and he also comes to hate her and this second husband also gives her divorce papers, puts them in her hand, and sends her off, or if he should die, then the first husband who divorced her can't marry her again. She has made herself ritually unclean, and her remarriage would be an abomination in the Presence of GOD and defile the land with sin, this land that GOD, your God, is giving you as an inheritance.

5   When a man takes a new wife, he is not to go out with the army or be given any business or work duties. He gets one year off simply to be at home making his wife happy.

6   Don't seize a handmill or an upper millstone as collateral for a loan. You'd be seizing someone's very life.

7   If a man is caught kidnapping one of his kinsmen, someone of the People of Israel, to enslave or sell him, the kidnapper must die. Purge that evil from among you.

8-9   Warning! If a serious skin disease breaks out, follow exactly the rules set down by the Levitical priests. Follow them precisely as I commanded them. Don't forget what GOD, your God, did to Miriam on your way out of Egypt.

10-13   When you make a loan of any kind to your neighbor, don't enter his house to claim his pledge. Wait outside. Let the man to whom you made the pledge bring the pledge to you outside. And if he is destitute, don't use his cloak as a bedroll; return it to him at nightfall so that he can sleep in his cloak and bless you. In the sight of GOD, your God, that will be viewed as a righteous act.

14-15   Don't abuse a laborer who is destitute and needy, whether he is a fellow Israelite living in your land and in your city. Pay him at the end of each workday; he's living from hand to mouth and needs it now. If you hold back his pay, he'll protest to GOD and you'll have sin on your books.

16   Parents shall not be put to death for their children, nor children for their parents. Each person shall be put to death for his own sin.

17-18   Make sure foreigners and orphans get their just rights. Don't take the cloak of a widow as security for a loan. Don't ever forget that you were once slaves in Egypt and GOD, your God, got you out of there. I command you: Do what I'm telling you.

19-22   When you harvest your grain and forget a sheaf back in the field, don't go back and get it; leave it for the foreigner, the orphan, and the widow so that GOD, your God, will bless you in all your work. When you shake the olives off your trees, don't go back over the branches and strip them bare — what's left is for the foreigner, the orphan, and the widow. And when you cut the grapes in your vineyard, don't take every last grape — leave a few for the foreigner, the orphan, and the widow. Don't ever forget that you were a slave in Egypt. I command you: Do what I'm telling you.

1-3   ## 25

When men have a legal dispute, let them go to court; the judges will decide between them, declaring one innocent and the other guilty. If the guilty one deserves punishment, the judge will have him prostrate himself before him and lashed as many times as his crime deserves, but not more than forty. If you hit him more than forty times, you will degrade him to something less than human.

4   Don't muzzle an ox while it is threshing.

5-6   When brothers are living together and one of them dies without having had a son, the widow of the dead brother shall not marry a stranger from outside the family; her husband's brother is to come to her and marry her and do the brother-in-law's duty by her. The first son that she bears shall be named after her dead husband so his name won't die out in Israel.

7-10   But if the brother doesn't want to marry his sister-in-law, she is to go to the leaders at the city gate and say, "My brother-in-law refuses to keep his brother's name alive in Israel; he won't agree to do the brother-in-law's duty by me." Then the leaders will call for the brother and confront him. If he stands there defiant and says, "I don't want her," his sister-in-law is to pull his sandal off his foot, spit in his face, and say, "This is what happens to the man who refuses to build up the family of his brother — his name in Israel will be Family-No-Sandal."

11-12   When two men are in a fight and the wife of the one man, trying to rescue her husband, grabs the genitals of the man hitting him, you are to cut off her hand. Show no pity.

13-16   Don't carry around with you two weights, one heavy and the other light, and don't keep two measures at hand, one large and the other small. Use only one weight, a true and honest weight, and one measure, a true and honest measure, so that you will live a long time on the land that GOD, your God, is giving you. Dishonest weights and measures are an abomination to GOD, your God — all this corruption in business deals!

17-19   Don't forget what Amalek did to you on the road after you left Egypt, how he attacked you when you were tired, barely able to put one foot in front of another, mercilessly cut off your stragglers, and had no regard for God. When GOD, your God, gives you rest from all the enemies that surround you in the inheritance-land GOD, your God, is giving you to possess, you are to wipe the name of Amalek from off the Earth. Don't forget!

1-5   ## 26

Once you enter the land that GOD, your God, is giving you as an inheritance and take it over and settle down, you are to take some of all the firstfruits of what you grow in the land that GOD, your God, is giving you, put them in a basket and go to the place GOD, your

God, sets apart for you to worship him. At that time, go to the priest who is there and say, "I announce to GOD, your God, today that I have entered the land that GOD promised our ancestors that he'd give to us." The priest will take the basket from you and place it on the Altar of GOD, your God. And there in the Presence of GOD, your God, you will recite:

5-10
A wandering Aramean was my father,
he went down to Egypt and sojourned there,
he and just a handful of his brothers at first, but soon
they became a great nation, mighty and many.
The Egyptians abused and battered us,
in a cruel and savage slavery.
We cried out to GOD, the God-of-Our-Fathers:
He listened to our voice, he saw
our destitution, our trouble, our cruel plight.
And GOD took us out of Egypt
with his strong hand and long arm, terrible and great,
with signs and miracle-wonders.
And he brought us to this place,
gave us this land flowing with milk and honey.
So here I am. I've brought the firstfruits
of what I've grown on this ground you gave me, O GOD.

10-11
Then place it in the Presence of GOD, your God. Prostrate yourselves in the Presence of GOD, your God. And rejoice! Celebrate all the good things that GOD, your God, has given you and your family; you and the Levite and the foreigner who lives with you.

12-14
Every third year, the year of the tithe, give a tenth of your produce to the Levite, the foreigner, the orphan, and the widow so that they may eat their fill in your cities. And then, in the Presence of GOD, your God, say this:

I have brought the sacred share,
I've given it to the Levite, foreigner, orphan, and widow.
What you commanded, I've done.
I haven't detoured around your commands,
I haven't forgotten a single one.
I haven't eaten from the sacred share while mourning,
I haven't removed any of it while ritually unclean,
I haven't used it in funeral feasts.
I have listened obediently to the Voice of GOD, my God,
I have lived the way you commanded me.

15
Look down from your holy house in Heaven!
Bless your people Israel and the ground you gave us,
just as you promised our ancestors you would,
this land flowing with milk and honey.

16-17 This very day GOD, your God, commands you to follow these rules and regulations, to live them out with everything you have in you. You've renewed your vows today that GOD is your God, that you'll live the way he shows you; do what he tells you in the rules, regulations, and commandments; and listen obediently to him.

18-19 And today GOD has reaffirmed that you are dearly held treasure just as he promised, a people entrusted with keeping his commandments, a people set high above all other nations that he's made, high in praise, fame, and honor: you're a people holy to GOD, your God. That's what he has promised.

1-3 **27** Moses commanded the leaders of Israel and charged the people: Keep every commandment that I command you today. On the day you cross the Jordan into the land that GOD, your God, is giving you, erect large stones and coat them with plaster. As soon as you cross over the river, write on the stones all the words of this Revelation so that you'll enter the land that GOD, your God, is giving you, that land flowing with milk and honey that GOD, the God-of-Your-Fathers, promised you.

4-7 So when you've crossed the Jordan, erect these stones on Mount Ebal. Then coat them with plaster. Build an Altar of stones for GOD, your God, there on the mountain. Don't use an iron tool on the stones; build the Altar to GOD, your God, with uncut stones and offer your Whole-Burnt-Offerings on it to GOD, your God. When you sacrifice your Peace-Offerings you will also eat them there, rejoicing in the Presence of GOD, your God.

8 Write all the words of this Revelation on the stones. Incise them sharply.

9-10 Moses and the Levitical priests addressed all Israel: Quiet. Listen obediently, Israel. This very day you have become the people of GOD, your God. Listen to the Voice of GOD, your God. Keep his commandments and regulations that I'm commanding you today.

11-13 That day Moses commanded: After you've crossed the Jordan, these tribes will stand on Mount Gerizim to bless the people: Simeon, Levi, Judah, Issachar, Joseph, and Benjamin. And these will stand on Mount Ebal for the curse: Reuben, Gad, Asher, Zebulun, Dan, and Naphtali.

14-26 The Levites, acting as spokesmen and speaking loudly, will address Israel:

GOD's curse on anyone who carves or casts a god-image — an abomination to GOD made by a craftsman — and sets it up in secret.
    All respond: *Yes. Absolutely.*
GOD's curse on anyone who demeans a parent.
    All respond: *Yes. Absolutely.*
GOD's curse on anyone who moves his neighbor's boundary marker.
    All respond: *Yes. Absolutely.*
GOD's curse on anyone who misdirects a blind man on the road.
    All respond: *Yes. Absolutely.*
GOD's curse on anyone who interferes with justice due the foreigner, orphan, or widow.
    All respond: *Yes. Absolutely.*

GOD's curse on anyone who has sex with his father's wife; he has violated the woman who belongs to his father.

All respond: *Yes. Absolutely.*

GOD's curse on anyone who has sex with an animal.

All respond: *Yes. Absolutely.*

GOD's curse on anyone who has sex with his sister, the daughter of his father or mother.

All respond: *Yes. Absolutely.*

GOD's curse on anyone who has sex with his mother-in-law.

All respond: *Yes. Absolutely.*

GOD's curse on anyone who kills his neighbor in secret.

All respond: *Yes. Absolutely.*

GOD's curse on anyone who takes a bribe to kill an innocent person.

All respond: *Yes. Absolutely.*

GOD's curse on whoever does not give substance to the words of this Revelation by living them.

All respond: *Yes. Absolutely.*

28 **1-6** If you listen obediently to the Voice of GOD, your God, and heartily obey all his commandments that I command you today, GOD, your God, will place you on high, high above all the nations of the world. All these blessings will come down on you and spread out beyond you because you have responded to the Voice of GOD, your God:

> GOD's blessing inside the city,
> GOD's blessing in the country;
> GOD's blessing on your children,
> > the crops of your land,
> > the young of your livestock,
> > the calves of your herds,
> > the lambs of your flocks.
> GOD's blessing on your basket and bread bowl;
> GOD's blessing in your coming in,
> GOD's blessing in your going out.

7 GOD will defeat your enemies who attack you. They'll come at you on one road and run away on seven roads.

8 GOD will order a blessing on your barns and workplaces; he'll bless you in the land that GOD, your God, is giving you.

9 GOD will form you as a people holy to him, just as he promised you, if you keep the commandments of GOD, your God, and live the way he has shown you.

10 All the peoples on Earth will see you living under the Name of GOD and hold you in respectful awe.

11-14 GOD will lavish you with good things: children from your womb, offspring from your animals, and crops from your land, the land that GOD promised your ancestors that he would give you. GOD will throw open the doors of his sky vaults and pour rain on your land on schedule and bless the work you take in hand. You will lend to many nations but you yourself won't have to take out a loan. GOD will make you the head, not the tail; you'll always be the top dog, never the bottom dog, as you obediently listen to and diligently keep the commands of GOD, your God, that I am commanding you today. Don't swerve an inch to the right or left from the words that I command you today by going off following and worshiping other gods.

15-19   Here's what will happen if you don't obediently listen to the Voice of GOD, your God, and diligently keep all the commandments and guidelines that I'm commanding you today. All these curses will come down hard on you:

GOD's curse in the city,
GOD's curse in the country;
GOD's curse on your basket and bread bowl;
GOD's curse on your children,
    the crops of your land,
    the young of your livestock,
    the calves of your herds,
    the lambs of your flocks.
GOD's curse in your coming in,
GOD's curse in your going out.

20   GOD will send The Curse, The Confusion, The Contrariness down on everything you try to do until you've been destroyed and there's nothing left of you — all because of your evil pursuits that led you to abandon me.

21   GOD will infect you with The Disease, wiping you right off the land that you're going in to possess.

22   GOD will set consumption and fever and rash and seizures and dehydration and blight and jaundice on you. They'll hunt you down until they kill you.

23-24   The sky over your head will become an iron roof, the ground under your feet, a slab of concrete. From out of the skies GOD will rain ash and dust down on you until you suffocate.

25-26   GOD will defeat you by enemy attack. You'll come at your enemies on one road and run away on seven roads. All the kingdoms of Earth will see you as a horror. Carrion birds and animals will boldly feast on your dead body with no one to chase them away.

27-29   GOD will hit you hard with the boils of Egypt, hemorrhoids, scabs, and an incurable itch. He'll make you go crazy and blind and senile. You'll grope around in the middle of the day like a blind person feeling his way through a lifetime of darkness; you'll never get to where you're going. Not a day will go by that you're not abused and robbed. And no one is going to help you.

30-31   You'll get engaged to a woman and another man will take her for his mistress; you'll build a house and never live in it; you'll plant a garden and never eat so much as a carrot; you'll watch your ox get butchered and not get a single steak from it; your donkey will be stolen from in front of you and you'll never see it again; your sheep will be sent off to your enemies and no one will lift a hand to help you.

32-34   Your sons and daughters will be shipped off to foreigners; you'll wear your eyes out looking vainly for them, helpless to do a thing. Your crops and everything you work for will be eaten and used by foreigners; you'll spend the rest of your lives abused and knocked around. What you see will drive you crazy.

35   GOD will hit you with painful boils on your knees and legs and no healing or relief from head to foot.

36-37   GOD will lead you and the king you set over you to a country neither you nor your ancestors have heard of; there you'll worship other gods, no-gods of wood and stone. Among all the peoples where GOD will take you, you'll be treated as a lesson or a proverb — a horror!

38-42   You'll plant sacks and sacks of seed in the field but get almost nothing — the grasshoppers will devour it. You'll plant and hoe and prune vineyards but won't drink or put up any wine — the worms will devour them. You'll have groves of olive trees everywhere, but you'll have no oil to rub on your face or hands — the olives will have fallen off. You'll have sons and daughters but they won't be yours for long — they'll go off to captivity. Locusts will take over all your trees and crops.

43-44   The foreigner who lives among you will climb the ladder, higher and higher, while you go deeper and deeper into the hole. He'll lend to you; you won't lend to him. He'll be the head; you'll be the tail.

45-46   All these curses are going to come on you. They're going to hunt you down and get you until there's nothing left of you because you didn't obediently listen to the Voice of GOD, your God, and diligently keep his commandments and guidelines that I commanded you. The curses will serve as signposts, warnings to your children ever after.

47-48   Because you didn't serve GOD, your God, out of the joy and goodness of your heart in the great abundance, you'll have to serve your enemies whom GOD will send against you. Life will be famine and drought, rags and wretchedness; then he'll put an iron yoke on your neck until he's destroyed you.

48-52   Yes, GOD will raise up a faraway nation against you, swooping down on you like an eagle, a nation whose language you can't understand, a mean-faced people, cruel to grandmothers and babies alike. They'll ravage the young of your animals and the crops from your fields until you're destroyed. They'll leave nothing behind: no grain, no wine, no oil, no calves, no lambs — and finally, no *you*. They'll lay siege to you while you're huddled behind your town gates. They'll knock those high, proud walls flat, those walls behind which you felt so safe. They'll lay siege to your fortified cities all over the country, this country that GOD, your God, has given you.

53-55   And you'll end up cannibalizing your own sons and daughters that GOD, your God, has given you. When the suffering from the siege gets extreme, you're going to eat your own babies. The most gentle and caring man among you will turn hard, his eye evil, against his own brother, his cherished wife, and even the rest of his children who are still alive, refusing to share with them a scrap of meat from the cannibal child-stew he is eating. He's lost everything, even his humanity, in the suffering of the siege that your enemy mounts against your fortified towns.

56-57   And the most gentle and caring woman among you, a woman who wouldn't step on a wildflower, will turn hard, her eye evil, against her cherished husband, against her son, against her daughter, against even the afterbirth of her newborn infants; she plans to eat them in secret — she does eat them! — because she has lost everything, even her humanity, in the suffering of the siege that your enemy mounts against your fortified towns.

58-61 If you don't diligently keep all the words of this Revelation written in this book, living in holy awe before This Name glorious and terrible, GOD, your God, then GOD will pound you with catastrophes, you and your children, huge interminable catastrophes, hideous interminable illnesses. He'll bring back and stick you with every old Egyptian malady that once terrorized you. And yes, every disease and catastrophe imaginable — things not even written in the Book of this Revelation — GOD will bring on you until you're destroyed.

62 Because you didn't listen obediently to the Voice of GOD, your God, you'll be left with a few pitiful stragglers in place of the dazzling stars-in-the-heavens multitude you had become.

63-66 And this is how things will end up: Just as GOD once enjoyed you, took pleasure in making life good for you, giving you many children, so GOD will enjoy getting rid of you, clearing you off the Earth. He'll weed you out of the very soil that you are entering in to possess. He'll scatter you to the four winds, from one end of the Earth to the other. You'll worship all kinds of other gods, gods neither you nor your parents ever heard of, wood and stone no-gods. But you won't find a home there, you'll not be able to settle down. GOD will give you a restless heart, longing eyes, a homesick soul. You will live in constant jeopardy, terrified of every shadow, never knowing what you'll meet around the next corner.

67 In the morning you'll say, "I wish it were evening." In the evening you'll say, "I wish it were morning." Afraid, terrorized at what's coming next, afraid of the unknown, because of the sights you've witnessed.

68 GOD will ship you back to Egypt by a road I promised you'd never see again. There you'll offer yourselves for sale, both men and women, as slaves to your enemies. And not a buyer to be found.

1 **29** These are the terms of the Covenant that GOD commanded Moses to make with the People of Israel in the land of Moab, renewing the Covenant he made with them at Horeb.

MOSES BLESSES ISRAEL ON THE PLAINS OF MOAB

2-4 Moses called all Israel together and said, You've seen with your own eyes everything that GOD did in Egypt to Pharaoh and his servants, and to the land itself — the massive trials to which you were eyewitnesses, the great signs and miracle-wonders. But GOD didn't give you an understanding heart or perceptive eyes or attentive ears until right now, this very day.

5-6 I took you through the wilderness for forty years and through all that time the clothes on your backs didn't wear out, the sandals on your feet didn't wear out, and you lived well without bread and wine and beer, proving to you that I am in fact GOD, your God.

7-8 When you arrived here in this place, Sihon king of Heshbon and Og king of Bashan met us primed for war but we beat them. We took their land and gave it as an inheritance to the Reubenites, the Gadites, and the half-tribe of Manasseh.

9 Diligently keep the words of this Covenant. Do what they say so that you will live well and wisely in every detail.

10-13   You are all standing here today in the Presence of GOD, your God—the heads of your tribes, your leaders, your officials, all Israel: your babies, your wives, the resident foreigners in your camps who fetch your firewood and water—ready to cross over into the solemnly sworn Covenant that GOD, your God, is making with you today, the Covenant that this day confirms that you are his people and he is GOD, your God, just as he promised you and your ancestors Abraham, Isaac, and Jacob.

14-21   I'm not making this Covenant and its oath with you alone. I *am* making it with you who are standing here today in the Presence of GOD, our God, yes, but also with those who are not here today. You know the conditions in which we lived in Egypt and how we crisscrossed through nations in our travels. You got an eyeful of their obscenities, their wood and stone, silver and gold junk-gods. Don't let down your guard lest even now, today, someone—man or woman, clan or tribe—gets sidetracked from GOD, our God, and gets involved with the no-gods of the nations; lest some poisonous weed sprout and spread among you, a person who hears the words of the Covenant-oath but exempts himself, thinking, "I'll live just the way I please, thank you," and ends up ruining life for everybody. GOD won't let him off the hook. GOD's anger and jealousy will erupt like a volcano against that person. The curses written in this book will bury him. GOD will delete his name from the records. GOD will separate him out from all the tribes of Israel for special punishment, according to all the curses of the Covenant written in this Book of Revelation.

22-23   The next generation, your children who come after you and the foreigner who comes from a far country, will be appalled when they see the widespread devastation, how GOD made the whole land sick. They'll see a fire-blackened wasteland of brimstone and salt flats, nothing planted, nothing growing, not so much as a blade of grass anywhere—like the overthrow of Sodom and Gomorrah, Admah and Zeboiim, which GOD overthrew in fiery rage.

24   All the nations will ask, "Why did GOD do this to this country? What on earth could have made him this angry?"

25-28   Your children will answer, "Because they abandoned the Covenant of the GOD of their ancestors that he made with them after he got them out of Egypt; they went off and worshiped other gods, submitted to gods they'd never heard of before, gods they had no business dealing with. So GOD's anger erupted against that land and all the curses written in this book came down on it. GOD, furiously angry, pulled them, roots and all, out of their land and dumped them in another country, as you can see."

29   GOD, our God, will take care of the hidden things but the revealed things are our business. It's up to us and our children to attend to all the terms in this Revelation.

1-5   30 Here's what will happen. While you're out among the nations where GOD has dispersed you and the blessings and curses come in just the way I have set them before you, and you and your children take them seriously and come back to GOD, your God, and obey him with your whole heart and soul according to everything that I command you today, GOD, your God, will restore everything you lost; he'll have compassion on you; he'll come back and pick up the pieces from all the places where you were scattered. No matter how far away you end up, GOD, your God, will get you out of there and bring you back to the land your ancestors once possessed. It will be yours again. He will give you a good life and make you more numerous than your ancestors.

6-7 GOD, your God, will cut away the thick calluses on your heart and your children's hearts, freeing you to love GOD, your God, with your whole heart and soul and live, really live. GOD, your God, will put all these curses on your enemies who hated you and were out to get you.

8-9 And you will make a new start, listening obediently to GOD, keeping all his commandments that I'm commanding you today. GOD, your God, will outdo himself in making things go well for you: you'll have babies, get calves, grow crops, and enjoy an all-around good life. Yes, GOD will start enjoying you again, making things go well for you just as he enjoyed doing it for your ancestors.

10 But only if you listen obediently to GOD, your God, and keep the commandments and regulations written in this Book of Revelation. Nothing halfhearted here; you must return to GOD, your God, totally, heart and soul, holding nothing back.

11-14 This commandment that I'm commanding you today isn't too much for you, it's not out of your reach. It's not on a high mountain — you don't have to get mountaineers to climb the peak and bring it down to your level and explain it before you can live it. And it's not across the ocean — you don't have to send sailors out to get it, bring it back, and then explain it before you can live it. No. The word is right here and now — as near as the tongue in your mouth, as near as the heart in your chest. Just do it!

15 Look at what I've done for you today: I've placed in front of you
    Life and Good
    Death and Evil.

16 And I command you today: Love GOD, your God. Walk in his ways. Keep his commandments, regulations, and rules so that you will live, really live, live exuberantly, blessed by GOD, your God, in the land you are about to enter and possess.

17-18 But I warn you: If you have a change of heart, refuse to listen obediently, and willfully go off to serve and worship other gods, you will most certainly die. You won't last long in the land that you are crossing the Jordan to enter and possess.

19-20 I call Heaven and Earth to witness against you today: I place before you Life and Death, Blessing and Curse. Choose life so that you and your children will live. And love GOD, your God, listening obediently to him, firmly embracing him. Oh yes, he is life itself, a long life settled on the soil that GOD, your God, promised to give your ancestors, Abraham, Isaac, and Jacob.

THE CHARGE

1-2 **31** Moses went on and addressed these words to all Israel. He said, "I'm 120 years old today. I can't get about as I used to. And GOD told me, 'You're not going to cross this Jordan River.'

3-5 "GOD, your God, will cross the river ahead of you and destroy the nations in your path so that you may dispossess them. (And Joshua will cross the river before you, as GOD said he would.) GOD will give the nations the same treatment he gave the kings of the Amorites, Sihon and Og, and their land; he'll destroy them. GOD will hand the nations over to you, and you'll treat them exactly as I have commanded you.

6 "Be strong. Take courage. Don't be intimidated. Don't give them a second thought because GOD, your God, is striding ahead of you. He's right there with you. He won't let you down; he won't leave you."

7-8 Then Moses summoned Joshua. He said to him with all Israel watching, "Be strong. Take courage. You will enter the land with this people, this land that GOD promised their ancestors that he'd give them. You will make them the proud possessors of it. GOD is striding ahead of you. He's right there with you. He won't let you down; he won't leave you. Don't be intimidated. Don't worry."

9-13 Moses wrote out this Revelation and gave it to the priests, the sons of Levi, who carried the Chest of the Covenant of GOD, and to all the leaders of Israel. And he gave these orders: "At the end of every seven years, the Year-All-Debts-Are-Canceled, during the pilgrim Festival of Booths when everyone in Israel comes to appear in the Presence of GOD, your God, at the place he designates, read out this Revelation to all Israel, with everyone listening. Gather the people together — men, women, children, and the foreigners living among you — so they can listen well, so they may learn to live in holy awe before GOD, your God, and diligently keep everything in this Revelation. And do this so that their children, who don't yet know all this, will also listen and learn to live in holy awe before GOD, your God, for as long as you live on the land that you are crossing over the Jordan to possess."

14-15 GOD spoke to Moses: "You are about to die. So call Joshua. Meet me in the Tent of Meeting so that I can commission him."

So Moses and Joshua went and stationed themselves in the Tent of Meeting. GOD appeared in the Tent in a Pillar of Cloud. The Cloud was near the entrance of the Tent of Meeting.

16-18 GOD spoke to Moses: "You're about to die and be buried with your ancestors. You'll no sooner be in the grave than this people will be up and whoring after the foreign gods of this country that they are entering. They will abandon me and violate my Covenant that I've made with them. I'll get angry, oh so angry! I'll walk off and leave them on their own, won't so much as look back at them. Then many calamities and disasters will devastate them because they are defenseless. They'll say, 'Isn't it because our God wasn't here that all this evil has come upon us?' But I'll stay out of their lives, keep looking the other way because of all their evil: they took up with other gods!

19-21 "But for right now, copy down this song and teach the People of Israel to sing it by heart. They'll have it then as my witness against them. When I bring them into the land that I promised to their ancestors, a land flowing with milk and honey, and they eat and become full and get fat and then begin fooling around with other gods and worshiping them, and then things start falling apart, many terrible things happening, this song will be there with them as a witness to who they are and what went wrong. Their children won't forget this song; they'll be singing it. Don't think I don't know what they are already scheming to do, and they're not even in the land yet, this land I promised them."

22 So Moses wrote down this song that very day and taught it to the People of Israel.

23 Then GOD commanded Joshua son of Nun saying, "Be strong. Take courage. You will lead the People of Israel into the land I promised to give them. And I'll be right there with you."

24-26 After Moses had finished writing down the words of this Revelation in a book, right down to the last word, he ordered the Levites who were responsible for carrying the Chest of the Covenant of GOD, saying, "Take this Book of Revelation and place it alongside the Chest of the Covenant of GOD, your God. Keep it there as a witness.

27-29 "I know what rebels you are, how stubborn and willful you can be. Even today, while I'm still alive and present with you, you're rebellious against GOD. How much worse when I've died! So gather the leaders of the tribes and the officials here. I have something I need to say directly to them with Heaven and Earth as witnesses. I know that after I die you're going to make a mess of things, abandoning the way I commanded, inviting all kinds of evil consequences in the days ahead. You're determined to do evil in defiance of GOD—I know you are—deliberately provoking his anger by what you do."

30 So with everyone in Israel gathered and listening, Moses taught them the words of this song, from start to finish.

THE SONG

1-5 **32** Listen, Heavens, I have something to tell you.
    Attention, Earth, I've got a mouth full of words.
    My teaching, let it fall like a gentle rain,
    my words arrive like morning dew,
Like a sprinkling rain on new grass,
    like spring showers on the garden.
For it's GOD's Name I'm preaching—
    respond to the greatness of our God!
The Rock: His works are perfect,
    and the way he works is fair and just;
A God you can depend upon, no exceptions,
    a straight-arrow God.
His messed-up, mixed-up children, his non-children,
    throw mud at him but none of it sticks.

6-7 Don't you realize it is GOD you are treating like this?
    This is crazy; don't you have any sense of reverence?
Isn't this your father who created you,
    who made you and gave you a place on Earth?
Read up on what happened before you were born;
    dig into the past, understand your roots.
Ask your parents what it was like before you were born;
    ask the old-ones, they'll tell you a thing or two.

8-9 When the High God gave the nations their stake,
    gave them their place on Earth,
He put each of the peoples within boundaries
    under the care of divine guardians.
But GOD himself took charge of his people,

took Jacob on as his personal concern.

10-14 He found him out in the wilderness,
　　in an empty, windswept wasteland.
He threw his arms around him, lavished attention on him,
　　guarding him as the apple of his eye.
He was like an eagle hovering over its nest,
　　overshadowing its young,
Then spreading its wings, lifting them into the air,
　　teaching them to fly.
GOD alone led him;
　　there was not a foreign god in sight.
GOD lifted him onto the hilltops,
　　so he could feast on the crops in the fields.
He fed him honey from the rock,
　　oil from granite crags,
Curds of cattle and the milk of sheep,
　　the choice cuts of lambs and goats,
Fine Bashan rams, high-quality wheat,
　　and the blood of grapes: you drank good wine!

15-18 Jeshurun put on weight and bucked;
　　you got fat, became obese, a tub of lard.
He abandoned the God who made him,
　　he mocked the Rock of his salvation.
They made him jealous with their foreign newfangled gods,
　　and with obscenities they vexed him no end.
They sacrificed to no-god demons,
　　gods they knew nothing about,
The latest in gods, fresh from the market,
　　gods your ancestors would never call "gods."
You walked out on the Rock who gave you your life,
　　forgot the birth-God who brought you into the world.

19-25 GOD saw it and turned on his heel,
　　angered and hurt by his sons and daughters.
He said, "From now on I'm looking the other way.
　　Wait and see what happens to them.
Oh, they're a turned-around, upside-down generation!
　　Who knows what they'll do from one moment to the next?
They've goaded me with their no-gods,
　　infuriated me with their hot-air gods;
I'm going to goad them with a no-people,
　　with a hollow nation incense them.
My anger started a fire,
　　a wildfire burning deep down in Sheol,
Then shooting up and devouring the Earth and its crops,
　　setting all the mountains, from bottom to top, on fire.
I'll pile catastrophes on them,
　　I'll shoot my arrows at them:
Starvation, blistering heat, killing disease;

I'll send snarling wild animals to attack from the forest
and venomous creatures to strike from the dust.
Killing in the streets,
terror in the houses,
Young men and virgins alike struck down,
and yes, breast-feeding babies and gray-haired old men."

26-27 I could have said, "I'll hack them to pieces,
wipe out all trace of them from the Earth,"
Except that I feared the enemy would grab the chance
to take credit for all of it,
Crowing, "Look what we did!
GOD had nothing to do with this."

28-33 They are a nation of ninnies,
they don't know enough to come in out of the rain.
If they had any sense at all, they'd know this;
they would see what's coming down the road.
How could one soldier chase a thousand enemies off,
or two men run off two thousand,
Unless their Rock had sold them,
unless GOD had given them away?
For their rock is nothing compared to our Rock;
even our enemies say that.
They're a vine that comes right out of Sodom,
who they are is rooted in Gomorrah;
Their grapes are poison grapes,
their grape-clusters bitter.
Their wine is rattlesnake venom,
mixed with lethal cobra poison.

34-35 Don't you realize that I have my shelves
well stocked, locked behind iron doors?
I'm in charge of vengeance and payback,
just waiting for them to slip up;
And the day of their doom is just around the corner,
sudden and swift and sure.

36-38 Yes, GOD will judge his people,
but oh how compassionately he'll do it.
When he sees their weakened plight
and there is no one left, slave or free,
He'll say, "So where are their gods,
the rock in which they sought refuge,
The gods who feasted on the fat of their sacrifices
and drank the wine of their drink-offerings?
Let them show their stuff and help you,
let them give you a hand!

39-42 "Do you see it now? Do you see that I'm the one?
Do you see that there's no other god beside me?

I bring death and I give life, I wound and I heal—
    there is no getting away from or around me!
I raise my hand in solemn oath;
    I say, 'I'm always around. By that very life I promise:
When I sharpen my lightning sword
    and execute judgment,
I take vengeance on my enemies
    and pay back those who hate me.
I'll make my arrows drunk with blood,
    my sword will gorge itself on flesh,
Feasting on slain and captive alike,
    the proud and vain enemy corpses.'"

43   Celebrate, nations, join the praise of his people.
    He avenges the deaths of his servants,
Pays back his enemies with vengeance,
    and cleanses his land for his people.

44-47   Moses came and recited all the words of this song in the hearing of the people, he and Joshua son of Nun. When Moses had finished saying all these words to all Israel, he said, "Take to heart all these words to which I give witness today and urgently command your children to put them into practice, every single word of this Revelation. Yes. This is no small matter for you; it's your life. In keeping this word you'll have a good and long life in this land that you're crossing the Jordan to possess."

48-50   That same day GOD spoke to Moses: "Climb the Abarim Mountains to Mount Nebo in the land of Moab, overlooking Jericho, and view the land of Canaan that I'm giving the People of Israel to have and hold. Die on the mountain that you climb and join your people in the ground, just as your brother Aaron died on Mount Hor and joined his people.

51-52   "This is because you broke faith with me in the company of the People of Israel at the Waters of Meribah Kadesh in the Wilderness of Zin—you didn't honor my Holy Presence in the company of the People of Israel. You'll look at the land spread out before you but you won't enter it, this land that I am giving to the People of Israel."

THE BLESSING

1-5   **33** Moses, man of God, blessed the People of Israel with this blessing before his death. He said,

GOD came down from Sinai,
    he dawned from Seir upon them;
He radiated light from Mount Paran,
    coming with ten thousand holy angels
And tongues of fire
    streaming from his right hand.
Oh, how you love the people,
    all his holy ones are palmed in your left hand.
They sit at your feet,
    honoring your teaching,

The Revelation commanded by Moses,
  as the assembly of Jacob's inheritance.
Thus GOD became king in Jeshurun
  as the leaders and tribes of Israel gathered.

6   Reuben:
"Let Reuben live and not die,
  but just barely, in diminishing numbers."

7   Judah:
"Listen, GOD, to the Voice of Judah,
  bring him to his people;
Strengthen his grip,
  be his helper against his foes."

8-11   Levi:
"Let your Thummim and Urim
  belong to your loyal saint;
The one you tested at Massah,
  whom you fought with at the Waters of Meribah,
Who said of his father and mother,
  'I no longer recognize them.'
He turned his back on his brothers
  and neglected his children,
Because he was guarding your sayings
  and watching over your Covenant.
Let him teach your rules to Jacob
  and your Revelation to Israel,
Let him keep the incense rising to your nostrils
  and the Whole-Burnt-Offerings on your Altar.
GOD bless his commitment,
  stamp your seal of approval on what he does;
Disable the loins of those who defy him,
  make sure we've heard the last from those who hate him."

12   Benjamin:
"GOD's beloved;
  GOD's permanent residence.
Encircled by GOD all day long,
  within whom GOD is at home."

13-17   Joseph:
"Blessed by GOD be his land:
  The best fresh dew from high heaven,
  and fountains springing from the depths;
The best radiance streaming from the sun
  and the best the moon has to offer;
Beauty pouring off the tops of the mountains
  and the best from the everlasting hills;
The best of Earth's exuberant gifts,
  the smile of the Burning-Bush Dweller.

All this on the head of Joseph,
    on the brow of the consecrated one among his brothers.
In splendor he's like a firstborn bull,
    his horns the horns of a wild ox;
He'll gore the nations with those horns,
    push them all to the ends of the Earth.
Ephraim by the ten thousands will do this,
    Manasseh by the thousands will do this."

18-19   Zebulun and Issachar:
"Celebrate, Zebulun, as you go out,
    and Issachar, as you stay home.
They'll invite people to the Mountain
    and offer sacrifices of right worship,
For they will have hauled riches in from the sea
    and gleaned treasures from the beaches."

20-21   Gad:
"Blessed is he who makes Gad large.
    Gad roams like a lion,
    tears off an arm, rips open a skull.
He took one look and grabbed the best place for himself,
    the portion just made for someone in charge.
He took his place at the head,
    carried out GOD's right ways
    and his rules for life in Israel."

22   Dan:
"Dan is a lion's cub
    leaping out of Bashan."

23   Naphtali:
"Naphtali brims with blessings,
    spills over with GOD's blessings
As he takes possession
    of the sea and southland."

24-25   Asher:
"Asher, best blessed of the sons!
    May he be the favorite of his brothers,
    his feet massaged in oil.
Safe behind iron-clad doors and gates,
    your strength like iron as long as you live."

26-28   There is none like God, Jeshurun,
    riding to your rescue through the skies,
    his dignity haloed by clouds.
The ancient God is home
    on a foundation of everlasting arms.
He drove out the enemy before you

and commanded, "Destroy!"
Israel lived securely,
    the fountain of Jacob undisturbed
In grain and wine country
    and, oh yes, his heavens drip dew.

29   Lucky Israel! Who has it as good as you?
    A people *saved* by GOD!
The Shield who defends you,
    the Sword who brings triumph.
Your enemies will come crawling on their bellies
    and you'll march on their backs.

THE DEATH OF MOSES

1-3   **34** Moses climbed from the Plains of Moab to Mount Nebo, the peak of Pisgah facing Jericho. GOD showed him all the land from Gilead to Dan, all Naphtali, Ephraim, and Manasseh; all Judah reaching to the Mediterranean Sea; the Negev and the plains which encircle Jericho, City of Palms, as far south as Zoar.

4   Then and there GOD said to him, "This is the land I promised to your ancestors, to Abraham, Isaac, and Jacob with the words 'I will give it to your descendants.' I've let you see it with your own eyes. There it is. But you're not going to go in."

5-6   Moses died there in the land of Moab, Moses the servant of GOD, just as GOD said. God buried him in the valley in the land of Moab opposite Beth Peor. No one knows his burial site to this very day.

7-8   Moses was 120 years old when he died. His eyesight was sharp; he still walked with a spring in his step. The People of Israel wept for Moses in the Plains of Moab thirty days. Then the days of weeping and mourning for Moses came to an end.

9   Joshua son of Nun was filled with the spirit of wisdom because Moses had laid his hands on him. The People of Israel listened obediently to him and did the same as when GOD had commanded Moses.

10-12   No prophet has risen since in Israel like Moses, whom GOD knew face-to-face. Never since has there been anything like the signs and miracle-wonders that GOD sent him to do in Egypt, to Pharaoh, to all his servants, and to all his land—nothing to compare with that all-powerful hand of his and all the great and terrible things Moses did as every eye in Israel watched.

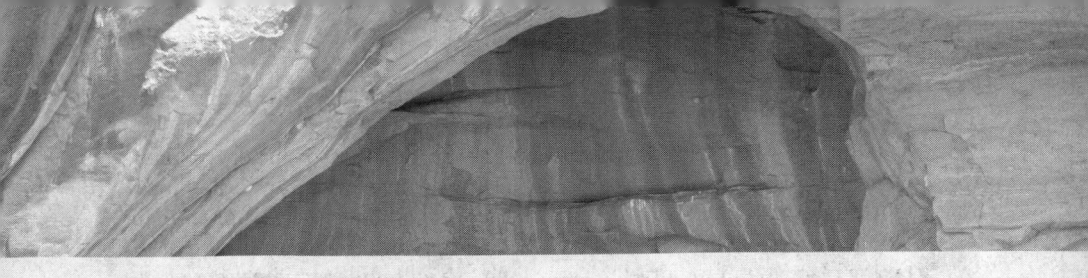

THE HISTORY BOOKS

The biblical books stretching from Joshua to 2 Maccabees are conventionally designated "the history books." But the word "history" doesn't tell the whole story, for this is history attentive to the conditions in which people encounter and experience God. The Hebrew people were intent on observing and participating in what happened in and around them because they believed that God was personally alive and active in the world, in their community, and in them.

Life could not be accounted for by something less than the life of God, no matter how impressive and mysterious their experience was, whether an eclipse of the sun, spots on the liver of a goat, or the hiss of steam from a fissure in the earth. God could not be reduced to astronomical, physiological, geological, or psychological phenomena; God was alive, always and everywhere working his will, challenging people with his call, evoking faith and obedience, shaping a worshiping community, showing his love and compassion, and working out judgments on sin. And none of this "in general" or "at large," but at particular times, in specific places, with named persons: history.

For biblical people, God is not an idea for philosophers to discuss or a force for priests to manipulate. God is not a part of creation that can be studied and observed and managed. God is person — a person to be worshiped or defied, believed or rejected, loved or hated, in time and place. That is why these books immerse us in dates and events, in persons and circumstances — in history. God meets us in the ordinary and extraordinary occurrences that make up the stuff of our daily lives. It never seemed to have occurred to our biblical ancestors that they could deal better with God by escaping from history, "getting away from it all" as we say. History is the medium in which God works salvation, just as paint and canvas is the medium in which Rembrandt made created works of art. We cannot get closer to God by distancing ourselves from the mess of history.

This deeply pervasive sense of history — the dignity of their place in history, the presence of God in history — accounts for the way in which the Hebrew people talked and wrote. They did not, as was the fashion in the ancient world, make up and embellish fanciful stories. Their writings did not entertain or explain; they revealed the ways of God with men and women and the world. They gave narrative shape to actual people and circumstances in their dealings with God, and in God's dealings with them.

But for the Hebrews there simply was no secular history. None. Everything that happened, happened in a world penetrated by God. Since they do not talk a lot about God in their storytelling, it is easy to forget that God is always the invisible and mostly silent presence in everything that is taking place. But if we forget for very long, we will understand neither what is written nor the way it is written. God is never absent from these narratives and never peripheral to them. As far as these writers were concerned, the only reason for paying attention to people and events was to stay alert to God.

This is a difficult mindset for us to acquire, for we are used to getting our history from so-called historians, scholars, and journalists for whom God is not involved or present in what they study and write. We are thoroughly trained by our schools, daily newspapers, and telecasts to read history solely in terms of politics and economics, human interest and environmental conditions. If we have a mind for it, we can go ahead and fit God in somewhere or other. These historical books — Joshua through 2 Maccabees — are radically and refreshingly different. They pull us into a way of reading history that involves us and everyone around us in all the operations of God.

JOSHUA

Land. Land flowing with milk and honey. Promised land. Holy land. Canaan land. The land. Joshua, Moses' successor as leader of Israel, was poised at the River Jordan to enter and take possession of Canaan, an unremarkable stretch of territory sandwiched between massive and already ancient civilizations. It would have been unimaginable to anyone at the time that anything of significance could take place on that land. This narrow patch had never been significant economically or culturally, but only as a land bridge between the two great cultures and economies of Egypt and Mesopotamia. But it was about to become important in the religious consciousness of humankind. In significant ways, this land would come to dwarf everything that had gone on before and around it.

The People of Israel had been landless for nearly five hundred years. The "fathers" — Abraham, Isaac, Jacob and his twelve sons — had been nomads in the land of Canaan. That was followed by a long period of slavery in Egypt (over four hundred years!), a miraculous deliverance into freedom led by Moses, and then forty years of testing and training for living as a free people under God's guidance and blessing.

The company camped at the Jordan on the day that opens the book of Joshua had nearly half a millennium of slavery behind them. They were a dispossessed, ragtag crew — and only very recently set free. The transition from being landless slaves to landholding free men and women was huge. Joshua leads the transition, first in taking the land (chapters 1 through 12), then in distributing it among the twelve tribes (chapters 13 through 22), and concluding with a solemn covenant-witness (chapters 23 through 24) that bound the people to the gift of land and the worship of the God from whom they received it.

For most modern readers of Joshua, the toughest barrier to embracing this story as sacred is the military strategy of "holy war," what I have translated as the "holy curse" — killing everyone in the conquered cities and totally destroying all the plunder, both animals and goods. Massacre and destruction. "No survivors" is the recurrent refrain. We look back from our time in history and think, "How horrible." But if we were able to put ourselves back in the thirteenth century B.C., we might see it differently, for that Canaanite culture was a snake pit of child sacrifice and sacred prostitution, practices ruthlessly devoted to using the most innocent and vulnerable members of the community (babies and virgins) to manipulate God or gods for gain.

As the book of Joshua takes the story of salvation forward from the leadership and teaching of Moses, it continues to keep us grounded in places and connected to persons: place names, personal names — hundreds of them. What we often consider to be the subjects of religion — ideas, truths, prayers, promises, beliefs — are never permitted to have a life of their own apart from particular persons and actual places. Biblical religion has a low tolerance for "great ideas" or "sublime truths" or "inspirational thoughts" apart from the people and places in which they occur. God's great love and purposes for us are worked out in the messes, storms and sins, blue skies, daily work, and dreams of our common lives, working with us as we are and not as we should be.

People who want God as an escape from reality, from the often hard conditions of this life, don't find this much to their liking. But to the man or woman wanting more reality, not less — this continuation of the salvation story — Joshua's fierce and devout determination to win land for his people and his extraordinary attention to getting all the tribes and their families name by name assigned to their own place, is good news indeed. Joshua lays a firm foundation for a life that is grounded.

JOSHUA

¹⁻⁹ **1** After the death of Moses the servant of GOD, GOD spoke to Joshua, Moses' assistant:

"Moses my servant is dead. Get going. Cross this Jordan River, you and all the people. Cross to the country I'm giving to the People of Israel. I'm giving you every square inch of the land you set your foot on—just as I promised Moses. From the wilderness and this Lebanon east to the Great River, the Euphrates River—all the Hittite country—and then west to the Great Sea. It's all yours. All your life, no one will be able to hold out against you. In the same way I was with Moses, I'll be with you. I won't give up on you; I won't leave you. Strength! Courage! You are going to lead this people to inherit the land that I promised to give their ancestors. Give it everything you have, heart and soul. Make sure you carry out The Revelation that Moses commanded you, every bit of it. Don't get off track, either left or right, so as to make sure you get to where you're going. And don't for a minute let this Book of The Revelation be out of mind. Ponder and meditate on it day and night, making sure you practice everything written in it. Then you'll get where you're going; then you'll succeed. Haven't I commanded you? Strength! Courage! Don't be timid; don't get discouraged. GOD, your God, is with you every step you take."

THE TAKING OF THE LAND

¹⁰⁻¹¹ Then Joshua gave orders to the people's leaders: "Go through the camp and give this order to the people: 'Pack your bags. In three days you will cross this Jordan River to enter and take the land GOD, your God, is giving you to possess.'"

¹²⁻¹⁵ Then Joshua addressed the Reubenites, the Gadites, and the half-tribe of Manasseh. He said, "Remember what Moses the servant of GOD commanded you: GOD, your God, gives you rest and he gives you this land. Your wives, your children, and your livestock can stay here east of the Jordan, the country Moses gave you; but you, tough soldiers all, must cross the River in battle formation, leading your brothers, helping them until GOD, your God, gives your brothers a place of rest just as he has done for you. They also will take possession of the land that GOD, your God, is giving them. Then you will be free to return to your possession, given to you by Moses the servant of GOD, across the Jordan to the east."

¹⁶⁻¹⁸ They answered Joshua: "Everything you commanded us, we'll do. Wherever you send us, we'll go. We obeyed Moses to the letter; we'll also obey you—we just pray that GOD, your God, will be with you as he was with Moses. Anyone who questions what you say and refuses to obey whatever you command him will be put to death. Strength! Courage!"

RAHAB

¹ **2** Joshua son of Nun secretly sent out from Shittim two men as spies: "Go. Look over the land. Check out Jericho." They left and arrived at the house of a harlot named Rahab and stayed there.

² The king of Jericho was told, "We've just learned that men arrived tonight to spy out the land. They're from the People of Israel."

3   The king of Jericho sent word to Rahab: "Bring out the men who came to
you to stay the night in your house. They're spies; they've come to spy out
the whole country."

4-7   The woman had taken the two men and hidden them. She said, "Yes, two
men did come to me, but I didn't know where they'd come from. At dark,
when the gate was about to be shut, the men left. But I have no idea where
they went. Hurry up! Chase them — you can still catch them!" (She had
actually taken them up on the roof and hidden them under the stalks of
flax that were spread out for her on the roof.) So the men set chase down the
Jordan road toward the fords. As soon as they were gone, the gate was shut.

8-11   Before the spies were down for the night, the woman came up to them on
the roof and said, "I know that GOD has given you the land. We're all afraid.
Everyone in the country feels hopeless. We heard how GOD dried up the waters
of the Red Sea before you when you left Egypt, and what he did to the two
Amorite kings east of the Jordan, Sihon and Og, whom you put under a holy
curse and destroyed. We heard it and our hearts sank. We all had the wind
knocked out of us. And all because of you, you and GOD, your God, God of the
heavens above and God of the earth below.

12-13   "Now promise me by GOD. I showed you mercy; now show my family mercy.
And give me some tangible proof, a guarantee of life for my father and mother,
my brothers and sisters — everyone connected with my family. Save our souls
from death!"

14   "Our lives for yours!" said the men. "But don't tell anyone our business.
When GOD turns this land over to us, we'll do right by you in loyal mercy."

15-16   She lowered them down out a window with a rope because her house was
on the city wall to the outside. She told them, "Run for the hills so your
pursuers won't find you. Hide out for three days and give your pursuers
time to return. Then get on your way."

17-20   The men told her, "In order to keep this oath you made us swear, here is
what you must do: Hang this red rope out the window through which you
let us down and gather your entire family with you in your house — father,
mother, brothers, and sisters. Anyone who goes out the doors of your
house into the street and is killed, it's his own fault — we aren't responsible. But for everyone within the house we take full responsibility. If
anyone lays a hand on one of them, it's our fault. But if you tell anyone
of our business here, the oath you made us swear is canceled — we're no
longer responsible."

21   She said, "If that's what you say, that's the way it is," and sent them off.
They left and she hung the red rope out the window.

22   They headed for the hills and stayed there for three days until the pursuers
had returned. The pursuers had looked high and low but found nothing.

23-24   The men headed back. They came down out of the hills, crossed the river,
and returned to Joshua son of Nun and reported all their experiences.
They told Joshua, "Yes! GOD has given the whole country to us. Everybody
there is in a state of panic because of us."

THE JORDAN

1-4   **3** Joshua was up early and on his way from Shittim with all the People
of Israel with him. He arrived at the Jordan and camped before crossing over. After three days, leaders went through the camp and gave
out orders to the people: "When you see the Covenant-Chest of GOD, your

God, carried by the Levitical priests, start moving. Follow it. Make sure you keep a proper distance between you and it, about half a mile—be sure now to keep your distance!—and you'll see clearly the route to take. You've never been on this road before."

5 Then Joshua addressed the people: "Sanctify yourselves. Tomorrow GOD will work miracle-wonders among you."

6 Joshua instructed the priests, "Take up the Chest of the Covenant and step out before the people." So they took it up and processed before the people.

7-8 GOD said to Joshua, "This very day I will begin to make you great in the eyes of all Israel. They'll see for themselves that I'm with you in the same way that I was with Moses. You will command the priests who are carrying the Chest of the Covenant: 'When you come to the edge of the Jordan's waters, stand there on the river bank.'"

9-13 Then Joshua addressed the People of Israel: "Attention! Listen to what GOD, your God, has to say. This is how you'll know that God is alive among you—he will completely dispossess before you the Canaanites, Hittites, Hivites, Perizzites, Girgashites, Amorites, and Jebusites. Look at what's before you: the Chest of the Covenant. Think of it—the Master of the entire earth is crossing the Jordan as you watch. Now take twelve men from the tribes of Israel, one man from each tribe. When the soles of the feet of the priests carrying the Chest of GOD, Master of all the earth, touch the Jordan's water, the flow of water will be stopped—the water coming from upstream will pile up in a heap."

14-16 And that's what happened. The people left their tents to cross the Jordan, led by the priests carrying the Chest of the Covenant. When the priests got to the Jordan and their feet touched the water at the edge (the Jordan overflows its banks throughout the harvest), the flow of water stopped. It piled up in a heap—a long way off—at Adam, which is near Zarethan. The river went dry all the way down to the Arabah Sea (the Salt Sea). And the people crossed, facing Jericho.

17 And there they stood; those priests carrying the Chest of the Covenant stood firmly planted on dry ground in the middle of the Jordan while all Israel crossed on dry ground. Finally the whole nation was across the Jordan, and not one wet foot.

1-3 4 When the whole nation was finally across, GOD spoke to Joshua: "Select twelve men from the people, a man from each tribe, and tell them, 'From right here, the middle of the Jordan where the feet of the priests are standing firm, take twelve stones. Carry them across with you and set them down in the place where you camp tonight.'"

4-7 Joshua called out the twelve men whom he selected from the People of Israel, one man from each tribe. Joshua directed them, "Cross to the middle of the Jordan and take your place in front of the Chest of GOD, your God. Each of you heft a stone to your shoulder, a stone for each of the tribes of the People of Israel, so you'll have something later to mark the occasion. When your children ask you, 'What are these stones to you?' you'll say, 'The flow of the Jordan was stopped in front of the Chest of the Covenant of GOD as it crossed the Jordan—stopped in its tracks. These stones are a permanent memorial for the People of Israel.'"

8-9 The People of Israel did exactly as Joshua commanded: They took twelve stones from the middle of the Jordan—a stone for each of the twelve tribes, just as GOD had instructed Joshua—carried them across with them to the camp, and set them down there. Joshua set up the twelve stones taken from the middle of the Jordan that had marked the place where the priests who carried the Chest of the Covenant had stood. They are still there today.

10-11 The priests carrying the Chest continued standing in the middle of the Jordan until everything God had instructed Joshua to tell the people to do was done (confirming what Moses had instructed Joshua). The people crossed; no one dawdled. When the crossing of all the people was complete, they watched as the Chest of the Covenant and the priests crossed over.

12-13 The Reubenites, Gadites, and the half-tribe of Manasseh had crossed over in battle formation in front of the People of Israel, obedient to Moses' instructions. All told, about forty thousand armed soldiers crossed over before GOD to the plains of Jericho, ready for battle.

14 GOD made Joshua great that day in the sight of all Israel. They were in awe of him just as they had been in awe of Moses all his life.

15-16 GOD told Joshua, "Command the priests carrying the Chest of The Testimony to come up from the Jordan."

17 Joshua commanded the priests, "Come up out of the Jordan."

18 They did it. The priests carrying GOD's Chest of the Covenant came up from the middle of the Jordan. As soon as the soles of the priests' feet touched dry land, the Jordan's waters resumed their flow within the banks, just as before.

19-22 The people came up out of the Jordan on the tenth day of the first month. They set up camp at The Gilgal (The Circle) to the east of Jericho. Joshua erected a monument at The Gilgal, using the twelve stones that they had taken from the Jordan. And then he told the People of Israel, "In the days to come, when your children ask their fathers, 'What are these stones doing here?' tell your children this: 'Israel crossed over this Jordan on dry ground.'

23-24 "Yes, GOD, your God, dried up the Jordan's waters for you until you had crossed, just as GOD, your God, did at the Red Sea, which had dried up before us until we had crossed. This was so that everybody on earth would recognize how strong GOD's rescuing hand is and so that you would hold GOD in solemn reverence always."

1 When all the Amorite kings west of the Jordan and the Canaanite kings along the seacoast heard how GOD had stopped the Jordan River before the People of Israel until they had crossed over, their hearts sank; the courage drained out of them just thinking about the People of Israel.

2-3 At that time GOD said to Joshua, "Make stone knives and circumcise the People of Israel a second time." So Joshua made stone knives and circumcised the People of Israel at Foreskins Hill.

4-7 This is why Joshua conducted the circumcision. All the males who had left Egypt, the soldiers, had died in the wilderness on the journey out of Egypt. All the people who had come out of Egypt, of course, had been circumcised, but all those born in the wilderness along the way since leaving Egypt had not been. The fact is that the People of Israel had walked through that wilderness for forty years until the entire nation died out, all the men of military age who had come out of Egypt but had disobeyed the call of GOD. GOD vowed that these would never lay eyes on the land GOD had solemnly promised their ancestors to give us, a land flowing with milk and honey. But their children had replaced them. These are the ones Joshua circumcised. They had never been circumcised; no one had circumcised them along the way.

8   When they had completed the circumcising of the whole nation, they stayed where they were in camp until they were healed.

9   GOD said to Joshua, "Today I have rolled away the reproach of Egypt." That's why the place is called The Gilgal. It's still called that.

10   The People of Israel continued to camp at The Gilgal. They celebrated the Passover on the evening of the fourteenth day of the month on the plains of Jericho.

11-12   Right away, the day after the Passover, they started eating the produce of that country, unraised bread and roasted grain. And then no more manna; the manna stopped. As soon as they started eating food grown in the land, there was no more manna for the People of Israel. That year they ate from the crops of Canaan.

13   And then this, while Joshua was there near Jericho: He looked up and saw right in front of him a man standing, holding his drawn sword. Joshua stepped up to him and said, "Whose side are you on—ours or our enemies'?"

14   He said, "Neither. I'm commander of GOD's army. I've just arrived." Joshua fell, face to the ground, and worshiped. He asked, "What orders does my Master have for his servant?"

15   GOD's army commander ordered Joshua, "Take your sandals off your feet. The place you are standing is holy."

Joshua did it.

JERICHO

1   Jericho was shut up tight as a drum because of the People of Israel: no one going in, no one coming out.

2-5   GOD spoke to Joshua, "Look sharp now. I've already given Jericho to you, along with its king and its crack troops. Here's what you are to do: March around the city, all your soldiers. Circle the city once. Repeat this for six days. Have seven priests carry seven ram's horn trumpets in front of the Chest. On the seventh day march around the city seven times, the priests blowing away on the trumpets. And then, a long blast on the ram's horn—when you hear that, all the people are to shout at the top of their lungs. The city wall will collapse at once. All the people are to enter, every man straight on in."

6   So Joshua son of Nun called the priests and told them, "Take up the Chest of the Covenant. Seven priests are to carry seven ram's horn trumpets leading GOD's Chest."

7   Then he told the people, "Set out! March around the city. Have the armed guard march before the Chest of GOD."

8-9 And it happened. Joshua spoke, the people moved: Seven priests with their seven ram's horn trumpets set out before GOD. They blew the trumpets, leading GOD's Chest of the Covenant. The armed guard marched ahead of the trumpet-blowing priests; the rear guard was marching after the Chest, marching and blowing their trumpets.

10 Joshua had given orders to the people, "Don't shout. In fact, don't even speak — not so much as a whisper until you hear me say, 'Shout!' — then shout away!"

11-13 He sent the Chest of GOD on its way around the city. It circled once, came back to camp, and stayed for the night. Joshua was up early the next morning and the priests took up the Chest of GOD. The seven priests carrying the seven ram's horn trumpets marched before the Chest of GOD, marching and blowing the trumpets, with the armed guard marching before and the rear guard marching after. Marching and blowing of trumpets!

14 On the second day they again circled the city once and returned to camp. They did this six days.

15-17 When the seventh day came, they got up early and marched around the city this same way but seven times — yes, this day they circled the city seven times. On the seventh time around the priests blew the trumpets and Joshua signaled the people, "Shout! — GOD has given you the city! The city and everything in it is under a holy curse and offered up to GOD.

"Except for Rahab the harlot — she is to live, she and everyone in her house with her, because she hid the agents we sent.

18-19 "As for you, watch yourselves in the city under holy curse. Be careful that you don't covet anything in it and take something that's cursed, endangering the camp of Israel with the curse and making trouble for everyone. All silver and gold, all vessels of bronze and iron are holy to GOD. Put them in GOD's treasury."

20 The priests blew the trumpets.

When the people heard the blast of the trumpets, they gave a thunderclap shout. The wall fell at once. The people rushed straight into the city and took it.

21 They put everything in the city under the holy curse, killing man and woman, young and old, ox and sheep and donkey.

22-24 Joshua ordered the two men who had spied out the land, "Enter the house of the harlot and rescue the woman and everyone connected with her, just as you promised her." So the young spies went in and brought out Rahab, her father, mother, and brothers — everyone connected with her. They got the whole family out and gave them a place outside the camp of Israel. But they burned down the city and everything in it, except for the gold and silver and the bronze and iron vessels — all that they put in the treasury of GOD's house.

25 But Joshua let Rahab the harlot live — Rahab and her father's household and everyone connected to her. She is still alive and well in Israel because she hid the agents whom Joshua sent to spy out Jericho.

26 Joshua swore a solemn oath at that time:

Cursed before GOD is the man
    who sets out to rebuild this city Jericho.
He'll pay for the foundation with his firstborn son,
    he'll pay for the gates with his youngest son.

27   GOD was with Joshua. He became famous all over the land.

ACHAN

1   7Then the People of Israel violated the holy curse. Achan son of Carmi, the son of Zabdi, the son of Zerah of the tribe of Judah, took some of the cursed things. GOD became angry with the People of Israel.

2   Joshua sent men from Jericho to Ai (The Ruin), which is near Beth Aven just east of Bethel. He instructed them, "Go up and spy out the land." The men went up and spied out Ai.

3   They returned to Joshua and reported, "Don't bother sending a lot of people—two or three thousand men are enough to defeat Ai. Don't wear out the whole army; there aren't that many people there."

4-5   So three thousand men went up—and then fled in defeat before the men of Ai! The men of Ai killed thirty-six—chased them from the city gate as far as The Quarries, killing them at the descent. The heart of the people sank, all spirit knocked out of them.

6   Joshua ripped his clothes and fell on his face to the ground before the Chest of GOD, he and the leaders throwing dirt on their heads, prostrate until evening.

7-9   Joshua said, "Oh, oh, oh . . . Master, GOD. Why did you insist on bringing this people across the Jordan? To make us victims of the Amorites? To wipe us out? Why didn't we just settle down on the east side of the Jordan? Oh, Master, what can I say after this, after Israel has been run off by its enemies? When the Canaanites and all the others living here get wind of this, they'll gang up on us and make short work of us—and then how will you keep up *your* reputation?"

10-12   GOD said to Joshua, "Get up. Why are you groveling? Israel has sinned: They've broken the covenant I commanded them; they've taken forbidden plunder—stolen and then covered up the theft, squirreling it away with their own stuff. The People of Israel can no longer look their enemies in the eye—they themselves are plunder. I can't continue with you if you don't rid yourselves of the cursed things.

13   "So get started. Purify the people. Tell them: Get ready for tomorrow by purifying yourselves. For this is what GOD, the God of Israel, says: There are cursed things in the camp. You won't be able to face your enemies until you have gotten rid of these cursed things.

14-15   "First thing in the morning you will be called up by tribes. The tribe GOD names will come up clan by clan; the clan GOD names will come up family by family; and the family GOD names will come up man by man. The person found with the cursed things will be burned, he and everything he has, because he broke GOD's covenant and did this despicable thing in Israel."

16-18   Joshua was up at the crack of dawn and called Israel up tribe by tribe. The tribe of Judah was singled out. Then he called up the clans and singled out the Zerahites. He called up the Zerahite families and singled out the Zabdi family. He called up the family members one by one and singled out Achan son of Carmi, the son of Zabdi, the son of Zerah of the tribe of Judah.

19   Joshua spoke to Achan, "My son, give glory to GOD, the God of Israel. Make your confession to him. Tell me what you did. Don't keep back anything from me."

20-21 Achan answered Joshua, "It's true. I sinned against GOD, the God of Israel. This is how I did it. In the plunder I spotted a beautiful Shinar robe, two hundred shekels of silver, and a fifty-shekel bar of gold, and I coveted and took them. They are buried in my tent with the silver at the bottom."

22-23 Joshua sent off messengers. They ran to the tent. And there it was, buried in the tent with the silver at the bottom. They took the stuff from the tent and brought it to Joshua and to all the People of Israel and spread it out before GOD.

24 Joshua took Achan son of Zerah, took the silver, the robe, the gold bar, his sons and daughters, his ox, donkey, sheep, and tent—everything connected with him. All Israel was there. They led them off to the Valley of Achor (Trouble Valley).

25-26 Joshua said, "Why have you troubled us? GOD will now trouble you. Today!" And all Israel stoned him—burned him with fire and stoned him with stones. They piled a huge pile of stones over him. It's still there. Only then did GOD turn from his hot anger. That's how the place came to be called Trouble Valley right up to the present time.

AI

1 **8** GOD said to Joshua, "Don't be timid and don't so much as hesitate. Take all your soldiers with you and go back to Ai. I have turned the king of Ai over to you—his people, his city, and his land.

2 "Do to Ai and its king what you did to Jericho and its king. Only this time you may plunder its stuff and cattle to your heart's content. Set an ambush behind the city."

3-8 Joshua and all his soldiers got ready to march on Ai. Joshua chose thirty thousand men, tough, seasoned fighters, and sent them off at night with these orders: "Look sharp now. Lie in ambush behind the city. Get as close as you can. Stay alert. I and the troops with me will approach the city head-on. When they come out to meet us just as before, we'll turn and run. They'll come after us, leaving the city. As we are off and running, they'll say, 'They're running away just like the first time.' That's your signal to spring from your ambush and take the city. GOD, your God, will hand it to you on a platter. Once you have the city, burn it down. GOD says it, you do it. Go to it. I've given you your orders."

9 Joshua sent them off. They set their ambush and waited between Bethel and Ai, just west of Ai. Joshua spent the night with the people.

10-13 Joshua was up early in the morning and mustered his army. He and the leaders of Israel led the troops to Ai. The whole army, fighting men all, marched right up within sight of the city and set camp on the north side of Ai. There was a valley between them and Ai. He had taken about five thousand men and put them in ambush between Bethel and Ai, west of the city. They were all deployed, the main army to the north of the city and the ambush to the west. Joshua spent the night in the valley.

14 So it happened that when the king of Ai saw all this, the men of the city lost no time; they were out of there at the crack of dawn to join Israel in battle, the king and his troops, at a field en route to the Arabah. The king didn't know of the ambush set against him behind the city.

15-17 Joshua and all Israel let themselves be chased; they ran toward the wilderness. Everybody in the city was called to the chase. They pursued Joshua and were led away from the city. There wasn't a soul left in Ai or

Bethel who wasn't out there chasing after Israel. The city was left empty and undefended as they were chasing Israel down.

18-19   Then GOD spoke to Joshua: "Stretch out the javelin in your hand toward Ai—I'm giving it to you." Joshua stretched out the javelin in his hand toward Ai. At the signal the men in ambush sprang to their feet, ran to the city, took it, and quickly had it up in flames.

20-21   The men of Ai looked back and, oh! saw the city going up in smoke. They found themselves trapped with nowhere to run. The army on the run toward the wilderness did an about-face—Joshua and all Israel, seeing that the ambush had taken the city, saw it going up in smoke, turned and attacked the men of Ai.

22-23   Then the men in the ambush poured out of the city. The men of Ai were caught in the middle with Israelites on both sides—a real massacre. And not a single survivor. Except for the king of Ai; they took him alive and brought him to Joshua.

24-25   When it was all over, Israel had killed everyone in Ai, whether in the fields or in the wilderness where they had chased them. When the killing was complete, the Israelites returned to Ai and completed the devastation. The death toll that day came to twelve thousand men and women—everyone in Ai.

26-27   Joshua didn't lower his outstretched javelin until the sacred destruction of Ai and all its people was completed. Israel did get to take the livestock and loot left in the city; GOD's instructions to Joshua allowed for that.

28-29   Joshua burned Ai to the ground. A "heap" of nothing forever, a "no-place" —go see for yourself. He hanged the king of Ai from a tree. At evening, with the sun going down, Joshua ordered the corpse cut down. They dumped it at the entrance to the city and piled it high with stones—you can go see that also.

30-32   Then Joshua built an altar to the GOD of Israel on Mount Ebal. He built it following the instructions of Moses the servant of GOD to the People of Israel and written in the Book of The Revelation of Moses, an altar of whole stones that hadn't been chiseled or shaped by an iron tool. On it they offered to GOD Whole-Burnt-Offerings and sacrificed Peace-Offerings. He also wrote out a copy of The Revelation of Moses on the stones. He wrote it with the People of Israel looking on.

33   All Israel was there, foreigners and citizens alike, with their elders, officers, and judges, standing on opposite sides of the Chest, facing the Levitical priests who carry GOD's Covenant Chest. Half of the people stood with their backs to Mount Gerizim and half with their backs to Mount Ebal to bless the People of Israel, just as Moses the servant of GOD had instructed earlier.

34-35   After that, he read out everything written in The Revelation, the Blessing and the Curse, everything in the Book of The Revelation. There wasn't a word of all that Moses commanded that Joshua didn't read to the entire congregation—men, women, children, and foreigners who had been with them on the journey.

GIBEON

1-2 All the kings west of the Jordan in the hills and foothills and along the Mediterranean seacoast north toward Lebanon—the Hittites, Amorites, Canaanites, Perizzites, Hivites, Girgashites, and Jebusites—got the news. They came together in a coalition to fight against Joshua and Israel under a single command.

3-6 The people of Gibeon heard what Joshua had done to Jericho and Ai and cooked up a ruse. They posed as travelers: their donkeys loaded with patched sacks and mended wineskins, threadbare sandals on their feet, tattered clothes on their bodies, nothing but dry crusts and crumbs for food. They came to Joshua at Gilgal and spoke to the men of Israel, "We've come from a far-off country; make a covenant with us."

7 The men of Israel said to these Hivites, "How do we know you aren't local people? How could we then make a covenant with you?"

8 They said to Joshua, "We'll be your servants."

Joshua said, "Who are you now? Where did you come from?"

9-11 They said, "From a far-off country, very far away. Your servants came because we'd heard such great things about GOD, your God—all those things he did in Egypt! And the two Amorite kings across the Jordan, King Sihon of Heshbon and King Og of Bashan, who ruled in Ashtaroth! Our leaders and everybody else in our country told us, 'Pack up some food for the road and go meet them. Tell them, We're your servants; make a covenant with us.'

12-13 "This bread was warm from the oven when we packed it and left to come and see you. Now look at it—crusts and crumbs. And our cracked and mended wineskins, good as new when we filled them. And our clothes and sandals, in tatters from the long, hard traveling."

14 The men of Israel looked them over and accepted the evidence. But they didn't ask GOD about it.

15 So Joshua made peace with them and formalized it with a covenant to guarantee their lives. The leaders of the congregation swore to it.

16-18 And then, three days after making this covenant, they learned that they were next-door neighbors who had been living there all along! The People of Israel broke camp and set out; three days later they reached their towns—Gibeon, Kephirah, Beeroth, and Kiriath Jearim. But the People of Israel didn't attack them; the leaders of the congregation had given their word before the GOD of Israel. But the congregation was up in arms over their leaders.

19-21 The leaders were united in their response to the congregation: "We promised them in the presence of the GOD of Israel. We can't lay a hand on them now. But we can do this: We will let them live so we don't get blamed for breaking our promise." Then the leaders continued, "We'll let them live, but they will be woodcutters and water carriers for the entire congregation."

And that's what happened; the leaders' promise was kept.

22-23 But Joshua called the Gibeonites together and said, "Why did you lie to us, telling us, 'We live far, far away from you,' when you're our next-door neighbors? For that you are cursed. From now on it's menial labor for you—woodcutters and water carriers for the house of my God."

24-25 They answered Joshua, "We got the message loud and clear that GOD, your God, commanded through his servant Moses: to give you the whole country and destroy everyone living in it. We were terrified because of you; that's why we did this. That's it. We're at your mercy. Whatever you decide is right for us, do it."

26-27   And that's what they did. Joshua delivered them from the power of the People of Israel so they didn't kill them. But he made them woodcutters and water carriers for the congregation and for the Altar of GOD at the place GOD chooses. They still are.

THE FIVE KINGS

1-2   10 It wasn't long before My-Master-Zedek king of Jerusalem heard that Joshua had taken Ai and destroyed it and its king under a holy curse, just as he had done to Jericho and its king. He also learned that the people of Gibeon had come to terms with Israel and were living as neighbors. He and his people were alarmed: Gibeon was a big city—as big as any with a king and bigger than Ai—and all its men were seasoned fighters.

3-4   Adoni-Zedek king of Jerusalem sent word to Hoham king of Hebron, Piram king of Jarmuth, Japhia king of Lachish, and Debir king of Eglon: "Come and help me. Let's attack Gibeon; they've joined up with Joshua and the People of Israel."

5   So the five Amorite (Western) kings—the king of Jerusalem, the king of Hebron, the king of Jarmuth, the king of Lachish, and the king of Eglon—combined their armies and set out to attack Gibeon.

6   The men of Gibeon sent word to Joshua camped at Gilgal, "Don't let us down now! Come up here quickly! Save us! Help us! All the Amorite kings who live up in the hills have ganged up on us."

7-8   So Joshua set out from Gilgal, his whole army with him—all those tough soldiers! GOD told him, "Don't give them a second thought. I've put them under your thumb—not one of them will stand up to you."

9-11   Joshua marched all night from Gilgal and took them by total surprise. GOD threw them into total confusion before Israel, a major victory at Gibeon. Israel chased them along the ridge to Beth Horon and fought them all the way down to Azekah and Makkedah. As they ran from the People of Israel, down from the Beth Horon ridge and all the way to Azekah, GOD pitched huge stones on them out of the sky and many died. More died from the hailstones than the People of Israel killed with the sword.

12-13   The day GOD gave the Amorites up to Israel, Joshua spoke to GOD, with all Israel listening:

"Stop, Sun, over Gibeon;
Halt, Moon, over Aijalon Valley."
And Sun stopped,
Moon stood stock still
Until he defeated his enemies.

13-14   (You can find this written in the Book of Jashar.) The sun stopped in its tracks in mid sky; just sat there all day. There's never been a day like that before or since—GOD took orders from a human voice! Truly, GOD fought for Israel.

15   Then Joshua returned, all Israel with him, to the camp at Gilgal.

16-17 Meanwhile the five kings had hidden in the cave at Makkedah. Joshua was told, "The five kings have been found, hidden in the cave at Makkedah."

18-19 Joshua said, "Roll big stones against the mouth of the cave and post guards to keep watch. But don't you hang around—go after your enemies. Cut off their retreat. Don't let them back into their cities. GOD has given them to you."

20-21 Joshua and the People of Israel then finished them off, total devastation. Only a few got away to the fortified towns. The whole army then returned intact to the camp and to Joshua at Makkedah. There was no criticism that day from the People of Israel!

22 Then Joshua said, "Open the mouth of the cave and bring me those five kings."

23 They did it. They brought him the five kings from the cave: the king of Jerusalem, the king of Hebron, the king of Jarmuth, the king of Lachish, and the king of Eglon.

24 When they had them all there in front of Joshua, he called up the army and told the field commanders who had been with him, "Come here. Put your feet on the necks of these kings."

They stepped up and put their feet on their necks.

25 Joshua told them, "Don't hold back. Don't be timid. Be strong! Be confident! This is what GOD will do to all your enemies when you fight them."

26-27 Then Joshua struck and killed the kings. He hung them on five trees where they remained until evening. At sunset Joshua gave the command. They took them down from the trees and threw them into the cave where they had hidden. They put large stones at the mouth of the cave. The kings are still in there.

NO SURVIVORS

28 That same day Joshua captured Makkedah, a massacre that included the king. He carried out the holy curse. No survivors. Makkedah's king got the same treatment as Jericho's king.

29-30 Joshua, all Israel with him, moved on from Makkedah to Libnah and fought against Libnah. GOD gave Libnah to Israel. They captured city and king and massacred the lot. No survivors. Libnah's king got the same treatment as Jericho's king.

31-32 Joshua, all Israel with him, moved on from Libnah to Lachish. He set up camp nearby and attacked. GOD gave Lachish to Israel. Israel took it in two days and killed everyone. He carried out the holy curse, the same as with Libnah.

33 Horam, king of Gezer, arrived to help Lachish. Joshua attacked him and his army until there was nothing left of them. No survivors.

34-35 Joshua, all Israel with him, moved on from Lachish to Eglon. They set up camp and attacked. They captured it and killed everyone, carrying out the holy curse, the same as they had done with Lachish.

36-37 Joshua, all Israel with him, went up from Eglon to Hebron. He attacked and captured it. They killed everyone, including its king, its villages, and their people. No survivors, the same as with Eglon. They carried out the holy curse on city and people.

38-39 Then Joshua, all Israel with him, turned toward Debir and attacked it. He captured it, its king, and its villages. They killed everyone. They put everyone and everything under the holy curse. No survivors. Debir and its king got the same treatment as Hebron and its king, and Libnah and its king.

40-42 Joshua took the whole country: hills, desert, foothills, and mountain slopes, including all kings. He left no survivors. He carried out the holy curse on everything that breathed, just as GOD, the God of Israel, had commanded. Joshua's conquest stretched from Kadesh Barnea to Gaza and from the entire region of Goshen to Gibeon. Joshua took all these kings and their lands in a single campaign because GOD, the God of Israel, fought for Israel.

43 Then Joshua, all Israel with him, went back to the camp at Gilgal.

1-3 **11** When Jabin king of Hazor heard of all this, he sent word to Jobab king of Madon; to the king of Shimron; to the king of Acshaph; to all the kings in the northern mountains; to the kings in the valley south of Kinnereth; to the kings in the western foothills and Naphoth Dor; to the Canaanites both east and west; to the Amorites, Hittites, Perizzites, and Jebusites in the hill country; and to the Hivites below Hermon in the region of Mizpah.

4-5 They came out in full force, all their troops massed together—a huge army, in number like sand on an ocean beach—to say nothing of all the horses and chariots. All these kings met and set up camp together at the Waters of Merom, ready to fight against Israel.

6 GOD said to Joshua: "Don't worry about them. This time tomorrow I'll hand them over to Israel, all dead. You'll hamstring their horses. You'll set fire to their chariots."

7-9 Joshua, his entire army with him, took them by surprise, falling on them at the Waters of Merom. GOD gave them to Israel, who struck and chased them all the way to Greater Sidon, to Misrephoth Maim, and then to the Valley of Mizpah on the east. No survivors. Joshua treated them following GOD's instructions: he hamstrung their horses; he burned up their chariots.

10-11 Then Joshua came back and took Hazor, killing its king. Early on Hazor had been head of all these kingdoms. They killed every person there, carrying out the holy curse—not a breath of life left anywhere. Then he burned down Hazor.

12-14 Joshua captured and massacred all the royal towns with their kings, the holy curse commanded by Moses the servant of GOD. But Israel didn't burn the cities that were built on mounds, except for Hazor—Joshua did burn down Hazor. The People of Israel plundered all the loot, including the cattle, from these towns for themselves. But they killed the people— total destruction. They left nothing human that breathed.

15 Just as GOD commanded his servant Moses, so Moses commanded Joshua, and Joshua did it. He didn't leave incomplete one thing that GOD had commanded Moses.

16-20 Joshua took the whole country: the mountains, the southern desert, all of Goshen, the foothills, the valley (the Arabah), and the Israel mountains with their foothills, from Mount Halak, which towers over the region of Seir, all the way to Baal Gad in the Valley of Lebanon in the shadows of Mount Hermon. He captured their kings and then killed them. Joshua fought against these kings for a long time. Not one town made peace with the People of Israel, with the one exception of the Hivites who lived in Gibeon. Israel fought and took all the rest. It was GOD's idea that they all would stubbornly fight the Israelites so he could put them under the holy curse without mercy. That way he could destroy them just as GOD had commanded Moses.

21-22 Joshua came out at that time also to root out the Anakim from the hills, from Hebron, from Debir, from Anab, from the mountains of Judah, from the mountains of Israel. Joshua carried out the holy curse on them and their cities. No Anakim were left in the land of the People of Israel, except in Gaza, Gath, and Ashdod — there were a few left there.

23 Joshua took the whole region. He did everything that GOD had told Moses. Then he parceled it out as an inheritance to Israel according to their tribes.

And Israel had rest from war.

THE DEFEATED KINGS

1 **12** These are the kings that the People of Israel defeated and whose land they took on the east of the Jordan, from the Arnon Gorge to Mount Hermon, with the whole eastern side of the Arabah Valley.

2-3 Sihon king of the Amorites, who reigned from Heshbon: His rule extended from Aroer, which sits at the edge of the Arnon Gorge, from the middle of the gorge and over half of Gilead to the Gorge of the Jabbok River, which is the border of the Ammonites. His rule included the eastern Arabah Valley from the Sea of Kinnereth to the Arabah Sea (the Salt Sea), eastward toward Beth Jeshimoth and southward to the slopes of Pisgah.

4-5 And Og king of Bashan, one of the last of the Rephaim who reigned from Ashtaroth and Edrei: His rule extended from Mount Hermon and Salecah over the whole of Bashan to the border of the Geshurites and the Maacathites (the other half of Gilead) to the border of Sihon king of Heshbon.

6 Moses the servant of GOD and the People of Israel defeated them. And Moses the servant of GOD gave this land as an inheritance to the Reubenites, the Gadites, and half of the tribe of Manasseh.

7-24 And these are the kings of the land that Joshua and the People of Israel defeated in the country west of the Jordan, from Baal Gad in the Valley of Lebanon south to Mount Halak, which towers over Seir. Joshua gave this land to the tribes of Israel as a possession, according to their divisions: lands in the mountains, the western foothills, and the Arabah Valley, on the slopes, and in the wilderness and the Negev desert (lands on which Hittites, Amorites and Canaanites, Perizzites, Hivites, and Jebusites had lived). The kings were:

The king of Jericho	one
The king of Ai (near Bethel)	one
The king of Jerusalem	one
The king of Hebron	one

The king of Jarmuth	one
The king of Lachish	one
The king of Eglon	one
The king of Gezer	one
The king of Debir	one
The king of Geder	one
The king of Hormah	one
The king of Arad	one
The king of Libnah	one
The king of Adullam	one
The king of Makkedah	one
The king of Bethel	one
The king of Tappuah	one
The king of Hepher	one
The king of Aphek	one
The king of Lasharon	one
The king of Madon	one
The king of Hazor	one
The king of Shimron Meron	one
The king of Acshaph	one
The king of Taanach	one
The king of Megiddo	one
The king of Kedesh	one
The king of Jokneam in Carmel	one
The king of Dor (Naphoth Dor)	one
The king of Goyim in Gilgal	one
The king of Tirzah	one

A total of thirty-one kings.

THE RECEIVING OF THE LAND

1-6 **13** When Joshua had reached a venerable age, GOD said to him, "You've had a good, long life, but there is a lot of land still to be taken. This is the land that remains:

all the districts of the Philistines and Geshurites;

the land from the Shihor River east of Egypt to the border of Ekron up north, Canaanite country (there were five Philistine tyrants — in Gaza, in Ashdod, in Ashkelon, in Gath, in Ekron); also the Avvim from the south;

all the Canaanite land from Arah (belonging to the Sidonians) to Aphek at the Amorite border;

the country of the Gebalites;

all Lebanon eastward from Baal Gad in the shadow of Mount Hermon to the Entrance of Hamath;

all who live in the mountains, from Lebanon to Misrephoth Maim;

all the Sidonians.

6-7 "I myself will drive them out before the People of Israel. All you have to do is allot this land to Israel as an inheritance, as I have instructed you. Do it now: Allot this land as an inheritance to the nine tribes and the half-tribe of Manasseh."

LAND EAST OF THE JORDAN

8 The other half-tribe of Manasseh, with the Reubenites and Gadites, had been given their inheritance by Moses on the other side of the Jordan eastward. Moses the servant of GOD gave it to them.

9-13 This land extended from Aroer at the edge of the Arnon Gorge and the city in the middle of the valley, taking in the entire tableland of Medeba as far as Dibon, and all the towns of Sihon king of the Amorites, who ruled from Heshbon, and out to the border of the Ammonites. It also included Gilead, the country of the people of Geshur and Maacah, all of Mount Hermon, and all Bashan as far as Salecah — the whole kingdom of Og in Bashan, who reigned in Ashtaroth and Edrei. He was one of the last survivors of the Rephaim. Moses had defeated them and taken their land. The People of Israel never did drive out the Geshurites and the Maacathites — they're still there, living in Israel.

14 Levi was the only tribe that did not receive an inheritance. The Fire-Gift-Offerings to GOD, the God of Israel, are their inheritance, just as he told them.

REUBEN

15-22 To the tribe of Reuben, clan by clan, Moses gave:
the land from Aroer at the edge of the Arnon Gorge and the town in the
middle of the valley, including the tableland around Medeba;
Heshbon on the tableland with all its towns (Dibon, Bamoth Baal,
Beth Baal Meon, Jahaz, Kedemoth, Mephaath, Kiriathaim, Sibmah,
Zereth Shahar on Valley Mountain, Beth Peor, the slopes of Pisgah,
Beth Jeshimoth);
and all the cities of the tableland, the whole kingdom of Sihon king
of the Amorites, who ruled at Heshbon, whom Moses put to death
along with the princes of Midian: Evi, Rekem, Zur, Hur, and Reba,
who lived in that country, all puppets of Sihon. (In addition to those
killed in battle, Balaam son of Beor, the soothsayer, was put to death
by the People of Israel.)

23 The boundary for the Reubenites was the bank of the Jordan River. This was the inheritance of the Reubenites, their villages and cities, according to their clans.

GAD

24-27 To the tribe of Gad, clan by clan, Moses gave:
the territory of Jazer and all the towns of Gilead and half the Ammonite
country as far as Aroer near Rabbah;
the land from Heshbon to Ramath Mizpah and Betonim, and from
Mahanaim to the region of Debir;
in the valley: Beth Haram, Beth Nimrah, Succoth, and Zaphon, with
the rest of the kingdom of Sihon king of Heshbon (the east side of
the Jordan, north to the end of the Sea of Kinnereth).

28 This was the inheritance of the Gadites, their cities and villages, clan by clan.

HALF-TRIBE OF MANASSEH

29-31 To the half-tribe of Manasseh, clan by clan, Moses gave:
the land stretching out from Mahanaim;
all of Bashan, which is the entire kingdom of Og king of Bashan, and all
the settlements of Jair in Bashan—sixty towns in all.
Half of Gilead with Ashtaroth and Edrei, the royal cities of Og in
Bashan, belong to the descendants of Makir, a son of Manasseh (in
other words, the half-tribe of the children of Makir) for their clans.

32-33 This is the inheritance that Moses gave out when he was on the plains of
Moab across the Jordan east of Jericho. But Moses gave no inheritance to the
tribe of Levi. GOD, the God of Israel, is their inheritance, just as he told them.

LAND WEST OF THE JORDAN

1-2 **14** Here are the inheritance allotments that the People of Israel
received in the land of Canaan. Eleazar the priest, Joshua son
of Nun, and the heads of the family clans made the allotments.
Each inheritance was assigned by lot to the nine and a half tribes, just as GOD
had commanded Moses.

3-4 Moses had given the two and a half tribes their inheritance east of the
Jordan, but hadn't given an inheritance to the Levites, as he had to the
others. Because the sons of Joseph had become two tribes, Manasseh and
Ephraim, they gave no allotment to the Levites; but they did give them
cities to live in with pasture rights for their flocks and herds.

5 The People of Israel followed through exactly as GOD had commanded
Moses. They apportioned the land.

CALEB

6-12 The people of Judah came to Joshua at Gilgal. Caleb son of Jephunneh the
Kenizzite spoke: "You'll remember what GOD said to Moses the man of
God concerning you and me back at Kadesh Barnea. I was forty years old
when Moses the servant of GOD sent me from Kadesh Barnea to spy out the
land. And I brought back an honest and accurate report. My companions
who went with me discouraged the people, but I stuck to my guns, totally
with GOD, my God. That was the day that Moses solemnly promised, 'The
land on which your feet have walked will be your inheritance, you and your
children's, forever. Yes, you have lived totally for GOD.' Now look at me: GOD
has kept me alive, as he promised. It is now forty-five years since GOD spoke
this word to Moses, years in which Israel wandered in the wilderness. And
here I am today, eighty-five years old! I'm as strong as I was the day Moses
sent me out. I'm as strong as ever in battle, whether coming or going. So give
me this hill country that GOD promised me. You yourself heard the report,
that the Anakim were there with their great fortress cities. If GOD goes with
me, I will drive them out, just as GOD said."

13-14 Joshua blessed him. He gave Hebron to Caleb son of Jephunneh as an
inheritance. Hebron belongs to Caleb son of Jephunneh the Kenizzite still
today, because he gave himself totally to GOD, the God of Israel.

15 The name of Hebron used to be Kiriath Arba, named after Arba, the
greatest man among the Anakim.

And the land had rest from war.

J U D A H

15 The lot for the people of Judah, their clans, extended south to the border of Edom, to the wilderness of Zin in the extreme south. The southern border ran from the tip of the Salt Sea south of The Tongue; it ran southward from Scorpions Pass, went around Zin and just south of Kadesh Barnea; then it ran past Hezron, ascended to Addar, and curved around to Karka; from there it passed along to Azmon, came out at the Brook of Egypt, ending at the Sea. This is the southern boundary.

The eastern boundary: the Salt Sea up to the mouth of the Jordan.

The northern boundary started at the shallows of the Sea at the mouth of the Jordan, went up to Beth Hoglah and around to the north of Beth Arabah and to the Stone of Bohan son of Reuben. The border then ascended to Debir from Trouble Valley and turned north toward Gilgal, which lies opposite Red Pass, just south of the gorge. The border then followed the Waters of En Shemesh and ended at En Rogel. The border followed the Valley of Ben Hinnom along the southern slope of the Jebusite ridge (that is, Jerusalem). It ascended to the top of the mountain opposite Hinnom Valley on the west, at the northern end of Rephaim Valley; the border then took a turn at the top of the mountain to the spring, the Waters of Nephtoah, and followed the valley out to Mount Ephron, turned toward Baalah (that is, Kiriath Jearim), took another turn west of Baalah to Mount Seir, curved around to the northern shoulder of Mount Jearim (that is, Kesalon), descended to Beth Shemesh, and crossed to Timnah. The border then went north to the ridge of Ekron, turned toward Shikkeron, passed along to Mount Baalah, and came out at Jabneel. The border ended at the Sea.

The western border: the coastline of the Great Sea.

This is the boundary around the people of Judah for their clans.

Joshua gave Caleb son of Jephunneh a section among the people of Judah, according to GOD's command. He gave him Kiriath Arba, that is, Hebron. Arba was the ancestor of Anak.

Caleb drove out three Anakim from Hebron: Sheshai, Ahiman, and Talmai, all descendants of Anak. He marched up from there against the people of Debir. Debir used to be called Kiriath Sepher.

Caleb said, "Whoever attacks Kiriath Sepher and takes it, I'll give my daughter Acsah to him as his wife." Othniel son of Kenaz, Caleb's brother, took it; so Caleb gave him his daughter Acsah as his wife.

When she arrived she got him
    to ask for farmland from her father.
As she dismounted from her donkey
    Caleb asked her, "What would you like?"
She said, "Give me a marriage gift.
    You've given me desert land;
Now give me pools of water!"
    And he gave her the upper and the lower pools.

This is the inheritance of the tribe of the people of Judah, clan by clan.

The southern towns of the tribe of Judah in the Negev were near the boundary of Edom:

Kabzeel, Eder, Jagur,
Kinah, Dimonah, Adadah,
Kedesh, Hazor, Ithnan,
Ziph, Telem, Bealoth,
Hazor Hadattah, Kerioth Hezron (that is, Hazor),
Amam, Shema, Moladah,
Hazar Gaddah, Heshmon, Beth Pelet,
Hazar Shual, Beersheba, Biziothiah,
Baalah, Iim, Ezem,
Eltolad, Kesil, Hormah,
Ziklag, Madmannah, Sansannah,
Lebaoth, Shilhim, Ain, and Rimmon —
    a total of twenty-nine towns and their villages.

33-47 In the Shephelah (the western foothills) there were:
Eshtaol, Zorah, Ashnah,
Zanoah, En Gannim, Tappuah, Enam,
Jarmuth, Adullam, Socoh, Azekah,
Shaaraim, Adithaim, and Gederah (or Gederothaim) —
    fourteen towns and their villages.
Zenan, Hadashah, Migdal Gad,
Dilean, Mizpah, Joktheel,
Lachish, Bozkath, Eglon,
Cabbon, Lahmas, Kitlish,
Gederoth, Beth Dagon, Naamah, and Makkedah —
    sixteen towns and their villages.
Libnah, Ether, Ashan,
Iphtah, Ashnah, Nezib,
Keilah, Aczib, and Mareshah —
    nine towns and their villages.
Ekron with its towns and villages;
From Ekron, west to the sea, all that bordered Ashdod with its villages;
Ashdod with its towns and villages;
Gaza with its towns and villages all the way to the Brook of Egypt.
The Great Sea is the western border.

48-60 In the hill country:
Shamir, Jattir, Socoh,
Dannah, Kiriath Sannah (that is, Debir),
Anab, Eshtemoh, Anim,
Goshen, Holon, and Giloh —
    eleven towns and their villages.
Arab, Dumah, Eshan,
Janim, Beth Tappuah, Aphekah,
Humtah, Kiriath Arba (that is, Hebron), and Zior —
    nine towns and their villages.
Maon, Carmel, Ziph, Juttah,
Jezreel, Jokdeam, Zanoah,
Kain, Gibeah, and Timnah —
    ten towns and their villages.
Halhul, Beth Zur, Gedor,

Maarath, Beth Anoth, and Eltekon —
    six towns and their villages.
Kiriath Baal (that is, Kiriath Jearim) and Rabbah —
    two towns and their villages.

61-62 In the wilderness:
Beth Arabah, Middin, Secacah,
Nibshan, the City of Salt, and En Gedi —
    six towns and their villages.

63 The people of Judah couldn't get rid of the Jebusites who lived in Jerusalem. The Jebusites stayed put, living alongside the people of Judah. They are still living there in Jerusalem.

JOSEPH

1-3 **16** The lot for the people of Joseph went from the Jordan near Jericho, east of the spring of Jericho, north through the desert mountains to Bethel. It went on from Bethel (that is, Luz) to the territory of the Arkites in Ataroth. It then descended westward to the territory of the Japhletites to the region of Lower Beth Horon and on to Gezer, ending at the Sea.

4 This is the region from which the people of Joseph — Manasseh and Ephraim — got their inheritance.

5-9 Ephraim's territory by clans:
The boundary of their inheritance went from Ataroth Addar in the east to Upper Beth Horon and then west to the Sea. From Micmethath on the north it turned eastward to Taanath Shiloh and passed along, still eastward, to Janoah. The border then descended from Janoah to Ataroth and Naarah; it touched Jericho and came out at the Jordan. From Tappuah the border went westward to the Brook Kanah and ended at the Sea. This was the inheritance of the tribe of Ephraim by clans, including the cities set aside for Ephraim within the inheritance of Manasseh — all those towns and their villages.

10 But they didn't get rid of the Canaanites who were living in Gezer. Canaanites are still living among the people of Ephraim, but they are made to do forced labor.

1-2 **17** This is the lot that fell to the people of Manasseh, Joseph's firstborn. (Gilead and Bashan had already been given to Makir, Manasseh's firstborn and father of Gilead, because he was an outstanding fighter.) So the lot that follows went to the rest of the people of Manasseh and their clans, the clans of Abiezer, Helek, Asriel, Shechem, Hepher, and Shemida. These are the male descendants of Manasseh son of Joseph by their clans.

3-4 Zelophehad son of Hepher, the son of Gilead, the son of Makir, the son of Manasseh, had no sons, only daughters. Their names were Mahlah, Noah, Hoglah, Milcah, and Tirzah. They went to Eleazar the priest, Joshua son of Nun, and the leaders and said, "GOD commanded Moses to give us an inheritance among our kinsmen." And Joshua did it; he gave them, as GOD commanded, an inheritance amid their father's brothers.

5-6   Manasseh's lot came to ten portions, in addition to the land of Gilead and Bashan on the other side of the Jordan, because Manasseh's daughters got an inheritance along with his sons. The land of Gilead belonged to the rest of the people of Manasseh.

7-10   The boundary of Manasseh went from Asher all the way to Micmethath, just opposite Shechem, then ran southward to the people living at En Tappuah. (The land of Tappuah belonged to Manasseh, but Tappuah itself on the border of Manasseh belonged to the Ephraimites.) The boundary continued south to the Brook Kanah. (The cities there belonged to Ephraim although they lay among the cities of Manasseh.) The boundary of Manasseh ran north of the brook and ended at the Sea. The land to the south belonged to Ephraim; the land to the north to Manasseh, with the Sea as their western border; they meet Asher on the north and Issachar on the east.

11   Within Issachar and Asher, Manasseh also held Beth Shan, Ibleam, and the people of Dor, Endor, Taanach, and Megiddo, together with their villages, and the third in the list is Naphoth.

12-13   The people of Manasseh never were able to take over these towns—the Canaanites wouldn't budge. But later, when the Israelites got stronger, they put the Canaanites to forced labor. But they never did get rid of them.

14   The people of Joseph spoke to Joshua: "Why did you give us just one allotment, one solitary share? There are a lot of us, and growing—GOD has extravagantly blessed us."

15   Joshua responded, "Since there are so many of you, and you find the hill country of Ephraim too confining, climb into the forest and clear ground there for yourselves in the land of the Perizzites and the Rephaim."

16   But the people of Joseph said, "There's not enough hill country for us; and the Canaanites who live down in the plain, both those in Beth Shan and its villages and in the Valley of Jezreel, have iron chariots."

17-18   Joshua said to the family of Joseph (to Ephraim and Manasseh): "Yes, there are a lot of you, and you are very strong. One lot is not enough for you. You also get the hill country. It's nothing but trees now, but you will clear the land and make it your own from one end to the other. The powerful Canaanites, even with their iron chariots, won't stand a chance against you."

THE SHILOH SURVEY

1-2   **18** Then the entire congregation of the People of Israel got together at Shiloh. They put up the Tent of Meeting.
        The land was under their control but there were still seven Israelite tribes who had yet to receive their inheritance.

3-5   Joshua addressed the People of Israel: "How long are you going to sit around on your hands, putting off taking possession of the land that GOD, the God of your ancestors, has given you? Pick three men from each tribe so I can commission them. They will survey and map the land, showing the inheritance due each tribe, and report back to me. They will divide it into seven parts. Judah will stay in its territory in the south and the people of Joseph will keep to their place in the north.

6   "You are responsible for preparing a survey map showing seven portions.

Then bring it to me so that I can cast lots for you here in the presence of our GOD.

7 "Only the Levites get no portion among you because the priesthood of GOD is their inheritance. And Gad, Reuben, and the half-tribe of Manasseh already have their inheritance on the east side of the Jordan, given to them by Moses the servant of GOD."

8 So the men set out. As they went out to survey the land, Joshua charged them: "Go. Survey the land and map it. Then come back to me and I will cast lots for you here at Shiloh in the presence of GOD."

9 So off the men went. They covered the ground and mapped the country by towns in a scroll. Then they reported back to Joshua at the camp at Shiloh.

10 Joshua cast the lots for them at Shiloh in the presence of GOD. That's where Joshua divided up the land to the People of Israel, according to their tribal divisions.

BENJAMIN

11 The first lot turned up for the tribe of Benjamin with its clans. The border of the allotment went between the peoples of Judah and Joseph.

12-13 The northern border began at the Jordan, then went up to the ridge north of Jericho, ascending west into the hill country into the wilderness of Beth Aven. From there the border went around to Luz, to its southern ridge (that is, Bethel), and then down from Ataroth Addar to the mountain to the south of Lower Beth Horon.

14 There the border took a turn on the west side and swung south from the mountain to the south of Beth Horon and ended at Kiriath Baal (that is, Kiriath Jearim), a town of the people of Judah. This was the west side.

15-19 The southern border began at the edge of Kiriath Jearim on the west, then ran west until it reached the spring, the Waters of Nephtoah. It then descended to the foot of the mountain opposite the Valley of Ben Hinnom (which flanks the Valley of Rephaim to the north), descended to the Hinnom Valley, just south of the Jebusite ridge, and went on to En Rogel. From there it curved north to En Shemesh and Geliloth, opposite the Red Pass (Adummim), down to the Stone of Bohan the son of Reuben, continued toward the north flank of Beth Arabah, then plunged to the Arabah. It then followed the slope of Beth Hoglah north and came out at the northern bay of the Salt Sea — the south end of the Jordan. This was the southern border.

20 The east border was formed by the Jordan.

This was the inheritance of the people of Benjamin for their clans, marked by these borders on all sides.

21-28 The cities of the tribe of Benjamin, clan by clan, were:

Jericho, Beth Hoglah, Emek Keziz,
Beth Arabah, Zemaraim, Bethel,
Avvim, Parah, Ophrah,
Kephar Ammoni, Ophni, and Geba —
    twelve towns with their villages.
Gibeon, Ramah, Beeroth,
Mizpah, Kephirah, Mozah,
Rekem, Irpeel, Taralah,

Zelah, Haeleph, the Jebusite city (that is, Jerusalem), Gibeah, and Kiriath Jearim—
    fourteen cities with their villages.
This was the inheritance for Benjamin, according to its clans.

SIMEON

1-8 19 The second lot went to Simeon for its clans. Their inheritance was within the territory of Judah. In their inheritance they had:

Beersheba (or Sheba), Moladah,
Hazar Shual, Balah, Ezem,
Eltolad, Bethul, Hormah,
Ziklag, Beth Marcaboth, Hazar Susah,
Beth Lebaoth, and Sharuhen—
    thirteen towns and their villages.
Ain, Rimmon, Ether, and Ashan—
    four towns and their villages—plus all the villages around these towns as far as Baalath Beer, the Ramah of the Negev.

8-9   This is the inheritance of the tribe of Simeon according to its clans. The inheritance of Simeon came out of the share of Judah, because Judah's portion turned out to be more than they needed. That's how the people of Simeon came to get their lot from within Judah's portion.

ZEBULUN

10-15 The third lot went to Zebulun, clan by clan:
    The border of their inheritance went all the way to Sarid. It ran west to Maralah, met Dabbesheth, and then went to the brook opposite Jokneam. In the other direction from Sarid, the border ran east; it followed the sunrise to the border of Kisloth Tabor, on to Daberath and up to Japhia. It continued east to Gath Hepher and Eth Kazin, came out at Rimmon, and turned toward Neah. There the border went around on the north to Hannathon and ran out into the Valley of Iphtah El. It included Kattath, Nahalal, Shimron, Idalah, and Bethlehem—twelve cities with their villages.

16   This is the inheritance of the people of Zebulun for their clans—these towns and their villages.

ISSACHAR

17-21 The fourth lot went to Issachar, clan by clan. Their territory included:

Jezreel, Kesulloth, Shunem,
Hapharaim, Shion, Anaharath,
Rabbith, Kishion, Ebez,
Remeth, En Gannim, En Haddah, and Beth Pazzez.

22   The boundary touched Tabor, Shahazumah, and Beth Shemesh and ended at the Jordan—sixteen towns and their villages.
23   These towns with their villages were the inheritance of the tribe of Issachar, clan by clan.

24 The fifth lot went to the tribe of Asher, clan by clan:

25-30   Their territory included Helkath, Hali, Beten, Acshaph, Allammelech, Amad, and Mishal. The western border touched Carmel and Shihor Libnath, then turned east toward Beth Dagon, touched Zebulun and the Valley of Iphtah El, and went north to Beth Emek and Neiel, skirting Cabul on the left. It went on to Abdon, Rehob, Hammon, and Kanah, all the way to Greater Sidon. The border circled back toward Ramah, extended to the fort city of Tyre, turned toward Hosah, and came out at the Sea in the region of Aczib, Ummah, Aphek, and Rehob — twenty-two towns and their villages.

31   These towns and villages were the inheritance of the tribe of Asher, clan by clan.

32 The sixth lot came to Naphtali and its clans.

33   Their border ran from Heleph, from the oak at Zaanannim, passing Adami Nekeb and Jabneel to Lakkum and ending at the Jordan.

34   The border returned on the west at Aznoth Tabor and came out at Hukkok, meeting Zebulun on the south, Asher on the west, and the Jordan on the east. The fort cities were:

35-38   Ziddim, Zer, Hammath, Rakkath, Kinnereth,
    Adamah, Ramah, Hazor,
    Kedesh, Edrei, En Hazor,
    Iron, Migdal El, Horem, Beth Anath, and Beth Shemesh —
        nineteen towns and their villages.

39   This is the inheritance of the tribe of Naphtali, the cities and their villages, clan by clan.

40-46 The seventh lot fell to Dan. The territory of their inheritance included:

    Zorah, Eshtaol, Ir Shemesh,
    Shaalabbin, Aijalon, Ithlah,
    Elon, Timnah, Ekron,
    Eltekeh, Gibbethon, Baalath,
    Jehud, Bene Berak, Gath Rimmon,
    Me Jarkon, and Rakkon, with the region facing Joppa.

47   But the people of Dan failed to get rid of the Westerners (Amorites), who pushed them back into the hills. The Westerners kept them out of the plain and they didn't have enough room. So the people of Dan marched up and attacked Leshem. They took it, killed the inhabitants, and settled in. They renamed it Leshem Dan after the name of Dan their ancestor.

48   This is the inheritance of the tribe of Dan, according to its clans, these towns with their villages.

49-50 They completed the dividing of the land as inheritance and the setting of its boundaries. The People of Israel then gave an inheritance among them to Joshua son of Nun. In obedience to GOD's word, they gave him the city which he had requested, Timnath Serah in the hill country of Ephraim. He rebuilt the city and settled there.

51 These are the inheritances which Eleazar the priest and Joshua son of Nun and the ancestral leaders assigned by lot to the tribes of Israel at Shiloh in the presence of GOD at the entrance of the Tent of Meeting. They completed the dividing of the land.

ASYLUM-CITIES

1-3 **20** Then GOD spoke to Joshua: "Tell the People of Israel: Designate the asylum-cities, as I instructed you through Moses, so that anyone who kills a person accidentally — that is, unintentionally — may flee there as a safe place of asylum from the avenger of blood.

4 "A person shall escape for refuge to one of these cities, stand at the entrance to the city gate, and lay out his case before the city's leaders. The leaders must then take him into the city among them and give him a place to live with them.

5-6 "If the avenger of blood chases after him, they must not give him up — he didn't intend to kill the person; there was no history of ill-feeling. He may stay in that city until he has stood trial before the congregation and until the death of the current high priest. Then he may go back to his own home in his hometown from which he fled."

7 They set apart Kedesh in Galilee in the hills of Naphtali, Shechem in the hills of Ephraim, and Kiriath Arba (that is, Hebron) in the hills of Judah.

8-9 On the other side of the Jordan, east of Jericho, they designated Bezer on the desert plateau from the tribe of Reuben, Ramoth in Gilead from the tribe of Gad, and Golan in Bashan from the tribe of Manasseh. These were the designated cities for the People of Israel and any resident foreigner living among them, so that anyone who killed someone unintentionally could flee there and not die by the hand of the avenger of blood without a fair trial before the congregation.

CITIES FOR THE LEVITES

1-2 **21** The ancestral heads of the Levites came to Eleazar the priest and Joshua son of Nun and to the heads of the other tribes of the People of Israel. This took place at Shiloh in the land of Canaan. They said, "GOD commanded through Moses that you give us cities to live in with access to pastures for our cattle."

3 So the People of Israel, out of their own inheritance, gave the Levites, just as GOD commanded, the following cities and pastures:

4-5 The lot came out for the families of the Kohathites this way: Levites descended from Aaron the priest received by lot thirteen cities out of the tribes of Judah, Simeon, and Benjamin. The rest of the Kohathites received by lot ten cities from the families of the tribes of Ephraim, Dan, and the half-tribe of Manasseh.

6 The Gershonites received by lot thirteen cities from the families of the tribes of Issachar, Asher, Naphtali, and the half-tribe of Manasseh in Bashan.

7 The families of the Merarites received twelve towns from the tribes

of Reuben, Gad, and Zebulun.

8   So the People of Israel gave these cities with their pastures to the Levites just as GOD had ordered through Moses, that is, by lot.

CITIES FOR THE DESCENDANTS OF AARON

9-10   They assigned from the tribes of Judah, Simeon, and Benjamin the following towns, here named individually (these were for the descendants of Aaron who were from the families of the Kohathite branch of Levi because the first lot fell to them):

11-12   Kiriath Arba (Arba was the ancestor of Anak), that is, Hebron, in the hills of Judah, with access to the pastures around it. The fields of the city and its open lands they had already given to Caleb son of Jephunneh as his possession.

13-16   To the descendants of Aaron the priest they gave Hebron (the asylum-city for the unconvicted killers), Libnah, Jattir, Eshtemoa, Holon, Debir, Ain, Juttah, and Beth Shemesh, all with their accompanying pastures — nine towns from these two tribes.

17-18   And from the tribe of Benjamin: Gibeon, Geba, Anathoth, and Almon, together with their pastures — four towns.

19   The total for the cities and pastures for the priests descended from Aaron came to thirteen.

20-22   The rest of the Kohathite families from the tribe of Levi were assigned their cities by lot from the tribe of Ephraim: Shechem (the asylum-city for the unconvicted killer) in the hills of Ephraim, Gezer, Kibzaim, and Beth Horon, with their pastures — four towns.

23-24   From the tribe of Dan they received Eltekeh, Gibbethon, Aijalon, and Gath Rimmon, all with their pastures — four towns.

25   And from the half-tribe of Manasseh they received Taanach and Gath Rimmon with their pastures — two towns.

26   All told, ten cities with their pastures went to the remaining Kohathite families.

27   The Gershonite families of the tribe of Levi were given from the half-tribe of Manasseh: Golan in Bashan (an asylum-city for the unconvicted killer), and Be Eshtarah, with their pastures — two cities.

28-29   And from the tribe of Issachar: Kishion, Daberath, Jarmuth, and En Gannim, with their pastures — four towns.

30-31   From the tribe of Asher: Mishal, Abdon, Helkath, and Rehob, with their pastures — four towns.

32   From the tribe of Naphtali: Kedesh in Galilee (an asylum-city for the unconvicted killer), Hammoth Dor, and Kartan, with their pastures — three towns.

33   For the Gershonites and their families: thirteen towns with their pastures.

34-35   The Merari families, the remaining Levites, were given from the tribe of Zebulun: Jokneam, Kartah, Dimnah, and Nahalal, with their pastures — four cities.

36-37   From the tribe of Reuben: Bezer, Jahaz, Kedemoth, and Mephaath, with their pastures — four towns.

38-39　　From the tribe of Gad: Ramoth in Gilead (an asylum-city for the unconvicted killer), Mahanaim, Heshbon, and Jazer, with their pastures—a
total of four towns.

40　　All these towns were assigned by lot to the Merarites, the remaining
Levites—twelve towns.

41-42　　The Levites held forty-eight towns with their accompanying pastures
within the territory of the People of Israel. Each of these towns had pastures surrounding it—this was the case for all these towns.

43-44　　And so GOD gave Israel the entire land that he had solemnly vowed to give to
their ancestors. They took possession of it and made themselves at home in it.
And GOD gave them rest on all sides, as he had also solemnly vowed to their
ancestors. Not a single one of their enemies was able to stand up to them—
GOD handed over all their enemies to them.

45　　Not one word failed from all the good words GOD spoke to the house of
Israel. Everything came out right.

1-5　　**22** Then Joshua called together the Reubenites, Gadites, and the
half-tribe of Manasseh. He said: "You have carried out everything Moses the servant of GOD commanded you, and you have
obediently done everything I have commanded you. All this time and right
down to this very day you have not abandoned your brothers; you've shouldered the task laid on you by GOD, your God. And now GOD, your God, has
given rest to your brothers just as he promised them. You're now free to go
back to your homes, the country of your inheritance that Moses the servant
of GOD gave you on the other side of the Jordan. Only this: Be vigilant in
keeping the Commandment and The Revelation that Moses the servant of
GOD laid on you: Love GOD, your God, walk in all his ways, do what he's commanded, embrace him, serve him with everything you are and have."

6-7　　Then Joshua blessed them and sent them on their way. They went home.
(To the half-tribe of Manasseh, Moses had assigned a share in Bashan.
To the other half, Joshua assigned land with their brothers west of the
Jordan.)

7-8　　When Joshua sent them off to their homes, he blessed them. He said:
"Go home. You're going home rich—great herds of cattle, silver and gold,
bronze and iron, huge piles of clothing. Share the wealth with your friends
and families—all this plunder from your enemies!"

9　　The Reubenites, Gadites, and the half-tribe of Manasseh left the People of
Israel at Shiloh in the land of Canaan to return to Gilead, the land of their
possession, which they had taken under the command of Moses as ordered
by GOD.

10　　They arrived at Geliloth on the Jordan (touching on Canaanite land).
There the Reubenites, Gadites, and the half-tribe of Manasseh built an
altar on the banks of the Jordan—a huge altar!

11　　The People of Israel heard of it: "What's this? The Reubenites, Gadites,
and the half-tribe of Manasseh have built an altar facing the land of

Canaan at Geliloth on the Jordan, across from the People of Israel!"

12-14 When the People of Israel heard this, the entire congregation mustered at Shiloh to go to war against them. They sent Phinehas son of Eleazar the priest to the Reubenites, Gadites, and the half-tribe of Manasseh (that is, to the land of Gilead). Accompanying him were ten chiefs, one chief for each of the ten tribes, each the head of his ancestral family. They represented the military divisions of Israel.

15-18 They went to the Reubenites, Gadites, and the half-tribe of Manasseh and spoke to them: "The entire congregation of GOD wants to know: What is this violation against the God of Israel that you have committed, turning your back on GOD and building your own altar—a blatant act of rebellion against GOD? Wasn't the crime of Peor enough for us? Why, to this day we aren't rid of it, still living with the fallout of the plague on the congregation of GOD! Look at you—turning your back on GOD! If you rebel against GOD today, tomorrow he'll vent his anger on all of us, the entire congregation of Israel.

19-20 "If you think the land of your possession isn't holy enough but somehow contaminated, come back over to GOD's possession, where GOD's Dwelling is set up, and take your land there, but don't rebel against GOD. And don't rebel against us by building your own altar apart from the Altar of our GOD. When Achan son of Zerah violated the holy curse, didn't anger fall on the whole congregation of Israel? He wasn't the only one to die for his sin."

21-22 The Reubenites, Gadites, and the half-tribe of Manasseh replied to the heads of the tribes of Israel:

> The God of Gods is GOD,
> The God of Gods is GOD!

22-23 "He knows and he'll let Israel know if this is a rebellious betrayal of GOD. And if it is, don't bother saving us. If we built ourselves an altar in rebellion against GOD, if we did it to present on it Whole-Burnt-Offerings or Grain-Offerings or to enact there sacrificial Peace-Offerings, let GOD decide.

24-25 "But that's not it. We did it because we cared. We were anxious lest someday your children should say to our children, 'You're not connected with GOD, the God of Israel! GOD made the Jordan a boundary between us and you. You Reubenites and Gadites have no part in GOD.' And then your children might cause our children to quit worshiping GOD.

26 "So we said to ourselves, 'Let's do something. Let's build an altar—but not for Whole-Burnt-Offerings, not for sacrifices.'

27 "We built this altar as a witness between us and you and our children coming after us, a witness to the Altar where we worship GOD in his Sacred Dwelling with our Whole-Burnt-Offerings and our sacrifices and our Peace-Offerings.

"This way, your children won't be able to say to our children in the future, 'You have no part in GOD.'

28 "We said to ourselves, 'If anyone speaks disparagingly to us or to our children in the future, we'll say: Look at this model of GOD's Altar which our ancestors made. It's not for Whole-Burnt-Offerings, not for sacrifices. It's a witness connecting us with you.'

29 "Rebelling against or turning our backs on GOD is the last thing on

our minds right now. We never dreamed of building an altar for Whole-Burnt-Offerings or Grain-Offerings to rival the Altar of our GOD in front of his Sacred Dwelling."

30 Phinehas the priest, all the heads of the congregation, and the heads of the military divisions of Israel who were also with him heard what the Reubenites, Gadites, and the half-tribe of Manasseh had to say. They were satisfied.

31 Priest Phinehas son of Eleazar said to Reuben, Gad, and Manasseh, "Now we're convinced that GOD is present with us since you haven't been disloyal to GOD in this matter. You saved the People of Israel from GOD's discipline."

32-33 Then Priest Phinehas son of Eleazar left the Reubenites, Gadites, and the half-tribe of Manasseh (from Gilead) and, with the chiefs, returned to the land of Canaan to the People of Israel and gave a full report. They were pleased with the report. The People of Israel blessed God—there was no more talk of attacking and destroying the land in which the Reubenites and Gadites were living.

34 Reuben and Gad named the altar:

A Witness Between Us.
GOD Alone Is God.

JOSHUA'S CHARGE

1-2 **23** A long time later, after GOD had given Israel rest from all their surrounding enemies, and Joshua was a venerable old man, Joshua called all Israel together—elders, chiefs, judges, and officers. Then he spoke to them:

2-3 "I'm an old man. I've lived a long time. You have seen everything that GOD has done to these nations because of you. He did it because he's GOD, your God. He fought for you.

4-5 "Stay alert: I have assigned to you by lot these nations that remain as an inheritance to your tribes—these in addition to the nations I have already cut down—from the Jordan to the Great Sea in the west. GOD, your God, will drive them out of your path until there's nothing left of them and you'll take over their land just as GOD, your God, promised you.

6-8 "Now, stay strong and steady. Obediently do everything written in the *Book of The Revelation of Moses*—don't miss a detail. Don't get mixed up with the nations that are still around. Don't so much as speak the names of their gods or swear by them. And by all means don't worship or pray to them. Hold tight to GOD, your God, just as you've done up to now.

9-10 "GOD has driven out superpower nations before you. And up to now, no one has been able to stand up to you. Think of it—one of you, single-handedly, putting a thousand on the run! Because GOD is GOD, your God. Because he fights for you, just as he promised you.

11-13 "Now, vigilantly guard your souls: Love GOD, your God. Because if you wander off and start taking up with these remaining nations still among you (intermarry, say, and have other dealings with them), know for certain that GOD, your God, will not get rid of these nations for you. They'll be nothing but trouble to you—horsewhips on your backs and sand in your eyes—until you're the ones who will be driven out of this good land that GOD, your God, has given you.

14 "As you can see, I'm about to go the way we all end up going. Know this with all your heart, with everything in you, that not one detail has failed of all the good things GOD, your God, promised you. It has all happened. Nothing's left undone—not so much as a word.

15-16 "But just as sure as everything good that GOD, your God, has promised has come true, so also GOD will bring to pass every bad thing until there's nothing left of you in this good land that GOD has given you. If you leave the path of the Covenant of GOD, your God, that he commanded you, go off and serve and worship other gods, GOD's anger will blaze out against you. In no time at all there'll be nothing left of you, no sign that you've ever been in this good land he gave you."

THE COVENANT AT SHECHEM

1-2 **24** Joshua called together all the tribes of Israel at Shechem. He called in the elders, chiefs, judges, and officers. They presented themselves before God. Then Joshua addressed all the people:

2-6 "This is what GOD, the God of Israel, says: A long time ago your ancestors, Terah and his sons Abraham and Nahor, lived to the east of the River Euphrates. They worshiped other gods. I took your ancestor Abraham from the far side of The River. I led him all over the land of Canaan and multiplied his descendants. I gave him Isaac. Then I gave Isaac Jacob and Esau. I let Esau have the mountains of Seir as home, but Jacob and his sons ended up in Egypt. I sent Moses and Aaron. I hit Egypt hard with plagues and then led you out of there. I brought your ancestors out of Egypt. You came to the sea, the Egyptians in hot pursuit with chariots and cavalry, to the very edge of the Red Sea!

7-10 "Then they cried out for help to GOD. He put a cloud between you and the Egyptians and then let the sea loose on them. It drowned them.

"You watched the whole thing with your own eyes, what I did to Egypt. And then you lived in the wilderness for a long time. I brought you to the country of the Amorites, who lived east of the Jordan, and they fought you. But I fought for you and you took their land. I destroyed them for you. Then Balak son of Zippor made his appearance. He was the king of Moab. He got ready to fight Israel by sending for Balaam son of Beor to come and curse you. But I wouldn't listen to Balaam—he ended up blessing you over and over! I saved you from him.

11 "You then crossed the Jordan and came to Jericho. The Jericho leaders ganged up on you as well as the Amorites, Perizzites, Canaanites, Hittites, Girgashites, Hivites, and Jebusites, but I turned them over to you.

12 "I sent the Hornet ahead of you. It drove out the two Amorite kings—did your work for you. You didn't have to do a thing, not so much as raise a finger.

13 "I handed you a land for which you did not work, towns you did not build. And here you are now living in them and eating from vineyards and olive groves you did not plant.

14 "So now: Fear GOD. Worship him in total commitment. Get rid of the gods your ancestors worshiped on the far side of The River (the Euphrates) and in Egypt. You, worship GOD.

15 "If you decide that it's a bad thing to worship GOD, then choose a god you'd rather serve—and do it today. Choose one of the gods your ancestors worshiped from the country beyond The River, or one of the gods of

the Amorites, on whose land you're now living. As for me and my family, we'll worship GOD."

16 The people answered, "We'd never forsake GOD! Never! We'd never leave GOD to worship other gods.

17-18 "GOD is our God! He brought up our ancestors from Egypt and from slave conditions. He did all those great signs while we watched. He has kept his eye on us all along the roads we've traveled and among the nations we've passed through. Just for us he drove out all the nations, Amorites and all, who lived in the land.

"Count us in: We too are going to worship GOD. He's our God."

19-20 Then Joshua told the people: "You can't do it; you're not able to worship GOD. He is a holy God. He is a jealous God. He won't put up with your fooling around and sinning. When you leave GOD and take up the worship of foreign gods, he'll turn right around and come down on you hard. He'll put an end to you—and after all the good he has done for you!"

21 But the people told Joshua: "No! No! We worship GOD!"

22 And so Joshua addressed the people: "You are witnesses against yourselves that you have chosen GOD for yourselves—to worship him."

And they said, "We are witnesses."

23 Joshua said, "Now get rid of all the foreign gods you have with you. Say an unqualified Yes to GOD, the God of Israel."

24 The people answered Joshua, "We will worship GOD. What he says, we'll do."

25-26 Joshua completed a Covenant for the people that day there at Shechem. He made it official, spelling it out in detail. Joshua wrote out all the directions and regulations into the Book of The Revelation of God. Then he took a large stone and set it up under the oak that was in the holy place of GOD.

27 Joshua spoke to all the people: "This stone is a witness against us. It has heard every word that GOD has said to us. It is a standing witness against you lest you cheat on your God."

28 Then Joshua dismissed the people, each to his own place of inheritance.

29-30 After all this, Joshua son of Nun, the servant of GOD, died. He was 110 years old. They buried him in the land of his inheritance at Timnath Serah in the mountains of Ephraim, north of Mount Gaash.

31 Israel served GOD through the lifetime of Joshua and of the elders who outlived him, who had themselves experienced all that GOD had done for Israel.

32 Joseph's bones, which the People of Israel had brought from Egypt, they buried in Shechem in the plot of ground that Jacob had purchased from the sons of Hamor (who was the father of Shechem). He paid a hundred silver coins for it. It belongs to the inheritance of the family of Joseph.

33 Eleazar son of Aaron died. They buried him at Gibeah, which had been allotted to his son Phinehas in the mountains of Ephraim.

JUDGES

Sex and violence, rape and massacre, brutality and deceit do not seem to be congenial materials for use in developing a story of salvation. Given the Bible's subject matter—God and salvation, living well and loving deeply—we quite naturally expect to find in its pages leaders for us who are good, noble, honorable men and women showing us the way. So it is always something of a shock to enter the pages of the book of Judges and find ourselves immersed in nearly unrelieved mayhem.

It might not gravel our sensibilities so much if these flawed and reprobate leaders were held up as negative moral examples, with lurid, hellfire descriptions of the punishing consequences of living such bad lives. But the story is not told quite that way. There is a kind of matter-of-fact indifference in the tone of the narration, almost as if God is saying, "Well, if this is all you're going to give me to work with, I'll use *these* men and women, just as they are, and get on with working out the story of salvation." These people are even given a measure of dignity as they find their place in the story; they are most certainly not employed for the sake of vilification or lampoon.

God, it turns out, does not require good people in order to do good work. He can and does work with us in whatever moral and spiritual condition he finds us. God, we are learning, does some of his best work using the most unlikely people. If God found a way to significantly include these leaders ("judges") in what we know is on its way to becoming a glorious conclusion, he can certainly use us along with our sometimes impossible friends and neighbors.

Twice in Judges (17:6 and 21:25) there is the telling refrain: "At that time there was no king in Israel. People did whatever they felt like doing." But we readers know that there *was* a king in Israel: *God* was king. And so, while the lack of an earthly king accounts for the moral and political anarchy, the presence of the sovereign God, however obscurely realized, means that the reality of the kingdom is never in doubt.

JUDGES

1 **1** A time came after the death of Joshua when the People of Israel asked GOD, "Who will take the lead in going up against the Canaanites to fight them?"

2 And GOD said, "Judah will go. I've given the land to him."

3 The men of Judah said to those of their brother Simeon, "Go up with us to our territory and we'll fight the Canaanites. Then we'll go with you to your territory." And Simeon went with them.

4 So Judah went up. GOD gave them the Canaanites and the Perizzites. They defeated them at Bezek—ten military units!

5-7 They caught up with My-Master-Bezek there and fought him. They smashed the Canaanites and the Perizzites. My-Master-Bezek ran, but they gave chase and caught him. They cut off his thumbs and big toes. My-Master-Bezek said, "Seventy kings with their thumbs and big toes cut off used to crawl under my table, scavenging. Now God has done to me what I did to them."

They brought him to Jerusalem and he died there.

8-10 The people of Judah attacked and captured Jerusalem, subduing the city by sword and then sending it up in flames. After that they had gone down to fight the Canaanites who were living in the hill country, the Negev, and the foothills. Judah had gone on to the Canaanites who lived in Hebron (Hebron used to be called Kiriath Arba) and brought Sheshai, Ahiman, and Talmai to their knees.

11-12 From there they had marched against the population of Debir (Debir used to be called Kiriath Sepher). Caleb had said, "Whoever attacks Kiriath Sepher and takes it, I'll give my daughter Acsah to him as his wife."

13 Othniel son of Kenaz, Caleb's brother, took it, so Caleb gave him his daughter Acsah as his wife.

14-15 When she arrived she got him
　　　to ask for farmland from her father.
As she dismounted from her donkey
　　　Caleb asked her, "What would you like?"
She said, "Give me a marriage gift.
　　　You've given me desert land;
Now give me pools of water!"
　　　And he gave her the upper and the lower pools.

16 The people of Hobab the Kenite, Moses' relative, went up with the people of Judah from the City of Palms to the wilderness of Judah at the descent of Arad. They settled down there with the Amalekites.

17 The people of Judah went with their kin the Simeonites and struck the Canaanites who lived in Zephath. They carried out the holy curse and named the city Curse-town.

18-19 But Judah didn't manage to capture Gaza, Ashkelon, and Ekron with their territories. GOD was certainly with Judah in that they took over the hill country. But they couldn't oust the people on the plain because they had iron chariots.

20   They gave Hebron to Caleb, as Moses had directed. Caleb drove out the three sons of Anak.

21   But the people of Benjamin couldn't get rid of the Jebusites living in Jerusalem. Benjaminites and Jebusites live side by side in Jerusalem to this day.

22-26   The house of Joseph went up to attack Bethel. GOD was with them. Joseph sent out spies to look the place over. Bethel used to be known as Luz. The spies saw a man leaving the city and said to him, "Show us a way into the city and we'll treat you well." The man showed them a way in. They killed everyone in the city but the man and his family. The man went to Hittite country and built a city. He named it Luz; that's its name to this day.

27-28   But Manasseh never managed to drive out Beth Shan, Taanach, Dor, Ibleam, and Megiddo with their territories. The Canaanites dug in their heels and wouldn't budge. When Israel became stronger they put the Canaanites to forced labor, but they never got rid of them.

29   Neither did Ephraim drive out the Canaanites who lived in Gezer. The Canaanites stuck it out and lived there with them.

30   Nor did Zebulun drive out the Canaanites in Kitron or Nahalol. They kept living there, but they were put to forced labor.

31-32   Nor did Asher drive out the people of Acco, Sidon, Ahlab, Aczib, Helbah, Aphek, and Rehob. Asher went ahead and settled down with the Canaanites since they could not get rid of them.

33   Naphtali fared no better. They couldn't drive out the people of Beth Shemesh or Beth Anath so they just moved in and lived with them. They did, though, put them to forced labor.

34-35   The Amorites pushed the people of Dan up into the hills and wouldn't let them down on the plains. The Amorites stubbornly continued to live in Mount Heres, Aijalon, and Shaalbim. But when the house of Joseph got the upper hand, they were put to forced labor.

36   The Amorite border extended from Scorpions' Pass and Sela upward.

1-2   GOD's angel went up from Gilgal to Bokim and said, "I brought you out of Egypt; I led you to the land that I promised to your fathers; and I said, I'll never break my covenant with you—never! And you're never to make a covenant with the people who live in this land. Tear down their altars! But you haven't obeyed me! What's this that you're doing?

3   "So now I'm telling you that I won't drive them out before you. They'll trip you up and their gods will become a trap."

4-5   When GOD's angel had spoken these words to all the People of Israel, they cried out—oh! how they wept! They named the place Bokim (Weepers). And there they sacrificed to GOD.

6-9   After Joshua had dismissed them, the People of Israel went off to claim their allotted territories and take possession of the land. The people worshiped GOD throughout the lifetime of Joshua and the time of the leaders who survived him, leaders who had been in on all of GOD's great work that he had done for Israel. Then Joshua son of Nun, the servant of GOD, died. He was 110 years old. They buried him in his allotted inheritance at Timnath Heres in the hills of Ephraim north of Mount Gaash.

¹⁰ Eventually that entire generation died and was buried. Then another generation grew up that didn't know anything of GOD or the work he had done for Israel.

¹¹⁻¹⁵ The People of Israel did evil in GOD's sight: they served Baal-gods; they deserted GOD, the God of their parents who had led them out of Egypt; they took up with other gods, gods of the peoples around them. They actually worshiped them! And oh, how they angered GOD as they worshiped god Baal and goddess Astarte! GOD's anger was hot against Israel: He handed them off to plunderers who stripped them; he sold them cheap to enemies on all sides. They were helpless before their enemies. Every time they walked out the door GOD was with them — but for evil, just as GOD had said, just as he had sworn he would do. They were in a bad way.

¹⁶⁻¹⁷ But then GOD raised up judges who saved them from their plunderers. But they wouldn't listen to their judges; they prostituted themselves to other gods — worshiped them! They lost no time leaving the road walked by their parents, the road of obedience to GOD's commands. They refused to have anything to do with it.

¹⁸⁻¹⁹ When GOD was setting up judges for them, he would be right there with the judge: He would save them from their enemies' oppression as long as the judge was alive, for GOD was moved to compassion when he heard their groaning because of those who afflicted and beat them. But when the judge died, the people went right back to their old ways — but even worse than their parents! — running after other gods, serving and worshiping them. Stubborn as mules, they didn't drop a single evil practice.

²⁰⁻²² And GOD's anger blazed against Israel. He said, "Because these people have thrown out my covenant that I commanded their parents and haven't listened to me, I'm not driving out one more person from the nations that Joshua left behind when he died. I'll use them to test Israel and see whether they stay on GOD's road and walk down it as their parents did."

²³ That's why GOD let those nations remain. He didn't drive them out or let Joshua get rid of them.

¹⁻⁴ **3** These are the nations that GOD left there, using them to test the Israelites who had no experience in the Canaanite wars. He did it to train the descendants of Israel, the ones who had no battle experience, in the art of war. He left the five Philistine tyrants, all the Canaanites, the Sidonians, and the Hivites living on Mount Lebanon from Mount Baal Hermon to Hamath's Pass. They were there to test Israel and see whether they would obey GOD's commands that were given to their parents through Moses.

⁵⁻⁶ But the People of Israel made themselves at home among the Canaanites, Hittites, Amorites, Perizzites, Hivites, and Jebusites. They married their daughters and gave their own daughters to their sons in marriage. And they worshiped their gods.

OTHNIEL

7-8 The People of Israel did evil in GOD's sight. They forgot their GOD and worshiped the Baal gods and Asherah goddesses. GOD's hot anger blazed against Israel. He sold them off to Cushan-Rishathaim king of Aram Naharaim. The People of Israel were in servitude to Cushan-Rishathaim for eight years.

9-10 The People of Israel cried out to GOD and GOD raised up a savior who rescued them: Caleb's nephew Othniel, son of his younger brother Kenaz. The Spirit of GOD came on him and he rallied Israel. He went out to war and GOD gave him Cushan-Rishathaim king of Aram Naharaim. Othniel made short work of him.

11 The land was quiet for forty years. Then Othniel son of Kenaz died.

EHUD

12-14 But the People of Israel went back to doing evil in GOD's sight. So GOD made Eglon king of Moab a power against Israel because they did evil in GOD's sight. He recruited the Ammonites and Amalekites and went out and struck Israel. They took the City of Palms. The People of Israel were in servitude to Eglon fourteen years.

15-19 The People of Israel cried out to GOD and GOD raised up for them a savior, Ehud son of Gera, a Benjaminite. He was left-handed. The People of Israel sent tribute by him to Eglon king of Moab. Ehud made himself a short two-edged sword and strapped it on his right thigh under his clothes. He presented the tribute to Eglon king of Moab. Eglon was grossly fat. After Ehud finished presenting the tribute, he went a little way with the men who had carried it. But when he got as far as the stone images near Gilgal, he went back and said, "I have a private message for you, O King."

The king told his servants, "Leave." They all left.

20-24 Ehud approached him — the king was now quite alone in his cool rooftop room — and said, "I have a word of God for you." Eglon stood up from his throne. Ehud reached with his left hand and took his sword from his right thigh and plunged it into the king's big belly. Not only the blade but the hilt went in. The fat closed in over it so he couldn't pull it out. Ehud slipped out by way of the porch and shut and locked the doors of the rooftop room behind him. Then he was gone.

When the servants came, they saw with surprise that the doors to the rooftop room were locked. They said, "He's probably relieving himself in the restroom."

25 They waited. And then they worried — no one was coming out of those locked doors. Finally, they got a key and unlocked them. There was their master, fallen on the floor, dead!

26-27 While they were standing around wondering what to do, Ehud was long gone. He got past the stone images and escaped to Seirah. When he got there, he sounded the trumpet on Mount Ephraim. The People of Israel came down from the hills and joined him. He took his place at their head.

28 He said, "Follow me, for GOD has given your enemies — yes, Moab! — to you." They went down after him and secured the fords of the Jordan against the Moabites. They let no one cross over.

29-30 At that time, they struck down about ten companies of Moabites, all of them well-fed and robust. Not one escaped. That day Moab was subdued under the hand of Israel.

The land was quiet for eighty years.

SHAMGAR

31 Shamgar son of Anath came after Ehud. Using a cattle prod, he killed six hundred Philistines single-handed. He too saved Israel.

DEBORAH

1-3 The People of Israel kept right on doing evil in GOD's sight. With Ehud dead, GOD sold them off to Jabin king of Canaan who ruled from Hazor. Sisera, who lived in Harosheth Haggoyim, was the commander of his army. The People of Israel cried out to GOD because he had cruelly oppressed them with his nine hundred iron chariots for twenty years.

4-5 Deborah was a prophet, the wife of Lappidoth. She was judge over Israel at that time. She held court under Deborah's Palm between Ramah and Bethel in the hills of Ephraim. The People of Israel went to her in matters of justice.

6-7 She sent for Barak son of Abinoam from Kedesh in Naphtali and said to him, "It has become clear that GOD, the God of Israel, commands you: Go to Mount Tabor and prepare for battle. Take ten companies of soldiers from Naphtali and Zebulun. I'll take care of getting Sisera, the leader of Jabin's army, to the Kishon River with all his chariots and troops. And I'll make sure you win the battle."

8 Barak said, "If you go with me, I'll go. But if you don't go with me, I won't go."

9-10 She said, "Of course I'll go with you. But understand that with an attitude like that, there'll be no glory in it for you. GOD will use a woman's hand to take care of Sisera."

Deborah got ready and went with Barak to Kedesh. Barak called Zebulun and Naphtali together at Kedesh. Ten companies of men followed him. And Deborah was with him.

11-13 It happened that Heber the Kenite had parted company with the other Kenites, the descendants of Hobab, Moses' in-law. He was now living at Zaanannim Oak near Kedesh. They told Sisera that Barak son of Abinoam had gone up to Mount Tabor. Sisera immediately called up all his chariots to the Kishon River—nine hundred iron chariots!—along with all his troops who were with him at Harosheth Haggoyim.

14 Deborah said to Barak, "Charge! This very day GOD has given you victory over Sisera. Isn't GOD marching before you?"

Barak charged down the slopes of Mount Tabor, his ten companies following him.

15-16 GOD routed Sisera—all those chariots, all those troops!—before Barak. Sisera jumped out of his chariot and ran. Barak chased the chariots and troops all the way to Harosheth Haggoyim. Sisera's entire fighting force was killed—not one man left.

17-18 Meanwhile Sisera, running for his life, headed for the tent of Jael, wife of Heber the Kenite. Jabin king of Hazor and Heber the Kenite were on good terms with one another. Jael stepped out to meet Sisera and said, "Come in, sir. Stay here with me. Don't be afraid."

So he went with her into her tent. She covered him with a blanket.

19 He said to her, "Please, a little water. I'm thirsty."

She opened a bottle of milk, gave him a drink, and then covered him up again.

20   He then said, "Stand at the tent flap. If anyone comes by and asks you, 'Is there anyone here?' tell him, 'No, not a soul.'"

21   Then while he was fast asleep from exhaustion, Jael wife of Heber took a tent peg and hammer, tiptoed toward him, and drove the tent peg through his temple and all the way into the ground. He convulsed and died.

22   Barak arrived in pursuit of Sisera. Jael went out to greet him. She said, "Come, I'll show you the man you're looking for." He went with her and there he was—Sisera, stretched out, dead, with a tent peg through his temple.

23-24   On that day God subdued Jabin king of Canaan before the People of Israel. The People of Israel pressed harder and harder on Jabin king of Canaan until there was nothing left of him.

1   **5** That day Deborah and Barak son of Abinoam sang this song:

2   When they let down their hair in Israel,
        they let it blow wild in the wind.
    The people volunteered with abandon,
        bless GOD!

3   Hear O kings! Listen O princes!
        To GOD, yes to GOD, I'll sing,
    Make music to GOD,
        to the God of Israel.

4-5   GOD, when you left Seir,
        marched across the fields of Edom,
    Earth quaked, yes, the skies poured rain,
        oh, the clouds made rivers.
    Mountains leapt before GOD, the Sinai God,
        before GOD, the God of Israel.

6-8   In the time of Shamgar son of Anath,
        and in the time of Jael,
    Public roads were abandoned,
        travelers went by backroads.
    Warriors became fat and sloppy,
        no fight left in them.
    Then you, Deborah, rose up;
        you got up, a mother in Israel.
    God chose new leaders,
        who then fought at the gates.
    And not a shield or spear to be seen
        among the forty companies of Israel.

9   Lift your hearts high, O Israel,
        with abandon, volunteering yourselves with the people—bless GOD!

10-11   You who ride on prize donkeys
        comfortably mounted on blankets

And you who walk down the roads,
  ponder, attend!
Gather at the town well
  and listen to them sing,
Chanting the tale of GOD's victories,
  his victories accomplished in Israel.

Then the people of GOD
  went down to the city gates.

12 Wake up, wake up, Deborah!
      Wake up, wake up, sing a song!
    On your feet, Barak!
      Take your prisoners, son of Abinoam!

13-18 Then the remnant went down to greet the brave ones.
        The people of GOD joined the mighty ones.
      The captains from Ephraim came to the valley,
        behind you, Benjamin, with your troops.
      Captains marched down from Makir,
        from Zebulun high-ranking leaders came down.
      Issachar's princes rallied to Deborah,
        Issachar stood fast with Barak,
        backing him up on the field of battle.
      But in Reuben's divisions there was much second-guessing.
        Why all those campfire discussions?
      Diverted and distracted,
        Reuben's divisions couldn't make up their minds.
      Gilead played it safe across the Jordan,
        and Dan, why did he go off sailing?
      Asher kept his distance on the seacoast,
        safe and secure in his harbors.
      But Zebulun risked life and limb, defied death,
        as did Naphtali on the battle heights.

19-23 The kings came, they fought,
        the kings of Canaan fought.
      At Taanach they fought, at Megiddo's brook,
        but they took no silver, no plunder.
      The stars in the sky joined the fight,
        from their courses they fought against Sisera.
      The torrent Kishon swept them away,
        the torrent attacked them, the torrent Kishon.
        Oh, you'll stomp on the necks of the strong!
      Then the hoofs of the horses pounded,
        charging, stampeding stallions.
      "Curse Meroz," says GOD's angel.
        "Curse, double curse, its people,
      Because they didn't come when GOD needed them,
        didn't rally to GOD's side with valiant fighters."

24-27

Most blessed of all women is Jael,
   wife of Heber the Kenite,
   most blessed of homemaking women.
He asked for water,
   she brought milk;
In a handsome bowl,
   she offered cream.
She grabbed a tent peg in her left hand,
   with her right hand she seized a hammer.
She hammered Sisera, she smashed his head,
   she drove a hole through his temple.
He slumped at her feet. He fell. He sprawled.
   He slumped at her feet. He fell.
   Slumped. Fallen. Dead.

28-30

Sisera's mother waited at the window,
   a weary, anxious watch.
"What's keeping his chariot?
   What delays his chariot's rumble?"
The wisest of her ladies-in-waiting answers
   with calm, reassuring words,
"Don't you think they're busy at plunder,
   dividing up the loot?
A girl, maybe two girls,
   for each man,
And for Sisera a bright silk shirt,
   a prize, fancy silk shirt!
And a colorful scarf — make it two scarves —
   to grace the neck of the plunderer."

31

Thus may all GOD's enemies perish,
   while his lovers be like the unclouded sun.

The land was quiet for forty years.

GIDEON

1-6

Yet again the People of Israel went back to doing evil in GOD's sight. GOD put them under the domination of Midian for seven years. Midian overpowered Israel. Because of Midian, the People of Israel made for themselves hideouts in the mountains — caves and forts. When Israel planted its crops, Midian and Amalek, the easterners, would invade them, camp in their fields, and destroy their crops all the way down to Gaza. They left nothing for them to live on, neither sheep nor ox nor donkey. Bringing their cattle and tents, they came in and took over, like an invasion of locusts. And their camels — past counting! They marched in and devastated the country. The People of Israel, reduced to grinding poverty by Midian, cried out to GOD for help.

7-10

One time when the People of Israel had cried out to GOD because of

Midian, GOD sent them a prophet with this message: "GOD, the God of Israel, says,

> I delivered you from Egypt,
>   I freed you from a life of slavery;
> I rescued you from Egypt's brutality
>   and then from every oppressor;
> I pushed them out of your way
>   and gave you their land.

"And I said to you, 'I am GOD, your God. Don't for a minute be afraid of the gods of the Amorites in whose land you are living.' But you didn't listen to me."

11-12   One day the angel of GOD came and sat down under the oak in Ophrah that belonged to Joash the Abiezrite, whose son Gideon was threshing wheat in the winepress, out of sight of the Midianites. The angel of GOD appeared to him and said, "GOD is with you, O mighty warrior!"

13   Gideon replied, "With *me*, my master? If GOD is with us, why has all this happened to us? Where are all the miracle-wonders our parents and grandparents told us about, telling us, 'Didn't GOD deliver us from Egypt?' The fact is, GOD has nothing to do with us — he has turned us over to Midian."

14   But GOD faced him directly: "Go in this strength that is yours. Save Israel from Midian. Haven't I just sent you?"

15   Gideon said to him, "*Me*, my master? How and with what could I ever save Israel? Look at me. My clan's the weakest in Manasseh and I'm the runt of the litter."

16   GOD said to him, "I'll be with you. Believe me, you'll defeat Midian as one man."

17-18   Gideon said, "If you're serious about this, do me a favor: Give me a sign to back up what you're telling me. Don't leave until I come back and bring you my gift."

He said, "I'll wait till you get back."

19   Gideon went and prepared a young goat and a huge amount of unraised bread (he used over half a bushel of flour!). He put the meat in a basket and the broth in a pot and took them back under the shade of the oak tree for a sacred meal.

20   The angel of God said to him, "Take the meat and unraised bread, place them on that rock, and pour the broth on them." Gideon did it.

21-22   The angel of GOD stretched out the tip of the stick he was holding and touched the meat and the bread. Fire broke out of the rock and burned up the meat and bread while the angel of God slipped away out of sight. And Gideon knew it was the angel of God!

Gideon said, "Oh no! Master, GOD! I have seen the angel of God face-to-face!"

23   But GOD reassured him, "Easy now. Don't panic. You won't die."

24   Then Gideon built an altar there to GOD and named it "GOD's Peace." It's still called that at Ophrah of Abiezer.

25-26   That night this happened. GOD said to him, "Take your father's best seven-year-old bull, the prime one. Tear down your father's Baal altar and chop down the Asherah fertility pole beside it. Then build an altar to

GOD, your God, on the top of this hill. Take the prime bull and present it as a Whole-Burnt-Offering, using firewood from the Asherah pole that you cut down."

27 Gideon selected ten men from his servants and did exactly what GOD had told him. But because of his family and the people in the neighborhood, he was afraid to do it openly, so he did it that night.

28 Early in the morning, the people in town were shocked to find Baal's altar torn down, the Asherah pole beside it chopped down, and the prime bull burning away on the altar that had been built.

29 They kept asking, "Who did this?"

Questions and more questions, and then the answer: "Gideon son of Joash did it."

30 The men of the town demanded of Joash: "Bring out your son! He must die! Why, he tore down the Baal altar and chopped down the Asherah tree!"

31 But Joash stood up to the crowd pressing in on him, "Are you going to fight Baal's battles for him? Are you going to save him? Anyone who takes Baal's side will be dead by morning. If Baal is a god in fact, let him fight his own battles and defend his own altar."

32 They nicknamed Gideon that day Jerub-Baal because after he had torn down the Baal altar, he had said, "Let Baal fight his own battles."

33-35 All the Midianites and Amalekites (the easterners) got together, crossed the river, and made camp in the Valley of Jezreel. GOD's Spirit came over Gideon. He blew his ram's horn trumpet and the Abiezrites came out, ready to follow him. He dispatched messengers all through Manasseh, calling them to the battle; also to Asher, Zebulun, and Naphtali. They all came.

36-37 Gideon said to God, "If this is right, if you are using me to save Israel as you've said, then look: I'm placing a fleece of wool on the threshing floor. If dew is on the fleece only, but the floor is dry, then I know that you will use me to save Israel, as you said."

38 That's what happened. When he got up early the next morning, he wrung out the fleece—enough dew to fill a bowl with water!

39 Then Gideon said to God, "Don't be impatient with me, but let me say one more thing. I want to try another time with the fleece. But this time let the fleece stay dry, while the dew drenches the ground."

40 God made it happen that very night. Only the fleece was dry while the ground was wet with dew.

1 Jerub-Baal (Gideon) got up early the next morning, all his troops right there with him. They set up camp at Harod's Spring. The camp of Midian was in the plain, north of them near the Hill of Moreh.

2-3 GOD said to Gideon, "You have too large an army with you. I can't turn Midian over to them like this—they'll take all the credit, saying, 'I did it all myself,' and forget about me. Make a public announcement: 'Anyone afraid, anyone who has any qualms at all, may leave Mount Gilead now and go home.'" Twenty-two companies headed for home. Ten companies were left.

4-5 GOD said to Gideon: "There are still too many. Take them down to the stream and I'll make a final cut. When I say, 'This one goes with you,' he'll go. When I say, 'This one doesn't go,' he won't go." So Gideon took the troops down to the stream.

5-6 GOD said to Gideon: "Everyone who laps with his tongue, the way a dog laps, set on one side. And everyone who kneels to drink, drinking with his face to the water, set to the other side." Three hundred lapped with their tongues from their cupped hands. All the rest knelt to drink.

7 GOD said to Gideon: "I'll use the three hundred men who lapped at the stream to save you and give Midian into your hands. All the rest may go home."

8 After Gideon took all their provisions and trumpets, he sent all the Israelites home. He took up his position with the three hundred. The camp of Midian stretched out below him in the valley.

9-12 That night, GOD told Gideon: "Get up and go down to the camp. I've given it to you. If you have any doubts about going down, go down with Purah your armor bearer; when you hear what they're saying, you'll be bold and confident." He and his armor bearer Purah went down near the place where sentries were posted. Midian and Amalek, all the easterners, were spread out on the plain like a swarm of locusts. And their camels! Past counting, like grains of sand on the seashore!

13 Gideon arrived just in time to hear a man tell his friend a dream. He said, "I had this dream: A loaf of barley bread tumbled into the Midianite camp. It came to the tent and hit it so hard it collapsed. The tent fell!"

14 His friend said, "This has to be the sword of Gideon son of Joash, the Israelite! God has turned Midian — the whole camp! — over to him."

15 When Gideon heard the telling of the dream and its interpretation, he went to his knees before God in prayer. Then he went back to the Israelite camp and said, "Get up and get going! GOD has just given us the Midianite army!"

16-18 He divided the three hundred men into three companies. He gave each man a trumpet and an empty jar, with a torch in the jar. He said, "Watch me and do what I do. When I get to the edge of the camp, do exactly what I do. When I and those with me blow the trumpets, you also, all around the camp, blow your trumpets and shout, 'For GOD and for Gideon!'"

19-22 Gideon and his hundred men got to the edge of the camp at the beginning of the middle watch, just after the sentries had been posted. They blew the trumpets, at the same time smashing the jars they carried. All three companies blew the trumpets and broke the jars. They held the torches in their left hands and the trumpets in their right hands, ready to blow, and shouted, "A sword for GOD and for Gideon!" They were stationed all around the camp, each man at his post. The whole Midianite camp jumped to its feet. They yelled and fled. When the three hundred blew the trumpets, GOD aimed each Midianite's sword against his companion, all over the camp. They ran for their lives — to Beth Shittah, toward Zererah, to the border of Abel Meholah near Tabbath.

23 Israelites rallied from Naphtali, from Asher, and from all over Manasseh. They had Midian on the run.

24 Gideon then sent messengers through all the hill country of Ephraim, urging them, "Come down against Midian! Capture the fords of the Jordan at Beth Barah."

25   So all the men of Ephraim rallied and captured the fords of the Jordan at Beth Barah. They also captured the two Midianite commanders Oreb (Raven) and Zeeb (Wolf). They killed Oreb at Raven Rock; Zeeb they killed at Wolf Winepress. And they pressed the pursuit of Midian. They brought the heads of Oreb and Zeeb to Gideon across the Jordan.

1   **8** Then the Ephraimites said to Gideon, "Why did you leave us out of this, not calling us when you went to fight Midian?" They were indignant and let him know it.

2-3   But Gideon replied, "What have I done compared to you? Why, even the gleanings of Ephraim are superior to the vintage of Abiezer. God gave you Midian's commanders, Oreb and Zeeb. What have I done compared with you?"

When they heard this, they calmed down and cooled off.

4-5   Gideon and his three hundred arrived at the Jordan and crossed over. They were bone-tired but still pressing the pursuit. He asked the men of Succoth, "Please, give me some loaves of bread for my troops I have with me. They're worn out, and I'm hot on the trail of Zebah and Zalmunna, the Midianite kings."

6   But the leaders in Succoth said, "You're on a wild goose chase; why should we help you on a fool's errand?"

7   Gideon said, "If you say so. But when GOD gives me Zebah and Zalmunna, I'll give you a thrashing, whip your bare flesh with desert thorns and thistles!"

8-9   He went from there to Peniel and made the same request. The men of Peniel, like the men of Succoth, also refused. Gideon told them, "When I return safe and sound, I'll demolish this tower."

10   Zebah and Zalmunna were in Karkor with an army of about fifteen companies, all that was left of the fighting force of the easterners — they had lost 120 companies of soldiers.

11-12   Gideon went up the caravan trail east of Nobah and Jogbehah, found and attacked the undefended camp. Zebah and Zalmunna fled, but he chased and captured the two kings of Midian. The whole camp had panicked.

13-15   Gideon son of Joash returned from the battle by way of the Heres Pass. He captured a young man from Succoth and asked some questions. The young man wrote down the names of the officials and leaders of Succoth, seventy-seven men. Then Gideon went to the men of Succoth and said, "Here are the wild geese, Zebah and Zalmunna, you said I'd never catch. You wouldn't give so much as a scrap of bread to my worn-out men; you taunted us, saying that we were on a fool's errand."

16-17   Then he took the seventy-seven leaders of Succoth and thrashed them with desert thorns and thistles. And he demolished the tower of Peniel and killed the men of the city.

18   He then addressed Zebah and Zalmunna: "Tell me about the men you killed at Tabor."

"They were men much like you," they said, "each one like a king's son."

19   Gideon said, "They were my brothers, my mother's sons. As GOD lives, if you had let them live, I would let you live."

20 Then he spoke to Jether, his firstborn: "Get up and kill them." But he couldn't do it, couldn't draw his sword. He was afraid—he was still just a boy.

21 Zebah and Zalmunna said, "Do it yourself—if you're man enough!" And Gideon did it. He stepped up and killed Zebah and Zalmunna. Then he took the crescents that hung on the necks of their camels.

22 The Israelites said, "Rule over us, you and your son and your grandson. You have saved us from Midian's tyranny."

23 Gideon said, "I most certainly will not rule over you, nor will my son. GOD will reign over you."

24 Then Gideon said, "But I do have one request. Give me, each of you, an earring that you took as plunder." Ishmaelites wore gold earrings, and the men all had their pockets full of them.

25-26 They said, "Of course. They're yours!"

They spread out a blanket and each man threw his plundered earrings on it. The gold earrings that Gideon had asked for weighed about forty-three pounds—and that didn't include the crescents and pendants, the purple robes worn by the Midianite kings, and the ornaments hung around the necks of their camels.

27 Gideon made the gold into a sacred ephod and put it on display in his hometown, Ophrah. All Israel prostituted itself there. Gideon and his family, too, were seduced by it.

28 Midian's tyranny was broken by the Israelites; nothing more was heard from them. The land was quiet for forty years in Gideon's time.

29-31 Jerub-Baal son of Joash went home and lived in his house. Gideon had seventy sons. He fathered them all—he had a lot of wives! His concubine, the one at Shechem, also bore him a son. He named him Abimelech.

32 Gideon son of Joash died at a good old age. He was buried in the tomb of his father Joash at Ophrah of the Abiezrites.

ABIMELECH

33-35 Gideon was hardly cool in the tomb when the People of Israel had gotten off track and were prostituting themselves to Baal—they made Baal-of-the-Covenant their god. The People of Israel forgot all about GOD, their God, who had saved them from all their enemies who had hemmed them in. And they didn't keep faith with the family of Jerub-Baal (Gideon), honoring all the good he had done for Israel.

1-2 Abimelech son of Jerub-Baal went to Shechem to his uncles and all his mother's relatives and said to them, "Ask all the leading men of Shechem, 'What do you think is best, that seventy men rule you—all those sons of Jerub-Baal—or that one man rule? You'll remember that I am your own flesh and blood.'"

3 His mother's relatives reported the proposal to the leaders of Shechem. They were inclined to take Abimelech. "Because," they said, "he is, after all, one of us."

4-5 They gave him seventy silver pieces from the shrine of Baal-of-the-Covenant. With the money he hired some reckless riffraff soldiers and they followed along after him. He went to his father's house in Ophrah and killed his half brothers, the sons of Jerub-Baal — seventy men! And on one stone! The youngest, Jotham son of Jerub-Baal, managed to hide, the only survivor.

6 Then all the leaders of Shechem and Beth Millo gathered at the Oak by the Standing Stone at Shechem and crowned Abimelech king.

7-9 When this was all told to Jotham, he climbed to the top of Mount Gerizim, raised his voice, and shouted:

> Listen to me, leaders of Shechem.
>> And let God listen to you!
> The trees set out one day
>> to anoint a king for themselves.
> They said to Olive Tree,
>> "Rule over us."
> But Olive Tree told them,
>> "Am I no longer good for making oil
> That gives glory to gods and men,
>> and to be demoted to waving over trees?"

10-11
> The trees then said to Fig Tree,
>> "You come and rule over us."
> But Fig Tree said to them,
>> "Am I no longer good for making sweets,
> My mouthwatering sweet fruits,
>> and to be demoted to waving over trees?"

12-13
> The trees then said to Vine,
>> "You come and rule over us."
> But Vine said to them,
>> "Am I no longer good for making wine,
> Wine that cheers gods and men,
>> and to be demoted to waving over trees?"

14-15
> All the trees then said to Tumbleweed,
>> "You come and reign over us."
> But Tumbleweed said to the trees:
>> "If you're serious about making me your king,
> Come and find shelter in my shade.
>> But if not, let fire shoot from Tumbleweed
>> and burn down the cedars of Lebanon!"

16-20 "Now listen: Do you think you did a right and honorable thing when you made Abimelech king? Do you think you treated Jerub-Baal and his family well, did for him what he deserved? My father fought for you, risked his own life, and rescued you from Midian's tyranny, and you have, just now, betrayed him. You massacred his sons — seventy men on a single stone! You made Abimelech, the son by his maidservant, king over

Shechem's leaders because he's your relative. If you think that this is an honest day's work, this way you have treated Jerub-Baal today, then enjoy Abimelech and let him enjoy you. But if not, let fire break from Abimelech and burn up the leaders of Shechem and Beth Millo. And let fire break from the leaders of Shechem and Beth Millo and burn up Abimelech."

21   And Jotham fled. He ran for his life. He went to Beer and settled down there, because he was afraid of his brother Abimelech.

22-24   Abimelech ruled over Israel for three years. Then God brought bad blood between Abimelech and Shechem's leaders, who now worked treacherously behind his back. Violence boomeranged: The murderous violence that killed the seventy brothers, the sons of Jerub-Baal, was now loose among Abimelech and Shechem's leaders, who had supported the violence.

25   To undermine Abimelech, Shechem's leaders put men in ambush on the mountain passes who robbed travelers on those roads. And Abimelech was told.

26-27   At that time Gaal son of Ebed arrived with his relatives and moved into Shechem. The leaders of Shechem trusted him. One day they went out into the fields, gathered grapes in the vineyards, and trod them in the winepress. Then they held a celebration in their god's temple, a feast, eating and drinking. And then they started putting down Abimelech.

28-29   Gaal son of Ebed said, "Who is this Abimelech? And who are we Shechemites to take orders from him? Isn't he the son of Jerub-Baal, and isn't this his henchman Zebul? We belong to the race of Hamor and bear the noble name of Shechem. Why should we be toadies of Abimelech? If I were in charge of this people, the first thing I'd do is get rid of Abimelech! I'd say, 'Show me your stuff, Abimelech—let's see who's boss here!'"

30-33   Zebul, governor of the city, heard what Gaal son of Ebed was saying and got angry. Secretly he sent messengers to Abimelech with the message, "Gaal son of Ebed and his relatives have come to Shechem and are stirring up trouble against you. Here's what you do: Tonight bring your troops and wait in ambush in the field. In the morning, as soon as the sun breaks, get moving and charge the city. Gaal and his troops will come out to you, and you'll know what to do next."

34-36   Abimelech and his troops, four companies of them, went up that night and waited in ambush approaching Shechem. Gaal son of Ebed had gotten up and was standing in the city gate. Abimelech and his troops left their cover. When Gaal saw them he said to Zebul, "Look at that, people coming down from the tops of the mountains!"

Zebul said, "That's nothing but mountain shadows; they just look like men." Gaal kept chattering away.

37   Then he said again, "Look at the troops coming down off Tabbur-erez (the Navel of the World)—and one company coming straight from the Oracle Oak."

38   Zebul said, "Where is that big mouth of yours now? You who said, 'And who is Abimelech that we should take orders from him?' Well, there he is with the troops you ridiculed. Here's your chance. Fight away!"

39-40   Gaal went out, backed by the leaders of Shechem, and did battle with Abimelech. Abimelech chased him, and Gaal turned tail and ran. Many fell wounded, right up to the city gate.

41   Abimelech set up his field headquarters at Arumah while Zebul kept Gaal and his relatives out of Shechem.

42-45   The next day the people went out to the fields. This was reported to Abimelech. He took his troops, divided them into three companies, and placed them in ambush in the fields. When he saw that the people were well out in the open, he sprang up and attacked them. Abimelech and the company with him charged ahead and took control of the entrance to the city gate; the other two companies chased down those who were in the open fields and killed them. Abimelech fought at the city all that day. He captured the city and massacred everyone in it. He leveled the city to the ground, then sowed it with salt.

46-49   When the leaders connected with Shechem's Tower heard this, they went into the fortified God-of-the-Covenant temple. This was reported to Abimelech that the Shechem's Tower bunch were gathered together. He and his troops climbed Mount Zalmon (Dark Mountain). Abimelech took his ax and chopped a bundle of firewood, picked it up, and put it on his shoulder. He said to his troops, "Do what you've seen me do, and quickly." So each of his men cut his own bundle. They followed Abimelech, piled their bundles against the Tower fortifications, and set the whole structure on fire. Everyone in Shechem's Tower died, about a thousand men and women.

50-54   Abimelech went on to Thebez. He camped at Thebez and captured it. The Tower-of-Strength stood in the middle of the city; all the men and women of the city along with the city's leaders had fled there and locked themselves in. They were up on the tower roof. Abimelech got as far as the tower and assaulted it. He came up to the tower door to set it on fire. Just then some woman dropped an upper millstone on his head and crushed his skull. He called urgently to his young armor bearer and said, "Draw your sword and kill me so they can't say of me, 'A woman killed him.'" His armor bearer drove in his sword, and Abimelech died.

55   When the Israelites saw that Abimelech was dead, they went home.

56-57   God avenged the evil Abimelech had done to his father, murdering his seventy brothers. And God brought down on the heads of the men of Shechem all the evil that they had done, the curse of Jotham son of Jerub-Baal.

TOLA

1-2   **10** Tola son of Puah, the son of Dodo, was next after Abimelech. He rose to the occasion to save Israel. He was a man of Issachar. He lived in Shamir in the hill country of Ephraim. He judged Israel for twenty-three years and then died and was buried at Shamir.

JAIR

3-5   After him, Jair the Gileadite stepped into leadership. He judged Israel for twenty-two years. He had thirty sons who rode on thirty donkeys and had thirty towns in Gilead. The towns are still called Jair's Villages. Jair died and was buried in Kamon.

6-8 And then the People of Israel went back to doing evil in GOD's sight. They worshiped the Baal gods and Ashtoreth goddesses: gods of Aram, Sidon, and Moab; gods of the Ammonites and the Philistines. They just walked off and left GOD, quit worshiping him. And GOD exploded in hot anger at Israel and sold them off to the Philistines and Ammonites, who, beginning that year, bullied and battered the People of Israel mercilessly. For eighteen years they had them under their thumb, all the People of Israel who lived east of the Jordan in the Amorite country of Gilead.

9 Then the Ammonites crossed the Jordan to go to war also against Judah, Benjamin, and Ephraim. Israel was in a bad way!

10 The People of Israel cried out to GOD for help: "We've sinned against you! We left our God and worshiped the Baal gods!"

11-14 GOD answered the People of Israel: "When the Egyptians, Amorites, Ammonites, Philistines, Sidonians — even Amalek and Midian! — oppressed you and you cried out to me for help, I saved you from them. And now you've gone off and betrayed me, worshiping other gods. I'm not saving you anymore. Go ahead! Cry out for help to the gods you've chosen — let them get you out of the mess you're in!"

15 The People of Israel said to GOD: "We've sinned. Do to us whatever you think best, but please, get us out of this!"

16 Then they cleaned house of the foreign gods and worshiped only GOD. And GOD took Israel's troubles to heart.

JEPHTHAH

17-18 The Ammonites prepared for war, setting camp in Gilead. The People of Israel set their rival camp in Mizpah. The leaders in Gilead said, "Who will stand up for us against the Ammonites? We'll make him head over everyone in Gilead!"

1-3 11 Jephthah the Gileadite was one tough warrior. He was the son of a whore, but Gilead was his father. Meanwhile Gilead's legal wife had given him other sons, and when they grew up, his wife's sons threw Jephthah out. They told him: "You're not getting any of our family inheritance — you're the son of another woman." So Jephthah fled from his brothers and went to live in the land of Tob. Some riffraff joined him and went around with him.

4-6 Some time passed. And then the Ammonites started fighting Israel. With the Ammonites at war with them, the elders of Gilead went to get Jephthah from the land of Tob. They said to Jephthah: "Come. Be our general and we'll fight the Ammonites."

7 But Jephthah said to the elders of Gilead: "But you hate me. You kicked me out of my family home. So why are you coming to me now? Because you are in trouble. Right?"

8 The elders of Gilead replied, "That's it exactly. We've come to you to get you to go with us and fight the Ammonites. You'll be the head of all of us, all the Gileadites."

9 Jephthah addressed the elders of Gilead, "So if you bring me back home to fight the Ammonites and GOD gives them to me, I'll be your head — is that right?"

10-11 They said, "GOD is witness between us; whatever you say, we'll do."

Jephthah went along with the elders of Gilead. The people made him their top man and general. And Jephthah repeated what he had said before GOD at Mizpah.

12 Then Jephthah sent messengers to the king of the Ammonites with a message: "What's going on here that you have come into my country picking a fight?"

13 The king of the Ammonites told Jephthah's messengers: "Because Israel took my land when they came up out of Egypt—from the Arnon all the way to the Jabbok and to the Jordan. Give it back peaceably and I'll go."

14-27 Jephthah again sent messengers to the king of the Ammonites with the message: "Jephthah's word: Israel took no Moabite land and no Ammonite land. When they came up from Egypt, Israel went through the desert as far as the Red Sea, arriving at Kadesh. There Israel sent messengers to the king of Edom saying, 'Let us pass through your land, please.' But the king of Edom wouldn't let them. Israel also requested permission from the king of Moab, but he wouldn't let them cross either. They were stopped in their tracks at Kadesh. So they traveled across the desert and circled around the lands of Edom and Moab. They came out east of the land of Moab and set camp on the other side of the Arnon—they didn't set foot in Moabite territory, for Arnon was the Moabite border. Israel then sent messengers to Sihon king of the Amorites at Heshbon the capital. Israel asked, 'Let us pass, please, through your land on the way to our country.' But Sihon didn't trust Israel to cut across his land; he got his entire army together, set up camp at Jahaz, and fought Israel. But GOD, the God of Israel, gave Sihon and all his troops to Israel. Israel defeated them. Israel took all the Amorite land, all Amorite land from Arnon to the Jabbok and from the desert to the Jordan. It was GOD, the God of Israel, who pushed out the Amorites in favor of Israel; so who do you think you are to try to take it over? Why don't you just be satisfied with what your god Chemosh gives you and we'll settle for what GOD, our God, gives us? Do you think you're going to come off better than Balak son of Zippor, the king of Moab? Did he get anywhere in opposing Israel? Did he risk war? All this time—it's been three hundred years now!—that Israel has lived in Heshbon and its villages, in Aroer and its villages, and in all the towns along the Arnon, why didn't you try to snatch them away then? No, I haven't wronged you. But this is an evil thing that you are doing to me by starting a fight. Today GOD the Judge will decide between the People of Israel and the people of Ammon."

28 But the king of the Ammonites refused to listen to a word that Jephthah had sent him.

29-31 GOD's Spirit came upon Jephthah. He went across Gilead and Manasseh, went through Mizpah of Gilead, and from there approached the Ammonites. Jephthah made a vow before GOD: "If you give me a clear victory over the Ammonites, then I'll give to GOD whatever comes out of the door of my house to meet me when I return in one piece from among the Ammonites—I'll offer it up in a sacrificial burnt offering."

32-33 Then Jephthah was off to fight the Ammonites. And GOD gave them to him. He beat them soundly, all the way from Aroer to the area around Minnith as far as Abel Keramim—twenty cities! A massacre! Ammonites brought to their knees by the People of Israel.

34-35   Jephthah came home to Mizpah. His daughter ran from the house to welcome him home — dancing to tambourines! She was his only child. He had no son or daughter except her. When he realized who it was, he ripped his clothes, saying, "Ah, dearest daughter — I'm dirt. I'm despicable. My heart is torn to shreds. I made a vow to GOD and I can't take it back!"

36   She said, "Dear father, if you made a vow to GOD, do to me what you vowed; GOD did his part and saved you from your Ammonite enemies."

37   And then she said to her father, "But let this one thing be done for me. Give me two months to wander through the hills and lament my virginity since I will never marry, I and my dear friends."

38-39   "Oh yes, go," he said. He sent her off for two months. She and her dear girlfriends went among the hills, lamenting that she would never marry. At the end of the two months, she came back to her father. He fulfilled the vow with her that he had made. She had never slept with a man.

39-40   It became a custom in Israel that for four days every year the young women of Israel went out to mourn for the daughter of Jephthah the Gileadite.

1   **12** The men of Ephraim mustered their troops, crossed to Zaphon, and said to Jephthah, "Why did you go out to fight the Ammonites without letting us go with you? We're going to burn your house down on you!"

2-3   Jephthah said, "I and my people had our hands full negotiating with the Ammonites. And I did call to you for help but you ignored me. When I saw that you weren't coming, I took my life in my hands and confronted the Ammonites myself. And GOD gave them to me! So why did you show up here today? Are you spoiling for a fight with me?"

4   So Jephthah got his Gilead troops together and fought Ephraim. And the men of Gilead hit them hard because they were saying, "Gileadites are nothing but half breeds and rejects from Ephraim and Manasseh."

5-6   Gilead captured the fords of the Jordan at the crossing to Ephraim. If an Ephraimite fugitive said, "Let me cross," the men of Gilead would ask, "Are you an Ephraimite?" and he would say, "No." And they would say, "Say, 'Shibboleth.'" But he would always say, "Sibboleth" — he couldn't say it right. Then they would grab him and kill him there at the fords of the Jordan. Forty-two Ephraimite divisions were killed on that occasion.

7   Jephthah judged Israel six years. Jephthah the Gileadite died and was buried in his city, Mizpah of Gilead.

IBZAN

8-9   After him, Ibzan of Bethlehem judged Israel. He had thirty sons and thirty daughters. He gave his daughters in marriage outside his clan and brought in thirty daughters-in-law from the outside for his sons.

10   He judged Israel seven years. Ibzan died and was buried in Bethlehem.

ELON

11-12   After him, Elon the Zebulunite judged Israel. He judged Israel ten years. Elon the Zebulunite died and was buried at Aijalon in the land of Zebulun.

ABDON

13-15 After him, Abdon son of Hillel the Pirathonite judged Israel. He had forty sons and thirty grandsons who rode on seventy donkeys. He judged Israel eight years. Abdon son of Hillel the Pirathonite died and was buried at Pirathon in the land of Ephraim in the Amalekite hill country.

SAMSON

1 **13** And then the People of Israel were back at it again, doing what was evil in GOD's sight. GOD put them under the domination of the Philistines for forty years.

2-5 At that time there was a man named Manoah from Zorah from the tribe of Dan. His wife was barren and childless. The angel of God appeared to her and told her, "I know that you are barren and childless, but you're going to become pregnant and bear a son. But take much care: Drink no wine or beer; eat nothing ritually unclean. You are, in fact, pregnant right now, carrying a son. No razor will touch his head — the boy will be God's Nazirite from the moment of his birth. He will launch the deliverance from Philistine oppression."

6-7 The woman went to her husband and said, "A man of God came to me. He looked like the angel of God — terror laced with glory! I didn't ask him where he was from and he didn't tell me his name, but he told me, 'You're pregnant. You're going to give birth to a son. Don't drink any wine or beer and eat nothing ritually unclean. The boy will be God's Nazirite from the moment of birth to the day of his death.'"

8 Manoah prayed to GOD: "Master, let the man of God you sent come to us again and teach us how to raise this boy who is to be born."

9-10 God listened to Manoah. God's angel came again to the woman. She was sitting in the field; her husband Manoah wasn't there with her. She jumped to her feet and ran and told her husband: "He's back! The man who came to me that day!"

11 Manoah got up and, following his wife, came to the man. He said to him, "Are you the man who spoke to my wife?"

He said, "I am."

12 Manoah said, "So. When what you say comes true, what do you have to tell us about this boy and his work?"

13-14 The angel of God said to Manoah, "Keep in mind everything I told the woman. Eat nothing that comes from the vine: Drink no wine or beer; eat no ritually unclean foods. She's to observe everything I commanded her."

15 Manoah said to the angel of God, "Please, stay with us a little longer; we'll prepare a meal for you — a young goat."

16 GOD's angel said to Manoah, "Even if I stay, I won't eat your food. But if you want to prepare a Whole-Burnt-Offering for GOD, go ahead — offer it!" Manoah had no idea that he was talking to the angel of God.

17 Then Manoah asked the angel of God, "What's your name? When your words come true, we'd like to honor you."

18 The angel of GOD said, "What's this? You ask for my name? You wouldn't understand — it's sheer wonder."

19-21 So Manoah took the kid and the Grain-Offering and sacrificed them on a rock altar to GOD who works wonders. As the flames leapt up from the altar to heaven, GOD's angel also ascended in the altar flames. When Manoah and his wife saw this, they fell facedown to the ground. Manoah and his wife never saw the angel of GOD again.

21-22 Only then did Manoah realize that this was GOD's angel. He said to his wife, "We're as good as dead! We've looked on God!"

23 But his wife said, "If GOD were planning to kill us, he wouldn't have accepted our Whole-Burnt-Offering and Grain-Offering, or revealed all these things to us—given us this birth announcement."

24-25 The woman gave birth to a son. They named him Samson. The boy grew and GOD blessed him. The Spirit of GOD began working in him while he was staying at a Danite camp between Zorah and Eshtaol.

※

1-2 14 Samson went down to Timnah. There in Timnah a woman caught his eye, a Philistine girl. He came back and told his father and mother, "I saw a woman in Timnah, a Philistine girl; get her for me as my wife."

3 His parents said to him, "Isn't there a woman among the girls in the neighborhood of our people? Do you have to go get a wife from the uncircumcised Philistines?"

But Samson said to his father, "Get her for me. She's the one I want—she's the right one."

4 (His father and mother had no idea that GOD was behind this, that he was arranging an opportunity against the Philistines. At the time the Philistines lorded it over Israel.)

5-6 Samson went down to Timnah with his father and mother. When he got to the vineyards of Timnah, a young lion came at him, roaring. The Spirit of GOD came on him powerfully and he ripped it open barehanded, like tearing a young goat. But he didn't tell his parents what he had done.

7 Then he went on down and spoke to the woman. In Samson's eyes, she was the one.

8-9 Some days later when he came back to get her, he made a little detour to look at what was left of the lion. And there a wonder: a swarm of bees in the lion's carcass—and honey! He scooped it up in his hands and kept going, eating as he went. He rejoined his father and mother and gave some to them and they ate. But he didn't tell them that he had scooped out the honey from the lion's carcass.

10-11 His father went on down to make arrangements with the woman, while Samson prepared a feast there. That's what the young men did in those days. Because the people were wary of him, they arranged for thirty friends to mingle with him.

12-13 Samson said to them: "Let me put a riddle to you. If you can figure it out during the seven days of the feast, I'll give you thirty linen garments and thirty changes of fine clothing. But if you can't figure it out then you'll give me thirty linen garments and thirty changes of fine clothing."

13-14 They said, "Put your riddle. Let's hear it." So he said,

From the eater came something to eat,
From the strong came something sweet.

14-15 They couldn't figure it out. After three days they were still stumped. On the fourth day they said to Samson's bride, "Worm the answer out of your husband or we'll burn you and your father's household. Have you invited us here to bankrupt us?"

16 So Samson's bride turned on the tears, saying to him, "You hate me. You don't love me. You've told a riddle to my people but you won't even tell me the answer."

He said, "I haven't told my own parents — why would I tell you?"

17 But she turned on the tears all the seven days of the feast. On the seventh day, worn out by her nagging, he told her. Then she went and told it to her people.

18 The men of the town came to him on the seventh day, just before sunset and said,

What is sweeter than honey?
What is stronger than a lion?

And Samson said,

If you hadn't plowed with my heifer,
You wouldn't have found out my riddle.

19-20 Then the Spirit of GOD came powerfully on him. He went down to Ashkelon and killed thirty of their men, stripped them, and gave their clothing to those who had solved the riddle. Stalking out, smoking with anger, he went home to his father's house. Samson's bride became the wife of the best man at his wedding.

❋

1-2 **15** Later on — it was during the wheat harvest — Samson visited his bride, bringing a young goat. He said, "Let me see my wife — show me her bedroom."

But her father wouldn't let him in. He said, "I concluded that by now you hated her with a passion, so I gave her to your best man. But her little sister is even more beautiful. Why not take her instead?"

3 Samson said, "That does it. This time when I wreak havoc on the Philistines, I'm blameless."

4-5 Samson then went out and caught three hundred jackals. He lashed the jackals' tails together in pairs and tied a torch between each pair of tails. He then set fire to the torches and let them loose in the Philistine fields of ripe grain. Everything burned, both stacked and standing grain, vineyards and olive orchards — everything.

6 The Philistines said, "Who did this?"

They were told, "Samson, son-in-law of the Timnite who took his bride and gave her to his best man."

The Philistines went up and burned both her and her father to death.

7 Samson then said, "If this is the way you're going to act, I swear I'll get even with you. And I'm not quitting till the job's done!"

8 With that he tore into them, ripping them limb from limb — a huge slaughter. Then he went down and stayed in a cave at Etam Rock.

❋

9-10 The Philistines set out and made camp in Judah, preparing to attack Lehi (Jawbone). When the men of Judah asked, "Why have you come up against us?" they said, "We're out to get Samson. We're going after Samson to do to him what he did to us."

11 Three companies of men from Judah went down to the cave at Etam Rock and said to Samson, "Don't you realize that the Philistines already bully and lord it over us? So what's going on with you, making things even worse?"

He said, "It was tit for tat. I only did to them what they did to me."

12 They said, "Well, we've come down here to tie you up and turn you over to the Philistines."

Samson said, "Just promise not to hurt me."

13 "We promise," they said. "We will tie you up and surrender you to them but, believe us, we won't kill you." They proceeded to tie him with new ropes and led him up from the Rock.

14-16 As he approached Lehi, the Philistines came to meet him, shouting in triumph. And then the Spirit of GOD came on him with great power. The ropes on his arms fell apart like flax on fire; the thongs slipped off his hands. He spotted a fresh donkey jawbone, reached down and grabbed it, and with it killed the whole company. And Samson said,

> With a donkey's jawbone
> I made heaps of donkeys of them.
> With a donkey's jawbone
> I killed an entire company.

17 When he finished speaking, he threw away the jawbone. He named that place Ramath Lehi (Jawbone Hill).

18-19 Now he was suddenly very thirsty. He called out to GOD, "You have given your servant this great victory. Are you going to abandon me to die of thirst and fall into the hands of the uncircumcised?" So God split open the rock basin in Lehi; water gushed out and Samson drank. His spirit revived—he was alive again! That's why it's called En Hakkore (Caller's Spring). It's still there at Lehi today.

20 Samson judged Israel for twenty years in the days of the Philistines.

1-2 **16** Samson went to Gaza and saw a prostitute. He went to her. The news got around: "Samson's here." They gathered around in hiding, waiting all night for him at the city gate, quiet as mice, thinking, "At sunrise we'll kill him."

3 Samson was in bed with the woman until midnight. Then he got up, seized the doors of the city gate and the two gateposts, bolts and all, hefted them on his shoulder, and carried them to the top of the hill that faces Hebron.

4-5 Some time later he fell in love with a woman in the Valley of Sorek (Grapes). Her name was Delilah. The Philistine tyrants approached her and said, "Seduce him. Discover what's behind his great strength and how we can tie him up and humble him. Each man's company will give you a hundred shekels of silver."

6 So Delilah said to Samson, "Tell me, dear, the secret of your great strength, and how you can be tied up and humbled."

7 Samson told her, "If they were to tie me up with seven bowstrings — the kind made from fresh animal tendons, not dried out — then I would become weak, just like anyone else."

8-9 The Philistine tyrants brought her seven bowstrings, not dried out, and she tied him up with them. The men were waiting in ambush in her room. Then she said, "The Philistines are on you, Samson!" He snapped the cords as though they were mere threads. The secret of his strength was still a secret.

10 Delilah said, "Come now, Samson — you're playing with me, making up stories. Be serious; tell me how you can be tied up."

11 He told her, "If you were to tie me up tight with new ropes, ropes never used for work, then I would be helpless, just like anybody else."

12 So Delilah got some new ropes and tied him up. She said, "The Philistines are on you, Samson!" The men were hidden in the next room. He snapped the ropes from his arms like threads.

13-14 Delilah said to Samson, "You're still playing games with me, teasing me with lies. Tell me how you can be tied up."

He said to her, "If you wove the seven braids of my hair into the fabric on the loom and drew it tight, then I would be as helpless as any other mortal."

When she had him fast asleep, Delilah took the seven braids of his hair and wove them into the fabric on the loom and drew it tight. Then she said, "The Philistines are on you, Samson!" He woke from his sleep and ripped loose from both the loom and fabric!

15 She said, "How can you say 'I love you' when you won't even trust me? Three times now you've toyed with me, like a cat with a mouse, refusing to tell me the secret of your great strength."

16-17 She kept at it day after day, nagging and tormenting him. Finally, he was fed up — he couldn't take another minute of it. He spilled it.

He told her, "A razor has never touched my head. I've been God's Nazirite from conception. If I were shaved, my strength would leave me; I would be as helpless as any other mortal."

18 When Delilah realized that he had told her his secret, she sent for the Philistine tyrants, telling them, "Come quickly — this time he's told me the truth." They came, bringing the bribe money.

19 When she got him to sleep, his head on her lap, she motioned to a man to cut off the seven braids of his hair. Immediately he began to grow weak. His strength drained from him.

20 Then she said, "The Philistines are on you, Samson!" He woke up, thinking, "I'll go out, like always, and shake free." He didn't realize that GOD had abandoned him.

21-22 The Philistines grabbed him, gouged out his eyes, and took him down to Gaza. They shackled him in irons and put him to the work of grinding in the prison. But his hair, though cut off, began to grow again.

23-24 The Philistine tyrants got together to offer a great sacrifice to their god Dagon. They celebrated, saying,

> Our god has given us
> Samson our enemy!

And when the people saw him, they joined in, cheering their god,

> Our god has given
> Our enemy to us,
> The one who ravaged our country,
> Piling high the corpses among us.

25-27 Then this: Everyone was feeling high and someone said, "Get Samson! Let him show us his stuff!" They got Samson from the prison and he put on a show for them.

They had him standing between the pillars. Samson said to the young man who was acting as his guide, "Put me where I can touch the pillars that hold up the temple so I can rest against them." The building was packed with men and women, including all the Philistine tyrants. And there were at least three thousand in the stands watching Samson's performance.

28 And Samson cried out to GOD:

> Master, GOD!
>   Oh, please, look on me again,
>   Oh, please, give strength yet once more.

> God!
>   With one avenging blow let me be avenged
>   On the Philistines for my two eyes!

29-30 Then Samson reached out to the two central pillars that held up the building and pushed against them, one with his right arm, the other with his left. Saying, "Let me die with the Philistines," Samson pushed hard with all his might. The building crashed on the tyrants and all the people in it. He killed more people in his death than he had killed in his life.

31 His brothers and all his relatives went down to get his body. They carried him back and buried him in the tomb of Manoah his father, between Zorah and Eshtaol.

He judged Israel for twenty years.

MICAH

1-2 **17** There was a man from the hill country of Ephraim named Micah. He said to his mother, "Remember that 1,100 pieces of silver that were taken from you? I overheard you when you pronounced your curse. Well, I have the money; I stole it. But now I've brought it back to you."

His mother said, "GOD bless you, my son!"

3-4 As he returned the 1,100 silver pieces to his mother, she said, "I had totally consecrated this money to GOD for my son to make a statue, a cast god." Then she took 200 pieces of the silver and gave it to a sculptor and he cast them into the form of a god.

5 This man, Micah, had a private chapel. He had made an ephod and some teraphim-idols and had ordained one of his sons to be his priest.

6 In those days there was no king in Israel. People did whatever they felt like doing.

※

7-8 Meanwhile there was a young man from Bethlehem in Judah and from a family of Judah. He was a Levite but was a stranger there. He left that town, Bethlehem in Judah, seeking his fortune. He got as far as the hill country of Ephraim and showed up at Micah's house.

9 Micah asked him, "So where are you from?"

He said, "I'm a Levite from Bethlehem in Judah. I'm on the road, looking for a place to settle down."

10 Micah said, "Stay here with me. Be my father and priest. I'll pay you ten pieces of silver a year, whatever clothes you need, and your meals."

11-12 The Levite agreed and moved in with Micah. The young man fit right in and became one of the family. Micah appointed the young Levite as his priest. This all took place in Micah's home.

13 Micah said, "Now I know that GOD will make things go well for me — why, I've got a Levite for a priest!"

※

1 **18** In those days there was no king in Israel. But also in those days, the tribe of Dan was looking for a place to settle down. They hadn't yet occupied their plot among the tribes of Israel.

2-3 The Danites sent out five robust warriors from Zorah and Eshtaol to look over the land and see what was out there suitable for their families. They said, "Go and explore the land."

They went into the hill country of Ephraim and got as far as the house of Micah. They camped there for the night. As they neared Micah's house, they recognized the voice of the young Levite. They went over and said to him, "How on earth did you get here? What's going on? What are you doing here?"

4 He said, "One thing led to another: Micah hired me and I'm now his priest."

5 They said, "Oh, good — inquire of God for us. Find out whether our mission will be a success."

6 The priest said, "Go assured. GOD's looking out for you all the way."

7 The five men left and headed north to Laish. They saw that the people there were living in safety under the umbrella of the Sidonians, quiet and unsuspecting. They had everything going for them. But the people lived a long way from the Sidonians to the west and had no treaty with the Arameans to the east.

8 When they got back to Zorah and Eshtaol, their brothers asked, "So, how did you find things?"

9-10 They said, "Let's go for it! Let's attack. We've seen the land and it is excellent. Are you going to just sit on your hands? Don't dawdle! Invade and conquer! When you get there, you'll find they're sitting ducks, totally unsuspecting. Wide open land — God is handing it over to you, everything you could ever ask for."

11-13 So six hundred Danite men set out from Zorah and Eshtaol, armed to the teeth. Along the way they made camp at Kiriath Jearim in Judah. That is why the place is still today called Dan's Camp—it's just west of Kiriath Jearim. From there they proceeded into the hill country of Ephraim and came to Micah's house.

14 The five men who earlier had explored the country of Laish told their companions, "Did you know there's an ephod, teraphim-idols, and a cast god-sculpture in these buildings? What do you think? Do you want to do something about it?"

15-18 So they turned off the road there, went to the house of the young Levite at Micah's place and asked how things had been with him. The six hundred Danites, all well-armed, stood guard at the entrance to the gate while the five scouts who had gone to explore the land went in and took the carved idol, the ephod, the teraphim-idols, and the god-sculpture. The priest was standing at the gate entrance with the six hundred armed men. When the five went into Micah's house and took the carved idol, the ephod, the teraphim-idols, and the sculpted god, the priest said to them, "What do you think you're doing?"

19 They said to him, "Hush! Don't make a sound. Come with us. Be our father and priest. Which is more important, that you be a priest to one man or that you become priest to a whole tribe and clan in Israel?"

20 The priest jumped at the chance. He took the ephod, the teraphim-idols, and the idol and fell in with the troops.

21-23 They turned away and set out, putting the children, the cattle, and the gear in the lead. They were well on their way from Micah's house before Micah and his neighbors got organized. But they soon overtook the Danites. They shouted at them. The Danites turned around and said, "So what's all the noise about?"

24 Micah said, "You took my god, the one I made, and you took my priest. And you marched off! What do I have left? How can you now say, 'What's the matter?'"

25 But the Danites answered, "Don't yell at us; you just might provoke some fierce, hot-tempered men to attack you, and you'll end up an army of dead men."

26 The Danites went on their way. Micah saw that he didn't stand a chance against their arms. He turned back and went home.

27 So they took the things that Micah had made, along with his priest, and they arrived at Laish, that city of quiet and unsuspecting people. They massacred the people and burned down the city.

28-29 There was no one around to help. They were a long way from Sidon and had no treaty with the Arameans. Laish was in the valley of Beth Rehob. When they rebuilt the city they renamed it Dan after their ancestor who was a son of Israel, but its original name was Laish.

30-31 The Danites set up the god-figure for themselves. Jonathan son of Gershom, the son of Moses, and his descendants were priests to the tribe of Dan down to the time of the land's captivity. All during the time that there was a sanctuary of God in Shiloh, they kept for their private use the god-figure that Micah had made.

THE LEVITE

1-4 **19** It was an era when there was no king in Israel. A Levite, living as a stranger in the backwoods hill country of Ephraim, got himself a concubine, a woman from Bethlehem in Judah. But she quarreled with him and left, returning to her father's house in Bethlehem in Judah. She was there four months. Then her husband decided to go after her and try to win her back. He had a servant and a pair of donkeys with him. When he arrived at her father's house, the girl's father saw him, welcomed him, and made him feel at home. His father-in-law, the girl's father, pressed him to stay. He stayed with him three days; they feasted and drank and slept.

5-6   On the fourth day, they got up at the crack of dawn and got ready to go. But the girl's father said to his son-in-law, "Strengthen yourself with a hearty breakfast and then you can go." So they sat down and ate breakfast together.

6-7   The girl's father said to the man, "Come now, be my guest. Stay the night — make it a holiday." The man got up to go, but his father-in-law kept after him, so he ended up spending another night.

8-9   On the fifth day, he was again up early, ready to go. The girl's father said, "You need some breakfast." They went back and forth, and the day slipped on as they ate and drank together. But the man and his concubine were finally ready to go. Then his father-in-law, the girl's father, said, "Look, the day's almost gone — why not stay the night? There's very little daylight left; stay another night and enjoy yourself. Tomorrow you can get an early start and set off for your own place."

10-11   But this time the man wasn't willing to spend another night. He got things ready, left, and went as far as Jebus (Jerusalem) with his pair of saddled donkeys, his concubine, and his servant. At Jebus, though, the day was nearly gone. The servant said to his master, "It's late; let's go into this Jebusite city and spend the night."

12-13   But his master said, "We're not going into any city of foreigners. We'll go on to Gibeah." He directed his servant, "Keep going. Let's go on ahead. We'll spend the night either at Gibeah or Ramah."

14-15   So they kept going. As they pressed on, the sun finally left them in the vicinity of Gibeah, which belongs to Benjamin. They left the road there to spend the night at Gibeah.

15-17   The Levite went and sat down in the town square, but no one invited them in to spend the night. Then, late in the evening, an old man came in from his day's work in the fields. He was from the hill country of Ephraim and lived temporarily in Gibeah where all the local citizens were Benjaminites. When the old man looked up and saw the traveler in the town square, he said, "Where are you going? And where are you from?"

18-19   The Levite said, "We're just passing through. We're coming from Bethlehem on our way to a remote spot in the hills of Ephraim. I come from there. I've just made a trip to Bethlehem in Judah and I'm on my way back home, but no one has invited us in for the night. We wouldn't be any trouble: We have food and straw for the donkeys, and bread and wine for the woman, the young man, and me — we don't need anything."

20-21   The old man said, "It's going to be all right; I'll take care of you. You aren't going to spend the night in the town square." He took them home and fed the donkeys. They washed up and sat down to a good meal.

22   They were relaxed and enjoying themselves when the men of the city, a gang of local hell-raisers all, surrounded the house and started pounding on the door. They yelled for the owner of the house, the old man, "Bring out the man who came to your house. We want to have sex with him."

23-24   He went out and told them, "No, brothers! Don't be obscene — this man is my guest. Don't commit this outrage. Look, my virgin daughter and his concubine are here. I'll bring them out for you. Abuse them if you must, but don't do anything so senselessly vile to this man."

25-26 But the men wouldn't listen to him. Finally, the Levite pushed his concubine out the door to them. They raped her repeatedly all night long. Just before dawn they let her go. The woman came back and fell at the door of the house where her master was sleeping. When the sun rose, there she was.

27 It was morning. Her master got up and opened the door to continue his journey. There she was, his concubine, crumpled in a heap at the door, her hands on the threshold.

28 "Get up," he said. "Let's get going." There was no answer.

29-30 He lifted her onto his donkey and set out for home. When he got home he took a knife and dismembered his concubine — cut her into twelve pieces. He sent her, piece by piece, throughout the country of Israel. And he ordered the men he sent out, "Say to every man in Israel: 'Has such a thing as this ever happened from the time the Israelites came up from the land of Egypt until now? Think about it! Talk it over. Do something!'"

1-2 **20** Then all the People of Israel came out. The congregation met in the presence of GOD at Mizpah. They were all there, from Dan to Beersheba, as one person! The leaders of all the people, representing all the tribes of Israel, took their places in the gathering of God's people. There were four hundred divisions of sword-wielding infantry.

3 Meanwhile the Benjaminites got wind that the Israelites were meeting at Mizpah.

The People of Israel said, "Now tell us. How did this outrageous evil happen?"

4-7 The Levite, the husband of the murdered woman, spoke: "My concubine and I came to spend the night at Gibeah, a Benjaminite town. That night the men of Gibeah came after me. They surrounded the house, intending to kill me. They gang-raped my concubine and she died. So I took my concubine, cut up her body, and sent her piece by piece — twelve pieces! — to every part of Israel's inheritance. This vile and outrageous crime was committed *in Israel*! So, Israelites, make up your minds. Decide on some action!"

8-11 All the people were at once and as one person on their feet. "None of us will go home; not a single one of us will go to his own house. Here's our plan for dealing with Gibeah: We'll march against it by drawing lots. We'll take ten of every hundred men from all the tribes of Israel (a hundred of every thousand, and a thousand of every ten thousand) to carry food for the army. When the troops arrive at Gibeah they will settle accounts for this outrageous and vile evil that was done in Israel." So all the men in Israel were gathered against the city, totally united.

12-13 The Israelite tribes sent messengers throughout the tribe of Benjamin saying, "What's the meaning of this outrage that took place among you? Surrender the men right here and now, these hell-raisers of Gibeah. We'll put them to death and burn the evil out of Israel."

13-16 But they wouldn't do it. The Benjaminites refused to listen to their brothers, the People of Israel. Instead they raised an army from all their cities and rallied at Gibeah to go to war against the People of Israel. In no time at all they had recruited from their cities twenty-six divisions of sword-wielding infantry. From Gibeah they got seven hundred hand-picked fighters, the best. There were another seven hundred supermarksmen who were ambidextrous—they could sling a stone at a hair and not miss.

17   The men of Israel, excluding Benjamin, mobilized four hundred divisions of sword-wielding fighting men.

18   They set out and went to Bethel to inquire of God. The People of Israel said, "Who of us shall be first to go into battle with the Benjaminites?"

GOD said, "Judah goes first."

19-21   The People of Israel got up the next morning and camped before Gibeah. The army of Israel marched out against Benjamin and took up their positions, ready to attack Gibeah. But the Benjaminites poured out of Gibeah and devastated twenty-two Israelite divisions on the ground.

22-23   The Israelites went back to the sanctuary and wept before GOD until evening. They again inquired of GOD, "Shall we again go into battle against the Benjaminites, our brothers?"

GOD said, "Yes. Attack."

24-25   The army took heart. The men of Israel took up the positions they had deployed on the first day.

On the second day, the Israelites again advanced against Benjamin. This time as the Benjaminites came out of the city, on this second day, they devastated another eighteen Israelite divisions, all swordsmen.

26   All the People of Israel, the whole army, were back at Bethel, weeping, sitting there in the presence of GOD. That day they fasted until evening. They sacrificed Whole-Burnt-Offerings and Peace-Offerings before GOD.

27-28   And they again inquired of GOD. The Chest of God's Covenant was there at that time with Phinehas son of Eleazar, the son of Aaron, as the ministering priest. They asked, "Shall we again march into battle against the Benjaminites, our brothers? Or should we call it quits?"

And GOD said, "Attack. Tomorrow I'll give you victory."

29-31   This time Israel placed men in ambush all around Gibeah. On the third day when Israel set out, they took up the same positions before the Benjaminites as before. When the Benjaminites came out to meet the army, they moved out from the city. Benjaminites began to cut down some of the troops just as they had before. About thirty men fell in the field and on the roads to Bethel and Gibeah.

32   The Benjaminites started bragging, "We're dropping them like flies, just as before!"

33   But the Israelites strategized: "Now let's retreat and pull them out of the city onto the main roads." So every Israelite moved farther out to Baal Tamar; at the same time the Israelite ambush rushed from its place west of Gibeah.

34-36   Ten crack divisions from all over Israel now arrived at Gibeah—intense, bloody fighting! The Benjaminites had no idea that they were about to go down in defeat—GOD routed them before Israel. The Israelites decimated twenty-five divisions of Benjamin that day—25,100 killed. They were all swordsmen. The Benjaminites saw that they were beaten.

The men of Israel acted like they were retreating before Benjamin, knowing that they could depend on the ambush they had prepared for Gibeah.

37-40 The ambush erupted and made quick work of Gibeah. The ambush spread out and massacred the city. The strategy for the main body of the ambush was that they send up a smoke signal from the city. Then the men of Israel would turn in battle. When that happened, Benjamin had killed about thirty Israelites and thought they were on their way to victory, yelling out, "They're on the run, just as in the first battle!" But then the signal went up from the city—a huge column of smoke. When the Benjaminites looked back, there it was, the whole city going up in smoke.

41-43 By the time the men of Israel had turned back on them, the men of Benjamin fell apart—they could see that they were trapped. Confronted by the Israelites, they tried to get away down the wilderness road, but by now the battle was everywhere. The men of Israel poured out of the towns, killing them right and left, hot on their trail, picking them off east of Gibeah.

44 Eighteen divisions of Benjaminites were wiped out, all their best fighters.

45 Five divisions turned to escape to the wilderness, to Rimmon Rock, but the Israelites caught and slaughtered them on roads.

Keeping the pressure on, the Israelites brought down two more divisions.

46 The total of the Benjaminites killed that day came to twenty-five divisions of infantry, their best swordsmen.

47 Six hundred men got away. They made it to Rimmon Rock in the wilderness and held out there for four months.

48 The men of Israel came back and killed all the Benjaminites who were left, all the men and animals they found in every town, and then torched the towns, sending them up in flames.

WIVES

1 Back at Mizpah the men of Israel had taken an oath: "No man among us will give his daughter to a Benjaminite in marriage."

2-3 Now, back in Bethel, the people sat in the presence of God until evening. They cried loudly; there was widespread lamentation. They said, "Why, O GOD, God of Israel, has this happened? Why do we find ourselves today missing one whole tribe from Israel?"

4 Early the next morning, the people got busy and built an altar. They sacrificed Whole-Burnt-Offerings and Peace-Offerings.

5 Then the Israelites said, "Who from all the tribes of Israel didn't show up as we gathered in the presence of GOD?" For they had all taken a sacred oath that anyone who had not gathered in the presence of GOD at Mizpah had to be put to death.

6-7 But the People of Israel were feeling sorry for Benjamin, their brothers. They said, "Today, one tribe is cut off from Israel. How can we get wives for those who are left? We have sworn by GOD not to give any of our daughters to them in marriage."

8-9 They said, "Which one of the tribes of Israel didn't gather before GOD at Mizpah?"

It turned out that no one had come to the gathering from Jabesh Gilead. When they took a roll call of the people, not a single person from Jabesh Gilead was there.

10-11 So the congregation sent twelve divisions of their top men there with the command, "Kill everyone of Jabesh Gilead, including women and children. These are your instructions: Every man and woman who has had sexual intercourse you must kill. But keep the virgins alive." And that's what they did.

12 And they found four hundred virgins among those who lived in Jabesh Gilead; they had never had sexual intercourse with a man. And they brought them to the camp at Shiloh, which is in the land of Canaan.

13-14 Then the congregation sent word to the Benjaminites who were at the Rimmon Rock and offered them peace. And Benjamin came. They gave them the women they had let live at Jabesh Gilead. But even then, there weren't enough for all the men.

15 The people felt bad for Benjamin; GOD had left out Benjamin — the missing piece from the Israelite tribes.

16-18 The elders of the congregation said, "How can we get wives for the rest of the men, since all the Benjaminite women have been killed? How can we keep the inheritance alive for the Benjaminite survivors? How can we prevent an entire tribe from extinction? We certainly can't give our own daughters to them as wives." (Remember, the Israelites had taken the oath: "Cursed is anyone who provides a wife to Benjamin.")

19 Then they said, "There is that festival of GOD held every year in Shiloh. It's north of Bethel, just east of the main road that goes up from Bethel to Shechem and a little south of Lebonah."

20-22 So they told the Benjaminites, "Go and hide in the vineyards. Stay alert — when you see the Shiloh girls come out to dance the dances, run out of the vineyards, grab one of the Shiloh girls for your wife, and then hightail it back to the country of Benjamin. When their fathers or brothers come to lay charges against us, we'll tell them, 'We did them a favor. After all we didn't go to war and kill to get wives for men. And it wasn't as if you were in on it by giving consent. But if you keep this up, you will incur blame.'"

23 And that's what the Benjaminites did: They carried off girls from the dance, wives enough for their number, got away, and went home to their inheritance. They rebuilt their towns and settled down.

24 From there the People of Israel dispersed, each man heading back to his own tribe and clan, each to his own plot of land.

25 At that time there was no king in Israel. People did whatever they felt like doing.

RUTH

As we read the broad, comprehensive biblical story of God at work in the world, most of us are entirely impressed: God speaking creation into being, God laying the foundations of the life of faith through great and definitive fathers and mothers, God saving a people out of a brutal slave existence and then forming them into lives of free and obedient love, God raising up leaders who direct and guide through the tangle of difficulties always involved in living joyfully and responsively before God.

Very impressive. So impressive, in fact, that many of us, while remaining impressed, feel left out. Our unimpressive, very ordinary lives make us feel like outsiders to such a star-studded cast. We disqualify ourselves. Guilt or willfulness or accident makes a loophole and we assume that what is true for everyone else is not true for us. We conclude that we are, somehow, "just not religious" and thus unfit to participate in the big story.

And then we turn a page and come on this small story of two widows and a farmer in their out-of-the-way village.

The outsider Ruth was not born into the faith and felt no natural part of it — like many of us. But she came to find herself gathered into the story and given a quiet and obscure part that proved critical to the way everything turned out.

Scripture is a vast tapestry of God's creating, saving, and blessing ways in this world. The great names in the plot that climaxes at Sinai (Abraham, Isaac, Jacob, Joseph, Moses) and the great names in the sequel (Joshua, Samuel, David, Solomon) can be intimidating to ordinary, random individuals: "Surely there is no way that I can have any significant part on such a stage." But the story of the widowed, impoverished, alien Ruth is proof to the contrary. She is the inconsequential outsider whose life turns out to be essential for telling the complete story of God's ways among us. The unassuming ending carries the punch line: "Boaz married Ruth, she had a son Obed, Obed was the father of Jesse, and Jesse the father of David."

David! In its artful telling of this "outsider" widow, uprooted and obscure, who turns out to be the great-grandmother of David and the ancestor of Jesus, the book of Ruth makes it possible for each of us to understand ourselves, however ordinary or "out of it," as irreplaceable in the full telling of God's story. We count — every last one of us — and what we do counts.

RUTH

¹⁻² Once upon a time—it was back in the days when judges led Israel—there was a famine in the land. A man from Bethlehem in Judah left home to live in the country of Moab, he and his wife and his two sons. The man's name was Elimelech; his wife's name was Naomi; his sons were named Mahlon and Kilion—all Ephrathites from Bethlehem in Judah. They all went to the country of Moab and settled there.

³⁻⁵ Elimelech died and Naomi was left, she and her two sons. The sons took Moabite wives; the name of the first was Orpah, the second Ruth. They lived there in Moab for the next ten years. But then the two brothers, Mahlon and Kilion, died. Now the woman was left without either her young men or her husband.

⁶⁻⁷ One day she got herself together, she and her two daughters-in-law, to leave the country of Moab and set out for home; she had heard that GOD had been pleased to visit his people and give them food. And so she started out from the place she had been living, she and her two daughters-in-law with her, on the road back to the land of Judah.

⁸⁻⁹ After a short while on the road, Naomi told her two daughters-in-law, "Go back. Go home and live with your mothers. And may GOD treat you as graciously as you treated your deceased husbands and me. May GOD give each of you a new home and a new husband!" She kissed them and they cried openly.

¹⁰ They said, "No, we're going on with you to your people."

¹¹⁻¹³ But Naomi was firm: "Go back, my dear daughters. Why would you come with me? Do you suppose I still have sons in my womb who can become your future husbands? Go back, dear daughters—on your way, please! I'm too old to get a husband. Why, even if I said, 'There's still hope!' and this very night got a man and had sons, can you imagine being satisfied to wait until they were grown? Would you wait that long to get married again? No, dear daughters; this is a bitter pill for me to swallow—more bitter for me than for you. GOD has dealt me a hard blow."

¹⁴ Again they cried openly. Orpah kissed her mother-in-law good-bye; but Ruth embraced her and held on.

¹⁵ Naomi said, "Look, your sister-in-law is going back home to live with her own people and gods; go with her."

¹⁶⁻¹⁷ But Ruth said, "Don't force me to leave you; don't make me go home. Where you go, I go; and where you live, I'll live. Your people are my people, your God is my god; where you die, I'll die, and that's where I'll be buried, so help me GOD—not even death itself is going to come between us!"

¹⁸⁻¹⁹ When Naomi saw that Ruth had her heart set on going with her, she gave in. And so the two of them traveled on together to Bethlehem.

When they arrived in Bethlehem the whole town was soon buzzing: "Is this really our Naomi? And after all this time!"

²⁰⁻²¹ But she said, "Don't call me Naomi; call me Bitter. The Strong One has dealt me a bitter blow. I left here full of life, and GOD has brought me back with nothing but the clothes on my back. Why would you call me Naomi?

God certainly doesn't. The Strong One ruined me."

22   And so Naomi was back, and Ruth the foreigner with her, back from the country of Moab. They arrived in Bethlehem at the beginning of the barley harvest.

1   2 It so happened that Naomi had a relative by marriage, a man promi-nent and rich, connected with Elimelech's family. His name was Boaz.

2   One day Ruth, the Moabite foreigner, said to Naomi, "I'm going to work; I'm going out to glean among the sheaves, following after some harvester who will treat me kindly."

Naomi said, "Go ahead, dear daughter."

3-4   And so she set out. She went and started gleaning in a field, following in the wake of the harvesters. Eventually she ended up in the part of the field owned by Boaz, her father-in-law Elimelech's relative. A little later Boaz came out from Bethlehem, greeting his harvesters, "GOD be with you!" They replied, "And GOD bless you!"

5   Boaz asked his young servant who was foreman over the farm hands, "Who is this young woman? Where did she come from?"

6-7   The foreman said, "Why, that's the Moabite girl, the one who came with Naomi from the country of Moab. She asked permission. 'Let me glean,' she said, 'and gather among the sheaves following after your harvesters.' She's been at it steady ever since, from early morning until now, without so much as a break."

8-9   Then Boaz spoke to Ruth: "Listen, my daughter. From now on don't go to any other field to glean — stay right here in this one. And stay close to my young women. Watch where they are harvesting and follow them. And don't worry about a thing; I've given orders to my servants not to harass you. When you get thirsty, feel free to go and drink from the water buckets that the servants have filled."

10   She dropped to her knees, then bowed her face to the ground. "How does this happen that you should pick me out and treat me so kindly — me, a foreigner?"

11-12   Boaz answered her, "I've heard all about you — heard about the way you treated your mother-in-law after the death of her husband, and how you left your father and mother and the land of your birth and have come to live among a bunch of total strangers. GOD reward you well for what you've done — and with a generous bonus besides from GOD, to whom you've come seeking protection under his wings."

13   She said, "Oh sir, such grace, such kindness — I don't deserve it. You've touched my heart, treated me like one of your own. And I don't even belong here!"

14   At the lunch break, Boaz said to her, "Come over here; eat some bread. Dip it in the wine."

So she joined the harvesters. Boaz passed the roasted grain to her. She ate her fill and even had some left over.

15-16   When she got up to go back to work, Boaz ordered his servants: "Let her glean where there's still plenty of grain on the ground — make it easy for her. Better yet, pull some of the good stuff out and leave it for her to glean. Give her special treatment."

17-18   Ruth gleaned in the field until evening. When she threshed out what she had gathered, she ended up with nearly a full sack of barley! She gathered up her gleanings, went back to town, and showed her mother-in-law the results of her day's work; she also gave her the leftovers from her lunch.

19 Naomi asked her, "So where did you glean today? Whose field? GOD bless whoever it was who took such good care of you!"

Ruth told her mother-in-law, "The man with whom I worked today? His name is Boaz."

20 Naomi said to her daughter-in-law, "Why, GOD bless that man! GOD hasn't quite walked out on us after all! He still loves us, in bad times as well as good!"

Naomi went on, "That man, Ruth, is one of our circle of covenant redeemers, a close relative of ours!"

21 Ruth the Moabitess said, "Well, listen to this: He also told me, 'Stick with my workers until my harvesting is finished.'"

22 Naomi said to Ruth, "That's wonderful, dear daughter! Do that! You'll be safe in the company of his young women; no danger now of being raped in some stranger's field."

23 So Ruth did it — she stuck close to Boaz's young women, gleaning in the fields daily until both the barley and wheat harvesting were finished. And she continued living with her mother-in-law.

1-2 **3** One day her mother-in-law Naomi said to Ruth, "My dear daughter, isn't it about time I arranged a good home for you so you can have a happy life? And isn't Boaz our close relative, the one with whose young women you've been working? Maybe it's time to make our move. Tonight is the night of Boaz's barley harvest at the threshing floor.

3-4 "Take a bath. Put on some perfume. Get all dressed up and go to the threshing floor. But don't let him know you're there until the party is well under way and he's had plenty of food and drink. When you see him slipping off to sleep, watch where he lies down and then go there. Lie at his feet to let him know that you are available to him for marriage. Then wait and see what he says. He'll tell you what to do."

5 Ruth said, "If you say so, I'll do it, just as you've told me."

6 She went down to the threshing floor and put her mother-in-law's plan into action.

7 Boaz had a good time, eating and drinking his fill — he felt great. Then he went off to get some sleep, lying down at the end of a stack of barley. Ruth quietly followed; she lay down to signal her availability for marriage.

8 In the middle of the night the man was suddenly startled and sat up. Surprise! This woman asleep at his feet!

9 He said, "And who are you?"

She said, "I am Ruth, your maiden; take me under your protecting wing. You're my close relative, you know, in the circle of covenant redeemers — you do have the right to marry me."

10-13 He said, "GOD bless you, my dear daughter! What a splendid expression of love! And when you could have had your pick of any of the young men around. And now, my dear daughter, don't you worry about a thing; I'll do all you could want or ask. Everybody in town knows what a courageous woman you are — a real prize! You're right, I am a close relative to you, but there is one even closer than I am. So stay the rest of the night. In the morning, if he wants to exercise his customary rights and responsibilities as the closest covenant redeemer, he'll have his chance; but if he isn't interested, as GOD lives, I'll do it. Now go back to sleep until morning."

14 Ruth slept at his feet until dawn, but she got up while it was still dark and wouldn't be recognized. Then Boaz said to himself, "No one must know that Ruth came to the threshing floor."

15 So Boaz said, "Bring the shawl you're wearing and spread it out."

She spread it out and he poured it full of barley, six measures, and put it on her shoulders. Then she went back to town.

16-17 When she came to her mother-in-law, Naomi asked, "And how did things go, my dear daughter?"

Ruth told her everything that the man had done for her, adding, "And he gave me all this barley besides — six quarts! He told me, 'You can't go back empty-handed to your mother-in-law!'"

18 Naomi said, "Sit back and relax, my dear daughter, until we find out how things turn out; that man isn't going to fool around. Mark my words, he's going to get everything wrapped up today."

1 **4** Boaz went straight to the public square and took his place there. Before long the "closer relative," the one mentioned earlier by Boaz, strolled by.

"Step aside, old friend," said Boaz. "Take a seat." The man sat down.

2 Boaz then gathered ten of the town elders together and said, "Sit down here with us; we've got some business to take care of." And they sat down.

3-4 Boaz then said to his relative, "The piece of property that belonged to our relative Elimelech is being sold by his widow Naomi, who has just returned from the country of Moab. I thought you ought to know about it. Buy it back if you want it — you can make it official in the presence of those sitting here and before the town elders. You have first redeemer rights. If you don't want it, tell me so I'll know where I stand. You're first in line to do this and I'm next after you."

He said, "I'll buy it."

5 Then Boaz added, "You realize, don't you, that when you buy the field from Naomi, you also get Ruth the Moabite, the widow of our dead relative, along with the redeemer responsibility to have children with her to carry on the family inheritance."

6 Then the relative said, "Oh, I can't do that — I'd jeopardize my own family's inheritance. You go ahead and buy it — you can have my rights — I can't do it."

7 In the olden times in Israel, this is how they handled official business regarding matters of property and inheritance: a man would take off his shoe and give it to the other person. This was the same as an official seal or personal signature in Israel.

8 So when Boaz's "redeemer" relative said, "Go ahead and buy it," he signed the deal by pulling off his shoe.

9-10 Boaz then addressed the elders and all the people in the town square that day: "You are witnesses today that I have bought from Naomi everything that belonged to Elimelech and Kilion and Mahlon, including responsibility for Ruth the foreigner, the widow of Mahlon — I'll take her as my wife and keep the name of the deceased alive along with his inheritance. The memory and reputation of the deceased is not going to disappear out of this family or from his hometown. To all this you are witnesses this very day."

11-12 All the people in the town square that day, backing up the elders, said, "Yes, we are witnesses. May GOD make this woman who is coming into your household like Rachel and Leah, the two women who built the family of Israel. May GOD make you a pillar in Ephrathah and famous in Bethlehem! With the children GOD gives you from this young woman, may your family rival the family of Perez, the son Tamar bore to Judah."

13 Boaz married Ruth. She became his wife. Boaz slept with her. By GOD's gracious gift she conceived and had a son.

14-15 The town women said to Naomi, "Blessed be GOD! He didn't leave you without family to carry on your life. May this baby grow up to be famous in Israel! He'll make you young again! He'll take care of you in old age. And this daughter-in-law who has brought him into the world and loves you so much, why, she's worth more to you than seven sons!"

16 Naomi took the baby and held him in her arms, cuddling him, cooing over him, waiting on him hand and foot.

17 The neighborhood women started calling him "Naomi's baby boy!" But his real name was Obed. Obed was the father of Jesse, and Jesse the father of David.

18-22 This is the family tree of Perez:
    Perez had Hezron,
    Hezron had Ram,
    Ram had Amminadab,
    Amminadab had Nahshon,
    Nahshon had Salmon,
    Salmon had Boaz,
    Boaz had Obed,
    Obed had Jesse,
    and Jesse had David.

1 & 2 SAMUEL

Four lives dominate the two-volume narrative, First and Second Samuel: Hannah, Samuel, Saul, and David. Chronologically, the stories are clustered around the year 1000 B.C., the millennial midpoint between the call of Abraham, the father of Israel, nearly a thousand years earlier (about 1800 B.C.) and the birth of Jesus, the Christ, a thousand years later.

These four lives become seminal for us at the moment we realize that our ego-bound experience is too small a context in which to understand and experience what it means to believe in God and follow his ways. For these are large lives — large because they live in the largeness of God. Not one of them can be accounted for in terms of cultural conditions or psychological dynamics; God is the country in which they live.

Most of us need to be reminded that these stories are not exemplary in the sense that we stand back and admire them, like statues in a gallery, knowing all the while that we will never be able to live either that gloriously or tragically ourselves. Rather they are immersions into the actual business of living itself: this is what it means to be human. Reading and praying our way through these pages, we get it; gradually but most emphatically we recognize that what it means to be a woman, a man, mostly has to do with God. These four stories do not show us how we should live but how in fact we do live, authenticating the reality of our daily experience as the stuff that God uses to work out his purposes of salvation in us and in the world.

The stories do not do this by talking about God, for there is surprisingly little explicit God talk here — whole pages sometimes without the name of God appearing. But as the narrative develops we realize that God is the commanding and accompanying presence that provides both plot and texture to every sentence. This cluster of interlocking stories trains us in perceptions of ourselves, our sheer and irreducible humanity, that cannot be reduced to personal feelings or ideas or circumstances. If we want a life other than mere biology, we must deal with God. There is no alternate way.

One of many welcome consequences in learning to "read" our lives in the lives of Hannah, Samuel, Saul, and David is a sense of affirmation and freedom: we don't have to fit into prefabricated moral or mental or religious boxes before we are admitted into the company of God — we are taken seriously just as we are and given a place in his story, for it is, after all, his story; none of us is the leading character in the story of our life.

For the biblical way is not so much to present us with a moral code and tell us "Live up to this"; nor is it to set out a system of doctrine and say, "Think like this and you will live well." The biblical way is to tell a story and invite us, "Live into this. This is what it looks like to be human; this is what is involved in entering and maturing as human beings." We do violence to the biblical revelation when we "use" it for what we can get out of it or what we think will provide color and spice to our otherwise bland lives. That results in a kind of "boutique spirituality"—God as decoration, God as enhancement. The Samuel narrative will not allow that. In the reading, as we submit our lives to what we read, we find that we are not being led to see God in our stories but to see our stories in God's. God is the larger context and plot in which our stories find themselves.

Such reading will necessarily be a prayerful reading—a God-listening, God-answering reading. The story, after all, is framed by prayer: Hannah's prayer at the beginning (1 Samuel 2), and David's near the end (2 Samuel 22–23).

1 SAMUEL

HANNAH POURS OUT HER HEART TO GOD

1-2 There once was a man who lived in Ramathaim. He was descended from the old Zuph family in the Ephraim hills. His name was Elkanah. (He was connected with the Zuphs from Ephraim through his father Jeroham, his grandfather Elihu, and his great-grandfather Tohu.) He had two wives. The first was Hannah; the second was Peninnah. Peninnah had children; Hannah did not.

3-7 Every year this man went from his hometown up to Shiloh to worship and offer a sacrifice to GOD-of-the-Angel-Armies. Eli and his two sons, Hophni and Phinehas, served as the priests of GOD there. When Elkanah sacrificed, he passed helpings from the sacrificial meal around to his wife Peninnah and all her children, but he always gave an especially generous helping to Hannah because he loved her so much, and because GOD had not given her children. But her rival wife taunted her cruelly, rubbing it in and never letting her forget that GOD had not given her children. This went on year after year. Every time she went to the sanctuary of GOD she could expect to be taunted. Hannah was reduced to tears and had no appetite.

8 Her husband Elkanah said, "Oh, Hannah, why are you crying? Why aren't you eating? And why are you so upset? Am I not of more worth to you than ten sons?"

9-11 So Hannah ate. Then she pulled herself together, slipped away quietly, and entered the sanctuary. The priest Eli was on duty at the entrance to GOD's Temple in the customary seat. Crushed in soul, Hannah prayed to GOD and cried and cried—inconsolably. Then she made a vow:

> Oh, GOD-of-the-Angel-Armies,
> If you'll take a good, hard look at my pain,
> If you'll quit neglecting me and go into action for me
> By giving me a son,
> I'll give him completely, unreservedly to you.
> I'll set him apart for a life of holy discipline.

12-14 It so happened that as she continued in prayer before GOD, Eli was watching her closely. Hannah was praying in her heart, silently. Her lips moved, but no sound was heard. Eli jumped to the conclusion that she was drunk. He approached her and said, "You're drunk! How long do you plan to keep this up? Sober up, woman!"

15-16 Hannah said, "Oh no, sir—please! I'm a woman hard used. I haven't been drinking. Not a drop of wine or beer. The only thing I've been pouring out is my heart, pouring it out to GOD. Don't for a minute think I'm a bad woman. It's because I'm so desperately unhappy and in such pain that I've stayed here so long."

17 Eli answered her, "Go in peace. And may the God of Israel give you what you have asked of him."

18 "Think well of me—and pray for me!" she said, and went her way. Then she ate heartily, her face radiant.

19   Up before dawn, they worshiped GOD and returned home to Ramah. Elkanah slept with Hannah his wife, and GOD began making the necessary arrangements in response to what she had asked.

DEDICATING THE CHILD TO GOD

20   Before the year was out, Hannah had conceived and given birth to a son. She named him Samuel, explaining, "I asked GOD for him."

21-22   When Elkanah next took his family on their annual trip to Shiloh to worship GOD, offering sacrifices and keeping his vow, Hannah didn't go. She told her husband, "After the child is weaned, I'll bring him myself and present him before GOD—and that's where he'll stay, for good."

23-24   Elkanah said to his wife, "Do what you think is best. Stay home until you have weaned him. Yes! Let GOD complete what he has begun!"

So she did. She stayed home and nursed her son until she had weaned him. Then she took him up to Shiloh, bringing also the makings of a generous sacrificial meal—a prize bull, flour, and wine. The child was so young to be sent off!

25-26   They first butchered the bull, then brought the child to Eli. Hannah said, "Excuse me, sir. Would you believe that I'm the very woman who was standing before you at this very spot, praying to GOD? I prayed for this child, and GOD gave me what I asked for. And now I have dedicated him to GOD. He's dedicated to GOD for life."

Then and there, they worshiped GOD.

1   **2** Hannah prayed:
I'm bursting with GOD-news!
     I'm walking on air.
I'm laughing at my rivals.
     I'm dancing my salvation.

2-5   Nothing and no one is holy like GOD,
     no rock mountain like our God.
Don't dare talk pretentiously—
     not a word of boasting, ever!
For GOD knows what's going on.
     He takes the measure of everything that happens.
The weapons of the strong are smashed to pieces,
     while the weak are infused with fresh strength.
The well-fed are out begging in the streets for crusts,
     while the hungry are getting second helpings.
The barren woman has a houseful of children,
     while the mother of many is bereft.

6-10   GOD brings death and GOD brings life,
     brings down to the grave and raises up.
GOD brings poverty and GOD brings wealth;
     he lowers, he also lifts up.
He puts poor people on their feet again;
     he rekindles burned-out lives with fresh hope,
Restoring dignity and respect to their lives—
     a place in the sun!

For the very structures of earth are GOD's;
>   he has laid out his operations on a firm foundation.
He protectively cares for his faithful friends, step by step,
>   but leaves the wicked to stumble in the dark.
No one makes it in this life by sheer muscle!
GOD's enemies will be blasted out of the sky,
>   crashed in a heap and burned.
GOD will set things right all over the earth,
>   he'll give strength to his king,
>   he'll set his anointed on top of the world!

11 Elkanah went home to Ramah. The boy stayed and served GOD in the company of Eli the priest.

SAMUEL SERVES GOD

12-17 Eli's own sons were a bad lot. They didn't know GOD and could not have cared less about the customs of priests among the people. Ordinarily, when someone offered a sacrifice, the priest's servant was supposed to come up and, while the meat was boiling, stab a three-pronged fork into the cooking pot. The priest then got whatever came up on the fork. But this is how Eli's sons treated all the Israelites who came to Shiloh to offer sacrifices to GOD. Before they had even burned the fat to GOD, the priest's servant would interrupt whoever was sacrificing and say, "Hand over some of that meat for the priest to roast. He doesn't like boiled meat; he likes his rare." If the man objected, "First let the fat be burned — God's portion! — then take all you want," the servant would demand, "No, I want it now. If you won't give it, I'll take it." It was a horrible sin these young servants were committing — and right in the presence of GOD! — desecrating the holy offerings to GOD.

18-20 In the midst of all this, Samuel, a boy dressed in a priestly linen tunic, served GOD. Additionally, every year his mother would make him a little robe cut to his size and bring it to him when she and her husband came for the annual sacrifice. Eli would bless Elkanah and his wife, saying, "GOD give you children to replace this child you have dedicated to GOD." Then they would go home.

21 GOD was most especially kind to Hannah. She had three more sons and two daughters! The boy Samuel stayed at the sanctuary and grew up with GOD.

A HARD LIFE WITH MANY TEARS

22-25 By this time Eli was very old. He kept getting reports on how his sons were ripping off the people and sleeping with the women who helped out at the sanctuary. Eli took them to task: "What's going on here? Why are you doing these things? I hear story after story of your corrupt and evil carrying on. Oh, my sons, this is not right! These are terrible reports I'm getting, stories spreading right and left among GOD's people! If you sin against another person, there's help — God's help. But if you sin against GOD, who is around to help?"

25-26 But they were far gone in disobedience and refused to listen to a thing their father said. So GOD, who was fed up with them, decreed their death. But the boy Samuel was very much alive, growing up, blessed by GOD and popular with the people.

27-30   A holy man came to Eli and said: "This is GOD's message: I revealed myself openly to your ancestors when they were Pharaoh's slaves in Egypt. Out of all the tribes of Israel, I chose your family to be my priests: to preside at the Altar, to burn incense, to wear the priestly robes in my presence. I put your ancestral family in charge of all the sacrificial offerings of Israel. So why do you now treat as mere loot these very sacrificial offerings that I commanded for my worship? Why do you treat your sons better than me, turning them loose to get fat on these offerings, and ignoring me? Therefore—this is GOD's word, the God of Israel speaking—I once said that you and your ancestral family would be my priests indefinitely, but now—GOD's word, remember!—there is no way this can continue.

> I honor those who honor me;
> those who scorn me I demean.

31-36   "Be well warned: It won't be long before I wipe out both your family and your future family. No one in your family will make it to old age! You'll see good things that I'm doing in Israel, but you'll see it and weep, for no one in your family will live to enjoy it. I will leave one person to serve at my Altar, but it will be a hard life, with many tears. Everyone else in your family will die before their time. What happens to your two sons, Hophni and Phinehas, will be the proof: Both will die the same day. Then I'll establish for myself a true priest. He'll do what I want him to do, be what I want him to be. I'll make his position secure and he'll do his work freely in the service of my anointed one. Survivors from your family will come to him begging for handouts, saying, 'Please, give me some priest work, just enough to put some food on the table.'"

"SPEAK, GOD. I'M READY TO LISTEN"

1-3   3 The boy Samuel was serving GOD under Eli's direction. This was at a time when the revelation of GOD was rarely heard or seen. One night Eli was sound asleep (his eyesight was very bad—he could hardly see). It was well before dawn; the sanctuary lamp was still burning. Samuel was still in bed in the Temple of GOD, where the Chest of God rested.

4-5   Then GOD called out, "Samuel, Samuel!"

Samuel answered, "Yes? I'm here." Then he ran to Eli saying, "I heard you call. Here I am."

Eli said, "I didn't call you. Go back to bed." And so he did.

6-7   GOD called again, "Samuel, Samuel!"

Samuel got up and went to Eli, "I heard you call. Here I am."

Again Eli said, "Son, I didn't call you. Go back to bed." (This all happened before Samuel knew GOD for himself. It was before the revelation of GOD had been given to him personally.)

8-9   GOD called again, "Samuel!"—the third time! Yet again Samuel got up and went to Eli, "Yes? I heard you call me. Here I am."

That's when it dawned on Eli that GOD was calling the boy. So Eli directed Samuel, "Go back and lie down. If the voice calls again, say, 'Speak, GOD. I'm your servant, ready to listen.'" Samuel returned to his bed.

10   Then GOD came and stood before him exactly as before, calling out, "Samuel! Samuel!"

Samuel answered, "Speak. I'm your servant, ready to listen."

11-14   GOD said to Samuel, "Listen carefully. I'm getting ready to do something in Israel that is going to shake everyone up and get their attention. The time has come for me to bring down on Eli's family everything I warned him of, every last word of it. I'm letting him know that the time's up. I'm bringing judgment on his family for good. He knew what was going on, that his sons were desecrating God's name and God's place, and he did nothing to stop them. This is my sentence on the family of Eli: The evil of Eli's family can never be wiped out by sacrifice or offering."

15   Samuel stayed in bed until morning, then rose early and went about his duties, opening the doors of the sanctuary, but he dreaded having to tell the vision to Eli.

16   But then Eli summoned Samuel: "Samuel, my son!"
Samuel came running: "Yes? What can I do for you?"

17   "What did he say? Tell it to me, all of it. Don't suppress or soften one word, as God is your judge! I want it all, word for word as he said it to you."

18   So Samuel told him, word for word. He held back nothing.
Eli said, "He is GOD. Let him do whatever he thinks best."

19-21   Samuel grew up. GOD was with him, and Samuel's prophetic record was flawless. Everyone in Israel, from Dan in the north to Beersheba in the south, recognized that Samuel was the real thing—a true prophet of GOD. GOD continued to show up at Shiloh, revealed through his word to Samuel at Shiloh.

THE CHEST OF GOD IS TAKEN

1-3   **4** Whatever Samuel said was broadcast all through Israel. Israel went to war against the Philistines. Israel set up camp at Ebenezer, the Philistines at Aphek. The Philistines marched out to meet Israel, the fighting spread, and Israel was badly beaten—about four thousand soldiers left dead on the field. When the troops returned to camp, Israel's elders said, "Why has GOD given us such a beating today by the Philistines? Let's go to Shiloh and get the Chest of GOD's Covenant. It will accompany us and save us from the grip of our enemies."

4   So the army sent orders to Shiloh. They brought the Chest of the Covenant of GOD, the GOD-of-the-Angel-Armies, the Cherubim-Enthroned-GOD. Eli's two sons, Hophni and Phinehas, accompanied the Chest of the Covenant of God.

5-6   When the Chest of the Covenant of GOD was brought into camp, everyone gave a huge cheer. The shouts were like thunderclaps shaking the very ground. The Philistines heard the shouting and wondered what on earth was going on: "What's all this shouting among the Hebrews?"

6-9   Then they learned that the Chest of GOD had entered the Hebrew camp. The Philistines panicked: "Their gods have come to their camp! Nothing like this has ever happened before. We're done for! Who can save us from the clutches of these supergods? These are the same gods who hit the Egyptians with all kinds of plagues out in the wilderness. On your feet, Philistines! Courage! We're about to become slaves to the Hebrews, just as they have been slaves to us. Show what you're made of! Fight for your lives!"

10-11   And did they ever fight! It turned into a rout. They thrashed Israel so mercilessly that the Israelite soldiers ran for their lives, leaving behind an incredible thirty thousand dead. As if that wasn't bad enough, the Chest of God was taken and the two sons of Eli—Hophni and Phinehas—were killed.

GLORY IS EXILED FROM ISRAEL

12-16 Immediately, a Benjaminite raced from the front lines back to Shiloh. Shirt torn and face smeared with dirt, he entered the town. Eli was sitting on his stool beside the road keeping vigil, for he was extremely worried about the Chest of God. When the man ran straight into town to tell the bad news, everyone wept. They were appalled. Eli heard the loud wailing and asked, "Why this uproar?" The messenger hurried over and reported. Eli was ninety-eight years old then, and blind. The man said to Eli, "I've just come from the front, barely escaping with my life."

"And so, my son," said Eli, "what happened?"

17 The messenger answered, "Israel scattered before the Philistines. The defeat was catastrophic, with enormous losses. Your sons Hophni and Phinehas died, and the Chest of God was taken."

18 At the words, "Chest of God," Eli fell backward off his stool where he sat next to the gate. Eli was an old man, and very fat. When he fell, he broke his neck and died. He had led Israel forty years.

19-20 His daughter-in-law, the wife of Phinehas, was pregnant and ready to deliver. When she heard that the Chest of God had been taken and that both her father-in-law and her husband were dead, she went to her knees to give birth, going into hard labor. As she was about to die, her midwife said, "Don't be afraid. You've given birth to a son!" But she gave no sign that she had heard.

21-22 The Chest of God gone, father-in-law dead, husband dead, she named the boy Ichabod (Glory's-Gone), saying, "Glory is exiled from Israel since the Chest of God was taken."

THREATENED WITH MASS DEATH

1-2 5 Once the Philistines had seized the Chest of God, they took it from Ebenezer to Ashdod, brought it into the shrine of Dagon, and placed it alongside the idol of Dagon.

3-5 Next morning when the citizens of Ashdod got up, they were shocked to find Dagon toppled from his place, flat on his face before the Chest of GOD. They picked him up and put him back where he belonged. First thing the next morning they found him again, toppled and flat on his face before the Chest of GOD. Dagon's head and arms were broken off, strewn across the entrance. Only his torso was in one piece. (That's why even today, the priests of Dagon and visitors to the Dagon shrine in Ashdod avoid stepping on the threshold.)

6 GOD was hard on the citizens of Ashdod. He devastated them by hitting them with tumors. This happened in both the town and the surrounding neighborhoods. He let loose rats among them. Jumping from ships there, rats swarmed all over the city! And everyone was deathly afraid.

7-8 When the leaders of Ashdod saw what was going on, they decided, "The chest of the god of Israel has got to go. We can't handle this, and neither can our god Dagon." They called together all the Philistine leaders and put it to them: "How can we get rid of the chest of the god of Israel?"

The leaders agreed: "Move it to Gath." So they moved the Chest of the God of Israel to Gath.

9 But as soon as they moved it there, GOD came down hard on that city, too. It was mass hysteria! He hit them with tumors. Tumors broke out on everyone in town, young and old.

10-12 So they sent the Chest of God on to Ekron, but as the Chest was being brought into town, the people shouted in protest, "You'll kill us all by bringing in this Chest of the God of Israel!" They called the Philistine leaders together and demanded, "Get it out of here, this Chest of the God of Israel. Send it back where it came from. We're threatened with mass death!" For everyone was scared to death when the Chest of God showed up. God was already coming down very hard on the place. Those who didn't die were hit with tumors. All over the city cries of pain and lament filled the air.

GOLD TUMORS AND RATS

1-2 After the Chest of GOD had been among the Philistine people for seven months, the Philistine leaders called together their religious professionals, the priests, and experts on the supernatural for consultation: "How can we get rid of this Chest of GOD, get it off our hands without making things worse? Tell us!"

3 They said, "If you're going to send the Chest of the God of Israel back, don't just dump it on them. Pay compensation. Then you will be healed. After you're in the clear again, God will let up on you. Why wouldn't he?"

4-6 "And what exactly would make for adequate compensation?"

"Five gold tumors and five gold rats," they said, "to match the number of Philistine leaders. Since all of you — leaders and people — suffered the same plague, make replicas of the tumors and rats that are devastating the country and present them as an offering to the glory of the God of Israel. Then maybe he'll ease up and not be so hard on you and your gods, and on your country. Why be stubborn like the Egyptians and Pharaoh? God didn't quit pounding on them until they let the people go. Only then did he let up.

7-9 "So here's what you do: Take a brand-new oxcart and two cows that have never been in harness. Hitch the cows to the oxcart and send their calves back to the barn. Put the Chest of GOD on the cart. Secure the gold replicas of the tumors and rats that you are offering as compensation in a sack and set them next to the Chest. Then send it off. But keep your eyes on it. If it heads straight back home to where it came from, toward Beth Shemesh, it is clear that this catastrophe is a divine judgment, but if not, we'll know that God had nothing to do with it — it was just an accident."

10-12 So that's what they did: They hitched two cows to the cart, put their calves in the barn, and placed the Chest of GOD and the sack of gold rats and tumors on the cart. The cows headed straight for home, down the road to Beth Shemesh, straying neither right nor left, mooing all the way. The Philistine leaders followed them to the outskirts of Beth Shemesh.

13-15 The people of Beth Shemesh were harvesting wheat in the valley. They looked up and saw the Chest. Jubilant, they ran to meet it. The cart came into the field of Joshua, a Beth Shemeshite, and stopped there beside a huge boulder. The harvesters tore the cart to pieces, then chopped up the wood and sacrificed the cows as a burnt offering to GOD. The Levites took charge of the Chest of GOD and the sack containing the gold offerings, placing them on the boulder. Offering the sacrifices, everyone in Beth Shemesh worshiped GOD most heartily that day.

16 When the five Philistine leaders saw what they came to see, they returned the same day to Ekron.

17-18 The five gold replicas of the tumors were offered by the Philistines in compensation for the cities of Ashdod, Gaza, Ashkelon, Gath, and Ekron.

The five gold rats matched the number of Philistine towns, both large and small, ruled by the five leaders. The big boulder on which they placed the Chest of GOD is still there in the field of Joshua of Beth Shemesh, a landmark.

IF YOU ARE SERIOUS ABOUT COMING BACK TO GOD

19-20   God struck some of the men of Beth Shemesh who, out of curiosity, irreverently peeked into the Chest of GOD. Seventy died. The whole town was in mourning, reeling under the hard blow from GOD, and questioning, "Who can stand before GOD, this holy God? And who can we get to take this Chest off our hands?"

21   They sent emissaries to Kiriath Jearim, saying, "The Philistines have returned the Chest of GOD. Come down and get it."

1   7 And they did. The men of Kiriath Jearim came and got the Chest of GOD and delivered it to the house of Abinadab on the hill. They ordained his son, Eleazar, to take responsibility for the Chest of GOD.

2   From the time that the Chest came to rest in Kiriath Jearim, a long time passed — twenty years it was — and throughout Israel there was a widespread, fearful movement toward GOD.

3   Then Samuel addressed the house of Israel: "If you are truly serious about coming back to GOD, clean house. Get rid of the foreign gods and fertility goddesses, ground yourselves firmly in GOD, worship him and him alone, and he'll save you from Philistine oppression."

4   They did it. They got rid of the gods and goddesses, the images of Baal and Ashtoreth, and gave their exclusive attention and service to GOD.

5   Next Samuel said, "Get everybody together at Mizpah and I'll pray for you."

6   So everyone assembled at Mizpah. They drew water from the wells and poured it out before GOD in a ritual of cleansing. They fasted all day and prayed, "We have sinned against GOD."

So Samuel prepared the Israelites for holy war there at Mizpah.

THE PLACE WHERE GOD HELPED US

7   When the Philistines heard that Israel was meeting at Mizpah, the Philistine leaders went on the offensive. Israel got the report and became frightened — Philistines on the move again!

8   They pleaded with Samuel, "Pray with all your might! And don't let up! Pray to GOD, our God, that he'll save us from the boot of the Philistines."

9   Samuel took a young lamb not yet weaned and offered it whole as a Whole-Burnt-Offering to GOD. He prayed fervently to GOD, interceding for Israel. And GOD answered.

10-12   While Samuel was offering the sacrifice, the Philistines came within range to fight Israel. Just then GOD thundered, a huge thunderclap exploding among the Philistines. They panicked — mass confusion! — and ran helter-skelter from Israel. Israel poured out of Mizpah and gave chase, killing Philistines right and left, to a point just beyond Beth Car. Samuel took a single rock and set it upright between Mizpah and Shen. He named it "Ebenezer" (Rock of Help), saying, "This marks the place where GOD helped us."

13-14   The Philistines learned their lesson and stayed home — no more border crossings. GOD was hard on the Philistines all through Samuel's lifetime.

All the cities from Ekron to Gath that the Philistines had taken from Israel were restored. Israel also freed the surrounding countryside from Philistine control. And there was peace between Israel and the Amorites.

15-17 Samuel gave solid leadership to Israel his entire life. Every year he went on a circuit from Bethel to Gilgal to Mizpah. He gave leadership to Israel in each of these places. But always he would return to Ramah, where he lived, and preside from there. That is where he built an altar to GOD.

REJECTING GOD AS THE KING

1-3 **8** When Samuel got to be an old man, he set his sons up as judges in Israel. His firstborn son was named Joel, the name of his second, Abijah. They were assigned duty in Beersheba. But his sons didn't take after him; they were out for what they could get for themselves, taking bribes, corrupting justice.

4-5 Fed up, all the elders of Israel got together and confronted Samuel at Ramah. They presented their case: "Look, you're an old man, and your sons aren't following in your footsteps. Here's what we want you to do: Appoint a king to rule us, just like everybody else."

6 When Samuel heard their demand — "Give us a king to rule us!" — he was crushed. How awful! Samuel prayed to GOD.

7-9 GOD answered Samuel, "Go ahead and do what they're asking. They are not rejecting you. They've rejected me as their King. From the day I brought them out of Egypt until this very day they've been behaving like this, leaving me for other gods. And now they're doing it to you. So let them have their own way. But warn them of what they're in for. Tell them the way kings operate, just what they're likely to get from a king."

10-18 So Samuel told them, delivered GOD's warning to the people who were asking him to give them a king. He said, "This is the way the kind of king you're talking about operates. He'll take your sons and make soldiers of them — chariotry, cavalry, infantry, regimented in battalions and squadrons. He'll put some to forced labor on his farms, plowing and harvesting, and others to making either weapons of war or chariots in which he can ride in luxury. He'll put your daughters to work as beauticians and waitresses and cooks. He'll conscript your best fields, vineyards, and orchards and hand them over to his special friends. He'll tax your harvests and vintage to support his extensive bureaucracy. Your prize workers and best animals he'll take for his own use. He'll lay a tax on your flocks and you'll end up no better than slaves. The day will come when you will cry in desperation because of this king you so much want for yourselves. But don't expect GOD to answer."

19-20 But the people wouldn't listen to Samuel. "No!" they said. "We will have a king to rule us! Then we'll be just like all the other nations. Our king will rule us and lead us and fight our battles."

21-22 Samuel took in what they said and rehearsed it with GOD. GOD told Samuel, "Do what they say. Make them a king."

Then Samuel dismissed the men of Israel: "Go home, each of you to your own city."

SAUL — HEAD AND SHOULDERS ABOVE THE CROWD

1-2 **9** There was a man from the tribe of Benjamin named Kish. He was the son of Abiel, grandson of Zeror, great-grandson of Becorath, great-great-grandson of Aphiah — a Benjaminite of stalwart character.

He had a son, Saul, a most handsome young man. There was none finer — he
literally stood head and shoulders above the crowd!

3-4   Some of Kish's donkeys got lost. Kish said to his son, "Saul, take one of
the servants with you and go look for the donkeys." Saul took one of the
servants and went to find the donkeys. They went into the hill country of
Ephraim around Shalisha, but didn't find them. Then they went over to
Shaalim — no luck. Then to Jabin, and still nothing.

5   When they got to Zuph, Saul said to the young man with him, "Enough
of this. Let's go back. Soon my father is going to forget about the donkeys and
start worrying about us."

6   He replied, "Not so fast. There's a holy man in this town. He carries a lot
of weight around here. What he says is always right on the mark. Maybe
he can tell us where to go."

7   Saul said, "If we go, what do we have to give him? There's no more bread in
our sacks. We've nothing to bring as a gift to the holy man. Do we have anything else?"

8-9   The servant spoke up, "Look, I just happen to have this silver coin! I'll
give it to the holy man and he'll tell us how to proceed!" (In former times
in Israel, a person who wanted to seek God's word on a matter would say,
"Let's visit the Seer," because the one we now call "the Prophet" used to
be called "the Seer.")

10   "Good," said Saul, "let's go." And they set off for the town where the holy
man lived.

11   As they were climbing up the hill into the town, they met some girls
who were coming out to draw water. They said to them, "Is this where the
Seer lives?"

12-13   They answered, "It sure is — just ahead. Hurry up. He's come today
because the people have prepared a sacrifice at the shrine. As soon as you
enter the town, you can catch him before he goes up to the shrine to eat.
The people won't eat until he arrives, for he has to bless the sacrifice. Only
then can everyone eat. So get going. You're sure to find him!"

14   They continued their climb and entered the city. And then there he
was — Samuel! — coming straight toward them on his way to the shrine!

15-16   The very day before, God had confided in Samuel, "This time tomorrow, I'm sending a man from the land of Benjamin to meet you. You're
to anoint him as prince over my people Israel. He will free my people
from Philistine oppression. Yes, I know all about their hard circumstances. I've heard their cries for help."

17   The moment Samuel laid eyes on Saul, God said, "He's the one, the man
I told you about. This is the one who will keep my people in check."

18   Saul came up to Samuel in the street and said, "Pardon me, but can you
tell me where the Seer lives?"

19-20   "I'm the Seer," said Samuel. "Accompany me to the shrine and eat
with me. In the morning I'll tell you all about what's on your mind, and
send you on your way. And by the way, your lost donkeys — the ones
you've been hunting for the last three days — have been found, so don't
worry about them. At this moment, Israel's future is in your hands."

21   Saul answered, "But I'm only a Benjaminite, from the smallest of
Israel's tribes, and from the most insignificant clan in the tribe at that.
Why are you talking to me like this?"

22-23   Samuel took Saul and his servant and led them into the dining hall at the shrine and seated them at the head of the table. There were about thirty guests. Then Samuel directed the chef, "Bring the choice cut I pointed out to you, the one I told you to reserve."

24 The chef brought it and placed it before Saul with a flourish, saying, "This meal was kept aside just for you. Eat! It was especially prepared for this time and occasion with these guests."

Saul ate with Samuel—a memorable day!

25 Afterward they went down from the shrine into the city. A bed was prepared for Saul on the breeze-cooled roof of Samuel's house.

26 They woke at the break of day. Samuel called to Saul on the roof, "Get up and I'll send you off." Saul got up and the two of them went out in the street.

27 As they approached the outskirts of town, Samuel said to Saul, "Tell your servant to go on ahead of us. You stay with me for a bit. I have a word of God to give you."

"You'll Be a New Person"

1-2 **10** Then Samuel took a flask of oil, poured it on Saul's head, and kissed him. He said, "Do you see what this means? GOD has anointed you prince over his people.

"This sign will confirm GOD's anointing of you as prince over his inheritance: After you leave me today, as you get closer to your home country of Benjamin, you'll meet two men near Rachel's Tomb. They'll say, 'The donkeys you went to look for are found. Your father has forgotten about the donkeys and is worried about you, wringing his hands—quite beside himself!'

3-4 "Leaving there, you'll arrive at the Oak of Tabor. There you'll meet three men going up to worship God at Bethel. One will be carrying three young goats, another carrying three sacks of bread, and the third a jug of wine. They'll say, 'Hello, how are you?' and offer you two loaves of bread, which you will accept.

5-6 "Next, you'll come to Gibeah of God, where there's a Philistine garrison. As you approach the town, you'll run into a bunch of prophets coming down from the shrine, playing harps and tambourines, flutes and drums. And they'll be prophesying. Before you know it, the Spirit of GOD will come on you and you'll be prophesying right along with them. And you'll be transformed. You'll be a new person!

7 "When these confirming signs are accomplished, you'll know that you're ready: Whatever job you're given to do, do it. God is with you!

8 "Now, go down to Gilgal and I will follow. I'll come down and join you in worship by sacrificing burnt offerings and peace offerings. Wait seven days. Then I'll come and tell you what to do next."

9 Saul turned and left Samuel. At that very moment God transformed him—made him a new person! And all the confirming signs took place the same day.

Saul Among the Prophets

10-12 When Saul and his party got to Gibeah, there were the prophets, right in front of them! Before he knew it, the Spirit of God came on Saul and he was prophesying right along with them. When those who had previously known Saul saw him prophesying with the prophets, they were totally surprised. "What's going on here? What's come over the son of Kish? How on earth did

Saul get to be a prophet?" One man spoke up and said, "Who started this? Where did these people ever come from?"

That's how the saying got started, "Saul among the prophets! Who would have guessed?!"

13-14   When Saul was done prophesying, he returned home. His uncle asked him and his servant, "So where have you two been all this time?"

"Out looking for the donkeys. We looked and looked and couldn't find them. And then we found Samuel!"

15   "So," said Saul's uncle, "what did Samuel tell you?"

16   Saul said, "He told us not to worry — the donkeys had been found." But Saul didn't breathe a word to his uncle of what Samuel said about the king business.

"WE WANT A KING!"

17-18   Samuel called the people to assemble before GOD at Mizpah. He addressed the children of Israel, "This is GOD's personal message to you:

18-19   "I brought Israel up out of Egypt. I delivered you from Egyptian oppression — yes, from all the bullying governments that made your life miserable. And now you want nothing to do with your God, the very God who has a history of getting you out of troubles of all sorts.

"And now you say, 'No! We want a king; give us a king!'

"Well, if that's what you want, that's what you'll get! Present yourselves formally before GOD, ranked in tribes and families."

20-21   After Samuel got all the tribes of Israel lined up, the Benjamin tribe was picked. Then he lined up the Benjamin tribe in family groups, and the family of Matri was picked. The family of Matri took its place in the lineup, and the name Saul, son of Kish, was picked. But when they went looking for him, he was nowhere to be found.

22   Samuel went back to GOD: "Is he anywhere around?"

GOD said, "Yes, he's right over there — hidden in that pile of baggage."

23   They ran and got him. He took his place before everyone, standing tall — head and shoulders above them.

24   Samuel then addressed the people, "Take a good look at whom GOD has chosen: the best! No one like him in the whole country!"

Then a great shout went up from the people: "Long live the king!"

25   Samuel went on to instruct the people in the rules and regulations involved in a kingdom, wrote it all down in a book, and placed it before GOD. Then Samuel sent everyone home.

26-27   Saul also went home to Gibeah, and with him some true and brave men whom GOD moved to join him. But the riffraff went off muttering, "Deliverer? Don't make me laugh!" They held him in contempt and refused to congratulate him. But Saul paid them no mind.

SAUL IS CROWNED KING

Nahash, king of the Ammonites, was brutalizing the tribes of Gad and Reuben, gouging out their right eyes and intimidating anyone who would come to Israel's help. There were very few Israelites living on the east side of the Jordan River who had not had their right eyes gouged out by Nahash. But seven thousand men had escaped from the Ammonites and were now living safely in Jabesh.

11 ¹ So Nahash went after them and prepared to go to war against Jabesh Gilead. The men of Jabesh petitioned Nahash: "Make a treaty with us and we'll serve you."

² Nahash said, "I'll make a treaty with you on one condition: that every right eye among you be gouged out! I'll humiliate every last man and woman in Israel before I'm done!"

³ The town leaders of Jabesh said, "Give us time to send messengers around Israel — seven days should do it. If no one shows up to help us, we'll accept your terms."

⁴⁻⁵ The messengers came to Saul's place at Gibeah and told the people what was going on. As the people broke out in loud wails, Saul showed up. He was coming back from the field with his oxen.

Saul asked, "What happened? Why is everyone crying?"

And they repeated the message that had come from Jabesh.

⁶⁻⁷ The Spirit of God came on Saul when he heard the report and he flew into a rage. He grabbed the yoke of oxen and butchered them on the spot. He sent the messengers throughout Israel distributing the bloody pieces with this message: "Anyone who refuses to join up with Saul and Samuel, let this be the fate of his oxen!"

⁷⁻⁸ The terror of GOD seized the people, and they came out, one and all, not a laggard among them. Saul took command of the people at Bezek. There were 300,000 men from Israel, another 30,000 from Judah.

⁹⁻¹¹ Saul instructed the messengers, "Tell this to the folk in Jabesh Gilead: 'Help is on the way. Expect it by noon tomorrow.'"

The messengers set straight off and delivered their message. Elated, the people of Jabesh Gilead sent word to Nahash: "Tomorrow we'll give ourselves up. You can deal with us on your terms." Long before dawn the next day, Saul had strategically placed his army in three groups. At first light they broke into the enemy camp and slaughtered Ammonites until noon. Those who were left ran for their lives, scattering every which way.

¹² The people came to Samuel then and said, "Where are those men who said, 'Saul is not fit to rule over us'? Hand them over. We'll kill them!"

¹³⁻¹⁴ But Saul said, "Nobody is going to be executed this day. This is the day GOD saved Israel! Come, let's go to Gilgal and there reconsecrate the kingship."

¹⁵ They all trooped out to Gilgal. Before GOD, they crowned Saul king at Gilgal. And there they worshiped, sacrificing peace offerings. Saul and all Israel celebrated magnificently.

"DON'T CHASE AFTER GHOST-GODS"

12 ¹⁻³ Samuel addressed all Israel: "I've listened to everything you've said to me, listened carefully to every word, and I've given you a king. See for yourself: Your king among you, leading you! But now look at me: I'm old and gray, and my sons are still here. I've led you faithfully from my youth until this very day. Look at me! Do you have any complaints to bring before GOD and his anointed? Have I ever stolen so much as an ox or a donkey? Have I ever taken advantage of you or exploited you? Have I ever taken a bribe or played fast and loose with the law? Bring your complaint and I'll make it right."

⁴ "Oh no," they said, "never. You've never done any of that — never abused us, never lined your own pockets."

5   "That settles it then," said Samuel. "GOD is witness, and his anointed is witness that you find nothing against me — no faults, no complaints."

6-8   And the people said, "He is witness."

Samuel continued, "This is the GOD who made Moses and Aaron your leaders and brought your ancestors out of Egypt. Take your stand before him now as I review your case before GOD in the light of all the righteous ways in which GOD has worked with you and your ancestors. When Jacob's sons entered Egypt, the Egyptians made life hard for them and they cried for help to GOD. GOD sent Moses and Aaron, who led your ancestors out of Egypt and settled them here in this place.

9   "They soon forgot their GOD, so he sold them off to Sisera, commander of Hazor's army, later to a hard life under the Philistines, and still later to the king of Moab. They had to fight for their lives.

10   "Then they cried for help to GOD. They confessed, 'We've sinned! We've gone off and left GOD and worshiped the fertility gods and goddesses of Canaan. Oh, deliver us from the brutalities of our enemies and we'll worship you alone.'

11   "So GOD sent Jerub-Baal (Gideon), Bedan (Barak), Jephthah, and Samuel. He saved you from that hard life surrounded by enemies, and you lived in peace.

12   "But when you saw Nahash, king of the Ammonites, preparing to attack you, you said to me, 'No more of this. We want a king to lead us.' And GOD was already your king!

13-15   "So here's the king you wanted, the king you asked for. GOD has let you have your own way, given you a king. If you fear GOD, worship and obey him, and don't rebel against what he tells you. If both you and your king follow GOD, no problem. GOD will be sure to save you. But if you don't obey him and rebel against what he tells you, king or no king, you will fare no better than your fathers.

16-17   "Pay attention! Watch this wonder that GOD is going to perform before you now! It's summer, as you well know, and the rainy season is over. But I'm going to pray to GOD. He'll send thunder and rain, a sign to convince you of the great wrong you have done to GOD by asking for a king."

18   Samuel prayed to GOD, and GOD sent thunder and rain that same day. The people were greatly afraid and in awe of GOD and of Samuel.

19   Then all the people begged Samuel, "Pray to your GOD for us, your servants. Pray that we won't die! On top of all our other sins, we've piled on one more — asking for a king!"

20-22   Samuel said to them, "Don't be fearful. It's true that you have done something very wrong. All the same, don't turn your back on GOD. Worship and serve him heart and soul! Don't chase after ghost-gods. There's nothing to them. They can't help you. They're nothing but ghost-gods! GOD, simply because of who he is, is not going to walk off and leave his people. GOD took delight in making you into his very own people.

23-25   "And neither will I walk off and leave you. That would be a sin against GOD! I'm staying right here at my post praying for you and teaching you the good and right way to live. But I beg of you, fear GOD and worship him honestly and heartily. You've seen how greatly he has worked among you! Be warned: If you live badly, both you and your king will be thrown out."

"GOD IS OUT LOOKING FOR YOUR REPLACEMENT"

1   **13** Saul was a young man when he began as king. He was king over Israel for many years.

2   Saul conscripted enough men for three companies of soldiers. He kept two companies under his command at Micmash and in the Bethel hills. The other company was under Jonathan at Gibeah in Benjamin. He sent the rest of the men home.

3-4   Jonathan attacked and killed the Philistine governor stationed at Geba (Gibeah). When the Philistines heard the news, they raised the alarm: "The Hebrews are in revolt!" Saul ordered the reveille trumpets blown throughout the land. The word went out all over Israel, "Saul has killed the Philistine governor — drawn first blood! The Philistines are stirred up and mad as hornets!" Summoned, the army came to Saul at Gilgal.

5   The Philistines rallied their forces to fight Israel: three companies of chariots, six companies of cavalry, and so many infantry they looked like sand on the seashore. They went up into the hills and set up camp at Micmash, east of Beth Aven.

6-7   When the Israelites saw that they were way outnumbered and in deep trouble, they ran for cover, hiding in caves and pits, ravines and brambles and cisterns — wherever. They retreated across the Jordan River, refugees fleeing to the country of Gad and Gilead. But Saul held his ground in Gilgal, his soldiers still with him but scared to death.

8   He waited seven days, the time set by Samuel. Samuel failed to show up at Gilgal, and the soldiers were slipping away, right and left.

9-10   So Saul took charge: "Bring me the burnt offering and the peace offerings!" He went ahead and sacrificed the burnt offering. No sooner had he done it than Samuel showed up! Saul greeted him.

11-12   Samuel said, "What on earth are you doing?"

Saul answered, "When I saw I was losing my army from under me, and that you hadn't come when you said you would, and that the Philistines were poised at Micmash, I said, 'The Philistines are about to come down on me in Gilgal, and I haven't yet come before GOD asking for his help.' So I took things into my own hands, and sacrificed the burnt offering."

13-14   "That was a fool thing to do," Samuel said to Saul. "If you had kept the appointment that your GOD commanded, by now GOD would have set a firm and lasting foundation under your kingly rule over Israel. As it is, your kingly rule is already falling to pieces. GOD is out looking for your replacement right now. This time he'll do the choosing. When he finds him, he'll appoint him leader of his people. And all because you didn't keep your appointment with GOD!"

15   At that, Samuel got up and left Gilgal. What army there was left followed Saul into battle. They went into the hills from Gilgal toward Gibeah in Benjamin. Saul looked over and assessed the soldiers still with him — a mere six hundred!

JONATHAN AND HIS ARMOR BEARER

16-18   Saul, his son Jonathan, and the soldiers who had remained made camp at Geba (Gibeah) of Benjamin. The Philistines were camped at Micmash. Three squads of raiding parties were regularly sent out from the Philistine camp. One squadron was assigned to the Ophrah road going toward Shual country; another was assigned to the Beth Horon road; the third took the border road that rimmed the Valley of Hyenas.

19-22 There wasn't a blacksmith to be found anywhere in Israel. The Philistines made sure of that—"Lest those Hebrews start making swords and spears." That meant that the Israelites had to go down among the Philistines to keep their farm tools — plowshares and mattocks, axes and sickles — sharp and in good repair. They charged a silver coin for the plowshares and mattocks, and half that for the rest. So when the battle of Micmash was joined, there wasn't a sword or spear to be found anywhere in Israel—except for Saul and his son Jonathan; they were both well-armed.

23 A patrol of Philistines took up a position at Micmash Pass.

1-3 **14** Later that day, Jonathan, Saul's son, said to his armor bearer, "Come on, let's go over to the Philistine garrison patrol on the other side of the pass." But he didn't tell his father. Meanwhile, Saul was taking it easy under the pomegranate tree at the threshing floor on the edge of town at Geba (Gibeah). There were about six hundred men with him. Ahijah, wearing the priestly Ephod, was also there. (Ahijah was the son of Ahitub, brother of Ichabod, son of Phinehas, who was the son of Eli the priest of GOD at Shiloh.) No one there knew that Jonathan had gone off.

4-5 The pass that Jonathan was planning to cross over to the Philistine garrison was flanked on either side by sharp rock outcroppings, cliffs named Bozez and Seneh. The cliff to the north faced Micmash; the cliff to the south faced Geba (Gibeah).

6 Jonathan said to his armor bearer, "Come on now, let's go across to these uncircumcised pagans. Maybe GOD will work for us. There's no rule that says GOD can only deliver by using a big army. No one can stop GOD from saving when he sets his mind to it."

7 His armor bearer said, "Go ahead. Do what you think best. I'm with you all the way."

8-10 Jonathan said, "Here's what we'll do. We'll cross over the pass and let the men see we're there. If they say, 'Halt! Don't move until we check you out,' we'll stay put and not go up. But if they say, 'Come on up,' we'll go right up — and we'll know GOD has given them to us. That will be our sign."

11 So they did it, the two of them. They stepped into the open where they could be seen by the Philistine garrison. The Philistines shouted out, "Look at that! The Hebrews are crawling out of their holes!"

12 Then they yelled down to Jonathan and his armor bearer, "Come on up here! We've got a thing or two to show you!"

13 Jonathan shouted to his armor bearer, "Up! Follow me! GOD has turned them over to Israel!" Jonathan scrambled up on all fours, his armor bearer right on his heels. When the Philistines came running up to them, he knocked them flat, his armor bearer right behind finishing them off, bashing their heads in with stones.

14-15 In this first bloody encounter, Jonathan and his armor bearer killed about twenty men. That set off a terrific upheaval in both camp and field, the soldiers in the garrison and the raiding squad badly shaken up, the ground itself shuddering — panic like you've never seen before!

STRAIGHT TO THE BATTLE

16-18 Saul's sentries posted back at Geba (Gibeah) in Benjamin saw the confusion and turmoil raging in the camp. Saul commanded, "Line up and take the roll. See who's here and who's missing." When they called the roll, Jonathan and his armor bearer turned up missing.

18-19 Saul ordered Ahijah, "Bring the priestly Ephod. Let's see what GOD has to say here." (Ahijah was responsible for the Ephod in those days.) While Saul was in conversation with the priest, the upheaval in the Philistine camp became greater and louder. Then Saul interrupted Ahijah: "Put the Ephod away."

20-23 Saul immediately called his army together and they went straight to the battle. When they got there they found total confusion — Philistines swinging their swords wildly, killing each other. Hebrews who had earlier defected to the Philistine camp came back. They now wanted to be with Israel under Saul and Jonathan. Not only that, but when all the Israelites who had been hiding out in the backwoods of Ephraim heard that the Philistines were running for their lives, they came out and joined the chase. GOD saved Israel! What a day!

The fighting moved on to Beth Aven. The whole army was behind Saul now — ten thousand strong! — with the fighting scattering into all the towns throughout the hills of Ephraim.

24 Saul did something really foolish that day. He addressed the army: "A curse on the man who eats anything before evening, before I've wreaked vengeance on my enemies!" None of them ate a thing all day.

25-27 There were honeycombs here and there in the fields. But no one so much as put his finger in the honey to taste it, for the soldiers to a man feared the curse. But Jonathan hadn't heard his father put the army under oath. He stuck the tip of his staff into some honey and ate it. Refreshed, his eyes lit up with renewed vigor.

28 A soldier spoke up, "Your father has put the army under solemn oath, saying, 'A curse on the man who eats anything before evening!' No wonder the soldiers are drooping!"

29-30 Jonathan said, "My father has imperiled the country. Just look how quickly my energy has returned since I ate a little of this honey! It would have been a lot better, believe me, if the soldiers had eaten their fill of whatever they took from the enemy. Who knows how much worse we could have whipped them!"

31-32 They killed Philistines that day all the way from Micmash to Aijalon, but the soldiers ended up totally exhausted. Then they started plundering. They grabbed anything in sight — sheep, cattle, calves — and butchered it where they found it. Then they glutted themselves — meat, blood, the works.

33-34 Saul was told, "Do something! The soldiers are sinning against GOD. They're eating meat with the blood still in it!"

Saul said, "You're biting the hand that feeds you! Roll a big rock over here — now!" He continued, "Disperse among the troops and tell them, 'Bring your oxen and sheep to me and butcher them properly here. Then you can feast to your heart's content. Please don't sin against GOD by eating meat with the blood still in it.'"

And so they did. That night each soldier, one after another, led his animal there to be butchered.

35   That's the story behind Saul's building an altar to God. It's the first altar to God that he built.

36   Saul said, "Let's go after the Philistines tonight! We can spend the night looting and plundering. We won't leave a single live Philistine!"

    "Sounds good to us," said the troops. "Let's do it!"

    But the priest slowed them down: "Let's find out what God thinks about this."

37   So Saul prayed to God, "Shall I go after the Philistines? Will you put them in Israel's hand?" God didn't answer him on that occasion.

38-39   Saul then said, "All army officers, step forward. Some sin has been committed this day. We're going to find out what it is and who did it! As God lives, Israel's Savior God, whoever sinned will die, even if it should turn out to be Jonathan, my son!"

    Nobody said a word.

40   Saul said to the Israelites, "You line up over on that side, and I and Jonathan my son will stand on this side."

    The army agreed, "Fine. Whatever you say."

41   Then Saul prayed to God, "O God of Israel, why haven't you answered me today? Show me the truth. If the sin is in me or Jonathan, then, O God, give the sign Urim. But if the sin is in the army of Israel, give the sign Thummim."

    The Urim sign turned up and pointed to Saul and Jonathan. That cleared the army.

42   Next Saul said, "Cast the lots between me and Jonathan — and death to the one God points to!"

    The soldiers protested, "No — this is not right. Stop this!" But Saul pushed on anyway. They cast the lots, Urim and Thummim, and the lot fell to Jonathan.

43   Saul confronted Jonathan. "What did you do? Tell me!"

    Jonathan said, "I licked a bit of honey off the tip of the staff I was carrying. That's it — and for that I'm to die?"

44   Saul said, "Yes. Jonathan most certainly will die. It's out of my hands — I can't go against God, can I?"

45   The soldiers rose up: "Jonathan — die? Never! He's just carried out this stunning salvation victory for Israel. As surely as God lives, not a hair on his head is going to be harmed. Why, he's been working hand-in-hand with God all day!" The soldiers rescued Jonathan and he didn't die.

46   Saul pulled back from chasing the Philistines, and the Philistines went home.

47-48   Saul extended his rule, capturing neighboring kingdoms. He fought enemies on every front — Moab, Ammon, Edom, the king of Zobah, the Philistines. Wherever he turned, he came up with a victory. He became invincible! He smashed Amalek, freeing Israel from the savagery and looting.

49-51   Saul's sons were Jonathan, Ishvi, and Malki-Shua. His daughters were Merab, the firstborn, and Michal, the younger. Saul's wife was Ahinoam, daughter of Ahimaaz. Abner son of Ner was commander of Saul's army (Ner was Saul's uncle). Kish, Saul's father, and Ner, Abner's father, were the sons of Abiel.

52 All through Saul's life there was war, bitter and relentless, with the Philistines. Saul conscripted every strong and brave man he laid eyes on.

1-2 **15** Samuel said to Saul, "GOD sent me to anoint you king over his people, Israel. Now, listen again to what GOD says. This is the GOD-of-the-Angel-Armies speaking:

2-3 "'I'm about to get even with Amalek for ambushing Israel when Israel came up out of Egypt. Here's what you are to do: Go to war against Amalek. Put everything connected with Amalek under a holy ban. And no exceptions! This is to be total destruction — men and women, children and infants, cattle and sheep, camels and donkeys — the works.'"

4-5 Saul called the army together at Telaim and prepared them to go to war — two hundred companies of infantry from Israel and another ten companies from Judah. Saul marched to Amalek City and hid in the canyon.

6 Then Saul got word to the Kenites: "Get out of here while you can. Evacuate the city right now or you'll get lumped in with the Amalekites. I'm warning you because you showed real kindness to the Israelites when they came up out of Egypt."

And they did. The Kenites evacuated the place.

7-9 Then Saul went after Amalek, from the canyon all the way to Shur near the Egyptian border. He captured Agag, king of Amalek, alive. Everyone else was killed under the terms of the holy ban. Saul and the army made an exception for Agag, and for the choice sheep and cattle. They didn't include them under the terms of the holy ban. But all the rest, which nobody wanted anyway, they destroyed as decreed by the holy ban.

10-11 Then GOD spoke to Samuel: "I'm sorry I ever made Saul king. He's turned his back on me. He refuses to do what I tell him."

11-12 Samuel was angry when he heard this. He prayed his anger and disappointment all through the night. He got up early in the morning to confront Saul but was told, "Saul's gone. He went to Carmel to set up a victory monument in his own honor, and then was headed for Gilgal."

By the time Samuel caught up with him, Saul had just finished an act of worship, having used Amalekite plunder for the burnt offerings sacrificed to GOD.

13 As Samuel came close, Saul called out, "GOD's blessings on you! I accomplished GOD's plan to the letter!"

14 Samuel said, "So what's this I'm hearing — this bleating of sheep, this mooing of cattle?"

15 "Only some Amalekite loot," said Saul. "The soldiers saved back a few of the choice cattle and sheep to offer up in sacrifice to GOD. But everything else we destroyed under the holy ban."

16 "Enough!" interrupted Samuel. "Let me tell you what GOD told me last night."

Saul said, "Go ahead. Tell me."

17-19 And Samuel told him. "When you started out in this, you were nothing — and you knew it. Then GOD put you at the head of Israel — made you king over Israel. Then GOD sent you off to do a job for him, ordering you, 'Go and put those sinners, the Amalekites, under a holy ban. Go to war against them until you have totally wiped them out.' So why did you not obey GOD? Why did you grab all this loot? Why, with GOD's eyes on you all the time, did you brazenly carry out this evil?"

20-21   Saul defended himself. "What are you talking about? I did obey GOD. I did the job GOD set for me. I brought in King Agag and destroyed the Amalekites under the terms of the holy ban. So the soldiers saved back a few choice sheep and cattle from the holy ban for sacrifice to GOD at Gilgal — what's wrong with that?"

22-23   Then Samuel said,

Do you think all GOD wants are sacrifices —
    empty rituals just for show?
He wants you to listen to him!
Plain listening is the thing,
    not staging a lavish religious production.
Not doing what GOD tells you
    is far worse than fooling around in the occult.
Getting self-important around GOD
    is far worse than making deals with your dead ancestors.
Because you said No to GOD's command,
    he says No to your kingship.

24-25   Saul gave in and confessed, "I've sinned. I've trampled roughshod over GOD's Word and your instructions. I cared more about pleasing the people. I let them tell me what to do. Oh, absolve me of my sin! Take my hand and lead me to the altar so I can worship GOD!"

26   But Samuel refused: "No, I can't come alongside you in this. You rejected GOD's command. Now GOD has rejected you as king over Israel."

27-29   As Samuel turned to leave, Saul grabbed at his priestly robe and a piece tore off. Samuel said, "GOD has just now torn the kingdom from you, and handed it over to your neighbor, a better man than you are. Israel's God-of-Glory doesn't deceive and he doesn't dither. He says what he means and means what he says."

30   Saul tried again, "I have sinned. But don't abandon me! Support me with your presence before the leaders and the people. Come alongside me as I go back to worship GOD."

31   Samuel did. He went back with him. And Saul went to his knees before GOD and worshiped.

32   Then Samuel said, "Present King Agag of Amalek to me." Agag came, dragging his feet, muttering that he'd be better off dead.

33   Samuel said, "Just as your sword made many a woman childless, so your mother will be childless among those women!" And Samuel cut Agag down in the presence of GOD right there in Gilgal.

34-35   Samuel left immediately for Ramah and Saul went home to Gibeah. Samuel had nothing to do with Saul from then on, though he grieved long and deeply over him. But GOD was sorry he had ever made Saul king in the first place.

GOD LOOKS INTO THE HEART

1   **16** GOD addressed Samuel: "So, how long are you going to mope over Saul? You know I've rejected him as king over Israel. Fill your flask with anointing oil and get going. I'm sending you to Jesse of Bethlehem. I've spotted the very king I want among his sons."

2-3 "I can't do that," said Samuel. "Saul will hear about it and kill me."

GOD said, "Take a heifer with you and announce, 'I've come to lead you in worship of GOD, with this heifer as a sacrifice.' Make sure Jesse gets invited. I'll let you know what to do next. I'll point out the one you are to anoint."

4 Samuel did what GOD told him. When he arrived at Bethlehem, the town fathers greeted him, but apprehensively. "Is there something wrong?"

5 "Nothing's wrong. I've come to sacrifice this heifer and lead you in the worship of GOD. Prepare yourselves, be consecrated, and join me in worship." He made sure Jesse and his sons were also consecrated and called to worship.

6 When they arrived, Samuel took one look at Eliab and thought, "Here he is! GOD's anointed!"

7 But GOD told Samuel, "Looks aren't everything. Don't be impressed with his looks and stature. I've already eliminated him. GOD judges persons differently than humans do. Men and women look at the face; GOD looks into the heart."

8 Jesse then called up Abinadab and presented him to Samuel. Samuel said, "This man isn't GOD's choice either."

9 Next Jesse presented Shammah. Samuel said, "No, this man isn't either."

10 Jesse presented his seven sons to Samuel. Samuel was blunt with Jesse, "GOD hasn't chosen any of these."

11 Then he asked Jesse, "Is this it? Are there no more sons?"

"Well, yes, there's the runt. But he's out tending the sheep."

Samuel ordered Jesse, "Go get him. We're not moving from this spot until he's here."

12 Jesse sent for him. He was brought in, the very picture of health—bright-eyed, good-looking.

GOD said, "Up on your feet! Anoint him! This is the one."

13 Samuel took his flask of oil and anointed him, with his brothers standing around watching. The Spirit of GOD entered David like a rush of wind, God vitally empowering him for the rest of his life.

Samuel left and went home to Ramah.

DAVID—AN EXCELLENT MUSICIAN

14 At that very moment the Spirit of GOD left Saul and in its place a black mood sent by GOD settled on him. He was terrified.

15-16 Saul's advisors said, "This awful tormenting depression from God is making your life miserable. O Master, let us help. Let us look for someone who can play the harp. When the black mood from God moves in, he'll play his music and you'll feel better."

17 Saul told his servants, "Go ahead. Find me someone who can play well and bring him to me."

18 One of the young men spoke up, "I know someone. I've seen him myself: the son of Jesse of Bethlehem, an excellent musician. He's also courageous, of age, well-spoken, and good-looking. And GOD is with him."

19 So Saul sent messengers to Jesse requesting, "Send your son David to me, the one who tends the sheep."

20-21 Jesse took a donkey, loaded it with a couple of loaves of bread, a flask of wine, and a young goat, and sent his son David with it to Saul. David came to Saul and stood before him. Saul liked him immediately and made him his right-hand man.

22   Saul sent word back to Jesse: "Thank you. David will stay here. He's just the one I was looking for. I'm very impressed by him."

23   After that, whenever the bad depression from God tormented Saul, David got out his harp and played. That would calm Saul down, and he would feel better as the moodiness lifted.

GOLIATH

1-3   **17** The Philistines drew up their troops for battle. They deployed them at Socoh in Judah, and set up camp between Socoh and Azekah at Ephes Dammim. Saul and the Israelites came together, camped at Oak Valley, and spread out their troops in battle readiness for the Philistines. The Philistines were on one hill, the Israelites on the opposing hill, with the valley between them.

4-7   A giant nearly ten feet tall stepped out from the Philistine line into the open, Goliath from Gath. He had a bronze helmet on his head and was dressed in armor — 126 pounds of it! He wore bronze shin guards and carried a bronze sword. His spear was like a fence rail — the spear tip alone weighed over fifteen pounds. His shield bearer walked ahead of him.

8-10   Goliath stood there and called out to the Israelite troops, "Why bother using your whole army? Am I not Philistine enough for you? And you're all committed to Saul, aren't you? So pick your best fighter and pit him against me. If he gets the upper hand and kills me, the Philistines will all become your slaves. But if I get the upper hand and kill him, you'll all become our slaves and serve us. I challenge the troops of Israel this day. Give me a man. Let us fight it out together!"

11   When Saul and his troops heard the Philistine's challenge, they were terrified and lost all hope.

12-15   Enter David. He was the son of Jesse the Ephrathite from Bethlehem in Judah. Jesse, the father of eight sons, was himself too old to join Saul's army. Jesse's three oldest sons had followed Saul to war. The names of the three sons who had joined up with Saul were Eliab, the firstborn; next, Abinadab; and third, Shammah. David was the youngest son. While his three oldest brothers went to war with Saul, David went back and forth from attending to Saul to tending his father's sheep in Bethlehem.

16   Each morning and evening for forty days, Goliath took his stand and made his speech.

17-19   One day, Jesse told David his son, "Take this sack of cracked wheat and these ten loaves of bread and run them down to your brothers in the camp. And take these ten wedges of cheese to the captain of their division. Check in on your brothers to see whether they are getting along all right, and let me know how they're doing — Saul and your brothers, and all the Israelites in their war with the Philistines in the Oak Valley."

20-23   David was up at the crack of dawn and, having arranged for someone to tend his flock, took the food and was on his way just as Jesse had directed him. He arrived at the camp just as the army was moving into battle formation, shouting the war cry. Israel and the Philistines moved into position, facing each other, battle-ready. David left his bundles of food in the care of a sentry, ran to the troops who were deployed, and greeted his brothers. While they were talking together, the Philistine champion, Goliath of Gath, stepped out from the front lines of the Philistines, and gave his usual challenge. David heard him.

24-25   The Israelites, to a man, fell back the moment they saw the giant — totally frightened. The talk among the troops was, "Have you ever seen anything like this, this man openly and defiantly challenging Israel? The man who kills the giant will have it made. The king will give him a huge reward, offer his daughter as a bride, and give his entire family a free ride."

FIVE SMOOTH STONES

26   David, who was talking to the men standing around him, asked, "What's in it for the man who kills that Philistine and gets rid of this ugly blot on Israel's honor? Who does he think he is, anyway, this uncircumcised Philistine, taunting the armies of God-Alive?"

27   They told him what everyone was saying about what the king would do for the man who killed the Philistine.

28   Eliab, his older brother, heard David fraternizing with the men and lost his temper: "What are you doing here! Why aren't you minding your own business, tending that scrawny flock of sheep? I know what you're up to. You've come down here to see the sights, hoping for a ringside seat at a bloody battle!"

29-30   "What is it with you?" replied David. "All I did was ask a question." Ignoring his brother, he turned to someone else, asked the same question, and got the same answer as before.

31   The things David was saying were picked up and reported to Saul. Saul sent for him.

32   "Master," said David, "don't give up hope. I'm ready to go and fight this Philistine."

33   Saul answered David, "You can't go and fight this Philistine. You're too young and inexperienced — and he's been at this fighting business since before you were born."

34-37   David said, "I've been a shepherd, tending sheep for my father. Whenever a lion or bear came and took a lamb from the flock, I'd go after it, knock it down, and rescue the lamb. If it turned on me, I'd grab it by the throat, wring its neck, and kill it. Lion or bear, it made no difference — I killed it. And I'll do the same to this Philistine pig who is taunting the troops of God-Alive. GOD, who delivered me from the teeth of the lion and the claws of the bear, will deliver me from this Philistine."

    Saul said, "Go. And GOD help you!"

38-39   Then Saul outfitted David as a soldier in armor. He put his bronze helmet on his head and belted his sword on him over the armor. David tried to walk but he could hardly budge.

    David told Saul, "I can't even move with all this stuff on me. I'm not used to this." And he took it all off.

40   Then David took his shepherd's staff, selected five smooth stones from the brook, and put them in the pocket of his shepherd's pack, and with his sling in his hand approached Goliath.

41-42   As the Philistine paced back and forth, his shield bearer in front of him, he noticed David. He took one look down on him and sneered — a mere youngster, apple-cheeked and peach-fuzzed.

43   The Philistine ridiculed David. "Am I a dog that you come after me with a stick?" And he cursed him by his gods.

44   "Come on," said the Philistine. "I'll make roadkill of you for the buzzards. I'll turn you into a tasty morsel for the field mice."

45-47   David answered, "You come at me with sword and spear and battle-ax. I come at you in the name of GOD-of-the-Angel-Armies, the God of Israel's troops, whom you curse and mock. This very day GOD is handing you over to me. I'm about to kill you, cut off your head, and serve up your body and the bodies of your Philistine buddies to the crows and coyotes. The whole earth will know that there's an extraordinary God in Israel. And everyone gathered here will learn that GOD doesn't save by means of sword or spear. The battle belongs to GOD—he's handing you to us on a platter!"

48-49   That roused the Philistine, and he started toward David. David took off from the front line, running toward the Philistine. David reached into his pocket for a stone, slung it, and hit the Philistine hard in the forehead, embedding the stone deeply. The Philistine crashed, facedown in the dirt.

50   That's how David beat the Philistine—with a sling and a stone. He hit him and killed him. No sword for David!

51   Then David ran up to the Philistine and stood over him, pulled the giant's sword from its sheath, and finished the job by cutting off his head. When the Philistines saw that their great champion was dead, they scattered, running for their lives.

52-54   The men of Israel and Judah were up on their feet, shouting! They chased the Philistines all the way to the outskirts of Gath and the gates of Ekron. Wounded Philistines were strewn along the Shaaraim road all the way to Gath and Ekron. After chasing the Philistines, the Israelites came back and looted their camp. David took the Philistine's head and brought it to Jerusalem. But the giant's weapons he placed in his own tent.

55   When Saul saw David go out to meet the Philistine, he said to Abner, commander of the army, "Tell me about this young man's family."

Abner said, "For the life of me, O King, I don't know."

56   The king said, "Well, find out the lineage of this raw youth."

57   As soon as David came back from killing the Philistine, Abner brought him, the Philistine's head still in his hand, straight to Saul.

58   Saul asked him, "Young man, whose son are you?"

"I'm the son of your servant Jesse," said David, "the one who lives in Bethlehem."

JONATHAN AND DAVID—SOUL FRIENDS

18 1   By the time David had finished reporting to Saul, Jonathan was deeply impressed with David—an immediate bond was forged between them. He became totally committed to David. From that point on he would be David's number-one advocate and friend.

2   Saul received David into his own household that day, no more to return to the home of his father.

3-4   Jonathan, out of his deep love for David, made a covenant with him. He formalized it with solemn gifts: his own royal robe and weapons—armor, sword, bow, and belt.

5   Whatever Saul gave David to do, he did it—and did it well. So well that Saul put him in charge of his military operations. Everybody, both the people in general and Saul's servants, approved of and admired David's leadership.

DAVID — THE NAME ON EVERYONE'S LIPS

6-9 As they returned home, after David had killed the Philistine, the women poured out of all the villages of Israel singing and dancing, welcoming King Saul with tambourines, festive songs, and lutes. In playful frolic the women sang,

> Saul kills by the thousand,
> David by the ten thousand!

This made Saul angry — very angry. He took it as a personal insult. He said, "They credit David with 'ten thousands' and me with only 'thousands.' Before you know it they'll be giving him the kingdom!" From that moment on, Saul kept his eye on David.

10-11 The next day an ugly mood was sent by God to afflict Saul, who became quite beside himself, raving. David played his harp, as he usually did at such times. Saul had a spear in his hand. Suddenly Saul threw the spear, thinking, "I'll nail David to the wall." David ducked, and the spear missed. This happened twice.

12-16 Now Saul feared David. It was clear that GOD was with David and had left Saul. So, Saul got David out of his sight by making him an officer in the army. David was in combat frequently. Everything David did turned out well. Yes, GOD was with him. As Saul saw David becoming more successful, he himself grew more fearful. He could see the handwriting on the wall. But everyone else in Israel and Judah loved David. They loved watching him in action.

17 One day Saul said to David, "Here is Merab, my eldest daughter. I want to give her to you as your wife. Be brave and bold for my sake. Fight GOD's battles!" But all the time Saul was thinking, "The Philistines will kill him for me. I won't have to lift a hand against him."

18 David, embarrassed, answered, "Do you really mean that? I'm from a family of nobodies! I can't be son-in-law to the king."

19 The wedding day was set, but as the time neared for Merab and David to be married, Saul reneged and married his daughter off to Adriel the Meholathite.

20-21 Meanwhile, Saul's daughter Michal was in love with David. When Saul was told of this, he rubbed his hands in anticipation. "Ah, a second chance. I'll use Michal as bait to get David out where the Philistines will make short work of him." So again he said to David, "You're going to be my son-in-law."

22 Saul ordered his servants, "Get David off by himself and tell him, 'The king is very taken with you, and everyone at court loves you. Go ahead, become the king's son-in-law!'"

23 The king's servants told all this to David, but David held back. "What are you thinking of? I can't do that. I'm a nobody; I have nothing to offer."

24-25 When the servants reported David's response to Saul, he told them to tell David this: "The king isn't expecting any money from you; only this: Go kill a hundred Philistines and bring evidence of your vengeance on the king's behalf. Avenge the king on his enemies." (Saul expected David to be killed in action.)

26-27   On receiving this message, David was pleased. There was something he could do for the king that would qualify him to be his son-in-law! He lost no time but went right out, he and his men, killed the hundred Philistines, brought their evidence back in a sack, and counted it out before the king — mission completed! Saul gave Michal his daughter to David in marriage.

28-29   As Saul more and more realized that GOD was with David, and how much his own daughter, Michal, loved him, his fear of David increased and settled into hate. Saul hated David.

30   Whenever the Philistine warlords came out to battle, David was there to meet them — and beat them, upstaging Saul's men. David's name was on everyone's lips.

THE BLACK MOOD OF SAUL

1-3   19 Saul called his son Jonathan together with his servants and ordered them to kill David. But because Jonathan treasured David, he went and warned him: "My father is looking for a way to kill you. Here's what you are to do. Tomorrow morning, hide and stay hidden. I'll go out with my father into the field where you are hiding. I'll talk about you with my father and we'll see what he says. Then I'll report back to you."

4-5   Jonathan brought up David with his father, speaking well of him. "Please," he said to his father, "don't attack David. He hasn't wronged you, has he? And just look at all the good he has done! He put his life on the line when he killed the Philistine. What a great victory GOD gave Israel that day! You were there. You saw it and were on your feet applauding with everyone else. So why would you even think of sinning against an innocent person, killing David for no reason whatever?"

6   Saul listened to Jonathan and said, "You're right. As GOD lives, David lives. He will not be killed."

7   Jonathan sent for David and reported to him everything that was said. Then he brought David back to Saul and everything was as it was before.

8   War broke out again and David went out to fight Philistines. He beat them badly, and they ran for their lives.

9-10   But then a black mood from God settled over Saul and took control of him. He was sitting at home, his spear in his hand, while David was playing music. Suddenly, Saul tried to skewer David with his spear, but David ducked. The spear stuck in the wall and David got away. It was night.

11-14   Saul sent men to David's house to stake it out and then, first thing in the morning, to kill him. But Michal, David's wife, told him what was going on. "Quickly now — make your escape tonight. If not, you'll be dead by morning!" She let him out of a window, and he made his escape. Then Michal took a dummy god and put it in the bed, placed a wig of goat's hair on its head, and threw a quilt over it. When Saul's men arrived to get David, she said, "He's sick in bed."

15-16   Saul sent his men back, ordering them, "Bring him, bed and all, so I can kill him." When the men entered the room, all they found in the bed was the dummy god with its goat-hair wig!

17   Saul stormed at Michal: "How could you play tricks on me like this? You sided with my enemy, and now he's gotten away!"

18   Michal said, "He threatened me. He said, 'Help me out of here or I'll kill you.'"

David made good his escape and went to Samuel at Ramah and told him everything Saul had done to him. Then he and Samuel withdrew to the privacy of Naioth.

19-20   Saul was told, "David's at Naioth in Ramah." He immediately sent his men to capture him. They saw a band of prophets prophesying with Samuel presiding over them. Before they knew it, the Spirit of God was on them, too, and they were ranting and raving right along with the prophets!

21   That was reported back to Saul, and he dispatched more men. They, too, were soon prophesying. So Saul tried a third time—a third set of men— and they ended up mindlessly raving as well!

22   Fed up, Saul went to Ramah himself. He came to the big cistern at Secu and inquired, "Where are Samuel and David?"

A bystander said, "Over at Naioth in Ramah."

23-24   As he headed out for Naioth in Ramah, the Spirit of God was on him, too. All the way to Naioth he was caught up in a babbling trance! He ripped off his clothes and lay there rambling gibberish before Samuel for a day and a night, stretched out naked. People are still talking about it: "Saul among the prophets! Who would have guessed?"

A COVENANT FRIENDSHIP IN GOD'S NAME

1   20 David got out of Naioth in Ramah alive and went to Jonathan. "What do I do now? What wrong have I inflicted on your father that makes him so determined to kill me?"

2   "Nothing," said Jonathan. "You've done nothing wrong. And you're not going to die. Really, you're not! My father tells me everything. He does nothing, whether big or little, without confiding in me. So why would he do this behind my back? It can't be."

3   But David said, "Your father knows that we are the best of friends. So he says to himself, 'Jonathan must know nothing of this. If he does, he'll side with David.' But it's true—as sure as GOD lives, and as sure as you're alive before me right now—he's determined to kill me."

4   Jonathan said, "Tell me what you have in mind. I'll do anything for you."

5-8   David said, "Tomorrow marks the New Moon. I'm scheduled to eat dinner with the king. Instead, I'll go hide in the field until the evening of the third. If your father misses me, say, 'David asked if he could run down to Bethlehem, his hometown, for an anniversary reunion, and worship with his family.' If he says, 'Good!' then I'm safe. But if he gets angry, you'll know for sure that he's made up his mind to kill me. Oh, stick with me in this. You've entered into a covenant of GOD with me, remember! If I'm in the wrong, go ahead and kill me yourself. Why bother giving me up to your father?"

9   "Never!" exclaimed Jonathan. "I'd never do that! If I get the slightest hint that my father is fixated on killing you, I'll tell you."

10   David asked, "And whom will you get to tell me if your father comes back with a harsh answer?"

11-17   "Come outside," said Jonathan. "Let's go to the field." When the two of them were out in the field, Jonathan said, "As GOD, the God of Israel, is my witness, by this time tomorrow I'll get it out of my father how he feels about you. Then I'll let you know what I learn. May GOD do his worst to me if I let you down! If my father still intends to kill you, I'll tell you and get you out of here in one piece. And GOD be with you as he's been with my father! If I make it through this alive, continue to be my covenant friend. And if I die, keep the covenant friendship with my family—forever. And when GOD finally rids the earth of David's enemies, stay loyal to Jonathan!" Jonathan repeated his pledge of love and friendship for David. He loved David more than his own soul!

18-23   Jonathan then laid out his plan: "Tomorrow is the New Moon, and you'll be missed when you don't show up for dinner. On the third day, when they've quit expecting you, come to the place where you hid before, and wait beside that big boulder. I'll shoot three arrows in the direction of the boulder. Then I'll send off my servant, 'Go find the arrows.' If I yell after the servant, 'The arrows are on this side! Retrieve them!' that's the signal that you can return safely—as GOD lives, not a thing to fear! But if I yell, 'The arrows are farther out!' then run for it—GOD wants you out of here! Regarding all the things we've discussed, remember that GOD's in on this with us to the very end!"

24-26   David hid in the field. On the holiday of the New Moon, the king came to the table to eat. He sat where he always sat, the place against the wall, with Jonathan across the table and Abner at Saul's side. But David's seat was empty. Saul didn't mention it at the time, thinking, "Something's happened that's made him unclean. That's it—he's probably unclean for the holy meal."

27   But the day after the New Moon, day two of the holiday, David's seat was still empty. Saul asked Jonathan his son, "So where's that son of Jesse? He hasn't eaten with us either yesterday or today."

28-29   Jonathan said, "David asked my special permission to go to Bethlehem. He said, 'Give me leave to attend a family reunion back home. My brothers have ordered me to be there. If it seems all right to you, let me go and see my brothers.' That's why he's not here at the king's table."

30-31   Saul exploded in anger at Jonathan: "You son of a slut! Don't you think I know that you're in cahoots with the son of Jesse, disgracing both you and your mother? For as long as the son of Jesse is walking around free on this earth, your future in this kingdom is at risk. Now go get him. Bring him here. From this moment, he's as good as dead!"

32   Jonathan stood up to his father. "Why dead? What's he done?"

33   Saul threw his spear at him to kill him. That convinced Jonathan that his father was fixated on killing David.

34   Jonathan stormed from the table, furiously angry, and ate nothing the rest of the day, upset for David and smarting under the humiliation from his father.

35-39   In the morning, Jonathan went to the field for the appointment with David. He had his young servant with him. He told the servant, "Run and get the arrows I'm about to shoot." The boy started running and Jonathan shot an arrow way beyond him. As the boy came to the area where the arrow had been shot, Jonathan yelled out, "Isn't the arrow farther out?" He yelled again, "Hurry! Quickly! Don't just stand there!" Jonathan's servant then picked up the arrow and brought it to his master. The boy, of course, knew nothing of what was going on. Only Jonathan and David knew.

40-41   Jonathan gave his quiver and bow to the boy and sent him back to town. After the servant was gone, David got up from his hiding place beside the boulder, then fell on his face to the ground—three times prostrating himself! And then they kissed one another and wept, friend over friend, David weeping especially hard.

42 Jonathan said, "Go in peace! The two of us have vowed friendship in GOD's name, saying, 'GOD will be the bond between me and you, and between my children and your children forever!'"

DAVID PRETENDS TO GO CRAZY

1 **21** David went on his way and Jonathan returned to town.

David went to Nob, to Ahimelech the Priest. Ahimelech was alarmed as he went out to greet David: "What are you doing here all by yourself—and not a soul with you?"

2-3 David answered Ahimelech the Priest, "The king sent me on a mission and gave strict orders: 'This is top secret—not a word of this to a soul.' I've arranged to meet up with my men in a certain place. Now, what's there here to eat? Do you have five loaves of bread? Give me whatever you can scrounge up!"

4 "I don't have any regular bread on hand," said the priest. "I only have holy bread. If your men have not slept with women recently, it's yours."

5 David said, "None of us has touched a woman. I always do it this way when I'm on a mission: My men abstain from sex. Even when it is an ordinary mission we do that—how much more on this holy mission."

6 So the priest gave them the holy bread. It was the only bread he had, Bread of the Presence that had been removed from GOD's presence and replaced by fresh bread at the same time.

7 One of Saul's officials was present that day keeping a religious vow. His name was Doeg the Edomite. He was chief of Saul's shepherds.

8 David asked Ahimelech, "Do you have a spear or sword of any kind around here? I didn't have a chance to grab my weapons. The king's mission was urgent and I left in a hurry."

9 The priest said, "The sword of Goliath, the Philistine you killed at Oak Valley—that's here! It's behind the Ephod wrapped in a cloth. If you want it, take it. There's nothing else here."

10-11 "Oh," said David, "there's no sword like that! Give it to me!"

And at that, David shot out of there, running for his life from Saul. He went to Achish, king of Gath. When the servants of Achish saw him, they said, "Can this be David, the famous David? Is this the one they sing of at their dances?

> Saul kills by the thousand,
> David by the ten thousand!"

12-15 When David realized that he had been recognized, he panicked, fearing the worst from Achish, king of Gath. So right there, while they were looking at him, he pretended to go crazy, pounding his head on the city gate and foaming at the mouth, spit dripping from his beard. Achish took one look at him and said to his servants, "Can't you see he's crazy? Why did you let him in here? Don't you think I have enough crazy people to put up with as it is without adding another? Get him out of here!"

SAUL MURDERS THE PRIESTS OF GOD

1-2 **22** So David got away and escaped to the Cave of Adullam. When his brothers and others associated with his family heard where he was, they came down and joined him. Not only that, but all who were down on their luck came around—losers and vagrants and misfits of all sorts. David became their leader. There were about four hundred in all.

3-4   Then David went to Mizpah in Moab. He petitioned the king of Moab, "Grant asylum to my father and mother until I find out what God has planned for me." David left his parents in the care of the king of Moab. They stayed there all through the time David was hiding out.

5   The prophet Gad told David, "Don't go back to the cave. Go to Judah." David did what he told him. He went to the forest of Hereth.

6-8   Saul got word of the whereabouts of David and his men. He was sitting under the big oak on the hill at Gibeah at the time, spear in hand, holding court surrounded by his officials. He said, "Listen here, you Benjaminites! Don't think for a minute that you have any future with the son of Jesse! Do you think he's going to hand over choice land, give you all influential jobs? Think again. Here you are, conspiring against me, whispering behind my back—not one of you is man enough to tell me that my own son is making deals with the son of Jesse, not one of you who cares enough to tell me that my son has taken the side of this, this . . . outlaw!"

9-10   Then Doeg the Edomite, who was standing with Saul's officials, spoke up: "I saw the son of Jesse meet with Ahimelech son of Ahitub, in Nob. I saw Ahimelech pray with him for GOD's guidance, give him food, and arm him with the sword of Goliath the Philistine."

11   Saul sent for the priest Ahimelech son of Ahitub, along with the whole family of priests at Nob. They all came to the king.

12   Saul said, "You listen to me, son of Ahitub!"
    "Certainly, master," he said.

13   "Why have you ganged up against me with the son of Jesse, giving him bread and a sword, even praying with him for GOD's guidance, setting him up as an outlaw, out to get me?"

14-15   Ahimelech answered the king, "There's not an official in your administration as true to you as David, your own son-in-law and captain of your bodyguard. None more honorable either. Do you think that was the first time I prayed with him for God's guidance? Hardly! But don't accuse me of any wrongdoing, me or my family. I have no idea what you're trying to get at with this 'outlaw' talk."

16   The king said, "Death, Ahimelech! You're going to die—you and everyone in your family!"

17   The king ordered his henchmen, "Surround and kill the priests of GOD! They're hand in glove with David. They knew he was running away from me and didn't tell me." But the king's men wouldn't do it. They refused to lay a hand on the priests of GOD.

18-19   Then the king told Doeg, "You do it—massacre the priests!" Doeg the Edomite led the attack and slaughtered the priests, the eighty-five men who wore the sacred robes. He then carried the massacre into Nob, the city of priests, killing man and woman, child and baby, ox, donkey, and sheep—the works.

20-21   Only one son of Ahimelech son of Ahitub escaped: Abiathar. He got away and joined up with David. Abiathar reported to David that Saul had murdered the priests of GOD.

22-23   David said to Abiathar, "I knew it—that day I saw Doeg the Edomite there, I knew he'd tell Saul. I'm to blame for the death of everyone in your father's family. Stay here with me. Don't be afraid. The one out to kill you is out to kill me, too. Stick with me. I'll protect you."

LIVING IN DESERT HIDEOUTS

1-2 **23** It was reported to David that the Philistines were raiding Keilah and looting the grain. David went in prayer to GOD: "Should I go after these Philistines and teach them a lesson?" GOD said, "Go. Attack the Philistines and save Keilah."

3 But David's men said, "We live in fear of our lives right here in Judah. How can you think of going to Keilah in the thick of the Philistines?"

4 So David went back to GOD in prayer. GOD said, "Get going. Head for Keilah. I'm placing the Philistines in your hands."

5-6 David and his men went to Keilah and fought the Philistines. He scattered their cattle, beat them decisively, and saved the people of Keilah. After Abiathar took refuge with David, he joined David in the raid on Keilah, bringing the Ephod with him.

7-8 Saul learned that David had gone to Keilah and thought immediately, "Good! God has handed him to me on a platter! He's in a walled city with locked gates, trapped!" Saul mustered his troops for battle and set out for Keilah to lay siege to David and his men.

9-11 But David got wind of Saul's strategy to destroy him and said to Abiathar the priest, "Get the Ephod." Then David prayed to GOD: "God of Israel, I've just heard that Saul plans to come to Keilah and destroy the city because of me. Will the city fathers of Keilah turn me over to him? Will Saul come down and do what I've heard? O GOD, God of Israel, tell me!"

GOD replied, "He's coming down."

12 "And will the head men of Keilah turn me and my men over to Saul?"

And GOD said, "They'll turn you over."

13 So David and his men got out of there. There were about six hundred of them. They left Keilah and kept moving, going here, there, wherever — always on the move.

When Saul was told that David had escaped from Keilah, he called off the raid.

14-15 David continued to live in desert hideouts and the backcountry wilderness hills of Ziph. Saul was out looking for him day after day, but God never turned David over to him. David kept out of the way in the wilderness of Ziph, secluded at Horesh, since it was plain that Saul was determined to hunt him down.

16-18 Jonathan, Saul's son, visited David at Horesh and encouraged him in God. He said, "Don't despair. My father, Saul, can't lay a hand on you. You will be Israel's king and I'll be right at your side to help. And my father knows it." Then the two of them made a covenant before GOD. David stayed at Horesh and Jonathan went home.

19-20 Some Ziphites went to Saul at Gibeah and said, "Did you know that David is hiding out near us in the caves and canyons of Horesh? Right now he's at Hakilah Hill just south of Jeshimon. So whenever you're ready to come down, we'd count it an honor to hand him over to the king."

21-23 Saul said, "GOD bless you for thinking about me! Now go back and check everything out. Learn his routines. Observe his movements — where he goes, who he's with. He's very shrewd, you know. Scout out all his hiding places. Then meet me at Nacon and I'll go with you. If he is anywhere to be found in all the thousands of Judah, I'll track him down!"

24-27   So the Ziphites set out on their reconnaissance for Saul.

Meanwhile, David and his men were in the wilderness of Maon, in the desert south of Jeshimon. Saul and his men arrived and began their search. When David heard of it, he went south to Rock Mountain, camping out in the wilderness of Maon. Saul heard where he was and set off for the wilderness of Maon in pursuit. Saul was on one side of the mountain, David and his men on the other. David was in full retreat, running, with Saul and his men closing in, about to get him. Just then a messenger came to Saul and said, "Hurry! Come back! The Philistines have just attacked the country!"

28-29   So Saul called off his pursuit of David and went back to deal with the Philistines. That's how that place got the name Narrow Escape. David left there and camped out in the caves and canyons of En Gedi.

"I'M NO REBEL"

1-4   **24** When Saul came back after dealing with the Philistines, he was told, "David is now in the wilderness of En Gedi." Saul took three companies — the best he could find in all Israel — and set out in search of David and his men in the region of Wild Goat Rocks. He came to some sheep pens along the road. There was a cave there and Saul went in to relieve himself. David and his men were huddled far back in the same cave. David's men whispered to him, "Can you believe it? This is the day GOD was talking about when he said, 'I'll put your enemy in your hands. You can do whatever you want with him.'" Quiet as a cat, David crept up and cut off a piece of Saul's royal robe.

5-7   Immediately, he felt guilty. He said to his men, "GOD forbid that I should have done this to my master, GOD's anointed, that I should so much as raise a finger against him. He's GOD's anointed!" David held his men in check with these words and wouldn't let them pounce on Saul. Saul got up, left the cave, and went on down the road.

8-13   Then David stood at the mouth of the cave and called to Saul, "My master! My king!" Saul looked back. David fell to his knees and bowed in reverence. He called out, "Why do you listen to those who say 'David is out to get you'? This very day with your very own eyes you have seen that just now in the cave GOD put you in my hands. My men wanted me to kill you, but I wouldn't do it. I told them that I won't lift a finger against my master — he's GOD's anointed. Oh, my father, look at this, look at this piece that I cut from your robe. I could have cut you — killed you! — but I didn't. Look at the evidence! I'm not against you. I'm no rebel. I haven't sinned against you, and yet you're hunting me down to kill me. Let's decide which of us is in the right. GOD may avenge me, but it is in his hands, not mine. An old proverb says, 'Evil deeds come from evil people.' So be assured that my hand won't touch you.

14-15   "What does the king of Israel think he's doing? Who do you think you're chasing? A dead dog? A flea? GOD is our judge. He'll decide who is right. Oh, that he would look down right now, decide right now — and set me free of you!"

16-21   When David had finished saying all this, Saul said, "Can this be the voice of my son David?" and he wept in loud sobs. "You're the one in the right, not me," he continued. "You've heaped good on me; I've dumped evil on you. And now you've done it again—treated me generously. GOD put me in your hands and you didn't kill me. Why? When a man meets his enemy, does he send him down the road with a blessing? May GOD give you a bonus of blessings for what you've done for me today! I know now beyond doubt that you will rule as king. The kingdom of Israel is already in your grasp! Now promise me under GOD that you will not kill off my family or wipe my name off the books."

22   David promised Saul. Then Saul went home and David and his men went up to their wilderness refuge.

TO FIGHT GOD'S BATTLES

1   **25** Samuel died. The whole country came to his funeral. Everyone grieved over his death, and he was buried in his hometown of Ramah. Meanwhile, David moved again, this time to the wilderness of Maon.

2-3   There was a certain man in Maon who carried on his business in the region of Carmel. He was very prosperous—three thousand sheep and a thousand goats, and it was sheep-shearing time in Carmel. The man's name was Nabal (Fool), a Calebite, and his wife's name was Abigail. The woman was intelligent and good-looking, the man brutish and mean.

4-8   David, out in the backcountry, heard that Nabal was shearing his sheep and sent ten of his young men off with these instructions: "Go to Carmel and approach Nabal. Greet him in my name, 'Peace! Life and peace to you. Peace to your household, peace to everyone here! I heard that it's sheep-shearing time. Here's the point: When your shepherds were camped near us we didn't take advantage of them. They didn't lose a thing all the time they were with us in Carmel. Ask your young men—they'll tell you. What I'm asking is that you be generous with my men—share the feast! Give whatever your heart tells you to your servants and to me, David your son.'"

9-11   David's young men went and delivered his message word for word to Nabal. Nabal tore into them, "Who is this David? Who is this son of Jesse? The country is full of runaway servants these days. Do you think I'm going to take good bread and wine and meat freshly butchered for my sheepshearers and give it to men I've never laid eyes on? Who knows where they've come from?"

12-13   David's men got out of there and went back and told David what he had said. David said, "Strap on your swords!" They all strapped on their swords, David and his men, and set out, four hundred of them. Two hundred stayed behind to guard the camp.

14-17   Meanwhile, one of the young shepherds told Abigail, Nabal's wife, what had happened: "David sent messengers from the backcountry to salute our master, but he tore into them with insults. Yet these men treated us very well. They took nothing from us and didn't take advantage of us all the time we were in the fields. They formed a wall around us, protecting us day and night all the time we were out tending the sheep. Do something quickly because big trouble is ahead for our master and all of us. Nobody can talk to him. He's impossible—a real brute!"

18-19   Abigail flew into action. She took two hundred loaves of bread, two skins of wine, five sheep dressed out and ready for cooking, a bushel of roasted grain, a hundred raisin cakes, and two hundred fig cakes, and she had it all loaded on some donkeys. Then she said to her young servants, "Go ahead and pave the way for me. I'm right behind you." But she said nothing to her husband Nabal.

20-22   As she was riding her donkey, descending into a ravine, David and his men were descending from the other end, so they met there on the road. David had just said, "That sure was a waste, guarding everything this man had out in the wild so that nothing he had was lost — and now he rewards me with insults. A real slap in the face! May God do his worst to me if Nabal and every cur in his misbegotten brood aren't dead meat by morning!"

23-25   As soon as Abigail saw David, she got off her donkey and fell on her knees at his feet, her face to the ground in homage, saying, "My master, let me take the blame! Let me speak to you. Listen to what I have to say. Don't dwell on what that brute Nabal did. He acts out the meaning of his name: Nabal, Fool. Foolishness oozes from him.

25-27   "I wasn't there when the young men my master sent arrived. I didn't see them. And now, my master, as GOD lives and as you live, GOD has kept you from this avenging murder — and may your enemies, all who seek my master's harm, end up like Nabal! Now take this gift that I, your servant girl, have brought to my master, and give it to the young men who follow in the steps of my master.

28-29   "Forgive my presumption! But GOD is at work in my master, developing a rule solid and dependable. My master fights GOD's battles! As long as you live no evil will stick to you.

> If anyone stands in your way,
>   if anyone tries to get you out of the way,
> Know this: Your God-honored life is tightly bound
>   in the bundle of God-protected life;
> But the lives of your enemies will be hurled aside
>   as a stone is thrown from a sling.

30-31   "When GOD completes all the goodness he has promised my master and sets you up as prince over Israel, my master will not have this dead weight in his heart, the guilt of an avenging murder. And when GOD has worked things for good for my master, remember me."

32-34   And David said, "Blessed be GOD, the God of Israel. He sent you to meet me! And blessed be your good sense! Bless you for keeping me from murder and taking charge of looking out for me. A close call! As GOD lives, the God of Israel who kept me from hurting you, if you had not come as quickly as you did, stopping me in my tracks, by morning there would have been nothing left of Nabal but dead meat."

35   Then David accepted the gift she brought him and said, "Return home in peace. I've heard what you've said and I'll do what you've asked."

36-38   When Abigail got home she found Nabal presiding over a huge banquet. He was in high spirits — and very, very drunk. So she didn't tell him anything of what she'd done until morning. But in the morning, after Nabal had sobered up, she told him the whole story. Right then and there he had a heart attack and fell into a coma. About ten days later GOD finished him off and he died.

39-40 When David heard that Nabal was dead he said, "Blessed be GOD who has stood up for me against Nabal's insults, kept me from an evil act, and let Nabal's evil boomerang back on him."

Then David sent for Abigail to tell her that he wanted her for his wife. David's servants went to Abigail at Carmel with the message, "David sent us to bring you to marry him."

41 She got up, and then bowed down, face to the ground, saying, "I'm your servant, ready to do anything you want. I'll even wash the feet of my master's servants!"

42 Abigail didn't linger. She got on her donkey and, with her five maids in attendance, went with the messengers to David and became his wife.

43-44 David also married Ahinoam of Jezreel. Both women were his wives. Saul had married off David's wife Michal to Palti (Paltiel) son of Laish, who was from Gallim.

OBSESSED WITH A SINGLE FLEA

1-3 **26** Some Ziphites came to Saul at Gibeah and said, "Did you know that David is hiding out on the Hakilah Hill just opposite Jeshimon?" Saul was on his feet in a minute and on his way to the wilderness of Ziph, taking three thousand of his best men, the pick of the crop, to hunt for David in that wild desert. He camped just off the road at the Hakilah Hill, opposite Jeshimon.

3-5 David, still out in the backcountry, knew Saul had come after him. He sent scouts to determine his precise location. Then David set out and came to the place where Saul had set up camp and saw for himself where Saul and Abner, son of Ner, his general, were staying. Saul was safely inside the camp, encircled by the army.

6 Taking charge, David spoke to Ahimelech the Hittite and to Abishai son of Zeruiah, Joab's brother: "Who will go down with me and enter Saul's camp?"

Abishai whispered, "I'll go with you."

7 So David and Abishai entered the encampment by night, and there he was—Saul, stretched out asleep at the center of the camp, his spear stuck in the ground near his head, with Abner and the troops sound asleep on all sides.

8 Abishai said, "This is the moment! God has put your enemy in your grasp. Let me nail him to the ground with his spear. One hit will do it, believe me; I won't need a second!"

9 But David said to Abishai, "Don't you dare hurt him! Who could lay a hand on GOD's anointed and even think of getting away with it?"

10-11 He went on, "As GOD lives, either GOD will strike him, or his time will come and he'll die in bed, or he'll fall in battle, but GOD forbid that I should lay a finger on GOD's anointed. Now, grab the spear at his head and the water jug and let's get out of here."

12 David took the spear and water jug that were right beside Saul's head, and they slipped away. Not a soul saw. Not a soul knew. No one woke up! They all slept through the whole thing. A blanket of deep sleep from GOD had fallen on them.

13-14 Then David went across to the opposite hill and stood far away on the top of the mountain. With this safe distance between them, he shouted across to the army and Abner son of Ner, "Hey, Abner! How long do I have to wait for you to wake up and answer me?"

Abner said, "Who's calling?"

15-16   "Aren't you in charge there?" said David. "Why aren't you minding the store? Why weren't you standing guard over your master the king, when a soldier came to kill the king your master? Bad form! As GOD lives, your life should be forfeit, you and the entire bodyguard. Look what I have — the king's spear and water jug that were right beside his head!"

17-20   By now, Saul had recognized David's voice and said, "Is that you, my son David?"

David said, "Yes, it's me, O King, my master. Why are you after me, hunting me down? What have I done? What crime have I committed? Oh, my master, my king, listen to this from your servant: If GOD has stirred you up against me, then I gladly offer my life as a sacrifice. But if it's men who have done it, let them be banished from GOD's presence! They've expelled me from my rightful place in GOD's heritage, sneering, 'Out of here! Go get a job with some other god!' But you're not getting rid of me that easily; you'll not separate me from GOD in life or death. The absurdity! The king of Israel obsessed with a single flea! Hunting me down — a mere partridge — out in the hills!"

21   Saul confessed, "I've sinned! Oh, come back, my dear son David! I won't hurt you anymore. You've honored me this day, treating my life as most precious. And I've acted the fool — a moral dunce, a real clown."

22-24   David answered, "See what I have here? The king's spear. Let one of your servants come and get it. It's GOD's business to decide what to do with each of us in regard to what's right and who's loyal. GOD put your life in my hands today, but I wasn't willing to lift a finger against GOD's anointed. Just as I honored your life today, may GOD honor my life and rescue me from all trouble."

25   Saul said to David, "Bless you, dear son David! Yes, do what you have to do! And, yes, succeed in all you attempt!"

Then David went on his way, and Saul went home.

1   **27** David thought to himself, "Sooner or later, Saul's going to get me. The best thing I can do is escape to Philistine country. Saul will count me a lost cause and quit hunting me down in every nook and cranny of Israel. I'll be out of his reach for good."

2-4   So David left; he and his six hundred men went to Achish son of Maoch, king of Gath. They moved in and settled down in Gath, with Achish. Each man brought his household; David brought his two wives, Ahinoam of Jezreel and Abigail, widow of Nabal of Carmel. When Saul was told that David had escaped to Gath, he called off the hunt.

5   Then David said to Achish, "If it's agreeable to you, assign me a place in one of the rural villages. It doesn't seem right that I, your mere servant, should be taking up space in the royal city."

6-7   So Achish assigned him Ziklag. (This is how Ziklag got to be what it is now, a city of the kings of Judah.) David lived in Philistine country a year and four months.

8-9   From time to time David and his men raided the Geshurites, the Girzites, and the Amalekites — these people were longtime inhabitants of the land stretching toward Shur and on to Egypt. When David raided an area he left no one alive, neither man nor woman, but took everything else: sheep, cattle, donkeys, camels, clothing—the works. Then he'd return to Achish.

10-11 Achish would ask, "And whom did you raid today?"

David would tell him, "Oh, the Negev of Judah," or "The Negev of Jerahmeel," or "The Negev of the Kenites." He never left a single person alive lest one show up in Gath and report what David had really been doing. This is the way David operated all the time he lived in Philistine country.

12 Achish came to trust David completely. He thought, "He's made himself so repugnant to his people that he'll be in my camp forever."

1 **28** During this time the Philistines mustered their troops to make war on Israel. Achish said to David, "You can count on this: You're marching with my troops, you and your men."

2 And David said, "Good! Now you'll see for yourself what I can do!"

"Great!" said Achish. "I'm making you my personal bodyguard—for life!"

SAUL PRAYED, BUT GOD DIDN'T ANSWER

3 Samuel was now dead. All Israel had mourned his death and buried him in Ramah, his hometown. Saul had long since cleaned out all those who held séances with the dead.

4-5 The Philistines had mustered their troops and camped at Shunem. Saul had assembled all Israel and camped at Gilboa. But when Saul saw the Philistine troops, he shook in his boots, scared to death.

6 Saul prayed to GOD, but GOD didn't answer—neither by dream nor by sign nor by prophet.

7 So Saul ordered his officials, "Find me someone who can call up spirits so I may go and seek counsel from those spirits."

His servants said, "There's a witch at Endor."

8 Saul disguised himself by putting on different clothes. Then, taking two men with him, he went under the cover of night to the woman and said, "I want you to consult a ghost for me. Call up the person I name."

9 The woman said, "Just hold on now! You know what Saul did, how he swept the country clean of mediums. Why are you trying to trap me and get me killed?"

10 Saul swore solemnly, "As GOD lives, you won't get in any trouble for this."

11 The woman said, "So whom do you want me to bring up?"

"Samuel. Bring me Samuel."

12 When the woman saw Samuel, she cried out loudly to Saul, "Why did you lie to me? You're Saul!"

13 The king told her, "You have nothing to fear . . . but what do you see?"

"I see a spirit ascending from the underground."

14 "And what does he look like?" Saul asked.

"An old man ascending, robed like a priest."

Saul knew it was Samuel. He fell down, face to the ground, and worshiped.

15 Samuel said to Saul, "Why have you disturbed me by calling me up?"

"Because I'm in deep trouble," said Saul. "The Philistines are making war against me and God has deserted me—he doesn't answer me any more, either by prophet or by dream. And so I'm calling on you to tell me what to do."

16-19 "Why ask me?" said Samuel. "GOD has turned away from you and is now on the side of your neighbor. GOD has done exactly what he told you through me—ripped the kingdom right out of your hands and given it to your neighbor. It's because you did not obey GOD, refused to carry out his seething judgment on Amalek, that GOD does to you what he is doing today. Worse yet, GOD is turning Israel, along with you, over to the Philistines. Tomorrow you and your sons will be with me. And, yes, indeed, GOD is giving Israel's army up to the Philistines."

20-22 Saul dropped to the ground, felled like a tree, terrified by Samuel's words. There wasn't an ounce of strength left in him—he'd eaten nothing all day and all night. The woman, realizing that he was in deep shock, said to him, "Listen to me. I did what you asked me to do, put my life in your hands in doing it, carried out your instructions to the letter. It's your turn to do what I tell you: Let me give you some food. Eat it. It will give you strength so you can get on your way."

23-25 He refused. "I'm not eating anything."

But when his servants joined the woman in urging him, he gave in to their pleas, picked himself up off the ground, and sat on the bed. The woman moved swiftly. She butchered a grain-fed calf she had, and took some flour, kneaded it, and baked some flat bread. Then she served it all up for Saul and his servants. After dining handsomely, they got up from the table and were on their way that same night.

1-2 **29** The Philistines mustered all their troops at Aphek. Meanwhile Israel had made camp at the spring at Jezreel. As the Philistine warlords marched forward by regiments and divisions, David and his men were bringing up the rear with Achish.

3 The Philistine officers said, "What business do these Hebrews have being here?"

Achish answered the officers, "Don't you recognize David, ex-servant of King Saul of Israel? He's been with me a long time. I've found nothing to be suspicious of, nothing to complain about, from the day he defected from Saul until now."

4-5 Angry with Achish, the Philistine officers said, "Send this man back to where he came from. Let him stick to his normal duties. He's not going into battle with us. He'd switch sides in the middle of the fight! What better chance to get back in favor with his master than by stabbing us in the back! Isn't this the same David they celebrate at their parties, singing,

Saul kills by the thousand,
David by the ten thousand!"

6-7 So Achish had to send for David and tell him, "As GOD lives, you've been a trusty ally—excellent in all the ways you have worked with me, beyond reproach in the ways you have conducted yourself. But the warlords don't see it that way. So it's best that you leave peacefully, now. It's not worth it, displeasing the Philistine warlords."

8 "But what have I done?" said David. "Have you had a single cause for complaint from the day I joined up with you until now? Why can't I fight against the enemies of my master the king?"

9-10 "I agree," said Achish. "You're a good man—as far as I'm concerned,

God's angel! But the Philistine officers were emphatic: 'He's not to go with us into battle.' So get an early start, you and the men who came with you. As soon as you have light enough to travel, go."

11 David rose early, he and his men, and by daybreak they were on their way back to Philistine country. The Philistines went on to Jezreel.

DAVID'S STRENGTH WAS IN HIS GOD

1-3 **30** Three days later, David and his men arrived back in Ziklag. Amalekites had raided the Negev and Ziklag. They tore Ziklag to pieces and then burned it down. They captured all the women, young and old. They didn't kill anyone, but drove them like a herd of cattle. By the time David and his men entered the village, it had been burned to the ground, and their wives, sons, and daughters all taken prisoner.

4-6 David and his men burst out in loud wails — wept and wept until they were exhausted with weeping. David's two wives, Ahinoam of Jezreel and Abigail widow of Nabal of Carmel, had been taken prisoner along with the rest. And suddenly David was in even worse trouble. There was talk among the men, bitter over the loss of their families, of stoning him.

6-7 David strengthened himself with trust in his GOD. He ordered Abiathar the priest, son of Ahimelech, "Bring me the Ephod so I can consult God." Abiathar brought it to David.

8 Then David prayed to GOD, "Shall I go after these raiders? Can I catch them?"

The answer came, "Go after them! Yes, you'll catch them! Yes, you'll make the rescue!"

9-10 David went, he and the six hundred men with him. They arrived at the Brook Besor, where some of them dropped out. David and four hundred men kept up the pursuit, but two hundred of them were too fatigued to cross the Brook Besor, and stayed there.

11-12 Some who went on came across an Egyptian in a field and took him to David. They gave him bread and he ate. And he drank some water. They gave him a piece of fig cake and a couple of raisin muffins. Life began to revive in him. He hadn't eaten or drunk a thing for three days and nights!

13-14 David said to him, "Who do you belong to? Where are you from?"

"I'm an Egyptian slave of an Amalekite," he said. "My master walked off and left me when I got sick — that was three days ago. We had raided the Negev of the Kerethites, of Judah, and of Caleb. Ziklag we burned."

15 David asked him, "Can you take us to the raiders?"

"Promise me by God," he said, "that you won't kill me or turn me over to my old master, and I'll take you straight to the raiders."

16 He led David to them. They were scattered all over the place, eating and drinking, gorging themselves on all the loot they had plundered from Philistia and Judah.

17-20 David pounced. He fought them from before sunrise until evening of the next day. None got away except for four hundred of the younger men who escaped by riding off on camels. David rescued everything the Amalekites had taken. And he rescued his two wives! Nothing and no one was missing — young or old, son or daughter, plunder or whatever. David recovered the whole lot. He herded the sheep and cattle before them, and they all shouted, "David's plunder!"

21 Then David came to the two hundred who had been too tired to

continue with him and had dropped out at the Brook Besor. They came out to welcome David and his band. As he came near he called out, "Success!"

22 But all the mean-spirited men who had marched with David, the rabble element, objected: "They didn't help in the rescue, they don't get any of the plunder we recovered. Each man can have his wife and children, but that's it. Take them and go!"

23-25 "Families don't do this sort of thing! Oh no, my brothers!" said David as he broke up the argument. "You can't act this way with what GOD gave us! God kept us safe. He handed over the raiders who attacked us. Who would ever listen to this kind of talk? The share of the one who stays with the gear is the share of the one who fights—equal shares. Share and share alike!" From that day on, David made that the rule in Israel—and it still is.

26-31 On returning to Ziklag, David sent portions of the plunder to the elders of Judah, his neighbors, with a note saying, "A gift from the plunder of GOD's enemies!" He sent them to the elders in Bethel, Ramoth Negev, Jattir, Aroer, Siphmoth, Eshtemoa, Racal, Jerahmeelite cities, Kenite cities, Hormah, Bor Ashan, Athach, and Hebron, along with a number of other places David and his men went to from time to time.

SAUL AND JONATHAN, DEAD ON THE MOUNTAIN

1-2 **31** The Philistines made war on Israel. The men of Israel were in full retreat from the Philistines, falling left and right, wounded on Mount Gilboa. The Philistines caught up with Saul and his sons. They killed Jonathan, Abinadab, and Malki-Shua, Saul's sons.

3-4 The battle was hot and heavy around Saul. The archers got his range and wounded him badly. Saul said to his weapon bearer, "Draw your sword and put me out of my misery, lest these pagan pigs come and make a game out of killing me."

4-6 But his weapon bearer wouldn't do it. He was terrified. So Saul took the sword himself and fell on it. When the weapon bearer saw that Saul was dead, he too fell on his sword and died with him. So Saul, his three sons, and his weapon bearer—the men closest to him—died together that day.

7 When the Israelites in the valley opposite and those on the other side of the Jordan saw that their army was in full retreat and that Saul and his sons were dead, they left their cities and ran for their lives. The Philistines moved in and occupied the sites.

8-10 The next day, when the Philistines came to rob the dead, they found Saul and his three sons dead on Mount Gilboa. They cut off Saul's head and stripped off his armor. Then they spread the good news all through Philistine country in the shrines of their idols and among the people. They displayed his armor in the shrine of the Ashtoreth. They nailed his corpse to the wall at Beth Shan.

11-13 The people of Jabesh Gilead heard what the Philistines had done to Saul. Their valiant men sprang into action. They traveled all night, took the corpses of Saul and his three sons from the wall at Beth Shan, and carried them back to Jabesh and burned off the flesh. They then buried the bones under the tamarisk tree in Jabesh and fasted in mourning for seven days.

2 SAMUEL

¹⁻² Shortly after Saul died, David returned to Ziklag from his rout of the Amalekites. Three days later a man showed up unannounced from Saul's army camp.

²⁻³ Disheveled and obviously in mourning, he fell to his knees in respect before David. David asked, "What brings you here?"

He answered, "I've just escaped from the camp of Israel."

⁴ "So what happened?" said David. "What's the news?"

He said, "The Israelites have fled the battlefield, leaving a lot of their dead comrades behind. And Saul and his son Jonathan are dead."

⁵ David pressed the young soldier for details: "How do you know for sure that Saul and Jonathan are dead?"

⁶⁻⁸ "I just happened by Mount Gilboa and came on Saul, badly wounded and leaning on his spear, with enemy chariots and horsemen bearing down hard on him. He looked behind him, saw me, and called me to him. 'Yes sir,' I said, 'at your service.' He asked me who I was, and I told him, 'I'm an Amalekite.'"

⁹ "Come here," he said, "and put me out of my misery. I'm nearly dead already, but my life hangs on."

¹⁰ "So I did what he asked—I killed him. I knew he wouldn't last much longer anyway. I removed his royal headband and bracelet, and have brought them to my master. Here they are."

¹¹⁻¹² In lament, David ripped his clothes to ribbons. All the men with him did the same. They wept and fasted the rest of the day, grieving the death of Saul and his son Jonathan, and also the army of GOD and the nation Israel, victims in a failed battle.

¹³ Then David spoke to the young soldier who had brought the report: "Who are you, anyway?"

"I'm from an immigrant family—an Amalekite."

¹⁴⁻¹⁵ "Do you mean to say," said David, "that you weren't afraid to up and kill GOD's anointed king?" Right then he ordered one of his soldiers, "Strike him dead!" The soldier struck him, and he died.

¹⁶ "You asked for it," David told him. "You sealed your death sentence when you said you killed GOD's anointed king."

¹⁷⁻¹⁸ Then David sang this lament over Saul and his son Jonathan, and gave orders that everyone in Judah learn it by heart. Yes, it's even inscribed in The Book of Jashar.

¹⁹⁻²¹
Oh, oh, Gazelles of Israel, struck down on your hills,
    the mighty warriors—fallen, fallen!
Don't announce it in the city of Gath,
    don't post the news in the streets of Ashkelon.
Don't give those coarse Philistine girls
    one more excuse for a drunken party!
No more dew or rain for you, hills of Gilboa,
    and not a drop from springs and wells,
For there the warriors' shields were dragged through the mud,
    Saul's shield left there to rot.

22 Jonathan's bow was bold—
       the bigger they were the harder they fell.
    Saul's sword was fearless—
       once out of the scabbard, nothing could stop it.

23 Saul and Jonathan—beloved, beautiful!
       Together in life, together in death.
    Swifter than plummeting eagles,
       stronger than proud lions.

24-25 Women of Israel, weep for Saul.
       He dressed you in finest cottons and silks,
       spared no expense in making you elegant.
    The mighty warriors—fallen, fallen
       in the middle of the fight!
    Jonathan—struck down on your hills!

26 O my dear brother Jonathan,
       I'm crushed by your death.
    Your friendship was a miracle-wonder,
       love far exceeding anything I've known—
       or ever hope to know.

27 The mighty warriors—fallen, fallen.
       And the arms of war broken to bits.

1 **2** After all this, David prayed. He asked GOD, "Shall I move to one of the cities of Judah?"

GOD said, "Yes, move."

"And to which city?"

"To Hebron."

2-3 So David moved to Hebron, along with his two wives, Ahinoam of Jezreel and Abigail the widow of Nabal of Carmel. David's men, along with their families, also went with him and made their home in and around Hebron.

4-7 The citizens of Judah came to Hebron, and then and there made David king over the clans of Judah.

A report was brought to David that the men of Jabesh Gilead had given Saul a decent burial. David sent messengers to the men of Jabesh Gilead: "GOD bless you for this—for honoring your master, Saul, with a funeral. GOD honor you and be true to you—and I'll do the same, matching your generous act of goodness. Strengthen your resolve and do what must be done. Your master, Saul, is dead. The citizens of Judah have made me their king."

8-11 In the meantime, Abner son of Ner, commander of Saul's army, had taken Saul's son Ish-Bosheth to Mahanaim and made him king over Gilead, over Asher, over Jezreel, over Ephraim, over Benjamin—king, as it turns out, over all Israel. Ish-Bosheth Saul's son, was forty years old when he was made king over Israel. He lasted only two years. But the people of Judah stuck with David. David ruled the people of Judah from Hebron for seven and a half years.

12-13 One day Abner son of Ner set out from Mahanaim with the soldiers of Ish-Bosheth son of Saul, headed for Gibeon. Joab son of Zeruiah, with David's soldiers, also set out. They met at the Pool of Gibeon, Abner's group on one side, Joab's on the other.

14 Abner challenged Joab, "Put up your best fighters. Let's see them do their stuff."

Joab said, "Good! Let them go at it!"

15-16 So they lined up for the fight, twelve Benjaminites from the side of Ish-Bosheth son of Saul, and twelve soldiers from David's side. The men from each side grabbed their opponents' heads and stabbed them with their daggers. They all fell dead—the whole bunch together. So, they called the place Slaughter Park. It's right there at Gibeon.

17-19 The fighting went from bad to worse throughout the day. Abner and the men of Israel were beaten to a pulp by David's men. The three sons of Zeruiah were present: Joab, Abishai, and Asahel. Asahel, as fast as a wild antelope on the open plain, chased Abner, staying hard on his heels.

20 Abner turned and said, "Is that you, Asahel?"

"It surely is," he said.

21 Abner said, "Let up on me. Pick on someone you have a chance of beating and be content with those spoils!" But Asahel wouldn't let up.

22 Abner tried again, "Turn back. Don't force me to kill you. How would I face your brother Joab?"

23-25 When he refused to quit, Abner struck him in the belly with the blunt end of his spear so hard that it came out his back. Asahel fell to the ground and died at once. Everyone who arrived at the spot where Asahel fell and died stood and gaped—Asahel dead! But Joab and Abishai kept up the chase after Abner. As the sun began to set, they came to the hill of Ammah that faced Giah on the road to the backcountry of Gibeon. The Benjaminites had taken their stand with Abner there, deployed strategically on a hill.

26 Abner called out to Joab, "Are we going to keep killing each other till doomsday? Don't you know that nothing but bitterness will come from this? How long before you call off your men from chasing their brothers?"

27-28 "As God lives," said Joab, "if you hadn't spoken up, we'd have kept up the chase until morning!" Then he blew the ram's horn trumpet and the whole army of Judah stopped in its tracks. They quit chasing Israel and called off the fighting.

29 Abner and his soldiers marched all that night up the Arabah Valley. They crossed the Jordan and, after a long morning's march, arrived at Mahanaim.

30-32 After Joab returned from chasing Abner, he took a head count of the army. Nineteen of David's men (besides Asahel) were missing. David's men had cut down 360 of Abner's men, all Benjaminites—all dead. They brought Asahel and buried him in the family tomb in Bethlehem. Joab and his men then marched all night, arriving in Hebron as the dawn broke.

1 **3** The war between the house of Saul and the house of David dragged on and on. The longer it went on the stronger David became, with the house of Saul getting weaker.

✦

2-5   During the Hebron years, sons were born to David:
    Amnon, born of Ahinoam of Jezreel — the firstborn;
    Kileab, born of Abigail of Carmel, Nabal's widow — his second;
    Absalom, born of Maacah, daughter of Talmai, king of Geshur —
        the third;
    Adonijah, born of Haggith — the fourth;
    Shephatiah, born of Abital — the fifth;
    Ithream, born of Eglah — the sixth.
These six sons of David were born in Hebron.

✦

6-7   Abner took advantage of the continuing war between the house of Saul and the house of David to gain power for himself. Saul had had a concubine, Rizpah, the daughter of Aiah. One day Ish-Bosheth confronted Abner: "What business do you have sleeping with my father's concubine?"

8-10   Abner lost his temper with Ish-Bosheth, "Treat me like a dog, will you! Is this the thanks I get for sticking by the house of your father, Saul, and all his family and friends? I personally saved you from certain capture by David, and you make an issue out of my going to bed with a woman! What GOD promised David, I'll help accomplish — transfer the kingdom from the house of Saul and make David ruler over the whole country, both Israel and Judah, from Dan to Beersheba. If not, may God do his worst to me."

11   Ish-Bosheth, cowed by Abner's outburst, couldn't say another word.

12   Abner went ahead and sent personal messengers to David: "Make a deal with me and I'll help bring the whole country of Israel over to you."

13   "Great," said David. "It's a deal. But only on one condition: You're not welcome here unless you bring Michal, Saul's daughter, with you when you come to meet me."

14   David then sent messengers to Ish-Bosheth son of Saul: "Give me back Michal, whom I won as my wife at the cost of a hundred Philistine foreskins."

15-16   Ish-Bosheth ordered that she be taken from her husband Paltiel son of Laish. But Paltiel followed her, weeping all the way, to Bahurim. There Abner told him, "Go home." And he went home.

17-18   Abner got the elders of Israel together and said, "Only yesterday, it seems, you were looking for a way to make David your king. So do it — now! For GOD has given the go-ahead on David: 'By my servant David's hand, I'll save my people Israel from the oppression of the Philistines and all their other enemies.'"

19   Abner took the Benjaminites aside and spoke to them. Then he went to Hebron for a private talk with David, telling him everything that Israel in general and Benjamin in particular were planning to do.

20   When Abner and the twenty men who were with him met with David in Hebron, David laid out a feast for them.

21   Abner then said, "I'm ready. Let me go now to rally everyone in Israel for my master, the king. They'll make a treaty with you, authorizing you to rule them however you see fit." Abner was sent off with David's blessing.

22-23   Soon after that, David's men, led by Joab, came back from a field assignment. Abner was no longer in Hebron with David, having just been dismissed with

David's blessing. As Joab and his raiding party arrived, they were told that Abner the son of Ner had been there with David and had been sent off with David's blessing.

24-25   Joab went straight to the king: "What's this you've done? Abner shows up, and you let him walk away scot-free? You know Abner son of Ner better than that. This was no friendly visit. He was here to spy on you, figure out your comings and goings, find out what you're up to."

26-27   Joab left David and went into action. He sent messengers after Abner; they caught up with him at the well at Sirah and brought him back. David knew nothing of all this. When Abner got back to Hebron, Joab steered him aside at the gate for a personal word with him. There he stabbed him in the belly, killed him in cold blood for the murder of his brother Asahel.

28-30   Later on, when David heard what happened, he said, "Before GOD I and my kingdom are totally innocent of this murder of Abner son of Ner. Joab and his entire family will always be under the curse of this bloodguilt. May they forever be victims of crippling diseases, violence, and famine." (Joab and his brother, Abishai, murdered Abner because he had killed their brother Asahel at the battle of Gibeon.)

31-32   David ordered Joab and all the men under him, "Rip your cloaks into rags! Wear mourning clothes! Lead Abner's funeral procession with loud lament!" King David followed the coffin. They buried Abner in Hebron. The king's voice was loud in lament as he wept at the side of Abner's grave. All the people wept, too.

33-34   Then the king sang this tribute to Abner:

Can this be? Abner dead like a nameless bum?
You were a free man, free to go and do as you wished —
Yet you fell as a victim in a street brawl.

And all the people wept — a crescendo of crying!

35-37   They all came then to David, trying to get him to eat something before dark. But David solemnly swore, "I'll not so much as taste a piece of bread, or anything else for that matter, before sunset, so help me God!" Everyone at the funeral took notice — and liked what they saw. In fact everything the king did was applauded by the people. It was clear to everyone that day, including all Israel, that the king had nothing to do with the death of Abner son of Ner.

38-39   The king spoke to his servants: "You realize, don't you, that today a prince and hero fell victim to foul play in Israel? And I, though anointed king, was helpless to do anything about it. These sons of Zeruiah are too much for me. GOD, requite the criminal for his crime!"

THE MURDER OF ISH-BOSHETH

1   **4**Saul's son, Ish-Bosheth, heard that Abner had died in Hebron. His heart sank. The whole country was shaken.

2-3   Ish-Bosheth had two men who were captains of raiding bands — one was named Baanah, the other Recab. They were sons of Rimmon the Beerothite, a Benjaminite. (The people of Beeroth had been assigned to Benjamin ever since they escaped to Gittaim. They still live there as resident aliens.)

4   It so happened that Saul's son, Jonathan, had a son who was maimed in both feet. When he was five years old, the report on Saul and Jonathan

came from Jezreel. His nurse picked him up and ran, but in her hurry to get away she fell, and the boy was maimed. His name was Mephibosheth.

5-7   One day Baanah and Recab, the two sons of Rimmon, headed out for the house of Ish-Bosheth. They arrived at the hottest time of the day, just as he was taking his afternoon nap. They entered the house on a ruse, pretending official business. The maid guarding the bedroom had fallen asleep, so Recab and Baanah slipped by her and entered the room where Ish-Bosheth was asleep on his bed. They killed him and then cut off his head, carrying it off as a trophy. They traveled all night long, taking the route through the Arabah Valley.

8   They presented the head of Ish-Bosheth to David at Hebron, telling the king, "Here's the head of Ish-Bosheth, Saul's son, your enemy. He was out to kill you, but GOD has given vengeance to my master, the king—vengeance this very day on Saul and his children!"

9-11   David answered the brothers Recab and Baanah, sons of Rimmon the Beerothite, "As surely as GOD lives—the One who got me out of every trouble I've ever been in—when the messenger told me, 'Good news! Saul is dead!' supposing I'd be delighted, I arrested him and killed him on the spot in Ziklag. That's what he got for his so-called good news! And now you show up—evil men who killed an innocent man in cold blood, a man asleep in his own house! Don't think I won't find you guilty of murder and rid the country of you!"

12   David then issued orders to his soldiers. They killed the two—chopped off their hands and feet, and hung the corpses at the pool in Hebron. But Ish-Bosheth's head they took and buried in Abner's tomb in Hebron.

1-2   5 Before long all the tribes of Israel approached David in Hebron and said, "Look at us—your own flesh and blood! In time past when Saul was our king, you were the one who really ran the country. Even then GOD said to you, 'You will shepherd my people Israel and you'll be the prince.'"

3   All the leaders of Israel met with King David at Hebron, and the king made a treaty with them in the presence of GOD. And so they anointed David king over Israel.

4-5   David was thirty years old when he became king, and ruled for forty years. In Hebron he ruled Judah for seven and a half years. In Jerusalem he ruled all Israel and Judah for thirty-three years.

6   David and his men immediately set out for Jerusalem to take on the Jebusites, who lived in that country. But they said, "You might as well go home! Even the blind and the lame could keep you out. You can't get in here!" They had convinced themselves that David couldn't break through.

7-8   But David went right ahead and captured the fortress of Zion, known ever since as the City of David. That day David said, "To get the best of these Jebusites, one must target the water system, not to mention this so-called lame and blind bunch that David hates." (In fact, he was so sick and tired of it, people coined the expression, "No lame and blind allowed in the palace.")

9-10   David made the fortress city his home and named it "City of David." He developed the city from the outside terraces inward. David proceeded with a longer stride, a larger embrace since the GOD-of-the-Angel-Armies was with him.

11-12 It was at this time that Hiram, king of Tyre, sent messengers to David, along with timbers of cedar. He also sent carpenters and masons to build a house for David. David took this as a sign that GOD had confirmed him as king of Israel, giving his kingship world prominence for the sake of Israel, his people.

13-16 David took on more concubines and wives from Jerusalem after he left Hebron. And more sons and daughters were born to him. These are the names of those born to him in Jerusalem:

> Shammua,
> Shobab,
> Nathan,
> Solomon,
> Ibhar,
> Elishua,
> Nepheg,
> Japhia,
> Elishama,
> Eliada,
> Eliphelet.

17-18 When the Philistines got word that David had been made king over all Israel, they came on the hunt for him. David heard of it and went down to the stronghold. When the Philistines arrived, they deployed their forces in Rephaim Valley.

19 Then David prayed to GOD: "Shall I go up and fight the Philistines? Will you help me beat them?"

20-21 "Go up," GOD replied. "Count on me. I'll help you beat them."

David then went straight to Baal Perazim, and smashed them to pieces. Afterward David said, "GOD exploded on my enemies like a gush of water." That's why David named the place Baal Perazim (The-Master-Who-Explodes). The retreating Philistines dumped their idols, and David and his soldiers took them away.

22-23 Later there was a repeat performance. The Philistines came up again and deployed their troops in the Rephaim Valley. David again prayed to GOD.

23-24 This time GOD said, "Don't attack them head-on. Instead, circle around behind them and ambush them from the grove of sacred trees. When you hear the sound of shuffling in the trees, get ready to move out. It's a signal that GOD is going ahead of you to smash the Philistine camp."

25 David did exactly what GOD told him. He routed the Philistines all the way from Gibeon to Gezer.

1-2 6 David mustered the pick of the troops of Israel—thirty divisions of them. Together with his soldiers, David headed for Baalah to recover the Chest of God, which was called by the Name GOD-of-the-Angel-Armies, who was enthroned over the pair of angels on the Chest.

3-7 They placed the Chest of God on a brand-new oxcart and removed it from Abinadab's house on the hill. Uzzah and Ahio, Abinadab's sons, were driving the new cart loaded with the Chest of God, Ahio in the lead and

Uzzah alongside the Chest. David and the whole company of Israel were in the parade, singing at the top of their lungs and playing mandolins, harps, tambourines, castanets, and cymbals. When they came to the threshing floor of Nacon, the oxen stumbled, so Uzzah reached out and grabbed the Chest of God. God blazed in anger against Uzzah and struck him hard because he had profaned the Chest. Uzzah died on the spot, right alongside the Chest.

8-11 Then David got angry because of God's deadly outburst against Uzzah. That place is still called Perez Uzzah (The-Explosion-Against-Uzzah). David became fearful of God that day and said, "This Chest is too hot to handle. How can I ever get it back to the City of David?" He refused to take the Chest of God a step farther. Instead, David removed it off the road and to the house of Obed-Edom the Gittite. The Chest of God stayed at the house of Obed-Edom the Gittite for three months. And God prospered Obed-Edom and his entire household.

12-16 It was reported to King David that God had prospered Obed-Edom and his entire household because of the Chest of God. So David thought, "I'll get that blessing for myself," and went and brought up the Chest of God from the house of Obed-Edom to the City of David, celebrating extravagantly all the way, with frequent sacrifices of choice bulls. David, ceremonially dressed in priest's linen, danced with great abandon before God. The whole country was with him as he accompanied the Chest of God with shouts and trumpet blasts. But as the Chest of God came into the City of David, Michal, Saul's daughter, happened to be looking out a window. When she saw King David leaping and dancing before God, her heart filled with scorn.

17-19 They brought the Chest of God and set it in the middle of the tent pavilion that David had pitched for it. Then and there David worshiped, offering burnt offerings and peace offerings. When David had completed the sacrifices of burnt and peace offerings, he blessed the people in the name of God-of-the-Angel-Armies and handed out to each person in the crowd, men and women alike, a loaf of bread, a date cake, and a raisin cake. Then everyone went home.

20-22 David returned home to bless his family. Michal, Saul's daughter, came out to greet him: "How wonderfully the king has distinguished himself today—exposing himself to the eyes of the servants' maids like some burlesque street dancer!" David replied to Michal, "In God's presence I'll dance all I want! He chose me over your father and the rest of our family and made me prince over God's people, over Israel. Oh yes, I'll dance to God's glory—more recklessly even than this. And as far as I'm concerned . . . I'll gladly look like a fool . . . but among these maids you're so worried about, I'll be honored no end."

23 Michal, Saul's daughter, was barren the rest of her life.

God's Covenant with David

1-2 7 Before long, the king made himself at home and God gave him peace from all his enemies. Then one day King David said to Nathan the prophet, "Look at this: Here I am, comfortable in a luxurious house of cedar, and the Chest of God sits in a plain tent."

3 Nathan told the king, "Whatever is on your heart, go and do it. GOD is with you."

4-7 But that night, the word of GOD came to Nathan saying, "Go and tell my servant David: This is GOD's word on the matter: You're going to build a 'house' for me to live in? Why, I haven't lived in a 'house' from the time I brought the children of Israel up from Egypt till now. All that time I've moved about with nothing but a tent. And in all my travels with Israel, did I ever say to any of the leaders I commanded to shepherd Israel, 'Why haven't you built me a house of cedar?'

8-11 "So here is what you are to tell my servant David: The GOD-of-the-Angel-Armies has this word for you: I took you from the pasture, tagging along after sheep, and made you prince over my people Israel. I was with you everywhere you went and mowed your enemies down before you. Now I'm making you famous, to be ranked with the great names on earth. And I'm going to set aside a place for my people Israel and plant them there so they'll have their own home and not be knocked around any more. Nor will evil men afflict you as they always have, even during the days I set judges over my people Israel. Finally, I'm going to give you peace from all your enemies.

11-16 "Furthermore, GOD has this message for you: GOD himself will build you a house! When your life is complete and you're buried with your ancestors, then I'll raise up your child, your own flesh and blood, to succeed you, and I'll firmly establish his rule. He will build a house to honor me, and I will guarantee his kingdom's rule permanently. I'll be a father to him, and he'll be a son to me. When he does wrong, I'll discipline him in the usual ways, the pitfalls and obstacles of this mortal life. But I'll never remove my gracious love from him, as I removed it from Saul, who preceded you and whom I most certainly did remove. Your family and your kingdom are permanently secured. I'm keeping my eye on them! And your royal throne will always be there, rock solid."

17 Nathan gave David a complete and accurate account of everything he heard and saw in the vision.

18-21 King David went in, took his place before GOD, and prayed: "Who am I, my Master GOD, and what is my family, that you have brought me to this place in life? But that's nothing compared to what's coming, for you've also spoken of my family far into the future, given me a glimpse into tomorrow, my Master GOD! What can I possibly say in the face of all this? You know me, Master GOD, just as I am. You've done all this not because of who I am but because of who you are — out of your very heart! — but you've let me in on it.

22-24 "This is what makes you so great, Master GOD! There is none like you, no God but you, nothing to compare with what we've heard with our own ears. And who is like your people, like Israel, a nation unique in the earth, whom God set out to redeem for himself (and became most famous for it), performing great and fearsome acts, throwing out nations and their gods left and right as you saved your people from Egypt? You established for yourself a people — your very own Israel! — your people permanently. And you, GOD, became their God.

25-27 "So now, great GOD, this word that you have spoken to me and my family, guarantee it permanently! Do exactly what you've promised! Then your reputation will flourish always as people exclaim, 'The GOD-of-the-Angel-Armies is God over Israel!' And the house of your servant David will remain sure and solid in your watchful presence. For you, GOD-of-the-Angel-Armies, Israel's

God, told me plainly, 'I will build you a house.' That's how I was able to find the courage to pray this prayer to you.

28-29   "And now, Master GOD, being the God you are, speaking sure words as you do, and having just said this wonderful thing to me, please, just one more thing: Bless my family; keep your eye on them always. You've already as much as said that you would, Master GOD! Oh, may your blessing be on my family permanently!"

8 ¹ In the days that followed, David struck hard at the Philistines — brought them to their knees and took control of the countryside. ² He also fought and defeated Moab. He chose two-thirds of them randomly and executed them. The other third he spared. So the Moabites fell under David's rule and were forced to bring tribute.

3-4   On his way to restore his sovereignty at the River Euphrates, David next defeated Hadadezer son of Rehob the king of Zobah. He captured from him a thousand chariots, seven thousand cavalry, and twenty thousand infantry. He hamstrung all the chariot horses, but saved back a hundred.

5-6   When the Arameans from Damascus came to the aid of Hadadezer king of Zobah, David killed twenty-two thousand of them. David set up a puppet government in Aram-Damascus. The Arameans became subjects of David and were forced to bring tribute. GOD gave victory to David wherever he marched.

7-8   David plundered the gold shields that belonged to the servants of Hadadezer and brought them to Jerusalem. He also looted a great quantity of bronze from Tebah and Berothai, cities of Hadadezer.

9-12   Toi, king of Hamath, heard that David had struck down the entire army of Hadadezer. So he sent his son Joram to King David to greet and congratulate him for fighting and defeating them, for Toi and Hadadezer were old enemies. He brought with him gifts of silver, gold, and bronze. King David consecrated these along with the silver and gold from all the nations he had conquered — from Aram, Moab, the Ammonites, the Philistines, and from Amalek, along with the plunder from Hadadezer son of Rehob king of Zobah.

13-14   David built a victory monument on his return from defeating the Arameans.

Abishai son of Zeruiah fought and defeated the Edomites in the Salt Valley. Eighteen thousand of them were killed. David set up a puppet government in Edom, and the Edomites became subjects under David.

GOD gave David victory wherever he marched.

15   Thus David ruled over all of Israel. He ruled well — fair and even-handed in all his duties and relationships.

16   Joab son of Zeruiah was head of the army;
Jehoshaphat son of Ahilud was clerk;

17   Zadok son of Ahitub and Ahimelech son of Abiathar were priests;
Seraiah was secretary;

18   Benaiah son of Jehoiada was over the Kerethites and Pelethites;
And David's sons were priests.

AN OPEN TABLE FOR MEPHIBOSHETH

1 **9** One day David asked, "Is there anyone left of Saul's family? If so, I'd like to show him some kindness in honor of Jonathan."

2 It happened that a servant from Saul's household named Ziba was there. They called him into David's presence. The king asked him, "Are you Ziba?"

"Yes sir," he replied.

3 The king asked, "Is there anyone left from the family of Saul to whom I can show some godly kindness?"

Ziba told the king, "Yes, there is Jonathan's son, lame in both feet."

4 "Where is he?"

"He's living at the home of Makir son of Ammiel in Lo Debar."

5 King David didn't lose a minute. He sent and got him from the home of Makir son of Ammiel in Lo Debar.

6 When Mephibosheth son of Jonathan (who was the son of Saul), came before David, he bowed deeply, abasing himself, honoring David.

David spoke his name: "Mephibosheth."

"Yes sir?"

7 "Don't be frightened," said David. "I'd like to do something special for you in memory of your father Jonathan. To begin with, I'm returning to you all the properties of your grandfather Saul. Furthermore, from now on you'll take all your meals at my table."

8 Shuffling and stammering, not looking him in the eye, Mephibosheth said, "Who am I that you pay attention to a stray dog like me?"

9-10 David then called in Ziba, Saul's right-hand man, and told him, "Everything that belonged to Saul and his family, I've handed over to your master's grandson. You and your sons and your servants will work his land and bring in the produce, provisions for your master's grandson. Mephibosheth himself, your master's grandson, from now on will take all his meals at my table." Ziba had fifteen sons and twenty servants.

11-12 "All that my master the king has ordered his servant," answered Ziba, "your servant will surely do."

And Mephibosheth ate at David's table, just like one of the royal family. Mephibosheth also had a small son named Mica. All who were part of Ziba's household were now the servants of Mephibosheth.

13 Mephibosheth lived in Jerusalem, taking all his meals at the king's table. He was lame in both feet.

1-2 **10** Sometime after this, the king of the Ammonites died and Hanun, his son, succeeded him as king. David said, "I'd like to show some kindness to Hanun, the son of Nahash — treat him as well and as kindly as his father treated me." So David sent Hanun condolences regarding his father.

2-3 But when David's servants got to the land of the Ammonites, the Ammonite leaders warned Hanun, their head delegate, "Do you for a minute suppose that David is honoring your father by sending you comforters? Don't you think it's because he wants to snoop around the city and size it up that David has sent his emissaries to you?"

4 So Hanun seized David's men, shaved off half their beards, cut off their robes halfway up their buttocks, and sent them packing.

5   When all this was reported to David, he sent someone to meet them, for they were seriously humiliated. The king told them, "Stay in Jericho until your beards grow out. Only then come back."

6   When it dawned on the Ammonites that as far as David was concerned they stunk to high heaven, they hired Aramean soldiers from Beth-Rehob and Zobah — twenty thousand infantry — and a thousand men from the king of Maacah, and twelve thousand men from Tob.

7   When David heard of this, he dispatched Joab with his strongest fighters in full force.

8-12   The Ammonites marched out and arranged themselves in battle formation at the city gate. The Arameans of Zobah and Rehob and the men of Tob and Maacah took up a position out in the open fields. When Joab saw that he had two fronts to fight, before and behind, he took his pick of the best of Israel and deployed them to confront the Arameans. The rest of the army he put under the command of Abishai, his brother, and deployed them to confront the Ammonites. Then he said, "If the Arameans are too much for me, you help me. And if the Ammonites prove too much for you, I'll come and help you. Courage! We'll fight with might and main for our people and for the cities of our God. And GOD will do whatever he sees needs doing!"

13-14   But when Joab and his soldiers moved in to fight the Arameans, they ran off in full retreat. Then the Ammonites, seeing the Arameans run for dear life, took to their heels from Abishai and went into the city.

     So Joab left off fighting the Ammonites and returned to Jerusalem.

15-17   When the Arameans saw how badly they'd been beaten by Israel, they picked up the pieces and regrouped. Hadadezer sent for the Arameans who were across the River. They came to Helam. Shobach, commander of Hadadezer's army, led them. All this was reported to David.

17-19   So David mustered Israel, crossed the Jordan, and came to Helam. The Arameans went into battle formation, ready for David, and the fight was on. But the Arameans again scattered before Israel. David killed seven hundred chariot drivers and forty thousand cavalry. And he mortally wounded Shobach, the army commander, who died on the battlefield. When all the kings who were vassals of Hadadezer saw that they had been routed by Israel, they made peace and became Israel's vassals. The Arameans were afraid to help the Ammonites ever again.

DAVID'S SIN AND SORROW

1   **11** When that time of year came around again, the anniversary of the Ammonite aggression, David dispatched Joab and his fighting men of Israel in full force to destroy the Ammonites for good. They laid siege to Rabbah, but David stayed in Jerusalem.

2-5   One late afternoon, David got up from taking his nap and was strolling on the roof of the palace. From his vantage point on the roof he saw a woman bathing. The woman was stunningly beautiful. David sent to ask about her, and was told, "Isn't this Bathsheba, daughter of Eliam and wife of Uriah the Hittite?" David sent his agents to get her. After she arrived, he went to bed with her. (This occurred during the time of "purification" following her period.) Then she returned home. Before long she realized she was pregnant.

     Later she sent word to David: "I'm pregnant."

6   David then got in touch with Joab: "Send Uriah the Hittite to me." Joab sent him.

7-8   When he arrived, David asked him for news from the front — how things were going with Joab and the troops and with the fighting. Then he said to Uriah, "Go home. Have a refreshing bath and a good night's rest."

8-9   After Uriah left the palace, an informant of the king was sent after him. But Uriah didn't go home. He slept that night at the palace entrance, along with the king's servants.

10   David was told that Uriah had not gone home. He asked Uriah, "Didn't you just come off a hard trip? So why didn't you go home?"

11   Uriah replied to David, "The Chest is out there with the fighting men of Israel and Judah — in tents. My master Joab and his servants are roughing it out in the fields. So, how can I go home and eat and drink and enjoy my wife? On your life, I'll not do it!"

12-13   "All right," said David, "have it your way. Stay for the day and I'll send you back tomorrow." So Uriah stayed in Jerusalem the rest of the day.

The next day David invited him to eat and drink with him, and David got him drunk. But in the evening Uriah again went out and slept with his master's servants. He didn't go home.

14-15   In the morning David wrote a letter to Joab and sent it with Uriah. In the letter he wrote, "Put Uriah in the front lines where the fighting is the fiercest. Then pull back and leave him exposed so that he's sure to be killed."

16-17   So Joab, holding the city under siege, put Uriah in a place where he knew there were fierce enemy fighters. When the city's defenders came out to fight Joab, some of David's soldiers were killed, including Uriah the Hittite.

18-21   Joab sent David a full report on the battle. He instructed the messenger, "After you have given to the king a detailed report on the battle, if he flares in anger, say, 'And by the way, your servant Uriah the Hittite is dead.'"

22-24   Joab's messenger arrived in Jerusalem and gave the king a full report. He said, "The enemy was too much for us. They advanced on us in the open field, and we pushed them back to the city gate. But then arrows came hot and heavy on us from the city wall, and eighteen of the king's soldiers died."

25   When the messenger completed his report of the battle, David got angry at Joab. He vented it on the messenger: "Why did you get so close to the city? Didn't you know you'd be attacked from the wall? Didn't you remember how Abimelech son of Jerub-Besheth got killed? Wasn't it a woman who dropped a millstone on him from the wall and crushed him at Thebez? Why did you go close to the wall!"

"By the way," said Joab's messenger, "your servant Uriah the Hittite is dead."

Then David told the messenger, "Oh. I see. Tell Joab, 'Don't trouble yourself over this. War kills — sometimes one, sometimes another — you never know who's next. Redouble your assault on the city and destroy it.' Encourage Joab."

26-27   When Uriah's wife heard that her husband was dead, she grieved for her husband. When the time of mourning was over, David sent someone to bring her to his house. She became his wife and bore him a son.

27-3   **12** But GOD was not at all pleased with what David had done, and sent Nathan to David. Nathan said to him, "There were two men in the same city — one rich, the other poor. The rich man had huge flocks of sheep, herds of cattle. The poor man had nothing but one little female lamb, which he had bought and raised. It grew up with him and his children as a member of the family. It ate off his plate and drank from his cup and slept on his bed. It was like a daughter to him.

4 "One day a traveler dropped in on the rich man. He was too stingy to take an animal from his own herds or flocks to make a meal for his visitor, so he took the poor man's lamb and prepared a meal to set before his guest."

5-6 David exploded in anger. "As surely as GOD lives," he said to Nathan, "the man who did this ought to be lynched! He must repay for the lamb four times over for his crime and his stinginess!"

7-12 "You're the man!" said Nathan. "And here's what GOD, the God of Israel, has to say to you: I made you king over Israel. I freed you from the fist of Saul. I gave you your master's daughter and other wives to have and to hold. I gave you both Israel and Judah. And if that hadn't been enough, I'd have gladly thrown in much more. So why have you treated the word of GOD with brazen contempt, doing this great evil? You murdered Uriah the Hittite, then took his wife as your wife. Worse, you killed him with an Ammonite sword! And now, because you treated God with such contempt and took Uriah the Hittite's wife as your wife, killing and murder will continually plague your family. This is GOD speaking, remember! I'll make trouble for you out of your own family. I'll take your wives from right out in front of you. I'll give them to some neighbor, and he'll go to bed with them openly. You did your deed in secret; I'm doing mine with the whole country watching!"

13-14 Then David confessed to Nathan, "I've sinned against GOD."

Nathan pronounced, "Yes, but that's not the last word. GOD forgives your sin. You won't die for it. But because of your blasphemous behavior, the son born to you will die."

15-18 After Nathan went home, GOD afflicted the child that Uriah's wife bore to David, and he came down sick. David prayed desperately to God for the little boy. He fasted, wouldn't go out, and slept on the floor. The elders in his family came in and tried to get him off the floor, but he wouldn't budge. Nor could they get him to eat anything. On the seventh day the child died. David's servants were afraid to tell him. They said, "What do we do now? While the child was living he wouldn't listen to a word we said. Now, with the child dead, if we speak to him there's no telling what he'll do."

19 David noticed that the servants were whispering behind his back, and realized that the boy must have died.

He asked the servants, "Is the boy dead?"

"Yes," they answered. "He's dead."

20 David got up from the floor, washed his face and combed his hair, put on a fresh change of clothes, then went into the sanctuary and worshiped. Then he came home and asked for something to eat. They set it before him and he ate.

21 His servants asked him, "What's going on with you? While the child was alive you fasted and wept and stayed up all night. Now that he's dead, you get up and eat."

22-23 "While the child was alive," he said, "I fasted and wept, thinking GOD might have mercy on me and the child would live. But now that he's dead, why fast? Can I bring him back now? I can go to him, but he can't come to me."

24-25 David went and comforted his wife Bathsheba. And when he slept with
her, they conceived a son. When he was born they named him Solomon.
GOD had a special love for him and sent word by Nathan the prophet that
GOD wanted him named Jedidiah (God's Beloved).

26-30 Joab, at war in Rabbah against the Ammonites, captured the royal city. He
sent messengers to David saying, "I'm fighting at Rabbah, and I've just
captured the city's water supply. Hurry and get the rest of the troops
together and set up camp here at the city and complete the capture yourself. Otherwise, I'll capture it and get all the credit instead of you." So
David marshaled all the troops, went to Rabbah, and fought and captured
it. He took the crown from their king's head—very heavy with gold, and
with a precious stone in it. It ended up on David's head. And they plundered the city, carrying off a great quantity of loot.

31 David emptied the city of its people and put them to slave labor using
saws, picks, and axes, and making bricks. He did this to all the Ammonite
cities. Then David and the whole army returned to Jerusalem.

1-4 13 Some time later, this happened: Absalom, David's son, had a sister
who was very attractive. Her name was Tamar. Amnon, also
David's son, was in love with her. Amnon was obsessed with his
sister Tamar to the point of making himself sick over her. She was a virgin, so
he couldn't see how he could get his hands on her. Amnon had a good friend,
Jonadab, the son of David's brother Shimeah. Jonadab was exceptionally
streetwise. He said to Amnon, "Why are you moping around like this, day after
day—you, the son of the king! Tell me what's eating at you."

"In a word, Tamar," said Amnon. "My brother Absalom's sister. I'm in
love with her."

5 "Here's what you do," said Jonadab. "Go to bed and pretend you're sick.
When your father comes to visit you, say, 'Have my sister Tamar come
and prepare some supper for me here where I can watch her and she can
feed me.'"

6 So Amnon took to his bed and acted sick. When the king came to visit,
Amnon said, "Would you do me a favor? Have my sister Tamar come and
make some nourishing dumplings here where I can watch her and be fed
by her."

7 David sent word to Tamar who was home at the time: "Go to the house
of your brother Amnon and prepare a meal for him."

8-9 So Tamar went to her brother Amnon's house. She took dough, kneaded
it, formed it into dumplings, and cooked them while he watched from his
bed. But when she took the cooking pot and served him, he wouldn't eat.

9-11 Amnon said, "Clear everyone out of the house," and they all cleared out.
Then he said to Tamar, "Bring the food into my bedroom, where we can
eat in privacy." She took the nourishing dumplings she had prepared and
brought them to her brother Amnon in his bedroom. But when she got
ready to feed him, he grabbed her and said, "Come to bed with me, sister!"

12-13 "No, brother!" she said, "Don't hurt me! This kind of thing isn't done in
Israel! Don't do this terrible thing! Where could I ever show my face? And
you—you'll be out on the street in disgrace. Oh, please! Speak to the king—
he'll let you marry me."

14   But he wouldn't listen. Being much stronger than she, he raped her.

15   No sooner had Amnon raped her than he hated her — an immense hatred. The hatred that he felt for her was greater than the love he'd had for her. "Get up," he said, "and get out!"

16-18   "Oh no, brother," she said. "Please! This is an even worse evil than what you just did to me!"

    But he wouldn't listen to her. He called for his valet. "Get rid of this woman. Get her out of my sight! And lock the door after her." The valet threw her out and locked the door behind her.

18-19   She was wearing a long-sleeved gown. (That's how virgin princesses used to dress from early adolescence on.) Tamar poured ashes on her head, then she ripped the long-sleeved gown, held her head in her hands, and walked away, sobbing as she went.

20   Her brother Absalom said to her, "Has your brother Amnon had his way with you? Now, my dear sister, let's keep it quiet — a family matter. He is, after all, your brother. Don't take this so hard." Tamar lived in her brother Absalom's home, bitter and desolate.

21-22   King David heard the whole story and was enraged, but he didn't discipline Amnon. David doted on him because he was his firstborn. Absalom quit speaking to Amnon — not a word, whether good or bad — because he hated him for violating his sister Tamar.

23-24   Two years went by. One day Absalom threw a sheep-shearing party in Baal Hazor in the vicinity of Ephraim and invited all the king's sons. He also went to the king and invited him. "Look, I'm throwing a sheep-shearing party. Come, and bring your servants."

25   But the king said, "No, son — not this time, and not the whole household. We'd just be a burden to you." Absalom pushed, but David wouldn't budge. But he did give him his blessing.

26-27   Then Absalom said, "Well, if you won't come, at least let my brother Amnon come."

    "And why," said the king, "should he go with you?" But Absalom was so insistent that he gave in and let Amnon and all the rest of the king's sons go.

28   Absalom prepared a banquet fit for a king. Then he instructed his servants, "Look sharp, now. When Amnon is well into the sauce and feeling no pain, and I give the order 'Strike Amnon,' kill him. And don't be afraid — I'm the one giving the command. Courage! You can do it!"

29-31   Absalom's servants did to Amnon exactly what their master ordered. All the king's sons got out as fast as they could, jumped on their mules, and rode off. While they were still on the road, a rumor came to the king: "Absalom just killed all the king's sons — not one is left!" The king stood up, ripped his clothes to shreds, and threw himself on the floor. All his servants who were standing around at the time did the same.

32-33   Just then, Jonadab, his brother Shimeah's son, stepped up. "My master must not think that all the young men, the king's sons, are dead. Only Amnon is dead. This happened because of Absalom's outrage since the day that Amnon violated his sister Tamar. So my master, the king, mustn't make things worse than they are, thinking that all your sons are dead. Only Amnon is dead."

34   Absalom fled.

    Just then the sentry on duty looked up and saw a cloud of dust on the road from Horonaim alongside the mountain. He came and told the king, "I've just seen a bunch of men on the Horonaim road, coming around the mountain."

35-37 Then Jonadab exclaimed to the king, "See! It's the king's sons coming, just as I said!" He had no sooner said the words than the king's sons burst in — loud laments and weeping! The king joined in, along with all the servants — loud weeping, many tears. David mourned the death of his son a long time.

37-39 When Absalom fled, he went to Talmai son of Ammihud, king of Geshur. He was there three years. The king finally gave up trying to get back at Absalom. He had come to terms with Amnon's death.

1-3 **14** Joab son of Zeruiah knew that the king, deep down, still cared for Absalom. So he sent to Tekoa for a wise woman who lived there and instructed her, "Pretend you are in mourning. Dress in black and don't comb your hair, so you'll look like you've been grieving over a dead loved one for a long time. Then go to the king and tell him this . . . " Joab then told her exactly what to say.

4 The woman of Tekoa went to the king, bowed deeply before him in homage, and said, "O King, help!"

5-7 He said, "How can I help?"

"I'm a widow," she said. "My husband is dead. I had two sons. The two of them got into a fight out in the field and there was no one around to step between them. The one struck the other and killed him. Then the whole family ganged up against me and demanded, 'Hand over this murderer so we can kill him for the life of the brother he murdered!' They want to wipe out the heir and snuff out the one spark of life left to me. And then there would be nothing left of my husband — not so much as a name — on the face of the earth.

15-17 "So now I've dared come to the king, my master, about all this. They're making my life miserable, and I'm afraid. I said to myself, 'I'll go to the king. Maybe he'll do something! When the king hears what's going on, he'll step in and rescue me from the abuse of the man who would get rid of me and my son and God's inheritance — the works!' As your handmaid, I decided ahead of time, 'The word of my master, the king, will be the last word in this, for my master is like an angel of God in discerning good and evil.' GOD be with you!"

8 The king said, "Go home, and I'll take care of this for you."

9 "I'll take all responsibility for what happens," the woman of Tekoa said. "I don't want to compromise the king and his reputation."

10 "Bring the man who has been harassing you," the king continued. "I'll see to it that he doesn't bother you anymore."

11 "Let the king invoke the name of GOD," said the woman, "so this self-styled vigilante won't ruin everything, to say nothing of killing my son."

"As surely as GOD lives," he said, "not so much as a hair of your son's head will be lost."

12 Then she asked, "May I say one more thing to my master, the king?"

He said, "Go ahead."

13-14 "Why, then," the woman said, "have you done this very thing against God's people? In his verdict, the king convicts himself by not bringing home his exiled son. We all die sometime. Water spilled on the ground can't be gathered up again. But God does not take away life. He works out ways to get the exile back."

18   The king then said, "I'm going to ask you something. Answer me truthfully."

"Certainly," she said. "Let my master, the king, speak."

19-20   The king said, "Is the hand of Joab mixed up in this?"

"On your life, my master king, a body can't veer an inch right or left and get by with it in the royal presence! Yes, it was your servant Joab who put me up to this, and put these very words in my mouth. It was because he wanted to turn things around that your servant Joab did this. But my master is as wise as God's angels in knowing how to handle things on this earth."

21   The king spoke to Joab. "All right, I'll do it. Go and bring the young man Absalom back."

22   Joab bowed deeply in reverence and blessed the king. "I'm reassured to know that I'm still in your good graces and have your confidence, since the king is taking the counsel of his servant."

23-24   Joab got up, went to Geshur, and brought Absalom to Jerusalem. The king said, "He may return to his house, but he is not to see me face-to-face." So Absalom returned home, but was not permitted to see the king.

25-27   This Absalom! There wasn't a man in all Israel talked about so much for his handsome good looks—and not a blemish on him from head to toe! When he cut his hair—he always cut it short in the spring because it had grown so heavy—the weight of the hair from his head was over two pounds! Three sons were born to Absalom, and one daughter. Her name was Tamar—and she was a beauty.

28-31   Absalom lived in Jerusalem for two years, and not once did he see the king face-to-face. He sent for Joab to get him in to see the king, but Joab still wouldn't budge. He tried a second time and Joab still wouldn't. So he told his servants, "Listen. Joab's field adjoins mine, and he has a crop of barley in it. Go set fire to it." So Absalom's servants set fire to the field. That got him moving—Joab came to Absalom at home and said, "Why did your servants set my field on fire?"

32   Absalom answered him, "Listen, I sent for you saying, 'Come, and soon. I want to send you to the king to ask, "What's the point of my coming back from Geshur? I'd be better off still there!" Let me see the king face-to-face. If he finds me guilty, then he can put me to death.'"

33   Joab went to the king and told him what was going on. Absalom was then summoned—he came and bowed deeply in reverence before him. And the king kissed Absalom.

1-2   As time went on, Absalom took to riding in a horse-drawn chariot, with fifty men running in front of him. Early each morning he would take up his post beside the road at the city gate. When anyone showed up with a case to bring to the king for a decision, Absalom would call him over and say, "Where do you hail from?"

And the answer would come, "Your servant is from one of the tribes of Israel."

3-6   Then Absalom would say, "Look, you've got a strong case; but the king isn't going to listen to you." Then he'd say, "Why doesn't someone make me a judge for this country? Anybody with a case could bring it to me and I'd settle things fair and square." Whenever someone would treat him with special honor, he'd shrug it off and treat him like an equal, making him feel important. Absalom did this to everyone who came to do business with the king and stole the hearts of everyone in Israel.

7-8 After four years of this, Absalom spoke to the king, "Let me go to Hebron to pay a vow that I made to GOD. Your servant made a vow when I was living in Geshur in Aram saying, 'If GOD will bring me back to Jerusalem, I'll serve him with my life.'"

9 The king said, "Go with my blessing." And he got up and set off for Hebron.

10-12 Then Absalom sent undercover agents to all the tribes of Israel with the message, "When you hear the blast of the ram's horn trumpet, that's your signal: Shout, 'Absalom is king in Hebron!'" Two hundred men went with Absalom from Jerusalem. But they had been called together knowing nothing of the plot and made the trip innocently. While Absalom was offering sacrifices, he managed also to involve Ahithophel the Gilonite, David's advisor, calling him away from his hometown of Giloh. The conspiracy grew powerful and Absalom's supporters multiplied.

13 Someone came to David with the report, "The whole country has taken up with Absalom!"

14 "Up and out of here!" called David to all his servants who were with him in Jerusalem. "We've got to run for our lives or none of us will escape Absalom! Hurry, he's about to pull the city down around our ears and slaughter us all!"

15 The king's servants said, "Whatever our master, the king, says, we'll do; we're with you all the way!"

16-18 So the king and his entire household escaped on foot. The king left ten concubines behind to tend to the palace. And so they left, step by step by step, and then paused at the last house as the whole army passed by him—all the Kerethites, all the Pelethites, and the six hundred Gittites who had marched with him from Gath, went past.

19-20 The king called out to Ittai the Gittite, "What are you doing here? Go back with King Absalom. You're a stranger here and freshly uprooted from your own country. You arrived only yesterday, and am I going to let you take your chances with us as I live on the road like a gypsy? Go back, and take your family with you. And God's grace and truth go with you!"

21 But Ittai answered, "As GOD lives and my master the king lives, where my master is, that's where I'll be—whether it means life or death."

22 "All right," said David, "go ahead." And they went on, Ittai the Gittite with all his men and all the children he had with him.

23-24 The whole country was weeping in loud lament as all the people passed by. As the king crossed the Brook Kidron, the army headed for the road to the wilderness. Zadok was also there, the Levites with him, carrying GOD's Chest of the Covenant. They set the Chest of God down, Abiathar standing by, until all the people had evacuated the city.

25-26 Then the king ordered Zadok, "Take the Chest back to the city. If I get back in GOD's good graces, he'll bring me back and show me where the Chest has been set down. But if he says, 'I'm not pleased with you'—well, he can then do with me whatever he pleases."

27-30 The king directed Zadok the priest, "Here's the plan: Return to the city peacefully, with Ahimaaz your son and Jonathan, Abiathar's son, with you. I'll wait at a spot in the wilderness across the river, until I get word from you telling us what's up." So Zadok and Abiathar took the Chest of God back to Jerusalem and placed it there, while David went up the Mount of Olives weeping, head covered but barefooted, and the whole army was with him, heads covered and weeping as they ascended.

31   David was told, "Ahithophel has joined the conspirators with Absalom." He prayed, "Oh, GOD—turn Ahithophel's counsel to foolishness."

32-36   As David approached the top of the hill where God was worshiped, Hushai the Arkite, clothes ripped to shreds and dirt on his head, was there waiting for him. David said, "If you come with me, you'll be just one more piece of luggage. Go back to the city and say to Absalom, 'I'm ready to be your servant, O King; I used to be your father's servant, now I'm your servant.' Do that and you'll be able to confuse Ahithophel's counsel for me. The priests Zadok and Abiathar are already there; whatever information you pick up in the palace, tell them. Their two sons—Zadok's son Ahimaaz and Abiathar's son Jonathan—are there with them—anything you pick up can be sent to me by them."

37   Hushai, David's friend, arrived at the same time Absalom was entering Jerusalem.

1   **16** Shortly after David passed the crest of the hill, Mephibosheth's steward Ziba met him with a string of pack animals, saddled and loaded with a hundred loaves of bread, a hundred raisin cakes, a hundred baskets of fresh fruit, and a skin of wine.

2   The king said to Ziba, "What's all this?"

"The donkeys," said Ziba, "are for the king's household to ride, the bread and fruit are for the servants to eat, and the wine is for drinking, especially for those overcome by fatigue in the wilderness."

3   The king said, "And where is your master's grandson?"

"He stayed in Jerusalem," said Ziba. "He said, 'This is the day Israel is going to restore my grandfather's kingdom to me.'"

4   "Everything that belonged to Mephibosheth," said the king, "is now yours."

Ziba said, "How can I ever thank you? I'll be forever in your debt, my master and king; may you always look on me with such kindness!"

5-8   When the king got to Bahurim, a man appeared who had connections with Saul's family. His name was Shimei son of Gera. As he followed along he shouted insults and threw rocks right and left at David and his company, servants and soldiers alike. To the accompaniment of curses he shouted, "Get lost, get lost, you butcher, you hellhound! GOD has paid you back for all your dirty work in the family of Saul and for stealing his kingdom. GOD has given the kingdom to your son Absalom. Look at you now—ruined! And good riddance, you pathetic old man!"

9   Abishai son of Zeruiah said, "This mangy dog can't insult my master the king this way—let me go over and cut off his head!"

10   But the king said, "Why are you sons of Zeruiah always interfering and getting in the way? If he's cursing, it's because GOD told him, 'Curse David.' So who dares raise questions?"

11-12   "Besides," continued David to Abishai and the rest of his servants, "my own son, my flesh and bone, is right now trying to kill me; compared to that this Benjaminite is small potatoes. Don't bother with him; let him curse; he's preaching GOD's word to me. And who knows, maybe GOD will see the trouble I'm in today and exchange the curses for something good."

13 David and his men went on down the road, while Shimei followed along on the ridge of the hill alongside, cursing, throwing stones down on them, and kicking up dirt.

14 By the time they reached the Jordan River, David and all the men of the company were exhausted. There they rested and were revived.

15 By this time Absalom and all his men were in Jerusalem.
And Ahithophel was with them.

16 Soon after, Hushai the Arkite, David's friend, came and greeted Absalom, "Long live the king! Long live the king!"

17 Absalom said to Hushai, "Is this the way you show devotion to your good friend? Why didn't you go with your friend David?"

18-19 "Because," said Hushai, "I want to be with the person that GOD and this people and all Israel have chosen. And I want to stay with him. Besides, who is there to serve other than the son? Just as I served your father, I'm now ready to serve you."

20 Then Absalom spoke to Ahithophel, "Are you ready to give counsel? What do we do next?"

21-22 Ahithophel told Absalom, "Go and sleep with your father's concubines, the ones he left to tend to the palace. Everyone will hear that you have openly disgraced your father, and the morale of everyone on your side will be strengthened." So Absalom pitched a tent up on the roof in public view, and went in and slept with his father's concubines.

23 The counsel that Ahithophel gave in those days was treated as if God himself had spoken. That was the reputation of Ahithophel's counsel to David; it was the same with Absalom.

1-3 **17** Next Ahithophel advised Absalom, "Let me handpick twelve thousand men and go after David tonight. I'll come on him when he's bone tired and take him by complete surprise. The whole army will run off and I'll kill only David. Then I'll bring the army back to you—a bride brought back to her husband! You're only after one man, after all. Then everyone will be together in peace!"

4 Absalom thought it was an excellent strategy, and all the elders of Israel agreed.

5 But then Absalom said, "Call in Hushai the Arkite—let's hear what he has to say."

6 So Hushai came and Absalom put it to him, "This is what Ahithophel advised. Should we do it? What do you say?"

7-10 Hushai said, "The counsel that Ahithophel has given in this instance is not good. You know your father and his men, brave and bitterly angry—like a bear robbed of her cubs. And your father is an experienced fighter; you can be sure he won't be caught napping at a time like this. Even while we're talking, he's probably holed up in some cave or other. If he jumps your men from ambush, word will soon get back, 'A slaughter of Absalom's army!' Even if your men are valiant with hearts of lions, they'll fall apart at such news, for everyone in Israel knows the kind of fighting stuff your father's made of, and also the men with him.

11-13   "Here's what I'd advise: Muster the whole country, from Dan to Beersheba, an army like the sand of the sea, and you personally lead them. We'll smoke him out wherever he is, fall on him like dew falls on the earth, and, believe me, there won't be a single survivor. If he hides out in a city, then the whole army will bring ropes to that city and pull it down and into a gully—not so much as a pebble left of it!"

14   Absalom and all his company agreed that the counsel of Hushai the Arkite was better than the counsel of Ahithophel. (GOD had determined to discredit the counsel of Ahithophel so as to bring ruin on Absalom.)

15-16   Then Hushai told the priests Zadok and Abiathar, "Ahithophel advised Absalom and the elders of Israel thus and thus, and I advised them thus and thus. Now send this message as quickly as possible to David: 'Don't spend the night on this side of the river; cross immediately or the king and everyone with him will be swallowed up alive.'"

17-20   Jonathan and Ahimaaz were waiting around at En Rogel. A servant girl would come and give them messages and then they would go and tell King David, for it wasn't safe to be seen coming into the city. But a soldier spotted them and told Absalom, so the two of them got out of there fast and went to a man's house in Bahurim. He had a well in his yard and they climbed into it. The wife took a rug and covered the well, then spread grain on it so no one would notice anything out of the ordinary. Shortly, Absalom's servants came to the woman's house and asked her, "Have you seen Ahimaaz and Jonathan?"

The woman said, "They were headed toward the river."

They looked but didn't find them, and then went back to Jerusalem.

21   When the coast was clear, Ahimaaz and Jonathan climbed out of the well and went on to make their report to King David, "Get up and cross the river quickly; Ahithophel has given counsel against you!"

22   David and his whole army were soon up and moving and crossed the Jordan. As morning broke there was not a single person who had not made it across the Jordan.

23   When Ahithophel realized that his counsel was not followed, he saddled his donkey and left for his hometown. After making out his will and putting his house in order, he hanged himself and died. He was buried in the family tomb.

24-26   About the time David arrived at Mahanaim, Absalom crossed the Jordan, and the whole army of Israel with him. Absalom had made Amasa head of the army, replacing Joab. (Amasa was the son of a man named Ithra, an Ishmaelite who had married Abigail, daughter of Nahash and sister of Zeruiah, the mother of Joab.) Israel and Absalom set camp in Gilead.

27-29   When David arrived at Mahanaim, Shobi son of Nahash from Ammonite Rabbah, and Makir son of Ammiel from Lo Debar, and Barzillai the Gileadite from Rogelim brought beds and blankets, bowls and jugs filled with wheat, barley, flour, roasted grain, beans and lentils, honey, and curds and cheese from the flocks and herds. They presented all this to David and his army to eat, "because," they said, "the army must be starved and exhausted and thirsty out in this wilderness."

1-2   **18** David organized his forces. He appointed captains of thousands and captains of hundreds. Then David deployed his troops, a third under Joab, a third under Abishai son of Zeruiah, Joab's brother, and a third under Ittai the Gittite.

The king then announced, "I'm marching with you."

3 They said, "No, you mustn't march with us. If we're forced to retreat, the enemy won't give it a second thought. And if half of us die, they won't do so either. But you are worth ten thousand of us. It will be better for us if you stay in the city and help from there."

4 "If you say so," said the king. "I'll do what you think is best." And so he stood beside the city gate as the whole army marched out by hundreds and by thousands.

5 Then the king ordered Joab and Abishai and Ittai, "Deal gently for my sake with the young man Absalom." The whole army heard what the king commanded the three captains regarding Absalom.

6-8 The army took the field to meet Israel. It turned out that the battle was joined in the Forest of Ephraim. The army of Israel was beaten badly there that day by David's men, a terrific slaughter—twenty thousand men! There was fighting helter-skelter all over the place—the forest claimed more lives that day than the sword!

9-10 Absalom ran into David's men, but was out in front of them riding his mule, when the mule ran under the branches of a huge oak tree. Absalom's head was caught in the oak and he was left dangling between heaven and earth, the mule running right out from under him. A solitary soldier saw him and reported it to Joab, "I just saw Absalom hanging from an oak tree!"

11 Joab said to the man who told him, "If you saw him, why didn't you kill him then and there? I'd have rewarded you with ten pieces of silver and a fancy belt."

12-13 The man told Joab, "Even if I'd had a chance at a thousand pieces of silver, I wouldn't have laid a hand on the king's son. We all heard the king command you and Abishai and Ittai, 'For my sake, protect the young man Absalom.' Why, I'd be risking my life, for nothing is hidden from the king. And you would have just stood there!"

14-15 Joab said, "I can't waste my time with you." He then grabbed three knives and stabbed Absalom in the heart while he was still alive in the tree; by then Absalom was surrounded by ten of Joab's armor bearers; they hacked away at him and killed him.

16-17 Joab then blew the ram's horn trumpet, calling off the army in its pursuit of Israel. They took Absalom, dumped him into a huge pit in the forest, and piled an immense mound of rocks over him.

Meanwhile the whole army of Israel was in flight, each man making his own way home.

18 While alive, Absalom had erected for himself a pillar in the Valley of the King, "because," he said, "I have no son to carry on my name." He inscribed the pillar with his own name. To this day it is called "The Absalom Memorial."

19-20 Ahimaaz, Zadok's son, said, "Let me run to the king and bring him the good news that GOD has delivered him from his enemies." But Joab said, "You're not the one to deliver the good news today; some other day, maybe, but it's not 'good news' today." (This was because the king's son was dead.)

21 Then Joab ordered a Cushite, "You go. Tell the king what you've seen."

"Yes sir," said the Cushite, and ran off.

22 Ahimaaz son of Zadok kept at it, begging Joab, "What does it matter? Let me run, too, following the Cushite."

Joab said, "Why all this 'Run, run'? You'll get no thanks for it, I can tell you."

23 "I don't care; let me run."

"Okay," said Joab, "run." So Ahimaaz ran, taking the lower valley road, and passed the Cushite.

24-25 David was sitting between the two gates. The sentry had gone up to the top of the gate on the wall and looked around. He saw a solitary runner. The sentry called down and told the king. The king said, "If he's alone, it must be good news!"

25-26 As the runner came closer, the sentry saw another runner and called down to the gate, "Another runner all by himself."

And the king said, "This also must be good news."

27 Then the sentry said, "I can see the first man now; he runs like Ahimaaz son of Zadok."

"He's a good man," said the king. "He's bringing good news for sure."

28 Then Ahimaaz called out and said to the king, "Peace!" Then he bowed deeply before the king, his face to the ground. "Blessed be your GOD; he has handed over the men who rebelled against my master the king."

29 The king asked, "But is the young man Absalom all right?"

Ahimaaz said, "I saw a huge ruckus just as Joab was sending me off, but I don't know what it was about."

30 The king said, "Step aside and stand over there." So he stepped aside.

31 Then the Cushite arrived and said, "Good news, my master and king! GOD has given victory today over all those who rebelled against you!"

32 "But," said the king, "is the young man Absalom all right?"

And the Cushite replied, "Would that all of the enemies of my master the king and all who maliciously rose against you end up like that young man."

33 The king was stunned. Heartbroken, he went up to the room over the gate and wept. As he wept he cried out,

> O my son Absalom, my dear, dear son Absalom!
> Why not me rather than you, my death and not yours,
> O Absalom, my dear, dear son!

DAVID'S GRIEF FOR ABSALOM

1-4 **19** Joab was told that David was weeping and lamenting over Absalom. The day's victory turned into a day of mourning as word passed through the army, "David is grieving over his son." The army straggled back to the city that day demoralized, dragging their tails. And the king held his face in his hands and lamented loudly,

> O my son Absalom,
> Absalom my dear, dear son!

5-7 But in private Joab rebuked the king: "Now you've done it—knocked the wind out of your loyal servants who have just saved your life, to say nothing of the lives of your sons and daughters, wives and concubines. What is this— loving those who hate you and hating those who love you? Your actions give a clear message: officers and soldiers mean nothing to you. You know that if Absalom were alive right now, we'd all be dead—would that make you happy? Get hold of yourself; get out there and put some heart into your servants! I swear to God that if you don't go to them they'll desert; not a soldier will be left here by nightfall. And that will be the worst thing that has happened yet."

8 So the king came out and took his place at the city gate. Soon everyone knew: "Oh, look! The king has come out to receive us." And his whole army came and presented itself to the king. But the Israelites had fled the field of battle and gone home.

9-10 Meanwhile, the whole populace was now complaining to its leaders, "Wasn't it the king who saved us time and again from our enemies, and rescued us from the Philistines? And now he has had to flee the country on account of Absalom. And now this Absalom whom we made king is dead in battle. So what are you waiting for? Why don't you bring the king back?"

11-13 When David heard what was being said, he sent word to Zadok and Abiathar, the priests, "Ask the elders of Judah, 'Why are you so laggard in bringing the king back home? You're my brothers! You're my own flesh and blood! So why are you the last ones to bring the king back home?' And tell Amasa, 'You, too, are my flesh and blood. As God is my witness, I'm making you the permanent commander of the army in place of Joab.'"

14 He captured the hearts of everyone in Judah. They were unanimous in sending for the king: "Come back, you and all your servants."

15-18 So the king returned. He arrived at the Jordan just as Judah reached Gilgal on their way to welcome the king and escort him across the Jordan. Even Shimei son of Gera, the Benjaminite from Bahurim, hurried down to join the men of Judah so he could welcome the king, a thousand Benjaminites with him. And Ziba, Saul's steward, with his fifteen sons and twenty servants, waded across the Jordan to meet the king and brought his entourage across, doing whatever they could to make the king comfortable.

18-20 Shimei son of Gera bowed deeply in homage to the king as soon as he was across the Jordan and said, "Don't think badly of me, my master! Overlook my irresponsible outburst on the day my master the king left Jerusalem—don't hold it against me! I know I sinned, but look at me now—the first of all the tribe of Joseph to come down and welcome back my master the king!"

21 Abishai son of Zeruiah interrupted, "Enough of this! Shouldn't we kill him outright? Why, he cursed God's anointed!"

22 But David said, "What is it with you sons of Zeruiah? Why do you insist on being so contentious? Nobody is going to be killed today. I am again king over Israel!"

23 Then the king turned to Shimei, "You're not going to die." And the king gave him his word.

24-25 Next Mephibosheth grandson of Saul arrived from Jerusalem to welcome the king. He hadn't combed his hair or trimmed his beard or washed his clothes from the day the king left until the day he returned safe and sound. The king said, "And why didn't you come with me, Mephibosheth?"

26-28 "My master the king," he said, "my servant betrayed me. I told him to saddle my donkey so I could ride it and go with the king, for, as you know, I am lame. And then he lied to you about me. But my master the king has been like one of God's angels: he knew what was right and did it. Wasn't everyone in my father's house doomed? But you took me in and gave me a place at your table. What more could I ever expect or ask?"

29   "That's enough," said the king. "Say no more. Here's my decision: You and Ziba divide the property between you."

30   Mephibosheth said, "Oh, let him have it all! All I care about is that my master the king is home safe and sound!"

31-32   Barzillai the Gileadite had come down from Rogelim. He crossed the Jordan with the king to give him a good send-off. Barzillai was a very old man — eighty years old! He had supplied the king's needs all the while he was in Mahanaim since he was very wealthy.

33   "Join me in Jerusalem," the king said to Barzillai. "Let me take care of you."

34-37   But Barzillai declined the offer, "How long do you think I'd live if I went with the king to Jerusalem? I'm eighty years old and not much good anymore to anyone. Can't taste food; can't hear music. So why add to the burdens of my master the king? I'll just go a little way across the Jordan with the king. But why would the king need to make a great thing of that? Let me go back and die in my hometown and be buried with my father and mother. But my servant Kimham here; let him go with you in my place. But treat him well!"

38   The king said, "That's settled; Kimham goes with me. And I will treat him well! If you think of anything else, I'll do that for you, too."

39-40   The army crossed the Jordan but the king stayed. The king kissed and blessed Barzillai, who then returned home. Then the king, Kimham with him, crossed over at Gilgal.

40-41   The whole army of Judah and half the army of Israel processed with the king. The men of Israel came to the king and said, "Why have our brothers, the men of Judah, taken over as if they owned the king, escorting the king and his family and close associates across the Jordan?"

42   The men of Judah retorted, "Because the king is related to us, that's why! But why make a scene? You don't see us getting treated special because of it, do you?"

43   The men of Israel shot back, "We have ten shares in the king to your one. Besides we're the firstborn — so why are we having to play second fiddle? It was our idea to bring him back."

But the men of Judah took a harder line than the men of Israel.

1   **20** Just then a good-for-nothing named Sheba son of Bicri the Benjaminite blew a blast on the ram's horn trumpet, calling out,

We've got nothing to do with David,
    there's no future for us with the son of Jesse!
Let's get out of here, Israel — head for your tents!

2-3   So all the men of Israel deserted David and followed Sheba son of Bicri. But the men of Judah stayed committed, sticking with their king all the way from the Jordan to Jerusalem. When David arrived home in Jerusalem, the king took the ten concubines he had left to watch the palace and placed them in seclusion, under guard. He provided for their needs but didn't visit them. They were virtual prisoners until they died, widows as long as they lived.

4-10   The king ordered Amasa, "Muster the men of Judah for me in three days;

then report in." Amasa went to carry out his orders, but he was late reporting back. So David told Abishai, "Sheba son of Bicri is going to hurt us even worse than Absalom did. Take your master's servants and hunt him down before he gets holed up in some fortress city where we can't get to him." So under Abishai's command, all the best men — Joab's men and the Kerethites and Pelethites — left Jerusalem to hunt down Sheba son of Bicri. They were near the boulder at Gibeon when Amasa came their way. Joab was wearing a tunic with a sheathed sword strapped on his waist, but the sword slipped out and fell to the ground. Joab greeted Amasa, "How are you, brother?" and took Amasa's beard in his right hand as if to kiss him. Amasa didn't notice the sword in Joab's other hand. Joab stuck him in the belly and his guts spilled to the ground. A second blow wasn't needed; he was dead. Then Joab and his brother Abishai continued to chase Sheba son of Bicri.

11-14 One of Joab's soldiers took up his post over the body and called out, "Everyone who sides with Joab and supports David, follow Joab!" Amasa was lying in a pool of blood in the middle of the road; the man realized that the whole army was going to stop and take a look, so he pulled Amasa's corpse off the road into the field and threw a blanket over him so it wouldn't collect spectators. As soon as he'd gotten him off the road, the traffic flowed normally, following Joab in the chase after Sheba son of Bicri. Sheba passed through all the tribes of Israel as far as Abel Beth Maacah; all the Bicrites clustered and followed him into the city.

15 Joab's army arrived and laid siege to Sheba in Abel Beth Maacah. They built a siege-ramp up against the city's fortification. The plan was to knock down the wall.

16-17 But a shrewd woman called out from the city, "Listen, everybody! Please tell Joab to come close so I can talk to him." When he had come, the woman said, "Are you Joab?"

He said, "I am."

"Then," she said, "listen to what I have to say."

He said, "I'm listening."

18-19 "There's an old saying in these parts: 'If it's answers you want, come to Abel and get it straight.' We're a peaceful people here, and reliable. And here you are, trying to tear down one of Israel's mother cities. Why would you want to mess with GOD's legacy like that?"

20-21 Joab protested, "Believe me, you've got me all wrong. I'm not here to hurt anyone or destroy anything — not on your life! But a man from the hill country of Ephraim, Sheba son of Bicri by name, revolted against King David; hand him over, him only, and we'll get out of here."

The woman told Joab, "Sounds good. His head will be tossed to you from the wall."

22 The woman presented her strategy to the whole city and they did it: They cut off the head of Sheba son of Bicri and tossed it down to Joab. He then blew a blast on the ram's horn trumpet and the soldiers all went home. Joab returned to the king in Jerusalem.

23-26 Joab was again commander of the whole army of Israel. Benaiah son of Jehoiada was over the Kerethites and Pelethites; Adoniram over the work crews; Jehoshaphat son of Ahilud was clerk; Sheva was historian; Zadok and Abiathar were priests; Ira the Jairite was David's chaplain.

FAMINE AND WAR

21 ¹ There was a famine in David's time. It went on year after year after year—three years. David went to GOD seeking the reason. GOD said, "This is because there is blood on Saul and his house, from the time he massacred the Gibeonites."

² So the king called the Gibeonites together for consultation. (The Gibeonites were not part of Israel; they were what was left of the Amorites, and protected by a treaty with Israel. But Saul, a fanatic for the honor of Israel and Judah, tried to kill them off.)

³ David addressed the Gibeonites: "What can I do for you? How can I compensate you so that you will bless GOD's legacy of land and people?"

⁴ The Gibeonites replied, "We don't want any money from Saul and his family. And it's not up to us to put anyone in Israel to death."

But David persisted: "What are you saying I should do for you?"

⁵⁻⁶ Then they told the king, "The man who tried to get rid of us, who schemed to wipe us off the map of Israel—well, let seven of his sons be handed over to us to be executed—hanged before GOD at Gibeah of Saul, the holy mountain."

And David agreed, "I'll hand them over to you."

⁷⁻⁹ The king spared Mephibosheth son of Jonathan, the son of Saul, because of the promise David and Jonathan had spoken before GOD. But the king selected Armoni and Mephibosheth, the two sons that Rizpah daughter of Aiah had borne to Saul, plus the five sons that Saul's daughter Merab had borne to Adriel son of Barzillai the Meholathite. He turned them over to the Gibeonites who hanged them on the mountain before GOD—all seven died together. Harvest was just getting underway, the beginning of the barley harvest, when they were executed.

¹⁰ Rizpah daughter of Aiah took rough burlap and spread it out for herself on a rock from the beginning of the harvest until the heavy rains started. She kept the birds away from the bodies by day and the wild animals by night.

¹¹⁻¹⁴ David was told what she had done, this Rizpah daughter of Aiah and concubine of Saul. He then went and got the remains of Saul and Jonathan his son from the leaders at Jabesh Gilead (who had rescued them from the town square at Beth Shan where the Philistines had hung them after striking them down at Gilboa). He gathered up their remains and brought them together with the dead bodies of the seven who had just been hanged. The bodies were taken back to the land of Benjamin and given a decent burial in the tomb of Kish, Saul's father.

They did everything the king ordered to be done. That cleared things up: from then on God responded to Israel's prayers for the land.

¹⁵⁻¹⁷ War broke out again between the Philistines and Israel. David and his men went down to fight. David became exhausted. Ishbi-Benob, a warrior descended from Rapha, with a spear weighing nearly eight pounds and outfitted in brand-new armor, announced that he'd kill David. But Abishai son of Zeruiah came to the rescue, struck the Philistine, and killed him.

Then David's men swore to him, "No more fighting on the front-lines for you! Don't snuff out the lamp of Israel!"

¹⁸ Later there was another skirmish with the Philistines at Gob. That time Sibbecai the Hushathite killed Saph, another of the warriors descended from Rapha.

19   At yet another battle with the Philistines at Gob, Elhanan son of Jaar, the weaver of Bethlehem, killed Goliath the Gittite whose spear was as big as a flagpole.

20-21   Still another fight broke out in Gath. There was a giant there with six fingers on his hands and six toes on his feet — twenty-four fingers and toes! He was another of those descended from Rapha. He insulted Israel, and Jonathan son of Shimeah, David's brother, killed him.

22   These four were descended from Rapha in Gath. And they all were killed by David and his soldiers.

1   # 22

David prayed to GOD the words of this song after GOD saved him from all his enemies and from Saul.

2-3
GOD is bedrock under my feet,
>the castle in which I live,
>my rescuing knight.
My God — the high crag
>where I run for dear life,
>hiding behind the boulders,
>safe in the granite hideout;
My mountaintop refuge,
>he saves me from ruthless men.

4
I sing to GOD the Praise-Lofty,
>and find myself safe and saved.

5-6
The waves of death crashed over me,
>devil waters rushed over me.
Hell's ropes cinched me tight;
>death traps barred every exit.

7
A hostile world! I called to GOD,
>to my God I cried out.
From his palace he heard me call;
>my cry brought me right into his presence —
>a private audience!

8-16
Earth wobbled and lurched;
>the very heavens shook like leaves,
Quaked like aspen leaves
>because of his rage.
His nostrils flared, billowing smoke;
>his mouth spit fire.
Tongues of fire darted in and out;
>he lowered the sky.
He stepped down;
>under his feet an abyss opened up.
He rode a winged creature,
>swift on wind-wings.
He wrapped himself
>in a trenchcoat of black rain-cloud darkness.

But his cloud-brightness burst through,
    a grand comet of fireworks.
Then GOD thundered out of heaven;
    the High God gave a great shout.
God shot his arrows—pandemonium!
    He hurled his lightnings—a rout!
The secret sources of ocean were exposed,
    the hidden depths of earth lay uncovered
The moment GOD roared in protest,
    let loose his hurricane anger.

17-20
But me he caught—reached all the way
    from sky to sea; he pulled me out
Of that ocean of hate, that enemy chaos,
    the void in which I was drowning.
They hit me when I was down,
    but GOD stuck by me.
He stood me up on a wide-open field;
    I stood there saved—surprised to be loved!

21-25
GOD made my life complete
    when I placed all the pieces before him.
When I cleaned up my act,
    he gave me a fresh start.
Indeed, I've kept alert to GOD's ways;
    I haven't taken God for granted.
Every day I review the ways he works,
    I try not to miss a trick.
I feel put back together,
    and I'm watching my step.
GOD rewrote the text of my life
    when I opened the book of my heart to his eyes.

26-28
You stick by people who stick with you,
    you're straight with people who're straight with you,
You're good to good people,
    you shrewdly work around the bad ones.
You take the side of the down-and-out,
    but the stuck-up you take down a peg.

29-31
Suddenly, GOD, your light floods my path,
    GOD drives out the darkness.
I smash the bands of marauders,
    I vault the high fences.
What a God! His road
    stretches straight and smooth.
Every GOD-direction is road-tested.
    Everyone who runs toward him
Makes it.

32-46
Is there any god like GOD?

Are we not at bedrock?
Is not this the God who armed me well,
  then aimed me in the right direction?
Now I run like a deer;
  I'm king of the mountain.
He shows me how to fight;
  I can bend a bronze bow!
You protect me with salvation-armor;
  you touch me and I feel ten feet tall.
You cleared the ground under me
  so my footing was firm.
When I chased my enemies I caught them;
  I didn't let go till they were dead men.
I nailed them; they were down for good;
  then I walked all over them.
You armed me well for this fight;
  you smashed the upstarts.
You made my enemies turn tail,
  and I wiped out the haters.
They cried "uncle"
  but Uncle didn't come;
They yelled for GOD
  and got no for an answer.
I ground them to dust; they gusted in the wind.
  I threw them out, like garbage in the gutter.
You rescued me from a squabbling people;
  you made me a leader of nations.
People I'd never heard of served me;
  the moment they got wind of me they submitted.
They gave up; they came trembling from their hideouts.

47-51 Live, GOD! Blessing to my Rock,
  my towering Salvation-God!
This God set things right for me
  and shut up the people who talked back.
He rescued me from enemy anger.
  You pulled me from the grip of upstarts,
You saved me from the bullies.
  That's why I'm thanking you, GOD,
  all over the world.
That's why I'm singing songs
  that rhyme your name.
God's king takes the trophy;
  God's chosen is beloved.
I mean David and all his children —
  always.

1 **23** These are David's last words:

  The voice of the son of Jesse,
  the voice of the man God took to the top,

Whom the God of Jacob made king,
    and Israel's most popular singer!

2-7 GOD's Spirit spoke through me,
    his words took shape on my tongue.
The God of Israel spoke to me,
    Israel's Rock-Mountain said,
"Whoever governs fairly and well,
    who rules in the Fear-of-God,
Is like first light at daybreak
    without a cloud in the sky,
Like green grass carpeting earth,
    glistening under fresh rain."
And this is just how my regime has been,
    for God guaranteed his covenant with me,
Spelled it out plainly
    and kept every promised word—
My entire salvation,
    my every desire.
But the devil's henchmen are like thorns
    culled and piled as trash;
Better not try to touch them;
    keep your distance with a rake or hoe.
They'll make a glorious bonfire!

8 This is the listing of David's top men.

Josheb-Basshebeth, the Tahkemonite. He was chief of the Three. He once put his spear to work against eight hundred—killed them all in a day.

9-10 Eleazar son of Dodai the Ahohite was the next of the elite Three. He was with David when the Philistines poked fun at them at Pas Dammim. When the Philistines drew up for battle, Israel retreated. But Eleazar stood his ground and killed Philistines right and left until he was exhausted—but he never let go of his sword! A big win for GOD that day. The army then rejoined Eleazar, but all there was left to do was the cleanup.

11-12 Shammah son of Agee the Hararite was the third of the Three. The Philistines had mustered for battle at Lehi, where there was a field full of lentils. Israel fled before the Philistines, but Shammah took his stand at the center of the field, successfully defended it, and routed the Philistines. Another great victory for GOD!

13-17 One day during harvest, the Three parted from the Thirty and joined David at the Cave of Adullam. A squad of Philistines had set up camp in the Valley of Rephaim. While David was holed up in the Cave, the Philistines had their base camp in Bethlehem. David had a sudden craving and said, "Would I ever like a drink of water from the well at the gate of Bethlehem!" So the Three penetrated the Philistine lines, drew water from the well at the gate of Bethlehem, and brought it back to David. But David wouldn't drink it; he poured it out as an offering to GOD, saying, "There is no way, GOD, that I'll drink this! This isn't mere water, it's their life-blood—they risked their very lives to bring it!" So David refused to drink it.

This is the sort of thing that the Three did.

¹⁸⁻¹⁹ Abishai brother of Joab and son of Zeruiah was the head of the Thirty. He once got credit for killing three hundred with his spear, but he was never named in the same breath as the Three. He was the most respected of the Thirty and was their captain, but never got included among the Three.

²⁰⁻²¹ Benaiah son of Jehoiada from Kabzeel was a vigorous man who accomplished a great deal. He once killed two lion cubs in Moab. Another time, on a snowy day, he climbed down into a pit and killed a lion. Another time he killed a formidable Egyptian. The Egyptian was armed with a spear and Benaiah went against him with nothing but a walking stick; he seized the spear from his grip and killed him with his own spear.

²²⁻²³ These are the things that Benaiah son of Jehoiada is famous for. But neither did he ever get ranked with the Three. He was held in greatest respect among the Thirty, but he never got included with the Three. David put him in charge of his bodyguard.

THE THIRTY

²⁴⁻³⁹ "The Thirty" consisted of:
    Asahel brother of Joab;
    Elhanan son of Dodo of Bethlehem;
    Shammah the Harodite;
    Elika the Harodite;
    Helez the Paltite;
    Ira son of Ikkesh the Tekoite;
    Abiezer the Anathothite;
    Sibbecai the Hushathite;
    Zalmon the Ahohite;
    Maharai the Netophathite;
    Heled son of Baanah the Netophathite;
    Ithai son of Ribai from Gibeah of the Benjaminites;
    Benaiah the Pirathonite;
    Hiddai from the badlands of Gaash;
    Abi-Albon the Arbathite;
    Azmaveth the Barhumite;
    Eliahba the Shaalbonite;
    Jashen the Gizonite;
    Jonathan son of Shammah the Hararite;
    Ahiam son of Sharar the Urite;
    Eliphelet son of Ahasbai the Maacathite;
    Eliam son of Ahithophel the Gilonite;
    Hezro the Carmelite;
    Paarai the Arbite;
    Igal son of Nathan, commander of the army of Hagrites;
    Zelek the Ammonite;
    Naharai the Beerothite, weapon bearer of Joab son of Zeruiah;
    Ira the Ithrite;
    Gareb the Ithrite;
    Uriah the Hittite.
Thirty-seven, all told.

24 ¹⁻² Once again GOD's anger blazed out against Israel. He tested David by telling him, "Go and take a census of Israel and Judah." So David gave orders to Joab and the army officers under him, "Canvass all the tribes of Israel, from Dan to Beersheba, and get a count of the population. I want to know the number."

³ But Joab resisted the king: "May your GOD multiply people by the hundreds right before the eyes of my master the king, but why on earth would you do a thing like this?"

⁴⁻⁹ Nevertheless, the king insisted, and so Joab and the army officers left the king to take a census of Israel. They crossed the Jordan and began with Aroer and the town in the canyon of the Gadites near Jazer, proceeded through Gilead, passed Hermon, then on to Dan, but detoured Sidon. They covered Fort Tyre and all the Hivite and Canaanite cities, and finally reached the Negev of Judah at Beersheba. They canvassed the whole country and after nine months and twenty days arrived back in Jerusalem. Joab gave the results of the census to the king: 800,000 able-bodied fighting men in Israel; in Judah 500,000.

¹⁰ But when it was all done, David was overwhelmed with guilt because he had counted the people, replacing trust with statistics. And David prayed to GOD, "I have sinned badly in what I have just done. But now GOD forgive my guilt—I've been really stupid."

¹¹⁻¹² When David got up the next morning, the word of GOD had already come to Gad the prophet, David's spiritual advisor, "Go and give David this message: 'GOD has spoken thus: There are three things I can do to you; choose one out of the three and I'll see that it's done.'"

¹³ Gad came to deliver the message: "Do you want three years of famine in the land, or three months of running from your enemies while they chase you down, or three days of an epidemic on the country? Think it over and make up your mind. What shall I tell the one who sent me?"

¹⁴ David told Gad, "They're all terrible! But I'd rather be punished by GOD, whose mercy is great, than fall into human hands."

¹⁵⁻¹⁶ So GOD let loose an epidemic from morning until suppertime. From Dan to Beersheba seventy thousand people died. But when the angel reached out over Jerusalem to destroy it, GOD felt the pain of the terror and told the angel who was spreading death among the people, "Enough's enough! Pull back!"

The angel of GOD had just reached the threshing floor of Araunah the Jebusite. David looked up and saw the angel hovering between earth and sky, sword drawn and about to strike Jerusalem. David and the elders bowed in prayer and covered themselves with rough burlap.

¹⁷ When David saw the angel about to destroy the people, he prayed, "Please! I'm the one who sinned; I, the shepherd, did the wrong. But these sheep, what did they do wrong? Punish me and my family, not them."

¹⁸⁻¹⁹ That same day Gad came to David and said, "Go and build an altar on the threshing floor of Araunah the Jebusite." David did what Gad told him, what GOD commanded.

²⁰⁻²¹ Araunah looked up and saw David and his men coming his way; he met them, bowing deeply, honoring the king and saying, "Why has my master the king come to see me?"

"To buy your threshing floor," said David, "so I can build an altar to GOD here and put an end to this disaster."

22-23   "Oh," said Araunah, "let my master the king take and sacrifice whatever he wants. Look, here's an ox for the burnt offering and threshing paddles and ox-yokes for fuel — Araunah gives it all to the king! And may GOD, your God, act in your favor."

24-25   But the king said to Araunah, "No. I've got to buy it from you for a good price; I'm not going to offer GOD, my God, sacrifices that are no sacrifice."

So David bought the threshing floor and the ox, paying out fifty shekels of silver. He built an altar to GOD there and sacrificed burnt offerings and peace offerings. GOD was moved by the prayers and that was the end of the disaster.

1 & 2 KINGS

Sovereignty, *God's* sovereignty, is one of the most difficult things for people of faith to live out in everyday routines. But we have no choice: God is Sovereign. God rules. Not only in our personal affairs but in the cosmos. Not only in our times and places of worship but in office buildings, political affairs, factories, universities, hospitals—yes, even behind the scenes in saloons and rock concerts. It's a wild and extravagant notion, to be sure. But nothing in our Scriptures is attested to more frequently or emphatically.

Yet not much in our daily experience confirms it. Impersonal forces and arrogant egos compete for the last word in power. Most of us are knocked around much of the time by forces and wills that give no hint of God. Still, generation after generation, men and women of sound mind continue to give sober witness to God's sovereign rule. One of the enduring titles given to Jesus is "King."

So how do we manage to live believingly and obediently in and under this revealed sovereignty in a world that is mostly either ignorant or defiant of it?

Worship shaped by an obedient reading of Scripture is basic. We submit to having our imaginations and behaviors conditioned by the reality of God rather than by what is handed out in school curricula and media reporting. In the course of this worshipful listening, the books of Kings turn out to provide essential data on what we can expect as we live under God's sovereign rule.

The story of our ancestors, the Hebrew kings, began in the books of Samuel. This story makes it clear that it was not God's idea that the Hebrews have a king, but since they insisted, he let them have their way. But God never abdicated his sovereignty to any of the Hebrew kings; the idea was that they would represent *his* sovereignty, not that he would delegate his sovereignty to them.

But it never worked very well. After five hundred years and something over forty kings, there was not much to show for it. Even the bright spots — David and Hezekiah and Josiah — were not *very* bright. Human beings, no matter how well intentioned or gifted, don't seem to be able to represent God's rule anywhere close to satisfactory. The books of Kings, in that light, are a relentless exposition of failure — a relentless five-hundred-year documentation proving that the Hebrew demand of God to "have a king" was about the worst thing they could have asked for.

But through the centuries, readers of this text have commonly realized something else: In the midst of the incredible mess these kings are making of God's purposes, God continues to work his purposes and *uses them* in the work — doesn't discard them, doesn't detour around them; he uses them. They are part of his sovereign rule, whether they want to be or not, whether they know it or not. God's purposes *are* worked out in confrontation and revelation, in judgment and salvation, but they are worked out. God's rule is not imposed in the sense that he forces each man and woman into absolute conformity to justice and truth and righteousness. The rule is worked from within, much of the time invisible and unnoticed, but always patiently and resolutely *there*. The books of Kings provide a premier witness to the sovereignty of God carried out among some of the most unlikely and uncooperative people who have ever lived.

The benefit of reading these books is enormous. To begin with, our understanding and experience of God's sovereignty develops counter to all power-based and piety-based assumptions regarding God's effective rule. We quit spinning our wheels on utopian projects and dreams. Following that, we begin to realize that if God's sovereignty is never canceled out by the so deeply sin-flawed leaders ("kings") in both our culture and our church, we can quite cheerfully exult in God's sovereignty as it is being exercised (though often silently and hiddenly) in all the circumstantial details of the actual present.

ı KINGS

DAVID

¹⁻⁴ King David grew old. The years had caught up with him. Even though they piled blankets on him, he couldn't keep warm. So his servants said to him, "We're going to get a young virgin for our master the king to be at his side and look after him; she'll get in bed with you and arouse our master the king." So they searched the country of Israel for the most ravishing girl they could find; they found Abishag the Shunammite and brought her to the king. The girl was stunningly beautiful; she stayed at his side and looked after the king, but the king did not have sex with her.

⁵⁻⁶ At this time Adonijah, whose mother was Haggith, puffed himself up saying, "I'm the next king!" He made quite a splash, with chariots and riders and fifty men to run ahead of him. His father had spoiled him rotten as a child, never once reprimanding him. Besides that, he was very good-looking and the next in line after Absalom.

⁷⁻⁸ Adonijah talked with Joab son of Zeruiah and with Abiathar the priest, and they threw their weight on his side. But neither the priest Zadok, nor Benaiah son of Jehoiada, nor Nathan the prophet, nor Shimei and Rei, nor David's personal bodyguards supported Adonijah.

⁹⁻¹⁰ Next Adonijah held a coronation feast, sacrificing sheep, cattle, and grain-fed heifers at the Stone of Zoheleth near the Rogel Spring. He invited all his brothers, the king's sons, and everyone in Judah who had position and influence—but he did not invite the prophet Nathan, Benaiah, the bodyguards, or his brother Solomon.

¹¹⁻¹⁴ Nathan went to Bathsheba, Solomon's mother, "Did you know that Adonijah, Haggith's son, has taken over as king, and our master David doesn't know a thing about it? Quickly now, let me tell you how you can save both your own life and Solomon's. Go immediately to King David. Speak up: 'Didn't you, my master the king, promise me, "Your son Solomon will be king after me and sit on my throne"? So why is Adonijah now king?' While you're there talking with the king, I'll come in and corroborate your story."

¹⁵⁻¹⁶ Bathsheba went at once to the king in his palace bedroom. He was so old! Abishag was at his side making him comfortable. As Bathsheba bowed low, honoring the king, he said, "What do you want?"

¹⁷⁻²¹ "My master," she said, "you promised me in GOD's name, 'Your son Solomon will be king after me and sit on my throne.' And now look what's happened—Adonijah has taken over as king, and my master the king doesn't even know it! He has thrown a huge coronation feast—cattle and grain-fed heifers and sheep—inviting all the king's sons, the priest Abiathar, and Joab head of the army. But your servant Solomon was *not* invited. My master the king, every eye in Israel is watching you to see what you'll do—to see who will sit on the throne of my master the king after him. If you fail to act, the moment you're buried my son Solomon and I are as good as dead."

²²⁻²³ Abruptly, while she was telling the king all this, Nathan the prophet came in and was announced: "Nathan the prophet is here." He came before

the king, honoring him by bowing deeply, his face touching the ground.

24-27 "My master the king," Nathan began, "did you say, 'Adonijah shall be king after me and sit on my throne'? Because that's what's happening. He's thrown a huge coronation feast—cattle, grain-fed heifers, sheep—inviting all the king's sons, the army officers, and Abiathar the priest. They're having a grand time, eating and drinking and shouting, 'Long live King Adonijah!' But I wasn't invited, nor was the priest Zadok, nor Benaiah son of Jehoiada, nor your servant Solomon. Is this something that my master the king has done behind our backs, not telling your servants who you intended to be king after you?"

28 King David took action: "Get Bathsheba back in here." She entered and stood before the king.

29-30 The king solemnly promised, "As GOD lives, the God who delivered me from every kind of trouble, I'll do exactly what I promised in GOD's name, the God of Israel: Your son Solomon will be king after me and take my place on the throne. And I'll make sure it happens this very day."

31 Bathsheba bowed low, her face to the ground. Kneeling in reverence before the king she said, "Oh, may my master, King David, live forever!"

32 King David said, "Call Zadok the priest, Nathan the prophet, and Benaiah son of Jehoiada." They came to the king.

33-35 Then he ordered, "Gather my servants, then mount my son Solomon on my royal mule and lead him in procession down to Gihon. When you get there, Zadok the priest and Nathan the prophet will anoint him king over Israel. Then blow the ram's horn trumpet and shout, 'Long live King Solomon!' You will then accompany him as he enters and takes his place on my throne, succeeding me as king. I have named him ruler over Israel and Judah."

36-37 Benaiah son of Jehoiada backed the king: "Yes! And may GOD, the God of my master the king, confirm it! Just as GOD has been with my master the king, may he also be with Solomon and make his rule even greater than that of my master King David!"

38-40 Then Zadok the priest, Nathan the prophet, Benaiah son of Jehoiada, and the king's personal bodyguard (the Kerethites and Pelethites) went down, mounted Solomon on King David's mule, and paraded with him to Gihon. Zadok the priest brought a flask of oil from the sanctuary and anointed Solomon. They blew the ram's horn trumpet and everyone shouted, "Long live King Solomon!" Everyone joined the fanfare, the band playing and the people singing, the very earth reverberating to the sound.

41 Adonijah and his retinue of guests were just finishing their "coronation" feast when they heard it. When Joab heard the blast of the ram's horn trumpet he said, "What's going on here? What's all this uproar?"

42 Suddenly, in the midst of the questioning, Jonathan son of Abiathar the priest, showed up. Adonijah said, "Welcome! A brave and good man like you must have good news."

43-48 But Jonathan answered, "Hardly! Our master King David has just made Solomon king! And the king has surrounded him with Zadok the priest, Nathan the prophet, Benaiah son of Jehoiada, with the Kerethites and Pelethites; and they've mounted Solomon on the royal mule. Zadok the priest and Nathan the prophet have anointed him king at Gihon and the parade is headed up this way singing—a great fanfare! The city is rocking! That's what you're hearing. Here's the crowning touch—Solomon is

seated on the throne of the kingdom! And that's not all: The king's servants have come to give their blessing to our master King David saying,
'God make Solomon's name even more honored than yours, and make his
rule greater than yours!' On his deathbed the king worshiped God and
prayed, 'Blessed be GOD, Israel's God, who has provided a successor to my
throne, and I've lived to see it!'"

49-50 Panicked, Adonijah's guests got out of there, scattering every which way.
But Adonijah himself, afraid for his life because of Solomon, fled to the
sanctuary and grabbed the horns of the Altar.

51 Solomon was told, "Adonijah, fearful of King Solomon, has taken sanctuary and seized the horns of the Altar and is saying, 'I'm not leaving
until King Solomon promises that he won't kill me.'"

52-53 Solomon then said, "If he proves to be a man of honor, not a hair of his
head will be hurt; but if there is evil in him, he'll die." Solomon summoned
him and they brought him from the Altar. Adonijah came and bowed
down, honoring the king. Solomon dismissed him, "Go home."

1-4 2 When David's time to die approached, he charged his son Solomon,
saying, "I'm about to go the way of all the earth, but you — be strong;
show what you're made of! Do what GOD tells you. Walk in the paths
he shows you: Follow the life-map absolutely, keep an eye out for the signposts, his course for life set out in the revelation to Moses; then you'll get on
well in whatever you do and wherever you go. Then GOD will confirm what
he promised me when he said, 'If your sons watch their step, staying true to
me heart and soul, you'll always have a successor on Israel's throne.'

5-6 "And don't forget what Joab son of Zeruiah did to the two commanders
of Israel's army, to Abner son of Ner and to Amasa son of Jether. He murdered them in cold blood, acting in peacetime as if he were at war, and has
been stained with that blood ever since. Do what you think best with him,
but by no means let him get off scot-free — make him pay.

7 "But be generous to the sons of Barzillai the Gileadite — extend every
hospitality to them; that's the way they treated me when I was running for
my life from Absalom your brother.

8-9 "You also will have to deal with Shimei son of Gera the Benjaminite
from Bahurim, the one who cursed me so viciously when I was on my way
to Mahanaim. Later, when he welcomed me back at the Jordan, I promised
him under GOD, 'I won't put you to death.' But neither should you treat
him as if nothing ever happened. You're wise, you know how to handle
these things. You'll know what to do to make him pay before he dies."

10-12 Then David joined his ancestors. He was buried in the City of David.
David ruled Israel for forty years — seven years in Hebron and another
thirty-three in Jerusalem. Solomon took over on the throne of his father
David; he had a firm grip on the kingdom.

SOLOMON

13-14 Adonijah son of Haggith came to Bathsheba, Solomon's mother. She
said, "Do you come in peace?"

He said, "In peace." And then, "May I say something to you?"

"Go ahead," she said, "speak."

15-16　"You know that I had the kingdom right in my hands and everyone expected me to be king, and then the whole thing backfired and the kingdom landed in my brother's lap—GOD's doing. So now I have one request to ask of you; please don't refuse me."

"Go ahead, ask," she said.

17　"Ask King Solomon—he won't turn *you* down—to give me Abishag the Shunammite as my wife."

18　"Certainly," said Bathsheba. "I'll speak to the king for you."

19　Bathsheba went to King Solomon to present Adonijah's request. The king got up and welcomed her, bowing respectfully, and returned to his throne. Then he had a throne put in place for his mother, and she sat at his right hand.

20　She said, "I have a small favor to ask of you. Don't refuse me."

The king replied, "Go ahead, Mother; of course I won't refuse you."

21　She said, "Give Abishag the Shunammite to your brother Adonijah as his wife."

22　King Solomon answered his mother, "What kind of favor is this, asking that Abishag the Shunammite be given to Adonijah? Why don't you just ask me to hand over the whole kingdom to him on a platter since he is my older brother and has Abiathar the priest and Joab son of Zeruiah on his side!"

23-24　Then King Solomon swore under GOD, "May God do his worst to me if Adonijah doesn't pay for this with his life! As surely as GOD lives, the God who has set me firmly on the throne of my father David and has put me in charge of the kingdom just as he promised, Adonijah will die for this—today!"

25　King Solomon dispatched Benaiah son of Jehoiada; he struck Adonijah and he died.

26　The king then told Abiathar the priest, "You're exiled to your place in Anathoth. You deserve death but I'm not going to kill you—for now anyway—because you were in charge of the Chest of our ruling GOD in the company of David my father, and because you shared all the hard times with my father."

27　Solomon stripped Abiathar of his priesthood, fulfilling GOD's word at Shiloh regarding the family of Eli.

28-29　When this news reached Joab, this Joab who had conspired with Adonijah (although he had remained loyal in the Absalom affair), he took refuge in the sanctuary of GOD, seizing the horns of the Altar and holding on for dear life. King Solomon was told that Joab had escaped to the sanctuary of GOD and was clinging to the Altar; he immediately sent Benaiah son of Jehoiada with orders, "Kill him."

30　Benaiah went to the sanctuary of GOD and said, "King's orders: Come out."

He said, "No—I'll die right here."

Benaiah went back to the king and reported, "This was Joab's answer."

31-33　The king said, "Go ahead then, do what he says: Kill him and bury him. Absolve me and my father's family of the guilt from Joab's senseless murders. GOD is avenging those bloody murders on Joab's head. Two men he murdered, men better by far than he ever was: Behind my father's back he brutally murdered Abner son of Ner, commander of Israel's army, and Amasa son of Jether, commander of Judah's army. Responsibility for their murders is forever fixed on Joab and his descendants; but for David and his descendants, his family and kingdom, the final verdict is GOD's peace."

34-35 So Benaiah son of Jehoiada went back, struck Joab, and killed him. He was buried in his family plot out in the desert. The king appointed Benaiah son of Jehoiada over the army in place of Joab, and replaced Abiathar with Zadok the priest.

36-37 The king next called in Shimei and told him, "Build yourself a house in Jerusalem and live there, but you are not to leave the area. If you so much as cross the Brook Kidron, you're as good as dead—you will have decreed your own death sentence."

38 Shimei answered the king, "Oh, thank you! Your servant will do exactly as my master the king says." Shimei lived in Jerusalem a long time.

39-40 But it so happened that three years later, two of Shimei's slaves ran away to Achish son of Maacah, king of Gath. Shimei was told, "Your slaves are in Gath." Shimei sprang into action, saddled his donkey, and went to Achish in Gath looking for his slaves. And then he came back, bringing his slaves.

41 Solomon was told, "Shimei left Jerusalem for Gath, and now he's back."

42-43 Solomon then called for Shimei and said, "Didn't I make you promise me under GOD, and give you a good warning besides, that you would not leave this area? That if you left you would have decreed your own death sentence? And didn't you say, 'Oh, thank you—I'll do exactly as you say'? So why didn't you keep your sacred promise and do what I ordered?"

44-45 Then the king told Shimei, "Deep in your heart you know all the evil that you did to my father David; GOD will now avenge that evil on you. But King Solomon will be blessed and the rule of David will be a sure thing under GOD forever."

46 The king then gave orders to Benaiah son of Jehoiada; he went out and struck Shimei dead.

The kingdom was now securely in Solomon's grasp.

1-3 **3** Solomon arranged a marriage contract with Pharaoh, king of Egypt. He married Pharaoh's daughter and brought her to the City of David until he had completed building his royal palace and GOD's Temple and the wall around Jerusalem. Meanwhile, the people were worshiping at local shrines because at that time no temple had yet been built to the Name of GOD. Solomon loved GOD and continued to live in the God-honoring ways of David his father, except that he also worshiped at the local shrines, offering sacrifices and burning incense.

4-5 The king went to Gibeon, the most prestigious of the local shrines, to worship. He sacrificed a thousand Whole-Burnt-Offerings on that altar. That night, there in Gibeon, GOD appeared to Solomon in a dream: God said, "What can I give you? Ask."

6 Solomon said, "You were extravagantly generous in love with David my father, and he lived faithfully in your presence, his relationships were just and his heart right. And you have persisted in this great and generous love by giving him—and this very day!—a son to sit on his throne.

7-8 "And now here I am: GOD, my God, you have made me, your servant, ruler of the kingdom in place of David my father. I'm too young for this, a mere child! I don't know the ropes, hardly know the 'ins' and 'outs' of this job. And here I am, set down in the middle of the people you've chosen, a great people—far too many to ever count.

9 "Here's what I want: Give me a God-listening heart so I can lead your people well, discerning the difference between good and evil. For who on their own is capable of leading your glorious people?"

10-14 God, the Master, was delighted with Solomon's response. And God said to him, "Because you have asked for this and haven't grasped after a long life, or riches, or the doom of your enemies, but you have asked for the ability to lead and govern well, I'll give you what you've asked for — I'm giving you a wise and mature heart. There's never been one like you before; and there'll be no one after. As a bonus, I'm giving you both the wealth and glory you didn't ask for — there's not a king anywhere who will come up to your mark. And if you stay on course, keeping your eye on the life-map and the God-signs as your father David did, I'll also give you a long life."

15 Solomon woke up — what a dream! He returned to Jerusalem, took his place before the Chest of the Covenant of God, and worshiped by sacrificing Whole-Burnt-Offerings and Peace-Offerings. Then he laid out a banquet for everyone in his service.

16-21 The very next thing, two prostitutes showed up before the king. The one woman said, "My master, this woman and I live in the same house. While we were living together, I had a baby. Three days after I gave birth, this woman also had a baby. We were alone — there wasn't anyone else in the house except for the two of us. The infant son of this woman died one night when she rolled over on him in her sleep. She got up in the middle of the night and took my son — I was sound asleep, mind you! — and put him at her breast and put her dead son at my breast. When I got up in the morning to nurse my son, here was this dead baby! But when I looked at him in the morning light, I saw immediately that he wasn't my baby."

22 "Not so!" said the other woman. "The living one's mine; the dead one's yours."

The first woman countered, "No! Your son's the dead one; mine's the living one."

They went back and forth this way in front of the king.

23 The king said, "What are we to do? This woman says, 'The living son is mine and the dead one is yours,' and this woman says, 'No, the dead one's yours and the living one's mine.'"

24 After a moment the king said, "Bring me a sword." They brought the sword to the king.

25 Then he said, "Cut the living baby in two — give half to one and half to the other."

26 The real mother of the living baby was overcome with emotion for her son and said, "Oh no, master! Give her the whole baby alive; don't kill him!"

But the other one said, "If I can't have him, you can't have him — cut away!"

27 The king gave his decision: "Give the living baby to the first woman. Nobody is going to kill this baby. She is the real mother."

28 The word got around — everyone in Israel heard of the king's judgment. They were all in awe of the king, realizing that it was God's wisdom that enabled him to judge truly.

1-2 **4** King Solomon was off to a good start ruling Israel. These were the leaders in his government:

2-6 Azariah son of Zadok — the priest;

Elihoreph and Ahijah, sons of Shisha — secretaries;
Jehoshaphat son of Ahilud — historian;
Benaiah son of Jehoiada — commander of the army;
Zadok and Abiathar — priests;
Azariah son of Nathan — in charge of the regional managers;
Zabud son of Nathan — priest and friend to the king;
Ahishar — manager of the palace;
Adoniram son of Abda — manager of the slave labor.

7-19 Solomon had twelve regional managers distributed throughout Israel. They were responsible for supplying provisions for the king and his administration. Each was in charge of bringing supplies for one month of the year. These are the names:

Ben-Hur in the Ephraim hills;
Ben-Deker in Makaz, Shaalbim, Beth Shemesh, and Elon Bethhanan;
Ben-Hesed in Arubboth — this included Socoh and all of Hepher;
Ben-Abinadab in Naphoth Dor (he was married to Solomon's daughter Taphath);
Baana son of Ahilud in Taanach and Megiddo, all of Beth Shan next to Zarethan below Jezreel, and from Beth Shan to Abel Meholah over to Jokmeam;
Ben-Geber in Ramoth Gilead — this included the villages of Jair son of Manasseh in Gilead and the region of Argob in Bashan with its sixty large walled cities with bronze-studded gates;
Ahinadab son of Iddo in Mahanaim;
Ahimaaz in Naphtali (he was married to Solomon's daughter Basemath);
Baana son of Hushai in Asher and Aloth;
Jehoshaphat son of Paruah in Issachar;
Shimei son of Ela in Benjamin;
Geber son of Uri in Gilead — this was the country of Sihon king of the Amorites and also of Og king of Bashan; he managed the whole district by himself.

SOLOMON'S PROSPERITY

20-21 Judah and Israel were densely populated — like sand on an ocean beach! All their needs were met; they ate and drank and were happy. Solomon was sovereign over all the kingdoms from the River Euphrates in the east to the country of the Philistines in the west, all the way to the border of Egypt. They brought tribute and were vassals of Solomon all his life.

22-23 One day's food supply for Solomon's household was:

185 bushels of fine flour
375 bushels of meal
10 grain-fed cattle
20 range cattle
100 sheep

and miscellaneous deer, gazelles, roebucks, and choice fowl.

24-25 Solomon was sovereign over everything, countries and kings, west of the River Euphrates from Tiphsah to Gaza. Peace reigned everywhere. Throughout Solomon's life, everyone in Israel and Judah lived safe and sound, all of them from Dan in the north to Beersheba in the south — content with what they had.

26-28 Solomon had forty thousand stalls for chariot horses and twelve thousand horsemen. The district managers, each according to his assigned month, delivered food supplies for King Solomon and all who sat at the king's table; there was always plenty. They also brought to the designated place their assigned quota of barley and straw for the horses.

29-34 God gave Solomon wisdom—the deepest of understanding and the largest of hearts. There was nothing beyond him, nothing he couldn't handle. Solomon's wisdom outclassed the vaunted wisdom of wise men of the East, outshone the famous wisdom of Egypt. He was wiser than anyone— wiser than Ethan the Ezrahite, wiser than Heman, wiser than Calcol and Darda the sons of Mahol. He became famous among all the surrounding nations. He created 3,000 proverbs; his songs added up to 1,005. He knew all about plants, from the huge cedar that grows in Lebanon to the tiny hyssop that grows in the cracks of a wall. He understood everything about animals and birds, reptiles and fish. Sent by kings from all over the earth who had heard of his reputation, people came from far and near to listen to the wisdom of Solomon.

INTERNATIONAL FAME

1-4 **5** Hiram king of Tyre sent ambassadors to Solomon when he heard that he had been crowned king in David's place. Hiram had loved David his whole life. Solomon responded, saying, "You know that David my father was not able to build a temple in honor of GOD because of the wars he had to fight on all sides, until GOD finally put them down. But now GOD has provided peace all around—no one against us, nothing at odds with us.

5-6 "Now here is what I want to do: Build a temple in honor of GOD, *my* God, following the promise that GOD gave to David my father, namely, 'Your son whom I will provide to succeed you as king, he will build a house in my honor.' And here is how you can help: Give orders for cedars to be cut from the Lebanon forest; my loggers will work alongside yours and I'll pay your men whatever wage you set. We both know that there is no one like you Sidonians for cutting timber."

7 When Hiram got Solomon's message, he was delighted, exclaiming, "Blessed be GOD for giving David such a wise son to rule this flourishing people!"

8-9 Then he sent this message to Solomon: "I received your request for the cedars and cypresses. It's as good as done—your wish is my command. My lumberjacks will haul the timbers from the Lebanon forest to the sea, assemble them into log rafts, float them to the place you set, then have them disassembled for you to haul away. All I want from you is that you feed my crew."

10-12 In this way Hiram supplied all the cedar and cypress timber that Solomon wanted. In his turn, Solomon gave Hiram 125,000 bushels of wheat and 115,000 gallons of virgin olive oil. He did this every year. And GOD, for his part, gave Solomon wisdom, just as he had promised. The healthy peace between Hiram and Solomon was formalized by a treaty.

THE TEMPLE WORK BEGINS

13-18 King Solomon raised a workforce of thirty thousand men from all over Israel. He sent them in shifts of ten thousand each month to the Lebanon forest;

they would work a month in Lebanon and then be at home two months. Adoniram was in charge of the work crew. Solomon also had seventy thousand unskilled workers and another eighty thousand stonecutters up in the hills—plus thirty-three hundred foremen managing the project and supervising the work crews. Following the king's orders, they quarried huge blocks of the best stone—dressed stone for the foundation of The Temple. Solomon and Hiram's construction workers, assisted by the men of Gebal, cut and prepared the timber and stone for building The Temple.

1-6   6 Four hundred and eighty years after the Israelites came out of Egypt, in the fourth year of Solomon's rule over Israel, in the month of Ziv, the second month, Solomon started building The Temple of GOD. The Temple that King Solomon built to GOD was ninety feet long, thirty feet wide, and forty-five feet high. There was a porch across the thirty-foot width of The Temple that extended out fifteen feet. Within The Temple he made narrow, deep-silled windows. Against the outside walls he built a supporting structure in which there were smaller rooms: The lower floor was seven and a half feet wide, the middle floor nine feet, and the third floor ten and a half feet. He had projecting ledges built into the outside Temple walls to support the buttressing beams.

7   The stone blocks for the building of The Temple were all dressed at the quarry so that the building site itself was reverently quiet—no noise from hammers and chisels and other iron tools.

8-10   The entrance to the ground floor was at the south end of The Temple; stairs led to the second floor and then to the third. Solomon built and completed The Temple, finishing it off with roof beams and planks of cedar. The supporting structure along the outside walls was attached to The Temple with cedar beams and the rooms in it were seven and a half feet tall.

11-13   The word of GOD came to Solomon saying, "About this Temple you are building—what's important is that you *live* the way I've set out for you and *do* what I tell you, following my instructions carefully and obediently. Then I'll complete in you the promise I made to David your father. I'll personally take up my residence among the Israelites—I won't desert my people Israel."

14-18   Solomon built and completed The Temple. He paneled the interior walls from floor to ceiling with cedar planks; for flooring he used cypress. The thirty feet at the rear of The Temple he made into an Inner Sanctuary, cedar planks from floor to ceiling—the Holy of Holies. The Main Sanctuary area in front was sixty feet long. The entire interior of The Temple was cedar, with carvings of fruits and flowers. All cedar—none of the stone was exposed.

19-22   The Inner Sanctuary within The Temple was for housing the Chest of the Covenant of God. This Inner Sanctuary was a cube, thirty feet each way, all plated with gold. The Altar of cedar was also gold-plated. Everywhere you looked there was pure gold: gold chains strung in front of the gold-plated Inner Sanctuary—gold everywhere—walls, ceiling, floor, and Altar. Dazzling!

23-28   Then he made two cherubim, gigantic angel-like figures, from olivewood. Each was fifteen feet tall. The outstretched wings of the cherubim (they were identical in size and shape) measured another fifteen feet. He placed the two cherubim, their wings spread, in the Inner Sanctuary. The combined wingspread stretched the width of the room, the wing of one cherub touched one wall, the wing of the other the other wall, and the wings touched in the middle. The cherubim were gold-plated.

29-30 He then carved engravings of cherubim, palm trees, and flower blossoms on all the walls of both the Inner and the Main Sanctuary. And all the floors of both inner and outer rooms were gold-plated.

31-32 He constructed doors of olivewood for the entrance to the Inner Sanctuary; the lintel and doorposts were five-sided. The doors were also carved with cherubim, palm trees, and flowers, and then covered with gold leaf.

33-35 Similarly, he built the entrance to the Main Sanctuary using olivewood for the doorposts but these doorposts were four-sided. The doors were of cypress, split into two panels, each panel swinging separately. These also were carved with cherubim, palm trees, and flowers, and plated with finely hammered gold leaf.

36 He built the inner court with three courses of dressed stones topped with a course of planed cedar timbers.

37-38 The foundation for GOD's Temple was laid in the fourth year in the month of Ziv. It was completed in the eleventh year in the month of Bul (the eighth month) down to the last detail, just as planned. It took Solomon seven years to build it.

1-5 It took Solomon another thirteen years to finish building his own palace complex. He built the Palace of the Forest of Lebanon a hundred and fifty feet long, seventy-five feet wide, and forty-five feet high. There were four rows of cedar columns supporting forty-five cedar beams, fifteen in each row, and then roofed with cedar. Windows in groupings of three were set high in the walls on either side. All the doors were rectangular and arranged symmetrically.

6 He built a colonnaded courtyard seventy-five feet long and forty-five wide. It had a roofed porch at the front with ample eaves.

7 He built a court room, the Hall of Justice, where he would decide judicial matters, and paneled it with cedar.

8 He built his personal residence behind the Hall on a similar plan. Solomon also built another one just like it for Pharaoh's daughter, whom he had married.

9-12 No expense was spared—everything here, inside and out, from foundation to roof was constructed using high-quality stone, accurately cut and shaped and polished. The foundation stones were huge, ranging in size from twelve to fifteen feet, and of the very best quality. The finest stone was used above the foundation, shaped to size and trimmed with cedar. The courtyard was enclosed with a wall made of three layers of stone and topped with cedar timbers, just like the one in the porch of The Temple of GOD.

13-14 King Solomon sent to Tyre and asked Hiram (not the king; another Hiram) to come. Hiram's mother was a widow from the tribe of Naphtali. His father was a Tyrian and a master worker in bronze. Hiram was a real artist—he could do anything with bronze. He came to King Solomon and did all the bronze work.

15-22 First he cast two pillars in bronze, each twenty-seven feet tall and eighteen feet in circumference. He then cast two capitals in bronze to set on the pillars; each capital was seven and a half feet high and flared at the top in the shape of a lily. Each capital was dressed with an elaborate filigree of seven braided chains and a double row of two hundred pomegranates, setting the pillars off magnificently. He set the pillars up in the entrance porch to The Temple; the pillar to the south he named Security (Jachin) and the pillar to the north Stability (Boaz). The capitals were in the shape of lilies.

22-24 When the pillars were finished, Hiram's next project was to make the Sea — an immense round basin of cast metal fifteen feet in diameter, seven and a half feet tall, and forty-five feet in circumference. Just under the rim there were two bands of decorative gourds, ten gourds to each foot and a half. The gourds were cast in one piece with the Sea.

25-26 The Sea was set on twelve bulls, three facing north, three facing west, three facing south, and three facing east; the bulls faced outward supporting the Sea on their hindquarters. The Sea was three inches thick and flared at the rim like a cup, or like a lily. It held about 11,500 gallons.

27-33 Hiram also made ten washstands of bronze. Each was six feet square and four and a half feet tall. They were made like this: Panels were fastened to the uprights. Lions, bulls, and cherubim were represented on the panels and uprights. Beveled wreath-work bordered the lions and bulls above and below. Each stand was mounted on four bronze wheels with bronze axles. The uprights were cast with decorative relief work. Each stand held a basin on a circular engraved support a foot and a half deep set on a pedestal two and a quarter feet square. The washstand itself was square. The axles were attached under the stand and the wheels fixed to them. The wheels were twenty-seven inches in diameter; they were designed like chariot wheels. Everything — axles, rims, spokes, and hubs — was of cast metal.

34-37 There was a handle at the four corners of each washstand, the handles cast in one piece with the stand. At the top of the washstand there was a ring about nine inches deep. The uprights and handles were cast with the stand. Everything and every available surface was engraved with cherubim, lions, and palm trees, bordered by arabesques. The washstands were identical, all cast in the same mold.

38-40 He also made ten bronze washbasins, each six feet in diameter with a capacity of 230 gallons, one basin for each of the ten washstands. He arranged five stands on the south side of The Temple and five on the north. The Sea was placed at the southeast corner of The Temple. Hiram then fashioned the various utensils: buckets and shovels and bowls.

40-45 Hiram completed all the work he set out to do for King Solomon on The Temple of God:

> two pillars;
> two capitals on top of the pillars;
> two decorative filigrees for the capitals;
> four hundred pomegranates for the two filigrees
>   (a double row of pomegranates for each filigree);
> ten washstands each with its washbasin;
> one Sea;

twelve bulls under the Sea;
miscellaneous buckets, shovels, and bowls.

45-47 All these artifacts that Hiram made for King Solomon for The Temple of GOD were of burnished bronze. He cast them in clay in a foundry on the Jordan plain between Succoth and Zarethan. These artifacts were never weighed—there were far too many! Nobody has any idea how much bronze was used.

48-50 Solomon was also responsible for all the furniture and accessories in The Temple of GOD:

the gold Altar;
the gold Table that held the Bread of the Presence;
the pure gold candelabras, five to the right and five to the
    left in front of the Inner Sanctuary;
the gold flowers, lamps, and tongs;
the pure gold dishes, wick trimmers, sprinkling bowls, ladles, and
    censers;
the gold sockets for the doors of the Inner Sanctuary, the Holy of
    Holies, used also for the doors of the Main Sanctuary.

51 That completed all the work King Solomon did on The Temple of GOD. He then brought in the items consecrated by his father David, the silver and the gold and the artifacts. He placed them all in the treasury of GOD's Temple.

1-2 8Bringing all this to a climax, King Solomon called in the leaders of Israel, all the heads of the tribes and the family patriarchs, to bring up the Chest of the Covenant of GOD from Zion, the City of David. And they came, all Israel before King Solomon in the month of Ethanim, the seventh month, for the great autumn festival.

3-5 With all Israel's leaders present, the priests took up the Chest of GOD and carried up the Chest and the Tent of Meeting and all the holy vessels that went with the Tent. King Solomon and the entire congregation of Israel were there at the Chest worshiping and sacrificing huge numbers of sheep and cattle—so many that no one could keep track.

6-9 Then the priests brought the Chest of the Covenant of GOD to its place in the Inner Sanctuary, the Holy of Holies, under the wings of the cherubim. The outspread wings of the cherubim stretched over the Chest and its poles. The poles were so long that their ends could be seen from the entrance to the Inner Sanctuary, but were not noticeable farther out. They're still there today. There was nothing in the Chest but the two stone tablets that Moses had placed in it at Horeb where GOD made a covenant with Israel after bringing them up from Egypt.

THE TEMPLE FINISHED, DEDICATED, FILLED

10-11 When the priests left the Holy Place, a cloud filled The Temple of GOD. The priests couldn't carry out their priestly duties because of the cloud—the glory of GOD filled The Temple of GOD!

12-13   Then Solomon spoke:

> God has told us that he lives in the dark
>   where no one can see him;
> I've built this splendid Temple, O God,
>   to mark your invisible presence forever.

14   The king then turned to face the congregation and blessed them:

15-16   "Blessed be God, the God of Israel, who spoke personally to my father David. Now he has kept the promise he made when he said, 'From the day I brought my people Israel from Egypt, I haven't set apart one city among the tribes of Israel to build a Temple to fix my Name there. But I did choose David to rule my people Israel.'

17-19   "My father David had it in his heart to build a Temple honoring the Name of God, the God of Israel. But God told him 'It was good that you wanted to build a Temple in my honor—most commendable! But you are not the one to do it—your son will build it to honor my Name.'

20-21   "God has done what he said he would do: I have succeeded David my father and ruled over Israel just as God promised; and now I've built a Temple to honor God, the God of Israel, and I've secured a place for the Chest that holds the covenant of God, the covenant that he made with our ancestors when he brought them up from the land of Egypt."

22-25   Before the entire congregation of Israel, Solomon took a position before the Altar, spread his hands out before heaven, and prayed,

> O God, God of Israel, there is no God like you in the skies above or on the earth below who unswervingly keeps covenant with his servants and relentlessly loves them as they sincerely live in obedience to your way. You kept your word to David my father, your personal word. You did exactly what you promised—every detail. The proof is before us today!
>
> Keep it up, God, O God of Israel! Continue to keep the promises you made to David my father when you said, "You'll always have a descendant to represent my rule on Israel's throne, on the condition that your sons are as careful to live obediently in my presence as you have."

26   O God of Israel, let this all happen;
        confirm and establish it!

27-32   Can it be that God will actually move into our neighborhood? Why, the cosmos itself isn't large enough to give you breathing room, let alone this Temple I've built. Even so, I'm bold to ask: Pay attention to these my prayers, both intercessory and personal, O God, my God. Listen to my prayers, energetic and devout, that I'm setting before you right now. Keep your eyes open to this Temple night and day, this place of which you said, "My Name will be honored there," and listen to the prayers that I pray at this place.

Listen from your home in heaven
and when you hear, forgive.

When someone hurts a neighbor and promises to make things right, and then comes and repeats the promise before your Altar in this Temple, listen from heaven and act accordingly: Judge your servants, making the offender pay for his offense and setting the offended free of any charges.

33-34   When your people Israel are beaten by an enemy because they've sinned against you, but then turn to you and acknowledge your rule in prayers desperate and devout in this Temple,

Listen from your home in heaven,
forgive the sin of your people Israel,
return them to the land you gave their ancestors.

35-36   When the skies shrivel up and there is no rain because your people have sinned against you, but then they pray at this place, acknowledging your rule and quitting their sins because you have scourged them,

Listen from your home in heaven,
forgive the sins of your servants, your people Israel.

Then start over with them: Train them to live right and well; send rain on the land you gave your people as an inheritance.

37-40   When disasters strike, famine or catastrophe, crop failure or disease, locust or beetle, or when an enemy attacks their defenses — calamity of any sort — any prayer that's prayed from anyone at all among your people Israel, hearts penetrated by the disaster, hands and arms thrown out to this Temple for help,

Listen from your home in heaven.

Forgive and go to work on us. Give what each deserves, for you know each life from the inside (you're the only one with such "inside knowledge"!) so that they'll live before you in lifelong reverent and believing obedience on this land you gave our ancestors.

41-43   And don't forget the foreigner who is not a member of your people Israel but has come from a far country because of your reputation. People *are* going to be attracted here by your great reputation, your wonder-working power, who come to pray at this Temple.

Listen from your home in heaven.

Honor the prayers of the foreigner so that people all over the world will know who you are and what you're like and will live in reverent obedience before you, just as your own people Israel do; so they'll know that you personally make this Temple that I've built what it is.

44-51   When your people go to war against their enemies at the time and place you send them and they pray to GOD toward the city you chose and this Temple I've built to honor your Name,

Listen from heaven to what they pray and ask for,
and do what's right for them.

When they sin against you—and they certainly will; there's no
one without sin!—and in anger you turn them over to the enemy
and they are taken captive to the enemy's land, whether far or near,
but repent in the country of their captivity and pray with changed
hearts in their exile, "We've sinned; we've done wrong; we've been
most wicked," and turn back to you heart and soul in the land of the
enemy who conquered them, and pray to you toward their homeland, the land you gave their ancestors, toward the city you chose,
and this Temple I have built to the honor of your Name,

Listen from your home in heaven
to their prayers desperate and devout
and do what is best for them.

Forgive your people who have sinned against you; forgive their gross
rebellions and move their captors to treat them with compassion.
They are, after all, your people and your precious inheritance whom
you rescued from the heart of that iron-smelting furnace, Egypt!

52-53   O be alert and attentive to the needy prayers of me, your servant,
and your dear people Israel; listen every time they cry out to you! You
handpicked them from all the peoples on earth to be your very own
people, as you announced through your servant Moses when you, O
GOD, in your masterful rule, delivered our ancestors from Egypt.

54-55   Having finished praying to GOD—all these bold and passionate prayers—
Solomon stood up before GOD's Altar where he had been kneeling all this
time, his arms stretched upward to heaven. Standing, he blessed the whole
congregation of Israel, blessing them at the top of his lungs:

56-58   "Blessed be GOD, who has given peace to his people Israel just as he said
he'd do. Not one of all those good and wonderful words that he spoke
through Moses has misfired. May GOD, our very own God, continue to
be with us just as he was with our ancestors—may he never give up and
walk out on us. May he keep us centered and devoted to him, following the
life path he has cleared, watching the signposts, walking at the pace and
rhythms he laid down for our ancestors.

59-61   "And let these words that I've prayed in the presence of GOD be always
right there before him, day and night, so that he'll do what is right for me,
to guarantee justice for his people Israel day after day after day. Then all
the people on earth will know GOD is the true God; there is no other God.
And you, your lives must be totally obedient to GOD, our personal God,
following the life path he has cleared, alert and attentive to everything he
has made plain this day."

62-63   The king and all Israel with him then worshiped, offering sacrifices to
GOD. Solomon offered Peace-Offerings, sacrificing to GOD 22,000 cattle

and 120,000 sheep. This is how the king and all Israel dedicated The Temple of GOD.

⁶⁴ That same day, the king set apart the central area of the Courtyard in front of GOD's Temple for sacred use and there sacrificed the Whole-Burnt-Offerings, Grain-Offerings, and fat from the Peace-Offerings — the bronze Altar was too small to handle all these offerings.

⁶⁵⁻⁶⁶ This is how Solomon kept the great autumn feast, and all Israel with him, people there all the way from the far northeast (the Entrance to Hamath) to the far southwest (the Brook of Egypt) — a huge congregation. They started out celebrating for seven days — and then did it another seven days! Two solid weeks of celebration! Then he dismissed them. They blessed the king and went home, exuberant with heartfelt gratitude for all the good GOD had done for his servant David and for his people Israel.

¹⁻² **9** After Solomon had completed building The Temple of GOD and his own palace, all the projects he had set his heart on doing, GOD appeared to Solomon again, just as he had appeared to him at Gibeon.

³⁻⁵ And GOD said to him, "I've listened to and received all your prayers, your ever-so-passionate prayers. I've sanctified this Temple that you have built: My Name is stamped on it forever; my eyes are on it and my heart in it always. As for you, if you live in my presence as your father David lived, pure in heart and action, living the life I've set out for you, attentively obedient to my guidance and judgments, then I'll back your kingly rule over Israel, make it a sure thing on a solid foundation. The same guarantee I gave David your father I'm giving you: 'You can count on always having a descendant on Israel's throne.'

⁶⁻⁹ "But if you or your sons betray me, ignoring my guidance and judgments, taking up with alien gods by serving and worshiping them, then the guarantee is off: I'll wipe Israel right off the map and repudiate this Temple I've just sanctified to honor my Name. And Israel will become nothing but a bad joke among the peoples of the world. And this Temple, splendid as it now is, will become an object of contempt; visitors will shake their heads, saying, 'Whatever happened here? What's the story behind these ruins?' Then they'll be told, 'The people who used to live here betrayed their GOD, the very God who rescued their ancestors from Egypt; they took up with alien gods, worshiping and serving them. That's what's behind this GOD-visited devastation.'"

¹⁰⁻¹² At the end of twenty years, having built the two buildings, The Temple of GOD and his personal palace, Solomon rewarded Hiram king of Tyre with a gift of twenty villages in the district of Galilee. Hiram had provided him with all the cedar and cypress and gold that he had wanted. But when Hiram left Tyre to look over the villages that Solomon had given him, he didn't like what he saw.

¹³⁻¹⁴ He said, "What kind of reward is this, my friend? Twenty backwoods hick towns!" People still refer to them that way. This is all Hiram got from Solomon in exchange for four and a half tons of gold!

15   This is the work record of the labor force that King Solomon raised to build The Temple of God, his palace, the defense complex (the Millo), the Jerusalem wall, and the fortified cities of Hazor, Megiddo, and Gezer.

16-17   Pharaoh king of Egypt had come up and captured Gezer, torched it, and killed all the Canaanites who lived there. He gave it as a wedding present to his daughter, Solomon's wife. So Solomon rebuilt Gezer.

17-19   He also built Lower Beth Horon, Baalath, and Tamar in the desert, back-country storehouse villages, and villages for chariots and horses. Solomon built widely and extravagantly in Jerusalem, in Lebanon, and wherever he fancied.

20-23   The remnants from the original inhabitants of the land (Amorites, Hittites, Perizzites, Hivites, and Jebusites—all non-Israelites), survivors of the holy wars, were rounded up by Solomon for his gangs of slave labor, a policy still in effect. But true Israelites were not treated this way; they were used in his army and administration—government leaders and commanders of his chariots and charioteers. They were also the project managers responsible for Solomon's building operations—550 of them in charge of the workforce.

24   It was after Pharaoh's daughter ceremonially ascended from the City of David and took up residence in the house built especially for her that Solomon built the defense complex (the Millo).

25   Three times a year Solomon worshiped at the Altar of God, sacrificing Whole-Burnt-Offerings and Peace-Offerings, and burning incense in the presence of God. Everything that had to do with The Temple he did generously and well; he didn't skimp.

26-28   And ships! King Solomon also built ships at Ezion Geber, located near Elath in Edom on the Red Sea. Hiram sent seaworthy sailors to assist Solomon's men with the fleet. They embarked for Ophir, brought back sixteen tons of gold, and presented it to King Solomon.

The Queen of Sheba Visits

1-5   **10** The queen of Sheba heard about Solomon and his connection with the Name of God. She came to put his reputation to the test by asking tough questions. She made a grand and showy entrance into Jerusalem—camels loaded with spices, a huge amount of gold, and precious gems. She came to Solomon and talked about all the things that she cared about, emptying her heart to him. Solomon answered everything she put to him—nothing stumped him. When the queen of Sheba experienced for herself Solomon's wisdom and saw with her own eyes the palace he had built, the meals that were served, the impressive array of court officials and sharply dressed waiters, the lavish crystal, and the elaborate worship extravagant with Whole-Burnt-Offerings at the steps leading up to The Temple of God, it took her breath away.

6-9   She said to the king, "It's all true! Your reputation for accomplishment and wisdom that reached all the way to my country is confirmed. I wouldn't have believed it if I hadn't seen it for myself; they didn't exaggerate! Such wisdom and elegance—far more than I could ever have imagined. Lucky the men and women who work for you, getting to be around you every day and hear your wise words firsthand! And blessed be God, your God, who took such a liking to you and made you king. Clearly, God's love for Israel is behind this, making you king to keep a just order and nurture a God-pleasing people."

10 She then gave the king four and a half tons of gold, and also sack after sack of spices and expensive gems. There hasn't been a cargo of spices like that since that shipload the queen of Sheba brought to King Solomon.

11-12 The ships of Hiram also imported gold from Ophir along with tremendous loads of fragrant sandalwood and expensive gems. The king used the sandalwood for fine cabinetry in The Temple of GOD and the palace complex, and for making harps and dulcimers for the musicians. Nothing like that shipment of sandalwood has been seen since.

13 King Solomon for his part gave the queen of Sheba all her heart's desire—everything she asked for, on top of what he had already so generously given her. Satisfied, she returned home with her train of servants.

14-15 Solomon received twenty-five tons of gold in tribute annually. This was above and beyond the taxes and profit on trade with merchants and assorted kings and governors.

16-17 King Solomon crafted two hundred body-length shields of hammered gold—seven and a half pounds of gold to each shield—and three hundred smaller shields about half that size. He stored the shields in the House of the Forest of Lebanon.

18-20 The king built a massive throne of ivory accented with a veneer of gold. The throne had six steps leading up to it, its back shaped like an arch. The armrests on each side were flanked by lions. Lions, twelve of them, were placed at either end of the six steps. There was no throne like it in any of the surrounding kingdoms.

21 King Solomon's chalices and tankards were made of gold and all the dinnerware and serving utensils in the House of the Forest of Lebanon were pure gold—nothing was made of silver; silver was considered common and cheap.

22 The king had a fleet of ocean-going ships at sea with Hiram's ships. Every three years the fleet would bring in a cargo of gold, silver, and ivory, and apes and peacocks.

23-25 King Solomon was wiser and richer than all the kings of the earth—he surpassed them all. People came from all over the world to be with Solomon and drink in the wisdom God had given him. And everyone who came brought gifts—artifacts of gold and silver, fashionable robes and gowns, the latest in weapons, exotic spices, and horses and mules—parades of visitors, year after year.

26-29 Solomon collected chariots and horses: fourteen hundred chariots and twelve thousand horses! He stabled them in the special chariot cities as well as in Jerusalem. The king made silver as common as rocks and cedar as common as the fig trees in the lowland hills. His horses were brought in from Egypt and Cilicia, specially acquired by the king's agents. Chariots from Egypt went for fifteen pounds of silver and a horse for about three and three-quarters pounds of silver. Solomon carried on a brisk horse-trading business with the Hittite and Aramean royal houses.

1-5 **11** King Solomon was obsessed with women. Pharaoh's daughter was only the first of the many foreign women he loved—Moabite, Ammonite, Edomite, Sidonian, and Hittite. He took them from the surrounding pagan nations of which GOD had clearly warned Israel, "You must not marry them; they'll seduce you into infatuations with their gods." Solomon fell in love with them anyway, refusing to give them up. He had seven hundred royal wives and three hundred concubines—a thousand women in all! And they did seduce him away from God. As Solomon grew older, his wives beguiled him with their alien gods and he became unfaithful—he didn't stay true to his GOD as his father David had done. Solomon took up with Ashtoreth, the whore goddess of the Sidonians, and Molech, the horrible god of the Ammonites.

6-8   Solomon openly defied GOD; he did not follow in his father David's footsteps. He went on to build a sacred shrine to Chemosh, the horrible god of Moab, and to Molech, the horrible god of the Ammonites, on a hill just east of Jerusalem. He built similar shrines for all his foreign wives, who then polluted the countryside with the smoke and stench of their sacrifices.

9-10   GOD was furious with Solomon for abandoning the GOD of Israel, the God who had twice appeared to him and had so clearly commanded him not to fool around with other gods. Solomon faithlessly disobeyed GOD's orders.

11-13   GOD said to Solomon, "Since this is the way it is with you, that you have no intention of keeping faith with me and doing what I have commanded, I'm going to rip the kingdom from you and hand it over to someone else. But out of respect for your father David I won't do it in your lifetime. It's your son who will pay—I'll rip it right out of his grasp. Even then I won't take it all; I'll leave him one tribe in honor of my servant David and out of respect for my chosen city Jerusalem."

14-20   GOD incited Hadad, a descendant of the king of Edom, into hostile actions against Solomon. Years earlier, when David devastated Edom, Joab, commander of the army, on his way to bury the dead, massacred all the men of Edom. Joab and his army stayed there for six months, making sure they had killed every man in Edom. Hadad, just a boy at the time, had escaped with some of the Edomites who had worked for his father. Their escape route took them through Midian to Paran. They picked up some men in Paran and went on to Egypt and to Pharaoh king of Egypt, who gave Hadad a house, food, and even land. Pharaoh liked him so well that he gave him the sister of his wife, Queen Tahpenes, in marriage. She bore Hadad a son named Genubath who was raised like one of the royal family. Genubath grew up in the palace with Pharaoh's children.

21   While living in Egypt, Hadad heard that both David and Joab, commander of the army, were dead. He approached Pharaoh and said, "Send me off with your blessing—I want to return to my country."

22   "But why?" said Pharaoh. "Why would you want to leave here? Hasn't everything been to your liking?"

"Everything has been just fine," said Hadad, "but I want to go home— give me a good send-off!"

※

23-25   Then God incited another adversary against Solomon, Rezon son of Eliada, who had deserted from his master, Hadadezer king of Zobah. After David's slaughter of the Arameans, Rezon collected a band of outlaws and became their leader. They later settled in Damascus, where Rezon eventually took over as king. Like Hadad, Rezon was a thorn in Israel's side all of Solomon's life. He was king over Aram, and he hated Israel.

26 And then, the last straw: Jeroboam son of Nebat rebelled against the king. He was an Ephraimite from Zeredah, his mother a widow named Zeruah. He served in Solomon's administration.

27-28 This is why he rebelled. Solomon had built the outer defense system (the Millo) and had restored the fortifications that were in disrepair from the time of his father David. Jeroboam stood out during the construction as strong and able. When Solomon observed what a good worker he was, he put the young man in charge of the entire workforce of the tribe of Joseph.

29-30 One day Jeroboam was walking down the road out of Jerusalem. Ahijah the prophet of Shiloh, wearing a brand-new cloak, met him. The two of them were alone on that remote stretch of road. Ahijah took off the new cloak that he was wearing and ripped it into twelve pieces.

31-33 Then he said to Jeroboam, "Take ten of these pieces for yourself; this is by order of the GOD of Israel: See what I'm doing—I'm ripping the kingdom out of Solomon's hands and giving you ten of the tribes. In honor of my servant David and out of respect for Jerusalem, the city I especially chose, he will get one tribe. And here's the reason: He faithlessly abandoned me and went off worshiping Ashtoreth goddess of the Sidonians, Chemosh god of the Moabites, and Molech god of the Ammonites. He hasn't lived the way I have shown him, hasn't done what I have wanted, and hasn't followed directions or obeyed orders as his father David did.

34-36 "Still, I won't take the whole kingdom away from him. I'll stick with him through his lifetime because of my servant David whom I chose and who did follow my directions and obey my orders. But after that I'll remove the kingdom from his son's control and give you ten tribes. I'll leave one tribe to his son, to maintain a witness to my servant David in Jerusalem, the city I chose as a memorial to my Name.

37-39 "But I have taken you in hand. Rule to your heart's content! You are to be the king of Israel. If you listen to what I tell you and live the way I show you and do what pleases me, following directions and obeying orders as my servant David did, I'll stick with you no matter what. I'll build you a kingdom as solid as the one I built for David. Israel will be yours! I am bringing pain and trouble on David's descendants, but the trials won't last forever."

40 Solomon ordered the assassination of Jeroboam, but he got away to Egypt and found asylum there with King Shishak. He remained in exile there until Solomon died.

41-43 The rest of Solomon's life and rule, his work and his wisdom, you can read for yourself in *The Chronicles of Solomon*. Solomon ruled in Jerusalem over all Israel for forty years. He died and was buried in the City of David his father. His son Rehoboam was the next king.

REHOBOAM

1-2 **12** Rehoboam traveled to Shechem where all Israel had gathered to inaugurate him as king. Jeroboam had been in Egypt, where he had taken asylum from King Solomon; when he got the report of Solomon's death he had come back.

3-4 Rehoboam assembled Jeroboam and all the people. They said to Rehoboam, "Your father made life hard for us—worked our fingers to the bone. Give us a break; lighten up on us and we'll willingly serve you."

5   "Give me three days to think it over, then come back," Rehoboam said.

6   King Rehoboam talked it over with the elders who had advised his father when he was alive: "What's your counsel? How do you suggest that I answer the people?"

7   They said, "If you will be a servant to this people, be considerate of their needs and respond with compassion, work things out with them, they'll end up doing anything for you."

8-9   But he rejected the counsel of the elders and asked the young men he'd grown up with who were now currying his favor, "What do you think? What should I say to these people who are saying, 'Give us a break from your father's harsh ways—lighten up on us'?"

10-11   The young turks he'd grown up with said, "These people who complain, 'Your father was too hard on us; lighten up'—well, tell them this: 'My little finger is thicker than my father's waist. If you think life under my father was hard, you haven't seen the half of it. My father thrashed you with whips; I'll beat you bloody with chains!'"

12-14   Three days later Jeroboam and the people showed up, just as Rehoboam had directed when he said, "Give me three days to think it over, then come back." The king's answer was harsh and rude. He spurned the counsel of the elders and went with the advice of the younger set, "If you think life under my father was hard, you haven't seen the half of it. My father thrashed you with whips; I'll beat you bloody with chains!"

15   Rehoboam turned a deaf ear to the people. GOD was behind all this, confirming the message that he had given to Jeroboam son of Nebat through Ahijah of Shiloh.

16-17   When all Israel realized that the king hadn't listened to a word they'd said, they stood up to him and said,

> Get lost, David!
> We've had it with you, son of Jesse!
> Let's get out of here, Israel, and fast!
> From now on, David, mind your own business.

And with that, they left. But Rehoboam continued to rule those who lived in the towns of Judah.

18-19   When King Rehoboam next sent out Adoniram, head of the workforce, the Israelites ganged up on him, pelted him with stones, and killed him. King Rehoboam jumped in his chariot and fled to Jerusalem as fast as he could. Israel has been in rebellion against the Davidic regime ever since.

JEROBOAM OF ISRAEL

20   When the word was out that Jeroboam was back and available, the assembled people invited him and inaugurated him king over all Israel. The only tribe left to the Davidic dynasty was Judah.

21   When Rehoboam got back to Jerusalem, he called up the men of Judah and the tribe of Benjamin, 180,000 of their best soldiers, to go to war against Israel and recover the kingdom for Rehoboam son of Solomon.

22-24   At this time the word of God came to Shemaiah, a man of God: "Tell this to Rehoboam son of Solomon king of Judah, along with everyone in Judah and Benjamin and anyone else who is around: This is GOD's word: Don't march out; don't fight against your brothers the Israelites; go back home, every last one of you; *I'm* in charge here." And they did it; they did what GOD said and went home.

———※———

25 Jeroboam made a fort at Shechem in the hills of Ephraim, and made that his headquarters. He also built a fort at Penuel.

26-27 But then Jeroboam thought, "It won't be long before the kingdom is reunited under David. As soon as these people resume worship at The Temple of GOD in Jerusalem, they'll start thinking of Rehoboam king of Judah as their ruler. They'll then kill me and go back to King Rehoboam."

28-30 So the king came up with a plan: He made two golden calves. Then he announced, "It's too much trouble for you to go to Jerusalem to worship. Look at these—the gods who brought you out of Egypt!" He put one calf in Bethel; the other he placed in Dan. This was blatant sin. Think of it—people traveling all the way to Dan to worship a calf!

31-33 And that wasn't the end of it. Jeroboam built forbidden shrines all over the place and recruited priests from wherever he could find them, regardless of whether they were fit for the job or not. To top it off, he created a holy New Year festival to be held on the fifteenth day of the eighth month to replace the one in Judah, complete with worship offered on the Altar at Bethel and sacrificing before the calves he had set up there. He staffed Bethel with priests from the local shrines he had made. This was strictly his own idea to compete with the feast in Judah; and he carried it off with flair, a festival exclusively for Israel, Jeroboam himself leading the worship at the Altar.

1-3 **13** And then this happened: Just as Jeroboam was at the Altar, about to make an offering, a holy man came from Judah by GOD's command and preached (these were GOD's orders) to the Altar: "Altar, Altar! GOD's message! 'A son will be born into David's family named Josiah. The priests from the shrines who are making offerings on you, he will sacrifice—on you! Human bones burned on you!'" At the same time he announced a sign: "This is the proof GOD gives—the Altar will split into pieces and the holy offerings spill into the dirt."

4-5 When the king heard the message the holy man preached against the Altar at Bethel, he reached out to grab him, yelling, "Arrest him!" But his arm was paralyzed and hung useless. At the same time the Altar broke apart and the holy offerings all spilled into the dirt—the very sign the holy man had announced by GOD's command.

6 The king pleaded with the holy man, "Help me! Pray to your GOD for the healing of my arm." The holy man prayed for him and the king's arm was healed—as good as new!

7 Then the king invited the holy man, "Join me for a meal; I have a gift for you."

8-10 The holy man told the king, "Not on your life! You couldn't pay me enough to get me to sit down with you at a meal in this place. I'm here under GOD's orders, and he commanded, 'Don't eat a crumb, don't drink a drop, and don't go back the way you came.'" Then he left by a different road than the one on which he had walked to Bethel.

¹¹ There was an old prophet who lived in Bethel. His sons came and told him the story of what the holy man had done that day in Bethel, told him everything that had happened and what the holy man had said to the king.

¹² Their father said, "Which way did he go?" His sons pointed out the road that the holy man from Judah had taken.

¹³⁻¹⁴ He told his sons, "Saddle my donkey." When they had saddled it, he got on and rode after the holy man. He found him sitting under an oak tree.

He asked him, "Are you the holy man who came from Judah?"

"Yes, I am," he said.

¹⁵ "Well, come home with me and have a meal."

¹⁶⁻¹⁷ "Sorry, I can't do that," the holy man said. "I can neither go back with you nor eat with you in this country. I'm under strict orders from GOD: 'Don't eat a crumb; don't drink a drop; and don't come back the way you came.'"

¹⁸⁻¹⁹ But he said, "I am also a prophet, just like you. And an angel came to me with a message from GOD: 'Bring him home with you, and give him a good meal!'" But the man was lying. So the holy man went home with him and they had a meal together.

²⁰⁻²² There they were, sitting at the table together, when the word of GOD came to the prophet who had brought him back. He confronted the holy man who had come from Judah: "GOD's word to you: You disobeyed GOD's command; you didn't keep the strict orders your GOD gave you; you came back and sat down to a good meal in the very place GOD told you, 'Don't eat a crumb; don't drink a drop.' For that you're going to die far from home and not be buried in your ancestral tomb."

²³⁻²⁵ When the meal was over, the prophet who had brought him back saddled his donkey for him. Down the road a way, a lion met him and killed him. His corpse lay crumpled on the road, the lion on one side and the donkey on the other. Some passersby saw the corpse in a heap on the road, with the lion standing guard beside it. They went to the village where the old prophet lived and told what they had seen.

²⁶ When the prophet who had gotten him off track heard it, he said, "It's the holy man who disobeyed GOD's strict orders. GOD turned him over to the lion who knocked him around and killed him, just as GOD had told him."

²⁷⁻³⁰ The prophet told his sons, "Saddle my donkey." They did it. He rode out and found the corpse in a heap in the road, with the lion and the donkey standing there. The lion hadn't bothered either the corpse or the donkey. The old prophet loaded the corpse of the holy man on his donkey and returned it to his own town to give it a decent burial. He placed the body in his own tomb. The people mourned, saying, "A sad day, brother!"

³¹⁻³² After the funeral, the prophet said to his sons, "When I die, bury me in the same tomb where the holy man is buried, my bones alongside his bones. The message that he preached by GOD's command against the Altar at Bethel and against all the sex-and-religion shrines in the towns of Samaria will come true."

³³⁻³⁴ After this happened, Jeroboam kept right on doing evil, recruiting priests for the forbidden shrines indiscriminately—anyone who wanted to could be a priest at one of the local shrines. This was the root sin of Jeroboam's government. And it was this that ruined him.

14 At about this time Jeroboam's son Abijah came down sick. Jeroboam said to his wife, "Do something. Disguise yourself so no one will know you are the queen and go to Shiloh. Ahijah the prophet lives there, the same Ahijah who told me I'd be king over this people. Take along ten loaves of bread, some sweet rolls, and a jug of honey. Make a visit to him and he'll tell you what's going on with our boy."

Jeroboam's wife did as she was told; she went straight to Shiloh and to Ahijah's house. Ahijah was an old man at this time, and blind, but GOD had warned Ahijah, "Jeroboam's wife is on her way to consult with you regarding her sick son; tell her this and this and this."

When she came in she was disguised. Ahijah heard her come through the door and said, "Welcome, wife of Jeroboam! But why the deception? I've got bad news for you. Go and deliver this message I received firsthand from GOD, the God of Israel, to Jeroboam: I raised you up from obscurity and made you the leader of my people Israel. I ripped the kingdom from the hands of David's family and gave it to you, but you weren't at all like my servant David who did what I told him and lived from his undivided heart, pleasing me. Instead you've set a new record in works of evil by making alien gods—tin gods! Pushing me aside and turning your back— you've made me mighty angry.

"And I'll not put up with it: I'm bringing doom on the household of Jeroboam, killing the lot of them right down to the last male wretch in Israel, whether slave or free. They've become nothing but garbage and I'm getting rid of them. The ones who die in the city will be eaten by stray dogs; the ones who die out in the country will be eaten by carrion crows. GOD's decree!

"And that's it. Go on home—the minute you step foot in town, the boy will die. Everyone will come to his burial, mourning his death. He is the only one in Jeroboam's family who will get a decent burial; he's the only one for whom GOD, the God of Israel, has a good word to say.

"Then GOD will appoint a king over Israel who will wipe out Jeroboam's family, wipe them right off the map—doomsday for Jeroboam! He will hit Israel hard, as a storm slaps reeds about; he'll pull them up by the roots from this good land of their inheritance, weeding them out, and then scatter them to the four winds. And why? Because they made GOD so angry with Asherah sex-and-religion shrines. He'll wash his hands of Israel because of Jeroboam's sins, which have led Israel into a life of sin."

Jeroboam's wife left and went home to Tirzah. The moment she stepped through the door, the boy died. They buried him and everyone mourned his death, just as GOD had said through his servant the prophet Ahijah.

The rest of Jeroboam's life, the wars he fought and the way he ruled, is written in *The Chronicles of the Kings of Israel*. He ruled for twenty-two years. He died and was buried with his ancestors. Nadab his son was king after him.

Rehoboam son of Solomon was king in Judah. He was forty-one years old when he took the throne and was king for seventeen years in Jerusalem, the city GOD selected from all the tribes of Israel for the worship of his

Name. Rehoboam's mother was Naamah, an Ammonite. Judah was openly wicked before GOD, making him very angry. They set new records in sin, surpassing anything their ancestors had done. They built Asherah sex-and-religion shrines and set up sacred stones all over the place—on hills, under trees, wherever you looked. Worse, they had male sacred prostitutes, polluting the country outrageously—all the stuff that GOD had gotten rid of when he brought Israel into the land.

25-28   In the fifth year of King Rehoboam's rule, Shishak king of Egypt made war against Jerusalem. He plundered The Temple of GOD and the royal palace of their treasures, cleaned them out—even the gold shields that Solomon had made. King Rehoboam replaced them with bronze shields and outfitted the royal palace guards with them. Whenever the king went to GOD's Temple, the guards carried the shields but always returned them to the guardroom.

29-31   The rest of Rehoboam's life, what he said and did, is all written in *The Chronicles of the Kings of Judah*. There was war between Rehoboam and Jeroboam the whole time. Rehoboam died and was buried with his ancestors in the City of David. His mother was Naamah, an Ammonite. His son Abijah ruled after him.

ABIJAH OF JUDAH

1-6   **15** In the eighteenth year of the rule of Jeroboam son of Nebat, Abijah took over the throne of Judah. He ruled in Jerusalem three years. His mother was Maacah daughter of Absalom. He continued to sin just like his father before him. He was not truehearted to GOD as his great-grandfather David had been. But despite that, out of respect for David, his GOD graciously gave him a lamp, a son to follow him and keep Jerusalem secure. For David had lived an exemplary life before GOD all his days, not going off on his own in willful defiance of GOD's clear directions (except for that time with Uriah the Hittite). But war continued between Abijah and Jeroboam the whole time.

7-8   The rest of Abijah's life, everything he did, is written in *The Chronicles of the Kings of Judah*. But the war with Jeroboam was the dominant theme. Abijah died and was buried with his ancestors in the City of David. His son Asa was king after him.

ASA OF JUDAH

9-10   In the twentieth year of Jeroboam king of Israel, Asa began his rule over Judah. He ruled for forty-one years in Jerusalem. His grandmother's name was Maacah.

11-15   Asa conducted himself well before GOD, reviving the ways of his ancestor David. He cleaned house: He got rid of the sacred prostitutes and threw out all the idols his predecessors had made. Asa spared nothing and no one; he went so far as to remove Queen Maacah from her position because she had built a shockingly obscene memorial to the whore goddess Asherah. Asa tore it down and burned it up in the Kidron Valley. Unfortunately, he didn't get rid of the local sex-and-religion shrines. But he was well-intentioned—his heart was in the right place, in tune with GOD. All the gold and silver vessels and artifacts that he and his father had consecrated for holy use he installed in The Temple.

16-17   But through much of his reign there was war between Asa and Baasha king of Israel. Baasha king of Israel started it by building a fort at Ramah and closing the border between Israel and Judah so no one could enter or leave Judah.

18-19 Asa took all the silver and gold that was left in the treasuries of The Temple of GOD and the royal palace, gave it to his servants, and sent them to Ben-Hadad son of Tabrimmon, the son of Hezion king of Aram, who was ruling in Damascus, with this message: "Let's make a treaty like the one between our fathers. I'm showing my good faith with this gift of silver and gold. Break your deal with Baasha king of Israel so he'll quit fighting against me."

20-21 Ben-Hadad went along with King Asa and sent out his troops against the towns of Israel. He attacked Ijon, Dan, Abel Beth Maacah, and the entire region of Kinnereth, including Naphtali. When Baasha got the report he quit fortifying Ramah and pulled back to Tirzah.

22 Then King Asa issued orders to everyone in Judah — no exemptions — to haul away the logs and stones Baasha had used in the fortification of Ramah and use them to fortify Geba in Benjamin and Mizpah.

23-24 A full account of Asa's life, all the great things he did and the fortifications he constructed, is written in *The Chronicles of the Kings of Judah*. In his old age he developed severe gout. Then Asa died and was buried with his ancestors in the City of David. His son Jehoshaphat became king after him.

NADAB OF ISRAEL

25-26 Nadab son of Jeroboam became king over Israel in the second year of Asa's rule in Judah. He was king of Israel two years. He was openly evil before GOD — he followed in the footsteps of his father who both sinned and made Israel sin.

27-28 Baasha son of Ahijah of the tribe of Issachar ganged up on him and attacked him at the Philistine town of Gibbethon while Nadab and the Israelites were doing battle there. Baasha killed Nadab in the third year of Asa king of Judah and became Israel's next king.

29-30 As soon as he was king he killed everyone in Jeroboam's family. There wasn't a living soul left to the name of Jeroboam; Baasha wiped them out totally, just as GOD's servant Ahijah of Shiloh had prophesied — punishment for Jeroboam's sins and for making Israel sin, for making the GOD of Israel thoroughly angry.

31-32 The rest of Nadab's life, everything else he did, is written in *The Chronicles of the Kings of Israel*. There was continuous war between Asa and Baasha king of Israel.

BAASHA OF ISRAEL

33-34 In the third year of Asa king of Judah, Baasha son of Ahijah became king in Tirzah over all Israel. He ruled twenty-four years. He was openly evil before GOD, walking in the footsteps of Jeroboam, who both sinned and made Israel sin.

1-4 **16** The word of GOD came to Jehu son of Hanani with this message for Baasha: "I took you from nothing — a complete nobody — and set you up as the leader of my people Israel, but you plodded along in the rut of Jeroboam, making my people Israel sin and making me seethe over their sin. And now the consequences — I will burn Baasha and his regime to cinders, the identical fate of Jeroboam son of Nebat. Baasha's people who die in the city will be eaten by scavenger dogs; carrion crows will eat the ones who die in the country."

5-6 The rest of Baasha's life, the record of his regime, is written in *The Chronicles of the Kings of Israel.* Baasha died and was buried with his ancestors in Tirzah. His son Elah was king after him.

7 That's the way it was with Baasha: Through the prophet Jehu son of Hanani, GOD's word came to him and his regime because of his life of open evil before GOD and his making GOD so angry — a chip off the block of Jeroboam, even though GOD had destroyed him.

ELAH OF ISRAEL

8-10 In the twenty-sixth year of Asa king of Judah, Elah son of Baasha began his rule. He was king in Tirzah only two years. One day when he was at the house of Arza the palace manager, drinking himself drunk, Zimri, captain of half his chariot-force, conspired against him. Zimri slipped in, knocked Elah to the ground, and killed him. This happened in the twenty-seventh year of Asa king of Judah. Zimri then became the king.

11-13 Zimri had no sooner become king than he killed everyone connected with Baasha, got rid of them all like so many stray dogs — relatives and friends alike. Zimri totally wiped out the family of Baasha, just as GOD's word delivered by the prophet Jehu had said — wages for the sins of Baasha and his son Elah; not only for their sins but for dragging Israel into their sins and making the GOD of Israel angry with their stupid idols.

14 The rest of Elah's life, what he said and did, is written in *The Chronicles of the Kings of Israel.*

ZIMRI OF ISRAEL

15-19 Zimri was king in Tirzah for all of seven days during the twenty-seventh year of the reign of Asa king of Judah. The Israelite army was on maneuvers near the Philistine town of Gibbethon at the time. When they got the report, "Zimri has conspired against the king and killed him," right there in the camp they made Omri, commander of the army, king. Omri and the army immediately left Gibbethon and attacked Tirzah. When Zimri saw that he was surrounded and as good as dead, he entered the palace citadel, set the place on fire, and died. It was a fit end for his sins, for living a flagrantly evil life before GOD, walking in the footsteps of Jeroboam, sinning and then dragging Israel into his sins.

20 As for the rest of Zimri's life, along with his infamous conspiracy, it's all written in *The Chronicles of the Kings of Israel.*

OMRI OF ISRAEL

21-22 After that the people of Israel were split right down the middle: Half favored Tibni son of Ginath as king, and half wanted Omri. Eventually the Omri side proved stronger than the Tibni side. Tibni ended up dead and Omri king.

23-24 Omri took over as king of Israel in the thirty-first year of the reign of Asa king of Judah. He ruled for twelve years, the first six in Tirzah. He then bought the hill Samaria from Shemer for 150 pounds of silver. He developed the hill and named the city that he built Samaria, after its original owner Shemer.

25-26　　But as far as GOD was concerned, Omri lived an evil life—set new records in evil. He walked in the footsteps of Jeroboam son of Nebat, who not only sinned but dragged Israel into his sins, making GOD angry—such an empty-headed, empty-hearted life!

27-28　　The rest of Omri's life, the mark he made on his times, is written in *The Chronicles of the Kings of Israel*. Omri died and was buried in Samaria. His son Ahab was the next king after him.

AHAB OF ISRAEL

29-33　　Ahab son of Omri became king of Israel in the thirty-eighth year of Asa king of Judah. Ahab son of Omri was king over Israel for twenty-two years. He ruled from Samaria. Ahab son of Omri did even more open evil before GOD than anyone yet—a new champion in evil! It wasn't enough for him to copy the sins of Jeroboam son of Nebat; no, he went all out, first by marrying Jezebel daughter of Ethbaal king of the Sidonians, and then by serving and worshiping the god Baal. He built a temple for Baal in Samaria, and then furnished it with an altar for Baal. Worse, he went on and built a shrine to the sacred whore Asherah. He made the GOD of Israel angrier than all the previous kings of Israel put together.

34　　It was under Ahab's rule that Hiel of Bethel refortified Jericho, but at a terrible cost: He ritually sacrificed his firstborn son Abiram at the laying of the foundation, and his youngest son Segub at the setting up of the gates. This is exactly what Joshua son of Nun said would happen.

1　　**17** And then this happened: Elijah the Tishbite, from among the settlers of Gilead, confronted Ahab: "As surely as GOD lives, the God of Israel before whom I stand in obedient service, the next years are going to see a total drought—not a drop of dew or rain unless I say otherwise."

2-4　　GOD then told Elijah, "Get out of here, and fast. Head east and hide out at the Kerith Ravine on the other side of the Jordan River. You can drink fresh water from the brook; I've ordered the ravens to feed you."

5-6　　Elijah obeyed GOD's orders. He went and camped in the Kerith canyon on the other side of the Jordan. And sure enough, ravens brought him his meals, both breakfast and supper, and he drank from the brook.

7-9　　Eventually the brook dried up because of the drought. Then GOD spoke to him: "Get up and go to Zarephath in Sidon and live there. I've instructed a woman who lives there, a widow, to feed you."

10-11　　So he got up and went to Zarephath. As he came to the entrance of the village he met a woman, a widow, gathering firewood. He asked her, "Please, would you bring me a little water in a jug? I need a drink." As she went to get it, he called out, "And while you're at it, would you bring me something to eat?"

12　　She said, "I swear, as surely as your GOD lives, I don't have so much as a biscuit. I have a handful of flour in a jar and a little oil in a bottle; you found me scratching together just enough firewood to make a last meal for my son and me. After we eat it, we'll die."

13-14　　Elijah said to her, "Don't worry about a thing. Go ahead and do what you've said. But first make a small biscuit for me and bring it back here. Then go ahead and make a meal from what's left for you and your son.

This is the word of the GOD of Israel: 'The jar of flour will not run out and the bottle of oil will not become empty before GOD sends rain on the land and ends this drought.'"

15-16   And she went right off and did it, did just as Elijah asked. And it turned out as he said — daily food for her and her family. The jar of meal didn't run out and the bottle of oil didn't become empty: GOD's promise fulfilled to the letter, exactly as Elijah had delivered it!

17   Later on the woman's son became sick. The sickness took a turn for the worse — and then he stopped breathing.

18   The woman said to Elijah, "Why did you ever show up here in the first place — a holy man barging in, exposing my sins, and killing my son?"

19-20   Elijah said, "Hand me your son."

He then took him from her bosom, carried him up to the loft where he was staying, and laid him on his bed. Then he prayed, "O GOD, my God, why have you brought this terrible thing on this widow who has opened her home to me? Why have you killed her son?"

21-23   Three times he stretched himself out full-length on the boy, praying with all his might, "GOD, my God, put breath back into this boy's body!" GOD listened to Elijah's prayer and put breath back into his body — he was alive! Elijah picked the boy up, carried him downstairs from the loft, and gave him to his mother. "Here's your son," said Elijah, "alive!"

24   The woman said to Elijah, "I see it all now — you *are* a holy man. When you speak, GOD speaks — a true word!"

1-2   **18** A long time passed. Then GOD's word came to Elijah. The drought was now in its third year. The message: "Go and present yourself to Ahab; I'm about to make it rain on the country." Elijah set out to present himself to Ahab. The drought in Samaria at the time was most severe.

3-4   Ahab called for Obadiah, who was in charge of the palace. Obadiah feared GOD — he was very devout. Earlier, when Jezebel had tried to kill off all the prophets of GOD, Obadiah had hidden away a hundred of them in two caves, fifty in a cave, and then supplied them with food and water.

5-6   Ahab ordered Obadiah, "Go through the country; locate every spring and every stream. Let's see if we can find enough grass to keep our horses and mules from dying." So they divided the country between them for the search — Ahab went one way, Obadiah the other.

7   Obadiah went his way and suddenly there he was — Elijah! Obadiah fell on his knees, bowing in reverence, and exclaimed, "Is it really you — my master Elijah?"

8   "Yes," said Elijah, "the real me. Now go and tell your boss, 'I've seen Elijah.'"

9-14   Obadiah said, "But what have I done to deserve this? Ahab will kill me. As surely as your GOD lives, there isn't a country or kingdom where my master hasn't sent out search parties looking for you. And if they said, 'We can't find him; we've looked high and low,' he would make that country or kingdom swear that you were not to be found. And now you're telling me, 'Go and tell your master Elijah's found!' The minute I leave you the Spirit of GOD will whisk you away to who knows where. Then when I report to Ahab, you'll have disappeared and Ahab will kill me. And I've served GOD devoutly since I was a boy! Hasn't anyone told you what I did when

Jezebel was out to kill the prophets of GOD, how I risked my life by hiding a hundred of them, fifty to a cave, and made sure they got food and water? And now you're telling me to draw attention to myself by announcing to my master, 'Elijah's been found.' Why, he'll kill me for sure."

15 Elijah said, "As surely as GOD-of-the-Angel-Armies lives, and before whom I take my stand, I'll meet with your master face-to-face this very day."

16 So Obadiah went straight to Ahab and told him. And Ahab went out to meet Elijah.

17-19 The moment Ahab saw Elijah he said, "So it's you, old troublemaker!"

"It's not I who has caused trouble in Israel," said Elijah, "but you and your government — you've dumped GOD's ways and commands and run off after the local gods, the Baals. Here's what I want you to do: Assemble everyone in Israel at Mount Carmel. And make sure that the special pets of Jezebel, the four hundred and fifty prophets of the local gods, the Baals, and the four hundred prophets of the whore goddess Asherah, are there."

20 So Ahab summoned everyone in Israel, particularly the prophets, to Mount Carmel.

21 Elijah challenged the people: "How long are you going to sit on the fence? If GOD is the real God, follow him; if it's Baal, follow him. Make up your minds!"

Nobody said a word; nobody made a move.

22-24 Then Elijah said, "I'm the only prophet of GOD left in Israel; and there are 450 prophets of Baal. Let the Baal prophets bring up two oxen; let them pick one, butcher it, and lay it out on an altar on firewood — but don't ignite it. I'll take the other ox, cut it up, and lay it on the wood. But neither will I light the fire. Then you pray to your gods and I'll pray to GOD. The god who answers with fire will prove to be, in fact, God."

All the people agreed: "A good plan — do it!"

25 Elijah told the Baal prophets, "Choose your ox and prepare it. You go first, you're the majority. Then pray to your god, but don't light the fire."

26 So they took the ox he had given them, prepared it for the altar, then prayed to Baal. They prayed all morning long, "O Baal, answer us!" But nothing happened — not so much as a whisper of breeze. Desperate, they jumped and stomped on the altar they had made.

27-28 By noon, Elijah had started making fun of them, taunting, "Call a little louder — he is a god, after all. Maybe he's off meditating somewhere or other, or maybe he's gotten involved in a project, or maybe he's on vacation. You don't suppose he's overslept, do you, and needs to be waked up?" They prayed louder and louder, cutting themselves with swords and knives — a ritual common to them — until they were covered with blood.

29 This went on until well past noon. They used every religious trick and strategy they knew to make something happen on the altar, but nothing happened — not so much as a whisper, not a flicker of response.

30-35 Then Elijah told the people, "Enough of that — it's my turn. Gather around." And they gathered. He then put the altar back together for by now it was in ruins. Elijah took twelve stones, one for each of the tribes of Jacob, the same Jacob to whom GOD had said, "From now on your name is Israel." He built the stones into the altar in honor of GOD. Then Elijah dug a fairly wide trench around the altar. He laid firewood on the altar, cut up the ox, put it on the wood, and said, "Fill four buckets with water and drench both the ox and the firewood." Then he said, "Do it again," and they did it. Then he said, "Do it a third time," and they did it a third time. The altar was drenched and the trench was filled with water.

36-37 When it was time for the sacrifice to be offered, Elijah the prophet came up and prayed, "O GOD, God of Abraham, Isaac, and Israel, make it known right now that you are God in Israel, that I am your servant, and that I'm doing what I'm doing under your orders. Answer me, GOD; O answer me and reveal to this people that you are GOD, the true God, and that you are giving these people another chance at repentance."

38 Immediately the fire of GOD fell and burned up the offering, the wood, the stones, the dirt, and even the water in the trench.

39 All the people saw it happen and fell on their faces in awed worship, exclaiming, "GOD is the true God! GOD is the true God!"

40 Elijah told them, "Grab the Baal prophets! Don't let one get away!"

They grabbed them. Elijah had them taken down to the Brook Kishon and they massacred the lot.

41 Elijah said to Ahab, "Up on your feet! Eat and drink — celebrate! Rain is on the way; I hear it coming."

42-43 Ahab did it: got up and ate and drank. Meanwhile, Elijah climbed to the top of Carmel, bowed deeply in prayer, his face between his knees. Then he said to his young servant, "On your feet now! Look toward the sea."

He went, looked, and reported back, "I don't see a thing."

"Keep looking," said Elijah, "seven times if necessary."

44 And sure enough, the seventh time he said, "Oh yes, a cloud! But very small, no bigger than someone's hand, rising out of the sea."

"Quickly then, on your way. Tell Ahab, 'Saddle up and get down from the mountain before the rain stops you.'"

45-46 Things happened fast. The sky grew black with wind-driven clouds, and then a huge cloudburst of rain, with Ahab hightailing it in his chariot for Jezreel. And GOD strengthened Elijah mightily. Pulling up his robe and tying it around his waist, Elijah ran in front of Ahab's chariot until they reached Jezreel.

REVENGE FROM JEZEBEL

1-2 **19** Ahab reported to Jezebel everything that Elijah had done, including the massacre of the prophets. Jezebel immediately sent a messenger to Elijah with her threat: "The gods will get you for this and I'll get even with you! By this time tomorrow you'll be as dead as any one of those prophets."

3-5 When Elijah saw how things were, he ran for dear life to Beersheba, far in the south of Judah. He left his young servant there and then went on into the desert another day's journey. He came to a lone broom bush and collapsed in its shade, wanting in the worst way to be done with it all — to just die: "Enough of this, GOD! Take my life — I'm ready to join my ancestors in the grave!" Exhausted, he fell asleep under the lone broom bush.

Suddenly an angel shook him awake and said, "Get up and eat!"

6 He looked around and, to his surprise, right by his head were a loaf of bread baked on some coals and a jug of water. He ate the meal and went back to sleep.

7 The angel of GOD came back, shook him awake again, and said, "Get up and eat some more — you've got a long journey ahead of you."

8-9 He got up, ate and drank his fill, and set out. Nourished by that meal, he walked forty days and nights, all the way to the mountain of God, to Horeb. When he got there, he crawled into a cave and went to sleep.

Then the word of GOD came to him: "So Elijah, what are you doing here?"

10 "I've been working my heart out for the GOD-of-the-Angel-Armies," said Elijah. "The people of Israel have abandoned your covenant, destroyed the places of worship, and murdered your prophets. I'm the only one left, and now they're trying to kill me."

11-12 Then he was told, "Go, stand on the mountain at attention before GOD. GOD will pass by."

A hurricane wind ripped through the mountains and shattered the rocks before GOD, but GOD wasn't to be found in the wind; after the wind an earthquake, but GOD wasn't in the earthquake; and after the earthquake fire, but GOD wasn't in the fire; and after the fire a gentle and quiet whisper.

13-14 When Elijah heard the quiet voice, he muffled his face with his great cloak, went to the mouth of the cave, and stood there. A quiet voice asked, "So Elijah, now tell me, what are you doing here?" Elijah said it again, "I've been working my heart out for GOD, the GOD-of-the-Angel-Armies, because the people of Israel have abandoned your covenant, destroyed your places of worship, and murdered your prophets. I'm the only one left, and now they're trying to kill me."

15-18 GOD said, "Go back the way you came through the desert to Damascus. When you get there anoint Hazael; make him king over Aram. Then anoint Jehu son of Nimshi; make him king over Israel. Finally, anoint Elisha son of Shaphat from Abel Meholah to succeed you as prophet. Anyone who escapes death by Hazael will be killed by Jehu; and anyone who escapes death by Jehu will be killed by Elisha. Meanwhile, I'm preserving for myself seven thousand souls: the knees that haven't bowed to the god Baal, the mouths that haven't kissed his image."

19 Elijah went straight out and found Elisha son of Shaphat in a field where there were twelve pairs of yoked oxen at work plowing; Elisha was in charge of the twelfth pair. Elijah went up to him and threw his cloak over him.

20 Elisha deserted the oxen, ran after Elijah, and said, "Please! Let me kiss my father and mother good-bye — then I'll follow you."

"Go ahead," said Elijah, "but, mind you, don't forget what I've just done to you."

21 So Elisha left; he took his yoke of oxen and butchered them. He made a fire with the plow and tackle and then boiled the meat — a true farewell meal for the family. Then he left and followed Elijah, becoming his right-hand man.

1-3 **20** At about this same time Ben-Hadad king of Aram mustered his troops. He recruited in addition thirty-two local sheiks, all outfitted with horses and chariots. He set out in force and surrounded Samaria, ready to make war. He sent an envoy into the city to set his terms before Ahab king of Israel: "Ben-Hadad lays claim to your silver and gold, and to the pick of your wives and sons."

4 The king of Israel accepted the terms: "As you say, distinguished lord; I and everything I have is yours."

5-6 But then the envoy returned a second time, saying, "On second thought, I want it all — your silver and gold and *all* your wives and sons. Hand them over — the whole works. I'll give you twenty-four hours; then my servants will arrive to search your palace and the houses of your officials and loot them; anything that strikes their fancy, they'll take."

7   The king of Israel called a meeting of all his tribal elders. He said, "Look at this — outrageous! He's just looking for trouble. He means to clean me out, demanding all my women and children. And after I already agreed to pay him off handsomely!"

8   The elders, backed by the people, said, "Don't cave in to him. Don't give an inch."

9   So he sent an envoy to Ben-Hadad, "Tell my distinguished lord, 'I agreed to the terms you delivered the first time, but this I can't do — this I *won't* do!'"

The envoy went back and delivered the answer.

10   Ben-Hadad shot back his response: "May the gods do their worst to me, and then worse again, if there'll be anything left of Samaria but rubble."

11   The king of Israel countered, "Think about it — it's easier to start a fight than end one."

12   It happened that when Ben-Hadad heard this retort he was into some heavy drinking, boozing it up with the sheiks in their field shelters. Drunkenly, he ordered his henchmen, "Go after them!" And they attacked the city.

13   Just then a lone prophet approached Ahab king of Israel and said, "GOD's word: Have you taken a good look at this mob? Well, look again — I'm turning it over to you this very day. And you'll know, beyond the shadow of a doubt, that I am GOD."

14   Ahab said, "Really? And who is going to make this happen?"

GOD said, "The young commandos of the regional chiefs."

"And who," said Ahab, "will strike the first blow?"

GOD said, "You."

15   Ahab looked over the commandos of the regional chiefs; he counted 232. Then he assessed the available troops — 7,000.

16-17   At noon they set out after Ben-Hadad who, with his allies, the thirty-two sheiks, was busy at serious drinking in the field shelters. The commandos of the regional chiefs made up the vanguard.

A report was brought to Ben-Hadad: "Men are on their way from Samaria."

18   He said, "If they've come in peace, take them alive as hostages; if they've come to fight, the same — take them alive as hostages."

19-20   The commandos poured out of the city with the full army behind them. They hit hard in hand-to-hand combat. The Arameans scattered from the field, with Israel hard on their heels. But Ben-Hadad king of Aram got away on horseback, along with his cavalry.

21   The king of Israel cut down both horses and chariots — an enormous defeat for Aram.

22   Sometime later the prophet came to the king of Israel and said, "On the alert now — build up your army, assess your capabilities, and see what has to be done. Before the year is out, the king of Aram will be back in force."

23-25   Meanwhile the advisors to the king of Aram said, "Their god is a god of the mountains — we don't stand a chance against them there. So let's engage them on the plain where we'll have the advantage. Here's the strategy: Remove each sheik from his place of leadership and replace him with a seasoned officer. Then recruit a fighting force equivalent in size to the army that deserted earlier — horse for horse, chariot for chariot. And we'll fight them on the plain — we're sure to prove stronger than they are."

It sounded good to the king; he did what they advised.

26-27 As the new year approached, Ben-Hadad rallied Aram and they went up to Aphek to make war on Israel. The Israelite army prepared to fight and took the field to meet Aram. They moved into battle formation before Aram in two camps, like two flocks of goats. The plain was seething with Arameans.

28 Just then a holy man approached the king of Israel saying, "This is GOD's word: Because Aram said, 'GOD is a god of the mountains and not a god of the valleys,' I'll hand over this huge mob of an army to you. Then you'll know that I am GOD."

29-30 The two armies were poised in a standoff for seven days. On the seventh day fighting broke out. The Israelites killed 100,000 of the Aramean infantry in one day. The rest of the army ran for their lives back to the city, Aphek, only to have the city wall fall on 27,000 of the survivors.

30-31 Ben-Hadad escaped into the city and hid in a closet. Then his advisors told him, "Look, we've heard that the kings of Israel play by the rules; let's dress in old gunnysacks, carry a white flag of truce, and present ourselves to the king of Israel on the chance that he'll let you live."

32 So that's what they did. They dressed in old gunnysacks and carried a white flag, and came to the king of Israel saying, "Your servant Ben-Hadad said, 'Please let me live.'"

Ahab said, "You mean to tell me that he's still alive? If he's alive, he's my brother."

33 The men took this as a good sign and concluded that everything was going to be all right: "Ben-Hadad is most certainly your brother!"

The king said, "Go and get him." They went and brought him back by chariot.

34 Ahab said, "I am prepared to return the cities that my father took from your father. And you can set up your headquarters in Damascus just as my father did in Samaria; I'll send you home under safe conduct." Then he made a covenant with him and sent him off.

35 A man who was one of the prophets said to a bystander, "Hit me; wound me. Do it for GOD's sake — it's his command. Hit me; wound me." But the man wouldn't do it.

36 So he told him, "Because you wouldn't obey GOD's orders, as soon as you leave me a lion will attack you." No sooner had the man left his side than a lion met him and attacked.

37 He then found another man and said, "Hit me; wound me." That man did it — hit him hard in the face, drawing blood.

38-40 Then the prophet went and took a position along the road, with a bandage over his eyes, waiting for the king. It wasn't long before the king happened by. The man cried out to the king, "Your servant was in the thick of the battle when a man showed up and turned over a prisoner to me, saying, 'Guard this man with your life; if he turns up missing you'll pay dearly.' But I got busy doing one thing after another and the next time I looked he was gone."

The king of Israel said, "You've just pronounced your own verdict."

41   At that, the man ripped the bandage off his eyes and the king recognized who he was — one of the prophets!

42   The man said to the king, "GOD's word: Because you let a man go who was under sentence by GOD, it's now your life for his, your people for his."

43   The king of Israel went home in a sulk. He arrived in Samaria in a very bad mood.

1-2   21 And then, to top it off, came this: Naboth the Jezreelite owned a vineyard in Jezreel that bordered the palace of Ahab king of Samaria. One day Ahab spoke to Naboth, saying, "Give me your vineyard so I can use it as a kitchen garden; it's right next to my house — so convenient. In exchange I'll give you a far better vineyard, or if you'd prefer I'll pay you money for it."

3-4   But Naboth told Ahab, "Not on your life! So help me GOD, I'd never sell the family farm to you!" Ahab went home in a black mood, sulking over Naboth the Jezreelite's words, "I'll never turn over my family inheritance to you." He went to bed, stuffed his face in his pillow, and refused to eat.

5   Jezebel his wife came to him. She said, "What's going on? Why are you so out of sorts and refusing to eat?"

6   He told her, "Because I spoke to Naboth the Jezreelite. I said, 'Give me your vineyard — I'll pay you for it or, if you'd rather, I'll give you another vineyard in exchange.' And he said, 'I'll never give you my vineyard.'"

7   Jezebel said, "Is this any way for a king of Israel to act? Aren't you the boss? On your feet! Eat! Cheer up! I'll take care of this; I'll get the vineyard of this Naboth the Jezreelite for you."

8-10   She wrote letters over Ahab's signature, stamped them with his official seal, and sent them to the elders in Naboth's city and to the civic leaders. She wrote "Call for a fast day and put Naboth at the head table. Then seat a couple of stool pigeons across from him who, in front of everybody will say, 'You! You blasphemed God and the king!' Then they'll throw him out and stone him to death."

11-14   And they did it. The men of the city — the elders and civic leaders — followed Jezebel's instructions that she wrote in the letters sent to them. They called for a fast day and seated Naboth at the head table. Then they brought in two stool pigeons and seated them opposite Naboth. In front of everybody the two degenerates accused him, "He blasphemed God and the king!" The company threw him out in the street, stoned him mercilessly, and he died.

15   When Jezebel got word that Naboth had been stoned to death, she told Ahab, "Go for it, Ahab — take the vineyard of Naboth the Jezreelite for your own, the vineyard he refused to sell you. Naboth is no more; Naboth is dead."

16   The minute Ahab heard that Naboth was dead, he set out for the vineyard of Naboth the Jezreelite and claimed it for his own.

17-19   Then GOD stepped in and spoke to Elijah the Tishbite, "On your feet; go down and confront Ahab of Samaria, king of Israel. You'll find him in the vineyard of Naboth; he's gone there to claim it as his own. Say this to him: 'GOD's word: What's going on here? First murder, then theft?' Then tell him, 'GOD's verdict: The very spot where the dogs lapped up Naboth's blood, they'll lap up your blood — that's right, *your* blood.'"

20-22   Ahab answered Elijah, "My enemy! So, you've run me down!"

"Yes, I've found you out," said Elijah. "And because you've bought into the business of evil, defying GOD. 'I will most certainly bring doom upon you, make mincemeat of your descendants, kill off every sorry male wretch who's even remotely connected with the name Ahab. And I'll bring down on you the same fate that fell on Jeroboam son of Nebat and Baasha son of Ahijah—you've made me *that* angry by making Israel sin.'"

23-24 As for Jezebel, GOD said, "Dogs will fight over the flesh of Jezebel all over Jezreel. Anyone tainted by Ahab who dies in the city will be eaten by stray dogs; corpses in the country will be eaten by carrion crows."

25-26 Ahab, pushed by his wife Jezebel and in open defiance of GOD, set an all-time record in making big business of evil. He indulged in outrageous obscenities in the world of idols, copying the Amorites whom GOD had earlier kicked out of Israelite territory.

27 When Ahab heard what Elijah had to say, he ripped his clothes to shreds, dressed in penitential rough burlap, and fasted. He even slept in coarse burlap pajamas. He tiptoed around, quiet as a mouse.

28-29 Then GOD spoke to Elijah the Tishbite: "Do you see how penitently submissive Ahab has become to me? Because of his repentance I'll not bring the doom during his lifetime; Ahab's son, though, will get it."

1-3 **22** They enjoyed three years of peace—no fighting between Aram and Israel. In the third year, Jehoshaphat king of Judah had a meeting with the king of Israel. Israel's king remarked to his aides, "Do you realize that Ramoth Gilead belongs to us, and we're sitting around on our hands instead of taking it back from the king of Aram?"

4-5 He turned to Jehoshaphat and said, "Will you join me in fighting for Ramoth Gilead?"

Jehoshaphat said, "You bet. I'm with you all the way—my troops are your troops, my horses are your horses." He then continued, "But before you do anything, ask GOD for guidance."

6 The king of Israel got the prophets together—all four hundred of them—and put the question to them: "Should I attack Ramoth Gilead? Or should I hold back?"

"Go for it," they said. "GOD will hand it over to the king."

7 But Jehoshaphat dragged his heels: "Is there still another prophet of GOD around here we can consult?"

8 The king of Israel told Jehoshaphat, "As a matter of fact, there is still one such man. But I hate him. He never preaches anything good to me, only doom, doom, doom—Micaiah son of Imlah."

"The king shouldn't talk about a prophet like that," said Jehoshaphat.

9 So the king of Israel ordered one of his men, "On the double! Get Micaiah son of Imlah."

10-12 Meanwhile, the king of Israel and Jehoshaphat were seated on their thrones, dressed in their royal robes, resplendent in front of the Samaria city gates. All the prophets were staging a prophecy-performance for their benefit. Zedekiah son of Kenaanah had even made a set of iron horns, and brandishing them called out, "GOD's word! With these horns you'll gore Aram until there's nothing left of him!" All the prophets chimed in, "Yes! Go for Ramoth Gilead! An easy victory! GOD's gift to the king!"

13 The messenger who went to get Micaiah said, "The prophets have all said Yes to the king. Make it unanimous—vote Yes!"

14 But Micaiah said, "As surely as GOD lives, what GOD says, I'll say."

15 With Micaiah before him, the king asked him, "So Micaiah—do we attack Ramoth Gilead, or do we hold back?"

"Go ahead," he said. "An easy victory. GOD's gift to the king."

16 "Not so fast," said the king. "How many times have I made you promise under oath to tell me the truth and nothing but the truth?"

17 "All right," said Micaiah, "since you insist.

> I saw all of Israel scattered over the hills,
>   sheep with no shepherd.
> Then GOD spoke: 'These poor people
>   have no one to tell them what to do.
> Let them go home and do
>   the best they can for themselves.'"

18 Then the king of Israel turned to Jehoshaphat, "See! What did I tell you? He never has a good word for me from GOD, only doom."

19-23 Micaiah kept on: "I'm not done yet; listen to GOD's word:

> I saw GOD enthroned,
>   and all the angel armies of heaven
> Standing at attention
>   ranged on his right and his left.
> And GOD said, 'How can we seduce Ahab
>   into attacking Ramoth Gilead?'
> Some said this,
>   and some said that.
> Then a bold angel stepped out,
>   stood before GOD, and said,
> 'I'll seduce him.'
>   'And how will you do it?' said GOD.
> 'Easy,' said the angel,
>   'I'll get all the prophets to lie.'
> 'That should do it,' said GOD.
>   'On your way—seduce him!'

"And that's what has happened. GOD filled the mouths of your puppet prophets with seductive lies. GOD has pronounced your doom."

24 Just then Zedekiah son of Kenaanah came up and punched Micaiah in the nose, saying, "Since when did the Spirit of GOD leave me and take up with you?"

25 Micaiah said, "You'll know soon enough; you'll know it when you're frantically and futilely looking for a place to hide."

26-27 The king of Israel had heard enough: "Get Micaiah out of here! Turn him over to Amon the city magistrate and to Joash the king's son with this message, 'King's orders: Lock him up in jail; keep him on bread and water until I'm back in one piece.'"

28 Micaiah said, "If you ever get back in one piece, I'm no prophet of GOD." He added, "When it happens, O people, remember where you heard it!"

29-30 The king of Israel and Jehoshaphat king of Judah attacked Ramoth Gilead. The king of Israel said to Jehoshaphat, "Wear my kingly robe; I'm going into battle disguised." So the king of Israel entered the battle in disguise.

31 Meanwhile, the king of Aram had ordered his chariot commanders (there were thirty-two of them): "Don't bother with anyone, whether small or great; go after the king of Israel and him only."

32-33 When the chariot commanders saw Jehoshaphat they said, "There he is! The king of Israel!" and took after him. Jehoshaphat yelled out, and the chariot commanders realized they had the wrong man — it wasn't the king of Israel after all. They let him go.

34 Just then someone, without aiming, shot an arrow randomly into the crowd and hit the king of Israel in the chink of his armor. The king told his charioteer, "Turn back! Get me out of here — I'm wounded."

35-37 All day the fighting continued, hot and heavy. Propped up in his chariot, the king watched from the sidelines. He died that evening. Blood from his wound pooled in the chariot. As the sun went down, shouts reverberated through the ranks, "Abandon camp! Head for home! The king is dead!"

37-38 The king was brought to Samaria and there they buried him. They washed down the chariot at the pool of Samaria where the town whores bathed, and the dogs lapped up the blood, just as GOD's word had said.

39-40 The rest of Ahab's life — everything he did, the ivory palace he built, the towns he founded, and the defense system he built up — is all written up in *The Chronicles of the Kings of Israel*. He was buried in the family cemetery and his son Ahaziah was the next king.

JEHOSHAPHAT OF JUDAH

41-44 Jehoshaphat son of Asa became king of Judah in the fourth year of Ahab king of Israel. Jehoshaphat was thirty-five years old when he became king and he ruled for twenty-five years in Jerusalem. His mother was Azubah daughter of Shilhi. He continued the kind of life characteristic of his father Asa — no detours, no dead ends — pleasing GOD with his life. But he failed to get rid of the neighborhood sex-and-religion shrines. People continued to pray and worship at these idolatrous shrines. And he kept on good terms with the king of Israel.

45-46 The rest of Jehoshaphat's life, his achievements and his battles, is all written in *The Chronicles of the Kings of Judah*. Also, he got rid of the sacred prostitutes left over from the days of his father Asa.

47 Edom was kingless during his reign; a deputy was in charge.

48-49 Jehoshaphat built ocean-going ships to sail to Ophir for gold. But they never made it; they shipwrecked at Ezion Geber. During that time Ahaziah son of Ahab proposed a joint shipping venture, but Jehoshaphat wouldn't go in with him.

50 Then Jehoshaphat died and was buried in the family cemetery in the City of David his ancestor. Jehoram his son was the next king.

AHAZIAH OF ISRAEL

51-53 Ahaziah son of Ahab became king over Israel in Samaria in the seventeenth year of Jehoshaphat king of Judah. He ruled Israel for two years. As far as GOD was concerned, he lived an evil life, reproducing the bad life of his father and mother, repeating the pattern set down by Jeroboam son of Nebat, who led Israel into a life of sin. Worshiping at the Baal shrines, he made GOD, the God of Israel, angry, oh, so angry. If anything, he was worse than his father.

2 KINGS

1   1 After Ahab died, Moab rebelled against Israel.

2   One day Ahaziah fell through the balcony railing on the rooftop of his house in Samaria and was injured. He sent messengers off to consult Baal-Zebub, the god of Ekron, "Am I going to recover from this accident?"

3-4   GOD's angel spoke to Elijah the Tishbite: "Up on your feet! Go out and meet the messengers of the king of Samaria with this word, 'Is it because there's no God in Israel that you're running off to consult Baal-Zebub god of Ekron?' Here's a message from the GOD you've tried to bypass: 'You're not going to get out of that bed you're in—you're as good as dead already.'" Elijah delivered the message and was gone.

5   The messengers went back. The king said, "So why are you back so soon—what's going on?"

6   They told him, "A man met us and said, 'Turn around and go back to the king who sent you; tell him, GOD's message: Is it because there's no God in Israel that you're running off to consult Baal-Zebub god of Ekron? You needn't bother. You're not going to get out of that bed you're in—you're as good as dead already.'"

7   The king said, "Tell me more about this man who met you and said these things to you. What was he like?"

8   "Shaggy," they said, "and wearing a leather belt."
He said, "That has to be Elijah the Tishbite!"

9   The king sent a captain with fifty men to Elijah. Meanwhile Elijah was sitting, big as life, on top of a hill. The captain said, "O Holy Man! King's orders: Come down!"

10   Elijah answered the captain of the fifty, "If it's true that I'm a 'holy man,' lightning strike you and your fifty men!" Out of the blue lightning struck and incinerated the captain and his fifty.

11   The king sent another captain with his fifty men, "O Holy Man! King's orders: Come down. And right now!"

12   Elijah answered, "If it's true that I'm a 'holy man,' lightning strike you and your fifty men!" Immediately a divine lightning bolt struck and incinerated the captain and his fifty.

13-14   The king then sent a third captain with his fifty men. For a third time, a captain with his fifty approached Elijah. This one fell on his knees in supplication: "O Holy Man, have respect for my life and the souls of these fifty men! Twice now lightning from out of the blue has struck and incinerated captains with their fifty men; please, I beg you, respect my life!"

15   The angel of GOD told Elijah, "Go ahead; and don't be afraid." Elijah got up and went down with him to the king.

16   Elijah told him, "GOD's word: Because you sent messengers to consult Baal-Zebub the god of Ekron, as if there were no God in Israel to whom you could pray, you'll never get out of that bed alive—already you're as good as dead."

17   And he died, exactly as GOD's word spoken by Elijah had said.
Because Ahaziah had no son, his brother Joram became the next king. The succession took place in the second year of the reign of Jehoram son of Jehoshaphat king of Judah.

18 The rest of Ahaziah's life is recorded in *The Chronicles of the Kings of Israel.*

1-2 **2** Just before GOD took Elijah to heaven in a whirlwind, Elijah and Elisha were on a walk out of Gilgal. Elijah said to Elisha, "Stay here. GOD has sent me on an errand to Bethel."

Elisha said, "Not on your life! I'm not letting you out of my sight!" So they both went to Bethel.

3 The guild of prophets at Bethel met Elisha and said, "Did you know that GOD is going to take your master away from you today?"

"Yes," he said, "I know it. But keep it quiet."

4 Then Elijah said to Elisha, "Stay here. GOD has sent me on an errand to Jericho."

Elisha said, "Not on your life! I'm not letting you out of my sight!" So they both went to Jericho.

5 The guild of prophets at Jericho came to Elisha and said, "Did you know that GOD is going to take your master away from you today?"

"Yes," he said, "I know it. But keep it quiet."

6 Then Elijah said to Elisha, "Stay here. GOD has sent me on an errand to the Jordan."

Elisha said, "Not on your life! I'm not letting you out of my sight!" And so the two of them went their way together.

7 Meanwhile, fifty men from the guild of prophets gathered some distance away while the two of them stood at the Jordan.

8 Elijah took his cloak, rolled it up, and hit the water with it. The river divided and the two men walked through on dry land.

9 When they reached the other side, Elijah said to Elisha, "What can I do for you before I'm taken from you? Ask anything."

Elisha said, "Your life repeated in my life. I want to be a holy man just like you."

10 "That's a hard one!" said Elijah. "But if you're watching when I'm taken from you, you'll get what you've asked for. But only if you're watching."

11-14 And so it happened. They were walking along and talking. Suddenly a chariot and horses of fire came between them and Elijah went up in a whirlwind to heaven. Elisha saw it all and shouted, "My father, my father! You—the chariot and cavalry of Israel!" When he could no longer see anything, he grabbed his robe and ripped it to pieces. Then he picked up Elijah's cloak that had fallen from him, returned to the shore of the Jordan, and stood there. He took Elijah's cloak—all that was left of Elijah!—and hit the river with it, saying, "Now where is the GOD of Elijah? Where is he?"

When he struck the water, the river divided and Elisha walked through.

15 The guild of prophets from Jericho saw the whole thing from where they were standing. They said, "The spirit of Elijah lives in Elisha!" They welcomed and honored him.

16 They then said, "We're at your service. We have fifty reliable men here; let's send them out to look for your master. Maybe GOD's spirit has swept him off to some mountain or dropped him into a remote ravine."

Elisha said, "No. Don't send them."

17 But they pestered him until he caved in: "Go ahead then. Send them." So they sent the fifty men off. For three days they looked, searching high and low. Nothing.

18   Finally, they returned to Elisha in Jericho. He told them, "So there—didn't I tell you?"

19   One day the men of the city said to Elisha, "You can see for yourself, master, how well our city is located. But the water is polluted and nothing grows."

20   He said, "Bring me a brand-new bowl and put some salt in it." They brought it to him.

21-22   He then went to the spring, sprinkled the salt into it, and proclaimed, "GOD's word: I've healed this water. It will no longer kill you or poison your land." And sure enough, the water was healed—and remains so to this day, just as Elisha said.

23   Another time, Elisha was on his way to Bethel and some little kids came out from the town and taunted him, "What's up, old baldhead! Out of our way, skinhead!"

24   Elisha turned, took one look at them, and cursed them in the name of GOD. Two bears charged out of the underbrush and knocked them about, ripping them limb from limb—forty-two children in all!

25   Elisha went on to Mount Carmel, and then returned to Samaria.

JORAM OF ISRAEL

1-3   3 Joram son of Ahab began his rule over Israel in Samaria in the eighteenth year of Jehoshaphat king of Judah. He was king for twelve years. In GOD's sight he was a bad king. But he wasn't as bad as his father and mother—to his credit he destroyed the obscene Baal stone that his father had made. But he hung on to the sinful practices of Jeroboam son of Nebat, the ones that had corrupted Israel for so long. He wasn't about to give them up.

4-7   King Mesha of Moab raised sheep. He was forced to give the king of Israel 100,000 lambs and another 100,000 rams. When Ahab died, the king of Moab rebelled against the king of Israel. So King Joram set out from Samaria and prepared Israel for war. His first move was to send a message to Jehoshaphat king of Judah: "The king of Moab has rebelled against me. Would you join me and fight him?"

7-8   "I'm with you all the way," said Jehoshaphat. "My troops are your troops, my horses are your horses. Which route shall we take?"

       "Through the badlands of Edom."

9   The king of Israel, the king of Judah, and the king of Edom started out on what proved to be a looping detour. After seven days they had run out of water for both army and animals.

10   The king of Israel said, "Bad news! GOD has gotten us three kings out here to dump us into the hand of Moab."

11   But Jehoshaphat said, "Isn't there a prophet of GOD anywhere around through whom we can consult GOD?"

       One of the servants of the king of Israel said, "Elisha son of Shaphat is around somewhere—the one who was Elijah's right-hand man."

12   Jehoshaphat said, "Good! A man we can trust!" So the three of them—the king of Israel, Jehoshaphat, and the king of Edom—went to meet him.

13   Elisha addressed the king of Israel, "What do you and I have in common? Go consult the puppet-prophets of your father and mother."

"Never!" said the king of Israel. "It's GOD who has gotten us into this fix, dumping all three of us kings into the hand of Moab."

¹⁴⁻¹⁵ Elisha said, "As GOD-of-the-Angel-Armies lives, and before whom I stand ready to serve, if it weren't for the respect I have for Jehoshaphat king of Judah, I wouldn't give you the time of day. But considering—bring me a minstrel." (When a minstrel played, the power of GOD came on Elisha.)

¹⁶⁻¹⁹ He then said, "GOD's word: Dig ditches all over this valley. Here's what will happen—you won't hear the wind, you won't see the rain, but this valley is going to fill up with water and your army and your animals will drink their fill. This is easy for GOD to do; he will also hand over Moab to you. You will ravage the country: Knock out its fortifications, level the key villages, clear-cut the orchards, clog the springs, and litter the cultivated fields with stones."

²⁰ In the morning—it was at the hour of morning sacrifice—the water had arrived, water pouring in from the west, from Edom, a flash flood filling the valley with water.

²¹⁻²² By this time everyone in Moab had heard that the kings had come up to make war against them. Everyone who was able to handle a sword was called into service and took a stand at the border. They were up and ready early in the morning when the sun rose over the water. From where the Moabites stood, the water reflecting the sun looked red, like blood.

²³ "Blood! Look at the blood!" they said. "The kings must have fought each other—a bloody massacre! Go for the loot, Moab!"

²⁴⁻²⁵ When Moab entered the camp of Israel, the Israelites were up on their feet killing Moabites right and left, the Moabites running for their lives, Israelites relentless in pursuit—a slaughter. They leveled the towns, littered the cultivated fields with rocks, clogged the springs, and clear-cut the orchards. Only the capital, Kir Hareseth, was left intact, and that not for long; it too was surrounded and attacked with thrown and flung rocks.

²⁶⁻²⁷ When the king of Moab realized that he was fighting a losing battle, he took seven hundred swordsmen to hack a corridor past the king of Edom, but they didn't make it. Then he took his son, his firstborn who would succeed him as king, and sacrificed him on the city wall. That set off furious anger against Israel. Israel pulled back and returned home.

¹ **4** One day the wife of a man from the guild of prophets called out to Elisha, "Your servant my husband is dead. You well know what a good man he was, devoted to GOD. And now the man to whom he was in debt is on his way to collect by taking my two children as slaves."

² Elisha said, "I wonder how I can be of help. Tell me, what do you have in your house?"

"Nothing," she said. "Well, I do have a little oil."

³⁻⁴ "Here's what you do," said Elisha. "Go up and down the street and borrow jugs and bowls from all your neighbors. And not just a few—all you can get. Then come home and lock the door behind you, you and your sons. Pour oil into each container; when each is full, set it aside."

⁵⁻⁶ She did what he said. She locked the door behind her and her sons; as they brought the containers to her, she filled them. When all the jugs and bowls were full, she said to one of her sons, "Another jug, please."

He said, "That's it. There are no more jugs."

Then the oil stopped.

7 She went and told the story to the man of God. He said, "Go sell the oil and make good on your debts. Live, both you and your sons, on what's left."

※

8 One day Elisha passed through Shunem. A leading lady of the town talked him into stopping for a meal. And then it became his custom: Whenever he passed through, he stopped by for a meal.

9-10 "I'm certain," said the woman to her husband, "that this man who stops by with us all the time is a holy man of God. Why don't we add on a small room upstairs and furnish it with a bed and desk, chair and lamp, so that when he comes by he can stay with us?"

11 And so it happened that the next time Elisha came by he went to the room and lay down for a nap.

12 Then he said to his servant Gehazi, "Tell the Shunammite woman I want to see her." He called her and she came to him.

13 Through Gehazi Elisha said, "You've gone far beyond the call of duty in taking care of us; what can we do for you? Do you have a request we can bring to the king or to the commander of the army?"

She replied, "Nothing. I'm secure and satisfied in my family."

14 Elisha conferred with Gehazi: "There's got to be something we can do for her. But what?"

Gehazi said, "Well, she has no son, and her husband is an old man."

15 "Call her in," said Elisha. He called her and she stood at the open door.

16 Elisha said to her, "This time next year you're going to be nursing an infant son."

"O my master, O Holy Man," she said, "don't play games with me, teasing me with such fantasies!"

17 The woman conceived. A year later, just as Elisha had said, she had a son.

18-19 The child grew up. One day he went to his father, who was working with the harvest hands, complaining, "My head, my head!"

His father ordered a servant, "Carry him to his mother."

20 The servant took him in his arms and carried him to his mother. He lay on her lap until noon and died.

21 She took him up and laid him on the bed of the man of God, shut him in alone, and left.

22 She then called her husband, "Get me a servant and a donkey so I can go to the Holy Man; I'll be back as soon as I can."

23 "But why today? This isn't a holy day — it's neither New Moon nor Sabbath."

She said, "Don't ask questions; I need to go right now. Trust me."

24-25 She went ahead and saddled the donkey, ordering her servant, "Take the lead — and go as fast as you can; I'll tell you if you're going too fast." And so off she went. She came to the Holy Man at Mount Carmel.

25-26 The Holy Man, spotting her while she was still a long way off, said to his servant Gehazi, "Look out there; why, it's the Shunammite woman! Quickly now. Ask her, 'Is something wrong? Are you all right? Your husband? Your child?'"

She said, "Everything's fine."

27 But when she reached the Holy Man at the mountain, she threw herself at his feet and held tightly to him.

Gehazi came up to pull her away, but the Holy Man said, "Leave her alone—can't you see that she's in distress? But GOD hasn't let me in on why; I'm completely in the dark."

28 Then she spoke up: "Did I ask for a son, master? Didn't I tell you, 'Don't tease me with false hopes'?"

29 He ordered Gehazi, "Don't lose a minute—grab my staff and run as fast as you can. If you meet anyone, don't even take time to greet him, and if anyone greets you, don't even answer. Lay my staff across the boy's face."

30 The boy's mother said, "As sure as GOD lives and you live, you're not leaving me behind." And so Gehazi let her take the lead, and followed behind.

31 But Gehazi arrived first and laid the staff across the boy's face. But there was no sound—no sign of life. Gehazi went back to meet Elisha and said, "The boy hasn't stirred."

32-35 Elisha entered the house and found the boy stretched out on the bed dead. He went into the room and locked the door—just the two of them in the room—and prayed to GOD. He then got into bed with the boy and covered him with his body, mouth on mouth, eyes on eyes, hands on hands. As he was stretched out over him like that, the boy's body became warm. Elisha got up and paced back and forth in the room. Then he went back and stretched himself upon the boy again. The boy started sneezing—seven times he sneezed!—and opened his eyes.

36 He called Gehazi and said, "Get the Shunammite woman in here!" He called her and she came in.

Elisha said, "Embrace your son!"

37 She fell at Elisha's feet, face to the ground in reverent awe. Then she embraced her son and went out with him.

38 Elisha went back down to Gilgal. There was a famine there. While he was consulting with the guild of prophets, he told his servant, "Put a large pot on the fire and cook up some stew for the prophets."

39-40 One of the men went out into the field to get some herbs; he came across a wild vine and picked gourds from it, filling his gunnysack. He brought them back, sliced them up, and put them in the stew, even though no one knew what kind of plant it was. The stew was then served up for the men to eat. They started to eat, and then exclaimed, "Death in the pot, O man of God! Death in the pot!" Nobody could eat it.

Elisha ordered, "Get me some meal." Then he sprinkled it into the stew pot.

41 "Now serve it up to the men," he said. They ate it, and it was just fine—nothing wrong with *that* stew!

42 One day a man arrived from Baal Shalishah. He brought the man of God twenty loaves of fresh-baked bread from the early harvest, along with a few apples from the orchard.

Elisha said, "Pass it around to the people to eat."

43 · His servant said, "For a hundred men? There's not nearly enough!"

Elisha said, "Just go ahead and do it. GOD says there's plenty."

44 And sure enough, there was. He passed around what he had—they not only ate, but had leftovers.

1-3 **5** Naaman was general of the army under the king of Aram. He was important to his master, who held him in the highest esteem because it was by him that GOD had given victory to Aram: a truly great man, but afflicted with a grievous skin disease. It so happened that Aram, on one of its raiding expeditions against Israel, captured a young girl who became a maid to Naaman's wife. One day she said to her mistress, "Oh, if only my master could meet the prophet of Samaria, he would be healed of his skin disease."

4 Naaman went straight to his master and reported what the girl from Israel had said.

5 "Well then, go," said the king of Aram. "And I'll send a letter of introduction to the king of Israel."

So he went off, taking with him about 750 pounds of silver, 150 pounds of gold, and ten sets of clothes.

6 Naaman delivered the letter to the king of Israel. The letter read, "When you get this letter, you'll know that I've personally sent my servant Naaman to you; heal him of his skin disease."

7 When the king of Israel read the letter, he was terribly upset, ripping his robe to pieces. He said, "Am I a god with the power to bring death or life that I get orders to heal this man from his disease? What's going on here? That king's trying to pick a fight, that's what!"

8 Elisha the man of God heard what had happened, that the king of Israel was so distressed that he'd ripped his robe to shreds. He sent word to the king, "Why are you so upset, ripping your robe like this? Send him to me so he'll learn that there's a prophet in Israel."

9 So Naaman with his horses and chariots arrived in style and stopped at Elisha's door.

10 Elisha sent out a servant to meet him with this message: "Go to the River Jordan and immerse yourself seven times. Your skin will be healed and you'll be as good as new."

11-12 Naaman lost his temper. He turned on his heel saying, "I thought he'd personally come out and meet me, call on the name of GOD, wave his hand over the diseased spot, and get rid of the disease. The Damascus rivers, Abana and Pharpar, are cleaner by far than any of the rivers in Israel. Why not bathe in them? I'd at least get clean." He stomped off, mad as a hornet.

13 But his servants caught up with him and said, "Father, if the prophet had asked you to do something hard and heroic, wouldn't you have done it? So why not this simple 'wash and be clean'?"

14 So he did it. He went down and immersed himself in the Jordan seven times, following the orders of the Holy Man. His skin was healed; it was like the skin of a little baby. He was as good as new.

15 He then went back to the Holy Man, he and his entourage, stood before him, and said, "I now know beyond a shadow of a doubt that there is no God anywhere on earth other than the God of Israel. In gratitude let me give you a gift."

16 "As GOD lives," Elisha replied, "the God whom I serve, I'll take nothing from you." Naaman tried his best to get him to take something, but he wouldn't do it.

17-18 "If you won't take anything," said Naaman, "let me ask you for something: Give me a load of dirt, as much as a team of donkeys can carry, because I'm never again going to worship any god other than GOD. But there's one thing for which I need GOD's pardon: When my master, leaning on my arm, enters the shrine of Rimmon and worships there, and I'm with him there, worshiping Rimmon, may you see to it that GOD forgive me for this."

19-21 Elisha said, "Everything will be all right. Go in peace."

But he hadn't gone far when Gehazi, servant to Elisha the Holy Man, said to himself, "My master has let this Aramean Naaman slip through his fingers without so much as a thank-you. By the living GOD, I'm going after him to get something or other from him!" And Gehazi took off after Naaman.

Naaman saw him running after him and jumped down from his chariot to greet him, "Is something wrong?"

22 "Nothing's wrong, but something's come up. My master sent me to tell you: 'Two young men just showed up from the hill country of Ephraim, brothers from the guild of the prophets. Supply their needs with a gift of 75 pounds of silver and a couple of sets of clothes.'"

23 Naaman said, "Of course, how about 150 pounds?" Naaman insisted. He tied up the money in two sacks and gave him the two sets of clothes; he even gave him two servants to carry the gifts back with him.

24 When they got to the fort on the hill, Gehazi took the gifts from the servants, stored them inside, then sent the servants back.

25 He returned and stood before his master. Elisha said, "So what have you been up to, Gehazi?"

"Nothing much," he said.

26-27 Elisha said, "Didn't you know I was with you in spirit when that man stepped down from his chariot to greet you? Tell me, is this a time to look after yourself, lining your pockets with gifts? Naaman's skin disease will now infect you and your family, with no relief in sight."

Gehazi walked away, his skin flaky and white like snow.

1-2 One day the guild of prophets came to Elisha and said, "You can see that this place where we're living under your leadership is getting cramped—we have no elbow room. Give us permission to go down to the Jordan where each of us will get a log. We'll build a roomier place."

Elisha said, "Go ahead."

3 One of them then said, "Please! Come along with us!"

He said, "Certainly."

4-5 He went with them. They came to the Jordan and started chopping down trees. As one of them was felling a timber, his axhead flew off and sank in the river.

"Oh no, master!" he cried out. "And it was borrowed!"

6 The Holy Man said, "Where did it sink?"

The man showed him the place.

He cut off a branch and tossed it at the spot. The axhead floated up.

7 "Grab it," he said. The man reached out and took it.

8 One time when the king of Aram was at war with Israel, after consulting with his officers, he said, "At such and such a place I want an ambush set."

9 The Holy Man sent a message to the king of Israel: "Watch out when you're passing this place, because Aram has set an ambush there."

10 So the king of Israel sent word concerning the place of which the Holy Man had warned him.

This kind of thing happened all the time.

11 The king of Aram was furious over all this. He called his officers together and said, "Tell me, who is leaking information to the king of Israel? Who is the spy in our ranks?"

12 But one of his men said, "No, my master, dear king. It's not any of us. It's Elisha the prophet in Israel. He tells the king of Israel everything you say, even what you whisper in your bedroom."

13 The king said, "Go and find out where he is. I'll send someone and capture him."

The report came back, "He's in Dothan."

14 Then he dispatched horses and chariots, an impressive fighting force. They came by night and surrounded the city.

15 Early in the morning a servant of the Holy Man got up and went out. Surprise! Horses and chariots surrounding the city! The young man exclaimed, "Oh, master! What shall we do?"

16 He said, "Don't worry about it—there are more on our side than on their side."

17 Then Elisha prayed, "O GOD, open his eyes and let him see."

The eyes of the young man were opened and he saw. A wonder! The whole mountainside full of horses and chariots of fire surrounding Elisha!

18 When the Arameans attacked, Elisha prayed to GOD, "Strike these people blind!" And GOD struck them blind, just as Elisha said.

19 Then Elisha called out to them, "Not that way! Not this city! Follow me and I'll lead you to the man you're looking for." And he led them into Samaria.

20 As they entered the city, Elisha prayed, "O GOD, open their eyes so they can see where they are." GOD opened their eyes. They looked around—they were trapped in Samaria!

21 When the king of Israel saw them, he said to Elisha, "Father, shall I massacre the lot?"

22 "Not on your life!" said Elisha. "You didn't lift a hand to capture them, and now you're going to kill them? No sir, make a feast for them and send them back to their master."

23 So he prepared a huge feast for them. After they ate and drank their fill he dismissed them. Then they returned home to their master. The raiding bands of Aram didn't bother Israel anymore.

24-25 At a later time, this: Ben-Hadad king of Aram pulled together his troops and launched a siege on Samaria. This brought on a terrible famine, so bad that food prices soared astronomically. Eighty shekels for a donkey's head! Five shekels for a bowl of field greens!

26 One day the king of Israel was walking along the city wall. A woman cried out, "Help! Your majesty!"

27 He answered, "If GOD won't help you, where on earth can *I* go for help? To the granary? To the dairy?"

28-29 The king continued, "Tell me your story."

She said, "This woman came to me and said, 'Give up your son and we'll have him for today's supper; tomorrow we'll eat my son.' So we cooked my son and ate him. The next day I told her, 'Your turn—bring your son so we can have him for supper.' But she had hidden her son away."

30-31 When the king heard the woman's story he ripped apart his robe. Since he was walking on the city wall, everyone saw that next to his skin he was wearing coarse burlap. And he called out, "God do his worst to me—and more—if Elisha son of Shaphat still has a head on his shoulders at this day's end."

32 Elisha was sitting at home, the elders sitting with him. The king had already dispatched an executioner, but before the man arrived Elisha spoke to the elders: "Do you know that this murderer has just now sent a man to take off my head? Look, when the executioner arrives, shut the door and lock it. Don't I even now hear the footsteps of his master behind him?"

33 While he was giving his instructions, the king showed up, accusing, "This trouble is directly from GOD! And what's next? I'm fed up with GOD!"

1 7 Elisha said, "Listen! GOD's word! The famine's over. This time tomorrow food will be plentiful—a handful of meal for a shekel; two handfuls of grain for a shekel. The market at the city gate will be buzzing."

2 The attendant on whom the king leaned for support said to the Holy Man, "You expect us to believe that? Trapdoors opening in the sky and food tumbling out?"

"You'll watch it with your own eyes," he said, "but *you* will not eat so much as a mouthful!"

3-4 It happened that four lepers were sitting just outside the city gate. They said to one another, "What are we doing sitting here at death's door? If we enter the famine-struck city we'll die; if we stay here we'll die. So let's take our chances in the camp of Aram and throw ourselves on their mercy. If they receive us we'll live, if they kill us we'll die. We've got nothing to lose."

5-8 So after the sun went down they got up and went to the camp of Aram. When they got to the edge of the camp, surprise! Not a man in the camp! The Master had made the army of Aram hear the sound of horses and a mighty army on the march. They told one another, "The king of Israel hired the kings of the Hittites and the kings of Egypt to attack us!" Panicked, they ran for their lives through the darkness, abandoning tents, horses, donkeys—the whole camp just as it was—running for dear life. These four lepers entered the camp and went into a tent. First they ate and drank. Then they grabbed silver, gold, and clothing, and went off and hid it. They came back, entered another tent, and looted it, again hiding their plunder.

9 Finally they said to one another, "We shouldn't be doing this! This is a day of good news and we're making it into a private party! If we wait around until morning we'll get caught and punished. Come on! Let's go tell the news to the king's palace!"

10 So they went and called out at the city gate, telling what had happened: "We went to the camp of Aram and, surprise!—the place was deserted. Not a soul, not a sound! Horses and donkeys left tethered and tents abandoned just as they were."

11-12 The gatekeepers got the word to the royal palace, giving them the whole story. Roused in the middle of the night, the king told his servants, "Let me tell you what Aram has done. They knew that we were starving, so they left camp and have hid in the field, thinking, 'When they come out of the city, we'll capture them alive and take the city.'"

13 One of his advisors answered, "Let some men go and take five of the

horses left behind. The worst that can happen is no worse than what could happen to the whole city. Let's send them and find out what's happened."

14   They took two chariots with horses. The king sent them after the army of Aram with the orders, "Scout them out; find out what happened."

15   They went after them all the way to the Jordan. The whole way was strewn with clothes and equipment that Aram had dumped in their panicked flight. The scouts came back and reported to the king.

16   The people then looted the camp of Aram. Food prices dropped overnight—a handful of meal for a shekel; two handfuls of grain for a shekel—GOD's word to the letter!

17   The king ordered his attendant, the one he leaned on for support, to be in charge of the city gate. The people, turned into a mob, poured through the gate, trampling him to death. It was exactly what the Holy Man had said when the king had come to see him.

18-20   Every word of the Holy Man to the king—"A handful of meal for a shekel, two handfuls of grain for a shekel this time tomorrow in the gate of Samaria," with the attendant's sarcastic reply to the Holy Man, "You expect us to believe that? Trapdoors opening in the sky and food tumbling out?" followed by the response, "You'll watch it with your own eyes, but you won't eat so much as a mouthful"—proved true. The final stroke came when the people trampled the man to death at the city gate.

1-3   8 Years before, Elisha had told the woman whose son he had brought to life, "Leave here and go, you and your family, and live someplace else. GOD has ordered a famine in the land; it will last for seven years." The woman did what the Holy Man told her and left. She and her family lived as aliens in the country of Philistia for seven years. Then, when the seven years were up, the woman and her family came back. She went directly to the king and asked for her home and farm.

4-5   The king was talking with Gehazi, servant to the Holy Man, saying, "Tell me some stories of the great things Elisha did." It so happened that as he was telling the king the story of the dead person brought back to life, the woman whose son was brought to life showed up asking for her home and farm.

Gehazi said, "My master the king, this is the woman! And this is her son whom Elisha brought back to life!"

6   The king wanted to know all about it, and so she told him the story. The king assigned an officer to take care of her, saying, "Make sure she gets everything back that's hers, plus all profits from the farm from the time she left until now."

7   Elisha traveled to Damascus. Ben-Hadad, king of Aram, was sick at the time. He was told, "The Holy Man is in town."

8   The king ordered Hazael, "Take a gift with you and go meet the Holy Man. Ask GOD through him, 'Am I going to recover from this sickness?'"

9   Hazael went and met with Elisha. He brought with him every choice thing he could think of from Damascus—forty camel-loads of items! When he arrived he stood before Elisha and said, "Your son Ben-Hadad, king of Aram, sent me here to ask you, 'Am I going to recover from this sickness?'"

10-11 Elisha answered, "Go and tell him, 'Don't worry; you'll live.' The fact is, though—GOD showed me—that he's doomed to die." Elisha then stared hard at Hazael, reading his heart. Hazael felt exposed and dropped his eyes. Then the Holy Man wept.

12 Hazael said, "Why does my master weep?"

"Because," said Elisha, "I know what you're going to do to the children of Israel:

> burn down their forts,
> murder their youth,
> smash their babies,
> rip open their pregnant women."

13 Hazael said, "Am I a mongrel dog that I'd do such a horrible thing?"

"GOD showed me," said Elisha, "that you'll be king of Aram."

14 Hazael left Elisha and returned to his master, who asked, "So, what did Elisha tell you?"

"He told me, 'Don't worry; you'll live.'"

15 But the very next day, someone took a heavy quilt, soaked it in water, covered the king's face, and suffocated him.

Now Hazael was king.

JEHORAM OF JUDAH

16-19 In the fifth year of the reign of Joram son of Ahab king of Israel, Jehoram son of Jehoshaphat king of Judah became king. He was thirty-two years old when he began his rule, and was king for eight years in Jerusalem. He copied the way of life of the kings of Israel, marrying into the Ahab family and continuing the Ahab line of sin—from GOD's point of view, an evil man living an evil life. But despite that, because of his servant David, GOD was not ready to destroy Judah. He had, after all, promised to keep a lamp burning through David's descendants.

20-21 During Jehoram's reign, Edom revolted against Judah's rule and set up their own king. Jehoram responded by taking his army of chariots to Zair.

Edom surrounded him, but in the middle of the night he and his charioteers broke through the lines and hit Edom hard. But his infantry deserted him.

22 Edom continues in revolt against Judah right up to the present. Even little Libnah revolted at that time.

23-24 The rest of the life and times of Jehoram, the record of his rule, is written in *The Chronicles of the Kings of Judah*. Jehoram died and was buried in the family grave in the City of David. His son Ahaziah succeeded him as king.

AHAZIAH OF JUDAH

25-27 In the twelfth year of the reign of Joram son of Ahab king of Israel, Ahaziah son of Jehoram king of Judah began his reign. Ahaziah was twenty-two years old when he became king; he ruled only a year in Jerusalem. His mother was Athaliah, granddaughter of Omri king of Israel. He lived and ruled just like the Ahab family had done, continuing the same evil-in-GOD's-sight line of sin, related by both marriage and sin to the Ahab clan.

28-29   He joined Joram son of Ahab king of Israel in a war against Hazael king of Aram at Ramoth Gilead. The archers wounded Joram. Joram pulled back to Jezreel to convalesce from the injuries he had received in the fight with Hazael. Ahaziah son of Jehoram king of Judah paid a visit to Joram son of Ahab on his sickbed in Jezreel.

JEHU OF ISRAEL

1-3   9 One day Elisha the prophet ordered a member of the guild of prophets, "Get yourself ready, take a flask of oil, and go to Ramoth Gilead. Look for Jehu son of Jehoshaphat son of Nimshi. When you find him, get him away from his companions and take him to a back room. Take your flask of oil and pour it over his head and say, 'GOD's word: I anoint you king over Israel.' Then open the door and get out of there as fast as you can. Don't wait around."

4-5   The young prophet went to Ramoth Gilead. On arrival he found the army officers all sitting around. He said, "I have a matter of business with you, officer."

Jehu said, "Which one of us?"

"With you, officer."

6-10   He got up and went inside the building. The young prophet poured the oil on his head and said, "GOD's word, the God of Israel: I've anointed you to be king over the people of GOD, over Israel. Your assignment is to attack the regime of Ahab your master. I am avenging the massacre of my servants the prophets — yes, the Jezebel-massacre of all the prophets of GOD. The entire line of Ahab is doomed. I'm wiping out the entire bunch of that sad lot. I'll see to it that the family of Ahab experiences the same fate as the family of Jeroboam son of Nebat and the family of Baasha son of Ahijah. As for Jezebel, the dogs will eat her carcass in the open fields of Jezreel. No burial for her!" Then he opened the door and made a run for it.

11   Jehu went back out to his master's officers. They asked, "Is everything all right? What did that crazy fool want with you?"

He said, "You know that kind of man — all talk."

12   "That's a lie!" they said. "Tell us what's going on."

He said, "He told me this and this and this — in effect, 'GOD's word: I anoint you king of Israel!'"

13   They sprang into action. Each man grabbed his robe; they piled them at the top of the steps for a makeshift throne. Then they blew the trumpet and declared, "Jehu is king!"

14-15   That ignited the conspiracy of Jehu son of Jehoshaphat son of Nimshi against Joram.

Meanwhile, Joram and the entire army were defending Ramoth Gilead against Hazael king of Aram. Except that Joram had pulled back to Jezreel to convalesce from the injuries he got from the Arameans in the battle with Hazael king of Aram.

Jehu said, "If you really want me as king, don't let anyone sneak out of the city and blab the news in Jezreel."

16   Then Jehu mounted a chariot and rode to Jezreel, where Joram was in bed, resting. King Ahaziah of Judah had come down to visit Joram.

17   A sentry standing duty on the watchtower in Jezreel saw the company of Jehu arrive. He said, "I see a band of men."

Joram said, "Get a horseman and send him out to meet them and inquire, 'Is anything wrong?'"

18 The horseman rode out to meet Jehu and said, "The king wants to know if there's anything wrong."

Jehu said, "What's it to you whether things are right or wrong? Fall in behind me."

The sentry said, "The messenger reached them, but he's not returning."

19 The king then sent a second horseman. When he reached them he said, "The king wants to know if there's anything wrong."

Jehu said, "What's it to you whether things are right or wrong? Fall in behind me."

20 The sentry said, "The messenger reached them, but he's not returning. The driving is like the driving of Jehu son of Nimshi — crazy!"

21 Joram ordered, "Get my chariot ready!" They hitched up his chariot. Joram king of Israel and Ahaziah king of Judah, each in his own chariot, drove out to meet Jehu. They met in the field of Naboth of Jezreel.

22 When Joram saw Jehu he called out, "Good day, Jehu!"

Jehu answered, "What's good about it? How can there be anything good about it as long as the promiscuous whoring and sorceries of your mother Jezebel pollute the country?"

23 Joram wheeled his chariot around and fled, yelling to Ahaziah, "It's a trap, Ahaziah!"

24 Jehu pulled on his bow and released an arrow; it hit Joram between the shoulder blades and went right through his heart. He slumped to his knees in his chariot.

25-26 Jehu ordered Bidkar, his lieutenant, "Quick — throw him into the field of Naboth of Jezreel. Remember when you and I were driving our chariots behind Ahab his father? That's when GOD pronounced this doom upon him: 'As surely as I saw the blood of murdered Naboth and his sons yesterday, you'll pay for it on this exact piece of ground. GOD's word!' So take him and throw him out in the field. GOD's instructions carried out to the letter!"

27 Ahaziah king of Judah saw what was going on and made his escape on the road toward Beth Haggan. Jehu chased him, yelling out, "Get him, too!" Jehu's troops shot and wounded him in his chariot on the hill up to Gur, near Ibleam. He was able to make it as far as Megiddo; there he died.

28 His aides drove on to Jerusalem. They buried him in the family plot in the City of David.

29 In the eleventh year of the reign of Joram son of Ahab, Ahaziah had become king of Judah.

30-31 When Jezebel heard that Jehu had arrived in Jezreel, she made herself up — put on eyeshadow and arranged her hair — and posed seductively at the window. When Jehu came through the city gate, she called down, "So, how are things, 'Zimri,' you dashing king-killer?"

32 Jehu looked up at the window and called, "Is there anybody up there on my side?" Two or three palace eunuchs looked out.

33 He ordered, "Throw her down!" They threw her out the window. Her blood spattered the wall and the horses, and Jehu trampled her under his horse's hooves.

34 Then Jehu went inside and ate his lunch. During lunch he gave orders, "Take care of that damned woman; give her a decent burial — she is, after

all, a king's daughter."

35-36   They went out to bury her, but there was nothing left of her but skull, feet, and hands. They came back and told Jehu. He said, "It's GOD's word, the word spoken by Elijah the Tishbite:

In the field of Jezreel,
   dogs will eat Jezebel;

37   The body of Jezebel will be like
   dog-droppings on the ground in Jezreel.
Old friends and lovers will say,
   'I wonder, is *this* Jezebel?'"

1-2   **10** Ahab had seventy sons still living in Samaria. Jehu wrote letters addressed to the officers of Jezreel, the city elders, and those in charge of Ahab's sons, and posted them to Samaria. The letters read:

2-3   This letter is fair warning. You're in charge of your master's children, chariots, horses, fortifications, and weapons. Pick the best and most capable of your master's sons and put him on the throne. Prepare to fight for your master's position.

4   They were absolutely terrified at the letter. They said, "Two kings have already been wiped out by him; what hope do we have?"

5   So they sent the warden of the palace, the mayor of the city, the elders, and the guardians to Jehu with this message: "We are your servants. Whatever you say, we'll do. We're not making anyone king here. You're in charge—do what you think best."

6-7   Then Jehu wrote a second letter:

If you are on my side and are willing to follow my orders, here's what you do: Decapitate the sons of your master and bring the heads to me by this time tomorrow in Jezreel.

The king's sons numbered seventy. The leaders of the city had taken responsibility for them. When they got the letter, they took the king's sons and killed all seventy. Then they put the heads in baskets and sent them to Jehu in Jezreel.

8   A messenger reported to Jehu: "They've delivered the heads of the king's sons."

He said, "Stack them in two piles at the city gate until morning."

9-10   In the morning Jehu came out, stood before the people, and addressed them formally: "Do you realize that this very day you are participants in GOD's righteous workings? True, I am the one who conspired against my master and assassinated him. But who, do you suppose, is responsible for this pile of skulls? Know this for certain: Not a single syllable that GOD spoke in judgment on the family of Ahab is canceled; you're seeing it with your own eyes—GOD doing what, through Elijah, he said he'd do."

11   Then Jehu proceeded to kill everyone who had anything to do with Ahab's family in Jezreel—leaders, friends, priests. He wiped out the entire lot.

12-13   That done, he brushed himself off and set out for Samaria. Along the way, at Beth Eked (Binding House) of the Shepherds, he met up with some relatives of Ahaziah king of Judah.

Jehu said, "Who are you?"

They said, "We're relatives of Ahaziah and we've come down to a reunion of the royal family."

14 "Grab them!" ordered Jehu. They were taken and then massacred at the well of Beth Eked. Forty-two of them — no survivors.

15 He went on from there and came upon Jehonadab the Recabite who was on his way to meet him. Greeting him, he said, "Are we together and of one mind in this?"

Jehonadab said, "We are — count on me."

"Then give me your hand," said Jehu.

They shook hands on it and Jehonadab stepped up into the chariot with Jehu.

16 "Come along with me," said Jehu, "and witness my zeal for GOD." Together they proceeded in the chariot.

17 When they arrived in Samaria, Jehu massacred everyone left in Samaria who was in any way connected with Ahab — a mass execution, just as GOD had told Elijah.

18-19 Next, Jehu got all the people together and addressed them:

> Ahab served Baal small-time;
> Jehu will serve him big-time.

"Get all the prophets of Baal here — everyone who served him, all his priests. Get everyone here; don't leave anyone out. I have a great sacrifice to offer Baal. If you don't show up, you won't live to tell about it." (Jehu was lying, of course. He planned to destroy all the worshipers of Baal.)

20 Jehu ordered, "Make preparation for a holy convocation for Baal." They did and posted the date.

21 Jehu then summoned everyone in Israel. They came in droves — every worshiper of Baal in the country. Nobody stayed home. They came and packed the temple of Baal to capacity.

22 Jehu directed the keeper of the wardrobe, "Get robes for all the servants of Baal." He brought out their robes.

23-24 Jehu and Jehonadab the Recabite now entered the temple of Baal and said, "Double-check and make sure that there are no worshipers of GOD in here; only Baal-worshipers are allowed." Then they launched the worship, making the sacrifices and burnt offerings.

Meanwhile, Jehu had stationed eighty men outside with orders: "Don't let a single person escape; if you do, it's your life for his life."

25-27 When Jehu had finished with the sacrificial solemnities, he signaled to the officers and guards, "Enter and kill! No survivors!"

And the bloody slaughter began. The officers and guards threw the corpses outside and cleared the way to enter the inner shrine of Baal. They hauled out the sacred phallic stone from the temple of Baal and pulverized it. They smashed the Baal altars and tore down the Baal temple. It's been a public toilet ever since.

28 And that's the story of Jehu's wasting of Baal in Israel.

29 But for all that, Jehu didn't turn back from the sins of Jeroboam son of Nebat, the sins that had dragged Israel into a life of sin — the golden calves

in Bethel and Dan stayed.

30   GOD commended Jehu: "You did well to do what I saw was best. You did what I ordered against the family of Ahab. As reward, your sons will occupy the throne of Israel for four generations."

31   Even then, though, Jehu wasn't careful to walk in GOD's ways and honor the God of Israel from an undivided heart. He didn't turn back from the sins of Jeroboam son of Nebat, who led Israel into a life of sin.

32-33   It was about this time that GOD began to shrink Israel. Hazael hacked away at the borders of Israel from the Jordan to the east — all the territory of Gilead, Gad, Reuben, and Manasseh from Aroer near the Brook Arnon. In effect, all Gilead and Bashan.

34-36   The rest of the life and times of Jehu, his accomplishments and fame, are written in *The Chronicles of the Kings of Israel*. Jehu died and was buried in the family plot in Samaria. His son Jehoahaz was the next king. Jehu ruled Israel from Samaria for twenty-eight years.

ATHALIAH OF JUDAH

1-3   11 Athaliah was the mother of Ahaziah. When she saw that her son was dead, she took over. She began by massacring the entire royal family. But Jehosheba, daughter of King Jehoram and sister of Ahaziah, took Ahaziah's son Joash and kidnapped him from among the king's sons slated for slaughter. She hid him and his nurse in a private room away from Athaliah. He didn't get killed. He was there with her, hidden away for six years in The Temple of GOD. Athaliah, oblivious to his existence, ruled the country.

4   In the seventh year Jehoiada sent for the captains of the bodyguards and the Palace Security Force. They met him in The Temple of GOD. He made a covenant with them, swore them to secrecy, and only then showed them the young prince.

5-8   Then he commanded them, "These are your instructions: Those of you who come on duty on the Sabbath and guard the palace, and those of you who go off duty on the Sabbath and guard The Temple of GOD, are to join forces at the time of the changing of the guard and form a ring around the young king, weapons at the ready. Kill anyone who tries to break through your ranks. Your job is to stay with the king at all times and places, coming and going."

9-11   The captains obeyed the orders of Jehoiada the priest. Each took his men, those who came on duty on the Sabbath and those who went off duty on the Sabbath, and presented them to Jehoiada the priest. The priest armed the officers with spears and shields originally belonging to King David, stored in The Temple of GOD. Well-armed, the guards took up their assigned positions for protecting the king, from one end of The Temple to the other, surrounding both Altar and Temple.

12   Then the priest brought the prince into view, crowned him, handed him the scroll of God's covenant, and made him king. As they anointed him, everyone applauded and shouted, "Long live the king!"

13-14   Athaliah heard the shouting of guards and people and came to the crowd gathered at The Temple of GOD. Astonished, she saw the king standing beside the throne, flanked by the captains and heralds, with everybody beside themselves with joy, trumpets blaring. Athaliah ripped her robes in dismay and shouted, "Treason! Treason!"

15-16 Jehoiada the priest ordered the military officers, "Drag her outside and kill anyone who tries to follow her!" (The priest had said, "Don't kill her inside The Temple of GOD.") So they dragged her out to the palace's horse corral; there they killed her.

17 Jehoiada now made a covenant between GOD and the king and the people: They were GOD's people. Another covenant was made between the king and the people.

18-20 The people poured into the temple of Baal and tore it down, smashing altar and images to smithereens. They killed Mattan the priest in front of the altar.

Jehoiada then stationed sentries in The Temple of GOD. He arranged for the officers of the bodyguard and the palace security, along with the people themselves, to escort the king down from The Temple of GOD through the Gate of the Guards and into the palace. There he sat on the royal throne. Everybody celebrated the event. And the city was safe and undisturbed — they had killed Athaliah with the royal sword.

21 Joash was seven years old when he became king.

JOASH OF JUDAH

1 **12** In the seventh year of Jehu, Joash began his kingly rule. He was king for forty years in Jerusalem. His mother's name was Gazelle. She was from Beersheba.

2-3 Taught and trained by Jehoiada the priest, Joash did what pleased GOD for as long as he lived. (Even so, he didn't get rid of the sacred fertility shrines — people still frequented them, sacrificing and burning incense.)

4-5 Joash instructed the priests: "Take the money that is brought into The Temple of GOD for holy offerings — both mandatory offerings and freewill offerings — and, keeping a careful accounting, use them to renovate The Temple wherever it has fallen into disrepair."

6 But by the twenty-third year of Joash's rule, the priests hadn't done one thing — The Temple was as dilapidated as ever.

7 King Joash called Jehoiada the priest and the company of priests and said, "Why haven't you renovated this sorry-looking Temple? You are forbidden to take any more money for Temple repairs — from now on, hand over everything you get."

8 The priests agreed not to take any more money or to be involved in The Temple renovation.

9-16 Then Jehoiada took a single chest and bored a hole in the lid and placed it to the right of the main entrance into The Temple of GOD. All the offerings that were brought to The Temple of GOD were placed in the chest by the priests who guarded the entrance. When they saw that a large sum of money had accumulated in the chest, the king's secretary and the chief priest would empty the chest and count the offerings. They would give the money accounted for to the managers of The Temple project; they in turn would pay the carpenters, construction workers, masons, stoneworkers, and the buyers of timber and quarried stone for the repair and renovation of The Temple of GOD — any expenses connected with fixing up The Temple. But none of the money brought into The Temple of GOD was used for liturgical "extras" (silver chalices, candle snuffers, trumpets, various gold and silver vessels, etc.). It was given to the workmen to pay for their repairing GOD's Temple. And no one even had to check on the men who handled the money given for the project—they were honest men. Offerings designated for Compensation Offerings and Absolution Offerings didn't go into the building project—those went directly to the priests.

17-18 Around this time Hazael king of Aram ventured out and attacked Gath, and he captured it. Then he decided to try for Jerusalem. Joash king of Judah countered by gathering up all the sacred memorials—gifts dedicated for holy use by his ancestors, the kings of Judah, Jehoshaphat, Jehoram, and Ahaziah, along with the holy memorials he himself had received, plus all the gold that he could find in the temple and palace storerooms—and sent it to Hazael king of Aram. Appeased, Hazael went on his way and didn't bother Jerusalem.

19-21 The rest of the life and times of Joash and all that he did are written in *The Chronicles of the Kings of Judah*. At the last his palace staff formed a conspiracy and assassinated Joash as he was strolling along the ramp of the fortified outside city wall. Jozabad son of Shimeath and Jehozabad son of Shomer were the assassins. And so Joash died and was buried in the family plot in the City of David. His son Amaziah was king after him.

JEHOAHAZ OF ISRAEL

1-3 **13** In the twenty-third year of Joash son of Ahaziah king of Judah, Jehoahaz son of Jehu became king of Israel in Samaria—a rule of seventeen years. He lived an evil life before GOD, walking step for step in the tracks of Jeroboam son of Nebat who led Israel into a life of sin, swerving neither left or right. Exasperated, GOD was furious with Israel and turned them over to Hazael king of Aram and Ben-Hadad son of Hazael. This domination went on for a long time.

4-6 Then Jehoahaz prayed for a softening of GOD's anger, and GOD listened. He realized how wretched Israel had become under the brutalities of the king of Aram. So GOD provided a savior for Israel who brought them out from under Aram's oppression. The children of Israel were again able to live at peace in their own homes. But it didn't make any difference: They didn't change their lives, didn't turn away from the Jeroboam-sins that now characterized Israel, including the sex-and-religion shrines of Asherah still flourishing in Samaria.

7 Nothing was left of Jehoahaz's army after Hazael's oppression except for fifty cavalry, ten chariots, and ten thousand infantry. The king of Aram had decimated the rest, leaving behind him mostly chaff.

8-9 The rest of the life and times of Jehoahaz, the record of his accomplishments, are written in *The Chronicles of the Kings of Israel*. Jehoahaz died and was buried with his ancestors in Samaria. His son Jehoash succeeded him as king.

JEHOASH OF ISRAEL

10-11 In the thirty-seventh year of Joash king of Judah, Jehoash son of Jehoahaz became king of Israel in Samaria—a reign of sixteen years. In GOD's eyes he lived an evil life. He didn't deviate one bit from the sins of Jeroboam son of Nebat, who led Israel into a life of sin. He plodded along in the same tracks, step after step.

12-13 The rest of the life and times of Jehoash, the record of his accomplishments and his war against Amaziah king of Judah, are written in *The Chronicles of the Kings of Israel*. Jehoash died and joined his ancestors.

Jeroboam took over his throne. Jehoash was buried in Samaria in the royal cemetery.

14 Elisha came down sick. It was the sickness of which he would soon die. Jehoash king of Israel paid him a visit. When he saw him he wept openly, crying, "My father, my father! Chariot and horsemen of Israel!"

15 Elisha told him, "Go and get a bow and some arrows." The king brought him the bow and arrows.

16 Then he told the king, "Put your hand on the bow." He put his hand on the bow. Then Elisha put his hand over the hand of the king.

17 Elisha said, "Now open the east window." He opened it.

Then he said, "Shoot!" And he shot.

"The arrow of GOD's salvation!" exclaimed Elisha. "The arrow of deliverance from Aram! You will do battle against Aram until there's nothing left of it."

18 "Now pick up the other arrows," said Elisha. He picked them up.

Then he said to the king of Israel, "Strike the ground."

The king struck the ground three times and then quit.

19 The Holy Man became angry with him: "Why didn't you hit the ground five or six times? Then you would beat Aram until he was finished. As it is, you'll defeat him three times only."

20-21 Then Elisha died and they buried him.

Some time later, raiding bands of Moabites, as they often did, invaded the country. One day, some men were burying a man and spotted the raiders. They threw the man into Elisha's tomb and got away. When the body touched Elisha's bones, the man came alive, stood up, and walked out on his own two feet.

22-24 Hazael king of Aram badgered and bedeviled Israel all through the reign of Jehoahaz. But GOD was gracious and showed mercy to them. He stuck with them out of respect for his covenant with Abraham, Isaac, and Jacob. He never gave up on them, never even considered discarding them, even to this day. Hazael king of Aram died. His son Ben-Hadad was the next king.

25 Jehoash son of Jehoahaz turned things around and took back the cities that Ben-Hadad son of Hazael had taken from his father Jehoahaz. Jehoash went to war three times and defeated him each time, recapturing the cities of Israel.

AMAZIAH OF JUDAH

1-2 **14** In the second year of Jehoash son of Jehoahaz king of Israel, Amaziah son of Joash became king of Judah. He was twenty-five years old when he became king and he reigned for twenty-nine years in Jerusalem. His mother's name was Jehoaddin. She was from Jerusalem.

3-4 He lived the way GOD wanted and did the right thing. But he didn't come up to the standards of his ancestor David; instead he lived pretty much as his father Joash had; the local sex-and-religion shrines continued to stay in business with people frequenting them.

5-6 When he had the affairs of the kingdom well in hand, he executed the palace guard that had assassinated his father the king. But he didn't kill the sons of the assassins. He was obedient to what GOD commanded, written in the Word revealed to Moses, that parents shouldn't be executed for their children's sins, nor children for those of their parents. We each pay personally for our sins.

7   Amaziah roundly defeated Edom in the Valley of Salt to the tune of ten thousand dead. In another battle he took The Rock and renamed it Joktheel, the name it still bears.

8   One day Amaziah sent envoys to Jehoash son of Jehoahaz, the son of Jehu, king of Israel, challenging him to a fight: "Come and meet with me — dare you. Let's have it out face-to-face!"

9-10   Jehoash king of Israel replied to Amaziah king of Judah, "One day a thistle in Lebanon sent word to a cedar in Lebanon, 'Give your daughter to my son in marriage.' But then a wild animal of Lebanon passed by and stepped on the thistle, crushing it. Just because you've defeated Edom in battle, you now think you're a big shot. Go ahead and be proud, but stay home. Why press your luck? Why bring defeat on yourself and Judah?"

11   Amaziah wouldn't take No for an answer. So Jehoash king of Israel gave in and agreed to a battle between him and Amaziah king of Judah. They met at Beth Shemesh, a town of Judah.

12   Judah was thoroughly beaten by Israel — all their soldiers ran home in defeat.

13-14   Jehoash king of Israel captured Amaziah king of Judah, the son of Joash, the son of Ahaziah, at Beth Shemesh. But Jehoash didn't stop there; he went on to attack Jerusalem. He demolished the wall of Jerusalem all the way from the Ephraim Gate to the Corner Gate — a stretch of about six hundred feet. He looted the gold, silver, and furnishings — anything he found that was worth taking — from both the palace and The Temple of GOD. And, for good measure, he took hostages. Then he returned to Samaria.

15-16   The rest of the life and times of Jehoash, his significant accomplishments and the fight with Amaziah king of Judah, are all written in *The Chronicles of the Kings of Israel*. Jehoash died and was buried in Samaria in the cemetery of the kings of Israel. His son Jeroboam became the next king.

17-18   Amaziah son of Joash king of Judah continued as king fifteen years after the death of Jehoash son of Jehoahaz king of Israel. The rest of the life and times of Amaziah is written in *The Chronicles of the Kings of Judah*.

19-20   At the last they cooked up a plot against Amaziah in Jerusalem and he had to flee to Lachish. But they tracked him down in Lachish and killed him there. They brought him back on horseback and buried him in Jerusalem, with his ancestors in the City of David.

21-22   Azariah — he was only sixteen years old at the time — was the unanimous choice of the people of Judah to succeed his father Amaziah as king. Following his father's death, he rebuilt and restored Elath to Judah.

JEROBOAM II OF ISRAEL

23-25   In the fifteenth year of Amaziah son of Joash king of Judah, Jeroboam son of Jehoash became king of Israel in Samaria. He ruled for forty-one years. As far as GOD was concerned he lived an evil life, never deviating an inch from all the sin of Jeroboam son of Nebat, who led Israel into a life of sin. But he did restore the borders of Israel to Lebo Hamath in the far north and to the Dead Sea in the south, matching what GOD, the God of Israel, had pronounced through his servant Jonah son of Amittai, the prophet from Gath Hepher.

26-27 GOD was fully aware of the trouble in Israel, its bitterly hard times. No one was exempt, whether slave or citizen, and no hope of help anywhere was in sight. But GOD wasn't yet ready to blot out the name of Israel from history, so he used Jeroboam son of Jehoash to save them.

28-29 The rest of the life and times of Jeroboam, his victories in battle and how he recovered for Israel both Damascus and Hamath which had belonged to Judah, these are all written in *The Chronicles of the Kings of Israel*. Jeroboam died and was buried with his ancestors in the royal cemetery. His son Zechariah became the next king.

AZARIAH (UZZIAH) OF JUDAH

1-5 In the twenty-seventh year of Jeroboam king of Israel, Azariah son of Amaziah became king in Judah. He was sixteen years old when he began his rule and he was king for fifty-two years in Jerusalem. His mother's name was Jecoliah. She was from Jerusalem. He did well in the eyes of GOD, following in the footsteps of his father Amaziah. But he also failed to get rid of the local sex-and-religion shrines; they continued to be popular with the people. GOD afflicted the king with a bad skin disease until the day of his death. He lived in the palace but no longer acted as king; his son Jotham ran the government and ruled the country.

6-7 The rest of the life and times of Azariah, everything he accomplished, is written in *The Chronicles of the Kings of Judah*. Azariah died and was buried with his ancestors in the City of David. Jotham his son was king after him.

ZECHARIAH OF ISRAEL

8-9 In the thirty-eighth year of Azariah king of Judah, Zechariah son of Jeroboam became king over Israel in Samaria. He lasted only six months. He lived a bad life before GOD, no different from his ancestors. He continued in the line of Jeroboam son of Nebat who led Israel into a life of sin.

10 Shallum son of Jabesh conspired against him, assassinated him in public view, and took over as king.

11-12 The rest of the life and times of Zechariah is written plainly in *The Chronicles of the Kings of Israel*. That completed the word of GOD that was given to Jehu, namely, "For four generations your sons will sit on the throne of Israel." Zechariah was the fourth.

SHALLUM OF ISRAEL

13 Shallum son of Jabesh became king in the thirty-ninth year of Azariah king of Judah. He was king in Samaria for only a month.

14 Menahem son of Gadi came up from Tirzah to Samaria. He attacked Shallum son of Jabesh and killed him. He then became king.

15 The rest of the life and times of Shallum and the account of the conspiracy are written in *The Chronicles of the Kings of Israel*.

MENAHEM OF ISRAEL

16 Using Tirzah as his base, Menahem opened his reign by smashing Tiphsah, devastating both the town and its suburbs because they didn't welcome him with open arms. He savagely ripped open all the pregnant women.

17-18 In the thirty-ninth year of Azariah king of Judah, Menahem son of Gadi became king over Israel. He ruled from Samaria for ten years. As far as GOD was concerned he lived an evil life. Sin for sin, he repeated the sins of Jeroboam son of Nebat, who led Israel into a life of sin.

19-20 Then Tiglath-Pileser III king of Assyria showed up and attacked the country. But Menahem made a deal with him: He bought his support by handing over about thirty-seven tons of silver. He raised the money by making every landowner in Israel pay fifty shekels to the king of Assyria. That satisfied the king of Assyria, and he left the country.

21-22 The rest of the life and times of Menahem, everything he did, is written in *The Chronicles of the Kings of Israel*. Menahem died and joined his ancestors. His son Pekahiah became the next king.

PEKAHIAH OF ISRAEL

23-24 In the fiftieth year of Azariah king of Judah, Pekahiah son of Menahem became king of Israel. He ruled in Samaria for two years. In GOD's eyes he lived an evil life. He stuck to the old sin tracks of Jeroboam son of Nebat, who led Israel into a life of sin.

25 And then his military aide Pekah son of Remaliah conspired against him—killed him in cold blood while he was in his private quarters in the royal palace in Samaria. He also killed Argob and Arieh. Fifty Gadites were in on the conspiracy with him. After the murder he became the next king.

26 The rest of the life and times of Pekahiah, everything he did, is written in *The Chronicles of the Kings of Israel*.

PEKAH OF ISRAEL

27-28 In the fifty-second year of Azariah king of Judah, Pekah son of Remaliah became king of Israel in Samaria. He ruled for twenty years. In GOD's view he lived an evil life; he didn't deviate so much as a hair's breadth from the path laid down by Jeroboam son of Nebat, who led Israel into a life of sin.

29 During the reign of Pekah king of Israel, Tiglath-Pileser III king of Assyria invaded the country. He captured Ijon, Abel Beth Maacah, Janoah, Kedesh, Hazor, Gilead, Galilee—the whole country of Naphtali—and took everyone captive to Assyria.

30 But then Hoshea son of Elah mounted a conspiracy against Pekah son of Remaliah. He assassinated him and took over as king. This was in the twentieth year of Jotham son of Uzziah.

31 The rest of the life and times of Pekah, everything he did, is written in *The Chronicles of the Kings of Israel*.

JOTHAM OF JUDAH

32-35 In the second year of Pekah son of Remaliah king of Israel, Jotham son of Uzziah became king in Judah. He was twenty-five years old when he became king and reigned sixteen years in Jerusalem. His mother's name was Jerusha daughter of Zadok. He acted well in GOD's eyes, following in the steps of his father Uzziah. But he didn't interfere with the traffic to the neighborhood sex-and-religion shrines; they continued, as popular as ever. The construction of the High Gate to The Temple of GOD was his work.

36-38 The rest of the life and times of Jotham, the record of his work, is written in *The Chronicles of the Kings of Judah*. It was during these years that GOD began sending Rezin king of Aram and Pekah son of Remaliah to attack Judah. Jotham died and joined his ancestors. They buried him in the family cemetery in the City of David. His son Ahaz was the next king.

AHAZ OF JUDAH

1-4 **16** In the seventeenth year of Pekah son of Remaliah, Ahaz son of Jotham became king of Judah. Ahaz was twenty years old when he became king and he ruled for sixteen years in Jerusalem. He didn't behave in the eyes of his GOD; he wasn't at all like his ancestor David. Instead he followed in the track of the kings of Israel. He even indulged in the outrageous practice of "passing his son through the fire" — a truly abominable act he picked up from the pagans GOD had earlier thrown out of the country. He also participated in the activities of the neighborhood sex-and-religion shrines that flourished all over the place.

5 Then Rezin king of Aram and Pekah son of Remaliah king of Israel ganged up against Jerusalem, throwing a siege around the city, but they couldn't make further headway against Ahaz.

6 At about this same time and on another front, the king of Edom recovered the port of Elath and expelled the men of Judah. The Edomites occupied Elath and have been there ever since.

7-8 Ahaz sent envoys to Tiglath-Pileser king of Assyria with this message: "I'm your servant and your son. Come and save me from the heavy-handed invasion of the king of Aram and the king of Israel. They're attacking me right now." Then Ahaz robbed the treasuries of the palace and The Temple of GOD of their gold and silver and sent them to the king of Assyria as a bribe.

9 The king of Assyria responded to him. He attacked and captured Damascus. He deported the people to Nineveh as exiles. Rezin he killed.

10-11 King Ahaz went to meet Tiglath-Pileser king of Assyria in Damascus. The altar in Damascus made a great impression on him. He sent back to Uriah the priest a drawing and set of blueprints of the altar. Uriah the priest built the altar to the specifications that King Ahaz had sent from Damascus. By the time the king returned from Damascus, Uriah had completed the altar.

12-14 The minute the king saw the altar he approached it with reverence and arranged a service of worship with a full course of offerings: Whole-Burnt-Offerings with billows of smoke, Grain-Offerings, libations of Drink-Offerings, the sprinkling of blood from the Peace-Offerings — the works. But the old bronze Altar that signaled the presence of GOD he displaced from its central place and pushed it off to the side of his new altar.

15 Then King Ahaz ordered Uriah the priest: "From now on offer all the sacrifices on the new altar, the great altar: morning Whole-Burnt-Offerings, evening Grain-Offerings, the king's Whole-Burnt-Offerings and Grain-Offerings, the people's Whole-Burnt-Offerings and Grain-Offerings, and also their Drink-Offerings. Splash all the blood from the

burnt offerings and sacrifices against this altar. The old bronze Altar will be for my personal use.

16   The priest Uriah followed King Ahaz's orders to the letter.

17-18   Then King Ahaz proceeded to plunder The Temple furniture of all its bronze. He stripped the bronze from The Temple furnishings, even salvaged the four bronze oxen that supported the huge basin, The Sea, and set The Sea unceremoniously on the stone pavement. Finally, he removed any distinctive features from within The Temple that were offensive to the king of Assyria.

19-20   The rest of the life and times of Ahaz is written in *The Chronicles of the Kings of Judah*. Ahaz died and was buried with his ancestors in the City of David. His son Hezekiah became the next king.

HOSHEA OF ISRAEL

1-2   17 In the twelfth year of Ahaz king of Judah, Hoshea son of Elah became king of Israel. He ruled in Samaria for nine years. As far as GOD was concerned, he lived a bad life, but not nearly as bad as the kings who had preceded him.

3-5   Then Shalmaneser king of Assyria attacked. Hoshea was already a puppet of the Assyrian king and regularly sent him tribute, but Shalmaneser discovered that Hoshea had been operating traitorously behind his back—having worked out a deal with King So of Egypt. And, adding insult to injury, Hoshea was way behind on his annual payments of tribute to Assyria. So the king of Assyria arrested him and threw him in prison, then proceeded to invade the entire country. He attacked Samaria and threw up a siege against it. The siege lasted three years.

6   In the ninth year of Hoshea's reign the king of Assyria captured Samaria and took the people into exile in Assyria. He relocated them in Halah, in Gozan along the Habor River, and in the towns of the Medes.

7-12   The exile came about because of sin: The children of Israel sinned against GOD, their God, who had delivered them from Egypt and the brutal oppression of Pharaoh king of Egypt. They took up with other gods, fell in with the ways of life of the pagan nations GOD had chased off, and went along with whatever their kings did. They did all kinds of things on the sly, things offensive to their GOD, then openly and shamelessly built local sex-and-religion shrines at every available site. They set up their sex-and-religion symbols at practically every crossroads. Everywhere you looked there was smoke from their pagan offerings to the deities—the identical offerings that had gotten the pagan nations off into exile. They had accumulated a long list of evil actions and GOD was fed up, fed up with their persistent worship of gods carved out of deadwood or shaped out of clay, even though GOD had plainly said, "Don't do this—ever!"

13   GOD had taken a stand against Israel and Judah, speaking clearly through countless holy prophets and seers time and time again, "Turn away from your evil way of life. Do what I tell you and have been telling you in The Revelation I gave your ancestors and of which I've kept reminding you ever since through my servants the prophets."

14-15   But they wouldn't listen. If anything, they were even more bullheaded than their stubborn ancestors, if that's possible. They were contemptuous of his instructions, the solemn and holy covenant he had made with their ancestors, and of his repeated reminders and warnings. They lived a "nothing" life and became "nothings"—just like the pagan peoples all around them. They were well-warned: GOD said, "Don't!" but they did it anyway.

16-17   They threw out everything GOD, their God, had told them, and replaced him with two statue-gods shaped like bull-calves and then a phallic pole for the whore goddess Asherah. They worshiped cosmic forces — sky gods and goddesses — and frequented the sex-and-religion shrines of Baal. They even sank so low as to offer their own sons and daughters as sacrificial burnt offerings! They indulged in all the black arts of magic and sorcery. In short, they prostituted themselves to every kind of evil available to them. And GOD had had enough.

18-20   GOD was so thoroughly angry that he got rid of them, got them out of the country for good until only one tribe was left — Judah. (Judah, actually, wasn't much better, for Judah also failed to keep GOD's commands, falling into the same way of life that Israel had adopted.) GOD rejected everyone connected with Israel, made life hard for them, and permitted anyone with a mind to exploit them to do so. And then this final No as he threw them out of his sight.

21-23   Back at the time that God ripped Israel out of their place in the family of David, they had made Jeroboam son of Nebat king. Jeroboam debauched Israel — turned them away from serving GOD and led them into a life of total sin. The children of Israel went along with all the sins that Jeroboam did, never murmured so much as a word of protest. In the end, GOD spoke a final No to Israel and turned his back on them. He had given them fair warning, and plenty of time, through the preaching of all his servants the prophets. Then he exiled Israel from her land to Assyria. And that's where they are now.

24-25   The king of Assyria brought in people from Babylon, Cuthah, Avva, Hamath, and Sepharvaim, and relocated them in the towns of Samaria, replacing the exiled Israelites. They moved in as if they owned the place and made themselves at home. When the Assyrians first moved in, GOD was just another god to them; they neither honored nor worshiped him. Then GOD sent lions among them and people were mauled and killed.

26   This message was then sent back to the king of Assyria: "The people you brought in to occupy the towns of Samaria don't know what's expected of them from the god of the land, and now he's sent lions and they're killing people right and left because nobody knows what the god of the land expects of them."

27   The king of Assyria ordered, "Send back some priests who were taken into exile from there. They can go back and live there and instruct the people in what the god of the land expects of them."

28   One of the priests who had been exiled from Samaria came back and moved into Bethel. He taught them how to honor and worship GOD.

29-31   But each people that Assyria had settled went ahead anyway making its own gods and setting them up in the neighborhood sex-and-religion shrines that the citizens of Samaria had left behind — a local custom-made god for each people:

for Babylon, Succoth Benoth;
for Cuthah, Nergal;
for Hamath, Ashima;

for Avva, Nibhaz and Tartak;

for Sepharvaim, Adrammelech and Anammelech (people burned their children in sacrificial offerings to these gods!).

³²⁻³³ They honored and worshiped God, but not exclusively—they also appointed all sorts of priests, regardless of qualification, to conduct a variety of rites at the local fertility shrines. They honored and worshiped God, but they also kept up their devotions to the old gods of the places they had come from.

³⁴⁻³⁹ And they're still doing it, still worshiping any old god that has nostalgic appeal to them. They don't really worship God—they don't take seriously what he says regarding how to behave and what to believe, what he revealed to the children of Jacob whom he named Israel. God made a covenant with his people and ordered them, "Don't honor other gods: Don't worship them, don't serve them, don't offer sacrifices to them. Worship God, the God who delivered you from Egypt in great and personal power. Reverence and fear him. Worship him. Sacrifice to him. And only him! All the things he had written down for you, directing you in what to believe and how to behave—well, do them for as long as you live. And whatever you do, *don't worship other gods!* And the covenant he made with you, don't forget your part in that. *And don't worship other gods!* Worship God, and God only—he's the one who will save you from enemy oppression."

⁴⁰⁻⁴¹ But they didn't pay any attention. They kept doing what they'd always done. As it turned out, all the time these people were putting on a front of worshiping God, they were at the same time involved with their local idols. And they're still doing it. Like father, like son.

Hezekiah of Judah

¹⁻⁴ **18** In the third year of Hoshea son of Elah king of Israel, Hezekiah son of Ahaz began his rule over Judah. He was twenty-five years old when he became king and he ruled for twenty-nine years in Jerusalem. His mother's name was Abijah daughter of Zechariah. In God's opinion he was a good king; he kept to the standards of his ancestor David. He got rid of the local fertility shrines, smashed the phallic stone monuments, and cut down the sex-and-religion Asherah groves. As a final stroke he pulverized the ancient bronze serpent that Moses had made; at that time the Israelites had taken up the practice of sacrificing to it—they had even dignified it with a name, Nehushtan (The Old Serpent).

⁵⁻⁶ Hezekiah put his whole trust in the God of Israel. There was no king quite like him, either before or after. He held fast to God—never loosened his grip—and obeyed to the letter everything God had commanded Moses. And God, for his part, held fast to him through all his adventures.

⁷⁻⁸ He revolted against the king of Assyria; he refused to serve him one more day. And he drove back the Philistines, whether in sentry outposts or fortress cities, all the way to Gaza and its borders.

⁹⁻¹¹ In the fourth year of Hezekiah and the seventh year of Hoshea son of Elah king of Israel, Shalmaneser king of Assyria attacked Samaria. He threw a siege around it and after three years captured it. It was in the sixth year of Hezekiah and the ninth year of Hoshea that Samaria fell to Assyria. The king of Assyria took Israel into exile and relocated them in Halah, in Gozan on the Habor River, and in towns of the Medes.

12 All this happened because they wouldn't listen to the voice of their GOD and treated his covenant with careless contempt. They refused either to listen or do a word of what Moses, the servant of GOD, commanded.

13-14 In the fourteenth year of King Hezekiah, Sennacherib king of Assyria attacked all the outlying fortress cities of Judah and captured them. King Hezekiah sent a message to the king of Assyria at his headquarters in Lachish: "I've done wrong; I admit it. Pull back your army; I'll pay whatever tribute you set."

14-16 The king of Assyria demanded tribute from Hezekiah king of Judah — eleven tons of silver and a ton of gold. Hezekiah turned over all the silver he could find in The Temple of GOD and in the palace treasuries. Hezekiah even took down the doors of The Temple of GOD and the doorposts that he had overlaid with gold and gave them to the king of Assyria.

17 So the king of Assyria sent his top three military chiefs (the Tartan, the Rabsaris, and the Rabshakeh) from Lachish with a strong military force to King Hezekiah in Jerusalem. When they arrived at Jerusalem, they stopped at the aqueduct of the Upper Pool on the road to the laundry commons.

18 They called loudly for the king. Eliakim son of Hilkiah who was in charge of the palace, Shebna the royal secretary, and Joah son of Asaph the court historian went out to meet them.

19-22 The third officer, the Rabshakeh, was spokesman. He said, "Tell Hezekiah: A message from The Great King, the king of Assyria: You're living in a world of make-believe, of pious fantasy. Do you think that mere words are any substitute for military strategy and troops? Now that you've revolted against me, who can you expect to help you? You thought Egypt would, but Egypt's nothing but a paper tiger — one puff of wind and she collapses; Pharaoh king of Egypt is nothing but bluff and bluster. Or are you going to tell me, 'We rely on GOD'? But Hezekiah has just eliminated most of the people's access to God by getting rid of all the local God-shrines, ordering everyone in Judah and Jerusalem, 'You must worship at the Jerusalem altar only.'

23-24 "So be reasonable. Make a deal with my master, the king of Assyria. I'll give you two thousand horses if you think you can provide riders for them. You can't do it? Well, then, how do you think you're going to turn back even one raw buck private from my master's troops? How long are you going to hold on to that figment of your imagination, these hoped-for Egyptian chariots and horses?

25 "Do you think I've come up here to destroy this country without the express approval of GOD? The fact is that GOD expressly ordered me, 'Attack and destroy this country!'"

26 Eliakim son of Hilkiah and Shebna and Joah said to the Rabshakeh, "Please, speak to us in the Aramaic language. We understand Aramaic. Don't speak in Hebrew — everyone crowded on the city wall can hear you."

27 But the Rabshakeh said, "We weren't sent with a private message to your master and you; this is public — a message to everyone within earshot. After all, they're involved in this as well as you; if you don't come to terms, they'll be eating their own turds and drinking their own pee right along with you."

28-32 Then he stepped forward and spoke in Hebrew loud enough for everyone to hear, "Listen carefully to the words of The Great King, the king of Assyria: Don't let Hezekiah fool you; he can't save you. And don't let

Hezekiah give you that line about trusting in GOD, telling you, 'GOD will save us—this city will never be abandoned to the king of Assyria.' Don't listen to Hezekiah—he doesn't know what he's talking about. Listen to the king of Assyria—deal with me and live the good life; I'll guarantee everyone your own plot of ground—a garden and a well! I'll take you to a land sweeter by far than this one, a land of grain and wine, bread and vineyards, olive orchards and honey. You only live once—so live, really live!

32-35   "No. Don't listen to Hezekiah. Don't listen to his lies, telling you 'GOD will save us.' Has there ever been a god anywhere who delivered anyone from the king of Assyria? Where are the gods of Hamath and Arpad? Where are the gods of Sepharvaim, Hena, and Ivvah? And Samaria—did their gods save them? Can you name a god who saved anyone anywhere from me, the king of Assyria? So what makes you think that GOD can save Jerusalem from me?"

36   The people were silent. No one spoke a word for the king had ordered, "Don't anyone say a word—not one word!"

37   Then Eliakim son of Hilkiah, the palace administrator, and Shebna the royal secretary, and Joah son of Asaph the court historian went back to Hezekiah. They had ripped their robes in despair; they reported to Hezekiah the speech of the Rabshakeh.

1-3   **19** When Hezekiah heard it all, he too ripped his robes apart and dressed himself in rough burlap. Then he went into The Temple of GOD. He sent Eliakim, who was in charge of the palace, Shebna the secretary, and the senior priests, all of them dressed in rough burlap, to the prophet Isaiah son of Amoz. They said to him, "A message from Hezekiah: 'This is a black day, a terrible day—doomsday!

> Babies poised to be born,
> No strength to birth them.

4   " 'Maybe GOD, your God, has been listening to the blasphemous speech of the Rabshakeh who was sent by the king of Assyria, his master, to humiliate the living God; maybe GOD, your God, won't let him get by with such talk; and you, maybe you will lift up prayers for what's left of these people.' "

5   That's the message King Hezekiah's servants delivered to Isaiah.

6-7   Isaiah answered them, "Tell your master, 'GOD's word: Don't be at all concerned about what you've heard from the king of Assyria's bootlicking errand boys—these outrageous blasphemies. Here's what I'm going to do: Afflict him with self-doubt. He's going to hear a rumor and, frightened for his life, retreat to his own country. Once there, I'll see to it that he gets killed.' "

8-13   Then Rabshakeh left and found that the king of Assyria had pulled up stakes from Lachish and was now fighting against Libnah. Then Sennacherib heard that Tirhakah king of Cush was on his way to fight against him. So he sent another envoy with orders to deliver this message to Hezekiah king of Judah: "Don't let that god that you think so much of keep stringing you along with the line, 'Jerusalem will never fall to the king of Assyria.' That's a barefaced lie. You know the track record of the kings of Assyria—country after country laid waste, devastated. And what makes you think you'll be an exception? Take a good look at these wasted nations, destroyed by my ancestors; did their gods do them any good? Look at Gozan, Haran, Rezeph, the people of Eden at Tel Assar. Ruins. And what's left of the king of Hamath, the king of Arpad, the king of Sepharvaim, of Hena, of Ivvah? Bones."

14-15 Hezekiah took the letter from the envoy and read it. He went to The Temple of GOD and spread it out before GOD. And Hezekiah prayed—oh, how he prayed!

GOD, God of Israel, seated
    in majesty on the cherubim-throne.
You are the one and only God,
    sovereign over all kingdoms on earth,
Maker of heaven,
    maker of earth.
16 Open your ears, GOD, and listen,
    open your eyes and look.
Look at this letter Sennacherib has sent,
    a brazen insult to the living God!
17 The facts are true, O GOD: The kings of Assyria
    have laid waste countries and kingdoms.
18 Huge bonfires they made of their gods, their
    no-gods hand-made from wood and stone.
19 But now O GOD, *our* God,
    save us from raw Assyrian power;
Make all the kingdoms on earth know
    that you are GOD, the one and only God.

20-21 It wasn't long before Isaiah son of Amoz sent word to Hezekiah:

GOD's word: You've prayed to me regarding Sennacherib king of Assyria; I've heard your prayer. This is my response to him:

The Virgin Daughter of Zion
    holds you in utter contempt;
Daughter Jerusalem
    thinks you're nothing but scum.
22 Who do you think it is you've insulted?
    Who do you think you've been bad-mouthing?
Before whom do you suppose you've been strutting?
    The Holy One of Israel, that's who!
23 You dispatched your errand boys
    to humiliate the Master.
You bragged, "With my army of chariots
    I've climbed the highest mountains,
        snow-peaked alpine Lebanon mountains!
I've cut down its giant cedars,
    chopped down its prize pine trees.
I've traveled the world,
    visited the finest forest retreats.
24 I've dug wells in faraway places

and drunk their exotic waters;
I've waded and splashed barefoot
   in the rivers of Egypt."

25   Did it never occur to you
         that I'm behind all this?
Long, long ago I drew up the plans,
      and now I've gone into action,
Using you as a doomsday weapon,
      reducing proud cities to piles of rubble,
26   Leaving their people dispirited,
         slumped shoulders, limp souls.
Useless as weeds, fragile as grass,
      insubstantial as wind-blown chaff.
27   I know when you sit down, when you come
         and when you go;
And, yes, I've marked every one
      of your temper tantrums against me.
28   It's because of your temper,
         your blasphemous foul temper,
That I'm putting my hook in your nose
      and my bit in your mouth
And turning you back
         to where you came from.

29   And this, Hezekiah, will be for you the confirming sign:

This year you'll eat the gleanings, next year
      whatever you can beg, borrow, or steal;
But the third year you'll sow and harvest,
      plant vineyards and eat grapes.
30   A remnant of the family of Judah yet again
      will sink down roots and raise up fruit.
31   The remnant will come from Jerusalem,
         the survivors from Mount Zion.
The Zeal of GOD
      will make it happen.

32   To sum up, this is what GOD says regarding the king of Assyria:

He won't enter this city,
      nor shoot so much as a single arrow there;
Won't brandish a shield,
      won't even begin to set siege;
33   He'll go home by the same road he came;
      he won't enter this city. GOD's word!
34   I'll shield this city, I'll save this city,
      for my sake and for David's sake.

35   And it so happened that that very night an angel of GOD came and
massacred 185,000 Assyrians. When the people of Jerusalem got up next

morning, there it was—a whole camp of corpses!

36-37 Sennacherib king of Assyria got out of there fast, headed straight home for Nineveh, and stayed put. One day when he was worshiping in the temple of his god Nisroch, his sons Adrammelech and Sharezer murdered him and then escaped to the land of Ararat. His son Esarhaddon became the next king.

1 **20** Some time later Hezekiah became deathly sick. The prophet Isaiah son of Amoz paid him a visit and said, "Put your affairs in order; you're about to die—you haven't long to live."

2-3 Hezekiah turned from Isaiah and faced GOD, praying:

> Remember, O GOD, who I am, what I've done!
> I've lived an honest life before you,
> My heart's been true and steady,
> I've lived to please you; lived for your approval.

And then the tears flowed. Hezekiah wept.

4-6 Isaiah, leaving, was not halfway across the courtyard when the word of GOD stopped him: "Go back and tell Hezekiah, prince of my people, 'GOD's word, Hezekiah! From the God of your ancestor David: I've listened to your prayer and I've observed your tears. I'm going to heal you. In three days you will walk on your own legs into The Temple of GOD. I've just added fifteen years to your life; I'm saving you from the king of Assyria, and I'm covering this city with my shield—for my sake and my servant David's sake.'"

7 Isaiah then said, "Prepare a plaster of figs."

They prepared the plaster, applied it to the boil, and Hezekiah was on his way to recovery.

8 Hezekiah said to Isaiah, "How do I know whether this is of GOD and not just the fig plaster? What confirming sign is there that GOD is healing me and that in three days I'll walk into The Temple of GOD on my own legs?"

9 "This will be your sign from GOD," said Isaiah, "that GOD is doing what he said he'd do: Do you want the shadow to advance ten degrees on the sundial or go back ten degrees? You choose."

10 Hezekiah said, "It would be easy to make the sun's shadow advance ten degrees. Make it go back ten degrees."

11 So Isaiah called out in prayer to GOD, and the shadow went back ten degrees on Ahaz's sundial.

12-13 Shortly after this, Merodach-Baladan, the son of Baladan king of Babylon, having heard that the king was sick, sent a get-well card and a gift to Hezekiah. Hezekiah was pleased and showed the messengers around the place—silver, gold, spices, aromatic oils, his stockpile of weapons—a guided tour of all his prized possessions. There wasn't a thing in his palace or kingdom that Hezekiah didn't show them.

14 And then Isaiah the prophet showed up: "And just what were these men doing here? Where did they come from and why?"

Hezekiah said, "They came from far away—from Babylon."

15 "And what did they see in your palace?"

"Everything," said Hezekiah. "There isn't anything I didn't show them — I gave them the grand tour."

16-18 Then Isaiah spoke to Hezekiah, "Listen to what GOD has to say about this: The day is coming when everything you own and everything your ancestors have passed down to you, right down to the last cup and saucer, will be cleaned out of here — plundered and packed off to Babylon. GOD's word! Worse yet, your sons, the progeny of sons you've begotten, will end up as eunuchs in the palace of the king of Babylon."

19 Hezekiah said to Isaiah, "If GOD says it, it must be good." But he was thinking to himself, "It won't happen during my lifetime — I'll enjoy peace and security as long as I live."

20-21 The rest of the life and times of Hezekiah, along with his projects, especially the way he engineered the Upper Pool and brought water into the city, are written in *The Chronicles of the Kings of Judah*. Hezekiah died and was buried with his ancestors. His son Manasseh became the next king.

MANASSEH OF JUDAH

1-6 21 Manasseh was twelve years old when he became king. He ruled for fifty-five years in Jerusalem. His mother's name was Hephzibah. In GOD's judgment he was a bad king — an evil king. He reintroduced all the moral rot and spiritual corruption that had been scoured from the country when GOD dispossessed the pagan nations in favor of the children of Israel. He rebuilt all the sex-and-religion shrines that his father Hezekiah had torn down, and he built altars and phallic images for the sex god Baal and sex goddess Asherah, exactly what Ahaz king of Israel had done. He worshiped the cosmic powers, taking orders from the constellations. He even built these pagan altars in The Temple of GOD, the very Jerusalem Temple dedicated exclusively by GOD's decree ("in Jerusalem I place my Name") to GOD's Name. And he built shrines to the cosmic powers and placed them in both courtyards of The Temple of GOD. He burned his own son in a sacrificial offering. He practiced black magic and fortunetelling. He held séances and consulted spirits from the underworld. Much evil — in GOD's judgment, a career in evil. And GOD was angry.

7-8 As a last straw he placed the carved image of the sex goddess Asherah in The Temple of GOD, a flagrant and provocative violation of GOD's well-known statement to both David and Solomon, "In this Temple and in this city Jerusalem, my choice out of all the tribes of Israel, I place my Name — exclusively and forever. Never again will I let my people Israel wander off from this land I gave to their ancestors. But here's the condition: They must keep everything I've commanded in the instructions my servant Moses passed on to them."

9 But the people didn't listen. Manasseh led them off the beaten path into practices of evil even exceeding the evil of the pagan nations that GOD had earlier destroyed.

10-12 GOD, thoroughly fed up, sent word through his servants the prophets: "Because Manasseh king of Judah has committed these outrageous sins, eclipsing the sin-performance of the Amorites before him, setting new records in evil, using foul idols to debase Judah into a nation of sinners, this is my judgment, GOD's verdict: I, the God of Israel, will visit catastrophe on Jerusalem and Judah, a doom so terrible that when people hear of it they'll shake their heads in disbelief, saying, 'I can't believe it!'

13-15 "I'll visit the fate of Samaria on Jerusalem, a rerun of Ahab's doom. I'll wipe out Jerusalem as you would wipe out a dish, wiping it out and turning it over to dry. I'll get rid of what's left of my inheritance, dumping them on their enemies. If their enemies can salvage anything from them, they're welcome to it. They've been nothing but trouble to me from the day their ancestors left Egypt until now. They pushed me to my limit; I won't put up with their evil any longer."

16 The final word on Manasseh was that he was an indiscriminate murderer. He drenched Jerusalem with the innocent blood of his victims. That's on top of all the sins in which he involved his people. As far as GOD was concerned, he'd turned them into a nation of sinners.

17-18 The rest of the life and times of Manasseh, everything he did and his sorry record of sin, is written in *The Chronicles of the Kings of Judah.* Manasseh died and joined his ancestors. He was buried in the palace garden, the Garden of Uzza. His son Amon became the next king.

AMON OF JUDAH

19-22 Amon was twenty-two years old when he became king. He was king for two years in Jerusalem. His mother's name was Meshullemeth, the daughter of Haruz. She was from Jotbah. In GOD's opinion he lived an evil life, just like his father Manasseh. He followed in the footsteps of his father, serving and worshiping the same foul gods his father had served. He totally deserted the GOD of his ancestors; he did not live GOD's way.

23-24 Amon's servants revolted and assassinated him, killing the king right in his own palace. But the people, in their turn, killed the conspirators against King Amon and then crowned Josiah, Amon's son, as king.

25-26 The rest of the life and times of Amon is written in *The Chronicles of the Kings of Judah.* They buried Amon in his burial plot in the Garden of Uzza. His son Josiah became the next king.

JOSIAH OF JUDAH

1-2 **22** Josiah was eight years old when he became king. He ruled for thirty-one years in Jerusalem. His mother's name was Jedidah daughter of Adaiah; she was from Bozkath. He lived the way GOD wanted. He kept straight on the path blazed by his ancestor David, not one step to either left or right.

3-7 One day in the eighteenth year of his kingship, King Josiah sent the royal secretary Shaphan son of Azaliah, the son of Meshullam, to The Temple of GOD with instructions: "Go to Hilkiah the high priest and have him count the money that has been brought to The Temple of GOD that the doormen have collected from the people. Have them turn it over to the foremen who are managing the work on The Temple of GOD so they can pay the workers who are repairing GOD's Temple, all the carpenters, construction workers, and masons. Also, authorize them to buy the lumber and dressed stone for The Temple repairs. You don't need to get a receipt for the money you give them—they're all honest men."

8 The high priest Hilkiah reported to Shaphan the royal secretary, "I've just found the Book of GOD's Revelation, instructing us in GOD's ways. I found it in The Temple!" He gave it to Shaphan and Shaphan read it.

9   Then Shaphan the royal secretary came back to the king and gave him an account of what had gone on: "Your servants have bagged up the money that has been collected for The Temple; they have given it to the foremen to pay The Temple workers."

10   Then Shaphan the royal secretary told the king, "Hilkiah the priest gave me a book." Shaphan proceeded to read it to the king.

11-13   When the king heard what was written in the book, God's Revelation, he ripped his robes in dismay. And then he called for Hilkiah the priest, Ahikam son of Shaphan, Acbor son of Micaiah, Shaphan the royal secretary, and Asaiah the king's personal aide. He ordered them all: "Go and pray to GOD for me and for this people — for all Judah! Find out what we must do in response to what is written in this book that has just been found! GOD's anger must be burning furiously against us — our ancestors haven't obeyed a thing written in this book, followed none of the instructions directed to us."

14-17   Hilkiah the priest, Ahikam, Acbor, Shaphan, and Asaiah went straight to Huldah the prophetess. She was the wife of Shallum son of Tikvah, the son of Harhas, who was in charge of the palace wardrobe. She lived in Jerusalem in the Second Quarter. The five men consulted with her. In response to them she said, "GOD's word, the God of Israel: Tell the man who sent you here that I'm on my way to bring the doom of judgment on this place and this people. Every word written in the book read by the king of Judah will happen. And why? Because they've deserted me and taken up with other gods, made me thoroughly angry by setting up their god-making businesses. My anger is raging white-hot against this place and nobody is going to put it out.

18-20   "And also tell the king of Judah, since he sent you to ask GOD for direction; tell him this, GOD's comment on what he read in the book: 'Because you took seriously the doom of judgment I spoke against this place and people, and because you responded in humble repentance, tearing your robe in dismay and weeping before me, I'm taking you seriously. GOD's word: I'll take care of you. You'll have a quiet death and be buried in peace. You won't be around to see the doom that I'm going to bring upon this place.'"

The men took her message back to the king.

1-3   **23** The king acted immediately, assembling all the elders of Judah and Jerusalem. Then the king proceeded to The Temple of GOD, bringing everyone in his train — priests and prophets and people ranging from the famous to the unknown. Then he read out publicly everything written in the Book of the Covenant that was found in The Temple of GOD. The king stood by the pillar and before GOD solemnly committed them all to the covenant: to follow GOD believingly and obediently; to follow his instructions, heart and soul, on what to believe and do; to put into practice the entire covenant, all that was written in the book. The people stood in affirmation; their commitment was unanimous.

4-9   Then the king ordered Hilkiah the high priest, his associate priest, and The Temple sentries to clean house — to get rid of everything in The Temple of GOD that had been made for worshiping Baal and Asherah and the cosmic powers. He had them burned outside Jerusalem in the fields of Kidron and then disposed of the ashes in Bethel. He fired the pagan priests whom the kings of Judah had hired to supervise the local sex-and-religion shrines in the towns of Judah and neighborhoods of Jerusalem. In a stroke he swept the country clean of the polluting stench of the round-the-clock worship of Baal, sun and moon, stars — all the so-called cosmic powers. He took the obscene phallic Asherah pole from The Temple of GOD to the Valley of Kidron outside Jerusalem, burned it up, then ground up the ashes and scattered them in the cemetery. He tore out the rooms of the male sacred prostitutes that had been set up in The Temple of GOD; women also used these rooms for weavings for Asherah. He swept the outlying towns of Judah clean of priests and smashed the sex-and-religion shrines where they worked their trade from one end of the country to the other — all the way from Geba to Beersheba. He smashed the sex-and-religion shrine that had been set up just to the left of the city gate for the private use of Joshua, the city mayor. Even though these sex-and-religion priests did not defile the Altar in The Temple itself, they were part of the general priestly corruption and had to go.

10-11   Then Josiah demolished the Topheth, the iron furnace griddle set up in the Valley of Ben Hinnom for sacrificing children in the fire. No longer could anyone burn son or daughter to the god Molech. He hauled off the horse statues honoring the sun god that the kings of Judah had set up near the entrance to The Temple. They were in the courtyard next to the office of Nathan-Melech, the warden. He burned up the sun-chariots as so much rubbish.

12-15   The king smashed all the altars to smithereens — the altar on the roof shrine of Ahaz, the various altars the kings of Judah had made, the altars of Manasseh that littered the courtyard of The Temple — he smashed them all, pulverized the fragments, and scattered their dust in the Valley of Kidron. The king proceeded to make a clean sweep of all the sex-and-religion shrines that had proliferated east of Jerusalem on the south slope of Abomination Hill, the ones Solomon king of Israel had built to the obscene Sidonian sex goddess Ashtoreth, to Chemosh the dirty-old-god of the Moabites, and to Milcom the depraved god of the Ammonites. He tore apart the altars, chopped down the phallic Asherah-poles, and scattered old bones over the sites. Next, he took care of the altar at the shrine in Bethel that Jeroboam son of Nebat had built — the same Jeroboam who had led Israel into a life of sin. He tore apart the altar, burned down the shrine leaving it in ashes, and then lit fire to the phallic Asherah-pole.

16   As Josiah looked over the scene, he noticed the tombs on the hillside. He ordered the bones removed from the tombs and had them cremated on the ruined altars, desacralizing the evil altars. This was a fulfillment of the word of GOD spoken by the Holy Man years before when Jeroboam had stood by the altar at the sacred convocation.

17   Then the king said, "And *that* memorial stone — whose is that?"

The men from the city said, "That's the grave of the Holy Man who spoke the message against the altar at Bethel that you have just fulfilled."

18   Josiah said, "Don't trouble his bones." So they left his bones undisturbed, along with the bones of the prophet from Samaria.

19-20   But Josiah hadn't finished. He now moved through all the towns of Samaria where the kings of Israel had built neighborhood sex-and-religion shrines, shrines that had so angered GOD. He tore the shrines down and left them in ruins — just as at Bethel. He killed all the priests who had conducted the sacrifices and cremated them on their own altars, thus desacralizing the altars. Only then did Josiah return to Jerusalem.

21   The king now commanded the people, "Celebrate the Passover to GOD, your God, exactly as directed in this Book of the Covenant."

22-23   This commanded Passover had not been celebrated since the days that the judges judged Israel—none of the kings of Israel and Judah had celebrated it. But in the eighteenth year of the rule of King Josiah this very Passover was celebrated to GOD in Jerusalem.

24   Josiah scrubbed the place clean and trashed spirit-mediums, sorcerers, domestic gods, and carved figures—all the vast accumulation of foul and obscene relics and images on display everywhere you looked in Judah and Jerusalem. Josiah did this in obedience to the words of GOD's Revelation written in the book that Hilkiah the priest found in The Temple of GOD.

25   There was no king to compare with Josiah—neither before nor after—a king who turned in total and repentant obedience to GOD, heart and mind and strength, following the instructions revealed to and written by Moses. The world would never again see a king like Josiah.

26-27   But despite Josiah, GOD's hot anger did not cool; the raging anger ignited by Manasseh burned unchecked. And GOD, not swerving in his judgment, gave sentence: "I'll remove Judah from my presence in the same way I removed Israel. I'll turn my back on this city, Jerusalem, that I chose, and even from this Temple of which I said, 'My Name lives here.'"

28-30   The rest of the life and times of Josiah is written in *The Chronicles of the Kings of Judah*. Josiah's death came about when Pharaoh Neco king of Egypt marched out to join forces with the king of Assyria at the Euphrates River. When King Josiah intercepted him at the Plain of Megiddo, Neco killed him. Josiah's servants took his body in a chariot, returned him to Jerusalem, and buried him in his own tomb. By popular choice Jehoahaz son of Josiah was anointed and succeeded his father as king.

JEHOAHAZ OF JUDAH

31   Jehoahaz was twenty-three years old when he began to rule. He was king in Jerusalem for a mere three months. His mother's name was Hamutal daughter of Jeremiah. She came from Libnah.

32   In GOD's opinion, he was an evil king, reverting to the evil ways of his ancestors.

33-34   Pharaoh Neco captured Jehoahaz at Riblah in the country of Hamath and put him in chains, preventing him from ruling in Jerusalem. He demanded that Judah pay tribute of nearly four tons of silver and seventy-five pounds of gold. Then Pharaoh Neco made Eliakim son of Josiah the successor to Josiah, but changed his name to Jehoiakim. Jehoahaz was carted off to Egypt and eventually died there.

35   Meanwhile Jehoiakim, like a good puppet, dutifully paid out the silver and gold demanded by Pharaoh. He scraped up the money by gouging the people, making everyone pay an assessed tax.

JEHOIAKIM OF JUDAH

36-37   Jehoiakim was twenty-five years old when he began to rule; he was king for eleven years in Jerusalem. His mother's name was Zebidah daughter of Pedaiah. She had come from Rumah. In GOD's opinion he was an evil king, picking up on the evil ways of his ancestors.

24 It was during his reign that Nebuchadnezzar king of Babylon invaded the country. Jehoiakim became his puppet. But after three years he had had enough and revolted.

God dispatched a succession of raiding bands against him: Babylonian, Aramean, Moabite, and Ammonite. The strategy was to destroy Judah. Through the preaching of his servants and prophets, God had said he would do this, and now he was doing it. None of this was by chance — it was God's judgment as he turned his back on Judah because of the enormity of the sins of Manasseh — Manasseh, the killer-king, who made the Jerusalem streets flow with the innocent blood of his victims. God wasn't about to overlook such crimes.

The rest of the life and times of Jehoiakim is written in *The Chronicles of the Kings of Judah*. Jehoiakim died and was buried with his ancestors. His son Jehoiachin became the next king.

The threat from Egypt was now over — no more invasions by the king of Egypt — for by this time the king of Babylon had captured all the land between the Brook of Egypt and the Euphrates River, land formerly controlled by the king of Egypt.

JEHOIACHIN OF JUDAH

Jehoiachin was eighteen years old when he became king. His rule in Jerusalem lasted only three months. His mother's name was Nehushta daughter of Elnathan; she was from Jerusalem. In God's opinion he also was an evil king, no different from his father.

The next thing to happen was that the officers of Nebuchadnezzar king of Babylon attacked Jerusalem and put it under siege. While his officers were laying siege to the city, Nebuchadnezzar king of Babylon paid a personal visit. And Jehoiachin king of Judah, along with his mother, officers, advisors, and government leaders, surrendered.

In the eighth year of his reign Jehoiachin was taken prisoner by the king of Babylon. Nebuchadnezzar emptied the treasuries of both The Temple of God and the royal palace and confiscated all the gold furnishings that Solomon king of Israel had made for The Temple of God. This should have been no surprise — God had said it would happen. And then he emptied Jerusalem of people — all its leaders and soldiers, all its craftsmen and artisans. He took them into exile, something like ten thousand of them! The only ones he left were the very poor.

He took Jehoiachin into exile to Babylon. With him he took the king's mother, his wives, his chief officers, the community leaders, anyone who was anybody — in round numbers, seven thousand soldiers plus another thousand or so craftsmen and artisans, all herded off into exile in Babylon.

Then the king of Babylon made Jehoiachin's uncle, Mattaniah, his puppet king, but changed his name to Zedekiah.

ZEDEKIAH OF JUDAH

Zedekiah was twenty-one years old when he started out as king. He was king in Jerusalem for eleven years. His mother's name was Hamutal the daughter of Jeremiah. Her hometown was Libnah.

As far as God was concerned Zedekiah was just one more evil king, a carbon copy of Jehoiakim.

20   The source of all this doom to Jerusalem and Judah was God's anger —
God turned his back on them as an act of judgment. And then Zedekiah
revolted against the king of Babylon.

1-7   **25** The revolt dates from the ninth year and tenth month of
Zedekiah's reign. Nebuchadnezzar set out for Jerusalem immediately with a full army. He set up camp and sealed off the
city by building siege mounds around it. The city was under siege for nineteen months (until the eleventh year of Zedekiah). By the fourth month of
Zedekiah's eleventh year, on the ninth day of the month, the famine was so
bad that there wasn't so much as a crumb of bread for anyone. Then there was
a breakthrough. At night, under cover of darkness, the entire army escaped
through an opening in the wall (it was the gate between the two walls above
the King's Garden). They slipped through the lines of the Babylonians who
surrounded the city and headed for the Jordan on the Arabah Valley road.
But the Babylonians were in pursuit of the king and they caught up with
him in the Plains of Jericho. By then Zedekiah's army had deserted and was
scattered. The Babylonians took Zedekiah prisoner and marched him off
to the king of Babylon at Riblah, then tried and sentenced him on the spot.
Zedekiah's sons were executed right before his eyes; the summary murder
of his sons was the last thing he saw, for they then blinded him. Securely
handcuffed, he was hauled off to Babylon.

8-12   In the nineteenth year of Nebuchadnezzar king of Babylon, on the
seventh day of the fifth month, Nebuzaradan, the king of Babylon's chief
deputy, arrived in Jerusalem. He burned The Temple of God to the ground,
went on to the royal palace, and then finished off the city — burned the
whole place down. He put the Babylonian troops he had with him to work
knocking down the city walls. Finally, he rounded up everyone left in the
city, including those who had earlier deserted to the king of Babylon, and
took them off into exile. He left a few poor dirt farmers behind to tend the
vineyards and what was left of the fields.

13-15   The Babylonians broke up the bronze pillars, the bronze washstands, and
the huge bronze basin (the Sea) that were in The Temple of God and
hauled the bronze off to Babylon. They also took the various bronze-
crafted liturgical accessories used in the services of Temple worship, as
well as the gold and silver censers and sprinkling bowls. The king's deputy
didn't miss a thing — he took every scrap of precious metal he could find.

16-17   The amount of bronze they got from the two pillars, the Sea, and all the
washstands that Solomon had made for The Temple of God was enormous — they couldn't weigh it all! Each pillar stood twenty-seven feet
high, plus another four and a half feet for an ornate capital of bronze
filigree and decorative fruit.

18-21   The king's deputy took a number of special prisoners: Seraiah the chief
priest, Zephaniah the associate priest, three wardens, the chief remaining army officer, five of the king's counselors, the accountant, the chief
recruiting officer for the army, and sixty men of standing from among
the people. Nebuzaradan the king's deputy marched them all off to the
king of Babylon at Riblah. And there at Riblah, in the land of Hamath,
the king of Babylon killed the lot of them in cold blood.

Judah went into exile, orphaned from her land.

22-23 Regarding the common people who were left behind in Judah, this: Nebuchadnezzar king of Babylon appointed Gedaliah son of Ahikam, the son of Shaphan, as their governor. When veteran army officers among the people heard that the king of Babylon had appointed Gedaliah, they came to Gedaliah at Mizpah. Among them were Ishmael son of Nethaniah, Johanan son of Kareah, Seraiah son of Tanhumeth the Netophathite, Jaazaniah the son of the Maacathite, and some of their followers.

24 Gedaliah assured the officers and their men, giving them his word, "Don't be afraid of the Babylonian officials. Go back to your farms and families and respect the king of Babylon. Trust me, everything is going to be all right."

25 Some time later — it was in the seventh month — Ishmael son of Nethaniah, the son of Elishama (he had royal blood in him), came back with ten men and killed Gedaliah, the traitor Jews, and the Babylonian officials who were stationed at Mizpah — a bloody massacre.

26 But then, afraid of what the Babylonians would do, they all took off for Egypt, leaders and people, small and great.

27-30 When Jehoiachin king of Judah had been in exile for thirty-seven years, Evil-Merodach became king in Babylon and let Jehoiachin out of prison. This release took place on the twenty-seventh day of the twelfth month. The king treated him most courteously and gave him preferential treatment beyond anything experienced by the other political prisoners held in Babylon. Jehoiachin took off his prison garb and for the rest of his life ate his meals in company with the king. The king provided everything he needed to live comfortably.

1 & 2 CHRONICLES

There is always more than one way to tell a story. The story of Israel's kings is first narrated in the books of Samuel and Kings. Here is another telling of the same story, a hundred or so years later, by another voice and from another perspective: Chronicles. Some of the earlier narrative is omitted and there are substantial additions but it is recognizably the same story. But Israel's fortunes have changed considerably since the earlier authoritative writing (Genesis through Kings); God's people are in danger of losing touch with what made them God's people in the first place. In retrospect, from the low point in their history in which they now find themselves, it looks very much like a succession of world powers; Assyria and Egypt, Babylon and Persia, have been calling all the shots. The People of Israel are swamped by alien influences; they are also, it seems, mired in internal religious pettiness; will they be obliterated?

A new writer (it may have been Ezra) took it in hand to tell the old and by now familiar story but with a new slant. His task was to recover and restore Israel's confidence and obedience as God's people. Remarkably — and improbably, considering the political and cultural conditions of the time — this writer insisted, with very little "hometown" support, on the core identity of Israel as a worshiping people in the Davidic tradition. And he did it all by writing the book you are about to read. Israel did not finally disappear into the ancient Near East melting pot of violence and sex and religion.

Names launch this story, hundreds and hundreds of names, lists of names, page after page of names, *personal* names. There is no true storytelling without names, and this immersion in names calls attention to the individual, the unique, the personal, which is inherent in all spirituality. Name lists (genealogies) occur in other places in Scripture (Genesis, Numbers, Matthew, Luke) but none as extravagantly copious as here. Holy history is not constructed from impersonal forces or abstract ideas; it is woven from names — persons, each one unique. Chronicles erects a solid defense against depersonalized religion.

And Chronicles provides a witness to the essential and primary place of accurate worship in human life. The narrative backbone of Chronicles is worship — the place of worship (the Jerusalem Temple), the ministers of worship (the priests and Levites), the musical components of worship (both vocal and instrumental), and the authoritative role of King David, the master of worship, who maintains faithfulness and integrity in worship.

In the way this story of Israel's past is told, nothing takes precedence over worship in nurturing and protecting our identity as a people of God—not politics, not economics, not family life, not art. And nothing in the preparation for and conduct of worship is too small to be left to whim or chance—nothing in architecture, personnel, music, or theology.

Earlier threats to Israel's identity and survival as a people of God frequently came in the form of hostile outsiders—Egyptians, Canaanites, Philistines, Amalekites, and others; but in this assessment of what matters, right and faithful worship turns out to be what counts most of all. The people of God are not primarily a political entity or a military force or an economic power; they are a holy congregation diligent in worship. To lose touch with the Davidic (and Moses-based) life of worship is to disintegrate as a holy people. To be seduced by the popular pagan worship of the surrounding culture is to be obliterated as a holy people.

Not many readers of this text will find their names in the lists of names in this book. Few worshiping congregations will recognize architectural continuities between The Temple and their local church sanctuaries. Not many communities have access to a pool of Levites from which to recruit choirs and appoint leaders of worship. So, what's left?

Well, worship is left—and names. Accurate worship, defined and fed by the God who reveals himself in Jesus Christ. And personal names that add up to a people of God, a holy congregation. Christians have characteristically read and prayed themselves into Chronicles in order to stay alert to the irreducibly personal in all matters of faith and practice, and to maintain a critical awareness that the worship of God is the indispensable foundation for living whole and redeemed lives.

1 CHRONICLES

ISRAEL'S FAMILY TREE: THE TRUNK

1-4
1 Adam
Seth
Enosh
Kenan
Mahalalel
Jared
Enoch
Methuselah
Lamech
Noah
Shem, Ham, and Japheth.

THE JAPHETH BRANCH

5 Japheth had Gomer, Magog, Madai, Javan, Tubal, Meshech, and Tiras.

6 Gomer had Ashkenaz, Riphath, and Togarmah.

7 Javan had Elisha, Tarshish, Kittim, and Rodanim.

THE HAM BRANCH

8 Ham had Cush, Mizraim, Put, and Canaan.

9 Cush had Seba, Havilah, Sabta, Raamah, and Sabteca.
Raamah had Sheba and Dedan.

10 Cush had Nimrod, the first great hero on earth.

11-12 Mizraim was ancestor to the Ludim, the Anamim, the Lehabim, the Naphtuhim, the Pathrusim, the Casluhim, and the Caphtorim from whom the Philistines descended.

13-16 Canaan had Sidon (his firstborn) and Heth, and was ancestor to the Jebusites, the Amorites, the Girgashites, the Hivites, the Arkites, the Sinites, the Arvadites, the Zemarites, and the Hamathites.

THE SHEM BRANCH

17 Shem had Elam, Asshur, Arphaxad, Lud, Aram, Uz, Hul, Gether, and Meshech.

18-19 Arphaxad had Shelah and Shelah had Eber. Eber had two sons: Peleg (Division) because in his time the earth was divided up; his brother was Joktan.

20-23 Joktan had Almodad, Sheleph, Hazarmaveth, Jerah, Hadoram, Uzal, Diklah, Ebal, Abimael, Sheba, Ophir, Havilah, and Jobab — all sons of Joktan.

24-28 The three main branches in summary: Shem, Arphaxad, Shelah, Eber, Peleg, Reu, Serug, Nahor, Terah, and Abram (Abraham). And Abraham had Isaac and Ishmael.

THE FAMILY OF ABRAHAM

29-31 Abraham's family tree developed along these lines: Ishmael had Nebaioth (his firstborn), then Kedar, Adbeel, Mibsam, Mishma, Dumah, Massa, Hadad, Tema, Jetur, Naphish, and Kedemah — the Ishmael branch.

32-33 Keturah, Abraham's concubine, gave birth to Zimran, Jokshan, Medan, Midian, Ishbak, and Shuah. Then Jokshan had Sheba and Dedan. And Midian had Ephah, Epher, Hanoch, Abida, and Eldaah. These made up the Keturah branch.

34-37 Abraham had Isaac, and Isaac had Esau and Israel (Jacob). Esau had Eliphaz, Reuel, Jeush, Jalam, and Korah. Eliphaz had Teman, Omar, Zepho, Gatam, Kenaz, Timna, and Amalek. And Reuel had Nahath, Zerah, Shammah, and Mizzah.

38-42 Seir then had Lotan, Shobal, Zibeon, Anah, Dishon, Ezer, and Dishan. Lotan had Hori and Homam. Timna was Lotan's sister. Shobal had Alian, Manahath, Ebal, Shepho, and Onam. Zibeon had Aiah and Anah. Anah had Dishon. Dishon had Hemdan, Eshban, Ithran, and Keran. Ezer had Bilhan, Zaavan, and Akan. And Dishan had Uz and Aran.

THE EDOMITE KING LIST

43-51 A list of the kings who ruled in the country of Edom before Israel had a king:

Bela son of Beor; his city was Dinhabah.

Bela died; Jobab son of Zerah from Bozrah was the next king.

Jobab died; Husham from the country of the Temanites was the next king.

Husham died; Hadad son of Bedad, who defeated Midian in the country of Moab, was the next king; his city was Avith.

Hadad died; Samlah from Masrekah was the next king.

Samlah died; Shaul from Rehoboth-by-the-River was the next king.

Shaul died; Baal-Hanan son of Acbor was the next king.

Baal-Hanan died; Hadad was the next king; his city was Pau and his wife was Mehetabel daughter of Matred, the daughter of Me-Zahab.

Last of all Hadad died.

51-54 The chieftains of Edom after that were Chief Timna, Chief Alvah, Chief Jetheth, Chief Oholibamah, Chief Elah, Chief Pinon, Chief Kenaz, Chief Teman, Chief Mibzar, Chief Magdiel, and Chief Iram. These were the chieftains of Edom.

THE FAMILY OF ISRAEL (JACOB)

1-2 **2** Israel's (that is, Jacob's) sons: Reuben, Simeon, Levi, Judah, Issachar, Zebulun, Dan, Joseph, Benjamin, Naphtali, Gad, and Asher.

3-9 Judah had Er, Onan, and Shelah; their mother was Bathshua the Canaanite. Er, Judah's firstborn, was so bad before GOD that GOD killed him. Judah also had Perez and Zerah by his daughter-in-law Tamar—a total of five sons. Perez had Hezron and Hamul; Zerah had Zimri, Ethan, Heman, Calcol, and Darda—five sons. Carmi had Achar, who brought doom on Israel when he violated a holy ban. Ethan's son was Azariah. And Hezron had Jerahmeel, Ram, and Chelubai.

10-17 Ram had Amminadab and Amminadab had Nahshon, a prominent leader in the Judah family. Nahshon had Salmon and Salmon had Boaz. Boaz had Obed and Obed had Jesse. Jesse's firstborn was Eliab, followed by Abinadab, Shimea, Nethanel, Raddai, Ozem, and finally David; David was the seventh. Their sisters were Zeruiah and Abigail. Zeruiah gave birth to three sons: Abishai, Joab, and Asahel; Abigail was the mother of Amasa (the father was Jether the Ishmaelite).

THE FAMILY OF CALEB

18-24 Caleb son of Hezron had children by his wife Azubah and also by Jerioth. Azubah's sons were Jesher, Shobab, and Ardon. After Azubah died, Caleb married Ephrath, who gave birth to Hur. Hur had Uri and Uri had Bezalel. Some time later Hezron married the daughter of Makir the father of Gilead; he was sixty years old when he married her; she gave birth to Segub. Then Segub had Jair who owned twenty-three cities in the land of Gilead. Geshur and Aram captured the nomadic villages of Jair and Kenath and their satellite settlements — sixty towns. These all belonged to Makir the father of Gilead. After the death of Hezron, Caleb married Ephrathah the wife of his father Hezron; she then gave birth to Ashhur the father of Tekoa.

THE FAMILY OF JERAHMEEL

25-26 The sons of Jerahmeel, Hezron's firstborn: Ram his firstborn, followed by Bunah, Oren, Ozem, and Ahijah. Jerahmeel had another wife whose name was Atarah; she gave birth to Onam.

27   The sons of Ram, Jerahmeel's firstborn: Maaz, Jamin, and Eker.

28-29   The sons of Onam: Shammai and Jada.

The sons of Shammai: Nadab and Abishur. Abishur's wife was Abihail; she gave birth to Ahban and Molid.

30   Nadab had Seled and Appaim. Seled died leaving no sons.

31   Appaim had Ishi; Ishi had Sheshan; and Sheshan had Ahlai.

32   Jada, Shammai's brother, had Jether and Jonathan. Jether died leaving no sons.

33   Jonathan had Peleth and Zaza.

This is the family tree of the sons of Jerahmeel.

34-41 Sheshan had no sons, only daughters. But Sheshan had an Egyptian servant, Jarha. Sheshan married his daughter to Jarha and she gave birth to Attai. Attai had Nathan, Nathan had Zabad, Zabad had Ephlal, Ephlal had Obed, Obed had Jehu, Jehu had Azariah, Azariah had Helez, Helez had Eleasah, Eleasah had Sismai, Sismai had Shallum, Shallum had Jekamiah, and Jekamiah had Elishama.

42   Jerahmeel's brother Caleb had a son, his firstborn, named Mesha; Mesha had Ziph; Ziph's son was Mareshah the father of Hebron.

43-44   The sons of Hebron: Korah, Tappuah, Rekem, and Shema. Shema had Raham the father of Jorkeam; Rekem had Shammai.

45   Shammai's son was Maon and Maon was the father of Beth Zur.

46   Caleb's concubine Ephah gave birth to Haran, Moza, and Gazez; Haran had Gazez.

47   The sons of Jahdai: Regem, Jotham, Geshan, Pelet, Ephah, and Shaaph.

48-50   Another concubine of Caleb, Maacah, gave birth to Sheber and Tirhanah. She also bore Shaaph the father of Madmannah and Sheva the father of Macbenah and Gibea. Caleb's daughter was Acsah. These made up the Caleb branch of the family tree.

50-51   The sons of Hur, Ephrathah's firstborn: Shobal who had Kiriath Jearim, Salma who had Bethlehem, and Hareph father of Beth Gader.

52-53 The family of Shobal, father of Kiriath Jearim: Haroeh, half of the population of Manahath, the families of Kiriath Jearim, the Ithrites, the Puthites, the Shumathites, and the Mishraites. The Zorathites and Eshtaolites also came from this line.

54-55 The sons of Salma: Bethlehem, the Netophathites, Atroth Beth Joab, half of the Manahathites, the Zorites, and the families of Sopherim who lived at Jabez—the Tirathites, the Shimeathites, and the Sucathites. They made up the Kenites who came from Hammath the father of the house of Recab.

THE FAMILY OF DAVID

1-3 3 These are the sons that David had while he lived at Hebron:
His firstborn was Amnon by Ahinoam of Jezreel;
second, Daniel by Abigail of Carmel;
third, Absalom born of Maacah, daughter of Talmai king of Geshur;
fourth, Adonijah born of Haggith;
fifth, Shephatiah born of Abital;
sixth, Ithream born of his wife Eglah.

4-9 He had these six sons while he was in Hebron; he was king there for seven years and six months.

He went on to be king in Jerusalem for another thirty-three years. These are the sons he had in Jerusalem: first Shammua, then Shobab, Nathan, and Solomon. Bathsheba daughter of Ammiel was the mother of these four. And then there were another nine sons: Ibhar, Elishua, Eliphelet, Nogah, Nepheg, Japhia, Elishama, Eliada, Eliphelet—David's sons, plus Tamar their sister. There were other sons by his concubines.

10-14 In the next generation Solomon had Rehoboam, who had Abijah, who had Asa, who had Jehoshaphat, who had Jehoram, who had Ahaziah, who had Joash, who had Amaziah, who had Azariah, who had Jotham, who had Ahaz, who had Hezekiah, who had Manasseh, who had Amon, who had Josiah.

15 Josiah's firstborn was Johanan, followed by Jehoiakim, then Zedekiah, and finally Shallum.

16 Jehoiakim's sons were Jeconiah (Jehoiachin) and Zedekiah.

17-18 The sons of Jeconiah born while he was captive in Babylon: Shealtiel, Malkiram, Pedaiah, Shenazzar, Jekamiah, Hoshama, and Nedabiah.

19-20 Pedaiah had Zerubbabel and Shimei; Zerubbabel had Meshullam and Hananiah. Shelomith was their sister. And then five more—Hashubah, Ohel, Berekiah, Hasadiah, and Jushab-Hesed.

21 Hananiah's sons were Pelatiah and Jeshaiah. There were also sons of Rephaiah, sons of Arnan, sons of Obadiah, and sons of Shecaniah.

22 Shecaniah had Shemaiah who in his turn had Hattush, Igal, Bariah, Neariah, and Shaphat—six of them.

23 Neariah had three sons: Elioenai, Hizkiah, and Azrikam.

24 And Elioenai had seven sons: Hodaviah, Eliashib, Pelaiah, Akkub, Johanan, Delaiah, and Anani.

AN APPENDIX TO THE FAMILY OF JUDAH

1-2 4 Sons of Judah: Perez, Hezron, Carmi, Hur, and Shobal. Reaiah, Shobal's son, had Jahath; and Jahath had Ahumai and Lahad. These made up the families of the Zorathites.

3-4 Sons of Etam: Jezreel, Ishma, and Idbash. Their sister was named

Hazzelelponi. Penuel had Gedor and Ezer had Hushah. These were the sons of Hur, firstborn son of Ephrathah, who was the father of Bethlehem.

5-8   Ashhur the father of Tekoa had two wives, Helah and Naarah. Naarah gave birth to Ahuzzam, Hepher, Temeni, and Haahashtari — Naarah's children. Helah's sons were Zereth, Zohar, Ethnan, and Koz, who had Anub, Hazzobebah, and the families of Aharhel son of Harum.

9-10   Jabez was a better man than his brothers, a man of honor. His mother had named him Jabez (Oh, the pain!), saying, "A painful birth! I bore him in great pain!" Jabez prayed to the God of Israel: "Bless me, O bless me! Give me land, large tracts of land. And provide your personal protection — don't let evil hurt me." God gave him what he asked.

11-12   Kelub, Shuhah's brother, had Mehir; Mehir had Eshton; Eshton had Beth Rapha, Paseah, and Tehinnah, who founded Ir Nahash (City of Smiths). These were known as the men of Recah.

13   The sons of Kenaz: Othniel and Seraiah.

The sons of Othniel: Hathath and Meonothai.

14   Meonothai had Ophrah; Seraiah had Joab, the founder of Ge Harashim (Colony of Artisans).

15   The sons of Caleb son of Jephunneh: Iru, Elah, and Naam.

The son of Elah: Kenaz.

16   The sons of Jehallelel: Ziph, Ziphah, Tiria, and Asarel.

17-18   The sons of Ezrah: Jether, Mered, Epher, and Jalon. One of Mered's wives, Pharaoh's daughter Bithiah, gave birth to Miriam, Shammai, and Ishbah the father of Eshtemoa. His Judean wife gave birth to Jered father of Gedor, Heber father of Soco, and Jekuthiel father of Zanoah.

19   The sons of Hodiah's wife, Naham's sister: the father of Keilah the Garmite, and Eshtemoa the Maacathite.

20   The sons of Shimon: Amnon, Rinnah, Ben-Hanan, and Tilon.

The sons of Ishi: Zoheth and Ben-Zoheth.

21-23   The sons of Shelah son of Judah: Er the father of Lecah, Laadah the father of Mareshah and the family of linen workers at Beth Ashbea, Jokim, the men of Cozeba, and Joash and Saraph, who ruled in Moab and Jashubi Lehem. (These records are from very old traditions.) They were the potters who lived at Netaim and Gederah, resident potters who worked for the king.

THE FAMILY OF SIMEON

24-25   The Simeon family tree: Nemuel, Jamin, Jarib, Zerah, and Shaul; Shaul had Shallum, Shallum had Mibsam, and Mibsam had Mishma.

26   The sons of Mishma: Hammuel had Zaccur and Zaccur had Shimei.

27-33   Shimei had sixteen sons and six daughters, but his brothers were not nearly as prolific and never became a large family like Judah. They lived in Beersheba, Moladah, Hazar Shual, Bilhah, Ezem, Tolad, Bethuel, Hormah, Ziklag, Beth Marcaboth, Hazar Susim, Beth Biri, and Shaaraim. They lived in these towns until David became king. Other settlements in the vicinity were the five towns of Etam, Ain, Rimmon, Token, and Ashan, and all the villages around these towns as far as Baalath. These were their settlements. And they kept good family records.

34-40 Meshobab; Jamlech; Joshah the son of Amaziah; Joel; Jehu the son of Joshibiah, the son of Seraiah, the son of Asiel; Elioenai; Jaakobah; Jeshohaiah; Asaiah; Adiel; Jesimiel; Benaiah; and Ziza the son of Shiphi, the son of Allon, the son of Jedaiah, the son of Shimri, the son of Shemaiah — all these were the leaders in their families. They prospered and increased in numbers so that they had to go as far as Gedor (Gerar) to the east of the valley looking for pasture for their flocks. And they found it — lush pasture, lots of elbow room, peaceful and quiet.

40-43 Some Hamites had lived there in former times. But the men in these family trees came when Hezekiah was king of Judah and attacked the Hamites, tearing down their tents and houses. There was nothing left of them, as you can see today. Then they moved in and took over because of the great pastureland. Five hundred of these Simeonites went on and invaded the hill country of Seir, led by Pelatiah, Neariah, Rephaiah, and Uzziel, the sons of Ishi. They killed all the escaped Amalekites who were still around. And they still live there.

The Family of Reuben

1-2 5 The family of Reuben the firstborn of Israel: Though Reuben was Israel's firstborn, after he slept with his father's concubine, a defiling act, his rights as the firstborn were passed on to the sons of Joseph son of Israel. He lost his "firstborn" place in the family tree. And even though Judah became the strongest of his brothers and King David eventually came from that family, the firstborn rights stayed with Joseph.

3 The sons of Reuben, firstborn of Israel: Hanoch, Pallu, Hezron, and Carmi.

4-6 The descendants of Joel: Shemaiah his son, Gog his son, Shimei his son, Micah his son, Reaiah his son, Baal his son, and Beerah his son, whom Tiglath-Pileser king of Assyria took into exile. Beerah was the prince of the Reubenites.

7-10 Beerah's brothers are listed in the family tree by families: first Jeiel, followed by Zechariah: then Bela son of Azaz, the son of Shema, the son of Joel. Joel lived in the area from Aroer to Nebo and Baal Meon. His family occupied the land up to the edge of the desert that goes all the way to the Euphrates River, since their growing herds of livestock spilled out of Gilead. During Saul's reign they fought and defeated the Hagrites; they then took over their tents and lived in them on the eastern frontier of Gilead.

11-12 The family of Gad were their neighbors in Bashan, as far as Salecah: Joel was the chief, Shapham the second-in-command, and then Janai, the judge in Bashan.

13-15 Their brothers, by families, were Michael, Meshullam, Sheba, Jorai, Jacan, Zia, and Eber — seven in all. These were the sons of Abihail son of Huri, the son of Jaroah, the son of Gilead, the son of Michael, the son of Jeshishai, the son of Jahdo, the son of Buz. Ahi son of Abdiel, the son of Guni, was head of their family.

16 The family of Gad lived in Gilead and Bashan, including the outlying villages and extending as far as the pastures of Sharon.

17   They were all written into the official family tree during the reigns of Jotham king of Judah and Jeroboam king of Israel.

18-22 The families of Reuben, Gad, and the half-tribe of Manasseh had 44,760 men trained for war—physically fit and skilled in handling shield, sword, and bow. They fought against the Hagrites, Jetur, Naphish, and Nodab. God helped them as they fought. God handed the Hagrites and all their allies over to them, because they cried out to him during the battle. God answered their prayers because they trusted him. They plundered the Hagrite herds and flocks: 50,000 camels, 250,000 sheep, and 2,000 donkeys. They also captured 100,000 people. Many were killed, because the battle was God's. They lived in that country until the exile.

23-26 The half-tribe of Manasseh had a large population. They occupied the land from Bashan to Baal Hermon, that is, to Senir (Mount Hermon). The heads of their families were Epher, Ishi, Eliel, Azriel, Jeremiah, Hodaviah, and Jahdiel—brave warriors, famous, and heads of their families. But they were not faithful to the God of their ancestors. They took up with the ungodly gods of the peoples of the land whom God had gotten rid of before they arrived. So the God of Israel stirred up the spirit of Pul king of Assyria (Tiglath-Pileser king of Assyria) to take the families of Reuben, Gad, and the half-tribe of Manasseh into exile. He deported them to Halah, Habor, Hara, and the river of Gozan. They've been there ever since.

THE FAMILY OF LEVI

1-14 6The sons of Levi were Gershon, Kohath, and Merari. The sons of Kohath were Amram, Izhar, Hebron, and Uzziel. The children of Amram were Aaron, Moses, and Miriam. The sons of Aaron were Nadab, Abihu, Eleazar, and Ithamar. Eleazar had Phinehas, Phinehas had Abishua, Abishua had Bukki, Bukki had Uzzi, Uzzi had Zerahiah, Zerahiah had Meraioth, Meraioth had Amariah, Amariah had Ahitub, Ahitub had Zadok, Zadok had Ahimaaz, Ahimaaz had Azariah, Azariah had Johanan, and Johanan had Azariah (who served as priest in the temple Solomon built in Jerusalem). Azariah had Amariah, Amariah had Ahitub, Ahitub had Zadok, Zadok had Shallum, Shallum had Hilkiah, Hilkiah had Azariah, Azariah had Seraiah, and Seraiah had Jehozadak.

15   Jehozadak went off to exile when GOD used Nebuchadnezzar to take Judah and Jerusalem into exile.

16-30 The sons of Levi were Gershon, Kohath, and Merari. These are the names of the sons of Gershon: Libni and Shimei. The sons of Kohath were Amram, Izhar, Hebron, and Uzziel. The sons of Merari were Mahli and Mushi. These are the Levitical clans according to families: the sons of Gershon were Libni his son, Jehath his son, Zimmah his son, Joah his son, Iddo his son, Zerah his son, and Jeatherai his son. The sons of Kohath were Amminadab his son, Korah his son, Assir his son, Elkanah his son, Ebiasaph his son, Assir his son, Tahath his son, Uriel his son, Uzziah his son, and Shaul his son. The sons of Elkanah were Amasai and Ahimoth, Elkanah his son, Zophai his son, Nahath his son, Eliab his son, Jeroham his son, and Elkanah his son. The sons of Samuel were Joel his firstborn son and Abijah his second. The sons of Merari were Mahli, Libni his son, Shimei his son, Uzzah his son, Shimea his son, Haggiah his son, and Asaiah his son.

DAVID'S WORSHIP LEADERS

31-32   These are the persons David appointed to lead the singing in the house of GOD after the Chest was placed there. They were the ministers of music in the place of worship, which was the Tent of Meeting until Solomon built The Temple of GOD in Jerusalem. As they carried out their work, they followed the instructions given to them.

33-38   These are the persons, together with their sons, who served by preparing for and directing worship: from the family of the Kohathites was Heman the choirmaster, the son of Joel, the son of Samuel, the son of Elkanah, the son of Jeroham, the son of Eliel, the son of Toah, the son of Zuph, the son of Elkanah, the son of Mahath, the son of Amasai, the son of Elkanah, the son of Joel, the son of Azariah, the son of Zephaniah, the son of Tahath, the son of Assir, the son of Ebiasaph, the son of Korah, the son of Izhar, the son of Kohath, the son of Levi, the son of Israel.

39-43   Heman's associate Asaph stood at his right hand. Asaph was the son of Berekiah, the son of Shimea, the son of Michael, the son of Baaseiah, the son of Malkijah, the son of Ethni, the son of Zerah, the son of Adaiah, the son of Ethan, the son of Zimmah, the son of Shimei, the son of Jahath, the son of Gershon, the son of Levi.

44-47   Of the sons of Merari, the associates who stood at his left hand, was Ethan the son of Kishi, the son of Abdi, the son of Malluch, the son of Hashabiah, the son of Amaziah, the son of Hilkiah, the son of Amzi, the son of Bani, the son of Shemer, the son of Mahli, the son of Mushi, the son of Merari, the son of Levi.

48   The rest of the Levites were assigned to all the other work in the place of worship, the house of God.

49   Aaron and his sons offered the sacrifices on the Altar of Burnt Offering and the Altar of Incense; they were in charge of all the work surrounding the Holy of Holies. They made atonement for Israel following the instructions commanded by Moses, servant of God.

50-53   These are the sons of Aaron: Eleazar his son, Phinehas his son, Abishua his son, Bukki his son, Uzzi his son, Zerahiah his son, Meraioth his son, Amariah his son, Ahitub his son, Zadok his son, and Ahimaaz his son.

THE PRIESTLY CITIES

54-81   And these are the places where the priestly families were assigned to live. The first assignment went by lot to the sons of Aaron of the Kohathite family; they were given Hebron in the land of Judah and all the neighboring pastures. Caleb the son of Jephunneh got the fields and villages around the city. The family of Aaron was also given the cities of refuge, with pastures included: Hebron, Libnah, Jattir, Eshtemoa, Hilen, Debir, Ashan, and Beth Shemesh. They were also given Geba from the tribe of Benjamin, Alemeth, and Anathoth, all with pastures included. In all, thirteen cities were distributed among the Kohathite families. The rest of the Kohathites were given another ten cities, distributed by lot from the half-tribe of Manasseh. The sons of Gershon were given, family by family, thirteen cities from the tribes of Issachar, Asher, Naphtali, and Manasseh in Bashan. The sons of Merari, family by family, were assigned by lot twelve cities from the tribes of Reuben, Gad, and Zebulun. The sons of Israel gave the Levites both the cities and their pastures. They also distributed by lot cities from the tribes of Judah, Simeon, and Benjamin. Some of the Kohath families were given their cities from the tribe of Ephraim, cities of refuge: Shechem in the hill country of Ephraim, Gezer, Jokmeam, Beth Horon, Aijalon, and Gath Rimmon—all with their pastures. The rest of the sons of Kohath were given Aner and Bileam with their pastures from the half-tribe of Manasseh. The sons of Gershon were given, family by family, from the half-tribe of Manasseh, Golan in Bashan and Ashtaroth; from the tribe of Issachar, Kedesh, Daberath, Ramoth, and Anem; from the tribe of Asher, Mashal, Abdon, Hukok, and Rehob; from the tribe of Naphtali, Kedesh in Galilee, Hammon, and Kiriathaim. The rest of the sons of Merari got Rimmono and Tabor from the tribe of Zebulun; Bezer in the desert, Jahzah, Kedemoth, and Mephaath from the tribe of Reuben to the east of the Jordan; and Ramoth in Gilead, Mahanaim, Heshbon, and Jazer from the tribe of Gad. Pastures were included in all these towns.

THE FAMILY OF ISSACHAR

1-5 **7** The sons of Issachar were Tola, Puah, Jashub, and Shimron—four sons. The sons of Tola were Uzzi, Rephaiah, Jeriel, Jahmai, Ibsam, and Samuel—the chiefs of their families. During David's reign, the Tola family counted 22,600 warriors in their lineage. The son of Uzzi was Izrahiah; the sons of Izrahiah were Michael, Obadiah, Joel, and Isshiah—five sons and all of them chiefs. They counted 36,000 warriors in their lineage because they had more wives and sons than their brothers. The extended families of Issachar accounted for 87,000 warriors—all of them listed in the family tree.

THE FAMILY OF BENJAMIN

6-12 Benjamin had three sons: Bela, Beker, and Jediael. Bela had five: Ezbon, Uzzi, Uzziel, Jerimoth, and Iri, all of them chiefs and warriors. They counted 22,034 names in their family tree. Beker's sons were Zemirah, Joash, Eliezer, Elioenai, Omri, Jeremoth, Abijah, Anathoth, and Alemeth. Through these chiefs their family tree listed 20,200 warriors. Jediael's son was Bilhan and the sons of Bilhan were Jeush, Benjamin, Ehud, Kenaanah, Zethan, Tarshish, and Ahishahar—all sons of Jediael and family chiefs; they counted 17,200 combat-ready warriors. Shuppim and Huppim were the sons of Ir; Hushim were from the family of Aher.

THE FAMILY OF NAPHTALI

13 The sons of Naphtali were Jahziel, Guni, Jezer, and Shallum; they are listed under the maternal line of Bilhah, their grandfather's concubine.

THE FAMILY OF MANASSEH

14-19 Manasseh's sons, born of his Aramean concubine, were Asriel and Makir the father of Gilead. Makir got his wife from the Huppites and Shuppites. His sister's name was Maacah. Another son, Zelophehad, had only daughters. Makir's wife Maacah bore a son whom she named Peresh; his brother's name was Sheresh and his sons were Ulam and Rakem. Ulam's son was Bedan. This accounts for the sons of Gilead son of Makir, the son of Manasseh. His sister Hammoleketh gave birth to Ishdod, Abiezer, and Mahlah. The sons of Shemida were Ahian, Shechem, Likhi, and Aniam.

THE FAMILY OF EPHRAIM

20-24 The sons of Ephraim were Shuthelah, Bered his son, Tahath his son, Eleadah his son, Tahath his son, Zabad his son, Shuthelah his son, and Ezer and Elead, cattle-rustlers, killed on one of their raids by the natives of Gath. Their father Ephraim grieved a long time and his family gathered to give him comfort. Then he slept with his wife again. She conceived and produced a son. He named him Beriah (Unlucky), because of the bad luck that had come to his family. His daughter was Sheerah. She built Lower and Upper Beth Horon and Uzzen Sheerah.

25-29 Rephah was Ephraim's son and also Resheph; Telah was his son, Tahan his son, Ladan his son, Ammihud his son, Elishama his son, Nun his son, and Joshua his son. They occupied Bethel and the neighboring country from Naaran on the east to Gezer and its villages on the west, along with Shechem and its villages, and extending as far as Ayyah and its villages. Stretched along the borders of Manasseh were Beth Shan, Taanach, Megiddo, and Dor, together with their satellite villages. The families descended from Joseph son of Israel lived in all these places.

THE FAMILY OF ASHER

30-32 The sons of Asher were Imnah, Ishvah, Ishvi, and Beriah; Serah was their sister. The sons of Beriah were Heber and Malkiel, who had Birzaith. Heber had Japhlet, Shomer, Hotham, and Shua their sister.

33-40 Japhlet had Pasach, Bimhal, and Ashvath. His brother Shomer had Rohgah, Hubbah, and Aram. His brother Helem had Zophah, Imna, Shelesh, and Amal. Zophah had Suah, Harnepher, Shual, Beri, Imrah, Bezer, Hod, Shamma, Shilshah, Ithran, and Beera. Jether had Jephunneh, Pispah, and Ara. Ulla had Arah, Hanniel, and Rizia. These were Asher's sons, all of them responsible, excellent in character, and brave in battle — good leaders. They listed 26,000 combat-ready men in their family tree.

THE FAMILY OF BENJAMIN (CONTINUED)

1-5 8 Benjamin's firstborn son was Bela, followed by Ashbel, Aharah, Nohah, and Rapha — five in all. Bela's sons were Addar, Gera, Abihud, Abishua, Naaman, Ahoah, Gera, Shephuphan, and Huram.

6-7 These are the families of Ehud that lived in Geba and were exiled to Manahath: Naaman, Ahijah, and Gera, who led them to exile and had Uzza and Ahihud.

8-12 In the land of Moab, Shaharaim had children after he divorced his wives Hushim and Baara. From his new wife Hodesh he had Jobab, Zibia, Mesha, Malcam, Jeuz, Sakia, and Mirmah — sons who became heads of families. From his earlier wife Hushim he had Abitub and Elpaal. Elpaal's sons were Eber, Misham, and Shemed, who built Ono and Lod with all their villages.

13-28 Beriah and Shema were family chiefs who lived at Aijalon. They drove out the citizens of Gath. Their brothers were Shashak and Jeremoth. The sons of Beriah were Zebadiah, Arad, Eder, Michael, Ishpah, and Joha. The sons of Elpaal were Zebadiah, Meshullam, Hizki, Heber, Ishmerai, Izliah, and Jobab. The sons of Shimei were Jakim, Zicri, Zabdi, Elienai, Zillethai, Eliel, Adaiah, Beraiah, and Shimrath. The sons of Shashak were Ishpan, Eber, Eliel, Abdon, Zicri, Hanan, Hananiah, Elam, Anthothijah, Iphdeiah, and Penuel. The sons of Jeroham were Shamsherai, Shehariah, Athaliah, Jaareshiah, Elijah, and Zicri. These were the chiefs of the families as listed in their family tree. They lived in Jerusalem.

29-32   Jeiel the father of Gibeon lived in Gibeon. His wife's name was Maacah. Abdon was his firstborn son, followed by Zur, Kish, Baal, Nadab, Gedor, Ahio, Zeker, and Mikloth. Mikloth had Shimeah. They lived in the neighborhood of their extended families in Jerusalem.

33-40   Ner had Kish, Kish had Saul, and Saul had Jonathan, Malki-Shua, Abinadab, and Esh-Baal. Jonathan had Merib-Baal, and Merib-Baal had Micah. Micah's sons were Pithon, Melech, Tarea, and Ahaz. Ahaz had Jehoaddah and Jehoaddah had Alemeth, Azmaveth, and Zimri. Zimri had Moza and Moza had Binea. Raphah was his son, Eleasah his son, and Azel his son. Azel had six sons named Azrikam, Bokeru, Ishmael, Sheariah, Obadiah, and Hanan. His brother Eshek's sons were Ulam his firstborn, followed by Jeush and Eliphelet. Ulam's sons were warriors well known as archers. They had lots of sons and grandsons — at least 150. These were all in Benjamin's family tree.

1   9 This is the complete family tree for all Israel, recorded in the *Royal Annals of the Kings of Israel and Judah* at the time they were exiled to Babylon because of their unbelieving and disobedient lives.

THE BACK-FROM-EXILE COMMUNITY IN JERUSALEM

2   The first Israelites to return from exile to their homes and cities were the priests, the Levites, and the temple support staff.

3-6   Returning to Jerusalem from the families of Judah, Benjamin, Ephraim, and Manasseh were the following: Uthai son of Ammihud, the son of Omri, the son of Imri, the son of Bani, from the line of Perez son of Judah; from the Shilonites were Asaiah the firstborn and his sons; from the family of Zerah there was Jeuel. There were 690 in the Judah group.

7-9   From the family of Benjamin were Sallu son of Meshullam, the son of Hodaviah, the son of Hassenuah, and Ibneiah son of Jeroham, and Elah son of Uzzi, the son of Micri, and Meshullam son of Shephatiah, the son of Reuel, the son of Ibnijah. There were 956 in the Benjamin group. All these named were heads of families.

10-13   From the company of priests there were Jedaiah; Jehoiarib; Jakin; Azariah son of Hilkiah, the son of Meshullam, the son of Zadok, the son of Meraioth, the son of Ahitub, who was in charge of taking care of the house of God; Adaiah son of Jeroham, the son of Pashhur, the son of Malkijah; also Maasai son of Adiel, the son of Jahzerah, the son of Meshullam, the son of Meshillemith, the son of Immer. The priests, all of them heads of families, numbered 1,760, skilled and seasoned servants in the work of worshiping God.

14-16   From the Levites were Shemaiah son of Hasshub, the son of Azrikam, the son of Hashabiah, a Merarite; then Bakbakkar, Heresh, Galal, Mattaniah son of Mica, the son of Zicri, the son of Asaph; also Obadiah son of Shemaiah, the son of Galal, the son of Jeduthun; and finally

Berekiah son of Asa, the son of Elkanah, who lived in the villages of the Netophathites.

17-18 The security guards were Shallum, Akkub, Talmon, Ahiman, and their brothers. Shallum was the chief and up to now the security guard at the King's Gate on the east. They also served as security guards at the camps of Levite families.

19-25 Shallum son of Kore, the son of Ebiasaph, the son of Korah, along with his brothers in the Korahite family, were in charge of the services of worship as doorkeepers of the Tent, as their ancestors had guarded the entrance to the camp of God. In the early days, Phinehas son of Eleazar was in charge of the security guards—God be with him! Now Zechariah son of Meshelemiah was the security guard at the entrance of the Tent of Meeting. The number of those who had been chosen to be security guards was 212—they were officially registered in their own camps. David and Samuel the seer handpicked them for their dependability. They and their sons had the permanent responsibility for guarding the gates of God's house, the house of worship; the main security guards were posted at the four entrances, east, west, north, and south; their brothers in the villages were scheduled to give them relief weekly—the four main security guards were responsible for round-the-clock surveillance.

26-32 Being Levites, they were responsible for the security of all supplies and valuables in the house of God. They kept watch all through the night and had the key to open the doors each morning. Some were in charge of the articles used in The Temple worship—they counted them both when they brought them in and when they took them out. Others were in charge of supplies in the sanctuary—flour, wine, oil, incense, and spices. And some of the priests were assigned to mixing the oils for the perfume. The Levite Mattithiah, the firstborn son of Shallum the Korahite, was responsible for baking the bread for the services of worship. Some of the brothers, sons of the Kohathites, were assigned to preparing the bread set out on the table each Sabbath.

33-34 And then there were the musicians, all heads of Levite families. They had permanent living quarters in The Temple; because they were on twenty-four-hour duty, they were exempt from all other duties. These were the heads of Levite families as designated in their family tree. They lived in Jerusalem.

THE FAMILY OF SAUL

35-38 Jeiel the father of Gibeon lived at Gibeon; his wife was Maacah. His firstborn son was Abdon, followed by Zur, Kish, Baal, Ner, Nadab, Gedor, Ahio, Zechariah, and Mikloth. Mikloth had Shimeam. They lived in the same neighborhood as their relatives in Jerusalem.

39-44 Ner had Kish, Kish had Saul, Saul had Jonathan, Malki-Shua, Abinadab, and Esh-Baal. Merib-Baal was the son of Jonathan and Merib-Baal had Micah. Micah's sons were Pithon, Melech, and Tahrea. Ahaz had Jarah, Jarah had Alemeth, Azmaveth, and Zimri; Zimri had Moza, Moza had Binea, Rephaiah was his son, Eleasah was his son, and Azel was his son. Azel had six sons: Azrikam, Bokeru, Ishmael, Sheariah, Obadiah, and Hanan—the sons of Azel.

10 **1-5** The Philistines went to war against Israel; the Israelites ran for their lives from the Philistines but fell, slaughtered on Mount Gilboa. The Philistines zeroed in on Saul and his sons and killed his sons Jonathan, Abinadab, and Malki-Shua. The battle went hard against Saul—the archers found him and wounded him. Saul said to his armor bearer, "Draw your sword and finish me off before these pagan pigs get to me and make a sport of my body." But his armor bearer, restrained by both reverence and fear, wouldn't do it. So Saul took his own sword and killed himself. The armor bearer, panicked because Saul was dead, then killed himself.

6-7 So Saul and his three sons—all four the same day—died. When all the Israelites in the valley saw that the army had fled and that Saul and his sons were dead, they abandoned their cities and ran off; the Philistines came and moved in.

8-10 The next day the Philistines came to plunder the dead bodies and found Saul and his sons dead on Mount Gilboa. They stripped Saul, removed his head and his armor, and put them on exhibit throughout Philistia, reporting the victory news to their idols and the people. Then they put Saul's armor on display in the temple of their gods and placed his skull as a trophy in the temple of their god Dagon.

11-12 The people of Jabesh Gilead heard what the Philistines had done to Saul. All of their fighting men went into action—retrieved the bodies of Saul and his sons and brought them to Jabesh, gave them a dignified burial under the oak at Jabesh, and mourned their deaths for seven days.

13-14 Saul died in disobedience, disobedient to GOD. He didn't obey GOD's words. Instead of praying, he went to a witch to seek guidance. Because he didn't go to GOD for help, GOD took his life and turned the kingdom over to David son of Jesse.

KING DAVID

11 **1-3** Then all Israel assembled before David at Hebron. "Look at us," they said. "We're your very flesh and blood. In the past, yes, even while Saul was king, you were the real leader of Israel. GOD told you, 'You will shepherd my people Israel; you are to be the ruler of my people Israel.'" When all the elders of Israel came to the king at Hebron, David made a covenant with them in the presence of GOD at Hebron. Then they anointed David king over Israel exactly as GOD had commanded through Samuel.

4-6 David and all Israel went to Jerusalem (it was the old Jebus, where the Jebusites lived). The citizens of Jebus told David, "No trespassing—you can't come here." David came on anyway and captured the fortress of Zion, the City of David. David had said, "The first person to kill a Jebusite will be commander-in-chief." Joab son of Zeruiah was the first; and he became the chief.

7-9 David took up residence in the fortress city; that's how it got its name, "City of David." David fortified the city all the way around, both the outer bulwarks (the Millo) and the outside wall. Joab rebuilt the city gates. David's stride became longer, his embrace larger—yes, GOD-of-the-Angel-Armies was with him!

DAVID'S MIGHTY MEN

10-11 These are the chiefs of David's Mighty Men, the ones who linked arms with him as he took up his kingship, with all Israel joining in, helping him become king in just the way GOD had spoken regarding Israel. The list of David's Mighty Men:

Jashobeam son of Hacmoni was chief of the Thirty. Singlehandedly he killed three hundred men, killed them all in one skirmish.

12-14   Next was Eleazar son of Dodai the Ahohite, one of the Big Three of the Mighty Men. He was with David at Pas Dammim, where the Philistines had mustered their troops for battle. It was an area where there was a field of barley. The army started to flee from the Philistines and then took its stand right in that field — and turned the tide! They slaughtered the Philistines, GOD helping them — a huge victory.

15-19   The Big Three from the Thirty made a rocky descent to David at the Cave of Adullam while a company of Philistines was camped in the Valley of Rephaim. David was holed up in the Cave while the Philistines were prepared for battle at Bethlehem. David had a sudden craving: "What I wouldn't give for a drink of water from the well in Bethlehem, the one at the gate!" The Three penetrated the Philistine camp, drew water from the well at the Bethlehem gate, shouldered it, and brought it to David. And then David wouldn't drink it! He poured it out as a sacred offering to GOD, saying, "I'd rather be damned by God than drink this! It would be like drinking the lifeblood of these men — they risked their lives to bring it." So he refused to drink it. These are the kinds of things that the Big Three of the Mighty Men did.

20-21   Abishai brother of Joab was the chief of the Thirty. Singlehandedly he fought three hundred men, and killed the lot, but he never made it into the circle of the Three. He was highly honored by the Thirty — he was their chief — still, he didn't measure up to the Three.

22-25   Benaiah son of Jehoiada was a Mighty Man from Kabzeel with many exploits to his credit: he killed two famous Moabites; he climbed down into a pit and killed a lion on a snowy day; and he killed an Egyptian, a giant seven and a half feet tall. The Egyptian had a spear like a ship's boom but Benaiah went at him with a mere club, tore the spear from the Egyptian's hand, and killed him with it. These are some of the things Benaiah son of Jehoiada did. But he was never included with the Three. He was highly honored among the Thirty, but didn't measure up to the Three. David put him in charge of his personal bodyguard.

26-47   The Mighty Men of the military were Asahel brother of Joab, Elhanan son of Dodo of Bethlehem, Shammoth the Harorite, Helez the Pelonite, Ira son of Ikkesh the Tekoite, Abiezer the Anathothite, Sibbecai the Hushathite, Ilai the Ahohite, Maharai the Netophathite, Heled son of Baanah the Netophathite, Ithai son of Ribai from Gibeah of the Benjaminite, Benaiah the Pirathonite, Hurai from the ravines of Gaash, Abiel the Arbathite, Azmaveth the Baharumite, Eliahba the Shaalbonite, the sons of Hashem the Gizonite, Jonathan son of Shagee the Hararite, Ahiam son of Sacar the Haranite, Eliphal son of Ur, Hepher the Mekerathite, Ahijah the Pelonite, Hezro the Carmelite, Naarai son of Ezbai, Joel brother of Nathan, Mibhar son of Hagri, Zelek the Ammonite, Naharai the Berothite, the armor bearer of Joab son of Zeruiah, Ira the Ithrite, Gareb the Ithrite, Uriah the Hittite, Zabad son of Ahlai, Adina son of Shiza the Reubenite, the Reubenite chief of the Thirty, Hanan son of Maacah, Joshaphat the Mithnite, Uzzia the Ashterathite, Shama and Jeiel the sons of Hotham the Aroerite, Jediael son of Shimri, Joha the Tizite his brother, Eliel the Mahavite, Jeribai and Joshaviah the sons of Elnaam, Ithmah the Moabite, Eliel, Obed, and Jaasiel the Mezobaite.

1-2   **12** These are the men who joined David in Ziklag; it was during the time he was banished by Saul the son of Kish; they were among the Mighty Men, good fighters. They were armed with bows and could sling stones and shoot arrows either right- or left-handed. They hailed from Saul's tribe, Benjamin.

3-7   The first was Ahiezer; then Joash son of Shemaah the Gibeathite; Jeziel and Pelet the sons of Azmaveth; Beracah; Jehu the Anathothite; Ishmaiah the Gibeonite, a Mighty Man among the Thirty, a leader of the Thirty; Jeremiah; Jahaziel; Johanan; Jozabad the Gederathite; Eluzai; Jerimoth; Bealiah; Shemariah; Shephatiah the Haruphite; Elkanah; Isshiah; Azarel; Joezer; Jashobeam; the Korahites; and Joelah and Zebadiah, the sons of Jeroham from Gedor.

8-15   There were some Gadites there who had defected to David at his wilderness fortress; they were seasoned and eager fighters who knew how to handle shield and spear. They were wild in appearance, like lions, but as agile as gazelles racing across the hills. Ezer was the first, then Obadiah, Eliab, Mishmannah, Jeremiah, Attai, Eliel, Johanan, Elzabad, Jeremiah, and Macbannai—eleven of them. These Gadites were the cream of the crop—any one of them was worth a hundred lesser men, and the best of them were worth a thousand. They were the ones who crossed the Jordan when it was at flood stage in the first month, and put everyone in the lowlands to flight, both east and west.

16-17   There were also men from the tribes of Benjamin and Judah who joined David in his wilderness fortress. When David went out to meet them, this is what he said: "If you have come in peace and to help me, you are most welcome to join this company; but if you have come to betray me to my enemies, innocent as I am, the God of our ancestors will see through you and bring judgment on you."

18   Just then Amasai chief of the Thirty, moved by God's Spirit, said,

We're on your side, O David,
  We're committed, O son of Jesse;
All is well, yes, all is well with you,
  And all's well with whoever helps you.
Yes, for your God has helped and does help you.

So David took them on and assigned them a place under the chiefs of the raiders.

19   Some from the tribe of Manasseh also defected to David when he started out with the Philistines to go to war against Saul. In the end, they didn't actually fight because the Philistine leaders, after talking it over, sent them home, saying, "We can't trust them with our lives—they'll betray us to their master Saul."

20-22   The men from Manasseh who defected to David at Ziklag were Adnah, Jozabad, Jediael, Michael, Jozabad, Elihu, and Zillethai, all leaders among the families of Manasseh. They helped David in his raids against the desert bandits; they were all stalwart fighters and good leaders among his raiders. Hardly a day went by without men showing up to help—it wasn't long before his band seemed as large as God's own army!

※

23-37 Here are the statistics on the battle-seasoned warriors who came down from the north to David at Hebron to hand over Saul's kingdom, in accord with GOD's word: from Judah, carrying shield and spear, 6,800 battle-ready; from Simeon, 7,100 stalwart fighters; from Levi, 4,600, which included Jehoiada leader of the family of Aaron, bringing 3,700 men and the young and stalwart Zadok with twenty-two leaders from his family; from Benjamin, Saul's family, 3,000, most of whom had stuck it out with Saul until now; from Ephraim, 20,800, fierce fighters and famous in their hometowns; from the half-tribe of Manasseh, 18,000 elected to come and make David king; from Issachar, men who understood both the times and Israel's duties, 200 leaders with their families; from Zebulun, 50,000 well-equipped veteran warriors, unswervingly loyal; from Naphtali, 1,000 chiefs leading 37,000 men heavily armed; from Dan, 28,600 battle-ready men; from Asher, 40,000 veterans, battle-ready; and from East of Jordan, men from Reuben, Gad, and the half-tribe of Manasseh, heavily armed, 120,000.

38-40 All these soldiers came to David at Hebron, ready to fight if necessary; they were both united and determined to make David king over all Israel. And everyone else in Israel was of the same mind — "Make David king!" They were with David for three days of feasting celebration, with food and drink supplied by their families. Neighbors ranging from as far north as Issachar, Zebulun, and Naphtali arrived with donkeys, camels, mules, and oxen loaded down with food for the party: flour, fig cakes, raisin cakes, wine, oil, cattle, and sheep — joy in Israel!

DAVID GOES TO GET THE CHEST OF GOD

1-14 **13** David consulted with all of his leaders, the commanders of thousands and of hundreds. Then David addressed the entire assembly of Israel, "If it seems right to you, and it is GOD's will, let's invite all our relatives wherever they are throughout Israel, along with their relatives, including their priests and Levites from their cities and surrounding pastures, to join us. And let's bring the Chest of our God back — the Chest that was out of sight, out of mind during the days of Saul." The entire assembly of Israel agreed — everybody agreed that it was the right thing to do. So David gathered all Israel together, from Egypt's Pond of Horus in the southwest to the Pass of Hamath in the northeast, to go and get the Chest of God from Kiriath Jearim. Then David and all Israel went to Baalah (Kiriath Jearim) in Judah to bring back the Chest of God, the "Cherubim-Throne-of-GOD," where GOD's Name is invoked. They moved the Chest of God on a brand-new cart from the house of Abinadab with Uzzah and Ahio in charge. In procession with the Chest of God, David and all Israel worshiped exuberantly in song and dance, with a marching band of all kinds of instruments. When they were at the threshing floor of Kidon, the oxen stumbled and Uzzah grabbed the Chest to keep it from falling off. GOD erupted in anger against Uzzah and killed him because he grabbed the Chest. He died on the spot — in the presence of God. David lost his temper, angry because GOD exploded against Uzzah; the place is still called Perez Uzzah (Exploded Uzzah). David was terrified of God that day; he said, "How can I possibly continue this parade with the Chest of God?" So David called off the parade of the Chest to the City of David; instead he stored it in the house of Obed-Edom the Gittite. The Chest of God was in storage in the house of Obed-Edom for three months. GOD blessed the family of Obed-Edom and everything around him.

DAVID BUILDS

1-7   **14** King Hiram of Tyre sent an envoy to David, along with cedar lumber, masons, and carpenters to build him a royal palace. Then David knew for sure that GOD had confirmed him as king over Israel, because of the rising reputation that GOD was giving his kingdom for the benefit of his people Israel. David married more wives and had more children in Jerusalem. His children born in Jerusalem were Shammua, Shobab, Nathan, Solomon, Ibhar, Elishua, Elpelet, Nogah, Nepheg, Japhia, Elishama, Beeliada, and Eliphelet.

8-9   The minute the Philistines heard that David had been made king over a united Israel, they went out in force to capture David. When David got the report, he marched out to confront them. On their way, the Philistines stopped off to plunder the Valley of Rephaim.

10   David prayed to God: "Is this the right time to attack the Philistines? Will you give me the victory?"

GOD answered, "Attack; I'll give you the victory."

11-12   David attacked at Baal Perazim and slaughtered them. David said, "God exploded my enemies, as water explodes from a burst pipe." That's how the place got its name, Baal Perazim (Baal-Explosion). The Philistines left their gods behind and David ordered that they be burned up.

13-15   And then the Philistines were back at it again, plundering in the valley. David again prayed to God. God answered, "This time don't attack head-on; circle around and come at them out of the balsam grove. When you hear a sound like shuffling feet in the tops of the balsams, attack; God will be two steps ahead of you, slaughtering the Philistines."

16   David did exactly as God commanded, slaughtering Philistines all the way from Gibeon to Gezer.

17   David was soon famous all over the place, far and near; and GOD put the fear of God into the godless nations.

DAVID WORSHIPS

1-2   **15** After David built houses for himself in the City of David, he cleared a place for the Chest and pitched a tent for it. Then David gave orders: "No one carries the Chest of God except the Levites; GOD designated them and them only to carry the Chest of GOD and be available full time for service in the work of worship."

3-10   David then called everyone in Israel to assemble in Jerusalem to bring up the Chest of GOD to its specially prepared place. David also called in the family of Aaron and the Levites. From the family of Kohath, Uriel the head with 120 relatives; from the family of Merari, Asaiah the head with 220 relatives; from the family of Gershon, Joel the head with 130 relatives; from the family of Elizaphan, Shemaiah the head with 200 relatives; from the family of Hebron, Eliel the head with 80 relatives; from the family of Uzziel, Amminadab the head with 112 relatives.

11-13 Then David called in Zadok and Abiathar the priests, and Uriel, Asaiah, Joel, Shemaiah, Eliel, and Amminadab the Levites. He said, "You are responsible for the Levitical families; now consecrate yourselves, both you and your relatives, and bring up the Chest of the GOD of Israel to the place I have set aside for it. The first time we did this, you Levites did not carry it properly, and GOD exploded in anger at us because we didn't make proper preparation and follow instructions."

14-15 So the priests and Levites consecrated themselves to bring up the Chest of the GOD of Israel. The Levites carried the Chest of God exactly as Moses, instructed by GOD, commanded — carried it with poles on their shoulders, careful not to touch it with their hands.

16 David ordered the heads of the Levites to assign their relatives to sing in the choir, accompanied by a well-equipped marching band, and fill the air with joyful sound.

17-18 The Levites assigned Heman son of Joel, and from his family, Asaph son of Berekiah, then Ethan son of Kushaiah from the family of Merari, and after them in the second rank their brothers Zechariah, Jaaziel, Shemiramoth, Jehiel, Unni, Eliab, Benaiah, Maaseiah, Mattithiah, Eliphelehu, Mikneiah, Obed-Edom, and Jeiel as security guards.

19-22 The members of the choir and marching band were: Heman, Asaph, and Ethan with bronze cymbals; Zechariah, Aziel, Shemiramoth, Jehiel, Unni, Eliab, Maaseiah, and Benaiah with lyres carrying the melody; Mattithiah, Eliphelehu, Mikneiah, Obed-Edom, Jeiel, and Azaziah with harps filling in the harmony; Kenaniah, the Levite in charge of music, a very gifted musician, was music director.

23-24 Berekiah and Elkanah were porters for the Chest. The priests Shebaniah, Joshaphat, Nethanel, Amasai, Zechariah, Benaiah, and Eliezer blew the trumpets before the Chest of God. Obed-Edom and Jehiah were also porters for the Chest.

25-28 Now they were ready. David, the elders of Israel, and the commanders of thousands started out to get the Chest of the Covenant of GOD and bring it up from the house of Obed-Edom. And they went rejoicing. Because God helped the Levites, strengthening them as they carried the Chest of the Covenant of GOD, they paused to worship by sacrificing seven bulls and seven rams. They were all dressed in elegant linen — David, the Levites carrying the Chest, the choir and band, and Kenaniah who was directing the music. David also wore a linen prayer shawl (called an ephod). On they came, all Israel on parade bringing up the Chest of the Covenant of GOD, shouting and cheering, playing every kind of brass and percussion and string instrument.

29 When the Chest of the Covenant of GOD entered the City of David, Michal, Saul's daughter, was watching from a window. When she saw King David dancing ecstatically she was filled with contempt.

*

1-3 **16** They brought the Chest of God and placed it right in the center of the tent that David had pitched for it; then they worshiped by presenting burnt offerings and peace offerings to God. When David had completed the offerings of worship, he blessed the people in the name of GOD. Then he passed around to every one there, men and women alike, a loaf of bread, a slice of barbecue, and a raisin cake.

4-6   Then David assigned some of the Levites to the Chest of GOD to lead worship—to intercede, give thanks, and praise the GOD of Israel. Asaph was in charge; under him were Zechariah, Jeiel, Shemiramoth, Jehiel, Mattithiah, Eliab, Benaiah, Obed-Edom, and Jeiel, who played the musical instruments. Asaph was on percussion. The priests Benaiah and Jahaziel blew the trumpets before the Chest of the Covenant of God at set times through the day.

7   That was the day that David inaugurated regular worship of praise to GOD, led by Asaph and his company.

8-19   Thank GOD! Call out his Name!
         Tell the whole world who he is and what he's done!
     Sing to him! Play songs for him!
         Broadcast all his wonders!
     Revel in his holy Name,
         GOD-seekers, be jubilant!
     Study GOD and his strength,
         seek his presence day and night;
     Remember all the wonders he performed,
         the miracles and judgments that came out of his mouth.
     Seed of Israel his servant!
         Children of Jacob, his first choice!
     He is GOD, *our* God;
         wherever you go you come on his judgments and decisions.
     He keeps his commitments across thousands
         of generations, the covenant he commanded,
     The same one he made with Abraham,
         the very one he swore to Isaac;
     He posted it in big block letters to Jacob,
         this eternal covenant with Israel:
     "I give you the land of Canaan,
         this is your inheritance;
     Even though you're not much to look at,
         a few straggling strangers."

20-22   They wandered from country to country,
         camped out in one kingdom after another;
     But he didn't let anyone push them around,
         he stood up for them against bully-kings:
     "Don't you dare touch my anointed ones,
         don't lay a hand on my prophets."

23-27   Sing to GOD, everyone and everything!
         Get out his salvation news every day!
     Publish his glory among the godless nations,
         his wonders to all races and religions.
     And why? Because GOD is great—well worth praising!
         No god or goddess comes close in honor.
     All the popular gods are stuff and nonsense,
         but GOD made the cosmos!
     Splendor and majesty flow out of him,
         strength and joy fill his place.

28-29　Shout Bravo! to God, families of the peoples,
　　　in awe of the Glory, in awe of the Strength: Bravo!
　　Shout Bravo! to his famous Name,
　　　lift high an offering and enter his presence!
　　Stand resplendent in his robes of holiness!

30-33　God is serious business, take him seriously;
　　　he's put the earth in place and it's not moving.
　　So let Heaven rejoice, let Earth be jubilant,
　　　and pass the word among the nations, "God reigns!"
　　Let Ocean, all teeming with life, bellow,
　　　let Field and all its creatures shake the rafters;
　　Then the trees in the forest will add their applause
　　　to all who are pleased and present before God
　　　—he's on his way to set things right!

34-36　Give thanks to God—he is good
　　　and his love never quits.
　　Say, "Save us, Savior God,
　　　round us up and get us out of these godless places,
　　So we can give thanks to your holy Name,
　　　and bask in your life of praise."
　　Blessed be God, the God of Israel,
　　　from everlasting to everlasting.

　　Then everybody said, "Yes! Amen!" and "Praise God!"

37-42　David left Asaph and his coworkers with the Chest of the Covenant of God and in charge of the work of worship; they were responsible for the needs of worship around the clock. He also assigned Obed-Edom and his sixty-eight relatives to help them. Obed-Edom son of Jeduthun and Hosah were in charge of the security guards. The priest Zadok and his family of priests were assigned to the Tent of God at the sacred mound at Gibeon to make sure that the services of morning and evening worship were conducted daily, complete with Whole-Burnt-Offerings offered on the Altar of Burnt Offering, as ordered in the Law of God, which was the norm for Israel. With them were Heman, Jeduthun, and others specifically named, with the job description: "Give thanks to God, for his love never quits!" Heman and Jeduthun were also well equipped with trumpets, cymbals, and other instruments for accompanying sacred songs. The sons of Jeduthun formed the security guard.

43　　Arrangements completed, the people all left for home. And David went home to bless his family.

David Submits and Prays

1　**17** After the king had made himself at home, he said to Nathan the prophet, "Look at this: Here I am comfortable in a luxurious palace of cedar and the Chest of the Covenant of God sits under a tent."

2　　Nathan told David, "Whatever is on your heart, go and do it; God is with you."

3-6 But that night, the word of God came to Nathan, saying, "Go and tell my servant David, This is GOD's word on the matter: You will not build me a 'house' to live in. Why, I haven't lived in a 'house' from the time I brought up the children of Israel from Egypt till now; I've gone from one tent and makeshift shelter to another. In all my travels with all Israel, did I ever say to any of the leaders I commanded to shepherd Israel, 'Why haven't you built me a house of cedar?'

7-10 "So here is what you are to tell my servant David: The GOD-of-the-Angel-Armies has this word for you: I took you from the pasture, tagging after sheep, and made you prince over my people Israel. I was with you everywhere you went and mowed your enemies down before you; and now I'm about to make you famous, ranked with the great names on earth. I'm going to set aside a place for my people Israel and plant them there so they'll have their own home and not be knocked around anymore; nor will evil nations afflict them as they always have, even during the days I set judges over my people Israel. And finally, I'm going to conquer all your enemies.

10-14 "And now I'm telling you this: GOD himself will build *you* a house! When your life is complete and you're buried with your ancestors, then I'll raise up your child to succeed you, a child from your own body, and I'll firmly establish his rule. *He* will build a house to honor me, and I will guarantee his kingdom's rule forever. I'll be a father to him, and he'll be a son to me. I will never remove my gracious love from him as I did from the one who preceded you. I will set him over my house and my kingdom forever; his throne will always be there, rock solid."

15 Nathan gave David a complete and accurate report of everything he heard and saw in the vision.

16-27 King David went in, took his place before GOD, and prayed:

Who am I, my Master GOD, and what is my family, that you have brought me to this place in life? But that's nothing compared to what's coming, for you've also spoken of my family far into the future, given me a glimpse into tomorrow and looked on me, Master GOD, as a Somebody. What's left for David to say to this—to your honoring your servant, even though you know me, just as I am? O GOD, out of the goodness of your heart, you've taken your servant to do this great thing and put your great work on display. There's none like you, GOD, no *God* but you, nothing to compare with what we've heard with our own ears. And who is like your people, like Israel, a nation unique on earth, whom God set out to redeem as his own people (and became most famous for it), performing great and fearsome acts, throwing out nations and their gods left and right as you saved your people from Egypt? You established for yourself a people—your very own Israel!—your people forever. And you, GOD, became their God.

So now, great GOD, this word that you have spoken to me and my family, guarantee it forever! Do exactly what you've promised! Then your reputation will be confirmed and flourish always as people exclaim, "The GOD-of-the-Angel-Armies, the God over Israel, is Israel's God!" And the house of your servant David will remain rock solid under your watchful presence. You, my God, have told me plainly, "I will build you a house." That's how I was able to find the courage to pray this prayer to you. GOD, being the God you are, you have spoken all these wonderful words to me. As if that weren't enough, you've blessed my family so that it will continue in your presence always. Because you have blessed it, GOD, it's *really* blessed — blessed for good!

DAVID FIGHTS

18 In the days that followed, David struck hard at the Philistines, bringing them to their knees, captured Gath, and took control of the surrounding countryside.

2 He also fought and defeated Moab. The Moabites came under David's rule and paid regular tribute.

3-4 On his way to restore his sovereignty at the Euphrates River, David defeated Hadadezer king of Zobah (over toward Hamath). David captured a thousand chariots, seven thousand cavalry, and twenty thousand infantry from him. He hamstrung all the chariot horses, but saved back a hundred.

5-6 When the Arameans from Damascus came to the aid of Hadadezer king of Zobah, David killed twenty-two thousand of them. David set up a puppet government in Aram-Damascus. The Arameans became subjects of David and were forced to bring tribute. GOD gave victory to David wherever he marched.

7-8 David plundered the gold shields that belonged to the servants of Hadadezer and brought them to Jerusalem. He also looted Tebah and Cun, cities of Hadadezer, of a huge quantity of bronze that Solomon later used to make the Great Bronze Sea, the Pillars, and bronze equipment in The Temple.

9-11 Tou king of Hamath heard that David had struck down the entire army of Hadadezer king of Zobah. He sent his son Hadoram to King David to greet and congratulate him for fighting and defeating Hadadezer. Tou and Hadadezer were old enemies. Hadoram brought David various things made of silver, gold, and bronze. King David consecrated these things along with the silver and gold that he had plundered from other nations: Edom, Moab, the Ammonites, the Philistines, and Amalek.

12-13 Abishai son of Zeruiah fought and defeated the Edomites in the Valley of Salt — eighteen thousand of them. He set up a puppet government in Edom and the Edomites became subjects under David.

GOD gave David victory wherever he marched.

14-17 Thus David ruled over all of Israel. He ruled well, fair and evenhanded in all his duties and relationships.

Joab son of Zeruiah was head of the army;
Jehoshaphat son of Ahilud was in charge of public records;
Zadok son of Ahitub and Abimelech son of Abiathar were priests;
Shavsha was secretary;
Benaiah son of Jehoiada was over the special forces, the Kerethites and Pelethites;
And David's sons held high positions, close to the king.

1-2 **19** Some time after this Nahash king of the Ammonites died and his son succeeded him as king. David said, "I'd like to show some kindness to Hanun son of Nahash—treat him as well and as kindly as his father treated me." So David sent condolences about his father's death.

2-3 But when David's servants arrived in Ammonite country and came to Hanun to bring condolences, the Ammonite leaders warned Hanun, "Do you for a minute suppose that David is honoring your father by sending you comforters? Don't you know that he's sent these men to snoop around the city and size it up so that he can capture it?"

4 So Hanun seized David's men, shaved them clean, cut off their robes halfway up their buttocks, and sent them packing.

5 When this was all reported to David, he sent someone to meet them, for they were seriously humiliated. The king told them, "Stay in Jericho until your beards grow out; only then come back."

6-7 When it dawned on the Ammonites that as far as David was concerned, they stank to high heaven, they hired, at a cost of a thousand talents of silver (thirty-seven and a half tons!), chariots and horsemen from the Arameans of Naharaim, Maacah, and Zobah—thirty-two thousand chariots and drivers; plus the king of Maacah with his troops who came and set up camp at Medeba; the Ammonites, too, were mobilized from their cities and got ready for battle.

8 When David heard this, he dispatched Joab with his strongest fighters in full force.

9-13 The Ammonites marched out and spread out in battle formation at the city gate; the kings who had come as allies took up a position in the open fields. When Joab saw that he had two fronts to fight, before and behind, he took his pick of the best of Israel and deployed them to confront the Arameans. The rest of the army he put under the command of Abishai, his brother, and deployed them to deal with the Ammonites. Then he said, "If the Arameans are too much for me, you help me; and if the Ammonites prove too much for you, I'll come and help you. Courage! We'll fight might and main for our people and for the cities of our God. And GOD will do whatever he sees needs doing!"

14-15 But when Joab and his soldiers moved in to fight the Arameans, they ran off in full retreat. Then the Ammonites, seeing the Arameans run for dear life, took to their heels and ran from Abishai into the city.

So Joab withdrew from the Ammonites and returned to Jerusalem.

16 When the Arameans saw how badly they'd been beaten by Israel, they picked up the pieces and regrouped; they sent for the Arameans who were across the river; Shophach, commander of Hadadezer's army, led them.

17-19 When all this was reported to David, he mustered all Israel, crossed the Jordan, advanced, and prepared to fight. The Arameans went into battle formation, ready for David, and the fight was on. But the Arameans again scattered before Israel. David killed seven thousand chariot drivers and forty thousand infantry. He also killed Shophach, the army commander. When all the kings who were vassals of Hadadezer saw that they had been routed by Israel, they made peace with David and served him. The Arameans were afraid to help the Ammonites ever again.

20 ¹⁻³ That spring, the time when kings usually go off to war, Joab led the army out and ravaged the Ammonites. He then set siege to Rabbah. David meanwhile was back in Jerusalem. Joab hit Rabbah hard and left it in ruins. David took the crown off the head of their king. Its weight was found to be a talent of gold and set with a precious stone. It was placed on David's head. He hauled great quantities of loot from the city and put the people to hard labor with saws and picks and axes. This is what he did to all the Ammonites. Then David and his army returned to Jerusalem.

⁴⁻⁸ Later war broke out with the Philistines at Gezer. That was the time Sibbecai the Hushathite killed Sippai of the clan of giants. The Philistines had to eat crow. In another war with the Philistines, Elhanan son of Jair killed Lahmi, the brother of Goliath the Gittite whose spear was like a ship's boom. And then there was the war at Gath that featured a hulking giant who had twenty-four fingers and toes, six on each hand and foot — yet another from the clan of giants. When he mocked Israel, Jonathan son of Shimea, David's brother, killed him. These came from the clan of giants and were killed by David and his men.

DAVID, SATAN, AND ARAUNAH

21 ¹⁻² Now Satan entered the scene and seduced David into taking a census of Israel. David gave orders to Joab and the army officers under him, "Canvass all the tribes of Israel, from Dan to Beersheba, and get a count of the population. I want to know the number."

³ Joab resisted: "May GOD multiply his people by hundreds! Don't they all belong to my master the king? But why on earth would you do a thing like this — why risk getting Israel into trouble with God?"

⁴⁻⁷ But David wouldn't take no for an answer, so Joab went off and did it — canvassed the country and then came back to Jerusalem and reported the results of the census: There were 1,100,000 fighting men; of that total, Judah accounted for 470,000. Joab, disgusted by the command — it, in fact, turned his stomach! — protested by leaving Levi and Benjamin out of the census-taking. And God, offended by the whole thing, punished Israel.

⁸ Then David prayed, "I have sinned badly in what I have just done, substituting statistics for trust; forgive my sin — I've been really stupid."

⁹⁻¹⁰ GOD answered by speaking to Gad, David's pastor: "Go and give David this message: 'GOD's word: You have your choice of three punishments; choose one and I'll do the rest.'"

¹¹⁻¹² Gad delivered the message to David: "Do you want three years of famine, three months of running from your enemies while they chase you down, or three days of the sword of GOD — an epidemic unleashed on the country by an angel of GOD? Think it over and make up your mind. What shall I tell the One who sent me?"

¹³ David told Gad, "They're all terrible! But I'd rather be punished by GOD whose mercy is great, than fall into human hands."

¹⁴⁻¹⁵ So GOD unleashed an epidemic in Israel — seventy thousand Israelites died. God then sent the angel to Jerusalem but when he saw the destruction about to begin, he compassionately changed his mind and ordered the death angel, "Enough's enough! Pull back!"

¹⁵⁻¹⁶ The angel of GOD had just reached the threshing floor of Araunah the Jebusite. David looked up and saw the angel hovering between earth and sky, sword drawn and about to strike Jerusalem. David and the elders

bowed in prayer and covered themselves with rough burlap.

17   David prayed, "Please! I'm the one who sinned; I'm the one at fault. But these sheep, what did they do wrong? Punish me, not them, me and my family; don't take it out on them."

18-19   The angel of GOD ordered Gad to tell David to go and build an altar to GOD on the threshing floor of Araunah the Jebusite. David did what Gad told him in obedience to GOD's command.

20-21   Meanwhile Araunah had quit threshing the wheat and was watching the angel; his four sons took cover and hid. David came up to Araunah. When Araunah saw David, he left the threshing floor and bowed deeply before David, honoring the king.

22   David said to Araunah, "Give me the site of the threshing floor so I can build an altar to GOD. Charge me the market price; we're going to put an end to this disaster."

23   "O Master, my king," said Araunah, "just take it; do whatever you want with it! Look, here's an ox for the burnt offering and threshing paddles for the fuel and wheat for the meal offering — it's all yours!"

24-27   David replied to Araunah, "No. I'm *buying* it from you, and at the full market price. I'm not going to offer GOD sacrifices that are no sacrifice." So David bought the place from Araunah for six hundred shekels of gold. He built an altar to GOD there and sacrificed Whole-Burnt-Offerings and Peace-Offerings. He called out to GOD and GOD answered by striking the altar of Whole-Burnt-Offering with lightning. Then GOD told the angel to put his sword back into its scabbard.

28   And that's the story of what happened when David saw that GOD answered him on the threshing floor of Araunah the Jebusite at the time he offered the sacrifice.

29-30   At this time the Tabernacle that Moses had constructed in the desert, and with it the Altar of Burnt Offering, were set up at the worship center at Gibeon. But David, terrified by the angel's sword, wouldn't go there to

1   pray to God anymore. So David declared, "From now on, *this* is the site for the worship of GOD; *this* is the place for Israel's Altar of Burnt Offering."

DAVID CHARGES SOLOMON TO BUILD THE TEMPLE

2-4   **22** David ordered all the resident aliens in the land to come together; he sent them to the stone quarries to cut dressed stone to build The Temple of God. He also stockpiled a huge quantity of iron for nails and bracings for the doors of the gates, more bronze than could be weighed, and cedar logs past counting (the Sidonians and Tyrians shipped in huge loads of cedar logs for David).

5-6   David was thinking, "My son Solomon is too young to plan ahead for this. But the sanctuary that is to be built for GOD has to be the greatest, the talk of all the nations; so I'll get the construction materials together." That's why David prepared this huge stockpile of building materials before he died. Then he called in Solomon his son and commanded him to build a sanctuary for the GOD of Israel.

7-10   David said to Solomon, "I wanted in the worst way to build a sanctuary to honor my GOD. But GOD prevented me, saying, 'You've killed too many people, fought too many wars. You are not the one to honor me by building a sanctuary—you've been responsible for too much killing, too much bloodshed. But you are going to have a son and he will be a quiet and peaceful man, and I will calm his enemies down on all sides. His very name will speak peace—that is, Solomon, which means Peace—and I'll give peace and rest under his rule. He will be the one to build a sanctuary in my honor. He'll be my royal adopted son and I'll be his father; and I'll make sure that the authority of his kingdom over Israel lasts forever.'

11-16 "So now, son, GOD be with you. GOD-speed as you build the sanctuary for your GOD, the job God has given you. And may GOD also give you discernment and understanding when he puts you in charge of Israel so that you will rule in reverent obedience under GOD's Revelation. That's what will make you successful, following the directions and doing the things that GOD commanded Moses for Israel. Courage! Take charge! Don't be timid; don't hold back. Look at this—I've gone to a lot of trouble to stockpile materials for the sanctuary of GOD: a hundred thousand talents (3,775 tons) of gold, a million talents (37,750 tons) of silver, tons of bronze and iron—too much to weigh—and all this timber and stone. And you're free to add more. And workers both plentiful and prepared: stonecutters, masons, carpenters, artisans in gold and silver, bronze and iron. You're all set—get to work! And GOD-speed!"

17-19 David gave orders to all of Israel's leaders to help his son Solomon, saying, "Isn't it obvious that your GOD is present with you; that he has given you peaceful relations with everyone around? My part in this was to put down the enemies, subdue the land to GOD and his people; your part is to give yourselves, heart and soul, to praying to your GOD. So get moving—build the sacred house of worship to GOD! Then bring the Chest of the Covenant of GOD and all the holy furnishings for the worship of God into the sanctuary built in honor of GOD."

PREPARATIONS FOR WORSHIP

1 **23** When David got to be an old man, he made his son Solomon king over Israel.

2-5 At the same time he brought together all the leaders of Israel, the priests, and the Levites. The Levites thirty years and older were counted; the total was thirty-eight thousand. David sorted them into work groups: "Twenty-four thousand are in charge of administering worship in the sanctuary; six thousand are officials and judges; four thousand are security guards; and four thousand are to serve in the orchestra, praising GOD with instruments that I have provided for praise."

6 David then divided the Levites into groupings named after the sons of Levi: Gershon, Kohath, and Merari.

7-11 The Gershonites: Ladan and Shimei. The three sons of Ladan: Jehiel, Zetham, and Joel. The three sons of Shimei: Shelomoth, Haziel, and Haran, all heads of the families of Ladan. The four sons of Shimei: Jahath, Ziza, Jeush, and Beriah. Jahath came first, followed by Ziza. Jeush and Beriah did not have many sons so they were counted as one family with one task.

12-14 The four sons of Kohath: Amram, Izhar, Hebron, and Uzziel. The sons of Amram: Aaron and Moses. Aaron was especially ordained to work in the Holy of Holies, to burn incense before GOD, to serve God and bless his Name always. This was a permanent appointment for Aaron and his sons.

Moses and his sons were counted in the tribe of Levi.

15-17   The sons of Moses: Gershom and Eliezer. Shubael was the first son of Gershom. Rehabiah was the first and only son of Eliezer; but though Eliezer had no other sons, Rehabiah had many sons.

18-23   Shelomith was the first son of Izhar. Hebron had four sons: Jeriah, Amariah, Jahaziel, and Jekameam. Uzziel had two sons: Micah and Isshiah. The sons of Merari: Mahli and Mushi. The sons of Mahli: Eleazar and Kish. Eleazar died without any sons, only daughters. Their cousins, the sons of Kish, married the daughters. Mushi had three sons: Mahli, Eder, and Jerimoth.

24   These are the sons of Levi twenty years and older, divided up according to families and heads of families and listed in the work groups that took care of the worship in the sanctuary of GOD.

25-27   David said, "Now that the GOD of Israel has given rest to his people and made Jerusalem his permanent home, the Levites no longer have to carry the Tabernacle and all the furniture required for the work of worship." These last words of David referred only to Levites twenty years old and above.

28-31   From now on the assigned work of the Levites was to assist Aaron's sons in the work of worship in GOD's house: maintain courtyards and closets, keep the furniture and utensils of worship clean, take care of any extra work needed in the work of worship, and provide bread for the table and flour for the Meal Offerings and the unraised wafers—all baking and mixing, all measuring and weighing. Also they were to be present for morning prayers, thanking and praising GOD, for evening prayers, and at the service of Whole-Burnt-Offerings to GOD on Sabbath, at New Moons, and at all festivals. They were on regular duty to serve GOD according to their assignment and the required number.

32   In short, the Levites, with the sons of Aaron as their companions in the ministry of holy worship, were responsible for everything that had to do with worship: the place and times and ordering of worship.

1-5   **24** The family of Aaron was grouped as follows: Aaron's sons were Nadab, Abihu, Eleazar, and Ithamar. Nadab and Abihu died before their father and left no sons. So Eleazar and Ithamar filled the office of priest. David assigned Zadok from the family of Eleazar and Ahimelech from the family of Ithamar and assigned them to separate divisions for carrying out their appointed ministries. It turned out that there were more leaders in Eleazar's family than in Ithamar's and so they divided them proportionately: sixteen clan leaders from Eleazar's family and eight clan leaders from Ithamar's family. They assigned the leaders by lot, treating both families alike, for there were officials of the sanctuary and officials of God among both the Eleazar and Ithamar families.

6   The secretary Shemaiah son of Nethanel, a Levite, wrote down their names in the presence of the king, the officials, Zadok the priest, Ahimelech son of Abiathar, and the leaders of the priestly and Levitical families. They took turns: One family was selected from Eleazar and then one from Ithamar.

7-18   The first lot fell to Jehoiarib,
      the second to Jedaiah,
    the third to Harim,
      the fourth to Seorim,

the fifth to Malkijah,
the sixth to Mijamin,
the seventh to Hakkoz,
the eighth to Abijah,
the ninth to Jeshua,
the tenth to Shecaniah,
the eleventh to Eliashib,
the twelfth to Jakim,
the thirteenth to Huppah,
the fourteenth to Jeshebeab,
the fifteenth to Bilgah,
the sixteenth to Immer,
the seventeenth to Hezir,
the eighteenth to Happizzez,
the nineteenth to Pethahiah,
the twentieth to Jehezkel,
the twenty-first to Jakin,
the twenty-second to Gamul,
the twenty-third to Delaiah,
and the twenty-fourth to Maaziah.

19 They served in this appointed order when they entered The Temple of GOD, following the procedures laid down by their ancestor Aaron as GOD, the God of Israel, had commanded him.

20 The rest of the Levites are as follows:
From the sons of Amram: Shubael; from the sons of Shubael: Jehdeiah.

21 Concerning Rehabiah: from his sons, Isshiah was the first.

22 From the Izharites: Shelomoth; from the sons of Shelomoth: Jahath.

23 The sons of Hebron: Jeriah the first, Amariah the second, Jahaziel the third, and Jekameam the fourth.

24-25 The son of Uzziel: Micah, and from the sons of Micah: Shamir. The brother of Micah was Isshiah, and from the sons of Isshiah: Zechariah.

26-27 The sons of Merari: Mahli and Mushi. The son of Jaaziah: Beno. The sons of Merari from Jaaziah: Beno, Shoham, Zaccur, and Ibri.

28 From Mahli: Eleazar, who had no sons.

29 From Kish: Jerahmeel, the son of Kish.

30-31 And from the sons of Mushi: Mahli, Eder, and Jerimoth.

These were the Levites by their families. They also cast lots, the same as their kindred the sons of Aaron had done, in the presence of David the king, Zadok, Ahimelech, and the leaders of the priestly and Levitical families. The families of the oldest and youngest brothers were treated the same.

THE MUSICIANS FOR WORSHIP

1-7 **25** Next David and the worship leaders selected some from the family of Asaph, Heman, and Jeduthun for special service in preaching and music. Here is the roster of names and assignments: From the family of Asaph: Zaccur, Joseph, Nethaniah, and Asarelah; they were supervised by Asaph, who spoke for GOD backed up by the king's authority. From the family of Jeduthun there were six sons: Gedaliah, Zeri, Jeshaiah, Shimei, Hashabiah, and Mattithiah; they were supervised by their father Jeduthun, who preached and accompanied himself with the zither — he was responsible for leading the thanks and praise to GOD. From the family of Heman: Bukkiah, Mattaniah, Uzziel, Shubael, Jerimoth, Hananiah, Hanani, Eliathah, Giddalti, Romamti-Ezer, Joshbekashah, Mallothi, Hothir, and Mahazioth. These were the sons of Heman the king's seer; they supported and assisted him in his divinely appointed work. God gave Heman fourteen sons and three daughters. Under their father's supervision they were in charge of leading the singing and providing musical accompaniment in the work of worship in the sanctuary of God (Asaph, Jeduthun, and Heman took their orders directly from the king). They were well-trained in the sacred music, all of them masters. There were 288 of them.

8   They drew names at random to see who would do what. Nobody, whether young or old, teacher or student, was given preference or advantage over another.

9-31   The first name from Asaph's family was Joseph and his twelve sons and brothers; second, Gedaliah and his twelve sons and brothers; third, Zaccur and his twelve sons and brothers; fourth, Izri and his twelve sons and brothers; fifth, Nethaniah and his twelve sons and brothers; sixth, Bukkiah and his twelve sons and brothers; seventh, Jesarelah and his twelve sons and brothers; eighth, Jeshaiah and his twelve sons and brothers; ninth, Mattaniah and his twelve sons and brothers; tenth, Shimei and his twelve sons and brothers; eleventh, Azarel and his twelve sons and brothers; twelfth, Hashabiah and his twelve sons and brothers; thirteenth, Shubael and his twelve sons and brothers; fourteenth, Mattithiah and his twelve sons and brothers; fifteenth, Jerimoth and his twelve sons and brothers; sixteenth, Hananiah and his twelve sons and brothers; seventeenth, Joshbekashah and his twelve sons and brothers; eighteenth, Hanani and his twelve sons and brothers; nineteenth, Mallothi and his twelve sons and brothers; twentieth, Eliathah and his twelve sons and brothers; twenty-first, Hothir and his twelve sons and brothers; twenty-second, Giddalti and his twelve sons and brothers; twenty-third, Mahazioth and his twelve sons and brothers; twenty-fourth, Romamti-Ezer and his twelve sons and brothers.

THE SECURITY GUARDS

1-11   **26** The teams of security guards were from the family of Korah: Meshelemiah son of Kore (one of the sons of Asaph). Meshelemiah's sons were Zechariah, the firstborn, followed by Jediael, Zebadiah, Jathniel, Elam, Jehohanan, and Eliehoenai — seven sons. Obed-Edom's sons were Shemaiah, the firstborn, followed by Jehozabad, Joah, Sacar, Nethanel, Ammiel, Issachar, and Peullethai — God blessed him with eight sons. His son Shemaiah had sons who provided outstanding leadership in the family: Othni, Rephael, Obed, and Elzabad; his relatives Elihu and Semakiah were also exceptional. These all came from the line of Obed-Edom — all of them outstanding and strong. There were sixty-two of them. Meshelemiah had eighteen sons and relatives who were outstanding. The sons of Hosah the Merarite were Shimri (he was not the firstborn but his father made him first), then Hilkiah, followed by Tabaliah and Zechariah. Hosah accounted for thirteen.

12-16   These teams of security guards, supervised by their leaders, kept order in The Temple of GOD, keeping up the traditions of their ancestors. They were all assigned to their posts by the same method regardless of the prominence of their families — each picked his gate assignment from a hat. Shelemiah was assigned to the East Gate; his son Zechariah, a shrewd counselor, got the North Gate. Obed-Edom got the South Gate; and his sons pulled duty at the storehouse. Shuppim and Hosah were posted to the West Gate and the Shalleketh Gate on the high road.

16-18 The guards stood shoulder to shoulder: six Levites per day on the east, four per day on the north and on the south, and two at a time at the storehouse. At the open court to the west, four guards were posted on the road and two at the court.

19 These are the teams of security guards from the sons of Korah and Merari.

FINANCIAL AFFAIRS: ACCOUNTANTS AND BOOKKEEPERS

20-22 Other Levites were put in charge of the financial affairs of The Temple of God. From the family of Ladan (all Gershonites) came Jehieli, and the sons of Jehieli, Zetham and his brother Joel. They supervised the finances of the sanctuary of GOD.

23-28 From the Amramites, the Izharites, the Hebronites, and the Uzzielites: Shubael, descended from Gershom the son of Moses, was the chief financial officer. His relatives through Eliezer: his son Rehabiah, his son Jeshaiah, his son Joram, his son Zicri, and his son Shelomith. Shelomith and his relatives were in charge of valuables consecrated by David the king, family heads, and various generals and commanders from the army. They dedicated the plunder that they had gotten in war to the work of the worship of GOD. In addition, everything that had been dedicated by Samuel the seer, Saul son of Kish, Abner son of Ner, and Joab son of Zeruiah—anything that had been dedicated, ever, was the responsibility of Shelomith and his family.

29-30 From the family of the Izharites, Kenaniah and sons were appointed as officials and judges responsible for affairs outside the work of worship and sanctuary. From the family of the Hebronites, Hashabiah and his relatives—1,700 well-qualified men—were responsible for administration of matters related to the worship of GOD and the king's work in the territory west of the Jordan.

31-32 According to the family tree of the Hebronites, Jeriah held pride of place. In the fortieth year of David's reign (his last), the Hebron family tree was researched and outstanding men were found at Jazer in Gilead, namely, Jeriah and 2,700 men of his extended family: David the king made them responsible for administration of matters related to the worship of God and the work of the king in the territory east of the Jordan—the Reubenites, the Gadites, and the half-tribe of Manasseh.

MILITARY ORGANIZATION

1 **27** Here is the listing of the sons of Israel by family heads, commanders and captains, and other officers who served the king in everything military. Army divisions were on duty a month at a time for the twelve months of the year. Each division comprised 24,000 men.

2-3 First division, first month: Jashobeam son of Zabdiel was in charge with 24,000 men. He came from the line of Perez. He was over all the army officers during the first month.

4 The division for the second month: Dodai the Ahohite was in charge: 24,000 men; Mikloth was the leader of his division.

5-6 Commander for the third month: Benaiah son of Jehoiada the priest with 24,000 men. This was the same Benaiah who was a Mighty Man among the Thirty and their chief. His son Ammizabad was in charge of the division.

7 Fourth division for the fourth month: Asahel brother of Joab; his son Zebadiah succeeded him: 24,000 men.

8 Fifth division, fifth month: commander Shamhuth the Izrahite: 24,000 men.

9 Sixth division, sixth month: Ira son of Ikkesh the Tekoite: 24,000 men.

10 Seventh division, seventh month: Helez the Pelonite, an Ephraimite: 24,000 men.

11 Eighth division, eighth month: Sibbecai the Hushathite, a Zerahite: 24,000 men.

12 Ninth division, ninth month: Abiezer the Anathothite, a Benjaminite: 24,000 men.

13 Tenth division, tenth month: Maharai the Netophathite, a Zerahite: 24,000 men.

14 Eleventh division, eleventh month: Benaiah the Pirathomite, an Ephraimite: 24,000 men.

15 Twelfth division, twelfth month: Heldai the Netophathite from the family of Othniel: 24,000 men.

TRIBAL ADMINISTRATORS

16-22 Administrators of the affairs of the tribes:
  for Reuben: Eliezer son of Zicri;
  for Simeon: Shephatiah son of Maacah;
  for Levi: Hashabiah son of Kemuel;
  for Aaron: Zadok;
  for Judah: Elihu, David's brother;
  for Issachar: Omri son of Michael;
  for Zebulun: Ishmaiah son of Obadiah;
  for Naphtali: Jerimoth son of Azriel;
  for Ephraim: Hoshea son of Azaziah;
  for one half-tribe of Manasseh: Joel son of Pedaiah;
  for the half-tribe of Manasseh in Gilead: Iddo son of Zechariah;
  for Benjamin: Jaasiel son of Abner;
  for Dan: Azarel son of Jeroham.
  These are the administrative officers assigned to the tribes of Israel.

23-24 David didn't keep a count of men under the age of twenty, because GOD had promised to give Israel a population as numerous as the stars in the sky. Joab son of Zeruiah started out counting the men, but he never finished. God's anger broke out on Israel because of the counting. As it turned out, the numbers were never entered into the court records of King David.

SUPPLY OFFICERS

25 The king's storage facilities were supervised by Azmaveth son of Adiel. Jonathan son of Uzziah was responsible for the warehouses in the outlying areas.

26 Ezri son of Kelub was in charge of the field workers on the farms.

27 Shimei the Ramathite was in charge of the vineyards and Zabdi the Shiphmite was in charge of grapes for the wine vats.

28 Baal-Hanan the Gederite was in charge of the olive and sycamore-fig trees in the western hills, and Joash was in charge of the olive oil.

29 Shitrai the Sharonite was in charge of herds grazing in Sharon and Shaphat son of Adlai was in charge of herds in the valley.

30-31 Obil the Ishmaelite was in charge of the camels, Jehdeiah the Meronothite was in charge of the donkeys, and Jaziz the Hagrite was in charge of the flocks.

These were the ones responsible for taking care of King David's property.

DAVID'S COUNSELORS

32 Jonathan, David's uncle, a wise and literate counselor, and Jehiel son of Hacmoni, were responsible for rearing the king's sons.

33-34 Ahithophel was the king's counselor; Hushai the Arkite was the king's friend. Ahithophel was later replaced by Jehoiada son of Benaiah and by Abiathar.

Joab was commander of the king's army.

DAVID'S VALEDICTORY ADDRESS

1 28 David called together all the leaders of Israel—tribal administrators, heads of various governmental operations, military commanders and captains, stewards in charge of the property and livestock belonging to the king and his sons—everyone who held responsible positions in the kingdom.

2-7 King David stood tall and spoke: "Listen to me, my people: I fully intended to build a permanent structure for the Chest of the Covenant of GOD, God's footstool. But when I got ready to build it, God said to me, 'You may not build a house to honor me—you've done too much fighting—killed too many people.' GOD chose me out of my family to be king over Israel forever. First he chose Judah as the lead tribe, then he narrowed it down to my family, and finally he picked me from my father's sons, pleased to make me the king over all Israel. And then from all my sons—and GOD gave me many!—he chose my son Solomon to sit on the throne of GOD's rule over Israel. He went on to say, 'Your son Solomon will build my house and my courts: I have chosen him to be my royal adopted son; and I will be to him a father. I will guarantee that his kingdom will last if he continues to be as strong-minded in doing what I command and carrying out my decisions as he is doing now.'

8 "And now, in this public place, all Israel looking on and God listening in, as GOD's people, obey and study every last one of the commandments of your GOD so that you can make the most of living in this good land and pass it on intact to your children, insuring a good future.

9-10 "And you, Solomon my son, get to know well your father's God; serve him with a whole heart and eager mind, for GOD examines every heart and sees through every motive. If you seek him, he'll make sure you find him, but if you abandon him, he'll leave you for good. Look sharp now! GOD has chosen *you* to build his holy house. Be brave, determined! And do it!"

11-19 Then David presented his son Solomon with the plans for The Temple complex: porch, storerooms, meeting rooms, and the place for atoning sacrifice. He turned over the plans for everything that God's Spirit had brought to his mind: the design of the courtyards, the arrangements of rooms, and the closets for storing all the holy things. He gave him his plan for organizing the Levites and priests in their work of leading and ordering worship in the house of God, and for caring for the liturgical furnishings. He provided exact specifications for how much gold and silver was needed for each article used in the services of worship: the gold and silver Lampstands and lamps, the gold tables for consecrated bread, the silver tables, the gold forks, the bowls and the jars, and the Incense Altar. And he gave him the plan for sculpting the cherubs with their wings outstretched over the Chest of the Covenant of GOD—the cherubim throne. "Here are the blueprints for the whole project as GOD gave me to understand it," David said.

20-21　David continued to address Solomon: "Take charge! Take heart! Don't be anxious or get discouraged. GOD, my God, is with you in this; he won't walk off and leave you in the lurch. He's at your side until every last detail is completed for conducting the worship of GOD. You have all the priests and Levites standing ready to pitch in, and skillful craftsmen and artisans of every kind ready to go to work. Both leaders and people are ready. Just say the word."

THEY GET READY TO BUILD

1-5　**29** Then David the king addressed the congregation: "My son Solomon was singled out and chosen by God to do this. But he's young and untested and the work is huge—this is not just a place for people to meet each other, but a house for GOD to meet us. I've done my best to get everything together for building this house for my God, all the materials necessary: gold, silver, bronze, iron, lumber, precious and varicolored stones, and building stones—vast stockpiles. Furthermore, because my heart is in this, in addition to and beyond what I have gathered, I'm turning over my personal fortune of gold and silver for making this place of worship for my God: 3,000 talents (about 113 tons) of gold—all from Ophir, the best—and 7,000 talents (214 tons) of silver for covering the walls of the buildings, and for the gold and silver work by craftsmen and artisans.

"And now, how about you? Who among you is ready and willing to join in the giving?"

6-8　Ready and willing, the heads of families, leaders of the tribes of Israel, commanders and captains in the army, stewards of the king's affairs, stepped forward and gave willingly. They gave 5,000 talents (188 tons) and 10,000 darics (185 pounds) of gold, 10,000 talents of silver (377 tons), 18,000 talents of bronze (679 tons), and 100,000 talents (3,775 tons) of iron. Anyone who had precious jewels put them in the treasury for the building of The Temple of GOD in the custody of Jehiel the Gershonite.

9　And the people were full of a sense of celebration—all that giving! And all given willingly, freely! King David was exuberant.

10-13　David blessed GOD in full view of the entire congregation:

Blessed are you, GOD of Israel, our father
　　from of old and forever.
To you, O GOD, belong the greatness and the might,
　　the glory, the victory, the majesty, the splendor;
Yes! Everything in heaven, everything on earth;

the kingdom all yours! You've raised yourself high over all.
Riches and glory come from you,
    you're ruler over all;
You hold strength and power in the palm of your hand
    to build up and strengthen all.
And here we are, O God, our God, giving thanks to you,
    praising your splendid Name.

14-19   "But me—who am I, and who are these my people, that we should presume to be giving something to you? Everything comes from you; all we're doing is giving back what we've been given from your generous hand. As far as you're concerned, we're homeless, shiftless wanderers like our ancestors, our lives mere shadows, hardly anything to us. GOD, our God, all these materials—these piles of stuff for building a house of worship for you, honoring your Holy Name—it all came from you! It was all yours in the first place! I know, dear God, that you care nothing for the surface— you want *us,* our true selves—and so I have given from the heart, honestly and happily. And now see all these people doing the same, giving freely, willingly—what a joy! O GOD, God of our fathers Abraham, Isaac, and Israel, keep this generous spirit alive forever in these people always, keep their hearts set firmly in you. And give my son Solomon an uncluttered and focused heart so that he can obey what you command, live by your directions and counsel, and carry through with building The Temple for which I have provided."

20   David then addressed the congregation: "Bless GOD, your God!" And they did it, blessed GOD, the God of their ancestors, and worshiped reverently in the presence of GOD and the king.

21-22   The very next day they butchered the sacrificial animals and offered in the worship of Israel to GOD a thousand bulls, a thousand rams, a thousand sheep, and in addition drink offerings and many other sacrifices. They feasted all day, eating and drinking before GOD, exuberant with joy.

22-25   Then they ceremonially reenacted Solomon's coronation, anointing David's son before GOD as their leader, and Zadok as priest. Solomon sat on the throne of GOD as king in place of David his father. And everything went well; all Israel obeyed him. All the leaders of the people, including all the sons of King David, accepted Solomon as their king and promised their loyalty. Solomon rode high on a crest of popular acclaim—it was all GOD's doing. GOD gave him position and honor beyond any king in Israel before him.

26-30   David son of Jesse ruled over all Israel. He was king for forty years. He ruled from Hebron seven years and from Jerusalem thirty-three. He died at a ripe old age, full of days, wealth, and glory. His son Solomon ruled after him. The history of David the king, from start to finish, is written in the chronicles of Samuel the seer, Nathan the prophet, and Gad the seer, including a full account of his rule, his exploits, and the times through which he and Israel and the surrounding kingdoms passed.

2 CHRONICLES

KING SOLOMON

1-6 Solomon son of David took a firm grip on the reins of his kingdom. GOD was with him and gave him much help. Solomon addressed all Israel — the commanders and captains, the judges, every leader, and all the heads of families. Then Solomon and the entire company went to the worship center at Gibeon — that's where the Tent of Meeting of God was, the one that Moses the servant of GOD had made in the wilderness. The Chest of God, though, was in Jerusalem — David had brought it up from Kiriath Jearim, prepared a special place for it, and pitched a tent for it. But the Bronze Altar that Bezalel son of Uri, the son of Hur, had made was in Gibeon, in its place before the Tabernacle of GOD; and that is where Solomon and the congregation gathered to pray. Solomon worshiped GOD at the Bronze Altar in front of the Tent of Meeting; he sacrificed a thousand Whole-Burnt-Offerings on it.

7 That night God appeared to Solomon. God said, "What do you want from me? Ask."

8-10 Solomon answered, "You were extravagantly generous with David my father, and now you have made me king in his place. Establish, GOD, the words you spoke to my father, for you've given me a staggering task, ruling this mob of people. Yes, give me wisdom and knowledge as I come and go among this people — for who on his own is capable of leading these, your glorious people?"

11-12 God answered Solomon, "This is what has come out of your heart: You didn't grasp for money, wealth, fame, and the doom of your enemies; you didn't even ask for a long life. You asked for wisdom and knowledge so you could govern well my people over whom I've made you king. Because of this, you get what you asked for — wisdom and knowledge. And I'm presenting you the rest as a bonus — money, wealth, and fame beyond anything the kings before or after you had or will have."

13 Then Solomon left the worship center at Gibeon and the Tent of Meeting and went to Jerusalem. He set to work as king of Israel.

14-17 Solomon collected chariots and horses: fourteen hundred chariots and twelve thousand horses! He stabled them in the special chariot-cities as well as in Jerusalem. The king made silver and gold as common as rocks, and cedar as common as the fig trees in the lowland hills. His horses were brought in from Egypt and Cilicia, specially acquired by the king's agents. Chariots from Egypt went for fifteen pounds of silver and a horse for about three and three-quarters of a pound of silver. Solomon carried on a brisk horse-trading business with the Hittite and Aramean royal houses.

THE TEMPLE CONSTRUCTION BEGINS

1 Solomon gave orders to begin construction on the house of worship in honor of GOD and a palace for himself.

2 Solomon assigned seventy thousand common laborers, eighty thousand to work the quarries in the mountains, and thirty-six hundred foremen to manage the workforce.

3-4 Then Solomon sent this message to King Hiram of Tyre: "Send me cedar logs, the same kind you sent David my father for building his palace. I'm about to build a house of worship in honor of GOD, a holy place for burning perfumed incense, for setting out holy bread, for making Whole-Burnt-Offerings at morning and evening worship, and for Sabbath, New Moon, and Holy Day services of worship—the acts of worship required of Israel.

5-10 "The house I am building has to be the best, for our God is the best, far better than competing gods. But who is capable of building such a structure? Why, the skies—the entire cosmos!—can't begin to contain him. And me, who am I to think I can build a house adequate for God—burning incense to him is about all I'm good for! I need your help: Send me a master artisan in gold, silver, bronze, iron, textiles of purple, crimson, and violet, and who knows the craft of engraving; he will supervise the trained craftsmen in Judah and Jerusalem that my father provided. Also send cedar, cypress, and algum logs from Lebanon; I know you have lumberjacks experienced in the Lebanon forests. I'll send workers to join your crews to cut plenty of timber—I'm going to need a lot, for this house I'm building is going to be absolutely stunning—a showcase temple! I'll provide all the food necessary for your crew of lumberjacks and loggers: 130,000 bushels of wheat, 120,000 gallons of wine, and 120,000 gallons of olive oil."

11 Hiram king of Tyre wrote Solomon in reply: "It's plain that GOD loves his people—he made you king over them!"

12-14 He wrote on, "Blessed be the GOD of Israel, who made heaven and earth, and who gave King David a son so wise, so knowledgeable and shrewd, to build a temple for GOD and a palace for himself. I've sent you Huram-Abi—he's already on his way—he knows the construction business inside and out. His mother is from Dan and his father from Tyre. He knows how to work in gold, silver, bronze, iron, stone, and wood, in purple, violet, linen, and crimson textiles; he is also an expert engraver and competent to work out designs with your artists and architects, and those of my master David, your father.

15-16 "Go ahead and send the wheat, barley, olive oil, and wine you promised for my work crews. We'll log the trees you need from the Lebanon forests and raft them down to Joppa. You'll have to get the timber up to Jerusalem yourself."

17-18 Solomon then took a census of all the foreigners living in Israel, using the same census-taking method employed by his father. They numbered 153,600. He assigned 70,000 of them as common laborers, 80,000 to work the quarries in the mountains, and 3,600 as foremen to manage the work crews.

1-4 3 So Solomon broke ground, launched construction of the house of GOD in Jerusalem on Mount Moriah, the place where GOD had appeared to his father David. The precise site, the threshing floor of Araunah the Jebusite, had been designated by David. He broke ground on the second day in the second month of the fourth year of his rule. These are the dimensions that Solomon set for the construction of the house of God: ninety feet long and thirty feet wide. The porch in front stretched the width of the building, that is, thirty feet; and it was thirty feet high.

4-7 The interior was gold-plated. He paneled the main hall with cypress and veneered it with fine gold engraved with palm tree and chain designs.

He decorated the building with precious stones and gold from Parvaim. Everything was coated with gold veneer: rafters, doorframes, walls, and doors. Cherubim were engraved on the walls.

8-9 He made the Holy of Holies a cube, thirty feet wide, long, and high. It was veneered with six hundred talents (something over twenty-two tons) of gold. The gold nails weighed fifty shekels (a little over a pound). The upper rooms were also veneered in gold.

10-13 He made two sculptures of cherubim, gigantic angel-like figures, for the Holy of Holies, both veneered with gold. The combined wingspread of the side-by-side cherubim (each wing measuring seven and a half feet) stretched from wall to wall, thirty feet. They stood erect facing the main hall.

14 He fashioned the curtain of violet, purple, and crimson fabric and worked a cherub design into it.

15-17 He made two huge free-standing pillars, each fifty-two feet tall, their capitals extending another seven and a half feet. The top of each pillar was set off with an elaborate filigree of chains, like necklaces, from which hung a hundred pomegranates. He placed the pillars in front of The Temple, one on the right, and the other on the left. The right pillar he named Jakin (Security) and the left pillar he named Boaz (Stability).

TEMPLE FURNISHINGS

1 He made the Bronze Altar thirty feet long, thirty feet wide, and ten feet high.

2-5 He made a Sea—an immense round basin of cast metal fifteen feet in diameter, seven and a half feet high, and forty-five feet in circumference. Just under the rim, there were two parallel bands of something like bulls, ten to each foot and a half. The figures were cast in one piece with the Sea. The Sea was set on twelve bulls, three facing north, three facing west, three facing south, and three facing east. All the bulls faced outward and supported the Sea on their hindquarters. The Sea was three inches thick and flared at the rim like a cup, or a lily. It held about 18,000 gallons.

6 He made ten Washbasins, five set on the right and five on the left, for rinsing the things used for the Whole-Burnt-Offerings. The priests washed themselves in the Sea.

7 He made ten gold Lampstands, following the specified pattern, and placed five on the right and five on the left.

8 He made ten tables and set five on the right and five on the left. He also made a hundred gold bowls.

9 He built a Courtyard especially for the priests and then the great court and doors for the court. The doors were covered with bronze.

10 He placed the Sea on the right side of The Temple at the southeast corner.

11-16 He also made ash buckets, shovels, and bowls.

And that about wrapped it up: Huram completed the work he had contracted to do for King Solomon:

> two pillars;
> two bowl-shaped capitals for the tops of the pillars;
> two decorative filigrees for the capitals;
> four hundred pomegranates for the filigrees (a double row of pomegranates for each filigree);

ten washstands with their basins;
one Sea and the twelve bulls under it;
miscellaneous buckets, forks, shovels, and bowls.

16-18 All these artifacts that Huram-Abi made for King Solomon for The Temple of GOD were made of burnished bronze. The king had them cast in clay in a foundry on the Jordan plain between Succoth and Zarethan. These artifacts were never weighed—there were far too many! Nobody has any idea how much bronze was used.

19-22 Solomon was also responsible for the furniture and accessories in The Temple of God:

the gold Altar;
the tables that held the Bread of the Presence;
the Lampstands of pure gold with their lamps, to be lighted
before the Inner Sanctuary, the Holy of Holies;
the gold flowers, lamps, and tongs (all solid gold);
the gold wick trimmers, bowls, ladles, and censers;
the gold doors of The Temple, doors to the Holy of Holies, and the
doors to the main sanctuary.

1 5 That completed the work King Solomon did on The Temple of GOD. He then brought in the holy offerings of his father David, the silver and the gold and the artifacts. He placed them all in the treasury of God's Temple.

INSTALLING THE CHEST

2-3 Bringing all this to a climax, Solomon got all the leaders together in Jerusalem—all the chiefs of tribes and the family patriarchs—to move the Chest of the Covenant of GOD from Zion and install it in The Temple. All the men of Israel assembled before the king on the feast day of the seventh month, the Feast of Booths.

4-6 When all the leaders of Israel were ready, the Levites took up the Chest. They carried the Chest, the Tent of Meeting, and all the sacred things in the Tent used in worship. The priests, all Levites, carried them. King Solomon and the entire congregation of Israel were there before the Chest, worshiping and sacrificing huge numbers of sheep and cattle—so many that no one could keep track.

7-10 The priests brought the Chest of the Covenant of GOD to its place in the Inner Sanctuary, the Holy of Holies, under the wings of the cherubim. The outspread wings of the cherubim formed a canopy over the Chest and its poles. The ends of the poles were so long that they stuck out from the entrance of the Inner Sanctuary, but were not noticeable further out—they're still there today. There was nothing in the Chest itself but the two stone tablets that Moses had placed in it at Horeb where GOD made a covenant with Israel after bringing them up from Egypt.

11-13 The priests then left the Holy Place. All the priests there were consecrated, regardless of rank or assignment; and all the Levites who were musicians were there—Asaph, Heman, Jeduthun, and their families, dressed in their worship robes; the choir and orchestra assembled on the east side of the Altar and were joined by 120 priests blowing trumpets. The

choir and trumpets made one voice of praise and thanks to GOD—orchestra and choir in perfect harmony singing and playing praise to GOD:

> Yes! God is good!
> His loyal love goes on forever!

13-14   Then a billowing cloud filled The Temple of GOD. The priests couldn't
even carry out their duties because of the cloud—the glory of GOD!—that
filled The Temple of God.

SOLOMON'S DEDICATION AND PRAYER

1-2   **6** Then Solomon said,

> GOD said he would dwell in a cloud,
> But I've built a temple most splendid,
> A place for you to live in forever.

3   The king then turned to face the congregation that had come together
and blessed them:

4-6   "Blessed be GOD, the God of Israel, who spoke personally to my father
David. Now he has done what he promised when he said, 'From the day
I brought my people Israel up from Egypt, I haven't set apart one city
among the tribes of Israel in which to build a temple to honor my Name,
or chosen one person to be the leader. But now I have chosen both a city
and a person: Jerusalem for honoring my Name and David to lead my
people Israel.'

7-9   "My father David very much wanted to build a temple honoring the
Name of GOD, the God of Israel, but GOD told him, 'It was good that you
wanted to build a temple in my honor—most commendable! But you are
not the one to do it. Your son, who will carry on your dynasty, will build
it for my Name.'

10-11   "And now you see the promise completed. GOD has done what he said
he would do; I have succeeded David my father and now rule Israel; and
I have built a temple to honor GOD, the God of Israel, and have secured a
place for the Chest that holds the Covenant of GOD, the covenant he made
with the people of Israel."

12-16   Before the entire congregation of Israel, Solomon took his position at
the Altar of GOD and stretched out his hands. Solomon had made a bronze
dais seven and a half feet square and four and a half feet high and placed
it inside the court; that's where he now stood. Then he knelt in full view of
the whole congregation, stretched his hands to heaven, and prayed:

> GOD, O God of Israel, there is no God like you in the skies above
> or on the earth below, who unswervingly keeps covenant with
> his servants and unfailingly loves them while they sincerely live
> in obedience to your way. You kept your word to David my father,
> your promise. You did exactly what you promised—every detail. The
> proof is before us today!
>   Keep it up, GOD, O God of Israel! Continue to keep the promises
> you made to David my father when you said, "You'll always have
> a descendant to represent my rule on Israel's throne, on the one

condition that your sons are as careful to live obediently in my presence as you have."

17 O GOD, God of Israel, let this all happen —
confirm and establish it!

18-21 Can it be that God will actually move into our neighborhood? Why, the cosmos itself isn't large enough to give you breathing room, let alone this Temple I've built. Even so, I'm bold to ask: Pay attention to these my prayers, both intercessory and personal, O GOD, my God. Listen to my prayers, energetic and devout, that I'm setting before you right now. Keep your eyes open to this Temple day and night, this place you promised to dignify with your Name. And listen to the prayers that I pray in this place. And listen to your people Israel when they pray at this place.

Listen from your home in heaven
and when you hear, forgive.

22 When someone hurts a neighbor and promises to make things right, and then comes and repeats the promise before your Altar in this Temple,

23 Listen from heaven and act;
judge your servants, making the offender pay for the offense
And set the offended free,
dismissing all charges.

24-25 When your people Israel are beaten by an enemy because they've sinned against you, but then turn to you and acknowledge your rule in prayers desperate and devout in this Temple,

Listen from your home in heaven;
forgive the sin of your people Israel,
return them to the land you gave to them and their ancestors.

26-27 When the skies shrivel up and there is no rain because your people have sinned against you, but then they pray at this place, acknowledging your rule and quit their sins because you have scourged them,

Listen from your home in heaven,
forgive the sins of your servants, your people Israel.
Then start over with them;
train them to live right and well;
Send rain on the land
you gave as inheritance to your people.

28-31 When disasters strike, famine or catastrophe, crop failure or disease, locust or beetle, or when an enemy attacks their defenses — calamity of any sort — any prayer that's prayed from anyone at all

among your people Israel, their hearts penetrated by disaster, hands
and arms thrown out for help to this Temple,

Listen from your home in heaven, forgive and reward us:
    reward each life and circumstance,
For you know each life from the inside,
    (you're the only one with such inside knowledge!),
So they'll live before you in lifelong reverence and believing
    obedience on this land you gave our ancestors.

³²   And don't forget the foreigner who is not a member of your people
Israel but has come from a far country because of your reputation —
people are going to be attracted here by your great reputation, your
wonderworking power — and who come to pray to this Temple.

³³ Listen from your home in heaven
    and honor the prayers of the foreigner,
So that people all over the world
    will know who you are and what you're like,
And live in reverent obedience before you,
    just as your own people Israel do,
So they'll know that you personally
    make this Temple that I've built what it is.

³⁴⁻³⁵   When your people go to war against their enemies at the time and
place you send them and they pray to GOD toward the city you chose
and The Temple I've built to honor your Name,

Listen from heaven to what they pray and ask for
    and do what is right for them.

³⁶⁻³⁹   When they sin against you — and they certainly will; there's no
one without sin! — and in anger you turn them over to the enemy
and they are taken captive to the enemy's land, whether far or near,
but repent in the country of their captivity and pray with changed
hearts in their exile, "We've sinned; we've done wrong; we've been
most wicked," and turn back to you heart and soul in the land of the
enemy who conquered them, and pray to you toward their homeland, the land you gave their ancestors, toward the city you chose,
and this Temple I have built to the honor of your Name,

Listen from your home in heaven
    to their prayers desperate and devout;
Do what is best for them.
    Forgive your people who have sinned against you.

⁴⁰   And now, dear God, be alert and attentive to prayer, all prayer,
offered in this place.

⁴¹⁻⁴² Up, GOD, enjoy your new place of quiet repose,
    you and your mighty covenant Chest;

Dress your priests up in salvation clothes,
let your holy people celebrate goodness.
And don't, GOD, back out on your anointed ones,
keep in mind the love promised to David your servant.

THE TEMPLE DEDICATION

1-3 **7** When Solomon finished praying, a bolt of lightning out of heaven struck the Whole-Burnt-Offering and sacrifices and the Glory of GOD filled The Temple. The Glory was so dense that the priests couldn't get in—GOD so filled The Temple that there was no room for the priests! When all Israel saw the fire fall from heaven and the Glory of GOD fill The Temple, they fell on their knees, bowed their heads, and worshiped, thanking GOD:

Yes! God is good!
His love never quits!

4-6 Then the king and all Israel worshiped, offering sacrifices to GOD. King Solomon worshiped by sacrificing 22,000 cattle and 120,000 sheep at the dedication of The Temple. The priests were all on duty; the choir and orchestra of Levites that David had provided for singing and playing anthems to the praise and love of GOD were all there; across the courtyard the priests blew trumpets. All Israelites were on their feet.

7-10 Solomon set apart the central area of the courtyard in front of GOD's Temple for sacred use and there sacrificed the Whole-Burnt-Offerings, Grain-Offerings, and fat from the Peace-Offerings—the Bronze Altar was too small to handle all these offerings. This is how Solomon kept the great autumn Feast of Booths. For seven days there were people there all the way from the far northeast (the Entrance to Hamath) to the far southwest (the Brook of Egypt)—a huge congregation. They started out celebrating for seven days, and then did it for another seven days, a week for dedicating the Altar and another for the Feast itself—two solid weeks of celebration! On the twenty-third day of the seventh month Solomon dismissed his congregation. They left rejoicing, exuberant over all the good GOD had done for David and Solomon and his people Israel.

GOD'S CONFIRMATION

11 Solomon completed building The Temple of GOD and the royal palace—the projects he had set his heart on doing. Everything was done—success! Satisfaction!

12-18 GOD appeared to Solomon that very night and said, "I accept your prayer; yes, I have chosen this place as a temple for sacrifice, a house of worship. If I ever shut off the supply of rain from the skies or order the locusts to eat the crops or send a plague on my people, and my people, my God-defined people, respond by humbling themselves, praying, seeking my presence, and turning their backs on their wicked lives, I'll be there ready for you: I'll listen from heaven, forgive their sins, and restore their land to health. From now on I'm alert day and night to the prayers offered at this place. Believe me, I've chosen and sanctified this Temple that you have built: My Name is stamped on it forever; my eyes are on it and my heart in it always. As for you, if you live in my presence as your father David lived, pure in heart and action, living the life I've set out for you, attentively obedient to my guidance and judgments, then I'll back your kingly rule over Israel—make it a sure thing on a sure foundation. The same covenant guarantee I gave to David your father I'm giving to you, namely, 'You can count on always having a descendant on Israel's throne.'

19-22   "But if you or your sons betray me, ignoring my guidance and judgments, taking up with alien gods by serving and worshiping them, then the guarantee is off: I'll wipe Israel right off the map and repudiate this Temple I've just sanctified to honor my Name. And Israel will be nothing but a bad joke among the peoples of the world. And this Temple, splendid as it now is, will become an object of contempt; tourists will shake their heads, saying, 'What happened here? What's the story behind these ruins?' Then they'll be told, 'The people who used to live here betrayed their GOD, the very God who rescued their ancestors from Egypt; they took up with alien gods, worshiping and serving them. That's what's behind this God-visited devastation.'"

MORE ON SOLOMON

1-6   At the end of twenty years, Solomon had quite a list of accomplishments. He had:

built The Temple of GOD and his own palace;
rebuilt the cities that Hiram had given him and colonized them with Israelites;
marched on Hamath Zobah and took it;
fortified Tadmor in the desert and all the store-cities he had founded in Hamath;
built the fortress cities Upper Beth Horon and Lower Beth Horon, complete with walls, gates, and bars;
built Baalath and store-cities;
built chariot-cities for his horses.

Solomon built impulsively and extravagantly—whenever a whim took him. And in Jerusalem, in Lebanon—wherever he fancied.

7-10   The remnants from the original inhabitants of the land (Hittites, Amorites, Perizzites, Hivites, Jebusites—all non-Israelites), survivors of the holy wars, were rounded up by Solomon for his gangs of slave labor. The policy is in effect today. But true Israelites were not treated this way; they were used in his army and administration—government leaders and commanders of his chariots and charioteers. They were also the project managers responsible for Solomon's building operations—250 in all in charge of the workforce.

11   Solomon brought Pharaoh's daughter from the City of David to a house built especially for her, "Because," he said, "my wife cannot live in the house of David king of Israel, for the areas in which the Chest of GOD has entered are sacred."

12-13   Then Solomon offered Whole-Burnt-Offerings to GOD on the Altar of GOD that he had built in front of The Temple porch. He kept to the regular schedule of worship set down by Moses: Sabbaths, New Moons, and the three annual feasts of Unraised Bread (Passover), Weeks (Pentecost), and Booths.

14-15   He followed the practice of his father David in setting up groups of priests carrying out the work of worship, with the Levites assigned to lead the sacred music for praising God and to assist the priests in the daily worship; he assigned security guards to be on duty at each gate — that's what David the man of God had ordered. The king's directions to the priests and Levites and financial stewards were kept right down to the fine print — no innovations — including the treasuries.

16 All that Solomon set out to do, from the groundbreaking of The Temple of GOD to its finish, was now complete.

17-18 Then Solomon went to Ezion Geber and Elath on the coast of Edom. Hiram sent him ships and with them veteran sailors. Joined by Solomon's men they sailed to Ophir (in east Africa), loaded on fifteen tons of gold, and brought it back to King Solomon.

1-4 The queen of Sheba heard of Solomon's reputation and came to Jerusalem to put his reputation to the test, asking all the tough questions. She made a showy entrance — an impressive retinue of attendants and camels loaded with perfume and much gold and precious stones. She emptied her heart to Solomon, talking over everything she cared about. And Solomon answered everything she put to him — nothing stumped him. When the queen of Sheba experienced for herself Solomon's wisdom and saw with her own eyes the palace he had built, the meals that were served, the impressive array of court officials, the sharply dressed waiters, the cupbearers, and then the elaborate worship extravagant with Whole-Burnt-Offerings at The Temple of GOD, it all took her breath away.

5-8 She said to the king, "It's all true! Your reputation for accomplishment and wisdom that reached all the way to my country is confirmed. I wouldn't have believed it if I hadn't seen it for myself; they didn't exaggerate! Such wisdom and elegance — far more than I could ever have imagined. Lucky the men and women who work for you, getting to be around you every day and hear your wise words firsthand! And blessed be your GOD who has taken such a liking to you, making you king. Clearly, GOD's love for Israel is behind this, making you king to keep a just order and nurture a God-pleasing people."

9-11 She then gave the king four and a half tons of gold and sack after sack of spices and precious stones. There hasn't been a cargo of spices like the shipload the queen of Sheba brought to King Solomon. The ships of Hiram also imported gold from Ophir along with fragrant sandalwood and expensive gems. The king used the sandalwood for fine cabinetry in The Temple of GOD and the royal palace, and for making harps and dulcimers for the musicians. Nothing like that shipment of sandalwood has been seen since.

12 King Solomon, for his part, gave the queen of Sheba all her heart's desire — everything she asked for. She took away more than she brought. Satisfied, she returned home with her train of servants.

13-14 Solomon received twenty-five tons of gold annually. This was above and beyond the taxes and profit on trade with merchants and traders. All kings of Arabia and various and assorted governors also brought silver and gold to Solomon.

15-16 King Solomon crafted two hundred body-length shields of hammered gold — about fifteen pounds of gold to each shield — and about three hundred small shields about half that size. He stored the shields in the House of the Forest of Lebanon.

17-19   The king made a massive throne of ivory with a veneer of gold. The throne had six steps leading up to it with an attached footstool of gold. The armrests on each side were flanked by lions. Lions, twelve of them, were placed at either end of the six steps. There was no throne like it in any other kingdom.

20   King Solomon's chalices and tankards were made of gold, and all the dinnerware and serving utensils in the House of the Forest of Lebanon were pure gold. Nothing was made of silver; silver was considered common and cheap in the time of Solomon.

21   The king's ships, manned by Hiram's sailors, made a round trip to Tarshish every three years, returning with a cargo of gold, silver, and ivory, apes and peacocks.

22-24   King Solomon was richer and wiser than all the kings of the earth — he surpassed them all. Kings came from all over the world to be with Solomon and get in on the wisdom God had given him. Everyone who came brought gifts — artifacts of gold and silver, fashionable robes and gowns, the latest in weapons, exotic spices, horses, and mules — parades of visitors, year after year.

25-28   Solomon collected horses and chariots. He had four thousand stalls for horses and chariots, and twelve thousand horsemen in barracks in the chariot-cities and in Jerusalem. He ruled over all the kings from the River Euphrates in the east, throughout the Philistine country, and as far west as the border of Egypt. The king made silver as common as rocks and cedar as common as the fig trees in the lowland hills. He carried on a brisk horse-trading business with Egypt and other places.

29-31   The rest of Solomon's life and rule, from start to finish, one can read in the records of Nathan the prophet, the prophecy of Ahijah of Shiloh, and in the visions of Iddo the seer concerning Jeroboam son of Nebat. Solomon ruled in Jerusalem over all Israel for forty years. Solomon died and was buried in the City of David his father. His son Rehoboam was the next king.

KING REHOBOAM

1-2   **10** Rehoboam traveled to Shechem where all Israel had gathered to inaugurate him as king. Jeroboam was then in Egypt, where he had taken asylum from King Solomon; when he got the report of Solomon's death, he came back.

3-4   Summoned by Israel, Jeroboam and all Israel went to Rehoboam and said, "Your father made life hard for us — worked our fingers to the bone. Give us a break; lighten up on us and we'll willingly serve you."

5   "Give me," said Rehoboam, "three days to think it over; then come back." So the people left.

6   King Rehoboam talked it over with the elders who had advised his father when he was alive: "What's your counsel? How do you suggest that I answer the people?"

7   They said, "If you will be a servant to this people, be considerate of their needs and respond with compassion, work things out with them, they'll end up doing anything for you."

8-9   But he rejected the counsel of the elders and asked the young men he'd grown up with who were now currying his favor, "What do you think? What should I say to these people who are saying, 'Give us a break from your father's harsh ways—lighten up on us'?"

10-11 The young turks he'd grown up with said, "These people who complain, 'Your father was too hard on us; lighten up'—well, tell them this: 'My little finger is thicker than my father's waist. If you think life under my father was hard, you haven't seen the half of it. My father thrashed you with whips; I'll beat you bloody with chains!'"

12-14 Three days later Jeroboam and the people showed up, just as Rehoboam had directed when he said, "Give me three days to think it over; then come back." The king's answer was harsh and rude. He spurned the counsel of the elders and went with the advice of the younger set: "If you think life under my father was hard, you haven't seen the half of it: my father thrashed you with whips; I'll beat you bloody with chains!"

15 Rehoboam turned a deaf ear to the people. God was behind all this, confirming the message that he had given to Jeroboam son of Nebat through Ahijah of Shiloh.

16-17 When all Israel realized that the king hadn't listened to a word they'd said, they stood up to him and said,

Get lost, David!
We've had it with you, son of Jesse!
Let's get out of here, Israel, and fast!
From now on, David, mind your own business.

And with that they left. Rehoboam continued to rule only those who lived in the towns of Judah.

18-19 When King Rehoboam next sent out Adoniram, head of the workforce, the Israelites ganged up on him, pelted him with stones, and killed him. King Rehoboam jumped in his chariot and escaped to Jerusalem as fast as he could. Israel has been in rebellion against the Davidic dynasty ever since.

1 **11** When Rehoboam got back to Jerusalem he called up the men of the tribes of Judah and Benjamin, 180,000 of their best soldiers, to go to war against Israel and recover the kingdom.

2-4 At the same time the word of GOD came to Shemaiah, a holy man, "Tell this to Rehoboam son of Solomon, king of Judah, along with all the Israelites in Judah and Benjamin. This is GOD's word: Don't march out; don't fight against your brothers the Israelites. Go back home, every last one of you; *I'm* in charge here." And they did it; they did what GOD said and went home.

5-12 Rehoboam continued to live in Jerusalem but built up a defense system for Judah all around: in Bethlehem, Etam, Tekoa, Beth Zur, Soco, Adullam, Gath, Mareshah, Ziph, Adoraim, Lachish, Azekah, Zorah, Aijalon, and Hebron—a line of defense protecting Judah and Benjamin. He beefed up the fortifications, appointed commanders, and put in supplies of food, olive oil, and wine. He installed arms—large shields and spears—in all the forts, making them very strong. So Judah and Benjamin were secure for the time.

13-17 The priests and Levites from all over Israel came and made themselves available to Rehoboam. The Levites left their pastures and properties and moved to Judah and Jerusalem because Jeroboam and his sons had dismissed them from the priesthood of GOD and replaced them with his own priests to preside over the worship centers at which he had installed goat and calf demon-idols. Everyone from all the tribes of Israel who determined to seek the GOD of Israel migrated with the priests and Levites to Jerusalem to worship there, sacrificing to the GOD of their ancestors. That gave a tremendous boost to the kingdom of Judah. They stuck with Rehoboam son of Solomon for three years, loyal to the ways of David and Solomon for this period.

18-21   Rehoboam married Mahalath daughter of Jerimoth, David's son, and Abihail daughter of Eliab, Jesse's son. Mahalath bore him Jeush, Shemariah, and Zaham. Then he married Maacah, Absalom's daughter, and she bore him Abijah, Attai, Ziza, and Shelomith. Maacah was Rehoboam's favorite wife; he loved her more than all his other wives and concubines put together (and he had a lot — eighteen wives and sixty concubines who produced twenty-eight sons and sixty daughters!).

22-23   Rehoboam designated Abijah son of Maacah as the "first son" and leader of the brothers — he intended to make him the next king. He was shrewd in deploying his sons in all the fortress cities that made up his defense system in Judah and Benjamin; he kept them happy with much food and many wives.

1   12 By the time Rehoboam had secured his kingdom and was strong again, he, and all Israel with him, had virtually abandoned GOD and his ways.

2-4   In Rehoboam's fifth year, because he and the people were unfaithful to GOD, Shishak king of Egypt invaded as far as Jerusalem. He came with twelve hundred chariots and sixty thousand cavalry, and soldiers from all over — the Egyptian army included Libyans, Sukkites, and Ethiopians. They took the fortress cities of Judah and advanced as far as Jerusalem itself.

5   Then the prophet Shemaiah, accompanied by the leaders of Judah who had retreated to Jerusalem before Shishak, came to Rehoboam and said, "GOD's word: You abandoned me; now I abandon you to Shishak."

6   The leaders of Israel and the king were repentant and said, "GOD is right."

7-8   When GOD saw that they were humbly repentant, the word of GOD came to Shemaiah: "Because they are humble, I'll not destroy them — I'll give them a break; I won't use Shishak to express my wrath against Jerusalem. What I will do, though, is make them Shishak's subjects — they'll learn the difference between serving me and serving human kings."

9   Then Shishak king of Egypt attacked Jerusalem. He plundered the treasury of The Temple of GOD and the treasury of the royal palace — he took everything he could lay his hands on. He even took the gold shields that Solomon had made.

10-11   King Rehoboam replaced the gold shields with bronze shields and gave them to the guards who were posted at the entrance to the royal palace. Whenever the king went to GOD's Temple, the guards went with him carrying the shields, but they always returned them to the guardroom.

12   Because Rehoboam was repentant, GOD's anger was blunted, so he wasn't totally destroyed. The picture wasn't entirely bleak — there were

some good things going on in Judah.

13-14   King Rehoboam regrouped and reestablished his rule in Jerusalem. He was forty-one years old when he became king and continued as king for seventeen years in Jerusalem, the city GOD chose out of all the tribes of Israel as the special presence of his Name. His mother was Naamah from Ammon. But the final verdict on Rehoboam was that he was a bad king — GOD was not important to him; his heart neither cared for nor sought after GOD.

15-16   The history of Rehoboam, from start to finish, is written in the memoirs of Shemaiah the prophet and Iddo the seer that contain the family trees. There was war between Rehoboam and Jeroboam the whole time. Rehoboam died and was buried with his ancestors in the City of David. His son Abijah ruled after him.

KING ABIJAH

1-2   **13** In the eighteenth year of the rule of King Jeroboam, Abijah took over the throne of Judah. He ruled in Jerusalem three years. His mother was Maacah daughter of Uriel of Gibeah.

2-3   War broke out between Abijah and Jeroboam. Abijah started out with 400,000 of his best soldiers; Jeroboam countered with 800,000 of his best.

4-7   Abijah took a prominent position on Mount Zemaraim in the hill country of Ephraim and gave this speech: "Listen, Jeroboam and all Israel! Don't you realize that GOD, the one and only God of Israel, established David and his sons as the permanent rulers of Israel, ratified by a 'covenant of salt' — GOD's kingdom ruled by GOD's king? And what happened? Jeroboam, the son of Solomon's slave Nebat, rebelled against his master. All the riffraff joined his cause and were too much for Rehoboam, Solomon's true heir. Rehoboam didn't know his way around — besides he was a real wimp; he couldn't stand up against them.

8-9   "Taking advantage of that weakness, you are asserting yourself against the very rule of GOD that is delegated to David's descendants — you think you are so big with your huge army backed up by the golden-calf idols that Jeroboam made for you as gods! But just look at what you've done — you threw out the priests of GOD, the sons of Aaron, and the Levites, and made priests to suit yourselves, priests just like the pagans have. Anyone who shows up with enough money to pay for it can be a priest! A priest of No-God!

10-11   "But for the rest of us in Judah, we're sticking with GOD. We have not traded him in for the latest model — we're keeping the tried-and-true priests of Aaron to lead us to GOD and the Levites to lead us in worship by sacrificing Whole-Burnt-Offerings and aromatic incense to GOD at the daily morning and evening prayers, setting out fresh holy bread on a clean table, and lighting the lamps on the golden Lampstand every night. We continue doing what GOD told us to in the way he told us to do it; but you have rid yourselves of him.

12   "Can't you see the obvious? God is on our side; he's our leader. And his priests with trumpets are all ready to blow the signal to battle. O Israel — don't fight against GOD, the God of your ancestors. You will not win this battle."

13-18   While Abijah was speaking, Jeroboam had sent men around to take them by surprise from the rear: Jeroboam in front of Judah and the ambush behind. When Judah looked back, they saw they were attacked front and back. They prayed desperately to GOD, the priests blew their trumpets, and the soldiers of Judah shouted their battle cry. At the battle cry, God routed Jeroboam and all Israel before Abijah and Judah. The army of Israel scattered before Judah; God gave them the victory. Abijah and his troops slaughtered them—500,000 of Israel's best fighters were killed that day. The army of Israel fell flat on its face—a humiliating defeat. The army of Judah won hands down because they trusted GOD, the God of their ancestors.

19-21   Abijah followed up his victory by pursuing Jeroboam, taking the towns of Bethel, Jeshanah, and Ephron with their surrounding villages. Jeroboam never did recover from his defeat while Abijah lived. Later on GOD struck him down and he died. Meanwhile Abijah flourished; he married fourteen wives and ended up with a family of twenty-two sons and sixteen daughters.

22   The rest of the history of Abijah, what he did and said, is written in the study written by Iddo the prophet.

KING ASA

1   **14** Abijah died and was buried with his ancestors in the City of David. His son Asa became the next king.

    For ten years into Asa's reign the country was at peace.

2-6   Asa was a good king. He did things right in GOD's eyes. He cleaned house: got rid of the pagan altars and shrines, smashed the sacred stone pillars, and chopped down the sex-and-religion groves (Asherim). He told Judah to center their lives in GOD, the God of their fathers, to do what the law said, and to follow the commandments. Because he got rid of all the pagan shrines and altars in the cities of Judah, his kingdom was at peace. Because the land was quiet and there was no war, he was able to build up a good defense system in Judah. GOD kept the peace.

7   Asa said to his people, "While we have the chance and the land is quiet, let's build a solid defense system, fortifying our cities with walls, towers, gates, and bars. We have this peaceful land because we sought GOD; he has given us rest from all troubles." So they built and enjoyed prosperity.

8   Asa had an army of 300,000 Judeans, equipped with shields and spears, and another 280,000 Benjaminites who were shield bearers and archers. They were all courageous warriors.

9-11   Zerah the Ethiopian went to war against Asa with an army of a million plus three hundred chariots and got as far as Mareshah. Asa met him there and prepared to fight from the Valley of Zephathah near Mareshah. Then Asa prayed to GOD, "O GOD, you aren't impressed by numbers or intimidated by a show of force once you decide to help: Help us, O GOD; we have come out to meet this huge army because we trust in you and who you are. Don't let mere mortals stand against you!"

12-15   GOD defeated the Ethiopians before Asa and Judah; the Ethiopians ran for their lives. Asa and his men chased them as far as Gerar; so many of the Ethiopians were killed that there was no fight left in them—a massacre before GOD and his troops; Judah carted off loads of plunder. They devastated all the towns around Gerar whose people were helpless, paralyzed by the fear of GOD, and looted the country. They also attacked herdsmen and brought back a lot of sheep and camels to Jerusalem.

1-6 **15** Then Azariah son of Obed, moved by the Spirit of God, went out to meet Asa. He said, "Listen carefully, Asa, and listen Judah and Benjamin: GOD will stick with you as long as you stick with him. If you look for him he will let himself be found; but if you leave him he'll leave you. For a long time Israel didn't have the real God, nor did they have the help of priest or teacher or book. But when they were in trouble and got serious, and decided to seek GOD, the God of Israel, GOD let himself be found. At that time it was a dog-eat-dog world; life was constantly up for grabs—no one, regardless of country, knew what the next day might bring. Nation battered nation, city pummeled city. God let loose every kind of trouble among them.

7 "But it's different with you: Be strong. Take heart. Payday is coming!"

8-9 Asa heard the prophecy of Azariah son of Obed, took a deep breath, then rolled up his sleeves, and went to work: He cleaned out the obscene and polluting sacred shrines from the whole country of Judah and Benjamin and from the towns he had taken in the hill country of Ephraim. He spruced up the Altar of GOD that was in front of The Temple porch. Then he called an assembly for all Judah and Benjamin, including those from Ephraim, Manasseh, and Simeon who were living there at the time (for many from Israel had left their homes and joined forces with Asa when they saw that GOD was on his side).

10-15 They all arrived in Jerusalem in the third month of the fifteenth year of Asa's reign for a great assembly of worship. From their earlier plunder they offered sacrifices of seven hundred oxen and seven thousand sheep for the worship. Then they bound themselves in a covenant to seek GOD, the God of their fathers, wholeheartedly, holding nothing back. And they agreed that anyone who refused to seek GOD, the God of Israel, should be killed, no matter who it was, young or old, man or woman. They shouted out their promise to GOD, a joyful sound accompanied with blasts from trumpets and rams' horns. The whole country felt good about the covenant promise— they had given their promise joyfully from the heart. Anticipating the best, they had sought God—and he showed up, ready to be found. GOD gave them peace within and without—a most peaceable kingdom!

16-19 In his cleanup of the country, Asa went so far as to remove his mother, Queen Maacah, from her throne because she had built a shockingly obscene image of the sex goddess Asherah. Asa tore it down, smashed it, and burned it up in the Kidron Valley. Unfortunately he didn't get rid of the local sex-and-religion shrines. But he was well-intentioned—his heart was in the right place, loyal to GOD. All the gold and silver vessels and artifacts that he and his father had consecrated for holy use he installed in The Temple of God. There wasn't a trace of war up to the thirty-fifth year of Asa's reign.

1 **16** But in the thirty-sixth year of Asa's reign, Baasha king of Israel attacked. He started it by building a fort at Ramah and closing the border between Israel and Judah to keep Asa king of Judah from leaving or entering.

2-3 Asa took silver and gold from the treasuries of The Temple of GOD and the royal palace and sent it to Ben-Hadad, king of Aram who lived in Damascus, with this message: "Let's make a treaty like the one between our fathers. I'm showing my good faith with this gift of silver and gold. Break your deal with Baasha king of Israel so he'll quit fighting against me."

4-5 Ben-Hadad went along with King Asa and sent his troops against the towns of Israel. They sacked Ijon, Dan, Abel Maim, and all the store-cities of Naphtali. When Baasha got the report, he quit fortifying Ramah.

6 Then King Asa issued orders to his people in Judah to haul away the logs and stones Baasha had used in the fortification of Ramah and used them himself to fortify Geba and Mizpah.

7-9 Just after that, Hanani the seer came to Asa king of Judah and said, "Because you went for help to the king of Aram and didn't ask GOD for help, you've lost a victory over the army of the king of Aram. Didn't the Ethiopians and Libyans come against you with superior forces, completely outclassing you with their chariots and cavalry? But you asked GOD for help and he gave you the victory. GOD is always on the alert, constantly on the lookout for people who are totally committed to him. You were foolish to go for human help when you could have had God's help. Now you're in trouble—one round of war after another."

10 At that, Asa lost his temper. Angry, he put Hanani in the stocks. At the same time Asa started abusing some of the people.

11-14 A full account of Asa is written in *The Chronicles of the Kings of Judah*. In the thirty-ninth year of his reign Asa came down with a severe case of foot infection. He didn't ask GOD for help, but went instead to the doctors. Then Asa died; he died in the forty-first year of his reign. They buried him in a mausoleum that he had built for himself in the City of David. They laid him in a crypt full of aromatic oils and spices. Then they had a huge bonfire in his memory.

JEHOSHAPHAT OF JUDAH

1-6 17 Asa's son Jehoshaphat was the next king; he started out by working on his defense system against Israel. He put troops in all the fortress cities of Judah and deployed garrisons throughout Judah and in the towns of Ephraim that his father Asa had captured. GOD was on Jehoshaphat's side because he stuck to the ways of his father Asa's early years. He didn't fool around with the popular Baal religion—he was a seeker and follower of the God of his father and was obedient to him; he wasn't like Israel. And GOD secured the kingdom under his rule, gave him a firm grip on it. And everyone in Judah showed their appreciation by bringing gifts. Jehoshaphat ended up very rich and much honored. He was single-minded in following GOD; and he got rid of the local sex-and-religion shrines.

7-9 In the third year of his reign he sent his officials—excellent men, every one of them—Ben-Hail, Obadiah, Zechariah, Nethanel, and Micaiah on a teaching mission to the cities of Judah. They were accompanied by Levites—Shemaiah, Nethaniah, Zebadiah, Asahel, Shemiramoth, Jehonathan, Adonijah, Tobijah, and Tob-Adonijah; the priests Elishama and Jehoram were also in the company. They made a circuit of the towns of Judah, teaching the people and using the Book of The Revelation of GOD as their text.

10-12 There was a strong sense of the fear of GOD in all the kingdoms around Judah—they didn't dare go to war against Jehoshaphat. Some Philistines even brought gifts and a load of silver to Jehoshaphat, and the desert bedouin brought flocks—7,700 rams and 7,700 goats. So Jehoshaphat became stronger by the day, and constructed more and more forts and store-cities—an age of prosperity for Judah!

13-19 He also had excellent fighting men stationed in Jerusalem. The captains of the military units of Judah, classified according to families, were: Captain Adnah with 300,000 soldiers; his associate Captain Jehohanan with 280,000; his associate Amasiah son of Zicri, a volunteer for GOD, with 200,000. Officer Eliada represented Benjamin with 200,000 fully equipped with bow and shield; and his associate was Jehozabad with 180,000 armed and ready for battle. These were under the direct command of the king; in addition there were the troops assigned to the fortress cities spread all over Judah.

18 But even though Jehoshaphat was very rich and much honored, he made a marriage alliance with Ahab of Israel. Some time later he paid a visit to Ahab at Samaria. Ahab celebrated his visit with a feast — a huge barbecue with all the lamb and beef you could eat. But Ahab had a hidden agenda; he wanted Jehoshaphat's support in attacking Ramoth Gilead. Then Ahab brought it into the open: "Will you join me in attacking Ramoth Gilead?" Jehoshaphat said, "You bet. I'm with you all the way; you can count on me and my troops."

4 Then Jehoshaphat said, "But before you do anything, ask GOD for guidance."

5 The king of Israel got the prophets together — all four hundred of them — and put the question to them: "Should I attack Ramoth Gilead or should I hold back?"

"Go for it," they said. "God will hand it over to the king."

6 But Jehoshaphat dragged his feet, "Is there another prophet of GOD around here we can consult? Let's get a second opinion."

7 The king of Israel told Jehoshaphat, "As a matter of fact, there is another. But I hate him. He never preaches anything good to me, only doom, doom, doom — Micaiah son of Imlah."

"The king shouldn't talk about a prophet like that!" said Jehoshaphat.

8 So the king of Israel ordered one of his men, "Quickly, get Micaiah son of Imlah."

9-11 Meanwhile, the king of Israel and Jehoshaphat were seated on their thrones, dressed in their royal robes, resplendent in front of the Samaria city gates. All the prophets were staging a prophecy-performance for their benefit. Zedekiah son of Kenaanah had even made a set of iron horns, and brandishing them, called out, "GOD's word! With these horns you'll gore Aram until there's nothing left of them!" All the prophets chimed in, "Yes! Go for Ramoth Gilead! An easy victory! GOD's gift to the king!"

12 The messenger who went to get Micaiah told him, "The prophets have all said Yes to the king. Make it unanimous — vote Yes!"

13 But Micaiah said, "As sure as GOD lives, what God says, I'll say."

14 With Micaiah before him, the king asked him, "So, Micaiah — do we attack Ramoth Gilead? Or do we hold back?"

"Go ahead," he said, "an easy victory! God's gift to the king."

15 "Not so fast," said the king. "How many times have I made you promise under oath to tell me the truth and nothing but the truth?"

16 "All right," said Micaiah, "since you insist . . .

I saw all of Israel scattered over the hills,
    sheep with no shepherd.
Then GOD spoke, 'These poor people
    have no one to tell them what to do.

> Let them go home and do
>   the best they can for themselves.'"

17 The king of Israel turned to Jehoshaphat, "See! What did I tell you? He never has a good word for me from GOD, only doom."

18-21 Micaiah kept on, "I'm not done yet; listen to GOD's word:

> I saw GOD enthroned,
>   and all the Angel Armies of heaven
> standing at attention,
>   ranged on his right and his left.
> And GOD said, "How can we seduce Ahab
>   into attacking Ramoth Gilead?"
> Some said this,
>   and some said that.
> Then a bold angel stepped out,
>   stood before GOD, and said,
> "I'll seduce him."
>   "And how will you do it?" said GOD.
> "Easy," said the angel,
>   "I'll get all the prophets to lie."
> "That should do it," said GOD;
>   "On your way — seduce him!"

22 "And that's what has happened. GOD filled the mouths of your puppet prophets with seductive lies. GOD has pronounced your doom."

23 Just then Zedekiah son of Kenaanah came up and slapped Micaiah in the face, saying, "Since when did the Spirit of GOD leave me and take up with you?"

24 Micaiah said, "You'll know soon enough; you'll know it when you're frantically and futilely looking for a place to hide."

25-26 The king of Israel had heard enough: "Get Micaiah out of here! Turn him over to Amon the city magistrate and to Joash the king's son with this message: 'King's orders! Lock him up in jail; keep him on bread and water until I'm back in one piece.'"

27 Micaiah said,

> If you ever get back in one piece,
>   I'm no prophet of GOD.

He added,

> When it happens, O people,
>   remember where you heard it!

28-29 So the king of Israel and Jehoshaphat king of Judah went ahead and attacked Ramoth Gilead. The king of Israel said to Jehoshaphat, "Wear my kingly robe; I'm going into battle disguised." So the king of Israel entered the battle in disguise.

30 Meanwhile, the king of Aram had ordered his chariot commanders (there were thirty-two of them), "Don't bother with anyone whether small

or great; go after the king of Israel and him only."

31-32   When the chariot commanders saw Jehoshaphat, they said, "There he is! The king of Israel!" and took after him. Jehoshaphat yelled out, and the chariot commanders realized they had the wrong man — it wasn't the king of Israel after all. God intervened and they let him go.

33   Just then someone, without aiming, shot an arrow into the crowd and hit the king of Israel in the chink of his armor. The king told his charioteer, "Turn back! Get me out of here — I'm wounded."

34   All day the fighting continued, hot and heavy. Propped up in his chariot, the king watched from the sidelines. He died that evening.

1-3   **19** But Jehoshaphat king of Judah got home safe and sound. Jehu, son of Hanani the seer, confronted King Jehoshaphat: "You have no business helping evil, cozying up to GOD-haters. Because you did this, GOD is good and angry with you. But you're not all bad — you made a clean sweep of the polluting sex-and-religion shrines; and you were single-minded in seeking God."

4   Jehoshaphat kept his residence in Jerusalem but made a regular round of visits among the people, from Beersheba in the south to Mount Ephraim in the north, urging them to return to GOD, the God of their ancestors.

5-7   And he was diligent in appointing judges in the land — each of the fortress cities had its judge. He charged the judges: "This is serious work; do it carefully. You are not merely judging between men and women; these are GOD's judgments that you are passing on. Live in the fear of GOD — be most careful, for GOD hates dishonesty, partiality, and bribery."

8-10   In Jerusalem Jehoshaphat also appointed Levites, priests, and family heads to decide on matters that had to do with worship and mediating local differences. He charged them: "Do your work in the fear of GOD; be dependable and honest in your duties. When a case comes before you involving any of your fellow citizens, whether it seems large (like murder) or small (like matters of interpretation of the law), you are responsible for warning them that they are dealing with GOD. Make that explicit, otherwise both you and they are going to be dealing with GOD's wrath. Do your work well or you'll end up being as guilty as they are.

11   "Amariah the chief priest is in charge of all cases regarding the worship of GOD; Zebadiah son of Ishmael, the leader of the tribe of Judah, is in charge of all civil cases; the Levites will keep order in the courts. Be bold and diligent. And GOD be with you as you do your best."

1-2   **20** Some time later the Moabites and Ammonites, accompanied by Meunites, joined forces to make war on Jehoshaphat. Jehoshaphat received this intelligence report: "A huge force is on its way from beyond the Dead Sea to fight you. There's no time to waste — they're already at Hazazon Tamar, the oasis of En Gedi."

3-4   Shaken, Jehoshaphat prayed. He went to GOD for help and ordered a nationwide fast. The country of Judah united in seeking GOD's help — they came from all the cities of Judah to pray to GOD.

5-9   Then Jehoshaphat took a position before the assembled people of Judah and Jerusalem at The Temple of GOD in front of the new courtyard and said, "O GOD, God of our ancestors, are you not God in heaven above and ruler of all kingdoms below? You hold all power and might in your fist—no one stands a chance against you! And didn't you make the natives of this land leave as you brought your people Israel in, turning it over permanently to your people Israel, the descendants of Abraham your friend? They have lived here and built a holy house of worship to honor you, saying, 'When the worst happens—whether war or flood or disease or famine—and we take our place before this Temple (we know you are personally present in this place!) and pray out our pain and trouble, we know that you will listen and give victory.'

10-12 "And now it's happened: men from Ammon, Moab, and Mount Seir have shown up. You didn't let Israel touch them when we got here at first—we detoured around them and didn't lay a hand on them. And now they've come to kick us out of the country you gave us. O dear God, won't you take care of them? We're helpless before this vandal horde ready to attack us. We don't know what to do; we're looking to you."

13 Everyone in Judah was there—little children, wives, sons—all present and attentive to GOD.

14-17 Then Jahaziel was moved by the Spirit of GOD to speak from the midst of the congregation. (Jahaziel was the son of Zechariah, the son of Benaiah, the son of Jeiel, the son of Mattaniah the Levite of the Asaph clan.) He said, "Attention everyone—all of you from out of town, all you from Jerusalem, and you King Jehoshaphat—GOD's word: Don't be afraid; don't pay any mind to this vandal horde. This is God's war, not yours. Tomorrow you'll go after them; see, they're already on their way up the slopes of Ziz; you'll meet them at the end of the ravine near the wilderness of Jeruel. You won't have to lift a hand in this battle; just stand firm, Judah and Jerusalem, and watch GOD's saving work for you take shape. Don't be afraid, don't waver. March out boldly tomorrow—GOD is with you."

18-19 Then Jehoshaphat knelt down, bowing with his face to the ground. All Judah and Jerusalem did the same, worshiping GOD. The Levites (both Kohathites and Korahites) stood to their feet to praise GOD, the God of Israel; they praised at the top of their lungs!

20 They were up early in the morning, ready to march into the wilderness of Tekoa. As they were leaving, Jehoshaphat stood up and said, "Listen Judah and Jerusalem! Listen to what I have to say! Believe firmly in GOD, your God, and your lives will be firm! Believe in your prophets and you'll come out on top!"

21 After talking it over with the people, Jehoshaphat appointed a choir for GOD; dressed in holy robes, they were to march ahead of the troops, singing,

Give thanks to GOD,
His love never quits.

22-23 As soon as they started shouting and praising, GOD set ambushes against the men of Ammon, Moab, and Mount Seir as they were attacking Judah, and they all ended up dead. The Ammonites and Moabites mistakenly attacked those from Mount Seir and massacred them. Then, further confused, they went at each other, and all ended up killed.

24 As Judah came up over the rise, looking into the wilderness for the horde of barbarians, they looked on a killing field of dead bodies—not a

living soul among them.

25-26   When Jehoshaphat and his people came to carry off the plunder they found more loot than they could carry off — equipment, clothing, valuables. It took three days to cart it away! On the fourth day they came together at the Valley of Blessing (Beracah) and blessed GOD (that's how it got the name, Valley of Blessing).

27-28   Jehoshaphat then led all the men of Judah and Jerusalem back to Jerusalem — an exuberant parade. GOD had given them joyful relief from their enemies! They entered Jerusalem and came to The Temple of GOD with all the instruments of the band playing.

29-30   When the surrounding kingdoms got word that GOD had fought Israel's enemies, the fear of God descended on them. Jehoshaphat heard no more from them; as long as Jehoshaphat reigned, peace reigned.

31-33   That about sums up Jehoshaphat's reign over Judah. He was thirty-five years old when he became king and ruled as king in Jerusalem for twenty-five years. His mother was Azubah daughter of Shilhi. He continued the kind of life characteristic of his father Asa — no detours, no dead-ends — pleasing GOD with his life. But he failed to get rid of the neighborhood sex-and-religion shrines — people continued to pray and worship at these idolatrous god shops.

34   The rest of Jehoshaphat's life, from start to finish, is written in the memoirs of Jehu son of Hanani, which are included in the *Royal Annals of Israel's Kings*.

35-37   Late in life Jehoshaphat formed a trading syndicate with Ahaziah king of Israel — which was very wrong of him to do. He went in as partner with him to build ocean-going ships at Ezion Geber to trade with Tarshish. Eliezer son of Dodavahu of Mareshah preached against Jehoshaphat's venture: "Because you joined forces with Ahaziah, GOD has shipwrecked your work." The ships were smashed and nothing ever came of the trade partnership.

1   **21** Jehoshaphat died and was buried in the family cemetery in the City of David. Jehoram his son was the next king.

KING JEHORAM

2-4   Jehoram's brothers were Azariah, Jehiel, Zechariah, Azariahu, Michael, and Shephatiah — the sons of Jehoshaphat king of Judah. Their father had lavished them with gifts — silver, gold, and other valuables, plus the fortress cities in Judah. But Jehoram was his firstborn son and he gave him the kingdom of Judah. But when Jehoram had taken over his father's kingdom and had secured his position, he killed all his brothers along with some of the government officials.

5-7   Jehoram was thirty-two years old when he became king and ruled in Jerusalem for eight years. He imitated Israel's kings and married into the Ahab dynasty. GOD considered him an evil man. But despite that, because of his covenant with David, GOD was not yet ready to destroy the descendants of David; he had, after all, promised to keep a light burning for David and his sons.

8-9   During Jehoram's reign, Edom revolted from Judah's rule and set up their own king. Jehoram responded by setting out with his officers and chariots. Edom surrounded him, but in the middle of the night he and his charioteers broke through the lines and hit Edom hard.

10-11   Edom continues in revolt against Judah right up to the present. Even
little Libnah revolted at that time. The evidence accumulated: Since Jehoram
had abandoned GOD, the God of his ancestors, God was abandoning him. He
even went so far as to build pagan sacred shrines in the mountains of Judah.
He brazenly led Jerusalem away from God, seducing the whole country.

12-15   One day he got a letter from Elijah the prophet. It read, "From GOD, the
God of your ancestor David—a message: Because you have not kept to the
ways of Jehoshaphat your father and Asa your grandfather, kings of Judah,
but have taken up with the ways of the kings of Israel in the north, leading
Judah and Jerusalem away from God, going step by step down the apostate
path of Ahab and his crew—why, you even killed your own brothers, all
of them better men than you!—GOD is going to afflict your people, your
wives, your sons, and everything you have with a terrible plague. And you
are going to come down with a terrible disease of the colon, painful and
humiliating."

16-20   The trouble started with an invasion. GOD incited the Philistines and
the Arabs who lived near the Ethiopians to attack Jehoram. They came to
the borders of Judah, forced their way in, and plundered the place—robbing the royal palace of everything in it including his wives and sons. One
son, his youngest, Ahaziah, was left behind. The terrible and fatal disease
in his colon followed. After about two years he was totally incontinent
and died writhing in pain. His people didn't honor him by lighting a great
bonfire, as was customary with his ancestors. He was thirty-two years old
when he became king and reigned for eight years in Jerusalem. There were
no tears shed when he died—it was good riddance!—and they buried him
in the City of David, but not in the royal cemetery.

KING AHAZIAH

1-6   22 The people of Jerusalem made Ahaziah, Jehoram's youngest son,
king. Raiders from the desert, who had come with the Arabs
against the settlement, had killed all the older sons. That's how
Ahaziah son of Jehoram king of Judah became king. Ahaziah was twenty-
two years old when he became king, but reigned only one year in Jerusalem.
His mother was Athaliah, granddaughter of Omri. He lived and ruled just
like the Ahab family had done, his mother training him in evil ways. GOD
also considered him evil, related by both marriage and sin to the Ahab clan.
After the death of his father, he attended the sin school of Ahab, and gradu-
ated with a degree in doom. He did what they taught him, went with Joram
son of Ahab king of Israel in the war against Hazael king of Aram at Ramoth
Gilead. Joram, wounded by the Arameans, retreated to Jezreel to recover
from the wounds he received in Ramah in his war with Hazael king of Aram.
Ahaziah son of Jehoram king of Judah paid a visit to Joram son of Ahab on
his sickbed at Jezreel.

7-9   The fate of Ahaziah when he went to visit was God's judgment on him.
When Ahaziah arrived at Jezreel, he and Joram met with Jehu son of
Nimshi, whom GOD had already authorized to destroy the dynasty of
Ahab. Jehu, already at work, executing doom on the dynasty of Ahab,
came upon the captains of Judah and Ahaziah's nephews, part of the
Ahaziah delegation, and killed them outright. Then he sent out a search
party looking for Ahaziah himself. They found him hiding out in Samaria

and hauled him back to Jehu. And Jehu killed him.

They didn't, though, just leave his body there. Out of respect for his grandfather Jehoshaphat, famous as a sincere seeker after GOD, they gave him a decent burial. But there was no one left in Ahaziah's family capable of ruling the kingdom.

QUEEN ATHALIAH

10-12 When Ahaziah's mother Athaliah saw that her son was dead, she took over. She began by massacring the entire royal family. Jehosheba, daughter of King Jehoram, took Ahaziah's son Joash, and kidnapped him from among the king's sons slated for slaughter. She hid him and his nurse in a private room away from Athaliah. So Jehosheba, daughter of King Jehoram and Ahaziah's sister—she was also the wife of Jehoiada the priest—saved Joash from the murderous Queen Athaliah. He was there with her, hidden away for six years in The Temple of God. Athaliah, oblivious to his existence, ruled the country.

1-3 23 In the seventh year the priest Jehoiada decided to make his move and worked out a strategy with certain influential officers in the army. He picked Azariah son of Jeroham, Ishmael son of Jehohanan, Azariah son of Obed, Maaseiah son of Adaiah, and Elishaphat son of Zicri as his associates. They dispersed throughout Judah and called in the Levites from all the towns in Judah along with the heads of families. They met in Jerusalem. The gathering met in The Temple of God. They made a covenant there in The Temple.

3-7 The priest Jehoiada showed them the young prince and addressed them: "Here he is—the son of the king. He is going to rule just as GOD promised regarding the sons of David. Now this is what you must do: A third of you priests and Levites who come on duty on the Sabbath are to be posted as security guards at the gates; another third will guard the palace; and the other third will guard the foundation gate. All the people will gather in the courtyards of The Temple of GOD. No one may enter The Temple of GOD except the priests and designated Levites—they are permitted in because they've been consecrated, but all the people must do the work assigned them. The Levites are to form a ring around the young king, weapons at the ready. Kill anyone who tries to break through your ranks. Your job is to stay with the king at all times and places, coming and going."

8-10 All the Levites and officers obeyed the orders of Jehoiada the priest. Each took charge of his men, both those who came on duty on the Sabbath and those who went off duty on the Sabbath, for Jehoiada the priest hadn't exempted any of them from duty. Then the priest armed the officers with spears and the large and small shields originally belonging to King David that were stored in The Temple of God. Well-armed, the guards took up their assigned positions for protecting the king, from one end of The Temple to the other, surrounding both Altar and Temple.

11 Then the priest brought the prince into view, crowned him, handed him the scroll of God's covenant, and made him king. As Jehoiada and his sons anointed him they shouted, "Long live the king!"

12-13 Athaliah, hearing all the commotion, the people running around and praising the king, came to The Temple to see what was going on. Astonished, she saw the young king standing at the entrance flanked by the captains and heralds, with everybody beside themselves with joy, trumpets blaring, the choir and orchestra leading the praise. Athaliah ripped her robes in dismay and shouted, "Treason! Treason!"

14-15   Jehoiada the priest ordered the military officers, "Drag her outside — and kill anyone who tries to follow her!" (The priest had said, "Don't kill her inside The Temple of GOD.") So they dragged her out to the palace's horse corral and there they killed her.

16   Jehoiada now made a covenant between himself and the king and the people: they were to be GOD's special people.

17   The people poured into the temple of Baal and tore it down, smashing altar and images to smithereens. They killed Mattan the priest of Baal in front of the altar.

18-21   Jehoiada turned the care of GOD's Temple over to the priests and Levites, the way David had directed originally. They were to offer the Whole-Burnt-Offerings of GOD as set out in The Revelation of Moses, and with praise and song as directed by David. He also assigned security guards at the gates of GOD's Temple so that no one who was unprepared could enter. Then he got everyone together — officers, nobles, governors, and the people themselves — and escorted the king down from The Temple of GOD, through the Upper Gate, and placed him on the royal throne. Everybody celebrated the event. And the city was safe and undisturbed — Athaliah had been killed; no more Athaliah terror.

KING JOASH

1   **24** Joash was seven years old when he became king; he was king for forty years in Jerusalem. His mother's name was Gazelle (Zibiah). She was from Beersheba.

2-3   Taught and trained by Jehoiada the priest, Joash did what pleased GOD throughout Jehoiada's lifetime. Jehoiada picked out two wives for him; he had a family of both sons and daughters.

4-6   The time came when Joash determined to renovate The Temple of GOD. He got the priests and Levites together and said, "Circulate through the towns of Judah every year and collect money from the people to repair The Temple of your God. You are in charge of carrying this out." But the Levites dragged their feet and didn't do anything.

7   Then the king called in Jehoiada the chief priest and said, "Why haven't you made the Levites bring in from Judah and Jerusalem the tax Moses, servant of GOD and the congregation, set for the upkeep of the place of worship? You can see how bad things are — wicked Queen Athaliah and her sons let The Temple of God go to ruin and took all its sacred artifacts for use in Baal worship."

8-9   Following the king's orders, they made a chest and placed it at the entrance to The Temple of GOD. Then they sent out a tax notice throughout Judah and Jerusalem: "Pay the tax that Moses the servant of GOD set when Israel was in the wilderness."

10   The people and their leaders were glad to do it and cheerfully brought their money until the chest was full.

11-14   Whenever the Levites brought the chest in for a royal audit and found it to be full, the king's secretary and the official of the chief priest would empty the chest and put it back in its place. Day after day they did this and collected a lot of money. The king and Jehoiada gave the money to the managers of The Temple project; they in turn paid the masons and carpenters for the repair work on The Temple of GOD. The construction workers kept at their jobs steadily until the restoration was complete—the house of GOD as good as new! When they had finished the work, they returned the surplus money to the king and Jehoiada, who used the money for making sacred vessels for Temple worship, vessels for the daily worship, for the Whole-Burnt-Offerings, bowls, and other gold and silver liturgical artifacts.

14-16 Whole-Burnt-Offerings were made regularly in The Temple of GOD throughout Jehoiada's lifetime. He died at a ripe old age—130 years old! They buried him in the royal cemetery because he had such a distinguished life of service to Israel and God and God's Temple.

17-19 But after the death of Jehoiada things fell apart. The leaders of Judah made a formal presentation to the king and he went along with them. Things went from bad to worse; they deserted The Temple of GOD and took up with the cult of sex goddesses. An angry cloud hovered over Judah and Jerusalem because of this sin. GOD sent prophets to straighten them out, warning of judgment. But nobody paid attention.

20 Then the Spirit of God moved Zechariah son of Jehoiada the priest to speak up: "God's word: Why have you deliberately walked away from GOD's commandments? You can't live this way! If you walk out on GOD, he'll walk out on you."

21-22 But they worked out a plot against Zechariah, and with the complicity of the king—he actually gave the order!—they murdered him, pelting him with rocks, right in the court of The Temple of GOD. That's the thanks King Joash showed the loyal Jehoiada, the priest who had made him king. He murdered Jehoiada's son. Zechariah's last words were, "Look, GOD! Make them pay for this!"

23-24 A year or so later Aramean troops attacked Joash. They invaded Judah and Jerusalem, massacred the leaders, and shipped all their plunder back to the king in Damascus. The Aramean army was quite small, but GOD used them to wipe out Joash's large army—their punishment for deserting GOD, the God of their ancestors. Arameans implemented God's judgment against Joash.

25-27 They left Joash badly wounded and his own servants finished him off—it was a palace conspiracy, avenging the murder of the son of Jehoiada the priest. They killed him in his bed. Afterward they buried him in the City of David, but he was not honored with a grave in the royal cemetery. The temple conspirators were Zabad, whose mother was Shimeath from Ammon, and Jehozabad, whose mother was Shimrith from Moab. The story of his sons, the many sermons preached to Joash, and the account of his repairs on The Temple of God can be found contained in the commentary on the royal history.

Amaziah, Joash's son, was the next king.

KING AMAZIAH

1-4 **25** Amaziah was twenty-five years old when he became king and reigned twenty-nine years in Jerusalem. His mother was Jehoaddin from Jerusalem. He lived well before GOD, doing the right thing for the most part. But he wasn't wholeheartedly devoted to God. When he had the affairs of the kingdom well in hand, he executed the palace guard who had assassinated his father the king. But he didn't kill the sons of the assassins — he was mindful of what GOD commanded in The Revelation of Moses, that parents shouldn't be executed for their childrens' sins, nor children for their parents'. We each pay personally for our sins.

5-6 Amaziah organized Judah and sorted out Judah and Benjamin by families and by military units. Men twenty years and older had to register — they ended up with 300,000 judged capable of military service. In addition he hired 100,000 soldiers from Israel in the north at a cost of about four and a half tons of silver.

7-8 A holy man showed up and said, "No, O King — don't let those northern Israelite soldiers into your army; GOD is not on their side, nor with any of the Ephraimites. Instead, you go by yourself and be strong. God and God only has the power to help or hurt your cause."

9 But Amaziah said to the holy man, "But what about all this money — these tons of silver I have already paid out to hire these men?"

"GOD's help is worth far more to you than that," said the holy man.

10 So Amaziah fired the soldiers he had hired from the north and sent them home. They were very angry at losing their jobs and went home seething.

11-12 But Amaziah was optimistic. He led his troops into the Valley of Salt and killed ten thousand men of Seir. They took another ten thousand as prisoners, led them to the top of the Rock, and pushed them off a cliff. They all died in the fall, smashed on the rocks.

13 But the troops Amaziah had dismissed from his army, angry over their lost opportunity for plunder, rampaged through the towns of Judah all the way from Samaria to Beth Horon, killing three thousand people and taking much plunder.

14-15 On his return from the destruction of the Edomites, Amaziah brought back the gods of the men of Seir and installed them as his own gods, worshiping them and burning incense to them. *That* ignited GOD's anger; a fiery blast of GOD's wrath put into words by a God-sent prophet: "What is this? Why on earth would you pray to inferior gods who couldn't so much as help their own people from you — gods weaker than Amaziah?"

16 Amaziah interrupted him, "Did I ask for your opinion? Shut up or get thrown out!"

The prophet quit speaking, but not before he got in one last word: "I have it on good authority: God has made up his mind to throw *you* out because of what you've done, and because you wouldn't listen to me."

17 One day Amaziah sent envoys to Jehoash son of Jehoahaz, the son of Jehu, king of Israel, challenging him to a fight: "Come and meet with me, I dare you. Let's have it out face-to-face!"

18-19 Jehoash king of Israel replied to Amaziah king of Judah, "One day a thistle in Lebanon sent word to a cedar in Lebanon, 'Give your daughter to my son in marriage.' But then a wild animal of Lebanon passed by and stepped on the thistle, crushing it. Just because you've defeated Edom in battle, you now think you're a big shot. Go ahead and be proud, but stay home. Why press your luck? Why bring defeat on yourself and Judah?"

20-22 Amaziah wouldn't take no for an answer — God had already decided to let Jehoash defeat him because he had defected to the gods of Edom.

So Jehoash king of Israel came on ahead and confronted Amaziah king of Judah. They met at Beth Shemesh, a town of Judah. Judah was thoroughly beaten by Israel—all the soldiers straggled home in defeat.

23-24 Jehoash king of Israel captured Amaziah king of Judah, the son of Joash, the son of Ahaziah, at Beth Shemesh. But Jehoash didn't stop at that; he went on to attack Jerusalem. He demolished the Wall of Jerusalem all the way from the Ephraim Gate to the Corner Gate—a stretch of about six hundred feet. He looted the gold, silver, and furnishings—anything he found that was worth taking—from both the palace and The Temple of God—and, for good measure, he took hostages. Then he returned to Samaria.

25-26 Amaziah son of Joash king of Judah continued as king fifteen years after the death of Jehoash son of Jehoahaz king of Israel. The rest of the life and times of Amaziah from start to finish is written in the *Royal Annals of the Kings of Judah and Israel.*

27-28 During those last days, after Amaziah had defected from GOD, they cooked up a plot against Amaziah in Jerusalem, and he had to flee to Lachish. But they tracked him down in Lachish and killed him there. They brought him back on horseback and buried him in Jerusalem with his ancestors in the City of David.

KING UZZIAH

1-2 **26** The people of Judah then took Uzziah, who was only sixteen years old, and made him king in place of his father Amaziah. The first thing he did after his father was dead and buried was to recover Elath for Judah and rebuild it.

3-5 Uzziah was sixteen years old when he became king and reigned for fifty-two years in Jerusalem. His mother was Jecoliah from Jerusalem. He behaved well in the eyes of GOD, following in the footsteps of his father Amaziah. He was a loyal seeker of God. He was well trained by his pastor and teacher Zechariah to live in reverent obedience before God, and for as long as Zechariah lived, Uzziah lived a godly life. And God prospered him.

6-8 He ventured out and fought the Philistines, breaking into the fortress cities of Gath, Jabneh, and Ashdod. He also built settlements around Ashdod and other Philistine areas. God helped him in his wars with the Philistines, the Arabs in Gur Baal, and the Meunites. The Ammonites also paid tribute. Uzziah became famous, his reputation extending all the way to Egypt. He became quite powerful.

9-10 Uzziah constructed defense towers in Jerusalem at the Corner Gate, the Valley Gate, and at the corner of the wall. He also built towers and dug cisterns out in the country. He had herds of cattle down in the foothills and out on the plains, had farmers and vinedressers at work in the hills and fields—he loved growing things.

11-15 On the military side, Uzziah had a well-prepared army ready to fight. They were organized by companies under the direction of Jeiel the secretary, Maaseiah the field captain, and Hananiah of the general staff. The roster of family leaders over the fighting men accounted for 2,600. Under them were reinforcement troops numbering 307,000, with 500 of them on constant alert—a strong royal defense against any attack. Uzziah had them well-armed with shields, spears, helmets, armor, bows, and slingshots. He also installed the latest in military technology on the towers and corners of Jerusalem for shooting arrows and hurling stones. He became well known for all this — a famous king. Everything seemed to go his way.

16-18   But then the strength and success went to his head. Arrogant and proud, he fell. One day, contemptuous of GOD, he walked into The Temple of GOD like he owned it and took over, burning incense on the Incense Altar. The priest Azariah, backed up by eighty brave priests of GOD, tried to prevent him. They confronted Uzziah: "You must not, you *cannot* do this, Uzziah — only the Aaronite priests, especially consecrated for the work, are permitted to burn incense. Get out of God's Temple; you are unfaithful and a disgrace!"

19-21   But Uzziah, censer in hand, was already in the middle of doing it and angrily rebuffed the priests. He lost his temper; angry words were exchanged — and then, even as they quarreled, a skin disease appeared on his forehead. As soon as they saw it, the chief priest Azariah and the other priests got him out of there as fast as they could. He hurried out — he knew that GOD then and there had given him the disease. Uzziah had his skin disease for the rest of his life and had to live in quarantine; he was not permitted to set foot in The Temple of GOD. His son Jotham, who managed the royal palace, took over the government of the country.

22-23   The rest of the history of Uzziah, from start to finish, was written by the prophet Isaiah son of Amoz. When Uzziah died, they buried him with his ancestors in a field next to the royal cemetery. His skin disease disqualified him from burial in the royal cemetery. His son Jotham became the next king.

KING JOTHAM

1-2   **27** Jotham was twenty-five years old when he became king; he reigned sixteen years at Jerusalem. His mother was Jerusha the daughter of Zadok. In GOD's eyes he lived a good life, following the path marked out by his father Uzziah. Unlike his father, though, he didn't desecrate The Temple of GOD. But the people pushed right on in their lives of corruption.

3-6   Jotham constructed the Upper Gate of The Temple of GOD, considerably extended the Wall of the Ophel, and built cities in the high country of Judah and forts and towers down in the forests. He fought and beat the king of the Ammonites — that year the Ammonites turned over three and a quarter tons of silver and about 65,000 bushels of wheat, and another 65,000 bushels of barley. They repeated this for the next two years. Jotham's strength was rooted in his steady and determined life of obedience to GOD.

7-9   The rest of the history of Jotham, including his wars and achievements, are all written in the *Royal Annals of the Kings of Israel and Judah*. He was twenty-five years old when he became king; he reigned for sixteen years at Jerusalem. Jotham died and was buried in the City of David. His son Ahaz became the next king.

KING AHAZ

1-4   **28** Ahaz was twenty years old when he became king and reigned sixteen years in Jerusalem. He didn't live right in the eyes of GOD; he wasn't at all like his ancestor David. Instead he followed in the track of Israel in the north, even casting metal figurines for worshiping the pagan Baal gods. He participated in the outlawed burning of incense in the Valley of Ben Hinnom and — incredibly! — indulged in the outrageous practice of "passing his sons through the fire," a truly abominable thing he picked up from the pagans GOD had earlier thrown out of the country. He also joined in the activities of the neighborhood sex-and-religion shrines that flourished all over the place.

5-8   GOD, fed up, handed him over to the king of Aram, who beat him badly and took many prisoners to Damascus. God also let the king of Israel loose on him and that resulted in a terrible slaughter: Pekah son of Remaliah killed 120,000 in one day, all of them first-class soldiers, and all because they had deserted GOD, the God of their ancestors. Furthermore, Zicri, an Ephraimite hero, killed the king's son Maaseiah, Azrikam the palace steward, and Elkanah, second in command to the king. And that wasn't the end of it — the Israelites captured 200,000 men, women, and children, besides huge cartloads of plunder that they took to Samaria.

9-11   GOD's prophet Oded was in the neighborhood. He met the army when it entered Samaria and said, "Stop right where you are and listen! GOD, the God of your ancestors, was angry with Judah and used you to punish them; but you took things into your own hands and used *your* anger, uncalled for and irrational, to turn your brothers and sisters from Judah and Jerusalem into slaves. Don't you see that this is a terrible sin against your GOD? Careful now; do exactly what I say — return these captives, every last one of them. If you don't, you'll find out how real anger, GOD's anger, works."

12-13   Some of their Ephraimite leaders — Azariah son of Jehohanan, Berekiah son of Meshillemoth, Jehizkiah son of Shallum, and Amasa son of Hadlai — stood up against the returning army and said, "Don't bring the captives here! We've already sinned against GOD; and now you are about to compound our sin and guilt. We're guilty enough as it is, enough to set off an explosion of divine anger."

14-15   So the soldiers turned over both the captives and the plunder to the leaders and the people. Personally designated men gathered the captives together, dressed the ones who were naked using clothing from the stores of plunder, put shoes on their feet, gave them all a square meal, provided first aid to the injured, put the weak ones on donkeys, and then escorted them to Jericho, the City of Palms, restoring them to their families. Then they went back to Samaria.

16-21   At about that time King Ahaz sent to the king of Assyria asking for personal help. The Edomites had come back and given Judah a bad beating, taking off a bunch of captives. Adding insult to injury the Philistines raided the cities in the foothills to the west and the southern desert and captured Beth Shemesh, Aijalon, and Gederoth, along with Soco, Timnah, and Gimzo, with their surrounding villages, and moved in, making themselves at home. Arrogant King Ahaz, acting as if he could do without God's help, had unleashed an epidemic of depravity. Judah, brought to its knees by GOD, was now reduced to begging for a handout. But the king of Assyria, Tiglath-Pileser, wouldn't help — he came instead and humiliated Ahaz even more by attacking and bullying him. Desperate, Ahaz ransacked The Temple of GOD, the royal palace, and every other place he could think of, scraping together everything he could, and gave it to the king of Assyria — and got nothing in return, not a bit of help.

22-25   But King Ahaz didn't learn his lesson — at the very time that everyone was turning against him, he continued to be against GOD! He offered sacrifices to the gods of Damascus. He had just been defeated by Damascus; he thought, "If I worship the gods who helped Damascus, those gods just might help me, too." But things only went from bad to worse: first Ahaz in ruins and then the country. He cleaned out The Temple of God of everything useful and valuable, boarded up the doors of The Temple, and then went out and set up pagan shrines for his own use all over Jerusalem. And not only in Jerusalem, but all over Judah — neighborhood shrines for worshiping any and every god on sale. And was GOD ever angry!

26-27 The rest of Ahaz's infamous life, all that he did from start to finish, is written in the *Royal Annals of the Kings of Judah and Israel*. When Ahaz died, they buried him in Jerusalem, but he was not honored with a burial in the cemetery of the kings. His son Hezekiah was the next king.

KING HEZEKIAH

1-2 **29** Hezekiah became king when he was twenty-five years old and was king in Jerusalem for twenty-nine years. His mother was Abijah daughter of Zechariah. In GOD's opinion he was a good king; he kept to the standards of his ancestor David.

3-9 In the first month of the first year of his reign, Hezekiah, having first repaired the doors of The Temple of GOD, threw them open to the public. He assembled the priests and Levites in the court on the east side and said, "Levites, listen! Consecrate yourselves and consecrate The Temple of GOD — give this much-defiled place a good housecleaning. Our ancestors went wrong and lived badly before GOD — they discarded him, turned away from this house where we meet with GOD, and walked off. They boarded up the doors, turned out the lights, and canceled all the acts of worship of the GOD of Israel in the holy Temple. And because of that, GOD's anger flared up and he turned those people into a public exhibit of disaster, a moral history lesson — look and read! This is why our ancestors were killed, and this is why our wives and sons and daughters were taken prisoner and made slaves.

10-11 "I have decided to make a covenant with the GOD of Israel and turn history around so that GOD will no longer be angry with us. Children, don't drag your feet in this! GOD has chosen you to take your place before him to serve in conducting and leading worship — *this* is your life work; make sure you do it and do it well."

12-17 The Levites stood at attention: Mahath son of Amasai and Joel son of Azariah from the Kohathites; Kish son of Abdi and Azariah son of Jehallelel from the Merarites; Joah son of Zimmah and Eden son of Joah from the Gershonites; Shimri and Jeiel sons of Elizaphan; Zechariah and Mattaniah sons of Asaph; Jehiel and Shimei of the family of Heman; Shemaiah and Uzziel of the family of Jeduthun. They presented themselves and their brothers, consecrated themselves, and set to work cleaning up The Temple of GOD as the king had directed — as GOD directed! The priests started from the inside and worked out; they emptied the place of the accumulation of defiling junk — pagan rubbish that had no business in that holy place — and the Levites hauled it off to the Kidron Valley. They began the Temple cleaning on the first day of the first month and by the eighth day they had worked their way out to the porch — eight days it took them to clean and consecrate The Temple itself, and in eight more days they had finished with the entire Temple complex.

18-19 Then they reported to Hezekiah the king, "We have cleaned up the entire Temple of GOD, including the Altar of Whole-Burnt-Offering and the Table of the Bread of the Presence with their furnishings. We have also cleaned up and consecrated all the vessels which King Ahaz had gotten rid of during his misrule. Take a look; we have repaired them. They're all there in front of the Altar of GOD."

20-24 Then Hezekiah the king went to work: He got all the leaders of the city together and marched to The Temple of GOD. They brought with them seven bulls, seven rams, seven lambs, and seven he-goats to sacrifice as an Absolution-Offering for the royal family, for the Sanctuary, and for Judah as a whole; he directed the Aaronite priests to sacrifice them on the Altar of GOD. The priests butchered the bulls and then took the blood and sprinkled it on the Altar, and then the same with the rams and lambs. Finally they brought the goats up; the king and congregation laid their hands upon them. The priests butchered them and made an Absolution-Offering with their blood at the Altar to atone for the sin of all Israel — the king had ordered that the Whole-Burnt-Offering and the Absolution-Offering be for all Israel.

25-26 The king ordered the Levites to take their places in The Temple of GOD with their musical instruments — cymbals, harps, zithers — following the original instructions of David, Gad the king's seer, and Nathan the prophet; this was GOD's command conveyed by his prophets. The Levites formed the orchestra of David, while the priests took up the trumpets.

27-30 Then Hezekiah gave the signal to begin: The Whole-Burnt-Offering was offered on the Altar; at the same time the sacred choir began singing, backed up by the trumpets and the David orchestra while the entire congregation worshiped. The singers sang and the trumpeters played all during the sacrifice of the Whole-Burnt-Offering. When the offering of the sacrifice was completed, the king and everyone there knelt to the ground and worshiped. Then Hezekiah the king and the leaders told the Levites to finish things off with anthems of praise to GOD using lyrics by David and Asaph the seer. They sang their praises with joy and reverence, kneeling in worship.

31-35 Hezekiah then made this response: "The dedication is complete — you're consecrated to GOD. Now you're ready: Come forward and bring your sacrifices and Thank-Offerings to The Temple of GOD."

And come they did. Everyone in the congregation brought sacrifices and Thank-Offerings and some, overflowing with generosity, even brought Whole-Burnt-Offerings, a generosity expressed in seventy bulls, a hundred rams, and two hundred lambs — all for Whole-Burnt-Offerings for GOD! The total number of animals consecrated for sacrifice that day amounted to six hundred bulls and three thousand sheep. They ran out of priests qualified to slaughter all the Whole-Burnt-Offerings so their brother Levites stepped in and helped out while other priests consecrated themselves for the work. It turned out that the Levites had been more responsible in making sure they were properly consecrated than the priests had been. Besides the overflow of Whole-Burnt-Offerings there were also choice pieces for the Peace-Offerings and lavish libations that went with the Whole-Burnt-Offerings. The worship in The Temple of GOD was on a firm footing again!

36 Hezekiah and the congregation celebrated: God had established a firm foundation for the lives of the people — and so quickly!

1-5 **30** Then Hezekiah invited all of Israel and Judah, with personal letters to Ephraim and Manasseh, to come to The Temple of GOD in Jerusalem to celebrate the Passover to Israel's God. The king and his officials and the congregation in Jerusalem had decided to celebrate Passover in the second month. They hadn't been able to celebrate it at the regular time because not enough of the priests were yet personally prepared and the people hadn't had time to gather in Jerusalem. Under these circumstances, the revised date was approved by both king and people and they sent out the invitation from one end of the country to the other, from Beersheba in the south to Dan in the north: "Come and celebrate the Passover to Israel's God in Jerusalem." No one living had ever celebrated it properly.

6-9 The king gave the orders, and the couriers delivered the invitations from the king and his leaders throughout Israel and Judah. The invitation read: "O Israelites! Come back to GOD, the God of Abraham, Isaac, and Israel, so that he can return to you who have survived the predations of the kings of Assyria. Don't repeat the sins of your ancestors who turned their backs on GOD, the God of their ancestors who then brought them to ruin—you can see the ruins all around you. Don't be pigheaded as your ancestors were. Clasp GOD's outstretched hand. Come to his Temple of holy worship, consecrated for all time. Serve GOD, *your* God. You'll no longer be in danger of his hot anger. If you come back to GOD, your captive relatives and children will be treated compassionately and allowed to come home. Your GOD is gracious and kind and won't snub you—come back and he'll welcome you with open arms."

10-12 So the couriers set out, going from city to city through the country of Ephraim and Manasseh, as far north as Zebulun. But the people poked fun at them, treated them as a joke. But not all; some from Asher, Manasseh, and Zebulun weren't too proud to accept the invitation and come to Jerusalem. It was better in Judah—God worked powerfully among them to make it unanimous, responding to the orders sent out by the king and his officials, orders backed up by the word of GOD.

13-17 It turned out that there was a tremendous crowd of people when the time came in the second month to celebrate the Passover (sometimes called the Feast of Unraised Bread). First they went to work and got rid of all the pagan altars that were in Jerusalem—hauled them off and dumped them in the Kidron Valley. Then, on the fourteenth day of the second month, they slaughtered the Passover lambs. The priests and Levites weren't ready; but now, embarrassed in their laziness, they consecrated themselves and brought Whole-Burnt-Offerings to The Temple of GOD. Ready now, they stood at their posts as designated by The Revelation of Moses the holy man; the priests sprinkled the blood the Levites handed to them. Because so many in the congregation had not properly prepared themselves by consecration and so were not qualified, the Levites took charge of the slaughter of the Passover lambs so that they would be properly consecrated to GOD.

18-19 There were a lot of people, especially those from Ephraim, Manasseh, Issachar, and Zebulun, who did not eat the Passover meal because they had not prepared themselves adequately. Hezekiah prayed for these as follows: "May GOD who is all good, pardon and forgive everyone who sincerely desires GOD, the God of our ancestors. Even—especially!—these who do not meet the literal conditions stated for access to The Temple."

20   GOD responded to Hezekiah's prayer and healed the people.

21-22   All the Israelites present in Jerusalem celebrated the Passover (Feast of Unraised Bread) for seven days, celebrated exuberantly. The Levites and priests praised GOD day after day, filling the air with praise sounds of percussion and brass. Hezekiah commended the Levites for the superb way in which they had led the people in the worship of GOD.

22-23   When the feast and festival — that glorious seven days of worship, the making of offerings, and the praising of GOD, the God of their ancestors — were over, the tables cleared and the floors swept, they all decided to keep going for another seven days! So they just kept on celebrating, and as joyfully as they began.

24-26   Hezekiah king of Judah gave one thousand bulls and seven thousand sheep for the congregation's worship; the officials gave an additional one thousand bulls and ten thousand sheep. And there turned out to be plenty of consecrated priests — qualified and well-prepared. The whole congregation of Judah, the priests and Levites, the congregation that came in from Israel, and the resident aliens from both Israel and Judah, were all in on the joyous celebration. Jerusalem was bursting with joy — nothing like this had taken place in Jerusalem since Solomon son of David king of Israel had built and dedicated The Temple.

27   The priests and Levites had the last word: they stood and blessed the people. And God listened, listened as the ascending sound of their prayers entered his holy heaven.

1   **31** After the Passover celebration, they all took off for the cities of Judah and smashed the phallic stone monuments, chopped down the sacred Asherah groves, and demolished the neighborhood sex-and-religion shrines and local god shops. They didn't stop until they had been all through Judah, Benjamin, Ephraim, and Manasseh. Then they all went back home and resumed their everyday lives.

2   Hezekiah organized the groups of priests and Levites for their respective tasks, handing out job descriptions for conducting the services of worship: making the various offerings, and making sure that thanks and praise took place wherever and whenever GOD was worshiped.

3   He also designated his personal contribution for the Whole-Burnt-Offerings for the morning and evening worship, for Sabbaths, for New Moon festivals, and for the special worship days set down in The Revelation of GOD.

4   In addition, he asked the people who lived in Jerusalem to be responsible for providing for the priests and Levites so they, without distraction or concern, could give themselves totally to The Revelation of GOD.

5-7   As soon as Hezekiah's orders had gone out, the Israelites responded generously: firstfruits of the grain harvest, new wine, oil, honey — everything they grew. They didn't hold back, turning over a tithe of everything. They also brought in a tithe of their cattle, sheep, and anything else they owned that had been dedicated to GOD. Everything was sorted and piled in mounds. They started doing this in the third month and didn't finish until the seventh month.

8-9   When Hezekiah and his leaders came and saw the extent of the mounds of gifts, they praised GOD and commended God's people Israel. Hezekiah then consulted the priests and Levites on how to handle the abundance of offerings.

10   Azariah, chief priest of the family of Zadok, answered, "From the moment of this huge outpouring of gifts to The Temple of GOD, there has been plenty to eat for everyone with food left over. GOD has blessed his people — just look at the evidence!"

11-18   Hezekiah then ordered storerooms to be prepared in The Temple of GOD. When they were ready, they brought in all the offerings of tithes and sacred gifts. They put Conaniah the Levite in charge with his brother Shimei as assistant. Jehiel, Azaziah, Nahath, Asahel, Jerimoth, Jozabad, Eliel, Ismakiah, Mahath, and Benaiah were project managers under the direction of Conaniah and Shimei, carrying out the orders of King Hezekiah and Azariah the chief priest of The Temple of God. Kore son of Imnah the Levite, security guard of the East Gate, was in charge of the Freewill-Offerings of God and responsible for distributing the offerings and sacred gifts. Faithful support out in the priestly cities was provided by Eden, Miniamin, Jeshua, Shemaiah, Amariah, and Shecaniah. They were even-handed in their distributions to their coworkers (all males thirty years and older) in each of their respective divisions as they entered The Temple of GOD each day to do their assigned work (their work was all organized by divisions). The divisions comprised officially registered priests by family and Levites twenty years and older by job description. The official family tree included everyone in the entire congregation — their small children, wives, sons, and daughters. The ardent dedication they showed in bringing themselves and their gifts to worship was total — no one was left out.

19   The Aaronites, the priests who lived out on the pastures that belonged to the priest-cities, had reputable men on hand to distribute regular rations to every priest — everyone listed in the official family tree of the Levites.

20-21   Hezekiah carried out this work and kept it up everywhere in Judah. He was the very best — good, right, and true before his GOD. Everything he took up, whether it had to do with worship in God's Temple or the carrying out of God's Law and Commandments, he did well in a spirit of prayerful worship. He was a great success.

※

1   **32** And then, after this exemplary track record, this: Sennacherib king of Assyria came and attacked Judah. He put the fortified cities under siege, determined to take them.

2-4   When Hezekiah realized that Sennacherib's strategy was to take Jerusalem, he talked to his advisors and military leaders about eliminating all the water supplies outside the city; they thought it was a good idea. There was a great turnout of people to plug the springs and tear down the aqueduct. They said, "Why should the kings of Assyria march in and be furnished with running water?"

5-6   Hezekiah also went to work repairing every part of the city wall that was damaged, built defensive towers on it, built another wall of defense further out, and reinforced the defensive rampart (the Millo) of the old City of David. He also built up a large store of armaments — spears and shields. He then appointed military officers to be responsible for the people and got them all together at the public square in front of the city gate.

6-8   Hezekiah rallied the people, saying, "Be strong! Take courage! Don't be intimidated by the king of Assyria and his troops — there are more on our side than on their side. He only has a bunch of mere men; we have our GOD to help us and fight for us!"

Morale surged. Hezekiah's words put steel in their spines.

9-15   Later on, Sennacherib, who had set up camp a few miles away at Lachish, sent messengers to Jerusalem, addressing Judah through Hezekiah: "A proclamation of Sennacherib king of Assyria: You poor people — do you think you're safe in that so-called fortress of Jerusalem? You're sitting ducks. Do you think Hezekiah will save you? Don't be stupid — Hezekiah has fed you a pack of lies. When he says, 'GOD will save us from the power of the king of Assyria,' he's lying — you're all going to end up dead. Wasn't it Hezekiah who cleared out all the neighborhood worship shrines and told you, 'There is only one legitimate place to worship'? Do you have any idea what I and my ancestors have done to all the countries around here? Has there been a single god anywhere strong enough to stand up against me? Can you name one god among all the nations that either I or my ancestors have ravaged that so much as lifted a finger against me? So what makes you think you'll make out any better with your god? Don't let Hezekiah fool you; don't let him get by with his barefaced lies; don't trust him. No god of any country or kingdom ever has been one bit of help against me or my ancestors — what kind of odds does that give your god?"

16   The messengers felt free to throw in their personal comments, putting down both GOD and God's servant Hezekiah.

17   Sennacherib continued to send letters insulting the GOD of Israel: "The gods of the nations were powerless to help their people; the god of Hezekiah is no better, probably worse."

18-19   The messengers would come up to the wall of Jerusalem and shout up to the people standing on the wall, shouting their propaganda in Hebrew, trying to scare them into demoralized submission. They contemptuously lumped the God of Jerusalem in with the handmade gods of other peoples.

20-21   King Hezekiah, joined by the prophet Isaiah son of Amoz, responded by praying, calling up to heaven. GOD answered by sending an angel who wiped out everyone in the Assyrian camp, both warriors and officers. Sennacherib was forced to return home in disgrace, tail between his legs. When he went into the temple of his god, his own sons killed him.

22-23   GOD saved Hezekiah and the citizens of Jerusalem from Sennacherib king of Assyria and everyone else. And he continued to take good care of them. People streamed into Jerusalem bringing offerings for the worship of GOD and expensive presents to Hezekiah king of Judah. All the surrounding nations were impressed — Hezekiah's stock soared.

24   Some time later Hezekiah became deathly sick. He prayed to GOD and was given a reassuring sign.

25-26   But the sign, instead of making Hezekiah grateful, made him arrogant. This made GOD angry, and his anger spilled over on Judah and Jerusalem. But then Hezekiah, and Jerusalem with him, repented of his arrogance, and GOD withdrew his anger while Hezekiah lived.

27-31   Hezekiah ended up very wealthy and much honored. He built treasuries for all his silver, gold, precious stones, spices, shields, and valuables, barns for the grain, new wine, and olive oil, stalls for his various breeds of cattle, and pens for his flocks. He founded royal cities for himself and built up huge stocks of sheep and cattle. God saw to it that he was extravagantly rich. Hezekiah was also responsible for diverting the upper outlet of the Gihon spring and rerouting the water to the west side of the City of David. Hezekiah succeeded in everything he did. But when the rulers of Babylon sent emissaries to find out about the sign from God that had taken place earlier, God left him on his own to see what he would do; he wanted to test his heart.

32-33 The rest of the history of Hezekiah and his life of loyal service, you can read for yourself—it's written in the vision of the prophet Isaiah son of Amoz in the *Royal Annals of the Kings of Judah and Israel.* When Hezekiah died, they buried him in the upper part of the King David cemetery. Everyone in Judah and Jerusalem came to the funeral. He was buried in great honor.

Manasseh his son was the next king.

KING MANASSEH

1-6 33 Manasseh was twelve years old when he became king. He ruled for fifty-five years in Jerusalem. In GOD's opinion he was a bad king—an evil king. He reintroduced all the moral rot and spiritual corruption that had been scoured from the country when GOD dispossessed the pagan nations in favor of the children of Israel. He rebuilt the sex-and-religion shrines that his father Hezekiah had torn down, he built altars and phallic images for the sex god Baal and the sex goddess Asherah and worshiped the cosmic powers, taking orders from the constellations. He built shrines to the cosmic powers and placed them in both courtyards of The Temple of GOD, the very Jerusalem Temple dedicated exclusively by GOD's decree to GOD's Name ("in Jerusalem I place my Name"). He burned his own sons in a sacrificial rite in the Valley of Ben Hinnom. He practiced witchcraft and fortunetelling. He held séances and consulted spirits from the underworld. Much evil—in GOD's view a career in evil. And GOD was angry.

7-8 As a last straw he placed a carved image of the sex goddess Asherah that he had commissioned in The Temple of God, a flagrant and provocative violation of God's well-known command to both David and Solomon, "In this Temple and in this city Jerusalem, my choice out of all the tribes of Israel, I place my Name—exclusively and forever." He had promised, "Never again will I let my people Israel wander off from this land I've given to their ancestors. But on this condition, that they keep everything I've commanded in the instructions my servant Moses passed on to them."

9-10 But Manasseh led Judah and the citizens of Jerusalem off the beaten path into practices of evil exceeding even the evil of the pagan nations that GOD had earlier destroyed. When GOD spoke to Manasseh and his people about this, they ignored him.

11-13 Then GOD directed the leaders of the troops of the king of Assyria to come after Manasseh. They put a hook in his nose, shackles on his feet, and took him off to Babylon. Now that he was in trouble, he went to his knees in prayer asking for help—total repentance before the God of his ancestors. As he prayed, GOD was touched; GOD listened and brought him back to Jerusalem as king. That convinced Manasseh that GOD was in control.

14-17 After that Manasseh rebuilt the outside defensive wall of the City of David to the west of the Gihon spring in the valley. It went from the Fish Gate and around the hill of Ophel. He also increased its height. He tightened up the defense system by posting army captains in all the fortress cities of Judah. He also did a good spring cleaning on The Temple, carting out the pagan idols and the goddess statue. He took all the altars he had set up on The Temple hill and throughout Jerusalem and dumped them outside the city. He put the Altar of GOD back in working order and restored worship, sacrificing Peace-Offerings and Thank-Offerings. He issued orders to the people: "You shall serve and worship GOD, the God of Israel." But the people didn't take him seriously—they used the name "GOD" but kept on going to the old pagan neighborhood shrines and doing the same old things.

18-19 The rest of the history of Manasseh—his prayer to his God, and the sermons the prophets personally delivered by authority of GOD, the God of Israel—this is all written in *The Chronicles of the Kings of Israel*. His prayer and how God was touched by his prayer, a list of all his sins and the things he did wrong, the actual places where he built the pagan shrines, the installation of the sex-goddess Asherah sites, and the idolatrous images that he worshiped previous to his conversion—this is all described in the records of the prophets.

20 When Manasseh died, they buried him in the palace garden. His son Amon was the next king.

KING AMON

21-23 Amon was twenty-two years old when he became king. He was king for two years in Jerusalem. In GOD's opinion he lived an evil life, just like his father Manasseh, but he never did repent to GOD as Manasseh repented. He just kept at it, going from one thing to another.

24-25 In the end Amon's servants revolted and assassinated him—killed the king right in his own palace. The citizens in their turn then killed the king's assassins. The citizens then crowned Josiah, Amon's son, as king.

KING JOSIAH

1-2 **34** Josiah was eight years old when he became king. He ruled for thirty-one years in Jerusalem. He behaved well before GOD. He kept straight on the path blazed by his ancestor David, not one step to the left or right.

3-7 When he had been king for eight years—he was still only a teenager—he began to seek the God of David his ancestor. Four years later, the twelfth year of his reign, he set out to cleanse the neighborhood of sex-and-religion shrines, and get rid of the sacred Asherah groves and the god and goddess figurines, whether carved or cast, from Judah. He wrecked the Baal shrines, tore down the altars connected with them, and scattered the debris and ashes over the graves of those who had worshiped at them. He burned the bones of the priests on the same altars they had used when alive. He scrubbed the place clean, Judah and Jerusalem, clean inside and out. The cleanup campaign ranged outward to the cities of Manasseh, Ephraim,

Simeon, and the surrounding neighborhoods—as far north as Naphtali. Throughout Israel he demolished the altars and Asherah groves, pulverized the god and goddess figures, chopped up the neighborhood shrines into firewood. With Israel once more intact, he returned to Jerusalem.

8-13   One day in the eighteenth year of his kingship, with the cleanup of country and Temple complete, King Josiah sent Shaphan son of Azaliah, Maaseiah the mayor of the city, and Joah son of Joahaz the historian to renovate The Temple of GOD. First they turned over to Hilkiah the high priest all the money collected by the Levitical security guards from Manasseh and Ephraim and the rest of Israel, and from Judah and Benjamin and the citizens of Jerusalem. It was then put into the hands of the foremen managing the work on The Temple of GOD who then passed it on to the workers repairing GOD's Temple—the carpenters, construction workers, and masons—so they could buy the lumber and dressed stone for rebuilding the foundations the kings of Judah had allowed to fall to pieces. The workmen were honest and diligent. Their foremen were Jahath and Obadiah, the Merarite Levites, and Zechariah and Meshullam from the Kohathites—these managed the project. The Levites—they were all skilled musicians—were in charge of the common laborers and supervised the workers as they went from job to job. The Levites also served as accountants, managers, and security guards.

14-17   While the money that had been given for The Temple of GOD was being received and dispersed, Hilkiah the high priest found a copy of The Revelation of Moses. He reported to Shaphan the royal secretary, "I've just found the Book of GOD's Revelation, instructing us in GOD's way—found it in The Temple!" He gave it to Shaphan, who then gave it to the king. And along with the book, he gave this report: "The job is complete—everything you ordered done is done. They took all the money that was collected in The Temple of GOD and handed it over to the managers and workers."

18   And then Shaphan told the king, "Hilkiah the priest gave me a book." Shaphan proceeded to read it out to the king.

19-21   When the king heard what was written in the book, GOD's Revelation, he ripped his robes in dismay. And then he called for Hilkiah, Ahikam son of Shaphan, Abdon son of Micah, Shaphan the royal secretary, and Asaiah the king's personal aide. He ordered them all: "Go and pray to GOD for me and what's left of Israel and Judah. Find out what we must do in response to what is written in this book that has just been found! GOD's anger must be burning furiously against us—our ancestors haven't obeyed a thing written in this book of GOD, followed none of the instructions directed to us."

22-25   Hilkiah and those picked by the king went straight to Huldah the prophetess. She was the wife of Shallum son of Tokhath, the son of Hasrah, who was in charge of the palace wardrobe. She lived in Jerusalem in the Second Quarter. The men consulted with her. In response to them she said, "GOD's word, the God of Israel: Tell the man who sent you here, 'GOD has spoken, I'm on my way to bring the doom of judgment on this place and this people. Every word written in the book read by the king of Judah will happen. And why? Because they've deserted me and taken up with other gods; they've made me thoroughly angry by setting up their god-making businesses. My anger is raging white-hot against this place and nobody is going to put it out.'

26-28 "And also tell the king of Judah, since he sent you to ask GOD for direction, GOD's comment on what he read in the book: 'Because you took seriously the doom of judgment I spoke against this place and people, and because you responded in humble repentance, tearing your robe in dismay and weeping before me, I'm taking you seriously. GOD's word. I'll take care of you; you'll have a quiet death and be buried in peace. You won't be around to see the doom that I'm going to bring upon this place and people.'"

The men took her message back to the king.

29-31 The king acted immediately, assembling all the elders of Judah and Jerusalem, and then proceeding to The Temple of GOD bringing everyone in his train—priests and prophets and people ranging from the least to the greatest. Then he read out publicly everything written in the Book of the Covenant that was found in The Temple of GOD. The king stood by his pillar and before GOD solemnly committed himself to the covenant: to follow GOD believingly and obediently; to follow his instructions, heart and soul, on what to believe and do; to confirm with his life the entire covenant, all that was written in the book.

32 Then he made everyone in Jerusalem and Benjamin commit themselves. And they did it. They committed themselves to the covenant of God, the God of their ancestors.

33 Josiah did a thorough job of cleaning up the pollution that had spread throughout Israelite territory and got everyone started fresh again, serving and worshiping their GOD. All through Josiah's life the people kept to the straight and narrow, obediently following GOD, the God of their ancestors.

1-4 **35** Josiah celebrated the Passover to GOD in Jerusalem. They killed the Passover lambs on the fourteenth day of the first month. He gave the priests detailed instructions and encouraged them in the work of leading worship in The Temple of GOD. He also told the Levites who were in charge of teaching and guiding Israel in all matters of worship (they were especially consecrated for this), "Place the sacred Chest in The Temple that Solomon son of David, the king of Israel, built. You don't have to carry it around on your shoulders any longer! Serve GOD and God's people Israel. Organize yourselves by families for your respective responsibilities, following the instructions left by David king of Israel and Solomon his son.

5-6 "Take your place in the sanctuary—a team of Levites for every grouping of your fellow citizens, the laity. Your job is to kill the Passover lambs, then consecrate yourselves and prepare the lambs so that everyone will be able to keep the Passover exactly as GOD commanded through Moses."

7-9 Josiah personally donated thirty thousand sheep, lambs, and goats and three thousand bulls—everything needed for the Passover celebration was there. His officials also pitched in on behalf of the people, including the priests and the Levites. Hilkiah, Zechariah, and Jehiel, leaders in The Temple of God, gave twenty-six hundred lambs and three hundred bulls to the priests for the Passover offerings. Conaniah, his brothers Shemaiah and Nethanel, along with the Levitical chiefs Hashabiah, Jeiel, and Jozabad, donated five thousand lambs and five hundred bulls to the Levites for the Passover offerings.

10-13   Preparations were complete for the service of worship; the priests took up their positions and the Levites were at their posts as instructed by the king. They killed the Passover lambs, and while the priests sprinkled the blood from the lambs, the Levites skinned them out. Then they set aside the Whole-Burnt-Offering for presentation to the family groupings of the people so that each group could offer it to GOD following the instructions in the Book of Moses. They did the same with the cattle. They roasted the Passover lamb according to the instructions and boiled the consecrated offerings in pots and kettles and pans and promptly served the people.

14   After the people had eaten the holy meal, the Levites served themselves and the Aaronite priests—the priests were busy late into the night making the offerings at the Altar.

15   The Asaph singers were all in their places following the instructions of David, Asaph, Heman, and Jeduthun the king's seer. The security guards were on duty at each gate—the Levites also served them because they couldn't leave their posts.

16-19   Everything went without a hitch in the worship of GOD that day as they celebrated the Passover and the offering of the Whole-Burnt-Offering on the Altar of GOD. It went just as Josiah had ordered. The Israelites celebrated the Passover, also known as the Feast of Unraised Bread, for seven days. The Passover hadn't been celebrated like this since the days of Samuel the prophet. None of the kings had done it. But Josiah, the priests, the Levites, all Judah and Israel who were there that week, plus the citizens of Jerusalem—*they* did it. In the eighteenth year of the rule of King Josiah, this Passover was celebrated.

20   Some time later, after Josiah's reformation of The Temple, Neco king of Egypt marched out toward Carchemish on the Euphrates River on his way to war. Josiah went out to fight him.

21   Neco sent messengers to Josiah saying, "What do we have against each other, O King of Judah? I haven't come to fight against you but against the country with whom I'm at war. God commanded me to hurry, so don't get in my way; you'll only interfere with God, who is on my side in this, and he'll destroy you."

22-23   But Josiah was spoiling for a fight and wouldn't listen to a thing Neco said (in actuality it was God who said it). Though King Josiah disguised himself when they met on the plain of Megiddo, archers shot him anyway.

The king said to his servants, "Get me out of here—I'm badly wounded."

24-25   So his servants took him out of his chariot and laid him down in an ambulance chariot and drove him back to Jerusalem. He died there and was buried in the family cemetery. Everybody in Judah and Jerusalem attended the funeral. Jeremiah composed an anthem of lament for Josiah. The anthem is still sung by the choirs of Israel to this day. The anthem is written in the Laments.

26-1   The rest of the history of Josiah, his exemplary and devout life, conformed to The Revelation of GOD. The whole story, from start to finish, is written in the *Royal Annals of the Kings of Israel and Judah*. By popular choice, Jehoahaz son of Josiah was made king at Jerusalem, succeeding his father.

KING JEHOAHAZ

2-3 **36** Jehoahaz was twenty-three years old when he began to rule. He was king in Jerusalem for a mere three months. The king of Egypt dethroned him and forced the country to pay him nearly four tons of silver and seventy-five pounds of gold.

KING JEHOIAKIM

4 Neco king of Egypt then made Eliakim, Jehoahaz's brother, king of Judah and Jerusalem, but changed his name to Jehoiakim; then he took Jehoahaz back with him to Egypt.

5 Jehoiakim was twenty-five years old when he began to rule; he was king for eleven years in Jerusalem. In GOD's opinion he was an evil king.

6-7 Nebuchadnezzar king of Babylon made war against him, and bound him in bronze chains, intending to take him prisoner to Babylon. Nebuchadnezzar also took things from The Temple of GOD to Babylon and put them in his royal palace.

8 The rest of the history of Jehoiakim, the outrageous sacrilege he committed and what happened to him as a consequence, is all written in the *Royal Annals of the Kings of Israel and Judah.*

Jehoiachin his son became the next king.

KING JEHOIACHIN

9-10 Jehoiachin was eighteen years old when he became king. But he ruled for only three months and ten days in Jerusalem. In GOD's opinion he was an evil king. In the spring King Nebuchadnezzar ordered him brought to Babylon along with the valuables remaining in The Temple of GOD. Then he made his uncle Zedekiah a puppet king over Judah and Jerusalem.

KING ZEDEKIAH

11-13 Zedekiah was twenty-one years old when he started out as king. He was king in Jerusalem for eleven years. As far as GOD was concerned, he was just one more evil king; there wasn't a trace of contrition in him when the prophet Jeremiah preached GOD's word to him. Then he compounded his troubles by rebelling against King Nebuchadnezzar, who earlier had made him swear in God's name that he would be loyal. He became set in his own stubborn ways—he never gave GOD a thought; repentance never entered his mind.

14 The evil mindset spread to the leaders and priests and filtered down to the people—it kicked off an epidemic of evil, repeating the abominations of the pagans and polluting The Temple of GOD so recently consecrated in Jerusalem.

15-17 GOD, the God of their ancestors, repeatedly sent warning messages to them. Out of compassion for both his people and his Temple he wanted to give them every chance possible. But they wouldn't listen; they poked fun at God's messengers, despised the message itself, and in general treated the prophets like idiots. GOD became more and more angry until there was no turning back—GOD called in Nebuchadnezzar king of Babylon, who came and killed indiscriminately—and right in The Temple itself; it was a ruthless massacre: young men and virgins, the elderly and weak—they were all the same to him.

18-20   And then he plundered The Temple of everything valuable, cleaned it out completely; he emptied the treasuries of The Temple of God, the treasuries of the king and his officials, and hauled it all, people and possessions, off to Babylon. He burned The Temple of God to the ground, knocked down the wall of Jerusalem, and set fire to all the buildings — everything valuable was burned up. Any survivor was taken prisoner into exile in Babylon and made a slave to Nebuchadnezzar and his family. The exile and slavery lasted until the kingdom of Persia took over.

21   This is exactly the message of GOD that Jeremiah had preached: the desolate land put to an extended sabbath rest, a seventy-year Sabbath rest making up for all the unkept Sabbaths.

KING CYRUS

22-23   In the first year of Cyrus king of Persia — this fulfilled the message of GOD preached by Jeremiah — GOD moved Cyrus king of Persia to make an official announcement throughout his kingdom; he wrote it out as follows: "From Cyrus king of Persia a proclamation: GOD, the God of the heavens, has given me all the kingdoms of the earth. He has also assigned me to build him a Temple of worship at Jerusalem in Judah. All who belong to GOD's people are urged to return — and may your GOD be with you! Move forward!"

EZRA

History had not treated the People of Israel well and they were in decline. A superpower military machine, Babylon, had battered them and then, leaving their city and temple a mound of rubble, hauled them off into exile. Now, 128 years later, a few Jews back in Jerusalem had been trying to put the pieces back together decade after weary decade. But it was not going well at all. They were hanging on by their fingernails. And then Ezra arrived.

This is an extreme case of a familiar story, repeated with variations in most centuries and in most places in the world. Men and women who find their basic identity in God, as God reveals himself in Israel and Messiah, don't find an easy time of it. They never have. They never will. Their identity is under constant challenge and threat — sometimes by hostile assault, at other times by subtle and smiling seductions. Whether by assault or seduction, the People of God have come perilously close to obliteration several times. We are never out of danger.

Because of Ezra, Israel made it through. God didn't leave Ezra to do this single-handedly; he gave him substantial and critical help in the rescue operation in the person of Nehemiah, whose work providentially converged with his. (Important details of the Ezra story are in the memoirs of Nehemiah, the book that follows this one.) The People-of-God identity was recovered and preserved. Ezra used Worship and Text to do it. Ezra engaged them in the worship of God, the most all-absorbing, comprehensive act in which men and women can engage. This is how our God-formed identities become most deeply embedded in us. And Ezra led them into an obedient listening to the text of Scripture. Listening and following God's revelation are the primary ways in which we keep attentively obedient to the living presence of God among us.

Ezra made his mark: Worship and Text continue to be foundational for recovering and maintaining identity as the People of God.

EZRA

CYRUS KING OF PERSIA: "BUILD THE TEMPLE OF GOD!"

1-4   **1** In the first year of Cyrus king of Persia—this fulfilled the Message of GOD preached by Jeremiah—GOD prodded Cyrus king of Persia to make an official announcement throughout his kingdom. He wrote it out as follows:

From Cyrus king of Persia, a Proclamation: GOD, the God of the heavens, has given me all the kingdoms of the earth. He has also assigned me to build him a Temple of worship in Jerusalem, Judah. Who among you belongs to his people? God be with you! Go to Jerusalem which is in Judah and build The Temple of GOD, the God of Israel, Jerusalem's God. Those who stay behind, wherever they happen to live, will support them with silver, gold, tools, and pack animals, along with Freewill-Offerings for The Temple of God in Jerusalem.

5-6   The heads of the families of Judah and Benjamin, along with the priests and Levites—everyone, in fact, God prodded—set out to build The Temple of GOD in Jerusalem. Their neighbors rallied behind them enthusiastically with silver, gold, tools, pack animals, expensive gifts, and, over and above these, Freewill-Offerings.

7-10   Also, King Cyrus turned over to them all the vessels and utensils from The Temple of GOD that Nebuchadnezzar had hauled from Jerusalem and put in the temple of his gods. Cyrus king of Persia put Mithredath the treasurer in charge of the transfer; he provided a full inventory for Sheshbazzar the prince of Judah, including the following:

30 gold dishes
  1,000 silver dishes
  29 silver pans
  30 gold bowls
  410 duplicate silver bowls
  1,000 miscellaneous items.

11   All told, there were 5,400 gold and silver articles that Sheshbazzar took with him when he brought the exiles back from Babylon to Jerusalem.

1-58   **2** These are the people from the province who now returned from the captivity, exiles whom Nebuchadnezzar king of Babylon had carried off captive. They returned to Jerusalem and Judah, each to his hometown. They came in company with Zerubbabel, Jeshua, Nehemiah, Seraiah, Reelaiah, Mordecai, Bilshan, Mispar, Bigvai, Rehum, and Baanah.

The numbers of the returning Israelites by families of origin were as follows:

Parosh, 2,172
Shephatiah, 372

Arah, 775
Pahath-Moab (sons of Jeshua and Joab), 2,812
Elam, 1,254
Zattu, 945
Zaccai, 760
Bani, 642
Bebai, 623
Azgad, 1,222
Adonikam, 666
Bigvai, 2,056
Adin, 454
Ater (sons of Hezekiah), 98
Bezai, 323
Jorah, 112
Hashum, 223
Gibbar, 95.

Israelites identified by place of origin were as follows:
Bethlehem, 123
Netophah, 56
Anathoth, 128
Azmaveth, 42
Kiriath Jearim, Kephirah, and Beeroth, 743
Ramah and Geba, 621
Micmash, 122
Bethel and Ai, 223
Nebo, 52
Magbish, 156
Elam (the other one), 1,254
Harim, 320
Lod, Hadid, and Ono, 725
Jericho, 345
Senaah, 3,630.

Priestly families:
Jedaiah (sons of Jeshua), 973
Immer, 1,052
Pashhur, 1,247
Harim, 1,017.

Levitical families:
Jeshua and Kadmiel (sons of Hodaviah), 74.

Singers:
Asaph's family line, 128.

Security guard families:
Shallum, Ater, Talmon, Akkub, Hatita, and Shobai, 139.

Families of temple support staff:
Ziha, Hasupha, Tabbaoth,
Keros, Siaha, Padon,
Lebanah, Hagabah, Akkub,
Hagab, Shalmai, Hanan,
Giddel, Gahar, Reaiah,
Rezin, Nekoda, Gazzam,
Uzza, Paseah, Besai,

Asnah, Meunim, Nephussim,
Bakbuk, Hakupha, Harhur,
Bazluth, Mehida, Harsha,
Barkos, Sisera, Temah,
Neziah, and Hatipha.
Families of Solomon's servants:
Sotai, Hassophereth, Peruda,
Jaala, Darkon, Giddel,
Shephatiah, Hattil, Pokereth-Hazzebaim, and Ami.
Temple support staff and Solomon's servants added up to 392.

59-60   These are those who came from Tel Melah, Tel Harsha, Kerub, Addon, and Immer. They weren't able to prove their ancestry, whether they were true Israelites or not:

61   Delaiah, Tobiah, and Nekoda, 652 in all.
Likewise with these priestly families:
Hobaiah, Hakkoz, and Barzillai, who had married a daughter of
Barzillai the Gileadite and took that name.

62-63   They had thoroughly searched for their family records but couldn't find them. And so they were barred from priestly work as ritually unclean. The governor ruled that they could not eat from the holy food until a priest could determine their status with the Urim and Thummim.

64-67   The total count for the congregation was 42,360. That did not include the male and female slaves, which numbered 7,337. There were also 200 male and female singers, and they had 736 horses, 245 mules, 435 camels, and 6,720 donkeys.

68-69   Some of the heads of families, on arriving at The Temple of GOD in Jerusalem, made Freewill-Offerings toward the rebuilding of The Temple of God on its site. They gave to the building fund as they were able, about 1,100 pounds of gold, about three tons of silver, and 100 priestly robes.

70   The priests, Levites, and some of the people lived in Jerusalem. The singers, security guards, and temple support staff found places in their hometowns. All the Israelites found a place to live.

THE BUILDING BEGUN: "THE FOUNDATION OF THE TEMPLE WAS LAID"

1-2   3 When the seventh month came and the Israelites had settled into their towns, the people assembled together in Jerusalem. Jeshua son of Jozadak and his brother priests, along with Zerubbabel, the son of Shealtiel, and his relatives, went to work and built the Altar of the God of Israel to offer Whole-Burnt-Offerings on it as written in The Revelation of Moses the man of God.

3-5   Even though they were afraid of what their non-Israelite neighbors might do, they went ahead anyway and set up the Altar on its foundations and offered Whole-Burnt-Offerings on it morning and evening. They also celebrated the Festival of Booths as prescribed and the daily Whole-Burnt-Offerings set for each day. And they presented the regular Whole-Burnt-Offerings for Sabbaths, New Moons, and GOD's Holy

Festivals, as well as Freewill-Offerings for GOD.

6   They began offering Whole-Burnt-Offerings to GOD from the very first day of the seventh month, even though The Temple of GOD's foundation had not yet been laid.

7   They gave money to hire masons and carpenters. They gave food, drink, and oil to the Sidonians and Tyrians in exchange for the cedar lumber they had brought by sea from Lebanon to Joppa, a shipment authorized by Cyrus the king of Persia.

8-9   In the second month of the second year after their arrival at The Temple of God in Jerusalem, Zerubbabel son of Shealtiel, and Jeshua son of Jozadak, in company with their brother priests and Levites and everyone else who had come back to Jerusalem from captivity, got started. They appointed the Levites twenty years of age and older to direct the rebuilding of The Temple of GOD. Jeshua and his family joined Kadmiel, Binnui, and Hodaviah, along with the extended family of Henadad — all Levites — to direct the work crew on The Temple of God.

10-11   When the workers laid the foundation of The Temple of GOD, the priests in their robes stood up with trumpets, and the Levites, sons of Asaph, with cymbals, to praise GOD in the tradition of David king of Israel. They sang antiphonally praise and thanksgiving to GOD:

Yes! GOD is good!
Oh yes — he'll never quit loving Israel!

11-13   All the people boomed out hurrahs, praising GOD as the foundation of The Temple of GOD was laid. As many were noisily shouting with joy, many of the older priests, Levites, and family heads who had seen the first Temple, when they saw the foundations of this Temple laid, wept loudly for joy. People couldn't distinguish the shouting from the weeping. The sound of their voices reverberated for miles around.

THE BUILDING STOPPED: "CEASE REBUILDING IN THAT CITY"

1-2   4 Old enemies of Judah and Benjamin heard that the exiles were building The Temple of the GOD of Israel. They came to Zerubbabel and the family heads and said, "We'll help you build. We worship your God the same as you. We've been offering sacrifices to him since Esarhaddon king of Assyria brought us here."

3   Zerubbabel, Jeshua, and the rest of the family heads of Israel said to them, "Nothing doing. Building The Temple of our God is not the same thing to you as to us. We alone will build for the GOD of Israel. We're the ones King Cyrus of Persia commanded to do it."

4-5   So these people started beating down the morale of the people of Judah, harassing them as they built. They even hired propagandists to sap their resolve. They kept this up for about fifteen years, throughout the lifetime of Cyrus king of Persia and on into the reign of Darius king of Persia.

6   In fact, in the reign of Xerxes, at the beginning of his reign, they wrote an accusation against those living in Judah and Jerusalem.

7   Again later, in the time of Artaxerxes, Bishlam, Mithredath, Tabeel, and their associates wrote regarding the Jerusalem business to Artaxerxes

king of Persia. The letter was written in Aramaic and translated. (What follows is written in Aramaic.)

8-16   Rehum the commanding officer and Shimshai the secretary wrote a letter against Jerusalem to Artaxerxes the king as follows:

> From: Rehum the commanding officer and Shimshai the secretary, backed by the rest of their associates, the judges and officials over the people from Tripolis, Persia, Erech, and Babylon, Elamites of Susa, and all the others whom the great and honorable Ashurbanipal deported and settled in the city of Samaria and other places in the land across the Euphrates.

(This is the copy of the letter they sent to him.)

> To: King Artaxerxes from your servants from the land across the Euphrates.
>
> We are here to inform the king that the Jews who came from you to us have arrived in Jerusalem and have set about rebuilding that rebellious and evil city. They are busy at work finishing the walls and rebuilding the foundations. The king needs to know that once that city is rebuilt and the wall completed they will no longer pay a penny of tribute, tax, or duty. The royal treasury will feel the loss. We're loyal to the king and cannot sit idly by while our king is being insulted — that's why we are passing this information on. We suggest that you look into the court records of your ancestors; you'll learn from those books that that city is a rebellious city, a thorn in the side to kings and provinces, a historic center of unrest and revolt. That's why the city was wiped out. We are letting the king know that if that city gets rebuilt and its walls restored, you'll end up with nothing in your province beyond the Euphrates.

17-22   The king sent his reply to Rehum the commanding officer, Shimshai the secretary, and the rest of their associates who lived in Samaria and other places beyond the Euphrates.

> Peace be with you. The letter that you sent has been translated and read to me. I gave orders to search the records, and sure enough it turns out that this city has revolted against kings time and again — rebellion is an old story there. I find that they've had their share of strong kings who have taken over beyond the Euphrates and exacted taxes, tribute, and duty. So do this: Order these men to stop work immediately — not a lick of rebuilding in that city unless I order it. Act quickly and firmly; they've done enough damage to kings!

23   The letter of King Artaxerxes was read to Rehum and Shimshai the secretary and their associates. They lost no time. They went to the Jews in Jerusalem and made them quit work.

24   That put a stop to the work on The Temple of God in Jerusalem. Nothing more was done until the second year of the reign of Darius king of Persia.

THE BUILDING RESUMED:
"HELP THE LEADERS IN THE REBUILDING"

1-2 5 Meanwhile the prophets Haggai and Zechariah son of Iddo were preaching to the Jews in Judah and Jerusalem in the authority of the God of Israel who ruled them. And so Zerubbabel son of Shealtiel and Jeshua son of Jozadak started again, rebuilding The Temple of God in Jerusalem. The prophets of God were right there helping them.

3-4 Tattenai was governor of the land beyond the Euphrates at this time. Tattenai, Shethar-Bozenai, and their associates came to the Israelites and asked, "Who issued you a permit to rebuild this Temple and restore it to use?" Then we told them the names of the men responsible for this construction work.

5 But God had his eye on the leaders of the Jews, and the work wasn't stopped until a report could reach Darius and an official reply be returned.

6-7 Tattenai, governor of the land beyond the Euphrates, and Shethar-Bozenai and his associates—the officials of that land—sent a letter to Darius the king. This is what they wrote to him:

To Darius the king. Peace and blessing!

8 We want to report to the king that we went to the province of Judah, to The Temple of the great God that is being rebuilt with large stones. Timbers are being fitted into the walls; the work is going on with great energy and in good time.

9-10 We asked the leaders, "Who issued you the permit to rebuild this Temple and restore it to use?" We also asked for their names so we could pass them on to you and have a record of the men at the head of the construction work.

11-12 This is what they told us: "We are servants of the God of the heavens and the earth. We are rebuilding The Temple that was built a long time ago. A great king of Israel built it, the entire structure. But our ancestors made the God of the heavens really angry and he turned them over to Nebuchadnezzar, king of Babylon, the Chaldean, who knocked this Temple down and took the people to Babylon in exile.

13-16 "But when Cyrus became king of Babylon, in his first year he issued a building permit to rebuild this Temple of God. He also gave back the gold and silver vessels of The Temple of God that Nebuchadnezzar had carted off and put in the Babylon temple. Cyrus the king removed them from the temple of Babylon and turned them over to Sheshbazzar, the man he had appointed governor. He told him, 'Take these vessels and place them in The Temple of Jerusalem and rebuild The Temple of God on its original site.' And Sheshbazzar did it. He laid the foundation of The Temple of God in Jerusalem. It has been under construction ever since but it is not yet finished."

17 So now, if it please the king, look up the records in the royal archives in Babylon and see if it is indeed a fact that Cyrus the king issued an official building permit authorizing the rebuilding of The Temple of God in Jerusalem. And then send the king's ruling on this matter to us.

1-3 **6** So King Darius ordered a search through the records in the archives in Babylon. Eventually a scroll was turned up in the fortress of Ecbatana over in the province of Media, with this writing on it:

Memorandum

In his first year as king, Cyrus issued an official decree regarding The Temple of God in Jerusalem, as follows:

3-5   The Temple where sacrifices are offered is to be rebuilt on new foundations. It is to be ninety feet high and ninety feet wide with three courses of large stones topped with one course of timber. The cost is to be paid from the royal bank. The gold and silver vessels from The Temple of God that Nebuchadnezzar carried to Babylon are to be returned to The Temple at Jerusalem, each to its proper place; place them in The Temple of God.

6-7   Now listen, Tattenai governor of the land beyond the Euphrates, Shethar-Bozenai, associates, and all officials of that land: Stay out of their way. Leave the governor and leaders of the Jews alone so they can work on that Temple of God as they rebuild it.

8-10   I hereby give official orders on how you are to help the leaders of the Jews in the rebuilding of that Temple of God:

    1. All construction costs are to be paid to these men from the royal bank out of the taxes coming in from the land beyond the Euphrates. And pay them on time, without delays.
    2. Whatever is required for their worship — young bulls, rams, and lambs for Whole-Burnt-Offerings to the God-of-Heaven; and whatever wheat, salt, wine, and anointing oil the priests of Jerusalem request — is to be given to them daily without delay so that they may make sacrifices to the God-of-Heaven and pray for the life of the king and his sons.

11-12   I've issued an official decree that anyone who violates this order is to be impaled on a timber torn out of his own house, and the house itself made a manure pit. And may the God who put his Name on that place wipe out any king or people who dares to defy this decree and destroy The Temple of God at Jerusalem.

    I, Darius, have issued an official decree. Carry it out precisely and promptly.

13   Tattenai governor of the land across the Euphrates, Shethar-Bozenai, and their associates did it: They carried out the decree of Darius precisely and promptly.

THE BUILDING COMPLETED:
"EXUBERANTLY CELEBRATED THE DEDICATION"

14-15 So the leaders of the Jews continued to build; the work went well under the preaching of the prophets Haggai and Zechariah son of Iddo. They completed the rebuilding under orders of the God of Israel and authorization by Cyrus, Darius, and Artaxerxes, kings of Persia. The Temple was completed on the third day of the month Adar in the sixth year of the reign of King Darius.

16-18   And then the Israelites celebrated—priests, Levites, every last exile, exuberantly celebrated the dedication of The Temple of God. At the dedication of this Temple of God they sacrificed a hundred bulls, two hundred rams, and four hundred lambs—and, as an Absolution-Offering for all Israel, twelve he-goats, one for each of the twelve tribes of Israel. They placed the priests in their divisions and the Levites in their places for the service of God at Jerusalem—all as written out in the Book of Moses.

19   On the fourteenth day of the first month, the exiles celebrated the Passover.

20   All the priests and Levites had purified themselves—all, no exceptions. They were all ritually clean. The Levites slaughtered the Passover lamb for the exiles, their brother priests, and themselves.

21-22   Then the Israelites who had returned from exile, along with everyone who had removed themselves from the defilements of the nations to join them and seek GOD, the God of Israel, ate the Passover. With great joy they celebrated the Feast of Unraised Bread for seven days. GOD had plunged them into a sea of joy; he had changed the mind of the king of Assyria to back them in rebuilding The Temple of God, the God of Israel.

EZRA ARRIVES

1-5   After all this, Ezra. It was during the reign of Artaxerxes king of Persia. Ezra was the son of Seraiah, son of Azariah, son of Hilkiah, son of Shallum, son of Zadok, son of Ahitub, son of Amariah, son of Azariah, son of Meraioth, son of Zerahiah, son of Uzzi, son of Bukki, son of Abishua, son of Phinehas, son of Eleazar, son of Aaron the high priest.

6-7   That's Ezra. He arrived from Babylon, a scholar well-practiced in the Revelation of Moses that the GOD of Israel had given. Because GOD's hand was on Ezra, the king gave him everything he asked for. Some of the Israelites—priests, Levites, singers, temple security guards, and temple slaves—went with him to Jerusalem. It was in the seventh year of Artaxerxes the king.

8-10   They arrived at Jerusalem in the fifth month of the seventh year of the king's reign. Ezra had scheduled their departure from Babylon on the first day of the first month; they arrived in Jerusalem on the first day of the fifth month under the generous guidance of his God. Ezra had committed himself to studying the Revelation of GOD, to living it, and to teaching Israel to live its truths and ways.

11   What follows is the letter that King Artaxerxes gave Ezra, priest and scholar, expert in matters involving the truths and ways of GOD concerning Israel:

12-20   Artaxerxes, King of Kings, to Ezra the priest, a scholar of the Teaching of the God-of-Heaven.

Peace. I hereby decree that any of the people of Israel living in my kingdom who want to go to Jerusalem, including their priests and Levites, may go with you. You are being sent by the king and his seven advisors to carry out an investigation of Judah and Jerusalem in relation to the Teaching of your God that you are carrying with you. You are also authorized to take the silver and gold that the king and his advisors are giving for the God of Israel, whose residence is in Jerusalem, along with all the silver and gold that has been collected from the generously donated offerings all over Babylon, including that from the people and the priests, for The Temple of their God in Jerusalem. Use this money carefully to buy bulls, rams, lambs, and the ingredients for Grain-Offerings and Drink-Offerings and then offer them on the Altar of The Temple of your God in Jerusalem. You are free to use whatever is left over from the silver and gold for what you and your brothers decide is in keeping with the will of your God. Deliver to the God of Jerusalem the vessels given to you for the services of worship in The Temple of your God. Whatever else you need for The Temple of your God you may pay for out of the royal bank.

21-23   I, Artaxerxes the king, have formally authorized and ordered all the treasurers of the land across the Euphrates to give Ezra the priest, scholar of the Teaching of the God-of-Heaven, the full amount of whatever he asks for up to 100 talents of silver, 650 bushels of wheat, and 607 gallons each of wine and olive oil. There is no limit on the salt. Everything the God-of-Heaven requires for The Temple of God must be given without hesitation. Why would the king and his sons risk stirring up his wrath?

24   Also, let it be clear that no one is permitted to impose tribute, tax, or duty on any priest, Levite, singer, temple security guard, temple servant, or any other worker connected with The Temple of God.

25   I authorize you, Ezra, exercising the wisdom of God that you have in your hands, to appoint magistrates and judges so they can administer justice among all the people of the land across the Euphrates who live by the Teaching of your God. Anyone who does not know the Teaching, you teach them.

26   Anyone who does not obey the Teaching of your God and the king must be tried and sentenced at once—death, banishment, a fine, prison, whatever.

EZRA: "I WAS READY TO GO"

27-28   Blessed be GOD, the God-of-Our-Fathers, who put it in the mind of the king to beautify The Temple of GOD in Jerusalem! Not only that, he caused the king and all his advisors and influential officials actually to like me and back me. My God was on my side and I was ready to go. And I organized all the leaders of Israel to go with me.

1-14   **8** These are the family heads and those who signed up to go up with me from Babylon in the reign of Artaxerxes the king:

From the family of Phinehas: Gershom
Family of Ithamar: Daniel
Family of David: Hattush
Family of Shecaniah
Family of Parosh: Zechariah, and with him 150 men signed up
Family of Pahath-Moab: Eliehoenai son of Zerahiah, and 200 men
Family of Zattu: Shecaniah son of Jahaziel, and 300 men
Family of Adin: Ebed son of Jonathan, and 50 men

Family of Elam: Jeshaiah son of Athaliah, and 70 men
Family of Shephatiah: Zebadiah son of Michael, and 80 men
Family of Joab: Obadiah son of Jehiel, and 218 men
Family of Bani: Shelomith son of Josiphiah, and 160 men
Family of Bebai: Zechariah son of Bebai, and 28 men
Family of Azgad: Johanan son of Hakkatan, and 110 men
Family of Adonikam (bringing up the rear): their names were
    Eliphelet, Jeuel, Shemaiah, and 60 men
Family of Bigvai: Uthai and Zaccur, and 70 men.

15-17   I gathered them together at the canal that runs to Ahava. We camped there three days. I looked them over and found that they were all laymen and priests but no Levites. So I sent for the leaders Eliezer, Ariel, Shemaiah, Elnathan, Jarib, Elnathan, Nathan, Zechariah, and Meshullam, and for the teachers Joiarib and Elnathan. I then sent them to Iddo, who is head of the town of Casiphia, and told them what to say to Iddo and his relatives who lived there in Casiphia: "Send us ministers for The Temple of God."

18-20   Well, the generous hand of our God was on us, and they brought back to us a wise man from the family of Mahli son of Levi, the son of Israel. His name was Sherebiah. With sons and brothers they numbered eighteen. They also brought Hashabiah and Jeshaiah of the family of Merari, with brothers and their sons, another twenty. And then there were 220 temple servants, descendants of the temple servants that David and the princes had assigned to help the Levites in their work. They were all signed up by name.

21-22   I proclaimed a fast there beside the Ahava Canal, a fast to humble ourselves before our God and pray for wise guidance for our journey—all our people and possessions. I was embarrassed to ask the king for a cavalry bodyguard to protect us from bandits on the road. We had just told the king, "Our God lovingly looks after all those who seek him, but turns away in disgust from those who leave him."

23   So we fasted and prayed about these concerns. And he listened.

24-27   Then I picked twelve of the leading priests—Sherebiah and Hashabiah with ten of their brothers. I weighed out for them the silver, the gold, the vessels, and the offerings for The Temple of our God that the king, his advisors, and all the Israelites had given:

    25 tons of silver
    100 vessels of silver valued at three and three-quarter tons of gold
    20 gold bowls weighing eighteen and a half pounds
    2 vessels of bright red copper, as valuable as gold.

28-29   I said to them, "You are holy to GOD and these vessels are holy. The silver and gold are Freewill-Offerings to the GOD of your ancestors. Guard them with your lives until you're able to weigh them out in a secure place in The Temple of our God for the priests and Levites and family heads who are in charge in Jerusalem."

30   The priests and Levites took charge of all that had been weighed out to them, and prepared to deliver it to Jerusalem to The Temple of our God.

31 We left the Ahava Canal on the twelfth day of the first month to travel to Jerusalem. God was with us all the way and kept us safe from bandits and highwaymen.

32-34 We arrived in Jerusalem and waited there three days. On the fourth day the silver and gold and vessels were weighed out in The Temple of our God into the hands of Meremoth son of Uriah, the priest. Eleazar son of Phinehas was there with him, also the Levites Jozabad son of Jeshua and Noadiah son of Binnui. Everything was counted and weighed and the totals recorded.

35 When they arrived, the exiles, now returned from captivity, offered Whole-Burnt-Offerings to the God of Israel:

> 12 bulls, representing all Israel
> 96 rams
> 77 lambs
> 12 he-goats as an Absolution-Offering.

All of this was sacrificed as a Whole-Burnt-Offering to GOD.

36 They also delivered the king's orders to the king's provincial administration assigned to the land beyond the Euphrates. They, in turn, gave their support to the people and The Temple of God.

EZRA PRAYS: "LOOK AT US . . . GUILTY BEFORE YOU"

1-2 9 After all this was done, the leaders came to me and said, "The People of Israel, priests and Levites included, have not kept themselves separate from the neighboring people around here with all their vulgar obscenities—Canaanites, Hittites, Perizzites, Jebusites, Ammonites, Moabites, Egyptians, Amorites. They have given some of their daughters in marriage to them and have taken some of their daughters for marriage to their sons. The holy seed is now all mixed in with these other peoples. And our leaders have led the way in this betrayal."

3 When I heard all this, I ripped my clothes and my cape; I pulled hair from my head and out of my beard; I slumped to the ground, appalled.

4-6 Many were in fear and trembling because of what God was saying about the betrayal by the exiles. They gathered around me as I sat there in despair, waiting for the evening sacrifice. At the evening sacrifice I picked myself up from my utter devastation, and in my ripped clothes and cape fell to my knees and stretched out my hands to GOD, my God. And I prayed:

6-7 "My dear God, I'm so totally ashamed, I can't bear to face you. O my God—our iniquities are piled up so high that we can't see out; our guilt touches the skies. We've been stuck in a muck of guilt since the time of our ancestors until right now; we and our kings and priests, because of our sins, have been turned over to foreign kings, to killing, to captivity, to looting, and to public shame—just as you see us now.

8-9 "Now for a brief time GOD, our God, has allowed us, this battered band, to get a firm foothold in his holy place so that our God may brighten our eyes and lighten our burdens as we serve out this hard sentence. We were slaves; yet even as slaves, our God didn't abandon us. He has put us in the good graces of the kings of Persia and given us the heart to build The

Temple of our God, restore its ruins, and construct a defensive wall in Judah and Jerusalem.

¹⁰⁻¹² "And now, our God, after all this what can we say for ourselves? For we have thrown your commands to the wind, the commands you gave us through your servants the prophets. They told us, 'The land you're taking over is a polluted land, polluted with the obscene vulgarities of the people who live there; they've filled it with their moral rot from one end to the other. Whatever you do, don't give your daughters in marriage to their sons nor marry your sons to their daughters. Don't cultivate their good opinion; don't make over them and get them to like you so you can make a lot of money and build up a tidy estate to hand down to your children.'

¹³⁻¹⁵ "And now this, on top of all we've already suffered because of our evil ways and accumulated guilt, even though you, dear God, punished us far less than we deserved and even went ahead and gave us this present escape. Yet here we are, at it again, breaking your commandments by intermarrying with the people who practice all these obscenities! Are you angry to the point of wiping us out completely, without even a few stragglers, with no way out at all? You are the righteous GOD of Israel. We are, right now, a small band of escapees. Look at us, openly standing here, guilty before you. No one can last long like this."

EZRA TAKES CHARGE

10 ¹ Ezra wept, prostrate in front of The Temple of God. As he prayed and confessed, a huge number of the men, women, and children of Israel gathered around him. All the people were now weeping as if their hearts would break.

²⁻³ Shecaniah son of Jehiel of the family of Elam, acting as spokesman, said to Ezra: "We betrayed our God by marrying foreign wives from the people around here. But all is not lost; there is still hope for Israel. Let's make a covenant right now with our God, agreeing to get rid of all these wives and their children, just as my master and those who honor God's commandment are saying. It's what The Revelation says, so let's do it.

⁴ "Now get up, Ezra. Take charge—we're behind you. Don't back down."

⁵ So Ezra stood up and had the leaders of the priests, the Levites, and all Israel solemnly swear to do what Shecaniah proposed. And they did it.

⁶ Then Ezra left the plaza in front of The Temple of God and went to the home of Jehohanan son of Eliashib where he stayed, still fasting from food and drink, continuing his mourning over the betrayal by the exiles.

⁷⁻⁸ A notice was then sent throughout Judah and Jerusalem ordering all the exiles to meet in Jerusalem. Anyone who failed to show up in three days, in compliance with the ruling of the leaders and elders, would have all his possessions confiscated and be thrown out of the congregation of the returned exiles.

⁹ All the men of Judah and Benjamin met in Jerusalem within the three days. It was the twentieth day of the ninth month. They all sat down in the plaza in front of The Temple of God. Because of the business before them, and aggravated by the buckets of rain coming down on them, they were restless, uneasy, and anxious.

¹⁰⁻¹¹ Ezra the priest stood up and spoke: "You've broken trust. You've

married foreign wives. You've piled guilt on Israel. Now make your confession to GOD, the God of your ancestors, and do what he wants you to do: Separate yourselves from the people of the land and from your foreign wives."

12 The whole congregation responded with a shout, "Yes, we'll do it — just the way you said it!"

13-14 They also said, "But look, do you see how many people there are out here? And it's the rainy season; you can't expect us to stand out here soaking wet until this is done — why, it will take days! A lot of us are deeply involved in this transgression. Let our leaders act on behalf of the whole congregation. Have everybody who lives in cities and who has married a foreign wife come at an appointed time, accompanied by the elders and judges of each city. We'll keep at this until the hot anger of our God over this thing is turned away."

15-17 Only Jonathan son of Asahel and Jahzeiah son of Tikvah, supported by Meshullam and Shabbethai the Levite, opposed this. So the exiles went ahead with the plan. Ezra the priest picked men who were family heads, each one by name. They sat down together on the first day of the tenth month to pursue the matter. By the first day of the first month they had finished dealing with every man who had married a foreign wife.

18-19 Among the families of priests, the following were found to have married foreign wives:

The family of Jeshua son of Jozadak and his brothers: Maaseiah, Eliezer, Jarib, and Gedaliah. They all promised to divorce their wives and sealed it with a handshake. For their guilt they brought a ram from the flock as a Compensation-Offering.

20 The family of Immer: Hanani and Zebadiah.

21 The family of Harim: Maaseiah, Elijah, Shemaiah, Jehiel, and Uzziah.

22 The family of Pashhur: Elioenai, Maaseiah, Ishmael, Nethanel, Jozabad, and Elasah.

23 From the Levites: Jozabad, Shimei, Kelaiah — that is, Kelita — Pethahiah, Judah, and Eliezer.

24 From the singers: Eliashib.

From the temple security guards: Shallum, Telem, and Uri.

25 And from the other Israelites:

The family of Parosh: Ramiah, Izziah, Malkijah, Mijamin, Eleazar, Malkijah, and Benaiah.

26 The family of Elam: Mattaniah, Zechariah, Jehiel, Abdi, Jeremoth, and Elijah.

27 The family of Zattu: Elioenai, Eliashib, Mattaniah, Jeremoth, Zabad, and Aziza.

28 The family of Bebai: Jehohanan, Hananiah, Zabbai, and Athlai.

29 The family of Bani: Meshullam, Malluch, Adaiah, Jashub, Sheal, and Jeremoth.

30 The family of Pahath-Moab: Adna, Kelal, Benaiah, Maaseiah, Mattaniah, Bezalel, Binnui, and Manasseh.

31-32 The family of Harim: Eliezer, Ishijah, Malkijah, Shemaiah, Shimeon, Benjamin, Malluch, and Shemariah.

33 The family of Hashum: Mattenai, Mattattah, Zabad, Eliphelet, Jeremai, Manasseh, and Shimei.

34-37   The family of Bani: Maadai, Amram, Uel, Benaiah, Bedeiah, Keluhi, Vaniah, Meremoth, Eliashib, Mattaniah, Mattenai, and Jaasu.

38-42   The family of Binnui: Shimei, Shelemiah, Nathan, Adaiah, Macnadebai, Shashai, Sharai, Azarel, Shelemiah, Shemariah, Shallum, Amariah, and Joseph.

43   The family of Nebo: Jeiel, Mattithiah, Zabad, Zebina, Jaddai, Joel, and Benaiah.

44   All these had married foreign wives and some had also had children by them.

NEHEMIAH

Separating life into distinct categories of "sacred" and "secular" damages, sometimes irreparably, any attempt to live a whole and satisfying life, a coherent life with meaning and purpose, a life lived to the glory of God. Nevertheless, the practice is widespread. But where did all these people come up with the habit of separating themselves and the world around them into these two camps? It surely wasn't from the Bible. The Holy Scriptures, from beginning to end, strenuously resist such a separation.

The damage to life is most obvious when the separation is applied to daily work. It is common for us to refer to the work of pastors, priests, and missionaries as "sacred," and that of lawyers, farmers, and engineers as "secular." It is also wrong. Work, by its very nature, is holy. The biblical story is dominated by people who have jobs in gardening, shepherding, the military, politics, carpentry, tent making, homemaking, fishing, and more.

Nehemiah is one of these. He started out as a government worker in the employ of a foreign king. Then he became—and this is the work he tells us of in these memoirs—a building contractor, called in to rebuild the walls of Jerusalem. His coworker Ezra was a scholar and teacher, working with the Scriptures. Nehemiah worked with stones and mortar. The stories of the two men are interwoven in a seamless fabric of vocational holiness. Neither job was more or less important or holy than the other. Nehemiah needed Ezra; Ezra needed Nehemiah. God's people needed the work of both of them. We still do.

NEHEMIAH

1-2 The memoirs of Nehemiah son of Hacaliah.

It was the month of Kislev in the twentieth year. At the time I was in the palace complex at Susa. Hanani, one of my brothers, had just arrived from Judah with some fellow Jews. I asked them about the conditions among the Jews there who had survived the exile, and about Jerusalem.

3 They told me, "The exile survivors who are left there in the province are in bad shape. Conditions are appalling. The wall of Jerusalem is still rubble; the city gates are still cinders."

4 When I heard this, I sat down and wept. I mourned for days, fasting and praying before the God-of-Heaven.

5-6 I said, "GOD, God-of-Heaven, the great and awesome God, loyal to his covenant and faithful to those who love him and obey his commands: Look at me, listen to me. Pay attention to this prayer of your servant that I'm praying day and night in intercession for your servants, the People of Israel, confessing the sins of the People of Israel. And I'm including myself, I and my ancestors, among those who have sinned against you.

7-9 "We've treated you like dirt: We haven't done what you told us, haven't followed your commands, and haven't respected the decisions you gave to Moses your servant. All the same, remember the warning you posted to your servant Moses: 'If you betray me, I'll scatter you to the four winds, but if you come back to me and do what I tell you, I'll gather up all these scattered peoples from wherever they ended up and put them back in the place I chose to mark with my Name.'

10-11 "Well, there they are—your servants, your people whom you so powerfully and impressively redeemed. O Master, listen to me, listen to your servant's prayer—and yes, to all your servants who delight in honoring you—and make me successful today so that I get what I want from the king."

I was cupbearer to the king.

2 It was the month of Nisan in the twentieth year of Artaxerxes the king. At the hour for serving wine I brought it in and gave it to the king. I had never been hangdog in his presence before, so he asked me, "Why the long face? You're not sick are you? Or are you depressed?"

2-3 That made me all the more agitated. I said, "Long live the king! And why shouldn't I be depressed when the city, the city where all my family is buried, is in ruins and the city gates have been reduced to cinders?"

4-5 The king then asked me, "So what do you want?"

Praying under my breath to the God-of-Heaven, I said, "If it please the king, and if the king thinks well of me, send me to Judah, to the city where my family is buried, so that I can rebuild it."

6 The king, with the queen sitting alongside him, said, "How long will your work take and when would you expect to return?"

I gave him a time, and the king gave his approval to send me.

7-8 Then I said, "If it please the king, provide me with letters to the governors across the Euphrates that authorize my travel through to Judah; and also an order to Asaph, keeper of the king's forest, to supply me with timber for the beams of The Temple fortress, the wall of the city, and the house where I'll be living."

8-9   The generous hand of my God was with me in this and the king gave them to me. When I met the governors across The River (the Euphrates) I showed them the king's letters. The king even sent along a cavalry escort.

10   When Sanballat the Horonite and Tobiah the Ammonite official heard about this, they were very upset, angry that anyone would come to look after the interests of the People of Israel.

"COME — LET'S BUILD THE WALL OF JERUSALEM"

11-12   And so I arrived in Jerusalem. After I had been there three days, I got up in the middle of the night, I and a few men who were with me. I hadn't told anyone what my God had put in my heart to do for Jerusalem. The only animal with us was the one I was riding.

13-16   Under cover of night I went past the Valley Gate toward the Dragon's Fountain to the Dung Gate looking over the walls of Jerusalem, which had been broken through and whose gates had been burned up. I then crossed to the Fountain Gate and headed for the King's Pool but there wasn't enough room for the donkey I was riding to get through. So I went up the valley in the dark continuing my inspection of the wall. I came back in through the Valley Gate. The local officials had no idea where I'd gone or what I was doing — I hadn't breathed a word to the Jews, priests, nobles, local officials, or anyone else who would be working on the job.

17-18   Then I gave them my report: "Face it: we're in a bad way here. Jerusalem is a wreck; its gates are burned up. Come — let's build the wall of Jerusalem and not live with this disgrace any longer." I told them how God was supporting me and how the king was backing me up.

They said, "We're with you. Let's get started." They rolled up their sleeves, ready for the good work.

19   When Sanballat the Horonite, Tobiah the Ammonite official, and Geshem the Arab heard about it, they laughed at us, mocking, "Ha! What do you think you're doing? Do you think you can cross the king?"

20   I shot back, "The God-of-Heaven will make sure we succeed. We're his servants and we're going to work, rebuilding. You can keep your nose out of it. You get no say in this — Jerusalem's none of your business!"

3
1-2   The high priest Eliashib and his fellow priests were up and at it: They went to work on the Sheep Gate; they repaired it and hung its doors, continuing on as far as the Tower of the Hundred and the Tower of Hananel. The men of Jericho worked alongside them; and next to them, Zaccur son of Imri.

3-5   The Fish Gate was built by the Hassenaah brothers; they repaired it, hung its doors, and installed its bolts and bars. Meremoth son of Uriah, the son of Hakkoz, worked; next to him Meshullam son of Berekiah, the son of Meshezabel; next to him Zadok son of Baana; and next to him the Tekoites (except for their nobles, who wouldn't work with their master and refused to get their hands dirty with such work).

6-8   The Jeshanah Gate was rebuilt by Joiada son of Paseah and Meshullam son of Besodeiah; they repaired it, hung its doors, and installed its bolts and bars. Melatiah the Gibeonite, Jadon the Meronothite, and the men of Gibeon and Mizpah, which was under the rule of the governor from across the Euphrates, worked alongside them. Uzziel son of Harhaiah of the goldsmiths' guild worked next to him, and next to him Hananiah, one of the perfumers. They rebuilt the wall of Jerusalem as far as the Broad Wall.

9-10 The next section was worked on by Rephaiah son of Hur, mayor of a half-district of Jerusalem. Next to him Jedaiah son of Harumaph rebuilt the front of his house; Hattush son of Hashabneiah worked next to him.

11-12 Malkijah son of Harim and Hasshub son of Pahath-Moab rebuilt another section that included the Tower of Furnaces. Working next to him was Shallum son of Hallohesh, mayor of the other half-district of Jerusalem, along with his daughters.

13 The Valley Gate was rebuilt by Hanun and villagers of Zanoah; they repaired it, hung its doors, and installed its bolts and bars. They went on to repair 1,500 feet of the wall, as far as the Dung Gate.

14 The Dung Gate itself was rebuilt by Malkijah son of Recab, the mayor of the district of Beth Hakkerem; he repaired it, hung its doors, and installed its bolts and bars.

15 The Fountain Gate was rebuilt by Shallun son of Col-Hozeh, mayor of the Mizpah district; he repaired it, roofed it, hung its doors, and installed its bolts and bars. He also rebuilt the wall of the Pool of Siloam at the King's Garden as far as the steps that go down from the City of David.

16 After him came Nehemiah son of Azbuk, mayor of half the district of Beth Zur. He worked from just in front of the Tomb of David as far as the Pool and the House of Heroes.

17-18 Levites under Rehum son of Bani were next in line. Alongside them, Hashabiah, mayor of half the district of Keilah, represented his district in the rebuilding. Next to him their brothers continued the rebuilding under Binnui son of Henadad, mayor of the other half-district of Keilah.

19-23 The section from in front of the Ascent to the Armory as far as the Angle was rebuilt by Ezer son of Jeshua, the mayor of Mizpah. From the Angle to the door of the house of Eliashib the high priest was done by Baruch son of Zabbai. Meremoth son of Uriah, the son of Hakkoz, took it from the door of Eliashib's house to the end of Eliashib's house. Priests from the neighborhood went on from there. Benjamin and Hasshub worked on the wall in front of their house, and Azariah son of Maaseiah, the son of Ananiah, did the work alongside his house.

24-27 The section from the house of Azariah to the Angle at the Corner was rebuilt by Binnui son of Henadad. Palal son of Uzai worked opposite the Angle and the tower that projects from the Upper Palace of the king near the Court of the Guard. Next to him Pedaiah son of Parosh and The Temple support staff who lived on the hill of Ophel worked up to the point opposite the Water Gate eastward and the projecting tower. The men of Tekoa did the section from the great projecting tower as far as the wall of Ophel.

28-30 Above the Horse Gate the priests worked, each priest repairing the wall in front of his own house. After them Zadok son of Immer rebuilt in front of his house and after him Shemaiah son of Shecaniah, the keeper of the East Gate; then Hananiah son of Shelemiah and Hanun, the sixth son of

Zalaph; then Meshullam son of Berekiah rebuilt the wall in front of his storage shed.

31-32   Malkijah the goldsmith repaired the wall as far as the house of The Temple support staff and merchants, up to the Inspection Gate, and the Upper Room at the Corner. The goldsmiths and the merchants made the repairs between the Upper Room at the Corner and the Sheep Gate.

"I STATIONED ARMED GUARDS"

1-2   **4** When Sanballat heard that we were rebuilding the wall he exploded in anger, vilifying the Jews. In the company of his Samaritan cronies and military he let loose: "What are these miserable Jews doing? Do they think they can get everything back to normal overnight? Make building stones out of make-believe?"

3   At his side, Tobiah the Ammonite jumped in and said, "That's right! What do they think they're building? Why, if a fox climbed that wall, it would fall to pieces under his weight."

4-5   Nehemiah prayed, "Oh listen to us, dear God. We're so despised: Boomerang their ridicule on their heads; have their enemies cart them off as war trophies to a land of no return; don't forgive their iniquity, don't wipe away their sin — they've insulted the builders!"

6   We kept at it, repairing and rebuilding the wall. The whole wall was soon joined together and halfway to its intended height because the people had a heart for the work.

7-9   When Sanballat, Tobiah, the Arabs, the Ammonites, and the Ashdodites heard that the repairs of the walls of Jerusalem were going so well — that the breaks in the wall were being fixed — they were absolutely furious. They put their heads together and decided to fight against Jerusalem and create as much trouble as they could. We countered with prayer to our God and set a round-the-clock guard against them.

10   But soon word was going around in Judah,

> The builders are pooped,
>   the rubbish piles up;
> We're in over our heads,
>   we can't build this wall.

11-12   And all this time our enemies were saying, "They won't know what hit them. Before they know it we'll be at their throats, killing them right and left. *That* will put a stop to the work!" The Jews who were their neighbors kept reporting, "They have us surrounded; they're going to attack!" If we heard it once, we heard it ten times.

13-14   So I stationed armed guards at the most vulnerable places of the wall and assigned people by families with their swords, lances, and bows. After looking things over I stood up and spoke to the nobles, officials, and everyone else: "Don't be afraid of them. Put your minds on the Master, great and awesome, and then fight for your brothers, your sons, your daughters, your wives, and your homes."

15-18   Our enemies learned that we knew all about their plan and that God had frustrated it. And we went back to the wall and went to work. From then on half of my young men worked while the other half stood guard with lances, shields, bows, and mail armor. Military officers served as backup for everyone in Judah who was at work rebuilding the wall. The common laborers held a tool in one hand and a spear in the other. Each of the builders had a sword strapped to his side as he worked. I kept the trumpeter at my side to sound the alert.

19-20   Then I spoke to the nobles and officials and everyone else: "There's a lot of work going on and we are spread out all along the wall, separated from each other. When you hear the trumpet call, join us there; our God will fight for us."

21   And so we kept working, from first light until the stars came out, half of us holding lances.

22   I also instructed the people, "Each person and his helper is to stay inside Jerusalem — guards by night and workmen by day."

23   We all slept in our clothes — I, my brothers, my workmen, and the guards backing me up. And each one kept his spear in his hand, even when getting water.

THE "GREAT PROTEST"

1-2   **5** A great protest was mounted by the people, including the wives, against their fellow Jews. Some said, "We have big families, and we need food just to survive."

3   Others said, "We're having to mortgage our fields and vineyards and homes to get enough grain to keep from starving."

4-5   And others said, "We're having to borrow money to pay the royal tax on our fields and vineyards. Look: We're the same flesh and blood as our brothers here; our children are just as good as theirs. Yet here we are having to sell our children off as slaves — some of our daughters have already been sold — and we can't do anything about it because our fields and vineyards are owned by somebody else."

6-7   I got really angry when I heard their protest and complaints. After thinking it over, I called the nobles and officials on the carpet. I said, "Each one of you is gouging his brother."

7-8   Then I called a big meeting to deal with them. I told them, "We did everything we could to buy back our Jewish brothers who had to sell themselves as slaves to foreigners. And now you're selling these same brothers back into debt slavery! Does that mean that we have to buy them back again?"

They said nothing. What could they say?

9   "What you're doing is wrong. Is there no fear of God left in you? Don't you care what the nations around here, our enemies, think of you?

10-11   "I and my brothers and the people working for me have also loaned them money. But this gouging them with interest has to stop. Give them back their foreclosed fields, vineyards, olive groves, and homes right now. And forgive your claims on their money, grain, new wine, and olive oil."

12-13   They said, "We'll give it all back. We won't make any more demands on them. We'll do everything you say."

Then I called the priests together and made them promise to keep their word. Then I emptied my pockets, turning them inside out, and said, "So may God empty the pockets and house of everyone who doesn't keep this promise — turned inside out and emptied."

Everyone gave a wholehearted "Yes, we'll do it!" and praised GOD. And the people did what they promised.

"Rᴇᴍᴇᴍʙᴇʀ ɪɴ Mʏ Fᴀᴠᴏʀ, O Mʏ Gᴏᴅ"

14-16 From the time King Artaxerxes appointed me as their governor in the land of Judah — from the twentieth to the thirty-second year of his reign, twelve years — neither I nor my brothers used the governor's food allowance. Governors who had preceded me had oppressed the people by taxing them forty shekels of silver (about a pound) a day for food and wine while their underlings bullied the people unmercifully. But out of fear of God I did none of that. I had work to do; I worked on this wall. All my men were on the job to do the work. We didn't have time to line our own pockets.

17-18 I fed 150 Jews and officials at my table in addition to those who showed up from the surrounding nations. One ox, six choice sheep, and some chickens were prepared for me daily, and every ten days a large supply of wine was delivered. Even so, I didn't use the food allowance provided for the governor — the people had it hard enough as it was.

19 Remember in my favor, O my God,
Everything I've done for these people.

"I'ᴍ Dᴏɪɴɢ ᴀ Gʀᴇᴀᴛ Wᴏʀᴋ; I Cᴀɴ'ᴛ Cᴏᴍᴇ Dᴏᴡɴ"

1-2 6When Sanballat, Tobiah, Geshem the Arab, and the rest of our enemies heard that I had rebuilt the wall and that there were no more breaks in it — even though I hadn't yet installed the gates — Sanballat and Geshem sent this message: "Come and meet with us at Kephirim in the valley of Ono."

2-3 I knew they were scheming to hurt me so I sent messengers back with this: "I'm doing a great work; I can't come down. Why should the work come to a standstill just so I can come down to see you?"

4 Four times they sent this message and four times I gave them my answer.

5-6 The fifth time — same messenger, same message — Sanballat sent an unsealed letter with this message:

6-7 "The word is out among the nations — and Geshem says it's true — that you and the Jews are planning to rebel. That's why you are rebuilding the wall. The word is that you want to be king and that you have appointed prophets to announce in Jerusalem, 'There's a king in Judah!' The king is going to be told all this — don't you think we should sit down and have a talk?"

8 I sent him back this: "There's nothing to what you're saying. You've made it all up."

9 They were trying to intimidate us into quitting. They thought, "They'll give up; they'll never finish it."
I prayed, "Give me strength."

10 Then I met secretly with Shemaiah son of Delaiah, the son of Mehetabel, at his house. He said:

Let's meet at the house of God,
    inside The Temple;
Let's find safety behind locked doors

because they're coming to kill you,
Yes, coming by night to kill you.

¹¹ I said, "Why would a man like me run for cover? And why would a man like me use The Temple as a hideout? I won't do it."

¹²⁻¹³ I sensed that God hadn't sent this man. The so-called prophecy he spoke to me was the work of Tobiah and Sanballat; they had hired him. He had been hired to scare me off — trick me — a layman, into desecrating The Temple and ruining my good reputation so they could accuse me.

¹⁴ "O my God, don't let Tobiah and Sanballat get by with all the mischief they've done. And the same goes for the prophetess Noadiah and the other prophets who have been trying to undermine my confidence."

¹⁵⁻¹⁶ The wall was finished on the twenty-fifth day of Elul. It had taken fifty-two days. When all our enemies heard the news and all the surrounding nations saw it, our enemies totally lost their nerve. They knew that God was behind this work.

¹⁷⁻¹⁹ All during this time letters were going back and forth constantly between the nobles of Judah and Tobiah. Many of the nobles had ties to him because he was son-in-law to Shecaniah son of Arah and his son Jehohanan had married the daughter of Meshullam son of Berekiah. They kept telling me all the good things he did and then would report back to him anything I would say. And then Tobiah would send letters to intimidate me.

THE WALL REBUILT: NAMES AND NUMBERS

¹⁻² After the wall was rebuilt and I had installed the doors, and the security guards, the singers, and the Levites were appointed, I put my brother Hanani, along with Hananiah the captain of the citadel, in charge of Jerusalem because he was an honest man and feared God more than most men.

³ I gave them this order: "Don't open the gates of Jerusalem until the sun is up. And shut and bar the gates while the guards are still on duty. Appoint the guards from the citizens of Jerusalem and assign them to posts in front of their own homes."

⁴ The city was large and spacious with only a few people in it and the houses not yet rebuilt.

⁵ God put it in my heart to gather the nobles, the officials, and the people in general to be registered. I found the genealogical record of those who were in the first return from exile. This is the record I found:

⁶⁻⁶⁰ These are the people of the province who returned from the captivity of the Exile, the ones Nebuchadnezzar king of Babylon had carried off captive; they came back to Jerusalem and Judah, each going to his own town. They came back in the company of Zerubbabel, Jeshua, Nehemiah, Azariah, Raamiah, Nahamani, Mordecai, Bilshan, Mispereth, Bigvai, Nehum, and Baanah.

The numbers of the men of the People of Israel by families of origin:
Parosh, 2,172
Shephatiah, 372
Arah, 652

Pahath-Moab (sons of Jeshua and Joab), 2,818
Elam, 1,254
Zattu, 845
Zaccai, 760
Binnui, 648
Bebai, 628
Azgad, 2,322
Adonikam, 667
Bigvai, 2,067
Adin, 655
Ater (sons of Hezekiah), 98
Hashum, 328
Bezai, 324
Hariph, 112
Gibeon, 95.
Israelites identified by place of origin:
Bethlehem and Netophah, 188
Anathoth, 128
Beth Azmaveth, 42
Kiriath Jearim, Kephirah, and Beeroth, 743
Ramah and Geba, 621
Micmash, 122
Bethel and Ai, 123
Nebo (the other one), 52
Elam (the other one), 1,254
Harim, 320
Jericho, 345
Lod, Hadid, and Ono, 721
Senaah, 3,930.
Priestly families:
Jedaiah (sons of Jeshua), 973
Immer, 1,052
Pashhur, 1,247
Harim, 1,017.
Levitical families:
Jeshua (sons of Kadmiel and of Hodaviah), 74.
Singers:
Asaph's family line, 148.
Security guard families:
Shallum, Ater, Talmon, Akkub, Hatita, and Shobai, 138.
Families of support staff:
Ziha, Hasupha, Tabbaoth,
Keros, Sia, Padon,
Lebana, Hagaba, Shalmai,
Hanan, Giddel, Gahar,
Reaiah, Rezin, Nekoda,
Gazzam, Uzza, Paseah,
Besai, Meunim, Nephussim,
Bakbuk, Hakupha, Harhur,
Bazluth, Mehida, Harsha,
Barkos, Sisera, Temah,

Neziah, and Hatipha.
Families of Solomon's servants:
Sotai, Sophereth, Perida,
Jaala, Darkon, Giddel,
Shephatiah, Hattil, Pokereth-Hazzebaim, and Amon.
The Temple support staff and Solomon's servants added up to 392.

61-63 These are those who came from Tel Melah, Tel Harsha, Kerub, Addon, and Immer. They weren't able to prove their ancestry, whether they were true Israelites or not:

The sons of Delaiah, Tobiah, and Nekoda, 642.
Likewise with these priestly families:
The sons of Hobaiah, Hakkoz, and Barzillai, who had married a daughter of Barzillai the Gileadite and took that name.

64-65 They looked high and low for their family records but couldn't find them. And so they were barred from priestly work as ritually unclean. The governor ruled that they could not eat from the holy food until a priest could determine their status by using the Urim and Thummim.

66-69 The total count for the congregation was 42,360. That did not include the male and female slaves who numbered 7,337. There were also 245 male and female singers. And there were 736 horses, 245 mules, 435 camels, and 6,720 donkeys.

70-72 Some of the heads of families made voluntary offerings for the work. The governor made a gift to the treasury of 1,000 drachmas of gold (about nineteen pounds), 50 bowls, and 530 garments for the priests. Some of the heads of the families made gifts to the treasury for the work; it came to 20,000 drachmas of gold and 2,200 minas of silver (about one and a third tons). Gifts from the rest of the people totaled 20,000 drachmas of gold (about 375 pounds), 2,000 minas of silver, and 67 garments for the priests.

73 The priests, Levites, security guards, singers, and Temple support staff, along with some others, and the rest of the People of Israel, all found a place to live in their own towns.

EZRA AND THE REVELATION

1 By the time the seventh month arrived, the People of Israel were settled in their towns. Then all the people gathered as one person in the town square in front of the Water Gate and asked the scholar Ezra to bring the Book of The Revelation of Moses that GOD had commanded for Israel.

2-3 So Ezra the priest brought The Revelation to the congregation, which was made up of both men and women — everyone capable of understanding. It was the first day of the seventh month. He read it facing the town square at the Water Gate from early dawn until noon in the hearing of the men and women, all who could understand it. And all the people listened — they were all ears — to the Book of The Revelation.

4 The scholar Ezra stood on a wooden platform constructed for the occasion. He was flanked on the right by Mattithiah, Shema, Anaiah, Uriah, Hilkiah, and Maaseiah, and on the left by Pedaiah, Mishael, Malkijah, Hashum, Hashbaddanah, Zechariah, and Meshullam.

5-6   Ezra opened the book. Every eye was on him (he was standing on the raised platform) and as he opened the book everyone stood. Then Ezra praised GOD, the great God, and all the people responded, "Oh Yes! Yes!" with hands raised high. And then they fell to their knees in worship of GOD, their faces to the ground.

7-8   Jeshua, Bani, Sherebiah, Jamin, Akkub, Shabbethai, Hodiah, Maaseiah, Kelita, Azariah, Jozabad, Hanan, and Pelaiah, all Levites, explained The Revelation while people stood, listening respectfully. They translated the Book of The Revelation of God so the people could understand it and then explained the reading.

9   Nehemiah the governor, along with Ezra the priest and scholar and the Levites who were teaching the people, said to all the people, "This day is holy to GOD, your God. Don't weep and carry on." They said this because all the people were weeping as they heard the words of The Revelation.

10   He continued, "Go home and prepare a feast, holiday food and drink; and share it with those who don't have anything: This day is holy to God. Don't feel bad. The joy of GOD is your strength!"

11   The Levites calmed the people, "Quiet now. This is a holy day. Don't be upset."

12   So the people went off to feast, eating and drinking and including the poor in a great celebration. Now they got it; they understood the reading that had been given to them.

13-15   On the second day of the month the family heads of all the people, the priests, and the Levites gathered around Ezra the scholar to get a deeper understanding of the words of The Revelation. They found written in The Revelation that GOD commanded through Moses that the People of Israel are to live in booths during the festival of the seventh month. So they published this decree and had it posted in all their cities and in Jerusalem: "Go into the hills and collect olive branches, pine branches, myrtle branches, palm branches, and any other leafy branches to make booths, as it is written."

16-17   So the people went out, brought in branches, and made themselves booths on their roofs, courtyards, the courtyards of The Temple of God, the Water Gate plaza, and the Ephraim Gate plaza. The entire congregation that had come back from exile made booths and lived in them. The People of Israel hadn't done this from the time of Joshua son of Nun until that very day—a terrific day! Great joy!

18   Ezra read from the Book of The Revelation of God each day, from the first to the last day—they celebrated the feast for seven days. On the eighth day they held a solemn assembly in accordance with the decree.

1-3   **9** Then on the twenty-fourth day of this month, the People of Israel gathered for a fast, wearing burlap and faces smudged with dirt as signs of repentance. The Israelites broke off all relations with foreigners, stood up, and confessed their sins and the iniquities of their parents. While they stood there in their places, they read from the Book of The Revelation of GOD, their God, for a quarter of the day. For another quarter of the day they confessed and worshiped their GOD.

4-5   A group of Levites—Jeshua, Bani, Kadmiel, Shebaniah, Bunni, Sherebiah, Bani, and Kenani—stood on the platform and cried out to GOD, their God, in a loud voice. The Levites Jeshua, Kadmiel, Bani, Hashabneiah, Sherebiah, Hodiah, Shebaniah, and Pethahiah said, "On your feet! Bless GOD, your God, for ever and ever!"

5-6   Blessed be your glorious name,
     exalted above all blessing and praise!
  You're the one,
     GOD, you alone;
  You made the heavens,
     the heavens of heavens, and all angels;
  The earth and everything on it,
     the seas and everything in them;
  You keep them all alive;
     heaven's angels worship you!

7-8   You're the one, GOD, *the* God
     who chose Abram
  And brought him from Ur of the Chaldees
     and changed his name to Abraham.
  You found his heart to be steady and true to you
     and signed a covenant with him,
  A covenant to give him the land of the Canaanites,
     the Hittites, and the Amorites,
  The Perizzites, Jebusites, and Girgashites,
     —to give it to his descendants.
  And you kept your word
     because you are righteous.

9-15   You saw the anguish of our parents in Egypt.
     You heard their cries at the Red Sea;
  You amazed Pharaoh, his servants, and the people of his land
     with wonders and miracle-signs.
  You knew their bullying arrogance against your people;
     you made a name for yourself that lasts to this day.
  You split the sea before them;
     they crossed through and never got their feet wet;
  You pitched their pursuers into the deep;
     they sank like a rock in the storm-tossed sea.
  By day you led them with a Pillar of Cloud,
     and by night with a Pillar of Fire
  To show them the way
     they were to travel.
  You came down onto Mount Sinai,
     you spoke to them out of heaven;
  You gave them instructions on how to live well,
     true teaching, sound rules and commands;
  You introduced them
     to your Holy Sabbath;
  Through your servant Moses you decreed

commands, rules, and instruction.
You gave bread from heaven for their hunger,
    you sent water from the rock for their thirst.
You told them to enter and take the land,
    which you promised to give them.

16-19 But they, our ancestors, were arrogant;
    bullheaded, they wouldn't obey your commands.
They turned a deaf ear, they refused
    to remember the miracles you had done for them;
They turned stubborn, got it into their heads
    to return to their Egyptian slavery.
And you, a forgiving God,
    gracious and compassionate,
Incredibly patient, with tons of love—
    you didn't dump them.
Yes, even when they cast a sculpted calf
    and said, "This is your god
Who brought you out of Egypt,"
    and continued from bad to worse,
You in your amazing compassion
    didn't walk off and leave them in the desert.
The Pillar of Cloud didn't leave them;
    daily it continued to show them their route;
The Pillar of Fire did the same by night,
    showed them the right way to go.

20-23 You gave them your good Spirit
    to teach them to live wisely.
You never stinted with your manna,
    gave them plenty of water to drink.
You supported them forty years in that desert;
    they had everything they needed;
Their clothes didn't wear out
    and their feet never blistered.
You gave them kingdoms and peoples,
    establishing generous boundaries.
They took over the country of Sihon king of Heshbon
    and the country of Og king of Bashan.
You multiplied children for them,
    rivaling the stars in the night skies,
And you brought them into the land
    that you promised their ancestors
    they would get and own.

24-25 Well, they entered all right,
    they took it and settled in.
The Canaanites who lived there
    you brought to their knees before them.
You turned over their land, kings, and peoples
    to do with as they pleased.

They took strong cities and fertile fields,
 they took over well-furnished houses,
Cisterns, vineyards, olive groves,
 and lush, extensive orchards.
And they ate, grew fat on the fat of the land;
 they reveled in your bountiful goodness.

26-31 But then they mutinied, rebelled against you,
 threw out your laws and killed your prophets,
The very prophets who tried to get them back on your side—
 and then things went from bad to worse.
You turned them over to their enemies,
 who made life rough for them.
But when they called out for help in their troubles
 you listened from heaven;
And in keeping with your bottomless compassion
 you gave them saviors:
Saviors who saved them
 from the cruel abuse of their enemies.
But as soon as they had it easy again
 they were right back at it—more evil.
So you turned away and left them again to their fate,
 to the enemies who came right back.
They cried out to you again; in your great compassion
 you heard and helped them again.
 This went on over and over and over.
You warned them to return to your Revelation,
 they responded with haughty arrogance:
They flouted your commands, spurned your rules
 —the very words by which men and women live!
They set their jaws in defiance,
 they turned their backs on you and didn't listen.
You put up with them year after year
 and warned them by your spirit through your prophets;
But when they refused to listen
 you abandoned them to foreigners.
Still, because of your great compassion,
 you didn't make a total end to them.
You didn't walk out and leave them for good;
 yes, you *are* a God of grace and compassion.

32-37 And now, our God, the great God,
 God majestic and terrible, loyal in covenant and love,
Don't treat lightly the trouble that has come to us,
 to our kings and princes, our priests and prophets,
Our ancestors, and all your people from the time
 of the Assyrian kings right down to today.
You are not to blame
 for all that has come down on us;
You did everything right,
 we did everything wrong.

> None of our kings, princes, priests, or ancestors
>   followed your Revelation;
> They ignored your commands,
>   dismissed the warnings you gave them.
> Even when they had their own kingdom
>   and were enjoying your generous goodness,
> Living in that spacious and fertile land
>   that you spread out before them,
> They didn't serve you
>   or turn their backs on the practice of evil.
> And here we are, slaves again today;
>   and here's the land you gave our ancestors
> So they could eat well and enjoy a good life,
>   and now look at us—no better than slaves on this land.
> Its wonderful crops go to the kings
>   you put over us because of our sins;
> They act like they own our bodies
>   and do whatever they like with our cattle.
>   We're in deep trouble.

38   "Because of all this we are drawing up a binding pledge, a sealed document signed by our princes, our Levites, and our priests."

⁂

1-8 **10** The sealed document bore these signatures:
         Nehemiah the governor, son of Hacaliah,
         Zedekiah, Seraiah, Azariah, Jeremiah,
     Pashhur, Amariah, Malkijah,
     Hattush, Shebaniah, Malluch,
     Harim, Meremoth, Obadiah,
     Daniel, Ginnethon, Baruch,
     Meshullam, Abijah, Mijamin,
     Maaziah, Bilgai, and Shemaiah.
     These were the priests.

9-13 The Levites:
      Jeshua son of Azaniah, Binnui of the sons of Henadad, Kadmiel,
      and their kinsmen: Shebaniah, Hodiah, Kelita, Pelaiah, Hanan,
      Mica, Rehob, Hashabiah,
      Zaccur, Sherebiah, Shebaniah,
      Hodiah, Bani, and Beninu.

14-27 The heads of the people:
       Parosh, Pahath-Moab, Elam, Zattu, Bani,
       Bunni, Azgad, Bebai,
       Adonijah, Bigvai, Adin,
       Ater, Hezekiah, Azzur,
       Hodiah, Hashum, Bezai,
       Hariph, Anathoth, Nebai,
       Magpiash, Meshullam, Hezir,
       Meshezabel, Zadok, Jaddua,

Pelatiah, Hanan, Anaiah,
Hoshea, Hananiah, Hasshub,
Hallohesh, Pilha, Shobek,
Rehum, Hashabnah, Maaseiah,
Ahiah, Hanan, Anan,
Malluch, Harim, and Baanah.

28-30 The rest of the people, priests, Levites, security guards, singers, Temple staff, and all who separated themselves from the foreign neighbors to keep The Revelation of God, together with their wives, sons, daughters — everyone old enough to understand — all joined their noble kinsmen in a binding oath to follow The Revelation of God given through Moses the servant of God, to keep and carry out all the commandments of GOD our Master, all his decisions and standards. Thus:

We will not marry our daughters to our foreign neighbors nor let our sons marry their daughters.

31 When the foreign neighbors bring goods or grain to sell on the Sabbath we won't trade with them — not on the Sabbath or any other holy day.

Every seventh year we will leave the land fallow and cancel all debts.

32-33 We accept the responsibility for paying an annual tax of one-third of a shekel (about an eighth ounce) for providing The Temple of our God with
bread for the Table
regular Grain-Offerings
regular Whole-Burnt-Offerings
offerings for the Sabbaths, New Moons, and appointed feasts
Dedication-Offerings
Absolution-Offerings to atone for Israel
maintenance of The Temple of our God.

34 We — priests, Levites, and the people — have cast lots to see when each of our families will bring wood for burning on the Altar of our God, following the yearly schedule set down in The Revelation.

35-36 We take responsibility for delivering annually to The Temple of God the firstfruits of our crops and our orchards, our firstborn sons and cattle, and the firstborn from our herds and flocks for the priests who serve in The Temple of our God — just as it is set down in The Revelation.

37-39 We will bring the best of our grain, of our contributions, of the fruit of every tree, of wine, and of oil to the priests in the storerooms of The Temple of our God.

We will bring the tithes from our fields to the Levites, since the Levites are appointed to collect the tithes in the towns where we work. We'll see to it that a priest descended from Aaron will supervise the Levites as they collect the tithes and make sure that they take a tenth of the tithes to the treasury in The Temple of our God. We'll see to it that the People of Israel and Levites bring the grain, wine, and oil to the storage rooms where the vessels of the Sanctuary are kept and where the priests who serve, the security guards, and the choir meet.

We will not neglect The Temple of our God.

11 The leaders of the people were already living in Jerusalem, so the rest of the people drew lots to get one out of ten to move to Jerusalem, the holy city, while the other nine remained in their towns. The people applauded those who voluntarily offered to live in Jerusalem.

These are the leaders in the province who resided in Jerusalem (some Israelites, priests, Levites, Temple staff, and descendants of Solomon's slaves lived in the towns of Judah on their own property in various towns; others from both Judah and Benjamin lived in Jerusalem):

From the family of Judah:

Athaiah son of Uzziah, the son of Zechariah, the son of Amariah, the son of Shephatiah, the son of Mahalalel, from the family line of Perez; Maaseiah son of Baruch, the son of Col-Hozeh, the son of Hazaiah, the son of Adaiah, the son of Joiarib, the son of Zechariah, the son of the Shilonite. The descendants of Perez who lived in Jerusalem numbered 468 valiant men.

From the family of Benjamin:

Sallu son of Meshullam, the son of Joed, the son of Pedaiah, the son of Kolaiah, the son of Maaseiah, the son of Ithiel, the son of Jeshaiah, and his brothers Gabbai and Sallai: 928 men. Joel son of Zicri was their chief and Judah son of Hassenuah was second in command over the city.

From the priests:

Jedaiah son of Joiarib; Jakin; Seraiah son of Hilkiah, the son of Meshullam, the son of Zadok, the son of Meraioth, the son of Ahitub, supervisor of The Temple of God, along with their associates responsible for work in The Temple: 822 men. Also Adaiah son of Jeroham, the son of Pelaliah, the son of Amzi, the son of Zechariah, the son of Pashhur, the son of Malkijah, and his associates who were heads of families: 242 men; Amashsai son of Azarel, the son of Ahzai, the son of Meshillemoth, the son of Immer, and his associates, all valiant men: 128 men. Their commander was Zabdiel son of Haggedolim.

From the Levites:

Shemaiah son of Hasshub, the son of Azrikam, the son of Hashabiah, the son of Bunni; Shabbethai and Jozabad, two of the leaders of the Levites who were in charge of the outside work of The Temple of God; Mattaniah son of Mica, the son of Zabdi, the son of Asaph, the director who led in thanksgiving and prayer; Bakbukiah, second among his associates; and Abda son of Shammua, the son of Galal, the son of Jeduthun. The Levites in the holy city totaled 284.

From the security guards:

Akkub, Talmon, and their associates who kept watch over the gates: 172 men.

The rest of the Israelites, priests, and Levites were in all the towns of Judah, each on his own family property.

The Temple staff lived on the hill Ophel. Ziha and Gishpa were responsible for them.

The chief officer over the Levites in Jerusalem was Uzzi son of Bani, the son of Hashabiah, the son of Mattaniah, the son of Mica. Uzzi was one of Asaph's descendants, singers who led worship in The Temple of God. The singers got their orders from the king, who drew up their daily schedule.

24   Pethahiah son of Meshezabel, a descendant of Zerah son of Judah, represented the people's concerns at the royal court.

25-30   Some of the Judeans lived in the villages near their farms:
>   Kiriath Arba (Hebron) and suburbs
>   Dibon and suburbs
>   Jekabzeel and suburbs
>   Jeshua
>   Moladah
>   Beth Pelet
>   Hazar Shual
>   Beersheba and suburbs
>   Ziklag
>   Meconah and suburbs
>   En Rimmon
>   Zorah
>   Jarmuth
>   Zanoah
>   Adullam and their towns
>   Lachish and its fields
>   Azekah and suburbs.

They were living all the way from Beersheba to the Valley of Hinnom.

31-36   The Benjaminites from Geba lived in:
>   Micmash
>   Aijah
>   Bethel and its suburbs
>   Anathoth
>   Nob and Ananiah
>   Hazor
>   Ramah and Gittaim
>   Hadid, Zeboim, and Neballat
>   Lod and Ono and the Valley of the Craftsmen.

Also some of the Levitical groups of Judah were assigned to Benjamin.

1-7   **12** These are the priests and Levites who came up with Zerubbabel son of Shealtiel and with Jeshua:
>   Seraiah, Jeremiah, Ezra,
>   Amariah, Malluch, Hattush,
>   Shecaniah, Rehum, Meremoth,
>   Iddo, Ginnethon, Abijah,
>   Mijamin, Moadiah, Bilgah,
>   Shemaiah, Joiarib, Jedaiah,
>   Sallu, Amok, Hilkiah, and Jedaiah.

These were the leaders of the priests during the time of Jeshua.

8-9   And the Levites:
>   Jeshua, Binnui, Kadmiel, Sherebiah, Judah;
>   Mattaniah, with his brothers, was in charge of songs of praise, and their brothers Bakbukiah and Unni stood opposite them in the services of worship.

10-11
> Jeshua fathered Joiakim,
> Joiakim fathered Eliashib,
> Eliashib fathered Joiada,
> Joiada fathered Jonathan,
> and Jonathan fathered Jaddua.

12-21
During the time of Joiakim, these were the heads of the priestly families:
> of the family of Seraiah, Meraiah;
> of Jeremiah, Hananiah;
> of Ezra, Meshullam;
> of Amariah, Jehohanan;
> of Malluch, Jonathan;
> of Shecaniah, Joseph;
> of Harim, Adna;
> of Meremoth, Helkai;
> of Iddo, Zechariah;
> of Ginnethon, Meshullam;
> of Abijah, Zicri;
> of Miniamin and Moadiah, Piltai;
> of Bilgah, Shammua;
> of Shemaiah, Jehonathan;
> of Joiarib, Mattenai;
> of Jedaiah, Uzzi;
> of Sallu, Kallai;
> of Amok, Eber;
> of Hilkiah, Hashabiah;
> and of Jedaiah, Nethanel.

22
During the time of Eliashib, Joiada, Johanan, and Jaddua, the Levites were registered as heads of families. During the reign of Darius the Persian, the priests were registered.

23-24
The Levites who were heads of families were registered in the Book of the Chronicles until the time of Johanan son of Eliashib. These were:
> Hashabiah,
> Sherebiah,
> and Jeshua son of Kadmiel.

Their brothers stood opposite them to give praise and thanksgiving, one side responding to the other, as had been directed by David the man of God.

25-26
The security guards included:
> Mattaniah,
> Bakbukiah,
> Obadiah,
> Meshullam,
> Talmon,
> and Akkub.

They guarded the storerooms at the gates. They lived during the time of Joiakim son of Jeshua, the son of Jozadak, the time of Nehemiah the governor and of Ezra the priest and scholar.

DEDICATION OF THE WALL

²⁷⁻²⁹ When it came time for the dedication of the wall, they tracked down and brought in the Levites from all their homes in Jerusalem to carry out the dedication exuberantly: thanksgiving hymns, songs, cymbals, harps, and lutes. The singers assembled from all around Jerusalem, from the villages of the Netophathites, from Beth Gilgal, from the farms at Geba and Azmaveth—the singers had built villages for themselves all around Jerusalem.

³⁰ The priests and Levites ceremonially purified themselves; then they did the same for the people, the gates, and the wall.

³¹⁻³⁶ I had the leaders of Judah come up on the wall, and I appointed two large choirs. One proceeded on the wall to the right toward the Dung Gate. Hashaiah and half the leaders of Judah followed them, including Azariah, Ezra, Meshullam, Judah, Benjamin, Shemaiah, and Jeremiah. Some of the young priests had trumpets. Next, playing the musical instruments of David the man of God, came Zechariah son of Jonathan, the son of Shemaiah, the son of Mattaniah, the son of Micaiah, the son of Zaccur, the son of Asaph, and his brothers Shemaiah, Azarel, Milalai, Gilalai, Maai, Nethanel, Judah, and Hanani. Ezra the scholar led them.

³⁷ At the Fountain Gate they went straight ahead, up the steps of the City of David using the wall stairway above the house of David to the Water Gate on the east.

³⁸⁻³⁹ The other choir proceeded to the left. I and half of the people followed them on the wall from the Tower of Furnaces to the Broad Wall, over the Ephraim Gate, the Jeshanah Gate, the Fish Gate, the Tower of Hananel, and the Tower of the Hundred as far as the Sheep Gate, stopping at the Prison Gate.

⁴⁰⁻⁴² The two choirs then took their places in The Temple of God. I was there with half of the officials, along with the priests Eliakim, Maaseiah, Miniamin, Micaiah, Elioenai, Zechariah, and Hananiah with their trumpets. Also Maaseiah, Shemaiah, Eleazar, Uzzi, Jehohanan, Malkijah, Elam, and Ezer. The singers, directed by Jezrahiah, made the rafters ring.

⁴³ That day they offered great sacrifices, an exuberant celebration because God had filled them with great joy. The women and children raised their happy voices with all the rest. Jerusalem's jubilation was heard far and wide.

⁴⁴⁻⁴⁶ That same day men were appointed to be responsible for the storerooms for the offerings, the firstfruits, and the tithes. They saw to it that the portion directed by The Revelation for the priests and Levites was brought in from the farms connected to the towns. Judah was so appreciative of the priests and Levites and their service; they, along with the singers and security guards, had done everything so well, conducted the worship of their God and the ritual of ceremonial cleansing in a way that would have made David and his son Solomon proud. That's the way it was done in the olden days, the days of David and Asaph, when they had choir directors for singing songs of praise and thanksgiving to God.

⁴⁷ During the time of Zerubbabel and Nehemiah, all Israel contributed the daily allowances for the singers and security guards. They also set

aside what was dedicated to the Levites, and the Levites did the same for
the Aaronites.

¹⁻³ 13 Also on that same day there was a reading from the Book of
Moses in the hearing of the people. It was found written there
that no Ammonite or Moabite was permitted to enter the congregation of God, because they hadn't welcomed the People of Israel with
food and drink; they even hired Balaam to work against them by cursing
them, but our God turned the curse into a blessing. When they heard the
reading of The Revelation, they excluded all foreigners from Israel.

⁴⁻⁵ Some time before this, Eliashib the priest had been put in charge of the
storerooms of The Temple of God. He was close to Tobiah and had made
available to him a large storeroom that had been used to store Grain-
Offerings, incense, worship vessels, and the tithes of grain, wine, and
oil for the Levites, singers, and security guards, and the offerings for the
priests.

⁶⁻⁹ When this was going on I wasn't there in Jerusalem; in the thirty-second
year of Artaxerxes king of Babylon, I had traveled back to the king. But
later I asked for his permission to leave again. I arrived in Jerusalem and
learned of the wrong that Eliashib had done in turning over to him a room
in the courts of The Temple of God. I was angry, really angry, and threw
everything in the room out into the street, all of Tobiah's stuff. Then I
ordered that they ceremonially cleanse the room. Only then did I put back
the worship vessels of The Temple of God, along with the Grain-Offerings
and the incense.

¹⁰⁻¹³ And then I learned that the Levites hadn't been given their regular
food allotments. So the Levites and singers who led the services of worship
had all left and gone back to their farms. I called the officials on the carpet, "Why has The Temple of God been abandoned?" I got everyone back
again and put them back on their jobs so that all Judah was again bringing in the tithe of grain, wine, and oil to the storerooms. I put Shelemiah
the priest, Zadok the scribe, and a Levite named Pedaiah in charge of
the storerooms. I made Hanan son of Zaccur, the son of Mattaniah, their
right-hand man. These men had a reputation for honesty and hard work.
They were responsible for distributing the rations to their brothers.

¹⁴ Remember me, O my God, for this. Don't ever forget the devoted
work I have done for The Temple of God and its worship.

¹⁵⁻¹⁶ During those days, while back in Judah, I also noticed that people treaded
wine presses, brought in sacks of grain, and loaded up their donkeys on the
Sabbath. They brought wine, grapes, figs, and all kinds of stuff to sell on
the Sabbath. So I spoke up and warned them about selling food on that day.
Tyrians living there brought in fish and whatever else, selling it to Judeans — *in
Jerusalem*, mind you! — on the Sabbath.

¹⁷⁻¹⁸ I confronted the leaders of Judah: "What's going on here? This evil!
Profaning the Sabbath! Isn't this exactly what your ancestors did? And
because of it didn't God bring down on us and this city all this misery?

And here you are adding to it — accumulating more wrath on Jerusalem by profaning the Sabbath."

19   As the gates of Jerusalem were darkened by the shadows of the approaching Sabbath, I ordered the doors shut and not to be opened until the Sabbath was over. I placed some of my servants at the gates to make sure that nothing to be sold would get in on the Sabbath day.

20-21   Traders and dealers in various goods camped outside the gates once or twice. But I took them to task. I said, "You have no business camping out here by the wall. If I find you here again, I'll use force to drive you off."

And that did it; they didn't come back on the Sabbath.

22   Then I directed the Levites to ceremonially cleanse themselves and take over as guards at the gates to keep the sanctity of the Sabbath day.

> Remember me also for this, my God. Treat me with mercy according to your great and steadfast love.

23-27   Also in those days I saw Jews who had married women from Ashdod, Ammon, and Moab. Half the children couldn't even speak the language of Judah; all they knew was the language of Ashdod or some other tongue. So I took those men to task, gave them a piece of my mind, even slapped some of them and jerked them by the hair. I made them swear to God: "Don't marry your daughters to their sons; and don't let their daughters marry your sons — and don't you yourselves marry them! Didn't Solomon the king of Israel sin because of women just like these? Even though there was no king quite like him, and God loved him and made him king over all Israel, foreign women were his downfall. Do you call this obedience — engaging in this extensive evil, showing yourselves faithless to God by marrying foreign wives?"

28   One of the sons of Joiada, the son of Eliashib the high priest, was a son-in-law of Sanballat the Horonite; I drove him out of my presence.

29   > Remember them, O my God, how they defiled the priesthood and the covenant of the priests and Levites.

30-31   All in all I cleansed them from everything foreign. I organized the orders of service for the priests and Levites so that each man knew his job. I arranged for a regular supply of altar wood at the appointed times and for the firstfruits.

> Remember me, O my God, for good.

TOBIT

This cautionary tale about fidelity to God and family was probably written down in the form we have it in the second century B.C., but the story took place centuries earlier. Tobit came from the tribe of Naphtali, aggressive bruisers with not a hand-wringer among them, who thought they were good people. But they were not nearly good enough for God, and so they were easily and often overrun by their enemies. They probably wore a lot of baubles and bangles, because they ended up worshiping not the austere God of their forebears but the flashy gods of their neighbors.

While the people of Naphtali were tough, they weren't necessarily all that virtuous—with the sole exception of Tobit, or so the Book of Tobit would have us believe. He offered regular sacrifices to God as prescribed; he tithed; and in general he kept the faith when all around him were abandoning it. For this he was blessed by God and given a high place in the Gentile government, even though he and his people were in exile.

Tobit made a point of giving his people a proper Jewish burial, which got him in all kinds of trouble, even after the exile was over. He'd also squirreled away money for a rainy day, and eventually sent his son Tobias or Tobiah—let's call him Toby to differentiate him from his father—to fetch it, which makes up most of the narrative.

Tobit and his family, apparently alone of their tribe, kept God's word. God rewarded this observance by sending them a stranger with a huge physique to protect and heal them—a mysterious fellow named Azariah, who seemed to know more than he let on, an angelic presence who revealed his true self only at the end of the narrative. He was really the archangel Raphael, one of only three angels called by name in the Scriptures—along with Michael and Gabriel.

The two main women in the story are memorable as well: smart, strong, and attractive. Anna put her finger on her saintly husband Tobit's sole spiritual defect—pride in his own generosity—and he howled to the heavens as if he had been accused of murder. Sarah had to endure a series of seven marriages to various male relatives, each one ending in the death of her husband on the wedding night before he could even make love to her.

There's also Sarah's father and mother, Raguel and Edna, who cared deeply about their daughter's welfare and were trying to get her married off to someone who wouldn't kick the bucket on his wedding night.

The archangel not only protected Toby on his journey and set him up with his bride-to-be, he also drove out the demon who was killing off Sarah's new husbands. In addition, he concocted a cure for Tobit's blindness with body parts from a dead fish. For these reasons, Raphael is recognized today as a patron saint of travelers, medical workers, and matchmakers.

In the twenty-first century, it isn't all that easy for any of us—Christian, Jew, Muslim, Hindu, Buddhist, or "none of the above"—to be virtuous either. If we want to rate our behavior against Tobit's, we can run down the several lists of dos and don'ts found in the book bearing his name. Most of us would have an embarrassingly low score. We could improve it, though, by taking Tobit's main life lesson to heart: Work harder at becoming better. (WG)

TOBIT

THE WORLD ACCORDING TO TOBIT

1-2 This is the world according to Tobit, a collection of tales about a character of the same name. My grasp of genealogy isn't all that good, but I'd say that he descended through his father Tobiel from the likes of Hananiel, Aduel, Gabael, Raphael, and Raguel of the line of Asiel, tribe of Naphtali.

My history is no better than my genealogy, but I'd say that Tobit lived during the reign of the Assyrian king Shalmaneser, if that were possible. He was taken into captivity and forced to march from his home in Thisbe, which I'm given to understand was right in the middle of nowhere. This is his story.

3 My name is Tobit, and I've walked the straight and narrow all the days of my life. I've been free with my fortune—my relatives will attest to that—and my people, fellow prisoners on the exile to Nineveh, will declare that I was able to provide them some small comforts along the way.

4-5 A bit about my own history. When I was a lad who called the land of Israel home, the whole tribe of Naphtali, every last one of them, bolted from the house of David. While observant Israelites offered sacrifice in the Temple of God in Jerusalem, my people offered sacrifice in the mountain chapels that Jeroboam commissioned in the city of Dan when he was king of Israel.

6-7 As for myself, unlike my embarrassing relatives, I never stopped celebrating the holy days, as the written Law of Moses required. Off I'd go to Jerusalem, bringing with me the firsts of everything—the crops, the flocks, the herds, the wools. These I'd give to the priests, the sons of Aaron, for presentation at the altar.

8 Over and above that, I tithed, but in the old-fashioned way. First, for the Levites' table, a tenth of my grains, wines, oils, fruits. Second, except for sabbatical years when I did more, a tenth of my liquid assets for general distribution. Third, every three years, a third of my assets for distribution to the orphans, widows, and converts. That was what the Law of Moses prescribed, and that was what my father, Tobiel, would have drilled into me if he hadn't died young; my grandmother Deborah took his place, and I can still hear her voice.

9 As for marriage, after I came of age, I married a woman named Anna, a relative of mine; with her I fathered a son and affectionately called him Toby.

10 Back to Nineveh, capital of Assyria. I lived the life of a captive, doing hard time there. All my generation who'd made the forced march abandoned the Jewish dietary laws, preferring to order from the Gentile menu. They fell for the cuisine of Nineveh, and so would I if I hadn't stood sentinel over my ravenous soul.

11-13 Yes, I was unbending on this one point of the Mosaic Law, and for that the All-High rewarded me. Even though I was an Israelite, he put me in the good graces of King Shalmaneser, who in turn came to know that I excelled in financial affairs. He put me in charge of his purse; his every wish became my every purchase.

14-15   Once, on royal business to Media, I made a side trip to Rages for a personal reason. I deposited with Gabael, the son of Gabri, a sizable amount of my earnings for a rainy day—pouches containing a considerable amount of silver, hefty in weight and value. Access to it would later prove difficult. After Shalmaneser died, his son Sennacherib succeeded to the throne, and the highway to Media was policed. Further trips, business or otherwise, were out of the question.

16-17   Back in the days of Shalmaneser, when I was flush, I made numerous gifts to my family and friends. My pantry I opened to the hungry. Donations from my modest wardrobe the down-and-out received from time to time. Later, whenever his son Sennacherib exercised his rage against one of my people, usually a refugee from the horrors in Judea, I hung about until I could snatch the body and bury it properly under cover of night.

18-20   Sennacherib was a terror in those days, visiting upon the Israelites the horrors that God was visiting upon him. He knew unburied bodies were disappearing from the dump outside the city walls, but he never knew why or how or by whom until a Ninevite told the king that I was the body-snatcher. I had to make myself scarce, knowing that the king would send the troops to find me and do me in. Everything I'd worked for in Nineveh, which was rather substantial by now, was confiscated, leaving not a handkerchief behind, and hauled off to the king's treasury. Everything, that is, except my truest treasures—my wife, Anna, and my son, Toby.

21-22   Fortunately for me, the wicked king died within forty days, assassinated by two of his sons, who then fled to the mountain area of Ararat. Another son, Esarhaddon, succeeded his father. Among his first appointments was Ahiqar, my brother Anael's son; he became chief of the kingdom's internal revenue. One of his first acts was to seek me out and give me special protection so I could return to Nineveh. As it turned out, Ahiqar had been chief taxer, procurator, and keeper of the symbols of authority when Sennacherib was alive. The king's son had the wisdom to reappoint him. He was quite a fellow, my nephew!

ONE MORE BURIAL

1-2   I returned to my home in Nineveh, and Anna and Toby were restored to me. On Pentecost, the Feast of Weeks, a grand dinner was prepared. I relaxed and reclined, looking forward to the eats and drinks. The table was set with everything—condiments galore, chilies, and chutneys without end—a feast for a king. Just one thing was missing. I said to my son, "We need a guest, somebody special. Head out and comb the crowd for one of our people, a fellow exile if possible, someone who'd like to celebrate the Feast of Pentecost but doesn't have the wherewithal to do so. Bring him back; drag him here if you have to. We'll dine together like a couple of kings. Hurry up. I won't start until you come back."

3   Toby leaped to the task and returned almost immediately.

"No luck?"

"Oh, I found someone all right."

"Where is he?"

"He's dead, strangled to death with a rope, and his body tossed right into the middle of the marketplace."

4   Before I knew what I was doing, I left the dining room in a sorrowful rage and went right to the body in the street. I picked it up and brought it back to one of the rooms in our house. I intended to bury the man properly as soon as the sun set.

5-7   Returning to the banquet, I purified my hands and then sat at the table and dipped them into the gorgeous spread. But I couldn't stop thinking of my fallen kinsman. I'd helped myself to sweet relish, but the taste that lingered was sour. Words of the prophet Amos came to my mind, the time he spoke against Bethel:

> Your feasts will turn into funerals,
>   your lullabies into laments.

My eyes filled with tears before my stomach was full of food. After the sun settled down in the evening, I went outside, dug the grave, and buried the poor fellow quickly and quietly, as the Law required.

8   My Gentile neighbors thought I was crazy.

"This man was caught once for burying his people; he was charged and found guilty. And yet he keeps on doing it!"

TOBIT LOSES HIS SIGHT

9-10   When I came back from the grave, it was still dark. I bathed and then went to the courtyard. It was hot, so hot that I didn't have the strength to cover my face against the insects. I fell asleep against the garden wall. I didn't know at the time that sparrows were perched along the top. Droppings still hot from their bowels fell into my eyes, woke me up, and affected my vision; everything seemed covered in a milky white film.

To try to clear my vision I went to the doctors, but they only made things worse. I could no longer distinguish one object from another. Everything appeared white. My whole family felt sorry for me, but there was nothing left to do. Ahiqar helped take care of me for two years, but then he had to meet a commitment in Elam.

11-12 During this hard time, my wife, Anna, earned money for us. She worked like a slave alongside other honest women churning out woolen fabrics. The finished work she brought to her Gentile product managers, and they paid her for her efforts—that was the deal. Once, in the middle of winter, she finished weaving her bolt of fabric and brought it to her managers. In return, more than satisfied with her work, they paid her what they promised with no deductions, hidden or otherwise, and tossed in a goat for good measure.

13-14 Well, I didn't know any of this. All I knew was that a goat wandered into my house and licked my ear. I called to my wife, "Where did this goat come from? Return it at once to its owners before they think you stole it! I mean, I like goat meat as much as the next fellow, but not if it's stolen."

"The goat was given to me," she said, "as a bonus over and above my pay."

I just couldn't bring myself to believe that, so I kept after her to return the goat at once. And when she didn't, I really got mad, but she held her ground.

"So, husband, it's okay for you to treat others generously and to be more than fair with complete strangers, but when someone treats me justly, even generously, that's not okay? Who do you think you are, the only virtuous man in the world?"

Anna had called me on my pride, and I deserved it.

TOBIT'S LAMENT

3 In the midst of my troubles, as was my custom when feeling sorry for myself, I burst into tears and lapsed into an overblown lament.

1-6   "You're just, O Lord. All your works are just. All your ways demonstrate mercy and truth. You're the judge of the world; take up my case and rule leniently. Don't take the rod to me for the sins and negligence of me and my forebears that were committed right under your very nose. We didn't obey the letter of your Law, so you handed us over to pillagers and plunderers. You kicked us out of the land you promised our ancestors, landing us where we knew nobody. You made us a joke to the Gentiles.

"Now your judgments are upon us, many and true, wringing from me and my people the precise amount of punishment our sins deserved; you wouldn't have had to do that if we'd acted properly and walked justly in your presence. Now do with me what you want; take my life if you will; whisk me from the face of the earth. It's better for me to die than to live. Only sadness flows in my veins. Only complaints flow from my mouth. See to it, Lord, that I get released from my anguish. Send me off to that hovel at the far end of the heavenly estate. Don't turn your face from me now!"

SEVEN SORROWFUL MARRIAGES

7-8 So much for Tobit's story in Nineveh. Simultaneously in Ecbatana, Media, somebody's ear was getting scorched. Sarah, the daughter of Raguel and Edna, had to listen to a diatribe from one of the female staff in her parents' house.

"You're just the sort of girl who suffocates her husbands! Serves you right. You've had seven and enjoyed none. So what gives you the right to whip us when you should be whipping yourself? You're the one who killed them. Why don't you kill yourself and leave us with the happiness of never having to deal with your sons and daughters?"

9-10 Sarah had been given in marriage—consecutively—to seven different men. Before each of them had made love to her even once, however, Asmodeus, the wickedest of all demons, claimed her for himself, killing each of the husbands in turn before they could reach the marriage bed.

Never had Sarah been so viciously attacked by the tongue of another. Teary-eyed, she climbed the stairs to the upper room of her parents' house, fully intending to put her head into a noose and hang herself.

Then she had second thoughts.

"If I do this, they'll never let my parents forget it: *You had one darling daughter, but she hanged herself when things went bad.* I'd lead them in their old age right to the gates of Hades. It would be far better for them if I pray to the Lord for a natural death; that way they wouldn't have to listen to the sort of reproach that would surely be tossed over the fence by their neighbors."

11-15 With her hands raised toward Jerusalem, Sarah offered her prayer.

"Bountiful and merciful are you, Lord; honored and revered is your name down through the ages. May all your works bless you! And now, to the heart of my prayer. I look up to you as you look down upon me. Grant me what I wish. Send me to the underworld. I can't stand one more snide remark about my marriages! You know that I'm pure; I've never consummated any of my marriages; I've never tarnished my own name nor that of my parents throughout this entire situation. I'm my father's only child; he doesn't have a son to leave an inheritance to; he doesn't have a brother or close relative who might need me as a replacement wife. I've been married to seven men; why should I wait around for an eighth? But if killing me isn't the sort of thing you want to be associated with, then look kindly upon me and render me deaf, plug up my ears, do anything that will prevent me from hearing the verbal slings and arrows of my enemies!"

SIMULTANEOUS ANSWERS TO SEPARATE PRAYERS

16-17 As it happened, at the same exact moment, the prayers of Tobit and Sarah were delivered into the presence of God, and God responded by sending the archangel Raphael with a healing touch for both. For Tobit, the cure was to remove the white scales that covered his eyes so that he could clearly see the light of God. For Sarah, it was to meet Toby, Tobit's son, who was, in fact, the closest relative eligible to marry her, even though she didn't even know he existed. But Raphael had a third mission, which was to pack up and drive off, once and for all, Asmodeus, the wickedest of demons.

So simultaneously, in two different cities, Tobit left the courtyard and entered his house in Nineveh and Sarah descended from the upper room to the ground floor of her parents' house in Ecbatana. Their prayers were about to be answered.

THE MONEY REMEMBERED

1-4 **4** That very same day, for some unknown reason, Tobit suddenly recalled the money he'd left with Gabael in Rages. "I've just asked God to take my life as soon as possible," he said to himself, "and I may be living on borrowed time. I'd better give my son the full particulars on this stash of funds." Tobit called Toby in and, never one to get right to the point, first gave his son a rambling list of dos and don'ts.

PATERNAL ADVICE

"Son, I'm going to die soon. Do give me a proper burial. Take care of your mother. Don't dismantle the household and leave her behind. Let her do what she wants. Don't upset her in any way. Many are the perils she underwent while she was carrying you about. When she dies, bury her with me in the same grave.

5-6 "In the days you have left in your own life, dear boy, always keep the Lord in mind. Don't get sidetracked into sin. Don't sidestep God's word. Do things because they're right. Walk hand in hand with truth. Then, your journey will prosper and your business will thrive.

7-11 "From your hoard, give all you can. Don't grind your teeth when you meet a pauper and God won't hold his nose when he meets you. Don't give until you impoverish yourself, but do make sure you feel the pinch. On a good day, give more; on a bad day, still give what you can. All the while you do this, know that you're depositing treasure against the day you'll need it. Charitable giving has its side benefits. It frees you from death, or at least from some of its pangs. One thing is sure; it'll prevent you from the Final Darkness. Giving to the lowest of the low is also a gift to the Highest of the High.

12 "Don't let extramarital sex undermine your virtue. Take a good wife— one from the family line, not a foreigner. Remember, we're children of prophets like Noah, Abraham, Jacob, and Isaac, and we want our own offspring to be prophets, too. They married within the family; they were blessed with lots of children; their descendants will inherit the earth.

13 "Don't let your affection for your family fade. Don't get estranged from them and their children; they're our people; find your spouse from among them. Beware of thinking that you're better than they are. That's how spiritual dry rot sets in: Good humor disappears and poverty arrives; everything's a joke and nothing seems to matter.

14 "Pay your employees what they're worth, and pay on time, not the day after. Do that, and your own eternal reward won't be delayed. Serve God in truth, and you'll get instant credit. In everything you do or say, show wisdom.

15 "What you'd hate to happen to you, don't dare do to another. Do drink wine, but don't stagger down the lane with a bottle in your hand.

16 "From your pantry always find something for the hungry. From your wardrobe always find something for the ragged. When you're flush with funds, give until you're back at the break-even point; and don't have second thoughts about your giving, as if there will be a monetary crash around every corner.

17 "If you visit the cemetery, break bread and pour wine on the graves of the just; the graves of the unjust you can pass on by.

18 "When you bump into people of wisdom, don't hesitate to consult them. Weed through their sometimes overwhelming verbiage until you find something worthwhile.

19-21 "Bless the Lord, but at the same time demand from him a map with proper highways and by-ways highlighted and a handbook on how to make the most of your life journey. You have to watch yourself in foreign countries—their signage isn't always reliable, but the Lord will see you round the detours. He helps those who ask and dumps those who consider themselves beyond his help.

"Try to make sense out of the lives your mother and I have led. They've been rather modest from the material point of view, but from the spiritual point of view they've been quite prosperous, what with our living in awe of God, avoiding sin for the most part, and generally behaving ourselves in the presence of God.

"Well, my boy, so much for my final words of advice. Hope I haven't been too fervent. Imprint them on your heart.

"And, oh yes, there's a stash of silver on deposit with Gabael, son of Gabria, in Rages, Media."

FINAL INSTRUCTIONS

1-2 5 "Of course I'll follow your advice, father dearest," Toby responded. "Why wouldn't I? But what's this about a stash of silver? How do I get in touch with the man who has the money? He doesn't know me, and I don't know him. Do you have a receipt? I could use that. Another thing. How do I get to Media? Can you give me directions?"

3 "He did indeed give me a receipt, made out in duplicate," Tobit replied. "We both signed; I have one copy; the other copy is tucked away with the money in a safe deposit box. That was twenty years ago. Now's a good time to collect. Find a trustworthy fellow to go with you. We'll pay his fee. Just get that money back while I'm still alive."

ANGELIC COMPANIONSHIP

4 Toby went out to find a bodyguard, though he didn't know how to choose honest from dishonest. In the first few minutes, however, he bumped into a fellow lounging about; he was certainly large and strong enough for the job, but there was something in his eyes that was unsettling.

5 "Where do you hail from?" asked Toby.

"From the children of Israel, your kind of people, and I'm looking for work," the man replied.

"Do you know the way to Media?"

6 "Been there many times, staying with a relative of mine, Gabael, who lives in Rages. Let's see. From Ecbatana to Rages—that's a trip from the plains to the mountains."

7 "Hold on, sir. I have to go in and consult with my father. But you're just the sort of person we're looking for, and we'll pay the going rate."

8 "Okay, but I don't have all day."

9 Toby told his father about the muscular fellow outside. "He's one of us, the children of Israel. He said he'd go with me."

"Ask him to come in," replied Tobit. "I'd like to know a few things. Whom is he kin to? What's his tribe? Can he be trusted?"

10 Toby went back outside and told the man, "My father has a question or two for you."

In the large fellow went, and before he could speak Tobit greeted him: "Welcome, my good man!"

The man returned the greeting: "Joy to you, my friend, and joy again!"

"What do I have to be joyful about?" Tobit complained. "I have eyes but can't see the light of day. I'm a dead man in the dark."

"What you need, sir, is a divine cure," replied the man. "God will heal you soon. In the meantime, you need to stand strong."

"From your lips to God's ear," Tobit said, and then he changed the subject. "My son, Toby, has to go to Media and needs a guide."

"I can do it blindfolded; I know all the routes."

11 "Sir, where do you come from? What family? What tribe?"

12 "What's that got to do with my doing my job?"

"I just want to know who you are and what your name is."

13 "My name is Azariah, son of the great Hananiah. I'm a distant relative of yours."

14-16 "Don't be upset with me for wanting to be sure about your family," replied Tobit. "I know both Hananiah and Nathan, the two sons of Shemaiah the Great; we used to go to Jerusalem and sacrifice in the Temple together; they were always straight-and-narrow fellows. Your family comes of good stock, the best. In this house, you're family to me. Joy! Now about your fee; we'll pay you a fair wage, plus expenses, and there'll be a little something extra at the end."

17 "Agreed. I'll go with your son," said Azariah. "You can stop worrying about him right now. We'll leave in one piece and return the same way. The road is safe, at least when I'm around."

"Thank you, brother, for taking on this assignment," said Tobit to Azariah. Then he turned to his son. "Toby, pack what you need for the journey, then get on the road with this new cousin of yours. May God in heaven protect you and bring you back to me safe." Then Tobit added an innocent, if prescient, blessing: "May God's angel accompany you!"

TOBY TAKES OFF

His baggage ready, Toby kissed his father and mother good-bye. Tobit cried out after him, "Take care! Have a good trip!"

18-20 Then Tobit's wife, Anna, turned her grief on him.

"Why did you send our only child off on this wild goose chase? Isn't it enough for Toby to be the staff we lean on as he makes his daily rounds for us? As for money, don't we have enough already? And as for the money in Rages, why can't we consider it a ransom we have to pay to keep our son here at home? Shouldn't his life, which God gave us, be enough for us at this stage in our lives?"

21-22 "Stop trying to fight it," Tobit said to Anna. "It isn't just a matter of numbers. Our son needs to have a big success at something, but I feel he's somehow safe and sound in the company of Azariah. Just keep your eyes peeled, and someday soon you'll see him coming home down the same road on which he just left."

A BIG FISH STORY

6 Anna stopped crying after her husband's assurances and turned to watch her son as he disappeared on his adventure.

2-3 Toby and Azariah were in the middle distance now, heading for the horizon. Trailing along after them was the family dog. They'd covered a good bit of territory before night overtook them and they set up camp by the Tigris. Toby went down to the bank to wash his feet. But as soon as he dipped a tentative toe into the water, he jumped back. A huge fish rose up and tried to swallow his foot!

4 "Grab the fish!" shouted Azariah with a laugh.

Toby grabbed it by the gills and wrestled it onto the bank.

5   "Fillet the fish," said Azariah, "but keep the gall, heart, and liver; they have medicinal value. As for the rest of the innards, give them a pitch."

6   Toby did just that, then cooked the fish over a fire and served it for the evening meal. What they couldn't eat, they salted for another day. When morning came, they continued their trip to the outskirts of Media. Meanwhile, an obvious question arose.

7   "So, what if any medicinal qualities do fish organs have?" Toby asked.

8-9   "The heart and liver you have to smoke, but not just anywhere," replied Azariah. "You have to do it in the presence of a man or woman who's run afoul of the wickedest demon or spirit. Whoever that demon is, he'll flee that person, never to return again, even at the end of the world. As for the gall, it's good for clouded vision. You gently dab the eyes of the patient with it. It'll clear away the milky whiteness, and the person's vision will return to normal."

10-13   Then they entered the city limits of Media and were coming close to Ecbatana when Azariah made an announcement.

"We'll have to stay at Raguel and Edna's home tonight. They're relatives of yours with an only child, a beautiful daughter named Sarah.

"When it comes to marriage, you should be the first in the relational line, and she has all the ancestral qualifications. As for her personal qualities, she's smart, strong, and attractive. What's more, she's the apple of her father's eye.

"It's okay for you to marry her. I'll speak with her father tonight. Of course, Raguel may want to deny you this privilege, but he can't. He knows Moses' rule: If a father gives his daughter to another man who is not a relative, that poor fellow will be punished by death. That means marrying kin is always superior to marrying someone right off the street or from a foreign country or with a different religion.

"Pay attention now to what I'm saying. Let's discuss all this with them tonight and set up the engagement between you and her. Then, when we return home from Rages, we can bring her to your house with all deliberate ceremony."

14-15   "Slow down, Azariah," responded Toby, "not so fast! What about that rumor making the rounds that she's been married seven times and in each she got to the bedchamber but not to the bed, her husband dying before the couple enjoyed marital relations. And then there's another rumor to the effect that if she didn't do in her husbands then a demon did. If the demon did it, he'll surely kill me if I'm the eighth husband. I, too, am an only child and don't want to die and have my parents grieve over my grave. I'm supposed to bury them, not the other way round."

16   "Don't you remember your father's list of dos and don'ts?" asked Azariah. "Didn't he want you to take a wife from the family line, not some pretty foreigner from God-knows-where? Listen to me. Forget about the demon. Just marry Sarah. I'll make it happen. This very night she'll be given to you as your wife.

17   "Here's what you do. When you enter the bridal chamber, place the heart and the liver of the fish on the embers in the incense burner. Before you know it, they'll stink up the room and affect the nose of the demon in such a way that it'll never return, even at the end of the world.

18   "I know I'm running on like your father often does, but one last tip. When you're alone with her at last, but before the foreplay, the first thing

both of you should do is pray to the Lord of Heaven that he may grant you both mercy and health.

"Have no fear; Sarah was destined to be yours before all time. You'll save her from her shame, and she'll love you and accompany you anywhere. No doubt you'll have lots of children with her; they'll make up for the siblings neither of you ever had. Now I know you have loads more to ask, but don't. Enough's enough."

Despite his serious reservations regarding death and demons, Toby was delighted with the prospect of meeting and marrying Sarah, especially since she was in the family line. Indeed, his heart began to beat faster as they approached her home.

WEDDING FEAST

1 "So this is Ecbatana. What's the quickest way to Raguel's house?" an eager Toby asked Azariah.

They soon found the old gentleman sitting by his courtyard gate. They greeted him, and he returned the greeting. "Had a good trip?" he asked. "Looks as though you boys arrived in one piece." Raguel led the way into the house, chattering right along. "Do come in."

2 To his wife, Edna, he whispered, "The small one, doesn't he remind you of my long-lost relative, Tobit?"

3 "Where are you boys from?" asked Edna.

"From the tribe of Naphtali, most of whom are still exiles back in Nineveh," Toby responded.

4-5 "We have a relative there. Would you happen to know him? His name is Tobit."

"He's my father."

"Unbelievable! How is he?"

"Alive and kicking!"

6 Raguel embraced Toby, tears coming into his eyes. Affectionately he asked his young relative about Tobit.

7-8 "Bless you, boy, son of the best of fathers! That blindness of his, what a bit of bad luck! Has it slowed him down? Is he still a justice-making, generous man?"

Through the tears, he kissed Toby on both cheeks. Edna was crying by this time, too, and their daughter, Sarah, joined the teary chorus as well.

9 Then Raguel absented himself, went to his flock, singled out a fine ram, butchered it, and field-dressed it for a feast. The visitors bathed, purified themselves, and reclined at the table. Then Toby gave Azariah a nudge.

"Have you told our host you have a plan for his daughter?" he whispered.

10 Raguel overheard the young man and gave an instant reply. "Eat, drink, relax, Toby—that's my advice. The evening yawns before us. As for marrying my daughter, my dear boy, there's no one else I'd rather give her to. Of course, I could give her to a stranger, someone I don't know from a place I've never heard of, but that wouldn't be right. You're a relative and fit all the qualifications. That's how I see it.

11 "But, my boy, we've had a bit of history with her. There have been seven bridegrooms before you, all relatives of mine. Each, as he was approaching

the wedding bed, dropped dead. But that was then, and this is now. Eat and drink, my boys. The Lord will take care of you both."

"From this moment on," replied Toby recklessly when he could get a word in, "I'm not going to eat or drink a thing until you make it official!"

"Now's as good a time as any, I guess" replied Raguel. "According to Moses, in a judgment handed down from heaven, she's mine to give and yours to receive. From today on and forever, she's your wife and you're her husband. And the Lord of Heaven knows what's best for you both this night. You'll make love. He'll make mercy and peace."

12 Raguel summoned Sarah. She came into the room. He took her by the hand and gave her to Toby.

"According to the rule written by Moses, take her as your wife. Bring her safe and sound to your father. May the God of Heaven give you a comfortable, uneventful journey!"

13 Raguel called his wife, Edna, to bring some paper. He made out the marriage contract, in which he covered the details according to the Mosaic Law, and signed it.

14 From that moment on they all resumed eating and drinking with great joy.

15 Raguel told his wife, "Turn the extra bedroom into a bridal chamber again and lead our lovely Sarah to it."

16 As the father instructed, so the mother did. Then, the final touch: Edna brought her daughter to the room. Tears swept the mother's face like a sudden squall; she dried her eyes and had some words for her daughter, the same as she had done seven times before.

17 "For all the sorrow you've endured, daughter, may the good Lord reward you with great joy! Be strong."

Then her mother left Sarah to face her fate for the eighth time.

A WEDDING NIGHT TO REMEMBER

1-3 **8** When the eating and drinking concluded, they led Toby to the room where the bride was waiting. He was no sooner inside than he remembered his bodyguard's admonition. He took out the two fish parts and placed them on the incense burner. As they blackened, the room was filled with such a stink that, with a whoosh, the demon Asmodeus was forced to flee to Upper Egypt. Azariah caught up with the wickedest of demons there, bound him up securely, never to escape, and returned to Ecbatana in one continuous sweep.

4 Back in the bridal bedroom, Raguel and Edna closed the door behind them. Then, mindful that Sarah's marriage bed had been a death trap seven times before, Toby followed Azariah's advice again. Breaking from the traditional wedding sequence, he got up from the bed.

"Get up, sister dearest. Let's use prayer to defeat the demon that has plagued you. Let's pray, beseech, and besiege our Lord to grant us tolerance and deliverance."

5-8 She did so, and he began to pray.

"Blessed are you, God of our fathers! Blessed be your name forever and ever! May the heavens and all your creatures bless you from age to age! You made Adam and gave him Eve. From both came the human race. You said, did you not, that it was not good for man to be alone? That he needed a helper, a look-alike? And so you provided. Now I take this woman, my cousin, as my lawful wedded wife, not to quiet my lust but to awaken my love. Keep our best interests at heart. We want to have children and grow old together."

"Amen," he said, and "Amen," she said.

9 Back to bed they went and continued the betrothal sequence they'd interrupted for the prayer.

JUST IN CASE

But Raguel couldn't sleep. Instead, he rose, rounded up some servants, and went outside to dig a grave.

10-14 "Just in case," he told his servants. "And if this Toby doesn't work out, if he dies tonight like the others, I don't want the neighbors to even know about it. I can't take any more of their mocking and false sympathy!"

When the grave was deep enough, he returned to his house and summoned his wife.

"Let's send the maid to see if the newlyweds are still breathing. If the boy's dead, we'll put him into the grave and no one else will be the wiser."

So they lit a lamp, opened the bedroom door, and pushed the maid in. She tiptoed to the bed and found the couple sleeping in each other's arms. She snuck back out to announce that the groom was alive and nothing bad had happened.

15-17 Both father and mother praised the Lord of Heaven.

"Bless you, God! May every blessing, pure and simple, rain down upon you! May all your saints bless you, and all your holy creation, too; and may all your angels and your chosen ones bless you, time without end! Bless you who blessed us and turned us into joyful persons. You didn't lay a hand on us when you could've punished us with death; instead, you enfolded us in great merciful wings. Bless you who blessed these two children, our children, your children. Find a place in your heart for them, as they'll find a place in their hearts for you. Fill their lives with mercy and joy."

18 Then Raguel ordered his servants to fill the grave in before first light, lest the neighbors find something to laugh about in the morning.

WEDDING PARTY

19-21 Raguel told Edna to light the ovens and start the baking. He went out to his flocks and herds, picked two cows and four rams, then slaughtered and dressed them. With all the ingredients in hand, the servants began preparing for the banquet. He summoned Toby and spoke to him in a paternal, no-nonsense sort of way.

"For fourteen days I want you to be my guest. Stay with us for that time. I want to fatten you up with food and drink, and you should want to comfort my daughter, who's had such a terrible time in the past and is now redeemed. Something else. I'm gathering all my assets and intend to give you half. When my wife and I die, the other half will be yours and Sarah's as well. Be strong, my boy! I'm now your father too, and Edna's now your mother. We're your and Sarah's parents, now and forever. You're not to worry ever again. Be happy!"

A Visit to and from the Banker

¹⁻⁴ **9** Faced with a fourteen-day celebration, Toby decided to have Azariah pick up the money from Gabael in Rages.

"My father's counting the days, you know, and if I'm a day late, he'll go into a funk. But you see how Raguel has set up the fourteen-day celebration? I just can't cut it short.

"You'll need four servants and two camels for the trip. Go to Gabael's house and show him the deposit receipt; it's for ten bags of silver. Load up the camels for the return trip, and while you're at it, why don't you bring Gabael and his household back for the wedding reception?"

⁵ So Azariah left with his entourage and headed for Rages, where he was received warmly by Gabael. He produced the deposit slip, saying he was acting in behalf of Toby, son of Tobit. Gabael promptly produced ten leather bags with their seals untouched and matched the deposit slip with its duplicate. Then he had the bags hoisted and secured upon the camels.

Finally, Azariah told Gabael the news about Toby's having married the daughter of Raguel and issued Toby's invitation for him and his household to come to the reception.

⁶ There wasn't much sleeping that night in Rages. In the morning, the entire family, including servants, all traveled to Ecbatana and found Toby reclining at table. The young man jumped up and saluted Gabael. The old man responded with tears and blessings.

"Blessed be the Lord who gave you peace. You're the son of a good and just man, a generous man. May the Lord bless your new wife and your father and mother and your wife's father and mother. And blessed be God because I now can love Toby, a second cousin of mine, once removed, much like I do his father, my first cousin!"

The Return to Nineveh

¹⁻² **10** Back in Nineveh, Tobit had been ticking off the days until his son returned. Already the boy was overdue, he pointed out to his wife. "Why is he taking longer than I planned? Could Gabael have died? Was there no one to return the money I left there?"

³⁻⁵ Anna began to cry, for she expected the worst. "My son's dead! He's nowhere to be found! What's keeping him?" And she kept up a doleful chorus, emitting a series of miserable mumbles: "Woe is me, dearest son! Why did I ever allow you to go, light of my eyes?"

⁶ As usual, Tobit chimed in.

"Shush, shush, Anna. Don't count the reasons why he's dead! Think of all the reasons he's still alive! Obviously, there's just been a delay somewhere along the route. He'll come back. Just you watch."

⁷ "Don't shush me! Shush yourself! My son has perished, died the death, and we'll never see him again!"

Anna couldn't sit down, getting up to check the road, coming back to worry some more; nothing would satisfy her. When the sun went down, she went inside and brought her grief to her bed, where she mourned all night long.

Meanwhile, back in Ecbatana, the fourteen-day wedding festival ran its course. Then Toby had a definitive word with his father-in-law Raguel.

"It's time for me to go. My father and mother are worried to death about me. I'm days overdue. So I ask you, my new father, to give me your blessing and send me off."

8 Raguel tried to argue. "Stay, my son. Remain with me and mine. I'll send messengers to your father, Tobit. They'll tell all the news about you."

9 But Toby fired right back. "Messengers won't do. Please send me back now."

10-11 So Raguel rose and put Sarah's hand in Toby's. Then he rounded up half of his estate: slaves, flocks and herds, donkeys and camels, clothing, currency, and household furniture. He had prepared quite a dowry. Then he made his good-byes to his son-in-law.

"Take care! Be good! Keep the faith! May the Lord of the heavens patrol the roads. And I want to see some grandchildren before I die."

12 Raguel kissed his daughter Sarah and had a good-bye message for her.

"Daughter dearest, treat your in-laws with respect. They're your parents now every bit as much as your mother and me. Go in peace! And I look forward to hearing good reports about you as long as I live."

He kissed her. Then it was Edna's turn. She had a message for Toby.

"Beloved son, may the Lord of Heaven bring you back to your home. And I too look forward to the grandchildren. Go in peace. I'm your new mother, and Sarah's your new sister. May we all travel with the Lord all the days of our lives."

Edna kissed them both and waved good-bye.

13 But first, for his in-laws, Toby had a parting word.

"May I honor you as parents for the rest of your lives!"

Then, rejoicing and counting the blessings of the Lord of Heaven, he gave the signal *Nineveh ho!* and the caravan groaned forward.

HOME AGAIN

1-3 **11** At last they were on their way. As they neared Kaserin, which wasn't all that far from Nineveh, Azariah had a suggestion. "You know, we left your father in a terrible state. Let's trot on ahead of the caravan and help prepare his household for the grand arrival. I hope you brought the fish gall with you."

4 Trotting along behind them, as throughout the whole trip, was the faithful family dog.

5-6 As they approached the home, there was Anna sitting by the side of the road, sweeping the horizon for sight of her son. She recognized his silhouette in the distance and cried out to his father. "Look, your son is coming, and the man who went with him."

7-8 As they approached, Azariah had some last-minute instructions for Toby.

"I know something you don't. Your father's eyes will be opened. Just squirt the fish gall into them; it will act as a medication, shrinking the white film to the point where it can be peeled off. Then he should be able to see the light."

9   Anna ran out to meet her son and flung her arms around his neck. "You're alive! I can see you with my own eyes! Now I can die, I'm so happy!" She cried and cried.

10-13   From the courtyard, the blind Tobit arose and shuffled toward the door. There Toby met him, fish gall in hand. He stopped his father and, holding him firmly by the shoulders, blew into his eyes.

"Hang on, father—don't faint on me now!" Toby said. He squirted the gall into his father's eyes. Then, with both hands, he managed to peel off the film. Seeing his son's face, the old man threw his arms around his neck. He too cried a river of tears.

14-15   "I see you, son, the light of my eyes! Blessed be God! Blessed be his great name! Blessed be all the holy angels forever! He's the one who laid the lash on me more than once, but he's also the one who returned my son to me!"

Tobit and Anna, father and mother, entered the house, joyfully shouting and blessing God at the top of their voices. Toby made clear to his father that the journey had been a complete success, thanks to the Lord God. Yes, he brought back the money and, yes, he'd taken a wife, Sarah, the daughter of Raguel. At that very moment, she was approaching the gate of Nineveh. A joyful shout went up from Tobit and Anna.

16-18   Tobit went out to the city gate to meet his daughter-in-law. Walking on his own, with no one on either side, he amazed the Ninevites who knew his frailty. He confessed in a loud voice that it was all God's doing, that God had been merciful and opened his eyes. Then he saw her, Sarah, his son's wife.

"I trust you had a safe journey, daughter dearest. May the God of Israel bless you. He's the one who led you to us. And blessings all round, on your parents and on my son and on your very pretty self. Come into your house in joyful blessing. Do come!"

It was a happy day for all the Israelites who lived in Nineveh. Ahiqar and his nephew Nadin showed up for the reception, which lasted for seven days. The bride and groom were showered with gifts.

SETTLING ACCOUNTS

1   **12** After the singing and dancing and the eating and drinking had come to an end, Tobit called Toby aside and told him, "The gentleman who went with you, Azariah, let's thank him, settle up accounts, and send him on his way."

2-3   "Father, I wouldn't mind giving him half of what I brought back on the trip," said his son. "He looked after me, helped me get a wife, recovered your money, and brought back your sight."

4-5   "I think that amount is just about right," agreed the father.

Then Toby approached his traveling companion. "Half of what we brought back, would that be fair?"

AZARIAH'S DOS AND DON'TS

6   Azariah thought it was time for a private chat with both father and son. He began with a prayer and a list of his own dos and don'ts.

"Bless God and confess him in front of all the living! You owe your prosperity to him. Bless and sing his name at every opportunity. Don't be ashamed of his name. Don't hesitate to proclaim him."

7 And then he got to the heart of the matter, if in a roundabout way.

"The mystery surrounding a king one should be slow to dispel. But to reveal the works of God and confess the words of God—they're very good things to do indeed. Do them, and evil will never have its way with you.

8 "Prayer with fasting is good, and so is generosity with justice. Better a little justice than a bundle of injustice. Giving is better than saving.

9 "Charitable giving frees us from death and purges every sin. The person who makes a habit of giving money to the poor will end up with more goods than he can handle.

10 "The person who befriends sin makes an enemy of his very own soul.

11 "Now all this is preamble to the truth, the whole truth, and nothing but the truth. As I just said, the mystery shrouding a king one should be slow to dispel, but the works of God should be shouted from the rooftops— that's the honorable thing to do.

THE BACKSTORY

12 "And now for the backstory. When you prayed, Tobit, Sarah was praying at the same time. I memorized everything you both said, brought it to God, and recited it in his presence. Also, whenever you properly buried unburied Israelites, despite the danger to you, I brought that to God's immediate attention.

13 "You remember, don't you, the time just before I showed up when you bounced up from the dinner table to bury a person whose body was found in the streets? That was my doing. God wanted to see if you were the real thing.

14 "Again, at God's behest, I intruded twice more in your lives, when I found a cure for you, Tobit, and a wife for you, Toby.

15 "You know me by the name of Azariah, but my real name is Raphael. I'm one of the seven holy angels who have multiple duties in the presence of God."

16-20 Both men were absolutely dumbfounded. The best they could do in response was fall on their face in front of the archangel. They were afraid of what was going to happen next. Raphael spoke again.

"No need to be afraid. Peace to you. Praise to God forevermore. The time I've spent with you—that was at God's behest, not mine. That's why you should bless him all the days of your lives.

"Recall, if you will, that whenever I was with you, I ate and drank as much as the next fellow, or at least I gave you that impression. But I had no need of either. It was an apparition.

"Bless the Lord on earth by confessing the God of Heaven. Watch me ascend to him and return to my own true home. As for our experiences together, write them all down."

And then he was gone.

21-22 When father and son finally dragged themselves off the ground, Raphael was nowhere to be seen. Because a real angel had appeared to them, they pranced about, blessing God in word and song for all his great works.

A Joyful Prayer

1 **13** Tobit sat down and wrote this joyful prayer for the Israelites in exile:

2 "Bless the living God forever,
Bless all his kingdom.
Both merciless and merciful,
he's the highway to Hades and back.
Swiping us from the jaws of hell,
his majesty saves us from our travesty.
No one escapes the movements of his hand.

3 Confess him to the Gentiles, children of Israel,
even though he's led you into the wilderness.

4 Exalt him in front of every living being;
he's your Lord, your Father,
your God for all time.

5 He laid the lash on your shoulders,
but he rubbed balm in your wounds;
he rounded you up from among the Gentiles,
wherever you were lost in the crowd.

6 When you turned toward him
by doing the right thing,
he turned toward you,
becoming totally yours,
face-to-face once more.
Just look at what he's done for you;
shout it from the rooftops!
Bless the Lord of Justice,
exalt the King of Eternity!
A captive on this earth, I confess him.
A sinner among sinners, I praise him.
Change your lives, stop your sins, do the just thing.
Who knows, he may do the just thing back to you.

7 My soul and I, we sing joyful things to the Lord of Heaven;
my soul rejoices all the days of my life.

8 Bless the Lord, you chosen ones,
all praise his majesty!
Confess him for all he's worth!"

Hymn to Jerusalem

Then Tobit wrote a second prayer for Jerusalem:

9 "O Jerusalem, holiest of cities,
The Lord will flay you alive for your wrongdoing,
but he'll reward you for your righteousness.

10 Praise the Lord for his good works,

bless the King of Eternity.
May he rebuild the Tabernacle,
but this time in your heart.
May he cheer up all the captives among you,
comfort all the miserable.

11 O Jerusalem, you're a beacon seen from the ends of the earth;
many nations will come to you from afar;
your name will echo from the hollows of the earth;
they'll come with gifts in their hands.
Generation after generation will give you joy.
Your reputation, O Jerusalem, will last forever.

12 Enemies will say harsh words about you.
They will pull you down, destroy your walls,
topple your towers, and torch your homes.
But blessed be everyone who keeps faith to the end.

13 Then will rejoice the children of the just,
assembling again to bless the Lord.
Happy are those who love you, O Jerusalem,
and happy are those who rejoice in your peace.

14 Bless the humankind who grieve
your every sorrow and loss;
they'll also experience every joy of yours.

15 My soul, bless the Lord, the great King;
16 he'll build his house in Jerusalem,
and it will last until the end of the world.
Happy I'll be if the remains of my seed
will see your charity with clarity
and proclaim your majesty, O Jerusalem.
Your gates will be studded
with sapphire and emerald,
the walls with precious stone,
the towers with gold plate,
the battlements with solid gold.

17 The streets will be cobbled with rubies
and paved with stones from Ophir;

18 the gates will sing canticles of joy;
the people will shout Alleluia!
Bless the God of Israel,
bless those who bless his name
from here to eternity!"

LAST WILL AND TESTAMENT

1-2 **14** That was the world according to Tobit. He had a peaceful death at the age of 112—or was it 118? He was buried with some flourish in Nineveh. He was about sixty when his eyes failed. After his sight was restored, he lived a fairly prosperous life, gave liberally to the poor, and confessed the wonderful generosity of God.

FINAL DOS AND DON'TS

3-4 As he lay dying, Tobit had yet one more list of dos and don'ts.

"Toby, take your children and return to Media. I have it on the authority of God, as it was spoken to Nahum in Nineveh, that all the prophecies made about Assyria and Nineveh will come to pass; we have to thank for this the prophets of Israel whom God sent to us. Everything will happen, neither more nor less, and right on schedule. If safety there be, it'll be in Media, not in Assyria or Babylon.

"Our relatives in the land of Israel, all of them, will be dispersed, scattered, driven in all directions from the best of all possible lands. The whole land of Israel will be deserted, not an Israelite in sight. No Israelites on the streets of Samaria or Jerusalem. Our Temple will be burned to the ground; our tears won't put out the flames. The holy city will become a wasteland, going out with a whimper, but it will come back with a bang.

5 "Again God will pour mercy on the Israelites and make them merry once again. Again he'll return them to the land of their ancestors. Again he'll build his house, but not with the same design and not until all the bad prophecies have come to pass.

"When they do return from captivity, everyone will participate in the rebuilding of Jerusalem and consider it an honor to do so. The house of the Lord will rise again, just as the prophets have promised.

6 "The nations of the world will be united and converted. They'll fear God, but in a good way. Their idols, which had promised so much and delivered so little, they'll leave behind.

7 "They'll bless the eternal God in justice. May all the children of Israel, who'll be liberated in those days, remember that God is truth. They'll gather together and come to Jerusalem. They'll live forever with a feeling of security in the land of Abraham. The day will come when the land is deeded to the Israelites. The people who love God will abound. The ones who love evildoing will be abandoned.

8 "Now, my children, I command your attention. Serve God in the truth, and act so pleasingly in the Lord's presence that he'll applaud your efforts. And pass the word on to your children to do the just thing until things are just for all, and to give until it hurts. It's a sign that they're mindful of God. And they should bless his name with truth and strength.

LEAVING HOME AGAIN

9-10 "Now, Toby my son, it's time for you to prepare for your departure from Nineveh. Don't hang back. There's no time to reminisce.

"The day your mother dies, bury her next to me. That very same day pack up your things and leave the city behind in the dust. Why? Wickedness abounds in the city everywhere you turn. Corruption has been developed into a fine art. The people subsidize it, even swim about in it.

"In our own family, for example, take the case of Ahiqar and Nadin; the elder brought him up; the younger did him in; then the Lord did the younger in. But God threw this infamy into the younger's face; the elder, however, found his way into the light; Nadin slipped and fell and ended up in eternal darkness; that's what he got for trying to kill Ahiqar. Because the elder gave liberally to the poor, he escaped the noose of death that Nadin had set for him. As a matter of fact, Nadin, in a moment of carelessness, stepped into that very same trap and it killed him.

11   "So you see, my children, the moral of the story is that generosity saves and iniquity kills."

And on that prophetic note, Tobit died. They laid him out on his bed, confirmed his death, and gave him a respectable burial, like the ones reserved for an honored citizen.

12-13   When his mother died, Toby buried her next to his father. Then he and his wife, Sarah, and their children left for Media, where they would live with his father-in-law Raguel and mother-in-law Edna in Ecbatana. Toby took good care of his in-laws, treating them with dignity and respect. Their final resting place was in their hometown. According to the will of both his father and his father-in-law, Toby and Sarah received both inheritances.

As for Toby himself, he lived to the ripe old age of 117—or was it 127? Before he breathed his last, news of the destruction of Nineveh reached him. Lines of prisoners from the city wound their way through Media, led by King Cyaxares of Media. In everything that happened to the children of Nineveh and Assyria, Toby found God's hand. He blessed the Lord God from here to eternity.

JUDITH

Passover is the Jewish religious festival commemorating the time when an avenging angel struck down the firstborn males of the Egyptians and Moses eventually led the Hebrews out of bondage; the story is found in Exodus 12. Passover has come to commemorate also the other times in Jewish history in which the Hebrews were enslaved or faced total annihilation.

Throughout the third century B.C., storytellers and writers created and polished a work on this subject that has come to be named the Book of Judith. Its history and geography are kind of wobbly, and hence it must be considered an imaginative tale.

It appealed to the men in the synagogue because it contained larger-than-life villains: Nebuchadnezzar, the evil king who defeated all the lesser gods and then proclaimed himself the one true god; and Holofernes, his hairy commander-in-chief, who defeated all the tribes and nations of his time except one, the Israelites.

The second half of the tale certainly must have appealed to the women. One of their own rose up—a middle-aged, well-to-do widow still mourning the passing of her husband. Judith was her name; in Hebrew it meant "Jewess." By tale's end, she has become a sort of Everywoman, a superheroine representing all Israelite women. In the title of the hymn at the end of the work, she's called Mother Israel.

The Assyrians were on the attack and had surrounded the town of Bethulia. The Israelite elders on the hilltop felt they could hold out for only five more days before they would have to surrender to the Assyrians. On hearing this, Judith summoned those elders and told them she had a plan. In the middle of the night she and Abra, her faithful female companion, slipped down from the hilltop to the plain. Within five days, they returned with mission accomplished.

The storytelling is rather refined. The performers who recited the work to gatherings of all sorts, and later the scribes who committed the story to parchment, credited all action to the hand of God; the hands of the two holy women couldn't have accomplished the outlandish plan if God's hand had not been joined to theirs.

In addition, the authors of the work put into the story many small, telling details that make it read like modern fiction.

Rapid dialogue exchange, known as stichomythia—it's a sort of verbal Ping Pong—may be found in many modern works of fiction, and it abounds in Judith, as well as in the better Greek plays.

Some critics have said that since Judith's behavior in carrying out her plan involved deception on her part, she shouldn't be held up as a model of grace under fire. In her defense, it may be said that her only protection and indeed her only weapon in her confrontation with Holofernes was deception. Not only did her actions in this regard save her from rape, but also they resulted in no Israelite casualties in the final battle with the Assyrians.

To Christians in the twenty-first century, the Book of Judith is a joy to read. It entertains and yet at the same time instructs us to beware false gods, to retain historical practices rather than ditching them for modernity's sake, and to pray always for God's help. (WG)

JUDITH

CLASH OF THE GENTILE KINGS

1 **1** Pick a king, any king, and put him in the story. Nebuchadnezzar of Assyria in the twelfth year of his reign will do; his capital was the grand city of Nineveh.

Pick another king, any other king, and put him in the same story. Arphaxad who reigned in Media, a provincial kingdom of the Persian Empire, will do; his capital was the great city of Ecbatana.

2-4 Arphaxad encircled his city with walls of hand-hewn stones of uniform cut; each stone was three feet wide and six feet long. The wall rose seventy feet high and was fifty feet wide. Each gateway had its own tower, one hundred feet high with a base sixty feet wide. The gates themselves he made seventy feet high; the opening, forty feet wide, wide enough for his cavalry to gallop out and his infantry to march through in formation.

5-6 The inevitable happened. The kings clashed on a plain, the one bordering Ragau; it was large enough to accommodate two major armies in classic conflict. Fighting on Nebuchadnezzar's side were all the mountain people; all the river people in the area of the Tigris, Euphrates, and Hydaspes; and Arioch, king of the Elamites. A united, if mixed, force of Chaldean stock.

7-10 To add to the force assembling on the plain, Nebuchadnezzar sent messengers to rally his other allies, among them the Persians and, for that matter, all who lived to the west: Cilicians, Damascenes, Lebanese, Antilebanese, and all the seacoast peoples; those from Carmel, Gileadites, Upper Galileans, and the plains people of Esdraelon; Transjordanians, all the way to Jerusalem, Bethany, Chelous, Kadesh, and the river of Egypt; Tahpanhes, Raamses, Goshen and, continuing westward, Tanis and Memphis; everyone who lived in Egypt, all the way to the borders of Ethiopia.

11 Unfortunately for Nebuchadnezzar, from all of his messengers to the west he got not one positive reply; in fact, quite the opposite. In the eyes of these westerners, he might be the king of Assyria, but not a god; he was just another human being with few—if any—real friends. His ambassadors came home empty-handed with a defeated look on their faces.

12 Well, the king knew an insult when he saw one. He became indignant and didn't care who knew it. He threw a fit, fell into a rage, rearranged the furniture, and swore to take revenge on every Cilician, Damascene, and Syrian; every Moabite, Ammonite, Judean, and Egyptian; indeed everybody between the two seas.

13-16 Meanwhile, in the seventeenth year of his reign, Nebuchadnezzar threw all his strength against Arphaxad; the Median caved, his cavalry and chariots unable to hold their ground. When the air cleared and the uproar quieted down, Nebuchadnezzar had won and Arphaxad had lost. The Assyrian continued his sweep toward Ecbatana. He took possession of the towers and seized the markets, thereby destroying its golden reputation as a capital city. As for the Median king, he was captured in the mountains of Ragau; the Assyrian spear and javelin throwers used the poor fellow for target practice. Good sport while it lasted; he was a sieve by the time it ended. Nebuchadnezzar returned to Nineveh with his armed forces for rest and relaxation. He and his troops lazed about for the next four months.

HOLOFERNES PUNISHES THE LOSERS

1-3 2 In the eighteenth year, first month, twenty-second day of the reign of Nebuchadnezzar, king of the Assyrians, Nineveh was abuzz. At last the scourge of the west that the king had been promising for years was about to begin. He convened his administrative officials and military officers. First, he warned that what they heard in that room was strictly classified, for their ears only. Then, ticking off all the evils of the region that had upset him, he conveyed to them his master plan. As a body, they agreed with the king's analysis and approved his remedy—that every last one of those who had been called to support the king against his enemies but had not done so should be exterminated.

4-5 And so that's what was supposed to happen. The king put the finishing touches on his strategic plan, then called his second-in-command, named Holofernes, whom he appointed supreme allied commander. These were the king's instructions to his general.

5-6 "I speak in my capacity as great king and lord of all things. It's time to assemble the invasion, 120,000 infantry and 12,000 cavalry. Provide special training where necessary. Then it's westward, ho! That's where our enemies lie waiting.

7-9 "To each of my so-called allies you'll deliver this ultimatum. I'm giving them two options.

"First option: unmerciful death. I'm bringing full wrath down upon them. They'll hear the tramp of my infantry's boots long before those very same boots trample them underfoot. Their fields will be covered with the wounded; their streams bloated with the dead. The survivors I'll send on death marches to prison camps at the ends of the earth.

10-11 "Second option: unconditional surrender to you in advance of my coming, the prisoners to await their fate in the prison camps until I come to pronounce final judgment on them. Those who choose to fight are the ones you will conquer first; then, turn them over to your troops for amusement. Don't feel sorry for them, they knew what to expect; steel yourselves for this bloody job.

12 "Be of good cheer. I'm the king of them all, the lord of everything, and I conquered the world by my own hand. Who'll deny that?

13 "As for you, Holofernes, Assyrian with a Persian name, remember what I've said this day and carry it out to the very last letter, beginning now!"

14-16 Holofernes made the appropriate exit from the king's presence and briefed the commanders of the imperial war machine. He picked out the officers who would train the expeditionary force (120,000 foot, 12,000 horse) and briefed them on the king's orders. Then he set about assembling the forces for the western front.

17-18 For transportation of their everyday baggage he chose camels, donkeys, and mules; for renewable food he chose sheep, oxen, and goats. His goal was a month's rations for everyone in the horde; what the army couldn't provide, it would forage or plunder. Where some delicacy was desired, he could always pay with gold and silver from the palace treasury, a vast shipment of which could be found in the baggage train.

19-20 Then Holofernes, the general of generals, finally hit the road with his force at full strength; the king would follow when he chose. Leading such an elite force prepared for special operations, he knew how many of everything he was supposed to have, but looking at it from his horse he had no way of actually counting it. They reminded him of locusts at lunch in a field or grains of sand on an arena floor.

21-23 After a three-day march, the army reached the neighborhood of Bectileth. There they camped at the foot of the mountain north of Upper Cilicia. The following day, Holofernes took his force up into the mountains, where he cut to pieces the people of Put and Lud and looted the Rassisites and Ishmaelites. Then he went back down to the desert fringe in the south, where he did the Chelleans in.

24-26 Next, he traveled along the Euphrates River, crossed Mesopotamia, and knocked off each fortified town along the brook Abron, which was burbling its way to the sea. They surrounded the periphery of Cilicia and killed everyone who raised a finger of complaint. He went farther, to the southern borders of Japheth, until the dunes of Arabia appeared on the horizon. He surrounded the Midianites, set fire to their tents, and in the embers roasted lambs swiped from the local folds.

27-28 At harvest time, he descended to the Damascus plain where he torched the grain, slaughtered the livestock, looted the towns, trashed the fields, and murdered all the young men. Is it any wonder that fear and trembling filled the peoples along the seacoast—Sidon and Tyre, Sur and Ocina, Jamnia, Azotus, Ascalon, and Gaza?

THE PUNISHED SEEK A TRUCE

1 3 The reluctant allies of the Assyrian king finally got the message. They should have responded when Nebuchadnezzar originally called for help. All they could do now was send envoys to try to sweet-talk Holofernes out of their horrific predicament.

2-5 "Enough already! We should have come when we were called, but here we are now, wanting to become children of Nebuchadnezzar. We stand in your presence. How may we serve you? Our homes are yours. Our buildings are yours. Our crops, flocks, herds are yours. Our tent cities are yours. Use them in good health. Come see them for yourself; it will do your eyes good." This or something very much like this was said to him.

6-7 Holofernes left the hill country for the seacoast, where his armed forces took possession of the fortified towns. In each he created a police force, drawing from the low lifes among the locals. Everywhere they went the invaders found themselves surrounded with victory and celebration, with garlands and dances and tambourines.

8 But their orders were to destroy the tented cities and deforest the woodland shrines. The word came from above to destroy—nay, exterminate—all gods and all religions. That done, Nebuchadnezzar clouded his own mind into thinking that he was the last god standing, entitled to full religious recognition from all tribes.

9-10   Next, the armed forces proceeded eastward to the plain of Esdraelon near Dothan, with the Judean mountains in the near distance. Between Geba and Scythopolis, they pitched camp in order to resupply their provisions; that alone took a month.

ISRAELITES SOUND THE ALARM

1-2   **4** The Israelites who were living in Judea at the time had heard the bad news about the Assyrians and were paralyzed with fear and trembling. Yes, they concluded, they would be next. Things didn't look good for Jerusalem or the Temple of the Lord God. There was no defense against the invaders.

3-4   What was so sad about this was that the Israelites were just coming out of a long period of captivity, collecting their scattered people from all over and merging them again into one nation. And then there was the Temple. They had just finished restoring the altar and refurbishing the furnishings, scrubbing the sacrileges of the previous invaders from the holy precincts. About the only thing the Israelites could do was alert Samaria and the environs of Kona, Beth Horon, Belmain, Jericho, Choba, Aesora, and Salem.

5   With the bad news came a set of instructions from headquarters. The locals were to man all the high ground, build walls around their towns, and deploy food to central locations against the possibility of a siege. From one point of view, at least, it was the best possible time for a siege; they'd just completed their harvests.

6-7   The high priest in Jerusalem at the time was Joakim. He was the one who composed the message and had it sent to the inhabitants of Bethulia and Betomesthaim, which overlooked the plain of Esdraelon-near-Dothan. His message was simple. The easiest spots to repel the invaders were the mountain passes, some so narrow that only two abreast could pass through at any one time.

8-9   The Israelites followed the instructions to the letter. They supported the communiqué issued by the high priest and the elders of the whole people of Israel, who were sitting in session in Jerusalem. Every man, woman, and child took the warning seriously and cried out to God for help. Then they humbled their souls by fasting with their bodies.

10-11   Everyone who lived in Jerusalem—that would include resident aliens, hired hands, privately owned slaves—all put away their everyday professional attire and pulled out their ceremonial sackcloth, the unfinished fabric made from goatskins, guaranteed to annoy the skin but please the Lord. Thus attired and cinctured, everyone went to the Temple and dusted their heads with ashes; then they prostrated themselves for prayer and penance, the harsh and hairy fabric between themselves and the ground.

12   The priests even removed the altar cloths and replaced them with sackcloth, crying out in unison to the Lord God of Israel. Why? They didn't want to surrender their children and wives to the invaders, nor lose their historical towns, nor have the holy places defamed and defiled merely for the entertainment and, alas, the perverse pleasure of the Gentiles.

13-15   For days the Israelites in Jerusalem and the rest of Judea prayed this way. During this time, even as the invaders approached, Joakim the high priest and all the other priests dressed in sackcloth and ashes and kept to the daily Temple schedule, making and accepting the required offerings. With ashes on their linen turbans, sweating profusely in their uncomfortable attire, they never ceased crying out to the Lord from the bottom of their souls that he might visit some good upon the whole house of Israel. The Lord heard their voice and saw the distress they were in.

INTELLIGENCE REPORTS

1-2   **5** The news that the Israelites had prepared themselves for battle— virtually shutting down the mountain passes and setting up a crazy quilt of barricades on the lower approaches—got back to Holofernes. He wasn't at all pleased. As a matter of fact, he exploded with anger, demanding a command appearance from the princes he'd just subdued—princes of Moab, leaders of Ammon, and magistrates from the seacoast communities. He quizzed them sternly.

3-4   "You're all Canaanites, aren't you? Don't you hate the Israelites as much as I do? So tell me, who are those people up there in the hill country? What kind of towns do they have? Where are their strongholds? Do they have armies? What kind of weapons do they have? Do they have a king? A general? Why have they, of all the peoples I've met in the west, turned their backs on me and refused to negotiate with me?"

5-9   Achior, the Ammonite ruler, proposed an answer.

"If you really want to know, I'll give you the lowdown on the 'hilltoppers,' as I call them. I know I'm one of your new servants, but if you listen to me, you won't be sorry.

"These Israelites, as they call themselves, descend from the Chaldeans. Religious refugees you might call them. They didn't like all those gods their ancestors had set up. So they pulled out and hit the road, landing in Mesopotamia where they lived for quite a while. There they worshiped a single deity instead of the loads of gods and goddesses they had worshiped back home. As they tell the story, he heard their prayers and advised them to make a farther move, from Mesopotamia to the land of Canaan.

"That's how they got here, and it's unlikely that they're going to leave anytime soon. They're traders, good ones, with a lot of gold, silver, and cattle to show for it."

10-12   "Didn't I hear they left for a while?" asked Holofernes.

"Yes, there was a famine and it was bad. They had to move westward again, this time landing in Egypt. There they stayed as long as there was food, but it was at a great price: All they did was work like slaves during the day and make babies at night. Soon they outnumbered the Egyptians. What else could the Egyptians do but fully enslave them? Soon the Israelites found themselves up to their noses in mud and water. Swallowing their pride, they started making bricks first with straw, then without it. At the same time they cried out to their divine protector, and he replied. He whipped Egypt with plagues, one after another. The Egyptians searched for antidotes but weren't able to find any, except ridding their land of Israelites altogether.

13-16   "When they got as far as the Red Sea, they had to stop. For them to get across, their protector had to part the waters. Then he led them through the Sinai and Kadesh Barnea. Along the way they met settled bedouin encampments but managed to disperse them without too much difficulty. Eventually, they entered the land of the Amorites. The Heshbonites objected, but the Israelites had military might enough to drive them off the land. Then they crossed the Jordan River, and the hill country was theirs. The Canaanites, Perizzites, Jebusites, Shechemites, and Gergesites all retreated, leaving the Israelites to enjoy centuries of peace and prosperity.

17-19 "The good times would continue, their God told them, as long as they didn't sin in his sight. If there was anything their God hated, it was sin. But sin the people did, and when they departed from the straight and narrow, their military touch disappeared. They lost one battle after another, finally ending up in captivity in a land not their own, having left their Temple in rubble and their hometowns occupied by their enemies. When the Israelites came back to their God, however, they were able to return from their far-flung diaspora. They repossessed Jerusalem where their Sanctuary had been and resettled in the hill country, which was then deserted.

20-21 "And so, my new master and lord, having made a short story long, the conclusion is simply this: If you want to subdue these people, all you have to do is wait till they sin again and their God abandons them. Then you can stroll up the mountain paths and their towns will be yours. But if you can't wait and must invade, then you'll find their Lord and God fighting on the battle line alongside them. And then, if I may say it, lord and master, you'll have made a fool of yourself on the world stage."

22 Before uttering that last sentiment, Achior should have thought twice. It caused an uproar. Holofernes' people began to call Achior names and insult him outrageously, ready to send him to the executioner right on the spot.

23 "We're not afraid of the Israelites!"

"They should be afraid of us!"

"They don't have the guts to come down to the plains and go man to man!"

24 "So if they don't come down to us, we'll go up to them and eat them for dinner. What do you think of that?"

HOLOFERNES ROARS

1 **6** When everyone calmed down, Holofernes had these words to say, addressing not only Achior but all Canaanites, non-Assyrians, and Moabites present.

2-4 "Just who do you think you are, Achior, you and your scruffy mercenaries from Ephraim? What kind of prophet are you, standing here and telling us not to fight the Israelites because they have some deity who'll defend them? Just the opposite is true. Yes, there's only one god, but he's going to defend *us*. His name is Nebuchadnezzar, lord of the universe. He'll send his power and might against the hill people and scatter them to the winds. And their divine protector won't be able to save them from that fate. Yes, we're the servants of just one person, just one god, and we plan to beat the living daylights out of the Israelites! Do you think those crazies on the hill can stop our cavalry when they storm up the mountain passes? We'll swamp them in their positions. The mountaintops will blot up the blood flow. The fields will be piled high with their dead. We'll sweep them away, leaving not a footprint of theirs behind. Don't look so skeptical! It's their own perversity that does them in. It didn't have to be this way.

"That's what Nebuchadnezzar, lord of the universe, would say to you if he were here, and nothing ever gets in the way of his words coming to pass."

Holofernes went on.

5-9 "But you, Achior, you little Ammonite mouse, you dare to speak to me that way? Take a good look at me. Next time you see me, I will have pulverized those bricklayers up there, the weepers and whiners who crawled out of Egypt. When you see me again, it will be your last day. My family members will pierce your body as though it were a pincushion. But for now, my slaves are going to deliver you to the hill country and place you in one of the towns near the passes. Not a scratch will befall you until you're killed with the citizens of that town. You'll die when they die. No need to look sad yet, my dear Achior. Perhaps, as you say, we'll lose on the mountains. But then again, perhaps we won't. That's my prediction, and my predictions always come true."

10-11 Holofernes ordered his attendants to bind Achior's hands, take him to Bethulia, and toss him to the Israelites. They secured the Ammonite leader, led him out of the tent, and crossed the plain to the base of the mountain pass, a spot made pleasant by subterranean springs.

12-14 When the Israelite lookouts saw the Assyrian party below, they called for their best warriors, who grabbed their slings and, aiming straight down, let go with a shower of stone. Hugging the mountain down below, the Assyrians had second thoughts. They tied Achior down and slipped off as best they could. The Israelites took this opportunity to scramble down to the mountain floor, cut Achior loose, and lead him up to Bethulia, where they promptly presented him to the local magistrates.

15-17 At the time, the magistrates were Uzziah, son of Micah of the tribe of Simeon; Chabris, son of Gothoniel; and Charmis, son of Melchiel. A town meeting was called in the assembly tent. Achior occupied the place of attention. Uzziah quizzed him about the latest happenings, and Achior was more than willing to talk. He told them about the session in Holofernes' tent, who was there, what was said, ending up with the general's boast that the house of Israel was headed for extinction.

18-19 Suddenly, it was prayer time in the mountain tent. Everyone fell down and cried out to God.

"Lord God of Heaven, consider the pride of our oppressors! Have mercy on our fragile condition! Look kindly on those of us who have bound ourselves to you."

20-21 Then they turned to Achior and saw to his needs. Uzziah took him from the assembly tent and brought him to his own house, where he had a meal prepared for him and the elders. Their continuing prayer that night was to the God of Israel, reminding him of his many promises to help his people.

INVASION PLANS

1-3   7 The following day, Holofernes issued orders to his armed forces to prepare themselves for a mountain assault that would be both the first and final battle in the campaign against the Israelites. The Assyrians and their allies made a spectacular sight. They were now up to 170,000 infantry, 12,000 cavalry, and that's not counting the baggage train run by supply corps personnel. On the eve of the battle, they pitched camp in the valley by the springs just below Bethulia. In breadth, they presented a front from Dothan to Balbaim; in depth, from Bethulia back to Cyamon, which faced Esdraelon.

4-5   When the Israelites looked down and saw enemy forces massing below, they began to shiver. The talk along the mountain line went something like this: "Look at them, as far as the eye can see. They'll crush everything underfoot; mountains, valleys, hills will be reduced to dust under their weight!" As night approached, each checked out his personal arms. The guards in the towers looked for enemy activity in the passes.

6-8   The next day, Holofernes paraded his cavalry on the plain for the mountain people to see. He personally visited the springs, something of a garden spot, inspected the entry points of the mountain passes, and set sentinels around both the paths and the water source. Then he leisurely returned to his camp.

The elders of the sons of Esau and the leaders of the Moabites and the maritime magistrates—none of them could wait to give the general the benefit of their limited military experience.

9-15   "May we have a word, lord and master? It'll be worth your while. We want to prevent you from suffering even one casualty. Those people don't really rely on their spears and slings to stop enemy troops from working their way up the passes. No, mountain fighting is different from fighting a battle on a plain. To beat them you have to fight like the mountaineers themselves. That way you won't lose a man.

"Here's what we mean. Just stay in camp and keep your military strength intact. Let your troops watch the springs; that's where the Bethulians get their water. If they can't get it, they'll die of thirst. Either that or they'll surrender the town. In the meantime, our people will ascend the nearby mountains on both sides of the city to prevent their escape that way. Famine and thirst will strike their fighting men down. Then the wives and the children after them. Their bodies will clog the streets. This will happen long before they'd ever taste the blade of a sword. You'll just be repaying them for their lack of gratitude; they shouldn't have refused to meet you when you wanted to parley for peace."

16-19   This strategy had a pleasant ring to Holofernes and the rest in the assembly tent. So it was ordered. The Moabites as well as 5,000 Assyrians removed their camp from Esdraelon to Dothan, where they put the Israelite springs under tight security. The Edomites and Ammonites secured positions on the mountain heights near Dothan. Another contingent did the same on the far side of Bethulia, to the south and east, toward Egrebel near Chusi on Mochmur. The rest of the Assyrian forces, with supply corps and supplies, remained right where they were, covering the ground for as far as the eye could see. Seeing themselves cut off on every side, the Israelites cried to the Lord God.

20-23 For the next thirty-four days no one moved—not the Israelites, not the Assyrians. On the thirty-fifth day, all the water jars on the hills were dangerously low. The cisterns were dry as a bone, not a drop left. Infants were fussing; women were moaning; children were fainting; people were falling in the streets. Those who had any strength left struggled to Uzziah's house, where he was sitting with the elders, and made their complaints known.

24-28 "May God choose between you and us! Why? Because you've done us a bad deed. You should have talked to the Assyrians, tried to find some peaceful way out of this mess! Now there's no one to help us. God has sold us out, sent us into the hands of our enemies. Now's the time to call a meeting and hand the town over to Holofernes. It's better to be captured by them than killed by them. We'll become slaves, yes, but we'll be alive. At least we won't have to see our babies shrivel, our women and children breathing their last in the massacre to come. We call you to account before Heaven and earth and before their gods and our God, who is making us pay for our sins and the sins of our forebears by allowing this terrible thing to happen to us today."

29-32 There was nothing left to do but weep to the high heavens, raising their many voices as one great voice. Uzziah had made an oath to persevere, but what else could he say? "Don't be so quick to give up, my brothers and sisters! Let's hang on for just five more days. God can't forget us forever. Surely in this short time he'll see the error of his ways and smile on us again. If not, if he no longer cares for us, I'll do what you want."

Uzziah ushered the people out and asked the men to return to their posts along the walls and towers of the city. The women and children he sent back to their homes. A great depression settled on the town.

JUDITH HAS A PLAN

1 **8** In Bethulia at that time there lived a widow named Judith, a woman with a respectable genealogy covering multiple generations. She was daughter of Merari, son of Ox, son of Joseph, son of Oziel, son of Elkiah, son of Ananias, son of Gideon, son of Raphain, son of Ahitub, son of Elijah, son of Hilkiah, son of Eliab, son of Nathanael, son of Salamiel, son of Sarasadai, son of Simeon, son of Israel.

2-3 Her husband was Manasseh, from the same tribe and lineage; he died during a barley harvest. As a foreman, it was his duty to supervise the binding of the sheaves in the field; apparently, sunstroke overcame him. They took him to his house in Bethulia and put him to bed, where he died. He was buried in the family plot, a field between Dothan and Balamon.

4-7 That was three years, four months earlier.

Judith remained in her home, mostly in the living area on the roof, where she erected an airy, breezy prayer tent for herself. Her undergarments were made of sackcloth for mourning; her outer clothing of finer, more finished fabric, in colors suitable for widows with a fashion sense. She kept the widow's fast; that is to say, she mourned on every day but the Sabbath and Sabbath eve, on the day before the New Moon, on the day of the New Moon, and in general on any joyful festival of the house of Israel.

She had a good figure, and her face hadn't lost its beauty. There was sentiment in her heart and common sense in her head, and in her garden she grew honesty.

Her husband had a decent lineage himself, having been a son of Joseph, Ahitub, Melchis, Eliab, Nathanael, Sarasadai, Israel. Upon his death, Manasseh had left his wife rather well off. There was a modicum of gold and silver, a few slaves, some livestock, and arable fields. Judith remained on the property and ran them all from her house.

8-10 As for Judith's reputation, no one could lay a finger on her because she was a God-fearing person. She'd heard about the rough words spoken to Uzziah—something to do with the lack of water. And she'd heard his response—that he swore he'd hand the town over to the Assyrians in five days.

So Judith sent her chief maid, Abra, a woman of no small talent herself, to invite Uzziah and the other elders of the city, Chabris and Charmis, to pay her mistress a visit. Judith had been helpful to them in the past, and hence they had no trouble accepting the invitation.

11-27 "Hear me out, gentlemen!" Judith announced. "What you said to the people today wasn't quite right. You made a deal with God that if he didn't come through for us you'd hand the place over to the enemy, am I right?"

They nodded.

"Well, who are you to swing a deal with the divinity above? Are you some kind of divinity here on earth? If you really tried to do that, then you don't have a brain in your head. If you yourselves can't appreciate the height of the human mind and don't understand the depth of the human heart, how do you expect to make sense of God?

"You haven't a ghost of a chance, my dear brothers. You want my advice? Stop ruffling the divine feathers! If God doesn't help us in five days, it doesn't mean that he hasn't the power to do so. But if he does want to help us, he can do it in five days—or a hundred and five days. And did you ever think that it just might be the divine will to do away with us right in front of our enemies?

"You shouldn't try to make deals with our Lord God. Why? Because the Divine Being isn't like a mere mortal who can be terrorized with threats or argued into a corner. I know I'm repeating myself, but if we expect help from God let's continue to invoke his name. He'll hear our voice if he wants to. In the past, people paid their respects to, bowed before, and worshiped gods cooked up by human minds and made by human hands. Other peoples did that, and we did that too, at least in the beginning. That's why our ancestors were abandoned to the sword and had a catastrophic end right in front of their enemies; indeed, *we* were our own worst enemies.

"But things are different today. We know a fake god from a real one, a God who won't forget us in our time of need. If we're captured, then the rest of Judea will be defeated and our holy places will fall prey to the looters. What then? God will charge us with the crime and punish us accordingly. The death of our people and the captivity of our land and the desertion of our heritage will fall on our own heads, be our own fault—at least that's how the Gentiles whom we'll be serving as slaves will interpret it. Our disgraceful conduct will even appear on our record and make us less desirable for decent positions as slaves.

"And even if we should earn favor with our masters, our Lord God would find a way to turn that against us. So here we are now, dear brothers. Let's show our friends and relatives how it should be done. Their lives depend on what we do today. The welfare of our shrines, homes, and sanctuaries lies in our hands. In spite of the obstacles facing us, let's give thanks to our Lord God.

"He tests us, yes, but no more than he did our ancestors. Remember how much he did for Abraham and Isaac, and for Jacob in Syrian Mesopotamia as he was shepherding sheep for Laban, his mother's brother. God put the torch to our forebears to force them to confess what was in their hearts; at least he hasn't done that to us yet. Although the Lord has been known to give the lash to those who love him the most, he does it not to punish his people but to keep them honest."

28-31 In reply, Uzziah had a few things to say.

"Everything you've said makes complete sense, and no one would want to contradict you. Nor is this the first time your wisdom has shed light on a particularly difficult issue. From your earliest days, everyone has known your generous heart.

"But our people are dying of thirst. That's what made us do what we did, swear to what we knew shouldn't be done. Now pray for us. Perhaps our God will listen to you. You're a holy woman. Ask him for rain to fill our cisterns. At least that would get rid of our dizziness; that would allow us to walk the streets without fear of fainting."

32-33 Judith decided on a more practical tack. "I have a different plan. I'm about to give you a heart attack, but it will give our heirs and biographers something to write about! Tonight stand by the city gate and give the command to open it when I tell you. My maid and I will slip through. And before the five-day limit has passed, the Lord God will visit Israel."

"And just how will that happen?" the three men asked.

34 "Don't try to guess. I'm not going to tell you how I plan to pull it off. But I'll give you one clue and one only. My hand will be the instrument."

35-36 What else could Uzziah and the others say?

"Go in peace. May the Lord precede you as you go about exacting revenge upon our enemies."

Then they staggered down from the lovely tent on the rooftop and resumed their positions at the gates and on the turrets.

※

THE PRAYER OF JUDITH

1 9 Left to herself, Judith knew that God favored the prayers of widows. First, she dusted her head with ashes and undressed down to her sackcloth. Then, assuming the prayer position, she fell on her face. Meanwhile, at the same time in Jerusalem, the holy city, it was incense time or thereabouts in the Temple—a perfect time for her to cry out to the Lord in Bethulia.

2 "Lord, God of my ancestor Simeon. He was the one to whom you gave a sword to exact revenge against the foreigners. They were the ones who raped Dinah, undoing her clothes and revealing her thighs, which no man had a right to see, and breaching the virginal barrier to plant their ugly seed in her secret garden. Hadn't you said, O Lord, 'Nothing like that should ever happen,' but it did, didn't it?

3 "So, Lord God, you gave up the rulers of the Hivites for execution. The

very bed they stained with virginal blood was stained again with their own lifeblood. As for the slaves, mid-level officials, and throne-room hangers-on who were involved at whatever level in the shameful acts perpetrated against the virgin Dinah—you beat all of them to a pulp.

4 "Their wives you rounded up and passed around; their daughters you led into captivity. The objects of any value that were left behind you gave to your own people who had protected Dinah and invoked you for help.

"Are you there, God? It's me, Judith, a widow!

5 "Yes, you did all these things in the past, as well as continue to do them in the present. And no doubt you'll do them in the future. You've thought about justice, and what you've conceived you've put into action.

6 "The things you have wanted to happen did indeed happen—make no mistake about that. Our enemies marched right in and said: 'Here we are, Lord. We're your agents. You've pre-planned us, and everything we will do is already pre-known to you.'

7 "So look now, Lord! The Assyrians are strutting their stuff on the plains below. They're parading their cavalry. They're marching their infantry. They're putting their hope in their weapons. What they don't know is that the one who lurks over us all—that's you, O Lord—is the one who'll win the war for us with a wave of your hand.

8 "*Lord* is your name—act like a lord. Cut their number, sap their strength, reduce their bravery with your wrath. They want to pollute your Holy Place, defile the Tabernacle in which your holy name resides, and whack the decorative horns off the altar corners with a blade swung in anger.

9-11 "You know my plan. Just give my poor widow's hand the strength to carry it off. As I'm sweet-talking the enemy, whispering sweet nothings in his ear, strike him down and his followers with him. Use my weak hand to quash their better-than-thou attitude.

"You can do that, can't you? Your strength doesn't rest in my physical power. You're God of the humble, helper of the weak, upholder of the infirm, protector of the abject, savior of the desperate.

12-14 "Hear my prayer, God of my father, God of the Israelites, Dominator of all things, Creator of the waters, King of the universe; hear my prayer! May my silken words whispered into the enemies' ears cause ruin among their ranks. Right from the start they've been against your covenant and your Temple, Mount Zion, the hilltop home you keep for us. Let your whole nation and the tribes that compose it know that you're the God of Universal Power and Might and not just one of those random rulers that come along from time to time."

NIGHT ON THE TOWN

1-2 **10** Face down, Judith prayed this prayer to the face of God above. Then she arose and called for Abra as she went downstairs into her house where she spent the joyous Sabbaths and festivals.

3-4 She stepped out of her sackcloth and bathed with what little water she had left. A dab of perfume in all the right places, a comb through the hair, a tiara to hold it in place, and she was ready to dress. She picked out something sportive, even provocative, reminiscent of the sort of fashionable clothes she wore when her husband was alive. On her feet she put sandals with anklets that went ding-ding-a-ling. For accessories she chose bright bracelets that went jing-jing-a-ling. In other words, she did herself up as though she were stepping out for a night on the town.

5 Into a picnic basket she and Abra put a five-day supply: a bottle of wine, a cruet of oil, barley and fig cakes, bread, cheese, and a set of dishes. Heavy, yes, but not so heavy that Abra couldn't carry it over rough terrain. Whatever might happen, Judith would keep kosher.

6-8 They found Uzziah and the other elders, Chabris and Charmis, waiting for them at the gate. When they saw Judith approaching, they couldn't believe their eyes. She certainly didn't look like a widow anymore. They said, "May the God of our forebears go with you. May he bless your plan and bring it to a successful conclusion."

9-10 Adoring God, she prayed face down, then had some words of parting: "It's time to do what we agreed should be done."

The elders gave the order to the young men in charge of the gate to open it. As they did so, Judith and Abra slipped through. The men kept track of them as they careened down the pass. But at the bottom, as they started crossing the plain, the lookouts lost sight of them.

11-13 The two women made a beeline for the enemy encampment, the bells giving away their position, and they were soon intercepted by an Assyrian patrol that started asking pointed questions: "Who are you?" "Where have you come from?" "Where do you think you're going?"

Judith replied, "I'm a daughter of the Hebrews, but I'm fleeing from them now, running away because God is about to turn them over to your wrath."

"So?"

"So I want to see your general, Holofernes, and tell him what's really going on up there. Also I want to show him a way up the mountain. He can climb it, defeat the Israelites, and take a commanding position over the plain without losing a man."

14-16 Feasting their eyes on Judith's beauty, the hardened soldiers heard her out before they replied.

"Looks like you just saved your life, little lady, by hurrying down here to give the good news to Holofernes. We'll take you to him. A word, if we may. When you get to see him, no need to be afraid. Just say what you have to say, and everything will be okay."

17-19 How to get the two women safely through to the general's quarters was a problem. An escort would be needed. Everyone volunteered. A hundred were picked. The group caused quite a stir as it made its way through the streets of the tent city. At Holofernes' canvas compound, the household guards surrounded the two women, waiting for their identities to be checked and their purpose evaluated. Sizing up Judith's beauty, the men liked what they saw, as their raucous compliments revealed.

"Hey, beautiful lady, are there any more like you up there? If so, their men are dead, dead as a doornail!"

20-23 When the guard got the go-ahead from within, members of the general's family came out to receive the women and usher them just inside the tent housing the throne room. Holofernes was at the back, reclining on his couch, which was under a rather flashy canopy, purple and gold with emeralds and other precious stones sewn on. When Judith was announced, he rose and, with a parade of silver lamps preceding him, came to the front of the tent. His male relatives couldn't help but remark in their own language that, although a matron and a widow, the woman was still gorgeous! Paying her respects, Judith knelt face down in front of him. At his nod, the servants helped her back to her feet.

JUDITH AND HOLOFERNES MEET

11 Holofernes spoke first.

1-4 "No need to be alarmed, dear lady. No need to be frightened. I've never harmed anyone who wanted to serve Nebuchadnezzar, universal king of the universe. But that doesn't prevent me from getting right to the point. Tell me about your people in the hill country. You know, I wouldn't have lifted a blade against them if they hadn't insulted me first. I don't find crudeness attractive, do you?

"So tell me why you've defected from them and come to us now. Is it that you consider us a safe haven? Please calm down. You're not going to die tonight, if that's what you're worried about, or tomorrow night, or the night after that. No one's going to lay a finger on you. I'll treat you well, as well as I treat all those who serve my lord and king."

5-19 It was Judith's turn to speak.

"Do take what I'm about to say to you at face value. If you do, you'll accomplish everything you want, with their God fighting at your side, and you won't lose so much as a whisker in the process. Nebuchadnezzar lives, king of all he surveys, marshal of his many armies! His general, Holofernes, lives, putting everyone who doesn't believe in Nebuchadnezzar on the straight and narrow! Through your efforts not only do human beings follow the king, but also wild animals and livestock, even birds of the air wander after him—and all this with Nebuchadnezzar gloriously reigning. We've heard of your wisdom and your rather extraordinary intentions. And we know you're fully capable of carrying them out.

"I could rattle on more about your impressive accomplishments to date, but I won't. I want to come right to the point.

"We've heard from Achior, the Ammonite leader. Yes, the people of Bethulia welcomed him, took him in, gave him their sympathy. In return, he gave us a blow-by-blow on what was said and done in your council. May I say that everything he said to you was correct? It's time you came to grips with that. Our people are impervious to defeat, nor will they be ruled by another's sword, unless, of course, they sin against God. That's the loophole.

"But, and this is my message to you, my lord, don't be frustrated. The Israelites are about to commit a great sin, a sin that will end all agreements between them and their God. At the precise moment that happens, they'll fall into your arms.

"They're out of food and water now. They plan to kill the cattle and eat anything and everything they can swallow, regardless of the dietary laws God gave them. They've decided to consume the firstfruits of the grain harvest and withhold the tithes of wine and oil ordinarily saved for the priests who preside in Jerusalem—stuff that no one's supposed to touch, let alone eat and drink.

"By the way, the people in Jerusalem are in the same predicament we are. They've broken God's Law and allowed exceptions to the dietary laws. We've sent messages to the Jewish Council there for permission for us to do the same. When the messengers return, which should be soon, and our people on the hilltop begin to swill down the forbidden food and drink, that's the moment their demise will begin.

"When I learned this, that's when I fled from their company. God sent me to make a deal with you that will amaze the world when it hears about it. But make no mistake, I still worship my God and serve him night and day. And now that I've had my say, I hope I may remain in your presence and enjoy your hospitality.

"One further thing, though. Every night I will leave the camp and go out into the field and pray that my God will send me a sign that the sinning has begun. Then I'll return to you with the news. At the right time, you can gear up your forces and advance unimpeded through the mountain passes.

"If you want, I'll lead your procession through Judea all the way to Jerusalem. I'll crown you ruler in the middle of the city. You'll lead the people like a shepherd leads his sheep. How do I know all this? It came to me in a dream. I'm merely passing it on to you."

20-23 Holofernes and his family members liked what they heard from the woman. Her beauty and her wisdom didn't hurt her message: "There's not another woman like her in the whole world." "So beautiful." "So wise."

Holofernes had this to say to her.

"Your God has done well to send you here to me and my family. You've strengthened our hands in our attempt to destroy those who insulted us. Over and above that, you're lovely to look at, delightful to hear. If things turn out the way you say they will, your God will become my God, you'll have rank in the palace of King Nebuchadnezzar, and our reputations will spread throughout the world."

The Banquet

1 **12** Holofernes informed Bagoas, his eunuch, chief of staff, and overall righthand man, that the lady would be dining in the silver room and that she'd be having caviar from his pantry and wine from his special collection.

2 "No caviar for me," said Judith, "but I do have a request. I won't be eating or drinking from your menu. That would give scandal. In this basket I've brought along enough kosher food to keep me and my maid going."

3 "As you wish," the general replied, "but if you should run out of anything, where may we find more? You're the only Israelite in our tent city."

4 "I've brought provisions enough to last me, my lord," she replied. *At least until my Lord signals that it's time to begin my plan,* she thought to herself.

5-6 Then the household staff led her to a secure tent. She slept the sleep of the just until midnight, when she arose and sent a note to Holofernes.

"Will my lord now issue an order permitting his new handmaid to go out into the valley to pray?"

7-9 Holofernes obliged, and she received a pass granting her in-and-out privileges. She used this for three days, each time leaving by night and going to the Bethulian springs outside the city, where she bathed. Rising from the waters, she recited prayers to the Lord God of Israel for the next step in the exaltation of her people. Returning refreshed, she entered her tent and remained there for the rest of the day. Toward evening, she had something to eat and drink.

10-12 On the fourth day, Holofernes decided to give a banquet for his household, leaving his high command on orange alert. For Bagoas he had a special word.

"Find the Hebrew woman who's somewhere among us and invite her to dinner. We don't want word getting around that I entertained such an international beauty and bade her farewell without seducing her. I'd never hear the end of it."

13 Bagoas knew all too well what that meant. He knew where to find Judith and offered her the grand invitation.

"It would be improper for a mature woman such as you to enter my lord's house and then refuse to sit opposite him as an honored guest, enjoying the wines, and then perhaps taking the honored place among the Assyrian women who assist in the palace of Nebuchadnezzar."

14 "Who am I," Judith replied, "to refuse such an invitation from my lord? His wish is my wish also and will be so until the day of my death."

15-16 Rising, she prettied herself with some bangles and baubles she'd brought along just in case. Abra preceded her, carrying the lambskins Bagoas had given her to recline on during her visit. She laid them down facing the general's place at his table.

Holofernes was already reclining at the table when Judith made a dramatic entrance he thought he'd never forget. Rising to his feet, he wanted to seduce her at once, but he restrained himself.

17 "Please have some wine," he said sweetly. "Nothing can liven up a party like good wine, I always say."

18 "I shall have a sip, my lord, but from my own wine, for this is the high point of my life so far."

19-20 She ate and drank the food and wine Abra had prepared from the Bethulian basket. Holofernes enjoyed his own wine, which, he noticed for the first time, was a fruity blend with a supple finish! As sommelier for the evening, Bagoas kept his master's glass full. In no time the supreme allied commander, having a very good time, was drunk.

BEHEADING IS BECOMING

1-3 **13** When the hour grew late, that was the cue for the servants to clean up and clear out. Bagoas shut the tent from the outside, secured the flap, and then dismissed the household staff. It was bedtime for all; everyone was exhausted. A lot of wine had been consumed. Only Judith and her maid remained in the tent with Holofernes, who was now stretched out on his own bed. Before he'd finished pulling all his clothes off, he'd sailed into a drunken slumber.

Judith asked Abra to leave the tent and wait for her to come out later for prayer in the fields, as was the two women's custom since they'd arrived in the camp. She'd told the same thing to Bagoas.

4-5 So there she was at last, standing over the Assyrian general.

"Lord, Lord God of all strength, at this horrid moment look kindly on what my hands are about to do; horrid, yes, but I'm doing it for Jerusalem. Now's the time for you to recover your heritage on earth. Now's the time for you to use my poor hands to quash the enemy who would destroy us."

6-8 She approached the head of the bed and unsheathed the heavy scimitar hanging there. Approaching closer, she grabbed Holofernes' hair to expose the neck and prayed again.

"Lord God of Israel, give me the strength to do what I have to do now."

With such force as her tiny hands could muster, she brought the blade down as hard as she could, not once but twice, before the head came loose and fell on the floor. She rolled the body off the bed and pulled the canopy, along with the mosquito netting, down in a heap.

9-10 A little tidying up, and then Judith handed the head and the mosquito net out the door of the tent to Abra, who quickly put them into the picnic basket and closed the lid. Then both women left, allowing those few still awake to suppose they were off to the valley for prayers as usual. They passed through the guard easily enough and, taking a circuitous route, eventually arrived at the mountain pass. Up they went to Bethulia, eventually approaching the gates of the city.

11-13 Judith called out to the Israelite sentries.

"Open up! Open up the gate! God's with us, our God's with us! Today's the day the Lord God has made good on his promise to help Israel and repulse our enemies!"

The guards heard her voice; some rushed back into town to rouse the elders and call anyone else who was still awake. A diverse crowd quickly gathered at the gate. They couldn't believe that Judith had come back alive. They opened the gate and welcomed her and her maid. A fire was kindled; everyone huddled around it.

14-16 Judith spoke up for all to hear.

"Praise our Lord, praise him. He hasn't taken his protection away from us, as we'd thought. Instead, he's dealt a terrible blow to our enemies by virtue of my hand this very night."

Opening the picnic basket, she pulled out Holofernes' grizzly head, which was still sporting a drunken smile, and held it up for all to see.

"Yes, this is the head of Holofernes, commander-in-chief of the Assyrian armies. Here also is the mosquito netting of the bed where I found him, unconscious from drinking too much wine. Yes, the Lord struck him down, though it was my hand on the handle.

"The Lord lives! He has protected me in the path I chose. But one thing I'd like to make clear. As soon as Holofernes looked at me, I knew he was mine. Which is another way of saying that he didn't seduce me; I seduced him! Which is yet another way of saying that he didn't lay a hand on me; I laid my hand on him!"

17 The people around the fire didn't know what to say. They bowed down and adored God, praying as one.

"Blessed are you, Lord, for annihilating the enemies of our people, reducing them to nothing on this very day."

18-20 Uzziah spoke for the rest of them.

"It was the Most High who blessed you and made you first among women on the face of the earth. Yes, it was he—the one who created

Heaven and earth—who directed your hand to do the bloody deed.

"May your praise never leave the hearts of humankind, who will remember the strength of our God for ever and ever. May God exalt the memory of your risking your life for your people, even when they'd been humiliated by their enemies. You diverted our ruin while remaining in the straight and narrow yourself."

To that the crowd around the fire said, "Amen, amen."

HANGING THE HEAD FOR ALL TO SEE

14 1-5 A final word from Judith.

"Hear me, friends. Take this head and hang it on the battlement facing the plain. When dawn comes and the sun rises, pick up your weapons and make as though you are about to descend the pass and engage the first line of Assyrian defense in battle. That's to say, do everything up to but not including the descent down the pass. As for the Assyrians, they'll grab their arms and return to their tent city. They'll rouse their officers, who'll run to the general's tent and find only his dead, headless body there. Panic will seize them, and they'll flee from you as fast as they can. That's when Israelites and would-be Israelites should descend to the floor of the valley and take up hot pursuit, slaying the enemy as you overtake them.

"But before you carry out that scenario, call Achior the Ammonite. I want to see him. He has to confirm the identity of the one who spat on the house of Israel, the same one who sent him to us in the hope that he'd die with us."

6-9 They called for Achior, who was staying at Uzziah's house. When the Ammonite ruler came to the bonfire and saw Holofernes' head held up by one of the men there, he fainted and fell on his face. After he came to, they helped him up. When he saw Judith, he fell at her feet, expressing his admiration for what she'd done.

"Blessed are you in every tent in Judah! As for the rest of the world, may they tremble when they hear your name! Now tell me, how did you do it?"

Judith told the story again, skipping none of the details. When she came to the end, shouts of joy went up once more from the listeners.

10 Achior had just gotten a good dose of what it meant to be a Jew, and he liked what he heard. He submitted himself for circumcision. Thus, he became a member of the house of Israel from that day to this.

11-12 First light came, and they hung the head of Holofernes high upon the city wall. Then they strapped on their arms and headed for all the mountain passes. When the Assyrian outposts got an eyeful of the Israelites from below, they sent messages up and down the line and back to Holofernes' headquarters.

13-15 There the messengers approached Bagoas the chamberlain.

"Rouse our leader right away! The Israelites have declared war on us. Even as we speak, they're in full battle garb and descending the passes to the valley floor, where it looks like they mean to fight to the death."

Bagoas entered the outer room of Holofernes but stopped short of the inner room. He made a noise at the curtain, suspecting that Holofernes was still sleeping with Judith. When there was no response, he peeked; there was the general's body sprawled over a footstool. Stone cold, hardly a stitch on it, and minus a head.

16-18　Bagoas let out a scream, went on a tear, and carried on as though it were the end of the world. He ran to the guest tent where Judith had been staying—she wasn't there. Out of control now, he cried out: "That wretched slave did it! That Hebrew woman is the culprit! With one blow she's brought down the house of King Nebuchadnezzar! Holofernes is dead on the ground, and his head is nowhere to be found!"

19　When they heard these words, the military officers lost their composure and tore their tunics, unable to understand how a surprise attack could have happened right under their noses. Consternation and imprecation rose from the valley floor. Yes, noted the hill people, the Assyrians were making quite a racket down there!

Assyrians Flee, Israelites Follow

1-3　**15** As the ghastly news spread through the tent city, everyone—Assyrian and non-Assyrian alike—was disoriented. Terror spread like the morning breeze. It was every man for himself. They upped and fled in every direction. Those Assyrians flanking the Israelites on the mountaintops also hit the road as fast as they could, with Israelites in hot pursuit.

4-5　Uzziah sent messengers to Betomasthaim, Choba, Kona, and everywhere else in the land of Israel to relay the good news and alert them to the possibility of enemy soldiers passing through their environs. How to deal with them? Death was the only way, said Uzziah.

When these Israelite enclaves got the news, they quickly dispatched any enemy regulars and mercenaries that showed up. When the people in and around Jerusalem got the news, they reacted fiercely. Those in Gilead and Galilee, who were flanking the escaping force, delivered major casualties, pursuing the enemy all the way to Damascus.

6　As for the Bethulians themselves, they flooded the plain and made short work of those dazed Assyrians who stayed to fight. By nightfall, all that was left on the plain was the rather ragged but still valuable baggage train that Holofernes no longer needed. The Bethulians claimed it as their own and, after a quick appraisal, concluded that they were considerably richer at dusk than they had been at dawn!

7　Returning from the slaughter, they inventoried the spoils of war that they hauled up the mountain passes and then divided up. No Bethulian was left out; every Bethulian's personal wealth was increased that day.

8-10　Joakim, the high priest in Jerusalem, with the elders of the Israelites and other inquisitive citizens of Jerusalem, came to visit. They toured the battlefield and saw all the good things the Israelite soldiery had done—that is, what the Lord God of Israel had done. They also met with Judith and expressed their appreciation and blessed her.

"You're the glory of Jerusalem, the glory of Israel, the glory of the Israelites! You did it all with your own hand; you did it for the good for Israel; you did it to please God. Blessed are you, woman, in the presence of Almighty God for all time."

"Amen, amen!" said the Bethulians to that.

11 It took thirty days for the Israelite accountants to divvy up the Assyrian booty from the valley. Holofernes' tent was given to Judith; they said it would look good on her rooftop. She also got his silver table settings, beds, food and liquid containers, and all his furniture. The cartage and haulage she had to supply herself; in this the Assyrian mules were especially helpful.

12-14 Needless to say, all the Israelite women wanted to meet their new heroine—to bless her, to entertain her, to dance for her. Wands wrapped with ivy were the favorite gift to her. Judith was overwhelmed with them and passed them out to her new women friends. For these women-only get-togethers, coronets of olive leaves were the favored attire for the head. Sporting the same, Judith did not hesitate to join the chorus of women singing and dancing in the streets; and the men followed. The song, by the way, was one of thanks to Israel and praise to God.

HYMN OF PRAISE FOR MOTHER ISRAEL

1 **16** In a new song for my God,
begin with tambourines!
Begin for my Lord with cymbals!
Work up for him a new psalm!
Exult and call upon his name!

2 You're a God who wages war against wars.
You pitch your tent in the central park.
You rescue me from those who'd do me in.

3 Came the Assyrian from the mountains to the north,
came by the thousands his army did;
they swarmed across rivers;
they galloped across hills.

4 He said he'd torch my country,
put my young men to the sword,
slam my babies on the rocks,
abuse our virgins for their pleasure.

5 But our omnipotent God scattered them,
confused them, sent them round in circles—
using a woman's hand to do it!

6 Strong Holofernes didn't fall
at the hands of our young men,
nor did the sons of the Titans do it,
nor did the giants gang up on him.
It was Judith, daughter of Merari,
who did him in,
with beauty as her only weapon!

7 She was a widow but smartly dressed,
who brought him to a shameful end,
much to the delight of poor Israel!
She powdered her nose, perfumed herself,

8 and gathered her hair with combs,

put on a sporty linen—
all to catch his lecherous eye!

9 Her sandals turned his head,
her beauty captivated him,
but her blade cut him from ear to ear!

10 The Persians were dismayed by her audacity;
the Medes, daunted by her constancy.

11 My people, whom they'd pounded into the ground,
howled as though they would wake the dead.
Those the enemy thought were too weak cried out,
and the enemy was terrified instead.
My people lifted up their voices on high,
and scared the bad guys silly.

12 Sons of slave girls speared the army regulars,
wounded them like runaway slaves.
All perished at the hands of the army of my Lord!

13 I'll praise my God with a new hymn:
"Lord, great and bright, invincible, unbeatable.

14 May every creature serve you!
You spoke over the void; creation appeared.
You breathed on creation; beings began to move.
Who will tell you 'no'?

15 Under your unhesitating gaze,
mountains quivered, boulders sagged.
But those who feared you will feel your warmth.

16 Great sacrifices may emit heavenly aromas,
but small sacrifice still has something to offer the Lord!
Just take the Lord at his word,
and you'll feel his warmth forever.

17 Gentile nations who would attack us should beware.
Our omnipotent God will vindicate us,
and punish them in the day of justice.
He'll introduce fire and worm to their flesh!"

AND SO IT ENDED

18-20 The people went to Jerusalem where they adored their God. They purified themselves in the Temple and made all the appropriate offerings. Judith brought to the Temple all the furniture and furnishings from Holofernes' tent—the people had given them to her as gifts, especially the tasteless canopy from his bedroom. She consecrated it all to the Lord. Judith stayed for the festivities; the party continued for three months.

21-23 When things quieted down, everyone headed for home. Judith headed for Bethulia and settled in on her own property. As time passed, her reputation spread. Many wanted to visit her; some desired to marry her; but she enjoyed widowhood and spent the rest of her life in her husband's house. She honored Abra—that extraordinary woman who over the years had been her head maid, personal assistant, chief steward, closest confidante, and admitted co-conspirator—making her a free woman. Judith died in Bethulia at the age of 105 and was buried next to her husband.

²⁴⁻²⁵ All Israel went into mourning for seven days when Judith died. As for her goods and property, she'd parceled them out to her relatives before she died. But her memory lived on. No neighboring country dared set foot in the land of Israel, let alone touch an Israelite.

ESTHER

The Jews in exile never hesitated to write about their wretched condition, but the writings that survived are far from wretched. In the Book of Esther, the writing appears to be more fiction than history, although it may well be inspired by past events; it's not so much a recording of those events as plotting the details of a fiction work that would not only inform but also entertain. It makes its moral points and has its entertaining moments. Even by today's standards, the story is remarkable.

It is set in ancient Susa, one of the capital cities of the Persian Empire. It was a large city on a flat plain, with high walls around the royal precincts. It would have been a crossroads of sorts for commercial travelers. As it was in most cities of the ancient Mediterranean world, the Jewish exile population of Susa was fairly large, no doubt living uneasily in the Jewish quarter.

Susa was the perfect setting for this sometimes pious, sometimes breathless, sometimes ruthless tale of betrayal and redemption. Mordecai and Esther, a father-daughter dynamic duo, single-handedly bring the great Persian populace to its knees. Their secret weapons? Not the sword, spear, and arrow but faith and love. It's the sort of uplifting story Jews in exile would share when they quietly gathered for their holy festivals. Indeed it would lead to the establishment of a new festival itself: Purim.

The Book of Esther has all the ingredients of a bestseller: mysterious dreams about the future; a rich-as-Croesus king; garden parties and royal banquets; a trophy wife who tells her drunken husband where to get off; a feminist movement aborted; eunuchs galore; priority mail at its best; hunting for virgins to send to the palace finishing school; a beautiful Jewish girl hiding her nationality; a Persian king trying to pick his next wife; a surrogate father with chutzpah enough to confess his Jewish faith despite the threat of peril; an extermination planned for the Jews; the villain eventually unmasked and then immediately hanged; and, at least for this one moment, exoneration and happiness for the Jews—followed by some inevitable blood and guts, of course.

The key to understanding the ending is that when a king back then made a decree, it lasted forever and could not be rescinded. He could make a new edict that counteracted the first edict, however, and then let the two sides fight it out, which is what happens in the Book of Esther.

This is truly a book that would be welcomed into the literature of any language. It was a story told and retold in many places and eventually committed to print by multiple scribes. As one might expect, no two versions were exactly alike.

The original versions of the Book of Esther were in Hebrew and had ten chapters. Later versions in Greek appeared with additional material. When Jerome translated the Greek version into Latin for the Vulgate Bible, he converted the additions into chapters 11–16. When the New Vulgate appeared in 1998, however, the additions were cut into snippets, which were then stitched in wherever they seemed to belong. The book was back to ten chapters, and the result is a smoother narrative that reads well enough, although some of the verse numbers are different from those in other translations. Every now and then there's a speed bump, but not one so high you would have to stop reading.

The Book of Esther was meant to be an encouragement to the Jews in exile at the time it was written. Its moral was that the Jews (and, by extension, we Christians today) should believe and practice the faith no matter what. But the book has a surprise, if bloody, ending. It encourages us also to look at the bright side of things and not be surprised when everything turns out all right.

For those readers who like to know if what they're reading at any point is from the Hebrew or the Greek manuscripts, the New Vulgate numbering system will help. The Hebrew text is numbered with traditional Arabic numerals; for example, 17, 18, 19. The Greek text is numbered with Arabic numerals plus, where required, letters of the alphabet; for example, 17a, 17b, 17c; 17aa, 17bb, 17cc. Please note, however, that in the sequence of alphabetical letters in the Latin language there is no *j* or *w*, so there is none here either. (WG)

ESTHER

1a-1i It was the second year of the reign of Xerxes the Great, first day of the month Nisan. Mordecai—of the Benjamin, Kish, Shimei, and Jair line—had a dream. He was a Jew in a Gentile city; nonetheless he had climbed the ladder to a low-level executive job in the royal palace. Here's the dream in his own words.

"It was weird: thunder, earthquake, screams, confusion, and panic in the streets. Two dragons came out of nowhere, ready for a knock-down, drag-out battle with each other. They clashed with a roar that could be heard around the world. Frightened, all the nations thought they were being attacked and prepared to fight back. Every creature felt sure the end had come. It was a dark and drizzly day. Vicious animals roamed the streets. Everyone and everything feared the end of civilization as they knew it. They cried out to God. At the height of their fervor, a spring gurgled into view. It was small, but it turned into a mighty river overflowing its banks. Daybreak then sunrise—the lowly had survived. They'd been taken prisoner by the haughty; now they returned the favor, imprisoning the upper class."

1k That was Mordecai's dream. When it was over, he untangled himself from the covers and rose, trying to figure out just what God was trying to tell him. He couldn't get the dream out of his mind all day, and yet he still had no idea what it meant as the sun set.

THE BACKSTORY

1-4 The background to this story revolves around King Xerxes, whose realm ranged from India all the way to Ethiopia—127 provinces in all. In the third year of his rule, when he was wintering in Susa, one of the capitals of Persia, he threw a banquet for his provincial officials; that's to say, the very best of the Persian and Mede nobles and the governors of his provinces. The king wanted to reward and honor them, but he also had another motive. He wanted to give them some idea of his wealth and splendor; he felt he had earned the bragging rights to do so. The celebration seemed to go on forever—180 days to be precise.

5-8 Near the end of the festival, Xerxes gathered within the walls of the city the whole crowd from the highest to the lowest. The occasion was a large garden party on the royal grounds; it alone lasted seven days. Everywhere people looked there were hangings made of the finest cotton in hyacinth and purple held by linen cords and festooned through silver rings from one marble column to another. The garden walkways were paved with mosaic-sized precious stones, mostly green and white, but there were other colors too. The guests drank from gold cups—no two alike. As for the wine from the king's cellar, it was first growth of the highest quality and came from seemingly bottomless vessels. No one was forced to drink, but neither was anyone cut off. It was the king's pleasure, passed down through the stewards, to make every one of his guests feel comfortable in the unusual surroundings.

9-15 The women were not to be ignored. Queen Vashti threw a separate but equal party for the women inside the royal palace where Xerxes had his apartments.

On the seventh day, the king, aglow from the wine, ordered his seven personal eunuchs—Mehuman, Biztha, Harbona, Bigtha, Abagtha, Zethar, and Carcas, the men who saw to his every need—to summon the queen. They were to tell her to wear her crown, because he wanted to show off his trophy wife to the male guests. The eunuchs were not to take no for an answer.

When they found the queen, however, she declined, ordering the eunuchs to tell the king that she refused to come in no uncertain terms.

The king blew his top. He asked his advisors to rummage through the laws for a suitable punishment for her. The advisors were Carshena, Shethar, Admatha, Tarshish, Meres, Marsena, and Memucan. These seven were Persian or Mede officials who had the ear of the king, chaired his advisory committees, and held first rank in the kingdom. "So," asked the king, "what law has Queen Vashti violated by not coming when I called for her?"

16-20   Memucan, who was the lead counsel in this affair, responded.

"Queen Vashti not only has broken many laws but also has caused great confusion in all the officials and people. The queen's negative response to a direct royal command will set a precedent; news of it will spread like wildfire among the women. They'll think they don't have to obey their husbands anymore. All they'll have to say is, 'Well, if a queen can say no to a king, then I can say no to my husband!' Persians and Medes alike will fear that their women will get word of this and act accordingly. If and when that happens, nothing good can follow—only depression and loss of face among every single male in your realm.

"To conclude, Your Majesty, if it should please you, issue a decree that may not be revoked. It should be written according to the laws of both the Persians and the Medes so it will apply across country borders. The wording we suggest is as follows. 'Queen Vashti shall never cross the king's threshold again. She shall hereby vacate her royal position in favor of another queen, who will possess the qualities of humility and submissiveness so lacking in her predecessor.' Once this decree is approved and published, all the wives of whatever level of society will restore to their husbands the honor due them."

21-22   This advice had a calming effect on the king. He ordered that Memucan's ideas be put into writing immediately. He'd send letters to all the provincial governors in diverse tongues and scripts, in print and by mouth. If it wasn't law before, it was law now: All husbands from now until forever would rule their own roosts, and there wouldn't be a thing their wives could do about it.

A NEW WIFE FOR THE KING

1-4   **2** With the threat to his power and masculinity dealt with, King Xerxes calmed down. He even began to have second thoughts about Vashti and the punishment he had decreed for her act of defiance. But his personal advisors proposed another course of action.

"The best thing we can do for the king right now is round up some good-looking young women who are still virgins and let him take his pick."

So they appointed subcommittees throughout the provinces to flush out a bevy of beautiful prospects. Those who passed the first interview were shipped to the harem at Susa. There Hegai, the king's eunuch in charge of the finishing school, welcomed the naïve girls, hoping he could turn them into sophisticated young women. The plan was that the one who most pleased the king would take Vashti's place on the throne.

5-7 At the same time in Susa, there was a Jew named Mordecai who came from a long line of the house of Israel; he was son of Jair, son of Shimei, son of Kish, of the tribe of Benjamin. How did he find his way from Jerusalem to Susa? He came when Jeconiah, king of Judah, and the other captives were deported by Nebuchadnezzar. He was foster father to his own father's brother's daughter, that is to say, to his young cousin, whose parents had both died. Her Jewish name was Hadassah, but they called her Esther in Greek. She had a lovely look about her and made a great first impression. On the death of her parents, Mordecai had taken Esther into his house and raised her as his daughter.

8-14 When the campaign to find a new wife for King Xerxes began, Esther was swept up with other young women and deposited in the king's palace in Susa, where she was sent to the finishing school under the eunuch Hegai's supervision. Esther caught the eunuch's eye and gained favor with him, so he put her name on the top of the list for the king's attention and began providing her with perfume and cosmetics. One day he simply picked her out of class, assigned her seven maids-in-waiting from the king's female staff, and moved them all into the best apartment reserved for the king's harem.

Upon the advice of Mordecai, Esther had guarded her anonymity carefully, revealing neither her nationality nor her family history. Every day Mordecai walked by her residence in the hope of greeting his daughter and learning what the next step in the royal consort contest would be.

Here's how the system worked. The year-long program was divided into two terms: six months focused on body oils and skin creams and six months on cosmetics and perfumes. On completion of the program, the young women were ready for an invitation to be presented to the king for a solo audition. Each was allowed to bring personal items for the overnight, but not too many.

The routine was always the same. A young woman entered the palace in the evening and in the morning was returned to the harem, which was under the supervision of the royal eunuch, Shaashgaz. As for the girl, she couldn't get a second chance with the king unless he asked for her by name, although she was most likely no longer a virgin.

15-18 Eventually, it was time for Esther, daughter of Abihail and adopted daughter of Mordecai, to be presented to the king. She took with her the basic minimum of things recommended by Hegai. Those who saw her en route thought she was graceful and attractive. Her visit to the royal chamber was a date to remember. It was Tebeth, the tenth month of the seventh year of Xerxes' reign.

The king was immediately taken by the young woman. She was by far the best of all the candidates who had been brought to him. He placed the queen's crown on her head and sat her on the queen's throne. Vashti was forgotten; the king was finally done with her.

He ordered a magnificent banquet in honor of Esther to be prepared, with all his ministers and officials from throughout the kingdom invited. The king was so happy that he allowed all the provinces to skip their next tax payment to him and lavished gifts upon everyone he met.

AN ASSASSINATION FOILED

19-23 In the meantime, Mordecai kept watch outside the King's Gate, waiting for the explosion that would surely take place when Esther was discovered to be a Jew. Inside the palace, Esther retained her ethnic anonymity as she'd been advised by Mordecai, but she continued performing her Jewish religious practices privately, as she had done since she was a child.

For Mordecai, the gate area was the perfect place to pick up the gossip of the day. One such tidbit alarmed him tremendously and he resolved to do something about it. Two of the king's eunuchs, Bigthana and Teresh, who were in charge of the gates, had turned on the king and planned to assassinate him. Mordecai heard about the conspiracy and sent a quick message to Queen Esther, who passed it on immediately to the king, giving the credit to Mordecai.

An inquiry was launched; the plot was confirmed; the two eunuchs were hanged. The events were noted in the official royal chronicles and would prove to be important later.

"THE JEWS MUST DIE"

1-4 3 King Xerxes promoted Haman, son of Hammedatha the Agagite, to the post of prime minister. Haman was now second-in-command to the king. The rest of the officials all reported to him. Whenever Haman entered and left the royal estate, the king's staff stationed at the King's Gate had to bend their knee or bow at the waist out of respect. Everyone did this; everyone, that is, except Mordecai.

"Why don't you observe the king's law when his prime minister comes and goes?" asked the king's men. "You've got to do it."

Sometimes Mordecai pretended not to hear them; other times he explained that he was a Jew and Jews bowed only before God. The gate-keepers sent a message to Haman requesting further instructions on how to respond to this strange behavior.

5-7 Next time through the gates, Haman paid special attention to Mordecai. He noticed the man didn't kneel or bow from the waist as he went by, which outraged him. He had Mordecai arrested, but he felt that punishing only a single man was beneath him. He figured if one Jew didn't bow to him, pretty soon all Jews would stop bowing to him; therefore, all Jews would have to pay the price for Mordecai's insubordination.

So Haman decided that all the Jews throughout the king's territories should be killed on a single day. But what day? In Nisan, the first month of the twelfth year of the reign of Xerxes, lots (called *pur* in Greek) were cast into an urn to determine the Day of Death for the Jews, the day on which the extermination would happen. The date drawn was the thirteenth of Adar, the twelfth month.

8-11 For King Xerxes' sake, Haman reviewed the rationale for the massive destruction he was proposing.

"Living among us are a people who aren't like us; they observe their own laws, not ours. You as king have nothing to gain by giving them royal protection. If you think it is appropriate, draw up the papers ordering that all Jews in your kingdom be killed immediately. To finance the operation, I'll pay for it myself and deposit 375 tons of silver in your treasury."

Then the king took off his signet ring and gave it to Haman, son of Hammedatha the Agagite and the archenemy of the Jews, giving the prime minister the power to act in the king's name.

"It's your money, Prime Minister," Xerxes proclaimed. "Do what you like with the Jews."

12-13 So on the thirteenth day of the first month the royal scribes were called in. Haman dictated the orders. Copies were made informing the governors and other provincial leaders what was to happen, in clear languages they could understand. Copies were sealed with the king's ring. The message was sent by couriers to all parts of the kingdom: The Jews were to be destroyed, killed, demolished—every last one of them, including young and old, mothers and infants—all on one day, the thirteenth day of Adar, the twelfth month. As for the worldly goods of the Jews, they'd be up for grabs.

13a-13h The text of the letter reads as follows.

"Xerxes the Great, king of 127 provinces from India to Ethiopia, writes the following to all who are subject to his imperial authority. I wish you well.

"When I first assumed power over a host of tribes and brought them under my authority, I had not the slightest intention of taking advantage of them. I always intended to act respectfully toward my people, to steer them away from terror, to offer them a calm existence as well as open borders in all directions. In a word, I wanted to restore peace to all.

"While in consultation with my advisors on just how to carry this out, one of them stood out from the others; his prudence, goodwill, and ability to focus were clearly superior. Haman is his name; he is now my prime minister, second in the kingdom after me. He has pointed out to me that while we have many different races in our varying provinces who live in harmony, one of them is hostile to all the others. These people obey their own laws, not the laws the rest of us obey. Hence, the concord among us has a fatal flaw that needs to be addressed.

"We finally have come to grips with all this and brought it out into the open. This tribe has rebelled against all the others and intends to impose their customs and laws on the rest of us, thus fracturing the harmony of our peaceable kingdom.

"Therefore, by this letter we decree that Haman, who is in charge of public affairs and whom we cherish as our second father, has addressed the problem and proposed the solution. This troublesome tribe, including their wives and children, should be thoroughly rooted out and disposed of as enemies of the people.

"We further decree that we should not shed a tear at this necessary cleansing from our realm of those who would do us all harm.

"We finally decree that the thirteenth day of Adar, the twelfth month of the present year, will be the Day of Death for the Jews. No longer will they be able to exhibit signs of hostility towards the rest of us. On that day they all shall make the violent descent into the netherworld. Only then will peace and quiet return to the many and diverse corners of our kingdom.

"Subjects who have clung to and concealed their Jewish identity will no longer be tolerated within our borders. They are best burned in the holy bonfire. As for their belongings, they are to be gathered at various collection centers until further notice.

"I have the honor to be, and so forth . . . "

14-15   Copies of the letter had to be circulated and posted; the provinces needed to know the law and what was expected of them on the Day of Death. Couriers hastened to carry the imperial edict far and wide. When it was publicly posted on the streets in Susa, the people—Jew and non-Jew alike—were confused and alarmed. Inside the palace, however, Haman and the king partied together to celebrate the finality of their solution.

IMPACT OF THE DECREES

15a-15i   On receiving the news, the various tribes making up the empire of Xerxes weren't all that upset; some even held Day of Death rallies. Wherever the edict was posted, however, the Jewish people were stunned and began to cry out. They implored the God of their forebears.

"Lord God alone in your high heavens, there's no other God except you. If we'd kept your Law, we'd be living out our lives in security and peace. Now, however, because we haven't followed your word to the letter, we've had one set of troubles after another. You're all our hopes rolled up into one, Lord. All your judgments have been right on the mark. Don't let our men become slaves or our women prostitutes. From our escape from Egypt right down to now, you've been nothing but kind and merciful to us. Don't let our legacy from you turn into our infamy! Don't allow our enemies to dominate and destroy us!"

MORDECAI AND ESTHER REACT TO THE NEWS

1-3   **4** When Mordecai learned the awful news about the Day of Death for the Jews, he tore off his clothes, put on sackcloth, and sprinkled his head with ashes. Then he walked down the main street of the city, crying out with a loud but sad voice all the way to the King's Gate. The guards barred his entrance because of his attire.

The same thing happened throughout the provinces. When the king's proclamation was posted, the sound of overwhelming grief rose from the Jewish quarters. There was fasting, crying, mourning; the main Jewish attire became sackcloth and ashes.

4-6   As for Esther, her maids and eunuchs rushed to tell her what was going on in the streets. The news was so bad she couldn't comprehend it. She sent Mordecai some clothes with the strict order that he take off the sackcloth and ashes immediately.

"Thanks, but no thanks," was his reply.

Then she summoned the eunuch named Hathach, whom the king had appointed to her personal staff. She sent him to Mordecai to find out why her adoptive father was self-destructing. Hathach found Mordecai making a spectacle of himself at the King's Gate.

7-8   Mordecai told Hathach all the bad news he was receiving from his sources in the government. Especially galling was the extraordinary bribe Haman had deposited in the royal bank to finance the slaughtering of the Jews. He gave Hathach a copy of the proclamation that had been posted right in Susa and asked the eunuch to show it to the queen to prove the king meant business. Then, in his own hand, he pleaded in writing for Esther to demand an interview with the king and try to intercede on behalf of the Jews.

8a "Recall the simple life you and I lived before you started hanging around with royalty," Mordecai said in his note. "The reason I am asking you to intervene is that Haman, the second-in-command in the kingdom, is the one pushing the idea of wiping us all out. First, pray earnestly to our Lord; then speak earnestly to your lord on our behalf. Only you can save us all from death."

9-11 Hathach returned to the queen with Mordecai's letter. Esther immediately dictated a response to her adoptive father.

"The king's servants and anyone who is subject to his authority in the provinces know this rule: Whoever enters the king's presence without an invitation, whether man or woman or even his queen, will be killed right on the spot. Of course, the king can extend his golden scepter and that would save the uninvited interloper's life. As for me, I haven't been asked to be in the king's presence for the last thirty days."

12-14 When Mordecai heard her reply, he sent back a reply, which was really a command.

"My daughter, don't think that because you're part of the king's household you will escape this purge. You'll die too. If you don't say something now, the liberation and salvation of the Jews will come eventually from another source, but meanwhile you and I and our people will die. But perhaps that was what God had in mind for you, a Jew, when you entered the royal family."

15-16 Again, Esther dictated a response.

"Father, go ahead and collect all the Jews living in Susa. Tell them to fast in my behalf. No food, no drink for three days and nights. I and my handmaids will do the same. After that, I'll go to the king, even though I'll break the law in doing so. If I die, I die."

17-17a So Mordecai went and did what Queen Esther asked. The Jewish elders did the same, and so they all prayed from dawn to dusk.

MORDECAI'S PRAYER

17b-17m "God of Abraham, God of Isaac, God of Jacob, give us your blessing. Lord, King Omnipotent, you who've furnished the universe, if you wanted to decree the salvation of Israel, who or what could get in your way? You've made Heaven and earth and all the other remarkable objects in the celestial confines. You are Lord of all; there is no one who can outshine your majesty.

"You know, Lord, that I would freely have kissed the soles of Haman's feet if it meant the salvation of Israel. I didn't do that, however, because that would put the praise of a human above the glory that is yours alone. I don't adore anyone or anything except you, my Lord God! I'm not being arrogant when I say these things nor am I trying to draw attention to myself.

"Surprise everyone, Lord! Show them your power! It's time, God of Abraham, Isaac, and Jacob, to spare us, your chosen ones, because our enemies want to destroy your inheritance to us. Don't abandon the promise you made that we would always be your people and you would always be our God. You paid a great price to get us out of the land of Egypt. Don't let that investment be in vain.

"Open your ears and hear my prayers. Convert our tears of sadness into tears of joy. Turn our dying into living; don't close the mouths of those who continue to praise your name."

All the Jews in the land, down to the very last one, cried out to the Lord in confidence with all their strength, even as death was staring them in the face.

17n-17p Queen Esther herself turned to the Lord. She too feared the danger of imminent death, not only for herself but for her people. She hung up her royal garments and put on the clothes of grief. In place of expensive hair conditioners, she massaged her scalp with ashes and subjected her body to fasting. She fell upon the ground with her maids and prayed from dawn to dusk.

ESTHER'S PRAYER

17q-17kk "God of Abraham, God of Isaac, God of Jacob, look favorably upon me. I have no one to help me, no one to defend me, except you, O Lord. I'm in grave peril the minute I approach the king.

"I've read in the books of my ancestors that you saved Noah from drowning in the flood.

"I've heard from the same books that you handed over to Abraham— accompanied by 318 of his militia's finest—the nine kings.

"I've heard from the same books that you freed Jonah from the belly of a whale.

"I've heard from the same books that you rescued from the fire Hananiah, Azariah, and Mishael.

"I've heard from the same books that you rescued Daniel from the lions' den.

"I've heard from the same books that you had mercy on Hezekiah, king of the Jews, who was condemned to die and was praying for his life.

"I've heard from the same books that you gave Hannah the son she was praying for.

"I've heard from the same books that you freed all those who stayed with you to the end.

"Now help me, a solitary woman, who has no one but you, my Lord and my God, to save me and my people.

"You know, O God, that your handmaid has loathed the bed of the uncircumcised, that I haven't eaten from the table of the unclean nor sipped the wine of their unholy sacrifices, that from the day I arrived at court I haven't been happy, except with you alone.

"You know, O God, that I'm forced to wear this crown in public and would rather wear last month's menstrual cloth instead! When I'm alone in my rooms, I toss the crown on the floor.

"Come to me, a mere orphan, O God, and tell me what to say when it's my turn to face the lion. Make me persuasive in the king's presence. Convert his heart to our side and convince him to destroy Haman and those who line up behind him. Free us from the deadly hand of our enemies; convert our grief into joy.

"There are those who'd trample on your promises to us, O God; it's time for you to set the record straight. Don't hide from us, Lord. It's time for you to reveal yourself as our protector."

※

BREAKING THE RULE

5 1-2 At the end of the third day, Esther resumed her regal finery. Soon she found herself standing in the atrium of the royal palace with the king sitting by himself at the far end of the cabinet room. And this is how it happened. He looked up and saw his queen standing in the doorway. His eyes smiled. He extended his golden scepter, the sign allowing her to enter. Approaching she touched the tip of the scepter.

ANOTHER ACCOUNT OF THE MEETING

2a-2p After Esther had prayed to God, the Savior of All, for three days, she dressed in all her royal splendor. Then she found she couldn't walk alone but needed the help of two maids. On one she leaned for support, trying not to give the appearance of someone about to faint; the other followed her, managing the train and trying to keep it from dragging on the ground.

The queen's face glowed, her flashing eyes hiding a sad soul that feared death. She passed through all the portals, finally standing in the doorway of the king's cabinet room. She was facing the king; his throne was the only seat in the room; his attire was regal—fine cloth, precious stones, and all the royal finery that inspired awe. With his piercing eyes and his golden scepter, he could make suppliants choke in fear just by looking at them.

When Xerxes looked up, he reacted at first like a raging bull. His first thought was to kill Esther right on the spot. But his voice had an ambivalent quality about it.

"Who dares enter the presence of the king without an invitation?"

Esther immediately fainted, her blush turning pale, her head falling on her maid's shoulder. At this moment the God of the Jews, the Lord of the Universe, apparently softened the spirit of the king. He had bolted from his throne in anger, but by the time he reached his wife he was cradling her in his arms, whispering into her ear, trying to get her to return to her senses.

"What do you want, my queen, my sister, my consort on the throne? I'm your brother. There's nothing to be afraid of. You're not going to die. The rules aren't meant for you, just for ordinary people. Come back to me!"

Raising the golden scepter he ran it slowly along her neck, all the while kissing her and whispering to her: "Speak to me. Say something."

Esther finally responded: "I see you, my lord. You look like an angel. My poor heart races in fear at your glory. You're a living wonder, my lord, and your face is full of grace."

As she was speaking, however, she fainted again; she looked for a moment as though she'd stopped breathing. The king was distraught, as were his cabinet ministers, who by then were wandering into the room to see what was happening.

3-5 Esther opened her eyes and the king said to her, "What do you want, my Esther, my queen? Half my kingdom? Is that what you want? It's yours."

Finally she responded, "If it pleases you, and only if it pleases you, my lord, I want you to visit me later today and bring Haman. I'll prepare dinner for both of you."

The king seemed a little surprised at the request, but he responded instantly and forcefully: "Call Prime Minister Haman at once. Esther must have her request granted!"

And that was how the king and Haman found themselves in the queen's dining hall that night.

THE TWO BANQUETS

6-14 After the king had sampled the dinner Esther had prepared, he said to her, "Whatever you want, it's yours. You name it. Even if it's half my kingdom."

Esther said, "My petition—my prayer—is simply this: If I find grace in the sight of the king, and only if it pleases you, then I want you both to come to dinner again tomorrow night, when I'll tell you what I want."

The king agreed readily, although he seemed a little confused. Haman looked forward to another meal with only him and the king in attendance.

But while heading back to his home, Haman saw something that turned his stomach. There was Mordecai, sitting by the King's Gate as usual. When the man once again failed to properly acknowledge Haman, the second-in-command to the king, the prime minister was furious.

Haman managed to disguise his irritation in public, but in private he called some of his friends and his wife Zeresh for a meeting. He went on at some length about his personal wealth and his large number of sons and how the king had elevated him over all other officials and advisors in the kingdom.

"Queen Esther called me to dine alone with her and the king not only today, but also tomorrow. That's how important I am. Yet even though all these great honors have come my way, every time I pass that Jew Mordecai he shows me no respect. He just sits outside the King's Gate as if he owned the place."

His wife Zeresh and friends responded.

"You can solve this immediately, Haman. Simply construct a hanging platform; seventy-five feet high should do it. Then tomorrow morning, ask the king to hang Mordecai. After that you can go to the banquet and have a good time."

That sounded like a good plan, and Haman gave the order for the gallows to be built early the next day.

QUITE A TURN OF EVENTS

1-3 6 That night the king had a hard time going to sleep. Perhaps a bit of reading might help. He asked that the volume of the history of the empire covering the early years of his reign be read to him. When the reader came to the name Mordecai, the king asked him to stop.

"Wasn't that the fellow who tipped us off that Bigthana and Teresh, the two eunuchs in charge of the King's Gate, were planning to kill me?"

It was the very one, the reader confirmed.

"Was Mordecai offered a reward at the time?"

Further investigation of the book revealed that Mordecai had been offered an appropriate reward but had refused to accept it.

4-10 Early the following morning the king went to his court and asked if there were anyone in the waiting room. In fact, Haman had been the first one in line. He planned to urge the king to hang Mordecai on the gallows that were just now being constructed.

"Haman wants to see you," said a junior official.

"Send him in," replied the king.

When Haman entered, the king put this question right to him: "What should I do for a man who deserves to be honored?"

Thinking in his heart that the king wanted to honor him and not somebody else, Haman gave this self-serving opinion:

"The person the king wants to honor ought to be clothed with a cloak from the king's own closet and mounted on a horse from the king's own stable. Then have your highest-ranking official dress and lead this honoree through the streets of the city, crying out: *This is how the king honors a special hero!*"

"Then that's what I want you to do," said the king to Haman. "Get the cloak and the horse, and make this work right down to the smallest detail. You know that Jewish fellow Mordecai, the one who's always sitting at the King's Gate? He richly deserves to be honored for something he did for me years ago."

11-14   Haman was completely flabbergasted and didn't know what to say or do, so he rounded up the cloak and a saddle, put the king's garment on Mordecai and Mordecai on the king's horse, and then led him through the streets of Susa, crying out, "This is how the king honors a special hero!"

After the mini-parade, Mordecai resumed his customary seat at the King's Gate, but Haman hurried off, trying to reach home so he could cover his head in shame and explode in grief. He told the whole story to his wife and close friends. They offered in return some wise if difficult counsel.

"If Mordecai has Jewish roots, think of what this means. You can't prevail against him. Indeed the one you want to hang is going to gloat when you're the one who's hanged instead."

While they were still talking, the king's eunuchs arrived to escort Haman with all deliberate haste to the second banquet being prepared by Queen Esther.

Hanging from the Gallows He Built

1-10   **7** At the invitation of Queen Esther, the king and his prime minister, Haman, entered her personal quarters for the second time. After tasting the wine, the king put the question to his queen again. "What's your pleasure? I'll grant it in advance, whatever it may be. Even if you ask for half the kingdom, know in advance that it's yours."

Esther replied: "If I find grace in your eyes, dearest king, and only if it pleases you, please give me my life and give my people their lives—that's what I pray for today. Why do I ask? My people and I have been set up, sold out, handed over for annihilation. Our future has been torn to shreds. It would have been one thing if we were merely going to be sent into slavery, but we are about to be massacred. I've been silent up till now, but I can hold my peace no longer. The wreckage to you and your reputation, which will surely come from this, is more than any king can sustain."

"Who's the person who dares to do such a thing?" asked the king. "And where is he now?"

"The author of the threat to us and indeed the king's very own worst enemy," replied Esther, "is sitting right here. It is no other than Haman, your trusted prime minister."

On hearing this, Haman got physically ill right in front of the king and queen. Disgusted and enraged, the king rose and left the banquet for some fresh air. Haman also rose, but he approached Esther on her couch, begging her to spare his life. Apparently, the extermination decree he'd ordered in the king's name wasn't turning out to be such a good idea after all.

When the king returned from the garden, he found Haman groveling on his knees in front of the queen. "Is this your plan," the king shouted, "to molest the queen in the presence of the king in his very own palace?"

That was the last word from the king's mouth on the subject. A hangman's hood was quickly slipped over Haman's head, and he was led off.

Harbona, one of the eunuchs on duty during the dinner, came forward and said, "You know, Your Majesty, I probably shouldn't be saying this, but Haman has just constructed a gallows outside his own home from which he planned to hang Mordecai; he even gave the odd specification that it should be seventy-five feet high."

"Hang Haman from it!" shouted the king.

And so Haman hung at the end of the very rope he'd prepared for Mordecai.

After that, the king slowly began to return to normal.

REVERSING THE EDICT

8 ¹⁻² Later that very same day, several other important things happened in Susa. King Xerxes gave Queen Esther the house that Haman, the archenemy of the Jews, had lived in; and Esther revealed to her husband that Mordecai the Jew was her adoptive father. Xerxes called for Mordecai at once. The king took the signet ring, the one he'd given to Haman, and passed it on to Mordecai. Esther then put her father in charge of Haman's estate.

³⁻⁴ Esther spoke to her husband again. This time she fell upon his feet, weeping and praying that he'd undo the death sentence Haman had inflicted upon the Jews. Before answering her, the king followed the custom of extending the golden scepter to her; she rose with it and stood before him.

⁵⁻⁶ "If it please the king, and if I find grace in his presence, and if my deprecation to him doesn't affect an already pre-existing law, and if I'm still the apple of his eye, I beg him—you—to hear my plea. The proclamation sent by Haman in which he ordered the Day of Death for the Jews in all the provinces has to be revoked and new letters sent countermanding it. How can I stand by and let my people suffer? How can I sit still while my relatives are being slaughtered?"

⁷⁻⁸ The king acknowledged her requests.

"I've found Haman guilty of raising his hand unjustly against the Jews. I've ordered him hanged from the gallows. I've assigned his house to you. Now it's your turn. Have Mordecai write a new order as you see fit. Put his words over my name as king and seal the letters with my ring, which will guarantee the contents of the edict."

Parenthetically, any order written in the king's name and sealed with his signet ring is irreversible, and so the original edict written by Haman could only be countermanded, not revoked.

9-10 The royal scribes were gathered; it was Sivan, the third month, the twenty-third day. Mordecai dictated the wording, which reversed the previous decree that had been sent out by Haman. The new edict regarding the fate of the Jews was sent to the Persian and Mede nobles as well as to the governors and other officials presiding over 127 provinces ranging from India to Ethiopia, each province receiving it in its own language and each people reading it in their own script. Copies were sent in the name of the king and bore the king's seal; couriers on mounts from the king's stables carried them to the four corners of the empire.

11-12c One of the provisions in the letter gave royal permission for the Jews to live wherever they chose and to arm and defend themselves. That would allow them to kill anyone who conspired to attack them based on the earlier decree—their wives and children included—and to confiscate all their property. All provisions of the new decree were to take effect on the Day of Death for the Jews, which had now been turned into the Day of Life for the Jews. Furthermore, the edict urged the Jews to use its provisions to their advantage on that one day: the thirteenth day of Adar in the twelfth month.

Here is a copy of the letter.

12d-12cc "Xerxes, the great king from India to Ethiopia, 127 provinces with governors and all others who respect our authority, wishes you well.

"Many who have enjoyed the king's bountiful generosity have abused the king's authority. Not only do they seek to oppress his subjects but they also plot against the very one who gave them the authority in the first place. They downgrade the good things people do; they even upgrade the evil things they themselves do by thinking them not so bad.

"Many in positions of importance, with the help of local officials, become accomplices to attempted extermination. These are the sort of persons who look for the loopholes in a good law when they want to pursue their own unlawful ends. We do not have to harken back to incidents in ancient history for crimes committed by people while they were in office. We have only to recall crimes committed in our own time.

"From now on we shall make peace a top priority in all the provinces. If we pay attention to the variables in governing, we will err more on the good side than the bad. A case in point is Haman, son of Hammedatha. He was a Macedonian, which meant he had no Persian bloodline and not a drop of our national virtue in him. He was just a guest of ours, enjoying our hospitality.

"He made himself expert in the humane diplomacy that we exercise with every country. So much so that our father the king brought this to public notice and eventually paid him the respect due to the second-in-command to the king.

"In reality, though, Haman was a viper seeking whom he might devour next. He recommended the death penalty for the Jew named Mordecai, who turned out to be our real savior and permanent benefactor of all the Jewish communities in this vast kingdom. He is the adoptive father of our Queen Esther, the wife of King Xerxes.

"Haman's plan, so far as we could detect it, was that once the Jews were eliminated he would somehow transfer the kingdom from the Persians to the Macedonians. But there was a flaw, a fatal flaw. The Jews were law-abiding citizens; children of the Living God, the Most High and Greatest Ever, who has watched over our kingdom in the best way possible. Therefore, the letter that Haman, son of Hammedatha, directed to you is now null and void. Additionally, the prosecutor who framed the defendant is now hanging on the gallows by the city gate—yet another instance of the God who oversees all things justly overturning a false guilty verdict.

"Copies of this edict are now being posted in all cities; the Jews henceforth will be allowed to follow their own customs. Please feel free to help your Jewish friends and neighbors defend themselves if and when they're attacked on that fast-approaching day of tribulation: the thirteenth day of the twelfth month, Adar.

"That day, destined to be one of death, God has turned into one of life for the Jews. Therefore, we also will consider this day as one of solemn observance on our own calendar and celebrate it with all joy. May this day be to all Persians what it is to your Jewish friends and neighbors, a day of salvation. May those who plotted the extermination remember it as the day of their own demise.

"Finally, any city, state, or province that is unwilling to follow this decree will perish in wrath by sword and fire; no habitat for civil society will remain nor will the habitats of bird and beast survive.

"I have the honor to be, and so forth . . ."

13-15   A copy of the decree was posted prominently in all the provinces; all could read it for themselves or hear it read to them. The couriers left Susa with a clatter, copies of the edict in their saddlebags. Needless to say, the edict was posted all over the city in which it was written. This assured that the Jews would be in a state of readiness should their enemies attack on the appointed day.

In conclusion, Mordecai made an appearance with the king outside the palace. Now a royal staff member, his colorful attire matched his new position. On his head, a gold crown; over his shoulders, a purple linen cloak.

16-17   As for the Jews, it was the birth of a brand new day, a joy, an honor—something to dance in the streets about. Whenever and wherever the edict arrived, it was festival time. Throughout the realm, there were banquets and parties; street venders were on every corner.

The joy was infectious. The Persians were glad for their Jewish neighbors; some even curious. The Jews explained what they were all about and were asked if others could become Jews.

Of course they could, was the answer! And some did. Now that the Jews were in the ascendancy, the Persians were learning what it was like to live in fear of them and their God.

BLOODY AFTERMATH

1-4   **9** On the thirteenth day of the twelfth month, Adar, the very day on which the new edict of the king—written by Mordecai—became law, some of the enemies of the Jews were still hoping to kill them, based on the authority granted by the original edict, written by Haman. The exact opposite happened, however; the Jews came out on top. In preparation for the Day of Death, the Jews in each community had originally planned to gather together to offer some token resistance. But as the day arrived, there wasn't a peep from their persecutors, just a sigh of relief from the general public.

Governors and other public officials throughout the king's realm with a shred of sense backed the Jews, if for no other reason than out of fear of Mordecai. He was the one they recognized now as the Prince of the Palace; he had plenty of authority to back up his version of the king's decree. Rumor increased his authority with every passing day.

5-10   What happened instead was the sweep of the Jewish swords, which resulted in slaughter and destruction for their enemies based on the right to protect themselves given to the Jews in the second edict. In Susa, Jews killed five hundred of their most virulent enemies; they did the same to Haman's ten sons. Here's a list of their names: Parshandatha, Dalphon, Aspatha, Poratha, Adalia, Aridatha, Parmashta, Arisai, Aridai, and Vaizatha.

When the Jews had mopped up those who had planned to exterminate them, they called it a day. As for their enemy's possessions, they didn't touch them, for this was about safety, not plunder.

11-12   In Susa, the body count was immediately reported to King Xerxes. He passed it on to the queen.

"In the city of Susa alone the Jews killed five hundred men and Haman's ten sons. Think of how many more they killed in the rest of the kingdom. Is there anything else you want me to do? You know I can order anything."

13-14   "If it pleases the king," Esther replied, "may power be granted to the Jews who are in Susa, that they can do the same for one more day tomorrow. And it would be appropriate as a warning to others if the bodies of Haman's sons were put on display from the gallows he constructed by his home."

So the king ordered, and the ten corpses were left dangling for all to see.

15-17   On the next day, the fourteenth day of the month of Adar, the Jews rounded up and killed another three hundred of those who had conspired against them. As for these people's belongings, again the Jews left them untouched.

In the rest of the provinces, the story was pretty much the same, although it only took one day. The Jews rounded up seventy-five thousand of their persecutors and killed them; once again they didn't lay a finger on the plunder that rightfully would have been theirs. All of this occurred in the countryside on the thirteenth day of the month of Adar, the day on which the Day of Death for the Jews had been set to start. On the fourteenth day of the month, then, the Jews in the provinces rested; it was time to feast and to be festive.

18-19   Back in Susa, however, since the Jews did their bloody work there on both the thirteenth and fourteenth, it was on the fifteenth they rested, had solemn commemorations, and held victory dinners.

This explains why the Jews who lived in the countryside celebrated on the fourteenth, while those who lived in the capital celebrated on the fifteenth. Both became days of banquets and presents and generally joyous behavior.

19a   The bottom line was that when the second edict had been posted most of the officials and general population of the kingdom began to honor the Jewish God. They had feared Haman; now it was Mordecai they feared.

20-22   Mordecai chronicled these remarkable events in a book, copies of which he sent to the Jewish communities throughout the kingdom and around the known world. In it he urged all Jews keep both the fourteenth and fifteenth of Adar as sacred, festive days every year. The feast would commemorate the days on which the Jews had fought back to save themselves from imminent extinction. Indeed he urged that the whole month of Adar became a time for Jews to banish grieving and sadness and replace them with hilarity and joyfulness. Food and gifts of all kinds were plentiful for friends and the poor alike.

23 So the Jews took all these practices and turned them into a solemn ritual, which they repeated year after year. That satisfied the mandate that Mordecai had put into his book.

MORDECAI'S BOOK IN SUMMARY

24-32 According to Mordecai, Haman, son of Hammedatha the Agagite, was an adversary to Jews and all things Jewish and thought the Jews were evil enough to rid the kingdom of every single one of them. To add some divine legitimacy to his diabolical plan, he used *pur,* the casting of lots, to pick the date of his Day of Death for the Jews.

At this point in the book, enter Queen Esther to speak to the king; she convinces him to allow a decree to be sent to contradict what Haman had written some time before—that the Jews were so bad they should be exterminated. Indeed the Jews turned out to be good; it was Haman who was evil. He was so wrong that he ended up being hanged from the gallows he had constructed to execute Mordecai.

And so from that time to this, these days have been called *Phuray* or *Purim,* the word for "lot," because the date of the events had been chosen by chance. All of Mordecai's adventures and experiences may be found in his book. They're the basis of the annual two-day Festival of Purim, as he had hoped. And he wished that the solemn feast should never be changed by future generations, no matter what.

And so these days of Purim are commemorated and celebrated down the ages and across the world. There's not a Jewish community that doesn't observe these holy days.

Later Queen Esther, daughter of Abihail and adopted daughter of Mordecai, added her account to her adoptive father's, confirming the authenticity of Purim. Mordecai and Esther, having confirmed the days of celebrating Purim, also prescribed days for fasting and special prayer.

They sent the volume to all Jewish communities living in the 127 provinces of King Xerxes, thus confirming an age of peace and truth throughout the kingdom.

THE END

10 1-3 King Xerxes' coffers filled with taxes from the vast mainland all the way to the great sea. After Mordecai the Jew was made prime minister, he exhibited the qualities of fortitude, authority, dignity, and ingenuity; proof of that may be found in various histories of the kings of Medes and Persians. They record how an ordinary Jew—albeit a presence in Jewish councils and a popular fellow with his people—became the second-in-command after the king. Mordecai's formula was simple: he merely sought the good of all the people and sowed the seeds of peace wherever he went.

3a-3k

His opening words to his fellow Jews were always the same: "This is the work of the Lord God!" Then he'd recount a futuristic dream he had as a young man in which a number of strange things were graphically portrayed; later each one of them actually occurred.

"A trickling stream of water became a roaring rapid. Light, sun, and water drenched the entire dream. The water represented my adopted daughter Esther, whom the king later took as his wife and welcomed as his queen. Two dragons also appeared—that would be Haman and me. The entire nation gathered to destroy our people.

"Our tribe—that's to say, the house of Israel—made a racket; it was not a political protest but a noisy prayer to the Lord. It was the Lord who took care of us, freed us from the evil about to be visited upon us, and made extravagant promises to us that he has kept—promises he didn't make to others.

"There were two lots, one for the people of God and one for the rest of humankind. Each lot had its own timetable, determined by the justice of God. God drew his own people's lot and then worked to justify his own choice.

"To conclude, these days will be observed every year in the month of Adar, on the fourteenth and fifteenth. It should be a two-day festival that is jumping with joy, because God is with us.

"Our generation began the festival; future generations will continue it."

1 MACCABEES

Of all the countries, towns, and city-states in the Middle East in the second century B.C., the land of the Jews was often ranked right at the bottom. Ruling the roost at one time or another were Syrians, Egyptians, Greeks, Persians, and others.

All these peoples were alike in many ways, but there were important differences between the Jews and the others. The Jews believed in one God, the others in many gods. The Jews believed they were the chosen people; the others felt they were the ones destined to rule the world. Jewish leaders never thought they were God; the others, especially the kings, felt they themselves were not only *godlike* but also literally gods worthy of worship. Both sides knew they couldn't co-exist.

Both could assemble an army of thousands, apparently without breaking a sweat. Both could ease on down a narrow road with a very large force in the middle of the night. At daybreak, horse, foot, elephant would face one another on a plain, with cheap red wine used to rouse the elephants. Both sides would raise their voices, for one cannot fight without yelling and screaming first. It was an explosion waiting to happen. And it did indeed happen, many times, with Israel losing more often than winning.

In about 167 B.C., however, one of the Gentiles who'd won a previous battle against Israel approached a Jewish priest named Mattathias and politely demanded that he sacrifice to Zeus right there on the street in front of everyone. In a calm but firm way, the king's agent explained the options: Sacrifice to Zeus or die. Overhearing the conversation and judging where the power currently resided, one Jew walked right in front of everyone and began to worship Zeus. Without a second thought but energized by a lifetime of fidelity to God's word, Mattathias drew his sword and whacked both the gentlemanly agent and the idolatrous Jew to death.

This priest had to flee for his life. He later returned with his five sons—known collectively as the Maccabees—to lead a revolt against the outside invaders and their Jewish collaborators that lasted thirty years. This resulted in—if only for a brief shining moment—the house of Israel being a free country, kingdom, nation.

A Jewish archivist put these history pieces together, patched in some appropriate documents, and produced a readable account that he hoped would inspire national pride and personal piety. He was careful to distinguish between *Judea,* literally and generically "the land of the Jewish people," which was a much larger and amorphous area, and *Judah,* the immediate and well-defined territory around Jerusalem. The tale unfolds . . . (WG)

1 MACCABEES

ALEXANDER THE CONQUERER

1-4 Alexander the Great, son of Philip the Macedonian and king of Greece, left Pella, Macedonia, taking a leisurely march southward along the coast of the Great Sea. He ended up in Cyprus, where he pulverized Darius III, king of the Persians and Medes. Whenever, wherever, he could, Alexander fought battles, stormed strongholds, and killed kings. He traveled to the ends of the earth, picking up spoils along the way, until there was nothing left to pick up. The silence was deafening; his heart pounded; he felt good about himself. As he went, he gathered military strength to the point of overkill. Rather than fight, tribes and nations paid him tribute on sight.

END OF AN ERA

5-7 When Alexander realized that death was approaching, he lay down on his bed and summoned his nobles—friends from childhood whom he'd promoted from courtiers to princes—and divided his kingdom among them. *Not a bad ride*, he thought, looking back on his twelve-year career as king; and then he breathed his last.

8-10 Alexander's heirs and aids took possession of his territories. They arranged their own crownings, making sure the white diadems fit just right. Their sons went on to inherit and rule the same territories for generations. Their reigns were marked by ever-decreasing public virtue and ever-increasing crime.

From that foul soil rose Antiochus IV, called Epiphanes, or Godlike, but we called him Flashman. He was son of King Antiochus III, called the Great. Flashman had been a hostage at Rome; in year 137 of the Greek calendar, he became a client king appointed by Rome.

ACCOMMODATION WITH THE GENTILES

11-12 In those days in the land of Israel, there arose some upstart Jewish insurgents who weren't happy about the theological conservatism of their leaders. They developed an argument that went like this: "Let's approach the Gentiles, who live all around us, and try to negotiate a treaty without using the words *One God* or *One Lord* in it. Why? Because they have lots of gods, and since we started distancing ourselves more and more from the Gentiles, bad things have begun to happen to us." This argument was persuasive to a lot of Jews.

13-15 These disgruntled Jews did approach Antiochus. The king was amenable but on one condition: Jews would have to abide by Gentile laws. And so the two sides agreed. The accommodators returned to Jerusalem and built a stadium, the sort one would find in every major Gentile city. They sported in the nude; hence, they felt they had to be de-circumcised. They withdrew from the holy covenant with God and generally enjoyed their Gentile life. In other words, they sold out. Nothing good came out of it, however, and the result was more bad news for the Jews.

THE EGYPTIAN CONNIPTION

16-20 Time came when Antiochus IV wanted to rule in Egypt. It was such a plum, and he figured ruling two kingdoms would be better than one. He entered Egypt with an overwhelming force: chariots, elephants, cavalry, ships, the works. He amassed his forces against Ptolemy VI, called Philometor, or Mother's Boy, king of Egypt. The Egyptian blinked first. Ptolemy turned and fled; bloodshed was inevitable; a great many were wounded; a great number died. The fortified cities in Egypt fell. Antiochus plundered his way across the country. In year 143 of the Greek calendar, he'd flattened everything Egyptian except the pyramids.

Turning, he headed eastward and upward to Jerusalem with a fearsome force.

SPOILING AND DESPOILING

21-24 Antiochus entered the Sanctuary in the Temple and with pride announced that all this was his. His men started dismantling: altar, lampstands, candlesticks, vessels of all sorts, offering table, censers, curtains, crowns, anything and everything that had gold or silver in it or on it. Decorations were stripped from the walls; hidden treasures were spirited out of their hiding places. This was stuff the eyes lusted for, and they hauled it off by the cartful. After the grand sweep, Antiochus left for home, slaughtering anyone who got in his way.

25-28 There was great mourning in Israel, lamentation rising up from every corner of the land. Princes and elders mourned; young men and women who survived were traumatized; all beauty vanished from their faces. Brides sat on their beds and wept; grooms stood by their beds and wept. The land was shaken because of what happened. The house of Jacob was shrouded with sorrow.

TAXATION WITHOUT REPRESENTATION

29-32 Two years passed before Antiochus sent his chief financial officer and tax collector, Apollonius, to the cities of Judah. Apollonius didn't come alone; he was accompanied by numerous accountants and other hangers-on.

The first words of Apollonius to the people were promising, so they let their guard down. Indeed, his words were honeyed right up to the moment he gave the doomsday command. His men cut down everyone in sight; with swiftness he tore the city apart; he destroyed the people of Israel. Everything that had any value he took; then he set fire to the city, destroying all the structures, leaving not a wall standing. The women and children he took captive; the cattle, well, they didn't know the difference.

CITY WITHIN A CITY

33-35 Then the invaders built another city within the city of David. The walls were thick and high; there were turrets galore. In a word, they turned the new headquarters, a miniature city in itself really, into one large fort located on the highest part of the Temple mount. It was dubbed Akra, or the Heights. That's where that sinful nation parked; they tucked themselves in rather nicely and comfortably. The huge structure wasn't only the barracks for a retaliatory force; it was also an arsenal housing the spoils and the arms needed to control the Jews. Outside, the building looked like a peaceable kingdom; inside, it was an explosion waiting to happen.

FATE OF THE TEMPLE

36-40 There was a plot behind the plot; the Sanctuary of the Temple was in the direct line of fire from the Heights. A diabolic evil if there ever was one in Israel! Deliberately, the invaders spilled innocent human blood around the Sanctuary and defiled the Holy Place in every possible way.

Needless to say, the Jerusalemites fled; their place had been taken over by the foreigners. The Jews were now at the mercy of the outsiders and their Jewish collaborators. The Temple's Sanctuary became a desperate, roach-ridden place; feast days turned into days of mourning; the Sabbath was a day of shame; honor had been turned into dishonor. Once glorious, the Temple's reputation had been tarnished beyond polish; the sublime buildings had decayed into a disaster area.

FORCED ACCULTURATION

41-42 At this point, Antiochus prepared a proclamation for his whole kingdom. His theme? That all the peoples were now one; that all his subjects must abandon *their* home laws for *his* home laws; that all tribes were now Gentile tribes and were subject to Gentile laws—as interpreted by himself, of course.

43-50 Many Jews went along with this new pagan cult, even to the point of sacrificing to idols and violating the Sabbath. By messengers into Jerusalem and the other cities of Judah, the king sent the proclamation that they should follow Gentile laws; that burnt offerings, sacrifices, and atonements of all kinds were banned from the Temple of God; that Sabbath and solemn feast days would now be secularized. The proclamation further ordered that new altars, temples, and idols should be built; that pigs as well as cattle should be offered in the same sacrifice; that boys should not be circumcised but brainwashed to receive the new doctrines and the new laws—all this to eliminate God's word among the house of Israel and the Law Moses had created to reinforce it. Whoever disobeyed the laws according to Antiochus would be condemned to death.

51-53 The proclamation was spread around the entire kingdom of Antiochus, delivered by royally appointed caretaker governments here and there.

Particularly loathsome was the mandate that the citizens of Judah had to offer sacrifices to idols in every town. This forced many of the Jewish people into line with those who'd already left God's word behind. Evils grew like wildly successful plants. This drove the faithful people of Israel to the fringes of society and made them into fugitives.

FROM CITIZENS TO FUGITIVES

54-59   On the fifteenth day of the month Kislev in the year Casleu, King Antiochus delivered the symbol of obscene desecration—the idol of idols, the abomination of abominations, the ugliest of the ugly, the worst of the worst—upon the altar of God. In every city of Judah, a replica of the abomination was made. The Jews were expected to sacrifice to it anywhere and everywhere—in their doorways, on the streets, and so on. On the twenty-fifth day of each month, the sacrifices were to be given in honor of the king's birthday.

When the invaders found remaindered copies of the Torah, they tore them to shreds and then set them on fire. Anyone caught observing God's Law was killed. These punishments were inflicted upon the Jews by this foreign power during monthly sweeps through the cities.

60-64   Women who circumcised their boys were killed according to the new laws (the unfortunate infants were hanged by the neck), and those who performed the circumcision rite were hanged in their own houses.

Many of the Jews, consulting themselves and others, decided not to follow these laws. They chose to die rather than eat pork, for example, which would profane the holy covenant with God. All of which is to say, the Jews angered just about every Gentile they met.

BIRTH OF A NATION

1-5   Back in those days, Mattathias, son of John, son of Simeon, a priest of the family of Joarib, abandoned Jerusalem and moved to Modein, a distance of twenty miles. It was a pleasant town halfway between Jerusalem and the Great Sea; it was also the family seat. He had five sons. John, called the Zealous Guide; Simon, called the Treasure; Judas, called the Hammer; Eleazar, called the Piercer; and Jonathan, called the Wary.

6-14   When Mattathias saw the blasphemies and sacrileges taking place in Judah and Jerusalem, he launched into a dirge.

"Why was I born to see the destruction of my people and my holy city? Why do my sons just sit there while she's in enemy hands, the Sanctuary fondled by foreign fingers?

"The Temple looks like a disaster area. Its irreplaceable ornaments have been carried off; our little children, slaughtered in the streets; our young men, cut to pieces with the enemy's blade.

"What nation has occupied a kingdom and not helped itself to the spoils? Everything's been carried off, right down to the last decoration; what was once ours is now in the hands of the invaders.

"Anyone can see that our holy things, our beautiful things, our glorious things have been degraded; the Gentiles have polluted them.

"What's left to live for?"

Mattathias and his sons tore their clothes; they covered themselves with sackcloth; they sent up a terrible wail.

FIRST SPLINTER GROUP

15-18   Tracing these dissenting Jews, who came to be called the Maccabees, to Modein, the king's henchmen came. Their purpose was to coax the family to offer public sacrifice for all to see. They drew a crowd in the street, including a goodly number of Jews, Mattathias and his sons among them. The king's man addressed the entire crowd but focused on Mattathias.

"You're a leader, a great and noble citizen, not to mention your sons and family. That's why we want you to be the first in your town to obey the order of the king. What we're asking you to do is no more than the Gentile nations have already done; and that would include most of the men of Judah and all those who remain in Jerusalem. But when you do so, you and your sons among others will be numbered among the special Friends of the King. As such, you'll be entitled to receive silver and gold ornaments and medals, purple hats and robes, and other rewards."

19-22   Mattathias responded, shouting to be sure he was heard.

"I don't care if all the nations obey the king! I don't care if everyone else has abandoned God's word and consented to the king's commands. I and my sons and family will continue under the Law of our ancestors. May the Lord continue to be merciful to us as we refuse to obey the king's laws and all that it implies. We've heard the king's message that we should swerve to the right or to the left in our holy observance, but we have no intention of doing so."

MATTATHIAS LOSES HIS COOL

23-28   As Mattathias spoke, a Jew walked right up to the front of the crowd, unfolded a collapsible altar, and began the pagan sacrifice. Mattathias, a nice man but with a short fuse, couldn't believe what he was seeing. His face turned red; his stomach churned. Suddenly, in defense of God's Law, he charged the man and killed him right on the false altar. In the same swoop, he felled the king's man. Then he overturned the altar.

It was a costly deed, but observance of the Law was worth more to Mattathias than the cost to himself. Hadn't Phinehas done the same to Zimri, son of Salu? Mattathias was ranting by this time.

"Listen, everybody! If you have a grain of love left for our beloved Law, follow me out of this city!" He and his sons fled toward the mountains, leaving their belongings behind.

SECOND SPLINTER GROUP

29-38   Another collection of faithful Jews, a splinter group sympathetic to the Maccabees, descended from the mountains to the desert, where they settled down—men, women, children, cattle—all refugees from the evils that pursued them. Antiochus IV learned that this particular group of Jews had ignored his commands and moved to the desert in hope of disappearing altogether. Orders were sent to the army encamped in Jerusalem, city of David. Apparently, the group of defectors was large enough for the army to find rather easily. It was the Sabbath. What better day to attack? Messengers were exchanged.

"Where can you hide now?" asked the king's men. "Drop your arms, do what the king says, and you'll live to pray another day!"

A spokesperson for the Jews replied. "We're not going anywhere. We won't obey the king's command, but we won't violate the Sabbath either."

That was that. The army rushed forward; the battle began; it was a massacre.

The Jews held their ground but didn't respond to the attack; they didn't toss a spear or hurl a stone; they didn't fall back for protective cover. Their spokesperson gave the cue: "Let us die before we sin. Heaven and earth will know what we did on this day." The battle heated up. The Jewish men were all slaughtered, and with them their wives, children, and cattle. Afterward, according to enemy estimates, a thousand bodies lay on the bloody sand.

Changing the Sabbath Rules

39-41   When Mattathias and his friends in the hills learned of the slaughter, a great mourning went up. One man was overheard telling his neighbor, "If we all do what our brothers did, or not do what the enemy wants us to do, then we're next on the king's timetable."

The conclusion was obvious: "Next time an armed force challenges us on the Sabbath, let's return fire! We don't want to die passive and helpless like the others!"

Third Splinter Group

42-44   Then another party of zealots, the Hasideans, showed up in the Maccabee camp. They were pious fellows, big and strong, from all over the land of Israel. Every one of them was a lover of God's word; every one of them had escaped the king's evils. More joined every day; every day they became more formidable. The ragtag assembly soon turned into an armed force, policing and punishing Jewish collaborators with the enemy. The foreign king's men came in for a licking, too. Encounters with them always turned into a rout for the Jews.

Surprise Raids

45-48   Elsewhere, Mattathias and his family and friends made surprise attacks in the king's domain. Chief target was the pagan altars. Commandos swarmed everywhere, and everywhere the bodies piled up.

The secondary target was circumcision. The raiders checked all the local boys for circumcision—there were many who were not—and circumcised them without request or permission; they tracked the young males down and did the deed with all deliberate haste.

Eventually the chosen wrested themselves from the pagans; they got their land back and their city back and their Law back. Most importantly, victory was denied the sinners.

A Father's Final Words

49-68 As it will to all, death came to Mattathias, but not before he uttered some final words to his sons.

"In your lifetimes you have come up against pride and punishment, destruction and defeat. Now, my sons, it's your time to be examples of how to live out God's word and continue the covenant we have with him.

"Remember the accomplishments of our ancestors during their lifetimes; if you do the same, you'll be remembered until the end of time.

"Abraham—wasn't he tested by temptation but only to improve his fidelity? Wasn't he remembered for his justice?

"Joseph—didn't he, during a time of severe trial, keep God's commandments? Didn't he become lord of Egypt?

"Phinehas, our father—didn't he outdo himself in pursuit of God? Didn't he receive the covenant of eternal priesthood?

"Joshua—didn't he keep his word and lead an important mission? Didn't he become a judge for Israel?

"Caleb—didn't he testify for the Lord? Didn't he receive an inheritance?

"David—wasn't he pious? Didn't he receive a throne for the ages?

"Elijah—didn't he out-do his enemies with his zeal? Wasn't he welcomed in Heaven?

"Hananiah, Azariah, and Mishael—weren't they faithful to the end? Weren't they rescued from the flame?

"Daniel—didn't he live a life of innocence? Wasn't he freed from the mouth of the lion?

"And so it was through all the generations that everyone who hoped in the Lord triumphed.

"No matter what sinners say, you need never be afraid of them, for they're full of deceit and decay.

"Today sinners are remembered and tomorrow they're forgotten; their death turns them into dust; their big plans die with them.

"My sons, comfort one another; act like men in the observance of God's word; you'll be glorified because of it.

"Now look at Simon your brother. I know him to be a man of good counsel; always listen to what he has to say; he will take my place as father.

"Judas has been a strong man from the time he was a youth; he'll be your military strategist and lead your wars.

"You'll all observe God's word in all its niceties; you'll all avenge God's chosen people.

"As for the Gentiles, treat them fairly at all times and in light of God's commandments."

END OF ANOTHER ERA

69-70 Then Mattathias blessed his sons and said good-bye, even as he was being gathered up to his forebears. He died in his hundred-and-forty-sixth year and was buried in the tomb of his ancestors in Modein. In all parts of Israel, the mourning was loud and long.

THE HAMMER

1-2 **3** Taking over Mattathias's military duties was his son Judas, but everyone called him Maccabeus, or the Hammer. His brothers and everyone else who had ties with his father promised to stand by him; with joy in their hearts, they undertook the battle with the Gentiles.

ODE IN PRAISE OF JUDAS

3 9 "Judas the Hammer made the Jews feel good about themselves.

"With a swagger he donned the breastplate as though he were a giant; he slapped the rest of his armament on; he made battle plans; he stood sentinel with his sword drawn.

"When he was on duty he was very much like a lion, prowling, growling, like a young cat on the hunt.

"He pursued the wicked and hunted them down—those who disturbed society and tried to burn it down.

"He drove his enemies underground; all of a sudden enemy operatives were no longer to be seen.

"He was a living rebuke to the pagan kings in the region; our forefather Jacob himself would have enjoyed that turn of events; just the thought of Judas was enough to restore calm to the land.

"Touring the cities of Judah, the Hammer dispatched the unholy; he polished Israel's reputation as a power.

"His own reputation spread to the ends of the earth; he was especially known for his courage in the face of death and dying."

JUDAS SWATS ANTIOCHUS

10-12 The Gentiles were marshaled by Apollonius, former chief financial advisor to Antiochus IV, now governor of Samaria; he led a great force from Samaria to wage war against Israel. When Judas Maccabeus learned of this, he met Apollonius half way; he whipped the army and killed its marshal. The wounded fell; those who still had legs fled; spoils were gathered. Judas accepted the sword of Apollonius and for the rest of his life fought with that sword as if it were his own.

SMACKDOWN IN SYRIA

13-16 | A general of the Syrian army, Seron, received alarming reports about an agitator named Judas Maccabeus who'd rustled up a ragtag bunch that were faithful enough or crazy enough to follow him into a battle.

These were Seron's words: "I need to make a name for myself, make a splash around the kingdom, and this supposed Hammer is the perfect place to start. I'll put an end to him once and for all, and those with him. How dare they spurn the edict of the king!"

To avenge beatings that the Maccabees had laid upon new Greek immigrants in Samaria, Seron, a pagan of another sort, readied his army of unholy ones. They marched up Beth Horon to the plain where the Jews were encamped. When he reached the top, he was met by Judas and a handful of his men.

17-24 | Getting a closer look at the immense enemy army, the squad of Jews had second thoughts.

"How can we few fight against an overwhelming force like that? They're fresh as daisies; we're fading fast, like dandelions in the hot sun, from our all-day fast."

But Judas rallied his troops.

"It's easy for a few to overcome the many if Heaven is on our side. Numbers make no difference to God. Victory in war comes from above, not from below. They'll come toward us in a wave, cursing and swearing to destroy us and take our property. What we're going to do is fight for our lives and for God's word. The Lord himself will destroy them right before our very eyes; so there's really nothing for us to fear."

When he stopped talking, the Hammer rushed toward the enemy, and Seron and his army fell into a disorderly retreat. Judas and his men pursued him from Beth Horon all the way down to his encampment on the plain, killing eight hundred of them on the way, Seron among them. The rest fled to the land of the Philistines.

IT TAKES MONEY TO WAGE WAR

25-31 | Word sped through the neighboring nations that Judas Maccabeus and his brothers were not to be underestimated. The name Judas, as well as the mountain of Gentile spoils he'd amassed, came to the attention of Antiochus IV. He exploded and immediately alerted all his forces and activated them for duty. Soon his fortified encampment was bursting with recruits.

In order to speed up the recruitment process, Antiochus paid in advance. His paymaster doled out packets of coins for a year's service on an emergency basis. That left what seemed like a permanent dent in the royal treasury. Tributes from satellite states were at an all-time low due to clerical confusion and poor collection. (Back in those days, substituting one currency for another was the real culprit.)

Antiochus feared he didn't have enough left over to provide the amenities for visiting celebrities; even his frugal forebears always had enough for showy displays of wealth. His best shot was to attack Persian territory, where he could extract some tribute from the locals. He was right; he increased his silver holdings by an immense amount.

Military Might Cut in Half

32-34   While he was away, Antiochus IV left Lysias in charge; he was a nobleman from a royal family and currently manager of royal affairs and governor of the territory that extended from the Euphrates westward to the Nile. His governmental title was Kinsman to the King.

Antiochus left behind his son, Antiochus V, called Eupator, or Wellborn, in the care of Lysias until he returned. The king also left half his army and all his elephants with Lysias to allow him to deal with Judah and Jerusalem.

35-37   Lysias had a commission to send an armed force to seek and destroy and break—once and for all—Israel and what was left of Jerusalem, leaving not a stone upon a stone, sweeping the ground clean, leaving not a memory behind. Then Lysias was to repopulate the city with immigrants and foreigners only, parceling out lots by lottery.

Meanwhile, Antiochus took his half of everything and left Antioch, the capital of his kingdom, crossed the Euphrates, and headed for higher country.

Knavery and Slavery

38-41   For his own generals, Lysias picked Ptolemy, son of Dorymenes, and Nicanor and Gorgias, all competent, reliable men from the king's inner circle. Under their command, Lysias sent an army of forty thousand foot and seven thousand horse to the land of Judah to carry out the king's command. They set out with pomp and purpose, eventually pitching camp in the plain near Emmaus. Forces from Idumea and Philistia joined them there.

The rumor mill alerted merchants in the area; they packed up their silver and gold, boxed some handcuffs and shackles, and headed to the encampment. There they hoped to turn a quick profit, buying Israelite captives and reselling them as slaves for twice the price.

Low Self-Esteem Never Won a War

42-44   As for Judas and his brothers, bad things began to happen. Foreign armies were encroaching on their borders. Perhaps their enemies might succeed in killing them off and wiping their memory from the face of the earth. The Maccabees began to spread the word throughout the Israelite camp.

"Let's raise our low expectations! Let's fight for our people and what we hold holy!"

A group gathered; an assembly was called. They agreed to prepare for battle; they prayed and sought mercy and pardon.

LAMENT FOR JERUSALEM

45 Jerusalem was uninhabited; it had become something of a desert or wilderness. People went in and out of the place, but none were Jews. The Sanctuary had been flattened, and the Heights were occupied by foreigners and collaborators.

Joy had fled from the house of Jacob; there were harps and kitharas lying about, but not a note came from them.

PIETY BEFORE THE FRAY

46-54 The Jews moved to Mizpah, near Jerusalem, where they knew they could find a place of prayer. There they fasted, tore their garments, put on sackcloth, and poured ashes on their heads. They unrolled the scroll of the Lord—the scroll the Gentiles scrutinized trying in vain to find their own pagan idols in it—and brought out their ornamented priestly attire, firstfruits, and tithes.

Then they called together the Nazirites, the ones who'd been preparing themselves for a life consecrated to God and implored the heavens.

"Oh God, what shall we do with these candidates? Where shall we lead them? For your Sanctuary has been trampled and contaminated; your priests are paralyzed with grief and shame. Look, Gentile nations converge against us; they want to destroy us. But you already know what they want to do with us. How shall we resist their attack if you don't help us?"

They sounded their trumpets and cried out with loud voices.

ONCE MORE INTO THE BREACH

55-60 After this prayer ceremony, Judas Maccabeus appointed civic leaders for groups of thousands, hundreds, fifties, and tens. There were the usual exceptions according to the Law: those who were building houses, marrying wives, planting vines, or just plain scared. The Jews moved their camp to a place south of Emmaus.

When the time came, Judas spoke.

"Let's gear up! Let's show them what we're made of! They've come to destroy us and all we hold dear. In the morning, let's return the favor! It's better for us to die in battle than live to see the evil our enemies have done to us and God's holy Sanctuary. What Heaven wants will be done on earth."

GORGIAS

1-7 General Gorgias assumed command of an elite force: five thousand foot, one thousand horse. They broke camp during the night. The plan was to approach the Jewish camp under cover of darkness, surprise the Jews, and cut them to pieces before they knew what was happening. Positioning the invaders' troops were some men from the Heights who knew the terrain.

But Judas got advance word, rose from his bed, silently alerted his men, and began a counter move. It took some time, but his men tiptoed from the camp. It was still dark when Gorgias entered the Jewish encampment, but no one was there. They'd fled to higher ground, thought Gorgias, but when day broke, Judas was discovered in the plain below. Standing with him were three thousand men, but there weren't enough arms and armament to go around. Looking up they could now see the enemy: well-armed, protected by cavalry, all experienced troops.

8-11   Judas spoke to his men.

"Don't be afraid of their numbers! Don't worry about their attack. Remember who saved our ancestors from the Red Sea when Pharaoh followed them with his army. Now's the time to shout to high Heaven! He will have mercy on us. He'll remember our covenant with God. He'll destroy the enemy right under our very nose. Now the Gentiles will know that the one and only God forgives and frees Israel!"

A ROUT

12-16   Once the enemy spotted them, the Jews began their charge; trumpets blaring, both sides clashed head on. The Gentiles were routed; they retreated to their campsite. Judas pursued them, killing the stragglers by sword, driving the enemy force back to Gazara and the plains of Idumea, even as far as Azotus and Jamnia. After-battle report: three thousand Gentiles killed. Judas and his men returned to their camp after the slaughter.

17-22   "There's good news and bad," Judas told his people. "Yes, there's plunder; but don't get too excited, the war isn't over yet. Gorgias and his army aren't that far away. We have to stand firm against them. We have to defeat them completely first. Then we can enjoy the spoils of war without worry."

After Judas said this, however, he noticed a remnant of the Gentile force returning to their camp. Suddenly, the camp was on fire. That told the Jews all they needed to know: The Gentiles weren't waiting for Judas to attack them—they were retreating. They split and slipped away through the neighboring towns.

23-25   Judas and his men visited the abandoned Gentile camp and picked up a fair amount of the spoils of war: gold, silver, some blue and crimson silk, piles of unusual but expensive trinkets. Returning to their base camp, the Jews sang songs and blessed Heaven.

"God is good; his mercy is forever!"

From that day forward there was a great sense of security in Israel for quite a while.

PRAY TO WIN

26-33   The enemy troops who had escaped with their lives returned to Lysias and told him everything. He was infuriated. Things in Israel hadn't gone as King Antiochus IV had commanded. So Lysias hatched another plan. This time he'd gather and train an overwhelming force: sixty thousand foot, five thousand horse.

Of course, that would take some time. A year passed before the enemy troops could march into Idumea and pitch their tents in Beth Zur.

By that time, Judas was waiting for them with ten thousand men. He prayed for victory.

"Blessed are you, Savior of Israel! You broke a superior force with a stone's throw by David! You delivered the foreigners into the hands of Jonathan, son of Saul, and his adjutant!

"Crush, then, the enemy before us; confound the army and its cavalry.

"Fill our enemy with fear; dissipate their ferocity; make them quake as they get pounded down.

"Slap them down with the sword of those who love you.

"May everyone know your name and raise their voice in praise and hymns."

THE FRUITS OF VICTORY

34-35   **B**oth sides clashed and, at battle's end, Lysias received the Gentile body count: five thousand. He saw the remainder of his force dissolve into the woods and hills. Grudgingly, he marveled at Judas's audacity, his willingness to live strongly and die bravely. The only thing Lysias could do was leave immediately for Antioch and prepare for another confrontation in Judea.

36-40   Judas and his brothers summed up their victory.

"Behold our enemy has been pulverized. It's time to return to the holy city and the Temple. We need to straighten things out and clear things up."

They gathered up their troops and returned to Mount Zion. The Temple mount was a ruin. The Sanctuary was still there, but no living creature was about. The altar had been profaned, the gates burned, the porticos overgrown, the sacristies and side rooms caved in. Forest shrubbery and mountain weeds had taken over. Visibly upset, the Jews tore their garments, let out a great wail, and covered themselves with ashes. They fell face down on the ground, sounded the horns of grief, and cried out to Heaven.

41-48   Judas ordered his men to scrub and purify the holy places, but first they had to drive out the enemy lingering in the Heights. After that, he chose priests with spotless reputations, those who put God's word ahead of everything else. They cleaned up the holy places and lugged the symbol of obscene desecration to the dump where it belonged.

The altar of burnt offerings proved a special problem; it too had been profaned and defaced, but what to do with it? One idea was to save it and purify it. Who'd know it was the same table? Another idea was to pull it down. They ended up stacking the stones in the Temple warehouse until they could get a prophet's recommendation for what to do next. Eventually, they took uncut stones and built a new altar out of them according to the original plans. They reconstructed the holy rooms and recast the holy things and sanctified the porticos.

DEDICATION

49-55 When the major work was done, new sacred cups were brought in, as well as a lampstand, incense, altar, and table. On the altar they burned incense and lit the candles. They placed bread on the table, hung the veil, put final touches on everything.

Next day, before dawn, they arose at five. It was the twenty-fifth day of Kislev, the ninth month on the Jewish calendar, in year 148 of the Greek calendar. They offered sacrifice according to the Law on the new altar on what happened to be the second anniversary of the day the Gentiles had made the Temple unclean.

Now the whole place had been renovated. Music was heard again, with canticles and psalms accompanied by harps, lutes, and cymbals. All the people fell on their face, adored God, and asked for heavenly blessings.

56-59 For eight days the joyous dedication celebration continued with burnt offerings and sacrifices of salvation and praise. They decorated the face of the Temple with golden crowns, ornamented the portals and side rooms, hung the massive doors. Great joy was written on the faces of the people; there wasn't a Gentile fingerprint left in the whole place. Judas, his brothers, and everyone else in Israel decreed that Dedication Day should be preserved and observed with joy and gladness in the same season every year for eight days within the range from the fifth to the twentieth day of Kislev.

60-61 During that time, they built up Mount Zion with high walls and strong turrets all around; that, they hoped, would discourage another unwanted visit by the Gentiles. Judas stationed a garrison there to defend the Temple; he also secured Beth Zur against an attack from Idumea.

JUDAS DEALS WITH THE GENTILES

1-5 **5** The Gentile nations in the region eventually noticed that the altar had been rebuilt and the Holy of Holies had been rededicated, perfect replicas of both, down to the last detail. It made their blood boil. They felt they had to do what they had done before—try to destroy the current descendants of Jacob. They began by chipping away, roughing up a few people here, whacking a few people there. Yes, it was time for the current descendents of Esau to get down to their nefarious business.

First, they blockaded the Israelites, especially in Idumea, but Judas Maccabeus broke through at Akrabattene and pounded them with swift strikes, capturing them, stripping them clean.

Records showed that along the highways he ambushed the sons of Baean, a notoriously bad bunch who'd been doing a bit of ambushing themselves against the Jews. The Gentiles were forced to retreat to towers and granaries. Judas locked them in, cursed them out loud, then set the structures on fire; there were no survivors.

6-8 Next on Judas's itinerary were the Ammonites. They were a well-organized people with a large population; their leader was Timotheus. Judas engaged them militarily, skirmishing at first, then pounding them into submission as much as he could. He captured the city of Jazer and her surrounding townships, then returned to Judea.

⁹⁻¹³ The Gentile residents of Gilead presented a united front, picking off Jews within their confines; the Jews withdrew to a stronghold in Dathema. Some of them managed to smuggle letters to Judas and his brothers. Their messages were short and to the point.

"The Gentiles have us surrounded and are about to destroy us . . ."

"We're stuck in a fairly fortified place, which they're about to storm. Timotheus is their general. That should tell you we don't have much time left . . ."

"Come quickly! Rescue us! Many of us have died already . . ."

"All the brothers living among the Tobiads have been killed, their wives and children carried off, their property listed as spoils . . ."

"Final tally of the dead: as many as a thousand . . ."

Special Operations

¹⁴⁻²⁰ While these communiqués were read and digested, other messengers, their clothes torn, arrived from Galilee bearing bad news. Ptolemais, Tyre, and Sidon were no longer friendly places. Galilee was flooded with unfriendly foreigners. Everyone was out to get the Jews.

Judas reacted immediately. He held a great convocation to think through their next step. Surrender and extinction were both unacceptable. He turned to his brother Simon and ordered: "Put together a strike force whose only goal is freeing our brothers in Galilee. Our brother Jonathan and I will do the same in Gilead."

Judas left two civic leaders—Joseph, son of Zechariah, and Azariah—to tend to home affairs and defense of the region: "You're in charge now. Exercise leadership. Don't engage the enemy until we return."

Three thousand men were allotted to Simon—enough to handle Galilee; for Judas and Jonathan to handle Gilead, eight thousand men.

²¹⁻²³ Simon headed for Galilee, where he got involved in one battle after another with the enemy. He made great inroads, or so it appeared; he followed them all the way to the gates of Ptolemais. Body count: three thousand Gentiles. And then there were the spoils. He gathered those of Israel in Galilee and Arbatta—with wives, children, property—and led them to Judea with a sense of great accomplishment.

²⁴⁻²⁷ Meanwhile, Judas and his brother Jonathan crossed the Jordan and went three days into the desert. There they met up with the Nabateans, who welcomed them in peace. The Nabateans related that many of the Jews' kinsmen were being held for execution by Gentiles in Bozrah, Bosor near Alema, Chaspho, Maked, and Carnaim—large, well-defended cities, as all Gilead cities were. And the word was that Timotheus was planning to attack Dathema, where many Jews had sought refuge, and kill them.

²⁸⁻³⁴ So Judas made a sudden turn, putting his men on the desert road to Bozrah. When they got there, they occupied the city, killing all Gentile males by the edge of razor-sharp swords. They rounded up everything valuable, rescued the Jews there, then set the city afire.

When night came, Judas made his next move, silently approaching the fortress at Dathema. Next morning, he looked out and saw a huge number of Timotheus's troops carrying ladders and moving engines to storm the fortress and kill the Jews within. The fight had begun; the cries of the citizenry within the walls ascended to high Heaven like trumpet blasts. To his men Judas shouted, "Fight today for your brothers and sisters!"

With three companies of men, he attacked the attackers from the rear, trumpets blasting, prayers rising with the screams. When Timotheus realized that it was Judas Maccabeus, he and his men fled as best they could. The Maccabees hit them hard. Enemy body count: eight thousand or thereabouts.

35-36   Next Judas turned his attention toward Alema; he assaulted it and captured it—killing every Gentile male, freeing the Jews, collecting spoils, then setting the city on fire. Next stops: Chaspho, Maked, Bosor, and the other cities of Gilead.

TIMOTHEUS REGROUPS

37-39   After reading reports of these setbacks, Timotheus gathered another army and pitched camp opposite Raphon, on the other side of the stream, which were really whitewater rapids.

Judas sent spies to size up the Gentile army; their report wasn't encouraging.

"It's a massive force made up of companies from all the Gentile nations in the region. And there are mercenaries, Arabs hired for the occasion. They pitched camp on the other side of the rapids. They're battle ready."

But so was Judas; he went to meet them head-on.

40-41   Timotheus addressed his top officers: "If Judas's army makes it to the middle of the rapids, we're done for; but if he's afraid to chance the crossing and camps on the other side, we'll cross the river and drive him back to defeat."

42-45   Judas made the first move; he stationed scribes by the rapids and gave them their orders: "Everyone crosses; no one stays behind. Your job is to make note of those who don't or won't cross!"

Judas was the first to dip a toe in the whitewater; his men followed him, sloshing through it and up onto the other side. The Gentile forces crumbled, threw down their arms, and ran for the shrine enclosure at Carnaim. The Jews took that city, burning the shrine and everything in it. Having lost the will to fight anymore, Carnaim was demilitarized.

Judas rounded up all the strays of Israel who were in Gilead, highbrow and lowbrow—wives, children, possessions included—and accompanied them and his great army on the triumphant road back to the land of Judah.

EPHRON, NO LAUGHING MATTER

46-50   The highway home passed through Ephron, which was a large, well-fortified city; there was no way around it. Because of advance word, the citizens had withdrawn inside the city walls; the gates were made impassable by piles of stones.

There was one thing Judas could do. He sent a peaceable note to the city officials: "We're on our way home, but to do so we have to go through your city. No harm will come to you. We'll ramble through peacefully on foot only."

The citizens found the note less than convincing, however, so Judas had a proclamation read throughout his army. He was going to order an attack on the city. Each man was to stay put and support the assault from that point. The siege machinery would do the heavy lifting.

The Jewish soldiers did as they were told. The assault began and lasted all day and all night; morning came, and the citizens opened their gates.

51-54 What followed wasn't pretty. Every Ephronite that day tasted the Israelite sword. The Jews picked up what spoils they could carry and, stepping over the dead, marched through the city to the far side.

Finally, they crossed the Jordan to the great plain of Beth Shan, where they camped overnight. The stragglers Judas rounded up every day, exhorting them to finish the trip; it was always "only a few more steps" before they arrived in the land of Judah. When they came to Mount Zion, they climbed with great joy and offered sacrifices because not one of them had been slain. They'd returned safely, and peace had been restored.

The Gentiles Win One

55-58 While Judas and Jonathan were in Gilead, Simon was in Galilee facing off against the enemy at Ptolemais. Meanwhile, Joseph, son of Zechariah, and Azariah—more civic leaders than generals—heard of the heroic deeds of the Maccabees and came to a conclusion: "We can do that, too. Let's fight the enemy here at home." They announced to the home guard that they were advancing to Jamnia.

59-64 Gorgias, the general for Lysias, led his army out to face the Jews. Joseph and Azariah didn't fare as well as the brothers Maccabee; they were routed by the enemy all the way back to the borders of Judah. Jewish casualties: two thousand dead.

Not a good day for those of Israel. These civic leaders had been ordered to stay at home but, thinking they were as valiant as the Maccabees, disobeyed that order, much to their sorrow. From another point of view, though, no harm was done. These men and their seed weren't in direct line with the ones into whose hands the salvation of the nation had been promised.

Unfinished Business

Judas Maccabeus and his brothers became known all over the land of Israel. To the enemy's chagrin, they also were getting to know the Maccabees. Wherever people gathered, great tales about the brothers were told.

65 There was a bit of unfinished business having to do with the Gentiles in the south. The Maccabees went to take care of that. They pummeled Hebron and its villages; they destroyed the armory; they burned the turrets around the barracks.

66-67 Then they moved camp to Samaria, a land of aliens and immigrants, an altogether unwholesome lot, and did a quick campaign to straighten things out there as well.

One notable episode. Some priests, who weren't supposed to fight but did indeed enter the fight, fell in battle with the Maccabees. The poor clerics meant to do the manly thing, but they just didn't have the muscle to pull it off.

68   Next on Judas's short list was Azotus; it was flooded with foreigners and undesirables. He went down there and destroyed their altars, burned their statues, and carted off their spoils. After that, there was nothing left for Judas and his brothers to do but return to Judah.

QUIRKY KING EASILY REBUFFED

1-4   **6** King Antiochus IV, called Flashman, was passing through the high country, wondering what his next move should be. One suggestion was Elam, a city in Persia famous for its wealth, with holdings in silver and gold. The temple there was something of a depository, housing cloth-of-gold garments, ceremonial breastplates, and ornamental shields, all of which had been left there by Alexander the Great, son of Philip, first king of the Greeks. Apparently, the articles were for sale or for rent. Elam it was then. Antiochus wanted to capture the city and clean the temple out, but he couldn't pull it off. The citizens had advance warning; they rose up in defense. The king had to withdraw quickly, which didn't make him happy. He decided to return to Babylon.

BAD NEWS FROM THE JEWISH FRONT

5-6   While still in Persian territory, Antiochus received a message informing him that his army in Judah had been defeated. That meant only one thing. Lysias, though he had a superior force, had fought face-to-face with the Jews and lost. As if that weren't bad enough, the Jews picked up lots of arms and cartloads of loot before they wrecked the Gentile encampment.

7   Further news. The Jews smashed the symbol of obscene desecration sitting on the exact same spot as the altar of the Jewish Sanctuary. They also surrounded the Temple with high walls, as well as occupying the king's very own city of Beth Zur. That didn't sit well with Antiochus either.

FLASHMAN DIES

8-16   When he digested the full report, Antiochus began to tremble and couldn't stop; *delirium tremens* at its worst. He lay down on his bed, a jellied mass rolling from one side to the other. None of his plans had turned out the way he wanted. The depression lasted for some days; it opened old wounds; he thought was going to die. He called for his advisory board, Friends of the King. It was time for some last words.

"I close my eyes, but I can't sleep. Stress has torn my heart to pieces. I ask myself what caused all this tribulation, where this flood of tears came from. I was happy once. I had power and people loved me for it! Now the evils I did in Jerusalem have come back to haunt me. I looted the city's gold and silver, and I doomed the citizens without cause. Now I am paying the price as I lay dying a sad death in a foreign land."

Antiochus asked for Philip, one of his advisors, and made him interim executive in charge of the Antiochine-empire enterprises. He gave him crown, robe, and ring, asking him to deliver them to his son, also named Antiochus, the "fifth" king, soon to succeed the "fourth." He also asked Philip to become regent to his son and raise him to be a king. Parenthetically, for what happened to Philip, see later in the story.

And that was the end of that. Antiochus IV, called Epiphanes, or Flashman, died in year 149 of the Greek calendar. Barely a soul noticed.

17   Except Lysias noticed. When he learned that the king had died, he immediately installed as the new king the young man he'd been in charge of raising: Antiochus V, called Eupator, or Wellborn.

FOCUSING ON THE HEIGHTS

18-27   A year after the inauguration, the foreigners and collaborators who still occupied the Heights were harassing the faithful Jews around the Sanctuary. Trying to keep the Gentile presence from totally disappearing from Jerusalem, they opposed the followers of God's word whenever they could.

Judas Maccabeus decided that the Heights crowd had to go. He assembled his troops; siege appeared to be the best course of action. Immediately they surrounded the Heights. This all took place in year 150 of the Greek calendar.

The Jews brought into play giant slings and battering rams. Some of the Jewish collaborators escaped and went to the young king Antiochus V. This was their urgent message.

"How come you're not doing anything about our brothers in Jerusalem, Your Highness? You should be avenging them! Yes, we're Jews, but we'd declared ourselves to serve your father. You have to look at things from his point of view. You should be pushing his edicts. This very moment our people in the Heights are being besieged; we have nothing in common with these Jews. They hunt us down and kill us. We have properties in the country, but the Jews grab those as well. They've attacked us not only in Jerusalem but throughout Judea. They've approached not only the Heights in Jerusalem with a view to kicking us out, but they've also attacked your fortress in Beth Zur. This may seem like a pretty small deal to you now, but unless you prevail against them sooner than later, they'll do something worse. And then there'll be no stopping them."

BOY KING BEEFS UP FORCES

28-33   That message got the young king's attention; he was outraged. He called his advisors to review civic as well as military assets; the latter included military vehicles (chariots, horses, and elephants).

Recruitment reached out to other kingdoms and the maritime provinces; mercenaries from all over responded. Final figures were impressive: one hundred thousand foot, twenty thousand horse, thirty-two battle-hardened elephants.

The king's armed forces moved through Idumea and pulled up at Beth

Zur. They fought for many days; every time they attempted to make war engines, the Jews sallied forth and burned them. It was a fierce show.

Judas left the Heights and moved his encampment to Beth Zechariah. The king rose before dawn, aroused his army, and headed for the same spot. The opposing armies readied themselves for the battle of battles. At trumpets' sound, the clash began.

34-41   Cheap red wine got the elephants into the right mood as their handlers readied them for combat. The king's generals divvied up the beasts—one elephant for each thousand infantry, breast-plated and helmeted, accompanied by five hundred cavalry, mounted and in position. The orders: *Wherever the elephant goes, the military goes with him. No exceptions!*

Each elephant was outfitted with a wooden tower housing one military engine or another; the beast was mounted by two muscular military men and one spindly fellow, an Indus, who was the handler, called a *mahout*.

Cavalry was stationed at the elephants' flanks; its job was to urge the infantry on and protect their backs. When the sun rose, golden rays bounced off the brass shields, glittering like candle lights on the hillside. Half the king's army advanced on the mountain road, the other half on the plain; slowly and carefully, yet noisily, they moved: thousands of voices, hundreds of trumpets, the clink of armor, the stink of beasts. A mighty force was lumbering toward the Jews.

How Not to Kill an Elephant

42-46   Judas made ready; the army entered the fray. First casualties: six hundred enemy. One of Judas's brothers, Eleazar, aptly called the Piercer, noticed that the harness of one of the elephants, higher than the others, had the king's insignia. Could it be the king himself was astride? Trying to inspire his people, Eleazar exposed himself to the enemy, then did something to ensure his name would go down in history.

Boldly, recklessly, he sailed right into the enemy line, swinging his sword right and left, the bodies falling on both sides. Finally, he got under the elephant, planted his feet, and thrust his spear upward, killing the beast—but killing himself as well as the beast collapsed upon him.

47-54   Seeing the strength of the royal forces and feeling the momentum of their military, Judas decided to retreat. The king's army headed toward Jerusalem. The king was aiming for Judea and Mount Zion, but first he made peace with those in Beth Zur. The poor people in that community had run out of food behind their walls; the pickings outside the walls weren't all that good either, since it was the year in which the land was resting.

The king posted occupying troops there, then moved on to take Jerusalem, where he set up his ballistics and mechanicals, flame throwers and stone hurlers, slings and catapults. Each side made machines to match the other's; the battle went on for many days.

The granaries, however, ran out, the seventh year being the fallow one. There was some grain around the city, but the king's men rounded it all up for themselves. Only a few of the Jews remained in the Sanctuary; hunger had driven the rest of them out. It was every man for himself.

UPSETTING NEWS

55-63   At just that time, Lysias got a piece of disturbing news about Philip, whom Antiochus IV had appointed to act as regent for his young son. Upon returning from Persia and Media with his own army, Phillip had decided that he himself should be king. After all, the new king was only nine years old.

So Lysias made haste to go home and personally tell the boy, whom he had already crowned king, and his commanders and advisors that it was time to give up the battle against the Maccabees.

"We lose a little every day; we're running out of food. We have the place under siege but haven't been able to gain entrance. Now's a good time to make peace with those Jews. Let's make a treaty with them. They can live according to what they call God's Law. The only reason they fight is that we despise their beliefs."

The proposal to make peace pleased the young king. Overtures were made to the Jews and they agreed to a truce; the peace document was circulated on both sides. The various officials ratified the plan, and the peace conference, which was held in the Heights, concluded.

Right afterwards, however, the king strolled from the Heights to Mount Zion itself, where he marveled at the fortifications around the Sanctuary. Suddenly he had second thoughts. He broke his oath and ordered the destruction of the outer wall.

After that, he left Jerusalem quickly, returning to Antioch, where he found Philip trying to usurp his throne. But the king's army made short work of Philip, and the young Antiochus V reclaimed his throne.

RISE OF DEMETRIUS

1-4   In year 151 of the Greek calendar, Demetrius, son of Seleucus, escaped from prison in Rome, where he'd been held hostage for sixteen years. Not long afterward, he reappeared with a few men in Tripolis, or Tri-City, a maritime city not far from Antioch, which he made the center of his operations for the invasion to come. And it did indeed come. His army entered the house of the king of his ancestors, grabbed Antiochus V and Lysias, and brought them as prisoners to Demetrius. Demetrius was notified of their arrival but said, "Don't bring them in; I don't want to see their faces."

The army executed them; Demetrius I, called Soter, or Savior of One and All, assumed the throne of their kingdom.

5-7   His first audience was with a group of Jewish collaborators—wicked, godless people. Alcimus acted as spokesman; he wanted to be appointed high priest. But first, he had a list of accusations a mile long.

"Judas Maccabeus and his brothers have destroyed all your throne's friends and our friends, kicking us out of our land. You need to send an observer, someone you trust, to tour Judah and assess the genocide inflicted upon us, our kingdom, and the region. My mission: to punish the perpetrators and all those who assisted them."

8-11   Demetrius agreed and chose Bacchides, one of his senior advisors, to act for him. His diplomatic experience included being governor of Greater Syria across the Orontes River. He had a decent reputation around the kingdom, and his loyalty to the new king was unquestioned. He was the right one to send. Accompanying him would be Alcimus the impious one, who'd succeeded in getting himself appointed high priest by the king. Their mission was to destroy the faithful ones of Israel.

After extensive preparations, they were able to launch a great army into the land of Judah. Alcimus sent envoys to Judas and his brothers; the messages, if read one way, meant peace, and if read another way, meant war.

Hardly peace, thought the Maccabees. Doves mean peace. Elephants mean war.

12-18 Upon their arrival in Judah, Alcimus and Bacchides were visited by local scribes who hoped to reconcile differences. The Hasideans were the first to seek peace. Their reasoning was flawed: "A priest of the line of Aaron, which Alcimus is, has come with a great army. Why would he deceive us?"

The invaders' response went something like this: "Why would we harm you? We're friends! You have our word, our solemn oath!"

An oath was an oath, thought the Hasideans, but before day's end sixty of them had been executed. Which makes one mindful of a Scripture passage:

> The bodies of your saints lie in the streets of Jerusalem;
> their blood flows in the gutters.
> Is there no one to bury them?

Fear and tremor grew throughout Judea; the whole population shook. "There's no truth or justice in this new regime," went the general sentiment. "They've broken their agreements and violated their oaths."

19-22 Bacchides struck camp, marched four miles up the Jerusalem road to Beth Zaith, and pitched camp. There he found a good many deserters from his army. Some of the locals he killed for show and left the bodies where they fell.

Bacchides entrusted the region to Alcimus; he left behind a military presence for protection. As for himself, he was off to see the king. Alcimus's hold on his position as high priest was shaky at best, so he had the theory that to keep the population under control he had to harass everyone continually. Some people willingly served him, and with their help he kept Judah under his thumb and caused great consternation in the house of Israel.

WARS AND RUMORS OF WARS

23-27 Everywhere Judas Maccabeus looked, he saw encroachment. The Israelite insurgents were becoming more of a problem than the Gentiles. He toured the trouble spots and took vengeance on the insurgents—deserters really—and that stopped them in their tracks. Alcimus had second thoughts. He saw that Judas had tightened home security. Perhaps he couldn't beat him on the field, but he could best him by way of rumor and insinuation.

Alcimus returned to King Demetrius and accused Judas of crimes against humanity. The king selected a highly placed advisor to respond, Nicanor was his name. There was no love lost between him and the children of Israel; in fact, he'd taken part in exercises against their land. His commission was to wipe out the Jews once and forever.

The king sent Nicanor off with a sizable force toward Jerusalem, but first he sent Judas and his brothers a message with lots of honeyed words and flowery phrases. It was too sweet to be believed.

EXCERPT OF LETTER FROM DEMETRIUS TO JUDAS MACCABEUS

28 "Should we two really be warring against each other? I don't think so. With far less effort on both our parts, we could become quite good friends. Hope you don't mind if I send my senior diplomatic officer, Nicanor, for a visit. He'll have a few men with him, mostly junior diplomats. He'll pay our respects, drop off a few gifts, that sort of thing. He looks forward to the pleasure of meeting you face-to-face."

MISSED SIGNALS

29-33 And that's what happened. Nicanor did go to meet the Hammer. They greeted each other with great civility. Parked not that far away, Judas knew, was Nicanor's army, awaiting the word to search and destroy. So when Nicanor asked for a second visit, Judas refused kindly; truth to tell, he was terrified.

Nicanor knew it was time to attack. Both sides clashed at a dull spot, Capharsalama; it was good for nothing except perhaps a nice battle. The first skirmish resulted in Nicanor losing five hundred men; the rest, including Nicanor himself, ran to the Heights for refuge.

From the Gentile stronghold, pretending he was out for a stroll, Nicanor went to Mount Zion. Having heard that he was on a mission of mercy, priests of the Sanctuary and senior elders greeted him warmly. They even showed him the offering that had been made that morning on behalf of King Demetrius.

34-35 All of a sudden, however, the mood changed. Nicanor mocked them, spit at them, subjected them to verbal abuse. He spoke as though he'd won the battle once and for all. He ended his string of insults by swearing an oath: "If Judas and his army aren't handed over to me by tomorrow, I'll burn this dump down!" That said, he wheeled around and went off in a huff.

36-38 The surviving priests went inside and stood facing the altar, weeping, and pleading to God in prayer.

"You yourself, Lord, chose this Temple to invoke your holy name herein, thus making it a house of praying and offering. Wreak vengeance on this bad man and his army! Swipe them with the sword! Remember their blasphemies! There's no room in your mansions for people like them!"

SURPRISE ENCOUNTER

39-42 Nicanor left Jerusalem for his stronghold at Beth Horon, where he planned to meet with Syrian reinforcements. Seven miles down the road, at Adasa, a surprise awaited him: Judas and his three-thousand-man army. Before the clash, Judas led his troops in this prayer.

"Remember, Lord, when the emissaries from King Sennacherib said one thing but meant another? Your angel swept down and slew them—one hundred and eighty-five thousand of them. So, Lord, do the same for us! Destroy that army in our sight today! Let the world know that Nicanor blasphemed in your Sanctuary and suffered the same sad end as Sennacherib!"

43-46 Both sides charged. It was the thirteenth day of the month Adar. Nicanor was the first to fall. His army, now without a leader, dropped their arms and fled. Judas followed them from Adasa all the way to Gazara, trumpets blasting to flush out the fugitives. The pursuing force went from town to town, stronghold to stronghold, slaying the enemy where they stood. Every man died by the sword; there wasn't one left standing.

47-50 Spoils were passed around. Nicanor's head was cut off, as was his right hand—the one that made the oath he broke a short time after it had been made. The bloody pieces were hung up in Jerusalem for all to see.

There was dancing in the streets. If there was anything the populace needed, it was a great celebration. And there was universal agreement that Defeat-of-Nicanor Day be celebrated every year on the same date, the thirteenth of Adar. At last there was peace throughout the land of Judah, if only for a while.

ROME, SOLUTION OR PROBLEM?

1-4 8 Judas Maccabeus gathered some interesting reports about the Romans. They were powerful, resourceful, and, it seemed, agreeable. They'd help anyone and everyone who asked. Every crisis they saw as an opportunity to make a new friend.

Did I say the Romans were powerful? They told never-ending stories about their victories on the battlefield. Then they told after-battle stories, listing all the good things they did for the defeated. In return, all the defeated had to do was send a lump sum once a year to a regional office.

Then there was Hispania. All the people there had to do was surrender. In return for not being killed, they graciously handed over management of their silver and gold mines.

The overall Roman strategy for other countries was as simple as it was careful, no matter how near or far from Rome it was. The king of a country they were approaching had two choices: to hand over his nation or to die; the same went for the locals. There was a third choice—to resist—but that would only cause pain. The Romans were good at inflicting pain, but they preferred collecting tribute. It was easier on everybody concerned.

5-10 The Romans whipped Philip and his son Perseus, king of the Macedonians. No matter how formidable the foes, the Romans always came out on top. Next, Antiochus III the Great, king of Asia. Though he fielded one hundred and twenty elephants in addition to cavalry, chariots, and infantry as far as the eye could see, his army was sent packing. As for himself, he was easy pickings; the Romans captured him alive and turned him from an independent king into a client king who'd work for the Romans and their successors. He paid tribute and offered up the hostages required by the Romans.

Next victims were Lycia, Mysia, and Lydia and an archipelago of petite but pearly regions. The Romans treated them as a group, subjecting them to a comparatively stable client king, Eumenes II of Pergamum.

Next, the Greeks. They decided to try their luck at independence, but Roman intelligence picked up word of their plans. Rome sent out a single general and his troops to straighten them out, and the Greek body count was high. The Romans captured wives and children, stripped the country bare, and destroyed its defenses. To this day, the Greeks have remained in the servant class.

11-13 There were other kingdoms, other islands, who became upstarts from time to time. The Romans were never amused. On the other hand, whoever welcomed the Roman presence found friendship with their conquerors. Nonetheless, whether near or far, these new client kings were a nervous bunch during the day; during the night they had bad dreams.

Those who weren't kings but wanted to be, the Romans supported. But those kings who wanted no Roman presence, the Romans deposed and made disappear. The more this distressing news spread, the better the Romans liked it.

14-16 None of the Roman senators sported a real crown, but that didn't stop them from acting as if they were real rulers. No one wore the purple, yet every one of them paraded around like a king. Three hundred or so senators would gather daily, assess the needs of the people, and generally see to the common welfare. Generally speaking, the senators entrusted relations with other countries to one man, who would serve only a one-year term. His executive powers covered the whole empire—a nice job but a nasty one. No one envied the position.

17-22 As emissaries to Rome, Judas chose Eupolemus, called Goodwar, of clan Accos, and Jason, son of Eleazar; both were fluent in Latin and Greek. Judas sent them to Rome to establish diplomatic relations and open a consulate. His immediate concern—and his emissaries would testify to this—was to free himself and his country from the greedy hands of the

Greeks. The way the Jews looked at it—and his emissaries would stress this point—was that their present situation was tantamount to slavery.

The legates set off for Rome. It was a far journey but worth it. When they finally entered the Roman senate house, their papers were checked. Finally, they delivered their message to the senators.

"Judas Maccabeus, his brothers, and the people of Israel have sent us to you. We wish to establish courteous and cordial relations with you. And we would like nothing better than your welcoming Judah as a client kingdom and Jews as your allies and friends."

The proposal was well received. The senators were polled and, in the opinion of the chair, the ayes had it and the issue passed. A document affirming a new era of peace and alliance was drawn up and styled upon brass tablets. The original was deposited in Rome; a less ornate facsimile was sent to Jerusalem.

WHAT THE AGREEMENT SAID

23-28   "All hail the Romans and the Jews, on land and sea, forever and a day, with sword or without! If war is thrust upon the Romans or the Jews or any of their allies in their dominions, the Jews will help, time permitting, wholeheartedly trying. They will not give aid to the warring parties, such aid being construed as wheat, weapons, money, ships, and so forth—as defined by Rome. They will fulfill their obligations accordingly and bear the costs thereof. In like manner, if war is thrust upon the Jews, the Romans will come to their aid, with heart overflowing, and do what they can, time permitting. The Romans will not give aid to the warring parties, that being construed as wheat, weapons, money, ships, and so forth—as defined by Rome. The Jewish people will obey Rome's orders without exception or deceit."

29-30   Thus read the treaty drawn up to express the new relationship between the Romans and the Jews. The agreement could be altered by addition or subtraction, all changes being subject to mutual ratification. As for the evils and perils inflicted upon the Jews, the Romans wrote a stern letter of reprimand to King Demetrius I of Antioch that began as follows.

LETTER FROM THE ROMANS TO DEMETRIUS

31-32   "Why are you trying to crush our new friends and allies, the Jews? If our Jewish friends and allies come to us again with the same complaint, we won't look kindly; we won't look the other way; we'll intervene. We'll find you and fight you on land or sea. In a word, don't mess with the Romans!"

THE RETURN OF BACCHIDES AND ALCIMUS

1-4   **9** In the meantime, Demetrius heard that Nicanor and his army had fallen. Again he sent Bacchides and Alcimus back to the land of Judea, this time with the Syrian wing of his army, which amounted to half his infantry. They traveled the road leading to Galilee, eventually pitching camp at the cliffs of Mesaloth by Arbela. Not willing to pass up an opportunity when it presented itself, they took over the town, killing a lot of the locals. In the first month of year 152 of the Greek calendar, they moved their camp to the neighborhood of Jerusalem. Next they headed for Berea with a substantial entourage—twenty thousand foot, two thousand horse.

FAMOUS LAST WORDS

5-8 Judas, with three thousand elite troops, was already encamped at nearby Elasa. When his men saw the enemy lumbering toward them, however, they saw it was an overwhelming force and meant business. As the day ended, a fair number of Jews had deserted their camp; during the night most of the rest of his army slipped away. At dawn, if he was lucky, Judas had eight hundred left. His crack force had shrunk at the worst possible time, just as the battle was about to begin. Judas could have rounded up the deserters, but time had run out and he was desperate. For the men still with him, he had some final words. "Let's meet this challenge head on! Let's bring the battle to the enemy!"

9 "No way!" his men replied. "We can't win here, but we can save our lives! Let's get out of here and find our brothers. Then we can take a stand and trade the enemy blow for blow."

10 "How can we justify retreat?" Judas asked them. "If our time has come, then die we must and die we shall. That's what our people have always done when caught in tight situations. Let's not lose our golden reputation at this late date!"

11-13 Not far away, the enemy army moved into position. The cavalry divided into two troops—one on each side of infantry, slingers and archers in the front. They were seasoned warriors all, none afraid to die. As trumpets tuned up, Bacchides was on the right flank, protected on each side by his best fighters. Opposite, Judas and his eight hundred men moved forward. Suddenly the earth was shaken by the trumpets and war cries of the combatants; the clangor wouldn't end till it was dark.

JUDAS FALLS, JONATHAN RISES

14-18 Judas saw that Bacchides was stronger on the right, so that's where he sent his veterans; they fought brilliantly, pushing the enemy back to Mount Azotus. The enemy's right wing bore the brunt of the fight. Trying to take advantage, the enemy's left wing wheeled about, disappearing from Judas's front only to reappear at his back. The battle worsened for both sides, the wounded and dying falling all over the battlefield. Then Judas himself fell. Those of his troops who were still standing with him looked at one another and ran off while they still could.

19-22 After the battle was lost, Jonathan and Simon carried their brother Judas off the field. Eventually, they buried him in the family grave in Modein. The people of Israel wept, moaning and mourning with deep grief; it lasted for many days. At the funeral services the question went round: "He saved us so many times! Why couldn't we have saved him?" Others remembered the Hammer's many victorious battles. Only a few of these have been recorded; most have been forgotten.

23-26 After the death of Judas, the wicked came out of the woodwork all over Judea, pretending to be the disadvantaged class in Jewish society. They staged public demonstrations, destroyed private property, rioted in the streets. Add to that, a great cloud of famine darkened the land. There was little the Maccabees could do. To fill the vacuum, the renegades rushed in.

For the executive positions in Judea, Bacchides turned to the locals he trusted, who were the dregs of the house of Israel. These functionaries made inquiries and hunted down all known associates of Judas Maccabeus. These were brought to Bacchides, found guilty, and tortured.

27-31 The entire country went into an uproar, the likes of which hadn't been seen since the disappearance of prophets and their prophecies. Finally, friends of Judas met privately with his brother Jonathan.

"Since the Hammer died, we haven't found anybody to fill his shoes who will take on Bacchides, the domestic insurgents, and our foreign enemies. Now today, whether you like it or not, we choose you to pick up where Judas left off, to be our king and our general in fighting the war of wars."

Jonathan, aptly called the Wary, overcame his natural hesitancy and agreed to take his brother's place as leader in all the affairs of Israel.

CLANDESTINE OPERATIONS

32-35 At that meeting, however, Bacchides had eyes and ears. He immediately put out an order to find and kill Jonathan. Jonathan and his brother Simon both knew there was at least one spy, probably many spies, at the meeting, so they quickly rounded up their supporters and headed for the little known desert resort of Tekoa. One of its tourist attractions was the pool of Asphar. Bacchides was immediately updated by his anonymous spies and mobilized his army. Even though it was the Sabbath, he marched to the Jordan.

PIRACY ON THE HIGH DUNES

But I'm getting ahead of my story. Meanwhile, Jonathan had sent another of his brothers, John, now a captain of the people and member of Jonathan's new administration, to their friends, the Nabatean Arabs. Since the two groups were at peace at the time, John was to make a bold request of them. Since those of Israel were about to begin battle, would the Nabateans stash the Jews' personal and professional baggage for them until the fighting was over?

36-37 On the road, however, John was met by some Jambrites, marauders from Medaba, and therein lies a tale. These pirates would appear on the road, travel with a group for a while to gain the people's trust, and then steal their stuff and carry them off to slavery—or worse. That was the bloody fate of John.

Word raced back to Jonathan and Simon. Not long thereafter, Jambrites were spotted at a wedding ceremony, escorting energetically the bride, a daughter of one of the great princes of Canaan, to the bridal chamber.

38-42 Jonathan and Simon, remembering the blood of their brother John, planned their revenge. They climbed up a hill and took cover under the trees and behind the brush. When they looked down, what a scene they saw: much ado about everything; a lot of processions and partying; drums beating, pipes whistling, weapons being brandished. And there was the Jambrite bridegroom, with family and friends and baggage.

Suddenly, the Maccabees rose from their ambush and swooped down. They killed some and wounded others; the rest fled into the mountains. The spoils were especially lavish; much of it looked familiar because it had been stolen from John.

The marriage had turned into a funeral; the lively music, into a dirge. Having avenged the murder of their brother, Jonathan and Simon returned to the bank of the Jordan.

SLAUGHTER ON THE SABBATH

43-46   Back to the main story. Bacchides was after Jonathan. He marched his army in great force from Jerusalem all the way to the Jordan River, even though it was the Sabbath. Jonathan said to his own people: "Yesterday and the day before we didn't have to rise and fight, but today we do. Look around you. We can't escape. There's water all around us: the river, marshes, soggy woods. Let's turn around and fight! Now's the time to cry to high Heaven to free us from the hand of our enemies!"

47-49   Jonathan found himself within arm's length of Bacchides and was about to strike him when the Syrian backed off, ducking the confrontation. Jonathan and his men brought the battle to the enemy and then swam across the Jordan to escape. By end of day, Bacchides had lost a thousand men. So much for Plan A. Bacchides thought it best to return to Jerusalem, where he began to implement Plan B.

50-53   Bacchides ordered all cities in Judea to increase their fortifications—higher walls, stouter gates, that sort of thing. First he built the Jericho stronghold, then ones in Emmaus, Beth Horon, Bethel, Timnath, Pharathon, and Tephon. In each of these, Bacchides placed a substantial garrison, more than enough to make the daily lives of the locals miserable. In addition, he fortified the cities of Beth Zur, Gazara, and Jerusalem and manned them with lots of soldiers and provisions. He demanded hostages, preferably the children of the local office holders, and housed them in the Heights, as his stronghold in Jerusalem was called.

ALCIMUS FALLS

54-57   In month two of year 153 of the Greek calendar, the Bacchides-installed high priest, Alcimus, ordered the wall of the Holy of Holies to be dismantled piece by piece and the writings of the prophets destroyed.

Almost as soon as the destruction began, however, it came to a halt. Alcimus had a real medical emergency; he was felled by a stroke, lost his voice, and couldn't move his limbs. Hence, there was no communication from him at work or at home. Dying, and in great pain of mind and body, his time had come. When Bacchides heard that his subservient high priest had died under such circumstances, he returned back home to his king for further instructions.

And so for Judah, a quiet descended upon the land; it lasted for two years.

One Step Ahead

58-61 Meanwhile, all the godless insurgents got together to hatch a plan.

"This Jonathan, he and everyone with him, are keeping a low profile, which isn't a bad idea for them, considering the circumstances. But just suppose we bring Bacchides back here. He'd catch all of them in one night, before they knew what hit them."

That was the plan; they brought it to Bacchides for his consideration and he liked the idea. While he started putting together an overwhelming force, he sent secret letters to his associates already in Judea. The message? To arrest Jonathan and his gang on sight.

They tried, but they couldn't get it done. Apparently there had been a leak; Jonathan was able to stay one step ahead of the assassins. In fact, he turned the tables on Bacchides by running down his spies, fifty of them. They died a miserable death—but then, spies have never been promised a long life.

Deadlock

62-64 Jonathan and Simon withdrew to the ramshackle desert town of Bethbasi where they had to spend their first days rebuilding the ruins and fortifying the outer wall. When Bacchides learned this, he recruited a large number and sent word to his operatives from all over Judea—those who had survived—to join him. When the general arrived in the desert, he pitched camp outside of Bethbasi. Fighting lasted for days to neither side's advantage. Bacchides had expected rapid dominance, but as time dragged on he had to resort to the drudgery of building siege machines from scratch.

65-69 Jonathan slipped out of town, leaving his brother Simon in charge. But he soon returned with reinforcements in the form of local mercenaries. On the way back, he hit Odomera and Phasiron, nomadic tribes sleeping in their tents. The more enemies Jonathan killed, the more volunteers he seemed to draw.

Simon did his part. Every day the enemy worked on the siege machines, and every night Simon and a few good men slipped out and torched the day's work.

Jonathan and Simon fought against Bacchides daily, raiding the fringes, chipping away at the edges. That unsettled Bacchides and prevented him from planning and focusing. So he did what leaders facing failure have always done—blamed those under him. He had his advisors executed and, to make his point, the executions were public. Then it was time for him to go home.

Peace, The Only Way to Win a War

70-73 Jonathan got wind of Bacchides' withdrawal and sent representatives to Bacchides to propose a peace plan and an exchange of prisoners. Bacchides accepted the plan and, to his credit, observed its terms. He swore that he'd do no more harm to Jonathan and those of the house of Israel as long as he lived. He released prisoners, mostly the ones he'd captured in Judah. He went back to his own country, never to return across the border again. So much for the sword that had been hanging over the Jews for so long.

Jonathan established residence in Michmash, where he took up the quiet duties of judge. He even managed to weed out the most troublesome traitors from the land.

DEMETRIUS PROPOSES AN ALLIANCE

1-5 **10** In year 160 of the Greek calendar, Alexander Epiphanes, called Alexander Balas, reputed son of Antiochus IV, made his appearance on the historical scene. He occupied Ptolemais, a thriving port city and commercial center on the Great Sea. The people didn't seem to mind; he reigned there for a while.

When King Demetrius I got wind of the new developments, he rallied an overwhelming force and began a march to Ptolemais. But before he did, he sent a diplomatic note full of complimentary phrases to Jonathan to the effect that Jonathan must now be accounted among the premier rulers in the region. The king thought to himself along these lines: *Alexander Balas may be a problem for us if he gets Jonathan on his side. Let's do something preemptive. Let's make peace with Jonathan before he remembers all the evils we have slapped on him and his brethren and his country in the past.*

6 So Demetrius said he would give Jonathan the power to raise an army and procure weaponry; he proposed they become allies. To sweeten the pot further, Demetrius promised to release all the Jewish hostages in the Heights, that dark stronghold in Jerusalem that had been reinforced by Bacchides.

JONATHAN RESPONDS

7-11 Finally officially recognized, Jonathan went to Jerusalem, where he read out loud to the people, including those in the Heights, the letter from Demetrius. Popular response was mostly negative. The people didn't want Jonathan to get too involved with the civil war between Demetrius and Alexander Balas, at least to the point where he had to raise an army.

Nonetheless, the child hostages being held in the Heights were handed over to Jonathan, and he delivered them to their parents. The second thing he did was take up residence in Jerusalem. The third thing he did was begin repairing and restoring the city, which had been laid low by Lysias. What he wanted the consulting architects to do was fortify it; that meant walls enclosing the city, squared stones only. They set to work.

12-14 In the Heights, there were still a few foreigners left, a skeleton staff, but they too began to pull out and head for home. Only in Beth Zur could one find a pocket of godless people who refused to accept God's word and follow his life-maps. It was their last stand.

Alexander Balas

15-17 Alexander Balas got wind of the promises Demetrius had made to Jonathan. "Jonathan did this," "Jonathan did that"—was all Balas heard, and it made him think: *Where can we find a stronger leader than this Jonathan? Nowhere! Then let's make friends with the original. Let us be the ones to become his allies!*

So Alexander wrote king-to-king to Jonathan.

Letter from Alexander Balas to Jonathan

18-20 "King Alexander sends greetings to his brother King Jonathan. We've heard golden reports about you. Your personal strength and your military strength have come to our attention. Hence it should come as no surprise that we invite you to become our Friend and Ally. Over and above that, we'd like to appoint you, as of today, to be high priest of your people. Enclosed please find a purple robe and golden crown.

"In return, what would we expect from you? We'd simply appreciate your thinking as we think on the great issues of the day; we'd like your friendship toward us to match our friendship toward you."

21 Thus it happened in month seven of year 160 of the Greek calendar, the Feast of Booths on the Hebrew calendar, that Jonathan donned the sacred garments of the high priest for the first time. He also went on to recruit an army and establish an industry to turn out arms and armaments.

Demetrius in the Doldrums

22-24 When word of this got back to Demetrius, he was upset that his plan hadn't worked.

Alexander has preempted us with the Jews, he thought. *He doesn't care about the Jews; he only did this to protect himself. I'll write to the Jews myself, paying my respects and offering our gifts, which will be better gifts than Alexander gave, with the understanding that the Jews will help us in an hour of need.*

The following letter contains Demetrius's desperate offer, which he made to the entire Jewish nation.

Letter from Demetrius to the Jewish Nation

25-45 "King Demetrius sends greetings to Jonathan and the Jewish nation. You have kept your word with us and remained in our friendship when it comes to our enemies. Or so we have heard, and we have taken great comfort in this. Persevere in our alliance. Keep your faith in us, and we will pay you back for any and all expenses you have incurred along these lines. Once we sign a treaty, you will be eligible for further gifts.

"Over and above that, I now release you and indeed all Jews from ever paying food taxes, salt taxes, crown taxes, and the like. In addition, you no longer have to pay us a third of your corn seed or half your fruit crop from this day forward and forever after. I hereby resign my financial interests throughout Judah and the three towns that have been added to it from Samaria.

"As for Jerusalem, it will be a holy and free city, secure within its own borders. Tithes and tributes raised within the city limits will be controlled solely by your officials. I will cede to you control of the Heights, which is in Jerusalem. I grant ownership to the high priest; he may use it any way he wishes.

"All Jews in one or another of my prisons I hereby release—without the usual exit fee. The captives will be absolved of all taxes and tributes so long as they live.

"All solemn feasts, Sabbaths, New Moons, memorials—as well as the three days before and after each solemn occasion—will be days of immunity and exemption. This applies to all the Jews in my kingdom. No one will transact business or disturb tranquility with them, no matter what the cause.

"Thirty thousand Jews will be inducted into our royal army. I'll guarantee their salary and pay for their equipment. All-Jewish squadrons will serve in our major fortresses. Your beasts of burden will no longer be subject to military duty.

"Some Jews will be placed in high positions requiring knowledge, experience, and fidelity. The Jews may choose their own leaders and governors; they can follow their own laws as commanded by the king of the land of Judah.

"Three towns of Samaria—Aphairema, Lydda, Rathamin—will be annexed to Judea and considered as one entity, subject to no power but that of the high priest.

"The town of Ptolemais I give as a gift to the Jewish Temple in Jerusalem, to be used to defray operational expenses. In addition, every year I will give the Temple fifteen thousand silver coins from the king's personal accounts. The overage, which used to be spread among my officials, will now be dedicated funds for your Temple's expenses. Of the silver, five thousand coins will be remitted to the Temple priests for use at their discretion.

"Those who flee to your Temple in Jerusalem seeking sanctuary from the king, avoiding debt, or claiming bankruptcy shall be released, their debts forgiven, their assets safe from collections.

"For rebuilding and maintaining your Temple, bills will be paid from the royal account. Expenses for fortifying Jerusalem will also come from royal revenues; the same holds for building protective walls throughout Judea."

RESPONSE TO THE LETTER FROM DEMETRIUS

46-50 When the letter arrived, Jonathan and his people didn't believe it, nor could they accept it. They remembered the time of the Great Malice, when Demetrius and his lieutenants had caused terrible pain in the house of Israel. So this letter made them tremble in its potential for treachery.

But they did put some faith in the promises of Alexander Balas, who had been the first to approach them promoting peace instead of war. Now it was the other way round; he was promoting war instead of peace, but it was on their behalf.

Alexander gathered a great army and stationed it near that of Demetrius. The two kings went at it. Demetrius got the worst of it and ordered his troops to retreat. Alexander pursued them and, as the day progressed, he prevailed. When the sun finally set on the landscape, Demetrius fell in a heap on the battlefield.

On the Egyptian Front

51   Next, Alexander Balas sent some ambassadors with a message to the Egyptian king, Ptolemy VI, called Philometor, or Mother's Boy.

Letter from Alexander Balas to Ptolemy

52-54   "I've just returned to my kingdom. I'm now sitting on the throne of my fathers. The kingdom is mine. Demetrius is no more. The land is all mine. I did battle with him. The great man was killed and his army with him. His throne is more comfortable than I thought. So I've just removed the last obstacle to our friendship. Send me your daughter, and I'll marry her. I'll be your son-in-law gladly. I'll shower you with gifts appropriate to your lofty position, and I'll treat her as though she were you."

Letter from Ptolemy to Alexander Balas

55-56   "Returning to the land of your forebears and sitting on their throne—that must be a happy day for you! As for your request, I am mostly agreeable. But why don't we meet at Ptolemais? Let's get to know each other. As for becoming your father-in-law—if things go well, so it will be."

A Wedding Party

57-58   Eventually it came to be that in year 162 of the Greek calendar, King Ptolemy VI and his daughter Cleopatra III, called Thea, or the Goddess, left Egypt and went to Ptolemais, a city on the coast near Galilee. Alexander Balas met him there. The Egyptian king gave Alexander his daughter in marriage, and the two kings shared in a splendid celebration of their new alliance.

59-60   Alexander had written to Jonathan, inviting him to attend the wedding in his neighborhood. When the Jewish king-and-high-priest arrived, with much pomp and circumstance and not a little swagger, he met the two great kings and distributed gifts not only to the bride—ring, bracelets, necklaces—but also to both kings—jewelry, timepieces, accessories in silver and gold. Needless to say, the bride was grateful and the kings pleased.

61-66   While Jonathan was there, however, some malcontents from Judea staged a public demonstration outside the wedding reception against him, charging him with all sorts of infractions. Alexander paid them no mind. Instead, the king ordered Jonathan's garments replaced with purple robes and had him sit on the throne next to him. Then he said to his top officers: "Take Jonathan to the middle of the city and proclaim that no one may charge him with any wrongdoing while he is with us as a guest."

When the noisy insurgents saw Jonathan sporting the purple and parading about with the king's blessing, they got out of town fast. The king further elevated Jonathan, enrolling him among his First Friends, promoting him to general, and appointing him governor and partaker of his domain. When Jonathan returned to Jerusalem, he had peace and joy in his heart.

ENTER DEMETRIUS II

67-69 In year 165 of the Greek calendar, however, Demetrius II came from Crete to the land of his ancestors. When Alexander Balas heard this, he was distressed and felt he had to return immediately to Antioch.

Demetrius II approached Apollonius, the governor of Coelesyria, with an evil proposal that Apollonius quickly accepted. He was appointed one of Demetrius's generals, and as soon as he'd assembled an overwhelming force, he put his plan to conquer Judah underway. Apollonius parked his army temporarily at the port city of Jamnia while he sent a letter to Jonathan, the king and high priest of the Jews.

LETTER FROM APOLLONIUS TO JONATHAN

70-73 "You alone resist me. You've made me a laughingstock. I'm up to my nose in shame. Why do you lord it over the rest of us from your lofty perch in the hills? If you had any pride, you'd come down to the plain and confer. But be warned: I have the resources of the cities behind me. Ask around; learn who I am and who my warriors are.

"As for you, the word around our camp isn't flattering: 'Jonathan can't see his foot in front of his face' and 'Twice his people have been routed from their own land!' In your present shape, you can't withstand an attack by a real army. Down here there isn't a rock or tree to hide behind, you coward!"

ENTERING A HOSTILE CITY

74-76 Jonathan was successfully provoked and accepted the challenge. He proceeded to recruit ten thousand men and began the march down from Jerusalem. His brother Simon joined him on the way. They intended to enter the port city of Joppa, but the gates were slammed shut, locked, and barred because there was a small unit of Apollonius's troops in that city. Jonathan demanded entry.

But inside the city, the citizens were of two minds: afraid to let the Jews in and afraid to keep them out. Eventually, however, they just allowed Jonathan and his men to walk through the front gate and take possession of the city.

THE BATTLE OF AZOTUS

⁷⁷⁻⁷⁹ When Apollonius heard the news of the fall of Joppa, he put three thousand horse and overwhelming foot on the road. Instead of heading north toward Joppa, however, he headed south—away from Jamnia—toward the city of Azotus, as though he were simply taking his troops on meaningless military maneuvers. He appeared to be so confident that he even let his light cavalry break rank and spill all over the plain, which was where he wanted the fight to occur because of his great superiority in cavalry.

Jonathan waited at first for Apollonius and his army in Joppa, but when they didn't come, he too headed south to Azotus, where the two forces met on the plain, as Apollonius wanted. At some point, Apollonius stole out of his campsite with a thousand cavalry to prepare an ambush.

⁸⁰⁻⁸³ Mid-battle, Jonathan felt something wasn't quite right. He'd walked into a trap he hadn't seen. Suddenly arrows rained from the heavens. There was no place to go; he was surrounded.

His men held their ground, as Jonathan ordered, and eventually the enemy's horses became confused and fatigued—rearing, snorting, throwing their riders off. Seeing the enemy in disarray, Simon took the offensive, charging head-on into the breach. He won the day, although there were few captives because most of the enemy foot soldiers had run from the field and the cavalry gave its horses full rein as they galloped toward Azotus. The retreating troops ran into Beth Dagon, a pagan temple housing Dagon, an idol they hoped would save them.

⁸⁴⁻⁸⁷ After plundering piles of spoils, Jonathan destroyed Azotus and the towns around it. As for the temple of Dagon, he torched the building, burning the men inside to death. Final Gentile body count: eight thousand or thereabouts. Causes of death: sword and fire.

Jonathan then headed for Askalon, where he encamped and was given a hero's welcome. From there he returned to Jerusalem, his army breaking their backs as they hauled carts of loot up the hills of Judea.

ADDED HONORS

⁸⁸⁻⁸⁹ When Alexander Balas heard the news of the victory at Azotus, he added to the honors he'd already conferred on Jonathan. He sent him a ceremonial buckle made of gold, the kind that only the king's Most-Favored Friends were allowed to wear. And he presented him with a nice piece of territory, Ekron, as his personal possession.

MUSICAL THRONES

¹⁻⁵ **11** The king of Egypt, Ptolemy VI—sometimes called Philopator, or Father's Boy, sometimes Philometor, or Mother's Boy—gathered an army that seemed as numerous as the grains of sand on a beach. He assembled a navy that was uncountable on the horizon. His plan? To acquire the kingdom of Alexander Balas by any means necessary

and add it to his own. Spouting words of peace and harmony, he went to Syria.

The cities opened their gates and gave him a royal welcome, as Alexander had ordered. What else could he do? The Egyptian was his father-in-law. Ptolemy pretended he was making the grand tour of a number of cities, but under some pretext or another he left behind in each a number of soldiers.

In Azotus at the time, the most popular tourist attractions were the ruins of the Dagon temple and the desolation of the surrounding neighborhood caused by Jonathan and his troops. The streets were strewn with still-unburied bodies that were mainly those of local civilians who had gotten caught in the carnage; the dead military had graves of their own. The official tour guide told the king that Jonathan had been the villain, but Ptolemy did not tip his hand either way.

6-7 Not long thereafter, Ptolemy invited Jonathan to visit him in Joppa. At the port city, which was something of a resort, they greeted each other with great ceremony and spent some time together. When Ptolemy began the next phase of his grand tour, Jonathan accompanied him as far as the Eleutherus, or the Freedom River. Then Jonathan returned to Jerusalem.

8-10 Quietly but maliciously, Ptolemy proclaimed dominion over the seaside cities all the way to Seleucia Maritima, or Seleucia-by-the-Sea. Next step in his plan for world conquest was to send representatives with a message to Demetrius II.

LETTER FROM PTOLEMY TO DEMETRIUS

"It's time we made an agreement, don't you think? I'll give you my daughter, whom Alexander now has as his wife, and you'll reign over the entire kingdom of your father. It pains me to think I gave my daughter to a man who wants to kill me."

THE END OF ALEXANDER BALAS AND PTOLEMY

11-12 The charge wasn't true, of course, but it would do in a pinch, especially if one wanted to topple the other fellow's kingdom. Ptolemy VI took away his daughter Cleopatra III, called Thea, or the Goddess, and gave her to Demetrius II; that permanently alienated Ptolemy from Alexander Balas. All pleasantries between the two men came to an abrupt end.

13-17 Ptolemy entered Antioch, Alexander's capital city, wearing two crowns: Egypt and Asia.

Where was Alexander when all this was happening? He was in Cilicia quieting a rebellion among the locals. When he got the news from home, he immediately returned, ready for war. But what he met was a superior force produced by the Egyptian king from the numerous troops he'd stashed all around the country. The two former in-laws met head to head in a plain northeast of Antioch. Ptolemy prevailed, and Alexander fled to Arabia, where he asked for asylum.

Back in Antioch and victorious, Ptolemy was enjoying himself immensely. In Arabia, Sheik Zabdiel cut off Alexander's head and sent it to Ptolemy for display, private or public.

18-19   Three days later, however, Ptolemy suddenly died. The locals immediately slaughtered his troops in the cities where he had stashed them.

And that's how, in year 160 of the Greek calendar, Demetrius II became king of Syria.

Taking on Demetrius

20-22   Then Jonathan gathered those who were from Judah and gave them instructions to destroy the Heights. The first step was to construct siege engines and build other pieces of military apparatus.

But a group of Jewish malcontents sent messages to Demetrius II, informing the new king that Jonathan was about to destroy the king's stronghold at the top of Jerusalem. When Demetrius read this, his anger went through the roof. He broke camp and went directly to the town of Ptolemais, where he wrote Jonathan a scathing letter ordering him not to destroy the Heights before he had talked with him at Ptolemais. Jonathan was to come with all possible haste.

23-27   Upon reading the king's edict, though, Jonathan accelerated the destruction of the Heights. At the same time, he chose some distinguished elders and priests to visit the Syrian king with him, putting both them and him in harm's way. Arming themselves with silver and gold, finery and jewelry, they went to Ptolemais and met Demetrius II, who gave them a surprisingly warm welcome. Protestors from Jerusalem, of course, made a public disturbance, hurling charges against Jonathan, but Demetrius paid no attention to them. Rather, he received Jonathan in the same grand manner as he did other kings. Moreover, he added Jonathan to his list of personal friends, elevating him from Friend of the King to Grand Friend of the King. Most importantly, Demetrius confirmed Jonathan's high priesthood and other titles.

28-37   Jonathan had one request to the king: Please exempt Judea and its three annexed towns in Samaria from tribute. In return Jonathan himself would pay 10 tons of silver. The king agreed and wrote Jonathan a letter of agreement containing all these items and more.

Letter from Demetrius to Jonathan

"King Demetrius sends greetings to Jonathan and the Jewish nation. We are sending you a copy of the letters we wrote to our prime minister and kinsman, Lasthenes, about you in order to bring you up to date."

Copy of Letter Announcing Truce

"King Demetrius sends greetings to his kinsman Lasthenes. Upon the nation of Jews, our friends, who keep the just obligations between us, we look fondly. And we appreciate their good will toward us. Therefore, to all concerned, we have determined that the territories of Judea and the three districts—Aphairema, Lydda, Ramathaim—which have been annexed to Judea from Samaria, and all their dependencies, should be exempt from the following royal taxes: tithes and tributes, food taxes, salt taxes, and crown taxes. All of these we concede. None of these grants or exemptions may be revoked now or in the future. In conclusion, take care to make a copy of the appropriate documents and send them to Jonathan on the holy mountain for deposit in a conspicuous place."

DEMOBILIZATION AND DESTABILIZATION

38 When King Demetrius realized that there was a quiet over the land, with no new wars threatening, he dismantled his military and sent them home. I'm talking about his domestic army; his foreign legions he kept intact. This did not sit well with the unemployed soldiers.

39-40 A certain Diodotus, called Gift of Zeus, traveling under the name Trypho, called the Magnificent, got his start on the historical scene as a member of Alexander Balas's entourage. Now he heard complaints bouncing around among the troops about the downsizing of Demetrius's military and knew the end was near for the king. So he went to the Arab Imalkue, who was tutor to Alexander's son, Antiochus. Trypho planned to take the young man and install him as his father's successor. He also told Imalkue about the pacifist decrees of Demetrius and the grumblings of the military. Trypho's scheme was rejected, but he had time; he'd hang around until he got a yes.

41-43 Meanwhile, Jonathan wrote to Demetrius, saying that he wanted to downsize the Heights and other strongholds that made life miserable in Judea. Demetrius replied as follows.

EMERGENCY REQUEST FROM DEMETRIUS TO JONATHAN

"I will not only do this for you and your nation, but also I'll treat you as royalty and your citizens as well as soon as the opportunity presents itself. Now you can do a favor for me—send me a regiment or two from your army, since my army I sent home."

44-48 So Jonathan sent three thousand seasoned veterans to Demetrius II in Antioch. When they arrived outside the city, Demetrius was delighted, for a mob of one hundred and twenty thousand people was roaming the streets, waiting for a chance to get their hands on the royals. The king fled to his palace and locked himself in; the streets belonged to the rioters. Demetrius called the Jewish troops into the city to restore the peace, which they did quickly and efficiently. They went street by street, door to door, at a great cost to the residents. The tally: one hundred thousand, mostly citizens, dead. In the end the Jews torched the city, but not before they amassed plenty of spoils and freed the king.

49-53 When the surviving citizens of Antioch returned to the streets and saw the great slaughter and wholesale looting, they died another sort of death. They even appealed to the king to give them a second chance to make a good impression. "Give us peace!" they shouted. "Stop the killing by the Jews!" The survivors threw their weapons down and surrendered.

In the sight of Demetrius, however, the Jewish military could do no wrong. The survivors even applauded them, but only when they were on their way out of town. As for the Jews, it had been a profitable venture, with their returning home with more loot than they could carry.

Once again Demetrius II could sit on the throne of the kingdom as a quiet spread over the land. But eventually he reneged on all his promises to the house of Israel and alienated Jonathan in a hundred other ways.

EXIT THE OLD KING, ENTER THE NEW KING

54-56 After all this, Trypho returned with the young Antiochus in tow. The boy was made king—Antiochus VI, also called Dionysus. The crown would have slipped down around his neck if it hadn't been for his ears.

All the military personnel who'd been laid off by Demetrius in the past now gathered with Trypho against him; he couldn't possibly win. He turned his back and fled, leaving his elephants behind. Trypho corralled them and took control of Antioch.

57-59 Before things got too antagonistic with his Jewish neighbors, Trypho had Antiochus drop a note to Jonathan: "I confirm your high priesthood, and I affirm your authority over the four regions as a Friend of the King."

With the letter, Antiochus sent Jonathan a set of gold vessels for use during the Temple services. He affirmed the high priest's right to drink from gold cups and wear the purple in public and sport the ceremonial gold buckle wherever he wanted. He also appointed Jonathan's brother Simon governor of the territory from Tyre to the Egyptian border.

SOMETIMES WELCOMED, SOMETIMES NOT

60-62 Secured in power, Jonathan hit the road again heading south, marching across the Euphrates and into the cities of Syria and Phoenicia; at several intervals Syrian armies joined the march. On arrival at Askalon, Jonathan received a decent welcome at the perimeter of the city. But when he got to Gaza, that wasn't the case. The citizens had barricaded themselves in. This was not a good move, for Jonathan immediately laid siege. Once inside, he torched the place; there were spoils galore, but most were singed. The Gazarenes surrendered, and he gave them the usual signs of peace, but not before accepting young hostages from them, which he sent to Jerusalem. Then Jonathan continued his triumphant tour of the surrounding land, eventually reaching Damascus.

THE BROTHERS PULL OFF MORE MILITARY VICTORIES

63-74 Then Jonathan heard from eyewitnesses that the generals of Demetrius II were in Kadesh, Galilee, intending to eliminate him as a player in the region. Jonathan rushed to confront them, leaving his brother Simon back at home.

Simon then besieged Beth Zur, battering the city for many days. Some pleaded for peace, and Simon granted it to them. Those who wanted to fight on, he captured or killed. He took complete control of the city and installed his own administrators.

Back to Jonathan. He pitched camp near Gennesaret and at daybreak woke and led his troops to the plain of Hazor. Standing there waiting for them was Demetrius's foreign army, which had not been dismantled. They approached each other on the plain. Meanwhile, companies of the enemy soldiers had been posted in the mountains, an ambush force if necessary. In mid-battle they sailed down from the hills and tilted the outcome of the battle. Jonathan's men fled, every one of them; not one was left except Mattathias, son of Absalom, and Judas, son of Chalphi, generals of Jonathan's army.

Jonathan gave his clothes a ceremonial rip, he bowed down until his head brushed the earth, and he prayed aloud. Then he rose and returned to battle, swinging his sword right and left like a madman. No one on the other side wanted to challenge him in this state; they turned and ran. Those who'd deserted him had second thoughts, returning to the ranks. Together they followed the enemy all the way back to their camp at Kadesh. Jonathan launched a final attack. By day's end, three thousand foreign troops had been killed. It was time for Jonathan to return to his home in Jerusalem.

DIPLOMATIC OVERTURES

1-5 **12** Jonathan saw that the time was right to reach out to major allies. He delegated several of his closest advisors and sent them to Rome with a diplomatic letter aimed at renewing friendly relations with the Romans. To Sparta and other places he sent similar letters and ambassadors.

When the representatives arrived in Rome, they entered the senate house and delivered the greeting: "Jonathan, our high priest, and the entire Jewish nation sent us to renew the friendship and alliance we once had." The senators received the delegation with respect and issued them letters of safe passage for their return.

When the delegation got to Sparta, this is the letter from Jonathan they delivered.

LETTER FROM JONATHAN TO THE SPARTANS

6-18 "The high priest Jonathan, the elders of the Jewish nation, its priests and people send greetings to our Spartan brothers and sisters. Long ago, letters were sent to Onias, our high priest, by Arias, your king, proposing that our countries should have a relationship, as the attached copy of one of the documents shows. Onias received your ambassadors with appropriate ceremony and accepted letters detailing our alliance.

"Therefore, although we are not asking for any specific help—we have holy books in hand that give us our strength and direction—we do boldly seek to renew our friendship. If we don't, we fear you'll forget about us, since so much time has passed since we last heard from you. Even so, every day since, on solemn occasions and at not-so-solemn observances, we have been mindful of you in our offerings and prayers. When it came to your great city, it was the right and decent thing to do.

"We've been thrilled to watch as your fame and glory have increased. As for us, many troubles have been visited upon us and many battles have embroiled us. We remain the perpetual targets of the petty kings surrounding our land. We don't want to bother you or our other foreign friends with these embarrassments. With the help of Heaven, we have freed ourselves from them and humbled our enemies in the process.

"Still, we have sent Numenius, son of Antiochus, and Antipater, son of Jason, to Rome to renew our longtime relationship with the Roman people. We also mandated these men to visit you and deliver letters concerning our renewed interest in our age-old connection. We patiently await your response to our overtures."

ARCHIVAL DOCUMENT

19-23   What follows is a copy of the original letter from Sparta to the Israelites.

"Arius, king of the Spartans, sends greetings to Onias, the high priest of the Jews. Found in our literature are references indicating that our nations are descended from the tribe of Abraham. That seems to imply we have mutual interests, so we would appreciate your bringing us up to date on your situation. Meanwhile, your possessions are ours and ours are yours. To conclude, we've told our ambassadors to bring you up to date about us."

BACK TO JONATHAN AND DEMETRIUS

24-32   Jonathan heard that the generals of Demetrius II had fielded against him an armed force much larger than before. To prevent them from reaching his country, he left Jerusalem and met them in the land of Hamath. He sent spies into their camp, who learned the enemy was already drawing into battle formation for a night attack. When the sun fell, Jonathan ordered that no campfires be lit, no one should doze off, and sentinels should be posted around the perimeter.

The enemy's spies reported back that Jonathan was waiting and ready for them. Fear and trembling ran through their ranks. Instead of attacking, Demetrius's troops lit their campfires and then withdrew from the encampment without a sound. Jonathan didn't learn the enemy had changed its mind until morning; all that was left of their encampment was the ash of a thousand fires. He followed them, but they had too much of a head start; they'd already crossed the river Eleutherus, or Freedom River.

That the day might not be a total loss, Jonathan turned aside and attacked the first town he came across, an Arab town inhabited by Zabadeans. He overwhelmed them and plundered the town, although the spoils were meager. On the march again, Jonathan went inland to Damascus and left his footprint all over the territory.

33-34   Simon, meanwhile, went in a different direction to the seacoast town of Askalon and the nearby fortresses dotting the coastal plain. He stopped in Joppa and left some troops there, because he'd heard that Demetrius was interested in taking over that strategic city.

35-38   When Jonathan arrived back in Jerusalem, he consulted with his senior advisors. He proposed—and they concurred—that they focus on building fortresses of their own in Judea, including reinforcing the city walls in Jerusalem and erecting an earthen mound around the Heights, which was the stronghold used by foreign rulers to control the city. This would isolate the Heights from the rest of the city and leave its defenders no way to obtain their wants and needs. The masons went to work. Especially in need of repair was a stretch of the eastern wall along the Kidron Valley and a patch of the wall holding the Chaphenatha gate.

Simon, for his part, saw to the repair and fortifications of Adida, a town in the foothills, mainly installing gates and bars for the windows and doors.

Trypho's Triumph and Jonathan's Demise

39-45 Trypho, called the Magnificent, at least by his supporters, sought to have himself crowned ruler of Asia and do away with the boy Antiochus as king. Jonathan was a problem for him, however. Trypho feared that perhaps the powerful Jewish king and high priest wouldn't like his grand plan and would perhaps even try to prevent it from succeeding. So the best thing to do was to arrest Jonathan and kill him. To that end, Trypho went to Beth Shan. Jonathan saw him coming and, with forty thousand crack troops of his own, met him face-to-face. Trypho sized up the situation. He too had a large force, but he was afraid to use it in case he should lose it. Instead, he received Jonathan with great honor, introducing him to his entourage and giving him gifts. Trypho also told his underlings to obey Jonathan as they obeyed him. But he did ask Jonathan one question.

"Why did you amass such an army if you didn't want to start a war? There's no need to have so many men on active duty; send most of them home. Pick a few of them and come with me to Ptolemais. I'll introduce you to the city, the neighboring military installations, all the people of authority. I'm returning home. Peace is the reason I came to Beth Shan in the first place."

46-52 Jonathan believed the so-called "Magnificent" and did what he asked. He dismissed the bulk of his army and sent them back to the land of Judah. He kept three thousand men for himself: two thousand he left in Galilee and one thousand accompanied him to Ptolemais. When they arrived, the gates were opened for them, but as soon as Jonathan's troops entered the city, the gates were sealed behind them and they were all slaughtered.

Then Trypho sent a force of foot and horse to Galilee, where he found the two thousand Jews encamped on the plain.

When the Jewish force realized that Jonathan and his men had been betrayed, they energized themselves for the final onslaught. Trypho, however, saw the Jews were prepared for the battle of their lives and retired from the field. The two thousand troops returned to the land of Judah, where all the people mourned for Jonathan and his slain men, the entire nation wrestling with great grief.

53-54 As for the Gentiles in the region, they rejoiced while the house of Israel grieved. They realized the Jews had no leader. Why not attack them now? There would never be a better time. These were their fighting words: "The Jews don't have a prince or second-in-command. Now's the time to do them in, once and for all. Let's make the world forget they ever existed."

1-6 **13** Simon, the last of the Maccabee brothers, heard that Trypho had gathered together a good-sized army to attack Jerusalem and tear the place apart, leaving nothing standing. Knowing that the Jews would panic at the prospect, Simon went to Jerusalem and rallied the people.

"You know how many battles my brothers and I have fought and how many sacrifices we have made defending our land and the Law. All my brothers have died for the cause; I'm the only one left. Far be it from me at this moment of great threat to spare my own life when my brothers gave theirs. I'll remain true to my family's legacy and fight to protect all that's holy, including your wives and children. Why? Because the Gentiles of this world want to destroy us out of pure malice, and I won't let them."

7-10 The people responded to Simon's oration with a great shout: "Judas and Jonathan are gone; you are our leader now. Take care of us and we'll take care of you!"

Simon, with warriors doing the heavy lifting, accelerated the repair of the wall of Jerusalem and the defense fortifications of the perimeter.

11-14 He then sent a different Jonathan, the son of Absalom, with a great force to Joppa, where they threw the inhabitants out and settled in themselves. Trypho countered by moving his large army from Ptolemais to the land of Judah. Numbered among his captives was Jonathan, the high priest and supreme commander of the Jews, who was still alive. Simon countered by pitching his camp at Adida, facing the great plain. Trypho blanched when he learned that the force shadowing his every move was led by Simon, Jonathan's brother and the last of the Maccabees. Perhaps, he thought, it wasn't too late to send a couple of representatives with an offer.

LETTER FROM TRYPHO TO SIMON

15-19 "We have detained your brother Jonathan for the money he owes to the king's treasury. But if you send three and a half tons of silver in reparation, we'll release him to you, but only if you also send his two sons as hostages. We don't want him leading the fight against us."

THE DEATH AND BURIAL OF JONATHAN

Simon knew that Trypho wasn't to be trusted, no matter what he said. But on the chance that Jonathan was still alive and Trypho might really release him, Simon sent the money and the hostages. If he didn't, he knew what the people would say: "Because Simon didn't send the money or the hostages, Jonathan was executed." So he sent Trypho the two boys and the ransom. But of course Trypho had lied once again; he didn't release Jonathan as he had promised.

20-24 After this latest betrayal, Trypho entered the region around Jerusalem with the full intention of tearing the city down. He went by way of the Adora road; Simon followed. Every move Trypho made, Simon countered.

The Gentiles stranded in the Heights managed to smuggle out some messengers to Trypho. They urged him to send provisions because they were starving to death. The desert road, they suggested, would be the longer but speedier route.

Trypho readied his cavalry, but that night there was a blinding storm, making the route impossible to take. He changed his plans, going to Gilead instead.

On the approach to Baskama, however, Trypho realized that Jonathan, his celebrity hostage, was causing him problems in many ways. So he had Jonathan summarily executed, buried him in an unmarked grave, and then turned around and quickly returned to his own land.

25-30 Simon somehow retrieved the bones of his brother and had him buried in Modein, the city of his fathers. All Israel was engulfed in sorrow and would be moaning and mourning Jonathan for a very long time.

Simon built an impressive monument for his family with polished stone on front and back. He constructed seven markers in the form of pyramids for his father, mother, four brothers, and himself. He also improvised a machine to hoist huge pillars or columns. On the fringe around the tops were carved suits of armor and at the very top were sculpted ships large enough to be seen from the sea. He wanted people to remember that Jonathan had won battles on sea as well as land. The sepulcher in Modein is still standing to this day.

DISPATCHING YOUNG ANTIOCHUS

31-32 While traveling home, Trypho pondered what he should do with King Antiochus VI, called Dionysus, a mere seven-year-old boy who was blocking his way to the throne. He knew that he'd have to kill the boy eventually—the sooner, the better. And so he did, without losing a step, without so much as slowing down. But he did take the trouble to make it look like an accident. Then he crowned himself king of Asia and covered his bloated kingdom with a thick layer of malice.

RETROFITTING

33-36 During this same time, Simon toughened the strongholds all over Judea, fortifying them with high towers, uncommonly thick walls, and gates with unbreakable bars. And he provisioned all of them to withstand a siege of some weeks.

Simon picked some delegates and sent them to King Demetrius II to ask him to grant immunity to the region. After all, it wasn't the locals who were causing the chaos—it was Trypho. Demetrius responded to the message in written form.

Letter from Demetrius II to Simon

36-40 "King Demetrius sends greetings to Simon, high priest and friend of kings, and to the elders of the Jewish nation. We have received the golden crown and palm branch you sent. In return, we are prepared to make a grand gesture and offer you a firm peace. And I will put in writing to my treasurers what I am telling you today.

"Whatever other arrangements and privileges we may have made in the past shall remain in force. The strongholds you have recently built shall remain yours. We shall forgive and forget all your debts and obligations to us to date, including the crown tax and the city tax. We shall welcome into our armed forces any of you who want to enlist. We shall consider this an act of peace."

Free Again

41-42 Year 170 of the Greek calendar was indeed a miraculous one. Israel had thrown off the foreign yoke and was free again. The people of Israel began to date their public and private documents from that year: "Year 1, under Simon, the high priest, the supreme commander, the prince of the Jews!"

On the Road Again

43-48 Simon pitched tents in Gaza-by-the-Sea. He surrounded the city walls, breached one turret, and the whole city was theirs. Those operating the siege machine jumped down inside the city and caused mayhem in the streets.

The Gazarenes, together with their wives and children, climbed up on their parapets and tore their tunics, shouting at the top of their lungs, begging mercy, asking Simon to give them clemency: "Don't destroy us the way we tried to destroy you; be merciful to us the way we should have been merciful to you."

Simon consented and didn't seek revenge for their defending themselves. But he did throw them out of the city and purify any structures housing idols. He wanted to make a grand entrance into the empty city, with lots of singing and praying. So once the deportation and ritual cleansing was taken care of, he found some followers of God's word and resettled them in the city. He then fortified it and finally entered it with pomp and circumstance and established a residence there.

End of Yet Another Era

49-54 Back in Jerusalem, those few Gentiles left on duty at the Heights were barred from leaving or entering the buildings, which prevented them from buying or selling anything. Everyone was hungry; a starvation watch went into effect; many died of hunger. They clamored to Simon for clemency. He gave it to them, but then threw them out. He purified the Heights from the complete contamination it had experienced. On day 23 of month two of year 171 of the Greek calendar, the Jews entered the Heights, really a city within a city, with praises and palms, with harps, cymbals, and lyres, with hymns and psalms, because the Great Menace had finally been driven out of their country.

Simon declared that this festival should be celebrated annually with great joy. He fortified the hill surrounding the Temple and made the Heights his new home and the home of those closest to him.

To round out this story, Simon saw his son John Hyrcanus grow up and perform well in military excursions. Finally, he promoted him in charge of all armed forces, with his headquarters and home in Gazara.

DEMETRIUS CAPTURED

1-3 **14** In year 172 of the Greek calendar, King Demetrius II gathered his own army and went to Media to gear up for the fight against Trypho, no longer so Magnificent, who had been seriously weakened. Arsaces VI, king of Persia and Media, also called Mithridates, or the Philanthropist, heard reports that Demetrius had crossed his borders and sent one of his generals to take him alive. The Persian general found a tent city of unknown origin. He pounced, found Demetrius, slapped him with chains, and led him back to Arsaces in Hyrcania, near the Caspian Sea, where he was put on display.

LAUDATORY POEM FOR SIMON

4-15 A great calm fell upon Judah
for the rest of Simon's term.
He put the nation before himself;
his reign pleased the people.
His golden reputation served him well.
His crowning glory was a daring battle;
he took Port Joppa on the Great Sea.
He opened the way to the Grecian isles.
He expanded the boundaries of his nation;
he was master of his population.
He herded captives into prison camps;
he ruled over Gazara,
Beth Zur, and the Heights.
He cleaned up after contaminations.
No one resisted him; nobody stood in his way.
All tilled their land in peace.
Fruits from below picked from the plants;
fruits from above plucked from the trees.
Elders could sit by the gates,
solving the problems of the world.
Young adults in military dress
paraded with medals and decorations.
He fed the cities, fortified the forts.

He had a golden reputation
all over the world.
He made peace on earth;
in the house of Israel he made great joy.
People could doze off
under their grapes or figs
without fear for their life.
Soldiers became farmers;
upstart kings became bad jokes.
To the down and outs
he gave hope and strength.
He reinstated God's Law and
enforced its remedies.
He restored the glory of the Sanctuary
and personally donated all the altar vessels.

NEWS OF JONATHAN'S DEATH SPREADS

16-23　When Rome and Sparta learned that Jonathan was dead, the mourning there was heartfelt. When they heard his brother Simon had taken his place as high priest in the cities of Judah, the Spartans wrote to Simon on brass tablets to renew the friendships and alliances they had made with Jonathan and the Maccabees. The Spartan document was read at a public assembly in Jerusalem. Here's a copy of the contents of that letter.

LETTER FROM THE SPARTANS TO THE JEWS

"We, the principals of the Spartans and the Spartan nation itself, send warmest greetings to your high priest, Simon, his advisors, his priests, and the rest of his Jewish people, all of whom we consider our relatives. The ambassadors you sent to our people have told us about your reputation and the respect it has received. Their presence has given us much joy. Our people's council has met, proposed, and agreed on a number of directives. Here is a copy of what was dictated in the council: 'Numenius of Antioch and Antipater, son of Jason, ambassadors of the Jews, have come to us to renew our former mutual friendship. Our people gave your representatives a cordial welcome. Please place a copy of their words in the public records as a reminder of the past. A copy of these words we have already sent to Simon, your high priest.'"

AMBASSADOR SENT TO ROME

24　After this mission to Sparta, Antipater returned home but, as Simon had ordered, Numenius continued on to Rome. His mission was the same: to rekindle the mutual friendship between the Jews and Rome. His trip was slowed because of the huge gift from Jerusalem to Rome: a thousand-pound shield made of gold. Professional movers with international connections had to be hired.

PROCLAMATION HONORING SIMON THE HIGH PRIEST

²⁵⁻⁴⁵ When the people of Israel heard the words from Sparta, they said: "How shall we thank Simon and his sons? They and his father and brothers have protected our homes, driven out our enemies, established our freedom."

A transcript of an official proclamation was transferred to brass tablets and posted on the top of Mount Zion. Here is a true copy of what it said.

"On the eighteenth day of Elul, year 172, in the third year under Simon, the high priest, in Asaramel, in the courtyard of the people of God, a great convention of priests and people, leaders and elders of the kingdom, has approved the following proclamation.

"Whereas, battles have been fought in our kingdom and Simon, son of Mattathias, descendant of Joarib, and his brethren put themselves in harm's way, resisting the enemies, saving the Sanctuary, restoring the Law, and doing other marvelous things for their country, and

"Whereas, Simon's brother Jonathan was cited for his valor and rewarded with high priesthood and after his death laid to rest by his people and became part of their history, and

"Whereas, our enemies wanted to stamp us out, deport us, and terrorize our entire region, finally laying hands on the Sanctuary, and

"Whereas, Simon resisted and fought for our nation, personally arming our valiant security forces and paying each soldier a decent wage for his efforts, and

"Whereas, Simon fortified the cities, including Beth Zur, that are within the borders of Judea, which former enemies had used as arms depots but under him Jewish soldiers were put in place to protect the armories, and

"Whereas, Simon fortified Joppa-by-the-Sea and Gazara, which was in the hills of Azotus, where many of the enemy formerly dwelled, and encouraged Jewish settlers to move there and donated all the money they would need to succeed, and

"Whereas, we saw loyalty in Simon and envisioned the glorious fruit his efforts would bear and made him supreme commander and high priest, and

"Whereas, all things in Simon's hands prospered and the foreign invaders disappeared from the region—especially those in Jerusalem and particularly in the Heights who had caused mammoth contamination of the Sanctuary, bringing much harm to our integrity, and

"Whereas, Simon rallied us to fortify the city and increase the strength of Jerusalem's outer walls, and

"Whereas, King Demetrius II conferred upon Simon the high priesthood and made him a Friend of the King, a flattering honor, and covered him with medals and decorations, and

"Whereas, the king did this because the Jews and the Romans are friends, allies, and distant relatives and he had no recourse but to receive Simon's ambassadors with diplomatic ceremony, and

"Whereas, back in Jerusalem the people and the priests were of one mind when we named Simon leader and high priest forever, or at least until another prophet appears, and

"Whereas, Simon had the Sanctuary restored and appointed officials to keep the local and regional governments running and to supervise the arms depots and the strongholds, and

"Whereas, Simon should continue to maintain the holy places and be obeyed in all things and his name should appear on all the documents of the country and he may wear the purple and display the gold anytime he wants, therefore

"Be it resolved that no one—priests or people—should annul or overturn the above privileges or call an assembly without Simon's knowledge and approval or criticize him for wearing the purple and displaying the gold, and

"Be it further resolved that whoever violates this resolution or ridicules it in public will be immediately arrested."

PROPOSITION APPROVED

46-49   All the people agreed with all of the above and put the proclamation into effect at once. Simon accepted the entire package. It pleased him to function as high priest, supreme commander, and ruler of the Jewish people and priests. He was completely in charge; he had the last word on everything; responsibility stopped at him. This proclamation they engraved on brass tablets that were posted in the wall of the inner Sanctuary. A copy of the above was also deposited in the Temple archives but was available only to Simon and his sons.

LETTER FROM ANTIOCHUS VII TO SIMON THE HIGH PRIEST

1-9   **15** King Antiochus VII, called Euergertes, or Goodman—also called Sidetes or Sidewinder, since he was born in Side, Pamphylia, a port town on the Great Sea; son of Demetrius I and younger brother of Demetrius II; third husband to Cleopatra III, called Thea, or the Goddess, her previous husbands having been Alexander Balas and Demetrius II—this Antiochus sent letters from the island of Rhodes to Simon, high priest and ruler of the tribe of Jews and all other peoples in Judea.

"King Antiochus sends greetings to Simon the high priest, principal of the Jewish nation.

"Whereas, certain enemies have usurped the kingdom of my forebears, I want to vindicate their names and restore their kingdom as it was before. To that end I have recruited a huge army and built a multitude of warships. My plan is to go through the country, avenging when I can those who have corrupted our nation and ruined our cities.

"Now, therefore, I confirm all the exemptions and special privileges previously remitted to you by the kings of my house who came before me; whatever gifts you may have received from them are yours forever. I myself give you leave to mint bronze coins for use in your country. I declare Jerusalem and the holy places free forever. All the arms you made and all the strongholds you built are yours and will remain so. All the income due to the royal treasury, now and in the future, are yours instead.

"I promise that when I recover my kingdom, your nation and your temple will share in a glory great enough for all the world to see."

TRYPHO ON THE RUN

10-14   In year 174 of the Greek calendar, Antiochus VII, called Goodman, entered
the land of his fathers. Most of Trypho's military had already deserted
and joined Antiochus, leaving the usurper with a token force. Antiochus
followed him all the way to Dor-by-the-Sea. All the evils on this earth
had come to be symbolized in that one tyrant, Trypho, now the Not-So-
Magnificent—which was why his military left him in the lurch.

Antiochus pitched camp, occupying a substantial amount of ground
above Dor with 100,000 battle-hardened foot and 8,000, war-trained
horse. His army surrounded the city; his navy blockaded the port. No one
was allowed to enter or leave.

JEWISH LEGATES LEAVE ROME

15   Meanwhile, Numenius entered the scene, showing up with his diplomatic
party. He had letters from Rome for the kings in the region. The one to
the Egyptian king, Ptolemy VII, called Neos Philopator, or the Young One
Who Loved His Father, son of Ptolemy VI and Cleopatra II, read as follows.

LETTER FROM CONSUL LUCIUS TO PTOLEMY VII

16-21   "Lucius Caecilius Metellus, Consul of Rome, sends greetings to Ptolemy, king
of Egypt. The Jewish ambassadors sent by Simon, high priest and commander of the people, came to us, wishing to renew old ties of friendship
and alliance. They brought with them a shield of gold weighing a thousand
pounds. It pleases us to write to other kings and kingdoms urging them
not to harm the Jews or meddle with the Jews, their cities, regions, and territories. Nor should you give aid and comfort to those who pick a fight with
them. It was our pleasure to accept the gift of the shield from them. If Jewish
renegades who flee the Jewish state end up in your domains, hand them over
to Simon, their high priest; he will see to it that they are punished according
to their laws."

22-24   Antiochus VII sent copies of the Roman letter to kings Demetrius II,
Attalus, Ariarthes, and Arsaces; he also copied the regions of Sampsames,
Sparta, Delos, Myndos, Sicyon, Caria, Samos, Pamphylia, Lycia,
Halicarnassus, Rhodes, Phaselis, Cos, Side, Aradus, Gortyna, Cnidus,
Cyprus, and Cyrene. Finally, a copy was sent to Simon, high priest and su-
preme commander of Israel.

DOUBLE CROSS

25-31   On the second day after his arrival home, Antiochus forced Trypho back
inch by inch, moving men and machines until they had cornered him.
Trypho had no way out.

Simon sent Antiochus two thousand men, an elite group, plus help in the form of silver and gold and equipment of all sorts. The king, however, turned the help away, breaking all previous ties to Simon and threatening him. In a letter delivered by Athenobius, a Friend of the King, Antiochus had a strong and disturbing message for Simon.

LETTER FROM ANTIOCHUS TO SIMON

"You hold Joppa, Gazara, and the Heights located in Jerusalem; they are *my cities in my kingdom.* You have disrespected my borders, done a lot of damage, and tried to usurp many of the places I am king. Now it's time for you to hand back the cities you occupy and return the local tributes you have collected. If you don't, here's an alternative. For the desolation you caused, you can pay me eighteen tons of silver. For the taxes you've skipped, another eighteen tons. If you don't pay up, there's another alternative, the final alternative: We'll hunt you down and exterminate you."

ENCOUNTERS OF MANY KINDS

32-36   When Athenobius arrived in Jerusalem, he had to blink from the glare. Simon's display of precious metals was shameless. Everything was gold and silver right down to the flatware, to the tiniest spoon for the salt dish. The Syrian was overcome by the dazzling display of opulence, even before his audience with the Jewish king and high priest.

Simon greeted him and responded to the accusations in the king's letter.

"We haven't taken other people's land nor do we hold anything that doesn't belong to us; we merely reclaimed our ancestral inheritance that had been stolen by our enemies. Now that we have control, we're not giving it up. Now in the case of foreign towns like Joppa and Gazara, those people regularly harassed our people until we took them over. For them I'll pay you a three and a half tons of silver."

Athenobius was enraged at Simon's attitude. The ambassador returned to his king, Antiochus, and reported word for word: Simon said this; then Simon said that.

Athenobius then embarked on a rambling critique of the Jewish leader. Simon's attire was truly atrocious—a sickening combination of gaudy fabric and poor tailoring. His recliners were over-upholstered; his pillows were overstuffed; his lampstands and flower pedestals were haphazard; nothing was in the right place—clearly the portrait of a man not in control.

Antiochus flew into a rage.

CENDEBEUS AGAINST THE JEWS

37-39   Back to Trypho, the former Magnificent. He had made it to a ship, run the blockade, and against foul winds and swelling seas fled to Orthosia, a few miles north of Tripolis, or Tri-City, which was still loyal to him. King Antiochus commandeered the next warship and went after him.

Meanwhile, Antiochus had appointed Cendebeus commander-in-chief of the coast guard and supplied him with an army of both foot and horse. The king ordered him to occupy Kedron, which faced Gazara, and reinforce its city gates. From there he was to declare war and move against the inhabitants of Judea.

40-41 So when Cendebeus arrived in Jamnia, he began to harass the people and launched a full-frontal attack on Judea, capturing and killing people at random. Having fortified Kedron, he stationed cavalry and infantry there. From that point he could control the highways and byways of Judea. What Antiochus had ordered, Cendebeus obeyed right down to the tiniest detail.

THE NEXT GENERATION OF MACCABEES GOES TO WAR

1-3 **16** John, son of Simon, called John Hyrcanus, arrived from Gazara and told his father what horrible things Cendebeus was doing to the people. As a result, Simon had a heart-to-heart talk with John and Judas, his two oldest sons.

"Listen, boys. I, my brothers, my father's house have fought the enemies of Israel from the time we were children right down to the present day. Things have gone well in our hands more often than not. Now I'm old. It's your turn now; you're old enough. Take my place and my brothers' places. Go out and fight for the nation. May Heaven's help be with you."

SIMON'S SON TAKES OVER

4-10 John Hyrcanus recruited from the region twenty thousand battle-hardened men, horse as well as foot, all crack troops and cavalry. They set out to confront Cendebeus; they spent the night in Modein. In the morning when they woke up, they went to the plain. There waiting for them was an overwhelming force. Separating the two armies was a stream through the meadow, the brook of Ayalon, or the place of the deer—a noisy, whitewater torrent.

John's force moved into position, with both sides staring at each other, John eye to eye with Cendebeus. Some of John's men had second thoughts about sloshing across the water and being killed in midstream, but John had no such fear; he plunged in and without looking back made his way across. The men dipped a tentative toe, then plunged in after their leader.

John divided his force, cavalry in the middle flanked on both sides by infantry, because the opposing cavalry greatly outnumbered his own. Horns blew till the trumpeters turned blue! Next thing John knew, Cendebeus and his men were retreating. Many of them fell wounded, and the rest made it back to their stronghold. On his own side, John's brother Judas had been wounded. All the more reason for him to pursue the enemy to Kedron, which Cendebeus had fortified. Some of the enemy fled all the way to the fields of Azotus, where they hid in the silos; but John torched the structures, killing two thousand men.

Then he returned to Judea in peace.

A TREACHEROUS PLOT

11-13   Ptolemy, son of Abubus and son-in-law of Simon, was appointed governor of the plain of Jericho. The young man was well-to-do, if his silver and gold decorations were any indication. But his heart turned to evil; his ego inflated. He wanted to get control of the entire region and rule it himself. His plan was to blindside Simon and his sons and pick them apart.

14-17   Where was Simon during all this? He was visiting the cities in his region, restoring order where necessary. He finally went down to Jericho with two of his sons, Mattathias and Judas. The year was 177 of the Greek calendar; the month, 11. Ptolemy greeted his in-laws in a bunker of the stronghold he'd built called Dok, near Jericho. He entertained them with a lavish banquet, but the attentive, splendidly attired servers weren't real waiters— they were Ptolemy's own undercover thugs.

Simon and his sons were relaxing and drinking wine when Ptolemy gave the signal and the "servers" assassinated Simon, his two sons, and some of their servants. By his treacherous act, Ptolemy had repaid good with evil.

18-20   Ptolemy wrote down what he had done and sent it to Antiochus VII. He asked the king to send reinforcements and promised that the cities would be his. He sent men to Gazara to take down John Hyrcanus and invited other commanders to come over to him, assuring them that silver and gold and gifts would be theirs. He dispatched troops to occupy Jerusalem and the Temple.

21-22   Before Ptolemy's assassins arrived in Gazara, however, a runner had brought the news to John Hyrcanus that his father and brothers had been murdered.

"You're the next to die," said the messenger.

The news made John gasp, but he decided to act first. Better them than me, he thought. Eventually, the would-be assassins showed up, pretending to be his friends, but they were immediately arrested and put to death.

THE END

23-24   As for the rest of John's history after he succeeded his father—his wars, heroism, leadership, achievements, and accomplishments—they were fortunately written down in the *Book of Days of the High Priesthood*.

2 MACCABEES

The First Book of Maccabees and the Second Book of Maccabees could easily be assumed to be volumes I and II—or least parts one and two—of the same story. They're not. Though they cover much of the same material, the two books were written at different times and by different authors who had no apparent access to the other's material. In fact, cross-referencing them is not a rewarding experience, but it turns out that it doesn't matter. Judas Maccabeus, his brothers, and followers appear full blown in both books, and the books have the same basic theme with different angles and emphases that make them equally interesting and worth reading.

Who was the author of 2 Maccabees? We know *what* he was—an erudite copyist, abridger, anthologizer; something of a historian and intellectual—but we don't know *who* he was.

He was an editor in the sense that he cut and pasted seemingly unconnected pieces into some sort of logical sequence and turned the project into a rather decent volume that biblical scholars can't do without. Every now and then we can hear his voice as he inserts a personal comment or two.

He was also a condenser. He took a five-volume work gathering dust on a shelf in the Temple library—*The Maccabean Memoirs* by Jason of Cyrene—and condensed it into one volume, which we call the Second Book of Maccabees, or simply 2 Maccabees. Here's what he had to say about his task:

> The original author was like a general contractor building an entirely new house—doing the heavy lifting, framing the whole structure, covering the exterior with something sturdy. All the interior designer had to do was arrange the pottery, position the furniture, and worry about which shade of beige is best. Roughly, the latter is what I did.

The editor also did some product engineering, however; he converted a difficult read into an easy read: "I've also kept in mind the readership—both those who read for pleasure and those who read for serious scholarship. Which means I've tried to make the condensed version attractive to both audiences."

The important readership for the book, of course, was the Jewish people, especially those dispersed throughout much of what is now the Middle East and Europe. Many of them were poor and oppressed, although a few had risen higher in Gentile societies; all had gaps in their religious experience. Hence, 1 and 2 Maccabees went a long way in restoring their identity and history.

The editor was finally a modest man; we know that from the end of the last chapter. "If my work is judged to be well thought out and well written, I'll be delighted. If it's thought to be mediocre and second rate, I can live with that!"

In 2 Maccabees there's a huge cast. There are good guys (Judas, Onias, Eleazar) and bad guys (Jason, Menelaus, Alcimus). There are hundreds of thousands of enemy troops who suffer massive casualties. There are thousands of Jewish troops, usually—according to the author—with no casualties at all! There is one special character: God himself making a special guest appearance, fighting side by side with the Jewish regulars. There are mysterious horsemen playing a version of military polo in the streets and some handsome but fearsome angels with experience in what we would call today "special operations." Finally, there are martyrs galore: male and female, old and young.

When it isn't one battlefield or another, the chief location is Jerusalem; especially the tract of land housing—among other buildings—the Temple, the heart of Jewish life.

As for the theme of the work, it's a perennial for Jews and Christians alike: *No matter where, no matter what, keep the faith.* (WG)

2 MACCABEES

LETTER 1

FROM THE JEWS IN JERUSALEM TO THE JEWS IN EGYPT

1 From the Jews in Jerusalem and Judea to the Jews in Egypt.

"We send you warm greetings and wish you great peace.

2-6 "May God bless you! May he remember his covenant with you, which he spoke to Abraham, Isaac, and Jacob, faithful servants all. May he give you the courage to worship him as your ancestors always have. May you do his will with great heart and willing souls. May you open your heart to God's word and his life-maps, and may that bring you peace. May he hear your prayers in good times and not desert you in bad times. Here in your ancient homeland we are praying for you continuously.

7-9 "In the year 169 of the Greek calendar, during the reign of Demetrius II in Syria, we Jews wrote to you about the storm and stress around us. Those were the years when Jason and his men revolted against the holy land and the Lord. Remember how he set fire to the gatehouse of the Temple and spilled the blood of innocent bystanders? When we prayed to God, he heard our prayers. We offered the sacrifices and donated the grains; we lit the Temple lamps and laid out the loaves. Now we write to remind you not to forget the Feast of Booths, also known as Dedication, in the month of Kislev."

10 The letter above is dated 188 of the Greek calendar.

LETTER 2

FROM THE JEWS IN JERUSALEM TO A PROMINENT EGYPTIAN JEW

From the Jews in Jerusalem and Judas Maccabeus, the Jewish senate and those in Judea, to Aristobulus, a descendant of priests and current prime minister to Ptolemy VI, king of Egypt.

"We send warm greetings and good wishes for your continued health.

11-13 "Freed by God from the great dangers, we give profound thanks; but we confess that we were ready to commit to battle before God was ready to commit to us. It is God himself who deserves all the credit for beating those who fought against the holy city. Here's how he did it. Antiochus IV—called Epiphanes, or Godlike by those who respected him and Flashman by those of us who didn't—was both king and commander-in-chief of his army. When he arrived in Persia with an overwhelming force, he seemed unbeatable. But he and his top aides were cut to pieces in the temple of Nanea after they'd been lured there by priests traitorous to him.

14-17 "The king had come to this backwater town under the pretext of 'marrying' the goddess Nanea, but it was really to collect her rather large dowry. Some of the Temple priests came out to invite the king and his staff to come in for an appraisal of the riches. As the king and his entourage entered, however, the priests locked the doors and fled. Other priests on the roof opened a trapdoor in the ceiling and stoned the enemy below till all were dead. Quickly, the first priests came back in and cut off the heads of the king and his people and tossed them out the front door. Praise God who handed such a good beating to our enemy!

18 "On the twenty-fifth day of Kislev we will celebrate the rededication and purification of the Temple that we call the Feast of Booths, and we felt we should alert you to do the same. In this way you'll also recall the fire that appeared when Nehemiah rebuilt the walls of Jerusalem and offered sacrifices on the altar of the Temple after our exile.

19-23 "As you may remember, when our ancestors were shipped off to Babylon, a few Temple priests stole some fire from the altar and hid it at the bottom of a dry well whose whereabouts were known only by a few. As the years passed, and only when it pleased the Lord, the king of Persia commissioned Nehemiah to send the surviving relatives to find the hidden fire. They came back empty-handed, but reported that they did find in the general area a well at the bottom of which was nothing but inky black water. Nehemiah ordered them back to the site for a sample of the muck. When they returned, Nehemiah ordered sacrifices prepared, then he ordered the priest to sprinkle the cloudy liquid on the sacrifice. At first nothing happened, but as time passed the sun came out from behind a cloud and suddenly a great fire rose up, consuming the sacrifice to the amazement of those present. While the sacrifice was burning, first Jonathan and then the priests began to pray; all the rest responded with Nehemiah.

THE PRAYER OF NEHEMIAH

24-25 "'Lord, Lord God, Creator of everyone and everything, awesome and magnificent, just and merciful, you alone are good. You're the one and only, gracious, just, omnipotent, eternal. You freed Israel from every evil. You picked our forebears to be your chosen people and made them holy.

26-29 "'Accept this sacrifice for your people, Israel, wherever they are. Stand by your people, and they'll stand by you. Gather up the scattered, the Jews in the hinterlands. You'll find many of them are poor and oppressed, slaving for the Gentiles. Please look kindly on them. Let the Gentiles know that you're our God. Strike back at those who kick us when we're down and spit in our face. Plant your people in your Holy Place, as Moses promised you would do.'

30-33 "Then the priests sang their hymns. When the sacrificial fire was almost out, Nehemiah ordered the rest of the liquid to be poured on the embers. The embers flamed up, but the glow was hardly noticed because of the dazzling light emanating from the high altar. The news spread fast that the actual well in which the fire had been hidden for so long still existed. Nehemiah had worked a wonder!

34-35 "The king of the Persians, by the way, confirmed the miracle, fenced off the area around the well, and declared it a pilgrimage site. His original investment in the shrine was repaid many times over, because no one objected to the admission charge, which he shared with his favored friends.

36 "For your information, Nehemiah and his friends named the liquid 'nephthar,' but visitors to the shrine insist on calling it 'naphtha.'

1-3   **2** "Records from a long time ago show that Jeremiah ordered some of the Jews to capture a few flickers from the aforementioned flame for their march into exile. The prophet had his reasons. He was afraid that once the chosen people were in a foreign country they'd forget to follow God's life-maps; they'd be wowed by the idols, the gold and silver splashing everywhere. So he wanted to help them keep God's word in their heart.

4-5   "The same records also document that the prophet, in response to a divine nudge, brought the Lord's tent, the chest, and the altar of incense all the way to the mountain where Moses had ascended empty-handed to God and then descended with the tablets in his hands. Jeremiah climbed that same slope and found a cave in which there was a cavity large enough to store the sacred articles. When he left, he sealed the cavity and concealed the entrance to the cave. Then he and his disciples climbed back down the mountain.

6-8   "Later, some of Jeremiah's followers tried to mark the path from memory, climbing the twists and turns of the mountain paths, but they never could find the cave. When the prophet heard of their efforts, he angrily chastised them. He told them he wanted the place to remain hidden until the day God would gather his people back in Israel again and shower them with mercy. At that time, he said, the Lord would disclose everything that had been done and reveal his majesty; and there would be signs in the clouds as was the case with Moses and also when Solomon prayed that his holy Temple be sanctified with all splendors possible.

9-12   "It is related that that Solomon in all his wisdom offered sacrifices at the dedication and completion of the Temple and that what had happened to Moses also happened to him. When each of them prayed to the Lord, a flame descended from the sky and consumed the sacrifices. This was how Moses had explained it: 'Because it was an absolution-offering, the meat was not to be eaten by anyone, including the priests, and instead was allowed to burn until it disappeared.' Solomon's festival ran for eight days.

13-15   "Similar historical material was found in the narratives and commentaries in Nehemiah's memoirs, *Rebuilding the Walls of the Holy City.* In that volume, he told how he established a library, an archive of writings about prophets, the royal correspondence of the House of David, inventories of donations, and other documents long thought lost.

"With the same enthusiasm for setting the record straight, our very own Judas, called Maccabeus, or the Hammer, collected all sorts of books scattered over the countryside because of the exile and war; we have this collection now in our possession. All of which brings us to our main point: If and when you have need of any of these historical materials, just send a messenger with a copy of this note.

16-18   "And so, as we write to you on the eve of the Feast of Booths, you'd do well to keep holy those two days on which we salute God, who freed his people and returned our heritage and restored our kingdom, priesthood, and ceremonies, just as he promised he would. For our hope is that after the great evils have passed the Lord will have mercy on us and gather all of us together in Jerusalem, where he will have purged the Temple and scoured the holy places."

THE MACCABEAN MEMOIRS
INTRODUCTION

19-22   This is the story of Judas, called Maccabeus, or the Hammer, and his brothers: *The Maccabean Memoirs*, as it were. There is a chapter on the purification of the great Temple in Jerusalem and the rededication of the altar. Another covers the military campaigns against Antiochus IV, called Epiphanes, or Godlike, and his son Antiochus V, called Eupator, or Wellborn—but some of us just refer to them as "like father, like son." There is a description of angels saluting those who fought so bravely for Judea during the wars, whose military assets were few but they forged ahead anyway, routing enemies who had more military power than they knew how to use effectively. Other chapters recount how the Jews recovered the world-famous Temple, freed the city of Jerusalem, and restored the Law of Moses, which had been about to be abolished. All this, of course, was done with the generous assistance of the Lord.

EDITORIAL NOTE

23-25   A more comprehensive treatment of this material may be found in the library under the name Jason of Cyrene; his version of events encompasses five full volumes. I have condensed his five into one volume. In doing so, I've taken into consideration the mountain of statistical and historical documents he faced and the difficulty of wading through them. I've also kept in mind the readership—both those who read for pleasure and those who read for serious scholarship. Which means I've tried to make the condensed version attractive to both audiences.

26-29   Producing an acceptable abridged version of the work wasn't an easy task; it caused me long days and sleepless nights. It was like preparing a banquet for a hundred people, each of whom has a different idea about what tastes good. Still I tried to do my job well; satisfied readers and an inspired community made the entire effort worth it.

The crucial details I took word for word from the original author; the rest I condensed. The original author was like a general contractor, building an entirely new house—doing the heavy lifting, framing the whole structure, covering the exterior with something sturdy. All the interior designer had to do was arrange the pottery, position the furniture, and worry about which shade of beige is best. Roughly, the latter is what I did.

30-31   The original historian took his time with the material. He paced off the outline and then dug in and began writing. His was not a quick rummage but a slow plough through miles of verbiage.

As the condenser, on the other hand, I didn't have the luxury of slowly strolling through a manuscript; mine was a fast-paced run-through, a speed-reading trip through the manuscript with more than half the verbiage hitting the cutting room floor.

32   But enough of this introduction; it wouldn't do if it ran longer than the rest of the book itself!

TROUBLE AT THE TREASURY

¹⁻³ **3** The Jews were living peacefully in Jerusalem. Reverence for God was at its highest; the crime rate was at its lowest. Onias the Third, son of Simon, was high priest at the time. His holiness was legendary; he preached against evil whenever he could. That's when it happened. Foreign kings, of all people, began honoring the Temple complex with extraordinary gifts. For example, the king of Asia—Seleucus IV, called Philopator, or Loving Father—paid with his own revenues many of the costs of the priestly services in Jerusalem.

⁴⁻⁶ But all was not well. Simon, of the tribe of Benjamin, by appointment the superintendent of the Temple, had a disagreement with the high priest over irregularities in Simon's supervision of the city marketplace. He couldn't convince Onias of his innocence, so he went to Apollonius of Tarsus, governor of Coelesyria and Phoenicia, and told him the Temple treasury in Jerusalem was overflowing, the accountants were months behind in their work, and millions had yet to be entered in their books. In other words there was more than enough to meet the everyday needs of the Temple. With some sophisticated accounting, the king could bring the entire treasury under his control.

⁷⁻⁸ Apollonius brought the matter up with King Seleucus. The king summoned Heliodorus, his prime minister, who drew up the necessary documents for the transfer of money from one treasury to another. Immediately, Heliodorus set out on his journey, ostensibly to inspect the cities of Coelesyria and Phoenicia, but that was only his cover; in reality, it was to check the Temple treasury and carry out the king's order to transfer the funds to him.

⁹ On his arrival in Jerusalem, the prime minister was welcomed warmly by Onias, the high priest, who had no idea of Simon's treachery. As soon as they sat down, however, Heliodorus explained the situation. "Rumor has it," he said, "that the Temple has more money than it needs; if this is true, the rest should be put in a more secure depository."

"Of course it isn't true," said the high priest. "You must have been listening to that rogue Simon. He's always spouting drivel."

TREASURY TOUR

¹⁰⁻¹³ The high priest decided a fiscal tour of the treasury was in order. One group of seemingly unaccounted-for assets were in reality relief funds in a special account reserved for helping widows and orphans; another were the personal accounts of a very wealthy businessman, Hyrcanus, son of Tobias. His balance at the moment was about a ton and a half of silver and three quarters of a ton of gold.

"This is preposterous," exclaimed the high priest. "You can't just walk in here unannounced and cart away whatever you want. We have depositors who believe in the honesty and trustworthiness of the Temple treasury. It's unthinkable! We have a worldwide reputation to maintain."

"Don't get mad at me," said Heliodorus smoothly. "I'm just obeying orders."

OBEYING ORDERS

14-17　A day was picked and Heliodorus's staff entered the Treasury and began to inventory its entire holdings. The priests, however, were most unhappy. They put on their ceremonial robes and threw themselves at the foot of the altar. They prayed, imploring God to answer them. They'd followed the Law concerning deposits, and now God himself seemed to be breaking that Law by allowing the funds to be carted off.

Those who got a look at the high priest's face were alarmed. His color had drained, leaving behind the sadness of his soul. His whole frame shook with fear; his heart had broken.

PANIC IN THE STREETS

18-23　When news of the raid on the Treasury got out, people ran from their houses and rallied around their priests, for the Temple was about to be profaned. Women were pulling on their sackcloth and ashes as they flooded the streets; cloistered virgins left their houses for the first time; other women ran to the windows to stare out in disbelief. All raised their hands in prayer.

The sight of the high priest face down before the altar, delirious and trembling, was pitiful. All were begging God to protect the money in their treasury. Inside however, the enemy accountants went methodically about their job.

THE VISION

24-30　When Heliodorus arrived and went into the Treasury, the Lord put on a demonstration of power featuring some of his angelic spirits. Those inside were overcome with fear. As in a vision they saw, or thought they saw, a horse with a richly decorated bridle and a horseman wearing strikingly fine gold armor. The horse charged at Heliodorus, reared, then with great force planted his hooves on the prime minister's chest.

Then two men, handsome and strong and in rather flashy attire themselves, attacked Heliodorus, one on each side. They whipped him badly, leaving stripes and welts all over his body.

Heliodorus fell to the floor as complete darkness enveloped the Treasury. A couple of his aides did their best; they picked him up, put him on a stretcher, and carried him out into the light of day. The rest of his staff stumbled out after him. They were of no help, because they could hardly help themselves; they recognized that they had just experienced the power of God.

As for Heliodorus, he just lay there, speechless, without any hope of recovery. The Jews, who were begging the Lord for help one minute, were giving praise the next because the Lord answered their urgent cries for help.

HEALING PRAYER

31-32 Some of Heliodorus's people approached the high priest and begged him to intercede with his Lord for Heliodorus, who was at death's door. At first Onias thought to refuse and let him suffer the fate he deserved, but then he realized that if Heliodorus were returned home in a coffin, the king would suspect the Jews had done it themselves and retaliate accordingly. So instead Onias offered sacrifice for the return of good health to the man.

33-34 As the high priest was praying, the same two who'd beat Heliodorus so badly approached the prime minister on his deathbed, one on each side again, and whispered to him: "You can thank Onias the high priest for giving you your life back. He prayed to God that you might be spared. Go back to your king and tell him and all the world that it was the Lord of Heaven who has done all this!" With these words the magnificent heroes disappeared.

35-36 What could Heliodorus do but offer sacrifices to the God of the Jews, promising great things to the one who saved his life and saluting Onias for his compassion? With that the prime minister and his entourage returned home. Everyone he met on the way he bothered with his story: "It happened right in front of my very eyes; it had to be the work of the great God."

37-40 Back home King Seleucus interrogated Heliodorus: "If I were to send another man to follow up, who would that be?"

"If you have an enemy or a traitor you'd like to get rid of," said Heliodorus, "send him, and he'll be whipped to within an inch of his life. A spirited and powerful force resides in that Temple. His home is in the heavens, but his presence protects the Temple. If anyone you send enters with malice in his heart, that person will be met with swipes and stripes."

That's the story of Prime Minister Heliodorus and the attempt to appropriate the Temple treasury.

THE ROOT OF ALL EVIL

1-2 **4** Back to the traitor Simon, the one who had instigated the attempted raid on the Temple treasury in Jerusalem. Now he was spreading the rumor that Onias the high priest was the mastermind who had instigated the entire affair, encouraging and helping Heliodorus to try to steal the money. Simon dared to say this about a benefactor of the city, the spiritual director of the nation, a man who lived God's word as well as preached it.

3-6 At first, Onias didn't take Simon all that seriously, but things reached the point where Simon's henchmen starting killing people connected to Onias. The opposition against the high priest was increasing. Perhaps Apollonius, son of Menestheus, leader of Coelesyria and Phoenicia, was using Simon to further his own causes. It was time for Onias to pay a visit to the king, not to point the finger at an accuser who was one of his own but as a diplomat representing the public as well as the personal interests of the Jews. Without the king's cooperation, peace would be impossible, and Simon would never be stopped.

HIGH PRIESTHOOD FOR SALE

7-10   The royal situation, however, changed drastically. Seleucus died, some say murdered by Heliodorus, and Antiochus IV, called Epiphanes, or Godlike, the dead king's younger son, took over the throne. In the process, Onias's brother, who had changed his Jewish name, Joshua, to the Greek, Jason, became high priest. Perhaps it would be more accurate to say that he bought the high priesthood.

Here's how things went down: Jason, through a third party, promised King Antiochus to pay, out of his own pocket, about thirteen tons of silver and, from another source, three tons. For five or six more cartloads of cash, Jason would get to build a sports complex along Greek lines. He'd train student athletes and he'd convert Jerusalemites to Antiochenes; that is, fans of the Greek Antiochene dynasty.

How could the new king turn down a deal like that? He gave his approval, and Jason became the high priest. He immediately introduced the easy-going Greek way of life to the strictly observant Jews in Jerusalem; a non-kosher menu wasn't far behind.

GOING GREEK

11   Jason began by removing the legal amenities gained by previous generations of Jews through John, father of Eupolemus; the father was the one who went on an official visit to Rome to express friendship and alliance and to request some concessions. Jason proclaimed these to be null and void; in their place he initiated Grecian customs that were contrary to the Law.

12-13   Next, at the foot of Temple hill, he built a sports complex where the best young Jewish athletes could train until they earned the coveted Greek laurel by playing like a Greek team. Greek small talk became the rage; Greek customs became the fashion. Jason was to blame; there wasn't a hint of true high priesthood about him.

14-15   The Temple priests spent less and less time in their ceremonial and sacrificial duties; instead they rushed off to the sports arenas from the start of the discus events to the naked wrestling matches, something definitely prohibited by the Law. They no longer marveled at the accomplishments of their forebears; all they were interested in were Greek laurels.

16   But their infatuation with all things Greek cloaked the fact that the Greeks themselves were becoming their oppressors.

FUNDS DIVERTED FROM WORSHIP TO WARSHIPS

17   It's easy to break the Law of God, but one does so at one's peril, as the following episode will show.

18-20   When the athletics games held every five years were celebrated in Tyre, the king was present, as one might expect. Jason, up to his old tricks, sent from Jerusalem a party of Jewish collaborators as spectators; they carried with them 300 silver coins as an offering to Hercules. But the envoys decided that wasn't the best use for the money and looked for a better destination for the cash. They came up with the construction of sleek, fast-moving, three-decker warships.

21-22 Apollonius, son of Menestheus, had been sent as an ambassador to the coronation of Ptolemy VI, called Philometor, or Mother's Boy. Antiochus IV was on the way too, but when he learned that he wasn't on the Egyptian's Friends-of-the-King short list, he turned around and headed for Joppa and from there to Jerusalem. When he arrived, he was greeted by Jason, the new high priest and given a magnificent welcome with a torchlight parade and welcoming speeches. Next stop for Antiochus and his army was Phoenicia.

MENELAUS OUTBIDS JASON

23-24 Three years later, that same Jason sent Menelaus, brother of Simon the Rogue, with tribute and other monies to Antiochus IV, to conduct some routine business and planning sessions. When he was introduced to the king, however, Menelaus impressed the king so much that he appointed him, instead of Jason, as high priest of Jerusalem. It didn't hurt that Menelaus outbid what Jason had paid the king three years earlier by ten to twelve tons of silver!

25-26 Dressing up in the ceremonial robes for the first time, Menelaus looked nothing like a high priest; he had the cruel but cool look of a tyrant and the wild-eyed look of a tiger about to spring. As for Jason, he had cheated his brother to get the office and another man had cheated him to take it away. Making the best of the bad choices he had, Jason headed to the land of the Ammonites for safety.

THE DEAL TURNS SOUR

27-28 Back to Menelaus. He had indeed made a deal for the office of high priest, but he failed to make a down payment or follow a repayment schedule. Sostratus, the commander of Jerusalem's foreign-controlled citadel—called the Heights—and the clearing agent for the royal transfer of large amounts of money, tried to collect the bribe, but without success.

29-31 When the nonpayment was brought to the king's attention, he summoned Menelaus and Sostratus to explain themselves. During Menelaus's absence, he left his brother Lysimachus in charge; Sostratus left the Cypriot, Crates, commander of the mercenaries from Cyprus, as his replacement.

Meanwhile, at another flash point of the empire, people in the Cilician cities of Tarsus and Mallus revolted because the king had given the two cities to his concubine, Antiochis. Quickly the king hurried off to Cilicia to quiet things there, leaving Andronicus, one of his high officials, in charge in Jerusalem.

32-33 Menelaus took advantage of the interlude to steal and then present to Andronicus some rather nice gold-plated ornaments and utensils that he had stolen from the Temple—similar items to the ones he sold to the shady pawn shops along the maritime coast.

When Onias had news of the theft of Temple property verified, he publicly accused Menelaus of fraud and then withdrew near Antioch, where he claimed inviolable sanctuary at the temple of Daphne.

HIRED ASSASSIN

34-35 When Menelaus got wind of this, he asked Andronicus to kill Onias. When Andronicus met Onias in the temple, he spoke to him warmly, sincerely, and without a hint of what was to come. With their right hands joined, Andronicus convinced the old man he no longer needed sanctuary, so Onias left the safe candlelight of the temple for the dangerous sunlight of the outdoors. Whereupon the assassin killed Onias in cold blood right on the temple steps.

The Jews and Gentiles were outraged at this cold-blooded killing; many from neighboring nations expressed grief at the murder of an innocent man.

36-38 When the king returned from the Cilician cities, he was bombarded with complaints about this by the Jews at Antioch and the Greeks in the locale, all of whom detested the senseless killing of Onias. Antiochus was moved to tears and filled with sorrow, especially when he thought of the deceased Onias and his modest, well-ordered life. He became incensed; he stripped the royal purple ribbons from Andronicus, tore off his clothes, and marched him naked through the streets until they reached the exact same spot where Andronicus had done the dirty deed, and then he had the assassin's throat slit.

It was the perfect retribution for the foul deed, engineered by the Lord himself.

LOOTING THE TEMPLE

39-43 Meanwhile, under the guidance of Menelaus, Lysimachus had been committing any number of sacrileges, and golden ornaments and utensils were disappearing at an alarming rate. When this was made known to the public, a large crowd gathered, looking for the thief. But Lysimachus sent an armed force of 3,000 troops through the streets to restore order, led by Auranus, an elderly officer who was as foolish as he was out of touch.

The people weren't intimidated. They began to throw stones, wood, ashes—anything they could get their hands on at Lysimachus and his troops. Many of the soldiers were wounded and some killed; they panicked and fled.

As for Lysimachus, he was left standing near the Treasury, surrounded by the enraged crowd; they killed him on the spot. The ultimate result of this public outcry was that charges were now brought against Menelaus himself, who was the real culprit.

BRIBERY AT THE TRIAL

44-46 When the king came to Tyre, three prosecuting attorneys argued the case against Menelaus. When the defendant saw that he was losing, he whispered to Ptolemy, son of Dorymenes, a provincial governor who was representing him, that perhaps they should take another approach. Money talked, and Menelaus had a seemingly endless supply that had been taken from others. Ptolemy nodded and asked for a recess.

Then the lawyer asked the king if he wouldn't like to leave the stuffy courtroom for a cooling stroll along the colonnade. The money was persuasive; the king changed his mind. He absolved Menelaus, acquitting him of all charges against him.

JUSTICE UPSIDE DOWN

47-50 What happened to the three lawyers who led the prosecution? They were found guilty of Menelaus's crimes and sentenced to death. They were unjustly charged and unjustly punished. The people of Tyre sympathized with them and gave them a great funeral. Because of the greed of the king and others, Menelaus went free and actually increased his output of evil, establishing himself as the kingpin of organized crime and public enemy number one.

PHANTOMS IN THE STREETS

1-4 About the time that Antiochus IV sent his second expedition into Egypt to try to conquer it, something strange happened throughout Jerusalem. For almost forty days, phantom horsemen had charge of the streets; they wore cloth of gold, brandished sharpened spears, and looked menacing; their swords were unsheathed and they meant business. They broke into bands and lined up at the ends of streets, then with arrows flying and spears hurtling, they charged one another, shields rattling, sunlight dancing on their armor.

Were the eerie maneuvers a good omen of something? The citizens certainly hoped and prayed they were, and not the opposite.

JEW AGAINST JEW

5 Rumor had it that Antiochus was dead; later this proved false, but in the heat of the moment Jason, the former high priest, gathered a thousand men outside the walls of his own city and gave the order to charge. The defenders on the walls fell back, the gates opened, and Jerusalem fell. Menelaus, who had replaced Jason as high priest by offering the king a bigger bribe, fled to the stronghold called the Heights, near the Treasury.

6-10 Jason and his men waded into their own kinsmen; it was Jew against Jew. But something was terribly wrong; wiping out his own people wasn't the sort of trophy Jason wanted on his mantelpiece. Confused and bewildered, he suddenly turned and fled back to Ammonite country. In the end it was just another black mark on his reputation; he had failed miserably once again.

Aretas, king of the Arabs, called Jason to account; but he fled from city to city. No one offered him sanctuary; he was loathsome because he was lawless, disgusting because he'd slaughtered his own kind. He hurried through Egypt. He who'd expelled people from their own countries was himself a runaway—a fugitive.

Jason crossed the great sea to Sparta, hoping they'd take him in because he had diplomatic relations with them; but there he died, alone and ignominiously. He who'd left bodies strewn on the streets of Jerusalem ended up dead on a street himself. There was no family, no mourning, no funeral, and no tomb.

11-14 When news of Jason's death reached Jerusalem, Antiochus the king feared that all of Judea would revolt against his rule and he went on a rampage like a wild animal. He set out from Egypt and took Jerusalem by storm. Troops went house to house with orders to kill; no one was spared. The old and the young, women and their children, women who had never married and infants without their parents—everyone was slaughtered. In three days' time 80,000 were lost: 40,000 meeting a violent death and 40,000 corralled for the slave market.

LOOTING THE TEMPLE

15-18 Not satisfied with this, Antiochus entered the Temple, the holiest place on earth, and who should be his guide but Menelaus, the greatest villain of them all. With his filthy paws the king took the holy utensils used for worship and made off with gifts from kings and other cities that had been sent to help finish the interior decoration of the Temple.

Antiochus was puffed up with his power, but he had no idea that his ransacking of the Temple was allowed by the Lord because of the sinfulness of the Jews. If they hadn't been up to their noses in sin, he would have been stopped in his tracks just as Heliodorus, sent by King Seleucus to steal money from the treasury not long before, had been.

19-20 The divine principle was simple: God didn't choose the people because of the Temple; he supported the Temple because of the people. The fortunes of the Temple were directly tied to the highs and lows of the people's faithfulness to God. Whenever they abandoned him, he removed his protection from the Temple. And he restored the Temple in all its glory whenever they returned to him.

21-24 Antiochus made off with over sixty-five tons of silver. In his mind, he'd pulled off a great victory. It made him so delusional that he began to think he could sail ships on dry ground or march soldiers across water.

In each place he controlled he left behind governors who were instructed to keep survivors in a state of high agitation. In Jerusalem he appointed Philip, a Phrygian with a barbarian's record. At Mount Gerizim, it was Andronicus.

And in Jerusalem he left Menelaus, his appointed high priest, who had the worst leadership record of all time. Because of his disdain for the Jews, Antiochus sent Apollonius with a Mysian force of 22,000 to finish Jerusalem off by killing the remaining men and selling their women and children into slavery.

SLAUGHTER ON THE SABBATH

25-27 When the new general arrived, he pretended he was on a peace mission. Then on the Sabbath, the day of quiet, when Jewish men were at prayer, he paraded his troops through the streets with weapons drawn. Those who rushed out of the Temple to see what was happening were cut down on sight. Then the soldiers ran wild through the city, killing as many as they could. Some escaped to the hill country—Judas Maccabeus and nine others were among them. They survived like animals, eating only what they could forage.

ATHENS VERSUS JERUSALEM

1-2 6 Not long after the Sabbath Slaughter, Antiochus IV sent an elderly but experienced Athenian diplomat to Jerusalem; his mission was to force the Jews to transfer allegiance from the Jewish God to the Greek gods. He also intended to rededicate the Temple to the Olympian god Zeus, also known as Jupiter by the Romans. The place of travelers and strangers, Mount Gerizim, would become a shrine to Zeus, the Host of the Strangers, and so on throughout Judea.

3-5 This all-out attack on Jewish life and beliefs was universally considered the worst ever. The Temple was turned into a night club complete with cocktail parties, pork cooked on the altar burners, all-nighters, female escorts, sex on demand. If it was against the Law, it was on the Temple menu now.

6-7 In the sacred precincts, Sabbath observance was out of the question; feast days and festivals were gone forever; it was better, safer, if you didn't admit you were a Jew.

Each month when the king's birthday was celebrated, the Jews were required to choke down non-kosher food such as the innards of sacrificial beasts. When the Greek god Bacchus's holiday rolled around, the Jews had to dress up, put on crowns of laurel, and parade around like the drunken god.

PRESSURING THE JEWS IN OTHER COUNTRIES

8-10 At the suggestion of the citizens of Ptolemais, a decree went out to the neighboring cities with Greek populations that they should put pressure on the local Jews until they sacrificed to the pagan gods. Every Jew who refused to do so should be killed.

Instant misery followed. Two Jewish women who had their babies circumcised were brought up on charges and paraded around the city with their babies hanging from their breasts; then the mothers and the children were tossed off the high city walls.

11 Some Jews celebrated the Sabbath with stealth; nearby caves offered a nice cover. But someone tipped the governor off, and he had the offenders burned alive as they prayed. Jewish devotion to God's word was such that

even as their community was being decimated, they debated whether or not they should defend themselves on the day of rest commanded by God. The result was ashes and embers.

DISCLAIMER

12-17 Please don't think, dear reader, that because *The Maccabean Memoirs* begins so badly for the Jews it will end up that way. The Lord is simply disciplining the Jews, not destroying them. It's a great blessing when consequences arrive quickly after the crime; to wait a long time for the inevitable is no favor at all. As for the other nations, the Lord treats them in a different way. He lets them wallow awhile, letting their sins pile up; then he gives them a whopping judgment at the end. His chosen ones he punishes right away, before they get carried away by their sins, so he doesn't have to punish them later. So the Lord has his own ways of being merciful to his own people. On the other hand, no matter what the catastrophe, he never leaves them without help. These remarks have been something of a digression, so let's get on with the story.

ELEAZAR, BEST OF THE JEWS

18-20 Eleazar, a prominent scribe, an elderly and respected fellow, had his mouth forcibly opened and pork thrust down his throat. Rather than swallow it, he coughed it up and spat it out. He preferred an honorable death to a life of disgrace and walked without support toward the torture chamber. To spit the pork out was an important gesture; a Jew couldn't eat unclean meat even if it were the last morsel of food left on earth.

21-22 The Gentiles who were in charge of the pork sacrifices were longtime admirers of Eleazar. They had taken him aside for a word. "Next time," they had whispered, "bring along some meat that looks like pork but isn't; we'll heat it up and you'll eat it and the interrogators will be none the wiser. You'd no longer face the death penalty, and we'd have done our good deed for the day."

23 Nice as the offer had been, Eleazar could not accept it. He not only was obliged not to eat pork but also not to give even the impression he was eating pork. He'd learned that as a child, and here he was now grown wiser with age. The choice as he saw it was to do the will of God now or eventually be condemned to the world of shadows below. Immediately he gave this reply to his Gentile friends.

24-28 "It's not right for a man of my age and reputation to do something like that," he proclaimed to them. "I'm ninety years old, and I'd be sending the wrong message to the younger men. It's not okay to offer pagan sacrifice at any time. If I pretend it's okay just to gain a few days more before I die, I will have wasted a lifetime of virtue and end everything poorly. It would be a mistake for me to escape punishment now, only to incur punishment from the Almighty hereafter. But if I do the virtuous thing now, I'll finish my life well and set a good example for those who follow. Yes, there comes a time when the only right thing to do leads to death."

Then he shuffled off toward the torture chamber, from which he wouldn't return.

29-31 His Gentile admirers, however, were not impressed; they were offended that he turned down their kind offer. To them he was just another old man who was out of his mind. He wouldn't know a kindness if it were handed to him on a silver platter. In the torture chamber they beat the old man to the point of death.

"Lord, you know this already!" Eleazar cried out. "My body groans, but my soul yearns for you and no one else."

And so this great man's life ended, leaving behind an example of strength and a memorial of virtue for young and old alike.

EIGHT MARTYRS

1 **7** Another historical item; another story from the past.

A Jewish mother and her seven sons were apprehended by thugs sent by Antiochus IV, known by his fans as Godlike, which he certainly was not. After refusing to eat pork, which was against the Law, the boys were bullied and whipped to try to force them to even touch it.

FIRST MARTYR

2 One of the young men, the eldest of them, spoke up. "Why are you beating us? Why do you care whether we eat pork or not? One thing we'll tell you; we'd rather die than break the dietary rules that were given to us by our ancestors."

3-4 "Nobody speaks to me like that," said the king, "and this fellow won't either." He ordered life-sized skillets and cauldrons to be put on the fire. While they were heating up, he summoned the young man, ordered his tongue cut out, his head scalped, his hands and feet chopped off. He gave the mother and the rest of her sons front-row seats for the bloody show.

5-6 What was left of the young man was dumped into the pan to be fried; he suffered terribly. The mother and her other sons encouraged one another to act with dignity when it was their turn: "The Lord God sees us, and our faithful devotion is a consolation to him."

This was Moses' prayer, and they prayed it with him: "In his servants he will be well pleased."

SECOND MARTYR

7-9 When the first son was dead, they brought up the second and made a mockery of him; he too was scalped. Once again the pork demand was made; again it was refused, but this time by the boy in Hebrew instead of Greek. Again he was placed in the frying pan. His last words were: "You wretched excuse for a king! You can snuff the life out of us now, but not in eternity; the king of the world will raise us up."

THIRD MARTYR

10 They then made sport with the third young man. When it came time for them to do their blade work, he stretched out his hands and stuck out his tongue, but not before he said a few last words.

11 "These I have from heaven, but I love God's word more than my hands and tongue; besides he'll give them back to me in the future."

12 The king was impressed by the young man's resilience, but he was also annoyed that he thought death by torture was no great deal.

FOURTH MARTYR

13-14 After the third came the fourth. He too had some last words.

"Being put to death by human beings is nothing; to be raised up by God, that's something to look forward to. You kill me, but you have nothing to look forward to."

FIFTH MARTYR

15-17 The fifth son endured the same result. This young fellow had his parting words as well.

"You have power on earth, and you can move the pieces around the board. Just don't think you can drive our people away from God; that would be a grave mistake for you. Stick around awhile. Sooner or later you'll bump into God. He'll be crushing your toes, and your sons and your sons' sons will stumble on deformed feet forever after."

SIXTH MARTYR

18-19 Son number six followed with his swan song.

"Make no mistake about it, we suffer as a people for the sins we've committed against our God; that is the only reason these shocking things are allowed to happen to us. But don't think you'll go unpunished; you can't fight against God and not expect blow-by-blow payback."

THE MOTHER'S WISDOM

20-21 What about the mother? She was a remarkable woman, worthwhile remembering in this account. As her sons were perishing right before her eyes, she kept her cool, for she had hope in the Lord. One by one she encouraged them in Hebrew, although Antiochus understood only Greek. She gave a woman's tender voice to her sons' rock-hard courage with these words of wisdom.

22-23 "I don't know how you all appeared in my womb; I wasn't the one who gave you life and breath, and I didn't give you shape and form. The Creator of the world did that. He's the one who made the first human and everything else in the universe; he's the one who'll restore all of you, body and soul, because you loved him more than your lives."

SEVENTH MARTYR

24 Antiochus suspected insult in her words, so he tried a different tack with the youngest of the seven, a boy just reaching puberty, by trying to win him over. The king was a smooth talker, and he sent a barrage of promises the young man's way and confirmed them with an oath. He said he could make the youngster a rich and happy man. All he had to do was abandon his ancestral ways, and was that so bad? Over and above that, he promised to give him the prestigious Friend-of-the-King medal, with the assurance of a political career when he grew up.

25-26 The boy wasn't impressed. The king turned toward the mother and said, "Listen, if you want to save his life, tell him to give in." She pretended not to hear the king at first, but when he yelled at her, she said she'd give it a try.

27-29 She turned to her youngest son and once again in her own language, Hebrew not Greek, told him the opposite of what the king had suggested.

"Son, have pity on me. I carried you in my womb for nine months. I breast-fed you for three years; I've nourished you and brought you to the present age. I'm your maid, your servant, your mother. So I beg you to raise your gaze from the earth to the heavens, taking in everything you see. God made them all out of nothing, including humankind. So what about this king? No need to fear him; he's just a butcher. I want you to be worthy of your brothers and join them in their death. As for me, I look forward to seeing you all in the time of divine mercy to come."

30-38 When she'd spoken her piece, the youngster turned to the king.

"No need to drag this out. I'm not going to obey you. I've cast my lot with God's word, given to my ancestors through Moses. As we Jews couldn't escape your murderous hand, so you won't escape the righteous hand of God. We've endured the suffering because we committed the sins. Yes, God's angry with our people, but it's for our own good and only for a little while; then we'll be reconciled with him again.

"You scoundrel and most disgusting thug! While your hand was raised in rage against my family, you didn't have anything to fear from us. But you won't escape from the punishing hand of God. My brothers have undergone a few moments of pain; now they've begun the long joy. You're now enjoying the short joy of tyranny; your long pain awaits. Like my brothers, I offer up my body and soul in observance of our ancestral customs. I invoke God to hasten his mercy; the stripes and welts are my confession that he's the Lord, the one and only. My family deserves the punishment of the Almighty for our sins and the sins of our people, but it shall soon be over for us. But not for you."

39-40 Antiochus blew his top when this teenager had the nerve to berate him, one insult after another. And so he returned the favor, inflicting one pain after another on the young boy's tender flesh, slowly extending the torture far beyond that of his brothers. And so this last brother, too young to sin, died confident in his trust of God.

EIGHTH MARTYR

41-42 Last but not least, of course, was the mother; she too ended up in the frying pan and was tortured like her sons.

But that's enough description of these monstrous cruelties—seemingly inflicted over the simple issue of dietary laws but really about who was in charge. I will add no more.

MOUNTAIN WARFARE

1-4 ⁸Judas, called Maccabeus, or the Hammer, and some of the other Jewish refugees slipped into country towns at night and picked up volunteers, but these had to pass the test. The Maccabees, as they were called collectively, had to know the recruits personally and the new fighters had to be practicing Jews. Soon the force would grow to six thousand. The group offered a prayer to the Lord.

"O Lord, please do something about the deplorable condition of your people and the wretched condition of your Temple. Please send relief to this city, which is being ruined and leveled. Please listen to the bleeding voices rising up to you. Please show disgust with the killing of small children and please counter all the blasphemies hurled at your holy name."

5-7 In response to the prayer of the Maccabees, God redirected his anger from the Jews to the Gentiles; the foreign occupiers became no match for the Jewish forces. The Jews overcame the enemy strongholds and entered their cities at will, burning their buildings to the ground. Everywhere they went, the Jews ran them out of the territory of the house of Israel. Night raids were particularly effective, and Judas was becoming something of a hero.

THE GENTILES CRY FOR HELP

8-9 Philip, the governor, could see the guerilla warriors slowly closing in on Jerusalem; his troops were no match for them. What he needed was massive and immediate military aid. He sent an alert and a request to Ptolemy, governor of Coelesyria and Phoenicia. Ptolemy responded quickly, sending Nicanor, son of Patroclus, one of the Friends of the King, with a force of 20,000 men to destroy the Jews. He also assigned to him Gorgias, a well-decorated general with lots of tactical fighting experience.

10-11 There was a hitch, however. Nicanor first had to raise seventy-five tons of silver owed by the king as an agreed-upon tribute payment to the Romans. The easiest way to do that was to sell captive Jews at a favorable price; but these Jews had yet to be captured.

Right away, Nicanor contacted the maritime cities and alerted them that he would be offering fresh Jewish slaves for sale at the bargain price of ninety slaves for one percent of a ton of silver. This was an incredible deal, of course, but there was a hidden cost to the buyers and the sellers—not in monetary but in punitive terms. God would extract a terrible price from them for each one of his people sold as a slave. Nicanor promised delivery of the slaves at the end of the next major battle with the Maccabees, which would be soon.

THE JEWS RESPOND

¹²⁻¹⁵ When Judas Maccabeus was tipped off that Nicanor's arrival was imminent, he spread the word throughout the Jewish encampment. Some of the new troops, who weren't sure where God stood in all this, lost their nerve and went absent without leave. Others sold whatever they had and gave it to the Lord, hoping he'd be on their side in the battle. If he wasn't, they knew, Nicanor had already sold them into slavery before he even caught them. Still others entreated God to remember the divine assurances he had given their ancestors in the past.

¹⁶⁻¹⁸ Judas rallied his troops, still about 6,000 strong, and told them not to worry; yes, they were outnumbered, but God was on their side, fighting side by side with the men around him, just like one of them.

"Just remember the shameful condition of the Temple and the terrible living conditions in Jerusalem. Think of our time-honored customs that have already been subverted. The only thing our enemies trust is their weapons and their battle screams. We, however, pray to and solely rely on the Almighty God, who at his discretion can destroy an entire army—the whole world for that matter—with a nod of his head."

¹⁹⁻²⁰ Judas told his troops to take courage from the many times God had bailed out their forebears.

"Remember Sennacherib? God destroyed his forces. Enemy body count: 185,000. Jewish body count: none. Remember the Galatians in Babylon? The Jewish force didn't top 8,000, but they joined in the battle against the Macedonians, who outnumbered them a hundred to one. But our side prevailed. Enemy body count: 120,000. Jewish body count: none. They couldn't have survived without God's help; and there were plenty of the spoils of war to go around as well."

READY TO DIE FOR GOD

²¹⁻²⁵ The Maccabean force welcomed these words of encouragement; now they were ready to die for God and country.

Judas divided the army in four parts. He commissioned his three brothers—Simon, Joseph, and Jonathan—with the field rank of captain, each with a division of 1,500 men. Judas asked their fifth brother, Eleazar, to read from the holy book. Then the Hammer shouted the battle cry for the day—"God and Victory"—and personally led the first division against Nicanor.

God did indeed help. Enemy body count: 9,000, not including those wounded. Jewish body count: none. What remained of Nicanor's large army retreated. The Jews even seized the very money from the slave dealers that had been intended to purchase them as slaves.

SABBATH

26-27 The Jews pursued their enemies, but could only go so far. The Sabbath service began at sunset, and they hurried to get back. Lugging the enemy's armor, weapons, and as much loot as they could carry, they returned just barely in time. They raised their voices in prayer, blessed the Lord for helping them be victorious. It was the beginning of a brand new era of the Lord's mercy on the house of Israel.

28-29 After the Sabbath was over, they took what they had accumulated from the enemy around the city, sharing it with those who had been tortured and with the widowed and orphaned; the rest they kept for themselves and their servants. Then they offered in common another prayer: that their complete and final reconciliation with the merciful God would come sooner rather than later.

30-32 Parenthetically, in addition to this fight, the Jews later attacked forces led by Timotheus and Bacchides. Enemy body count: 20,000. Jewish body count: none. The high strongholds weren't that hard to take. Again the Jews divided the spoils after each battle, giving equal portions to themselves and the locals, who were made up of those who had been tortured, orphans, widows, and the elderly.

After each battle they diligently collected the enemy's weapons and stashed them in secure locations; the remaining loot they dragged back to Jerusalem. They executed the commander-in-chief of Timotheus's army—a horrific human being; he had planned most of the attacks against the Jews.

DANCING AGAIN IN JERUSALEM

33 When the final victory celebration took place in the holy city, they took care of the enemies who had torched the city gates by tossing them into a fire. The same fate awaited Callisthenes, who hid himself in a house; he died as he lived—by the flame.

34-36 As for Nicanor, the mastermind of it all, he'd invited a thousand slave dealers to witness the battle, but the outcome ruined his career. He was taken down by the very Jews he'd hope to sell. He stripped off his designer clothes and slipped into some anonymous rags. Like a runaway slave he made his way along the fugitive route to the Great Sea, then north to Antioch, where he arrived alone and broke—the single remaining reminder of his rather splendid army.

His plan to sell the Jews into slavery had fallen through; he'd promised today to pay what he'd earn tomorrow, but his big discount on the price of slaves turned into a really bad deal for him. He admitted to everyone that the Jews had a protector, much like the Roman god Jupiter, only better. The Jews had followed the life-maps set out by their God, and that's why they had won and Nicanor had lost.

1 **9** Here is the story of final episode in the life of Antiochus IV. When he left Persia, he did so in disgrace and disarray.

2 His first stop was Persepolis. He tried to loot the Temple there and take over the city, but the citizens issued a call to arms and Antiochus had to retreat. In wretched condition, he and his army decided to live to fight another day.

3 Next stop was Ecbatana, where he caught up with the bad news about the rout of Nicanor and Timotheus in Jerusalem.

4 That was one defeat too many for the king some called Flashman behind his back. Antiochus exploded with anger; the Jews had made him look silly once again, and he would make them pay for what others had been doing to him. "I'll turn Jerusalem into a cemetery!" he said, and he ordered his charioteer to drive straight through to Judea. But then he was struck down.

5-6 With divine peripheral vision, the Lord God of Israel saw and heard what was happening and hit Antiochus hard. There were no external symptoms, but the pain in his bowels was crippling; a bowel movement might have helped, but none was forthcoming. Somehow that punishment seemed particularly appropriate, given the king's custom of disemboweling others.

FLAT OUT

7-8 After he recovered, Antiochus's arrogance drove him on. Full of pride and breathing fire, fanning his hatred of the Jews, his chariot careened down the road, an accident waiting to happen. And when it did, it threw him out of the vehicle and broke every bone in his body; the pain was unbearable. He who felt he could command the waves of the sea and control the mountaintops, who liked to be called Godlike, was now completely down and out. His aides got him on a horse-drawn litter and carted him off to the field hospital. Yes, there was a God in Heaven!

9-10 There wasn't much they could do for this unholy man. The body was still alive, but tiny maggots, omens of the imminent death to come, wormed their way from his eyes. His bruised skin blackened, his scraped skin fell off, gangrene set in. The odor was so bad that the entire army could smell it. Moments before, he thought he could touch the stars; now no one wanted to touch him because of the stink.

11-13 But the king wasn't dead yet. His pride had been destroyed at last, and there was a moment of self-reflection left. He finally realized that no human beings should ever act as though they were divine. When the smell of his own rotting flesh finally got to him, he proclaimed: "It's okay to be slapped around by God, but it's not okay to slap others around as though you were God."

Then this disgusting excuse for a man, who felt his death coming on, began to pray to the one true Lord.

REFLECTIONS ON APPROACHING DEATH

14   As for Jerusalem, the city Antiochus had threatened to turn into a cemetery, he now wanted to turn it into a free state.

15   As for the Jews, whose bodies he had thought weren't even worthy to be given a proper burial but should be fed to the birds and beasts who would lick their plates clean, to these he now gave all the rights and privileges Athenians enjoyed.

16   As for the holy Temple he'd looted many times over, he'd restore it to its original beauty, replace twice over the furnishings and sacred utensils he'd stolen, and pay the annual sacrifice expenses for everyone.

17   Over and above that, he'd go all the way and become a Jew himself! He'd travel all over the world, praising the God of Israel.

18   Of course that never happened. As the king's pains increased as his breathing decreased, he felt the judgment of God nearing and dictated one last letter to the Jews in an attempt to solidify their support for the claim to the throne of his son. He sent similar letters to all his other subjects.

THE LETTER

19   To my distinguished subjects, the Jews.

"Your king and leader Antiochus sends you greetings and wishes you well.

20-22   "It is my hope your children are doing fine, and your plans are going nicely; I give thanks to your God for that, and my hopes are in Heaven. As for me I'm not at all well, but I remember you kindly. I'm returning from Persia where I got a disabling disease; I haven't got long to live; hence, it's time for me to make some farewell decisions. Of course, I haven't despaired of getting well; perhaps I will, but probably not.

23-24   "I want to do what my father did. Before he departed on a dangerous mission in the high country, he appointed his successor. I want to do the same so that when I die, you'll know whom to turn to.

25   "The princes in the neighboring countries consider the death of the king an opportunity to move up one place; of course, they all want to be the one who advances by hook or by crook. I'll save them the trouble. I'm proud to announce that my successor will be my son, Antiochus V. Many of you in the provinces have met him already; he travels around from place to place as my ambassador and already knows what's in my will. He'll receive a copy of this letter.

26-27   "And so I beg you to be mindful of the many favors I bestowed on you from time to time and to be faithful to my son. I trust he'll behave modestly and humanely and will follow my specific instruction to be kind to you."

DEATH AND THE ATTEMPTED COUP

28-29   And so this murderer and blasphemer died a miserable death in the hills of a foreign country. He died in great pain, like the pain he had inflicted on so many others.

Parenthetically, Philip, one of the dead king's close friends in peace and in war, who was like a brother to him, brought the body of the king back home. But Philip didn't trust the new king, Antiochus V, and tried to overthrow him. When he failed, Philip then headed for Egypt, where a spacious, desert-view home in lovely Exile Estates awaited him, courtesy of Ptolemy VI, called Philometor or Mother's Boy.

TEMPLE PURIFICATION

1-3 **10** Judas, called Maccabeus, or the Hammer, and his troops occupied the city and the Temple, following the leadership of the Lord. The pagan altars in the marketplace they tore down; the temples of the idols they demolished. Once the Temple was scoured, they built a brand new altar since the old one had been violated; they even kindled new fire from struck stones. Then they offered the first sacrifices offered in over two years, burned incense and lighted lamps, and laid out the Bread of the Presence, unraised but consecrated bread.

4 When the preparations were completed, they prostrated themselves and prayed to God that they'd seen the last of a long chain of evil. They even had the courage to ask the Lord that if they should sin again could the punishment be of a more lenient nature and not at the hands of such deviant brutes.

5-8 On the very anniversary of the day the Temple had first been polluted— that is, day twenty-five of month Kislev—it was purified. This became the first day of the joyful eight-day Feast of Booths. Just the previous year, the feast had been celebrated in the woods of the surrounding hills, where they had lived like animals in caves. Now they brought the forest indoors, carrying branches, palms, and greenery; they sang hymns to him who had helped scour the place. The joyful Jews in Jerusalem decided to send a message to Jews dispersed around the world, asking them to observe these days every year.

EDITORIAL NOTE

9-10 And so ends the story of Antiochus IV, called Epiphanes or Godlike, but to us he was always Flashman. For reading purposes, I have abridged his crimes and those of his son, Antiochus V, called Eupator or Wellborn. Suffice it to say, "Like father, like son." I leave a lot out, but the theme is clear: Wars, all wars, are evil.

THE TROUBLES BEGIN AGAIN

11-13 When Antiochus V received the crown, he made several appointments. The first was Lysias of Coelesyria and Phoenicia to be his new prime minister. Lysias replaced Ptolemy, called Macron, or Large Head, who had been the first to recognize Jews as a political entity after so many years of oppression; he dealt peacefully with them, but because of that he wasn't popular in his own court. Some Friends of the King said his loyalty was suspect because he had abandoned his allegiance to Ptolemy VI of Egypt when Macron was governor of Cyprus and gone over to the side of Antiochus IV, the father of the new king. No longer able to maintain the respect he felt he needed at the new court to carry out his high office, Macron did the Greek thing and ended his own life by taking poison.

14-15   In contrast to that good man, Gorgias was appointed by the new king as the governor of the region that included Judea. He maintained a group of hired thugs whose orders were to attack Jews whenever or wherever possible. The Idumeans, who had several strongholds in the district, harassed the Jews, welcomed fugitives who fled Jerusalem, and pushed Gorgias to wage all-out war on Judea.

16-18   After praying and petitioning God, Judas Maccabeus and his companions attacked the Idumean outposts. Pushing hard, they overran the enemy on the walls and killed anyone else they encountered on the way in. Enemy body count: 20,000. Jewish body count: none. Some Idumeans, about 9,000, took refuge in two towers, which were well fortified and provisioned enough to withstand a siege.

BRIBERY, EXECUTION, AND CARNAGE

19-23   Judas left the situation in the hands of his brothers, Simon and Joseph, along with a man named Zacchaeus and his forces, and headed to another, more pressing front.

Meanwhile, some of Simon's men at Idumea with empty pockets were prone to bribery; for about 75,000 coins, they let some prisoners escape.

When Judas heard this news, he returned, assembled the officers in charge of the division, and accused them of putting their fellow Jews at risk by letting Gentiles go who would be free to attack them again. The Hammer executed these Jews for treason.

Then he made a successful assault on the towers. To show his troops he meant business, he killed everyone inside. Enemy body count: 20,000. Jewish body count: none.

A FINAL DEFEAT FOR TIMOTHEUS

24   Timotheus, who had suffered defeat at the hands of the Jews once already, assembled a massive force of soldiers hired from Asia, infantry as well as cavalry. One day he showed up in Judea, obviously planning to take the region back over.

25-28   Judas and his troops, before making contact with Timotheus, prayed to the Lord, sprinkling ashes on their heads and wearing sackcloth as a sign of penitence. Then they lay prostrate at the foot of the altar and asked that the Lord become an enemy to their enemy, an adversary to their adversary. The prayers said, they picked up their weapons and left the city walls. When they spotted the enemy, they stopped for the night, but at first light the two sides went at it—one side feeling virtuous and confident in receiving the Lord's help, the other side relying solely on their superior numbers and weapons.

29-32   At the height of the battle, but appearing somehow above the fray, five men on horseback, their gold bridles flashing in the sun, appeared on the battlefield in support of the Jews. Two of them protected Judas Maccabeus, shielding him from incoming projectiles. The other three returned fire with thunderbolts. The enemy was bowled over; some were blinded with fear, others with smoke. Enemy body count: 20,500 foot; 600 horse. Jewish body count: none. Timotheus fled to Gazara and was happy to escape to that town, because his brother Chaereas was in charge of the stronghold there.

33-37 The Maccabees kept the pressure on Gazara for four days. The enemy inside the fortification were confident, perhaps over-confident; they threw all kinds of things at the Jewish troops and insulted the Maccabees and cursed their God.

At the dawn of the fifth day, twenty muscular young Jews, outraged more at the insults and curses than the incoming missiles, finally got to the wall and scaled it with ladders. Others repeated the maneuver on the far side of the fortress. Up the wall they went, eventually torching the towers and the gates. The blasphemers died blaspheming.

The Maccabees poured in and occupied the city once thought invincible. Timotheus they found hiding in an open well. They killed him on the spot, as well as his brother Chaereas and a fellow named Apollophanes.

38 When things quieted down, the Jewish fighters sang hymns and songs and praised the Lord who had performed magnificently, giving the victory to his people.

Lycias Takes Over

1-4 **11** At the height of his career, Lysias, who was prime minister and happened to be a cousin of the king, wasn't happy with this turn of affairs. He activated 80,000 men from his standing armies, saddled his entire cavalry, and launched them against the Jews. This, he thought, would be more than enough force to retake the city of Jerusalem and finally turn it into a Greek capital.

To pay for all this, Lysias planned to tax the Jewish Temple, just as he did those of the Greeks, and put the high priesthood up for auction every year. In his planning, though, he never considered that the powerful God of Israel might be his real adversary. For Lysias's idea of power was an overwhelming number of cavalry, even more infantry, and at least eighty elephants, and God didn't have any of those!

Beth Zur

5-7 Lysias invaded Judea and headed for Beth Zur, a fortified place situated only twenty miles south of Jerusalem on a narrow strip of land, where he opened up his offensive. When the Jews learned that Lysias was besieging one of their top fortifications, they took to prayer with pleas and tears. They asked the Lord to send an experienced angel to save them yet again.

Judas Maccabeus, as usual, was the first one to take up arms and urged others to do the same to help save their embattled kin. His force set out toward Beth Zur for a counterattack.

A Solitary Horseman

8-12 As the Maccabees were just leaving Jerusalem, they saw, or thought they saw, a solitary horseman dressed in white and wielding a gold sword leading the way. They blessed the Lord up and down; they felt their courage return to the point where they could do just about anything from taming a ferocious beast to walking through a solid wall. The troops continued in battle formation with an angel at the front and the Lord covering their back. Like lions they charged against Lysias and his troops. Enemy body count: 11,000 foot; 1,600 horse. Jewish body count: none. The rest of the enemy ran for their lives, and many were wounded and disarmed. As for Lysias, losing face but saving his life, he escaped like the coward he was.

Making the Best of a Bad Situation

13-15 Lysias had suffered a great loss and he didn't have a prayer of beating the Jews as long as they had the all-powerful God backing them up. The best thing he could do is what all losing generals do: dictate a letter saying he'd agree to just terms and encourage his king to think of the Jews as his newfound friends.

Judas Maccabeus replied, checking the small print and hoping he was doing what was best for his people. Lysias liked what he read in the Hammer's reply. Here for the record are some of the official letters that went back and forth.

Letter from Lysias to the Jews

16 From Lysias to the Jews.

"I send you greetings and wish you good health.

17-20 "Your envoys, John and Absalom, have returned a revised version of your original document, and we have gone over the points made. Some of them require the king's approval; he's seen them and agreed. If you're true to the document, I'll be the same; further details can be worked out by our representatives.

21 "I have the honor to be, and so forth . . ."

Dated year 148 of the Greek calendar, the month Jupiter Corinthius, day 24.

Letter from Antiochus V to Lysias

22 From King Antiochus to his honorable brother Lysias.

"I send you greetings.

23 "Since our father has passed into the company of the gods, it has been our wish that our subjects may attend to their own lives and interests without tumultuous interference.

24 "Also I have heard that the Jews did not agree with my father's order to switch from the Jewish calendar and culture to the Greek; they preferred to continue to observe the Jewish customs already in place.

25 "Desirous that the Jews should not have to endure the aforementioned tumultuous interference, we decide officially that the Temple be restored to them and that their right to observe Jewish laws be restored also.

26 "Therefore, you would do well if you would grant them the peace they want. Assure them that this is my wish and that I will implement all articles of the peace agreement. Reassure them that I am of sound mind and that they may resume the good life in their holy city."

LETTER FROM ANTIOCHUS V TO THE JEWS

27 From King Antiochus to the leaders of the Jews and the Jewish people.
"We send you greetings.

28 "We hope this finds you well. That is our wish for you. And we ourselves are well.

29-32 "Menelaus has made it clear that you want to return to your own country and resume your old jobs. Consider these duly noted. Therefore, those of you who leave for Jerusalem in the next thirty days, the month of Xanthicus, will have safe conduct with nothing to fear. You may prepare your age-old cuisine and observe your traditional customs. No doubt there have been misunderstandings, but no one will be punished for these. In any event, we have sent you Menelaus to iron out the rough spots.

33 "I have the honor to be, and so forth . . ."
Dated year 148 of the Greek calendar, the month Xanthicus, day 15.

LETTER FROM THE ROMANS TO THE JEWS

34 The Romans also sent the Jews a letter, supposedly dated the same as that of Antiochus but probably later.
"Quintus Memmius, Titus Manius, Roman Legates, send greetings to the Jewish people.

35-37 "Whatsoever Lysias the Honorable has conceded to you, we will grant you. About the matters that Lysias referred to the king, please study them with a view to bringing us up to date; we would like to second the motions. We leave for Antioch today. Do put this request on top of your pile and attend to it at once. We don't want to make a mistake.

38 "We have the honor to be, and so forth . . ."
Dated year 148 of the Greek calendar, the month Xanthicus, day 15.

TROUBLE SPOTS

1-2 **12** When the agreements had all been signed and sealed, Lysias returned to Antiochus and the Jewish armies went back to farming and agriculture. But certain Gentile leaders—Timotheus; Apollonius, son of Gennaeus; Hieronymus; Demophon; and above all Nicanor, commander-in-chief of the Cyprians—weren't going to let the Jews get away with a thing; they harassed them whenever and wherever they wanted. Below is a list of various campaigns. Parenthetically, included is another account of the pursuit of Timotheus and his army.

JOPPA AND JAMNIA

3-4   Some Joppa-by-the-Sea citizens supposedly changed their minds about the Jews, and invited 200 of them in their neighborhood for a summer sail in the harbor. Yes, the peace treaty was already in effect. The Jews wanted peace too, so they agreed to come; what did they have to lose? When the boats got beyond the mouth of the harbor, they headed for deep water. Suddenly the Joppanites dumped their guests overboard and stayed to make sure they all drowned.

5   When Judas Maccabeus heard this unspeakable cruelty to his own people, he rounded up his best fighters; together again they invoked the Just Judge—God himself.

6-7   After making inquiries in Joppa, he learned where the murderers were. He and his band made a midnight raid on the harbor, torched the boathouse, and ran their swords through the murderers as they tried to escape.

Then the Maccabees turned their wrath on the city, but it had already closed its gates. Judas raised his voice, letting it be known that he'd be returning soon to kill the rest of them.

8-9   But meanwhile, the Maccabees picked up news of more mayhem against the Jews, this time in Jamnia, about twelve miles south. Again they made a midnight raid on the harbor near the city, this time burning all the ships. People said the fire could be seen as far away as Jerusalem, in the hills some thirty miles distant.

ARAB AMBUSH

10-12   Onward the Maccabees marched, looking for Timotheus, but they were ambushed by an Arabian force: 5,000 foot; 500 horse.

It was a hard fight, but those with Judas fought side by side with God and were victorious. The nomads petitioned Judas for peace, promising pastures and assistance in a variety of ways. Judas could see they might be helpful in the future. They joined hands and promised peace. After that the desert dwellers returned to their tents.

CASPIN

13-16   Judas wanted to send a message to the many nationalities in Caspin, a fortified city with bridges and walls surrounding. He made a frontal attack. The rowdy defenders looked down. They could have returned fire; instead they laughed at the Jews below, calling them names, mocking their beliefs, and generally filling the air with off-color language. Their walls were thick; their food supplies were plentiful; they could hold out forever.

But those with Judas invoked the great Lord and Architect of the Universe, who in the time of Joshua ferociously assaulted fortified walls without the usual instruments of war such as battering rams and siege engines. The Lord helped out Joshua and Judas, and they captured their cities, slaughtering their way through to the far side. Human blood ran through the gutters like rainwater, eventually pooling into a red lake.

CHARAX

17-20 Next stop: ninety-five miles away, the town of Charax, a settlement of Jews who were called Toubiani, although no one is sure why. Timotheus had been there, did nothing in particular, then left, leaving behind a rather impressive fortress. Two captains in the Maccabean force, Dositheus and Sosipater, made short work of the stronghold. Enemy body count: 10,000. Jewish body count: none.

For his next march Judas split his force into divisions: 6,000 standing. The enemy force was impressive: 120,000 foot; 2,500 horse.

KARNION

21-23 When Timotheus heard that Judas was closing in, he sent his women and children with their baggage to a place called Karnion. It was comfortable, dependable, and defensible; its approach was narrow.

When the first Maccabean division came into sight, fear spread among the enemy in the compact field. Sensing the presence of the Lord and Architect of the Universe, they panicked and began to run, trampling each other, tripping over their weapons, afflicting casualties on their own forces.

Judas, on the other hand, pushed forward, methodically cutting the foreign forces down. Enemy body count: 30,000. Jewish body count: none.

24-25 Timotheus was captured and brought to Dositheus and Sosipater, where he pleaded like a child for his life. When he finally got hold of himself, he tried to put together a deal. His force had many Jews as prisoners— relatives of men in the Maccabean army. If Timotheus died, they would surely die too; but if he lived, he swore under oath, he'd free all Jewish prisoners. That made sense to Judas, and he let the villain go untouched.

26 Next stop, Karnion itself and the shrine of the goddess Atargatis, where he overwhelmed the stronghold and killed its inhabitants. Enemy body count: 25,000. Jewish body count: none.

EPHRON

27-28 Next stop: Ephron, where there was a fortified city with a diverse population. The robust young fighters manning the parapets there put up a good fight; the prize inside the walls was rumored to be a military supply depot with siege machines, missiles, and such. It was a formidable place to conquer, but the Maccabees invoked the help of their Almighty God, who could break the back of an opposing army with the blink of his eye. Enemy body count: 25,000. Jewish body count: none.

SCYTHOPOLIS

29-32   From here the Maccabees moved quickly to Scythopolis, some seventy miles from Jerusalem. There they were met by Jews from the city who testified that the Gentiles there respected them and treated them well, even in bad times. The Maccabees gave their kin thanks and urged the Gentiles to continue their friendly neighbor policy toward the Jews.

Then the Maccabees marched to Jerusalem, arriving in time for the Feast of Weeks. By the end of the harvest festival, Pentecost, they were ready to hit the road again, this time for Idumea; they had some scores to settle with Gorgias the governor.

IDUMEA

33-35   There they were met in the field by only a moderate-sized force of 3,000 foot; 400 horse. In the battle that ensued, however, the Maccabees suffered their first battlefield casualties against the Gentiles.

In the heat of battle at Idumea, Dositheus, a Maccabean horseman with upper-body strength, riding in the ranks of an officer named Bacenor's cavalry, grabbed Gorgias by the cloak, yanked him off his horse, and by sheer force dragged him along the ground hoping to take him alive. Fast approaching, however, was a Thracian cavalry man, who with one sweep of his sword cut the Jew at the shoulder, thus freeing the governor, who was last seen heading for Marisa.

36-37   There were only so many enemies a Maccabean soldier could kill in a day before fatigue set in and he was killed himself. One of the Jewish leaders, Esdris, and his men found themselves in that predicament and began to fall. All Judas could do was invoke the Lord to make his presence known and power felt on the battlefield. He raised his voice in a Hebrew hymn that became the battle cry as the Maccabees surprised the enemy and began to push back; but the army of Gorgias had suffered enough death of their own for one day and fled the field.

ADULLAM

38-39   Judas gave the order to retire to the city of Adullam, arriving just in time for the beginning of the Sabbath; the Jews purified themselves and spent the holy day there. The following day they returned to the battlefield to pick up their dead and transport them to the tombs of their forebears.

40   As they identified their dead comrades, they found something odd. On the inside of every one of their cloaks was pinned a tiny image of one of the pagan idols, most likely picked up during the battle at Jamnia. For a Jew to wear one of these was the equivalent of religious treason. When all the dead Jewish bodies were found, it became quite clear that the ones who had died all wore the pagan insignia, probably in case the enemy had won and the Jews had lost.

41-42 Yes, the Lord's hand had been at work on the battlefield. The Maccabees blessed this divine act of judgment; yet they also begged the Lord to forgive the transgression of their fallen compatriots. Judas exhorted his troops to stay strong in the Lord. As he put it, if you weren't a hundred percent for the Lord, the Lord couldn't be a hundred percent for you.

43-46 Yet Judas collected 2,000 silver coins and sent the sum to Jerusalem as a sacrifice for forgiveness for his beloved, if wayward, soldiers. Yes, the Hammer believed in the resurrection of the dead; if he didn't, why would he have prayed and sacrificed for them? And yes, Judas thought that since these men had died for a just cause, a special reward would still be awaiting them. In his own pious way, Judas tried to compensate as best he could for the sins committed by his dead soldiers.

THE CHILD KING

1-3 **13** In year 149 of the Greek calendar, the Maccabees made note of the fact that the army of the boy Antiochus V, called Eupator or Wellborn, was making its way in great numbers toward the Jews. The new king was accompanied by Lysias, his regent and prime minister, and they each had separate but equal military assets: 110,000 foot; 5,000 horse, 22 elephants, 300 chariots with hooks.

At some point, Menelaus the high priest joined the march; his interests weren't so much military as political. Using every argument in the book, he tried to convince the young Antiochus that he, Menelaus, should remain in office in Jerusalem. He did not have the interests of his own people at heart at all.

MENELAUS MEETS A JUST END

4-5 At this moment God, the real King of all kings, inserted himself into the discussion by enlightening the boy king of the true nature of this traitor to his own people. Lysias informed the king that Menelaus was the source of all their problems with the Jews: political, social, military. Everyone who knew the high priest agreed.

The young king ordered Menelaus arrested and sent to the town of Beroea, also called Aleppo. There was a tower in that place, seventy-five feet high, with a mechanism at the top that could swing a person out over a pit full of glowing embers. When a condemned criminal was dropped into the pit, the ashes would flame up and consume the person entirely. Not a piece of flesh or bone remained.

6-8 That is how Menelaus the lawbreaker was executed. He was dropped into the fire, and every time he'd try to crawl out, he was pushed back in. There was not enough left of his body to bury. Some say it was truly a just end for a man who consistently committed so many sins in front of the altar of the Temple, with its holy fire and ashes, to die consumed by fire and ash. The punishment fit his crimes.

PRAYER BEFORE THE STORM

9   The young king was subject to sudden anger, often with reckless results. Although he was called Eupator or Wellborn, he turned out worse than his father as far as the Jews were concerned.

10-11   As soon as Judas Maccabeus recognized the coming peril, he ordered the people to invoke the Lord day and night. God had saved them in the past; perhaps he'd save them now, for it was a real possibility that the Jews would be deprived of their Law and Temple once and for all. The Maccabean winning streak had given the people something of a breather and provided a sort of Jewish resurgence, but they knew at any moment they could be returned to subjugation by the pagan nations.

12   So the Jews all prayed together, asking for the Lord's protection with tears, fasts, and vigils. They had but a short time to prepare for what might happen in the immediate future. The prayer lasted for three consecutive days without breaks.

13-14   Afterward, feeling certain they'd enlisted the Lord once again in their ranks, Judas consulted his advisors. Should they wait for the enemy to invade Judea, which would surely come in time, or should they make a preemptive strike against the enemy now?

Preemptive strike it was. With the Lord and Architect of the Universe on their side and Judas urging all to fight to the death for God and country, they marched to Modein, where they dug in.

COMMANDO RAID

15-17   Judas announced the battle cry for the day: "God's the Victor!" Then he picked an elite squad of highly trained young men. In the middle of the night they stole into the enemy camp and ran roughshod through the king's quarters. Enemy body count: 2,000 men; one elephant. Jewish body count: none.

After that the whole enemy encampment was filled with fear and confusion. The Maccabean squad had made good their escape by daybreak; they couldn't have done it without the protection of the Lord.

18-21   Young Antiochus survived the commando raid. He didn't appreciate the results, but he was impressed by its audacity and courage. He could be daring too, but he had to pick his spot; then he'd give the Jews a taste of their own medicine.

The Jewish stronghold of Beth Zur was first. Antiochus had more than enough military assets to take the place, but his troops were beaten back and driven off. In the preceding months, Judas had seen to it that a steady stream of supplies had been sent to the stronghold so it could hold out against almost any attack, but a spy known today only by his Persian name Rhodocus, then one of the Jewish army regulars, leaked precious information to the enemy that weakened the defenses. When he lost his cover, however, he was arrested and confined by the Maccabees.

A SUDDEN PEACE

21-23 Again the boy king changed his approach. He proposed a truce if not a peace with those in the Beth Zur compound. Then he withdrew his vast military forces.

Accidentally, however, Antiochus ran into the Maccabean army, and the two forces went head to head. The Jews won a decisive victory.

The king would have probably regrouped and attacked again if it weren't for the bad news he received from Antioch. Philip, the caretaker of the government in the king's absence, had rebelled. In order to free himself to counter this attempted coup, the king was forced to do the unthinkable. He approached the Jews and formally surrendered, with few terms and conditions. He vowed to honor Jewish customs and religious practices. Sacrifice could light up the Temple again; civility could return to daily life in the holy city.

24-25 To that end Antiochus V formally received Judas, called Maccabeus, or the Hammer. He appointed Hegemonides military and civil governor of territory ranging from Ptolemais to the region of the Gerrhenes, that is, the entire coastal plain. When the king passed through Ptolemais, however, he found the citizenry up in arms. How could the Jews ever be their friends or conduct business with them? They wanted the treaty annulled.

26 Lysias himself had to get up on a podium and explain. He pointed out the reasonableness of the mutual agreements, speaking persuasively, answering all questions, and generally restoring the people's confidence. Then he and the king returned to Antioch, leaving the details to the people.

So much for the comings and goings of Antiochus V, called Eupator or Wellborn, although the Jews just said, "Like father, like son."

DEMETRIUS AND ALCIMUS

1-2 # 14

Three years later, Demetrius, son of Seleucus IV, entered the port of Tripolis or Tri-City with a large fleet bearing a very large army. He usurped the throne and did away with Antiochus V and Lysias, the king's prime minister.

3 One of the supplicants to the new king was Alcimus, at one time a high priest of the Jewish Temple appointed by Antiochus after Menelaus was executed. He had consorted with the heathens and been defrocked of his position by the Maccabees and no longer had access to the holy altar and its benefits.

4-5 In year 151 of the Greek calendar, the disbarred priest went to Demetrius with a plan. First, he left off some presents: a gold crown, a palm, and some olive branches customarily found at the Temple. He left the king no message; he just put his name on the visitors' list. Then he sat down and waited.

While he did so, Alcimus wove the details of his far-fetched plan in his mind. When his name finally was called, he entered the new king's chamber. Demetrius asked for a report on the Jews, how they were doing, what they were thinking—that sort of thing.

BAD-MOUTHING THE JEWS

6-8   This is a summary of what Alcimus said.

"Among the Jewish people there's a group called Hasideans, or the Devoted Ones; Judas is their leader, as well as heading up his own warlike tribe. In battle they're all comfortable; in peacetime they're all restless. I have laid aside my ancestral position—that is, the high priesthood—to warn you about what is happening in my country.

"I come to you about matters concerning your kingdom, which has always been my top concern, and out of concern for my fellow citizens and my country. This evil man Judas, called the Hammer, should be put under constant royal surveillance.

9-10   "As king, of course, you know all things and have the care of our region and our nation at heart; but be on the lookout—you can't be too careful about this man. As long as he's on a winning streak, peace with the Jews will be impossible and commerce with them will remain stagnant."

11-13   So much for Alcimus's bad-mouthing report. Demetrius's advisors chimed in, confirming Alcimus's analysis. The king grew angry and felt he had to act quickly to save face and bring these upstart people into line. Nicanor would be his man in Judea; he was commander of the king's crack elephant brigade and was now appointed temporary governor of Judea with orders to kill Judas and drive the rest of the Jews to the ends of the earth. Then Alcimus would be restored to his rightful place as high priest in the holy city.

14   On hearing this change in royal policy, the Gentiles who'd been driven from their cities by the Maccabees flocked to join the army being assembled. They saw it as a chance to return home and exact revenge on a few Jews along the way.

MULTINATIONAL MILITARY

15   When the Jews learned the Gentiles had formed a multinational army under the leadership of Nicanor and were already on the way, they sprinkled ashes on their heads and prayed to the God who'd chosen them to be his people and had favored them many times with signs of his affection and protection.

16-19   Then, under the command of Judas, they set out for Adasa, a town in which the battle had already begun. There the Hammer's brother, Simon, had been surprised by Nicanor. There had been a skirmish; both parties had withdrawn and were waiting for the other to make the next move.

But Nicanor was no fool; he'd heard of his enemy's strength and valor when fighting for God and country. Perhaps, he thought, the sword wasn't the best way to approach Judas. The best course might be to send Posidonius, Theodotus, and Mattathias to see if both sides could meet together.

TRUCE AND FRIENDSHIP

20-22 Initial discussions were intense; both sides withdrew several times for consultations, but a consensus was finally reached. A day was picked for the official signing ceremony; chairs were set out. As a precaution, Judas had deployed squads of troops around the clearing but out of sight. But the meeting went off without a hitch and an agreement was made.

23-25 Nicanor surprised everyone by remaining in Jerusalem; he behaved himself, even demobilizing the regional army he'd just activated. He kept in regular touch with Judas; they had a number of things in common. He urged the great Maccabee to marry and have children. This Judas did; and the two men lived near each other. Both found that life was good and peace wasn't all that bad.

26 Alcimus, however, seeing the mutual goodwill between the two men and the respectful understanding they exhibited toward each other, went to Demetrius and told him at some length that Nicanor had sold out to Jewish interests. His proof was that Nicanor had designated as his successor that very Judas Maccabeus who was a onetime conspirator against the kingdom and, as far as anyone knew, was still conspiring.

27-29 The king was incensed and wrote to Nicanor expressing his displeasure about his cozy relationship with Judas. He ordered his governor to arrest the Maccabee immediately and escort him back to Antioch personally.

When he got the letter, Nicanor didn't know what to do. He wasn't used to breaking his agreements without cause, especially with someone who had become a friend. Of course, he couldn't disobey the king outright, but he could wait for an opportunity for things to sort themselves out. Perhaps he would catch Judas in an act of disloyalty and move on him then.

END OF AN IMPERFECT FRIENDSHIP

30 But Judas wasn't a fool after all these years of dealing with others. He could see his friendship with Nicanor deteriorating. When they met now, Nicanor didn't have a kind word to say to him. The friendship had run its course. So Judas gathered a few of his men, headed once again for the hills, and was seen no more.

31-33 When Nicanor learned that Judas had disappeared, he thought he knew where he was. He went to the Temple and ordered the priests, who were right in the middle of holding services, to hand him over. The priests, however, swore under oath that they didn't know where Judas was. Nicanor raised his right hand and pointed at the Temple.

"If you don't deliver this man into my hands, I'll level this glorious Temple of yours and replace it on this very site with a new, more glamorous temple that I'll consecrate to Dionysus, Greek god of chaos and misrule."

34 Nicanor left. The priests, stretching their hands upward to Heaven, called upon the real defender of their nation.

35-36 "Lord and Architect of the Universe, it was with your permission that we built this Temple. Holy One, Lord of Everything Sacred, you saved it once; now save it again."

THE MARTYRDOM OF RAZIS

37 Someone had tipped off Nicanor regarding Razis, a Gentile convert who had become one of the pillars of Jerusalem. He was a lover of the city with a good reputation and was affectionately known as a father to the Jews.

38 Before the revolt, when Gentiles never mingled with Jews, somebody publicly accused Razis of following God's word. He readily admitted it, risking his body and soul to proclaim the Lord. He knew he might someday die for his beliefs, but he wanted nothing more than to finish his life well.

39-40 Nicanor now wanted to do something drastic that would express his utter hatred for the Jews. Perhaps he could find this man, Razis, and make a public spectacle of him. Nicanor sent 500 troops to find the old man and arrest him for treason. Yes, his capture would shatter the Jews.

41-42 The battering ram team broke through the gates, smashed through the door, and were about to torch the place when they saw Razis on the floor of his home; he'd fallen on his own sword. He preferred to die with honor rather than live in disgrace; in either event he was going to die, if not by his own sword then in their torture chamber.

43-46 But the elderly man wasn't dead; it wasn't a mortal wound because he'd failed to point the sword at one of his vital organs. He got to his feet and holding his hands over his groin ran up to the roof and threw himself over the wall. The crowd parted as he fell, and he hit the ground hard. He was hardly breathing, but his determination was strong. Razis got up again and, with blood pouring from his groin and trying to hold his entrails in, he ran through the streets and up a high rock. At the top, he fished out his bowels and threw them down at the crowd. Then screaming as loud as he could, he asked the Healer of Body and Soul to return his body parts to him when next they met!

THE DREAM COMES TRUE

1-6 **15** When Nicanor learned that the Maccabees were encamped near Samaria, he picked the Sabbath, the day of quiet and repose, to attack. He'd have the jump on them; and he knew they wouldn't counterattack on the Sabbath.

Jews who were members of his army warned Nicanor: "The Sabbath's not a day to attack ferociously; only animals and barbarians do that. Respect the sanctity of the day and honor our God, who beholds all things."

Nicanor asked them if they believed there really was a Jewish deity in Heaven and, if so, did he make one day of the week better than the other six?

"Yes, the Lord lives," the men replied. "He abides in Heaven and runs the universe from there. He's the one who ordered us to refrain from any activity except worship on the seventh day."

"But I'm the strongman here on earth," Nicanor replied defiantly. "I run the king's army and take care of the king's business!" After thumping his chest, though, the insecure man decided he too could use a day of rest and postponed the attack. Instead he amused himself by planning to erect a public statue of himself as a reward for beating the Jews in a battle that hadn't yet been fought.

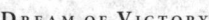

DREAM OF VICTORY

7-9 As for Judas Maccabeus, his confidence in God never flagged. He urged his men, exhorting them not to fear the upcoming battle with the multinational army. If they remember all the divine help they had received in the past and concentrate on the battle at hand, he told them, victory would surely be theirs. He further motivated the troops by stories about God and his prophets that cheered them up considerably.

10-11 Judas went on, denouncing the enemy as truth benders and oath breakers. He armed every single one of his followers not with spear and shield, which they already had, but with words and pep talks. Then he told them of a dream he just had.

12 "First, I saw a high priest named Onias; he was an honest man and good, somewhat bashful, modest in manner, and well spoken. From childhood he learned all the domestic virtues, even how to pray with arms extended for all the Jewish people.

13-16 "Then I saw another person, silver haired, majestic, finely clothed. Onias said to me, 'This is a lover of our people; he has prayed much for them and the holy city; his name is Jeremiah, prophet of God.'

"Jeremiah extended his right arm to me and then gave me a golden sword. 'Accept this sword,' Jeremiah said. 'It's a gift from God; use it well, and it will destroy your adversaries.'"

17-19 The soldiers got the message; Judas's dream had hit the target. The Maccabees decided not to fight defensively but to advance to the front, itching for the fight. At stake was their valor, not to mention the salvation of the holy city and the Temple. Of course, the young men feared for their wives and children, for their fellow soldiers and relatives; but their greatest fear was reserved for the fate of the Temple. And of course, the people in Jerusalem worried about their troops in battle.

ARMOR DOESN'T WIN BATTLES

20 At last the past and the future met in the present. Both parties were committed to the field, elephants in the middle, cavalry at both wings.

21 As Judas surveyed the scene, he saw crowds of men restless before the charge; armor of all sorts glistening in the sun; drunken elephants raring to go any which way. Then he raised his hands to the heavens and called upon the Lord, who worked on a grand scale as a matter of course. The Lord knew that armor never won battles; they were won by valor and goodness. Then he prayed.

THE PRAYER OF JUDAS

22-24 "Lord, you've done this before; you sent your angel to meet Sennacherib's army in the days of King Hezekiah of Judea. Enemy body count: 185,000 foot and horse. That was then, but this is now, Dominator of the Heavens. To lead us, I ask that you send an experienced angel, one whose very sight will kindle fear and trembling in the enemy. With a sweep of your broad hand you can destroy those who come in hatred of your holy people."

THE BATTLE BEGINS

25-27   Those on Nicanor's side of the battle line moved forward with horns blaring and fight songs screaming; the Maccabees, calling upon the Lord, met the enemy head on in hand-to-hand combat, fighting the enemy on the field while praying to God in their hearts. Needless to say, the Jews won the day, but they couldn't have done it without God fighting by their side. Enemy body count: 35,000 foot and horse. Jewish body count: none.

28-30   When the action ceased on the battlefield and the Jews were rejoicing, they recognized the body of Nicanor slain on the field in his full armor. With shouts and song, the troops blessed the Almighty in Hebrew, the language of their ancestors.

Judas—always the first to hit the enemy battle line, always willing to give his life for his people, always supportive of his fellow freedom fighters—gave the order to cut off Nicanor's head and his right arm, beginning at the shoulder; he wanted them for display in Jerusalem.

31-33   When the Maccabees arrived in the holy city, Judas made an appearance on the steps of the Temple altar, summoning the high priests, the citizens, the military, even the frightened residents in the foreign stronghold in Jerusalem called the Heights. He held up Nicanor's ugly head for all to see. Then he had the tongue cut out, to be fed to the birds. As for the arm, it would look nice hanging on any of the magnificent Temple walls that Nicanor had threatened—with that same arm—to tear down.

34   Then a general blessing went up from every voice. "Blessed is God, who once again has rescued the Temple from contamination!"

35   The head and arm ended up on the tower of the citadel, where everyone could see it. Nicanor's body parts symbolized the many ways God had provided help to his people.

36   The Jews at the celebration had their say. They wanted this solemn remembrance to happen every year. The date picked was the thirteenth day of the month of Adar in Aramaic, or the day before the Feast of Purim begins.

EDITOR'S FINAL WORDS

37   That was the end for Nicanor. As for the Jews, they retained possession of Jerusalem and the story of the Maccabees continued.

All these chapters having been written; however, it's time for me, the editor of *The Maccabean Memoirs*, to conclude my remarks.

38   If my work is judged to be well thought out and well written, I'll be delighted. If it's thought to be mediocre and second rate, I can live with that!

39   A final comparison. One can drink wine as it is and swallow hard or one can drink it mixed with water and enjoy it; hence, a book is good when it's written, but it's better when it's read. And so it is with mine.

WISDOM BOOKS

There is a distinctive strain of writing in the Bible that more or less specializes in dealing with human experience — as is. *This* is what is involved in being human, and don't you forget it. "Wisdom" is the common designation given to this aspect of biblical witness and writing.

The word in this context refers more to a kind of attitude, a distinctive stance, than to any particular ideas or doctrines or counsel. As such, Wisdom is wide-ranging, collecting under its umbrella diverse and unlikely fellow travelers. What keeps the feet of these faith-travelers on common ground is Wisdom's unrelenting insistence that nothing in human experience can be omitted or slighted if we decide to take God seriously and respond to him believingly.

God and God's ways provide the comprehensive plot and sovereign action in the Holy Scriptures, but human beings — every last man and woman of us, including every last detail involved in our daily living — are invited and honored participants in all of it. There are no spectator seats provided for the drama of salvation. There is no "bench" for incompetent players.

It is fairly common among people who get interested in religion or God to get proportionately *dis*interested in their jobs and families, their communities and their colleagues — the more of God, the less of the human. But that is not the way God intends it. Wisdom counters this tendency by giving witness to the precious nature of human experience in all its forms, whether or not it feels or appears "spiritual."

The seven Wisdom books, including the deuterocanonical books of Wisdom and Sirach, serve as our primary witnesses to biblical wisdom. It is not as if wisdom is confined to these books, for its influence is pervasive throughout Scripture. But in these books human experience as the arena in which God is present and working is placed front and center.

The comprehensiveness of these seven witnesses becomes evident when we set Psalms at the center of the Wisdom literature and view the other six as three sets of two, each revolving around it: first Job and Proverbs, then Ecclesiastes and the Song of Songs, and finally Wisdom and Sirach.

Psalms is a magnetic center, pulling every scrap and dimension of human experience into the presence of God. The Psalms are indiscriminate in their subject matter—complaint and thanks, doubt and anger, outcries of pain and outbursts of joy, quiet reflection and boisterous worship. If it's *human*, it qualifies. Any human experience, feeling, or thought can be prayed. Eventually it all *must* be prayed if it is to retain—or recover—its essential humanity. The totality of God's concern with the totality of our humanity is then elaborated by means of the other three pairs of books.

Job and Proverbs set the crisis experience of extreme suffering opposite the routine experience of getting along as best we can in the ordinary affairs of work and family, money and sex, the use of language and the expression of emotions. The life of faith has to do with extraordinary experience; the life of faith has to do with ordinary experience. Neither cancels out the other; neither takes precedence over the other. As Job rages in pain and protest, we find that the worst that can happen to us has been staked out as God's territory. As the pithy Proverbs sharpen our observations and insights regarding what is going on all around us, we realize that all this unobtrusive, undramatic dailiness is also God's country.

Song of Songs and Ecclesiastes set the ecstatic experience of love in tension with the boredom of the same old round. The life of faith has to do with the glories of discovering far more in life that we ever dreamed of; the life of faith has to do with doggedly putting one flat foot in front of the other, wondering what the point of it all is. Neither cancels out the other; neither takes precedence of the other. As we sing and pray the lyrics of the Song of Songs, we become convinced that God blesses the best that human experience is capable of; as we ponder the sardonic verses of Ecclesiastes, we recognize the limits inherent in all human experience, appreciate it for what it is, but learn not to confuse it with God.

Wisdom and Sirach are much later writings from the intertestamental period. By this time, Wisdom had been clearly personified as "Lady Wisdom," and she was a practical guide to living a good life by following God's life-maps. These two books continue the theme of finding God in both the extraordinary and the ordinary events of human existence and point to a better world where divine Wisdom rules.

In such ways, these Wisdom writers keep us honest with and attentive to the entire range of human experience that God the Spirit uses to fashion a life of holy salvation in each of us.

JOB

Job suffered. His name is synonymous with suffering. He asked, "Why?" He asked, "Why me?" And he put his questions to God. He asked his questions persistently, passionately, and eloquently. He refused to take silence for an answer. He refused to take clichés for an answer. He refused to let God off the hook.

Job did not take his sufferings quietly or piously. He disdained going for a second opinion to outside physicians or philosophers. Job took his stance before *God*, and there he protested his suffering, protested mightily.

It is not only because Job suffered that he is important to us. It is because he suffered in the same ways that *we* suffer—in the vital areas of family, personal health, and material things. Job is also important to us because he searchingly questioned and boldly protested his suffering. Indeed, he went "to the top" with his questions.

It is not suffering as such that troubles us. It is undeserved suffering.

Almost all of us in our years of growing up have the experience of disobeying our parents and getting punished for it. When that discipline was connected with wrongdoing, it had a certain sense of justice to it: *When we do wrong, we get punished*.

One of the surprises as we get older, however, is that we come to see that there is no real correlation between the amount of wrong we commit and the amount of pain we experience. An even larger surprise is that very often there is something quite the opposite: We do right and get knocked down. We do the best we are capable of doing, and just as we are reaching out to receive our reward we are hit from the blind side and sent reeling.

This is the suffering that first bewilders and then outrages us. This is the kind of suffering that bewildered and outraged Job, for Job was doing everything right when suddenly everything went wrong. And it is this kind of suffering to which Job gives voice when he protests to God.

Job gives voice to his sufferings so well, so accurately and honestly, that anyone who has ever suffered—which includes every last one of us—can recognize his or her personal pain in the voice of Job. Job says boldly what some of us are too timid to say. He makes poetry out of what in many of us is only a tangle of confused whimpers. He shouts out to God what a lot of us mutter behind our sleeves. He refuses to accept the role of a defeated victim.

It is also important to note what Job does *not* do, lest we expect something from him that he does not intend. Job does not curse God as his wife suggests he should do, getting rid of the problem by getting rid of God. But neither does Job *explain* suffering. He does not instruct us in how to live so that we can avoid suffering. Suffering is a mystery, and Job comes to respect the mystery.

In the course of facing, questioning, and respecting suffering, Job finds himself in an even larger mystery—the mystery of God. Perhaps the greatest mystery in suffering is how it can bring a person into the presence of God in a state of worship, full of wonder, love, and praise. Suffering does not inevitably do that, but it does it far more often than we would expect. It certainly did that for Job. Even in his answer to his wife he speaks the language of an uncharted irony, a dark and difficult kind of truth: "We take the good days from God—why not also the bad days?"

But there is more to the book of Job than Job. There are Job's friends. The moment we find ourselves in trouble of any kind—sick in the hospital, bereaved by a friend's death, dismissed from a job or relationship, depressed or bewildered—people start showing up telling us exactly what is wrong with us and what we must do to get better. Sufferers attract fixers the way roadkills attract vultures. At first we are impressed that they bother with us and amazed at their facility with answers. They know so much! How did they get to be such experts in living?

More often than not, these people use the Word of God frequently and loosely. They are full of spiritual diagnosis and prescription. It all sounds so hopeful. But then we begin to wonder, "Why is it that for all their apparent compassion we feel worse instead of better after they've said their piece?"

The book of Job is not only a witness to the dignity of suffering and God's presence in our suffering but is also our primary biblical protest against religion that has been reduced to explanations or "answers." Many of the answers that Job's so-called friends give him are technically true. But it is the "technical" part that ruins them. They are answers without personal relationship, intellect without intimacy. The answers are slapped onto Job's ravaged life like labels on a specimen bottle. Job rages against this secularized wisdom that has lost touch with the living realities of God.

In every generation there are men and women who pretend to be able to instruct us in a way of life that guarantees that we will be "healthy, wealthy, and wise." According to the propaganda of these people, anyone who lives intelligently and morally is exempt from suffering. From their point of view, it is lucky for us that they are now at hand to provide the intelligent and moral answers we need.

On behalf of all of us who have been misled by the platitudes of the nice people who show up to tell us everything is going to be just all right if we simply think such-and-such and do such-and-such, Job issues an anguished rejoinder. He rejects the kind of advice and teaching that has God all figured out, that provides glib explanations for every circumstance. Job's honest defiance continues to be the best defense against the clichés of positive thinkers and the prattle of religious small talk.

The honest, innocent Job is placed in a setting of immense suffering and then surrounded by the conventional religious wisdom of the day in the form of speeches by Eliphaz, Bildad, Zophar, and Elihu. The contrast is unforgettable. The counselors methodically and pedantically recite their bookish precepts to Job. At first Job rages in pain and roars out his protests, but then he becomes silent in awestruck faith before God, who speaks from out of a storm — a "whirlwind" of Deity. Real faith cannot be reduced to spiritual bromides and merchandised in success stories. It is refined in the fires and the storms of pain.

The book of Job does not reject answers as such. There *is* content to biblical religion. It is the *secularization* of answers that is rejected — answers severed from their Source, the living God, the Word that both batters us and heals us. We cannot have truth *about* God divorced from the mind and heart *of* God.

In our compassion, we don't like to see people suffer. And so our instincts are aimed at preventing and alleviating suffering. No doubt that is a good impulse. But if we really want to reach out to others who are suffering, we should be careful not to be like Job's friends, not to do our "helping" with the presumption that we can fix things, get rid of them, or make them "better." We may look at our suffering friends and imagine how they could have better marriages, better-behaved children, better mental and emotional health. But when we rush in to fix suffering, we need to keep in mind several things.

First, no matter how insightful we may be, we don't *really* understand the full nature of our friends' problems. Second, our friends may not *want* our advice. Third, the ironic fact of the matter is that more often than not, people do not suffer *less* when they are committed to following God, but *more*. When these people go through suffering, their lives are often transformed, deepened, marked with beauty and holiness, in remarkable ways that could never have been anticipated before the suffering.

So, instead of continuing to focus on preventing suffering — which we simply won't be very successful at anyway — perhaps we should begin *entering* the suffering, participating insofar as we are able — entering the mystery and looking around for God. In other words, we need to quit feeling sorry for people who suffer and instead look up to them, learn from them, and — if they will let us — join them in protest and prayer. Pity can be nearsighted and condescending; shared suffering can be dignifying and life-changing. As we look at Job's suffering and praying and worshiping, we see that he has already blazed a trail of courage and integrity for us to follow.

But sometimes it's hard to know just how to follow Job's lead when we feel so alone in our suffering, unsure of what God wants us to do. What we must realize during those times of darkness is that the God who appeared to Job in the whirlwind is calling out to all of us. Although God may not appear to us in a vision, he makes himself known to us in all the many ways that he describes to Job — from the macro to the micro, from the wonders of the galaxies to the little things we take for granted. He is the Creator of the unfathomable universe all around us — and he is also the Creator of the universe inside of us. And so we gain hope—not from the darkness of our suffering, not from pat answers in books, but from the God who sees our suffering and shares our pain.

Reading Job prayerfully and meditatively leads us to face the questions that arise when our lives don't turn out the way we expect them to. First we hear all the stock answers. Then we ask the questions again, with variations—and hear the answers again, with variations. Over and over and over. Every time we let Job give voice to our own questions, our suffering gains in dignity and we are brought a step closer to the threshold of the voice and mystery of God. Every time we persist with Job in rejecting the quick-fix counsel of people who see us and hear us but do not understand us, we deepen our availability and openness to the revelation that comes only out of the tempest. The mystery of God eclipses the darkness and the struggle. We realize that suffering calls *our* lives into question, not God's. The tables are turned: God-Alive is present to us. God is speaking to us. And so Job's experience is confirmed and repeated once again in our suffering and our vulnerable humanity.

JOB

¹⁻³ 1 Job was a man who lived in Uz. He was honest inside and out, a man of his word, who was totally devoted to God and hated evil with a passion. He had seven sons and three daughters. He was also very wealthy — seven thousand head of sheep, three thousand camels, five hundred teams of oxen, five hundred donkeys, and a huge staff of servants — the most influential man in all the East!

⁴⁻⁵ His sons used to take turns hosting parties in their homes, always inviting their three sisters to join them in their merrymaking. When the parties were over, Job would get up early in the morning and sacrifice a burnt offering for each of his children, thinking, "Maybe one of them sinned by defying God inwardly." Job made a habit of this sacrificial atonement, just in case they'd sinned.

THE FIRST TEST: FAMILY AND FORTUNE

⁶⁻⁷ One day when the angels came to report to GOD, Satan, who was the Designated Accuser, came along with them. GOD singled out Satan and said, "What have you been up to?"

Satan answered GOD, "Going here and there, checking things out on earth."

⁸ GOD said to Satan, "Have you noticed my friend Job? There's no one quite like him — honest and true to his word, totally devoted to God and hating evil."

⁹⁻¹⁰ Satan retorted, "So do you think Job does all that out of the sheer goodness of his heart? Why, no one ever had it so good! You pamper him like a pet, make sure nothing bad ever happens to him or his family or his possessions, bless everything he does — he can't lose!

¹¹ "But what do you think would happen if you reached down and took away everything that is his? He'd curse you right to your face, that's what."

¹² GOD replied, "We'll see. Go ahead — do what you want with all that is his. Just don't hurt *him*." Then Satan left the presence of GOD.

¹³⁻¹⁵ Sometime later, while Job's children were having one of their parties at the home of the oldest son, a messenger came to Job and said, "The oxen were plowing and the donkeys grazing in the field next to us when Sabeans attacked. They stole the animals and killed the field hands. I'm the only one to get out alive and tell you what happened."

¹⁶ While he was still talking, another messenger arrived and said, "Bolts of lightning struck the sheep and the shepherds and fried them — burned them to a crisp. I'm the only one to get out alive and tell you what happened."

¹⁷ While he was still talking, another messenger arrived and said, "Chaldeans coming from three directions raided the camels and massacred the camel drivers. I'm the only one to get out alive and tell you what happened."

¹⁸⁻¹⁹ While he was still talking, another messenger arrived and said, "Your children were having a party at the home of the oldest brother when a tornado swept in off the desert and struck the house. It collapsed on the young people and they died. I'm the only one to get out alive and tell you what happened."

²⁰ Job got to his feet, ripped his robe, shaved his head, then fell to the ground and worshiped:

21 Naked I came from my mother's womb,
    naked I'll return to the womb of the earth.
GOD gives, GOD takes.
    God's name be ever blessed.

22   Not once through all this did Job sin; not once did he blame God.

THE SECOND TEST: HEALTH

1-3 2 One day when the angels came to report to GOD, Satan also showed up. GOD singled out Satan, saying, "And what have you been up to?" Satan answered GOD, "Oh, going here and there, checking things out." Then GOD said to Satan, "Have you noticed my friend Job? There's no one quite like him, is there — honest and true to his word, totally devoted to God and hating evil? He still has a firm grip on his integrity! You tried to trick me into destroying him, but it didn't work."

4-5   Satan answered, "A human would do anything to save his life. But what do you think would happen if you reached down and took away his health? He'd curse you to your face, that's what."

6   GOD said, "All right. Go ahead — you can do what you like with him. But mind you, don't kill him."

7-8   Satan left GOD and struck Job with terrible sores. Job was ulcers and scabs from head to foot. They itched and oozed so badly that he took a piece of broken pottery to scrape himself, then went and sat on a trash heap, among the ashes.

9   His wife said, "Still holding on to your precious integrity, are you? Curse God and be done with it!"

10   He told her, "You're talking like an empty-headed fool. We take the good days from God — why not also the bad days?"
    Not once through all this did Job sin. He said nothing against God.

JOB'S THREE FRIENDS

11-13 Three of Job's friends heard of all the trouble that had fallen on him. Each traveled from his own country — Eliphaz from Teman, Bildad from Shuhah, Zophar from Naamath — and went together to Job to keep him company and comfort him. When they first caught sight of him, they couldn't believe what they saw — they hardly recognized him! They cried out in lament, ripped their robes, and dumped dirt on their heads as a sign of their grief. Then they sat with him on the ground. Seven days and nights they sat there without saying a word. They could see how rotten he felt, how deeply he was suffering.

JOB CRIES OUT
WHAT'S THE POINT OF LIFE?

1-2 3 Then Job broke the silence. He spoke up and cursed his fate:

3-10   "Obliterate the day I was born.
    Blank out the night I was conceived!
Let it be a black hole in space.
    May God above forget it ever happened.
    Erase it from the books!
May the day of my birth be buried in deep darkness,

shrouded by the fog,
    swallowed by the night.
And the night of my conception — the devil take it!
    Rip the date off the calendar,
    delete it from the almanac.
Oh, turn that night into pure nothingness —
    no sounds of pleasure from that night, ever!
May those who are good at cursing curse that day.
    Unleash the sea beast, Leviathan, on it.
May its morning stars turn to black cinders,
    waiting for a daylight that never comes,
    never once seeing the first light of dawn.
And why? Because it released me from my mother's womb
    into a life with so much trouble.

11-19   "Why didn't I die at birth,
    my first breath out of the womb my last?
Why were there arms to rock me,
    and breasts for me to drink from?
I could be resting in peace right now,
    asleep forever, feeling no pain,
In the company of kings and statesmen
    in their royal ruins,
Or with princes resplendent
    in their gold and silver tombs.
Why wasn't I stillborn and buried
    with all the babies who never saw light,
Where the wicked no longer trouble anyone
    and bone-weary people get a long-deserved rest?
Prisoners sleep undisturbed,
    never again to wake up to the bark of the guards.
The small and the great are equals in that place,
    and slaves are free from their masters.

20-23   "Why does God bother giving light to the miserable,
    why bother keeping bitter people alive,
Those who want in the worst way to die, and can't,
    who can't imagine anything better than death,
Who count the day of their death and burial
    the happiest day of their life?
What's the point of life when it doesn't make sense,
    when God blocks all the roads to meaning?

24-26   "Instead of bread I get groans for my supper,
    then leave the table and vomit my anguish.
The worst of my fears has come true,
    what I've dreaded most has happened.
My repose is shattered, my peace destroyed.
    No rest for me, ever — death has invaded life."

ELIPHAZ SPEAKS OUT
Now *You're* the One in Trouble

1-6 Then Eliphaz from Teman spoke up:

"Would you mind if I said something to you?
Under the circumstances it's hard to keep quiet.
You yourself have done this plenty of times, spoken words
that clarify, encouraged those who were about to quit.
Your words have put stumbling people on their feet,
put fresh hope in people about to collapse.
But now *you're* the one in trouble — you're hurting!
You've been hit hard and you're reeling from the blow.
But shouldn't your devout life give you confidence now?
Shouldn't your exemplary life give you hope?

7-11 "Think! Has a truly innocent person ever ended up on the scrap heap?
Do genuinely upright people ever lose out in the end?
It's my observation that those who plow evil
and sow trouble reap evil and trouble.
One breath from God and they fall apart,
one blast of his anger and there's nothing left of them.
The mighty lion, king of the beasts, roars mightily,
but when he's toothless he's useless —
No teeth, no prey — and the cubs
wander off to fend for themselves.

12-16 "A word came to me in secret —
a mere whisper of a word, but I heard it clearly.
It came in a scary dream one night,
after I had fallen into a deep, deep sleep.
Dread stared me in the face, and Terror.
I was scared to death — I shook from head to foot.
A spirit glided right in front of me —
the hair on my head stood on end.
I couldn't tell what it was that appeared there —
a blur . . . and then I heard a muffled voice:

17-21 "'How can mere mortals be more righteous than God?
How can humans be purer than their Creator?
Why, God doesn't even trust his own servants,
doesn't even cheer his angels,
So how much less these bodies composed of mud,
fragile as moths?
These bodies of ours are here today and gone tomorrow,
and no one even notices — gone without a trace.
When the tent stakes are ripped up, the tent collapses —
we die and are never the wiser for having lived.'"

DON'T BLAME FATE WHEN THINGS GO WRONG

1-7 5 "Call for help, Job, if you think anyone will answer!
To which of the holy angels will you turn?
The hot temper of a fool eventually kills him,
the jealous anger of a simpleton does her in.
I've seen it myself — seen fools putting down roots,
and then, suddenly, their houses are cursed.
Their children out in the cold, abused and exploited,
with no one to stick up for them.
Hungry people off the street plunder their harvests,
cleaning them out completely, taking thorns and all,
insatiable for everything they have.
Don't blame fate when things go wrong —
trouble doesn't come from nowhere.
It's human! Mortals are born and bred for trouble,
as certainly as sparks fly upward.

WHAT A BLESSING WHEN GOD CORRECTS YOU!

8-16 "If I were in your shoes, I'd go straight to God,
I'd throw myself on the mercy of God.
After all, he's famous for great and unexpected acts;
there's no end to his surprises.
He gives rain, for instance, across the wide earth,
sends water to irrigate the fields.
He raises up the down-and-out,
gives firm footing to those sinking in grief.
He aborts the schemes of conniving crooks,
so that none of their plots come to term.
He catches the know-it-alls in their conspiracies —
all that intricate intrigue swept out with the trash!
Suddenly they're disoriented, plunged into darkness;
they can't see to put one foot in front of the other.
But the downtrodden are saved by God,
saved from the murderous plots, saved from the iron fist.
And so the poor continue to hope,
while injustice is bound and gagged.

17-19 "So, what a blessing when God steps in and corrects you!
Mind you, don't despise the discipline of Almighty God!
True, he wounds, but he also dresses the wound;
the same hand that hurts you, heals you.
From one disaster after another he delivers you;
no matter what the calamity, the evil can't touch you —

20-26 "In famine, he'll keep you from starving,
in war, from being gutted by the sword.
You'll be protected from vicious gossip
and live fearless through any catastrophe.
You'll shrug off disaster and famine,
and stroll fearlessly among wild animals.

You'll be on good terms with rocks and mountains;
    wild animals will become your good friends.
You'll know that your place on earth is safe,
    you'll look over your goods and find nothing amiss.
You'll see your children grow up,
    your family lovely and lissome as orchard grass.
You'll arrive at your grave ripe with many good years,
    like sheaves of golden grain at harvest.

27   "Yes, this is the way things are—my word of honor!
    Take it to heart and you won't go wrong."

JOB REPLIES TO ELIPHAZ
God Has Dumped the Works on Me

1-7   **6** Job answered:

"If my misery could be weighed,
    if you could pile the whole bitter load on the scales,
It would be heavier than all the sand of the sea!
    Is it any wonder that I'm screaming like a caged cat?
The arrows of God Almighty are in me,
    poison arrows—and I'm poisoned all through!
    God has dumped the whole works on me.
Donkeys bray and cows moo when they run out of pasture—
    so don't expect me to keep quiet in this.
Do you see what God has dished out for me?
    It's enough to turn anyone's stomach!
Everything in me is repulsed by it—
    it makes me sick.

Pressed Past the Limits

8-13   "All I want is an answer to one prayer,
    a last request to be honored:
Let God step on me—squash me like a bug,
    and be done with me for good.
I'd at least have the satisfaction
    of not having blasphemed the Holy God,
    before being pressed past the limits.
Where's the strength to keep my hopes up?
    What future do I have to keep me going?
Do you think I have nerves of steel?
    Do you think I'm made of iron?
Do you think I can pull myself up by my bootstraps?
    Why, I don't even have any boots!

My So-Called Friends

14-23   "When desperate people give up on God Almighty,
    their friends, at least, should stick with them.
But my brothers are fickle as a gulch in the desert—
    one day they're gushing with water
From melting ice and snow

cascading out of the mountains,
But by midsummer they're dry,
gullies baked dry in the sun.
Travelers who spot them and go out of their way for a drink
end up in a waterless gulch and die of thirst.
Merchant caravans from Tema see them and expect water,
tourists from Sheba hope for a cool drink.
They arrive so confident — but what a disappointment!
They get there, and their faces fall!
And you, my so-called friends, are no better —
there's nothing to you!
One look at a hard scene and you shrink in fear.
It's not as though I asked you for anything —
I didn't ask you for one red cent —
Nor did I beg you to go out on a limb for me.
So why all this dodging and shuffling?

24-27 "Confront me with the truth and I'll shut up,
show me where I've gone off the track.
Honest words never hurt anyone,
but what's the point of all this pious bluster?
You pretend to tell me what's wrong with my life,
but treat my words of anguish as so much hot air.
Are people mere things to you?
Are friends just items of profit and loss?

28-30 "Look me in the eyes!
Do you think I'd lie to your face?
Think it over — no double-talk!
Think carefully — my integrity is on the line!
Can you detect anything false in what I say?
Don't you trust me to discern good from evil?"

THERE'S NOTHING TO MY LIFE

1-6 7 "Human life is a struggle, isn't it?
It's a life sentence to hard labor.
Like field hands longing for quitting time
and working stiffs with nothing to hope for but payday,
I'm given a life that meanders and goes nowhere —
months of aimlessness, nights of misery!
I go to bed and think, 'How long till I can get up?'
I toss and turn as the night drags on — and I'm fed up!
I'm covered with maggots and scabs.
My skin gets scaly and hard, then oozes with pus.
My days come and go swifter than the click of knitting needles,
and then the yarn runs out — an unfinished life!

7-10 "God, don't forget that I'm only a puff of air!
These eyes have had their last look at goodness.
And your eyes have seen the last of me;
even while you're looking, there'll be nothing left to look at.

When a cloud evaporates, it's gone for good;
   those who go to the grave never come back.
They don't return to visit their families;
   never again will friends drop in for coffee.

11-16   "And so I'm not keeping one bit of this quiet,
   I'm laying it all out on the table;
      my complaining to high heaven is bitter, but honest.
Are you going to put a muzzle on me,
   the way you quiet the sea and still the storm?
If I say, 'I'm going to bed, then I'll feel better.
   A little nap will lift my spirits,'
You come and so scare me with nightmares
   and frighten me with ghosts
That I'd rather strangle in the bedclothes
   than face this kind of life any longer.
I hate this life! Who needs any more of this?
   Let me alone! There's nothing to my life — it's nothing
      but smoke.

17-21   "What are mortals anyway, that you bother with them,
   that you even give them the time of day?
That you check up on them every morning,
   looking in on them to see how they're doing?
Let up on me, will you?
   Can't you even let me spit in peace?
Even suppose I'd sinned — how would that hurt you?
   You're responsible for every human being.
Don't you have better things to do than pick on me?
   Why make a federal case out of me?
Why don't you just forgive my sins
   and start me off with a clean slate?
The way things are going, I'll soon be dead.
   You'll look high and low, but I won't be around."

BILDAD'S RESPONSE
DOES GOD MESS UP?

1-7   **8** Bildad from Shuhah was next to speak:

   "How can you keep on talking like this?
   You're talking nonsense, and noisy nonsense at that.
Does God mess up?
   Does God Almighty ever get things backward?
It's plain that your children sinned against him —
   otherwise, why would God have punished them?
Here's what you must do — and don't put it off any longer:
   Get down on your knees before God Almighty.
If you're as innocent and upright as you say,
   it's not too late — he'll come running;
      he'll set everything right again, reestablish your fortunes.

Even though you're not much right now,
     you'll end up better than ever.

To Hang Your Life from One Thin Thread

8-19 "Put the question to our ancestors,
     study what they learned from their ancestors.
For we're newcomers at this, with a lot to learn,
     and not too long to learn it.
So why not let the ancients teach you, tell you what's what,
     instruct you in what they knew from experience?
Can mighty pine trees grow tall without soil?
     Can luscious tomatoes flourish without water?
Blossoming flowers look great before they're cut or picked,
     but without soil or water they wither more quickly than grass.
That's what happens to all who forget God—
     all their hopes come to nothing.
They hang their life from one thin thread,
     they hitch their fate to a spider web.
One jiggle and the thread breaks,
     one jab and the web collapses.
Or they're like weeds springing up in the sunshine,
     invading the garden,
Spreading everywhere, overtaking the flowers,
     getting a foothold even in the rocks.
But when the gardener rips them out by the roots,
     the garden doesn't miss them one bit.
The sooner the godless are gone, the better;
     then good plants can grow in their place.

20-22 "There's no way that God will reject a good person,
     and there is no way he'll help a bad one.
God will let you laugh again;
     you'll raise the roof with shouts of joy,
With your enemies thoroughly discredited,
     their house of cards collapsed."

JOB CONTINUES
How Can Mere Mortals Get Right with God?

1-13 9 Job continued by saying:

"So what's new? I know all this.
     The question is, 'How can mere mortals get right with God?'
If we wanted to bring our case before him,
     what chance would we have? Not one in a thousand!
God's wisdom is so deep, God's power so immense,
     who could take him on and come out in one piece?
He moves mountains before they know what's happened,
     flips them on their heads on a whim.
He gives the earth a good shaking up,
     rocks it down to its very foundations.
He tells the sun, 'Don't shine,' and it doesn't;

he pulls the blinds on the stars.
All by himself he stretches out the heavens
  and strides on the waves of the sea.
He designed the Big Dipper and Orion,
  the Pleiades and Alpha Centauri.
We'll never comprehend all the great things he does;
  his miracle-surprises can't be counted.
Somehow, though he moves right in front of me, I don't see him;
  quietly but surely he's active, and I miss it.
If he steals you blind, who can stop him?
  Who's going to say, 'Hey, what are you doing?'
God doesn't hold back on his anger;
  even dragon-bred monsters cringe before him.

14-20 "So how could I ever argue with him,
  construct a defense that would influence God?
Even though I'm innocent I could never prove it;
  I can only throw myself on the Judge's mercy.
If I called on God and he himself answered me,
  then, and only then, would I believe that he'd heard me.
As it is, he knocks me about from pillar to post,
  beating me up, black-and-blue, for no good reason.
He won't even let me catch my breath,
  piles bitterness upon bitterness.
If it's a question of who's stronger, he wins, hands down!
  If it's a question of justice, who'll serve him the subpoena?
Even though innocent, anything I say incriminates me;
  blameless as I am, my defense just makes me sound worse.

If God's Not Responsible, Who Is?

21-24 "Believe me, I'm blameless.
  I don't understand what's going on.
  I hate my life!
Since either way it ends up the same, I can only conclude
  that God destroys the good right along with the bad.
When calamity hits and brings sudden death,
  he folds his arms, aloof from the despair of the innocent.
He lets the wicked take over running the world,
  he installs judges who can't tell right from wrong.
  If he's not responsible, who is?

25-31 "My time is short — what's left of my life races off
  too fast for me to even glimpse the good.
My life is going fast, like a ship under full sail,
  like an eagle plummeting to its prey.
Even if I say, 'I'll put all this behind me,
  I'll look on the bright side and force a smile,'
All these troubles would still be like grit in my gut
  since it's clear you're not going to let up.
The verdict has already been handed down — 'Guilty!' —
  so what's the use of protests or appeals?

Even if I scrub myself all over
and wash myself with the strongest soap I can find,
It wouldn't last — you'd push me into a pigpen, or worse,
so nobody could stand me for the stink.

32-35   "God and I are not equals; I can't bring a case against him.
We'll never enter a courtroom as peers.
How I wish we had an arbitrator
to step in and let me get on with life —
To break God's death grip on me,
to free me from this terror so I could breathe again.
Then I'd speak up and state my case boldly.
As things stand, there is no way I can do it."

To Find Some Skeleton in My Closet

1   10 "I can't stand my life — I hate it!
I'm putting it all out on the table,
all the bitterness of my life — I'm holding back nothing."

2-7   Job prayed:

"Here's what I want to say:
Don't, God, bring in a verdict of guilty
without letting me know the charges you're bringing.
How does this fit into what you once called 'good' —
giving me a hard time, spurning me,
a life you shaped by your very own hands,
and then blessing the plots of the wicked?
You don't look at things the way we mortals do.
You're not taken in by appearances, are you?
Unlike us, you're not working against a deadline.
You have all eternity to work things out.
So what's this all about, anyway — this compulsion
to dig up some dirt, to find some skeleton in my closet?
You know good and well I'm not guilty.
You also know no one can help me.

8-12   "You made me like a handcrafted piece of pottery —
and now are you going to smash me to pieces?
Don't you remember how beautifully you worked my clay?
Will you reduce me now to a mud pie?
Oh, that marvel of conception as you stirred together
semen and ovum —
What a miracle of skin and bone,
muscle and brain!
You gave me life itself, and incredible love.
You watched and guarded every breath I took.

13-17   "But you never told me about this part.
I should have known that there was more to it —
That if I so much as missed a step, you'd notice and pounce,

wouldn't let me get by with a thing.
If I'm truly guilty, I'm doomed.
But if I'm innocent, it's no better — I'm still doomed.
My belly is full of bitterness.
I'm up to my ears in a swamp of affliction.
I try to make the best of it, try to brave it out,
but you're too much for me,
relentless, like a lion on the prowl.
You line up fresh witnesses against me.
You compound your anger
and pile on the grief and pain!

18-22 "So why did you have me born?
I wish no one had ever laid eyes on me!
I wish I'd never lived — a stillborn,
buried without ever having breathed.
Isn't it time to call it quits on my life?
Can't you let up, and let me smile just once
Before I die and am buried,
before I'm nailed into my coffin, sealed in the ground,
And banished for good to the land of the dead,
blind in the final dark?"

ZOPHAR'S COUNSEL
How Wisdom Looks from the Inside

1-6 **11** Now it was the turn of Zophar from Naamath:

"What a flood of words! Shouldn't we put a stop to it?
Should this kind of loose talk be permitted?
Job, do you think you can carry on like this and we'll say nothing?
That we'll let you rail and mock and not step in?
You claim, 'My doctrine is sound
and my conduct impeccable.'
How I wish God would give you a piece of his mind,
tell you what's what!
I wish he'd show you how wisdom looks from the inside,
for true wisdom is mostly 'inside.'
But you can be sure of this,
you haven't gotten half of what you deserve.

7-12 "Do you think you can explain the mystery of God?
Do you think you can diagram God Almighty?
God is far higher than you can imagine,
far deeper than you can comprehend,
Stretching farther than earth's horizons,
far wider than the endless ocean.
If he happens along, throws you in jail
then hauls you into court, can you do anything about it?
He sees through vain pretensions,
spots evil a long way off —
no one pulls the wool over *his* eyes!

Hollow men, hollow women, will wise up
    about the same time mules learn to talk.

REACH OUT TO GOD

13-20 "Still, if you set your heart on God
    and reach out to him,
If you scrub your hands of sin
    and refuse to entertain evil in your home,
You'll be able to face the world unashamed
    and keep a firm grip on life, guiltless and fearless.
You'll forget your troubles;
    they'll be like old, faded photographs.
Your world will be washed in sunshine,
    every shadow dispersed by dayspring.
Full of hope, you'll relax, confident again;
    you'll look around, sit back, and take it easy.
Expansive, without a care in the world,
    you'll be hunted out by many for your blessing.
But the wicked will see none of this.
    They're headed down a dead-end road
    with nothing to look forward to — nothing."

JOB ANSWERS ZOPHAR
PUT YOUR EAR TO THE EARTH

1-3 **12** Job answered:

"I'm sure you speak for all the experts,
    and when you die there'll be no one left to tell us how to live.
But don't forget that I also have a brain —
    I don't intend to play second fiddle to you.
    It doesn't take an expert to know these things.

4-6 "I'm ridiculed by my friends:
    'So that's the man who had conversations with God!'
Ridiculed without mercy:
    'Look at the man who never did wrong!'
It's easy for the well-to-do to point their fingers in blame,
    for the well-fixed to pour scorn on the strugglers.
Crooks reside safely in high-security houses,
    insolent blasphemers live in luxury;
    they've bought and paid for a god who'll protect them.

7-12 "But ask the animals what they think — let them teach you;
    let the birds tell you what's going on.
Put your ear to the earth — learn the basics.
    Listen — the fish in the ocean will tell you their stories.
Isn't it clear that they all know and agree
    that GOD is sovereign, that he holds all things in his hand —
Every living soul, yes,
    every breathing creature?
Isn't this all just common sense,

as common as the sense of taste?
Do you think the elderly have a corner on wisdom,
    that you have to grow old before you understand life?

FROM GOD WE LEARN HOW TO LIVE

13-25 "True wisdom and real power belong to God;
    from him we learn how to live,
    and also what to live for.
If he tears something down, it's down for good;
    if he locks people up, they're locked up for good.
If he holds back the rain, there's a drought;
    if he lets it loose, there's a flood.
Strength and success belong to God;
    both deceived and deceiver must answer to him.
He strips experts of their vaunted credentials,
    exposes judges as witless fools.
He divests kings of their royal garments,
    then ties a rag around their waists.
He strips priests of their robes,
    and fires high officials from their jobs.
He forces trusted sages to keep silence,
    deprives elders of their good sense and wisdom.
He dumps contempt on famous people,
    disarms the strong and mighty.
He shines a spotlight into caves of darkness,
    hauls deepest darkness into the noonday sun.
He makes nations rise and then fall,
    builds up some and abandons others.
He robs world leaders of their reason,
    and sends them off into no-man's-land.
They grope in the dark without a clue,
    lurching and staggering like drunks."

I'M TAKING MY CASE TO GOD

1-5 **13** "Yes, I've seen all this with my own eyes,
    heard and understood it with my very own ears.
Everything you know, I know,
    so I'm not taking a backseat to any of you.
I'm taking my case straight to God Almighty;
    I've had it with you — I'm going directly to God.
You graffiti my life with lies.
    You're a bunch of pompous quacks!
I wish you'd shut your mouths —
    silence is your only claim to wisdom.

6-12 "Listen now while I make my case,
    consider my side of things for a change.
Or are you going to keep on lying 'to do God a service'?
    to make up stories 'to get him off the hook'?
Why do you always take his side?
    Do you think he needs a lawyer to defend himself?

How would you fare if you were in the dock?
　　Your lies might convince a jury — but would they
　　　　convince *God*?
He'd reprimand you on the spot
　　if he detected a bias in your witness.
Doesn't his splendor put you in awe?
　　Aren't you afraid to speak cheap lies before him?
Your wise sayings are knickknack wisdom,
　　good for nothing but gathering dust.

13-19　"So hold your tongue while I have my say,
　　then I'll take whatever I have coming to me.
Why do I go out on a limb like this
　　and take my life in my hands?
Because even if he killed me, I'd keep on hoping.
　　I'd defend my innocence to the very end.
Just wait, this is going to work out for the best — my salvation!
　　If I were guilt-stricken do you think I'd be doing this —
　　laying myself on the line before God?
You'd better pay attention to what I'm telling you,
　　listen carefully with both ears.
Now that I've laid out my defense,
　　I'm sure that I'll be acquitted.
Can anyone prove charges against me?
　　I've said my piece. I rest my case.

WHY DOES GOD STAY HIDDEN AND SILENT?

20-27　"Please, God, I have two requests;
　　grant them so I'll know I count with you:
First, lay off the afflictions;
　　the terror is too much for me.
Second, address me directly so I can answer you,
　　or let me speak and then you answer me.
How many sins have been charged against me?
　　Show me the list — how bad is it?
Why do you stay hidden and silent?
　　Why treat me like I'm your enemy?
Why kick me around like an old tin can?
　　Why beat a dead horse?
You compile a long list of mean things about me,
　　even hold me accountable for the sins of my youth.
You hobble me so I can't move about.
　　You watch every move I make,
　　and brand me as a dangerous character.

28　"Like something rotten, human life fast decomposes,
　　like a moth-eaten shirt or a mildewed blouse."

IF WE DIE, WILL WE LIVE AGAIN?

¹⁻¹⁷ **14** "We're all adrift in the same boat:
　　　too few days, too many troubles.
　　We spring up like wildflowers in the desert and then wilt,
　　transient as the shadow of a cloud.
Do you occupy your time with such fragile wisps?
　　Why even bother hauling me into court?
There's nothing much to us to start with;
　　how do you expect us to amount to anything?
Mortals have a limited life span.
　　You've already decided how long we'll live —
　　you set the boundary and no one can cross it.
So why not give us a break? Ease up!
　　Even ditchdiggers get occasional days off.
For a tree there is always hope.
　　Chop it down and it still has a chance —
　　its roots can put out fresh sprouts.
Even if its roots are old and gnarled,
　　its stump long dormant,
At the first whiff of water it comes to life,
　　buds and grows like a sapling.
But men and women? They die and stay dead.
　　They breathe their last, and that's it.
Like lakes and rivers that have dried up,
　　parched reminders of what once was,
So mortals lie down and never get up,
　　never wake up again — never.
Why don't you just bury me alive,
　　get me out of the way until your anger cools?
But don't leave me there!
　　Set a date when you'll see me again.
If we humans die, will we live again? That's my question.
　　All through these difficult days I keep hoping,
　　waiting for the final change — for resurrection!
Homesick with longing for the creature you made,
　　you'll call — and I'll answer!
You'll watch over every step I take,
　　but you won't keep track of my missteps.
My sins will be stuffed in a sack
　　and thrown into the sea — sunk in deep ocean.

¹⁸⁻²² "Meanwhile, mountains wear down
　　and boulders break up,
Stones wear smooth
　　and soil erodes,
　　as you relentlessly grind down our hope.
You're too much for us.
　　As always, you get the last word.
We don't like it and our faces show it,
　　but you send us off anyway.

If our children do well for themselves, we never know it;
    if they do badly, we're spared the hurt.
Body and soul, that's it for us —
    a lifetime of pain, a lifetime of sorrow."

ELIPHAZ ATTACKS AGAIN
You Trivialize Religion

15 Eliphaz of Teman spoke a second time:

1-16

"If you were truly wise, would you sound so much like a
    windbag, belching hot air?
Would you talk nonsense in the middle of a serious argument,
    babbling baloney?
Look at you! You trivialize religion,
    turn spiritual conversation into empty gossip.
It's your sin that taught you to talk this way.
    You chose an education in fraud.
Your own words have exposed your guilt.
    It's nothing I've said — you've incriminated yourself!
Do you think you're the first person to have to deal with
        these things?
    Have you been around as long as the hills?
Were you listening in when God planned all this?
    Do you think you're the only one who knows anything?
What do you know that we don't know?
    What insights do you have that we've missed?
Gray beards and white hair back us up —
    old folks who've been around a lot longer than you.
Are God's promises not enough for you,
    spoken so gently and tenderly?
Why do you let your emotions take over,
    lashing out and spitting fire,
Pitting your whole being against God
    by letting words like this come out of your mouth?
Do you think it's possible for any mere mortal to be sinless
        in God's sight,
    for anyone born of a human mother to get it all together?
Why, God can't even trust his holy angels.
    He sees the flaws in the very heavens themselves,
So how much less we humans, smelly and foul,
    who lap up evil like water?

ALWAYS AT ODDS WITH GOD

17-26

"I've a thing or two to tell you, so listen up!
    I'm letting you in on my views;
It's what wise men and women have always taught,
    holding nothing back from what *they* were taught
By their parents, back in the days
    when they had this land all to themselves:
Those who live by their own rules, not God's, can expect
        nothing but trouble,

and the longer they live, the worse it gets.
Every little sound terrifies them.
Just when they think they have it made, disaster strikes.
They despair of things ever getting better —
they're on the list of people for whom things always turn out
for the worst.
They wander here and there,
never knowing where the next meal is coming from —
every day is doomsday!
They live in constant terror,
always with their backs up against the wall
Because they insist on shaking their fists at God,
defying God Almighty to his face,
Always and ever at odds with God,
always on the defensive.

27-35   "Even if they're the picture of health,
trim and fit and youthful,
They'll end up living in a ghost town
sleeping in a hovel not fit for a dog,
a ramshackle shack.
They'll never get ahead,
never amount to a hill of beans.
And then death — don't think they'll escape that!
They'll end up shriveled weeds,
brought down by a puff of God's breath.
There's a lesson here: Whoever invests in lies,
gets lies for interest,
Paid in full before the due date.
Some investment!
They'll be like fruit frost-killed before it ripens,
like buds sheared off before they bloom.
The godless are fruitless — a barren crew;
a life built on bribes goes up in smoke.
They have sex with sin and give birth to evil.
Their lives are wombs for breeding deceit."

JOB DEFENDS HIMSELF
IF YOU WERE IN MY SHOES

1-5   **16** Then Job defended himself:

"I've had all I can take of your talk.
What a bunch of miserable comforters!
Is there no end to your windbag speeches?
What's your problem that you go on and on like this?
If you were in my shoes,
I could talk just like you.
I could put together a terrific harangue
and really let you have it.
But I'd never do that. I'd console and comfort,
make things better, not worse!

6-14   "When I speak up, I feel no better;
    if I say nothing, that doesn't help either.
I feel worn down.
    God, you have wasted me totally — me and my family!
You've shriveled me like a dried prune,
    showing the world that you're against me.
My gaunt face stares back at me from the mirror,
    a mute witness to your treatment of me.
Your anger tears at me,
    your teeth rip me to shreds,
    your eyes burn holes in me — God, my enemy!
People take one look at me and gasp.
    Contemptuous, they slap me around
    and gang up against me.
And God just stands there and lets them do it,
    lets wicked people do what they want with me.
I was contentedly minding my business when God beat me up.
    He grabbed me by the neck and threw me around.
He set me up as his target,
    then rounded up archers to shoot at me.
Merciless, they shot me full of arrows;
    bitter bile poured from my gut to the ground.
He burst in on me, onslaught after onslaught,
    charging me like a mad bull.

15-17   "I sewed myself a shroud and wore it like a shirt;
    I lay facedown in the dirt.
Now my face is blotched red from weeping;
    look at the dark shadows under my eyes,
Even though I've never hurt a soul
    and my prayers are sincere!

THE ONE WHO REPRESENTS MORTALS BEFORE GOD

18-22   "O Earth, don't cover up the wrong done to me!
    Don't muffle my cry!
There must be Someone in heaven who knows the truth about me,
    in highest heaven, some Attorney who can clear my name —
My Champion, my Friend,
    while I'm weeping my eyes out before God.
I appeal to the One who represents mortals before God
    as a neighbor stands up for a neighbor.

"Only a few years are left
    before I set out on the road of no return."

1-2   **17** "My spirit is broken,
    my days used up,
    my grave dug and waiting.
See how these mockers close in on me?
    How long do I have to put up with their insolence?

3-5 "O God, pledge your support for me.
　　　Give it to me in writing, with your signature.
　　　You're the only one who can do it!
　　These people are so useless!
　　　You know firsthand how stupid they can be.
　　　You wouldn't let them have the last word, would you?
　　Those who betray their own friends
　　　leave a legacy of abuse to their children.

6-8 "God, you've made me the talk of the town —
　　　people spit in my face;
　　I can hardly see from crying so much;
　　　I'm nothing but skin and bones.
　　Decent people can't believe what they're seeing;
　　　the good-hearted wake up and insist I've given up on God.

9 "But principled people hold tight, keep a firm grip on life,
　　　sure that their clean, pure hands will get stronger and stronger!

10-16 "Maybe you'd all like to start over,
　　　to try it again, the bunch of you.
　　So far I haven't come across one scrap
　　　of wisdom in anything you've said.
　　My life's about over. All my plans are smashed,
　　　all my hopes are snuffed out —
　　My hope that night would turn into day,
　　　my hope that dawn was about to break.
　　If all I have to look forward to is a home in the graveyard,
　　　if my only hope for comfort is a well-built coffin,
　　If a family reunion means going six feet under,
　　　and the only family that shows up is worms,
　　Do you call that hope?
　　　Who on earth could find any hope in that?
　　No. If hope and I are to be buried together,
　　　I suppose you'll all come to the double funeral!"

BILDAD'S SECOND ATTACK
PLUNGED FROM LIGHT INTO DARKNESS

1-4 **18** Bildad from Shuhah chimed in:

　　　"How monotonous these word games are getting!
　　　Get serious! We need to get down to business.
　　Why do you treat your friends like slow-witted animals?
　　　You look down on us as if we don't know anything.
　　Why are you working yourself up like this?
　　　Do you want the world redesigned to suit you?
　　　Should reality be suspended to accommodate you?

5-21 "Here's the rule: The light of the wicked is put out.
　　　Their flame dies down and is extinguished.
　　Their house goes dark —

every lamp in the place goes out.
Their strong strides weaken, falter;
  they stumble into their own traps.
They get all tangled up
  in their own red tape,
Their feet are grabbed and caught,
  their necks in a noose.
They trip on ropes they've hidden,
  and fall into pits they've dug themselves.
Terrors come at them from all sides.
  They run helter-skelter.
The hungry grave is ready
  to gobble them up for supper,
To lay them out for a gourmet meal,
  a treat for ravenous Death.
They are snatched from their home sweet home
  and marched straight to the death house.
Their lives go up in smoke;
  acid rain soaks their ruins.
Their roots rot
  and their branches wither.
They'll never again be remembered —
  nameless in unmarked graves.
They are plunged from light into darkness,
  banished from the world.
And they leave empty-handed — not one single child —
  nothing to show for their life on this earth.
Westerners are aghast at their fate,
  easterners are horrified:
'Oh no! So this is what happens to perverse people.
  This is how the God-ignorant end up!'"

JOB ANSWERS BILDAD
I Call for Help and No One Bothers

19 Job answered:

"How long are you going to keep battering away at me,
  pounding me with these harangues?
Time after time after time you jump all over me.
  Do you have no conscience, abusing me like this?
Even if I have, somehow or other, gotten off the track,
  what business is that of yours?
Why do you insist on putting me down,
  using my troubles as a stick to beat me?
Tell it to God — he's the one behind all this,
  he's the one who dragged me into this mess.

"Look at me — I shout 'Murder!' and I'm ignored;
  I call for help and no one bothers to stop.
God threw a barricade across my path — I'm stymied;
  he turned out all the lights — I'm stuck in the dark.

He destroyed my reputation,
    robbed me of all self-respect.
He tore me apart piece by piece — I'm ruined!
    Then he yanked out hope by the roots.
He's angry with me — oh, how he's angry!
    He treats me like his worst enemy.
He has launched a major campaign against me,
    using every weapon he can think of,
    coming at me from all sides at once.

I KNOW THAT GOD LIVES

13-20 "God alienated my family from me;
    everyone who knows me avoids me.
My relatives and friends have all left;
    houseguests forget I ever existed.
The servant girls treat me like a bum off the street,
    look at me like they've never seen me before.
I call my attendant and he ignores me,
    ignores me even though I plead with him.
My wife can't stand to be around me anymore.
    I'm repulsive to my family.
Even street urchins despise me;
    when I come out, they taunt and jeer.
Everyone I've ever been close to abhors me;
    my dearest loved ones reject me.
I'm nothing but a bag of bones;
    my life hangs by a thread.

21-22 "Oh, friends, dear friends, take pity on me.
    God has come down hard on me!
Do you have to be hard on me, too?
    Don't you ever tire of abusing me?

23-27 "If only my words were written in a book —
    better yet, chiseled in stone!
Still, I know that God lives — the One who gives me back my life —
    and eventually he'll take his stand on earth.
And I'll see him — even though I get skinned alive! —
    see God myself, with my very own eyes.
    Oh, how I long for that day!

28-29 "If you're thinking, 'How can we get through to him,
    get him to see that his trouble is all his own fault?'
Forget it. Start worrying about *yourselves*.
    Worry about your own sins and God's coming judgment,
    for judgment is most certainly on the way."

ZOPHAR ATTACKS JOB — THE SECOND ROUND
SAVORING EVIL AS A DELICACY

1-3

20

Zophar from Naamath again took his turn:

"I can't believe what I'm hearing!
    You've put my teeth on edge, my stomach in a knot.
How dare you insult my intelligence like this!
    Well, here's a piece of my mind!

4-11

"Don't you even know the basics,
        how things have been since the earliest days,
        when Adam and Eve were first placed on earth?
The good times of the wicked are short-lived;
        godless joy is only momentary.
The evil might become world famous,
        strutting at the head of the celebrity parade,
But still end up in a pile of dung.
        Acquaintances look at them with disgust and say, 'What's that?'
They fly off like a dream that can't be remembered,
        like a shadowy illusion that vanishes in the light.
Though once notorious public figures, now they're nobodies,
        unnoticed, whether they come or go.
Their children will go begging on skid row,
        and they'll have to give back their ill-gotten gain.
Right in the prime of life,
        and youthful and vigorous, they'll die.

12-19

"They savor evil as a delicacy,
        roll it around on their tongues,
Prolong the flavor, a dalliance in decadence —
        real gourmets of evil!
But then they get stomach cramps,
        a bad case of food poisoning.
They gag on all that rich food;
        God makes them vomit it up.
They gorge on evil, make a diet of that poison —
        a deadly diet — and it kills them.
No quiet picnics for them beside gentle streams
        with fresh-baked bread and cheese, and tall, cool drinks.
They spit out their food half-chewed,
        unable to relax and enjoy anything they've worked for.
And why? Because they exploited the poor,
        took what never belonged to them.

20-29

"Such God-denying people are never content with what they have
            or who they are;
        their greed drives them relentlessly.
They plunder everything
        but they can't hold on to any of it.
Just when they think they have it all, disaster strikes;

they're served up a plate full of misery.
When they've filled their bellies with that,
    God gives them a taste of his anger,
    and they get to chew on that for a while.
As they run for their lives from one disaster,
    they run smack into another.
They're knocked around from pillar to post,
    beaten to within an inch of their lives.
They're trapped in a house of horrors,
    and see their loot disappear down a black hole.
Their lives are a total loss—
    not a penny to their name, not so much as a bean.
God will strip them of their sin-soaked clothes
    and hang their dirty laundry out for all to see.
Life is a complete wipeout for them,
    nothing surviving God's wrath.
There! That's God's blueprint for the wicked—
    what they have to look forward to."

JOB'S RESPONSE
Why Do the Wicked Have It So Good?

1-3 **21** Job replied:

"Now listen to me carefully, please listen,
    at least do me the favor of listening.
Put up with me while I have my say—
    then you can mock me later to your heart's content.

4-16 "It's not *you* I'm complaining to—it's *God*.
    Is it any wonder I'm getting fed up with his silence?
Take a good look at me. Aren't you appalled by what's happened?
    No! Don't say anything. I can do without your comments.
When I look back, I go into shock,
    my body is racked with spasms.
Why do the wicked have it so good,
    live to a ripe old age and get rich?
They get to see their children succeed,
    get to watch and enjoy their grandchildren.
Their homes are peaceful and free from fear;
    they never experience God's disciplining rod.
Their bulls breed with great vigor
    and their cows calve without fail.
They send their children out to play
    and watch them frolic like spring lambs.
They make music with fiddles and flutes,
    have good times singing and dancing.
They have a long life on easy street,
    and die painlessly in their sleep.
They say to God, 'Get lost!
    We've no interest in you or your ways.
Why should we have dealings with God Almighty?

What's there in it for us?'
But they're wrong, dead wrong — they're not gods.
It's beyond me how they can carry on like this!

17-21 "Still, how often does it happen that the wicked fail,
or disaster strikes,
or they get their just deserts?
How often are they blown away by bad luck?
Not very often.
You might say, 'God is saving up the punishment for their children.'
I say, 'Give it to them right now so they'll know what
they've done!'
They deserve to experience the effects of their evil,
feel the full force of God's wrath firsthand.
What do they care what happens to their families
after they're safely tucked away in the grave?

FANCY FUNERALS WITH ALL THE TRIMMINGS

22-26 "But who are we to tell God how to run his affairs?
He's dealing with matters that are way over our heads.
Some people die in the prime of life,
with everything going for them —
fat and sassy.
Others die bitter and bereft,
never getting a taste of happiness.
They're laid out side by side in the cemetery,
where the worms can't tell one from the other.

27-33 "I'm not deceived. I know what you're up to,
the plans you're cooking up to bring me down.
Naively you claim that the castles of tyrants fall to pieces,
that the achievements of the wicked collapse.
Have you ever asked world travelers how they see it?
Have you not listened to their stories
Of evil men and women who got off scot-free,
who never had to pay for their wickedness?
Did anyone ever confront them with their crimes?
Did they ever have to face the music?
Not likely — they're given fancy funerals
with all the trimmings,
Gently lowered into expensive graves,
with everyone telling lies about how wonderful they were.

34 "So how do you expect me to get any comfort from your nonsense?
Your so-called comfort is a tissue of lies."

ELIPHAZ ATTACKS JOB — THE THIRD ROUND
COME TO TERMS WITH GOD

1-11 **22** Once again Eliphaz the Temanite took up his theme:

"Are any of us strong enough to give God a hand,

or smart enough to give him advice?
So what if you were righteous — would God Almighty even notice?
    Even if you gave a perfect performance, do you think
        he'd applaud?
Do you think it's because he cares about your purity
    that he's disciplining you, putting you on the spot?
Hardly! It's because you're a first-class moral failure,
    because there's no end to your sins.
When people came to you for help,
    you took the shirts off their backs, exploited their helplessness.
You wouldn't so much as give a drink to the thirsty,
    or food, not even a scrap, to the hungry.
And there you sat, strong and honored by everyone,
    surrounded by immense wealth!
You turned poor widows away from your door;
    heartless, you crushed orphans.
Now *you're* the one trapped in terror, paralyzed by fear.
    Suddenly the tables have turned!
How do you like living in the dark, sightless,
    up to your neck in flood waters?

12-14   "You agree, don't you, that God is in charge?
    He runs the universe — just look at the stars!
Yet you dare raise questions: 'What does God know?
    From that distance and darkness, how can he judge?
He roams the heavens wrapped in clouds,
    so how can he see us?'

15-18   "Are you going to persist in that tired old line
    that wicked men and women have always used?
Where did it get them? They died young,
    flash floods sweeping them off to their doom.
They told God, 'Get lost!
    What good is God Almighty to us?'
And yet it was God who gave them everything they had.
    It's beyond me how they can carry on like this!

19-20   "Good people see bad people crash, and call for a celebration.
    Relieved, they crow,
'At last! Our enemies — wiped out.
    Everything they had and stood for is up in smoke!'

21-25   "Give in to God, come to terms with him
    and everything will turn out just fine.
Let him tell you what to do;
    take his words to heart.
Come back to God Almighty
    and he'll rebuild your life.
Clean house of everything evil.
    Relax your grip on your money
    and abandon your gold-plated luxury.

God Almighty will be your treasure,
  more wealth than you can imagine.

26-30 "You'll take delight in God, the Mighty One,
  and look to him joyfully, boldly.
You'll pray to him and he'll listen;
  he'll help you do what you've promised.
You'll decide what you want and it will happen;
  your life will be bathed in light.
To those who feel low you'll say, 'Chin up! Be brave!'
  and God will save them.
Yes, even the guilty will escape,
  escape through God's grace in your life."

JOB'S DEFENSE
I'M COMPLETELY IN THE DARK

1-7 **23** Job replied:

"I'm not letting up — I'm standing my ground.
  My complaint is legitimate.
God has no right to treat me like this —
  it isn't fair!
If I knew where on earth to find him,
  I'd go straight to him.
I'd lay my case before him face-to-face,
  give him all my arguments firsthand.
I'd find out exactly what he's thinking,
  discover what's going on in his head.
Do you think he'd dismiss me or bully me?
  No, he'd take me seriously.
He'd see a straight-living man standing before him;
  my Judge would acquit me for good of all charges.

8-9 "I travel East looking for him — I find no one;
  then West, but not a trace;
I go North, but he's hidden his tracks;
  then South, but not even a glimpse.

10-12 "But he knows where I am and what I've done.
  He can cross-examine me all he wants, and I'll pass the test
    with honors.
I've followed him closely, my feet in his footprints,
  not once swerving from his way.
I've obeyed every word he's spoken,
  and not just obeyed his advice — I've *treasured* it.

13-17 "But he is singular and sovereign. Who can argue with him?
  He does what he wants, when he wants to.
He'll complete in detail what he's decided about me,
  and whatever else he determines to do.
Is it any wonder that I dread meeting him?

Whenever I think about it, I get scared all over again.
God makes my heart sink!
   God Almighty gives me the shudders!
I'm completely in the dark,
   I can't see my hand in front of my face."

AN ILLUSION OF SECURITY

1-12   "But if Judgment Day isn't hidden from the Almighty,
24   why are we kept in the dark?
      There are people out there getting by with murder —
stealing and lying and cheating.
They rip off the poor
   and exploit the unfortunate,
Push the helpless into the ditch,
   bully the weak so that they fear for their lives.
The poor, like stray dogs and cats,
   scavenge for food in back alleys.
They sort through the garbage of the rich,
   eke out survival on handouts.
Homeless, they shiver through cold nights on the street;
   they've no place to lay their heads.
Exposed to the weather, wet and frozen,
   they huddle in makeshift shelters.
Nursing mothers have their babies snatched from them;
   the infants of the poor are kidnapped and sold.
They go about patched and threadbare;
   even the hard workers go hungry.
No matter how backbreaking their labor,
   they can never make ends meet.
People are dying right and left, groaning in torment.
   The wretched cry out for help
   and God does nothing, acts like nothing's wrong!

13-17   "Then there are those who avoid light at all costs,
   who scorn the light-filled path.
When the sun goes down, the murderer gets up —
   kills the poor and robs the defenseless.
Sexual predators can't wait for nightfall,
   thinking, 'No one can see us now.'
Burglars do their work at night,
   but keep well out of sight through the day.
   They want nothing to do with light.
Deep darkness is morning for that bunch;
   they make the terrors of darkness their companions in crime.

18-25   "They are scraps of wood floating on the water —
   useless, cursed junk, good for nothing.
As surely as snow melts under the hot, summer sun,
   sinners disappear in the grave.
The womb has forgotten them, worms have relished them —
   nothing that is evil lasts.

Unscrupulous,
    they prey on those less fortunate.
However much they strut and flex their muscles,
    there's nothing to them. They're hollow.
They may have an illusion of security,
    but God has his eye on them.
They may get their brief successes,
    but then it's over, nothing to show for it.
Like yesterday's newspaper,
    they're used to wrap up the garbage.
You're free to try to prove me a liar,
    but you won't be able to do it."

BILDAD'S THIRD ATTACK
EVEN THE STARS AREN'T PERFECT IN GOD'S EYES

25 1-6 Bildad the Shuhite again attacked Job:

"God is sovereign, God is fearsome —
    everything in the cosmos fits and works in his plan.
Can anyone count his angel armies?
    Is there any place where his light doesn't shine?
How can a mere mortal presume to stand up to God?
    How can an ordinary person pretend to be guiltless?
Why, even the moon has its flaws,
    even the stars aren't perfect in God's eyes,
So how much less, plain men and women —
    slugs and maggots by comparison!"

JOB'S DEFENSE
GOD SETS A BOUNDARY BETWEEN LIGHT AND DARKNESS

26 1-4 Job answered:

"Well, you've certainly been a great help to a helpless man!
    You came to the rescue just in the nick of time!
What wonderful advice you've given to a mixed-up man!
    What amazing insights you've provided!
Where in the world did you learn all this?
    How did you become so inspired?

5-14 "All the buried dead are in torment,
    and all who've been drowned in the deep, deep sea.
Hell is ripped open before God,
    graveyards dug up and exposed.
He spreads the skies over unformed space,
    hangs the earth out in empty space.
He pours water into cumulus cloud-bags
    and the bags don't burst.
He makes the moon wax and wane,
    putting it through its phases.
He draws the horizon out over the ocean,
    sets a boundary between light and darkness.

Thunder crashes and rumbles in the skies.
    Listen! It's God raising his voice!
By his power he stills sea storms,
    by his wisdom he tames sea monsters.
With one breath he clears the sky,
    with one finger he crushes the sea serpent.
And this is only the beginning,
    a mere whisper of his rule.
    Whatever would we do if he *really* raised his voice!"

No Place to Hide

27 Having waited for Zophar, Job now resumed his defense:

1-6
    "God-Alive! He's denied me justice!
God Almighty! He's ruined my life!
But for as long as I draw breath,
    and for as long as God breathes life into me,
I refuse to say one word that isn't true.
    I refuse to confess to any charge that's false.
There is no way I'll ever agree to your accusations.
    I'll not deny my integrity even if it costs me my life.
I'm holding fast to my integrity and not loosening my grip—
    and, believe me, I'll never regret it.

7-10
"Let my enemy be exposed as wicked!
    Let my adversary be proven guilty!
What hope do people without God have when life is cut short?
    when God puts an end to life?
Do you think God will listen to their cry for help
    when disaster hits?
What interest have they ever shown in the Almighty?
    Have they ever been known to pray before?

11-12
"I've given you a clear account of God in action,
    suppressed nothing regarding God Almighty.
The evidence is right before you. You can all see it for yourselves,
    so why do you keep talking nonsense?

13-23
"I'll quote your own words back to you:

"'This is how God treats the wicked,
    this is what evil people can expect from God Almighty:
Their children—all of them—will die violent deaths;
    they'll never have enough bread to put on the table.
They'll be wiped out by the plague,
    and none of the widows will shed a tear when they're gone.
Even if they make a lot of money
    and are resplendent in the latest fashions,
It's the good who will end up wearing the clothes
    and the decent who will divide up the money.
They build elaborate houses

that won't survive a single winter.
They go to bed wealthy
    and wake up poor.
Terrors pour in on them like flash floods —
    a tornado snatches them away in the middle of the night,
A cyclone sweeps them up — gone!
    Not a trace of them left, not even a footprint.
Catastrophes relentlessly pursue them;
    they run this way and that, but there's no place to hide —
Pummeled by the weather,
    blown to kingdom come by the storm.'"

Where Does Wisdom Come From?

28 1-11 "We all know how silver seams the rocks,
    we've seen the stuff from which gold is refined,
We're aware of how iron is dug out of the ground
and copper is smelted from rock.
Miners penetrate the earth's darkness,
    searching the roots of the mountains for ore,
    digging away in the suffocating darkness.
Far from civilization, far from the traffic,
    they cut a shaft,
    and are lowered into it by ropes.
Earth's surface is a field for grain,
    but its depths are a forge
Firing sapphires from stones
    and chiseling gold from rocks.
Vultures are blind to its riches,
    hawks never lay eyes on it.
Wild animals are oblivious to it,
    lions don't know it's there.
Miners hammer away at the rock,
    they uproot the mountains.
They tunnel through the rock
    and find all kinds of beautiful gems.
They discover the origins of rivers,
    and bring earth's secrets to light.

12-19 "But where, oh where, will they find Wisdom?
    Where does Insight hide?
Mortals don't have a clue,
    haven't the slightest idea where to look.
Earth's depths say, 'It's not here';
    ocean deeps echo, 'Never heard of it.'
It can't be bought with the finest gold;
    no amount of silver can get it.
Even famous Ophir gold can't buy it,
    not even diamonds and sapphires.
Neither gold nor emeralds are comparable;
    extravagant jewelry can't touch it.
Pearl necklaces and ruby bracelets — why bother?

None of this is even a down payment on Wisdom!
Pile gold and African diamonds as high as you will,
    they can't hold a candle to Wisdom.

20-22 "So where does Wisdom come from?
    And where does Insight live?
It can't be found by looking, no matter
    how deep you dig, no matter how high you fly.
If you search through the graveyard and question the dead,
    they say, 'We've only heard rumors of it.'

23-28 "God alone knows the way to Wisdom,
    he knows the exact place to find it.
He knows where everything is on earth,
    he sees everything under heaven.
After he commanded the winds to blow
    and measured out the waters,
Arranged for the rain
    and set off explosions of thunder and lightning,
He focused on Wisdom,
    made sure it was all set and tested and ready.
Then he addressed the human race: 'Here it is!
    Fear-of-the-Lord — that's Wisdom,
    and Insight means shunning evil.'"

WHEN GOD WAS STILL BY MY SIDE

1-6 **29** Job now resumed his response:

"Oh, how I long for the good old days,
    when God took such very good care of me.
He always held a lamp before me
    and I walked through the dark by its light.
Oh, how I miss those golden years
    when God's friendship graced my home,
When the Mighty One was still by my side
    and my children were all around me,
When everything was going my way,
    and nothing seemed too difficult.

7-20 "When I walked downtown
    and sat with my friends in the public square,
Young and old greeted me with respect;
    I was honored by everyone in town.
When I spoke, everyone listened;
    they hung on my every word.
People who knew me spoke well of me;
    my reputation went ahead of me.
I was known for helping people in trouble
    and standing up for those who were down on their luck.
The dying blessed me,
    and the bereaved were cheered by my visits.

All my dealings with people were good.
  I was known for being fair to everyone I met.
I was eyes to the blind
  and feet to the lame,
Father to the needy,
  and champion of abused aliens.
I grabbed street thieves by the scruff of the neck
  and made them give back what they'd stolen.
I thought, 'I'll die peacefully in my own bed,
  grateful for a long and full life,
A life deep-rooted and well-watered,
  a life limber and dew-fresh,
My soul suffused with glory
  and my body robust until the day I die.'

21-25   "Men and women listened when I spoke,
  hung expectantly on my every word.
After I spoke, they'd be quiet,
  taking it all in.
They welcomed my counsel like spring rain,
  drinking it all in.
When I smiled at them, they could hardly believe it;
  their faces lit up, their troubles took wing!
I was their leader, establishing the mood
  and setting the pace by which they lived.
  Where I led, they followed."

THE PAIN NEVER LETS UP

1-8   **30** "But no longer. Now I'm the butt of their jokes —
  young ruffians! whippersnappers!
  Why, I considered their fathers
  mere inexperienced pups.
But they are worse than dogs — good for nothing,
  stray, mangy animals,
Half-starved, scavenging the back alleys,
  howling at the moon;
Homeless guttersnipes
  chewing on old bones and licking old tin cans;
Outcasts from the community,
  cursed as dangerous delinquents.
Nobody would put up with them;
  they were driven from the neighborhood.
You could hear them out there at the edge of town,
  yelping and barking, huddled in junkyards,
A gang of beggars and no-names,
  thrown out on their ears.

9-15   "But now I'm the one they're after,
  mistreating me, taunting and mocking.
They abhor me, they abuse me.
  How dare those scoundrels — they spit in my face!

Now that God has undone me and left me in a heap,
    they hold nothing back. Anything goes.
They come at me from my blind side,
    trip me up, then jump on me while I'm down.
They throw every kind of obstacle in my path,
    determined to ruin me —
    and no one lifts a finger to help me!
They violate my broken body,
    trample through the rubble of my ruined life.
Terrors assault me —
    my dignity in shreds,
    salvation up in smoke.

16-19   "And now my life drains out,
    as suffering seizes and grips me hard.
Night gnaws at my bones;
    the pain never lets up.
I am tied hand and foot, my neck in a noose.
    I twist and turn.
Thrown facedown in the muck,
    I'm a muddy mess, inside and out.

WHAT DID I DO TO DESERVE THIS?

20-23   "I shout for help, God, and get nothing, no answer!
    I stand to face you in protest, and you give me a blank stare!
You've turned into my tormenter —
    you slap me around, knock me about.
You raised me up so I was riding high
    and then dropped me, and I crashed.
I know you're determined to kill me,
    to put me six feet under.

24-31   "What did I do to deserve this?
    Did I ever hit anyone who was calling for help?
Haven't I wept for those who live a hard life,
    been heartsick over the lot of the poor?
But where did it get me?
    I expected good but evil showed up.
    I looked for light but darkness fell.
My stomach's in a constant churning, never settles down.
    Each day confronts me with more suffering.
I walk under a black cloud. The sun is gone.
    I stand in the congregation and protest.
I howl with the jackals,
    I hoot with the owls.
I'm black-and-blue all over,
    burning up with fever.
My fiddle plays nothing but the blues;
    my mouth harp wails laments."

WHAT CAN I EXPECT FROM GOD?

31 1-4 "I made a solemn pact with myself
      never to undress a girl with my eyes.
So what can I expect from God?
What do I deserve from God Almighty above?
Isn't calamity reserved for the wicked?
      Isn't disaster supposed to strike those who do wrong?
Isn't God looking, observing how I live?
      Doesn't he mark every step I take?

5-8 "Have I walked hand in hand with falsehood,
      or hung out in the company of deceit?
Weigh me on a set of honest scales
      so God has proof of my integrity.
If I've strayed off the straight and narrow,
      wanted things I had no right to,
      messed around with sin,
Go ahead, then —
      give my portion to someone who deserves it.

9-12 "If I've let myself be seduced by a woman
      and conspired to go to bed with her,
Fine, my wife has every right to go ahead
      and sleep with anyone she wants to.
For disgusting behavior like that,
      I'd deserve the worst punishment you could hand out.
Adultery is a fire that burns the house down;
      I wouldn't expect anything I count dear to survive it.

13-15 "Have I ever been unfair to my employees
      when they brought a complaint to me?
What, then, will I do when God confronts me?
      When God examines my books, what can I say?
Didn't the same God who made me, make them?
      Aren't we all made of the same stuff, equals before God?

16-18 "Have I ignored the needs of the poor,
      turned my back on the indigent,
Taken care of my own needs and fed my own face
      while they languished?
Wasn't my home always open to them?
      Weren't they always welcome at my table?

19-20 "Have I ever left a poor family shivering in the cold
      when they had no warm clothes?
Didn't the poor bless me when they saw me coming,
      knowing I'd brought coats from my closet?

21-23 "If I've ever used my strength and influence
      to take advantage of the unfortunate,

Go ahead, break both my arms,
    cut off all my fingers!
The fear of God has kept me from these things —
    how else could I ever face him?

IF ONLY SOMEONE WOULD GIVE ME A HEARING!

24-28   "Did I set my heart on making big money
    or worship at the bank?
Did I boast about my wealth,
    show off because I was well-off?
Was I ever so awed by the sun's brilliance
    and moved by the moon's beauty
That I let myself become seduced by them
    and worshiped them on the sly?
If so, I would deserve the worst of punishments,
    for I would be betraying God himself.

29-30   "Did I ever crow over my enemy's ruin?
    Or gloat over my rival's bad luck?
No, I never said a word of detraction,
    never cursed them, even under my breath.

31-34   "Didn't those who worked for me say,
    'He fed us well. There were always second helpings'?
And no stranger ever had to spend a night in the street;
    my doors were always open to travelers.
Did I hide my sin the way Adam did,
    or conceal my guilt behind closed doors
Because I was afraid what people would say,
    fearing the gossip of the neighbors so much
That I turned myself into a recluse?
    You know good and well that I didn't.

35-37   "Oh, if only someone would give me a hearing!
    I've signed my name to my defense — let the
      Almighty One answer!
    I want to see my indictment in writing.
Anyone's welcome to read my defense;
    I'll write it on a poster and carry it around town.
I'm prepared to account for every move I've ever made —
    to anyone and everyone, prince or pauper.

38-40   "If the very ground that I farm accuses me,
    if even the furrows fill with tears from my abuse,
If I've ever raped the earth for my own profit
    or dispossessed its rightful owners,
Then curse it with thistles instead of wheat,
    curse it with weeds instead of barley."

The words of Job to his three friends were finished.

ELIHU SPEAKS
GOD'S SPIRIT MAKES WISDOM POSSIBLE

1-5

32 Job's three friends now fell silent. They were talked out, stymied because Job wouldn't budge an inch — wouldn't admit to an ounce of guilt. Then Elihu lost his temper. (Elihu was the son of Barakel the Buzite from the clan of Ram.) He blazed out in anger against Job for pitting his righteousness against God's. He was also angry with the three friends because they had neither come up with an answer nor proved Job wrong. Elihu had waited with Job while they spoke because they were all older than he. But when he saw that the three other men had exhausted their arguments, he exploded with pent-up anger.

6-10   This is what Elihu, son of Barakel the Buzite, said:

"I'm a young man,
    and you are all old and experienced.
That's why I kept quiet
    and held back from joining the discussion.
I kept thinking, 'Experience will tell.
    The longer you live, the wiser you become.'
But I see I was wrong — it's God's Spirit in a person,
    the breath of the Almighty One, that makes wise human insight possible.
The experts have no corner on wisdom;
    getting old doesn't guarantee good sense.
So I've decided to speak up. Listen well!
    I'm going to tell you exactly what I think.

11-14   "I hung on your words while you spoke,
    listened carefully to your arguments.
While you searched for the right words,
    I was all ears.
And now what have you proved? Nothing.
    Nothing you say has even touched Job.
And don't excuse yourselves by saying, 'We've done our best.
    Now it's up to God to talk sense into him.'
Job has yet to contend with me.
    And rest assured, I won't be using *your* arguments!

15-22   "Do you three have nothing else to say?
    Of *course* you don't! You're total frauds!
Why should I wait any longer,
    now that you're stopped dead in your tracks?
I'm ready to speak my piece. That's right!
    It's my turn — and it's about time!
I've got a lot to say,
    and I'm bursting to say it.
The pressure has built up, like lava beneath the earth.
    I'm a volcano ready to blow.
I *have* to speak — I have no choice.
    I have to say what's on my heart,
And I'm going to say it straight —

the truth, the whole truth, and nothing but the truth.
I was never any good at bootlicking;
   my Maker would make short work of me if I started in now!"

1-4   **33** "So please, Job, hear me out,
   honor me by listening to me.
   What I'm about to say
has been carefully thought out.
I have no ulterior motives in this;
   I'm speaking honestly from my heart.
The Spirit of God made me what I am,
   the breath of God Almighty gave me life!

God Always Answers, One Way or Another

5-7   "And if you think you can prove me wrong, do it.
   Lay out your arguments. Stand up for yourself!
Look, I'm human — no better than you;
   we're both made of the same kind of mud.
So let's work this through together;
   don't let my aggressiveness overwhelm you.

8-11   "Here's what you said.
   I heard you say it with my own ears.
You said, 'I'm pure — I've done nothing wrong.
   Believe me, I'm clean — my conscience is clear.
But God keeps picking on me;
   he treats me like I'm his enemy.
He's thrown me in jail;
   he keeps me under constant surveillance.'

12-14   "But let me tell you, Job, you're wrong, dead wrong!
   God is far greater than any human.
So how dare you haul him into court,
   and then complain that he won't answer your charges?
God always answers, one way or another,
   even when people don't recognize his presence.

15-18   "In a dream, for instance, a vision at night,
   when men and women are deep in sleep,
   fast asleep in their beds —
God opens their ears
   and impresses them with warnings
To turn them back from something bad they're planning,
   from some reckless choice,
And keep them from an early grave,
   from the river of no return.

19-22   "Or, God might get their attention through pain,
   by throwing them on a bed of suffering,
So they can't stand the sight of food,
   have no appetite for their favorite treats.

They lose weight, wasting away to nothing,
  reduced to a bag of bones.
They hang on the cliff-edge of death,
  knowing the next breath may be their last.

23-25 "But even then an angel could come,
  a champion — there are thousands of them! —
  to take up your cause,
A messenger who would mercifully intervene,
  canceling the death sentence with the words:
  'I've come up with the ransom!'
Before you know it, you're healed,
  the very picture of health!

26-28 "Or, you may fall on your knees and pray — to God's delight!
  You'll see God's smile and celebrate,
  finding yourself set right with God.
You'll sing God's praises to everyone you meet,
  testifying, 'I messed up my life —
  and let me tell you, it wasn't worth it.
But God stepped in and saved me from certain death.
  I'm alive again! Once more I see the light!'

29-30 "This is the way God works.
  Over and over again
He pulls our souls back from certain destruction
  so we'll see the light — and *live* in the light!

31-33 "Keep listening, Job.
  Don't interrupt — I'm not finished yet.
But if you think of anything I should know, tell me.
  There's nothing I'd like better than to see your name cleared.
Meanwhile, keep listening. Don't distract me with interruptions.
  I'm going to teach you the basics of wisdom."

ELIHU'S SECOND SPEECH
IT'S IMPOSSIBLE FOR GOD TO DO EVIL

1-4 # 34 Elihu continued:

"So, my fine friends — listen to me,
  and see what you think of this.
Isn't it just common sense —
  as common as the sense of taste —
To put our heads together
  and figure out what's going on here?

5-9 "We've all heard Job say, 'I'm in the right,
  but God won't give me a fair trial.
When I defend myself, I'm called a liar to my face.
  I've done nothing wrong, and I get punished anyway.'
Have you ever heard anything to beat this?

Does nothing faze this man Job?
Do you think he's spent too much time in bad company,
  hanging out with the wrong crowd,
So that now he's parroting their line:
  'It doesn't pay to try to please God'?

10-15 "You're veterans in dealing with these matters;
  certainly we're of one mind on this.
It's impossible for God to do anything evil;
  no way can the Mighty One do wrong.
He makes us pay for exactly what we've done — no more, no less.
  Our chickens always come home to roost.
It's impossible for God to do anything wicked,
  for the Mighty One to subvert justice.
He's the one who runs the earth!
  He cradles the whole world in his hand!
If he decided to hold his breath,
  every man, woman, and child would die for lack of air.

GOD IS WORKING BEHIND THE SCENES

16-20 "So, Job, use your head;
  this is all pretty obvious.
Can someone who hates order, keep order?
  Do you dare condemn the righteous, mighty God?
Doesn't God always tell it like it is,
  exposing corrupt rulers as scoundrels and criminals?
Does he play favorites with the rich and famous and slight the poor?
  Isn't he equally responsible to everybody?
Don't people who deserve it die without notice?
  Don't wicked rulers tumble to their doom?
When the so-called great ones are wiped out,
  we know God is working behind the scenes.

21-28 "He has his eyes on every man and woman.
  He doesn't miss a trick.
There is no night dark enough, no shadow deep enough,
  to hide those who do evil.
God doesn't need to gather any more evidence;
  their sin is an open-and-shut case.
He deposes the so-called high and mighty without asking questions,
  and replaces them at once with others.
Nobody gets by with anything; overnight,
  judgment is signed, sealed, and delivered.
He punishes the wicked for their wickedness
  out in the open where everyone can see it,
Because they quit following him,
  no longer even thought about him or his ways.
Their apostasy was announced by the cry of the poor;
  the cry of the afflicted got God's attention.

BECAUSE YOU REFUSE TO LIVE ON GOD'S TERMS

29-30   "If God is silent, what's that to you?
      If he turns his face away, what can you do about it?
  But whether silent or hidden, he's there, ruling,
      so that those who hate God won't take over
      and ruin people's lives.

31-33   "So why don't you simply confess to God?
      Say, 'I sinned, but I'll sin no more.
  Teach me to see what I still don't see.
      Whatever evil I've done, I'll do it no more.'
  Just because you refuse to live on God's terms,
      do you think he should start living on yours?
  You choose. I can't do it for you.
      Tell me what you decide.

34-37   "All right-thinking people say —
      and the wise who have listened to me concur —
  'Job is an ignoramus.
      He talks utter nonsense.'
  Job, you need to be pushed to the wall and called to account
      for wickedly talking back to God the way you have.
  You've compounded your original sin
      by rebelling against God's discipline,
  Defiantly shaking your fist at God,
      piling up indictments against the Almighty One."

ELIHU'S THIRD SPEECH
WHEN GOD MAKES CREATION A CLASSROOM

1-3   **35**   Elihu lit into Job again:

      "Does this kind of thing make any sense?
  First you say, 'I'm perfectly innocent before God.'
  And then you say, 'It doesn't make a bit of difference
      whether I've sinned or not.'

4-8   "Well, I'm going to show you
      that you don't know what you're talking about,
      neither you nor your friends.
  Look up at the sky. Take a long hard look.
      See those clouds towering above you?
  If you sin, what difference could that make to God?
      No matter how much you sin, will it matter to him?
  Even if you're good, what would God get out of that?
      Do you think he's dependent on your accomplishments?
  The only ones who care whether you're good or bad
      are your family and friends and neighbors.
      God's not dependent on your behavior.

9-15   "When times get bad, people cry out for help.

They cry for relief from being kicked around,
But never give God a thought when things go well,
    when God puts spontaneous songs in their hearts,
When God sets out the entire creation as a science classroom,
    using birds and beasts to teach wisdom.
People are arrogantly indifferent to God—
    until, of course, they're in trouble,
    and then God is indifferent to them.
There's nothing behind such prayers except panic;
    the Almighty pays them no mind.
So why would he notice you
    just because you say you're tired of waiting to be heard,
Or waiting for him to get good and angry
    and do something about the world's problems?

16   "Job, you talk sheer nonsense—
    nonstop nonsense!"

THOSE WHO LEARN FROM THEIR SUFFERING

1-4   **36** Here Elihu took a deep breath, but kept going:

"Stay with me a little longer. I'll convince you.
    There's still more to be said on God's side.
I learned all this firsthand from the Source;
    everything I know about justice I owe to my Maker himself.
Trust me, I'm giving you undiluted truth;
    believe me, I know these things inside and out.

5-15   "It's true that God is all-powerful,
    but he doesn't bully innocent people.
For the wicked, though, it's a different story—
    he doesn't give them the time of day,
    but champions the rights of their victims.
He never takes his eyes off the righteous;
    he honors them lavishly, promotes them endlessly.
When things go badly,
    when affliction and suffering descend,
God tells them where they've gone wrong,
    shows them how their pride has caused their trouble.
He forces them to heed his warning,
    tells them they must repent of their bad life.
If they obey and serve him,
    they'll have a good, long life on easy street.
But if they disobey, they'll be cut down in their prime
    and never know the first thing about life.
Angry people without God pile grievance upon grievance,
    always blaming others for their troubles.
Living it up in sexual excesses,
    virility wasted, they die young.
But those who learn from their suffering,
    God delivers from their suffering.

Obsessed with Putting the Blame on God

16-21 "Oh, Job, don't you see how God's wooing you
  from the jaws of danger?
How he's drawing you into wide-open places —
  inviting you to feast at a table laden with blessings?
And here you are laden with the guilt of the wicked,
  obsessed with putting the blame on *God*!
Don't let your great riches mislead you;
  don't think you can bribe your way out of this.
Did you plan to buy your way out of this?
  Not on your life!
And don't think that night,
  when people sleep off their troubles,
  will bring you any relief.
Above all, don't make things worse with more evil —
  that's what's behind your suffering as it is!

22-25 "Do you have any idea how powerful God is?
  Have you ever heard of a teacher like him?
Has anyone ever had to tell him what to do,
  or correct him, saying, 'You did that all wrong!'?
Remember, then, to praise his workmanship,
  which is so often celebrated in song.
Everybody sees it;
  nobody is too far away to see it.

No One Can Escape from God

26 "Take a long, hard look. See how great he is — infinite,
  greater than anything you could ever imagine or figure out!

27-33 "He pulls water up out of the sea,
  distills it, and fills up his rain-cloud cisterns.
Then the skies open up
  and pour out soaking showers on everyone.
Does anyone have the slightest idea how this happens?
  How he arranges the clouds, how he speaks in thunder?
Just look at that lightning, his sky-filling light show
  illumining the dark depths of the sea!
These are the symbols of his sovereignty,
  his generosity, his loving care.
He hurls arrows of light,
  taking sure and accurate aim.
The High God roars in the thunder,
  angry against evil."

1-13 37 "Whenever this happens, my heart stops —
  I'm stunned, I can't catch my breath.
  Listen to it! Listen to his thunder,
  the rolling, rumbling thunder of his voice.
He lets loose his lightnings from horizon to horizon,

lighting up the earth from pole to pole.
In their wake, the thunder echoes his voice,
    powerful and majestic.
He lets out all the stops, he holds nothing back.
    No one can mistake that voice —
His word thundering so wondrously,
    his mighty acts staggering our understanding.
He orders the snow, 'Blanket the earth!'
    and the rain, 'Soak the whole countryside!'
No one can escape the weather — it's *there*.
    And no one can escape from God.
Wild animals take shelter,
    crawling into their dens,
When blizzards roar out of the north
    and freezing rain crusts the land.
It's God's breath that forms the ice,
    it's God's breath that turns lakes and rivers solid.
And yes, it's God who fills clouds with rainwater
    and hurls lightning from them every which way.
He puts them through their paces — first this way, then that —
    commands them to do what he says all over the world.
Whether for discipline or grace or extravagant love,
    he makes sure they make their mark.

A TERRIBLE BEAUTY STREAMS FROM GOD

14-18 "Job, are you listening? Have you noticed all this?
    Stop in your tracks! Take in God's miracle-wonders!
Do you have any idea how God does it all,
    how he makes bright lightning from dark storms,
How he piles up the cumulus clouds —
    all these miracle-wonders of a perfect Mind?
Why, you don't even know how to keep cool
    on a sweltering hot day,
So how could you even dream
    of making a dent in that hot-tin-roof sky?

19-22 "If you're so smart, give us a lesson in how to address God.
    We're in the dark and can't figure it out.
Do you think I'm dumb enough to challenge God?
    Wouldn't that just be asking for trouble?
No one in his right mind stares straight at the sun
    on a clear and cloudless day.
As gold comes from the northern mountains,
    so a terrible beauty streams from God.

23-24 "Mighty God! Far beyond our reach!
    Unsurpassable in power and justice!
    It's unthinkable that he'd treat anyone unfairly.
So bow to him in deep reverence, one and all!
    If you're wise, you'll most certainly worship him."

GOD CONFRONTS JOB
HAVE YOU GOTTEN TO THE BOTTOM OF THINGS?

38 And now, finally, GOD answered Job from the eye of a violent
storm. He said:

1-11

"Why do you confuse the issue?
Why do you talk without knowing what you're talking about?
Pull yourself together, Job!
Up on your feet! Stand tall!
I have some questions for you,
and I want some straight answers.
Where were you when I created the earth?
Tell me, since you know so much!
Who decided on its size? Certainly you'll know that!
Who came up with the blueprints and measurements?
How was its foundation poured,
and who set the cornerstone,
While the morning stars sang in chorus
and all the angels shouted praise?
And who took charge of the ocean
when it gushed forth like a baby from the womb?
That was me! I wrapped it in soft clouds,
and tucked it in safely at night.
Then I made a playpen for it,
a strong playpen so it couldn't run loose,
And said, 'Stay here, this is your place.
Your wild tantrums are confined to this place.'

12-15

"And have you ever ordered Morning, 'Get up!'
told Dawn, 'Get to work!'
So you could seize Earth like a blanket
and shake out the wicked like cockroaches?
As the sun brings everything to light,
brings out all the colors and shapes,
The cover of darkness is snatched from the wicked —
they're caught in the very act!

16-18

"Have you ever gotten to the true bottom of things,
explored the labyrinthine caves of deep ocean?
Do you know the first thing about death?
Do you have one clue regarding death's dark mysteries?
And do you have any idea how large this earth is?
Speak up if you have even the beginning of an answer.

19-21

"Do you know where Light comes from
and where Darkness lives
So you can take them by the hand
and lead them home when they get lost?
Why, of *course* you know that.
You've known them all your life,
grown up in the same neighborhood with them!

22-30
"Have you ever traveled to where snow is made,
    seen the vault where hail is stockpiled,
The arsenals of hail and snow that I keep in readiness
    for times of trouble and battle and war?
Can you find your way to where lightning is launched,
    or to the place from which the wind blows?
Who do you suppose carves canyons
    for the downpours of rain, and charts
    the route of thunderstorms
That bring water to unvisited fields,
    deserts no one ever lays eyes on,
Drenching the useless wastelands
    so they're carpeted with wildflowers and grass?
And who do you think is the father of rain and dew,
    the mother of ice and frost?
You don't for a minute imagine
    these marvels of weather just happen, do you?

31-33
"Can you catch the eye of the beautiful Pleiades sisters,
    or distract Orion from his hunt?
Can you get Venus to look your way,
    or get the Great Bear and her cubs to come out and play?
Do you know the first thing about the sky's constellations
    and how they affect things on Earth?

34-35
"Can you get the attention of the clouds,
    and commission a shower of rain?
Can you take charge of the lightning bolts
    and have them report to you for orders?

WHAT DO YOU HAVE TO SAY FOR YOURSELF?

36-38
"Who do you think gave weather-wisdom to the ibis,
    and storm-savvy to the rooster?
Does anyone know enough to number all the clouds
    or tip over the rain barrels of heaven
When the earth is cracked and dry,
    the ground baked hard as a brick?

39-41
"Can you teach the lioness to stalk her prey
    and satisfy the appetite of her cubs
As they crouch in their den,
    waiting hungrily in their cave?
And who sets out food for the ravens
    when their young cry to God,
    fluttering about because they have no food?"

1-4
39 "Do you know the month when mountain goats give birth?
    Have you ever watched a doe bear her fawn?
    Do you know how many months she is pregnant?
Do you know the season of her delivery,
    when she crouches down and drops her offspring?

Her young ones flourish and are soon on their own;
  they leave and don't come back.

5-8 "Who do you think set the wild donkey free,
  opened the corral gates and let him go?
I gave him the whole wilderness to roam in,
  the rolling plains and wide-open places.
He laughs at his city cousins, who are harnessed and harried.
  He's oblivious to the cries of teamsters.
He grazes freely through the hills,
  nibbling anything that's green.

9-12 "Will the wild buffalo condescend to serve you,
  volunteer to spend the night in your barn?
Can you imagine hitching your plow to a buffalo
  and getting him to till your fields?
He's hugely strong, yes, but could you trust him,
  would you dare turn the job over to him?
You wouldn't for a minute depend on him, would you,
  to do what you said when you said it?

13-18 "The ostrich flaps her wings futilely—
  all those beautiful feathers, but useless!
She lays her eggs on the hard ground,
  leaves them there in the dirt, exposed to the weather,
Not caring that they might get stepped on and cracked
  or trampled by some wild animal.
She's negligent with her young, as if they weren't even hers.
  She cares nothing about anything.
She wasn't created very smart, that's for sure,
  wasn't given her share of good sense.
But when she runs, oh, how she runs,
  laughing, leaving horse and rider in the dust.

19-25 "Are you the one who gave the horse his prowess
  and adorned him with a shimmering mane?
Did you create him to prance proudly
  and strike terror with his royal snorts?
He paws the ground fiercely, eager and spirited,
  then charges into the fray.
He laughs at danger, fearless,
  doesn't shy away from the sword.
The banging and clanging
  of quiver and lance don't faze him.
He quivers with excitement, and at the trumpet blast
  races off at a gallop.
At the sound of the trumpet he neighs mightily,
  smelling the excitement of battle from a long way off,
  catching the rolling thunder of the war cries.

26-30 "Was it through your know-how that the hawk learned to fly,

soaring effortlessly on thermal updrafts?
Did you command the eagle's flight,
    and teach her to build her nest in the heights,
Perfectly at home on the high cliff face,
    invulnerable on pinnacle and crag?
From her perch she searches for prey,
    spies it at a great distance.
Her young gorge themselves on carrion;
    wherever there's a roadkill, you'll see her circling."

40 ¹⁻² GOD then confronted Job directly:

"Now what do you have to say for yourself?
Are you going to haul me, the Mighty One, into court and press
    charges?"

JOB ANSWERS GOD
I'M READY TO SHUT UP AND LISTEN

³⁻⁵ Job answered:

"I'm speechless, in awe — words fail me.
    I should never have opened my mouth!
I've talked too much, way too much.
    I'm ready to shut up and listen."

GOD'S SECOND SET OF QUESTIONS
I WANT STRAIGHT ANSWERS

⁶⁻⁷ GOD addressed Job next from the eye of the storm, and this is what he said:

"I have some more questions for you,
    and I want straight answers.

⁸⁻¹⁴ "Do you presume to tell me what I'm doing wrong?
    Are you calling me a sinner so you can be a saint?
Do you have an arm like my arm?
    Can you shout in thunder the way I can?
Go ahead, show your stuff.
    Let's see what you're made of, what you can do.
Unleash your outrage.
    Target the arrogant and lay them flat.
Target the arrogant and bring them to their knees.
    Stop the wicked in their tracks — make mincemeat of them!
Dig a mass grave and dump them in it —
    faceless corpses in an unmarked grave.
I'll gladly step aside and hand things over to you —
    you can surely save yourself with no help from me!

¹⁵⁻²⁴ "Look at the land beast, Behemoth. I created him as well as you.
    Grazing on grass, docile as a cow —
Just look at the strength of his back,
    the powerful muscles of his belly.

His tail sways like a cedar in the wind;
    his huge legs are like beech trees.
His skeleton is made of steel,
    every bone in his body hard as steel.
Most magnificent of all my creatures,
    but I still lead him around like a lamb!
The grass-covered hills serve him meals,
    while field mice frolic in his shadow.
He takes afternoon naps under shade trees,
    cools himself in the reedy swamps,
Lazily cool in the leafy shadows
    as the breeze moves through the willows.
And when the river rages he doesn't budge,
    stolid and unperturbed even when the Jordan goes wild.
But you'd never want him for a pet —
    you'd never be able to housebreak him!"

I Run This Universe

1-11   **41**   "Or can you pull in the sea beast, Leviathan, with a fly rod
        and stuff him in your creel?
        Can you lasso him with a rope,
    or snag him with an anchor?
Will he beg you over and over for mercy,
    or flatter you with flowery speech?
Will he apply for a job with you
    to run errands and serve you the rest of your life?
Will you play with him as if he were a pet goldfish?
    Will you make him the mascot of the neighborhood children?
Will you put him on display in the market
    and have shoppers haggle over the price?
Could you shoot him full of arrows like a pin cushion,
    or drive harpoons into his huge head?
If you so much as lay a hand on him,
    you won't live to tell the story.
What hope would you have with such a creature?
    Why, one look at him would do you in!
If you can't hold your own against his glowering visage,
    how, then, do you expect to stand up to *me*?
Who could confront me and get by with it?
    I'm *in charge* of all this — I *run* this universe!

12-17   "But I've more to say about Leviathan, the sea beast,
    his enormous bulk, his beautiful shape.
Who would even dream of piercing that tough skin
    or putting those jaws into bit and bridle?
And who would dare knock at the door of his mouth
    filled with row upon row of fierce teeth?
His pride is invincible;
    nothing can make a dent in that pride.
Nothing can get through that proud skin —
    impervious to weapons and weather,

The thickest and toughest of hides,
    impenetrable!

18-34 "He snorts and the world lights up with fire,
    he blinks and the dawn breaks.
Comets pour out of his mouth,
    fireworks arc and branch.
Smoke erupts from his nostrils
    like steam from a boiling pot.
He blows and fires blaze;
    flames of fire stream from his mouth.
All muscle he is — sheer and seamless muscle.
    To meet him is to dance with death.
Sinewy and lithe,
    there's not a soft spot in his entire body —
As tough inside as out,
    rock-hard, invulnerable.
Even angels run for cover when he surfaces,
    cowering before his tail-thrashing turbulence.
Javelins bounce harmlessly off his hide,
    harpoons ricochet wildly.
Iron bars are so much straw to him,
    bronze weapons beneath notice.
Arrows don't even make him blink;
    bullets make no more impression than raindrops.
A battle ax is nothing but a splinter of kindling;
    he treats a brandished harpoon as a joke.
His belly is armor-plated, inexorable —
    unstoppable as a barge.
He roils deep ocean the way you'd boil water,
    he whips the sea like you'd whip an egg into batter.
With a luminous trail stretching out behind him,
    you might think Ocean had grown a gray beard!
There's nothing on this earth quite like him,
    not an ounce of fear in *that* creature!
He surveys all the high and mighty —
    king of the ocean, king of the deep!"

JOB WORSHIPS GOD
I Babbled on About Things Far Beyond Me

1-6 ## 42 Job answered God:

"I'm convinced: You can do anything and everything.
    Nothing and no one can upset your plans.
You asked, 'Who is this muddying the water,
    ignorantly confusing the issue, second-guessing my purposes?'
I admit it. I was the one. I babbled on about things far beyond me,
    made small talk about wonders way over my head.
You told me, 'Listen, and let me do the talking.
    Let me ask the questions. *You* give the answers.'
I admit I once lived by rumors of you;

now I have it all firsthand — from my own eyes and ears!
I'm sorry — forgive me. I'll never do that again, I promise!
I'll never again live on crusts of hearsay, crumbs of rumor."

GOD RESTORES JOB
I WILL ACCEPT HIS PRAYER

7-8 After GOD had finished addressing Job, he turned to Eliphaz the Temanite and said, "I've had it with you and your two friends. I'm fed up! You haven't been honest either with me or about me — not the way my friend Job has. So here's what you must do. Take seven bulls and seven rams, and go to my friend Job. Sacrifice a burnt offering on your own behalf. My friend Job will pray for you, and I will accept his prayer. He will ask me not to treat you as you deserve for talking nonsense about me, and for not being honest with me, as he has."

9 They did it. Eliphaz the Temanite, Bildad the Shuhite, and Zophar the Naamathite did what GOD commanded. And GOD accepted Job's prayer.

10-11 After Job had interceded for his friends, GOD restored his fortune — and then doubled it! All his brothers and sisters and friends came to his house and celebrated. They told him how sorry they were, and consoled him for all the trouble GOD had brought him. Each of them brought generous house-warming gifts.

12-15 GOD blessed Job's later life even more than his earlier life. He ended up with fourteen thousand sheep, six thousand camels, one thousand teams of oxen, and one thousand donkeys. He also had seven sons and three daughters. He named the first daughter Dove, the second, Cinnamon, and the third, Darkeyes. There was not a woman in that country as beautiful as Job's daughters. Their father treated them as equals with their brothers, providing the same inheritance.

16-17 Job lived on another 140 years, living to see his children and grand-children — four generations of them! Then he died — an old man, a full life.

PSALMS

Most Christians for most of the Christian centuries have learned to pray by praying the Psalms. The Hebrews, with several centuries of a head start on us in matters of prayer and worship, provided us with this prayer book that gives us a language adequate for responding to the God who speaks to us.

The stimulus to paraphrase the Psalms into a contemporary idiom comes from my lifetime of work as a pastor. As a pastor I was charged with, among other things, teaching people to pray, helping them to give voice to the entire experience of being human, and to do it both honestly and thoroughly. I found that it was not as easy as I expected. Getting started is easy enough. The impulse to pray is deep within us, at the very center of our created being, and so practically anything will do to get us started — "Help" and "Thanks!" are our basic prayers. But honesty and thoroughness don't come quite as spontaneously.

Faced with the prospect of conversation with a holy God who speaks worlds into being, it is not surprising that we have trouble. We feel awkward and out of place: "I'm not good enough for this. I'll wait until I clean up my act and prove that I am a decent person." Or we excuse ourselves on the grounds that our vocabulary is inadequate: "Give me a few months — or years! — to practice prayers that are polished enough for such a sacred meeting. Then I won't feel so stuttery and ill at ease."

My usual response when presented with these difficulties is to put the Psalms in a person's hand and say, "Go home and pray these. You've got wrong ideas about prayer; the praying you find in these Psalms will dispel the wrong ideas and introduce you to the real thing." A common response of those who do what I ask is surprise — they don't expect this kind of thing in the Bible. And then I express surprise at their surprise: "Did you think these would be the prayers of *nice* people? Did you think the psalmists' language would be polished and polite?"

Untutored, we tend to think that prayer is what good people do when they are doing their best. It is not. Inexperienced, we suppose that there must be an "insider" language that must be acquired before God takes us seriously in our prayer. There is not. Prayer is elemental, not advanced, language. It is the means by which our language becomes honest, true, and personal in response to God. It is the means by which we get everything in our lives out in the open before God.

But even with the Psalms in their hands and my pastoral encouragement, people often tell me that they still don't get it. In English translation, the Psalms often sound smooth and polished, sonorous with Elizabethan rhythms and diction. As literature, they are beyond compare. But as *prayer*, as the utterances of men and women passionate for God in moments of anger and praise and lament, these translations miss something. *Grammatically*, they are accurate. The scholarship undergirding the translations is superb and devout. But as *prayers* they are not quite right. The Psalms in Hebrew are earthy and rough. They are not genteel. They are not the prayers of nice people, couched in cultured language.

And so in my pastoral work of teaching people to pray, I started paraphrasing the Psalms into the rhythms and idiom of contemporary English. I wanted to provide men and women access to the immense range and the terrific energies of prayer in the kind of language that is most immediate to them, which also happens to be the language in which these psalm prayers were first expressed and written by David and his successors.

I continue to want to do that, convinced that only as we develop raw honesty and detailed thoroughness in our praying do we become whole, truly human in Jesus Christ, who also prayed the Psalms.

PSALMS

1 **1** How well God must like you —
  you don't hang out at Sin Saloon,
  you don't slink along Dead-End Road,
  you don't go to Smart-Mouth College.

2-3 Instead you thrill to GOD's Word,
  you chew on Scripture day and night.
You're a tree replanted in Eden,
  bearing fresh fruit every month,
Never dropping a leaf,
  always in blossom.

4-5 You're not at all like the wicked,
  who are mere windblown dust —
Without defense in court,
  unfit company for innocent people.

6 GOD charts the road you take.
The road *they* take is Skid Row.

1-6 **2** Why the big noise, nations?
  Why the mean plots, peoples?
  Earth-leaders push for position,
Demagogues and delegates meet for summit talks,
The God-deniers, the Messiah-defiers:
"Let's get free of God!
Cast loose from Messiah!"
Heaven-throned God breaks out laughing.
At first he's amused at their presumption;
Then he gets good and angry.
Furiously, he shuts them up:
"Don't you know there's a King in Zion? A coronation banquet
Is spread for him on the holy summit."

7-9 Let me tell you what GOD said next.
He said, "You're my son,
And today is your birthday.
What do you want? Name it:
Nations as a present? continents as a prize?
You can command them all to dance for you,
Or throw them out with tomorrow's trash."

10-12 So, rebel-kings, use your heads;
Upstart-judges, learn your lesson:
Worship GOD in adoring embrace,
Celebrate in trembling awe. Kiss Messiah!

Your very lives are in danger, you know;
His anger is about to explode,
But if you make a run for God — you won't regret it!

1-2 **3** GOD! Look! Enemies past counting!
Enemies sprouting like mushrooms,
Mobs of them all around me, roaring their mockery:
"Hah! No help for *him* from God!"

3-4 But you, GOD, shield me on all sides;
You ground my feet, you lift my head high;
With all my might I shout up to GOD,
His answers thunder from the holy mountain.

5-6 I stretch myself out. I sleep.
Then I'm up again — rested, tall and steady,
Fearless before the enemy mobs
Coming at me from all sides.

7 Up, GOD! My God, help me!
Slap their faces,
First this cheek, then the other,
Your fist hard in their teeth!

8 Real help comes from GOD.
Your blessing clothes your people!

1 **4** When I call, give me answers. God, take my side!
Once, in a tight place, you gave me room;
Now I'm in trouble again: grace me! hear me!

2 You rabble — how long do I put up with your scorn?
How long will you lust after lies?
How long will you live crazed by illusion?

3 Look at this: look
Who got picked by GOD!
He listens the split second I call to him.

4-5 Complain if you must, but don't lash out.
Keep your mouth shut, and let your heart do the talking.
Build your case before God and wait for his verdict.

6-7 Why is everyone hungry for *more*? "More, more," they say.
"More, more."
I have God's more-than-enough,
More joy in one ordinary day

7-8 Than they get in all their shopping sprees.
At day's end I'm ready for sound sleep,
For you, GOD, have put my life back together.

A DAVID PSALM

1-3 **5** Listen, GOD! Please, pay attention!
    Can you make sense of these ramblings,
    my groans and cries?
    King-God, I need your help.
Every morning
    you'll hear me at it again.
Every morning
    I lay out the pieces of my life
    on your altar
    and watch for fire to descend.

4-6 You don't socialize with Wicked,
    or invite Evil over as your houseguest.
Hot-Air-Boaster collapses in front of you;
    you shake your head over Mischief-Maker.
GOD destroys Lie-Speaker;
    Blood-Thirsty and Truth-Bender disgust you.

7-8 And here I am, your invited guest —
    it's incredible!
I enter your house; here I am,
    prostrate in your inner sanctum,
Waiting for directions
    to get me safely through enemy lines.

9-10 Every word they speak is a land mine;
    their lungs breathe out poison gas.
Their throats are gaping graves,
    their tongues slick as mudslides.
Pile on the guilt, God!
    Let their so-called wisdom wreck them.
Kick them out! They've had their chance.

11-12 But you'll welcome us with open arms
    when we run for cover to you.
Let the party last all night!
    Stand guard over our celebration.
You are famous, GOD, for welcoming God-seekers,
    for decking us out in delight.

A DAVID PSALM

1-2 **6** Please, GOD, no more yelling,
    no more trips to the woodshed.
Treat me nice for a change;
    I'm so starved for affection.

2-3 Can't you see I'm black-and-blue,
    beat up badly in bones and soul?
GOD, how long will it take
    for you to let up?

4-5 Break in, GOD, and break up this fight;
    if you love me at all, get me out of here.
I'm no good to you dead, am I?
    I can't sing in your choir if I'm buried in some tomb!

6-7 I'm tired of all this — so tired. My bed
    has been floating forty days and nights
On the flood of my tears.
    My mattress is soaked, soggy with tears.
The sockets of my eyes are black holes;
    nearly blind, I squint and grope.

8-9 Get out of here, you Devil's crew:
    at last GOD has heard my sobs.
My requests have all been granted,
    my prayers are answered.

10 Cowards, my enemies disappear.
Disgraced, they turn tail and run.

A DAVID PSALM

1-2 **7** GOD! God! I am running to you for dear life;
    the chase is wild.
  If they catch me, I'm finished:
ripped to shreds by foes fierce as lions,
    dragged into the forest and left
    unlooked for, unremembered.

3-5 GOD, if I've done what they say —
    betrayed my friends,
    ripped off my enemies —
If my hands are really that dirty,
    let them get me, walk all over me,
    leave me flat on my face in the dirt.

6-8 Stand up, GOD; pit your holy fury
    against my furious enemies.
Wake up, God. My accusers have packed
    the courtroom; it's judgment time.
Take your place on the bench, reach for your gavel,
    throw out the false charges against me.
I'm ready, confident in your verdict:
    "Innocent."

9-11 Close the book on Evil, GOD,
    but publish your mandate for us.

You get us ready for life:
    you probe for our soft spots,
    you knock off our rough edges.
And I'm feeling so fit, so safe:
    made right, kept right.
God in solemn honor does things right,
    but his nerves are sandpapered raw.

11-13   Nobody gets by with anything.
    God is already in action —
Sword honed on his whetstone,
    bow strung, arrow on the string,
Lethal weapons in hand,
    each arrow a flaming missile.

14   Look at that guy!
    He had sex with sin,
    he's pregnant with evil.
Oh, look! He's having
    the baby — a Lie-Baby!

15-16   See that man shoveling day after day,
    digging, then concealing, his man-trap
    down that lonely stretch of road?
Go back and look again — you'll see him in it headfirst,
    legs waving in the breeze.
That's what happens:
    mischief backfires;
    violence boomerangs.

17   I'm thanking God, who makes things right.
I'm singing the fame of heaven-high GOD.

A DAVID PSALM

1   GOD, brilliant Lord,
    yours is a household name.

2   Nursing infants gurgle choruses about you;
    toddlers shout the songs
That drown out enemy talk,
    and silence atheist babble.

3-4   I look up at your macro-skies, dark and enormous,
    your handmade sky-jewelry,
Moon and stars mounted in their settings.
    Then I look at my micro-self and wonder,
Why do you bother with us?
    Why take a second look our way?

5-8   Yet we've so narrowly missed being gods,
    bright with Eden's dawn light.

You put us in charge of your handcrafted world,
    repeated to us your Genesis-charge,
Made us lords of sheep and cattle,
    even animals out in the wild,
Birds flying and fish swimming,
    whales singing in the ocean deeps.

9   GOD, brilliant Lord,
    your name echoes around the world.

A DAVID PSALM

1-2 **9** I'm thanking you, GOD, from a full heart,
    I'm writing the book on your wonders.
    I'm whistling, laughing, and jumping for joy;
I'm singing your song, High God.

3-4 The day my enemies turned tail and ran,
    they stumbled on you and fell on their faces.
You took over and set everything right;
    when I needed you, you were there, taking charge.

5-6 You blow the whistle on godless nations;
    you throw dirty players out of the game,
    wipe their names right off the roster.
Enemies disappear from the sidelines,
    their reputation trashed,
    their names erased from the halls of fame.

7-8 GOD holds the high center,
    he sees and sets the world's mess right.
He decides what is right for us earthlings,
    gives people their just deserts.

9-10 GOD's a safe-house for the battered,
    a sanctuary during bad times.
The moment you arrive, you relax;
    you're never sorry you knocked.

11-12 Sing your songs to Zion-dwelling GOD,
    tell his stories to everyone you meet:
How he tracks down killers
    yet keeps his eye on us,
    registers every whimper and moan.

13-14 Be kind to me, GOD;
    I've been kicked around long enough.
Once you've pulled me back
    from the gates of death,
I'll write the book on Hallelujahs;
    on the corner of Main and First
    I'll hold a street meeting;

I'll be the song leader; we'll fill the air
    with salvation songs.

15-16   They're trapped, those godless countries,
        in the very snares they set,
Their feet all tangled
    in the net they spread.
They have no excuse;
    the way God works is well-known.
The cunning machinery made by the wicked
    has maimed their own hands.

17-20   The wicked bought a one-way
        ticket to hell.
No longer will the poor be nameless —
    no more humiliation for the humble.
Up, GOD! Aren't you fed up with their empty strutting?
    Expose these grand pretensions!
Shake them up, GOD!
    Show them how silly they look.

1-2   **10** GOD, are you avoiding me?
        Where are you when I need you?
        Full of hot air, the wicked
are hot on the trail of the poor.
Trip them up, tangle them up
    in their fine-tuned plots.

3-4   The wicked are windbags,
        the swindlers have foul breath.
The wicked snub GOD,
    their noses stuck high in the air.
Their graffiti are scrawled on the walls:
    "Catch us if you can!" "God is dead."

5-6   They care nothing for what you think;
        if you get in their way, they blow you off.
They live (they think) a charmed life:
    "We can't go wrong. This is our lucky year!"

7-8   They carry a mouthful of hexes,
        their tongues spit venom like adders.
They hide behind ordinary people,
    then pounce on their victims.

9   They mark the luckless,
        then wait like a hunter in a blind;
When the poor wretch wanders too close,
    they stab him in the back.

10-11   The hapless fool is kicked to the ground,

the unlucky victim is brutally axed.
He thinks God has dumped him,
    he's sure that God is indifferent to his plight.

12-13   Time to get up, GOD — get moving.
    The luckless think they're Godforsaken.
They wonder why the wicked scorn God
    and get away with it,
Why the wicked are so cocksure
    they'll never come up for audit.

14   But you know all about it —
    the contempt, the abuse.
I dare to believe that the luckless
    will get lucky someday in you.
You won't let them down:
    orphans won't be orphans forever.

15-16   Break the wicked right arms,
    break all the evil left arms.
Search and destroy
    every sign of crime.
GOD's grace and order wins;
    godlessness loses.

17-18   The victim's faint pulse picks up;
    the hearts of the hopeless pump red blood
    as you put your ear to their lips.
Orphans get parents,
    the homeless get homes.
The reign of terror is over,
    the rule of the gang lords is ended.

A DAVID PSALM

1-3   **11** I've already run for dear life
    straight to the arms of GOD.
    So why would I run away now
when you say,

"Run to the mountains; the evil
    bows are bent, the wicked arrows
Aimed to shoot under cover of darkness
    at every heart open to God.
The bottom's dropped out of the country;
    good people don't have a chance"?

4-6   But GOD hasn't moved to the mountains;
    his holy address hasn't changed.
He's in charge, as always, his eyes
    taking everything in, his eyelids
Unblinking, examining Adam's unruly brood

inside and out, not missing a thing.
He tests the good and the bad alike;
  if anyone cheats, God's outraged.
Fail the test and you're out,
  out in a hail of firestones,
Drinking from a canteen
  filled with hot desert wind.

7 GOD's business is putting things right;
  he loves getting the lines straight,
Setting us straight. Once we're standing tall,
  we can look him straight in the eye.

A DAVID PSALM

1-2 **12** Quick, GOD, I need your helping hand!
  The last decent person just went down,
  All the friends I depended on gone.
Everyone talks in lie language;
Lies slide off their oily lips.
They doubletalk with forked tongues.

3-4 Slice their lips off their faces! Pull
The braggart tongues from their mouths!
I'm tired of hearing, "We can talk anyone into anything!
Our lips manage the world."

5 Into the hovels of the poor,
Into the dark streets where the homeless groan, God speaks:
"I've had enough; I'm on my way
To heal the ache in the heart of the wretched."

6-8 God's words are pure words,
Pure silver words refined seven times
In the fires of his word-kiln,
Pure on earth as well as in heaven.
GOD, keep us safe from their lies,
From the wicked who stalk us with lies,
From the wicked who collect honors
For their wonderful lies.

A DAVID PSALM

1-2 **13** Long enough, GOD —
    you've ignored me long enough.
    I've looked at the back of your head
  long enough. Long enough
I've carried this ton of trouble,
  lived with a stomach full of pain.
Long enough my arrogant enemies
  have looked down their noses at me.

3-4 Take a good look at me, GOD, my God;

I want to look life in the eye,
So no enemy can get the best of me
    or laugh when I fall on my face.

5-6 I've thrown myself headlong into your arms—
        I'm celebrating your rescue.
I'm singing at the top of my lungs,
        I'm so full of answered prayers.

A DAVID PSALM

1 **14** Bilious and bloated, they gas,
        "God is gone."
        Their words are poison gas,
    fouling the air; they poison
Rivers and skies;
        thistles are their cash crop.

2 GOD sticks his head out of heaven.
        He looks around.
He's looking for someone not stupid—
        one man, even, God-expectant,
        just one God-ready woman.

3 He comes up empty. A string
        of zeros. Useless, unshepherded
Sheep, taking turns pretending
        to be Shepherd.
The ninety and nine
        follow their fellow. ·

4 Don't they know anything,
        all these impostors?
Don't they know
        they can't get away with this—
Treating people like a fast-food meal
        over which they're too busy to pray?

5-6 Night is coming for them, and nightmares,
        for God takes the side of victims.
Do you think you can mess
        with the dreams of the poor?
You can't, for God
        makes their dreams come true.

7 Is there anyone around to save Israel?
        Yes. God is around; GOD turns life around.
Turned-around Jacob skips rope,
        turned-around Israel sings laughter.

15 1 God, who gets invited
to dinner at your place?
How do we get on your guest list?

2 "Walk straight,
act right,
tell the truth.

3-4 "Don't hurt your friend,
don't blame your neighbor;
despise the despicable.

5 "Keep your word even when it costs you,
make an honest living,
never take a bribe.

"You'll never get
blacklisted
if you live like this."

16 1-2 Keep me safe, O God,
I've run for dear life to you.
I say to God, "Be my Lord!"
Without you, nothing makes sense.

3 And these God-chosen lives all around—
what splendid friends they make!

4 Don't just go shopping for a god.
Gods are not for sale.
I swear I'll never treat god-names
like brand-names.

5-6 My choice is you, God, first and only.
And now I find I'm *your* choice!
You set me up with a house and yard.
And then you made me your heir!

7-8 The wise counsel God gives when I'm awake
is confirmed by my sleeping heart.
Day and night I'll stick with God;
I've got a good thing going and I'm not letting go.

9-10 I'm happy from the inside out,
and from the outside in, I'm firmly formed.
You canceled my ticket to hell—
that's not my destination!

11 Now you've got my feet on the life path,
        all radiant from the shining of your face.
    Ever since you took my hand,
        I'm on the right way.

1-2 **17** Listen while I build my case, GOD,
            the most honest prayer you'll ever hear.
            Show the world I'm innocent —
        in your heart you know I am.

3   Go ahead, examine me from inside out,
        surprise me in the middle of the night —
    You'll find I'm just what I say I am.
        My words don't run loose.

4-5 I'm not trying to get my way
        in the world's way.
    I'm trying to get *your* way,
        your Word's way.
    I'm staying on your trail;
        I'm putting one foot
    In front of the other.
        I'm not giving up.

6-7 I call to you, God, because I'm sure of an answer.
        So — answer! bend your ear! listen sharp!
    Paint grace-graffiti on the fences;
        take in your frightened children who
    Are running from the neighborhood bullies
        straight to you.

8-9 Keep your eye on me;
        hide me under your cool wing feathers
    From the wicked who are out to get me,
        from mortal enemies closing in.

10-14 Their hearts are hard as nails,
        their mouths blast hot air.
    They are after me, nipping my heels,
        determined to bring me down,
    Lions ready to rip me apart,
        young lions poised to pounce.
    Up, GOD: beard them! break them!
        By your sword, free me from their clutches;
    Barehanded, GOD, break these mortals,
        these flat-earth people who can't think beyond today.

    I'd like to see their bellies
        swollen with famine food,
    The weeds they've sown

harvested and baked into famine bread,
With second helpings for their children
    and crusts for their babies to chew on.

15 And me? I plan on looking
        you full in the face. When I get up,
    I'll see your full stature
        and live heaven on earth.

A DAVID SONG, WHICH HE SANG TO GOD AFTER BEING
SAVED FROM ALL HIS ENEMIES AND FROM SAUL

1-2 **18** I love you, GOD —
        you make me strong.
    GOD is bedrock under my feet,
    the castle in which I live,
        my rescuing knight.
    My God — the high crag
        where I run for dear life,
        hiding behind the boulders,
        safe in the granite hideout.

3 I sing to GOD, the Praise-Lofty,
        and find myself safe and saved.

4-5 The hangman's noose was tight at my throat;
        devil waters rushed over me.
    Hell's ropes cinched me tight;
        death traps barred every exit.

6 A hostile world! I call to GOD,
        I cry to God to help me.
    From his palace he hears my call;
        my cry brings me right into his presence —
        a private audience!

7-15 Earth wobbles and lurches;
        huge mountains shake like leaves,
    Quake like aspen leaves
        because of his rage.
    His nostrils flare, bellowing smoke;
        his mouth spits fire.
    Tongues of fire dart in and out;
        he lowers the sky.
    He steps down;
        under his feet an abyss opens up.
    He's riding a winged creature,
        swift on wind-wings.
    Now he's wrapped himself
        in a trenchcoat of black-cloud darkness.
    But his cloud-brightness bursts through,
        spraying hailstones and fireballs.

Then GOD thundered out of heaven;
    the High God gave a great shout,
    spraying hailstones and fireballs.
God shoots his arrows — pandemonium!
    He hurls his lightnings — a rout!
The secret sources of ocean are exposed,
    the hidden depths of earth lie uncovered
The moment you roar in protest,
    let loose your hurricane anger.

16-19   But me he caught — reached all the way
    from sky to sea; he pulled me out
Of that ocean of hate, that enemy chaos,
    the void in which I was drowning.
They hit me when I was down,
    but GOD stuck by me.
He stood me up on a wide-open field;
    I stood there saved — surprised to be loved!

20-24   GOD made my life complete
    when I placed all the pieces before him.
When I got my act together,
    he gave me a fresh start.
Now I'm alert to GOD's ways;
    I don't take God for granted.
Every day I review the ways he works;
    I try not to miss a trick.
I feel put back together,
    and I'm watching my step.
GOD rewrote the text of my life
    when I opened the book of my heart to his eyes.

25-27   The good people taste your goodness,
The whole people taste your health,
The true people taste your truth,
The bad ones can't figure you out.
You take the side of the down-and-out,
But the stuck-up you take down a peg.

28-29   Suddenly, GOD, you floodlight my life;
    I'm blazing with glory, God's glory!
I smash the bands of marauders,
    I vault the highest fences.

30   What a God! His road
    stretches straight and smooth.
Every GOD-direction is road-tested.
    Everyone who runs toward him
Makes it.

31-42   Is there any god like GOD?

Are we not at bedrock?
Is not this the God who armed me,
    then aimed me in the right direction?
Now I run like a deer;
    I'm king of the mountain.
He shows me how to fight;
    I can bend a bronze bow!
You protect me with salvation-armor;
    you hold me up with a firm hand,
    caress me with your gentle ways.
You cleared the ground under me
    so my footing was firm.
When I chased my enemies I caught them;
    I didn't let go till they were dead men.
I nailed them; they were down for good;
    then I walked all over them.
You armed me well for this fight,
    you smashed the upstarts.
You made my enemies turn tail,
    and I wiped out the haters.
They cried "uncle"
    but Uncle didn't come;
They yelled for GOD
    and got no for an answer.
I ground them to dust; they gusted in the wind.
    I threw them out, like garbage in the gutter.

43-45   You rescued me from a squabbling people;
    you made me a leader of nations.
People I'd never heard of served me;
    the moment they got wind of me they listened.
The foreign devils gave up; they came
    on their bellies, crawling from their hideouts.

46-48   Live, GOD! Blessings from my Rock,
    my free and freeing God, towering!
This God set things right for me
    and shut up the people who talked back.
He rescued me from enemy anger,
    he pulled me from the grip of upstarts,
He saved me from the bullies.

49-50   That's why I'm thanking you, GOD,
    all over the world.
That's why I'm singing songs
    that rhyme your name.
God's king takes the trophy;
    God's chosen is beloved.
I mean David and all his children —
    always.

A DAVID PSALM

19
1-2 God's glory is on tour in the skies,
      God-craft on exhibit across the horizon.
      Madame Day holds classes every morning,
Professor Night lectures each evening.

3-4 Their words aren't heard,
      their voices aren't recorded,
But their silence fills the earth:
      unspoken truth is spoken everywhere.

4-5 God makes a huge dome
      for the sun — a superdome!
The morning sun's a new husband
      leaping from his honeymoon bed,
The daybreaking sun an athlete
      racing to the tape.

6 That's how God's Word vaults across the skies
      from sunrise to sunset,
Melting ice, scorching deserts,
      warming hearts to faith.

7-9 The revelation of GOD is whole
      and pulls our lives together.
The signposts of GOD are clear
      and point out the right road.
The life-maps of GOD are right,
      showing the way to joy.
The directions of GOD are plain
      and easy on the eyes.
GOD's reputation is twenty-four-carat gold,
      with a lifetime guarantee.
The decisions of GOD are accurate
      down to the nth degree.

10 God's Word is better than a diamond,
      better than a diamond set between emeralds.
You'll like it better than strawberries in spring,
      better than red, ripe strawberries.

11-14 There's more: God's Word warns us of danger
      and directs us to hidden treasure.
Otherwise how will we find our way?
      Or know when we play the fool?
Clean the slate, God, so we can start the day fresh!
      Keep me from stupid sins,
      from thinking I can take over your work;
Then I can start this day sun-washed,
      scrubbed clean of the grime of sin.

These are the words in my mouth;
>   these are what I chew on and pray.
Accept them when I place them
>   on the morning altar,
O God, my Altar-Rock,
>   God, Priest-of-My-Altar.

20

1-4 GOD answer you on the day you crash,
>   The name God-of-Jacob put you out of harm's reach,
>   Send reinforcements from Holy Hill,
Dispatch from Zion fresh supplies,
Exclaim over your offerings,
Celebrate your sacrifices,
Give you what your heart desires,
Accomplish your plans.

5 When you win, we plan to raise the roof
>   and lead the parade with our banners.
May all your wishes come true!

6 That clinches it — help's coming,
>   an answer's on the way,
>   everything's going to work out.

7-8 See those people polishing their chariots,
>   and those others grooming their horses?
>   But we're making garlands for GOD our God.
The chariots will rust,
>   those horses pull up lame —
>   and we'll be on our feet, standing tall.

9 Make the king a winner, GOD;
>   the day we call, give us your answer.

21

1-7 Your strength, GOD, is the king's strength.
>   Helped, he's hollering Hosannas.
>   You gave him exactly what he wanted;
you didn't hold back.
You filled his arms with gifts;
>   you gave him a right royal welcome.
He wanted a good life; you gave it to him,
>   and then made it a *long* life as a bonus.
You lifted him high and bright as a cumulus cloud,
>   then dressed him in rainbow colors.
You pile blessings on him;
>   you make him glad when you smile.
Is it any wonder the king loves GOD?
>   that he's sticking with the Best?

8-12 With a fistful of enemies in one hand
    and a fistful of haters in the other,
You radiate with such brilliance
    that they cringe as before a furnace.
Now the furnace swallows them whole,
    the fire eats them alive!
You purge the earth of their progeny,
    you wipe the slate clean.
All their evil schemes, the plots they cook up,
    have fizzled — every one.
You sent them packing;
    they couldn't face you.

13 Show your strength, GOD, so no one can miss it.
    We are out singing the good news!

A DAVID PSALM

1-2 **22** God, God . . . my God!
        Why did you dump me
        miles from nowhere?
Doubled up with pain, I call to God
    all the day long. No answer. Nothing.
I keep at it all night, tossing and turning.

3-5 And you! Are you indifferent, above it all,
    leaning back on the cushions of Israel's praise?
We know you were there for our parents:
    they cried for your help and you gave it;
    they trusted and lived a good life.

6-8 And here I am, a nothing — an earthworm,
    something to step on, to squash.
Everyone pokes fun at me;
    they make faces at me, they shake their heads:
"Let's see how GOD handles this one;
    since God likes him so much, let *him* help him!"

9-11 And to think you were midwife at my birth,
    setting me at my mother's breasts!
When I left the womb you cradled me;
    since the moment of birth you've been my God.
Then you moved far away
    and trouble moved in next door.
I need a neighbor.

12-13 Herds of bulls come at me,
    the raging bulls stampede,
Horns lowered, nostrils flaring,
    like a herd of buffalo on the move.

14-15 I'm a bucket kicked over and spilled,

every joint in my body has been pulled apart.
My heart is a blob
    of melted wax in my gut.
I'm dry as a bone,
    my tongue black and swollen.
They have laid me out for burial
    in the dirt.

16-18   Now packs of wild dogs come at me;
    thugs gang up on me.
They pin me down hand and foot,
    and lock me in a cage — a bag
Of bones in a cage, stared at
    by every passerby.
They take my wallet and the shirt off my back,
    and then throw dice for my clothes.

19-21   You, GOD — don't put off my rescue!
    Hurry and help me!
Don't let them cut my throat;
    don't let those mongrels devour me.
If you don't show up soon,
    I'm done for — gored by the bulls,
    meat for the lions.

22-24   Here's the story I'll tell my friends when they come to worship,
    and punctuate it with Hallelujahs:
Shout Hallelujah, you God-worshipers;
    give glory, you sons of Jacob;
    adore him, you daughters of Israel.
He has never let you down,
    never looked the other way
    when you were being kicked around.
He has never wandered off to do his own thing;
    he has been right there, listening.

25-26   Here in this great gathering for worship
    I have discovered this praise-life.
And I'll do what I promised right here
    in front of the God-worshipers.
Down-and-outers sit at GOD's table
    and eat their fill.
Everyone on the hunt for God
    is here, praising him.
"Live it up, from head to toe.
    Don't ever quit!"

27-28   From the four corners of the earth
    people are coming to their senses,
    are running back to GOD.
Long-lost families

are falling on their faces before him.
God has taken charge;
     from now on he has the last word.

29 All the power-mongers are before him
          — worshiping!
All the poor and powerless, too
          — worshiping!
Along with those who never got it together
          — worshiping!

30-31 Our children and their children
          will get in on this
As the word is passed along
     from parent to child.
Babies not yet conceived
     will hear the good news —
     that God does what he says.

A DAVID PSALM

1-3 **23** God, my shepherd!
          I don't need a thing.
          You have bedded me down in lush meadows,
     you find me quiet pools to drink from.
True to your word,
     you let me catch my breath
     and send me in the right direction.

4 Even when the way goes through
     Death Valley,
I'm not afraid
     when you walk at my side.
Your trusty shepherd's crook
     makes me feel secure.

5 You serve me a six-course dinner
     right in front of my enemies.
You revive my drooping head;
     my cup brims with blessing.

6 Your beauty and love chase after me
     every day of my life.
I'm back home in the house of God
     for the rest of my life.

A DAVID PSALM

1-2 **24** God claims Earth and everything in it,
          God claims World and all who live on it.
          He built it on Ocean foundations,
     laid it out on River girders.

3-4   Who can climb Mount GOD?
        Who can scale the holy north-face?
    Only the clean-handed,
        only the pure-hearted;
    Men who won't cheat,
        women who won't seduce.

5-6   GOD is at their side;
        with GOD's help they make it.
    This, Jacob, is what happens
        to God-seekers, God-questers.

7   Wake up, you sleepyhead city!
    Wake up, you sleepyhead people!
        King-Glory is ready to enter.

8   Who is this King-Glory?
        GOD, armed
        and battle-ready.

9   Wake up, you sleepyhead city!
    Wake up, you sleepyhead people!
        King-Glory is ready to enter.

10   Who is this King-Glory?
        GOD-of-the-Angel-Armies:
        he is King-Glory.

A DAVID PSALM

1-2   **25** My head is high, GOD, held high;
        I'm looking to you, GOD;
        No hangdog skulking for me.

3   I've thrown in my lot with you;
    You won't embarrass me, will you?
    Or let my enemies get the best of me?

    Don't embarrass any of us
    Who went out on a limb for you.
    It's the traitors who should be humiliated.

4   Show me how you work, GOD;
    School me in your ways.

5   Take me by the hand;
    Lead me down the path of truth.
    You are my Savior, aren't you?

6   Mark the milestones of your mercy and love, GOD;
    Rebuild the ancient landmarks!

7 Forget that I sowed wild oats;
Mark me with your sign of love.
Plan only the best for me, GOD!

8 GOD is fair and just;
He corrects the misdirected,
Sends them in the right direction.

9 He gives the rejects his hand,
And leads them step-by-step.

10 From now on every road you travel
Will take you to GOD.
Follow the Covenant signs;
Read the charted directions.

11 Keep up your reputation, GOD;
Forgive my bad life;
It's been a very bad life.

12 My question: What are God-worshipers like?
Your answer: Arrows aimed at God's bull's-eye.

13 They settle down in a promising place;
Their kids inherit a prosperous farm.

14 God-friendship is for God-worshipers;
They are the ones he confides in.

15 If I keep my eyes on GOD,
I won't trip over my own feet.

16 Look at me and help me!
I'm all alone and in big trouble.

17 My heart and kidneys are fighting each other;
Call a truce to this civil war.

18 Take a hard look at my life of hard labor,
Then lift this ton of sin.

19 Do you see how many people
Have it in for me?
How viciously they hate me?

20 Keep watch over me and keep me out of trouble;
Don't let me down when I run to you.

21 Use all your skill to put me together;
I wait to see your finished product.

22 GOD, give your people a break
From this run of bad luck.

A DAVID PSALM

1 **26** Clear my name, GOD;
I've kept an honest shop.
I've thrown in my lot with you, GOD, and
I'm not budging.

2 Examine me, GOD, from head to foot,
order your battery of tests.
Make sure I'm fit
inside and out

3 So I never lose
sight of your love,
But keep in step with you,
never missing a beat.

4-5 I don't hang out with tricksters,
I don't pal around with thugs;
I hate that pack of gangsters,
I don't deal with double-dealers.

6-7 I scrub my hands with purest soap,
then join hands with the others in the great circle,
dancing around your altar, GOD,
Singing God-songs at the top of my lungs,
telling God-stories.

8-10 GOD, I love living with you;
your house glows with your glory.
When it's time for spring cleaning,
don't sweep me out with the quacks and crooks,
Men with bags of dirty tricks,
women with purses stuffed with bribe-money.

11-12 You know I've been aboveboard with you;
now be aboveboard with me.
I'm on the level with you, GOD;
I bless you every chance I get.

A DAVID PSALM

1 **27** Light, space, zest—
that's GOD!
So, with him on my side I'm fearless,
afraid of no one and nothing.

2 When vandal hordes ride down
ready to eat me alive,
Those bullies and toughs
fall flat on their faces.

3 When besieged,
     I'm calm as a baby.
   When all hell breaks loose,
     I'm collected and cool.

4 I'm asking GOD for one thing,
     only one thing:
   To live with him in his house
     my whole life long.
   I'll contemplate his beauty;
     I'll study at his feet.

5 That's the only quiet, secure place
     in a noisy world,
   The perfect getaway,
     far from the buzz of traffic.

6 God holds me head and shoulders
     above all who try to pull me down.
   I'm headed for his place to offer anthems
     that will raise the roof!
   Already I'm singing God-songs;
     I'm making music to GOD.

7-9 Listen, GOD, I'm calling at the top of my lungs:
       "Be good to me! Answer me!"
     When my heart whispered, "Seek God,"
       my whole being replied,
     "I'm seeking him!"
       Don't hide from me now!

9-10 You've always been right there for me;
        don't turn your back on me now.
      Don't throw me out, don't abandon me;
        you've always kept the door open.
      My father and mother walked out and left me,
        but GOD took me in.

11-12 Point me down your highway, GOD;
         direct me along a well-lighted street;
         show my enemies whose side you're on.
       Don't throw me to the dogs,
         those liars who are out to get me,
         filling the air with their threats.

13-14 I'm sure now I'll see God's goodness
         in the exuberant earth.
       Stay with GOD!
         Take heart. Don't quit.
       I'll say it again:
         Stay with GOD.

A DAVID PSALM

1 **28** Don't turn a deaf ear
         when I call you, GOD.
         If all I get from you is
deafening silence,
I'd be better off
    in the Black Hole.

2 I'm letting you know what I need,
       calling out for help
And lifting my arms
       toward your inner sanctum.

3-4 Don't shove me into
       the same jail cell with those crooks,
With those who are
       full-time employees of evil.
They talk a good line of "peace,"
       then moonlight for the Devil.

Pay them back for what they've done,
       for how bad they've been.
Pay them back for their long hours
       in the Devil's workshop;
Then cap it with a huge bonus.

5 Because they have no idea how God works
       or what he is up to,
God will smash them to smithereens
       and walk away from the ruins.

6-7 Blessed be GOD —
       he heard me praying.
He proved he's on my side;
       I've thrown my lot in with him.

Now I'm jumping for joy,
       and shouting and singing my thanks to him.

8-9 GOD is all strength for his people,
       ample refuge for his chosen leader;
Save your people
       and bless your heritage.
Care for them;
       carry them like a good shepherd.

A DAVID PSALM

1-2 **29** Bravo, GOD, bravo!
         Gods and all angels shout, "Encore!"
         In awe before the glory,

in awe before God's visible power.
Stand at attention!
Dress your best to honor him!

3   GOD thunders across the waters,
Brilliant, his voice and his face, streaming brightness—
GOD, across the flood waters.

4   GOD's thunder tympanic,
GOD's thunder symphonic.

5   GOD's thunder smashes cedars,
GOD topples the northern cedars.

6   The mountain ranges skip like spring colts,
The high ridges jump like wild kid goats.

7-8   GOD's thunder spits fire.
GOD thunders, the wilderness quakes;
He makes the desert of Kadesh shake.

9   GOD's thunder sets the oak trees dancing
A wild dance, whirling; the pelting rain strips their branches.
We fall to our knees—we call out, "Glory!"

10   Above the floodwaters is GOD's throne
from which his power flows,
from which he rules the world.

11   GOD makes his people strong.
GOD gives his people peace.

A DAVID PSALM

1 **30** I give you all the credit, GOD—
you got me out of that mess,
you didn't let my foes gloat.

2-3   GOD, my God, I yelled for help
and you put me together.
GOD, you pulled me out of the grave,
gave me another chance at life
when I was down-and-out.

4-5   All you saints! Sing your hearts out to GOD!
Thank him to his face!
He gets angry once in a while, but across
a lifetime there is only love.
The nights of crying your eyes out
give way to days of laughter.

6-7
When things were going great
  I crowed, "I've got it made.
I'm GOD's favorite.
  He made me king of the mountain."
Then you looked the other way
  and I fell to pieces.

8-10
I called out to you, GOD;
  I laid my case before you:
"Can you sell me for a profit when I'm dead?
  auction me off at a cemetery yard sale?
When I'm 'dust to dust' my songs
  and stories of you won't sell.
So listen! and be kind!
  Help me out of this!"

11-12
You did it: you changed wild lament
  into whirling dance;
You ripped off my black mourning band
  and decked me with wildflowers.
I'm about to burst with song;
  I can't keep quiet about you.
GOD, my God,
  I can't thank you enough.

A DAVID PSALM

1-2
31 I run to you, GOD; I run for dear life.
  Don't let me down!
  Take me seriously this time!
Get down on my level and listen,
  and please — no procrastination!
Your granite cave a hiding place,
  your high cliff aerie a place of safety.

3-5
You're my cave to hide in,
  my cliff to climb.
Be my safe leader,
  be my true mountain guide.
Free me from hidden traps;
  I want to hide in you.
I've put my life in your hands.
  You won't drop me,
  you'll never let me down.

6-13
I hate all this silly religion,
  but you, GOD, I trust.
I'm leaping and singing in the circle of your love;
  you saw my pain,
  you disarmed my tormentors,
You didn't leave me in their clutches
  but gave me room to breathe.

Be kind to me, GOD —
    I'm in deep, deep trouble again.
I've cried my eyes out;
    I feel hollow inside.
My life leaks away, groan by groan;
    my years fade out in sighs.
My troubles have worn me out,
    turned my bones to powder.
To my enemies I'm a monster;
    I'm ridiculed by the neighbors.
My friends are horrified;
    they cross the street to avoid me.
They want to blot me from memory,
    forget me like a corpse in a grave,
    discard me like a broken dish in the trash.
The street-talk gossip has me
    "criminally insane"!
Behind locked doors they plot
    how to ruin me for good.

14-18   Desperate, I throw myself on you:
    you are my God!
Hour by hour I place my days in your hand,
    safe from the hands out to get me.
Warm me, your servant, with a smile;
    save me because you love me.
Don't embarrass me by not showing up;
    I've given you plenty of notice.
Embarrass the wicked, stand them up,
    leave them stupidly shaking their heads
    as they drift down to hell.
Gag those loudmouthed liars
    who heckle me, your follower,
    with jeers and catcalls.

19-22   What a stack of blessing you have piled up
    for those who worship you,
Ready and waiting for all who run to you
    to escape an unkind world.
You hide them safely away
    from the opposition.
As you slam the door on those oily, mocking faces,
    you silence the poisonous gossip.
Blessed GOD!
    His love is the wonder of the world.
Trapped by a siege, I panicked.
    "Out of sight, out of mind," I said.
But you heard me say it,
    you heard and listened.

23 Love GOD, all you saints;
GOD takes care of all who stay close to him,
But he pays back in full
those arrogant enough to go it alone.

24 Be brave. Be strong. Don't give up.
Expect GOD to get here soon.

A DAVID PSALM

1 **32** Count yourself lucky, how happy you must be—
you get a fresh start,
your slate's wiped clean.

2 Count yourself lucky—
GOD holds nothing against you
and you're holding nothing back from him.

3 When I kept it all inside,
my bones turned to powder,
my words became daylong groans.

4 The pressure never let up;
all the juices of my life dried up.

5 Then I let it all out;
I said, "I'll make a clean breast of my failures to GOD."

Suddenly the pressure was gone—
my guilt dissolved,
my sin disappeared.

6 These things add up. Every one of us needs to pray;
when all hell breaks loose and the dam bursts
we'll be on high ground, untouched.

7 GOD's my island hideaway,
keeps danger far from the shore,
throws garlands of hosannas around my neck.

8 Let me give you some good advice;
I'm looking you in the eye
and giving it to you straight:

9 "Don't be ornery like a horse or mule
that needs bit and bridle
to stay on track."

10 God-defiers are always in trouble;
GOD-affirmers find themselves loved
every time they turn around.

11   Celebrate GOD.
          Sing together — everyone!
          All you honest hearts, raise the roof!

1-3   **33** Good people, cheer GOD!
              Right-living people sound best when praising.
              Use guitars to reinforce your Hallelujahs!
          Play his praise on a grand piano!
      Invent your own new song to him;
          give him a trumpet fanfare.

4-5   For GOD's Word is solid to the core;
          everything he makes is sound inside and out.
      He loves it when everything fits,
          when his world is in plumb-line true.
      Earth is drenched
          in GOD's affectionate satisfaction.

6-7   The skies were made by GOD's command;
          he breathed the word and the stars popped out.
      He scooped Sea into his jug,
          put Ocean in his keg.

8-9   Earth-creatures, bow before GOD;
          world-dwellers — down on your knees!
      Here's why: he spoke and there it was,
          in place the moment he said so.

10-12 GOD takes the wind out of Babel pretense,
          he shoots down the world's power-schemes.
      GOD's plan for the world stands up,
          all his designs are made to last.
      Blessed is the country with GOD for God;
          blessed are the people he's put in his will.

13-15 From high in the skies GOD looks around,
          he sees all Adam's brood.
      From where he sits
          he overlooks all us earth-dwellers.
      He has shaped each person in turn;
          now he watches everything we do.

16-17 No king succeeds with a big army alone,
          no warrior wins by brute strength.
      Horsepower is not the answer;
          no one gets by on muscle alone.

18-19 Watch this: God's eye is on those who respect him,
          the ones who are looking for his love.
      He's ready to come to their rescue in bad times;
          in lean times he keeps body and soul together.

20-22 We're depending on God;
  he's everything we need.
What's more, our hearts brim with joy
  since we've taken for our own his holy name.
Love us, God, with all you've got —
  that's what we're depending on.

A D a v i d P s a l m , W h e n H e O u t w i t t e d
A b i m e l e c h a n d G o t A w a y

1 **34** I bless God every chance I get;
  my lungs expand with his praise.

2 I live and breathe God;
  if things aren't going well, hear this and be happy:

3 Join me in spreading the news;
  together let's get the word out.

4 God met me more than halfway,
  he freed me from my anxious fears.

5 Look at him; give him your warmest smile.
  Never hide your feelings from him.

6 When I was desperate, I called out,
  and God got me out of a tight spot.

7 God's angel sets up a circle
  of protection around us while we pray.

8 Open your mouth and taste, open your eyes and see —
  how good God is.
Blessed are you who run to him.

9 Worship God if you want the best;
  worship opens doors to all his goodness.

10 Young lions on the prowl get hungry,
  but God-seekers are full of God.

11 Come, children, listen closely;
  I'll give you a lesson in God worship.

12 Who out there has a lust for life?
  Can't wait each day to come upon beauty?

13 Guard your tongue from profanity,
  and no more lying through your teeth.

14 Turn your back on sin; do something good.
  Embrace peace — don't let it get away!

15   GOD keeps an eye on his friends,
      his ears pick up every moan and groan.

16   GOD won't put up with rebels;
      he'll cull them from the pack.

17   Is anyone crying for help? GOD is listening,
      ready to rescue you.

18   If your heart is broken, you'll find GOD right there;
      if you're kicked in the gut, he'll help you catch your breath.

19   Disciples so often get into trouble;
      still, GOD is there every time.

20   He's your bodyguard, shielding every bone;
      not even a finger gets broken.

21   The wicked commit slow suicide;
      they waste their lives hating the good.

22   GOD pays for each slave's freedom;
      no one who runs to him loses out.

A DAVID PSALM

1-3   **35** Harass these hecklers, GOD,
          punch these bullies in the nose.
          Grab a weapon, anything at hand;
      stand up for me!
      Get ready to throw the spear, aim the javelin,
          at the people who are out to get me.
      Reassure me; let me hear you say,
          "I'll save you."

4-8   When those thugs try to knife me in the back,
          make them look foolish.
      Frustrate all those
          who are plotting my downfall.
      Make them like cinders in a high wind,
          with GOD's angel working the bellows.
      Make their road lightless and mud-slick,
          with GOD's angel on their tails.
      Out of sheer cussedness they set a trap to catch me;
          for no good reason they dug a ditch to stop me.
      Surprise them with your ambush —
          catch them in the very trap they set,
          the disaster they planned for me.

9-10 But let me run loose and free,
          celebrating GOD's great work,
      Every bone in my body laughing, singing, "GOD,
          there's no one like you.

You put the down-and-out on their feet
    and protect the unprotected from bullies!"

11-12   Hostile accusers appear out of nowhere,
        they stand up and badger me.
They pay me back misery for mercy,
    leaving my soul empty.

13-14   When they were sick, I dressed in black;
        instead of eating, I prayed.
My prayers were like lead in my gut,
    like I'd lost my best friend, my brother.
I paced, distraught as a motherless child,
    hunched and heavyhearted.

15-16   But when I was down
        they threw a party!
All the nameless riffraff of the town came
    chanting insults about me.
Like barbarians desecrating a shrine,
    they destroyed my reputation.

17-18   GOD, how long are you going
        to stand there doing nothing?
Save me from their brutalities;
        everything I've got is being thrown to the lions.
I will give you full credit
    when everyone gathers for worship;
When the people turn out in force
    I will say my Hallelujahs.

19-21   Don't let these liars, my enemies,
        have a party at my expense,
Those who hate me for no reason,
        winking and rolling their eyes.
No good is going to come
    from that crowd;
They spend all their time cooking up gossip
    against those who mind their own business.
They open their mouths
    in ugly grins,
Mocking, "Ha-ha, ha-ha, thought you'd get away with it?
    We've caught you hands down!"

22   Don't you see what they're doing, GOD?
        You're not going to let them
Get by with it, are you? Not going to walk off
    without *doing* something, are you?

23-26   Please get up — wake up! Tend to my case.
        My God, my Lord — my life is on the line.

Do what you think is right, GOD, my God,
   but don't make me pay for their good time.
Don't let them say to themselves,
   "Ha-ha, we got what we wanted."
Don't let them say,
   "We've chewed him up and spit him out."
Let those who are being hilarious
   at my expense
Be made to look ridiculous.
   Make them wear donkey's ears;
Pin them with the donkey's tail,
   who made themselves so high and mighty!

27-28　But those who want
      the best for me,
Let them have the last word — a glad shout! —
   and say, over and over and over,
"GOD is great — everything works
   together for good for his servant."
I'll tell the world how great and good you are,
   I'll shout Hallelujah all day, every day.

A DAVID PSALM

1-4　**36** The God-rebel tunes in to sedition —
         all ears, eager to sin.
         He has no regard for God,
   he stands insolent before him.
He has smooth-talked himself
   into believing
That his evil
   will never be noticed.
Words gutter from his mouth,
   dishwater dirty.
Can't remember when he
   did anything decent.
Every time he goes to bed,
   he fathers another evil plot.
When he's loose on the streets,
   nobody's safe.
He plays with fire
   and doesn't care who gets burned.

5-6　God's love is meteoric,
      his loyalty astronomic,
His purpose titanic,
   his verdicts oceanic.
Yet in his largeness
   nothing gets lost;
Not a man, not a mouse,
   slips through the cracks.

7-9 How exquisite your love, O God!
>How eager we are to run under your wings,
To eat our fill at the banquet you spread
>as you fill our tankards with Eden spring water.
You're a fountain of cascading light,
>and you open our eyes to light.

10-12 Keep on loving your friends;
>do your work in welcoming hearts.
Don't let the bullies kick me around,
>the moral midgets slap me down.
Send the upstarts sprawling
>flat on their faces in the mud.

A DAVID PSALM

1-2 **37** Don't bother your head with braggarts
>or wish you could succeed like the wicked.
In no time they'll shrivel like grass clippings
and wilt like cut flowers in the sun.

3-4 Get insurance with GOD and do a good deed,
>settle down and stick to your last.
Keep company with GOD,
>get in on the best.

5-6 Open up before GOD, keep nothing back;
>he'll do whatever needs to be done:
He'll validate your life in the clear light of day
>and stamp you with approval at high noon.

7 Quiet down before GOD,
>be prayerful before him.
Don't bother with those who climb the ladder,
>who elbow their way to the top.

8-9 Bridle your anger, trash your wrath,
>cool your pipes — it only makes things worse.
Before long the crooks will be bankrupt;
>GOD-investors will soon own the store.

10-11 Before you know it, the wicked will have had it;
>you'll stare at his once famous place and — nothing!
Down-to-earth people will move in and take over,
>relishing a huge bonanza.

12-13 Bad guys have it in for the good guys,
>obsessed with doing them in.
But GOD isn't losing any sleep; to him
>they're a joke with no punch line.

14-15 Bullies brandish their swords,
>pull back on their bows with a flourish.

They're out to beat up on the harmless,
    or mug that nice man out walking his dog.
A banana peel lands them flat on their faces —
    slapstick figures in a moral circus.

16-17   Less is more and more is less.
    One righteous will outclass fifty wicked,
For the wicked are moral weaklings
    but the righteous are GOD-strong.

18-19   GOD keeps track of the decent folk;
    what they do won't soon be forgotten.
In hard times, they'll hold their heads high;
    when the shelves are bare, they'll be full.

20   God-despisers have had it;
    GOD's enemies are finished —
Stripped bare like vineyards at harvest time,
    vanished like smoke in thin air.

21-22   Wicked borrows and never returns;
    Righteous gives and gives.
Generous gets it all in the end;
    Stingy is cut off at the pass.

23-24   Stalwart walks in step with GOD;
    his path blazed by GOD, he's happy.
If he stumbles, he's not down for long;
    GOD has a grip on his hand.

25-26   I once was young, now I'm a graybeard —
    not once have I seen an abandoned believer,
    or his kids out roaming the streets.
Every day he's out giving and lending,
    his children making him proud.

27-28   Turn your back on evil,
    work for the good and don't quit.
GOD loves this kind of thing,
    never turns away from his friends.

28-29   Live this way and you've got it made,
    but bad eggs will be tossed out.
The good get planted on good land
    and put down healthy roots.

30-31   Righteous chews on wisdom like a dog on a bone,
    rolls virtue around on his tongue.
His heart pumps God's Word like blood through his veins;
    his feet are as sure as a cat's.

32-33   Wicked sets a watch for Righteous,
        he's out for the kill.
    GOD, alert, is also on watch —
        Wicked won't hurt a hair of his head.

34   Wait passionately for GOD,
        don't leave the path.
    He'll give you your place in the sun
        while you watch the wicked lose it.

35-36   I saw Wicked bloated like a toad,
        croaking pretentious nonsense.
    The next time I looked there was nothing —
        a punctured bladder, vapid and limp.

37-38   Keep your eye on the healthy soul,
        scrutinize the straight life;
    There's a future
        in strenuous wholeness.
    But the willful will soon be discarded;
        insolent souls are on a dead-end street.

39-40   The spacious, free life is from GOD,
        it's also protected and safe.
    GOD-strengthened, we're delivered from evil —
        when we run to him, he saves us.

A DAVID PSALM

1-2   **38** Take a deep breath, GOD; calm down —
        don't be so hasty with your punishing rod.
    Your sharp-pointed arrows of rebuke draw blood;
    my backside smarts from your caning.

3-4   I've lost twenty pounds in two months
        because of your accusation.
    My bones are brittle as dry sticks
        because of my sin.
    I'm swamped by my bad behavior,
        collapsed under gunnysacks of guilt.

5-8   The cuts in my flesh stink and grow maggots
        because I've lived so badly.
    And now I'm flat on my face
        feeling sorry for myself morning to night.
    All my insides are on fire,
        my body is a wreck.
    I'm on my last legs; I've had it —
        my life is a vomit of groans.

9-16   Lord, my longings are sitting in plain sight,
        my groans an old story to you.

My heart's about to break;
    I'm a burned-out case.
Cataracts blind me to God and good;
    old friends avoid me like the plague.
My cousins never visit,
    my neighbors stab me in the back.
My competitors blacken my name,
    devoutly they pray for my ruin.
But I'm deaf and mute to it all,
    ears shut, mouth shut.
I don't hear a word they say,
    don't speak a word in response.
What I do, GOD, is wait for you,
    wait for my Lord, my God — you *will* answer!
I wait and pray so they won't laugh me off,
    won't smugly strut off when I stumble.

17-20   I'm on the edge of losing it —
    the pain in my gut keeps burning.
I'm ready to tell my story of failure,
    I'm no longer smug in my sin.
My enemies are alive and in action,
    a lynch mob after my neck.
I give out good and get back evil
    from God-haters who can't stand a God-lover.

21-22   Don't dump me, GOD;
    my God, don't stand me up.
Hurry and help me;
    I want some wide-open space in my life!

A DAVID PSALM

1-3   **39** I'm determined to watch steps and tongue
        so they won't land me in trouble.
    I decided to hold my tongue
as long as Wicked is in the room.
"Mum's the word," I said, and kept quiet.
    But the longer I kept silence
The worse it got —
    my insides got hotter and hotter.
My thoughts boiled over;
    I spilled my guts.

4-6   "Tell me, what's going on, GOD?
        How long do I have to live?
        Give me the bad news!
You've kept me on pretty short rations;
    my life is string too short to be saved.
Oh! we're all puffs of air.
    Oh! we're all shadows in a campfire.

Oh! we're just spit in the wind.
We make our pile, and then we leave it.

7-11 "What am I doing in the meantime, Lord?
Hoping, that's what I'm doing — hoping
You'll save me from a rebel life,
save me from the contempt of dunces.
I'll say no more, I'll shut my mouth,
since you, Lord, are behind all this.
But I can't take it much longer.
When you put us through the fire
to purge us from our sin,
our dearest idols go up in smoke.
Are we also nothing but smoke?

12-13 "Ah, GOD, listen to my prayer, my
cry — open your ears.
Don't be callous;
just look at these tears of mine.
I'm a stranger here. I don't know my way —
a migrant like my whole family.
Give me a break, cut me some slack
before it's too late and I'm out of here."

A DAVID PSALM

1-3 **40** I waited and waited and waited for GOD.
At last he looked; finally he listened.
He lifted me out of the ditch,
pulled me from deep mud.
He stood me up on a solid rock
to make sure I wouldn't slip.
He taught me how to sing the latest God-song,
a praise-song to our God.
More and more people are seeing this:
they enter the mystery,
abandoning themselves to GOD.

4-5 Blessed are you who give yourselves over to GOD,
turn your backs on the world's "sure thing,"
ignore what the world worships;
The world's a huge stockpile
of GOD-wonders and God-thoughts.
Nothing and no one
comes close to you!
I start talking about you, telling what I know,
and quickly run out of words.
Neither numbers nor words
account for you.

6 Doing something for you, bringing something to you —
that's not what you're after.

Being religious, acting pious—
    that's not what you're asking for.
You've opened my ears
    so I can listen.

7-8   So I answered, "I'm coming.
    I read in your letter what you wrote about me,
And I'm coming to the party
    you're throwing for me."
That's when God's Word entered my life,
    became part of my very being.

9-10   I've preached you to the whole congregation,
    I've kept back nothing, GOD—you know that.
I didn't keep the news of your ways
    a secret, didn't keep it to myself.
I told it all, how dependable you are, how thorough.
    I didn't hold back pieces of love and truth
For myself alone. I told it all,
    let the congregation know the whole story.

11-12   Now GOD, don't hold out on me,
    don't hold back your passion.
Your love and truth
    are all that keeps me together.
When troubles ganged up on me,
    a mob of sins past counting,
I was so swamped by guilt
    I couldn't see my way clear.
More guilt in my heart than hair on my head,
    so heavy the guilt that my heart gave out.

13-15   Soften up, GOD, and intervene;
    hurry and get me some help,
So those who are trying to kidnap my soul
    will be embarrassed and lose face,
So anyone who gets a kick out of making me miserable
    will be heckled and disgraced,
So those who pray for my ruin
    will be booed and jeered without mercy.

16-17   But all who are hunting for you—
    oh, let them sing and be happy.
Let those who know what you're all about
    tell the world you're great and not quitting.
And me? I'm a mess. I'm nothing and have nothing:
    make something of me.
You can do it; you've got what it takes—
    but God, don't put it off.

A DAVID PSALM

41

1-3 Dignify those who are down on their luck;
    you'll feel good — *that's* what GOD does.
    GOD looks after us all,
makes us robust with life —
Lucky to be in the land,
    we're free from enemy worries.
Whenever we're sick and in bed,
    GOD becomes our nurse,
    nurses us back to health.

4-7 I said, "GOD, be gracious!
    Put me together again —
    my sins have torn me to pieces."
My enemies are wishing the worst for me;
    they make bets on what day I will die.
If someone comes to see me,
    he mouths empty platitudes,
All the while gathering gossip about me
    to entertain the street-corner crowd.
These "friends" who hate me
    whisper slanders all over town.
They form committees
    to plan misery for me.

8-9 The rumor goes out, "He's got some dirty,
    deadly disease. The doctors
    have given up on him."
Even my best friend, the one I always told everything
    — he ate meals at my house all the time! —
    has bitten my hand.

10 GOD, give grace, get me up on my feet.
    I'll show them a thing or two.

11-12 Meanwhile, I'm sure you're on my side —
    no victory shouts yet from the enemy camp!
You know me inside and out, you hold me together,
    you never fail to stand me tall in your presence
    so I can look you in the eye.

13 Blessed is GOD, Israel's God,
    always, always, always.
    Yes. Yes. Yes.

A PSALM OF THE SONS OF KORAH

42

1-3 A white-tailed deer drinks
    from the creek;
I want to drink God,
deep draughts of God.

I'm thirsty for God-alive.
I wonder, "Will I ever make it —
    arrive and drink in God's presence?"
I'm on a diet of tears —
    tears for breakfast, tears for supper.
All day long
    people knock at my door,
Pestering,
    "Where is this God of yours?"

4   These are the things I go over and over,
    emptying out the pockets of my life.
I was always at the head of the worshiping crowd,
    right out in front,
Leading them all,
    eager to arrive and worship,
Shouting praises, singing thanksgiving —
    celebrating, all of us, God's feast!

5   Why are you down in the dumps, dear soul?
    Why are you crying the blues?
Fix my eyes on God —
    soon I'll be praising again.
He puts a smile on my face.
    He's my God.

6-8   When my soul is in the dumps, I rehearse
    everything I know of you,
From Jordan depths to Hermon heights,
    including Mount Mizar.
Chaos calls to chaos,
    to the tune of whitewater rapids.
Your breaking surf, your thundering breakers
    crash and crush me.
Then GOD promises to love me all day,
    sing songs all through the night!
    My life is God's prayer.

9-10   Sometimes I ask God, my rock-solid God,
    "Why did you let me down?
Why am I walking around in tears,
    harassed by enemies?"
They're out for the kill, these
    tormentors with their obscenities,
Taunting day after day,
    "Where is this God of yours?"

11   Why are you down in the dumps, dear soul?
    Why are you crying the blues?
Fix my eyes on God —
    soon I'll be praising again.

He puts a smile on my face.
He's my God.

43 Clear my name, God; stick up for me
against these loveless, immoral people.
Get me out of here, away
from these lying degenerates.
I counted on you, God.
Why did you walk out on me?
Why am I pacing the floor, wringing my hands
over these outrageous people?

3-4 Give me your lantern and compass,
give me a map,
So I can find my way to the sacred mountain,
to the place of your presence,
To enter the place of worship,
meet my exuberant God,
Sing my thanks with a harp,
magnificent God, my God.

5 Why are you down in the dumps, dear soul?
Why are you crying the blues?
Fix my eyes on God —
soon I'll be praising again.
He puts a smile on my face.
He's my God.

A PSALM OF THE SONS OF KORAH

44 We've been hearing about this, God,
all our lives.
Our fathers told us the stories
their fathers told them,
How single-handedly you weeded out the godless
from the fields and planted us,
How you sent those people packing
but gave us a fresh start.
We didn't fight for this land;
we didn't work for it — it was a gift!
You gave it, smiling as you gave it,
delighting as you gave it.

4-8 You're my King, O God —
command victories for Jacob!
With your help we'll wipe out our enemies,
in your name we'll stomp them to dust.
I don't trust in weapons;
my sword won't save me —
But it's you, you who saved us from the enemy;
you made those who hate us lose face.

All day we parade God's praise—
    we thank you by name over and over.

9-12   But now you've walked off and left us,
    you've disgraced us and won't fight for us.
You made us turn tail and run;
    those who hate us have cleaned us out.
You delivered us as sheep to the butcher,
    you scattered us to the four winds.
You sold your people at a discount—
    you made nothing on the sale.

13-16   You made people on the street,
    urchins, poke fun and call us names.
You made us a joke among the godless,
    a cheap joke among the rabble.
Every day I'm up against it,
    my nose rubbed in my shame—
Gossip and ridicule fill the air,
    people out to get me crowd the street.

17-19   All this came down on us,
    and we've done nothing to deserve it.
We never betrayed your Covenant: our hearts
    were never false, our feet never left your path.
Do we deserve torture in a den of jackals?
    or lockup in a black hole?

20-22   If we had forgotten to pray to our God
    or made fools of ourselves with store-bought gods,
Wouldn't God have figured this out?
    We can't hide things from him.
No, you decided to make us martyrs,
    lambs assigned for sacrifice each day.

23-26   Get up, GOD! Are you going to sleep all day?
    Wake up! Don't you care what happens to us?
Why do you bury your face in the pillow?
    Why pretend things are just fine with us?
And here we are—flat on our faces in the dirt,
    held down with a boot on our necks.
Get up and come to our rescue.
    If you love us so much, *Help us!*

A WEDDING SONG OF THE SONS OF KORAH

1   **45** My heart bursts its banks,
    spilling beauty and goodness.
    I pour it out in a poem to the king,
shaping the river into words:

2-4 "You're the handsomest of men;
 every word from your lips is sheer grace,
 and God has blessed you, blessed you so much.
Strap your sword to your side, warrior!
 Accept praise! Accept due honor!
 Ride majestically! Ride triumphantly!
Ride on the side of truth!
 Ride for the righteous meek!

4-5 "Your instructions are glow-in-the-dark;
 you shoot sharp arrows
Into enemy hearts; the king's
 foes lie down in the dust, beaten.

6-7 "Your throne is God's throne,
 ever and always;
The scepter of your royal rule
 measures right living.
You love the right
 and hate the wrong.
And that is why God, your very own God,
 poured fragrant oil on your head,
Marking you out as king
 from among your dear companions.

8-9 "Your ozone-drenched garments
 are fragrant with mountain breeze.
Chamber music — from the throne room —
 makes you want to dance.
Kings' daughters are maids in your court,
 the Bride glittering with golden jewelry.

10-12 "Now listen, daughter, don't miss a word:
 forget your country, put your home behind you.
Be *here* — the king is wild for you.
 Since he's your lord, adore him.
Wedding gifts pour in from Tyre;
 rich guests shower you with presents."

13-15 (Her wedding dress is dazzling,
 lined with gold by the weavers;
All her dresses and robes
 are woven with gold.
She is led to the king,
 followed by her virgin companions.
A procession of joy and laughter!
 a grand entrance to the king's palace!)

16-17 "Set your mind now on sons —
 don't dote on father and grandfather.

You'll set your sons up as princes
    all over the earth.
I'll make you famous for generations;
    you'll be the talk of the town
    for a long, long time."

A SONG OF THE SONS OF KORAH

46 God is a safe place to hide,
    ready to help when we need him.
We stand fearless at the cliff-edge of doom,
    courageous in seastorm and earthquake,
Before the rush and roar of oceans,
    the tremors that shift mountains.

1-3

Jacob-wrestling God fights for us,
GOD-of-Angel-Armies protects us.

4-6 River fountains splash joy, cooling God's city,
    this sacred haunt of the Most High.
God lives here, the streets are safe,
    God at your service from crack of dawn.
Godless nations rant and rave, kings and kingdoms threaten,
    but Earth does anything he says.

7 Jacob-wrestling God fights for us,
GOD-of-Angel-Armies protects us.

8-10 Attention, all! See the marvels of GOD!
    He plants flowers and trees all over the earth,
Bans war from pole to pole,
    breaks all the weapons across his knee.
"Step out of the traffic! Take a long,
    loving look at me, your High God,
    above politics, above everything."

11 Jacob-wrestling God fights for us,
GOD-of-Angel-Armies protects us.

A PSALM OF THE SONS OF KORAH

47 Applause, everyone. Bravo, bravissimo!
    Shout God-songs at the top of your lungs!
GOD Most High is stunning,
    astride land and ocean.
He crushes hostile people,
    puts nations at our feet.
He set us at the head of the line,
    prize-winning Jacob, his favorite.
Loud cheers as God climbs the mountain,
    a ram's horn blast at the summit.
Sing songs to God, sing out!
    Sing to our King, sing praise!

1-9

He's Lord over earth,
    so sing your best songs to God.
God is Lord of godless nations—
    sovereign, he's King of the mountain.
Princes from all over are gathered,
    people of Abraham's God.
The powers of earth are God's—
    he soars over all.

A PSALM OF THE SONS OF KORAH

1-3 **48** GOD majestic,
    praise abounds in our God-city!
His sacred mountain,
    breathtaking in its heights—earth's joy.
Zion Mountain looms in the North,
    city of the world-King.
God in his citadel peaks
    impregnable.

4-6 The kings got together,
    they united and came.
They took one look and shook their heads,
    they scattered and ran away.
They doubled up in pain
    like a woman having a baby.

7-8 You smashed the ships of Tarshish
    with a storm out of the East.
We heard about it, then we saw it
    with our eyes—
In GOD's city of Angel Armies,
    in the city our God
Set on firm foundations,
    firm forever.

9-10 We pondered your love-in-action, God,
    waiting in your temple:
Your name, God, evokes a train
    of Hallelujahs wherever
It is spoken, near and far;
    your arms are heaped with goodness-in-action.

11 Be glad, Zion Mountain;
    Dance, Judah's daughters!
    He does what he said he'd do!

12-14 Circle Zion, take her measure,
    count her fortress peaks,
Gaze long at her sloping bulwark,
    climb her citadel heights—
Then you can tell the next generation

detail by detail the story of God,
Our God forever,
who guides us till the end of time.

A PSALM OF THE SONS OF KORAH

49 Listen, everyone, listen —
earth-dwellers, don't miss this.
All you haves
and have-nots,
All together now: listen.

1-2

3-4 I set plainspoken wisdom before you,
my heart-seasoned understandings of life.
I fine-tuned my ear to the sayings of the wise,
I solve life's riddle with the help of a harp.

5-6 So why should I fear in bad times,
hemmed in by enemy malice,
Shoved around by bullies,
demeaned by the arrogant rich?

7-9 Really! There's no such thing as self-rescue,
pulling yourself up by your bootstraps.
The cost of rescue is beyond our means,
and even then it doesn't guarantee
Life forever, or insurance
against the Black Hole.

10-11 Anyone can see that the brightest and best die,
wiped out right along with fools and dunces.
They leave all their prowess behind,
move into their new home, The Coffin,
The cemetery their permanent address.
And to think they named counties after themselves!

12 We aren't immortal. We don't last long.
Like our dogs, we age and weaken. And die.

13-15 This is what happens to those who live for the moment,
who only look out for themselves:
Death herds them like sheep straight to hell;
they disappear down the gullet of the grave;
They waste away to nothing —
nothing left but a marker in a cemetery.
But me? God snatches me from the clutch of death,
he reaches down and grabs me.

16-19 So don't be impressed with those who get rich
and pile up fame and fortune.
They can't take it with them;
fame and fortune all get left behind.

Just when they think they've arrived
and folks praise them because they've made good,
They enter the family burial plot
where they'll never see sunshine again.

20 We aren't immortal. We don't last long.
Like our dogs, we age and weaken. And die.

AN ASAPH PSALM

1-3 **50** The God of gods — it's GOD! — speaks out, shouts, "Earth!"
welcomes the sun in the east,
farewells the disappearing sun in the west.
From the dazzle of Zion,
God blazes into view.
Our God makes his entrance,
he's not shy in his coming.
Starbursts of fireworks precede him.

4-5 He summons heaven and earth as a jury,
he's taking his people to court:
"Round up my saints who swore
on the Bible their loyalty to me."

6 The whole cosmos attests to the fairness of this court,
that here *God* is judge.

7-15 "Are you listening, dear people? I'm getting ready to speak;
Israel, I'm about ready to bring you to trial.
This is God, your God,
speaking to you.
I don't find fault with your acts of worship,
the frequent burnt sacrifices you offer.
But why should I want your blue-ribbon bull,
or more and more goats from your herds?
Every creature in the forest is mine,
the wild animals on all the mountains.
I know every mountain bird by name;
the scampering field mice are my friends.
If I get hungry, do you think I'd tell you?
All creation and its bounty are mine.
Do you think I feast on venison?
or drink draughts of goats' blood?
Spread for me a banquet of praise,
serve High God a feast of kept promises,
And call for help when you're in trouble —
I'll help you, and you'll honor me."

16-21 Next, God calls up the wicked:

"What are you up to, quoting my laws,
talking like we are good friends?

You never answer the door when I call;
　　you treat my words like garbage.
If you find a thief, you make him your buddy;
　　adulterers are your friends of choice.
Your mouth drools filth;
　　lying is a serious art form with you.
You stab your own brother in the back,
　　rip off your little sister.
I kept a quiet patience while you did these things;
　　you thought I went along with your game.
I'm calling you on the carpet, *now*,
　　laying your wickedness out in plain sight.

22-23　"Time's up for playing fast and
　　　loose with me.
I'm ready to pass sentence,
　　and there's no help in sight!
It's the praising life that honors me.
　　As soon as you set your foot on the Way,
I'll show you my salvation."

A DAVID PSALM, AFTER HE WAS CONFRONTED BY NATHAN ABOUT THE AFFAIR WITH BATHSHEBA

1-3　**51** Generous in love — God, give grace!
　　　　Huge in mercy — wipe out my bad record.
　　　　Scrub away my guilt,
　　soak out my sins in your laundry.
I know how bad I've been;
　　my sins are staring me down.

4-6　You're the One I've violated, and you've seen
　　　it all, seen the full extent of my evil.
You have all the facts before you;
　　whatever you decide about me is fair.
I've been out of step with you for a long time,
　　in the wrong since before I was born.
What you're after is truth from the inside out.
　　Enter me, then; conceive a new, true life.

7-15　Soak me in your laundry and I'll come out clean,
　　　scrub me and I'll have a snow-white life.
Tune me in to foot-tapping songs,
　　set these once-broken bones to dancing.
Don't look too close for blemishes,
　　give me a clean bill of health.
God, make a fresh start in me,
　　shape a Genesis week from the chaos of my life.
Don't throw me out with the trash,
　　or fail to breathe holiness in me.
Bring me back from gray exile,
　　put a fresh wind in my sails!

Give me a job teaching rebels your ways
    so the lost can find their way home.
Commute my death sentence, God, my salvation God,
    and I'll sing anthems to your life-giving ways.
Unbutton my lips, dear God;
    I'll let loose with your praise.

16-17 Going through the motions doesn't please you,
    a flawless performance is nothing to you.
I learned God-worship
    when my pride was shattered.
Heart-shattered lives ready for love
    don't for a moment escape God's notice.

18-19 Make Zion the place you delight in,
    repair Jerusalem's broken-down walls.
Then you'll get real worship from us,
    acts of worship small and large,
Including all the bulls
    they can heave onto your altar!

A DAVID PSALM, WHEN DOEG THE EDOMITE REPORTED TO SAUL,
"DAVID'S AT AHIMELECH'S HOUSE"

1-4 **52** Why do you brag of evil, "Big Man"?
    God's mercy carries the day.
    You scheme catastrophe;
your tongue cuts razor-sharp,
    artisan in lies.
You love evil more than good,
    you call black white.
You love malicious gossip,
    you foul-mouth.

5 God will tear you limb from limb,
    sweep you up and throw you out,
Pull you up by the roots
    from the land of life.

6-7 Good people will watch and
    worship. They'll laugh in relief:
"Big Man bet on the wrong horse,
    trusted in big money,
    made his living from catastrophe."

8 And I'm an olive tree,
    growing green in God's house.
I trusted in the generous mercy
    of God then and now.

9 I thank you always
    that you went into action.

And I'll stay right here,
  your good name my hope,
  in company with your faithful friends.

A DAVID PSALM

53

1-2 Bilious and bloated, they gas,
      "God is gone."
    It's poison gas —
  they foul themselves, they poison
Rivers and skies;
  thistles are their cash crop.
God sticks his head out of heaven.
  He looks around.
He's looking for someone not stupid —
  one man, even, God-expectant,
  just one God-ready woman.

3 He comes up empty. A string
    of zeros. Useless, unshepherded
Sheep, taking turns pretending
    to be Shepherd.
The ninety and nine
    follow the one.

4 Don't they know anything,
    all these impostors?
Don't they know
    they can't get away with this,
Treating people like a fast-food meal
    over which they're too busy to pray?

5 Night is coming for them, and nightmare —
    a nightmare they'll never wake up from.
God will make hash of these squatters,
    send them packing for good.

6 Is there anyone around to save Israel?
    God turns life around.
Turned-around Jacob skips rope,
    turned-around Israel sings laughter.

A DAVID PSALM, WHEN THE ZIPHITES REPORTED TO SAUL,
"DAVID IS HIDING OUT WITH US"

54

1-2 God, for your sake, help me!
      Use your influence to clear me.
    Listen, God — I'm desperate.
  Don't be too busy to hear me.

3 Outlaws are out to get me,
    hit men are trying to kill me.

Nothing will stop them;
    God means nothing to them.

4-5   Oh, look! God's right here helping!
        GOD's on my side,
    Evil is looping back on my enemies.
        Don't let up! Finish them off!

6-7   I'm ready now to worship, so ready.
        I thank you, GOD — you're so good.
    You got me out of every scrape,
        and I saw my enemies get it.

A DAVID PSALM

1-3 **55** Open your ears, God, to my prayer;
        don't pretend you don't hear me knocking.
    Come close and whisper your answer.
    I really need you.
    I shudder at the mean voice,
        quail before the evil eye,
    As they pile on the guilt,
        stockpile angry slander.

4-8   My insides are turned inside out;
        specters of death have me down.
    I shake with fear,
        I shudder from head to foot.
    "Who will give me wings," I ask —
        "wings like a dove?"
    Get me out of here on dove wings;
        I want some peace and quiet.
    I want a walk in the country,
        I want a cabin in the woods.
    I'm desperate for a change
        from rage and stormy weather.

9-11   Come down hard, Lord — slit their tongues.
        I'm appalled how they've split the city
    Into rival gangs
        prowling the alleys
    Day and night spoiling for a fight,
        trash piled in the streets,
    Even shopkeepers gouging and cheating
        in broad daylight.

12-14   This isn't the neighborhood bully
        mocking me — I could take that.
    This isn't a foreign devil spitting
        invective — I could tune that out.
    It's *you*! We grew up together!
        You! My best friend!

Those long hours of leisure as we walked
    arm in arm, God a third party to our conversation.

15   Haul my betrayers off alive to hell — let them
    experience the horror, let them
    feel every desolate detail of a damned life.

16-19   I call to God;
    GOD will help me.
At dusk, dawn, and noon I sigh
    deep sighs — he hears, he rescues.
My life is well and whole, secure
    in the middle of danger
Even while thousands
    are lined up against me.
God hears it all, and from his judge's bench
    puts them in their place.
But, set in their ways, they won't change;
    they pay him no mind.

20-21   And this, my best friend, betrayed his best friends;
    his life betrayed his word.
All my life I've been charmed by his speech,
    never dreaming he'd turn on me.
His words, which were music to my ears,
    turned to daggers in my heart.

22-23   Pile your troubles on GOD's shoulders —
    he'll carry your load, he'll help you out.
He'll never let good people
    topple into ruin.
But you, God, will throw the others
    into a muddy bog,
Cut the lifespan of assassins
    and traitors in half.

And I trust in you.

A DAVID PSALM, WHEN HE WAS CAPTURED
BY THE PHILISTINES IN GATH

1-4   **56** Take my side, God — I'm getting kicked around,
    stomped on every day.
    Not a day goes by
but somebody beats me up;
They make it their duty
    to beat me up.
When I get really afraid
    I come to you in trust.
I'm proud to praise God;
    fearless now, I trust in God.
    What can mere mortals do?

5-6　They don't let up —
　　　　they smear my reputation
　　　　and huddle to plot my collapse.
　　　They gang up,
　　　　sneak together through the alleys
　　　To take me by surprise,
　　　　wait their chance to get me.

7　Pay them back in evil!
　　　Get angry, God!
　　　Down with these people!

8　You've kept track of my every toss and turn
　　　through the sleepless nights,
　　　Each tear entered in your ledger,
　　　each ache written in your book.

9　If my enemies run away,
　　　turn tail when I yell at them,
　　　Then I'll know
　　　that God is on my side.

10-11　I'm proud to praise God,
　　　proud to praise GOD.
　　　Fearless now, I trust in God;
　　　what can mere mortals do to me?

12-13　God, you did everything you promised,
　　　and I'm thanking you with all my heart.
　　　You pulled me from the brink of death,
　　　my feet from the cliff-edge of doom.
　　　Now I stroll at leisure with God
　　　in the sunlit fields of life.

A DAVID PSALM, WHEN HE HID IN A CAVE FROM SAUL

1-3　**57** Be good to me, God — and now!
　　　　I've run to you for dear life.
　　　　I'm hiding out under your wings
　　　until the hurricane blows over.
　　　I call out to High God,
　　　　the God who holds me together.
　　　He sends orders from heaven and saves me,
　　　　he humiliates those who kick me around.
　　　God delivers generous love,
　　　　he makes good on his word.

4　I find myself in a pride of lions
　　　who are wild for a taste of human flesh;
　　　Their teeth are lances and arrows,
　　　their tongues are sharp daggers.

5 Soar high in the skies, O God!
  Cover the whole earth with your glory!

6 They booby-trapped my path;
  I thought I was dead and done for.
 They dug a mantrap to catch me,
  and fell in headlong themselves.

7-8 I'm ready, God, so ready,
  ready from head to toe,
 Ready to sing, ready to raise a tune:
  "Wake up, soul!
 Wake up, harp! wake up, lute!
  Wake up, you sleepyhead sun!"

9-10 I'm thanking you, GOD, out loud in the streets,
  singing your praises in town and country.
 The deeper your love, the higher it goes;
  every cloud is a flag to your faithfulness.

11 Soar high in the skies, O God!
  Cover the whole earth with your glory!

A DAVID PSALM

1-2 **58** Is this any way to run a country?
   Is there an honest politician in the house?
   Behind the scenes you brew cauldrons of evil,
 behind closed doors you make deals with demons.

3-5 The wicked crawl from the wrong side of the cradle;
  their first words out of the womb are lies.
 Poison, lethal rattlesnake poison,
  drips from their forked tongues—
 Deaf to threats, deaf to charm,
  decades of wax built up in their ears.

6-9 God, smash their teeth to bits,
  leave them toothless tigers.
 Let their lives be buckets of water spilled,
  all that's left, a damp stain in the sand.
 Let them be trampled grass
  worn smooth by the traffic.
 Let them dissolve into snail slime,
  be a miscarried fetus that never sees sunlight.
 Before what they cook up is half-done, God,
  throw it out with the garbage!

10-11 The righteous will call up their friends
  when they see the wicked get their reward,
 Serve up their blood in goblets
  as they toast one another,

Everyone cheering, "It's worth it to play by the rules!
  God's handing out trophies and tending the earth!"

1-2
59 My God! Rescue me from my enemies,
    defend me from these mutineers.
  Rescue me from their dirty tricks,
save me from their hit men.

3-4
Desperadoes have ganged up on me,
  they're hiding in ambush for me.
I did nothing to deserve this, GOD,
  crossed no one, wronged no one.
All the same, they're after me,
  determined to get me.

4-5
Wake up and see for yourself! You're GOD,
  GOD-of-Angel-Armies, Israel's God!
Get on the job and take care of these pagans,
  don't be soft on these hard cases.

6-7
They return when the sun goes down,
They howl like coyotes, ringing the city.
Then suddenly they're all at the gate,
Snarling invective, drawn daggers in their teeth.
They think they'll never get caught.

8-10
But you, GOD, break out laughing;
  you treat the godless nations like jokes.
Strong God, I'm watching you do it,
  I can always count on you.
God in dependable love shows up on time,
  shows me my enemies in ruin.

11-13
Don't make quick work of them, GOD,
  lest my people forget.
Bring them down in slow motion,
  take them apart piece by piece.
Let all their mean-mouthed arrogance
  catch up with them,
Catch them out and bring them down
  — every muttered curse
  — every barefaced lie.
Finish them off in fine style!
  Finish them off for good!
Then all the world will see
  that God rules well in Jacob,
  everywhere that God's in charge.

14-15   They return when the sun goes down,
    They howl like coyotes, ringing the city.
    They scavenge for bones,
    And bite the hand that feeds them.

16-17   And me? I'm singing your prowess,
    shouting at cockcrow your largesse,
For you've been a safe place for me,
    a good place to hide.
Strong God, I'm watching you do it,
    I can always count on you—
God, my dependable love.

A DAVID PSALM, WHEN HE FOUGHT AGAINST
ARAM-NAHARAIM AND ARAM-ZOBAH AND JOAB KILLED
TWELVE THOUSAND EDOMITES AT THE VALLEY OF SALT

1-2   **60** God! you walked off and left us,
    kicked our defenses to bits
    And stalked off angry.
Come back. Oh please, come back!

You shook earth to the foundations,
    ripped open huge crevasses.
Heal the breaks! Everything's
    coming apart at the seams.

3-5   You made your people look doom in the face,
    then gave us cheap wine to drown our troubles.
Then you planted a flag to rally your people,
    an unfurled flag to look to for courage.
Now do something quickly, answer right now,
    so the one you love best is saved.

6-8   That's when God spoke in holy splendor,
    "Bursting with joy,
I make a present of Shechem,
    I hand out Succoth Valley as a gift.
Gilead's in my pocket,
    to say nothing of Manasseh.
Ephraim's my hard hat,
    Judah my hammer;
Moab's a scrub bucket,
    I mop the floor with Moab,
Spit on Edom,
    rain fireworks all over Philistia."

9-10   Who will take me to the thick of the fight?
    Who'll show me the road to Edom?
You aren't giving up on us, are you, God?
    refusing to go out with our troops?

11-12 Give us help for the hard task;
     human help is worthless.
In God we'll do our very best;
     he'll flatten the opposition for good.

A DAVID PSALM

1-2 **61** God, listen to me shout,
     bend an ear to my prayer.
When I'm far from anywhere,
down to my last gasp,
I call out, "Guide me
     up High Rock Mountain!"

3-5 You've always given me breathing room,
     a place to get away from it all,
A lifetime pass to your safe-house,
     an open invitation as your guest.
You've always taken me seriously, God,
     made me welcome among those who know and love you.

6-8 Let the days of the king add up
     to years and years of good rule.
Set his throne in the full light of God;
     post Steady Love and Good Faith as lookouts,
And I'll be the poet who sings your glory—
     and live what I sing every day.

A DAVID PSALM

1-2 **62** God, the one and only—
     I'll wait as long as he says.
Everything I need comes from him,
so why not?
He's solid rock under my feet,
     breathing room for my soul,
An impregnable castle:
     I'm set for life.

3-4 How long will you gang up on me?
     How long will you run with the bullies?
There's nothing to you, any of you—
     rotten floorboards, worm-eaten rafters,
Anthills plotting to bring down mountains,
     far gone in make-believe.
You talk a good line,
     but every "blessing" breathes a curse.

5-6 God, the one and only—
     I'll wait as long as he says.
Everything I hope for comes from him,
     so why not?
He's solid rock under my feet,

breathing room for my soul,
An impregnable castle:
   I'm set for life.

7-8 My help and glory are in God
     —granite-strength and safe-harbor-God—
So trust him absolutely, people;
   lay your lives on the line for him.
   God is a safe place to be.

9 Man as such is smoke,
   woman as such, a mirage.
Put them together, they're nothing;
   two times nothing is nothing.

10 And a windfall, if it comes—
   don't make too much of it.

11 God said this once and for all;
   how many times
Have I heard it repeated?
   "Strength comes
Straight from God."

12 Love to you, Lord God!
   You pay a fair wage for a good day's work!

A DAVID PSALM, WHEN HE WAS OUT IN THE JUDEAN WILDERNESS

1 **63** God—you're my God!
     I can't get enough of you!
     I've worked up such hunger and thirst for God,
traveling across dry and weary deserts.

2-4 So here I am in the place of worship, eyes open,
   drinking in your strength and glory.
In your generous love I am really living at last!
   My lips brim praises like fountains.
I bless you every time I take a breath;
   My arms wave like banners of praise to you.

5-8 I eat my fill of prime rib and gravy;
   I smack my lips. It's time to shout praises!
If I'm sleepless at midnight,
   I spend the hours in grateful reflection.
Because you've always stood up for me,
   I'm free to run and play.
I hold on to you for dear life,
   and you hold me steady as a post.

9-11 Those who are out to get me are marked for doom,
   marked for death, bound for hell.

They'll die violent deaths;
    jackals will tear them limb from limb.
But the king is glad in God;
    his true friends spread the joy,
While small-minded gossips
    are gagged for good.

A DAVID PSALM

64

1 Listen and help, O God.
    I'm reduced to a whine
    And a whimper, obsessed
with feelings of doomsday.

2-6 Don't let them find me —
    the conspirators out to get me,
Using their tongues as weapons,
    flinging poison words,
    poison-tipped arrow-words.
They shoot from ambush,
    shoot without warning,
    not caring who they hit.
They keep fit doing calisthenics
    of evil purpose,
They keep lists of the traps
    they've secretly set.
They say to each other,
    "No one can catch us,
    no one can detect our perfect crime."
The Detective detects the mystery
    in the dark of the cellar heart.

7-8 The God of the Arrow shoots!
    They double up in pain,
Fall flat on their faces
    in full view of the grinning crowd.

9-10 Everyone sees it. God's
    work is the talk of the town.
Be glad, good people! Fly to GOD!
    Good-hearted people, make praise your habit.

A DAVID PSALM

65

1-2 Silence is praise to you,
    Zion-dwelling God,
    And also obedience.
You hear the prayer in it all.

2-8 We all arrive at your doorstep sooner
    or later, loaded with guilt,
Our sins too much for us —
    but you get rid of them once and for all.

Blessed are the chosen! Blessed the guest
    at home in your place!
We expect our fill of good things
    in your house, your heavenly manse.
All your salvation wonders
    are on display in your trophy room.
Earth-Tamer, Ocean-Pourer,
    Mountain-Maker, Hill-Dresser,
Muzzler of sea storm and wave crash,
    of mobs in noisy riot —
Far and wide they'll come to a stop,
    they'll stare in awe, in wonder.
Dawn and dusk take turns
    calling, "Come and worship."

9-13   Oh, visit the earth,
    ask her to join the dance!
Deck her out in spring showers,
    fill the God-River with living water.
Paint the wheat fields golden.
    Creation was made for this!
Drench the plowed fields,
    soak the dirt clods
With rainfall as harrow and rake
    bring her to blossom and fruit.
Snow-crown the peaks with splendor,
    scatter rose petals down your paths,
All through the wild meadows, rose petals.
    Set the hills to dancing,
Dress the canyon walls with live sheep,
    a drape of flax across the valleys.
Let them shout, and shout, and shout!
    Oh, oh, let them sing!

1-4   **66** All together now — applause for God!
    Sing songs to the tune of his glory,
    set glory to the rhythms of his praise.
Say of God, "We've never seen anything like him!"
    When your enemies see you in action,
    they slink off like scolded dogs.
The whole earth falls to its knees —
    it worships you, sings to you,
    can't stop enjoying your name and fame.

5-6   Take a good look at God's wonders —
    they'll take your breath away.
He converted sea to dry land;
    travelers crossed the river on foot.
    Now isn't that cause for a song?

7 Ever sovereign in his high tower, he keeps
    his eye on the godless nations.
Rebels don't dare
    raise a finger against him.

8-12 Bless our God, O peoples!
    Give him a thunderous welcome!
Didn't he set us on the road to life?
    Didn't he keep us out of the ditch?
He trained us first,
    passed us like silver through refining fires,
Brought us into hardscrabble country,
    pushed us to our very limit,
Road-tested us inside and out,
    took us to hell and back;
Finally he brought us
    to this well-watered place.

13-15 I'm bringing my prizes and presents to your house.
    I'm doing what I said I'd do,
What I solemnly swore I'd do
    that day when I was in so much trouble:
The choicest cuts of meat
    for the sacrificial meal;
Even the fragrance
    of roasted lamb is like a meal!
Or make it an ox
    garnished with goat meat!

16-20 All believers, come here and listen,
    let me tell you what God did for me.
I called out to him with my mouth,
    my tongue shaped the sounds of music.
If I had been cozy with evil,
    the Lord would never have listened.
But he most surely *did* listen,
    he came on the double when he heard my prayer.
Blessed be God: he didn't turn a deaf ear,
    he stayed with me, loyal in his love.

1-7 **67** God, mark us with grace
    and blessing! Smile!
The whole country will see how you work,
    all the godless nations see how you save.
God! Let people thank and enjoy you.
    Let all people thank and enjoy you.
Let all far-flung people become happy
    and shout their happiness because
You judge them fair and square,
    you tend the far-flung peoples.
God! Let people thank and enjoy you.

Let all people thank and enjoy you.
Earth, display your exuberance!
You mark us with blessing, O God, our God.
You mark us with blessing, O God.
Earth's four corners — honor him!

A David Psalm

68
1-4
Up with God!
    Down with his enemies!
        Adversaries, run for the hills!
Gone like a puff of smoke,
    like a blob of wax in the fire —
        one look at God and the wicked vanish.
When the righteous see God in action
    they'll laugh, they'll sing,
        they'll laugh and sing for joy.
Sing hymns to God;
    all heaven, sing out;
        clear the way for the coming of Cloud-Rider.
Enjoy God,
    cheer when you see him!

5-6
Father of orphans,
    champion of widows,
        is God in his holy house.
God makes homes for the homeless,
    leads prisoners to freedom,
        but leaves rebels to rot in hell.

7-10
God, when you took the lead with your people,
    when you marched out into the wild,
Earth shook, sky broke out in a sweat;
    God was on the march.
Even Sinai trembled at the sight of God on the move,
    at the sight of Israel's God.
You pour out rain in buckets, O God;
    thorn and cactus become an oasis
For your people to camp in and enjoy.
    You set them up in business;
        they went from rags to riches.

11-14
The Lord gave the word;
    thousands called out the good news:
"Kings of the armies
    are on the run, on the run!"
While housewives, safe and sound back home,
    divide up the plunder,
        the plunder of Canaanite silver and gold.
On that day that Shaddai scattered the kings,
    snow fell on Black Mountain.

<table>
<tr><td>15-16</td><td>

You huge mountains, Bashan mountains,
    mighty mountains, dragon mountains.
All you mountains not chosen,
    sulk now, and feel sorry for yourselves,
For this is the mountain God has chosen to live on;
    he'll rule from this mountain forever.

</td></tr>
</table>

15-16

You huge mountains, Bashan mountains,
    mighty mountains, dragon mountains.
All you mountains not chosen,
    sulk now, and feel sorry for yourselves,
For this is the mountain God has chosen to live on;
    he'll rule from this mountain forever.

17-18

The chariots of God, twice ten thousand,
    and thousands more besides,
The Lord in the lead, riding down Sinai —
    straight to the Holy Place!
You climbed to the High Place, captives in tow,
    your arms full of booty from rebels,
And now you sit there in state,
    GOD, sovereign GOD!

19-23

Blessed be the Lord —
    day after day he carries us along.
He's our Savior, our God, oh yes!
    He's God-for-us, he's God-who-saves-us.
Lord GOD knows all
    death's ins and outs.
What's more, he made heads roll,
    split the skulls of the enemy
As he marched out of heaven,
    saying, "I tied up the Dragon in knots,
    put a muzzle on the Deep Blue Sea."
You can wade through your enemies' blood,
    and your dogs taste of your enemies from your boots.

24-31

See God on parade
    to the sanctuary, my God,
    my King on the march!
Singers out front, the band behind,
    maidens in the middle with castanets.
The whole choir blesses God.
    Like a fountain of praise, Israel blesses GOD.
Look — little Benjamin's out
    front and leading
Princes of Judah in their royal robes,
    princes of Zebulon, princes of Naphtali.
Parade your power, O God,
    the power, O God, that made us what we are.
Your temple, High God, is Jerusalem;
    kings bring gifts to you.
Rebuke that old crocodile, Egypt,
    with her herd of wild bulls and calves,
Rapacious in her lust for silver,
    crushing peoples, spoiling for a fight.
Let Egyptian traders bring blue cloth
    and Cush come running to God, her hands outstretched.

32-34 Sing, O kings of the earth!
    Sing praises to the Lord!
There he is: Sky-Rider,
    striding the ancient skies.
Listen — he's calling in thunder,
    rumbling, rolling thunder.
Call out "Bravo!" to God,
    the High God of Israel.
His splendor and strength
    rise huge as thunderheads.

35 A terrible beauty, O God,
    streams from your sanctuary.
It's Israel's strong God! He gives
    power and might to his people!
O you, his people — bless God!

A DAVID PSALM

1 **69** God, God, save me!
    I'm in over my head,

2 Quicksand under me, swamp water over me;
I'm going down for the third time.

3 I'm hoarse from calling for help,
Bleary-eyed from searching the sky for God.

4 I've got more enemies than hairs on my head;
Sneaks and liars are out to knife me in the back.

What I never stole
Must I now give back?

5 God, you know every sin I've committed;
My life's a wide-open book before you.

6 Don't let those who look to you in hope
Be discouraged by what happens to me,
Dear Lord! GOD of the armies!

Don't let those out looking for you
Come to a dead end by following me —
Please, dear God of Israel!

7 Because of you I look like an idiot,
I walk around ashamed to show my face.

8 My brothers shun me like a bum off the street;
My family treats me like an unwanted guest.

9   I love you more than I can say.
    Because I'm madly in love with you,
    They blame me for everything they dislike about you.

10 When I poured myself out in prayer and fasting,
    All it got me was more contempt.

11 When I put on a sad face,
    They treated me like a clown.

12 Now drunks and gluttons
    Make up drinking songs about me.

13 And me? I pray.
    GOD, it's time for a break!

    God, answer in love!
    Answer with your sure salvation!

14 Rescue me from the swamp,
    Don't let me go under for good,

    Pull me out of the clutch of the enemy;
    This whirlpool is sucking me down.

15 Don't let the swamp be my grave, the Black Hole
    Swallow me, its jaws clenched around me.

16 Now answer me, GOD, because you love me;
    Let me see your great mercy full-face.

17 Don't look the other way; your servant can't take it.
    I'm in trouble. Answer right now!

18 Come close, God; get me out of here.
    Rescue me from this deathtrap.

19 You know how they kick me around—
    Pin on me the donkey's ears, the dunce's cap.

20 I'm broken by their taunts,
    Flat on my face, reduced to a nothing.

    I looked in vain for one friendly face. Not one.
    I couldn't find one shoulder to cry on.

21 They put poison in my soup,
    Vinegar in my drink.

22 Let their supper be bait in a trap that snaps shut;
    May their best friends be trappers who'll skin them alive.

23 Make them become blind as bats,
Give them the shakes from morning to night.

24 Let them know what you think of them,
Blast them with your red-hot anger.

25 Burn down their houses,
Leave them desolate with nobody at home.

26 They gossiped about the one you disciplined,
Made up stories about anyone wounded by God.

27 Pile on the guilt,
Don't let them off the hook.

28 Strike their names from the list of the living;
No rock-carved honor for them among the righteous.

29 I'm hurt and in pain;
Give me space for healing, and mountain air.

30 Let me shout God's name with a praising song,
Let me tell his greatness in a prayer of thanks.

31 For GOD, this is better than oxen on the altar,
Far better than blue-ribbon bulls.

32 The poor in spirit see and are glad —
Oh, you God-seekers, take heart!

33 For GOD listens to the poor,
He doesn't walk out on the wretched.

34 You heavens, praise him; praise him, earth;
Also ocean and all things that swim in it.

35 For God is out to help Zion,
Rebuilding the wrecked towns of Judah.

Guess who will live there —
The proud owners of the land?

36 No, the children of his servants will get it,
The lovers of his name will live in it.

A DAVID PRAYER

1-3 70 God! Please hurry to my rescue!
GOD, come quickly to my side!
Those who are out to get me —
let them fall all over themselves.
Those who relish my downfall —

send them down a blind alley.
    Give them a taste of their own medicine,
        those gossips off clucking their tongues.

4 Let those on the hunt for you
        sing and celebrate.
Let all who love your saving way
        say over and over, "God is mighty!"

5 But I've lost it. I'm wasted.
        God—quickly, quickly!
Quick to my side, quick to my rescue!
        GOD, don't lose a minute.

1-3 **71** I run for dear life to GOD,
        I'll never live to regret it.
        Do what you do so well:
get me out of this mess and up on my feet.
Put your ear to the ground and listen,
        give me space for salvation.
Be a guest room where I can retreat;
        you said your door was always open!
You're my salvation—my vast, granite fortress.

4-7 My God, free me from the grip of Wicked,
        from the clutch of Bad and Bully.
You keep me going when times are tough—
        my bedrock, GOD, since my childhood.
I've hung on you from the day of my birth,
        the day you took me from the cradle;
        I'll never run out of praise.
Many gasp in alarm when they see me,
        but you take me in stride.

8-11 Just as each day brims with your beauty,
        my mouth brims with praise.
But don't turn me out to pasture when I'm old
        or put me on the shelf when I can't pull my weight.
My enemies are talking behind my back,
        watching for their chance to knife me.
The gossip is: "God has abandoned him.
        Pounce on him now; no one will help him."

12-16 God, don't just watch from the sidelines.
        Come on! Run to my side!
My accusers—make them lose face.
        Those out to get me—make them look
Like idiots, while I stretch out, reaching for you,
        and daily add praise to praise.
I'll write the book on your righteousness,
        talk up your salvation the livelong day,

never run out of good things to write or say.
I come in the power of the Lord GOD,
    I post signs marking his right-of-way.

17-24   You got me when I was an unformed youth,
    God, and taught me everything I know.
Now I'm telling the world your wonders;
    I'll keep at it until I'm old and gray.
God, don't walk off and leave me
    until I get out the news
Of your strong right arm to this world,
    news of your power to the world yet to come,
Your famous and righteous
    ways, O God.
God, you've done it all!
    Who is quite like you?
You, who made me stare trouble in the face,
    Turn me around;
Now let me look life in the face.
    I've been to the bottom;
Bring me up, streaming with honors;
    turn to me, be tender to me,
And I'll take up the lute and thank you
    to the tune of your faithfulness, God.
I'll make music for you on a harp,
    Holy One of Israel.
When I open up in song to you,
    I let out lungsful of praise,
    my rescued life a song.
All day long I'm chanting
    about you and your righteous ways,
While those who tried to do me in
    slink off looking ashamed.

A SOLOMON PSALM

1-8   **72** Give the gift of wise rule to the king, O God,
    the gift of just rule to the crown prince.
    May he judge your people rightly,
be honorable to your meek and lowly.
Let the mountains give exuberant witness;
    shape the hills with the contours of right living.
Please stand up for the poor,
    help the children of the needy,
    come down hard on the cruel tyrants.
Outlast the sun, outlive the moon —
    age after age after age.
Be rainfall on cut grass,
    earth-refreshing rain showers.
Let righteousness burst into blossom
    and peace abound until the moon fades to nothing.

Rule from sea to sea,
    from the River to the Rim.

9-14   Foes will fall on their knees before God,
    his enemies lick the dust.
Kings remote and legendary will pay homage,
    kings rich and resplendent will turn over their wealth.
All kings will fall down and worship,
    and godless nations sign up to serve him,
Because he rescues the poor at the first sign of need,
    the destitute who have run out of luck.
He opens a place in his heart for the down-and-out,
    he restores the wretched of the earth.
He frees them from tyranny and torture —
    when they bleed, he bleeds;
    when they die, he dies.

15-17   And live! Oh, let him live!
    Deck him out in Sheba gold.
Offer prayers unceasing to him,
    bless him from morning to night.
Fields of golden grain in the land,
    cresting the mountains in wild exuberance,
Cornucopias of praise, praises
    springing from the city like grass from the earth.
May he never be forgotten,
    his fame shine on like sunshine.
May all godless people enter his circle of blessing
    and bless the One who blessed them.

18-20   Blessed God, Israel's God,
    the one and only wonder-working God!
Blessed always his blazing glory!
    All earth brims with his glory.
Yes and Yes and Yes.

AN ASAPH PSALM

1-5   **73** No doubt about it! God is good —
    good to good people, good to the good-hearted.
But I nearly missed it,
    missed seeing his goodness.
I was looking the other way,
    looking up to the people
At the top,
    envying the wicked who have it made,
Who have nothing to worry about,
    not a care in the whole wide world.

6-10   Pretentious with arrogance,
    they wear the latest fashions in violence,
Pampered and overfed,

decked out in silk bows of silliness.
They jeer, using words to kill;
 they bully their way with words.
They're full of hot air,
 loudmouths disturbing the peace.
People actually listen to them — can you believe it?
 Like thirsty puppies, they lap up their words.

11-14 What's going on here? Is God out to lunch?
 Nobody's tending the store.
The wicked get by with everything;
 they have it made, piling up riches.
I've been stupid to play by the rules;
 what has it gotten me?
A long run of bad luck, that's what —
 a slap in the face every time I walk out the door.

15-20 If I'd have given in and talked like this,
 I would have betrayed your dear children.
Still, when I tried to figure it out,
 all I got was a splitting headache . . .
Until I entered the sanctuary of God.
 Then I saw the whole picture:
The slippery road you've put them on,
 with a final crash in a ditch of delusions.
In the blink of an eye, disaster!
 A blind curve in the dark, and — nightmare!
We wake up and rub our eyes. . . . Nothing.
 There's nothing to them. And there never was.

21-24 When I was beleaguered and bitter,
 totally consumed by envy,
I was totally ignorant, a dumb ox
 in your very presence.
I'm still in your presence,
 but you've taken my hand.
You wisely and tenderly lead me,
 and then you bless me.

25-28 You're all I want in heaven!
 You're all I want on earth!
When my skin sags and my bones get brittle,
 GOD is rock-firm and faithful.
Look! Those who left you are falling apart!
 Deserters, they'll never be heard from again.
But I'm in the very presence of God —
 oh, how refreshing it is!
I've made Lord GOD my home.
 God, I'm telling the world what you do!

AN ASAPH PSALM

74 You walked off and left us, and never looked back.
God, how could you do that?
We're your very own sheep;
how can you stomp off in anger?

2-3 Refresh your memory of us — you bought us a long time ago.
Your most precious tribe — you paid a good price for us!
Your very own Mount Zion — you actually lived here once!
Come and visit the site of disaster,
see how they've wrecked the sanctuary.

4-8 While your people were at worship, your enemies barged in,
brawling and scrawling graffiti.
They set fire to the porch;
axes swinging, they chopped up the woodwork,
Beat down the doors with sledgehammers,
then split them into kindling.
They burned your holy place to the ground,
violated the place of worship.
They said to themselves, "We'll wipe them all out,"
and burned down all the places of worship.

9-17 There's not a sign or symbol of God in sight,
nor anyone to speak in his name,
no one who knows what's going on.
How long, God, will barbarians blaspheme,
enemies curse and get by with it?
Why don't you do something? How long are you going
to sit there with your hands folded in your lap?
God is my King from the very start;
he works salvation in the womb of the earth.
With one blow you split the sea in two,
you made mincemeat of the dragon Tannin.
You lopped off the heads of Leviathan,
then served them up in a stew for the animals.
With your finger you opened up springs and creeks,
and dried up the wild floodwaters.
You own the day, you own the night;
you put stars and sun in place.
You laid out the four corners of earth,
shaped the seasons of summer and winter.

18-21 Mark and remember, GOD, all the enemy
taunts, each idiot desecration.
Don't throw your lambs to the wolves;
after all we've been through, don't forget us.
Remember your promises;
the city is in darkness, the countryside violent.
Don't leave the victims to rot in the street;
make them a choir that sings your praises.

22-23 On your feet, O God —
   stand up for yourself!
Do you hear what they're saying about you,
   all the vile obscenities?
Don't tune out their malicious filth,
   the brawling invective that never lets up.

AN ASAPH PSALM

1 **75** We thank you, God, we thank you —
   your Name is our favorite word;
   your mighty works are all we talk about.

2-4 You say, "I'm calling this meeting to order,
   I'm ready to set things right.
When the earth goes topsy-turvy
   And nobody knows which end is up,
I nail it all down,
   I put everything in place again.
I say to the smart alecks, 'That's enough,'
   to the bullies, 'Not so fast.'"

5-6 Don't raise your fist against High God.
   Don't raise your voice against Rock of Ages.
He's the One from east to west;
   from desert to mountains, he's the One.

7-8 God rules: he brings this one down to his knees,
   pulls that one up on her feet.
GOD has a cup in his hand,
   a bowl of wine, full to the brim.
He draws from it and pours;
   it's drained to the dregs.
Earth's wicked ones drink it all,
   drink it down to the last bitter drop!

9-10 And I'm telling the story of God Eternal,
   singing the praises of Jacob's God.
The fists of the wicked
   are bloody stumps,
The arms of the righteous
   are lofty green branches.

AN ASAPH PSALM

1-3 **76** God is well-known in Judah;
   in Israel, he's a household name.
He keeps a house in Salem,
   his own suite of rooms in Zion.
That's where, using arrows for kindling,
   he made a bonfire of weapons of war.

4-6 Oh, how bright you shine!
    Outshining their huge piles of loot!
The warriors were plundered
    and left there impotent.
And now there's nothing to them,
    nothing to show for their swagger and threats.
Your sudden roar, God of Jacob,
    knocked the wind out of horse and rider.

7-10 Fierce you are, and fearsome!
    Who can stand up to your rising anger?
From heaven you thunder judgment;
    earth falls to her knees and holds her breath.
God stands tall and makes things right,
    he saves all the wretched on earth.
Instead of smoldering rage — God-praise!
    All that sputtering rage — now a garland for God!

11-12 Do for GOD what you said you'd do —
    he is, after all, your God.
Let everyone in town bring offerings
    to the One Who Watches our every move.
Nobody gets by with anything,
    no one plays fast and loose with him.

AN ASAPH PSALM

1 **77** I yell out to my God, I yell with all my might,
    I yell at the top of my lungs. He listens.

2-6 I found myself in trouble and went looking for my Lord;
    my life was an open wound that wouldn't heal.
When friends said, "Everything will turn out all right,"
    I didn't believe a word they said.
I remember God — and shake my head.
    I bow my head — then wring my hands.
I'm awake all night — not a wink of sleep;
    I can't even say what's bothering me.
I go over the days one by one,
    I ponder the years gone by.
I strum my lute all through the night,
    wondering how to get my life together.

7-10 Will the Lord walk off and leave us for good?
    Will he never smile again?
Is his love worn threadbare?
    Has his salvation promise burned out?
Has God forgotten his manners?
    Has he angrily stalked off and left us?
"Just my luck," I said. "The High God goes out of business
    just the moment I need him."

11-12 Once again I'll go over what God has done,
      lay out on the table the ancient wonders;
I'll ponder all the things you've accomplished,
      and give a long, loving look at your acts.

13-15 O God! Your way is holy!
      No god is great like God!
You're the God who makes things happen;
      you showed everyone what you can do—
You pulled your people out of the worst kind of trouble,
      rescued the children of Jacob and Joseph.

16-19 Ocean saw you in action, God,
      saw you and trembled with fear;
      Deep Ocean was scared to death.
Clouds belched buckets of rain,
      Sky exploded with thunder,
      your arrows flashing this way and that.
From Whirlwind came your thundering voice,
      Lightning exposed the world,
      Earth reeled and rocked.
You strode right through Ocean,
      walked straight through roaring Ocean,
      but nobody saw you come or go.

20 Hidden in the hands of Moses and Aaron,
   You led your people like a flock of sheep.

AN ASAPH PSALM

1-4 **78** Listen, dear friends, to God's truth,
      bend your ears to what I tell you.
      I'm chewing on the morsel of a proverb;
I'll let you in on the sweet old truths,
Stories we heard from our fathers,
      counsel we learned at our mother's knee.
We're not keeping this to ourselves,
      we're passing it along to the next generation—
God's fame and fortune,
      the marvelous things he has done.

5-8 He planted a witness in Jacob,
      set his Word firmly in Israel,
Then commanded our parents
      to teach it to their children
So the next generation would know,
      and all the generations to come—
Know the truth and tell the stories
      so their children can trust in God,
Never forget the works of God
      but keep his commands to the letter.
Heaven forbid they should be like their parents,

> bullheaded and bad,
> A fickle and faithless bunch
>   who never stayed true to God.

9-16
> The Ephraimites, armed to the teeth,
>   ran off when the battle began.
> They were cowards to God's Covenant,
>   refused to walk by his Word.
> They forgot what he had done —
>   marvels he'd done right before their eyes.
> He performed miracles in plain sight of their parents
>   in Egypt, out on the fields of Zoan.
> He split the Sea and they walked right through it;
>   he piled the waters to the right and the left.
> He led them by day with a cloud,
>   led them all the night long with a fiery torch.
> He split rocks in the wilderness,
>   gave them all they could drink from underground springs;
> He made creeks flow out from sheer rock,
>   and water pour out like a river.

17-20
> All they did was sin even more,
>   rebel in the desert against the High God.
> They tried to get their own way with God,
>   clamored for favors, for special attention.
> They whined like spoiled children,
>   "Why can't God give us a decent meal in this desert?
> Sure, he struck the rock and the water flowed,
>   creeks cascaded from the rock.
> But how about some fresh-baked bread?
>   How about a nice cut of meat?"

21-31
> When God heard that, he was furious —
>   his anger flared against Jacob,
>   he lost his temper with Israel.
> It was clear they didn't believe God,
>   had no intention of trusting in his help.
> But God helped them anyway, commanded the clouds
>   and gave orders that opened the gates of heaven.
> He rained down showers of manna to eat,
>   he gave them the Bread of Heaven.
> They ate the bread of the mighty angels;
>   he sent them all the food they could eat.
> He let East Wind break loose from the skies,
>   gave a strong push to South Wind.
> This time it was birds that rained down —
>   succulent birds, an abundance of birds.
> He aimed them right for the center of their camp;
>   all round their tents there were birds.
> They ate and had their fill;
>   he handed them everything they craved on a platter.

But their greed knew no bounds;
    they stuffed their mouths with more and more.
Finally, God was fed up, his anger erupted —
    he cut down their brightest and best,
    he laid low Israel's finest young men.

32-37   And — can you believe it? — they kept right on sinning;
    all those wonders and they still wouldn't believe!
So their lives dribbled off to nothing —
    nothing to show for their lives but a ghost town.
When he cut them down, they came running for help;
    they turned and pled for mercy.
They gave witness that God was their rock,
    that High God was their redeemer,
But they didn't mean a word of it;
    they lied through their teeth the whole time.
They could not have cared less about him,
    wanted nothing to do with his Covenant.

38-55   And God? Compassionate!
    Forgave the sin! Didn't destroy!
Over and over he reined in his anger,
    restrained his considerable wrath.
He knew what they were made of;
    he knew there wasn't much to them,
How often in the desert they had spurned him,
    tried his patience in those wilderness years.
Time and again they pushed him to the limit,
    provoked Israel's Holy God.
How quickly they forgot what he'd done,
    forgot their day of rescue from the enemy,
When he did miracles in Egypt,
    wonders on the plain of Zoan.
He turned the River and its streams to blood —
    not a drop of water fit to drink.
He sent flies, which ate them alive,
    and frogs, which bedeviled them.
He turned their harvest over to caterpillars,
    everything they had worked for to the locusts.
He flattened their grapevines with hail;
    a killing frost ruined their orchards.
He pounded their cattle with hail,
    let thunderbolts loose on their herds.
His anger flared,
    a wild firestorm of havoc,
An advance guard of disease-carrying angels
    to clear the ground, preparing the way before him.
He didn't spare those people,
    he let the plague rage through their lives.
He killed all the Egyptian firstborns,
    lusty infants, offspring of Ham's virility.

Then he led his people out like sheep,
    took his flock safely through the wilderness.
He took good care of them; they had nothing to fear.
    The Sea took care of their enemies for good.
He brought them into his holy land,
    this mountain he claimed for his own.
He scattered everyone who got in their way;
    he staked out an inheritance for them —
    the tribes of Israel all had their own places.

56-64   But they kept on giving him a hard time,
    rebelled against God, the High God,
    refused to do anything he told them.
They were worse, if that's possible, than their parents:
    traitors — crooked as a corkscrew.
Their pagan orgies provoked God's anger,
    their obscene idolatries broke his heart.
When God heard their carryings-on, he was furious;
    he posted a huge No over Israel.
He walked off and left Shiloh empty,
    abandoned the shrine where he had met with Israel.
He let his pride and joy go to the dogs,
    turned his back on the pride of his life.
He turned them loose on fields of battle;
    angry, he let them fend for themselves.
Their young men went to war and never came back;
    their young women waited in vain.
Their priests were massacred,
    and their widows never shed a tear.

65-72   Suddenly the Lord was up on his feet
    like someone roused from deep sleep,
    shouting like a drunken warrior.
He hit his enemies hard, sent them running,
    yelping, not daring to look back.
He disqualified Joseph as leader,
    told Ephraim he didn't have what it takes,
And chose the Tribe of Judah instead,
    Mount Zion, which he loves so much.
He built his sanctuary there, resplendent,
    solid and lasting as the earth itself.
Then he chose David, his servant,
    handpicked him from his work in the sheep pens.
One day he was caring for the ewes and their lambs,
    the next day God had him shepherding Jacob,
    his people Israel, his prize possession.
His good heart made him a good shepherd;
    he guided the people wisely and well.

AN ASAPH PSALM

1-4
79
God! Barbarians have broken into your home,
  violated your holy temple,
  left Jerusalem a pile of rubble!
They've served up the corpses of your servants
  as carrion food for birds of prey,
Threw the bones of your holy people
  out to the wild animals to gnaw on.
They dumped out their blood
  like buckets of water.
All around Jerusalem, their bodies
  were left to rot, unburied.
We're nothing but a joke to our neighbors,
  graffiti scrawled on the city walls.

5-7
How long do we have to put up with this, GOD?
  Do you have it in for us for good?
  Will your smoldering rage never cool down?
If you're going to be angry, be angry
  with the pagans who care nothing about you,
  or your rival kingdoms who ignore you.
They're the ones who ruined Jacob,
  who wrecked and looted the place where he lived.

8-10
Don't blame us for the sins of our parents.
  Hurry up and help us; we're at the end of our rope.
You're famous for helping; God, give *us* a break.
  Your reputation is on the line.
Pull us out of this mess, forgive us our sins—
  do what you're famous for doing!
Don't let the heathen get by with their sneers:
  "Where's your God? Is he out to lunch?"
Go public and show the godless world
  that they can't kill your servants and get by with it.

11-13
Give groaning prisoners a hearing;
  pardon those on death row from their doom—you can do it!
Give our jeering neighbors what they've got coming to them;
  let their God-taunts boomerang and knock them flat.
Then we, your people, the ones you love and care for,
  will thank you over and over and over.
We'll tell everyone we meet
  how wonderful you are, how praiseworthy you are!

AN ASAPH PSALM

1-2
80
Listen, Shepherd, Israel's Shepherd—
  get all your Joseph sheep together.
Throw beams of light
from your dazzling throne
So Ephraim, Benjamin, and Manasseh

can see where they're going.
Get out of bed — you've slept long enough!
 Come on the run before it's too late.

3 God, come back!
 Smile your blessing smile:
 That will be our salvation.

4-6 GOD, God-of-the-Angel-Armies,
  how long will you smolder like a sleeping volcano
  while your people call for fire and brimstone?
 You put us on a diet of tears,
  bucket after bucket of salty tears to drink.
 You make us look ridiculous to our friends;
  our enemies poke fun day after day.

7 God-of-the-Angel-Armies, come back!
 Smile your blessing smile:
 That will be our salvation.

8-18 Remember how you brought a young vine from Egypt,
  cleared out the brambles and briers
  and planted your very own vineyard?
 You prepared the good earth,
  you planted her roots deep;
  the vineyard filled the land.
 Your vine soared high and shaded the mountains,
  even dwarfing the giant cedars.
 Your vine ranged west to the Sea,
  east to the River.
 So why do you no longer protect your vine?
  Trespassers pick its grapes at will;
 Wild pigs crash through and crush it,
  and the mice nibble away at what's left.
 God-of-the-Angel-Armies, turn our way!
  Take a good look at what's happened
  and attend to this vine.
 Care for what you once tenderly planted —
  the vine you raised from a shoot.
 And those who dared to set it on fire —
  give them a look that will kill!
 Then take the hand of your once-favorite child,
  the child you raised to adulthood.
 We will never turn our back on you;
  breathe life into our lungs so we can shout your name!

19 GOD, God-of-the-Angel-Armies, come back!
 Smile your blessing smile:
 That will be our salvation.

AN ASAPH PSALM

81 1-5

A song to our strong God!
a shout to the God of Jacob!
Anthems from the choir, music from the band,
sweet sounds from lute and harp,
Trumpets and trombones and horns:
it's festival day, a feast to God!
A day decreed by God,
solemnly ordered by the God of Jacob.
He commanded Joseph to keep this day
so we'd never forget what he did in Egypt.

I hear this most gentle whisper from One
I never guessed would speak to me:

6-7

"I took the world off your shoulders,
freed you from a life of hard labor.
You called to me in your pain;
I got you out of a bad place.
I answered you from where the thunder hides,
I proved you at Meribah Fountain.

8-10

"Listen, dear ones—get this straight;
O Israel, don't take this lightly.
Don't take up with strange gods,
don't worship the latest in gods.
I'm GOD, your God, the very God
who rescued you from doom in Egypt,
Then fed you all you could eat,
filled your hungry stomachs.

11-12

"But my people didn't listen,
Israel paid no attention;
So I let go of the reins and told them, 'Run!
Do it your own way!'

13-16

"Oh, dear people, will you listen to me now?
Israel, will you follow my map?
I'll make short work of your enemies,
give your foes the back of my hand.
I'll send the GOD-haters cringing like dogs,
never to be heard from again.
You'll feast on my fresh-baked bread
spread with butter and rock-pure honey."

AN ASAPH PSALM

82 1

God calls the judges into his courtroom,
he puts all the judges in the dock.

2-4 "Enough! You've corrupted justice long enough,
    you've let the wicked get away with murder.
You're here to defend the defenseless,
    to make sure that underdogs get a fair break;
Your job is to stand up for the powerless,
    and prosecute all those who exploit them."

5 Ignorant judges! Head-in-the-sand judges!
    They haven't a clue to what's going on.
And now everything's falling apart,
    the world's coming unglued.

6-7 "I commissioned you judges, each one of you,
    deputies of the High God,
But you've betrayed your commission
    and now you're stripped of your rank, busted."

8 O God, give them their just deserts!
    You've got the whole world in your hands!

A N A S A P H P S A L M

1-5 **83** GOD, don't shut me out;
    don't give me the silent treatment, O God.
    Your enemies are out there whooping it up,
the God-haters are living it up;
They're plotting to do your people in,
    conspiring to rob you of your precious ones.
"Let's wipe this nation from the face of the earth,"
    they say; "scratch Israel's name off the books."
And now they're putting their heads together,
    making plans to get rid of you.

6-8 Edom and the Ishmaelites,
    Moab and the Hagrites,
    Gebal and Ammon and Amalek,
    Philistia and the Tyrians,
    And now Assyria has joined up,
    Giving muscle to the gang of Lot.

9-12 Do to them what you did to Midian,
    to Sisera and Jabin at Kishon Brook;
They came to a bad end at Endor,
    nothing but dung for the garden.
Cut down their leaders as you did Oreb and Zeeb,
    their princes to nothings like Zebah and Zalmunna,
With their empty brags, "We're grabbing it all,
    grabbing God's gardens for ourselves."

13-18 My God! I've had it with them!
    Blow them away!
Tumbleweeds in the desert waste,

charred sticks in the burned-over ground.
Knock the breath right out of them, so they're gasping
for breath, gasping, "GOD."
Bring them to the end of their rope,
and leave them there dangling, helpless.
Then they'll learn your name: "GOD,"
the one and only High God on earth.

A KORAH PSALM

84 What a beautiful home, GOD-of-the-Angel-Armies!
I've always longed to live in a place like this,
Always dreamed of a room in your house,
where I could sing for joy to God-alive!

3-4 Birds find nooks and crannies in your house,
sparrows and swallows make nests there.
They lay their eggs and raise their young,
singing their songs in the place where we worship.
GOD-of-the-Angel-Armies! King! God!
How blessed they are to live and sing there!

5-7 And how blessed all those in whom you live,
whose lives become roads you travel;
They wind through lonesome valleys, come upon brooks,
discover cool springs and pools brimming with rain!
God-traveled, these roads curve up the mountain, and
at the last turn — Zion! God in full view!

8-9 GOD-of-the-Angel-Armies, listen:
O God of Jacob, open your ears — I'm praying!
Look at our shields, glistening in the sun,
our faces, shining with your gracious anointing.

10-12 One day spent in your house, this beautiful place of worship,
beats thousands spent on Greek island beaches.
I'd rather scrub floors in the house of my God
than be honored as a guest in the palace of sin.
All sunshine and sovereign is GOD,
generous in gifts and glory.
He doesn't scrimp with his traveling companions.
It's smooth sailing all the way with GOD-of-the-Angel-Armies.

A KORAH PSALM

85 GOD, you smiled on your good earth!
You brought good times back to Jacob!
You lifted the cloud of guilt from your people,
you put their sins far out of sight.
You took back your sin-provoked threats,
you cooled your hot, righteous anger.

4-7 Help us again, God of our help;
don't hold a grudge against us forever.

You aren't going to keep this up, are you?
scowling and angry, year after year?
Why not help us make a fresh start — a resurrection life?
Then your people will laugh and sing!
Show us how much you love us, GOD!
Give us the salvation we need!

8-9   I can't wait to hear what he'll say.
GOD's about to pronounce his people well,
The holy people he loves so much,
so they'll never again live like fools.
See how close his salvation is to those who fear him?
Our country is home base for Glory!

10-13   Love and Truth meet in the street,
Right Living and Whole Living embrace and kiss!
Truth sprouts green from the ground,
Right Living pours down from the skies!
Oh yes! GOD gives Goodness and Beauty;
our land responds with Bounty and Blessing.
Right Living strides out before him,
and clears a path for his passage.

A DAVID PSALM

1-7   # 86
Bend an ear, GOD; answer me.
I'm one miserable wretch!
Keep me safe — haven't I lived a good life?
Help your servant — I'm depending on you!
You're my God; have mercy on me.
I count on you from morning to night.
Give your servant a happy life;
I put myself in your hands!
You're well-known as good and forgiving,
bighearted to all who ask for help.
Pay attention, GOD, to my prayer;
bend down and listen to my cry for help.
Every time I'm in trouble I call on you,
confident that you'll answer.

8-10   There's no one quite like you among the gods, O Lord,
and nothing to compare with your works.
All the nations you made are on their way,
ready to give honor to you, O Lord,
Ready to put your beauty on display,
parading your greatness,
And the great things you do —
God, you're the one, there's no one but you!

11-17   Train me, GOD, to walk straight;
then I'll follow your true path.
Put me together, one heart and mind;

then, undivided, I'll worship in joyful fear.
From the bottom of my heart I thank you, dear Lord;
    I've never kept secret what you're up to.
You've always been great toward me — what love!
    You snatched me from the brink of disaster!
God, these bullies have reared their heads!
    A gang of thugs is after me —
    and they don't care a thing about you.
But you, O God, are both tender and kind,
    not easily angered, immense in love,
    and you never, never quit.
So look me in the eye and show kindness,
    give your servant the strength to go on,
    save your dear, dear child!
Make a show of how much you love me
    so the bullies who hate me will stand there slack-jawed,
As you, GOD, gently and powerfully
    put me back on my feet.

A KORAH PSALM

1-3
87 He founded Zion on the Holy Mountain —
    and oh, how GOD loves his home!
    Loves it far better than all
the homes of Jacob put together!
God's hometown — oh!
    everyone there is talking about you!

4 I name them off, those among whom I'm famous:
    Egypt and Babylon,
    also Philistia,
    even Tyre, along with Cush.
Word's getting around; they point them out:
    "This one was born again here!"

5 The word's getting out on Zion:
    "Men and women, right and left,
    get born again in her!"

6 GOD registers their names in his book:
    "This one, this one, and this one —
    born again, right here."

7 Singers and dancers give credit to Zion:
    "All my springs are in you!"

A KORAH PRAYER OF HEMAN

1-9
88 GOD, you're my last chance of the day.
    I spend the night on my knees before you.
    Put me on your salvation agenda;
    take notes on the trouble I'm in.
I've had my fill of trouble;

I'm camped on the edge of hell.
I'm written off as a lost cause,
  one more statistic, a hopeless case.
Abandoned as already dead,
  one more body in a stack of corpses,
And not so much as a gravestone —
  I'm a black hole in oblivion.
You've dropped me into a bottomless pit,
  sunk me in a pitch-black abyss.
I'm battered senseless by your rage,
  relentlessly pounded by your waves of anger.
You turned my friends against me,
  made me horrible to them.
I'm caught in a maze and can't find my way out,
  blinded by tears of pain and frustration.

9-12 I call to you, GOD; all day I call.
  I wring my hands, I plead for help.
Are the dead a live audience for your miracles?
  Do ghosts ever join the choirs that praise you?
Does your love make any difference in a graveyard?
  Is your faithful presence noticed in the corridors of hell?
Are your marvelous wonders ever seen in the dark,
  your righteous ways noticed in the Land of No Memory?

13-18 I'm standing my ground, GOD, shouting for help,
  at my prayers every morning, on my knees each daybreak.
Why, GOD, do you turn a deaf ear?
  Why do you make yourself scarce?
For as long as I remember I've been hurting;
  I've taken the worst you can hand out, and I've had it.
Your wildfire anger has blazed through my life;
  I'm bleeding, black-and-blue.
You've attacked me fiercely from every side,
  raining down blows till I'm nearly dead.
You made lover and neighbor alike dump me;
  the only friend I have left is Darkness.

AN ETHAN PRAYER

1-4 **89** Your love, GOD, is my song, and I'll sing it!
  I'm forever telling everyone how faithful you are.
  I'll never quit telling the story of your love —
how you built the cosmos
and guaranteed everything in it.
Your love has always been our lives' foundation,
  your fidelity has been the roof over our world.
You once said, "I joined forces with my chosen leader,
  I pledged my word to my servant, David, saying,
'Everyone descending from you is guaranteed life;
  I'll make your rule as solid and lasting as rock.'"

5-18　GOD! Let the cosmos praise your wonderful ways,
　　　　the choir of holy angels sing anthems to your faithful ways!
　　　Search high and low, scan skies and land,
　　　　you'll find nothing and no one quite like GOD.
　　　The holy angels are in awe before him;
　　　　he looms immense and august over everyone around him.
　　　GOD-of-the-Angel-Armies, who is like you,
　　　　powerful and faithful from every angle?
　　　You put the arrogant ocean in its place
　　　　and calm its waves when they turn unruly.
　　　You gave that old hag Egypt the back of your hand,
　　　　you brushed off your enemies with a flick of your wrist.
　　　You own the cosmos — you made everything in it,
　　　　everything from atom to archangel.
　　　You positioned the North and South Poles;
　　　　the mountains Tabor and Hermon sing duets to you.
　　　With your well-muscled arm and your grip of steel —
　　　　nobody trifles with you!
　　　The Right and Justice are the roots of your rule;
　　　　Love and Truth are its fruits.
　　　Blessed are the people who know the passwords of praise,
　　　　who shout on parade in the bright presence of GOD.
　　　Delighted, they dance all day long; they know
　　　　who you are, what you do — they can't keep it quiet!
　　　Your vibrant beauty has gotten inside us —
　　　　you've been so good to us! We're walking on air!
　　　All we are and have we owe to GOD,
　　　　Holy God of Israel, our King!

19-37　A long time ago you spoke in a vision,
　　　　you spoke to your faithful beloved:
　　　"I've crowned a hero,
　　　　I chose the best I could find;
　　　I found David, my servant,
　　　　poured holy oil on his head,
　　　And I'll keep my hand steadily on him,
　　　　yes, I'll stick with him through thick and thin.
　　　No enemy will get the best of him,
　　　　no scoundrel will do him in.
　　　I'll weed out all who oppose him,
　　　　I'll clean out all who hate him.
　　　I'm with him for good and I'll love him forever;
　　　　I've set him on high — he's riding high!
　　　I've put Ocean in his one hand, River in the other;
　　　　he'll call out, 'Oh, my Father — my God, my Rock of Salvation!'
　　　Yes, I'm setting him apart as the First of the royal line,
　　　　High King over all of earth's kings.
　　　I'll preserve him eternally in my love,
　　　　I'll faithfully do all I so solemnly promised.
　　　I'll guarantee his family tree
　　　　and underwrite his rule.

If his children refuse to do what I tell them,
  if they refuse to walk in the way I show them,
If they spit on the directions I give them
  and tear up the rules I post for them—
I'll rub their faces in the dirt of their rebellion
  and make them face the music.
But I'll never throw them out,
  never abandon or disown them.
Do you think I'd withdraw my holy promise?
  or take back words I'd already spoken?
I've given my word, my whole and holy word;
  do you think I would lie to David?
His family tree is here for good,
  his sovereignty as sure as the sun,
Dependable as the phases of the moon,
  inescapable as weather."

³⁸⁻⁵¹ But GOD, you did walk off and leave us,
  you lost your temper with the one you anointed.
You tore up the promise you made to your servant,
  you stomped his crown in the mud.
You blasted his home to kingdom come,
  reduced his city to a pile of rubble
Picked clean by wayfaring strangers,
  a joke to all the neighbors.
You declared a holiday for all his enemies,
  and they're celebrating for all they're worth.
Angry, you opposed him in battle,
  refused to fight on his side;
You robbed him of his splendor, humiliated this warrior,
  ground his kingly honor in the dirt.
You took the best years of his life
  and left him an impotent, ruined husk.
How long do we put up with this, GOD?
  Are you gone for good? Will you hold this grudge forever?
Remember my sorrow and how short life is.
  Did you create men and women for nothing but this?
We'll see death soon enough. Everyone does.
  And there's no back door out of hell.
So where is the love you're so famous for, Lord?
  What happened to your promise to David?
Take a good look at your servant, dear Lord;
  I'm the butt of the jokes of all nations,
The taunting jokes of your enemies, GOD,
  as they dog the steps of your dear anointed.

  Blessed be GOD forever and always!
    Yes. Oh, yes.

A PRAYER OF MOSES, MAN OF GOD

1-2 **90** God, it seems you've been our home forever;
        long before the mountains were born,
        Long before you brought earth itself to birth,
    from "once upon a time" to "kingdom come" — you are God.

3-11 So don't return us to mud, saying,
        "Back to where you came from!"
    Patience! You've got all the time in the world — whether
        a thousand years or a day, it's all the same to you.
    Are we no more to you than a wispy dream,
        no more than a blade of grass
    That springs up gloriously with the rising sun
        and is cut down without a second thought?
    Your anger is far and away too much for us;
        we're at the end of our rope.
    You keep track of all our sins; every misdeed
        since we were children is entered in your books.
    All we can remember is that frown on your face.
        Is that all we're ever going to get?
    We live for seventy years or so
        (with luck we might make it to eighty),
    And what do we have to show for it? Trouble.
        Toil and trouble and a marker in the graveyard.
    Who can make sense of such rage,
        such anger against the very ones who fear you?

12-17 Oh! Teach us to live well!
        Teach us to live wisely and well!
    Come back, GOD — how long do we have to wait? —
        and treat your servants with kindness for a change.
    Surprise us with love at daybreak;
        then we'll skip and dance all the day long.
    Make up for the bad times with some good times;
        we've seen enough evil to last a lifetime.
    Let your servants see what you're best at —
        the ways you rule and bless your children.
    And let the loveliness of our Lord, our God, rest on us,
        confirming the work that we do.
        Oh, yes. Affirm the work that we do!

1-13 **91** You who sit down in the High God's presence,
        spend the night in Shaddai's shadow,
        Say this: "GOD, you're my refuge.
    I trust in you and I'm safe!"
    That's right — he rescues you from hidden traps,
        shields you from deadly hazards.
    His huge outstretched arms protect you —
        under them you're perfectly safe;
        his arms fend off all harm.

Fear nothing — not wild wolves in the night,
    not flying arrows in the day,
Not disease that prowls through the darkness,
    not disaster that erupts at high noon.
Even though others succumb all around,
    drop like flies right and left,
    no harm will even graze you.
You'll stand untouched, watch it all from a distance,
    watch the wicked turn into corpses.
Yes, because GOD's your refuge,
    the High God your very own home,
Evil can't get close to you,
    harm can't get through the door.
He ordered his angels
    to guard you wherever you go.
If you stumble, they'll catch you;
    their job is to keep you from falling.
You'll walk unharmed among lions and snakes,
    and kick young lions and serpents from the path.

14-16 "If you'll hold on to me for dear life," says GOD,
    "I'll get you out of any trouble.
I'll give you the best of care
    if you'll only get to know and trust me.
Call me and I'll answer, be at your side in bad times;
    I'll rescue you, then throw you a party.
I'll give you a long life,
    give you a long drink of salvation!"

A SABBATH SONG

1-3 **92** What a beautiful thing, GOD, to give thanks,
    to sing an anthem to you, the High God!
To announce your love each daybreak,
    sing your faithful presence all through the night,
Accompanied by dulcimer and harp,
    the full-bodied music of strings.

4-9 You made me so happy, GOD.
    I saw your work and I shouted for joy.
How magnificent your work, GOD!
    How profound your thoughts!
Dullards never notice what you do;
    fools never do get it.
When the wicked popped up like weeds
    and all the evil men and women took over,
You mowed them down,
    finished them off once and for all.
You, GOD, are High and Eternal.
    Look at your enemies, GOD!
Look at your enemies — ruined!
    Scattered to the winds, all those hirelings of evil!

10-14 But you've made me strong as a charging bison,
 you've honored me with a festive parade.
The sight of my critics going down is still fresh,
 the rout of my malicious detractors.
My ears are filled with the sounds of promise:
 "Good people will prosper like palm trees,
Grow tall like Lebanon cedars;
 transplanted to GOD's courtyard,
They'll grow tall in the presence of God,
 lithe and green, virile still in old age."

15 Such witnesses to upright GOD!
 My Mountain, my huge, holy Mountain!

1-2 **93** GOD is King, robed and ruling,
 GOD is robed and surging with strength.

And yes, the world is firm, immovable,
Your throne ever firm — you're Eternal!

3-4 Sea storms are up, GOD,
Sea storms wild and roaring,
Sea storms with thunderous breakers.

Stronger than wild sea storms,
Mightier than sea-storm breakers,
Mighty GOD rules from High Heaven.

5 What you say goes — it always has.
"Beauty" and "Holy" mark your palace rule,
GOD, to the very end of time.

1-2 **94** GOD, put an end to evil;
 avenging God, show your colors!
Judge of the earth, take your stand;
throw the book at the arrogant.

3-4 GOD, the wicked get away with murder —
 how long will you let this go on?
They brag and boast
 and crow about their crimes!

5-7 They walk all over your people, GOD,
 exploit and abuse your precious people.
They take out anyone who gets in their way;
 if they can't use them, they kill them.
They think, "GOD isn't looking,
 Jacob's God is out to lunch."

8-11 Well, think again, you idiots,
 fools — how long before you get smart?

Do you think Ear-Maker doesn't hear,
    Eye-Shaper doesn't see?
Do you think the trainer of nations doesn't correct,
    the teacher of Adam doesn't know?
GOD knows, all right —
    knows your stupidity,
    sees your shallowness.

12-15 How blessed the man you train, GOD,
    the woman you instruct in your Word,
Providing a circle of quiet within the clamor of evil,
    while a jail is being built for the wicked.
GOD will never walk away from his people,
    never desert his precious people.
Rest assured that justice is on its way
    and every good heart put right.

16-19 Who stood up for me against the wicked?
    Who took my side against evil workers?
If GOD hadn't been there for me,
    I never would have made it.
The minute I said, "I'm slipping, I'm falling,"
    your love, GOD, took hold and held me fast.
When I was upset and beside myself,
    you calmed me down and cheered me up.

20-23 Can Misrule have anything in common with you?
    Can Troublemaker pretend to be on your side?
They ganged up on good people,
    plotted behind the backs of the innocent.
But GOD became my hideout,
    God was my high mountain retreat,
Then boomeranged their evil back on them:
    for their evil ways he wiped them out,
    our GOD cleaned them out for good.

95

1-2 Come, let's shout praises to GOD,
    raise the roof for the Rock who saved us!
Let's march into his presence singing praises,
    lifting the rafters with our hymns!

3-5 And why? Because GOD is the best,
    High King over all the gods.
In one hand he holds deep caves and caverns,
    in the other hand grasps the high mountains.
He made Ocean — he owns it!
    His hands sculpted Earth!

6-7 So come, let us worship: bow before him,
    on your knees before GOD, who made us!
Oh yes, he's our God,
    and we're the people he pastures, the flock he feeds.

7-11 Drop everything and listen, listen as he speaks:
  "Don't turn a deaf ear as in the Bitter Uprising,
As on the day of the Wilderness Test,
  when your ancestors turned and put *me* to the test.
For forty years they watched me at work among them,
  as over and over they tried my patience.
And I was provoked — oh, was I provoked!
  'Can't they keep their minds on God for five minutes?
  Do they simply refuse to walk down my road?'
Exasperated, I exploded,
  'They'll never get where they're headed,
  never be able to sit down and rest.'"

1-2 **96** Sing God a brand-new song!
Earth and everyone in it, sing!
Sing to God — *worship* God!

2-3 Shout the news of his victory from sea to sea,
Take the news of his glory to the lost,
News of his wonders to one and all!

4-5 For God is great, and worth a thousand Hallelujahs.
His terrible beauty makes the gods look cheap;
Pagan gods are mere tatters and rags.

5-6 God made the heavens —
Royal splendor radiates from him,
A powerful beauty sets him apart.

7 Bravo, God, Bravo!
Everyone join in the great shout: Encore!
In awe before the beauty, in awe before the might.

8-9 Bring gifts and celebrate,
Bow before the beauty of God,
Then to your knees — everyone worship!

10 Get out the message — God Rules!
He put the world on a firm foundation;
He treats everyone fair and square.

11 Let's hear it from Sky,
With Earth joining in,
And a huge round of applause from Sea.

12 Let Wilderness turn cartwheels,
Animals, come dance,
Put every tree of the forest in the choir —

13 An extravaganza before God as he comes,
As he comes to set everything right on earth,
Set everything right, treat everyone fair.

97

1 GOD rules: *there's* something to shout over!
On the double, mainlands and islands — celebrate!

2 Bright clouds and storm clouds circle 'round him;
Right and justice anchor his rule.

3 Fire blazes out before him,
Flaming high up the craggy mountains.

4 His lightnings light up the world;
Earth, wide-eyed, trembles in fear.

5 The mountains take one look at GOD
And melt, melt like wax before earth's Lord.

6 The heavens announce that he'll set everything right,
And everyone will see it happen — glorious!

7-8 All who serve handcrafted gods will be sorry —
And they were so proud of their ragamuffin gods!

On your knees, all you gods — worship him!
And Zion, you listen and take heart!

Daughters of Zion, sing your hearts out:
GOD has done it all, has set everything right.

9 You, GOD, are High God of the cosmos,
Far, far higher than any of the gods.

10 GOD loves all who hate evil,
And those who love him he keeps safe,
Snatches them from the grip of the wicked.

11 Light-seeds are planted in the souls of God's people,
Joy-seeds are planted in good heart-soil.

12 So, God's people, shout praise to GOD,
Give thanks to our Holy God!

98

1 Sing to GOD a brand-new song.
He's made a world of wonders!

He rolled up his sleeves,
He set things right.

2 GOD made history with salvation,
He showed the world what he could do.

3 He remembered to love us, a bonus
To his dear family, Israel — indefatigable love.

The whole earth comes to attention.
Look — God's work of salvation!

4   Shout your praises to GOD, everybody!
     Let loose and sing! Strike up the band!

5   Round up an orchestra to play for GOD,
     Add on a hundred-voice choir.

6   Feature trumpets and big trombones,
     Fill the air with praises to King GOD.

7   Let the sea and its fish give a round of applause,
     With everything living on earth joining in.

8   Let ocean breakers call out, "Encore!"
     And mountains harmonize the finale —

9   A tribute to GOD when he comes,
     When he comes to set the earth right.

     He'll straighten out the whole world,
     He'll put the world right, and everyone in it.

1-3 **99** GOD rules. On your toes, everybody!
     He rules from his angel throne — take notice!
     GOD looms majestic in Zion,
     He towers in splendor over all the big names.
     Great and terrible your beauty: let everyone praise you!
          Holy. Yes, holy.

4-5 Strong King, lover of justice,
     You laid things out fair and square;
     You set down the foundations in Jacob,
     Foundation stones of just and right ways.
     Honor GOD, our God; worship his rule!
          Holy. Yes, holy.

6-9 Moses and Aaron were his priests,
     Samuel among those who prayed to him.
     They prayed to GOD and he answered them;
     He spoke from the pillar of cloud.
     And they did what he said; they kept the law he gave them.
     And then GOD, our God, answered them
     (But you were never soft on their sins).
     Lift high GOD, our God; worship at his holy mountain.
          Holy. Yes, holy is GOD our God.

A THANKSGIVING PSALM

100 ¹⁻²
On your feet now—applaud GOD!
Bring a gift of laughter,
sing yourselves into his presence.

3 Know this: GOD is God, and God, GOD.
He made us; we didn't make him.
We're his people, his well-tended sheep.

4 Enter with the password: "Thank you!"
Make yourselves at home, talking praise.
Thank him. Worship him.

5 For GOD is sheer beauty,
all-generous in love,
loyal always and ever.

A DAVID PSALM

101 ¹⁻⁸
My theme song is God's love and justice,
and I'm singing it right to you, GOD.
I'm finding my way down the road of right living,
but how long before you show up?
I'm doing the very best I can,
and I'm doing it at home, where it counts.
I refuse to take a second look
at corrupting people and degrading things.
I reject made-in-Canaan gods,
stay clear of contamination.
The crooked in heart keep their distance;
I refuse to shake hands with those who plan evil.
I put a gag on the gossip
who bad-mouths his neighbor;
I can't stand arrogance.
But I have my eye on salt-of-the-earth people—
they're the ones I want working with me;
Men and women on the straight and narrow—
these are the ones I want at my side.
But no one who traffics in lies
gets a job with me; I have no patience with liars.
I've rounded up all the wicked like cattle
and herded them right out of the country.
I purged GOD's city
of all who make a business of evil.

A PRAYER OF ONE WHOSE LIFE IS FALLING TO PIECES, AND WHO LETS GOD KNOW JUST HOW BAD IT IS

102 ¹⁻²
GOD, listen! Listen to my prayer,
listen to the pain in my cries.
Don't turn your back on me

just when I need you so desperately.
Pay attention! This is a cry for *help*!
    And hurry — this can't wait!

3-11 I'm wasting away to nothing,
    I'm burning up with fever.
I'm a ghost of my former self,
    half-consumed already by terminal illness.
My jaws ache from gritting my teeth;
    I'm nothing but skin and bones.
I'm like a buzzard in the desert,
    a crow perched on the rubble.
Insomniac, I twitter away,
    mournful as a sparrow in the gutter.
All day long my enemies taunt me,
    while others just curse.
They bring in meals — casseroles of ashes!
    I draw drink from a barrel of my tears.
And all because of your furious anger;
    you swept me up and threw me out.
There's nothing left of me —
    a withered weed, swept clean from the path.

12-17 Yet you, GOD, are sovereign still,
    always and ever sovereign.
You'll get up from your throne and help Zion —
    it's time for compassionate help.
Oh, how your servants love this city's rubble
    and weep with compassion over its dust!
The godless nations will sit up and take notice
    — see your glory, worship your name —
When GOD rebuilds Zion,
    when he shows up in all his glory,
When he attends to the prayer of the wretched.
    He won't dismiss their prayer.

18-22 Write this down for the next generation
    so people not yet born will praise GOD:
"GOD looked out from his high holy place;
    from heaven he surveyed the earth.
He listened to the groans of the doomed,
    he opened the doors of their death cells."
Write it so the story can be told in Zion,
    so GOD's praise will be sung in Jerusalem's streets
And wherever people gather together
    along with their rulers to worship him.

23-28 GOD sovereignly brought me to my knees,
    he cut me down in my prime.
"Oh, don't," I prayed, "please don't let me die.
    You have more years than you know what to do with!

You laid earth's foundations a long time ago,
  and handcrafted the very heavens;
You'll still be around when they're long gone,
  threadbare and discarded like an old suit of clothes.
You'll throw them away like a worn-out coat,
  but year after year you're as good as new.
Your servants' children will have a good place to live
  and their children will be at home with you."

A DAVID PSALM

1-2   **103** O my soul, bless GOD.
        From head to toe, I'll bless his holy name!
      O my soul, bless GOD,
  don't forget a single blessing!

3-5   He forgives your sins — every one.
      He heals your diseases — every one.
      He redeems you from hell — saves your life!
      He crowns you with love and mercy — a paradise crown.
      He wraps you in goodness — beauty eternal.
      He renews your youth — you're always young in his presence.

6-18 GOD makes everything come out right;
        he puts victims back on their feet.
      He showed Moses how he went about his work,
        opened up his plans to all Israel.
      GOD is sheer mercy and grace;
        not easily angered, he's rich in love.
      He doesn't endlessly nag and scold,
        nor hold grudges forever.
      He doesn't treat us as our sins deserve,
        nor pay us back in full for our wrongs.
      As high as heaven is over the earth,
        so strong is his love to those who fear him.
      And as far as sunrise is from sunset,
        he has separated us from our sins.
      As parents feel for their children,
        GOD feels for those who fear him.
      He knows us inside and out,
        keeps in mind that we're made of mud.
      Men and women don't live very long;
        like wildflowers they spring up and blossom,
      But a storm snuffs them out just as quickly,
        leaving nothing to show they were here.
      GOD's love, though, is ever and always,
        eternally present to all who fear him,
      Making everything right for them and their children
        as they follow his Covenant ways
        and remember to do whatever he said.

19-22 GOD has set his throne in heaven;
  he rules over us all. He's the King!
So bless GOD, you angels,
  ready and able to fly at his bidding,
  quick to hear and do what he says.
Bless GOD, all you armies of angels,
  alert to respond to whatever he wills.
Bless GOD, all creatures, wherever you are —
  everything and everyone made by GOD.

And you, O my soul, bless GOD!

1-14 **104** O my soul, bless GOD!

  GOD, my God, how great you are!
  beautifully, gloriously robed,
Dressed up in sunshine,
  and all heaven stretched out for your tent.
You built your palace on the ocean deeps,
  made a chariot out of clouds and took off on wind-wings.
You commandeered winds as messengers,
  appointed fire and flame as ambassadors.
You set earth on a firm foundation
  so that nothing can shake it, ever.
You blanketed earth with ocean,
  covered the mountains with deep waters;
Then you roared and the water ran away —
  your thunder crash put it to flight.
Mountains pushed up, valleys spread out
  in the places you assigned them.
You set boundaries between earth and sea;
  never again will earth be flooded.
You started the springs and rivers,
  sent them flowing among the hills.
All the wild animals now drink their fill,
  wild donkeys quench their thirst.
Along the riverbanks the birds build nests,
  ravens make their voices heard.
You water the mountains from your heavenly cisterns;
  earth is supplied with plenty of water.
You make grass grow for the livestock,
  hay for the animals that plow the ground.

14-23 Oh yes, God brings grain from the land,
  wine to make people happy,
Their faces glowing with health,
  a people well-fed and hearty.
GOD's trees are well-watered —
  the Lebanon cedars he planted.
Birds build their nests in those trees;
  look — the stork at home in the treetop.

Mountain goats climb about the cliffs;
    badgers burrow among the rocks.
The moon keeps track of the seasons,
    the sun is in charge of each day.
When it's dark and night takes over,
    all the forest creatures come out.
The young lions roar for their prey,
    clamoring to God for their supper.
When the sun comes up, they vanish,
    lazily stretched out in their dens.
Meanwhile, men and women go out to work,
    busy at their jobs until evening.

24-30   What a wildly wonderful world, GOD!
    You made it all, with Wisdom at your side,
    made earth overflow with your wonderful creations.
Oh, look — the deep, wide sea,
    brimming with fish past counting,
    sardines and sharks and salmon.
Ships plow those waters,
    and Leviathan, your pet dragon, romps in them.
All the creatures look expectantly to you
    to give them their meals on time.
You come, and they gather around;
    you open your hand and they eat from it.
If you turned your back,
    they'd die in a minute —
Take back your Spirit and they die,
    revert to original mud;
Send out your Spirit and they spring to life —
    the whole countryside in bloom and blossom.

31-32   The glory of GOD — let it last forever!
    Let GOD enjoy his creation!
He takes one look at earth and triggers an earthquake,
    points a finger at the mountains, and volcanoes erupt.

33-35   Oh, let me sing to GOD all my life long,
    sing hymns to my God as long as I live!
Oh, let my song please him;
    I'm so pleased to be singing to GOD.
But clear the ground of sinners —
    no more godless men and women!

O my soul, bless GOD!

1-6   **105** Hallelujah!

Thank GOD! Pray to him by name!
    Tell everyone you meet what he has done!
Sing him songs, belt out hymns,

translate his wonders into music!
Honor his holy name with Hallelujahs,
    you who seek GOD. Live a happy life!
Keep your eyes open for GOD, watch for his works;
    be alert for signs of his presence.
Remember the world of wonders he has made,
    his miracles, and the verdicts he's rendered —
        O seed of Abraham, his servant,
        O child of Jacob, his chosen.

7-15   He's GOD, our God,
    in charge of the whole earth.
And he remembers, remembers his Covenant —
    for a thousand generations he's been as good as his word.
It's the Covenant he made with Abraham,
    the same oath he swore to Isaac,
The very statute he established with Jacob,
    the eternal Covenant with Israel,
Namely, "I give you the land.
    Canaan is your hill-country inheritance."
When they didn't count for much,
    a mere handful, and strangers at that,
Wandering from country to country,
    drifting from pillar to post,
He permitted no one to abuse them.
    He told kings to keep their hands off:
"Don't you dare lay a hand on my anointed,
    don't hurt a hair on the heads of my prophets."

16-22   Then he called down a famine on the country,
    he broke every last blade of wheat.
But he sent a man on ahead:
    Joseph, sold as a slave.
They put cruel chains on his ankles,
    an iron collar around his neck,
Until God's word came to the Pharaoh,
    and GOD confirmed his promise.
God sent the king to release him.
    The Pharaoh set Joseph free;
He appointed him master of his palace,
    put him in charge of all his business
To personally instruct his princes
    and train his advisors in wisdom.

23-42   Then Israel entered Egypt,
    Jacob immigrated to the Land of Ham.
God gave his people lots of babies;
    soon their numbers alarmed their foes.
He turned the Egyptians against his people;
    they abused and cheated God's servants.
Then he sent his servant Moses,

and Aaron, whom he also chose.
They worked marvels in that spiritual wasteland,
    miracles in the Land of Ham.
He spoke, "Darkness!" and it turned dark —
    they couldn't see what they were doing.
He turned all their water to blood
    so that all their fish died;
He made frogs swarm through the land,
    even into the king's bedroom;
He gave the word and flies swarmed,
    gnats filled the air.
He substituted hail for rain,
    he stabbed their land with lightning;
He wasted their vines and fig trees,
    smashed their groves of trees to splinters;
With a word he brought in locusts,
    millions of locusts, armies of locusts;
They consumed every blade of grass in the country
    and picked the ground clean of produce;
He struck down every firstborn in the land,
    the first fruits of their virile powers.
He led Israel out, their arms filled with loot,
    and not one among his tribes even stumbled.
Egypt was glad to have them go —
    they were scared to death of them.
God spread a cloud to keep them cool through the day
    and a fire to light their way through the night;
They prayed and he brought quail,
    filled them with the bread of heaven;
He opened the rock and water poured out;
    it flowed like a river through that desert —
All because he remembered his Covenant,
    his promise to Abraham, his servant.

43-45   Remember this! He led his people out singing for joy;
    his chosen people marched, singing their hearts out!
He made them a gift of the country they entered,
    helped them seize the wealth of the nations
So they could do everything he told them —
    could follow his instructions to the letter.

Hallelujah!

1-3   **106** Hallelujah!
    Thank GOD! And why?
      Because he's good, because his love lasts.
But who on earth can do it —
    declaim GOD's mighty acts, broadcast all his praises?
You're one happy man when you do what's right,
    one happy woman when you form the habit of justice.

4-5 Remember me, GOD, when you enjoy your people;
    include me when you save them;
I want to see your chosen succeed,
    celebrate with your celebrating nation,
    join the Hallelujahs of your pride and joy!

6-12 We've sinned a lot, both we and our parents;
    We've fallen short, hurt a lot of people.
After our parents left Egypt,
    they took your wonders for granted,
    forgot your great and wonderful love.
They were barely beyond the Red Sea
    when they defied the High God
    — the very place he saved them!
    — the place he revealed his amazing power!
He rebuked the Red Sea so that it dried up on the spot
    — he paraded them right through!
    — no one so much as got wet feet!
He saved them from a life of oppression,
    pried them loose from the grip of the enemy.
Then the waters flowed back on their oppressors;
    there wasn't a single survivor.
Then they believed his words were true
    and broke out in songs of praise.

13-18 But it wasn't long before they forgot the whole thing,
    wouldn't wait to be told what to do.
They only cared about pleasing themselves in that desert,
    provoked God with their insistent demands.
He gave them exactly what they asked for —
    but along with it they got an empty heart.
One day in camp some grew jealous of Moses,
    also of Aaron, holy priest of GOD.
The ground opened and swallowed Dathan,
    then buried Abiram's gang.
Fire flared against that rebel crew
    and torched them to a cinder.

19-22 They cast in metal a bull calf at Horeb
    and worshiped the statue they'd made.
They traded the Glory
    for a cheap piece of sculpture — a grass-chewing bull!
They forgot God, their very own Savior,
    who turned things around in Egypt,
Who created a world of wonders in the Land of Ham,
    who gave that stunning performance at the Red Sea.

23-27 Fed up, God decided to get rid of them —
    and except for Moses, his chosen, he would have.
But Moses stood in the gap and deflected God's anger,
    prevented it from destroying them utterly.

They went on to reject the Blessed Land,
    didn't believe a word of what God promised.
They found fault with the life they had
    and turned a deaf ear to GOD's voice.
Exasperated, God swore
    that he'd lay them low in the desert,
Scattering their children hither and yon,
    strewing them all over the earth.

28-31   Then they linked up with Baal Peor,
    attending funeral banquets and eating idol food.
That made God so angry
    that a plague spread through their ranks;
Phinehas stood up and pled their case
    and the plague was stopped.
This was counted to his credit;
    his descendants will never forget it.

32-33   They angered God again at Meribah Springs;
    this time Moses got mixed up in their evil;
Because they defied GOD yet again,
    Moses exploded and lost his temper.

34-39   They didn't wipe out those godless cultures
    as ordered by GOD;
Instead they intermarried with the heathen,
    and in time became just like them.
They worshiped their idols,
    were caught in the trap of idols.
They sacrificed their sons and daughters
    at the altars of demon gods.
They slit the throats of their babies,
    murdered their infant girls and boys.
They offered their babies to Canaan's gods;
    the blood of their babies stained the land.
Their way of life stank to high heaven;
    they lived like whores.

40-43   And GOD was furious — a wildfire anger;
    he couldn't stand even to look at his people.
He turned them over to the heathen
    so that the people who hated them ruled them.
Their enemies made life hard for them;
    they were tyrannized under that rule.
Over and over God rescued them, but they never learned —
    until finally their sins destroyed them.

44-46   Still, when God saw the trouble they were in
    and heard their cries for help,
He remembered his Covenant with them,
    and, immense with love, took them by the hand.

He poured out his mercy on them
  while their captors looked on, amazed.

47 Save us, GOD, our God!
  Gather us back out of exile
So we can give thanks to your holy name
  and join in the glory when you are praised!

Blessed be GOD, Israel's God!
Bless now, bless always!
Oh! Let everyone say Amen!
Hallelujah!

1-3 **107** Oh, thank GOD — he's so good!
  His love never runs out.
  All of you set free by GOD, tell the world!
Tell how he freed you from oppression,
Then rounded you up from all over the place,
  from the four winds, from the seven seas.

4-9 Some of you wandered for years in the desert,
  looking but not finding a good place to live,
Half-starved and parched with thirst,
  staggering and stumbling, on the brink of exhaustion.
Then, in your desperate condition, you called out to GOD.
  He got you out in the nick of time;
He put your feet on a wonderful road
  that took you straight to a good place to live.
So thank GOD for his marvelous love,
  for his miracle mercy to the children he loves.
He poured great draughts of water down parched throats;
  the starved and hungry got plenty to eat.

10-16 Some of you were locked in a dark cell,
  cruelly confined behind bars,
Punished for defying God's Word,
  for turning your back on the High God's counsel —
A hard sentence, and your hearts so heavy,
  and not a soul in sight to help.
Then you called out to GOD in your desperate condition;
  he got you out in the nick of time.
He led you out of your dark, dark cell,
  broke open the jail and led you out.
So thank GOD for his marvelous love,
  for his miracle mercy to the children he loves;
He shattered the heavy jailhouse doors,
  he snapped the prison bars like matchsticks!

17-22 Some of you were sick because you'd lived a bad life,
  your bodies feeling the effects of your sin;
You couldn't stand the sight of food,

so miserable you thought you'd be better off dead.
Then you called out to GOD in your desperate condition;
    he got you out in the nick of time.
He spoke the word that healed you,
    that pulled you back from the brink of death.
So thank GOD for his marvelous love,
    for his miracle mercy to the children he loves;
Offer thanksgiving sacrifices,
    tell the world what he's done — sing it out!

23-32   Some of you set sail in big ships;
    you put to sea to do business in faraway ports.
Out at sea you saw GOD in action,
    saw his breathtaking ways with the ocean:
With a word he called up the wind —
    an ocean storm, towering waves!
You shot high in the sky, then the bottom dropped out;
    your hearts were stuck in your throats.
You were spun like a top, you reeled like a drunk,
    you didn't know which end was up.
Then you called out to GOD in your desperate condition;
    he got you out in the nick of time.
He quieted the wind down to a whisper,
    put a muzzle on all the big waves.
And you were so glad when the storm died down,
    and he led you safely back to harbor.
So thank GOD for his marvelous love,
    for his miracle mercy to the children he loves.
Lift high your praises when the people assemble,
    shout Hallelujah when the elders meet!

33-41   GOD turned rivers into wasteland,
    springs of water into sunbaked mud;
Luscious orchards became alkali flats
    because of the evil of the people who lived there.
Then he changed wasteland into fresh pools of water,
    arid earth into springs of water,
Brought in the hungry and settled them there;
    they moved in — what a great place to live!
They sowed the fields, they planted vineyards,
    they reaped a bountiful harvest.
He blessed them and they prospered greatly;
    their herds of cattle never decreased.
But abuse and evil and trouble declined
    as he heaped scorn on princes and sent them away.
He gave the poor a safe place to live,
    treated their clans like well-cared-for sheep.

42-43   Good people see this and are glad;
    bad people are speechless, stopped in their tracks.

If you are really wise, you'll think this over —
    it's time you appreciated GOD's deep love.

A DAVID PRAYER

1-2 **108** I'm ready, God, so ready,
        ready from head to toe.
Ready to sing,
ready to raise a God-song:
"Wake, soul! Wake, lute!
    Wake up, you sleepyhead sun!"

3-6 I'm thanking you, GOD, out in the streets,
    singing your praises in town and country.
The deeper your love, the higher it goes;
    every cloud's a flag to your faithfulness.
Soar high in the skies, O God!
    Cover the whole earth with your glory!
And for the sake of the one you love so much,
    reach down and help me — answer me!

7-9 That's when God spoke in holy splendor:
    "Brimming over with joy,
I make a present of Shechem,
    I hand out Succoth Valley as a gift.
Gilead's in my pocket,
    to say nothing of Manasseh.
Ephraim's my hard hat,
    Judah my hammer.
Moab's a scrub bucket —
    I mop the floor with Moab,
Spit on Edom,
    rain fireworks all over Philistia."

10-11 Who will take me to the thick of the fight?
    Who'll show me the road to Edom?
You aren't giving up on us, are you, God?
    refusing to go out with our troops?

12-13 Give us help for the hard task;
    human help is worthless.
In God we'll do our very best;
    he'll flatten the opposition for good.

A DAVID PRAYER

1-5 **109** My God, don't turn a deaf ear to my hallelujah prayer.
    Liars are pouring out invective on me;
    Their lying tongues are like a pack of dogs out to get me,
barking their hate, nipping my heels — and for no reason!
I loved them and now they slander me — yes, me! —
    and treat my prayer like a crime;
They return my good with evil,
    they return my love with hate.

6-20
Send the Evil One to accuse my accusing judge;
    dispatch Satan to prosecute him.
When he's judged, let the verdict be "Guilty,"
    and when he prays, let his prayer turn to sin.
Give him a short life,
    and give his job to somebody else.
Make orphans of his children,
    dress his wife in widow's weeds;
Turn his children into begging street urchins,
    evicted from their homes — homeless.
May the bank foreclose and wipe him out,
    and strangers, like vultures, pick him clean.
May there be no one around to help him out,
    no one willing to give his orphans a break.
Chop down his family tree
    so that nobody even remembers his name.
But erect a memorial to the sin of his father,
    and make sure his mother's name is there, too —
Their sins recorded forever before GOD,
    but they themselves sunk in oblivion.
That's all he deserves since he was never once kind,
    hounded the afflicted and heartbroken to their graves.
Since he loved cursing so much,
    let curses rain down;
Since he had no taste for blessing,
    let blessings flee far from him.
He dressed up in curses like a fine suit of clothes;
    he drank curses, took his baths in curses.
So give him a gift — a costume of curses;
    he can wear curses every day of the week!
That's what they'll get, those out to get me —
    an avalanche of just deserts from GOD.

21-25
Oh, GOD, my Lord, step in;
    work a miracle for me — you can do it!
Get me out of here — your love is so great! —
    I'm at the end of my rope, my life in ruins.
I'm fading away to nothing, passing away,
    my youth gone, old before my time.
I'm weak from hunger and can hardly stand up,
    my body a rack of skin and bones.
I'm a joke in poor taste to those who see me;
    they take one look and shake their heads.

26-29
Help me, oh help me, GOD, my God,
    save me through your wonderful love;
Then they'll know that your hand is in this,
    that you, GOD, have been at work.
Let them curse all they want;
    you do the blessing.
Let them be jeered by the crowd when they stand up,

followed by cheers for me, your servant.
Dress my accusers in clothes dirty with shame,
discarded and humiliating old ragbag clothes.

30-31 My mouth's full of great praise for GOD,
I'm singing his hallelujahs surrounded by crowds,
For he's always at hand to take the side of the needy,
to rescue a life from the unjust judge.

A DAVID PRAYER

1-3 **110** The word of GOD to my Lord:
"Sit alongside me here on my throne
until I make your enemies a stool for your feet."
You were forged a strong scepter by GOD of Zion;
now rule, though surrounded by enemies!
Your people will freely join you, resplendent in holy armor
on the great day of your conquest,
Join you at the fresh break of day,
join you with all the vigor of youth.

4-7 GOD gave his word and he won't take it back:
you're the permanent priest, the Melchizedek priest.
The Lord stands true at your side,
crushing kings in his terrible wrath,
Bringing judgment on the nations,
handing out convictions wholesale,
crushing opposition across the wide earth.
The King-Maker put his King on the throne;
the True King rules with head held high!

1-10 **111** Hallelujah!
I give thanks to GOD with everything I've got —
Wherever good people gather, and in the congregation.
GOD's works are so great, worth
A lifetime of study — endless enjoyment!
Splendor and beauty mark his craft;
His generosity never gives out.
His miracles are his memorial —
This GOD of Grace, this GOD of Love.
He gave food to those who fear him,
He remembered to keep his ancient promise.
He proved to his people that he could do what he said:
Hand them the nations on a platter — a gift!
He manufactures truth and justice;
All his products are guaranteed to last —
Never out-of-date, never obsolete, rust-proof.
All that he makes and does is honest and true:
He paid the ransom for his people,
He ordered his Covenant kept forever.
He's so personal and holy, worthy of our respect.
The good life begins in the fear of GOD —

Do that and you'll know the blessing of GOD.
His Hallelujah lasts forever!

1-10

112

Hallelujah!
    Blessed man, blessed woman, who fear GOD,
    Who cherish and relish his commandments,
Their children robust on the earth,
And the homes of the upright — how blessed!
Their houses brim with wealth
And a generosity that never runs dry.
Sunrise breaks through the darkness for good people —
God's grace and mercy and justice!
The good person is generous and lends lavishly;
No shuffling or stumbling around for this one,
But a sterling and solid and lasting reputation.
Unfazed by rumor and gossip,
Heart ready, trusting in GOD,
Spirit firm, unperturbed,
Ever blessed, relaxed among enemies,
They lavish gifts on the poor —
A generosity that goes on, and on, and on.
An honored life! A beautiful life!
Someone wicked takes one look and rages,
Blusters away but ends up speechless.
There's nothing to the dreams of the wicked. Nothing.

1-3

113

Hallelujah!
    You who serve GOD, praise GOD!
        Just to speak his name is praise!
Just to remember GOD is a blessing —
    now and tomorrow and always.
From east to west, from dawn to dusk,
    keep lifting all your praises to GOD!

4-9

GOD is higher than anything and anyone,
    outshining everything you can see in the skies.
Who can compare with GOD, our God,
    so majestically enthroned,
Surveying his magnificent
    heavens and earth?
He picks up the poor from out of the dirt,
    rescues the wretched who've been thrown out with the trash,
Seats them among the honored guests,
    a place of honor among the brightest and best.
He gives childless couples a family,
    gives them joy as the parents of children.
Hallelujah!

1-8

114

After Israel left Egypt,
    the clan of Jacob left those barbarians behind;
Judah became holy land for him,

Israel the place of holy rule.
Sea took one look and ran the other way;
 River Jordan turned around and ran off.
The mountains turned playful and skipped like rams,
 the hills frolicked like spring lambs.
What's wrong with you, Sea, that you ran away?
 and you, River Jordan, that you turned and ran off?
And mountains, why did you skip like rams?
 and you, hills, frolic like spring lambs?
Tremble, Earth! You're in the Lord's presence!
 in the presence of Jacob's God.
He turned the rock into a pool of cool water,
 turned flint into fresh spring water.

1-2
115
Not for our sake, GOD, no, not for our sake,
 but for your name's sake, show your glory.
 Do it on account of your merciful love,
do it on account of your faithful ways.
Do it so none of the nations can say,
 "Where now, oh where is their God?"

3-8 Our God is in heaven
 doing whatever he wants to do.
Their gods are metal and wood,
 handmade in a basement shop:
Carved mouths that can't talk,
 painted eyes that can't see,
Tin ears that can't hear,
 molded noses that can't smell,
Hands that can't grasp, feet that can't walk or run,
 throats that never utter a sound.
Those who make them have become just like them,
 have become just like the gods they trust.

9-11 But you, Israel: put your trust in GOD!
 —trust your Helper! trust your Ruler!
Clan of Aaron, trust in GOD!
 —trust your Helper! trust your Ruler!
You who fear GOD, trust in GOD!
 —trust your Helper! trust your Ruler!

12-16 O GOD, remember us and bless us,
 bless the families of Israel and Aaron.
And let GOD bless all who fear GOD —
 bless the small, bless the great.
Oh, let GOD enlarge your families —
 giving growth to you, growth to your children.
May you be blessed by GOD,
 by GOD, who made heaven and earth.
The heaven of heavens is for GOD,
 but he put us in charge of the earth.

17-18
Dead people can't praise GOD—
   not a word to be heard from those buried in the ground.
But we bless GOD, oh yes—
   we bless him now, we bless him always!
Hallelujah!

1-6
116 I love GOD because he listened to me,
      listened as I begged for mercy.
      He listened so intently
   as I laid out my case before him.
Death stared me in the face,
   hell was hard on my heels.
Up against it, I didn't know which way to turn;
   then I called out to GOD for help:
"Please, GOD!" I cried out.
   "Save my life!"
GOD is gracious—it is he who makes things right,
   our most compassionate God.
GOD takes the side of the helpless;
   when I was at the end of my rope, he saved me.

7-8
I said to myself, "Relax and rest.
   GOD has showered you with blessings.
   Soul, you've been rescued from death;
   Eye, you've been rescued from tears;
   And you, Foot, were kept from stumbling."

9-11
I'm striding in the presence of GOD,
   alive in the land of the living!
I stayed faithful, though bedeviled,
   and despite a ton of bad luck,
Despite giving up on the human race,
   saying, "They're all liars and cheats."

12-19
What can I give back to GOD
   for the blessings he's poured out on me?
I'll lift high the cup of salvation—a toast to GOD!
   I'll pray in the name of GOD;
I'll complete what I promised GOD I'd do,
   and I'll do it together with his people.
When they arrive at the gates of death,
   GOD welcomes those who love him.
Oh, GOD, here I am, your servant,
   your faithful servant: set me free for your service!
I'm ready to offer the thanksgiving sacrifice
   and pray in the name of GOD.
I'll complete what I promised GOD I'd do,
   and I'll do it in company with his people,
In the place of worship, in GOD's house,
   in Jerusalem, GOD's city.
Hallelujah!

117 1-2 **P**raise GOD, everybody!
Applaud GOD, all people!
His love has taken over our lives;
GOD's faithful ways are eternal.
Hallelujah!

118 1-4 **T**hank GOD because he's good,
because his love never quits.
Tell the world, Israel,
"His love never quits."
And you, clan of Aaron, tell the world,
"His love never quits."
And you who fear GOD, join in,
"His love never quits."

5-16 Pushed to the wall, I called to GOD;
from the wide open spaces, he answered.
GOD's now at my side and I'm not afraid;
who would dare lay a hand on me?
GOD's my strong champion;
I flick off my enemies like flies.
Far better to take refuge in GOD
than trust in people;
Far better to take refuge in GOD
than trust in celebrities.
Hemmed in by barbarians,
in GOD's name I rubbed their faces in the dirt;
Hemmed in and with no way out,
in GOD's name I rubbed their faces in the dirt;
Like swarming bees, like wild prairie fire, they hemmed me in;
in GOD's name I rubbed their faces in the dirt.
I was right on the cliff-edge, ready to fall,
when GOD grabbed and held me.
GOD's my strength, he's also my song,
and now he's my salvation.
Hear the shouts, hear the triumph songs
in the camp of the saved?
"The hand of GOD has turned the tide!
The hand of GOD is raised in victory!
The hand of GOD has turned the tide!"

17-20 I didn't die. I *lived*!
And now I'm telling the world what GOD did.
GOD tested me, he pushed me hard,
but he didn't hand me over to Death.
Swing wide the city gates—the *righteous* gates!
I'll walk right through and thank GOD!
This Temple Gate belongs to GOD,
so the victors can enter and praise.

21-25
Thank you for responding to me;
   you've truly become my salvation!
The stone the masons discarded as flawed
   is now the capstone!
This is GOD's work.
   We rub our eyes — we can hardly believe it!
This is the very day GOD acted —
   let's celebrate and be festive!
Salvation now, GOD. Salvation now!
   Oh yes, GOD — a free and full life!

26-29
Blessed are you who enter in GOD's name —
   from GOD's house we bless you!
GOD is God,
   he has bathed us in light.
Festoon the shrine with garlands,
   hang colored banners above the altar!
You're my God, and I thank you.
   O my God, I lift high your praise.
Thank GOD — he's so good.
   His love never quits!

1-8
119
You're blessed when you stay on course,
   walking steadily on the road revealed by GOD.
You're blessed when you follow his directions,
   doing your best to find him.
That's right — you don't go off on your own;
   you walk straight along the road he set.
You, GOD, prescribed the right way to live;
   now you expect us to live it.
Oh, that my steps might be steady,
   keeping to the course you set;
Then I'd never have any regrets
   in comparing my life with your counsel.
I thank you for speaking straight from your heart;
   I learn the pattern of your righteous ways.
I'm going to do what you tell me to do;
   don't ever walk off and leave me.

9-16
How can a young person live a clean life?
   By carefully reading the map of your Word.
I'm single-minded in pursuit of you;
   don't let me miss the road signs you've posted.
I've banked your promises in the vault of my heart
   so I won't sin myself bankrupt.
Be blessed, GOD;
   train me in your ways of wise living.
I'll transfer to my lips
   all the counsel that comes from your mouth;
I delight far more in what you tell me about living

than in gathering a pile of riches.
I ponder every morsel of wisdom from you,
    I attentively watch how you've done it.
I relish everything you've told me of life,
    I won't forget a word of it.

17-24   Be generous with me and I'll live a full life;
    not for a minute will I take my eyes off your road.
Open my eyes so I can see
    what you show me of your miracle-wonders.
I'm a stranger in these parts;
    give me clear directions.
My soul is starved and hungry, ravenous! —
    insatiable for your nourishing commands.
And those who think they know so much,
    ignoring everything you tell them — let them have it!
Don't let them mock and humiliate me;
    I've been careful to do just what you said.
While bad neighbors maliciously gossip about me,
    I'm absorbed in pondering your wise counsel.
Yes, your sayings on life are what give me delight;
    I listen to them as to good neighbors!

25-32   I'm feeling terrible — I couldn't feel worse!
    Get me on my feet again. You promised, remember?
When I told my story, you responded;
    train me well in your deep wisdom.
Help me understand these things inside and out
    so I can ponder your miracle-wonders.
My sad life's dilapidated, a falling-down barn;
    build me up again by your Word.
Barricade the road that goes Nowhere;
    grace me with your clear revelation.
I choose the true road to Somewhere,
    I post your road signs at every curve and corner.
I grasp and cling to whatever you tell me;
    GOD, don't let me down!
I'll run the course you lay out for me
    if you'll just show me how.

33-40   GOD, teach me lessons for living
    so I can stay the course.
Give me insight so I can do what you tell me —
    my whole life one long, obedient response.
Guide me down the road of your commandments;
    I love traveling this freeway!
Give me a bent for your words of wisdom,
    and not for piling up loot.

Divert my eyes from toys and trinkets,
    invigorate me on the pilgrim way.
Affirm your promises to me —
    promises made to all who fear you.
Deflect the harsh words of my critics —
    but what you say is always so good.
See how hungry I am for your counsel;
    preserve my life through your righteous ways!

41-48   Let your love, GOD, shape my life
    with salvation, exactly as you promised;
Then I'll be able to stand up to mockery
    because I trusted your Word.
Don't ever deprive me of truth, not ever —
    your commandments are what I depend on.
Oh, I'll guard with my life what you've revealed to me,
    guard it now, guard it ever;
And I'll stride freely through wide open spaces
    as I look for your truth and your wisdom;
Then I'll tell the world what I find,
    speak out boldly in public, unembarrassed.
I cherish your commandments — oh, how I love them! —
    relishing every fragment of your counsel.

49-56   Remember what you said to me, your servant —
    I hang on to these words for dear life!
These words hold me up in bad times;
    yes, your promises rejuvenate me.
The insolent ridicule me without mercy,
    but I don't budge from your revelation.
I watch for your ancient landmark words,
    and know I'm on the right track.
But when I see the wicked ignore your directions,
    I'm beside myself with anger.
I set your instructions to music
    and sing them as I walk this pilgrim way.
I meditate on your name all night, GOD,
    treasuring your revelation, O GOD.
Still, I walk through a rain of derision
    because I live by your Word and counsel.

57-64   Because you have satisfied me, GOD, I promise
    to do everything you say.
I beg you from the bottom of my heart: smile,
    be gracious to me just as you promised.
When I took a long, careful look at your ways,
    I got my feet back on the trail you blazed.
I was up at once, didn't drag my feet,

was quick to follow your orders.
The wicked hemmed me in — there was no way out —
    but not for a minute did I forget your plan for me.
I get up in the middle of the night to thank you;
    your decisions are so right, so true — I can't wait till morning!
I'm a friend and companion of all who fear you,
    of those committed to living by your rules.
Your love, GOD, fills the earth!
    Train me to live by your counsel.

65-72   Be good to your servant, GOD;
    be as good as your Word.
Train me in good common sense;
    I'm thoroughly committed to living your way.
Before I learned to answer you, I wandered all over the place,
    but now I'm in step with your Word.
You are good, and the source of good;
    train me in your goodness.
The godless spread lies about me,
    but I focus my attention on what you are saying;
They're bland as a bucket of lard,
    while I dance to the tune of your revelation.
My troubles turned out all for the best —
    they forced me to learn from your textbook.
Truth from your mouth means more to me
    than striking it rich in a gold mine.

73-80   With your very own hands you formed me;
    now breathe your wisdom over me so I can understand you.
When they see me waiting, expecting your Word,
    those who fear you will take heart and be glad.
I can see now, GOD, that your decisions are right;
    your testing has taught me what's true and right.
Oh, love me — and right now! — hold me tight!
    just the way you promised.
Now comfort me so I can live, really live;
    your revelation is the tune I dance to.
Let the fast-talking tricksters be exposed as frauds;
    they tried to sell me a bill of goods,
    but I kept my mind fixed on your counsel.
Let those who fear you turn to me
    for evidence of your wise guidance.
And let me live whole and holy, soul and body,
    so I can always walk with my head held high.

81-88   I'm homesick — longing for your salvation;
    I'm waiting for your word of hope.
My eyes grow heavy watching for some sign of your promise;

how long must I wait for your comfort?
There's smoke in my eyes — they burn and water,
    but I keep a steady gaze on the instructions you post.
How long do I have to put up with all this?
    How long till you haul my tormentors into court?
The arrogant godless try to throw me off track,
    ignorant as they are of God and his ways.
Everything you command is a sure thing,
    but they harass me with lies. Help!
They've pushed and pushed — they never let up —
    but I haven't relaxed my grip on your counsel.
In your great love revive me
    so I can alertly obey your every word.

89-96   What you say goes, GOD,
    and *stays*, as permanent as the heavens.
Your truth never goes out of fashion;
    it's as up-to-date as the earth when the sun comes up.
Your Word and truth are dependable as ever;
    that's what you ordered — you set the earth going.
If your revelation hadn't delighted me so,
    I would have given up when the hard times came.
But I'll never forget the advice you gave me;
    you saved my life with those wise words.
Save me! I'm all yours.
    I look high and low for your words of wisdom.
The wicked lie in ambush to destroy me,
    but I'm only concerned with your plans for me.
I see the limits to everything human,
    but the horizons can't contain your commands!

97-104   Oh, how I love all you've revealed;
    I reverently ponder it all the day long.
Your commands give me an edge on my enemies;
    they never become obsolete.
I've even become smarter than my teachers
    since I've pondered and absorbed your counsel.
I've become wiser than the wise old sages
    simply by doing what you tell me.
I watch my step, avoiding the ditches and ruts of evil
    so I can spend all my time keeping your Word.
I never make detours from the route you laid out;
    you gave me such good directions.
Your words are so choice, so tasty;
    I prefer them to the best home cooking.
With your instruction, I understand life;
    that's why I hate false propaganda.

105-112 By your words I can see where I'm going;
    they throw a beam of light on my dark path.
I've committed myself and I'll never turn back
    from living by your righteous order.
Everything's falling apart on me, GOD;
    put me together again with your Word.
Festoon me with your finest sayings, GOD;
    teach me your holy rules.
My life is as close as my own hands,
    but I don't forget what you have revealed.
The wicked do their best to throw me off track,
    but I don't swerve an inch from your course.
I inherited your book on living; it's mine forever —
    what a gift! And how happy it makes me!
I concentrate on doing exactly what you say —
    I always have and always will.

113-120 I hate the two-faced,
    but I love your clear-cut revelation.
You're my place of quiet retreat;
    I wait for your Word to renew me.
Get out of my life, evildoers,
    so I can keep my God's commands.
Take my side as you promised; I'll live then for sure.
    Don't disappoint all my grand hopes.
Stick with me and I'll be all right;
    I'll give total allegiance to your definitions of life.
Expose all who drift away from your sayings;
    their casual idolatry is lethal.
You reject earth's wicked as so much rubbish;
    therefore I lovingly embrace everything you say.
I shiver in awe before you;
    your decisions leave me speechless with reverence.

121-128 I stood up for justice and the right;
    don't leave me to the mercy of my oppressors.
Take the side of your servant, good God;
    don't let the godless take advantage of me.
I can't keep my eyes open any longer, waiting for you
    to keep your promise to set everything right.
Let your love dictate how you deal with me;
    teach me from your textbook on life.
I'm your servant — help me understand what that means,
    the inner meaning of your instructions.
It's time to act, GOD;
    they've made a shambles of your revelation!
Yea-Saying God, I love what you command,
    I love it better than gold and gemstones;

Yea-Saying God, I honor everything you tell me,
  I despise every deceitful detour.

129-136 Every word you give me is a miracle word —
  how could I help but obey?
Break open your words, let the light shine out,
  let ordinary people see the meaning.
Mouth open and panting,
  I wanted your commands more than anything.
Turn my way, look kindly on me,
  as you always do to those who personally love you.
Steady my steps with your Word of promise
  so nothing malign gets the better of me.
Rescue me from the grip of bad men and women
  so I can live life your way.
Smile on me, your servant;
  teach me the right way to live.
I cry rivers of tears
  because nobody's living by your book!

137-144 You *are* right and you *do* right, GOD;
  your decisions are right on target.
You rightly instruct us in how to live
  ever faithful to you.
My rivals nearly did me in,
  they persistently ignored your commandments.
Your promise has been tested through and through,
  and I, your servant, love it dearly.
I'm too young to be important,
  but I don't forget what you tell me.
Your righteousness is eternally right,
  your revelation is the only truth.
Even though troubles came down on me hard,
  your commands always gave me delight.
The way you tell me to live is always right;
  help me understand it so I can live to the fullest.

145-152 I call out at the top of my lungs,
  "GOD! Answer! I'll do whatever you say."
I called to you, "Save me
  so I can carry out all your instructions."
I was up before sunrise,
  crying for help, hoping for a word from you.
I stayed awake all night,
  prayerfully pondering your promise.
In your love, listen to me;
  in your justice, GOD, keep me alive.
As those out to get me come closer and closer,

they go farther and farther from the truth you reveal;
But you're the closest of all to me, GOD,
    and all your judgments true.
I've known all along from the evidence of your words
    that you meant them to last forever.

153-160 Take a good look at my trouble, and help me—
    I haven't forgotten your revelation.
Take my side and get me out of this;
    give me back my life, just as you promised.
"Salvation" is only gibberish to the wicked
    because they've never looked it up in your dictionary.
Your mercies, GOD, run into the billions;
    following your guidelines, revive me.
My antagonists are too many to count,
    but I don't swerve from the directions you gave.
I took one look at the quitters and was filled with loathing;
    they walked away from your promises so casually!
Take note of how I love what you tell me;
    out of your life of love, prolong my life.
Your words all add up to the sum total: Truth.
    Your righteous decisions are eternal.

161-168 I've been slandered unmercifully by the politicians,
    but my awe at your words keeps me stable.
I'm ecstatic over what you say,
    like one who strikes it rich.
I hate lies—can't stand them!—
    but I love what you have revealed.
Seven times each day I stop and shout praises
    for the way you keep everything running right.
For those who love what you reveal, everything fits—
    no stumbling around in the dark for them.
I wait expectantly for your salvation;
    GOD, I do what you tell me.
My soul guards and keeps all your instructions—
    oh, how much I love them!
I follow your directions, abide by your counsel;
    my life's an open book before you.

169-176 Let my cry come right into your presence, GOD;
    provide me with the insight that comes only from your Word.
Give my request your personal attention,
    rescue me on the terms of your promise.
Let praise cascade off my lips;
    after all, you've taught me the truth about life!
And let your promises ring from my tongue;
    every order you've given is right.

Put your hand out and steady me
  since I've chosen to live by your counsel.
I'm homesick, GOD, for your salvation;
  I love it when you show yourself!
Invigorate my soul so I can praise you well,
  use your decrees to put iron in my soul.
And should I wander off like a lost sheep—seek me!
  I'll recognize the sound of your voice.

A PILGRIM SONG

1-2 **120** I'm in trouble. I cry to GOD,
      desperate for an answer:
      "Deliver me from the liars, GOD!
They smile so sweetly but lie through their teeth."

3-4 Do you know what's next, can you see what's coming,
  all you barefaced liars?
Pointed arrows and burning coals
  will be your reward.

5-7 I'm doomed to live in Meshech,
  cursed with a home in Kedar,
My whole life lived camping
  among quarreling neighbors.
I'm all for peace, but the minute
  I tell them so, they go to war!

A PILGRIM SONG

1-2 **121** I look up to the mountains;
      does my strength come from mountains?
      No, my strength comes from GOD,
who made heaven, and earth, and mountains.

3-4 He won't let you stumble,
  your Guardian God won't fall asleep.
Not on your life! Israel's
  Guardian will never doze or sleep.

5-6 GOD's your Guardian,
  right at your side to protect you—
Shielding you from sunstroke,
  sheltering you from moonstroke.

7-8 GOD guards you from every evil,
  he guards your very life.
He guards you when you leave and when you return,
  he guards you now, he guards you always.

1-2 **122** When they said, "Let's go to the house of GOD,"
  my heart leaped for joy.
And now we're here, O Jerusalem,
  inside Jerusalem's walls!

3-5 Jerusalem, well-built city,
  built as a place for worship!
The city to which the tribes ascend,
  all GOD's tribes go up to worship,
To give thanks to the name of GOD —
  this is what it means to be Israel.
Thrones for righteous judgment
  are set there, famous David-thrones.

6-9 Pray for Jerusalem's peace!
  Prosperity to all you Jerusalem-lovers!
Friendly insiders, get along!
  Hostile outsiders, keep your distance!
For the sake of my family and friends,
  I say it again: live in peace!
For the sake of the house of our God, GOD,
  I'll do my very best for you.

1-4 **123** I look to you, heaven-dwelling God,
  look up to you for help.
Like servants, alert to their master's commands,
  like a maiden attending her lady,
We're watching and waiting, holding our breath,
  awaiting your word of mercy.
Mercy, GOD, mercy!
  We've been kicked around long enough,
Kicked in the teeth by complacent rich men,
  kicked when we're down by arrogant brutes.

1-5 **124** If GOD hadn't been for us
  —all together now, Israel, sing out! —
If GOD hadn't been for us
  when everyone went against us,
We would have been swallowed alive
  by their violent anger,
Swept away by the flood of rage,
  drowned in the torrent;
We would have lost our lives
  in the wild, raging water.

6 Oh, blessed be GOD!
  He didn't go off and leave us.

He didn't abandon us defenseless,
    helpless as a rabbit in a pack of snarling dogs.

7   We've flown free from their fangs,
    free of their traps, free as a bird.
Their grip is broken;
    we're free as a bird in flight.

8   GOD's strong name is our help,
    the same GOD who made heaven and earth.

A PILGRIM SONG

1-5 **125** Those who trust in GOD
    are like Zion Mountain:
    Nothing can move it, a rock-solid mountain
you can always depend on.
Mountains encircle Jerusalem,
    and GOD encircles his people—
    always has and always will.
The fist of the wicked
    will never violate
What is due the righteous,
    provoking wrongful violence.
Be good to your good people, GOD,
    to those whose hearts are right!
GOD will round up the backsliders,
    corral them with the incorrigibles.
Peace over Israel!

A PILGRIM SONG

1-3 **126** It seemed like a dream, too good to be true,
    when GOD returned Zion's exiles.
    We laughed, we sang,
we couldn't believe our good fortune.
We were the talk of the nations—
    "GOD was wonderful to them!"
GOD *was* wonderful to us;
    we are one happy people.

4-6 And now, GOD, do it again—
    bring rains to our drought-stricken lives
So those who planted their crops in despair
    will shout hurrahs at the harvest,
So those who went off with heavy hearts
    will come home laughing, with armloads of blessing.

A PILGRIM SONG OF SOLOMON

1-2 **127** If GOD doesn't build the house,
    the builders only build shacks.
    If GOD doesn't guard the city,
the night watchman might as well nap.

It's useless to rise early and go to bed late,
    and work your worried fingers to the bone.
Don't you know he enjoys
    giving rest to those he loves?

3-5   Don't you see that children are GOD's best gift?
    the fruit of the womb his generous legacy?
Like a warrior's fistful of arrows
    are the children of a vigorous youth.
Oh, how blessed are you parents,
    with your quivers full of children!
Your enemies don't stand a chance against you;
    you'll sweep them right off your doorstep.

A PILGRIM SONG

1-2   **128** All you who fear GOD, how blessed you are!
    how happily you walk on his smooth straight road!
You worked hard and deserve all you've got coming.
Enjoy the blessing! Revel in the goodness!

3-4   Your wife will bear children as a vine bears grapes,
    your household lush as a vineyard,
The children around your table
    as fresh and promising as young olive shoots.
Stand in awe of God's Yes.
    Oh, how he blesses the one who fears GOD!

5-6   Enjoy the good life in Jerusalem
    every day of your life.
And enjoy your grandchildren.
    Peace to Israel!

A PILGRIM SONG

1-4   **129** "They've kicked me around ever since I was young"
    — this is how Israel tells it —
    "They've kicked me around ever since I was young,
but they never could keep me down.
Their plowmen plowed long furrows
    up and down my back;
But GOD wouldn't put up with it,
    he sticks with us.
Then GOD ripped the harnesses
    of the evil plowmen to shreds."

5-8   Oh, let all those who hate Zion
    grovel in humiliation;
Let them be like grass in shallow ground
    that withers before the harvest,
Before the farmhands can gather it in,
    the harvesters get in the crop,
Before the neighbors have a chance to call out,

"Congratulations on your wonderful crop!
We bless you in GOD's name!"

A PILGRIM SONG

1-2 **130** Help, GOD — the bottom has fallen out of my life!
         Master, hear my cry for help!
         Listen hard! Open your ears!
Listen to my cries for mercy.

3-4 If you, GOD, kept records on wrongdoings,
      who would stand a chance?
As it turns out, forgiveness is your habit,
      and that's why you're worshiped.

5-6 I pray to GOD — my life a prayer —
      and wait for what he'll say and do.
My life's on the line before God, my Lord,
      waiting and watching till morning,
      waiting and watching till morning.

7-8 O Israel, wait and watch for GOD —
      with GOD's arrival comes love,
      with GOD's arrival comes generous redemption.
No doubt about it — he'll redeem Israel,
      buy back Israel from captivity to sin.

A PILGRIM SONG

1 **131** GOD, I'm not trying to rule the roost,
         I don't want to be king of the mountain.
         I haven't meddled where I have no business
or fantasized grandiose plans.

2 I've kept my feet on the ground,
      I've cultivated a quiet heart.
Like a baby content in its mother's arms,
      my soul is a baby content.

3 Wait, Israel, for GOD. Wait with hope.
      Hope now; hope always!

A PILGRIM SONG

1-5 **132** O GOD, remember David,
         remember all his troubles!
         And remember how he promised GOD,
made a vow to the Strong God of Jacob,
"I'm not going home,
      and I'm not going to bed,
I'm not going to sleep,
      not even take time to rest,
Until I find a home for GOD,
      a house for the Strong God of Jacob."

6-7 Remember how we got the news in Ephrathah,
    learned all about it at Jaar Meadows?
We shouted, "Let's go to the shrine dedication!
    Let's worship at God's own footstool!"

8-10 Up, GOD, enjoy your new place of quiet repose,
    you and your mighty covenant ark;
Get your priests all dressed up in justice;
    prompt your worshipers to sing this prayer:
"Honor your servant David;
    don't disdain your anointed one."

11-18 GOD gave David his word,
    he won't back out on this promise:
"One of your sons
    I will set on your throne;
If your sons stay true to my Covenant
    and learn to live the way I teach them,
Their sons will continue the line —
    always a son to sit on your throne.
Yes — I, GOD, chose Zion,
    the place I wanted for my shrine;
This will always be my home;
    this is what I want, and I'm here for good.
I'll shower blessings on the pilgrims who come here,
    and give supper to those who arrive hungry;
I'll dress my priests in salvation clothes;
    the holy people will sing their hearts out!
Oh, I'll make the place radiant for David!
    I'll fill it with light for my anointed!
I'll dress his enemies in dirty rags,
    but I'll make his crown sparkle with splendor."

A PILGRIM SONG OF DAVID

1-3 **133** How wonderful, how beautiful,
    when brothers and sisters get along!
It's like costly anointing oil
flowing down head and beard,
Flowing down Aaron's beard,
    flowing down the collar of his priestly robes.
It's like the dew on Mount Hermon
    flowing down the slopes of Zion.
Yes, that's where GOD commands the blessing,
    ordains eternal life.

A PILGRIM SONG

1-3 **134** Come, bless GOD,
    all you servants of GOD!
You priests of GOD, posted to the nightwatch
in GOD's shrine,
Lift your praising hands to the Holy Place,

and bless GOD.
In turn, may GOD of Zion bless you —
    GOD who made heaven and earth!

1-4
135 Hallelujah!
    Praise the name of GOD,
        praise the works of GOD.
All you priests on duty in GOD's temple,
    serving in the sacred halls of our God,
Shout "Hallelujah!" because GOD's so good,
    sing anthems to his beautiful name.
And why? Because GOD chose Jacob,
    embraced Israel as a prize possession.

5-12
I, too, give witness to the greatness of GOD,
    our Lord, high above all other gods.
He does just as he pleases —
    however, wherever, whenever.
He makes the weather — clouds and thunder,
    lightning and rain, wind pouring out of the north.
He struck down the Egyptian firstborn,
    both human and animal firstborn.
He made Egypt sit up and take notice,
    confronted Pharaoh and his servants with miracles.
Yes, he struck down great nations,
    he slew mighty kings —
Sihon king of the Amorites, also Og of Bashan —
    every last one of the Canaanite kings!
Then he turned their land over to Israel,
    a gift of good land to his people.

13-18
GOD, your name is eternal,
    GOD, you'll never be out-of-date.
GOD stands up for his people,
    GOD holds the hands of his people.
The gods of the godless nations are mere trinkets,
    made for quick sale in the markets:
Chiseled mouths that can't talk,
    painted eyes that can't see,
Carved ears that can't hear —
    dead wood! cold metal!
Those who make and trust them
    become like them.

19-21
Family of Israel, bless GOD!
    Family of Aaron, bless GOD!
Family of Levi, bless GOD!
    You who fear GOD, bless GOD!
Oh, blessed be GOD of Zion,
    First Citizen of Jerusalem!
Hallelujah!

136 ¹⁻³ Thank GOD! He deserves your thanks.
    His love never quits.
Thank the God of all gods,
    His love never quits.
Thank the Lord of all lords.
    His love never quits.

⁴⁻²² Thank the miracle-working God,
    His love never quits.
The God whose skill formed the cosmos,
    His love never quits.
The God who laid out earth on ocean foundations,
    His love never quits.
The God who filled the skies with light,
    His love never quits.
The sun to watch over the day,
    His love never quits.
Moon and stars as guardians of the night,
    His love never quits.
The God who struck down the Egyptian firstborn,
    His love never quits.
And rescued Israel from Egypt's oppression,
    His love never quits.
Took Israel in hand with his powerful hand,
    His love never quits.
Split the Red Sea right in half,
    His love never quits.
Led Israel right through the middle,
    His love never quits.
Dumped Pharaoh and his army in the sea,
    His love never quits.
The God who marched his people through the desert,
    His love never quits.
Smashed huge kingdoms right and left,
    His love never quits.
Struck down the famous kings,
    His love never quits.
Struck Sihon the Amorite king,
    His love never quits.
Struck Og the Bashanite king,
    His love never quits.
Then distributed their land as booty,
    His love never quits.
Handed the land over to Israel.
    His love never quits.

²³⁻²⁶ God remembered us when we were down,
    His love never quits.
Rescued us from the trampling boot,
    His love never quits.
Takes care of everyone in time of need.

His love never quits.
Thank God, who did it all!
His love never quits!

137 1-3 Alongside Babylon's rivers
we sat on the banks; we cried and cried,
remembering the good old days in Zion.
Alongside the quaking aspens
we stacked our unplayed harps;
That's where our captors demanded songs,
sarcastic and mocking:
"Sing us a happy Zion song!"

4-6 Oh, how could we ever sing GOD's song
in this wasteland?
If I ever forget you, Jerusalem,
let my fingers wither and fall off like leaves.
Let my tongue swell and turn black
if I fail to remember you,
If I fail, O dear Jerusalem,
to honor you as my greatest.

7-9 GOD, remember those Edomites,
and remember the ruin of Jerusalem,
That day they yelled out,
"Wreck it, smash it to bits!"
And you, Babylonians — ravagers!
A reward to whoever gets back at you
for all you've done to us;
Yes, a reward to the one who grabs your babies
and smashes their heads on the rocks!

A DAVID PSALM

138 1-3 Thank you! Everything in me says "Thank you!"
Angels listen as I sing my thanks.
I kneel in worship facing your holy temple
and say it again: "Thank you!"
Thank you for your love,
thank you for your faithfulness;
Most holy is your name,
most holy is your Word.
The moment I called out, you stepped in;
you made my life large with strength.

4-6 When they hear what you have to say, GOD,
all earth's kings will say "Thank you."
They'll sing of what you've done:
"How great the glory of GOD!"
And here's why: GOD, high above, sees far below;
no matter the distance, he knows everything about us.

7-8 When I walk into the thick of trouble,
    keep me alive in the angry turmoil.
With one hand
    strike my foes,
With your other hand
    save me.
Finish what you started in me, GOD.
    Your love is eternal—don't quit on me now.

A DAVID PSALM

139 GOD, investigate my life;
    get all the facts firsthand.
    I'm an open book to you;

1-6 even from a distance, you know what I'm thinking.
You know when I leave and when I get back;
    I'm never out of your sight.
You know everything I'm going to say
    before I start the first sentence.
I look behind me and you're there,
    then up ahead and you're there, too—
    your reassuring presence, coming and going.
This is too much, too wonderful—
    I can't take it all in!

7-12 Is there anyplace I can go to avoid your Spirit?
    to be out of your sight?
If I climb to the sky, you're there!
    If I go underground, you're there!
If I flew on morning's wings
    to the far western horizon,
You'd find me in a minute—
    you're already there waiting!
Then I said to myself, "Oh, he even sees me in the dark!
    At night I'm immersed in the light!"
It's a fact: darkness isn't dark to you;
    night and day, darkness and light, they're all the same to you.

13-16 Oh yes, you shaped me first inside, then out;
    you formed me in my mother's womb.
I thank you, High God—you're breathtaking!
    Body and soul, I am marvelously made!
    I worship in adoration—what a creation!
You know me inside and out,
    you know every bone in my body;
You know exactly how I was made, bit by bit,
    how I was sculpted from nothing into something.
Like an open book, you watched me grow from conception to birth;
    all the stages of my life were spread out before you,
The days of my life all prepared
    before I'd even lived one day.

17-22
Your thoughts — how rare, how beautiful!
  God, I'll never comprehend them!
I couldn't even begin to count them —
  any more than I could count the sand of the sea.
Oh, let me rise in the morning and live always with you!
  And please, God, do away with wickedness for good!
And you murderers — out of here! —
  all the men and women who belittle you, God,
  infatuated with cheap god-imitations.
See how I hate those who hate you, GOD,
  see how I loathe all this godless arrogance;
I hate it with pure, unadulterated hatred.
  Your enemies are my enemies!

23-24
Investigate my life, O God,
  find out everything about me;
Cross-examine and test me,
  get a clear picture of what I'm about;
See for yourself whether I've done anything wrong —
  then guide me on the road to eternal life.

A DAVID PSALM

1-5
140 GOD, get me out of here, away from this evil;
      protect me from these vicious people.
    All they do is think up new ways to be bad;
  they spend their days plotting war games.
They practice the sharp rhetoric of hate and hurt,
  speak venomous words that maim and kill.
GOD, keep me out of the clutch of these wicked ones,
  protect me from these vicious people;
Stuffed with self-importance, they plot ways to trip me up,
  determined to bring me down.
These crooks invent traps to catch me
  and do their best to incriminate me.

6-8
I prayed, "GOD, you're my God!
  Listen, GOD! Mercy!
GOD, my Lord, Strong Savior,
  protect me when the fighting breaks out!
Don't let the wicked have their way, GOD,
  don't give them an inch!"

9-11
These troublemakers all around me —
  let them drown in their own verbal poison.
Let God pile hellfire on them,
  let him bury them alive in crevasses!
These loudmouths —
  don't let them be taken seriously;
These savages —
  let the Devil hunt them down!

12-13 I know that you, GOD, are on the side of victims,
    that you care for the rights of the poor.
And I know that the righteous personally thank you,
    that good people are secure in your presence.

A DAVID PSALM

1-2 **141** GOD, come close. Come quickly!
    Open your ears — it's my voice you're hearing!
    Treat my prayer as sweet incense rising;
my raised hands are my evening prayers.

3-7 Post a guard at my mouth, GOD,
    set a watch at the door of my lips.
Don't let me so much as dream of evil
    or thoughtlessly fall into bad company.
And these people who only do wrong —
    don't let them lure me with their sweet talk!
May the Just One set me straight,
    may the Kind One correct me,
Don't let sin anoint my head.
    I'm praying hard against their evil ways!
Oh, let their leaders be pushed off a high rock cliff;
    make them face the music.
Like a rock pulverized by a maul,
    let their bones be scattered at the gates of hell.

8-10 But GOD, dear Lord,
    I only have eyes for you.
Since I've run for dear life to you,
    take good care of me.
Protect me from their evil scheming,
    from all their demonic subterfuge.
Let the wicked fall flat on their faces,
    while I walk off without a scratch.

A DAVID PRAYER — WHEN HE WAS IN THE CAVE

1-2 **142** I cry out loudly to GOD,
    loudly I plead with GOD for mercy.
    I spill out all my complaints before him,
and spell out my troubles in detail:

3-7 "As I sink in despair, my spirit ebbing away,
    you know how I'm feeling,
Know the danger I'm in,
    the traps hidden in my path.
Look right, look left —
    there's not a soul who cares what happens!
I'm up against it, with no exit —
    bereft, left alone.
I cry out, GOD, call out:
    'You're my last chance, my only hope for life!'

Oh listen, please listen;
    I've never been this low.
Rescue me from those who are hunting me down;
    I'm no match for them.
Get me out of this dungeon
    so I can thank you in public.
Your people will form a circle around me
    and you'll bring me showers of blessing!"

A DAVID PSALM

143

1-2
Listen to this prayer of mine, GOD;
    pay attention to what I'm asking.
Answer me — you're famous for your answers!
    Do what's right for me.
But don't, please don't, haul me into court;
    not a person alive would be acquitted there.

3-6
The enemy hunted me down;
    he kicked me and stomped me within an inch of my life.
He put me in a black hole,
    buried me like a corpse in that dungeon.
I sat there in despair, my spirit draining away,
    my heart heavy, like lead.
I remembered the old days,
    went over all you've done, pondered the ways you've worked,
Stretched out my hands to you,
    as thirsty for you as a desert thirsty for rain.

7-10
Hurry with your answer, GOD!
    I'm nearly at the end of my rope.
Don't turn away; don't ignore me!
    That would be certain death.
If you wake me each morning with the sound of your loving voice,
    I'll go to sleep each night trusting in you.
Point out the road I must travel;
    I'm all ears, all eyes before you.
Save me from my enemies, GOD —
    you're my only hope!
Teach me how to live to please you,
    because you're my God.
Lead me by your blessed Spirit
    into cleared and level pastureland.

11-12
Keep up your reputation, God — give me life!
    In your justice, get me out of this trouble!
In your great love, vanquish my enemies;
    make a clean sweep of those who harass me.
And why? Because I'm your servant.

A DAVID PSALM

1-2 144 Blessed be GOD, my mountain,
 who trains me to fight fair and well.
He's the bedrock on which I stand,
 the castle in which I live,
 my rescuing knight,
The high crag where I run for dear life,
 while he lays my enemies low.

3-4 I wonder why you care, GOD —
 why do you bother with us at all?
All we are is a puff of air;
 we're like shadows in a campfire.

5-8 Step down out of heaven, GOD;
 ignite volcanoes in the hearts of the mountains.
Hurl your lightnings in every direction;
 shoot your arrows this way and that.
Reach all the way from sky to sea:
 pull me out of the ocean of hate,
 out of the grip of those barbarians
Who lie through their teeth,
 who shake your hand
 then knife you in the back.

9-10 O God, let me sing a new song to you,
 let me play it on a twelve-string guitar —
A song to the God who saved the king,
 the God who rescued David, his servant.

11 Rescue me from the enemy sword,
 release me from the grip of those barbarians
Who lie through their teeth,
 who shake your hand
 then knife you in the back.

12-14 Make our sons in their prime
 like sturdy oak trees,
Our daughters as shapely and bright
 as fields of wildflowers.
Fill our barns with great harvest,
 fill our fields with huge flocks;
Protect us from invasion and exile —
 eliminate the crime in our streets.

15 How blessed the people who have all this!
How blessed the people who have GOD for God!

DAVID'S PRAISE

1 **145** I lift you high in praise, my God, O my King!
and I'll bless your name into eternity.

2 I'll bless you every day,
and keep it up from now to eternity.

3 GOD is magnificent; he can never be praised enough.
There are no boundaries to his greatness.

4 Generation after generation stands in awe of your work;
each one tells stories of your mighty acts.

5 Your beauty and splendor have everyone talking;
I compose songs on your wonders.

6 Your marvelous doings are headline news;
I could write a book full of the details of your greatness.

7 The fame of your goodness spreads across the country;
your righteousness is on everyone's lips.

8 GOD is all mercy and grace —
not quick to anger, is rich in love.

9 GOD is good to one and all;
everything he does is suffused with grace.

10-11 Creation and creatures applaud you, GOD;
your holy people bless you.

They talk about the glories of your rule,
they exclaim over your splendor,

12 Letting the world know of your power for good,
the lavish splendor of your kingdom.

13 Your kingdom is a kingdom eternal;
you never get voted out of office.

GOD always does what he says,
and is gracious in everything he does.

14 GOD gives a hand to those down on their luck,
gives a fresh start to those ready to quit.

15 All eyes are on you, expectant;
you give them their meals on time.

16 Generous to a fault,
you lavish your favor on all creatures.

17   Everything GOD does is right—
      the trademark on all his works is love.

18   GOD's there, listening for all who pray,
      for all who pray and mean it.

19   He does what's best for those who fear him—
      hears them call out, and saves them.

20   GOD sticks by all who love him,
      but it's all over for those who don't.

21   My mouth is filled with GOD's praise.
      Let everything living bless him,
      bless his holy name from now to eternity!

1-2   ## 146 Hallelujah!
      O my soul, praise GOD!
      All my life long I'll praise GOD,
   singing songs to my God as long as I live.

3-9   Don't put your life in the hands of experts
      who know nothing of life, of *salvation* life.
   Mere humans don't have what it takes;
      when they die, their projects die with them.
   Instead, get help from the God of Jacob,
      put your hope in GOD and know real blessing!
   GOD made sky and soil,
      sea and all the fish in it.
   He always does what he says—
      he defends the wronged,
      he feeds the hungry.
   GOD frees prisoners—
      he gives sight to the blind,
      he lifts up the fallen.
   GOD loves good people, protects strangers,
      takes the side of orphans and widows,
      but makes short work of the wicked.

10   GOD's in charge—*always.*
      Zion's God is God for good!
      Hallelujah!

1   ## 147 Hallelujah!
      It's a good thing to sing praise to our God;
      praise is beautiful, praise is fitting.

2-6   GOD's the one who rebuilds Jerusalem,
      who regathers Israel's scattered exiles.
   He heals the heartbroken
      and bandages their wounds.

He counts the stars
　　and assigns each a name.
Our Lord is great, with limitless strength;
　　we'll never comprehend what he knows and does.
GOD puts the fallen on their feet again
　　and pushes the wicked into the ditch.

7-11 Sing to GOD a thanksgiving hymn,
　　play music on your instruments to God,
Who fills the sky with clouds,
　　preparing rain for the earth,
Then turning the mountains green with grass,
　　feeding both cattle and crows.
He's not impressed with horsepower;
　　the size of our muscles means little to him.
Those who fear GOD get GOD's attention;
　　they can depend on his strength.

12-18 Jerusalem, worship GOD!
　　Zion, praise your God!
He made your city secure,
　　he blessed your children among you.
He keeps the peace at your borders,
　　he puts the best bread on your tables.
He launches his promises earthward —
　　how swift and sure they come!
He spreads snow like a white fleece,
　　he scatters frost like ashes,
He broadcasts hail like birdseed —
　　who can survive his winter?
Then he gives the command and it all melts;
　　he breathes on winter — suddenly it's spring!

19-20 He speaks the same way to Jacob,
　　speaks words that work to Israel.
He never did this to the other nations;
　　they never heard such commands.
Hallelujah!

1-5 **148** Hallelujah!
　　Praise GOD from heaven,
　　　　praise him from the mountaintops;
Praise him, all you his angels,
　　praise him, all you his warriors,
Praise him, sun and moon,
　　praise him, you morning stars;
Praise him, high heaven,
　　praise him, heavenly rain clouds;
Praise, oh let them praise the name of GOD —
　　he spoke the word, and there they were!

6 He set them in place
from all time to eternity;
He gave his orders,
and that's it!

7-12 Praise GOD from earth,
you sea dragons, you fathomless ocean deeps;
Fire and hail, snow and ice,
hurricanes obeying his orders;
Mountains and all hills,
apple orchards and cedar forests;
Wild beasts and herds of cattle,
snakes, and birds in flight;
Earth's kings and all races,
leaders and important people,
Robust men and women in their prime,
and yes, graybeards and little children.

13-14 Let them praise the name of GOD—
it's the only Name worth praising.
His radiance exceeds anything in earth and sky;
he's built a monument—his very own people!

Praise from all who love GOD!
Israel's children, intimate friends of GOD.
Hallelujah!

1-4 **149** Hallelujah!
Sing to GOD a brand-new song,
praise him in the company of all who love him.
Let all Israel celebrate their Sovereign Creator,
Zion's children exult in their King.
Let them praise his name in dance;
strike up the band and make great music!
And why? Because GOD delights in his people,
festoons plain folk with salvation garlands!

5-9 Let true lovers break out in praise,
sing out from wherever they're sitting,
Shout the high praises of God,
brandish their swords in the wild sword-dance—
A portent of vengeance on the God-defying nations,
a signal that punishment's coming,
Their kings chained and hauled off to jail,
their leaders behind bars for good,
The judgment on them carried out to the letter
—and all who love God in the seat of honor!
Hallelujah!

1-6

150

Hallelujah!
Praise God in his holy house of worship,
    praise him under the open skies;
Praise him for his acts of power,
    praise him for his magnificent greatness;
Praise with a blast on the trumpet,
    praise by strumming soft strings;
Praise him with castanets and dance,
    praise him with banjo and flute;
Praise him with cymbals and a big bass drum,
    praise him with fiddles and mandolin.
Let every living, breathing creature praise GOD!
    Hallelujah!

PROVERBS

Many people think that what's written in the Bible has mostly to do with getting people into heaven — getting right with God, saving their eternal souls. It does have to do with that, of course, but not mostly. It is equally concerned with living on this earth — living well, living in robust sanity. In our Scriptures, heaven is not the primary concern, to which earth is a tagalong afterthought. "On earth *as* it is in heaven" is Jesus' prayer.

"Wisdom" is the biblical term for this on-earth-as-it-is-in-heaven everyday living. Wisdom is the art of living skillfully in whatever actual conditions we find ourselves. It has virtually nothing to do with information as such, with knowledge as such. A college degree is no certification of wisdom—nor is it primarily concerned with keeping us out of moral mud puddles, although it does have a profound moral effect upon us.

Wisdom has to do with becoming skillful in honoring our parents and raising our children, handling our money and conducting our sexual lives, going to work and exercising leadership, using words well and treating friends kindly, eating and drinking healthily, cultivating emotions within ourselves and attitudes toward others that make for peace. Threaded through all these items is the insistence that the way we think of and respond to God is the most practical thing we do. In matters of everyday practicality, nothing, absolutely nothing, takes precedence over God.

Proverbs concentrates on these concerns more than any other book in the Bible. Attention to the here and now is everywhere present in the stories and legislation, the prayers and the sermons, that are spread over the thousands of pages of the Bible. Proverbs distills it all into riveting images and aphorisms that keep us connected in holy obedience to the ordinary.

PROVERBS

WISE SAYINGS OF SOLOMON
A MANUAL FOR LIVING

1-6 These are the wise sayings of Solomon,
    David's son, Israel's king—
Written down so we'll know how to live well and right,
    to understand what life means and where it's going;
A manual for living,
    for learning what's right and just and fair;
To teach the inexperienced the ropes
    and give our young people a grasp on reality.
There's something here also for seasoned men and women,
    still a thing or two for the experienced to learn—
Fresh wisdom to probe and penetrate,
    the rhymes and reasons of wise men and women.

START WITH GOD

7 Start with GOD—the first step in learning is bowing down to GOD;
    only fools thumb their noses at such wisdom and learning.

8-19 Pay close attention, friend, to what your father tells you;
    never forget what you learned at your mother's knee.
Wear their counsel like flowers in your hair,
    like rings on your fingers.
Dear friend, if bad companions tempt you,
    don't go along with them.
If they say—"Let's go out and raise some hell.
    Let's beat up some old man, mug some old woman.
Let's pick them clean
    and get them ready for their funerals.
We'll load up on top-quality loot.
    We'll haul it home by the truckload.
Join us for the time of your life!
    With us, it's share and share alike!"—
Oh, friend, don't give them a second look;
    don't listen to them for a minute.
They're racing to a very bad end,
    hurrying to ruin everything they lay hands on.
Nobody robs a bank
    with everyone watching,
Yet that's what these people are doing—
    they're doing themselves in.
When you grab all you can get, that's what happens:
    the more you get, the less you are.

LADY WISDOM

20-21 Lady Wisdom goes out in the street and shouts.
    At the town center she makes her speech.

In the middle of the traffic she takes her stand.
>At the busiest corner she calls out:

22-24 "Simpletons! How long will you wallow in ignorance?
>Cynics! How long will you feed your cynicism?
Idiots! How long will you refuse to learn?
>About face! I can revise your life.
Look, I'm ready to pour out my spirit on you;
>I'm ready to tell you all I know.
As it is, I've called, but you've turned a deaf ear;
>I've reached out to you, but you've ignored me.

25-28 "Since you laugh at my counsel
>and make a joke of my advice,
How can I take you seriously?
>I'll turn the tables and joke about *your* troubles!
What if the roof falls in,
>and your whole life goes to pieces?
What if catastrophe strikes and there's nothing
>to show for your life but rubble and ashes?
You'll need me then. You'll call for me, but don't expect
>an answer.
>No matter how hard you look, you won't find me.

29-33 "Because you hated Knowledge
>and had nothing to do with the Fear-of-God,
Because you wouldn't take my advice
>and brushed aside all my offers to train you,
Well, you've made your bed — now lie in it;
>you wanted your own way — now, how do you like it?
Don't you see what happens, you simpletons, you idiots?
>Carelessness kills; complacency is murder.
First pay attention to me, and then relax.
>Now you can take it easy — you're in good hands."

MAKE INSIGHT YOUR PRIORITY

1-5 **2** Good friend, take to heart what I'm telling you;
>collect my counsels and guard them with your life.
Tune your ears to the world of Wisdom;
>set your heart on a life of Understanding.
That's right — if you make Insight your priority,
>and won't take no for an answer,
Searching for it like a prospector panning for gold,
>like an adventurer on a treasure hunt,
Believe me, before you know it Fear-of-God will be yours;
>you'll have come upon the Knowledge of God.

6-8 And here's why: GOD gives out Wisdom free,
>is plainspoken in Knowledge and Understanding.
He's a rich mine of Common Sense for those who live well,
>a personal bodyguard to the candid and sincere.

He keeps his eye on all who live honestly,
    and pays special attention to his loyally committed ones.

9-15   So now you can pick out what's true and fair,
    find all the good trails!
Lady Wisdom will be your close friend,
    and Brother Knowledge your pleasant companion.
Good Sense will scout ahead for danger,
    Insight will keep an eye out for you.
They'll keep you from making wrong turns,
    or following the bad directions
Of those who are lost themselves
    and can't tell a trail from a tumbleweed,
These losers who make a game of evil
    and throw parties to celebrate perversity,
Traveling paths that go nowhere,
    wandering in a maze of detours and dead ends.

16-19   Wise friends will rescue you from the Temptress —
    that smooth-talking Seductress
Who's faithless to the husband she married years ago,
    never gave a second thought to her promises before God.
Her whole way of life is doomed;
    every step she takes brings her closer to hell.
No one who joins her company ever comes back,
    ever sets foot on the path to real living.

20-22   So — join the company of good men and women,
    keep your feet on the tried-and-true paths.
It's the men who walk straight who will settle this land,
    the women with integrity who will last here.
The corrupt will lose their lives;
    the dishonest will be gone for good.

DON'T ASSUME YOU KNOW IT ALL

1-2   **3** Good friend, don't forget all I've taught you;
    take to heart my commands.
They'll help you live a long, long time,
    a long life lived full and well.

3-4   Don't lose your grip on Love and Loyalty.
    Tie them around your neck; carve their initials on your heart.
Earn a reputation for living well
    in God's eyes and the eyes of the people.

5-12   Trust GOD from the bottom of your heart;
    don't try to figure out everything on your own.
Listen for GOD's voice in everything you do, everywhere you go;
    he's the one who will keep you on track.
Don't assume that you know it all.
    Run to GOD! Run from evil!

Your body will glow with health,
  your very bones will vibrate with life!

Honor GOD with everything you own;
  give him the first and the best.
Your barns will burst,
  your wine vats will brim over.
But don't, dear friend, resent GOD's discipline;
  don't sulk under his loving correction.
It's the child he loves that GOD corrects;
  a father's delight is behind all this.

THE VERY TREE OF LIFE

13-18 You're blessed when you meet Lady Wisdom,
  when you make friends with Madame Insight.
She's worth far more than money in the bank;
  her friendship is better than a big salary.
Her value exceeds all the trappings of wealth;
  nothing you could wish for holds a candle to her.
With one hand she gives long life,
  with the other she confers recognition.
Her manner is beautiful,
  her life wonderfully complete.
She's the very Tree of Life to those who embrace her.
  Hold her tight — and be blessed!

19-20 With Lady Wisdom, GOD formed Earth;
  with Madame Insight, he raised Heaven.
They knew when to signal rivers and springs to the surface,
  and dew to descend from the night skies.

NEVER WALK AWAY

21-26 Dear friend, guard Clear Thinking and Common Sense with your life;
  don't for a minute lose sight of them.
They'll keep your soul alive and well,
  they'll keep you fit and attractive.
You'll travel safely,
  you'll neither tire nor trip.
You'll take afternoon naps without a worry,
  you'll enjoy a good night's sleep.
No need to panic over alarms or surprises,
  or predictions that doomsday's just around the corner,
Because GOD will be right there with you;
  he'll keep you safe and sound.

27-29 Never walk away from someone who deserves help;
  your hand is *God's* hand for that person.
Don't tell your neighbor "Maybe some other time"
  or "Try me tomorrow"
  when the money's right there in your pocket.
Don't figure ways of taking advantage of your neighbor
  when he's sitting there trusting and unsuspecting.

30-32
Don't walk around with a chip on your shoulder,
    always spoiling for a fight.
Don't try to be like those who shoulder their way through life.
    Why be a bully?
"Why not?" you say. Because GOD can't stand twisted souls.
    It's the straightforward who get his respect.

33-35
GOD's curse blights the house of the wicked,
    but he blesses the home of the righteous.
He gives proud skeptics a cold shoulder,
    but if you're down on your luck, he's right there to help.
Wise living gets rewarded with honor;
    stupid living gets the booby prize.

YOUR LIFE IS AT STAKE

1-2
4 Listen, friends, to some fatherly advice;
    sit up and take notice so you'll know how to live.
I'm giving you good counsel;
    don't let it go in one ear and out the other.

3-9
When I was a boy at my father's knee,
    the pride and joy of my mother,
He would sit me down and drill me:
    "Take this to heart. Do what I tell you — live!
Sell everything and buy Wisdom! Forage for Understanding!
    Don't forget one word! Don't deviate an inch!
Never walk away from Wisdom — she guards your life;
    love her — she keeps her eye on you.
Above all and before all, do this: Get Wisdom!
    Write this at the top of your list: Get Understanding!
Throw your arms around her — believe me, you won't regret it;
    never let her go — she'll make your life glorious.
She'll garland your life with grace,
    she'll festoon your days with beauty."

10-15
Dear friend, take my advice;
    it will add years to your life.
I'm writing out clear directions to Wisdom Way,
    I'm drawing a map to Righteous Road.
I don't want you ending up in blind alleys,
    or wasting time making wrong turns.
Hold tight to good advice; don't relax your grip.
    Guard it well — your life is at stake!
Don't take Wicked Bypass;
    don't so much as set foot on that road.
Stay clear of it; give it a wide berth.
    Make a detour and be on your way.

16-17
Evil people are restless
    unless they're making trouble;
They can't get a good night's sleep

unless they've made life miserable for somebody.
Perversity is their food and drink,
    violence their drug of choice.

18-19 The ways of right-living people glow with light;
    the longer they live, the brighter they shine.
But the road of wrongdoing gets darker and darker —
    travelers can't see a thing; they fall flat on their faces.

LEARN IT BY HEART

20-22 Dear friend, listen well to my words;
    tune your ears to my voice.
Keep my message in plain view at all times.
    Concentrate! Learn it by heart!
Those who discover these words live, really live;
    body and soul, they're bursting with health.

23-27 Keep vigilant watch over your heart;
    that's where life starts.
Don't talk out of both sides of your mouth;
    avoid careless banter, white lies, and gossip.
Keep your eyes straight ahead;
    ignore all sideshow distractions.
Watch your step,
    and the road will stretch out smooth before you.
Look neither right nor left;
    leave evil in the dust.

NOTHING BUT SIN AND BONES

1-2 5 Dear friend, pay close attention to this, my wisdom;
    listen very closely to the way I see it.
Then you'll acquire a taste for good sense;
    what I tell you will keep you out of trouble.

3-6 The lips of a seductive woman are oh so sweet,
    her soft words are oh so smooth.
But it won't be long before she's gravel in your mouth,
    a pain in your gut, a wound in your heart.
She's dancing down the primrose path to Death;
    she's headed straight for Hell and taking you with her.
She hasn't a clue about Real Life,
    about who she is or where she's going.

7-14 So, my friend, listen closely;
    don't treat my words casually.
Keep your distance from such a woman;
    absolutely stay out of her neighborhood.
You don't want to squander your wonderful life,
    to waste your precious life among the hardhearted.
Why should you allow strangers to take advantage of you?
    Why be exploited by those who care nothing for you?

You don't want to end your life full of regrets,
　　nothing but sin and bones,
Saying, "Oh, why didn't I do what they told me?
　　Why did I reject a disciplined life?
Why didn't I listen to my mentors,
　　or take my teachers seriously?
My life is ruined!
　　I haven't one blessed thing to show for my life!"

NEVER TAKE LOVE FOR GRANTED

15-16　Do you know the saying, "Drink from your own rain barrel,
　　draw water from your own spring-fed well"?
It's true. Otherwise, you may one day come home
　　and find your barrel empty and your well polluted.

17-20　Your spring water is for you and you only,
　　not to be passed around among strangers.
Bless your fresh-flowing fountain!
　　Enjoy the wife you married as a young man!
Lovely as an angel, beautiful as a rose —
　　don't ever quit taking delight in her body.
　　Never take her love for granted!
Why would you trade enduring intimacies for cheap thrills with a whore?
　　for dalliance with a promiscuous stranger?

21-23　Mark well that GOD doesn't miss a move you make;
　　he's aware of every step you take.
The shadow of your sin will overtake you;
　　you'll find yourself stumbling all over yourself in the dark.
Death is the reward of an undisciplined life;
　　your foolish decisions trap you in a dead end.

LIKE A DEER FROM THE HUNTER

1-5　6 Dear friend, if you've gone into hock with your neighbor
　　　or locked yourself into a deal with a stranger,
If you've impulsively promised the shirt off your back
　　and now find yourself shivering out in the cold,
Friend, don't waste a minute, get yourself out of that mess.
　　You're in that man's clutches!
　　Go, put on a long face; act desperate.
Don't procrastinate —
　　there's no time to lose.
Run like a deer from the hunter,
　　fly like a bird from the trapper!

A LESSON FROM THE ANT

6-11　You lazy fool, look at an ant.
　　Watch it closely; let it teach you a thing or two.
Nobody has to tell it what to do.
　　All summer it stores up food;
　　at harvest it stockpiles provisions.

So how long are you going to laze around doing nothing?
　　How long before you get out of bed?
A nap here, a nap there, a day off here, a day off there,
　　sit back, take it easy — do you know what comes next?
Just this: You can look forward to a dirt-poor life,
　　poverty your permanent houseguest!

ALWAYS COOKING UP SOMETHING NASTY

12-15　Riffraff and rascals
　　talk out of both sides of their mouths.
They wink at each other, they shuffle their feet,
　　they cross their fingers behind their backs.
Their perverse minds are always cooking up something nasty,
　　always stirring up trouble.
Catastrophe is just around the corner for them,
　　a total smashup, their lives ruined beyond repair.

SEVEN THINGS GOD HATES

16-19　Here are six things GOD hates,
　　and one more that he loathes with a passion:

　　　　eyes that are arrogant,
　　　　a tongue that lies,
　　　　hands that murder the innocent,
　　　　a heart that hatches evil plots,
　　　　feet that race down a wicked track,
　　　　a mouth that lies under oath,
　　　　a troublemaker in the family.

WARNING ON ADULTERY

20-23　Good friend, follow your father's good advice;
　　don't wander off from your mother's teachings.
Wrap yourself in them from head to foot;
　　wear them like a scarf around your neck.
Wherever you walk, they'll guide you;
　　whenever you rest, they'll guard you;
　　when you wake up, they'll tell you what's next.
For sound advice is a beacon,
　　good teaching is a light,
　　moral discipline is a life path.

24-35　They'll protect you from wanton women,
　　from the seductive talk of some temptress.
Don't lustfully fantasize on her beauty,
　　nor be taken in by her bedroom eyes.
You can buy an hour with a whore for a loaf of bread,
　　but a wanton woman may well eat *you* alive.
Can you build a fire in your lap
　　and not burn your pants?
Can you walk barefoot on hot coals
　　and not get blisters?

It's the same when you have sex with your neighbor's wife:
    Touch her and you'll pay for it. No excuses.
Hunger is no excuse
    for a thief to steal;
When he's caught he has to pay it back,
    even if he has to put his whole house in hock.
Adultery is a brainless act,
    soul-destroying, self-destructive;
Expect a bloody nose, a black eye,
    and a reputation ruined for good.
For jealousy detonates rage in a cheated husband;
    wild for revenge, he won't make allowances.
Nothing you say or pay will make it all right;
    neither bribes nor reason will satisfy him.

D RESSED TO S EDUCE

1-5

7 Dear friend, do what I tell you;
    treasure my careful instructions.
    Do what I say and you'll live well.
My teaching is as precious as your eyesight — guard it!
Write it out on the back of your hands;
    etch it on the chambers of your heart.
Talk to Wisdom as to a sister.
    Treat Insight as your companion.
They'll be with you to fend off the Temptress —
    that smooth-talking, honey-tongued Seductress.

6-12

As I stood at the window of my house
    looking out through the shutters,
Watching the mindless crowd stroll by,
    I spotted a young man without any sense
Arriving at the corner of the street where she lived,
    then turning up the path to her house.
It was dusk, the evening coming on,
    the darkness thickening into night.
Just then, a woman met him —
    she'd been lying in wait for him, dressed to seduce him.
Brazen and brash she was,
    restless and roaming, never at home,
Walking the streets, loitering in the mall,
    hanging out at every corner in town.

13-20

She threw her arms around him and kissed him,
    boldly took his arm and said,
"I've got all the makings for a feast —
    today I made my offerings, my vows are all paid,
So now I've come to find you,
    hoping to catch sight of your face — and here you are!
I've spread fresh, clean sheets on my bed,
    colorful imported linens.
My bed is aromatic with spices

and exotic fragrances.
Come, let's make love all night,
    spend the night in ecstatic lovemaking!
My husband's not home; he's away on business,
    and he won't be back for a month."

21-23   Soon she has him eating out of her hand,
    bewitched by her honeyed speech.
Before you know it, he's trotting behind her,
    like a calf led to the butcher shop,
Like a stag lured into ambush
    and then shot with an arrow,
Like a bird flying into a net
    not knowing that its flying life is over.

24-27   So, friends, listen to me,
    take these words of mine most seriously.
Don't fool around with a woman like that;
    don't even stroll through her neighborhood.
Countless victims come under her spell;
    she's the death of many a poor man.
She runs a halfway house to hell,
    fits you out with a shroud and a coffin.

LADY WISDOM CALLS OUT

1-11   8 Do you hear Lady Wisdom calling?
    Can you hear Madame Insight raising her voice?
    She's taken her stand at First and Main,
    at the busiest intersection.
Right in the city square
    where the traffic is thickest, she shouts,
"You — I'm talking to all of you,
    everyone out here on the streets!
Listen, you idiots — learn good sense!
    You blockheads — shape up!
Don't miss a word of this — I'm telling you how to live well,
    I'm telling you how to live at your best.
My mouth chews and savors and relishes truth —
    I can't stand the taste of evil!
You'll only hear true and right words from my mouth;
    not one syllable will be twisted or skewed.
You'll recognize this as true — you with open minds;
    truth-ready minds will see it at once.
Prefer my life-disciplines over chasing after money,
    and God-knowledge over a lucrative career.
For Wisdom is better than all the trappings of wealth;
    nothing you could wish for holds a candle to her.

12-21   "I am Lady Wisdom, and I live next to Sanity;
    Knowledge and Discretion live just down the street.
The Fear-of-God means hating Evil,

whose ways I hate with a passion —
    pride and arrogance and crooked talk.
Good counsel and common sense are my characteristics;
    I am both Insight and the Virtue to live it out.
With my help, leaders rule,
    and lawmakers legislate fairly;
With my help, governors govern,
    along with all in legitimate authority.
I love those who love me;
    those who look for me find me.
Wealth and Glory accompany me —
    also substantial Honor and a Good Name.
My benefits are worth more than a big salary, even a *very* big salary;
    the returns on me exceed any imaginable bonus.
You can find me on Righteous Road — that's where I walk —
    at the intersection of Justice Avenue,
Handing out life to those who love me,
    filling their arms with life — armloads of life!

22-31   "God sovereignly made me — the first, the basic —
    before he did anything else.
I was brought into being a long time ago,
    well before Earth got its start.
I arrived on the scene before Ocean,
    yes, even before Springs and Rivers and Lakes.
Before Mountains were sculpted and Hills took shape,
    I was already there, newborn;
Long before God stretched out Earth's Horizons,
    and tended to the minute details of Soil and Weather,
And set Sky firmly in place,
    I was there.
When he mapped and gave borders to wild Ocean,
    built the vast vault of Heaven,
    and installed the fountains that fed Ocean,
When he drew a boundary for Sea,
    posted a sign that said NO TRESPASSING,
And then staked out Earth's Foundations,
    I was right there with him, making sure everything fit.
Day after day I was there, with my joyful applause,
    always enjoying his company,
Delighted with the world of things and creatures,
    happily celebrating the human family.

32-36   "So, my dear friends, listen carefully;
    those who embrace these my ways are most blessed.
Mark a life of discipline and live wisely;
    don't squander your precious life.
Blessed the man, blessed the woman, who listens to me,
    awake and ready for me each morning,
    alert and responsive as I start my day's work.
When you find me, you find life, real life,

to say nothing of God's good pleasure.
But if you wrong me, you damage your very soul;
    when you reject me, you're flirting with death."

LADY WISDOM GIVES A DINNER PARTY

¹⁻⁶ **9** Lady Wisdom has built and furnished her home;
    it's supported by seven hewn timbers.
The banquet meal is ready to be served: lamb roasted,
wine poured out, table set with silver and flowers.
Having dismissed her serving maids,
    Lady Wisdom goes to town, stands in a prominent place,
    and invites everyone within sound of her voice:
"Are you confused about life, don't know what's going on?
    Come with me, oh come, have dinner with me!
I've prepared a wonderful spread — fresh-baked bread,
    roast lamb, carefully selected wines.
Leave your impoverished confusion and *live*!
    Walk up the street to a life with meaning."

⁷⁻¹² If you reason with an arrogant cynic, you'll get slapped in the face;
    confront bad behavior and get a kick in the shins.
So don't waste your time on a scoffer;
    all you'll get for your pains is abuse.
But if you correct those who care about life,
    that's different — they'll love you for it!
Save your breath for the wise — they'll be wiser for it;
    tell good people what you know — they'll profit from it.
Skilled living gets its start in the Fear-of-God,
    insight into life from knowing a Holy God.
It's through me, Lady Wisdom, that your life deepens,
    and the years of your life ripen.
Live wisely and wisdom will permeate your life;
    mock life and life will mock you.

MADAME WHORE CALLS OUT, TOO

¹³⁻¹⁸ Then there's this other woman, Madame Whore —
    brazen, empty-headed, frivolous.
She sits on the front porch
    of her house on Main Street,
And as people walk by minding
    their own business, calls out,
"Are you confused about life, don't know what's going on?
    Steal off with me, I'll show you a good time!
    No one will ever know — I'll give you the time of your life."
But they don't know about all the skeletons in her closet,
    that all her guests end up in hell.

THE WISE SAYINGS OF SOLOMON
AN HONEST LIFE IS IMMORTAL

1 **10** Wise son, glad father;
stupid son, sad mother.

2 Ill-gotten gain gets you nowhere;
an honest life is immortal.

3 GOD won't starve an honest soul,
but he frustrates the appetites of the wicked.

4 Sloth makes you poor;
diligence brings wealth.

5 Make hay while the sun shines — that's smart;
go fishing during harvest — that's stupid.

6 Blessings accrue on a good and honest life,
but the mouth of the wicked is a dark cave of abuse.

7 A good and honest life is a blessed memorial;
a wicked life leaves a rotten stench.

8 A wise heart takes orders;
an empty head will come unglued.

9 Honesty lives confident and carefree,
but Shifty is sure to be exposed.

10 An evasive eye is a sign of trouble ahead,
but an open, face-to-face meeting results in peace.

11 The mouth of a good person is a deep, life-giving well,
but the mouth of the wicked is a dark cave of abuse.

12 Hatred starts fights,
but love pulls a quilt over the bickering.

13 You'll find wisdom on the lips of a person of insight,
but the shortsighted needs a slap in the face.

14 The wise accumulate knowledge — a true treasure;
know-it-alls talk too much — a sheer waste.

THE ROAD TO LIFE IS A DISCIPLINED LIFE

15 The wealth of the rich is their bastion;
the poverty of the indigent is their ruin.

16 The wage of a good person is exuberant life;
an evil person ends up with nothing but sin.

17 The road to life is a disciplined life;
   ignore correction and you're lost for good.

18 Liars secretly hoard hatred;
   fools openly spread slander.

19 The more talk, the less truth;
   the wise measure their words.

20 The speech of a good person is worth waiting for;
   the blabber of the wicked is worthless.

21 The talk of a good person is rich fare for many,
   but chatterboxes die of an empty heart.

FEAR-OF-GOD EXPANDS YOUR LIFE

22 GOD's blessing makes life rich;
   nothing we do can improve on God.

23 An empty-head thinks mischief is fun,
   but a mindful person relishes wisdom.

24 The nightmares of the wicked come true;
   what the good people desire, they get.

25 When the storm is over, there's nothing left of the wicked;
   good people, firm on their rock foundation, aren't even fazed.

26 A lazy employee will give you nothing but trouble;
   it's vinegar in the mouth, smoke in the eyes.

27 The Fear-of-GOD expands your life;
   a wicked life is a puny life.

28 The aspirations of good people end in celebration;
   the ambitions of bad people crash.

29 GOD is solid backing to a well-lived life,
   but he calls into question a shabby performance.

30 Good people *last* — they can't be moved;
   the wicked are here today, gone tomorrow.

31 A good person's mouth is a clear fountain of wisdom;
   a foul mouth is a stagnant swamp.

32 The speech of a good person clears the air;
   the words of the wicked pollute it.

1 **11** GOD hates cheating in the marketplace;
he loves it when business is aboveboard.

2 The stuck-up fall flat on their faces,
but down-to-earth people stand firm.

3 The integrity of the honest keeps them on track;
the deviousness of crooks brings them to ruin.

4 A thick bankroll is no help when life falls apart,
but a principled life can stand up to the worst.

5 Moral character makes for smooth traveling;
an evil life is a hard life.

6 Good character is the best insurance;
crooks get trapped in their sinful lust.

7 When the wicked die, that's it —
the story's over, end of hope.

8 A good person is saved from much trouble;
a bad person runs straight into it.

9 The loose tongue of the godless spreads destruction;
the common sense of the godly preserves them.

10 When it goes well for good people, the whole town cheers;
when it goes badly for bad people, the town celebrates.

11 When right-living people bless the city, it flourishes;
evil talk turns it into a ghost town in no time.

12 Mean-spirited slander is heartless;
quiet discretion accompanies good sense.

13 A gadabout gossip can't be trusted with a secret,
but someone of integrity won't violate a confidence.

14 Without good direction, people lose their way;
the more wise counsel you follow, the better your chances.

15 Whoever makes deals with strangers is sure to get burned;
if you keep a cool head, you'll avoid rash bargains.

16 A woman of gentle grace gets respect,
but men of rough violence grab for loot.

A GOD-SHAPED LIFE

17 When you're kind to others, you help yourself;
   when you're cruel to others, you hurt yourself.

18 Bad work gets paid with a bad check;
   good work gets solid pay.

19 Take your stand with God's loyal community and live,
   or chase after phantoms of evil and die.

20 GOD can't stand deceivers,
   but oh how he relishes integrity.

21 Count on this: The wicked won't get off scot-free,
   and God's loyal people will triumph.

22 Like a gold ring in a pig's snout
   is a beautiful face on an empty head.

23 The desires of good people lead straight to the best,
   but wicked ambition ends in angry frustration.

24 The world of the generous gets larger and larger;
   the world of the stingy gets smaller and smaller.

25 The one who blesses others is abundantly blessed;
   those who help others are helped.

26 Curses on those who drive a hard bargain!
   Blessings on all who play fair and square!

27 The one who seeks good finds delight;
   the student of evil becomes evil.

28 A life devoted to things is a dead life, a stump;
   a God-shaped life is a flourishing tree.

29 Exploit or abuse your family, and end up with a fistful of air;
   common sense tells you it's a stupid way to live.

30 A good life is a fruit-bearing tree;
   a violent life destroys souls.

31 If good people barely make it,
   what's in store for the bad!

IF YOU LOVE LEARNING

12

1 If you love learning, you love the discipline that goes with it —
   how shortsighted to refuse correction!

2   A good person basks in the delight of GOD,
      and he wants nothing to do with devious schemers.

3   You can't find firm footing in a swamp,
      but life rooted in God stands firm.

4   A hearty wife invigorates her husband,
      but a frigid woman is cancer in the bones.

5   The thinking of principled people makes for justice;
      the plots of degenerates corrupt.

6   The words of the wicked kill;
      the speech of the upright saves.

7   Wicked people fall to pieces — there's nothing to them;
      the homes of good people hold together.

8   A person who talks sense is honored;
      airheads are held in contempt.

9   Better to be ordinary and work for a living
      than act important and starve in the process.

10   Good people are good to their animals;
      the "good-hearted" bad people kick and abuse them.

11   The one who stays on the job has food on the table;
      the witless chase whims and fancies.

12   What the wicked construct finally falls into ruin,
      while the roots of the righteous give life, and more life.

WISE PEOPLE TAKE ADVICE

13   The gossip of bad people gets them in trouble;
      the conversation of good people keeps them out of it.

14   Well-spoken words bring satisfaction;
      well-done work has its own reward.

15   Fools are headstrong and do what they like;
      wise people take advice.

16   Fools have short fuses and explode all too quickly;
      the prudent quietly shrug off insults.

17   Truthful witness by a good person clears the air,
      but liars lay down a smoke screen of deceit.

18   Rash language cuts and maims,
      but there is healing in the words of the wise.

19 Truth lasts;
    lies are here today, gone tomorrow.

20 Evil scheming distorts the schemer;
    peace-planning brings joy to the planner.

21 No evil can overwhelm a good person,
    but the wicked have their hands full of it.

22 God can't stomach liars;
    he loves the company of those who keep their word.

23 Prudent people don't flaunt their knowledge;
    talkative fools broadcast their silliness.

24 The diligent find freedom in their work;
    the lazy are oppressed by work.

25 Worry weighs us down;
    a cheerful word picks us up.

26 A good person survives misfortune,
    but a wicked life invites disaster.

27 A lazy life is an empty life,
    but "early to rise" gets the job done.

28 Good men and women travel right into life;
    sin's detours take you straight to hell.

WALK WITH THE WISE

13 Intelligent children listen to their parents;
    foolish children do their own thing.

2 The good acquire a taste for helpful conversation;
    bullies push and shove their way through life.

3 Careful words make for a careful life;
    careless talk may ruin everything.

4 Indolence wants it all and gets nothing;
    the energetic have something to show for their lives.

5 A good person hates false talk;
    a bad person wallows in gibberish.

6 A God-loyal life keeps you on track;
    sin dumps the wicked in the ditch.

7 A pretentious, showy life is an empty life;
    a plain and simple life is a full life.

8 The rich can be sued for everything they have,
  but the poor are free of such threats.

9 The lives of good people are brightly lit streets;
  the lives of the wicked are dark alleys.

10 Arrogant know-it-alls stir up discord,
  but wise men and women listen to each other's counsel.

11 Easy come, easy go,
  but steady diligence pays off.

12 Unrelenting disappointment leaves you heartsick,
  but a sudden good break can turn life around.

13 Ignore the Word and suffer;
  honor God's commands and grow rich.

14 The teaching of the wise is a fountain of life,
  so, no more drinking from death-tainted wells!

15 Sound thinking makes for gracious living,
  but liars walk a rough road.

16 A commonsense person *lives* good sense;
  fools litter the country with silliness.

17 Irresponsible talk makes a real mess of things,
  but a reliable reporter is a healing presence.

18 Refuse discipline and end up homeless;
  embrace correction and live an honored life.

19 Souls who follow their hearts thrive;
  fools bent on evil despise matters of soul.

20 Become wise by walking with the wise;
  hang out with fools and watch your life fall to pieces.

21 Disaster entraps sinners,
  but God-loyal people get a good life.

22 A good life gets passed on to the grandchildren;
  ill-gotten wealth ends up with good people.

23 Banks foreclose on the farms of the poor,
  or else the poor lose their shirts to crooked lawyers.

24 A refusal to correct is a refusal to love;
  love your children by disciplining them.

25 An appetite for good brings much satisfaction,
   but the belly of the wicked always wants more.

A WAY THAT LEADS TO HELL

1 **14** Lady Wisdom builds a lovely home;
   Sir Fool comes along and tears it down brick by brick.

2 An honest life shows respect for GOD;
   a degenerate life is a slap in his face.

3 Frivolous talk provokes a derisive smile;
   wise speech evokes nothing but respect.

4 No cattle, no crops;
   a good harvest requires a strong ox for the plow.

5 A true witness never lies;
   a false witness makes a business of it.

6 Cynics look high and low for wisdom — and never find it;
   the open-minded find it right on their doorstep!

7 Escape quickly from the company of fools;
   they're a waste of your time, a waste of your words.

8 The wisdom of the wise keeps life on track;
   the foolishness of fools lands them in the ditch.

9 The stupid ridicule right and wrong,
   but a moral life is a favored life.

10 The person who shuns the bitter moments of friends
   will be an outsider at their celebrations.

11 Lives of careless wrongdoing are tumbledown shacks;
   holy living builds soaring cathedrals.

12-13 There's a way of life that looks harmless enough;
   look again — it leads straight to hell.
   Sure, those people appear to be having a good time,
   but all that laughter will end in heartbreak.

SIFT AND WEIGH EVERY WORD

14 A mean person gets paid back in meanness,
   a gracious person in grace.

15 The gullible believe anything they're told;
   the prudent sift and weigh every word.

16 The wise watch their steps and avoid evil;
   fools are headstrong and reckless.

17 The hotheaded do things they'll later regret;
the coldhearted get the cold shoulder.

18 Foolish dreamers live in a world of illusion;
wise realists plant their feet on the ground.

19 Eventually, evil will pay tribute to good;
the wicked will respect God-loyal people.

20 An unlucky loser is shunned by all,
but everyone loves a winner.

21 It's criminal to ignore a neighbor in need,
but compassion for the poor — what a blessing!

22 Isn't it obvious that conspirators lose out,
while the thoughtful win love and trust?

23 Hard work always pays off;
mere talk puts no bread on the table.

24 The wise accumulate wisdom;
fools get stupider by the day.

25 Souls are saved by truthful witness
and betrayed by the spread of lies.

26 The Fear-of-God builds up confidence,
and makes a world safe for your children.

27 The Fear-of-God is a spring of living water
so you won't go off drinking from poisoned wells.

28 The mark of a good leader is loyal followers;
leadership is nothing without a following.

29 Slowness to anger makes for deep understanding;
a quick-tempered person stockpiles stupidity.

30 A sound mind makes for a robust body,
but runaway emotions corrode the bones.

31 You insult your Maker when you exploit the powerless;
when you're kind to the poor, you honor God.

32 The evil of bad people leaves them out in the cold;
the integrity of good people creates a safe place for living.

33 Lady Wisdom is at home in an understanding heart —
fools never even get to say hello.

34 God-devotion makes a country strong;
   God-avoidance leaves people weak.

35 Diligent work gets a warm commendation;
   shiftless work earns an angry rebuke.

GOD DOESN'T MISS A THING

1 **15** A gentle response defuses anger,
   but a sharp tongue kindles a temper-fire.

2 Knowledge flows like spring water from the wise;
   fools are leaky faucets, dripping nonsense.

3 GOD doesn't miss a thing—
   he's alert to good and evil alike.

4 Kind words heal and help;
   cutting words wound and maim.

5 Moral dropouts won't listen to their elders;
   welcoming correction is a mark of good sense.

6 The lives of God-loyal people flourish;
   a misspent life is soon bankrupt.

7 Perceptive words spread knowledge;
   fools are hollow—there's nothing to them.

8 GOD can't stand pious poses,
   but he delights in genuine prayers.

9 A life frittered away disgusts GOD;
   he loves those who run straight for the finish line.

10 It's a school of hard knocks for those who leave God's path,
   a dead-end street for those who hate God's rules.

11 Even hell holds no secrets from GOD—
   do you think he can't read human hearts?

LIFE ASCENDS TO THE HEIGHTS

12 Know-it-alls don't like being told what to do;
   they avoid the company of wise men and women.

13 A cheerful heart brings a smile to your face;
   a sad heart makes it hard to get through the day.

14 An intelligent person is always eager to take in more truth;
   fools feed on fast-food fads and fancies.

15 A miserable heart means a miserable life;
  a cheerful heart fills the day with song.

16 A simple life in the Fear-of-GOD
  is better than a rich life with a ton of headaches.

17 Better a bread crust shared in love
  than a slab of prime rib served in hate.

18 Hot tempers start fights;
  a calm, cool spirit keeps the peace.

19 The path of lazy people is overgrown with briers;
  the diligent walk down a smooth road.

20 Intelligent children make their parents proud;
  lazy students embarrass their parents.

21 The empty-headed treat life as a plaything;
  the perceptive grasp its meaning and make a go of it.

22 Refuse good advice and watch your plans fail;
  take good counsel and watch them succeed.

23 Congenial conversation — what a pleasure!
  The right word at the right time — beautiful!

24 Life ascends to the heights for the thoughtful —
  it's a clean about-face from descent into hell.

25 GOD smashes the pretensions of the arrogant;
  he stands with those who have no standing.

26 GOD can't stand evil scheming,
  but he puts words of grace and beauty on display.

27 A greedy and grasping person destroys community;
  those who refuse to exploit live and let live.

28 Prayerful answers come from God-loyal people;
  the wicked are sewers of abuse.

29 GOD keeps his distance from the wicked;
  he closely attends to the prayers of God-loyal people.

30 A twinkle in the eye means joy in the heart,
  and good news makes you feel fit as a fiddle.

31 Listen to good advice if you want to live well,
  an honored guest among wise men and women.

32 An undisciplined, self-willed life is puny;
an obedient, God-willed life is spacious.

33 Fear-of-God is a school in skilled living—
first you learn humility, then you experience glory.

EVERYTHING WITH A PLACE AND A PURPOSE

1 **16** Mortals make elaborate plans,
but GOD has the last word.

2 Humans are satisfied with whatever looks good;
GOD probes for what *is* good.

3 Put GOD in charge of your work,
then what you've planned will take place.

4 GOD made everything with a place and purpose;
even the wicked are included—but for *judgment*.

5 GOD can't stomach arrogance or pretense;
believe me, he'll put those upstarts in their place.

6 Guilt is banished through love and truth;
Fear-of-God deflects evil.

7 When GOD approves of your life,
even your enemies will end up shaking your hand.

8 Far better to be right and poor
than to be wrong and rich.

9 We plan the way we want to live,
but only GOD makes us able to live it.

IT PAYS TO TAKE LIFE SERIOUSLY

10 A good leader motivates,
doesn't mislead, doesn't exploit.

11 GOD cares about honesty in the workplace;
your business is his business.

12 Good leaders abhor wrongdoing of all kinds;
sound leadership has a moral foundation.

13 Good leaders cultivate honest speech;
they love advisors who tell them the truth.

14 An intemperate leader wreaks havoc in lives;
you're smart to stay clear of someone like that.

15 Good-tempered leaders invigorate lives;
   they're like spring rain and sunshine.

16 Get wisdom — it's worth more than money;
   choose insight over income every time.

17 The road of right living bypasses evil;
   watch your step and save your life.

18 First pride, then the crash —
   the bigger the ego, the harder the fall.

19 It's better to live humbly among the poor
   than to live it up among the rich and famous.

20 It pays to take life seriously;
   things work out when you trust in GOD.

21 A wise person gets known for insight;
   gracious words add to one's reputation.

22 True intelligence is a spring of fresh water,
   while fools sweat it out the hard way.

23 They make a lot of sense, these wise folks;
   whenever they speak, their reputation increases.

24 Gracious speech is like clover honey —
   good taste to the soul, quick energy for the body.

25 There's a way that looks harmless enough;
   look again — it leads straight to hell.

26 Appetite is an incentive to work;
   hunger makes you work all the harder.

27 Mean people spread mean gossip;
   their words smart and burn.

28 Troublemakers start fights;
   gossips break up friendships.

29 Calloused climbers betray their very own friends;
   they'd stab their own grandmothers in the back.

30 A shifty eye betrays an evil intention;
   a clenched jaw signals trouble ahead.

31 Gray hair is a mark of distinction,
   the award for a God-loyal life.

32 Moderation is better than muscle,
    self-control better than political power.

33 Make your motions and cast your votes,
    but GOD has the final say.

A WHACK ON THE HEAD OF A FOOL

1 **17** A meal of bread and water in contented peace
    is better than a banquet spiced with quarrels.

2 A wise servant takes charge of an unruly child
    and is honored as one of the family.

3 As silver in a crucible and gold in a pan,
    so our lives are assayed by GOD.

4 Evil people relish malicious conversation;
    the ears of liars itch for dirty gossip.

5 Whoever mocks poor people insults their Creator;
    gloating over misfortune is a punishable crime.

6 Old people are distinguished by grandchildren;
    children take pride in their parents.

7 We don't expect eloquence from fools,
    nor do we expect lies from our leaders.

8 Receiving a gift is like getting a rare gemstone;
    any way you look at it, you see beauty refracted.

9 Overlook an offense and bond a friendship;
    fasten on to a slight and—good-bye, friend!

10 A quiet rebuke to a person of good sense
    does more than a whack on the head of a fool.

11 Criminals out looking for nothing but trouble
    won't have to wait long—they'll meet it coming and going!

12 Better to meet a grizzly robbed of her cubs
    than a fool hellbent on folly.

13 Those who return evil for good
    will meet their own evil returning.

14 The start of a quarrel is like a leak in a dam,
    so stop it before it bursts.

15 Whitewashing bad people and throwing mud on good people
    are equally abhorrent to GOD.

16   What's this? Fools out shopping for wisdom!
      They wouldn't recognize it if they saw it!

One Who Knows Much Says Little

17   Friends love through all kinds of weather,
      and families stick together in all kinds of trouble.

18   It's stupid to try to get something for nothing,
      or run up huge bills you can never pay.

19   The person who courts sin marries trouble;
      build a wall, invite a burglar.

20   A bad motive can't achieve a good end;
      double-talk brings you double trouble.

21   Having a fool for a child is misery;
      it's no fun being the parent of a dolt.

22   A cheerful disposition is good for your health;
      gloom and doom leave you bone-tired.

23   The wicked take bribes under the table;
      they show nothing but contempt for justice.

24   The perceptive find wisdom in their own front yard;
      fools look for it everywhere but right here.

25   A surly, stupid child is sheer pain to a father,
      a bitter pill for a mother to swallow.

26   It's wrong to penalize good behavior,
      or make good citizens pay for the crimes of others.

27   The one who knows much says little;
      an understanding person remains calm.

28   Even dunces who keep quiet are thought to be wise;
      as long as they keep their mouths shut, they're smart.

Words Kill, Words Give Life

18 Loners who care only for themselves
      spit on the common good.

2   Fools care nothing for thoughtful discourse;
      all they do is run off at the mouth.

3   When wickedness arrives, shame's not far behind;
      contempt for life is contemptible.

4   Many words rush along like rivers in flood,
      but deep wisdom flows up from artesian springs.

5   It's not right to go easy on the guilty,
      or come down hard on the innocent.

6   The words of a fool start fights;
      do him a favor and gag him.

7   Fools are undone by their big mouths;
      their souls are crushed by their words.

8   Listening to gossip is like eating cheap candy;
      do you really want junk like that in your belly?

9   Slack habits and sloppy work
      are as bad as vandalism.

10   GOD's name is a place of protection —
      good people can run there and be safe.

11   The rich think their wealth protects them;
      they imagine themselves safe behind it.

12   Pride first, then the crash,
      but humility is precursor to honor.

13   Answering before listening
      is both stupid and rude.

14   A healthy spirit conquers adversity,
      but what can you do when the spirit is crushed?

15   Wise men and women are always learning,
      always listening for fresh insights.

16   A gift gets attention;
      it buys the attention of eminent people.

17   The first speech in a court case is always convincing —
      until the cross-examination starts!

18   You may have to draw straws
      when faced with a tough decision.

19   Do a favor and win a friend forever;
      nothing can untie that bond.

20   Words satisfy the mind as much as fruit does the stomach;
      good talk is as gratifying as a good harvest.

21   Words kill, words give life;
      they're either poison or fruit — you choose.

22   Find a good spouse, you find a good life —
      and even more: the favor of God!

23   The poor speak in soft supplications;
      the rich bark out answers.

24   Friends come and friends go,
      but a true friend sticks by you like family.

If You Quit Listening

1   **19** Better to be poor and honest
      than a rich person no one can trust.

2   Ignorant zeal is worthless;
      haste makes waste.

3   People ruin their lives by their own stupidity,
      so why does God always get blamed?

4   Wealth attracts friends as honey draws flies,
      but poor people are avoided like a plague.

5   Perjury won't go unpunished.
      Would you let a liar go free?

6   Lots of people flock around a generous person;
      everyone's a friend to the philanthropist.

7   When you're down on your luck, even your family avoids you —
      yes, even your best friends wish you'd get lost.
   If they see you coming, they look the other way —
      out of sight, out of mind.

8   Grow a wise heart — you'll do yourself a favor;
      keep a clear head — you'll find a good life.

9   The person who tells lies gets caught;
      the person who spreads rumors is ruined.

10   Blockheads shouldn't live on easy street
      any more than workers should give orders to their boss.

11   Smart people know how to hold their tongue;
      their grandeur is to forgive and forget.

12   Mean-tempered leaders are like mad dogs;
      the good-natured are like fresh morning dew.

13 A parent is worn to a frazzle by a stupid child;
      a nagging spouse is a leaky faucet.

14 House and land are handed down from parents,
      but a congenial spouse comes straight from GOD.

15 Life collapses on loafers;
      lazybones go hungry.

16 Keep the rules and keep your life;
      careless living kills.

17 Mercy to the needy is a loan to GOD,
      and GOD pays back those loans in full.

18 Discipline your children while you still have the chance;
      indulging them destroys them.

19 Let angry people endure the backlash of their own anger;
      if you try to make it better, you'll only make it worse.

20 Take good counsel and accept correction —
      that's the way to live wisely and well.

21 We humans keep brainstorming options and plans,
      but GOD's purpose prevails.

22 It's only human to want to make a buck,
      but it's better to be poor than a liar.

23 Fear-of-GOD is life itself,
      a full life, and serene — no nasty surprises.

24 Some people dig a fork into the pie
      but are too lazy to raise it to their mouth.

25 Punish the insolent — make an example of them.
      Who knows? Somebody might learn a good lesson.

26 Kids who lash out against their parents
      are an embarrassment and disgrace.

27 If you quit listening, dear child, and strike off on your own,
      you'll soon be out of your depth.

28 An unprincipled witness desecrates justice;
      the mouths of the wicked spew malice.

29 The irreverent have to learn reverence the hard way;
      only a slap in the face brings fools to attention.

DEEP WATER IN THE HEART

20 1 Wine makes you mean, beer makes you quarrelsome —
a staggering drunk is not much fun.

2 Quick-tempered leaders are like mad dogs —
cross them and they bite your head off.

3 It's a mark of good character to avert quarrels,
but fools love to pick fights.

4 A farmer too lazy to plant in the spring
has nothing to harvest in the fall.

5 Knowing what is right is like deep water in the heart;
a wise person draws from the well within.

6 Lots of people claim to be loyal and loving,
but where on earth can you find one?

7 God-loyal people, living honest lives,
make it much easier for their children.

8-9 Leaders who know their business and care
keep a sharp eye out for the shoddy and cheap,
For who among us can be trusted
to be always diligent and honest?

10 Switching price tags and padding the expense account
are two things GOD hates.

11 Young people eventually reveal by their actions
if their motives are on the up and up.

DRINKING FROM THE CHALICE OF KNOWLEDGE

12 Ears that hear and eyes that see —
we get our basic equipment from GOD!

13 Don't be too fond of sleep; you'll end up in the poorhouse.
Wake up and get up; then there'll be food on the table.

14 The shopper says, "That's junk — I'll take it off your hands,"
then goes off boasting of the bargain.

15 Drinking from the beautiful chalice of knowledge
is better than adorning oneself with gold and rare gems.

16 Hold tight to collateral on any loan to a stranger;
beware of accepting what a transient has pawned.

17 Stolen bread tastes sweet,
   but soon your mouth is full of gravel.

18 Form your purpose by asking for counsel,
   then carry it out using all the help you can get.

19 Gossips can't keep secrets,
   so never confide in blabbermouths.

20 Anyone who curses father and mother
   extinguishes light and exists benighted.

THE VERY STEPS WE TAKE

21 A bonanza at the beginning
   is no guarantee of blessing at the end.

22 Don't ever say, "I'll get you for that!"
   Wait for GOD; he'll settle the score.

23 GOD hates cheating in the marketplace;
   rigged scales are an outrage.

24 The very steps we take come from GOD;
   otherwise how would we know where we're going?

25 An impulsive vow is a trap;
   later you'll wish you could get out of it.

26 After careful scrutiny, a wise leader
   makes a clean sweep of rebels and dolts.

27 GOD is in charge of human life,
   watching and examining us inside and out.

28 Love and truth form a good leader;
   sound leadership is founded on loving integrity.

29 Youth may be admired for vigor,
   but gray hair gives prestige to old age.

30 A good thrashing purges evil;
   punishment goes deep within us.

GOD EXAMINES OUR MOTIVES

21

1 Good leadership is a channel of water controlled by GOD;
   he directs it to whatever ends he chooses.

2 We justify our actions by appearances;
   GOD examines our motives.

3   Clean living before God and justice with our neighbors
    mean far more to GOD than religious performance.

4   Arrogance and pride — distinguishing marks in the wicked —
    are just plain sin.

5   Careful planning puts you ahead in the long run;
    hurry and scurry puts you further behind.

6   Make it to the top by lying and cheating;
    get paid with smoke and a promotion — to death!

7   The wicked get buried alive by their loot
    because they refuse to use it to help others.

8   Mixed motives twist life into tangles;
    pure motives take you straight down the road.

DO YOUR BEST, PREPARE FOR THE WORST

9   Better to live alone in a tumbledown shack
    than share a mansion with a nagging spouse.

10   Wicked souls love to make trouble;
    they feel nothing for friends and neighbors.

11   Simpletons only learn the hard way,
    but the wise learn by listening.

12   A God-loyal person will see right through the wicked
    and undo the evil they've planned.

13   If you stop your ears to the cries of the poor,
    your cries will go unheard, unanswered.

14   A quietly given gift soothes an irritable person;
    a heartfelt present cools a hot temper.

15   Good people celebrate when justice triumphs,
    but for the workers of evil it's a bad day.

16   Whoever wanders off the straight and narrow
    ends up in a congregation of ghosts.

17   You're addicted to thrills? What an empty life!
    The pursuit of pleasure is never satisfied.

18   What a bad person plots against the good, boomerangs;
    the plotter gets it in the end.

19   Better to live in a tent in the wild
    than with a cross and petulant spouse.

20 Valuables are safe in a wise person's home;
      fools put it all out for yard sales.

21 Whoever goes hunting for what is right and kind
      finds life itself — *glorious* life!

22 One sage entered a whole city of armed soldiers —
      their trusted defenses fell to pieces!

23 Watch your words and hold your tongue;
      you'll save yourself a lot of grief.

24 You know their names — Brash, Impudent, Blasphemer —
      intemperate hotheads, every one.

25 Lazy people finally die of hunger
      because they won't get up and go to work.

26 Sinners are always wanting what they don't have;
      the God-loyal are always giving what they do have.

27 Religious performance by the wicked stinks;
      it's even worse when they use it to get ahead.

28 A lying witness is unconvincing;
      a person who speaks truth is respected.

29 Unscrupulous people fake it a lot;
      honest people are sure of their steps.

30 Nothing clever, nothing conceived, nothing contrived,
      can get the better of GOD.

31 Do your best, prepare for the worst —
      then trust GOD to bring victory.

THE CURE COMES THROUGH DISCIPLINE

1 **22** A sterling reputation is better than striking it rich;
      a gracious spirit is better than money in the bank.

2 The rich and the poor shake hands as equals —
      GOD made them both!

3 A prudent person sees trouble coming and ducks;
      a simpleton walks in blindly and is clobbered.

4 The payoff for meekness and Fear-of-GOD
      is plenty and honor and a satisfying life.

5 The perverse travel a dangerous road, potholed and mud-slick;
      if you know what's good for you, stay clear of it.

6   Point your kids in the right direction —
     when they're old they won't be lost.

7   The poor are always ruled over by the rich,
     so don't borrow and put yourself under their power.

8   Whoever sows sin reaps weeds,
     and bullying anger sputters into nothing.

9   Generous hands are blessed hands
     because they give bread to the poor.

10   Kick out the troublemakers and things will quiet down;
     you need a break from bickering and griping!

11   GOD loves the pure-hearted and well-spoken;
     good leaders also delight in their friendship.

12   GOD guards knowledge with a passion,
     but he'll have nothing to do with deception.

13   The loafer says, "There's a lion on the loose!
     If I go out I'll be eaten alive!"

14   The mouth of a whore is a bottomless pit;
     you'll fall in that pit if you're on the outs with GOD.

15   Young people are prone to foolishness and fads;
     the cure comes through tough-minded discipline.

16   Exploit the poor or glad-hand the rich — whichever,
     you'll end up the poorer for it.

THE THIRTY PRECEPTS OF THE SAGES
DON'T MOVE BACK THE BOUNDARY LINES

17-21   Listen carefully to my wisdom;
     take to heart what I can teach you.
You'll treasure its sweetness deep within;
     you'll give it bold expression in your speech.
To make sure your foundation is trust in GOD,
     I'm laying it all out right now just for you.
I'm giving you thirty sterling principles —
     tested guidelines to live by.
Believe me — these are truths that work,
     and will keep you accountable
     to those who sent you.

1

22-23   Don't walk on the poor just because they're poor,
     and don't use your position to crush the weak,

Because GOD will come to their defense;
　　the life you took, he'll take from you and give back to them.

2

24-25　Don't hang out with angry people;
　　don't keep company with hotheads.
Bad temper is contagious —
　　don't get infected.

3

26-27　Don't gamble on the pot of gold at the end of the rainbow,
　　hocking your house against a lucky chance.
The time will come when you have to pay up;
　　you'll be left with nothing but the shirt on your back.

4

28　Don't stealthily move back the boundary lines
　　staked out long ago by your ancestors.

5

29　Observe people who are good at their work —
　　skilled workers are always in demand and admired;
　　they don't take a backseat to anyone.

RESTRAIN YOURSELF

6

1-3　**23** When you go out to dinner with an influential person,
　　　　mind your manners:
　　　Don't gobble your food,
　　don't talk with your mouth full.
And don't stuff yourself;
　　bridle your appetite.

7

4-5　Don't wear yourself out trying to get rich;
　　restrain yourself!
Riches disappear in the blink of an eye;
　　wealth sprouts wings
　　and flies off into the wild blue yonder.

8

6-8　Don't accept a meal from a tightwad;
　　don't expect anything special.
He'll be as stingy with you as he is with himself;
　　he'll say, "Eat! Drink!" but won't mean a word of it.
His miserly serving will turn your stomach
　　when you realize the meal's a sham.

9

9　Don't bother talking sense to fools;
　　they'll only poke fun at your words.

10

10-11 Don't stealthily move back the boundary lines
　　or cheat orphans out of their property,
For they have a powerful Advocate
　　who will go to bat for them.

11

12 Give yourselves to disciplined instruction;
　　open your ears to tested knowledge.

12

13-14 Don't be afraid to correct your young ones;
　　a spanking won't kill them.
A good spanking, in fact, might save them
　　from something worse than death.

13

15-16 Dear child, if you become wise,
　　I'll be one happy parent.
My heart will dance and sing
　　to the tuneful truth you'll speak.

14

17-18 Don't for a minute envy careless rebels;
　　soak yourself in the Fear-of-God —
That's where your future lies.
　　Then you won't be left with an armload of nothing.

15

19-21 Oh listen, dear child — become wise;
　　point your life in the right direction.
Don't drink too much wine and get drunk;
　　don't eat too much food and get fat.
Drunks and gluttons will end up on skid row,
　　in a stupor and dressed in rags.

Buy Wisdom, Education, Insight

16

22-25 Listen with respect to the father who raised you,
　　and when your mother grows old, don't neglect her.
Buy truth — don't sell it for love or money;
　　buy wisdom, buy education, buy insight.
Parents rejoice when their children turn out well;
　　wise children become proud parents.
So make your father happy!
　　Make your mother proud!

17

26 Dear child, I want your full attention;
　　please do what I show you.

27-28 A whore is a bottomless pit;
     a loose woman can get you in deep trouble fast.
She'll take you for all you've got;
     she's worse than a pack of thieves.

18

29-35 Who are the people who are always crying the blues?
     Who do you know who reeks of self-pity?
Who keeps getting beat up for no reason at all?
     Whose eyes are bleary and bloodshot?
It's those who spend the night with a bottle,
     for whom drinking is serious business.
Don't judge wine by its label,
     or its bouquet, or its full-bodied flavor.
Judge it rather by the hangover it leaves you with—
     the splitting headache, the queasy stomach.
Do you really prefer seeing double,
     with your speech all slurred,
Reeling and seasick,
     drunk as a sailor?
"They hit me," you'll say, "but it didn't hurt;
     they beat on me, but I didn't feel a thing.
When I'm sober enough to manage it,
     bring me another drink!"

INTELLIGENCE OUTRANKS MUSCLE

19

1-2 **24** Don't envy bad people;
     don't even want to be around them.
All they think about is causing a disturbance;
all they talk about is making trouble.

20

3-4 It takes wisdom to build a house,
     and understanding to set it on a firm foundation;
It takes knowledge to furnish its rooms
     with fine furniture and beautiful draperies.

21

5-6 It's better to be wise than strong;
     intelligence outranks muscle any day.
Strategic planning is the key to warfare;
     to win, you need a lot of good counsel.

22

7 Wise conversation is way over the head of fools;
     in a serious discussion they haven't a clue.

23

8-9 The person who's always cooking up some evil
     soon gets a reputation as prince of rogues.

Fools incubate sin;
    cynics desecrate beauty.

RESCUE THE PERISHING

24

10 If you fall to pieces in a crisis,
    there wasn't much to you in the first place.

25

11-12 Rescue the perishing;
    don't hesitate to step in and help.
If you say, "Hey, that's none of my business,"
    will that get you off the hook?
Someone is watching you closely, you know—
    Someone not impressed with weak excuses.

26

13-14 Eat honey, dear child—it's good for you—
    and delicacies that melt in your mouth.
Likewise knowledge,
    and wisdom for your soul—
Get that and your future's secured,
    your hope is on solid rock.

27

15-16 Don't interfere with good people's lives;
    don't try to get the best of them.
No matter how many times you trip them up,
    God-loyal people don't stay down long;
Soon they're up on their feet,
    while the wicked end up flat on their faces.

28

17-18 Don't laugh when your enemy falls;
    don't crow over his collapse.
GOD might see, and become very provoked,
    and then take pity on his plight.

29

19-20 Don't bother your head with braggarts
    or wish you could succeed like the wicked.
Those people have no future at all;
    they're headed down a dead-end street.

30

21-22 Fear GOD, dear child—respect your leaders;
    don't be defiant or mutinous.
Without warning your life can turn upside down,
    and who knows how or when it might happen?

MORE SAYINGS OF THE WISE
AN HONEST ANSWER

23 It's wrong, very wrong,
    to go along with injustice.

24-25 Whoever whitewashes the wicked
    gets a black mark in the history books,
But whoever exposes the wicked
    will be thanked and rewarded.

26 An honest answer
    is like a warm hug.

27 First plant your fields;
    then build your barn.

28-29 Don't talk about your neighbors behind their backs—
    no slander or gossip, please.
Don't say to anyone, "I'll get back at you for what you did to me.
    I'll make you pay for what you did!"

30-34 One day I walked by the field of an old lazybones,
    and then passed the vineyard of a lout;
They were overgrown with weeds,
    thick with thistles, all the fences broken down.
I took a long look and pondered what I saw;
    the fields preached me a sermon and I listened:
"A nap here, a nap there, a day off here, a day off there,
    sit back, take it easy—do you know what comes next?
Just this: You can look forward to a dirt-poor life,
    with poverty as your permanent houseguest!"

FURTHER WISE SAYINGS OF SOLOMON
THE RIGHT WORD AT THE RIGHT TIME

1 25 There are also these proverbs of Solomon,
    collected by scribes of Hezekiah, king of Judah.

2 God delights in concealing things;
    scientists delight in discovering things.

3 Like the horizons for breadth and the ocean for depth,
    the understanding of a good leader is broad and deep.

4-5 Remove impurities from the silver
    and the silversmith can craft a fine chalice;
Remove the wicked from leadership
    and authority will be credible and God-honoring.

6-7 Don't work yourself into the spotlight;
    don't push your way into the place of prominence.

It's better to be promoted to a place of honor
    than face humiliation by being demoted.

8   Don't jump to conclusions — there may be
    a perfectly good explanation for what you just saw.

9-10   In the heat of an argument,
    don't betray confidences;
Word is sure to get around,
    and no one will trust you.

11-12   The right word at the right time
    is like a custom-made piece of jewelry,
And a wise friend's timely reprimand
    is like a gold ring slipped on your finger.

13   Reliable friends who do what they say
    are like cool drinks in sweltering heat — refreshing!

14   Like billowing clouds that bring no rain
    is the person who talks big but never produces.

15   Patient persistence pierces through indifference;
    gentle speech breaks down rigid defenses.

A PERSON WITHOUT SELF-CONTROL

16-17   When you're given a box of candy, don't gulp it all down;
    eat too much chocolate and you'll make yourself sick;
And when you find a friend, don't outwear your welcome;
    show up at all hours and he'll soon get fed up.

18   Anyone who tells lies against the neighbors
    in court or on the street is a loose cannon.

19   Trusting a double-crosser when you're in trouble
    is like biting down on an abscessed tooth.

20   Singing light songs to the heavyhearted
    is like pouring salt in their wounds.

21-22   If you see your enemy hungry, go buy him lunch;
    if he's thirsty, bring him a drink.
Your generosity will surprise him with goodness,
    and GOD will look after you.

23   A north wind brings stormy weather,
    and a gossipy tongue stormy looks.

24   Better to live alone in a tumbledown shack
    than share a mansion with a nagging spouse.

25 Like a cool drink of water when you're worn out and weary
    is a letter from a long-lost friend.

26 A good person who gives in to a bad person
    is a muddied spring, a polluted well.

27 It's not smart to stuff yourself with sweets,
    nor is glory piled on glory good for you.

28 A person without self-control
    is like a house with its doors and windows knocked out.

FOOLS RECYCLE SILLINESS

1 **26** We no more give honors to fools
    than pray for snow in summer or rain during harvest.

2 You have as little to fear from an undeserved curse
    as from the dart of a wren or the swoop of a swallow.

3 A whip for the racehorse, a tiller for the sailboat—
    and a stick for the back of fools!

4 Don't respond to the stupidity of a fool;
    you'll only look foolish yourself.

5 Answer a fool in simple terms
    so he doesn't get a swelled head.

6 You're only asking for trouble
    when you send a message by a fool.

7 A proverb quoted by fools
    is limp as a wet noodle.

8 Putting a fool in a place of honor
    is like setting a mud brick on a marble column.

9 To ask a moron to quote a proverb
    is like putting a scalpel in the hands of a drunk.

10 Hire a fool or a drunk
    and you shoot yourself in the foot.

11 As a dog eats its own vomit,
    so fools recycle silliness.

12 See that man who thinks he's so smart?
    You can expect far more from a fool than from him.

13 Loafers say, "It's dangerous out there!
    Tigers are prowling the streets!"
    and then pull the covers back over their heads.

14 Just as a door turns on its hinges,
　　so a lazybones turns back over in bed.

15 A shiftless sluggard puts his fork in the pie,
　　but is too lazy to lift it to his mouth.

LIKE GLAZE ON CRACKED POTTERY

16 Dreamers fantasize their self-importance;
　　they think they are smarter
　　than a whole college faculty.

17 You grab a mad dog by the ears
　　when you butt into a quarrel that's none of your business.

18-19 People who shrug off deliberate deceptions,
　　saying, "I didn't mean it, I was only joking,"
　Are worse than careless campers
　　who walk away from smoldering campfires.

20 When you run out of wood, the fire goes out;
　　when the gossip ends, the quarrel dies down.

21 A quarrelsome person in a dispute
　　is like kerosene thrown on a fire.

22 Listening to gossip is like eating cheap candy;
　　do you want junk like that in your belly?

23 Smooth talk from an evil heart
　　is like glaze on cracked pottery.

24-26 Your enemy shakes hands and greets you like an old friend,
　　all the while conniving against you.
　When he speaks warmly to you, don't believe him for a minute;
　　he's just waiting for the chance to rip you off.
　No matter how cunningly he conceals his malice,
　　eventually his evil will be exposed in public.

27 Malice backfires;
　　spite boomerangs.

28 Liars hate their victims;
　　flatterers sabotage trust.

YOU DON'T KNOW TOMORROW

27 1 Don't brashly announce what you're going to do tomorrow;
　　you don't know the first thing about tomorrow.

2 Don't call attention to yourself;
　　let others do that for you.

3   Carrying a log across your shoulders
          while you're hefting a boulder with your arms
     Is nothing compared to the burden
          of putting up with a fool.

4   We're blasted by anger and swamped by rage,
          but who can survive jealousy?

5   A spoken reprimand is better
          than approval that's never expressed.

6   The wounds from a lover are worth it;
          kisses from an enemy do you in.

7   When you've stuffed yourself, you refuse dessert;
          when you're starved, you could eat a horse.

8   People who won't settle down, wandering hither and yon,
          are like restless birds, flitting to and fro.

9   Just as lotions and fragrance give sensual delight,
          a sweet friendship refreshes the soul.

10   Don't leave your friends or your parents' friends
          and run home to your family when things get rough;
     Better a nearby friend
          than a distant family.

11   Become wise, dear child, and make me happy;
          then nothing the world throws my way will upset me.

12   A prudent person sees trouble coming and ducks;
          a simpleton walks in blindly and is clobbered.

13   Hold tight to collateral on any loan to a stranger;
          be wary of accepting what a transient has pawned.

14   If you wake your friend in the early morning
          by shouting "Rise and shine!"
     It will sound to him
          more like a curse than a blessing.

15-16 A nagging spouse is like
          the drip, drip, drip of a leaky faucet;
     You can't turn it off,
          and you can't get away from it.

YOUR FACE MIRRORS YOUR HEART

17   You use steel to sharpen steel,
          and one friend sharpens another.

18   If you care for your orchard, you'll enjoy its fruit;
      if you honor your boss, you'll be honored.

19   Just as water mirrors your face,
      so your face mirrors your heart.

20   Hell has a voracious appetite,
      and lust just never quits.

21   The purity of silver and gold is tested
      by putting them in the fire;
   The purity of human hearts is tested
      by giving them a little fame.

22   Pound on a fool all you like—
      you can't pound out foolishness.

23-27   Know your sheep by name;
      carefully attend to your flocks;
   (Don't take them for granted;
      possessions don't last forever, you know.)
   And then, when the crops are in
      and the harvest is stored in the barns,
   You can knit sweaters from lambs' wool,
      and sell your goats for a profit;
   There will be plenty of milk and meat
      to last your family through the winter.

IF YOU DESERT GOD'S LAW

28 The wicked are edgy with guilt, ready to run off
      even when no one's after them;
   Honest people are relaxed and confident,
   bold as lions.

2   When the country is in chaos,
      everybody has a plan to fix it—
   But it takes a leader of real understanding
      to straighten things out.

3   The wicked who oppress the poor
      are like a hailstorm that beats down the harvest.

4   If you desert God's law, you're free to embrace depravity;
      if you love God's law, you fight for it tooth and nail.

5   Justice makes no sense to the evilminded;
      those who seek GOD know it inside and out.

6   It's better to be poor and direct
      than rich and crooked.

7 Practice God's law — get a reputation for wisdom;
   hang out with a loose crowd — embarrass your family.

8 Get as rich as you want
      through cheating and extortion,
   But eventually some friend of the poor
      is going to give it all back to them.

9 God has no use for the prayers
      of the people who won't listen to him.

10 Lead good people down a wrong path
       and you'll come to a bad end;
       do good and you'll be rewarded for it.

11 The rich think they know it all,
       but the poor can see right through them.

12 When good people are promoted, everything is great,
       but when the bad are in charge, watch out!

13 You can't whitewash your sins and get by with it;
       you find mercy by admitting and leaving them.

14 A tenderhearted person lives a blessed life;
       a hardhearted person lives a hard life.

15 Lions roar and bears charge —
       and the wicked lord it over the poor.

16 Among leaders who lack insight, abuse abounds,
       but for one who hates corruption, the future is bright.

17 A murderer haunted by guilt
       is doomed — there's no helping him.

18 Walk straight — live well and be saved;
       a devious life is a doomed life.

DOING GREAT HARM IN SEEMINGLY HARMLESS WAYS

19 Work your garden — you'll end up with plenty of food;
       play and party — you'll end up with an empty plate.

20 Committed and persistent work pays off;
       get-rich-quick schemes are ripoffs.

21 Playing favorites is always a bad thing;
       you can do great harm in seemingly harmless ways.

22 A miser in a hurry to get rich
       doesn't know that he'll end up broke.

23 In the end, serious reprimand is appreciated
  far more than bootlicking flattery.

24 Anyone who robs father and mother
  and says, "So, what's wrong with that?"
  is worse than a pirate.

25 A grasping person stirs up trouble,
  but trust in GOD brings a sense of well-being.

26 If you think you know it all, you're a fool for sure;
  real survivors learn wisdom from others.

27 Be generous to the poor — you'll never go hungry;
  shut your eyes to their needs, and run a gauntlet of curses.

28 When corruption takes over, good people go underground,
  but when the crooks are thrown out, it's safe to come out.

IF PEOPLE CAN'T SEE WHAT GOD IS DOING

1 **29** For people who hate discipline
  and only get more stubborn,
  There'll come a day when life tumbles in and they break,
  but by then it'll be too late to help them.

2 When good people run things, everyone is glad,
  but when the ruler is bad, everyone groans.

3 If you love wisdom, you'll delight your parents,
  but you'll destroy their trust if you run with whores.

4 A leader of good judgment gives stability;
  an exploiting leader leaves a trail of waste.

5 A flattering neighbor is up to no good;
  he's probably planning to take advantage of you.

6 Evil people fall into their own traps;
  good people run the other way, glad to escape.

7 The good-hearted understand what it's like to be poor;
  the hardhearted haven't the faintest idea.

8 A gang of cynics can upset a whole city;
  a group of sages can calm everyone down.

9 A sage trying to work things out with a fool
  gets only scorn and sarcasm for his trouble.

10 Murderers hate honest people;
  moral folks encourage them.

11   A fool lets it all hang out;
      a sage quietly mulls it over.

12   When a leader listens to malicious gossip,
      all the workers get infected with evil.

13   The poor and their abusers have at least something in common:
      they can both *see* — their sight, GOD's gift!

14   Leadership gains authority and respect
      when the voiceless poor are treated fairly.

15   Wise discipline imparts wisdom;
      spoiled adolescents embarrass their parents.

16   When degenerates take charge, crime runs wild,
      but the righteous will eventually observe their collapse.

17   Discipline your children; you'll be glad you did —
      they'll turn out delightful to live with.

18   If people can't see what God is doing,
      they stumble all over themselves;
   But when they attend to what he reveals,
      they are most blessed.

19   It takes more than talk to keep workers in line;
      mere words go in one ear and out the other.

20   Observe the people who always talk before they think —
      even simpletons are better off than they are.

21   If you let people treat you like a doormat,
      you'll be quite forgotten in the end.

22   Angry people stir up a lot of discord;
      the intemperate stir up trouble.

23   Pride lands you flat on your face;
      humility prepares you for honors.

24   Befriend an outlaw
      and become an enemy to yourself.
   When the victims cry out,
      you'll be included in their curses
      if you're a coward to their cause in court.

25   The fear of human opinion disables;
      trusting in GOD protects you from that.

26 Everyone tries to get help from the leader,
  but only God will give us justice.

27 Good people can't stand the sight of deliberate evil;
  the wicked can't stand the sight of well-chosen goodness.

THE WORDS OF AGUR BEN YAKEH
God? Who Needs Him?

1-2 30 The skeptic swore, "There is no God!
  No God! — I can do anything I want!
  I'm more animal than human;
  so-called human intelligence escapes me.

3-4 "I flunked 'wisdom.'
  I see no evidence of a holy God.
Has anyone ever seen Anyone
  climb into Heaven and take charge?
  grab the winds and control them?
  gather the rains in his bucket?
  stake out the ends of the earth?
Just tell me his name, tell me the names of his sons.
  Come on now — tell me!"

5-6 The believer replied, "Every promise of God proves true;
  he protects everyone who runs to him for help.
So don't second-guess him;
  he might take you to task and show up your lies."

7-9 And then he prayed, "God, I'm asking for two things
  before I die; don't refuse me —
Banish lies from my lips
  and liars from my presence.
Give me enough food to live on,
  neither too much nor too little.
If I'm too full, I might get independent,
  saying, 'God? Who needs him?'
If I'm poor, I might steal
  and dishonor the name of my God."

10 Don't blow the whistle on your fellow workers
  behind their backs;
They'll accuse you of being underhanded,
  and then *you'll* be the guilty one!

11 Don't curse your father
  or fail to bless your mother.

12 Don't imagine yourself to be quite presentable
  when you haven't had a bath in weeks.

13 Don't be stuck-up
  and think you're better than everyone else.

14 Don't be greedy,
  merciless and cruel as wolves,
  Tearing into the poor and feasting on them,
  shredding the needy to pieces only to discard them.

15-16 A leech has twin daughters
  named "Gimme" and "Gimme more."

FOUR INSATIABLES

Three things are never satisfied,
  no, there are four that never say, "That's enough, thank you!" —

  hell,
  a barren womb,
  a parched land,
  a forest fire.

17 An eye that disdains a father
  and despises a mother —
that eye will be plucked out by wild vultures
  and consumed by young eagles.

FOUR MYSTERIES

18-19 Three things amaze me,
  no, four things I'll never understand —

  how an eagle flies so high in the sky,
  how a snake glides over a rock,
  how a ship navigates the ocean,
  why adolescents act the way they do.

20 Here's how a prostitute operates:
  she has sex with her client,
Takes a bath,
  then asks, "Who's next?"

FOUR INTOLERABLES

21-23 Three things are too much for even the earth to bear,
  yes, four things shake its foundations —

  when the janitor becomes the boss,
  when a fool gets rich,
  when a whore is voted "woman of the year,"
  when a "girlfriend" replaces a faithful wife.

FOUR SMALL WONDERS

²⁴⁻²⁸ There are four small creatures,
　　wisest of the wise they are —

　　　　ants — frail as they are,
　　　　　　get plenty of food in for the winter;
　　　　marmots — vulnerable as they are,
　　　　　　manage to arrange for rock-solid homes;
　　　　locusts — leaderless insects,
　　　　　　yet they strip the field like an army regiment;
　　　　lizards — easy enough to catch,
　　　　　　but they sneak past vigilant palace guards.

FOUR DIGNITARIES

²⁹⁻³¹ There are three solemn dignitaries,
　　four that are impressive in their bearing —

　　　　a lion, king of the beasts, deferring to none;
　　　　a rooster, proud and strutting;
　　　　a billy goat;
　　　　a head of state in stately procession.

³²⁻³³ If you're dumb enough to call attention to yourself
　　by offending people and making rude gestures,
Don't be surprised if someone bloodies your nose.
　　Churned milk turns into butter;
　　riled emotions turn into fist fights.

SPEAK OUT FOR JUSTICE

¹ **31** The words of King Lemuel,
　　　　the strong advice his mother gave him:

²⁻³ "Oh, son of mine, what can you be thinking of!
　　Child whom I bore! The son I dedicated to God!
Don't dissipate your virility on fortune-hunting women,
　　promiscuous women who shipwreck leaders.

⁴⁻⁷ "Leaders can't afford to make fools of themselves,
　　gulping wine and swilling beer,
Lest, hung over, they don't know right from wrong,
　　and the people who depend on them are hurt.
Use wine and beer only as sedatives,
　　to kill the pain and dull the ache
Of the terminally ill,
　　for whom life is a living death.

⁸⁻⁹ "Speak up for the people who have no voice,
　　for the rights of all the down-and-outers.

Speak out for justice!
  Stand up for the poor and destitute!"

Hymn to a Good Wife

10-31 A good woman is hard to find,
  and worth far more than diamonds.
Her husband trusts her without reserve,
  and never has reason to regret it.
Never spiteful, she treats him generously
  all her life long.
She shops around for the best yarns and cottons,
  and enjoys knitting and sewing.
She's like a trading ship that sails to faraway places
  and brings back exotic surprises.
She's up before dawn, preparing breakfast
  for her family and organizing her day.
She looks over a field and buys it,
  then, with money she's put aside, plants a garden.
First thing in the morning, she dresses for work,
  rolls up her sleeves, eager to get started.
She senses the worth of her work,
  is in no hurry to call it quits for the day.
She's skilled in the crafts of home and hearth,
  diligent in homemaking.
She's quick to assist anyone in need,
  reaches out to help the poor.
She doesn't worry about her family when it snows;
  their winter clothes are all mended and ready to wear.
She makes her own clothing,
  and dresses in colorful linens and silks.
Her husband is greatly respected
  when he deliberates with the city fathers.
She designs gowns and sells them,
  brings the sweaters she knits to the dress shops.
Her clothes are well-made and elegant,
  and she always faces tomorrow with a smile.
When she speaks she has something worthwhile to say,
  and she always says it kindly.
She keeps an eye on everyone in her household,
  and keeps them all busy and productive.
Her children respect and bless her;
  her husband joins in with words of praise:
"Many women have done wonderful things,
  but you've outclassed them all!"
Charm can mislead and beauty soon fades.
  The woman to be admired and praised
  is the woman who lives in the Fear-of-God.
Give her everything she deserves!
  Festoon her life with praises!

ECCLESIASTES

Unlike the animals, who seem quite content to simply be themselves, we humans are always looking for ways to be more than or other than what we find ourselves to be. We explore the countryside for excitement, search our souls for meaning, shop the world for pleasure. We try this. Then we try that. The usual fields of endeavor are money, sex, power, adventure, and knowledge.

Everything we try is so promising at first! But nothing ever seems to amount to very much. We intensify our efforts — but the harder we work at it, the less we get out of it. Some people give up early and settle for a humdrum life. Others never seem to learn, and so they flail away through a lifetime, becoming less and less human by the year, until by the time they die there is hardly enough humanity left to compose a corpse.

Ecclesiastes is a famous — maybe the world's most famous — witness to this experience of futility. The acerbic wit catches our attention. The stark honesty compels notice. And people do notice — oh, how they notice! Nonreligious and religious alike notice. Unbelievers and believers notice. More than a few of them are surprised to find this kind of thing in the Bible.

But it is most emphatically and necessarily in the Bible in order to call a halt to our various and futile attempts to make something of our lives, so that we can give our full attention to God — who God is and what he does to make something of us. Ecclesiastes actually doesn't say that much about God; the author leaves that to the other sixty-five books of the Bible. His task is to expose our total incapacity to find the meaning and completion of our lives on our own.

It is our propensity to go off on our own, trying to be human by our own devices and desires, that makes Ecclesiastes necessary reading. Ecclesiastes sweeps our souls clean of all "lifestyle" spiritualities so that we can be ready for God's visitation revealed in Jesus Christ. Ecclesiastes is a John-the-Baptist kind of book. It functions not as a meal but as a bath. It is not nourishment; it is cleansing. It is repentance. It is purging. We read Ecclesiastes to get scrubbed clean from illusion and sentiment, from ideas that are idolatrous and feelings that cloy. It is an exposé and rejection of every arrogant and ignorant expectation that we can live our lives by ourselves on our own terms.

Ecclesiastes challenges the naive optimism that sets a goal that appeals to us and then goes after it with gusto, expecting the result to be a good life. The author's cool skepticism, a refreshing negation to the lush and seductive suggestions swirling around us, promising everything but delivering nothing, clears the air. And once the air is cleared, we are ready for reality — for God.

["Ecclesiastes" is a Greek word that is usually translated "the Preacher" or "the Teacher." Because of the experiential stance of the writing in this book, giving voice to what is so basic among men and women throughout history, I have translated it "the Quester."]

ECCLESIASTES

THE QUESTER

1 These are the words of the Quester, David's son and king in Jerusalem:

2-11 Smoke, nothing but smoke. [That's what the Quester says.]
    There's nothing to anything — it's all smoke.
What's there to show for a lifetime of work,
    a lifetime of working your fingers to the bone?
One generation goes its way, the next one arrives,
    but nothing changes — it's business as usual for old
        planet earth.
The sun comes up and the sun goes down,
    then does it again, and again — the same old round.
The wind blows south, the wind blows north.
    Around and around and around it blows,
    blowing this way, then that — the whirling, erratic wind.
All the rivers flow into the sea,
    but the sea never fills up.
The rivers keep flowing to the same old place,
    and then start all over and do it again.
Everything's boring, utterly boring —
    no one can find any meaning in it.
Boring to the eye,
    boring to the ear.
What was will be again,
    what happened will happen again.
There's nothing new on this earth.
    Year after year it's the same old thing.
Does someone call out, "Hey, *this* is new"?
    Don't get excited — it's the same old story.
Nobody remembers what happened yesterday.
    And the things that will happen tomorrow?
Nobody'll remember them either.
    Don't count on being remembered.

I'VE SEEN IT ALL

12-14 Call me "the Quester." I've been king over Israel in Jerusalem. I looked most carefully into everything, searched out all that is done on this earth. And let me tell you, there's not much to write home about. God hasn't made it easy for us. I've seen it all and it's nothing but smoke — smoke, and spitting into the wind.

15   Life's a corkscrew that can't be straightened,
    A minus that won't add up.

16-17 I said to myself, "I know more and I'm wiser than anyone before me in Jerusalem. I've stockpiled wisdom and knowledge." What I've finally concluded is that so-called wisdom and knowledge are mindless and witless — nothing but spitting into the wind.

18   Much learning earns you much trouble.
    The more you know, the more you hurt.

1-3   **2** I said to myself, "Let's go for it — experiment with pleasure, have a good time!" But there was nothing to it, nothing but smoke.

What do I think of the fun-filled life? Insane! Inane!
    My verdict on the pursuit of happiness? Who needs it?
With the help of a bottle of wine
    and all the wisdom I could muster,
I tried my level best
    to penetrate the absurdity of life.
I wanted to get a handle on anything useful we mortals might do
    during the years we spend on this earth.

I Never Said No to Myself

4-8   Oh, I did great things:
    built houses,
    planted vineyards,
    designed gardens and parks
        and planted a variety of fruit trees in them,
    made pools of water
        to irrigate the groves of trees.
I bought slaves, male and female,
        who had children, giving me even more slaves;
    then I acquired large herds and flocks,
        larger than any before me in Jerusalem.
I piled up silver and gold,
        loot from kings and kingdoms.
I gathered a chorus of singers to entertain me with song,
    and — most exquisite of all pleasures —
    voluptuous maidens for my bed.

9-10   Oh, how I prospered! I left all my predecessors in Jerusalem far behind, left them behind in the dust. What's more, I kept a clear head through it all. Everything I wanted I took — I never said no to myself. I gave in to every impulse, held back nothing. I sucked the marrow of pleasure out of every task — my reward to myself for a hard day's work!

I Hate Life

11   Then I took a good look at everything I'd done, looked at all the sweat and hard work. But when I looked, I saw nothing but smoke. Smoke and spitting into the wind. There was nothing to any of it. Nothing.

12-14   And then I took a hard look at what's smart and what's stupid. What's left to do after you've been king? That's a hard act to follow. You just do what you can, and that's it. But I did see that it's better to be smart than stupid, just as light is better than darkness. Even so, though the smart ones see where they're going and the stupid ones grope in the dark, they're all the same in the end. One fate for all — and that's it.

15-16   When I realized that my fate's the same as the fool's, I had to ask myself, "So why bother being wise?" It's all smoke, nothing but smoke. The smart and the stupid both disappear out of sight. In a day or two they're both forgotten. Yes, both the smart and the stupid die, and that's it.

17 I hate life. As far as I can see, what happens on earth is a bad business. It's smoke — and spitting into the wind.

18-19 And I hated everything I'd accomplished and accumulated on this earth. I can't take it with me — no, I have to leave it to whoever comes after me. Whether they're worthy or worthless — and who's to tell? — they'll take over the earthly results of my intense thinking and hard work. Smoke.

20-23 That's when I called it quits, gave up on anything that could be hoped for on this earth. What's the point of working your fingers to the bone if you hand over what you worked for to someone who never lifted a finger for it? Smoke, that's what it is. A bad business from start to finish. So what do you get from a life of hard labor? Pain and grief from dawn to dusk. Never a decent night's rest. Nothing but smoke.

24-26 The best you can do with your life is have a good time and get by the best you can. The way I see it, that's it — divine fate. Whether we feast or fast, it's up to God. God may give wisdom and knowledge and joy to his favorites, but sinners are assigned a life of hard labor, and end up turning their wages over to God's favorites. Nothing but smoke — and spitting into the wind.

THERE'S A RIGHT TIME FOR EVERYTHING

1 **3** There's an opportune time to do things, a right time for everything on the earth:

2-8 A right time for birth and another for death,
A right time to plant and another to reap,
A right time to kill and another to heal,
A right time to destroy and another to construct,
A right time to cry and another to laugh,
A right time to lament and another to cheer,
A right time to make love and another to abstain,
A right time to embrace and another to part,
A right time to search and another to count your losses,
A right time to hold on and another to let go,
A right time to rip out and another to mend,
A right time to shut up and another to speak up,
A right time to love and another to hate,
A right time to wage war and another to make peace.

9-13 But in the end, does it really make a difference what anyone does? I've had a good look at what God has given us to do — busywork, mostly. True, God made everything beautiful in itself and in its time — but he's left us in the dark, so we can never know what God is up to, whether he's coming or going. I've decided that there's nothing better to do than go ahead and have a good time and get the most we can out of life. That's it — eat, drink, and make the most of your job. It's God's gift.

14 I've also concluded that whatever God does, that's the way it's going to be, always. No addition, no subtraction. God's done it and that's it. That's so we'll quit asking questions and simply worship in holy fear.

15 Whatever was, is.
Whatever will be, is.
That's how it always is with God.

GOD'S TESTING US

16-18 I took another good look at what's going on: The very place of judgment—corrupt! The place of righteousness—corrupt! I said to myself, "God will judge righteous and wicked." There's a right time for every thing, every deed—and there's no getting around it. I said to myself regarding the human race, "God's testing the lot of us, showing us up as nothing but animals."

19-22 Humans and animals come to the same end—humans die, animals die. We all breathe the same air. So there's really no advantage in being human. None. Everything's smoke. We all end up in the same place—we all came from dust, we all end up as dust. Nobody knows for sure that the human spirit rises to heaven or that the animal spirit sinks into the earth. So I made up my mind that there's nothing better for us men and women than to have a good time in whatever we do—that's our lot. Who knows if there's anything else to life?

SLOW SUICIDE

1-3 Next I turned my attention to all the outrageous violence that takes place on this planet—the tears of the victims, no one to comfort them; the iron grip of oppressors, no one to rescue the victims from them. So I congratulated the dead who are already dead instead of the living who are still alive. But luckier than the dead or the living is the person who has never even been, who has never seen the bad business that takes place on this earth.

4 Then I observed all the work and ambition motivated by envy. What a waste! Smoke. And spitting into the wind.

5 The fool sits back and takes it easy,
His sloth is slow suicide.

6 One handful of peaceful repose
Is better than two fistfuls of worried work—
More spitting into the wind.

WHY AM I WORKING LIKE A DOG?

7-8 I turned my head and saw yet another wisp of smoke on its way to nothingness: a solitary person, completely alone—no children, no family, no friends—yet working obsessively late into the night, compulsively greedy for more and more, never bothering to ask, "Why am I working like a dog, never having any fun? And who cares?" More smoke. A bad business.

9-10 It's better to have a partner than go it alone.
Share the work, share the wealth.
And if one falls down, the other helps,
But if there's no one to help, tough!

11   Two in a bed warm each other.
         Alone, you shiver all night.

12   By yourself you're unprotected.
         With a friend you can face the worst.
         Can you round up a third?
         A three-stranded rope isn't easily snapped.

13-16   A poor youngster with some wisdom is better off than an old but foolish king who doesn't know which end is up. I saw a youth just like this start with nothing and go from rags to riches, and I saw everyone rally to the rule of this young successor to the king. Even so, the excitement died quickly, the throngs of people soon lost interest. Can't you see it's only smoke? And spitting into the wind?

GOD'S IN CHARGE, NOT YOU

1   5 Watch your step when you enter God's house.
          Enter to learn. That's far better than mindlessly offering
            a sacrifice,
        Doing more harm than good.

2   Don't shoot off your mouth, or speak before you think.
         Don't be too quick to tell God what you think he wants to hear.
         God's in charge, not you — the less you speak, the better.

3   Overwork makes for restless sleep.
         Overtalk shows you up as a fool.

4-5   When you tell God you'll do something, do it — now.
         God takes no pleasure in foolish gabble. Vow it, then do it.
         Far better not to vow in the first place than to vow and not pay up.

6   Don't let your mouth make a total sinner of you.
         When called to account, you won't get by with
           "Sorry, I didn't mean it."
         Why risk provoking God to angry retaliation?

7   But against all illusion and fantasy and empty talk
         There's always this rock foundation: Fear God!

A SALARY OF SMOKE

8-9   Don't be too upset when you see the poor kicked around, and justice and right violated all over the place. Exploitation filters down from one petty official to another. There's no end to it, and nothing can be done about it. But the good earth doesn't cheat anyone — even a bad king is honestly served by a field.

10   The one who loves money is never satisfied with money,
         Nor the one who loves wealth with big profits. More smoke.

11   The more loot you get, the more looters show up.
       And what fun is that — to be robbed in broad daylight?

12   Hard and honest work earns a good night's sleep,
       Whether supper is beans or steak.
       But a rich man's belly gives him insomnia.

13-17   Here's a piece of bad luck I've seen happen:
       A man hoards far more wealth than is good for him
       And then loses it all in a bad business deal.
       He fathered a child but hasn't a cent left to give him.
       He arrived naked from the womb of his mother;
       He'll leave in the same condition — with nothing.
       This is bad luck, for sure — naked he came, naked he went.
       So what was the point of working for a salary of smoke?
       All for a miserable life spent in the dark?

MAKE THE MOST OF WHAT GOD GIVES

18-20   After looking at the way things are on this earth, here's what I've decided is the best way to live: Take care of yourself, have a good time, and make the most of whatever job you have for as long as God gives you life. And that's about it. That's the human lot. Yes, we should make the most of what God gives, both the bounty and the capacity to enjoy it, accepting what's given and delighting in the work. It's God's gift! God deals out joy in the present, the *now*. It's useless to brood over how long we might live.

THINGS ARE BAD

1-2   **6** I looked long and hard at what goes on around here, and let me tell you, things are bad. And people feel it. There are people, for instance, on whom God showers everything — money, property, reputation — all they ever wanted or dreamed of. And then God doesn't let them enjoy it. Some stranger comes along and has all the fun. It's more of what I'm calling *smoke*. A bad business.

3-5   Say a couple have scores of children and live a long, long life but never enjoy themselves — even though they end up with a big funeral! I'd say that a stillborn baby gets the better deal. It gets its start in a mist and ends up in the dark — unnamed. It sees nothing and knows nothing, but is better off by far than anyone living.

6   Even if someone lived a thousand years — make it two thousand! — but didn't enjoy anything, what's the point? Doesn't everyone end up in the same place?

7   We work to feed our appetites;
       Meanwhile our souls go hungry.

8-9   So what advantage has a sage over a fool, or over some poor wretch who barely gets by? Just grab whatever you can while you can; don't assume something better might turn up by and by. All it amounts to anyway is smoke. And spitting into the wind.

10   Whatever happens, happens. Its destiny is fixed.
You can't argue with fate.

11-12   The more words that are spoken, the more smoke there is in the air. And who is any better off? And who knows what's best for us as we live out our meager smoke-and-shadow lives? And who can tell any of us the next chapter of our lives?

Don't Take Anything for Granted

1   **7** A good reputation is better than a fat bank account.
Your death date tells more than your birth date.

2   You learn more at a funeral than at a feast —
After all, that's where we'll end up. We might discover
    something from it.

3   Crying is better than laughing.
It blotches the face but it scours the heart.

4   Sages invest themselves in hurt and grieving.
Fools waste their lives in fun and games.

5   You'll get more from the rebuke of a sage
Than from the song and dance of fools.

6   The giggles of fools are like the crackling of twigs
Under the cooking pot. And like smoke.

7   Brutality stupefies even the wise
And destroys the strongest heart.

8   Endings are better than beginnings.
Sticking to it is better than standing out.

9   Don't be quick to fly off the handle.
Anger boomerangs. You can spot a fool by the lumps on his head.

10   Don't always be asking, "Where are the good old days?"
Wise folks don't ask questions like that.

11-12   Wisdom is better when it's paired with money,
Especially if you get both while you're still living.
Double protection: wisdom and wealth!
Plus this bonus: Wisdom energizes its owner.

13   Take a good look at God's work.
Who could simplify and reduce Creation's curves and angles
To a plain straight line?

14   On a good day, enjoy yourself;
On a bad day, examine your conscience.

God arranges for both kinds of days
So that we won't take anything for granted.

STAY IN TOUCH WITH BOTH SIDES

15-17 I've seen it all in my brief and pointless life — here a good person cut down in the middle of doing good, there a bad person living a long life of sheer evil. So don't knock yourself out being good, and don't go overboard being wise. Believe me, you won't get anything out of it. But don't press your luck by being bad, either. And don't be reckless. Why die needlessly?

18 It's best to stay in touch with both sides of an issue. A person who fears God deals responsibly with all of reality, not just a piece of it.

19 Wisdom puts more strength in one wise person
Than ten strong men give to a city.

20 There's not one totally good person on earth,
Not one who is truly pure and sinless.

21-22 Don't eavesdrop on the conversation of others.
What if the gossip's about you and you'd rather not hear it?
You've done that a few times, haven't you — said things
Behind someone's back you wouldn't say to his face?

HOW TO INTERPRET THE MEANING OF LIFE

23-25 I tested everything in my search for wisdom. I set out to be wise, but it was beyond me, far beyond me, and deep — oh so deep! Does anyone ever find it? I concentrated with all my might, studying and exploring and seeking wisdom — the meaning of life. I also wanted to identify evil and stupidity, foolishness and craziness.

26-29 One discovery: A woman can be a bitter pill to swallow, full of seductive scheming and grasping. The lucky escape her; the undiscerning get caught. At least this is my experience — what I, the Quester, have pieced together as I've tried to make sense of life. But the wisdom I've looked for I haven't found. I didn't find one man or woman in a thousand worth my while. Yet I did spot one ray of light in this murk: God made men and women true and upright; *we're* the ones who've made a mess of things.

1 8 There's nothing better than being wise,
Knowing how to interpret the meaning of life.
Wisdom puts light in the eyes,
And gives gentleness to words and manners.

NO ONE CAN CONTROL THE WIND

2-7 Do what your king commands; you gave a sacred oath of obedience. Don't worryingly second-guess your orders or try to back out when the task is unpleasant. You're serving his pleasure, not yours. The king has the last word. Who dares say to him, "What are you doing?" Carrying out orders won't hurt you a bit; the wise person obeys promptly and accurately. Yes, there's a right time and way for everything, even though, unfortunately, we miss it for the most part. It's true that no one knows what's going to happen, or when. Who's around to tell us?

8   No one can control the wind or lock it in a box.
No one has any say-so regarding the day of death.
No one can stop a battle in its tracks.
No one who does evil can be saved by evil.

9   All this I observed as I tried my best to understand all that's going on in this world. As long as men and women have the power to hurt each other, this is the way it is.

ONE FATE FOR EVERYBODY

10   One time I saw wicked men given a solemn burial in holy ground. When the people returned to the city, they delivered flowery eulogies — and in the very place where wicked acts were done by those very men! More smoke. Indeed.

11   Because the sentence against evil deeds is so long in coming, people in general think they can get by with murder.

12-13   Even though a person sins and gets by with it hundreds of times throughout a long life, I'm still convinced that the good life is reserved for the person who fears God, who lives reverently in his presence, and that the evil person will not experience a "good" life. No matter how many days he lives, they'll all be as flat and colorless as a shadow — because he doesn't fear God.

14   Here's something that happens all the time and makes no sense at all: Good people get what's coming to the wicked, and bad people get what's coming to the good. I tell you, this makes no sense. It's smoke.

15   So, I'm all for just going ahead and having a good time — the best possible. The only earthly good men and women can look forward to is to eat and drink well and have a good time — compensation for the struggle for survival these few years God gives us on earth.

16-17   When I determined to load up on wisdom and examine everything taking place on earth, I realized that if you keep your eyes open day and night without even blinking, you'll still never figure out the meaning of what God is doing on this earth. Search as hard as you like, you're not going to make sense of it. No matter how smart you are, you won't get to the bottom of it.

1-3   Well, I took all this in and thought it through, inside and out. Here's what I understood: The good, the wise, and all that they do are in God's hands — but, day by day, whether it's love or hate they're dealing with, they don't know.

Anything's possible. It's one fate for everybody — righteous and wicked, good people, bad people, the nice and the nasty, worshipers and non-worshipers, committed and uncommitted. I find this outrageous — the worst thing about living on this earth — that everyone's lumped together in one fate. Is it any wonder that so many people are obsessed with evil? Is it any wonder that people go crazy right and left? Life leads to death. That's it.

SEIZE LIFE!

4-6   Still, anyone selected out for life has hope, for, as they say, "A living dog is better than a dead lion." The living at least know *something*, even if it's only that they're going to die. But the dead know nothing and get nothing. They're a minus that no one remembers. Their loves, their hates, yes, even their dreams, are long gone. There's not a trace of them left in the affairs of this earth.

7-10
Seize life! Eat bread with gusto,
Drink wine with a robust heart.
Oh yes—God takes pleasure in *your* pleasure!
Dress festively every morning.
Don't skimp on colors and scarves.
Relish life with the spouse you love
Each and every day of your precarious life.
Each day is God's gift. It's all you get in exchange
For the hard work of staying alive.
Make the most of each one!
Whatever turns up, grab it and do it. And heartily!
This is your last and only chance at it,
For there's neither work to do nor thoughts to think
In the company of the dead, where you're most certainly headed.

11
I took another walk around the neighborhood and realized that on this earth as it is—

The race is not always to the swift,
Nor the battle to the strong,
Nor satisfaction to the wise,
Nor riches to the smart,
Nor grace to the learned.
Sooner or later bad luck hits us all.

12
No one can predict misfortune.
Like fish caught in a cruel net or birds in a trap,
So men and women are caught
By accidents evil and sudden.

WISDOM IS BETTER THAN MUSCLE

13-15
One day as I was observing how wisdom fares on this earth, I saw something that made me sit up and take notice. There was a small town with only a few people in it. A strong king came and mounted an attack, building trenches and attack posts around it. There was a poor but wise man in that town whose wisdom saved the town, but he was promptly forgotten. (He was only a poor man, after all.)

16
All the same, I still say that wisdom is better than muscle, even though the wise poor man was treated with contempt and soon forgotten.

17
The quiet words of the wise are more effective
Than the ranting of a king of fools.

18
Wisdom is better than warheads,
But one hothead can ruin the good earth.

10 ¹ Dead flies in perfume make it stink,
And a little foolishness decomposes much wisdom.

² Wise thinking leads to right living;
Stupid thinking leads to wrong living.

³ Fools on the road have no sense of direction.
The way they walk tells the story: "There goes the fool again!"

⁴ If a ruler loses his temper against you, don't panic;
A calm disposition quiets intemperate rage.

⁵⁻⁷ Here's a piece of bad business I've seen on this earth,
An error that can be blamed on whoever is in charge:
Immaturity is given a place of prominence,
While maturity is made to take a backseat.
I've seen unproven upstarts riding in style,
While experienced veterans are put out to pasture.

⁸ Caution: The trap you set might catch you.
Warning: Your accomplice in crime might double-cross you.

⁹ Safety first: Quarrying stones is dangerous.
Be alert: Felling trees is hazardous.

¹⁰ Remember: The duller the ax the harder the work;
Use your head: The more brains, the less muscle.

¹¹ If the snake bites before it's been charmed,
What's the point in then sending for the charmer?

¹²⁻¹³ The words of a wise person are gracious.
The talk of a fool self-destructs—
He starts out talking nonsense
And ends up spouting insanity and evil.

¹⁴ Fools talk way too much,
Chattering stuff they know nothing about.

¹⁵ A decent day's work so fatigues fools
That they can't find their way back to town.

¹⁶⁻¹⁷ Unlucky the land whose king is a young pup,
And whose princes party all night.
Lucky the land whose king is mature,
Where the princes behave themselves
And don't drink themselves silly.

18   A shiftless man lives in a tumbledown shack;
A lazy woman ends up with a leaky roof.

19   Laughter and bread go together,
And wine gives sparkle to life —
But it's money that makes the world go around.

20   Don't bad-mouth your leaders, not even under your breath,
And don't abuse your betters, even in the privacy of your home.
Loose talk has a way of getting picked up and spread around.
Little birds drop the crumbs of your gossip far and wide.

1   **11** Be generous: Invest in acts of charity.
Charity yields high returns.

2   Don't hoard your goods; spread them around.
Be a blessing to others. This could be your last night.

3-4   When the clouds are full of water, it rains.
When the wind blows down a tree, it lies where it falls.
Don't sit there watching the wind. Do your own work.
Don't stare at the clouds. Get on with your life.

5   Just as you'll never understand
the mystery of life forming in a pregnant woman,
So you'll never understand
the mystery at work in all that God does.

6   Go to work in the morning
and stick to it until evening without watching the clock.
You never know from moment to moment
how your work will turn out in the end.

BEFORE THE YEARS TAKE THEIR TOLL

7-8   Oh, how sweet the light of day,
And how wonderful to live in the sunshine!
Even if you live a long time, don't take a single day for granted.
Take delight in each light-filled hour,
Remembering that there will also be many dark days
And that most of what comes your way is smoke.

9   You who are young, make the most of your youth.
Relish your youthful vigor.
Follow the impulses of your heart.
If something looks good to you, pursue it.
But know also that not just anything goes;
You have to answer to God for every last bit of it.

10 Live footloose and fancy-free —
You won't be young forever.
Youth lasts about as long as smoke.

1-2 **12** Honor and enjoy your Creator while you're still young,
Before the years take their toll and your vigor wanes,
Before your vision dims and the world blurs
And the winter years keep you close to the fire.

3-5 In old age, your body no longer serves you so well.
Muscles slacken, grip weakens, joints stiffen.
The shades are pulled down on the world.
You can't come and go at will. Things grind to a halt.
The hum of the household fades away.
You are wakened now by bird-song.
Hikes to the mountains are a thing of the past.
Even a stroll down the road has its terrors.
Your hair turns apple-blossom white,
Adorning a fragile and impotent matchstick body.
Yes, you're well on your way to eternal rest,
While your friends make plans for your funeral.

6-7 Life, lovely while it lasts, is soon over.
Life as we know it, precious and beautiful, ends.
The body is put back in the same ground it came from.
The spirit returns to God, who first breathed it.

8 It's all smoke, nothing but smoke.
The Quester says that everything's smoke.

THE FINAL WORD

9-10 Besides being wise himself, the Quester also taught others knowledge. He weighed, examined, and arranged many proverbs. The Quester did his best to find the right words and write the plain truth.

11 The words of the wise prod us to live well.
They're like nails hammered home, holding life together.
They are given by God, the one Shepherd.

12-13 But regarding anything beyond this, dear friend, go easy. There's no end to the publishing of books, and constant study wears you out so you're no good for anything else. The last and final word is this:

Fear God.
Do what he tells you.

14 And that's it. Eventually God will bring everything that we do out into the open and judge it according to its hidden intent, whether it's good or evil.

SONG OF SONGS

We don't read very far in the Song of Songs before we realize two things: one, it contains exquisite love lyrics, and two, it is very explicit sexually. The Song, in other words, makes a connection between conjugal love and sex — a very important and very biblical connection to make. There are some who would eliminate sex when they speak of love, supposing that they are making it more holy. Others, when they think of sex, never think of love. The Song proclaims an integrated wholeness that is at the center of Christian teaching on committed, wedded love for a world that seems to specialize in loveless sex.

The Song is a convincing witness that men and women were created physically, emotionally, and spiritually to live in love. At the outset of Scripture we read, "It is not good for man to live alone." The Song of Songs elaborates on the Genesis story by celebrating the union of two diverse personalities in love.

We read Genesis and learn that this is the created pattern of joy and mutuality. We read the Song and see the goal and ideal toward which we all press for fulfillment. Despite our sordid failures in love, we see here what we are created for, what God intends for us in the ecstasy and fulfillment that is celebrated in the lyricism of the Song.

Christians read the Song on many levels: as the intimacy of marital love between man and woman, God's deep love for his people, Christ's Bridegroom love for his church, the Christian's love for his or her Lord. It is a prism in which all the love of God in all the world, and all the responses of those who love and whom God loves, gathers and then separates into individual colors.

SONG OF SONGS

1 The Song—best of all songs—Solomon's song!

THE WOMAN

2-3 Kiss me—full on the mouth!
  Yes! For your love is better than wine,
  headier than your aromatic oils.
The syllables of your name murmur like a meadow brook.
  No wonder everyone loves to say your name!

4 Take me away with you! Let's run off together!
  An elopement with my King-Lover!
We'll celebrate, we'll sing,
  we'll make great music.
Yes! For your love is better than vintage wine.
  Everyone loves you—of course! And why not?

5-6 I am weathered but still elegant,
  oh, dear sisters in Jerusalem,
Weather-darkened like Kedar desert tents,
  time-softened like Solomon's Temple hangings.
Don't look down on me because I'm dark,
  darkened by the sun's harsh rays.
My brothers ridiculed me and sent me to work in the fields.
  They made me care for the face of the earth,
  but I had no time to care for my own face.

7 Tell me where you're working
  —I love you so much—
Tell me where you're tending your flocks,
  where you let them rest at noontime.
Why should I be the one left out,
  outside the orbit of your tender care?

THE MAN

8 If you can't find me, loveliest of all women,
  it's all right. Stay with your flocks.
Lead your lambs to good pasture.
  Stay with your shepherd neighbors.

9-11 You remind me of Pharaoh's
  well-groomed and satiny mares.
Pendant earrings line the elegance of your cheeks;
  strands of jewels illumine the curve of your throat.
I'm making jewelry for you, gold and silver jewelry
  that will mark and accent your beauty.

THE WOMAN

12-14 When my King-Lover lay down beside me,
       my fragrance filled the room.
His head resting between my breasts —
       the head of my lover was a sachet of sweet myrrh.
My beloved is a bouquet of wildflowers
       picked just for me from the fields of En Gedi.

THE MAN

15 Oh, my dear friend! You're so beautiful!
       And your eyes so beautiful — like doves!

THE WOMAN

16-17 And you, my dear lover — you're so handsome!
       And the bed we share is like a forest glen.
We enjoy a canopy of cedars
       enclosed by cypresses, fragrant and green.

1 I'm just a wildflower picked from the plains of Sharon,
       a lotus blossom from the valley pools.

THE MAN

2 A lotus blossoming in a swamp of weeds —
       that's my dear friend among the girls in the village.

THE WOMAN

3-4 As an apricot tree stands out in the forest,
       my lover stands above the young men in town.
All I want is to sit in his shade,
       to taste and savor his delicious love.
He took me home with him for a festive meal,
       but his eyes feasted on *me*!

5-6 Oh! Give me something refreshing to eat — and quickly!
       Apricots, raisins — anything. I'm about to faint with love!
His left hand cradles my head,
       and his right arm encircles my waist!

7 Oh, let me warn you, sisters in Jerusalem,
       by the gazelles, yes, by all the wild deer:
Don't excite love, don't stir it up,
       until the time is ripe — and you're ready.

8-10 Look! Listen! There's my lover!
       Do you see him coming?
Vaulting the mountains,
       leaping the hills.
My lover is like a gazelle, graceful;
       like a young stag, virile.
Look at him there, on tiptoe at the gate,

all ears, all eyes — ready!
My lover has arrived
and he's speaking to me!

THE MAN

10-14 Get up, my dear friend,
fair and beautiful lover — come to me!
Look around you: Winter is over;
the winter rains are over, gone!
Spring flowers are in blossom all over.
The whole world's a choir — and singing!
Spring warblers are filling the forest
with sweet arpeggios.
Lilacs are exuberantly purple and perfumed,
and cherry trees fragrant with blossoms.
Oh, get up, dear friend,
my fair and beautiful lover — come to me!
Come, my shy and modest dove —
leave your seclusion, come out in the open.
Let me see your face,
let me hear your voice.
For your voice is soothing
and your face is ravishing.

THE WOMAN

15 Then you must protect me from the foxes,
foxes on the prowl,
Foxes who would like nothing better
than to get into our flowering garden.

16-17 My lover is mine, and I am his.
Nightly he strolls in our garden,
Delighting in the flowers
until dawn breathes its light and night slips away.

Turn to me, dear lover.
Come like a gazelle.
Leap like a wild stag
on delectable mountains!

1-4 **3** Restless in bed and sleepless through the night,
I longed for my lover.
I wanted him desperately. His absence was painful.
So I got up, went out and roved the city,
hunting through streets and down alleys.
I wanted my lover in the worst way!
I looked high and low, and didn't find him.
And then the night watchmen found me
as they patrolled the darkened city.
"Have you seen my dear lost love?" I asked.
No sooner had I left them than I found him,

found my dear lost love.
I threw my arms around him and held him tight,
wouldn't let him go until I had him home again,
safe at home beside the fire.

5 Oh, let me warn you, sisters in Jerusalem,
by the gazelles, yes, by all the wild deer:
Don't excite love, don't stir it up,
until the time is ripe — and you're ready.

6-10 What's this I see, approaching from the desert,
raising clouds of dust,
Filling the air with sweet smells
and pungent aromatics?
Look! It's Solomon's carriage,
carried and guarded by sixty soldiers,
sixty of Israel's finest,
All of them armed to the teeth,
trained for battle,
ready for anything, anytime.
King Solomon once had a carriage built
from fine-grained Lebanon cedar.
He had it framed with silver and roofed with gold.
The cushions were covered with a purple fabric,
the interior lined with tooled leather.

11 Come and look, sisters in Jerusalem.
Oh, sisters of Zion, don't miss this!
My King-Lover,
dressed and garlanded for his wedding,
his heart full, bursting with joy!

THE MAN

1-5 **4** You're so beautiful, my darling,
so beautiful, and your dove eyes are veiled
By your hair as it flows and shimmers,
like a flock of goats in the distance
streaming down a hillside in the sunshine.
Your smile is generous and full —
expressive and strong and clean.
Your lips are jewel red,
your mouth elegant and inviting,
your veiled cheeks soft and radiant.
The smooth, lithe lines of your neck
command notice — all heads turn in awe and admiration!
Your breasts are like fawns,
twins of a gazelle, grazing among the first spring flowers.

6-7 The sweet, fragrant curves of your body,
the soft, spiced contours of your flesh
Invite me, and I come. I stay

until dawn breathes its light and night slips away.
You're beautiful from head to toe, my dear love,
    beautiful beyond compare, absolutely flawless.

8-15 Come with me from Lebanon, my bride.
    Leave Lebanon behind, and come.
Leave your high mountain hideaway.
    Abandon your wilderness seclusion,
Where you keep company with lions
    and panthers guard your safety.
You've captured my heart, dear friend.
    You looked at me, and I fell in love.
    One look my way and I was hopelessly in love!
How beautiful your love, dear, dear friend —
    far more pleasing than a fine, rare wine,
    your fragrance more exotic than select spices.
The kisses of your lips are honey, my love,
    every syllable you speak a delicacy to savor.
Your clothes smell like the wild outdoors,
    the ozone scent of high mountains.
Dear lover and friend, you're a secret garden,
    a private and pure fountain.
Body and soul, you are paradise,
    a whole orchard of succulent fruits —
Ripe apricots and peaches,
    oranges and pears;
Nut trees and cinnamon,
    and all scented woods;
Mint and lavender,
    and all herbs aromatic;
A garden fountain, sparkling and splashing,
    fed by spring waters from the Lebanon mountains.

THE WOMAN

16 Wake up, North Wind,
    get moving, South Wind!
Breathe on my garden,
    fill the air with spice fragrance.

Oh, let my lover enter his garden!
    Yes, let him eat the fine, ripe fruits.

THE MAN

1 **5** I went to my garden, dear friend, best lover!
    breathed the sweet fragrance.
  I ate the fruit and honey,
  I drank the nectar and wine.

Celebrate with me, friends!
    Raise your glasses — "To life! To love!"

2   I was sound asleep, but in my dreams I was wide awake.
      Oh, listen! It's the sound of my lover knocking, calling!

THE MAN

"Let me in, dear companion, dearest friend,
      my dove, consummate lover!
I'm soaked with the dampness of the night,
      drenched with dew, shivering and cold."

THE WOMAN

3   "But I'm in my nightgown — do you expect me to get dressed?
      I'm bathed and in bed — do you want me to get dirty?"

4-7   But my lover wouldn't take no for an answer,
      and the longer he knocked, the more excited I became.
I got up to open the door to my lover,
      sweetly ready to receive him,
Desiring and expectant
      as I turned the door handle.
But when I opened the door he was gone.
      My loved one had tired of waiting and left.
And I died inside — oh, I felt so bad!
      I ran out looking for him
But he was nowhere to be found.
      I called into the darkness — but no answer.
The night watchmen found me
      as they patrolled the streets of the city.
They slapped and beat and bruised me,
      ripping off my clothes,
These watchmen,
      who were supposed to be guarding the city.

8   I beg you, sisters in Jerusalem —
      if you find my lover,
Please tell him I want him,
      that I'm heartsick with love for him.

THE CHORUS

9   What's so great about your lover, fair lady?
What's so special about him that you beg for our help?

THE WOMAN

10-16   My dear lover glows with health —
      red-blooded, radiant!
He's one in a million.
      There's no one quite like him!
My golden one, pure and untarnished,
      with raven black curls tumbling across his shoulders.
His eyes are like doves, soft and bright,

but deep-set, brimming with meaning, like wells of water.
His face is rugged, his beard smells like sage,
    His voice, his words, warm and reassuring.
Fine muscles ripple beneath his skin,
    quiet and beautiful.
His torso is the work of a sculptor,
    hard and smooth as ivory.
He stands tall, like a cedar,
    strong and deep-rooted,
A rugged mountain of a man,
    aromatic with wood and stone.
His words are kisses, his kisses words.
    Everything about him delights me, thrills me
        through and through!

That's my lover, that's my man,
    dear Jerusalem sisters.

THE CHORUS

1 6 So where has this love of yours gone,
        fair one?
    Where on earth can he be?
Can we help you look for him?

THE WOMAN

2-3 Never mind. My lover is already on his way to his garden,
    to browse among the flowers, touching the colors and forms.
I am my lover's and my lover is mine.
    He caresses the sweet-smelling flowers.

THE MAN

4-7 Dear, dear friend and lover,
    you're as beautiful as Tirzah, city of delights,
Lovely as Jerusalem, city of dreams,
    the ravishing visions of my ecstasy.
Your beauty is too much for me — I'm in over my head.
    I'm not used to this! I can't take it in.
Your hair flows and shimmers
    like a flock of goats in the distance
    streaming down a hillside in the sunshine.
Your smile is generous and full —
    expressive and strong and clean.
Your veiled cheeks
    are soft and radiant.

8-9 There's no one like her on earth,
    never has been, never will be.
She's a woman beyond compare.
    My dove is perfection,
Pure and innocent as the day she was born,
    and cradled in joy by her mother.

Everyone who came by to see her
    exclaimed and admired her —
All the fathers and mothers, the neighbors and friends,
    blessed and praised her:

10   "Has anyone ever seen anything like this —
    dawn-fresh, moon-lovely, sun-radiant,
    ravishing as the night sky with its galaxies of stars?"

11-12   One day I went strolling through the orchard,
    looking for signs of spring,
Looking for buds about to burst into flower,
    anticipating readiness, ripeness.
Before I knew it my heart was raptured,
    carried away by lofty thoughts!

13   Dance, dance, dear Shulammite, Angel-Princess!
    Dance, and we'll feast our eyes on your grace!
Everyone wants to see the Shulammite dance
    her victory dances of love and peace.

1-9   **7** Shapely and graceful your sandaled feet,
    and queenly your movement —
    Your limbs are lithe and elegant,
    the work of a master artist.
Your body is a chalice,
    wine-filled.
Your skin is silken and tawny
    like a field of wheat touched by the breeze.
Your breasts are like fawns,
    twins of a gazelle.
Your neck is carved ivory, curved and slender.
    Your eyes are wells of light, deep with mystery.
    Quintessentially feminine!
Your profile turns all heads,
    commanding attention.
The feelings I get when I see the high mountain ranges
    — stirrings of desire, longings for the heights —
Remind me of you,
    and I'm spoiled for anyone else!
Your beauty, within and without, is absolute,
    dear lover, close companion.
You are tall and supple, like the palm tree,
    and your full breasts are like sweet clusters of dates.
I say, "I'm going to climb that palm tree!
    I'm going to caress its fruit!"
Oh yes! Your breasts
    will be clusters of sweet fruit to me,
Your breath clean and cool like fresh mint,
    your tongue and lips like the best wine.

T H E W O M A N

9-12   Yes, and yours are, too — my love's kisses
      flow from his lips to mine.
I am my lover's.
      I'm all he wants. I'm all the world to him!
Come, dear lover —
      let's tramp through the countryside.
Let's sleep at some wayside inn,
      then rise early and listen to bird-song.
Let's look for wildflowers in bloom,
      blackberry bushes blossoming white,
Fruit trees festooned
      with cascading flowers.
And there I'll give myself to you,
      my love to your love!

13   Love-apples drench us with fragrance,
      fertility surrounds, suffuses us,
Fruits fresh and preserved
      that I've kept and saved just for you, my love.

1-2   **8** I wish you'd been my twin brother,
      sharing with me the breasts of my mother,
      Playing outside in the street,
      kissing in plain view of everyone,
      and no one thinking anything of it.
I'd take you by the hand and bring you home
      where I was raised by my mother.
You'd drink my wine
      and kiss my cheeks.

3-4   Imagine! His left hand cradling my head,
      his right arm around my waist!
Oh, let me warn you, sisters in Jerusalem:
      Don't excite love, don't stir it up,
      until the time is ripe — and you're ready.

T H E C H O R U S

5   Who is this I see coming up from the country,
      arm in arm with her lover?

T H E M A N

I found you under the apricot tree,
      and woke you up to love.
Your mother went into labor under that tree,
      and under that very tree she bore you.

T H E W O M A N

6-8   Hang my locket around your neck,
      wear my ring on your finger.

Love is invincible facing danger and death.
    Passion laughs at the terrors of hell.
The fire of love stops at nothing—
    it sweeps everything before it.
Flood waters can't drown love,
    torrents of rain can't put it out.
Love can't be bought, love can't be sold—
    it's not to be found in the marketplace.
My brothers used to worry about me:

8-9   "Our little sister has no breasts.
    What shall we do with our little sister
    when men come asking for her?
She's a virgin and vulnerable,
    and we'll protect her.
If they think she's a wall, we'll top it with barbed wire.
    If they think she's a door, we'll barricade it."

10   Dear brothers, I'm a walled-in virgin still,
    but my breasts are full—
And when my lover sees me,
    he knows he'll soon be satisfied.

THE MAN

11-12   King Solomon may have vast vineyards
    in lush, fertile country,
Where he hires others to work the ground.
    People pay anything to get in on that bounty.
But *my* vineyard is all mine,
    and I'm keeping it to myself.
You can have your vast vineyards, Solomon,
    you and your greedy guests!

13   Oh, lady of the gardens,
    my friends are with me listening.
    Let me hear your voice!

THE WOMAN

14   Run to me, dear lover.
    Come like a gazelle.
Leap like a wild stag
    on the spice mountains.

WISDOM

This particular Wisdom book instructs, advises, and urges, but it also entertains.

Part of the entertainment value is due to the fact that the text leads the reader, ancient or modern, on a merry chase rather than following a well-worn biblical or philosophical, Jewish or Gentile path. It has a polished literary style full of well-turned Greek and Hebrew phrases and waxes eloquent on the fairly dry subject of wisdom. Also, the author introduces a variety of interesting characters.

There are two Solomons: first, the greatest of the Israelite kings (tenth century B.C.); second, the narrator of this book masking as the great king and wise judge (second century B.C.).

There's Lady Wisdom, who is an abstract virtue personified by the author and also represents Justice, Temperance, Prudence, and Fortitude when they're not referred to specifically. These happy four would be recognized in later centuries as the cardinal or moral virtues—ways of living empowered by reason as well as revelation.

There are the Israelites: the godly, the wise, the educated; that's to say, the good side. And then there are the Egyptians: the ungodly, the wicked, the ignorant; that's to say, the bad side.

There's the God of Revelation, and there's the God of Reason. Finally, there's a whittler and a potter, appearing as rather lively illustrations of two producers of the handmade idols the author portrays as the root of all evil.

The Book of Wisdom is a remarkably sophisticated book, written sometime between 200 and 100 B.C. in Alexandria, Egypt, a thriving port city on the Mediterranean near the mouth of the Nile. The metropolis sported a 445-feet-high lighthouse, a population approaching a million that included the largest aggregation of Jews outside of Jerusalem, and a library that grew to 400,000 volumes.

Each incoming ship was met by local stevedores as well as by strong-armed librarians looking to buy manuscripts, quick-copy them, or trade them for copies of other manuscripts. These bibliophiles were not to be denied.

Down on the docks, the most precious cargo being off-loaded was the learning of the Greeks. Their philosophy was already trumpeting the power of reason to arrive at some rather extraordinary conclusions.

The Book of Wisdom's anonymous author is thought to have been a pious, well-educated Jew of the time. The task as he saw it was to write something that would appeal to his urban yet cosmopolitan community. What he came up with was a kind of "pocket history" of the Israelites and a packet of wise sayings for successful administrators.

In Hebrew, the book was titled *The Book of the Great Wisdom of Solomon*; in Old Latin, *The Wisdom of Solomon*; in Greek, it was *Sophia*.

The finished work was copied many times in the library and translated into other languages. Also on the copyist's bench were such biblical titles as *Ecclesiasticus,* or *The Wisdom of Jesus, Son of Sirach,* and the translation of the Bible from Hebrew into Greek known as the *Septuagint*.

The value of the Book of Wisdom was that it could be read aloud or recited in the many synagogues of the Jewish quarter of the city. The eager young Solomons in the congregations were especially interested. They were the upwardly mobile intellectuals, brought up in the old traditions according to the old laws, but they wanted to know where they fit in this exciting new world. But Wisdom was also the sort of book that could be the subject of seminars held in and around the library, which was something of a safe place for Jewish and Gentile agnostics to gather. Under this guise, the Book of Wisdom was more of a book-club selection than an expression of faith.

The Book of Wisdom was also the sort of book that could be read aloud or recited, and perhaps enjoyed with liquid refreshment at the cafés and taverns in the Greek and Egyptian quarters of the city. There the clientele was interested not so much in the would-be Solomons as in the would-be Alexanders. Alexander the Great had conquered a fair amount of the world before his death; he founded the city in 332 B.C. When the Book of Wisdom appeared in 132 B.C. or thereabouts, these young Alexanders were poised to manage the Mediterranean world and needed all the wisdom they could get.

The Book of Wisdom should be required reading for chief executive officers around the world—Solomons and Alexanders alike. And it should be casual reading for the rest of us. The Book of Wisdom promotes the virtuous life, whether it's based on rational moral virtues or faith-filled theological virtues. It supports faith seeking reason and reason seeking faith.

Reading the Book of Wisdom today is still a pious exercise. Its witty presentation contains as much fruit for Christians today as for the Jews who read it two thousand years ago. (WG)

WISDOM

MANAGEMENT OF WORLD AFFAIRS

1-2 Those who manage world affairs—the young would-be Alexanders in today's society—should look long and hard at justice; they should take a no-nonsense attitude toward that moral virtue; they should seek the Lord in the simplicity of their heart. If managers want to find the Lord, they don't have to hunt him down; he'll walk in from the woods when he's good and ready.

3-4 Thinking crooked thoughts means walking crooked miles; that's no way to find God. Proven virtue, on the other hand, whistles down the straight and narrow, whisking the non-virtuous right off the road. No, Lady Wisdom doesn't enter the malevolent soul, nor does she take up residence in a body mildewed with sin.

SPIRIT OF WISDOM

5-7 The spirit of discipline flees the fictional, leaves behind the nonsensical, and won't be corrupted by the spirit of the age. Lady Wisdom smiles upon humankind, but she doesn't have a good thing to say about lips that lie, liars who cheat, or cheaters who take the name of the Lord in vain. Divine surveillance misses nothing; it picks up every move, hears every word; it scrutinizes hearts and scours souls. The Lord has no need of directions to find anyone, nor does he need an ear trumpet to hear everything.

TRASHING WISDOM

8-11 Those who trash Wisdom have nowhere to hide; a thorough search will flush them out. The suspect will be interrogated; the Lord will audit the interview; penalties for iniquities will be assessed. Hidden microphones pick up everything; stage whispers can be deafening. Mumbling won't help; cheap shots are beneath contempt. Make a living on lies and *you'll* sully *your* reputation.

SCANDALOUS WAYS

12-15 Your scandalous ways flirt with death; your mischievous hands play with explosives. God didn't make death, nor does he enjoy punishment. He created everything, gave everything its being. Generations have enjoyed good health; there isn't a poisonous flower in the garden, not a punishing plant on earth. Justice outlives our lives.

16 The not-so-pious in word and deed—they're the ones who invited death. Somehow they imagined death as a friend; they even made a pact with death to put as good a face on it as possible. This type was meant for one another.

GODLESS LOGIC

1 Here's how the godless think. "Life is too short, too tedious. We have nothing to look forward to at the end, no refreshment, no consolation, no anything; and no one's come back from the dead with a different tale."

2 Or, "We come out of nowhere, make a brief appearance, then disappear without a trace. What we inhale are fumes; what we exhale are sparks."

3 Or, "When the sparks are no more and the body has turned to dust, then our spirit will dissolve in the summer breeze."

4 Or, "Over time our names will be forgotten. Our reputations will slip from history—like a wisp of cloud, a shroud of fog fleeing the rays of sun, aggravated by the heat of day."

5 Or, "Our life will pass like shadows on a wall; we can't rewind our life— our death day isn't a movable feast; no one comes back alive."

GODLESS ALIBIS

6 "Let's enjoy the good things of life; let's use creatures with the devil-may-care attitude of youth!"

7-8 Or, "Let's splurge on vintage wines and intoxicating scents! Let's trip through the meadows bursting with flowers! Let's crown ourselves with rosebuds while we may!"

9 Or, "Let's roll in the flower beds, make love on the petals. Crushed blossoms will be the relics of our joy; this is our life, our generation, our destiny."

LIFELESS LIFE PLANS

10 "Let's kick the poor in the pants! Let's pinch the widows on their bottoms! Let's spit in the faces of senior citizens."

11 And, "Since we're in the majority, we'll redefine the law to suit ourselves! Those who can't stand up to us will just have to do what we say."

12 And, "Let's give the just the run-around; they're no good to us. They're always underfoot, always better-than-thou when it comes to observance of God's word. What they accuse us of amounts to nothing more than a few white lies."

13-14 And, "The just are so certain that they know God personally; they even have the audacity to label themselves children of God. They have made themselves a living reproach to us. To see them approach gives most of us the hives."

15-16 And, "The just are odd, strange, different; we don't know what they'll do next. They rank us socially just above forbidden pork; they tiptoe around us as if to avoid contagion; they say they'll die happily and we'll die miserably; they brag that God's their refuge."

17   And, "Let's see if the words of the just are true; they have to die just as we do."

18   And, "If they claim they're true children of God, let's put them to the test; let's see if God will take up their cause and prevent them from getting hurt."

19   And, "Let's interrogate them endlessly and torment them mercilessly; then we'll see how faithful they really are; let's stretch their piety to the breaking point."

20   And, "Let's condemn them to a really messy death and see if, as their very words always promise, God comes to save them."

FATAL FLAWS

21-22   These were the ravings and ramblings of the godless; but they have a fatal flaw. Malice prevents them from seeing the truth. They haven't a clue about their obligations to God, nor do they know that holiness is its own reward, nor do they reckon the honor that awaits lives lived in fidelity.

23-24   God created humanity in mint condition, with his own face on the coin. The devil was envious of God; that's how death entered the world; and those on earth who think the same as the Great Deceiver are the ones who'll die the death of deaths.

THE JUST VERSUS THE UNJUST

1-4   3 As for the souls of the just, they're in the hands of God; the torment of death never lays a finger on them. In the eyes of the not-so-just, the just seem to have died and gone to hell; but such affliction as they may have suffered was merely their exit fee from this world to the next. Their departure was misinterpreted as their demise; in reality they're at peace. Yes, the just suffer as much as the unjust during the death process; but their passing is full of hope and the promise of immortality.

REWARDS AFTER DEATH FOR THE JUST

5-9   Such punishments as the just incur are few, but their rewards are great. God puts them to the test, and they always pass with flying colors. Like gold ore in the furnace the Lord refines them; like burnt offering from the sacrificial fire he receives them.

When it's Final Awards Day, you'll be able to pick them out; they're the sparks dancing about in the harvest after death, the final, burn-the-stubble bonfire. They'll govern the nations and lord it over nationalities; their Lord will reign forever.

Those who put their faith in the Lord will understand truth; those who are faithful will enjoy eternal rest. He showers grace and mercy on those who are committed to him. From time to time he even drops by for a personal chat with them.

REWARDS AFTER DEATH FOR THE UNJUST

10-12 The unjust, on the other hand, if their ideas are to be taken seriously, face punishment; they're slackers caring not a fig for justice or the Lord. Without wisdom and understanding, their life's a bust. There's ambition but nothing to hope for; there's sweat but no equity; stuff is made, but there's no market for it. Their wives don't have a brain in their heads; their children are disasters waiting to happen; their generation—there's not a good word to say for it.

13-14 By way of contrast, on Judgment Day the woman who couldn't bear a child and was never bedded in sin—she'll be considered to have led a fruitful and productive life. The eunuch who worked lawfully with his hands but kept them ritually clean and never had a wicked thought about God will be decorated for his fidelity under fire; in fact, he'll end up with quite a nice spot in the ultimate Temple of the Lord.

THE FATE OF BAD SEED

15-19 For most people, hard labor produces the fruit of a glorious reputation and is the fount of undeniable wisdom. But seed spent on adulterous beds produces only genealogical outsiders; seed spent on the wrong side of the sheets will only stain life, not sustain it. Should the odious offspring of extramarital trysts manage to live a long life, they won't amount to much; their hope will grow gray hair, and that's about all it will grow.

Dying young doesn't matter for them; they have nothing to aspire to, not even at Final Awards Day, when all the medals will be handed out to somebody else. Yes, these illegitimate children are a lost generation and will be reckoned as such at the End of Days.

CHILDREN, WISDOM, AND OLD AGE

1 Better to have no children if that's your fate; you can still live a virtuous life without them; and your virtue will outlive your life. God knows this, and you know it too.

2 Incidentally, when Lady Wisdom slides like a swan into a room, eyes turn toward her; when she sweeps majestically out of the room, the good feelings noticeably lessen. Wherever she drops in, she's treated royally; as belle of the ball, she lives up to her reputation.

3-7 Back to children. A litter of illegitimate children won't help. Faking family histories doesn't right a wrong; half fact, half fiction—you can't base a family on these. Seedlings may branch quite stunningly at first; but if poorly planted they'll bend in the first breeze; in the first bluster they'll topple. Immature branches will break off; the fruit will be too hard to bite, not even fit for jams or jellies. Children conceived on sour sheets will be witnesses for the prosecution of their parents at the Last Tribunal.

The children of the just and temperate, on the other hand, even if they should die before their time, will find eternal rest.

8-9   Old age is remarkable, not because it seems to go on forever, not because it ticks off the decades, but because the white hair signifies wisdom and a spotless way of life.

ENOCH

10-14   Enoch, for example, a favorite of God's who lived among sinners, was swept away by God; he was snatched up lest mischief muss up his intellect, or make-believe mess up his soul, or double-talk obscure his real goal, or lust seduce his innocent soul. He died relatively young for back then (some say he lived only a couple hundred years); yet he lived a full life. God liked what Enoch did with his time and talents; and that's why he plucked him from the maelstrom of malice. However, the general population missed the point; they had no precedent for dealing with someone disappearing from the face of the earth.

THE LAST LAUGH

15-18   Grace and mercy have always been showered upon the elect; God has always kept track of his favorites. Even when the godly die, they are a living reproach to the ungodly who survive. The callow youth who reaches spiritual maturity early will be the living reproach to the callous old fool who's acquired no spiritual maturity at all. The foolish see the wise drop like flies and don't have a clue as to what God had in mind for the just, nor do they know why God rescued them from oblivion. The secular crowd will see their lives and dismiss them outright; but—please pardon the gallows humor—God will have the last laugh.

19-20   When the godless die, their remains go unnoticed, but their reputations remain notorious. An angry God roughs them up like rag dolls, tearing them from seam to seam. They're sentenced to desolation without consolation—no more pleasure, just pain—and their memory will eventually fade. At the Final Tally they'll stand at the back, their own sins singling them out, pointing the finger, accusing them on the spot.

GODLY VERSUS UNGODLY

1-3   5 Then the just will stand with great confidence against those who've narrowed their influence and belittled their labors. On seeing the godly square off against them, the ungodly will feel the shakes coming on; their eyes will pop at the swiftness of God's rescue of those they persecuted. Beating up on themselves, croaking under the pressure from within, but bursting to speak, the wicked interrupt one another.

4   "Here he is, the guy we used to make fun of, the butt of our jokes!"
        Or, "How were we to know? We thought her life made no sense at all."
        Or, "When they died, we thought that was the end of them."

5   Or, "How come these were counted as children of God and we weren't?"
        Or, "How did they worm their way into the inner circle of God?"

6   Or, "What else can we say, except that we made a terrible mistake?"

Or, "It was high noon for them; the light of truth shone down upon them; apparently, the sun never rose on us."

7 Or, "We were involved right up to our eyebrows with destruction and deceit."

Or, "We dragged ourselves across forbidden deserts; God was nowhere to be found on our maps and charts."

8 Or, "We have our pride, and we have our wealth, but what have they done for us lately?"

9 Or, "All our possessions pass like shadows on a wall, like long-distance messengers; now you see them, now you don't."

Unlikeable Likenesses

10 "Like a ship in high swells leaving behind a wake then no wake at all, the keel cutting its way through the water, the water repairing the cut, leaving not a scar behind."

11 Or, "Like a bird laboring across the skies, following a route invisible to those below; just its wings slapping the winds, leaving no sign of its passing."

12 Or, "Like an arrow whipping toward a target, momentarily parting the air, leaving not a trace behind."

13 "So it is with us. We're born and, not long after, we're gone; not a whiff of our virtue hangs in the air; just the rank odor of our vice.

14 "Such hopes as the ungodly have are like filaments in the wind; like frothy designs on a calm sea, only to be dissolved by a light chop; like smoke helpless before the wind; like house guests here one day, gone the next."

Medals and Decorations

15-16 But the godly don't disappear; they live forever; their reward is in the Lord; their landlord is the Most High. That's why they receive decorations for meritorious service: the Gold Pendant, the Legion of Merit, awarded by the Lord himself. His right hand protects them; his left hand defends them.

The Lord as Warrior

17-23 The Lord arms himself with zeal; he'll arm creation for the ultimate destruction of his enemies. For a breastplate he'll strap on justice; for a helmet he'll don justice without prejudice; for a shield he'll uphold rectitude; his anger will sharpen his spear.

With all creation for allies he'll fight against the ignorant. Lightning bolts will seek their target like arrows drawn to the bull's-eye; hailstones the size of boulders will rain down from the heavens; oceans will glow white with rage; rivers will turn into rapids; rising water will roam where it wants. Powerful storms will be thrown against the wicked; hurricane-force winds will blow them down. Their own lawlessness will run rampant; their malfeasance will make governments fall.

WOULD-BE SOLOMONS AND ALEXANDERS

¹⁻² **6** In conclusion, young Solomons and Alexanders of the world, open your good ear and listen to what I have to say! Those who manage the affairs of the world, hear this! If you're responsible for the fate of millions, if you pride yourselves on your principalities, then lend me your ear!

³⁻⁴ Such power as you may have really isn't yours—it's the Lord's, given to you as a gift; your domination comes from the Most High. He keeps a check on your ways and means; he oversees your principles and practices. You may be administrators of your kingdoms, but you've been caught cooking the books! God is going one way, but you're going in the opposite direction.

⁵⁻⁸ It won't be pretty, but it will be sudden—God's breaking down the door and calling you to account! Life without parole—that's the sentence for executives at the top of the heap. Mercy is conceded, but only to the down and out; those at the top will be subjected to rigorous investigation. God will not stand down before any of them, nor will he be distracted by a flash of finery. Obviously, he's the one who made the great and small, providing the necessities of life for every single person. But for the top of the heap he'll make a forensic examination of each and every act.

⁹⁻¹¹ My words are directed to you, Solomons and Alexanders of the world. Put wisdom first; it will cut your mistakes in half. Those who manage to the best of their ability will be rewarded justly; those who teach justice will mount a successful defense of their stewardship. In conclusion, keep my words in a warm spot; take them to heart—that's where they'll do you the most good.

LADY WISDOM, CEO

¹²⁻¹⁵ Lady Wisdom is smartly spoken, impeccably dressed; her door is always open; she's quick to make friends. These last she surprises, addressing them by name; no name tags for her. Those who join the line to meet her don't have long to wait. As the sun rises, there she is, sitting on her porch. You have only to look at her to get the picture; her smile eases tension, lifts depression.

¹⁶⁻¹⁷ Those who need her the most become her pets. That has resulted in some hilarious encounters, every one of which she treats as providential. Getting to know her is entry-level education; getting to love her is continuing education.

¹⁸⁻²¹ If you truly love her, you'll observe the laws; if you truly observe the laws, you'll enjoy immortality. Immortality brings one closer to God. Therefore, yearning leads to the ultimate kingdom. If you're the type who takes delight in thrones and oval offices, then honor Wisdom; she'll get you where you want to go.

WISDOM'S EXECUTIVE BIO

²²⁻²⁴ Just who is Wisdom and how did she come to be? I'll tell you. There's no secret about God's arrangements. I'll take her from her birth at the creation and

place her in the light of today's knowledge—no fibs, no white lies, no equivocations, no mental reservations! I could keep her history to myself, but I won't—that wouldn't be serving her best interests. The wiser the world, the safer the population; the wiser the kings, the more stable the kingdoms. To conclude, accept my invitation to meet Wisdom—you've got nothing to lose.

RECREATING KING SOLOMON

1 7 Who am I that I should address you so?
My name is Solomon, greatest of the kings of Israel.
But more importantly, I'm just another person, no different from anyone else; I too am descended from Adam and Eve.

2-3 Of my own parents' intercourse, I'm the happy result; it took ten lunar months for me to grow full term. When my head emerged from my mother's womb, I breathed the same air as everyone else. When the rest of me dropped, I took a tumble, as happens when the mother is in the squatting position. My first sound was a cry, the noise heard in nurseries since the beginning of time.

4-6 At once I was swept up, swaddled, and suckled. No regal babe has had a better beginning or indeed a better end; the door in is also the door out— that's all there is to life.

NANNY EXTRAORDINAIRE

7-10 For this very reason I prayed, trying to make sense of it all. I cried out for Wisdom, and she responded to my call. When she came to sit, I preferred her lap to the laps of other royals. I compared Wealth with Wisdom, and Wisdom was the clear winner. I could have compared her with the finest jewels, but why would I? Gold dust is no more precious than yellow sand; the same could be said of silver. Health and Beauty take a back seat to Wisdom. She sheds more light than the sun; they merely reflect and refract.

11-13 As if the wonderfulness of Wisdom weren't enough, she didn't come empty-handed; she brought gifts for everybody; each one wore her label or bore her mark.

How was I to know she had her own boutique? I'm not going to hide the fact that I enjoyed her gifts immensely; I won't hesitate to recommend them to others.

14 Humankind won't exhaust her inventory; her fastest moving article is education. Those who make good use of her gifts will have something to talk about with God.

DIVINE CO-CONSPIRATOR

15-16 I'll need God's help if I'm to speak in complete sentences and express thoughts worthy of Wisdom's students. He can do it because he's taught Wisdom all she knows, and personally supervises her continuing seminars for the would-be wise. He's taught us how to speak and what to say; he knows what everything is and how everything works.

17-20 No wonder he introduced her to the various branches of knowledge: geography of the earth and names of the elements; measurement of times and calculation of calendars, seasons and cycles, festival and ferial days; planets and stars; animal husbandry and animal behavior; wind power and reason power; horticulture and pharmacology.

21 The general body of knowledge I mastered; then I entered into serious research. Who directed my dissertation? None other than Lady Wisdom herself.

INQUIRING MIND

22-23 She had this inquiring mind coupled with dedication. She was one of a kind, able to multitask and keep an edge; nimble in argument, able to conduct three conversations at the same time; kept a clean record, always had her wits about her; wouldn't hurt a fly; was drawn to the good; sharp as a tack, nothing got past her; always had an orange in her pocket; cordial with humans, kind to animals; mature, confident—could hold her own in male company. She was a model of virtue, didn't miss a trick; she could discern the movements of the soul—whether intellectual or moral, subtle or not-so-subtle.

24-26 Wisdom has moves that motion doesn't have. Her purity points to the kernel of any argument. Wisdom is the breath of God, breathing out and breathing in; an unfiltered emanation of the Omnipotent; there is no bad breath from her. She's the mirror image of eternal light, a reflection of the potency and goodness of God.

27 Yes, Wisdom is one, but she can interact with everyone else; she never needs to renovate, yet she doesn't hesitate to innovate; she influences one generation after another, turning them into friends of God and the prophets.

28 God loves no one more than the person who's spent a semester with her.

29-30 She is more splendid than the sun; but like the stars, she prefers spot lighting—bright but not blinding, which is good after dark; owlish about evil, she can spot mischief at midnight.

EXECUTIVE SUMMARY

1 **8** Lady Wisdom has a wide acquaintance, extending from one end of the world to the other; she's overcommitted but seems to manage smoothly.

2 This woman I've loved from my earliest days; marriage was what I had in mind; it was love at first sight.

3-4 She enjoyed spending time with God; he returned her affection. She studied under the master and became a central figure in his projects.

5-6 If the rich and famous don't number Lady Wisdom among their closest friends, it's their loss. Wisdom—she's what makes the world go around. To put it another way, if knowledge is what makes the world go around, who's the master mechanic but Wisdom herself?

7 If anyone loves Justice, know that Wisdom laid the groundwork for that virtue some centuries ago. Along with Justice she teaches Temperance, Prudence, and Fortitude; these four are the chief moral virtues, the virtues human beings have relied on since the beginning.

8   If someone wants to consult an expert on a subject, Wisdom's the one; she knows the past and can surmise the future. She knows the ins and outs of rhetoric, and the ups and downs of riddles. She is kept advised of coming catastrophes and looks forward to coming attractions.

Marriage Proposal

9-10 That's why I proposed to her and suggested we marry each other. She'd be a fount of good advice and a source of great comfort. To be seen in public with her would enhance my reputation; oldsters would admire me even though I was a youngster.

11   They'd think I was on the cutting edge when I presided in court; those in office would recognize me as an up-and-comer.

12   Before I spoke, they'd hold their tongues; when I spoke up, they'd respect what I say; when I got carried away, they'd hide their yawns.

13   Through her I'd have an immortality of sorts, happily remembered by those who come after me.

14-15 Populations would do as I say; nations would bow to me; despots and dictators who inspired horror would get the shivers when they came face-to-face with me. I'd be popular in peace time and celebrated in war time.

16   Entering my house, I'd find rest and recreation with her; no sore points would come up in our conversation; with her around there'd never be a dull moment.

17-18 When I reflect on these things and go over them in my heart, I think our marriage will last forever. Being friends with her is an absolute delight; her handiwork is meticulous. When arguing, she gives better than she gets; her rhetoric is dizzying and dazzling. Is it any wonder that I wanted to marry her?

The Path Through Prudence

19-20 As a child I was rather precocious, but I grew up well-rounded—or was it the other way around? I was a *prima donna* in school but became well adjusted.

21   What else can I say, except that there was only one way to get Wisdom's attention. I had to speak with our mutual friend, Prudence; getting that far was quite a leap; then I approached the Lord and talked myself silly.

This is what I said from the bottom of my heart.

King Solomon's Prayer

1-4   **9** "God of my ancestors, Lord of my mercies! When you spoke, all creation broke loose. After consulting Lady Wisdom you appointed humankind to ride herd on the creatures you'd made and to manage the world with commitment and justice, erring more on the side of the heart than the mind. Grant me access to Lady Wisdom, and count me as one of your children.

5   "I worked for you; my mother Bathsheba worked for you also. But now

I'm not all that well, and I'm getting on in years; I still haven't mastered the ins and outs of law and order.

6-8   "When someone pretends to have wisdom in public, I know it is worldly wisdom, not yours, and will be reckoned as such. Yet you chose me to rule your people, to educate your sons and daughters. Build a Temple on your holy mountain, you told me; construct an altar in the city where you live; copy the Tabernacle made some centuries ago.

9-12   "Lady Wisdom knows what you've done; she was with you from the beginning; she learned how to please you and how not to alter your life-maps. Send her as emissary from your holy heavens; tell her to leave your broad expanse and come to me. I need her if I'm to finish my work right; I want to meet your expectations.

    "She knows everything and misunderstands nothing; she'll prevent me from making mistakes; her reputation will protect me. May all my efforts be properly appraised, O Lord; may I treat your people in a just and fair manner; may I be a worthy successor to my father, David."

SOME REFLECTIONS ON THE MIND OF GOD

13-18   How does the mind of God work? Who can follow the directions from the Lord's recipe? Our reasoning processes are cumbersome; our philosophical constructs are complicated; our bodies grind the soul down; our existence messes the mind up. It's hard to make sense out of what's going on in the world; harder still to understand what's happening right under our noses.

    As for what's in the heavens, who'll figure it out? Who'll know what your counsel might be? We won't, unless you send your divine spirit by sharing Wisdom with us. How else will you keep us on the straight and narrow? Lady Wisdom has helped us know your pleasure throughout history.

POCKET HISTORY OF THE ISRAELITES
SEVEN JUST MEN

1-2   **10** Over the centuries, Lady Wisdom has come to the rescue of seven just men.
    First was Adam, the first of the created beings, father of the rest. Wisdom got him back on his feet after he'd been floored by the first sin; from a loser she turned him into a contender.

3   Cain should have been second. But he tore himself away from Wisdom when he killed his brother Abel.

4   So second was Noah. As background, punishment for Cain's sin was a flood that submerged the earth; but again Lady Wisdom came to the rescue, steadying the tiller of the *Two-by-Two*—the leaky ship manned by Noah.

5   Third was Abraham. As background, when the nations of the world came together in unholy alliance only to find that nobody could agree with anybody else, Lady Wisdom singled out Abraham, recommending him without reservation to God. She's the one who fortified his hand when he was willing to sacrifice his son Isaac.

6-9   Fourth was Lot; Lady Wisdom snatched him as he was fleeing from the wicked, who were dropping like flies as fire descended upon the Pentapolis. Among the reminders of that wickedness are a crater smoldering, an orchard bearing fruit that doesn't ripen, and a statuesque figure of Lot's unbelieving wife.

Getting back to that fateful day in the five-city area, passersby snubbed Lady Wisdom, choosing their own way over hers, only to fall catastrophically, leaving behind enough ruins to draw the curious for centuries to come. But on that fateful day, she'd been able to rescue all those who were observant.

10-12   Fifth was Jacob. As background, Lady Wisdom was there for him when he fled from his brother's deadly embrace. She gave him a peek at the kingdom of God and an introduction to theology; she commended him for his labors and helped him achieve his goals. Those who would defraud and oppress him thought Jacob didn't have what it takes to win, but she saw to it that he prospered. She insulated him from his enemies and put him into protective custody; eventually, he bested his attackers. In the meantime, she'd given him a tip: *In a brawl, piety packs more power than a punch.*

13-14   Sixth was Joseph. As background, just men were being sold into slavery; Lady Wisdom ransomed them from the slavery of sin. Joseph was among them, and with him she descended into the dungeon where he was chained; she didn't leave his side until she was able to offer him the governorship of a kingdom, as well as power over those who'd thrown him into prison. She demonstrated that the charges against him were lies, cleared his record, and gave him the highest decoration the next world had to offer.

15-20   Seventh was Moses. As background, Lady Wisdom once rescued the Israelites, an observant and unoffending people, from a nation that wanted to imprison them. To that end she introduced herself to a servant of the Lord named Moses; she held her ground against a furious pharaoh, her only weapons being signs and wonders.

The holy people she rewarded for their labors by leading them on a great escape, hiding them by day, moving them by night. She led them across the Red Sea, wading with them through deep water; their enemies she drowned in the same water, their bloated corpses rising up to the surface. The living salvaged what they could from the dead; then, Lord, they filled the air with praises of your holy name; with one voice they praised your victorious hand.

21   As for Lady Wisdom, she gave voice to the voiceless. And, as if that weren't gift enough, she topped off their prayers and songs with a touch of eloquence.

POCKET HISTORY OF THE ISRAELITES
LADY WISDOM HELPS MOSES

1-3   11 Lady Wisdom preserved the Israelites.
She put them in the hands of Moses, a holy prophet. Then they wandered through deserts, not a nomad in sight; they camped where no bedouin had tented before. They held their ground when attacked; they took revenge where appropriate.

4-8   When they ran out of water, they called out to you, O Lord; then a waterfall burst from above. Who'd have thought drought relief would come from rock?

The Egyptians suffered from lack of drinking water; the Israelites survived with plenty of it. It wasn't that the Egyptians didn't have enough water; it was that it was polluted with blood from the slaughter of the Israelite infants. The current in the Nile ran swiftly enough, but the water was undrinkable.

Back in the desert, at one point you cut off the water supply from the Israelites to give them a taste of the death-dealing thirst you could inflict upon your enemies.

9-12   You put the Israelite spirit to the ultimate test, but your lash tickled them rather than sliced them to ribbons; from it they learned that your friends fared far better than your enemies.

You, O Lord, were just being a parent to the Israelites, giving them correct advice. But to the Egyptians you came across as a heartless king, a grand inquisitor who'd turned torture into a fine art. But it didn't matter whether the Egyptians were present or absent; the Israelite still could feel your sting. The painful burden of thirst was dumped on your people, but they realized that you were still on their side.

13-14   The second drought was more powerful than the first, but the Israelite thirst was less than the Egyptian thirst; that's when the Egyptians sensed the presence of the Israelites' God. The Egyptians had great fun at the expense of Moses. They thought he was a fraud, then threw him out; but in the final analysis they had to admire him, for his thirst was less devastating than theirs.

15   As for the Egyptians, not a brain existed among them. They were afflicted with some really bad ideas; for example, they worshiped the dumbest creatures in the garden. As a reward, the Lord God of the Israelites sent hordes of insects to plague them.

16-20   The lesson of the Lord was that each sin, no matter how lovely it appeared at first, contained its own unique punishment. For the Lord this was no big deal. With the wave of his hand he'd created the world and everything in it.

With another wave, Lord, you could have afflicted the enemy population with a multitude of bears or fierce lions; or perhaps with a menagerie of imaginary animals snorting fire and smoke with horrendous sparks coming from their eyes. Such creatures as these could kill with the swipe of a paw or the crunch of a jaw; just the sight of them would scare a person to death. Even without these powerful weapons they could wither an adversary with just a whiff of their bad breath. Of course, you could have wrought ultimate justice with just a wave of your mighty arm.

Instead, Lord, you decided to proceed with greater precision. You'd do your calculations according to your own weights and measures.

21   It's not a bad thing, flashing some muscle from time to time; but after you do, who'd want to arm wrestle you again?

22-24   Like a speck of dust on a scale—that's how the whole world weighs in before you—like a drop of morning dew. But have mercy on us all. You can do that; pay no attention to our sins—we're already doing the penance. You look upon created things with delight; you dislike nothing you've created. Honestly, if you dislike something you shouldn't have created it in the first place.

25 How could the china keep from chipping if you hadn't made it unbreakable in the first place?

Likewise, how could something not called into existence by you last forever?

26 Spare us, O Lord; we come from your collection; we wear your label; we bear your mark.

POCKET HISTORY OF THE ISRAELITES
DIGRESSION ON GOD'S MERCY AND JUSTICE

1-2 **12** In all created beings, O Lord, you find a spark of your own immortal spirit. To those who wander from the straight and narrow, you provide mid-course correction. To those who sin against you, you give a sharp warning plus a hopeful word; you want everyone to leave the wicked life behind and believe in you.

3-7 An example from the distant past, if I may. Those ancient Canaanites who lived in your holy land—you detested them, thought them beneath your dignity. It has to do with their despicable religious practices, their sorceries and sacrifices. Without giving it a second thought, they sacrificed their children and dined on their tripe; they banqueted on their neighbors' flesh and blood and enjoyed their chops; they participated in the initiation rites and reveled in the secret and unholy mysteries. These were the people you authorized our ancestors to throttle until dead. That would restore dignity to the land you hold most holy and intended for people who were your own.

8-10 But you spared the Canaanites from divine annihilation, sending instead blitz after blitz of wasps and hornets whose only mission was to sting every last one of them. That's not to say you couldn't have wiped the enemy out with your army, served them up as lunch at the zoo, slain them with your arguments, or cut them dead in public. Instead, you judged them gently. You gave them time to repent and think things through. You did this even though you knew they weren't your kind of people. Evil seemed to be ingrained in them. They wouldn't change their way of thinking even when you gave them the chance.

11-12 They were bad seeds right from the start, but you forgave their sins even though they didn't repent. Did you realize, however, the sort of insults they'd throw at you for doing that?

"What right did you have to destroy us? What kind of an unjust judge are you anyway?"

13-14 But you, Lord, are free to destroy the nations you create. There's no other God but you, and no one takes care of everybody the way you do. Your record is unimpeachable, so who would impeach you? Neither tyrant nor dictator dare accuse you of anything, let alone of unjust decisions and actions.

15-16 Since you're justice itself, your sentences can't be anything but just. You never punish the innocent. Your strength is the beginning of your justice; as we know, you're the God of all, but you act sparingly with each and every one.

17-20 You show your resolve by not overreacting when your jurisdiction is challenged; you don't blow your top every time your existence is denied. On the contrary, you judge with clemency; you govern with indulgence, even though you can dump us anytime you want! Your conduct on the judicial bench has taught your people that justice must always be kind; your conduct as a parent has given your children hope in forgiveness. You didn't have to rank reconciliation over sin, but you did. You did indeed castigate the enemies of your people, and they deserved to die, but you gave them plenty of space to repent and change their wicked ways.

21-22 With your own people you've been both strict and lenient; you gave our forebears all sorts of covenants, assurances, and once-in-a-lifetime deals. For every lash you gave to discipline us, you gave two or three to our enemies. Before we judge others, we should meditate on your goodness; when our turn to be judged comes, we should hope for the same mercy.

BACK TO THE EGYPTIANS

23-27 Take the example of the Egyptians. Those who sinned more from carelessness than anything else you punished by confronting them with their own abominations. They spent much of their lives wandering around in error, believing among other things that certain animals made good gods. They must have been in their second childhood to think that. Because of this you rendered your judgment on them in mocking tones, as if they were delinquents in juvenile court. Most of them understood the punishment all too well; those who didn't, you punished much more severely. When they did accept their suffering with dignity, they turned on the false gods who deceived them and began to see that the God they once denied was indeed the one, true God.

POCKET HISTORY OF THE ISRAELITES
THE IGNORANT

1-2 **13** All of our enemies come by their stupidity honestly; it's built into their nature. The subject of God just doesn't come up; when confronted by all the good things in the world, these ignorant people can't wrap their mind around Him-Who-Is, nor would they recognize the architect of the world if they bumped into him in the parking lot. The best they can do when it comes to gods are fire, wind, tornado, hurricane, even the celestial candelabra.

3-5 Granted, there's some dark beauty or deep divinity in all these, but how much better it would be to find in them the real Lord God; he's the author of all created things.

Admiring the power and performance of created things is one thing, but it should point to the one who made them, the one who's more powerful than they. From the magnitude and beauty of created things one can reasonably expect to see the Creator himself.

6-7 But perhaps they aren't as dense as we think; even as they err, they're looking for God and want to find him. Wandering around creation they make inquiries, but for them seeing is believing, and there are so many curious things to see.

8-10 Ultimately, though, ignorance is no excuse. Even the ignorant are able to learn and apply that knowledge to the world; hence, finding the Lord of Creation should have been a comparatively easy task. How unhappy they must be, putting their hopes in things that have no life! Too quickly they put the Made-in-Heaven sticker onto all sorts of bric-a-brac: gold and silver jewelry, animal sculpture, a random stone turned into a piece of art by an ancient hand.

The Whittler

11-13   A good example of this type of believer would be a certain master carpenter who whittled in his spare time. He picked out a tree and cut it down; he stripped off the bark in no time and, blade flashing, made a common article he could use in his daily rounds. Some of the scrap he put on the fire which he used to heat up a nice meal. The rest he was going to leave behind, but he picked up one piece. Being curvy and knotty, it had little promise, but he began to whittle; from it there appeared the image of a human being.

14-16   Another piece of wood he turned into an animal. Then he painted it or stained it until he covered every imperfection on the surface. He had a place for it on his wall and hung it on a nail. He made sure the artifact wouldn't fall, knowing that if it couldn't prevent itself from falling, which it couldn't, it would need all the external help it could get just to stay up.

17-19   When the whittler prayed out loud to these lifeless images about possessions and marriage and children, he felt unembarrassed. When he prayed for health, he addressed a piece of wood that was dead. When he prayed for life, he prayed to something that had no spirit. When he prayed for help, he invoked a helpless image. When he prayed for good journey, he petitioned something that couldn't walk. When he prayed for a helping hand in earning money or doing business or producing product, he approached an image that had no hands.

Pocket History of the Israelites
Accessory Before and After

1-5   **14** Let me put it another way. A man wants to set sail, but the waves are too high. So what does he do? He calls on his lucky image for protection, a piece of wood more fragile than the boat he's in! He'd be better off putting his trust in the boat builder, whose motive was to sell his product for profit; toward that end the manufacturer did what was necessary to make a good boat.

   But you, Father, your providence pilots the craft; yours is the firm hand on the tiller in smooth seas and rough. With you at the helm, even the first-time sailor who doesn't know fore from aft can feel safe. Your general principle? A boat should rely on your wisdom, not skip your wisdom altogether. With this mindset, humankind has forever been relying on a few slats of wood to put to sea, survive the surf, and eventually beach our raft safely.

6-7   This has been so from the beginning of history. An example was when a race of proud giants was dying out. Noah, the hope of the world, and his people hit the sea in a big boat, leaving behind the seed of a new generation.

They made it safely due to your firm hand on the tiller. Blessed is that wooden boat, Noah's transport, *Two-by-Two,* on which the most precious piece of cargo was justice itself.

8-13 As for a figurine masking as a god, it should be disavowed and those who whittled it denounced; it was just a piece of wood, but they proclaimed it a god.

Equally odious to God are godless people and the godlessness they represent. Punishment with torment awaits both the makers and their work.

From this it follows that the judgment of God will visit the pagan idols; though part of creation, they've been turned into an abomination that tries our souls and trips our minds. Messing with idols eventually leads to fooling around with marital infidelity, which in turn is the ruination of family life. The idols weren't around at the beginning, nor will they last forever.

THE INVENTION OF IDOLS

14-16 Idol worship first appeared in human history not long after Adam, but while it remains in fashion, it will not last forever.

An example of idol-creation was a grieving couple, not long after the death of their child, having an image made of the little girl. Overcome with grief, they reverenced that image as though it were a god. They even developed sorceries and sacrifices that those who were part of their household were supposed to attend. The practice caught on as time passed, and what began as an unhealthy step in the grieving process for a single family became the law of the land.

17-18 Still another example was when those away from home couldn't reverence their royals in person. They made images of their rulers and honored them from afar. The artist-hustlers who specialized in producing these images made them so attractive that they became collectibles in other countries.

19-20 Then there were the conniving craftspeople who coined images of the powerful that were more flattering than the originals. No doubt the images had a charm about them; perhaps that explains their popularity; but the person supposed to be *remembered* by such an image was now being *reverenced* as a god.

21 These were tragic deceptions, a manipulation of the human mind that had a terrible result. The gullible among the grief-ridden or civic-minded began trying to impose on the wooden or stone images the word that shouldn't be said or read aloud: *God.*

22-27 Moving right along, as if it weren't enough to make a blunder with regard to *God,* they made a blunder with regard to *peace* itself, thinking that their being out of control was a good thing for the rest of us. They sacrificed their own children, offered secret sacrifices, met at midnight for exotic rituals. They no longer lived their lives virtuously or kept their marriages holy; instead, they set deadly traps of unnatural sexuality between one another. Everything was out of control; chaos ruled. Violence and murder, theft and deceit, corruption and infidelity, riot and perjury ran rampant. Values were violated, favors forgotten, souls seduced, bestiality experimented with, marriages broken, adultery promoted.

My point is that idols aren't to be invoked or worshiped; they're the beginning, cause, and end of every evil.

28-31 Another example is when idol worshipers carry on until they fall into a trance or assume a prophetic stance and mouth some nonsense; they live a life without justice and can't avoid committing perjury. They put their trust in idols, which can't return the trust; they retaliate against others, but expect no retaliation in return.

But transgressions will catch up with them for two reasons; first, they chose idols over God; second, they swore unjust oaths and told lies. It's not the powerlessness of idols but the punishment of sinners that stalks the steps of the unjust.

POCKET HISTORY OF THE ISRAELITES
THE TRINKETRY OF IDOLATRY

1-4 **15** Yes, God of ours, you're persuasive but never abrasive, slow to anger yet quick to comfort when it comes to us poor sinners. Even if we sin, we're yours, knowing your great tolerance for sinners; the fact that you're counting us as friends is a compliment. To know you is to come face-to-face with justice; meeting your power first hand is the beginning of immortality. In making our decision we haven't been dazzled by a fast talker, nor fooled by a portrait artist, nor lured by a prideful statue.

5-6 Idols bring out goose bumps on the skin of the ignorant; they much prefer a bric-a-brac god to a live one. These are the kind of people who go crazy over the trinketry of idolatry; they fall into three categories: those who make them, those who can't live without them, those who worship them.

THE POTTER

7 A potter works her clay hard to fashion for our use a one-of-a-kind vase; or, using the same clay, she makes pots that can be put to good use or bad. But all the pots are the same size and shape; the one who determines which pot goes where and does what is the potter herself.

8-9 Suppose the very same potter using the very same clay, but with a very different intention, made a god object—a flashy, life-like doll. The potter would do well to remember that she had come from clay herself and, after comparatively few years, would return to that very same clay, thus concluding the very short lease she had on her body. But no, the potter's concern was elsewhere. She was worrying not that she'd have a short working life but that in the life she had left she'd be in stiff competition with others who work wood or precious metals into religious objects. She's quite good at it, making flashy articles look like gods; and she doesn't mind advertising her wares.

10-13 Alas, the potter's heart is ash; her hope is hopeless; her life is not worth the clay in her pottery barn. That is because she ignored the one who fashioned her, who put her on the wheel of life and molded her. Instead, the potter's experience taught her that life was arbitrary and capricious, that her daily work was a sport with a prize that she needed to win by doing whatever was necessary. And yet she knew she sinned when she made both beautiful objects and evil idols from the clay of the same earth.

Mischievous Hands

14-17 All those who oppress people with idols are uneducated and unhappy, churlish and childish. All their idols they pretend are gods have eyes that can't see, a nose that can't breathe, ears that can't hear, fingers that can't feel, feet that can't walk. Why? Because a human being made them, a human being whose own breath was borrowed from God. Humans can make idols look like themselves, but they can't make idols come alive the way God made all of us come alive.

Although the whittler and the potter are mortal, the figurines they create with their mischievous hands are dead on arrival. Even idol makers are better than the figurines they worship, because evil people are truly alive, while their evil idols never will be.

Odd Thing

18-19 Odd thing, though, is that the animals people have worshiped as idols over the years have been among the least attractive in the garden; they had nothing in common with human beings; they were nothing short of hideous. If they were supposed to be gods, don't you think they should have been easier to look at? How could that have happened? I can only guess that the idol animals must have missed God's blessing for good looks at the dawn of creation.

Pocket History of the Israelites
A New Cuisine

1-4 **16** You punished the Egyptians for their animal idolatry, Lord. How fitting the punishment included the flies and fleas you sent! Of course, you could have punished your own people that way, but instead you upgraded their menu to include quail. But when meal time came for the idolaters, they lost their appetite when presented with entrees of reptiles and insects. But your people, Lord, after undergoing a short period of hunger, were introduced to a brand-new cuisine. It was part of your divine plan, wasn't it, to oppress the oppressors and show your own people that you were systematically annihilating their enemies?

5-9 Not that the Israelites were let off the hook completely; but when your people were plagued by poisonous snakes, for example, it was only a short time before your wrath petered out. In fact, the hardships they endured were more of a warning than a punishment, a demonstration that your Law had teeth in it. To remind them of that, you gave them a sign, a bronze serpent, which became a medicine of sorts. To be cured of snakebite all one of our people had to do was face the symbol. Of course, the fake snake didn't do it; you, the Savior of us all, were the Divine Doctor!

By this display of your power, you showed the Egyptians that you were the one who delivered your people from evil. The Egyptians, in contrast, continued to die from the plagues you visited on them. No remedies presented themselves to them, and not one of them shed a tear for their predicament; they deserved what they got.

SOME REFLECTIONS ON HOW GOD OPERATES

10-13 None of your people died of the venom; you arrived just in time to save their skins. Our ancestors were poisoned to death, almost, but it was more vaccination than poison; they recovered quickly before they could forget who it was that saved them. They tried herbals and wraps, but to no effect; it was your word, O Lord, that did the trick. You have the power of life and death; you led our people on a merry chase to the gates of hell and back.

14-15 This isn't remotely possible for humans who kill someone. Try though they may, they can never bring the victim back to life again; nor can they retrieve the soul of their victim once it's been consigned to the netherworld. The conclusion is obvious: There's no matching or avoiding *your* power, Lord.

16-21 The ungodly Egyptians deny you are the One True God. For that they've felt the strength of your lash; you persecuted them with flood and with fire. Especially remarkable was the fact that twice the water didn't extinguish the fire; fire didn't melt the hailstones that fell on the wicked or consume the angel bread that appeared for your people; fire must have meant that the just were vindicated.

There was a time, though, when you turned the fire down in Egypt; you didn't want to burn the locusts assailing the Egyptians. At the same time you didn't want them to forget that they were being punished by fire.

At another time, in the middle of the river your fiery judgment burned out of control; the result was that the Egyptian crops were torched by lightning. But to your own people you introduced angel bread; it was bread from the vaults of heaven, ready to eat, a wholesome and satisfying bread appealing to all different taste buds. This sort of divine gift revealed to your children your sweet side. The bread was presented in one flavor, but it satisfied every palate.

SOME MORE OBSERVATIONS ON DIVINE METHODS

22-23 Snow and ice held up well against the fire; they didn't melt away. The Egyptians got the message; lightning burned their crops to a crisp; neither rain nor hail put out the flame. Yet here again, that the just might be nourished, you downgraded the fire.

24-26 You knew what you were doing; you're the Creator. You used your might to give the unjust a loud slap; but to your own people you offered a light tap. You served up a nutritious blend of graces; using a sort of sliding scale, you saw to it that all received their minimum daily requirement. This taught your children you loved them, Lord. After all, it's not crop production that feeds the people; it's your word that sustains the world.

27-29 For example, the angel bread, which couldn't be destroyed by fire, simply melted away in sunlight. Which was another way of telling our ancestors that if they wanted to enjoy your bounty, they'd better get up and be at prayer before sunrise! Remember, the hope of the ungrateful is like an icicle in spring melting and floating as dirty water right down the drain.

POCKET HISTORY OF THE ISRAELITES
EGYPTIANS MISREAD THE SIGNS

1-3 **17** Your judgments are comprehensive and hard to sum up; that's why they made no sense to the Egyptians. They preferred to cloud their own minds into thinking they were the lords of our holy nation. In reality, they were captives of the darkness, prisoners of the night, huddled in their own houses, hiding from perpetual providence. They thought they'd hidden their sins from the public eye; but under a moonless sky they'd been discovered, quaking in their boots, afraid of the dark.

4-7 Their homes weren't a safe haven from their fear; things that went bump in the night rattled them—phantoms with sad faces silently flaunted them. They had no light source; no stars lit the horrid night. Suddenly a fire full of fear flared up; they'd imagined the worst, but this was worse still. They knew magic when they saw it, but this was real; nothing in their experience could explain it.

8-9 Supposedly, the Egyptians had a cure for every sickness of the soul, but nothing in their flimsy pharmacopeia could help. They couldn't put their finger on what was terrifying them—herds thundering, snakes hissing—they shriveled up scared to death. They just shut their eyes, trying to lock their fears out; instead they locked them inside with them.

NIGHTMARES

10-12 Wickedness would be proud if it weren't its own worst enemy; a battered conscience always has a guilty look. There's no fear quite like the refusal to accept a reasonable explanation; the less one relies on reason, the more one clings to unreason, which is a torment all its own.

13-15 Some of our enemies slept without dreams; others slept through dreams of hell; but both slept the same sleep. Sometimes they were agitated by imagined monsters; sometimes they fainted dead away; sometimes they were swamped by fear. If they collapsed, they awoke to find themselves right in the same spot but bound in solitary confinement in a prison without bars.

16-18 If farmers or shepherds or laborers faced an emergency they couldn't flee, they'd find themselves chained to others in darkness. Whether it was a whistling wind, the sweet sound of birds in the trees, the rhythmic racket of a rising stream, the thumping of a falling rock, the rumbling of herds on the hoof, the trumpeting of carnivores at play, an echo bouncing off a canyon wall—whatever the sound, it froze them in their tracks.

19-20 The next day often proved to be an ordinary day like any other; it was business as usual for most. But those who'd felt the tortures of the damned at night went about with a cloud inside their heads, sure that death was waiting for them right around the corner. The Egyptians were their own worst enemies; they lived in a place that was darker than dark.

18

1-4 During the exodus from Egypt, while it was always high noon for your friends, Lord, it was always midnight for your foes. The Egyptians were close enough to hear your people's voices, but not close enough to get a glimpse of them.

The enemy suffered from the plagues, and they wondered why your people hadn't. But the Egyptians had something to be thankful for: that your people weren't trying to right past wrongs in the present. In fact, the Egyptians sought a truce that would allow your people to leave the area. Then you presented the Israelites with a flaming pillar of fire that would light the way into a new territory; it was a hot but harmless sun and added a sense of dignity to their flight.

But the enemy had no such light. They muddled along in the dark; they'd boxed in your people every chance they had. Darkness it would be for them, then, until your people revealed the unfailing light of God's word.

5-6 Decades before, when Egypt had decided to kill the innocent infants of your people, Lord, one of the babies, Moses, was overlooked and then saved. Years later, you dispatched a multitude of Egyptian firstborns and did the same to the Egyptian army, drowning them in a sudden flood. Our ancestors had some intimation of what would happen the night of that first Passover, but they had confidence in their commitments to you and were confident in yours to them. When things actually happened as you had said, it brought them some measure of relief, stiffening their resolve to rely on the promises you'd already made them.

7-9 Thus a measure of justice was restored and the enemies of your people were being annihilated. You punished them and rewarded your people in one fell swoop; indeed, you went out of your way to do it. All during this wretched time, your good people maintained their sacrificial schedule; they even managed to get complete agreement on the Law of Moses. They'd be faithful in good times and bad, and they'd retain the ancient hymns of praise.

10-12 Coming from the enemy camp, however, was anything but music; howling echoed across the wasteland; mothers bewailed the slaughter of their children. Master and slave, king and commoner—no one escaped the punishment. Death faced them all, leaving no one to count the bodies, no one to bury them all. In a flash a whole generation was wiped out!

13-20 No one believed their firstborn would be wiped out; nothing in their menagerie of magic gave the slightest hint that this could happen. When it did, the enemy had to admit that your people, not they, were the favorites of the one true God.

It was midnight when it happened; all was calm, all was clear, when all hell broke out. From the royal throne room of Heaven your almighty word fell upon that doomed land like a heavily armed warrior brandishing a sharp sword to carry out your command. With feet on the ground and head in the sky, this Avenging Angel delivered death with every swing. The next-to-die froze with fear, their desperate lives parading before them. Half-dead, half-alive, mumbling their last excuses, they knew they were done for; their dreams had told them so.

Now it is true that the just were also touched by death; an epidemic hit your people in the desert and swept many of them away. Fortunately for them, Lord, your wrath toward them had a short timeline.

21-23 One man, a priest and utterly blameless fellow named Aaron, took up the mantle of his office; that is to say, he did what a priest was supposed to do. He prayed, offered incense, begged forgiveness—all to withstand the wrath of God and put an end to the slaughter; there was no mistaking he was a servant of yours.

He made your wrath grind to a halt. He didn't use physical force or force of arms; he just prayed until the Avenging Angel terminated the destruction. Aaron's only weapons were the religious commitments of his ancestors. The dead were falling on one another, wave after wave of them, but Aaron intervened and broke the momentum of the Avenger's attack on the living.

24-25 Aaron dressed for the occasion. His long, white, priestly vestment was decorated with the symbols of our ancestors—four rows of engraved stones on the front—and his head was topped by a majestic turban. Confronted by the high priest, the Avenger stopped in his tracks and paid his respects. Aaron had braved the wrath of God, but that was about as much as he dared do.

POCKET HISTORY OF THE ISRAELITES
WRATH WITHOUT MERCY

1-2 **19** For the Egyptians, right down to the present day, Lord, yours has been wrath without mercy. You always knew what would happen; their fate was no mystery to you. The Egyptians offered safe passage to the Israelites and sent them off with some ceremony; but you knew our enemies would renege and set out in hot pursuit. How did it happen?

3-5 While the Egyptians were dealing with their grief, making a fine funereal racket at the gravesites of their dead, they came up with the idea that their newly made "friends" in the wasteland were in reality fugitives and had to be pursued. On the one hand, the fact that your people were a danger worth considering drew them to this conclusion; on the other hand, they forgot what the real danger was. They'd suffered, but not enough; they deserved more. So, at the same time the Egyptians were meeting with another round of death, your people were undertaking a remarkable journey.

6-9 All creation was reconfigured anew along the guidelines you'd set up with a view to protect your children from harm. The cloud that followed your people every day parked over their campsite every night. When they got to the Red Sea, the fast current momentarily parted, revealing dry land and allowing them to cross without even getting their feet wet; on the other side was a grassy plain.

The whole nation of Israel passed through, their every step protected by your hand, and they experienced what their eyes had never seen before. On the other side they ran around like horses grazing on a plain or lambs flocking about on a hill. They all glorified the one who had helped them escape.

10-13   They couldn't help but remember how things had been in Egypt: Livestock were bred, but only flies were born; fisheries were stocked, but only frogs were produced. Surviving on what was no better than prison fare, the wanderers craved a better menu; and that was when a new and exotic species of bird appeared. God answered their prayer with quail, migratory seabirds that began to follow them.

As for the Egyptians, punishments for their sins dogged their every step; thunder heralded the hard times that lay ahead. The punishments fit their transgressions, the most wicked of which was their abandonment of hospitality toward strangers.

ANOTHER EXAMPLE OF NOT WELCOMING STRANGERS

14-17   This reminds me of the residents of Sodom, way back in history, who didn't welcome strangers into their homes; others of them welcomed guests, even benefactors of theirs, but when these strangers' backs were turned, they were forced into slavery. Still others—and they'll be punished for this—brought a violent end to strangers who showed up at their door.

Hosts in that town who received guests cordially and treated them with complete etiquette were even punished by their neighbors for doing so. But when these unwelcoming neighbors went to the door of a just man named Lot to complain about his hospitality to strangers, they were blinded; each had to find his way back to his own door.

THE END

18-21   The entire pocket history of the Jews can be summed up like this: The natural elements should have been in harmony, but they weren't. A harp string should have sounded a note and, in combination with notes produced by other strings, a melody should have been composed. This was what should have taken place, but didn't.

Instead, livestock were changed into fish; what swam in water began to walk on land. Fire could burn under water, even though water is supposed to snuff fire out. Flame for its part couldn't cook the food or melt the manna from above.

22   Yet all things considered, Lord, you magnified your people; you honored them; you didn't give up on them; you assisted them at all the right times and in all the right places.

SIRACH

Unlike most other books of the Bible, Sirach has an introduction or prologue of its own, provided by the fellow who discovered the manuscript. He was a young Egyptian Jew who, in the middle of the second century B.C., was rummaging in the shelves and bins of the library at Alexandria and came across an interesting work, a sort of encyclopedia of Judaica written by, of all people, his grandfather, Jesus, son of Eleazar, son of Sirach. The young man was enthralled and decided to carry the work one step further; he translated it from Hebrew into Greek, the common language of Mediterranean intellectuals, especially the Egyptian and Greek Jews, whose Judaism was apparently rather thin.

The work has much in common with the various Wisdom-personified books of the Bible, especially the Book of Ecclesiastes and the deuterocanonical Book of Wisdom. There's a grand opening introducing God, Wisdom, and the fear of the Lord. There follows a list of actual situations, many of which contain embarrassing moments, and a sage's analysis of each. It ends with another grand parade of Wisdom and a short history of the Jews, sometimes called "the chosen," from Enoch to Simeon II.

Much of the advice offered to the Mediterranean Jews a couple of centuries before Christ still has meaning and insight to Christians and others over two millennia later, especially the author's focus on fidelity to the Law ("God's word") and the commandments and precepts ("God's life-maps").

From the first centuries of the Christian era, this book of the Bible was commonly referred to as *Ecclesiasticus Liber* or *Liber Ecclesiasticus (Church Book)* or as just plain *Ecclesiasticus*; it was easily attainable and appropriate for liturgies. It is also called *The Wisdom of Ben Sira* in some modern translations. (WG)

SIRACH

Many great things have come down through God's word and the teachings of the prophets and in the commentaries on them. For the doctrine and wisdom contained therein, we have the house of Israel to thank and praise.

Those who read and understand such writing have studied the subject matter and, to a great extent, have mastered it. Those of us for whom the matter was beyond our comprehension have depended upon scholars to simplify and break it down for us.

My grandfather Jesus was one of these great popularizers. He devoted a good part of his life to poring over the sacred texts. He would never say he'd mastered the material, but he did feel that he'd acquired a certain proficiency. Is it any wonder then that he wanted to add a bit of his own wisdom—this book—to the growing literature, something to help teachers teach and followers of wisdom live the sort of life described in God's word?

That's just what my grandfather did two generations ago, and that's what I do now. All I've done, however, is translate his work from the old Hebrew into everyday modern Greek. No doubt you've heard rumors of the original; now you have a chance to read it in your own language. That's why I urge and encourage you, dear reader, to approach his work without fear and read it with care.

About my translation. My Hebrew isn't perfect, nor is my Greek. In some places I've stumbled; in others I've fallen flat. But don't worry, you'll get the drift right from the start. The various translations of God's word and the teachings of the prophets have fared better, but not by much, in my opinion.

Who am I, who addresses you in this prologue? I arrived in Egypt thirty-eight years ago, during the reign of Ptolemy VIII, Euergetes II, or Benefactor (behind his back—Physcon, or Potbelly). Browsing in the Library of Alexandria archives, I came across a manuscript in the Hebrew section—not a scroll, more like a codex or bound book. A riffle or two, and I soon realized it was not the turgid prose one usually finds on the dusty shelves. I spent some time with it and came to the conclusion that this was just the sort of book the Jews in the Diaspora needed. That's when I decided to translate it from Hebrew into Greek.

I burned many a candle working day and night on the project—translating, editing, writing, and publishing the work myself. All the while I kept in mind the audience who would most appreciate the work: those who wished to school themselves in the customs and practices of the Israelites and live the life of God's word as in Jerusalem.

1-5

1 All wisdom comes from the Lord God and has been with the Lord God from the first, even before there was a calendar to count. Grains of sand, drops of rain, number of days since time began, who's been counting? Height of sky, girth of earth, depth of sea, who's been measuring? How come the wisdom of God came first, before there was a first, and is anyone looking

into this? Before all creation, Lady Wisdom was wise, and with her stood intellect and prudence. Source of Wisdom? Best guess: the word of God Most High, his activities and eternal mandates.

6-10 Root of Wisdom—who's leaking her secret? And her nimbleness—who's trying to match it? The discipline, the science of wisdom—who grasps it? Her multifold experience—who's got a handle on it? The only one who knows all this is the Most High, omnipotent Creator, powerful King. You can't be in awe enough of God, sitting on his throne and lording it over all. Wisdom he created, breathing her into existence. Her he saw and sized up; her he fitted into all his works; every human being he arranged according to her size and weight; her he introduced to all his friends.

WISDOM IS ANCIENT AND LIVELY

11-20 Fear of the Lord—it's worthy of praise, sudden and unexpected joy, the crowning glory of the universe! Fear of the Lord will tickle your heart, produce quality days, extend your life. Fear the Lord and death will go well; you'll be blessed as you breathe your last.

Loving God for the right reason is Wisdom. She's appeared to some; the Lord's appeared with her wherever his great works are shown. Fear of the Lord—that's how Wisdom began. She uses human beings as her accomplices; in fact she is with them in the womb before they are born. From the first couple in the first garden, her insight has been paired with human intelligence, and it always will be.

Fear of God has everything to do with knowledge. Reverence of God and knowledge will guard and indeed justify hearts; it will produce a cheerful and joyful atmosphere. To fear God—that's Wisdom in her full blossom, a fruity wine with a crisp, clean finish.

21-25 Wisdom fills houses and rearranges the furniture; she stuffs attics with memories and closets with traditions. Fear of the Lord is the crown of Wisdom, the power of peace, and the fruit of salvation—all are gifts of God. Wisdom in the form of knowledge, intellect, and prudence drench like the rain; those who held fast to her rose in her estimation. To fear the Lord—that's the foundation and fountain of wisdom; her branches are ancient, but her leaves are lively.

26-32 In a wisdom collection, the faithful find the body and soul of knowledge; the sinner finds only a collection of incomprehensible expressions: "Fear of the Lord drives sin out; whenever it's present, virtue prevails." "No one who lacks fear of the Lord is justified." "Anger is an outlet for some but an outrage for others." "The patient endure for quite a while." "Pleasure always follows pain." "Good sense sometimes doesn't get good press, but others will live to tell the backstory."

In a treasury of wisdom there is a cornucopia of knowledge, but when wisdom is tossed into a trash can, there's no room for devotion to God.

FAITH AND HUMILITY

33-40 So, my children, if you desire wisdom, keep an eye on justice; God will reward you with wisdom. Fear of the Lord—that's wisdom and education.

They're not the only things that please God; there's faith and humility. Don't think the fear of the Lord is impossible, but don't seek access to the Lord unless you've made up your mind. Don't be a hypocrite in public. Watch out for that mouth of yours.

Don't trumpet your good deeds; you may fall on your face; your reputation may be dragged through the mud. God might leak your secrets to the public and reveal your true self right in the middle of the synagogue. Remember that you came to the Lord in a bad state of soul; your heart was full of tricks and lies.

WISDOM FOR BEGINNERS

1-6 2 So, my child, you want to serve God? Then get your life in order, respect others, and prepare your soul for the trials that will surely come. Tell your heart what to think; don't go to sleep on the job. Bend your ear; listen to your mind. When times get rough, keep your cool. Take a tip from God. Join hands with him. Don't slip-slide. Don't go it alone. Do the wise thing; make smart choices.

Grief will come. Bear up, and the pain will pass. Humility and patience are your virtues here. That's how gold and silver are purified; that's how the chosen are toughened and strengthened. Believe in God and he'll help you recover. Invest your hope in him and he'll lead the way. Respect God and expect one beautiful friendship.

7-13 Fear the Lord. His mercy is never far away. Don't wander off and get lost. Fear the Lord, but believe in him; your reward is safe with him. Fear the Lord, but look on the bright side; there'll be blessings and mercies galore. You who fear the Lord, love him. He'll light your candles.

Cast your eye behind you, my children, and what do you see? Some who were hopefully infused; others who were hopelessly confused. Some who were comfortable with God's word; others to whom God's word gave hives. Some who invoked the Lord; others who choked on the Lord.

The Lord won't forget. He's fond and forgiving. He'll take care of your sins at the Final Inspection. He protects all who seek the truth.

WOES AND MORE WOES

14-17 Woe to the waffling heart, the quivering lip, the pointing finger! Woe to the sinners who don't know whether they're coming or going! Woe to the faint of heart; they don't believe and won't protect themselves! Woe to you who didn't set aside provisions! Woe to you who lost your bearings! What will you do when the Lord comes looking?

18-23 Those who fear the Lord hear his word. Those who love him keep the highway in good repair. Those who fear the Lord find out what he likes. Those who love him enjoy his teachings. Those who fear the Lord prepare their hearts and humble their souls in his presence. Those who fear the Lord follow his life-maps; they don't care when the Final Inspection will come.

"If we don't do penance for our sins now," these good people say, "we'll receive the Lord's punishment, not his mercy." The Lord is great, but make no mistake about it: When his verdict is "guilty," the sentence is harsh. But then, of course, there's always his forgiveness.

PARENTS AND CHILDREN

1-10 **3** Children of Wisdom are counted among the just; their generations are known for obedience and love.

Yes, you children, listen to the advice of your parents. Follow it and you'll be saved. Parents should be honored and respected by their children. Honor your mother and father and God will wipe out your past sins; he'll help you deal with the occasions of present sins; he'll hear your daily prayer. Honor your mother and it's like putting money in the bank. Honor your father and your own children will honor you. Your prayers will be answered. You'll live a longer life. Obey your father and your mother will rest well. Those who fear the Lord honor their parents; they slave for the ones who brought them into the world. In everything you do or say, make your parents proud. They'll bless you for it.

11-18 A father's blessing enriches his children's homes; a mother's curse does major damage to a family. If your father messes up, don't spread the news; his shame does no good for you. A man's reputation comes from his father. A mother's disgrace filters down to her daughter. Child, support your father in his old age; don't do something that will make him sad. If he shows signs of senility, give him a pass. Don't turn from him in his last days. Caring for a father won't go unnoticed. If your mother lashes out, give her some space. Your reputation will increase. In the day of trial you'll be remembered and your sins will melt like ice in the sun. Dump your father, and people won't forget it; make your mother mad, and God won't forget it.

MORE ON HUMILITY

19-26 Child, work hard but don't trumpet your success; you'll be ranked above the one who gives but expects something in return. No matter how great you become, humble yourself at every opportunity; you'll find appreciation in the presence of God. Many think they're high and mighty, but God reveals his mysteries to the humble.

God's power is great, and yet he's honored by the humble. Things beyond your reach—don't spend much time on. Things too complicated for you—don't waste energy on. Things God asks of you—always give some thought to. God has many varied works, but you don't have to poke into every one of them. You don't have to see with your own eyes everything that's been hidden from you. Don't get lost in endless divine detail. A whole bunch of things already have been shown to you, even though they're beyond your comprehension. Much human time has been wasted trying to figure out the universe. Judging things solely on how they appear on the surface has its limits. There's no light without an inner eye, no wisdom without a contemplative mind.

HEART CONDITION

27-32 A hard heart comes to a bad end. An adventurous heart dies of danger. An undecided heart chokes at the fork in the road. A depraved heart is victimized by the scandal sheets. A sick heart will be weighed down with pain. A sinful heart heaps sin upon sin. A proud heart has no remedy. A fruitless heart suffers from canker and rot.

But there's a remedy. The wise heart understands the words of the wise, the cocked ear desires wisdom. The well-instructed heart refrains from sin; in works of justice it meets with success.

CARE FOR THE DOWN-AND-OUTERS

33-34 Water puts out fire; charitable giving pays off sins. God looks out for those who are grateful. He won't forget them in the future; in emergencies they'll find sure footing.

1-11 4 Child, don't defraud paupers of a charitable gift; don't turn up your nose when a poor person passes. Don't make the hungry cry for their supper; don't refuse to acknowledge the presence of people just because they're broke. Don't make the homeless feel bad; don't make the beggar beg. Don't blow up at a supplicant's simple request; don't insult the borrower with your disdain. Don't take your eyes off the powerless when you are upset with them; don't curse them; don't give them cause to curse you back. If they hold you responsible for their misfortune, the Creator should handle their complaint—not you.

Make yourself approachable to everyone in your house of worship. Humble yourself to the leaders; bow your head to your betters. Incline your ear to the less fortunate. Don't patronize them, but give them their due. Respond courteously to them with non-inflammatory words; protect them from those who'd do them harm. Don't be afraid to make snap decisions in this regard: To the orphan be a parent; to the widow or widower be a spouse.

Do all these, and you'll be obedient to the Most High. God himself will cradle you more than any mother does her child.

REWARDS OF WISDOM

12-22 Lady Wisdom breathes life into her children and takes care of those who seek her out. To love her is to love life. Those who wait in line for her experience sweetness from the Lord. Anyone who won't let go of her will inherit glory. Wherever she makes a grand entrance, God gives a blessing.

Wisdom's regulars are in the service of the Holy One. Those who love her also love God and God loves them. Those who listen and learn from her will judge nations. If they get a good look at her, they will remain confident in the midst of adversity. Whoever believes in her will have her forever—they will pass her on to their heirs.

When Wisdom picks out a person for special instruction, there's a trial period. She induces fear and terror in first-timers—just to see them in action and test them under fire—until she's embedded herself in their thoughts and knows she can rely on them. She'll strengthen them, shape them, lighten their steps with joy. She'll reveal her secrets to them and confer upon them the jewels of knowledge and justice.

If they mess up, however, she'll leave them behind, even hand them over to their enemies.

DOS AND DON'TS

23-36   Child, do make good use of your time and do go out of your way to avoid evil. For your soul's sake, don't become bamboozled. There'll be confusion, yes—sometimes about sin, sometimes about glory and grace. Don't let anyone face you down and don't let anyone lie about your reputation.

Don't respect the neighbor who tells white lies. Don't refrain from speaking wisdom when the occasion presents itself. Don't dress up your wisdom in clever disguise.

People recognize wisdom when they hear it—they understand it in the give and take of language. Don't whittle away at the truth. Don't trip up on what you don't know. Don't freeze up when you confess your sins. Don't collaborate with another to commit a sin.

Don't resist the current when it carries you downstream; don't try to swim back upstream. Don't let a day pass in the fight against your enemies—God will knock their blocks off. Don't be quick to speak or slow to act. Don't be like a lion in your household, rousting your domestic servants, rampaging against your family. Don't open your hand when it's time to receive; don't close your hand when it's time to give.

1-11   **5** Don't rely on your assets. Don't say, "I have enough to live comfortably for the rest of my life."

There's no need to be a long-distance runner, no need to take a stroll through the garden of evil.

Don't say, "I'm not a pushover for anybody" or "Who'll topple me from my pedestal?" Why? Because a vindictive God will knock *your* block off.

Don't say, "I've sinned and I'm already forgiven!" The Most High will reward your confession when he's good and ready. Don't be over-confident about forgiveness, and for sure don't commit another sin just because you can. Don't say, "The Lord's capacity for forgiveness is great, more than enough to forgive my own sins." Why? Because the Lord can deliver his wrath quickly, while sinners are notoriously slow-moving targets.

So don't be slow when turning toward the Lord; don't put it off until tomorrow. His wrath will be pre-emptive; you'll never see it coming. Don't set your heart on your stash of ill-gotten goods, for on the day of calamity your financial empire will crash. Don't set sail every time a breeze comes up. Don't wander in just any direction. Every sinner speaks with a false tongue.

12-17   Do, on the other hand, stay on the straight and narrow. Rely on your senses, your discernment, and your knowledge. And may peace and justice be your constant guides.

Be quick to hear the words of others and get their drift, but slow to offer a response. If you have an informed opinion, respond to your neighbor; if not, keep your mouth shut, lest you embarrass yourself.

You can be either mean or nice in your conversation. Remember that words can be your downfall. When you gossip, everything is ruined; the first victim of gossip is yourself. You can tell thieves by the guilt written all over their faces and you can tell gossipers by their whispers—nobody wants to be around them.

GOOD FRIENDS AND BAD

1-4 6Words can cause both major damage and minor damage, so be careful not to turn your friends into enemies by your words. The descendants after you will inherit your name and your shame. That's what happens to every greedy, trash-talking braggart. Don't cloud your mind into thinking you're something special, lest your self-image trip you up. That would be like a worm eating your foliage, ruining your fruit, leaving you like a dead tree in the middle of nowhere. A nasty soul will destroy itself, much to the joy of the person's enemies and the laughter of the godless.

5-12 Good mouths multiply fans and mollify enemies; a cordial tongue wins friends and influences people. A thousand people may get to know you, but bare your soul to only a few. If you have a friend in the making, don't rush to bare your innermost thoughts. A chance friend may not be a friend for all seasons, especially when it comes to the Final Inspection.

There's the friend who turns amity to enmity, revealing all your confidences. There's the friend who loves to join you at the table but is nowhere to be found on the day of necessity. There are good-times-only friends who act like your long-lost relative, hithering and thithering your domestics as though they were theirs. If you suffer financial reversals, however, they all turn against you—all of a sudden they're history and nowhere to be found.

13-17 Get rid of these "friends" and pay attention to your real ones. There's the faithful friend, a strong protection against the storm. Find a friend like that, and you've found a treasure. There's no substitute for a faithful friend; they have a goodness money can't buy. The faithful friend is a life-extender, an elixir of life. Those who fear God know such a friend when they meet one.

Fear God and you'll discover a unique friendship, for the friend you find will be God himself.

THE PAYOFF FOR FOLLOWING WISDOM

18-37 Child, go search for Lady Wisdom while you're young; when you're old, you'll know where to find her. Think of her as one who ploughs and sows; in good time, the fruit will ripen. In making this happen, you'll have to put in some sweat equity, but in the end you'll enjoy fruits beyond compare. To the unschooled, Wisdom is too hard; they'll spend as little time with her as possible. To them Wisdom is a menace—the sooner they get rid of her, the better. *Discipline* is her second name, and for that reason few of them have made her acquaintance. For those who do come to know her, though, she's the ticket to the presence of God.

Listen, child, and take my advice; don't ignore Wisdom or toss her in the closet. Instead, slip your foot into her shackles and your neck into her chain; put your shoulder under her and carry her aloft; don't make a fuss over the constraints. Approach her with all your soul; use all your strength to follow her ways. Where is she? Flush her out and you'll find her; embrace her and never let her go. In the end you'll find rest in her and she will be an absolute delight. Her fetters rather than her formidable jewelry will be her protection; her choker will·be turned into a pearl necklace. Her décor is golden; her chains are really purple ribbons. You too should don her designer gown and wear her joyful crown.

Child, pay attention to me and you'll learn something. If you adjust your soul, you'll be wise. If you love to learn, you'll welcome the education. If you bend an ear, you'll hear something important. Take your stand in the middle of the synagogue leaders. Join the crowd of Wisdom followers. Fulfill your vocation to hear her every erudite discourse and understand her every wordy proverb. If you discover Wisdom experts, take them to lunch; may your feet wear down the steps in front of their residence.

Finally, child, keep your thoughts on the life-maps of the Lord. Be a stickler where divine directions are concerned. God will firm up your desire to get to know Wisdom, and it will be granted.

EVILS TO AVOID

7 Don't do bad stuff and bad stuff won't do you in.

1-17
Leave Sin City behind; it'll get along without you. Child, don't plant seeds of injustice; you'll only harvest sevenfold of that awful stuff. Don't look for a seat of power from the Lord; don't seek a seat of honor from the king. Don't tell the Deity how good you are; he's read your heart already.

Don't appear before a public official as a know-it-all. Don't enter the judicial track unless you're fit to fight the politics. Don't let a potentate stare you down. Keep scandal out of your resume. Don't shame yourself on public occasions or embarrass yourself in one-on-one situations.

Don't become a serial sinner—one sin's enough to punish you forever. Don't pussyfoot around on difficult social justice issues. Don't look down on praying or charitable giving. Don't say, "God will be amazed at the number of gifts I bring to the bargaining table. And when it's my turn to make a deal with him, he'll just love my offerings." Don't ridicule another human being who's brought no cash to the table. God's the one who praises and punishes.

Don't plant a lie against your brother or sister; don't breathe a falsehood against your friend. Don't spout one lie after another—that's a very bad habit. Don't talk nonstop when you're addressing your betters; and especially don't pray nonstop when you're addressing God. Don't hate laborious work or day-laborers, certainly not the agricultural ones down on the farm; they're created by the Most High. Don't show off among the uneducated.

The funny thing about the disdain of others: Sometimes you see it coming, but mostly you don't. Instead of puffing yourself up, humble your spirit and then humble it again. Otherwise, all you've got to look forward to is fire and worms.

DOMESTIC AND PASTORAL ADVICE

18-30 Don't exchange a friend for a bag of coins. Don't sell your sibling for a sack of gold from the port of Ophir. Don't discard a spouse who's sensible and tasteful; you picked your husband or wife out with the Lord's help, and that's more valuable than all the gold in Ophir. Don't abuse the day-laborer who does an honest day's work for an honest day's pay. Don't undervalue your slaves; don't defraud them of their liberty; don't dump them without any resources.

Do you have livestock? Keep an eye on them. There's no need to thin the herd; if they are dependable they have value.

Where are your sons? Show them who's boss; break them in as though they were bred from the herd. Any daughters? Keep them under lock and key; don't be indulgent with them; don't give in to their petty requests. Hand a daughter over in marriage with all ceremony, but only give her to a man of some sensibility. If you have a decent wife, don't divorce her. If she's not all that decent, however, don't trust her for a minute. With your whole heart honor your father. Don't forget to mourn your mother. Remember, but for your parents you'd never have seen the light of day. What tribute can you give to them who gave you so much?

31-36 Fear the Lord with your whole soul. Revere and respect his priests. With your whole strength love him who made you. Don't dump on his ministers. Honor God by honoring the priests and giving them that portion of the tithes due them: firstfruits, purifications, a few things you could use yourself. Give them the best part of the sacrificial animal and don't forget all the other oblations and offerings.

Then, to culminate your propitiation and benediction, turn your complete attention to the poor.

37-40 Give generously to all the living and don't be less generous to all the dead. Do spend quality time when consoling the inconsolable and don't hesitate to weep with them. Don't be reluctant to visit the sick and infirm; they'll inspire you more than you help them.

Finally, remember, the last day will come when it will come. That—if nothing else—should prevent you from sinning again.

CAUTIONS AND PRECAUTIONS

1-7 **8** Don't challenge the powerful; you may find yourself the target. Don't mess with the rich; the rich will always trump the poor. Gold has stopped the heart of Midas; silver has turned the heart of the mighty. Don't browbeat loudmouths; you'll only fan their flame. Don't treat people who are slow of mind as fools; their brilliant offspring may well return the compliment to yours. Don't despise people who repent and turn away from sin, or call them "losers" or worse; we're all subject to making mistakes and seeking forgiveness.

8-12 Don't spurn senior citizens; some of them may live a lot longer than you do. Don't point out the flaws in their wise sayings; familiarize yourself with their proverbs and learn from their wisdom. Don't consider their stories to be pure drivel; they learned them from their forebears. You can gain real understanding from them, things to draw on when you're on the spot. So don't dance on the graves of the elderly if you don't want them to dance on yours.

13-18 Don't light a fire in sinners by arguing with them; a spark from their flame might turn you into a torch. Don't square off against known liars; they'll turn your words against you. Don't lend to a person who has more than you or guarantee a loan for someone else (and if you've already done so, you might as well write it off as a loss). Don't try to score style points with judges; they prefer rational arguments that make sense. Don't take to the road with people with rage in their heart; you're the one who will suffer. They'll leave you by the wayside and you'll perish because of their folly. Don't joke around with angry people or agree to go off with them; they're happiest when blood flows and might overcome you when you're alone.

Don't reveal your inmost soul to fools; they'll broadcast your secrets to the world. While with strangers, don't let slip a secret; there's no telling whom they'll leak it to next. Don't open your heart to just anybody; that very person may rob you of your happiness.

ADVICE TO MEN

1-13 9 Don't be jealous of the wife you married; she may return the compliment. Don't give a woman the key to your heart; she slips into something silk and saps your strength. Don't approach a woman of the world; she'll sweet-talk you into her bed. Don't approach a liar with a lyre; you'll soon be singing her song. Don't stare at a virgin in a crowd; don't get caught with her in the powder room. Don't fool around with prostitutes; they may snatch your soul as well as your money. Don't prowl the streets of the city at night; don't stand on the corner watching the girls go by. Avert your face when you see a well-turned-out woman; don't give her the impression you're shopping around. Many a man has been ruined by a beautiful woman; lust leaps into life like a spark into fire. Don't recline at the table with someone else's wife; don't sip wine with her propped next to you. Your heart may fall into her lap; your blood may tip you in her direction.

VARIOUS PIECES OF GOOD ADVICE

14-15 Don't toss an old friendship away; your new friend may not measure up. A new friendship is like a wine; the older it becomes, the better it tastes.

16-17 Don't envy the celebrity and wealth of sinners; you don't know what comeuppance awaits them. Don't be troubled by the prosperity of wrong-doers; they won't enjoy a moment's peace on the road to perdition.

18-20 You may be waylaid by someone who means to kill you, but you'll never be waylaid by fear of death. If gangsters happen by, make no sudden moves; they'll take your life as easily as look at you. You're walking across a field of traps and snares; you're walking on nets about to be yanked.

21-22 Pass the time of day with your good neighbors; enter into conversation with the wise and prudent. Argue with smart people about the great issues; pursue trains of thought leading to the Most High.

23   Invite like-minded people to your dinner parties. Take pride in your mutual fear of the Lord. Let the high point of the evening be your awe at creation.

24   Artists will be praised for their artifacts; princes will be remembered for their speeches; elders will be honored for their proverbs.

25   In a civilized society, the blabbermouth is a curse. Worse is the one who shoots from the lip.

THE PERFECT GOVERNMENT

1-5   10 A lackluster leader will weaken a nation, but it will be stiffened if its leaders are strong. Power on earth lies in the hand of God; he'll raise up a suitable ruler every time. Human prosperity resides in the hand of God; that honor will be reflected in the work of good government. The courts will educate the people; the administrators will see to the public order. Public officials will be model citizens; the ruler will fare no better than the ruled.

PRIDE AND PREJUDICE

6-11   Don't try to get even with neighbors for their past faults; don't do anything out of pride. Before both God and human beings, pride is hateful; every deadly sin is equally detestable.

Revolutions take place; power changes hands; bribery, embezzlement, injustice are the main causes. No one is grubbier, shabbier than the greedy; their soul is always for sale to the highest bidder. Not even earth and ash should be proud; every day everything dies a little. A long illness makes doctors sad; a short illness makes them happy. Every potentate has a short life; a king is alive one day and dead the next. When people breathe their last, their body attracts snakes, beasts, and worms.

12-21   Pride's the sin when you storm out of God's presence; you've withdrawn your affections from your Creator. The beginning of all sin is pride. When you're up to your nose in self-righteousness, pride will pull you under in the end.

The Lord has created plagues, customizing them to destroy the proud forever. In the empty seats of power God has placed the meek and the mild. The roots of proud nations God has uprooted; in their place he's sown humility. The lands of the Gentiles were ploughed under by God, leaving not a trace behind. He has parched them, dried them out, erased them from collective human memory. With the proud, he's buried their history; with the humble, he's preserved their memory.

22-25   Men and women created pride and anger, not God. Human seed is an admirable commodity, but only if it fears God. It quickly loses its potency when it strays from the life-maps of God. Leaders are honored when they follow them; ordinary people who follow them should be likewise acknowledged. The traveler, the foreigner, the pauper—Lady Wisdom is accessible to each and every one of them.

26-30   Don't look down upon honest people if they're poor; don't look up to sinful people if they're rich. The magnate, the judge, the politician—they're held in high esteem, but in no higher esteem than a person who fears the Lord. The one who's free and ignorant is in second place to the slave who's educated. The wise won't whine when they're reproved. Don't blow your own horn in good times; don't apologize for your failings in bad times. Better, the person who works hard and has enough to eat; worse, the one who loafs a lot and has nothing to eat.

31-34   Child, honor your soul and keep your dignity intact; give them room and board and a proper education. Who'll think twice about those who sin against themselves? Who'll honor those who dishonor their own soul? The poor may be honored because of their education and fear of the Lord, and the rich may be honored for their wealth; but whoever's honored though poor may well be honored again upon becoming wealthy, while whoever's dishonored though rich may well be dishonored again upon becoming poor.

1   **11** Lady Wisdom will raise up the heads of those bowed low; she'll seat them at the head table with the world's great magnates.

Miscellaneous Bits of Wisdom

2-6   Don't praise people for their good looks or blame them for their plain looks; the life of a bee is but a flit, a buzz, but her homemade honey is heavenly.

Don't wear flashy clothes; don't prance around as if it were Awards Day. Such awards as there are belong to the Most High; he has medals and decorations, but not for display.

Many tyrants have been bumped from their thrones only to be replaced by people nobody knows. Many politicians have fallen into utter disgrace; many celebrities have been victimized by rumor mills.

7-9   Before you interrogate, keep an open mind; after you've interrogated, make the right decision. Until you've heard a party out, don't interrupt; when someone else is speaking, don't break in. In an affair that doesn't affect you, don't get involved; don't be a party to a venture cooked up by crooks.

10   Don't overcommit yourself. No matter how fast you go, you still can't outrun disaster; if you are in hot pursuit, you still won't catch up; if you're the one being followed, you won't get away.

11-13   Some people labor and hustle and sacrifice, but their lives are none the richer for it. Others are feeble and without defense, have lots of physical complaints and more poverty than they can handle, but the eye of God can spot some goodness in them; he helps them up, dusts them off, and raises their heads. Many people are astonished at this divinely inspired change.

14-17   Good and bad, life and death, poverty and honesty—all come from God. Wisdom, education, knowledge of God's word—these too are the provenance of the Lord. Error and darkness have been created by sinners; those who wallow in evil will grow old with evil. God gives his gifts to the just; he'll welcome them into eternity.

18-20 One can become rich just by spending little; the accumulated wealth is its own reward. That rich person says, "At last I can rest, take some time off. Now I can eat well, but not too well, even though I still eat alone." But the rich sometimes forget that time passes and death approaches. They'll have to leave everything behind and die, just like everyone else. The moral? Stand firm in your commitment to Wisdom and know what's involved—that is the work of a lifetime.

21 Don't be bowled over by the lifestyle of sinners; it's more stylish to confide in the Lord and enjoy life with him. As God sees it, anytime he wants to he could swoop down on the poor and fill their pockets with gold.

22-27 God's blessing may come upon us as a swift reward; it may bloom faster than we expect. When you get such a blessing don't say, "What am I going to do with this?" or "What's in this for me?" or "I've got quite enough of this already!" or "This is just more clutter." In good times don't forget the bad times; in bad times don't forget the good times.

28-30 When death comes to call, God draws up the final tally on each person in a fair and just way. The affliction of this final hour can make us forget a lifetime of delights. At the end, we all leave behind a lot of baggage. So don't praise people before their death; we are fully known only at life's end.

31-36 Finally, don't bring total strangers into your house; they can fleece you in a thousand different ways. Such con-artistry is like a partridge being lured by crumbs into a cage, like a deer drawn by a scent into a trap, like a salesperson closing a deal on an unsuspecting customer. That's how scammers work—worming their way into your confidence. But ultimately they give themselves away, turning good into bad, pinning their calling card on the corpse. A bonfire can leap from a single spark; blood can spurt from a single scratch; the spy lies in wait for the final betrayal. Keep an eye on your malevolent guests; they give you a choice of delicious evils—pick one and you'll be punished forever. Admit an interloper into your house and you'll be subverted into a whirlwind; you'll be turned into the bad guy. Then you're the one who'll be tossed out of your own house.

1-12 **12** On the other hand, do good deeds for strangers—get to know them; there'll be gratitude enough to go round. Do good to a person who deserves it and you'll be recompensed big time—if not by the person then by the Lord.

No good reputation, however, is due cheapskates. They're misers when it comes to charitable gifts; there is no affection for them from the Most High. If they did penance, of course, it would help their case.

Give to the merciful but not the sinful; the ungodly have something else coming their way—punishment. Give to the good; don't bother with the bad. Be kind to the humble, but not to the proud. Keep the instruments of war out of bad people's reach; they'll turn them against you. Do sinners a good deed and they'll do you two bad deeds.

Truly the Most High has no affection for sinners; what he does have for them is a surprise at the Final Inspection.

In prosperity everyone's your friend; in adversity everyone's your enemy. In good times enemies make good friends; in bad times so-called friends are the first to disappear. Never believe a thing your enemies say; their word is like green rust on a copper pan. If they play humble and pretend they're nobody, alert your soul and keep your distance; to them you're a living reproach. They polish the pot as hard as they can, but they can't rub off the rust entirely.

Don't stand next to them; don't let them sit on your right. They'll just slip by you and ask if the place is reserved.

That's the end of my little advice list. Go and do what I did.

FRIENDLY ENEMIES

13 When a snake bites a snake charmer, who feels sorry? When a lion bites a lion tamer, who is surprised? That's what happens when you hang out with a felon: You're guilty by association, but your punishment is postponed until the Final Inspection. "Friendly enemies" stick with you for an hour; if you flinch, they flee. They say one thing to your face, but in their heart they think the opposite; they plan to dump you in the nearest ditch. They shed tears when they want, but given the chance they'll go for your jugular. If bad stuff happens to you, they're at your side; but their help does more harm than good. They nod, offer a reassuring hand, and whisper sympathetically, but their villainous faces send another message.

SUFFERING RICH FOOLS NOT-SO-GLADLY

1-11 **13** Touch tar, and you'll sport it till it wears off; hang with a proud person, and you'll learn prideful ways. Don't carry more than your weight class; that is, don't hang with the rich and famous. What'll the clay pot say to the black kettle? When they meet, the pot will break.

When the rich steal, they yell their innocence; when the poor are hurt, they have to apologize. If you have what the rich want, they'll take it from you; if you have nothing, they'll drop you like a hot potato. If you have anything valuable, they'll move in with you, take over the house, remove its contents, and won't bat an eyelash. If they need you long-term, they'll feign congeniality, deceive you with hope, give you small presents. "What are your needs?"—that's what they'll ask. They'll kill you with hospitality, but eventually they'll scare the living daylights out of you. In the end, they'll have no respect for you. When they see you on the street, they'll look the other way, shaking their head at what a wretch you turned out to be.

Humble yourself before God; in return you can expect a helpful hand. Don't allow yourself to be humbled by a rich fool. Don't let a rich fool ridicule wisdom; don't be seduced by a rich fool into doing something foolish.

12-17 If you're invited by a person from the upper class, decline; that will surely provoke more invitations. Don't approach the rich directly, because they might think you are a stranger, but don't stray far, or they just might forget you. Don't affect familiarity with the rich. Take what they say with a grain of salt. Shoot your mouth off and they'll slowly pick your argument apart. Their "rugged individual" rhetoric will slice you and dice you; their evil charm will drape you with chains. Watch your step; take seriously the danger you are in. The street you're going down is more perilous than you think. If you hear a sound in your sleep, rouse yourself from your dreams of upward mobility.

PREYING ON THE POOR

18-25 Love God; invoke his name; he'll come save your life. Every animal likes to hang out with its own kind; every human likes to socialize with another human. Every species forms its own herd or pride; every human has a family, race, nation. What would a wolf have to say to a lamb? What would a sinner have in common with a saint? What peace does the hyena offer a dog? What do the rich have to offer the poor?

As the lion stalks the wild ass of the desert, so the rich prey on the poor. The proud hold the poor in contempt; the poor disgust the rich. When the rich crash, their friends rush to help; when the humble tumble, everyone passes by. When a rich swindler has been swindled, there's no shortage of consolers; they even join in trash-talking the perpetrator. When the humble are deceived, however, they're roundly denounced; when they tell the truth, no one believes them. When the rich speak, there isn't a boo or a catcall; the audience breaks into thunderous applause. But if a poor person speaks to the same audience, they ask, "Who is this simpleton?" If the poor make fools of themselves, they're drowned out with jeers.

Wealth is good only when the conscience is sinless; poverty is bad only when the conscience is sinful. You can tell a good person from a bad person by the expression on their respective faces. A happy face is the sign of a good heart; such a thing exists, but it's hard to find.

THE HAPPY AND THE UNHAPPY

1-10 **14** Blessed are those who haven't committed a blooper and bitten their tongue in instant remorse. Happy are those whose conscience is clear and who don't cut themselves off from hope.

Unhappy the misers who always want another million—or just "more" than the next person. At some level, they realize they are gathering things for other people who will enjoy them after their death. So if these hoarders can't feel good about their possessions, how can they possibly do any good for others? They never enjoy their own wealth, so they feel cheated; nothing is worse than that. It is a pitiful punishment for a life of miserliness. If ever these sad people did a good act, they can't remember it; maybe they will near the end, but then it will be too late! Their spiritual eye is livid, ashen, black and blue; they avert their glance; they despise everyone else. As rich as they are, they can't begin to satisfy themselves. They consume everything in sight, but whatever they swallow doesn't satisfy them. They lose their taste buds; nothing looks good on the menu.

DEATH IS ON ITS WAY

11-21 If you do have a stash of cash, of course take care of yourself and your family; but then make the appropriate offerings to God. Remember, death approaches, never missing a step. The list of the hell-bound hasn't been finalized, so there's hope still for you, but it's fading fast.

Before death comes, do a kindness to a friend; extend a hand to the poor; do what you can for someone else. Don't miss your fair share of the good things in life; enjoy the smallest blessings while you can.

Don't forget to make your will and divide the fruits of your labors equally among your family and friends. Engage with others; take some time for yourself. While you're still alive, don't forget the joy of justice; when you're dead, you won't have to worry about it—there'll be nothing left you can do.

Flesh wrinkles, clothes sag, fruit drops in the orchard, everything withers—so goes the generation of flesh and blood. One thing dies, another is born. The corruptible crumble in the end; artists die with their art. Yet every significant work will be labeled; every artisan will be identified.

BUNDLE OF BLESSINGS

22-27 Blessed is the one who lingers with Lady Wisdom, who meditates on justice, who contemplates the eye of God. Blessed are those who thread their way through Wisdom's heart, flush out her hidden places, track her down, find her route and stick to it, peek through her window, listen at her door, take up rest near her house, attach their residence to hers. There a bundle of blessings may always be found. They'll enroll their children under her roof and reside under her branches; in her shade, protected from the heat, they'll rest in her glory.

THE SEARCH FOR WISDOM

1-6 **15** Those who respect God will always do the right things; those who study God's word will always judge well. They'll meet Lady Wisdom as an honored mother; she'll receive them as a virgin bride. She'll serve them an end from the wisdom loaf and pour them a draft from the wisdom well. They'll lean on her lest they go all limp; they'll listen to her and nod in agreement. She'll buck them up in front of their neighbors. In the middle of common prayer, she'll help them speak. She'll fill them with the spirit of wisdom and knowledge. She'll vest them with a robe of glory. She'll fuss over them, clothing them in joy and power. She'll make a reservation for each of them under their eternal name.

7-10 The oblivious people bump into Wisdom without recognizing her, just as most of the smart ones do. The sinners see her but don't like her. The arrogant are far from her because of their painful pride. The liars say they remember her, but they really don't.

It is the honest who hang out with her. They make progress with her help as they trundle toward the Final Inspection.

Fountains of praise for her won't be coming from a sinner's mouth; such praise comes from God's mouth, from the throats of the wise praise for her will rise.

WHAT ARE THE CHOICES?

11-22 Don't say, "My sin is God's fault." That's a hateful thing to say; besides, it's not true. Don't say, "He made me do it!" That's not true either; God has no need of you. The Lord hates every expression of error, and those who respect God don't like errors either. God was there at the creation. He created humankind with thoughts and ideas, likes and dislikes. He added his life-maps, then topped it off with intelligence and understanding. If you follow God's life-maps, they'll take care of you; if you keep the faith, you'll live God's life. He puts water and fire at your disposal; do with it what you want. The choices are life and death, good and bad—pick one and you'll have it. God's wisdom is great; his strength, massive; his surveillance, continuous and extensive. God has his eye on those who respect him; he knows who does what; he commands that no one carouse; he's given no one a license to sin. Who'd want a hoard of feckless and faithless children?

GODLESS CHILDREN AND GRANDCHILDREN

1-4 **16** Don't take pride in your godless children. If the grandchildren are just as bad, don't coddle them either, for they have no respect for God. Don't expect too much from them; don't comment on their accomplishments. Better is one child who respects God than a thousand who don't. It's better to die without children than leave behind godless children.

GOD'S JUDGMENT

5-11 From one wise person you can grow a country; with one tribe of godless people you can bring a country down. My eyes have seen much; my ears have heard even more. In any collection of sinners, fire will flicker; in an unbelieving nation, fire will flare up.

For example, the fabled giants of old weren't pardoned for their sins. Those muscle-bound mercenaries thought they had the upper hand. But God didn't spare Lot's neighbors; he took them down for being so proud. He didn't shed a tear for the outlaw tribe; he slaughtered the sinners with their boots on. The body count reached six hundred thousand hard-hearted battlers, who fought side by side. If one stiff neck among them survived, it would be surprising.

12-15 Mercy and anger are both on God's side: mercy upholding, sustaining; anger flooding, overflowing. His mercy is mammoth; he adjusts it to fit the situation, judging human beings by what they do and not what they say. Sinners won't get far with their plunder; the purveyor of justice won't be embarrassed in the end. There'll be a reward for every merciful act done; all will get precisely what they deserve and what makes sense given our shared earthly pilgrimage. The Lord dimmed the heart of Pharaoh lest he dazzle him with his powerful works. The Lord's mercy is apparent to all worldly creatures. He separated the light from the dark for his children.

16-23 Look at the heavens, and the heavens beyond that! Look at the awesome deep and abundant world! All things will come together at the Final Inspection—mountains, hills, plains, plates of the earth. When God sizes them up, he'll shake them till they tremble. The human mind can't make any sense of this. Who understands God's ways? Who sees God's storms coming? Many, many of God's works are hidden, so who'll keep the populace abreast of all his justice events? God's decree is far from complete; his interrogation will continue until everything's recorded.

But some people talk this way: "In the midst of all this, God will forget all about me. Nobody on high will remember who I am or what I've done. In such a mighty crowd I'll go unremembered and unrecognized. I'm just an ant in this immense creation!"

Who has thoughts like this? The ill-informed.

24-31 Hear me, child, and I'll tell you how it really is. I'll speak knowledge with prudence, fair and balanced; I'll try to tell the story of Lady Wisdom faithfully. Listen to my words; they come from the heart. I'll speak in equity of spirit about the the virtues that God put into his creation from the start. I'll announce his knowledge; I'll impart his wisdom.

When God created his vast array of creation at the beginning, he divided it into meaningful parts and personages. He beautified his works in eternity; he identified the artisans and their creations in each generation. They neither ate nor drank but still maintained their strength. There was plenty of space for them to stand side by side without feeling the slightest pinch. From here to eternity they didn't question anything he said. After all this, God looked at the earth, assessed his work, and put on some finishing touches. Every blessed, vital, living, created thing went on parade, after which they returned to their proper place.

THE STORY OF CREATION FROM THE BEGINNING

1-21 **17** God created the first human being, a man, out of earth. He styled him along his own lines and then deposited him back onto earth. He outfitted him with characteristics very much like his own. He gave him a long life span. He put him in charge of the whole earthly enterprise. He demanded that the second human being, a woman, respect the man and vice versa. He commanded all beasts and birds to respect the first couple. God gave the two human beings wisdom and language, with eyes and ears to figure out how to use them. He filled them with intellectual knowledge and curiosity. He introduced them to the life of the spirit. He filled their hearts with sensations.

God taught the first couple the difference between good and evil; he made it clear to them that he meant business. He gave them the grand tour of his wonderful garden, allowing them time to absorb and admire its wonderful features. The first couple praised to the sky this holy place; both would pass the word about it to the next generation.

God instructed them on how to get the most out of the various wonders; he told them the secrets of how to live righteously. Theirs would be an arrangement that would last forever. He showed them justice and how it worked.

The first couple couldn't believe their eyes; their ears heard God's sonorous voice: "Steer clear of all iniquity." He told them in no uncertain terms how to behave.

No one could make a turn without God's knowing it; no one could hide from his surveillance. He installed a leader in every Gentile nation; he created a little bit of himself in the house of Israel. All the action on earth to him was like the noonday sun; he saw everything as though the sun never slept. The humans' iniquities were plain as day; their sins couldn't be stashed out of sight. He thought charitable giving was an especially good sign; generosity was especially pleasing to his eye.

After this life's over, God will show up for the Final Inspection; then he'll return all of us to the earth from which we came. To repeat offenders he'll give reprieves; to those quaking in their boots he'll give forgiveness. There will be plenty of awards for good behavior to go around.

WHAT THE CREATION STORY MEANS

22-31 Turn away from your sinful life; turn toward the Lord. Cut your sin production in half; pray before the Lord. Avert injustice; embrace justice. If the Most High doesn't like it, you don't like it. God wrote the book on justice; read it.

Don't give up as you wait in line for the final disposition and prayer. Can those in the grave praise the Most High? Which of the dead can pray better than the living, at least the ones who believe in God? Don't wallow in the error of the ungodly.

Repent before death comes; after death, repentance is too late. Confess your sins while you're living; confess while you still have your wits about you. Praise God, and you'll glory in his commiseration. How massive is the mercy of God! How great is the compassion of the Lord!

Not everything can be done by mortals; the child of mortals isn't immortal. What's brighter than the sun? Yet even the sun has eclipses. What's more wicked than what flesh and blood can cook up? There's power in High Heaven; all the rest is earth and ash.

And that's about as clear as it gets.

THE CREATURES GOD MADE

1-5 **18** The one who lives in time-without-time created everything in one fell swoop. Who could tell the story of these eternal happenings or explore the divine wonderland or explain its vast magnitude? Who would know if anything were missing? Who could inventory the total creativity of God? God alone is the undisputed King and will remain King in time-without-time!

6-11 When human beings come to the end of the timeline, they begin again; when they stop, they become anxious. What are human beings? Why are they defective? What are they good for? Can they do good; can they do evil? Average age, a hundred years, human time; mere drops in the sea, mere grains on the beach, when compared to time-without-time.

Because of the time differential, God is patient with humans; he showers his mercy upon them. He sees that their hearts are off kilter, and that's not good. He recognizes their imperfection because it sticks out. So, what's lacking he quickly resupplies; he restores them to a state of grace.

MORE PRACTICAL ADVICE

12-14   Should humans be merciful toward their neighbors? Of course! They should do what God does for them. He takes them to task, teaches them, guides them like a shepherd leading his flock. He's pleased when those who learn the ins and outs of mercy put them to work right away.

15-28   When you do good, child, don't make a big deal out of it. Every time you give a charitable gift, don't add a wisecrack or a put-down. Doesn't your insult negate the good intention? Isn't a kind word better than the gift itself? When givers are gracious, they give both. The smart aleck will always say something edgy; the self-promoter will always give something gaudy to be noticed.

Before you're judged, judge yourself. Before you speak, learn what to say. Before you fall ill, take a preventative. Before you're questioned, question yourself. In the process of visiting someone, find atonement. Before you boast, eat humble pie. Surrounded by sin, show your conversion is real. Let nothing get in the way of your praying on schedule.

Don't be slow to prepare for death; the mercy of God will be found on the far side of time. Sunrise, noon, sunset—time is such a drag for humans. But for God, time is just a flash. Before that prayer, prepare your soul; don't be tempted to tempt the Lord. Remember God's choice at the Final Inspection; when your turn comes, he can look either way.

When you eat a lot, remember famine; when you have a lot, remember poverty.

Wise people find danger in everything; on Sin Street they keep their nose clean.

Alert people know Lady Wisdom when they meet her; they'll praise anyone who bumps into her.

29   Those who have mastered language have done a wise thing; they've taken the trouble to understand truth and justice. From them wise epigrams and epithets fall like the rain.

SOME FINAL NOTES ON SELF-RESTRAINT

30-33   On self-restraint, a few thoughts. Contain your desires; curb your pleasures. If you swamp your soul with desires, your enemies will give you a standing ovation. Don't delight in all-night banquets; they'll bankrupt you before you know it. Don't eat or drink to excess when you don't have a coin to your name; you'll become your own worst enemy.

✹

WORDS TO LIVE BY

1-6 **19** Workers who show up drunk every day will never get rich; whoever skips the small things slips a little each day. Wine and sex make wise people act silly. Whoever patronizes prostitutes will die; flies and worms will feast on the carcass. The brave soul kills the fearful body; such people will be singled out of the crowd and extolled as great examples. Whoever believes too quickly will never amount to a thing; whoever sins against the soul will never appear sweet and innocent. Whoever enjoys carousing will get a deserved reputation. Those who bristle at being corrected don't care much what others think. Those who hate to be gossiped about should put a lid on their own malice.

7-12 Don't let a wicked or harsh word pass your lips; your reputation will not be lessened for holding back. Don't tell on friends or foes who have committed a sin and give them up to the crowd; people may judge you instead and end up avoiding you completely. Have you heard a bad word against your neighbor? Swallow it. Don't worry, it won't explode. A fool can't wait to pop off a juicy bit of news; it is like a woman in labor who can't wait for the baby to come out. A pointed piece of gossip in a fool's heart is like an arrow in someone's thigh—it's got to come out.

13-31 On the other hand, don't hesitate to confront friends and neighbors if you think they might have done something wrong; give them a clue what you think is going on. For starters, perhaps they didn't do what they are accused of doing—say, gossiping. If they did do it—and the crime rate on calumny *is* high—they might do it again, but perhaps they won't become repeat offenders if you say something. Try to straighten your neighbors out privately before you bring them up on charges. Don't believe everything you hear. A slip of the tongue isn't necessarily a slip of the soul. Who is there who hasn't said something regrettable?

Fear of the Lord is all the wisdom there is, because all wisdom is found in the fulfillment of God's word. So make room for it in your life. Wisdom isn't the exercise of malice, nor is there always prudence in counseling sinners who want to play around with wise sayings. Better the simpleton who thinks wisdom is a word game than the intellectual who knowingly transgresses God's word.

There's often a certain method in the madness of sinners. Those who buy a jury, why are they the ones who are always depressed and brokenhearted and stressed out? Then there are those who adopt extravagant acts of humility. They look you in the eye and pretend to be unworthy, but if you don't see them coming, they'll take advantage of you in a second. People who don't know how to sin may, given the opportunity, still manage to do so quite nicely.

A regular person usually has a smooth appearance; a wise person has a wrinkled brow. What people wear, how they smile, and how they walk—these tell a lot about them.

Once in a while, correction misses the mark; sometimes there's a hint that a verdict has been rigged. In a case like this, it's best not to say a thing. That's the prudent way.

✺

ABOUT WISE MEN AND FOOLS

1-19 **20** A kind word of correction is better than blowing one's top. Don't interrupt a person who's admitting a fault. A eunuch undressing a maiden with his eyes across a crowded floor is creepy; that's a man protesting his own castration. How good it is when sinners show repentance; that takes the wind out of the sin. The wise one enjoys quiet time; the blabbermouth can't keep his trap shut. There's the person who *doesn't* know when to speak; there's the person who *does* know when to speak. The wise won't interrupt others; they're not fools. Nobody can interrupt fools; they talk nonstop. One who uses two words where one would do or always demands the floor is a bore and impossible to like. The wise make their important points with a few choice words; the foolish take to a dictionary to try to make their insignificant points seem erudite. People with no self-control are moving in the wrong direction; they're going to end up in a blind alley or dead-end street.

Sometimes doing good dents your reputation, whereas doing tiny acts of kindness puffs it up. For example, you may buy a large amount of stuff, but you can spread the money over several businesses that need it.

Most gifts are welcome; others, the kind that come with strings attached, are most unwelcome. A huge gift from someone with no taste is something you can never use; the giver uses eyes over brains. Such people specialize in ostentation; they carry on about how great the cheap trinkets they give are, sounding off like the town crier addressing the world at large.

A lender lends one day and the next day cancels the loan; no wonder that lender is so lonely.

The foolish say, "We have no friends. We do good, but what good is good if we can't tell somebody about it?" Their dinner table is never empty—freeloaders all, who make fun of their clueless hosts behind their backs: "This food isn't served the right way" or "When the wine runs out, they have no idea what to do about it."

20-28 Better a slip on the pavement than a slip of the tongue; the final slip isn't that far away.

A person without charm is like a story without an end; it just goes on and on and on. If a foolish person tells a story with a moral, you won't get it; it's never right at the end.

Sinners who avoid sin when there's no sin available sleep with a smile on their face.

You can mess up your soul in three ways: be poorly informed; have a bad friend give you good advice; have a good friend give you bad advice.

You can make a promise to a friend, but it may not be the promise the friend wanted.

A lie is a blot on anyone's reputation; those without reputation spout lies all the time. A thief has a better reputation than a liar; no matter, they're both on a slippery slope. Chronic liars lie to themselves that they're charming; truth is, they can't remember where one lie ends and another begins.

A FINAL FEW BROMIDES

29-33 The wise use good ideas to get ahead; the ambitious just hobnob with their betters.

Those who plow the land will pile the crops up; those who work in justice will get their sweet desserts; those who follow directions won't veer off into a ditch.

Favors and gifts blind the eyes of the recipients; they prevent them from seeing the truth and telling it to the givers.

When wisdom is hidden and treasure tucked away, what's the good of either?

If you have to get rid of one of them, bury boredom before wisdom.

A COLLECTION OF SINNERS

1-14 **21** Child, have you sinned today? Don't do it again. As for your previous sins, pray they've been forgiven. Consider sin a snake; once you spot it, run for your life. Come too close, and it'll lunge and bite. Its teeth, like a lion's, will puncture and pierce, preparing to dine on you and others. Every iniquity is like a two-edged sword, a wound from which there's no recovery. Chronic injuries soon put a hole in your fortune; your proud mansion is nibbled away by termites—not a trace of the once-proud structure will be found. Requests from the mouths of the poor seem slow to reach God's ears, but the response from the mouth of God is always swift and direct. The sinner who doesn't fear God does not take correction well; the sinner who does fear God takes correction to heart. A collection of sinners is like a heap of flax; it's the best thing to start a fire with.

Cobbles on Sin Street have been worn down smooth; traffic has been heavy, nonstop, over the years. Anyone who keeps God's word comes to understand it; God's earmarks are wisdom and understanding. Whoever has poor judgment is unteachable.

The brawny can stop an opponent with their voice; the wise can stop the brawny with a whisper.

Building a house with other people's money is like collecting stones for your own funeral mound.

15-20 Street smarts are prerequisites for one thing only: evil. Education can't take place when the atmosphere is bitter. The words of the wise should flow like a flood; wise counsel should spout like the fountain of life. The heart of a fool is like a cracked urn—fill it to the brim with wisdom and it all leaks out. If saints hear words of wisdom, they praise them and try to do something good because of them. If sinners hear the same words of wisdom, they refuse to listen; they turn their hearing aids off. To fools, wise sayings are as heavy as a student backpack; to the wise, they're as light as a goose-down pillow. A voice well tuned to wisdom is needed in every house of worship; it provokes holy thoughts in people's hearts.

21-31 To fools, wisdom is a mansion in ruins, only good for architectural salvage. To spiritual dropouts, wisdom is a bundle of unpronounceable words. To fools, wisdom lessons are like fetters on their feet; wisdom readings are like manacles on their hands. The foolish person out-laughs everyone in the room; the wise person never laughs, just smiles or chuckles politely. To the wise, learning is a gold ornament; it is a bracelet on the right arm. Fools have one foot in the house next door; the wise welcome people into their home. Fools stare out from behind the curtains of their home; the wise take their regular spot in the marketplace. Fools try to eavesdrop at the door; the wise get their information directly from the source. The lips of fools tell silly jokes; the words of the wise are taken seriously. Fools locate their heart in their mouth, where it is easily accessible for them to speak whatever they feel at the time; but the wise embed their mouth in their heart, where it speaks only what has been carefully considered. Fools curse the devil; the devil curses the wise. Foolish informers dig up dirt on everyone; they and their associates are the lowest of the low. The ones who are honored are the quiet, respectable, wise ones who mind their own business.

ON FOOLISH CHILDREN AND FRIENDS

1-5 **22** Foolish slackers are about as exciting as a pet stone; booing and hissing, everyone makes fun of them. Foolish sluggards are about as interesting as a cow pie; all who come in contact with them have to wash their hands. A father can't communicate with a son who's uneducated; a foolish daughter without discipline has no value on the marriage market. A wise daughter will bring a tidy sum to her husband; a foolish daughter who messes up is no good to her father. A foolish woman with a big mouth is an embarrassment to both father and husband; they'll dishonor her, maybe even disown her.

6-13 Music has no place during the mourning period; discipline and doctrine, on the other hand, are never out of date. Teaching a fool is like piecing together smithereens; it's like telling a story to the hard of hearing or shaking awake a deep sleeper. Speaking to a snoring man wastes wisdom on one dead to the world; when the fellow wakes up, his first words are: "Who are you?" and "What are you doing here?"

Mourn for the dead, for their light has gone out; but weep more for fools, for their light was never turned on. Spare tears for the dead, because they're already at rest; spare no tears for fools, because their minds were never really alive. For the dead, mourn seven days; for fools, mourn the rest of their lives.

14-18 Don't waste time with the foolish; keep your guard up. Fools mean trouble; associating with them does no good to your reputation. Brush the foolish off and you'll keep out of trouble. You know more than you need to about their stupidity. What's heavier than lead? Isn't "lead" another name for fool? Sand, salt, iron—they're easier to lug about than the imprudent, unreliable, unholy fool.

19-23 A well-framed house won't come apart. Just as firm is the well-counseled heart; no huffing or puffing will blow the soul down. A firm heart in the act of intelligence is like a bright ornament on a white-washed wall; a flimsy fence and cheap cement job won't stand up to a strong wind. A mousy heart and anxious mind will never withstand a decent argument.

24-27 Poking the eyes produces tears, piercing the heart causes heartbreak;

both can end a friendship. Throwing a stone at pigeons sends them flying; insulting friends or acquaintances sends them fleeing. Drawing a sword against a friend isn't the end of everything; you can always sheathe the sword. If you say something necessary but sad to a friend, don't give up; there may be reconciliation—as long as insult, indecency, pride, leaking secrets, or treachery don't end the friendship!

28-33 Keep the faith with friends when they're a coin short; they'll keep faith with you when their ship comes in. When the going gets rough, stick with them; they'll stick with you when the good times roll.

As surely as fire precedes smoke—so curses, abuse, and threats precede bloodshed between friends.

Don't snub your friends on the street or look the other way and pretend you didn't see them if they snub you. When word gets around that they did, it won't help their reputation or hurt yours.

A SHORT PRAYER

"Lord, Father, and Ruler of my life, who'll guard my mouth? Who'll seal my lips? Who'll shield me from my own tongue?

1-6 **23** "Lord, Father, and Ruler of my life, don't let me listen to them; don't let me fall in with them. Who else but you will tear my thought process to shreds? Who'll discipline the doctrine in my heart? Who won't ignore my ignorance? Who won't cover up my derelictions? Who'll prevent my ignorance from increasing, my shortcomings from multiplying, my sins from overflowing?

"Otherwise, I will surely drop in the sight of my adversaries. My enemies will rejoice over my death.

"Lord, Father, and Ruler of my life, don't leave me in their hands. Don't let my eyes get that highbrow look; don't let my eyelashes get that lowbrow look. Rescue me from my huge appetites; release me from my lusts; don't let me turn into a fool."

SINS OF THE MOUTH

7-21 Child, here's what I want to teach you about your speech. If you heed my teaching, you won't run off at the mouth or be scandalized by the language of the street.

The sinner's lips are a sure giveaway; foul mouths and proud mouths say scandalous things. Don't let swearing and the use of abusive language become a habit; many can't break it, no matter how hard they try.

Don't use the name of God casually; don't trifle with the names of the saints; don't think you're immune from the punishment for that sin. Under continued questioning a slave will acquire a bruise or two, so every soul who takes the name of God in vain will rack up a lash or two.

Habitual users of abusive language fill themselves with iniquity; they fill their house with plague. Even if they empty their house, the sin is still on their clothes. If they try to cover it up, they double their trouble. If they swear in vain, they'll be judged; everyone in their household will suffer.

There are blasphemies worthy of the death penalty. You know what they are. May they never be uttered by the children of the Lord. All evils of the mouth are remote from the devout; they won't seriously wallow in such dereliction. Don't talk trash; yes, it's sinful.

Remember your father and mother, and mind your manners when you're sitting with the high and mighty. Everybody is waiting for you to make a mistake. The new street language isn't helping your case; it will make you bad-mouth the day you were born. If you become a person with a foul mouth, you'll never change as long as you live. There are many ways to sin with the mouth, but there are only a couple of ways to pay the price: God's anger and your personal perdition.

On the Near Side of the Bed

22-31 A hot soul is like a roaring fire; it won't go out until it's burned everything in sight. The sexually immoral have a fire inside, and death is the only sure way to douse it. For them, life is biscuits and honey, wine and roses, until the day they die, but those who sin against marriage put a permanent mark on their soul.

"What, me worry?" they ask themselves. "Who's looking?" They do their deed in the dark; no one else is in the room except them.

"What have we got to lose by having a little fling?" they rationalize. "The Most High can't keep track of every person's sins."

They don't understand that God sees everything; they fear others, but they don't fear God. Reflected in the eyes of every person should be the fear of God, but the sexually immoral don't understand that the eyes of God are many times brighter than the sun, scanning all the movement on land and sea, peeking in the hidden folds of human hearts. Before creation God knew every detail; after creation everything was in the perfect place for God to observe.

The sexually immoral will be arrested in the city streets or they'll bolt from the city to the country. It was supposed to be a "safe" house, but there they will be taken into custody. Everyone will know their names.

What was it about the fear of the Lord that they didn't understand?

On the Far Side of the Bed

32-38 This is the predicament of the woman who abandons her marriage bed for the bed of an illicit lover. First, she didn't know what God's word said; second, she sinned against her husband; third, she gained "sexually immoral" notoriety; fourth, she might conceive children who will have to be raised by someone else.

This woman will be brought into the assembly; her friends and family will be witnesses against her. Any illegitimate children won't appear in her genealogy, nor will they create genealogies of their own. She'll leave behind a wretched past; the blot will remain on her permanent record.

Those who look back at such proceedings know that nothing is better than the fear of God and nothing sweeter than the life-maps of the Lord. Following the Lord is a great adventure—the journey of a lifetime.

WISDOM SPEAKS

24 ¹⁻⁴ It's fanfares, ruffles, and flourishes—hail to Lady Wisdom! God echoes her praises, and so do all the people. The presence of the Most High she's well acquainted with; in plain view of God she conducts herself nicely. In the assembly of the most low she feels at home; in the holy places she's well received. In the company of the elect she's welcome; among the blessed she's a role model.

Lady Wisdom has this to say.

⁵⁻¹³ "I exited the mouth of the Most High, entering existence as the first of his creations. I saw to it that a nightlight should hang in the heavens; as an accessory I draped the earth in a tinted scarf. I've lived in the shadow of the Most High; my throne was atop a pillar of cloud. I've floated about the heavens; I've strolled the ocean bottoms. I've stood in the waves of the sea and on the hills and the plains. I've held the number-one slot wherever I've visited. I've tiptoed through the hearts of both the high and the low.

"In all my travels I was really looking for a dwelling place. It isn't that I didn't have offers, but where would I really feel at home? Then the Creator of All, with a note of authority, chimed in. Knowing I wanted a quiet, well-lighted place, he gave me a tent of my own. His words to me were: 'Move in with the house of Jacob. Cast your lot with Israel. Plant your roots with the people I've chosen.'

¹⁴⁻¹⁶ "Before the beginning, I was on the job; after the ending, I'll still be finishing up. I've done my best work in the presence of the Most High, surrounded by that tent. Likewise, I had a residence on the holy mount; Jerusalem had a comfortable, home-like feeling. I settled in with the chosen; that's what the Lord wanted me to do. There were a lot of them, but they felt like family to me.

¹⁷⁻²⁵ "I'm a mighty cedar of Lebanon, a cypress on Mount Hermon, a royal palm in En Gedi, a rose plantation in Jericho, an olive stand in the middle of a field, a palm tree full grown near the water. In the cinnamon and the balsam, I am the scent. In fine myrrh, I'm the sweet smell. Gum of storax, gum of galbanum, oil of onycha—I'm the perfume. In the censer, I'm the frankincense. In the terebinth, I'm the branches; I'm the honor and grace. On the vine, I'm the grape; in the garden, I'm the foliage. Of fair love and fear, knowledge and hope, I'm the mother. To grace and truth, I'm the way; to hope and virtue, I'm the path.

²⁶⁻³¹ "Come over here to me, one and all, who can't wait to see me. Have I got something for you! I've got bushels and bushels from my garden of virtues. My teaching is ultimate honey; my heritage is sweet milk. Who eats me satisfies a hunger; who drinks me quenches a thirst; who hears me fulfills a longing; who works with me won't commit a sin; who makes sense out of me will have eternal life."

THE SOURCE OF WISDOM

³²⁻³⁷ All these truths may be found in the covenant with the Most High, God's word that Moses commanded us to obey; it's the inheritance of the house

of Jacob. God positioned his servant David to become the king firmly sitting on the throne of honor forever. God's word, from which wisdom flows, is like the Pishon in Eden, like the Tigris in fruit-picking time, like the Euphrates at the end of growing season, like the Jordan at harvest time, like the Nile at overflow, like the Gihon at vintage time.

38-39   For the first human beings, Wisdom was a casual acquaintance; they were in no hurry to get to know her better. As for her, her audience was broader than the sea, her thoughts deeper than the ocean.

WISDOM SPEAKS AGAIN

40-47   "I, Wisdom, am a stream; from a mighty river I started like a rivulet, like a channel from the river of paradise. I said, 'I'll water the plants in my garden. I'll flood the grains in my meadow.' Lo and behold, my trickle turned into a torrent; my abundance flowed down to the sea. I begin my story well before dawn and finish it well past dark each day. I visit the unknown peoples, the ones who aren't on the maps. I take a peek at all the sleepers, rough and smooth. I illuminate all who hope in the Lord. I keep the teachings coming like prophecy; I leave them for generations to come. I instruct the progeny all the way to the holy time.

"So you see, I don't do this for myself alone. I do it for everybody who wants to find the truth."

FAVORITE AND UNFAVORITE THINGS

1-4   **25** Three things make my soul happy, as God is my witness: nations that respect each other; neighbors who are nice to each other; spouses that stick it out with each other.

These next three things make my soul unhappy; in fact, they drive me crazy: poor people who are proud of poverty; rich people who lie about being rich; old people who didn't go to school when they had the chance.

5-8   Misspend your junior years and you'll have nothing to spend in your senior years. Gray is beautiful when it comes to good judgment; counsel is handsome when elders philosophize. How appealing the wisdom of the veterans in the ranks! How sound the counsel of the proven heroes in command! A life of experience—that's the crown of the seniors among us. The fear of God—that's the glory of those who've already lived a lifetime.

9-16   I've identified nine types of humans who find happiness in their hearts; there's a tenth, which is always number one on my tongue. Those who play with their children. Those who live to see their enemies dead. Those who marry their equals. Those who don't yoke an ox with an ass. Those who keep a rein on their tongue. Those who work for someone smarter than themselves. Those who find real friends. Those who tell stories with happy endings. Those who find wisdom and knowledge. Those who fear the Lord.

Fear of the Lord is tenth on the list but first among created things. Do you know anyone who practices it? Fear of the Lord is the beginning of God's love; following fast is faith and sticking to it.

THE WICKED WOMAN

17-36 Sadness of the heart strikes everyone; and equally, no one likes to bump into a wicked woman. Any pain but the pain of the heart; any wickedness but the wickedness of a woman; any misery but the misery of the hateful; any revenge but the revenge of the enemy; any poison but the poison of a snake; any wrath but the wrath of a woman.

Better camp with a lion or dragon than bed with an evil woman. Wickedness changes her very looks; her normal face turns into that of a female bear. At dinner with her husband and their neighbors she does her thing; trying to swallow his pride, he sighs silently. There's no malice like a wicked wife's malice; truly it's a sinner's life for her. An old trooper marching barefoot in desert sand, that's a quiet man reading a book while his garrulous wife chatters on and on. Don't be distracted by a wicked woman's looks or wealth; don't fall for her wiles. Her anger, irreverence, and confusion are overwhelming, especially if she's the one who wears the pants in the family. Feigning humility and pretending sadness—that's a wicked woman for you. Hands trembling, knees buckling—that's how a wicked wife makes her husband feel. She's like the woman who committed the first sin; she's like the woman who did us all in.

You wouldn't let your cistern leak, so why would you let your wife go flirting about by herself? If she refuses to go out for a walk with you, your enemies will die laughing. Cut the wicked woman off. Sever the connection. Kick her out of the house.

THE GOOD WIFE

1-4 **26** Happy the man who's got a good wife: He'll live twice as long; she'll double his life. A strong wife puts a sparkle in her husband; she'll fill his life with peace. A good wife is a good deal; she's the reward to a man who fears God. Rich or poor, she's good for his heart. She keeps a perpetual smile on his face.

THE JEALOUS WIFE

5-7 Alas, my heart fears three things; but there's a fourth that turns my face white. The three are gossip of the citizenry; demonstrations in the streets, and lying under oath. All are worse than death.

8-11 The fourth is a wife who's mistakenly jealous of another woman. She is a pain in a husband's heart and a cause for his grief; her words are a scourge to everyone in earshot.

As a cattle yoke slips and slides, so a jealous wife shifts and changes; reining her in is like squeezing a scorpion.

A jealous wife makes everyone mad and sad; in no way can the wreckage she causes be covered up.

THE CHEATING WIFE

12-15 A cheating wife can't hide her unfaithfulness; her guilt gives her away. If you have a strong-willed wife, watch out. Given the opportunity, she may do herself harm; her actions will tell the sad tale. Don't be surprised if she no longer looks you in the eye. Like a thirsty traveler drinking from every font, she sits at every tent, opening her quiver for any and all to deposit their arrows until she can take no more.

BACK TO THE GOOD WIFE

16-24 The charm of a devoted wife will delight her husband and put some meat on his bones by virtue of her diligence. A gift from God is a wife with an open mind and a closed mouth; a wife with wisdom wouldn't be a bad thing. There's no grace like a wife who's faithful and modest; all the treasures in the world are as nothing when compared with the dignity of her continent soul. As the sun is an ornament in the sky, so the good wife lights up her husband's home. As the splendid candles on the candelabra, so the facial beauty upon a shapely form. As golden columns on silver bases, so strong legs on pretty feet. As the eternal foundation upon solid rock, so the life-map of God written on the heart of the holy woman.

THINGS I DON'T LIKE

25-27 Two things sadden my heart; a third thing makes me angry. The first two: a warrior who's fallen upon hard times and a wise person who's held in contempt. The third: one who betrays justice for sin. God will punish that one for treason.

28 Two difficult and dangerous types to look out for: a merchant negotiating in bad faith and a shopkeeper hawking a bad product.

PRACTICAL WISDOM

1-3 27 Because of worldly gain, many commit sin; anyone who seeks to be rich has a wandering eye. In masonry, shims are placed between the stones; in the marketplace, sins are slipped between buying and selling.

4-16 If you don't hold yourself firm in the fear of the Lord, your house will suffer tremors and edge off its foundations. As sifting flour leaves dust behind, so sifting ideas leave lint of their own. As pottery needs a furnace, so the just need suffering. As fruit trees need pruning, so people's words need censoring. Hear people out before you praise them; opinions reveal real values. Follow Lady Wisdom and she'll never be out of sight. Put her justice on like a priestly robe. Dwell with her, and she'll protect you forever.

As birds hang with birds, so truth sticks to those who don't tell lies. As the lion lies in wait for lunch, so the hunter of iniquity lies in wait for the kill. As the wise remain unchanged like the sun, so the foolish change like the moon.

Among the uneducated, limit your time. In the company of thinkers, linger for a while. The conversation of the lowlife is coarse; they laugh at raunchy jokes. Those who swear nonstop raise the hair on your head; their petty quarrels are ridiculous. Their arguments often lead to bloodshed; their cursing is hard on the ears.

17-24 Unveil the innermost thoughts of friends and you'll lose them; you'll never find others like them. Love your friends; keep faith with them. They have secrets, but if you reveal them, don't expect to hang with them anymore. Killing a friendship with your neighbor is like bringing about your own death. As you let go of a bird in hand, you lose a friendly neighbor, never to return. Don't bother following them; they're long gone. They've escaped like a gazelle from a trap, but not before sustaining a wound to their soul. You can no longer hunt them down. Maledictions can be mollified; reconciliations do take place. However, broadcasting the mysteries of a friend, that's just about the lowest of the low.

25-33 A person with shifty eyes is cooking up evil for sure; the best strategy is to rush off in the opposite direction. When you meet such people, they say nice things and compliment your opinions, but at the last minute their lips curl and the knives come out. I've disliked many things, and I've never liked unfaithful friends. Even the Lord dislikes them.

As a stone tossed in the air will fall on your head, so a lie that wounds another will also wound you. Whoever digs a hole will fall into it; whoever tries to trip up another will be tripped up; whoever sets a snare for another will step on it.

Make a wicked judgment and it'll return to haunt you; you won't know where it came from. Illusion and impropriety belong to the proud; vengeance lies in wait for them like a lion. Take pleasure when the just fail and you'll be caught by the same trap. Anger and furor are both detestable, yet the sinner holds on to them for dear life.

EXPECTING FORGIVENESS

1-5 **28** If you seek revenge upon another, you'll get your comeuppance from the Lord; the Lord already has you on the Revenge Watch List. Forgive your neighbors on the near side when they sin against you; in return, your neighbors on the far side will do the same. Should anyone harbor anger against another and expect to be forgiven? If you don't show mercy toward another, should the Lord still show mercy to you? Can human beings keep their anger on high and still expect forgiveness from the Lord?

ANTICIPATE DEATH AND DYING

6-10 Plan for the end times; quit stirring things up. Remember death and dying; don't forget the life-maps of the Lord. With these in mind, don't rile your neighbor and you'll do the smart thing with the Most High. So what if your neighbors are not all that smart? Quit finding fault with them and your own sin count will go down.

MOUTHING OFF

11-14 The angry person is always looking for a fight; the sinful person will always upset the apple cart; the troublemaker will always make a mess of things. The more the wood, the greater the fire; the stronger the fighter, the wilder the rage; the richer the sinner, the hotter the flame.

It doesn't take much to start a fire. A sudden disagreement can lead to bloodshed; a tongue testifying in court can lead to death. If you blow on a spark, you may light a fire; if you spit on the fire, you may put it out. The mouth blows where it may.

THE THIRD EVIL TONGUE

15-25 The first evil tongue whispers and the second double-talks—both are cursed, both wreak havoc with the peace of many. The third evil tongue sows discord, causing much commotion, dividing the peaceful people of one nation from those of another.

The third evil tongue destroys walled cities of the rich, demolishes houses of the high and mighty, cuts off people's resources, dissolves whole nations. It makes short work of the valiant; it separates them from the fruits of their labors. Those spotted by the third evil tongue won't have a moment's peace, nor will they have anyone in whom they can confide.

Strokes from a whip leave stripes on the skin, but a tongue-lashing will break a human spirit. Many have died by a sword in the mouth, but not as many as those destroyed by words of the third evil tongue. Blessed are you if you've been shielded from it, haven't walked into the third tongue's rage or been seized for its yoke or thrust into its chains. Its yoke is a yoke of iron; its chains are of brass. Death by the third tongue—death while alive—is the worst kind, worse than death in the underworld, the death after death.

FINAL SLIP OF THE TONGUE

26-30 The power of the just will not survive, but at least it won't go up in flames. Those who leave God behind fall into the fire; they'll burn, but they won't burn out. The fire will hurl itself at them like a lion; like a leopard it will tear them to pieces.

Plug your ears with thorns; don't listen to evil things; make doors and then locks for the doors. Melt down your gold and your silver; weigh your words; bridle your tongue. Focus yourself so your tongue doesn't slip at the end and you fall in the sight of your hidden enemies—the fall that causes terminal damage and ultimate death.

LENDERS AND BORROWERS

1-3 It's a kindness to lend to a neighbor; it's a way to follow the life-maps of the Lord. Lend to your neighbors when they're having a hard time; repay them on time when they give you a loan. Your word is your bond. Deal fairly with others. You have nothing to lose.

4-10 Many recipients think a loan is a gift; that doesn't make lenders happy. When you borrow from neighbors, thank them profusely and speak kindly of their financial holdings. When your loan falls due, don't grimace and grumble and ask for more time.

If you can pay in full but don't, at least offer to pay half; your neighbors will consider themselves fortunate. If you can't repay, you defraud your neighbors twice; they acquire a new enemy and receive no money back at all. You return their kindness with curses and insults; your neighbors expect honor and thanks, but all they get is a pie in the face. Many don't lend to anyone—not because they're afraid of being defrauded but because they're afraid they'll be abused.

11-26 Lend money to friends, even if they're losers; then pretend you hid it under a rock and forgot where you hid it.

When it comes to the poor, take the most generous approach. Whatever you do, don't keep them waiting for a handout. Offer a helping hand; that's the life-map. Don't send the poor away empty-handed.

The great life-maps of the Lord, that's where your real treasure lies; they'll provide you with more profit than gold. Store your treasure in the hearts of the poor; it'll be safe from evil there. Shield and spear are good against the human enemy, but charitable giving is a better weapon against the devil.

Good people make loans to their neighbors; bad people default on loans from their neighbors. Don't forget the trust your neighbors have in you; they're putting their credit rating on the line for you. Sinners spend the money they should pay back; ingrates abandon the one offering financial protection. The failed promise to repay has destroyed many; it tosses them about like the waves of the sea, turns them into fugitives or vagabonds.

Sinners who don't follow the life-maps of the Lord default on their promissory note. They diversify their debts but end up in debtors' court.

HOSPITALITY ADVICE

27-35 Give relief to your neighbors, but not beyond your means; help them along the way so they don't falter.

What human beings need most in life is water, bread, clothing, and a roof to protect them against the weather. Better the food fare of the poor under even a leaky roof than the splendid banquet of the rich but no place to hang one's hat.

Small plate, large plate—it should all be the same to you; don't listen to those who tout the ostentatious life.

On the other hand, it's a miserable life begging from house to house.

Where you find hospitality, you sometimes feel uneasy; you don't want to say the wrong thing.

When you offer hospitality, serve it with food and drink without cost; then sit down and listen to the complaints: "Hop to it! If you're the host, then be the host and set the table!" or "If that's bread in your hands, give it to me!" or "Don't sit there; I'm saving it for the guest of honor!" or "Clear the room; I'm inviting all my relatives in!"

There are two pretty hard things for hosts of some sensitivity to abide: complaints about their hospitality and degradation of lending as a profession.

BRINGING UP A SON

1-6 **30** If you love your son, keep a good set of disciplines at the ready; he'll thank you for it when he grows up. If you engage your son as a young man, you'll enjoy him when he grows up; he'll be the favorite of your household. Teach your son, and you'll send your enemy into a tizzy; he'll be the favorite of your friends. When you die, you won't be truly dead; you'll leave behind a reasonable facsimile of yourself.

While you're here, you and your son will have good times together. When you're gone, he won't die of grief nor will he appear disoriented to his enemies. You'll leave behind a host of the hearth; your enemies won't be welcome, but your friends will.

7-13 Spoil your son, and you'll be his nursemaid forever; respond to his every call, and he'll grow up a crybaby. An unbroken horse is hard to handle; an unbroken son thinks he knows it all. Pamper your son, and he'll take over the house; indulge him, and he'll disappoint you every time. Don't laugh with him till it hurts; when he grows up, he'll make your teeth grind. Don't let him do what he wants; don't overlook his peccadilloes. Tell him who's boss right from the start. Discipline the infant regularly before he can speak; if you don't, he'll grow up stubborn and not believe a thing you say; he'll be a thorn in your side. Spend time with your son. Work him hard. Don't let him embarrass you in public.

RANDOM ADVICE

14-17 Better off is the poor intellectual who's healthy and strong than the rich fool who's racked with disease. A healthy body is better than gold and silver; a healthy soul is better than a fat wallet. There's no treasure greater than corporeal health; no delight greater than spiritual health. A happy death is preferable to an unhappy life; eternal rest is preferable to lingering depression.

18-25 Fine foods that no one eats are like funereal sweets left at a tomb. What does it profit an idol who's offered food? What a shame the idol can't eat or smell!

You may try to flee from the Lord, but you can't leave your sinful baggage behind. A eunuch may embrace a virgin, but all he can muster is a sigh. Don't spread sorrow on your soul; don't tie yourself down with too many restrictions.

What makes a person tick is a heart of joy, a treasure trove of sanctity;

what makes someone happy is length of days. Indulge your soul and take care of your heart; repel all sadness trying to board your soul. Sadness causes many deaths; what's the goodness in that? Envy and anger shorten a life; brooding speeds up old age. An honest heart produces a good attitude, just as a fine meal induces a good appetite.

WELL-TO-DO AND ILL-TO-DO

1-7 **31** Round-the-clock financial management destroys the health of the rich; fretting about investments prevents a decent night's sleep; stressing leads to insomnia; insomnia leads to apnea and worse. Well-to-do people who have labored hard to acquire their wealth—if and when they take time off, they'll enjoy their perks. The ill-to-do, working just as hard, can't climb out of poverty. If and when they take time off, they're poorer when they get back than when they left on vacation. A taste for gold isn't a ticket to heaven; if the rich think that, they've made a serious mistake. The allure of gold has ruined many people; it's the surface beauty of gold that does them in. Those who give up all for gold will be sorry; every shallow person will be captured by it.

8-11 Happy are the rich who haven't a smudge on their record. Gold wasn't the only thing in their lives; they didn't put all their hopes in money and wealth. Who are these people? They deserve a toast; they have a deserved reputation for philanthropy. They've run the course and won the race; they'll be remembered forever. They could have transgressed but didn't! They could have caused major damage but didn't! Their wealth is secure in the eyes of the Lord; their reputation is secure in the history of the saints.

MANNERS MATTER

12-25 Do you ever get invited to a sumptuous banquet? Don't be the first to say the obvious: "I've never seen so much food in all my life!"

A sharp eye is good, but an evil eye isn't so good; God is not fond of the evil eye. What in creation causes more evil than the eye? The eye can weep both real tears and make-believe tears. So don't be the first to give a banquet table the once-over; don't look for the best place to dig in; don't let your runaway appetite make a fool of you; don't rush to be the first hand in the deep dish. Watch your neighbors' manners, then do what they do. Think before you act.

Don't carry on when a plate is put before you; if you stuff your cheeks, nobody will speak to you. Make believe you have manners, even if you don't. If you make a pig of yourself, nobody will sit next to you.

If you sit in the middle of the banquet hall, don't wave your hand to summon a servant. Don't be the first to ask, "Where are the drinks?" Make a small glass of wine last through the meal; a small glass won't keep you awake or upset your stomach. Anyone who's restless, cranky, and dyspeptic after a banquet is someone who's lost control. Those who are smart about eating look forward to nighttime; they all sleep soundly and each individual's soul is refreshed. If you're forced to eat more than you want, leave the table and vomit; that will cool you off. The last thing you want to do is get sick over the food.

SOME ADVICE ON MODERATION

26-29 Listen to me, child. Don't think I'm a quack. In the end, you'll thank me.

Don't boast; don't blow your work out of all proportion. That way nothing bad will happen to you. People will bless your business if it's open to charity; your philanthropy will be officially noted. The public will curse your business if it's closed to charity; that too will be officially noted.

30-42 Don't blame the vintner; the imbiber is the one to blame for getting drunk. Dipping hot iron into cold water will seal a sharp edge; likewise, soaking your tummy in wine will ensure your drunkenness. Wine is the elixir of life—if you drink it in moderation.

What would life be without wine? Can wine cheat us out of life? No, but death can. Wine is meant for enjoyment, not for drunkenness, right from the start.

Wine sets the soul a-sail with joy and pleasure, but be sure to trim the sails when the wind turns. Health of mind and body comes from drinking soberly. Wine drunk in excess creates irritable bowels, arouses anger, ruins the drinker's health. Excessive wine-drinking sours the soul, offends others, destroys the drinker's reputation. Drunkenness of the imprudent drinker makes the drunkard a target for everything you can think of; it saps strength and opens wounds.

Don't argue with your neighbors about the quality of the wine at a fine feast at their house; don't ruin the meal for them. Don't insult them. Don't make a scene. Don't embarrass them in front of others.

HOSTING ADVICE

1-9 **32** Who made you presider of the feast? Who put you at the number-one table? Mix with the crowd as if you are one of them. Take care of them all. See that everyone is properly placed and only then find your own seat. At that point, you can enjoy yourself and appreciate their praise and the recognition that goes with it. As the eldest person present, extend the formal welcome. Say a few words of introduction but know when to stop; get to the music as quick as you can. And when the music stops is no time for you to go on and on about how wonderful you are.

As a gorgeous red stone in a gold setting, so is a recital at a wine tasting. As an emerald on a golden ring, so is a string quartet accompanied by a pleasant wine. Enjoy the music even if you don't know what it means.

MORE PARENTAL ADVICE

10-23 So, child, don't let the conversation center on you. If asked a question, keep your answer short. In conversation always summarize; appear knowledgeable yet reticent. Don't attempt to impress the powerful; don't bore your elders to tears. Modesty precedes people's approval as lightning precedes thunder. When business is over, don't hang around. Head for home and shut the door behind you; freshen up, relax, and enjoy. Turn to your hobbies and other distractions, but don't sin and don't spout off as a know-it-all. To top all this, bless the Lord who made you and rewards you from his own special reserve. Those who fear the Lord absorb his teaching; those who arrive early at his gate get a special blessing. Whoever obeys God's word will be refreshed by it; whoever violates God's word will be strangled by it. Those who fear the Lord will receive just judgment; they who receive just judgment light a lamp for the Lord. The truly sinful can't abide correction; they always seem to cook up an excuse. Don't ignore the counsel of others; there's nothing to fear in their opinions but fear of opinion itself.

24-28   Don't do anything I wouldn't do; then whatever happens, it won't be your fault. Don't go the way of all ruin. Don't trip on the same stone twice. Don't take a road you don't know. Don't roll a boulder in front of your soul. Pay attention to your children. Don't overlook your household staff.

In everything you do, put your faith on alert; this is how you follow God's life-maps. Those who put their faith in God's word won't lose out at the end.

REFLECTIONS OF ALL SORTS

1-5   **33** Nothing bad will happen to those who fear the Lord—except temptation, from which God will always save them. The intelligent obey commandments and directives; they don't wreck themselves like a ship against the rocks. An educated lawyer, for example, believes in God's word; that word informs the jurist when called to plead a case. Prudent and pious lawyers will prepare their arguments and then relax and pray they'll be sharp in court; they'll review the literature, then respond—confident and well-rested—to the judge's questions.

6   The heart of a fool is like the wheel of a cart; the mind of a fool goes round and round in circles. A comedian who insults others is like someone riding a wild stallion; no matter who's in the saddle, the horse laughs last.

7-14   Why does night come after day if the light from the sun is always on? The Lord separated night from day because he could; he divided time into seasons with holidays and holy days because he decided to. Some of these God magnified to high holy days; in between was called "ordinary" time. He created humans from the earth, starting with Adam. The Lord separated the peoples because he could; he sent them off in all directions because he decided to. Some he blessed and raised up; some of these he made holy and sat near him. Others he cursed and humbled; he bounced them out of their cozy spots. Potters hold a dripping mess in their hand; they shape it, fire it, then dispose of it any way they want. So the Lord holds a dripping mess in his hand; he shapes it according to an original design.

15-18   As good is set against bad, life is set against death and sin is set against justice. So all the works of the Most High come in pairs, one set against the other. I was last in the line to go through the vineyard—after the grape-pickers, the harvesters, the vintners; but the Lord bumped me to the top of the list. I roared through the vineyard and filled my winepress. Please note that I didn't labor for myself alone but for all who labor to learn wisdom.

19-24   Leaders of the people, hear what I have to say! Rulers of the faithful, lend me your ears! While you're alive, don't give power of attorney to your son or wife, your friend or acquaintance; and don't entrust your estate to somebody else. You may have second thoughts and want it back. While you're alive and well, make no changes in your final preparations. Better your children ask you for something than the other way round. In all your works, stay in charge. Don't give up control as the end of your life nears; only at death and not before should your inheritance be distributed.

25-33   An ass's life is fodder, whip, hard work; a slave's life is bread, whip, hard work. Keep your slaves exhausted and all they will have energy for is to take a nap. When slaves are bored and twiddling their thumbs, they are thinking of liberty. Yoke and lash make a stubborn neck bend; a full workload keeps a slave's neck bent. Idle slaves are just asking for trouble; send them to work. Don't let them have a minute to themselves; leisure leads to mischief. Keep their nose to the grindstone; work's the only thing they're supposed to do. If a slave shows attitude, slap the fetters on—but not tight enough to break the skin. Always think twice before handing out major punishment.

    On the other hand, if you have particularly good slaves, consider them to be your soul mates. If they're really good, treat them like blood relatives. Remember, if you hurt slaves for no reason, they're justified in running away. If they turn against you and take to the road, you won't know which direction to turn to find them.

HOPES AND DREAMS

1-8   **34** The foolish have thoughts and hopes, but what good are they? Dreams play tricks on the lackadaisical. Those who bump into shadows or chase after the wind find their truth in bad dreams and nightmares. What we see in a dream is a picture of a face; what we see in a mirror is a real face. Can our face come clean with a dirty rag? Can our soul come clean with a dirty lie? Divinations and omens are a waste of time; the heart in pain suffers fantasies like a woman in labor. Unless you're sure your vision is sent by the Most High, don't give up your heart to it. Dreams have tripped up a lot of people. Don't put your hope in them; they deceive.

    God's word will do its duty; Lady Wisdom will do her duty.

MISCELLANEOUS REFLECTIONS

9-13   A traveler has learned many things and an adventurer has experienced many places; they have the stories to prove it. A stay-at-home has knowledge of only a few things, but a traveler's knowledge has been increased a hundredfold. I've seen many things in my travels; I've heard quite a few stories. Several times I've been in danger of death; just as many times I've been saved.

14-21   The spirit of those who fear God will live; in this respect, they'll be blessed. Their hope is in the one saving them; God has his eye on those who love him. Those who fear the Lord have nothing to fear; God is their hope and their happiness. To whom do they look? Whom do they lean on? God, and God alone. Those who fear the Lord have their eyes constantly on him; he's the powerful protector, the strong foundation, the shade of a tent, the umbrella under the midday heat. He's the guard against a fall, the nurse after a fall, the lifter of souls, the opener of eyes, the giver of health, life, and blessings. The Lord draws the life-maps for those on the road to truth and justice.

22-27   Gifts of dubious origin don't make good offerings to the Lord; they aren't well received by him. Gifts from sinners aren't pleasing to the Most High, nor are offerings from convicts and criminals. If a hundred such gifts aren't satisfactory, would a thousand be better? It's not the number that counts. When a poor person makes a humble offering, on the other hand, it's like a parent sacrificing a child.

Bread is the lifeblood of the poor; anyone who defrauds the pauper is a bloodthirsty bandit. Those who swipe the meager bread earned by the sweat of the needy might as well have murdered their next-door neighbor.

Much the same as the killer is the defrauder for hire.

28-31   The poor build, crooks destroy; what's fair in that? The poor pray, crooks curse; whose voice does the Lord hear?

If a person washes after touching the dead but then touches the dead again, what benefit was the washing? If a sinner fasts to make up for sins but then goes and sins again, who'll answer that person's prayer?

SPIRITUAL REWARDS

1-9   **35** Keep God's word, and you'll be making a peace offering; follow his life-maps, and you'll reach your destination sooner. Being thankful is like offering God fine flour; being generous is equivalent to giving him high praise. When the number of misdemeanors is down, the Lord is pleased; when the number of felonies declines, he receives that as a prayer. When you appear before the Lord, don't come empty-handed; by following God's life-maps, you are bringing a gift. The altars of the just groan under their many offerings; their sacrifices give off a heavenly aroma. The good deeds of the just are welcomed by the Lord; he won't forget who gave what.

10-19   Open your good eye if you want to give glory to the Lord. Don't downsize your offerings; they should be the firstfruits from your land. Every time you give a gift, do it with a smile; don't be a grouch when you turn in your tithes. Give to the Most High a good portion of what he's given you; open your heart and give what you can afford. Do the Lord a favor and give him the gifts he deserves; he'll return the favor seven times over. Don't offer God gifts of questionable origin; he won't accept them. Don't offer money you've received from bribes or extortion, for example. Why? Because the Lord is the God of Justice.

The poor who've been wronged shouldn't complain when the prayers of the rich-but-wronged are also heard. On the other hand, the rich shouldn't think poorly of the wails of an orphan or the cries of a widow. Don't the tears running down their faces cry out against the killer of their father and husband? Their prayers of grief rise all the way to the heavens.

20-26   The prayers of those who adore God will be warmly welcomed; their humble prayers will reach the clouds. Their prayers must arrive before they can be acted upon, but they won't be discarded before they're reviewed. The Most High will take the proper action, if any is needed; he'll get to it as soon as possible. The Lord is like a warrior who won't rest until he's crushed the cruel, avenged the innocent, scattered the proud, broken the wicked. He will reward his faithful people for doing their part. That's to say, he will render the judgment of judgments on them and shower them with mercy. In the time of great trouble, his mercy will come like clouds of rain in a time of drought.

A Prayer for Victory

36

1-19   "Have mercy on us, God of all; look kindly upon us and show us the light of your compassion. Extend your fear upon the Gentile nations; they've never given you a thought. They don't know there's no God but you, but they too should recognize your wonders. Raise your hand over their lands; they should see whom they're dealing with. They'll see the holy things you've done for us, just as we'll see the holy things you've done for them. They'll come to know what we know now: There's no God but you, Lord. Create new signage; do new wonders. Show off your fist; swing your sword arm; taunt them; toss thunder and lightning at them; confront our enemies; bring the battle to them. Hasten the final victory, for time is running out. Remember the end game, for your storied wonders need to be made known. Throw your flame at their fugitives; bring destruction to those who devastate us. Make mincemeat out of the enemy princes, the ones who say, "There's no one else but us!" Gather together all the tribes of Jacob. They'll be yours now, as though they've never stopped being yours. Have mercy upon your people, who invoke your name; upon the house of Israel, whom you've named your firstborn. Have mercy on the city you have made holy, Jerusalem, a residential place of peace and quiet. Fill Zion with your majesty and the Temple with your glory. Reintroduce the prophets, who were your creations; breathe new life into the prophecies they spoke in your name. Reward those who've kept their faith intact; may they find your word still relevant. Hear the prayers of your servants; be gracious to us as you promised in the blessing of Aaron. Lead us down Justice Road so that every last inhabitant on earth will know that you, and you alone, are the God of the Ages."

Musings on Food and Good Wives

20-22   We can swallow any food, but one food is better than all the others. The discerning palate knows when meat is venison; the wise heart knows when words are lies. The deceitful heart invites Sadness to a party; the honest heart sends Joy the invitation.

23-28   A woman can conceive no matter who her husband is, but one woman makes a better wife than another for the man. The beauty of a good wife lights up the face of her husband; it lights up something else, his sexual desire for her. Over and above that, if she has a voice that calms and charms and understands, then he becomes one happy guy. A good woman is something more than a wife; she's a wise partner, a faithful helpmate, a colossal support.

Where there's no hedge, the vineyard is vulnerable; where there's no wife, a man has no moorings. Who'd put their trust in a man who had no nest, checking into rough houses off the beaten path like a light-footed thief slipping from town to town?

PERFECT FRIENDSHIP

1-6 **37** Every friend of yours would say, "We have the perfect friendship!" But in reality some people are friends in name only. It's painful, isn't it, when a true friend of yours is proven false and you become sworn enemies? You say to yourself, "My friend, were you created only to cover the earth with the mud of your malice?"

False friends like to hide among your true friends; in times of trouble, however, the false is at the throat of the true. A true friend will offer sound counsel on difficult matters and, if necessary, go to court to help you argue your cause. So keep your true friends in mind; don't forget to count them among your most precious assets.

THE PITFALLS OF ADVICE

7-11 Don't seek advice from those who'll try to impede your progress. Don't share your innermost thoughts with those who want to profit from your troubles. Some counselors are in it only for personal gain. Protect your soul from them; ask for references beforehand—what's hiding behind that smile? Bad advisors can cast a spell over you, asking but not really caring: "Are you doing all right?" When something bad happens, they just stand there watching you suffer.

12-14 In fact, don't seek advice from anyone who acts suspicious or hostile; keep your soul hidden from anyone who is jealous of you or has a hidden agenda. For example: Don't consult with one woman about another, a coward concerning war, a merchant about business forecasts, a buyer about inventory, the tight-lipped about how to show gratitude, the vulgar about piety, the dishonest about honesty, a casual laborer about getting a job done right, a migrant about the international economic picture, or the methodical about multi-tasking.

15-22 Instead, meet regularly with the God-fearing—those who follow his life-maps, whose souls are compatible with yours. When you trip in the dark, these people will come to your aid.

Listen first to your own heart, the best counsel comes from there. A good conscience can see further than any guard on the highest rampart.

And don't forget to pray to the Most High; he'll direct your journey to the truth.

Before beginning every project, describe it to someone you trust in accurate detail. Before taking every step, seek sound counsel. Good advice streams from the knowledge of good and evil, life and death.

Keep all this in mind.

THE WISE

23-29 Over a lifetime the wise instruct many; yet sometimes for their own souls they haven't got a clue. They speak in a loving manner, but there's nothing lovable about them. The Lord stops the flow of grace; they lose their taste for food just as they lose their taste for wisdom.

When the wise know their own souls, however, they wear their wisdom well. When they teach other people, they are blessed with many blessings.

The days in each person's life have already been counted; the days of the house of Israel's existence are beyond counting. So the truly wise will leave behind a legacy; their name will live on for eternity.

MORE PARENTAL ADVICE

30-34 Child, look closely at your soul. Examine your life. If you come across something obnoxious, stop doing it.

Not every food appeals to everyone; not every taste suits every palette. So at dinner don't be glutinous; don't get carried away trying every single thing on the menu. Some foods aren't fresh and are beginning to turn; food poisoning will result in nausea and vomiting. Besides, overeating is overrated; it's shortened the lives of many. Undereating, on the other hand, is underrated; it's lengthened a lot of lives.

MEDICAL AND MOURNING ADVICE

1-8 **38** Take doctors to lunch; one day you'll need one of them, so thank the Most High for creating them. God sends them to medical school, and the government pays the bill. Their profession gives them prominence in the community; among the rulers they're well regarded.

The Most High has extracted from the earth a pharmacopoeia of medications; the prudent endure them, even if they sting or taste bad. Wasn't bad water once upon a time sweetened with a twig so that we might recognize the power of the Lord? The Most High gives us little bits of knowledge about medicine because he wants nature to be appreciated and respected. This allows the doctors to ease our pain and the pharmacists to make their oils and balms. God's natural gifts to us will never run out; they bring health and peace for all the world!

9-15 Child, when you're sick, don't be slow to call the doctor. But also pray to the Lord, for he has his own medicine cabinet. First, turn away from dirty sin; when you wash your hands, wash the sins right out of your heart. If you're poor, offer a bloodless, sweet-smelling prayer with flour and incense; make a bloody, crisp, fat-smelling offering only if you can afford it.

Then call a doctor. The Lord knows their credentials. Don't let them rush in and rush out. They've got what you need, but it may take a while. There's a time in all our lives when we need the comfort of trained healing hands, but good doctors will also pray to the Lord for us that they make the correct diagnosis to allow us to recover.

And here's another suggestion. When you sin in the sight of the Lord, call on the Divine Doctor to heal you at once.

16-24　Child, if a person you know dies, it's okay to cry; it's time to begin the lament. Pretend to be sad if you have to. According to ritual, cover the body and see that it gets a decent burial. After that, you can turn off your tears. Make a show of public grief, but nothing fancy; one day, two days— that should satisfy most observers.

If your sadness remains, however, try to console yourself. Be careful— sadness has a stress all its own, reminding us that our own death may arrive ahead of schedule. This depressing thought can break the strongest person. As you leave the cemetery, sadness may follow, but unresolved grief may drive you to despair. In this case, you have to forget about the deceased and drive out the memory of your loved one.

If that doesn't work, imagine your own final days. Remember your loved one's judgment is today. It's going to be the same for you tomorrow.

If you wallow in your grief, you won't bring the person back. Instead, you'll just mess up yourself. Let the dead rest; bury your memories with the body. The deceased is gone; you are still alive.

OTHER IMPORTANT OCCUPATIONS

25-27　Wisdom in the life of a scribe comes from quiet time. Writers who downsize their workload upsize their wisdom output.

Which farmer is filled with wisdom? The one who speed-plows the field? Who prods the oxen and drives his cattle and beasts of burden to hurry up? No, it is the one who takes the time as long as the sun shines to plow the straightest furrows and then spends the evening feeding and fattening the livestock.

28　That's what good engravers do, too. Working assiduously, they cut designs from a pattern, then change the details in each. They put their whole heart into a piece until the image is exactly right, staying up all night if necessary.

29-31　That's what good blacksmiths do, too. Standing facing the anvil, they focus on bending the iron just so. The fiery heat wrinkles their skin; they feed the forge even as the heat pushes them back. The noise of the hammer dings their ears. Their eyes stay fixed on the product they're making. They give everything they have to finish the job on time, working deep into the night to polish the metal just right.

32-34　That's what good potters do, too. Sitting on a stool, peddling the wheel with their feet, they have to sit just so and focus on their work. The entire operation is aimed at producing both quality and quantity. Potters need strong arms to handle the clay and stout legs to soften it. They throw their heart into the glazing and keep the oven burning at a steady heat far into the night.

35-39　In all these examples, the workers' lives are in their own hands; they are artists in their chosen field. Without people like these, you can't build or live in or walk around a city. The citizens can't meet in assemblies, and even if they could they'd have no place to gather. There would be no judges and no seats for judges; no one to process the judges' decisions; no formality, no finality. Worst of all, there would be nowhere to go to hear religious parables and sacred texts proclaimed.

If it weren't for the skilled laborers and artisans, the world would fall apart. Their work is their prayer; their prayer is their work.

WHAT THE PIOUS SAY AND DO

1-11 **39** Those who are comfortable with the fear of the Lord and have no trouble meditating on God's word—they're the sort who seek the wisdom of the prophets of old and steep themselves in timeless prophecies. They enjoy the parade of the sacred writers; they enter the nooks and crannies of the timeless texts. They eke out the meanings hidden in the proverbs; they poke around the cracks and crevices of the parables.

Such people are at home with the powerful of this world. They argue cases before the highest courts. They travel as ambassadors into neighboring countries, assessing the good and evil in their populations. Yet at break of every day they hand over their hearts to the Lord who made them; they pray constantly in the presence of the Most High. They open their mouths in prayer; they confess their sins. The Lord's wisdom drops on them like rain in the breeze; the Lord's forgiveness sprouts in them like flowers in the field. With the grace of the Lord they are filled with the spirit of piety and understanding. They channel God's counsel and discipline; they contemplate his secrets. They make public the discipline of God's life-maps; they are never embarrassed by God's word.

12-15 Many praise such pious people in public; their reputation will live on. Their memory won't fade; their name will ring bells from generation to generation. The poets will recite their wisdom; the holy will praise their prayer. As long as they're around, they're one in a thousand; when they decide to call it quits, their memory lingers.

MEDITATION ON GOOD AND EVIL

16-26 From this point on, I'll meditate and tell you the fruits of my meditation; I'm as full of light as a full moon.

Listen to me, my child. Like roses on the riverbanks, your complexion will blossom; like frankincense in the forest, your sweetness will abound; like wild lilies in the field, your garden will flourish. Raise your voice. Chant the canticles. Bless the Lord in all his works. Surround his name with magnificence. Confess him in your public prayer. In your hymns raise voice and lute. This is what you should say: "All the works of the Lord are very, very good! Everything God has promised will come in its own time."

There's no need to ask, "What's this for?" or "What's that for?" Everything that's supposed to happen will happen, but in its own time. God just has to say it and standing water will start flowing; if he wants it to, river water will form a reservoir. When the Lord speaks, he conveys a certain calm, because nobody's threatening his existence. All the works of human beings are set before him, not a hair is hidden from his eye. His gaze turns from eternity on the left to eternity on the right; nothing he sees amazes him. There's no need to say, "This is not as good as that." Everything God created has its own purpose.

27-29   This blessing is like a river overflowing, a flood soaking the earth. With righteous anger, however, the Lord will disperse those people who didn't seek him out and listen to him; he'll turn their fresh water into salt marsh. His good deeds and intentions are directed to the holy, but to the wicked his words and actions are incomprehensible.

30-35   From the start, good things were created for good people; for the bad people, of course, some things were good but became bad. Among the human necessities are water, fire, and iron; salt, milk, and wheat for bread; honey and grapes for wine; olive oil; cloth. All these necessities are promised for the good, but not necessarily for those who fail to follow God's life-maps.

There are spirits who are created for vengeance, furies who bring their own punishments with them. At the time of the Final Inspection, the one who made all the good will let the bad waters flow. Hail, fire, famine, death—all these he created to set things straight.

36-41   There will be a horrifying scene full of wild beasts with frontal incisors, sticky stingers, and forked tongues; the avenging sword will swing right and left, felling the wicked. Then the holy will rejoice in the life-maps they chose; they'll have been filled with the necessities of life. When the time comes, their obedience to the Lord will be rewarded.

How and why do I know this? Because the Lord has told me: "That was my intention right from the start. I conceived it. I ordered it. I put it down in writing. All my works are good; they're planned right down to the final second and the last detail."

So you see, there's no reason to ask, "What's this for?" or "What's that for?" or to say, "This is not as good as that." Everything has its own time slot. And now, at the end of this meditation, I ask that every heart and mouth praise and bless the name of the Lord for what he has done for all of us.

LIFE AFTER PARADISE

1-16   **40** No more lounging around in the garden of the Lord. We children of Adam and Eve have to hustle from the moment we emerge from our mother's womb to the moment we return to Mother Earth. Our thoughts, fears, wild imaginings of things to come— from the one who warms the highest seat to the one who's never had a seat to warm; from the wearer of royal purple to the wearer of coarse cloth—all will be subject to anger, greed, growling, anxiety, fear of death, outrageous behavior, confrontational outbursts.

During the night, in the quiet of our sleep, nightmares do their ugly dance. No real rest can be found. We wake up as tired as when we went to sleep. Our sleeping hearts, once so sure of their clear vision, are blurred; we feel as though we just returned from battle. But when we wake up, we're amazed that all our fears have fled.

All this happens from humans down to animals. Upon sinners, it's seven times worse. For them, to the list above add death, blood, war, sword, oppressions, occupations, invasions, incursions—all these have been created specifically for the wicked, and that would include the ultimate destruction when everything that came from the earth will return to the earth and everything that came from the sea will return to the sea.

Every corruption and every iniquity will be wiped out. Faith, however, will remain standing in its rightful place. Wealth gotten by stealth will turn to dry riverbed; a great crack of thunder, a sudden wash of rain, and that dust will be swept away forever. The rush of water will be joyful and cleansing to the virtuous, but by the time it reaches the cheaters and double-dealers it will become only a trickle. Descendants of the wicked won't add branches to their family tree; lifeless roots can't get a grip on hard rock. The green growth along the river will be dead before harvest time.

EVEN BETTER

17-28 Grace and goodness are the same outside as they are inside the original garden; honesty and mercy will flourish anywhere. Life for the laborers who are at peace with their lot can be sweet—some would say it's a treasure. The building of a family or a city will create a memorable name for yourself, but even better would be building a virtuous life. Wine and music lighten the heart; wisdom enlightens the soul. Flutes with harps make music smooth; smoother still is a kind tongue. The eye desires to see goodness and beauty; even better, the green plantings in the field. Two friends have a good time when they get together; even better is a happy wife and husband. Brothers are helpers in time of trouble; even better, mercy to strangers that knows no bounds. Gold and silver afford good backing; even better, wisdom that provides sure footing. Intellectual capacity and moral strength make the heart dance; even better, though, is fear of the Lord. Fear of the Lord isn't the absence of something, nor is it an engine with a missing a part. Fear of the Lord is the tree in the original garden; all glory flourishes in its shade.

ADVICE ON BEGGING

29-32 Child, the one thing to avoid in life is indigence; it's better to die than beg. Sneaking a peek at the table of the rich isn't the sort of life to choose; another's feast will only upset your own stomach. Those who are disciplined and educated take care of themselves. Begging does seem to have a certain sweetness, but in reality it sours the stomach.

THOUGHTS ON DEATH AND PARENTING

1-4 **41** O Death, how bitter the thought of you must be to those who acquired their wealth honestly—the quiet sort, successful in every way, who still have the strength to enjoy life's pleasures! O Death, how sweet the thought of you must be to the homeless who have lost all strength—totally dependent, with no trust or patience left!

5-15 Don't fear the judgment of death. It has embraced everyone who went before us and will claim everyone who comes after us. Death is the judgment from God on every single human being; why would we want to resist the Most High? No matter how old we are—ten, one hundred, one thousand—when we die it's because we have no further business on earth.

The children of sinners learn from their parents. They gather where their elders hung out. They have no reputation for good to leave behind. Their descendants slip into perpetual shame. The children complain about their reprobate parents, but they're the reason their own offspring are in disgrace.

You who give up on God's word, your children will fall under the general curse; when you die, you'll have your own personal curse. Everything that came from nothing will be returned to nothing; that's how the wicked are punished.

People mourn the loss of their bodies, but they can never lose their bad reputations. Take good care of your personal legacy; it will remain with you a long time, a precious treasure for a thousand years.

16-20 A good life has a sure and certain number of days; a good reputation lasts forever. Better those who hide their stupidity than those who hide their wisdom. Hidden wisdom and invisible treasure, what's the good of either? Child, keep discipline tight but not to the breaking point. Respect my judgment; I know what I'm talking about. Not every good thing is worthy of respect; not every shame is justifiable.

THINGS TO BE ASHAMED OF

21-28 There are many things to be ashamed of: describing your sexual escapades to your father and mother; lying before a judge or magistrate; breaking the law of a prince or judge; disrupting a civil or religious gathering; cheating a friend or companion; disgracing the place where you live; stealing what's not yours; denying the truth or bearing false witness before God; putting elbows on the dinner table; short-changing the short-sighted; not returning a greeting; giving a prostitute the once-over; not acknowledging the presence of a relative; taking but not restoring; admiring another man's wife; exchanging glances with a handmaid and then visiting her bed chamber; telling dirty stories to your friends; insulting a stranger, then saying it was a joke.

MORE THINGS TO BE ASHAMED OF

1 42 Gossiping about things heard but not seen; revealing things told to you in confidence—don't do these two things and you'll never be lonely. You'll find welcome wherever human beings are found.

THINGS NOT TO BE ASHAMED OF

2-8 Upholding God's word and covenant; using the judicial process to render judgment on the godless; mediating disputes between citizens and out-of-towners; transferring inheritances to foreigners; fairly calibrating weights and balances; estimating the value of acquisitions large and small; fighting price-fixing by merchants; correcting children in public; bloodying the side of a wicked slave; restricting a wicked wife; locking prying fingers out of your possessions; labeling merchandise with correct number and weight; accurately describing contents of incoming and outgoing parcels; teaching the uneducated and intellectually challenged; supporting the elders who pass judgment on those who have sex outside of marriage—do all these and truth will be well served. You'll never sin to save face; you'll be welcomed anywhere in the land of the living.

Caring for a Daughter

9-14 A daughter must be kept under constant watch by her parents; their anxiety about her should keep them awake at night. When she is young, they watch so that she doesn't lose her virginity; after she is married, they watch so that she doesn't become a hateful hag. That's to say, they don't want her to get pregnant before she gets married, be unfaithful to her husband after the wedding, or be infertile even if she is faithful.

A flirtatious daughter deserves a strict custodian. She can make you look negligent to your enemies, silly to your friends in the city, or hopelessly out of touch among her peers; that's to say, she can make your life miserable in any number of ways.

A beautiful girl like her isn't easy to find, so you won't find one on a street corner watching all the boys go by or hanging around with a bunch of married women. Just as a moth flies suddenly out of a garment, harm can happen to her in a flash. Better a parent's early reprimand than a daughter who charges for her favors or a woman trapped in a life of prostitution.

Trumpeting the Lord's Museum

15-20 I will therefore be mindful of the works of the Lord; I'll trumpet the things I've seen; you'll recognize the Lord by his works. The sun lights up and shines down upon all things; it is God's works that are illumined. And weren't the prophets appointed to tell his story, even though they failed in capturing the full wonder of the Lord? These witnesses have been given the strength to stand at attention before his glory. He has plumbed the depths of the human heart; he has uncovered its deepest secrets. He can do this because he knows all there is to know; he's read all the signs and symbols of the world; he's kept a record of what has happened and what will happen; he can reveal all the cracks and crevices. No thoughts escape him; no words hide from him.

21-26 He has arranged the *magnum opus* of his wisdom collection—unique before there was unique; unique after there was unique; nothing unique has been added; nothing unique has been taken away. As for a curator, he's reserved that position for himself. How desirable is his collection! What we see is only a spark, a speck, of the originals! All of these things have a life of their own and will live forever. For every emergency there's a divine tool in the kit; each one different, not one duplicate. Yet nothing goes wrong; nothing needs a fix; each confirms the good of the other. Who'd tire of visiting a brilliant museum like this?

CYCLE OF CREATION

43 **1-28** Glory on high and purity too, a little bit of heaven above, a glimpse of glory!

The sun appearing, announcing the day, a blazing ceramic, the work of the Most High. At high noon the earth's on fire. Everyone can feel it; who can withstand it? Three times as hot as air from a furnace, it burns the mountains and fills the air with smoke; it illuminates the world but with blinding rays. How great you are who made the sun and at whose word it keeps to its course!

The moon has its own seasons. It ticks off the time; the world counts on it. It marks the festival days as they roll around; in its course, it increases and decreases. True to its name, the Crescent, it does the same thing the next month. It's a cluster of encampments in the highest skies, burning brightly in the heavenly meadows.

The fires are the stars, the beauties of the heavens, illuminating the sky of the Most High. The Holy One keeps them on their track so they don't fall asleep during their watches at night.

Look quickly for the rainbow. Bless the one who made it; its colorful ribbon is pleasing in its splendor. It circles the heavens leading a parade, following the route the Most High has traced.

He has only to speak and it begins to snow; he has only to judge and his decisions are like lightning. When he opens the heavenly vaults, the clouds fly out like birds. A word from him and the clouds turn into hail. He has only to speak and thunder shivers the earth. He has only to look and the mountains tremble. He exhales and the south wind whistles and the north wind howls and tornadoes roar. The snow flies like flocks of birds and settles on the ground like swarms of locusts. It gives off a blinding whiteness that boggles the mind. He spreads frost upon the earth as if it were salt; when it freezes, the field is a carpet of nails. The frigid north wind blows at his command, and wherever water is found ice covers it, protecting it like a breastplate. Freezing cold devours the mountains, destroys the wilderness, and extinguishes the greenery.

What's God's remedy? Sun shining, gentle dew dropping, frost thawing, and the earth regaining its cheer. He has only to think it and the sea calms and islands emerge like plants.

Those who navigate the sea tell of its perils; when we hear these tales, however, we celebrate God's genius. The sea is full of exceptional and wonderful creations. Under his direction, his angel completes the cycle of life; at his word and right on time, the cycle ends and then begins again.

29-37 I have much more to report, but words will fail me. To simplify, "God is all there is!" We want to glorify him, but we don't have the strength. After all, he's the one who made all this happen. He's an awesome Lord and doesn't care who knows it; his power is full of marvels. If you want to glorify the Lord, don't hesitate. You can praise him, but you can't overpraise him. If you're going to praise him, put your shoulder into it. Don't give up too soon; you'll never praise too much. Who's seen him? Who'll tell the tale? Who can capture him as he was at the beginning? Much of what he's done, especially the big secrets of the universe, is still unknown to us. What we've been able to see to date is pitifully small. To make a long story short, God made everything, but he gave the wisdom to appreciate it only to his friends.

PRAISE THE GIANTS, SUNG AND UNSUNG

1-8 **44** Let's praise the giants who've gone before us and our parents who've begotten us. The Lord has provided us such a splash of talent since we left the garden!

Let's remember the early governors and judges, men and women of great authority, empowered by their own prudence, encouraging the prophets. They ruled the people with good counsel, knowledge gained from Scripture, words of wisdom from everyday life—accompanied by lots of singing and psalms and Scripture stories.

We have had famous leaders known for their ability, and yet they ruled with a sense of beauty, living quietly in their homes.

All these gained fame in their own generation. They were held in high esteem, and their children left behind the same sort of reputation.

9-15 Then there were those who have no memorials; they died, and their reputation died with them. They were born, yet it's as though they were never born. The same happened to their children. But these were people of mercy; their pious practices were not in vain. Their real wealth is with us still in their descendants. When the genes are good, the inheritance has to be good.

God made covenants with these people; and because of this their children and their children's children will live forever—their glory won't be dimmed. Their bodies rest in peace; their reputations will live forever. They appear, by name or anonymously, in the wisdom collection. Their praises will be sung wherever religious people gather.

Finally, there were these.

16 Enoch pleased God so much he was taken up to be with the Lord; he became a model of repentance to the tribes of Israel.

17-19 Noah was a model of good behavior; back in the days of the flood he obeyed the Lord and became the instrument to bring God and humankind back together. Because of Noah's faithfulness, there were survivors when the flood came. To the covenant between God and Noah there was a codicil: Never again would God destroy the world.

20-23 Abraham, the grand progenitor of many peoples—there wasn't a blot on his reputation. He kept God's word; the Lord entered into covenant with him. He was a living witness to that covenant; yes, he was tested and tempted, yet he remained faithful. With solemn promise the Lord assured him that his children would be blessed and increase like dust particles, outnumbering the stars, and that their inheritance would span from sea to sea, from one end of the earth to the other.

24-27 Isaac was accorded the same promises by the Lord as those his father, Abraham, had received, and he became a blessing to all the nations. And after Isaac, God transferred the rights of the firstborn onto Jacob. He acknowledged the descendants of Jacob, dividing them into twelve tribes. From him and his line sprang a man of mercy who found grace in the people's eyes.

※

MOSES, AARON, PHINEHAS

1-6 **45** It is Moses, beloved of God and by the people, whose memory we hold in the highest of all regard. The Lord treated Moses as a saint in glory; he put the fear of God into Moses' enemies; he turned Israel's history around through his actions. The Lord put him on a par with kings, gave him his word for the people, and let him have a glimpse of the heavenly glory. The Lord brought Moses up to speed in faith and patience. He made him stand out from the rest of the Israelites, heard his prayers, and led him into a cloud. Face-to-face, the Lord gave Moses the life-maps—God's word of knowledge and wisdom—to make the guidelines for human behavior crystal clear for the descendants of Israel.

7-27 The Lord elevated one other person to the same heights—Moses' brother, Aaron, from the tribe of Levi—and made an unending promise to him. He conferred upon Aaron and his posterity the priesthood of the nation and dressed him in perfect clothing and ornaments. The Lord put around his middle a sash of glory. The rest of his apparel was correct down to the last stitch: his crown, topped with symbols of virtue; ornamental trousers, tunic, shoulders; embroidered pomegranates dominating the decor; strings of golden bells draping around him, loud enough to be heard in the Temple, signaling a grand entrance about to be made, an audible memorial to all the children of the chosen.

Next for Aaron, a holy robe of gold, blue, purple, the work of a master weaver; a sash of twisted scarlet, work of an expert stylist; precious gems sewn over the breastpiece in settings of gold, the work of a jeweler; inscriptions about the twelve tribes, the work of an engraver; on the headpiece a crown of gold, inside of which was engraved the word *holiness*. The crown was an honorable symbol, a dazzler to the eye, a real beauty to the connoisseur of sacred objects. Aaron made a stunning figure, not seen since the garden! His garments were meant to be worn not by non-Israelites but by Israelites only, by Aaron's children and grandchildren for the rest of time.

The high priesthood was given to Aaron for all time so he and his descendants could lead and bless the people. His bloodline was to hold the office for as long as Heaven exists. Moses poured oil on his brother Aaron's hands, anointing them for holy use. His sacrifices were to be consumed by fire every day, twice a day, forever. The Lord chose him to offer sacrifice and incense with a decent smell, a good aroma to associate with memorials of important events that would satisfy the people. The Lord gave him strength to enforce the life-maps and knowledge of the details of God's promises in order to educate the children of Jacob in God's word and bring its light to the people of Israel.

Some, however, took exception to Aaron and rose against him out of envy. They included those with Dathan and Abiram; joining the defiance was the band of Korah. They rose up against Aaron and his followers in the desert wilderness. The Lord God saw this, and it upset him mightily. Matching his wrath to that of the rebels, he consumed them with fire. They attacked, he counterattacked, and they were wiped out.

That divine gesture increased Aaron's stature and earned him and his descendants their only inheritance—the firstfruits of the land, the best portions of the prepared bread and sacrificial meats. These God gave to Aaron and his bloodline forever. Aaron himself and his descendants wouldn't inherit any land (the other tribes inherited that), but the Lord gave Aaron's house a special slice of the divine inheritance as the high priests of Israel.

28-31   Third in glory after Moses and Aaron was Phinehas, son of Eleazar. His fear of the Lord was legendary. When the spirit of the chosen collapsed, he emerged as a force. With hope and without hesitation, he stood up for the house of Israel. God was so pleased that he made a covenant of peace with Phinehas—he and his descendants would be in charge of the Sanctuary and of the people; the dignity of Aaron's priesthood would rest with them forever. Please note there was also a covenant with King David, son of Jesse of the tribe of Judah. This was an individual heritage through one son alone, but the heritage of Aaron through Phinehas is for all their descendants for all time.

So, may God give the descendants of Phinehas the wisdom to lead the people. May the good they have already achieved not be forgotten. May the glory of the chosen last forever.

JOSHUA, CALEB, SAMUEL

1-8   **46** Also earning a reputation in war was Joshua, son of Nun, successor to Moses in the line of prophets. His name, which means "savior," gives some hint of his importance. His efforts in saving so many of God's elect were monumental. He overran the enemy with the hope of helping Israel realize its inheritance. How adept he was in the swing of his sword and the toss of his javelin against the insurgents! Who could stop him? Who could slow him down? After all, he was the Lord's choice to lead the charge. Wasn't it his hand that stopped the sun in its tracks, making one day last 48 hours? He invoked the powerful Most High in opposing the enemies of Israel on all sides. The great Lord heard his prayer and pelted them with hailstones hard as rocks. Joshua engaged the enemy, destroying them on the slopes of the hills. These doomed nations bore the brunt of his military supremacy, all the while learning what it meant to wage war against the one true God. Yes, Joshua followed the Powerful One, who at all times was watching his back.

9-12   In the days of Moses, Joshua had pleaded for mercy for the chosen. He and Caleb, son of Jephunneh, stood up against a rebellious crowd, dispelling one rumor after another and averting God's anger from the people. Out of six hundred thousand Jewish soldiers at the time, only these two were allowed to lead the chosen into the land that had been promised to them, a place where milk streamed and honey oozed.

To Caleb, the Lord gave strength enough to battle deep into his old age so that he might finally take possession of his inheritance; his descendants took it from there. He wanted all of the children of Israel to see that doing what the Lord asked was a good thing.

13-15   Then came the judges. They were well known; their hearts hadn't been corrupted and they hadn't turned away from the Lord. Their memory was blessed; their bones rose up, sprang forth from where they fell. Their names were dusted off by their children and restored to their proper place.

16-23 One of these judges picked by God was Samuel, a prophet of the Lord, who got a government going and anointed the leaders to run it. Now, God's word provided those governors with guidance through its life-maps, but the God of Jacob still checked in from time to time to see how things were going. Samuel was faithful to the Lord's vision and was soon recognized as a prophet. He invoked the Lord for help in opposing the enemies around them, offering up a suckling lamb. The Lord spoke up from Heaven, his booming voice making himself heard. He pulverized the princes of Tyre and the lords of the Philistines.

Before Samuel laid down for his final rest, he confessed in the presence of the Lord and his anointed: "Never in my life did I accept from anybody so much as a pair of shoes, let alone a lot of money!"

No one came forward to say otherwise. After that, Samuel slept the sleep of sleeps, but he had one last thing to do. He returned in a dream with a message for the king, warning him to rid the nation of its godlessness.

NATHAN, DAVID, SOLOMON

1-13 **47** After Samuel, there arose Nathan, a prophet who served David well. That's all I'll say about Nathan.

Regarding David, as the tastiest part of a sacred sacrifice is the first cut, so David was the first pick of the children of Israel. He played with lions as well as lambs; he frolicked with wild bears and tame sheep. Wasn't he the youngster who knocked off the giant Goliath and wiped clean the shame of his people? Goliath was mouthing off when David, with the flick of his wrist, let loose his sling, hitting the proud warrior right between the eyes. David, invoking the name of the Lord Most High, found enough strength in his right hand to take the strong man down, as well as ten thousand more of his compatriots. For this he was mightily praised, heaped high with the Lord's blessings, and offered the crown of glory. He laid low the enemies on all sides. He humiliated the Philistines, who had the upper hand at the time; he destroyed their supposed supremacy.

In everything David did, with every word he spoke, he gave thanks to the Holy and the High; with his whole heart he praised the Lord. Simply speaking, he loved the Lord. David organized a choir around the Lord's altar, where songs and psalms filled the air. They added class to the festivals; they celebrated the seasons. Right to the end of David's life, the choir began each day filling the air with song praising the holy name of the Lord.

The Lord wiped clean his sins. He declared David's supremacy, giving him the covenant of the kingdom and the royal throne in Israel.

14-25 Then David's son Solomon—renowned for his wise decisions—appeared on the scene. Because of him, people were able to live in security. His rule was marked by peace. Thanks to God, there was not much stress during the day; during the night, no bad dreams. Solomon built a structure suitable for the Lord; everyone thought the Temple would last forever.

How wise was Solomon when he was young! Like water his wisdom covered half the earth; like a carpet his knowledge covered the other half. He furnished the world with a game room complete with puzzles. His reputation reached the far-off isles. He was renowned for peace. His traditional songs and sayings, parables and interpretations, the other nations admired. In the name of the Lord God, also known as the God of Israel, he amassed gold, which was hard to get, as though it were bronze, which was easy to get; the same with silver, as though it were common lead.

But Solomon also amassed women as though they were a cheap commodity; the ruler became subject to his lust. He destroyed his reputation; he scattered his seed all over the landscape. His children felt ashamed of him; they felt their father was just another doddering fool and made him divide his kingdom among them when he didn't have to.

The rebel kingdom that emerged was the opposite of everything the chosen ones stood for. Obviously, God could have dumped Solomon at this point, but he didn't. The Lord didn't mess with Solomon's mind or take away his wisdom; he didn't expel his children from the line of David or bring it to an end. So Solomon dedicated what was left of his kingdom to the memory of Jacob and kept it in the Davidic line.

26-28 When Solomon went to rest with his fathers, he left behind a son, Rehoboam, a witless wonder if there ever was one. In a word, he didn't have a clue. This young man ruled over a country of his own making called Ephraim, but it certainly wasn't Israel.

29-31 Next, Jeroboam, son of Nebat, appeared on the scene. He taught both Israel and Ephraim to sin; soon what used to be considered a sin was a sin no longer. The result was that God allowed the expulsion of the sinners from their own country. Yet even in exile, these descendants of David and Solomon gravitated toward sinful cities until their iniquities finally caught up with them.

ELIJAH, ELISHA, HEZEKIAH, ISAIAH

1-12 **48** Next there arose like a flame a prophet whose word burned like a torch. The first thing he did was inflict a famine on the people. Many grew envious of his power, but most of these he weeded out. With the Lord's advice and consent, he turned the rain off and the fire on—blitzing the earth three times. He was, of course, Elijah, and his ability to do miraculous things increased exponentially. Who had a reputation like his? With the Lord's approval, he raised from his final resting place a dead child. Kings he toppled from their thrones, bounced them from their beds, smashed their fragile power into smithereens. At Sinai he went on the defense; at Horeb he recovered his courage and went on the offense. He brought kings to their knees in repentance; he schooled prophets who'd follow him.

Elijah was caught up by a whirlwind, horses of fire pulling his chariot up and away. According to tradition, he is the one in the final days who'll dampen the fiery wrath of the Lord, soften the Lord's heart toward his wayward children, and restore the tribes of Jacob. Blessed are those who make friends with him; they sleep the better because of their friendship. Like Elijah, we all have only one life to live; unlike him we all have to die and don't have his reputation to leave behind.

13-18 Elijah was indeed swept up in a whirlwind, but he left behind his spirit in Elisha. Elisha was fearless when facing a prince. No one was more powerful than he; no one bested him when faced with word-to-word combat. After his death his body continued to prophesy. Alive, he did wonders; dead, wonders continued to be attributed to him. And yet, for all his efforts, dead or alive, the people didn't repent. They didn't pull back from their sinful lives, even while they were being ejected from the land and exiled all over the face of the earth. What was left of the chosen was a pitiful few in Judah; they had one leader, a king from the house of David. Even then, only some did what pleased God; the rest kept on sinning.

19-25 That king was Hezekiah. He fortified Jerusalem, tunneling under the city wall, breaking rock with iron, allowing water to flow from outside to inside; he built a well for the water. During his reign, Sennacherib the Assyrian made his presence known; he sent his ambassador, Rabshekah, to see Hezekiah. After his aide returned, Sennacherib raised his hand against Zion. He bragged about his ability to maneuver his military anywhere he wanted. Within Jerusalem's walls, heads turned, hearts trembled. They moaned and mourned like mothers in the throes of childbirth. They invoked the merciful Lord, spreading their arms and lifting them up to the heavens.

The Holy One turned to hear their prayer; he fortunately hadn't used indelible ink when noting their sins. He didn't turn them over to their enemies, but he did turn them over to the holy prophet Isaiah, who saw to the purification process. The Lord pounded the Assyrian camps; his angel did the dirty work, cleaning up afterward. That was how Hezekiah made God smile. His head held high, Hezekiah walked the walk of David and his bloodline. That was the path strongly recommended by Isaiah, a great and faithful prophet.

26-28 Then miraculously, the sun backed up, adding a day, or so it seemed; it also added a year to Hezekiah's life. Isaiah saw the big picture of what was to come. He consoled the doleful hearts in Zion. He got a glimpse of what would happen in the future; he knew what would happen next before it happened.

ASSORTED PROPHETS

1-9 **49** The memory of Josiah lingers, like fragrance in a perfumery, like the aftertaste of honey, like haunting music at a banquet. He had a divine directive to bring repentance to his nation. He abolished the abomination of godlessness; he directed his heart toward the Lord. Surrounded by sinners, he shored up religious practices where he could. Everyone was wicked at the time—David, Hezekiah, and Josiah were the exceptions.

The kings of Judah abandoned God's word. Fear of the Lord was a joke to them. They ended up giving their kingdom to others; they gave away their power to an alien nation. They set the torch to the chosen city of holiness; they emptied the streets.

Jeremiah had predicted all this. They treated him like trash, though he'd been consecrated a prophet while in his mother's womb. His task was to overwhelm, overthrow, oversee. That done, he had to rebuild, replant, renew.

10-12 It was Ezekiel who saw the vision of glory; it was shown to him in a chariot full of angelic-like figures. He blessed those who kept to the straight and narrow as Job had done.

The bones of the Twelve Prophets spring back to life again! They were the ones who kept the descendants of Jacob going by preserving his faith and rescuing his people.

13-14 How may we recover the history of Zerubbabel? He was like a signet ring on the right hand of God. The same with Jeshua, Jozadak's son. They built the house of God, dedicated the holy structure to the Lord, and designed it to give God glory forever.

15 Then there was Nehemiah, long and happily remembered. From the rubble he rebuilt the city's walls. He restored our houses, right down to the doors and the locks on the doors.

16 Enoch was one of a kind; earthbound, he was eventually lifted up from the earth.

17-18 There was also Joseph, born a mere human. He became leader of his people and cornerstone of his nation. His relics were a pilgrim destination that continued to be a source of piety and strength.

19 Seth and Shem created decent reputations, but for best of the best we have to look all the way back to the beginning: Adam.

SIMEON

1-23 **50** Next is Simeon II, called the Righteous, son of Jochanan, high priest in his lifetime. He renovated the house of God, strengthening the structure and doubling the size of the Temple. He calculated the height of the building from the substructure to the top of the wall. He dug a reservoir; when full, it looked like a lake, a calm sea. His first concern was the security of the citizens; his second, the city's fortification against a siege.

How splendid he looked as he came out from behind the curtain of the Holy of Holies! He was outfitted like the morning star emerging from a cloud, like a full moon at festival time, like the sun at high noon shining upon the Temple of God, like a rainbow on a cloudy day, like roses in springtime, like water lilies on riverbanks, like whiffs of frankincense in the breeze, like a fire giving rise to incense, like a vase of beaten gold studded with precious gems, like an olive tree bending under the fruit, like a regal cypress poking holes in the clouds—that's what Simeon looked like when he donned the vestments of the high priest. He was the epitome of splendor.

He ascended to the holy altar where he circled, incensing the place. He accepted portions of the sacrifice from the hands of the other priests, then he stood next to the altar, ringed by his brethren. They looked like a stand of cedars on Mount Lebanon. Like branches of palm they stood around him—all the sons of Aaron in all their glory, raising their hands in offering in the presence of the entire assembly of Israel. Completing the prayers at the altar, he prepared the sacrificial offerings to the Most High. He extended his hand for the ceremonial cup, then poured out the blood of the grape. He emptied it out at the foot of the altar, sending up a heavenly aroma to the heavens.

Then the sons of Aaron cried out a holy shout and blew the hammered horns making a great noise, loud enough to be heard by the Most High God of Israel. The people in the Temple were quick to fall facedown on the floor to adore the Lord himself, offering prayers to the All-Powerful. They raised their musical instruments and played, their voices praying as they sang; a great chant arose, smoothing and soothing. The people petitioned the Merciful One until the service in his honor was finished. Then descending, Simeon put his hands upon the whole congregation of the children of Israel, blessing them out loud to the glory of the holy name. He repeated this until everyone had received the blessing of the Lord God.

GLORIFY GOD

24-26 At last, dear reader, glorify the God of all. He made all the great treasures all over the world, exalting our days right from the time we emerged from the womb, helping us grow with an eye toward what was best for us. May there be peace in the land of Israel now, and may it remain forever. May God entrust his mercy to all of us and free us in our own lifetimes.

A FINAL ASIDE

27-28 Three nations I have absolutely no use for—and one of them isn't a nation at all. They are those who were smart enough to live in Seir and Philistia, and those who were foolish enough to live in Shechem.

CONCLUSION

29-31 Wisdom, what it is and how it works—that's what Jesus, son of Sirach, a Jerusalemite, has put down in this book. Mercy, it was said, flowed from his heart and his pen. You'd do well to familiarize yourself with this book. Keep these words close to your heart. If you do what they say, you'll be able to do everything else. But remember, the first step is fear of the Lord.

PRAYER OF JESUS, SON OF SIRACH

1-17 **51** "I'll call out to you, my Lord and King. I'll join the choir of praise, my God and Savior. I'll call out your name.

"You helped me. You protected me. You saved my body from falling apart, my tongue from gossiping, my lips from lying. You rescued me from insurgents, from the traps of those who'd eat me for lunch, from the hands of those hunting me down, from the worries troubling me, from the heat of the flame that surrounds me, from the middle of the fire I didn't start, from the depth of the belly of hell, from the demeanor's tongue and the liar's word, from the sting of insult.

"You rescued my soul as it approached death; you saved my life from the inferno below. My enemies surround me on all sides; there was no one to help. I looked around, but there wasn't a soul. Then it was that I remembered your mercy, Lord, your kind words and works since the garden.

"You've delivered those who depended on you, Lord; you freed them from the grimy grasp of the wicked. I raised my supplication from the earth; I prayed for death to take a holiday. I invoked the Lord: 'You are my Father; don't abandon me in the day of trouble; don't leave me without help amidst storms and dangers.' I'll praise your name without stop; I'll join in the general confession. You've freed me from dangerous times; you've rescued me from wicked times. I'll call out to you; I'll pray to you; I'll bless the name of the Lord."

FINAL WORDS TO THE READER

18-30 From the time I was young, before I sinned for the first time, I sought wisdom openly in my prayer. I demanded it right in front of the Temple. Right down to the present day I inquired after it; eventually, it opened like a flower, like a grape before its time. My heart leapt like a leopard; my foot stayed on the straight and narrow. From my youth I'd been searching for it; I inclined my ear a little and there she was, Lady Wisdom. She was more than enough for me, and since discovering her I've progressed a great deal.

To the one who gave wisdom, I'll return the glory. I made a plan, I kept to the plan, and I wasn't disappointed. My soul wrestled with wisdom; I followed the rules of engagement with the Lord. I extended my hands on high; the things I couldn't understand I came to understand. I directed my soul to wisdom; I found it had a purifying effect; I had it in my heart right from the beginning; right from the start I knew it couldn't be left behind. Looking for wisdom and not finding it upset me terribly; looking for wisdom and finding it calmed me wonderfully. For my reward, the Lord gave me the gift of language. With it I praise him back.

31-38 Come to me, those who don't know; gather round, those who want to know. Why have you been so slow to apply to the School of Wisdom when your minds thirst for knowledge? Here are a few tips. Put yourself on an extreme budget. Commit yourself to the program. Don't let your mind wander. Next thing you know, you'll have found wisdom. You can see, I've worked at it for a while and found time to reflect. Higher education costs a lot of money, but you'll find much gold in your studies. Relax your mind in the Lord; keep your prayers simple. Work yourself silly in your own good time. The Lord will reward you nicely in his own good time.

PROPHETS

Over a period of several hundred years, the Hebrew people gave birth to an extraordinary number of prophets—men and women distinguished by the power and skill with which they presented the reality of God. They delivered God's commands and promises and living presence to communities and nations who had been living on god-fantasies and god-lies.

Everyone more or less believes in God. But most of us do our best to keep God on the margins of our lives or, failing that, refashion God to suit our convenience. Prophets insist that God is the sovereign center, not off in the wings awaiting our beck and call. And prophets insist that we deal with God as God reveals himself, not as we imagine him to be.

These men and women woke people up to the sovereign presence of God in their lives. They yelled, they wept, they rebuked, they soothed, they challenged, they comforted. They used words with power and imagination, whether blunt or subtle.

Seventeen of these prophets wrote what they spoke. We call them "the writing prophets." They comprise the section from Isaiah to Malachi in this Bible that also includes the unattributed Book of Lamentations. These Hebrew prophets provide the help we so badly need if we are to stay alert and knowledgeable regarding the conditions in which we cultivate faithful and obedient lives before God. For the ways of the world—its assumptions, its values, its methods of going about its work—are never on the side of God. Never.

The prophets purge our imaginations of this world's assumptions on how life is lived and what counts in life. Over and over again, God the Holy Spirit uses these prophets to separate his people from the cultures in which they live, putting them back on the path of simple faith and obedience and worship in defiance of all that the world admires and rewards. Prophets train us in discerning the difference between the ways of the world and the ways of the gospel, keeping us present to the Presence of God.

We don't read very many pages into the Prophets before realizing that there was nothing easygoing about them. Prophets were not popular figures. They never achieved celebrity status. They were decidedly uncongenial to the temperaments and dispositions of the people with whom they lived. And the centuries have not mellowed them. It's understandable that we should have a difficult time coming to terms with them. They aren't particularly sensitive to our feelings. They have very modest, as we would say, "relationship skills." We like leaders, especially religious leaders, who understand our problems ("come alongside us" is our idiom for it), leaders with a touch of glamour, leaders who look good on posters and on television.

The hard-rock reality is that prophets don't fit into our way of life.

For a people who are accustomed to "fitting God" into their lives, or, as we like to say, "making room for God," the prophets are hard to take and easy to dismiss. The God of whom the prophets speak is far too large to fit into our lives. If we want anything to do with God, we have to fit into him.

The prophets are not "reasonable," accommodating themselves to what makes sense to us. They are not diplomatic, tactfully negotiating an agreement that allows us a "say" in the outcome. What they do is haul us unceremoniously into a reality far too large to be accounted for by our explanations and expectations. They plunge us into mystery, immense and staggering.

Their words and visions penetrate the illusions with which we cocoon ourselves from reality. We humans have an enormous capacity for denial and for self-deceit. We incapacitate ourselves from dealing with the consequences of sin, for facing judgment, for embracing truth. Then the prophets step in and help us to first recognize and then enter the new life God has for us, the life that hope in God opens up.

They don't explain God. They shake us out of old conventional habits of small-mindedness, of trivializing god-gossip, and set us on our feet in wonder and obedience and worship. If we insist on understanding them before we live into them, we will never get it.

※

Basically, the prophets did two things: They worked to get people to accept the worst as *God's* judgment—not a religious catastrophe or a political disaster, but *judgment*. If what seems like the worst turns out to be *God's* judgment, it can be embraced, not denied or avoided, for God is good and intends our salvation. So judgment, while certainly not what we human beings anticipate in our planned future, can never be the worst that can happen. It is the best, for it is the work of God to set the world, and us, right.

And the prophets worked to get people who were beaten down to open themselves up to hope in God's future. In the wreckage of exile and death and humiliation and sin, the prophet ignited hope, opening lives to the new work of salvation that God is about at all times and everywhere.

※

One of the bad habits that we pick up early in our lives is separating things and people into secular and sacred. We assume that the secular is what we are more or less in charge of: our jobs, our time, our entertainment, our government, our social relations. The sacred is what God has charge of: worship and the Bible, heaven and hell, church and prayers. We then contrive to set aside a sacred place for God, designed, we say, to honor God but really intended to keep God in his place, leaving us free to have the final say about everything else that goes on.

Prophets will have none of this. They contend that everything, absolutely everything, takes place on sacred ground. God has something to say about every aspect of our lives: The way we feel and act in the so-called privacy of our hearts and homes, the way we make our money and the way we spend it, the politics we embrace, the wars we fight, the catastrophes we endure, the people we hurt and the people we help. Nothing is hidden from the scrutiny of God, nothing is exempt from the rule of God, nothing escapes the purposes of God. Holy, holy, holy.

Prophets make it impossible to evade God or make detours around God. Prophets insist on receiving God in every nook and cranny of life. For a prophet, God is more real than the next-door neighbor.

ISAIAH

For Isaiah, words are watercolors and melodies and chisels to make truth and beauty and goodness. Or, as the case may be, hammers and swords and scalpels to *unmake* sin and guilt and rebellion. Isaiah does not merely convey information. He creates visions, delivers revelation, arouses belief. He is a poet in the most fundamental sense — a *maker*, making God present and that presence urgent. Isaiah is the supreme poet-prophet to come out of the Hebrew people.

Isaiah is a large presence in the lives of people who live by faith in God, who submit themselves to being shaped by the Word of God and are on the lookout for the holy. *The Holy.* The characteristic name for God in Isaiah is "The Holy." As we read this large and comprehensive gathering of messages that were preached to the ancient people of Israel, we find ourselves immersed in both the presence and the action of The Holy.

The more hours we spend pondering the words of Isaiah, the more the word "holy" changes in our understanding. If "holy" was ever a pious, pastel-tinted word in our vocabularies, the Isaiah-preaching quickly turns it into something blazing. Holiness is the most attractive quality, the most intense experience we ever get of sheer *life* — authentic, firsthand living, not life looked at and enjoyed from a distance. We find ourselves in on the operations of God himself, not talking about them or reading about them. Holiness is a furnace that transforms the men and women who enter it. "Holy, Holy, Holy" is not needlepoint. It is the banner of a revolution, *the* revolution.

The book of Isaiah is expansive, dealing with virtually everything that is involved in being a people of God on this planet Earth. The impressive art of Isaiah involves taking the stuff of our ordinary and often disappointing human experience and showing us how it is the very stuff that God uses to create and save and give hope. As this vast panorama opens up before us, it turns out that nothing is unusable by God. He uses everything and everybody as material for his work, which is the remaking of the mess we have made of our lives.

"Symphony" is the term many find useful to capture the fusion of simplicity and complexity presented in the book of Isaiah. The major thrust is clearly God's work of salvation: "The Salvation Symphony" (the name Isaiah means "God Saves"). The prominent themes repeated and developed throughout this vast symphonic work are judgment, comfort, and hope. All three elements are present on nearly every page, but each also gives distinction to the three "movements" of the book that so powerfully enact salvation: Messages of Judgment (chapters 1–39), Messages of Comfort (chapters 40–55), and Messages of Hope (chapters 56–66).

ISAIAH

MESSAGES OF JUDGMENT
QUIT YOUR WORSHIP CHARADES

1 The vision that Isaiah son of Amoz saw regarding Judah and Jerusalem during the times of the kings of Judah: Uzziah, Jotham, Ahaz, and Hezekiah.

2-4 Heaven and earth, you're the jury.
    Listen to GOD's case:
"I had children and raised them well,
    and they turned on me.
The ox knows who's boss,
    the mule knows the hand that feeds him,
But not Israel.
    My people don't know up from down.
Shame! Misguided GOD-dropouts,
    staggering under their guilt-baggage,
Gang of miscreants,
    band of vandals —
My people have walked out on me, their GOD,
    turned their backs on The Holy of Israel,
    walked off and never looked back.

5-9 "Why bother even trying to do anything with you
    when you just keep to your bullheaded ways?
You keep beating your heads against brick walls.
    Everything within you protests against you.
From the bottom of your feet to the top of your head,
    nothing's working right.
Wounds and bruises and running sores —
    untended, unwashed, unbandaged.
Your country is laid waste,
    your cities burned down.
Your land is destroyed by outsiders while you watch,
    reduced to rubble by barbarians.
Daughter Zion is deserted —
    like a tumbledown shack on a dead-end street,
Like a tarpaper shanty on the wrong side of the tracks,
    like a sinking ship abandoned by the rats.
If GOD-of-the-Angel-Armies hadn't left us a few survivors,
    we'd be as desolate as Sodom, doomed just like Gomorrah.

10 "Listen to my Message,
    you Sodom-schooled leaders.
Receive God's revelation,
    you Gomorrah-schooled people.

11-12 "Why this frenzy of sacrifices?"
    GOD's asking.
"Don't you think I've had my fill of burnt sacrifices,
    rams and plump grain-fed calves?
Don't you think I've had my fill
    of blood from bulls, lambs, and goats?
When you come before me,
    whoever gave you the idea of acting like this,
Running here and there, doing this and that—
    all this sheer *commotion* in the place provided for worship?

13-17 "Quit your worship charades.
    I can't stand your trivial religious games:
Monthly conferences, weekly Sabbaths, special meetings—
    meetings, meetings, meetings—I can't stand one more!
Meetings for this, meetings for that. I hate them!
    You've worn me out!
I'm sick of your religion, religion, religion,
    while you go right on sinning.
When you put on your next prayer-performance,
    I'll be looking the other way.
No matter how long or loud or often you pray,
    I'll not be listening.
And do you know why? Because you've been tearing
    people to pieces, and your hands are bloody.
Go home and wash up.
    Clean up your act.
Sweep your lives clean of your evildoings
    so I don't have to look at them any longer.
Say no to wrong.
    Learn to do good.
Work for justice.
    Help the down-and-out.
Stand up for the homeless.
    Go to bat for the defenseless.

LET'S ARGUE THIS OUT

18-20 "Come. Sit down. Let's argue this out."
    This is GOD's Message:
"If your sins are blood-red,
    they'll be snow-white.
If they're red like crimson,
    they'll be like wool.
If you'll willingly obey,
    you'll feast like kings.
But if you're willful and stubborn,
    you'll die like dogs."
That's right. GOD says so.

THOSE WHO WALK OUT ON GOD

21-23 Oh! Can you believe it? The chaste city
    has become a whore!
She was once all justice,
    everyone living as good neighbors,
And now they're all
    at one another's throats.
Your coins are all counterfeits.
    Your wine is watered down.
Your leaders are turncoats
    who keep company with crooks.
They sell themselves to the highest bidder
    and grab anything not nailed down.
They never stand up for the homeless,
    never stick up for the defenseless.

24-31 This Decree, therefore, of the Master, GOD-of-the-Angel-Armies,
    the Strong One of Israel:
"This is it! I'll get my oppressors off my back.
    I'll get back at my enemies.
I'll give you the back of my hand,
    purge the junk from your life, clean you up.
I'll set honest judges and wise counselors among you
    just like it was back in the beginning.
Then you'll be renamed
    City-That-Treats-People-Right, the True-Blue City."
GOD's right ways will put Zion right again.
    GOD's right actions will restore her penitents.
But it's curtains for rebels and GOD-traitors,
    a dead end for those who walk out on GOD.
"Your dalliances in those oak grove shrines
    will leave you looking mighty foolish,
All that fooling around in god and goddess gardens
    that you thought was the latest thing.
You'll end up like an oak tree
    with all its leaves falling off,
Like an unwatered garden,
    withered and brown.
'The Big Man' will turn out to be dead bark and twigs,
    and his 'work,' the spark that starts the fire
That exposes man and work both
    as nothing but cinders and smoke."

CLIMB GOD'S MOUNTAIN

1-5 The Message Isaiah got regarding Judah and Jerusalem:

There's a day coming
    when the mountain of GOD's House
Will be The Mountain —
    solid, towering over all mountains.

All nations will river toward it,
  people from all over set out for it.
They'll say, "Come,
  let's climb GOD's Mountain,
  go to the House of the God of Jacob.
He'll show us the way he works
  so we can live the way we're made."
Zion's the source of the revelation.
  GOD's Message comes from Jerusalem.
He'll settle things fairly between nations.
  He'll make things right between many peoples.
They'll turn their swords into shovels,
  their spears into hoes.
No more will nation fight nation;
  they won't play war anymore.
Come, family of Jacob,
  let's live in the light of GOD.

6-9   GOD, you've walked out on your family Jacob
  because their world is full of hokey religion,
Philistine witchcraft, and pagan hocus-pocus,
  a world rolling in wealth,
Stuffed with things,
  no end to its machines and gadgets,
And gods — gods of all sorts and sizes.
  These people make their own gods and worship what they make.
A degenerate race, facedown in the gutter.
  Don't bother with them! They're not worth forgiving!

PRETENTIOUS EGOS BROUGHT DOWN TO EARTH

10   Head for the hills,
  hide in the caves
From the terror of GOD,
  from his dazzling presence.

11-17   People with a big head are headed for a fall,
  pretentious egos brought down a peg.
It's GOD alone at front-and-center
  on the Day we're talking about,
The Day that GOD-of-the-Angel-Armies
  is matched against all big-talking rivals,
  against all swaggering big names;
Against all giant sequoias
  hugely towering,
  and against the expansive chestnut;
Against Kilimanjaro and Annapurna,
  against the ranges of Alps and Andes;
Against every soaring skyscraper,
  against all proud obelisks and statues;
Against ocean-going luxury liners,
  against elegant three-masted schooners.

The swelled big heads will be punctured bladders,
    the pretentious egos brought down to earth,
Leaving GOD alone at front-and-center
    on the Day we're talking about.

18   And all those sticks and stones
        dressed up to look like gods
        will be gone for good.

19   Clamber into caves in the cliffs,
        duck into any hole you can find.
Hide from the terror of GOD,
    from his dazzling presence,
When he assumes his full stature on earth,
    towering and terrifying.

20-21   On that Day men and women will take
        the sticks and stones
They've decked out in gold and silver
    to look like gods and then worshiped,
And they will dump them
    in any ditch or gully,
Then run for rock caves
    and cliff hideouts
To hide from the terror of GOD,
    from his dazzling presence,
When he assumes his full stature on earth,
    towering and terrifying.

22   Quit scraping and fawning over mere humans,
        so full of themselves, so full of hot air!
        Can't you see there's nothing to them?

JERUSALEM ON ITS LAST LEGS

1-7   **3** The Master, GOD-of-the-Angel-Armies,
        is emptying Jerusalem and Judah
    Of all the basic necessities,
    plain bread and water to begin with.
He's withdrawing police and protection,
    judges and courts,
    pastors and teachers,
    captains and generals,
    doctors and nurses,
    and, yes, even the repairmen and jacks-of-all-trades.
He says, "I'll put little kids in charge of the city.
    Schoolboys and schoolgirls will order everyone around.
People will be at each other's throats,
    stabbing one another in the back:
Neighbor against neighbor, young against old,
    the no-account against the well-respected.
One brother will grab another and say,

'You look like you've got a head on your shoulders.
Do something!
    Get us out of this mess.'
And he'll say, 'Me? Not me! I don't have a clue.
    Don't put me in charge of anything.'

8-9   "Jerusalem's on its last legs.
    Judah is soon down for the count.
Everything people say and do
    is at cross-purposes with GOD,
    a slap in my face.
Brazen in their depravity,
    they flaunt their sins like degenerate Sodom.
Doom to their eternal souls! They've made their bed;
    now they'll sleep in it.

10-11   "Reassure the righteous
    that their good living will pay off.
But doom to the wicked! Disaster!
    Everything they did will be done to them.

12   "Skinny kids terrorize my people.
    Silly girls bully them around.
My dear people! Your leaders are taking you down a blind alley.
    They're sending you off on a wild-goose chase."

A CITY BROUGHT TO HER KNEES BY HER SORROWS

13-15   GOD enters the courtroom.
    He takes his place at the bench to judge his people.
GOD calls for order in the court,
    hauls the leaders of his people into the dock:
"You've played havoc with this country.
    Your houses are stuffed with what you've stolen from the poor.
What is this anyway? Stomping on my people,
    grinding the faces of the poor into the dirt?"
That's what the Master,
    GOD-of-the-Angel-Armies, says.

16-17   GOD says, "Zion women are stuck-up,
    prancing around in their high heels,
Making eyes at all the men in the street,
    swinging their hips,
Tossing their hair,
    gaudy and garish in cheap jewelry."
The Master will fix it so those Zion women
    will all turn bald —
Scabby, bald-headed women.
    The Master will do it.

18-23   The time is coming when the Master will strip them of their fancy
baubles — the dangling earrings, anklets and bracelets, combs and mirrors

and silk scarves, diamond brooches and pearl necklaces, the rings on their fingers and the rings on their toes, the latest fashions in hats, exotic perfumes and aphrodisiacs, gowns and capes, all the world's finest in fabrics and design.

24 Instead of wearing seductive scents,
    these women are going to smell like rotting cabbages;
Instead of modeling flowing gowns,
    they'll be sporting rags;
Instead of their stylish hairdos,
    scruffy heads;
Instead of beauty marks,
    scabs and scars.

25-26 Your finest fighting men will be killed,
    your soldiers left dead on the battlefield.
The entrance gate to Zion will be clotted
    with people mourning their dead—
A city stooped under the weight of her loss,
    brought to her knees by her sorrows.

1 **4** That will be the day when seven women
    will gang up on one man, saying,
    "We'll take care of ourselves,
get our own food and clothes.
Just give us a child. Make us pregnant
    so we'll have something to live for!"

GOD'S BRANCH

2-4 And that's when GOD's Branch will sprout green and lush. The produce of the country will give Israel's survivors something to be proud of again. Oh, they'll hold their heads high! Everyone left behind in Zion, all the discards and rejects in Jerusalem, will be reclassified as "holy"—alive and therefore precious. GOD will give Zion's women a good bath. He'll scrub the bloodstained city of its violence and brutality, purge the place with a firestorm of judgment.

5-6 Then GOD will bring back the ancient pillar of cloud by day and the pillar of fire by night and mark Mount Zion and everyone in it with his glorious presence, his immense, protective presence, shade from the burning sun and shelter from the driving rain.

LOOKING FOR A CROP OF JUSTICE

1-2 **5** I'll sing a ballad to the one I love,
    a love ballad about his vineyard:
    The one I love had a vineyard,
a fine, well-placed vineyard.
He hoed the soil and pulled the weeds,
    and planted the very best vines.
He built a lookout, built a winepress,
    a vineyard to be proud of.

He looked for a vintage yield of grapes,
　　but for all his pains he got junk grapes.

3-4　"Now listen to what I'm telling you,
　　you who live in Jerusalem and Judah.
What do you think is going on
　　between me and my vineyard?
Can you think of anything I could have done
　　to my vineyard that I didn't do?
When I expected good grapes,
　　why did I get bitter grapes?

5-6　"Well now, let me tell you
　　what I'll do to my vineyard:
I'll tear down its fence
　　and let it go to ruin.
I'll knock down the gate
　　and let it be trampled.
I'll turn it into a patch of weeds, untended, uncared for—
　　thistles and thorns will take over.
I'll give orders to the clouds:
　　'Don't rain on that vineyard, ever!'"

7　Do you get it? The vineyard of GOD-of-the-Angel-Armies
　　is the country of Israel.
All the men and women of Judah
　　are the garden he was so proud of.
He looked for a crop of justice
　　and saw them murdering each other.
He looked for a harvest of righteousness
　　and heard only the moans of victims.

YOU WHO CALL EVIL GOOD AND GOOD EVIL

8-10　Doom to you who buy up all the houses
　　and grab all the land for yourselves—
Evicting the old owners,
　　posting NO TRESPASSING signs,
Taking over the country,
　　leaving everyone homeless and landless.
I overheard GOD-of-the-Angel-Armies say:
"Those mighty houses will end up empty.
　　Those extravagant estates will be deserted.
A ten-acre vineyard will produce a pint of wine,
　　a fifty-pound sack of seed, a quart of grain."

11-17　Doom to those who get up early
　　and start drinking booze before breakfast,
Who stay up all hours of the night
　　drinking themselves into a stupor.
They make sure their banquets are well-furnished
　　with harps and flutes and plenty of wine,

But they'll have nothing to do with the work of GOD,
    pay no mind to what he is doing.
Therefore my people will end up in exile
    because they don't know the score.
Their "big men" will starve to death
    and the common people die of thirst.
Sheol developed a huge appetite,
    swallowing people nonstop!
Big people and little people alike
    down that gullet, to say nothing of all the drunks.
The down-and-out on a par
    with the high-and-mighty,
Windbag boasters crumpled,
    flaccid as a punctured bladder.
But by working justice,
    GOD-of-the-Angel-Armies will be a mountain.
By working righteousness,
    Holy God will show what "holy" is.
And lambs will graze
    as if they owned the place,
Kids and calves
    right at home in the ruins.

18-19 Doom to you who use lies to sell evil,
    who haul sin to market by the truckload,
Who say, "What's God waiting for?
    Let him get a move on so we can see it.
Whatever The Holy of Israel has cooked up,
    we'd like to check it out."

20 Doom to you who call evil good
    and good evil,
Who put darkness in place of light
    and light in place of darkness,
Who substitute bitter for sweet
    and sweet for bitter!

21-23 Doom to you who think you're so smart,
    who hold such a high opinion of yourselves!
All you're good at is drinking—champion boozers
    who collect trophies from drinking bouts
And then line your pockets with bribes from the guilty
    while you violate the rights of the innocent.

24 But they won't get by with it. As fire eats stubble
    and dry grass goes up in smoke,
Their souls will atrophy,
    their achievements crumble into dust,
Because they said no to the revelation
    of GOD-of-the-Angel-Armies,
Would have nothing to do

with The Holy of Israel.

25-30
That's why GOD flamed out in anger against his people,
    reached out and knocked them down.
The mountains trembled
    as their dead bodies piled up in the streets.
But even after that, he was still angry,
    his fist still raised, ready to hit them again.
He raises a flag, signaling a distant nation,
    whistles for people at the ends of the earth.
And here they come —
    on the run!
None drag their feet, no one stumbles,
    no one sleeps or dawdles.
Shirts are on and pants buckled,
    every boot is spit-polished and tied.
Their arrows are sharp,
    bows strung,
The hooves of their horses shod,
    chariot wheels greased.
Roaring like a pride of lions,
    the full-throated roars of young lions,
They growl and seize their prey,
    dragging it off — no rescue for that one!
They'll roar and roar and roar on that Day,
    like the roar of ocean billows.
Look as long and hard as you like at that land,
    you'll see nothing but darkness and trouble.
Every light in the sky
    will be blacked out by the clouds.

HOLY, HOLY, HOLY!

1-8
6 In the year that King Uzziah died, I saw the Master sitting on a throne — high, exalted! — and the train of his robes filled the Temple. Angel-seraphs hovered above him, each with six wings. With two wings they covered their faces, with two their feet, and with two they flew. And they called back and forth one to the other,

Holy, Holy, Holy is GOD-of-the-Angel-Armies.
    His bright glory fills the whole earth.

The foundations trembled at the sound of the angel voices, and then the whole house filled with smoke. I said,

"Doom! It's Doomsday!
    I'm as good as dead!
Every word I've ever spoken is tainted —
    blasphemous even!
And the people I live with talk the same way,
    using words that corrupt and desecrate.
And here I've looked God in the face!

The King! GOD-of-the-Angel-Armies!"

Then one of the angel-seraphs flew to me. He held a live coal that he
had taken with tongs from the altar. He touched my mouth with the coal
and said,

"Look. This coal has touched your lips.
    Gone your guilt,
        your sins wiped out."
And then I heard the voice of the Master:
    "Whom shall I send?
    Who will go for us?"
I spoke up,
    "I'll go.
    Send me!"

9-10 He said, "Go and tell this people:

"'Listen hard, but you aren't going to get it;
    look hard, but you won't catch on.'
Make these people blockheads,
    with fingers in their ears and blindfolds on their eyes,
So they won't see a thing,
    won't hear a word,
So they won't have a clue about what's going on
    and, yes, so they won't turn around and be made whole."

11-13 Astonished, I said,
    "And Master, how long is this to go on?"
He said, "Until the cities are emptied out,
    not a soul left in the cities—
Houses empty of people,
    countryside empty of people.
Until I, GOD, get rid of everyone, sending them off,
    the land totally empty.
And even if some should survive, say a tenth,
    the devastation will start up again.
The country will look like pine and oak forest
    with every tree cut down—
Every tree a stump, a huge field of stumps.
    But there's a holy seed in those stumps."

A VIRGIN WILL BEAR A SON

1-2 During the time that Ahaz son of Jotham, son of Uzziah, was king
of Judah, King Rezin of Aram and King Pekah son of Remaliah
of Israel attacked Jerusalem, but the attack sputtered out. When
the Davidic government learned that Aram had joined forces with Ephraim
(that is, Israel), Ahaz and his people were badly shaken. They shook like trees
in the wind.

3-6 Then GOD told Isaiah, "Go and meet Ahaz. Take your son Shear-jashub (A-Remnant-Will-Return) with you. Meet him south of the city at the end of the aqueduct where it empties into the upper pool on the road to the public laundry. Tell him, Listen, calm down. Don't be afraid. And don't panic over these two burnt-out cases, Rezin of Aram and the son of Remaliah. They talk big but there's nothing to them. Aram, along with Ephraim's son of Remaliah, have plotted to do you harm. They've conspired against you, saying, 'Let's go to war against Judah, dismember it, take it for ourselves, and set the son of Tabeel up as a puppet king over it.'

7-9 But GOD, the Master, says,

"It won't happen.
    Nothing will come of it
Because the capital of Aram is Damascus
    and the king of Damascus is a mere man, Rezin.
As for Ephraim, in sixty-five years
    it will be rubble, nothing left of it.
The capital of Ephraim is Samaria,
    and the king of Samaria is the mere son of Remaliah.
If you don't take your stand in faith,
    you won't have a leg to stand on."

10-11 GOD spoke again to Ahaz. This time he said, "Ask for a sign from your GOD. Ask anything. Be extravagant. Ask for the moon!"

12 But Ahaz said, "I'd never do that. I'd never make demands like that on GOD!"

13-17 So Isaiah told him, "Then listen to this, government of David! It's bad enough that you make people tired with your pious, timid hypocrisies, but now you're making God tired. So the Master is going to give you a sign anyway. Watch for this: A girl who is presently a virgin will get pregnant. She'll bear a son and name him Immanuel (God-With-Us). By the time the child is twelve years old, able to make moral decisions, the threat of war will be over. Relax, those two kings that have you so worried will be out of the picture. But also be warned: GOD will bring on you and your people and your government a judgment worse than anything since the time the kingdom split, when Ephraim left Judah. The king of Assyria is coming!"

18-19 That's when GOD will whistle for the flies at the headwaters of Egypt's Nile, and whistle for the bees in the land of Assyria. They'll come and infest every nook and cranny of this country. There'll be no getting away from them.

20 And that's when the Master will take the razor rented from across the Euphrates — the king of Assyria no less! — and shave the hair off your heads and genitals, leaving you shamed, exposed, and denuded. He'll shave off your beards while he's at it.

21-22 It will be a time when survivors will count themselves lucky to have a cow and a couple of sheep. At least they'll have plenty of milk! Whoever's left in the land will learn to make do with the simplest foods — curds, whey, and honey.

23-25 But that's not the end of it. This country that used to be covered with fine vineyards — thousands of them, worth millions! — will revert to a weed patch. Weeds and thornbushes everywhere! Good for nothing except, perhaps, hunting rabbits. Cattle and sheep will forage as best they can in the fields of weeds — but there won't be a trace of all those fertile and well-tended gardens and fields.

1   Then GOD told me, "Get a big sheet of paper and write in indelible ink, 'This belongs to Maher-shalal-hash-baz (Spoil-Speeds-Plunder-Hurries).'"

2-3   I got two honest men, Uriah the priest and Zechariah son of Jeberekiah, to witness the document. Then I went home to my wife, the prophetess. She conceived and gave birth to a son.

3-4   GOD told me, "Name him Maher-shalal-hash-baz. Before that baby says 'Daddy' or 'Mamma' the king of Assyria will have plundered the wealth of Damascus and the riches of Samaria."

5-8   GOD spoke to me again, saying:

"Because this people has turned its back
    on the gently flowing stream of Shiloah
And gotten all excited over Rezin
    and the son of Remaliah,
I'm stepping in and facing them with
    the wild floodwaters of the Euphrates,
The king of Assyria and all his fanfare,
    a river in flood, bursting its banks,
Pouring into Judah, sweeping everything before it,
    water up to your necks,
A huge wingspan of a raging river,
    O Immanuel, spreading across your land."

9-10   But face the facts, all you oppressors, and then wring your hands.
    Listen, all of you, far and near.
Prepare for the worst and wring your hands.
    Yes, prepare for the worst and wring your hands!
Plan and plot all you want — nothing will come of it.
    All your talk is mere talk, empty words,
Because when all is said and done,
    the last word is Immanuel — God-With-Us.

A BOULDER BLOCKING YOUR WAY

11-15   GOD spoke strongly to me, grabbed me with both hands and warned me not to go along with this people. He said:

"Don't be like this people,
    always afraid somebody is plotting against them.
Don't fear what they fear.
    Don't take on their worries.

If you're going to worry,
>   worry about The Holy. Fear GOD-of-the-Angel-Armies.
The Holy can be either a Hiding Place
>   or a Boulder blocking your way,
The Rock standing in the willful way
>   of both houses of Israel,
A barbed-wire Fence preventing trespass
>   to the citizens of Jerusalem.
Many of them are going to run into that Rock
>   and get their bones broken,
Get tangled up in that barbed wire
>   and not get free of it."

16-18   Gather up the testimony,
>   preserve the teaching for my followers,
While I wait for GOD as long as he remains in hiding,
>   while I wait and hope for him.
I stand my ground and hope,
>   I and the children GOD gave me as signs to Israel,
Warning signs and hope signs from GOD-of-the-Angel-Armies,
>   who makes his home in Mount Zion.

19-22   When people tell you, "Try out the fortunetellers.
>   Consult the spiritualists.
Why not tap into the spirit-world,
>   get in touch with the dead?"
Tell them, "No, we're going to study the Scriptures."
>   People who try the other ways get nowhere—a dead end!
Frustrated and famished,
>   they try one thing after another.
When nothing works out they get angry,
>   cursing first this god and then that one,
Looking this way and that,
>   up, down, and sideways — and seeing nothing,
A blank wall, an empty hole.
>   They end up in the dark with nothing.

A CHILD HAS BEEN BORN—FOR US!

1   But there'll be no darkness for those who were in trouble. Earlier he did bring the lands of Zebulun and Naphtali into disrepute, but the time is coming when he'll make that whole area glorious — the road along the Sea, the country past the Jordan, international Galilee.

2-7   The people who walked in darkness
>   have seen a great light.
For those who lived in a land of deep shadows—
>   light! sunbursts of light!
You repopulated the nation,
>   you expanded its joy.
Oh, they're so glad in your presence!

Festival joy!
The joy of a great celebration,
    sharing rich gifts and warm greetings.
The abuse of oppressors and cruelty of tyrants—
    all their whips and cudgels and curses—
Is gone, done away with, a deliverance
    as surprising and sudden as Gideon's old victory over Midian.
The boots of all those invading troops,
    along with their shirts soaked with innocent blood,
Will be piled in a heap and burned,
    a fire that will burn for days!
For a child has been born—for us!
    the gift of a son—for us!
He'll take over
    the running of the world.
His names will be: Amazing Counselor,
    Strong God,
Eternal Father,
    Prince of Wholeness.
His ruling authority will grow,
    and there'll be no limits to the wholeness he brings.
He'll rule from the historic David throne
    over that promised kingdom.
He'll put that kingdom on a firm footing
    and keep it going
With fair dealing and right living,
    beginning now and lasting always.
The zeal of GOD-of-the-Angel-Armies
    will do all this.

GOD ANSWERED FIRE WITH FIRE

8-10 The Master sent a message against Jacob.
    It landed right on Israel's doorstep.
All the people soon heard the message,
    Ephraim and the citizens of Samaria.
But they were a proud and arrogant bunch.
    They dismissed the message, saying,
"Things aren't that bad.
    We can handle anything that comes.
If our buildings are knocked down,
    we'll rebuild them bigger and finer.
If our forests are cut down,
    we'll replant them with finer trees."

11-12 So GOD incited their adversaries against them,
    stirred up their enemies to attack:
From the east, Arameans; from the west, Philistines.
    They made hash of Israel.
But even after that, he was still angry,
    his fist still raised, ready to hit them again.

13-17 But the people paid no mind to him who hit them,
  didn't seek GOD-of-the-Angel-Armies.
So GOD hacked off Israel's head and tail,
  palm branch and reed, both on the same day.
The big-head elders were the head,
  the lying prophets were the tail.
Those who were supposed to lead this people
  led them down blind alleys,
And those who followed the leaders
  ended up lost and confused.
That's why the Master lost interest in the young men,
  had no feeling for their orphans and widows.
All of them were godless and evil,
  talking filth and folly.
And even after that, he was still angry,
  his fist still raised, ready to hit them again.

18-21 Their wicked lives raged like an out-of-control fire,
  the kind that burns everything in its path —
Trees and bushes, weeds and grasses —
  filling the skies with smoke.
GOD-of-the-Angel-Armies answered fire with fire,
  set the whole country on fire,
Turned the people into consuming fires,
  consuming one another in their lusts —
Appetites insatiable, stuffing and gorging
  themselves left and right with people and things.
But still they starved. Not even their children
  were safe from their rapacious hunger.
Manasseh ate Ephraim, and Ephraim Manasseh,
  and then the two ganged up against Judah.
And after that, he was still angry,
  his fist still raised, ready to hit them again.

YOU WHO LEGISLATE EVIL

1-4 **10** Doom to you who legislate evil,
  who make laws that make victims —

Laws that make misery for the poor,
  that rob my destitute people of dignity,
Exploiting defenseless widows,
  taking advantage of homeless children.
What will you have to say on Judgment Day,
  when Doomsday arrives out of the blue?
Who will you get to help you?
  What good will your money do you?
A sorry sight you'll be then, huddled with the prisoners,
  or just some corpses stacked in the street.

Even after all this, God is still angry,
  his fist still raised, ready to hit them again.

D O O M T O A S S Y R I A !

5-11   "Doom to Assyria, weapon of my anger.
  My wrath is a cudgel in his hands!
I send him against a godless nation,
  against the people I'm angry with.
I command him to strip them clean, rob them blind,
  and then push their faces in the mud and leave them.
But Assyria has another agenda;
  he has something else in mind.
He's out to destroy utterly,
  to stamp out as many nations as he can.
Assyria says, 'Aren't my commanders all kings?
  Can't they do whatever they like?
Didn't I destroy Calno as well as Carchemish?
  Hamath as well as Arpad? Level Samaria as I did Damascus?
I've eliminated kingdoms full of gods
  far more impressive than anything in Jerusalem and Samaria.
So what's to keep me from destroying Jerusalem
  in the same way I destroyed Samaria and all her god-idols?'"

12-13   When the Master has finished dealing with Mount Zion and Jerusalem, he'll say, "Now it's Assyria's turn. I'll punish the bragging arrogance of the king of Assyria, his high and mighty posturing, the way he goes around saying,

13-14   "'I've done all this by myself.
  I know more than anyone.
I've wiped out the boundaries of whole countries.
  I've walked in and taken anything I wanted.
I charged in like a bull
  and toppled their kings from their thrones.
I reached out my hand and took all that they treasured
  as easily as a boy taking a bird's eggs from a nest.
Like a farmer gathering eggs from the henhouse,
  I gathered the world in my basket,
And no one so much as fluttered a wing
  or squawked or even chirped.'"

15-19   Does an ax take over from the one who swings it?
  Does a saw act more important than the sawyer?
As if a shovel did its shoveling by using a ditch digger!
  As if a hammer used the carpenter to pound nails!
Therefore the Master, GOD-of-the-Angel-Armies,
  will send a debilitating disease on his robust Assyrian fighters.
Under the canopy of God's bright glory
  a fierce fire will break out.
Israel's Light will burst into a conflagration.
  The Holy will explode into a firestorm,

And in one day burn to cinders
    every last Assyrian thornbush.
GOD will destroy the splendid trees and lush gardens.
    The Assyrian body and soul will waste away to nothing
    like a disease-ridden invalid.
A child could count what's left of the trees
    on the fingers of his two hands.

20-23   And on that Day also, what's left of Israel, the ragtag survivors of Jacob, will no longer be fascinated by abusive, battering Assyria. They'll lean on GOD, The Holy — yes, truly. The ragtag remnant — what's left of Jacob — will come back to the Strong God. Your people Israel were once like the sand on the seashore, but only a scattered few will return. Destruction is ordered, brimming over with righteousness. For the Master, GOD-of-the-Angel-Armies, will finish here what he started all over the globe.

24-27   Therefore the Master, GOD-of-the-Angel-Armies, says: "My dear, dear people who live in Zion, don't be terrorized by the Assyrians when they beat you with clubs and threaten you with rods like the Egyptians once did. In just a short time my anger against you will be spent and I'll turn my destroying anger on them. I, GOD-of-the-Angel-Armies, will go after them with a cat-o'-nine-tails and finish them off decisively — as Gideon downed Midian at the rock Oreb, as Moses turned the tables on Egypt. On that day, Assyria will be pulled off your back, and the yoke of slavery lifted from your neck."

27-32   Assyria's on the move: up from Rimmon,
    on to Aiath,
through Migron,
    with a bivouac at Micmash.
They've crossed the pass,
    set camp at Geba for the night.
Ramah trembles with fright.
    Gibeah of Saul has run off.
Cry for help, daughter of Gallim!
    Listen to her, Laishah!
    Do something, Anathoth!
Madmenah takes to the hills.
    The people of Gebim flee in panic.
The enemy's soon at Nob — nearly there!
    In sight of the city he shakes his fist
At the mount of dear daughter Zion,
    the hill of Jerusalem.

33-34   But now watch this: The Master, GOD-of-the-Angel-Armies,
    swings his ax and lops the branches,
Chops down the giant trees,
    lays flat the towering forest-on-the-march.
His ax will make toothpicks of that forest,
    that Lebanon-like army reduced to kindling.

A GREEN SHOOT FROM JESSE'S STUMP

¹⁻⁵ **11** A green Shoot will sprout from Jesse's stump,
from his roots a budding Branch.
The life-giving Spirit of GOD will hover over him,
the Spirit that brings wisdom and understanding,
The Spirit that gives direction and builds strength,
the Spirit that instills knowledge and Fear-of-GOD.
Fear-of-GOD
will be all his joy and delight.
He won't judge by appearances,
won't decide on the basis of hearsay.
He'll judge the needy by what is right,
render decisions on earth's poor with justice.
His words will bring everyone to awed attention.
A mere breath from his lips will topple the wicked.
Each morning he'll pull on sturdy work clothes and boots,
and build righteousness and faithfulness in the land.

A LIVING KNOWLEDGE OF GOD

⁶⁻⁹ The wolf will romp with the lamb,
the leopard sleep with the kid.
Calf and lion will eat from the same trough,
and a little child will tend them.
Cow and bear will graze the same pasture,
their calves and cubs grow up together,
and the lion eat straw like the ox.
The nursing child will crawl over rattlesnake dens,
the toddler stick his hand down the hole of a serpent.
Neither animal nor human will hurt or kill
on my holy mountain.
The whole earth will be brimming with knowing God-Alive,
a living knowledge of God ocean-deep, ocean-wide.

¹⁰ On that day, Jesse's Root will be raised high, posted as a rallying banner
for the peoples. The nations will all come to him. His headquarters will be
glorious.

¹¹ Also on that day, the Master for the second time will reach out to bring
back what's left of his scattered people. He'll bring them back from Assyria,
Egypt, Pathros, Ethiopia, Elam, Sinar, Hamath, and the ocean islands.

¹²⁻¹⁶ And he'll raise that rallying banner high, visible to all nations,
gather in all the scattered exiles of Israel,
Pull in all the dispersed refugees of Judah
from the four winds and the seven seas.
The jealousy of Ephraim will dissolve,
the hostility of Judah will vanish —
Ephraim no longer the jealous rival of Judah,
Judah no longer the hostile rival of Ephraim!
Blood brothers united, they'll pounce on the Philistines in the west,

join forces to plunder the people in the east.
They'll attack Edom and Moab.
　　The Ammonites will fall into line.
GOD will once again dry up Egypt's Red Sea,
　　making for an easy crossing.
He'll send a blistering wind
　　down on the great River Euphrates,
Reduce it to seven mere trickles.
　　None even need get their feet wet!
In the end there'll be a highway all the way from Assyria,
　　easy traveling for what's left of God's people —
A highway just like the one Israel had
　　when he marched up out of Egypt.

MY STRENGTH AND SONG

1　**12** And you will say in that day,
　　　　"I thank you, GOD.
　　　　You were angry
　　but your anger wasn't forever.
You withdrew your anger
　　and moved in and comforted me.

2　"Yes, indeed — God is my salvation.
　　I trust, I won't be afraid.
GOD — yes GOD! — is my strength and song,
　　best of all, my salvation!"

3-4　Joyfully you'll pull up buckets of water
　　from the wells of salvation.
And as you do it, you'll say,
　　"Give thanks to GOD.
Call out his name.
　　Ask him anything!
Shout to the nations, tell them what he's done,
　　spread the news of his great reputation!

5-6　"Sing praise-songs to GOD. He's done it all!
　　Let the whole earth know what he's done!
Raise the roof! Sing your hearts out, O Zion!
　　The Greatest lives among you: The Holy of Israel."

BABYLON IS DOOMED!

1　**13** The Message on Babylon. Isaiah son of Amoz saw it:

2-3　"Run up a flag on an open hill.
　　Yell loud. Get their attention.
Wave them into formation.
　　Direct them to the nerve center of power.
I've taken charge of my special forces,
　　called up my crack troops.
They're bursting with pride and passion
　　to carry out my angry judgment."

₄₋₅ Thunder rolls off the mountains
　　like a mob huge and noisy —
Thunder of kingdoms in an uproar,
　　nations assembling for war.
GOD-of-the-Angel-Armies is calling
　　his army into battle formation.
They come from far-off countries,
　　they pour in across the horizon.
It's GOD on the move with the weapons of his wrath,
　　ready to destroy the whole country.

₆₋₈ Wail! GOD's Day of Judgment is near —
　　an avalanche crashing down from the Strong God!
Everyone paralyzed in the panic,
　　hysterical and unstrung,
Doubled up in pain
　　like a woman giving birth to a baby.
Horrified — everyone they see
　　is like a face out of a nightmare.

₉₋₁₆ "Watch now. GOD's Judgment Day comes.
　　Cruel it is, a day of wrath and anger,
A day to waste the earth
　　and clean out all the sinners.
The stars in the sky, the great parade of constellations,
　　will be nothing but black holes.
The sun will come up as a black disk,
　　and the moon a blank nothing.
I'll put a full stop to the evil on earth,
　　terminate the dark acts of the wicked.
I'll gag all braggarts and boasters — not a peep anymore from them —
　　and trip strutting tyrants, leave them flat on their faces.
Proud humanity will disappear from the earth.
　　I'll make mortals rarer than hens' teeth.
And yes, I'll even make the sky shake,
　　and the earth quake to its roots
Under the wrath of GOD-of-the-Angel-Armies,
　　the Judgment Day of his raging anger.
Like a hunted white-tailed deer,
　　like lost sheep with no shepherd,
People will huddle with a few of their own kind,
　　run off to some makeshift shelter.
But tough luck to stragglers — they'll be killed on the spot,
　　throats cut, bellies ripped open,
Babies smashed on the rocks
　　while mothers and fathers watch,
Houses looted,
　　wives raped.

₁₇₋₂₂ "And now watch this:

Against Babylon, I'm inciting the Medes,
A ruthless bunch indifferent to bribes,
the kind of brutality that no one can blunt.
They massacre the young,
wantonly kick and kill even babies.
And Babylon, most glorious of all kingdoms,
the pride and joy of Chaldeans,
Will end up smoking and stinking like Sodom,
and, yes, like Gomorrah, when God had finished with them.
No one will live there anymore,
generation after generation a ghost town.
Not even Bedouins will pitch tents there.
Shepherds will give it a wide berth.
But strange and wild animals will like it just fine,
filling the vacant houses with eerie night sounds.
Skunks will make it their home,
and unspeakable night hags will haunt it.
Hyenas will curdle your blood with their laughing,
and the howling of coyotes will give you the shivers.

"Babylon is doomed.
It won't be long now."

Now You Are Nothing

1-2 **14** But not so with Jacob. GOD will have compassion on Jacob. Once again he'll choose Israel. He'll establish them in their own country. Outsiders will be attracted and throw their lot in with Jacob. The nations among whom they lived will actually escort them back home, and then Israel will pay them back by making slaves of them, men and women alike, possessing them as slaves in GOD's country, capturing those who had captured them, ruling over those who had abused them.

3-4 When GOD has given you time to recover from the abuse and trouble and harsh servitude that you had to endure, you can amuse yourselves by taking up this satire, a taunt against the king of Babylon:

4-6 Can you believe it? The tyrant is gone!
The tyranny is over!
GOD has broken the rule of the wicked,
the power of the bully-rulers
That crushed many people.
A relentless rain of cruel outrage
Established a violent rule of anger
rife with torture and persecution.

7-10 And now it's over, the whole earth quietly at rest.
Burst into song! Make the rafters ring!
Ponderosa pine trees are happy,
giant Lebanon cedars are relieved, saying,
"Since you've been cut down,
there's no one around to cut us down."
And the underworld dead are all excited,

preparing to welcome you when you come.
Getting ready to greet you are the ghostly dead,
    all the famous names of earth.
All the buried kings of the nations
    will stand up on their thrones
With well-prepared speeches,
    royal invitations to death:
"Now you are as nothing as we are!
    Make yourselves at home with us dead folks!"

11   This is where your pomp and fine music led you, Babylon,
    to your underworld private chambers,
A king-size mattress of maggots for repose
    and a quilt of crawling worms for warmth.

12   What a comedown this, O Babylon!
    Daystar! Son of Dawn!
Flat on your face in the underworld mud,
    you, famous for flattening nations!

13-14   You said to yourself,
    "I'll climb to heaven.
I'll set my throne
    over the stars of God.
I'll run the assembly of angels
    that meets on sacred Mount Zaphon.
I'll climb to the top of the clouds.
    I'll take over as King of the Universe!"

15-17   But you didn't make it, did you?
    Instead of climbing up, you came down—
Down with the underground dead,
    down to the abyss of the Pit.
People will stare and muse:
    "Can this be the one
Who terrorized earth and its kingdoms,
    turned earth to a moonscape,
Wasted its cities,
    shut up his prisoners to a living death?"

18-20   Other kings get a decent burial,
    honored with eulogies and placed in a tomb.
But you're dumped in a ditch unburied,
    like a stray dog or cat,
Covered with rotting bodies,
    murdered and indigent corpses.
Your dead body desecrated, mutilated—
    no state funeral for you!
You've left your land in ruins,
    left a legacy of massacre.
The progeny of your evil life

will never be named. Oblivion!

21   Get a place ready to slaughter the sons of the wicked
        and wipe out their father's line.
    Unthinkable that they should own a square foot of land
        or desecrate the face of the world with their cities!

22-23   "I will confront them"—Decree of GOD-of-the-Angel-Armies—"and strip Babylon of name and survivors, children and grandchildren." GOD'S Decree. "I'll make it a worthless swamp and give it as a prize to the hedgehog. And then I'll bulldoze it out of existence." Decree of GOD-of-the-Angel-Armies.

WHO COULD EVER CANCEL SUCH PLANS?

24-27   GOD-of-the-Angel-Armies speaks:

"Exactly as I planned,
    it will happen.
Following my blueprints,
    it will take shape.
I will shatter the Assyrian who trespasses my land
    and stomp him into the dirt on my mountains.
I will ban his taking and making of slaves
    and lift the weight of oppression from all shoulders."
This is the plan,
    planned for the whole earth,
And this is the hand that will do it,
    reaching into every nation.
GOD-of-the-Angel-Armies has planned it.
    Who could ever cancel such plans?
His is the hand that's reached out.
    Who could brush it aside?

28-31   In the year King Ahaz died, this Message came:

Hold it, Philistines! It's too soon to celebrate
    the defeat of your cruel oppressor.
From the death throes of that snake a worse snake will come,
    and from that, one even worse.
The poor won't have to worry.
    The needy will escape the terror.
But you Philistines will be plunged into famine,
    and those who don't starve, God will kill.
Wail and howl, proud city!
    Fall prostrate in fear, Philistia!
On the northern horizon, smoke from burned cities,
    the wake of a brutal, disciplined destroyer.

32   What does one say to
        outsiders who ask questions?
Tell them, "GOD has established Zion.

Those in need and in trouble find refuge in her."

POIGNANT CRIES REVERBERATE THROUGH MOAB

15

1-4 A Message concerning Moab:

Village Ar of Moab is in ruins,
    destroyed in a night raid.
Village Kir of Moab is in ruins,
    destroyed in a night raid.
Village Dibon climbs to its chapel in the hills,
    goes up to lament.
Moab weeps and wails
    over Nebo and Medba.
Every head is shaved bald,
    every beard shaved clean.
They pour into the streets wearing black,
    go up on the roofs, take to the town square,
Everyone in tears,
    everyone in grief.
Towns Heshbon and Elealeh cry long and loud.
    The sound carries as far as Jahaz.
Moab sobs, shaking in grief.
    The soul of Moab trembles.

5-9 Oh, how I grieve for Moab!
    Refugees stream to Zoar
    and then on to Eglath-shelishiyah.
Up the slopes of Luhith they weep;
    on the road to Horonaim they cry their loss.
The springs of Nimrim are dried up —
    grass brown, buds stunted, nothing grows.
They leave, carrying all their possessions
    on their backs, everything they own,
Making their way as best they can
    across Willow Creek to safety.
Poignant cries reverberate
    all through Moab,
Gut-wrenching sobs as far as Eglaim,
    heart-racking sobs all the way to Beer-elim.
The banks of the Dibon crest with blood,
    but God has worse in store for Dibon:
A lion — a lion to finish off the fugitives,
    to clean up whoever's left in the land.

A NEW GOVERNMENT IN THE DAVID TRADITION

16

1-4 "Dispatch a gift of lambs," says Moab,
    "to the leaders in Jerusalem —
    Lambs from Sela sent across the desert
to buy the goodwill of Jerusalem.
The towns and people of Moab
    are at a loss,

New-hatched birds knocked from the nest,
　　fluttering helplessly
At the banks of the Arnon River,
　　unable to cross:
'Tell us what to do,
　　help us out!
Protect us,
　　hide us!
Give the refugees from Moab
　　sanctuary with you.
Be a safe place for those on the run
　　from the killing fields.'"

4-5　"When this is all over," Judah answers,
　　　"the tyrant toppled,
The killing at an end,
　　all signs of these cruelties long gone,
A new government of love will be established
　　in the venerable David tradition.
A Ruler you can depend upon
　　will head this government,
A Ruler passionate for justice,
　　a Ruler quick to set things right."

6-12　We've heard — everyone's heard! — of Moab's pride,
　　　world-famous for pride —
Arrogant, self-important, insufferable,
　　full of hot air.
So now let Moab lament for a change,
　　with antiphonal mock-laments from the neighbors!
What a shame! How terrible!
　　No more fine fruitcakes and Kir-hareseth candies!
All those lush Heshbon fields dried up,
　　the rich Sibmah vineyards withered!
Foreign thugs have crushed and torn out
　　the famous grapevines
That once reached all the way to Jazer,
　　right to the edge of the desert,
Ripped out the crops in every direction
　　as far as the eye can see.
I'll join the weeping. I'll weep right along with Jazer,
　　weep for the Sibmah vineyards.
And yes, Heshbon and Elealeh,
　　I'll mingle my tears with your tears!
The joyful shouting at harvest is gone.
　　Instead of song and celebration, dead silence.
No more boisterous laughter in the orchards,
　　no more hearty work songs in the vineyards.
Instead of the bustle and sound of good work in the fields,
　　silence — deathly and deadening silence.

My heartstrings throb like harp strings for Moab,
  my soul in sympathy for sad Kir-heres.
When Moab trudges to the shrine to pray,
  he wastes both time and energy.
Going to the sanctuary and praying for relief
  is useless. Nothing ever happens.

13-14   This is GOD's earlier Message on Moab. GOD's updated Message is, "In three years, no longer than the term of an enlisted soldier, Moab's impressive presence will be gone, that splendid hot-air balloon will be punctured, and instead of a vigorous population, just a few shuffling bums cadging handouts."

DAMASCUS: A PILE OF DUST AND RUBBLE

1-3   **17** A Message concerning Damascus:

"Watch this: Damascus undone as a city,
  a pile of dust and rubble!
Her towns emptied of people.
  The sheep and goats will move in
And take over the towns
  as if they owned them — which they will!
Not a sign of a fort is left in Ephraim,
  not a trace of government left in Damascus.
What's left of Aram?
  The same as what's left of Israel — not much."
    Decree of GOD-of-the-Angel-Armies.

THE DAY IS COMING

4-6   "The Day is coming when Jacob's robust splendor goes pale
  and his well-fed body turns skinny.
The country will be left empty, picked clean
  as a field harvested by field hands.
She'll be like a few stalks of barley left standing
  in the lush Valley of Rephaim after harvest,
Or like the couple of ripe olives overlooked
  in the top of the olive tree,
Or the four or five apples
  that the pickers couldn't reach in the orchard."
    Decree of the GOD of Israel.

7-8   Yes, the Day is coming when people will notice The One Who Made Them, take a long hard look at The Holy of Israel. They'll lose interest in all the stuff they've made — altars and monuments and rituals, their home-made, handmade religion — however impressive it is.

9   And yes, the Day is coming when their fortress cities will be abandoned — the very same cities that the Hivites and Amorites abandoned when Israel invaded! And the country will be empty, desolate.

10-11 And why? Because you have forgotten God-Your-Salvation,
     not remembered your Rock-of-Refuge.
And so, even though you are very religious,
     planting all sorts of bushes and herbs and trees
     to honor and influence your fertility gods,
And even though you make them grow so well,
     bursting with buds and sprouts and blossoms,
Nothing will come of them. Instead of a harvest
     you'll get nothing but grief and pain, pain, pain.

12-13 Oh my! Thunder! A thundering herd of people!
     Thunder like the crashing of ocean waves!
Nations roaring, roaring,
     like the roar of a massive waterfall,
Roaring like a deafening Niagara!
     But God will silence them with a word,
And then he'll blow them away like dead leaves off a tree,
     like down from a thistle.

14 At bedtime, terror fills the air.
     By morning it's gone — not a sign of it anywhere!
This is what happens to those who would ruin us,
     this is the fate of those out to get us.

1-2 **18** Doom to the land of flies and mosquitoes
     beyond the Ethiopian rivers,
Shipping emissaries all over the world,
down rivers and across seas.

Go, swift messengers,
     go to this people tall and handsome,
This people held in respect everywhere,
     this people mighty and merciless,
     from the land crisscrossed with rivers.

3 Everybody everywhere,
     all earth-dwellers:
When you see a flag flying on the mountain, look!
     When you hear the trumpet blown, listen!

4-6 For here's what GOD told me:

"I'm not going to say anything,
     but simply look on from where I live,
Quiet as warmth that comes from the sun,
     silent as dew during harvest."
And then, just before harvest, after the blossom
     has turned into a maturing grape,

He'll step in and prune back the new shoots,
     ruthlessly hack off all the growing branches.
He'll leave them piled on the ground
     for birds and animals to feed on —
Fodder for the summering birds,
     fodder for the wintering animals.

7 Then tribute will be brought to GOD-of-the-Angel-Armies,
     brought from this people tall and handsome,
This people once held in respect everywhere,
     this people once mighty and merciless,
From the land crisscrossed with rivers,
     to Mount Zion, GOD's place.

ANARCHY AND CHAOS AND KILLING!

1 **19** A Message concerning Egypt:

Watch this! GOD riding on a fast-moving cloud,
     moving in on Egypt!
The god-idols of Egypt shudder and shake,
     Egyptians paralyzed by panic.

2-4 God says, "I'll make Egyptian fight Egyptian,
     brother fight brother, neighbor fight neighbor,
City fight city, kingdom fight kingdom —
     anarchy and chaos and killing!
I'll knock the wind out of the Egyptians.
     They won't know coming from going.
They'll go to their god-idols for answers;
     they'll conjure ghosts and hold séances, desperate for answers.
But I'll turn the Egyptians
     over to a tyrant most cruel.
I'll put them under the rule of a mean, merciless king."
     Decree of the Master, GOD-of-the-Angel-Armies.

5-10 The River Nile will dry up,
     the riverbed baked dry in the sun.
The canals will become stagnant and stink,
     every stream touching the Nile dry up.
River vegetation will rot away
     the banks of the Nile-baked clay,
The riverbed hard and smooth,
     river grasses dried up and gone with the wind.
Fishermen will complain
     that the fishing's been ruined.
Textile workers will be out of work, all weavers
     and workers in linen and cotton and wool
Dispirited, depressed in their forced idleness —
     everyone who works for a living, jobless.

11-15 The princes of Zoan are fools,
     the advisors of Pharaoh stupid.

How could any of you dare tell Pharaoh,
    "Trust me: I'm wise. I know what's going on.
    Why, I'm descended from the old wisdom of Egypt"?
There's not a wise man or woman left in the country.
    If there were, one of them would tell you
    what GOD-of-the-Angel-Armies has in mind for Egypt.
As it is, the princes of Zoan are all fools
    and the princes of Memphis, dunces.
The honored pillars of your society
    have led Egypt into detours and dead ends.
GOD has scrambled their brains,
    Egypt's become a falling-down-in-his-own-vomit drunk.
Egypt's hopeless, past helping,
    a senile, doddering old fool.

16-17   On that Day, Egyptians will be like hysterical schoolgirls, screaming at the first hint of action from GOD-of-the-Angel-Armies. Little Judah will strike terror in Egyptians! Say "Judah" to an Egyptian and see panic. The word triggers fear of the GOD-of-the-Angel-Armies' plan against Egypt.

18   On that Day, more than one city in Egypt will learn to speak the language of faith and promise to follow GOD-of-the-Angel-Armies. One of these cities will be honored with the title "City of the Sun."

19-22   On that Day, there will be a place of worship to GOD in the center of Egypt and a monument to GOD at its border. It will show how the GOD-of-the-Angel-Armies has helped the Egyptians. When they cry out in prayer to GOD because of oppressors, he'll send them help, a savior who will keep them safe and take care of them. GOD will openly show himself to the Egyptians and they'll get to know him on that Day. They'll worship him seriously with sacrifices and burnt offerings. They'll make vows and keep them. GOD will wound Egypt, first hit and then heal. Egypt will come back to GOD, and GOD will listen to their prayers and heal them, heal them from head to toe.

23   On that Day, there will be a highway all the way from Egypt to Assyria: Assyrians will have free range in Egypt and Egyptians in Assyria. No longer rivals, they'll worship together, Egyptians and Assyrians!

24-25   On that Day, Israel will take its place alongside Egypt and Assyria, sharing the blessing from the center. GOD-of-the-Angel-Armies, who blessed Israel, will generously bless them all: "Blessed be Egypt, my people! . . . Blessed be Assyria, work of my hands! . . . Blessed be Israel, my heritage!"

EXPOSED TO MOCKERY AND JEERS

1-2   **20** In the year the field commander, sent by King Sargon of Assyria, came to Ashdod and fought and took it, GOD told Isaiah son of Amoz, "Go, take off your clothes and sandals," and Isaiah did it, going about naked and barefooted.

3-6   Then GOD said, "Just as my servant Isaiah has walked around town naked and barefooted for three years as a warning sign to Egypt and Ethiopia, so the king of Assyria is going to come and take the Egyptians as captives and the Ethiopians as exiles. He'll take young and old alike and march them out of there naked and barefooted, exposed to mockery and jeers — the bared buttocks of Egypt on parade! Everyone who has put hope in Ethiopia and expected help from Egypt will be thrown into confusion. Everyone who lives along this coast will say, 'Look at them! Naked and barefooted, shuffling off to exile! And we thought they were our best hope, that they'd rescue us from the king of Assyria. *Now* what's going to happen to us? How are we going to get out of this?'"

The Betrayer Betrayed

21 A Message concerning the desert at the sea:

1-4

As tempests drive through the Negev Desert,
    coming out of the desert, that terror-filled place,
A hard vision is given me:
    The betrayer betrayed, the plunderer plundered.
Attack, Elam!
    Lay siege, Media!
Persians, attack!
    Attack, Babylon!
I'll put an end to
    all the moaning and groaning.
Because of this news I'm doubled up in pain,
    writhing in pain like a woman having a baby,
Baffled by what I hear,
    undone by what I see.
Absolutely stunned,
    horror-stricken,
I had hoped for a relaxed evening,
    but it has turned into a nightmare.

5 The banquet is spread,
    the guests reclining in luxurious ease,
Eating and drinking, having a good time,
    and then, "To arms, princes! The fight is on!"

6-9 The Master told me, "Go, post a lookout.
    Have him report whatever he spots.
When he sees horses and wagons in battle formation,
    lines of donkeys and columns of camels,
Tell him to keep his ear to the ground,
    note every whisper, every rumor."
Just then, the lookout shouted,
    "I'm at my post, Master,
Sticking to my post day after day
    and all through the night!
I watched them come,
    the horses and wagons in battle formation.
I heard them call out the war news in headlines:
    'Babylon fallen! Fallen!
And all its precious god-idols
    smashed to pieces on the ground.'"

10   Dear Israel, you've been through a lot,
       you've been put through the mill.
     The good news I get from God-of-the-Angel-Armies,
       the God of Israel, I now pass on to you.

11-12   A Message concerning Edom:

        A voice calls to me
          from the Seir mountains in Edom,
        "Night watchman! How long till daybreak?
          How long will this night last?"
        The night watchman calls back,
          "Morning's coming,
        But for now it's still night.
          If you ask me again, I'll give the same answer."

13-15   A Message concerning Arabia:

        You'll have to camp out in the desert badlands,
          you caravans of Dedanites.
        Haul water to the thirsty,
          greet fugitives with bread.
        Show your desert hospitality,
          you who live in Tema.
        The desert's swarming with refugees
          escaping the horrors of war.

16-17   The Master told me, "Hang on. Within one year—I'll sign a contract on it!—the arrogant brutality of Kedar, those hooligans of the desert, will be over, nothing much left of the Kedar toughs." The God of Israel says so.

A Country of Cowards

1-3   **22** A Message concerning the Valley of Vision:

        What's going on here anyway?
          All this partying and noisemaking,
        Shouting and cheering in the streets,
          the city noisy with celebrations!
        You have no brave soldiers to honor,
          no combat heroes to be proud of.
        Your leaders were all cowards,
          captured without even lifting a sword,
        A country of cowards
          captured escaping the battle.

You Looked, but You Never Looked to Him

4-8   In the midst of the shouting, I said, "Let me alone.
       Let me grieve by myself.
     Don't tell me it's going to be all right.

These people are doomed. It's *not* all right."
For the Master, GOD-of-the-Angel-Armies,
    is bringing a day noisy with mobs of people,
Jostling and stampeding in the Valley of Vision,
    knocking down walls
    and hollering to the mountains, "Attack! Attack!"
Old enemies Elam and Kir arrive armed to the teeth —
    weapons and chariots and cavalry.
Your fine valleys are noisy with war,
    chariots and cavalry charging this way and that.
    God has left Judah exposed and defenseless.

8-11   You assessed your defenses that Day, inspected your arsenal of weapons in the Forest Armory. You found the weak places in the city walls that needed repair. You secured the water supply at the Lower Pool. You took an inventory of the houses in Jerusalem and tore down some to get bricks to fortify the city wall. You built a large cistern to ensure plenty of water.

You looked and looked and looked, but you never looked to him who gave you this city, never once consulted the One who has long had plans for this city.

12-13   The Master, GOD-of-the-Angel-Armies,
    called out on that Day,
Called for a day of repentant tears,
    called you to dress in somber clothes of mourning.
But what do *you* do? You throw a party!
    Eating and drinking and dancing in the streets!
You barbecue bulls and sheep, and throw a huge feast —
    slabs of meat, kegs of beer.
"Seize the day! Eat and drink!
    Tomorrow we die!"

14   GOD-of-the-Angel-Armies whispered to me his verdict on this frivolity: "You'll pay for this outrage until the day you die." The Master, GOD-of-the-Angel-Armies, says so.

THE KEY OF THE DAVIDIC HERITAGE

15-19   The Master, GOD-of-the-Angel-Armies, spoke: "Come. Go to this steward, Shebna, who is in charge of all the king's affairs, and tell him: What's going on here? You're an outsider here and yet you act like you own the place, make a big, fancy tomb for yourself where everyone can see it, making sure everyone will think you're important. GOD is about to sack you, to throw you to the dogs. He'll grab you by the hair, swing you round and round dizzyingly, and then let you go, sailing through the air like a ball, until you're out of sight. Where you'll land, nobody knows. And there you'll die, and all the stuff you've collected heaped on your grave. You've disgraced your master's house! You're fired — and good riddance!

20-24   "On that Day I'll replace Shebna. I will call my servant Eliakim son of Hilkiah. I'll dress him in your robe. I'll put your belt on him. I'll give him your authority. He'll be a father-leader to Jerusalem and the government of

Judah. I'll give him the key of the Davidic heritage. He'll have the run of the place—open any door and keep it open, lock any door and keep it locked. I'll pound him like a nail into a solid wall. He'll secure the Davidic tradition. Everything will hang on him—not only the fate of Davidic descendants but also the detailed daily operations of the house, including cups and cutlery.

25   "And then the Day will come," says GOD-of-the-Angel-Armies, "when that nail will come loose and fall out, break loose from that solid wall—and everything hanging on it will go with it." That's what will happen. GOD says so.

IT WAS ALL NUMBERS, DEAD NUMBERS, PROFIT AND LOSS

1-4   23 Wail, ships of Tarshish,
        your strong seaports all in ruins!
     When the ships returned from Cyprus,
   they saw the destruction.
Hold your tongue, you who live on the seacoast,
   merchants of Sidon.
Your people sailed the deep seas,
   buying and selling,
Making money on wheat from Shihor,
   grown along the Nile—
   multinational broker in grains!
Hang your head in shame, Sidon. The Sea speaks up,
   the powerhouse of the ocean says,
"I've never had labor pains, never had a baby,
   never reared children to adulthood,
Never gave life, never worked with life.
   It was all numbers, dead numbers, profit and loss."

5   When Egypt gets the report on Tyre,
   what wailing! what wringing of hands!

NOTHING LEFT HERE TO BE PROUD OF

6-12   Visit Tarshish, you who live on the seacoast.
        Take a good, long look and wail—yes, cry buckets of tears!
     Is this the city you remember as energetic and alive,
        bustling with activity, this historic old city,
     Expanding throughout the globe,
        buying and selling all over the world?
     And who is behind the collapse of Tyre,
        the Tyre that controlled the world markets?
     Tyre's merchants were the business tycoons.
        Tyre's traders called all the shots.
     GOD-of-the-Angel-Armies ordered the crash
        to show the sordid backside of pride
        and puncture the inflated reputations.
     Sail for home, O ships of Tarshish.
        There are no docks left in this harbor.
     GOD reached out to the sea and sea traders,
        threw the sea kingdoms into turmoil.

GOD ordered the destruction
    of the seacoast cities, the centers of commerce.
GOD said, "There's nothing left here to be proud of,
    bankrupt and bereft Sidon.
Do you want to make a new start in Cyprus?
    Don't count on it. Nothing there will work out for you either."

13   Look at what happened to Babylon: There's nothing left of it. Assyria turned it into a desert, into a refuge for wild dogs and stray cats. They brought in their big siege engines, tore down the buildings, and left nothing behind but rubble.

14   Wail, ships of Tarshish,
    your strong seaports all in ruins!

15-16   For the next seventy years, a king's lifetime, Tyre will be forgotten. At the end of the seventy years, Tyre will stage a comeback, but it will be the comeback of a worn-out whore, as in the song:

"Take a harp, circle the city,
    unremembered whore.
Sing your old songs, your many old songs.
    Maybe someone will remember."

17-18   At the end of the seventy years, GOD will look in on Tyre. She'll go back to her old whoring trade, selling herself to the highest bidder, doing anything with anyone — promiscuous with all the kingdoms of earth — for a fee. But everything she gets, all the money she takes in, will be turned over to GOD. It will not be put in banks. Her profits will be put to the use of GOD-Aware, GOD-Serving-People, providing plenty of food and the best of clothing.

THE LANDSCAPE WILL BE A MOONSCAPE

1-3   **24** Danger ahead! GOD's about to ravish the earth
        and leave it in ruins,
    Rip everything out by the roots
and send everyone scurrying:
    priests and laypeople alike,
    owners and workers alike,
    celebrities and nobodies alike,
    buyers and sellers alike,
    bankers and beggars alike,
    the haves and have-nots alike.
The landscape will be a moonscape,
    totally wasted.
And why? Because GOD says so.
    He's issued the orders.

4   The earth turns gaunt and gray,
    the world silent and sad,

sky and land lifeless, colorless.

EARTH POLLUTED BY ITS VERY OWN PEOPLE

5-13 Earth is polluted by its very own people,
    who have broken its laws,
Disrupted its order,
    violated the sacred and eternal covenant.
Therefore a curse, like a cancer,
    ravages the earth.
Its people pay the price of their sacrilege.
    They dwindle away, dying out one by one.
No more wine, no more vineyards,
    no more songs or singers.
The laughter of castanets is gone,
    the shouts of celebrants, gone,
    the laughter of fiddles, gone.
No more parties with toasts of champagne.
    Serious drinkers gag on their drinks.
The chaotic cities are unlivable. Anarchy reigns.
    Every house is boarded up, condemned.
People riot in the streets for wine,
    but the good times are gone forever —
    no more joy for this old world.
The city is dead and deserted,
    bulldozed into piles of rubble.
That's the way it will be on this earth.
    This is the fate of all nations:
An olive tree shaken clean of its olives,
    a grapevine picked clean of its grapes.

14-16 But there are some who will break into glad song.
    Out of the west they'll shout of GOD's majesty.
Yes, from the east GOD's glory will ascend.
    Every island of the sea
Will broadcast GOD's fame,
    the fame of the God of Israel.
From the four winds and the seven seas we hear the singing:
    "All praise to the Righteous One!"

16-20 But I said, "That's all well and good for somebody,
    but all I can see is doom, doom, and more doom."
All of them at one another's throats,
    yes, all of them at one another's throats.
Terror and pits and booby traps
    are everywhere, whoever you are.
If you run from the terror,
    you'll fall into the pit.
If you climb out of the pit,
    you'll get caught in the trap.
Chaos pours out of the skies.
    The foundations of earth are crumbling.

Earth is smashed to pieces,
    earth is ripped to shreds,
    earth is wobbling out of control,
Earth staggers like a drunk,
    sways like a shack in a high wind.
Its piled-up sins are too much for it.
    It collapses and won't get up again.

21-23   That's when GOD will call on the carpet
    rebel powers in the skies and
Rebel kings on earth.
    They'll be rounded up like prisoners in a jail,
Corralled and locked up in a jail,
    and then sentenced and put to hard labor.
Shamefaced moon will cower, humiliated,
    red-faced sun will skulk, disgraced,
Because GOD-of-the-Angel-Armies will take over,
    ruling from Mount Zion and Jerusalem,
Splendid and glorious
    before all his leaders.

GOD'S HAND RESTS ON THIS MOUNTAIN

1-5   **25** GOD, you are *my* God.
    I celebrate you. I praise you.
    You've done your share of miracle-wonders,
    well-thought-out plans, solid and sure.
Here you've reduced the city to rubble,
    the strong city to a pile of stones.
The enemy Big City is a non-city,
    never to be a city again.
Superpowers will see it and honor you,
    brutal oppressors bow in worshipful reverence.
They'll see that you take care of the poor,
    that you take care of poor people in trouble,
Provide a warm, dry place in bad weather,
    provide a cool place when it's hot.
Brutal oppressors are like a winter blizzard
    and vicious foreigners like high noon in the desert.
But you, shelter from the storm and shade from the sun,
    shut the mouths of the big-mouthed bullies.

6-8   But here on this mountain, GOD-of-the-Angel-Armies
    will throw a feast for all the people of the world,
A feast of the finest foods, a feast with vintage wines,
    a feast of seven courses, a feast lavish with gourmet desserts.
And here on this mountain, GOD will banish
    the pall of doom hanging over all peoples,
The shadow of doom darkening all nations.
    Yes, he'll banish death forever.
And GOD will wipe the tears from every face.
    He'll remove every sign of disgrace

From his people, wherever they are.
   Yes! GOD says so!

9-10 Also at that time, people will say,
   "Look at what's happened! This is our God!
We waited for him and he showed up and saved us!
   This GOD, the one we waited for!
Let's celebrate, sing the joys of his salvation.
   GOD's hand rests on this mountain!"

10-12 As for the Moabites, they'll be treated like refuse,
   waste shoveled into a cesspool.
Thrash away as they will,
   like swimmers trying to stay afloat,
They'll sink in the sewage.
   Their pride will pull them under.
Their famous fortifications will crumble to nothing,
   those mighty walls reduced to dust.

STRETCH THE BORDERS OF LIFE

1-6 **26** At that time, this song
   will be sung in the country of Judah:
We have a strong city, Salvation City,
   built and fortified with salvation.
Throw wide the gates
   so good and true people can enter.
People with their minds set on you,
   you keep completely whole,
Steady on their feet,
   because they keep at it and don't quit.
Depend on GOD and keep at it
   because in the LORD GOD you have a sure thing.
Those who lived high and mighty
   he knocked off their high horse.
He used the city built on the hill
   as fill for the marshes.
All the exploited and outcast peoples
   build their lives on the reclaimed land.

7-10 The path of right-living people is level.
   The Leveler evens the road for the right-living.
We're in no hurry, GOD. We're content to linger
   in the path sign-posted with your decisions.
Who you are and what you've done
   are all we'll ever want.
Through the night my soul longs for you.
   Deep from within me my spirit reaches out to you.
When your decisions are on public display,
   everyone learns how to live right.
If the wicked are shown grace,
   they don't seem to get it.

In the land of right living, they persist in wrong living,
    blind to the splendor of GOD.

11-15   You hold your hand up high, GOD,
    but they don't see it.
Open their eyes to what you do,
    to see your zealous love for your people.
Shame them. Light a fire under them.
    Get the attention of these enemies of yours.
GOD, order a peaceful and whole life for us
    because everything we've done, you've done for us.
O GOD, our God, we've had other masters rule us,
    but you're the only Master we've ever known.
The dead don't talk,
    ghosts don't walk,
Because you've said, "Enough — that's all for you,"
    and wiped them off the books.
But the living you make larger than life.
    The more life you give, the more glory you display,
    and stretch the borders to accommodate more living!

16-18   O GOD, they begged you for help when they were in trouble,
    when your discipline was so heavy
    they could barely whisper a prayer.
Like a woman having a baby,
    writhing in distress, screaming her pain
    as the baby is being born,
That's how we were because of you, O GOD.
    We were pregnant full-term.
We writhed in labor but bore no baby.
    We gave birth to wind.
Nothing came of our labor.
    We produced nothing living.
    We couldn't save the world.

19   But friends, your dead will live,
    your corpses will get to their feet.
All you dead and buried,
    wake up! Sing!
Your dew is morning dew
    catching the first rays of sun,
The earth bursting with life,
    giving birth to the dead.

20-21   Come, my people, go home
    and shut yourselves in.
Go into seclusion for a while
    until the punishing wrath is past,
Because GOD is sure to come from his place
    to punish the wrong of the people on earth.
Earth itself will point out the bloodstains;

it will show where the murdered have been hidden away.

SELECTED GRAIN BY GRAIN

27 At that time GOD will unsheathe his sword,
      his merciless, massive, mighty sword.
      He'll punish the serpent Leviathan as it flees,
the serpent Leviathan thrashing in flight.
He'll kill that old dragon
    that lives in the sea.

"At that same time, a fine vineyard will appear.
    There's something to sing about!
I, GOD, tend it.
    I keep it well-watered.
I keep careful watch over it
    so that no one can damage it.
I'm not angry. I care.
    Even if it gives me thistles and thornbushes,
I'll just pull them out
    and burn them up.
Let that vine cling to me for safety,
    let it find a good and whole life with me,
    let it hold on for a good and whole life."

The days are coming when Jacob
    shall put down roots,
Israel blossom and grow fresh branches,
    and fill the world with its fruit.

Has GOD knocked them to the ground
    as he knocked down those who hit them? Oh, no.
Were they killed
    as their killers were killed? Again, no.
He was hard on them all right. The exile was a harsh sentence.
    He blew them away on a fierce blast of wind.
But the good news is that through this experience
    Jacob's guilt was taken away.
    The evidence that his sin is removed will be this:
He will tear down the alien altars,
    take them apart stone by stone,
And then crush the stones into gravel
    and clean out all the sex-and-religion shrines.
For there's nothing left of that pretentious grandeur.
    Nobody lives there anymore. It's unlivable.
But animals do just fine,
    browsing and bedding down.
And it's not a bad place to get firewood.
    Dry twigs and dead branches are plentiful.
It's the leavings of a people with no sense of God.
    So, the God who made them
Will have nothing to do with them.

He who formed them will turn his back on them.

12-13 At that time GOD will thresh
from the River Euphrates to the Brook of Egypt,
And you, people of Israel,
will be selected grain by grain.
At that same time a great trumpet will be blown,
calling home the exiles from Assyria,
Welcoming home the refugees from Egypt
to come and worship GOD on the holy mountain, Jerusalem.

GOD WILL SPEAK IN BABY TALK

1-4 **28** Doom to the pretentious drunks of Ephraim,
shabby and washed out and seedy—
Tipsy, sloppy-fat, beer-bellied parodies
of a proud and handsome past.
Watch closely: GOD has someone picked out,
someone tough and strong to flatten them.
Like a hailstorm, like a hurricane, like a flash flood,
one-handed he'll throw them to the ground.
Samaria, the party hat on Israel's head,
will be knocked off with one blow.
It will disappear quicker than
a piece of meat tossed to a dog.

5-6 At that time, GOD-of-the-Angel-Armies will be
the beautiful crown on the head of what's left of his people:
Energy and insights of justice to those who guide and decide,
strength and prowess to those who guard and protect.

7-8 These also, the priest and prophet, stagger from drink,
weaving, falling-down drunks,
Besotted with wine and whiskey,
can't see straight, can't talk sense.
Every table is covered with vomit.
They *live* in vomit.

9-10 "Is that so? And who do you think you are to teach us?
Who are you to lord it over us?
We're not babies in diapers
to be talked down to by such as you—
'Da, da, da, da,
blah, blah, blah, blah.
That's a good little girl,
that's a good little boy.'"

11-12 But that's exactly how you will be addressed.
God will speak to this people
In baby talk, one syllable at a time—
and he'll do it through foreign oppressors.
He said before, "This is the time and place to rest,

to give rest to the weary.
This is the place to lay down your burden."
But they won't listen.

13 So GOD will start over with the simple basics
and address them in baby talk, one syllable at a time —
"Da, da, da, da,
blah, blah, blah, blah.
That's a good little girl,
that's a good little boy."
And like toddlers, they will get up and fall down,
get bruised and confused and lost.

14-15 Now listen to GOD's Message, you scoffers,
you who rule this people in Jerusalem.
You say, "We've taken out good life insurance.
We've hedged all our bets, covered all our bases.
No disaster can touch us. We've thought of everything.
We're advised by the experts. We're set."

THE MEANING OF THE STONE

16-17 But the Master, GOD, has something to say to this:

"Watch closely. I'm laying a foundation in Zion,
a solid granite foundation, squared and true.
And this is the meaning of the stone:
A TRUSTING LIFE WON'T TOPPLE.
I'll make justice the measuring stick
and righteousness the plumb line for the building.
A hailstorm will knock down the shantytown of lies,
and a flash flood will wash out the rubble.

18-22 "Then you'll see that your precious life insurance policy
wasn't worth the paper it was written on.
Your careful precautions against death
were a pack of illusions and lies.
When the disaster happens,
you'll be crushed by it.
Every time disaster comes, you'll be in on it —
disaster in the morning, disaster at night."
Every report of disaster
will send you cowering in terror.
There will be no place where you can rest,
nothing to hide under.
GOD will rise to full stature,
raging as he did long ago on Mount Perazim
And in the valley of Gibeon against the Philistines.
But this time it's against *you*.
Hard to believe, but true.
Not what you'd expect, but it's coming.
Sober up, friends, and don't scoff.

Scoffing will just make it worse.
I've heard the orders issued for destruction, orders from
GOD-of-the-Angel-Armies—ending up in an international disaster.

23-26 Listen to me now.
Give me your closest attention.
Do farmers plow and plow and do nothing but plow?
Or harrow and harrow and do nothing but harrow?
After they've prepared the ground, don't they plant?
Don't they scatter dill and spread cumin,
Plant wheat and barley in the fields
and raspberries along the borders?
They know exactly what to do and when to do it.
Their God is their teacher.

27-29 And at the harvest, the delicate herbs and spices,
the dill and cumin, are treated delicately.
On the other hand, wheat is threshed and milled, but still not endlessly.
The farmer knows how to treat each kind of grain.
He's learned it all from GOD-of-the-Angel-Armies,
who knows everything about when and how and where.

BLIND YOURSELVES SO THAT YOU SEE NOTHING

1-4 **29** Doom, Ariel, Ariel,
the city where David set camp!
Let the years add up,
let the festivals run their cycles,
But I'm not letting up on Jerusalem.
The moaning and groaning will continue.
Jerusalem to me is an Ariel.
Like David, I'll set up camp against you.
I'll set siege, build towers,
bring in siege engines, build siege ramps.
Driven into the ground, you'll speak,
you'll mumble words from the dirt—
Your voice from the ground, like the muttering of a ghost.
Your speech will whisper from the dust.

5-8 But it will be your enemies who are beaten to dust,
the mob of tyrants who will be blown away like chaff.
Because, surprise, as if out of nowhere,
a visit from GOD-of-the-Angel-Armies,
With thunderclaps, earthquakes, and earsplitting noise,
backed up by hurricanes, tornadoes, and lightning strikes,
And the mob of enemies at war with Ariel,
all who trouble and hassle and torment her,
will turn out to be a bad dream, a nightmare.
Like a hungry man dreaming he's eating steak
and wakes up hungry as ever,
Like a thirsty woman dreaming she's drinking iced tea

and wakes up thirsty as ever,
So that mob of nations at war against Mount Zion
  will wake up and find they haven't shot an arrow,
  haven't killed a single soul.

9-10   Drug yourselves so you feel nothing.
  Blind yourselves so you see nothing.
Get drunk, but not on wine.
  Black out, but not from whiskey.
For GOD has rocked you into a deep, deep sleep,
  put the discerning prophets to sleep,
  put the farsighted seers to sleep.

YOU HAVE EVERYTHING BACKWARD

11-12   What you've been shown here is somewhat like a letter in a sealed envelope. If you give it to someone who can read and tell her, "Read this," she'll
say, "I can't. The envelope is sealed." And if you give it to someone who can't
read and tell him, "Read this," he'll say, "I can't read."

13-14   The Master said:

"These people make a big show of saying the right thing,
  but their hearts aren't in it.
Because they act like they're worshiping me
  but don't mean it,
I'm going to step in and shock them awake,
  astonish them, stand them on their ears.
The wise ones who had it all figured out
  will be exposed as fools.
The smart people who thought they knew everything
  will turn out to know nothing."

15-16   Doom to you! You pretend to have the inside track.
  You shut GOD out and work behind the scenes,
Plotting the future as if you knew everything,
  acting mysterious, never showing your hand.
You have everything backward!
  You treat the potter as a lump of clay.
Does a book say to its author,
  "He didn't write a word of me"?
Does a meal say to the woman who cooked it,
  "She had nothing to do with this"?

17-21   And then before you know it,
  and without you having anything to do with it,
Wasted Lebanon will be transformed into lush gardens,
  and Mount Carmel reforested.
At that time the deaf will hear
  word-for-word what's been written.
After a lifetime in the dark,

the blind will see.
The castoffs of society will be laughing and dancing in GOD,
    the down-and-outs shouting praise to The Holy of Israel.
For there'll be no more gangs on the street.
    Cynical scoffers will be an extinct species.
Those who never missed a chance to hurt or demean
    will never be heard of again:
Gone the people who corrupted the courts,
    gone the people who cheated the poor,
    gone the people who victimized the innocent.

22-24 And finally this, GOD's Message for the family of Jacob,
    the same GOD who redeemed Abraham:
"No longer will Jacob hang his head in shame,
    no longer grow gaunt and pale with waiting.
For he's going to see his children,
    my personal gift to him — lots of children.
And these children will honor me
    by living holy lives.
In holy worship they'll honor the Holy One of Jacob
    and stand in holy awe of the God of Israel.
Those who got off-track will get back on-track,
    and complainers and whiners learn gratitude."

ALL SHOW, NO SUBSTANCE

1-5 **30** "Doom, rebel children!"
    GOD's Decree.
    "You make plans, but not mine.
You make deals, but not in my Spirit.
You pile sin on sin,
    one sin on top of another,
Going off to Egypt
    without so much as asking me,
Running off to Pharaoh for protection,
    expecting to hide out in Egypt.
Well, some protection Pharaoh will be!
    Some hideout, Egypt!
They look big and important, true,
    with officials strategically established in
Zoan in the north and Hanes in the south,
    but there's nothing to them.
Anyone stupid enough to trust them
    will end up looking stupid —
All show, no substance,
    an embarrassing farce."

6-7 And this note on the animals of the Negev
    encountered on the road to Egypt:
A most dangerous, treacherous route,
    menaced by lions and deadly snakes.
And you're going to lug all your stuff down *there,*

your donkeys and camels loaded down with bribes,
Thinking you can buy protection
    from that hollow farce of a nation?
Egypt is all show, no substance.
    My name for her is Toothless Dragon.

THIS IS A REBEL GENERATION

8-11 So, go now and write all this down.
    Put it in a book
So that the record will be there
    to instruct the coming generations,
Because this is a rebel generation,
    a people who lie,
A people unwilling to listen
    to anything GOD tells them.
They tell their spiritual leaders,
    "Don't bother us with irrelevancies."
They tell their preachers,
    "Don't waste our time on impracticalities.
Tell us what makes us feel better.
    Don't bore us with obsolete religion.
That stuff means nothing to us.
    Quit hounding us with The Holy of Israel."

12-14 Therefore, The Holy of Israel says this:
    "Because you scorn this Message,
Preferring to live by injustice
    and shape your lives on lies,
This perverse way of life
    will be like a towering, badly built wall
That slowly, slowly tilts and shifts,
    and then one day, without warning, collapses—
Smashed to bits like a piece of pottery,
    smashed beyond recognition or repair,
Useless, a pile of debris
    to be swept up and thrown in the trash."

GOD TAKES THE TIME TO DO EVERYTHING RIGHT

15-17 GOD, the Master, The Holy of Israel,
    has this solemn counsel:
"Your salvation requires you to turn back to me
    and stop your silly efforts to save yourselves.
Your strength will come from settling down
    in complete dependence on me—
The very thing
    you've been unwilling to do.
You've said, 'Nothing doing! We'll rush off on horseback!'
    You'll rush off, all right! Just not far enough!
You've said, 'We'll ride off on fast horses!'
    Do you think your pursuers ride old nags?
Think again: A thousand of you will scatter before one attacker.

Before a mere five you'll all run off.
There'll be nothing left of you —
  a flagpole on a hill with no flag,
  a signpost on a roadside with the sign torn off."

18 But God's not finished. He's waiting around to be gracious to you.
  He's gathering strength to show mercy to you.
God takes the time to do everything right — everything.
  Those who wait around for him are the lucky ones.

19-22   Oh yes, people of Zion, citizens of Jerusalem, your time of tears is over. Cry for help and you'll find it's grace and more grace. The moment he hears, he'll answer. Just as the Master kept you alive during the hard times, he'll keep your teacher alive and present among you. Your teacher will be right there, local and on the job, urging you on whenever you wander left or right: "This is the right road. Walk down this road." You'll scrap your expensive and fashionable god-images. You'll throw them in the trash as so much garbage, saying, "Good riddance!"

23-26   God will provide rain for the seeds you sow. The grain that grows will be abundant. Your cattle will range far and wide. Oblivious to war and earthquake, the oxen and donkeys you use for hauling and plowing will be fed well near running brooks that flow freely from mountains and hills. Better yet, on the Day God heals his people of the wounds and bruises from the time of punishment, moonlight will flare into sunlight, and sunlight, like a whole week of sunshine at once, will flood the land.

27-28 Look, God's on his way,
  and from a long way off!
Smoking with anger,
  immense as he comes into view,
Words steaming from his mouth,
  searing, indicting words!
A torrent of words, a flash flood of words
  sweeping everyone into the vortex of his words.
He'll shake down the nations in a sieve of destruction,
  herd them into a dead end.

29-33 But *you* will sing,
  sing through an all-night holy feast!
Your hearts will burst with song,
  make music like the sound of flutes on parade,
En route to the mountain of God,
  on the way to the Rock of Israel.
God will sound out in grandiose thunder,
  display his hammering arm,
Furiously angry, showering sparks —
  cloudburst, storm, hail!
Oh yes, at God's thunder
  Assyria will cower under the clubbing.
Every blow God lands on them with his club

is in time to the music of drums and pipes,
GOD in all-out, two-fisted battle,
    fighting against them.
Topheth's fierce fires are well prepared,
    ready for the Assyrian king.
The Topheth furnace is deep and wide,
    well stoked with hot-burning wood.
GOD's breath, like a river of burning pitch,
    starts the fire.

IMPRESSED BY MILITARY MATHEMATICS

1-3   **31**   Doom to those who go off to Egypt
    thinking that horses can help them,
    Impressed by military mathematics,
awed by sheer numbers of chariots and riders—
And to The Holy of Israel, not even a glance,
    not so much as a prayer to GOD.
Still, he must be reckoned with,
    a most wise God who knows what he's doing.
He can call down catastrophe.
    He's a God who does what he says.
He intervenes in the work of those who do wrong,
    stands up against interfering evildoers.
Egyptians are mortal, not God,
    and their horses are flesh, not Spirit.
When GOD gives the signal, helpers and helped alike
    will fall in a heap and share the same dirt grave.

4-5   This is what GOD told me:

"Like a lion, king of the beasts,
    that gnaws and chews and worries its prey,
Not fazed in the least by a bunch of shepherds
    who arrive to chase it off,
So GOD-of-the-Angel-Armies comes down
    to fight on Mount Zion, to make war from its heights.
And like a huge eagle hovering in the sky,
    GOD-of-the-Angel-Armies protects Jerusalem.
I'll protect and rescue it.
    Yes, I'll hover and deliver."

6-7   Repent, return, dear Israel, to the One you so cruelly abandoned. On the day you return, you'll throw away—every last one of you—the no-gods your sinful hands made from metal and wood.

8-9   "Assyrians will fall dead,
    killed by a sword-thrust but not by a soldier,
    laid low by a sword not swung by a mortal.
Assyrians will run from that sword, run for their lives,
    and their prize young men made slaves.

Terrorized, that rock-solid people will fall to pieces,
    their leaders scatter hysterically."
GOD's Decree on Assyria.
    His fire blazes in Zion,
    his furnace burns hot in Jerusalem.

SAFE HOUSES, QUIET GARDENS

1-8 **32** But look! A king will rule in the right way,
    and his leaders will carry out justice.
    Each one will stand as a shelter from high winds,
    provide safe cover in stormy weather.
Each will be cool running water in parched land,
    a huge granite outcrop giving shade in the desert.
Anyone who looks will see,
    anyone who listens will hear.
The impulsive will make sound decisions,
    the tongue-tied will speak with eloquence.
No more will fools become celebrities,
    nor crooks be rewarded with fame.
For fools are fools and that's that,
    thinking up new ways to do mischief.
They leave a wake of wrecked lives
    and lies about GOD,
Turning their backs on the homeless hungry,
    ignoring those dying of thirst in the streets.
And the crooks? Underhanded sneaks they are,
    inventive in sin and scandal,
Exploiting the poor with scams and lies,
    unmoved by the victimized poor.
But those who are noble make noble plans,
    and stand for what is noble.

9-14 Take your stand, indolent women!
    Listen to me!
Indulgent, indolent women,
    listen closely to what I have to say.
In just a little over a year from now,
    you'll be shaken out of your lazy lives.
The grape harvest will fail,
    and there'll be no fruit on the trees.
Oh tremble, you indolent women.
    Get serious, you pampered dolls!
Strip down and discard your silk fineries.
    Put on funeral clothes.
Shed honest tears for the lost harvest,
    the failed vintage.
Weep for my people's gardens and farms
    that grow nothing but thistles and thornbushes.
Cry tears, real tears, for the happy homes no longer happy,
    the merry city no longer merry.

The royal palace is deserted,
 the bustling city quiet as a morgue,
The emptied parks and playgrounds
 taken over by wild animals,
 delighted with their new home.

15-20 Yes, weep and grieve until the Spirit is poured
  down on us from above
And the badlands desert grows crops
  and the fertile fields become forests.
Justice will move into the badlands desert.
  Right will build a home in the fertile field.
And where there's Right, there'll be Peace
  and the progeny of Right: quiet lives and endless trust.
My people will live in a peaceful neighborhood—
  in safe houses, in quiet gardens.
The forest of your pride will be clear-cut,
  the city showing off your power leveled.
But you will enjoy a blessed life,
  planting well-watered fields and gardens,
  with your farm animals grazing freely.

THE GROUND UNDER OUR FEET MOURNS

1 **33** Doom to you, Destroyer,
   not yet destroyed;
  And doom to you, Betrayer,
 not yet betrayed.
When you finish destroying,
 your turn will come—destroyed!
When you quit betraying,
 your turn will come—betrayed!

2-4 GOD, treat us kindly. You're our only hope.
  First thing in the morning, be there for us!
  When things go bad, help us out!
You spoke in thunder and everyone ran.
  You showed up and nations scattered.
Your people, for a change, got in on the loot,
  picking the field clean of the enemy spoils.

5-6 GOD is supremely esteemed. His center holds.
  Zion brims over with all that is just and right.
GOD keeps your days stable and secure—
  salvation, wisdom, and knowledge in surplus,
  and best of all, Zion's treasure, Fear-of-GOD.

7-9 But look! Listen!
  Tough men weep openly.
  Peacemaking diplomats are in bitter tears.
The roads are empty—
  not a soul out on the streets.

The peace treaty is broken,
 its conditions violated,
 its signers reviled.
The very ground under our feet mourns,
 the Lebanon mountains hang their heads,
Flowering Sharon is a weed-choked gully,
 and the forests of Bashan and Carmel? Bare branches.

10-12   "Now I'm stepping in," GOD says.
 "From now on, I'm taking over.
 The gloves come off. Now see how mighty I am.
There's nothing to you.
 Pregnant with chaff, you produce straw babies;
 full of hot air, you self-destruct.
You're good for nothing but fertilizer and fuel.
 Earth to earth — and the sooner the better.

13-14   "If you're far away,
 get the reports on what I've done,
And if you're in the neighborhood,
 pay attention to my record.
The sinners in Zion are rightly terrified;
 the godless are at their wit's end:
'Who among us can survive this firestorm?
 Who of us can get out of this purge with our lives?'"

15-16   The answer's simple:
 Live right,
 speak the truth,
 despise exploitation,
 refuse bribes,
 reject violence,
 avoid evil amusements.
This is how you raise your standard of living!
 A safe and stable way to live.
 A nourishing, satisfying way to live.

GOD MAKES ALL THE DECISIONS HERE

17-19   Oh, you'll see the king — a beautiful sight!
 And you'll take in the wide vistas of land.
In your mind you'll go over the old terrors:
 "What happened to that Assyrian inspector who condemned and
 confiscated?
And the one who gouged us of taxes?
 And that cheating moneychanger?"
Gone! Out of sight forever! Their insolence
 nothing now but a fading stain on the carpet!
No more putting up with a language you can't understand,
 no more sounds of gibberish in your ears.

20-22   Just take a look at Zion, will you?

Centering our worship in festival feasts!
Feast your eyes on Jerusalem,
    a quiet and permanent place to live.
No more pulling up stakes and moving on,
    no more patched-together lean-tos.
Instead, GOD! GOD majestic, God himself the place
    in a country of broad rivers and streams,
But rivers blocked to invading ships,
    off-limits to predatory pirates.
For GOD makes all the decisions here. GOD is our king.
    GOD runs this place and he'll keep us safe.

23   Ha! Your sails are in shreds,
    your mast wobbling,
    your hold leaking.
The plunder is free for the taking, free for all —
    for weak and strong, insiders and outsiders.

24   No one in Zion will say, "I'm sick."
    Best of all, they'll all live guilt-free.

THE FIRES BURNING DAY AND NIGHT

1   **34** Draw in close now, nations. Listen carefully,
    you people. Pay attention!
    Earth, you, too, and everything in you.
World, and all that comes from you.

2-4   And here's why: GOD is angry,
    good and angry with all the nations,
So blazingly angry at their arms and armies
    that he's going to rid earth of them, wipe them out.
The corpses, thrown in a heap,
    will stink like the town dump in midsummer,
Their blood flowing off the mountains
    like creeks in spring runoff.
Stars will fall out of the sky
    like overripe, rotting fruit in the orchard,
And the sky itself will be folded up like a blanket
    and put away in a closet.
All that army of stars, shriveled to nothing,
    like leaves and fruit in autumn, dropping and rotting!

5-7   "Once I've finished with earth and sky,
    I'll start in on Edom.
I'll come down hard on Edom,
    a people I've slated for total termination."
GOD has a sword, thirsty for blood and more blood,
    a sword hungry for well-fed flesh,
Lamb and goat blood,
    the suet-rich kidneys of rams.
Yes, GOD has scheduled a sacrifice in Bozrah, the capital,

the whole country of Edom a slaughterhouse.
A wholesale slaughter, wild animals
    and farm animals alike slaughtered.
The whole country soaked with blood,
    all the ground greasy with fat.

8-15 It's GOD's scheduled time for vengeance,
    the year all Zion's accounts are settled.
Edom's streams will flow sluggish, thick with pollution,
    the soil sterile, poisoned with waste,
The whole country
    a smoking, stinking garbage dump—
The fires burning day and night,
    the skies black with endless smoke.
Generation after generation of wasteland—
    no more travelers through this country!
Vultures and skunks will police the streets;
    owls and crows will feel at home there.
God will reverse creation. Chaos!
    He will cancel fertility. Emptiness!
Leaders will have no one to lead.
    They'll name it No Kingdom There,
A country where all kings
    and princes are unemployed.
Thistles will take over, covering the castles,
    fortresses conquered by weeds and thornbushes.
Wild dogs will prowl the ruins,
    ostriches have the run of the place.
Wildcats and hyenas will hunt together,
    demons and devils dance through the night.
The night-demon Lilith, evil and rapacious,
    will establish permanent quarters.
Scavenging carrion birds will breed and brood,
    infestations of ominous evil.

16-17 Get and read GOD's book:
    None of this is going away,
    this breeding, brooding evil.
GOD has personally commanded it all.
    His Spirit set it in motion.
GOD has assigned them their place,
    decreed their fate in detail.
This is permanent—
    generation after generation, the same old thing.

THE VOICELESS BREAK INTO SONG

1-2 **35** Wilderness and desert will sing joyously,
    the badlands will celebrate and flower—
    Like the crocus in spring, bursting into blossom,
    a symphony of song and color.
Mountain glories of Lebanon—a gift.

Awesome Carmel, stunning Sharon—gifts.
GOD's resplendent glory, fully on display.
GOD awesome, GOD majestic.

3-4 Energize the limp hands,
strengthen the rubbery knees.
Tell fearful souls,
"Courage! Take heart!
GOD is here, right here,
on his way to put things right
And redress all wrongs.
He's on his way! He'll save you!"

5-7 Blind eyes will be opened,
deaf ears unstopped,
Lame men and women will leap like deer,
the voiceless break into song.
Springs of water will burst out in the wilderness,
streams flow in the desert.
Hot sands will become a cool oasis,
thirsty ground a splashing fountain.
Even lowly jackals will have water to drink,
and barren grasslands flourish richly.

8-10 There will be a highway
called the Holy Road.
No one rude or rebellious
is permitted on this road.
It's for GOD's people exclusively—
impossible to get lost on this road.
Not even fools can get lost on it.
No lions on this road,
no dangerous wild animals—
Nothing and no one dangerous or threatening.
Only the redeemed will walk on it.
The people GOD has ransomed
will come back on this road.
They'll sing as they make their way home to Zion,
unfading halos of joy encircling their heads,
Welcomed home with gifts of joy and gladness
as all sorrows and sighs scurry into the night.

IT'S THEIR FATE THAT'S AT STAKE

1-3 **36** In the fourteenth year of King Hezekiah, Sennacherib king of Assyria made war on all the fortress cities of Judah and took them. Then the king of Assyria sent his general, the "Rabshekah," accompanied by a huge army, from Lachish to Jerusalem to King Hezekiah. The general stopped at the aqueduct where it empties into the upper pool on the road to the public laundry. Three men went out to meet him: Eliakim son of Hilkiah, in charge of the palace; Shebna the secretary; and Joah son of Asaph, the official historian.

4-7   The Rabshekah said to them, "Tell Hezekiah that the Great King, the king of Assyria, says this: 'What kind of backing do you think you have against me? You're bluffing and I'm calling your bluff. Your words are no match for my weapons. What kind of backup do you have now that you've rebelled against me? Egypt? Don't make me laugh. Egypt is a rubber crutch. Lean on Egypt and you'll end up flat on your face. That's all Pharaoh king of Egypt is to anyone who leans on him. And if you try to tell me, "We're leaning on our GOD," isn't it a bit late? Hasn't Hezekiah just gotten rid of all the places of worship, telling you, "You've got to worship at *this* altar"?

8-9   "'Be reasonable. Face the facts: My master the king of Assyria will give you two thousand horses if you can put riders on them. You can't do it, can you? So how do you think, depending on flimsy Egypt's chariots and riders, you can stand up against even the lowest-ranking captain in my master's army?

10   "'And besides, do you think I came all this way to destroy this land without first getting GOD's blessing? It was your GOD who told me, Make war on this land. Destroy it.'"

11   Eliakim, Shebna, and Joah answered the Rabshekah, "Please talk to us in Aramaic. We understand Aramaic. Don't talk to us in Hebrew within earshot of all the people gathered around."

12   But the Rabshekah replied, "Do you think my master has sent me to give this message to your master and you but not also to the people clustered here? It's their fate that's at stake. They're the ones who are going to end up eating their own excrement and drinking their own urine."

13-15   Then the Rabshekah stood up and called out loudly in Hebrew, the common language, "Listen to the message of the great king, the king of Assyria! Don't listen to Hezekiah's lies. He can't save you. And don't pay any attention to Hezekiah's pious sermons telling you to lean on GOD, telling you 'GOD will save us, depend on it. GOD won't let this city fall to the king of Assyria.'

16-20   "Don't listen to Hezekiah. Listen to the king of Assyria's offer: 'Make peace with me. Come and join me. Everyone will end up with a good life, with plenty of land and water, and eventually something far better. I'll turn you loose in wide open spaces, with more than enough fertile and productive land for everyone.' Don't let Hezekiah mislead you with his lies, 'GOD will save us.' Has that ever happened? Has any god in history ever gotten the best of the king of Assyria? Look around you. Where are the gods of Hamath and Arpad? The gods of Sepharvaim? Did the gods do anything for Samaria? Name one god that has ever saved its countries from me. So what makes you think that GOD could save Jerusalem from me?'"

21   The three men were silent. They said nothing, for the king had already commanded, "Don't answer him."

22   Then Eliakim son of Hilkiah, the palace administrator, Shebna the secretary, and Joah son of Asaph, the court historian, tearing their clothes in defeat and despair, went back and reported what the Rabshekah had said to Hezekiah.

THE ONLY GOD THERE IS

1-2   **37** When King Hezekiah heard the report, he also tore his clothes and dressed in rough, penitential burlap gunnysacks, and went into the sanctuary of GOD. He sent Eliakim the palace administrator, Shebna the secretary, and the senior priests, all of them also dressed in penitential burlap, to the prophet Isaiah son of Amoz.

3-4 They said to him, "Hezekiah says, 'This is a black day. We're in crisis. We're like pregnant women without even the strength to have a baby! Do you think your GOD heard what the Rabshekah said, sent by his master the king of Assyria to mock the living God? And do you think your GOD will do anything about it? Pray for us, Isaiah. Pray for those of us left here holding the fort!'"

5-7 Then King Hezekiah's servants came to Isaiah. Isaiah said, "Tell your master this, 'GOD's Message: Don't be upset by what you've heard, all those words the servants of the Assyrian king have used to mock me. I personally will take care of him. I'll arrange it so that he'll get a rumor of bad news back home and rush home to take care of it. And he'll die there. Killed—a violent death.'"

8 The Rabshekah left and found the king of Assyria fighting against Libnah. (He had gotten word that the king had left Lachish.)

9-13 Just then the Assyrian king received an intelligence report on King Tirhakah of Ethiopia: "He is on his way to make war on you."

On hearing that, he sent messengers to Hezekiah with instructions to deliver this message: "Don't let your GOD, on whom you so naively lean, deceive you, promising that Jerusalem won't fall to the king of Assyria. Use your head! Look around at what the kings of Assyria have done all over the world—one country after another devastated! And do you think you're going to get off? Have any of the gods of any of these countries ever stepped in and saved them, even one of these nations my predecessors destroyed—Gozan, Haran, Rezeph, and the people of Eden who lived in Telassar? Look around. Do you see anything left of the king of Hamath, the king of Arpad, the king of the city of Sepharvaim, the king of Hena, the king of Ivvah?"

14 Hezekiah took the letter from the hands of the messengers and read it. Then he went into the sanctuary of GOD and spread the letter out before GOD.

15-20 Then Hezekiah prayed to GOD: "GOD-of-the-Angel-Armies, enthroned over the cherubim-angels, you are God, the only God there is, God of all kingdoms on earth. You *made* heaven and earth. Listen, O GOD, and hear. Look, O GOD, and see. Mark all these words of Sennacherib that he sent to mock the living God. It's quite true, O GOD, that the kings of Assyria have devastated all the nations and their lands. They've thrown their gods into the trash and burned them—no great achievement since they were no-gods anyway, gods made in workshops, carved from wood and chiseled from rock. An end to the no-gods! But now step in, O GOD, our God. Save us from him. Let all the kingdoms of earth know that you and you alone are GOD."

21-25 Then Isaiah son of Amoz sent this word to Hezekiah: "GOD's Message, the God of Israel: Because you brought King Sennacherib of Assyria to me in prayer, here is my answer, GOD's answer:

"'She has no use for you, Sennacherib, nothing but contempt,

this virgin daughter Zion.
She spits at you and turns on her heel,
    this daughter Jerusalem.

"'Who do you think you've been mocking and reviling
    all these years?
Who do you think you've been jeering
    and treating with such utter contempt
All these years?
    The Holy of Israel!
You've used your servants to mock the Master.
    You've bragged, "With my fleet of chariots
I've gone to the highest mountain ranges,
    penetrated the far reaches of Lebanon,
Chopped down its giant cedars,
    its finest cypresses.
I conquered its highest peak,
    explored its deepest forest.
I dug wells
    and drank my fill.
I emptied the famous rivers of Egypt
    with one kick of my foot.

26-27   "'Haven't you gotten the news
    that I've been behind this all along?
This is a longstanding plan of mine
    and I'm just now making it happen,
using you to devastate strong cities,
    turning them into piles of rubble
and leaving their citizens helpless,
    bewildered, and confused,
drooping like unwatered plants,
    stunted like withered seedlings.

28-29   "'I know all about your pretentious poses,
    your officious comings and goings,
    and, yes, the tantrums you throw against me.
Because of all your wild raging against me,
    your unbridled arrogance that I keep hearing of,
I'll put my hook in your nose
    and my bit in your mouth.
I'll show you who's boss. I'll turn you around
    and take you back to where you came from.

30-32   "'And this, Hezekiah, will be your confirming sign: This year's crops will be slim pickings, and next year it won't be much better. But in three years, farming will be back to normal, with regular sowing and reaping, planting and harvesting. What's left of the people of Judah will put down roots and make a new start. The people left in Jerusalem will get moving again. Mount Zion survivors will take hold again. The zeal of GOD-of-the-Angel-Armies will do all this.'

33-35 "Finally, this is GOD's verdict on the king of Assyria:

"'Don't worry, he won't enter this city,
    won't let loose a single arrow,
Won't brandish so much as one shield,
    let alone build a siege ramp against it.
He'll go back the same way he came.
    He won't set a foot in this city.
        GOD's Decree.
I've got my hand on this city
    to save it,
Save it for my very own sake,
    but also for the sake of my David dynasty.'"

36-38 Then the Angel of GOD arrived and struck the Assyrian camp—185,000 Assyrians died. By the time the sun came up, they were all dead—an army of corpses! Sennacherib, king of Assyria, got out of there fast, back home to Nineveh. As he was worshiping in the sanctuary of his god Nisroch, he was murdered by his sons Adrammelech and Sharezer. They escaped to the land of Ararat. His son Esar-haddon became the next king.

TIME SPENT IN DEATH'S WAITING ROOM

1 **38** At that time, Hezekiah got sick. He was about to die. The prophet Isaiah son of Amoz visited him and said, "GOD says, 'Prepare your affairs and your family. This is it: You're going to die. You're not going to get well.'"

2-3 Hezekiah turned away from Isaiah and, facing the wall, prayed to GOD: "GOD, please, I beg you: Remember how I've lived my life. I've lived faithfully in your presence, lived out of a heart that was totally yours. You've seen how I've lived, the good that I have done." And Hezekiah wept as he prayed—painful tears.

4-6 Then GOD told Isaiah, "Go and speak with Hezekiah. Give him this Message from me, GOD, the God of your ancestor David: 'I've heard your prayer. I have seen your tears. Here's what I'll do: I'll add fifteen years to your life. And I'll save both you and this city from the king of Assyria. I have my hand on this city.

7-8 "'And this is your confirming sign, confirming that I, GOD, will do exactly what I have promised. Watch for this: As the sun goes down and the shadow lengthens on the sundial of Ahaz, I'm going to reverse the shadow ten notches on the dial.'" And that's what happened: The declining sun's shadow reversed ten notches on the dial.

9-15 This is what Hezekiah king of Judah wrote after he'd been sick and then recovered from his sickness:

In the very prime of life
    I have to leave.

Whatever time I have left
    is spent in death's waiting room.
No more glimpses of God
    in the land of the living,
No more meetings with my neighbors,
    no more rubbing shoulders with friends.
This body I inhabit is taken down
    and packed away like a camper's tent.
Like a weaver, I've rolled up the carpet of my life
    as God cuts me free of the loom
And at day's end sweeps up the scraps and pieces.
    I cry for help until morning.
Like a lion, God pummels and pounds me,
    relentlessly finishing me off.
I squawk like a doomed hen,
    moan like a dove.
My eyes ache from looking up for help:
    "Master, I'm in trouble! Get me out of this!"
But what's the use? God himself gave me the word.
    He's done it to me.
I can't sleep —
    I'm that upset, that troubled.

16-19 O Master, these are the conditions in which people live,
      and yes, in these very conditions my spirit is still alive —
      fully recovered with a fresh infusion of life!
It seems it was good for me
    to go through all those troubles.
Throughout them all you held tight to my lifeline.
    You never let me tumble over the edge into nothing.
But my sins you let go of,
    threw them over your shoulder — good riddance!
The dead don't thank you,
    and choirs don't sing praises from the morgue.
Those buried six feet under
    don't witness to your faithful ways.
It's the living — live men, live women — who thank you,
    just as I'm doing right now.
Parents give their children
    full reports on your faithful ways.

20 God saves and will save me.
    As fiddles and mandolins strike up the tunes,
We'll sing, oh we'll sing, sing,
    for the rest of our lives in the Sanctuary of God.

21-22 Isaiah had said, "Prepare a poultice of figs and put it on the boil so he may recover."

Hezekiah had said, "What is my cue that it's all right to enter again the Sanctuary of God?"

THERE WILL BE NOTHING LEFT

39 ¹ Sometime later, King Merodach-baladan son of Baladan of Babylon sent messengers with greetings and a gift to Hezekiah. He had heard that Hezekiah had been sick and was now well.

² Hezekiah received the messengers warmly. He took them on a tour of his royal precincts, proudly showing them all his treasures: silver, gold, spices, expensive oils, all his weapons — everything out on display. There was nothing in his house or kingdom that Hezekiah didn't show them.

³ Later the prophet Isaiah showed up. He asked Hezekiah, "What were these men up to? What did they say? And where did they come from?"

Hezekiah said, "They came from a long way off, from Babylon."

⁴ "And what did they see in your palace?"

"Everything," said Hezekiah. "I showed them the works, opened all the doors and impressed them with it all."

⁵⁻⁷ Then Isaiah said to Hezekiah, "Now listen to this Message from GOD-of-the-Angel-Armies: I have to warn you, the time is coming when everything in this palace, along with everything your ancestors accumulated before you, will be hauled off to Babylon. GOD says that there will be nothing left. Nothing. And not only your things but your *sons*. Some of your sons will be taken into exile, ending up as eunuchs in the palace of the king of Babylon."

⁸ Hezekiah replied to Isaiah, "Good. If GOD says so, it's good." Within himself he was thinking, "But surely nothing bad will happen in my lifetime. I'll enjoy peace and stability as long as I live."

MESSAGES OF COMFORT
PREPARE FOR GOD'S ARRIVAL

40 ¹⁻² "Comfort, oh comfort my people,"
    says your God.
"Speak softly and tenderly to Jerusalem,
    but also make it very clear
That she has served her sentence,
    that her sin is taken care of — forgiven!
She's been punished enough and more than enough,
    and now it's over and done with."

³⁻⁵ Thunder in the desert!
    "Prepare for GOD's arrival!
Make the road straight and smooth,
    a highway fit for our God.
Fill in the valleys,
    level off the hills,
Smooth out the ruts,
    clear out the rocks.
Then GOD's bright glory will shine
    and everyone will see it.
    Yes. Just as GOD has said."

6-8　A voice says, "Shout!"
　　　　I said, "What shall I shout?"

　　　"These people are nothing but grass,
　　　　　their love fragile as wildflowers.
　　　The grass withers, the wildflowers fade,
　　　　　if GOD so much as puffs on them.
　　　　　Aren't these people just so much grass?
　　　True, the grass withers and the wildflowers fade,
　　　　　but our God's Word stands firm and forever."

9-11　Climb a high mountain, Zion.
　　　　　You're the preacher of good news.
　　　Raise your voice. Make it good and loud, Jerusalem.
　　　　　You're the preacher of good news.
　　　　　Speak loud and clear. Don't be timid!
　　　Tell the cities of Judah,
　　　　　"Look! Your God!"
　　　Look at him! GOD, the Master, comes in power,
　　　　　ready to go into action.
　　　He is going to pay back his enemies
　　　　　and reward those who have loved him.
　　　Like a shepherd, he will care for his flock,
　　　　　gathering the lambs in his arms,
　　　Hugging them as he carries them,
　　　　　leading the nursing ewes to good pasture.

THE CREATOR OF ALL YOU CAN SEE OR IMAGINE

12-17　Who has scooped up the ocean
　　　　　in his two hands,
　　　　　or measured the sky between his thumb and little finger,
　　　Who has put all the earth's dirt in one of his baskets,
　　　　　weighed each mountain and hill?
　　　Who could ever have told GOD what to do
　　　　　or taught him his business?
　　　What expert would he have gone to for advice,
　　　　　what school would he attend to learn justice?
　　　What god do you suppose might have taught him what he knows,
　　　　　showed him how things work?
　　　Why, the nations are but a drop in a bucket,
　　　　　a mere smudge on a window.
　　　Watch him sweep up the islands
　　　　　like so much dust off the floor!
　　　There aren't enough trees in Lebanon
　　　　　nor enough animals in those vast forests
　　　　　to furnish adequate fuel and offerings for his worship.
　　　All the nations add up to simply nothing before him —
　　　　　less than nothing is more like it. A minus.

18-20　So who even comes close to being like God?
　　　　　To whom or what can you compare him?

Some no-god idol? Ridiculous!
    It's made in a workshop, cast in bronze,
Given a thin veneer of gold,
    and draped with silver filigree.
Or, perhaps someone will select a fine wood—
    olive wood, say—that won't rot,
Then hire a woodcarver to make a no-god,
    giving special care to its base so it won't tip over!

21-24　Have you not been paying attention?
    Have you not been listening?
Haven't you heard these stories all your life?
    Don't you understand the foundation of all things?
God sits high above the round ball of earth.
    The people look like mere ants.
He stretches out the skies like a canvas—
    yes, like a tent canvas to live under.
He ignores what all the princes say and do.
    The rulers of the earth count for nothing.
Princes and rulers don't amount to much.
    Like seeds barely rooted, just sprouted,
They shrivel when God blows on them.
    Like flecks of chaff, they're gone with the wind.

25-26　"So—who is like me?
    Who holds a candle to me?" says The Holy.
Look at the night skies:
    Who do you think made all this?
Who marches this army of stars out each night,
    counts them off, calls each by name
—so magnificent! so powerful!—
    and never overlooks a single one?

27-31　Why would you ever complain, O Jacob,
    or, whine, Israel, saying,
"GOD has lost track of me.
    He doesn't care what happens to me"?
Don't you know anything? Haven't you been listening?
GOD doesn't come and go. God *lasts*.
    He's Creator of all you can see or imagine.
He doesn't get tired out, doesn't pause to catch his breath.
    And he knows *everything,* inside and out.
He energizes those who get tired,
    gives fresh strength to dropouts.
For even young people tire and drop out,
    young folk in their prime stumble and fall.
But those who wait upon GOD get fresh strength.
    They spread their wings and soar like eagles,
They run and don't get tired,
    they walk and don't lag behind.

Do You Feel Like a Lowly Worm?

¹
41

"Quiet down, far-flung ocean islands. Listen!
　　Sit down and rest, everyone. Recover your strength.
　　Gather around me. Say what's on your heart.
Together let's decide what's right.

2-3
"Who got things rolling here,
　　got this champion from the east on the move?
Who recruited him for this job,
　　then rounded up and corralled the nations
　　so he could run roughshod over kings?
He's off and running,
　　pulverizing nations into dust,
　　leaving only stubble and chaff in his wake.
He chases them and comes through unscathed,
　　his feet scarcely touching the path.

4
"Who did this? Who made it happen?
　　Who always gets things started?
I did. God. I'm first on the scene.
　　I'm also the last to leave.

5-7
"Far-flung ocean islands see it and panic.
　　The ends of the earth are shaken.
　　Fearfully they huddle together.
They try to help each other out,
　　making up stories in the dark.
The godmakers in the workshops
　　go into overtime production, crafting new models of no-gods,
Urging one another on—'Good job!' 'Great design!'—
　　pounding in nails at the base
　　so that the things won't tip over.

8-10
"But you, Israel, are my servant.
　　You're Jacob, my first choice,
　　descendants of my good friend Abraham.
I pulled you in from all over the world,
　　called you in from every dark corner of the earth,
Telling you, 'You're my servant, serving on my side.
　　I've picked you. I haven't dropped you.'
Don't panic. I'm with you.
　　There's no need to fear for I'm your God.
I'll give you strength. I'll help you.
　　I'll hold you steady, keep a firm grip on you.

11-13
"Count on it: Everyone who had it in for you
　　will end up out in the cold—
　　real losers.
Those who worked against you
　　will end up empty-handed—

nothing to show for their lives.
When you go out looking for your old adversaries
    you won't find them —
Not a trace of your old enemies,
    not even a memory.
That's right. Because I, your GOD,
    have a firm grip on you and I'm not letting go.
I'm telling you, 'Don't panic.
    I'm right here to help you.'

14-16 "Do you feel like a lowly worm, Jacob?
    Don't be afraid.
Feel like a fragile insect, Israel?
    I'll help you.
I, GOD, want to reassure you.
    The God who buys you back, The Holy of Israel.
I'm transforming you from worm to harrow,
    from insect to iron.
As a sharp-toothed harrow you'll smooth out the mountains,
    turn those tough old hills into loamy soil.
You'll open the rough ground to the weather,
    to the blasts of sun and wind and rain.
But you'll be confident and exuberant,
    expansive in The Holy of Israel!

17-20 "The poor and homeless are desperate for water,
    their tongues parched and no water to be found.
But *I'm* there to be found, I'm there for them,
    and I, God of Israel, will not leave them thirsty.
I'll open up rivers for them on the barren hills,
    spout fountains in the valleys.
I'll turn the baked-clay badlands into a cool pond,
    the waterless waste into splashing creeks.
I'll plant the red cedar in that treeless wasteland,
    also acacia, myrtle, and olive.
I'll place the cypress in the desert,
    with plenty of oaks and pines.
Everyone will see this. No one can miss it —
    unavoidable, indisputable evidence
That I, GOD, personally did this.
    It's created and signed by The Holy of Israel.

21-24 "Set out your case for your gods," says GOD.
    "Bring your evidence," says the King of Jacob.
"Take the stand on behalf of your idols, offer arguments,
    assemble reasons.
Spread out the facts before us
    so that we can assess them ourselves.
Ask them, 'If you are gods, explain what the past means —
    or, failing that, tell us what will happen in the future.
Can't do that?

How about doing something—anything!
Good or bad—whatever.
Can you hurt us or help us? Do we need to be afraid?'
They say nothing, because they *are* nothing—
sham gods, no-gods, fool-making gods.

25-29 "I, God, started someone out from the north and he's come.
He was called out of the east by name.
He'll stomp the rulers into the mud
the way a potter works the clay.
Let me ask you, Did anyone guess that this might happen?
Did anyone tell us earlier so we might confirm it
with 'Yes, he's right!'?
No one mentioned it, no one announced it,
no one heard a peep out of you.
But I told Zion all about this beforehand.
I gave Jerusalem a preacher of good news.
But around here there's no one—
no one who knows what's going on.
I ask, but no one can tell me the score.
Nothing here. It's all smoke and hot air—
sham gods, hollow gods, no-gods."

GOD'S SERVANT WILL SET EVERYTHING RIGHT

1-4 **42** "Take a good look at my servant.
I'm backing him to the hilt.
He's the one I chose,
and I couldn't be more pleased with him.
I've bathed him with my Spirit, my *life*.
He'll set everything right among the nations.
He won't call attention to what he does
with loud speeches or gaudy parades.
He won't brush aside the bruised and the hurt
and he won't disregard the small and insignificant,
but he'll steadily and firmly set things right.
He won't tire out and quit. He won't be stopped
until he's finished his work—to set things right on earth.
Far-flung ocean islands
wait expectantly for his teaching."

THE GOD WHO MAKES US ALIVE WITH HIS OWN LIFE

5-9 GOD'S Message,
the God who created the cosmos, stretched out the skies,
laid out the earth and all that grows from it,
Who breathes life into earth's people,
makes them alive with his own life:
"I am GOD. I have called you to live right and well.
I have taken responsibility for you, kept you safe.
I have set you among my people to bind them to me,
and provided you as a lighthouse to the nations,
To make a start at bringing people into the open, into light:

opening blind eyes,
    releasing prisoners from dungeons,
    emptying the dark prisons.
I am GOD. That's my name.
    I don't franchise my glory,
    don't endorse the no-god idols.
Take note: The earlier predictions of judgment have been fulfilled.
    I'm announcing the new salvation work.
Before it bursts on the scene,
    I'm telling you all about it."

10-16 Sing to GOD a brand-new song,
    sing his praises all over the world!
Let the sea and its fish give a round of applause,
    with all the far-flung islands joining in.
Let the desert and its camps raise a tune,
    calling the Kedar nomads to join in.
Let the villagers in Sela round up a choir
    and perform from the tops of the mountains.
Make GOD's glory resound;
    echo his praises from coast to coast.
GOD steps out like he means business.
    You can see he's primed for action.
He shouts, announcing his arrival;
    he takes charge and his enemies fall into line:
"I've been quiet long enough.
    I've held back, biting my tongue.
But now I'm letting loose, letting go,
    like a woman who's having a baby—
Stripping the hills bare,
    withering the wildflowers,
Drying up the rivers,
    turning lakes into mudflats.
But I'll take the hand of those who don't know the way,
    who can't see where they're going.
I'll be a personal guide to them,
    directing them through unknown country.
I'll be right there to show them what roads to take,
    make sure they don't fall into the ditch.
These are the things I'll be doing for them—
    sticking with them, not leaving them for a minute."

17 But those who invested in the no-gods
    are bankrupt—dead broke.

YOU'VE SEEN A LOT, BUT LOOKED AT NOTHING

18-25 Pay attention! Are you deaf?
    Open your eyes! Are you blind?
You're my servant, and you're not looking!
    You're my messenger, and you're not listening!
The very people I depended upon, servants of GOD,

blind as a bat — willfully blind!
You've seen a lot, but looked at nothing.
  You've heard everything, but listened to nothing.
GOD intended, out of the goodness of his heart,
  to be lavish in his revelation.
But this is a people battered and cowed,
  shut up in attics and closets,
Victims licking their wounds,
  feeling ignored, abandoned.
But is anyone out there listening?
  Is anyone paying attention to what's coming?
Who do you think turned Jacob over to the thugs,
  let loose the robbers on Israel?
Wasn't it GOD himself, this God against whom we've sinned —
  not doing what he commanded,
  not listening to what he said?
Isn't it God's anger that's behind all this,
  God's punishing power?
Their whole world collapsed but they still didn't get it;
  their life is in ruins but they don't take it to heart.

WHEN YOU'RE BETWEEN A ROCK AND A HARD PLACE

1-4

43 But now, GOD's Message,
  the God who made you in the first place, Jacob,
  the One who got you started, Israel:
"Don't be afraid, I've redeemed you.
  I've called your name. You're mine.
When you're in over your head, I'll be there with you.
  When you're in rough waters, you will not go down.
When you're between a rock and a hard place,
  it won't be a dead end —
Because I am GOD, your personal God,
  The Holy of Israel, your Savior.
I paid a huge price for you:
  all of Egypt, with rich Cush and Seba thrown in!
That's how much you mean to me!
  That's how much I love you!
I'd sell off the whole world to get you back,
  trade the creation just for you.

5-7

"So don't be afraid: I'm with you.
  I'll round up all your scattered children,
  pull them in from east and west.
I'll send orders north and south:
  'Send them back.
Return my sons from distant lands,
  my daughters from faraway places.
I want them back, every last one who bears my name,
  every man, woman, and child
Whom I created for my glory,
  yes, personally formed and made each one.'"

8-13 Get the blind and deaf out here and ready—
the blind (though there's nothing wrong with their eyes)
and the deaf (though there's nothing wrong with their ears).
Then get the other nations out here and ready.
Let's see what they have to say about this,
how they account for what's happened.
Let them present their expert witnesses
and make their case;
let them try to convince us what they say is true.
"But *you* are my witnesses." GOD's Decree.
"You're my handpicked servant
So that you'll come to know and trust me,
understand both *that* I am and *who* I am.
Previous to me there was no such thing as a god,
nor will there be after me.
I, yes I, am GOD.
I'm the only Savior there is.
I spoke, I saved, I told you what existed
long before these upstart gods appeared on the scene.
And you know it, you're my witnesses,
you're the evidence." GOD's Decree.
"Yes, I am God.
I've always been God
and I always will be God.
No one can take anything from me.
I make; who can unmake it?"

YOU DIDN'T EVEN DO THE MINIMUM

14-15 GOD, your Redeemer,
The Holy of Israel, says:
"Just for you, I will march on Babylon.
I'll turn the tables on the Babylonians.
Instead of whooping it up,
they'll be wailing.
I am GOD, your Holy One,
Creator of Israel, your King."

16-21 This is what GOD says,
the God who builds a road right through the ocean,
who carves a path through pounding waves,
The God who summons horses and chariots and armies—
they lie down and then can't get up;
they're snuffed out like so many candles:
"Forget about what's happened;
don't keep going over old history.
Be alert, be present. I'm about to do something brand-new.
It's bursting out! Don't you see it?
There it is! I'm making a road through the desert,
rivers in the badlands.

Wild animals will say 'Thank you!'
— the coyotes and the buzzards —
Because I provided water in the desert,
rivers through the sun-baked earth,
Drinking water for the people I chose,
the people I made especially for myself,
a people custom-made to praise me.

22-24 "But you didn't pay a bit of attention to me, Jacob.
You so quickly tired of me, Israel.
You wouldn't even bring sheep for offerings in worship.
You couldn't be bothered with sacrifices.
It wasn't that I asked that much from you.
I didn't expect expensive presents.
But you didn't even do the minimum —
so stingy with me, so closefisted.
Yet you haven't been stingy with your sins.
You've been plenty generous with them — and I'm fed up.

25 "But I, yes I, am the one
who takes care of your sins — that's what I do.
I don't keep a list of your sins.

26-28 "So, make your case against me. Let's have this out.
Make your arguments. Prove you're in the right.
Your original ancestor started the sinning,
and everyone since has joined in.
That's why I had to disqualify the Temple leaders,
repudiate Jacob and discredit Israel."

PROUD TO BE CALLED ISRAEL

1-5 44 "But for now, dear servant Jacob, listen —
yes, you, Israel, my personal choice.
GOD who made you has something to say to you;
the God who formed you in the womb wants to help you.
Don't be afraid, dear servant Jacob,
Jeshurun, the one I chose.
For I will pour water on the thirsty ground
and send streams coursing through the parched earth.
I will pour my Spirit into your descendants
and my blessing on your children.
They shall sprout like grass on the prairie,
like willows alongside creeks.
This one will say, 'I am GOD's,'
and another will go by the name Jacob;
That one will write on his hand 'GOD's property' —
and be proud to be called Israel."

6-8 GOD, King of Israel,
your Redeemer, GOD-of-the-Angel-Armies, says:
"I'm first, I'm last, and everything in between.

I'm the only God there is.
Who compares with me?
    Speak up. See if you measure up.
From the beginning, who else has always announced what's coming?
    So what is coming next? Anybody want to venture a try?
Don't be afraid, and don't worry:
    Haven't I always kept you informed, told you what was going on?
You're my eyewitnesses:
    Have you ever come across a God, a real God, other than me?
    There's no Rock like me that I know of."

LOVER OF EMPTINESS

9-11   All those who make no-god idols don't amount to a thing, and what they work so hard at making is nothing. Their little puppet-gods see nothing and know nothing—they're total embarrassments! Who would bother making gods that can't do anything, that can't *"god"*? Watch all the no-god worshipers hide their faces in shame. Watch the no-god makers slink off humiliated when their idols fail them. Get them out here in the open. Make them face God-reality.

12   The blacksmith makes his no-god, works it over in his forge, hammering it on his anvil—such hard work! He works away, fatigued with hunger and thirst.

13-17   The woodworker draws up plans for his no-god, traces it on a block of wood. He shapes it with chisels and planes into human shape—a beautiful woman, a handsome man, ready to be placed in a chapel. He first cuts down a cedar, or maybe picks out a pine or oak, and lets it grow strong in the forest, nourished by the rain. Then it can serve a double purpose: Part he uses as firewood for keeping warm and baking bread; from the other part he makes a god that he worships—carves it into a god shape and prays before it. With half he makes a fire to warm himself and barbecue his supper. He eats his fill and sits back satisfied with his stomach full and his feet warmed by the fire: "Ah, this is the life." And he still has half left for a god, made to his personal design—a handy, convenient no-god to worship whenever so inclined. Whenever the need strikes him he prays to it, "Save me. You're my god."

18-19   Pretty stupid, wouldn't you say? Don't they have eyes in their heads? Are their brains working at all? Doesn't it occur to them to say, "Half of this tree I used for firewood: I baked bread, roasted meat, and enjoyed a good meal. And now I've used the rest to make an abominable no-god. Here I am praying to a stick of wood!"

20   This lover of emptiness, of nothing, is so out of touch with reality, so far gone, that he can't even look at what he's doing, can't even look at the no-god stick of wood in his hand and say, "This is crazy."

21-22   "Remember these things, O Jacob.
    Take it seriously, Israel, that you're my servant.
I made you, *shaped* you: You're my servant.
    O Israel, I'll never forget you.
I've wiped the slate of all your wrongdoings.
    There's nothing left of your sins.

Come back to me, come back.
I've redeemed you."

23 High heavens, sing!
GOD has done it.
Deep earth, shout!
And you mountains, sing!
A forest choir of oaks and pines and cedars!
GOD has redeemed Jacob.
GOD's glory is on display in Israel.

24 GOD, your Redeemer,
who shaped your life in your mother's womb, says:
"I am GOD. I made all that is.
With no help from you I spread out the skies
and laid out the earth."

25-28 He makes the magicians look ridiculous
and turns fortunetellers into jokes.
He makes the experts look trivial
and their latest knowledge look silly.
But he backs the word of his servant
and confirms the counsel of his messengers.
He says to Jerusalem, "Be inhabited,"
and to the cities of Judah, "Be rebuilt,"
and to the ruins, "I raise you up."
He says to Ocean, "Dry up.
I'm drying up your rivers."
He says to Cyrus, "My shepherd —
everything I want, you'll do it."
He says to Jerusalem, "Be built,"
and to the Temple, "Be established."

THE GOD WHO FORMS LIGHT AND DARKNESS

1-7 **45** GOD's Message to his anointed,
to Cyrus, whom he took by the hand
To give the task of taming the nations,
of terrifying their kings —
He gave him free rein,
no restrictions:
"I'll go ahead of you,
clearing and paving the road.
I'll break down bronze city gates,
smash padlocks, kick down barred entrances.
I'll lead you to buried treasures,
secret caches of valuables —
Confirmations that it is, in fact, I, GOD,
the God of Israel, who calls you by your name.
It's because of my dear servant Jacob,
Israel my chosen,
That I've singled you out, called you by name,

and given you this privileged work.
  And you don't even know me!
I am GOD, the only God there is.
  Besides me there are no real gods.
I'm the one who armed you for this work,
  though you don't even know me,
So that everyone, from east to west, will know
  that I have no god-rivals.
  I am GOD, the only God there is.
I form light and create darkness,
  I make harmonies and create discords.
  I, GOD, do all these things.

8-10   "Open up, heavens, and rain.
  Clouds, pour out buckets of my goodness!
Loosen up, earth, and bloom salvation;
  sprout right living.
  I, GOD, generate all this.
But doom to you who fight your Maker—
  you're a pot at odds with the potter!
Does clay talk back to the potter:
  'What are you doing? What clumsy fingers!'
Would a sperm say to a father,
  'Who gave you permission to use me to make a baby?'
Or a fetus to a mother,
  'Why have you cooped me up in this belly?'"

11-13   Thus GOD, The Holy of Israel, Israel's Maker, says:
  "Do you question who or what I'm making?
  Are you telling me what I can or cannot do?
I made earth,
  and I created man and woman to live on it.
I handcrafted the skies
  and direct all the constellations in their turnings.
And now I've got Cyrus on the move.
  I've rolled out the red carpet before him.
He will build my city.
  He will bring home my exiles.
I didn't hire him to do this. I *told* him.
  I, GOD-of-the-Angel-Armies."

14   GOD says:

"The workers of Egypt, the merchants of Ethiopia,
  and those statuesque Sabeans
Will all come over to you—all yours.
  Docile in chains, they'll follow you,
Hands folded in reverence, praying before you:
  'Amazing! God is with you!
  There is no other God—none.'"

LOOK AT THE EVIDENCE

15-17 Clearly, you are a God who works behind the scenes,
       God of Israel, Savior God.
Humiliated, all those others
       will be ashamed to show their faces in public.
Out of work and at loose ends, the makers of no-god idols
       won't know what to do with themselves.
The people of Israel, though, are saved by you, GOD,
       saved with an eternal salvation.
They won't be ashamed,
       they won't be at loose ends, ever.

18-24 GOD, Creator of the heavens —
       he is, remember, *God.*
Maker of earth —
       he put it on its foundations, built it from scratch.
He didn't go to all that trouble
       to just leave it empty, nothing in it.
       He made it to be lived in.

       This GOD says:

"I am GOD,
       the one and only.
I don't just talk to myself
       or mumble under my breath.
I never told Jacob,
       'Seek me in emptiness, in dark nothingness.'
I am GOD. I work out in the open,
       saying what's right, setting things right.
So gather around, come on in,
       all you refugees and castoffs.
They don't seem to know much, do they —
       those who carry around their no-god blocks of wood,
       praying for help to a dead stick?
So tell me what you think. Look at the evidence.
       Put your heads together. Make your case.
Who told you, and a long time ago, what's going on here?
       Who made sense of things for you?
Wasn't I the one? GOD?
       It had to be me. I'm the only God there is —
The only God who does things right
       and knows how to help.
So turn to me and be helped — saved! —
       everyone, whoever and wherever you are.
I am GOD,
       the only God there is, the one and only.
I promise in my own name:
       Every word out of my mouth does what it says.
       I never take back what I say.

Everyone is going to end up kneeling before me.
>   Everyone is going to end up saying of me,
>   'Yes! Salvation and strength are in GOD!'"

24-25 All who have raged against him
>   will be brought before him,
>   disgraced by their unbelief.
> And all who are connected with Israel
>   will have a robust, praising, good life in GOD!

THIS IS SERIOUS BUSINESS, REBELS

1-2 **46** The god Bel falls down, god Nebo slumps.
>   The no-god hunks of wood are loaded on mules
>   And have to be hauled off,
> wearing out the poor mules—
> Dead weight, burdens who can't bear burdens,
>   hauled off to captivity.

3-4 "Listen to me, family of Jacob,
>   everyone that's left of the family of Israel.
> I've been carrying you on my back
>   from the day you were born,
> And I'll keep on carrying you when you're old.
>   I'll be there, bearing you when you're old and gray.
> I've done it and will keep on doing it,
>   carrying you on my back, saving you.

5-7 "So to whom will you compare me, the Incomparable?
>   Can you picture me without reducing me?
> People with a lot of money
>   hire craftsmen to make them gods.
> The artisan delivers the god,
>   and they kneel and worship it!
> They carry it around in holy parades,
>   then take it home and put it on a shelf.
> And there it sits, day in and day out,
>   a dependable god, always right where you put it.
> Say anything you want to it, it never talks back.
>   Of course, it never *does* anything either!

8-11 "Think about this. Wrap your minds around it.
>   This is serious business, rebels. Take it to heart.
> Remember your history,
>   your long and rich history.
> I am GOD, the only God you've had or ever will have—
>   incomparable, irreplaceable—
> From the very beginning
>   telling you what the ending will be,
> All along letting you in
>   on what is going to happen,
> Assuring you, 'I'm in this for the long haul,

I'll do exactly what I set out to do,'
Calling that eagle, Cyrus, out of the east,
    from a far country the man I chose to help me.
I've said it, and I'll most certainly do it.
    I've planned it, so it's as good as done.

12-13   "Now listen to me:
    You're a hardheaded bunch and hard to help.
I'm ready to help you right now.
    Deliverance is not a long-range plan.
    Salvation isn't on hold.
I'm putting salvation to work in Zion now,
    and glory in Israel."

THE PARTY'S OVER

1-3 **47** "Get off your high horse and sit in the dirt,
        virgin daughter of Babylon.
        No more throne for you—sit on the ground,
    daughter of the Chaldeans.
Nobody will be calling you 'charming'
    and 'alluring' anymore. Get used to it.
Get a job, any old job:
    Clean gutters, scrub toilets.
Hock your gowns and scarves,
    put on overalls—the party's over.
Your nude body will be on public display,
    exposed to vulgar taunts.
It's vengeance time, and I'm taking vengeance.
    No one gets let off the hook."

YOU'RE ACTING LIKE THE CENTER OF THE UNIVERSE

4-13 Our Redeemer speaks,
    named GOD-of-the-Angel-Armies, The Holy of Israel:
"Shut up and get out of the way,
    daughter of Chaldeans.
You'll no longer be called
    'First Lady of the Kingdoms.'
I was fed up with my people,
    thoroughly disgusted with my progeny.
I turned them over to you,
    but you had no compassion.
You put old men and women
    to cruel, hard labor.
You said, 'I'm the First Lady.
    I'll always be the pampered darling.'
You took nothing seriously, took nothing to heart,
    never gave tomorrow a thought.
Well, start thinking, playgirl.
    You're acting like the center of the universe,
Smugly saying to yourself, 'I'm Number One. There's nobody but me.
    I'll never be a widow, I'll never lose my children.'

Those two things are going to hit you both at once,
    suddenly, on the same day:
Spouse and children gone, a total loss,
    despite your many enchantments and charms.
You were so confident and comfortable in your evil life,
    saying, 'No one sees me.'
You thought you knew so much, had everything figured out.
    What delusion!
    Smugly telling yourself, 'I'm Number One. There's nobody but me.'
Ruin descends —
    you can't charm it away.
Disaster strikes —
    you can't cast it off with spells.
Catastrophe, sudden and total —
    and you're totally at sea, totally bewildered!
But don't give up. From your great repertoire
    of enchantments there must be one you haven't yet tried.
You've been at this a long time.
    Surely *something* will work.
I know you're exhausted trying out remedies,
    but don't give up.
Call in the astrologers and stargazers.
    They're good at this. Surely they can work up something!

14-15 "Fat chance. You'd be grasping at straws
    that are already in the fire,
A fire that is even now raging.
    Your 'experts' are in it and won't get out.
It's not a fire for cooking venison stew,
    not a fire to warm you on a winter night!
That's the fate of your friends in sorcery, your magician buddies
    you've been in cahoots with all your life.
They reel, confused, bumping into one another.
    None of them bother to help you."

TESTED IN THE FURNACE OF AFFLICTION

1-11 **48** "And now listen to this, family of Jacob,
    you who are called by the name Israel:
Who got you started in the loins of Judah,
    you who use GOD's name to back up your promises
    and pray to the God of Israel?
But do you mean it?
    Do you live like it?
You claim to be citizens of the Holy City;
    you act as though you lean on the God of Israel,
    named GOD-of-the-Angel-Armies.
For a long time now, I've let you in on the way I work:
    I told you what I was going to do beforehand,
    then I did it and it was done, and that's that.
I know you're a bunch of hardheads,
    obstinate and flint-faced,

So I got a running start and began telling you
    what was going on before it even happened.
That is why you can't say,
    'My god-idol did this.'
    'My favorite god-carving commanded this.'
You have all this evidence
    confirmed by your own eyes and ears.
    Shouldn't you be talking about it?
And that was just the beginning.
    I have a lot more to tell you,
    things you never knew existed.
This isn't a variation on the same old thing.
    This is new, brand-new,
    something you'd never guess or dream up.
When you hear this you won't be able to say,
    'I knew that all along.'
You've never been good listeners to me.
    You have a history of ignoring me,
A sorry track record of fickle attachments—
    rebels from the womb.
But out of the sheer goodness of my heart,
    because of who I am,
I keep a tight rein on my anger and hold my temper.
    I don't wash my hands of you.
Do you see what I've done?
    I've refined you, but not without fire.
    I've tested you like silver in the furnace of affliction.
Out of myself, simply because of who I am, I do what I do.
    I have my reputation to keep up.
    I'm not playing second fiddle to either gods or people.

12-13   "Listen, Jacob. Listen, Israel—
    I'm the One who named you!
I'm the One.
    I got things started and, yes, I'll wrap them up.
Earth is my work, handmade.
    And the skies—I made them, too, horizon to horizon.
When I speak, they're on their feet, at attention.

14-16   "Come everybody, gather around, listen:
    Who among the gods has delivered the news?
I, GOD, love this man Cyrus, and I'm using him
    to do what I want with Babylon.
I, yes I, have spoken. I've called him.
    I've brought him here. He'll be successful.
Come close, listen carefully:
    I've never kept secrets from you.
    I've always been present with you."

YOUR PROGENY, LIKE GRAINS OF SAND

16-19 And now, the Master, GOD, sends me and his Spirit
with this Message from GOD
your Redeemer, The Holy of Israel:
"I am GOD, your God,
who teaches you how to live right and well.
I show you what to do, where to go.
If you had listened all along to what I told you,
your life would have flowed full like a river,
blessings rolling in like waves from the sea.
Children and grandchildren are like sand,
your progeny like grains of sand.
There would be no end of them,
no danger of losing touch with me."

20 Get out of Babylon! Run from the Babylonians!
Shout the news. Broadcast it.
Let the world know, the whole world.
Tell them, "GOD redeemed his dear servant Jacob!"

21 They weren't thirsty when he led them through the deserts.
He made water pour out of the rock;
he split the rock and the water gushed.

22 "There is no peace," says GOD, "for the wicked."

A LIGHT FOR THE NATIONS

1-3 **49** Listen, far-flung islands,
pay attention, faraway people:
GOD put me to work from the day I was born.
The moment I entered the world he named me.
He gave me speech that would cut and penetrate.
He kept his hand on me to protect me.
He made me his straight arrow
and hid me in his quiver.
He said to me, "You're my dear servant,
Israel, through whom I'll shine."

4 But I said, "I've worked for nothing.
I've nothing to show for a life of hard work.
Nevertheless, I'll let GOD have the last word.
I'll let him pronounce his verdict."

5-6 "And now," GOD says,
this God who took me in hand
from the moment of birth to be his servant,
To bring Jacob back home to him,
to set a reunion for Israel—
What an honor for me in GOD's eyes!
That God should be my strength!

He says, "But that's not a big enough job for my servant —
    just to recover the tribes of Jacob,
      merely to round up the strays of Israel.
I'm setting you up as a light for the *nations*
    so that my salvation becomes *global*!"

7   GOD, Redeemer of Israel, The Holy of Israel,
    says to the despised one, kicked around by the nations,
      slave labor to the ruling class:
"Kings will see, get to their feet — the princes, too —
    and then fall on their faces in homage
Because of GOD, who has faithfully kept his word,
    The Holy of Israel, who has chosen you."

8-12   GOD also says:

"When the time's ripe, I answer you.
    When victory's due, I help you.
I form you and use you
    to reconnect the people with me,
To put the land in order,
    to resettle families on the ruined properties.
I tell prisoners, 'Come on out. You're free!'
    and those huddled in fear, 'It's all right. It's safe now.'
There'll be foodstands along all the roads,
    picnics on all the hills —
Nobody hungry, nobody thirsty,
    shade from the sun, shelter from the wind,
For the Compassionate One guides them,
    takes them to the best springs.
I'll make all my mountains into roads,
    turn them into a superhighway.
Look: These coming from far countries,
    and those, out of the north,
These streaming in from the west,
    and those from all the way down the Nile!"

13   Heavens, raise the roof! Earth, wake the dead!
    Mountains, send up cheers!
GOD has comforted his people.
    He has tenderly nursed his beaten-up, beaten-down people.

14   But Zion said, "I don't get it. GOD has left me.
    My Master has forgotten I even exist."

15-18   "Can a mother forget the infant at her breast,
    walk away from the baby she bore?
But even if mothers forget,
    I'd never forget you — never.
Look, I've written your names on the backs of my hands.
    The walls you're rebuilding are never out of my sight.

Your builders are faster than your wreckers.
  The demolition crews are gone for good.
Look up, look around, look well!
  See them all gathering, coming to you?
As sure as I am the living God" — GOD's Decree —
  "you're going to put them on like so much jewelry,
  you're going to use them to dress up like a bride.

19-21   "And your ruined land?
  Your devastated, decimated land?
Filled with more people than you know what to do with!
  And your barbarian enemies, a fading memory.
The children born in your exile will be saying,
  'It's getting too crowded here. I need more room.'
And you'll say to yourself,
  'Where on earth did these children come from?
I lost everything, had nothing, was exiled and penniless.
  So who reared these children?
  How did these children get here?'"

22-23   The Master, GOD, says:

"Look! I signal to the nations,
  I raise my flag to summon the people.
Here they'll come: women carrying your little boys in their arms,
  men carrying your little girls on their shoulders.
Kings will be your babysitters,
  princesses will be your nursemaids.
They'll offer to do all your drudge work —
  scrub your floors, do your laundry.
You'll know then that I am GOD.
  No one who hopes in me ever regrets it."

24-26   Can plunder be retrieved from a giant,
  prisoners of war gotten back from a tyrant?
But GOD says, "Even if a giant grips the plunder
  and a tyrant holds my people prisoner,
I'm the one who's on your side,
  defending your cause, rescuing your children.
And your enemies, crazed and desperate, will turn on themselves,
  killing each other in a frenzy of self-destruction.
Then everyone will know that I, GOD,
  have saved you — I, the Mighty One of Jacob."

WHO OUT THERE FEARS GOD?

1-3   **50** GOD says:

"Can you produce your mother's divorce papers
  proving I got rid of her?
Can you produce a receipt
  proving I sold you?

Of course you can't.
    It's your sins that put you here,
    your wrongs that got you shipped out.
So why didn't anyone come when I knocked?
    Why didn't anyone answer when I called?
Do you think I've forgotten how to help?
    Am I so decrepit that I can't deliver?
I'm as powerful as ever,
    and can reverse what I once did:
I can dry up the sea with a word,
    turn river water into desert sand,
And leave the fish stinking in the sun,
    stranded on dry land . . .
Turn all the lights out in the sky
    and pull down the curtain."

4-9   The Master, GOD, has given me
    a well-taught tongue,
So I know how to encourage tired people.
    He wakes me up in the morning,
Wakes me up, opens my ears
    to listen as one ready to take orders.
The Master, GOD, opened my ears,
    and I didn't go back to sleep,
    didn't pull the covers back over my head.
I followed orders,
    stood there and took it while they beat me,
    held steady while they pulled out my beard,
Didn't dodge their insults,
    faced them as they spit in my face.
And the Master, GOD, stays right there and helps me,
    so I'm not disgraced.
Therefore I set my face like flint,
    confident that I'll never regret this.
My champion is right here.
    Let's take our stand together!
Who dares bring suit against me?
    Let him try!
Look! the Master, GOD, is right here.
    Who would dare call me guilty?
Look! My accusers are a clothes bin of threadbare
    socks and shirts, fodder for moths!

10-11   Who out there fears GOD,
    actually listens to the voice of his servant?
For anyone out there who doesn't know where you're going,
    anyone groping in the dark,
Here's what: Trust in GOD.
    Lean on your God!

But if all you're after is making trouble,
    playing with fire,
Go ahead and see where it gets you.
    Set your fires, stir people up, blow on the flames,
But don't expect me to just stand there and watch.
    I'll hold your feet to those flames.

COMMITTED TO SEEKING GOD

1-3   **51** "Listen to me, all you who are serious about right living
        and committed to seeking GOD.
    Ponder the rock from which you were cut,
    the quarry from which you were dug.
Yes, ponder Abraham, your father,
    and Sarah, who bore you.
Think of it! One solitary man when I called him,
    but once I blessed him, he multiplied.
Likewise I, GOD, will comfort Zion,
    comfort all her mounds of ruins.
I'll transform her dead ground into Eden,
    her moonscape into the garden of GOD,
A place filled with exuberance and laughter,
    thankful voices and melodic songs.

4-6   "Pay attention, my people.
    Listen to me, nations.
Revelation flows from me.
    My decisions light up the world.
My deliverance arrives on the run,
    my salvation right on time.
    I'll bring justice to the peoples.
Even faraway islands will look to me
    and take hope in my saving power.
Look up at the skies,
    ponder the earth under your feet.
The skies will fade out like smoke,
    the earth will wear out like work pants,
    and the people will die off like flies.
But my salvation will last forever,
    my setting-things-right will never be obsolete.

7-8   "Listen now, you who know right from wrong,
    you who hold my teaching inside you:
Pay no attention to insults, and when mocked
    don't let it get you down.
Those insults and mockeries are moth-eaten,
    from brains that are termite-ridden,
But my setting-things-right lasts,
    my salvation goes on and on and on."

9-11   Wake up, wake up, flex your muscles, GOD!
    Wake up as in the old days, in the long ago.

Didn't you once make mincemeat of Rahab,
    dispatch the old chaos-dragon?
And didn't you once dry up the sea,
    the powerful waters of the deep,
And then made the bottom of the ocean a road
    for the redeemed to walk across?
In the same way GOD's ransomed will come back,
    come back to Zion cheering, shouting,
Joy eternal wreathing their heads,
    exuberant ecstasies transporting them —
    and not a sign of moans or groans.

WHAT ARE YOU AFRAID OF — OR WHO?

12-16   "I, I'm the One comforting you.
    What are you afraid of — or who?
Some man or woman who'll soon be dead?
    Some poor wretch destined for dust?
You've forgotten me, GOD, who made you,
    who unfurled the skies, who founded the earth.
And here you are, quaking like an aspen
    before the tantrums of a tyrant
    who thinks he can kick down the world.
But what will come of the tantrums?
    The victims will be released before you know it.
They're not going to die.
    They're not even going to go hungry.
For I am GOD, your very own God,
    who stirs up the sea and whips up the waves,
    named GOD-of-the-Angel-Armies.
I teach you how to talk, word by word,
    and personally watch over you,
Even while I'm unfurling the skies,
    setting earth on solid foundations,
    and greeting Zion: 'Welcome, my people!'"

17-20   So wake up! Rub the sleep from your eyes!
    Up on your feet, Jerusalem!
You've drunk the cup GOD handed you,
    the strong drink of his anger.
You drank it down to the last drop,
    staggered and collapsed, dead-drunk.
And nobody to help you home,
    no one among your friends or children
    to take you by the hand and put you in bed.
You've been hit with a double dose of trouble
    — does anyone care?
Assault and battery, hunger and death
    — will anyone comfort?
Your sons and daughters have passed out,
    strewn in the streets like stunned rabbits,
Sleeping off the strong drink of GOD's anger,

the rage of your God.

21-23 Therefore listen, please,
　　you with your splitting headaches,
You who are nursing the hangovers
　　that didn't come from drinking wine.
Your Master, your GOD, has something to say,
　　your God has taken up his people's case:
"Look, I've taken back the drink that sent you reeling.
　　No more drinking from that jug of my anger!
I've passed it over to your abusers to drink, those who ordered you,
　　'Down on the ground so we can walk all over you!'
And you had to do it. Flat on the ground,
　　you were the dirt under their feet."

GOD IS LEADING YOU OUT OF HERE

1-2 **52** Wake up, wake up! Pull on your boots, Zion!
　　　　Dress up in your Sunday best, Jerusalem, holy city!
　　　　Those who want no part of God have been culled out.
They won't be coming along.
Brush off the dust and get to your feet, captive Jerusalem!
　　Throw off your chains, captive daughter of Zion!

3 GOD says, "You were sold for nothing. You're being bought back for nothing."

4-6 Again, the Master, GOD, says, "Early on, my people went to Egypt and lived, strangers in the land. At the other end, Assyria oppressed them. And now, what have I here?" GOD's Decree. "My people are hauled off again for no reason at all. Tyrants on the warpath, whooping it up, and day after day, incessantly, my reputation blackened. Now it's time that my people know who I am, what I'm made of—yes, that I have something to say. Here I am!"

7-10 How beautiful on the mountains
　　are the feet of the messenger bringing good news,
Breaking the news that all's well,
　　proclaiming good times, announcing salvation,
　　telling Zion, "Your God reigns!"
Voices! Listen! Your scouts are shouting, thunderclap shouts,
　　shouting in joyful unison.
They see with their own eyes
　　GOD coming back to Zion.
Break into song! Boom it out, ruins of Jerusalem:
　　"GOD has comforted his people!
　　He's redeemed Jerusalem!"
GOD has rolled up his sleeves.
　　All the nations can see his holy, muscled arm.
Everyone, from one end of the earth to the other,
　　sees him at work, doing his salvation work.

11-12 Out of here! Out of here! Leave this place!
　　Don't look back. Don't contaminate yourselves with plunder.

Just leave, but leave clean. Purify yourselves
    in the process of worship, carrying the holy vessels of GOD.
But you don't have to be in a hurry.
    You're not running from anybody!
GOD is leading you out of here,
    and the God of Israel is also your rear guard.

IT WAS OUR PAINS HE CARRIED

13-15 "Just watch my servant blossom!
    Exalted, tall, head and shoulders above the crowd!
But he didn't begin that way.
    At first everyone was appalled.
He didn't even look human—
    a ruined face, disfigured past recognition.
Nations all over the world will be in awe, taken aback,
    kings shocked into silence when they see him.
For what was unheard of they'll see with their own eyes,
    what was unthinkable they'll have right before them."

1 **53** Who believes what we've heard and seen?
    Who would have thought GOD's saving power would
       look like this?

2-6 The servant grew up before God—a scrawny seedling,
    a scrubby plant in a parched field.
There was nothing attractive about him,
    nothing to cause us to take a second look.
He was looked down on and passed over,
    a man who suffered, who knew pain firsthand.
One look at him and people turned away.
    We looked down on him, thought he was scum.
But the fact is, it was *our* pains he carried—
    our disfigurements, all the things wrong with *us*.
We thought he brought it on himself,
    that God was punishing him for his own failures.
But it was our sins that did that to him,
    that ripped and tore and crushed him—*our sins!*
He took the punishment, and that made us whole.
    Through his bruises we get healed.
We're all like sheep who've wandered off and gotten lost.
    We've all done our own thing, gone our own way.
And GOD has piled all our sins, everything we've done wrong,
    on him, on him.

7-9 He was beaten, he was tortured,
    but he didn't say a word.
Like a lamb taken to be slaughtered
    and like a sheep being sheared,
    he took it all in silence.
Justice miscarried, and he was led off—
    and did anyone really know what was happening?

He died without a thought for his own welfare,
    beaten bloody for the sins of my people.
They buried him with the wicked,
    threw him in a grave with a rich man,
Even though he'd never hurt a soul
    or said one word that wasn't true.

10   Still, it's what GOD had in mind all along,
    to crush him with pain.
The plan was that he give himself as an offering for sin
    so that he'd see life come from it — life, life, and more life.
    And GOD's plan will deeply prosper through him.

11-12   Out of that terrible travail of soul,
    he'll see that it's worth it and be glad he did it.
Through what he experienced, my righteous one, my servant,
    will make many "righteous ones,"
    as he himself carries the burden of their sins.
Therefore I'll reward him extravagantly —
    the best of everything, the highest honors —
Because he looked death in the face and didn't flinch,
    because he embraced the company of the lowest.
He took on his own shoulders the sin of the many,
    he took up the cause of all the black sheep.

SPREAD OUT! THINK BIG!

1-6 **54** "Sing, barren woman, who has never had a baby.
    Fill the air with song, you who've never experienced
    childbirth!
You're ending up with far more children
    than all those childbearing women." GOD says so!
"Clear lots of ground for your tents!
    Make your tents large. Spread out! Think big!
Use plenty of rope,
    drive the tent pegs deep.
You're going to need lots of elbow room
    for your growing family.
You're going to take over whole nations;
    you're going to resettle abandoned cities.
Don't be afraid — you're not going to be embarrassed.
    Don't hold back — you're not going to come up short.
You'll forget all about the humiliations of your youth,
    and the indignities of being a widow will fade from memory.
For your Maker is your bridegroom,
    his name, GOD-of-the-Angel-Armies!
Your Redeemer is The Holy of Israel,
    known as God of the whole earth.
You were like an abandoned wife, devastated with grief,
    and GOD welcomed you back,
Like a woman married young
    and then left," says your God.

7-8 Your Redeemer GOD says:

"I left you, but only for a moment.
    Now, with enormous compassion, I'm bringing you back.
In an outburst of anger I turned my back on you—
    but only for a moment.
It's with lasting love
    that I'm tenderly caring for you.

9-10 "This exile is just like the days of Noah for me:
    I promised then that the waters of Noah
    would never again flood the earth.
I'm promising now no more anger,
    no more dressing you down.
For even if the mountains walk away
    and the hills fall to pieces,
My love won't walk away from you,
    my covenant commitment of peace won't fall apart."
    The GOD who has compassion on you says so.

11-17 "Afflicted city, storm-battered, unpitied:
    I'm about to rebuild you with stones of turquoise,
Lay your foundations with sapphires,
    construct your towers with rubies,
Your gates with jewels,
    and all your walls with precious stones.
All your children will have GOD for their teacher—
    what a mentor for your children!
You'll be built solid, grounded in righteousness,
    far from any trouble—nothing to fear!
    far from terror—it won't even come close!
If anyone attacks you,
    don't for a moment suppose that I sent them,
And if any should attack,
    nothing will come of it.
I create the blacksmith
    who fires up his forge
    and makes a weapon designed to kill.
I also create the destroyer—
    but no weapon that can hurt you has ever been forged.
Any accuser who takes you to court
    will be dismissed as a liar.
This is what GOD's servants can expect.
    I'll see to it that everything works out for the best."
        GOD's Decree.

BUY WITHOUT MONEY

1-5 **55** "Hey there! All who are thirsty,
        come to the water!
    Are you penniless?
    Come anyway—buy and eat!

Come, buy your drinks, buy wine and milk.
　　Buy without money — everything's free!
Why do you spend your money on junk food,
　　your hard-earned cash on cotton candy?
Listen to me, listen well: Eat only the best,
　　fill yourself with only the finest.
Pay attention, come close now,
　　listen carefully to my life-giving, life-nourishing words.
I'm making a lasting covenant commitment with you,
　　the same that I made with David: sure, solid, enduring love.
I set him up as a witness to the nations,
　　made him a prince and leader of the nations,
And now I'm doing it to you:
　　You'll summon nations you've never heard of,
and nations who've never heard of you
　　will come running to you
Because of me, your GOD,
　　because The Holy of Israel has honored you."

6-7　Seek GOD while he's here to be found,
　　pray to him while he's close at hand.
Let the wicked abandon their way of life
　　and the evil their way of thinking.
Let them come back to GOD, who is merciful,
　　come back to our God, who is lavish with forgiveness.

8-11　"I don't think the way you think.
　　The way you work isn't the way I work."
　　　　GOD's Decree.
"For as the sky soars high above earth,
　　so the way I work surpasses the way you work,
　　and the way I think is beyond the way you think.
Just as rain and snow descend from the skies
　　and don't go back until they've watered the earth,
Doing their work of making things grow and blossom,
　　producing seed for farmers and food for the hungry,
So will the words that come out of my mouth
　　not come back empty-handed.
They'll do the work I sent them to do,
　　they'll complete the assignment I gave them.

12-13　"So you'll go out in joy,
　　you'll be led into a whole and complete life.
The mountains and hills will lead the parade,
　　bursting with song.
All the trees of the forest will join the procession,
　　exuberant with applause.
No more thistles, but giant sequoias,
　　no more thornbushes, but stately pines —
Monuments to me, to GOD,
　　living and lasting evidence of GOD."

MESSAGES OF HOPE
SALVATION IS JUST AROUND THE CORNER

1-3

56
GOD's Message:

"Guard my common good:
   Do what's right and do it in the right way,
For salvation is just around the corner,
   my setting-things-right is about to go into action.
How blessed are you who enter into these things,
   you men and women who embrace them,
Who keep Sabbath and don't defile it,
   who watch your step and don't do anything evil!
Make sure no outsider who now follows GOD
   ever has occasion to say, 'GOD put me in second-class.
   I don't really belong.'
And make sure no physically mutilated person
   is ever made to think, 'I'm damaged goods.
   I don't really belong.'"

4-5

For GOD says:

"To the mutilated who keep my Sabbaths
   and choose what delights me
   and keep a firm grip on my covenant,
I'll provide them an honored place
   in my family and within my city,
   even more honored than that of sons and daughters.
I'll confer permanent honors on them
   that will never be revoked.

6-8

"And as for the outsiders who now follow me,
   working for me, loving my name,
   and wanting to be my servants—
All who keep Sabbath and don't defile it,
   holding fast to my covenant—
I'll bring them to my holy mountain
   and give them joy in my house of prayer.
They'll be welcome to worship the same as the 'insiders,'
   to bring burnt offerings and sacrifices to my altar.
Oh yes, my house of worship
   will be known as a house of prayer for all people."
The Decree of the Master, GOD himself,
   who gathers in the exiles of Israel:
"I will gather others also,
   gather them in with those already gathered."

9-12

A call to the savage beasts: Come on the run.
   Come, devour, beast barbarians!
For Israel's watchmen are blind, the whole lot of them.

They have no idea what's going on.
They're dogs without sense enough to bark,
    lazy dogs, dreaming in the sun—
But hungry dogs, they do know how to eat,
    voracious dogs, with never enough.
And these are Israel's shepherds!
    They know nothing, understand nothing.
They all look after themselves,
    grabbing whatever's not nailed down.
"Come," they say, "let's have a party.
    Let's go out and get drunk!"
And tomorrow, more of the same:
    "Let's live it up!"

NEVER TIRED OF TRYING NEW RELIGIONS

57 1-2 Meanwhile, right-living people die
    and no one gives them a thought.
    God-fearing people are carted off
and no one even notices.
The right-living people are out of their misery,
    they're finally at rest.
They lived well and with dignity
    and now they're finally at peace.

3-10 "But you, children of a witch, come here!
    Sons of a slut, daughters of a whore.
What business do you have taunting,
    sneering, and sticking out your tongue?
Do you have any idea what wretches you've turned out to be?
    A race of rebels, a generation of liars.
You satisfy your lust any place you find some shade
    and fornicate at whim.
You kill your children at any convenient spot—
    any cave or crevasse will do.
You take stones from the creek
    and set up your sex-and-religion shrines.
You've chosen your fate.
    Your worship will be your doom.
You've climbed a high mountain
    to practice your foul sex-and-death religion.
Behind closed doors
    you assemble your precious gods and goddesses.
Deserting me, you've gone all out, stripped down
    and made your bed your place of worship.
You've climbed into bed with the 'sacred' whores
    and loved every minute of it,
    adoring every curve of their naked bodies.
You anoint your king-god with ointments
    and lavish perfumes on yourselves.
You send scouts to search out the latest in religion,

send them all the way to hell and back.
You wear yourselves out trying the new and the different,
    and never see what a waste it all is.
You've always found strength for the latest fad,
    never got tired of trying new religions.

11-13   "Who talked you into the pursuit of this nonsense,
    leaving me high and dry,
      forgetting you ever knew me?
Because I don't yell and make a scene
    do you think I don't exist?
I'll go over, detail by detail, all your 'righteous' attempts at religion,
    and expose the absurdity of it all.
Go ahead, cry for help to your collection of no-gods:
    A good wind will blow them away.
    They're smoke, nothing but smoke.

"But anyone who runs to me for help
    will inherit the land,
    will end up owning my holy mountain!"

14   Someone says: "Build, build! Make a road!
    Clear the way, remove the rocks
    from the road my people will travel."

15-21   A Message from the high and towering God,
    who lives in Eternity,
    whose name is Holy:
"I live in the high and holy places,
    but also with the low-spirited, the spirit-crushed,
And what I do is put new spirit in them,
    get them up and on their feet again.
For I'm not going to haul people into court endlessly,
    I'm not going to be angry forever.
Otherwise, people would lose heart.
    These souls I created would tire out and give up.
I *was* angry, good and angry, because of Israel's sins.
    I struck him hard and turned away in anger,
    while he kept at his stubborn, willful ways.
When I looked again and saw what he was doing,
    I decided to heal him, lead him, and comfort him,
    creating a new language of praise for the mourners.
Peace to the far-off, peace to the near-at-hand," says GOD —
    "and yes, I will heal them.
But the wicked are storm-battered seas
    that can't quiet down.
    The waves stir up garbage and mud.
There's no peace," God says, "for the wicked."

YOUR PRAYERS WON'T GET OFF THE GROUND

58 ¹⁻³ "Shout! A full-throated shout!
Hold nothing back—a trumpet-blast shout!
Tell my people what's wrong with their lives,
face my family Jacob with their sins!
They're busy, busy, busy at worship,
and love studying all about me.
To all appearances they're a nation of right-living people—
law-abiding, God-honoring.
They ask me, 'What's the right thing to do?'
and love having me on their side.
But they also complain,
'Why do we fast and you don't look our way?
Why do we humble ourselves and you don't even notice?'

3-5   "Well, here's why:

"The bottom line on your 'fast days' is profit.
You drive your employees much too hard.
You fast, but at the same time you bicker and fight.
You fast, but you swing a mean fist.
The kind of fasting you do
won't get your prayers off the ground.
Do you think this is the kind of fast day I'm after:
a day to show off humility?
To put on a pious long face
and parade around solemnly in black?
Do you call *that* fasting,
a fast day that I, GOD, would like?

6-9   "This is the kind of fast day I'm after:
to break the chains of injustice,
get rid of exploitation in the workplace,
free the oppressed,
cancel debts.
What I'm interested in seeing you do is:
sharing your food with the hungry,
inviting the homeless poor into your homes,
putting clothes on the shivering ill-clad,
being available to your own families.
Do this and the lights will turn on,
and your lives will turn around at once.
Your righteousness will pave your way.
The GOD of glory will secure your passage.
Then when you pray, GOD will answer.
You'll call out for help and I'll say, 'Here I am.'

A FULL LIFE IN THE EMPTIEST OF PLACES

9-12   "If you get rid of unfair practices,
quit blaming victims,

quit gossiping about other people's sins,
If you are generous with the hungry
and start giving yourselves to the down-and-out,
Your lives will begin to glow in the darkness,
your shadowed lives will be bathed in sunlight.
I will always show you where to go.
I'll give you a full life in the emptiest of places—
firm muscles, strong bones.
You'll be like a well-watered garden,
a gurgling spring that never runs dry.
You'll use the old rubble of past lives to build anew,
rebuild the foundations from out of your past.
You'll be known as those who can fix anything,
restore old ruins, rebuild and renovate,
make the community livable again.

13-14 "If you watch your step on the Sabbath
and don't use my holy day for personal advantage,
If you treat the Sabbath as a day of joy,
GOD's holy day as a celebration,
If you honor it by refusing 'business as usual,'
making money, running here and there—
Then you'll be free to enjoy GOD!
Oh, I'll make you ride high and soar above it all.
I'll make you feast on the inheritance of your ancestor Jacob."
Yes! GOD says so!

WE LONG FOR LIGHT BUT SINK INTO DARKNESS

1-8 **59** Look! Listen!
GOD's arm is not amputated—he can still save.
GOD's ears are not stopped up—he can still hear.
There's nothing wrong with God; the wrong is in *you*.
Your wrongheaded lives caused the split between you and God.
Your sins got between you so that he doesn't hear.
Your hands are drenched in blood,
your fingers dripping with guilt,
Your lips smeared with lies,
your tongue swollen from muttering obscenities.
No one speaks up for the right,
no one deals fairly.
They trust in illusion, they tell lies,
they get pregnant with mischief and have sin-babies.
They hatch snake eggs and weave spider webs.
Eat an egg and die; break an egg and get a snake!
The spider webs are no good for shirts or shawls.
No one can wear these weavings!
They weave wickedness,
they hatch violence.
They compete in the race to do evil
and run to be the first to murder.
They plan and plot evil, think and breathe evil,

and leave a trail of wrecked lives behind them.
They know nothing about peace
  and less than nothing about justice.
They make tortuously twisted roads.
  No peace for the wretch who walks down those roads!

9-11 Which means that we're a far cry from fair dealing,
  and we're not even close to right living.
We long for light but sink into darkness,
  long for brightness but stumble through the night.
Like the blind, we inch along a wall,
  groping eyeless in the dark.
We shuffle our way in broad daylight,
  like the dead, but somehow walking.
We're no better off than bears, groaning,
  and no worse off than doves, moaning.
We look for justice — not a sign of it;
  for salvation — not so much as a hint.

12-15 Our wrongdoings pile up before you, God,
  our sins stand up and accuse us.
Our wrongdoings stare us down;
  we know in detail what we've done:
Mocking and denying GOD,
  not following our God,
Spreading false rumors, inciting sedition,
  pregnant with lies, muttering malice.
Justice is beaten back,
  Righteousness is banished to the sidelines,
Truth staggers down the street,
  Honesty is nowhere to be found,
Good is missing in action.
  Anyone renouncing evil is beaten and robbed.

15-19 GOD looked and saw evil looming on the horizon —
  so much evil and no sign of Justice.
He couldn't believe what he saw:
  not a soul around to correct this awful situation.
So he did it himself, took on the work of Salvation,
  fueled by his own Righteousness.
He dressed in Righteousness, put it on like a suit of armor,
  with Salvation on his head like a helmet,
Put on Judgment like an overcoat,
  and threw a cloak of Passion across his shoulders.
He'll make everyone pay for what they've done:
  fury for his foes, just deserts for his enemies.
  Even the far-off islands will get paid off in full.
In the west they'll fear the name of GOD,
  in the east they'll fear the glory of GOD,
For he'll arrive like a river in flood stage,
  whipped to a torrent by the wind of GOD.

20 "I'll arrive in Zion as Redeemer,
    to those in Jacob who leave their sins."
      GOD's Decree.

21   "As for me," GOD says, "this is my covenant with them: My Spirit that I've placed upon you and the words that I've given you to speak, they're not going to leave your mouths nor the mouths of your children nor the mouths of your grandchildren. You will keep repeating these words and won't ever stop." GOD's orders.

PEOPLE RETURNING FOR THE REUNION

1-7
60
"Get out of bed, Jerusalem!
    Wake up. Put your face in the sunlight.
    GOD's bright glory has risen for you.
The whole earth is wrapped in darkness,
    all people sunk in deep darkness,
But GOD rises on you,
    his sunrise glory breaks over you.
Nations will come to your light,
    kings to your sunburst brightness.
Look up! Look around!
    Watch as they gather, watch as they approach you:
Your sons coming from great distances,
    your daughters carried by their nannies.
When you see them coming you'll smile — big smiles!
    Your heart will swell and, yes, burst!
All those people returning by sea for the reunion,
    a rich harvest of exiles gathered in from the nations!
And then streams of camel caravans as far as the eye can see,
    young camels of nomads in Midian and Ephah,
Pouring in from the south from Sheba,
    loaded with gold and frankincense,
    preaching the praises of GOD.
And yes, a great roundup
    of flocks from the nomads in Kedar and Nebaioth,
Welcome gifts for worship at my altar
    as I bathe my glorious Temple in splendor.

WHAT'S THAT WE SEE IN THE DISTANCE?

8-22
"What's that we see in the distance,
    a cloud on the horizon, like doves darkening the sky?
It's ships from the distant islands,
    the famous Tarshish ships
Returning your children from faraway places,
    loaded with riches, with silver and gold,
And backed by the name of your GOD, The Holy of Israel,
    showering you with splendor.
Foreigners will rebuild your walls,
    and their kings assist you in the conduct of worship.
When I was angry I hit you hard.
    It's my desire now to be tender.

Your Jerusalem gates will always be open
   — open house day and night! —
Receiving deliveries of wealth from all nations,
   and their kings, the delivery boys!
Any nation or kingdom that doesn't deliver will perish;
   those nations will be totally wasted.
The rich woods of Lebanon will be delivered
   — all that cypress and oak and pine —
To give a splendid elegance to my Sanctuary,
   as I make my footstool glorious.
The descendants of your oppressor
   will come bowing and scraping to you.
All who looked down at you in contempt
   will lick your boots.
They'll confer a title on you: City of GOD,
   Zion of The Holy of Israel.
Not long ago you were despised refuse —
   out-of-the-way, unvisited, ignored.
But now I've put you on your feet,
   towering and grand forever, a joy to look at!
When you suck the milk of nations
   and the breasts of royalty,
You'll know that I, GOD, am your Savior,
   your Redeemer, Champion of Jacob.
I'll give you only the best — no more hand-me-downs!
   Gold instead of bronze, silver instead of iron,
   bronze instead of wood, iron instead of stones.
I'll install Peace to run your country,
   make Righteousness your boss.
There'll be no more stories of crime in your land,
   no more robberies, no more vandalism.
You'll name your main street Salvation Way,
   and install Praise Park at the center of town.
You'll have no more need of the sun by day
   nor the brightness of the moon at night.
GOD will be your eternal light,
   your God will bathe you in splendor.
Your sun will never go down,
   your moon will never fade.
I will be your eternal light.
   Your days of grieving are over.
All your people will live right and well,
   in permanent possession of the land.
They're the green shoot that I planted,
   planted with my own hands to display my glory.
The runt will become a great tribe,
   the weakling become a strong nation.
I am GOD.
   At the right time I'll make it happen."

ANNOUNCE FREEDOM TO ALL CAPTIVES

61 1-7

The Spirit of GOD, the Master, is on me
        because GOD anointed me.
He sent me to preach good news to the poor,
    heal the heartbroken,
Announce freedom to all captives,
    pardon all prisoners.
GOD sent me to announce the year of his grace —
    a celebration of God's destruction of our enemies —
    and to comfort all who mourn,
To care for the needs of all who mourn in Zion,
    give them bouquets of roses instead of ashes,
Messages of joy instead of news of doom,
    a praising heart instead of a languid spirit.
Rename them "Oaks of Righteousness"
    planted by GOD to display his glory.
They'll rebuild the old ruins,
    raise a new city out of the wreckage.
They'll start over on the ruined cities,
    take the rubble left behind and make it new.
You'll hire outsiders to herd your flocks
    and foreigners to work your fields,
But you'll have the title "Priests of GOD,"
    honored as ministers of our God.
You'll feast on the bounty of nations,
    you'll bask in their glory.
Because you got a double dose of trouble
    and more than your share of contempt,
Your inheritance in the land will be doubled
    and your joy go on forever.

8-9

"Because I, GOD, love fair dealing
    and hate thievery and crime,
I'll pay your wages on time and in full,
    and establish my eternal covenant with you.
Your descendants will become well-known all over.
    Your children in foreign countries
Will be recognized at once
    as the people I have blessed."

10-11

I will sing for joy in GOD,
    explode in praise from deep in my soul!
He dressed me up in a suit of salvation,
    he outfitted me in a robe of righteousness,
As a bridegroom who puts on a tuxedo
    and a bride a jeweled tiara.
For as the earth bursts with spring wildflowers,
    and as a garden cascades with blossoms,
So the Master, GOD, brings righteousness into full bloom
    and puts praise on display before the nations.

LOOK, YOUR SAVIOR COMES!

¹⁻⁵ **62** Regarding Zion, I can't keep my mouth shut,
  regarding Jerusalem, I can't hold my tongue,
  Until her righteousness blazes down like the sun
and her salvation flames up like a torch.
Foreign countries will see your righteousness,
  and world leaders your glory.
You'll get a brand-new name
  straight from the mouth of GOD.
You'll be a stunning crown in the palm of GOD's hand,
  a jeweled gold cup held high in the hand of your God.
No more will anyone call you Rejected,
  and your country will no more be called Ruined.
You'll be called Hephzibah (My Delight),
  and your land Beulah (Married),
Because GOD delights in you
  and your land will be like a wedding celebration.
For as a young man marries his virgin bride,
  so your builder marries you,
And as a bridegroom is happy in his bride,
  so your God is happy with you.

⁶⁻⁷ I've posted watchmen on your walls, Jerusalem.
  Day and night they keep at it, praying, calling out,
  reminding GOD to remember.
They are to give him no peace until he does what he said,
  until he makes Jerusalem famous as the City of Praise.

⁸⁻⁹ GOD has taken a solemn oath,
  an oath he means to keep:
"Never again will I open your grain-filled barns
  to your enemies to loot and eat.
Never again will foreigners drink the wine
  that you worked so hard to produce.
No. The farmers who grow the food will eat the food
  and praise GOD for it.
And those who make the wine will drink the wine
  in my holy courtyards."

¹⁰⁻¹² Walk out of the gates. Get going!
  Get the road ready for the people.
Build the highway. Get at it!
  Clear the debris,
  hoist high a flag, a signal to all peoples!
Yes! GOD has broadcast to all the world:
  "Tell daughter Zion, 'Look! Your Savior comes,
Ready to do what he said he'd do,
  prepared to complete what he promised.'"
Zion will be called new names: Holy People, GOD-Redeemed,
  Sought-Out, City-Not-Forsaken.

WHO GOES THERE?

63
1 The watchmen call out,
"Who goes there, marching out of Edom,
out of Bozrah in clothes dyed red?
Name yourself, so splendidly dressed,
advancing, bristling with power!"

"It is I: I speak what is right,
I, mighty to save!"

2 "And why are your robes so red,
your clothes dyed red like those who tread grapes?"

3-6 "I've been treading the winepress alone.
No one was there to help me.
Angrily, I stomped the grapes;
raging, I trampled the people.
Their blood spurted all over me—
all my clothes were soaked with blood.
I was set on vengeance.
The time for redemption had arrived.
I looked around for someone to help
—no one.
I couldn't believe it
—not one volunteer.
So I went ahead and did it myself,
fed and fueled by my rage.
I trampled the people in my anger,
crushed them under foot in my wrath,
soaked the earth with their lifeblood."

ALL THE THINGS GOD HAS DONE THAT NEED PRAISING

7-9 I'll make a list of GOD's gracious dealings,
all the things GOD has done that need praising,
All the generous bounties of GOD,
his great goodness to the family of Israel—
Compassion lavished,
love extravagant.
He said, "Without question these are my people,
children who would never betray me."
So he became their Savior.
In all their troubles,
he was troubled, too.
He didn't send someone else to help them.
He did it himself, in person.
Out of his own love and pity
he redeemed them.
He rescued them and carried them along
for a long, long time.

10 But they turned on him;
    they grieved his Holy Spirit.
So he turned on them,
    became their enemy and fought them.

11-14 Then they remembered the old days,
    the days of Moses, God's servant:
"Where is he who brought the shepherds of his flock
    up and out of the sea?
And what happened to the One who set
    his Holy Spirit within them?
Who linked his arm with Moses' right arm,
    divided the waters before them,
Making him famous ever after,
    and led them through the muddy abyss
    as surefooted as horses on hard, level ground?
Like a herd of cattle led to pasture,
    the Spirit of GOD gave them rest."

14-19 *That's* how you led your people!
    That's how you became so famous!
Look down from heaven, look at us!
    Look out the window of your holy and magnificent house!
Whatever happened to your passion,
    your famous mighty acts,
Your heartfelt pity, your compassion?
    Why are you holding back?
You are our Father.
    Abraham and Israel are long dead.
    They wouldn't know us from Adam.
But you're our *living* Father,
    our Redeemer, famous from eternity!
Why, GOD, did you make us wander from your ways?
    Why did you make us cold and stubborn
    so that we no longer worshiped you in awe?
Turn back for the sake of your servants.
    You own us! We belong to you!
For a while your holy people had it good,
    but now our enemies have wrecked your holy place.
For a long time now, you've paid no attention to us.
    It's like you never knew us.

CAN WE BE SAVED?

1-7 **64** Oh, that you would rip open the heavens and descend,
    make the mountains shudder at your presence—
    As when a forest catches fire,
as when fire makes a pot to boil—
To shock your enemies into facing you,
    make the nations shake in their boots!
You did terrible things we never expected,
    descended and made the mountains shudder at your presence.

Since before time began
　　no one has ever imagined,
No ear heard, no eye seen, a God like you
　　who works for those who wait for him.
You meet those who happily do what is right,
　　who keep a good memory of the way you work.
But how angry you've been with us!
　　We've sinned and kept at it so long!
　　Is there any hope for us? Can we be saved?
We're all sin-infected, sin-contaminated.
　　Our best efforts are grease-stained rags.
We dry up like autumn leaves—
　　sin-dried, we're blown off by the wind.
No one prays to you
　　or makes the effort to reach out to you
Because you've turned away from us,
　　left us to stew in our sins.

8-12　Still, GOD, you are our Father.
　　We're the clay and you're our potter:
　　All of us are what you made us.
Don't be too angry with us, O GOD.
　　Don't keep a permanent account of wrongdoing.
　　Keep in mind, please, we *are* your people—all of us.
Your holy cities are all ghost towns:
　　Zion's a ghost town,
　　Jerusalem's a field of weeds.
Our holy and beautiful Temple,
　　which our ancestors filled with your praises,
Was burned down by fire,
　　all our lovely parks and gardens in ruins.
In the face of all this,
　　are you going to sit there unmoved, GOD?
Aren't you going to say something?
　　Haven't you made us miserable long enough?

The People Who Bothered to Reach Out to God

1-7　**65** "I've made myself available
　　　　to those who haven't bothered to ask.
　　　　I'm here, ready to be found
　　by those who haven't bothered to look.
I kept saying 'I'm here, I'm right here'
　　to a nation that ignored me.
I reached out day after day
　　to a people who turned their backs on me,
People who make wrong turns,
　　who insist on doing things their own way.
They get on my nerves,
　　are rude to my face day after day,
Make up their own kitchen religion,
　　a potluck religious stew.

They spend the night in tombs
    to get messages from the dead,
Eat forbidden foods
    and drink a witch's brew of potions and charms.
They say, 'Keep your distance.
    Don't touch me. I'm holier than thou.'
These people gag me.
    I can't stand their stench.
Look at this! Their sins are all written out—
    I have the list before me.
I'm not putting up with this any longer.
    I'll pay them the wages
They have coming for their sins.
    And for the sins of their parents lumped in,
    a bonus." GOD says so.
"Because they've practiced their blasphemous worship,
    mocking me at their hillside shrines,
I'll let loose the consequences
    and pay them in full for their actions."

8-10   GOD's Message:

"But just as one bad apple doesn't ruin the whole bushel,
    there are still plenty of good apples left.
So I'll preserve those in Israel who obey me.
    I won't destroy the whole nation.
I'll bring out my true children from Jacob
    and the heirs of my mountains from Judah.
My chosen will inherit the land,
    my servants will move in.
The lush valley of Sharon in the west
    will be a pasture for flocks,
And in the east, the valley of Achor,
    a place for herds to graze.
These will be for the people
    who bothered to reach out to me, who wanted me in their lives,
    who actually bothered to look for me.

11-12   "But you who abandon me, your GOD,
    who forget the holy mountains,
Who hold dinners for Lady Luck
    and throw cocktail parties for Sir Fate,
Well, you asked for it. Fate it will be:
    your destiny, Death.
For when I invited you, you ignored me;
    when I spoke to you, you brushed me off.
You did the very things I exposed as evil;
    you chose what I hate."

13-16 Therefore, this is the Message from the Master, GOD:

"My servants will eat,
  and you'll go hungry;
My servants will drink,
  and you'll go thirsty;
My servants will rejoice,
  and you'll hang your heads.
My servants will laugh from full hearts,
  and you'll cry out heartbroken,
  yes, wail from crushed spirits.
Your legacy to my chosen
  will be your name reduced to a cussword.
I, GOD, will put you to death
  and give a new name to my servants.
Then whoever prays a blessing in the land
  will use my faithful name for the blessing,
And whoever takes an oath in the land
  will use my faithful name for the oath,
Because the earlier troubles are gone and forgotten,
  banished far from my sight.

New Heavens and a New Earth

17-25 "Pay close attention now:
  I'm creating new heavens and a new earth.
All the earlier troubles, chaos, and pain
  are things of the past, to be forgotten.
Look ahead with joy.
  Anticipate what I'm creating:
I'll create Jerusalem as sheer joy,
  create my people as pure delight.
I'll take joy in Jerusalem,
  take delight in my people:
No more sounds of weeping in the city,
  no cries of anguish;
No more babies dying in the cradle,
  or old people who don't enjoy a full lifetime;
One-hundredth birthdays will be considered normal—
  anything less will seem like a cheat.
They'll build houses
  and move in.
They'll plant fields
  and eat what they grow.
No more building a house
  that some outsider takes over,
No more planting fields
  that some enemy confiscates,
For my people will be as long-lived as trees,
  my chosen ones will have satisfaction in their work.
They won't work and have nothing come of it,
  they won't have children snatched out from under them.

For they themselves are plantings blessed by GOD,
    with their children and grandchildren likewise GOD-blessed.
Before they call out, I'll answer.
    Before they've finished speaking, I'll have heard.
Wolf and lamb will graze the same meadow,
    lion and ox eat straw from the same trough,
    but snakes—they'll get a diet of dirt!
Neither animal nor human will hurt or kill
    anywhere on my Holy Mountain," says GOD.

LIVING WORSHIP TO GOD

66 1-2 GOD's Message:

    "Heaven's my throne,
earth is my footstool.
What sort of house could you build for me?
    What holiday spot reserve for me?
I made all this! I own all this!"
    GOD's Decree.
"But there *is* something I'm looking for:
    a person simple and plain,
    reverently responsive to what I say.

3-4 "Your acts of worship
    are acts of sin:
Your sacrificial slaughter of the ox
    is no different from murdering the neighbor;
Your offerings for worship,
    no different from dumping pig's blood on the altar;
Your presentation of memorial gifts,
    no different from honoring a no-god idol.
You choose self-serving worship,
    you delight in self-centered worship—disgusting!
Well, I choose to expose your nonsense
    and let you realize your worst fears,
Because when I invited you, you ignored me;
    when I spoke to you, you brushed me off.
You did the very things I exposed as evil,
    you chose what I hate."

5 But listen to what GOD has to say
    to you who reverently respond to his Word:
"Your own families hate you
    and turn you out because of me.
They taunt you, 'Let us see GOD's glory!
    If God's so great, why aren't you happy?'
But they're the ones
    who are going to end up shamed."

6   Rumbles of thunder from the city!
      A voice out of the Temple!
GOD's voice,
      handing out judgment to his enemies:

7-9   "Before she went into labor,
      she had the baby.
Before the birth pangs hit,
      she delivered a son.
Has anyone ever heard of such a thing?
      Has anyone seen anything like this?
A country born in a day?
      A nation born in a flash?
But Zion was barely in labor
      when she had her babies!
Do I open the womb
      and not deliver the baby?
Do I, the One who delivers babies,
      shut the womb?

10-11   "Rejoice, Jerusalem,
      and all who love her, celebrate!
And all you who have shed tears over her,
      join in the happy singing.
You newborns can satisfy yourselves
      at her nurturing breasts.
Yes, delight yourselves and drink your fill
      at her ample bosom."

12-13   GOD's Message:

"I'll pour robust well-being into her like a river,
      the glory of nations like a river in flood.
You'll nurse at her breasts,
      nestle in her bosom,
      and be bounced on her knees.
As a mother comforts her child,
      so I'll comfort you.
You will be comforted in Jerusalem."

14-16   You'll see all this and burst with joy
      — you'll feel ten feet tall —
As it becomes apparent that GOD is on your side
      and against his enemies.
For GOD arrives like wildfire
      and his chariots like a tornado,
A furious outburst of anger,
      a rebuke fierce and fiery.
For it's by fire that GOD brings judgment,
      a death sentence on the human race.

Many, oh so many,
    are under GOD's sentence of death:

17   "All who enter the sacred groves for initiation in those unholy rituals that climaxed in that foul and obscene meal of pigs and mice will eat together and then die together." GOD's Decree.

18-21   "I know everything they've ever done or thought. I'm going to come and then gather everyone — all nations, all languages. They'll come and see my glory. I'll set up a station at the center. I'll send the survivors of judgment all over the world: Spain and Africa, Turkey and Greece, and the far-off islands that have never heard of me, who know nothing of what I've done nor who I am. I'll send them out as missionaries to preach my glory among the nations. They'll return with all your long-lost brothers and sisters from all over the world. They'll bring them back and offer them in living worship to GOD. They'll bring them on horses and wagons and carts, on mules and camels, straight to my holy mountain Jerusalem," says GOD. "They'll present them just as Israelites present their offerings in a ceremonial vessel in the Temple of GOD. I'll even take some of them and make them priests and Levites," says GOD.

22-23   "For just as the new heavens and new earth
    that I am making will stand firm before me"
      — GOD's Decree —
"So will your children
    and your reputation stand firm.
Month after month and week by week,
    everyone will come to worship me," GOD says.

24   "And then they'll go out and look at what happened
    to those who rebelled against me. Corpses!
Maggots endlessly eating away on them,
    an endless supply of fuel for fires.
Everyone who sees what's happened
    and smells the stench retches."

JEREMIAH

Jeremiah's life and Jeremiah's book are a single piece. He wrote what he lived, he lived what he wrote. There is no dissonance between his life and his book. Some people write better than they live; others live better than they write. Jeremiah, writing or living, was the same Jeremiah.

This is important to know because Jeremiah is the prophet of choice for many when we find ourselves having to live through difficult times and want some trustworthy help in knowing what to think, how to pray, how to carry on. We'd like some verification of credentials. This book provides the verification.

We live in disruptive times. The decades preceding and following the pivotal third millennium are not exactly unprecedented. There have certainly been comparable times of disruption in the past that left everyone reeling, wondering what on earth and in heaven was going on. But whatever their occasion or size, troubles require attention.

Jeremiah's troubled life spanned one of the most troublesome periods in Hebrew history, the decades leading up to the fall of Jerusalem in 587 B.C., followed by the Babylonian exile. Everything that could go wrong *did* go wrong. And Jeremiah was in the middle of all of it, sticking it out, praying and preaching, suffering and striving, writing and believing. He lived through crushing storms of hostility and furies of bitter doubt. Every muscle in his body was stretched to the limit by fatigue; every thought in his mind was subjected to questioning; every feeling in his heart was put through fires of ridicule. He experienced it all agonizingly and wrote it all magnificently.

What happens when everything you believe in and live by is smashed to bits by circumstances? Sometimes the reversals of what we expect from God come to us as individuals, other times as entire communities. When it happens, does catastrophe work to re-form our lives to conform to who God actually is and not the way we imagined or wished him to be? Does it lead to an abandonment of God? Or, worse, does it trigger a stubborn grasping to the old collapsed system of belief, holding on for dear life to an illusion?

Anyone who lives in disruptive times looks for companions who have been through them earlier, wanting to know how they went through it, how they made it, what it was like. In looking for a companion who has lived through catastrophic disruption and survived with grace, biblical people more often than not come upon Jeremiah and receive him as a true, honest, and God-revealing companion for the worst of times.

JEREMIAH

DEMOLISH, AND THEN START OVER

1-4 The Message of Jeremiah son of Hilkiah of the family of priests who lived in Anathoth in the country of Benjamin. GOD's Message began to come to him during the thirteenth year that Josiah son of Amon reigned over Judah. It continued to come to him during the time Jehoiakim son of Josiah reigned over Judah. And it continued to come to him clear down to the fifth month of the eleventh year of the reign of Zedekiah son of Josiah over Judah, the year that Jerusalem was taken into exile. This is what GOD said:

5 "Before I shaped you in the womb,
   I knew all about you.
Before you saw the light of day,
   I had holy plans for you:
A prophet to the nations —
   that's what I had in mind for you."

6 But I said, "Hold it, Master GOD! Look at me.
   I don't know anything. I'm only a boy!"

7-8 GOD told me, "Don't say, 'I'm only a boy.'
   I'll tell you where to go and you'll go there.
I'll tell you what to say and you'll say it.
   Don't be afraid of a soul.
I'll be right there, looking after you."
   GOD's Decree.

9-10 GOD reached out, touched my mouth, and said,
   "Look! I've just put my words in your mouth — hand-delivered!
See what I've done? I've given you a job to do
   among nations and governments — a red-letter day!
Your job is to pull up and tear down,
   take apart and demolish,
And then start over,
   building and planting."

STAND UP AND SAY YOUR PIECE

11-12 GOD's Message came to me: "What do you see, Jeremiah?"
   I said, "A walking stick — that's all."
And GOD said, "Good eyes! I'm sticking with you.
   I'll make every word I give you come true."

13-15 GOD's Message came again: "So what do you see now?"
   I said, "I see a boiling pot, tipped down toward us."
Then GOD told me, "Disaster will pour out of the north
   on everyone living in this land.
Watch for this: I'm calling all the kings out of the north."
   GOD's Decree.

15-16   "They'll come and set up headquarters
             facing Jerusalem's gates,
         Facing all the city walls,
             facing all the villages of Judah.
         I'll pronounce my judgment on the people of Judah
             for walking out on me — what a terrible thing to do! —
         And courting other gods with their offerings,
             worshiping as gods sticks they'd carved, stones they'd painted.

17   "But you — up on your feet and get dressed for work!
             Stand up and say your piece. Say exactly what I tell you to say.
         Don't pull your punches
             or I'll pull you out of the lineup.

18-19   "Stand at attention while I prepare you for your work.
             I'm making you as impregnable as a castle,
         Immovable as a steel post,
             solid as a concrete block wall.
         You're a one-man defense system
             against this culture,
         Against Judah's kings and princes,
             against the priests and local leaders.
         They'll fight you, but they won't
             even scratch you.
         I'll back you up every inch of the way."
             GOD'S Decree.

ISRAEL WAS GOD'S HOLY CHOICE

1-3   2 GOD'S Message came to me. It went like this:

         "Get out in the streets and call to Jerusalem,
             'GOD'S Message!
         I remember your youthful loyalty,
             our love as newlyweds.
         You stayed with me through the wilderness years,
             stuck with me through all the hard places.
         Israel was GOD'S holy choice,
             the pick of the crop.
         Anyone who laid a hand on her
             would soon wish he hadn't!'"
             GOD'S Decree.

4-6   Hear GOD'S Message, House of Jacob!
             Yes, you — House of Israel!
         GOD'S Message: "What did your ancestors find fault with in me
             that they drifted so far from me,
         Took up with Sir Windbag
             and turned into windbags themselves?
         It never occurred to them to say, 'Where's GOD,
             the God who got us out of Egypt,

Who took care of us through thick and thin, those rough-and-tumble
    wilderness years of parched deserts and death valleys,
A land that no one who enters comes out of,
    a cruel, inhospitable land?'

7-8 "I brought you to a garden land
    where you could eat lush fruit.
But you barged in and polluted my land,
    trashed and defiled my dear land.
The priests never thought to ask, 'Where's GOD?'
    The religion experts knew nothing of me.
The rulers defied me.
    The prophets preached god Baal
And chased empty god-dreams and silly god-schemes.

9-11 "Because of all this, I'm bringing charges against you"
    — GOD's Decree —
    "charging you and your children and your grandchildren.
Look around. Have you ever seen anything quite like this?
    Sail to the western islands and look.
Travel to the Kedar wilderness and look.
    Look closely. Has this ever happened before,
That a nation has traded in its gods
    for gods that aren't even close to gods?
But my people have traded my Glory
    for empty god-dreams and silly god-schemes.

12-13 "Stand in shock, heavens, at what you see!
    Throw up your hands in disbelief — this can't be!"
      GOD's Decree.
"My people have committed a compound sin:
    they've walked out on me, the fountain
Of fresh flowing waters, and then dug cisterns —
    cisterns that leak, cisterns that are no better than sieves.

14-17 "Isn't Israel a valued servant,
    born into a family with place and position?
So how did she end up a piece of meat
    fought over by snarling and roaring lions?
There's nothing left of her but a few old bones,
    her towns trashed and deserted.
Egyptians from the cities of Memphis and Tahpanhes
    have broken your skulls.
And why do you think all this has happened?
    Isn't it because you walked out on your God
    just as he was beginning to lead you in the right way?

18-19 "And now, what do you think you'll get by going off to Egypt?
    Maybe a cool drink of Nile River water?
Or what do you think you'll get by going off to Assyria?
    Maybe a long drink of Euphrates River water?

Your evil ways will get you a sound thrashing, that's what you'll get.
    You'll pay dearly for your disloyal ways.
Take a long, hard look at what you've done and its bitter results.
    Was it worth it to have walked out on your God?"
        GOD'S Decree, Master GOD-of-the-Angel-Armies.

ADDICTED TO ALIEN GODS

20-22   "A long time ago you broke out of the harness.
    You shook off all restraints.
You said, 'I will not serve!'
    and off you went,
Visiting every sex-and-religion shrine on the way,
    like a common whore.
You were a select vine when I planted you
    from completely reliable stock.
And look how you've turned out—
    a tangle of rancid growth, a poor excuse for a vine.
Scrub, using the strongest soaps.
    Scour your skin raw.
The sin-grease won't come out. I can't stand to even look at you!"
    GOD'S Decree, the Master's Decree.

23-24   "How dare you tell me, 'I'm not stained by sin.
    I've never chased after the Baal sex gods'!
Well, look at the tracks you've left behind in the valley.
    How do you account for what is written in the desert dust—
Tracks of a camel in heat, running this way and that,
    tracks of a wild donkey in rut,
Sniffing the wind for the slightest scent of sex.
    Who could possibly corral her!
On the hunt for sex, sex, and more sex—
    insatiable, indiscriminate, promiscuous.

25   "Slow down. Take a deep breath. What's the hurry?
    Why wear yourself out? Just what are you after anyway?
But you say, 'I can't help it.
    I'm addicted to alien gods. I can't quit.'

26-28   "Just as a thief is chagrined, but only when caught,
    so the people of Israel are chagrined,
Caught along with their kings and princes,
    their priests and prophets.
They walk up to a tree and say, 'My father!'
    They pick up a stone and say, 'My mother! You bore me!'
All I ever see of them is their backsides.
    They never look me in the face.
But when things go badly, they don't hesitate to come running,
    calling out, 'Get a move on! Save us!'
Why not go to your handcrafted gods you're so fond of?
    Rouse them. Let them save you from your bad times.

You've got more gods, Judah,
    than you know what to do with.

TRYING OUT ANOTHER SIN-PROJECT

29-30   "What do you have against me,
    running off to assert your 'independence'?"
       GOD's Decree.
"I've wasted my time trying to train your children.
    They've paid no attention to me, ignored my discipline.
And you've gotten rid of your God-messengers,
    treating them like dirt and sweeping them away.

31-32   "What a generation you turned out to be!
    Didn't I tell you? Didn't I warn you?
Have I let you down, Israel?
    Am I nothing but a dead-end street?
Why do my people say, 'Good riddance!
    From now on we're on our own'?
Young women don't forget their jewelry, do they?
    Brides don't show up without their veils, do they?
But my people forget me.
    Day after day after day they never give me a thought.

33-35   "What an impressive start you made
    to get the most out of life.
You founded schools of sin,
    taught graduate courses in evil!
And now you're sending out graduates, resplendent in cap and gown—
    except the gowns are stained with the blood of your victims!
All that blood convicts you.
    You cut and hurt a lot of people to get where you are.
And yet you have the gall to say, 'I've done nothing wrong.
    God doesn't mind. He hasn't punished me, has he?'
Don't look now, but judgment's on the way,
    aimed at you who say, 'I've done nothing wrong.'

36-37   "You think it's just a small thing, don't you,
    to try out another sin-project when the first one fails?
But Egypt will leave you in the lurch
    the same way that Assyria did.
You're going to walk away from there
    wringing your hands.
I, GOD, have blacklisted those you trusted.
    You'll get not a lick of help from them."

YOUR SEX-AND-RELIGION OBSESSIONS

1   **3** GOD's Message came to me as follows:

"If a man's wife
    walks out on him

And marries another man,
 can he take her back as if nothing had happened?
Wouldn't that raise a huge stink
 in the land?
And isn't that what you've done —
 'whored' your way with god after god?
And now you want to come back as if nothing had happened."
 GOD's Decree.

2-5 "Look around at the hills.
 Where have you *not* had sex?
You've camped out like hunters stalking deer.
 You've solicited many lover-gods,
Like a streetwalking whore
 chasing after other gods.
And so the rain has stopped.
 No more rain from the skies!
But it doesn't even faze you. Brazen as whores,
 you carry on as if you've done nothing wrong.
Then you have the nerve to call out, 'My father!
 You took care of me when I was a child. Why not now?
Are you going to keep up your anger nonstop?'
 That's your line. Meanwhile you keep sinning nonstop."

ADMIT YOUR GOD-DEFIANCE

6-10 GOD spoke to me during the reign of King Josiah: "You have noticed, haven't you, how fickle Israel has visited every hill and grove of trees as a whore at large? I assumed that after she had gotten it out of her system, she'd come back, but she didn't. Her flighty sister, Judah, saw what she did. She also saw that because of fickle Israel's loose morals I threw her out, gave her her walking papers. But that didn't faze flighty sister Judah. She went out, big as you please, and took up a whore's life also. She took up cheap sex-and-religion as a sideline diversion, an indulgent recreation, and used anything and anyone, flouting sanity and sanctity alike, stinking up the country. And not once in all this did flighty sister Judah even give me a nod, although she made a show of it from time to time." GOD's Decree.

11-12 Then GOD told me, "Fickle Israel was a good sight better than flighty Judah. Go and preach this message. Face north toward Israel and say:

12-15 " 'Turn back, fickle Israel.
 I'm not just hanging back to punish you.
I'm committed in love to you.
 My anger doesn't seethe nonstop.
Just admit your guilt.
 Admit your God-defiance.
Admit to your promiscuous life with casual partners,
 pulling strangers into the sex-and-religion groves
While turning a deaf ear to me.' "
 GOD's Decree.
"Come back, wandering children!"
 GOD's Decree.

"I, yes I, am your true husband.
   I'll pick you out one by one —
This one from the city, these two from the country —
   and bring you to Zion.
I'll give you good shepherd-rulers who rule my way,
   who rule you with intelligence and wisdom.

16 "And this is what will happen: You will increase and prosper in the land.
The time will come" — GOD's Decree! — "when no one will say any longer,
'Oh, for the good old days! Remember the Ark of the Covenant?' It won't
even occur to anyone to say it — 'the good old days.' The so-called good old
days of the Ark are gone for good.

17 "Jerusalem will be the new Ark — 'GOD's Throne.' All the godless
nations, no longer stuck in the ruts of their evil ways, will gather there to
honor GOD.

18 "At that time, the House of Judah will join up with the House of Israel.
Holding hands, they'll leave the north country and come to the land I willed to
your ancestors.

19-20 "I planned what I'd say if you returned to me:
   'Good! I'll bring you back into the family.
I'll give you choice land,
   land that the godless nations would die for.'
And I imagined that you would say, 'Dear father!'
   and would never again go off and leave me.
But no luck. Like a false-hearted woman walking out on her husband,
   you, the whole family of Israel, have proven false to me."
         GOD's Decree.

21-22 The sound of voices comes drifting out of the hills,
   the unhappy sound of Israel's crying,
Israel lamenting the wasted years,
   never once giving her God a thought.
"Come back, wandering children!
   I can heal your wanderlust!"

22-25 "We're here! We've come back to you.
   You're our own true GOD!
All that popular religion was a cheap lie,
   duped crowds buying up the latest in gods.
We're back! Back to our true GOD,
   the salvation of Israel.
The Fraud picked us clean, swindled us
   of what our ancestors bequeathed us,
Gypped us out of our inheritance —
   God-blessed flocks and God-given children.
We made our bed and now lie in it,
   all tangled up in the dirty sheets of dishonor.
All because we sinned against our GOD,

we and our fathers and mothers.
From the time we took our first steps, said our first words,
we've been rebels, disobeying the voice of our GOD."

4 **1-2** "If you want to come back, O Israel,
you must really come back to me.
You must get rid of your stinking sin paraphernalia
and not wander away from me anymore.
Then you can say words like, 'As GOD lives . . .'
and have them mean something true and just and right.
And the godless nations will get caught up in the blessing
and find something in Israel to write home about."

3-4 Here's another Message from GOD
to the people of Judah and Jerusalem:
"Plow your unplowed fields,
but then don't plant weeds in the soil!
Yes, circumcise your *lives* for God's sake.
Plow your unplowed hearts,
all you people of Judah and Jerusalem.
Prevent fire — the fire of my anger —
for once it starts it can't be put out.
Your wicked ways
are fuel for the fire.

GOD'S SLEDGEHAMMER ANGER

5-8 "Sound the alarm in Judah,
broadcast the news in Jerusalem.
Say, 'Blow the ram's horn trumpet through the land!'
Shout out — a bullhorn bellow! —
'Close ranks!
Run for your lives to the shelters!'
Send up a flare warning Zion:
'Not a minute to lose! Don't sit on your hands!'
Disaster's descending from the north. I set it off!
When it lands, it will shake the foundations.
Invaders have pounced like a lion from its cover,
ready to rip nations to shreds,
Leaving your land in wrack and ruin,
your cities in rubble, abandoned.
Dress in funereal black.
Weep and wail,
For GOD's sledgehammer anger
has slammed into us head-on.

9 "When this happens"
— GOD's Decree —
"King and princes will lose heart;
priests will be baffled and prophets stand dumbfounded."

10   Then I said, "Alas, Master God!
           You've fed lies to this people, this Jerusalem.
       You assured them, 'All is well, don't worry,'
           at the very moment when the sword was at their throats."

11-12 At that time, this people, yes, this very Jerusalem,
           will be told in plain words:
       "The northern hordes are sweeping in
           from the desert steppes—
       A wind that's up to no good, a gale-force wind.
           I ordered this wind.
       I'm pronouncing
           my hurricane judgment on my people."

Your Evil Life Is Piercing Your Heart

13-14 Look at them! Like banks of storm clouds,
           racing, tumbling, their chariots a tornado,
       Their horses faster than eagles!
           Woe to us! We're done for!
       Jerusalem! Scrub the evil from your lives
           so you'll be fit for salvation.
       How much longer will you harbor
           devious and malignant designs within you?

15-17 What's this? A messenger from Dan?
           Bad news from Ephraim's hills!
       Make the report public.
           Broadcast the news to Jerusalem:
       "Invaders from far off are
           raising war cries against Judah's towns.
       They're all over her, like a dog on a bone.
           And why? Because she rebelled against me."
               God's Decree.

18   "It's the way you've lived
           that's brought all this on you.
       The bitter taste is from your evil life.
           That's what's piercing your heart."

19-21 I'm doubled up with cramps in my belly—
           a poker burns in my gut.
       My insides are tearing me up,
           never a moment's peace.
       The ram's horn trumpet blast rings in my ears,
           the signal for all-out war.
       Disaster hard on the heels of disaster,
           the whole country in ruins!
       In one stroke my home is destroyed,
           the walls flattened in the blink of an eye.

How long do I have to look at the warning flares,
   listen to the siren of danger?

EXPERTS AT EVIL

22   "What fools my people are!
         They have no idea who I am.
      A company of half-wits,
         dopes and donkeys all!
      Experts at evil
         but klutzes at good."

23-26   I looked at the earth —
            it was back to pre-Genesis chaos and emptiness.
         I looked at the skies,
            and not a star to be seen.
         I looked at the mountains —
            they were trembling like aspen leaves,
         And all the hills
            rocking back and forth in the wind.
         I looked — what's this! Not a man or woman in sight,
            and not a bird to be seen in the skies.
         I looked — this can't be! Every garden and orchard shriveled up.
            All the towns were ghost towns.
         And all this because of GOD,
            because of the blazing anger of GOD.

27-28   Yes, this is GOD's Word on the matter:

         "The whole country will be laid waste —
            still it won't be the end of the world.
         The earth will mourn
            and the skies lament
         Because I've given my word and won't take it back.
            I've decided and won't change my mind."

YOU'RE NOT GOING TO SEDUCE ANYONE

29   Someone shouts, "Horsemen and archers!"
         and everybody runs for cover.
      They hide in ditches,
         they climb into caves.
      The cities are emptied,
         not a person left anywhere.

30-31   And you, what do you think you're up to?
            Dressing up in party clothes,
         Decking yourselves out in jewelry,
            putting on lipstick and rouge and mascara!
         Your primping goes for nothing.
            You're not going to seduce anyone. They're out to *kill* you!
         And what's that I hear? The cry of a woman in labor,
            the screams of a mother giving birth to her firstborn.

It's the cry of Daughter Zion, gasping for breath,
> reaching out for help:
"Help, oh help me! I'm dying!
> The killers are on me!"

SINS ARE PILED SKY-HIGH

1-2 **5** "Patrol Jerusalem's streets.
> Look around. Take note.
> Search the market squares.
> See if you can find one man, one woman,
A single soul who does what is right
> and tries to live a true life.
> I want to forgive that person."
> > GOD's Decree.
"But if all they do is say, 'As sure as GOD lives . . .'
> they're nothing but a bunch of liars."

3-6 But you, GOD,
> you have an eye for truth, don't you?
You hit them hard, but it didn't faze them.
> You disciplined them, but they refused correction.
Hardheaded, harder than rock,
> they wouldn't change.
Then I said to myself, "Well, these are just poor people.
> They don't know any better.
They were never taught anything about GOD.
> They never went to prayer meetings.
I'll find some people from the best families.
> I'll talk to them.
They'll know what's going on, the way GOD works.
> They'll know the score."
But they were no better! Rebels all!
> Off doing their own thing.
The invaders are ready to pounce and kill,
> like a mountain lion, a wilderness wolf,
Panthers on the prowl.
> The streets aren't safe anymore.
And why? Because the people's sins are piled sky-high;
> their betrayals are past counting.

7-9 "Why should I even bother with you any longer?
> Your children wander off, leaving me,
Taking up with gods
> that aren't even gods.
I satisfied their deepest needs, and then they went off with the 'sacred' whores,
> left me for orgies in sex shrines!
A bunch of well-groomed, lusty stallions,
> each one pawing and snorting for his neighbor's wife.
Do you think I'm going to stand around and do nothing?"
> GOD's Decree.

"Don't you think I'll take serious measures
    against a people like this?

EYES THAT DON'T REALLY LOOK,
EARS THAT DON'T REALLY LISTEN

10-11   "Go down the rows of vineyards and rip out the vines,
    but not all of them. Leave a few.
Prune back those vines!
    That growth didn't come from GOD!
They've betrayed me over and over again,
    Judah and Israel both."
      GOD's Decree.

12-13   "They've spread lies about GOD.
    They've said, 'There's nothing to him.
Nothing bad will happen to us,
    neither famine nor war will come our way.
The prophets are all windbags.
    They speak nothing but nonsense.'"

14   Therefore, this is what GOD said to me, GOD-of-the-Angel-Armies:

"Because they have talked this way,
    they are going to eat those words.
Watch now! I'm putting my words
    as fire in your mouth.
And the people are a pile of kindling
    ready to go up in flames.

15-17   "Attention! I'm bringing a far-off nation
    against you, O house of Israel."
      GOD's Decree.
"A solid nation,
    an ancient nation,
A nation that speaks another language.
    You won't understand a word they say.
When they aim their arrows, you're as good as dead.
    They're a nation of real fighters!
They'll clean you out of house and home,
    rob you of crops and children alike.
They'll feast on your sheep and cattle,
    strip your vines and fig trees.
And the fortresses that made you feel so safe—
    leveled with a stroke of the sword!

18-19   "Even then, as bad as it will be"—GOD's Decree!—"it will not be the
end of the world for you. And when people ask, 'Why did our GOD do all this
to us?' you must say to them, 'It's tit for tat. Just as you left me and served
foreign gods in your own country, so now you must serve foreigners in their
own country.'

20-25   "Tell the house of Jacob this,
     put out this bulletin in Judah:
  Listen to this,
     you scatterbrains, airheads,
  With eyes that see but don't really look,
     and ears that hear but don't really listen.
  Why don't you honor me?
     Why aren't you in awe before me?
  Yes, *me*, who made the shorelines
     to contain the ocean waters.
  I drew a line in the sand
     that cannot be crossed.
  Waves roll in but cannot get through;
     breakers crash but that's the end of them.
  But this people—what a people!
     Uncontrollable, untameable runaways.
  It never occurs to them to say,
     'How can we honor our GOD with our lives,
  The God who gives rain in both spring and autumn
     and maintains the rhythm of the seasons,
  Who sets aside time each year for harvest
     and keeps everything running smoothly for us?'
  Of course you don't! Your bad behavior blinds you to all this.
     Your sins keep my blessings at a distance.

TO STAND FOR NOTHING AND STAND UP FOR NO ONE

26-29   "My people are infiltrated by wicked men,
     unscrupulous men on the hunt.
  They set traps for the unsuspecting.
     Their victims are innocent men and women.
  Their houses are stuffed with ill-gotten gain,
     like a hunter's bag full of birds.
  Pretentious and powerful and rich,
     hugely obese, oily with rolls of fat.
  Worse, they have no conscience.
     Right and wrong mean nothing to them.
  They stand for nothing, stand up for no one,
     throw orphans to the wolves, exploit the poor.
  Do you think I'll stand by and do nothing about this?"
     GOD's Decree.
  "Don't you think I'll take serious measures
     against a people like this?

30-31   "Unspeakable! Sickening!
     What's happened in this country?
  Prophets preach lies
     and priests hire on as their assistants.
  And my people love it. They eat it up!
     But what will you do when it's time to pick up the pieces?"

A City Full of Lies

1-5 6 "Run for your lives, children of Benjamin!
    Get out of Jerusalem, and now!
    Give a blast on the ram's horn in Blastville.
Send up smoke signals from Smoketown.
Doom pours out of the north—
    massive terror!
I have likened my dear daughter Zion
    to a lovely meadow.
Well, now 'shepherds' from the north have discovered her
    and brought in their flocks of soldiers.
They've pitched camp all around her,
    and plan where they'll 'graze.'
And then, 'Prepare to attack! The fight is on!
    To arms! We'll strike at noon!
Oh, it's too late? Day is dying?
    Evening shadows are upon us?
Well, up anyway! We'll attack by night
    and tear apart her defenses stone by stone.'"

6-8   GOD-of-the-Angel-Armies gave the orders:

"Chop down her trees.
    Build a siege ramp against Jerusalem,
A city full of brutality,
    bursting with violence.
Just as a well holds a good supply of water,
    she supplies wickedness nonstop.
The streets echo the cries: 'Violence! Rape!'
    Victims, bleeding and moaning, lie all over the place.
You're in deep trouble, Jerusalem.
    You've pushed me to the limit.
You're on the brink of being wiped out,
    being turned into a ghost town."

9   More orders from GOD-of-the-Angel-Armies:

"Time's up! Harvest the grapes for judgment.
    Salvage what's left of Israel.
Go back over the vines.
    Pick them clean, every last grape.

Is Anybody Listening?

10-11 "I've got something to say. Is anybody listening?
    I've a warning to post. Will anyone notice?
It's hopeless! Their ears are stuffed with wax—
    deaf as a post, blind as a bat.
It's hopeless! They've tuned out GOD.
    They don't want to hear from me.
But I'm bursting with the wrath of GOD.

I can't hold it in much longer.

11-12 "So dump it on the children in the streets.
    Let it loose on the gangs of youth.
For no one's exempt: Husbands and wives will be taken,
    the old and those ready to die;
Their homes will be given away —
    all they own, even their loved ones —
When I give the signal
    against all who live in this country."
        GOD's Decree.

13-15 "Everyone's after the dishonest dollar,
    little people and big people alike.
Prophets and priests and everyone in between
    twist words and doctor truth.
My people are broken — shattered! —
    and they put on Band-Aids,
Saying, 'It's not so bad. You'll be just fine.'
    But things are not 'just fine'!
Do you suppose they are embarrassed
    over this outrage?
No, they have no shame.
    They don't even know how to blush.
There's no hope for them. They've hit bottom
    and there's no getting up.
As far as I'm concerned,
    they're finished."
        GOD has spoken.

DEATH IS ON THE PROWL

16-20 GOD's Message yet again:

"Go stand at the crossroads and look around.
    Ask for directions to the old road,
The tried-and-true road. Then take it.
    Discover the right route for your souls.
But they said, 'Nothing doing.
    We aren't going that way.'
I even provided watchmen for them
    to warn them, to set off the alarm.
But the people said, 'It's a false alarm.
    It doesn't concern us.'
And so I'm calling in the nations as witnesses:
    'Watch, witnesses, what happens to them!'
And, 'Pay attention, Earth!
    Don't miss these bulletins.'
I'm visiting catastrophe on this people, the end result
    of the games they've been playing with me.
They've ignored everything I've said,
    had nothing but contempt for my teaching.

What would I want with incense brought in from Sheba,
  rare spices from exotic places?
Your burnt sacrifices in worship give me no pleasure.
  Your religious rituals mean nothing to me."

21 So listen to this. Here's GOD's verdict on your way of life:

"Watch out! I'm putting roadblocks and barriers
  on the road you're taking.
They'll send you sprawling,
  parents and children, neighbors and friends—
  and that will be the end of the lot of you."

22-23 And listen to this verdict from GOD:

"Look out! An invasion from the north,
  a mighty power on the move from a faraway place:
Armed to the teeth,
  vicious and pitiless,
Booming like sea storm and thunder—tramp, tramp, tramp—
  riding hard on war horses,
In battle formation
  against you, dear Daughter Zion!"

24-25 We've heard the news,
  and we're as limp as wet dishrags.
We're paralyzed with fear.
  Terror has a death grip on our throats.
Don't dare go outdoors!
  Don't leave the house!
Death is on the prowl.
  Danger everywhere!

26 "Dear Daughter Zion: Dress in black.
  Blacken your face with ashes.
Weep most bitterly,
  as for an only child.
The countdown has begun . . .
  six, five, four, three . . .
  The Terror is on us!"

27-30 GOD gave me this task:

"I have made you the examiner of my people,
  to examine and weigh their lives.
They're a thickheaded, hard-nosed bunch,
  rotten to the core, the lot of them.
Refining fires are cranked up to white heat,
  but the ore stays a lump, unchanged.
It's useless to keep trying any longer.

Nothing can refine evil out of them.
Men will give up and call them 'slag,'
thrown on the slag heap by me, their GOD."

THE NATION THAT WOULDN'T OBEY GOD

1-2 The Message from GOD to Jeremiah: "Stand in the gate of GOD's Temple and preach this Message.

2-3 "Say, 'Listen, all you people of Judah who come through these gates to worship GOD. GOD-of-the-Angel-Armies, Israel's God, has this to say to you:

3-7 "'Clean up your act—the way you live, the things you do—so I can make my home with you in this place. Don't for a minute believe the lies being spoken here—"This is GOD's Temple, GOD's Temple, GOD's Temple!" Total nonsense! Only if you clean up your act (the way you live, the things you do), only if you do a total spring cleaning on the way you live and treat your neighbors, only if you quit exploiting the street people and orphans and widows, no longer taking advantage of innocent people on this very site and no longer destroying your souls by using this Temple as a front for other gods—only *then* will I move into your neighborhood. Only then will this country I gave your ancestors be my permanent home, my Temple.

8-11 "'Get smart! Your leaders are handing you a pack of lies, and you're swallowing them! Use your heads! Do you think you can rob and murder, have sex with the neighborhood wives, tell lies nonstop, worship the local gods, and buy every novel religious commodity on the market—and then march into this Temple, set apart for my worship, and say, "We're safe!" thinking that the place itself gives you a license to go on with all this outrageous sacrilege? A cave full of criminals! Do you think you can turn this Temple, set apart for my worship, into something like that? Well, think again. I've got eyes in my head. I can see what's going on.'" GOD's Decree!

12 "'Take a trip down to the place that was once in Shiloh, where I met my people in the early days. Take a look at those ruins, what I did to it because of the evil ways of my people Israel.

13-15 "'So now, because of the way you have lived and failed to listen, even though time and again I took you aside and talked seriously with you, and because you refused to change when I called you to repent, I'm going to do to this Temple, set aside for my worship, this place you think is going to keep you safe no matter what, this place I gave as a gift to your ancestors and you, the same as I did to Shiloh. And as for you, I'm going to get rid of you, the same as I got rid of those old relatives of yours around Shiloh, your fellow Israelites in that former kingdom to the north.'

16-18 "And you, Jeremiah, don't waste your time praying for this people. Don't offer to make petitions or intercessions. Don't bother me with them. I'm not listening. Can't you see what they're doing in all the villages of Judah and in the Jerusalem streets? Why, they've got the children gathering wood while the fathers build fires and the mothers make bread to be offered to 'the Queen of Heaven'! And as if that weren't bad enough, they go around pouring out libations to any other gods they come across, just to hurt me.

19 "But is it me they're hurting?" GOD's Decree! "Aren't they just hurting themselves? Exposing themselves shamefully? Making themselves ridiculous?

20 "Here's what the Master GOD has to say: 'My white-hot anger is about to

descend on this country and everything in it — people and animals, trees in the field and vegetables in the garden — a raging wildfire that no one can put out.'

21-23   "The Message from GOD-of-the-Angel-Armies, Israel's God: 'Go ahead! Put your burnt offerings with all your other sacrificial offerings and make a good meal for yourselves. *I* sure don't want them! When I delivered your ancestors out of Egypt, I never said anything to them about wanting burnt offerings and sacrifices as such. But I did say this, *commanded* this: "Obey me. Do what I say and I will be your God and you will be my people. Live the way I tell you. Do what I command so that your lives will go well."

24-26   "'But do you think they listened? Not a word of it. They did just what they wanted to do, indulged any and every evil whim and got worse day by day. From the time your ancestors left the land of Egypt until now, I've supplied a steady stream of my servants the prophets, but do you think the people listened? Not once. Stubborn as mules and worse than their ancestors!'

27-28   "Tell them all this, but don't expect them to listen. Call out to them, but don't expect an answer. Tell them, 'You are the nation that wouldn't obey GOD, that refused all discipline. Truth has disappeared. There's not a trace of it left in your mouths.

29   "'So shave your heads.
     Go bald to the hills and lament,
For GOD has rejected and left
     this generation that has made him so angry.'

30-31   "The people of Judah have lived evil lives while I've stood by and watched." GOD's Decree. "In deliberate insult to me, they've set up their obscene god-images in the very Temple that was built to honor me. They've constructed Topheth altars for burning babies in prominent places all through the valley of Ben-hinnom, altars for burning their sons and daughters alive in the fire — a shocking perversion of all that I am and all I command.

32-34   "But soon, very soon" — GOD's Decree! — "the names Topheth and Ben-hinnom will no longer be used. They'll call the place what it is: Murder Meadow. Corpses will be stacked up in Topheth because there's no room left to bury them! Corpses abandoned in the open air, fed on by crows and coyotes, who have the run of the place. And I'll empty both smiles and laughter from the villages of Judah and the streets of Jerusalem. No wedding songs, no holiday sounds. *Dead* silence."

1-2   8 "And when the time comes" — GOD's Decree! — "I'll see to it that they dig up the bones of the kings of Judah, the bones of the princes and priests and prophets, and yes, even the bones of the common people. They'll dig them up and spread them out like a congregation at worship before sun, moon, and stars, all those sky gods they've been so infatuated with all these years, following their 'lucky stars' in doglike devotion. The bones will be left scattered and exposed, to reenter the soil as fertilizer, like manure.

3   "Everyone left — all from this evil generation unlucky enough to still be alive in whatever godforsaken place I will have driven them to — will

wish they were dead." Decree of GOD-of-the-Angel-Armies.

TO KNOW EVERYTHING BUT GOD'S WORD

4-7   "Tell them this, GOD's Message:

"'Do people fall down and not get up?
    Or take the wrong road and then just keep going?
So why does this people go backward,
    and just keep on going — *backward*!
They stubbornly hold on to their illusions,
    refuse to change direction.
I listened carefully
    but heard not so much as a whisper.
No one expressed one word of regret.
    Not a single "I'm sorry" did I hear.
They just kept at it, blindly and stupidly
    banging their heads against a brick wall.
Cranes know when it's time
    to move south for winter.
And robins, warblers, and bluebirds
    know when it's time to come back again.
But my people? My people know nothing,
    not the first thing of GOD and his rule.

8-9   "'How can you say, "We know the score.
    We're the proud owners of GOD's revelation"?
Look where it's gotten you — stuck in illusion.
    Your religion experts have taken you for a ride!
Your know-it-alls will be unmasked,
    caught and shown up for what they are.
Look at them! They know everything but GOD's Word.
    Do you call that "knowing"?

10-12   "'So here's what will happen to the know-it-alls:
    I'll make them wifeless and homeless.
Everyone's after the dishonest dollar,
    little people and big people alike.
Prophets and priests and everyone in between
    twist words and doctor truth.
My dear Daughter — my people — broken, shattered,
    and yet they put on Band-Aids,
Saying, "It's not so bad. You'll be just fine."
    But things are not "just fine"!
Do you suppose they are embarrassed
    over this outrage?
Not really. They have no shame.
    They don't even know how to blush.
There's no hope for them. They've hit bottom
    and there's no getting up.
As far as I'm concerned,
    they're finished.'" GOD has spoken.

〰

13   "'I went out to see if I could salvage anything'"
      —GOD's Decree—
      "'but found nothing:
Not a grape, not a fig,
      just a few withered leaves.
I'm taking back
      everything I gave them.'"

14-16   So why are we sitting here, doing nothing?
      Let's get organized.
Let's go to the big city
      and at least die fighting.
We've gotten GOD's ultimatum:
      We're damned if we do and damned if we don't—
      damned because of our sin against him.
We hoped things would turn out for the best,
      but it didn't happen that way.
We were waiting around for healing—
      and terror showed up!
From Dan at the northern borders
      we hear the hooves of horses,
Horses galloping, horses neighing.
      The ground shudders and quakes.
They're going to swallow up the whole country.
      Towns and people alike—fodder for war.

17   "'What's more, I'm dispatching
      poisonous snakes among you,
Snakes that can't be charmed,
      snakes that will bite you and kill you.'"
       GOD's Decree!

ADVANCING FROM ONE EVIL TO THE NEXT

18-22   I drown in grief.
      I'm heartsick.
Oh, listen! Please listen! It's the cry of my dear people
      reverberating through the country.
Is GOD no longer in Zion?
      Has the King gone away?
Can you tell me why they flaunt their plaything-gods,
      their silly, imported no-gods before me?
The crops are in, the summer is over,
      but for us nothing's changed.
      We're still waiting to be rescued.
For my dear broken people, I'm heartbroken.
      I weep, seized by grief.
Are there no healing ointments in Gilead?
      Isn't there a doctor in the house?
So why can't something be done

to heal and save my dear, dear people?

¹⁻² **9** I wish my head were a well of water
   and my eyes fountains of tears
So I could weep day and night
 for casualties among my dear, dear people.
At times I wish I had a wilderness hut,
 a backwoods cabin,
Where I could get away from my people
 and never see them again.
They're a faithless, feckless bunch,
 a congregation of degenerates.

³⁻⁶ "Their tongues shoot out lies
 like a bow shoots arrows —
A mighty army of liars,
 the sworn enemies of truth.
They advance from one evil to the next,
 ignorant of me."
  GOD's Decree.
"Be wary of even longtime neighbors.
 Don't even trust your grandmother!
Brother schemes against brother,
 like old cheating Jacob.
Friend against friend
 spreads malicious gossip.
Neighbors gyp neighbors,
 never telling the truth.
They've trained their tongues to tell lies,
 and now they can't tell the truth.
They pile wrong upon wrong, stack lie upon lie,
 and refuse to know me."
  GOD's Decree.

⁷⁻⁹ Therefore, GOD-of-the-Angel-Armies says:

"Watch this! I'll melt them down
 and see what they're made of.
What else can I do
 with a people this wicked?
Their tongues are poison arrows!
 Deadly lies stream from their mouths.
Neighbor greets neighbor with a smile,
 'Good morning! How're things?'
 while scheming to do away with him.
Do you think I'm going to stand around and do nothing?"
  GOD's Decree.
"Don't you think I'll take serious measures
 against a people like this?

10-11 "I'm lamenting the loss of the mountain pastures.
  I'm chanting dirges for the old grazing grounds.
They've become deserted wastelands too dangerous for travelers.
  No sounds of sheep bleating or cattle mooing.
Birds and wild animals, all gone.
  Nothing stirring, no sounds of life.
I'm going to make Jerusalem a pile of rubble,
  fit for nothing but stray cats and dogs.
I'm going to reduce Judah's towns to piles of ruins
  where no one lives!"

---

12 I asked, "Is there anyone around bright enough to tell us what's going on here? Anyone who has the inside story from GOD and can let us in on it?

  "Why is the country wasted?

  "Why no travelers in this desert?"

13-15 GOD's answer: "Because they abandoned my plain teaching. They wouldn't listen to anything I said, refused to live the way I told them to. Instead they lived any way they wanted and took up with the Baal gods, who they thought would give them what they wanted—following the example of their parents." And this is the consequence. GOD-of-the-Angel-Armies says so:

  "I'll feed them with pig slop.
  "I'll give them poison to drink.
16 "Then I'll scatter them far and wide among godless peoples that neither they nor their parents have ever heard of, and I'll send Death in pursuit until there's nothing left of them."

A Life That Is All Outside but No Inside

17-19 A Message from GOD-of-the-Angel-Armies:

"Look over the trouble we're in and call for help.
  Send for some singers who can help us mourn our loss.
Tell them to hurry—
  to help us express our loss and lament,
Help us get our tears flowing,
  make tearful music of our crying.
Listen to it!
  Listen to that torrent of tears out of Zion:
'We're a ruined people,
  we're a shamed people!
We've been driven from our homes
  and must leave our land!' "

20-21 Mourning women! Oh, listen to GOD's Message!
  Open your ears. Take in what he says.
Teach your daughters songs for the dead
  and your friends the songs of heartbreak.
Death has climbed in through the window,

broken into our bedrooms.
Children on the playgrounds drop dead,
   and young men and women collapse at their games.

22   Speak up! "GOD's Message:

" 'Dead bodies everywhere, scattered at random
   like sheep and goat dung in the fields,
Like wheat cut down by reapers
   and left to rot where it falls.' "

23-24   GOD's Message:

"Don't let the wise brag of their wisdom.
   Don't let heroes brag of their exploits.
Don't let the rich brag of their riches.
   If you brag, brag of this and this only:
That you understand and know me.
   I'm GOD, and I act in loyal love.
I do what's right and set things right and fair,
   and delight in those who do the same things.
These are my trademarks."
   GOD's Decree.

25-26   "Stay alert! It won't be long now"—GOD's Decree!—"when I will
personally deal with everyone whose life is all outside but no inside: Egypt,
Judah, Edom, Ammon, Moab. All these nations are big on performance
religion—including Israel, who is no better."

THE STICK GODS

1-5   **10** Listen to the Message that GOD is sending your way, House
         of Israel. Listen most carefully:

"Don't take the godless nations as your models.
   Don't be impressed by their glamour and glitz,
   no matter how much they're impressed.
The religion of these peoples
   is nothing but smoke.
An idol is nothing but a tree chopped down,
   then shaped by a woodsman's ax.
They trim it with tinsel and balls,
   use hammer and nails to keep it upright.
It's like a scarecrow in a cabbage patch—can't talk!
   Deadwood that has to be carried—can't walk!
Don't be impressed by such stuff.
   It's useless for either good or evil."

6-9   All this is nothing compared to you, O GOD.
   You're wondrously great, famously great.
Who can fail to be impressed by you, King of the nations?

It's your very nature to be worshiped!
Look far and wide among the elite of the nations.
    The best they can come up with is nothing compared to you.
Stupidly, they line them up — a lineup of sticks,
    good for nothing but making smoke.
Gilded with silver foil from Tarshish,
    covered with gold from Uphaz,
Hung with violet and purple fabrics —
    no matter how fancy the sticks, they're still sticks.

10   But GOD is the real thing —
        the living God, the eternal King.
    When he's angry, Earth shakes.
        Yes, and the godless nations quake.

11-15   "Tell them this, 'The stick gods
        who made nothing, neither sky nor earth,
    Will come to nothing
        on the earth and under the sky.'"
    But it is God whose power made the earth,
        whose wisdom gave shape to the world,
        who crafted the cosmos.
    He thunders, and rain pours down.
        He sends the clouds soaring.
    He embellishes the storm with lightnings,
        launches wind from his warehouse.
    Stick-god worshipers looking mighty foolish,
        god-makers embarrassed by their handmade gods!
    Their gods are frauds — dead sticks,
        deadwood gods, tasteless jokes.
        When the fires of judgment come, they'll be ashes.

16   But the Portion-of-Jacob is the real thing.
        He put the whole universe together
    And pays special attention to Israel.
        His name? GOD-of-the-Angel-Armies!

17-18   Grab your bags,
        all you who are under attack.
    GOD has given notice:
        "Attention! I'm evicting
    Everyone who lives here,
        And right now — yes, right now!
    I'm going to press them to the limit,
        squeeze the life right out of them."

19-20   But it's a black day for me!
        Hopelessly wounded,
    I said, "Why, oh why

did I think I could bear it?"
My house is ruined—
    the roof caved in.
Our children are gone—
    we'll never see them again.
No one left to help in rebuilding,
    no one to make a new start!

21   It's because our leaders are stupid.
    They never asked GOD for counsel,
And so nothing worked right.
    The people are scattered all over.

22   But listen! Something's coming!
    A big commotion from the northern borders!
Judah's towns about to be smashed,
    left to all the stray dogs and cats!

23-25   I know, GOD, that mere mortals
    can't run their own lives,
That men and women
    don't have what it takes to take charge of life.
So correct us, GOD, as you see best.
    Don't lose your temper. That would be the end of us.
Vent your anger on the godless nations,
    who refuse to acknowledge you,
And on the people
    who won't pray to you—
The very ones who've made hash out of Jacob,
    yes, made hash
And devoured him whole,
    people and pastures alike.

THE TERMS OF THIS COVENANT

1   **11** The Message that came to Jeremiah from GOD:

2-4   "Preach to the people of Judah and citizens of Jerusalem. Tell them this: 'This is GOD's Message, the Message of Israel's God to you. Anyone who does not keep the terms of this covenant is cursed. The terms are clear. I made them plain to your ancestors when I delivered them from Egypt, out of the iron furnace of suffering.

4-5   "'Obey what I tell you. Do exactly what I command you. Your obedience will close the deal. You'll be mine and I'll be yours. This will provide the conditions in which I will be able to do what I promised your ancestors: to give them a fertile and lush land. And, as you know, that's what I did.'"

"Yes, GOD," I replied. "That's true."

6-8   GOD continued: "Preach all this in the towns of Judah and the streets of Jerusalem. Say, 'Listen to the terms of this covenant and carry them out! I warned your ancestors when I delivered them from Egypt and I've kept up the warnings. I haven't quit warning them for a moment. I warned them from morning to night: "Obey me or else!" But they didn't obey. They paid no attention to me. They did whatever they wanted to do, whenever they wanted to do it, until finally I stepped in and ordered the punishments set out in the covenant, which, despite all my warnings, they had ignored.'"

9-10 Then GOD said, "There's a conspiracy among the people of Judah and the citizens of Jerusalem. They've plotted to reenact the sins of their ancestors—the ones who disobeyed me and decided to go after other gods and worship them. Israel and Judah are in this together, mindlessly breaking the covenant I made with their ancestors.

11-13 "Well, your God has something to say about this: Watch out! I'm about to visit doom on you, and no one will get out of it. You're going to cry for help but I won't listen. Then all the people in Judah and Jerusalem will start praying to the gods you've been sacrificing to all these years, but it won't do a bit of good. You've got as many gods as you have villages, Judah! And you've got enough altars for sacrifices to that impotent sex god Baal to put one on every street corner in Jerusalem!

14 "And as for you, Jeremiah, I don't want you praying for this people. Nothing! Not a word of petition. Indeed, I'm not going to listen to a single syllable of their crisis-prayers."

PROMISES AND PIOUS PROGRAMS

15-16 "What business do the ones I love have figuring out
    how to get off the hook? And right in the house of worship!
Do you think making promises and devising pious programs
    will save you from doom?
Do you think you can get out of this
    by becoming more religious?
A mighty oak tree, majestic and glorious—
    that's how I once described you.
But it will only take a clap of thunder and a bolt of lightning
    to leave you a shattered wreck.

17 "I, GOD-of-the-Angel-Armies, who planted you—yes, I have pronounced doom on you. Why? Because of the disastrous life you've lived, Israel and Judah alike, goading me to anger with your continuous worship and offerings to that sorry god Baal."

18-19 GOD told me what was going on. That's how I knew.
    You, GOD, opened my eyes to their evil scheming.
I had no idea what was going on—naive as a lamb
    being led to slaughter!
I didn't know they had it in for me,
    didn't know of their behind-the-scenes plots:
"Let's get rid of the preacher.
    That will stop the sermons!
Let's get rid of him for good.
    He won't be remembered for long."

20 Then I said, "GOD-of-the-Angel-Armies,
    you're a fair judge.
You examine and cross-examine
    human actions and motives.

I want to see these people shown up and put down!
    I'm an open book before you. Clear my name."

²¹⁻²³ That sent a signal to GOD, who spoke up: "Here's what I'll do to the men of Anathoth who are trying to murder you, the men who say, 'Don't preach to us in GOD's name or we'll kill you.' Yes, it's GOD-of-the-Angel-Armies speaking. Indeed! I'll call them to account: Their young people will die in battle, their children will die of starvation, and there will be no one left at all, none. I'm visiting the men of Anathoth with doom. Doomsday!"

WHAT MAKES YOU THINK YOU CAN RACE AGAINST HORSES?

¹⁻⁴ # 12
You are right, O GOD, and you set things right.
    I can't argue with that. But I do have some questions:
    Why do bad people have it so good?
Why do con artists make it big?
You planted them and they put down roots.
    They flourished and produced fruit.
They talk as if they're old friends with you,
    but they couldn't care less about you.
Meanwhile, you know *me* inside and out.
    You don't let me get by with a thing!
Make them pay for the way they live,
    pay with their lives, like sheep marked for slaughter.
How long do we have to put up with this—
    the country depressed, the farms in ruin—
And all because of wickedness, these wicked lives?
    Even animals and birds are dying off
Because they'll have nothing to do with God
    and think God has nothing to do with them.

⁵⁻⁶ "So, Jeremiah, if you're worn out in this footrace with men,
    what makes you think you can race against horses?
And if you can't keep your wits during times of calm,
    what's going to happen when troubles break loose
        like the Jordan in flood?
Those closest to you, your own brothers and cousins,
    are working against you.
They're out to get you. They'll stop at nothing.
    Don't trust them, especially when they're smiling.

⁷⁻¹¹ "I will abandon the House of Israel,
    walk away from my beloved people.
I will turn over those I most love
    to those who are her enemies.
She's been, this one I held dear,
    like a snarling lion in the jungle,
Growling and baring her teeth at me—
    and I can't take it anymore.
Has this one I hold dear become a preening peacock?

But isn't she under attack by vultures?
Then invite all the hungry animals at large,
    invite them in for a free meal!
Foreign, scavenging shepherds
    will loot and trample my fields,
Turn my beautiful, well-cared-for fields
    into vacant lots of tin cans and thistles.
They leave them littered with junk—
    a ruined land, a land in lament.
The whole countryside is a wasteland,
    and no one will really care.

12-13   "The barbarians will invade,
    swarm over hills and plains.
The judgment sword of GOD will take its toll
    from one end of the land to the other.
    Nothing living will be safe.
They will plant wheat and reap weeds.
    Nothing they do will work out.
They will look at their meager crops and wring their hands.
    All this the result of GOD's fierce anger!"

14-17   GOD's Message: "Regarding all the bad neighbors who abused the land I gave to Israel as their inheritance: I'm going to pluck them out of their lands, and then pluck Judah out from among them. Once I've pulled the bad neighbors out, I will relent and take them tenderly to my heart and put them back where they belong, put each of them back in their home country, on their family farms. Then if they will get serious about living my way and pray to me as well as they taught my people to pray to that god Baal, everything will go well for them. But if they won't listen, then I'll pull them out of their land by the roots and cart them off to the dump. Total destruction!" GOD's Decree.

PEOPLE WHO DO ONLY WHAT THEY WANT TO DO

1-2   **13** GOD told me, "Go and buy yourself some linen shorts. Put them on and keep them on. Don't even take them off to wash them." So I bought the shorts as GOD directed and put them on.

3-5   Then GOD told me, "Take the shorts that you bought and go straight to Perath and hide them there in a crack in the rock." So I did what GOD told me and hid them at Perath.

6-7   Next, after quite a long time, GOD told me, "Go back to Perath and get the linen shorts I told you to hide there." So I went back to Perath and dug them out of the place where I had hidden them. The shorts by then had rotted and were worthless.

8-11   GOD explained, "This is the way I am going to ruin the pride of Judah and the great pride of Jerusalem—a wicked bunch of people who won't obey me, who do only what they want to do, who chase after all kinds of no-gods and worship them. They're going to turn out as rotten as these old shorts. Just as shorts clothe and protect, so I kept the whole family of Israel under my care"—GOD's Decree—"so that everyone could see they were my people, a people I could show off to the world and be proud of. But they refused to do a thing I said.

12 "And then tell them this, 'GOD's Message, personal from the God of Israel: Every wine jug should be full of wine.'

"And they'll say, 'Of course. We know that. Every wine jug should be full of wine!'

13-14 "Then you'll say, 'This is what GOD says: Watch closely. I'm going to fill every person who lives in this country—the kings who rule from David's throne, the priests, the prophets, the citizens of Jerusalem—with wine that will make them drunk. And then I'll smash them, smash the wine-filled jugs—old and young alike. Nothing will stop me. Not an ounce of pity or mercy or compassion will slow me down. Every last drunken jug of them will be smashed!'"

THE LIGHT YOU ALWAYS TOOK FOR GRANTED

15-17 Then I said, Listen. Listen carefully: Don't stay stuck in your ways!
  It's GOD's Message we're dealing with here.
Let your lives glow bright before GOD
  before he turns out the lights,
Before you trip and fall
  on the dark mountain paths.
The light you always took for granted will go out
  and the world will turn black.
If you people won't listen,
  I'll go off by myself and weep over you,
Weep because of your stubborn arrogance,
  bitter, bitter tears,
Rivers of tears from my eyes,
  because GOD's sheep will end up in exile.

18-19 Tell the king and the queen-mother,
  "Come down off your high horses.
Your dazzling crowns
  will tumble off your heads."
The villages in the Negev will be surrounded,
  everyone trapped,
And Judah dragged off to exile,
  the whole country dragged to oblivion.

20-22 Look, look, Jerusalem!
  Look at the enemies coming out of the north!
What will become of your flocks of people,
  the beautiful flocks in your care?
How are you going to feel when the people
  you've played up to, looked up to all these years
Now look down on you? You didn't expect this?
  Surprise! The pain of a woman having a baby!
Do I hear you saying,

"What's going on here? Why me?"
The answer's simple: You're guilty,
    hugely guilty.
Your guilt has your life endangered,
    your guilt has you writhing in pain.

23   Can an African change skin?
        Can a leopard get rid of its spots?
    So what are the odds on you doing good,
        you who are so long-practiced in evil?

24-27 "I'll blow these people away —
        like wind-blown leaves.
    You have it coming to you.
        I've measured it out precisely."
            GOD's Decree.
    "It's because you forgot me
        and embraced the Big Lie,
        that so-called god Baal.
    I'm the one who will rip off your clothes,
        expose and shame you before the watching world.
    Your obsessions with gods, gods, and more gods,
        your goddess affairs, your god-adulteries.
    Gods on the hills, gods in the fields —
        every time I look you're off with another god.
    O Jerusalem, what a sordid life!
        Is there any hope for you!"

TIME AND AGAIN WE'VE BETRAYED GOD

1-6   **14** GOD's Message that came to Jeremiah regarding the drought:

    "Judah weeps,
        her cities mourn.
    The people fall to the ground, moaning,
        while sounds of Jerusalem's sobs rise up, up.
    The rich people sent their servants for water.
        They went to the cisterns, but the cisterns were dry.
    They came back with empty buckets,
        wringing their hands, shaking their heads.
    All the farm work has stopped.
        Not a drop of rain has fallen.
    The farmers don't know what to do.
        They wring their hands, they shake their heads.
    Even the doe abandons her fawn in the field
        because there is no grass —
    Eyes glazed over, on her last legs,
        nothing but skin and bones."

7-9   We know we're guilty. We've lived bad lives —
        but do something, GOD. Do it for *your* sake!
    Time and time again we've betrayed you.

No doubt about it—we've sinned against you.
Hope of Israel! Our only hope!
 Israel's last chance in this trouble!
Why are you acting like a tourist,
 taking in the sights, here today and gone tomorrow?
Why do you just stand there and stare,
 like someone who doesn't know what to do in a crisis?
But GOD, you are, in fact, *here,* here *with us!*
 You know who we are—you named us!
 Don't leave us in the lurch.

10 Then GOD said of these people:

"Since they loved to wander this way and that,
 never giving a thought to where they were going,
I will now have nothing more to do with them—
 except to note their guilt and punish their sins."

THE KILLING FIELDS

11-12 GOD said to me, "Don't pray that everything will turn out all right for this people. When they skip their meals in order to pray, I won't listen to a thing they say. When they redouble their prayers, bringing all kinds of offerings from their herds and crops, I'll not accept them. I'm finishing them off with war and famine and disease."

13 I said, "But Master, GOD! Their preachers have been telling them that everything is going to be all right—no war and no famine—that there's nothing to worry about."

14 Then GOD said, "These preachers are liars, and they use my name to cover their lies. I never sent them, I never commanded them, and I don't talk with them. The sermons they've been handing out are sheer illusion, tissues of lies, whistlings in the dark.

15-16 "So this is my verdict on them: All the preachers who preach using my name as their text, preachers I never sent in the first place, preachers who say, 'War and famine will never come here'—these preachers will die in war and by starvation. And the people to whom they've been preaching will end up as corpses, victims of war and starvation, thrown out in the streets of Jerusalem unburied—no funerals for them or their wives or their children! I'll make sure they get the full brunt of all their evil.

17-18 "And you, Jeremiah, will say this to them:

"'My eyes pour out tears.
 Day and night, the tears never quit.
My dear, dear people are battered and bruised,
 hopelessly and cruelly wounded.
I walk out into the fields,
 shocked by the killing fields strewn with corpses.
I walk into the city,
 shocked by the sight of starving bodies.
And I watch the preachers and priests
 going about their business as if nothing's happened!'"

19-22 God, have you said your final No to Judah?
    Can you simply not stand Zion any longer?
If not, why have you treated us like this,
    beaten us nearly to death?
We hoped for peace —
    nothing good came from it;
We looked for healing —
    and got kicked in the stomach.
We admit, O GOD, how badly we've lived,
    and our ancestors, how bad they were.
We've sinned, they've sinned,
    we've all sinned against you!
Your reputation is at stake! Don't quit on us!
    Don't walk out and abandon your glorious Temple!
Remember your covenant.
    Don't break faith with us!
Can the no-gods of the godless nations cause rain?
    Can the sky water the earth by itself?
You're the one, O GOD, who does this.
    So you're the one for whom we wait.
You made it all,
    you do it all.

1-2 **15** Then GOD said to me: "Jeremiah, even if Moses and Samuel stood here and made their case, I wouldn't feel a thing for this people. Get them out of here. Tell them to get lost! And if they ask you, 'So where do we go?' tell them GOD says,

"'If you're assigned to die, go and die;
    if assigned to war, go and get killed;
If assigned to starve, go starve;
    if assigned to exile, off to exile you go!'

3-4 "I've arranged for four kinds of punishment: death in battle, the corpses dropped off by killer dogs, the rest picked clean by vultures, the bones gnawed by hyenas. They'll be a sight to see, a sight to shock the whole world — and all because of Manasseh son of Hezekiah and all he did in Jerusalem.

5 "Who do you think will feel sorry for you, Jerusalem?
    Who do you think will waste tears on you?
Who will bother to take the time to ask,
    'So, how are things going?'

6-9 "*You* left *me*, remember?" GOD's Decree.
    "You turned your back and walked out.
So I will grab you and hit you hard.
    I'm tired of letting you off the hook.
I threw you to the four winds
    and let the winds scatter you like leaves.
I made sure you'll lose everything,

since nothing makes you change.
I created more widows among you
    than grains of sand on the ocean beaches.
At noon mothers will get the news
    of their sons killed in action.
Sudden anguish for the mothers—
    all those terrible deaths.
A mother of seven falls to the ground,
    gasping for breath,
Robbed of her children in their prime.
    Her sun sets at high noon!
Then I'll round up any of you that are left alive
    and see that you're killed by your enemies."
        GOD's Decree.

GIVING EVERYTHING AWAY FOR NOTHING

10-11 Unlucky mother—that you had me as a son,
    given the unhappy job of indicting the whole country!
I've never hurt or harmed a soul,
    and yet everyone is out to get me.
But, GOD knows, I've done everything I could to help them,
    prayed for them and against their enemies.
I've always been on their side, trying to stave off disaster.
    God knows how I've tried!

12-14 "O Israel, O Judah, what are your chances
    against the iron juggernaut from the north?
In punishment for your sins, I'm giving away
    everything you've got, giving it away for nothing.
I'll make you slaves to your enemies
    in a strange and far-off land.
My anger is blazing and fierce,
    burning in hot judgment against you."

15-18 You know where I am, GOD! Remember what I'm doing here!
    Take my side against my detractors.
Don't stand back while they ruin me.
    Just look at the abuse I'm taking!
When your words showed up, I ate them—
    swallowed them whole. What a feast!
What delight I took in being yours,
    O GOD, GOD-of-the-Angel-Armies!
I never joined the party crowd
    in their laughter and their fun.
Led by you, I went off by myself.
    You'd filled me with indignation. Their sin had me seething.
But why, why this chronic pain,
    this ever worsening wound and no healing in sight?
You're nothing, GOD, but a mirage,

a lovely oasis in the distance — and then nothing!

19-21 This is how God answered me:

"Take back those words, and I'll take you back.
    Then you'll stand tall before me.
Use words truly and well. Don't stoop to cheap whining.
    Then, but only then, you'll speak for me.
Let your words change *them*.
    Don't change your words to suit them.
I'll turn you into a steel wall,
    a thick steel wall, impregnable.
They'll attack you but won't put a dent in you
    because I'm at your side, defending and delivering."
        God's Decree.
"I'll deliver you from the grip of the wicked.
    I'll get you out of the clutch of the ruthless."

Can Mortals Manufacture Gods?

1   16 God's Message to me:

2-4   "Jeremiah, don't get married. Don't raise a family here. I have signed the death warrant on all the children born in this country, the mothers who bear them and the fathers who beget them — an epidemic of death. Death unlamented, the dead unburied, dead bodies decomposing and stinking like dung, all the killed and starved corpses served up as meals for carrion crows and mongrel dogs!"

5-7   God continued: "Don't enter a house where there's mourning. Don't go to the funeral. Don't sympathize. I've quit caring about what happens to this people." God's Decree. "No more loyal love on my part, no more compassion. The famous and obscure will die alike here, unlamented and unburied. No funerals will be conducted, no one will give them a second thought, no one will care, no one will say, 'I'm sorry,' no one will so much as offer a cup of tea, not even for the mother or father.

8   "And if there happens to be a feast celebrated, don't go there either to enjoy the festivities."

9   God-of-the-Angel-Armies, the God of Israel, says, "Watch this! I'm about to banish smiles and laughter from this place. No more brides and bridegrooms celebrating. And I'm doing it in your lifetime, before your very eyes.

10-13   "When you tell this to the people and they ask, 'Why is God talking this way, threatening us with all these calamities? We're not criminals, after all. What have we done to our God to be treated like this?' tell them this: 'It's because your ancestors left me, walked off and never looked back. They took up with the no-gods, worshiped and doted on them, and ignored me and wouldn't do a thing I told them. And *you're* even *worse*! Take a good look in the mirror — each of you doing whatever you want, whenever you want, refusing to pay attention to me. And for this I'm getting rid of you, throwing you out in the cold, into a far and strange country. You can worship your precious no-gods there to your heart's content. Rest assured, I won't bother you anymore.'

14-15 "On the other hand, don't miss this: The time is coming when no one will say any longer, 'As sure as GOD lives, the God who delivered Israel from Egypt.' What they'll say is, 'As sure as GOD lives, the God who brought Israel back from the land of the north, brought them back from all the places where he'd scattered them.' That's right, I'm going to bring them back to the land I first gave to their ancestors.

16-17 "Now, watch for what comes next: I'm going to assemble a bunch of fisher-men." GOD's Decree! "They'll go fishing for my people and pull them in for judgment. Then I'll send out a party of hunters, and they'll hunt them out in all the mountains, hills, and caves. I'm watching their every move. I haven't lost track of a single one of them, neither them nor their sins.

18 "They won't get by with a thing. They'll pay double for everything they did wrong. They've made a complete mess of things, littering their lives with their obscene no-gods, leaving piles of stinking god-junk all over the place."

19-20 GOD, my strength, my stronghold,
　　my safe retreat when trouble descends:
The godless nations will come
　　from earth's four corners, saying,
"Our ancestors lived on lies,
　　useless illusions, all smoke."
Can mortals manufacture gods?
　　Their factories turn out no-gods!

21 "Watch closely now. I'm going to teach these wrongheaded people.
　　Starting right now, I'm going to teach them
Who I am and what I do,
　　teach them the meaning of my name, GOD — 'I A M.'"

THE HEART IS HOPELESSLY DARK AND DECEITFUL

1-2 **17** "Judah's sin is engraved
　　　　with a steel chisel,
　　　A steel chisel with a diamond point —
engraved on their granite hearts,
　　engraved on the stone corners of their altars.
The evidence against them is plain to see:
　　sex-and-religion altars and sacred sex shrines
Anywhere there's a grove of trees,
　　anywhere there's an available hill.

3-4 "I'll use your mountains as roadside stands
　　for giving away everything you have.
All your 'things' will serve as reparations
　　for your sins all over the country.
You'll lose your gift of land,
　　The inheritance I gave you.
I'll make you slaves of your enemies
　　in a far-off and strange land.

My anger is hot and blazing and fierce,
    and no one will put it out."

5-6   G<small>OD</small>'s Message:

"Cursed is the strong one
    who depends on mere humans,
Who thinks he can make it on muscle alone
    and sets G<small>OD</small> aside as dead weight.
He's like a tumbleweed on the prairie,
    out of touch with the good earth.
He lives rootless and aimless
    in a land where nothing grows.

7-8   "But blessed is the man who trusts me, G<small>OD</small>,
    the woman who sticks with G<small>OD</small>.
They're like trees replanted in Eden,
    putting down roots near the rivers—
Never a worry through the hottest of summers,
    never dropping a leaf,
Serene and calm through droughts,
    bearing fresh fruit every season.

9-10   "The heart is hopelessly dark and deceitful,
    a puzzle that no one can figure out.
But I, G<small>OD</small>, search the heart
    and examine the mind.
I get to the heart of the human.
    I get to the root of things.
I treat them as they really are,
    not as they pretend to be."

11   Like a cowbird that cheats by laying its eggs
    in another bird's nest
Is the person who gets rich by cheating.
    When the eggs hatch, the deceit is exposed.
What a fool he'll look like then!

12-13   From early on your Sanctuary was set high,
    a throne of glory, exalted!
O G<small>OD</small>, you're the hope of Israel.
    All who leave you end up as fools,
Deserters with nothing to show for their lives,
    who walk off from G<small>OD</small>, fountain of living waters—
    and wind up dead!

14-18　Goᴅ, pick up the pieces.
　　Put me back together again.
　　You are my praise!
Listen to how they talk about me:
　　"So where's this 'Word of Goᴅ'?
　　We'd like to see something happen!"
But it wasn't my idea to call for Doomsday.
　　I never wanted trouble.
You know what I've said.
　　It's all out in the open before you.
Don't add to my troubles.
　　Give me some relief!
Let those who harass me be harassed, not me.
　　Let *them* be disgraced, not me.
Bring down upon them the day of doom.
　　Lower the boom. *Boom*!

Keep the Sabbath Day Holy

19-20　Goᴅ's Message to me: "Go stand in the People's Gate, the one used by Judah's kings as they come and go, and then proceed in turn to all the gates of Jerusalem. Tell them, 'Listen, you kings of Judah, listen to Goᴅ's Message — and all you people who go in and out of these gates, you listen!

21-23　"'This is Goᴅ's Message. Be careful, if you care about your lives, not to desecrate the Sabbath by turning it into just another workday, lugging stuff here and there. Don't use the Sabbath to do business as usual. Keep the Sabbath day holy, as I commanded your ancestors. They never did it, as you know. They paid no attention to what I said and went about their own business, refusing to be guided or instructed by me.

24-26　"'But now, take seriously what I tell you. Quit desecrating the Sabbath by busily going about your own work, and keep the Sabbath day holy by not doing business as usual. Then kings from the time of David and their officials will continue to ride through these gates on horses or in chariots. The people of Judah and citizens of Jerusalem will continue to pass through them, too. Jerusalem will always be filled with people. People will stream in from all over Judah, from the province of Benjamin, from the Jerusalem suburbs, from foothills and mountains and deserts. They'll come to worship, bringing all kinds of offerings — animals, grains, incense, expressions of thanks — into the Sanctuary of Goᴅ.

27　"'But if you won't listen to me, won't keep the Sabbath holy, won't quit using the Sabbath for doing your own work, busily going in and out of the city gates on your self-important business, then I'll burn the gates down. In fact, I'll burn the whole city down, palaces and all, with a fire nobody will be able to put out!'"

To Worship the Big Lie

1-2　**18** Goᴅ told Jeremiah, "Up on your feet! Go to the potter's house. When you get there, I'll tell you what I have to say."

3-4　So I went to the potter's house, and sure enough, the potter was there, working away at his wheel. Whenever the pot the potter was working on turned out badly, as sometimes happens when you are working with clay, the potter would simply start over and use the same clay to make another pot.

5-10 Then GOD's Message came to me: "Can't I do just as this potter does, people of Israel?" GOD's Decree! "Watch this potter. In the same way that this potter works his clay, I work on you, people of Israel. At any moment I may decide to pull up a people or a country by the roots and get rid of them. But if they repent of their wicked lives, I will think twice and start over with them. At another time I might decide to plant a people or country, but if they don't cooperate and won't listen to me, I will think again and give up on the plans I had for them.

11 "So, tell the people of Judah and citizens of Jerusalem my Message: 'Danger! I'm shaping doom against you, laying plans against you. Turn back from your doomed way of life. Straighten out your lives.'

12 "But they'll just say, 'Why should we? What's the point? We'll live just the way we've always lived, doom or no doom.'"

13-17 GOD's Message:

"Ask around.
    Survey the godless nations.
Has anyone heard the likes of this?
    Virgin Israel has become a slut!
Does snow disappear from the Lebanon peaks?
    Do alpine streams run dry?
But my people have left me
    to worship the Big Lie.
They've gotten off the track,
    the old, well-worn trail,
And now bushwhack through underbrush
    in a tangle of roots and vines.
Their land's going to end up a mess—
    a fool's memorial to be spit on.
Travelers passing through
    will shake their heads in disbelief.
I'll scatter my people before their enemies,
    like autumn leaves in a high wind.
On their day of doom, they'll stare at my back as I walk away,
    catching not so much as a glimpse of my face."

18 Some of the people said, "Come on, let's cook up a plot against Jeremiah. We'll still have the priests to teach us the law, wise counselors to give us advice, and prophets to tell us what God has to say. Come on, let's discredit him so we don't have to put up with him any longer."

19-23 And I said to GOD:

"GOD, listen to me!
    Just listen to what my enemies are saying.
Should I get paid evil for good?

That's what they're doing. They've made plans to kill me!
Remember all the times I stood up for them before you,
    speaking up for them,
    trying to soften your anger?
But enough! Let their children starve!
    Let them be massacred in battle!
Let their wives be childless and widowed,
    their friends die and their proud young men be killed.
Let cries of panic sound from their homes
    as you surprise them with war parties!
They're all set to lynch me.
    The noose is practically around my neck!
But you know all this, GOD.
    You know they're determined to kill me.
Don't whitewash their crimes,
    don't overlook a single sin!
Round the bunch of them up before you.
    Strike while the iron of your anger is hot!"

SMASHING THE CLAY POT

1-2 **19** GOD said to me, "Go, buy a clay pot. Then get a few leaders from the people and a few of the leading priests and go out to the Valley of Ben-hinnom, just outside the Potsherd Gate, and preach there what I tell you.

3-5 "Say, 'Listen to GOD's Word, you kings of Judah and people of Jerusalem! This is the Message from GOD-of-the-Angel-Armies, the God of Israel. I'm about to bring doom crashing down on this place. Oh, and will ears ever ring! Doom—because they've walked off and left me, and made this place strange by worshiping strange gods, gods never heard of by them, their parents, or the old kings of Judah. Doom—because they have massacred innocent people. Doom—because they've built altars to that no-god Baal, and burned their own children alive in the fire as offerings to Baal, an atrocity I never ordered, never so much as hinted at!

6-9 "'And so it's payday, and soon'—GOD's Decree!—'this place will no longer be known as Topheth or Valley of Ben-hinnom, but Massacre Meadows. I'm canceling all the plans Judah and Jerusalem had for this place, and I'll have them killed by their enemies. I'll stack their dead bodies to be eaten by carrion crows and wild dogs. I'll turn this city into such a museum of atrocities that anyone coming near will be shocked speechless by the savage brutality. The people will turn into cannibals. Dehumanized by the pressure of the enemy siege, they'll eat their own children! Yes, they'll eat one another, family and friends alike.'

10-13 "Say all this, and then smash the pot in front of the men who have come with you. Then say, 'This is what GOD-of-the-Angel-Armies says: I'll smash this people and this city like a man who smashes a clay pot into so many pieces it can never be put together again. They'll bury bodies here in Topheth until there's no more room. And the whole city will become a Topheth. The city will be turned by people and kings alike into a center for worshiping the star gods and goddesses, turned into an open grave, the whole city an open grave, stinking like a sewer, like Topheth.'"

14-15 Then Jeremiah left Topheth, where GOD had sent him to preach the sermon, and took his stand in the court of GOD's Temple and said to the people, "This is the Message from GOD-of-the-Angel-Armies to you: 'Warning! Danger! I'm bringing down on this city and all the surrounding towns the doom that I have pronounced. They're set in their ways and won't budge. They refuse to do a thing I say.'"

LIFE'S BEEN NOTHING BUT TROUBLE AND TEARS

1-5 **20** The priest Pashur son of Immer was the senior priest in GOD's Temple. He heard Jeremiah preach this sermon. He whipped Jeremiah the prophet and put him in the stocks at the Upper Benjamin Gate of GOD's Temple. The next day Pashur came and let him go. Jeremiah told him, "GOD has a new name for you: not Pashur but Danger-Everywhere, because GOD says, 'You're a danger to yourself and everyone around you. All your friends are going to get killed in battle while you stand there and watch. What's more, I'm turning all of Judah over to the king of Babylon to do whatever he likes with them—haul them off into exile, kill them at whim. Everything worth anything in this city, property and possessions along with everything in the royal treasury—I'm handing it all over to the enemy. They'll rummage through it and take what they want back to Babylon.

6 "'And you, Pashur, you and everyone in your family will be taken prisoner into exile—that's right, exile in Babylon. You'll die and be buried there, you and all your cronies to whom you preached your lies.'"

7-10 You pushed me into this, GOD, and I let you do it.
    You were too much for me.
And now I'm a public joke.
    They all poke fun at me.
Every time I open my mouth
    I'm shouting, "Murder!" or "Rape!"
And all I get for my GOD-warnings
    are insults and contempt.
But if I say, "Forget it!
    No more GOD-Messages from me!"
The words are fire in my belly,
    a burning in my bones.
I'm worn out trying to hold it in.
    I can't do it any longer!
Then I hear whispering behind my back:
    "There goes old 'Danger-Everywhere.' Shut him up! Report him!"
Old friends watch, hoping I'll fall flat on my face:
    "One misstep and we'll have him. We'll get rid of him for good!"

11 But GOD, a most fierce warrior, is at my side.
    Those who are after me will be sent sprawling—
Slapstick buffoons falling all over themselves,
    a spectacle of humiliation no one will ever forget.

12 Oh, GOD-of-the-Angel-Armies, no one fools you.
    You see through everyone, everything.

I want to see you pay them back for what they've done.
  I rest my case with you.

13 Sing to God! All praise to God!
  He saves the weak from the grip of the wicked.

14-18 Curse the day
  I was born!
The day my mother bore me—
  a curse on it, I say!
And curse the man who delivered
  the news to my father:
"You've got a new baby—a boy baby!"
  (How happy it made him.)
Let that birth notice be blacked out,
  deleted from the records,
And the man who brought it haunted to his death
  with the bad news he brought.
He should have killed me before I was born,
  with that womb as my tomb,
My mother pregnant for the rest of her life
  with a baby dead in her womb.
Why, oh why, did I ever leave that womb?
  Life's been nothing but trouble and tears,
  and what's coming is more of the same.

Start Each Day with a Sense of Justice

1-2 **21** God's Message to Jeremiah when King Zedekiah sent Pashur son of Malkijah and the priest Zephaniah son of Maaseiah to him with this request: "Nebuchadnezzar, king of Babylon, has waged war against us. Pray to God for us. Ask him for help. Maybe God will intervene with one of his famous miracles and make him leave."

3-7 But Jeremiah said, "Tell Zedekiah: 'This is the God of Israel's Message to you: You can say good-bye to your army, watch morale and weapons flushed down the drain. I'm going to personally lead the king of Babylon and the Chaldeans, against whom you're fighting so hard, right into the city itself. I'm joining *their* side and fighting against *you*, fighting all-out, holding nothing back. And in fierce anger. I'm prepared to wipe out the population of this city, people and animals alike, in a raging epidemic. And then I will personally deliver Zedekiah king of Judah, his princes, and any survivors left in the city who haven't died from disease, been killed, or starved. I'll deliver them to Nebuchadnezzar, king of Babylon—yes, hand them over to their enemies, who have come to kill them. He'll kill them ruthlessly, showing no mercy.'

8-10 "And then tell the people at large, 'God's Message to you is this: Listen carefully. I'm giving you a choice: life or death. Whoever stays in this city will die—either in battle or by starvation or disease. But whoever goes out and surrenders to the Chaldeans who have surrounded the city will live. You'll lose everything—but not your life. I'm determined to see this city destroyed. I'm that angry with this place! God's Decree. I'm going to give it to the king of Babylon, and he's going to burn it to the ground.'

11-14 "To the royal house of Judah, listen to GOD's Message!
　　House of David, listen — GOD's Message to you:
'Start each day by dealing with justice.
　　Rescue victims from their exploiters.
Prevent fire — the fire of my anger —
　　for once it starts, it can't be put out.
Your evil regime
　　is fuel for my anger.
Don't you realize that I'm against you,
　　yes, *against* you.
You think you've got it made,
　　all snug and secure.
You say, "Who can possibly get to us?
　　Who can crash our party?"
Well, I can — and will!
　　I'll punish your evil regime.
I'll start a fire that will rage unchecked,
　　burn everything in sight to cinders.'"

WALKING OUT ON THE COVENANT OF GOD

1-3 **22** GOD's orders: "Go to the royal palace and deliver this Message. Say, 'Listen to what GOD says, O King of Judah, you who sit on David's throne — you and your officials and all the people who go in and out of these palace gates. This is GOD's Message: Attend to matters of justice. Set things right between people. Rescue victims from their exploiters. Don't take advantage of the homeless, the orphans, the widows. Stop the murdering!

4-5 　　"'If you obey these commands, then kings who follow in the line of David will continue to go in and out of these palace gates mounted on horses and riding in chariots — they and their officials and the citizens of Judah. But if you don't obey these commands, then I swear — GOD's Decree! — this palace will end up a heap of rubble.'"

6-7 This is GOD's verdict on Judah's royal palace:

"I number you among my favorite places —
　　like the lovely hills of Gilead,
　　like the soaring peaks of Lebanon.
Yet I swear I'll turn you into a wasteland,
　　as empty as a ghost town.
I'll hire a demolition crew,
　　well-equipped with sledgehammers and wrecking bars,
Pound the country to a pulp
　　and burn it all up.

8-9 　　"Travelers from all over will come through here and say to one another, 'Why would GOD do such a thing to this wonderful city?' They'll be told, 'Because they walked out on the covenant of their GOD, took up with other gods and worshiped them.'"

BUILDING A FINE HOUSE BUT DESTROYING LIVES

¹⁰ Don't weep over dead King Josiah.
 Don't waste your tears.
Weep for his exiled son:
 He's gone for good.
 He'll never see home again.

¹¹⁻¹² For this is GOD's Word on Shallum son of Josiah, who succeeded his father as king of Judah: "He's gone from here, gone for good. He'll die in the place they've taken him to. He'll never see home again."

¹³⁻¹⁷ "Doom to him who builds palaces but bullies people,
 who makes a fine house but destroys lives,
Who cheats his workers
 and won't pay them for their work,
Who says, 'I'll build me an elaborate mansion
 with spacious rooms and fancy windows.
I'll bring in rare and expensive woods
 and the latest in interior decor.'
So, that makes you a king—
 living in a fancy palace?
Your father got along just fine, didn't he?
 He did what was right and treated people fairly,
And things went well with him.
 He stuck up for the down-and-out,
And things went well for Judah.
 Isn't this what it means to know me?"
  GOD's Decree!
"But you're blind and brainless.
 All you think about is yourself,
Taking advantage of the weak,
 bulldozing your way, bullying victims."

¹⁸⁻¹⁹ This is God's epitaph on Jehoiakim son of Josiah king of Judah:
 "Doom to this man!
Nobody will shed tears over him,
 'Poor, poor brother!'
Nobody will shed tears over him,
 'Poor, poor master!'
They'll give him a donkey's funeral,
 drag him out of the city and dump him.

YOU'VE MADE A TOTAL MESS OF YOUR LIFE

²⁰⁻²³ "People of Jerusalem, climb a Lebanon peak and weep,
 climb a Bashan mountain and wail,
Climb the Abarim ridge and cry—
 you've made a total mess of your life.
I spoke to you when everything was going your way.

You said, 'I'm not interested.'
You've been that way as long as I've known you,
   never listened to a thing I said.
All your leaders will be blown away,
   all your friends end up in exile,
And you'll find yourself in the gutter,
   disgraced by your evil life.
You big-city people thought you were so important,
   thought you were 'king of the mountain'!
You're soon going to be doubled up in pain,
   pain worse than the pangs of childbirth.

24-26   "As sure as I am the living God"—God's Decree—"even if you, Jehoiachin son of Jehoiakim king of Judah, were the signet ring on my right hand, I'd pull you off and give you to those who are out to kill you, to Nebuchadnezzar king of Babylon and the Chaldeans, and then throw you, both you and your mother, into a foreign country, far from your place of birth. There you'll both die.

27   "You'll be homesick, desperately homesick, but you'll never get home again."

28-30   Is Jehoiachin a leaky bucket,
   a rusted-out pail good for nothing?
Why else would he be thrown away, he and his children,
   thrown away to a foreign place?
O land, land, land,
   listen to God's Message!
This is God's verdict:
"Write this man off as if he were childless,
   a man who will never amount to anything.
Nothing will ever come of his life.
   He's the end of the line, the last of the kings."

An Authentic David-Branch

1-4   **23** "Doom to the shepherd-leaders who butcher and scatter my sheep!" God's Decree. "So here is what I, God, Israel's God, say to the shepherd-leaders who misled my people: 'You've scattered my sheep. You've driven them off. You haven't kept your eye on them. Well, let me tell you, I'm keeping my eye on *you*, keeping track of your criminal behavior. I'll take over and gather what's left of my sheep, gather them in from all the lands where I've driven them. I'll bring them back where they belong, and they'll recover and flourish. I'll set shepherd-leaders over them who will take good care of them. They won't live in fear or panic anymore. All the lost sheep rounded up!' God's Decree.

5-6   "Time's coming" — God's Decree —
   "when I'll establish a truly righteous David-Branch,
A ruler who knows how to rule justly.
   He'll make sure of justice and keep people united.
In his time Judah will be secure again

and Israel will live in safety.
This is the name they'll give him:
'GOD-Who-Puts-Everything-Right.'

7-8 "So watch for this. The time's coming" — GOD's Decree — "when no one will say, 'As sure as GOD lives, the God who brought the Israelites out of Egypt,' but, 'As sure as GOD lives, the God who brought the descendants of Israel back from the north country and from the other countries where he'd driven them, so that they can live on their own good earth.'"

THE "EVERYTHING WILL TURN OUT FINE" SERMON

9 My head is reeling,
my limbs are limp,
I'm staggering like a drunk,
seeing double from too much wine —
And all because of GOD,
because of his holy words.

10-12 Now for what GOD says regarding the lying prophets:

"Can you believe it? A country teeming with adulterers!
faithless, promiscuous idolater-adulterers!
They're a curse on the land.
The land's a wasteland.
Their unfaithfulness
is turning the country into a cesspool,
Prophets and priests devoted to desecration.
They have nothing to do with me as their God.
My very own Temple, mind you —
mud-spattered with their crimes." GOD's Decree.
"But they won't get by with it.
They'll find themselves on a slippery slope,
Careening into the darkness,
somersaulting into the pitch-black dark.
I'll make them pay for their crimes.
It will be the Year of Doom." GOD's Decree.

13-14 "Over in Samaria I saw prophets
acting like silly fools — shocking!
They preached using that no-god Baal for a text,
messing with the minds of my people.
And the Jerusalem prophets are even worse — horrible! —
sex-driven, living a lie,
Subsidizing a culture of wickedness,
and never giving it a second thought.
They're as bad as those wretches in old Sodom,
the degenerates of old Gomorrah."

15 So here's the Message to the prophets from GOD-of-the-Angel-Armies:

"I'll cook them a supper of maggoty meat
    with after-dinner drinks of strychnine.
The Jerusalem prophets are behind all this.
    They're the cause of the godlessness polluting this country."

16-17   A Message from GOD-of-the-Angel-Armies:

"Don't listen to the sermons of the prophets.
    It's all hot air. Lies, lies, and more lies.
They make it all up.
    Not a word they speak comes from me.
They preach their 'Everything Will Turn Out Fine' sermon
    to congregations with no taste for God,
Their 'Nothing Bad Will Ever Happen to You' sermon
    to people who are set in their own ways.

18-20   "Have any of these prophets bothered to meet with me,
        the true GOD?
    bothered to take in what *I* have to say?
    listened to and then *lived out* my Word?
Look out! GOD's hurricane will be let loose—
    my hurricane blast,
Spinning the heads of the wicked like tops!
    God's raging anger won't let up
Until I've made a clean sweep,
    completing the job I began.
When the job's done,
    you'll see that it's been well done.

QUIT THE "GOD TOLD ME THIS" KIND OF TALK

21-22   "I never sent these prophets,
    but they ran anyway.
I never spoke to them,
    but they preached away.
If they'd have bothered to sit down and meet with me,
    they'd have preached my Message to my people.
They'd have gotten them back on the right track,
    gotten them out of their evil ruts.

23-24   "Am I not a God near at hand"—GOD's Decree—
    "and not a God far off?
Can anyone hide out in a corner
    where I can't see him?"
        GOD's Decree.
"Am I not present everywhere,
    whether seen or unseen?"
        GOD's Decree.

25-27 "I know what they're saying, all these prophets who preach lies using me as their text, saying 'I had this dream! I had this dream!' How long do I have to put up with this? Do these prophets give two cents about me as they preach their lies and spew out their grandiose delusions? They swap dreams with one another, feed on each other's delusive dreams, trying to distract my people from me just as their ancestors were distracted by the no-god Baal.

28-29 "You prophets who do nothing but dream —
    go ahead and tell your silly dreams.
But you prophets who have a message from me —
    tell it truly and faithfully.
What does straw have in common with wheat?
    Nothing else is like GOD's Decree.
Isn't my Message like fire?" GOD's Decree.
    "Isn't it like a sledgehammer busting a rock?"

30-31 "I've had it with the 'prophets' who get all their sermons secondhand from each other. Yes, I've had it with them. They make up stuff and then pretend it's a real sermon.

32 "Oh yes, I've had it with the prophets who preach the lies they dream up, spreading them all over the country, ruining the lives of my people with their cheap and reckless lies.

"I never sent these prophets, never authorized a single one of them. They do nothing for this people — *nothing*!" GOD's Decree.

33 "And anyone, including prophets and priests, who asks, 'What's GOD got to say about all this, what's troubling him?' tell him, 'You, you're the trouble, and I'm getting rid of you.'" GOD's Decree.

34 "And if anyone, including prophets and priests, goes around saying glibly 'GOD's Message! GOD's Message!' I'll punish him and his family.

35-36 "Instead of claiming to know what GOD says, ask questions of one another, such as 'How do we understand GOD in this?' But don't go around pretending to know it all, saying 'God told me this . . . God told me that. . . .' I don't want to hear it anymore. Only the person I authorize speaks for me. Otherwise, my Message gets twisted, the Message of the living GOD-of-the-Angel-Armies.

37-38 "You can ask the prophets, 'How did GOD answer you? What did he tell you?' But don't pretend that you know all the answers yourselves and talk like you know it all. I'm telling you: Quit the 'God told me this . . . God told me that . . .' kind of talk.

39-40 "Are you paying attention? You'd better, because I'm about to take you in hand and throw you to the ground, you and this entire city that I gave to your ancestors. I've had it with the lot of you. You're never going to live this down. You're going down in history as a disgrace."

TWO BASKETS OF FIGS

1-2 **24** GOD showed me two baskets of figs placed in front of the Temple of GOD. This was after Nebuchadnezzar king of Babylon had taken Jehoiachin son of Jehoiakim king of Judah from Jerusalem into exile in Babylon, along with the leaders of Judah, the craftsmen, and the skilled laborers. In one basket the figs were of the finest quality, ripe and ready to eat. In the other basket the figs were rotten, so rotten they couldn't be eaten.

3   GOD said to me, "Jeremiah, what do you see?"

"Figs," I said. "Excellent figs of the finest quality, and also rotten figs, so rotten they can't be eaten."

4-6   Then GOD told me, "This is the Message from the GOD of Israel: The exiles from here that I've sent off to the land of the Babylonians are like the good figs, and I'll make sure they get good treatment. I'll keep my eye on them so that their lives are good, and I'll bring them back to this land. I'll build them up, not tear them down; I'll plant them, not uproot them.

7   "And I'll give them a heart to know me, GOD. They'll be my people and I'll be their God, for they'll have returned to me with all their hearts.

8-10   "But like the rotten figs, so rotten they can't be eaten, is Zedekiah king of Judah. Rotten figs — that's how I'll treat him and his leaders, along with the survivors here and those down in Egypt. I'll make them something that the whole world will look on as disgusting — repugnant outcasts, their names used as curse words wherever in the world I drive them. And I'll make sure they die like flies — from war, starvation, disease, whatever — until the land I once gave to them and their ancestors is completely rid of them."

DON'T FOLLOW THE GOD-FADS OF THE DAY

1   25 This is the Message given to Jeremiah for all the people of Judah. It came in the fourth year of Jehoiakim son of Josiah king of Judah. It was the first year of Nebuchadnezzar king of Babylon.

2   Jeremiah the prophet delivered the Message to all the people of Judah and citizens of Jerusalem:

3   From the thirteenth year of Josiah son of Amon king of Judah right up to the present day — twenty-three years it's been! — GOD's Word has come to me, and from early each morning to late every night I've passed it on to you. And you haven't listened to a word of it!

4-6   Not only that but GOD also sent a steady stream of prophets to you who were just as persistent as me, and you never listened. They told you, "Turn back — right now, each one of you! — from your evil way of life and bad behavior, and live in the land GOD gave you and your ancestors, the land he intended to give you forever. Don't follow the god-fads of the day, taking up and worshiping these no-gods. Don't make me angry with your god-businesses, making and selling gods — a dangerous business!

7   "You refused to listen to any of this, and now I am really angry. These god-making businesses of yours are your doom."

8-11   The verdict of GOD-of-the-Angel-Armies on all this: "Because you have refused to listen to what I've said, I'm stepping in. I'm sending for the armies out of the north headed by Nebuchadnezzar king of Babylon, my servant in this, and I'm setting them on this land and people and even the surrounding countries. I'm devoting the whole works to total destruction — a horror to top all the horrors in history. And I'll banish every sound of joy — singing, laughter, marriage festivities, genial workmen, candlelit suppers. The whole landscape will be one vast wasteland. These countries will be in subjection to the king of Babylon for seventy years.

12-14   "Once the seventy years is up, I'll punish the king of Babylon and the whole nation of Babylon for their sin. Then *they'll* be the wasteland. Everything that I said I'd do to that country, I'll do — everything that's written in this book, everything Jeremiah preached against all the godless nations. Many nations and great kings will make slaves of the Babylonians, paying them back for everything they've done to others. They won't get by with anything." GOD's Decree.

GOD PUTS THE HUMAN RACE ON TRIAL

15-16 This is a Message that the GOD of Israel gave me: "Take this cup filled with the wine of my wrath that I'm handing to you. Make all the nations where I send you drink it down. They'll drink it and get drunk, staggering in delirium because of the killing that I'm going to unleash among them."

17-26 I took the cup from GOD's hand and made them drink it, all the nations to which he sent me:

Jerusalem and the towns of Judah, along with their kings and leaders, turning them into a vast wasteland, a horror to look at, a cussword — which, in fact, they now are;

Pharaoh king of Egypt with his attendants and leaders, plus all his people and the melting pot of foreigners collected there;

All the kings of Uz;

All the kings of the Philistines from Ashkelon, Gaza, Ekron, and what's left of Ashdod;

Edom, Moab, and the Ammonites;

All the kings of Tyre, Sidon, and the coastlands across the sea;

Dedan, Tema, Buz, and the nomads on the fringe of the desert;

All the kings of Arabia and the various Bedouin sheiks and chieftains wandering about in the desert;

All the kings of Zimri, Elam, and the Medes;

All the kings from the north countries near and far, one by one;

All the kingdoms on planet Earth . . .

And the king of Sheshak (that is, Babylon) will be the last to drink.

27 "Tell them, 'These are orders from GOD-of-the-Angel-Armies, the God of Israel: Drink and get drunk and vomit. Fall on your faces and don't get up again. You're slated for a massacre.'

28 "If any of them refuse to take the cup from you and drink it, say to them, 'GOD-of-the-Angel-Armies has ordered you to drink. So drink!

29 "'Prepare for the worst! I'm starting off the catastrophe in the city that I claim as my own, so don't think you are going to get out of it. No, you're not getting out of anything. It's the sword and nothing but the sword against everyone everywhere!'" The GOD-of-the-Angel-Armies' Decree.

30-31 "Preach it all, Jeremiah. Preach the entire Message to them. Say:

"'GOD roars like a lion from high heaven;
    thunder rolls out from his holy dwelling —
Ear-splitting bellows against his people,
    shouting hurrahs like workers in harvest.
The noise reverberates all over the earth;
    everyone everywhere hears it.
GOD makes his case against the godless nations.

He's about to put the human race on trial.
For the wicked the verdict is clear-cut:
  death by the sword.'" GOD's Decree.

32 A Message from GOD-of-the-Angel-Armies:

"Prepare for the worst! Doomsday!
  Disaster is spreading from nation to nation.
A huge storm is about to rage
  all across planet Earth."

33 Laid end to end, those killed in GOD's judgment that day will stretch
from one end of the earth to the other. No tears will be shed and no burials
conducted. The bodies will be left where they fall, like so much horse dung
fertilizing the fields.

34-38 Wail, shepherds! Cry out for help!
  Grovel in the dirt, you masters of flocks!
Time's up—you're slated for the slaughterhouse,
  like a choice ram with its throat cut.
There's no way out for the rulers,
  no escape for those shepherds.
Hear that? Rulers crying for help,
  shepherds of the flock wailing!
GOD is about to ravage their fine pastures.
  The peaceful sheepfolds will be silent with death,
  silenced by GOD's deadly anger.
God will come out into the open
  like a lion leaping from its cover,
And the country will be torn to pieces,
  ripped and ravaged by his anger.

CHANGE THE WAY YOU'RE LIVING

1 **26** At the beginning of the reign of Jehoiakim son of Josiah king
of Judah, this Message came from GOD to Jeremiah:

2-3 "GOD's Message: Stand in the court of GOD's Temple and
preach to the people who come from all over Judah to worship in GOD's
Temple. Say everything I tell you to say to them. Don't hold anything back.
Just maybe they'll listen and turn back from their bad lives. Then I'll reconsider the disaster that I'm planning to bring on them because of their evil
behavior.

4-6 "Say to them, 'This is GOD's Message: If you refuse to listen to me and
live by my teaching that I've revealed so plainly to you, and if you continue
to refuse to listen to my servants the prophets that I tirelessly keep on sending to you—but you've never listened! Why would you start now?—then
I'll make this Temple a pile of ruins like Shiloh, and I'll make this city nothing but a bad joke worldwide.'"

7-9 Everybody there—priests, prophets, and people—heard Jeremiah preaching this Message in the Temple of GOD. When Jeremiah had finished his sermon, saying everything God had commanded him to say, the priests and prophets and people all grabbed him, yelling, "Death! You're going to die for this! How dare you preach—and using GOD's name!—saying that this Temple will become a heap of rubble like Shiloh and this city be wiped out without a soul left in it!"

All the people mobbed Jeremiah right in the Temple itself.

※

10 Officials from the royal court of Judah were told of this. They left the palace immediately and came to GOD's Temple to investigate. They held court on the spot, at the New Gate entrance to GOD's Temple.

11 The prophets and priests spoke first, addressing the officials, but also the people: "Death to this man! He deserves nothing less than death! He has preached against this city—you've heard the evidence with your own ears."

12-13 Jeremiah spoke next, publicly addressing the officials before the crowd: "GOD sent me to preach against both this Temple and city everything that's been reported to you. So do something about it! Change the way you're living, change your behavior. Listen obediently to the Message of your GOD. Maybe GOD will reconsider the disaster he has threatened.

14-15 "As for me, I'm at your mercy—do whatever you think is best. But take warning: If you kill me, you're killing an innocent man, and you and the city and the people in it will be liable. I didn't say any of this on my own. GOD sent me and told me what to say. You've been listening to GOD speak, not Jeremiah."

16 The court officials, backed by the people, then handed down their ruling to the priests and prophets: "Acquittal. No death sentence for this man. He has spoken to us with the authority of our GOD."

17-18 Then some of the respected leaders stood up and addressed the crowd: "In the reign of Hezekiah king of Judah, Micah of Moresheth preached to the people of Judah this sermon: This is GOD-of-the-Angel-Armies' Message for you:

"'Because of people like you,
    Zion will be turned back into farmland,
Jerusalem end up as a pile of rubble,
    and instead of the Temple on the mountain,
    a few scraggly scrub pines.'

19 "Did King Hezekiah or anyone else in Judah kill Micah of Moresheth because of that sermon? Didn't Hezekiah honor him and pray for mercy from GOD? And then didn't GOD call off the disaster he had threatened?

"Friends, we're at the brink of bringing a terrible calamity upon ourselves."

※

20-23 (At another time there had been a man, Uriah son of Shemaiah from Kiriath-jearim, who had preached similarly in the name of GOD. He preached against this same city and country just as Jeremiah did. When King Jehoiakim and his royal court heard his sermon, they determined to kill him. Uriah, afraid for his life, went into hiding in Egypt. King Jehoiakim sent Elnathan son of Achbor with a posse of men after him. They brought him back from Egypt and presented him to the king. And the king had him killed. They dumped his body unceremoniously outside the city.

24 But in Jeremiah's case, Ahikam son of Shaphan stepped forward and took his side, preventing the mob from lynching him.)

HARNESS YOURSELVES UP TO THE YOKE

1-4 27 Early in the reign of Zedekiah son of Josiah king of Judah, Jeremiah received this Message from GOD: "Make a harness and a yoke and then harness yourself up. Send a message to the kings of Edom, Moab, Ammon, Tyre, and Sidon. Send it through their ambassadors who have come to Jerusalem to see Zedekiah king of Judah. Give them this charge to take back to their masters: 'This is a Message from GOD-of-the-Angel-Armies, the God of Israel. Tell your masters:

5-8 "'I'm the one who made the earth, man and woman, and all the animals in the world. I did it on my own without asking anyone's help and I hand it out to whomever I will. Here and now I give all these lands over to my servant Nebuchadnezzar king of Babylon. I have made even the wild animals subject to him. All nations will be under him, then his son, and then his grandson. Then his country's time will be up and the tables will be turned: *Babylon* will be the underdog servant. But until then, any nation or kingdom that won't submit to Nebuchadnezzar king of Babylon must take the yoke of the king of Babylon and harness up. I'll punish that nation with war and starvation and disease until I've got them where I want them.

9-11 "'So don't for a minute listen to all your prophets and spiritualists and fortunetellers, who claim to know the future and who tell you not to give in to the king of Babylon. They're handing you a line of lies, barefaced lies, that will end up putting you in exile far from home. I myself will drive you out of your lands, and that'll be the end of you. But the nation that accepts the yoke of the king of Babylon and does what he says, I'll let that nation stay right where it is, minding its own business.'"

12-15 Then I gave this same message to Zedekiah king of Judah: "Harness yourself up to the yoke of the king of Babylon. Serve him and his people. Live a long life! Why choose to get killed or starve to death or get sick and die, which is what GOD has threatened to any nation that won't throw its lot in with Babylon? Don't listen to the prophets who are telling you not to submit to the king of Babylon. They're telling you lies, *preaching* lies. GOD's Word on this is, 'I didn't send those prophets, but they keep preaching lies, claiming I sent them. If you listen to them, I'll end up driving you out of here and that will be the end of you, both you and the lying prophets.'"

16-22 And finally I spoke to the priests and the people at large: "This is GOD's Message: Don't listen to the preaching of the prophets who keep telling you, 'Trust us: The furnishings, plundered from GOD's Temple, are going to be returned from Babylon any day now.' That's a lie. Don't listen to them. Submit to the king of Babylon and live a long life. Why do something that will destroy this city and leave it a heap of rubble? If they are real prophets and have a Message from GOD, let them come to GOD-of-the-Angel-Armies in prayer so that the furnishings that are still left in GOD's Temple, the king's palace, and Jerusalem aren't also lost to Babylon. That's because GOD-of-the-Angel-Armies has already spoken about the Temple furnishings that remain—the pillars, the great bronze basin, the stands, and all the other bowls and chalices that Nebuchadnezzar king of Babylon didn't take when he took Jehoiachin son of Jehoiakim off to Babylonian exile along with all the leaders of Judah and Jerusalem. He said that the furnishings left behind in the Temple of GOD and in the royal palace and in Jerusalem will be taken off to Babylon and stay there until, in GOD's words, 'I take the matter up again and bring them back where they belong.'"

FROM A WOODEN TO AN IRON YOKE

1-2 **28** Later that same year (it was in the fifth month of King Zedekiah's fourth year) Hananiah son of Azzur, a prophet from Gibeon, confronted Jeremiah in the Temple of GOD in front of the priests and all the people who were there. Hananiah said:

2-4 "This Message is straight from GOD-of-the-Angel-Armies, the God of Israel: 'I will most certainly break the yoke of the king of Babylon. Before two years are out I'll have all the furnishings of GOD's Temple back here, all the things that Nebuchadnezzar king of Babylon plundered and hauled off to Babylon. I'll also bring back Jehoiachin son of Jehoiakim king of Judah and all the exiles who were taken off to Babylon.' GOD's Decree. 'Yes, I will break the king of Babylon's yoke. You'll no longer be in harness to him.'"

5-9 Prophet Jeremiah stood up to prophet Hananiah in front of the priests and all the people who were in GOD's Temple that day. Prophet Jeremiah said, "Wonderful! Would that it were true—that GOD would validate your preaching by bringing the Temple furnishings and all the exiles back from Babylon. But listen to me, listen closely. Listen to what I tell both you and all the people here today: The old prophets, the ones before our time, preached judgment against many countries and kingdoms, warning of war and disaster and plague. So any prophet who preaches that everything is just fine and there's nothing to worry about stands out like a sore thumb. We'll wait and see. If it happens, it happens—and then we'll know that GOD sent him."

10-11 At that, Hananiah grabbed the yoke from Jeremiah's shoulders and smashed it. And then he addressed the people: "This is GOD's Message: In just this way I will smash the yoke of the king of Babylon and get him off the neck of all the nations—and within two years."

Jeremiah walked out.

12-14 Later, sometime after Hananiah had smashed the yoke from off his shoulders, Jeremiah received this Message from GOD: "Go back to Hananiah and tell him, 'This is GOD's Message: You smashed the wooden yoke-bars; now you've got iron yoke-bars. This is a Message from GOD-of-the-Angel-Armies, Israel's own God: I've put an iron yoke on all these nations. They're harnessed to Nebuchadnezzar king of Babylon. They'll do just what he tells them. Why, I'm even putting him in charge of the wild animals.'"

15-16 So prophet Jeremiah told prophet Hananiah, "Hold it, Hananiah! GOD never sent you. You've talked the whole country into believing a pack of lies! And so GOD says, 'You claim to be sent? I'll send you all right—right off the face of the earth! Before the year is out, you'll be dead because you fomented sedition against GOD.'"

17 Prophet Hananiah died that very year, in the seventh month.

PLANS TO GIVE YOU THE FUTURE YOU HOPE FOR

1-2 **29** This is the letter that the prophet Jeremiah sent from Jerusalem to what was left of the elders among the exiles, to the priests and prophets and all the exiles whom Nebuchadnezzar had taken to Babylon from Jerusalem, including King Jehoiachin, the queen mother, the government leaders, and all the skilled laborers and craftsmen.

3 The letter was carried by Elasah son of Shaphan and Gemariah son of Hilkiah, whom Zedekiah king of Judah had sent to Nebuchadnezzar king of Babylon. The letter said:

4 This is the Message from GOD-of-the-Angel-Armies, Israel's God, to all the exiles I've taken from Jerusalem to Babylon:

5 "Build houses and make yourselves at home.

"Put in gardens and eat what grows in that country.

6 "Marry and have children. Encourage your children to marry and have children so that you'll thrive in that country and not waste away.

7 "Make yourselves at home there and work for the country's welfare.

"Pray for Babylon's well-being. If things go well for Babylon, things will go well for you."

8-9 Yes. Believe it or not, this is the Message from GOD-of-the-Angel-Armies, Israel's God: "Don't let all those so-called preachers and know-it-alls who are all over the place there take you in with their lies. Don't pay any attention to the fantasies they keep coming up with to please you. They're a bunch of liars preaching lies—and claiming I sent them! I never sent them, believe me." GOD's Decree!

10-11 This is GOD's Word on the subject: "As soon as Babylon's seventy years are up and not a day before, I'll show up and take care of you as I promised and bring you back home. I know what I'm doing. I have it all planned out—plans to take care of you, not abandon you, plans to give you the future you hope for.

12 "When you call on me, when you come and pray to me, I'll listen.

13-14 "When you come looking for me, you'll find me.

"Yes, when you get serious about finding me and want it more than anything else, I'll make sure you won't be disappointed." GOD's Decree.

"I'll turn things around for you. I'll bring you back from all the countries into which I drove you"—GOD's Decree—"bring you home to the place from which I sent you off into exile. You can count on it.

15-19 "But for right now, because you've taken up with these new-fangled prophets who set themselves up as 'Babylonian specialists,' spreading the word 'GOD sent them just for us!' GOD is setting the record straight: As for the king still sitting on David's throne and all the people left in Jerusalem who didn't go into exile with you, they're facing bad times. GOD-of-the-Angel-Armies says, 'Watch this! Catastrophe is on the way: war, hunger, disease! They're a barrel of rotten apples. I'll rid the country of them through war and hunger and disease. The whole world is going to hold its nose at the smell, shut its eyes at the horrible sight. They'll end up in slum ghettos because they wouldn't listen to a thing I said when I sent my servant-prophets preaching tirelessly and urgently. No, they wouldn't listen to a word I said.'" GOD's Decree.

20-23   "And you — you exiles whom I sent out of Jerusalem to Babylon — listen to GOD's Message to you. As far as Ahab son of Kolaiah and Zedekiah son of Maaseiah are concerned, the 'Babylonian specialists' who are preaching lies in my name, I will turn them over to Nebuchadnezzar king of Babylon, who will kill them while you watch. The exiles from Judah will take what they see at the execution and use it as a curse: 'GOD fry you to a crisp like the king of Babylon fried Zedekiah and Ahab in the fire!' Those two men, sex predators and prophet-impostors, got what they deserved. They pulled every woman they got their hands on into bed — their neighbors' wives, no less — and preached lies claiming it was my Message. I never sent those men. I've never had anything to do with them." GOD's Decree.

"They won't get away with a thing. I've witnessed it all."

24-26   And this is the Message for Shemaiah the Nehelamite: "GOD-of-the-Angel-Armies, the God of Israel, says: You took it on yourself to send letters to all the people in Jerusalem and to the priest Zephaniah son of Maaseiah and the company of priests. In your letter you told Zephaniah that GOD set you up as priest replacing priest Jehoiadah. He's put you in charge of GOD's Temple and made you responsible for locking up any crazy fellow off the street who takes it into his head to be a prophet.

27-28   "So why haven't you done anything about muzzling Jeremiah of Anathoth, who's going around posing as a prophet? He's gone so far as to write to us in Babylon, 'It's going to be a long exile, so build houses and make yourselves at home. Plant gardens and prepare Babylonian recipes.'"

29   The priest Zephaniah read that letter to the prophet Jeremiah.

30-32   Then GOD told Jeremiah, "Send this Message to the exiles. Tell them what GOD says about Shemaiah the Nehelamite: Shemaiah is preaching lies to you. I didn't send him. He is seducing you into believing lies. So this is GOD's verdict: I will punish Shemaiah the Nehelamite and his whole family. He's going to end up with nothing and no one. No one from his family will be around to see any of the good that I am going to do for my people because he has preached rebellion against me." GOD's Decree.

DON'T DESPAIR, ISRAEL

1-2   **30** This is the Message Jeremiah received from GOD: "GOD's Message, the God of Israel: 'Write everything I tell you in a book.

3   "'Look. The time is coming when I will turn everything around for my people, both Israel and Judah. I, GOD, say so. I'll bring them back to the land I gave their ancestors, and they'll take up ownership again.'"

4   This is the way GOD put it to Israel and Judah:

5-7   "GOD's Message:

" 'Cries of panic are being heard.
    The peace has been shattered.
Ask around! Look around!
    Can men bear babies?
So why do I see all these he-men
    holding their bellies like women in labor,
Faces contorted,
    pale as death?
The blackest of days,
    no day like it ever!
A time of deep trouble for Jacob —
    but he'll come out of it alive.

8-9   " 'And then I'll enter the darkness.
    I'll break the yoke from their necks,
Cut them loose from the harness.
    No more slave labor to foreigners!
They'll serve their GOD
    and the David-King I'll establish for them.

10-11   " 'So fear no more, Jacob, dear servant.
    Don't despair, Israel.
Look up! I'll save you out of faraway places,
    I'll bring your children back from exile.
Jacob will come back and find life good,
    safe and secure.
I'll be with you. I'll save you.
    I'll finish off all the godless nations
Among which I've scattered you,
    but I won't finish you off.
I'll punish you, but fairly.
    I won't send you off with just a slap on the wrist.'

12-15   "This is GOD's Message:

" 'You're a burned-out case,
    as good as dead.
Everyone has given up on you.
    You're hopeless.
All your fair-weather friends have skipped town
    without giving you a second thought.
But I delivered the knockout blow,
    a punishment you will never forget,
Because of the enormity of your guilt,
    the endless list of your sins.
So why all this self-pity, licking your wounds?
    You deserve all this, and more.
Because of the enormity of your guilt,
    the endless list of your sins,

I've done all this to you.

16-17 "'Everyone who hurt you will be hurt;
        your enemies will end up as slaves.
Your plunderers will be plundered;
        your looters will become loot.
As for you, I'll come with healing,
        curing the incurable,
Because they all gave up on you
        and dismissed you as hopeless—
        that good-for-nothing Zion.'

18-21 "Again, GOD's Message:

"'I'll turn things around for Jacob.
        I'll compassionately come in and rebuild homes.
The town will be rebuilt on its old foundations;
        the mansions will be splendid again.
Thanksgivings will pour out of the windows;
        laughter will spill through the doors.
Things will get better and better.
        Depression days are over.
They'll thrive, they'll flourish.
        The days of contempt will be over.
They'll look forward to having children again,
        to being a community in which I take pride.
I'll punish anyone who hurts them,
        and their prince will come from their own ranks.
One of their own people shall be their leader.
        Their ruler will come from their own ranks.
I'll grant him free and easy access to me.
        Would anyone dare to do that on his own,
        to enter my presence uninvited?' GOD's Decree.

22 "'And that's it: You'll be my very own people,
        I'll be your very own God.'"

23-24 Look out! GOD's hurricane is let loose,
        his hurricane blast,
Spinning the heads of the wicked like dust devils!
        God's raging anger won't let up
Until he's made a clean sweep
        completing the job he began.
When the job's done
        you'll see it's been well done.

1 31 "And when that happens"—GOD's Decree—
        "it will be plain as the sun at high noon:
        I'll be the God of every man, woman, and child in Israel
and they shall be my very own people."

2-6 This is the way God put it:

"They found grace out in the desert,
    these people who survived the killing.
Israel, out looking for a place to rest,
    met God out looking for them!"
God told them, "I've never quit loving you and never will.
    Expect love, love, and more love!
And so now I'll start over with you and build you up again,
    dear virgin Israel.
You'll resume your singing,
    grabbing tambourines and joining the dance.
You'll go back to your old work of planting vineyards
    on the Samaritan hillsides,
And sit back and enjoy the fruit—
    oh, how you'll enjoy those harvests!
The time's coming when watchmen will call out
    from the hilltops of Ephraim:
'On your feet! Let's go to Zion,
    go to meet our God!'"

7 Oh yes, God says so:

"Shout for joy at the top of your lungs for Jacob!
    Announce the good news to the number-one nation!
Raise cheers! Sing praises. Say,
    'God has saved his people,
    saved the core of Israel.'

8   "Watch what comes next:

"I'll bring my people back
    from the north country
And gather them up from the ends of the earth,
    gather those who've gone blind
And those who are lame and limping,
    gather pregnant women,
Even the mothers whose birth pangs have started,
    bring them all back, a huge crowd!

9 "Watch them come! They'll come weeping for joy
    as I take their hands and lead them,
Lead them to fresh flowing brooks,
    lead them along smooth, uncluttered paths.
Yes, it's because I'm Israel's Father
    and Ephraim's my firstborn son!

10-14 "Hear this, nations! God's Message!

Broadcast this all over the world!
Tell them, 'The One who scattered Israel
    will gather them together again.
From now on he'll keep a careful eye on them,
    like a shepherd with his flock.'
I, GOD, will pay a stiff ransom price for Jacob;
    I'll free him from the grip of the Babylonian bully.
The people will climb up Zion's slopes shouting with joy,
    their faces beaming because of GOD's bounty—
Grain and wine and oil,
    flocks of sheep, herds of cattle.
Their lives will be like a well-watered garden,
    never again left to dry up.
Young women will dance and be happy,
    young men and old men will join in.
I'll convert their weeping into laughter,
    lavishing comfort, invading their grief with joy.
I'll make sure that their priests get three square meals a day
    and that my people have more than enough.'" GOD's Decree.

15-17   Again, GOD's Message:

"Listen to this! Laments coming out of Ramah,
    wild and bitter weeping.
It's Rachel weeping for her children,
    Rachel refusing all solace.
Her children are gone,
    gone—long gone into exile."
But GOD says, "Stop your incessant weeping,
    hold back your tears.
Collect wages from your grief work." GOD's Decree.
    "They'll be coming back home!
There's hope for your children." GOD's Decree.

18-19   "I've heard the contrition of Ephraim.
    Yes, I've heard it clearly, saying,
'You trained me well.
    You broke me, a wild yearling horse, to the saddle.
Now put me, trained and obedient, to use.
    You are my GOD.
After those years of running loose, I repented.
    After you trained me to obedience,
I was ashamed of my past, my wild, unruly past.
    Humiliated, I beat on my chest.
Will I ever live this down?'

20   "Oh! Ephraim is my dear, dear son,
    my child in whom I take pleasure!
Every time I mention his name,
    my heart bursts with longing for him!

Everything in me cries out for him.
    Softly and tenderly I wait for him." GOD's Decree.

21-22 "Set up signposts to mark your trip home.
    Get a good map.
Study the road conditions.
    The road out is the road back.
Come back, dear virgin Israel,
    come back to your hometowns.
How long will you flit here and there, indecisive?
    How long before you make up your fickle mind?
GOD will create a new thing in this land:
    A transformed woman will embrace the transforming GOD!"

23-24 A Message from Israel's GOD-of-the-Angel-Armies: "When I've turned everything around and brought my people back, the old expressions will be heard on the streets: 'GOD bless you!' . . . 'O True Home!' . . . 'O Holy Mountain!' All Judah's people, whether in town or country, will get along just fine with each other.

25   I'll refresh tired bodies;
    I'll restore tired souls.

26   Just then I woke up and looked around — what a pleasant and satisfying sleep!

27-28 "Be ready. The time's coming" — GOD's Decree — "when I will plant people and animals in Israel and Judah, just as a farmer plants seed. And in the same way that earlier I relentlessly pulled up and tore down, took apart and demolished, so now I am sticking with them as they start over, building and planting.

29   "When that time comes you won't hear the old proverb anymore,

        Parents ate the green apples,
        their children got the stomachache.

30 "No, each person will pay for his own sin. You eat green apples, you're the one who gets sick.

31-32 "That's right. The time is coming when I will make a brand-new covenant with Israel and Judah. It won't be a repeat of the covenant I made with their ancestors when I took their hand to lead them out of the land of Egypt. They broke that covenant even though I did my part as their Master." GOD's Decree.

33-34   "This is the brand-new covenant that I will make with Israel when the time comes. I will put my law within them — write it on their hearts! — and be their God. And they will be my people. They will no longer go around setting up schools to teach each other about GOD. They'll know me firsthand, the dull and the bright, the smart and the slow. I'll wipe the slate clean for each of them. I'll forget they ever sinned!" GOD's Decree.

IF THIS ORDERED COSMOS EVER FELL TO PIECES

35 GOD's Message, from the God who lights up the day with sun and
　　brightens the night with moon and stars,
Who whips the ocean into a billowy froth,
　　whose name is GOD-of-the-Angel-Armies:

36 "If this ordered cosmos ever fell to pieces,
　　fell into chaos before me" — GOD's Decree —
"Then and only then might Israel fall apart
　　and disappear as a nation before me."

37 GOD's Message:

"If the skies could be measured with a yardstick
　　and the earth explored to its core,
Then and only then would I turn my back on Israel,
　　disgusted with all they've done." GOD's Decree.

38-40 "The time is coming" — it's GOD's Decree — "when GOD's city will be rebuilt, rebuilt all the way from the Citadel of Hanamel to the Corner Gate. The master plan will extend west to Gareb Hill and then around to Goath. The whole valley to the south where incinerated corpses are dumped — a death valley if there ever was one! — and all the terraced fields out to the Brook Kidron on the east as far north as the Horse Gate will be consecrated to me as a holy place.

　　"This city will never again be torn down or destroyed."

KILLING AND DISEASE ARE ON OUR DOORSTEP

1-5 **32** The Message Jeremiah received from GOD in the tenth year of Zedekiah king of Judah. It was the eighteenth year of Nebuchadnezzar. At that time the army of the king of Babylon was holding Jerusalem under siege. Jeremiah was shut up in jail in the royal palace. Zedekiah, king of Judah, had locked him up, complaining, "How dare you preach, saying, 'GOD says, I'm warning you: I will hand this city over to the king of Babylon and he will take it over. Zedekiah king of Judah will be handed over to the Chaldeans right along with the city. He will be handed over to the king of Babylon and forced to face the music. He'll be hauled off to Babylon where he'll stay until I deal with him. GOD's Decree. Fight against the Babylonians all you want — it won't get you anywhere.'"

6-7 Jeremiah said, "GOD's Message came to me like this: Prepare yourself! Hanamel, your uncle Shallum's son, is on his way to see you. He is going to say, 'Buy my field in Anathoth. You have the legal right to buy it.'

8 "And sure enough, just as GOD had said, my cousin Hanamel came to me while I was in jail and said, 'Buy my field in Anathoth in the territory of Benjamin, for you have the legal right to keep it in the family. Buy it. Take it over.'

"That did it. I knew it was GOD's Message.

9-12 "So I bought the field at Anathoth from my cousin Hanamel. I paid him seventeen silver shekels. I followed all the proper procedures: In the presence of witnesses I wrote out the bill of sale, sealed it, and weighed out the money on the scales. Then I took the deed of purchase—the sealed copy that contained the contract and its conditions and also the open copy—and gave them to Baruch son of Neriah, the son of Mahseiah. All this took place in the presence of my cousin Hanamel and the witnesses who had signed the deed, as the Jews who were at the jail that day looked on.

13-15 "Then, in front of all of them, I told Baruch, 'These are orders from GOD-of-the-Angel-Armies, the God of Israel: Take these documents—both the sealed and the open deeds—and put them for safekeeping in a pottery jar. For GOD-of-the-Angel-Armies, the God of Israel, says, "Life is going to return to normal. Homes and fields and vineyards are again going to be bought in this country."'

16-19 "And then, having handed over the legal documents to Baruch son of Neriah, I prayed to GOD, 'Dear GOD, my Master, you created earth and sky by your great power—by merely stretching out your arm! There is nothing you can't do. You're loyal in your steadfast love to thousands upon thousands—but you also make children live with the fallout from their parents' sins. Great and powerful God, named GOD-of-the-Angel-Armies, determined in purpose and relentless in following through, you see everything that men and women do and respond appropriately to the way they live, to the things they do.

20-23 "'You performed signs and wonders in the country of Egypt and continue to do so right into the present, right here in Israel and everywhere else, too. You've made a reputation for yourself that doesn't diminish. You brought your people Israel out of Egypt with signs and wonders—a powerful deliverance!—by merely stretching out your arm. You gave them this land and solemnly promised to their ancestors a bountiful and fertile land. But when they entered the land and took it over, they didn't listen to you. They didn't do what you commanded. They wouldn't listen to a thing you told them. And so you brought this disaster on them.

24-25 "'Oh, look at the siege ramps already set in place to take the city. Killing and starvation and disease are on our doorstep. The Babylonians are attacking! The Word you spoke is coming to pass—it's daily news! And yet you, GOD, the Master, even though it is certain that the city will be turned over to the Babylonians, also told me, Buy the field. Pay for it in cash. And make sure there are witnesses.'"

26-30 Then GOD's Message came again to Jeremiah: "Stay alert! I am GOD, the God of everything living. Is there anything I can't do? So listen to GOD's Message: No doubt about it, I'm handing this city over to the Babylonians and Nebuchadnezzar king of Babylon. He'll take it. The attacking Chaldeans will break through and burn the city down: All those houses whose roofs were used as altars for offerings to Baal and the worship of who knows how many other gods provoked me. It isn't as if this were the first time they had provoked me. The people of Israel and Judah have been doing this for a long time—doing what I hate, making me angry by the way they live." GOD's Decree.

31-35 "This city has made me angry from the day they built it, and now I've had my fill. I'm destroying it. I can't stand to look any longer at the wicked lives of the people of Israel and Judah, deliberately making me angry, the whole lot of them — kings and leaders and priests and preachers, in the country and in the city. They've turned their backs on me — won't even look me in the face! — even though I took great pains to teach them how to live. They refused to listen, refused to be taught. Why, they even set up obscene god and goddess statues in the Temple built in my honor — an outrageous desecration! And then they went out and built shrines to the god Baal in the valley of Hinnom, where they burned their children in sacrifice to the god Molech — I can hardly conceive of such evil! — turning the whole country into one huge act of sin.

36 "But there is also this Message from me, the GOD of Israel, to this city of which you have said, 'In killing and starvation and disease this city will be delivered up to the king of Babylon':

37-40 "'Watch for this! I will collect them from all the countries to which I will have driven them in my anger and rage and indignation. Yes, I'll bring them all back to this place and let them live here in peace. They will be my people, I will be their God. I'll make them of one mind and heart, always honoring me, so that they can live good and whole lives, they and their children after them. What's more, I'll make a covenant with them that will last forever, a covenant to stick with them no matter what, and work for their good. I'll fill their hearts with a deep respect for me so they'll not even *think* of turning away from me.

41 "'Oh how I'll rejoice in them! Oh how I'll delight in doing good things for them! Heart and soul, I'll plant them in this country and keep them here!'

42-44 "Yes, this is GOD's Message: 'I will certainly bring this huge catastrophe on this people, but I will also usher in a wonderful life of prosperity. I promise. Fields are going to be bought here again, yes, in this very country that you assume is going to end up desolate — gone to the dogs, unlivable, wrecked by the Babylonians. Yes, people will buy farms again, and legally, with deeds of purchase, sealed documents, proper witnesses — and right here in the territory of Benjamin, and in the area around Jerusalem, around the villages of Judah and the hill country, the Shephelah and the Negev. I will restore everything that was lost.' GOD's Decree."

THINGS YOU COULD NEVER FIGURE OUT ON YOUR OWN

1 **33** While Jeremiah was still locked up in jail, a second Message from GOD was given to him:

2-3 "This is GOD's Message, the God who made earth, made it livable and lasting, known everywhere as GOD: 'Call to me and I will answer you. I'll tell you marvelous and wondrous things that you could never figure out on your own.'

4-5 "This is what GOD, the God of Israel, has to say about what's going on in this city, about the homes of both people and kings that have been demolished, about all the ravages of war and the killing by the Chaldeans, and about the streets littered with the dead bodies of those killed because of my raging anger — about all that's happened because the evil actions in this city have turned my stomach in disgust.

6-9 "But now take another look. I'm going to give this city a thorough renovation, working a true healing inside and out. I'm going to show them life
whole, life brimming with blessings. I'll restore everything that was lost to
Judah and Jerusalem. I'll build everything back as good as new. I'll scrub
them clean from the dirt they've done against me. I'll forgive everything
they've done wrong, forgive all their rebellions. And Jerusalem will be a
center of joy and praise and glory for all the countries on earth. They'll get
reports on all the good I'm doing for her. They'll be in awe of the blessings
I am pouring on her.

10-11 "Yes, GOD's Message: 'You're going to look at this place, these empty
and desolate towns of Judah and streets of Jerusalem, and say, "A wasteland.
Unlivable. Not even a dog could live here." But the time is coming when you're
going to hear laughter and celebration, marriage festivities, people exclaiming, "Thank GOD-of-the-Angel-Armies. He's so good! His love never quits," as
they bring thank offerings into GOD's Temple. I'll restore everything that was
lost in this land. I'll make everything as good as new.' I, GOD, say so.

12-13 "GOD-of-the-Angel-Armies says: 'This coming desolation, unfit for
even a stray dog, is once again going to become a pasture for shepherds
who care for their flocks. You'll see flocks everywhere — in the mountains
around the towns of the Shephelah and Negev, all over the territory of
Benjamin, around Jerusalem and the towns of Judah — flocks under the
care of shepherds who keep track of each sheep.' GOD says so.

A FRESH AND TRUE SHOOT FROM THE DAVID-TREE

14-18 "'Watch for this: The time is coming' — GOD's Decree — 'when I will keep
the promise I made to the families of Israel and Judah. When that time
comes, I will make a fresh and true shoot sprout from the David-Tree. He
will run this country honestly and fairly. He will set things right. That's
when Judah will be secure and Jerusalem live in safety. The motto for the
city will be, "GOD Has Set Things Right for Us." GOD has made it clear that
there will always be a descendant of David ruling the people of Israel and
that there will always be Levitical priests on hand to offer burnt offerings,
present grain offerings, and carry on the sacrificial worship in my honor.'"

19-22 GOD's Message to Jeremiah: "GOD says, 'If my covenant with day and my
covenant with night ever fell apart so that day and night became
haphazard and you never knew which was coming and when, then and only
then would my covenant with my servant David fall apart and his descendants no longer rule. The same goes for the Levitical priests who serve me.
Just as you can't number the stars in the sky nor measure the sand on the
seashore, neither will you be able to account for the descendants of David
my servant and the Levites who serve me.'"

23-24 GOD's Message to Jeremiah: "Have you heard the saying that's making
the rounds: 'The two families GOD chose, Israel and Judah, he disowned'?
And have you noticed that my people are treated with contempt, with
rumors afoot that there's nothing to them anymore?

25-26 "Well, here's GOD's response: 'If my covenant with day and night wasn't in working order, if sky and earth weren't functioning the way I set them going, then, but only then, you might think I had disowned the descendants of Jacob and of my servant David, and that I wouldn't set up any of David's descendants over the descendants of Abraham, Isaac, and Jacob. But as it is, I will give them back everything they've lost. The last word is, I will have mercy on them.'"

FREEDOM TO THE SLAVES

1   GOD's Message to Jeremiah at the time King Nebuchadnezzar of Babylon mounted an all-out attack on Jerusalem and all the towns around it with his armies and allies and everyone he could muster:

2-3   "I, GOD, the God of Israel, direct you to go and tell Zedekiah king of Judah: 'This is GOD's Message. Listen to me. I am going to hand this city over to the king of Babylon, and he is going to burn it to the ground. And don't think you'll get away. You'll be captured and be his prisoner. You will have a personal confrontation with the king of Babylon and be taken off with him, captive, to Babylon.

4-5   "'But listen, O Zedekiah king of Judah, to the rest of the Message of GOD. You won't be killed. You'll die a peaceful death. They will honor you with funeral rites as they honored your ancestors, the kings who preceded you. They will properly mourn your death, weeping, "Master, master!" This is a solemn promise. GOD's Decree.'"

6-7   The prophet Jeremiah gave this Message to Zedekiah king of Judah in Jerusalem, gave it to him word for word. It was at the very time that the king of Babylon was mounting his all-out attack on Jerusalem and whatever cities in Judah that were still standing—only Lachish and Azekah, as it turned out (they were the only fortified cities left in Judah).

8-10 GOD delivered a Message to Jeremiah after King Zedekiah made a covenant with the people of Jerusalem to decree freedom to the slaves who were Hebrews, both men and women. The covenant stipulated that no one in Judah would own a fellow Jew as a slave. All the leaders and people who had signed the covenant set free the slaves, men and women alike.

11   But a little while later, they reneged on the covenant, broke their promise and forced their former slaves to become slaves again.

12-14 Then Jeremiah received this Message from GOD: "GOD, the God of Israel, says, 'I made a covenant with your ancestors when I delivered them out of their slavery in Egypt. At the time I made it clear: "At the end of seven years, each of you must free any fellow Hebrew who has had to sell himself to you. After he has served six years, set him free." But your ancestors totally ignored me.

15-16 "'And now, *you*—what have you done? First you turned back to the right way and did the right thing, decreeing freedom for your brothers and sisters—and you made it official in a solemn covenant in my Temple. And then you turned right around and broke your word, making a mockery of both me and the covenant, and made them all slaves again, these men and women you'd just set free. You forced them back into slavery.

17-20 "'So here is what I, GOD, have to say: You have not obeyed me and set your brothers and sisters free. Here is what I'm going to do: I'm going to set *you* free — GOD's Decree — free to get killed in war or by disease or by starvation. I'll make you a spectacle of horror. People all over the world will take one look at you and shudder. Everyone who violated my covenant, who didn't do what was solemnly promised in the covenant ceremony when they split the young bull into two halves and walked between them, all those people that day who walked between the two halves of the bull — leaders of Judah and Jerusalem, palace officials, priests, and all the rest of the people — I'm handing the lot of them over to their enemies who are out to kill them. Their dead bodies will be carrion food for vultures and stray dogs.

21-22   "'As for Zedekiah king of Judah and his palace staff, I'll also hand them over to their enemies, who are out to kill them. The army of the king of Babylon has pulled back for a time, but not for long, for I'm going to issue orders that will bring them back to this city. They'll attack and take it and burn it to the ground. The surrounding cities of Judah will fare no better. I'll turn them into ghost towns, unlivable and unlived in.'" GOD's Decree.

MEETING IN GOD'S TEMPLE

1   **35** The Message that Jeremiah received from GOD ten years earlier, during the time of Jehoiakim son of Josiah king of Israel:

2   "Go visit the Recabite community. Invite them to meet with you in one of the rooms in GOD's Temple. And serve them wine."

3-4   So I went and got Jaazaniah son of Jeremiah, son of Habazziniah, along with all his brothers and sons — the whole community of the Recabites as it turned out — and brought them to GOD's Temple and to the meeting room of Hanan son of Igdaliah, a man of God. It was next to the meeting room of the Temple officials and just over the apartment of Maaseiah son of Shallum, who was in charge of Temple affairs.

5   Then I set out chalices and pitchers of wine for the Recabites and said, "A toast! Drink up!"

6-7   But they wouldn't do it. "We don't drink wine," they said. "Our ancestor Jonadab son of Recab commanded us, 'You are not to drink wine, you or your children, ever. Neither shall you build houses or settle down, planting fields and gardens and vineyards. Don't own property. Live in tents as nomads so that you will live well and prosper in a wandering life.'

8-10   "And we've done it, done everything Jonadab son of Recab commanded. We and our wives, our sons and daughters, drink no wine at all. We don't build houses. We don't have vineyards or fields or gardens. We live in tents as nomads. We've listened to our ancestor Jonadab and we've done everything he commanded us.

11   "But when Nebuchadnezzar king of Babylon invaded our land, we said, 'Let's go to Jerusalem and get out of the path of the Chaldean and Aramean armies, find ourselves a safe place.' That's why we're living in Jerusalem right now."

WHY WON'T YOU LEARN YOUR LESSON?

12-15   Then Jeremiah received this Message from GOD: "GOD-of-the-Angel-Armies, the God of Israel, wants you to go tell the people of Judah and the citizens of Jerusalem that I say, 'Why won't you learn your lesson and do what I tell you?' GOD's Decree. 'The commands of Jonadab son of Recab to his sons have been carried out to the letter. He told them not to drink wine, and they haven't touched a drop to this very day. They honored and obeyed their ancestor's command. But look at you! I have gone to a lot of trouble to get your attention, and you've ignored me. I sent prophet after prophet to you, all of them my servants, to tell you from early morning to late at night to change your life, make a clean break with your evil past and do what is right, to not take up with every Tom, Dick, and Harry of a god that comes down the pike, but settle down and be faithful in this country I gave your ancestors.

15-16 " 'And what do I get from you? Deaf ears. The descendants of Jonadab son of Recab carried out to the letter what their ancestor commanded them, but this people ignores me.'

17 "So here's what is going to happen. GOD-of-the-Angel-Armies, the God of Israel, says, 'I will bring calamity down on the heads of the people of Judah and Jerusalem — the very calamity I warned you was coming — because you turned a deaf ear when I spoke, turned your backs when I called.' "

18-19 Then, turning to the Recabite community, Jeremiah said, "And this is what GOD-of-the-Angel-Armies, the God of Israel, says to you: 'Because you have done what Jonadab your ancestor told you, obeyed his commands and followed through on his instructions, receive this Message from GOD-of-the-Angel-Armies, the God of Israel: There will always be a descendant of Jonadab son of Recab at my service! Always!' "

READING GOD'S MESSAGE

1 **36** In the fourth year of Jehoiakim son of Josiah king of Judah, Jeremiah received this Message from GOD:

2 "Get a scroll and write down everything I've told you regarding Israel and Judah and all the other nations from the time I first started speaking to you in Josiah's reign right up to the present day.

3 "Maybe the community of Judah will finally get it, finally understand the catastrophe that I'm planning for them, turn back from their bad lives, and let me forgive their perversity and sin."

4 So Jeremiah called in Baruch son of Neriah. Jeremiah dictated and Baruch wrote down on a scroll everything that GOD had said to him.

5-6 Then Jeremiah told Baruch, "I'm blacklisted. I can't go into GOD's Temple, so you'll have to go in my place. Go into the Temple and read everything you've written at my dictation. Wait for a day of fasting when everyone is there to hear you. And make sure that all the people who come from the Judean villages hear you.

7 "Maybe, just maybe, they'll start praying and GOD will hear their prayers. Maybe they'll turn back from their bad lives. This is no light matter. GOD has certainly let them know how angry he is!"

8 Baruch son of Neriah did everything Jeremiah the prophet told him to do. In the Temple of GOD he read the Message of GOD from the scroll.

9 It came about in December of the fifth year of Jehoiakim son of Josiah king of Judah that all the people of Jerusalem, along with all the people from the Judean villages, were there in Jerusalem to observe a fast to GOD.

10 Baruch took the scroll to the Temple and read out publicly the words of Jeremiah. He read from the meeting room of Gemariah son of Shaphan the secretary of state, which was in the upper court right next to the New Gate of GOD's Temple. Everyone could hear him.

11-12 The moment Micaiah the son of Gemariah heard what was being read from the scroll — GOD's Message! — he went straight to the palace and to the chambers of the secretary of state where all the government officials were holding a meeting: Elishama the secretary, Delaiah son of Shemaiah, Elnathan son of Achbor, Gemariah son of Shaphan, Zedekiah son of Hananiah, and all the other government officials.

13 Micaiah reported everything he had heard Baruch read from the scroll as the officials listened.

14 Immediately they dispatched Jehudi son of Nethaniah, son of Semaiah, son of Cushi, to Baruch, ordering him, "Take the scroll that you have read to the people and bring it here." So Baruch went and retrieved the scroll.

15 The officials told him, "Sit down. Read it to us, please." Baruch read it.

16 When they had heard it all, they were upset. They talked it over. "We've got to tell the king all this."

17 They asked Baruch, "Tell us, how did you come to write all this? Was it at Jeremiah's dictation?"

18 Baruch said, "That's right. Every word right from his own mouth. And I wrote it down, word for word, with pen and ink."

19 The government officials told Baruch, "You need to get out of here. Go into hiding, you and Jeremiah. Don't let anyone know where you are!"

20-21 The officials went to the court of the palace to report to the king, having put the scroll for safekeeping in the office of Elishama the secretary of state. The king sent Jehudi to get the scroll. He brought it from the office of Elishama the secretary. Jehudi then read it to the king and the officials who were in the king's service.

22-23 It was December. The king was sitting in his winter quarters in front of a charcoal fire. After Jehudi would read three or four columns, the king would cut them off the scroll with his pocketknife and throw them in the fire. He continued in this way until the entire scroll had been burned up in the fire.

24-26 Neither the king nor any of his officials showed the slightest twinge of conscience as they listened to the messages read. Elnathan, Delaiah, and Gemariah tried to convince the king not to burn the scroll, but he brushed them off. He just plowed ahead and ordered Prince Jerahameel, Seraiah son of Azriel, and Shelemiah son of Abdeel to arrest Jeremiah the prophet and his secretary Baruch. But GOD had hidden them away.

27-28 After the king had burned the scroll that Baruch had written at Jeremiah's dictation, Jeremiah received this Message from GOD: "Get another blank scroll and do it all over again. Write out everything that was in that first scroll that Jehoiakim king of Judah burned up.

29 "And send this personal message to Jehoiakim king of Judah: 'GOD says, You had the gall to burn this scroll and then the nerve to say, "What kind of nonsense is this written here — that the king of Babylon will come and destroy this land and kill everything in it?"

30-31 "'Well, do you want to know what GOD says about Jehoiakim king of Judah? This: No descendant of his will ever rule from David's throne. His corpse will be thrown in the street and left unburied, exposed to the hot sun and the freezing night. I will punish him and his children and the officials in his government for their blatant sin. I'll let loose on them and everyone in

Jerusalem the doomsday disaster of which I warned them but they spit at.'"

32 So Jeremiah went and got another scroll and gave it to Baruch son of Neriah, his secretary. At Jeremiah's dictation he again wrote down everything that Jehoiakim king of Judah had burned in the fire. There were also generous additions, but of the same kind of thing.

IN AN UNDERGROUND DUNGEON

1-2 **37** King Zedekiah son of Josiah, a puppet king set on the throne by Nebuchadnezzar king of Babylon in the land of Judah, was now king in place of Jehoiachin son of Jehoiakim. But neither he nor his officials nor the people themselves paid a bit of attention to the Message GOD gave by Jeremiah the prophet.

3 However, King Zedekiah sent Jehucal son of Shelemiah, and Zephaniah the priest, son of Maaseiah, to Jeremiah the prophet, saying, "Pray for us — pray hard! — to the Master, our GOD."

4-5 Jeremiah was still moving about freely among the people in those days. This was before he had been put in jail. Pharaoh's army was marching up from Egypt. The Chaldeans fighting against Jerusalem heard that the Egyptians were coming and pulled back.

6-10 Then Jeremiah the prophet received this Message from GOD: "I, the GOD of Israel, want you to give this Message to the king of Judah, who has just sent you to me to find out what he should do. Tell him, 'Get this: Pharaoh's army, which is on its way to help you, isn't going to stick it out. No sooner will they get here than they'll leave and go home to Egypt. And then the Babylonians will come back and resume their attack, capture this city and burn it to the ground. I, GOD, am telling you: Don't kid yourselves, reassuring one another, "The Babylonians will leave in a few days." I tell you, they aren't leaving. Why, even if you defeated the entire attacking Chaldean army and all that was left were a few wounded soldiers in their tents, the wounded would still do the job and burn this city to the ground.'"

11-13 When the Chaldean army pulled back from Jerusalem, Jeremiah left Jerusalem to go over to the territory of Benjamin to take care of some personal business. When he got to the Benjamin Gate, the officer on guard there, Irijah son of Shelemiah, son of Hananiah, grabbed Jeremiah the prophet, accusing him, "You're deserting to the Chaldeans!"

14-16 "That's a lie," protested Jeremiah. "I wouldn't think of deserting to the Chaldeans."

But Irijah wouldn't listen to him. He arrested him and took him to the police. The police were furious with Jeremiah. They beat him up and threw him into jail in the house of Jonathan the secretary of state. (They were using the house for a prison cell.) So Jeremiah entered an underground cell in a cistern turned into a dungeon. He stayed there a long time.

17 Later King Zedekiah had Jeremiah brought to him. The king questioned him privately, "Is there a Message from GOD?"

"There certainly is," said Jeremiah. "You're going to be turned over to the king of Babylon."

18-20 Jeremiah continued speaking to King Zedekiah: "Can you tell me why you threw me into prison? What crime did I commit against you or your officials or this people? And tell me, whatever has become of your prophets who preached all those sermons saying that the king of Babylon would never attack you or this land? Listen to me, please, my master—my king! Please don't send me back to that dungeon in the house of Jonathan the secretary. I'll die there!"

21 So King Zedekiah ordered that Jeremiah be assigned to the courtyard of the palace guards. He was given a loaf of bread from Bakers' Alley every day until all the bread in the city was gone. And that's where Jeremiah remained—in the courtyard of the palace guards.

FROM THE DUNGEON TO THE PALACE

1 **38** Shaphatiah son of Mattan, Gedaliah son of Pashur, Jehucal son of Shelemiah, and Pashur son of Malkijah heard what Jeremiah was telling the people, namely:

2 "This is GOD's Message: 'Whoever stays in this town will die—will be killed or starve to death or get sick and die. But those who go over to the Babylonians will save their necks and live.'

3 "And, GOD's sure Word: 'This city is destined to fall to the army of the king of Babylon. He's going to take it over.'"

4 These officials told the king, "Please, kill this man. He's got to go! He's ruining the resolve of the soldiers who are still left in the city, as well as the people themselves, by spreading these words. This man isn't looking after the good of this people. He's trying to ruin us!"

5 King Zedekiah caved in: "If you say so. Go ahead, handle it your way. You're too much for me."

6 So they took Jeremiah and threw him into the cistern of Malkijah the king's son that was in the courtyard of the palace guard. They lowered him down with ropes. There wasn't any water in the cistern, only mud. Jeremiah sank into the mud.

7-9 Ebed-melek the Ethiopian, a court official assigned to the royal palace, heard that they had thrown Jeremiah into the cistern. While the king was holding court in the Benjamin Gate, Ebed-melek went immediately from the palace to the king and said, "My master, O king—these men are committing a great crime in what they're doing, throwing Jeremiah the prophet into the cistern and leaving him there to starve. He's as good as dead. There isn't a scrap of bread left in the city."

10 So the king ordered Ebed-melek the Ethiopian, "Get three men and pull Jeremiah the prophet out of the cistern before he dies."

11-12 Ebed-melek got three men and went to the palace wardrobe and got some scraps of old clothing, which they tied together and lowered down with ropes to Jeremiah in the cistern. Ebed-melek the Ethiopian called down to Jeremiah, "Put these scraps of old clothing under your armpits and around the ropes."

Jeremiah did what he said.

13 And so they pulled Jeremiah up out of the cistern by the ropes. But he was still confined in the courtyard of the palace guard.

14 Later, King Zedekiah sent for Jeremiah the prophet and had him brought to the third entrance of the Temple of GOD. The king said to Jeremiah, "I'm going to ask you something. Don't hold anything back from me."

15 Jeremiah said, "If I told you the whole truth, you'd kill me. And no matter what I said, you wouldn't pay any attention anyway."

16 Zedekiah swore to Jeremiah right there, but in secret, "As sure as GOD

lives, who gives *us* life, I won't kill you, nor will I turn you over to the men who are trying to kill you."

17-18 So Jeremiah told Zedekiah, "This is the Message from GOD, GOD-of-the-Angel-Armies, the God of Israel: 'If you will turn yourself over to the generals of the king of Babylon, you will live, this city won't be burned down, and your family will live. But if you don't turn yourself over to the generals of the king of Babylon, this city will go into the hands of the Chaldeans and they'll burn it down. And don't for a minute think there's any escape for you.'"

19 King Zedekiah said to Jeremiah, "But I'm afraid of the Judeans who have already deserted to the Chaldeans. If they get hold of me, they'll rough me up good."

20-22 Jeremiah assured him, "They won't get hold of you. Listen, please. Listen to GOD's voice. I'm telling you this for your own good so that you'll live. But if you refuse to turn yourself over, this is what GOD has shown me will happen: Picture this in your mind — all the women still left in the palace of the king of Judah, led out to the officers of the king of Babylon, and as they're led out they are saying:

"'They lied to you and did you in,
    those so-called friends of yours;
And now you're stuck, about knee-deep in mud,
    and your "friends," where are they now?'

23 "They'll take all your wives and children and give them to the Chaldeans. And you, don't think you'll get out of this — the king of Babylon will seize you and then burn this city to the ground."

24-26 Zedekiah said to Jeremiah, "Don't let anyone know of this conversation, if you know what's good for you. If the government officials get wind that I've been talking with you, they may come and say, 'Tell us what went on between you and the king, what you said and what he said. Hold nothing back and we won't kill you.' If this happens, tell them, 'I presented my case to the king so that he wouldn't send me back to the dungeon of Jonathan to die there.'"

27 And sure enough, all the officials came to Jeremiah and asked him. He responded as the king had instructed. So they quit asking. No one had overheard the conversation.

28 Jeremiah lived in the courtyard of the palace guards until the day that Jerusalem was captured.

BAD NEWS, NOT GOOD NEWS

1-2 **39** In the ninth year and tenth month of Zedekiah king of Judah, Nebuchadnezzar king of Babylon came with his entire army and laid siege to Jerusalem. In the eleventh year and fourth month, on the ninth day of Zedekiah's reign, they broke through into the city.

3 All the officers of the king of Babylon came and set themselves up as a ruling council from the Middle Gate: Nergal-sharezer of Simmagar, Nebushazban the Rabsaris, Nergal-sharezer the Rabmag, along with all the other officials of the king of Babylon.

4-7 When Zedekiah king of Judah and his remaining soldiers saw this, they ran for their lives. They slipped out at night on a path in the king's garden through the gate between two walls and headed for the wilderness, toward the Jordan Valley. The Babylonian army chased them and caught Zedekiah in the wilderness of Jericho. They seized him and took him to Nebuchadnezzar king of Babylon at Riblah in the country of Hamath. Nebuchadnezzar decided his fate. The king of Babylon killed all the sons of Zedekiah in Riblah right before his eyes and then killed all the nobles of Judah. After Zedekiah had seen the slaughter, Nebuchadnezzar blinded him, chained him up, and then took him off to Babylon.

8-10   Meanwhile, the Babylonians burned down the royal palace, the Temple, and all the homes of the people. They leveled the walls of Jerusalem. Nebuzaradan, commander of the king's bodyguard, rounded up everyone left in the city, along with those who had surrendered to him, and herded them off to exile in Babylon. He didn't bother taking the few poor people who had nothing. He left them in the land of Judah to eke out a living as best they could in the vineyards and fields.

11-12   Nebuchadnezzar king of Babylon gave Nebuzaradan captain of the king's bodyguard special orders regarding Jeremiah: "Look out for him. Make sure nothing bad happens to him. Give him anything he wants."

13-14   So Nebuzaradan, chief of the king's bodyguard, along with Nebushazban the Rabsaris, Nergal-sharezer the Rabmag, and all the chief officers of the king of Babylon, sent for Jeremiah, taking him from the courtyard of the royal guards and putting him under the care of Gedaliah son of Ahikam, the son of Shaphan, to be taken home. And so he was able to live with the people.

15-18   Earlier, while Jeremiah was still in custody in the courtyard of the royal guards, GOD's Message came to him: "Go and speak with Ebed-melek the Ethiopian. Tell him, 'GOD-of-the-Angel-Armies, the God of Israel, says, Listen carefully: I will do exactly what I said I would do to this city—bad news, not good news. When it happens, you will be there to see it. But I'll deliver you on that doomsday. You won't be handed over to those men whom you have good reason to fear. Yes, I'll most certainly save you. You won't be killed. You'll walk out of there safe and sound because you trusted me.'" GOD's Decree.

GO AND LIVE WHEREVER YOU WISH

1   **40** GOD's Message to Jeremiah after Nebuzaradan captain of the bodyguard set him free at Ramah. When Nebuzaradan came upon him, he was in chains, along with all the other captives from Jerusalem and Judah who were being herded off to exile in Babylon.

2-3   The captain of the bodyguard singled out Jeremiah and said to him, "Your GOD pronounced doom on this place. GOD came and did what he had warned he'd do because you all sinned against GOD and wouldn't do what he told you. So now you're all suffering the consequences.

4-5   "But today, Jeremiah, I'm setting you free, taking the chains off your hands. If you'd like to come to Babylon with me, come along. I'll take good care of you. But if you don't want to come to Babylon with me, that's just fine, too. Look, the whole land stretches out before you. Do what you like. Go and live wherever you wish. If you want to stay home, go back to Gedaliah son of Ahikam, son of Shaphan. The king of Babylon made him governor of the cities of Judah. Stay with him and your people. Or go wherever you'd like. It's up to you."

The captain of the bodyguard gave him food for the journey and a parting gift, and sent him off.

6 Jeremiah went to Gedaliah son of Ahikam at Mizpah and made his home with him and the people who were left behind in the land.

TAKE CARE OF THE LAND

7-8 When the army leaders and their men, who had been hiding out in the fields, heard that the king of Babylon had appointed Gedaliah son of Ahikam as governor of the land, putting him in charge of the men, women, and children of the poorest of the poor who hadn't been taken off to exile in Babylon, they came to Gedaliah at Mizpah: Ishmael son of Nethaniah, Johanan and Jonathan the sons of Kareah, Seraiah son of Tanhumeth, the sons of Ephai the Netophathite, and Jaazaniah son of the Maacathite, accompanied by their men.

9 Gedaliah son of Ahikam, the son of Shaphan, promised them and their men, "You have nothing to fear from the Chaldean officials. Stay here on the land. Be subject to the king of Babylon. You'll get along just fine.

10 "My job is to stay here in Mizpah and be your advocate before the Chaldeans when they show up. Your job is to take care of the land: Make wine, harvest the summer fruits, press olive oil. Store it all in pottery jugs and settle into the towns that you have taken over."

11-12 The Judeans who had escaped to Moab, Ammon, Edom, and other countries heard that the king of Babylon had left a few survivors in Judah and made Gedaliah son of Ahikam, son of Shaphan, governor over them. They all started coming back to Judah from all the places where they'd been scattered. They came to Judah and to Gedaliah at Mizpah and went to work gathering in a huge supply of wine and summer fruits.

13-14 One day Johanan son of Kareah and all the officers of the army who had been hiding out in the backcountry came to Gedaliah at Mizpah and told him, "You know, don't you, that Baaliss king of Ammon has sent Ishmael son of Nethaniah to kill you?" But Gedaliah son of Ahikam didn't believe them.

15 Then Johanan son of Kareah took Gedaliah aside privately in Mizpah: "Let me go and kill Ishmael son of Nethaniah. No one needs to know about it. Why should we let him kill you and plunge the land into anarchy? Why let everyone you've taken care of be scattered and what's left of Judah destroyed?"

16 But Gedaliah son of Ahikam told Johanan son of Kareah, "Don't do it. I forbid it. You're spreading a false rumor about Ishmael."

MURDER

41 1-3 But in the seventh month, Ishmael son of Nethaniah, son of Elishama, came. He had royal blood in his veins and had been one of the king's high-ranking officers. He paid a visit to Gedaliah son of Ahikam at Mizpah with ten of his men. As they were

eating together, Ishmael and his ten men jumped to their feet and knocked Gedaliah down and killed him, killed the man the king of Babylon had appointed governor of the land. Ishmael also killed all the Judeans who were with Gedaliah in Mizpah, as well as the Chaldean soldiers who were stationed there.

⁴⁻⁵ On the second day after the murder of Gedaliah—no one yet knew of it—men arrived from Shechem, Shiloh, and Samaria, eighty of them, with their beards shaved, their clothing ripped, and gashes on their bodies. They were pilgrims carrying grain offerings and incense on their way to worship at the Temple in Jerusalem.

⁶ Ishmael son of Nethaniah went out from Mizpah to welcome them, weeping ostentatiously. When he greeted them he invited them in: "Come and meet Gedaliah son of Ahikam."

⁷⁻⁸ But as soon as they were inside the city, Ishmael son of Nethaniah and his henchmen slaughtered the pilgrims and dumped the bodies in a cistern. Ten of the men talked their way out of the massacre. They bargained with Ishmael, "Don't kill us. We have a hidden store of wheat, barley, olive oil, and honey out in the fields." So he held back and didn't kill them with their fellow pilgrims.

⁹ Ishmael's reason for dumping the bodies into a cistern was to cover up the earlier murder of Gedaliah. The cistern had been built by king Asa as a defense against Baasha king of Israel. This was the cistern that Ishmael son of Nethaniah filled with the slaughtered men.

¹⁰ Ishmael then took everyone else in Mizpah, including the king's daughters entrusted to the care of Gedaliah son of Ahikam by Nebuzaradan the captain of the bodyguard, as prisoners. Rounding up the prisoners, Ishmael son of Nethaniah proceeded to take them over into the country of Ammon.

¹¹⁻¹² Johanan son of Kareah and all the army officers with him heard about the atrocities committed by Ishmael son of Nethaniah. They set off at once after Ishmael son of Nethaniah. They found him at the large pool at Gibeon.

¹³⁻¹⁵ When all the prisoners from Mizpah who had been taken by Ishmael saw Johanan son of Kareah and the army officers with him, they couldn't believe their eyes. They were so happy! They all rallied around Johanan son of Kareah and headed back home. But Ishmael son of Nethaniah got away, escaping from Johanan with eight men into the land of Ammon.

¹⁶ Then Johanan son of Kareah and the army officers with him gathered together what was left of the people whom Ishmael son of Nethaniah had taken prisoner from Mizpah after the murder of Gedaliah son of Ahikam—men, women, children, eunuchs—and brought them back from Gibeon.

¹⁷⁻¹⁸ They set out at once for Egypt to get away from the Chaldeans, stopping on the way at Geruth-kimham near Bethlehem. They were afraid of what the Chaldeans might do in retaliation of Ishmael son of Nethaniah's murder of Gedaliah son of Ahikam, whom the king of Babylon had appointed as governor of the country.

What You Fear Will Catch Up with You

¹⁻³ **42** All the army officers, led by Johanan son of Kareah and Jezaniah son of Hoshaiah, accompanied by all the people, small and great, came to Jeremiah the prophet and said, "We have a request. Please listen. Pray to your God for us, what's left of us. You can see

for yourself how few we are! Pray that your GOD will tell us the way we should go and what we should do."

4 Jeremiah the prophet said, "I hear your request. And I will pray to your GOD as you have asked. Whatever GOD says, I'll pass on to you. I'll tell you everything, holding nothing back."

5-6 They said to Jeremiah, "Let GOD be our witness, a true and faithful witness against us, if we don't do everything that your GOD directs you to tell us. Whether we like it or not, we'll do it. We'll obey whatever our GOD tells us. Yes, count on us. We'll do it."

7-8 Ten days later GOD's Message came to Jeremiah. He called together Johanan son of Kareah and all the army officers with him, including all the people, regardless of how much clout they had.

9-12 He then spoke: "This is the Message from GOD, the God of Israel, to whom you sent me to present your prayer. He says, 'If you are ready to stick it out in this land, I will build you up and not drag you down, I will plant you and not pull you up like a weed. I feel deep compassion on account of the doom I have visited on you. You don't have to fear the king of Babylon. Your fears are for nothing. I'm on your side, ready to save and deliver you from anything he might do. I'll pour mercy on you. What's more, *he* will show you mercy! He'll let you come back to your very own land.'

13-17 "But do not say, 'We're not staying around this place,' refusing to obey the command of your GOD and saying instead, 'No! We're off to Egypt, where things are peaceful — no wars, no attacking armies, plenty of food. We're going to live there.' If what's left of Judah is headed down that road, then listen to GOD's Message. This is what GOD-of-the-Angel-Armies says: 'If you have determined to go to Egypt and make that your home, then the very wars you fear will catch up with you in Egypt and the starvation you dread will track you down in Egypt. You'll die there! Every last one of you who is determined to go to Egypt and make it your home will either be killed, starve, or get sick and die. No survivors, not one! No one will escape the doom that I'll bring upon you.'

18 "This is the Message from GOD-of-the-Angel-Armies, the God of Israel: 'In the same way that I swept the citizens of Jerusalem away with my anger and wrath, I'll do the same thing all over again in Egypt. You'll end up being cursed, reviled, ridiculed, and mocked. And you'll never see your homeland again.'

19-20 "GOD has plainly told you, you leftovers from Judah, 'Don't go to Egypt.' Could anything be plainer? I warn you this day that you are living out a fantasy. You're making a fatal mistake.

"Didn't you just now send me to your GOD, saying, 'Pray for us to our GOD. Tell us everything that GOD says and we'll do it all'?

21-22 "Well, now I've told you, told you everything he said, and you haven't obeyed a word of it, not a single word of what your GOD sent me to tell you. So now let me tell you what will happen next: You'll be killed, you'll starve to death, you'll get sick and die in the wonderful country where you've determined to go and live."

DEATH! EXILE! SLAUGHTER!

1-3 **43** When Jeremiah finished telling all the people the whole Message that their GOD had sent him to give them — all these words — Azariah son of Hoshaiah and Johanan son of Kareah, backed by all the self-important men, said to Jeremiah, "Liar! Our GOD never sent you with this message telling us not to go to Egypt and live there. Baruch son of Neriah is behind this. He has turned you against us. He's playing into the hands of the Babylonians so we'll either end up being killed or taken off to exile in Babylon."

4   Johanan son of Kareah and the army officers, and the people along with them, wouldn't listen to GOD's Message that they stay in the land of Judah and live there.

5-7   Johanan son of Kareah and the army officers gathered up everyone who was left from Judah, who had come back after being scattered all over the place—the men, women, and children, the king's daughters, all the people that Nebuzaradan captain of the bodyguard had left in the care of Gedaliah son of Ahikam, the son of Shaphan, and last but not least, Jeremiah the prophet and Baruch son of Neriah. They entered the land of Egypt in total disobedience of GOD's Message and arrived at the city of Tahpanhes.

8-9   While in Tahpanhes, GOD's Word came to Jeremiah: "Pick up some large stones and cover them with mortar in the vicinity of the pavement that leads up to the building set aside for Pharaoh's use in Tahpanhes. Make sure some of the men of Judah are watching.

10-13   "Then address them: 'This is what GOD-of-the-Angel-Armies says: Be on the lookout! I'm sending for and bringing Nebuchadnezzar the king of Babylon—my servant, mind you!—and he'll set up his throne on these very stones that I've had buried here and he'll spread out his canopy over them. He'll come and absolutely smash Egypt, sending each to his assigned fate: death, exile, slaughter. He'll burn down the temples of Egypt's gods. He'll either burn up the gods or haul them off as booty. Like a shepherd who picks lice from his robes, he'll pick Egypt clean. And then he'll walk away without a hand being laid on him. He'll shatter the sacred obelisks at Egypt's House of the Sun and make a huge bonfire of the temples of Egypt's gods.'"

THE SAME FATE WILL FALL UPON ALL

1-6   **44** The Message that Jeremiah received for all the Judeans who lived in the land of Egypt, who had their homes in Migdol, Tahpanhes, Noph, and the land of Pathros: "This is what GOD-of-the-Angel-Armies, the God of Israel, says: 'You saw with your own eyes the terrible doom that I brought down on Jerusalem and the Judean cities. Look at what's left: ghost towns of rubble and smoking ruins, and all because they took up with evil ways, making me angry by going off to offer sacrifices and worship the latest in gods—no-gods that neither they nor you nor your ancestors knew the first thing about. Morning after morning and long into the night I kept after you, sending you all those prophets, my servants, begging you, "Please, please—don't do this, don't fool around in this loathsome gutter of gods that I hate with a passion." But do you think anyone paid the least bit of attention or repented of evil or quit offering sacrifices to the no-gods? Not one. So I let loose with my anger, a firestorm of wrath in the cities of Judah and the streets of Jerusalem, and left them in ruins and wasted. And they're *still* in ruins and wasted.'

7-8   "This is the Message of GOD, GOD-of-the-Angel-Armies, the God of Israel: 'So why are you ruining your lives by amputating yourselves—man, woman, child, and baby—from the life of Judah, leaving yourselves isolated, unconnected? And why do you deliberately make me angry by what you do, offering sacrifices to these no-gods in the land of Egypt where you've come to live? You'll only destroy yourselves and make yourselves an example used in curses and an object of ridicule among all the nations of the earth.

⁹⁻¹¹ "'Have you so soon forgotten the evil lives of your ancestors, the evil lives of the kings of Judah and their wives, to say nothing of your own evil lives, you and your wives, the evil you flaunted in the land of Judah and the streets of Jerusalem? And to this day, there's not a trace of remorse, not a sign of reverence, nobody caring about living by what I tell them or following my instructions that I've set out so plainly before you and your parents! So this is what GOD-of-the-Angel-Armies decrees:

¹¹⁻¹⁴ "'Watch out! I've decided to bring doom on you and get rid of everyone connected with Judah. I'm going to take what's left of Judah, those who have decided to go to Egypt and live there, and finish them off. In Egypt they will either be killed or starve to death. The same fate will fall upon both the obscure and the important. Regardless of their status, they will either be killed or starve. You'll end up cursed, reviled, ridiculed, and mocked. I'll give those who are in Egypt the same medicine I gave those in Jerusalem: massacre, starvation, and disease. None of those who managed to get out of Judah alive and get away to Egypt are going to make it back to the Judah for which they're so homesick. None will make it back, except maybe a few fugitives.'"

MAKING GODDESS COOKIES

¹⁵⁻¹⁸ The men who knew that their wives had been burning sacrifices to the no-gods, joined by a large crowd of women, along with virtually everyone living in Pathros of Egypt, answered Jeremiah: "We're having nothing to do with what you tell us is GOD's Message. We're going to go right on offering sacrifices to the Queen of Heaven and pouring out drink offerings to her, keeping up the traditions set by our ancestors, our kings and government leaders in the cities of Judah and the streets of Jerusalem in the good old days. We had a good life then — lots of food, rising standard of living, and no bad luck. But the moment we quit sacrificing to the Queen of Heaven and pouring out offerings to her, everything fell apart. We've had nothing but massacres and starvation ever since."

¹⁹ And then the women chimed in: "Yes! Absolutely! We're going to keep at it, offering sacrifices to the Queen of Heaven and pouring out offerings to her. Aren't our husbands behind us? They like it that we make goddess cookies and pour out our offerings to her."

²⁰⁻²³ Then Jeremiah spoke up, confronting the men and the women, all the people who had answered so insolently. He said, "The sacrifices that you and your parents, your kings, your government officials, and the common people of the land offered up in the cities of Judah and the streets of Jerusalem — don't you think GOD noticed? He noticed, all right. And he got fed up. Finally, he couldn't take your evil behavior and your disgusting acts any longer. Your land became a wasteland, a death valley, a horror story, a ghost town. And it continues to be just that. This doom has come upon you because you kept offering all those sacrifices, and you sinned against GOD! You refused to listen to him, wouldn't live the way he directed, ignored the covenant conditions."

²⁴⁻²⁵ Jeremiah kept going, but now zeroed in on the women: "Listen, all you

who are from Judah and living in Egypt — please, listen to GOD's Word. GOD-of-the-Angel-Armies, the God of Israel, says: 'You women! You said it and then you did it. You said, "We're going to keep the vows we made to sacrifice to the Queen of Heaven and pour out offerings to her, and nobody's going to stop us!"'

25-27   "Well, go ahead. Keep your vows. Do it up big. But also listen to what GOD has to say about it, all you who are from Judah but live in Egypt: 'I swear by my great name, backed by everything I am — this is GOD speaking! — that never again shall my name be used in vows, such as "As sure as the Master, GOD, lives!" by anyone in the whole country of Egypt. I've targeted each one of you for doom. The good is gone for good.

27-28   "'All the Judeans in Egypt will die off by massacre or starvation until they're wiped out. The few who get out of Egypt alive and back to Judah will be *very* few, hardly worth counting. Then that ragtag bunch that left Judah to live in Egypt will know who had the last word.

29-30   "'And this will be the evidence: I will bring punishment right here, and by this you'll know that the decrees of doom against you are the real thing. Watch for this sign of doom: I will give Pharaoh Hophra king of Egypt over to his enemies, those who are out to kill him, exactly as I gave Zedekiah king of Judah to his enemy Nebuchadnezzar, who was after him.'"

GOD'S PILING ON THE PAIN

1   **45** This is what Jeremiah told Baruch one day in the fourth year of Jehoiakim's reign as he was taking dictation from the prophet:

2-3   "These are the words of GOD, the God of Israel, to you, Baruch. You say, 'These are bad times for me! It's one thing after another. GOD is piling on the pain. I'm worn out and there's no end in sight.'

4-5   "But GOD says, 'Look around. What I've built I'm about to wreck, and what I've planted I'm about to rip up. And I'm doing it everywhere — all over the whole earth! So forget about making any big plans for yourself. Things are going to get worse before they get better. But don't worry. I'll keep you alive through the whole business.'"

YOU VAINLY COLLECT MEDICINES

1   **46** GOD's Messages through the prophet Jeremiah regarding the godless nations.

2-5   The Message to Egypt and the army of Pharaoh Neco king of Egypt at the time it was defeated by Nebuchadnezzar king of Babylon while camped at Carchemish on the Euphrates River in the fourth year of the reign of Jehoiakim king of Judah:

" 'Present arms!
    March to the front!
Harness the horses!
    Up in the saddles!
Battle formation! Helmets on,
    spears sharpened, armor in place!'
But what's this I see?
    They're scared out of their wits!
They break ranks and run for cover.

Their soldiers panic.
They run this way and that,
    stampeding blindly.
It's total chaos, total confusion, danger everywhere!"
    GOD's Decree.

6   "The swiftest runners won't get away,
        the strongest soldiers won't escape.
    In the north country, along the River Euphrates,
        they'll stagger, stumble, and fall.

7-9   "Who is this like the Nile in flood?
        like its streams torrential?
    Why, it's Egypt like the Nile in flood,
        like its streams torrential,
    Saying, 'I'll take over the world.
        I'll wipe out cities and peoples.'
    Run, horses!
        Roll, chariots!
    Advance, soldiers
        from Cush and Put with your shields,
    Soldiers from Lud,
        experts with bow and arrow.

10   "But it's not your day. It's the Master's, me, GOD-of-the-Angel-Armies —
        the day when I have it out with my enemies,
    The day when Sword puts an end to my enemies,
        when Sword exacts vengeance.
    I, the Master, GOD-of-the-Angel-Armies,
        will pile them on an altar — a huge sacrifice! —
    In the great north country,
        along the mighty Euphrates.

11-12   "Oh, virgin Daughter Egypt,
        climb into the mountains of Gilead, get healing balm.
    You will vainly collect medicines,
        for nothing will be able to cure what ails you.
    The whole world will hear your anguished cries.
        Your wails fill the earth,
    As soldier falls against soldier
        and they all go down in a heap."

EGYPT'S ARMY SLITHERS LIKE A SNAKE

13   The Message that GOD gave to the prophet Jeremiah when Nebuchadnezzar
king of Babylon was on his way to attack Egypt:

14   "Tell Egypt, alert Migdol,
        post warnings in Noph and Tahpanhes:
    'Wake up! Be prepared!
        War's coming!'

15-19 "Why will your bull-god Apis run off?
             Because GOD will drive him off.
        Your ragtag army will fall to pieces.
             The word is passing through the ranks,
        'Let's get out of here while we still can.
             Let's head for home and save our skins.'
        When they get home they'll nickname Pharaoh
             'Big-Talk-Bad-Luck.'
        As sure as I am the living God"
             — the King's Decree, GOD-of-the-Angel-Armies is his name —
        "A conqueror is coming: like Tabor, singular among mountains;
             like Carmel, jutting up from the sea!
        So pack your bags for exile,
             you coddled daughters of Egypt,
        For Memphis will soon be nothing,
             a vacant lot grown over with weeds.

20-21 "Too bad, Egypt, a beautiful sleek heifer
             attacked by a horsefly from the north!
        All her hired soldiers are stationed to defend her —
             like well-fed calves they are.
        But when their lives are on the line, they'll run off,
             cowards every one.
        When the going gets tough,
             they'll take the easy way out.

22-24 "Egypt will slither and hiss like a snake
             as the enemy army comes in force.
        They will rush in, swinging axes
             like lumberjacks cutting down trees.
        They'll level the country" — GOD's Decree — "nothing
             and no one standing for as far as you can see.
        The invaders will be a swarm of locusts,
             innumerable, past counting.
        Daughter Egypt will be ravished,
             raped by vandals from the north."

25-26   GOD-of-the-Angel-Armies, the God of Israel, says, "Watch out when I
        visit doom on the god Amon of Thebes, Egypt and its gods and kings,
        Pharaoh and those who trust in him. I'll turn them over to those who are
        out to kill them, to Nebuchadnezzar and his military. Egypt will be set back
        a thousand years. Eventually people will live there again." GOD's Decree.

27-28 "But you, dear Jacob my servant, you have nothing to fear.
             Israel, there's no need to worry.
        Look up! I'll save you from that far country,
             I'll get your children out of the land of exile.
        Things are going to be normal again for Jacob,
             safe and secure, smooth sailing.
        Yes, dear Jacob my servant, you have nothing to fear.

Depend on it, I'm on your side.
I'll finish off all the godless nations
   among which I've scattered you,
But I won't finish you off.
   I have more work left to do on you.
I'll punish you, but fairly.
   No, I'm not finished with you yet."

IT'S DOOMSDAY FOR PHILISTINES

47 1-5 GOD's Message to the prophet Jeremiah regarding the Philistines just before Pharaoh attacked Gaza. This is what GOD says:

"Look out! Water will rise in the north country,
   swelling like a river in flood.
The torrent will flood the land,
   washing away city and citizen.
Men and women will scream in terror,
   wails from every door and window,
As the thunder from the hooves of the horses will be heard,
   the clatter of chariots, the banging of wheels.
Fathers, paralyzed by fear,
   won't even grab up their babies
Because it will be doomsday for Philistines, one and all,
   no hope of help for Tyre and Sidon.
GOD will finish off the Philistines,
   what's left of those from the island of Crete.
Gaza will be shaved bald as an egg,
   Ashkelon struck dumb as a post.
You're on your last legs.
   How long will you keep flailing?

6 "Oh, Sword of GOD,
   how long will you keep this up?
Return to your scabbard.
   Haven't you had enough? Can't you call it quits?

7 "But how can it quit
   when I, GOD, command the action?
I've ordered it to cut down
   Ashkelon and the seacoast."

GET OUT WHILE YOU CAN!

48 1-10 The Message on Moab from GOD-OF-THE-ANGEL-ARMIES, the God of Israel:

"Doom to Nebo! Leveled to the ground!
   Kiriathaim demeaned and defeated,
The mighty fortress reduced to a molehill,
   Moab's glory—dust and ashes.
Conspirators plot Heshbon's doom:
   'Come, let's wipe Moab off the map.'

Dungface Dimon will loudly lament,
   as killing follows killing.
Listen! A cry out of Horonaim:
   'Disaster — doom and more doom!'
Moab will be shattered.
   Her cries will be heard clear down in Zoar.
Up the ascent of Luhith
   climbers weep,
And down the descent from Horonaim,
   cries of loss and devastation.
Oh, run for your lives! Get out while you can!
   Survive by your wits in the wild!
You trusted in thick walls and big money, yes?
   But it won't help you now.
Your big god Chemosh will be hauled off,
   his priests and managers with him.
A wrecker will wreck every city.
   Not a city will survive.
The valley fields will be ruined,
   the plateau pastures destroyed, just as I told you.
Cover the land of Moab with salt.
   Make sure nothing ever grows here again.
Her towns will all be ghost towns.
   Nobody will ever live here again.
Sloppy work in GOD's name is cursed,
   and cursed all halfhearted use of the sword.

11-17 "Moab has always taken it easy —
   lazy as a dog in the sun,
Never had to work for a living,
   never faced any trouble,
Never had to grow up,
   never once worked up a sweat.
But those days are a thing of the past.
   I'll put him to work at hard labor.
That will wake him up to the world of hard knocks.
   That will smash his illusions.
Moab will be as ashamed of god Chemosh
   as Israel was ashamed of her Bethel calf-gods,
   the calf-gods she thought were so great.
For how long do you think you'll be saying, 'We're tough.
   We can beat anyone anywhere'?
The destruction of Moab has already begun.
   Her choice young soldiers are lying dead right now."
The King's Decree —
   his full name, GOD-of-the-Angel-Armies.
"Yes. Moab's doom is on countdown,
   disaster targeted and launched.
Weep for Moab, friends and neighbors,
   all who know how famous he's been.
Lament, 'His mighty scepter snapped in two like a toothpick,

that magnificent royal staff!'

18-20 "Come down from your high horse, pampered beauty of Dibon.
　　Sit in dog dung.
The destroyer of Moab will come against you.
　　He'll wreck your safe, secure houses.
Stand on the roadside,
　　pampered women of Aroer.
Interview the refugees who are running away.
　　Ask them, 'What's happened? And why?'
Moab will be an embarrassing memory, nothing left of the place.
　　Wail and weep your eyes out!
Tell the bad news along the Arnon river.
　　Tell the world that Moab is no more.

21-24 　"My judgment will come to the plateau cities: on Holon, Jahzah, and
Mephaath; on Dibon, Nebo, and Beth-diblathaim; on Kiriathaim, Beth-
gamul, and Beth-meon; on Kerioth, Bozrah, and all the cities of Moab, far
and near.

25 "Moab's link to power is severed.
　　Moab's arm is broken." GOD's Decree.

THE SHEER NOTHINGNESS OF MOAB

26-27 "Turn Moab into a drunken sot, drunk on the wine of my wrath, a dung-
faced drunk, filling the country with vomit — Moab a falling-down drunk,
a joke in bad taste. Wasn't it you, Moab, who made crude jokes over Israel?
And when they were caught in bad company, didn't you cluck and gossip
and snicker?

28 "Leave town! Leave! Look for a home in the cliffs,
　　you who grew up in Moab.
Try living like a dove
　　who nests high in the river gorge.

29-33 "We've all heard of Moab's pride,
　　that legendary pride,
The strutting, bullying, puffed-up pride,
　　the insufferable arrogance.
I know" — GOD's Decree — "his rooster-crowing pride,
　　the inflated claims, the sheer nothingness of Moab.
But I will weep for Moab,
　　yes, I will mourn for the people of Moab.
　　I will even mourn for the people of Kir-heres.
I'll weep for the grapevines of Sibmah
　　and join Jazer in her weeping —
Grapevines that once reached the Dead Sea
　　with tendrils as far as Jazer.
Your summer fruit and your bursting grapes
　　will be looted by brutal plunderers,
Lush Moab stripped

of song and laughter.
And yes, I'll shut down the winepresses,
　stop all the shouts and hurrahs of harvest.

34　　"Heshbon and Elealeh will cry out, and the people in Jahaz will hear
the cries. They will hear them all the way from Zoar to Horonaim and
Eglath-shelishiyah. Even the waters of Nimrim will be dried up.

35　　"I will put a stop in Moab"—GOD's Decree—"to all hiking to the high
places to offer burnt sacrifices to the gods.

36　　"My heart moans for Moab, for the men of Kir-heres, like soft flute
sounds carried by the wind. They've lost it all. They've got nothing.

37　　"Everywhere you look are signs of mourning:
　heads shaved, beards cut,
Hands scratched and bleeding,
　clothes ripped and torn.

38　　"In every house in Moab there'll be loud lamentation, on every street in
Moab, loud lamentation. As with a pottery jug that no one wants, I'll smash
Moab to bits." GOD's Decree.

39　"Moab ruined!
　Moab shamed and ashamed to be seen!
Moab a cruel joke!
　The stark horror of Moab!"

40-42　GOD's verdict on Moab. Indeed!

"Look! An eagle is about to swoop down
　and spread its wings over Moab.
The towns will be captured,
　the fortresses taken.
Brave warriors will double up in pain, helpless to fight,
　like a woman giving birth to a baby.
There'll be nothing left of Moab, nothing at all,
　because of his defiant arrogance against me.

43-44　"Terror and pit and trap
　are what you have facing you, Moab." GOD's Decree.
"A man running in terror
　will fall into a trap.
A man climbing out of a pit
　will be caught in a trap.
This is my agenda for Moab
　on doomsday." GOD's Decree.

45-47　"On the outskirts of Heshbon,
　refugees will pull up short, worn out.
Fire will flame high from Heshbon,
　a firestorm raging from the capital of Sihon's kingdom.

It will burn off Moab's eyebrows,
will scorch the skull of the braggarts.
That's all for you, Moab!
You worshipers of Chemosh will be finished off!
Your sons will be trucked off to prison camps;
your daughters will be herded into exile.
But yet there's a day that's coming
when I'll put things right in Moab.

"For now, that's the judgment on Moab."

YOU'RE A BROKEN-DOWN HAS-BEEN

1-6

49 GOD's Message on the Ammonites:

"Doesn't Israel have any children,
no one to step into her inheritance?
So why is the god Milcom taking over Gad's land,
his followers moving into its towns?
But not for long! The time's coming"
— GOD's Decree —
"When I'll fill the ears of Rabbah, Ammon's big city,
with battle cries.
She'll end up a pile of rubble,
all her towns burned to the ground.
Then Israel will kick out the invaders.
I, GOD, say so, and it will *be* so.
Wail Heshbon, Ai is in ruins.
Villages of Rabbah, wring your hands!
Dress in mourning, weep buckets of tears.
Go into hysterics, run around in circles!
Your god Milcom will be hauled off to exile,
and all his priests and managers right with him.
Why do you brag of your once-famous strength?
You're a broken-down has-been, a castoff
Who fondles his trophies and dreams of glory days
and vainly thinks, 'No one can lay a hand on me.'
Well, think again. I'll face you with terror from all sides."
Word of the Master, GOD-of-the-Angel-Armies.
"You'll be stampeded headlong,
with no one to round up the runaways.
Still, the time will come
when I will make things right with Ammon." GOD's Decree.

STRUTTING ACROSS THE STAGE OF HISTORY

7-11

The Message of GOD-of-the-Angel-Armies on Edom:

"Is there nobody wise left in famous Teman?
no one with a sense of reality?
Has their wisdom gone wormy and rotten?
Run for your lives! Get out while you can!
Find a good place to hide,

you who live in Dedan!
I'm bringing doom to Esau.
   It's time to settle accounts.
When harvesters work your fields,
   don't they leave gleanings?
When burglars break into your house,
   don't they take only what they want?
But I'll strip Esau clean.
   I'll search out every nook and cranny.
I'll destroy everything connected with him,
   children and relatives and neighbors.
There'll be no one left who will be able to say,
   'I'll take care of your orphans.
   Your widows can depend on me.'"

12-13   Indeed. GOD says, "I tell you, if there are people who have to drink the cup of God's wrath even though they don't deserve it, why would you think you'd get off? You won't get off. You'll drink it. Oh yes, you'll drink every drop. And as for Bozrah, your capital, I swear by all that I am"—GOD's Decree—"that that city will end up a pile of charred ruins, a stinking garbage dump, an obscenity—and all her daughter-cities with her."

14   I've just heard the latest from GOD.
   He's sent an envoy to the nations:
"Muster your troops and attack Edom.
   Present arms! Go to war!"

15-16   "Ah, Edom, I'm dropping you to last place among nations,
   the bottom of the heap, kicked around.
You think you're so great—
   strutting across the stage of history,
Living high in the impregnable rocks,
   acting like king of the mountain.
You think you're above it all, don't you,
   like an eagle in its aerie?
Well, you're headed for a fall.
   I'll bring you crashing to the ground." GOD's Decree.

17-18   "Edom will end up trash. Stinking, despicable trash. A wonder of the world in reverse. She'll join Sodom and Gomorrah and their neighbors in the sewers of history." GOD says so.

"No one will live there,
   no mortal soul move in there.

19   "Watch this: Like a lion coming up
   from the thick jungle of the Jordan
Looking for prey in the mountain pastures,
   I will come upon Edom and pounce.
I'll take my pick of the flock—and who's to stop me?
   The shepherds of Edom are helpless before me."

20-22 So, listen to this plan that GOD has worked out against Edom, the blueprint of what he's prepared for those who live in Teman:

"Believe it or not, the young, the vulnerable —
    mere lambs and kids — will be dragged off.
Believe it or not, the flock
    in shock, helpless to help, will watch it happen.
The very earth will shudder because of their cries,
    cries of anguish heard at the distant Red Sea.
Look! An eagle soars, swoops down,
    spreads its wings over Bozrah.
Brave warriors will double up in pain, helpless to fight,
    like a woman giving birth to a baby."

THE BLOOD WILL DRAIN FROM THE FACE OF DAMASCUS

23-27 The Message on Damascus:

"Hamath and Arpad will be in shock
    when they hear the bad news.
Their hearts will melt in fear
    as they pace back and forth in worry.
The blood will drain from the face of Damascus
    as she turns to flee.
Hysterical, she'll fall to pieces,
    disabled, like a woman in childbirth.
And now how lonely — bereft, abandoned!
    The once famous city, the once happy city.
Her bright young men dead in the streets,
    her brave warriors silent as death.
On that day" — Decree of GOD-of-the-Angel-Armies —
    "I'll start a fire at the wall of Damascus
    that will burn down all of Ben-hadad's forts."

FIND A SAFE PLACE TO HIDE

28-33 The Message on Kedar and the sheikdoms of Hazor who were attacked
by Nebuchadnezzar king of Babylon. This is GOD's Message:

"On your feet! Attack Kedar!
    Plunder the Bedouin nomads from the east.
    Grab their blankets and pots and pans.
Steal their camels.
    Traumatize them, shouting, 'Terror! Death! Doom!
Danger everywhere!'
    Oh, run for your lives,
You nomads from Hazor." GOD's Decree.
    "Find a safe place to hide.
Nebuchadnezzar king of Babylon
    has plans to wipe you out,
    to go after you with a vengeance:
'After them,' he says. 'Go after these relaxed nomads
    who live free and easy in the desert,

Who live in the open with no doors to lock,
    who live off by themselves.'
Their camels are there for the taking,
    their herds and flocks, easy picking.
I'll scatter them to the four winds,
    these defenseless nomads on the fringes of the desert.
I'll bring terror from every direction.
    They won't know what hit them." GOD's Decree.
"Jackals will take over the camps of Hazor,
    camps abandoned to wind and sand.
No one will live there,
    no mortal soul move in there."

THE WINDS WILL BLOW AWAY ELAM

34-39 GOD's Message to the prophet Jeremiah on Elam at the outset of the reign of Zedekiah king of Judah. This is what GOD-of-the-Angel-Armies says:

"Watch this! I'll break Elam's bow,
    her weapon of choice, across my knee.
Then I'll let four winds loose on Elam,
    winds from the four corners of earth.
I'll blow them away in all directions,
    landing homeless Elamites in every country on earth.
They'll live in constant fear and terror
    among enemies who want to kill them.
I'll bring doom on them,
    my anger-fueled doom.
I'll set murderous hounds on their heels
    until there's nothing left of them.
And then I'll set up my throne in Elam,
    having thrown out the king and his henchmen.
But the time will come when I make
    everything right for Elam again." GOD's Decree.

GET OUT OF BABYLON AS FAST AS YOU CAN

1-3 **50** The Message of GOD through the prophet Jeremiah on Babylon, land of the Chaldeans:

"Get the word out to the nations! Preach it!
    Go public with this, broadcast it far and wide:
Babylon taken, god-Bel hanging his head in shame,
    god-Marduk exposed as a fraud.
All her god-idols shuffling in shame,
    all her play-gods exposed as cheap frauds.
For a nation will come out of the north to attack her,
    reduce her cities to rubble.
Empty of life — no animals, no people —
    not a sound, not a movement, not a breath.

4-5 "In those days, at that time" — GOD's Decree —

"the people of Israel will come,
  And the people of Judah with them.
    Walking and weeping, they'll seek me, their GOD.
They'll ask directions to Zion
  and set their faces toward Zion.
They'll come and hold tight to GOD,
  bound in a covenant eternal they'll never forget.

6-7 "My people were lost sheep.
    Their shepherds led them astray.
They abandoned them in the mountains
  where they wandered aimless through the hills.
They lost track of home,
  couldn't remember where they came from.
Everyone who met them took advantage of them.
  Their enemies had no qualms:
'Fair game,' they said. 'They walked out on GOD.
  They abandoned the True Pasture, the hope of their parents.'

8-10 "But now, get out of Babylon as fast as you can.
    Be rid of that Babylonian country.
On your way. Good sheepdogs lead, but don't you be led.
  Lead the way home!
Do you see what I'm doing?
  I'm rallying a host of nations against Babylon.
They'll come out of the north,
  attack and take her.
Oh, they know how to fight, these armies.
  They never come home empty-handed.
Babylon is ripe for picking!
  All her plunderers will fill their bellies!" GOD's Decree.

11-16 "You Babylonians had a good time while it lasted, didn't you?
    You lived it up, exploiting and using my people,
Frisky calves romping in lush pastures,
  wild stallions out having a good time!
Well, your mother would hardly be proud of you.
  The woman who bore you wouldn't be pleased.
Look at what's come of you! A nothing nation!
  Rubble and garbage and weeds!
Emptied of life by my holy anger,
  a desert of death and emptiness.
Travelers who pass by Babylon will gasp, appalled,
  shaking their heads at such a comedown.
Gang up on Babylon! Pin her down!
  Throw everything you have against her.
Hold nothing back. Knock her flat.
  She's sinned — oh, how she's sinned, against me!
Shout battle cries from every direction.
  All the fight has gone out of her.
Her defenses have been flattened,

her walls smashed.
'Operation GOD's Vengeance.'
  Pile on the vengeance!
Do to her as she has done.
  Give her a good dose of her own medicine!
Destroy her farms and farmers,
  ravage her fields, empty her barns.
And you captives, while the destruction rages,
  get out while the getting's good,
  get out fast and run for home.

17 "Israel is a scattered flock,
  hunted down by lions.
The king of Assyria started the carnage.
  The king of Babylon, Nebuchadnezzar,
Has completed the job,
  gnawing the bones clean."

18-20 And now this is what GOD-of-the-Angel-Armies,
  the God of Israel, has to say:
"Just watch! I'm bringing doom on the king of Babylon and his land,
  the same doom I brought on the king of Assyria.
But Israel I'll bring home to good pastures.
  He'll graze on the hills of Carmel and Bashan,
On the slopes of Ephraim and Gilead.
  He will eat to his heart's content.
In those days and at that time" — GOD's Decree —
  "they'll look high and low for a sign of Israel's guilt — nothing;
Search nook and cranny for a trace of Judah's sin — nothing.
  These people that I've saved will start out with a clean slate.

21 "Attack Merathaim, land of rebels!
  Go after Pekod, country of doom!
Hunt them down. Make a clean sweep." GOD's Decree.
  "These are my orders. Do what I tell you.

22-24 "The thunderclap of battle
  shakes the foundations!
The Hammer has been hammered,
  smashed and splintered,
Babylon pummeled
  beyond recognition.
I set out a trap and you were caught in it.
  O Babylon, you never knew what hit you,
Caught and held in the steel grip of that trap!
  That's what you get for taking on GOD.

25-28 "I, GOD, opened my arsenal.
  I brought out my weapons of wrath.

The Master, GOD-of-the-Angel-Armies,
    has a job to do in Babylon.
Come at her from all sides!
    Break into her granaries!
Shovel her into piles and burn her up.
    Leave nothing! Leave no one!
Kill all her young turks.
    Send them to their doom!
Doom to them! Yes, Doomsday!
    The clock has finally run out on them.
And here's a surprise:
    Runaways and escapees from Babylon
Show up in Zion reporting the news of GOD's vengeance,
    taking vengeance for my own Temple.

29-30 "Call in the troops against Babylon,
    anyone who can shoot straight!
Tighten the noose!
    Leave no loopholes!
Give her back as good as she gave,
    a dose of her own medicine!
Her brazen insolence is an outrage
    against GOD, The Holy of Israel.
And now she pays: her young strewn dead in the streets,
    her soldiers dead, silent forever." GOD's Decree.

31-32 "Do you get it, Mister Pride? I'm your enemy!"
    Decree of the Master, GOD-of-the-Angel-Armies.
"Time's run out on you:
    That's right: It's Doomsday.
Mister Pride will fall flat on his face.
    No one will offer him a hand.
I'll set his towns on fire.
    The fire will spread wild through the country."

33-34 And here's more from GOD-of-the-Angel-Armies:

"The people of Israel are beaten down,
    the people of Judah along with them.
Their oppressors have them in a grip of steel.
    They won't let go.
But the Rescuer is strong:
    GOD-of-the-Angel-Armies.
Yes, I will take their side,
    I'll come to their rescue.
I'll soothe their land,
    but rough up the people of Babylon.

35-40 "It's all-out war in Babylon" — GOD's Decree —
    "total war against people, leaders, and the wise!

War to the death on her boasting pretenders, fools one and all!
    War to the death on her soldiers, cowards to a man!
War to the death on her hired killers, gutless wonders!
    War to the death on her banks—looted!
War to the death on her water supply—drained dry!
    A land of make-believe gods gone crazy—hobgoblins!
The place will be haunted with jackals and scorpions,
    night-owls and vampire bats.
No one will ever live there again.
    The land will reek with the stench of death.
It will join Sodom and Gomorrah and their neighbors,
    the cities I did away with." GOD's Decree.
"No one will live there again.
    No one will again draw breath in that land, ever.

41-43 "And now, watch this! People pouring
    out of the north, hordes of people,
A mob of kings stirred up
    from far-off places.
Flourishing deadly weapons,
    barbarians they are, cruel and pitiless.
Roaring and relentless, like ocean breakers,
    they come riding fierce stallions,
In battle formation, ready to fight
    you, Daughter Babylon!
Babylon's king hears them coming.
    He goes white as a ghost, limp as a dishrag.
Terror-stricken, he doubles up in pain, helpless to fight,
    like a woman giving birth to a baby.

44 "And now watch this: Like a lion coming up
    from the thick jungle of the Jordan,
Looking for prey in the mountain pastures,
    I'll take over and pounce.
I'll take my pick of the flock—and who's to stop me?
    All the so-called shepherds are helpless before me."

45-46 So, listen to this plan that GOD has worked out against Babylon, the blueprint of what he's prepared for dealing with Chaldea:

Believe it or not, the young,
    the vulnerable—mere lambs and kids—will be dragged off.
Believe it or not, the flock
    in shock, helpless to help, watches it happen.
When the shout goes up, "Babylon's down!"
    the very earth will shudder at the sound.
    The news will be heard all over the world.

HURRICANE PERSIA

51 ¹⁻⁵ There's more. GOD says more:

"Watch this:
  I'm whipping up
A death-dealing hurricane against Babylon — 'Hurricane Persia' —
  against all who live in that perverse land.
I'm sending a cleanup crew into Babylon.
  They'll clean the place out from top to bottom.
When they get through there'll be nothing left of her
  worth taking or talking about.
They won't miss a thing.
  A total and final Doomsday!
Fighters will fight with everything they've got.
  It's no-holds-barred.
They will spare nothing and no one.
  It's final and wholesale destruction — the end!
Babylon littered with the wounded,
  streets piled with corpses.
It turns out that Israel and Judah
  are not widowed after all.
As their God, GOD-of-the-Angel-Armies, I am still alive and well,
  committed to them even though
They filled their land with sin
  against Israel's most Holy God.

6-8 "Get out of Babylon as fast as you can.
  Run for your lives! Save your necks!
Don't linger and lose your lives to my vengeance on her
  as I pay her back for her sins.
Babylon was a fancy gold chalice
  held in my hand,
Filled with the wine of my anger
  to make the whole world drunk.
The nations drank the wine
  and they've all gone crazy.
Babylon herself will stagger and crash,
  senseless in a drunken stupor — tragic!
Get anointing balm for her wound.
  Maybe she can be cured."

9 "We did our best, but she can't be helped.
  Babylon is past fixing.
Give her up to her fate.
  Go home.
The judgment on her will be vast,
  a skyscraper-memorial of vengeance.

Your Lifeline Is Cut

10　"God has set everything right for us.
　　　Come! Let's tell the good news
　　Back home in Zion.
　　　Let's tell what our God did to set things right.

11-13　"Sharpen the arrows!
　　　Fill the quivers!
　　God has stirred up the kings of the Medes,
　　　infecting them with war fever: 'Destroy Babylon!'
　　God's on the warpath.
　　　He's out to avenge his Temple.
　　Give the signal to attack Babylon's walls.
　　　Station guards around the clock.
　　Bring in reinforcements.
　　　Set men in ambush.
　　God will do what he planned,
　　　what he said he'd do to the people of Babylon.
　　You have more water than you need,
　　　you have more money than you need —
　　But your life is over,
　　　your lifeline cut."

14　God-of-the-Angel-Armies has solemnly sworn:
　　　"I'll fill this place with soldiers.
　　They'll swarm through here like locusts
　　　chanting victory songs over you."

15-19　By his power he made earth.
　　　His wisdom gave shape to the world.
　　　He crafted the cosmos.
　　He thunders and rain pours down.
　　　He sends the clouds soaring.
　　He embellishes the storm with lightnings,
　　　launches the wind from his warehouse.
　　Stick-god worshipers look mighty foolish!
　　　god-makers embarrassed by their handmade gods!
　　Their gods are frauds, dead sticks —
　　　deadwood gods, tasteless jokes.
　　They're nothing but stale smoke.
　　　When the smoke clears, they're gone.
　　But the Portion-of-Jacob is the real thing;
　　　he put the whole universe together,
　　With special attention to Israel.
　　　His name? God-of-the-Angel-Armies!

They'll Sleep and Never Wake Up

20-23　God says, "You, Babylon, are my hammer,

my weapon of war.
I'll use you to smash godless nations,
    use you to knock kingdoms to bits.
I'll use you to smash horse and rider,
    use you to smash chariot and driver.
I'll use you to smash man and woman,
    use you to smash the old man and the boy.
I'll use you to smash the young man and young woman,
    use you to smash shepherd and sheep.
I'll use you to smash farmer and yoked oxen,
    use you to smash governors and senators.

24   "Judeans, you'll see it with your own eyes. I'll pay Babylon and all the Chaldeans back for all the evil they did in Zion." GOD's Decree.

25-26 "I'm your enemy, Babylon, Mount Destroyer,
    you ravager of the whole earth.
I'll reach out, I'll take you in my hand,
    and I'll crush you till there's no mountain left.
I'll turn you into a gravel pit—
    no more cornerstones cut from you,
No more foundation stones quarried from you!
    Nothing left of you but gravel." GOD's Decree.

27-28 "Raise the signal in the land,
    blow the shofar-trumpet for the nations.
Consecrate the nations for holy work against her.
    Call kingdoms into service against her.
    Enlist Ararat, Minni, and Ashkenaz.
Appoint a field marshal against her,
    and round up horses, locust hordes of horses!
Consecrate the nations for holy work against her—
    the king of the Medes, his leaders and people.

29-33 "The very land trembles in terror, writhes in pain,
    terrorized by my plans against Babylon,
Plans to turn the country of Babylon
    into a lifeless moonscape—a wasteland.
Babylon's soldiers have quit fighting.
    They hide out in ruins and caves—
Cowards who've given up without a fight,
    exposed as cowering milksops.
Babylon's houses are going up in flames,
    the city gates torn off their hinges.
Runner after runner comes racing in,
    each on the heels of the last,
Bringing reports to the king of Babylon
    that his city is a lost cause.
The fords of the rivers are all taken.
    Wildfire rages through the swamp grass.

Soldiers desert left and right.
  I, GOD-of-the-Angel-Armies, said it would happen:
'Daughter Babylon is a threshing floor
  at threshing time.
Soon, oh very soon, her harvest will come
  and then the chaff will fly!'

34-37   "Nebuchadnezzar king of Babylon
  chewed up my people and spit out the bones.
He wiped his dish clean, pushed back his chair,
  and belched — a huge gluttonous belch.
Lady Zion says,
  'The brutality done to me be done to Babylon!'
And Jerusalem says,
  'The blood spilled from me be charged to the Chaldeans!'
Then I, GOD, step in and say,
  'I'm on your side, taking up your cause.
I'm your Avenger. You'll get your revenge.
  I'll dry up her rivers, plug up her springs.
Babylon will be a pile of rubble,
  scavenged by stray dogs and cats,
A dumping ground for garbage,
  a godforsaken ghost town.'

38-40   "The Babylonians will be like lions and their cubs,
  ravenous, roaring for food.
I'll fix them a meal, all right — a banquet, in fact.
  They'll drink themselves falling-down drunk.
Dead drunk, they'll sleep — and sleep, and sleep . . .
  and they'll never wake up." GOD's Decree.
"I'll haul these 'lions' off to the slaughterhouse
  like the lambs, rams, and goats,
    never to be heard of again.

41-48   "Babylon is finished —
  the pride of the whole earth is flat on her face.
What a comedown for Babylon,
  to end up inglorious in the sewer!
Babylon drowned in chaos,
  battered by waves of enemy soldiers.
Her towns stink with decay and rot,
  the land empty and bare and sterile.
No one lives in these towns anymore.
  Travelers give them a wide berth.
I'll bring doom on the glutton god-Bel in Babylon.
  I'll make him vomit up all he gulped down.
No more visitors stream into this place,
  admiring and gawking at the wonders of Babylon.

The wonders of Babylon are no more.
Run for your lives, my dear people!
Run, and don't look back!
Get out of this place while you can,
this place torched by GOD's raging anger.
Don't lose hope. Don't ever give up
when the rumors pour in hot and heavy.
One year it's this, the next year it's that—
rumors of violence, rumors of war.
Trust me, the time is coming
when I'll put the no-gods of Babylon in their place.
I'll show up the whole country as a sickening fraud,
with dead bodies strewn all over the place.
Heaven and earth, angels and people,
will throw a victory party over Babylon
When the avenging armies from the north
descend on her." GOD's Decree!

REMEMBER GOD IN YOUR LONG AND DISTANT EXILE

49-50 "Babylon must fall—
compensation for the war dead in Israel.
Babylonians will be killed
because of all that Babylonian killing.
But you exiles who have escaped a Babylonian death,
get out! And fast!
Remember GOD in your long and distant exile.
Keep Jerusalem alive in your memory."

51 How we've been humiliated, taunted and abused,
kicked around for so long that we hardly know who we are!
And we hardly know what to think—
our old Sanctuary, GOD's house, desecrated by strangers.

52-53 "I know, but trust me: The time is coming"
—GOD's Decree—
"When I will bring doom on her no-god idols,
and all over this land her wounded will groan.
Even if Babylon climbed a ladder to the moon
and pulled up the ladder so that no one could get to her,
That wouldn't stop me.
I'd make sure my avengers would reach her."
GOD's Decree.

54-56 "But now listen! Do you hear it? A cry out of Babylon!
An unearthly wail out of Chaldea!
GOD is taking his wrecking bar to Babylon.
We'll be hearing the last of her noise—
Death throes like the crashing of waves,
death rattles like the roar of cataracts.
The avenging destroyer is about to enter Babylon:
Her soldiers are taken, her weapons are trashed.

Indeed, GOD is a God who evens things out.
    All end up with their just deserts.

57 "I'll get them drunk, the whole lot of them —
    princes, sages, governors, soldiers.
Dead drunk, they'll sleep — and sleep and sleep . . .
    and never wake up." The King's Decree.
His name? GOD-of-the-Angel-Armies!

58   GOD-of-the-Angel-Armies speaks:

"The city walls of Babylon — those massive walls! —
    will be flattened.
And those city gates — huge gates! —
    will be set on fire.
The harder you work at this empty life,
    the less you are.
Nothing comes of ambition like this
    but ashes."

59 Jeremiah the prophet gave a job to Seraiah son of Neriah, son of Mahseiah, when Seraiah went with Zedekiah king of Judah to Babylon. It was in the fourth year of Zedekiah's reign. Seraiah was in charge of travel arrangements.

60-62 Jeremiah had written down in a little booklet all the bad things that would come down on Babylon. He told Seraiah, "When you get to Babylon, read this out in public. Read, 'You, O GOD, said that you would destroy this place so that nothing could live here, neither human nor animal — a wasteland to top all wastelands, an eternal nothing.'

63-64 "When you've finished reading the page, tie a stone to it, throw it into the River Euphrates, and watch it sink. Then say, 'That's how Babylon will sink to the bottom and stay there after the disaster I'm going to bring upon her.'"

THE DESTRUCTION OF JERUSALEM AND EXILE OF JUDAH

1 **52** Zedekiah was twenty-one years old when he started out as king. He was king in Jerusalem for eleven years. His mother's name was Hamutal, the daughter of Jeremiah. Her hometown was Libnah.

2 As far as GOD was concerned, Zedekiah was just one more evil king, a carbon copy of Jehoiakim.

3-5 The source of all this doom to Jerusalem and Judah was GOD's anger. GOD turned his back on them as an act of judgment.

Zedekiah revolted against the king of Babylon. Nebuchadnezzar set out for Jerusalem with a full army. He set up camp and sealed off the city by building siege mounds around it. He arrived on the ninth year and tenth month of Zedekiah's reign. The city was under siege for nineteen months (until the eleventh year of Zedekiah).

6-8 By the fourth month of Zedekiah's eleventh year, on the ninth day of the month, the famine was so bad that there wasn't so much as a crumb of bread for anyone. Then the Babylonians broke through the city walls. Under cover of the night darkness, the entire Judean army fled through an opening in the wall (it was the gate between the two walls above the King's Garden). They slipped through the lines of the Babylonians who surrounded the city and headed for the Jordan into the Arabah Valley, but the Babylonians were in full pursuit. They caught up with them in the Plains of Jericho. But by then Zedekiah's army had deserted and was scattered.

9-11 The Babylonians captured Zedekiah and marched him off to the king of Babylon at Riblah in Hamath, who tried and sentenced him on the spot. The king of Babylon then killed Zedekiah's sons right before his eyes. The summary murder of his sons was the last thing Zedekiah saw, for they then blinded him. The king of Babylon followed that up by killing all the officials of Judah. Securely handcuffed, Zedekiah was hauled off to Babylon. The king of Babylon threw him in prison, where he stayed until the day he died.

12-16 In the nineteenth year of Nebuchadnezzar king of Babylon on the seventh day of the fifth month, Nebuzaradan, the king of Babylon's chief deputy, arrived in Jerusalem. He burned the Temple of GOD to the ground, went on to the royal palace, and then finished off the city. He burned the whole place down. He put the Babylonian troops he had with him to work knocking down the city walls. Finally, he rounded up everyone left in the city, including those who had earlier deserted to the king of Babylon, and took them off into exile. He left a few poor dirt farmers behind to tend the vineyards and what was left of the fields.

17-19 The Babylonians broke up the bronze pillars, the bronze washstands, and the huge bronze basin (the Sea) that were in the Temple of GOD, and hauled the bronze off to Babylon. They also took the various bronze-crafted liturgical accessories, as well as the gold and silver censers and sprinkling bowls, used in the services of Temple worship. The king's deputy didn't miss a thing. He took every scrap of precious metal he could find.

20-23 The amount of bronze they got from the two pillars, the Sea, the twelve bronze bulls that supported the Sea, and the ten washstands that Solomon had made for the Temple of GOD was enormous. They couldn't weigh it all! Each pillar stood twenty-seven feet high with a circumference of eighteen feet. The pillars were hollow, the bronze a little less than an inch thick. Each pillar was topped with an ornate capital of bronze pomegranates and filigree, which added another seven and a half feet to its height. There were ninety-six pomegranates evenly spaced—in all, a hundred pomegranates worked into the filigree.

24-27 The king's deputy took a number of special prisoners: Seraiah the chief priest, Zephaniah the associate priest, three wardens, the chief remaining army officer, seven of the king's counselors who happened to be in the city, the chief recruiting officer for the army, and sixty men of standing from among the people who were still there. Nebuzaradan the king's deputy marched them all off to the king of Babylon at Riblah. And there at Riblah, in the land of Hamath, the king of Babylon killed the lot of them in cold blood.

Judah went into exile, orphaned from her land.

28 3,023 men of Judah were taken into exile by Nebuchadnezzar in the seventh year of his reign.

29   832 from Jerusalem were taken in the eighteenth year of his reign.

30   745 men from Judah were taken off by Nebuzaradan, the king's chief deputy, in Nebuchadnezzar's twenty-third year.

The total number of exiles was 4,600.

31-34   When Jehoiachin king of Judah had been in exile for thirty-seven years, Evil-Merodach became king in Babylon and let Jehoiachin out of prison. This release took place on the twenty-fifth day of the twelfth month. The king treated him most courteously and gave him preferential treatment beyond anything experienced by the political prisoners held in Babylon. Jehoiachin took off his prison garb and from then on ate his meals in company with the king. The king provided everything he needed to live comfortably for the rest of his life.

LAMENTATIONS

Lamentations is a concentrated and intense biblical witness to suffering. Suffering is a huge, unavoidable element in the human condition. To be human is to suffer. No one gets an exemption. It comes as no surprise then to find that our Holy Scriptures, immersed as they are in the human condition, provide extensive witness to suffering.

There are two polar events in the history of the Hebrew people: the Exodus from Egypt and the Exile into Babylon. Exodus is the definitive story of salvation into a free life. God delivered his people from Egyptian slavery (in about 1200 B.C.). It is a story of freedom. It's accompanied by singing and dancing—an exuberant experience. Exile is the definitive story of judgment accompanied by immense suffering. God's people are taken into Babylonian slavery (the fall of Jerusalem in 587 B.C. marks the event). It is a time of devastation and lament. It is a terrible experience. The two events, Exodus and Exile, are bookends holding together the wide-ranging experiences of God's people that fall between the exuberance that accompanies salvation and the suffering associated with judgment.

Lamentations, written out of the Exile experience, provides the community of faith with a form and vocabulary for dealing with loss and pain. The precipitating event, the fall of Jerusalem, is told in 2 Kings 25 and Jeremiah 52. It is impossible to overstate either the intensity or the complexity of the suffering that came to a head in the devastation of Jerusalem and then continued on into the seventy years of exile in Babylon. Loss was total. Carnage was rampant. Cannibalism and sacrilege were twin horrors stalking the streets of destroyed Jerusalem. The desperate slaying of innocent children showed complete loss of respect for human worth, and the angry murder of priests showed absolute loss of respect for divine will. The worst that can happen to body and spirit, to person and nation, happened here—a nadir of suffering. And throughout the world the suffering continues, both in large-scale horrors and in personal agonies.

Neither explaining suffering nor offering a program for the elimination of suffering, Lamentations keeps company with the extensive biblical witness that gives dignity to suffering by insisting that God enters our suffering and is companion to our suffering.

LAMENTATIONS

WORTHLESS, CHEAP, ABJECT!

1 **1** Oh, oh, oh . . .
How empty the city, once teeming with people.
   A widow, this city, once in the front rank of nations,
once queen of the ball, she's now a drudge in the kitchen.

2 She cries herself to sleep each night, tears soaking her pillow.
   No one's left among her lovers to sit and hold her hand.
   Her friends have all dumped her.

3 After years of pain and hard labor, Judah has gone into exile.
   She camps out among the nations, never feels at home.
   Hunted by all, she's stuck between a rock and a hard place.

4 Zion's roads weep, empty of pilgrims headed to the feasts.
   All her city gates are deserted, her priests in despair.
   Her virgins are sad. How bitter her fate.

5 Her enemies have become her masters. Her foes are living it up
   because GOD laid her low, punishing her repeated rebellions.
   Her children, prisoners of the enemy, trudge into exile.

6 All beauty has drained from Daughter Zion's face.
   Her princes are like deer famished for food,
   chased to exhaustion by hunters.

7 Jerusalem remembers the day she lost everything,
   when her people fell into enemy hands, and not a soul there to help.
   Enemies looked on and laughed, laughed at her helpless silence.

8 Jerusalem, who outsinned the whole world, is an outcast.
   All who admired her despise her now that they see beneath the surface.
   Miserable, she groans and turns away in shame.

9 She played fast and loose with life, she never considered tomorrow,
   and now she's crashed royally, with no one to hold her hand:
   "Look at my pain, O GOD! And how the enemy cruelly struts."

10 The enemy reached out to take all her favorite things. She watched
   as pagans barged into her Sanctuary, those very people for whom
   you posted orders: KEEP OUT: THIS ASSEMBLY OFF-LIMITS.

11 All the people groaned, so desperate for food, so desperate to stay alive
   that they bartered their favorite things for a bit of breakfast:
   "O GOD, look at me! Worthless, cheap, abject!

12 "And you passersby, look at me! Have you ever seen anything like this?
   Ever seen pain like my pain, seen what he did to me,
   what GOD did to me in his rage?

13 "He struck me with lightning, skewered me from head to foot,
   then he set traps all around so I could hardly move.
   He left me with nothing—left me sick, and sick of living.

14 "He wove my sins into a rope
   and harnessed me to captivity's yoke.
   I'm goaded by cruel taskmasters.

15 "The Master piled up my best soldiers in a heap,
   then called in thugs to break their fine young necks.
   The Master crushed the life out of fair virgin Judah.

16 "For all this I weep, weep buckets of tears,
   and not a soul within miles around cares for my soul.
   My children are wasted, my enemy got his way."

17 Zion reached out for help, but no one helped.
   GOD ordered Jacob's enemies to surround him,
   and now no one wants anything to do with Jerusalem.

18 "GOD has right on his side. I'm the one who did wrong.
   Listen everybody! Look at what I'm going through!
   My fair young women, my fine young men, all herded into exile!

19 "I called to my friends; they betrayed me.
   My priests and my leaders only looked after themselves,
   trying but failing to save their own skins.

20 "O GOD, look at the trouble I'm in! My stomach in knots,
   my heart wrecked by a life of rebellion.
   Massacres in the streets, starvation in the houses.

21 "Oh, listen to my groans. No one listens, no one cares.
   When my enemies heard of the trouble you gave me, they cheered.
   Bring on Judgment Day! Let them get what I got!

22 "Take a good look at their evil ways and give it to them!
   Give them what you gave me for my sins.
   Groaning in pain, body and soul, I've had all I can take."

GOD WALKED AWAY FROM HIS HOLY TEMPLE

2 Oh, oh, oh . . .
  How the Master has cut down Daughter Zion
     from the skies, dashed Israel's glorious city to earth,
  in his anger treated his favorite as throwaway junk.

2   The Master, without a second thought, took Israel in one gulp.
      Raging, he smashed Judah's defenses,
      made hash of her king and princes.

3   His anger blazing, he knocked Israel flat,
      broke Israel's arm and turned his back just as the enemy approached,
      came on Jacob like a wildfire from every direction.

4   Like an enemy, he aimed his bow, bared his sword,
      and killed our young men, our pride and joy.
      His anger, like fire, burned down the homes in Zion.

5   The Master became the enemy. He had Israel for supper.
      He chewed up and spit out all the defenses.
      He left Daughter Judah moaning and groaning.

6   He plowed up his old trysting place, trashed his favorite rendezvous.
      GOD wiped out Zion's memories of feast days and Sabbaths,
      angrily sacked king and priest alike.

7   GOD abandoned his altar, walked away from his holy Temple
      and turned the fortifications over to the enemy.
      As they cheered in GOD's Temple, you'd have thought it was a feast day!

8   GOD drew up plans to tear down the walls of Daughter Zion.
      He assembled his crew, set to work and went at it.
      Total demolition! The stones wept!

9   Her city gates, iron bars and all, disappeared in the rubble:
      her kings and princes off to exile — no one left to instruct or lead;
      her prophets useless — they neither saw nor heard anything from GOD.

10   The elders of Daughter Zion sit silent on the ground.
      They throw dust on their heads, dress in rough penitential burlap —
      the young virgins of Jerusalem, their faces creased with the dirt.

11   My eyes are blind with tears, my stomach in a knot.
      My insides have turned to jelly over my people's fate.
      Babies and children are fainting all over the place,

12   Calling to their mothers, "I'm hungry! I'm thirsty!"
      then fainting like dying soldiers in the streets,
      breathing their last in their mothers' laps.

13   How can I understand your plight, dear Jerusalem?
      What can I say to give you comfort, dear Zion?
      Who can put you together again? This bust-up is past understanding.

14   Your prophets courted you with sweet talk.
      They didn't face you with your sin so that you could repent.
      Their sermons were all wishful thinking, deceptive illusions.

15 Astonished, passersby can't believe what they see.
They rub their eyes, they shake their heads over Jerusalem.
Is this the city voted "Most Beautiful" and "Best Place to Live"?

16 But now your enemies gape, slack-jawed.
Then they rub their hands in glee: "We've got them!
We've been waiting for this! Here it is!"

17 GOD did carry out, item by item, exactly what he said he'd do.
He always said he'd do this. Now he's done it — torn the place down.
He's let your enemies walk all over you, declared them world champions!

18 Give out heart-cries to the Master, dear repentant Zion.
Let the tears roll like a river, day and night,
and keep at it — no time-outs. Keep those tears flowing!

19 As each night watch begins, get up and cry out in prayer.
Pour your heart out face-to-face with the Master.
Lift high your hands. Beg for the lives of your children
who are starving to death out on the streets.

20 "Look at us, GOD. Think it over. Have you ever treated *anyone* like this?
Should women eat their own babies, the very children they raised?
Should priests and prophets be murdered in the Master's own Sanctuary?

21 "Boys and old men lie in the gutters of the streets,
my young men and women killed in their prime.
Angry, you killed them in cold blood, cut them down without mercy.

22 "You invited, like friends to a party, men to swoop down in attack
so that on the big day of GOD's wrath no one would get away.
The children I loved and reared — gone, gone, gone."

GOD LOCKED ME UP IN DEEP DARKNESS

1-3 **3** I'm the man who has seen trouble,
trouble coming from the lash of GOD's anger.
He took me by the hand and walked me
into pitch-black darkness.
Yes, he's given me the back of his hand
over and over and over again.

4-6 He turned me into a scarecrow
of skin and bones, then broke the bones.
He hemmed me in, ganged up on me,
poured on the trouble and hard times.
He locked me up in deep darkness,
like a corpse nailed inside a coffin.

7-9 He shuts me in so I'll never get out,
manacles my hands, shackles my feet.
Even when I cry out and plead for help,

he locks up my prayers and throws away the key.
He sets up blockades with quarried limestone.
    He's got me cornered.

10-12   He's a prowling bear tracking me down,
            a lion in hiding ready to pounce.
        He knocked me from the path and ripped me to pieces.
            When he finished, there was nothing left of me.
        He took out his bow and arrows
            and used me for target practice.

13-15   He shot me in the stomach
            with arrows from his quiver.
        Everyone took me for a joke,
            made me the butt of their mocking ballads.
        He forced rotten, stinking food down my throat,
            bloated me with vile drinks.

16-18   He ground my face into the gravel.
            He pounded me into the mud.
        I gave up on life altogether.
            I've forgotten what the good life is like.
        I said to myself, "This is it. I'm finished.
            GOD is a lost cause."

IT'S A GOOD THING TO HOPE FOR HELP FROM GOD

19-21   I'll never forget the trouble, the utter lostness,
            the taste of ashes, the poison I've swallowed.
        I remember it all — oh, how well I remember —
            the feeling of hitting the bottom.
        But there's one other thing I remember,
            and remembering, I keep a grip on hope:

22-24   GOD's loyal love couldn't have run out,
            his merciful love couldn't have dried up.
        They're created new every morning.
            How great your faithfulness!
        I'm sticking with GOD (I say it over and over).
            He's all I've got left.

25-27   GOD proves to be good to the man who passionately waits,
            to the woman who diligently seeks.
        It's a good thing to quietly hope,
            quietly hope for help from GOD.
        It's a good thing when you're young
            to stick it out through the hard times.

28-30   When life is heavy and hard to take,
            go off by yourself. Enter the silence.
        Bow in prayer. Don't ask questions:
            Wait for hope to appear.

Don't run from trouble. Take it full-face.
The "worst" is never the worst.

31-33 Why? Because the Master won't ever
walk out and fail to return.
If he works severely, he also works tenderly.
His stockpiles of loyal love are immense.
He takes no pleasure in making life hard,
in throwing roadblocks in the way:

34-36 Stomping down hard
on luckless prisoners,
Refusing justice to victims
in the court of High God,
Tampering with evidence —
the Master does not approve of such things.

GOD SPEAKS BOTH GOOD THINGS AND HARD THINGS INTO BEING

37-39 Who do you think "spoke and it happened"?
It's the Master who gives such orders.
Doesn't the High God speak everything,
good things and hard things alike, into being?
And why would anyone gifted with life
complain when punished for sin?

40-42 Let's take a good look at the way we're living
and reorder our lives under GOD.
Let's lift our hearts and hands at one and the same time,
praying to God in heaven:
"We've been contrary and willful,
and you haven't forgiven.

43-45 "You lost your temper with us, holding nothing back.
You chased us and cut us down without mercy.
You wrapped yourself in thick blankets of clouds
so no prayers could get through.
You treated us like dirty dishwater,
threw us out in the backyard of the nations.

46-48 "Our enemies shout abuse,
their mouths full of derision, spitting invective.
We've been to hell and back.
We've nowhere to turn, nowhere to go.
Rivers of tears pour from my eyes
at the smashup of my dear people.

49-51 "The tears stream from my eyes,
an artesian well of tears,
Until you, GOD, look down from on high,
look and see my tears.
When I see what's happened to the young women in the city,
the pain breaks my heart.

52-54 "Enemies with no reason to be enemies
          hunted me down like a bird.
They threw me into a pit,
          then pelted me with stones.
Then the rains came and filled the pit.
          The water rose over my head. I said, 'It's all over.'

55-57 "I called out your name, O GOD,
          called from the bottom of the pit.
You listened when I called out, 'Don't shut your ears!
          Get me out of here! Save me!'
You came close when I called out.
          You said, 'It's going to be all right.'

58-60 "You took my side, Master;
          you brought me back alive!
GOD, you saw the wrongs heaped on me.
          Give me my day in court!
Yes, you saw their mean-minded schemes,
          their plots to destroy me.

61-63 "You heard, GOD, their vicious gossip,
          their behind-my-back plots to ruin me.
They never quit, these enemies of mine, dreaming up mischief,
          hatching out malice, day after day after day.
Sitting down or standing up — just look at them! —
          they mock me with vulgar doggerel.

64-66 "Make them pay for what they've done, GOD.
          Give them their just deserts.
Break their miserable hearts!
          Damn their eyes!
Get good and angry. Hunt them down.
          Make a total demolition here under your heaven!"

WAKING UP WITH NOTHING

1 4Oh, oh, oh . . .
          How gold is treated like dirt,
             the finest gold thrown out with the garbage,
Priceless jewels scattered all over,
          jewels loose in the gutters.

2 And the people of Zion, once prized,
          far surpassing their weight in gold,
Are now treated like cheap pottery,
          like everyday pots and bowls mass-produced by a potter.

3 Even wild jackals nurture their babies,
          give them their breasts to suckle.
But my people have turned cruel to their babies,
          like an ostrich in the wilderness.

4   Babies have nothing to drink.
     Their tongues stick to the roofs of their mouths.
  Little children ask for bread
     but no one gives them so much as a crust.

5   People used to the finest cuisine
     forage for food in the streets.
  People used to the latest in fashions
     pick through the trash for something to wear.

6   The evil guilt of my dear people
     was worse than the sin of Sodom —
  The city was destroyed in a flash,
     and no one around to help.

7   The splendid and sacred nobles
     once glowed with health.
  Their bodies were robust and ruddy,
     their beards like carved stone.

8   But now they are smeared with soot,
     unrecognizable in the street,
  Their bones sticking out,
     their skin dried out like old leather.

9   Better to have been killed in battle
     than killed by starvation.
  Better to have died of battle wounds
     than to slowly starve to death.

10   Nice and kindly women
     boiled their own children for supper.
  This was the only food in town
     when my dear people were broken.

11   GOD let all his anger loose, held nothing back.
     He poured out his raging wrath.
  He set a fire in Zion
     that burned it to the ground.

12   The kings of the earth couldn't believe it.
     World rulers were in shock,
  Watching old enemies march in big as you please,
     right through Jerusalem's gates.

13   Because of the sins of her prophets
     and the evil of her priests,
  Who exploited good and trusting people,
     robbing them of their lives,

14 These prophets and priests blindly grope their way through the streets,
   grimy and stained from their dirty lives,
Wasted by their wasted lives,
   shuffling from fatigue, dressed in rags.

15 People yell at them, "Get out of here, dirty old men!
   Get lost, don't touch us, don't infect us!"
They have to leave town. They wander off.
   Nobody wants them to stay here.
Everyone knows, wherever they wander,
   that they've been kicked out of their own hometown.

16 GOD himself scattered them.
   No longer does he look out for them.
He has nothing to do with the priests;
   he cares nothing for the elders.

17 We watched and watched,
   wore our eyes out looking for help. And nothing.
We mounted our lookouts and looked
   for the help that never showed up.

18 They tracked us down, those hunters.
   It wasn't safe to go out in the street.
Our end was near, our days numbered.
   We were doomed.

19 They came after us faster than eagles in flight,
   pressed us hard in the mountains, ambushed us in the desert.

20 Our king, our life's breath, the anointed of GOD,
   was caught in their traps—
Our king under whose protection
   we always said we'd live.

21 Celebrate while you can, O Edom!
   Live it up in Uz!
For it won't be long before you drink this cup, too.
   You'll find out what it's like to drink God's wrath,
Get drunk on God's wrath
   and wake up with nothing, stripped naked.

22 And that's it for you, Zion. The punishment's complete.
   You won't have to go through this exile again.
But Edom, your time is coming:
   He'll punish your evil life, put all your sins on display.

GIVE US A FRESH START

5 1-22 "Remember, GOD, all we've been through.
Study our plight, the black mark we've made in history.
Our precious land has been given to outsiders,
our homes to strangers.
Orphans we are, not a father in sight,
and our mothers no better than widows.
We have to pay to drink our own water.
Even our firewood comes at a price.
We're nothing but slaves, bullied and bowed,
worn out and without any rest.
We sold ourselves to Assyria and Egypt
just to get something to eat.
Our parents sinned and are no more,
and now we're paying for the wrongs they did.
Slaves rule over us;
there's no escape from their grip.
We risk our lives to gather food
in the bandit-infested desert.
Our skin has turned black as an oven,
dried out like old leather from the famine.
Our wives were raped in the streets in Zion,
and our virgins in the cities of Judah.
They hanged our princes by their hands,
dishonored our elders.
Strapping young men were put to women's work,
mere boys forced to do men's work.
The city gate is empty of wise elders.
Music from the young is heard no more.
All the joy is gone from our hearts.
Our dances have turned into dirges.
The crown of glory has toppled from our head.
Woe! Woe! Would that we'd never sinned!
Because of all this we're heartsick;
we can't see through the tears.
On Mount Zion, wrecked and ruined,
jackals pace and prowl.
And yet, GOD, you're sovereign still,
your throne intact and eternal.
So why do you keep forgetting us?
Why dump us and leave us like this?
Bring us back to you, GOD — we're ready to come back.
Give us a fresh start.
As it is, you've cruelly disowned us.
You've been so very angry with us."

BARUCH

The "Book" of Baruch is composed of bits and pieces; each chapter has a life of its own and an author of its own. They may have belonged to longer pieces, but these six chapters—a hint of history, a couple of poems, a couple of prayers, and a letter to end all letters—are scraps that must have fallen to the proverbial cutting room floor.

Some wise Jewish editors, writers, and copyists in the last couple of centuries B.C. must have picked the scraps up and realized they'd have value if they were joined together, however roughly, even though the result would have a patchwork quilt kind of look. They knew if they didn't put these fragments into a single manuscript, they'd be lost forever. So the Book of Baruch had a convoluted beginning but a noble ending with its inclusion as one of the deuterocanonical books of the Bible.

In a way, the Hebrew editors did what the idol makers mentioned in the Letter of Jeremiah (chapter 6) did. Those craftspeople made intricate idols but needed something to tie them all together, so they decided to make a crown for each idol out of bits and pieces of broken jewelry. That produced uniformity, if not classical unity.

That's what the editors of this book achieved. They had an intricate manuscript they had developed, and they put Baruch's name on the cover to tie it all together. Baruch was Jeremiah's friend and secretary, so naming the book after him was an obvious choice. But some of the pieces were written after Baruch's death. Not that this would have bothered anyone back then—nor would it now for that matter. Baruch was the *honorary* author. Besides, Jeremiah's Baruch wasn't the only Baruch in the Hebrew world who could read and write, and perhaps edit and publish. So, the Book of Baruch it is.

That being said, the various pieces of the short book do have a unity of sorts. They're addressed to the Jews in exile, mainly in Babylon in the sixth century B.C. The author or authors acknowledge that it was hard under those circumstances to keep the faith, to think well of the God who had allowed his own people to suffer great harm, to resist the fanciful idolatry in a colorful city, even to refrain from cannibalizing their own when they were starving to death.

First, there's a historical introduction that sets a dark mood indicating that all was not well in the Jewish community. Second, there's a penitential prayer in praise of divine wisdom. Third, there's a lament and song of consolation. Fourth, there's the Letter of Jeremiah about idol worship.

The Letter of Jeremiah is an exhortation offering the Jews consolation in their exile and urging their commitment to keeping the faith of their forebears. It begins with a number of logical illustrations and ends with a rant against idols and the gods they represent.

The letter is pious and rational—smoothly, even elegantly, written. For much of it the writer reduces the proposition that idols are "real" to the absurd; he then goes even further by reducing the absurd to the ridiculous. By letter's end, the attack on idols is actually pretty entertaining, which is sad but true.

The general audience for this work when it was first written was all the Jews in exile, whether in Babylon or elsewhere. Their world had fallen apart, and they were scattered like slaves all over the known world. Prophets had promised the house of Israel a glorious future: God would be with them every step of the way. When their world crumbled, however, the people crumpled; and the authors of the Book of Baruch were trying to pick them up and get them back on track.

The particular audience for the work today is mostly Christians, many of whom find themselves exiles in their own countries. Their beliefs have been watered down; their societies mock their values; their governments belie the assumption that certain commonly accepted moral or just behaviors are possible or even desirable. They are beset by idols such as sex, money, power, celebrity, and violence. One biblical scholar has summed up the Book of Baruch as "spirituality for displaced persons." Isn't that what we need right now? (WG)

BARUCH

DONATIONS AND VESSELS

1-2 This is the book that Baruch, son of Neriah, son of Mahseiah, son of Zedekiah, son of Hasadiah, son of Hilkiah, wrote while he was in Babylon. The timing is a little murky, but it was sometime after the Chaldeans captured Jerusalem and torched the city.

3-7 A good while later, when Baruch was heading home to Jerusalem, he read the complete work to King Jeconiah, son of Jehoiakim, and others in the hall—the king's staff, his family, his senior advisors, and so on. From there, the reports of the document spread to the Jews who called Babylon their home. They cried and fasted and prayed in the sight of the Lord; they took up a collection, and everyone contributed what they could. They sent the total amount to Jerusalem, where it was gladly received by Jehoiakim, a member of the high priestly family, son of Hilkiah and grandson of Shallum, as well as by the other priests and the people.

8-9 At the same time, the vessels of the Lord for the Temple in Jerusalem that had been missing were returned to their rightful place. Zedekiah, son of King Josiah, had commissioned replacements after Nebuchadnezzar, king of Babylon, had dragged Jeconiah and his people from Jerusalem to Babylon. The vessels that had been removed from the Temple were returned on the tenth day of the month of Sivan.

A note accompanied the donations.

LETTER FROM THE JEWS IN BABYLON TO THE JEWS IN JERUSALEM

10-14 "We took up a collection and here's what we were able to raise. It's not much, but use it for burnt sacrifices, pounds of incense, and the various offerings of the season, and place them upon the altar of the Lord our God.

"And pray for Nebuchadnezzar, king of Babylon, and for his son, Belshazzar, that they'll live as long as the heavens hold up. The Lord will give inner strength to us and open our eyes to the realities; we'll live under the protection of Nebuchadnezzar and Belshazzar. We'll display our loyalty and find favor in their sight.

"Also pray for us to our Lord God, because we have sinned against him. His anger and indignation against us haven't cooled as yet. We are sending this confession of our sinfulness to you so that it could be read aloud in the house of the Lord on the great feast day and all the other holy days in the calendar.

CONFESSION OF SINFULNESS

15-17 "When we look at our Lord God, we see justice; when we look in the mirror, we see confusion; when we look through the window, we see shame on the faces of the people of Judah and the citizens of Jerusalem. Our king, leaders, priests, prophets, ancestors are all ashamed to death. We've sinned before the Lord, and we've lost our credibility with him.

18-19 "We haven't heard the voice of our Lord God recently; we haven't obeyed the commandments, even though they were presented to us face-to-face. From the day the Lord led our ancestors from the land of Egypt down to this very day we've gone out of our way to do the wrong thing; that's why we tiptoe about, lest our Lord God hear where we are.

20-22 "Evil and rumors of evil have damaged the splendid reputation the Lord conferred upon his servant Moses. That was the day on which he led our forebears out of the land of Egypt to the land of milk and honey. Since that day we haven't obeyed God, even though he sent prophet after prophet to warn us. Instead we flirted with idols; we've done nothing but evil right under God's nose.

LETTER FROM THE JEWS IN BABYLON: CONTINUED

1-5 2 "The Lord made good on his word; he spoke against us and our judges, against our kings and leaders, against every person in Israel and Judah. He put us in evil situations that have never been heard of before. If the writings of Moses are to be believed, all of us would one day eat the flesh of our own son or daughter! He subjected us to all the kings in the vicinity; he scattered us every which way; we were ashamed, desolate—out of our minds. Our faces were rubbed in the dirt, not raised up to the sky. Why? Because we sinned against our God by not obeying his voice.

6-8 "As we said, when we look at our Lord God, we see justice; when we look in the mirror, we see confusion. That's as true today as it was in the past. That's why the Lord found us guilty; that's why he sentenced us to all these evils. Still, we could have looked longingly toward the face of the Lord; but we turned our wretched hearts in the opposite direction.

9-10 "The Lord kept track of our adversities and laid them upon us; he made sure we got only what we deserved, not a tiny bit more. We didn't obey his voice; we sidestepped every commandment he gave us face-to-face.

PRAYER FOR GOD'S MERCY

11-15 "Then, Lord God of Israel, you led your people from the land of Egypt with signs and portents, with great strength and power.

"We've gone out of our way to sin, Lord God, even though we knew where the straight and narrow was. Would you think of giving us a second chance? We're just a few lost souls in a thriving metropolis; nobody knows our names. We've turned away from you, yes, but look at it from our enemies' point of view. They think you turned away from us. We pray that you prove them wrong by granting us the favor of your presence again. All the world would then know that you're our God; your name will be invoked wherever the house of Israel is dispersed.

16-19 "Lord, reach down from your lofty spot and choose us once again as your favorites. Allow our petitions another hearing. See that it's not the dead who'll give proper glory and honor to your name. It's people like us, who are still alive but have been profoundly humbled, whose back is bent and whose walk is slow, whose eyes are failing, whose soul is parched—we're the ones who'll garner you the recognition you deserve. Our prayers aren't based on the just deeds of our ancestors or our kings; our prayers are our own. We bow before you today. Give us another chance!

20-23 "We can't say your prophets didn't warn us. 'Put your shoulder into it and serve the king of Babylon,' they said, 'and God says you'll earn a ticket back to the land he promised to your ancestors. The voice of the Lord is in the voice of the king of Babylon, and if you don't listen to it the Lord will lose his interest in Judah and Jerusalem. Joy and happiness will disappear. The sighs of the bridegroom and the murmurs of the bride will be no more. There won't be a Jewish footprint left on the face of your homeland; there won't even be any evidence that there ever were any footprints.'

24-26 "We didn't listen to your voice by serving the king of Babylon; and you fulfilled the threat you made through the prophets that the bones of our kings and ancestors would be left unburied and suffer the heat of the sun and the frost of the night. They died in pain, starving to death, succumbing to disease. Your own house, the Temple of God, you've reduced to rubble because of the malice of the house of Israel and the house of Judah.

27-28 "But the truth is, Lord God, you have been with us in every trial and tribulation; that's what you promised us through Moses on the day you commanded him to write down your Law in the presence of the children of Israel.

29-35 "This is what the Lord God had Moses write: 'If you don't listen to my voice, you will surely be dispersed in ragged groups throughout the nations. But surely in your captivity you'll come to your senses. Then you'll know that I am the Lord God and have a knowing heart and a sharp ear; you'll praise me in the land of your captivity and you'll remember my name. You'll turn back to me, hard though it may be, from your evil mischief, and you'll remember the ways of your ancestors—of Abraham, Isaac, and Jacob; you'll possess the earth, and I'll multiply you and clear the air of threats. I'll restore my covenant with you. I will be your God; you will be my people. From that point forward, I won't remove you from the land I gave you.'

※

LETTER FROM THE JEWS IN BABYLON: CONCLUDING SUMMARY

1-5 **3** "All-Powerful Lord, God of Israel, the stressful soul and the anxious spirit cry out to you non-stop. Hear us, O Lord. You've got the vantage point of eternity from which to judge things, but we feel we are failing miserably and need your mercy.

"Our ancestors sinned in your sight and died the slow death; they didn't listen to your voice and their evil deeds have left a mark on us. So please look beyond the sins of our forebears and remember who you are and how highly we think of you now.

6-8 "You're our Lord God; we praised you once; we will praise you again. When we did, we had a proper fear of you in our hearts and could invoke your holy name. Our captivity has eliminated the sins of our parents and grandparents from our hearts. You've scattered us in exile over the known world, where our enemies have covered us with shame and bad-mouthed us to anyone who'd listen. All this has been to punish us for the iniquities of our ancestors, who turned their back on you!"

※

POEM ABOUT WISDOM
FIRST STANZA

9 Hear, O Israel, the commandments of life; keep your ears open, and you'll pick up some wisdom.

10   What's your story, O Israel? How come you find yourself in enemy territory so often?

11   You've grown gray hairs in a foreign land; you're as good as dead; you're
written off as though you were already dwelling in the world below.

12   You've left behind the fountain of Lady Wisdom!

13   If you walked in the way of God, you'd live in peace forever.

14   Learn how to find prudence, fortitude, and understanding; once they are
discovered, you'll know what life means, what wisdom means, what peace is.

SECOND STANZA

15   Has anyone found where Lady Wisdom hangs out? Has anyone dipped a
tentative hand into her treasury of insights?

16   Where are the rulers of the nations? Where are the lion tamers?

17   Where are the bird watchers?

18   Who are the millionaires, and where do they get their information? The
millionaires want to become billionaires; nothing else interests them. But in
the end, they die like everybody else, leaving not a trace behind.

19   When they breathed their last, they descended into the land of shadows
and others took their place on earth.

20   One generation after another has taken up residence on earth, but they
never seemed to find the way of Lady Wisdom.

21   They always took the wrong turn at every fork in the road. Their children
didn't think the search for her was worth their while; they didn't even get
out of bed to look for her in the next room.

22   Lady Wisdom wasn't heard in Canaan, nor was she seen in Teman.

23   The sons of Hagar sought her on earth, as did the merchants of Medan
and Teman, and the storytellers and the schoolmasters; however, they didn't
know the way to her. For them, she wasn't worth thinking about.

THIRD STANZA

24   O Israel, how expansive is God's residence! It has more furniture than one
could use in a lifetime of sitting and sleeping!

25   As for God, he doesn't meet himself on the road; he's already there—high
as the sky, broad as the horizon.

26   From the very beginning there were giants; they knew how to flex their
muscles and make their wars.

27   God could have chosen them, but he didn't; he could have given them the
life-maps, but he didn't.

28   They died because they didn't discover wisdom; they made one foolish
mistake after another.

FOURTH STANZA

29   Who has risen to the heavens, kidnapped Lady Wisdom, and brought her
down from the clouds?

30   Who has roamed the sea in search of her and carried enough gold to buy
her back?

31   No one knows the way to her; she's off the maps and charts.

32   But there's one person who truly knows where she is; he's the one who
made the earth and filled it with four-footed beasts.

33   He turns the sun on and turns the sun off; it follows the path laid down
for it; it dares not wander.

34 Stars twinkle and blink and seem quite happy in his company.

35 When he calls, they say, "We're already here," blinking and twinkling with joy at the one who made them.

36-37 This is our God; there's not another like him; he laid out the pathways to Lady Wisdom and gave the directions to Jacob his faithful servant and Israel his beloved son.

38 Since then, she's been spotted regularly on earth, pausing now and then to chat with her admirers.

FIFTH STANZA

1 4 Lady Wisdom is an eternal book that contains the life-maps of God, which are also the Law of God. Everyone who follows the life-maps will live; those who don't will die.

2 Turn your life around, tribe of Jacob. Welcome Lady Wisdom while you can; let her be your lighthouse in the storm.

3 Don't waste your worship on some other god; don't spend your good offerings on a bad altar.

4 We're blessed, people of Israel, because we know what pleases God.

POEM OF CONSOLATION
EXHORTATION

5 O Israel, be confident; fear not; never forget to keep Lady Wisdom in the front of your mind.

6-7 Yes, you've been sold off to the nations, but to be purified, not destroyed.

You brought it on yourself by your infidelity; you were handed over to your adversaries because you exasperated him who made you.

What were you thinking, sacrificing to demons and idols who are no gods at all?

8 You forgot the God who breast-fed you; you offended Jerusalem, the city that nourished you.

JERUSALEM PERSONIFIED

9 The holy city saw wrathful clouds coming across the skies toward you; she said as much to you: "Listen to me, neighbors of Zion; God has brought great grief upon me.

10 "I saw my own sons and daughters marched off into captivity; it was a penalty slapped on them by the Eternal One.

11 "It was a great joy to bring them up; it was a great grief to let them go.

12 "Let no one rejoice in my sorrow; I'm a widow now, and all my friends have left me.

"I'm a city with no children; they sinned and have paid the price for it.

13 "My children had no concept why I did things the way I did; they failed to follow God's life-maps and tiptoed around the pathways of Lady Wisdom.

14 "Let the neighbors of Zion come. Help them understand what it means to lose one's sons and daughters as a punishment from the Eternal One.

15 "To carry out the penalty, he pressed into divine service a distant nation with a questionable history and an unintelligible language. They didn't honor the old, nor did they have any pity on the young.

16 "They abducted my beloved sons and dragged off my beautiful daughters, leaving me as the sole survivor.

ADDRESS TO THE EXILES

17 "I am Jerusalem; there's no way I can help.

18 "God's the one who threw you to the dogs; he's the one who'll rescue you from the dogs.

19 "Fly, my children, fly while you can! And don't look back at the derelict city you've left behind.

20 "I'm taking off my peacetime fashions and putting on my prayer-time sackcloth, and I will spend the rest of my life crying out to the Eternal One.

21 "Have faith, my children; you too should call to God. He'll rescue you from the hand of your enemies.

22 "My fervent prayer is that you'll be freed soon by the Eternal One, and lately I have felt a hint of consolation, the gentlest breeze of hope.

23 "I sent you off with grief and tears, but God will return you to me with tears of joy forever.

24 "Your next-door neighbors who saw you hustled off into captivity will see you returning soon, safe and sound, with splendor and glory.

25 "Children, be patient; put up with the punishment God has sent you. Your enemy has persecuted you, but soon you'll see them in captivity with ropes around their necks.

26 "My sweet children, you have walked the rough roads; you were led into captivity like a flock of sheep rustled in the middle of the night.

27 "Keep the faith, my children, and cry out to God. He'll surely remember you, and he'll rescue you on his own timetable.

28 "Remember, with no effort at all you willingly wandered off from God; now make ten times the effort to get back to him.

29 "Eventually, he who sent you into exile will bring you home to me, to my eternal joy."

BARUCH COMFORTS JERUSALEM

30 Have faith, Jerusalem! He who gave you the name City of Peace will console you.

31 Sorry will be those who mishandled you and mocked you as you fell!

32 Babylon, the city in which your children were enslaved, will become a wretched place.

33 She rejoiced in your ruin and celebrated your fall. It's her turn next time; desolation is on its way.

34 The Lord will cut short the exuberance of the city; their joy will turn to grief.

35 Fire will come upon them, spread by the Eternal One himself; it will last a long time; the only inhabitants left will be demons.

36 Look toward the east, Jerusalem; see the joy of God coming toward you.

37 Your children, the ones you sent away, are gathering from one end of the horizon to the other, rejoicing in the glory of God.

❋

RETURN OF THE EXILES PROPHESIED

1 **5** Jerusalem, get rid of the dull clothes of grief and put on your best dress, the clothes of glory meant for you from all eternity.

2 Wrap yourself in a lovely layered cloak; pick one from the justice collection. On your head put a crown in honor of the Eternal One.

3 God wants to show off how splendid you can look.

4 As of now, your name will be on the permanent divine invitation list; look under the headings of Peace and Justice and the Glory of God's Worship.

5 Arise, Jerusalem, and take your stand on high; look to the east, and you'll see your children gathering, rejoicing in the memory of God.

6 They were abducted a long time ago by their enemies and led away, made to walk the many miles on foot. God, however, will lead them back to you, carried with glory as though on a royal throne.

7 God has decided to level the mountains, turning the hard rock into gravel; the gorges and valleys he has ordered filled and leveled. He will do this so that the house of Israel may make the return trip to you in the security of the glory of the Most High.

8 At the command of God, forests and fragrant woods will spring up to provide shade for the returning pilgrims.

9 God will lead Israel home with joy, lighting the way with the majesty, mercy, and justice only he can command.

❋

LETTER OF JEREMIAH AGAINST IDOLATRY

1-2 **6** Because of the sins you've committed before God, you're about to be conducted into Babylon as captives of Nebuchadnezzar, king of the Babylonians. Once there, you won't be returning home soon— after seven generations, actually. After that, God will walk you out of captivity without a shot being fired.

3-6 While in Babylon, you'll see silver, gold, and wooden gods in the streets being lugged about on portable thrones; the intent is to put fear into the common people. Watch your step, therefore, and don't be intimidated by this crude and ugly show. When you get caught up in one of these idol parades, with the crowd chanting their adoration, just say to yourself, "It's you, O Lord, whom I adore and worship."

Remember, my angel will be parading with you every step of the way.

7-10 As for the idols, their tongues look realistic, sanded smooth by the carpenters, but they can't say a word. The wooden figures are plated with gold and silver; they're lifelike but not alive. These are just statues that can't walk or talk.

Their creators turn these idols out in great numbers. As though they were giddy young schoolgirls, they make crowns for their dolls out of precious bits and pieces of broken jewelry. They even dress the idols up with clothes from their own closets. Finally, there's a crowning ceremony of sorts and the idols are ready to go to market.

Behind the scenes, though, priests sometimes strip the gods of their silver and gold and spend the money on themselves. Like big shots they toss a coin or two to the prostitutes working the pagan temple terrace.

11-15 These idols, however, are mere dust catchers; at no moment are they free of rust and termites. As for the purple garments, they're magisterial in cut and color, but the faces of the idols have to be wiped clean like any other statue.

The statues have scepters as though they were real rulers like judges of the region, but they have no judicial power over anyone. There's a sword in the right hand and an ax in the left—weapons they'll never use. Imagine an idol swinging one about in a war, let alone a robbery. Thus it's plain to everybody that these idols aren't gods and there's absolutely no need to be afraid of them. Like a chipped cup or a cracked mirror, they've lost their usefulness; so much for the "gods" of other nations.

16-22 The idols are installed in the Gentile temples; their eye sockets are a favorite depository of the dirt kicked up by tourists coming and going.

The courtyards of these "temples" are walled—an appropriate place for one guilty of a capital crime. Fearing a nighttime burglary, the priests fortify their buildings with gates, locks, and crossbars; then they light candles— more for the idols than themselves, even though the idols can't see.

The idols are rugged, but they have no more life than the beams in the temple roof. Worms eat the idols' hearts out; moths feast on the garments, but the idols don't feel a thing. Black candle smoke hangs in the temple air, darkening their facial features. Owls and sparrows find a convenient perch on their heads and shoulders; cats climb all over them.

All of this shows the gods aren't real and there's nothing to fear from them.

23-26 The gold exterior of an idol has a certain smart look about it, but someone has to polish it, get the grime off; as for the idol, it doesn't feel a thing. No matter how expensive it is, there's not a breath of life in it. An idol has feet of its own but can't move an inch; it has to be carried everywhere. No wonder those who worship them are a bit confused. If an idol takes a tumble, it can't get up by itself. If someone puts it on a pedestal, it can't move. When gifts and offerings are placed on the floor in front of it, it can't bend over to pick them up.

27-29 The priests sell or put to their own use the offerings that people bring to the idols. The priests' wives also get their fingers in the collections, taking and salting the meat offerings for their personal use. But they give nothing to the poor or the sick as they claim they do. The uncleanliness of menstruation and childbearing should prevent women from touching genuine sacrifices, but their husbands look the other way when they do. These women know the idols aren't real gods, and they have nothing to fear from them. That's because the idols are just pieces of gold, silver, and wood.

30-39 The priests are equally impious. They sit in their temples in old, dirty, torn clothing, with shaved heads and beards, and no covering on their heads. They roar and carry on in front of their gods as though they were at a feast for the dead. Any clothing left for the idols as offerings the priests bring home for their wives and children. What kinds of priests are these?

When an idol gets a compliment, it can't say thank you. When someone punches it in the nose, it can't swing back. An idol can't play kingmaker or lead a revolution. It can't print money or leave an inheritance. If anyone asks an idol for a favor, it can't grant it. An idol can't prevent a person from dying or rescue someone from being captured. It can't restore sight to a person who is blind or even stop someone blind from walking into a pole. It can't bring comfort to widows or do something nice for orphans. These gods in their silver, gold, and wooden trappings are no better than rock carvings on a mountainside; those who worship them are in a total fog.

How is it, then, that these sad dolls are thought to be gods?

40-41 The Chaldeans don't have sense enough not to take their idols seriously. When they bump into someone who can't hear or speak, they haul the person off to their god Bel—as if an idol who can't speak or hear could make a human being speak or hear! But these Chaldeans can't think for themselves; if they could, they'd have left their idols long ago. As it is, they don't have an intelligent thought in their heads.

42-43 Here's a word about their temple prostitutes. They wear ceremonial wreathes—the sign of their profession—and sit by the entrance burning cheap incense and trying to attract customers. A coin in her lap and she's ready for service. When she returns to her spot, she heckles the woman next to her, saying she couldn't get a decent customer in a million years. How's that for creating a pious atmosphere for worshiping the idols?

44-47 Everything about the idols is false; therefore, how could anyone think or say they're real? It's not the fault of the carpenters, whittlers, and the various smithies; they produce a product according to the blueprints given to them by the priests. As it will to all of us, death will come to the creative artists. But how, then, could they make gods that will live forever? The idols they leave behind convey nothing but mortality. Eternity is the realm of the wise, not the foolish.

48-51 For example, when war or natural disaster threatens, the pagan priests have only two thoughts: how to save their own skins and how to preserve the idols that have proved so profitable to them. How can anyone in this situation continue to think the idols are real gods? They can't even save themselves, much less anyone else. The idols are merely wooden dolls with a gold and silver veneer. It's common knowledge throughout the entire world that they're frauds. They're the work of talented human hands, which is to say they're not the work of God. Is there anyone who doesn't understand this by now?

52-57 These idols can't raise up a king or bring rain down upon the people. They can't legislate or relieve those who suffer injury. They actually can't do a thing on their own; they're like crows flying about in midair with no place to land. When fire hits the temple in which an idol is enshrined, the priests flee to save themselves; the idol, however, just stands there, waiting to go up in smoke along with the wooden timbers.

If idols can't resist a king or stop a war, how can they be considered gods? If they can't defend themselves against burglars, what good are they in protecting other people's possessions? When they're the very things being burgled—covered as they are in precious metals and fine fabrics—they can't cry for help. And if they can't cry for help for themselves, why should anyone cry to them for help?

58 A strong king or a useful tool, for example, are both good things to have around. They're certainly more helpful than a false god! Even a locked door is better than an idol, because at least it protects the valuables inside. A beam supporting a roof is more reliable than a false god being asked to hold up a palace or a house.

59-63 Sun, moon, stars—they're splendid. They give off light when they're supposed to; they follow the rules laid down for them. Likewise with lightning—when it appears, it can be seen for miles. The same with wind—when it blows, it cools us. As for clouds, when God commands them to overshadow the world, they do so. And fire, when God commands it to burn the forest and mountains, it does so.

But idols can't do these things or anything like them. How can anyone think or say that idols are gods when they can't even make a judgment or do a favor?

64-67 Now you know, dear reader, if you didn't know before, that idols aren't gods and you have nothing to fear from them. As for kings, idols can't say a thing good or bad about them. Idols can't move the stars or the sun or the moon, interfering with orbits established by the one and only real God.

Even wild beasts are more powerful than idols; they at least flee instinctively to find shelter when a storm comes; idols just stand there in the rain.

68-71 Seriously, there's no escape from the argument that idols aren't gods and we have nothing to fear from them. An idol is like a scarecrow in a garden of cucumbers—it scares nobody and nobody cares. Idols are like thornbushes—they look intimidating to us, but not to the birds who sit on the thorns. An idol is like a dead body thrown by the wayside. Moths nibble at an idol's royal purple and scarlet clothes; termites feast on its wooden body. That wouldn't happen if they were gods, would it?

72 Here is my conclusion: It is better for the just to eschew all idols in their lives; that way they'll have nothing silly or disgraceful to answer for.

EZEKIEL

Catastrophe strikes and a person's world falls apart. People respond variously, but two of the more common responses are denial and despair. Denial refuses to acknowledge the catastrophe. It shuts its eyes tight or looks the other way; it manages to act as if everything is going to be just fine; it takes refuge in distractions and lies and fantasies. Despair is paralyzed by the catastrophe and accepts it as the end of the world. It is unwilling to do anything, concluding that life for all intents and purposes is over. Despair listlessly closes its eyes to a world in which all the color has drained out, a world gone dead.

Among biblical writers, Ezekiel is our master at dealing with catastrophe. When catastrophe struck — it was the sixth-century B.C. invasion of Israel by Babylon — denial was the primary response. Ezekiel found himself living among a people of God who (astonishingly similar to us!) stubbornly refused to see what was right before their eyes (the denial crowd). There were also some who were unwilling to see anything other than what was right before their eyes (the despair crowd).

But Ezekiel saw. He saw what the people with whom he lived either couldn't or wouldn't see. He saw in wild and unforgettable images, elaborated in exuberant detail — God at work in a catastrophic era. The denial people refused to see that the catastrophe was in fact catastrophic. How could it be? God wouldn't let anything that bad happen to them. Ezekiel showed them. He showed them that, yes, there *was* catastrophe, but God was at work in the catastrophe, sovereignly *using* the catastrophe. He showed them so that they would be able to embrace God in the worst of times.

The despair people, overwhelmed by the devastation, refused to see that life was worth living. How could it be? They had lost everything, or would soon — country, Temple, freedom, and many, many lives. Ezekiel showed them. He showed them that God was and would be at work in the wreckage and rubble, sovereignly *using* the disaster to create a new people of God.

Whether through denial or despair, the people of God nearly lost their identity as a people of God. But they didn't. God's people emerged from that catastrophic century robust and whole. And the reason, in large part, was Ezekiel.

EZEKIEL

WHEELS WITHIN WHEELS, LIKE A GYROSCOPE

1 When I was thirty years of age, I was living with the exiles on the Kebar River. On the fifth day of the fourth month, the sky opened up and I saw visions of God.

2-3 (It was the fifth day of the month in the fifth year of the exile of King Jehoiachin that GOD's Word came to Ezekiel the priest, the son of Buzi, on the banks of the Kebar River in the country of Babylon. GOD's hand came upon him that day.)

4-9 I looked: I saw an immense dust storm come from the north, an immense cloud with lightning flashing from it, a huge ball of fire glowing like bronze. Within the fire were what looked like four creatures vibrant with life. Each had the form of a human being, but each also had four faces and four wings. Their legs were as sturdy and straight as columns, but their feet were hoofed like those of a calf and sparkled from the fire like burnished bronze. On all four sides under their wings they had human hands. All four had both faces and wings, with the wings touching one another. They turned neither one way nor the other; they went straight forward.

10-12 Their faces looked like this: In front a human face, on the right side the face of a lion, on the left the face of an ox, and in back the face of an eagle. So much for the faces. The wings were spread out with the tips of one pair touching the creature on either side; the other pair of wings covered its body. Each creature went straight ahead. Wherever the spirit went, they went. They didn't turn as they went.

13-14 The four creatures looked like a blazing fire, or like fiery torches. Tongues of fire shot back and forth between the creatures, and out of the fire, bolts of lightning. The creatures flashed back and forth like strikes of lightning.

15-16 As I watched the four creatures, I saw something that looked like a wheel on the ground beside each of the four-faced creatures. This is what the wheels looked like: They were identical wheels, sparkling like diamonds in the sun. It looked like they were wheels within wheels, like a gyroscope.

17-21 They went in any one of the four directions they faced, but straight, not veering off. The rims were immense, circled with eyes. When the living creatures went, the wheels went; when the living creatures lifted off, the wheels lifted off. Wherever the spirit went, they went, the wheels sticking right with them, for the spirit of the living creatures was in the wheels. When the creatures went, the wheels went; when the creatures stopped, the wheels stopped; when the creatures lifted off, the wheels lifted off, because the spirit of the living creatures was in the wheels.

22-24 Over the heads of the living creatures was something like a dome, shimmering like a sky full of cut glass, vaulted over their heads. Under the dome one set of wings was extended toward the others, with another set of wings covering their bodies. When they moved I heard their wings — it was like the roar of a great waterfall, like the voice of The Strong God, like the noise of a battlefield. When they stopped, they folded their wings.

25-28 And then, as they stood with folded wings, there was a voice from above the dome over their heads. Above the dome there was something that looked like a throne, sky-blue like a sapphire, with a humanlike figure towering above the throne. From what I could see, from the waist up he looked like burnished bronze and from the waist down like a blazing fire. Brightness everywhere! The way a rainbow springs out of the sky on a rainy day — that's what it was like. It turned out to be the Glory of GOD!

When I saw all this, I fell to my knees, my face to the ground. Then I heard a voice.

1   It said, "Son of man, stand up. I have something to say to you."

2   The moment I heard the voice, the Spirit entered me and put me on my feet. As he spoke to me, I listened.

3-7   He said, "Son of man, I'm sending you to the family of Israel, a rebellious nation if there ever was one. They and their ancestors have fomented rebellion right up to the present. They're a hard case, these people to whom I'm sending you — hardened in their sin. Tell them, 'This is the Message of GOD, the Master.' They are a defiant bunch. Whether or not they listen, at least they'll know that a prophet's been here. But don't be afraid of them, son of man, and don't be afraid of anything they say. Don't be afraid when living among them is like stepping on thorns or finding scorpions in your bed. Don't be afraid of their mean words or their hard looks. They're a bunch of rebels. Your job is to speak to them. Whether they listen is not your concern. They're hardened rebels.

8   "Only take care, son of man, that you don't rebel like these rebels. Open your mouth and eat what I give you."

9-10   When I looked he had his hand stretched out to me, and in the hand a book, a scroll. He unrolled the scroll. On both sides, front and back, were written lamentations and mourning and doom.

WARN THESE PEOPLE

1   He told me, "Son of man, eat what you see. Eat this book. Then go and speak to the family of Israel."

2-3   As I opened my mouth, he gave me the scroll to eat, saying, "Son of man, eat this book that I am giving you. Make a full meal of it!"

So I ate it. It tasted so good — just like honey.

4-6   Then he told me, "Son of man, go to the family of Israel and speak my Message. Look, I'm not sending you to a people who speak a hard-to-learn language with words you can hardly pronounce. If I had sent you to such people, their ears would have perked up and they would have listened immediately.

7-9   "But it won't work that way with the family of Israel. They won't listen to you because they won't listen to me. They are, as I said, a hard case, hardened in their sin. But I'll make you as hard in your way as they are in theirs. I'll make your face as hard as rock, harder than granite. Don't let them intimidate you. Don't be afraid of them, even though they're a bunch of rebels."

10-11   Then he said, "Son of man, get all these words that I'm giving you inside you. Listen to them obediently. Make them your own. And now go. Go to the exiles, your people, and speak. Tell them, 'This is the Message of GOD, the Master.' Speak your piece, whether they listen or not."

12-13   Then the Spirit picked me up. Behind me I heard a great commotion—"Blessed be the Glory of GOD in his Sanctuary!"—the wings of the living creatures beating against each other, the whirling wheels, the rumble of a great earthquake.

14-15   The Spirit lifted me and took me away. I went bitterly and angrily. I didn't want to go. But GOD had me in his grip. I arrived among the exiles who lived near the Kebar River at Tel Aviv. I came to where they were living and sat there for seven days, appalled.

16   At the end of the seven days, I received this Message from GOD:

17-19   "Son of man, I've made you a watchman for the family of Israel. Whenever you hear me say something, warn them for me. If I say to the wicked, 'You are going to die,' and you don't sound the alarm warning them that it's a matter of life or death, they will die and it will be your fault. I'll hold you responsible. But if you warn the wicked and they keep right on sinning anyway, they'll most certainly die for their sin, but *you* won't die. You'll have saved your life.

20-21   "And if the righteous turn back from living righteously and take up with evil when I step in and put them in a hard place, they'll die. If you haven't warned them, they'll die because of their sins, and none of the right things they've done will count for anything—and I'll hold you responsible. But if you warn these righteous people not to sin and they listen to you, they'll live because they took the warning—and again, you'll have saved your life."

22   GOD grabbed me by the shoulder and said, "Get up. Go out on the plain. I want to talk with you."

23   So I got up and went out on the plain. I couldn't believe my eyes: the Glory of GOD! Right there! It was like the Glory I had seen at the Kebar River. I fell to the ground, prostrate.

24-26   Then the Spirit entered me and put me on my feet. He said, "Go home and shut the door behind you." And then something odd: "Son of man: They'll tie you hand and foot with ropes so you can't leave the house. I'll make your tongue stick to the roof of your mouth so you won't be able to talk and tell the people what they're doing wrong, even though they are a bunch of rebels.

27   "But then when the time is ripe, I'll free your tongue and you'll say, 'This is what GOD, the Master, says: . . .' From then on it's up to them. They can listen or not listen, whichever they like. They *are* a bunch of rebels!"

THIS IS WHAT SIN DOES

1-3   4 "Now, son of man, take a brick and place it before you. Draw a picture of the city Jerusalem on it. Then make a model of a military siege against the brick: Build siege walls, construct a ramp, set up army camps, lay in battering rams around it. Then get an iron skillet and place it upright between you and the city—an iron wall. Face the model: The city shall be under siege and you shall be the besieger. This is a sign to the family of Israel.

4-5   "Next lie on your left side and place the sin of the family of Israel on yourself. You will bear their sin for as many days as you lie on your side. The number of days you bear their sin will match the number of years of their sin, namely, 390. For 390 days you will bear the sin of the family of Israel.

6-7   "Then, after you have done this, turn over and lie down on your right side and bear the sin of the family of Judah. Your assignment this time is to lie there for forty days, a day for each year of their sin. Look straight at the siege of Jerusalem. Roll up your sleeve, shake your bare arm, and preach against her.

8   "I will tie you up with ropes, tie you so you can't move or turn over until you have finished the days of the siege.

9-12   "Next I want you to take wheat and barley, beans and lentils, dried millet and spelt, and mix them in a bowl to make a flat bread. This is your food ration for the 390 days you lie on your side. Measure out about half a pound for each day and eat it on schedule. Also measure out your daily ration of about a pint of water and drink it on schedule. Eat the bread as you would a muffin. Bake the muffins out in the open where everyone can see you, using dried human dung for fuel."

13   GOD said, "This is what the people of Israel are going to do: Among the pagan nations where I will drive them, they will eat foods that are strictly taboo to a holy people."

14   I said, "GOD, my Master! Never! I've never contaminated myself with food like that. Since my youth I've never eaten anything forbidden by law, nothing found dead or violated by wild animals. I've never taken a single bite of forbidden food."

15   "All right," he said. "I'll let you bake your bread over cow dung instead of human dung."

16-17   Then he said to me, "Son of man, I'm going to cut off all food from Jerusalem. The people will live on starvation rations, worrying where the next meal's coming from, scrounging for the next drink of water. Famine conditions. People will look at one another, see nothing but skin and bones, and shake their heads. This is what sin does."

A JEALOUS GOD, NOT TO BE TRIFLED WITH

1-2   5 "Now, son of man, take a sharp sword and use it as a straight razor, shaving your head and your beard. Then, using a set of balancing scales, divide the hair into thirds. When the days of the siege are over, take one-third of the hair and burn it inside the city. Take another third, chop it into bits with the sword and sprinkle it around the city. The final third you'll throw to the wind. Then I'll go after them with a sword.

3-4   "Retrieve a few of the hairs and slip them into your pocket. Take some of them and throw them into the fire — burn them up. From them, fire will spread to the whole family of Israel.

5-6   "This is what GOD, the Master, says: This means *Jerusalem*. I set her at the center of the world, all the nations ranged around her. But she rebelled against my laws and ordinances, rebelled far worse than the nations ranged around her — sheer wickedness! — refused my guidance, ignored my directions.

7   "Therefore this is what GOD, the Master, says: You've been more headstrong and willful than any of the nations around you, refusing my guidance, ignoring my directions. You've sunk to the gutter level of those around you.

8-10   "Therefore this is what GOD, the Master, says: I'm setting myself against you — yes, against you, Jerusalem. I'm going to punish you in full sight of the nations. Because of your disgusting no-god idols, I'm going to do something to you that I've never done before and will never do again: turn families into cannibals — parents eating children, children eating parents!

Punishment indeed. And whoever's left over I'll throw to the winds.

11-12 "Therefore, as sure as I am the living God — Decree of GOD, the Master — because you've polluted my Sanctuary with your obscenities and disgusting no-god idols, I'm pulling out. Not an ounce of pity will I show you. A third of your people will die of either disease or hunger inside the city, a third will be killed outside the city, and a third will be thrown to the winds and chased by killers.

13 "Only then will I calm down and let my anger cool. Then you'll know that I was serious about this all along, that I'm a jealous God and not to be trifled with.

14-15 "When I get done with you, you'll be a pile of rubble. Nations who walk by will make coarse jokes. When I finish my angry punishment and searing rebukes, you'll be reduced to an object of ridicule and mockery, turned into a horror story circulating among the surrounding nations. I, GOD, have spoken.

16-17 "When I shoot my lethal famine arrows at you, I'll shoot to kill. Then I'll step up the famine and cut off food supplies. Famine and more famine — and then I'll send in the wild animals to finish off your children. Epidemic disease, unrestrained murder, death — and I will have sent it! I, GOD, have spoken."

TURN ISRAEL INTO WASTELAND

1-7 6 Then the Word of GOD came to me: "Son of man, now turn and face the mountains of Israel and preach against them: 'O Mountains of Israel, listen to the Message of GOD, the Master. GOD, the Master, speaks to the mountains and hills, to the ravines and the valleys: I'm about to destroy your sacred god and goddess shrines. I'll level your altars, bust up your sun-god pillars, and kill your people as they bow down to your no-god idols. I'll stack the dead bodies of Israelites in front of your idols and then scatter your bones around your shrines. Every place where you've lived, the towns will be torn down and the pagan shrines demolished — altars busted up, idols smashed, all your custom-made sun-god pillars in ruins. Corpses everywhere you look! Then you'll know that I am GOD.

8-10 "'But I'll let a few escape the killing as you are scattered through other lands and nations. In the foreign countries where they're taken as prisoners of war, they'll remember me. They'll realize how devastated I was by their betrayals, by their voracious lust for gratifying themselves in their idolatries. They'll be disgusted with their evil ways, disgusting to God in the way they've lived. They'll know that I am GOD. They'll know that my judgment against them was no empty threat.

11-14 "'This is what GOD, the Master, says: Clap your hands, stamp your feet, yell out, "No, no, no!" because of all the evil obscenities rife in Israel. They're going to be killed, dying of hunger, dying of disease — death everywhere you look, people dropping like flies, people far away dying, people nearby dying, and whoever's left in the city starving to death. Why? Because I'm angry, furiously angry. They'll realize that I am GOD when they see their people's corpses strewn over and around all their ruined sex-and-religion shrines on the bare hills and in the lush fertility groves, in all the places where they indulged their sensual rites. I'll bring my hand down hard on them, demolish the country wherever they live, turn it into wasteland from one end to the other, from the wilderness to Riblah. Then they'll know that I am GOD!'"

₁₋₄ 7 GOD's Word came to me, saying, "You, son of man—GOD, the Master, has this Message for the land of Israel:

" 'Endtime.
    The end of business as usual for everyone.
It's all over. The end is upon you.
    I've launched my anger against you.
I've issued my verdict on the way you live.
    I'll make you pay for your disgusting obscenities.
I won't look the other way,
    I won't feel sorry for you.
I'll make you pay for the way you've lived:
    Your disgusting obscenities will boomerang on you,
    and you'll realize that I am GOD.'

₅₋₉ "I, GOD, the Master, say:
    'Disaster after disaster! Look, it comes!
Endtime—
    the end comes.
The end is ripe. Watch out, it's coming!
    This is your fate, you who live in this land.
Time's up.
    It's zero hour.
No dragging of feet now,
    no bargaining for more time.
Soon now I'll pour my wrath on you,
    pay out my anger against you,
Render my verdict on the way you've lived,
    make you pay for your disgusting obscenities.
I won't look the other way,
    I won't feel sorry for you.
I'll make you pay for the way you've lived.
    Your disgusting obscenities will boomerang on you.
Then you'll realize
    that it is I, GOD, who have hit you.

₁₀₋₁₃ " 'Judgment Day!
    Fate has caught up with you.
The scepter outsized and pretentious,
    pride bursting all bounds,
Violence strutting,
    brandishing the evil scepter.
But there's nothing to them,
    and nothing will be left of them.
Time's up.
    Countdown: five, four, three, two . . .
Buyer, don't crow; seller, don't worry:
    Judgment wrath has turned the world topsy-turvy.
The bottom has dropped out of buying and selling.

It will never be the same again.
But don't fantasize an upturn in the market.
  The country is bankrupt because of its sins,
  and it's not going to get any better.

14-16 " 'The trumpet signals the call to battle:
    "Present arms!"
But no one marches into battle.
    My wrath has them paralyzed!
On the open roads you're killed,
    or else you go home and die of hunger and disease.
Either get murdered out in the country
    or die of sickness or hunger in town.
Survivors run for the hills.
    They moan like doves in the valleys,
Each one moaning
    for his own sins.

17-18 " 'Every hand hangs limp,
    every knee turns to rubber.
They dress in rough burlap —
    sorry scarecrows,
Shifty and shamefaced,
    with their heads shaved bald.

19-27 " 'They throw their money into the gutters.
    Their hard-earned cash stinks like garbage.
They find that it won't buy a thing
    they either want or need on Judgment Day.
They tripped on money
    and fell into sin.
Proud and pretentious with their jewels,
    they deck out their vile and vulgar no-gods in finery.
    I'll make those god-obscenities a stench in their nostrils.
I'll give away their religious junk —
    strangers will pick it up for free,
    the godless spit on it and make jokes.
I'll turn my face so I won't have to look
    as my treasured place and people are violated,
As violent strangers walk in
    and desecrate place and people —
A bloody massacre,
    as crime and violence fill the city.
I'll bring in the dregs of humanity
    to move into their houses.
I'll put a stop to the boasting and strutting
    of the high-and-mighty,
And see to it that there'll be nothing holy
    left in their holy places.
Catastrophe descends. They look for peace,
    but there's no peace to be found —

Disaster on the heels of disaster,
    one rumor after another.
They clamor for the prophet to tell them what's up,
    but nobody knows anything.
Priests don't have a clue;
    the elders don't know what to say.
The king holds his head in despair;
    the prince is devastated.
The common people are paralyzed.
    Gripped by fear, they can't move.
I'll deal with them where they are,
    judge them on their terms.
They'll know that I am GOD.'"

THE SPIRIT CARRIED ME IN VISIONS

1-4 In the sixth year, in the sixth month and the fifth day, while I was sitting at home meeting with the leaders of Judah, it happened that the hand of my Master, GOD, gripped me. When I looked, I was astonished. What I saw looked like a man—from the waist down like fire and from the waist up like highly burnished bronze. He reached out what looked like a hand and grabbed me by the hair. The Spirit swept me high in the air and carried me in visions of God to Jerusalem, to the entrance of the north gate of the Temple's inside court where the image of the sex goddess that makes God so angry had been set up. Right before me was the Glory of the God of Israel, exactly like the vision I had seen out on the plain.

5 He said to me, "Son of man, look north." I looked north and saw it: Just north of the entrance loomed the altar of the sex goddess, Asherah, that makes God so angry.

6 Then he said, "Son of man, do you see what they're doing? Outrageous obscenities! And doing them right here! It's enough to drive me right out of my own Temple. But you're going to see worse yet."

7 He brought me to the door of the Temple court. I looked and saw a gaping hole in the wall.

8 He said, "Son of man, dig through the wall."
I dug through the wall and came upon a door.

9 He said, "Now walk through the door and take a look at the obscenities they're engaging in."

10-11 I entered and looked. I couldn't believe my eyes: Painted all over the walls were pictures of reptiles and animals and monsters—the whole pantheon of Egyptian gods and goddesses—being worshiped by Israel. In the middle of the room were seventy of the leaders of Israel, with Jaazaniah son of Shaphan standing in the middle. Each held his censer with the incense rising in a fragrant cloud.

12 He said, "Son of man, do you see what the elders are doing here in the dark, each one before his favorite god-picture? They tell themselves, 'GOD doesn't see us. GOD has forsaken the country.'"

13 Then he said, "You're going to see worse yet."

14-15 He took me to the entrance at the north gate of the Temple of GOD. I saw women sitting there, weeping for Tammuz, the Babylonian fertility god. He said, "Have you gotten an eyeful, son of man? You're going to see worse yet."

16 Finally, he took me to the inside court of the Temple of GOD. There between the porch and the altar were about twenty-five men. Their backs were to GOD's Temple. They were facing east, bowing in worship to the sun.

17-18 He said, "Have you seen enough, son of man? Isn't it bad enough that Judah engages in these outrageous obscenities? They fill the country with violence and now provoke me even further with their obscene gestures. That's it. They have an angry God on their hands! From now on, no mercy. They can shout all they want, but I'm not listening."

A MARK ON THE FOREHEAD

1 **9** Then I heard him call out loudly, "Executioners, come! And bring your deadly weapons with you."

2 Six men came down the road from the upper gate that faces north, each carrying his lethal weapon. With them was a man dressed in linen with a writing case slung from his shoulder. They entered and stood by the bronze altar.

3-4 The Glory of the God of Israel ascended from his usual place above the cherubim-angels, moved to the threshold of the Temple, and called to the man with the writing case who was dressed in linen: "Go through the streets of Jerusalem and put a mark on the forehead of everyone who is in anguish over the outrageous obscenities being done in the city."

5-6 I listened as he went on to address the executioners: "Follow him through the city and kill. Feel sorry for no one. Show no compassion. Kill old men and women, young men and women, mothers and children. But don't lay a hand on anyone with the mark. Start at my Temple."

They started with the leaders in front of the Temple.

7-8 He told the executioners, "Desecrate the Temple. Fill it with corpses. Then go out and continue the killing." So they went out and struck the city.

While the massacre went forward, I was left alone. I fell on my face in prayer: "Oh, oh, GOD, my Master! Are you going to kill everyone left in Israel in this pouring out of your anger on Jerusalem?"

9-10 He said, "The guilt of Israel and Judah is enormous. The land is swollen with murder. The city is bloated with injustice. They all say, 'GOD has forsaken the country. He doesn't see anything we do.' Well, I do see, and I'm not feeling sorry for any of them. They're going to pay for what they've done."

11 Just then, the man dressed in linen and carrying the writing case came back and reported, "I've done what you told me."

THE TEMPLE, FILLED WITH THE PRESENCE OF GOD

1 **10** When I next looked, oh! Above the dome over the heads of the cherubim-angels was what looked like a throne, sky-blue, like a sapphire!

2-5 GOD said to the man dressed in linen, "Enter the place of the wheels under the cherubim-angels. Fill your hands with burning coals from beneath the cherubim and scatter them over the city."

I watched as he entered. The cherubim were standing on the south side of the Temple when the man entered. A cloud filled the inside courtyard. Then the Glory of GOD ascended from the cherubim and moved to the threshold of the Temple. The cloud filled the Temple. Court and Temple were both filled with the blazing presence of the Glory of GOD. And the sound! The wings of the cherubim were audible all the way to the outer court—the sound of the voice was like The Strong God in thunder.

6-8 When GOD commanded the man dressed in linen, "Take fire from among the wheels, from between the cherubim," he went in and stood beside a wheel. One of the cherubim reached into the fire, took some coals, and put them in the hands of the man dressed in linen. He took them and went out. Something that looked like a human hand could be seen under the wings of the cherubim.

9-13 And then I saw four wheels beside the cherubim, one beside each cherub. The wheels radiating were sparkling like diamonds in the sun. All four wheels looked alike, each like a wheel within a wheel. When they moved, they went in any of the four directions but in a perfectly straight line. Where the cherubim went, the wheels went straight ahead. The cherubim were full of eyes in their backs, hands, and wings. The wheels likewise were full of eyes. I heard the wheels called "wheels within wheels."

14 Each of the cherubim had four faces: the first, of an angel; the second, a human; the third, a lion; the fourth, an eagle.

15-17 Then the cherubim ascended. They were the same living creatures I had seen at the Kebar River. When the cherubim moved, the wheels beside them moved. When the cherubim spread their wings to take off from the ground, the wheels stayed right with them. When the cherubim stopped, the wheels stopped. When the cherubim rose, the wheels rose, because the spirit of the living creatures was also in the wheels.

18-19 Then the Glory of GOD left the Temple entrance and hovered over the cherubim. I watched as the cherubim spread their wings and left the ground, the wheels right with them. They stopped at the entrance of the east gate of the Temple. The Glory of the God of Israel was above them.

20-22 These were the same living creatures I had seen previously beneath the God of Israel at the Kebar River. I recognized them as cherubim. Each had four faces and four wings. Under their wings were what looked like human hands. Their faces looked exactly like those I had seen at the Kebar River. Each went straight ahead.

A NEW HEART AND A NEW SPIRIT

1 Then the Spirit picked me up and took me to the gate of the Temple that faces east. There were twenty-five men standing at the gate. I recognized the leaders, Jaazaniah son of Azzur and Pelatiah son of Benaiah.

2-3 GOD said, "Son of man, these are the men who draw up blueprints for sin, who think up new programs for evil in this city. They say, 'We can make anything happen here. We're the best. We're the choice pieces of meat in the soup pot.'

4 "Oppose them, son of man. Preach against them."

5-6 Then the Spirit of GOD came upon me and told me what to say: "This is what GOD says: 'That's a fine public speech, Israel, but I know what you are thinking. You've murdered a lot of people in this city. The streets are piled high with corpses.'

7-12 "Therefore this is what GOD, the Master, says: 'The corpses that you've piled in the streets are the meat and this city is the soup pot, and *you're* not even in the pot! I'm throwing you out! You fear war, but war is what you're going to get. I'm bringing war against you. I'm throwing you out of this city, giving you over to foreigners, and punishing you good. You'll be killed in battle. I'll carry out judgment on you at the borders of Israel. Then you'll realize that I am GOD. This city will not be your soup pot and you won't be the choice pieces of meat in it either. Hardly. I will carry out judgment on you at the borders of Israel and you'll realize that I am GOD, for you haven't followed my statutes and ordinances. Instead of following my ways, you've sunk to the level of the laws of the nations around you.' "

13 Even while I was preaching, Pelatiah son of Benaiah died. I fell down, face to the ground, and prayed loudly, "O Master, GOD! Will you completely wipe out what's left of Israel?"

14-15 The answer from GOD came back: "Son of man, your brothers — I mean the whole people of Israel who are in exile with you — are the people of whom the citizens of Jerusalem are saying, 'They're in the far country, far from GOD. This land has been given to us to own.'

16-20 "Well, tell them this, 'This is your Message from GOD, the Master. True, I sent you to the far country and scattered you through other lands. All the same, I've provided you a temporary sanctuary in the countries where you've gone. I will gather you back from those countries and lands where you've been scattered and give you back the land of Israel. You'll come back and clean house, throw out all the rotten images and obscene idols. I'll give you a new heart. I'll put a new spirit in you. I'll cut out your stone heart and replace it with a red-blooded, firm-muscled heart. Then you'll obey my statutes and be careful to obey my commands. You'll be my people! I'll be your God!

21 " 'But not those who are self-willed and addicted to their rotten images and obscene idols! I'll see that they're paid in full for what they've done.' Decree of GOD, the Master."

22-23 Then the cherubim spread their wings, with the wheels beside them and the Glory of the God of Israel hovering over them. The Glory of GOD ascended from within the city and rested on the mountain to the east of the city.

24-25 Then, still in the vision given me by the Spirit of God, the Spirit took me and carried me back to the exiles in Babylon. And then the vision left me. I told the exiles everything that GOD had shown me.

PUT THE BUNDLE ON YOUR SHOULDER
AND WALK INTO THE NIGHT

1-6 **12** GOD's Message came to me: "Son of man, you're living with a bunch of rebellious people. They have eyes but don't see a thing, they have ears but don't hear a thing. They're rebels all. So, son of man, pack up your exile duffel bags. Leave in broad daylight with everyone watching and go off, as if into exile. Maybe then they'll understand what's going on, rebels though they are. You'll take up your baggage while they watch, a bundle of the bare necessities of someone going into exile, and toward evening leave, just like a person going off into exile. As they watch, dig through the wall of the house and carry your bundle through it. In full sight of the people, put the bundle on your shoulder and walk out into the night. Cover your face so you won't have to look at what you'll never see again. I'm using you as a sign for the family of Israel."

7 I did exactly as he commanded me. I got my stuff together and brought it out in the street where everyone could see me, bundled it up the way someone being taken off into exile would, and then, as the sun went down, made a hole in the wall of the house with my hands. As it grew dark and as they watched, I left, throwing my bundle across my shoulders.

8-10 The next morning GOD spoke to me: "Son of man, when anyone in Israel, that bunch of rebels, asks you, 'What are you doing?' Tell them, 'GOD, the Master, says that this Message especially concerns the prince in Jerusalem — Zedekiah — but includes all the people of Israel.'

11 "Also tell them, 'I am drawing a picture for you. As I am now doing, it will be done to all the people of Israel. They will go into exile as captives.'

12-15 "The prince will put his bundle on his shoulders in the dark and leave. He'll dig through the wall of the house, covering his face so he won't have to look at the land he'll never see again. But I'll make sure he gets caught and is taken to Babylon. Blinded, he'll never see that land in which he'll die. I'll scatter to the four winds those who helped him escape, along with his troops, and many will die in battle. They'll realize that I am GOD when I scatter them among foreign countries.

16 "I'll permit a few of them to escape the killing, starvation, and deadly sickness so that they can confess among the foreign countries all the disgusting obscenities they've been involved in. They will realize that I am GOD."

17-20 GOD's Message came to me: "Son of man, eat your meals shaking in your boots, drink your water trembling with fear. Tell the people of this land, everyone living in Jerusalem and Israel, GOD's Message: 'You'll eat your meals shaking in your boots and drink your water in terror because your land is going to be stripped bare as punishment for the brutality rampant in it. All the cities and villages will be emptied out and the fields destroyed. Then you'll realize that I am GOD.'"

21-22 GOD's Message came to me: "Son of man, what's this proverb making the rounds in the land of Israel that says, 'Everything goes on the same as ever; all the prophetic warnings are false alarms'?

23-25 "Tell them, 'GOD, the Master, says, This proverb's going to have a short life!'

"Tell them, 'Time's about up. Every warning is about to come true. False alarms and easygoing preaching are a thing of the past in the life of Israel. I, GOD, am doing the speaking. What I say happens. None of what I say is on hold. What I say, I'll do — and soon, you rebels!' Decree of GOD the Master."

26-28 GOD's Message came to me: "Son of man, do you hear what Israel is saying: that the alarm the prophet raises is for a long time off, that he's preaching about the far-off future? Well, tell them, 'GOD, the Master, says, "Nothing of what I say is on hold. What I say happens."' Decree of GOD, the Master."

PEOPLE WHO LOVE LISTENING TO LIES

1-2 **13** GOD's Message came to me: "Son of man, preach against the prophets of Israel who are making things up out of their own heads and calling it 'prophesying.'

2-6 "Preach to them the real thing. Tell them, 'Listen to GOD's Message!' GOD, the Master, pronounces doom on the empty-headed prophets who do their own thing and know nothing of what's going on! Your prophets, Israel, are like jackals scavenging through the ruins. They haven't lifted a finger to repair the defenses of the city and have risked nothing to help Israel stand on GOD's Day of Judgment. All they do is fantasize comforting illusions and preach lying sermons. They say 'GOD says . . .' when GOD hasn't so much as breathed in their direction. And yet they stand around thinking that something they said is going to happen.

7-9 "Haven't you fantasized sheer nonsense? Aren't your sermons tissues of lies, saying 'GOD says . . .' when I've done nothing of the kind? Therefore—and this is the Message of GOD, the Master, remember—I'm dead set against prophets who substitute illusions for visions and use sermons to tell lies. I'm going to ban them from the council of my people, remove them from membership in Israel, and outlaw them from the land of Israel. Then you'll realize that I am GOD, the Master.

10-12 "The fact is that they've lied to my people. They've said, 'No problem; everything's just fine,' when things are not at all fine. When people build a wall, they're right behind them slapping on whitewash. Tell those who are slapping on the whitewash, 'When a torrent of rain comes and the hailstones crash down and the hurricane sweeps in and the wall collapses, what's the good of the whitewash that you slapped on so liberally, making it look so good?'

13-14 "And that's exactly what will happen. I, GOD, the Master, say so: 'I'll let the hurricane of my wrath loose, a torrent of my hailstone-anger. I'll make that wall you've slapped with whitewash collapse. I'll level it to the ground so that only the foundation stones will be left. And in the ruin you'll all die. You'll realize then that I am GOD.

15-16 "'I'll dump my wrath on that wall, all of it, and on those who plastered it with whitewash. I will say to them, There is no wall, and those who did such a good job of whitewashing it wasted their time, those prophets of Israel who preached to Jerusalem and announced all their visions telling us things were just fine when they weren't at all fine. Decree of GOD, the Master.'

17-19 "And the women prophets—son of man, take your stand against the women prophets who make up stuff out of their own minds. Oppose them. Say 'Doom' to the women who sew magic bracelets and head scarves to suit every taste, devices to trap souls. Say, 'Will you kill the souls of my people, use living souls to make yourselves rich and popular? You have profaned me among my people just to get ahead yourselves, used me to make yourselves look good—killing souls who should never have died and coddling souls who shouldn't live. You've lied to people who love listening to lies.'

20-21 "Therefore GOD says, 'I am against all the devices and techniques you use to hunt down souls. I'll rip them out of your hands. I'll free the souls you're trying to catch. I'll rip your magic bracelets and scarves to shreds and deliver my people from your influence so they'll no longer be victimized by you. That's how you'll come to realize that I am GOD.

22-23 "'Because you've confounded and confused good people, unsuspecting and innocent people, with your lies, and because you've made it easy for others to persist in evil so that it wouldn't even dawn on them to turn to me so I could save them, as of now you're finished. No more delusion-mongering from you, no more sermonic lies. I'm going to rescue my people from your clutches. And you'll realize that I am God.'"

Idols in Their Hearts

1-5 **14** Some of the leaders of Israel approached me and sat down with me. God's Message came to me: "Son of Man, these people have installed idols in their hearts. They have embraced the wickedness that will ruin them. Why should I even bother with their prayers? Therefore tell them, 'The Message of God, the Master: All in Israel who install idols in their hearts and embrace the wickedness that will ruin them and still have the gall to come to a prophet, be on notice: I, God, will step in and personally answer them as they come dragging along their mob of idols. I am ready to go to work on the hearts of the house of Israel, all of whom have left me for their idols.'

6-8 "Therefore, say to the house of Israel: 'God, the Master, says, Repent! Turn your backs on your no-god idols. Turn your backs on all your outrageous obscenities. To every last person from the house of Israel, including any of the resident aliens who live in Israel—all who turn their backs on me and embrace idols, who install the wickedness that will ruin them at the center of their lives and then have the gall to go to the prophet to ask me questions—I, God, will step in and give the answer myself. I'll oppose those people to their faces, make an example of them—a warning lesson—and get rid of them so you will realize that I am God.

9-11 "'If a prophet is deceived and tells these idolaters the lies they want to hear, I, God, get blamed for those lies. He won't get by with it. I'll grab him by the scruff of the neck and get him out of there. They'll be equally guilty, the prophet and the one who goes to the prophet, so that the house of Israel will never again wander off my paths and make themselves filthy in their rebellions, but will rather be my people, just as I am their God. Decree of God, the Master.'"

12-14 God's Message came to me: "Son of man, when a country sins against me by living faithlessly and I reach out and destroy its food supply by bringing on a famine, wiping out humans and animals alike, even if Noah, Daniel, and Job—the Big Three—were alive at the time, it wouldn't do the population any good. Their righteousness would only save their own lives." Decree of God, the Master.

15-16 "Or, if I make wild animals go through the country so that everyone has to leave and the country becomes wilderness and no one dares enter it anymore because of the wild animals, even if these three men were living there, as sure as I am the living God, neither their sons nor daughters would be rescued, but only those three, and the country would revert to wilderness.

17-18 "Or, if I bring war on that country and give the order, 'Let the killing begin!' leaving both people and animals dead, even if those three men were alive at the time, as sure as I am the living God, neither sons nor daughters would be rescued, but only these three.

19-20 "Or, if I visit a deadly disease on that country, pouring out my lethal anger, killing both people and animals, and Noah, Daniel, and Job happened to be alive at the time, as sure as I am the living God, not a son, not a daughter, would be rescued. Only these three would be delivered because of their righteousness.

21-23 "Now then, that's the picture," says GOD, the Master, "once I've sent my four catastrophic judgments on Jerusalem—war, famine, wild animals, disease—to kill off people and animals alike. But look! Believe it or not, there'll be survivors. Some of their sons and daughters will be brought out. When they come out to you and their salvation is right in your face, you'll see for yourself the life they've been saved from. You'll know that this severe judgment I brought on Jerusalem was worth it, that it had to be. Yes, when you see in detail the kind of lives they've been living, you'll feel much better. You'll see the reason behind all that I've done in Jerusalem." Decree of GOD, the Master.

USED AS FUEL FOR THE FIRE

1-3 **15** GOD's Message came to me: "Son of man, how would you compare the wood of a vine with the branches of any tree you'd find in the forest? Is vine wood ever used to make anything? Is it used to make pegs to hang things from?

4 "I don't think so. At best it's good for fuel. Look at it: A flimsy piece of vine, thrown in the fire and then rescued—the ends burned off and the middle charred. Now is it good for anything?

5 "Hardly. When it was whole it wasn't good for anything. Half-burned is no improvement. What's it good for?

6-8 "So here's the Message of GOD, the Master: Like the wood of the vine I selected from among the trees of the forest and used as fuel for the fire, just so I'll treat those who live in Jerusalem. I am dead set against them. Even though at one time they got out of the fire charred, the fire's going to burn them up. When I take my stand against them, you'll realize that I am GOD. I'll turn this country into a wilderness because they've been faithless." Decree of GOD, the Master.

YOUR BEAUTY WENT TO YOUR HEAD

1-3 **16** GOD's Message came to me: "Son of man, confront Jerusalem with her outrageous violations. Say this: 'The Message of GOD, the Master, to Jerusalem: You were born and bred among Canaanites. Your father was an Amorite and your mother a Hittite.

4-5 "'On the day you were born your umbilical cord was not cut, you weren't bathed and cleaned up, you weren't rubbed with salt, you weren't wrapped in a baby blanket. No one cared a fig for you. No one did one thing to care for you tenderly in these ways. You were thrown out into a vacant lot and left there, dirty and unwashed—a newborn nobody wanted.

6-7 "'And then I came by. I saw you all miserable and bloody. Yes, I said to you, lying there helpless and filthy, "Live! Grow up like a plant in the field!" And you did. You grew up. You grew tall and matured as a woman, full-breasted, with flowing hair. But you were naked and vulnerable, fragile and exposed.

8-14 "'I came by again and saw you, saw that you were ready for love and a lover. I took care of you, dressed you and protected you. I promised you my love and entered the covenant of marriage with you. I, God, the Master, gave my word. You became mine. I gave you a good bath, washing off all that old blood, and anointed you with aromatic oils. I dressed you in a colorful gown and put leather sandals on your feet. I gave you linen blouses and a fashionable wardrobe of expensive clothing. I adorned you with jewelry: I placed bracelets on your wrists, fitted you out with a necklace, emerald rings, sapphire earrings, and a diamond tiara. You were provided with everything precious and beautiful: with exquisite clothes and elegant food, garnished with honey and oil. You were absolutely stunning. You were a queen! You became world-famous, a legendary beauty brought to perfection by my adornments. Decree of God, the Master.

15-16 "'But your beauty went to your head and you became a common whore, grabbing anyone coming down the street and taking him into your bed. You took your fine dresses and made "tents" of them, using them as brothels in which you practiced your trade. This kind of thing should never happen, never.

What a Sick Soul!

17-19 "'And then you took all that fine jewelry I gave you, my gold and my silver, and made pornographic images of them for your brothels. You decorated your beds with fashionable silks and cottons, and perfumed them with my aromatic oils and incense. And then you set out the wonderful foods I provided—the fresh breads and fruits, with fine herbs and spices, which were my gifts to you—and you served them as delicacies in your whorehouses. That's what happened, says God, the Master.

20-21 "'And then you took your sons and your daughters, whom you had given birth to as my children, and you killed them, sacrificing them to idols. Wasn't it bad enough that you had become a whore? And now you're a murderer, killing my children and sacrificing them to idols.

22 "'Not once during these years of outrageous obscenities and whorings did you remember your infancy, when you were naked and exposed, a blood-smeared newborn.

23-24 "'And then to top off all your evil acts, you built your bold brothels in every town square. Doom! Doom to you, says God, the Master! At every major intersection you built your bold brothels and exposed your sluttish sex, spreading your legs for everyone who passed by.

25-27 "'And then you went international with your whoring. You fornicated with the Egyptians, seeking them out in their sex orgies. The more promiscuous you became, the angrier I got. Finally, I intervened, reduced your borders and turned you over to the rapacity of your enemies. Even the Philistine women—can you believe it?—were shocked at your sluttish life.

28-29 "'You went on to fornicate with the Assyrians. Your appetite was insatiable. But still you weren't satisfied. You took on the Babylonians, a country of businessmen, and *still* you weren't satisfied.

30-31 "'What a sick soul! Doing all this stuff—the champion whore! You built your bold brothels at every major intersection, opened up your whorehouses in every neighborhood, but you were different from regular whores in that you wouldn't accept a fee.

32-34 "'Wives who are unfaithful to their husbands accept gifts from their lovers. And men commonly pay their whores. But you pay your lovers! You bribe men from all over to come to bed with you! You're just the opposite of the regular whores who get paid for sex. Instead, you pay men for *their* favors! You even pervert whoredom!

35-38 " 'Therefore, whore, listen to GOD's Message: I, GOD, the Master, say, Because you've been unrestrained in your promiscuity, stripped down for every lover, flaunting your sex, and because of your pornographic idols and all the slaughtered children you offered to them, therefore, because of all this, I'm going to get all your lovers together, all those you've used for your own pleasure, the ones you loved and the ones you loathed. I'll assemble them as a courtroom of spectators around you. In broad daylight I'll strip you naked before them — they'll see what you *really* look like. Then I'll sentence you to the punishment for an adulterous woman and a murderous woman. I'll give you a taste of my wrath!

39-41 " 'I'll gather all your lovers around you and turn you over to them. They'll tear down your bold brothels and sex shrines. They'll rip off your clothes, take your jewels, and leave you naked and exposed. Then they'll call for a mass meeting. The mob will stone you and hack you to pieces with their swords. They'll burn down your houses. A massive judgment — with all the women watching!

41-42 " 'I'll have put a full stop to your whoring life — no more paying lovers to come to your bed! By then my anger will be played out. My jealousy will subside.

43 " 'Because you didn't remember what happened when you were young but made me angry with all this behavior, I'll make you pay for your waywardness. Didn't you just exponentially compound your outrageous obscenities with all your sluttish ways?

44-45 " 'Everyone who likes to use proverbs will use this one: "Like mother, like daughter." You're the daughter of your mother, who couldn't stand her husband and children. And you're a true sister of your sisters, who couldn't stand their husbands and children. Your mother was a Hittite and your father an Amorite.

46-48 " 'Your older sister is Samaria. She lived to the north of you with her daughters. Your younger sister is Sodom, who lived to the south of you with her daughters. Haven't you lived just like they did? Haven't you engaged in outrageous obscenities just like they did? In fact, it didn't take you long to catch up and pass them! As sure as I am the living God! — Decree of GOD, the Master — your sister Sodom and her daughters never even came close to what you and your daughters have done.

49-50 " 'The sin of your sister Sodom was this: She lived with her daughters in the lap of luxury — proud, gluttonous, and lazy. They ignored the oppressed and the poor. They put on airs and lived obscene lives. And you know what happened: I did away with them.

51-52 " 'And Samaria. Samaria didn't sin half as much as you. You've committed far more obscenities than she ever did. Why, you make your two sisters look good in comparison with what you've done! Face it, your sisters look mighty good compared with you. Because you've outsinned them so completely, you've actually made them look righteous. Aren't you ashamed? But you're going to have to live with it. What a reputation to carry into history: outsinning your two sisters!

53-58 " 'But I'm going to reverse their fortunes, the fortunes of Sodom and her daughters and the fortunes of Samaria and her daughters. And — get this — *your* fortunes right along with them! Still, you're going to have to live with your shame. And by facing and accepting your shame, you're going to provide some comfort to your two sisters. Your sisters, Sodom with her daughters and Samaria with her daughters, will become what they were before, and you will become what you were before. Remember the days when you were putting on airs, acting so high and mighty, looking down on sister Sodom? That was before your evil ways were exposed. And now *you're* the butt of contempt, despised by the Edomite women, the Philistine women, and everybody else around. But you have to face it, to accept the shame of your obscene and vile life. Decree of GOD, the Master.

59-63   "'GOD, the Master, says, I'll do to you just as you have already done, you who have treated my oath with contempt and broken the covenant. All the same, I'll remember the covenant I made with you when you were young and I'll make a new covenant with you that will last forever. You'll remember your sorry past and be properly contrite when you receive back your sisters, both the older and the younger. I'll give them to you as daughters, but not as participants in your covenant. I'll firmly establish my covenant with you and you'll know that I am GOD. You'll remember your past life and face the shame of it, but when I make atonement for you, make everything right after all you've done, it will leave you speechless.'" Decree of GOD, the Master.

THE GREAT TREE IS MADE SMALL AND THE SMALL TREE GREAT

1-6   **17** GOD's Message came to me: "Son of man, make a riddle for the house of Israel. Tell them a story. Say, 'GOD, the Master, says:

"'A great eagle
    with a huge wingspan and long feathers,
In full plumage and bright colors,
    came to Lebanon
And took the top off a cedar,
    broke off the top branch,
Took it to a land of traders,
    and set it down in a city of shopkeepers.
Then he took a cutting from the land
    and planted it in good, well-watered soil,
    like a willow on a riverbank.
It sprouted into a flourishing vine,
    low to the ground.
Its branches grew toward the eagle
    and the roots became established —
A vine putting out shoots,
    developing branches.

7-8   "'There was another great eagle
    with a huge wingspan and thickly feathered.
This vine sent out its roots toward him
    from the place where it was planted.
Its branches reached out to him
    so he could water it
    from a long distance.
It had been planted
    in good, well-watered soil,

And it put out branches and bore fruit,
   and became a noble vine.

9-10   "'GOD, the Master, says,
   Will it thrive?
Won't he just pull it up by the roots
   and leave the grapes to rot
And the branches to shrivel up,
   a withered, dead vine?
It won't take much strength
   or many hands to pull it up.
Even if it's transplanted,
   will it thrive?
When the hot east wind strikes it,
   won't it shrivel up?
Won't it dry up and blow away
   from the place where it was planted?'"

11-12   GOD's Message came to me: "Tell this house of rebels, 'Do you get it? Do you know what this means?'

12-14   "Tell them, 'The king of Babylon came to Jerusalem and took its king and its leaders back to Babylon. He took one of the royal family and made a covenant with him, making him swear his loyalty. The king of Babylon took all the top leaders into exile to make sure that this kingdom stayed weak—didn't get any big ideas of itself—and kept the covenant with him so that it would have a future.

15   "'But he rebelled and sent emissaries to Egypt to recruit horses and a big army. Do you think that's going to work? Are they going to get by with this? Does anyone break a covenant and get off scot-free?

16-18   "'As sure as I am the living God, this king who broke his pledge of loyalty and his covenant will die in that country, in Babylon. Pharaoh with his big army—all those soldiers!—won't lift a finger to fight for him when Babylon sets siege to the city and kills everyone inside. Because he broke his word and broke the covenant, even though he gave his solemn promise, because he went ahead and did all these things anyway, he won't escape.

19-21   "'Therefore, GOD, the Master, says, As sure as I am the living God, because the king despised my oath and broke my covenant, I'll bring the consequences crashing down on his head. I'll send out a search party and catch him. I'll take him to Babylon and have him brought to trial because of his total disregard for me. All his elite soldiers, along with the rest of the army, will be killed in battle, and whoever is left will be scattered to the four winds. Then you'll realize that I, GOD, have spoken.

22-24   "'GOD, the Master, says, I personally will take a shoot from the top of the towering cedar, a cutting from the crown of the tree, and plant it on a high and towering mountain, on the high mountain of Israel. It will grow, putting out branches and fruit—a majestic cedar. Birds of every sort and kind will live under it. They'll build nests in the shade of its branches. All the trees of the field will recognize that I, GOD, made the great tree small and the small tree great, made the green tree turn dry and the dry tree sprout green branches. I, GOD, said it—and I did it.'"

Judged According to the Way You Live

1-2

18

God's Message to me: "What do you people mean by going around the country repeating the saying,

The parents ate green apples,
The children got the stomachache?

3-4

"As sure as I'm the living God, you're not going to repeat this saying in Israel any longer. Every soul—man, woman, child—belongs to me, parent and child alike. You die for your own sin, not another's.

5-9

"Imagine a person who lives well, treating others fairly, keeping good relationships—

> doesn't eat at the pagan shrines,
> doesn't worship the idols so popular in Israel,
> doesn't seduce a neighbor's spouse,
> doesn't indulge in casual sex,
> doesn't bully anyone,
> doesn't pile up bad debts,
> doesn't steal,
> doesn't refuse food to the hungry,
> doesn't refuse clothing to the ill-clad,
> doesn't exploit the poor,
> doesn't live by impulse and greed,
> doesn't treat one person better than another,
> But lives by my statutes and faithfully
> honors and obeys my laws.
> This person who lives upright and well
> shall live a full and true life.
> Decree of God, the Master.

10-13

"But if this person has a child who turns violent and murders and goes off and does any of these things, even though the parent has done none of them—

> eats at the pagan shrines,
> seduces his neighbor's spouse,
> bullies the weak,
> steals,
> piles up bad debts,
> admires idols,
> commits outrageous obscenities,
> exploits the poor

"—do you think this person, the child, will live? Not a chance! Because he's done all these vile things, he'll die. And his death will be his own fault.

14-17

"Now look: Suppose that this child has a child who sees all the sins done by his parent. The child sees them, but doesn't follow in the parent's footsteps—

doesn't eat at the pagan shrines,
doesn't worship the popular idols of Israel,
doesn't seduce his neighbor's spouse,
doesn't bully anyone,
doesn't refuse to loan money,
doesn't steal,
doesn't refuse food to the hungry,
doesn't refuse to give clothes to the ill-clad,
doesn't live by impulse and greed,
doesn't exploit the poor.

He does what I say;
he performs my laws and lives by my statutes.

17-18 "This person will not die for the sins of the parent; he will live truly and well. But the parent will die for what the parent did, for the sins of—

oppressing the weak,
robbing brothers and sisters,
doing what is dead wrong in the community.

19-20 "Do you need to ask, 'So why does the child not share the guilt of the parent?'

"Isn't it plain? It's because the child did what is fair and right. Since the child was careful to do what is lawful and right, the child will live truly and well. The soul that sins is the soul that dies. The child does not share the guilt of the parent, nor the parent the guilt of the child. If you live upright and well, you get the credit; if you live a wicked life, you're guilty as charged.

21-23 "But a wicked person who turns his back on that life of sin and keeps all my statutes, living a just and righteous life, he'll live, really live. He won't die. I won't keep a list of all the things he did wrong. He will live. Do you think I take any pleasure in the death of wicked men and women? Isn't it my pleasure that they turn around, no longer living wrong but living right — really living?

24 "The same thing goes for a good person who turns his back on an upright life and starts sinning, plunging into the same vile obscenities that the wicked person practices. Will this person live? I don't keep a list of all the things this person did right, like money in the bank he can draw on. Because of his defection, because he accumulates sin, he'll die.

25-28 "Do I hear you saying, 'That's not fair! God's not fair!'?

"Listen, Israel. I'm not fair? You're the ones who aren't fair! If a good person turns away from his good life and takes up sinning, he'll die for it. He'll die for his own sin. Likewise, if a bad person turns away from his bad life and starts living a good life, a fair life, he will save his life. Because he faces up to all the wrongs he's committed and puts them behind him, he will live, really live. He won't die.

29 "And yet Israel keeps on whining, 'That's not fair! God's not fair.'

"I'm not fair, Israel? You're the ones who aren't fair.

30-32 "The upshot is this, Israel: I'll judge each of you according to the way you live. So turn around! Turn your backs on your rebellious living so that sin won't drag you down. Clean house. No more rebellions, please. Get a

new heart! Get a new spirit! Why would you choose to die, Israel? I take no
pleasure in anyone's death. Decree of GOD, the Master.

"Make a clean break! Live!"

A STORY OF TWO LIONS

₁₋₄ **19** Sing the blues over the princes of Israel. Say:

What a lioness was your mother
among lions!
She crouched in a pride of young lions.
Her cubs grew large.
She reared one of her cubs to maturity,
a robust young lion.
He learned to hunt.
He ate men.
Nations sounded the alarm.
He was caught in a trap.
They took him with hooks
and dragged him to Egypt.

₅₋₉ When the lioness saw she was luckless,
that her hope for that cub was gone,
She took her other cub
and made him a strong young lion.
He prowled with the lions,
a robust young lion.
He learned to hunt.
He ate men.
He rampaged through their defenses,
left their cities in ruins.
The country and everyone in it
was terrorized by the roars of the lion.
The nations got together to hunt him.
Everyone joined the hunt.
They set out their traps
and caught him.
They put a wooden collar on him
and took him to the king of Babylon.
No more would that voice be heard
disturbing the peace in the mountains of Israel!

₁₀₋₁₄ Here's another way to put it:
Your mother was like a vine in a vineyard,
transplanted alongside streams of water,
Luxurious in branches and grapes
because of the ample water.
It grew sturdy branches
fit to be carved into a royal scepter.
It grew high, reaching into the clouds.
Its branches filled the horizon,
and everyone could see it.

Then it was ripped up in a rage
  and thrown to the ground.
The hot east wind shriveled it up
  and stripped its fruit.
The sturdy branches dried out,
  fit for nothing but kindling.
Now it's a stick stuck out in the desert,
  a bare stick in a desert of death,
Good for nothing but making fires,
  campfires in the desert.
Not a hint now of those sturdy branches
  fit for use as a royal scepter!

(This is a sad song, a text for singing the blues.)

Get Rid of All the Things You've Become Addicted To

¹ **20** In the seventh year, the fifth month, on the tenth day of the month, some of the leaders of Israel came to ask for guidance from God. They sat down before me.

²⁻³ Then God's Message came to me: "Son of man, talk with the leaders of Israel. Tell them, 'God, the Master, says, "Have you come to ask me questions? As sure as I am the living God, I'll not put up with questions from you. Decree of God, the Master."'

⁴⁻⁵ "Son of man, why don't *you* do it? Yes, go ahead. Hold them accountable. Confront them with the outrageous obscenities of their parents. Tell them that God, the Master, says:

⁵⁻⁶ "'On the day I chose Israel, I revealed myself to them in the country of Egypt, raising my hand in a solemn oath to the people of Jacob, in which I said, "I am God, your personal God." On the same day that I raised my hand in the solemn oath, I promised them that I would take them out of the country of Egypt and bring them into a country that I had searched out just for them, a country flowing with milk and honey, a jewel of a country.

⁷ "'At that time I told them, "Get rid of all the vile things that you've become addicted to. Don't make yourselves filthy with the Egyptian no-god idols. I *alone* am God, your God."

⁸⁻¹⁰ "'But they rebelled against me, wouldn't listen to a word I said. None got rid of the vile things they were addicted to. They held on to the no-gods of Egypt as if for dear life. I seriously considered inflicting my anger on them in force right there in Egypt. Then I thought better of it. I acted out of who I was, not by how I felt. And I acted in a way that would evoke honor, not blasphemy, from the nations around them, nations who had seen me reveal myself by promising to lead my people out of Egypt. And then I did it: I led them out of Egypt into the desert.

¹¹⁻¹² "'I gave them laws for living, showed them how to live well and obediently before me. I also gave them my weekly holy rest days, my "Sabbaths," a kind of signpost erected between me and them to show them that I, God, am in the business of making them holy.

¹³⁻¹⁷ "'But Israel rebelled against me in the desert. They didn't follow my statutes. They despised my laws for living well and obediently in the ways I had set out. And they totally desecrated my holy Sabbaths. I seriously considered unleashing my anger on them right there in the desert. But I thought better

of it and acted out of who I was, not by what I felt, so that I might be honored and not blasphemed by the nations who had seen me bring them out. But I did lift my hand in a solemn oath there in the desert and promise them that I would not bring them into the country flowing with milk and honey that I had chosen for them, that jewel among all lands. I canceled my promise because they despised my laws for living obediently, wouldn't follow my statutes, and went ahead and desecrated my holy Sabbaths. They preferred living by their no-god idols. But I didn't go all the way: I didn't wipe them out, didn't finish them off in the desert.

18-20   " 'Then I addressed myself to their children in the desert: "Don't do what your parents did. Don't take up their practices. Don't make yourselves filthy with their no-god idols. I myself am GOD, your God: Keep my statutes and live by my laws. Keep my Sabbaths as holy rest days, signposts between me and you, signaling that I am GOD, *your* God."

21-22   " 'But the children also rebelled against me. They neither followed my statutes nor kept my laws for living upright and well. And they desecrated my Sabbaths. I seriously considered dumping my anger on them, right there in the desert. But I thought better of it and acted out of who I was, not by what I felt, so that I might be honored and not blasphemed by the nations who had seen me bring them out.

23-26   " 'But I did lift my hand in solemn oath there in the desert, and swore that I would scatter them all over the world, disperse them every which way because they didn't keep my laws nor live by my statutes. They desecrated my Sabbaths and remained addicted to the no-god idols of their parents. Since they were determined to live bad lives, I myself gave them statutes that could not produce goodness and laws that did not produce life. I abandoned them. Filthy in the gutter, they perversely sacrificed their firstborn children in the fire. The very horror should have shocked them into recognizing that I am GOD.'

27-29   "Therefore, speak to Israel, son of man. Tell them that GOD says, 'As if that wasn't enough, your parents further insulted me by betraying me. When I brought them into that land that I had solemnly promised with my upraised hand to give them, every time they saw a hill with a sex-and-religion shrine on it or a grove of trees where the sacred whores practiced, they were there, buying into the whole pagan system. I said to them, "What hill do you go to?"' (It's still called 'Whore Hills.')

30-31   "Therefore, say to Israel, 'The Message of GOD, the Master: You're making your lives filthy by copying the ways of your parents. In repeating their vile practices, you've become whores yourselves. In burning your children as sacrifices, you've become as filthy as your no-god idols—as recently as today!

" 'Am I going to put up with questions from people like you, Israel? As sure as I am the living God, I, GOD, the Master, refuse to be called into question by you!

32   " 'What you're secretly thinking is never going to happen. You're thinking, "We're going to be like everybody else, just like the other nations. We're going to worship gods we can make and control."

33-35   " 'As sure as I am the living God, says GOD, the Master, think again! With a mighty show of strength and a terrifying rush of anger, I will be King over you! I'll bring you back from the nations, collect you out of the countries to which you've been scattered, with a mighty show of strength and a terrifying rush of anger. I'll bring you to the desert of nations and haul you into court, where you'll be face-to-face with judgment.

36-38 "'As I faced your parents with judgment in the desert of Egypt, so I'll face you with judgment. I'll scrutinize and search every person as you arrive, and I'll bring you under the bond of the covenant. I'll cull out the rebels and traitors. I'll lead them out of their exile, but I won't bring them back to Israel.

"'Then you'll realize that I am GOD.

39-43 "'But you, people of Israel, this is the Message of GOD, the Master, to you: Go ahead, serve your no-god idols! But later, you'll think better of it and quit throwing filth and mud on me with your pagan offerings and no-god idols. For on my holy mountain, the high mountain of Israel, I, GOD, the Master, tell you that the entire people of Israel will worship me. I'll receive them there with open arms. I'll demand your best gifts and offerings, all your holy sacrifices. What's more, I'll receive you as the best kind of offerings when I bring you back from all the lands and countries in which you've been scattered. I'll demonstrate in the eyes of the world that I am The Holy. When I return you to the land of Israel, the land that I solemnly promised with upraised arm to give to your parents, you'll realize that I am GOD. Then and there you'll remember all that you've done, the way you've lived that has made you so filthy—and you'll loathe yourselves.

44 "'But, dear Israel, you'll also realize that I am GOD when I respond to you out of who I am, not by what I feel about the evil lives you've lived, the corrupt history you've compiled. Decree of GOD, the Master.'"

NOBODY WILL PUT OUT THE FIRE

45-46 GOD's Message came to me: "Son of man, face south. Let the Message roll out against the south. Prophesy against the wilderness forest of the south.

47-48 "Tell the forest of the south, 'Listen to the Message of GOD! GOD, the Master, says, I'll set a fire in you that will burn up every tree, dead trees and live trees alike. Nobody will put out the fire. The whole country from south to north will be blackened by it. Everyone is going to see that I, GOD, started the fire and that it's not going to be put out.'"

49 And I said, "O GOD, everyone is saying of me, 'He just makes up stories.'"

A SWORD! A SWORD!

1-5 21 GOD's Message came to me: "Son of man, now face Jerusalem and let the Message roll out against the Sanctuary. Prophesy against the land of Israel. Say, 'GOD's Message: I'm against you. I'm pulling my sword from its sheath and killing both the wicked and the righteous. Because I'm treating everyone the same, good and bad, everyone from south to north is going to feel my sword! Everyone will know that I mean business.'

6 "So, son of man, groan! Double up in pain. Make a scene!

7 "When they ask you, 'Why all this groaning, this carrying on?' say, 'Because of the news that's coming. It'll knock the breath out of everyone. Hearts will stop cold, knees turn to rubber. Yes, it's coming. No stopping it. Decree of GOD, the Master.'"

8-10 GOD's Message to me: "Son of man, prophesy. Tell them, 'The Master says:

> "'A sword! A sword!
>   razor-sharp and polished,
> Sharpened to kill,
>   polished to flash like lightning!
>
> "'My child, you've despised the scepter of Judah
>   by worshiping every tree-idol.

11 > "'The sword is made to glisten,
>   to be held and brandished.
> It's sharpened and polished,
>   ready to be brandished by the killer.'

12 > "Yell out and wail, son of man.
>   The sword is against my people!
> The princes of Israel
>   and my people—abandoned to the sword!
> Wring your hands!
>   Tear out your hair!

13 > "'Testing comes.
>   Why have you despised discipline?
> You can't get around it.
>   Decree of God, the Master.'

14-17 > "So, prophesy, son of man!
>   Clap your hands. Get their attention.
> Tell them that the sword's coming down
>   once, twice, three times.
> It's a sword to kill,
>   a sword for a massacre,
> A sword relentless,
>   a sword inescapable—
> People collapsing right and left,
>   going down like dominoes.
> I've stationed a murderous sword
>   at every gate in the city,
> Flashing like lightning,
>   brandished murderously.
> Cut to the right, thrust to the left,
>   murderous, sharp-edged sword!
> Then I'll clap my hands,
>   a signal that my anger is spent.
>   I, God, have spoken."

18-22 God's Message came to me: "Son of man, lay out two roads for the sword of the king of Babylon to take. Start them from the same place. Place a signpost at the beginning of each road. Post one sign to mark the road of the sword to Rabbah of the Ammonites. Post the other to mark the road to Judah and Fort

Jerusalem. The king of Babylon stands at the fork in the road and he decides by divination which of the two roads to take. He draws straws, he throws god-dice, he examines a goat liver. He opens his right hand: The omen says, 'Head for Jerusalem!' So he's on his way with battering rams, roused to kill, sounding the battle cry, pounding down city gates, building siege works.

23 "To the Judah leaders, who themselves have sworn oaths, it will seem like a false divination, but he will remind them of their guilt, and so they'll be captured.

24 "So this is what GOD, the Master, says: 'Because your sin is now out in the open so everyone can see what you've been doing, you'll be taken captive.

25-27 "'O Zedekiah, blasphemous and evil prince of Israel: Time's up. It's "punishment payday." GOD says, Take your royal crown off your head. No more "business as usual." The underdog will be promoted and the top dog will be demoted. Ruins, ruins, ruins! I'll turn the whole place into ruins. And ruins it will remain until the one comes who has a right to it. Then I'll give it to him.'

28-32 "But, son of man, your job is to prophesy. Tell them, 'This is the Message from GOD, the Master, against the Ammonites and against their cruel taunts:

"'A sword! A sword!
    Bared to kill,
Sharp as a razor,
    flashing like lightning.
Despite false sword propaganda
    circulated in Ammon,
The sword will sever Ammonite necks,
    for whom it's punishment payday.
Return the sword to the sheath! I'll judge you in your home country,
    in the land where you grew up.
I'll empty out my wrath on you,
    breathe hot anger down your neck.
I'll give you to vicious men
    skilled in torture.
You'll end up as stove-wood.
    Corpses will litter your land.
Not so much as a memory will be left of you.
    I, GOD, have said so.'"

THE SCARECROW OF THE NATIONS

1-5 **22** GOD's Message came to me: "Son of man, are you going to judge this bloody city or not? Come now, are you going to judge her? Do it! Face her with all her outrageous obscenities. Tell her, 'This is what GOD, the Master, says: You're a city murderous at the core, just asking for punishment. You're a city obsessed with no-god idols, making yourself filthy. In all your killing, you've piled up guilt. In all your idol-making, you've become filthy. You've forced a premature end to your existence. I'll put you on exhibit as the scarecrow of the nations, the world's worst joke. From far and near they'll deride you as infamous in filth, notorious for chaos.

6-12 "'Your leaders, the princes of Israel among you, compete in crime. You're a community that's insolent to parents, abusive to outsiders, oppressive against orphans and widows. You treat my holy things with contempt and desecrate my Sabbaths. You have people spreading lies and spilling blood, flocking to the hills to the sex shrines and fornicating unrestrained. Incest is common. Men force themselves on women regardless of whether they're ready or willing. Sex is now anarchy. Anyone is fair game: neighbor, daughter-in-law, sister. Murder is for hire, usury is rampant, extortion is commonplace.

"'And you've forgotten *me*. Decree of GOD, the Master.

13-14   "'Now look! I've clapped my hands, calling everyone's attention to your rapacious greed and your bloody brutalities. Can you stick with it? Will you be able to keep at this once I start dealing with you?

14-16   "'I, GOD, have spoken. I'll put an end to this. I'll throw you to the four winds. I'll scatter you all over the world. I'll put a full stop to your filthy living. You will be defiled, spattered with your own mud in the eyes of the nations. And you'll recognize that I am GOD.'"

17-22   GOD's Message came to me: "Son of man, the people of Israel are slag to me, the useless byproduct of refined copper, tin, iron, and lead left at the smelter—a worthless slag heap. So tell them, 'GOD, the Master, has spoken: Because you've all become worthless slag, you're on notice: I'll assemble you in Jerusalem. As men gather silver, copper, iron, lead, and tin into a furnace and blow fire on it to melt it down, so in my wrath I'll gather you and melt you down. I'll blow on you with the fire of my wrath to melt you down in the furnace. As silver is melted down, you'll be melted down. That should get through to you. Then you'll recognize that I, GOD, have let my wrath loose on you.'"

23-25   GOD's Message came to me: "Son of man, tell her, 'You're a land that during the time I was angry with you got no rain, not so much as a spring shower. The leaders among you became desperate, like roaring, ravaging lions killing indiscriminately. They grabbed and looted, leaving widows in their wake.

26-29   "'Your priests violated my law and desecrated my holy things. They can't tell the difference between sacred and secular. They tell people there's no difference between right and wrong. They're contemptuous of my holy Sabbaths, profaning me by trying to pull me down to their level. Your politicians are like wolves prowling and killing and rapaciously taking whatever they want. Your preachers cover up for the politicians by pretending to have received visions and special revelations. They say, "This is what GOD, the Master, says . . ." when GOD hasn't said so much as one word. Extortion is rife, robbery is epidemic, the poor and needy are abused, outsiders are kicked around at will, with no access to justice.'

30-31   "I looked for someone to stand up for me against all this, to repair the defenses of the city, to take a stand for me and stand in the gap to protect this land so I wouldn't have to destroy it. I couldn't find anyone. Not one. So I'll empty out my wrath on them, burn them to a crisp with my hot anger, serve them with the consequences of all they've done. Decree of GOD, the Master."

WILD WITH LUST

1-4   **23** GOD's Message came to me: "Son of man, there were two women, daughters of the same mother. They became whores in Egypt, whores from a young age. Their breasts were fondled, their young bosoms caressed. The older sister was named Oholah, the younger was Oholibah. They were my daughters, and they gave birth to sons and daughters.

"Oholah is Samaria and Oholibah is Jerusalem.

5-8 "Oholah started whoring while she was still mine. She lusted after Assyrians as lovers: military men smartly uniformed in blue, ambassadors and governors, good-looking young men mounted on fine horses. Her lust was unrestrained. She was a whore to the Assyrian elite. She compounded her filth with the idols of those to whom she gave herself in lust. She never slowed down. The whoring she began while young in Egypt she continued, sleeping with men who played with her breasts and spent their lust on her.

9-10 "So I left her to her Assyrian lovers, for whom she was so obsessed with lust. They ripped off her clothes, took away her children, and then, the final indignity, killed her. Among women her name became Shame—history's judgment on her.

11-18 "Her sister Oholibah saw all this, but she became even worse than her sister in lust and whoring, if you can believe it. She also went crazy with lust for Assyrians: ambassadors and governors, military men smartly dressed and mounted on fine horses—the Assyrian elite. And I saw that she also had become incredibly filthy. Both women followed the same path. But Oholibah surpassed her sister. When she saw figures of Babylonians carved in relief on the walls and painted red, fancy belts around their waists, elaborate turbans on their heads, all of them looking important—famous Babylonians!—she went wild with lust and sent invitations to them in Babylon. The Babylonians came on the run, fornicated with her, made her dirty inside and out. When they had thoroughly debased her, she lost interest in them. Then she went public with her fornication. She exhibited her sex to the world.

18-21 "I turned my back on her just as I had on her sister. But that didn't slow her down. She went at her whoring harder than ever. She remembered when she was young, just starting out as a whore in Egypt. That whetted her appetite for more virile, vulgar, and violent lovers—stallions obsessive in their lust. She longed for the sexual prowess of her youth back in Egypt, where her firm young breasts were caressed and fondled.

22-27 "'Therefore, Oholibah, this is the Message from GOD, the Master: I will incite your old lovers against you, lovers you got tired of and left in disgust. I'll bring them against you from every direction, Babylonians and all the Chaldeans, Pekod, Shoa, and Koa, and all Assyrians—good-looking young men, ambassadors and governors, elite officers and celebrities—all of them mounted on fine, spirited horses. They'll come down on you out of the north, armed to the teeth, bringing chariots and troops from all sides. I'll turn over the task of judgment to them. They'll punish you according to their rules. I'll stand totally and relentlessly against you as they rip into you furiously. They'll mutilate you, cutting off your ears and nose, killing at random. They'll enslave your children—and anybody left over will be burned. They'll rip off your clothes and steal your jewelry. I'll put a stop to your sluttish sex, the whoring life you began in Egypt. You won't look on whoring with fondness anymore. You won't think back on Egypt with stars in your eyes.

28-30 "'A Message from GOD, the Master: I'm at the point of abandoning you to those you hate, to those by whom you're repulsed. They'll treat you hatefully, leave you publicly naked, your whore's body exposed in the cruel glare of the sun. Your sluttish lust will be exposed. Your lust has brought you to this condition because you whored with pagan nations and made yourself filthy with their no-god idols.

31-34 " 'You copied the life of your sister. Now I'll let you drink the cup she drank.

" 'This is the Message of GOD, the Master:

" 'You'll drink your sister's cup,
   a cup canyon-deep and ocean-wide.
You'll be shunned and taunted
   as you drink from that cup, full to the brim.
You'll be falling-down-drunk and the tears will flow
   as you drink from that cup titanic with terror:
   It's the cup of your sister Samaria.
You'll drink it dry,
   then smash it to bits and eat the pieces,
   and end up tearing at your breasts.
I've given the word—
   Decree of GOD, the Master.

35 " 'Therefore GOD, the Master, says, Because you've forgotten all about me, pushing me into the background, you now must pay for what you've done—pay for your sluttish sex and whoring life.' "

36-39 Then GOD said to me, "Son of man, will you confront Oholah and Oholibah with what they've done? Make them face their outrageous obscenities, obscenities ranging from adultery to murder. They committed adultery with their no-god idols, sacrificed the children they bore me in order to feed their idols! And there is also this: They've defiled my holy Sanctuary and desecrated my holy Sabbaths. The same day that they sacrificed their children to their idols, they walked into my Sanctuary and defiled it. That's what they did—in *my* house!

40-42 "Furthermore, they even sent out invitations by special messenger to men far away—and, sure enough, they came. They bathed themselves, put on makeup and provocative lingerie. They reclined on a sumptuous bed, aromatic with incense and oils—*my* incense and oils! The crowd gathered, jostling and pushing, a drunken rabble. They adorned the sisters with bracelets on their arms and tiaras on their heads.

43-44 "I said, 'She's burned out on sex!' but that didn't stop them. They kept banging on her doors night and day as men do when they're after a whore. That's how they used Oholah and Oholibah, the worn-out whores.

45 "Righteous men will pronounce judgment on them, giving out sentences for adultery and murder. That was their lifework: adultery and murder."

46-47 "GOD says, 'Let a mob loose on them: Terror! Plunder! Let the mob stone them and hack them to pieces—kill all their children, burn down their houses!

48-49 " 'I'll put an end to sluttish sex in this country so that all women will be well warned and not copy you. You'll pay the price for all your obsessive sex. You'll pay in full for your promiscuous affairs with idols. And you'll realize that I am GOD, the Master.' "

BRING THE POT TO A BOIL

24 ¹⁻⁵ The Message of GOD came to me in the ninth year, the tenth month, and the tenth day of the month: "Son of man, write down this date. The king of Babylon has laid siege to Jerusalem this very day. Tell this company of rebels a story:

"'Put on the soup pot.
    Fill it with water.
Put chunks of meat into it,
    all the choice pieces—loin and brisket.
Pick out the best soup bones
    from the best of the sheep in the flock.
Pile wood beneath the pot.
    Bring it to a boil
    and cook the soup.

⁶   "'GOD, the Master, says:

"'Doom to the city of murder,
    to the pot thick with scum,
    thick with a filth that can't be scoured.
Empty the pot piece by piece;
    don't bother who gets what.

⁷⁻⁸   "'The blood from murders
    has stained the whole city;
Blood runs bold on the street stones,
    with no one bothering to wash it off—
Blood out in the open to public view
    to provoke my wrath,
    to trigger my vengeance.

⁹⁻¹²   "'Therefore, this is what GOD, the Master, says:

"'Doom to the city of murder!
    I, too, will pile on the wood.
Stack the wood high,
    light the match,
Cook the meat, spice it well, pour out the broth,
    and then burn the bones.
Then I'll set the empty pot on the coals
    and heat it red-hot so the bronze glows,
So the germs are killed
    and the corruption is burned off.
But it's hopeless. It's too far gone.
    The filth is too thick.

¹³⁻¹⁴   "'Your encrusted filth is your filthy sex. I wanted to clean you up, but you wouldn't let me. I'll make no more attempts at cleaning you up until my anger quiets down. I, GOD, have said it, and I'll do it. I'm not holding

back. I've run out of compassion. I'm not changing my mind. You're getting exactly what's coming to you. Decree of GOD, the Master.'"

No Tears

15-17   GOD's Message came to me: "Son of man, I'm about to take from you the delight of your life — a real blow, I know. But, please, no tears. Keep your grief to yourself. No public mourning. Get dressed as usual and go about your work — none of the usual funeral rituals."

18   I preached to the people in the morning. That evening my wife died. The next morning I did as I'd been told.

19   The people came to me, saying, "Tell us why you're acting like this. What does it mean, anyway?"

20-21   So I told them, "GOD's Word came to me, saying, 'Tell the family of Israel, This is what GOD, the Master, says: I will desecrate my Sanctuary, your proud impregnable fort, the delight of your life, your heart's desire. The children you left behind will be killed.

22-24   "'Then you'll do exactly as I've done. You'll perform none of the usual funeral rituals. You'll get dressed as usual and go about your work. No tears. But your sins will eat away at you from within and you'll groan among yourselves. Ezekiel will be your example. The way he did it is the way you'll do it.

"'When this happens you'll recognize that I am GOD, the Master.'"

25-27   "And you, son of man: The day I take away the people's refuge, their great joy, the delight of their life, what they've most longed for, along with all their children — on that very day a survivor will arrive and tell you what happened to the city. You'll break your silence and start talking again, talking to the survivor. Again, you'll be an example for them. And they'll recognize that I am GOD."

ACTS OF VENGEANCE

1-5   **25** GOD's Message came to me:

"Son of man, face Ammon and preach against the people: Listen to the Message of GOD, the Master. This is what GOD has to say: Because you cheered when my Sanctuary was desecrated and the land of Judah was devastated and the people of Israel were taken into exile, I'm giving you over to the people of the east. They'll move in and make themselves at home, eating the food right off your tables and drinking your milk. I'll turn your capital, Rabbah, into pasture for camels and all your villages into corrals for flocks. Then you'll realize that I am GOD.

6-7   "GOD, the Master, says, Because you clapped and cheered, venting all your malicious contempt against the land of Israel, I'll step in and hand you out as loot — first come, first served. I'll cross you off the roster of nations. There'll be nothing left of you. And you'll realize that I am GOD."

8-11   "GOD, the Master, says: Because Moab said, 'Look, Judah's nothing special,' I'll lay wide open the flank of Moab by exposing its lovely frontier villages to attack: Beth-jeshimoth, Baal-meon, and Kiriathaim. I'll lump Moab in with Ammon and give them to the people of the east for the taking. Ammon won't be heard from again. I'll punish Moab severely. And they'll realize that I am GOD."

12-14   "GOD, the Master, says: Because Edom reacted against the people of Judah in spiteful revenge and was so criminally vengeful against them, therefore I, GOD, the Master, will oppose Edom and kill the lot of them, people and animals both. I'll waste it—corpses stretched from Teman to Dedan. I'll use my people Israel to bring my vengeance down on Edom. My wrath will fuel their action. And they'll realize it's *my* vengeance. Decree of GOD the Master."

15-17   "GOD, the Master, says: Because the Philistines were so spitefully vengeful—all those centuries of stored-up malice!—and did their best to destroy Judah, therefore I, GOD, the Master, will oppose the Philistines and cut down the Cretans and anybody else left along the seacoast. Huge acts of vengeance, massive punishments! When I bring vengeance, they'll realize that I am GOD."

As the Waves of the Sea, Surging Against the Shore

1-2   **26** In the eleventh year, on the first day of the month, GOD's Message came to me: "Son of man, Tyre cheered when they got the news of Jerusalem, exclaiming,

"'Good! The gateway city is smashed!
    Now all her business comes my way.
She's in ruins
    and I'm in clover.'

3-6   "Therefore, GOD, the Master, has this to say:

"'I'm against you, Tyre,
    and I'll bring many nations surging against you,
    as the waves of the sea surging against the shore.
They'll smash the city walls of Tyre
    and break down her towers.
I'll wash away the soil
    and leave nothing but bare rock.
She'll be an island of bare rock in the ocean,
    good for nothing but drying fishnets.
Yes, I've said so.' Decree of GOD, the Master.
    'She'll be loot, free pickings for the nations!
Her surrounding villages will be butchered.
    Then they'll realize that I am GOD.'

7-14   "GOD, the Master, says: Look! Out of the north I'm bringing Nebuchadnezzar king of Babylon, a king's king, down on Tyre. He'll come with chariots and horses and riders—a huge army. He'll massacre your surrounding villages and lay siege to you. He'll build siege ramps against your walls. A forest of shields will advance against you! He'll pummel your walls with his battering rams and shatter your towers with his iron weapons. You'll be covered with dust from his horde of horses—a thundering herd of war horses pouring through the breaches, pulling chariots. Oh, it will be an earthquake of an army and a city in shock! Horses will stampede through the streets. Your people will be slaughtered and your huge pillars strewn like matchsticks. The invaders will steal and loot—all that wealth, all that stuff! They'll knock down your fine houses and dump the stone and timber rubble into the sea. And your parties, your famous good-time parties, will be no more. No more songs, no more lutes. I'll reduce you to an island of bare rock, good for nothing but drying fishnets. You'll never be rebuilt. I, GOD, have said so. Decree of GOD, the Master.

INTRODUCED TO THE TERRORS OF DEATH

15   "This is the Message of GOD, the Master, to Tyre: Won't the ocean islands shake at the crash of your collapse, at the groans of your wounded, at your mayhem and massacre?

16-18   "All up and down the coast, the princes will come down from their thrones, take off their royal robes and fancy clothes, and wrap themselves in sheer terror. They'll sit on the ground, shaken to the core, horrified at you. Then they'll begin chanting a funeral song over you:

"'Sunk! Sunk to the bottom of the sea,
    famous city on the sea!
Power of the seas,
    you and your people,
Intimidating everyone
    who lived in your shadows.
But now the islands are shaking
    at the sound of your crash,
Ocean islands in tremors
    from the impact of your fall.'

19-21   "The Message of GOD, the Master: 'When I turn you into a wasted city, a city empty of people, a ghost town, and when I bring up the great ocean deeps and cover you, then I'll push you down among those who go to the grave, the long, long dead. I'll make you live there, in the grave in old ruins, with the buried dead. You'll never see the land of the living again. I'll introduce you to the terrors of death and that'll be the end of you. They'll send out search parties for you, but you'll never be found. Decree of GOD, the Master.'"

TYRE, GATEWAY TO THE SEA

1-9   **27** GOD's Message came to me: "You, son of man, raise a funeral song over Tyre. Tell Tyre, gateway to the sea, merchant to the world, trader among the far-off islands, 'This is what GOD, the Master, says:

"'You boast, Tyre:
    "I'm the perfect ship—stately, handsome."
You ruled the high seas from

a real beauty, crafted to perfection.
Your planking came from
    Mount Hermon junipers.
A Lebanon cedar
    supplied your mast.
They made your oars
    from sturdy Bashan oaks.
Cypress from Cyprus inlaid with ivory
    was used for the decks.
Your sail and flag were of colorful
    embroidered linen from Egypt.
Your purple deck awnings
    also came from Cyprus.
Men of Sidon and Arvad pulled the oars.
    Your seasoned seamen, O Tyre, were the crew.
Ship's carpenters
    were old salts from Byblos.
All the ships of the sea and their sailors
    clustered around you to barter for your goods.

10-11   "'Your army was composed of soldiers
    from Paras, Lud, and Put,
Elite troops in uniformed splendor.
    They put you on the map!
Your city police were imported from
    Arvad, Helech, and Gammad.
They hung their shields from the city walls,
    a final, perfect touch to your beauty.

12   "'Tarshish carried on business with you because of your great wealth. They worked for you, trading in silver, iron, tin, and lead for your products.

13   "'Greece, Tubal, and Meshech did business with you, trading slaves and bronze for your products.

14   "'Beth-togarmah traded work horses, war horses, and mules for your products.

15   "'The people of Rhodes did business with you. Many far-off islands traded with you in ivory and ebony.

16   "'Edom did business with you because of all your goods. They traded for your products with agate, purple textiles, embroidered cloth, fine linen, coral, and rubies.

17   "'Judah and Israel did business with you. They traded for your products with premium wheat, millet, honey, oil, and balm.

18   "'Damascus, attracted by your vast array of products and well-stocked warehouses, carried on business with you, trading in wine from Helbon and wool from Zahar.

19   "'Danites and Greeks from Uzal traded with you, using wrought iron, cinnamon, and spices.

20   "'Dedan traded with you for saddle blankets.

21   "'Arabia and all the Bedouin sheiks of Kedar traded lambs, rams, and goats with you.

22   "'Traders from Sheba and Raamah in South Arabia carried on business

with you in premium spices, precious stones, and gold.

23-24   "'Haran, Canneh, and Eden from the east in Assyria and Media traded with you, bringing elegant clothes, dyed textiles, and elaborate carpets to your bazaars.

25   "'The great Tarshish ships were your freighters, importing and exporting. Oh, it was big business for you, trafficking the seaways!

26-32   "'Your sailors row mightily,
          taking you into the high seas.
        Then a storm out of the east
          shatters your ship in the ocean deep.
        Everything sinks — your rich goods and products,
          sailors and crew, ship's carpenters and soldiers,
        Sink to the bottom of the sea.
          Total shipwreck.
        The cries of your sailors
          reverberate on shore.
        Sailors everywhere abandon ship.
          Veteran seamen swim for dry land.
        They cry out in grief,
          a choir of bitter lament over you.
        They smear their faces with ashes,
          shave their heads,
        Wear rough burlap,
          wildly keening their loss.
        They raise their funeral song:
          "Who on the high seas is like Tyre!"

33-36   "'As you crisscrossed the seas with your products,
          you satisfied many peoples.
        Your worldwide trade
          made earth's kings rich.
        And now you're battered to bits by the waves,
          sunk to the bottom of the sea,
        And everything you've bought and sold
          has sunk to the bottom with you.
        Everyone on shore looks on in terror.
          The hair of kings stands on end,
          their faces drawn and haggard!
        The buyers and sellers of the world
          throw up their hands:
        This horror can't happen!
          Oh, this *has* happened!'"

THE MONEY HAS GONE TO YOUR HEAD

1-5   **28** GOD's Message came to me, "Son of man, tell the prince of Tyre, 'This is what GOD, the Master, says:

"'Your heart is proud,
          going around saying, "I'm a god.
        I sit on God's divine throne,

ruling the sea" —
You, a mere mortal,
   not even close to being a god,
A mere mortal
   trying to be a god.
Look, you think you're smarter than Daniel.
   No enigmas can stump you.
Your sharp intelligence
   made you world-wealthy.
You piled up gold and silver
   in your banks.
You used your head well,
   worked good deals, made a lot of money.
But the money has gone to your head,
   swelled your head — what a big head!

6-11   "'Therefore, God, the Master, says:

"'Because you're acting like a god,
   pretending to *be* a god,
I'm giving fair warning: I'm bringing strangers down on you,
   the most vicious of all nations.
They'll pull their swords and make hash
   of your reputation for knowing it all.
They'll puncture the balloon
   of your god-pretensions.
They'll bring you down from your self-made pedestal
   and bury you in the deep blue sea.
Will you protest to your assassins,
   "You can't do that! I'm a god"?
To them you're a mere mortal.
   They're killing a man, not a god.
You'll die like a stray dog,
   killed by strangers —
Because I said so.
   Decree of God, the Master.'"

11-19   God's Message came to me: "Son of man, raise a funeral song over the king of Tyre. Tell him, A Message from God, the Master:

"You had everything going for you.
   You were in Eden, God's garden.
You were dressed in splendor,
   your robe studded with jewels:
Carnelian, peridot, and moonstone,
   beryl, onyx, and jasper,
Sapphire, turquoise, and emerald,
   all in settings of engraved gold.
A robe was prepared for you
   the same day you were created.
You were the anointed cherub.

I placed you on the mountain of God.
You strolled in magnificence
  among the stones of fire.
From the day of your creation
  you were sheer perfection . . .
  and then imperfection — evil! — was detected in you.
In much buying and selling
  you turned violent, you sinned!
I threw you, disgraced, off the mountain of God.
  I threw you out — you, the anointed angel-cherub.
  No more strolling among the gems of fire for you!
Your beauty went to your head.
  You corrupted wisdom
  by using it to get worldly fame.
I threw you to the ground,
  sent you sprawling before an audience of kings
  and let them gloat over your demise.
By sin after sin after sin,
  by your corrupt ways of doing business,
  you defiled your holy places of worship.
So I set a fire around and within you.
  It burned you up. I reduced you to ashes.
All anyone sees now
  when they look for you is ashes,
  a pitiful mound of ashes.
All who once knew you
  now throw up their hands:
'This can't have happened!
  This *has* happened!'"

20-23 God's Message came to me: "Son of man, confront Sidon. Preach against it. Say, 'Message from God, the Master:

"'Look! I'm against you, Sidon.
  I intend to be known for who I truly am among you.'
They'll know that I am God
  when I set things right
  and reveal my holy presence.
I'll order an epidemic of disease there,
  along with murder and mayhem in the streets.
People will drop dead right and left,
  as war presses in from every side.
Then they'll realize that I mean business,
  that I am God.

24 "No longer will Israel have to put up with
  their thistle-and-thorn neighbors
Who have treated them so contemptuously.
  And they also will realize that I am God."

25-26   GOD, the Master, says, "When I gather Israel from the peoples among whom they've been scattered and put my holiness on display among them with all the nations looking on, then they'll live in their own land that I gave to my servant Jacob. They'll live there in safety. They'll build houses. They'll plant vineyards, living in safety. Meanwhile, I'll bring judgment on all the neighbors who have treated them with such contempt. And they'll realize that I am GOD."

NEVER A WORLD POWER AGAIN

1-6   **29** In the tenth year, in the tenth month, on the twelfth day, GOD's Message came to me: "Son of man, confront Pharaoh king of Egypt. Preach against him and all the Egyptians. Tell him, 'GOD, the Master, says:

"'Watch yourself, Pharaoh, king of Egypt.
    I'm dead set against you,
You lumbering old dragon,
    lolling and flaccid in the Nile,
Saying, "It's my Nile.
    I made it. It's mine."
I'll set hooks in your jaw;
    I'll make the fish of the Nile stick to your scales.
I'll pull you out of the Nile,
    with all the fish stuck to your scales.
Then I'll drag you out into the desert,
    you and all the Nile fish sticking to your scales.
You'll lie there in the open, rotting in the sun,
    meat to the wild animals and carrion birds.
Everybody living in Egypt
    will realize that I am GOD.

6-9   "'Because you've been a flimsy reed crutch to Israel so that when they gripped you, you splintered and cut their hand, and when they leaned on you, you broke and sent them sprawling — Message of GOD, the Master — I'll bring war against you, do away with people and animals alike, and turn the country into an empty desert so they'll realize that I am GOD.

9-11   "'Because you said, "It's my Nile. I made it. It's all mine," therefore I am against you and your rivers. I'll reduce Egypt to an empty, desolate waste-land all the way from Migdol in the north to Syene and the border of Ethiopia in the south. Not a human will be seen in it, nor will an animal move through it. It'll be just empty desert, empty for forty years.

12   "'I'll make Egypt the most desolate of all desolations. For forty years I'll make her cities the most wasted of all wasted cities. I'll scatter Egyptians to the four winds, send them off every which way into exile.

13-16   "'But,' says GOD, the Master, 'that's not the end of it. After the forty years, I'll gather up the Egyptians from all the places where they've been scattered. I'll put things back together again for Egypt. I'll bring her back to Pathros where she got her start long ago. There she'll start over again from scratch. She'll take her place at the bottom of the ladder and there she'll stay, never to climb that ladder again, never to be a world power again. Never again will Israel be tempted to rely on Egypt. All she'll be to

Israel is a reminder of old sin. Then Egypt will realize that I am God, the
Master.'"

※

17-18   In the twenty-seventh year, in the first month, on the first day of the
month, God's Message came to me: "Son of man, Nebuchadnezzar, king of
Babylon, has worn out his army against Tyre. They've worked their fingers
to the bone and have nothing to show for it.

19-20   "Therefore, God, the Master, says, 'I'm giving Egypt to Nebuchadnezzar
king of Babylon. He'll haul away its wealth, pick the place clean. He'll pay
his army with Egyptian plunder. He's been working for me all these years
without pay. This is his pay: Egypt. Decree of God, the Master.

21   "'And then I'll stir up fresh hope in Israel—the dawn of deliverance!—
and I'll give you, Ezekiel, bold and confident words to speak. And they'll
realize that I am God.'"

Egypt on Fire

1-5   **30** God, the Master, spoke to me: "Son of man, preach. Give them
the Message of God, the Master. Wail:

"'Doomsday!'
    Time's up!
    God's big day of judgment is near.
Thick clouds are rolling in.
    It's doomsday for the nations.
Death will rain down on Egypt.
    Terror will paralyze Ethiopia
When they see the Egyptians killed,
    their wealth hauled off,
    their foundations demolished,
And Ethiopia, Put, Lud, Arabia, Libya
    —all of Egypt's old allies—
    killed right along with them.

6-8   "'God says:

"'Egypt's allies will fall
    and her proud strength will collapse—
From Migdol in the north to Syene in the south,
    a great slaughter in Egypt!
    Decree of God, the Master.
Egypt, most desolate of the desolate,
    her cities wasted beyond wasting,
Will realize that I am God
    when I burn her down
    and her helpers are knocked flat.

9   "'When that happens, I'll send out messengers by ship to sound the
alarm among the easygoing Ethiopians. They'll be terrorized. Egypt's
doomed! Judgment's coming!

10-12 "'GOD, the Master, says:

"'I'll put a stop to Egypt's arrogance.
    I'll use Nebuchadnezzar king of Babylon to do it.
He and his army, the most brutal of nations,
    shall be used to destroy the country.
They'll brandish their swords
    and fill Egypt with corpses.
I'll dry up the Nile
    and sell off the land to a bunch of crooks.
I'll hire outsiders to come in
    and waste the country, strip it clean.
    I, GOD, have said so.

13-19 "'And now this is what GOD, the Master, says:

"'I'll smash all the no-god idols;
    I'll topple all those huge statues in Memphis.
The prince of Egypt will be gone for good,
    and in his place I'll put *fear*—fear throughout Egypt!
I'll demolish Pathros,
    burn Zoan to the ground, and punish Thebes,
Pour my wrath on Pelusium, Egypt's fort,
    and knock Thebes off its proud pedestal.
I'll set Egypt on fire:
    Pelusium will writhe in pain,
Thebes blown away,
    Memphis raped.
The young warriors of On and Pi-beseth
    will be killed and the cities exiled.
A dark day for Tahpanhes
    when I shatter Egypt,
When I break Egyptian power
    and put an end to her arrogant oppression!
She'll disappear in a cloud of dust,
    her cities hauled off as exiles.
That's how I'll punish Egypt,
    and that's how she'll realize that I am GOD.'"

20 In the eleventh year, on the seventh day of the first month, GOD's Message came to me:

21 "Son of man, I've broken the arm of Pharaoh king of Egypt. And look! It hasn't been set. No splint has been put on it so the bones can knit and heal, so he can use a sword again.

22-26 "Therefore, GOD, the Master, says, I am dead set against Pharaoh king of Egypt and will go ahead and break his other arm—both arms broken! There's no way he'll ever swing a sword again. I'll scatter Egyptians all over the world. I'll make the arms of the king of Babylon strong and put my sword in his hand, but I'll break the arms of Pharaoh and he'll groan like one who is mortally wounded. I'll make the arms of the king of Babylon strong, but the arms of Pharaoh shall go limp. The Egyptians will realize that I am GOD when I place my sword in the hand of the king of Babylon. He'll wield it against Egypt and I'll scatter Egyptians all over the world. Then they'll realize that I am GOD."

THE FUNERAL OF THE BIG TREE

1-9   **31** In the eleventh year, on the first day of the third month, GOD's Message came to me: "Son of man, tell Pharaoh king of Egypt, that pompous old goat:

" 'Who do you, astride the world,
     think you really are?
Look! Assyria was a Big Tree, huge as a Lebanon cedar,
     beautiful limbs offering cool shade,
Skyscraper high,
     piercing the clouds.
The waters gave it drink,
     the primordial deep lifted it high,
Gushing out rivers around
     the place where it was planted,
And then branching out in streams
     to all the trees in the forest.
It was immense,
     dwarfing all the trees in the forest —
Thick boughs, long limbs,
     roots delving deep into earth's waters.
All the birds of the air
     nested in its boughs.
All the wild animals
     gave birth under its branches.
All the mighty nations
     lived in its shade.
It was stunning in its majesty —
     the reach of its branches!
     the depth of its water-seeking roots!
Not a cedar in God's garden came close to it.
     No pine tree was anything like it.
Mighty oaks looked like bushes
     growing alongside it.
Not a tree in God's garden
     was in the same class of beauty.
I made it beautiful,
     a work of art in limbs and leaves,
The envy of every tree in Eden,
     every last tree in God's garden.' "

10-13   Therefore, GOD, the Master, says, " 'Because it skyscrapered upward, piercing the clouds, swaggering and proud of its stature, I turned it over to a world-famous leader to call its evil to account. I'd had enough. Outsiders, unbelievably brutal, felled it across the mountain ranges. Its branches were strewn through all the valleys, its leafy boughs clogging all the streams and rivers. Because its shade was gone, everybody walked off. No longer a tree—just a log. On that dead log birds perch. Wild animals burrow under it.

14 "'That marks the end of the "big tree" nations. No more trees nourished from the great deep, no more cloud-piercing trees, no more earthborn trees taking over. They're all slated for death—back to earth, right along with men and women, for whom it's "dust to dust."

15-17 "'The Message of GOD, the Master: On the day of the funeral of the Big Tree, I threw the great deep into mourning. I stopped the flow of its rivers, held back great seas, and wrapped the Lebanon mountains in black. All the trees of the forest fainted and fell. I made the whole world quake when it crashed, and threw it into the underworld to take its place with all else that gets buried. All the trees of Eden and the finest and best trees of Lebanon, well-watered, were relieved—they had descended to the underworld with it—along with everyone who had lived in its shade and all who had been killed.

18 "'Which of the trees of Eden came anywhere close to you in splendor and size? But you're slated to be cut down to take your place in the underworld with the trees of Eden, to be a dead log stacked with all the other dead logs, among the other uncircumcised who are dead and buried.

"'This means Pharaoh, the pompous old goat.

"'Decree of GOD, the Master.'"

A CLOUD ACROSS THE SUN

1-2 **32** In the twelfth year, on the first day of the twelfth month, GOD's Message came to me: "Son of man, sing a funeral lament over Pharaoh king of Egypt. Tell him:

"'You think you're a young lion
  prowling through the nations.
You're more like a dragon in the ocean,
  snorting and thrashing about.

3-10 "'GOD, the Master, says:

"'I'm going to throw my net over you
  —many nations will get in on this operation—
  and haul you out with my dragnet.
I'll dump you on the ground
  out in an open field
And bring in all the crows and vultures
  for a sumptuous carrion lunch.
I'll invite wild animals from all over the world
  to gorge on your guts.
I'll scatter hunks of your meat in the mountains
  and strew your bones in the valleys.
The country, right up to the mountains,
  will be drenched with your blood,
  your blood filling every ditch and channel.
When I blot you out,
  I'll pull the curtain on the skies

and shut out the stars.
I'll throw a cloud across the sun
    and turn off the moonlight.
I'll turn out every light in the sky above you
    and put your land in the dark.
        Decree of GOD, the Master.
I'll shake up everyone worldwide
    when I take you off captive to strange and far-off countries.
I'll shock people with you.
    Kings will take one look and shudder.
I'll shake my sword
    and they'll shake in their boots.
On the day you crash, they'll tremble,
    thinking, "That could be me!"

To Lay Your Pride Low

11-15   " 'GOD, the Master, says:

" 'The sword of the king of Babylon
    is coming against you.
I'll use the swords of champions
    to lay your pride low,
Use the most brutal of nations
    to knock Egypt off her high horse,
    to puncture that hot-air pomposity.
I'll destroy all their livestock
    that graze along the river.
Neither human foot nor animal hoof
    will muddy those waters anymore.
I'll clear their springs and streams,
    make their rivers flow clean and smooth.
        Decree of GOD, the Master.
When I turn Egypt back to the wild
    and strip her clean of all her abundant produce,
When I strike dead all who live there,
    then they'll realize that I am GOD.'

16   "This is a funeral song. Chant it.
    Daughters of the nations, chant it.
Chant it over Egypt for the death of its pomp."
    Decree of GOD, the Master.

17-19   In the twelfth year, on the fifteenth day of the first month, GOD's Message
came to me:

"Son of man, lament over Egypt's pompous ways.
    Send her on her way.
Dispatch Egypt
    and her proud daughter nations
To the underworld,
    down to the country of the dead and buried.

Say, 'You think you're so high and mighty?
  Down! Take your place with the heathen in that unhallowed grave!'

20-21 "She'll be dumped in with those killed in battle. The sword is bared. Drag her off in all her proud pomp! All the big men and their helpers down among the dead and buried will greet them: 'Welcome to the grave of the heathen! Join the ranks of the victims of war!'

22-23 "Assyria is there and its congregation, the whole nation a cemetery. Their graves are in the deepest part of the underworld, a congregation of graves, all killed in battle, these people who terrorized the land of the living.

24-25 "Elam is there in all her pride, a cemetery — all killed in battle, dumped in her heathen grave with the dead and buried, these people who terrorized the land of the living. They carry their shame with them, along with the others in the grave. They turned Elam into a resort for the pompous dead, landscaped with heathen graves, slaughtered in battle. They once terrorized the land of the living. Now they carry their shame down with the others in deep earth. They're in the section set aside for the slain in battle.

26-27 "Meshech-tubal is there in all her pride, a cemetery in uncircumcised ground, dumped in with those slaughtered in battle — just deserts for terrorizing the land of the living. Now they carry their shame down with the others in deep earth. They're in the section set aside for the slain. They're segregated from the heroes, the old-time giants who entered the grave in full battle dress, their swords placed under their heads and their shields covering their bones, those heroes who spread terror through the land of the living.

28 "And you, Egypt, will be dumped in a heathen grave, along with all the rest, in the section set aside for the slain.

29 "Edom is there, with her kings and princes. In spite of her vaunted greatness, she is dumped in a heathen grave with the others headed for the grave.

30 "The princes of the north are there, the whole lot of them, and all the Sidonians who carry their shame to their graves — all that terror they spread with their brute power! — dumped in unhallowed ground with those killed in battle, carrying their shame with the others headed for deep earth.

31 "Pharaoh will see them all and, pompous old goat that he is, take comfort in the company he'll keep — Pharaoh and his slaughtered army. Decree of GOD, the Master.

32 "I used him to spread terror in the land of the living and now I'm dumping him in heathen ground with those killed by the sword — Pharaoh and all his pomp. Decree of GOD, the Master."

YOU ARE THE WATCHMAN

1-5 **33** GOD's Message came to me: "Son of man, speak to your people. Tell them, 'If I bring war on this land and the people take one of their citizens and make him their watchman, and if the watchman sees war coming and blows the trumpet, warning the people, then if anyone hears the sound of the trumpet and ignores it and war comes and takes him off, it's his own fault. He heard the alarm, he ignored it — it's his own fault. If he had listened, he would have saved his life.

6 "'But if the watchman sees war coming and doesn't blow the trumpet, warning the people, and war comes and takes anyone off, I'll hold the watchman responsible for the bloodshed of any unwarned sinner.'

7-9 "You, son of man, are the watchman. I've made you a watchman for Israel. The minute you hear a message from me, warn them. If I say to the wicked, 'Wicked man, wicked woman, you're on the fast track to death!' and you don't speak up and warn the wicked to change their ways, the wicked will die unwarned in their sins and I'll hold you responsible for their bloodshed. But if you warn the wicked to change their ways and they don't do it, they'll die in their sins well-warned and at least you will have saved your own life.

10 "Son of man, speak to Israel. Tell them, 'You've said, "Our rebellions and sins are weighing us down. We're wasting away. How can we go on living?"'

11 "Tell them, 'As sure as I am the living God, I take no pleasure from the death of the wicked. I want the wicked to change their ways and live. Turn your life around! Reverse your evil ways! Why *die*, Israel?'

12-13 "There's more, son of man. Tell your people, 'A good person's good life won't save him when he decides to rebel, and a bad person's bad life won't prevent him from repenting of his rebellion. A good person who sins can't expect to live when he chooses to sin. It's true that I tell good people, "Live! Be alive!" But if they trust in their good deeds and turn to evil, that good life won't amount to a hill of beans. They'll die for their evil life.

14-16 "'On the other hand, if I tell a wicked person, "You'll die for your wicked life," and he repents of his sin and starts living a righteous and just life—being generous to the down-and-out, restoring what he had stolen, cultivating life-nourishing ways that don't hurt others—he'll live. He won't die. None of his sins will be kept on the books. He's doing what's right, living a good life. He'll live.

17-19 "'Your people say, "The Master's way isn't fair." But it's the way *they're* living that isn't fair. When good people turn back from living good lives and plunge into sin, they'll die for it. And when a wicked person turns away from his wicked life and starts living a just and righteous life, he'll come alive.

20 "'Still, you keep on saying, "The Master's way isn't fair." We'll see, Israel. I'll decide on each of you exactly according to how you live.'"

21 In the twelfth year of our exile, on the fifth day of the tenth month, a survivor from Jerusalem came to me and said, "The city's fallen."

22 The evening before the survivor arrived, the hand of GOD had been on me and restored my speech. By the time he arrived in the morning I was able to speak. I could talk again.

23-24 GOD's Message came to me: "Son of man, those who are living in the ruins back in Israel are saying, 'Abraham was only one man and he owned the whole country. But there are *lots* of us. Our ownership is even more certain.'

25-26 "So tell them, 'GOD the Master says, You eat flesh that contains blood, you worship no-god idols, you murder at will—and you expect to own this land? You rely on the sword, you engage in obscenities, you indulge in sex at random—anyone, anytime. And you still expect to own this land?'

27-28 "Tell them this, Ezekiel: 'The Message of GOD, the Master. As sure as I am the living God, those who are still alive in the ruins will be killed.

Anyone out in the field I'll give to wild animals for food. Anyone hiding out in mountain forts and caves will die of disease. I'll make this country an empty wasteland—no more arrogant bullying! Israel's mountains will become dangerously desolate. No one will dare pass through them.'

29 "They'll realize that I am GOD when I devastate the country because of all the obscenities they've practiced.

30-32 "As for you, son of man, you've become quite the talk of the town. Your people meet on street corners and in front of their houses and say, 'Let's go hear the latest news from GOD.' They show up, as people tend to do, and sit in your company. They listen to you speak, but don't do a thing you say. They flatter you with compliments, but all they care about is making money and getting ahead. To them you're merely entertainment—a country singer of sad love songs, playing a guitar. They love to hear you talk, but nothing comes of it.

33 "But when all this happens—and it is going to happen!—they'll realize that a prophet was among them."

WHEN THE SHEEP GET SCATTERED

1-6 **34** GOD's Message came to me: "Son of man, prophesy against the shepherd-leaders of Israel. Yes, prophesy! Tell those shepherds, 'GOD, the Master, says: Doom to you shepherds of Israel, feeding your own mouths! Aren't shepherds supposed to feed sheep? You drink the milk, you make clothes from the wool, you roast the lambs, but you don't feed the sheep. You don't build up the weak ones, don't heal the sick, don't doctor the injured, don't go after the strays, don't look for the lost. You bully and badger them. And now they're scattered every which way because there was no shepherd—scattered and easy pickings for wolves and coyotes. Scattered—*my sheep!*—exposed and vulnerable across mountains and hills. My sheep scattered all over the world, and no one out looking for them!

7-9 "'Therefore, shepherds, listen to the Message of GOD: As sure as I am the living God—Decree of GOD, the Master—because my sheep have been turned into mere prey, into easy meals for wolves because you shepherds ignored them and only fed yourselves, listen to what GOD has to say:

10 "'Watch out! I'm coming down on the shepherds and taking my sheep back. They're fired as shepherds of my sheep. No more shepherds who just feed themselves! I'll rescue my sheep from their greed. They're not going to feed off my sheep any longer!

11-16 "'GOD, the Master, says: From now on, *I myself* am the shepherd. I'm going looking for them. As shepherds go after their flocks when they get scattered, I'm going after my sheep. I'll rescue them from all the places they've been scattered to in the storms. I'll bring them back from foreign peoples, gather them from foreign countries, and bring them back to their home country. I'll feed them on the mountains of Israel, along the streams, among their own people. I'll lead them into lush pasture so they can roam the mountain pastures of Israel, graze at leisure, feed in the rich pastures on the mountains of Israel. And I myself will be the shepherd of my sheep. I myself will make sure they get plenty of rest. I'll go after the lost, I'll collect the strays, I'll doctor the injured, I'll build up the weak ones and oversee the strong ones so they're not exploited.

17-19 "'And as for you, my dear flock, I'm stepping in and judging between one sheep and another, between rams and goats. Aren't you satisfied to feed in good pasture without taking over the whole place? Can't you be satisfied to drink from the clear stream without muddying the water with your feet? Why do the rest of my sheep have to make do with grass that's trampled down and water that's been muddied?

20-22 " 'Therefore, GOD, the Master, says: I myself am stepping in and making things right between the plump sheep and the skinny sheep. Because you forced your way with shoulder and rump and butted at all the weaker animals with your horns till you scattered them all over the hills, I'll come in and save my dear flock, no longer let them be pushed around. I'll step in and set things right between one sheep and another.

23-24 " 'I'll appoint one shepherd over them all: my servant David. He'll feed them. He'll be their shepherd. And I, GOD, will be their God. My servant David will be their prince. I, GOD, have spoken.

25-27 " 'I'll make a covenant of peace with them. I'll banish fierce animals from the country so the sheep can live safely in the wilderness and sleep in the forest. I'll make them and everything around my hill a blessing. I'll send down plenty of rain in season—showers of blessing! The trees in the orchards will bear fruit, the ground will produce, they'll feel content and safe on their land, and they'll realize that I am GOD when I break them out of their slavery and rescue them from their slave masters.

28-29 " 'No longer will they be exploited by outsiders and ravaged by fierce beasts. They'll live safe and sound, fearless and free. I'll give them rich gardens, lavish in vegetables—no more living half-starved, no longer taunted by outsiders.

30-31 " 'They'll know, beyond doubting, that I, GOD, am their God, that I'm with them and that they, the people Israel, are my people. Decree of GOD, the Master:

You are my dear flock,
     the flock of my pasture, my human flock,
And I am your God.
     Decree of GOD, the Master.' "

A PILE OF RUBBLE

1-4 **35** GOD's Message came to me: "Son of man, confront Mount Seir. Prophesy against it! Tell them, 'GOD, the Master, says:

" 'I'm coming down hard on you, Mount Seir.
     I'm stepping in and turning you to a pile of rubble.
I'll reduce your towns to piles of rocks.
     There'll be nothing left of you.
     Then you'll realize that I am GOD.

5-9 " 'I'm doing this because you've kept this age-old grudge going against Israel: You viciously attacked them when they were already down, looking their final punishment in the face. Therefore, as sure as I am the living God, I'm lining you up for a real bloodbath. Since you loved blood so much, you'll be chased by rivers of blood. I'll reduce Mount Seir to a heap of rubble. No one will either come or go from that place! I'll blanket your mountains with corpses. Massacred bodies will cover your hills and fill up your valleys and ditches. I'll reduce you to ruins and all your towns will be ghost towns — population zero. Then you'll realize that I am God.

10-13   "'Because you said, "These two nations, these two countries, are mine. I'm taking over" (even though God is right there watching, right there listening), I'll turn your hate-bloated anger and rage right back on you. You'll know I mean business when I bring judgment on you. You'll realize then that I, God, have overheard all the vile abuse you've poured out against the mountains of Israel, saying, "They're roadkill and we're going to eat them up." You've strutted around, talking so big, insolently pitting yourselves against me. And I've heard it all.

14-15   "'This is the verdict of God, the Master: With the whole earth applauding, I'll demolish you. Since you danced in the streets, thinking it was so wonderful when Israel's inheritance was demolished, I'll give you the same treatment: demolition. Mount Seir demolished — yes, every square inch of Edom. Then they'll realize that I am God!'"

BACK TO YOUR OWN LAND

1-5   **36** "And now, son of man, prophesy to the mountains of Israel. Say, 'Mountains of Israel, listen to God's Message. God, the Master, says, Because the enemy crowed over you, "Good! Those old hills are now ours!" now here is a prophecy in the name of God, the Master: Because nations came at you from all sides, ripping and plundering, hauling pieces of you off every which way, and you've become the butt of cheap gossip and jokes, therefore, Mountains of Israel, listen to the Message of God, the Master. My Message to mountains and hills, to ditches and valleys, to the heaps of rubble and the emptied towns that are looted for plunder and turned into jokes by all the surrounding nations: Therefore, says God, the Master, now I'm speaking in a fiery rage against the rest of the nations, but especially against Edom, who in an orgy of violence and shameless insolence robbed me of my land, grabbed it for themselves.'

6-7   "Therefore prophesy over the land of Israel, preach to the mountains and hills, to every ditch and valley: 'The Message of God, the Master: Look! Listen! I'm angry — and I care. I'm speaking to you because you've been humiliated among the nations. Therefore I, God, the Master, am telling you that I've solemnly sworn that the nations around you are next. It's their turn to be humiliated.

8-12   "'But you, Mountains of Israel, will burst with new growth, putting out branches and bearing fruit for my people Israel. My people are coming home! Do you see? I'm back again. I'm on your side. You'll be plowed and planted as before! I'll see to it that your population grows all over Israel, that the towns fill up with people, that the ruins are rebuilt. I'll make this place teem with life — human and animal. The country will burst into life, life, and more life, your towns and villages full of people just as in the old days. I'll treat you better than I ever have. And you'll realize that I am God. I'll put people over you — my own people Israel! They'll take care of you and you'll be their inheritance. Never again will you be a harsh and unforgiving land to them.

13-15   "'God, the Master, says: Because you have a reputation of being a land that eats people alive and makes women barren, I'm now telling you that you'll never eat people alive again nor make women barren. Decree of God, the Master. And I'll never again let the taunts of outsiders be heard over you nor permit nations to look down on you. You'll no longer be a land that makes women barren. Decree of GOD, the Master.'"

16-21 GOD's Message came to me: "Son of man, when the people of Israel lived in their land, they polluted it by the way they lived. I poured out my anger on them because of the polluted blood they poured out on the ground. And so I got thoroughly angry with them polluting the country with their wanton murders and dirty gods. I kicked them out, exiled them to other countries. I sentenced them according to how they had lived. Wherever they went, they gave me a bad name. People said, 'These are GOD's people, but they got kicked off his land.' I suffered much pain over my holy reputation, which the people of Israel blackened in every country they entered.

22-23 "Therefore, tell Israel, 'Message of GOD, the Master: I'm not doing this for you, Israel. I'm doing it for me, to save my character, my holy name, which you've blackened in every country where you've gone. I'm going to put my great and holy name on display, the name that has been ruined in so many countries, the name that you blackened wherever you went. Then the nations will realize who I really am, that I am GOD, when I show my holiness through you so that they can see it with their own eyes.

24-28 "'For here's what I'm going to do: I'm going to take you out of these countries, gather you from all over, and bring you back to your own land. I'll pour pure water over you and scrub you clean. I'll give you a new heart, put a new spirit in you. I'll remove the stone heart from your body and replace it with a heart that's God-willed, not self-willed. I'll put my Spirit in you and make it possible for you to do what I tell you and live by my commands. You'll once again live in the land I gave your ancestors. You'll be my people! I'll be your God!

29-30 "'I'll pull you out of that stinking pollution. I'll give personal orders to the wheat fields, telling them to grow bumper crops. I'll send no more famines. I'll make sure your fruit trees and field crops flourish. Other nations won't be able to hold you in contempt again because of famine.

31 "'And then you'll think back over your terrible lives—the evil, the shame—and be thoroughly disgusted with yourselves, realizing how badly you've lived—all those obscenities you've carried out.

32 "'I'm not doing this for you. Get this through your thick heads! Shame on you. What a mess you made of things, Israel!

33-36 "'Message of GOD, the Master: On the day I scrub you clean from all your filthy living, I'll also make your cities livable. The ruins will be rebuilt. The neglected land will be worked again, no longer overgrown with weeds and thistles, worthless in the eyes of passersby. People will exclaim, "Why, this weed patch has been turned into a Garden of Eden! And the ruined cities, smashed into oblivion, are now thriving!" The nations around you that are still in existence will realize that I, GOD, rebuild ruins and replant empty waste places. I, GOD, said so, and I'll do it.

37-38 "'Message of GOD, the Master: Yet again I'm going to do what Israel asks. I'll increase their population as with a flock of sheep. Like the milling flocks of sheep brought for sacrifices in Jerusalem during the appointed feasts, the ruined cities will be filled with flocks of people. And they'll realize that I am GOD.'"

BREATH OF LIFE

¹⁻² **37** GOD grabbed me. GOD's Spirit took me up and set me down in the middle of an open plain strewn with bones. He led me around and among them — a lot of bones! There were bones all over the plain — dry bones, bleached by the sun.

³ He said to me, "Son of man, can these bones live?"

I said, "Master GOD, only you know that."

⁴ He said to me, "Prophesy over these bones: 'Dry bones, listen to the Message of GOD!'"

⁵⁻⁶ GOD, the Master, told the dry bones, "Watch this: I'm bringing the breath of life to you and you'll come to life. I'll attach sinews to you, put meat on your bones, cover you with skin, and breathe life into you. You'll come alive and you'll realize that I am GOD!"

⁷⁻⁸ I prophesied just as I'd been commanded. As I prophesied, there was a sound and, oh, rustling! The bones moved and came together, bone to bone. I kept watching. Sinews formed, then muscles on the bones, then skin stretched over them. But they had no breath in them.

⁹ He said to me, "Prophesy to the breath. Prophesy, son of man. Tell the breath, 'GOD, the Master, says, Come from the four winds. Come, breath. Breathe on these slain bodies. Breathe life!'"

¹⁰ So I prophesied, just as he commanded me. The breath entered them and they came alive! They stood up on their feet, a huge army.

¹¹ Then God said to me, "Son of man, these bones are the whole house of Israel. Listen to what they're saying: 'Our bones are dried up, our hope is gone, there's nothing left of us.'

¹²⁻¹⁴ "Therefore, prophesy. Tell them, 'GOD, the Master, says: I'll dig up your graves and bring you out alive — O my people! Then I'll take you straight to the land of Israel. When I dig up graves and bring you out as my people, you'll realize that I am GOD. I'll breathe my life into you and you'll live. Then I'll lead you straight back to your land and you'll realize that I am GOD. I've said it and I'll do it. GOD's Decree.'"

¹⁵⁻¹⁷ GOD's Message came to me: "You, son of man: Take a stick and write on it, 'For Judah, with his Israelite companions.' Then take another stick and write on it, 'For Joseph — Ephraim's stick, together with all his Israelite companions.' Then tie the two sticks together so that you're holding one stick.

¹⁸⁻¹⁹ "When your people ask you, 'Are you going to tell us what you're doing?' tell them, 'GOD, the Master, says, Watch me! I'll take the Joseph stick that is in Ephraim's hand, with the tribes of Israel connected with him, and lay the Judah stick on it. I'll make them into one stick. I'm holding one stick.'

²⁰⁻²⁴ "Then take the sticks you've inscribed and hold them up so the people can see them. Tell them, 'GOD, the Master, says, Watch me! I'm taking the Israelites out of the nations in which they've been exiled. I'll gather them in from all directions and bring them back home. I'll make them one nation in the land, on the mountains of Israel, and give them one king — one king over all of them. Never again will they be divided into two nations, two kingdoms. Never again will they pollute their lives with their no-god idols and all those vile obscenities and rebellions. I'll save them out of all their

old sinful haunts. I'll clean them up. They'll be my people! I'll be their God! My servant David will be king over them. They'll all be under one shepherd.

24-27 "'They'll follow my laws and keep my statutes. They'll live in the same land I gave my servant Jacob, the land where your ancestors lived. They and their children and their grandchildren will live there forever, and my servant David will be their prince forever. I'll make a covenant of peace with them that will hold everything together, an everlasting covenant. I'll make them secure and place my holy place of worship at the center of their lives forever. I'll live right there with them. I'll be their God! They'll be my people!

28 "'The nations will realize that I, GOD, make Israel holy when my holy place of worship is established at the center of their lives forever.'"

GOD AGAINST GOG

1-6 **38** GOD's Message came to me: "Son of man, confront Gog from the country of Magog, head of Meshech and Tubal. Prophesy against him. Say, 'GOD, the Master, says: Be warned, Gog. I am against you, head of Meshech and Tubal. I'm going to turn you around, put hooks in your jaws, and drag you off with your whole army, your horses and riders in full armor — all those shields and bucklers and swords — fighting men armed to the teeth! Persia and Cush and Put will be in the ranks, also well-armed, as will Gomer and its army and Beth-togarmah out of the north with its army. Many nations will be with you!

7-9 "'Get ready to fight, you and the whole company that's been called out. Take charge and wait for orders. After a long time, you'll be given your orders. In the distant future you'll arrive at a country that has recovered from a devastating war. People from many nations will be gathered there on the mountains of Israel, for a long time now a wasteland. These people have been brought back from many countries and now live safe and secure. You'll rise like a thunderstorm and roll in like clouds and cover the land, you and the massed troops with you.

10-12 "'Message of GOD, the Master: At that time you'll start thinking things over and cook up an evil plot. You'll say, "I'm going to invade a country without defenses, attack an unsuspecting, carefree people going about their business — no gates to their cities, no locks on their doors. And I'm going to plunder the place, march right in and clean them out, this rebuilt country risen from the ashes, these returned exiles and their booming economy centered down at the navel of the earth."

13 "'Sheba and Dedan and Tarshish, traders all out to make a fast buck, will say, "So! You've opened a new market for plunder! You've brought in your troops to get rich quick!"'

14-16 "Therefore, son of man, prophesy! Tell Gog, 'A Message from GOD, the Master: When my people Israel are established securely, will you make your move? Will you come down out of the far north, you and that mob of armies, charging out on your horses like a tidal wave across the land, and invade my people Israel, covering the country like a cloud? When the time's ripe, I'll unleash you against my land in such a way that the nations will recognize me, realize that through you, Gog, in full view of the nations, I am putting my holiness on display.

17-22 "'A Message of GOD, the Master: Years ago when I spoke through my servants, the prophets of Israel, wasn't it you I was talking about? Year after year they prophesied that I would bring you against them. And when the day comes, Gog, you will attack that land of Israel. Decree of GOD, the Master. My raging anger will erupt. Fueled by blazing jealousy, I tell you that then there will be an earthquake that rocks the land of Israel. Fish and birds and wild animals — even ants and beetles! — and every human being will tremble and shake before me. Mountains will disintegrate, terraces will crumble. I'll order all-out war against you, Gog — Decree of GOD, the Master — Gog killing Gog on all the mountains of Israel. I'll deluge Gog with judgment: disease and massacre, torrential rain and hail, volcanic lava pouring down on you and your mobs of troops and people.

23 "'I'll show you how great I am, how holy I am. I'll make myself known all over the world. Then you'll realize that I am GOD.'"

CALL THE WILD ANIMALS!

1-5 **39** "Son of man, prophesy against Gog. Say, 'A Message of GOD, the Master: I'm against you, Gog, head of Meshech and Tubal. I'm going to turn you around and drag you out, drag you out of the far north and down on the mountains of Israel. Then I'll knock your bow out of your left hand and your arrows from your right hand. On the mountains of Israel you'll be slaughtered, you and all your troops and the people with you. I'll serve you up as a meal to carrion birds and scavenging animals. You'll be killed in the open field. I've given my word. Decree of GOD, the Master.'

6 "I'll set fire to Magog and the far-off islands, where people are so seemingly secure. And they'll realize that I am GOD.

7 "I'll reveal my holy name among my people Israel. Never again will I let my holy name be dragged in the mud. Then the nations will realize that I, GOD, am The Holy in Israel.

8 "It's coming! Yes, it will happen! This is the day I've been telling you about.

9-10 "People will come out of the cities of Israel and make a huge bonfire of the weapons of war, piling on shields large and small, bows and arrows, clubs and spears, a fire they'll keep going for seven years. They won't need to go into the woods to get fuel for the fire. There'll be plenty of weapons to keep it going. They'll strip those who stripped them. They'll rob those who robbed them. Decree of GOD, the Master.

11 "At that time I'll set aside a burial ground for Gog in Israel at Traveler's Rest, just east of the sea. It will obstruct the route of travelers, blocking their way, the mass grave of Gog and his mob of an army. They'll call the place Gog's Mob.

12-16 "Israel will bury the corpses in order to clean up the land. It will take them seven months. All the people will turn out to help with the burials. It will be a big day for the people when it's all done and I'm given my due. Men will be hired full-time for the cleanup burial operation and will go through the country looking for defiling, decomposing corpses. At the end of seven months, there'll be an all-out final search. Anyone who sees a bone will mark the place with a stick so the buriers can get it and bury it in the mass burial site, Gog's Mob. (A town nearby is called Mobville, or Hamonah.) That's how they'll clean up the land.

17-20 "Son of man, GOD, the Master, says: Call the birds! Call the wild animals! Call out, 'Gather and come, gather around my sacrificial meal that I'm preparing for you on the mountains of Israel. You'll eat meat and drink blood. You'll eat off the bodies of great heroes and drink the blood of famous princes as if they were so many rams and lambs, goats and bulls, the choicest grain-fed animals of Bashan. At the sacrificial meal I'm fixing for you, you'll eat fat till you're stuffed and drink blood till you're drunk. At the table I set for you, you'll stuff yourselves with horses and riders, heroes and fighters of every kind.' Decree of GOD, the Master.

21-24 "I'll put my glory on display among the nations and they'll all see the judgment I execute, see me at work handing out judgment. From that day on, Israel will realize that I am their GOD. And the nations will get the message that it was because of their sins that Israel went into exile. They were disloyal to me and I turned away from them. I turned them over to their enemies and they were all killed. I treated them as their polluted and sin-sated lives deserved. I turned away from them, refused to look at them.

25-29 "But now I will return Jacob back from exile, I'll be compassionate with all the people of Israel, and I'll be zealous for my holy name. Eventually the memory will fade, the memory of their shame over their betrayals of me when they lived securely in their own land, safe and unafraid. Once I've brought them back from foreign parts, gathered them in from enemy territories, I'll use them to demonstrate my holiness with all the nations watching. Then they'll realize for sure that I am their GOD, for even though I sent them off into exile, I will gather them back to their own land, leaving not one soul behind. After I've poured my Spirit on Israel, filled them with my life, I'll no longer turn away. I'll look them full in the face. Decree of GOD, the Master."

MEASURING THE TEMPLE COMPLEX

1-3 **40** In the twenty-fifth year of our exile, at the beginning of the year on the tenth of the month — it was the fourteenth year after the city fell — GOD touched me and brought me here. He brought me in divine vision to the land of Israel and set me down on a high mountain. To the south there were buildings that looked like a city. He took me there and I met a man deeply tanned, like bronze. He stood at the entrance holding a linen cord and a measuring stick.

4 The man said to me, "Son of man, look and listen carefully. Pay close attention to everything I'm going to show you. That's why you've been brought here. And then tell Israel everything you see."

5 First I saw a wall around the outside of the Temple complex. The measuring stick in the man's hand was about ten feet long. He measured the thickness of the wall: about ten feet. The height was also about ten feet.

6-7 He went into the gate complex that faced the east and went up the seven steps. He measured the depth of the outside threshold of the gate complex: ten feet. There were alcoves flanking the gate corridor, each ten feet square, each separated by a wall seven and a half feet thick. The inside threshold of the gate complex that led to the porch facing into the Temple courtyard was ten feet deep.

8-9 He measured the inside porch of the gate complex: twelve feet deep, flanked by pillars three feet thick. The porch opened onto the Temple courtyard.

10   Inside this east gate complex were three alcoves on each side. Each room was the same size and the separating walls were identical.

11   He measured the outside entrance to the gate complex: fifteen feet wide and nineteen and a half feet deep.

12   In front of each alcove was a low wall eighteen inches high. The alcoves were ten feet square.

13   He measured the width of the gate complex from the outside edge of the alcove roof on one side to the outside edge of the alcove roof on the other: thirty-seven and a half feet from one top edge to the other.

14   He measured the inside walls of the gate complex: ninety feet to the porch leading into the courtyard.

15   The distance from the entrance of the gate complex to the far end of the porch was seventy-five feet.

16   The alcoves and their connecting walls inside the gate complex were topped by narrow windows all the way around. The porch also. All the windows faced inward. The doorjambs between the alcoves were decorated with palm trees.

17-19   The man then led me to the outside courtyard and all its rooms. A paved walkway had been built connecting the courtyard gates. Thirty rooms lined the courtyard. The walkway was the same length as the gateways. It flanked them and ran their entire length. This was the walkway for the outside courtyard. He measured the distance from the front of the entrance gateway across to the entrance of the inner court: one hundred fifty feet.

19-23   Then he took me to the north side. Here was another gate complex facing north, exiting the outside courtyard. He measured its length and width. It had three alcoves on each side. Its gateposts and porch were the same as in the first gate: eighty-seven and a half feet by forty-three and three-quarters feet. The windows and palm trees were identical to the east gateway. Seven steps led up to it, and its porch faced inward. Opposite this gate complex was a gate complex to the inside courtyard, on the north as on the east. The distance between the two was one hundred seventy-five feet.

24-27   Then he took me to the south side, to the south gate complex. He measured its gateposts and its porch. It was the same size as the others. The porch with its windows was the same size as those previously mentioned. It also had seven steps up to it. Its porch opened onto the outside courtyard, with palm trees decorating its gateposts on both sides. Opposite to it, the gate complex for the inner court faced south. He measured the distance across the courtyard from gate to gate: one hundred seventy-five feet.

28-31   He led me into the inside courtyard through the south gate complex. He measured it and found it the same as the outside ones. Its alcoves, connecting walls, and vestibule were the same. The gate complex and porch, windowed all around, measured eighty-seven and a half by forty-three and three-quarters feet. The vestibule of each of the gate complexes leading to the inside courtyard was forty-three and three-quarters by eight and three-quarters feet. Each vestibule faced the outside courtyard. Palm trees were carved on its doorposts. Eight steps led up to it.

32-34   He then took me to the inside courtyard on the east and measured the gate complex. It was identical to the others—alcoves, connecting walls, and vestibule all the same. The gate complex and vestibule had windows all around. It measured eighty-seven and a half by forty-three and three-quarters feet. Its porch faced the outside courtyard. There were palm trees on the doorposts on both sides. And it had eight steps.

35-37   He brought me to the gate complex to the north and measured it: same measurements. The alcoves, connecting walls, and vestibule with its windows: eighty-seven and a half by forty-three and three-quarters feet. Its porch faced the outside courtyard. There were palm trees on its doorposts on both sides. And it had eight steps.

38-43   There was a room with a door at the vestibule of the gate complex where the burnt offerings were cleaned. Two tables were placed within the vestibule, one on either side, on which the animals for burnt offerings, sin offerings, and guilt offerings were slaughtered. Two tables were also placed against both outside walls of the vestibule—four tables inside and four tables outside, eight tables in all for slaughtering the sacrificial animals. The four tables used for the burnt offerings were thirty-one and a half inches square and twenty-one inches high. The tools for slaughtering the sacrificial animals and other sacrifices were kept there. Meat hooks, three inches long, were fastened to the walls. The tables were for the sacrificial animals.

44-46   Right where the inside gate complex opened onto the inside courtyard there were two rooms, one at the north gate facing south and the one at the south gate facing north. The man told me, "The room facing south is for the priests who are in charge of the Temple. And the room facing north is for the priests who are in charge of the altar. These priests are the sons of Zadok, the only sons of Levi permitted to come near to GOD to serve him."

47   He measured the inside courtyard: a hundred seventy-five feet square. The altar was in front of the Temple.

48-49   He led me to the porch of the Temple and measured the gateposts of the porch: eight and three-quarters feet high on both sides. The entrance to the gate complex was twenty-one feet wide and its connecting walls were four and a half feet thick. The vestibule itself was thirty-five feet wide and twenty-one feet deep. Ten steps led up to the porch. Columns flanked the gateposts.

1-2   **41** He brought me into the Temple itself and measured the doorposts on each side. Each was ten and a half feet thick. The entrance was seventeen and a half feet wide. The walls on each side were eight and three-quarters feet thick.

He also measured the Temple Sanctuary: seventy feet by thirty-five feet.

3-4   He went further in and measured the doorposts at the entrance: Each was three and a half feet thick. The entrance itself was ten and a half feet wide, and the entrance walls were twelve and a quarter feet thick. He measured the inside Sanctuary, thirty-five feet square, set at the end of the main Sanctuary. He told me, "This is The Holy of Holies."

5-7   He measured the wall of the Temple. It was ten and a half feet thick. The side rooms around the Temple were seven feet wide. There were three floors of these side rooms, thirty rooms on each of the three floors. There were supporting beams around the Temple wall to hold up the side rooms, but they were freestanding, not attached to the wall itself. The side rooms around the Temple became wider from first floor to second floor to third floor. A staircase went from the bottom floor, through the middle, and then to the top floor.

8-11   I observed that the Temple had a ten-and-a-half-foot-thick raised base around it, which provided a foundation for the side rooms. The outside walls of the side rooms were eight and three-quarters feet thick. The open area between the side rooms of the Temple and the priests' rooms was a thirty-five-foot-wide strip all around the Temple. There were two entrances to the side rooms from the open area, one placed on the north side, the other on the south. There were eight and three-quarters feet of open space all around.

12   The house that faced the Temple courtyard to the west was one hundred twenty-two and a half feet wide, with eight-and-three-quarters-foot-thick walls. The length of the wall and building was one hundred fifty-seven and a half feet.

13-14   He measured the Temple: one hundred seventy-five feet long. The Temple courtyard and the house, including its walls, measured a hundred seventy-five feet. The breadth of the front of the Temple and the open area to the east was a hundred seventy-five feet.

15-18   He measured the length of the house facing the courtyard at the back of the Temple, including the shelters on each side: one hundred seventy-five feet. The main Sanctuary, the inner Sanctuary, and the vestibule facing the courtyard were paneled with wood, and had window frames and door frames in all three sections. From floor to windows the walls were paneled. Above the outside entrance to the inner Sanctuary and on the walls at regular intervals all around the inner Sanctuary and the main Sanctuary, angel-cherubim and palm trees were carved in alternating sequence.

18-20   Each angel-cherub had two faces: a human face toward the palm tree on the right and the face of a lion toward the palm tree on the left. They were carved around the entire Temple. The cherubim–palm tree motif was carved from floor to door height on the wall of the main Sanctuary.

21-22   The main Sanctuary had a rectangular doorframe. In front of the Holy Place was something that looked like an altar of wood, five and a quarter feet high and three and a half feet square. Its corners, base, and sides were of wood. The man said to me, "This is the table that stands before GOD."

23-26   Both the main Sanctuary and the Holy Place had double doors. Each door had two leaves: two hinged leaves for each door, one set swinging inward and the other set outward. The doors of the main Sanctuary were carved with angel-cherubim and palm trees. There was a canopy of wood in front of the vestibule outside. There were narrow windows alternating with carved palm trees on both sides of the porch.

42 1-9 The man led me north into the outside courtyard and brought me to the rooms that are in front of the open space and the house facing north. The length of the house on the north was one hundred seventy-five feet, and its width eighty-seven and a half feet. Across the thirty-five feet that separated the inside courtyard from the paved walkway at the edge of the outside courtyard, the rooms rose level by level for three stories. In front of the rooms on the inside was a hallway seventeen and a half feet wide and one hundred seventy-five feet long. Its entrances were from the north. The upper rooms themselves were narrower, their galleries being wider than on the first and second floors of the building. The rooms on the third floor had no pillars like the pillars in the outside courtyard and were smaller than the rooms on the first and second floors. There was an outside wall parallel to the rooms and the outside courtyard. It fronted the rooms for eighty-seven and a half feet. The row of rooms facing the outside courtyard was eighty-seven and a half feet long. The row on the side nearest the Sanctuary was one hundred seventy-five feet long. The first-floor rooms had their entrance from the east, coming in from the outside courtyard.

10-12 On the south side along the length of the courtyard's outside wall and fronting on the Temple courtyard were rooms with a walkway in front of them. These were just like the rooms on the north — same exits and dimensions — with the main entrance from the east leading to the hallway and the doors to the rooms the same as those on the north side. The design on the south was a mirror image of that on the north.

13-14 Then he said to me, "The north and south rooms adjacent to the open area are holy rooms where the priests who come before GOD eat the holy offerings. There they place the holy offerings — grain offerings, sin offerings, and guilt offerings. These are set-apart rooms, holy space. After the priests have entered the Sanctuary, they must not return to the outside courtyard and mingle among the people until they change the sacred garments in which they minister and put on their regular clothes."

15-16 After he had finished measuring what was inside the Temple area, he took me out the east gate and measured it from the outside. Using his measuring stick, he measured the east side: eight hundred seventy-five feet.

17 He measured the north side: eight hundred seventy-five feet.

18 He measured the south side: eight hundred seventy-five feet.

19 Last of all he went to the west side and measured it: eight hundred seventy-five feet.

20 He measured the wall on all four sides. Each wall was eight hundred seventy-five feet. The walls separated the holy from the ordinary.

THE MEANING OF THE TEMPLE

43 1-3 The man brought me to the east gate. Oh! The bright Glory of the God of Israel rivered out of the east sounding like the roar of floodwaters, and the earth itself glowed with the bright Glory. It looked just like what I had seen when he came to destroy the city, exactly like what I had seen earlier at the Kebar River. And again I fell, face to the ground.

4-5   The bright Glory of GOD poured into the Temple through the east gate. The Spirit put me on my feet and led me to the inside courtyard and—oh! the bright Glory of GOD filled the Temple!

6-9   I heard someone speaking to me from inside the Temple while the man stood beside me. He said, "Son of man, this is the place for my throne, the place I'll plant my feet. This is the place where I'll live with the Israelites forever. Neither the people of Israel nor their kings will ever again drag my holy name through the mud with their whoring and the no-god idols their kings set up at all the wayside shrines. When they set up their worship shrines right alongside mine with only a thin wall between them, they dragged my holy name through the mud with their obscene and vile worship. Is it any wonder that I destroyed them in anger? So let them get rid of their whoring ways and the stinking no-god idols introduced by their kings and I'll move in and live with them forever.

10-11   "Son of man, tell the people of Israel all about the Temple so they'll be dismayed by their wayward lives. Get them to go over the layout. That will bring them up short. Show them the whole plan of the Temple, its ins and outs, the proportions, the regulations, and the laws. Draw a picture so they can see the design and meaning and live by its design and intent.

12   "This is the law of the Temple: As it radiates from the top of the mountain, everything around it becomes holy ground. Yes, this is law, the meaning, of the Temple.

13-14   "These are the dimensions of the altar, using the long (twenty-one-inch) ruler. The gutter at its base is twenty-one inches deep and twenty-one inches wide, with a four-inch lip around its edge.

14-15   "The height of the altar is three and a half feet from the base to the first ledge and twenty inches wide. From the first ledge to the second ledge it is seven feet high and twenty-one inches wide. The altar hearth is another seven feet high. Four horns stick upward from the hearth twenty-one inches high.

16-17   "The top of the altar, the hearth, is square, twenty-one by twenty-one feet. The upper ledge is also square, twenty-four and a half feet on each side, with a ten-and-a-half-inch lip and a twenty-one-inch-wide gutter all the way around.

    "The steps of the altar ascend from the east."

18   Then the man said to me, "Son of man, GOD, the Master, says: 'These are the ordinances for conduct at the altar when it is built, for sacrificing burnt offerings and sprinkling blood on it.

19-21   "'For a sin offering, give a bull to the priests, the Levitical priests who are from the family of Zadok who come into my presence to serve me. Take some of its blood and smear it on the four horns of the altar that project from the four corners of the top ledge and all around the lip. That's to purify the altar and make it fit for the sacrifice. Then take the bull for the sin offerings and burn it in the place set aside for this in the courtyard outside the Sanctuary.

22-24   "'On the second day, offer a male goat without blemish for a sin offering. Purify the altar the same as you purified it for the bull. Then, when you have purified it, offer a bull without blemish and a ram without blemish from the flock. Present them before GOD. Sprinkle salt on them and offer them as a burnt offering to GOD.

25-26 "'For seven days, prepare a goat for a sin offering daily, and also a bull and a ram from the flock, animals without blemish. For seven days the priests are to get the altar ready for its work, purifying it. This is how you dedicate it.

27 "'After these seven days of dedication, from the eighth day on, the priests will present your burnt offerings and your peace offerings. And I'll accept you with pleasure, with delight! Decree of GOD, the Master.'"

SANCTUARY RULES

1 **44** Then the man brought me back to the outside gate complex of the Sanctuary that faces east. But it was shut.

2-3 GOD spoke to me: "This gate is shut and it's to stay shut. No one is to go through it because GOD, the God of Israel, has gone through it. It stays shut. Only the prince, because he's the prince, may sit there to eat in the presence of GOD. He is to enter the gate complex through the porch and leave by the same way."

4 The man led me through the north gate to the front of the Temple. I looked, and — oh! — the bright Glory of GOD filling the Temple of GOD! I fell on my face in worship.

5 GOD said to me, "Son of man, get a grip on yourself. Use your eyes, use your ears, pay careful attention to everything I tell you about the ordinances of this Temple of GOD, the way all the laws work, instructions regarding it and all the entrances and exits of the Sanctuary.

6-9 "Tell this bunch of rebels, this family Israel, 'Message of GOD, the Master: No more of these vile obscenities, Israel, dragging irreverent and unrepentant outsiders, uncircumcised in heart and flesh, into my Sanctuary, feeding them the sacrificial offerings as if it were the food for a neighborhood picnic. With all your vile obscenities, you've broken trust with me, the solemn covenant I made with you. You haven't taken care of my holy things. You've hired out the work to foreigners who care nothing for this place, my Sanctuary. No irreverent and unrepentant aliens, uncircumcised in heart or flesh, not even the ones who live among Israelites, are to enter my Sanctuary.'

10-14 "The Levites who walked off and left me, along with everyone else — all Israel — who took up with all the no-god idols, will pay for everything they did wrong. From now on they'll do only the menial work in the Sanctuary: guard the gates and help out with the Temple chores — and also kill the sacrificial animals for the people and serve them. Because they acted as priests to the no-god idols and made my people Israel stumble and fall, I've taken an oath to punish them. Decree of GOD, the Master. Yes, they'll pay for what they've done. They're fired from the priesthood. No longer will they come into my presence and take care of my holy things. No more access to The Holy Place! They'll have to live with what they've done, carry the shame of their vile and obscene lives. From now on, their job is to sweep up and run errands. That's it.

15-16 "But the Levitical priests who descend from Zadok, who faithfully took care of my Sanctuary when everyone else went off and left me, are going to come into my presence and serve me. They are going to carry out the priestly work of offering the solemn sacrifices of worship. Decree of GOD, the Master. They're the only ones permitted to enter my Sanctuary. They're the only ones to approach my table and serve me, accompanying me in my work.

17-19   "When they enter the gate complex of the inside courtyard, they are to dress in linen. No woolens are to be worn while serving at the gate complex of the inside courtyard or inside the Temple itself. They're to wear linen turbans on their heads and linen underclothes — nothing that makes them sweat. When they go out into the outside courtyard where the people gather, they must first change out of the clothes they have been serving in, leaving them in the sacred rooms where they change to their everyday clothes, so that they don't trivialize their holy work by the way they dress.

20   "They are to neither shave their heads nor let their hair become unkempt, but must keep their hair trimmed and neat.

21   "No priest is to drink on the job — no wine while in the inside courtyard.

22   "Priests are not to marry widows or divorcees, but only Israelite virgins or widows of priests.

23   "Their job is to teach my people the difference between the holy and the common, to show them how to discern between unclean and clean.

24   "When there's a difference of opinion, the priests will arbitrate. They'll decide on the basis of my judgments, laws, and statutes. They are in charge of making sure the appointed feasts are honored and my Sabbaths kept holy in the ways I've commanded.

25-27   "A priest must not contaminate himself by going near a corpse. But when the dead person is his father or mother, son or daughter, brother or unmarried sister, he can approach the dead. But after he has been purified, he must wait another seven days. Then, when he returns to the inside courtyard of the Sanctuary to do his priestly work in the Sanctuary, he must first offer a sin offering for himself. Decree of GOD, the Master.

28-30   "As to priests owning land, I am their inheritance. Don't give any land in Israel to them. *I* am their 'land,' their inheritance. They'll take their meals from the grain offerings, the sin offerings, and the guilt offerings. Everything in Israel offered to GOD in worship is theirs. The best of everything grown, plus all special gifts, comes to the priests. All that is given in worship to GOD goes to them. Serve them first. Serve from your best and your home will be blessed.

31   "Priests are not to eat any meat from bird or animal unfit for ordinary human consumption, such as carcasses found dead on the road or in the field."

SACRED SPACE FOR GOD

1-4   "When you divide up the inheritance of the land, you must set aside part of the land as sacred space for GOD: approximately seven miles long by six miles wide, all of it holy ground. Within this rectangle, reserve a seven-hundred-fifty-foot square for the Sanctuary with a seventy-five-foot buffer zone surrounding it. Mark off within the sacred reserve a section seven miles long by three miles wide. The Sanctuary with its Holy of Holies will be placed there. This is where the priests will live, those who lead worship in the Sanctuary and serve GOD there. Their houses will be there along with The Holy Place.

5   "To the north of the sacred reserve, an area roughly seven miles long and two and a quarter miles wide will be set aside as land for the villages of the Levites who administer the affairs of worship in the Sanctuary.

6 "To the south of the sacred reserve, measure off a section seven miles long and about a mile and a half wide for the city itself, an area held in common by the whole family of Israel.

7-8 "The prince gets the land abutting the seven-mile east and west borders of the central sacred square, extending eastward toward the Jordan and westward toward the Mediterranean. This is the prince's possession in Israel. My princes will no longer bully my people, running roughshod over them. They'll respect the land as it has been allotted to the tribes.

9-12 "This is the Message of GOD, the Master: 'I've put up with you long enough, princes of Israel! Quit bullying and taking advantage of my people. Do what's just and right for a change. Use honest scales — honest weights and honest measures. Every pound must have sixteen ounces. Every gallon must measure four quarts. The ounce is the basic measure for both. And your coins must be honest — no wooden nickels!

EVERYONE IN THE LAND MUST CONTRIBUTE

13-15 "'These are the prescribed offerings you are to supply: one-sixtieth part of your wheat, one-sixtieth part of your barley, one-hundredth part of your oil, one sheep out of every two hundred from the lush pastures of Israel. These will be used for the grain offerings, burnt offerings, and peace offerings for making the atonement sacrifices for the people. Decree of GOD, the Master.

16-17 "'Everyone in the land must contribute to these special offerings that the prince in Israel will administer. It's the prince's job to provide the burnt offerings, grain offerings, and drink offerings at the Holy Festivals, the New Moons, and the Sabbaths — all the commanded feasts among the people of Israel. Sin offerings, grain offerings, burnt offerings, and peace offerings for making atonement for the people of Israel are his responsibility.

18-20 "'This is the Message from GOD, the Master: On the first day of the first month, take an unblemished bull calf and purify the Sanctuary. The priest is to take blood from the sin offerings and rub it on the doorposts of the Temple, on the four corners of the ledge of the altar, and on the gate entrance to the inside courtyard. Repeat this ritual on the seventh day of the month for anyone who sins without knowing it. In this way you make atonement for the Temple.

21 "'On the fourteenth day of the first month, you will observe the Passover, a feast of seven days. During the feast you will eat bread made without yeast.

22-23 "'On Passover, the prince supplies a bull as a sin offering for himself and all the people of the country. Each day for each of the seven days of the feast, he will supply seven bulls and seven rams unblemished as a burnt offering to GOD, and also each day a male goat.

24 "'He will supply about five and a half gallons of grain offering and a gallon of oil for each bull and each ram.

25 "'On the fifteenth day of the seventh month, and on each of the seven days of the feast, he is to supply the same materials for sin offerings, burnt offerings, grain offerings, and oil.'"

1-3 **46** "'Message from GOD, the Master: The gate of the inside courtyard on the east is to be shut on the six working days, but open on the Sabbath. It is also to be open on the New Moon. The prince will enter through the entrance area of the gate complex and stand at the gateposts as the priests present his burnt offerings and peace offerings while he worships there on the porch. He will then leave, but the gate won't be shut until evening. On Sabbaths and New Moons, the people are to worship before GOD at the outside entrance to that gate complex.

4-5 "'The prince supplies for GOD the burnt offering for the Sabbath — six unblemished lambs and an unblemished ram. The grain offering to go with the ram is about five and a half gallons plus a gallon of oil, and a handful of grain for each lamb.

6-7 "'At the New Moon he is to supply a bull calf, six lambs, and a ram, all without blemish. He will also supply five and a half gallons of grain offering and a gallon of oil for both ram and bull, and a handful of grain offering for each lamb.

8 "'When the prince enters, he will go through the entrance vestibule of the gate complex and leave the same way.

9-10 "'But when the people of the land come to worship GOD at the commanded feasts, those who enter through the north gate will exit from the south gate, and those who enter though the south gate will exit from the north gate. You don't exit the gate through which you enter, but through the opposite gate. The prince is to be there, mingling with them, going in and out with them.

11 "'At the festivals and the commanded feasts, the appropriate grain offering is five and a half gallons, with a gallon of oil for the bull and ram and a handful of grain for each lamb.

12 "'When the prince brings a freewill offering to GOD, whether a burnt offering or a peace offering, the east gate is to be opened for him. He offers his burnt or peace offering the same as he does on the Sabbath. Then he leaves, and after he is out, the gate is shut.

13-15 "'Every morning you are to bring a yearling lamb unblemished for a burnt offering to GOD. Also, every morning bring a grain offering of about a gallon of grain with a quart or so of oil to moisten it. Presenting this grain offering to GOD is standard procedure. The lamb, the grain offering, and the oil for the burnt offering are a regular daily ritual.

16-18 "'A Message from GOD, the Master: If the prince deeds a gift from his inheritance to one of his sons, it stays in the family. But if he deeds a gift from his inheritance to a servant, the servant keeps it only until the year of liberation (the Jubilee year). After that, it comes back to the prince. His inheritance is only for his sons. It stays in the family. The prince must not take the inheritance from any of the people, dispossessing them of their land. He can give his sons only what he himself owns. None of my people are to be run off their land.'"

19-20 Then the man brought me through the north gate into the holy chambers assigned to the priests and showed me a back room to the west. He said, "This is the kitchen where the priests will cook the guilt offering and sin offering and bake the grain offering so that they won't have to do it in the outside courtyard and endanger the unprepared people out there with The Holy."

21-23 He proceeded to take me to the outside courtyard and around to each of its four corners. In each corner I observed another court. In each of the four corners of the outside courtyard were smaller courts sixty by forty-five feet, each the same size. On the inside walls of the courts was a stone shelf, and beneath the shelves, hearths for cooking.

24   He said, "These are the kitchens where those who serve in the Temple will cook the sacrifices of the people."

TREES ON BOTH SIDES OF THE RIVER

1-2   **47** Now he brought me back to the entrance to the Temple. I saw water pouring out from under the Temple porch to the east (the Temple faced east). The water poured from the south side of the Temple, south of the altar. He then took me out through the north gate and led me around the outside to the gate complex on the east. The water was gushing from under the south front of the Temple.

3-5   He walked to the east with a measuring tape and measured off fifteen hundred feet, leading me through water that was ankle-deep. He measured off another fifteen hundred feet, leading me through water that was knee-deep. He measured off another fifteen hundred feet, leading me through water waist-deep. He measured off another fifteen hundred feet. By now it was a river over my head, water to swim in, water no one could possibly walk through.

6-7   He said, "Son of man, have you had a good look?"

Then he took me back to the riverbank. While sitting on the bank, I noticed a lot of trees on both sides of the river.

8-10   He told me, "This water flows east, descends to the Arabah and then into the sea, the sea of stagnant waters. When it empties into those waters, the sea will become fresh. Wherever the river flows, life will flourish — great schools of fish — because the river is turning the salt sea into fresh water. Where the river flows, life abounds. Fishermen will stand shoulder to shoulder along the shore from En Gedi all the way north to En-eglaim, casting their nets. The sea will teem with fish of all kinds, like the fish of the Great Mediterranean.

11   "The swamps and marshes won't become fresh. They'll stay salty.

12   "But the river itself, on both banks, will grow fruit trees of all kinds. Their leaves won't wither, the fruit won't fail. Every month they'll bear fresh fruit because the river from the Sanctuary flows to them. Their fruit will be for food and their leaves for healing."

DIVIDE UP THIS LAND

13-14   A Message from GOD, the Master: "These are the boundaries by which you are to divide up the inheritance of the land for the twelve tribes of Israel, with Joseph getting two parcels. It is to be divided up equally. I swore in a solemn oath to give it to your ancestors, swore that this land would be your inheritance.

15-17   "These are the boundaries of the land:

"The northern boundary runs from the Great Mediterranean Sea along the Hethlon road to where you turn off to the entrance of Hamath, Zedad, Berothah, and Sibraim, which lies between the territory of Damascus and the territory of Hamath, and on to Hazor-hatticon on the border of Hauran. The boundary runs from the Sea to Hazor-enon, with the territories of Damascus and Hamath to the north. That is the northern boundary.

18   "The eastern boundary runs between Damascus and Hauran, down along the Jordan between Gilead and the land of Israel to the Eastern Sea as

far as Tamar. This is the eastern boundary.

19 "The southern boundary runs west from Tamar to the waters of Meribah-kadesh, along the Brook of Egypt, and out to the Great Mediterranean Sea. This is the southern boundary.

20 "The western boundary is formed by the Great Mediterranean Sea north to where the road turns east toward the entrance to Hamath. This is the western boundary.

21-23 "Divide up this land among the twelve tribes of Israel. Divide it up as your inheritance, and include in it the resident aliens who have made themselves at home among you and now have children. Treat them as if they were born there, just like yourselves. They also get an inheritance among the tribes of Israel. In whatever tribe the resident alien lives, there he gets his inheritance. Decree of GOD, the Master."

THE SANCTUARY OF GOD AT THE CENTER

1 48 "These are the tribes:

"Dan: one portion, along the northern boundary, following the Hethlon road that turns off to the entrance of Hamath as far as Hazor-enon so that the territory of Damascus lies to the north alongside Hamath, the northern border stretching from east to west.

2 "Asher: one portion, bordering Dan from east to west.

3 "Naphtali: one portion, bordering Asher from east to west.

4 "Manasseh: one portion, bordering Naphtali from east to west.

5 "Ephraim: one portion, bordering Manasseh from east to west.

6 "Reuben: one portion, bordering Ephraim from east to west.

7 "Judah: one portion, bordering Reuben from east to west.

8-9 "Bordering Judah from east to west is the consecrated area that you will set aside as holy: a square approximately seven by seven miles, with the Sanctuary set at the center. The consecrated area reserved for GOD is to be seven miles long and a little less than three miles wide.

10-12 "This is how it will be parceled out. The priest will get the area measuring seven miles on the north and south boundaries, with a width of a little more than three miles at the east and west boundaries. The Sanctuary of GOD will be at the center. This is for the consecrated priests, the Zadokites who stayed true in their service to me and didn't get off track as the Levites did when Israel wandered off the main road. This is their special gift, a gift from the land itself, most holy ground, bordering the section of the Levites.

13-14 "The Levites get a section equal in size to that of the priests, roughly seven by three miles. They are not permitted to sell or trade any of it. It's the choice part of the land, to say nothing of being holy to GOD.

15-19 "What's left of the 'sacred square'—each side measures out at seven miles by a mile and a half—is for ordinary use: the city and its buildings with open country around it, but the city at the center. The north, south, east, and west sides of the city are each about a mile and a half in length. A strip of pasture, one hundred twenty-five yards wide, will border the city on all sides. The remainder of this portion, three miles of countryside to the east and to the west of the sacred precinct, is for farming. It will supply food for the city. Workers from all the tribes of Israel will serve as field hands to farm the land.

20 "This dedicated area, set apart for holy purposes, will be a square, seven miles by seven miles, a 'holy square,' which includes the part set aside for the city.

21-22 "The rest of this land, the country stretching east to the Jordan and west to the Mediterranean from the seven-mile sides of the 'holy square,' belongs to the prince. His land is sandwiched between the tribal portions north and south, and goes out both east and west from the 'sacred square' with its Temple at the center. The land set aside for the Levites on one side and the city on the other is in the middle of the territory assigned to the prince. The 'sacred square' is flanked east and west by the prince's land and bordered on the north and south by the territories of Judah and Benjamin, respectively.

23 "And then the rest of the tribes:
"Benjamin: one portion, stretching from the eastern to the western boundary.

24 "Simeon: one portion, bordering Benjamin from east to west.

25 "Issachar: one portion, bordering Simeon from east to west.

26 "Zebulun: one portion, bordering Issachar from east to west.

27 "Gad: one portion, bordering Zebulun from east to west.

28 "The southern boundary of Gad will run south from Tamar to the waters of Meribah-kadesh, along the Brook of Egypt and then out to the Great Mediterranean Sea.

29 "This is the land that you are to divide up among the tribes of Israel as their inheritance. These are their portions." Decree of GOD, the Master.

30-31 "These are the gates of the city. On the north side, which is 2,250 yards long (the gates of the city are named after the tribes of Israel), three gates: the gate of Reuben, the gate of Judah, the gate of Levi.

32 "On the east side, measuring 2,250 yards, three gates: the gate of Joseph, the gate of Benjamin, the gate of Dan.

33 "On the south side, measuring 2,250 yards, three gates: the gate of Simeon, the gate of Issachar, the gate of Zebulun.

34 "On the west side, measuring 2,250 yards, three gates: the gate of Gad, the gate of Asher, the gate of Naphtali.

35 "The four sides of the city measure to a total of nearly six miles.

"From now on the name of the city will be YAHWEH-SHAMMAH:

"GOD-IS-THERE."

DANIEL

Images generated by the Book of Daniel have been percolating through the daily experiences of the people of God for well over two thousand years now, producing a richly aromatic brew stimulating God's people to obey and trust their sovereign God.

Obedience to God in the pressures and stresses of day-by-day living and trust in God's ways in the large sweep of history are always at risk, but especially in times of suffering and persecution. Obedience to God is difficult when we are bullied into compliance to the God-ignoring culture out of sheer survival. Trust in God is likewise at risk of being abandoned in favor of the glamorous seductions of might and size.

Daniel was written out of just such times. There was little or no observable evidence in the circumstances to commend against-the-stream obedience or overarching trust. But Daniel's stories and visions have supplied what that society did not — could not — give. Century after century, Daniel has shot adrenaline into the veins of God-obedience and put backbone into God-trust.

Daniel is composed, in approximately equal parts, of stories and visions—eight chapters of stories (1–6 and 13–14) and six of visions (7–12). The stories tell of souls living faithfully in obedience to God in a time of adversity. The visions are wide-screen renditions of God's sovereignty worked out among nations who couldn't care less about him.

The soul-survival stories nourish a commitment to integrity and perseverance right now. Very few of us live in settings congenial to God-loyalty and among people who affirm a costly discipleship. Hardly a day goes by that we do not have to choose between compliance to what is expedient and loyalty to our Lord. The stories keep us alert to what is at stake day by day, hour by hour.

The visions of God's history-saving ways nourish hope in God during times when world events seem to put God in eclipse. The visions are difficult to understand, written as they are in a deliberately cryptic style (apocalyptic). From time to time they have been subjected to intense study and explanation. But for a first reading, perhaps it is better simply to let the strange symbolic figures give witness to the large historical truth that eclipses the daily accumulation of historical facts reported by our news media, namely, that God is sovereign. In the course of all the noise and shuffling, strutting and posing, of arrogant rulers and nations that we call history, with the consequent troubles to us all, God is serenely sovereign; we can trust him to bring all things and people under his rule.

There are always some of us who want to concentrate on the soul, and others of us who want to deal with the big issues of history. Daniel is one of our primary documents for keeping it all together — the personal and the political, the present and the future, the soul and society. (EP)

Note on the Additional Writings in Daniel

There are several stories not found in the original Hebrew versions of the Book of Daniel. Because they seemed to fit the overall themes of the initial work, they have always been added to Bibles in the Roman Catholic and several other Christian traditions.

They start with The Prayer of Azariah and the Song of the Three Young Men. The first is a national lament that Azariah (also called Abednego) proclaims while encountering an angel of the Lord after being thrown into a fiery furnace with two other friends of Daniel. The second is a litany said by Shadrach (also called Hananiah), Meshach (also called Mishael), and Abednego (also called Azariah) as they sat warming their feet until the king let them out of the furnace and gave them a promotion.

These two poems are inserted between the original verses 23 and 24 of chapter 3 of the Book of Daniel. Together they are 67 verses long. So, after verse 90, the Hebrew narrative as translated by Eugene Peterson returns. The reader will notice that the final 7 verses of this edition now have two sets of numerals: the first continuing the narrative of the insert (91–97); the second continuing the narrative as though there had been no insert (24–30).

Chapter 13, the Song of Susanna, is something of a "whodunit" that includes a courtroom scene worthy of a modern detective novel. A beautiful woman is accused of adultery by two judges, but she turns out to be an attempted-rape victim. Even though the story takes place within a Jewish community located in a non-Jewish country, it urges its intended Jewish audience or readership to be faithful to their religious identity and practice.

The two separate stories in chapter 14, one of the god Bel and the other of a god who is a dragon, are pieces of short fiction that teach a lesson. They were not really intended as history; thus they were not included in the original prophecy of Daniel. But because Daniel's name was found in them, the stories were added to the end of the Book of Daniel as the final chapter. (WG)

DANIEL

DANIEL WAS GIFTED BY GOD

1-2 It was the third year of King Jehoiakim's reign in Judah when King Nebuchadnezzar of Babylon declared war on Jerusalem and besieged the city. The Master handed King Jehoiakim of Judah over to him, along with some of the furnishings from the Temple of God. Nebuchadnezzar took king and furnishings to the country of Babylon, the ancient Shinar. He put the furnishings in the sacred treasury.

3-5 The king told Ashpenaz, head of the palace staff, to get some Israelites from the royal family and nobility — young men who were healthy and handsome, intelligent and well-educated, good prospects for leadership positions in the government, perfect specimens! — and indoctrinate them in the Babylonian language and the lore of magic and fortunetelling. The king then ordered that they be served from the same menu as the royal table — the best food, the finest wine. After three years of training they would be given positions in the king's court.

6-7 Four young men from Judah — Daniel, Hananiah, Mishael, and Azariah — were among those selected. The head of the palace staff gave them Babylonian names: Daniel was named Belteshazzar, Hananiah was named Shadrach, Mishael was named Meshach, Azariah was named Abednego.

8-10 But Daniel determined that he would not defile himself by eating the king's food or drinking his wine, so he asked the head of the palace staff to exempt him from the royal diet. The head of the palace staff, by God's grace, liked Daniel, but he warned him, "I'm afraid of what my master the king will do. He is the one who assigned this diet and if he sees that you are not as healthy as the rest, he'll have my head!"

11-13 But Daniel appealed to a steward who had been assigned by the head of the palace staff to be in charge of Daniel, Hananiah, Mishael, and Azariah: "Try us out for ten days on a simple diet of vegetables and water. Then compare us with the young men who eat from the royal menu. Make your decision on the basis of what you see."

14-16 The steward agreed to do it and fed them vegetables and water for ten days. At the end of the ten days they looked better and more robust than all the others who had been eating from the royal menu. So the steward continued to exempt them from the royal menu of food and drink and served them only vegetables.

17-19 God gave these four young men knowledge and skill in both books and life. In addition, Daniel was gifted in understanding all sorts of visions and dreams. At the end of the time set by the king for their training, the head of the royal staff brought them in to Nebuchadnezzar. When the king interviewed them, he found them far superior to all the other young men. None were a match for Daniel, Hananiah, Mishael, and Azariah.

19-20 And so they took their place in the king's service. Whenever the king consulted them on anything, on books or on life, he found them ten times better than all the magicians and enchanters in his kingdom put together.

21 Daniel continued in the king's service until the first year in the reign of King Cyrus.

1-3 2 In the second year of his reign, King Nebuchadnezzar started having dreams that disturbed him deeply. He couldn't sleep. He called in all the Babylonian magicians, enchanters, sorcerers, and fortunetellers to interpret his dreams for him. When they came and lined up before the king, he said to them, "I had a dream that I can't get out of my mind. I can't sleep until I know what it means."

4 The fortunetellers, speaking in the Aramaic language, said, "Long live the king! Tell us the dream and we will interpret it."

5-6 The king answered the fortunetellers, "This is my decree: If you can't tell me both the dream itself and its interpretation, I'll have you ripped to pieces, limb from limb, and your homes torn down. But if you tell me both the dream and its interpretation, I'll lavish you with gifts and honors. So go to it: Tell me the dream and its interpretation."

7 They answered, "If it please your majesty, tell us the dream. We'll give the interpretation."

8-9 But the king said, "I know what you're up to—you're just playing for time. You know you're up a tree. You know that if you can't tell me my dream, you're doomed. I see right through you—you're going to cook up some fancy stories and confuse the issue until I change my mind. Nothing doing! First tell me the dream, then I'll know that you're on the up and up with the interpretation and not just blowing smoke in my eyes."

10-11 The fortunetellers said, "Nobody anywhere can do what you ask. And no king, great or small, has ever demanded anything like this from any magician, enchanter, or fortuneteller. What you're asking is impossible unless some god or goddess should reveal it—and they don't hang around with people like us."

12-13 That set the king off. He lost his temper and ordered the whole company of Babylonian wise men killed. When the death warrant was issued, Daniel and his companions were included. They also were marked for execution.

14-15 When Arioch, chief of the royal guards, was making arrangements for the execution, Daniel wisely took him aside and quietly asked what was going on: "Why this all of a sudden?"

15-16 After Arioch filled in the background, Daniel went to the king and asked for a little time so that he could interpret the dream.

17-18 Daniel then went home and told his companions Hananiah, Mishael, and Azariah what was going on. He asked them to pray to the God of heaven for mercy in solving this mystery so that the four of them wouldn't be killed along with the whole company of Babylonian wise men.

D R E A M   I N T E R P R E T A T I O N :   A   S T O R Y   O F   F I V E   K I N G D O M S

19-23 That night the answer to the mystery was given to Daniel in a vision. Daniel blessed the God of heaven, saying,

"Blessed be the name of God,
        forever and ever.
He knows all, does all:
        He changes the seasons and guides history,
He raises up kings and also brings them down,
        he provides both intelligence and discernment,

He opens up the depths, tells secrets,
    sees in the dark — light spills out of him!
God of all my ancestors, all thanks! all praise!
    You made me wise and strong.
And now you've shown us what we asked for.
    You've solved the king's mystery."

24   So Daniel went back to Arioch, who had been put in charge of the execution. He said, "Call off the execution! Take me to the king and I'll interpret his dream."

25   Arioch didn't lose a minute. He ran to the king, bringing Daniel with him, and said, "I've found a man from the exiles of Judah who can interpret the king's dream!"

26   The king asked Daniel (renamed in Babylonian, Belteshazzar), "Are you sure you can do this — tell me the dream I had and interpret it for me?"

27-28   Daniel answered the king, "No mere human can solve the king's mystery, I don't care who it is — no wise man, enchanter, magician, diviner. But there is a God in heaven who solves mysteries, and he has solved this one. He is letting King Nebuchadnezzar in on what is going to happen in the days ahead. This is the dream you had when you were lying on your bed, the vision that filled your mind:

29-30   "While you were stretched out on your bed, O king, thoughts came to you regarding what is coming in the days ahead. The Revealer of Mysteries showed you what will happen. But the interpretation is given through me, not because I'm any smarter than anyone else in the country, but so that you will know what it means, so that you will understand what you dreamed.

31-36   "What you saw, O king, was a huge statue standing before you, striking in appearance. And terrifying. The head of the statue was pure gold, the chest and arms were silver, the belly and hips were bronze, the legs were iron, and the feet were an iron-ceramic mixture. While you were looking at this statue, a stone cut out of a mountain by an invisible hand hit the statue, smashing its iron-ceramic feet. Then the whole thing fell to pieces — iron, tile, bronze, silver, and gold, smashed to bits. It was like scraps of old newspapers in a vacant lot in a hot dry summer, blown every which way by the wind, scattered to oblivion. But the stone that hit the statue became a huge mountain, dominating the horizon. This was your dream.

36-40   "And now we'll interpret it for the king. You, O king, are the most powerful king on earth. The God of heaven has given you the works: rule, power, strength, and glory. He has put you in charge of men and women, wild animals and birds, all over the world — you're the head ruler, you are the head of gold. But your rule will be taken over by another kingdom, inferior to yours, and that one by a third, a bronze kingdom, but still ruling the whole land, and after that by a fourth kingdom, ironlike in strength. Just as iron smashes things to bits, breaking and pulverizing, it will bust up the previous kingdoms.

41-43   "But then the feet and toes that ended up as a mixture of ceramic and iron will deteriorate into a mongrel kingdom with some remains of iron in it. Just as the toes of the feet were part ceramic and part iron, it will end up a mixed bag of the breakable and unbreakable. That kingdom won't bond, won't hold together any more than iron and clay hold together.

44-45   "But throughout the history of these kingdoms, the God of heaven will be building a kingdom that will never be destroyed, nor will this king-dom ever fall under the domination of another. In the end it will crush the other kingdoms and finish them off and come through it all standing strong and eternal. It will be like the stone cut from the mountain by the invisible hand that crushed the iron, the bronze, the ceramic, the silver, and the gold.

"The great God has let the king know what will happen in the years to come. This is an accurate telling of the dream, and the interpretation is also accurate."

46-47　　When Daniel finished, King Nebuchadnezzar fell on his face in awe before Daniel. He ordered the offering of sacrifices and burning of incense in Daniel's honor. He said to Daniel, "Your God is beyond question the God of all gods, the Master of all kings. And he solves all mysteries, I know, because you've solved this mystery."

48-49　　Then the king promoted Daniel to a high position in the kingdom, lav-ished him with gifts, and made him governor over the entire province of Babylon and the chief in charge of all the Babylonian wise men. At Daniel's request the king appointed Shadrach, Meshach, and Abednego to admin-istrative posts throughout Babylon, while Daniel governed from the royal headquarters.

Four Men in the Furnace

1-3　　**3** King Nebuchadnezzar built a gold statue, ninety feet high and nine feet thick. He set it up on the Dura plain in the province of Babylon. He then ordered all the important leaders in the province, everybody who was anybody, to the dedication ceremony of the statue. They all came for the dedication, all the important people, and took their places before the statue that Nebuchadnezzar had erected.

4-6　　A herald then proclaimed in a loud voice: "Attention, everyone! Every race, color, and creed, listen! When you hear the band strike up — all the trum-pets and trombones, the tubas and baritones, the drums and cymbals — fall to your knees and worship the gold statue that King Nebuchadnezzar has set up. Anyone who does not kneel and worship shall be thrown immediately into a roaring furnace."

7　　The band started to play, a huge band equipped with all the musical instruments of Babylon, and everyone — every race, color, and creed — fell to their knees and worshiped the gold statue that King Nebuchadnezzar had set up.

8-12　　Just then, some Babylonian fortunetellers stepped up and accused the Jews. They said to King Nebuchadnezzar, "Long live the king! You gave strict orders, O king, that when the big band started playing, everyone had to fall to their knees and worship the gold statue, and whoever did not go to their knees and worship it had to be pitched into a roaring furnace. Well, there are some Jews here — Shadrach, Meshach, and Abednego — whom you have placed in high positions in the province of Babylon. These men are ignoring you, O king. They don't respect your gods and they won't worship the gold statue you set up."

13-15　　Furious, King Nebuchadnezzar ordered Shadrach, Meshach, and Abednego to be brought in. When the men were brought in, Nebuchadnezzar asked, "Is it true, Shadrach, Meshach, and Abednego, that you don't respect my gods and refuse to worship the gold statue that I have set up? I'm giving you a second chance — but from now on, when the big band strikes up you must go to your knees and worship the statue I have made. If you don't worship it, you will be pitched into a roaring furnace, no questions asked. Who is the god who can rescue you from my power?"

16-18   Shadrach, Meshach, and Abednego answered King Nebuchadnezzar, "Your threat means nothing to us. If you throw us in the fire, the God we serve can rescue us from your roaring furnace and anything else you might cook up, O king. But even if he doesn't, it wouldn't make a bit of difference, O king. We still wouldn't serve your gods or worship the gold statue you set up."

19-23   Nebuchadnezzar, his face purple with anger, cut off Shadrach, Meshach, and Abednego. He ordered the furnace fired up seven times hotter than usual. He ordered some strong men from the army to tie them up, hands and feet, and throw them into the roaring furnace. Shadrach, Meshach, and Abednego, bound hand and foot, fully dressed from head to toe, were pitched into the roaring fire. Because the king was in such a hurry and the furnace was so hot, flames from the furnace killed the men who carried Shadrach, Meshach, and Abednego to it, while the fire raged around Shadrach, Meshach, and Abednego.

THE PRAYER OF AZARIAH

24-25   The three young men danced in the middle of the flames, praising God and blessing the Lord. One of them, Azariah, also called Abednego, stopped for a moment and, as the flames were licking his lips, raised his voice in prayer.

26   "Blessed are you, O Lord, God of our ancestors! You alone are praiseworthy, and your name will be blessed forever!

27   "For you've done what is just—in general and in every particular; your ways are the right ways.

28   "Your judgments in regard to all phases of our conduct in Jerusalem, the holy city of our forebears, have the ring of truth; under the circumstances, you've done the best for us that we could have expected.

29   "For we failed to follow your life-maps and acted with arrogance; with each new sin we drew farther away from you. We've failed in just about every way we could.

30   "We were deaf and didn't follow your verbal directions, even though you ordered us to obey you for our own good.

31   "Tough love you gave us, but it was right on target.

32   "Eventually, you handed us over to our enemies—like this unjust king here, the worst of his kind—who are all evil personified, the fruit of bad seed, undesirables in every conceivable way.

33   "Now we can't open our mouths, your own servants who worship you, because we've embarrassed and shamed ourselves.

34   "Don't ever, we beg you, abandon us—you have promised us otherwise, so please don't water down your covenant.

35   "Don't pry your mercy from our grasp; Abraham, your beloved friend, wouldn't want that, nor would his son Isaac or his grandson Israel.

36   "You promised that their seed would multiply like the stars in the sky, like the grains of sand on the beach.

37   "So why, O Lord, are we now the least favored nation? Why are we ranked lowest of the low? It has to be because of our sins.

38   "How can we find favor with you if we don't have a prince or a prophet

or a leader? We have no altar on which to offer you sacrifices, offerings, incense, the firstfruits of our fields.

³⁹⁻⁴⁰ "In spite of all this, look upon our contrite heart and humble spirit, as though we ourselves were rams and bulls or fatted lambs being offered to you. Let our bodies be our sacrifice in your sight today, so that we can follow you perfectly—perfectly in the sense that those who put their faith in you are never wrong.

⁴¹ "We follow you with our whole heart; fearing you still, we want to look upon your face.

⁴² "Don't let us die in shame. Treat us the way you always have; massage us with your usual gentility; smother us with your inexhaustible mercy.

⁴³ "Wrap us in your wondrous ways; restore glory to your name, O Lord.

⁴⁴ "Confound those who persecute your servants; break the hold they have on us; shatter their strength against our weakness.

⁴⁵ "Let them know you're the Lord, the one and only God, gloriously reigning over the whole world."

SONG OF THE THREE YOUNG MEN

⁴⁶⁻⁵¹ Those who had imprisoned the three, malicious ministers of the king, didn't rest for a minute from fueling the furnace with roughage, debris, and dead wood. The fire rose about eight feet above the furnace floor and spread laterally, burning to death some Chaldeans who happened to be standing nearby. But inside the fire, an angel of the Lord descended upon Azariah and his friends and snuffed the fiery flames, leaving behind a light summer breeze.

Apparently, the fire hadn't touched the young men at all or caused them any pain. Then the happy three, as if in one voice, began glorifying the Lord with a praise list, even as they stood in the furnace that was perfectly comfortable to them.

⁵² "Blessed are you, O Lord, God of our ancestors! You alone are praiseworthy and high above us, and your name will be blessed forever!

⁵³ "Blessed are you in the Temple of your glory; you are praiseworthy and high above us forever.

⁵⁴ "Blessed are you on the throne of your glory; you are praiseworthy and high above us forever.

⁵⁵ "Blessed are you who take time to observe what is going on here below; you are praiseworthy and high above us forever.

⁵⁶ "Blessed are you for always seeing the big picture; you are praiseworthy and high above us forever.

⁵⁷ "All creation, bless the Lord; praise and honor him forever.

⁵⁸ "Everything above creation, bless the Lord; praise and honor him forever.

⁵⁹ "Angels of all ranks, bless the Lord; praise and honor him forever.

⁶⁰ "Waterfalls and waterways, bless the Lord; praise and honor him forever.

⁶¹ "Every virtuous being, bless the Lord; praise and honor him forever.

⁶² "Sun and moon, bless the Lord; praise and honor him forever.

⁶³ "Stars of the sky, bless the Lord; praise and honor him forever.

⁶⁴ "Dew and fog, bless the Lord; praise and honor him forever.

⁶⁵ "Hurricanes and tornadoes, bless the Lord; praise and honor him forever.

⁶⁶ "Fire and heat, bless the Lord; praise and honor him forever.

⁶⁷ "Hot and cold, bless the Lord; praise and honor him forever.

68 "Snow and hail, bless the Lord; praise and honor him forever.

69 "Freezing rain and frostbite, bless the Lord; praise and honor him forever.

70 "Ice and snow, bless the Lord; praise and honor him forever.

71 "Nights and days, bless the Lord; praise and honor him forever.

72 "Light and darkness, bless the Lord; praise and honor him forever.

73 "Thunder and lightning, bless the Lord; praise and honor him forever.

74 "All the earth, bless the Lord; praise and honor him forever.

75 "Mountains and hills, bless the Lord; praise and honor him forever.

76 "Plants and herbs, bless the Lord; praise and honor him forever.

77 "Seas and streams, bless the Lord; praise and honor him forever.

78 "Lakes and rivers, bless the Lord; praise and honor him forever.

79 "Water mammals and fish, bless the Lord; praise and honor him forever.

80 "All creatures that fly, bless the Lord; praise and honor him forever.

81 "All beasts tame and wild, bless the Lord; praise and honor him forever.

82 "All the offspring of the world, bless the Lord; praise and honor him forever.

83 "House of Israel, bless the Lord; praise and honor him forever.

84 "Priests and prophets, bless the Lord, praise and honor him forever.

85 "All people of God, bless the Lord; praise and honor him forever.

86 "Souls of the just, bless the Lord; praise and honor him forever.

87 "All who are holy and humble of heart, bless the Lord; praise and honor him forever.

88 "Hananiah, Azariah, Mishael—we bless the Lord; we praise and honor him forever.

"For he rescued us from the world below and saved us from the hand of death; he freed us from the fiery furnace.

89 "Stand up and proclaim the greatness of the Lord; he is goodness itself and his mercy never quits.

90 "All who are in awe of the God of gods, bless the Lord; stand up and proclaim him, for his mercy never quits."

91/24 Suddenly King Nebuchadnezzar jumped up in alarm and said, "Didn't we throw three men, bound hand and foot, into the fire?"

"That's right, O king," they said.

92/25 "But look!" he said. "I see four men, walking around freely in the fire, completely unharmed! And the fourth man looks like a son of the gods!"

93/26 Nebuchadnezzar went to the door of the roaring furnace and called in, "Shadrach, Meshach, and Abednego, servants of the High God, come out here!"

Shadrach, Meshach, and Abednego walked out of the fire.

94/27 All the important people, the government leaders and king's counselors, gathered around to examine them and discovered that the fire hadn't so much as touched the three men — not a hair singed, not a scorch mark on their clothes, not even the smell of smoke on them!

95/28 Nebuchadnezzar said, "Blessed be the God of Shadrach, Meshach, and Abednego! He sent his angel and rescued his servants who trusted in him. They ignored the king's orders and laid their bodies on the line rather than serve or worship any god but their own.

96/29 "Therefore I issue this decree: Anyone anywhere, of any race, color, or creed, who says anything against the God of Shadrach, Meshach, and

Abednego will be ripped to pieces, limb from limb, and their houses torn down. There has never been a god who can pull off a rescue like this."

97/ 30   Then the king promoted Shadrach, Meshach, and Abednego in the province of Babylon.

A Dream of a Chopped-Down Tree

1-2   4 King Nebuchadnezzar to everyone, everywhere — every race, color, and creed: "Peace and prosperity to all! It is my privilege to report to you the gracious miracles that the High God has done for me.

3   "His miracles are staggering,
   his wonders are surprising.
His kingdom lasts and lasts,
   his sovereign rule goes on forever.

4-7   "I, Nebuchadnezzar, was at home taking it easy in my palace, without a care in the world. But as I was stretched out on my bed I had a dream that scared me — a nightmare that shook me. I sent for all the wise men of Babylon so that they could interpret the dream for me. When they were all assembled — magicians, enchanters, fortunetellers, witches — I told them the dream. None could tell me what it meant.

8   "And then Daniel came in. His Babylonian name is Belteshazzar, named after my god, a man full of the divine Holy Spirit. I told him my dream.

9   "'Belteshazzar,' I said, 'chief of the magicians, I know that you are a man full of the divine Holy Spirit and that there is no mystery that you can't solve. Listen to this dream that I had and interpret it for me.

10-12   "'This is what I saw as I was stretched out on my bed. I saw a big towering tree at the center of the world. As I watched, the tree grew huge and strong. Its top reached the sky and it could be seen from the four corners of the earth. Its leaves were beautiful, its fruit abundant — enough food for everyone! Wild animals found shelter under it, birds nested in its branches, everything living was fed and sheltered by it.

13-15   "'And this also is what I saw as I was stretched out on my bed. I saw a holy watchman descend from heaven, and call out:

Chop down the tree, lop off its branches,
   strip its leaves and scatter its fruit.
Chase the animals from beneath it
   and shoo the birds from its branches.
But leave the stump and roots in the ground,
   belted with a strap of iron and bronze in the grassy meadow.

15-16   Let him be soaked in heaven's dew
   and take his meals with the animals that graze.
Let him lose his mind
   and get an animal's mind in exchange,
And let this go on
   for seven seasons.

17   The angels announce this decree,
   the holy watchmen bring this sentence,

So that everyone living will know
    that the High God rules human kingdoms.
He arranges kingdom affairs however he wishes,
    and makes leaders out of losers.

⁂

18 "'This is what I, King Nebuchadnezzar, dreamed. It's your turn, Belteshazzar—interpret it for me. None of the wise men of Babylon could make heads or tails of it, but I'm sure you can do it. You're full of the divine Holy Spirit.'"

"You Will Graze on the Grass Like an Ox"

19 At first Daniel, who had been renamed Belteshazzar in Babylon, was upset. The thoughts that came swarming into his mind terrified him.

"Belteshazzar," the king said, "stay calm. Don't let the dream and its interpretation scare you."

"My master," said Belteshazzar, "I wish this dream were about your enemies and its interpretation for your foes.

20-22 "The tree you saw that grew so large and sturdy with its top touching the sky, visible from the four corners of the world; the tree with the luxuriant foliage and abundant fruit, enough for everyone; the tree under which animals took cover and in which birds built nests—you, O king, are that tree.

"You have grown great and strong. Your royal majesty reaches sky-high, and your sovereign rule stretches to the four corners of the world.

23-25 "But the part about the holy angel descending from heaven and proclaiming, 'Chop down the tree, destroy it, but leave stump and roots in the ground belted with a strap of iron and bronze in the grassy meadow; let him be soaked with heaven's dew and take his meals with the grazing animals for seven seasons'—this, O king, also refers to you. It means that the High God has sentenced my master the king: You will be driven away from human company and live with the wild animals. You will graze on grass like an ox. You will be soaked in heaven's dew. This will go on for seven seasons, and you will learn that the High God rules over human kingdoms and that he arranges all kingdom affairs.

26 "The part about the tree stump and roots being left means that your kingdom will still be there for you after you learn that it is heaven that runs things.

27 "So, king, take my advice: Make a clean break with your sins and start living for others. Quit your wicked life and look after the needs of the down-and-out. Then *you* will continue to have a good life."

The Loss and Regaining of a Mind and a Kingdom

28-30 All this happened to King Nebuchadnezzar. Just twelve months later, he was walking on the balcony of the royal palace in Babylon and boasted, "Look at this, Babylon the great! And I built it all by myself, a royal palace adequate to display my honor and glory!"

31-32 The words were no sooner out of his mouth than a voice out of heaven spoke, "This is the verdict on you, King Nebuchadnezzar: Your kingdom is taken from you. You will be driven out of human company and live with the wild animals. You will eat grass like an ox. The sentence is for seven seasons, enough time to learn that the High God rules human kingdoms and puts whomever he wishes in charge."

33 It happened at once. Nebuchadnezzar was driven out of human company, ate grass like an ox, and was soaked in heaven's dew. His hair grew like the feathers of an eagle and his nails like the claws of a hawk.

34-35 "At the end of the seven years, I, Nebuchadnezzar, looked to heaven. I was given my mind back and I blessed the High God, thanking and glorifying God, who lives forever:

"His sovereign rule lasts and lasts,
    his kingdom never declines and falls.
Life on this earth doesn't add up to much,
    but God's heavenly army keeps everything going.
No one can interrupt his work,
    no one can call his rule into question.

36-37 "At the same time that I was given back my mind, I was also given back my majesty and splendor, making my kingdom shine. All the leaders and important people came looking for me. I was reestablished as king in my kingdom and became greater than ever. And that's why I'm singing — I, Nebuchadnezzar — singing and praising the King of Heaven:

"Everything he does is right,
    and he does it the right way.
He knows how to turn a proud person
    into a humble man or woman."

THE WRITING OF A DISEMBODIED HAND

1-4 **5** King Belshazzar held a great feast for his one thousand nobles. The wine flowed freely. Belshazzar, heady with the wine, ordered that the gold and silver chalices his father Nebuchadnezzar had stolen from God's Temple of Jerusalem be brought in so that he and his nobles, his wives and concubines, could drink from them. When the gold and silver chalices were brought in, the king and his nobles, his wives and his concubines, drank wine from them. They drank the wine and drunkenly praised their gods made of gold and silver, bronze and iron, wood and stone.

5-7 At that very moment, the fingers of a human hand appeared and began writing on the lamp-illumined, whitewashed wall of the palace. When the king saw the disembodied hand writing away, he went white as a ghost, scared out of his wits. His legs went limp and his knees knocked. He yelled out for the enchanters, the fortunetellers, and the diviners to come. He told these Babylonian magi, "Anyone who can read this writing on the wall and tell me what it means will be famous and rich — purple robe, the great gold chain — and be third-in-command in the kingdom."

8-9 One after the other they tried, but could make no sense of it. They could neither read what was written nor interpret it to the king. So now the king was really frightened. All the blood drained from his face. The nobles were in a panic.

10-12 The queen heard of the hysteria among the king and his nobles and came to the banquet hall. She said, "Long live the king! Don't be upset. Don't sit around looking like ghosts. There is a man in your kingdom who is full of the divine Holy Spirit. During your father's time he was well known for his intellectual brilliance and spiritual wisdom. He was so good that your father, King Nebuchadnezzar, made him the head of all the magicians, enchanters, fortunetellers, and diviners. There was no one quite like him. He could do anything—interpret dreams, solve mysteries, explain puzzles. His name is Daniel, but he was renamed Belteshazzar by the king. Have Daniel called in. He'll tell you what is going on here."

13-16   So Daniel was called in. The king asked him, "Are you the Daniel who was one of the Jewish exiles my father brought here from Judah? I've heard about you—that you're full of the Holy Spirit, that you've got a brilliant mind, that you are incredibly wise. The wise men and enchanters were brought in here to read this writing on the wall and interpret it for me. They couldn't figure it out—not a word, not a syllable. But I've heard that you interpret dreams and solve mysteries. So—if you can read the writing and interpret it for me, you'll be rich and famous—a purple robe, the great gold chain around your neck—and third-in-command in the kingdom."

17   Daniel answered the king, "You can keep your gifts, or give them to someone else. But I will read the writing for the king and tell him what it means.

18-21   "Listen, O king! The High God gave your father Nebuchadnezzar a great kingdom and a glorious reputation. Because God made him so famous, people from everywhere, whatever their race, color, and creed, were totally intimidated by him. He killed or spared people on whim. He promoted or humiliated people capriciously. He developed a big head and a hard spirit. Then God knocked him off his high horse and stripped him of his fame. He was thrown out of human company, lost his mind, and lived like a wild animal. He ate grass like an ox and was soaked by heaven's dew until he learned his lesson: that the High God rules human kingdoms and puts anyone he wants in charge.

22-23   "You are his son and have known all this, yet you're as arrogant as he ever was. Look at you, setting yourself up in competition against the Master of heaven! You had the sacred chalices from his Temple brought into your drunken party so that you and your nobles, your wives and your concubines, could drink from them. You used the sacred chalices to toast your gods of silver and gold, bronze and iron, wood and stone—blind, deaf, and imbecile gods. But you treat with contempt the living God who holds your entire life from birth to death in his hand.

24-26   "God sent the hand that wrote on the wall, and this is what is written: MENE, TEQEL, and PERES. This is what the words mean:

"*Mene*: God has numbered the days of your rule and they don't add up.

27   "*Teqel*: You have been weighed on the scales and you don't weigh much.

28   "*Peres*: Your kingdom has been divided up and handed over to the Medes and Persians."

29   Belshazzar did what he had promised. He robed Daniel in purple, draped the great gold chain around his neck, and promoted him to third-in-charge in the kingdom.

30-31   That same night the Babylonian king Belshazzar was murdered. Darius the Mede was sixty-two years old when he succeeded him as king.

DANIEL IN THE LIONS' DEN

6 1-3 Darius reorganized his kingdom. He appointed one hundred twenty governors to administer all the parts of his realm. Over them were three vice-regents, one of whom was Daniel. The governors reported to the vice-regents, who made sure that everything was in order for the king. But Daniel, brimming with spirit and intelligence, so completely outclassed the other vice-regents and governors that the king decided to put him in charge of the whole kingdom.

4-5 The vice-regents and governors got together to find some old scandal or skeleton in Daniel's life that they could use against him, but they couldn't dig up anything. He was totally exemplary and trustworthy. They could find no evidence of negligence or misconduct. So they finally gave up and said, "We're never going to find anything against this Daniel unless we can cook up something religious."

6-7 The vice-regents and governors conspired together and then went to the king and said, "King Darius, live forever! We've convened your vice-regents, governors, and all your leading officials, and have agreed that the king should issue the following decree:

For the next thirty days no one is to pray to any god or mortal except you, O king. Anyone who disobeys will be thrown into the lions' den.

8 "Issue this decree, O king, and make it unconditional, as if written in stone like all the laws of the Medes and the Persians."

9 King Darius signed the decree.

10 When Daniel learned that the decree had been signed and posted, he continued to pray just as he had always done. His house had windows in the upstairs that opened toward Jerusalem. Three times a day he knelt there in prayer, thanking and praising his God.

11-12 The conspirators came and found him praying, asking God for help. They went straight to the king and reminded him of the royal decree that he had signed. "Did you not," they said, "sign a decree forbidding anyone to pray to any god or man except you for the next thirty days? And anyone caught doing it would be thrown into the lions' den?"

"Absolutely," said the king. "Written in stone, like all the laws of the Medes and Persians."

13 Then they said, "Daniel, one of the Jewish exiles, ignores you, O king, and defies your decree. Three times a day he prays."

14 At this, the king was very upset and tried his best to get Daniel out of the fix he'd put him in. He worked at it the whole day long.

15 But then the conspirators were back: "Remember, O king, it's the law of the Medes and Persians that the king's decree can never be changed."

16 The king caved in and ordered Daniel brought and thrown into the lions' den. But he said to Daniel, "Your God, to whom you are so loyal, is going to get you out of this."

17 A stone slab was placed over the opening of the den. The king sealed the cover with his signet ring and the signet rings of all his nobles, fixing Daniel's fate.

18 The king then went back to his palace. He refused supper. He couldn't sleep. He spent the night fasting.

19-20   At daybreak the king got up and hurried to the lions' den. As he approached the den, he called out anxiously, "Daniel, servant of the living God, has your God, whom you serve so loyally, saved you from the lions?"

21-22   "O king, live forever!" said Daniel. "My God sent his angel, who closed the mouths of the lions so that they would not hurt me. I've been found innocent before God and also before you, O king. I've done nothing to harm you."

23   When the king heard these words, he was happy. He ordered Daniel taken up out of the den. When he was hauled up, there wasn't a scratch on him. He had trusted his God.

24   Then the king commanded that the conspirators who had informed on Daniel be thrown into the lions' den, along with their wives and children. Before they hit the floor, the lions had them in their jaws, tearing them to pieces.

25-27   King Darius published this proclamation to every race, color, and creed on earth:

> Peace to you! Abundant peace!
>   I decree that Daniel's God shall be worshiped and feared
> in all parts of my kingdom.
>   He is the living God, world without end. His kingdom
> never falls.
>   His rule continues eternally.
>   He is a savior and rescuer.
>   He performs astonishing miracles in heaven and on earth.
>   He saved Daniel from the power of the lions.

28   From then on, Daniel was treated well during the reign of Darius, and also in the following reign of Cyrus the Persian.

A Vision of Four Animals

1   In the first year of the reign of King Belshazzar of Babylon, Daniel had a dream. What he saw as he slept in his bed terrified him — a real nightmare. Then he wrote out his dream:

2-3   "In my dream that night I saw the four winds of heaven whipping up a great storm on the sea. Four huge animals, each different from the others, ascended out of the sea.

4   "The first animal looked like a lion, but it had the wings of an eagle. While I watched, its wings were pulled off. It was then pulled erect so that it was standing on two feet like a man. Then a human heart was placed in it.

5   "Then I saw a second animal that looked like a bear. It lurched from side to side, holding three ribs in its jaws. It was told, 'Attack! Devour! Fill your belly!'

6   "Next I saw another animal. This one looked like a panther. It had four birdlike wings on its back. This animal had four heads and was made to rule.

7   "After that, a fourth animal appeared in my dream. This one was a grisly horror — hideous. It had huge iron teeth. It crunched and swallowed its victims. Anything left over, it trampled into the ground. It was different from the other animals — this one was a real monster. It had ten horns.

8   "As I was staring at the horns and trying to figure out what they meant, another horn sprouted up, a little horn. Three of the original horns

were pulled out to make room for it. There were human eyes in this little horn, and a big mouth speaking arrogantly.

9-10 "As I was watching all this,

"Thrones were set in place
  and The Old One sat down.
His robes were white as snow,
  his hair was white like wool.
His throne was flaming with fire,
  its wheels blazing.
A river of fire
  poured out of the throne.
Thousands upon thousands served him,
  tens of thousands attended him.
The courtroom was called to order,
  and the books were opened.

11-13 "I kept watching. The little horn was speaking arrogantly. Then, as I watched, the monster was killed and its body cremated in a roaring fire. The other animals lived on for a limited time, but they didn't really do anything, had no power to rule. My dream continued.

13-14 "I saw a human form, a son of man,
  arriving in a whirl of clouds.
He came to The Old One
  and was presented to him.
He was given power to rule — all the glory of royalty.
  Everyone — race, color, and creed — had to serve him.
His rule would be forever, never ending.
  His kingly rule would never be replaced.

15-16 "But as for me, Daniel, I was disturbed. All these dream-visions had me agitated. So I went up to one of those standing by and asked him the meaning of all this. And he told me, interpreting the dream for me:

17-18 "'These four huge animals,' he said, 'mean that four kingdoms will appear on earth. But eventually the holy people of the High God will be given the kingdom and have it ever after — yes, forever and ever.'

19-22 "But I wanted to know more. I was curious about the fourth animal, the one so different from the others, the hideous monster with the iron teeth and the bronze claws, gulping down what it ripped to pieces and trampling the leftovers into the dirt. And I wanted to know about the ten horns on its head and the other horn that sprouted up while three of the original horns were removed. This new horn had eyes and a big mouth and spoke arrogantly, dominating the other horns. I watched as this horn was making war on God's holy people and getting the best of them. But then The Old One intervened and decided things in favor of the people of the High God. In the end, God's holy people took over the kingdom.

23-25 "The bystander continued, telling me this: 'The fourth animal is a fourth kingdom that will appear on earth. It will be different from the first three kingdoms, a monster kingdom that will chew up everyone in sight and spit them out. The ten horns are ten kings, one after another, that will come from this kingdom. But then another king will arrive. He will be different from the earlier kings. He will begin by toppling three kings. Then he will blaspheme the High God, persecute the followers of the High God, and try to get rid of sacred worship and moral practice. God's holy people will be persecuted by him for a time, two times, half a time.

26-27 "'But when the court comes to order, the horn will be stripped of its power and totally destroyed. Then the royal rule and the authority and the glory of all the kingdoms under heaven will be handed over to the people of the High God. Their royal rule will last forever. All other rulers will serve and obey them.'

28 "And there it ended. I, Daniel, was in shock. I was like a man who had seen a ghost. But I kept it all to myself."

A VISION OF A RAM AND A BILLY GOAT

1 8 "In King Belshazzar's third year as king, another vision came to me, Daniel. This was now the second vision.

2-4 "In the vision, I saw myself in Susa, the capital city of the province Elam, standing at the Ulai Canal. Looking around, I was surprised to see a ram also standing at the gate. The ram had two huge horns, one bigger than the other, but the bigger horn was the last to appear. I watched as the ram charged: first west, then north, then south. No beast could stand up to him. He did just as he pleased, strutting as if he were king of the beasts.

5-7 "While I was watching this, wondering what it all meant, I saw a billy goat with an immense horn in the middle of its forehead come up out of the west and fly across the whole country, not once touching the ground. The billy goat approached the double-horned ram that I had earlier seen standing at the gate and, enraged, charged it viciously. I watched as, mad with rage, it charged the ram and hit it so hard that it broke off its two horns. The ram didn't stand a chance against it. The billy goat knocked the ram to the ground and stomped all over it. Nothing could have saved the ram from the goat.

8-12 "Then the billy goat swelled to an enormous size. At the height of its power its immense horn broke off and four other big horns sprouted in its place, pointing to the four points of the compass. And then from one of these big horns another horn sprouted. It started small, but then grew to an enormous size, facing south and east — toward lovely Palestine. The horn grew tall, reaching to the stars, the heavenly army, and threw some of the stars to the earth and stomped on them. It even dared to challenge the power of God, Prince of the Celestial Army! And then it threw out daily worship and desecrated the Sanctuary. As judgment against their sin, the holy people of God got the same treatment as the daily worship. The horn cast God's Truth aside. High-handed, it took over everything and everyone.

13 "Then I overheard two holy angels talking. One asked, 'How long is what we see here going to last — the abolishing of daily worship, this devastating judgment against sin, the kicking around of God's holy people and the Sanctuary?'

14 "The other answered, 'Over the course of 2,300 sacrifices, evening and morning. Then the Sanctuary will be set right again.'

15 "While I, Daniel, was trying to make sense of what I was seeing, suddenly there was a humanlike figure standing before me.

16-17   "Then I heard a man's voice from over by the Ulai Canal calling out, 'Gabriel, tell this man what is going on. Explain the vision to him.' He came up to me, but when he got close I became terrified and fell facedown on the ground.

17-18   "He said, 'Understand that this vision has to do with the time of the end.' As soon as he spoke, I fainted, my face in the dirt. But he picked me up and put me on my feet.

19   "And then he continued, 'I want to tell you what is going to happen as the judgment days of wrath wind down, for there is going to be an end to all this.

20-22   "'The double-horned ram you saw stands for the two kings of the Medes and Persians. The billy goat stands for the kingdom of the Greeks. The huge horn on its forehead is the first Greek king. The four horns that sprouted after it was broken off are the four kings that come after him, but without his power.

23-26   "'As their kingdoms cool down
    and rebellions heat up,
A king will show up,
    hard-faced, a master trickster.
His power will swell enormously.
    He'll talk big, high-handedly,
Doing whatever he pleases,
    knocking off heroes and holy ones left and right.
He'll plot and scheme to make crime flourish —
    and oh, how it will flourish!
He'll think he's invincible
    and get rid of anyone who gets in his way.
But when he takes on the Prince of all princes,
    he'll be smashed to bits —
    but not by human hands.
This vision of the 2,300 sacrifices, evening and morning,
    is accurate but confidential.
Keep it to yourself.
    It refers to the far future.'

27   "I, Daniel, walked around in a daze, unwell for days. Then I got a grip on myself and went back to work taking care of the king's affairs. But I continued to be upset by the vision. I couldn't make sense of it."

God's Covenant Commitment

1-4   9 "Darius, son of Ahasuerus, born a Mede, became king over the land of Babylon. In the first year of his reign, I, Daniel, was meditating on the Scriptures that gave, according to the Word of God to the prophet Jeremiah, the number of years that Jerusalem had to lie in ruins, namely, seventy. I turned to the Master God, asking for an answer — praying earnestly, fasting from meals, wearing rough penitential burlap, and kneeling in the ashes. I poured out my heart, baring my soul to God, my God:

4-8   "'O Master, great and august God. You never waver in your covenant commitment, never give up on those who love you and do what you say. Yet we have sinned in every way imaginable. We've done evil things, rebelled, dodged and taken detours around your clearly marked paths. We've turned a deaf ear to your servants the prophets, who preached your Word to our kings and leaders, our parents, and all the people in the land. You have done everything right, Master, but all we have to show for our lives is guilt and shame, the whole lot of us — people of Judah, citizens of Jerusalem, Israel at home and Israel in exile in all the places we've been banished to because of our betrayal of you. Oh yes, GOD, we've been exposed in our shame, all of us — our kings, leaders, parents — before the whole world. And deservedly so, because of our sin.

9-12 "'Compassion is our only hope, the compassion of you, the Master, our God, since in our rebellion we've forfeited our rights. We paid no attention to you when you told us how to live, the clear teaching that came through your servants the prophets. All of us in Israel ignored what you said. We defied your instructions and did what we pleased. And now we're paying for it: The solemn curse written out plainly in the revelation to God's servant Moses is now doing its work among us, the wages of our sin against you. You did to us and our rulers what you said you would do: You brought this catastrophic disaster on us, the worst disaster on record — and in Jerusalem!

13-14 "'Just as written in God's revelation to Moses, the catastrophe was total. Nothing was held back. We kept at our sinning, never giving you a second thought, oblivious to your clear warning, and so you had no choice but to let the disaster loose on us in full force. You, our GOD, had a perfect right to do this since we persistently and defiantly ignored you.

15-17 "'Master, you are our God, for you delivered your people from the land of Egypt in a show of power — people are still talking about it! We confess that we have sinned, that we have lived bad lives. Following the lines of what you have always done in setting things right, setting *people* right, please stop being so angry with Jerusalem, your very own city, your holy mountain. We know it's our fault that this has happened, all because of our sins and our parents' sins, and now we're an embarrassment to everyone around us. We're a blot on the neighborhood. So listen, God, to this determined prayer of your servant. Have mercy on your ruined Sanctuary. Act out of who you are, not out of what we are.

18 "'Turn your ears our way, God, and listen. Open your eyes and take a long look at our ruined city, this city named after you. We know that we don't deserve a hearing from you. Our appeal is to your compassion. This prayer is our last and only hope:

19 "'Master, listen to us!
Master, forgive us!
Master, look at us and do something!
Master, don't put us off!
Your city and your people are named after you:
You have a stake in us!'

SEVENTY SEVENS

20-21 "While I was pouring out my heart, baring my sins and the sins of my people Israel, praying my life out before my GOD, interceding for the holy mountain of my God — while I was absorbed in this praying, the humanlike

Gabriel, the one I had seen in an earlier vision, approached me, flying in like a bird about the time of evening worship.

22-23 "He stood before me and said, 'Daniel, I have come to make things plain to you. You had no sooner started your prayer when the answer was given. And now I'm here to deliver the answer to you. You are much loved! So listen carefully to the answer, the plain meaning of what is revealed:

24 "'Seventy sevens are set for your people and for your holy city to throttle rebellion, stop sin, wipe out crime, set things right forever, confirm what the prophet saw, and anoint The Holy of Holies.

25-26 "'Here is what you must understand: From the time the word goes out to rebuild Jerusalem until the coming of the Anointed Leader, there will be seven sevens. The rebuilding will take sixty-two sevens, including building streets and digging a moat. Those will be rough times. After the sixty-two sevens, the Anointed Leader will be killed—the end of him. The city and Sanctuary will be laid in ruins by the army of the newly arriving leader. The end will come in a rush, like a flood. War will rage right up to the end, desolation the order of the day.

27 "'Then for one seven, he will forge many and strong alliances, but halfway through the seven he will banish worship and prayers. At the place of worship, a desecrating obscenity will be set up and remain until finally the desecrator himself is decisively destroyed.'"

A VISION OF A BIG WAR

1 **10** In the third year of the reign of King Cyrus of Persia, a message was made plain to Daniel, whose Babylonian name was Belteshazzar. The message was true. It dealt with a big war. He understood the message, the understanding coming by revelation:

2-3 "During those days, I, Daniel, went into mourning over Jerusalem for three weeks. I ate only plain and simple food, no seasoning or meat or wine. I neither bathed nor shaved until the three weeks were up.

4-6 "On the twenty-fourth day of the first month I was standing on the bank of the great river, the Tigris. I looked up and to my surprise saw a man dressed in linen with a belt of pure gold around his waist. His body was hard and glistening, as if sculpted from a precious stone, his face radiant, his eyes bright and penetrating like torches, his arms and feet glistening like polished bronze, and his voice, deep and resonant, sounded like a huge choir of voices.

7-8 "I, Daniel, was the only one to see this. The men who were with me, although they didn't see it, were overcome with fear and ran off and hid, fearing the worst. Left alone after the appearance, abandoned by my friends, I went weak in the knees, the blood drained from my face.

9-10 "I heard his voice. At the sound of it I fainted, fell flat on the ground, face in the dirt. A hand touched me and pulled me to my hands and knees.

11 "'Daniel,' he said, 'man of quality, listen carefully to my message. And get up on your feet. Stand at attention. I've been sent to bring you news.'

"When he had said this, I stood up, but I was still shaking.

12-14 "'Relax, Daniel,' he continued, 'don't be afraid. From the moment you decided to humble yourself to receive understanding, your prayer was heard, and I set out to come to you. But I was waylaid by the angel-prince of the kingdom of Persia and was delayed for a good three weeks. But then Michael, one of the chief angel-princes, intervened to help me. I left him there with the prince of the kingdom of Persia. And now I'm here to help you understand what will eventually happen to your people. The vision has to do with what's ahead.'

15-17 "While he was saying all this, I looked at the ground and said nothing. Then I was surprised by something like a human hand that touched my lips. I opened my mouth and started talking to the messenger: 'When I saw you, master, I was terror-stricken. My knees turned to water. I couldn't move. How can I, a lowly servant, speak to you, my master? I'm paralyzed. I can hardly breathe!'

18-19 "Then this humanlike figure touched me again and gave me strength. He said, 'Don't be afraid, friend. Peace. Everything is going to be all right. Take courage. Be strong.'

"Even as he spoke, courage surged up within me. I said, 'Go ahead, let my master speak. You've given me courage.'

20-21 "He said, 'Do you know why I've come here to you? I now have to go back to fight against the angel-prince of Persia, and when I get him out of the way, the angel-prince of Greece will arrive. But first let me tell you what's written in The True Book. No one helps me in my fight against these beings except Michael, your angel-prince.'"

1 11 "'And I, in my turn, have been helping him out as best I can ever since the first year in the reign of Darius the Mede.'

THE KINGS OF THE SOUTH AND THE NORTH

2 "But now let me tell you the truth of how things stand: Three more kings of Persia will show up, and then a fourth will become richer than all of them. When he senses that he is powerful enough as a result of his wealth, he will go to war against the entire kingdom of Greece.

3-4 "'Then a powerful king will show up and take over a huge territory and run things just as he pleases. But at the height of his power, with everything seemingly under control, his kingdom will split into four parts, like the four points of the compass. But his heirs won't get in on it. There will be no continuity with his kingship. Others will tear it to pieces and grab whatever they can get for themselves.

5-6 "'Next the king of the south will grow strong, but one of his princes will grow stronger than he and rule an even larger territory. After a few years, the two of them will make a pact, and the daughter of the king of the south will marry the king of the north to cement the peace agreement. But her influence will weaken and her child will not survive. She and her servants, her child, and her husband will be betrayed.

6-9 "'Sometime later a member of the royal family will show up and take over. He will take command of his army and invade the defenses of the king of the north and win a resounding victory. He will load up their tin gods and all the gold and silver trinkets that go with them and cart them off to Egypt. Eventually, the king of the north will recover and invade the country of the king of the south, but unsuccessfully. He will have to retreat.

10 "'But then his sons will raise a huge army and rush down like a flood, a torrential attack, on the defenses of the south.

11-13 "'Furious, the king of the south will come out and engage the king of the north and his huge army in battle and rout them. As the corpses are cleared from the field, the king, inflamed with bloodlust, will go on a blood-letting rampage, massacring tens of thousands. But his victory won't last long, for the king of the north will put together another army bigger than the last one, and after a few years he'll come back to do battle again with his immense army and endless supplies.

14 "'In those times, many others will get into the act and go off to fight against the king of the south. Hotheads from your own people, drunk on dreams, will join them. But they'll sputter out.

15-17 "'When the king of the north arrives, he'll build siege works and capture the outpost fortress city. The armies of the south will fall to pieces before him. Not even their famous commando shock troops will slow down the attacker. He'll march in big as you please, as if he owned the place. He'll take over that beautiful country, Palestine, and make himself at home in it. Then he'll proceed to get everything, lock, stock, and barrel, in his control. He'll cook up a peace treaty and even give his daughter in marriage to the king of the south in a plot to destroy him totally. But the plot will fizzle. It won't succeed.

18-19 "'Later, he'll turn his attention to the coastal regions and capture a bunch of prisoners, but a general will step in and put a stop to his bullying ways. The bully will be bullied! He'll go back home and tend to his own military affairs. But by then he'll be washed up and soon will be heard of no more.

20 "'He will be replaced shortly by a real loser, his rule, reputation, and authority already in shreds. And he won't last long. He'll slip out of history quietly, without even a fight.

21-24 "'His place will be taken by a reject, a man spurned and passed over for advancement. He'll surprise everyone, seemingly coming out of nowhere, and will seize the kingdom. He'll come in like a steamroller, flattening the opposition. Even the Prince of the Covenant will be crushed. After nego-tiating a cease-fire, he'll betray its terms. With a few henchmen, he'll take total control. Arbitrarily and impulsively, he'll invade the richest provinces. He'll surpass all his ancestors, near and distant, in his rape of the country, grabbing and looting, living with his cronies in corrupt and lavish luxury.

24-26 "'He will make plans against the fortress cities, but they'll turn out to be shortsighted. He'll get a great army together, all charged up to fight the king of the south. The king of the south in response will get his army—an even greater army—in place, ready to fight. But he won't be able to sustain that intensity for long because of the treacherous intrigue in his own ranks, his court having been honeycombed with vicious plots. His army will be smashed, the battlefield filled with corpses.

27 "'The two kings, each with evil designs on the other, will sit at the con-ference table and trade lies. Nothing will come of the treaty, which is noth-ing but a tissue of lies anyway. But that's not the end of it. There's more to this story.

28 "'The king of the north will go home loaded down with plunder, but his mind will be set on destroying the holy covenant as he passes through the country on his way home.

29-32 "'One year later he will mount a fresh invasion of the south. But the second invasion won't compare to the first. When the Roman ships arrive, he will turn tail and go back home. But as he passes through the country, he will be filled with anger at the holy covenant. He will take up with all those who betray the holy covenant, favoring them. The bodyguards surrounding him will march in and desecrate the Sanctuary and citadel. They'll throw out the daily worship and set up in its place the obscene sacrilege. The king of the north will play up to those who betray the holy covenant, corrupting them even further with his seductive talk, but those who stay courageously loyal to their God will take a strong stand.

33-35 "'Those who keep their heads on straight will teach the crowds right from wrong by their example. They'll be put to severe testing for a season: some killed, some burned, some exiled, some robbed. When the testing is intense, they'll get some help, but not much. Many of the helpers will be halfhearted at best. The testing will refine, cleanse, and purify those who keep their heads on straight and stay true, for there is still more to come.

36-39 "'Meanwhile, the king of the north will do whatever he pleases. He'll puff himself up and posture himself as greater than any god. He will even dare to brag and boast in defiance of the God of gods. And he'll get by with it for a while — until this time of wrathful judgment is completed, for what is decreed must be done. He will have no respect for the gods of his ancestors, not even that popular favorite among women, Adonis. Contemptuous of every god and goddess, the king of the north will puff himself up greater than all of them. He'll even stoop to despising the God of the holy ones, and in the place where God is worshiped he will put on exhibit, with a lavish show of silver and gold and jewels, a new god that no one has ever heard of. Marching under the banner of a strange god, he will attack the key fortresses. He will promote everyone who falls into line behind this god, putting them in positions of power and paying them off with grants of land.

40-45 "'In the final wrap-up of this story, the king of the south will confront him. But the king of the north will come at him like a tornado. Unleashing chariots and horses and an armada of ships, he'll blow away anything in his path. As he enters the beautiful land, people will fall before him like dominoes. Only Edom, Moab, and a few Ammonites will escape. As he reaches out, grabbing country after country, not even Egypt will be exempt. He will confiscate the treasuries of Egyptian gold and silver and other valuables. The Libyans and Ethiopians will fall in with him. Then disturbing reports will come in from the north and east that will throw him into a panic. Towering in rage, he'll rush to stamp out the threat. But he'll no sooner have pitched camp between the Mediterranean Sea and the Holy Mountain — all those royal tents! — than he'll meet his end. And not a soul around who can help!'"

THE WORST TROUBLE THE WORLD HAS EVER SEEN

1-2 **12** "'That's when Michael, the great angel-prince, champion of your people, will step in. It will be a time of trouble, the worst trouble the world has ever seen. But your people will be saved from the trouble, every last one found written in the Book. Many who have been long dead and buried will wake up, some to eternal life, others to eternal shame.

3 "'Men and women who have lived wisely and well will shine brilliantly, like the cloudless, star-strewn night skies. And those who put others on the right path to life will glow like stars forever.

4   "'This is a confidential report, Daniel, for your eyes and ears only. Keep it secret. Put the book under lock and key until the end. In the interim there is going to be a lot of frantic running around, trying to figure out what's going on.'

5-6   "As I, Daniel, took all this in, two figures appeared, one standing on this bank of the river and one on the other bank. One of them asked a third man who was dressed in linen and who straddled the river, 'How long is this astonishing story to go on?'

7   "The man dressed in linen, who straddled the river, raised both hands to the skies. I heard him solemnly swear by the Eternal One that it would be a time, two times, and half a time, that when the oppressor of the holy people was brought down the story would be complete.

8   "I heard all this plainly enough, but I didn't understand it. So I asked, 'Master, can you explain this to me?'

9-10   "'Go on about your business, Daniel,' he said. 'The message is confidential and under lock and key until the end, until things are about to be wrapped up. The populace will be washed clean and made like new. But the wicked will just keep on being wicked, without a clue about what is happening. Those who live wisely and well will understand what's going on.'

11   "From the time that the daily worship is banished from the Temple and the obscene desecration is set up in its place, there will be 1,290 days.

12   "Blessed are those who patiently make it through the 1,335 days.

13   "And you? Go about your business without fretting or worrying. Relax. When it's all over, you will be on your feet to receive your reward."

THE SONG OF SUSANNA

1-4   **13** There was a man who lived in Babylon whose name was Joakim. He married the daughter of Hilkiah. A model of beauty and piety, she was considered quite a catch in her time; her name was Susanna. Her parents were devout Jews and educated their children according to God's word.

Joakim himself was quite wealthy; his manor house was attractively situated on a tract of land with an enclosed orchard and garden. There was constant traffic to and from the place by the Jewish locals, for they considered him more honorable than the rest. And therein lies a tale.

5   The people elected two elderly men as judges of this small Jewish community. Parenthetically, what the Lord said about evil being Babylon's only export could certainly be applied to these two men. They were supposed to serve and protect the people who elected them, but as you will hear, they abused their power and almost brought down an innocent woman.

6-7   These two held court regularly in the public rooms of Joakim's manor house, presiding and deciding the cases of the people. These meetings rarely ran beyond noon, after which the crowd returned to town and the judges took advantage of Joakim's hospitality.

About that time each day, Susanna strolled in her husband's orchard and garden.

₈₋₁₃ The two noticed that this beautiful woman took the same walk every day. At first it aroused their curiosity, then their unholy lust. They suppressed their consciences, turned their eyes away from justice, and abandoned the virtues they so urgently advocated for others in their judicial pronouncements.

The very sight of Susanna made them feel like love-struck teenage boys, although they didn't admit it to each other. They were too ashamed to acknowledge they each wanted to have sex with her. Every day they shadowed Susanna as she walked; every day they ended their surveillance with the same words: "Let's go home; it's time for dinner." They both agreed and went off in different directions.

₁₄ One day, however, they both retraced their steps at the same time and spotted the other lurking in the garden shrubbery. Both demanded to know just what was going on. Then they admitted they were aroused every time they saw Susanna in her garden. So they decided to join forces and make a plan to have her. The first thing to do was to pinpoint where and when they could find her alone.

₁₅₋₁₈ Just such an opportunity presented itself one day. Susanna had entered the main gate, accompanied by two female servants. The heat was intolerable; perhaps a bath would help. As far as she could tell, nobody was around; she had no idea that peeping through the shrubbery were two dirty old men who were stalking her.

"Would you go and get my bath oils and perfumes?" she asked her two maid servants. Off they went on their errand, locking the main gate from within and exiting through a side gardener's gate that locked behind them. They did not know that two rapists were lurking in the foliage inside the walls.

₁₉₋₂₁ The moment the girls left, the two judges rose and made their move and said to the startled woman: "We have you now, Susanna! The gates are locked. No one will see us or hear us. You know what we want. Don't put up a fight. We intend to have you, whether you want it or not. If you don't submit, we'll destroy you in court. We'll swear that you sent your servants off so you could have sex with some young boy."

₂₂₋₂₃ Susanna cried out: "I'm pinned in on all sides! You have me right where you want me. If I give in, I'll be brought to trial and stoned for adultery. If I don't give in, you'll rape me and then abandon me to a life of shame. Better, though, that I shouldn't give in and sin before the Lord."

₂₄₋₂₅ So Susanna started shouting at the top of her lungs; the old men shouted back, ran to the main gate, unlocked it from inside, and fled.

₂₆₋₂₇ When the servants in the house heard the clamor, they rushed to the main gate of the garden, only to meet the two frazzled men on their way out who told their lying story about Susanna and the fictional young man. The two ladies-in-waiting just stood by in disbelief; they'd never heard a story like that about their mistress.

₂₈₋₃₁ Next day the two men made their way to Joakim's house; they were still outraged that their plan had failed. They demanded that Susanna, daughter of Hilkiah, Joakim's wife, be brought in front of the entire community.

Susanna entered the public room with her parents and children and all her relatives. She was a beautiful woman, but something about her now made her seem fragile.

32-33 The two judges ordered her to take off her veil; they wanted to see her cringe under their attack. Everyone in the room was crying; everyone except the accusers, that is.

34-40 The two would-be rapists rose from their chairs and went to her and laid their unclean hands on Susanna's head. With tears in her eyes, she looked up to heaven; she had complete faith in the Lord. The two judges spoke to everyone assembled.

"We were ambling around Joakim's garden, the two of us, when who should come in but this woman with her two maids; she dismissed the maids and locked the gate from the inside. Then a young man came to her; he must have been hiding in the shrubbery. He lay down with her and made love to her.

"Where were we while all this was happening? We were in a corner of the garden behind a tree, but we could see and hear everything. We ran to them, but it was too late; we saw that they were already having sex. We grabbed the young man but he was too strong for us; he slipped out of our hands and fled through the gardener's gate. But we were able to get hold of her; we questioned her and demanded the young man's name, but we couldn't get a peep out of her. All we can say now is that we saw and heard everything."

41 The people assembled believed the two men; after all, they were respected seniors in the community and judges to boot. What else could the crowd do but condemn Suzanna to death?

42-43 Susanna, however, raised a prayer in a confident voice:

"Eternal God, you who know all secrets, who knew everything before it was something, you know these men have brought false testimony against me. It is the law that I must die if I did what they claim, but I've done none of the things they accuse me of. They made it all up!"

44-45 The Lord heard her cry. As they were leading Susanna away to her execution, God strengthened the spirit of a young man, a junior prophet if you will; his name was Daniel.

46-49 Daniel stepped in front of the crowd and spoke up: "I will not be a party to her death."

The crowd answered him: "What are you saying?"

He stood his ground in their midst.

"People of the house of Israel, how unjust can you be? What evidence did the two accusers actually present? Has anybody corroborated their charges? Are you willing to condemn a faithful daughter of Israel without proof of her guilt? Reopen the case, and you'll find that the testimony of the two accusers against her is tainted."

50 The people were convinced enough to return to the court, along with Susanna, her supporters, and the two prosecutors. The crowd said to Daniel: "Come, sit in our midst, young man, and tell us what you know. God seems to have given youth the wisdom that usually comes with age."

51-54 "Separate the two accusers from each other," directed Daniel, "and I'll interrogate them one at a time in front of you."

They put the two men in different rooms where they could not hear the other's testimony. Daniel then questioned the first one.

"You veteran old sinner, your sins have come back to haunt you. You've churned out unjust judgments; you've oppressed the poor; you've freed the guilty. All the while you quoted what the Lord has commanded: 'Don't sentence the innocent and just to death!'

"Now, more to the point, if you did indeed see Susanna committing adultery, tell us—*precisely*—where you and your partner in crime were standing in the garden when you supposedly saw her and her lover together."

55 "Behind a small gum tree," the man responded, beads of sweat starting to form on his upper lip.

"You're lying through your teeth," Daniel said. "Behold the angel of the Lord! Once your sentence has been rendered by God, the angel will cut you in two with one swift stroke!"

56-58 That judge was taken out of the room, and the other one brought in. Daniel spoke first.

"Are you really a Jew? Your actions seem more like those of a Canaanite to me. Beauty has tempted you; lust has led you to sin. You're not used to being refused by daughters of Israel, are you? You intimidate them with threats and insults, then steal their virtue.

"Now, more to the point, answer me this: What tree—*precisely*—were you and your partner in crime standing behind when you supposedly saw the young man whispering sweet nothings into Susanna's ear?"

"Behind a large oak tree," the man said, his eyes darting around the room.

59 "You're lying through your teeth," Daniel said. "The angel of God with sword in hand is waiting, ready to separate your top from your bottom, and that will be the end of you."

60-64 The congregation let out a shout, blessing the God who always saves those who put their hope in him. They rose up against the two judges. Daniel had convinced them that both had given false testimony under oath. Their punishment would be the same as the one they had pronounced against Susanna: according to the Law of Moses, they had to be stoned to death. And so it happened. Innocent blood was spared that day, but guilty blood was not. Hilkiah and his wife praised the Lord for their daughter Susanna, who had her reputation restored, along with that of her husband Joakim and their relatives, thanks to the budding prophet.

Daniel's reputation rose in the eyes of the people on that day, and it remained so for the rest of his life.

※

BEL CONFOUNDED

1-2 **14** When King Astyages joined his ancestors in death, Cyrus the Persian succeeded to his throne. Daniel, a close friend of the new king and one deserving many commendations, also moved up one place.

3-4 At that time, the Babylonians had an idol by the name of Bel, whose daily worship requirements included the delivery of flour (twelve Egyptian measures), sheep (forty strong), and wine (six liquid measures). King Cyrus was a daily visitor to the shrine.

At the same time every day that the king was worshiping, however, his close friend and companion Daniel prayed to his own God. The question was bound to come up. "Why," the king asked Daniel, "aren't you paying your respects to Bel?"

5   "I don't worship a handmade idol," Daniel replied. "I worship the living God, the God who created Heaven and earth, the God who has power over all creatures."

6   "Doesn't Bel seem to you to be living?" asked the king. "Don't you see how much he eats and drinks every day?"

7   Daniel laughed. "Don't make a mistake, dear king. Bel is made of clay, then bronzed over; it doesn't eat a thing or drink a drop."

8-9   The king exploded with anger. He summoned his priests and put it to them.

"Under pain of death, tell me who eats and drinks the daily offerings! If it's Bel, Daniel will die; blasphemy is a capital crime."

Daniel chimed in: "I wouldn't have it any other way."

10-12   There were seventy priests attending Bel, not counting their wives and children. The king went with Daniel to the temple of Bel for his answer. "Here's what we propose," one of the priests told the king. "All the priests will leave the temple. You yourself can present the sacred food and drink and place them on the altar of Bel; then leave, shutting the door behind you and putting your royal seal on the lock. Return tomorrow morning and enter the temple. If you don't find that all the food was eaten and all the drink was drunk, we'll all gladly die the death. If there's not a crumb or drop left on the altar, then Daniel should die the death for his lies against us."

13-14   The priests were confident, even arrogant, for they themselves had constructed a trapdoor under the altar through which they carted off all the daily offerings and divided them among themselves.

After the priests left, the king himself placed the offerings before Bel. But Daniel took the precaution of asking that a thin layer of ash be spread all over the floor, to which the king didn't object. Then they both left, the king affixing his seal on the outside of the locked door.

15   Following their usual practice, the priests entered the sanctuary at night through the trapdoor, their wives and children with them, and made short work of the food and drink.

16-20   At first light the king rose and took Daniel with him to the temple. "Are the doors still sealed, Daniel?" he asked.

"Yes, they're sealed," Daniel acknowledged.

Then the king broke the seal and opened the door. Immediately he saw that the temple was empty and the food and drink were totally gone. He exclaimed at the top of his lungs, "How great thou art, O Bel! There's not a whiff of godly trickery, no sign of priestly impropriety."

Daniel, however, just laughed and held the king back from entering. "Look at the floor, Your Highness. Footprints in the ash all over the place. Whose could they be?"

"I see the footprints of men and women and signs of children," the king said and realized what had happened. Then he blew his top!

21-22   He issued warrants for the immediate arrest of the priests and their families. For their part, in the hope for mercy, they showed him the secret door through which they'd passed every night to eat and make merry. But the king still ordered their immediate execution.

As for the statue and temple of Bel, the king told Daniel to take care of it. Daniel saw that the idol was smashed to smithereens and the temple flattened.

THE DRAGON COMETH

23-26 There was a colossal dragon whom the Babylonians worshiped. "You can't say this god is not living," King Cyrus pointed out to Daniel, "and therefore, you should have no difficulty in worshiping it."

"I adore the Lord my God because he's the ever-living God. Your dragon I could kill without sword or club."

"Go ahead and try," said the king.

27 Then Daniel took some sticky substance, some fat, and some hair and brought them to a boil; then he spooned the mixture into the dragon's mouth, which apparently couldn't get enough of it. When the beast could swallow no more, it burst into a thousand pieces.

"So," Daniel asked the king, "is this the god you worship?"

THE FALLOUT

28-29 When the Babylonian people heard all this, they were highly indignant and took to the streets.

"The king's becoming a Jew! Daniel destroyed Bel. He killed the dragon and had the priests executed."

When the king gave the dissenters an audience, they said, "Hand Daniel over to us. If you don't, we'll kill you and your family."

30-32 The king, seeing they meant business, handed over his friend. They dropped Daniel into a pit of lions and left him there for six days. There were seven lions in the pit. Their daily diet consisted of two human carcasses dead or alive and two live sheep. But after Daniel's forced visit to their den, no food was given to the lions in the hope that they'd devour Daniel right away.

33-36 At that time in Judea, there was a prophet, Habakkuk by name, who owned a farm. To make lunch for the reapers in his fields, he cooked up stew topped with bread crumbs. One day an angel of the Lord said to Habakkuk, "Bring the meal you have cooked to Babylon, where Daniel is in the lions' den."

"Lord, I don't know how to get to Babylon," Habakkuk replied, "and I certainly don't know where to find any lions' den." But with the whisper of a wind the angel of the Lord picked the prophet up by the hair on his head and set him down in Babylon at the edge of the lions' den.

37-39 "Daniel, Daniel!" Habakkuk cried out. "Take the lunch God sent you!"

Daniel replied with a prayer: "You've heard me, O Lord, and loved me; you've not abandoned me."

While Daniel ate the food, the angel of the Lord returned Habakkuk home with all deliberate haste.

40 On the seventh day of the ordeal, the king came to the prison to mourn his friend's passing. When he looked into the cell, he expected to see a

corpse or just a few bones; instead he saw a very live Daniel sitting comfortably among the lions.

41-42   The king cried out with great voice: "Thou art great, O Lord, God of Daniel! You're one of a kind and true to yourself and your people."

The troublemakers who'd instigated Daniel's punishment by threatening to overthrow the king were themselves thrown into the lions' den, where they were immediately enjoyed by the same starving lions that wouldn't touch Daniel.

HOSEA

We live in a world awash in love stories. Most of them are lies. They are not love stories at all—they are lust stories, sex-fantasy stories, domination stories. From the cradle we are fed on lies about love.

This would be bad enough if it only messed up human relationships—man and woman, parent and child, friend and friend—but it also messes up God-relationships. The huge, mountainous reality of all existence is that God is love, that God loves the world. Each single detail of the real world that we face and deal with day after day is permeated by this love.

But when our minds and imaginations are crippled with lies about love, we have a hard time understanding this fundamental ingredient of daily living, "love," either as a noun or as a verb. And if the basic orienting phrase "God is love" is plastered over with cultural graffiti that obscure and deface the truth of the way the world is, we are not going to get very far in living well. We require true stories of love if we are to live truly.

Hosea is the prophet of love, but not love as we imagine or fantasize it. He was a parable of God's love for his people lived out as God revealed and enacted it—a lived parable. It is an astonishing story: a prophet commanded to marry a common whore and have children with her. It is an even more astonishing message: God loves us in just this way—goes after us at our worst, keeps after us until he gets us, and makes lovers of men and women who know nothing of real love. Once we absorb this story and the words that flow from it, we will know God far more accurately. And we will be well on our way to being cured of all the sentimentalized and neurotic distortions of love that incapacitate us from dealing with the God who loves us and loving the neighbors who don't love us.

HOSEA

1 This is God's Message to Hosea son of Beeri. It came to him during the royal reigns of Judah's kings Uzziah, Jotham, Ahaz, and Hezekiah. This was also the time that Jeroboam son of Joash was king over Israel.

THIS WHOLE COUNTRY HAS BECOME A WHOREHOUSE

2 The first time GOD spoke to Hosea he said:

"Find a whore and marry her.
  Make this whore the mother of your children.
And here's why: This whole country
  has become a whorehouse, unfaithful to me, GOD."

3 Hosea did it. He picked Gomer daughter of Diblaim. She got pregnant and gave him a son.

4-5 Then GOD told him:

"Name him Jezreel. It won't be long now before
  I'll make the people of Israel pay for the massacre at Jezreel.
  I'm calling it quits on the kingdom of Israel.
Payday is coming! I'm going to chop Israel's bows and arrows
  into kindling in the valley of Jezreel."

6-7 Gomer got pregnant again. This time she had a daughter. GOD told Hosea:

"Name this one No-Mercy. I'm fed up with Israel.
  I've run out of mercy. There's no more forgiveness.
Judah's another story. I'll continue having mercy on them.
  I'll save them. It will be their GOD who saves them,
Not their armaments and armies,
  not their horsepower and manpower."

8-9 After Gomer had weaned No-Mercy, she got pregnant yet again and had a son. GOD said:

"Name him Nobody. You've become nobodies to me,
  and I, GOD, am a nobody to you.

10-11 "But down the road the population of Israel is going to explode past counting, like sand on the ocean beaches. In the very place where they were once named Nobody, they will be named God's Somebody. Everybody in Judah and everybody in Israel will be assembled as one people. They'll choose a single leader. There'll be no stopping them—a great day in Jezreel!"

1 2 "Rename your brothers 'God's Somebody.'
Rename your sisters 'All Mercy.'

WILD WEEKENDS AND UNHOLY HOLIDAYS

2-13 "Haul your mother into court. Accuse her!
She's no longer my wife.
I'm no longer her husband.
Tell her to quit dressing like a whore,
displaying her breasts for sale.
If she refuses, I'll rip off her clothes
and expose her, naked as a newborn.
I'll turn her skin into dried-out leather,
her body into a badlands landscape,
a rack of bones in the desert.
I'll have nothing to do with her children,
born one and all in a whorehouse.
Face it: Your mother's been a whore,
bringing bastard children into the world.
She said, 'I'm off to see my lovers!
They'll wine and dine me,
Dress and caress me,
perfume and adorn me!'
But I'll fix her: I'll dump her in a field of thistles,
then lose her in a dead-end alley.
She'll go on the hunt for her lovers
but not bring down a single one.
She'll look high and low
but won't find a one. Then she'll say,
'I'm going back to my husband, the one I started out with.
That was a better life by far than this one.'
She didn't know that it was I all along
who wined and dined and adorned her,
That I was the one who dressed her up
in the big-city fashions and jewelry
that she wasted on wild Baal-orgies.
I'm about to bring her up short: No more wining and dining!
Silk lingerie and gowns are a thing of the past.
I'll expose her genitals to the public.
All her fly-by-night lovers will be helpless to help her.
Party time is over. I'm calling a halt to the whole business,
her wild weekends and unholy holidays.
I'll wreck her sumptuous gardens and ornamental fountains,
of which she bragged, 'Whoring paid for all this!'
They will soon be dumping grounds for garbage,
feeding grounds for stray dogs and cats.
I'll make her pay for her indulgence in promiscuous religion—
all that sensuous Baal worship
And all the promiscuous sex that went with it,
stalking her lovers, dressed to kill,
And not a thought for me."
GOD's Message!

To Start All Over Again

14-15　"And now, here's what I'm going to do:
　　　I'm going to start all over again.
I'm taking her back out into the wilderness
　　　where we had our first date, and I'll court her.
I'll give her bouquets of roses.
　　　I'll turn Heartbreak Valley into Acres of Hope.
She'll respond like she did as a young girl,
　　　those days when she was fresh out of Egypt.

16-20　"At that time" — this is God's Message still —
　　　"you'll address me, 'Dear husband!'
Never again will you address me,
　　　'My slave-master!'
I'll wash your mouth out with soap,
　　　get rid of all the dirty false-god names,
　　　not so much as a whisper of those names again.
At the same time I'll make a peace treaty between you
　　　and wild animals and birds and reptiles,
And get rid of all weapons of war.
　　　Think of it! Safe from beasts and bullies!
And then I'll marry you for good — forever!
　　　I'll marry you true and proper, in love and tenderness.
Yes, I'll marry you and neither leave you nor let you go.
　　　You'll know me, God, for who I really am.

21-23　"On the very same day, I'll answer" — this is God's Message —
　　　"I'll answer the sky, sky will answer earth,
Earth will answer grain and wine and olive oil,
　　　and they'll all answer Jezreel.
I'll plant her in the good earth.
　　　I'll have mercy on No-Mercy.
I'll say to Nobody, 'You're my dear Somebody,'
　　　and he'll say 'You're my God!'"

In Time They'll Come Back

1　3 Then God ordered me, "Start all over: Love your wife again,
　　　your wife who's in bed with her latest boyfriend, your
　　　cheating wife.
Love her the way I, God, love the Israelite people,
　　　even as they flirt and party with every god that takes their fancy."

2-3　I did it. I paid good money to get her back.
　　　It cost me the price of a slave.
Then I told her, "From now on you're living with me.
　　　No more whoring, no more sleeping around.
　　　You're living with me and I'm living with you."

4-5 The people of Israel are going to live a long time
    stripped of security and protection,
without religion and comfort,
    godless and prayerless.
But in time they'll come back, these Israelites,
    come back looking for their GOD and their David-King.
They'll come back chastened to reverence
    before GOD and his good gifts, ready for the End of the story of his love.

NO ONE IS FAITHFUL

1-3 **4** Attention all Israelites! GOD's Message!
    GOD indicts the whole population:
    "No one is faithful. No one loves.
No one knows the first thing about God.
All this cussing and lying and killing, theft and loose sex,
    sheer anarchy, one murder after another!
And because of all this, the very land itself weeps
    and everything in it is grief-stricken—
animals in the fields and birds on the wing,
    even the fish in the sea are listless, lifeless.

4-10 "But don't look for someone to blame.
    No finger pointing!
You, priest, are the one in the dock.
    You stumble around in broad daylight,
And then the prophets take over and stumble all night.
    Your mother is as bad as you.
My people are ruined
    because they don't know what's right or true.
Because you've turned your back on knowledge,
    I've turned my back on you priests.
Because you refuse to recognize the revelation of God,
    I'm no longer recognizing your children.
The more priests, the more sin.
    They traded in their glory for shame.
They pig out on my people's sins.
    They can't wait for the latest in evil.
The result: You can't tell the people from the priests,
    the priests from the people.
I'm on my way to make them both pay
    and take the consequences of the bad lives they've lived.
They'll eat and be as hungry as ever,
    have sex and get no satisfaction.
They walked out on me, their GOD,
    for a life of rutting with whores.

THEY MAKE A PICNIC OUT OF RELIGION

11-14 "Wine and whiskey
    leave my people in a stupor.
They ask questions of a dead tree,

expect answers from a sturdy walking stick.
Drunk on sex, they can't find their way home.
    They've replaced their God with their genitals.
They worship on the tops of mountains,
    make a picnic out of religion.
Under the oaks and elms on the hills
    they stretch out and take it easy.
Before you know it, your daughters are whores
    and the wives of your sons are sleeping around.
But I'm not going after your whoring daughters
    or the adulterous wives of your sons.
It's the men who pick up the whores that I'm after,
    the men who worship at the holy whorehouses —
    a stupid people, ruined by whores!

15-19   "You've ruined your own life, Israel —
    but don't drag Judah down with you!
Don't go to the sex shrine at Gilgal,
    don't go to that sin city Bethel,
Don't go around saying 'GOD bless you' and not mean it,
    taking God's name in vain.
Israel is stubborn as a mule.
    How can GOD lead him like a lamb to open pasture?
Ephraim is addicted to idols.
    Let him go.
When the beer runs out,
    it's sex, sex, and more sex.
Bold and sordid debauchery —
    how they love it!
The whirlwind has them in its clutches.
    Their sex-worship leaves them finally impotent."

THEY WOULDN'T RECOGNIZE GOD IF THEY SAW HIM

1-2   5 "Listen to this, priests!
    Attention, people of Israel!
  Royal family — all ears!
    You're in charge of justice around here.
But what have you done? Exploited people at Mizpah,
    ripped them off on Tabor,
Victimized them at Shittim.
    I'm going to punish the lot of you.

3-4   "I know you, Ephraim, inside and out.
    Yes, Israel, I see right through you!
Ephraim, you've played your sex-and-religion games long enough.
    All Israel is thoroughly polluted.
They couldn't turn to God if they wanted to.
    Their evil life is a bad habit.
Every breath they take is a whore's breath.
    They wouldn't recognize GOD if they saw me.

5-7　"Bloated by arrogance, big as a house,
　　　　they're a public disgrace,
　　The lot of them — Israel, Ephraim, Judah —
　　　　lurching and weaving down their guilty streets.
　　When they decide to get their lives together
　　　　and go off looking for GOD once again,
　　They'll find it's too late.
　　　　I, GOD, will be long gone.
　　They've played fast and loose with me for too long,
　　　　filling the country with their bastard offspring.
　　A plague of locusts will
　　　　devastate their violated land.

8-9　"Blow the ram's horn shofar in Gibeah,
　　　　the bugle in Ramah!
　　Signal the invasion of Sin City!
　　　　Scare the daylights out of Benjamin!
　　Ephraim will be left wasted,
　　　　a lifeless moonscape.
　　I'm telling it straight, the unvarnished truth,
　　　　to the tribes of Israel.

10　"Israel's rulers are crooks and thieves,
　　　　cheating the people of their land,
　　And I'm angry, good and angry.
　　　　Every inch of their bodies is going to feel my anger.

11-12　"Brutal Ephraim is himself brutalized —
　　　　a taste of his own medicine!
　　He was so determined
　　　　to do it his own worthless way.
　　Therefore I'm pus to Ephraim,
　　　　dry rot in the house of Judah.

13　"When Ephraim saw he was sick
　　　　and Judah saw his pus-filled sores,
　　Ephraim went running to Assyria,
　　　　went for help to the big king.
　　But he can't heal you.
　　　　He can't cure your oozing sores.

14-15　"I'm a grizzly charging Ephraim,
　　　　a grizzly with cubs charging Judah.
　　I'll rip them to pieces — yes, I will!
　　　　No one can stop me now.
　　I'll drag them off.
　　　　No one can help them.
　　Then I'll go back to where I came from
　　　　until they come to their senses.
　　When they finally hit rock bottom,
　　　　maybe they'll come looking for me."

GANGS OF PRIESTS ASSAULTING WORSHIPERS

¹⁻³ 6 "Come on, let's go back to GOD.
  He hurt us, but he'll heal us.
  He hit us hard,
but he'll put us right again.
In a couple of days we'll feel better.
  By the third day he'll have made us brand-new,
Alive and on our feet,
  fit to face him.
We're ready to study GOD,
  eager for God-knowledge.
As sure as dawn breaks,
  so sure is his daily arrival.
He comes as rain comes,
  as spring rain refreshing the ground."

⁴⁻⁷ "What am I to do with you, Ephraim?
  What do I make of you, Judah?
Your declarations of love last no longer
  than morning mist and predawn dew.
That's why I use prophets to shake you to attention,
  why my words cut you to the quick:
To wake you up to my judgment
  blazing like light.
I'm after love that lasts, not more religion.
  I want you to know GOD, not go to more prayer meetings.
You broke the covenant — just like Adam!
  You broke faith with me — ungrateful wretches!

⁸⁻⁹ "Gilead has become Crime City —
  blood on the sidewalks, blood on the streets.
It used to be robbers who mugged pedestrians.
  Now it's gangs of priests
Assaulting worshipers on their way to Shechem.
  Nothing is sacred to them.

¹⁰ "I saw a shocking thing in the country of Israel:
  Ephraim worshiping in a religious whorehouse,
  and Israel in the mud right there with him.

¹¹ "You're as bad as the worst of them, Judah.
  You've been sowing wild oats. Now it's harvest time."

DESPITE ALL THE SIGNS, ISRAEL IGNORES GOD

¹⁻² 7 "Every time I gave Israel a fresh start,
  wiped the slate clean and got them going again,
  Ephraim soon filled the slate with new sins,
the treachery of Samaria written out in bold print.
Two-faced and double-tongued,

they steal you blind, pick you clean.
It never crosses their mind
that I keep account of their every crime.
They're mud-spattered head to toe with the residue of sin.
I see who they are and what they've done.

3-7 "They entertain the king with their evil circus,
delight the princes with their acrobatic lies.
They're a bunch of overheated adulterers,
like an oven that holds its heat
From the kneading of the dough
to the rising of the bread.
On the royal holiday the princes get drunk
on wine and the frenzy of the mocking mob.
They're like wood stoves,
red-hot with lust.
Through the night their passion is banked;
in the morning it blazes up, flames hungrily licking.
Murderous and volcanic,
they incinerate their rulers.
Their kings fall one by one,
and no one pays any attention to me.

8-10 "Ephraim mingles with the pagans, dissipating himself.
Ephraim is half-baked.
Strangers suck him dry
but he doesn't even notice.
His hair has turned gray —
he doesn't notice.
Bloated by arrogance, big as a house,
Israel's a public disgrace.
Israel lumbers along oblivious to GOD,
despite all the signs, ignoring GOD.

11-16 "Ephraim is bird-brained,
mindless, clueless,
First chirping after Egypt,
then fluttering after Assyria.
I'll throw my net over them. I'll clip their wings.
I'll teach them to mind me!
Doom! They've run away from home.
Now they're *really* in trouble! They've *defied* me.
And I'm supposed to help them
while they feed me a line of lies?
Instead of crying out to me in heartfelt prayer,
they whoop it up in bed with their whores,
Gash themselves bloody in their sex-and-religion orgies,
but turn their backs on me.
I'm the one who gave them good minds and healthy bodies,
and how am I repaid? With evil scheming!
They turn, but not to me —

turn here, then there, like a weather vane.
Their rulers will be cut down, murdered—
    just deserts for their mocking blasphemies.
And the final sentence?
    Ridicule in the court of world opinion."

A L T A R S   F O R   S I N N I N G

1-3   **8** "Blow the trumpet! Sound the alarm!
    Vultures are circling over God's people
    Who have broken my covenant
and defied my revelation.
Predictably, Israel cries out, 'My God! We know you!'
    But they don't act like it.
Israel will have nothing to do with what's good,
    and now the enemy is after them.

4-10   "They crown kings, but without asking me.
    They set up princes but don't let me in on it.
Instead, they make idols, using silver and gold,
    idols that will be their ruin.
Throw that gold calf-god on the trash heap, Samaria!
    I'm seething with anger against that rubbish!
How long before they shape up?
    And they're Israelites!
A sculptor made that thing—
    it's not God.
That Samaritan calf
    will be broken to bits.
Look at them! Planting wind-seeds,
    they'll harvest tornadoes.
Wheat with no head
    produces no flour.
And even if it did,
    strangers would gulp it down.
Israel is swallowed up and spit out.
    Among the pagans they're a piece of junk.
They trotted off to Assyria:
    Why, even wild donkeys stick to their own kind,
    but donkey-Ephraim goes out and *pays* to get lovers.
Now, because of their whoring life among the pagans,
    I'm going to gather them together and confront them.
They're going to reap the consequences soon,
    feel what it's like to be oppressed by the big king.

11-14   "Ephraim has built a lot of altars,
    and then uses them for sinning.
    Can you believe it? Altars for sinning!
I write out my revelation for them in detail
    and they pretend they can't read it.
They offer sacrifices to me
    and then they feast on the meat.

GOD is not pleased!
I'm fed up—I'll keep remembering their guilt.
    I'll punish their sins
    and send them back to Egypt.
Israel has forgotten his Maker
    and gotten busy making palaces.
    Judah has gone in for a lot of fortress cities.
I'm sending fire on their cities
    to burn down their fortifications."

STARVED FOR GOD

1-6 **9** Don't waste your life in wild orgies, Israel.
        Don't party away your life with the heathen.
        You walk away from your God at the drop of a hat
    and like a whore sell yourself promiscuously
    at every sex-and-religion party on the street.
All that party food won't fill you up.
    You'll end up hungrier than ever.
At this rate you'll not last long in GOD's land:
    Some of you are going to end up bankrupt in Egypt.
    Some of you will be disillusioned in Assyria.
As refugees in Egypt and Assyria,
    you won't have much chance to worship GOD—
Sentenced to rations of bread and water,
    and your souls polluted by the spirit-dirty air.
You'll be starved for GOD,
    exiled from GOD's own country.
Will you be homesick for the old Holy Days?
    Will you miss festival worship of GOD?
Be warned! When you escape from the frying pan of disaster,
    you'll fall into the fire of Egypt.
    Egypt will give you a fine funeral!
What use will all your god-inspired silver be then
    as you eke out a living in a field of weeds?

7-9 Time's up. Doom's at the doorstep.
    It's payday!
Did Israel bluster, "The prophet is crazy!
    The 'man of the Spirit' is nuts!"?
Think again. Because of your great guilt,
    you're in big trouble.
The prophet is looking out for Ephraim,
    working under God's orders.
But everyone is trying to trip him up.
    He's hated right in God's house, of all places.
The people are going from bad to worse,
    rivaling that ancient and unspeakable crime at Gibeah.
God's keeping track of their guilt.
    He'll make them pay for their sins.

10-13
"Long ago when I came upon Israel,
  it was like finding grapes out in the desert.
When I found your ancestors, it was like finding
  a fig tree bearing fruit for the first time.
But when they arrived at Baal-peor, that pagan shrine,
  they took to sin like a pig to filth,
  wallowing in the mud with their newfound friends.
Ephraim is fickle and scattered, like a flock of blackbirds,
  their beauty dissipated in confusion and clamor,
Frenetic and noisy, frigid and barren,
  and nothing to show for it—neither conception nor childbirth.
Even if they did give birth, I'd declare them
  unfit parents and take away their children!
Yes indeed—a black day for them
  when I turn my back and walk off!
I see Ephraim letting his children run wild.
  He might just as well take them and kill them outright!"

14
Give it to them, God! But what?
  Give them a dried-up womb and shriveled breasts.

15-16
"All their evil came out into the open
  at the pagan shrine at Gilgal. Oh, how I hated them there!
Because of their evil practices,
  I'll kick them off my land.
I'm wasting no more love on them.
  Their leaders are a bunch of rebellious adolescents.
Ephraim is hit hard—
  roots withered, no more fruit.
Even if by some miracle they had children,
  the dear babies wouldn't live—I'd make sure of that!"

17
My God has washed his hands of them.
  They wouldn't listen.
They're doomed to be wanderers,
  vagabonds among the godless nations.

1-2
10
Israel was once a lush vine,
    bountiful in grapes.
    The more lavish the harvest,
  the more promiscuous the worship.
The more money they got,
  the more they squandered on gods-in-their-own-image.
Their sweet smiles are sheer lies.
  They're guilty as sin.
God will smash their worship shrines,
  pulverize their god-images.

3-4   They go around saying,
         "Who needs a king?
      We couldn't care less about GOD,
         so why bother with a king?
         What difference would he make?"
      They talk big,
         lie through their teeth,
         make deals.
      But their high-sounding words
         turn out to be empty words, litter in the gutters.

5-6   The people of Samaria travel over to Crime City
         to worship the golden calf-god.
      They go all out, prancing and hollering,
         taken in by their showmen priests.
      They act so important around the calf-god,
         but are oblivious to the sham, the shame.
      They have plans to take it to Assyria,
         present it as a gift to the great king.
      And so Ephraim makes a fool of himself,
         disgraces Israel with his stupid idols.

7-8   Samaria is history. Its king
         is a dead branch floating down the river.
      Israel's favorite sin centers
         will all be torn down.
      Thistles and crabgrass
         will decorate their ruined altars.
      Then they'll say to the mountains, "Bury us!"
         and to the hills, "Fall on us!"

9-10 You got your start in sin at Gibeah —
         that ancient, unspeakable, shocking sin —
      And you've been at it ever since.
         And Gibeah will mark the end of it
         in a war to end all the sinning.
      I'll come to teach them a lesson.
         Nations will gang up on them,
      Making them learn the hard way
         the sum of Gibeah plus Gibeah.

11-15 Ephraim was a trained heifer
         that loved to thresh.
      Passing by and seeing her strong, sleek neck,
         I wanted to harness Ephraim,
      Put Ephraim to work in the fields —
         Judah plowing, Jacob harrowing:
      Sow righteousness,
         reap love.
      It's time to till the ready earth,
         it's time to dig in with GOD,

Until he arrives
   with righteousness ripe for harvest.
But instead you plowed wicked ways,
   reaped a crop of evil and ate a salad of lies.
You thought you could do it all on your own,
   flush with weapons and manpower.
But the volcano of war will erupt among your people.
   All your defense posts will be leveled
As viciously as king Shalman
   leveled the town of Beth-arba,
When mothers and their babies
   were smashed on the rocks.
That's what's ahead for you, you so-called people of God,
   because of your off-the-charts evil.
Some morning you're going to wake up
   and find Israel, king and kingdom, a blank — nothing.

ISRAEL PLAYED AT RELIGION WITH TOY GODS

1-9
11

"When Israel was only a child, I loved him.
   I called out, 'My son!' — called him out of Egypt.
   But when others called him,
   he ran off and left me.
He worshiped the popular sex gods,
   he played at religion with toy gods.
Still, I stuck with him. I led Ephraim.
   I rescued him from human bondage,
But he never acknowledged my help,
   never admitted that I was the one pulling his wagon,
That I lifted him, like a baby, to my cheek,
   that I bent down to feed him.
Now he wants to go *back* to Egypt or go over to Assyria —
   anything but return to me!
That's why his cities are unsafe — the murder rate skyrockets
   and every plan to improve things falls to pieces.
My people are hell-bent on leaving me.
   They pray to god Baal for help.
   He doesn't lift a finger to help them.
But how can I give up on you, Ephraim?
   How can I turn you loose, Israel?
How can I leave you to be ruined like Admah,
   devastated like luckless Zeboim?
I can't bear to even think such thoughts.
   My insides churn in protest.
And so I'm not going to act on my anger.
   I'm not going to destroy Ephraim.
And why? Because I am God and not a human.
   I'm The Holy One and I'm here — in your very midst.

10-12
"The people will end up following GOD.
   I will roar like a lion —
Oh, how I'll roar!

My frightened children will come running from the west.
Like frightened birds they'll come from Egypt,
from Assyria like scared doves.
I'll move them back into their homes."
GOD's Word!

SOUL-DESTROYING LIES

Ephraim tells lies right and left.
Not a word of Israel can be trusted.
Judah, meanwhile, is no better,
addicted to cheap gods.

1-5 Ephraim, obsessed with god-fantasies,
chases ghosts and phantoms.
He tells lies nonstop,
soul-destroying lies.
Both Ephraim and Judah made deals with Assyria
and tried to get an inside track with Egypt.
GOD is bringing charges against Israel.
Jacob's children are hauled into court to be punished.
In the womb, that heel, Jacob, got the best of his brother.
When he grew up, he tried to get the best of GOD.
But GOD would not be bested.
GOD bested him.
Brought to his knees,
Jacob wept and prayed.
GOD found him at Bethel.
That's where he spoke with him.
GOD is GOD-of-the-Angel-Armies,
GOD-Revealed, GOD-Known.

6 What are you waiting for? Return to your God!
Commit yourself in love, in justice!
Wait for your God,
and don't give up on him — ever!

7-8 The businessmen engage in wholesale fraud.
They love to rip people off!
Ephraim boasted, "Look, I'm rich!
I've made it big!
And look how well I've covered my tracks:
not a hint of fraud, not a sign of sin!"

9-11 "But not so fast! I'm GOD, *your* God!
Your God from the days in Egypt!
I'm going to put you back to living in tents,
as in the old days when you worshiped in the wilderness.
I speak through the prophets
to give clear pictures of the way things are.

Using prophets, I tell revealing stories.
I show Gilead rampant with religious scandal
    and Gilgal teeming with empty-headed religion.
I expose their worship centers as
    stinking piles of garbage in their gardens."

₁₂₋₁₄ Are you going to repeat the life of your ancestor Jacob?
    He ran off guilty to Aram,
Then sold his soul to get ahead,
    and made it big through treachery and deceit.
Your real identity is formed through God-sent prophets,
    who led you out of Egypt and served as faithful pastors.
As it is, Ephraim has continually
    and inexcusably insulted God.
Now he has to pay for his life-destroying ways.
    His Master will do to him what *he* has done.

RELIGION CUSTOMIZED TO TASTE

₁₋₃ **13** God once let loose against Ephraim
    a terrifying sentence against Israel:
    Caught and convicted
in the lewd sex-worship of Baal—they died!
And now they're back in the sin business again,
    manufacturing god-images they can use,
Religion customized to taste. Professionals see to it:
    Anything you want in a god you can get.
Can you believe it? They sacrifice live babies to these dead gods—
    kill living babies and kiss golden calves!
And now there's nothing left to these people:
    hollow men, desiccated women,
Like scraps of paper blown down the street,
    like smoke in a gusty wind.

₄₋₆ "I'm still your GOD,
    the God who saved you out of Egypt.
I'm the only real God you've ever known.
    I'm the one and only God who delivers.
I took care of you during the wilderness hard times,
    those years when you had nothing.
I took care of you, took care of all your needs,
    gave you everything you needed.
You were spoiled. You thought you didn't need me.
    You forgot me.

₇₋₁₂ "I'll charge them like a lion,
    like a leopard stalking in the brush.
I'll jump them like a sow grizzly robbed of her cubs.
    I'll rip out their guts.
Coyotes will make a meal of them.
    Crows will clean their bones.
I'm going to destroy you, Israel.

Who is going to stop me?
Where is your trusty king you thought would save you?
    Where are all the local leaders you wanted so badly?
All these rulers you insisted on having,
    demanding, 'Give me a king! Give me leaders!'?
Well, long ago I gave you a king, but I wasn't happy about it.
    Now, fed up, I've gotten rid of him.
I have a detailed record of your infidelities—
    Ephraim's sin documented and stored in a safe-deposit box.

13-15   "When birth pangs signaled it was time to be born,
    Ephraim was too stupid to come out of the womb.
When the passage into life opened up,
    he didn't show.
Shall I intervene and pull them into life?
    Shall I snatch them from a certain death?
Who is afraid of you, Death?
    Who cares about your threats, Tomb?
In the end I'm abolishing regret,
    banishing sorrow,
Even though Ephraim ran wild,
    the black sheep of the family.

15-16   "GOD's tornado is on its way,
    roaring out of the desert.
It will devastate the country,
    leaving a trail of ruin and wreckage.
The cities will be gutted,
    dear possessions gone for good.
Now Samaria has to face the charges
    because she has rebelled against her God:
Her people will be killed, babies smashed on the rocks,
    pregnant women ripped open."

COME BACK! RETURN TO YOUR GOD!

1-3   **14** O Israel, come back! Return to your GOD!
    You're down but you're not out.
    Prepare your confession
and come back to GOD.
Pray to him, "Take away our sin,
    accept our confession.
Receive as restitution
    our repentant prayers.
Assyria won't save us;
    horses won't get us where we want to go.
We'll never again say 'our god'
    to something we've made or made up.
You're our last hope. Is it not true
    that in you the orphan finds mercy?"

4-8 "I will heal their waywardness.
  I will love them lavishly. My anger is played out.
I will make a fresh start with Israel.
  He'll burst into bloom like a crocus in the spring.
He'll put down deep oak tree roots,
  he'll become a forest of oaks!
He'll become splendid — like a giant sequoia,
  his fragrance like a grove of cedars!
Those who live near him will be blessed by him,
  be blessed and prosper like golden grain.
Everyone will be talking about them,
  spreading their fame as the vintage children of God.
Ephraim is finished with gods that are no-gods.
  From now on I'm the one who answers and satisfies him.
I am like a luxuriant fruit tree.
  Everything you need is to be found in me."

9 If you want to live well,
  make sure you understand all of this.
If you know what's good for you,
  you'll learn this inside and out.
GOD's paths get you where you want to go.
  Right-living people walk them easily;
  wrong-living people are always tripping and stumbling.

JOEL

When disaster strikes, understanding of God is at risk. Unexpected illness or death, national catastrophe, social disruption, personal loss, plague or epidemic, devastation by flood or drought, turn men and women who haven't given God a thought in years into instant theologians. Rumors fly: "God is absent" . . . "God is angry" . . . "God is playing favorites, and I'm not the favorite" . . . "God is ineffectual" . . . "God is holding a grudge from a long time ago, and now we're paying for it" . . .

It is the task of the prophet to stand up at such moments of catastrophe and clarify who God is and how he acts. If the prophet is good — that is, accurate and true — the disaster becomes a lever for prying people's lives loose from their sins and setting them free for God. Joel is one of the good ones: He used a current event in Israel as a text to call his people to an immediate awareness that there wasn't a day that went by that they weren't dealing with God. We are always dealing with God.

The event that Joel used as his text was a terrible locust plague that was devastating the crops of Israel, creating an agricultural disaster of major proportions. He compared it to a massive military invasion. But any catastrophe would have served him as well. He projected it onto a big screen and used it to focus the reality of God in the lives of his people. Then he expanded the focus to include everything and everyone *everywhere* — the whole world crowded into Decision Valley for God's verdict. This powerful picture has kept God's people alert to the eternal consequences of their decisions for many centuries.

There is a sense in which catastrophe doesn't introduce anything new into our lives. It simply exposes the moral or spiritual reality that already exists but was hidden beneath an overlay of routine, self-preoccupation, and business as usual. Then suddenly, there it is before us: a moral universe in which our accumulated decisions — on what we say and do, on how we treat others, on whether or not we will obey God's commands — are set in the stark light of God's judgment.

In our everyday experience, right and wrong and the decisions we make about them seldom come to us neatly packaged and precisely defined. Joel's prophetic words continue to reverberate down through the generations, making the ultimate connection between anything, small or large, that disrupts our daily routine, and God, giving us fresh opportunity to reorient our lives in faithful obedience. Joel gives us opportunity for "deathbed repentance" before we die, while there is still time and space for a lot of good living to the glory of God.

JOEL

GET IN TOUCH WITH REALITY—AND WEEP!

1-3 **1** GOD's Message to Joel son of Pethuel:

Attention, elder statesmen! Listen closely,
    everyone, whoever and wherever you are!
Have you ever heard of anything like this?
    Has anything like this ever happened before—ever?
Make sure you tell your children,
    and your children tell their children,
And their children *their* children.
    Don't let this message die out.

4 What the chewing locust left,
    the gobbling locust ate;
What the gobbling locust left,
    the munching locust ate;
What the munching locust left,
    the chomping locust ate.

5-7 Sober up, you drunks!
    Get in touch with reality—and weep!
Your supply of booze is cut off.
    You're on the wagon, like it or not.
My country's being invaded
    by an army invincible, past numbering,
Teeth like those of a lion,
    fangs like those of a tiger.
It has ruined my vineyards,
    stripped my orchards,
And clear-cut the country.
    The landscape's a moonscape.

8-10 Weep like a young virgin dressed in black,
    mourning the loss of her fiancé.
Without grain and grapes,
    worship has been brought to a standstill
    in the Sanctuary of GOD.
The priests are at a loss.
    GOD's ministers don't know what to do.
The fields are sterile.
    The very ground grieves.
The wheat fields are lifeless,
    vineyards dried up, olive oil gone.

11-12 Dirt farmers, despair!
    Grape growers, wring your hands!
Lament the loss of wheat and barley.

All crops have failed.
Vineyards dried up,
    fig trees withered,
Pomegranates, date palms, and apple trees—
    deadwood everywhere!
And joy is dried up and withered
    in the hearts of the people.

NOTHING'S GOING ON IN THE PLACE OF WORSHIP

13-14 And also you priests,
    put on your robes and join the outcry.
You who lead people in worship,
    lead them in lament.
Spend the night dressed in gunnysacks,
    you servants of my God.
Nothing's going on in the place of worship,
    no offerings, no prayers—nothing.
Declare a holy fast, call a special meeting,
    get the leaders together,
Round up everyone in the country.
    Get them into GOD's Sanctuary for serious prayer to GOD.

15-18 What a day! Doomsday!
    GOD's Judgment Day has come.
The Strong God has arrived.
    This is serious business!
Food is just a memory at our tables,
    as are joy and singing from God's Sanctuary.
The seeds in the field are dead,
    barns deserted,
Grain silos abandoned.
    Who needs them? The crops have failed!
The farm animals groan—oh, how they groan!
    The cattle mill around.
There's nothing for them to eat.
    Not even the sheep find anything.

19-20 GOD! I pray, I cry out to you!
    The fields are burning up,
The country is a dust bowl,
    forest and prairie fires rage unchecked.
Wild animals, dying of thirst,
    look to you for a drink.
Springs and streams are dried up.
    The whole country is burning up.

THE LOCUST ARMY

1-3 **2** Blow the ram's horn trumpet in Zion!
    Trumpet the alarm on my holy mountain!
  Shake the country up!
GOD's Judgment's on its way—the Day's almost here!

A black day! A Doomsday!
  Clouds with no silver lining!
Like dawn light moving over the mountains,
  a huge army is coming.
There's never been anything like it
  and never will be again.
Wildfire burns everything before this army
  and fire licks up everything in its wake.
Before it arrives, the country is like the Garden of Eden.
  When it leaves, it is Death Valley.
  Nothing escapes unscathed.

4-6 The locust army seems all horses—
  galloping horses, an army of horses.
It sounds like thunder
  leaping on mountain ridges,
Or like the roar of wildfire
  through grass and brush,
Or like an invincible army shouting for blood,
  ready to fight, straining at the bit.
At the sight of this army,
  the people panic, faces white with terror.

7-11 The invaders charge.
  They climb barricades. Nothing stops them.
Each soldier does what he's told,
  so disciplined, so determined.
They don't get in each other's way.
  Each one knows his job and does it.
Undaunted and fearless,
  unswerving, unstoppable.
They storm the city,
  swarm its defenses,
Loot the houses,
  breaking down doors, smashing windows.
They arrive like an earthquake,
  sweep through like a tornado.
Sun and moon turn out their lights,
  stars black out.
GOD himself bellows in thunder
  as he commands his forces.
Look at the size of that army!
  And the strength of those who obey him!
GOD's Judgment Day—great and terrible.
  Who can possibly survive this?

CHANGE YOUR LIFE

12 But there's also this, it's not too late—
  GOD's personal Message!—
"Come back to me and really mean it!
  Come fasting and weeping, sorry for your sins!"

13-14 Change your life, not just your clothes.
    Come back to GOD, *your* God.
And here's why: God is kind and merciful.
    He takes a deep breath, puts up with a lot,
This most patient God, extravagant in love,
    always ready to cancel catastrophe.
Who knows? Maybe he'll do it now,
    maybe he'll turn around and show pity.
Maybe, when all's said and done,
    there'll be blessings full and robust for your GOD!

15-17 Blow the ram's horn trumpet in Zion!
    Declare a day of repentance, a holy fast day.
Call a public meeting.
    Get everyone there. Consecrate the congregation.
Make sure the elders come,
    but bring in the children, too, even the nursing babies,
Even men and women on their honeymoon —
    interrupt them and get them there.
Between Sanctuary entrance and altar,
    let the priests, GOD's servants, weep tears of repentance.
Let them intercede: "Have mercy, GOD, on your people!
    Don't abandon your heritage to contempt.
Don't let the pagans take over and rule them
    and sneer, 'And so where is this God of theirs?'"

18-20 At that, GOD went into action to get his land back.
    He took pity on his people.
GOD answered and spoke to his people,
    "Look, listen — I'm sending a gift:
Grain and wine and olive oil.
    The fast is over — eat your fill!
I won't expose you any longer
    to contempt among the pagans.
I'll head off the final enemy coming out of the north
    and dump them in a wasteland.
Half of them will end up in the Dead Sea,
    the other half in the Mediterranean.
There they'll rot, a stench to high heaven.
    The bigger the enemy, the stronger the stench!"

THE TREES ARE BEARING FRUIT AGAIN

21-24 Fear not, Earth! Be glad and celebrate!
    GOD has done great things.
Fear not, wild animals!
    The fields and meadows are greening up.
The trees are bearing fruit again:
    a bumper crop of fig trees and vines!
Children of Zion, celebrate!

Be glad in your GOD.
He's giving you a teacher
    to train you how to live right—
Teaching, like rain out of heaven, showers of words
    to refresh and nourish your soul, just as he used to do.
And plenty of food for your body—silos full of grain,
    casks of wine and barrels of olive oil.

25-27   "I'll make up for the years of the locust,
    the great locust devastation—
Locusts savage, locusts deadly,
    fierce locusts, locusts of doom,
That great locust invasion
    I sent your way.
You'll eat your fill of good food.
    You'll be full of praises to your GOD,
The God who has set you back on your heels in wonder.
    Never again will my people be despised.
You'll know without question
    that I'm in the thick of life with Israel,
That I'm your GOD, yes, *your* GOD,
    the one and only real God.
Never again will my people be despised.

THE SUN TURNING BLACK AND THE MOON BLOOD-RED

28-32   "And that's just the beginning: After that—

"I will pour out my Spirit
    on every kind of people:
Your sons will prophesy,
    also your daughters.
Your old men will dream,
    your young men will see visions.
I'll even pour out my Spirit on the servants,
    men and women both.
I'll set wonders in the sky above
    and signs on the earth below:
Blood and fire and billowing smoke,
    the sun turning black and the moon blood-red,
Before the Judgment Day of GOD,
    the Day tremendous and awesome.
Whoever calls, 'Help, GOD!'
    gets help.
On Mount Zion and in Jerusalem
    there will be a great rescue—just as GOD said.
Included in the survivors
    are those that GOD calls."

GOD IS A SAFE HIDING PLACE

3 "In those days, yes, at that very time
> when I put life back together again for Judah and Jerusalem,
> I'll assemble all the godless nations.

1-3 I'll lead them down into Judgment Valley
And put them all on trial, and judge them one and all
> because of their treatment of my own people Israel.
They scattered my people all over the pagan world
> and grabbed my land for themselves.
They threw dice for my people
> and used them for barter.
They would trade a boy for a whore,
> sell a girl for a bottle of wine when they wanted a drink.

4-8 "As for you, Tyre and Sidon and Philistia,
> why should I bother with you?
Are you trying to get back at me
> for something I did to you?
If you are, forget it.
> I'll see to it that it boomerangs on you.
You robbed me, cleaned me out of silver and gold,
> carted off everything valuable to furnish your own temples.
You sold the people of Judah and Jerusalem
> into slavery to the Greeks in faraway places.
But I'm going to reverse your crime.
> I'm going to free those slaves.
I'll have done to you what you did to them:
> I'll sell your children as slaves to your neighbors,
And they'll sell them to the far-off Sabeans."
> GOD's Verdict.

9-11 Announce this to the godless nations:
> Prepare for battle!
Soldiers at attention!
> Present arms! Advance!
Turn your shovels into swords,
> turn your hoes into spears.
Let the weak one throw out his chest
> and say, "I'm tough, I'm a fighter."
Hurry up, pagans! Wherever you are, get a move on!
> Get your act together.
Prepare to be
> shattered by GOD!

12 Let the pagan nations set out
> for Judgment Valley.
There I'll take my place at the bench
> and judge all the surrounding nations.

13 "Swing the sickle —
　　　the harvest is ready.
Stomp on the grapes —
　　　the winepress is full.
The wine vats are full,
　　　overflowing with vintage evil.

14 "Mass confusion, mob uproar —
　　　in Decision Valley!
GOD's Judgment Day has arrived
　　　in Decision Valley.

15-17 "The sky turns black,
　　　sun and moon go dark, stars burn out.
GOD roars from Zion, shouts from Jerusalem.
　　　Earth and sky quake in terror.
But GOD is a safe hiding place,
　　　a granite safe house for the children of Israel.
Then you'll know for sure
　　　that I'm *your* GOD,
Living in Zion,
　　　my sacred mountain.
Jerusalem will be a sacred city,
　　　posted: 'NO TRESPASSING.'

MILK RIVERING OUT OF THE HILLS

18-21 "What a day!
　　　Wine streaming off the mountains,
Milk rivering out of the hills,
　　　water flowing everywhere in Judah,
A fountain pouring out of GOD's Sanctuary,
　　　watering all the parks and gardens!
But Egypt will be reduced to weeds in a vacant lot,
　　　Edom turned into barren badlands,
All because of brutalities to the Judean people,
　　　the atrocities and murders of helpless innocents.
Meanwhile, Judah will be filled with people,
　　　Jerusalem inhabited forever.
The sins I haven't already forgiven, I'll forgive."
　　　GOD has moved into Zion for good.

AMOS

More people are exploited and abused in the cause of religion than in any other way. Sex, money, and power all take a backseat to religion as a source of evil. Religion is the most dangerous energy source known to humankind. The moment a person (or government or religion or organization) is convinced that God is either ordering or sanctioning a cause or project, anything goes. The history, worldwide, of religion-fueled hate, killing, and oppression is staggering. The biblical prophets are in the front line of those doing something about it.

The biblical prophets continue to be the most powerful and effective voices ever heard on this earth for keeping religion honest, humble, and compassionate. Prophets sniff out injustice, especially injustice that is dressed up in religious garb. They sniff it out a mile away. Prophets see through hypocrisy, especially hypocrisy that assumes a religious pose. Prophets are not impressed by position or power or authority. They aren't taken in by numbers, size, or appearances of success.

They pay little attention to what men and women say about God or do for God. They listen to God and rigorously test all human language and action against what they hear. Among these prophets, Amos towers as defender of the downtrodden poor and accuser of the powerful rich who use God's name to legitimize their sin.

None of us can be trusted in this business. If we pray and worship God and associate with others who likewise pray and worship God, we absolutely must keep company with these biblical prophets. We are required to submit all our words and acts to their passionate scrutiny to prevent the perversion of our religion into something self-serving. A spiritual life that doesn't give a large place to the prophet-articulated justice will end up making us worse instead of better, separating us from God's ways instead of drawing us into them.

AMOS

1 The Message of Amos, one of the shepherds of Tekoa, that he received on behalf of Israel. It came to him in visions during the time that Uzziah was king of Judah and Jeroboam II son of Joash was king of Israel, two years before the big earthquake.

SWALLOWING THE SAME OLD LIES

2 The Message:

GOD roars from Zion,
    shouts from Jerusalem!
The thunderclap voice withers the pastures tended by shepherds,
    shrivels Mount Carmel's proud peak.

3-5 GOD's Message:

"Because of the three great sins of Damascus
    — make that four — I'm not putting up with her any longer.
She pounded Gilead to a pulp, pounded her senseless
    with iron hammers and mauls.
For that, I'm setting the palace of Hazael on fire.
    I'm torching Ben-hadad's forts.
I'm going to smash the Damascus gates
    and banish the crime king who lives in Sin Valley,
    the vice boss who gives orders from Paradise Palace.
The people of the land will be sent back
    to where they came from — to Kir."
        GOD's Decree.

6-8 GOD's Message:

"Because of the three great sins of Gaza
    — make that four — I'm not putting up with her any longer.
She deported whole towns
    and then sold the people to Edom.
For that, I'm burning down the walls of Gaza,
    burning up all her forts.
I'll banish the crime king from Ashdod,
    the vice boss from Ashkelon.
I'll raise my fist against Ekron,
    and what's left of the Philistines will die."
        GOD's Decree.

9-10 GOD's Message:

"Because of the three great sins of Tyre
    — make that four — I'm not putting up with her any longer.
She deported whole towns to Edom,
    breaking the treaty she had with her kin.

For that, I'm burning down the walls of Tyre,
    burning up all her forts."

11-12   GOD's Message:

"Because of the three great sins of Edom
    —make that four—I'm not putting up with her any longer.
She hunts down her brother to murder him.
    She has no pity, she has no heart.
Her anger rampages day and night.
    Her meanness never takes a timeout.
For that, I'm burning down her capital, Teman,
    burning up the forts of Bozrah."

13-15   GOD's Message:

"Because of the three great sins of Ammon
    —make that four—I'm not putting up with her any longer.
She ripped open pregnant women in Gilead
    to get more land for herself.
For that, I'm burning down the walls of her capital, Rabbah,
    burning up her forts.
Battle shouts! War whoops!
    with a tornado to finish things off!
The king has been carted off to exile,
    the king and his princes with him."
        GOD's Decree.

1-3 2 GOD's Message:

    "Because of the three great sins of Moab
        —make that four—I'm not putting up with her any longer.
She violated the corpse of Edom's king,
    burning it to cinders.
For that, I'm burning down Moab,
    burning down the forts of Kerioth.
Moab will die in the shouting,
    go out in the blare of war trumpets.
I'll remove the king from the center
    and kill all his princes with him."
        GOD's Decree.

4-5   GOD's Message:

"Because of the three great sins of Judah
    —make that four—I'm not putting up with them any longer.
They rejected GOD's revelation,
    refused to keep my commands.
But they swallowed the same old lies
    that got their ancestors onto dead-end roads.

For that, I'm burning down Judah,
    burning down all the forts of Jerusalem."

DESTROYED FROM THE ROOTS UP

6-8   GOD's Message:

"Because of the three great sins of Israel
    — make that four — I'm not putting up with them any longer.
They buy and sell upstanding people.
    People for them are only *things* — ways of making money.
They'd sell a poor man for a pair of shoes.
    They'd sell their own grandmother!
They grind the penniless into the dirt,
    shove the luckless into the ditch.
Everyone and his brother sleeps with the 'sacred whore' —
    a sacrilege against my Holy Name.
Stuff they've extorted from the poor
    is piled up at the shrine of their god,
While they sit around drinking wine
    they've conned from their victims.

9-11   "In contrast, I was always on your side.
    I destroyed the Amorites who confronted you,
Amorites with the stature of great cedars,
    tough as thick oaks.
I destroyed them from the top branches down.
    I destroyed them from the roots up.
And yes, I'm the One who delivered you from Egypt,
    led you safely through the wilderness for forty years
And then handed you the country of the Amorites
    like a piece of cake on a platter.
I raised up some of your young men to be prophets,
    set aside your best youth for training in holiness.
Isn't this so, Israel?"
    GOD's Decree.

12-13   "But you made the youth-in-training break training,
    and you told the young prophets, 'Don't prophesy!'
You're too much for me.
    I'm hard-pressed — to the breaking point.
I'm like a wagon piled high and overloaded,
    creaking and groaning.

14-15   "When I go into action, what will you do?
    There's no place to run no matter how fast you run.
The strength of the strong won't count.
    Fighters won't make it.
Skilled archers won't make it.
    Fast runners won't make it.
Chariot drivers won't make it.
    Even the bravest of all your warriors

Won't make it.
He'll run off for dear life, stripped naked."
GOD's Decree.

THE LION HAS ROARED

3 ¹ Listen to this, Israel. GOD is calling you to account—and I mean
all of you, everyone connected with the family that he delivered out
of Egypt. Listen!

² "Out of all the families on earth,
I picked *you*.
Therefore, because of your special calling,
I'm holding you responsible for all your sins."

3-7 Do two people walk hand in hand
if they aren't going to the same place?
Does a lion roar in the forest
if there's no carcass to devour?
Does a young lion growl with pleasure
if he hasn't caught his supper?
Does a bird fall to the ground
if it hasn't been hit with a stone?
Does a trap spring shut
if nothing trips it?
When the alarm goes off in the city,
aren't people alarmed?
And when disaster strikes the city,
doesn't GOD stand behind it?
The fact is, GOD, the Master, does nothing
without first telling his prophets the whole story.

8 The lion has roared—
who isn't frightened?
GOD has spoken—
what prophet can keep quiet?

9-11 Announce to the forts of Assyria,
announce to the forts of Egypt—
Tell them, "Gather on the Samaritan mountains, take a good, hard look:
what a snake pit of brutality and terror!
They can't—or won't—do one thing right." GOD said so.
"They stockpile violence and blight.
Therefore"—this is GOD's Word—"an enemy will surround the country.
He'll strip you of your power and plunder your forts."

12 GOD's Message:

"In the same way that a shepherd
trying to save a lamb from a lion
Manages to recover

just a pair of legs or the scrap of an ear,
So will little be saved of the Israelites
    who live in Samaria —
A couple of old chairs at most,
    the broken leg of a table.

13-15 "Listen and bring witness against Jacob's family" —
    this is God's Word, GOD-of-the-Angel-Armies!
"Note well! The day I make Israel pay for its sins,
    pay for the sin-altars of worship at Bethel,
The horned altars will all be dehorned
    and scattered around.
I'll tear down the winter palace,
    smash the summer palace — all your fancy buildings.
The luxury homes will be demolished,
    all those pretentious houses."
      GOD's Decree.

YOU NEVER GOT HUNGRY FOR GOD

1 **4** "Listen to this, you cows of Bashan
    grazing on the slopes of Samaria.
You women! Mean to the poor,
    cruel to the down-and-out!
Indolent and pampered, you demand of your husbands,
    'Bring us a tall, cool drink!'

2-3 "This is serious — I, GOD, have sworn by my holiness!
    Be well warned: Judgment Day is coming!
They're going to rope you up and haul you off,
    keep the stragglers in line with cattle prods.
They'll drag you through the ruined city walls,
    forcing you out single file,
And kick you to kingdom come."
      GOD's Decree.

4-5 "Come along to Bethel and sin!
    And then to Gilgal and sin some more!
Bring your sacrifices for morning worship.
    Every third day bring your tithe.
Burn pure sacrifices — thank offerings.
    Speak up — announce freewill offerings!
That's the sort of religious show
    you Israelites just love."
      GOD's Decree.

6 "You know, don't you, that I'm the One
    who emptied your pantries and cleaned out your cupboards,
Who left you hungry and standing in bread lines?
    But you never got hungry for me. You continued to ignore me."
      GOD's Decree.

7-8   "Yes, and I'm the One who stopped the rains
      three months short of harvest.
  I'd make it rain on one village
      but not on another.
  I'd make it rain on one field
      but not on another — and that one would dry up.
  People would stagger from village to village
      crazed for water and never quenching their thirst.
  But you never got thirsty for me.
      You ignored me."
        GOD's Decree.

9   "I hit your crops with disease
      and withered your orchards and gardens.
  Locusts devoured your olive and fig trees,
      but you continued to ignore me."
        GOD's Decree.

10   "I revisited you with the old Egyptian plagues,
      killed your choice young men and prize horses.
  The stink of rot in your camps was so strong
      that you held your noses —
  But you didn't notice me.
      You continued to ignore me."
        GOD's Decree.

11   "I hit you with earthquake and fire,
      left you devastated like Sodom and Gomorrah.
  You were like a burning stick
      snatched from the flames.
  But you never looked my way.
      You continued to ignore me."
        GOD's Decree.

12   "All this I have done to you, Israel,
      and this is why I have done it.
  Time's up, O Israel!
      Prepare to meet your God!"

13   Look who's here: Mountain-Shaper! Wind-Maker!
      He laid out the whole plot before Adam.
  He brings everything out of nothing,
      like dawn out of darkness.
  He strides across the alpine ridges.
      His name is GOD, God-of-the-Angel-Armies.

ALL SHOW, NO SUBSTANCE

1   **5** Listen to this, family of Israel,
      this Message I'm sending in bold print, this tragic warning:

2   "Virgin Israel has fallen flat on her face.
      She'll never stand up again.

She's been left where she's fallen.
No one offers to help her up."

3   This is the Message, GOD's Word:

"The city that marches out with a thousand
will end up with a hundred.
The city that marches out with a hundred
will end up with ten. Oh, family of Israel!"

4-5   GOD's Message to the family of Israel:

"Seek me and live.
Don't fool around at those shrines of Bethel,
Don't waste time taking trips to Gilgal,
and don't bother going down to Beer-sheba.
Gilgal is here today and gone tomorrow
and Bethel is all show, no substance."

6   So seek GOD and live! You don't want to end up
with nothing to show for your life
But a pile of ashes, a house burned to the ground.
For God will send just such a fire,
and the firefighters will show up too late.

RAW TRUTH IS NEVER POPULAR

7-9   Woe to you who turn justice to vinegar
and stomp righteousness into the mud.
Do you realize where you are? You're in a cosmos
star-flung with constellations by God,
A world God wakes up each morning
and puts to bed each night.
God dips water from the ocean
and gives the land a drink.
GOD, God-revealed, does all this.
And he can destroy it as easily as make it.
He can turn this vast wonder into total waste.

10-12   People hate this kind of talk.
Raw truth is never popular.
But here it is, bluntly spoken:
Because you run roughshod over the poor
and take the bread right out of their mouths,
You're never going to move into
the luxury homes you have built.
You're never going to drink wine
from the expensive vineyards you've planted.
I know precisely the extent of your violations,
the enormity of your sins. Appalling!
You bully right-living people,
taking bribes right and left and kicking the poor when they're down.

13 Justice is a lost cause. Evil is epidemic.
   Decent people throw up their hands.
Protest and rebuke are useless,
   a waste of breath.

14 Seek good and not evil —
   and live!
You talk about GOD, the God-of-the-Angel-Armies,
   being your best friend.
Well, *live* like it,
   and maybe it will happen.

15 Hate evil and love good,
   then work it out in the public square.
Maybe GOD, the God-of-the-Angel-Armies,
   will notice your remnant and be gracious.

16-17   Now again, my Master's Message, GOD, God-of-the-Angel-Armies:

"Go out into the streets and lament loudly!
   Fill the malls and shops with cries of doom!
Weep loudly, 'Not me! Not us, Not now!'
   Empty offices, stores, factories, workplaces.
Enlist everyone in the general lament.
   I want to hear it loud and clear when I make my visit."
      GOD's Decree.

TIME TO FACE HARD REALITY, NOT FANTASY

18-20 Woe to all of you who want GOD's Judgment Day!
   Why would you want to see GOD, want him to come?
When GOD comes, it will be bad news before it's good news,
   the worst of times, not the best of times.
Here's what it's like: A man runs from a lion
   right into the jaws of a bear.
A woman goes home after a hard day's work
   and is raped by a neighbor.
At GOD's coming we face hard reality, not fantasy —
   a black cloud with no silver lining.

21-24 "I can't stand your religious meetings.
   I'm fed up with your conferences and conventions.
I want nothing to do with your religion projects,
   your pretentious slogans and goals.
I'm sick of your fund-raising schemes,
   your public relations and image making.
I've had all I can take of your noisy ego-music.
   When was the last time you sang to *me*?
Do you know what I want?
   I want justice — oceans of it.
I want fairness — rivers of it.
   That's what I want. That's *all* I want.

25-27 "Didn't you, dear family of Israel, worship me faithfully for forty years in the wilderness, bringing the sacrifices and offerings I commanded? How is it you've stooped to dragging gimcrack statues of your so-called rulers around, hauling the cheap images of all your star-gods here and there? Since you like them so much, you can take them with you when I drive you into exile beyond Damascus." GOD's Message, God-of-the-Angel-Armies.

THOSE WHO LIVE ONLY FOR TODAY

1-2 6 Woe to you who think you live on easy street in Zion,
    who think Mount Samaria is the good life.
  You assume you're at the top of the heap,
    voted the number-one best place to live.
Well, wake up and look around. Get off your pedestal.
    Take a look at Calneh.
Go and visit Great Hamath.
    Look in on Gath of the Philistines.
Doesn't that take you off your high horse?
    Compared to them, you're not much, are you?

3-6 Woe to you who are rushing headlong to disaster!
    Catastrophe is just around the corner!
Woe to those who live in luxury
    and expect everyone else to serve them!
Woe to those who live only for today,
    indifferent to the fate of others!
Woe to the playboys, the playgirls,
    who think life is a party held just for them!
Woe to those addicted to feeling good—life without pain!
    those obsessed with looking good—life without wrinkles!
They could not care less
    about their country going to ruin.

7 But here's what's *really* coming:
    a forced march into exile.
They'll leave the country whining,
    a rag-tag bunch of good-for-nothings.

YOU'VE MADE A SHAMBLES OF JUSTICE

8 GOD, the Master, has sworn, and solemnly stands by his Word.
    The God-of-the-Angel-Armies speaks:

"I hate the arrogance of Jacob.
    I have nothing but contempt for his forts.
I'm about to hand over the city
    and everyone in it."

9-10 Ten men are in a house, all dead. A relative comes and gets the bodies to prepare them for a decent burial. He discovers a survivor huddled in a closet and asks, "Are there any more?" The answer: "Not a soul. But hush! GOD must not be mentioned in this desecrated place."

11 Note well: GOD issues the orders.

He'll knock large houses to smithereens.
He'll smash little houses to bits.

12-13 Do you hold a horse race in a field of rocks?
Do you plow the sea with oxen?
You'd cripple the horses
and drown the oxen.
And yet you've made a shambles of justice,
a bloated corpse of righteousness,
Bragging of your trivial pursuits,
beating up on the weak and crowing, "Look what I've done!"

14 "Enjoy it while you can, you Israelites.
I've got a pagan army on the move against you"
—this is your GOD speaking, God-of-the-Angel-Armies—
"And they'll make hash of you,
from one end of the country to the other."

TO DIE HOMELESS AND FRIENDLESS

1-2 **7** GOD, my Master, showed me this vision: He was preparing a locust swarm. The first cutting, which went to the king, was complete, and the second crop was just sprouting. The locusts ate everything green. Not even a blade of grass was left.

I called out, "GOD, my Master! Excuse me, but what's going to come of Jacob? He's so small."

3 GOD gave in.
"It won't happen," he said.

4 GOD showed me this vision: Oh! GOD, my Master GOD was calling up a firestorm. It burned up the ocean. Then it burned up the Promised Land.

5 I said, "GOD, my Master! Hold it—please! What's going to come of Jacob? He's so small."

6 GOD gave in.
"All right, this won't happen either," GOD, my Master, said.

7 GOD showed me this vision: My Master was standing beside a wall. In his hand he held a plumb line.

8-9 GOD said to me, "What do you see, Amos?"
I said, "A plumb line."
Then my Master said, "Look what I've done. I've hung a plumb line in the midst of my people Israel. I've spared them for the last time. This is it!

"Isaac's sex-and-religion shrines will be smashed,
Israel's unholy shrines will be knocked to pieces.
I'm raising my sword against the royal family of Jeroboam."

10 Amaziah, priest at the shrine at Bethel, sent a message to Jeroboam, king of Israel:
"Amos is plotting to get rid of you; and he's doing it as an insider, working from within Israel. His talk will destroy the country. He's got to be silenced.

Do you know what Amos is saying?

11   'Jeroboam will be killed.
        Israel is headed for exile.'"

12-13   Then Amaziah confronted Amos: "Seer, be on your way! Get out of
here and go back to Judah where you came from! Hang out there. Do your
preaching there. But no more preaching at Bethel! Don't show your face here
again. This is the king's chapel. This is a royal shrine."

14-15   But Amos stood up to Amaziah: "I never set up to be a preacher, never
had plans to be a preacher. I raised cattle and I pruned trees. Then GOD took
me off the farm and said, 'Go preach to my people Israel.'

16-17   "So listen to GOD's Word. You tell me, 'Don't preach to Israel. Don't say
anything against the family of Isaac.' But here's what GOD is telling you:

        Your wife will become a whore in town.
        Your children will get killed.
        Your land will be auctioned off.
        You will die homeless and friendless.
        And Israel will be hauled off to exile, far from *home*."

YOU WHO GIVE LITTLE AND TAKE MUCH

1   8   My Master GOD showed me this vision: A bowl of fresh fruit.
2   He said, "What do you see, Amos?"
        I said, "A bowl of fresh, ripe fruit."
GOD said, "Right. So, I'm calling it quits with my people Israel. I'm no
longer acting as if everything is just fine."

3   "The royal singers will wail when it happens."
        My Master GOD said so.
"Corpses will be strewn here, there, and everywhere.
        Hush!"

4-6   Listen to this, you who walk all over the weak,
        you who treat poor people as less than nothing,
Who say, "When's my next paycheck coming
        so I can go out and live it up?
How long till the weekend
        when I can go out and have a good time?"
Who give little and take much,
        and never do an honest day's work.
You exploit the poor, using them —
        and then, when they're used up, you discard them.

7-8   GOD swears against the arrogance of Jacob:
        "I'm keeping track of their every last sin."
God's oath will shake earth's foundations,
        dissolve the whole world into tears.
God's oath will sweep in like a river that rises,
        flooding houses and lands,
And then recedes,
        leaving behind a sea of mud.

9-10 "On Judgment Day, watch out!"
    These are the words of GOD, my Master.
"I'll turn off the sun at noon.
    In the middle of the day the earth will go black.
I'll turn your parties into funerals
    and make every song you sing a dirge.
Everyone will walk around in rags,
    with sunken eyes and bald heads.
Think of the worst that could happen
    — your only son, say, murdered.
That's a hint of Judgment Day
    — that and much more.

11-12 "Oh yes, Judgment Day is coming!"
    These are the words of my Master GOD.
"I'll send a famine through the whole country.
    It won't be food or water that's lacking, but my Word.
People will drift from one end of the country to the other,
    roam to the north, wander to the east.
They'll go anywhere, listen to anyone,
    hoping to hear GOD's Word — but they won't hear it.

13-14 "On Judgment Day,
    lovely young girls will faint of Word-thirst,
    robust young men will faint of God-thirst,
Along with those who take oaths at the Samaria Sin-and-Sex Center,
    saying, 'As the lord god of Dan is my witness!'
    and 'The lady goddess of Beer-sheba bless you!'
Their lives will fall to pieces.
    They'll never put it together again."

ISRAEL THROWN INTO A SIEVE

1-4 **9** I saw my Master standing beside the altar at the shrine. He said:

    "Hit the tops of the shrine's pillars,
    make the floor shake.
The roof's about to fall on the heads of the people,
    and whoever's still alive, I'll kill.
No one will get away,
    no runaways will make it.
If they dig their way down into the underworld,
    I'll find them and bring them up.
If they climb to the stars,
    I'll find them and bring them down.
If they hide out at the top of Mount Carmel,
    I'll find them and bring them back.
If they dive to the bottom of the ocean,
    I'll send Dragon to swallow them up.
If they're captured alive by their enemies,
    I'll send Sword to kill them.
I've made up my mind
    to hurt them, not help them."

5-6 My Master, GOD-of-the-Angel-Armies,
    touches the earth, a mere touch, and it trembles.
    The whole world goes into mourning.
Earth swells like the Nile at flood stage;
    then the water subsides, like the great Nile of Egypt.
God builds his palace—towers soaring high in the skies,
    foundations set on the rock-firm earth.
He calls ocean waters and they come,
    then he ladles them out on the earth.
        GOD, your God, does all this.

7-8 "Do you Israelites think you're any better than the far-off Cushites?"
GOD's Decree.

"Am I not involved with all nations? Didn't I bring Israel up from Egypt, the Philistines from Caphtor, the Arameans from Qir? But you can be sure that I, GOD, the Master, have my eye on the Kingdom of Sin. I'm going to wipe it off the face of the earth. Still, I won't totally destroy the family of Jacob." GOD's Decree.

9-10 "I'm still giving the orders around here. I'm throwing Israel into a sieve among all the nations and shaking them good, shaking out all the sin, all the sinners. No real grain will be lost, but all the sinners will be sifted out and thrown away, the people who say, 'Nothing bad will ever happen in our lifetime. It won't even come close.'

BLESSINGS LIKE WINE POURING OFF THE MOUNTAINS

11-12 "But also on that Judgment Day I will restore David's house that has fallen to pieces. I'll repair the holes in the roof, replace the broken windows, fix it up like new. David's people will be strong again and seize what's left of enemy Edom, plus everyone else under my sovereign judgment." GOD's Decree. He will do this.

13-15 "Yes indeed, it won't be long now." GOD's Decree.

"Things are going to happen so fast your head will swim, one thing fast on the heels of the other. You won't be able to keep up. Everything will be happening at once—and everywhere you look, blessings! Blessings like wine pouring off the mountains and hills. I'll make everything right again for my people Israel:

"They'll rebuild their ruined cities.
They'll plant vineyards and drink good wine.
They'll work their gardens and eat fresh vegetables.
And I'll plant *them*, plant them on their own land.
They'll never again be uprooted from the land I've given them."

GOD, your God, says so.

OBADIAH

It takes the entire Bible to read any part of the Bible. Even the brief walk-on appearance of Obadiah has its place. No one, whether in or out of the Bible, is without significance. It was Obadiah's assignment to give voice to God's word of judgment against Edom.

Back in the early stages of the biblical narrative, we are told the story of the twins Jacob and Esau (Genesis 25–36). They came out of the womb fighting. Jacob was ancestor to the people of Israel, Esau ancestor to the people of Edom. The two neighboring peoples, Israel mostly to the west of the Jordan River and Dead Sea and Edom to the southeast, never did get along. They had a long history of war and rivalry. When Israel was taken into exile — first the northern kingdom by the Assyrians in 721 B.C. and later the southern kingdom by the Babylonians in 586 B.C. — Edom stood across the fence and watched, glad to see her old relative get beat up.

At first reading, this brief but intense prophecy of Obadiah, targeted at Edom, is a broadside indictment of Edom's cruel injustice to God's chosen people. Edom is the villain and God's covenant people the victim.

But the last line of the prophecy takes a giant step out of the centuries of hate and rivalry and invective. Israel, so often a victim of Edomite aggression through the centuries, is suddenly revealed to be saved from the injustices of the past and taking up a position of rule over their ancient enemies the Edomites. But instead of doing to others what had been done to them and continuing the cycle of violence that they had been caught in, they are presented as taking over the reins of government and administering God's justice justly. They find themselves in a new context — God's kingdom — and realize that they have a new vocation — to represent God's rule. It is not much (one verse out of twenty-one!), but it is a glimmer (it is the final verse!).

On the Day of Judgment, dark retaliation and invective do not get the last word. Only the first rays of the light of justice appear here. But these rays will eventually add up to a kingdom of light, in which all nations will be judged justly from the eternal throne in heaven.

OBADIAH

YOUR WORLD WILL COLLAPSE

1 Obadiah's Message to Edom
   from GOD, the Master.
We got the news straight from GOD
   by a special messenger sent out to the godless nations:

"On your feet, prepare for battle;
   get ready to make war on Edom!

2-4 "Listen to this, Edom:
   I'm turning you to a no-account,
      the runt of the godless nations, despised.
You thought you were so great,
   perched high among the rocks, king of the mountain,
Thinking to yourself,
   'Nobody can get to me! Nobody can touch me!'
Think again. Even if, like an eagle,
   you hang out on a high cliff-face,
Even if you build your nest in the stars,
   I'll bring you down to earth."
      GOD'S sure Word.

5-14 "If thieves crept up on you,
   they'd rob you blind — isn't that so?
If they mugged you on the streets at night,
   they'd pick you clean — isn't that so?
Oh, they'll take Esau apart, piece by piece,
   empty his purse and pockets.
All your old partners will drive you to the edge.
   Your old friends will lie to your face.
Your old drinking buddies will stab you in the back.
   Your world will collapse. You won't know what hit you.
So don't be surprised" — it's GOD'S sure Word! —
   "when I wipe out all sages from Edom
   and rid the Esau mountains of its famous wise men.
Your great heroes will desert you, Teman.
   There'll be nobody left in Esau's mountains.
Because of the murderous history compiled
   against your brother Jacob,
You will be looked down on by everyone.
   You'll lose your place in history.
On that day you stood there and didn't do anything.
   Strangers took your brother's army into exile.
Godless foreigners invaded and pillaged Jerusalem.
   You stood there and watched.
   You were as bad as they were.

You shouldn't have gloated over your brother
    when he was down-and-out.
You shouldn't have laughed and joked at Judah's sons
    when they were facedown in the mud.
You shouldn't have talked so big
    when everything was so bad.
You shouldn't have taken advantage of my people
    when their lives had fallen apart.
You of all people should not have been amused
    by their troubles, their wrecked nation.
You shouldn't have taken the shirt off their back
    when they were knocked flat, defenseless.
And you shouldn't have stood waiting at the outskirts
    and cut off refugees,
And traitorously turned in helpless survivors
    who had lost everything.

15-18 "God's Judgment Day is near
    for all the godless nations.
As you have done, it will be done to you.
    What you did will boomerang back
    and hit your own head.
Just as you partied on my holy mountain,
    all the godless nations will drink God's wrath.
They'll drink and drink and drink —
    they'll drink themselves to death.
But not so on Mount Zion — there's respite there!
    a safe and holy place!
The family of Jacob will take back their possessions
    from those who took them from them.
That's when the family of Jacob will catch fire,
    the family of Joseph become fierce flame,
    while the family of Esau will be straw.
Esau will go up in flames,
    nothing left of Esau but a pile of ashes."
      God said it, and it is so.

19-21 People from the south will take over the Esau mountains;
    people from the foothills will overrun the Philistines.
They'll take the farms of Ephraim and Samaria,
    and Benjamin will take Gilead.
Earlier, Israelite exiles will come back
    and take Canaanite land to the north at Zarephath.
Jerusalem exiles from the far northwest in Sepharad
    will come back and take the cities in the south.
The remnant of the saved in Mount Zion
    will go into the mountains of Esau
And rule justly and fairly,
    a rule that honors God's kingdom.

JONAH

Everybody knows about Jonah. People who have never read the Bible know enough about Jonah to laugh at a joke about him and the "whale." Jonah has entered our folklore. There is a playful aspect to his story, a kind of slapstick clumsiness about Jonah as he bumbles his way along, trying, but always unsuccessfully, to avoid God.

But the playfulness is not frivolous. This is deadly serious. While we are smiling or laughing at Jonah, we drop the guard with which we are trying to keep God at a comfortable distance, and suddenly we find ourselves caught in the purposes and commands of God. All of us. No exceptions.

Stories are the most prominent biblical way of helping us see ourselves in "the God story," which always gets around to the story of God making and saving us. Stories, in contrast to abstract statements of truth, tease us into becoming participants in what is being said. We find ourselves involved in the action. We may start out as spectators or critics, but if the story is good (and the biblical stories are very good!), we find ourselves no longer just listening to but inhabiting the story.

One reason that the Jonah story is so enduringly important for nurturing the life of faith in us is that Jonah is not a hero too high and mighty for us to identify with—he doesn't do anything great. Instead of being held up as an ideal to admire, we find Jonah as a companion in our ineptness. Here is someone on our level. Even when Jonah does it right (like preaching, finally, in Nineveh) he does it wrong (by getting angry at God). But the whole time, God is working within and around Jonah's very ineptness and accomplishing his purposes in him. Most of us need a biblical friend or two like Jonah.

JONAH

RUNNING AWAY FROM GOD

1-2 One day long ago, GOD's Word came to Jonah, Amittai's son: "Up on your feet and on your way to the big city of Nineveh! Preach to them. They're in a bad way and I can't ignore it any longer."

3 But Jonah got up and went the other direction to Tarshish, running away from GOD. He went down to the port of Joppa and found a ship headed for Tarshish. He paid the fare and went on board, joining those going to Tarshish — as far away from GOD as he could get.

4-6 But GOD sent a huge storm at sea, the waves towering.

The ship was about to break into pieces. The sailors were terrified. They called out in desperation to their gods. They threw everything they were carrying overboard to lighten the ship. Meanwhile, Jonah had gone down into the hold of the ship to take a nap. He was sound asleep. The captain came to him and said, "What's this? Sleeping! Get up! Pray to your god! Maybe your god will see we're in trouble and rescue us."

7 Then the sailors said to one another, "Let's get to the bottom of this. Let's draw straws to identify the culprit on this ship who's responsible for this disaster."

So they drew straws. Jonah got the short straw.

8 Then they grilled him: "Confess. Why this disaster? What is your work? Where do you come from? What country? What family?"

9 He told them, "I'm a Hebrew. I worship GOD, the God of heaven who made sea and land."

10 At that, the men were frightened, really frightened, and said, "What on earth have you done!" As Jonah talked, the sailors realized that he was running away from GOD.

11 They said to him, "What are we going to do with you — to get rid of this storm?" By this time the sea was wild, totally out of control.

12 Jonah said, "Throw me overboard, into the sea. Then the storm will stop. It's all my fault. I'm the cause of the storm. Get rid of me and you'll get rid of the storm."

13 But no. The men tried rowing back to shore. They made no headway. The storm only got worse and worse, wild and raging.

14 Then they prayed to GOD, "O GOD! Don't let us drown because of this man's life, and don't blame us for his death. You are GOD. Do what you think is best."

15 They took Jonah and threw him overboard. Immediately the sea was quieted down.

16 The sailors were impressed, no longer terrified by the sea, but in awe of GOD. They worshiped GOD, offered a sacrifice, and made vows.

17 Then GOD assigned a huge fish to swallow Jonah. Jonah was in the fish's belly three days and nights.

AT THE BOTTOM OF THE SEA

1-9 Then Jonah prayed to his God from the belly of the fish.
He prayed:

"In trouble, deep trouble, I prayed to GOD.
   He answered me.
From the belly of the grave I cried, 'Help!'
   You heard my cry.
You threw me into ocean's depths,
   into a watery grave,
With ocean waves, ocean breakers
   crashing over me.
I said, 'I've been thrown away,
   thrown out, out of your sight.
I'll never again lay eyes
   on your Holy Temple.'
Ocean gripped me by the throat.
   The ancient Abyss grabbed me and held tight.
My head was all tangled in seaweed
   at the bottom of the sea where the mountains take root.
I was as far down as a body can go,
   and the gates were slamming shut behind me forever —
Yet you pulled me up from that grave alive,
   O GOD, my God!
When my life was slipping away,
   I remembered GOD,
And my prayer got through to you,
   made it all the way to your Holy Temple.
Those who worship hollow gods, god-frauds,
   walk away from their only true love.
But I'm worshiping you, GOD,
   calling out in thanksgiving!
And I'll do what I promised I'd do!
   Salvation belongs to GOD!"

10   Then GOD spoke to the fish, and it vomited up Jonah on the seashore.

MAYBE GOD WILL CHANGE HIS MIND

1-2   **3** Next, GOD spoke to Jonah a second time: "Up on your feet and on your way to the big city of Nineveh! Preach to them. They're in a bad way and I can't ignore it any longer."

3   This time Jonah started off straight for Nineveh, obeying GOD's orders to the letter.

Nineveh was a big city, very big — it took three days to walk across it.

4   Jonah entered the city, went one day's walk and preached, "In forty days Nineveh will be smashed."

5   The people of Nineveh listened, and trusted God. They proclaimed a citywide fast and dressed in burlap to show their repentance. Everyone did it — rich and poor, famous and obscure, leaders and followers.

6-9   When the message reached the king of Nineveh, he got up off his throne, threw down his royal robes, dressed in burlap, and sat down in the dirt. Then he issued a public proclamation throughout Nineveh, authorized by him and his leaders: "Not one drop of water, not one bite of food for man, woman, or animal, including your herds and flocks! Dress them all, both people and animals, in burlap, and send up a cry for help to God. Everyone must turn around, turn back from an evil life and the violent ways that stain their hands. Who knows? Maybe God will turn around and change his mind about us, quit being angry with us and let us live!"

10 God saw what they had done, that they had turned away from their evil lives. He *did* change his mind about them. What he said he would do to them he didn't do.

"I KNEW THIS WAS GOING TO HAPPEN!"

1-2 4 Jonah was furious. He lost his temper. He yelled at GOD, "GOD! I knew it — when I was back home, I knew this was going to happen! That's why I ran off to Tarshish! I knew you were sheer grace and mercy, not easily angered, rich in love, and ready at the drop of a hat to turn your plans of punishment into a program of forgiveness!

3 "So, GOD, if you won't kill them, kill *me*! I'm better off dead!"

4 GOD said, "What do you have to be angry about?"

5 But Jonah just left. He went out of the city to the east and sat down in a sulk. He put together a makeshift shelter of leafy branches and sat there in the shade to see what would happen to the city.

6 GOD arranged for a broad-leafed tree to spring up. It grew over Jonah to cool him off and get him out of his angry sulk. Jonah was pleased and enjoyed the shade. Life was looking up.

7-8 But then God sent a worm. By dawn of the next day, the worm had bored into the shade tree and it withered away. The sun came up and God sent a hot, blistering wind from the east. The sun beat down on Jonah's head and he started to faint. He prayed to die: "I'm better off dead!"

9 Then God said to Jonah, "What right do you have to get angry about this shade tree?"

Jonah said, "Plenty of right. It's made me angry enough to die!"

10-11 GOD said, "What's this? How is it that you can change your feelings from pleasure to anger overnight about a mere shade tree that you did nothing to get? You neither planted nor watered it. It grew up one night and died the next night. So, why can't I likewise change what I feel about Nineveh from anger to pleasure, this big city of more than 120,000 childlike people who don't yet know right from wrong, to say nothing of all the innocent animals?"

MICAH

Prophets use words to remake the world. The world — heaven and earth, men and women, animals and birds — was made in the first place by God's Word. Prophets, arriving on the scene and finding that world in ruins, finding a world of moral rubble and spiritual disorder, take up the work of words again to rebuild what human disobedience and mistrust demolished. These prophets learn their speech from God. Their words are God-grounded, God-energized, God-passionate. As their words enter the language of our communities, men and women find themselves in the presence of God, who enters the mess of human sin to rebuke and renew.

Left to ourselves we turn God into an object, something we can deal with, some *thing* we can use to our benefit, whether that thing is a feeling or an idea or an image. Prophets scorn all such stuff. They train us to respond to God's presence and voice.

Micah, the final member of that powerful quartet of writing prophets who burst on the world scene in the eighth century B.C. (Isaiah, Hosea, and Amos were the others), like virtually all his fellow prophets — those charged with keeping people alive to God and alert to listening to the voice of God — was a master of metaphor. This means that he used words not simply to define or identify what can be seen, touched, smelled, heard, or tasted, but to plunge us into a world of *presence*. To experience presence is to enter that far larger world of reality that our sensory experiences point to but cannot describe — the realities of love and compassion, justice and faithfulness, sin and evil . . . and God. Mostly God. The realities that are Word-evoked are where most of the world's action takes place. There are no "mere words."

MICAH

1 God's Message as it came to Micah of Moresheth. It came during the reigns of Jotham, Ahaz, and Hezekiah, kings of Judah. It had to do with what was going on in Samaria and Jerusalem.

God Takes the Witness Stand

2 Listen, people—all of you.
    Listen, earth, and everyone in it:
The Master, God, takes the witness stand against you,
    the Master from his Holy Temple.

3-5 Look, here he comes! God, from his place!
    He comes down and strides across mountains and hills.
Mountains sink under his feet,
    valleys split apart;
The rock mountains crumble into gravel,
    the river valleys leak like sieves.
All this because of Jacob's sin,
    because Israel's family did wrong.
You ask, "So what is Jacob's sin?"
    Just look at Samaria—isn't it obvious?
And all the sex-and-religion shrines in Judah—
    isn't Jerusalem responsible?

6-7 "I'm turning Samaria into a heap of rubble,
    a vacant lot littered with garbage.
I'll dump the stones from her buildings in the valley
    and leave her abandoned foundations exposed.
All her carved and cast gods and goddesses
    will be sold for stove wood and scrap metal,
All her sacred fertility groves
    burned to the ground,
All the sticks and stones she worshiped as gods,
    destroyed.
These were her earnings from her life as a whore.
    This is what happens to the fees of a whore."

8-9 This is why I lament and mourn.
    This is why I go around in rags and barefoot.
This is why I howl like a pack of coyotes,
    and moan like a mournful owl in the night.
God has inflicted punishing wounds;
    Judah has been wounded with no healing in sight.
Judgment has marched through the city gates.
    Jerusalem must face the charges.

10-16 Don't gossip about this in Telltown.
   Don't waste your tears.
In Dustville,
   roll in the dust.
In Alarmtown,
   the alarm is sounded.
The citizens of Exitburgh
   will never get out alive.
Lament, Last-Stand City:
   There's nothing in you left standing.
The villagers of Bittertown
   wait in vain for sweet peace.
Harsh judgment has come from GOD
   and entered Peace City.
All you who live in Chariotville,
   get in your chariots for flight.
You led the daughter of Zion
   into trusting not God but chariots.
Similar sins in Israel
   also got their start in you.
Go ahead and give your good-bye gifts
   to Good-byeville.
Miragetown beckoned
   but disappointed Israel's kings.
Inheritance City
   has lost its inheritance.
Glorytown
   has seen its last of glory.
Shave your heads in mourning
   over the loss of your precious towns.
Go bald as a goose egg—they've gone
   into exile and aren't coming back.

GOD HAS HAD ENOUGH

1-5 2 Doom to those who plot evil,
   who go to bed dreaming up crimes!
As soon as it's morning,
   they're off, full of energy, doing what they've planned.
They covet fields and grab them,
   find homes and take them.
They bully the neighbor and his family,
   see people only for what they can get out of them.
GOD has had enough. He says,
   "I have some plans of my own:
Disaster because of this interbreeding evil!
   Your necks are on the line.
You're not walking away from this.
   It's doomsday for you.
Mocking ballads will be sung of you,

and you yourselves will sing the blues:
'Our lives are ruined,
   our homes and lands auctioned off.
They take everything, leave us nothing!
   All is sold to the highest bidder.'"
And there'll be no one to stand up for you,
   no one to speak for you before GOD and his jury.

6-7 "Don't preach," say the preachers.
   "Don't preach such stuff.
Nothing bad will happen to us.
   Talk like *this* to the family of Jacob?
Does GOD lose his temper?
   Is this the way he acts?
Isn't he on the side of good people?
   Doesn't he help those who help themselves?"

8-11 "What do you mean, 'good people'!
   You're the enemy of my people!
You rob unsuspecting people
   out for an evening stroll.
You take their coats off their backs
   like soldiers who plunder the defenseless.
You drive the women of my people
   out of their ample homes.
You make victims of the children
   and leave them vulnerable to violence and vice.
Get out of here, the lot of you.
   You can't take it easy here!
You've polluted this place,
   and now *you're* polluted—ruined!
If someone showed up with a good smile and glib tongue
   and told lies from morning to night—
'I'll preach sermons that will tell you
   how you can get anything you want from God:
More money, the best wines . . . you name it'—
   you'd hire him on the spot as your preacher!

12-13 "I'm calling a meeting, Jacob.
   I want everyone back—all the survivors of Israel.
I'll get them together in one place—
   like sheep in a fold, like cattle in a corral—
   a milling throng of homebound people!
Then I, GOD, will burst all confinements
   and lead them out into the open.
They'll follow their King.
   I will be out in front leading them."

HATERS OF GOOD, LOVERS OF EVIL

1-3 **3** Then I said:

"Listen, leaders of Jacob, leaders of Israel:
Don't you know anything of justice?
Haters of good, lovers of evil:
Isn't justice in your job description?
But you skin my people alive.
You rip the meat off their bones.
You break up the bones, chop the meat,
and throw it in a pot for cannibal stew."

4 The time's coming, though, when these same leaders
will cry out for help to GOD, but he won't listen.
He'll turn his face the other way
because of their history of evil.

❋

5-7 Here is GOD's Message to the prophets,
the preachers who lie to my people:
"For as long as they're well paid and well fed,
the prophets preach, 'Isn't life wonderful! Peace to all!'
But if you don't pay up and jump on their bandwagon,
their 'God bless you' turns into 'God damn you.'
Therefore, you're going blind. You'll see nothing.
You'll live in deep shadows and know nothing.
The sun has set on the prophets.
They've had their day; from now on it's night.
Visionaries will be confused,
experts will be all mixed up.
They'll hide behind their reputations and make lame excuses
to cover up their God-ignorance."

❋

8 But me — I'm filled with GOD's power,
filled with GOD's Spirit of justice and strength,
Ready to confront Jacob's crime
and Israel's sin.

9-12 The leaders of Jacob and
the leaders of Israel are
Leaders contemptuous of justice,
who twist and distort right living,
Leaders who build Zion by killing people,
who expand Jerusalem by committing crimes.
Judges sell verdicts to the highest bidder,
priests mass-market their teaching,
prophets preach for high fees,
All the while posturing and pretending
dependence on GOD:

"We've got GOD on our side.
 He'll protect us from disaster."
Because of people like you,
 Zion will be turned back into farmland,
Jerusalem end up as a pile of rubble,
 and instead of the Temple on the mountain,
 a few scraggly scrub pines.

THE MAKING OF GOD'S PEOPLE

1-4 **4** But when all is said and done,
 GOD's Temple on the mountain,
 Firmly fixed, will dominate all mountains,
 towering above surrounding hills.
People will stream to it
 and many nations set out for it,
Saying, "Come, let's climb GOD's mountain.
 Let's go to the Temple of Jacob's God.
He will teach us how to live.
 We'll know how to live God's way."
True teaching will issue from Zion,
 GOD's revelation from Jerusalem.
He'll establish justice in the rabble of nations
 and settle disputes in faraway places.
They'll trade in their swords for shovels,
 their spears for rakes and hoes.
Nations will quit fighting each other,
 quit learning how to kill one another.
Each man will sit under his own shade tree,
 each woman in safety will tend her own garden.
GOD-of-the-Angel-Armies says so,
 and he means what he says.

5 Meanwhile, all the other people live however they wish,
 picking and choosing their gods.
But we live honoring GOD,
 and we're loyal to our God forever and ever.

6-7 "On that great day," GOD says,
 "I will round up all the hurt and homeless,
 everyone I have bruised or banished.
I will transform the battered into a company of the elite.
 I will make a strong nation out of the long lost,
A showcase exhibit of GOD's rule in action,
 as I rule from Mount Zion, from here to eternity.

8 "And you stragglers around Jerusalem,
 eking out a living in shantytowns:
The glory that once was will be again.
 Jerusalem's daughter will be the kingdom center."

9-10 So why the doomsday hysterics?
    You still have a king, don't you?
But maybe he's not doing his job
    and you're panicked like a woman in labor.
Well, go ahead—twist and scream, Daughter Jerusalem.
    You *are* like a woman in childbirth.
You'll soon be out of the city, on your way
    and camping in the open country.
And then you'll arrive in Babylon.
    What you lost in Jerusalem will be found in Babylon.
GOD will give you new life again.
    He'll redeem you from your enemies.

11-12 But for right now, they're ganged up against you,
    many godless peoples, saying,
"Kick her when she's down! Violate her!
    We want to see Zion grovel in the dirt."
These blasphemers have no idea
    what GOD is thinking and doing in this.
They don't know that this is the making of GOD's people,
    that they are wheat being threshed, gold being refined.

13 On your feet, Daughter of Zion! Be threshed of chaff,
    be refined of dross.
I'm remaking you into a people invincible,
    into God's juggernaut to crush the godless peoples.
You'll bring their plunder as holy offerings to GOD,
    their wealth to the Master of the earth.

THE LEADER WHO WILL SHEPHERD-RULE ISRAEL

1 5 But for now, prepare for the worst, victim daughter!
        The siege is set against us.
        They humiliate Israel's king,
    slapping him around like a rag doll.

2-4 But you, Bethlehem, David's country,
    the runt of the litter—
From you will come the leader
    who will shepherd-rule Israel.
He'll be no upstart, no pretender.
    His family tree is ancient and distinguished.
Meanwhile, Israel will be in foster homes
    until the birth pangs are over and the child is born,
And the scattered brothers come back
    home to the family of Israel.
He will stand tall in his shepherd-rule by GOD's strength,
    centered in the majesty of GOD-Revealed.
And the people will have a good and safe home,
    for the whole world will hold him in respect—
    Peacemaker of the world!

5-6
And if some bullying Assyrian shows up,
   invades and violates our land, don't worry.
We'll put him in his place, send him packing,
   and watch his every move.
Shepherd-rule will extend as far as needed,
   to Assyria and all other Nimrod-bullies.
Our shepherd-ruler will save us from old or new enemies,
   from anyone who invades or violates our land.

7
The purged and select company of Jacob will be
   like an island in the sea of peoples.
They'll be like dew from GOD,
   like summer showers
Not mentioned in the weather forecast,
   not subject to calculation or control.

8-9
Yes, the purged and select company of Jacob will be
   like an island in the sea of peoples,
Like the king of beasts among wild beasts,
   like a young lion loose in a flock of sheep,
Killing and devouring the lambs
   and no one able to stop him.
With your arms raised in triumph over your foes,
   your enemies will be no more!

10-15
"The day is coming"
   — GOD's Decree —
"When there will be no more war. None.
   I'll slaughter your war horses and demolish your chariots.
I'll dismantle military posts
   and level your fortifications.
I'll abolish your religious black markets,
   your underworld traffic in black magic.
I will smash your carved and cast gods
   and chop down your phallic posts.
No more taking control of the world,
   worshiping what you do or make.
I'll root out your sacred sex-and-power centers
   and destroy the God-defiant.
In raging anger, I'll make a clean sweep
   of godless nations who haven't listened."

WHAT GOD IS LOOKING FOR

1-2
6 Listen now, listen to GOD:

"Take your stand in court.
If you have a complaint, tell the mountains;
   make your case to the hills.
And now, Mountains, hear GOD's case;
   listen, Jury Earth —

For I am bringing charges against my people.
I am building a case against Israel.

3-5 "Dear people, how have I done you wrong?
Have I burdened you, worn you out? Answer!
I delivered you from a bad life in Egypt;
I paid a good price to get you out of slavery.
I sent Moses to lead you—
and Aaron and Miriam to boot!
Remember what Balak king of Moab tried to pull,
and how Balaam son of Beor turned the tables on him.
Remember all those stories about Shittim and Gilgal.
Keep all GOD's salvation stories fresh and present."

6-7 How can I stand up before GOD
and show proper respect to the high God?
Should I bring an armload of offerings
topped off with yearling calves?
Would GOD be impressed with thousands of rams,
with buckets and barrels of olive oil?
Would he be moved if I sacrificed my firstborn child,
my precious baby, to cancel my sin?

8 But he's already made it plain how to live, what to do,
what GOD is looking for in men and women.
It's quite simple: Do what is fair and just to your neighbor,
be compassionate and loyal in your love,
And don't take yourself too seriously—
take God seriously.

9 Attention! GOD calls out to the city!
If you know what's good for you, you'll listen.
So listen, all of you!
This is serious business.

10-16 "Do you expect me to overlook obscene wealth
you've piled up by cheating and fraud?
Do you think I'll tolerate shady deals
and shifty scheming?
I'm tired of the violent rich
bullying their way with bluffs and lies.
I'm fed up. Beginning now, you're finished.
You'll pay for your sins down to your last cent.
No matter how much you get, it will never be enough—
hollow stomachs, empty hearts.
No matter how hard you work, you'll have nothing to show for it—
bankrupt lives, wasted souls.
You'll plant grass
but never get a lawn.

You'll make jelly
    but never spread it on your bread.
You'll press apples
    but never drink the cider.
You have lived by the standards of your king, Omri,
    the decadent lifestyle of the family of Ahab.
Because you've slavishly followed their fashions,
    I'm forcing you into bankruptcy.
Your way of life will be laughed at, a tasteless joke.
    Your lives will be derided as futile and fake."

STICK AROUND TO SEE WHAT GOD WILL DO

1-6   7 I'm overwhelmed with sorrow!
    sunk in a swamp of despair!
    I'm like someone who goes to the garden
to pick cabbages and carrots and corn
And returns empty-handed,
    finds nothing for soup or sandwich or salad.
There's not a decent person in sight.
    Right-living humans are extinct.
They're all out for one another's blood,
    animals preying on each other.
They've all become experts in evil.
    Corrupt leaders demand bribes.
The powerful rich
    make sure they get what they want.
The best and brightest are thistles.
    The top of the line is crabgrass.
But no longer: It's exam time.
    Look at them slinking away in disgrace!
Don't trust your neighbor,
    don't confide in your friend.
Watch your words,
    even with your spouse.
Neighborhoods and families are falling to pieces.
    The closer they are — sons, daughters, in-laws —
The worse they can be.
    Your own family is the enemy.

7   But me, I'm not giving up.
    I'm sticking around to see what GOD will do.
I'm waiting for God to make things right.
    I'm counting on God to listen to me.

SPREADING YOUR WINGS

8-10   Don't, enemy, crow over me.
    I'm down, but I'm not out.
I'm sitting in the dark right now,
    but GOD is my light.
I can take GOD's punishing rage.
    I deserve it — I sinned.

But it's not forever. He's on my side
    and is going to get me out of this.
He'll turn on the lights and show me his ways.
    I'll see the whole picture and how right he is.
And my enemy will see it, too,
    and be discredited — yes, disgraced!
This enemy who kept taunting,
    "So where is this GOD of yours?"
I'm going to see it with these, my own eyes —
    my enemy disgraced, trash in the gutter.

11-13 Oh, that will be a day! A day for rebuilding your city,
    a day for stretching your arms, spreading your wings!
All your dispersed and scattered people will come back,
    old friends and family from faraway places,
From Assyria in the east to Egypt in the west,
    from across the seas and out of the mountains.
But there'll be a reversal for everyone else — massive depopulation —
    because of the way they lived, the things they did.

14-17 Shepherd, O GOD, your people with your staff,
    your dear and precious flock.
Uniquely yours in a grove of trees,
    centered in lotus land.
Let them graze in lush Bashan
    as in the old days in green Gilead.
Reproduce the miracle-wonders
    of our exodus from Egypt.
And the godless nations: Put them in their place —
    humiliated in their arrogance, speechless and clueless.
Make them slink like snakes, crawl like cockroaches,
    come out of their holes from under their rocks
And face our GOD.
    Fill them with holy fear and trembling.

18-20 Where is the god who can compare with you —
    wiping the slate clean of guilt,
Turning a blind eye, a deaf ear,
    to the past sins of your purged and precious people?
You don't nurse your anger and don't stay angry long,
    for mercy is your specialty. That's what you love most.
And compassion is on its way to us.
    You'll stamp out our wrongdoing.
You'll sink our sins
    to the bottom of the ocean.
You'll stay true to your word to Father Jacob
    and continue the compassion you showed Grandfather Abraham —
Everything you promised our ancestors
    from a long time ago.

NAHUM

The stage of history is large. Larger-than-life figures appear on this stage from time to time, swaggering about, brandishing weapons and money, terrorizing and bullying. These figures are not, as they suppose themselves to be, at the center of the stage — not, in fact, anywhere near the center. But they make a lot of noise and are able to call attention to themselves. They often manage to get a significant number of people watching and even admiring: big nations, huge armies, important people. At any given moment a few superpower nations and their rulers dominate the daily news. Every century a few of these names are left carved on its park benches, marking rather futile, and in retrospect pitiable, attempts at immortality.

The danger is that the noise of these pretenders to power will distract us from what is going on quietly at the center of the stage in the person and action of God. God's characteristic way of working is in quietness and through prayer. "I speak," says poet George Meredith, "of the unremarked forces that split the heart and make the pavement toss — forces concealed in quiet people and plants." If we are conditioned to respond to noise and size, we will miss God's word and action.

From time to time, God assigns someone to pay attention to one or another of these persons or nations or movements just long enough to get the rest of us to *quit* paying so much attention to them and get back to the main action: *God*! Nahum drew that assignment in the seventh century B.C. Assyria had the whole world terrorized. At the time that Nahum delivered his prophecy, Assyria (and its capital, Nineveh) appeared invincible. A world free of Assyrian domination was unimaginable. Nahum's task was to make it imaginable — to free God's people from Assyrian paralysis, free them to believe in and pray to a sovereign God. Nahum's preaching, his Spirit-born metaphors, his God-shaped syntax, knocked Assyria off her high horse and cleared the field of Nineveh-distraction so that Israel could see that despite her world reputation, Assyria didn't amount to much. Israel could now attend to what was *really* going on.

Because Nahum has a single message — doom to Nineveh/Assyria — it is easy to misunderstand the prophet as simply a Nineveh-hater. But Nahum writes and preaches out of the large context in which Israel's sins are denounced as vigorously as those of any of her enemies. The effect of Nahum is not to foment religious hate against the enemy but to say, "Don't admire or be intimidated by this enemy. They are going to be judged by the very same standards applied to us."

NAHUM

GOD IS SERIOUS BUSINESS

1 A report on the problem of Nineveh, the way God gave Nahum of Elkosh to see it:

2-6 GOD is serious business.
 He won't be trifled with.
He avenges his foes.
 He stands up against his enemies, fierce and raging.
But GOD doesn't lose his temper.
 He's powerful, but it's a patient power.
Still, no one gets by with anything.
 Sooner or later, everyone pays.
Tornadoes and hurricanes
 are the wake of his passage,
Storm clouds are the dust
 he shakes off his feet.
He yells at the sea: It dries up.
 All the rivers run dry.
The Bashan and Carmel mountains shrivel,
 the Lebanon orchards shrivel.
Mountains quake in their roots,
 hills dissolve into mud flats.
Earth shakes in fear of GOD.
 The whole world's in a panic.
Who can face such towering anger?
 Who can stand up to this fierce rage?
His anger spills out like a river of lava,
 his fury shatters boulders.

7-10 GOD is good,
 a hiding place in tough times.
He recognizes and welcomes
 anyone looking for help,
No matter how desperate the trouble.
 But cozy islands of escape
He wipes right off the map.
 No one gets away from God.
Why waste time conniving against GOD?
 He's putting an end to all such scheming.
For troublemakers, no second chances.
 Like a pile of dry brush,
Soaked in oil,
 they'll go up in flames.

A THINK TANK FOR LIES

11 Nineveh's an anthill
 of evil plots against GOD,

A think tank for lies
    that seduce and betray.

12-13   And GOD has something to say about all this:
        "Even though you're on top of the world,
    With all the applause and all the votes,
        you'll be mowed down flat.

    "I've afflicted you, Judah, true,
        but I won't afflict you again.
    From now on I'm taking the yoke from your neck
        and splitting it up for kindling.
    I'm cutting you free
        from the ropes of your bondage."

14 GOD's orders on Nineveh:

    "You're the end of the line.
        It's all over with Nineveh.
    I'm gutting your temple.
        Your gods and goddesses go in the trash.
    I'm digging your grave. It's an unmarked grave.
        You're nothing — no, you're *less* than nothing!"

15 Look! Striding across the mountains —
        a messenger bringing the latest good news: peace!
    A holiday, Judah! Celebrate!
        Worship and recommit to God!
    No more worries about *this* enemy.
        This one is history. Close the books.

ISRAEL'S BEEN TO HELL AND BACK

1   **2** The juggernaut's coming!
        Post guards, lay in supplies.
    Get yourselves together,
        get ready for the big battle.

2   GOD has restored the Pride of Jacob,
        the Pride of Israel.
    Israel's lived through hard times.
        He's been to hell and back.

3-12   Weapons flash in the sun,
        the soldiers splendid in battle dress,
    Chariots burnished and glistening,
        ready to charge,
    A spiked forest of brandished spears,
        lethal on the horizon.
    The chariots pour into the streets.

They fill the public squares,
Flaming like torches in the sun,
   like lightning darting and flashing.
The Assyrian king rallies his men,
   but they stagger and stumble.
They run to the ramparts
   to stem the tide, but it's too late.
Soldiers pour through the gates.
   The palace is demolished.
Soon it's all over:
   Nineveh stripped, Nineveh doomed,
Maids and slaves moaning like doves,
   beating their breasts.
Nineveh is a tub
   from which they've pulled the plug.
Cries go up, "Do something! Do something!"
   but it's too late. Nineveh's soon empty—nothing.
Other cries come: "Plunder the silver!
   Plunder the gold!
A bonanza of plunder!
   Take everything you want!"
Doom! Damnation! Desolation!
   Hearts sink,
   knees fold,
   stomachs retch,
   faces blanch.
So, what happened to the famous
   and fierce Assyrian lion
And all those cute Assyrian cubs?
   To the lion and lioness
Cozy with their cubs,
   fierce and fearless?
To the lion who always returned from the hunt
   with fresh kills for lioness and cubs,
The lion lair heaped with bloody meat,
   blood and bones for the royal lion feast?

13   "Assyria, I'm your enemy,"
   says GOD-of-the-Angel-Armies.
"I'll torch your chariots. They'll go up in smoke.
   'Lion Country' will be strewn with carcasses.
The war business is over—you're out of work:
   You'll have no more wars to report,
No more victories to announce.
   You're out of war work forever."

LET THE NATIONS GET THEIR FILL OF THE UGLY TRUTH

1-4 **3** Doom to Murder City—
   full of lies, bursting with loot, addicted to violence!
   Horns blaring, wheels clattering,

    horses rearing, chariots lurching,
Horsemen galloping,
    brandishing swords and spears,
Dead bodies rotting in the street,
    corpses stacked like cordwood,
Bodies in every gutter and alley,
    clogging every intersection!
And whores! Whores without end!
    Whore City,
Fatally seductive, you're the Witch of Seduction,
    luring nations to their ruin with your evil spells.

※

5-7   "I'm your enemy, Whore Nineveh —
    I, GOD-of-the-Angel-Armies!
I'll strip you of your seductive silk robes
    and expose you on the world stage.
I'll let the nations get their fill of the ugly truth
    of who you really are and have been all along.
I'll pelt you with dog dung
    and place you on a pedestal: 'Slut on Exhibit.'
Everyone who sees you will gag and say,
    'Nineveh's a pigsty:
What on earth did we ever see in her?
    Who would give her a second look? Ugh!'"

PAST THE POINT OF NO RETURN

8-13   Do you think you're superior to Egyptian Thebes,
    proudly invincible on the River Nile,
Protected by the great River,
    walled in by the River, secure?
Ethiopia stood guard to the south,
    Egypt to the north.
Put and Libya, strong friends,
    were ready to step in and help.
But you know what happened to her:
    The whole city was marched off to a refugee camp,
Her babies smashed to death
    in public view on the streets,
Her prize leaders auctioned off,
    her celebrities put in chain gangs.
Expect the same treatment, Nineveh.
    You'll soon be staggering like a bunch of drunks,
Wondering what hit you,
    looking for a place to sleep it off.
All your forts are like peach trees,
    the lush peaches ripe, ready for the picking.
One shake of the tree and they fall
    straight into hungry mouths.
Face it: Your warriors are wimps.
    You're sitting ducks.

Your borders are gaping doors, inviting
    your enemies in. And who's to stop them?

14-15 Store up water for the siege.
    Shore up your defenses.
Get down to basics: Work the clay
    and make bricks.
Sorry. Too late.
    Enemy fire will burn you up.
Swords will cut you to pieces.
    You'll be chewed up as if by locusts.

15-17 Yes, as if by locusts—a fitting fate,
    for you yourselves are a locust plague.
You've multiplied shops and shopkeepers—
    more buyers and sellers than stars in the sky!
A plague of locusts, cleaning out the neighborhood
    and then flying off.
Your bureaucrats are locusts,
    your brokers and bankers are locusts.
Early on, they're all at your service,
    full of smiles and promises,
But later when you return with questions or complaints,
    you'll find they've flown off and are nowhere to be found.

18-19 King of Assyria! Your shepherd-leaders,
    in charge of caring for your people,
Are busy doing everything else but.
    They're not doing their job,
And your people are scattered and lost.
    There's no one to look after them.
You're past the point of no return.
    Your wound is fatal.
When the story of your fate gets out,
    the whole world will applaud and cry "Encore!"
Your cruel evil has seeped
    into every nook and cranny of the world.
    Everyone has felt it and suffered.

HABAKKUK

Living by faith is a bewildering venture. We rarely know what's coming next, and not many things turn out the way we anticipate. It is natural to assume that since I am God's chosen and beloved, I will get favorable treatment from the God who favors me so extravagantly. It is not unreasonable to expect that from the time that I become his follower, I will be exempt from dead ends, muddy detours, and cruel treatment from the travelers I meet daily who are walking the other direction. That God-followers don't get preferential treatment in life always comes as a surprise. But it's also a surprise to find that there are a few men and women *within* the Bible who show up alongside us at such moments.

The prophet Habakkuk is one of them, and a most welcome companion he is. Most prophets, most of the time, speak God's Word *to us*. They are preachers calling us to listen to God's words of judgment and salvation, confrontation and comfort. They face us with God as he is, not as we imagine him to be. Most prophets are in-your-face assertive, not given to tact, not diplomatic, as they insist that we pay attention to God. But Habakkuk speaks our word *to God*. He gives voice to our bewilderment, articulates our puzzled attempts to make sense of things, faces God with our disappointment with God. He insists that God pay attention to us, and he insists with a prophet's characteristic no-nonsense bluntness.

The circumstance that aroused Habakkuk took place in the seventh century B.C. The prophet realized that God was going to use the godless military machine of Babylon to bring God's judgment on God's own people — using a godless nation to punish a godly nation! It didn't make sense, and Habakkuk was quick and bold to say so. He dared to voice his feelings that God didn't know his own God business. Not a day has passed since then that one of us hasn't picked up and repeated Habakkuk's bafflement: "God, you don't seem to make sense!"

But this prophet companion who stands at our side does something even more important: He waits and he listens. It is in his waiting and listening — which then turns into his praying — that he found himself inhabiting the large world of God's sovereignty. Only there did he eventually realize that the believing-in-God life, the steady trusting-in-God life, is the full life, the only real life. Habakkuk started out exactly where we start out with our puzzled complaints and God-accusations, but he didn't stay there. He ended up in a world, along with us, where every detail in our lives of love for God is worked into something good.

HABAKKUK

JUSTICE IS A JOKE

1-4 The problem as God gave Habakkuk to see it:

GOD, how long do I have to cry out for help
before you listen?
How many times do I have to yell, "Help! Murder! Police!"
before you come to the rescue?
Why do you force me to look at evil,
stare trouble in the face day after day?
Anarchy and violence break out,
quarrels and fights all over the place.
Law and order fall to pieces.
Justice is a joke.
The wicked have the righteous hamstrung
and stand justice on its head.

GOD SAYS, "LOOK!"

5-11 "Look around at the godless nations.
Look long and hard. Brace yourself for a shock.
Something's about to take place
and you're going to find it hard to believe.
I'm about to raise up Babylonians to punish you,
Babylonians, fierce and ferocious —
World-conquering Babylon,
grabbing up nations right and left,
A dreadful and terrible people,
making up its own rules as it goes.
Their horses run like the wind,
attack like bloodthirsty wolves.
A stampede of galloping horses
thunders out of nowhere.
They descend like vultures
circling in on carrion.
They're out to kill. Death is on their minds.
They collect victims like squirrels gathering nuts.
They mock kings,
poke fun at generals,
Spit on forts,
and leave them in the dust.
They'll all be blown away by the wind.
Brazen in sin, they call strength their god."

WHY IS GOD SILENT NOW?

12-13 GOD, you're from eternity, aren't you?
Holy God, we aren't going to die, are we?
GOD, you chose *Babylonians* for your judgment work?
Rock-Solid God, you gave *them* the job of discipline?

But you can't be serious!
    You can't condone evil!
So why don't you do something about this?
    Why are you silent *now*?
This outrage! Evil men swallow up the righteous
    and you stand around and *watch*!

                    ✼

14-16   You're treating men and women
    as so many fish in the ocean,
Swimming without direction,
    swimming but not getting anywhere.
Then this evil Babylonian arrives and goes fishing.
    He pulls in a good catch.
He catches his limit and fills his creel —
    a good day of fishing! He's happy!
He praises his rod and reel,
    piles his fishing gear on an altar and worships it!
It's made his day,
    and he's going to eat well tonight!

                    ✼

17   Are you going to let this go on and on?
    Will you let this Babylonian fisherman
Fish like a weekend angler,
    killing people as if they're nothing but fish?

                    ✼

1   **2** What's God going to say to my questions? I'm braced for the worst.
    I'll climb to the lookout tower and scan the horizon.
  I'll wait to see what God says,
    how he'll answer my complaint.

FULL OF SELF, BUT SOUL-EMPTY

2-3   And then GOD answered: "Write this.
    Write what you see.
Write it out in big block letters
    so that it can be read on the run.
This vision-message is a witness
    pointing to what's coming.
It aches for the coming — it can hardly wait!
    And it doesn't lie.
If it seems slow in coming, wait.
    It's on its way. It will come right on time.

                    ✼

4   "Look at that man, bloated by self-importance —
    full of himself but soul-empty.
But the person in right standing before God
    through loyal and steady believing
    is fully alive, *really* alive.

5-6 "Note well: Money deceives.
    The arrogant rich don't last.
They are more hungry for wealth
    than the grave is for cadavers.
Like death, they always want more,
    but the 'more' they get is dead bodies.
They are cemeteries filled with dead nations,
    graveyards filled with corpses.
Don't give people like this a second thought.
    Soon the whole world will be taunting them:

6-8 "'Who do you think you are—
    getting rich by stealing and extortion?
How long do you think
    you can get away with this?'
Indeed, how long before your victims wake up,
    stand up and make *you* the victim?
You've plundered nation after nation.
    Now you'll get a taste of your own medicine.
All the survivors are out to plunder you,
    a payback for all your murders and massacres.

9-11 "Who do you think you are—
    recklessly grabbing and looting,
Living it up, acting like king of the mountain,
    acting above it all, above trials and troubles?
You've engineered the ruin of your own house.
    In ruining others you've ruined yourself.
You've undermined your foundations,
    rotted out your own soul.
The bricks of your house will speak up and accuse you.
    The woodwork will step forward with evidence.

12-14 "Who do you think you are—
    building a town by murder, a city with crime?
Don't you know that GOD-of-the-Angel-Armies
    makes sure nothing comes of that but ashes,
Makes sure the harder you work
    at that kind of thing, the less you are?
Meanwhile the earth fills up
    with awareness of GOD's glory
    as the waters cover the sea.

15-17 "Who do you think you are—
    inviting your neighbors to your drunken parties,
Giving them too much to drink,
    roping them into your sexual orgies?
You thought you were having the time of your life.
    Wrong! It's a time of disgrace.
All the time you were drinking,
    you were drinking from the cup of God's wrath.

You'll wake up holding your throbbing head, hung over—
    hung over from Lebanon violence,
Hung over from animal massacres,
    hung over from murder and mayhem,
From multiple violations
    of place and people.

18-19 "What's the use of a carved god
    so skillfully carved by its sculptor?
What good is a fancy cast god
    when all it tells is lies?
What sense does it make to be a pious god-maker
    who makes gods that can't even talk?
Who do you think you are—
    saying to a stick of wood, 'Wake up,'
Or to a dumb stone, 'Get up'?
    Can they teach you anything about anything?
There's nothing to them but surface.
    There's nothing on the inside.

20 "But oh! GOD is in his holy Temple!
    Quiet everyone—a holy silence. Listen!"

GOD RACING ON THE CREST OF THE WAVES

1-2 **3** A prayer of the prophet Habakkuk, with orchestra:

    GOD, I've heard what our ancestors say about you,
    and I'm stopped in my tracks, down on my knees.
Do among us what you did among them.
    Work among us as you worked among them.
And as you bring judgment, as you surely must,
    remember mercy.

3-7 God's on his way again,
    retracing the old salvation route,
Coming up from the south through Teman,
    the Holy One from Mount Paran.
Skies are blazing with his splendor,
    his praises sounding through the earth,
His cloud-brightness like dawn, exploding, spreading,
    forked-lightning shooting from his hand—
    what power hidden in that fist!
Plague marches before him,
    pestilence at his heels!
He stops. He shakes Earth.
    He looks around. Nations tremble.
The age-old mountains fall to pieces;
    ancient hills collapse like a spent balloon.
The paths God takes are older
    than the oldest mountains and hills.

I saw everyone worried, in a panic:
  Old wilderness adversaries,
Cushan and Midian, were terrified,
  hoping he wouldn't notice them.

8-16 Gᴏᴅ, is it River you're mad at?
  Angry at old River?
Were you raging at Sea when you rode
  horse and chariot through to salvation?
You unfurled your bow
  and let loose a volley of arrows.
  You split Earth with rivers.
Mountains saw what was coming.
  They twisted in pain.
Flood Waters poured in.
  Ocean roared and reared huge waves.
Sun and Moon stopped in their tracks.
  Your flashing arrows stopped them,
  your lightning-strike spears impaled them.
Angry, you stomped through Earth.
  Furious, you crushed the godless nations.
You were out to save your people,
  to save your specially chosen people.
You beat the stuffing
  out of King Wicked,
Stripped him naked
  from head to toe,
Set his severed head on his own spear
  and blew away his army.
Scattered they were to the four winds —
  and ended up food for the sharks!
You galloped through the Sea on your horses,
  racing on the crest of the waves.
When I heard it, my stomach did flips.
  I stammered and stuttered.
My bones turned to water.
  I staggered and stumbled.
I sit back and wait for Doomsday
  to descend on our attackers.

17-19 Though the cherry trees don't blossom
  and the strawberries don't ripen,
Though the apples are worm-eaten
  and the wheat fields stunted,
Though the sheep pens are sheepless
  and the cattle barns empty,
I'm singing joyful praise to Gᴏᴅ.
  I'm turning cartwheels of joy to my Savior God.
Counting on Gᴏᴅ's Rule to prevail,

I take heart and gain strength.
I run like a deer.
I feel like I'm king of the mountain!

(For congregational use, with a full orchestra.)

ZEPHANIAH

We humans keep looking for a religion that will give us access to God without having to bother with people. We want to go to God for comfort and inspiration when we're fed up with the men and women and children around us. We want God to give us an edge in the dog-eat-dog competition of daily life.

This determination to get ourselves a religion that gives us an inside track with God, but leaves us free to deal with people however we like, is age-old. It is the sort of religion that has been promoted and marketed with both zeal and skill throughout human history. Business is always booming.

It is also the sort of religion that the biblical prophets are determined to root out. They are dead set against it.

Because the root of the solid spiritual life is embedded in a relationship between people and God, it is easy to develop the misunderstanding that my spiritual life is something personal between God and me—a private thing to be nurtured by prayers and singing, spiritual readings that comfort and inspire, and worship with like-minded friends. If we think this way for very long, we will assume that the way we treat the people we don't like or who don't like us has nothing to do with God.

That's when the prophets step in and interrupt us, insisting, "Everything you do or think or feel has to do with God. Every person you meet has to do with God." We live in a vast world of interconnectedness, and the connections have consequences, either in things or in people—and all the consequences come together in God. The biblical phrase for the coming together of the consequences is Judgment Day.

We can't be reminded too often or too forcefully of this reckoning. Zephaniah's voice in the choir of prophets sustains the intensity, the urgency.

ZEPHANIAH

NO LONGER GIVING GOD A THOUGHT OR A PRAYER

1 GOD's Message to Zephaniah son of Cushi, son of Gedaliah, son of Amariah, son of Hezekiah. It came during the reign of Josiah son of Amon, who was king of Judah:

2 "I'm going to make a clean sweep of the earth,
    a thorough housecleaning." GOD's Decree.

3 "Men and women and animals,
    including birds and fish—
Anything and everything that causes sin—will go,
    but especially people.

4-6 "I'll start with Judah
    and everybody who lives in Jerusalem.
I'll sweep the place clean of every trace
    of the sex-and-religion Baal shrines and their priests.
I'll get rid of the people who sneak up to their rooftops at night
    to worship the star gods and goddesses;
Also those who continue to worship GOD
    but cover their bases by worshiping other king-gods as well;
Not to mention those who've dumped GOD altogether,
    no longer giving him a thought or offering a prayer.

7-13 "Quiet now!
    Reverent silence before me, GOD, the Master!
Time's up. My Judgment Day is near:
    The Holy Day is all set, the invited guests made holy.
On the Holy Day, GOD's Judgment Day,
    I will punish the leaders and the royal sons;
I will punish those who dress up like foreign priests and priestesses,
    Who introduce pagan prayers and practices;
And I'll punish all who import pagan superstitions
    that turn holy places into hellholes.
Judgment Day!" GOD's Decree!
    "Cries of panic from the city's Fish Gate,
Cries of terror from the city's Second Quarter,
    sounds of great crashing from the hills!
Wail, you shopkeepers on Market Street!
    Moneymaking has had its day. The god Money is dead.
On Judgment Day,
    I'll search through every closet and alley in Jerusalem.
I'll find and punish those who are sitting it out, fat and lazy,
    amusing themselves and taking it easy,
Who think, 'GOD doesn't do anything, good or bad.

He isn't involved, so neither are we.'
But just wait. They'll lose everything they have,
    money and house and land.
They'll build a house and never move in.
    They'll plant vineyards and never taste the wine.

A DAY OF DARKNESS AT NOON

14-18 "The Great Judgment Day of GOD is almost here.
    It's countdown time: . . . seven, six, five, four . . .
Bitter and noisy cries on my Judgment Day,
    even strong men screaming for help.
Judgment Day is payday — my anger paid out:
    a day of distress and anguish,
    a day of catastrophic doom,
    a day of darkness at noon,
    a day of black storm clouds,
    a day of bloodcurdling war cries,
    as forts are assaulted,
    as defenses are smashed.
I'll make things so bad they won't know what hit them.
    They'll walk around groping like the blind.
    They've sinned against GOD!
Their blood will be poured out like old dishwater,
    their guts shoveled into slop buckets.
Don't plan on buying your way out.
    Your money is worthless for this.
This is the Day of GOD's Judgment — my *wrath*!
    I *care* about sin with fiery passion —
A fire to burn up the corrupted world,
    a wildfire finish to the corrupting people."

SEEK GOD

1-2 So get yourselves together. Shape up!
    You're a nation without a clue about what it wants.
    Do it before you're blown away
    like leaves in a windstorm,
Before GOD's Judgment-anger
    sweeps down on you,
Before GOD's Judgment Day wrath
    descends with full force.

3 Seek GOD, all you quietly disciplined people
    who live by GOD's justice.
Seek GOD's right ways. Seek a quiet and disciplined life.
    Perhaps you'll be hidden on the Day of GOD's anger.

ALL EARTH-MADE GODS WILL BLOW AWAY

4-5 Gaza is scheduled for demolition,
    Ashdod will be cleaned out by high noon,
    Ekron pulled out by the roots.

Doom to the seaside people,
the seafaring people from Crete!
The Word of GOD is bad news for you
who settled Canaan, the Philistine country:
"You're slated for destruction —
no survivors!"

6-7 The lands of the seafarers
will become pastureland,
A country for shepherds and sheep.
What's left of the family of Judah will get it.
Day after day they'll pasture by the sea,
and go home in the evening to Ashkelon to sleep.
Their very own GOD will look out for them.
He'll make things as good as before.

8-12 "I've heard the crude taunts of Moab,
the mockeries flung by Ammon,
The cruel talk they've used to put down my people,
their self-important strutting along Israel's borders.
Therefore, as sure as I am the living God," says
GOD-of-the-Angel-Armies,
Israel's personal God,
"Moab will become a ruin like Sodom,
Ammon a ghost town like Gomorrah,
One a field of rocks, the other a sterile salt flat,
a moonscape forever.
What's left of my people will finish them off,
will pick them clean and take over.
This is what they get for their bloated pride,
their taunts and mockeries of the people
of GOD-of-the-Angel-Armies.
GOD will be seen as truly terrible — a Holy Terror.
All earth-made gods will shrivel up and blow away;
And everyone, wherever they are, far or near,
will fall to the ground and worship him.
Also you Ethiopians,
you, too, will die — I'll see to it."

13-15 Then GOD will reach into the north
and destroy Assyria.
He will waste Nineveh,
leave her dry and treeless as a desert.
The ghost town of a city,
the haunt of wild animals,
Nineveh will be home to raccoons and coyotes —
they'll bed down in its ruins.
Owls will hoot in the windows, ravens will croak in the doorways —

all that fancy woodwork now a perch for birds.
Can this be the famous Fun City
 that had it made,
That boasted, "I'm the Number-One City!
 I'm King of the Mountain!"
So why is the place deserted,
 a lair for wild animals?
Passersby hardly give it a look;
 they dismiss it with a gesture.

SEWER CITY

1-5 **3** Doom to the rebellious city,
  the home of oppressors — Sewer City!
  The city that wouldn't take advice,
 wouldn't accept correction,
Wouldn't trust GOD,
 wouldn't even get close to her own god!
Her very own leaders
 are rapacious lions,
Her judges are rapacious timber wolves
 out every morning prowling for a fresh kill.
Her prophets are out for what they can get.
 They're opportunists — you can't trust them.
Her priests desecrate the Sanctuary.
 They use God's law as a weapon to maim and kill souls.
Yet GOD remains righteous in her midst,
 untouched by the evil.
He stays at it, day after day, meting out justice.
 At evening he's still at it, strong as ever.
But evil men and women, without conscience
 and without shame, persist in evil.

6 "So I cut off the godless nations.
 I knocked down their defense posts,
Filled her roads with rubble
 so no one could get through.
Her cities were bombed-out ruins,
 unlivable and unlived in.

7 "I thought, 'Surely she'll honor me now,
 accept my discipline and correction,
Find a way of escape from the trouble she's in,
 find relief from the punishment I'm bringing.'
But it didn't faze her. Bright and early
 she was up at it again, doing the same old things.

8 "Well, if that's what you want, stick around."
 GOD's Decree.
"Your day in court is coming,
 but remember I'll be there to bring evidence.

I'll bring all the nations to the courtroom,
    round up all the kingdoms,
And let them feel the brunt of my anger,
    my raging wrath.
My zeal is a fire
    that will purge and purify the earth.

God Is in Charge at the Center

9-13   "In the end I will turn things around for the people.
    I'll give them a language undistorted, unpolluted,
Words to address God in worship
    and, united, to serve me with their shoulders to the wheel.
They'll come from beyond the Ethiopian rivers,
    they'll come praying—
All my scattered, exiled people
    will come home with offerings for worship.
You'll no longer have to be ashamed
    of all those acts of rebellion.
I'll have gotten rid of your arrogant leaders.
    No more pious strutting on my holy hill!
I'll leave a core of people among you
    who are poor in spirit—
What's left of Israel that's really Israel.
    They'll make their home in God.
This core holy people
    will not do wrong.
They won't lie,
    won't use words to flatter or seduce.
Content with who they are and where they are,
    unanxious, they'll live at peace."

14-15   So sing, Daughter Zion!
    Raise the rafters, Israel!
Daughter Jerusalem,
    be happy! celebrate!
God has reversed his judgments against you
    and sent your enemies off chasing their tails.
From now on, God is Israel's king,
    in charge at the center.
There's nothing to fear from evil
    ever again!

God Is Present Among You

16-17   Jerusalem will be told:
    "Don't be afraid.
Dear Zion,
    don't despair.
Your God is present among you,
    a strong Warrior there to save you.
Happy to have you back, he'll calm you with his love

and delight you with his songs.

18-20 "The accumulated sorrows of your exile
    will dissipate.
I, your God, will get rid of them for you.
    You've carried those burdens long enough.
At the same time, I'll get rid of all those
    who've made your life miserable.
I'll heal the maimed;
    I'll bring home the homeless.
In the very countries where they were hated
    they will be venerated.
On Judgment Day
    I'll bring you back home — a great family gathering!
You'll be famous and honored
    all over the world.
You'll see it with your own eyes —
    all those painful partings turned into reunions!"
      GOD's Promise.

HAGGAI

Places of worship are a problem. And the problem does not seem to be architectural. Grand Gothic cathedrals that dominate a city don't ensure that the worship of God dominates that city. Unpainted, ramshackle, clapboard sheds perched precariously on the edge of a prairie don't guarantee a congregation of humble saints in denim.

As we look over the centuries of the many and various building projects in God's name — wilderness tabernacle, revival tent, Gothic cathedral, wayside chapel, synagogue, temple, meetinghouse, storefront mission, the catacombs — there doesn't seem to be any connection between the buildings themselves and the belief and behavior of the people who assemble in them.

In noticing this, it is not uncommon for us to be dismissive of the buildings themselves by saying, "A place of worship is not a building; it's people," or "I prefer worshiping God in the great cathedral of the outdoors." These pronouncements are often tagged with the scriptural punch line, "The God who made the universe doesn't live in custom-made shrines," which is supposed to end the discussion. God doesn't live in buildings — period. That's what we often say.

But then there is Haggai to account for. Haggai was dignified with the title "prophet" (therefore we must take him seriously). His single task, carried out in a three-and-a-half-month mission, was to get God's people to work at rebuilding God's Temple (the same Temple that had been destroyed by God's decree only seventy or so years earlier).

Compared with the great prophets who preached repentance and salvation, Haggai's message doesn't sound very "spiritual." But in God's economy it is perhaps unwise to rank our assigned work as either more or less spiritual. We are not angels; we inhabit space. Material — bricks and mortar, boards and nails — keeps us grounded and connected with the ordinary world in which we necessarily live out our extraordinary beliefs. Haggai keeps us in touch with those times in our lives when repairing the building where we worship is an act of obedience every bit as important as praying in that place of worship.

HAGGAI

CAUGHT UP WITH TAKING CARE OF YOUR OWN HOUSES

1 1 On the first day of the sixth month of the second year in the reign of King Darius of Persia, GOD's Message was delivered by the prophet Haggai to the governor of Judah, Zerubbabel son of Shealtiel, and to the high priest, Joshua son of Jehozadak:

2 A Message from GOD-of-the-Angel-Armies: "The people procrastinate. They say this isn't the right time to rebuild my Temple, the Temple of GOD."

3-4 Shortly after that, GOD said more and Haggai spoke it: "How is it that it's the 'right time' for you to live in your fine new homes while the Home, GOD's Temple, is in ruins?"

5-6 And then a little later, GOD-of-the-Angel-Armies spoke out again:

"Take a good, hard look at your life.
    Think it over.
You have spent a lot of money,
    but you haven't much to show for it.
You keep filling your plates,
    but you never get filled up.
You keep drinking and drinking and drinking,
    but you're always thirsty.
You put on layer after layer of clothes,
    but you can't get warm.
And the people who work for you,
    what are they getting out of it?
Not much—
    a leaky, rusted-out bucket, that's what."

7 That's why GOD-of-the-Angel-Armies said:

"Take a good, hard look at your life.
    Think it over."

8-9 Then GOD said:

"Here's what I want you to do:
    Climb into the hills and cut some timber.
Bring it down and rebuild the Temple.
    Do it just for me. Honor me.
You've had great ambitions for yourselves,
    but nothing has come of it.
The little you have brought to my Temple
    I've blown away—there was nothing to it.

9-11 "And why?" (This is a Message from GOD-of-the-Angel-Armies, remember.) "Because while you've run around, caught up with taking care of your own houses, my Home is in ruins. That's why. Because of your stinginess. And so I've given you a dry summer and a skimpy crop. I've matched your tight-fisted stinginess by decreeing a season of drought, drying up fields and hills, withering gardens and orchards, stunting vegetables and fruit. Nothing—not man or woman, not animal or crop—is going to thrive."

12 Then the governor, Zerubbabel son of Shealtiel, and the high priest, Joshua son of Jehozadak, and all the people with them listened, really listened, to the voice of their GOD. When GOD sent the prophet Haggai to them, they paid attention to him. In listening to Haggai, they honored GOD.

13 Then Haggai, GOD's messenger, preached GOD's Message to the people: "I am with you!" GOD's Word.

14-15 This is how GOD got Zerubbabel, Joshua, and all the people moving—got them working on the Temple of GOD-of-the-Angel-Armies. This happened on the twenty-fourth day of the sixth month in the second year of King Darius.

THIS TEMPLE WILL END UP BETTER THAN IT STARTED OUT

1-3 On the twenty-first day of the seventh month, the Word of GOD came through the prophet Haggai: "Tell Governor Zerubbabel son of Shealtiel and High Priest Joshua son of Jehozadak and all the people: 'Is there anyone here who saw the Temple the way it used to be, all glorious? And what do you see now? Not much, right?

4-5 "'So get to work, Zerubbabel!'—GOD is speaking.
"'Get to work, Joshua son of Jehozadak—high priest!'
"'Get to work, all you people!'—GOD is speaking.
"'Yes, get to work! For I am with you.' The GOD-of-the-Angel-Armies is speaking! 'Put into action the word I covenanted with you when you left Egypt. I'm living and breathing among you right now. Don't be timid. Don't hold back.'

6-7 "This is what GOD-of-the-Angel-Armies said: 'Before you know it, I will shake up sky and earth, ocean and fields. And I'll shake down all the godless nations. They'll bring bushels of wealth and I will fill this Temple with splendor.' GOD-of-the-Angel-Armies says so.

8 'I own the silver,
I own the gold.'
Decree of GOD-of-the-Angel-Armies.

9 "'This Temple is going to end up far better than it started out, a glorious beginning but an even more glorious finish: a place in which I will hand out wholeness and holiness.' Decree of GOD-of-the-Angel-Armies."

10-12 On the twenty-fourth day of the ninth month (again, this was in the second year of Darius), GOD's Message came to Haggai: "GOD-of-the-Angel-Armies speaks: Consult the priests for a ruling. If someone carries a piece of sacred meat in his pocket, meat that is set apart for sacrifice on the altar, and the pocket touches a loaf of bread, a dish of stew, a bottle of wine or oil, or any other food, will these foods be made holy by such contact?"

The priests said, "No."

13 Then Haggai said, "How about someone who is contaminated by touching a corpse—if that person touches one of these foods, will it be contaminated?"

The priests said, "Yes, it will be contaminated."

14 Then Haggai said, "'So, this people is contaminated. Their nation is contaminated. Everything they do is contaminated. Whatever they do for me is contaminated.' GOD says so.

15-17 "'Think back. Before you set out to lay the first foundation stones for the rebuilding of my Temple, how did it go with you? Isn't it true that your foot-dragging, halfhearted efforts at rebuilding the Temple of GOD were reflected in a sluggish, halfway return on your crops—half the grain you were used to getting, half the wine? I hit you with drought and blight and hail. Everything you were doing got hit. But it didn't seem to faze you. You continued to ignore me.' GOD's Decree.

18-19 "'Now think ahead from this same date—this twenty-fourth day of the ninth month. Think ahead from when the Temple rebuilding was launched. Has anything in your fields—vine, fig tree, pomegranate, olive tree—failed to flourish? From now on you can count on a blessing.'"

20-21 GOD's Message came a second time to Haggai on that most memorable day, the twenty-fourth day of the ninth month: "Speak to Zerubbabel, the governor of Judah:

21-23 "'I am about to shake up everything, to turn everything upside down and start over from top to bottom—overthrow governments, destroy foreign powers, dismantle the world of weapons and armaments, throw armies into confusion, so that they end up killing one another. And on that day'"—this is GOD's Message—"'I will take you, O Zerubbabel son of Shealtiel, as my personal servant and I will set you as a signet ring, the sign of my sovereign presence and authority. I've looked over the field and chosen you for this work.'" The Message of GOD-of-the-Angel-Armies.

ZECHARIAH

Zechariah shared with his contemporary Haggai the prophetic task of getting the people of Judah to rebuild their ruined Temple. Their preaching pulled the people out of self-preoccupation and got them working together as a people of God. There was a job to do, and the two prophets teamed up to make sure it got done.

But Zechariah did more than that. For the people were faced with more than a ruined Temple and city. Their self-identity as the people of God was in ruins. For a century they had been knocked around by the world powers, kicked and mocked, used and abused. This once-proud people, their glorious sacred history starred with the names of Abraham, Moses, Samuel, David, and Isaiah, had been treated with contempt for so long that they were in danger of losing all connection with that past, losing their magnificent identity as God's people.

Zechariah was a major factor in recovering the magnificence from the ruins of a degrading exile. Zechariah reinvigorated their imaginations with his visions and messages. The visions provided images of a sovereign God that worked their way into the lives of the people, countering the long ordeal of debasement and ridicule. The messages forged a fresh vocabulary that gave energy and credibility to the long-term purposes of God being worked out in their lives.

But that isn't the end of it. Zechariah's enigmatic visions, working at multiple levels, and his poetically charged messages are at work still, like time capsules in the lives of God's people, continuing to release insight and hope and clarity for the people whom God is using to work out his purposes in a world that has no language for God and the purposes of God.

ZECHARIAH

1-4 In the eighth month of the second year in the reign of Darius, GOD's Message came to the prophet Zechariah son of Berechiah, son of Iddo: "GOD was very angry with your ancestors. So give to the people this Message from GOD-of-the-Angel-Armies: 'Come back to me and I'll come back to you. Don't be like your parents. The old-time prophets called out to them, "A Message from GOD-of-the-Angel-Armies: Leave your evil life. Quit your evil practices." But they ignored everything I said to them, stubbornly refused to listen.'

5-6 "And where are your ancestors now? Dead and buried. And the prophets who preached to them? Also dead and buried. But the Message that my servants the prophets spoke, that isn't dead and buried. That Message did its work on your ancestors, did it not? It woke them up and they came back, saying, 'He did what he said he would do, sure enough. We didn't get by with a thing.'"

FIRST VISION: FOUR RIDERS

7 On the twenty-fourth day of the eleventh month in the second year of the reign of Darius, the Message of GOD was given to the prophet Zechariah son of Berechiah, son of Iddo:

8 One night I looked out and saw a man astride a red horse. He was in the shadows in a grove of birches. Behind him were more horses—a red, a chestnut, and a white.

9 I said, "Sir, what are these horses doing here? What's the meaning of this?"
The Angel-Messenger said, "Let me show you."

10 Then the rider in the birch grove spoke up, "These are the riders that GOD sent to check things out on earth."

11 They reported their findings to the Angel of GOD in the birch grove: "We have looked over the whole earth and all is well. Everything's under control."

12 The Angel of GOD reported back, "O GOD-of-the-Angel-Armies, how long are you going to stay angry with Jerusalem and the cities of Judah? When are you going to let up? Isn't seventy years long enough?"

13-15 GOD reassured the Angel-Messenger—good words, comforting words —who then addressed me: "Tell them this. Tell them that GOD-of-the-Angel-Armies has spoken. This is GOD's Message: 'I care deeply for Jerusalem and Zion. I feel very possessive of them. But I'm thoroughly angry with the godless nations that act as if they own the whole world. I was only moderately angry earlier, but now they've gone too far. I'm going into action.

16-17 "'I've come back to Jerusalem, but with compassion this time.'
    This is GOD speaking.
'I'll see to it that my Temple is rebuilt.'
    A Decree of GOD-of-the-Angel-Armies!
'The rebuilding operation is already staked out.'
    Say it again—a Decree of GOD-of-the-Angel-Armies:
'My cities will prosper again,
    GOD will comfort Zion again,
    Jerusalem will be back in my favor again.'"

SECOND VISION: FOUR HORNS AND FOUR BLACKSMITHS

18 I looked up, and was surprised by another vision: four horns!

19 I asked the Messenger-Angel, "And what's the meaning of this?"

He said, "These are the powers that have scattered Judah, Israel, and Jerusalem abroad."

20 Then GOD expanded the vision to include four blacksmiths.

21 I asked, "And what are these all about?"

He said, "Since the 'horns' scattered Judah so badly that no one had any hope left, these blacksmiths have arrived to combat the horns. They'll dehorn the godless nations who used their horns to scatter Judah to the four winds."

THIRD VISION: THE MAN WITH THE TAPE MEASURE

1-5 I looked up and was surprised to see
a man holding a tape measure in his hand.
I said, "What are you up to?"
"I'm on my way," he said, "to survey Jerusalem,
to measure its width and length."
Just then the Messenger-Angel on his way out
met another angel coming in and said,
"Run! Tell the Surveyor, 'Jerusalem will burst its walls—
bursting with people, bursting with animals.
And I'll be right there with her'—GOD's Decree—'a wall of fire
around unwalled Jerusalem and a radiant presence within.'"

6-7 "Up on your feet! Get out of there—and now!" GOD says so.
"Return from your far exile.
I scattered you to the four winds." GOD's Decree.
"Escape from Babylon, Zion, and come home—now!"

8-9 GOD-of-the-Angel-Armies, the One of Glory who sent me on my mission, commenting on the godless nations who stripped you and left you homeless, said, "Anyone who hits you, hits me—bloodies my nose, blackens my eye. Yes, and at the right time I'll give the signal and they'll be stripped and thrown out by their own servants." Then you'll know for sure that GOD-of-the-Angel-Armies sent me on this mission.

10 "Shout and celebrate, Daughter of Zion!
I'm on my way. I'm moving into your neighborhood!"
GOD's Decree.

11-12 Many godless nations will be linked up with GOD at that time. ("They will become my family! I'll live in their homes!") And then you'll know for sure that GOD-of-the-Angel-Armies sent me on this mission. GOD will reclaim his Judah inheritance in the Holy Land. He'll again make clear that Jerusalem is his choice.

⁕

13 Quiet, everyone! Shh! Silence before GOD. Something's afoot in his holy house. He's on the move!

FOURTH VISION: JOSHUA'S NEW CLOTHES

1-2 3 Next the Messenger-Angel showed me the high priest Joshua. He was standing before GOD's Angel where the Accuser showed up to accuse him. Then GOD said to the Accuser, "I, GOD, rebuke you, Accuser! I rebuke you and choose Jerusalem. Surprise! Everything is going up in flames, but I reach in and pull out Jerusalem!"

3-4 Joshua, standing before the angel, was dressed in dirty clothes. The angel spoke to his attendants, "Get him out of those filthy clothes," and then said to Joshua, "Look, I've stripped you of your sin and dressed you up in clean clothes."

5 I spoke up and said, "How about a clean new turban for his head also?" And they did it—put a clean new turban on his head. Then they finished dressing him, with GOD's Angel looking on.

6-7 GOD's Angel then charged Joshua, "Orders from GOD-of-the-Angel-Armies: 'If you live the way I tell you and remain obedient in my service, then you'll make the decisions around here and oversee my affairs. And all my attendants standing here will be at your service.

8-9 "'Careful, High Priest Joshua—both you and your friends sitting here with you, for your friends are in on this, too! Here's what I'm doing next: I'm introducing my servant Branch. And note this: This stone that I'm placing before Joshua, a single stone with seven eyes'—Decree of GOD-of-the-Angel-Armies—'I'll engrave with these words: "I'll strip this land of its filthy sin, all at once, in a single day."

10 "'At that time, everyone will get along with one another, with friendly visits across the fence, friendly visits on one another's porches.'"

FIFTH VISION: A LAMPSTAND AND TWO OLIVE TREES

1 4 The Messenger-Angel again called me to attention. It was like being wakened out of deep sleep.

2-3 He said, "What do you see?"

I answered, "I see a lampstand of solid gold with a bowl on top. Seven lamps, each with seven spouts, are set on the bowl. And there are two olive trees, one on either side of the bowl."

4 Then I asked the Messenger-Angel, "What does this mean, sir?"

5-7 The Messenger-Angel said, "Can't you tell?"

"No, sir," I said.

Then he said, "This is GOD's Message to Zerubbabel: 'You can't force these things. They only come about through my Spirit,' says GOD-of-the-Angel-Armies. 'So, big mountain, who do you think you are? Next to Zerubbabel you're nothing but a molehill. He'll proceed to set the Cornerstone in place, accompanied by cheers: Yes! Yes! Do it!'"

8-10 After that, the Word of GOD came to me: "Zerubbabel started rebuilding this Temple and he will complete it. That will be your confirmation that GOD-of-the-Angel-Armies sent me to you. Does anyone dare despise this day of small beginnings? They'll change their tune when they see Zerubbabel setting the last stone in place!"

Going back to the vision, the Messenger-Angel said, "The seven lamps are the eyes of GOD probing the dark corners of the world like searchlights."

11-12 "And the two olive trees on either side of the lampstand?" I asked. "What's the meaning of them? And while you're at it, the two branches of the olive trees that feed oil to the lamps — what do they mean?"

13 He said, "You haven't figured that out?"

I said, "No, sir."

14 He said, "These are the two who stand beside the Master of the whole earth and supply golden lamp oil worldwide."

SIXTH VISION: THE FLYING BOOK

1 5 I looked up again and saw — surprise! — a book on the wing! A book flying!

2 The Messenger-Angel said to me, "What do you see now?"

I said, "I see a book flying, a huge book — thirty feet long and fifteen wide!"

3-4 He told me, "This book is the verdict going out worldwide against thieves and liars. The first half of the book disposes of everyone who steals; the second half takes care of everyone who lies. I launched it" — Decree of GOD-of-the-Angel-Armies — "and so it will fly into the house of every thief and every liar. It will land in each house and tear it down, timbers and stones."

SEVENTH VISION: A WOMAN IN A BASKET

5 The Messenger-Angel appeared and said, "Look up. Tell me what you see."

6 I said, "What in the world is that?"

He said, "This is a bushel basket on a journey. It holds the sin of everyone, everywhere."

7 Then the lid made of lead was removed from the basket — and there was a woman sitting in it!

8 He said, "This is Miss Wicked." He pushed her back down into the basket and clamped the lead lid over her.

9 Then I looked up and to my surprise saw two women flying. On outstretched wings they airlifted the bushel basket into the sky.

10 I said to the Messenger-Angel, "Where are they taking the bushel basket?"

11 He said, "East to the land of Shinar. They will build a garage to house it. When it's finished, the basket will be stored there."

EIGHTH VISION: FOUR CHARIOTS

1 6 Once again I looked up — another strange sight! Four chariots charging out from between two mountains. The mountains were bronze.

2-3 The first chariot was drawn by red horses, the second chariot by black horses, the third chariot by white horses, and the fourth chariot by dappled horses. All the horses were powerful.

4 I asked the Messenger-Angel, "Sir, what's the meaning here?"

5-7 The angel answered, "These are the four winds of heaven, which originate with the Master of the whole earth. The black horses are headed north with the white ones right after them. The dappled horses are headed south." The powerful horses galloped out, bursting with energy, eager to patrol through the earth. The Messenger-Angel commanded: "On your way! Survey the earth!" and they were off in every direction.

8 Then he called to me and said, "Look at them go! The ones going north are conveying a sense of my Spirit, serene and secure. No more trouble from that direction."

A Man Named Branch

9-12 Then this Message from GOD came to me: "Take up a collection from the exiles. Target Heldai, Tobiah, and Jedaiah. They've just arrived from Babylon. You'll find them at the home of Josiah son of Zephaniah. Collect silver and gold from them and fashion crowns. Place one on the head of Joshua son of Jehozadak, the high priest, and give him this message:

12-13 "'A Message from GOD-of-the-Angel-Armies. Be alert. We have a man here whose name is Branch. He will branch out from where he is and build the Temple of GOD. Yes, he's the one. He'll build the Temple of GOD. Then he'll assume the role of royalty, take his place on the throne and rule—a priest sitting on the throne!—showing that king and priest can coexist in harmony.'

14 "The other crown will be in the Temple of GOD as a symbol of royalty, under the custodial care of Helem, Tobiah, Jedaiah, and Hen son of Zephaniah.

15 "People will come from faraway places to pitch in and rebuild the Temple of GOD. This will confirm that GOD-of-the-Angel-Armies did, in fact, send me to you. All this follows as you put your minds to a life of responsive obedience to the voice of your GOD."

"You're Interested in Religion, I'm Interested in People"

1 On the fourth day of the ninth month, in the fourth year of the reign of King Darius, GOD's Message again came to Zechariah.

2-3 The town of Bethel had sent a delegation headed by Sarezer and Regem-Melech to pray for GOD's blessing and to confer with the priests of the Temple of GOD-of-the-Angel-Armies, and also with the prophets. They posed this question: "Should we plan for a day of mourning and abstinence next August, the seventieth anniversary of Jerusalem's fall, as we have been doing all these years?"

4-6 GOD-of-the-Angel-Armies gave me this Message for them, for all the people and for the priests: "When you held days of fasting every fifth and seventh month all these seventy years, were you doing it for me? And when you held feasts, was that for me? Hardly. You're interested in religion, I'm interested in people.

7-10 "There's nothing new to say on the subject. Don't you still have the message of the earlier prophets from the time when Jerusalem was still a thriving, bustling city and the outlying countryside, the Negev and Shephelah, was populated? [This is the message that GOD gave Zechariah.] Well, the message hasn't changed. GOD-of-the-Angel-Armies said then and says now:

"'Treat one another justly.
Love your neighbors.
Be compassionate with each other.
Don't take advantage of widows, orphans, visitors, and the poor.
Don't plot and scheme against one another—that's evil.'

11-13 "But did your ancestors listen? No, they set their jaws in defiance. They shut their ears. They steeled themselves against GOD's revelation and the Spirit-filled sermons preached by the earlier prophets by order of GOD-of-the-Angel-Armies. And GOD became angry, really angry, because he told them everything plainly and they wouldn't listen to a word he said.

13-14 "So [this is what GOD-of-the-Angel-Armies said] if they won't listen to me, I won't listen to them. I scattered them to the four winds. They ended up strangers wherever they were. Their 'promised land' became a vacant lot—weeds and tin cans and thistles. Not a sign of life. They turned a dreamland into a wasteland."

REBUILDING THE TEMPLE

1-2 8 And then these Messages from GOD-of-the-Angel-Armies:

A Message from GOD-of-the-Angel-Armies:

"I am zealous for Zion—I *care*!
  I'm angry about Zion—I'm *involved*!"

GOD's Message:

3 "I've come back to Zion,
    I've moved back to Jerusalem.
Jerusalem's new names will be Truth City,
    and Mountain of GOD-of-the-Angel-Armies,
    and Mount Holiness."

4-5 A Message from GOD-of-the-Angel-Armies:
"Old men and old women will come back to Jerusalem, sit on benches on the streets and spin tales, move around safely with their canes—a good city to grow old in. And boys and girls will fill the public parks, laughing and playing—a good city to grow up in."

6 A Message from GOD-of-the-Angel-Armies:
"Do the problems of returning and rebuilding by just a few survivors seem too much? But is anything too much for me? Not if I have my say."

7-8 A Message from GOD-of-the-Angel-Armies:
"I'll collect my people from countries to the east and countries to the west. I'll bring them back and move them into Jerusalem. They'll be my people and I'll be their God. I'll stick with them and do right by them."

9-10 A Message from GOD-of-the-Angel-Armies:
"Get a grip on things. Hold tight, you who are listening to what I say through the preaching of the prophets. The Temple of GOD-of-the-Angel-Armies has been reestablished. The Temple is being rebuilt. We've come through a hard time: You worked for a pittance and were lucky to get that;

the streets were dangerous; you could never let down your guard; I had turned the world into an armed camp.

11-12 "But things have changed. I'm taking the side of my core of surviving people:

Sowing and harvesting will resume,
Vines will grow grapes,
Gardens will flourish,
Dew and rain will make everything green.

12-13 "My core survivors will get everything they need — and more. You've gotten a reputation as a bad-news people, you people of Judah and Israel, but I'm coming to save you. From now on, you're the good-news people. Don't be afraid. Keep a firm grip on what I'm doing."

KEEP YOUR LIVES SIMPLE AND HONEST

14-17 A Message from GOD-of-the-Angel-Armies:

"In the same way that I decided to punish you when your ancestors made me angry, and didn't pull my punches, at this time I've decided to bless Jerusalem and the country of Judah. Don't be afraid. And now here's what I want you to do: Tell the truth, the whole truth, when you speak. Do the right thing by one another, both personally and in your courts. Don't cook up plans to take unfair advantage of others. Don't do or say what isn't so. I hate all that stuff. Keep your lives simple and honest." Decree of GOD.

18-19 Again I received a Message from GOD-of-the-Angel-Armies:

"The days of mourning set for the fourth, fifth, seventh, and tenth months will be turned into days of feasting for Judah — celebration and holiday. Embrace truth! Love peace!"

20-21 A Message from GOD-of-the-Angel-Armies:

"People and their leaders will come from all over to see what's going on. The leaders will confer with one another: 'Shouldn't we try to get in on this? Get in on GOD's blessings? Pray to GOD-of-the-Angel-Armies? What's keeping us? Let's go!'

22 "Lots of people, powerful nations — they'll come to Jerusalem looking for what they can get from GOD-of-the-Angel-Armies, looking to get a blessing from GOD."

23 A Message from GOD-of-the-Angel-Armies:

"At that time, ten men speaking a variety of languages will grab the sleeve of one Jew, hold tight, and say, 'Let us go with you. We've heard that God is with you.'"

THE WHOLE WORLD HAS ITS EYES ON GOD

1-6 **9** War Bulletin:

GOD's Message challenges the country of Hadrach.

It will settle on Damascus.
The whole world has its eyes on GOD.
   Israel isn't the only one.
That includes Hamath at the border,
   and Tyre and Sidon, clever as they think they are.
Tyre has put together quite a kingdom for herself;
   she has stacked up silver like cordwood,
   piled gold high as haystacks.
But God will certainly bankrupt her;
   he will dump all that wealth into the ocean
   and burn up what's left in a big fire.
Ashkelon will see it and panic,
   Gaza will wring its hands,
   Ekron will face a dead end.
Gaza's king will die.
   Ashkelon will be emptied out,
   And a villain will take over in Ashdod.

6-8   "I'll take proud Philistia down a peg:
   I'll make him spit out his bloody booty
   and abandon his vile ways."
What's left will be all God's — a core of survivors,
   a family brought together in Judah —
But enemies like Ekron will go the way of the Jebusites,
   into the dustbin of history.
"I will set up camp in my home country
   and defend it against invaders.
Nobody is going to hurt my people ever again.
   I'm keeping my eye on them.

A HUMBLE KING RIDING A DONKEY

9-10   "Shout and cheer, Daughter Zion!
   Raise the roof, Daughter Jerusalem!
Your king is coming!
   a good king who makes all things right,
   a humble king riding a donkey,
   a mere colt of a donkey.
I've had it with war — no more chariots in Ephraim,
   no more war horses in Jerusalem,
   no more swords and spears, bows and arrows.
He will offer peace to the nations,
   a peaceful rule worldwide,
   from the four winds to the seven seas.

11-13   "And you, because of my blood covenant with you,
   I'll release your prisoners from their hopeless cells.
Come home, hope-filled prisoners!
   This very day I'm declaring a double bonus —
   everything you lost returned twice-over!
Judah is now my weapon, the bow I'll pull,
   setting Ephraim as an arrow to the string.

I'll wake up your sons, O Zion,
   to counter your sons, O Greece.
From now on
   people are my swords."

14-17 Then GOD will come into view,
   his arrows flashing like lightning!
Master GOD will blast his trumpet
   and set out in a whirlwind.
GOD-of-the-Angel-Armies will protect them—
   all-out war,
The war to end all wars,
   no holds barred.
Their GOD will save the day. He'll rescue them.
   They'll become like sheep, gentle and soft,
Or like gemstones in a crown,
   catching all the colors of the sun.
Then how they'll shine! shimmer! glow!
   the young men robust, the young women lovely!

GOD'S WORK OF REBUILDING

1 **10** Pray to GOD for rain—it's time for the spring rain—
   to GOD, the rainmaker,
   Spring thunderstorm maker,
maker of grain and barley.

2-3 "Store-bought gods babble gibberish.
   Religious experts spout rubbish.
They pontificate hot air.
   Their prescriptions are nothing but smoke.
And so the people wander like lost sheep,
   poor lost sheep without a shepherd.
I'm furious with the so-called shepherds.
   They're worse than billy goats, and I'll treat them like goats."

3-5 GOD-of-the-Angel-Armies will step in
   and take care of his flock, the people of Judah.
He'll revive their spirits,
   make them proud to be on God's side.
God will use them in his work of rebuilding,
   use them as foundations and pillars,
Use them as tools and instruments,
   use them to oversee his work.
They'll be a workforce to be proud of, working as one,
   their heads held high, striding through swamps and mud,
Courageous and vigorous because GOD is with them,
   undeterred by the world's thugs.

6-12 "I'll put muscle in the people of Judah;

I'll save the people of Joseph.
I know their pain and will make them good as new.
   They'll get a fresh start, as if nothing had ever happened.
And why? Because I am their very own GOD,
   I'll do what needs to be done for them.
The people of Ephraim will be famous,
   their lives brimming with joy.
Their children will get in on it, too —
   oh, let them feel blessed by GOD!
I'll whistle and they'll all come running.
   I've set them free — oh, how they'll flourish!
Even though I scattered them to the far corners of earth,
   they'll remember me in the faraway places.
They'll keep the story alive in their children,
   and they will come back.
I'll bring them back from the Egyptian west
   and round them up from the Assyrian east.
I'll bring them back to sweet Gilead,
   back to leafy Lebanon.
Every square foot of land
   will be marked by homecoming.
They'll sail through troubled seas, brush aside brash ocean waves.
   Roaring rivers will turn to a trickle.
Gaudy Assyria will be stripped bare,
   bully Egypt exposed as a fraud.
But my people — oh, I'll make them strong, GOD-strong!
   and they'll live my way." GOD says so!

1-4   **11** Open your borders to the immigrants, proud Lebanon!
      Your sentinel trees will burn.
      Weep, great pine trees! Mourn, you sister cedars!
   Your towering trees are cordwood.
Weep Bashan oak trees!
   Your thick forest is now a field of stumps.
Do you hear the wailing of shepherds?
   They've lost everything they once owned.
Do you hear the outrage of the lions?
   The mighty jungle of the Jordan is wasted.
Make room for the returning exiles!

BREAKING THE BEAUTIFUL COVENANT

4-5   GOD commanded me, "Shepherd the sheep that are soon to be slaughtered. The people who buy them will butcher them for quick and easy money. What's worse, they'll get away with it. The people who sell them will say, 'Lucky me! God's on my side; I've got it made!' They have shepherds who couldn't care less about them."

6   GOD's Decree: "I'm washing my hands of the people of this land. From now on they're all on their own. It's dog-eat-dog, survival of the fittest, and the devil take the hindmost. Don't look for help from me."

7-8   So I took over from the crass, money-grubbing owners, and shepherded the sheep marked for slaughter. I got myself two shepherd staffs. I named one Lovely and the other Harmony. Then I went to work shepherding the sheep. Within a month I got rid of the corrupt shepherds. I got tired of putting up with them—and they couldn't stand me.

9 And then I got tired of the sheep and said, "I've had it with you—no more shepherding from me. If you die, you die; if you're attacked, you're attacked. Whoever survives can eat what's left."

10-11 Then I took the staff named Lovely and broke it across my knee, breaking the beautiful covenant I had made with all the peoples. In one stroke, both staff and covenant were broken. The money-hungry owners saw me do it and knew GOD was behind it.

12 Then I addressed them: "Pay me what you think I'm worth." They paid me an insulting sum, counting out thirty silver coins.

13 GOD told me, "Throw it in the poor box." This stingy wage was all they thought of me and my work! So I took the thirty silver coins and threw them into the poor box in GOD's Temple.

14 Then I broke the other staff, Harmony, across my knee, breaking the concord between Judah and Israel.

15-16 GOD then said, "Dress up like a stupid shepherd. I'm going to install just such a shepherd in this land—a shepherd indifferent to victims, who ignores the lost, abandons the injured, and disdains decent citizens. He'll only be in it for what he can get out of it, using and abusing any and all.

17 "Doom to you, useless shepherd,
    walking off and leaving the sheep!
A curse on your arm!
    A curse on your right eye!
Your arm will hang limp and useless.
    Your right eye will go stone blind."

HOME AGAIN IN JERUSALEM

1-2 **12** War Bulletin:

GOD's Message concerning Israel, GOD's Decree—the very GOD who threw the skies into space, set earth on a firm foundation, and breathed his own life into men and women: "Watch for this: I'm about to turn Jerusalem into a cup of strong drink that will have the people who have set siege to Judah and Jerusalem staggering in a drunken stupor.

3 "On the Big Day, I'll turn Jerusalem into a huge stone blocking the way for everyone. All who try to lift it will rupture themselves. All the pagan nations will come together and try to get rid of it.

4-5 "On the Big Day"—this is GOD speaking—"I'll throw all the war horses into a crazed panic, and their riders along with them. But I'll keep my eye on Judah, watching out for her at the same time that I make the enemy horses go blind. The families of Judah will then realize, 'Why, our leaders are strong and able through GOD-of-the-Angel-Armies, their personal God.'

6 "On the Big Day, I'll turn the families of Judah into something like a burning match in a tinder-dry forest, like a fiercely flaming torch in a barn full of hay. They'll burn up everything and everyone in sight—people to the right, people to the left—while Jerusalem fills up with people moving in and making themselves at home—home again in Jerusalem.

7-8 "I, GOD, will begin by restoring the common households of Judah so that the glory of David's family and the leaders in Jerusalem won't over-shadow the ordinary people in Judah. On the Big Day, I'll look after every-one who lives in Jerusalem so that the lowliest, weakest person will be as glorious as David and the family of David itself will be godlike, like the Angel of GOD leading the people.

9 "On the Big Day, I'll make a clean sweep of all the godless nations that fought against Jerusalem.

10-14 "Next I'll deal with the family of David and those who live in Jerusalem. I'll pour a spirit of grace and prayer over them. They'll then be able to recognize me as the One they so grievously wounded—that piercing spear-thrust! And they'll weep—oh, how they'll weep! Deep mourning as of a parent grieving the loss of the firstborn child. The lamentation in Jerusalem that day will be massive, as famous as the lamentation over Hadad-Rimmon on the fields of Megiddo:

Everyone will weep and grieve,
    the land and everyone in it:
The family of David off by itself
    and their women off by themselves;
The family of Nathan off by itself
    and their women off by themselves;
The family of Levi off by itself
    and their women off by themselves;
The family of Shimei off by itself
    and their women off by themselves;
And all the rest of the families off by themselves
    and their women off by themselves."

WASHING AWAY SINS

1 # 13 "On the Big Day, a fountain will be opened for the family of David and all the leaders of Jerusalem for washing away their sins, for scrubbing their stained and soiled lives clean.

2-3 "On the Big Day"—this is GOD-of-the-Angel-Armies speaking—"I will wipe out the store-bought gods, erase their names from memory. People will forget they ever heard of them. And I'll get rid of the prophets who pol-luted the air with their diseased words. If anyone dares persist in spreading diseased, polluting words, his very own parents will step in and say, 'That's it! You're finished! Your lies about GOD put everyone in danger,' and then they'll stab him to death in the very act of prophesying lies about GOD—his own parents, mind you!

4-6 "On the Big Day, the lying prophets will be publicly exposed and humili-ated. Then they'll wish they'd never swindled people with their 'visions.' No more masquerading in prophet clothes. But they'll deny they've even heard of such things: 'Me, a prophet? Not me. I'm a farmer—grew up on the farm.' And if someone says, 'And so where did you get that black eye?' they'll say, 'I ran into a door at a friend's house.'

7-9 "Sword, get moving against my shepherd,
    against my close associate!"

Decree of GOD-of-the-Angel-Armies.
"Kill the shepherd! Scatter the sheep!
    The back of my hand against even the lambs!
All across the country" — GOD's Decree —
    "two-thirds will be devastated
    and one-third survive.
I'll deliver the surviving third to the refinery fires.
    I'll refine them as silver is refined,
    test them for purity as gold is tested.
Then they'll pray to me by name
    and I'll answer them personally.
I'll say, 'That's my people.'
    They'll say, 'GOD — my God!'"

THE DAY IS COMING

1-2   **14** Note well: GOD's Judgment Day is on the way:
    "Plunder will be piled high and handed out.
    I'm bringing all the godless nations
to war against Jerusalem —
Houses plundered,
    women raped,
Half the city taken into exile,
    the other half left behind."

3-5   But then GOD will march out against the godless nations and fight — a great war! That's the Day he'll take his stand on the Mount of Olives, facing Jerusalem from the east. The Mount of Olives will be split right down the middle, from east to west, leaving a wide valley. Half the mountain will shift north, the other half south. Then you will run for your lives down the valley, your escape route that will take you all the way to Azal. You'll run for your lives, just as you ran on the day of the great earthquake in the days of Uzziah, king of Judah. Then my GOD will arrive and all the holy angels with him.

6-7   What a Day that will be! No more cold nights — in fact, no more nights! The Day is coming — the timing is GOD's — when it will be continuous day. Every evening will be a fresh morning.

8   What a Day that will be! Fresh flowing rivers out of Jerusalem, half to the eastern sea, half to the western sea, flowing year-round, summer and winter!

9   GOD will be king over all the earth, one GOD and only one. What a Day that will be!

10-11   The land will stretch out spaciously around Jerusalem — to Geba in the north and Rimmon in the south, with Jerusalem towering at the center, and the commanding city gates — Gate of Benjamin to First Gate to Corner Gate to Hananel Tower to the Royal Winery — ringing the city full of people. Never again will Jerusalem be totally destroyed. From now on it will be a safe city.

12-14   But this is what will happen to all who fought against Jerusalem: GOD will visit them with a terrible plague. People's flesh will rot off their bones while they are walking around; their eyes will rot in their sockets and their tongues in their mouths; people will be dying on their feet! Mass hysteria when that happens—total panic! Fellow soldiers fighting and killing each other—holy terror! And then Judah will jump into the fray!

14-15 Treasures from all the nations will be piled high—gold, silver, the latest fashions. The plague will also hit the animals—horses, mules, camels, donkeys. Everything alive in the military camps will be hit by the plague.

16-19 All the survivors from the godless nations that fought against Jerusalem will travel to Jerusalem every year to worship the King, GOD-of-the-Angel-Armies, and celebrate the Feast of Booths. If any of these survivors fail to make the annual pilgrimage to Jerusalem to worship the King, GOD-of-the-Angel-Armies, there will be no rain. If the Egyptians don't make the pilgrimage and worship, there will be no rain for them. Every nation that does not go up to celebrate the Feast of Booths will be hit with the plague. Egypt and any other nation that does not make pilgrimage to celebrate the Feast of Booths gets punished.

20-21 On that Day, the Big Day, all the horses' harness bells will be inscribed "Holy to GOD." The cooking pots in the Temple of GOD will be as sacred as chalices and plates on the altar. In fact, all the pots and pans in all the kitchens of Jerusalem and Judah will be holy to GOD-of-the-Angel-Armies. People who come to worship, preparing meals and sacrifices, will use them. On that Big Day there will be no buying or selling in the Temple of GOD-of-the-Angel-Armies.

MALACHI

Most of life is not lived in crisis—which is a good thing. Not many of us would be able to sustain a life of perpetual pain or loss or ecstasy or challenge. But crisis has this to say for it: In time of crisis everything, absolutely everything, is important and significant. Life itself is on the line. No word is casual, no action marginal. And almost always, God and our relationship with God is on the front page.

But during the humdrum times, when things are, as we tend to say, "normal," our interest in God is crowded to the margins of our lives and we become preoccupied with ourselves. "Religion" during such times is trivialized into asking "God-questions"—calling God into question or complaining about him, treating the worship of God as a mere hobby or diversion, managing our personal affairs (such as marriage) for our own convenience and disregarding what God has to say about them, going about our usual activities as if God were not involved in such dailiness.

The prophecy of Malachi is made to order for just such conditions. Malachi creates a crisis at a time when we are unaware of crisis. He wakes us up to the crisis of God during the times when the only thing we are concerned with is us. He keeps us on our toes, listening for God, waiting in anticipation for God, ready to respond to God, who is always coming to us.

Malachi gets in the last word of Holy Scripture in the Old Testament. The final sentences in his message to us evoke the gigantic figures of Moses and Elijah—Moses to keep us rooted in what God has done and said in the past, Elijah to keep us alert to what God will do in the days ahead. By leaving us in the company of mighty Moses and fiery Elijah, Malachi considerably reduces the danger of our trivializing matters of God and the soul.

MALACHI

NO MORE OF THIS SO-CALLED WORSHIP!

1 A Message. GOD's Word to Israel through Malachi:

2-3 GOD said, "I love you."

You replied, "Really? How have you loved us?"

"Look at history" (this is GOD's answer). "Look at how differently I've treated you, Jacob, from Esau: I loved Jacob and hated Esau. I reduced pretentious Esau to a molehill, turned his whole country into a ghost town."

4 When Edom (Esau) said, "We've been knocked down, but we'll get up and start over, good as new," GOD-of-the-Angel-Armies said, "Just try it and see how far you get. When I knock you down, you stay down. People will take one look at you and say, 'Land of Evil!' and 'the GOD-cursed tribe!'

5 "Yes, take a good look. Then you'll see how faithfully I've loved you and you'll want even more, saying, 'May GOD be even greater, beyond the borders of Israel!'

6 "Isn't it true that a son honors his father and a worker his master? So if I'm your Father, where's the honor? If I'm your Master, where's the respect?" GOD-of-the-Angel-Armies is calling you on the carpet: "You priests despise me!

"You say, 'Not so! How do we despise you?'

"By your shoddy, sloppy, defiling worship.

"You ask, 'What do you mean, "defiling"? What's defiling about it?'

7-8 "When you say, 'The altar of GOD is not important anymore; worship of GOD is no longer a priority,' that's defiling. And when you offer worthless animals for sacrifices in worship, animals that you're trying to get rid of—blind and sick and crippled animals—isn't that defiling? Try a trick like that with your banker or your senator—how far do you think it will get you?" GOD-of-the-Angel-Armies asks you.

9 "Get on your knees and pray that I will be gracious to you. You priests have gotten everyone in trouble. With this kind of conduct, do you think I'll pay attention to you?" GOD-of-the-Angel-Armies asks you.

10 "Why doesn't one of you just shut the Temple doors and lock them? Then none of you can get in and play at religion with this silly, empty-headed worship. I am not pleased. The GOD-of-the-Angel-Armies is not pleased. And I don't want any more of this so-called worship!

OFFERING GOD SOMETHING HAND-ME-DOWN, BROKEN, OR USELESS

11 "I am honored all over the world. And there are people who know how to worship me all over the world, who honor me by bringing their best to me. They're saying it everywhere: 'God is greater, this GOD-of-the-Angel-Armies.'

12-13 "All except you. Instead of honoring me, you profane me. You profane me when you say, 'Worship is not important, and what we bring to worship is of no account,' and when you say, 'I'm bored—this doesn't do anything for me.' You act so superior, sticking your noses in the air—act superior to *me*, GOD-of-the-Angel-Armies! And when you do offer something to me, it's a hand-me-down, or broken, or useless. Do you think I'm going to accept it? This is GOD speaking to you!

14   "A curse on the person who makes a big show of doing something great for me — an expensive sacrifice, say — and then at the last minute brings in something puny and worthless! I'm a great king, GOD-of-the-Angel-Armies, honored far and wide, and I'll not put up with it!"

DESECRATING THE HOLINESS OF GOD

1-3   2 "And now this indictment, you priests! If you refuse to obediently listen, and if you refuse to honor me, GOD-of-the-Angel-Armies, in worship, then I'll put you under a curse. I'll exchange all your blessings for curses. In fact, the curses are already at work because you're not serious about honoring me. Yes, and the curse will extend to your children. I'm going to plaster your faces with rotting garbage, garbage thrown out from your feasts. That's what you have to look forward to!

4-6   "Maybe that will wake you up. Maybe then you'll realize that I'm indicting you in order to put new life into my covenant with the priests of Levi, the covenant of GOD-of-the-Angel-Armies. My covenant with Levi was to give life and peace. I kept my covenant with him, and he honored me. He stood in reverent awe before me. He taught the truth and did not lie. He walked with me in peace and uprightness. He kept many out of the ditch, kept them on the road.

7-9   "It's the job of priests to teach the truth. People are supposed to look to them for guidance. The priest is the messenger of GOD-of-the-Angel-Armies. But you priests have abandoned the way of priests. Your teaching has messed up many lives. You have corrupted the covenant of priest Levi. GOD-of-the-Angel-Armies says so. And so I am showing you up for who you are. Everyone will be disgusted with you and avoid you because you don't live the way I told you to live, and you don't teach my revelation truly and impartially."

10   Don't we all come from one Father? Aren't we all created by the same God? So why can't we get along? Why do we desecrate the covenant of our ancestors that binds us together?

11-12   Judah has cheated on GOD — a sickening violation of trust in Israel and Jerusalem: Judah has desecrated the holiness of GOD by falling in love and running off with foreign women, women who worship alien gods. GOD's curse on those who do this! Drive them out of house and home! They're no longer fit to be part of the community no matter how many offerings they bring to GOD-of-the-Angel-Armies.

13-15   And here's a second offense: You fill the place of worship with your whining and sniveling because you don't get what you want from GOD. Do you know why? Simple. Because GOD was there as a witness when you spoke your marriage vows to your young bride, and now you've broken those vows, broken the faith-bond with your vowed companion, your covenant wife. GOD, not you, made marriage. His Spirit inhabits even the smallest details of marriage. And what does he want from marriage? Children of God, that's what. So guard the spirit of marriage within you. Don't cheat on your spouse.

16   "I hate divorce," says the GOD of Israel. GOD-of-the-Angel-Armies says, "I hate the violent dismembering of the 'one flesh' of marriage." So watch yourselves. Don't let your guard down. Don't cheat.

17   You make GOD tired with all your talk.

"How do we tire him out?" you ask.

By saying, "GOD loves sinners and sin alike. GOD loves all." And also by saying, "Judgment? GOD's too nice to judge."

THE MASTER YOU'VE BEEN LOOKING FOR

1   **3** "Look! I'm sending my messenger on ahead to clear the way for me. Suddenly, out of the blue, the Leader you've been looking for will enter his Temple—yes, the Messenger of the Covenant, the one you've been waiting for. Look! He's on his way!" A Message from the mouth of GOD-of-the-Angel-Armies.

2-4   But who will be able to stand up to that coming? Who can survive his appearance?

He'll be like white-hot fire from the smelter's furnace. He'll be like the strongest lye soap at the laundry. He'll take his place as a refiner of silver, as a cleanser of dirty clothes. He'll scrub the Levite priests clean, refine them like gold and silver, until they're fit for GOD, fit to present offerings of righteousness. Then, and only then, will Judah and Jerusalem be fit and pleasing to GOD, as they used to be in the years long ago.

5   "Yes, I'm on my way to visit you with Judgment. I'll present compelling evidence against sorcerers, adulterers, liars, those who exploit workers, those who take advantage of widows and orphans, those who are inhospitable to the homeless—anyone and everyone who doesn't honor me." A Message from GOD-of-the-Angel-Armies.

6-7   "I am GOD—yes, I AM. I haven't changed. And because I haven't changed, you, the descendants of Jacob, haven't been destroyed. You have a long history of ignoring my commands. You haven't done a thing I've told you. Return to me so I can return to you," says GOD-of-the-Angel-Armies.

"You ask, 'But how do we return?'

8-11   "Begin by being honest. Do honest people rob God? But you rob me day after day.

"You ask, 'How have we robbed you?'

"The tithe and the offering—that's how! And now you're under a curse—the whole lot of you—because you're robbing me. Bring your full tithe to the Temple treasury so there will be ample provisions in my Temple. Test me in this and see if I don't open up heaven itself to you and pour out blessings beyond your wildest dreams. For my part, I will defend you against marauders, protect your wheat fields and vegetable gardens against plunderers." The Message of GOD-of-the-Angel-Armies.

12   "You'll be voted 'Happiest Nation.' You'll experience what it's like to be a country of grace." GOD-of-the-Angel-Armies says so.

THE DIFFERENCE BETWEEN SERVING GOD AND NOT SERVING HIM

13   GOD says, "You have spoken hard, rude words to me.

"You ask, 'When did we ever do that?'

14-15   "When you said, 'It doesn't pay to serve God. What do we ever get out of it? When we did what he said and went around with long faces, serious about GOD-of-the-Angel-Armies, what difference did it make? Those who take life into their own hands are the lucky ones. They break all the rules and get ahead anyway. They push God to the limit and get by with it.'"

16 Then those whose lives honored GOD got together and talked it over. GOD saw what they were doing and listened in. A book was opened in God's presence and minutes were taken of the meeting, with the names of the GOD-fearers written down, all the names of those who honored GOD's name.

17-18 GOD-of-the-Angel-Armies said, "They're mine, all mine. They'll get special treatment when I go into action. I treat them with the same consideration and kindness that parents give the child who honors them. Once more you'll see the difference it makes between being a person who does the right thing and one who doesn't, between serving God and not serving him."

THE SUN OF RIGHTEOUSNESS WILL DAWN

1-3 4 "Count on it: The day is coming, raging like a forest fire. All the arrogant people who do evil things will be burned up like stove wood, burned to a crisp, nothing left but scorched earth and ash — a black day. But for you, sunrise! The sun of righteousness will dawn on those who honor my name, healing radiating from its wings. You will be bursting with energy, like colts frisky and frolicking. And you'll tromp on the wicked. They'll be nothing but ashes under your feet on that Day." GOD-of-the-Angel-Armies says so.

4 "Remember and keep the revelation I gave through my servant Moses, the revelation I commanded at Horeb for all Israel, all the rules and procedures for right living.

5-6 "But also look ahead: I'm sending Elijah the prophet to clear the way for the Big Day of GOD — the decisive Judgment Day! He will convince parents to look after their children and children to look up to their parents. If they refuse, I'll come and put the land under a curse."

THE NEW TESTAMENT

THE NEW TESTAMENT

The arrival of Jesus signaled the beginning of a new era. God entered history in a personal way, and made it unmistakably clear that he is on our side, doing everything possible to save us. It was all presented and worked out in the life, death, and resurrection of Jesus. It was, and is, hard to believe — seemingly too good to be true.

But one by one, men and women did believe it, believed Jesus was God alive among them and for them. Soon they would realize that he also lived in them. To their great surprise they found themselves living in a world where God called all the shots — had the first word on everything; had the last word on everything. That meant that everything, quite literally every thing, had to be re-centered, re-imagined, and re-thought.

They went at it with immense gusto. They told stories of Jesus and arranged his teachings in memorable form. They wrote letters. They sang songs. They prayed. One of them wrote an extraordinary poem based on holy visions. There was no apparent organization to any of this; it was all more or less spontaneous and, to the eye of the casual observer, haphazard. Over the course of about fifty years, these writings added up to what would later be compiled by the followers of Jesus and designated "The New Testament."

Three kinds of writing — eyewitness stories, personal letters, and a visionary poem — make up the book. Five stories, twenty-one letters, one poem.

In the course of this writing and reading, collecting and arranging, with no one apparently in charge, the early Christians, whose lives were being changed and shaped by what they were reading, arrived at the conviction that there was, in fact, someone in charge — God's Holy Spirit was behind and in it all. In retrospect, they could see that it was not at all random or haphazard, that every word worked with every other word, and that all the separate documents worked in intricate harmony. There was nothing accidental in any of this, nothing merely circumstantial. They were bold to call what had been written "God's Word," and trusted their lives to it. They accepted its authority over their lives. Most of its readers since have been similarly convinced.

A striking feature in all this writing is that it was done in the street language of the day, the idiom of the playground and marketplace. In the Greek-speaking world of that day, there were two levels of language: formal and informal. Formal language was used to write philosophy and history, government decrees and epic poetry. If someone were to sit down and consciously write for posterity, it would of course be written in this formal language with its learned vocabulary and precise diction. But if the writing was routine — shopping lists, family letters, bills, and receipts — it was written in the common, informal idiom of everyday speech, street language.

And this is the language used throughout the New Testament. Some people are taken aback by this, supposing that language dealing with a holy God and holy things should be elevated — stately and ceremonial. But one good look at Jesus — his preference for down-to-earth stories and easy association with common people — gets rid of that supposition. For Jesus is the descent of God to our lives, just as they are, not the ascent of our lives to God, hoping he might approve when he sees how hard we try.

And that is why the followers of Jesus in their witness and preaching, translating and teaching, have always done their best to get the Message — the "good news" — into the language of whatever streets they happen to be living on. In order to understand the Message right, the language must be right — not a refined language that appeals to our aspirations after the best but a rough and earthy language that reveals God's presence and action where we least expect it, catching us when we are up to our elbows in the soiled ordinariness of our lives and God is the furthest thing from our minds.

This version of the New Testament in a contemporary idiom keeps the language of the Message current and fresh and understandable in the same language in which we do our shopping, talk with our friends, worry about world affairs, and teach our children their table manners. The goal is not to render a word-for-word conversion of Greek into English, but rather to convert the tone, the rhythm, the events, the ideas, into the way we actually think and speak.

In the midst of doing this work, I realized that this is exactly what I have been doing all my vocational life. For thirty-five years as a pastor I stood at the border between two languages, biblical Greek and everyday English, acting as a translator, providing the right phrases, getting the right words so that the men and women to whom I was pastor could find their way around and get along in this world where God has spoken so decisively and clearly in Jesus. I did it from the pulpit and in the kitchen, in hospitals and restaurants, on parking lots and at picnics, always looking for an English way to make the biblical text relevant to the conditions of the people.

MATTHEW

The story of Jesus doesn't begin with Jesus. God had been at work for a long time. Salvation, which is the main business of Jesus, is an old business. Jesus is the coming together in final form of themes and energies and movements that had been set in motion before the foundation of the world.

Matthew opens the New Testament by setting the local story of Jesus in its world historical context. He makes sure that as we read his account of the birth, life, death, and resurrection of Jesus, we see the connections with everything that has gone before. "Fulfilled" is one of Matthew's characteristic verbs: such and such happened "that it might be *fulfilled.*" Jesus is unique, but he is not odd.

Better yet, Matthew tells the story in such a way that not only is everything previous to us completed in Jesus; *we* are completed in Jesus. Every day we wake up in the middle of something that is already going on, that has been going on for a long time: genealogy and geology, history and culture, the cosmos — God. We are neither accidental nor incidental to the story. We get orientation, briefing, background, reassurance.

Matthew provides the comprehensive context by which we see all God's creation and salvation completed in Jesus, and all the parts of our lives — work, family, friends, memories, dreams — also completed in Jesus. Lacking such a context, we are in danger of seeing Jesus as a mere diversion from the concerns announced in the newspapers. Nothing could be further from the truth.

MATTHEW

1 The family tree of Jesus Christ, David's son, Abraham's son:

2-6 Abraham had Isaac,
Isaac had Jacob,
Jacob had Judah and his brothers,
Judah had Perez and Zerah (the mother was Tamar),
Perez had Hezron,
Hezron had Aram,
Aram had Amminadab,
Amminadab had Nahshon,
Nahshon had Salmon,
Salmon had Boaz (his mother was Rahab),
Boaz had Obed (Ruth was the mother),
Obed had Jesse,
Jesse had David,
    and David became king.

6-11 David had Solomon (Uriah's wife was the mother),
Solomon had Rehoboam,
Rehoboam had Abijah,
Abijah had Asa,
Asa had Jehoshaphat,
Jehoshaphat had Joram,
Joram had Uzziah,
Uzziah had Jotham,
Jotham had Ahaz,
Ahaz had Hezekiah,
Hezekiah had Manasseh,
Manasseh had Amon,
Amon had Josiah,
Josiah had Jehoiachin and his brothers,
    and then the people were taken into the Babylonian exile.

12-16 When the Babylonian exile ended,
Jeconiah had Shealtiel,
Shealtiel had Zerubbabel,
Zerubbabel had Abiud,
Abiud had Eliakim,
Eliakim had Azor,
Azor had Zadok,
Zadok had Achim,
Achim had Eliud,
Eliud had Eleazar,
Eleazar had Matthan,
Matthan had Jacob,
Jacob had Joseph, Mary's husband,
    the Mary who gave birth to Jesus,
    the Jesus who was called Christ.

17 There were fourteen generations from Abraham to David,
another fourteen from David to the Babylonian exile,
and yet another fourteen from the Babylonian exile to Christ.

THE BIRTH OF JESUS

18-19 The birth of Jesus took place like this. His mother, Mary, was engaged to be married to Joseph. Before they came to the marriage bed, Joseph discovered she was pregnant. (It was by the Holy Spirit, but he didn't know that.) Joseph, chagrined but noble, determined to take care of things quietly so Mary would not be disgraced.

20-23 While he was trying to figure a way out, he had a dream. God's angel spoke in the dream: "Joseph, son of David, don't hesitate to get married. Mary's pregnancy is Spirit-conceived. God's Holy Spirit has made her pregnant. She will bring a son to birth, and when she does, you, Joseph, will name him Jesus — 'God saves' — because he will save his people from their sins." This would bring the prophet's embryonic sermon to full term:

Watch for this — a virgin will get pregnant and bear a son;
They will name him Immanuel (Hebrew for "God is with us").

24-25 Then Joseph woke up. He did exactly what God's angel commanded in the dream: He married Mary. But he did not consummate the marriage until she had the baby. He named the baby Jesus.

SCHOLARS FROM THE EAST

1-2 2 After Jesus was born in Bethlehem village, Judah territory — this was during Herod's kingship — a band of scholars arrived in Jerusalem from the East. They asked around, "Where can we find and pay homage to the newborn King of the Jews? We observed a star in the eastern sky that signaled his birth. We're on pilgrimage to worship him."

3-4 When word of their inquiry got to Herod, he was terrified — and not Herod alone, but most of Jerusalem as well. Herod lost no time. He gathered all the high priests and religion scholars in the city together and asked, "Where is the Messiah supposed to be born?"

5-6 They told him, "Bethlehem, Judah territory. The prophet Micah wrote it plainly:

It's you, Bethlehem, in Judah's land,
no longer bringing up the rear.
From you will come the leader
who will shepherd-rule my people, my Israel."

7-8 Herod then arranged a secret meeting with the scholars from the East. Pretending to be as devout as they were, he got them to tell him exactly when the birth-announcement star appeared. Then he told them the prophecy about Bethlehem, and said, "Go find this child. Leave no stone unturned. As soon as you find him, send word and I'll join you at once in your worship."

9-10 Instructed by the king, they set off. Then the star appeared again, the same star they had seen in the eastern skies. It led them on until it hovered over the place of the child. They could hardly contain themselves: They were in the right place! They had arrived at the right time!

11 They entered the house and saw the child in the arms of Mary, his mother. Overcome, they kneeled and worshiped him. Then they opened their luggage and presented gifts: gold, frankincense, myrrh.

12 In a dream, they were warned not to report back to Herod. So they worked out another route, left the territory without being seen, and returned to their own country.

13 After the scholars were gone, God's angel showed up again in Joseph's dream and commanded, "Get up. Take the child and his mother and flee to Egypt. Stay until further notice. Herod is on the hunt for this child, and wants to kill him."

14-15 Joseph obeyed. He got up, took the child and his mother under cover of darkness. They were out of town and well on their way by daylight. They lived in Egypt until Herod's death. This Egyptian exile fulfilled what Hosea had preached: "I called my son out of Egypt."

16-18 Herod, when he realized that the scholars had tricked him, flew into a rage. He commanded the murder of every little boy two years old and under who lived in Bethlehem and its surrounding hills. (He determined that age from information he'd gotten from the scholars.) That's when Jeremiah's sermon was fulfilled:

A sound was heard in Ramah,
    weeping and much lament.
Rachel weeping for her children,
    Rachel refusing all solace,
Her children gone,
    dead and buried.

19-20 Later, when Herod died, God's angel appeared in a dream to Joseph in Egypt: "Up, take the child and his mother and return to Israel. All those out to murder the child are dead."

21-23 Joseph obeyed. He got up, took the child and his mother, and reentered Israel. When he heard, though, that Archelaus had succeeded his father, Herod, as king in Judea, he was afraid to go there. But then Joseph was directed in a dream to go to the hills of Galilee. On arrival, he settled in the village of Nazareth. This move was a fulfillment of the prophetic words, "He shall be called a Nazarene."

THUNDER IN THE DESERT!

1-2 While Jesus was living in the Galilean hills, John, called "the Baptizer," was preaching in the desert country of Judea. His message was simple and austere, like his desert surroundings: "Change your life. God's kingdom is here."

3 John and his message were authorized by Isaiah's prophecy:

Thunder in the desert!
Prepare for God's arrival!
Make the road smooth and straight!

4-6 John dressed in a camel-hair habit tied at the waist by a leather strap. He lived on a diet of locusts and wild field honey. People poured out of Jerusalem, Judea, and the Jordanian countryside to hear and see him in action. There at the Jordan River those who came to confess their sins were baptized into a changed life.

7-10 When John realized that a lot of Pharisees and Sadducees were show-ing up for a baptismal experience because it was becoming the popular thing to do, he exploded: "Brood of snakes! What do you think you're doing slith-ering down here to the river? Do you think a little water on your snakeskins is going to make any difference? It's your life that must change, not your skin! And don't think you can pull rank by claiming Abraham as father. Being a descendant of Abraham is neither here nor there. Descendants of Abraham are a dime a dozen. What counts is your life. Is it green and blos-soming? Because if it's deadwood, it goes on the fire.

11-12 "I'm baptizing you here in the river, turning your old life in for a king-dom life. The real action comes next: The main character in this dra-ma—compared to him I'm a mere stagehand—will ignite the kingdom life within you, a fire within you, the Holy Spirit within you, changing you from the inside out. He's going to clean house—make a clean sweep of your lives. He'll place everything true in its proper place before God; everything false he'll put out with the trash to be burned."

13-14 Jesus then appeared, arriving at the Jordan River from Galilee. He wanted John to baptize him. John objected, "I'm the one who needs to be baptized, not *you!*"

15 But Jesus insisted. "Do it. God's work, putting things right all these centuries, is coming together right now in this baptism." So John did it.

16-17 The moment Jesus came up out of the baptismal waters, the skies opened up and he saw God's Spirit—it looked like a dove—descending and land-ing on him. And along with the Spirit, a voice: "This is my Son, chosen and marked by my love, delight of my life."

THE TEST

1-3 **4** Next Jesus was taken into the wild by the Spirit for the Test. The Devil was ready to give it. Jesus prepared for the Test by fasting forty days and forty nights. That left him, of course, in a state of extreme hunger, which the Devil took advantage of in the first test: "Since you are God's Son, speak the word that will turn these stones into loaves of bread."

4 Jesus answered by quoting Deuteronomy: "It takes more than bread to stay alive. It takes a steady stream of words from God's mouth."

5-6 For the second test the Devil took him to the Holy City. He sat him on top of the Temple and said, "Since you are God's Son, jump." The Devil goaded him by quoting Psalm 91: "He has placed you in the care of angels. They will catch you so that you won't so much as stub your toe on a stone."

7 Jesus countered with another citation from Deuteronomy: "Don't you dare test the Lord your God."

8-9 For the third test, the Devil took him to the peak of a huge mountain. He gestured expansively, pointing out all the earth's kingdoms, how glori-ous they all were. Then he said, "They're yours—lock, stock, and barrel. Just go down on your knees and worship me, and they're yours."

10 Jesus' refusal was curt: "Beat it, Satan!" He backed his rebuke with a

third quotation from Deuteronomy: "Worship the Lord your God, and only him. Serve him with absolute single-heartedness."

11   The Test was over. The Devil left. And in his place, angels! Angels came and took care of Jesus' needs.

TEACHING AND HEALING

12-17   When Jesus got word that John had been arrested, he returned to Galilee. He moved from his hometown, Nazareth, to the lakeside village Capernaum, nestled at the base of the Zebulun and Naphtali hills. This move completed Isaiah's sermon:

> Land of Zebulun, land of Naphtali,
>   road to the sea, over Jordan,
>   Galilee, crossroads for the nations.
> People sitting out their lives in the dark
>   saw a huge light;
> Sitting in that dark, dark country of death,
>   they watched the sun come up.

This Isaiah-prophesied sermon came to life in Galilee the moment Jesus started preaching. He picked up where John left off: "Change your life. God's kingdom is here."

18-20   Walking along the beach of Lake Galilee, Jesus saw two brothers: Simon (later called Peter) and Andrew. They were fishing, throwing their nets into the lake. It was their regular work. Jesus said to them, "Come with me. I'll make a new kind of fisherman out of you. I'll show you how to catch men and women instead of perch and bass." They didn't ask questions, but simply dropped their nets and followed.

21-22   A short distance down the beach they came upon another pair of brothers, James and John, Zebedee's sons. These two were sitting in a boat with their father, Zebedee, mending their fishnets. Jesus made the same offer to them, and they were just as quick to follow, abandoning boat and father.

23-25   From there he went all over Galilee. He used synagogues for meeting places and taught people the truth of God. God's kingdom was his theme—that beginning right now they were under God's government, a good government! He also healed people of their diseases and of the bad effects of their bad lives. Word got around the entire Roman province of Syria. People brought anybody with an ailment, whether mental, emotional, or physical. Jesus healed them, one and all. More and more people came, the momentum gathering. Besides those from Galilee, crowds came from the "Ten Towns" across the lake, others up from Jerusalem and Judea, still others from across the Jordan.

YOU'RE BLESSED

1-2   **5** When Jesus saw his ministry drawing huge crowds, he climbed a hillside. Those who were apprenticed to him, the committed, climbed with him. Arriving at a quiet place, he sat down and taught his climbing companions. This is what he said:

3   "You're blessed when you're at the end of your rope. With less of you there is more of God and his rule.

4   "You're blessed when you feel you've lost what is most dear to you. Only

then can you be embraced by the One most dear to you.

5 "You're blessed when you're content with just who you are — no more, no less. That's the moment you find yourselves proud owners of everything that can't be bought.

6 "You're blessed when you've worked up a good appetite for God. He's food and drink in the best meal you'll ever eat.

7 "You're blessed when you care. At the moment of being 'care-full,' you find yourselves cared for.

8 "You're blessed when you get your inside world — your mind and heart — put right. Then you can see God in the outside world.

9 "You're blessed when you can show people how to cooperate instead of compete or fight. That's when you discover who you really are, and your place in God's family.

10 "You're blessed when your commitment to God provokes persecution. The persecution drives you even deeper into God's kingdom.

11-12 "Not only that — count yourselves blessed every time people put you down or throw you out or speak lies about you to discredit me. What it means is that the truth is too close for comfort and they are uncomfortable. You can be glad when that happens — give a cheer, even! — for though they don't like it, *I* do! And all heaven applauds. And know that you are in good company. My prophets and witnesses have always gotten into this kind of trouble.

SALT AND LIGHT

13 "Let me tell you why you are here. You're here to be salt-seasoning that brings out the God-flavors of this earth. If you lose your saltiness, how will people taste godliness? You've lost your usefulness and will end up in the garbage.

14-16 "Here's another way to put it: You're here to be light, bringing out the God-colors in the world. God is not a secret to be kept. We're going public with this, as public as a city on a hill. If I make you light-bearers, you don't think I'm going to hide you under a bucket, do you? I'm putting you on a light stand. Now that I've put you there on a hilltop, on a light stand — shine! Keep open house; be generous with your lives. By opening up to others, you'll prompt people to open up with God, this generous Father in heaven.

COMPLETING GOD'S LAW

17-18 "Don't suppose for a minute that I have come to demolish the Scriptures — either God's Law or the Prophets. I'm not here to demolish but to complete. I am going to put it all together, pull it all together in a vast panorama. God's Law is more real and lasting than the stars in the sky and the ground at your feet. Long after stars burn out and earth wears out, God's Law will be alive and working.

19-20 "Trivialize even the smallest item in God's Law and you will only have trivialized yourself. But take it seriously, show the way for others, and you will find honor in the kingdom. Unless you do far better than the Pharisees in the matters of right living, you won't know the first thing about entering the kingdom.

MURDER

21-22 "You're familiar with the command to the ancients, 'Do not murder.' I'm telling you that anyone who is so much as angry with a brother or sister is guilty of murder. Carelessly call a brother 'idiot!' and you just might find yourself hauled into court. Thoughtlessly yell 'stupid!' at a sister and you are on the brink of hellfire. The simple moral fact is that words kill.

23-24 "This is how I want you to conduct yourself in these matters. If you enter your place of worship and, about to make an offering, you suddenly remember a grudge a friend has against you, abandon your offering, leave immediately, go to this friend and make things right. Then and only then, come back and work things out with God.

25-26 "Or say you're out on the street and an old enemy accosts you. Don't lose a minute. Make the first move; make things right with him. After all, if you leave the first move to him, knowing his track record, you're likely to end up in court, maybe even jail. If that happens, you won't get out without a stiff fine.

ADULTERY AND DIVORCE

27-28 "You know the next commandment pretty well, too: 'Don't go to bed with another's spouse.' But don't think you've preserved your virtue simply by staying out of bed. Your *heart* can be corrupted by lust even quicker than your *body*. Those leering looks you think nobody notices—they also corrupt.

29-30 "Let's not pretend this is easier than it really is. If you want to live a morally pure life, here's what you have to do: You have to blind your right eye the moment you catch it in a lustful leer. You have to choose to live one-eyed or else be dumped on a moral trash pile. And you have to chop off your right hand the moment you notice it raised threateningly. Better a bloody stump than your entire being discarded for good in the dump.

31-32 "Remember the Scripture that says, 'Whoever divorces his wife, let him do it legally, giving her divorce papers and her legal rights'? Too many of you are using that as a cover for selfishness and whim, pretending to be righteous just because you are 'legal.' Please, no more pretending. If you divorce your wife, you're responsible for making her an adulteress (unless she has already made herself that by sexual promiscuity). And if you marry such a divorced adulteress, you're automatically an adulterer yourself. You can't use legal cover to mask a moral failure.

EMPTY PROMISES

33-37 "And don't say anything you don't mean. This counsel is embedded deep in our traditions. You only make things worse when you lay down a smoke screen of pious talk, saying, 'I'll pray for you,' and never doing it, or saying, 'God be with you,' and not meaning it. You don't make your words true by embellishing them with religious lace. In making your speech sound more religious, it becomes less true. Just say 'yes' and 'no.' When you manipulate words to get your own way, you go wrong.

LOVE YOUR ENEMIES

38-42 "Here's another old saying that deserves a second look: 'Eye for eye, tooth for tooth.' Is that going to get us anywhere? Here's what I propose: 'Don't hit back at all.' If someone strikes you, stand there and take it. If someone drags you into court and sues for the shirt off your back, giftwrap your best coat and make a present of it. And if someone takes unfair advantage of you, use the occasion to practice the servant life. No more tit-for-tat stuff. Live generously.

43-47   "You're familiar with the old written law, 'Love your friend,' and its un-written companion, 'Hate your enemy.' I'm challenging that. I'm telling you to love your enemies. Let them bring out the best in you, not the worst. When someone gives you a hard time, respond with the energies of prayer, for then you are working out of your true selves, your God-created selves. This is what God does. He gives his best — the sun to warm and the rain to nourish — to everyone, regardless: the good and bad, the nice and nasty. If all you do is love the lovable, do you expect a bonus? Anybody can do that. If you simply say hello to those who greet you, do you expect a medal? Any run-of-the-mill sinner does that.

48   "In a word, what I'm saying is, *Grow up*. You're kingdom subjects. Now live like it. Live out your God-created identity. Live generously and gra-ciously toward others, the way God lives toward you."

The World Is Not a Stage

1   6 "Be especially careful when you are trying to be good so that you don't make a performance out of it. It might be good theater, but the God who made you won't be applauding.

2-4   "When you do something for someone else, don't call attention to yourself. You've seen them in action, I'm sure — 'playactors' I call them — treating prayer meeting and street corner alike as a stage, acting com-passionate as long as someone is watching, playing to the crowds. They get applause, true, but that's all they get. When you help someone out, don't think about how it looks. Just do it — quietly and unobtrusively. That is the way your God, who conceived you in love, working behind the scenes, helps you out.

Pray with Simplicity

5   "And when you come before God, don't turn that into a theatrical pro-duction either. All these people making a regular show out of their prayers, hoping for stardom! Do you think God sits in a box seat?

6   "Here's what I want you to do: Find a quiet, secluded place so you won't be tempted to role-play before God. Just be there as simply and honestly as you can manage. The focus will shift from you to God, and you will begin to sense his grace.

7-13   "The world is full of so-called prayer warriors who are prayer-ignorant. They're full of formulas and programs and advice, peddling techniques for getting what you want from God. Don't fall for that nonsense. This is your Father you are dealing with, and he knows better than you what you need. With a God like this loving you, you can pray very simply. Like this:

Our Father in heaven,
Reveal who you are.
Set the world right;
Do what's best —
    as above, so below.
Keep us alive with three square meals.
Keep us forgiven with you and forgiving others.
Keep us safe from ourselves and the Devil.
You're in charge!
You can do anything you want!

You're ablaze in beauty!
Yes. Yes. Yes.

14-15 "In prayer there is a connection between what God does and what you do. You can't get forgiveness from God, for instance, without also forgiving others. If you refuse to do your part, you cut yourself off from God's part.

16-18 "When you practice some appetite-denying discipline to better concentrate on God, don't make a production out of it. It might turn you into a small-time celebrity but it won't make you a saint. If you 'go into training' inwardly, act normal outwardly. Shampoo and comb your hair, brush your teeth, wash your face. God doesn't require attention-getting devices. He won't overlook what you are doing; he'll reward you well.

A LIFE OF GOD-WORSHIP

19-21 "Don't hoard treasure down here where it gets eaten by moths and corroded by rust or — worse! — stolen by burglars. Stockpile treasure in heaven, where it's safe from moth and rust and burglars. It's obvious, isn't it? The place where your treasure is, is the place you will most want to be, and end up being.

22-23 "Your eyes are windows into your body. If you open your eyes wide in wonder and belief, your body fills up with light. If you live squinty-eyed in greed and distrust, your body is a dank cellar. If you pull the blinds on your windows, what a dark life you will have!

24 "You can't worship two gods at once. Loving one god, you'll end up hating the other. Adoration of one feeds contempt for the other. You can't worship God and Money both.

25-26 "If you decide for God, living a life of God-worship, it follows that you don't fuss about what's on the table at mealtimes or whether the clothes in your closet are in fashion. There is far more to your life than the food you put in your stomach, more to your outer appearance than the clothes you hang on your body. Look at the birds, free and unfettered, not tied down to a job description, careless in the care of God. And you count far more to him than birds.

27-29 "Has anyone by fussing in front of the mirror ever gotten taller by so much as an inch? All this time and money wasted on fashion — do you think it makes that much difference? Instead of looking at the fashions, walk out into the fields and look at the wildflowers. They never primp or shop, but have you ever seen color and design quite like it? The ten best-dressed men and women in the country look shabby alongside them.

30-33 "If God gives such attention to the appearance of wildflowers — most of which are never even seen — don't you think he'll attend to you, take pride in you, do his best for you? What I'm trying to do here is to get you to relax, to not be so preoccupied with *getting*, so you can respond to God's *giving*. People who don't know God and the way he works fuss over these things, but you know both God and how he works. Steep your life in God-reality, God-initiative, God-provisions. Don't worry about missing out. You'll find all your everyday human concerns will be met.

34 "Give your entire attention to what God is doing right now, and don't get worked up about what may or may not happen tomorrow. God will help you deal with whatever hard things come up when the time comes.

A SIMPLE GUIDE FOR BEHAVIOR

1-5 **7** "Don't pick on people, jump on their failures, criticize their faults — unless, of course, you want the same treatment. That critical spirit has a way of boomeranging. It's easy to see a smudge on your neighbor's face and be oblivious to the ugly sneer on your own. Do you have the nerve to say, 'Let me wash your face for you,' when your own face is distorted by contempt? It's this whole traveling road-show mentality all over again, playing a holier-than-thou part instead of just living your part. Wipe that ugly sneer off your own face, and you might be fit to offer a washcloth to your neighbor.

6 "Don't be flip with the sacred. Banter and silliness give no honor to God. Don't reduce holy mysteries to slogans. In trying to be relevant, you're only being cute and inviting sacrilege.

7-11 "Don't bargain with God. Be direct. Ask for what you need. This isn't a cat-and-mouse, hide-and-seek game we're in. If your child asks for bread, do you trick him with sawdust? If he asks for fish, do you scare him with a live snake on his plate? As bad as you are, you wouldn't think of such a thing. You're at least decent to your own children. So don't you think the God who conceived you in love will be even better?

12 "Here is a simple, rule-of-thumb guide for behavior: Ask yourself what you want people to do for you, then grab the initiative and do it for *them*. Add up God's Law and Prophets and this is what you get.

BEING AND DOING

13-14 "Don't look for shortcuts to God. The market is flooded with surefire, easy-going formulas for a successful life that can be practiced in your spare time. Don't fall for that stuff, even though crowds of people do. The way to life — to God! — is vigorous and requires total attention.

15-20 "Be wary of false preachers who smile a lot, dripping with practiced sincerity. Chances are they are out to rip you off some way or other. Don't be impressed with charisma; look for character. Who preachers *are* is the main thing, not what they say. A genuine leader will never exploit your emotions or your pocketbook. These diseased trees with their bad apples are going to be chopped down and burned.

21-23 "Knowing the correct password — saying 'Master, Master,' for instance — isn't going to get you anywhere with me. What is required is serious obedience — *doing* what my Father wills. I can see it now — at the Final Judgment thousands strutting up to me and saying, 'Master, we preached the Message, we bashed the demons, our God-sponsored projects had everyone talking.' And do you know what I am going to say? 'You missed the boat. All you did was use me to make yourselves important. You don't impress me one bit. You're out of here.'

24-25 "These words I speak to you are not incidental additions to your life, homeowner improvements to your standard of living. They are foundational words, words to build a life on. If you work these words into your life, you are like a smart carpenter who built his house on solid rock. Rain poured down, the river flooded, a tornado hit — but nothing moved that house. It was fixed to the rock.

26-27 "But if you just use my words in Bible studies and don't work them into your life, you are like a stupid carpenter who built his house on the sandy beach. When a storm rolled in and the waves came up, it collapsed like a house of cards."

28-29   When Jesus concluded his address, the crowd burst into applause. They had never heard teaching like this. It was apparent that he was living everything he was saying—quite a contrast to their religion teachers! This was the best teaching they had ever heard.

He Carried Our Diseases

1-2   8 Jesus came down the mountain with the cheers of the crowd still ringing in his ears. Then a leper appeared and went to his knees before Jesus, praying, "Master, if you want to, you can heal my body."

3-4   Jesus reached out and touched him, saying, "I want to. Be clean." Then and there, all signs of the leprosy were gone. Jesus said, "Don't talk about this all over town. Just quietly present your healed body to the priest, along with the appropriate expressions of thanks to God. Your cleansed and grateful life, not your words, will bear witness to what I have done."

5-6   As Jesus entered the village of Capernaum, a Roman captain came up in a panic and said, "Master, my servant is sick. He can't walk. He's in terrible pain."

7   Jesus said, "I'll come and heal him."

8-9   "Oh, no," said the captain. "I don't want to put you to all that trouble. Just give the order and my servant will be fine. I'm a man who takes orders and gives orders. I tell one soldier, 'Go,' and he goes; to another, 'Come,' and he comes; to my slave, 'Do this,' and he does it."

10-12   Taken aback, Jesus said, "I've yet to come across this kind of simple trust in Israel, the very people who are supposed to know all about God and how he works. This man is the vanguard of many outsiders who will soon be coming from all directions—streaming in from the east, pouring in from the west, sitting down at God's kingdom banquet alongside Abraham, Isaac, and Jacob. Then those who grew up 'in the faith' but had no faith will find themselves out in the cold, outsiders to grace and wondering what happened."

13   Then Jesus turned to the captain and said, "Go. What you believed could happen has happened." At that moment his servant became well.

14-15   By this time they were in front of Peter's house. On entering, Jesus found Peter's mother-in-law sick in bed, burning up with fever. He touched her hand and the fever was gone. No sooner was she up on her feet than she was fixing dinner for him.

16-17   That evening a lot of demon-afflicted people were brought to him. He relieved the inwardly tormented. He cured the bodily ill. He fulfilled Isaiah's well-known sermon:

He took our illnesses,
He carried our diseases.

Your Business Is Life, Not Death

18-19   When Jesus saw that a curious crowd was growing by the minute, he told his disciples to get him out of there to the other side of the lake. As they left, a religion scholar asked if he could go along. "I'll go with you, wherever," he said.

20   Jesus was curt: "Are you ready to rough it? We're not staying in the best inns, you know."

21   Another follower said, "Master, excuse me for a couple of days, please. I have my father's funeral to take care of."

22   Jesus refused. "First things first. Your business is life, not death. Follow me. Pursue life."

23-25   Then he got in the boat, his disciples with him. The next thing they knew, they were in a severe storm. Waves were crashing into the boat—and he was sound asleep! They roused him, pleading, "Master, save us! We're going down!"

26   Jesus reprimanded them. "Why are you such cowards, such faint-hearts?" Then he stood up and told the wind to be silent, the sea to quiet down: "Silence!" The sea became smooth as glass.

27   The men rubbed their eyes, astonished. "What's going on here? Wind and sea come to heel at his command!"

THE MADMEN AND THE PIGS

28-31   They landed in the country of the Gadarenes and were met by two madmen, victims of demons, coming out of the cemetery. The men had terrorized the region for so long that no one considered it safe to walk down that stretch of road anymore. Seeing Jesus, the madmen screamed out, "What business do you have giving us a hard time? You're the Son of God! You weren't supposed to show up here yet!" Off in the distance a herd of pigs was browsing and rooting. The evil spirits begged Jesus, "If you kick us out of these men, let us live in the pigs."

32-34   Jesus said, "Go ahead, but get out of here!" Crazed, the pigs stampeded over a cliff into the sea and drowned. Scared to death, the swineherds bolted. They told everyone back in town what had happened to the madmen and the pigs. Those who heard about it were angry about the drowned pigs. A mob formed and demanded that Jesus get out and not come back.

WHO NEEDS A DOCTOR?

1-3   9 Back in the boat, Jesus and the disciples recrossed the sea to Jesus' hometown. They were hardly out of the boat when some men carried a paraplegic on a stretcher and set him down in front of them. Jesus, impressed by their bold belief, said to the paraplegic, "Cheer up, son. I forgive your sins." Some religion scholars whispered, "Why, that's blasphemy!"

4-8   Jesus knew what they were thinking, and said, "Why this gossipy whispering? Which do you think is simpler: to say, 'I forgive your sins,' or, 'Get up and walk'? Well, just so it's clear that I'm the Son of Man and authorized to do either, or both. . . ." At this he turned to the paraplegic and said, "Get up. Take your bed and go home." And the man did it. The crowd was awestruck, amazed and pleased that God had authorized Jesus to work among them this way.

9   Passing along, Jesus saw a man at his work collecting taxes. His name was Matthew. Jesus said, "Come along with me." Matthew stood up and followed him.

10-11   Later when Jesus was eating supper at Matthew's house with his close followers, a lot of disreputable characters came and joined them. When the Pharisees saw him keeping this kind of company, they had a fit, and lit into Jesus' followers. "What kind of example is this from your Teacher, acting cozy with crooks and riffraff?"

12-13   Jesus, overhearing, shot back, "Who needs a doctor: the healthy or the sick? Go figure out what this Scripture means: 'I'm after mercy, not religion.' I'm here to invite outsiders, not coddle insiders."

KINGDOM COME

14   A little later John's followers approached, asking, "Why is it that we and the Pharisees rigorously discipline body and spirit by fasting, but your followers don't?"

15   Jesus told them, "When you're celebrating a wedding, you don't skimp on the cake and wine. You feast. Later you may need to pull in your belt, but not now. No one throws cold water on a friendly bonfire. This is Kingdom Come!"

16-17   He went on, "No one cuts up a fine silk scarf to patch old work clothes; you want fabrics that match. And you don't put your wine in cracked bottles."

JUST A TOUCH

18-19   As he finished saying this, a local official appeared, bowed politely, and said, "My daughter has just now died. If you come and touch her, she will live." Jesus got up and went with him, his disciples following along.

20-22   Just then a woman who had hemorrhaged for twelve years slipped in from behind and lightly touched his robe. She was thinking to herself, "If I can just put a finger on his robe, I'll get well." Jesus turned—caught her at it. Then he reassured her: "Courage, daughter. You took a risk of faith, and now you're well." The woman was well from then on.

23-26   By now they had arrived at the house of the town official, and pushed their way through the gossips looking for a story and the neighbors bringing in casseroles. Jesus was abrupt: "Clear out! This girl isn't dead. She's sleeping." They told him he didn't know what he was talking about. But when Jesus had gotten rid of the crowd, he went in, took the girl's hand, and pulled her to her feet—alive. The news was soon out, and traveled throughout the region.

BECOME WHAT YOU BELIEVE

27-28   As Jesus left the house, he was followed by two blind men crying out, "Mercy, Son of David! Mercy on us!" When Jesus got home, the blind men went in with him. Jesus said to them, "Do you really believe I can do this?" They said, "Why, yes, Master!"

29-31   He touched their eyes and said, "Become what you believe." It happened. They saw. Then Jesus became very stern. "Don't let a soul know how this happened." But they were hardly out the door before they started blabbing it to everyone they met.

32-33   Right after that, as the blind men were leaving, a man who had been struck speechless by an evil spirit was brought to Jesus. As soon as Jesus threw the evil tormenting spirit out, the man talked away just as if he'd been talking all his life. The people were up on their feet applauding: "There's never been anything like this in Israel!"

34   The Pharisees were left sputtering, "Hocus-pocus. It's nothing but hocus-pocus. He's probably made a pact with the Devil."

35-38   Then Jesus made a circuit of all the towns and villages. He taught in their meeting places, reported kingdom news, and healed their diseased bodies, healed their bruised and hurt lives. When he looked out over the crowds, his heart broke. So confused and aimless they were, like sheep with no shepherd. "What a huge harvest!" he said to his disciples. "How few workers! On your knees and pray for harvest hands!"

The Twelve Harvest Hands

1-4 **10** The prayer was no sooner prayed than it was answered. Jesus called twelve of his followers and sent them into the ripe fields. He gave them power to kick out the evil spirits and to tenderly care for the bruised and hurt lives. This is the list of the twelve he sent:

Simon (they called him Peter, or "Rock"),
Andrew, his brother,
James, Zebedee's son,
John, his brother,
Philip,
Bartholomew,
Thomas,
Matthew, the tax man,
James, son of Alphaeus,
Thaddaeus,
Simon, the Canaanite,
Judas Iscariot (who later turned on him).

5-8 Jesus sent his twelve harvest hands out with this charge: "Don't begin by traveling to some far-off place to convert unbelievers. And don't try to be dramatic by tackling some public enemy. Go to the lost, confused people right here in the neighborhood. Tell them that the kingdom is here. Bring health to the sick. Raise the dead. Touch the untouchables. Kick out the demons. You have been treated generously, so live generously.

9-10 "Don't think you have to put on a fund-raising campaign before you start. You don't need a lot of equipment. *You* are the equipment, and all you need to keep that going is three meals a day. Travel light.

11 "When you enter a town or village, don't insist on staying in a luxury inn. Get a modest place with some modest people, and be content there until you leave.

12-15 "When you knock on a door, be courteous in your greeting. If they welcome you, be gentle in your conversation. If they don't welcome you, quietly withdraw. Don't make a scene. Shrug your shoulders and be on your way. You can be sure that on Judgment Day they'll be mighty sorry—but it's no concern of yours now.

16 "Stay alert. This is hazardous work I'm assigning you. You're going to be like sheep running through a wolf pack, so don't call attention to yourselves. Be as cunning as a snake, inoffensive as a dove.

17-20 "Don't be naive. Some people will impugn your motives, others will smear your reputation—just because you believe in me. Don't be upset when they haul you before the civil authorities. Without knowing it, they've done you—and me—a favor, given you a platform for preaching the kingdom news! And don't worry about what you'll say or how you'll say it. The right words will be there; the Spirit of your Father will supply the words.

21-23 "When people realize it is the living God you are presenting and not some idol that makes them feel good, they are going to turn on you, even people in your own family. There is a great irony here: proclaiming so much love, experiencing so much hate! But don't quit. Don't cave in. It is all well worth it in the end. It is not success you are after in such times but survival. Be survivors! Before you've run out of options, the Son of Man will have arrived.

24-25 "A student doesn't get a better desk than her teacher. A laborer doesn't make more money than his boss. Be content — pleased, even — when you, my students, my harvest hands, get the same treatment I get. If they call me, the Master, 'Dungface,' what can the workers expect?

26-27 "Don't be intimidated. Eventually everything is going to be out in the open, and everyone will know how things really are. So don't hesitate to go public now.

28 "Don't be bluffed into silence by the threats of bullies. There's nothing they can do to your soul, your core being. Save your fear for God, who holds your entire life — body and soul — in his hands.

FORGET ABOUT YOURSELF

29-31 "What's the price of a pet canary? Some loose change, right? And God cares what happens to it even more than you do. He pays even greater attention to you, down to the last detail — even numbering the hairs on your head! So don't be intimidated by all this bully talk. You're worth more than a million canaries.

32-33 "Stand up for me against world opinion and I'll stand up for you before my Father in heaven. If you turn tail and run, do you think I'll cover for you?

34-37 "Don't think I've come to make life cozy. I've come to cut — make a sharp knife-cut between son and father, daughter and mother, bride and mother-in-law — cut through these cozy domestic arrangements and free you for God. Well-meaning family members can be your worst enemies. If you prefer father or mother over me, you don't deserve me. If you prefer son or daughter over me, you don't deserve me.

38-39 "If you don't go all the way with me, through thick and thin, you don't deserve me. If your first concern is to look after yourself, you'll never find yourself. But if you forget about yourself and look to me, you'll find both yourself and me.

40-42 "We are intimately linked in this harvest work. Anyone who accepts what you do, accepts me, the One who sent you. Anyone who accepts what I do accepts my Father, who sent me. Accepting a messenger of God is as good as being God's messenger. Accepting someone's help is as good as giving someone help. This is a large work I've called you into, but don't be overwhelmed by it. It's best to start small. Give a cool cup of water to someone who is thirsty, for instance. The smallest act of giving or receiving makes you a true apprentice. You won't lose out on a thing."

JOHN THE BAPTIZER

1 When Jesus finished placing this charge before his twelve disciples, he went on to teach and preach in their villages.

2-3 John, meanwhile, had been locked up in prison. When he got wind of what Jesus was doing, he sent his own disciples to ask, "Are you the

One we've been expecting, or are we still waiting?"

4-6   Jesus told them, "Go back and tell John what's going on:

The blind see,
The lame walk,
Lepers are cleansed,
The deaf hear,
The dead are raised,
The wretched of the earth learn that God is on their side.

"Is this what you were expecting? Then count yourselves most blessed!"

7-10   When John's disciples left to report, Jesus started talking to the crowd about John. "What did you expect when you went out to see him in the wild? A weekend camper? Hardly. What then? A sheik in silk pajamas? Not in the wilderness, not by a long shot. What then? A prophet? That's right, a prophet! Probably the best prophet you'll ever hear. He is the prophet that Malachi announced when he wrote, 'I'm sending my prophet ahead of you, to make the road smooth for you.'

11-14   "Let me tell you what's going on here: No one in history surpasses John the Baptizer; but in the kingdom he prepared you for, the lowliest person is ahead of him. For a long time now people have tried to force themselves into God's kingdom. But if you read the books of the Prophets and God's Law closely, you will see them culminate in John, teaming up with him in preparing the way for the Messiah of the kingdom. Looked at in this way, John is the 'Elijah' you've all been expecting to arrive and introduce the Messiah.

15   "Are you listening to me? Really listening?

16-19   "How can I account for this generation? The people have been like spoiled children whining to their parents, 'We wanted to skip rope, and you were always too tired; we wanted to talk, but you were always too busy.' John came fasting and they called him crazy. I came feasting and they called me a lush, a friend of the riffraff. Opinion polls don't count for much, do they? The proof of the pudding is in the eating."

The Unforced Rhythms of Grace

20   Next Jesus let fly on the cities where he had worked the hardest but whose people had responded the least, shrugging their shoulders and going their own way.

21-24   "Doom to you, Chorazin! Doom, Bethsaida! If Tyre and Sidon had seen half of the powerful miracles you have seen, they would have been on their knees in a minute. At Judgment Day they'll get off easy compared to you. And Capernaum! With all your peacock strutting, you are going to end up in the abyss. If the people of Sodom had had your chances, the city would still be around. At Judgment Day they'll get off easy compared to you."

25-26   Abruptly Jesus broke into prayer: "Thank you, Father, Lord of heaven and earth. You've concealed your ways from sophisticates and know-it-alls, but spelled them out clearly to ordinary people. Yes, Father, that's the way you like to work."

27   Jesus resumed talking to the people, but now tenderly. "The Father has given me all these things to do and say. This is a unique Father-Son

operation, coming out of Father and Son intimacies and knowledge. No one knows the Son the way the Father does, nor the Father the way the Son does. But I'm not keeping it to myself; I'm ready to go over it line by line with anyone willing to listen.

28-30   "Are you tired? Worn out? Burned out on religion? Come to me. Get away with me and you'll recover your life. I'll show you how to take a real rest. Walk with me and work with me—watch how I do it. Learn the unforced rhythms of grace. I won't lay anything heavy or ill-fitting on you. Keep company with me and you'll learn to live freely and lightly."

In Charge of the Sabbath

1-2   **12** One Sabbath, Jesus was strolling with his disciples through a field of ripe grain. Hungry, the disciples were pulling off the heads of grain and munching on them. Some Pharisees reported them to Jesus: "Your disciples are breaking the Sabbath rules!"

3-5   Jesus said, "Really? Didn't you ever read what David and his companions did when they were hungry, how they entered the sanctuary and ate fresh bread off the altar, bread that no one but priests were allowed to eat? And didn't you ever read in God's Law that priests carrying out their Temple duties break Sabbath rules all the time and it's not held against them?

6-8   "There is far more at stake here than religion. If you had any idea what this Scripture meant—'I prefer a flexible heart to an inflexible ritual'—you wouldn't be nitpicking like this. The Son of Man is no lackey to the Sabbath; he's in charge."

9-10   When Jesus left the field, he entered their meeting place. There was a man there with a crippled hand. They said to Jesus, "Is it legal to heal on the Sabbath?" They were baiting him.

11-14   He replied, "Is there a person here who, finding one of your lambs fallen into a ravine, wouldn't, even though it was a Sabbath, pull it out? Surely kindness to people is as legal as kindness to animals!" Then he said to the man, "Hold out your hand." He held it out and it was healed. The Pharisees walked out furious, sputtering about how they were going to ruin Jesus.

In Charge of Everything

15-21   Jesus, knowing they were out to get him, moved on. A lot of people followed him, and he healed them all. He also cautioned them to keep it quiet, following guidelines set down by Isaiah:

> Look well at my handpicked servant;
>   I love him so much, take such delight in him.
> I've placed my Spirit on him;
>   he'll decree justice to the nations.
> But he won't yell, won't raise his voice;
>   there'll be no commotion in the streets.
> He won't walk over anyone's feelings,
>   won't push you into a corner.
> Before you know it, his justice will triumph;
>   the mere sound of his name will signal hope, even
>   among far-off unbelievers.

NO NEUTRAL GROUND

22-23 Next a poor demon-afflicted wretch, both blind and deaf, was set down before him. Jesus healed him, gave him his sight and hearing. The people who saw it were impressed — "This has to be the Son of David!"

24 But the Pharisees, when they heard the report, were cynical. "Black magic," they said. "Some devil trick he's pulled from his sleeve."

25-27 Jesus confronted their slander. "A judge who gives opposite verdicts on the same person cancels himself out; a family that's in a constant squabble disintegrates; if Satan banishes Satan, is there any Satan left? If you're slinging devil mud at me, calling me a devil kicking out devils, doesn't the same mud stick to your own exorcists?

28-29 "But if it's by *God's* power that I am sending the evil spirits packing, then God's kingdom is here for sure. How in the world do you think it's possible in broad daylight to enter the house of an awake, able-bodied man and walk off with his possessions unless you tie him up first? Tie him up, though, and you can clean him out.

30 "This is war, and there is no neutral ground. If you're not on my side, you're the enemy; if you're not helping, you're making things worse.

31-32 "There's nothing done or said that can't be forgiven. But if you deliberately persist in your slanders against God's Spirit, you are repudiating the very One who forgives. If you reject the Son of Man out of some misunderstanding, the Holy Spirit can forgive you, but when you reject the Holy Spirit, you're sawing off the branch on which you're sitting, severing by your own perversity all connection with the One who forgives.

33 "If you grow a healthy tree, you'll pick healthy fruit. If you grow a diseased tree, you'll pick worm-eaten fruit. The fruit tells you about the tree.

34-37 "You have minds like a snake pit! How do you suppose what you say is worth anything when you are so foul-minded? It's your heart, not the dictionary, that gives meaning to your words. A good person produces good deeds and words season after season. An evil person is a blight on the orchard. Let me tell you something: Every one of these careless words is going to come back to haunt you. There will be a time of Reckoning. Words are powerful; take them seriously. Words can be your salvation. Words can also be your damnation."

JONAH-EVIDENCE

38 Later a few religion scholars and Pharisees got on him. "Teacher, we want to see your credentials. Give us some hard evidence that God is in this. How about a miracle?"

39-40 Jesus said, "You're looking for proof, but you're looking for the wrong kind. All you want is something to titillate your curiosity, satisfy your lust for miracles. The only proof you're going to get is what looks like the absence of proof: Jonah-evidence. Like Jonah, three days and nights in the fish's belly, the Son of Man will be gone three days and nights in a deep grave.

41-42 "On Judgment Day, the Ninevites will stand up and give evidence that will condemn this generation, because when Jonah preached to them they changed their lives. A far greater preacher than Jonah is here, and you squabble about 'proofs.' On Judgment Day, the Queen of Sheba will come forward and bring evidence that will condemn this generation, because she traveled from a far corner of the earth to listen to wise Solomon. Wisdom

far greater than Solomon's is right in front of you, and you quibble over
'evidence.'

43-45 "When a defiling evil spirit is expelled from someone, it drifts along
through the desert looking for an oasis, some unsuspecting soul it can
bedevil. When it doesn't find anyone, it says, 'I'll go back to my old haunt.'
On return it finds the person spotlessly clean, but vacant. It then runs out
and rounds up seven other spirits more evil than itself and they all move in,
whooping it up. That person ends up far worse off than if he'd never gotten
cleaned up in the first place.

"That's what this generation is like: You may think you have cleaned
out the junk from your lives and gotten ready for God, but you weren't hospitable to my kingdom message, and now all the devils are moving back in."

OBEDIENCE IS THICKER THAN BLOOD

46-47 While he was still talking to the crowd, his mother and brothers showed
up. They were outside trying to get a message to him. Someone told Jesus,
"Your mother and brothers are out here, wanting to speak with you."

48-50 Jesus didn't respond directly, but said, "Who do you think my mother
and brothers are?" He then stretched out his hand toward his disciples.
"Look closely. These are my mother and brothers. Obedience is thicker than
blood. The person who obeys my heavenly Father's will is my brother and
sister and mother."

A HARVEST STORY

1-3 **13** At about that same time Jesus left the house and sat on the
beach. In no time at all a crowd gathered along the shoreline, forcing him to get into a boat. Using the boat as a pulpit, he addressed
his congregation, telling stories.

3-8 "What do you make of this? A farmer planted seed. As he scattered the
seed, some of it fell on the road, and birds ate it. Some fell in the gravel;
it sprouted quickly but didn't put down roots, so when the sun came up
it withered just as quickly. Some fell in the weeds; as it came up, it was
strangled by the weeds. Some fell on good earth, and produced a harvest
beyond his wildest dreams.

9 "Are you listening to this? Really listening?"

WHY TELL STORIES?

10 The disciples came up and asked, "Why do you tell stories?"

11-15 He replied, "You've been given insight into God's kingdom. You know
how it works. Not everybody has this gift, this insight; it hasn't been given to
them. Whenever someone has a ready heart for this, the insights and understandings flow freely. But if there is no readiness, any trace of receptivity soon
disappears. That's why I tell stories: to create readiness, to nudge the people
toward receptive insight. In their present state they can stare till doomsday
and not see it, listen till they're blue in the face and not get it. I don't want
Isaiah's forecast repeated all over again:

Your ears are open but you don't hear a thing.
    Your eyes are awake but you don't see a thing.
The people are blockheads!
They stick their fingers in their ears

so they won't have to listen;
They screw their eyes shut
so they won't have to look,
so they won't have to deal with me face-to-face
and let me heal them.

16-17   "But you have God-blessed eyes—eyes that see! And God-blessed ears—ears that hear! A lot of people, prophets and humble believers among them, would have given anything to see what you are seeing, to hear what you are hearing, but never had the chance.

THE MEANING OF THE HARVEST STORY

18-19   "Study this story of the farmer planting seed. When anyone hears news of the kingdom and doesn't take it in, it just remains on the surface, and so the Evil One comes along and plucks it right out of that person's heart. This is the seed the farmer scatters on the road.

20-21   "The seed cast in the gravel—this is the person who hears and instantly responds with enthusiasm. But there is no soil of character, and so when the emotions wear off and some difficulty arrives, there is nothing to show for it.

22   "The seed cast in the weeds is the person who hears the kingdom news, but weeds of worry and illusions about getting more and wanting everything under the sun strangle what was heard, and nothing comes of it.

23   "The seed cast on good earth is the person who hears and takes in the News, and then produces a harvest beyond his wildest dreams."

24-26   He told another story. "God's kingdom is like a farmer who planted good seed in his field. That night, while his hired men were asleep, his enemy sowed thistles all through the wheat and slipped away before dawn. When the first green shoots appeared and the grain began to form, the thistles showed up, too.

27   "The farmhands came to the farmer and said, 'Master, that was clean seed you planted, wasn't it? Where did these thistles come from?'

28   "He answered, 'Some enemy did this.'

    "The farmhands asked, 'Should we weed out the thistles?'

29-30   "He said, 'No, if you weed the thistles, you'll pull up the wheat, too. Let them grow together until harvest time. Then I'll instruct the harvesters to pull up the thistles and tie them in bundles for the fire, then gather the wheat and put it in the barn.'"

31-32   Another story. "God's kingdom is like a pine nut that a farmer plants. It is quite small as seeds go, but in the course of years it grows into a huge pine tree, and eagles build nests in it."

33   Another story. "God's kingdom is like yeast that a woman works into the dough for dozens of loaves of barley bread—and waits while the dough rises."

34-35   All Jesus did that day was tell stories—a long storytelling afternoon. His storytelling fulfilled the prophecy:

I will open my mouth and tell stories;
I will bring out into the open
    things hidden since the world's first day.

THE CURTAIN OF HISTORY

36 Jesus dismissed the congregation and went into the house. His disciples came in and said, "Explain to us that story of the thistles in the field."

37-39 So he explained. "The farmer who sows the pure seed is the Son of Man. The field is the world, the pure seeds are subjects of the kingdom, the thistles are subjects of the Devil, and the enemy who sows them is the Devil. The harvest is the end of the age, the curtain of history. The harvest hands are angels.

40-43 "The picture of thistles pulled up and burned is a scene from the final act. The Son of Man will send his angels, weed out the thistles from his kingdom, pitch them in the trash, and be done with them. They are going to complain to high heaven, but nobody is going to listen. At the same time, ripe, holy lives will mature and adorn the kingdom of their Father.

"Are you listening to this? Really listening?

44 "God's kingdom is like a treasure hidden in a field for years and then accidentally found by a trespasser. The finder is ecstatic — what a find! — and proceeds to sell everything he owns to raise money and buy that field.

45-46 "Or, God's kingdom is like a jewel merchant on the hunt for excellent pearls. Finding one that is flawless, he immediately sells everything and buys it.

47-50 "Or, God's kingdom is like a fishnet cast into the sea, catching all kinds of fish. When it is full, it is hauled onto the beach. The good fish are picked out and put in a tub; those unfit to eat are thrown away. That's how it will be when the curtain comes down on history. The angels will come and cull the bad fish and throw them in the garbage. There will be a lot of desperate complaining, but it won't do any good."

51 Jesus asked, "Are you starting to get a handle on all this?"

They answered, "Yes."

52 He said, "Then you see how every student well-trained in God's kingdom is like the owner of a general store who can put his hands on anything you need, old or new, exactly when you need it."

53-57 When Jesus finished telling these stories, he left there, returned to his hometown, and gave a lecture in the meetinghouse. He made a real hit, impressing everyone. "We had no idea he was this good!" they said. "How did he get so wise, get such ability?" But in the next breath they were cutting him down: "We've known him since he was a kid; he's the carpenter's son. We know his mother, Mary. We know his brothers James and Joseph, Simon and Judas. All his sisters live here. Who does he think he is?" They got their noses all out of joint.

58 But Jesus said, "A prophet is taken for granted in his hometown and his family." He didn't do many miracles there because of their hostile indifference.

THE DEATH OF JOHN

1-2 At about this time, Herod, the regional ruler, heard what was being said about Jesus. He said to his servants, "This has to be John the Baptizer come back from the dead. That's why he's able to work miracles!"

3-5 Herod had arrested John, put him in chains, and sent him to prison to placate Herodias, his brother Philip's wife. John had provoked Herod by naming his relationship with Herodias "adultery." Herod wanted to kill him, but he was afraid because so many people revered John as a prophet of God.

6-12 But at his birthday celebration, he got his chance. Herodias's daughter provided the entertainment, dancing for the guests. She swept Herod away. In his drunken enthusiasm, he promised her on oath anything she wanted. Already coached by her mother, she was ready: "Give me, served up on a platter, the head of John the Baptizer." That sobered the king up fast. Unwilling to lose face with his guests, he did it—ordered John's head cut off and presented to the girl on a platter. She in turn gave it to her mother. Later, John's disciples got the body, gave it a reverent burial, and reported to Jesus.

SUPPER FOR FIVE THOUSAND

13-14 When Jesus got the news, he slipped away by boat to an out-of-the-way place by himself. But unsuccessfully—someone saw him and the word got around. Soon a lot of people from the nearby villages walked around the lake to where he was. When he saw them coming, he was overcome with pity and healed their sick.

15 Toward evening the disciples approached him. "We're out in the country and it's getting late. Dismiss the people so they can go to the villages and get some supper."

16 But Jesus said, "There is no need to dismiss them. You give them supper."

17 "All we have are five loaves of bread and two fish," they said.

18-21 Jesus said, "Bring them here." Then he had the people sit on the grass. He took the five loaves and two fish, lifted his face to heaven in prayer, blessed, broke, and gave the bread to the disciples. The disciples then gave the food to the congregation. They all ate their fill. They gathered twelve baskets of leftovers. About five thousand were fed.

WALKING ON THE WATER

22-23 As soon as the meal was finished, he insisted that the disciples get in the boat and go on ahead to the other side while he dismissed the people. With the crowd dispersed, he climbed the mountain so he could be by himself and pray. He stayed there alone, late into the night.

24-26 Meanwhile, the boat was far out to sea when the wind came up against them and they were battered by the waves. At about four o'clock in the morning, Jesus came toward them walking on the water. They were scared out of their wits. "A ghost!" they said, crying out in terror.

27 But Jesus was quick to comfort them. "Courage, it's me. Don't be afraid."

28 Peter, suddenly bold, said, "Master, if it's really you, call me to come to you on the water."

29-30 He said, "Come ahead."

Jumping out of the boat, Peter walked on the water to Jesus. But when he looked down at the waves churning beneath his feet, he lost his nerve and started to sink. He cried, "Master, save me!"

31 Jesus didn't hesitate. He reached down and grabbed his hand. Then he said, "Faint-heart, what got into you?"

32-33 The two of them climbed into the boat, and the wind died down. The disciples in the boat, having watched the whole thing, worshiped Jesus, saying, "This is it! You are God's Son for sure!"

34-36 On return, they beached the boat at Gennesaret. When the people got wind that he was back, they sent out word through the neighborhood and rounded up all the sick, who asked for permission to touch the edge of his coat. And whoever touched him was healed.

WHAT POLLUTES YOUR LIFE

1-2 **15** After that, Pharisees and religion scholars came to Jesus all the way from Jerusalem, criticizing, "Why do your disciples play fast and loose with the rules?"

3-9 But Jesus put it right back on them. "Why do you use your rules to play fast and loose with God's commands? God clearly says, 'Respect your father and mother,' and, 'Anyone denouncing father or mother should be killed.' But you weasel around that by saying, 'Whoever wants to, can say to father and mother, What I owed to you I've given to God.' That can hardly be called respecting a parent. You cancel God's command by your rules. Frauds! Isaiah's prophecy of you hit the bull's-eye:

> These people make a big show of saying the right thing,
>   but their heart isn't in it.
> They act like they're worshiping me,
>   but they don't mean it.
> They just use me as a cover
>   for teaching whatever suits their fancy."

10-11 He then called the crowd together and said, "Listen, and take this to heart. It's not what you swallow that pollutes your life, but what you vomit up."

12 Later his disciples came and told him, "Did you know how upset the Pharisees were when they heard what you said?"

13-14 Jesus shrugged it off. "Every tree that wasn't planted by my Father in heaven will be pulled up by its roots. Forget them. They are blind men leading blind men. When a blind man leads a blind man, they both end up in the ditch."

15 Peter said, "I don't get it. Put it in plain language."

16-20 Jesus replied, "You, too? Are you being willfully stupid? Don't you know that anything that is swallowed works its way through the intestines and is finally defecated? But what comes out of the mouth gets its start in the heart. It's from the heart that we vomit up evil arguments, murders, adulteries, fornications, thefts, lies, and cussing. That's what pollutes. Eating or not eating certain foods, washing or not washing your hands—that's neither here nor there."

HEALING THE PEOPLE

21-22 From there Jesus took a trip to Tyre and Sidon. They had hardly arrived when a Canaanite woman came down from the hills and pleaded, "Mercy, Master, Son of David! My daughter is cruelly afflicted by an evil spirit."

23 Jesus ignored her. The disciples came and complained, "Now she's bothering us. Would you please take care of her? She's driving us crazy."

24 Jesus refused, telling them, "I've got my hands full dealing with the lost sheep of Israel."

25 Then the woman came back to Jesus, went to her knees, and begged. "Master, help me."

26 He said, "It's not right to take bread out of children's mouths and throw it to dogs."

27 She was quick: "You're right, Master, but beggar dogs do get scraps from the master's table."

28 Jesus gave in. "Oh, woman, your faith is something else. What you want is what you get!" Right then her daughter became well.

29-31 After Jesus returned, he walked along Lake Galilee and then climbed a mountain and took his place, ready to receive visitors. They came, tons of them, bringing along the paraplegic, the blind, the maimed, the mute — all sorts of people in need — and more or less threw them down at Jesus' feet to see what he would do with them. He healed them. When the people saw the mutes speaking, the maimed healthy, the paraplegics walking around, the blind looking around, they were astonished and let everyone know that God was blazingly alive among them.

32 But Jesus wasn't finished with them. He called his disciples and said, "I hurt for these people. For three days now they've been with me, and now they have nothing to eat. I can't send them away without a meal — they'd probably collapse on the road."

33 His disciples said, "But where in this deserted place are you going to dig up enough food for a meal?"

34-39 Jesus asked, "How much bread do you have?"

"Seven loaves," they said, "plus a few fish." At that, Jesus directed the people to sit down. He took the seven loaves and the fish. After giving thanks, he divided it up and gave it to the people. Everyone ate. They had all they wanted. It took seven large baskets to collect the leftovers. Over four thousand people ate their fill at that meal. After Jesus sent them away, he climbed in the boat and crossed over to the Magadan hills.

SOME BAD YEAST

1-4 **16** Some Pharisees and Sadducees were on him again, pressing him to prove himself to them. He told them, "You have a saying that goes, 'Red sky at night, sailor's delight; red sky at morning, sailors take warning.' You find it easy enough to forecast the weather — why can't you read the signs of the times? An evil and wanton generation is always wanting signs and wonders. The only sign you'll get is the Jonah sign." Then he turned on his heel and walked away.

5-6 On their way to the other side of the lake, the disciples discovered they had forgotten to bring along bread. In the meantime, Jesus said to them, "Keep a sharp eye out for Pharisee-Sadducee yeast."

7-12 Thinking he was scolding them for forgetting bread, they discussed in whispers what to do. Jesus knew what they were doing and said, "Why all these worried whispers about forgetting the bread? Runt believers! Haven't you caught on yet? Don't you remember the five loaves of bread and the five thousand people, and how many baskets of fragments you picked up? Or the seven loaves that fed four thousand, and how many baskets of leftovers you collected? Haven't you realized yet that bread isn't the problem? The problem is yeast, Pharisee-Sadducee yeast." Then they got it: that he wasn't concerned about eating, but teaching — the Pharisee-Sadducee kind of teaching.

SON OF MAN, SON OF GOD

13 When Jesus arrived in the villages of Caesarea Philippi, he asked his disciples, "What are people saying about who the Son of Man is?"

14 They replied, "Some think he is John the Baptizer, some say Elijah, some Jeremiah or one of the other prophets."

15 He pressed them, "And how about you? Who do you say I am?"

16 Simon Peter said, "You're the Christ, the Messiah, the Son of the living God."

17-18 Jesus came back, "God bless you, Simon, son of Jonah! You didn't get that answer out of books or from teachers. My Father in heaven, God himself, let you in on this secret of who I really am. And now I'm going to tell you who you are, *really* are. You are Peter, a rock. This is the rock on which I will put together my church, a church so expansive with energy that not even the gates of hell will be able to keep it out.

19 "And that's not all. You will have complete and free access to God's kingdom, keys to open any and every door: no more barriers between heaven and earth, earth and heaven. A yes on earth is yes in heaven. A no on earth is no in heaven."

20 He swore the disciples to secrecy. He made them promise they would tell no one that he was the Messiah.

YOU'RE NOT IN THE DRIVER'S SEAT

21-22 Then Jesus made it clear to his disciples that it was now necessary for him to go to Jerusalem, submit to an ordeal of suffering at the hands of the religious leaders, be killed, and then on the third day be raised up alive. Peter took him in hand, protesting, "Impossible, Master! That can never be!"

23 But Jesus didn't swerve. "Peter, get out of my way. Satan, get lost. You have no idea how God works."

24-26 Then Jesus went to work on his disciples. "Anyone who intends to come with me has to let me lead. You're not in the driver's seat; *I* am. Don't run from suffering; embrace it. Follow me and I'll show you how. Self-help is no help at all. Self-sacrifice is the way, my way, to finding yourself, your true self. What kind of deal is it to get everything you want but lose yourself? What could you ever trade your soul for?

27-28 "Don't be in such a hurry to go into business for yourself. Before you know it the Son of Man will arrive with all the splendor of his Father, accompanied by an army of angels. You'll get everything you have coming to you, a personal gift. This isn't pie in the sky by and by. Some of you standing here are going to see it take place, see the Son of Man in kingdom glory."

SUNLIGHT POURED FROM HIS FACE

1-3 **17** Six days later, three of them saw that glory. Jesus took Peter and the brothers, James and John, and led them up a high mountain. His appearance changed from the inside out, right before their eyes. Sunlight poured from his face. His clothes were filled with light. Then they realized that Moses and Elijah were also there in deep conversation with him.

4 Peter broke in, "Master, this is a great moment! What would you think if I built three memorials here on the mountain—one for you, one for Moses, one for Elijah?"

5 While he was going on like this, babbling, a light-radiant cloud enveloped them, and sounding from deep in the cloud a voice: "This is my Son, marked by my love, focus of my delight. Listen to him."

6-8 When the disciples heard it, they fell flat on their faces, scared to death. But Jesus came over and touched them. "Don't be afraid." When they opened their eyes and looked around all they saw was Jesus, only Jesus.

9 Coming down the mountain, Jesus swore them to secrecy. "Don't breathe a word of what you've seen. After the Son of Man is raised from the dead, you are free to talk."

10 The disciples, meanwhile, were asking questions. "Why do the religion scholars say that Elijah has to come first?"

11-13 Jesus answered, "Elijah does come and get everything ready. I'm telling you, Elijah has already come but they didn't know him when they saw him. They treated him like dirt, the same way they are about to treat the Son of Man." That's when the disciples realized that all along he had been talking about John the Baptizer.

WITH A MERE KERNEL OF FAITH

14-16 At the bottom of the mountain, they were met by a crowd of waiting people. As they approached, a man came out of the crowd and fell to his knees begging, "Master, have mercy on my son. He goes out of his mind and suffers terribly, falling into seizures. Frequently he is pitched into the fire, other times into the river. I brought him to your disciples, but they could do nothing for him."

17-18 Jesus said, "What a generation! No sense of God! No focus to your lives! How many times do I have to go over these things? How much longer do I have to put up with this? Bring the boy here." He ordered the afflicting demon out — and it was out, gone. From that moment on the boy was well.

19 When the disciples had Jesus off to themselves, they asked, "Why couldn't we throw it out?"

20 "Because you're not yet taking *God* seriously," said Jesus. "The simple truth is that if you had a mere kernel of faith, a poppy seed, say, you would tell this mountain, 'Move!' and it would move. There is nothing you wouldn't be able to tackle."

22-23 As they were regrouping in Galilee, Jesus told them, "The Son of Man is about to be betrayed to some people who want nothing to do with God. They will murder him — and three days later he will be raised alive." The disciples felt terrible.

24 When they arrived at Capernaum, the tax men came to Peter and asked, "Does your teacher pay taxes?"

25 Peter said, "Of course."

But as soon as they were in the house, Jesus confronted him. "Simon, what do you think? When a king levies taxes, who pays — his children or his subjects?"

26-27 He answered, "His subjects."

Jesus said, "Then the children get off free, right? But so we don't upset them needlessly, go down to the lake, cast a hook, and pull in the first fish that bites. Open its mouth and you'll find a coin. Take it and give it to the tax men. It will be enough for both of us."

WHOEVER BECOMES SIMPLE AGAIN

1 18 At about the same time, the disciples came to Jesus asking, "Who gets the highest rank in God's kingdom?"

2-5 For an answer Jesus called over a child, whom he stood in the middle of the room, and said, "I'm telling you, once and for all, that unless you return to square one and start over like children, you're not even going to get a look at the kingdom, let alone get in. Whoever becomes simple and elemental again, like this child, will rank high in God's kingdom. What's more, when you receive the childlike on my account, it's the same as receiving me.

6-7 "But if you give them a hard time, bullying or taking advantage of their simple trust, you'll soon wish you hadn't. You'd be better off dropped in the middle of the lake with a millstone around your neck. Doom to the world for giving these God-believing children a hard time! Hard times are inevitable, but you don't have to make it worse — and it's doomsday to you if you do.

8-9 "If your hand or your foot gets in the way of God, chop it off and throw it away. You're better off maimed or lame and alive than the proud owners of two hands and two feet, godless in a furnace of eternal fire. And if your eye distracts you from God, pull it out and throw it away. You're better off one-eyed and alive than exercising your twenty-twenty vision from inside the fire of hell.

10 "Watch that you don't treat a single one of these childlike believers arrogantly. You realize, don't you, that their personal angels are constantly in touch with my Father in heaven?

WORK IT OUT BETWEEN YOU

12-14 "Look at it this way. If someone has a hundred sheep and one of them wanders off, doesn't he leave the ninety-nine and go after the one? And if he finds it, doesn't he make far more over it than over the ninety-nine who stay put? Your Father in heaven feels the same way. He doesn't want to lose even one of these simple believers.

15-17 "If a fellow believer hurts you, go and tell him — work it out between the two of you. If he listens, you've made a friend. If he won't listen, take one or two others along so that the presence of witnesses will keep things honest, and try again. If he still won't listen, tell the church. If he won't listen to the church, you'll have to start over from scratch, confront him with the need for repentance, and offer again God's forgiving love.

18-20 "Take this most seriously: A yes on earth is yes in heaven; a no on earth is no in heaven. What you say to one another is eternal. I mean this. When two of you get together on anything at all on earth and make a prayer of it, my Father in heaven goes into action. And when two or three of you are together because of me, you can be sure that I'll be there."

A STORY ABOUT FORGIVENESS

21 At that point Peter got up the nerve to ask, "Master, how many times do I forgive a brother or sister who hurts me? Seven?"

22 Jesus replied, "Seven! Hardly. Try seventy times seven.

23-25 "The kingdom of God is like a king who decided to square accounts with his servants. As he got under way, one servant was brought before him who had run up a debt of a hundred thousand dollars. He couldn't pay up, so the king ordered the man, along with his wife, children, and goods, to be auctioned off at the slave market.

26-27   "The poor wretch threw himself at the king's feet and begged, 'Give me a chance and I'll pay it all back.' Touched by his plea, the king let him off, erasing the debt.

28   "The servant was no sooner out of the room when he came upon one of his fellow servants who owed him ten dollars. He seized him by the throat and demanded, 'Pay up. Now!'

29-31   "The poor wretch threw himself down and begged, 'Give me a chance and I'll pay it all back.' But he wouldn't do it. He had him arrested and put in jail until the debt was paid. When the other servants saw this going on, they were outraged and brought a detailed report to the king.

32-35   "The king summoned the man and said, 'You evil servant! I forgave your entire debt when you begged me for mercy. Shouldn't you be compelled to be merciful to your fellow servant who asked for mercy?' The king was furious and put the screws to the man until he paid back his entire debt. And that's exactly what my Father in heaven is going to do to each one of you who doesn't forgive unconditionally anyone who asks for mercy."

DIVORCE

1-2   **19** When Jesus had completed these teachings, he left Galilee and crossed the region of Judea on the other side of the Jordan. Great crowds followed him there, and he healed them.

3   One day the Pharisees were badgering him: "Is it legal for a man to divorce his wife for any reason?"

4-6   He answered, "Haven't you read in your Bible that the Creator originally made man and woman for each other, male and female? And because of this, a man leaves father and mother and is firmly bonded to his wife, becoming one flesh—no longer two bodies but one. Because God created this organic union of the two sexes, no one should desecrate his art by cutting them apart."

7   They shot back in rebuttal, "If that's so, why did Moses give instructions for divorce papers and divorce procedures?"

8-9   Jesus said, "Moses provided for divorce as a concession to your hard heartedness, but it is not part of God's original plan. I'm holding you to the original plan, and holding you liable for adultery if you divorce your faithful wife and then marry someone else. I make an exception in cases where the spouse has committed adultery."

10   Jesus' disciples objected, "If those are the terms of marriage, we're stuck. Why get married?"

11-12   But Jesus said, "Not everyone is mature enough to live a married life. It requires a certain aptitude and grace. Marriage isn't for everyone. Some, from birth seemingly, never give marriage a thought. Others never get asked—or accepted. And some decide not to get married for kingdom reasons. But if you're capable of growing into the largeness of marriage, do it."

TO ENTER GOD'S KINGDOM

13-15   One day children were brought to Jesus in the hope that he would lay hands on them and pray over them. The disciples shooed them off. But Jesus intervened: "Let the children alone, don't prevent them from coming to me. God's kingdom is made up of people like these." After laying hands on them, he left.

16 Another day, a man stopped Jesus and asked, "Teacher, what good thing must I do to get eternal life?"

17 Jesus said, "Why do you question me about what's good? *God* is the One who is good. If you want to enter the life of God, just do what he tells you."

18-19 The man asked, "What in particular?"

Jesus said, "Don't murder, don't commit adultery, don't steal, don't lie, honor your father and mother, and love your neighbor as you do yourself."

20 The young man said, "I've done all that. What's left?"

21 "If you want to give it all you've got," Jesus replied, "go sell your possessions; give everything to the poor. All your wealth will then be in heaven. Then come follow me."

22 That was the last thing the young man expected to hear. And so, crestfallen, he walked away. He was holding on tight to a lot of things, and he couldn't bear to let go.

23-24 As he watched him go, Jesus told his disciples, "Do you have any idea how difficult it is for the rich to enter God's kingdom? Let me tell you, it's easier to gallop a camel through a needle's eye than for the rich to enter God's kingdom."

25 The disciples were staggered. "Then who has any chance at all?"

26 Jesus looked hard at them and said, "No chance at all if you think you can pull it off yourself. Every chance in the world if you trust God to do it."

27 Then Peter chimed in, "We left everything and followed you. What do we get out of it?"

28-30 Jesus replied, "Yes, you have followed me. In the re-creation of the world, when the Son of Man will rule gloriously, you who have followed me will also rule, starting with the twelve tribes of Israel. And not only you, but anyone who sacrifices home, family, fields — whatever — because of me will get it all back a hundred times over, not to mention the considerable bonus of eternal life. This is the Great Reversal: many of the first ending up last, and the last first."

A STORY ABOUT WORKERS

1-2 20 "God's kingdom is like an estate manager who went out early in the morning to hire workers for his vineyard. They agreed on a wage of a dollar a day, and went to work.

3-5 "Later, about nine o'clock, the manager saw some other men hanging around the town square unemployed. He told them to go to work in his vineyard and he would pay them a fair wage. They went.

5-6 "He did the same thing at noon, and again at three o'clock. At five o'clock he went back and found still others standing around. He said, 'Why are you standing around all day doing nothing?'

7 "They said, 'Because no one hired us.'

"He told them to go to work in his vineyard.

8 "When the day's work was over, the owner of the vineyard instructed his foreman, 'Call the workers in and pay them their wages. Start with the last hired and go on to the first.'

9-12 "Those hired at five o'clock came up and were each given a dollar. When those who were hired first saw that, they assumed they would get far more. But they got the same, each of them one dollar. Taking the dollar, they groused angrily to the manager, 'These last workers put in only one easy hour, and you just made them equal to us, who slaved all day under a scorching sun.'

13-15 "He replied to the one speaking for the rest, 'Friend, I haven't been unfair. We agreed on the wage of a dollar, didn't we? So take it and go. I decided to give to the one who came last the same as you. Can't I do what I want with my own money? Are you going to get stingy because I am generous?'

16 "Here it is again, the Great Reversal: many of the first ending up last, and the last first."

TO DRINK FROM THE CUP

17-19 Jesus, now well on the way up to Jerusalem, took the Twelve off to the side of the road and said, "Listen to me carefully. We are on our way up to Jerusalem. When we get there, the Son of Man will be betrayed to the religious leaders and scholars. They will sentence him to death. They will then hand him over to the Romans for mockery and torture and crucifixion. On the third day he will be raised up alive."

20 It was about that time that the mother of the Zebedee brothers came with her two sons and knelt before Jesus with a request.

21 "What do you want?" Jesus asked.

She said, "Give your word that these two sons of mine will be awarded the highest places of honor in your kingdom, one at your right hand, one at your left hand."

22 Jesus responded, "You have no idea what you're asking." And he said to James and John, "Are you capable of drinking the cup that I'm about to drink?"

They said, "Sure, why not?"

23 Jesus said, "Come to think of it, you *are* going to drink my cup. But as to awarding places of honor, that's not my business. My Father is taking care of that."

24-28 When the ten others heard about this, they lost their tempers, thoroughly disgusted with the two brothers. So Jesus got them together to settle things down. He said, "You've observed how godless rulers throw their weight around, how quickly a little power goes to their heads. It's not going to be that way with you. Whoever wants to be great must become a servant. Whoever wants to be first among you must be your slave. That is what the Son of Man has done: He came to serve, not be served—and then to give away his life in exchange for the many who are held hostage."

29-31 As they were leaving Jericho, a huge crowd followed. Suddenly they came upon two blind men sitting alongside the road. When they heard it was Jesus passing, they cried out, "Master, have mercy on us! Mercy, Son of David!" The crowd tried to hush them up, but they got all the louder, crying, "Master, have mercy on us! Mercy, Son of David!"

32 Jesus stopped and called over, "What do you want from me?"

33 They said, "Master, we want our eyes opened. We want to see!"

34 Deeply moved, Jesus touched their eyes. They had their sight back that very instant, and joined the procession.

THE ROYAL WELCOME

1-3 **21** When they neared Jerusalem, having arrived at Bethphage on Mount Olives, Jesus sent two disciples with these instructions: "Go over to the village across from you. You'll find a donkey tethered there, her colt with her. Untie her and bring them to me. If anyone asks what you're doing, say, 'The Master needs them!' He will send them with you."

4-5 This is the full story of what was sketched earlier by the prophet:

> Tell Zion's daughter,
> "Look, your king's on his way,
>   poised and ready, mounted
> On a donkey, on a colt,
>   foal of a pack animal."

6-9 The disciples went and did exactly what Jesus told them to do. They led the donkey and colt out, laid some of their clothes on them, and Jesus mounted. Nearly all the people in the crowd threw their garments down on the road, giving him a royal welcome. Others cut branches from the trees and threw them down as a welcome mat. Crowds went ahead and crowds followed, all of them calling out, "Hosanna to David's son!" "Blessed is he who comes in God's name!" "Hosanna in highest heaven!"

10 As he made his entrance into Jerusalem, the whole city was shaken. Unnerved, people were asking, "What's going on here? Who is this?"

11 The parade crowd answered, "This is the prophet Jesus, the one from Nazareth in Galilee."

HE KICKED OVER THE TABLES

12-14 Jesus went straight to the Temple and threw out everyone who had set up shop, buying and selling. He kicked over the tables of loan sharks and the stalls of dove merchants. He quoted this text:

> My house was designated a house of prayer;
> You have made it a hangout for thieves.

Now there was room for the blind and crippled to get in. They came to Jesus and he healed them.

15-16 When the religious leaders saw the outrageous things he was doing, and heard all the children running and shouting through the Temple, "Hosanna to David's Son!" they were up in arms and took him to task. "Do you hear what these children are saying?"

Jesus said, "Yes, I hear them. And haven't you read in God's Word, 'From the mouths of children and babies I'll furnish a place of praise'?"

17 Fed up, Jesus turned on his heel and left the city for Bethany, where he spent the night.

THE WITHERED FIG TREE

18-20 Early the next morning Jesus was returning to the city. He was hungry. Seeing a lone fig tree alongside the road, he approached it anticipating a breakfast of figs. When he got to the tree, there was nothing but fig leaves.

He said, "No more figs from this tree — ever!" The fig tree withered on the spot, a dry stick. The disciples saw it happen. They rubbed their eyes, saying, "Did we really see this? A leafy tree one minute, a dry stick the next?"

21-22 But Jesus was matter-of-fact: "Yes — and if you embrace this kingdom life and don't doubt God, you'll not only do minor feats like I did to the fig tree, but also triumph over huge obstacles. This mountain, for instance, you'll tell, 'Go jump in the lake,' and it will jump. Absolutely everything, ranging from small to large, as you make it a part of your believing prayer, gets included as you lay hold of God."

TRUE AUTHORITY

23 Then he was back in the Temple, teaching. The high priests and leaders of the people came up and demanded, "Show us your credentials. Who authorized you to teach here?"

24-25 Jesus responded, "First let me ask you a question. You answer my question and I'll answer yours. About the baptism of John — who authorized it: heaven or humans?"

25-27 They were on the spot and knew it. They pulled back into a huddle and whispered, "If we say 'heaven,' he'll ask us why we didn't believe him; if we say 'humans,' we're up against it with the people because they all hold John up as a prophet." They decided to concede that round to Jesus. "We don't know," they answered.

Jesus said, "Then neither will I answer your question.

THE STORY OF TWO SONS

28 "Tell me what you think of this story: A man had two sons. He went up to the first and said, 'Son, go out for the day and work in the vineyard.'

29 "The son answered, 'I don't want to.' Later on he thought better of it and went.

30 "The father gave the same command to the second son. He answered, 'Sure, glad to.' But he never went.

31-32 "Which of the two sons did what the father asked?"

They said, "The first."

Jesus said, "Yes, and I tell you that crooks and whores are going to precede you into God's kingdom. John came to you showing you the right road. You turned up your noses at him, but the crooks and whores believed him. Even when you saw their changed lives, you didn't care enough to change and believe him.

THE STORY OF THE GREEDY FARMHANDS

33-34 "Here's another story. Listen closely. There was once a man, a wealthy farmer, who planted a vineyard. He fenced it, dug a winepress, put up a watchtower, then turned it over to the farmhands and went off on a trip. When it was time to harvest the grapes, he sent his servants back to collect his profits.

35-37 "The farmhands grabbed the first servant and beat him up. The next one they murdered. They threw stones at the third but he got away. The owner tried again, sending more servants. They got the same treatment. The owner was at the end of his rope. He decided to send his son. 'Surely,' he thought, 'they will respect my son.'

38-39 "But when the farmhands saw the son arrive, they rubbed their hands in greed. 'This is the heir! Let's kill him and have it all for ourselves.' They grabbed him, threw him out, and killed him.

40 "Now, when the owner of the vineyard arrives home from his trip, what do you think he will do to the farmhands?"

41 "He'll kill them—a rotten bunch, and good riddance," they answered. "Then he'll assign the vineyard to farmhands who will hand over the profits when it's time."

42-44 Jesus said, "Right—and you can read it for yourselves in your Bibles:

> The stone the masons threw out
> is now the cornerstone.
> This is God's work;
> we rub our eyes, we can hardly believe it!

"This is the way it is with you. God's kingdom will be taken back from you and handed over to a people who will live out a kingdom life. Whoever stumbles on this Stone gets shattered; whoever the Stone falls on gets smashed."

45-46 When the religious leaders heard this story, they knew it was aimed at them. They wanted to arrest Jesus and put him in jail, but, intimidated by public opinion, they held back. Most people held him to be a prophet of God.

The Story of the Wedding Banquet

1-3 **22** Jesus responded by telling still more stories. "God's kingdom," he said, "is like a king who threw a wedding banquet for his son. He sent out servants to call in all the invited guests. And they wouldn't come!

4 "He sent out another round of servants, instructing them to tell the guests, 'Look, everything is on the table, the prime rib is ready for carving. Come to the feast!'

5-7 "They only shrugged their shoulders and went off, one to weed his garden, another to work in his shop. The rest, with nothing better to do, beat up on the messengers and then killed them. The king was outraged and sent his soldiers to destroy those thugs and level their city.

8-10 "Then he told his servants, 'We have a wedding banquet all prepared but no guests. The ones I invited weren't up to it. Go out into the busiest intersections in town and invite anyone you find to the banquet.' The servants went out on the streets and rounded up everyone they laid eyes on, good and bad, regardless. And so the banquet was on—every place filled.

11-13 "When the king entered and looked over the scene, he spotted a man who wasn't properly dressed. He said to him, 'Friend, how dare you come in here looking like that!' The man was speechless. Then the king told his servants, 'Get him out of here—fast. Tie him up and ship him to hell. And make sure he doesn't get back in.'

14 "That's what I mean when I say, 'Many get invited; only a few make it.'"

Paying Taxes

15-17 That's when the Pharisees plotted a way to trap him into saying something damaging. They sent their disciples, with a few of Herod's followers mixed in, to ask, "Teacher, we know you have integrity, teach the way of God accurately, are indifferent to popular opinion, and don't pander to your students. So tell us honestly: Is it right to pay taxes to Caesar or not?"

18-19 Jesus knew they were up to no good. He said, "Why are you playing these games with me? Why are you trying to trap me? Do you have a coin? Let me see it." They handed him a silver piece.

20 "This engraving—who does it look like? And whose name is on it?"

21 They said, "Caesar."

"Then give Caesar what is his, and give God what is his."

22 The Pharisees were speechless. They went off shaking their heads.

MARRIAGE AND RESURRECTION

23-28 That same day, Sadducees approached him. This is the party that denies any possibility of resurrection. They asked, "Teacher, Moses said that if a man dies childless, his brother is obligated to marry his widow and get her with child. Here's a case where there were seven brothers. The first brother married and died, leaving no child, and his wife passed to his brother. The second brother also left her childless, then the third—and on and on, all seven. Eventually the wife died. Now here's our question: At the resurrection, whose wife is she? She was a wife to each of them."

29-33 Jesus answered, "You're off base on two counts: You don't know your Bibles, and you don't know how God works. At the resurrection we're beyond marriage. As with the angels, all our ecstasies and intimacies then will be with God. And regarding your speculation on whether the dead are raised or not, don't you read your Bibles? The grammar is clear: God says, 'I am—not *was*—the God of Abraham, the God of Isaac, the God of Jacob.' The living God defines himself not as the God of dead men, but of the *living*." Hearing this exchange the crowd was much impressed.

THE MOST IMPORTANT COMMAND

34-36 When the Pharisees heard how he had bested the Sadducees, they gathered their forces for an assault. One of their religion scholars spoke for them, posing a question they hoped would show him up: "Teacher, which command in God's Law is the most important?"

37-40 Jesus said, "'Love the Lord your God with all your passion and prayer and intelligence.' This is the most important, the first on any list. But there is a second to set alongside it: 'Love others as well as you love yourself.' These two commands are pegs; everything in God's Law and the Prophets hangs from them."

DAVID'S SON AND MASTER

41-42 As the Pharisees were regrouping, Jesus caught them off balance with his own test question: "What do you think about the Christ? Whose son is he?" They said, "David's son."

43-45 Jesus replied, "Well, if the Christ is David's son, how do you explain that David, under inspiration, named Christ his 'Master'?

God said to my Master,
"Sit here at my right hand
until I make your enemies your footstool."

"Now if David calls him 'Master,' how can he at the same time be his son?"

46   That stumped them, literalists that they were. Unwilling to risk losing face again in one of these public verbal exchanges, they quit asking questions for good.

RELIGIOUS FASHION SHOWS

1-3   **23** Now Jesus turned to address his disciples, along with the crowd that had gathered with them. "The religion scholars and Pharisees are competent teachers in God's Law. You won't go wrong in following their teachings on Moses. But be careful about following *them*. They talk a good line, but they don't live it. They don't take it into their hearts and live it out in their behavior. It's all spit-and-polish veneer.

4-7   "Instead of giving you God's Law as food and drink by which you can banquet on God, they package it in bundles of rules, loading you down like pack animals. They seem to take pleasure in watching you stagger under these loads, and wouldn't think of lifting a finger to help. Their lives are perpetual fashion shows, embroidered prayer shawls one day and flowery prayers the next. They love to sit at the head table at church dinners, basking in the most prominent positions, preening in the radiance of public flattery, receiving honorary degrees, and getting called 'Doctor' and 'Reverend.'

8-10   "Don't let people do that to *you*, put you on a pedestal like that. You all have a single Teacher, and you are all classmates. Don't set people up as experts over your life, letting them tell you what to do. Save that authority for God; let *him* tell you what to do. No one else should carry the title of 'Father'; you have only one Father, and he's in heaven. And don't let people maneuver you into taking charge of them. There is only one Life-Leader for you and them — Christ.

11-12   "Do you want to stand out? Then step down. Be a servant. If you puff yourself up, you'll get the wind knocked out of you. But if you're content to simply be yourself, your life will count for plenty.

FRAUDS!

13   "I've had it with you! You're hopeless, you religion scholars, you Pharisees! Frauds! Your lives are roadblocks to God's kingdom. You refuse to enter, and won't let anyone else in either.

15   "You're hopeless, you religion scholars and Pharisees! Frauds! You go halfway around the world to make a convert, but once you get him you make him into a replica of yourselves, double-damned.

16-22   "You're hopeless! What arrogant stupidity! You say, 'If someone makes a promise with his fingers crossed, that's nothing; but if he swears with his hand on the Bible, that's serious.' What ignorance! Does the leather on the Bible carry more weight than the skin on your hands? And what about this piece of trivia: 'If you shake hands on a promise, that's nothing; but if you raise your hand that God is your witness, that's serious'? What ridiculous hairsplitting! What difference does it make whether you shake hands or raise hands? A promise is a promise. What difference does it make if you make your promise inside or outside a house of worship? A promise is a promise. God is present, watching and holding you to account regardless.

23-24   "You're hopeless, you religion scholars and Pharisees! Frauds! You keep meticulous account books, tithing on every nickel and dime you get, but on the meat of God's Law, things like fairness and compassion and commitment — the absolute basics! — you carelessly take it or leave it. Careful bookkeeping is commendable, but the basics are required. Do you have any idea how silly you look, writing a life story that's wrong from start to finish, nitpicking over commas and semicolons?

25-26 "You're hopeless, you religion scholars and Pharisees! Frauds! You burnish the surface of your cups and bowls so they sparkle in the sun, while the insides are maggoty with your greed and gluttony. Stupid Pharisee! Scour the insides, and then the gleaming surface will mean something.

27-28 "You're hopeless, you religion scholars and Pharisees! Frauds! You're like manicured grave plots, grass clipped and the flowers bright, but six feet down it's all rotting bones and worm-eaten flesh. People look at you and think you're saints, but beneath the skin you're total frauds.

29-32 "You're hopeless, you religion scholars and Pharisees! Frauds! You build granite tombs for your prophets and marble monuments for your saints. And you say that if you had lived in the days of your ancestors, no blood would have been on your hands. You protest too much! You're cut from the same cloth as those murderers, and daily add to the death count.

33-34 "Snakes! Reptilian sneaks! Do you think you can worm your way out of this? Never have to pay the piper? It's on account of people like you that I send prophets and wise guides and scholars generation after generation — and generation after generation you treat them like dirt, greeting them with lynch mobs, hounding them with abuse.

35-36 "You can't squirm out of this: Every drop of righteous blood ever spilled on this earth, beginning with the blood of that good man Abel right down to the blood of Zechariah, Barachiah's son, whom you murdered at his prayers, is on your head. All this, I'm telling you, is coming down on you, on your generation.

37-39 "Jerusalem! Jerusalem! Murderer of prophets! Killer of the ones who brought you God's news! How often I've ached to embrace your children, the way a hen gathers her chicks under her wings, and you wouldn't let me. And now you're so desolate, nothing but a ghost town. What is there left to say? Only this: I'm out of here soon. The next time you see me you'll say, 'Oh, God has blessed him! He's come, bringing God's rule!'"

ROUTINE HISTORY

1-2 **24** Jesus then left the Temple. As he walked away, his disciples pointed out how very impressive the Temple architecture was. Jesus said, "You're not impressed by all this sheer *size*, are you? The truth of the matter is that there's not a stone in that building that is not going to end up in a pile of rubble."

3 Later as he was sitting on Mount Olives, his disciples approached and asked him, "Tell us, when are these things going to happen? What will be the sign of your coming, that the time's up?"

4-8 Jesus said, "Watch out for doomsday deceivers. Many leaders are going to show up with forged identities, claiming, 'I am Christ, the Messiah.' They will deceive a lot of people. When reports come in of wars and rumored wars, keep your head and don't panic. This is routine history; this is no sign of the end. Nation will fight nation and ruler fight ruler, over and over. Famines and earthquakes will occur in various places. This is nothing compared to what is coming.

9-10   "They are going to throw you to the wolves and kill you, everyone hating you because you carry my name. And then, going from bad to worse, it will be dog-eat-dog, everyone at each other's throat, everyone hating each other.

11-12   "In the confusion, lying preachers will come forward and deceive a lot of people. For many others, the overwhelming spread of evil will do them in — nothing left of their love but a mound of ashes.

13-14   "Staying with it — that's what God requires. Stay with it to the end. You won't be sorry, and you'll be saved. All during this time, the good news — the Message of the kingdom — will be preached all over the world, a witness staked out in every country. And then the end will come.

THE MONSTER OF DESECRATION

15-20   "But be ready to run for it when you see the monster of desecration set up in the Temple sanctuary. The prophet Daniel described this. If you've read Daniel, you'll know what I'm talking about. If you're living in Judea at the time, run for the hills; if you're working in the yard, don't return to the house to get anything; if you're out in the field, don't go back and get your coat. Pregnant and nursing mothers will have it especially hard. Hope and pray this won't happen during the winter or on a Sabbath.

21-22   "This is going to be trouble on a scale beyond what the world has ever seen, or will see again. If these days of trouble were left to run their course, nobody would make it. But on account of God's chosen people, the trouble will be cut short.

THE ARRIVAL OF THE SON OF MAN

23-25   "If anyone tries to flag you down, calling out, 'Here's the Messiah!' or points, 'There he is!' don't fall for it. Fake Messiahs and lying preachers are going to pop up everywhere. Their impressive credentials and dazzling performances will pull the wool over the eyes of even those who ought to know better. But I've given you fair warning.

26-28   "So if they say, 'Run to the country and see him arrive!' or, 'Quick, get downtown, see him come!' don't give them the time of day. The Arrival of the Son of Man isn't something you go to see. He comes like swift lightning to you! Whenever you see crowds gathering, think of carrion vultures circling, moving in, hovering over a rotting carcass. You can be quite sure that it's not the living Son of Man pulling in those crowds.

29   "Following those hard times,

Sun will fade out,
   moon cloud over,
Stars fall out of the sky,
   cosmic powers tremble.

30-31   "Then, the Arrival of the Son of Man! It will fill the skies — no one will miss it. Unready people all over the world, outsiders to the splendor and power, will raise a huge lament as they watch the Son of Man blazing out of heaven. At that same moment, he'll dispatch his angels with a trumpet-blast summons, pulling in God's chosen from the four winds, from pole to pole.

32-35   "Take a lesson from the fig tree. From the moment you notice its buds form, the merest hint of green, you know summer's just around the corner. So it is with you: When you see all these things, you'll know he's at the door. Don't take this lightly. I'm not just saying this for some future generation, but for all of you. This age continues until all these things take place. Sky and earth will wear out; my words won't wear out.

36 "But the exact day and hour? No one knows that, not even heaven's angels, not even the Son. Only the Father knows.

37-39 "The Arrival of the Son of Man will take place in times like Noah's. Before the great flood everyone was carrying on as usual, having a good time right up to the day Noah boarded the ark. They knew nothing—until the flood hit and swept everything away.

39-44 "The Son of Man's Arrival will be like that: Two men will be working in the field—one will be taken, one left behind; two women will be grinding at the mill—one will be taken, one left behind. So stay awake, alert. You have no idea what day your Master will show up. But you do know this: You know that if the homeowner had known what time of night the burglar would arrive, he would have been there with his dogs to prevent the break-in. Be vigilant just like that. You have no idea when the Son of Man is going to show up.

45-47 "Who here qualifies for the job of overseeing the kitchen? A person the Master can depend on to feed the workers on time each day. Someone the Master can drop in on unannounced and always find him doing his job. A God-blessed man or woman, I tell you. It won't be long before the Master will put this person in charge of the whole operation.

48-51 "But if that person only looks out for himself, and the minute the Master is away does what he pleases—abusing the help and throwing drunken parties for his friends—the Master is going to show up when he least expects it and make hash of him. He'll end up in the dump with the hypocrites, out in the cold shivering, teeth chattering."

THE STORY OF THE VIRGINS

1-5 **25** "God's kingdom is like ten young virgins who took oil lamps and went out to greet the bridegroom. Five were silly and five were smart. The silly virgins took lamps, but no extra oil. The smart virgins took jars of oil to feed their lamps. The bridegroom didn't show up when they expected him, and they all fell asleep.

6 "In the middle of the night someone yelled out, 'He's here! The bridegroom's here! Go out and greet him!'

7-8 "The ten virgins got up and got their lamps ready. The silly virgins said to the smart ones, 'Our lamps are going out; lend us some of your oil.'

9 "They answered, 'There might not be enough to go around; go buy your own.'

10 "They did, but while they were out buying oil, the bridegroom arrived. When everyone who was there to greet him had gone into the wedding feast, the door was locked.

11 "Much later, the other virgins, the silly ones, showed up and knocked on the door, saying, 'Master, we're here. Let us in.'

12 "He answered, 'Do I know you? I don't think I know you.'

13 "So stay alert. You have no idea when he might arrive.

14-18   "It's also like a man going off on an extended trip. He called his servants together and delegated responsibilities. To one he gave five thousand dollars, to another two thousand, to a third one thousand, depending on their abilities. Then he left. Right off, the first servant went to work and doubled his master's investment. The second did the same. But the man with the single thousand dug a hole and carefully buried his master's money.

19-21   "After a long absence, the master of those three servants came back and settled up with them. The one given five thousand dollars showed him how he had doubled his investment. His master commended him: 'Good work! You did your job well. From now on be my partner.'

22-23   "The servant with the two thousand showed how he also had doubled his master's investment. His master commended him: 'Good work! You did your job well. From now on be my partner.'

24-25   "The servant given one thousand said, 'Master, I know you have high standards and hate careless ways, that you demand the best and make no allowances for error. I was afraid I might disappoint you, so I found a good hiding place and secured your money. Here it is, safe and sound down to the last cent.'

26-27   "The master was furious. 'That's a terrible way to live! It's criminal to live cautiously like that! If you knew I was after the best, why did you do less than the least? The least you could have done would have been to invest the sum with the bankers, where at least I would have gotten a little interest.'

28-30   "'Take the thousand and give it to the one who risked the most. And get rid of this "play-it-safe" who won't go out on a limb. Throw him out into utter darkness.'

T H E   S H E E P   A N D   T H E   G O A T S

31-33   "When he finally arrives, blazing in beauty and all his angels with him, the Son of Man will take his place on his glorious throne. Then all the nations will be arranged before him and he will sort the people out, much as a shepherd sorts out sheep and goats, putting sheep to his right and goats to his left.

34-36   "Then the King will say to those on his right, 'Enter, you who are blessed by my Father! Take what's coming to you in this kingdom. It's been ready for you since the world's foundation. And here's why:

> I was hungry and you fed me,
> I was thirsty and you gave me a drink,
> I was homeless and you gave me a room,
> I was shivering and you gave me clothes,
> I was sick and you stopped to visit,
> I was in prison and you came to me.'

37-40   "Then those 'sheep' are going to say, 'Master, what are you talking about? When did we ever see you hungry and feed you, thirsty and give you a drink? And when did we ever see you sick or in prison and come to you?' Then the King will say, 'I'm telling the solemn truth: Whenever you did one of these things to someone overlooked or ignored, that was me — you did it to me.'

41-43 "Then he will turn to the 'goats,' the ones on his left, and say, 'Get out, worthless goats! You're good for nothing but the fires of hell. And why? Because —

I was hungry and you gave me no meal,
I was thirsty and you gave me no drink,
I was homeless and you gave me no bed,
I was shivering and you gave me no clothes,
Sick and in prison, and you never visited.'

44 "Then those 'goats' are going to say, 'Master, what are you talking about? When did we ever see you hungry or thirsty or homeless or shivering or sick or in prison and didn't help?'

45 "He will answer them, 'I'm telling the solemn truth: Whenever you failed to do one of these things to someone who was being overlooked or ignored, that was me — you failed to do it to me.'

46 "Then those 'goats' will be herded to their eternal doom, but the 'sheep' to their eternal reward."

ANOINTED FOR BURIAL

1-2 **26** When Jesus finished saying these things, he told his disciples, "You know that Passover comes in two days. That's when the Son of Man will be betrayed and handed over for crucifixion."

3-5 At that very moment, the party of high priests and religious leaders was meeting in the chambers of the Chief Priest named Caiaphas, conspiring to seize Jesus by stealth and kill him. They agreed that it should not be done during Passover Week. "We don't want a riot on our hands," they said.

6-9 When Jesus was at Bethany, a guest of Simon the Leper, a woman came up to him as he was eating dinner and anointed him with a bottle of very expensive perfume. When the disciples saw what was happening, they were furious. "That's criminal! This could have been sold for a lot and the money handed out to the poor."

10-13 When Jesus realized what was going on, he intervened. "Why are you giving this woman a hard time? She has just done something wonderfully significant for me. You will have the poor with you every day for the rest of your lives, but not me. When she poured this perfume on my body, what she really did was anoint me for burial. You can be sure that wherever in the whole world the Message is preached, what she has just done is going to be remembered and admired."

14-16 That is when one of the Twelve, the one named Judas Iscariot, went to the cabal of high priests and said, "What will you give me if I hand him over to you?" They settled on thirty silver pieces. He began looking for just the right moment to hand him over.

THE TRAITOR

17 On the first of the Days of Unleavened Bread, the disciples came to Jesus and said, "Where do you want us to prepare your Passover meal?"

18-19 He said, "Enter the city. Go up to a certain man and say, 'The Teacher says, My time is near. I and my disciples plan to celebrate the Passover meal at your house.'" The disciples followed Jesus' instructions to the letter, and prepared the Passover meal.

20-21 After sunset, he and the Twelve were sitting around the table. During the meal, he said, "I have something hard but important to say to you: One of you is going to hand me over to the conspirators."

22 They were stunned, and then began to ask, one after another, "It isn't me, is it, Master?"

23-24 Jesus answered, "The one who hands me over is someone I eat with daily, one who passes me food at the table. In one sense the Son of Man is entering into a way of treachery well-marked by the Scriptures — no surprises here. In another sense that man who turns him in, turns traitor to the Son of Man — better never to have been born than do this!"

25 Then Judas, already turned traitor, said, "It isn't me, is it, Rabbi?"
Jesus said, "Don't play games with me, Judas."

THE BREAD AND THE CUP

26-29 During the meal, Jesus took and blessed the bread, broke it, and gave it to his disciples:

Take, eat.
This is my body.

Taking the cup and thanking God, he gave it to them:

Drink this, all of you.
This is my blood,
God's new covenant poured out for many people
    for the forgiveness of sins.

"I'll not be drinking wine from this cup again until that new day when I'll drink with you in the kingdom of my Father."

30 They sang a hymn and went directly to Mount Olives.

GETHSEMANE

31-32 Then Jesus told them, "Before the night's over, you're going to fall to pieces because of what happens to me. There is a Scripture that says,

I'll strike the shepherd;
helter-skelter the sheep will be scattered.

But after I am raised up, I, your Shepherd, will go ahead of you, leading the way to Galilee."

33 Peter broke in, "Even if everyone else falls to pieces on account of you, I won't."

34 "Don't be so sure," Jesus said. "This very night, before the rooster crows up the dawn, you will deny me three times."

35 Peter protested, "Even if I had to die with you, I would never deny you." All the others said the same thing.

36-38 Then Jesus went with them to a garden called Gethsemane and told his disciples, "Stay here while I go over there and pray." Taking along Peter and the two sons of Zebedee, he plunged into an agonizing sorrow. Then he said, "This sorrow is crushing my life out. Stay here and keep vigil with me."

39 Going a little ahead, he fell on his face, praying, "My Father, if there is any way, get me out of this. But please, not what I want. You, what do *you* want?"

40-41 When he came back to his disciples, he found them sound asleep. He said to Peter, "Can't you stick it out with me a single hour? Stay alert; be in prayer so you don't wander into temptation without even knowing you're in danger. There is a part of you that is eager, ready for anything in God. But there's another part that's as lazy as an old dog sleeping by the fire."

42 He then left them a second time. Again he prayed, "My Father, if there is no other way than this, drinking this cup to the dregs, I'm ready. Do it your way."

43-44 When he came back, he again found them sound asleep. They simply couldn't keep their eyes open. This time he let them sleep on, and went back a third time to pray, going over the same ground one last time.

45-46 When he came back the next time, he said, "Are you going to sleep on and make a night of it? My time is up, the Son of Man is about to be handed over to the hands of sinners. Get up! Let's get going! My betrayer is here."

WITH SWORDS AND CLUBS

47-49 The words were barely out of his mouth when Judas (the one from the Twelve) showed up, and with him a gang from the high priests and religious leaders brandishing swords and clubs. The betrayer had worked out a sign with them: "The one I kiss, that's the one — seize him." He went straight to Jesus, greeted him, "How are you, Rabbi?" and kissed him.

50-51 Jesus said, "Friend, why this charade?"

Then they came on him — grabbed him and roughed him up. One of those with Jesus pulled his sword and, taking a swing at the Chief Priest's servant, cut off his ear.

52-54 Jesus said, "Put your sword back where it belongs. All who use swords are destroyed by swords. Don't you realize that I am able right now to call to my Father, and twelve companies — more, if I want them — of fighting angels would be here, battle-ready? But if I did that, how would the Scriptures come true that say this is the way it has to be?"

55-56 Then Jesus addressed the mob: "What is this — coming out after me with swords and clubs as if I were a dangerous criminal? Day after day I have been sitting in the Temple teaching, and you never so much as lifted a hand against me. You've done it this way to confirm and fulfill the prophetic writings."

Then all the disciples cut and ran.

FALSE CHARGES

57-58 The gang that had seized Jesus led him before Caiaphas the Chief Priest, where the religion scholars and leaders had assembled. Peter followed at a safe distance until they got to the Chief Priest's courtyard. Then he slipped in and mingled with the servants, watching to see how things would turn out.

59-60 The high priests, conspiring with the Jewish Council, tried to cook up charges against Jesus in order to sentence him to death. But even though many stepped up, making up one false accusation after another, nothing was believable.

60-61 Finally two men came forward with this: "He said, 'I can tear down this Temple of God and after three days rebuild it.'"

62 The Chief Priest stood up and said, "What do you have to say to the accusation?"

63 Jesus kept silent.

Then the Chief Priest said, "I command you by the authority of the living God to say if you are the Messiah, the Son of God."

64 Jesus was curt: "You yourself said it. And that's not all. Soon you'll see it for yourself:

The Son of Man seated at the right hand of the Mighty One,
Arriving on the clouds of heaven."

65-66 At that, the Chief Priest lost his temper, ripping his robes, yelling, "He blasphemed! Why do we need witnesses to accuse him? You all heard him blaspheme! Are you going to stand for such blasphemy?"

They all said, "Death! That seals his death sentence."

67-68 Then they were spitting in his face and banging him around. They jeered as they slapped him: "Prophesy, Messiah: Who hit you that time?"

DENIAL IN THE COURTYARD

69 All this time, Peter was sitting out in the courtyard. One servant girl came up to him and said, "You were with Jesus the Galilean."

70 In front of everybody there, he denied it. "I don't know what you're talking about."

71 As he moved over toward the gate, someone else said to the people there, "This man was with Jesus the Nazarene."

72 Again he denied it, salting his denial with an oath: "I swear, I never laid eyes on the man."

73 Shortly after that, some bystanders approached Peter. "You've got to be one of them. Your accent gives you away."

74-75 Then he got really nervous and swore. "I don't know the man!"

Just then a rooster crowed. Peter remembered what Jesus had said: "Before the rooster crows, you will deny me three times." He went out and cried and cried and cried.

THIRTY SILVER COINS

1-2 **27** In the first light of dawn, all the high priests and religious leaders met and put the finishing touches on their plot to kill Jesus. Then they tied him up and paraded him to Pilate, the governor.

3-4 Judas, the one who betrayed him, realized that Jesus was doomed. Overcome with remorse, he gave back the thirty silver coins to the high priests, saying, "I've sinned. I've betrayed an innocent man."

They said, "What do we care? That's *your* problem!"

5 Judas threw the silver coins into the Temple and left. Then he went out and hung himself.

6-10 The high priests picked up the silver pieces, but then didn't know what to do with them. "It wouldn't be right to give this—a payment for murder!—as an offering in the Temple." They decided to get rid of it by buying the "Potter's Field" and use it as a burial place for the homeless. That's how the field got called "Murder Meadow," a name that has stuck to this day. Then Jeremiah's words became history:

> They took the thirty silver pieces,
> The price of the one priced by some sons of Israel,
> And they purchased the potter's field.

And so they unwittingly followed the divine instructions to the letter.

PILATE

11 Jesus was placed before the governor, who questioned him: "Are you the 'King of the Jews'?"

Jesus said, "If you say so."

12-14 But when the accusations rained down hot and heavy from the high priests and religious leaders, he said nothing. Pilate asked him, "Do you hear that long list of accusations? Aren't you going to say something?" Jesus kept silence — not a word from his mouth. The governor was impressed, really impressed.

15-18 It was an old custom during the Feast for the governor to pardon a single prisoner named by the crowd. At the time, they had the infamous Jesus Barabbas in prison. With the crowd before him, Pilate said, "Which prisoner do you want me to pardon: Jesus Barabbas, or Jesus the so-called Christ?" He knew it was through sheer spite that they had turned Jesus over to him.

19 While court was still in session, Pilate's wife sent him a message: "Don't get mixed up in judging this noble man. I've just been through a long and troubled night because of a dream about him."

20 Meanwhile, the high priests and religious leaders had talked the crowd into asking for the pardon of Barabbas and the execution of Jesus.

21 The governor asked, "Which of the two do you want me to pardon?"

They said, "Barabbas!"

22 "Then what do I do with Jesus, the so-called Christ?"

They all shouted, "Nail him to a cross!"

23 He objected, "But for what crime?"

But they yelled all the louder, "Nail him to a cross!"

24 When Pilate saw that he was getting nowhere and that a riot was imminent, he took a basin of water and washed his hands in full sight of the crowd, saying, "I'm washing my hands of responsibility for this man's death. From now on, it's in your hands. You're judge and jury."

25 The crowd answered, "We'll take the blame, we and our children after us."

26 Then he pardoned Barabbas. But he had Jesus whipped, and then handed over for crucifixion.

THE CRUCIFIXION

27-31 The soldiers assigned to the governor took Jesus into the governor's palace and got the entire brigade together for some fun. They stripped him and dressed him in a red toga. They plaited a crown from branches of a thornbush and set it on his head. They put a stick in his right hand for a scepter. Then they knelt before him in mocking reverence: "Bravo, King of the Jews!" they said. "Bravo!" Then they spit on him and hit him on the head with the stick. When they had had their fun, they took off the toga and put his own clothes back on him. Then they proceeded out to the crucifixion.

32-34 Along the way they came on a man from Cyrene named Simon and made him carry Jesus' cross. Arriving at Golgotha, the place they call "Skull

Hill," they offered him a mild painkiller (a mixture of wine and myrrh), but when he tasted it he wouldn't drink it.

³⁵⁻⁴⁰ After they had finished nailing him to the cross and were waiting for him to die, they whiled away the time by throwing dice for his clothes. Above his head they had posted the criminal charge against him: THIS IS JESUS, THE KING OF THE JEWS. Along with him, they also crucified two criminals, one to his right, the other to his left. People passing along the road jeered, shaking their heads in mock lament: "You bragged that you could tear down the Temple and then rebuild it in three days — so show us your stuff! Save yourself! If you're really God's Son, come down from that cross!"

⁴¹⁻⁴⁴ The high priests, along with the religion scholars and leaders, were right there mixing it up with the rest of them, having a great time poking fun at him: "He saved others — he can't save himself! King of Israel, is he? Then let him get down from that cross. We'll *all* become believers then! He was so sure of God — well, let him rescue his 'Son' now — if he wants him! He did claim to be God's Son, didn't he?" Even the two criminals crucified next to him joined in the mockery.

⁴⁵⁻⁴⁶ From noon to three, the whole earth was dark. Around mid-afternoon Jesus groaned out of the depths, crying loudly, "*Eli, Eli, lama sabachthani?*" which means, "My God, my God, why have you abandoned me?"

⁴⁷⁻⁴⁹ Some bystanders who heard him said, "He's calling for Elijah." One of them ran and got a sponge soaked in sour wine and lifted it on a stick so he could drink. The others joked, "Don't be in such a hurry. Let's see if Elijah comes and saves him."

⁵⁰ But Jesus, again crying out loudly, breathed his last.

⁵¹⁻⁵³ At that moment, the Temple curtain was ripped in two, top to bottom. There was an earthquake, and rocks were split in pieces. What's more, tombs were opened up, and many bodies of believers asleep in their graves were raised. (After Jesus' resurrection, they left the tombs, entered the holy city, and appeared to many.)

⁵⁴ The captain of the guard and those with him, when they saw the earthquake and everything else that was happening, were scared to death. They said, "This has to be the Son of God!"

⁵⁵⁻⁵⁶ There were also quite a few women watching from a distance, women who had followed Jesus from Galilee in order to serve him. Among them were Mary Magdalene, Mary the mother of James and Joseph, and the mother of the Zebedee brothers.

THE TOMB

⁵⁷⁻⁶¹ Late in the afternoon a wealthy man from Arimathea, a disciple of Jesus, arrived. His name was Joseph. He went to Pilate and asked for Jesus' body. Pilate granted his request. Joseph took the body and wrapped it in clean linens, put it in his own tomb, a new tomb only recently cut into the rock, and rolled a large stone across the entrance. Then he went off. But Mary Magdalene and the other Mary stayed, sitting in plain view of the tomb.

⁶²⁻⁶⁴ After sundown, the high priests and Pharisees arranged a meeting with Pilate. They said, "Sir, we just remembered that that liar announced while he was still alive, 'After three days I will be raised.' We've got to get that tomb sealed until the third day. There's a good chance his disciples will come and steal the corpse and then go around saying, 'He's risen from the dead.' Then we'll be worse off than before, the final deceit surpassing the first."

65-66 Pilate told them, "You will have a guard. Go ahead and secure it the best you can." So they went out and secured the tomb, sealing the stone and posting guards.

RISEN FROM THE DEAD

1-4 28 After the Sabbath, as the first light of the new week dawned, Mary Magdalene and the other Mary came to keep vigil at the tomb. Suddenly the earth reeled and rocked under their feet as God's angel came down from heaven, came right up to where they were standing. He rolled back the stone and then sat on it. Shafts of lightning blazed from him. His garments shimmered snow-white. The guards at the tomb were scared to death. They were so frightened, they couldn't move.

5-6 The angel spoke to the women: "There is nothing to fear here. I know you're looking for Jesus, the One they nailed to the cross. He is not here. He was raised, just as he said. Come and look at the place where he was placed.

7 "Now, get on your way quickly and tell his disciples, 'He is risen from the dead. He is going on ahead of you to Galilee. You will see him there.' That's the message."

8-10 The women, deep in wonder and full of joy, lost no time in leaving the tomb. They ran to tell the disciples. Then Jesus met them, stopping them in their tracks. "Good morning!" he said. They fell to their knees, embraced his feet, and worshiped him. Jesus said, "You're holding on to me for dear life! Don't be frightened like that. Go tell my brothers that they are to go to Galilee, and that I'll meet them there."

11-15 Meanwhile, the guards had scattered, but a few of them went into the city and told the high priests everything that had happened. They called a meeting of the religious leaders and came up with a plan: They took a large sum of money and gave it to the soldiers, bribing them to say, "His disciples came in the night and stole the body while we were sleeping." They assured them, "If the governor hears about your sleeping on duty, we will make sure you don't get blamed." The soldiers took the bribe and did as they were told. That story, cooked up in the Jewish High Council, is still going around.

16-17 Meanwhile, the eleven disciples were on their way to Galilee, headed for the mountain Jesus had set for their reunion. The moment they saw him they worshiped him. Some, though, held back, not sure about *worship*, about risking themselves totally.

18-20 Jesus, undeterred, went right ahead and gave his charge: "God authorized and commanded me to commission you: Go out and train everyone you meet, far and near, in this way of life, marking them by baptism in the threefold name: Father, Son, and Holy Spirit. Then instruct them in the practice of all I have commanded you. I'll be with you as you do this, day after day after day, right up to the end of the age."

MARK

Mark wastes no time in getting down to business—a single-sentence introduction, and not a digression to be found from beginning to end. An event has taken place that radically changes the way we look at and experience the world, and he can't wait to tell us about it. There's an air of breathless excitement in nearly every sentence he writes. The sooner we get the message, the better off we'll be, for the message is good, incredibly good: God is here, and he's on our side.

The bare announcement that God exists doesn't particularly qualify as news. Most people in most centuries have believed in the existence of God or gods. It may well be, in fact, that human beings in aggregate and through the centuries have given more attention and concern to divinity than to all their other concerns put together—food, housing, clothing, pleasure, work, family, whatever.

But that God is here right now, and on our side, actively seeking to help us in the way we most need help—*this* qualifies as news. For, common as belief in God is, there is also an enormous amount of guesswork and gossip surrounding the subject, which results in runaway superstition, anxiety, and exploitation. So Mark, understandably, is in a hurry to tell us what happened in the birth, life, death, and resurrection of Jesus—the Event that reveals the truth of God to us, so that we can live in reality and not illusion. He doesn't want us to waste a minute of these precious lives of ours ignorant of this most practical of all matters—that God is passionate to save us.

MARK

JOHN THE BAPTIZER

1-3 The good news of Jesus Christ — the Message! — begins here, following to the letter the scroll of the prophet Isaiah.

Watch closely: I'm sending my preacher ahead of you;
He'll make the road smooth for you.
Thunder in the desert!
Prepare for God's arrival!
Make the road smooth and straight!

4-6 John the Baptizer appeared in the wild, preaching a baptism of life-change that leads to forgiveness of sins. People thronged to him from Judea and Jerusalem and, as they confessed their sins, were baptized by him in the Jordan River into a changed life. John wore a camel-hair habit, tied at the waist with a leather belt. He ate locusts and wild field honey.

7-8 As he preached he said, "The real action comes next: The star in this drama, to whom I'm a mere stagehand, will change your life. I'm baptizing you here in the river, turning your old life in for a kingdom life. His baptism — a holy baptism by the Holy Spirit — will change you from the inside out."

9-11 At this time, Jesus came from Nazareth in Galilee and was baptized by John in the Jordan. The moment he came out of the water, he saw the sky split open and God's Spirit, looking like a dove, come down on him. Along with the Spirit, a voice: "You are my Son, chosen and marked by my love, pride of my life."

GOD'S KINGDOM IS HERE

12-13 At once, this same Spirit pushed Jesus out into the wild. For forty wilderness days and nights he was tested by Satan. Wild animals were his companions, and angels took care of him.

14-15 After John was arrested, Jesus went to Galilee preaching the Message of God: "Time's up! God's kingdom is here. Change your life and believe the Message."

16-18 Passing along the beach of Lake Galilee, he saw Simon and his brother Andrew net-fishing. Fishing was their regular work. Jesus said to them, "Come with me. I'll make a new kind of fisherman out of you. I'll show you how to catch men and women instead of perch and bass." They didn't ask questions. They dropped their nets and followed.

19-20 A dozen yards or so down the beach, he saw the brothers James and John, Zebedee's sons. They were in the boat, mending their fishnets. Right off, he made the same offer. Immediately, they left their father Zebedee, the boat, and the hired hands, and followed.

CONFIDENT TEACHING

21-22 Then they entered Capernaum. When the Sabbath arrived, Jesus lost no time in getting to the meeting place. He spent the day there teaching. They were surprised at his teaching — so forthright, so confident — not quibbling and quoting like the religion scholars.

23-24 Suddenly, while still in the meeting place, he was interrupted by a man who was deeply disturbed and yelling out, "What business do you have here with us, Jesus? Nazarene! I know what you're up to! You're the Holy One of God, and you've come to destroy us!"

25-26 Jesus shut him up: "Quiet! Get out of him!" The afflicting spirit threw the man into spasms, protesting loudly — and got out.

27-28 Everyone there was incredulous, buzzing with curiosity. "What's going on here? A new teaching that does what it says? He shuts up defiling, demonic spirits and sends them packing!" News of this traveled fast and was soon all over Galilee.

29-31 Directly on leaving the meeting place, they came to Simon and Andrew's house, accompanied by James and John. Simon's mother-in-law was sick in bed, burning up with fever. They told Jesus. He went to her, took her hand, and raised her up. No sooner had the fever left than she was up fixing dinner for them.

32-34 That evening, after the sun was down, they brought sick and evil-afflicted people to him, the whole city lined up at his door! He cured their sick bodies and tormented spirits. Because the demons knew his true identity, he didn't let them say a word.

THE LEPER

35-37 While it was still night, way before dawn, he got up and went out to a secluded spot and prayed. Simon and those with him went looking for him. They found him and said, "Everybody's looking for you."

38-39 Jesus said, "Let's go to the rest of the villages so I can preach there also. This is why I've come." He went to their meeting places all through Galilee, preaching and throwing out the demons.

40 A leper came to him, begging on his knees, "If you want to, you can cleanse me."

41-45 Deeply moved, Jesus put out his hand, touched him, and said, "I want to. Be clean." Then and there the leprosy was gone, his skin smooth and healthy. Jesus dismissed him with strict orders: "Say nothing to anyone. Take the offering for cleansing that Moses prescribed and present yourself to the priest. This will validate your healing to the people." But as soon as the man was out of earshot, he told everyone he met what had happened, spreading the news all over town. So Jesus kept to out-of-the-way places, no longer able to move freely in and out of the city. But people found him, and came from all over.

A PARAPLEGIC

1-5 After a few days, Jesus returned to Capernaum, and word got around that he was back home. A crowd gathered, jamming the entrance so no one could get in or out. He was teaching the Word. They brought a paraplegic to him, carried by four men. When they weren't able to get in because of the crowd, they removed part of the roof and lowered the paraplegic on his stretcher. Impressed by their bold belief, Jesus said to the paraplegic, "Son, I forgive your sins."

6-7 Some religion scholars sitting there started whispering among themselves, "He can't talk that way! That's blasphemy! God and only God can forgive sins."

8-12 Jesus knew right away what they were thinking, and said, "Why are you so skeptical? Which is simpler: to say to the paraplegic, 'I forgive your sins,' or say, 'Get up, take your stretcher, and start walking'? Well, just so it's clear that I'm the Son of Man and authorized to do either, or both . . ." (he looked now at the paraplegic), "Get up. Pick up your stretcher and go home." And the man did it—got up, grabbed his stretcher, and walked out, with everyone there watching him. They rubbed their eyes, incredulous—and then praised God, saying, "We've never seen anything like this!"

THE TAX COLLECTOR

13-14 Then Jesus went again to walk alongside the lake. Again a crowd came to him, and he taught them. Strolling along, he saw Levi, son of Alphaeus, at his work collecting taxes. Jesus said, "Come along with me." He came.

15-16 Later Jesus and his disciples were at home having supper with a collection of disreputable guests. Unlikely as it seems, more than a few of them had become followers. The religion scholars and Pharisees saw him keeping this kind of company and lit into his disciples: "What kind of example is this, acting cozy with the riffraff?"

17 Jesus, overhearing, shot back, "Who needs a doctor: the healthy or the sick? I'm here inviting the sin-sick, not the spiritually-fit."

FEASTING OR FASTING?

18 The disciples of John and the disciples of the Pharisees made a practice of fasting. Some people confronted Jesus: "Why do the followers of John and the Pharisees take on the discipline of fasting, but your followers don't?"

19-20 Jesus said, "When you're celebrating a wedding, you don't skimp on the cake and wine. You feast. Later you may need to pull in your belt, but not now. As long as the bride and groom are with you, you have a good time. No one throws cold water on a friendly bonfire. This is Kingdom Come!"

21-22 He went on, "No one cuts up a fine silk scarf to patch old work clothes; you want fabrics that match. And you don't put your wine in cracked bottles."

23-24 One Sabbath day he was walking through a field of ripe grain. As his disciples made a path, they pulled off heads of grain. The Pharisees told on them to Jesus: "Look, your disciples are breaking Sabbath rules!"

25-28 Jesus said, "Really? Haven't you ever read what David did when he was hungry, along with those who were with him? How he entered the sanctuary and ate fresh bread off the altar, with the Chief Priest Abiathar right there watching—holy bread that no one but priests were allowed to eat—and handed it out to his companions?" Then Jesus said, "The Sabbath was made to serve us; we weren't made to serve the Sabbath. The Son of Man is no lackey to the Sabbath. He's in charge!"

DOING GOOD ON THE SABBATH

1-3 **3** Then he went back in the meeting place where he found a man with a crippled hand. The Pharisees had their eyes on Jesus to see if he would heal him, hoping to catch him in a Sabbath infraction. He said to the man with the crippled hand, "Stand here where we can see you."

4 Then he spoke to the people: "What kind of action suits the Sabbath best? Doing good or doing evil? Helping people or leaving them helpless?" No one said a word.

5-6   He looked them in the eye, one after another, angry now, furious at their hard-nosed religion. He said to the man, "Hold out your hand." He held it out—it was as good as new! The Pharisees got out as fast as they could, sputtering about how they would join forces with Herod's followers and ruin him.

THE TWELVE APOSTLES

7-10   Jesus went off with his disciples to the sea to get away. But a huge crowd from Galilee trailed after them—also from Judea, Jerusalem, Idumea, across the Jordan, and around Tyre and Sidon—swarms of people who had heard the reports and had come to see for themselves. He told his disciples to get a boat ready so he wouldn't be trampled by the crowd. He had healed many people, and now everyone who had something wrong was pushing and shoving to get near and touch him.

11-12   Evil spirits, when they recognized him, fell down and cried out, "You are the Son of God!" But Jesus would have none of it. He shut them up, forbidding them to identify him in public.

13-19   He climbed a mountain and invited those he wanted with him. They climbed together. He settled on twelve, and designated them apostles. The plan was that they would be with him, and he would send them out to proclaim the Word and give them authority to banish demons. These are the Twelve:

> Simon (Jesus later named him Peter, meaning "Rock"),
> James, son of Zebedee,
> John, brother of James (Jesus nicknamed the Zebedee
>   brothers Boanerges, meaning "Sons of Thunder"),
> Andrew,
> Philip,
> Bartholomew,
> Matthew,
> Thomas,
> James, son of Alphaeus,
> Thaddaeus,
> Simon the Canaanite,
> Judas Iscariot (who betrayed him).

SATAN FIGHTING SATAN?

20-21   Jesus came home and, as usual, a crowd gathered—so many making demands on him that there wasn't even time to eat. His friends heard what was going on and went to rescue him, by force if necessary. They suspected he was getting carried away with himself.

22-27   The religion scholars from Jerusalem came down spreading rumors that he was working black magic, using devil tricks to impress them with spiritual power. Jesus confronted their slander with a story: "Does it make sense to send a devil to catch a devil, to use Satan to get rid of Satan? A constantly squabbling family disintegrates. If Satan were fighting Satan, there soon wouldn't be any Satan left. Do you think it's possible in broad daylight to enter the house of an awake, able-bodied man, and walk off with his possessions unless you tie him up first? Tie him up, though, and you can clean him out.

28-30 "Listen to this carefully. I'm warning you. There's nothing done or said that can't be forgiven. But if you persist in your slanders against God's Holy Spirit, you are repudiating the very One who forgives, sawing off the branch on which you're sitting, severing by your own perversity all connection with the One who forgives." He gave this warning because they were accusing him of being in league with Evil.

JESUS' MOTHER AND BROTHERS

31-32 Just then his mother and brothers showed up. Standing outside, they relayed a message that they wanted a word with him. He was surrounded by the crowd when he was given the message, "Your mother and brothers and sisters are outside looking for you."

33-35 Jesus responded, "Who do you think are my mother and brothers?" Looking around, taking in everyone seated around him, he said, "Right here, right in front of you—my mother and my brothers. Obedience is thicker than blood. The person who obeys God's will is my brother and sister and mother."

THE STORY OF THE SCATTERED SEED

1-2 4 He went back to teaching by the sea. A crowd built up to such a great size that he had to get into an offshore boat, using the boat as a pulpit as the people pushed to the water's edge. He taught by using stories, many stories.

3-8 "Listen. What do you make of this? A farmer planted seed. As he scattered the seed, some of it fell on the road and birds ate it. Some fell in the gravel; it sprouted quickly but didn't put down roots, so when the sun came up it withered just as quickly. Some fell in the weeds; as it came up, it was strangled among the weeds and nothing came of it. Some fell on good earth and came up with a flourish, producing a harvest exceeding his wildest dreams.

9 "Are you listening to this? Really listening?"

10-12 When they were off by themselves, those who were close to him, along with the Twelve, asked about the stories. He told them, "You've been given insight into God's kingdom—you know how it works. But to those who can't see it yet, everything comes in stories, creating readiness, nudging them toward receptive insight. These are people—

Whose eyes are open but don't see a thing,
Whose ears are open but don't understand a word,
Who avoid making an about-face and getting forgiven."

13 He continued, "Do you see how this story works? All my stories work this way.

14-15 "The farmer plants the Word. Some people are like the seed that falls on the hardened soil of the road. No sooner do they hear the Word than Satan snatches away what has been planted in them.

16-17 "And some are like the seed that lands in the gravel. When they first hear the Word, they respond with great enthusiasm. But there is such shallow soil of character that when the emotions wear off and some difficulty arrives, there is nothing to show for it.

18-19 "The seed cast in the weeds represents the ones who hear the kingdom news but are overwhelmed with worries about all the things they have to do and all the things they want to get. The stress strangles what they heard, and nothing comes of it.

20 "But the seed planted in the good earth represents those who hear the Word, embrace it, and produce a harvest beyond their wildest dreams."

GIVING, NOT GETTING

21-22 Jesus went on: "Does anyone bring a lamp home and put it under a wash-tub or beneath the bed? Don't you put it up on a table or on the mantel? We're not keeping secrets, we're telling them; we're not hiding things, we're bringing them out into the open.

23 "Are you listening to this? Really listening?

24-25 "Listen carefully to what I am saying — and be wary of the shrewd advice that tells you how to get ahead in the world on your own. Giving, not getting, is the way. Generosity begets generosity. Stinginess impoverishes."

NEVER WITHOUT A STORY

26-29 Then Jesus said, "God's kingdom is like seed thrown on a field by a man who then goes to bed and forgets about it. The seed sprouts and grows — he has no idea how it happens. The earth does it all without his help: first a green stem of grass, then a bud, then the ripened grain. When the grain is fully formed, he reaps — harvest time!

30-32 "How can we picture God's kingdom? What kind of story can we use? It's like a pine nut. When it lands on the ground it is quite small as seeds go, yet once it is planted it grows into a huge pine tree with thick branches. Eagles nest in it."

33-34 With many stories like these, he presented his message to them, fitting the stories to their experience and maturity. He was never without a story when he spoke. When he was alone with his disciples, he went over every-thing, sorting out the tangles, untying the knots.

THE WIND RAN OUT OF BREATH

35-38 Late that day he said to them, "Let's go across to the other side." They took him in the boat as he was. Other boats came along. A huge storm came up. Waves poured into the boat, threatening to sink it. And Jesus was in the stern, head on a pillow, sleeping! They roused him, saying, "Teacher, is it nothing to you that we're going down?"

39-40 Awake now, he told the wind to pipe down and said to the sea, "Quiet! Settle down!" The wind ran out of breath; the sea became smooth as glass. Jesus reprimanded the disciples: "Why are you such cowards? Don't you have any faith at all?"

41 They were in absolute awe, staggered. "Who is this, anyway?" they asked. "Wind and sea at his beck and call!"

THE MADMAN

1-5 They arrived on the other side of the sea in the country of the Gerasenes. As Jesus got out of the boat, a madman from the cemetery came up to him. He lived there among the tombs and graves. No one could restrain him — he couldn't be chained, couldn't be tied down. He had been tied up many times with chains and ropes, but he broke the chains, snapped the ropes. No one was strong enough to tame him. Night and day he roamed through the graves and the hills, screaming out and slashing himself with sharp stones.

6-8   When he saw Jesus a long way off, he ran and bowed in worship before him — then bellowed in protest, "What business do you have, Jesus, Son of the High God, messing with me? I swear to God, don't give me a hard time!" (Jesus had just commanded the tormenting evil spirit, "Out! Get out of the man!")

9-10   Jesus asked him, "Tell me your name."

He replied, "My name is Mob. I'm a rioting mob." Then he desperately begged Jesus not to banish them from the country.

11-13   A large herd of pigs was browsing and rooting on a nearby hill. The demons begged him, "Send us to the pigs so we can live in them." Jesus gave the order. But it was even worse for the pigs than for the man. Crazed, they stampeded over a cliff into the sea and drowned.

14-15   Those tending the pigs, scared to death, bolted and told their story in town and country. Everyone wanted to see what had happened. They came up to Jesus and saw the madman sitting there wearing decent clothes and making sense, no longer a walking madhouse of a man.

16-17   Those who had seen it told the others what had happened to the demon-possessed man and the pigs. At first they were in awe — and then they were upset, upset over the drowned pigs. They demanded that Jesus leave and not come back.

18-20   As Jesus was getting into the boat, the demon-delivered man begged to go along, but he wouldn't let him. Jesus said, "Go home to your own people. Tell them your story — what the Master did, how he had mercy on you." The man went back and began to preach in the Ten Towns area about what Jesus had done for him. He was the talk of the town.

A RISK OF FAITH

21-24 After Jesus crossed over by boat, a large crowd met him at the seaside. One of the meeting-place leaders named Jairus came. When he saw Jesus, he fell to his knees, beside himself as he begged, "My dear daughter is at death's door. Come and lay hands on her so she will get well and live." Jesus went with him, the whole crowd tagging along, pushing and jostling him.

25-29   A woman who had suffered a condition of hemorrhaging for twelve years — a long succession of physicians had treated her, and treated her badly, taking all her money and leaving her worse off than before — had heard about Jesus. She slipped in from behind and touched his robe. She was thinking to herself, "If I can put a finger on his robe, I can get well." The moment she did it, the flow of blood dried up. She could feel the change and knew her plague was over and done with.

30   At the same moment, Jesus felt energy discharging from him. He turned around to the crowd and asked, "Who touched my robe?"

31   His disciples said, "What are you talking about? With this crowd pushing and jostling you, you're asking, 'Who touched me?' Dozens have touched you!"

32-33   But he went on asking, looking around to see who had done it. The woman, knowing what had happened, knowing she was the one, stepped up in fear and trembling, knelt before him, and gave him the whole story.

34   Jesus said to her, "Daughter, you took a risk of faith, and now you're healed and whole. Live well, live blessed! Be healed of your plague."

35 While he was still talking, some people came from the leader's house and told him, "Your daughter is dead. Why bother the Teacher any more?"

36 Jesus overheard what they were talking about and said to the leader, "Don't listen to them; just trust me."

37-40 He permitted no one to go in with him except Peter, James, and John. They entered the leader's house and pushed their way through the gossips looking for a story and neighbors bringing in casseroles. Jesus was abrupt: "Why all this busybody grief and gossip? This child isn't dead; she's sleeping." Provoked to sarcasm, they told him he didn't know what he was talking about.

40-43 But when he had sent them all out, he took the child's father and mother, along with his companions, and entered the child's room. He clasped the girl's hand and said, "*Talitha koum*," which means, "Little girl, get up." At that, she was up and walking around! This girl was twelve years of age. They, of course, were all beside themselves with joy. He gave them strict orders that no one was to know what had taken place in that room. Then he said, "Give her something to eat."

JUST A CARPENTER

1-2 6 He left there and returned to his hometown. His disciples came along. On the Sabbath, he gave a lecture in the meeting place. He made a real hit, impressing everyone. "We had no idea he was this good!" they said. "How did he get so wise all of a sudden, get such ability?"

3 But in the next breath they were cutting him down: "He's just a carpenter—Mary's boy. We've known him since he was a kid. We know his brothers, James, Justus, Jude, and Simon, and his sisters. Who does he think he is?" They tripped over what little they knew about him and fell, sprawling. And they never got any further.

4-6 Jesus told them, "A prophet has little honor in his hometown, among his relatives, on the streets he played in as a child." Jesus wasn't able to do much of anything there—he laid hands on a few sick people and healed them, that's all. He couldn't get over their stubbornness. He left and made a circuit of the other villages, teaching.

THE TWELVE

7-8 Jesus called the Twelve to him, and sent them out in pairs. He gave them authority and power to deal with the evil opposition. He sent them off with these instructions:

8-9 "Don't think you need a lot of extra equipment for this. *You* are the equipment. No special appeals for funds. Keep it simple.

10 "And no luxury inns. Get a modest place and be content there until you leave.

11 "If you're not welcomed, not listened to, quietly withdraw. Don't make a scene. Shrug your shoulders and be on your way."

12-13 Then they were on the road. They preached with joyful urgency that life can be radically different; right and left they sent the demons packing; they brought wellness to the sick, anointing their bodies, healing their spirits.

THE DEATH OF JOHN

14 King Herod heard of all this, for by this time the name of Jesus was on everyone's lips. He said, "This has to be John the Baptizer come back from the dead—that's why he's able to work miracles!"

15 Others said, "No, it's Elijah."

Others said, "He's a prophet, just like one of the old-time prophets."

16 But Herod wouldn't budge: "It's John, sure enough. I cut off his head, and now he's back, alive."

17-20 Herod was the one who had ordered the arrest of John, put him in chains, and sent him to prison at the nagging of Herodias, his brother Philip's wife. For John had provoked Herod by naming his relationship with Herodias "adultery." Herodias, smoldering with hate, wanted to kill him, but didn't dare because Herod was in awe of John. Convinced that he was a holy man, he gave him special treatment. Whenever he listened to him he was miserable with guilt—and yet he couldn't stay away. Something in John kept pulling him back.

21-22 But a portentous day arrived when Herod threw a birthday party, inviting all the brass and bluebloods in Galilee. Herodias's daughter entered the banquet hall and danced for the guests. She dazzled Herod and the guests.

22-23 The king said to the girl, "Ask me anything. I'll give you anything you want." Carried away, he kept on, "I swear, I'll split my kingdom with you if you say so!"

24 She went back to her mother and said, "What should I ask for?"

"Ask for the head of John the Baptizer."

25 Excited, she ran back to the king and said, "I want the head of John the Baptizer served up on a platter. And I want it now!"

26-29 That sobered the king up fast. But unwilling to lose face with his guests, he caved in and let her have her wish. The king sent the executioner off to the prison with orders to bring back John's head. He went, cut off John's head, brought it back on a platter, and presented it to the girl, who gave it to her mother. When John's disciples heard about this, they came and got the body and gave it a decent burial.

SUPPER FOR FIVE THOUSAND

30-31 The apostles then rendezvoused with Jesus and reported on all that they had done and taught. Jesus said, "Come off by yourselves; let's take a break and get a little rest." For there was constant coming and going. They didn't even have time to eat.

32-34 So they got in the boat and went off to a remote place by themselves. Someone saw them going and the word got around. From the surrounding towns people went out on foot, running, and got there ahead of them. When Jesus arrived, he saw this huge crowd. At the sight of them, his heart broke—like sheep with no shepherd they were. He went right to work teaching them.

35-36 When his disciples thought this had gone on long enough—it was now quite late in the day—they interrupted: "We are a long way out in the country, and it's very late. Pronounce a benediction and send these folks off so they can get some supper."

37 Jesus said, "You do it. Fix supper for them."

They replied, "Are you serious? You want us to go spend a fortune on food for their supper?"

38 But he was quite serious. "How many loaves of bread do you have? Take an inventory."

That didn't take long. "Five," they said, "plus two fish."

39-44 Jesus got them all to sit down in groups of fifty or a hundred—they looked like a patchwork quilt of wildflowers spread out on the green grass! He took the five loaves and two fish, lifted his face to heaven in prayer, blessed, broke, and gave the bread to the disciples, and the disciples in turn gave it to the people. He did the same with the fish. They all ate their fill. The disciples gathered twelve baskets of leftovers. More than five thousand were at the supper.

WALKING ON THE SEA

45-46 As soon as the meal was finished, Jesus insisted that the disciples get in the boat and go on ahead across to Bethsaida while he dismissed the congregation. After sending them off, he climbed a mountain to pray.

47-49 Late at night, the boat was far out at sea; Jesus was still by himself on land. He could see his men struggling with the oars, the wind having come up against them. At about four o'clock in the morning, Jesus came toward them, walking on the sea. He intended to go right by them. But when they saw him walking on the sea, they thought it was a ghost and screamed, scared out of their wits.

50-52 Jesus was quick to comfort them: "Courage! It's me. Don't be afraid." As soon as he climbed into the boat, the wind died down. They were stunned, shaking their heads, wondering what was going on. They didn't understand what he had done at the supper. None of this had yet penetrated their hearts.

53-56 They beached the boat at Gennesaret and tied up at the landing. As soon as they got out of the boat, word got around fast. People ran this way and that, bringing their sick on stretchers to where they heard he was. Wherever he went, village or town or country crossroads, they brought their sick to the marketplace and begged him to let them touch the edge of his coat—that's all. And whoever touched him became well.

THE SOURCE OF YOUR POLLUTION

1-4 The Pharisees, along with some religion scholars who had come from Jerusalem, gathered around him. They noticed that some of his disciples weren't being careful with ritual washings before meals. The Pharisees—Jews in general, in fact—would never eat a meal without going through the motions of a ritual hand-washing, with an especially vigorous scrubbing if they had just come from the market (to say nothing of the scourings they'd give jugs and pots and pans).

5 The Pharisees and religion scholars asked, "Why do your disciples flout the rules, showing up at meals without washing their hands?"

6-8 Jesus answered, "Isaiah was right about frauds like you, hit the bull's-eye in fact:

These people make a big show of saying the right thing,
    but their heart isn't in it.
They act like they are worshiping me,
    but they don't mean it.

They just use me as a cover
    for teaching whatever suits their fancy,
Ditching God's command
    and taking up the latest fads."

9-13 He went on, "Well, good for you. You get rid of God's command so you won't be inconvenienced in following the religious fashions! Moses said, 'Respect your father and mother,' and, 'Anyone denouncing father or mother should be killed.' But you weasel out of that by saying that it's perfectly acceptable to say to father or mother, 'Gift! What I owed you I've given as a gift to God,' thus relieving yourselves of obligation to father or mother. You scratch out God's Word and scrawl a whim in its place. You do a lot of things like this."

14-15 Jesus called the crowd together again and said, "Listen now, all of you — take this to heart. It's not what you swallow that pollutes your life; it's what you vomit — that's the real pollution."

17 When he was back home after being with the crowd, his disciples said, "We don't get it. Put it in plain language."

18-19 Jesus said, "Are you being willfully stupid? Don't you see that what you swallow can't contaminate you? It doesn't enter your heart but your stomach, works its way through the intestines, and is finally flushed." (That took care of dietary quibbling; Jesus was saying that *all* foods are fit to eat.)

20-23 He went on: "It's what comes out of a person that pollutes: obscenities, lusts, thefts, murders, adulteries, greed, depravity, deceptive dealings, carousing, mean looks, slander, arrogance, foolishness — all these are vomit from the heart. *There* is the source of your pollution."

24-26 From there Jesus set out for the vicinity of Tyre. He entered a house there where he didn't think he would be found, but he couldn't escape notice. He was barely inside when a woman who had a disturbed daughter heard where he was. She came and knelt at his feet, begging for help. The woman was Greek, Syro-Phoenician by birth. She asked him to cure her daughter.

27 He said, "Stand in line and take your turn. The children get fed first. If there's any left over, the dogs get it."

28 She said, "Of course, Master. But don't dogs under the table get scraps dropped by the children?"

29-30 Jesus was impressed. "You're right! On your way! Your daughter is no longer disturbed. The demonic affliction is gone." She went home and found her daughter relaxed on the bed, the torment gone for good.

31-35 Then he left the region of Tyre, went through Sidon back to Galilee Lake and over to the district of the Ten Towns. Some people brought a man who could neither hear nor speak and asked Jesus to lay a healing hand on him. He took the man off by himself, put his fingers in the man's ears and some spit on the man's tongue. Then Jesus looked up in prayer, groaned mightily, and commanded, "*Ephphatha!* — Open up!" And it happened. The man's hearing was clear and his speech plain — just like that.

36-37 Jesus urged them to keep it quiet, but they talked it up all the more, beside themselves with excitement. "He's done it all and done it well. He gives hearing to the deaf, speech to the speechless."

A MEAL FOR FOUR THOUSAND

1-3 8 At about this same time he again found himself with a hungry crowd on his hands. He called his disciples together and said, "This crowd is breaking my heart. They have stuck with me for three days, and now they have nothing to eat. If I send them home hungry, they'll faint along the way — some of them have come a long distance."

4 His disciples responded, "What do you expect us to do about it? Buy food out here in the desert?"

5 He asked, "How much bread do you have?"

"Seven loaves," they said.

6-10 So Jesus told the crowd to sit down on the ground. After giving thanks, he took the seven bread loaves, broke them into pieces, and gave them to his disciples so they could hand them out to the crowd. They also had a few fish. He pronounced a blessing over the fish and told his disciples to hand them out as well. The crowd ate its fill. Seven sacks of leftovers were collected. There were well over four thousand at the meal. Then he sent them home. He himself went straight to the boat with his disciples and set out for Dalmanoutha.

11-12 When they arrived, the Pharisees came out and started in on him, badgering him to prove himself, pushing him up against the wall. Provoked, he said, "Why does this generation clamor for miraculous guarantees? If I have anything to say about it, you'll not get so much as a hint of a guarantee."

CONTAMINATING YEAST

13-15 He then left them, got back in the boat, and headed for the other side. But the disciples forgot to pack a lunch. Except for a single loaf of bread, there wasn't a crumb in the boat. Jesus warned, "Be very careful. Keep a sharp eye out for the contaminating yeast of Pharisees and the followers of Herod."

16-19 Meanwhile, the disciples were finding fault with each other because they had forgotten to bring bread. Jesus overheard and said, "Why are you fussing because you forgot bread? Don't you see the point of all this? Don't you get it at all? Remember the five loaves I broke for the five thousand? How many baskets of leftovers did you pick up?"

They said, "Twelve."

20 "And the seven loaves for the four thousand — how many bags full of leftovers did you get?"

"Seven."

21 He said, "Do you still not get it?"

22-23 They arrived at Bethsaida. Some people brought a sightless man and begged Jesus to give him a healing touch. Taking him by the hand, he led him out of the village. He put spit in the man's eyes, laid hands on him, and asked, "Do you see anything?"

24-26 He looked up. "I see men. They look like walking trees." So Jesus laid hands on his eyes again. The man looked hard and realized that he had recovered perfect sight, saw everything in bright, twenty-twenty focus. Jesus sent him straight home, telling him, "Don't enter the village."

THE MESSIAH

27 Jesus and his disciples headed out for the villages around Caesarea Philippi. As they walked, he asked, "Who do the people say I am?"

28 "Some say 'John the Baptizer,'" they said. "Others say 'Elijah.' Still others say 'one of the prophets.'"

29 He then asked, "And you — what are you saying about me? Who am I?"

Peter gave the answer: "You are the Christ, the Messiah."

30-32 Jesus warned them to keep it quiet, not to breathe a word of it to anyone. He then began explaining things to them: "It is necessary that the Son of Man proceed to an ordeal of suffering, be tried and found guilty by the elders, high priests, and religion scholars, be killed, and after three days rise up alive." He said this simply and clearly so they couldn't miss it.

32-33 But Peter grabbed him in protest. Turning and seeing his disciples wavering, wondering what to believe, Jesus confronted Peter. "Peter, get out of my way! Satan, get lost! You have no idea how God works."

34-37 Calling the crowd to join his disciples, he said, "Anyone who intends to come with me has to let me lead. You're not in the driver's seat; *I* am. Don't run from suffering; embrace it. Follow me and I'll show you how. Self-help is no help at all. Self-sacrifice is the way, my way, to saving yourself, your true self. What good would it do to get everything you want and lose you, the real you? What could you ever trade your soul for?

38 "If any of you are embarrassed over me and the way I'm leading you when you get around your fickle and unfocused friends, know that you'll be an even greater embarrassment to the Son of Man when he arrives in all the splendor of God, his Father, with an army of the holy angels."

1 **9** Then he drove it home by saying, "This isn't pie in the sky by and by. Some of you who are standing here are going to see it happen, see the kingdom of God arrive in full force."

IN A LIGHT-RADIANT CLOUD

2-4 Six days later, three of them *did* see it. Jesus took Peter, James, and John and led them up a high mountain. His appearance changed from the inside out, right before their eyes. His clothes shimmered, glistening white, whiter than any bleach could make them. Elijah, along with Moses, came into view, in deep conversation with Jesus.

5-6 Peter interrupted, "Rabbi, this is a great moment! Let's build three memorials — one for you, one for Moses, one for Elijah." He blurted this out without thinking, stunned as they all were by what they were seeing.

7 Just then a light-radiant cloud enveloped them, and from deep in the cloud, a voice: "This is my Son, marked by my love. Listen to him."

8 The next minute the disciples were looking around, rubbing their eyes, seeing nothing but Jesus, only Jesus.

9-10 Coming down the mountain, Jesus swore them to secrecy. "Don't tell a soul what you saw. After the Son of Man rises from the dead, you're free to talk." They puzzled over that, wondering what on earth "rising from the dead" meant.

11 Meanwhile they were asking, "Why do the religion scholars say that Elijah has to come first?"

12-13 Jesus replied, "Elijah does come first and get everything ready for the coming of the Son of Man. They treated this Elijah like dirt, much like they will treat the Son of Man, who will, according to Scripture, suffer terribly and be kicked around contemptibly."

There Are No Ifs

14-16 When they came back down the mountain to the other disciples, they saw a huge crowd around them, and the religion scholars cross-examining them. As soon as the people in the crowd saw Jesus, admiring excitement stirred them. They ran and greeted him. He asked, "What's going on? What's all the commotion?"

17-18 A man out of the crowd answered, "Teacher, I brought my mute son, made speechless by a demon, to you. Whenever it seizes him, it throws him to the ground. He foams at the mouth, grinds his teeth, and goes stiff as a board. I told your disciples, hoping they could deliver him, but they couldn't."

19-20 Jesus said, "What a generation! No sense of God! How many times do I have to go over these things? How much longer do I have to put up with this? Bring the boy here." They brought him. When the demon saw Jesus, it threw the boy into a seizure, causing him to writhe on the ground and foam at the mouth.

21-22 He asked the boy's father, "How long has this been going on?"

"Ever since he was a little boy. Many times it pitches him into fire or the river to do away with him. If you can do anything, do it. Have a heart and help us!"

23 Jesus said, "If? There are no 'ifs' among believers. Anything can happen."

24 No sooner were the words out of his mouth than the father cried, "Then I believe. Help me with my doubts!"

25-27 Seeing that the crowd was forming fast, Jesus gave the vile spirit its marching orders: "Dumb and deaf spirit, I command you — Out of him, and stay out!" Screaming, and with much thrashing about, it left. The boy was pale as a corpse, so people started saying, "He's dead." But Jesus, taking his hand, raised him. The boy stood up.

28 After arriving back home, his disciples cornered Jesus and asked, "Why couldn't we throw the demon out?"

29 He answered, "There is no way to get rid of this kind of demon except by prayer."

30-32 Leaving there, they went through Galilee. He didn't want anyone to know their whereabouts, for he wanted to teach his disciples. He told them, "The Son of Man is about to be betrayed to some people who want nothing to do with God. They will murder him. Three days after his murder, he will rise, alive." They didn't know what he was talking about, but were afraid to ask him about it.

So You Want First Place?

33 They came to Capernaum. When he was safe at home, he asked them, "What were you discussing on the road?"

34 The silence was deafening — they had been arguing with one another over who among them was greatest.

35 He sat down and summoned the Twelve. "So you want first place? Then take the last place. Be the servant of all."

36-37 He put a child in the middle of the room. Then, cradling the little one in his arms, he said, "Whoever embraces one of these children as I do embraces me, and far more than me — God who sent me."

38 John spoke up, "Teacher, we saw a man using your name to expel demons and we stopped him because he wasn't in our group."

39-41 Jesus wasn't pleased. "Don't stop him. No one can use my name to do something good and powerful, and in the next breath cut me down. If he's not an enemy, he's an ally. Why, anyone by just giving you a cup of water in my name is on our side. Count on it that God will notice.

42 "On the other hand, if you give one of these simple, childlike believers a hard time, bullying or taking advantage of their simple trust, you'll soon wish you hadn't. You'd be better off dropped in the middle of the lake with a millstone around your neck.

43-48 "If your hand or your foot gets in God's way, chop it off and throw it away. You're better off maimed or lame and alive than the proud owner of two hands and two feet, godless in a furnace of eternal fire. And if your eye distracts you from God, pull it out and throw it away. You're better off one-eyed and alive than exercising your twenty-twenty vision from inside the fire of hell.

49-50 "Everyone's going through a refining fire sooner or later, but you'll be well-preserved, protected from the *eternal* flames. Be preservatives yourselves. Preserve the peace."

DIVORCE

1-2 From there he went to the area of Judea across the Jordan. A crowd of people, as was so often the case, went along, and he, as he so often did, taught them. Pharisees came up, intending to give him a hard time. They asked, "Is it legal for a man to divorce his wife?"

3 Jesus said, "What did Moses command?"

4 They answered, "Moses gave permission to fill out a certificate of dismissal and divorce her."

5-9 Jesus said, "Moses wrote this command only as a concession to your hardhearted ways. In the original creation, God made male and female to be together. Because of this, a man leaves father and mother, and in marriage he becomes one flesh with a woman — no longer two individuals, but forming a new unity. Because God created this organic union of the two sexes, no one should desecrate his art by cutting them apart."

10-12 When they were back home, the disciples brought it up again. Jesus gave it to them straight: "A man who divorces his wife so he can marry someone else commits adultery against her. And a woman who divorces her husband so she can marry someone else commits adultery."

13-16 The people brought children to Jesus, hoping he might touch them. The disciples shooed them off. But Jesus was irate and let them know it: "Don't push these children away. Don't ever get between them and me. These children are at the very center of life in the kingdom. Mark this: Unless you accept God's kingdom in the simplicity of a child, you'll never get in." Then, gathering the children up in his arms, he laid his hands of blessing on them.

TO ENTER GOD'S KINGDOM

17 As he went out into the street, a man came running up, greeted him with great reverence, and asked, "Good Teacher, what must I do to get eternal life?"

18-19 Jesus said, "Why are you calling me good? No one is good, only God. You know the commandments: Don't murder, don't commit adultery, don't steal, don't lie, don't cheat, honor your father and mother."

20 He said, "Teacher, I have—from my youth—kept them all!"

21 Jesus looked him hard in the eye—and loved him! He said, "There's one thing left: Go sell whatever you own and give it to the poor. All your wealth will then be heavenly wealth. And come follow me."

22 The man's face clouded over. This was the last thing he expected to hear, and he walked off with a heavy heart. He was holding on tight to a lot of things, and not about to let go.

23-25 Looking at his disciples, Jesus said, "Do you have any idea how difficult it is for people who 'have it all' to enter God's kingdom?" The disciples couldn't believe what they were hearing, but Jesus kept on: "You can't imagine how difficult. I'd say it's easier for a camel to go through a needle's eye than for the rich to get into God's kingdom."

26 *That* set the disciples back on their heels. "Then who has any chance at all?" they asked.

27 Jesus was blunt: "No chance at all if you think you can pull it off by yourself. Every chance in the world if you let God do it."

28 Peter tried another angle: "We left everything and followed you."

29-31 Jesus said, "Mark my words, no one who sacrifices house, brothers, sisters, mother, father, children, land—whatever—because of me and the Message will lose out. They'll get it all back, but multiplied many times in homes, brothers, sisters, mothers, children, and land—but also in troubles. And then the bonus of eternal life! This is once again the Great Reversal: Many who are first will end up last, and the last first."

32-34 Back on the road, they set out for Jerusalem. Jesus had a head start on them, and they were following, puzzled and not just a little afraid. He took the Twelve and began again to go over what to expect next. "Listen to me carefully. We're on our way up to Jerusalem. When we get there, the Son of Man will be betrayed to the religious leaders and scholars. They will sentence him to death. Then they will hand him over to the Romans, who will mock and spit on him, give him the third degree, and kill him. After three days he will rise alive."

THE HIGHEST PLACES OF HONOR

35 James and John, Zebedee's sons, came up to him. "Teacher, we have something we want you to do for us."

36 "What is it? I'll see what I can do."

37 "Arrange it," they said, "so that we will be awarded the highest places of honor in your glory—one of us at your right, the other at your left."

38 Jesus said, "You have no idea what you're asking. Are you capable of drinking the cup I drink, of being baptized in the baptism I'm about to be plunged into?"

39-40 "Sure," they said. "Why not?"

Jesus said, "Come to think of it, you *will* drink the cup I drink, and be baptized in my baptism. But as to awarding places of honor, that's not my business. There are other arrangements for that."

41-45 When the other ten heard of this conversation, they lost their tempers with James and John. Jesus got them together to settle things down. "You've observed how godless rulers throw their weight around," he said, "and when people get a little power how quickly it goes to their heads. It's not going to be that way with you. Whoever wants to be great must become a servant. Whoever wants to be first among you must be your slave. That is what the Son of Man has done: He came to serve, not to be served—and then to give away his life in exchange for many who are held hostage."

46-48 They spent some time in Jericho. As Jesus was leaving town, trailed by his disciples and a parade of people, a blind beggar by the name of Bartimaeus, son of Timaeus, was sitting alongside the road. When he heard that Jesus the Nazarene was passing by, he began to cry out, "Son of David, Jesus! Mercy, have mercy on me!" Many tried to hush him up, but he yelled all the louder, "Son of David! Mercy, have mercy on me!"

49-50 Jesus stopped in his tracks. "Call him over."

They called him. "It's your lucky day! Get up! He's calling you to come!" Throwing off his coat, he was on his feet at once and came to Jesus.

51 Jesus said, "What can I do for you?"

The blind man said, "Rabbi, I want to see."

52 "On your way," said Jesus. "Your faith has saved and healed you."

In that very instant he recovered his sight and followed Jesus down the road.

ENTERING JERUSALEM ON A COLT

1-3 When they were nearing Jerusalem, at Bethphage and Bethany on Mount Olives, he sent off two of the disciples with instructions: "Go to the village across from you. As soon as you enter, you'll find a colt tethered, one that has never yet been ridden. Untie it and bring it. If anyone asks, 'What are you doing?' say, 'The Master needs him, and will return him right away.'"

4-7 They went and found a colt tied to a door at the street corner and untied it. Some of those standing there said, "What are you doing untying that colt?" The disciples replied exactly as Jesus had instructed them, and the people let them alone. They brought the colt to Jesus, spread their coats on it, and he mounted.

8-10 The people gave him a wonderful welcome, some throwing their coats on the street, others spreading out rushes they had cut in the fields. Running ahead and following after, they were calling out,

Hosanna!
Blessed is he who comes in God's name!
Blessed the coming kingdom of our father David!
Hosanna in highest heaven!

11 He entered Jerusalem, then entered the Temple. He looked around, taking it all in. But by now it was late, so he went back to Bethany with the Twelve.

THE CURSED FIG TREE

12-14 As they left Bethany the next day, he was hungry. Off in the distance he saw a fig tree in full leaf. He came up to it expecting to find something for breakfast, but found nothing but fig leaves. (It wasn't yet the season for figs.) He addressed the tree: "No one is going to eat fruit from you again — ever!" And his disciples overheard him.

15-17 They arrived at Jerusalem. Immediately on entering the Temple Jesus started throwing out everyone who had set up shop there, buying and sell-ing. He kicked over the tables of the bankers and the stalls of the pigeon merchants. He didn't let anyone even carry a basket through the Temple. And then he taught them, quoting this text:

My house was designated a house of prayer for the nations;
You've turned it into a hangout for thieves.

18 The high priests and religion scholars heard what was going on and plotted how they might get rid of him. They panicked, for the entire crowd was carried away by his teaching.

19 At evening, Jesus and his disciples left the city.

20-21 In the morning, walking along the road, they saw the fig tree, shriveled to a dry stick. Peter, remembering what had happened the previous day, said to him, "Rabbi, look — the fig tree you cursed is shriveled up!"

22-25 Jesus was matter-of-fact: "Embrace this God-life. Really embrace it, and nothing will be too much for you. This mountain, for instance: Just say, 'Go jump in the lake' — no shuffling or shilly-shallying — and it's as good as done. That's why I urge you to pray for absolutely everything, ranging from small to large. Include everything as you embrace this God-life, and you'll get God's everything. And when you assume the posture of prayer, remember that it's not all *asking*. If you have anything against someone, *forgive* — only then will your heavenly Father be inclined to also wipe your slate clean of sins."

HIS CREDENTIALS

27-28 Then when they were back in Jerusalem once again, as they were walk-ing through the Temple, the high priests, religion scholars, and leaders came up and demanded, "Show us your credentials. Who authorized you to speak and act like this?"

29-30 Jesus responded, "First let me ask you a question. Answer my question and then I'll present my credentials. About the baptism of John — who authorized it: heaven or humans? Tell me."

31-33 They were on the spot, and knew it. They pulled back into a huddle and whispered, "If we say 'heaven,' he'll ask us why we didn't believe John; if we say 'humans,' we'll be up against it with the people because they all hold John up as a prophet." They decided to concede that round to Jesus. "We don't know," they said.

Jesus replied, "Then I won't answer your question either."

THE STORY ABOUT A VINEYARD

1-2 **12** Then Jesus started telling them stories. "A man planted a vine-yard. He fenced it, dug a winepress, erected a watchtower, turned it over to the farmhands, and went off on a trip. At the time for harvest, he sent a servant back to the farmhands to collect his profits.

3-5 "They grabbed him, beat him up, and sent him off empty-handed. So he sent another servant. That one they tarred and feathered. He sent another and that one they killed. And on and on, many others. Some they beat up, some they killed.

6 "Finally there was only one left: a beloved son. In a last-ditch effort, he sent him, thinking, 'Surely they will respect my son.'

7-8 "But those farmhands saw their chance. They rubbed their hands together in greed and said, 'This is the heir! Let's kill him and have it all for ourselves.' They grabbed him, killed him, and threw him over the fence.

9-11 "What do you think the owner of the vineyard will do? Right. He'll come and clean house. Then he'll assign the care of the vineyard to others. Read it for yourselves in Scripture:

> That stone the masons threw out
>   is now the cornerstone!
> This is God's work;
>   we rub our eyes—we can hardly believe it!"

12 They wanted to lynch him then and there but, intimidated by public opinion, held back. They knew the story was about them. They got away from there as fast as they could.

PAYING TAXES TO CAESAR

13-14 They sent some Pharisees and followers of Herod to bait him, hoping to catch him saying something incriminating. They came up and said, "Teacher, we know you have integrity, that you are indifferent to public opinion, don't pander to your students, and teach the way of God accurately. Tell us: Is it lawful to pay taxes to Caesar or not?"

15-16 He knew it was a trick question, and said, "Why are you playing these games with me? Bring me a coin and let me look at it." They handed him one.

"This engraving—who does it look like? And whose name is on it?"

"Caesar," they said.

17 Jesus said, "Give Caesar what is his, and give God what is his."

Their mouths hung open, speechless.

OUR INTIMACIES WILL BE WITH GOD

18-23 Some Sadducees, the party that denies any possibility of resurrection, came up and asked, "Teacher, Moses wrote that if a man dies and leaves a wife but no child, his brother is obligated to marry the widow and have children. Well, there once were seven brothers. The first took a wife. He died childless. The second married her. He died, and still no child. The same with the third. All seven took their turn, but no child. Finally the wife died. When they are raised at the resurrection, whose wife is she? All seven were her husband."

24-27 Jesus said, "You're way off base, and here's why: One, you don't know your Bibles; two, you don't know how God works. After the dead are raised up, we're past the marriage business. As it is with angels now, all our ecstasies and intimacies then will be with God. And regarding the dead, whether or not they are raised, don't you ever read the Bible? How God at the bush said to Moses, 'I am — not *was* — the God of Abraham, the God of Isaac, and the God of Jacob'? The living God is God of the *living*, not the dead. You're way, way off base."

Tʜᴇ Mᴏsᴛ Iᴍᴘᴏʀᴛᴀɴᴛ Cᴏᴍᴍᴀɴᴅᴍᴇɴᴛ

28 One of the religion scholars came up. Hearing the lively exchanges of question and answer and seeing how sharp Jesus was in his answers, he put in his question: "Which is most important of all the commandments?"

29-31 Jesus said, "The first in importance is, 'Listen, Israel: The Lord your God is one; so love the Lord God with all your passion and prayer and intelligence and energy.' And here is the second: 'Love others as well as you love yourself.' There is no other commandment that ranks with these."

32-33 The religion scholar said, "A wonderful answer, Teacher! So lucid and accurate — that God is one and there is no other. And loving him with all passion and intelligence and energy, and loving others as well as you love yourself. Why, that's better than all offerings and sacrifices put together!"

34 When Jesus realized how insightful he was, he said, "You're almost there, right on the border of God's kingdom."

After that, no one else dared ask a question.

35-37 While he was teaching in the Temple, Jesus asked, "How is it that the religion scholars say that the Messiah is David's 'son,' when we all know that David, inspired by the Holy Spirit, said,

> God said to my Master,
> "Sit here at my right hand
>   until I put your enemies under your feet."

"David here designates the Messiah 'my Master' — so how can the Messiah also be his 'son'?"

The large crowd was delighted with what they heard.

38-40 He continued teaching. "Watch out for the religion scholars. They love to walk around in academic gowns, preening in the radiance of public flattery, basking in prominent positions, sitting at the head table at every church function. And all the time they are exploiting the weak and helpless. The longer their prayers, the worse they get. But they'll pay for it in the end."

41-44 Sitting across from the offering box, he was observing how the crowd tossed money in for the collection. Many of the rich were making large contributions. One poor widow came up and put in two small coins — a measly two cents. Jesus called his disciples over and said, "The truth is that this poor widow gave more to the collection than all the others put together. All the others gave what they'll never miss; she gave extravagantly what she couldn't afford — she gave her all."

Dᴏᴏᴍsᴅᴀʏ Dᴇᴄᴇɪᴠᴇʀs

1 **13** As he walked away from the Temple, one of his disciples said, "Teacher, look at that stonework! Those buildings!"

2 Jesus said, "You're impressed by this grandiose architecture?

There's not a stone in the whole works that is not going to end up in a heap of rubble."

3-4 Later, as he was sitting on Mount Olives in full view of the Temple, Peter, James, John, and Andrew got him off by himself and asked, "Tell us, when is this going to happen? What sign will we get that things are coming to a head?"

5-8 Jesus began, "Watch out for doomsday deceivers. Many leaders are going to show up with forged identities claiming, 'I'm the One.' They will deceive a lot of people. When you hear of wars and rumored wars, keep your head and don't panic. This is routine history, and no sign of the end. Nation will fight nation and ruler fight ruler, over and over. Earthquakes will occur in various places. There will be famines. But these things are nothing compared to what's coming.

9-10 "And watch out! They're going to drag you into court. And then it will go from bad to worse, dog-eat-dog, everyone at your throat because you carry my name. You're placed there as sentinels to truth. The Message has to be preached all across the world.

11 "When they bring you, betrayed, into court, don't worry about what you'll say. When the time comes, say what's on your heart—the Holy Spirit will make his witness in and through you.

12-13 "It's going to be brother killing brother, father killing child, children killing parents. There's no telling who will hate you because of me.

"Stay with it—that's what is required. Stay with it to the end. You won't be sorry; you'll be saved.

RUN FOR THE HILLS

14-18 "But be ready to run for it when you see the monster of desecration set up where it should *never* be. You who can read, make sure you understand what I'm talking about. If you're living in Judea at the time, run for the hills; if you're working in the yard, don't go back to the house to get anything; if you're out in the field, don't go back to get your coat. Pregnant and nursing mothers will have it especially hard. Hope and pray this won't happen in the middle of winter.

19-20 "These are going to be hard days—nothing like it from the time God made the world right up to the present. And there'll be nothing like it again. If he let the days of trouble run their course, nobody would make it. But because of God's chosen people, those he personally chose, he has already intervened.

NO ONE KNOWS THE DAY OR HOUR

21-23 "If anyone tries to flag you down, calling out, 'Here's the Messiah!' or points, 'There he is!' don't fall for it. Fake Messiahs and lying preachers are going to pop up everywhere. Their impressive credentials and dazzling performances will pull the wool over the eyes of even those who ought to know better. So watch out. I've given you fair warning.

24-25 "Following those hard times,

Sun will fade out,
   moon cloud over,
Stars fall out of the sky,
   cosmic powers tremble.

26-27 "And then they'll see the Son of Man enter in grand style, his Arrival filling the sky—no one will miss it! He'll dispatch the angels; they will pull in the chosen from the four winds, from pole to pole.

28-31 "Take a lesson from the fig tree. From the moment you notice its buds form, the merest hint of green, you know summer's just around the corner. And so it is with you. When you see all these things, you know he is at the door. Don't take this lightly. I'm not just saying this for some future generation, but for this one, too—these things will happen. Sky and earth will wear out; my words won't wear out.

32-37 "But the exact day and hour? No one knows that, not even heaven's angels, not even the Son. Only the Father. So keep a sharp lookout, for you don't know the timetable. It's like a man who takes a trip, leaving home and putting his servants in charge, each assigned a task, and commanding the gatekeeper to stand watch. So, stay at your post, watching. You have no idea when the homeowner is returning, whether evening, midnight, cockcrow, or morning. You don't want him showing up unannounced, with you asleep on the job. I say it to you, and I'm saying it to all: Stay at your post. Keep watch."

ANOINTING HIS HEAD

1-2 **14** In only two days the eight-day Festival of Passover and the Feast of Unleavened Bread would begin. The high priests and religion scholars were looking for a way they could seize Jesus by stealth and kill him. They agreed that it should not be done during Passover Week. "We don't want the crowds up in arms," they said.

3-5 Jesus was at Bethany, a guest of Simon the Leper. While he was eating dinner, a woman came up carrying a bottle of very expensive perfume. Opening the bottle, she poured it on his head. Some of the guests became furious among themselves. "That's criminal! A sheer waste! This perfume could have been sold for well over a year's wages and handed out to the poor." They swelled up in anger, nearly bursting with indignation over her.

6-9 But Jesus said, "Let her alone. Why are you giving her a hard time? She has just done something wonderfully significant for me. You will have the poor with you every day for the rest of your lives. Whenever you feel like it, you can do something for them. Not so with me. She did what she could when she could—she pre-anointed my body for burial. And you can be sure that wherever in the whole world the Message is preached, what she just did is going to be talked about admiringly."

10-11 Judas Iscariot, one of the Twelve, went to the cabal of high priests, determined to betray him. They couldn't believe their ears, and promised to pay him well. He started looking for just the right moment to hand him over.

TRAITOR TO THE SON OF MAN

12 On the first of the Days of Unleavened Bread, the day they prepare the Passover sacrifice, his disciples asked him, "Where do you want us to go and make preparations so you can eat the Passover meal?"

13-15 He directed two of his disciples, "Go into the city. A man carrying a water jug will meet you. Follow him. Ask the owner of whichever house he enters, 'The Teacher wants to know, Where is my guest room where I can eat the Passover meal with my disciples?' He will show you a spacious second-story room, swept and ready. Prepare for us there."

16 The disciples left, came to the city, found everything just as he had told them, and prepared the Passover meal.

17-18 After sunset he came with the Twelve. As they were at the supper table eating, Jesus said, "I have something hard but important to say to you: One of you is going to hand me over to the conspirators, one who at this moment is eating with me."

19 Stunned, they started asking, one after another, "It isn't me, is it?"

20-21 He said, "It's one of the Twelve, one who eats with me out of the same bowl. In one sense, it turns out that the Son of Man is entering into a way of treachery well-marked by the Scriptures — no surprises here. In another sense, the man who turns him in, turns traitor to the Son of Man — better never to have been born than do this!"

"This Is My Body"

22 In the course of their meal, having taken and blessed the bread, he broke it and gave it to them. Then he said,

> Take, this is my body.

23-24 Taking the chalice, he gave it to them, thanking God, and they all drank from it. He said,

> This is my blood,
> God's new covenant,
> Poured out for many people.

25 "I'll not be drinking wine again until the new day when I drink it in the kingdom of God."

26 They sang a hymn and then went directly to Mount Olives.

27-28 Jesus told them, "You're all going to feel that your world is falling apart and that it's my fault. There's a Scripture that says,

> I will strike the shepherd;
> The sheep will go helter-skelter.

"But after I am raised up, I will go ahead of you, leading the way to Galilee."

29 Peter blurted out, "Even if everyone else is ashamed of you when things fall to pieces, I won't be."

30 Jesus said, "Don't be so sure. Today, this very night in fact, before the rooster crows twice, you will deny me three times."

31 He blustered in protest, "Even if I have to die with you, I will never deny you." All the others said the same thing.

Gethsemane

32-34 They came to an area called Gethsemane. Jesus told his disciples, "Sit here while I pray." He took Peter, James, and John with him. He plunged into a sinkhole of dreadful agony. He told them, "I feel bad enough right now to die. Stay here and keep vigil with me."

35-36   Going a little ahead, he fell to the ground and prayed for a way out: "Papa, Father, you can — can't you? — get me out of this. Take this cup away from me. But please, not what I want — what do *you* want?"

37-38   He came back and found them sound asleep. He said to Peter, "Simon, you went to sleep on me? Can't you stick it out with me a single hour? Stay alert, be in prayer, so you don't enter the danger zone without even knowing it. Don't be naive. Part of you is eager, ready for anything in God; but another part is as lazy as an old dog sleeping by the fire."

39-40   He then went back and prayed the same prayer. Returning, he again found them sound asleep. They simply couldn't keep their eyes open, and they didn't have a plausible excuse.

41-42   He came back a third time and said, "Are you going to sleep all night? No — you've slept long enough. Time's up. The Son of Man is about to be betrayed into the hands of sinners. Get up. Let's get going. My betrayer has arrived."

A Gang of Ruffians

43-47   No sooner were the words out of his mouth when Judas, the one out of the Twelve, showed up, and with him a gang of ruffians, sent by the high priests, religion scholars, and leaders, brandishing swords and clubs. The betrayer had worked out a signal with them: "The one I kiss, that's the one — seize him. Make sure he doesn't get away." He went straight to Jesus and said, "Rabbi!" and kissed him. The others then grabbed him and roughed him up. One of the men standing there unsheathed his sword, swung, and came down on the Chief Priest's servant, lopping off the man's ear.

48-50   Jesus said to them, "What is this, coming after me with swords and clubs as if I were a dangerous criminal? Day after day I've been sitting in the Temple teaching, and you never so much as lifted a hand against me. What you in fact have done is confirm the prophetic writings." All the disciples cut and ran.

51-52   A young man was following along. All he had on was a bedsheet. Some of the men grabbed him but he got away, running off naked, leaving them holding the sheet.

Condemned to Death

53-54   They led Jesus to the Chief Priest, where the high priests, religious leaders, and scholars had gathered together. Peter followed at a safe distance until they got to the Chief Priest's courtyard, where he mingled with the servants and warmed himself at the fire.

55-59   The high priests conspiring with the Jewish Council looked high and low for evidence against Jesus by which they could sentence him to death. They found nothing. Plenty of people were willing to bring in false charges, but nothing added up, and they ended up canceling each other out. Then a few of them stood up and lied: "We heard him say, 'I am going to tear down this Temple, built by hard labor, and in three days build another without lifting a hand.'" But even they couldn't agree exactly.

60-61   In the middle of this, the Chief Priest stood up and asked Jesus, "What do you have to say to the accusation?" Jesus was silent. He said nothing.

     The Chief Priest tried again, this time asking, "Are you the Messiah, the Son of the Blessed?"

62   Jesus said, "Yes, I am, and you'll see it yourself:

> The Son of Man seated
> At the right hand of the Mighty One,
> Arriving on the clouds of heaven."

63-64   The Chief Priest lost his temper. Ripping his clothes, he yelled, "Did you hear that? After that do we need witnesses? You heard the blasphemy. Are you going to stand for it?"

They condemned him, one and all. The sentence: death.

65   Some of them started spitting at him. They blindfolded his eyes, then hit him, saying, "Who hit you? Prophesy!" The guards, punching and slapping, took him away.

THE ROOSTER CROWED

66-67   While all this was going on, Peter was down in the courtyard. One of the Chief Priest's servant girls came in and, seeing Peter warming himself there, looked hard at him and said, "You were with the Nazarene, Jesus."

68   He denied it: "I don't know what you're talking about." He went out on the porch. A rooster crowed.

69-70   The girl spotted him and began telling the people standing around, "He's one of them." He denied it again.

After a little while, the bystanders brought it up again. "You've *got* to be one of them. You've got 'Galilean' written all over you."

71-72   Now Peter got really nervous and swore, "I never laid eyes on this man you're talking about." Just then the rooster crowed a second time. Peter remembered how Jesus had said, "Before a rooster crows twice, you'll deny me three times." He collapsed in tears.

STANDING BEFORE PILATE

1   **15** At dawn's first light, the high priests, with the religious leaders and scholars, arranged a conference with the entire Jewish Council. After tying Jesus securely, they took him out and presented him to Pilate.

2-3   Pilate asked him, "Are you the 'King of the Jews'?"

He answered, "If you say so." The high priests let loose a barrage of accusations.

4-5   Pilate asked again, "Aren't you going to answer anything? That's quite a list of accusations." Still, he said nothing. Pilate was impressed, really impressed.

6-10   It was a custom at the Feast to release a prisoner, anyone the people asked for. There was one prisoner called Barabbas, locked up with the insurrectionists who had committed murder during the uprising against Rome. As the crowd came up and began to present its petition for him to release a prisoner, Pilate anticipated them: "Do you want me to release the King of the Jews to you?" Pilate knew by this time that it was through sheer spite that the high priests had turned Jesus over to him.

11-12   But the high priests by then had worked up the crowd to ask for the release of Barabbas. Pilate came back, "So what do I do with this man you call King of the Jews?"

13   They yelled, "Nail him to a cross!"

14 Pilate objected, "But for what crime?"

But they yelled all the louder, "Nail him to a cross!"

15 Pilate gave the crowd what it wanted, set Barabbas free and turned Jesus over for whipping and crucifixion.

16-20 The soldiers took Jesus into the palace (called Praetorium) and called together the entire brigade. They dressed him up in purple and put a crown plaited from a thornbush on his head. Then they began their mockery: "Bravo, King of the Jews!" They banged on his head with a club, spit on him, and knelt down in mock worship. After they had had their fun, they took off the purple cape and put his own clothes back on him. Then they marched out to nail him to the cross.

THE CRUCIFIXION

21 There was a man walking by, coming from work, Simon from Cyrene, the father of Alexander and Rufus. They made him carry Jesus' cross.

22-24 The soldiers brought Jesus to Golgotha, meaning "Skull Hill." They offered him a mild painkiller (wine mixed with myrrh), but he wouldn't take it. And they nailed him to the cross. They divided up his clothes and threw dice to see who would get them.

25-30 They nailed him up at nine o'clock in the morning. The charge against him — THE KING OF THE JEWS — was printed on a poster. Along with him, they crucified two criminals, one to his right, the other to his left. People passing along the road jeered, shaking their heads in mock lament: "You bragged that you could tear down the Temple and then rebuild it in three days — so show us your stuff! Save yourself! If you're really God's Son, come down from that cross!"

31-32 The high priests, along with the religion scholars, were right there mixing it up with the rest of them, having a great time poking fun at him: "He saved others — but he can't save himself! Messiah, is he? King of Israel? Then let him climb down from that cross. We'll all become believers then!" Even the men crucified alongside him joined in the mockery.

33-34 At noon the sky became extremely dark. The darkness lasted three hours. At three o'clock, Jesus groaned out of the depths, crying loudly, "*Eloi, Eloi, lama sabachthani?*" which means, "My God, my God, why have you abandoned me?"

35-36 Some of the bystanders who heard him said, "Listen, he's calling for Elijah." Someone ran off, soaked a sponge in sour wine, put it on a stick, and gave it to him to drink, saying, "Let's see if Elijah comes to take him down."

37-39 But Jesus, with a loud cry, gave his last breath. At that moment the Temple curtain ripped right down the middle. When the Roman captain standing guard in front of him saw that he had quit breathing, he said, "This has to be the Son of God!"

TAKEN TO A TOMB

40-41 There were women watching from a distance, among them Mary Magdalene, Mary the mother of the younger James and Joses, and Salome. When Jesus was in Galilee, these women followed and served him, and had come up with him to Jerusalem.

42-45 Late in the afternoon, since it was the Day of Preparation (that is, Sabbath eve), Joseph of Arimathea, a highly respected member of the Jewish

Council, came. He was one who lived expectantly, on the lookout for the kingdom of God. Working up his courage, he went to Pilate and asked for Jesus' body. Pilate questioned whether he could be dead that soon and called for the captain to verify that he was really dead. Assured by the captain, he gave Joseph the corpse.

46-47 Having already purchased a linen shroud, Joseph took him down, wrapped him in the shroud, placed him in a tomb that had been cut into the rock, and rolled a large stone across the opening. Mary Magdalene and Mary, mother of Joses, watched the burial.

THE RESURRECTION

1-3 **16** When the Sabbath was over, Mary Magdalene, Mary the mother of James, and Salome bought spices so they could embalm him. Very early on Sunday morning, as the sun rose, they went to the tomb. They worried out loud to each other, "Who will roll back the stone from the tomb for us?"

4-5 Then they looked up, saw that it had been rolled back—it was a huge stone—and walked right in. They saw a young man sitting on the right side, dressed all in white. They were completely taken aback, astonished.

6-7 He said, "Don't be afraid. I know you're looking for Jesus the Nazarene, the One they nailed on the cross. He's been raised up; he's here no longer. You can see for yourselves that the place is empty. Now—on your way. Tell his disciples and Peter that he is going on ahead of you to Galilee. You'll see him there, exactly as he said."

8 They got out as fast as they could, beside themselves, their heads swimming. Stunned, they said nothing to anyone.

9-11 [After rising from the dead, Jesus appeared early on Sunday morning to Mary Magdalene, whom he had delivered from seven demons. She went to his former companions, now weeping and carrying on, and told them. When they heard her report that she had seen him alive and well, they didn't believe her.

12-13 Later he appeared, but in a different form, to two of them out walking in the countryside. They went back and told the rest, but they weren't believed either.

14-16 Still later, as the Eleven were eating supper, he appeared and took them to task most severely for their stubborn unbelief, refusing to believe those who had seen him raised up. Then he said, "Go into the world. Go everywhere and announce the Message of God's good news to one and all. Whoever believes and is baptized is saved; whoever refuses to believe is damned.

17-18 "These are some of the signs that will accompany believers: They will throw out demons in my name, they will speak in new tongues, they will take snakes in their hands, they will drink poison and not be hurt, they will lay hands on the sick and make them well."

19-20 Then the Master Jesus, after briefing them, was taken up to heaven, and he sat down beside God in the place of honor. And the disciples went everywhere preaching, the Master working right with them, validating the Message with indisputable evidence.]

Note: Mark 16:9-20 [the portion in brackets] is contained only in later manuscripts.

LUKE

Most of us, most of the time, feel left out — misfits. We don't belong. Others seem to be so confident, so sure of themselves, "insiders" who know the ropes, old hands in a club from which we are excluded.

One of the ways we have of responding to this is to form our own club, or join one that will have us. Here is at least one place where we are "in" and the others "out." The clubs range from informal to formal in gatherings that are variously political, social, cultural, and economic. But the one thing they have in common is the principle of exclusion. Identity or worth is achieved by excluding all but the chosen. The terrible price we pay for keeping all those other people out so that we can savor the sweetness of being insiders is a reduction of reality, a shrinkage of life.

Nowhere is this price more terrible than when it is paid in the cause of religion. But religion has a long history of doing just that, of reducing the huge mysteries of God to the respectability of club rules, of shrinking the vast human community to a "membership." But with God there are no outsiders.

Luke is a most vigorous champion of the outsider. An outsider himself, the only Gentile in an all-Jewish cast of New Testament writers, he shows how Jesus includes those who typically were treated as outsiders by the religious establishment of the day: women, common laborers (sheepherders), the racially different (Samaritans), the poor. He will not countenance religion as a club. As Luke tells the story, all of us who have found ourselves on the outside looking in on life with no hope of gaining entrance (and who of us hasn't felt it?) now find the doors wide open, found and welcomed by God in Jesus.

LUKE

1-4 So many others have tried their hand at putting together a story of the wonderful harvest of Scripture and history that took place among us, using reports handed down by the original eyewitnesses who served this Word with their very lives. Since I have investigated all the reports in close detail, starting from the story's beginning, I decided to write it all out for you, most honorable Theophilus, so you can know beyond the shadow of a doubt the reliability of what you were taught.

A Childless Couple Conceives

5-7 During the rule of Herod, King of Judea, there was a priest assigned service in the regiment of Abijah. His name was Zachariah. His wife was descended from the daughters of Aaron. Her name was Elizabeth. Together they lived honorably before God, careful in keeping to the ways of the commandments and enjoying a clear conscience before God. But they were childless because Elizabeth could never conceive, and now they were quite old.

8-12 It so happened that as Zachariah was carrying out his priestly duties before God, working the shift assigned to his regiment, it came his one turn in life to enter the sanctuary of God and burn incense. The congregation was gathered and praying outside the Temple at the hour of the incense offering. Unannounced, an angel of God appeared just to the right of the altar of incense. Zachariah was paralyzed in fear.

13-15 But the angel reassured him, "Don't fear, Zachariah. Your prayer has been heard. Elizabeth, your wife, will bear a son by you. You are to name him John. You're going to leap like a gazelle for joy, and not only you — many will delight in his birth. He'll achieve great stature with God.

15-17 "He'll drink neither wine nor beer. He'll be filled with the Holy Spirit from the moment he leaves his mother's womb. He will turn many sons and daughters of Israel back to their God. He will herald God's arrival in the style and strength of Elijah, soften the hearts of parents to children, and kindle devout understanding among hardened skeptics — he'll get the people ready for God."

18 Zachariah said to the angel, "Do you expect me to believe this? I'm an old man and my wife is an old woman."

19-20 But the angel said, "I am Gabriel, the sentinel of God, sent especially to bring you this glad news. But because you won't believe me, you'll be unable to say a word until the day of your son's birth. Every word I've spoken to you will come true on time — *God's* time."

21-22 Meanwhile, the congregation waiting for Zachariah was getting restless, wondering what was keeping him so long in the sanctuary. When he came out and couldn't speak, they knew he had seen a vision. He continued speechless and had to use sign language with the people.

23-25 When the course of his priestly assignment was completed, he went back home. It wasn't long before his wife, Elizabeth, conceived. She went off by herself for five months, relishing her pregnancy. "So, this is how God acts to remedy my unfortunate condition!" she said.

A VIRGIN CONCEIVES

26-28 In the sixth month of Elizabeth's pregnancy, God sent the angel Gabriel to the Galilean village of Nazareth to a virgin engaged to be married to a man descended from David. His name was Joseph, and the virgin's name, Mary. Upon entering, Gabriel greeted her:

Good morning!
You're beautiful with God's beauty,
Beautiful inside and out!
God be with you.

29-33 She was thoroughly shaken, wondering what was behind a greeting like that. But the angel assured her, "Mary, you have nothing to fear. God has a surprise for you: You will become pregnant and give birth to a son and call his name Jesus.

He will be great,
be called 'Son of the Highest.'
The Lord God will give him
the throne of his father David;
He will rule Jacob's house forever —
no end, ever, to his kingdom."

34 Mary said to the angel, "But how? I've never slept with a man."
35 The angel answered,

The Holy Spirit will come upon you,
the power of the Highest hover over you;
Therefore, the child you bring to birth
will be called Holy, Son of God.

36-38 "And did you know that your cousin Elizabeth conceived a son, old as she is? Everyone called her barren, and here she is six months pregnant! Nothing, you see, is impossible with God."
And Mary said,

Yes, I see it all now:
I'm the Lord's maid, ready to serve.
Let it be with me
just as you say.

Then the angel left her.

BLESSED AMONG WOMEN

39-45 Mary didn't waste a minute. She got up and traveled to a town in Judah in the hill country, straight to Zachariah's house, and greeted Elizabeth. When Elizabeth heard Mary's greeting, the baby in her womb leaped. She was filled with the Holy Spirit, and sang out exuberantly,

You're so blessed among women,
 and the babe in your womb, also blessed!
And why am I so blessed that
 the mother of my Lord visits me?
The moment the sound of your
 greeting entered my ears,
The babe in my womb
 skipped like a lamb for sheer joy.
Blessed woman, who believed what God said,
 believed every word would come true!

46-55   And Mary said,

I'm bursting with God-news;
 I'm dancing the song of my Savior God.
God took one good look at me, and look what happened —
 I'm the most fortunate woman on earth!
What God has done for me will never be forgotten,
 the God whose very name is holy, set apart from all others.
His mercy flows in wave after wave
 on those who are in awe before him.
He bared his arm and showed his strength,
 scattered the bluffing braggarts.
He knocked tyrants off their high horses,
 pulled victims out of the mud.
The starving poor sat down to a banquet;
 the callous rich were left out in the cold.
He embraced his chosen child, Israel;
 he remembered and piled on the mercies, piled them high.
It's exactly what he promised,
 beginning with Abraham and right up to now.

56   Mary stayed with Elizabeth for three months and then went back to her own home.

THE BIRTH OF JOHN

57-58   When Elizabeth was full-term in her pregnancy, she bore a son. Her neighbors and relatives, seeing that God had overwhelmed her with mercy, celebrated with her.

59-60   On the eighth day, they came to circumcise the child and were calling him Zachariah after his father. But his mother intervened: "No. He is to be called John."

61-62   "But," they said, "no one in your family is named that." They used sign language to ask Zachariah what he wanted him named.

63-64   Asking for a tablet, Zachariah wrote, "His name is to be John." That took everyone by surprise. Surprise followed surprise — Zachariah's mouth was now open, his tongue loose, and he was talking, praising God!

65-66   A deep, reverential fear settled over the neighborhood, and in all that Judean hill country people talked about nothing else. Everyone who heard about it took it to heart, wondering, "What will become of this child? Clearly, God has his hand in this."

67-79 Then Zachariah was filled with the Holy Spirit and prophesied,

> Blessed be the Lord, the God of Israel;
>   he came and set his people free.
> He set the power of salvation in the center of our lives,
>   and in the very house of David his servant,
> Just as he promised long ago
>   through the preaching of his holy prophets:
> Deliverance from our enemies
>   and every hateful hand;
> Mercy to our fathers,
>   as he remembers to do what he said he'd do,
> What he swore to our father Abraham —
>   a clean rescue from the enemy camp,
> So we can worship him without a care in the world,
>   made holy before him as long as we live.
>
> And you, my child, "Prophet of the Highest,"
>   will go ahead of the Master to prepare his ways,
> Present the offer of salvation to his people,
>   the forgiveness of their sins.
> Through the heartfelt mercies of our God,
>   God's Sunrise will break in upon us,
> Shining on those in the darkness,
>   those sitting in the shadow of death,
> Then showing us the way, one foot at a time,
>   down the path of peace.

80 The child grew up, healthy and spirited. He lived out in the desert until the day he made his prophetic debut in Israel.

THE BIRTH OF JESUS

1-5 2 About that time Caesar Augustus ordered a census to be taken throughout the Empire. This was the first census when Quirinius was governor of Syria. Everyone had to travel to his own ancestral hometown to be accounted for. So Joseph went from the Galilean town of Nazareth up to Bethlehem in Judah, David's town, for the census. As a descendant of David, he had to go there. He went with Mary, his fiancée, who was pregnant.

6-7 While they were there, the time came for her to give birth. She gave birth to a son, her firstborn. She wrapped him in a blanket and laid him in a manger, because there was no room in the hostel.

AN EVENT FOR EVERYONE

8-12 There were sheepherders camping in the neighborhood. They had set night watches over their sheep. Suddenly, God's angel stood among them and God's glory blazed around them. They were terrified. The angel said, "Don't be afraid. I'm here to announce a great and joyful event that is meant for everybody, worldwide: A Savior has just been born in David's town, a Savior who is Messiah and Master. This is what you're to look for: a baby wrapped in a blanket and lying in a manger."

13-14 At once the angel was joined by a huge angelic choir singing God's praises:

> Glory to God in the heavenly heights,
> Peace to all men and women on earth who please him.

15-18 As the angel choir withdrew into heaven, the sheepherders talked it over. "Let's get over to Bethlehem as fast as we can and see for ourselves what God has revealed to us." They left, running, and found Mary and Joseph, and the baby lying in the manger. Seeing was believing. They told everyone they met what the angels had said about this child. All who heard the sheepherders were impressed.

19-20 Mary kept all these things to herself, holding them dear, deep within herself. The sheepherders returned and let loose, glorifying and praising God for everything they had heard and seen. It turned out exactly the way they'd been told!

BLESSINGS

21 When the eighth day arrived, the day of circumcision, the child was named Jesus, the name given by the angel before he was conceived.

22-24 Then when the days stipulated by Moses for purification were complete, they took him up to Jerusalem to offer him to God as commanded in God's Law: "Every male who opens the womb shall be a holy offering to God," and also to sacrifice the "pair of doves or two young pigeons" prescribed in God's Law.

25-32 In Jerusalem at the time, there was a man, Simeon by name, a good man, a man who lived in the prayerful expectancy of help for Israel. And the Holy Spirit was on him. The Holy Spirit had shown him that he would see the Messiah of God before he died. Led by the Spirit, he entered the Temple. As the parents of the child Jesus brought him in to carry out the rituals of the Law, Simeon took him into his arms and blessed God:

> God, you can now release your servant;
>   release me in peace as you promised.
> With my own eyes I've seen your salvation;
>   it's now out in the open for everyone to see:
> A God-revealing light to the non-Jewish nations,
>   and of glory for your people Israel.

33-35 Jesus' father and mother were speechless with surprise at these words. Simeon went on to bless them, and said to Mary his mother,

> This child marks both the failure and
>   the recovery of many in Israel,
> A figure misunderstood and contradicted —
>   the pain of a sword-thrust through you —
> But the rejection will force honesty,
>   as God reveals who they really are.

36-38 Anna the prophetess was also there, a daughter of Phanuel from the tribe of Asher. She was by now a very old woman. She had been married seven years and a widow for eighty-four. She never left the Temple area, worshiping night and day with her fastings and prayers. At the very time Simeon was praying, she showed up, broke into an anthem of praise to God, and talked about the child to all who were waiting expectantly for the freeing of Jerusalem.

39-40   When they finished everything required by God in the Law, they returned to Galilee and their own town, Nazareth. There the child grew strong in body and wise in spirit. And the grace of God was on him.

They Found Him in the Temple

41-45   Every year Jesus' parents traveled to Jerusalem for the Feast of Passover. When he was twelve years old, they went up as they always did for the Feast. When it was over and they left for home, the child Jesus stayed behind in Jerusalem, but his parents didn't know it. Thinking he was somewhere in the company of pilgrims, they journeyed for a whole day and then began looking for him among relatives and neighbors. When they didn't find him, they went back to Jerusalem looking for him.

46-48   The next day they found him in the Temple seated among the teachers, listening to them and asking questions. The teachers were all quite taken with him, impressed with the sharpness of his answers. But his parents were not impressed; they were upset and hurt.

His mother said, "Young man, why have you done this to us? Your father and I have been half out of our minds looking for you."

49-50   He said, "Why were you looking for me? Didn't you know that I had to be here, dealing with the things of my Father?" But they had no idea what he was talking about.

51-52   So he went back to Nazareth with them, and lived obediently with them. His mother held these things dearly, deep within herself. And Jesus matured, growing up in both body and spirit, blessed by both God and people.

A Baptism of Life-Change

1-6   In the fifteenth year of the rule of Caesar Tiberius—it was while Pontius Pilate was governor of Judea; Herod, ruler of Galilee; his brother Philip, ruler of Iturea and Trachonitis; Lysanias, ruler of Abilene; during the Chief-Priesthood of Annas and Caiaphas—John, Zachariah's son, out in the desert at the time, received a message from God. He went all through the country around the Jordan River preaching a baptism of life-change leading to forgiveness of sins, as described in the words of Isaiah the prophet:

Thunder in the desert!
"Prepare God's arrival!
Make the road smooth and straight!
Every ditch will be filled in,
Every bump smoothed out,
The detours straightened out,
All the ruts paved over.
Everyone will be there to see
The parade of God's salvation."

7-9 When crowds of people came out for baptism because it was the popular thing to do, John exploded: "Brood of snakes! What do you think you're doing slithering down here to the river? Do you think a little water on your snakeskins is going to deflect God's judgment? It's your *life* that must change, not your skin. And don't think you can pull rank by claiming Abraham as 'father.' Being a child of Abraham is neither here nor there—children of Abraham are a dime a dozen. God can make children from stones if he wants. What counts is your life. Is it green and blossoming? Because if it's deadwood, it goes on the fire."

10 The crowd asked him, "Then what are we supposed to do?"

11 "If you have two coats, give one away," he said. "Do the same with your food."

12 Tax men also came to be baptized and said, "Teacher, what should we do?"

13 He told them, "No more extortion—collect only what is required by law."

14 Soldiers asked him, "And what should we do?"

He told them, "No shakedowns, no blackmail—and be content with your rations."

15 The interest of the people by now was building. They were all beginning to wonder, "Could this John be the Messiah?"

16-17 But John intervened: "I'm baptizing you here in the river. The main character in this drama, to whom I'm a mere stagehand, will ignite the kingdom life, a fire, the Holy Spirit within you, changing you from the inside out. He's going to clean house—make a clean sweep of your lives. He'll place everything true in its proper place before God; everything false he'll put out with the trash to be burned."

18-20 There was a lot more of this—words that gave strength to the people, words that put heart in them. The Message! But Herod, the ruler, stung by John's rebuke in the matter of Herodias, his brother Philip's wife, capped his long string of evil deeds with this outrage: He put John in jail.

21-22 After all the people were baptized, Jesus was baptized. As he was praying, the sky opened up and the Holy Spirit, like a dove descending, came down on him. And along with the Spirit, a voice: "You are my Son, chosen and marked by my love, pride of my life."

SON OF ADAM, SON OF GOD

23-38 When Jesus entered public life he was about thirty years old, the son (in public perception) of Joseph, who was—

son of Heli,
son of Matthat,
son of Levi,
son of Melki,
son of Jannai,
son of Joseph,
son of Mattathias,
son of Amos,
son of Nahum,
son of Esli,
son of Naggai,

son of Maath,
son of Mattathias,
son of Semein,
son of Josech,
son of Joda,
son of Joanan,
son of Rhesa,
son of Zerubbabel,
son of Shealtiel,
son of Neri,
son of Melchi,
son of Addi,
son of Cosam,
son of Elmadam,
son of Er,
son of Joshua,
son of Eliezer,
son of Jorim,
son of Matthat,
son of Levi,
son of Simeon,
son of Judah,
son of Joseph,
son of Jonam,
son of Eliakim,
son of Melea,
son of Menna,
son of Mattatha,
son of Nathan,
son of David,
son of Jesse,
son of Obed,
son of Boaz,
son of Salmon,
son of Nahshon,
son of Amminadab,
son of Admin,
son of Arni,
son of Hezron,
son of Perez,
son of Judah,
son of Jacob,
son of Isaac,
son of Abraham,
son of Terah,
son of Nahor,
son of Serug,
son of Reu,
son of Peleg,
son of Eber,
son of Shelah,
son of Kenan,

son of Arphaxad,
son of Shem,
son of Noah,
son of Lamech,
son of Methuselah,
son of Enoch,
son of Jared,
son of Mahalaleel,
son of Kenan,
son of Enos,
son of Seth,
son of Adam,
son of God.

TESTED BY THE DEVIL

1-2 **4** Now Jesus, full of the Holy Spirit, left the Jordan and was led by the Spirit into the wild. For forty wilderness days and nights he was tested by the Devil. He ate nothing during those days, and when the time was up he was hungry.

3 The Devil, playing on his hunger, gave the first test: "Since you're God's Son, command this stone to turn into a loaf of bread."

4 Jesus answered by quoting Deuteronomy: "It takes more than bread to really live."

5-7 For the second test he led him up and spread out all the kingdoms of the earth on display at once. Then the Devil said, "They're yours in all their splendor to serve your pleasure. I'm in charge of them all and can turn them over to whomever I wish. Worship me and they're yours, the whole works."

8 Jesus refused, again backing his refusal with Deuteronomy: "Worship the Lord your God and only the Lord your God. Serve him with absolute single-heartedness."

9-11 For the third test the Devil took him to Jerusalem and put him on top of the Temple. He said, "If you are God's Son, jump. It's written, isn't it, that 'he has placed you in the care of angels to protect you; they will catch you; you won't so much as stub your toe on a stone'?"

12 "Yes," said Jesus, "and it's also written, 'Don't you dare tempt the Lord your God.'"

13 That completed the testing. The Devil retreated temporarily, lying in wait for another opportunity.

TO SET THE BURDENED FREE

14-15 Jesus returned to Galilee powerful in the Spirit. News that he was back spread through the countryside. He taught in their meeting places to everyone's acclaim and pleasure.

16-21 He came to Nazareth where he had been reared. As he always did on the Sabbath, he went to the meeting place. When he stood up to read, he was handed the scroll of the prophet Isaiah. Unrolling the scroll, he found the place where it was written,

God's Spirit is on me;
    he's chosen me to preach the Message of good news to
        the poor,

> Sent me to announce pardon to prisoners and
> recovery of sight to the blind,
> To set the burdened and battered free,
> to announce, "This is God's year to act!"

He rolled up the scroll, handed it back to the assistant, and sat down. Every eye in the place was on him, intent. Then he started in, "You've just heard Scripture make history. It came true just now in this place."

22 All who were there, watching and listening, were surprised at how well he spoke. But they also said, "Isn't this Joseph's son, the one we've known since he was a youngster?"

23-27 He answered, "I suppose you're going to quote the proverb, 'Doctor, go heal yourself. Do here in your hometown what we heard you did in Capernaum.' Well, let me tell you something: No prophet is ever welcomed in his hometown. Isn't it a fact that there were many widows in Israel at the time of Elijah during that three and a half years of drought when famine devastated the land, but the only widow to whom Elijah was sent was in Sarepta in Sidon? And there were many lepers in Israel at the time of the prophet Elisha but the only one cleansed was Naaman the Syrian."

28-30 That set everyone in the meeting place seething with anger. They threw him out, banishing him from the village, then took him to a mountain cliff at the edge of the village to throw him to his doom, but he gave them the slip and was on his way.

31-32 He went down to Capernaum, a village in Galilee. He was teaching the people on the Sabbath. They were surprised and impressed—his teaching was so forthright, so confident, so authoritative, not the quibbling and quoting they were used to.

33-34 In the meeting place that day there was a man demonically disturbed. He screamed, "Ho! What business do you have here with us, Jesus? Nazarene! I know what you're up to. You're the Holy One of God and you've come to destroy us!"

35 Jesus shut him up: "Quiet! Get out of him!" The demonic spirit threw the man down in front of them all and left. The demon didn't hurt him.

36-37 That set everyone back on their heels, whispering and wondering, "What's going on here? Someone whose words make things happen? Someone who orders demonic spirits to get out and they go?" Jesus was the talk of the town.

He Healed Them All

38-39 He left the meeting place and went to Simon's house. Simon's mother-in-law was running a high fever and they asked him to do something for her. He stood over her, told the fever to leave—and it left. Before they knew it, she was up getting dinner for them.

40-41 When the sun went down, everyone who had anyone sick with some ailment or other brought them to him. One by one he placed his hands on them and healed them. Demons left in droves, screaming, "Son of God! You're the Son of God!" But he shut them up, refusing to let them speak because they knew too much, knew him to be the Messiah.

42-44 He left the next day for open country. But the crowds went looking and, when they found him, clung to him so he couldn't go on. He told them, "Don't you realize that there are yet other villages where I have to tell the Message of God's kingdom, that this is the work God sent me to do?" Meanwhile he continued preaching in the meeting places of Galilee.

PUSH OUT INTO DEEP WATER

1-3 5 Once when he was standing on the shore of Lake Gennesaret, the crowd was pushing in on him to better hear the Word of God. He noticed two boats tied up. The fishermen had just left them and were out scrubbing their nets. He climbed into the boat that was Simon's and asked him to put out a little from the shore. Sitting there, using the boat for a pulpit, he taught the crowd.

4 When he finished teaching, he said to Simon, "Push out into deep water and let your nets out for a catch."

5-7 Simon said, "Master, we've been fishing hard all night and haven't caught even a minnow. But if you say so, I'll let out the nets." It was no sooner said than done — a huge haul of fish, straining the nets past capacity. They waved to their partners in the other boat to come help them. They filled both boats, nearly swamping them with the catch.

8-10 Simon Peter, when he saw it, fell to his knees before Jesus. "Master, leave. I'm a sinner and can't handle this holiness. Leave me to myself." When they pulled in that catch of fish, awe overwhelmed Simon and everyone with him. It was the same with James and John, Zebedee's sons, coworkers with Simon.

10-11 Jesus said to Simon, "There is nothing to fear. From now on you'll be fishing for men and women." They pulled their boats up on the beach, left them, nets and all, and followed him.

INVITATION TO A CHANGED LIFE

12 One day in one of the villages there was a man covered with leprosy. When he saw Jesus he fell down before him in prayer and said, "If you want to, you can cleanse me."

13 Jesus put out his hand, touched him, and said, "I want to. Be clean." Then and there his skin was smooth, the leprosy gone.

14-16 Jesus instructed him, "Don't talk about this all over town. Just quietly present your healed self to the priest, along with the offering ordered by Moses. Your cleansed and obedient life, not your words, will bear witness to what I have done." But the man couldn't keep it to himself, and the word got out. Soon a large crowd of people had gathered to listen and be healed of their ailments. As often as possible Jesus withdrew to out-of-the-way places for prayer.

17 One day as he was teaching, Pharisees and religion teachers were sitting around. They had come from nearly every village in Galilee and Judea, even as far away as Jerusalem, to be there. The healing power of God was on him.

18-20 Some men arrived carrying a paraplegic on a stretcher. They were looking for a way to get into the house and set him before Jesus. When they couldn't find a way in because of the crowd, they went up on the roof, removed some tiles, and let him down in the middle of everyone, right in front of Jesus. Impressed by their bold belief, he said, "Friend, I forgive your sins."

21 That set the religion scholars and Pharisees buzzing. "Who does he think he is? That's blasphemous talk! God and only God can forgive sins."

22-26   Jesus knew exactly what they were thinking and said, "Why all this gossipy whispering? Which is simpler: to say 'I forgive your sins,' or to say 'Get up and start walking'? Well, just so it's clear that I'm the Son of Man and authorized to do either, or both. . . ." He now spoke directly to the paraplegic: "Get up. Take your bedroll and go home." Without a moment's hesitation, he did it — got up, took his blanket, and left for home, giving glory to God all the way. The people rubbed their eyes, incredulous — and then also gave glory to God. Awestruck, they said, "We've never seen anything like that!"

27-28   After this he went out and saw a man named Levi at his work collecting taxes. Jesus said, "Come along with me." And he did — walked away from everything and went with him.

29-30   Levi gave a large dinner at his home for Jesus. Everybody was there, tax men and other disreputable characters as guests at the dinner. The Pharisees and their religion scholars came to his disciples greatly offended. "What is he doing eating and drinking with crooks and 'sinners'?"

31-32   Jesus heard about it and spoke up, "Who needs a doctor: the healthy or the sick? I'm here inviting outsiders, not insiders — an invitation to a changed life, changed inside and out."

33   They asked him, "John's disciples are well-known for keeping fasts and saying prayers. Also the Pharisees. But you seem to spend most of your time at parties. Why?"

34-35   Jesus said, "When you're celebrating a wedding, you don't skimp on the cake and wine. You feast. Later you may need to pull in your belt, but this isn't the time. As long as the bride and groom are with you, you have a good time. When the groom is gone, the fasting can begin. No one throws cold water on a friendly bonfire. This is Kingdom Come!

36-39   "No one cuts up a fine silk scarf to patch old work clothes; you want fabrics that match. And you don't put wine in old, cracked bottles; you get strong, clean bottles for your fresh vintage wine. And no one who has ever tasted fine aged wine prefers unaged wine."

IN CHARGE OF THE SABBATH

1-2   On a certain Sabbath Jesus was walking through a field of ripe grain. His disciples were pulling off heads of grain, rubbing them in their hands to get rid of the chaff, and eating them. Some Pharisees said, "Why are you doing that, breaking a Sabbath rule?"

3-4   But Jesus stood up for them. "Have you never read what David and those with him did when they were hungry? How he entered the sanctuary and ate fresh bread off the altar, bread that no one but priests were allowed to eat? He also handed it out to his companions."

5   Then he said, "The Son of Man is no slave to the Sabbath; he's in charge."

6-8   On another Sabbath he went to the meeting place and taught. There was a man there with a crippled right hand. The religion scholars and Pharisees had their eye on Jesus to see if he would heal the man, hoping to catch him in a Sabbath infraction. He knew what they were up to and spoke to the man with the crippled hand: "Get up and stand here before us." He did.

9   Then Jesus addressed them, "Let me ask you something: What kind of action suits the Sabbath best? Doing good or doing evil? Helping people or leaving them helpless?"

10-11   He looked around, looked each one in the eye. He said to the man, "Hold out your hand." He held it out — it was as good as new! They were beside themselves with anger, and started plotting how they might get even with him.

THE TWELVE APOSTLES

12-16   At about that same time he climbed a mountain to pray. He was there all night in prayer before God. The next day he summoned his disciples; from them he selected twelve he designated as apostles:

> Simon, whom he named Peter,
> Andrew, his brother,
> James,
> John,
> Philip,
> Bartholomew,
> Matthew,
> Thomas,
> James, son of Alphaeus,
> Simon, called the Zealot,
> Judas, son of James,
> Judas Iscariot, who betrayed him.

YOU'RE BLESSED

17-21   Coming down off the mountain with them, he stood on a plain surrounded by disciples, and was soon joined by a huge congregation from all over Judea and Jerusalem, even from the seaside towns of Tyre and Sidon. They had come both to hear him and to be cured of their ailments. Those disturbed by evil spirits were healed. Everyone was trying to touch him — so much energy surging from him, so many people healed! Then he spoke:

> You're blessed when you've lost it all.
> God's kingdom is there for the finding.
>
> You're blessed when you're ravenously hungry.
> Then you're ready for the Messianic meal.
>
> You're blessed when the tears flow freely.
> Joy comes with the morning.

22-23   "Count yourself blessed every time someone cuts you down or throws you out, every time someone smears or blackens your name to discredit me. What it means is that the truth is too close for comfort and that that person is uncomfortable. You can be glad when that happens — skip like a lamb, if you like! — for even though they don't like it, I do . . . and all heaven applauds. And know that you are in good company; my preachers and witnesses have always been treated like this.

GIVE AWAY YOUR LIFE

24   But it's trouble ahead if you think you have it made.
What you have is all you'll ever get.

25   And it's trouble ahead if you're satisfied with yourself.
Your *self* will not satisfy you for long.

And it's trouble ahead if you think life's all fun and games.
There's suffering to be met, and you're going to meet it.

26   "There's trouble ahead when you live only for the approval of others, saying what flatters them, doing what indulges them. Popularity contests are not truth contests—look how many scoundrel preachers were approved by your ancestors! Your task is to be true, not popular.

27-30   "To you who are ready for the truth, I say this: Love your enemies. Let them bring out the best in you, not the worst. When someone gives you a hard time, respond with the energies of prayer for that person. If someone slaps you in the face, stand there and take it. If someone grabs your shirt, giftwrap your best coat and make a present of it. If someone takes unfair advantage of you, use the occasion to practice the servant life. No more tit-for-tat stuff. Live generously.

31-34   "Here is a simple rule of thumb for behavior: Ask yourself what you want people to do for you; then grab the initiative and do it for *them*! If you only love the lovable, do you expect a pat on the back? Run-of-the-mill sinners do that. If you only help those who help you, do you expect a medal? Garden-variety sinners do that. If you only give for what you hope to get out of it, do you think that's charity? The stingiest of pawnbrokers does that.

35-36   "I tell you, love your enemies. Help and give without expecting a return. You'll never—I promise—regret it. Live out this God-created identity the way our Father lives toward us, generously and graciously, even when we're at our worst. Our Father is kind; you be kind.

37-38   "Don't pick on people, jump on their failures, criticize their faults—unless, of course, you want the same treatment. Don't condemn those who are down; that hardness can boomerang. Be easy on people; you'll find life a lot easier. Give away your life; you'll find life given back, but not merely given back—given back with bonus and blessing. Giving, not getting, is the way. Generosity begets generosity."

39-40   He quoted a proverb: "'Can a blind man guide a blind man?' Wouldn't they both end up in the ditch? An apprentice doesn't lecture the master. The point is to be careful who you follow as your teacher.

41-42   "It's easy to see a smudge on your neighbor's face and be oblivious to the ugly sneer on your own. Do you have the nerve to say, 'Let me wash your face for you,' when your own face is distorted by contempt? It's this I-know-better-than-you mentality again, playing a holier-than-thou part instead of just living your own part. Wipe that ugly sneer off your own face and you might be fit to offer a washcloth to your neighbor.

Work the Words into Your Life

43-45   "You don't get wormy apples off a healthy tree, nor good apples off a diseased tree. The health of the apple tells the health of the tree. You must begin with your own life-giving lives. It's who you are, not what you say and do, that counts. Your true being brims over into true words and deeds.

46-47   "Why are you so polite with me, always saying 'Yes, sir,' and 'That's right, sir,' but never doing a thing I tell you? These words I speak to you are not mere additions to your life, homeowner improvements to your standard of living. They are foundation words, words to build a life on.

48-49   "If you work the words into your life, you are like a smart carpenter who dug deep and laid the foundation of his house on bedrock. When the river burst its banks and crashed against the house, nothing could shake it; it was built to last. But if you just use my words in Bible studies and don't work them into your life, you are like a dumb carpenter who built a house but skipped the foundation. When the swollen river came crashing in, it collapsed like a house of cards. It was a total loss."

A PLACE OF HOLY MYSTERY

1-5   7 When he finished speaking to the people, he entered Capernaum. A Roman captain there had a servant who was on his deathbed. He prized him highly and didn't want to lose him. When he heard Jesus was back, he sent leaders from the Jewish community asking him to come and heal his servant. They came to Jesus and urged him to do it, saying, "He deserves this. He loves our people. He even built our meeting place."

6-8   Jesus went with them. When he was still quite far from the house, the captain sent friends to tell him, "Master, you don't have to go to all this trouble. I'm not that good a person, you know. I'd be embarrassed for you to come to my house, even embarrassed to come to you in person. Just give the order and my servant will get well. I'm a man under orders; I also give orders. I tell one soldier, 'Go,' and he goes; another, 'Come,' and he comes; my slave, 'Do this,' and he does it."

9-10   Taken aback, Jesus addressed the accompanying crowd: "I've yet to come across this kind of simple trust anywhere in Israel, the very people who are supposed to know about God and how he works." When the messengers got back home, they found the servant up and well.

11-15   Not long after that, Jesus went to the village Nain. His disciples were with him, along with quite a large crowd. As they approached the village gate, they met a funeral procession—a woman's only son was being carried out for burial. And the mother was a widow. When Jesus saw her, his heart broke. He said to her, "Don't cry." Then he went over and touched the coffin. The pallbearers stopped. He said, "Young man, I tell you: Get up." The dead son sat up and began talking. Jesus presented him to his mother.

16-17   They all realized they were in a place of holy mystery, that God was at work among them. They were quietly worshipful—and then noisily grateful, calling out among themselves, "God is back, looking to the needs of his people!" The news of Jesus spread all through the country.

IS THIS WHAT YOU WERE EXPECTING?

18-19   John's disciples reported back to him the news of all these events taking place. He sent two of them to the Master to ask the question, "Are you the One we've been expecting, or are we still waiting?"

20   The men showed up before Jesus and said, "John the Baptizer sent us to ask you, 'Are you the One we've been expecting, or are we still waiting?'"

21-23   In the next two or three hours Jesus healed many from diseases, distress, and evil spirits. To many of the blind he gave the gift of sight. Then he gave his answer: "Go back and tell John what you have just seen and heard:

The blind see,
The lame walk,

> Lepers are cleansed,
> The deaf hear,
> The dead are raised,
> The wretched of the earth
>   have God's salvation hospitality extended to them.

"Is this what you were expecting? Then count yourselves fortunate!"

24-27 After John's messengers left to make their report, Jesus said more about John to the crowd of people. "What did you expect when you went out to see him in the wild? A weekend camper? Hardly. What then? A sheik in silk pajamas? Not in the wilderness, not by a long shot. What then? A messenger from God? That's right, a messenger! Probably the greatest messenger you'll ever hear. He is the messenger Malachi announced when he wrote,

> I'm sending my messenger on ahead
> To make the road smooth for you.

28-30 "Let me lay it out for you as plainly as I can: No one in history surpasses John the Baptizer, but in the kingdom he prepared you for, the lowliest person is ahead of him. The ordinary and disreputable people who heard John, by being baptized by him into the kingdom, are the clearest evidence; the Pharisees and religious officials would have nothing to do with such a baptism, wouldn't think of giving up their place in line to their inferiors.

31-35 "How can I account for the people of this generation? They're like spoiled children complaining to their parents, 'We wanted to skip rope and you were always too tired; we wanted to talk but you were always too busy.' John the Baptizer came fasting and you called him crazy. The Son of Man came feasting and you called him a lush. Opinion polls don't count for much, do they? The proof of the pudding is in the eating."

ANOINTING HIS FEET

36-39 One of the Pharisees asked him over for a meal. He went to the Pharisee's house and sat down at the dinner table. Just then a woman of the village, the town harlot, having learned that Jesus was a guest in the home of the Pharisee, came with a bottle of very expensive perfume and stood at his feet, weeping, raining tears on his feet. Letting down her hair, she dried his feet, kissed them, and anointed them with the perfume. When the Pharisee who had invited him saw this, he said to himself, "If this man was the prophet I thought he was, he would have known what kind of woman this is who is falling all over him."

40 Jesus said to him, "Simon, I have something to tell you."

"Oh? Tell me."

41-42 "Two men were in debt to a banker. One owed five hundred silver pieces, the other fifty. Neither of them could pay up, and so the banker canceled both debts. Which of the two would be more grateful?"

43-47 Simon answered, "I suppose the one who was forgiven the most."

"That's right," said Jesus. Then turning to the woman, but speaking to Simon, he said, "Do you see this woman? I came to your home; you provided no water for my feet, but she rained tears on my feet and dried them with her hair. You gave me no greeting, but from the time I arrived she hasn't quit kissing my feet. You provided nothing for freshening up, but she has soothed my feet with perfume. Impressive, isn't it? She was forgiven many, many sins, and so she is very, very grateful. If the forgiveness is minimal, the gratitude is minimal."

48 Then he spoke to her: "I forgive your sins."

49 That set the dinner guests talking behind his back: "Who does he think he is, forgiving sins!"

50 He ignored them and said to the woman, "Your faith has saved you. Go in peace."

1-3 8 He continued according to plan, traveled to town after town, village after village, preaching God's kingdom, spreading the Message. The Twelve were with him. There were also some women in their company who had been healed of various evil afflictions and illnesses: Mary, the one called Magdalene, from whom seven demons had gone out; Joanna, wife of Chuza, Herod's manager; and Susanna—along with many others who used their considerable means to provide for the company.

The Story of the Seeds

4-8 As they went from town to town, a lot of people joined in and traveled along. He addressed them, using this story: "A farmer went out to sow his seed. Some of it fell on the road; it was tramped down and the birds ate it. Other seed fell in the gravel; it sprouted, but withered because it didn't have good roots. Other seed fell in the weeds; the weeds grew with it and strangled it. Other seed fell in rich earth and produced a bumper crop.

"Are you listening to this? Really listening?"

9 His disciples asked, "Why did you tell this story?"

10 He said, "You've been given insight into God's kingdom—you know how it works. There are others who need stories. But even with stories some of them aren't going to get it:

Their eyes are open but don't see a thing,
Their ears are open but don't hear a thing.

11-12 "This story is about some of those people. The seed is the Word of God. The seeds on the road are those who hear the Word, but no sooner do they hear it than the Devil snatches it from them so they won't believe and be saved.

13 "The seeds in the gravel are those who hear with enthusiasm, but the enthusiasm doesn't go very deep. It's only another fad, and the moment there's trouble it's gone.

14 "And the seed that fell in the weeds—well, these are the ones who hear, but then the seed is crowded out and nothing comes of it as they go about their lives worrying about tomorrow, making money, and having fun.

15 "But the seed in the good earth—these are the good-hearts who seize the Word and hold on no matter what, sticking with it until there's a harvest.

Misers of What You Hear

16-18 "No one lights a lamp and then covers it with a washtub or shoves it under the bed. No, you set it up on a lamp stand so those who enter the room can see their way. We're not keeping secrets; we're telling them. We're not hiding things; we're bringing *everything* out into the open. So be careful that you don't become misers of what you hear. Generosity begets generosity. Stinginess impoverishes."

19-20   His mother and brothers showed up but couldn't get through to him because of the crowd. He was given the message, "Your mother and brothers are standing outside wanting to see you."

21   He replied, "My mother and brothers are the ones who hear and do God's Word. Obedience is thicker than blood."

22-24   One day he and his disciples got in a boat. "Let's cross the lake," he said. And off they went. It was smooth sailing, and he fell asleep. A terrific storm came up suddenly on the lake. Water poured in, and they were about to capsize. They woke Jesus: "Master, Master, we're going to drown!"

Getting to his feet, he told the wind, "Silence!" and the waves, "Quiet down!" They did it. The lake became smooth as glass.

25   Then he said to his disciples, "Why can't you trust me?"

They were in absolute awe, staggered and stammering, "Who is this, anyway? He calls out to the winds and sea, and they do what he tells them!"

THE MADMAN AND THE PIGS

26-29   They sailed on to the country of the Gerasenes, directly opposite Galilee. As he stepped out onto land, a madman from town met him; he was a victim of demons. He hadn't worn clothes for a long time, nor lived at home; he lived in the cemetery. When he saw Jesus he screamed, fell before him, and bellowed, "What business do you have messing with me? You're Jesus, Son of the High God, but don't give me a hard time!" (The man said this because Jesus had started to order the unclean spirit out of him.) Time after time the demon threw the man into convulsions. He had been placed under constant guard and tied with chains and shackles, but crazed and driven wild by the demon, he would shatter the bonds.

30-31   Jesus asked him, "What is your name?"

"Mob. My name is Mob," he said, because many demons afflicted him. And they begged Jesus desperately not to order them to the bottomless pit.

32-33   A large herd of pigs was browsing and rooting on a nearby hill. The demons begged Jesus to order them into the pigs. He gave the order. It was even worse for the pigs than for the man. Crazed, they stampeded over a cliff into the lake and drowned.

34-36   Those tending the pigs, scared to death, bolted and told their story in town and country. People went out to see what had happened. They came to Jesus and found the man from whom the demons had been sent, sitting there at Jesus' feet, wearing decent clothes and making sense. It was a holy moment, and for a short time they were more reverent than curious. Then those who had seen it happen told how the demoniac had been saved.

37-39   Later, a great many people from the Gerasene countryside got together and asked Jesus to leave — too much change, too fast, and they were scared. So Jesus got back in the boat and set off. The man whom he had delivered from the demons asked to go with him, but he sent him back, saying, "Go home and tell everything God did in you." So he went back and preached all over town everything Jesus had done in him.

HIS TOUCH

40-42 On his return, Jesus was welcomed by a crowd. They were all there expecting him. A man came up, Jairus by name. He was president of the meeting place. He fell at Jesus' feet and begged him to come to his home because his twelve-year-old daughter, his only child, was dying. Jesus went with him, making his way through the pushing, jostling crowd.

43-45 In the crowd that day there was a woman who for twelve years had been afflicted with hemorrhages. She had spent every penny she had on doctors but not one had been able to help her. She slipped in from behind and touched the edge of Jesus' robe. At that very moment her hemorrhaging stopped. Jesus said, "Who touched me?"

When no one stepped forward, Peter said, "But Master, we've got crowds of people on our hands. Dozens have touched you."

46 Jesus insisted, "Someone touched me. I felt power discharging from me."

47 When the woman realized that she couldn't remain hidden, she knelt trembling before him. In front of all the people, she blurted out her story—why she touched him and how at that same moment she was healed.

48 Jesus said, "Daughter, you took a risk trusting me, and now you're healed and whole. Live well, live blessed!"

49 While he was still talking, someone from the leader's house came up and told him, "Your daughter died. No need now to bother the Teacher."

50-51 Jesus overheard and said, "Don't be upset. Just trust me and everything will be all right." Going into the house, he wouldn't let anyone enter with him except Peter, John, James, and the child's parents.

52-53 Everyone was crying and carrying on over her. Jesus said, "Don't cry. She didn't die; she's sleeping." They laughed at him. They knew she was dead.

54-56 Then Jesus, gripping her hand, called, "My dear child, get up." She was up in an instant, up and breathing again! He told them to give her something to eat. Her parents were ecstatic, but Jesus warned them to keep quiet. "Don't tell a soul what happened in this room."

KEEP IT SIMPLE

1-5 9 Jesus now called the Twelve and gave them authority and power to deal with all the demons and cure diseases. He commissioned them to preach the news of God's kingdom and heal the sick. He said, "Don't load yourselves up with equipment. Keep it simple; *you* are the equipment. And no luxury inns—get a modest place and be content there until you leave. If you're not welcomed, leave town. Don't make a scene. Shrug your shoulders and move on."

6 Commissioned, they left. They traveled from town to town telling the latest news of God, the Message, and curing people everywhere they went.

7-9 Herod, the ruler, heard of these goings on and didn't know what to think. There were people saying John had come back from the dead, others that Elijah had appeared, still others that some prophet of long ago had shown up. Herod said, "But I killed John—took off his head. So who is this that I keep hearing about?" Curious, he looked for a chance to see him in action.

10-11 The apostles returned and reported on what they had done. Jesus took them away, off by themselves, near the town called Bethsaida. But the crowds got wind of it and followed. Jesus graciously welcomed them and talked to them about the kingdom of God. Those who needed healing, he healed.

BREAD AND FISH FOR FIVE THOUSAND

12 As the day declined, the Twelve said, "Dismiss the crowd so they can go to the farms or villages around here and get a room for the night and a bite to eat. We're out in the middle of nowhere."

13-14 "You feed them," Jesus said.

They said, "We couldn't scrape up more than five loaves of bread and a couple of fish—unless, of course, you want us to go to town ourselves and buy food for everybody." (There were more than five thousand people in the crowd.)

14-17 But he went ahead and directed his disciples, "Sit them down in groups of about fifty." They did what he said, and soon had everyone seated. He took the five loaves and two fish, lifted his face to heaven in prayer, blessed, broke, and gave the bread and fish to the disciples to hand out to the crowd. After the people had all eaten their fill, twelve baskets of leftovers were gathered up.

DON'T RUN FROM SUFFERING

18 One time when Jesus was off praying by himself, his disciples nearby, he asked them, "What are the crowds saying about me, about who I am?"

19 They said, "John the Baptizer. Others say Elijah. Still others say that one of the prophets from long ago has come back."

20-21 He then asked, "And you—what are you saying about me? Who am I?"

Peter answered, "The Messiah of God." Jesus then warned them to keep it quiet. They were to tell no one what Peter had said.

22 He went on, "It is necessary that the Son of Man proceed to an ordeal of suffering, be tried and found guilty by the religious leaders, high priests, and religion scholars, be killed, and on the third day be raised up alive."

23-27 Then he told them what they could expect for themselves: "Anyone who intends to come with me has to let me lead. You're not in the driver's seat—I am. Don't run from suffering; embrace it. Follow me and I'll show you how. Self-help is no help at all. Self-sacrifice is the way, *my* way, to finding yourself, your true self. What good would it do to get everything you want and lose you, the real you? If any of you is embarrassed with me and the way I'm leading you, know that the Son of Man will be far more embarrassed with you when he arrives in all his splendor in company with the Father and the holy angels. This isn't, you realize, pie in the sky by and by. Some who have taken their stand right here are going to see it happen, see with their own eyes the kingdom of God."

JESUS IN HIS GLORY

28-31 About eight days after saying this, he climbed the mountain to pray, taking Peter, John, and James along. While he was in prayer, the appearance of his face changed and his clothes became blinding white. At once two men were there talking with him. They turned out to be Moses and Elijah—and what a glorious appearance they made! They talked over his exodus, the one Jesus was about to complete in Jerusalem.

32-33 Meanwhile, Peter and those with him were slumped over in sleep. When they came to, rubbing their eyes, they saw Jesus in his glory and the two men standing with him. When Moses and Elijah had left, Peter said to Jesus, "Master, this is a great moment! Let's build three memorials: one for you, one for Moses, and one for Elijah." He blurted this out without thinking.

34-35 While he was babbling on like this, a light-radiant cloud enveloped them. As they found themselves buried in the cloud, they became deeply aware of God. Then there was a voice out of the cloud: "This is my Son, the Chosen! Listen to him."

36 When the sound of the voice died away, they saw Jesus there alone. They were speechless. And they continued speechless, said not one thing to anyone during those days of what they had seen.

37-40 When they came down off the mountain the next day, a big crowd was there to meet them. A man called from out of the crowd, "Please, please, Teacher, take a look at my son. He's my only child. Often a spirit seizes him. Suddenly he's screaming, thrown into convulsions, his mouth foaming. And then it beats him black-and-blue before it leaves. I asked your disciples to deliver him but they couldn't."

41 Jesus said, "What a generation! No sense of God! No focus to your lives! How many times do I have to go over these things? How much longer do I have to put up with this? Bring your son here."

42-43 While he was coming, the demon slammed him to the ground and threw him into convulsions. Jesus stepped in, ordered the vile spirit gone, healed the boy, and handed him back to his father. They all shook their heads in wonder, astonished at God's greatness, God's majestic greatness.

YOUR BUSINESS IS LIFE

43-44 While they continued to stand around exclaiming over all the things he was doing, Jesus said to his disciples, "Treasure and ponder each of these next words: The Son of Man is about to be betrayed into human hands."

45 They didn't get what he was saying. It was like he was speaking a foreign language and they couldn't make heads or tails of it. But they were embarrassed to ask him what he meant.

46-48 They started arguing over which of them would be most famous. When Jesus realized how much this mattered to them, he brought a child to his side. "Whoever accepts this child as if the child were me, accepts me," he said. "And whoever accepts me, accepts the One who sent me. You become great by accepting, not asserting. Your spirit, not your size, makes the difference."

49 John spoke up, "Master, we saw a man using your name to expel demons and we stopped him because he wasn't of our group."

50 Jesus said, "Don't stop him. If he's not an enemy, he's an ally."

51-54 When it came close to the time for his Ascension, he gathered up his courage and steeled himself for the journey to Jerusalem. He sent messengers on ahead. They came to a Samaritan village to make arrangements for his hospitality. But when the Samaritans learned that his destination was Jerusalem, they refused hospitality. When the disciples James and John learned of it, they said, "Master, do you want us to call a bolt of lightning down out of the sky and incinerate them?"

55-56 Jesus turned on them: "Of course not!" And they traveled on to another village.

57 On the road someone asked if he could go along. "I'll go with you, wherever," he said.

58 Jesus was curt: "Are you ready to rough it? We're not staying in the best inns, you know."

Jesus said to another, "Follow me."

59 He said, "Certainly, but first excuse me for a couple of days, please. I have to make arrangements for my father's funeral."

60 Jesus refused. "First things first. Your business is life, not death. And life is urgent: Announce God's kingdom!"

61 Then another said, "I'm ready to follow you, Master, but first excuse me while I get things straightened out at home."

62 Jesus said, "No procrastination. No backward looks. You can't put God's kingdom off till tomorrow. Seize the day."

LAMBS IN A WOLF PACK

1-2 **10** Later the Master selected seventy and sent them ahead of him in pairs to every town and place where he intended to go. He gave them this charge:

"What a huge harvest! And how few the harvest hands. So on your knees; ask the God of the Harvest to send harvest hands.

3 "On your way! But be careful—this is hazardous work. You're like lambs in a wolf pack.

4 "Travel light. Comb and toothbrush and no extra luggage.

"Don't loiter and make small talk with everyone you meet along the way.

5-6 "When you enter a home, greet the family, 'Peace.' If your greeting is received, then it's a good place to stay. But if it's not received, take it back and get out. Don't impose yourself.

7 "Stay at one home, taking your meals there, for a worker deserves three square meals. Don't move from house to house, looking for the best cook in town.

8-9 "When you enter a town and are received, eat what they set before you, heal anyone who is sick, and tell them, 'God's kingdom is right on your doorstep!'

10-12 "When you enter a town and are not received, go out in the street and say, 'The only thing we got from you is the dirt on our feet, and we're giving it back. Did you have any idea that God's kingdom was right on your doorstep?' Sodom will have it better on Judgment Day than the town that rejects you.

13-14 "Doom, Chorazin! Doom, Bethsaida! If Tyre and Sidon had been given half the chances given you, they'd have been on their knees long ago, repenting and crying for mercy. Tyre and Sidon will have it easy on Judgment Day compared to you.

15 "And you, Capernaum! Do you think you're about to be promoted to heaven? Think again. You're on a mudslide to hell.

16 "The one who listens to you, listens to me. The one who rejects you, rejects me. And rejecting me is the same as rejecting God, who sent me."

17 The seventy came back triumphant. "Master, even the demons danced to your tune!"

18-20 Jesus said, "I know. I saw Satan fall, a bolt of lightning out of the sky. See what I've given you? Safe passage as you walk on snakes and scorpions, and protection from every assault of the Enemy. No one can put a hand on you. All the same, the great triumph is not in your authority over evil, but in God's authority over you and presence with you. Not what you do for God but what God does for you—that's the agenda for rejoicing."

21 At that, Jesus rejoiced, exuberant in the Holy Spirit. "I thank you, Father, Master of heaven and earth, that you hid these things from the know-it-alls and showed them to these innocent newcomers. Yes, Father, it pleased you to do it this way.

22 "I've been given it all by my Father! Only the Father knows who the Son is and only the Son knows who the Father is. The Son can introduce the Father to anyone he wants to."

23-24 He then turned in a private aside to his disciples. "Fortunate the eyes that see what you're seeing! There are plenty of prophets and kings who would have given their right arm to see what you are seeing but never got so much as a glimpse, to hear what you are hearing but never got so much as a whisper."

Defining "Neighbor"

25 Just then a religion scholar stood up with a question to test Jesus. "Teacher, what do I need to do to get eternal life?"

26 He answered, "What's written in God's Law? How do you interpret it?"

27 He said, "That you love the Lord your God with all your passion and prayer and muscle and intelligence—and that you love your neighbor as well as you do yourself."

28 "Good answer!" said Jesus. "Do it and you'll live."

29 Looking for a loophole, he asked, "And just how would you define 'neighbor'?"

30-32 Jesus answered by telling a story. "There was once a man traveling from Jerusalem to Jericho. On the way he was attacked by robbers. They took his clothes, beat him up, and went off leaving him half-dead. Luckily, a priest was on his way down the same road, but when he saw him he angled across to the other side. Then a Levite religious man showed up; he also avoided the injured man.

33-35 "A Samaritan traveling the road came on him. When he saw the man's condition, his heart went out to him. He gave him first aid, disinfecting and bandaging his wounds. Then he lifted him onto his donkey, led him to an inn, and made him comfortable. In the morning he took out two silver coins and gave them to the innkeeper, saying, 'Take good care of him. If it costs any more, put it on my bill—I'll pay you on my way back.'

36 "What do you think? Which of the three became a neighbor to the man attacked by robbers?"

37 "The one who treated him kindly," the religion scholar responded.
Jesus said, "Go and do the same."

Mary and Martha

38-40 As they continued their travel, Jesus entered a village. A woman by the name of Martha welcomed him and made him feel quite at home. She had a sister, Mary, who sat before the Master, hanging on every word he said. But Martha was pulled away by all she had to do in the kitchen. Later, she stepped in, interrupting them. "Master, don't you care that my sister has abandoned the kitchen to me? Tell her to lend me a hand."

41-42 The Master said, "Martha, dear Martha, you're fussing far too much and getting yourself worked up over nothing. One thing only is essential, and Mary has chosen it—it's the main course, and won't be taken from her."

ASK FOR WHAT YOU NEED

1 **11** One day he was praying in a certain place. When he finished, one of his disciples said, "Master, teach us to pray just as John taught his disciples."

2-4 So he said, "When you pray, say,

Father,
Reveal who you are.
Set the world right.
Keep us alive with three square meals.
Keep us forgiven with you and forgiving others.
Keep us safe from ourselves and the Devil."

5-6 Then he said, "Imagine what would happen if you went to a friend in the middle of the night and said, 'Friend, lend me three loaves of bread. An old friend traveling through just showed up, and I don't have a thing on hand.'

7 "The friend answers from his bed, 'Don't bother me. The door's locked; my children are all down for the night; I can't get up to give you anything.'

8 "But let me tell you, even if he won't get up because he's a friend, if you stand your ground, knocking and waking all the neighbors, he'll finally get up and get you whatever you need.

9 "Here's what I'm saying:

Ask and you'll get;
Seek and you'll find;
Knock and the door will open.

10-13 "Don't bargain with God. Be direct. Ask for what you need. This is not a cat-and-mouse, hide-and-seek game we're in. If your little boy asks for a serving of fish, do you scare him with a live snake on his plate? If your little girl asks for an egg, do you trick her with a spider? As bad as you are, you wouldn't think of such a thing—you're at least decent to your own children. And don't you think the Father who conceived you in love will give the Holy Spirit when you ask him?"

NO NEUTRAL GROUND

14-16 Jesus delivered a man from a demon that had kept him speechless. The demon gone, the man started talking a blue streak, taking the crowd by complete surprise. But some from the crowd were cynical. "Black magic," they said. "Some devil trick he's pulled from his sleeve." Others were skeptical, waiting around for him to prove himself with a spectacular miracle.

17-20 Jesus knew what they were thinking and said, "Any country in civil war for very long is wasted. A constantly squabbling family falls to pieces. If Satan cancels Satan, is there any Satan left? You accuse me of ganging up with the Devil, the prince of demons, to cast out demons, but if you're slinging devil mud at me, calling me a devil who kicks out devils, doesn't the same mud stick to your own exorcists? But if it's *God's* finger I'm pointing that sends the demons on their way, then God's kingdom is here for sure.

21-22   "When a strong man, armed to the teeth, stands guard in his front yard, his property is safe and sound. But what if a stronger man comes along with superior weapons? Then he's beaten at his own game, the arsenal that gave him such confidence hauled off, and his precious possessions plundered.

23   "This is war, and there is no neutral ground. If you're not on my side, you're the enemy; if you're not helping, you're making things worse.

24-26   "When a corrupting spirit is expelled from someone, it drifts along through the desert looking for an oasis, some unsuspecting soul it can bedevil. When it doesn't find anyone, it says, 'I'll go back to my old haunt.' On return, it finds the person swept and dusted, but vacant. It then runs out and rounds up seven other spirits dirtier than itself and they all move in, whooping it up. That person ends up far worse than if he'd never gotten cleaned up in the first place."

27   While he was saying these things, some woman lifted her voice above the murmur of the crowd: "Blessed the womb that carried you, and the breasts at which you nursed!"

28   Jesus commented, "Even more blessed are those who hear God's Word and guard it with their lives!"

KEEP YOUR EYES OPEN

29-30   As the crowd swelled, he took a fresh tack: "The mood of this age is all wrong. Everybody's looking for proof, but you're looking for the wrong kind. All you're looking for is something to titillate your curiosity, satisfy your lust for miracles. But the only proof you're going to get is the Jonah-proof given to the Ninevites, which looks like no proof at all. What Jonah was to Nineveh, the Son of Man is to this age.

31-32   "On Judgment Day the Ninevites will stand up and give evidence that will condemn this generation, because when Jonah preached to them they changed their lives. A far greater preacher than Jonah is here, and you squabble about 'proofs.' On Judgment Day the Queen of Sheba will come forward and bring evidence that condemns this generation, because she traveled from a far corner of the earth to listen to wise Solomon. Wisdom far greater than Solomon's is right in front of you, and you quibble over 'evidence.'

33-36   "No one lights a lamp, then hides it in a drawer. It's put on a lamp stand so those entering the room have light to see where they're going. Your eye is a lamp, lighting up your whole body. If you live wide-eyed in wonder and belief, your body fills up with light. If you live squinty-eyed in greed and distrust, your body is a dank cellar. Keep your eyes open, your lamp burning, so you don't get musty and murky. Keep your life as well-lighted as your best-lighted room."

FRAUDS!

37-41   When he finished that talk, a Pharisee asked him to dinner. He entered his house and sat right down at the table. The Pharisee was shocked and somewhat offended when he saw that Jesus didn't wash up before the meal. But the Master said to him, "I know you Pharisees burnish the surface of your cups and plates so they sparkle in the sun, but I also know your insides are maggoty with greed and secret evil. Stupid Pharisees! Didn't the One who made the outside also make the inside? Turn both your pockets and your hearts inside out and give generously to the poor; then your *lives* will be clean, not just your dishes and your hands.

42   "I've had it with you! You're hopeless, you Pharisees! Frauds! You keep meticulous account books, tithing on every nickel and dime you get, but manage to find loopholes for getting around basic matters of justice and God's love. Careful bookkeeping is commendable, but the basics are required.

43-44   "You're hopeless, you Pharisees! Frauds! You love sitting at the head table at church dinners, love preening yourselves in the radiance of public flattery. Frauds! You're just like unmarked graves: People walk over that nice, grassy surface, never suspecting the rot and corruption that is six feet under."

45   One of the religion scholars spoke up: "Teacher, do you realize that in saying these things you're insulting us?"

46   He said, "Yes, and I can be even more explicit. You're hopeless, you religion scholars! You load people down with rules and regulations, nearly breaking their backs, but never lift even a finger to help.

47-51   "You're hopeless! You build tombs for the prophets your ancestors killed. The tombs you build are monuments to your murdering ancestors more than to the murdered prophets. That accounts for God's Wisdom saying, 'I will send them prophets and apostles, but they'll kill them and run them off.' What it means is that every drop of righteous blood ever spilled from the time earth began until now, from the blood of Abel to the blood of Zechariah, who was struck down between altar and sanctuary, is on your heads. Yes, it's on the bill of this generation and this generation will pay.

52   "You're hopeless, you religion scholars! You took the key of knowledge, but instead of unlocking doors, you locked them. You won't go in yourself, and won't let anyone else in either."

53-54   As soon as Jesus left the table, the religion scholars and Pharisees went into a rage. They went over and over everything he said, plotting how they could trap him in something from his own mouth.

CAN'T HIDE BEHIND A RELIGIOUS MASK

1-3   **12** By this time the crowd, unwieldy and stepping on each other's toes, numbered into the thousands. But Jesus' primary concern was his disciples. He said to them, "Watch yourselves carefully so you don't get contaminated with Pharisee yeast, Pharisee phoniness. You can't keep your true self hidden forever; before long you'll be exposed. You can't hide behind a religious mask forever; sooner or later the mask will slip and your true face will be known. You can't whisper one thing in private and preach the opposite in public; the day's coming when those whispers will be repeated all over town.

4-5   "I'm speaking to you as dear friends. Don't be bluffed into silence or insincerity by the threats of religious bullies. True, they can kill you, but *then* what can they do? There's nothing they can do to your soul, your core being. Save your fear for God, who holds your entire life—body and soul—in his hands.

6-7   "What's the price of two or three pet canaries? Some loose change, right? But God never overlooks a single one. And he pays even greater attention to you, down to the last detail—even numbering the hairs on your head! So don't be intimidated by all this bully talk. You're worth more than a million canaries.

8-9   "Stand up for me among the people you meet and the Son of Man will stand up for you before all God's angels. But if you pretend you don't know me, do you think I'll defend you before God's angels?

10   "If you bad-mouth the Son of Man out of misunderstanding or ignorance, that can be overlooked. But if you're knowingly attacking God himself, taking aim at the Holy Spirit, that won't be overlooked.

11-12   "When they drag you into their meeting places, or into police courts and before judges, don't worry about defending yourselves—what you'll say or how you'll say it. The right words will be there. The Holy Spirit will give you the right words when the time comes."

THE STORY OF THE GREEDY FARMER

13   Someone out of the crowd said, "Teacher, order my brother to give me a fair share of the family inheritance."

14   He replied, "Mister, what makes you think it's any of my business to be a judge or mediator for you?"

15   Speaking to the people, he went on, "Take care! Protect yourself against the least bit of greed. Life is not defined by what you have, even when you have a lot."

16-19   Then he told them this story: "The farm of a certain rich man produced a terrific crop. He talked to himself: 'What can I do? My barn isn't big enough for this harvest.' Then he said, 'Here's what I'll do: I'll tear down my barns and build bigger ones. Then I'll gather in all my grain and goods, and I'll say to myself, Self, you've done well! You've got it made and can now retire. Take it easy and have the time of your life!'

20   "Just then God showed up and said, 'Fool! Tonight you die. And your barnful of goods—who gets it?'

21   "That's what happens when you fill your barn with Self and not with God."

STEEP YOURSELF IN GOD-REALITY

22-24   He continued this subject with his disciples. "Don't fuss about what's on the table at mealtimes or if the clothes in your closet are in fashion. There is far more to your inner life than the food you put in your stomach, more to your outer appearance than the clothes you hang on your body. Look at the ravens, free and unfettered, not tied down to a job description, carefree in the care of God. And you count far more.

25-28   "Has anyone by fussing before the mirror ever gotten taller by so much as an inch? If fussing can't even do that, why fuss at all? Walk into the fields and look at the wildflowers. They don't fuss with their appearance—but have you ever seen color and design quite like it? The ten best-dressed men and women in the country look shabby alongside them. If God gives such attention to the wildflowers, most of them never even seen, don't you think he'll attend to you, take pride in you, do his best for you?

29-32   "What I'm trying to do here is get you to relax, not be so preoccupied with *getting* so you can respond to God's *giving*. People who don't know God and the way he works fuss over these things, but you know both God and how he works. Steep yourself in God-reality, God-initiative, God-provisions. You'll find all your everyday human concerns will be met. Don't be afraid of missing out. You're my dearest friends! The Father wants to give you the very kingdom itself.

33-34   "Be generous. Give to the poor. Get yourselves a bank that can't go bankrupt, a bank in heaven far from bankrobbers, safe from embezzlers, a bank you can bank on. It's obvious, isn't it? The place where your treasure is, is the place you will most want to be, and end up being.

WHEN THE MASTER SHOWS UP

35-38   "Keep your shirts on; keep the lights on! Be like house servants waiting for their master to come back from his honeymoon, awake and ready to open the door when he arrives and knocks. Lucky the servants whom the master finds on watch! He'll put on an apron, sit them at the table, and serve them a meal, sharing his wedding feast with them. It doesn't matter what time of the night he arrives; they're awake—and so blessed!

39-40   "You know that if the house owner had known what night the burglar was coming, he wouldn't have stayed out late and left the place unlocked. So don't you be slovenly and careless. Just when you don't expect him, the Son of Man will show up."

41   Peter said, "Master, are you telling this story just for us? Or is it for everybody?"

42-46   The Master said, "Let me ask you: Who is the dependable manager, full of common sense, that the master puts in charge of his staff to feed them well and on time? He is a blessed man if when the master shows up he's doing his job. But if he says to himself, 'The master is certainly taking his time,' begins maltreating the servants and maids, throws parties for his friends, and gets drunk, the master will walk in when he least expects it, give him the thrashing of his life, and put him back in the kitchen peeling potatoes.

47-48   "The servant who knows what his master wants and ignores it, or insolently does whatever he pleases, will be thoroughly thrashed. But if he does a poor job through ignorance, he'll get off with a slap on the hand. Great gifts mean great responsibilities; greater gifts, greater responsibilities!

TO START A FIRE

49-53   "I've come to start a fire on this earth—how I wish it were blazing right now! I've come to change everything, turn everything rightside up—how I long for it to be finished! Do you think I came to smooth things over and make everything nice? Not so. I've come to disrupt and confront! From now on, when you find five in a house, it will be—

> Three against two,
>   and two against three;
> Father against son,
>   and son against father;
> Mother against daughter,
>   and daughter against mother;
> Mother-in-law against bride,
>   and bride against mother-in-law."

54-56 Then he turned to the crowd: "When you see clouds coming in from the west, you say, 'Storm's coming'—and you're right. And when the wind comes out of the south, you say, 'This'll be a hot one'—and you're right. Frauds! You know how to tell a change in the weather, so don't tell me you can't tell a change in the season, the God-season we're in right now.

57-59 "You don't have to be a genius to understand these things. Just use your common sense, the kind you'd use if, while being taken to court, you decided to settle up with your accuser on the way, knowing that if the case went to the judge you'd probably go to jail and pay every last penny of the fine. That's the kind of decision I'm asking you to make."

UNLESS YOU TURN TO GOD

1-5 **13** About that time some people came up and told him about the Galileans Pilate had killed while they were at worship, mixing their blood with the blood of the sacrifices on the altar. Jesus responded, "Do you think those murdered Galileans were worse sinners than all other Galileans? Not at all. Unless you turn to God, you, too, will die. And those eighteen in Jerusalem the other day, the ones crushed and killed when the Tower of Siloam collapsed and fell on them, do you think they were worse citizens than all other Jerusalemites? Not at all. Unless you turn to God, you, too, will die."

6-7 Then he told them a story: "A man had an apple tree planted in his front yard. He came to it expecting to find apples, but there weren't any. He said to his gardener, 'What's going on here? For three years now I've come to this tree expecting apples and not one apple have I found. Chop it down! Why waste good ground with it any longer?'

8-9 "The gardener said, 'Let's give it another year. I'll dig around it and fertilize, and maybe it will produce next year; if it doesn't, then chop it down.'"

HEALING ON THE SABBATH

10-13 He was teaching in one of the meeting places on the Sabbath. There was a woman present, so twisted and bent over with arthritis that she couldn't even look up. She had been afflicted with this for eighteen years. When Jesus saw her, he called her over. "Woman, you're free!" He laid hands on her and suddenly she was standing straight and tall, giving glory to God.

14 The meeting-place president, furious because Jesus had healed on the Sabbath, said to the congregation, "Six days have been defined as work days. Come on one of the six if you want to be healed, but not on the seventh, the Sabbath."

15-16 But Jesus shot back, "You frauds! Each Sabbath every one of you regularly unties your cow or donkey from its stall, leads it out for water, and thinks nothing of it. So why isn't it all right for me to untie this daughter of Abraham and lead her from the stall where Satan has had her tied these eighteen years?"

17 When he put it that way, his critics were left looking quite silly and red-faced. The congregation was delighted and cheered him on.

THE WAY TO GOD

18-19 Then he said, "How can I picture God's kingdom for you? What kind of story can I use? It's like a pine nut that a man plants in his front yard.

It grows into a huge pine tree with thick branches, and eagles build nests in it."

20-21 He tried again. "How can I picture God's kingdom? It's like yeast that a woman works into enough dough for three loaves of bread—and waits while the dough rises."

22 He went on teaching from town to village, village to town, but keeping on a steady course toward Jerusalem.

23-25 A bystander said, "Master, will only a few be saved?"

He said, "Whether few or many is none of your business. Put your mind on your life with God. The way to life—to God!—is vigorous and requires your total attention. A lot of you are going to assume that you'll sit down to God's salvation banquet just because you've been hanging around the neighborhood all your lives. Well, one day you're going to be banging on the door, wanting to get in, but you'll find the door locked and the Master saying, 'Sorry, you're not on my guest list.'

26-27 "You'll protest, 'But we've known you all our lives!' only to be interrupted with his abrupt, 'Your kind of knowing can hardly be called knowing. You don't know the first thing about me.'

28-30 "That's when you'll find yourselves out in the cold, strangers to grace. You'll watch Abraham, Isaac, Jacob, and all the prophets march into God's kingdom. You'll watch outsiders stream in from east, west, north, and south and sit down at the table of God's kingdom. And all the time you'll be outside looking in—and wondering what happened. This is the Great Reversal: the last in line put at the head of the line, and the so-called first ending up last."

31 Just then some Pharisees came up and said, "Run for your life! Herod's on the hunt. He's out to kill you!"

32-35 Jesus said, "Tell that fox that I've no time for him right now. Today and tomorrow I'm busy clearing out the demons and healing the sick; the third day I'm wrapping things up. Besides, it's not proper for a prophet to come to a bad end outside Jerusalem.

Jerusalem, Jerusalem, killer of prophets,
    abuser of the messengers of God!
How often I've longed to gather your children,
    gather your children like a hen,
Her brood safe under her wings—
    but you refused and turned away!
And now it's too late: You won't see me again
    until the day you say,
      'Blessed is he
      who comes in
      the name of God.'"

1-3 **14** One time when Jesus went for a Sabbath meal with one of the top leaders of the Pharisees, all the guests had their eyes on him, watching his every move. Right before him there was a man hugely swollen in his joints. So Jesus asked the religion scholars and Pharisees present, "Is it permitted to heal on the Sabbath? Yes or no?"

4-6   They were silent. So he took the man, healed him, and sent him on his way. Then he said, "Is there anyone here who, if a child or animal fell down a well, wouldn't rush to pull him out immediately, not asking whether or not it was the Sabbath?" They were stumped. There was nothing they could say to that.

INVITE THE MISFITS

7-9   He went on to tell a story to the guests around the table. Noticing how each had tried to elbow into the place of honor, he said, "When someone invites you to dinner, don't take the place of honor. Somebody more important than you might have been invited by the host. Then he'll come and call out in front of everybody, 'You're in the wrong place. The place of honor belongs to this man.' Red-faced, you'll have to make your way to the very last table, the only place left.

10-11   "When you're invited to dinner, go and sit at the last place. Then when the host comes he may very well say, 'Friend, come up to the front.' That will give the dinner guests something to talk about! What I'm saying is, If you walk around with your nose in the air, you're going to end up flat on your face. But if you're content to be simply yourself, you will become more than yourself."

12-14   Then he turned to the host. "The next time you put on a dinner, don't just invite your friends and family and rich neighbors, the kind of people who will return the favor. Invite some people who never get invited out, the misfits from the wrong side of the tracks. You'll be—and experience—a blessing. They won't be able to return the favor, but the favor will be returned—oh, how it will be returned!—at the resurrection of God's people."

THE STORY OF THE DINNER PARTY

15   That triggered a response from one of the guests: "How fortunate the one who gets to eat dinner in God's kingdom!"

16-17   Jesus followed up. "Yes. For there was once a man who threw a great dinner party and invited many. When it was time for dinner, he sent out his servant to the invited guests, saying, 'Come on in; the food's on the table.'

18   "Then they all began to beg off, one after another making excuses. The first said, 'I bought a piece of property and need to look it over. Send my regrets.'

19   "Another said, 'I just bought five teams of oxen, and I really need to check them out. Send my regrets.'

20   "And yet another said, 'I just got married and need to get home to my wife.'

21   "The servant went back and told the master what had happened. He was outraged and told the servant, 'Quickly, get out into the city streets and alleys. Collect all who look like they need a square meal, all the misfits and homeless and wretched you can lay your hands on, and bring them here.'

22   "The servant reported back, 'Master, I did what you commanded—and there's still room.'

23-24   "The master said, 'Then go to the country roads. Whoever you find, drag them in. I want my house full! Let me tell you, not one of those originally invited is going to get so much as a bite at my dinner party.'"

FIGURE THE COST

25-27 One day when large groups of people were walking along with him, Jesus turned and told them, "Anyone who comes to me but refuses to let go of father, mother, spouse, children, brothers, sisters — yes, even one's own self! — can't be my disciple. Anyone who won't shoulder his own cross and follow behind me can't be my disciple.

28-30 "Is there anyone here who, planning to build a new house, doesn't first sit down and figure the cost so you'll know if you can complete it? If you only get the foundation laid and then run out of money, you're going to look pretty foolish. Everyone passing by will poke fun at you: 'He started something he couldn't finish.'

31-32 "Or can you imagine a king going into battle against another king without first deciding whether it is possible with his ten thousand troops to face the twenty thousand troops of the other? And if he decides he can't, won't he send an emissary and work out a truce?

33 "Simply put, if you're not willing to take what is dearest to you, whether plans or people, and kiss it good-bye, you can't be my disciple.

34 "Salt is excellent. But if the salt goes flat, it's useless, good for nothing.

"Are you listening to this? Really listening?"

THE STORY OF THE LOST SHEEP

1-3 15 By this time a lot of men and women of doubtful reputation were hanging around Jesus, listening intently. The Pharisees and religion scholars were not pleased, not at all pleased. They growled, "He takes in sinners and eats meals with them, treating them like old friends." Their grumbling triggered this story.

4-7 "Suppose one of you had a hundred sheep and lost one. Wouldn't you leave the ninety-nine in the wilderness and go after the lost one until you found it? When found, you can be sure you would put it across your shoulders, rejoicing, and when you got home call in your friends and neighbors, saying, 'Celebrate with me! I've found my lost sheep!' Count on it — there's more joy in heaven over one sinner's rescued life than over ninety-nine good people in no need of rescue.

THE STORY OF THE LOST COIN

8-10 "Or imagine a woman who has ten coins and loses one. Won't she light a lamp and scour the house, looking in every nook and cranny until she finds it? And when she finds it you can be sure she'll call her friends and neighbors: 'Celebrate with me! I found my lost coin!' Count on it — that's the kind of party God's angels throw every time one lost soul turns to God."

THE STORY OF THE LOST SON

11-12 Then he said, "There was once a man who had two sons. The younger said to his father, 'Father, I want right now what's coming to me.'

12-16 "So the father divided the property between them. It wasn't long before the younger son packed his bags and left for a distant country. There, undisciplined and dissipated, he wasted everything he had. After he had gone through all his money, there was a bad famine all through that country and he began to hurt. He signed on with a citizen there who assigned him to his fields to slop the pigs. He was so hungry he would have eaten the corn-cobs in the pig slop, but no one would give him any.

17-20 "That brought him to his senses. He said, 'All those farmhands work-ing for my father sit down to three meals a day, and here I am starving to death. I'm going back to my father. I'll say to him, Father, I've sinned against God, I've sinned before you; I don't deserve to be called your son. Take me on as a hired hand.' He got right up and went home to his father.

20-21 "When he was still a long way off, his father saw him. His heart pound-ing, he ran out, embraced him, and kissed him. The son started his speech: 'Father, I've sinned against God, I've sinned before you; I don't deserve to be called your son ever again.'

22-24 "But the father wasn't listening. He was calling to the servants, 'Quick. Bring a clean set of clothes and dress him. Put the family ring on his finger and sandals on his feet. Then get a grain-fed heifer and roast it. We're going to feast! We're going to have a wonderful time! My son is here — given up for dead and now alive! Given up for lost and now found!' And they began to have a wonderful time.

25-27 "All this time his older son was out in the field. When the day's work was done he came in. As he approached the house, he heard the music and dancing. Calling over one of the houseboys, he asked what was going on. He told him, 'Your brother came home. Your father has ordered a feast — bar-becued beef! — because he has him home safe and sound.'

28-30 "The older brother stalked off in an angry sulk and refused to join in. His father came out and tried to talk to him, but he wouldn't listen. The son said, 'Look how many years I've stayed here serving you, never giv-ing you one moment of grief, but have you ever thrown a party for me and my friends? Then this son of yours who has thrown away your money on whores shows up and you go all out with a feast!'

31-32 "His father said, 'Son, you don't understand. You're with me all the time, and everything that is mine is yours — but this is a wonderful time, and we had to celebrate. This brother of yours was dead, and he's alive! He was lost, and he's found!'"

THE STORY OF THE CROOKED MANAGER

1-2 **16** Jesus said to his disciples, "There was once a rich man who had a manager. He got reports that the manager had been tak-ing advantage of his position by running up huge personal expenses. So he called him in and said, 'What's this I hear about you? You're fired. And I want a complete audit of your books.'

3-4 "The manager said to himself, 'What am I going to do? I've lost my job as manager. I'm not strong enough for a laboring job, and I'm too proud to beg. . . . Ah, I've got a plan. Here's what I'll do . . . then when I'm turned out into the street, people will take me into their houses.'

5 "Then he went at it. One after another, he called in the people who were in debt to his master. He said to the first, 'How much do you owe my master?'

6 "He replied, 'A hundred jugs of olive oil.'

"The manager said, 'Here, take your bill, sit down here — quick now — write fifty.'

7 "To the next he said, 'And you, what do you owe?'

"He answered, 'A hundred sacks of wheat.'

"He said, 'Take your bill, write in eighty.'

8-9   "Now here's a surprise: The master praised the crooked manager! And why? Because he knew how to look after himself. Streetwise people are smarter in this regard than law-abiding citizens. They are on constant alert, looking for angles, surviving by their wits. I want you to be smart in the same way—but for what is *right*—using every adversity to stimulate you to creative survival, to concentrate your attention on the bare essentials, so you'll live, really live, and not complacently just get by on good behavior."

GOD SEES BEHIND APPEARANCES

10-13   Jesus went on to make these comments:

> If you're honest in small things,
>   you'll be honest in big things;
> If you're a crook in small things,
>   you'll be a crook in big things.
> If you're not honest in small jobs,
>   who will put you in charge of the store?
> No worker can serve two bosses:
>   He'll either hate the first and love the second
> Or adore the first and despise the second.
>   You can't serve both God and the Bank.

14-18   When the Pharisees, a money-obsessed bunch, heard him say these things, they rolled their eyes, dismissing him as hopelessly out of touch. So Jesus spoke to them: "You are masters at making yourselves look good in front of others, but God knows what's behind the appearance.

> What society sees and calls monumental,
>   God sees through and calls monstrous.
> God's Law and the Prophets climaxed in John;
> Now it's all kingdom of God—the glad news
>   and compelling invitation to every man and woman.
> The sky will disintegrate and the earth dissolve
>   before a single letter of God's Law wears out.
> Using the legalities of divorce
>   as a cover for lust is adultery;
> Using the legalities of marriage
>   as a cover for lust is adultery.

THE RICH MAN AND LAZARUS

19-21   "There once was a rich man, expensively dressed in the latest fashions, wasting his days in conspicuous consumption. A poor man named Lazarus, covered with sores, had been dumped on his doorstep. All he lived for was to get a meal from scraps off the rich man's table. His best friends were the dogs who came and licked his sores.

22-24   "Then he died, this poor man, and was taken up by the angels to the lap of Abraham. The rich man also died and was buried. In hell and in torment, he looked up and saw Abraham in the distance and Lazarus in his lap. He called out, 'Father Abraham, mercy! Have mercy! Send Lazarus to dip his finger in water to cool my tongue. I'm in agony in this fire.'

25-26   "But Abraham said, 'Child, remember that in your lifetime you got the good things and Lazarus the bad things. It's not like that here. Here he's consoled and you're tormented. Besides, in all these matters there is a huge chasm set between us so that no one can go from us to you even if he wanted to, nor can anyone cross over from you to us.'

27-28   "The rich man said, 'Then let me ask you, Father: Send him to the house of my father where I have five brothers, so he can tell them the score and warn them so they won't end up here in this place of torment.'

29   "Abraham answered, 'They have Moses and the Prophets to tell them the score. Let them listen to them.'

30   "'I know, Father Abraham,' he said, 'but they're not listening. If someone came back to them from the dead, they would change their ways.'

31   "Abraham replied, 'If they won't listen to Moses and the Prophets, they're not going to be convinced by someone who rises from the dead.'"

A KERNEL OF FAITH

1-2   **17** He said to his disciples, "Hard trials and temptations are bound to come, but too bad for whoever brings them on! Better to wear a millstone necklace and take a swim in the deep blue sea than give even one of these dear little ones a hard time!

3-4   "Be alert. If you see your friend going wrong, correct him. If he responds, forgive him. Even if it's personal against you and repeated seven times through the day, and seven times he says, 'I'm sorry, I won't do it again,' forgive him."

5   The apostles came up and said to the Master, "Give us more faith."

6   But the Master said, "You don't need *more* faith. There is no 'more' or 'less' in faith. If you have a bare kernel of faith, say the size of a poppy seed, you could say to this sycamore tree, 'Go jump in the lake,' and it would do it.

7-10   "Suppose one of you has a servant who comes in from plowing the field or tending the sheep. Would you take his coat, set the table, and say, 'Sit down and eat'? Wouldn't you be more likely to say, 'Prepare dinner; change your clothes and wait table for me until I've finished my coffee; then go to the kitchen and have your supper'? Does the servant get special thanks for doing what's expected of him? It's the same with you. When you've done everything expected of you, be matter-of-fact and say, 'The work is done. What we were told to do, we did.'"

11-13   It happened that as he made his way toward Jerusalem, he crossed over the border between Samaria and Galilee. As he entered a village, ten men, all lepers, met him. They kept their distance but raised their voices, calling out, "Jesus, Master, have mercy on us!"

14-16   Taking a good look at them, he said, "Go, show yourselves to the priests."
They went, and while still on their way, became clean. One of them, when he realized that he was healed, turned around and came back, shouting his gratitude, glorifying God. He kneeled at Jesus' feet, so grateful. He couldn't thank him enough — and he was a Samaritan.

17-19   Jesus said, "Were not ten healed? Where are the nine? Can none be found to come back and give glory to God except this outsider?" Then he said to him, "Get up. On your way. Your faith has healed and saved you."

When the Son of Man Arrives

20-21 Jesus, grilled by the Pharisees on when the kingdom of God would come, answered, "The kingdom of God doesn't come by counting the days on the calendar. Nor when someone says, 'Look here!' or, 'There it is!' And why? Because God's kingdom is already among you."

22-24 He went on to say to his disciples, "The days are coming when you are going to be desperately homesick for just a glimpse of one of the days of the Son of Man, and you won't see a thing. And they'll say to you, 'Look over there!' or, 'Look here!' Don't fall for any of that nonsense. The arrival of the Son of Man is not something you go out to see. He simply comes.

24-25 "You know how the whole sky lights up from a single flash of lightning? That's how it will be on the Day of the Son of Man. But first it's necessary that he suffer many things and be turned down by the people of today.

26-27 "The time of the Son of Man will be just like the time of Noah — everyone carrying on as usual, having a good time right up to the day Noah boarded the ship. They suspected nothing until the flood hit and swept everything away.

28-30 "It was the same in the time of Lot — the people carrying on, having a good time, business as usual right up to the day Lot walked out of Sodom and a firestorm swept down and burned everything to a crisp. That's how it will be — sudden, total — when the Son of Man is revealed.

31-33 "When the Day arrives and you're out working in the yard, don't run into the house to get anything. And if you're out in the field, don't go back and get your coat. Remember what happened to Lot's wife! If you grasp and cling to life on your terms, you'll lose it, but if you let that life go, you'll get life on God's terms.

34-35 "On that Day, two men will be in the same boat fishing — one taken, the other left. Two women will be working in the same kitchen — one taken, the other left."

37 Trying to take all this in, the disciples said, "Master, where?"

He told them, "Watch for the circling of the vultures. They'll spot the corpse first. The action will begin around my dead body."

The Story of the Persistent Widow

1-3 **18** Jesus told them a story showing that it was necessary for them to pray consistently and never quit. He said, "There was once a judge in some city who never gave God a thought and cared nothing for people. A widow in that city kept after him: 'My rights are being violated. Protect me!'

4-5 "He never gave her the time of day. But after this went on and on he said to himself, 'I care nothing what God thinks, even less what people think. But because this widow won't quit badgering me, I'd better do something and see that she gets justice — otherwise I'm going to end up beaten black-and-blue by her pounding.'"

6-8 Then the Master said, "Do you hear what that judge, corrupt as he is, is saying? So what makes you think God won't step in and work justice for his chosen people, who continue to cry out for help? Won't he stick up for them? I assure you, he will. He will not drag his feet. But how much of that kind of persistent faith will the Son of Man find on the earth when he returns?"

The Story of the Tax Man and the Pharisee

9-12   He told his next story to some who were complacently pleased with themselves over their moral performance and looked down their noses at the common people: "Two men went up to the Temple to pray, one a Pharisee, the other a tax man. The Pharisee posed and prayed like this: 'Oh, God, I thank you that I am not like other people — robbers, crooks, adulterers, or, heaven forbid, like this tax man. I fast twice a week and tithe on all my income.'

13   "Meanwhile the tax man, slumped in the shadows, his face in his hands, not daring to look up, said, 'God, give mercy. Forgive me, a sinner.'"

14   Jesus commented, "This tax man, not the other, went home made right with God. If you walk around with your nose in the air, you're going to end up flat on your face, but if you're content to be simply yourself, you will become more than yourself."

15-17   People brought babies to Jesus, hoping he might touch them. When the disciples saw it, they shooed them off. Jesus called them back. "Let these children alone. Don't get between them and me. These children are the kingdom's pride and joy. Mark this: Unless you accept God's kingdom in the simplicity of a child, you'll never get in."

The Rich Official

18   One day one of the local officials asked him, "Good Teacher, what must I do to deserve eternal life?"

19-20   Jesus said, "Why are you calling me good? No one is good — only God. You know the commandments, don't you? No illicit sex, no killing, no stealing, no lying, honor your father and mother."

21   He said, "I've kept them all for as long as I can remember."

22   When Jesus heard that, he said, "Then there's only one thing left to do: Sell everything you own and give it away to the poor. You will have riches in heaven. Then come, follow me."

23   This was the last thing the official expected to hear. He was very rich and became terribly sad. He was holding on tight to a lot of things and not about to let them go.

24-25   Seeing his reaction, Jesus said, "Do you have any idea how difficult it is for people who have it all to enter God's kingdom? I'd say it's easier to thread a camel through a needle's eye than get a rich person into God's kingdom."

26   "Then who has any chance at all?" the others asked.

27   "No chance at all," Jesus said, "if you think you can pull it off by yourself. Every chance in the world if you trust God to do it."

28   Peter tried to regain some initiative: "We left everything we owned and followed you, didn't we?"

29-30   "Yes," said Jesus, "and you won't regret it. No one who has sacrificed home, spouse, brothers and sisters, parents, children — whatever — will lose out. It will all come back multiplied many times over in your lifetime. And then the bonus of eternal life!"

31-34 Then Jesus took the Twelve off to the side and said, "Listen carefully. We're on our way up to Jerusalem. Everything written in the Prophets about the Son of Man will take place. He will be handed over to the Romans, jeered at, made sport of, and spit on. Then, after giving him the third degree, they will kill him. In three days he will rise, alive." But they didn't get it, could make neither heads nor tails of what he was talking about.

35-37 He came to the outskirts of Jericho. A blind man was sitting beside the road asking for handouts. When he heard the rustle of the crowd, he asked what was going on. They told him, "Jesus the Nazarene is going by."

38 He yelled, "Jesus! Son of David! Mercy, have mercy on me!"

39 Those ahead of Jesus told the man to shut up, but he only yelled all the louder, "Son of David! Mercy, have mercy on me!"

40 Jesus stopped and ordered him to be brought over. When he had come near, Jesus asked, "What do you want from me?"

41 He said, "Master, I want to see again."

42-43 Jesus said, "Go ahead—see again! Your faith has saved and healed you!" The healing was instant: He looked up, seeing—and then followed Jesus, glorifying God. Everyone in the street joined in, shouting praise to God.

Zacchaeus

1-4 Then Jesus entered and walked through Jericho. There was a man there, his name Zacchaeus, the head tax man and quite rich. He wanted desperately to see Jesus, but the crowd was in his way—he was a short man and couldn't see over the crowd. So he ran on ahead and climbed up in a sycamore tree so he could see Jesus when he came by.

5-7 When Jesus got to the tree, he looked up and said, "Zacchaeus, hurry down. Today is my day to be a guest in your home." Zacchaeus scrambled out of the tree, hardly believing his good luck, delighted to take Jesus home with him. Everyone who saw the incident was indignant and grumped, "What business does he have getting cozy with this crook?"

8 Zacchaeus just stood there, a little stunned. He stammered apologetically, "Master, I give away half my income to the poor—and if I'm caught cheating, I pay four times the damages."

9-10 Jesus said, "Today is salvation day in this home! Here he is: Zacchaeus, son of Abraham! For the Son of Man came to find and restore the lost."

The Story About Investment

11 While he had their attention, and because they were getting close to Jerusalem by this time and expectation was building that God's kingdom would appear any minute, he told this story:

12-13 "There was once a man descended from a royal house who needed to make a long trip back to headquarters to get authorization for his rule and then return. But first he called ten servants together, gave them each a sum of money, and instructed them, 'Operate with this until I return.'

14 "But the citizens there hated him. So they sent a commission with a signed petition to oppose his rule: 'We don't want this man to rule us.'

15 "When he came back bringing the authorization of his rule, he called those ten servants to whom he had given the money to find out how they had done.

16 "The first said, 'Master, I doubled your money.'

17 "He said, 'Good servant! Great work! Because you've been trustworthy in this small job, I'm making you governor of ten towns.'

18 "The second said, 'Master, I made a fifty percent profit on your money.'

19 "He said, 'I'm putting you in charge of five towns.'

20-21 "The next servant said, 'Master, here's your money safe and sound. I kept it hidden in the cellar. To tell you the truth, I was a little afraid. I know you have high standards and hate sloppiness, and don't suffer fools gladly.'

22-23 "He said, 'You're right that I don't suffer fools gladly—and you've acted the fool! Why didn't you at least invest the money in securities so I would have gotten a little interest on it?'

24 "Then he said to those standing there, 'Take the money from him and give it to the servant who doubled my stake.'

25 "They said, 'But Master, he already has double . . .'

26 "He said, 'That's what I mean: Risk your life and get more than you ever dreamed of. Play it safe and end up holding the bag.

27 "'As for these enemies of mine who petitioned against my rule, clear them out of here. I don't want to see their faces around here again.'"

GOD'S PERSONAL VISIT

28-31 After saying these things, Jesus headed straight up to Jerusalem. When he got near Bethphage and Bethany at the mountain called Olives, he sent off two of the disciples with instructions: "Go to the village across from you. As soon as you enter, you'll find a colt tethered, one that has never been ridden. Untie it and bring it. If anyone says anything, asks, 'What are you doing?' say, 'His Master needs him.'"

32-33 The two left and found it just as he said. As they were untying the colt, its owners said, "What are you doing untying the colt?"

34 They said, "His Master needs him."

35-36 They brought the colt to Jesus. Then, throwing their coats on its back, they helped Jesus get on. As he rode, the people gave him a grand welcome, throwing their coats on the street.

37-38 Right at the crest, where Mount Olives begins its descent, the whole crowd of disciples burst into enthusiastic praise over all the mighty works they had witnessed:

> Blessed is he who comes,
>   the king in God's name!
> All's well in heaven!
>   Glory in the high places!

39 Some Pharisees from the crowd told him, "Teacher, get your disciples under control!"

40 But he said, "If they kept quiet, the stones would do it for them, shouting praise."

41-44 When the city came into view, he wept over it. "If you had only recognized this day, and everything that was good for you! But now it's too late. In the days ahead your enemies are going to bring up their heavy artillery and surround you, pressing in from every side. They'll smash you and your babies on the pavement. Not one stone will be left intact. All this because you didn't recognize and welcome God's personal visit."

45-46   Going into the Temple he began to throw out everyone who had set up shop, selling everything and anything. He said, "It's written in Scripture,

My house is a house of prayer;
You have turned it into a religious bazaar."

47-48   From then on he taught each day in the Temple. The high priests, religion scholars, and the leaders of the people were trying their best to find a way to get rid of him. But with the people hanging on every word he spoke, they couldn't come up with anything.

1-2   **20** One day he was teaching the people in the Temple, proclaiming the Message. The high priests, religion scholars, and leaders confronted him and demanded, "Show us your credentials. Who authorized you to speak and act like this?"

3-4   Jesus answered, "First, let me ask you a question: About the baptism of John—who authorized it, heaven or humans?"

5-7   They were on the spot, and knew it. They pulled back into a huddle and whispered, "If we say 'heaven,' he'll ask us why we didn't believe him; if we say 'humans,' the people will tear us limb from limb, convinced as they are that John was God's prophet." They agreed to concede that round to Jesus and said they didn't know.

8   Jesus said, "Then neither will I answer your question."

The Story of Corrupt Farmhands

9-12   Jesus told another story to the people: "A man planted a vineyard. He handed it over to farmhands and went off on a trip. He was gone a long time. In time he sent a servant back to the farmhands to collect the profits, but they beat him up and sent him off empty-handed. He decided to try again and sent another servant. That one they beat black-and-blue, and sent him off empty-handed. He tried a third time. They worked that servant over from head to foot and dumped him in the street.

13   "Then the owner of the vineyard said, 'I know what I'll do: I'll send my beloved son. They're bound to respect my son.'

14-15   "But when the farmhands saw him coming, they quickly put their heads together. 'This is our chance—this is the heir! Let's kill him and have it all to ourselves.' They killed him and threw him over the fence.

15-16   "What do you think the owner of the vineyard will do? Right. He'll come and clean house. Then he'll assign the care of the vineyard to others."

Those who were listening said, "Oh, no! He'd never do that!"

17-18   But Jesus didn't back down. "Why, then, do you think this was written:

That stone the masons threw out—
It's now the cornerstone!?

"Anyone falling over that stone will break every bone in his body; if the stone falls on anyone, it will be a total smashup."

19   The religion scholars and high priests wanted to lynch him on the spot, but they were intimidated by public opinion. They knew the story was about them.

PAYING TAXES

20-22 Watching for a chance to get him, they sent spies who posed as honest inquirers, hoping to trick him into saying something that would get him in trouble with the law. So they asked him, "Teacher, we know that you're honest and straightforward when you teach, that you don't pander to anyone but teach the way of God accurately. Tell us: Is it lawful to pay taxes to Caesar or not?"

23-24 He knew they were laying for him and said, "Show me a coin. Now, this engraving, who does it look like and what does it say?"

25 "Caesar," they said.

Jesus said, "Then give Caesar what is his and give God what is his."

26 Try as they might, they couldn't trap him into saying anything incriminating. His answer caught them off guard and left them speechless.

ALL INTIMACIES WILL BE WITH GOD

27-33 Some Sadducees came up. This is the Jewish party that denies any possibility of resurrection. They asked, "Teacher, Moses wrote us that if a man dies and leaves a wife but no child, his brother is obligated to take the widow to wife and get her with child. Well, there once were seven brothers. The first took a wife. He died childless. The second married her and died, then the third, and eventually all seven had their turn, but no child. After all that, the wife died. That wife, now—in the resurrection whose wife is she? All seven married her."

34-38 Jesus said, "Marriage is a major preoccupation here, but not there. Those who are included in the resurrection of the dead will no longer be concerned with marriage nor, of course, with death. They will have better things to think about, if you can believe it. All ecstasies and intimacies then will be with God. Even Moses exclaimed about resurrection at the burning bush, saying, 'God: God of Abraham, God of Isaac, God of Jacob!' God isn't the God of dead men, but of the living. To him all are alive."

39-40 Some of the religion scholars said, "Teacher, that's a great answer!" For a while, anyway, no one dared put questions to him.

41-44 Then he put a question to them: "How is it that they say that the Messiah is David's son? In the Book of Psalms, David clearly says,

> God said to my Master,
> "Sit here at my right hand
>   until I put your enemies under your feet."

"David here designates the Messiah as 'my Master'—so how can the Messiah also be his 'son'?"

45-47 With everybody listening, Jesus spoke to his disciples. "Watch out for the religion scholars. They love to walk around in academic gowns, preen in the radiance of public flattery, bask in prominent positions, sit at the head table at every church function. And all the time they are exploiting the weak and helpless. The longer their prayers, the worse they get. But they'll pay for it in the end."

1-4 **21** Just then he looked up and saw the rich people dropping offerings in the collection plate. Then he saw a poor widow put in two pennies. He said, "The plain truth is that this widow has given by far the largest offering today. All these others made offerings that they'll never miss; she gave extravagantly what she couldn't afford — she gave her all!"

WATCH OUT FOR DOOMSDAY DECEIVERS

5-6 One day people were standing around talking about the Temple, remarking how beautiful it was, the splendor of its stonework and memorial gifts. Jesus said, "All this you're admiring so much — the time is coming when every stone in that building will end up in a heap of rubble."

7 They asked him, "Teacher, when is this going to happen? What clue will we get that it's about to take place?"

8-9 He said, "Watch out for the doomsday deceivers. Many leaders are going to show up with forged identities claiming, 'I'm the One,' or, 'The end is near.' Don't fall for any of that. When you hear of wars and uprisings, keep your head and don't panic. This is routine history and no sign of the end."

10-11 He went on, "Nation will fight nation and ruler fight ruler, over and over. Huge earthquakes will occur in various places. There will be famines. You'll think at times that the very sky is falling.

12-15 "But before any of this happens, they'll arrest you, hunt you down, and drag you to court and jail. It will go from bad to worse, dog-eat-dog, everyone at your throat because you carry my name. You'll end up on the witness stand, called to testify. Make up your mind right now not to worry about it. I'll give you the words and wisdom that will reduce all your accusers to stammers and stutters.

16-19 "You'll even be turned in by parents, brothers, relatives, and friends. Some of you will be killed. There's no telling who will hate you because of me. Even so, every detail of your body and soul — even the hairs of your head! — is in my care; nothing of you will be lost. Staying with it — that's what is required. Stay with it to the end. You won't be sorry; you'll be saved.

VENGEANCE DAY

20-24 "When you see soldiers camped all around Jerusalem, then you'll know that she is about to be devastated. If you're living in Judea at the time, run for the hills. If you're in the city, get out quickly. If you're out in the fields, don't go home to get your coat. This is Vengeance Day — everything written about it will come to a head. Pregnant and nursing mothers will have it especially hard. Incredible misery! Torrential rage! People dropping like flies; people dragged off to prisons; Jerusalem under the boot of barbarians until the nations finish what was given them to do.

25-26 "It will seem like all hell has broken loose — sun, moon, stars, earth, sea, in an uproar and everyone all over the world in a panic, the wind knocked out of them by the threat of doom, the powers-that-be quaking.

27-28 "And then — then! — they'll see the Son of Man welcomed in grand style — a glorious welcome! When all this starts to happen, up on your feet. Stand tall with your heads high. Help is on the way!"

29-33 He told them a story. "Look at a fig tree. Any tree for that matter. When the leaves begin to show, one look tells you that summer is right around the corner. The same here — when you see these things happen, you know God's kingdom is about here. Don't brush this off: I'm not just saying this for some future generation, but for this one, too — these things will happen. Sky and earth will wear out; my words won't wear out.

34-36 "But be on your guard. Don't let the sharp edge of your expectation get dulled by parties and drinking and shopping. Otherwise, that Day is going to take you by complete surprise, spring on you suddenly like a trap, for it's going to come on everyone, everywhere, at once. So, whatever you do, don't go to sleep at the switch. Pray constantly that you will have the strength and wits to make it through everything that's coming and end up on your feet before the Son of Man."

37-38 He spent his days in the Temple teaching, but his nights out on the mountain called Olives. All the people were up at the crack of dawn to come to the Temple and listen to him.

THE PASSOVER MEAL

1-2 **22** The Feast of Unleavened Bread, also called Passover, drew near. The high priests and religion scholars were looking for a way to do away with Jesus but, fearful of the people, they were also looking for a way to cover their tracks.

3-6 That's when Satan entered Judas, the one called Iscariot. He was one of the Twelve. Leaving the others, he conferred with the high priests and the Temple guards about how he might betray Jesus to them. They couldn't believe their good luck and agreed to pay him well. He gave them his word and started looking for a way to betray Jesus, but out of sight of the crowd.

7-8 The Day of Unleavened Bread came, the day the Passover lamb was butchered. Jesus sent Peter and John off, saying, "Go prepare the Passover for us so we can eat it together."

9 They said, "Where do you want us to do this?"

10-12 He said, "Keep your eyes open as you enter the city. A man carrying a water jug will meet you. Follow him home. Then speak with the owner of the house: The Teacher wants to know, 'Where is the guest room where I can eat the Passover meal with my disciples?' He will show you a spacious second-story room, swept and ready. Prepare the meal there."

13 They left, found everything just as he told them, and prepared the Passover meal.

14-16 When it was time, he sat down, all the apostles with him, and said, "You've no idea how much I have looked forward to eating this Passover meal with you before I enter my time of suffering. It's the last one I'll eat until we all eat it together in the kingdom of God."

17-18 Taking the cup, he blessed it, then said, "Take this and pass it among you. As for me, I'll not drink wine again until the kingdom of God arrives."

19 Taking bread, he blessed it, broke it, and gave it to them, saying, "This is my body, given for you. Eat it in my memory."

20 He did the same with the cup after supper, saying, "This cup is the new covenant written in my blood, blood poured out for you.

21-22 "Do you realize that the hand of the one who is betraying me is at this moment on this table? It's true that the Son of Man is going down a path already marked out — no surprises there. But for the one who turns him in, turns traitor to the Son of Man, this is doomsday."

23 They immediately became suspicious of each other and began quizzing one another, wondering who might be about to do this.

24-26 Within minutes they were bickering over who of them would end up the greatest. But Jesus intervened: "Kings like to throw their weight around and people in authority like to give themselves fancy titles. It's not going to be that way with you. Let the senior among you become like the junior; let the leader act the part of the servant.

27-30 "Who would you rather be: the one who eats the dinner or the one who serves the dinner? You'd rather eat and be served, right? But I've taken my place among you as the one who serves. And you've stuck with me through thick and thin. Now I confer on you the royal authority my Father conferred on me so you can eat and drink at my table in my kingdom and be strengthened as you take up responsibilities among the congregations of God's people.

31-32 "Simon, stay on your toes. Satan has tried his best to separate all of you from me, like chaff from wheat. Simon, I've prayed for you in particular that you not give in or give out. When you have come through the time of testing, turn to your companions and give them a fresh start."

33 Peter said, "Master, I'm ready for anything with you. I'd go to jail for you. I'd *die* for you!"

34 Jesus said, "I'm sorry to have to tell you this, Peter, but before the rooster crows you will have three times denied that you know me."

35 Then Jesus said, "When I sent you out and told you to travel light, to take only the bare necessities, did you get along all right?"

"Certainly," they said, "we got along just fine."

36-37 He said, "This is different. Get ready for trouble. Look to what you'll need; there are difficult times ahead. Pawn your coat and get a sword. What was written in Scripture, 'He was lumped in with the criminals,' gets its final meaning in me. Everything written about me is now coming to a conclusion."

38 They said, "Look, Master, two swords!"

But he said, "Enough of that; no more sword talk!"

A DARK NIGHT

39-40 Leaving there, he went, as he so often did, to Mount Olives. The disciples followed him. When they arrived at the place, he said, "Pray that you don't give in to temptation."

41-44 He pulled away from them about a stone's throw, knelt down, and prayed, "Father, remove this cup from me. But please, not what I want. What do *you* want?" At once an angel from heaven was at his side, strengthening him. He prayed on all the harder. Sweat, wrung from him like drops of blood, poured off his face.

45-46 He got up from prayer, went back to the disciples and found them asleep, drugged by grief. He said, "What business do you have sleeping? Get up. Pray so you won't give in to temptation."

47-48 No sooner were the words out of his mouth than a crowd showed up, Judas, the one from the Twelve, in the lead. He came right up to Jesus to kiss him. Jesus said, "Judas, you would betray the Son of Man with a kiss?"

49-50 When those with him saw what was happening, they said, "Master, shall we fight?" One of them took a swing at the Chief Priest's servant and cut off his right ear.

51 Jesus said, "Let them be. Even in this." Then, touching the servant's ear, he healed him.

52-53 Jesus spoke to those who had come — high priests, Temple police, religion leaders: "What is this, jumping me with swords and clubs as if I were a dangerous criminal? Day after day I've been with you in the Temple and you've not so much as lifted a hand against me. But do it your way — it's a dark night, a dark hour."

A Rooster Crowed

54-56 Arresting Jesus, they marched him off and took him into the house of the Chief Priest. Peter followed, but at a safe distance. In the middle of the courtyard some people had started a fire and were sitting around it, trying to keep warm. One of the serving maids sitting at the fire noticed him, then took a second look and said, "This man was with him!"

57 He denied it, "Woman, I don't even know him."

58 A short time later, someone else noticed him and said, "You're one of them."

But Peter denied it: "Man, I am not."

59 About an hour later, someone else spoke up, really adamant: "He's got to have been with him! He's got 'Galilean' written all over him."

60-62 Peter said, "Man, I don't know what you're talking about." At that very moment, the last word hardly off his lips, a rooster crowed. Just then, the Master turned and looked at Peter. Peter remembered what the Master had said to him: "Before the rooster crows, you will deny me three times." He went out and cried and cried and cried.

Slapping Him Around

63-65 The men in charge of Jesus began poking fun at him, slapping him around. They put a blindfold on him and taunted, "Who hit you that time?" They were having a grand time with him.

66-67 When it was morning, the religious leaders of the people and the high priests and scholars all got together and brought him before their High Council. They said, "Are you the Messiah?"

67-69 He answered, "If I said yes, you wouldn't believe me. If I asked what you meant by your question, you wouldn't answer me. So here's what I have to say: From here on the Son of Man takes his place at God's right hand, the place of power."

70 They all said, "So you admit your claim to be the Son of God?"

"You're the ones who keep saying it," he said.

71 But they had made up their minds, "Why do we need any more evidence? We've all heard him as good as say it himself."

Pilate

1-2 **23** Then they all took Jesus to Pilate and began to bring up charges against him. They said, "We found this man undermining our law and order, forbidding taxes to be paid to Caesar, setting himself up as Messiah-King."

3 Pilate asked him, "Is this true that you're 'King of the Jews'?"

"Those are your words, not mine," Jesus replied.

4 Pilate told the high priests and the accompanying crowd, "I find nothing wrong here. He seems harmless enough to me."

5   But they were vehement. "He's stirring up unrest among the people with his teaching, disturbing the peace everywhere, starting in Galilee and now all through Judea. He's a dangerous man, endangering the peace."

6-7   When Pilate heard that, he asked, "So, he's a Galilean?" Realizing that he properly came under Herod's jurisdiction, he passed the buck to Herod, who just happened to be in Jerusalem for a few days.

8-10 Herod was delighted when Jesus showed up. He had wanted for a long time to see him, he'd heard so much about him. He hoped to see him do something spectacular. He peppered him with questions. Jesus didn't answer — not one word. But the high priests and religion scholars were right there, saying their piece, strident and shrill in their accusations.

11-12 Mightily offended, Herod turned on Jesus. His soldiers joined in, taunting and jeering. Then they dressed him up in an elaborate king costume and sent him back to Pilate. That day Herod and Pilate became thick as thieves. Always before they had kept their distance.

13-16 Then Pilate called in the high priests, rulers, and the others and said, "You brought this man to me as a disturber of the peace. I examined him in front of all of you and found there was nothing to your charge. And neither did Herod, for he has sent him back here with a clean bill of health. It's clear that he's done nothing wrong, let alone anything deserving death. I'm going to warn him to watch his step and let him go."

18-20 At that, the crowd went wild: "Kill him! Give us Barabbas!" (Barabbas had been thrown in prison for starting a riot in the city and for murder.) Pilate still wanted to let Jesus go, and so spoke out again.

21   But they kept shouting back, "Crucify! Crucify him!"

22   He tried a third time. "But for what crime? I've found nothing in him deserving death. I'm going to warn him to watch his step and let him go."

23-25 But they kept at it, a shouting mob, demanding that he be crucified. And finally they shouted him down. Pilate caved in and gave them what they wanted. He released the man thrown in prison for rioting and murder, and gave them Jesus to do whatever they wanted.

SKULL HILL

26-31 As they led him off, they made Simon, a man from Cyrene who happened to be coming in from the countryside, carry the cross behind Jesus. A huge crowd of people followed, along with women weeping and carrying on. At one point Jesus turned to the women and said, "Daughters of Jerusalem, don't cry for me. Cry for yourselves and for your children. The time is coming when they'll say, 'Lucky the women who never conceived! Lucky the wombs that never gave birth! Lucky the breasts that never gave milk!' Then they'll start calling to the mountains, 'Fall down on us!' calling to the hills, 'Cover us up!' If people do these things to a live, green tree, can you imagine what they'll do with deadwood?"

32   Two others, both criminals, were taken along with him for execution.

33   When they got to the place called Skull Hill, they crucified him, along with the criminals, one on his right, the other on his left.

34-35 Jesus prayed, "Father, forgive them; they don't know what they're doing."

Dividing up his clothes, they threw dice for them. The people stood there staring at Jesus, and the ringleaders made faces, taunting, "He saved others. Let's see him save himself! The Messiah of God — ha! The Chosen — ha!"

36-37   The soldiers also came up and poked fun at him, making a game of it. They toasted him with sour wine: "So you're King of the Jews! Save yourself!"

38   Printed over him was a sign: THIS IS THE KING OF THE JEWS.

39   One of the criminals hanging alongside cursed him: "Some Messiah you are! Save yourself! Save us!"

40-41   But the other one made him shut up: "Have you no fear of God? You're getting the same as him. We deserve this, but not him — he did nothing to deserve this."

42   Then he said, "Jesus, remember me when you enter your kingdom."

43   He said, "Don't worry, I will. Today you will join me in paradise."

44-46   By now it was noon. The whole earth became dark, the darkness lasting three hours — a total blackout. The Temple curtain split right down the middle. Jesus called loudly, "Father, I place my life in your hands!" Then he breathed his last.

47   When the captain there saw what happened, he honored God: "This man was innocent! A good man, and innocent!"

48-49   All who had come around as spectators to watch the show, when they saw what actually happened, were overcome with grief and headed home. Those who knew Jesus well, along with the women who had followed him from Galilee, stood at a respectful distance and kept vigil.

50-54   There was a man by the name of Joseph, a member of the Jewish High Council, a man of good heart and good character. He had not gone along with the plans and actions of the council. His hometown was the Jewish village of Arimathea. He lived in alert expectation of the kingdom of God. He went to Pilate and asked for the body of Jesus. Taking him down, he wrapped him in a linen shroud and placed him in a tomb chiseled into the rock, a tomb never yet used. It was the day before Sabbath, the Sabbath just about to begin.

55-56   The women who had been companions of Jesus from Galilee followed along. They saw the tomb where Jesus' body was placed. Then they went back to prepare burial spices and perfumes. They rested quietly on the Sabbath, as commanded.

LOOKING FOR THE LIVING ONE IN A CEMETERY

1-3   **24** At the crack of dawn on Sunday, the women came to the tomb carrying the burial spices they had prepared. They found the entrance stone rolled back from the tomb, so they walked in. But once inside, they couldn't find the body of the Master Jesus.

4-8   They were puzzled, wondering what to make of this. Then, out of nowhere it seemed, two men, light cascading over them, stood there. The women were awestruck and bowed down in worship. The men said, "Why are you looking for the Living One in a cemetery? He is not here, but raised up. Remember how he told you when you were still back in Galilee that he had to be handed over to sinners, be killed on a cross, and in three days rise up?" Then they remembered Jesus' words.

9-11   They left the tomb and broke the news of all this to the Eleven and the rest. Mary Magdalene, Joanna, Mary the mother of James, and the other women with them kept telling these things to the apostles, but the apostles didn't believe a word of it, thought they were making it all up.

12　　But Peter jumped to his feet and ran to the tomb. He stooped to look in and saw a few grave clothes, that's all. He walked away puzzled, shaking his head.

The Road to Emmaus

13-16　That same day two of them were walking to the village Emmaus, about seven miles out of Jerusalem. They were deep in conversation, going over all these things that had happened. In the middle of their talk and questions, Jesus came up and walked along with them. But they were not able to recognize who he was.

17-18　　He asked, "What's this you're discussing so intently as you walk along?"

They just stood there, long-faced, like they had lost their best friend. Then one of them, his name was Cleopas, said, "Are you the only one in Jerusalem who hasn't heard what's happened during the last few days?"

19-24　　He said, "What has happened?"

They said, "The things that happened to Jesus the Nazarene. He was a man of God, a prophet, dynamic in work and word, blessed by both God and all the people. Then our high priests and leaders betrayed him, got him sentenced to death, and crucified him. And we had our hopes up that he was the One, the One about to deliver Israel. And it is now the third day since it happened. But now some of our women have completely confused us. Early this morning they were at the tomb and couldn't find his body. They came back with the story that they had seen a vision of angels who said he was alive. Some of our friends went off to the tomb to check and found it empty just as the women said, but they didn't see Jesus."

25-27　　Then he said to them, "So thick-headed! So slow-hearted! Why can't you simply believe all that the prophets said? Don't you see that these things had to happen, that the Messiah had to suffer and only then enter into his glory?" Then he started at the beginning, with the Books of Moses, and went on through all the Prophets, pointing out everything in the Scriptures that referred to him.

28-31　　They came to the edge of the village where they were headed. He acted as if he were going on but they pressed him: "Stay and have supper with us. It's nearly evening; the day is done." So he went in with them. And here is what happened: He sat down at the table with them. Taking the bread, he blessed and broke and gave it to them. At that moment, open-eyed, wide-eyed, they recognized him. And then he disappeared.

32　　Back and forth they talked. "Didn't we feel on fire as he conversed with us on the road, as he opened up the Scriptures for us?"

A Ghost Doesn't Have Muscle and Bone

33-34　They didn't waste a minute. They were up and on their way back to Jerusalem. They found the Eleven and their friends gathered together, talking away: "It's really happened! The Master has been raised up — Simon saw him!"

35　　Then the two went over everything that happened on the road and how they recognized him when he broke the bread.

36-41　　While they were saying all this, Jesus appeared to them and said, "Peace be with you." They thought they were seeing a ghost and were scared half to death. He continued with them, "Don't be upset, and don't let all these doubting questions take over. Look at my hands; look at my feet — it's really me. Touch me. Look me over from head to toe. A ghost doesn't have muscle and bone like this." As he said this, he showed them his hands and feet. They still couldn't believe what they were seeing. It was too much; it seemed too good to be true.

41-43 He asked, "Do you have any food here?" They gave him a piece of leftover fish they had cooked. He took it and ate it right before their eyes.

You're the Witnesses

44 Then he said, "Everything I told you while I was with you comes to this: All the things written about me in the Law of Moses, in the Prophets, and in the Psalms have to be fulfilled."

45-49 He went on to open their understanding of the Word of God, showing them how to read their Bibles this way. He said, "You can see now how it is written that the Messiah suffers, rises from the dead on the third day, and then a total life-change through the forgiveness of sins is proclaimed in his name to all nations — starting from here, from Jerusalem! You're the first to hear and see it. You're the witnesses. What comes next is very important: I am sending what my Father promised to you, so stay here in the city until he arrives, until you're equipped with power from on high."

50-51 He then led them out of the city over to Bethany. Raising his hands he blessed them, and while blessing them, took his leave, being carried up to heaven.

52-53 And they were on their knees, worshiping him. They returned to Jerusalem bursting with joy. They spent all their time in the Temple praising God. Yes.

JOHN

In Genesis, the first book of the Bible, God is presented as speaking the creation into existence. God speaks the word and it happens: heaven and earth, ocean and stream, trees and grass, birds and fish, animals and humans. Everything, seen and unseen, called into being by God's spoken word.

In deliberate parallel to the opening words of Genesis, John presents God as speaking salvation into existence. This time God's word takes on human form and enters history in the person of Jesus. Jesus speaks the word and it happens: forgiveness and judgment, healing and illumination, mercy and grace, joy and love, freedom and resurrection. Everything broken and fallen, sinful and diseased, called into salvation by God's spoken word.

For, somewhere along the line things went wrong (Genesis tells that story, too) and are in desperate need of fixing. The fixing is all accomplished by speaking — God speaking salvation into being in the person of Jesus. Jesus, in this account, not only speaks the word of God; he *is* the Word of God.

Keeping company with these words, we begin to realize that our words are more important than we ever supposed. Saying "I believe," for instance, marks the difference between life and death. Our words accrue dignity and gravity in conversations with Jesus. For Jesus doesn't impose salvation as a solution; he *narrates* salvation into being through leisurely conversation, intimate personal relationships, compassionate responses, passionate prayer, and — putting it all together — a sacrificial death. We don't casually walk away from words like that.

JOHN

THE LIFE-LIGHT

1-2 The Word was first,
    the Word present to God,
God present to the Word.
The Word was God,
    in readiness for God from day one.

3-5 Everything was created through him;
    nothing — not one thing! —
    came into being without him.
What came into existence was Life,
    and the Life was Light to live by.
The Life-Light blazed out of the darkness;
    the darkness couldn't put it out.

6-8 There once was a man, his name John, sent by God to point out the way
to the Life-Light. He came to show everyone where to look, who to believe in.
John was not himself the Light; he was there to show the way to the Light.

9-13 The Life-Light was the real thing:
    Every person entering Life
    he brings into Light.
He was in the world,
    the world was there through him,
    and yet the world didn't even notice.
He came to his own people,
    but they didn't want him.
But whoever did want him,
    who believed he was who he claimed
    and would do what he said,
He made to be their true selves,
    their child-of-God selves.
These are the God-begotten,
    not blood-begotten,
    not flesh-begotten,
    not sex-begotten.

14 The Word became flesh and blood,
    and moved into the neighborhood.
We saw the glory with our own eyes,
    the one-of-a-kind glory,
    like Father, like Son,
Generous inside and out,
    true from start to finish.

15 John pointed him out and called, "This is the One! The One I told
you was coming after me but in fact was ahead of me. He has always been

ahead of me, has always had the first word."

16-18
> We all live off his generous bounty,
>> gift after gift after gift.
> We got the basics from Moses,
>> and then this exuberant giving and receiving,
> This endless knowing and understanding—
>> all this came through Jesus, the Messiah.
> No one has ever seen God,
>> not so much as a glimpse.
> This one-of-a-kind God-Expression,
>> who exists at the very heart of the Father,
>> has made him plain as day.

THUNDER IN THE DESERT

19-20 When Jews from Jerusalem sent a group of priests and officials to ask John who he was, he was completely honest. He didn't evade the question. He told the plain truth: "I am not the Messiah."

21 They pressed him, "Who, then? Elijah?"

"I am not."

"The Prophet?"

"No."

22 Exasperated, they said, "Who, then? We need an answer for those who sent us. Tell us something—anything!—about yourself."

23 "I'm thunder in the desert: 'Make the road straight for God!' I'm doing what the prophet Isaiah preached."

24-25 Those sent to question him were from the Pharisee party. Now they had a question of their own: "If you're neither the Messiah, nor Elijah, nor the Prophet, why do you baptize?"

26-27 John answered, "I only baptize using water. A person you don't recognize has taken his stand in your midst. He comes after me, but he is not in second place to me. I'm not even worthy to hold his coat for him."

28 These conversations took place in Bethany on the other side of the Jordan, where John was baptizing at the time.

THE GOD-REVEALER

29-31 The very next day John saw Jesus coming toward him and yelled out, "Here he is, God's Passover Lamb! He forgives the sins of the world! This is the man I've been talking about, 'the One who comes after me but is really ahead of me.' I knew nothing about who he was—only this: that my task has been to get Israel ready to recognize him as the God-Revealer. That is why I came here baptizing with water, giving you a good bath and scrubbing sins from your life so you can get a fresh start with God."

32-34 John clinched his witness with this: "I watched the Spirit, like a dove flying down out of the sky, making himself at home in him. I repeat, I know nothing about him except this: The One who authorized me to baptize with water told me, 'The One on whom you see the Spirit come down and stay, this One will baptize with the Holy Spirit.' That's exactly what I saw happen, and I'm telling you, there's no question about it: *This* is the Son of God."

COME, SEE FOR YOURSELF

35-36 The next day John was back at his post with two disciples, who were watching. He looked up, saw Jesus walking nearby, and said, "Here he is, God's Passover Lamb."

37-38 The two disciples heard him and went after Jesus. Jesus looked over his shoulder and said to them, "What are you after?"

They said, "Rabbi" (which means "Teacher"), "where are you staying?"

39 He replied, "Come along and see for yourself."

They came, saw where he was living, and ended up staying with him for the day. It was late afternoon when this happened.

40-42 Andrew, Simon Peter's brother, was one of the two who heard John's witness and followed Jesus. The first thing he did after finding where Jesus lived was find his own brother, Simon, telling him, "We've found the Messiah" (that is, "Christ"). He immediately led him to Jesus.

Jesus took one look up and said, "You're John's son, Simon? From now on your name is Cephas" (or Peter, which means "Rock").

43-44 The next day Jesus decided to go to Galilee. When he got there, he ran across Philip and said, "Come, follow me." (Philip's hometown was Bethsaida, the same as Andrew and Peter.)

45-46 Philip went and found Nathanael and told him, "We've found the One Moses wrote of in the Law, the One preached by the prophets. It's *Jesus*, Joseph's son, the one from Nazareth!" Nathanael said, "Nazareth? You've got to be kidding."

But Philip said, "Come, see for yourself."

47 When Jesus saw him coming he said, "There's a real Israelite, not a false bone in his body."

48 Nathanael said, "Where did you get that idea? You don't know me."

Jesus answered, "One day, long before Philip called you here, I saw you under the fig tree."

49 Nathanael exclaimed, "Rabbi! You are the Son of God, the King of Israel!"

50-51 Jesus said, "You've become a believer simply because I say I saw you one day sitting under the fig tree? You haven't seen anything yet! Before this is over you're going to see heaven open and God's angels descending to the Son of Man and ascending again."

FROM WATER TO WINE

1-3 Three days later there was a wedding in the village of Cana in Galilee. Jesus' mother was there. Jesus and his disciples were guests also. When they started running low on wine at the wedding banquet, Jesus' mother told him, "They're just about out of wine."

4 Jesus said, "Is that any of our business, Mother — yours or mine? This isn't my time. Don't push me."

5 She went ahead anyway, telling the servants, "Whatever he tells you, do it."

6-7 Six stoneware water pots were there, used by the Jews for ritual washings. Each held twenty to thirty gallons. Jesus ordered the servants, "Fill the pots with water." And they filled them to the brim.

8 "Now fill your pitchers and take them to the host," Jesus said, and they did.

9-10   When the host tasted the water that had become wine (he didn't know what had just happened but the servants, of course, knew), he called out to the bridegroom, "Everybody I know begins with their finest wines and after the guests have had their fill brings in the cheap stuff. But you've saved the best till now!"

11   This act in Cana of Galilee was the first sign Jesus gave, the first glimpse of his glory. And his disciples believed in him.

12   After this he went down to Capernaum along with his mother, brothers, and disciples, and stayed several days.

Tear Down This Temple . . .

13-14   When the Passover Feast, celebrated each spring by the Jews, was about to take place, Jesus traveled up to Jerusalem. He found the Temple teeming with people selling cattle and sheep and doves. The loan sharks were also there in full strength.

15-17   Jesus put together a whip out of strips of leather and chased them out of the Temple, stampeding the sheep and cattle, upending the tables of the loan sharks, spilling coins left and right. He told the dove merchants, "Get your things out of here! Stop turning my Father's house into a shopping mall!" That's when his disciples remembered the Scripture, "Zeal for your house consumes me."

18-19   But the Jews were upset. They asked, "What credentials can you present to justify this?" Jesus answered, "Tear down this Temple and in three days I'll put it back together."

20-22   They were indignant: "It took forty-six years to build this Temple, and you're going to rebuild it in three days?" But Jesus was talking about his body as the Temple. Later, after he was raised from the dead, his disciples remembered he had said this. They then put two and two together and believed both what was written in Scripture and what Jesus had said.

23-25   During the time he was in Jerusalem, those days of the Passover Feast, many people noticed the signs he was displaying and, seeing they pointed straight to God, entrusted their lives to him. But Jesus didn't entrust his life to them. He knew them inside and out, knew how untrustworthy they were. He didn't need any help in seeing right through them.

Born from Above

1-2   3 There was a man of the Pharisee sect, Nicodemus, a prominent leader among the Jews. Late one night he visited Jesus and said, "Rabbi, we all know you're a teacher straight from God. No one could do all the God-pointing, God-revealing acts you do if God weren't in on it."

3   Jesus said, "You're absolutely right. Take it from me: Unless a person is born from above, it's not possible to see what I'm pointing to—to God's kingdom."

4   "How can anyone," said Nicodemus, "be born who has already been born and grown up? You can't re-enter your mother's womb and be born again. What are you saying with this 'born-from-above' talk?"

5-6   Jesus said, "You're not listening. Let me say it again. Unless a person submits to this original creation—the 'wind-hovering-over-the-water' creation, the invisible moving the visible, a baptism into a new life—it's not possible to enter God's kingdom. When you look at a baby, it's just that: a body you can look at and touch. But the person who takes shape within is formed by something you can't see and touch — the Spirit — and becomes a living spirit.

7-8 "So don't be so surprised when I tell you that you have to be 'born from above' — out of this world, so to speak. You know well enough how the wind blows this way and that. You hear it rustling through the trees, but you have no idea where it comes from or where it's headed next. That's the way it is with everyone 'born from above' by the wind of God, the Spirit of God."

9 Nicodemus asked, "What do you mean by this? How does this happen?"

10-12 Jesus said, "You're a respected teacher of Israel and you don't know these basics? Listen carefully. I'm speaking sober truth to you. I speak only of what I know by experience; I give witness only to what I have seen with my own eyes. There is nothing secondhand here, no hearsay. Yet instead of facing the evidence and accepting it, you procrastinate with questions. If I tell you things that are plain as the hand before your face and you don't believe me, what use is there in telling you of things you can't see, the things of God?

13-15 "No one has ever gone up into the presence of God except the One who came down from that Presence, the Son of Man. In the same way that Moses lifted the serpent in the desert so people could have something to see and then believe, it is necessary for the Son of Man to be lifted up — and everyone who looks up to him, trusting and expectant, will gain a real life, eternal life.

16-18 "This is how much God loved the world: He gave his Son, his one and only Son. And this is why: so that no one need be destroyed; by believing in him, anyone can have a whole and lasting life. God didn't go to all the trouble of sending his Son merely to point an accusing finger, telling the world how bad it was. He came to help, to put the world right again. Anyone who trusts in him is acquitted; anyone who refuses to trust him has long since been under the death sentence without knowing it. And why? Because of that person's failure to believe in the one-of-a-kind Son of God when introduced to him.

19-21 "This is the crisis we're in: God-light streamed into the world, but men and women everywhere ran for the darkness. They went for the darkness because they were not really interested in pleasing God. Everyone who makes a practice of doing evil, addicted to denial and illusion, hates God-light and won't come near it, fearing a painful exposure. But anyone working and living in truth and reality welcomes God-light so the work can be seen for the God-work it is."

THE BRIDEGROOM'S FRIEND

22-26 After this conversation, Jesus went on with his disciples into the Judean countryside and relaxed with them there. He was also baptizing. At the same time, John was baptizing over at Aenon near Salim, where water was abundant. This was before John was thrown into jail. John's disciples got into an argument with the establishment Jews over the nature of baptism. They came to John and said, "Rabbi, you know the one who was with you on the other side of the Jordan? The one you authorized with your witness? Well, he's now competing with us. He's baptizing, too, and everyone's going to him instead of us."

27-29 John answered, "It's not possible for a person to succeed — I'm talking about *eternal* success — without heaven's help. You yourselves were there when I made it public that I was not the Messiah but simply the one sent ahead of him to get things ready. The one who gets the bride is, by definition, the bridegroom. And the bridegroom's friend, his 'best man' — that's me — in place at his side where he can hear every word, is genuinely happy. How could he be jealous when he knows that the wedding is finished and the marriage is off to a good start?

29-30 "That's why my cup is running over. This is the assigned moment for him to move into the center, while I slip off to the sidelines.

31-33 "The One who comes from above is head and shoulders over other messengers from God. The earthborn is earthbound and speaks earth language; the heavenborn is in a league of his own. He sets out the evidence of what he saw and heard in heaven. No one wants to deal with these facts. But anyone who examines this evidence will come to stake his life on this: that God himself is the truth.

34-36 "The One that God sent speaks God's words. And don't think he rations out the Spirit in bits and pieces. The Father loves the Son extravagantly. He turned everything over to him so he could give it away — a lavish distribution of gifts. That is why whoever accepts and trusts the Son gets in on everything, life complete and forever! And that is also why the person who avoids and distrusts the Son is in the dark and doesn't see life. All he experiences of God is darkness, and an angry darkness at that."

The Woman at the Well

1-3 4 Jesus realized that the Pharisees were keeping count of the baptisms that he and John performed (although his disciples, not Jesus, did the actual baptizing). They had posted the score that Jesus was ahead, turning him and John into rivals in the eyes of the people. So Jesus left the Judean countryside and went back to Galilee.

4-6 To get there, he had to pass through Samaria. He came into Sychar, a Samaritan village that bordered the field Jacob had given his son Joseph. Jacob's well was still there. Jesus, worn out by the trip, sat down at the well. It was noon.

7-8 A woman, a Samaritan, came to draw water. Jesus said, "Would you give me a drink of water?" (His disciples had gone to the village to buy food for lunch.)

9 The Samaritan woman, taken aback, asked, "How come you, a Jew, are asking me, a Samaritan woman, for a drink?" (Jews in those days wouldn't be caught dead talking to Samaritans.)

10 Jesus answered, "If you knew the generosity of God and who I am, you would be asking *me* for a drink, and I would give you fresh, living water."

11-12 The woman said, "Sir, you don't even have a bucket to draw with, and this well is deep. So how are you going to get this 'living water'? Are you a better man than our ancestor Jacob, who dug this well and drank from it, he and his sons and livestock, and passed it down to us?"

13-14 Jesus said, "Everyone who drinks this water will get thirsty again and again. Anyone who drinks the water I give will never thirst — not ever. The water I give will be an artesian spring within, gushing fountains of endless life."

15 The woman said, "Sir, give me this water so I won't ever get thirsty, won't ever have to come back to this well again!"

16 He said, "Go call your husband and then come back."

17-18 "I have no husband," she said.

"That's nicely put: 'I have no husband.' You've had five husbands, and the man you're living with now isn't even your husband. You spoke the truth there, sure enough."

19-20 "Oh, so you're a prophet! Well, tell me this: Our ancestors worshiped God at this mountain, but you Jews insist that Jerusalem is the only place for worship, right?"

21-23 "Believe me, woman, the time is coming when you Samaritans will worship the Father neither here at this mountain nor there in Jerusalem. You worship guessing in the dark; we Jews worship in the clear light of day. God's way of salvation is made available through the Jews. But the time is coming—it has, in fact, come—when what you're called will not matter and where you go to worship will not matter.

23-24 "It's who you are and the way you live that count before God. Your worship must engage your spirit in the pursuit of truth. That's the kind of people the Father is out looking for: those who are simply and honestly *themselves* before him in their worship. God is sheer being itself—Spirit. Those who worship him must do it out of their very being, their spirits, their true selves, in adoration."

25 The woman said, "I don't know about that. I do know that the Messiah is coming. When he arrives, we'll get the whole story."

26 "I am he," said Jesus. "You don't have to wait any longer or look any further."

27 Just then his disciples came back. They were shocked. They couldn't believe he was talking with that kind of a woman. No one said what they were all thinking, but their faces showed it.

28-30 The woman took the hint and left. In her confusion she left her water pot. Back in the village she told the people, "Come see a man who knew all about the things I did, who knows me inside and out. Do you think this could be the Messiah?" And they went out to see for themselves.

It's Harvest Time

31 In the meantime, the disciples pressed him, "Rabbi, eat. Aren't you going to eat?"

32 He told them, "I have food to eat you know nothing about."

33 The disciples were puzzled. "Who could have brought him food?"

34-35 Jesus said, "The food that keeps me going is that I do the will of the One who sent me, finishing the work he started. As you look around right now, wouldn't you say that in about four months it will be time to harvest? Well, I'm telling you to open your eyes and take a good look at what's right in front of you. These Samaritan fields are ripe. It's harvest time!

36-38 "The Harvester isn't waiting. He's taking his pay, gathering in this grain that's ripe for eternal life. Now the Sower is arm in arm with the Harvester, triumphant. That's the truth of the saying, 'This one sows, that one harvests.' I sent you to harvest a field you never worked. Without lifting a finger, you have walked in on a field worked long and hard by others."

39-42 Many of the Samaritans from that village committed themselves to him because of the woman's witness: "He knew all about the things I did. He knows me inside and out!" They asked him to stay on, so Jesus stayed two days. A lot more people entrusted their lives to him when they heard what he had to say. They said to the woman, "We're no longer taking this on your say-so. We've heard it for ourselves and know it for sure. He's the Savior of the world!"

☙

43-45 After the two days he left for Galilee. Now, Jesus knew well from experience that a prophet is not respected in the place where he grew up. So when he arrived in Galilee, the Galileans welcomed him, but only because they were impressed with what he had done in Jerusalem during the Passover Feast, not that they really had a clue about who he was or what he was up to.

46-48 Now he was back in Cana of Galilee, the place where he made the water into wine. Meanwhile in Capernaum, there was a certain official from the king's court whose son was sick. When he heard that Jesus had come from Judea to Galilee, he went and asked that he come down and heal his son, who was on the brink of death. Jesus put him off: "Unless you people are dazzled by a miracle, you refuse to believe."

49 But the court official wouldn't be put off. "Come down! It's life or death for my son."

50-51 Jesus simply replied, "Go home. Your son lives."

The man believed the bare word Jesus spoke and headed home. On his way back, his servants intercepted him and announced, "Your son lives!"

52-53 He asked them what time he began to get better. They said, "The fever broke yesterday afternoon at one o'clock." The father knew that that was the very moment Jesus had said, "Your son lives."

53-54 That clinched it. Not only he but his entire household believed. This was now the second sign Jesus gave after having come from Judea into Galilee.

EVEN ON THE SABBATH

1-6 5 Soon another Feast came around and Jesus was back in Jerusalem. Near the Sheep Gate in Jerusalem there was a pool, in Hebrew called *Bethesda*, with five alcoves. Hundreds of sick people — blind, crippled, paralyzed — were in these alcoves. One man had been an invalid there for thirty-eight years. When Jesus saw him stretched out by the pool and knew how long he had been there, he said, "Do you want to get well?"

7 The sick man said, "Sir, when the water is stirred, I don't have anybody to put me in the pool. By the time I get there, somebody else is already in."

8-9 Jesus said, "Get up, take your bedroll, start walking." The man was healed on the spot. He picked up his bedroll and walked off.

9-10 That day happened to be the Sabbath. The Jews stopped the healed man and said, "It's the Sabbath. You can't carry your bedroll around. It's against the rules."

11 But he told them, "The man who made me well told me to. He said, 'Take your bedroll and start walking.'"

12-13 They asked, "Who gave you the order to take it up and start walking?" But the healed man didn't know, for Jesus had slipped away into the crowd.

14 A little later Jesus found him in the Temple and said, "You look wonderful! You're well! Don't return to a sinning life or something worse might happen."

15-16 The man went back and told the Jews that it was Jesus who had made him well. That is why the Jews were out to get Jesus — because he did this kind of thing on the Sabbath.

17   But Jesus defended himself. "My Father is working straight through, even on the Sabbath. So am I."

18   That really set them off. The Jews were now not only out to expose him; they were out to *kill* him. Not only was he breaking the Sabbath, but he was calling God his own Father, putting himself on a level with God.

What the Father Does, the Son Does

19-20   So Jesus explained himself at length. "I'm telling you this straight. The Son can't independently do a thing, only what he sees the Father doing. What the Father does, the Son does. The Father loves the Son and includes him in everything he is doing.

20-23   "But you haven't seen the half of it yet, for in the same way that the Father raises the dead and creates life, so does the Son. The Son gives life to anyone he chooses. Neither he nor the Father shuts anyone out. The Father handed all authority to judge over to the Son so that the Son will be honored equally with the Father. Anyone who dishonors the Son, dishonors the Father, for it was the Father's decision to put the Son in the place of honor.

24   "It's urgent that you listen carefully to this: Anyone here who believes what I am saying right now and aligns himself with the Father, who has in fact put me in charge, has at this very moment the real, lasting life and is no longer condemned to be an outsider. This person has taken a giant step from the world of the dead to the world of the living.

25-27   "It's urgent that you get this right: The time has arrived—I mean right now!—when dead men and women will hear the voice of the Son of God and, hearing, will come alive. Just as the Father has life in himself, he has conferred on the Son life in himself. And he has given him the authority, simply because he is the Son of Man, to decide and carry out matters of Judgment.

28-29   "Don't act so surprised at all this. The time is coming when everyone dead and buried will hear his voice. Those who have lived the right way will walk out into a resurrection Life; those who have lived the wrong way, into a resurrection Judgment.

30-33   "I can't do a solitary thing on my own: I listen, then I decide. You can trust my decision because I'm not out to get my own way but only to carry out orders. If I were simply speaking on my own account, it would be an empty, self-serving witness. But an independent witness confirms me, the most reliable Witness of all. Furthermore, you all saw and heard John, and he gave expert and reliable testimony about me, didn't he?

34-38   "But my purpose is not to get your vote, and not to appeal to mere human testimony. I'm speaking to you this way so that you will be saved. John was a torch, blazing and bright, and you were glad enough to dance for an hour or so in his bright light. But the witness that really confirms me far exceeds John's witness. It's the work the Father gave me to complete. These very tasks, as I go about completing them, confirm that the Father, in fact, sent me. The Father who sent me, confirmed me. And you missed it. You never heard his voice, you never saw his appearance. There is nothing left in your memory of his Message because you do not take his Messenger seriously.

39-40   "You have your heads in your Bibles constantly because you think you'll find eternal life there. But you miss the forest for the trees. These Scriptures are all about *me*! And here I am, standing right before you, and you aren't willing to receive from me the life you say you want.

41-44 "I'm not interested in crowd approval. And do you know why? Because I know you and your crowds. I know that love, especially God's love, is not on your working agenda. I came with the authority of my Father, and you either dismiss me or avoid me. If another came, acting self-important, you would welcome him with open arms. How do you expect to get anywhere with God when you spend all your time jockeying for position with each other, ranking your rivals and ignoring God?

45-47 "But don't think I'm going to accuse you before my Father. Moses, in whom you put so much stock, is your accuser. If you believed, really believed, what Moses said, you would believe me. He wrote of me. If you won't take seriously what *he* wrote, how can I expect you to take seriously what *I* speak?"

BREAD AND FISH FOR ALL

1-4 6 After this, Jesus went across the Sea of Galilee (some call it Tiberias). A huge crowd followed him, attracted by the miracles they had seen him do among the sick. When he got to the other side, he climbed a hill and sat down, surrounded by his disciples. It was nearly time for the Feast of Passover, kept annually by the Jews.

5-6 When Jesus looked out and saw that a large crowd had arrived, he said to Philip, "Where can we buy bread to feed these people?" He said this to stretch Philip's faith. He already knew what he was going to do.

7 Philip answered, "Two hundred silver pieces wouldn't be enough to buy bread for each person to get a piece."

8-9 One of the disciples — it was Andrew, brother to Simon Peter — said, "There's a little boy here who has five barley loaves and two fish. But that's a drop in the bucket for a crowd like this."

10-11 Jesus said, "Make the people sit down." There was a nice carpet of green grass in this place. They sat down, about five thousand of them. Then Jesus took the bread and, having given thanks, gave it to those who were seated. He did the same with the fish. All ate as much as they wanted.

12-13 When the people had eaten their fill, he said to his disciples, "Gather the leftovers so nothing is wasted." They went to work and filled twelve large baskets with leftovers from the five barley loaves.

14-15 The people realized that God was at work among them in what Jesus had just done. They said, "This is the Prophet for sure, God's Prophet right here in Galilee!" Jesus saw that in their enthusiasm, they were about to grab him and make him king, so he slipped off and went back up the mountain to be by himself.

16-21 In the evening his disciples went down to the sea, got in the boat, and headed back across the water to Capernaum. It had grown quite dark and Jesus had not yet returned. A huge wind blew up, churning the sea. They were maybe three or four miles out when they saw Jesus walking on the sea, quite near the boat. They were scared senseless, but he reassured them, "It's me. It's all right. Don't be afraid." So they took him on board. In no time they reached land — the exact spot they were headed to.

22-24 The next day the crowd that was left behind realized that there had been only one boat, and that Jesus had not gotten into it with his disciples. They had seen them go off without him. By now boats from Tiberias had pulled up near where they had eaten the bread blessed by the Master. So when the crowd realized he was gone and wasn't coming back, they piled into the Tiberias boats and headed for Capernaum, looking for Jesus.

25   When they found him back across the sea, they said, "Rabbi, when did you get here?"

26   Jesus answered, "You've come looking for me not because you saw God in my actions but because I fed you, filled your stomachs—and for free.

THE BREAD OF LIFE

27   "Don't waste your energy striving for perishable food like that. Work for the food that sticks with you, food that nourishes your lasting life, food the Son of Man provides. He and what he does are guaranteed by God the Father to last."

28   To that they said, "Well, what do we do then to get in on God's works?"

29   Jesus said, "Throw your lot in with the One that God has sent. That kind of a commitment gets you in on God's works."

30-31   They waffled: "Why don't you give us a clue about who you are, just a hint of what's going on? When we see what's up, we'll commit ourselves. Show us what you can do. Moses fed our ancestors with bread in the desert. It says so in the Scriptures: 'He gave them bread from heaven to eat.'"

32-33   Jesus responded, "The real significance of that Scripture is not that Moses gave you bread from heaven but that my Father is right now offering you bread from heaven, the *real* bread. The Bread of God came down out of heaven and is giving life to the world."

34   They jumped at that: "Master, give us this bread, now and forever!"

35-38   Jesus said, "I am the Bread of Life. The person who aligns with me hungers no more and thirsts no more, ever. I have told you this explicitly because even though you have seen me in action, you don't really believe me. Every person the Father gives me eventually comes running to me. And once that person is with me, I hold on and don't let go. I came down from heaven not to follow my own whim but to accomplish the will of the One who sent me.

39-40   "This, in a nutshell, is that will: that everything handed over to me by the Father be completed—not a single detail missed—and at the wrap-up of time I have everything and everyone put together, upright and whole. This is what my Father wants: that anyone who sees the Son and trusts who he is and what he does and then aligns with him will enter *real* life, *eternal* life. My part is to put them on their feet alive and whole at the completion of time."

41-42   At this, because he said, "I am the Bread that came down from heaven," the Jews started arguing over him: "Isn't this the son of Joseph? Don't we know his father? Don't we know his mother? How can he now say, 'I came down out of heaven' and expect anyone to believe him?"

43-46   Jesus said, "Don't bicker among yourselves over me. You're not in charge here. The Father who sent me is in charge. He draws people to me—that's the only way you'll ever come. Only then do I do my work, putting people together, setting them on their feet, ready for the End. This is what the prophets meant when they wrote, 'And then they will all be personally taught by God.' Anyone who has spent any time at all listening to the Father, really listening and therefore learning, comes to me to be taught person- ally—to see it with his own eyes, hear it with his own ears, from me, since I have it firsthand from the Father. No one has seen the Father except the One who has his Being alongside the Father — and you can see *me*.

47-51 "I'm telling you the most solemn and sober truth now: Whoever believes in me has real life, eternal life. I am the Bread of Life. Your ancestors ate the manna bread in the desert and died. But now here is Bread that truly comes down out of heaven. Anyone eating this Bread will not die, ever. I am the Bread — living Bread! — who came down out of heaven. Anyone who eats this Bread will live — and forever! The Bread that I present to the world so that it can eat and live is myself, this flesh-and-blood self."

52 At this, the Jews started fighting among themselves: "How can this man serve up his flesh for a meal?"

53-58 But Jesus didn't give an inch. "Only insofar as you eat and drink flesh and blood, the flesh and blood of the Son of Man, do you have life within you. The one who brings a hearty appetite to this eating and drinking has eternal life and will be fit and ready for the Final Day. My flesh is real food and my blood is real drink. By eating my flesh and drinking my blood you enter into me and I into you. In the same way that the fully alive Father sent me here and I live because of him, so the one who makes a meal of me lives because of me. This is the Bread from heaven. Your ancestors ate bread and later died. Whoever eats this Bread will live always."

59 He said these things while teaching in the meeting place in Capernaum.

Too Tough to Swallow

60 Many among his disciples heard this and said, "This is tough teaching, too tough to swallow."

61-65 Jesus sensed that his disciples were having a hard time with this and said, "Does this throw you completely? What would happen if you saw the Son of Man ascending to where he came from? The Spirit can make life. Sheer muscle and willpower don't make anything happen. Every word I've spoken to you is a Spirit-word, and so it is life-making. But some of you are resisting, refusing to have any part in this." (Jesus knew from the start that some weren't going to risk themselves with him. He knew also who would betray him.) He went on to say, "This is why I told you earlier that no one is capable of coming to me on his own. You get to me only as a gift from the Father."

66-67 After this a lot of his disciples left. They no longer wanted to be associated with him. Then Jesus gave the Twelve their chance: "Do you also want to leave?"

68-69 Peter replied, "Master, to whom would we go? You have the words of real life, eternal life. We've already committed ourselves, confident that you are the Holy One of God."

70-71 Jesus responded, "Haven't I handpicked you, the Twelve? Still, one of you is a devil!" He was referring to Judas, son of Simon Iscariot. This man — one from the Twelve! — was even then getting ready to betray him.

1-2 7 Later Jesus was going about his business in Galilee. He didn't want to travel in Judea because the Jews there were looking for a chance to kill him. It was near the time of Tabernacles, a feast observed annually by the Jews.

3-5 His brothers said, "Why don't you leave here and go up to the Feast so your disciples can get a good look at the works you do? No one who intends to be publicly known does everything behind the scenes. If you're serious about what you are doing, come out in the open and show the world." His brothers were pushing him like this because they didn't believe in him either.

6-8 Jesus came back at them, "Don't crowd me. This isn't my time. It's your time—it's *always* your time; you have nothing to lose. The world has nothing against you, but it's up in arms against me. It's against me because I expose the evil behind its pretensions. You go ahead, go up to the Feast. Don't wait for me. I'm not ready. It's not the right time for me."

9-11 He said this and stayed on in Galilee. But later, after his family had gone up to the Feast, he also went. But he kept out of the way, careful not to draw attention to himself. The Jews were already out looking for him, asking around, "Where is that man?"

12-13 There was a lot of contentious talk about him circulating through the crowds. Some were saying, "He's a good man." But others said, "Not so. He's selling snake oil." This kind of talk went on in guarded whispers because of the intimidating Jewish leaders.

COULD IT BE THE MESSIAH?

14-15 With the Feast already half over, Jesus showed up in the Temple, teaching. The Jews were impressed, but puzzled: "How does he know so much without being schooled?"

16-19 Jesus said, "I didn't make this up. What I teach comes from the One who sent me. Anyone who wants to do his will can test this teaching and know whether it's from God or whether I'm making it up. A person making things up tries to make himself look good. But someone trying to honor the one who sent him sticks to the facts and doesn't tamper with reality. It was Moses, wasn't it, who gave you God's Law? But none of you are living it. So why are you trying to kill me?"

20 The crowd said, "You're crazy! Who's trying to kill you? You're demon-possessed."

21-24 Jesus said, "I did one miraculous thing a few months ago, and you're still standing around getting all upset, wondering what I'm up to. Moses prescribed circumcision—originally it came not from Moses but from his ancestors—and so you circumcise a man, dealing with one part of his body, even if it's the Sabbath. You do this in order to preserve one item in the Law of Moses. So why are you upset with me because I made a man's whole body well on the Sabbath? Don't be nitpickers; use your head—and heart!—to discern what is right, to test what is authentically right."

25-27 That's when some of the people of Jerusalem said, "Isn't this the one they were out to kill? And here he is out in the open, saying whatever he pleases, and no one is stopping him. Could it be that the rulers know that he is, in fact, the Messiah? And yet we know where this man came from. The Messiah is going to come out of nowhere. Nobody is going to know where he comes from."

28-29 That provoked Jesus, who was teaching in the Temple, to cry out, "Yes, you think you know me and where I'm from, but that's not where I'm from. I didn't set myself up in business. My true origin is in the One who sent me, and you don't know him at all. I come from him—that's how I know him. He sent me here."

30-31 They were looking for a way to arrest him, but not a hand was laid on him because it wasn't yet God's time. Many from the crowd committed themselves in faith to him, saying, "Will the Messiah, when he comes, provide better or more convincing evidence than this?"

32-34 The Pharisees, alarmed at this seditious undertow going through the crowd, teamed up with the high priests and sent their police to arrest him. Jesus rebuffed them: "I am with you only a short time. Then I go on to the One who sent me. You will look for me, but you won't find me. Where I am, you can't come."

35-36 The Jews put their heads together. "Where do you think he is going that we won't be able to find him? Do you think he is about to travel to the Greek world to teach the Jews? What is he talking about, anyway: 'You will look for me, but you won't find me,' and 'Where I am, you can't come'?"

37-39 On the final and climactic day of the Feast, Jesus took his stand. He cried out, "If anyone thirsts, let him come to me and drink. Rivers of living water will brim and spill out of the depths of anyone who believes in me this way, just as the Scripture says." (He said this in regard to the Spirit, whom those who believed in him were about to receive. The Spirit had not yet been given because Jesus had not yet been glorified.)

40-44 Those in the crowd who heard these words were saying, "This has to be the Prophet." Others said, "He is the Messiah!" But others were saying, "The Messiah doesn't come from Galilee, does he? Don't the Scriptures tell us that the Messiah comes from David's line and from Bethlehem, David's village?" So there was a split in the crowd over him. Some went so far as wanting to arrest him, but no one laid a hand on him.

45 That's when the Temple police reported back to the high priests and Pharisees, who demanded, "Why didn't you bring him with you?"

46 The police answered, "Have you heard the way he talks? We've never heard anyone speak like this man."

47-49 The Pharisees said, "Are you carried away like the rest of the rabble? You don't see any of the leaders believing in him, do you? Or any from the Pharisees? It's only this crowd, ignorant of God's Law, that is taken in by him — and damned."

50-51 Nicodemus, the man who had come to Jesus earlier and was both a ruler and a Pharisee, spoke up. "Does our Law decide about a man's guilt without first listening to him and finding out what he is doing?"

52-53 But they cut him off. "Are you also campaigning for the Galilean? Examine the evidence. See if any prophet ever comes from Galilee."

Then they all went home.

To Throw the Stone

1-2 **8** Jesus went across to Mount Olives, but he was soon back in the Temple again. Swarms of people came to him. He sat down and taught them.

3-6 The religion scholars and Pharisees led in a woman who had been caught in an act of adultery. They stood her in plain sight of everyone and said, "Teacher, this woman was caught red-handed in the act of adultery. Moses, in the Law, gives orders to stone such persons. What do you say?" They were trying to trap him into saying something incriminating so they could bring charges against him.

6-8 Jesus bent down and wrote with his finger in the dirt. They kept at him, badgering him. He straightened up and said, "The sinless one among you, go first: Throw the stone." Bending down again, he wrote some more in the dirt.

9-10   Hearing that, they walked away, one after another, beginning with the oldest. The woman was left alone. Jesus stood up and spoke to her. "Woman, where are they? Does no one condemn you?"

11   "No one, Master."

"Neither do I," said Jesus. "Go on your way. From now on, don't sin."

You're Missing God in All This

12   Jesus once again addressed them: "I am the world's Light. No one who follows me stumbles around in the darkness. I provide plenty of light to live in."

13   The Pharisees objected, "All we have is your word on this. We need more than this to go on."

14-18   Jesus replied, "You're right that you only have my word. But you can depend on it being true. I know where I've come from and where I go next. You don't know where I'm from or where I'm headed. You decide according to what you can see and touch. I don't make judgments like that. But even if I did, my judgment would be true because I wouldn't make it out of the narrowness of my experience but in the largeness of the One who sent me, the Father. That fulfills the conditions set down in God's Law: that you can count on the testimony of two witnesses. And that is what you have: You have my word and you have the word of the Father who sent me."

19   They said, "Where is this so-called Father of yours?"

Jesus said, "You're looking right at me and you don't see me. How do you expect to see the Father? If you knew me, you would at the same time know the Father."

20   He gave this speech in the Treasury while teaching in the Temple. No one arrested him because his time wasn't yet up.

21   Then he went over the same ground again. "I'm leaving and you are going to look for me, but you're missing God in this and are headed for a dead end. There is no way you can come with me."

22   The Jews said, "So, is he going to kill himself? Is that what he means by 'You can't come with me'?"

23-24   Jesus said, "You're tied down to the mundane; I'm in touch with what is beyond your horizons. You live in terms of what you see and touch. I'm living on other terms. I told you that you were missing God in all this. You're at a dead end. If you won't believe I am who I say I am, you're at the dead end of sins. You're missing God in your lives."

25-26   They said to him, "Just who are you anyway?"

Jesus said, "What I've said from the start. I have so many things to say that concern you, judgments to make that affect you, but if you don't accept the trustworthiness of the One who commanded my words and acts, none of it matters. That is who you are questioning—not me but the One who sent me."

27-29   They still didn't get it, didn't realize that he was referring to the Father. So Jesus tried again. "When you raise up the Son of Man, then you will know who I am—that I'm not making this up, but speaking only what the Father taught me. The One who sent me stays with me. He doesn't abandon me. He sees how much joy I take in pleasing him."

30   When he put it in these terms, many people decided to believe.

If the Son Sets You Free

31-32   Then Jesus turned to the Jews who had claimed to believe in him. "If you stick with this, living out what I tell you, you are my disciples for sure. Then you will experience for yourselves the truth, and the truth will free you."

33   Surprised, they said, "But we're descendants of Abraham. We've never been slaves to anyone. How can you say, 'The truth will free you'?"

34-38   Jesus said, "I tell you most solemnly that anyone who chooses a life of sin is trapped in a dead-end life and is, in fact, a slave. A slave is a transient, who can't come and go at will. The Son, though, has an established position, the run of the house. So if the Son sets you free, you are free through and through. I know you are Abraham's descendants. But I also know that you are trying to kill me because my message hasn't yet penetrated your thick skulls. I'm talking about things I have seen while keeping company with the Father, and you just go on doing what you have heard from your father."

39-41   They were indignant. "Our father is Abraham!"

Jesus said, "If you were Abraham's children, you would have been doing the things Abraham did. And yet here you are trying to kill me, a man who has spoken to you the truth he got straight from God! Abraham never did that sort of thing. You persist in repeating the works of your father."

They said, "We're not bastards. We have a legitimate father: the one and only God."

42-47   "If God were your father," said Jesus, "you would love me, for I came from God and arrived here. I didn't come on my own. He sent me. Why can't you understand one word I say? Here's why: You can't handle it. You're from your father, the Devil, and all you want to do is please him. He was a killer from the very start. He couldn't stand the truth because there wasn't a shred of truth in him. When the Liar speaks, he makes it up out of his lying nature and fills the world with lies. I arrive on the scene, tell you the plain truth, and you refuse to have a thing to do with me. Can any one of you convict me of a single misleading word, a single sinful act? But if I'm telling the truth, why don't you believe me? Anyone on God's side listens to God's words. This is why you're not listening — because you're not on God's side."

I Am Who I Am

48   The Jews then said, "That clinches it. We were right all along when we called you a Samaritan and said you were crazy — demon-possessed!"

49-51   Jesus said, "I'm not crazy. I simply honor my Father, while you dishonor me. I am not trying to get anything for myself. God intends something gloriously grand here and is making the decisions that will bring it about. I say this with absolute confidence. If you practice what I'm telling you, you'll never have to look death in the face."

52-53   At this point the Jews said, "Now we *know* you're crazy. Abraham died. The prophets died. And you show up saying, 'If you practice what I'm telling you, you'll never have to face death, not even a taste.' Are you greater than Abraham, who died? And the prophets died! Who do you think you are!"

54-56   Jesus said, "If I turned the spotlight on myself, it wouldn't amount to anything. But my Father, the same One you say is your Father, put me here at this time and place of splendor. You haven't recognized him in this. But I have. If I, in false modesty, said I didn't know what was going on, I would be as much of a liar as you are. But I do know, and I am doing what he says. Abraham — your 'father' — with jubilant faith looked down the corridors of history and saw my day coming. He saw it and cheered."

57   The Jews said, "You're not even fifty years old — and Abraham saw you?"

58   "Believe me," said Jesus, "*I am who I am* long before Abraham was anything."

59   That did it — pushed them over the edge. They picked up rocks to throw at him. But Jesus slipped away, getting out of the Temple.

TRUE BLINDNESS

1-2   **9** Walking down the street, Jesus saw a man blind from birth. His disciples asked, "Rabbi, who sinned: this man or his parents, causing him to be born blind?"

3-5   Jesus said, "You're asking the wrong question. You're looking for someone to blame. There is no such cause-effect here. Look instead for what God can do. We need to be energetically at work for the One who sent me here, working while the sun shines. When night falls, the workday is over. For as long as I am in the world, there is plenty of light. I am the world's Light."

6-7   He said this and then spit in the dust, made a clay paste with the saliva, rubbed the paste on the blind man's eyes, and said, "Go, wash at the Pool of Siloam" (Siloam means "Sent"). The man went and washed — and saw.

8   Soon the town was buzzing. His relatives and those who year after year had seen him as a blind man begging were saying, "Why, isn't this the man we knew, who sat here and begged?"

9   Others said, "It's him all right!"

But others objected, "It's not the same man at all. It just looks like him."

He said, "It's me, the very one."

10   They said, "How did your eyes get opened?"

11   "A man named Jesus made a paste and rubbed it on my eyes and told me, 'Go to Siloam and wash.' I did what he said. When I washed, I saw."

12   "So where is he?"

"I don't know."

13-15 They marched the man to the Pharisees. This day when Jesus made the paste and healed his blindness was the Sabbath. The Pharisees grilled him again on how he had come to see. He said, "He put a clay paste on my eyes, and I washed, and now I see."

16   Some of the Pharisees said, "Obviously, this man can't be from God. He doesn't keep the Sabbath."

Others countered, "How can a bad man do miraculous, God-revealing things like this?" There was a split in their ranks.

17   They came back at the blind man, "You're the expert. He opened *your* eyes. What do you say about him?"

He said, "He is a prophet."

18-19 The Jews didn't believe it, didn't believe the man was blind to begin with. So they called the parents of the man now bright-eyed with sight. They asked them, "Is this your son, the one you say was born blind? So how is it that he now sees?"

20-23 His parents said, "We know he is our son, and we know he was born blind. But we don't know how he came to see — haven't a clue about who opened his eyes. Why don't you ask him? He's a grown man and can speak for himself." (His parents were talking like this because they were intimidated by the Jewish leaders, who had already decided that anyone who took a stand that this was the Messiah would be kicked out of the meeting place. That's why his parents said, "Ask him. He's a grown man.")

24   They called the man back a second time—the man who had been blind—and told him, "Give credit to God. We know this man is an impostor."

25   He replied, "I know nothing about that one way or the other. But I know one thing for sure: I was blind . . . I now see."

26   They said, "What did he do to you? How did he open your eyes?"

27   "I've told you over and over and you haven't listened. Why do you want to hear it again? Are you so eager to become his disciples?"

28-29   With that they jumped all over him. "*You* might be a disciple of that man, but we're disciples of Moses. We know for sure that God spoke to Moses, but we have no idea where this man even comes from."

30-33   The man replied, "This is amazing! You claim to know nothing about him, but the fact is, he opened my eyes! It's well known that God isn't at the beck and call of sinners, but listens carefully to anyone who lives in reverence and does his will. That someone opened the eyes of a man born blind has never been heard of—ever. If this man didn't come from God, he wouldn't be able to do anything."

34   They said, "You're nothing but dirt! How dare you take that tone with us!" Then they threw him out in the street.

35   Jesus heard that they had thrown him out, and went and found him. He asked him, "Do you believe in the Son of Man?"

36   The man said, "Point him out to me, sir, so that I can believe in him."

37   Jesus said, "You're looking right at him. Don't you recognize my voice?"

38   "Master, I believe," the man said, and worshiped him.

39   Jesus then said, "I came into the world to bring everything into the clear light of day, making all the distinctions clear, so that those who have never seen will see, and those who have made a great pretense of seeing will be exposed as blind."

40   Some Pharisees overheard him and said, "Does that mean you're calling us blind?"

41   Jesus said, "If you were really blind, you would be blameless, but since you claim to see everything so well, you're accountable for every fault and failure."

He Calls His Sheep by Name

1-5   **10** "Let me set this before you as plainly as I can. If a person climbs over or through the fence of a sheep pen instead of going through the gate, you know he's up to no good—a sheep rustler! The shepherd walks right up to the gate. The gatekeeper opens the gate to him and the sheep recognize his voice. He calls his own sheep by name and leads them out. When he gets them all out, he leads them and they follow because they are familiar with his voice. They won't follow a stranger's voice but will scatter because they aren't used to the sound of it."

6-10   Jesus told this simple story, but they had no idea what he was talking about. So he tried again. "I'll be explicit, then. I am the Gate for the sheep. All those others are up to no good—sheep stealers, every one of them. But the sheep didn't listen to them. I am the Gate. Anyone who goes through me will be cared for—will freely go in and out, and find pasture. A thief is only there to steal and kill and destroy. I came so they can have real and eternal life, more and better life than they ever dreamed of.

11-13   "I am the Good Shepherd. The Good Shepherd puts the sheep before himself, sacrifices himself if necessary. A hired man is not a real shepherd. The sheep mean nothing to him. He sees a wolf come and runs for it, leaving the sheep to be ravaged and scattered by the wolf. He's only in it for the money. The sheep don't matter to him.

14-18   "I am the Good Shepherd. I know my own sheep and my own sheep know me. In the same way, the Father knows me and I know the Father. I put the sheep before myself, sacrificing myself if necessary. You need to know that I have other sheep in addition to those in this pen. I need to gather and bring them, too. They'll also recognize my voice. Then it will be one flock, one Shepherd. This is why the Father loves me: because I freely lay down my life. And so I am free to take it up again. No one takes it from me. I lay it down of my own free will. I have the right to lay it down; I also have the right to take it up again. I received this authority personally from my Father."

19-21   This kind of talk caused another split in the Jewish ranks. A lot of them were saying, "He's crazy, a maniac — out of his head completely. Why bother listening to him?" But others weren't so sure: "These aren't the words of a crazy man. Can a 'maniac' open blind eyes?"

22-24   They were celebrating Hanukkah just then in Jerusalem. It was winter. Jesus was strolling in the Temple across Solomon's Porch. The Jews, circling him, said, "How long are you going to keep us guessing? If you're the Messiah, tell us straight out."

25-30   Jesus answered, "I told you, but you don't believe. Everything I have done has been authorized by my Father, actions that speak louder than words. You don't believe because you're not my sheep. My sheep recognize my voice. I know them, and they follow me. I give them real and eternal life. They are protected from the Destroyer for good. No one can steal them from out of my hand. The Father who put them under my care is so much greater than the Destroyer and Thief. No one could ever get them away from him. I and the Father are one heart and mind."

31-32   Again the Jews picked up rocks to throw at him. Jesus said, "I have made a present to you from the Father of a great many good actions. For which of these acts do you stone me?"

33   The Jews said, "We're not stoning you for anything good you did, but for what you said — this blasphemy of calling yourself God."

34-38   Jesus said, "I'm only quoting your inspired Scriptures, where God said, 'I tell you — you are gods.' If God called your ancestors 'gods' — and Scripture doesn't lie — why do you yell, 'Blasphemer! Blasphemer!' at the unique One the Father consecrated and sent into the world, just because I said, 'I am the Son of God'? If I don't do the things my Father does, well and good; don't believe me. But if I am doing them, put aside for a moment what you hear me say about myself and just take the evidence of the actions that are right before your eyes. Then perhaps things will come together for you, and you'll see that not only are we doing the same thing, we *are* the same — Father and Son. He is in me; I am in him."

39-42   They tried yet again to arrest him, but he slipped through their fingers.

He went back across the Jordan to the place where John first baptized, and stayed there. A lot of people followed him over. They were saying, "John did no miracles, but everything he said about this man has come true." Many believed in him then and there.

THE DEATH OF LAZARUS

1-3   **11** A man was sick, Lazarus of Bethany, the town of Mary and her sister Martha. This was the same Mary who massaged the Lord's feet with aromatic oils and then wiped them with her hair. It was her brother Lazarus who was sick. So the sisters sent word to Jesus, "Master, the one you love so very much is sick."

4   When Jesus got the message, he said, "This sickness is not fatal. It will become an occasion to show God's glory by glorifying God's Son."

5-7   Jesus loved Martha and her sister and Lazarus, but oddly, when he heard that Lazarus was sick, he stayed on where he was for two more days. After the two days, he said to his disciples, "Let's go back to Judea."

8   They said, "Rabbi, you can't do that. The Jews are out to kill you, and you're going back?"

9-10   Jesus replied, "Are there not twelve hours of daylight? Anyone who walks in daylight doesn't stumble because there's plenty of light from the sun. Walking at night, he might very well stumble because he can't see where he's going."

11   He said these things, and then announced, "Our friend Lazarus has fallen asleep. I'm going to wake him up."

12-13   The disciples said, "Master, if he's gone to sleep, he'll get a good rest and wake up feeling fine." Jesus was talking about death, while his disciples thought he was talking about taking a nap.

14-15   Then Jesus became explicit: "Lazarus died. And I am glad for your sakes that I wasn't there. You're about to be given new grounds for believing. Now let's go to him."

16   That's when Thomas, the one called the Twin, said to his companions, "Come along. We might as well die with him."

17-20   When Jesus finally got there, he found Lazarus already four days dead. Bethany was near Jerusalem, only a couple of miles away, and many of the Jews were visiting Martha and Mary, sympathizing with them over their brother. Martha heard Jesus was coming and went out to meet him. Mary remained in the house.

21-22   Martha said, "Master, if you'd been here, my brother wouldn't have died. Even now, I know that whatever you ask God he will give you."

23   Jesus said, "Your brother will be raised up."

24   Martha replied, "I know that he will be raised up in the resurrection at the end of time."

25-26   "You don't have to wait for the End. I am, right now, Resurrection and Life. The one who believes in me, even though he or she dies, will live. And everyone who lives believing in me does not ultimately die at all. Do you believe this?"

27   "Yes, Master. All along I have believed that you are the Messiah, the Son of God who comes into the world."

28   After saying this, she went to her sister Mary and whispered in her ear, "The Teacher is here and is asking for you."

29-32   The moment she heard that, she jumped up and ran out to him. Jesus had not yet entered the town but was still at the place where Martha had met him. When her sympathizing Jewish friends saw Mary run off, they followed her, thinking she was on her way to the tomb to weep there. Mary came to where Jesus was waiting and fell at his feet, saying, "Master, if only you had been here, my brother would not have died."

33-34 When Jesus saw her sobbing and the Jews with her sobbing, a deep anger welled up within him. He said, "Where did you put him?"

34-35 "Master, come and see," they said. Now Jesus wept.

36 The Jews said, "Look how deeply he loved him."

37 Others among them said, "Well, if he loved him so much, why didn't he do something to keep him from dying? After all, he opened the eyes of a blind man."

38-39 Then Jesus, the anger again welling up within him, arrived at the tomb. It was a simple cave in the hillside with a slab of stone laid against it. Jesus said, "Remove the stone."

The sister of the dead man, Martha, said, "Master, by this time there's a stench. He's been dead four days!"

40 Jesus looked her in the eye. "Didn't I tell you that if you believed, you would see the glory of God?"

41-42 Then, to the others, "Go ahead, take away the stone."

They removed the stone. Jesus raised his eyes to heaven and prayed, "Father, I'm grateful that you have listened to me. I know you always do listen, but on account of this crowd standing here I've spoken so that they might believe that you sent me."

43-44 Then he shouted, "Lazarus, come out!" And he came out, a cadaver, wrapped from head to toe, and with a kerchief over his face.

Jesus told them, "Unwrap him and let him loose."

The Man Who Creates God-Signs

45-48 That was a turnaround for many of the Jews who were with Mary. They saw what Jesus did, and believed in him. But some went back to the Pharisees and told on Jesus. The high priests and Pharisees called a meeting of the Jewish ruling body. "What do we do now?" they asked. "This man keeps on doing things, creating God-signs. If we let him go on, pretty soon everyone will be believing in him and the Romans will come and remove what little power and privilege we still have."

49-52 Then one of them — it was Caiaphas, the designated Chief Priest that year — spoke up, "Don't you know anything? Can't you see that it's to our advantage that one man dies for the people rather than the whole nation be destroyed?" He didn't say this of his own accord, but as Chief Priest that year he unwittingly prophesied that Jesus was about to die sacrificially for the nation, and not only for the nation but so that all God's exile-scattered children might be gathered together into one people.

53-54 From that day on, they plotted to kill him. So Jesus no longer went out in public among the Jews. He withdrew into the country bordering the desert to a town called Ephraim and secluded himself there with his disciples.

55-56 The Jewish Passover was coming up. Crowds of people were making their way from the country up to Jerusalem to get themselves ready for the Feast. They were curious about Jesus. There was a lot of talk of him among those standing around in the Temple: "What do you think? Do you think he'll show up at the Feast or not?"

57 Meanwhile, the high priests and Pharisees gave out the word that anyone getting wind of him should inform them. They were all set to arrest him.

ANOINTING HIS FEET

1-3 **12** Six days before Passover, Jesus entered Bethany where Lazarus, so recently raised from the dead, was living. Lazarus and his sisters invited Jesus to dinner at their home. Martha served. Lazarus was one of those sitting at the table with them. Mary came in with a jar of very expensive aromatic oils, anointed and massaged Jesus' feet, and then wiped them with her hair. The fragrance of the oils filled the house.

4-6 Judas Iscariot, one of his disciples, even then getting ready to betray him, said, "Why wasn't this oil sold and the money given to the poor? It would have easily brought three hundred silver pieces." He said this not because he cared two cents about the poor but because he was a thief. He was in charge of their common funds, but also embezzled them.

7-8 Jesus said, "Let her alone. She's anticipating and honoring the day of my burial. You always have the poor with you. You don't always have me."

9-11 Word got out among the Jews that he was back in town. The people came to take a look, not only at Jesus but also at Lazarus, who had been raised from the dead. So the high priests plotted to kill Lazarus because so many of the Jews were going over and believing in Jesus on account of him.

SEE HOW YOUR KING COMES

12-15 The next day the huge crowd that had arrived for the Feast heard that Jesus was entering Jerusalem. They broke off palm branches and went out to meet him. And they cheered:

Hosanna!
Blessed is he who comes in God's name!
Yes! The King of Israel!

Jesus got a young donkey and rode it, just as the Scripture has it:

No fear, Daughter Zion:
See how your king comes,
riding a donkey's colt.

16 The disciples didn't notice the fulfillment of many Scriptures at the time, but after Jesus was glorified, they remembered that what was written about him matched what was done to him.

17-19 The crowd that had been with him when he called Lazarus from the tomb, raising him from the dead, was there giving eyewitness accounts. It was because they had spread the word of this latest God-sign that the crowd swelled to a welcoming parade. The Pharisees took one look and threw up their hands: "It's out of control. The world's in a stampede after him."

A GRAIN OF WHEAT MUST DIE

20-21 There were some Greeks in town who had come up to worship at the Feast. They approached Philip, who was from Bethsaida in Galilee: "Sir, we want to see Jesus. Can you help us?"

22-23 Philip went and told Andrew. Andrew and Philip together told Jesus. Jesus answered, "Time's up. The time has come for the Son of Man to be glorified.

24-25 "Listen carefully: Unless a grain of wheat is buried in the ground, dead to the world, it is never any more than a grain of wheat. But if it is buried, it sprouts and reproduces itself many times over. In the same way, anyone who holds on to life just as it is destroys that life. But if you let it go, reckless in your love, you'll have it forever, real and eternal.

26 "If any of you wants to serve me, then follow me. Then you'll be where I am, ready to serve at a moment's notice. The Father will honor and reward anyone who serves me.

27-28 "Right now I am storm-tossed. And what am I going to say? 'Father, get me out of this'? No, this is why I came in the first place. I'll say, 'Father, put your glory on display.'"

A voice came out of the sky: "I have glorified it, and I'll glorify it again."

29 The listening crowd said, "Thunder!"

Others said, "An angel spoke to him!"

30-33 Jesus said, "The voice didn't come for me but for you. At this moment the world is in crisis. Now Satan, the ruler of this world, will be thrown out. And I, as I am lifted up from the earth, will attract everyone to me and gather them around me." He put it this way to show how he was going to be put to death.

34 Voices from the crowd answered, "We heard from God's Law that the Messiah lasts forever. How can it be necessary, as you put it, that the Son of Man 'be lifted up'? Who is this 'Son of Man'?"

35-36 Jesus said, "For a brief time still, the light is among you. Walk by the light you have so darkness doesn't destroy you. If you walk in darkness, you don't know where you're going. As you have the light, believe in the light. Then the light will be within you, and shining through your lives. You'll be children of light."

THEIR EYES ARE BLINDED

36-40 Jesus said all this, and then went into hiding. All these God-signs he had given them and they still didn't get it, still wouldn't trust him. This proved that the prophet Isaiah was right:

> God, who believed what we preached?
> Who recognized God's arm, outstretched and ready to act?

First they wouldn't believe, then they *couldn't* — again, just as Isaiah said:

> Their eyes are blinded,
>   their hearts are hardened,
> So that they wouldn't see with their eyes
>   and perceive with their hearts,
> And turn to me, God,
>   so I could heal them.

41 Isaiah said these things after he got a glimpse of God's cascading brightness that would pour through the Messiah.

42-43 On the other hand, a considerable number from the ranks of the leaders did believe. But because of the Pharisees, they didn't come out in the open with it. They were afraid of getting kicked out of the meeting place. When push came to shove they cared more for human approval than for God's glory.

44-46 Jesus summed it all up when he cried out, "Whoever believes in me, believes not just in me but in the One who sent me. Whoever looks at me is looking, in fact, at the One who sent me. I am Light that has come into the world so that all who believe in me won't have to stay any longer in the dark.

47-50 "If anyone hears what I am saying and doesn't take it seriously, I don't reject him. I didn't come to reject the world; I came to save the world. But you need to know that whoever puts me off, refusing to take in what I'm saying, is willfully choosing rejection. The Word, the Word-made-flesh that I have spoken and that I am, *that* Word and no other is the last word. I'm not making any of this up on my own. The Father who sent me gave me orders, told me what to say and how to say it. And I know exactly what his command produces: real and eternal life. That's all I have to say. What the Father told me, I tell you."

WASHING HIS DISCIPLES' FEET

1-2 **13** Just before the Passover Feast, Jesus knew that the time had come to leave this world to go to the Father. Having loved his dear companions, he continued to love them right to the end. It was suppertime. The Devil by now had Judas, son of Simon the Iscariot, firmly in his grip, all set for the betrayal.

3-6 Jesus knew that the Father had put him in complete charge of everything, that he came from God and was on his way back to God. So he got up from the supper table, set aside his robe, and put on an apron. Then he poured water into a basin and began to wash the feet of the disciples, drying them with his apron. When he got to Simon Peter, Peter said, "Master, *you* wash *my* feet?"

7 Jesus answered, "You don't understand now what I'm doing, but it will be clear enough to you later."

8 Peter persisted, "You're not going to wash my feet — ever!"

Jesus said, "If I don't wash you, you can't be part of what I'm doing."

9 "Master!" said Peter. "Not only my feet, then. Wash my hands! Wash my head!"

10-12 Jesus said, "If you've had a bath in the morning, you only need your feet washed now and you're clean from head to toe. My concern, you understand, is holiness, not hygiene. So now you're clean. But not every one of you." (He knew who was betraying him. That's why he said, "Not every one of you.") After he had finished washing their feet, he took his robe, put it back on, and went back to his place at the table.

12-17 Then he said, "Do you understand what I have done to you? You address me as 'Teacher' and 'Master,' and rightly so. That is what I am. So if I, the Master and Teacher, washed your feet, you must now wash each other's feet. I've laid down a pattern for you. What I've done, you do. I'm only pointing out the obvious. A servant is not ranked above his master; an employee doesn't give orders to the employer. If you understand what I'm telling you, act like it — and live a blessed life.

THE ONE WHO ATE BREAD AT MY TABLE

18-20   "I'm not including all of you in this. I know precisely whom I've selected, so as not to interfere with the fulfillment of this Scripture:

> The one who ate bread at my table
> Turned on his heel against me.

"I'm telling you all this ahead of time so that when it happens you will believe that I am who I say I am. Make sure you get this right: Receiving someone I send is the same as receiving me, just as receiving me is the same as receiving the One who sent me."

21   After he said these things, Jesus became visibly upset, and then he told them why. "One of you is going to betray me."

22-25   The disciples looked around at one another, wondering who on earth he was talking about. One of the disciples, the one Jesus loved dearly, was reclining against him, his head on his shoulder. Peter motioned to him to ask who Jesus might be talking about. So, being the closest, he said, "Master, who?"

26-27   Jesus said, "The one to whom I give this crust of bread after I've dipped it." Then he dipped the crust and gave it to Judas, son of Simon the Iscariot. As soon as the bread was in his hand, Satan entered him.

"What you must do," said Jesus, "do. Do it and get it over with."

28-29   No one around the supper table knew why he said this to him. Some thought that since Judas was their treasurer, Jesus was telling him to buy what they needed for the Feast, or that he should give something to the poor.

30   Judas, with the piece of bread, left. It was night.

A NEW COMMAND

31-32   When he had left, Jesus said, "Now the Son of Man is seen for who he is, and God seen for who he is in him. The moment God is seen in him, God's glory will be on display. In glorifying him, he himself is glorified—glory all around!

33   "Children, I am with you for only a short time longer. You are going to look high and low for me. But just as I told the Jews, I'm telling you: 'Where I go, you are not able to come.'

34-35   "Let me give you a new command: Love one another. In the same way I loved you, you love one another. This is how everyone will recognize that you are my disciples—when they see the love you have for each other."

36   Simon Peter asked, "Master, just where are you going?"

Jesus answered, "You can't now follow me where I'm going. You will follow later."

37   "Master," said Peter, "why can't I follow now? I'll lay down my life for you!"

38   "Really? You'll lay down your life for me? The truth is that before the rooster crows, you'll deny me three times."

THE ROAD

1-4   **14** "Don't let this throw you. You trust God, don't you? Trust me. There is plenty of room for you in my Father's home. If that weren't so, would I have told you that I'm on my way to get a room ready for you? And if I'm on my way to get your room ready, I'll come back and get you so you can live where I live. And you already know the road I'm taking."

5 Thomas said, "Master, we have no idea where you're going. How do you expect us to know the road?"

6-7 Jesus said, "I am the Road, also the Truth, also the Life. No one gets to the Father apart from me. If you really knew me, you would know my Father as well. From now on, you do know him. You've even seen him!"

8 Philip said, "Master, show us the Father; then we'll be content."

9-10 "You've been with me all this time, Philip, and you still don't understand? To see me is to see the Father. So how can you ask, 'Where is the Father?' Don't you believe that I am in the Father and the Father is in me? The words that I speak to you aren't mere words. I don't just make them up on my own. The Father who resides in me crafts each word into a divine act.

11-14 "Believe me: I am in my Father and my Father is in me. If you can't believe that, believe what you see — these works. The person who trusts me will not only do what I'm doing but even greater things, because I, on my way to the Father, am giving you the same work to do that I've been doing. You can count on it. From now on, whatever you request along the lines of who I am and what I am doing, I'll do it. That's how the Father will be seen for who he is in the Son. I mean it. Whatever you request in this way, I'll do.

The Spirit of Truth

15-17 "If you love me, show it by doing what I've told you. I will talk to the Father, and he'll provide you another Friend so that you will always have someone with you. This Friend is the Spirit of Truth. The godless world can't take him in because it doesn't have eyes to see him, doesn't know what to look for. But you know him already because he has been staying with you, and will even be *in* you!

18-20 "I will not leave you orphaned. I'm coming back. In just a little while the world will no longer see me, but you're going to see me because I am alive and you're about to come alive. At that moment you will know absolutely that I'm in my Father, and you're in me, and I'm in you.

21 "The person who knows my commandments and keeps them, that's who loves me. And the person who loves me will be loved by my Father, and I will love him and make myself plain to him."

22 Judas (not Iscariot) said, "Master, why is it that you are about to make yourself plain to us but not to the world?"

23-24 "Because a loveless world," said Jesus, "is a sightless world. If anyone loves me, he will carefully keep my word and my Father will love him — we'll move right into the neighborhood! Not loving me means not keeping my words. The message you are hearing isn't mine. It's the message of the Father who sent me.

25-27 "I'm telling you these things while I'm still living with you. The Friend, the Holy Spirit whom the Father will send at my request, will make everything plain to you. He will remind you of all the things I have told you. I'm leaving you well and whole. That's my parting gift to you. Peace. I don't leave you the way you're used to being left — feeling abandoned, bereft. So don't be upset. Don't be distraught.

28 "You've heard me tell you, 'I'm going away, and I'm coming back.'

If you loved me, you would be glad that I'm on my way to the Father because the Father is the goal and purpose of my life.

29-31   "I've told you this ahead of time, before it happens, so that when it does happen, the confirmation will deepen your belief in me. I'll not be talking with you much more like this because the chief of this godless world is about to attack. But don't worry — he has nothing on me, no claim on me. But so the world might know how thoroughly I love the Father, I am carrying out my Father's instructions right down to the last detail.

"Get up. Let's go. It's time to leave here."

The Vine and the Branches

1-3   **15** "I am the Real Vine and my Father is the Farmer. He cuts off every branch of me that doesn't bear grapes. And every branch that is grape-bearing he prunes back so it will bear even more. You are already pruned back by the message I have spoken.

4   "Live in me. Make your home in me just as I do in you. In the same way that a branch can't bear grapes by itself but only by being joined to the vine, you can't bear fruit unless you are joined with me.

5-8   "I am the Vine, you are the branches. When you're joined with me and I with you, the relation intimate and organic, the harvest is sure to be abundant. Separated, you can't produce a thing. Anyone who separates from me is deadwood, gathered up and thrown on the bonfire. But if you make yourselves at home with me and my words are at home in you, you can be sure that whatever you ask will be listened to and acted upon. This is how my Father shows who he is — when you produce grapes, when you mature as my disciples.

9-10   "I've loved you the way my Father has loved me. Make yourselves at home in my love. If you keep my commands, you'll remain intimately at home in my love. That's what I've done — kept my Father's commands and made myself at home in his love.

11-15   "I've told you these things for a purpose: that my joy might be your joy, and your joy wholly mature. This is my command: Love one another the way I loved you. This is the very best way to love. Put your life on the line for your friends. You are my friends when you do the things I command you. I'm no longer calling you servants because servants don't understand what their master is thinking and planning. No, I've named you friends because I've let you in on everything I've heard from the Father.

16   "You didn't choose me, remember; I chose you, and put you in the world to bear fruit, fruit that won't spoil. As fruit bearers, whatever you ask the Father in relation to me, he gives you.

17   "But remember the root command: Love one another.

Hated by the World

18-19   "If you find the godless world is hating you, remember it got its start hating me. If you lived on the world's terms, the world would love you as one of its own. But since I picked you to live on God's terms and no longer on the world's terms, the world is going to hate you.

20   "When that happens, remember this: Servants don't get better treatment than their masters. If they beat on me, they will certainly beat on you. If they did what I told them, they will do what you tell them.

21-25   "They are going to do all these things to you because of the way they treated me, because they don't know the One who sent me. If I hadn't come and told them all this in plain language, it wouldn't be so bad. As it is, they have no excuse. Hate me, hate my Father — it's all the same. If I hadn't done what I have done among them, works no one has *ever* done, they wouldn't be to blame. But they saw the God-signs and hated anyway, both me and my Father. Interesting — they have verified the truth of their own Scriptures where it is written, 'They hated me for no good reason.'

26-27 "When the Friend I plan to send you from the Father comes — the Spirit of Truth issuing from the Father — he will confirm everything about me. You, too, from your side must give your confirming evidence, since you are in this with me from the start."

1-4 **16** "I've told you these things to prepare you for rough times ahead. They are going to throw you out of the meeting places. There will even come a time when anyone who kills you will think he's doing God a favor. They will do these things because they never really understood the Father. I've told you these things so that when the time comes and they start in on you, you'll be well-warned and ready for them.

THE FRIEND WILL COME

4-7 "I didn't tell you this earlier because I was with you every day. But now I am on my way to the One who sent me. Not one of you has asked, 'Where are you going?' Instead, the longer I've talked, the sadder you've become. So let me say it again, this truth: It's better for you that I leave. If I don't leave, the Friend won't come. But if I go, I'll send him to you.

8-11 "When he comes, he'll expose the error of the godless world's view of sin, righteousness, and judgment: He'll show them that their refusal to believe in me is their basic sin; that righteousness comes from above, where I am with the Father, out of their sight and control; that judgment takes place as the ruler of this godless world is brought to trial and convicted.

12-15 "I still have many things to tell you, but you can't handle them now. But when the Friend comes, the Spirit of the Truth, he will take you by the hand and guide you into all the truth there is. He won't draw attention to himself, but will make sense out of what is about to happen and, indeed, out of all that I have done and said. He will honor me; he will take from me and deliver it to you. Everything the Father has is also mine. That is why I've said, 'He takes from me and delivers to you.'

16 "In a day or so you're not going to see me, but then in another day or so you will see me."

JOY LIKE A RIVER OVERFLOWING

17-18 That stirred up a hornet's nest of questions among the disciples: "What's he talking about: 'In a day or so you're not going to see me, but then in another day or so you will see me'? And, 'Because I'm on my way to the Father'? What is this 'day or so'? We don't know what he's talking about."

19-20 Jesus knew they were dying to ask him what he meant, so he said, "Are you trying to figure out among yourselves what I meant when I said, 'In a day or so you're not going to see me, but then in another day or so you will see me'? Then fix this firmly in your minds: You're going to be in deep mourning while the godless world throws a party. You'll be sad, very sad, but your sadness will develop into gladness.

21-23 "When a woman gives birth, she has a hard time, there's no getting around it. But when the baby is born, there is joy in the birth. This new life in the world wipes out memory of the pain. The sadness you have right now is similar to that pain, but the coming joy is also similar. When I see you again, you'll be full of joy, and it will be a joy no one can rob from you. You'll no longer be so full of questions.

23-24 "This is what I want you to do: Ask the Father for whatever is in keeping with the things I've revealed to you. Ask in my name, according to my will, and he'll most certainly give it to you. Your joy will be a river overflowing its banks!

25-28 "I've used figures of speech in telling you these things. Soon I'll drop the figures and tell you about the Father in plain language. Then you can make your requests directly to him in relation to this life I've revealed to you. I won't continue making requests of the Father on your behalf. I won't need to. Because you've gone out on a limb, committed yourselves to love and trust in me, believing I came directly from the Father, the Father loves you directly. First, I left the Father and arrived in the world; now I leave the world and travel to the Father."

29-30 His disciples said, "Finally! You're giving it to us straight, in plain talk — no more figures of speech. Now we know that you know everything — it all comes together in you. You won't have to put up with our questions anymore. We're convinced you came from God."

31-33 Jesus answered them, "Do you finally believe? In fact, you're about to make a run for it — saving your own skins and abandoning me. But I'm not abandoned. The Father is with me. I've told you all this so that trusting me, you will be unshakable and assured, deeply at peace. In this godless world you will continue to experience difficulties. But take heart! I've conquered the world."

JESUS' PRAYER FOR HIS FOLLOWERS

1-5 **17** Jesus said these things. Then, raising his eyes in prayer, he said:

Father, it's time.
Display the bright splendor of your Son
So the Son in turn may show your bright splendor.
You put him in charge of everything human
So he might give real and eternal life to all in his charge.
And this is the real and eternal life:
That they know you,
The one and only true God,
And Jesus Christ, whom you sent.
I glorified you on earth
By completing down to the last detail
What you assigned me to do.
And now, Father, glorify me with your very own splendor,
The very splendor I had in your presence
Before there was a world.

6-12 I spelled out your character in detail
To the men and women you gave me.

They were yours in the first place;
Then you gave them to me,
And they have now done what you said.
They know now, beyond the shadow of a doubt,
That everything you gave me is firsthand from you,
For the message you gave me, I gave them;
And they took it, and were convinced
That I came from you.
They believed that you sent me.
I pray for them.
I'm not praying for the God-rejecting world
But for those you gave me,
For they are yours by right.
Everything mine is yours, and yours mine,
And my life is on display in them.
For I'm no longer going to be visible in the world;
They'll continue in the world
While I return to you.
Holy Father, guard them as they pursue this life
That you conferred as a gift through me,
So they can be one heart and mind
As we are one heart and mind.
As long as I was with them, I guarded them
In the pursuit of the life you gave through me;
I even posted a night watch.
And not one of them got away,
Except for the rebel bent on destruction
(the exception that proved the rule of Scripture).

13-19 Now I'm returning to you.
I'm saying these things in the world's hearing
So my people can experience
My joy completed in them.
I gave them your word;
The godless world hated them because of it,
Because they didn't join the world's ways,
Just as I didn't join the world's ways.
I'm not asking that you take them out of the world
But that you guard them from the Evil One.
They are no more defined by the world
Than I am defined by the world.
Make them holy — consecrated — with the truth;
Your word is consecrating truth.
In the same way that you gave me a mission in the world,
I give them a mission in the world.
I'm consecrating myself for their sakes
So they'll be truth-consecrated in their mission.

20-23
I'm praying not only for them
But also for those who will believe in me
Because of them and their witness about me.
The goal is for all of them to become one heart and mind —
Just as you, Father, are in me and I in you,
So they might be one heart and mind with us.
Then the world might believe that you, in fact, sent me.
The same glory you gave me, I gave them,
So they'll be as unified and together as we are —
I in them and you in me.
Then they'll be mature in this oneness,
And give the godless world evidence
That you've sent me and loved them
In the same way you've loved me.

24-26
Father, I want those you gave me
To be with me, right where I am,
So they can see my glory, the splendor you gave me,
Having loved me
Long before there ever was a world.
Righteous Father, the world has never known you,
But I have known you, and these disciples know
That you sent me on this mission.
I have made your very being known to them —
Who you are and what you do —
And continue to make it known,
So that your love for me
Might be in them
Exactly as I am in them.

SEIZED IN THE GARDEN AT NIGHT

1
18 Jesus, having prayed this prayer, left with his disciples and crossed over the brook Kidron at a place where there was a garden. He and his disciples entered it.

2-4
Judas, his betrayer, knew the place because Jesus and his disciples went there often. So Judas led the way to the garden, and the Roman soldiers and police sent by the high priests and Pharisees followed. They arrived there with lanterns and torches and swords. Jesus, knowing by now everything that was coming down on him, went out and met them. He said, "Who are you after?"

They answered, "Jesus the Nazarene."

5-6
He said, "That's me." The soldiers recoiled, totally taken aback. Judas, his betrayer, stood out like a sore thumb.

7
Jesus asked again, "Who are you after?"

They answered, "Jesus the Nazarene."

8-9
"I told you," said Jesus, "that's me. I'm the one. So if it's me you're after, let these others go." (This validated the words in his prayer, "I didn't lose one of those you gave.")

10
Just then Simon Peter, who was carrying a sword, pulled it from its sheath and struck the Chief Priest's servant, cutting off his right ear.

Malchus was the servant's name.

11 Jesus ordered Peter, "Put back your sword. Do you think for a minute I'm not going to drink this cup the Father gave me?"

12-14 Then the Roman soldiers under their commander, joined by the Jewish police, seized Jesus and tied him up. They took him first to Annas, father-in-law of Caiaphas. Caiaphas was the Chief Priest that year. It was Caiaphas who had advised the Jews that it was to their advantage that one man die for the people.

15-16 Simon Peter and another disciple followed Jesus. That other disciple was known to the Chief Priest, and so he went in with Jesus to the Chief Priest's courtyard. Peter had to stay outside. Then the other disciple went out, spoke to the doorkeeper, and got Peter in.

17 The young woman who was the doorkeeper said to Peter, "Aren't you one of this man's disciples?"

He said, "No, I'm not."

18 The servants and police had made a fire because of the cold and were huddled there warming themselves. Peter stood with them, trying to get warm.

THE INTERROGATION

19-21 Annas interrogated Jesus regarding his disciples and his teaching. Jesus answered, "I've spoken openly in public. I've taught regularly in meeting places and the Temple, where the Jews all come together. Everything has been out in the open. I've said nothing in secret. So why are you treating me like a conspirator? Question those who have been listening to me. They know well what I have said. My teachings have all been aboveboard."

22 When he said this, one of the policemen standing there slapped Jesus across the face, saying, "How dare you speak to the Chief Priest like that!"

23 Jesus replied, "If I've said something wrong, prove it. But if I've spoken the plain truth, why this slapping around?"

24 Then Annas sent him, still tied up, to the Chief Priest Caiaphas.

25 Meanwhile, Simon Peter was back at the fire, still trying to get warm. The others there said to him, "Aren't you one of his disciples?"

He denied it, "Not me."

26 One of the Chief Priest's servants, a relative of the man whose ear Peter had cut off, said, "Didn't I see you in the garden with him?"

27 Again, Peter denied it. Just then a rooster crowed.

THE KING OF THE JEWS

28-29 They led Jesus then from Caiaphas to the Roman governor's palace. It was early morning. They themselves didn't enter the palace because they didn't want to be disqualified from eating the Passover. So Pilate came out to them and spoke. "What charge do you bring against this man?"

30 They said, "If he hadn't been doing something evil, do you think we'd be here bothering you?"

31-32 Pilate said, "You take him. Judge him by *your* law."

The Jews said, "We're not allowed to kill anyone." (This would confirm Jesus' word indicating the way he would die.)

33 Pilate went back into the palace and called for Jesus. He said, "Are you the 'King of the Jews'?"

34 Jesus answered, "Are you saying this on your own, or did others tell

you this about me?"

35 Pilate said, "Do I look like a Jew? Your people and your high priests turned you over to me. What did you do?"

36 "My kingdom," said Jesus, "doesn't consist of what you see around you. If it did, my followers would fight so that I wouldn't be handed over to the Jews. But I'm not that kind of king, not the world's kind of king."

37 Then Pilate said, "So, are you a king or not?"

Jesus answered, "You tell me. Because I am King, I was born and entered the world so that I could witness to the truth. Everyone who cares for truth, who has any feeling for the truth, recognizes my voice."

38-39 Pilate said, "What is truth?"

Then he went back out to the Jews and told them, "I find nothing wrong in this man. It's your custom that I pardon one prisoner at Passover. Do you want me to pardon the 'King of the Jews'?"

40 They shouted back, "Not this one, but Barabbas!" Barabbas was a Jewish freedom fighter.

THE THORN CROWN OF THE KING

1-3 **19** So Pilate took Jesus and had him whipped. The soldiers, having braided a crown from thorns, set it on his head, threw a purple robe over him, and approached him with, "Hail, King of the Jews!" Then they greeted him with slaps in the face.

4-5 Pilate went back out again and said to them, "I present him to you, but I want you to know that I do not find him guilty of any crime." Just then Jesus came out wearing the thorn crown and purple robe.

Pilate announced, "Here he is: the Man."

6 When the high priests and police saw him, they shouted in a frenzy, "Crucify! Crucify!"

Pilate told them, "You take him. You crucify him. I find nothing wrong with him."

7 The Jews answered, "We have a law, and by that law he must die because he claimed to be the Son of God."

8-9 When Pilate heard this, he became even more scared. He went back into the palace and said to Jesus, "Where did you come from?"

Jesus gave no answer.

10 Pilate said, "You won't talk? Don't you know that I have the authority to pardon you, and the authority to — crucify you?"

11 Jesus said, "You haven't a shred of authority over me except what has been given you from heaven. That's why the one who betrayed me to you has committed a far greater fault."

12 At this, Pilate tried his best to pardon him, but the Jews shouted him down: "If you pardon this man, you're no friend of Caesar's. Anyone setting himself up as 'king' defies Caesar."

13-14 When Pilate heard those words, he led Jesus outside. He sat down at the judgment seat in the area designated Stone Court (in Hebrew, *Gabbatha*). It was the preparation day for Passover. The hour was noon. Pilate said to the Jews, "Here is your king."

15 They shouted back, "Kill him! Kill him! Crucify him!"

Pilate said, "I am to crucify your king?"

The high priests answered, "We have no king except Caesar."

16-19 Pilate caved in to their demand. He turned him over to be crucified.

THE CRUCIFIXION

They took Jesus away. Carrying his cross, Jesus went out to the place called Skull Hill (the name in Hebrew is *Golgotha*), where they crucified him, and with him two others, one on each side, Jesus in the middle. Pilate wrote a sign and had it placed on the cross. It read:

JESUS THE NAZARENE
THE KING OF THE JEWS.

20-21   Many of the Jews read the sign because the place where Jesus was crucified was right next to the city. It was written in Hebrew, Latin, and Greek. The Jewish high priests objected. "Don't write," they said to Pilate, "'The King of the Jews.' Make it, 'This man said, "I am the King of the Jews."'"

22   Pilate said, "What I've written, I've written."

23-24   When they crucified him, the Roman soldiers took his clothes and divided them up four ways, to each soldier a fourth. But his robe was seamless, a single piece of weaving, so they said to each other, "Let's not tear it up. Let's throw dice to see who gets it." This confirmed the Scripture that said, "They divided up my clothes among them and threw dice for my coat." (The soldiers validated the Scriptures!)

24-27   While the soldiers were looking after themselves, Jesus' mother, his aunt, Mary the wife of Clopas, and Mary Magdalene stood at the foot of the cross. Jesus saw his mother and the disciple he loved standing near her. He said to his mother, "Woman, here is your son." Then to the disciple, "Here is your mother." From that moment the disciple accepted her as his own mother.

28   Jesus, seeing that everything had been completed so that the Scripture record might also be complete, then said, "I'm thirsty."

29-30   A jug of sour wine was standing by. Someone put a sponge soaked with the wine on a javelin and lifted it to his mouth. After he took the wine, Jesus said, "It's done . . . complete." Bowing his head, he offered up his spirit.

31-34   Then the Jews, since it was the day of Sabbath preparation, and so the bodies wouldn't stay on the crosses over the Sabbath (it was a high holy day that year), petitioned Pilate that their legs be broken to speed death, and the bodies taken down. So the soldiers came and broke the legs of the first man crucified with Jesus, and then the other. When they got to Jesus, they saw that he was already dead, so they didn't break his legs. One of the soldiers stabbed him in the side with his spear. Blood and water gushed out.

35   The eyewitness to these things has presented an accurate report. He saw it himself and is telling the truth so that you, also, will believe.

36-37   These things that happened confirmed the Scripture, "Not a bone in his body was broken," and the other Scripture that reads, "They will stare at the one they pierced."

38   After all this, Joseph of Arimathea (he was a disciple of Jesus, but secretly, because he was intimidated by the Jews) petitioned Pilate to take the body of Jesus. Pilate gave permission. So Joseph came and took the body.

39-42   Nicodemus, who had first come to Jesus at night, came now in broad daylight carrying a mixture of myrrh and aloes, about seventy-five pounds. They took Jesus' body and, following the Jewish burial custom, wrapped it in linen with the spices. There was a garden near the place he was crucified, and in the garden a new tomb in which no one had yet been placed. So, because it was Sabbath preparation for the Jews and the tomb was convenient, they placed Jesus in it.

RESURRECTION!

1-2 **20** Early in the morning on the first day of the week, while it was still dark, Mary Magdalene came to the tomb and saw that the stone was moved away from the entrance. She ran at once to Simon Peter and the other disciple, the one Jesus loved, breathlessly panting, "They took the Master from the tomb. We don't know where they've put him."

3-10 Peter and the other disciple left immediately for the tomb. They ran, neck and neck. The other disciple got to the tomb first, outrunning Peter. Stooping to look in, he saw the pieces of linen cloth lying there, but he didn't go in. Simon Peter arrived after him, entered the tomb, observed the linen cloths lying there, and the kerchief used to cover his head not lying with the linen cloths but separate, neatly folded by itself. Then the other disciple, the one who had gotten there first, went into the tomb, took one look at the evidence, and believed. No one yet knew from the Scripture that he had to rise from the dead. The disciples then went back home.

11-13 But Mary stood outside the tomb weeping. As she wept, she knelt to look into the tomb and saw two angels sitting there, dressed in white, one at the head, the other at the foot of where Jesus' body had been laid. They said to her, "Woman, why do you weep?"

13-14 "They took my Master," she said, "and I don't know where they put him." After she said this, she turned away and saw Jesus standing there. But she didn't recognize him.

15 Jesus spoke to her, "Woman, why do you weep? Who are you looking for?"

She, thinking that he was the gardener, said, "Mister, if you took him, tell me where you put him so I can care for him."

16 Jesus said, "Mary."

Turning to face him, she said in Hebrew, "*Rabboni!*" meaning "Teacher!"

17 Jesus said, "Don't cling to me, for I have not yet ascended to the Father. Go to my brothers and tell them, 'I ascend to my Father and your Father, my God and your God.'"

18 Mary Magdalene went, telling the news to the disciples: "I saw the Master!" And she told them everything he said to her.

TO BELIEVE

19-20 Later on that day, the disciples had gathered together, but, fearful of the Jews, had locked all the doors in the house. Jesus entered, stood among them, and said, "Peace to you." Then he showed them his hands and side.

20-21 The disciples, seeing the Master with their own eyes, were exuberant. Jesus repeated his greeting: "Peace to you. Just as the Father sent me, I send you."

22-23 Then he took a deep breath and breathed into them. "Receive the Holy Spirit," he said. "If you forgive someone's sins, they're gone for good. If you don't forgive sins, what are you going to do with them?"

²⁴⁻²⁵ But Thomas, sometimes called the Twin, one of the Twelve, was not with them when Jesus came. The other disciples told him, "We saw the Master."

But he said, "Unless I see the nail holes in his hands, put my finger in the nail holes, and stick my hand in his side, I won't believe it."

²⁶ Eight days later, his disciples were again in the room. This time Thomas was with them. Jesus came through the locked doors, stood among them, and said, "Peace to you."

²⁷ Then he focused his attention on Thomas. "Take your finger and examine my hands. Take your hand and stick it in my side. Don't be unbelieving. Believe."

²⁸ Thomas said, "My Master! My God!"

²⁹ Jesus said, "So, you believe because you've seen with your own eyes. Even better blessings are in store for those who believe without seeing."

³⁰⁻³¹ Jesus provided far more God-revealing signs than are written down in this book. These are written down so you will believe that Jesus is the Messiah, the Son of God, and in the act of believing, have real and eternal life in the way he personally revealed it.

FISHING

¹⁻³ **21** After this, Jesus appeared again to the disciples, this time at the Tiberias Sea (the Sea of Galilee). This is how he did it: Simon Peter, Thomas (nicknamed "Twin"), Nathanael from Cana in Galilee, the brothers Zebedee, and two other disciples were together. Simon Peter announced, "I'm going fishing."

³⁻⁴ The rest of them replied, "We're going with you." They went out and got in the boat. They caught nothing that night. When the sun came up, Jesus was standing on the beach, but they didn't recognize him.

⁵ Jesus spoke to them: "Good morning! Did you catch anything for breakfast?"

They answered, "No."

⁶ He said, "Throw the net off the right side of the boat and see what happens."

They did what he said. All of a sudden there were so many fish in it, they weren't strong enough to pull it in.

⁷⁻⁹ Then the disciple Jesus loved said to Peter, "It's the Master!"

When Simon Peter realized that it was the Master, he threw on some clothes, for he was stripped for work, and dove into the sea. The other disciples came in by boat for they weren't far from land, a hundred yards or so, pulling along the net full of fish. When they got out of the boat, they saw a fire laid, with fish and bread cooking on it.

¹⁰⁻¹¹ Jesus said, "Bring some of the fish you've just caught." Simon Peter joined them and pulled the net to shore—153 big fish! And even with all those fish, the net didn't rip.

¹² Jesus said, "Breakfast is ready." Not one of the disciples dared ask, "Who are you?" They knew it was the Master.

¹³⁻¹⁴ Jesus then took the bread and gave it to them. He did the same with the fish. This was now the third time Jesus had shown himself alive to the disciples since being raised from the dead.

DO YOU LOVE ME?

15 After breakfast, Jesus said to Simon Peter, "Simon, son of John, do you love me more than these?"

"Yes, Master, you know I love you."

Jesus said, "Feed my lambs."

16 He then asked a second time, "Simon, son of John, do you love me?"

"Yes, Master, you know I love you."

Jesus said, "Shepherd my sheep."

17-19 Then he said it a third time: "Simon, son of John, do you love me?"

Peter was upset that he asked for the third time, "Do you love me?" so he answered, "Master, you know everything there is to know. You've got to know that I love you."

Jesus said, "Feed my sheep. I'm telling you the very truth now: When you were young you dressed yourself and went wherever you wished, but when you get old you'll have to stretch out your hands while someone else dresses you and takes you where you don't want to go." He said this to hint at the kind of death by which Peter would glorify God. And then he commanded, "Follow me."

20-21 Turning his head, Peter noticed the disciple Jesus loved following right behind. When Peter noticed him, he asked Jesus, "Master, what's going to happen to *him*?"

22-23 Jesus said, "If I want him to live until I come again, what's that to you? You — follow me." That is how the rumor got out among the brothers that this disciple wouldn't die. But that is not what Jesus said. He simply said, "If I want him to live until I come again, what's that to you?"

24 This is the same disciple who was eyewitness to all these things and wrote them down. And we all know that his eyewitness account is reliable and accurate.

25 There are so many other things Jesus did. If they were all written down, each of them, one by one, I can't imagine a world big enough to hold such a library of books.

ACTS

Because the story of Jesus is so impressive — God among us! God speaking a language we can understand! God acting in ways that heal and help and save us! — there is a danger that we will be impressed, but only be impressed. As the spectacular dimensions of this story slowly (or suddenly) dawn upon us, we could easily become enthusiastic spectators, and then let it go at that — become admirers of Jesus, generous with our oohs and ahs, and in our better moments inspired to imitate him.

It is Luke's task to prevent that, to prevent us from becoming mere spectators to Jesus, fans of the Message. Of the original quartet of writers on Jesus, Luke alone continues to tell the story as the apostles and disciples live it into the next generation. The remarkable thing is that it continues to be essentially the same story. Luke continues his narration with hardly a break, a pause perhaps to dip his pen in the inkwell, writing in the same style, using the same vocabulary.

The story of Jesus doesn't end with Jesus. It continues in the lives of those who believe in him. The supernatural does not stop with Jesus. Luke makes it clear that these Christians he wrote about were no more spectators of Jesus than Jesus was a spectator of God — they are *in* on the action of God, God acting *in* them, God living *in* them. Which also means, of course, in *us*.

ACTS

TO THE ENDS OF THE WORLD

¹⁻⁵ **1** Dear Theophilus, in the first volume of this book I wrote on everything that Jesus began to do and teach until the day he said good-bye to the apostles, the ones he had chosen through the Holy Spirit, and was taken up to heaven. After his death, he presented himself alive to them in many different settings over a period of forty days. In face-to-face meetings, he talked to them about things concerning the kingdom of God. As they met and ate meals together, he told them that they were on no account to leave Jerusalem but "must wait for what the Father promised: the promise you heard from me. John baptized in water; you will be baptized in the Holy Spirit. And soon."

⁶ When they were together for the last time they asked, "Master, are you going to restore the kingdom to Israel now? Is this the time?"

⁷⁻⁸ He told them, "You don't get to know the time. Timing is the Father's business. What you'll get is the Holy Spirit. And when the Holy Spirit comes on you, you will be able to be my witnesses in Jerusalem, all over Judea and Samaria, even to the ends of the world."

⁹⁻¹¹ These were his last words. As they watched, he was taken up and disappeared in a cloud. They stood there, staring into the empty sky. Suddenly two men appeared — in white robes! They said, "You Galileans! — why do you just stand here looking up at an empty sky? This very Jesus who was taken up from among you to heaven will come as certainly — and mysteriously — as he left."

RETURNING TO JERUSALEM

¹²⁻¹³ So they left the mountain called Olives and returned to Jerusalem. It was a little over half a mile. They went to the upper room they had been using as a meeting place:

Peter,
John,
James,
Andrew,
Philip,
Thomas,
Bartholomew,
Matthew,
James, son of Alphaeus,
Simon the Zealot,
Judas, son of James.

¹⁴ They agreed they were in this for good, completely together in prayer, the women included. Also Jesus' mother, Mary, and his brothers.

REPLACING JUDAS

¹⁵⁻¹⁷ During this time, Peter stood up in the company — there were about 120 of them in the room at the time — and said, "Friends, long ago the Holy

Spirit spoke through David regarding Judas, who became the guide to those who arrested Jesus. That Scripture had to be fulfilled, and now has been. Judas was one of us and had his assigned place in this ministry.

18-20 "As you know, he took the evil bribe money and bought a small farm. There he came to a bad end, rupturing his belly and spilling his guts. Everybody in Jerusalem knows this by now; they call the place Murder Meadow. It's exactly what we find written in the Psalms:

> Let his farm become haunted
> So no one can ever live there.

"And also what was written later:

> Let someone else take over his post.

21-22 "Judas must now be replaced. The replacement must come from the company of men who stayed together with us from the time Jesus was baptized by John up to the day of his ascension, designated along with us as a witness to his resurrection."

23-26 They nominated two: Joseph Barsabbas, nicknamed Justus, and Matthias. Then they prayed, "You, O God, know every one of us inside and out. Make plain which of these two men you choose to take the place in this ministry and leadership that Judas threw away in order to go his own way." They then drew straws. Matthias won and was counted in with the eleven apostles.

A Sound Like a Strong Wind

1-4 2 When the Feast of Pentecost came, they were all together in one place. Without warning there was a sound like a strong wind, gale force — no one could tell where it came from. It filled the whole building. Then, like a wildfire, the Holy Spirit spread through their ranks, and they started speaking in a number of different languages as the Spirit prompted them.

5-11 There were many Jews staying in Jerusalem just then, devout pilgrims from all over the world. When they heard the sound, they came on the run. Then when they heard, one after another, their own mother tongues being spoken, they were thunderstruck. They couldn't for the life of them figure out what was going on, and kept saying, "Aren't these all Galileans? How come we're hearing them talk in our various mother tongues?

> Parthians, Medes, and Elamites;
> Visitors from Mesopotamia, Judea, and Cappadocia,
> Pontus and Asia, Phrygia and Pamphylia,
> Egypt and the parts of Libya belonging to Cyrene;
> Immigrants from Rome, both Jews and proselytes;
> Even Cretans and Arabs!

"They're speaking our languages, describing God's mighty works!"

12 Their heads were spinning; they couldn't make head or tail of any of it. They talked back and forth, confused: "What's going on here?"

13 Others joked, "They're drunk on cheap wine."

PETER SPEAKS UP

¹⁴⁻²¹ That's when Peter stood up and, backed by the other eleven, spoke out with bold urgency: "Fellow Jews, all of you who are visiting Jerusalem, listen carefully and get this story straight. These people aren't drunk as some of you suspect. They haven't had time to get drunk—it's only nine o'clock in the morning. This is what the prophet Joel announced would happen:

> "In the Last Days," God says,
> "I will pour out my Spirit
>   on every kind of people:
> Your sons will prophesy,
>   also your daughters;
> Your young men will see visions,
>   your old men dream dreams.
> When the time comes,
>   I'll pour out my Spirit
> On those who serve me, men and women both,
>   and they'll prophesy.
> I'll set wonders in the sky above
>   and signs on the earth below,
> Blood and fire and billowing smoke,
>   the sun turning black and the moon blood-red,
> Before the Day of the Lord arrives,
>   the Day tremendous and marvelous;
> And whoever calls out for help
>   to me, God, will be saved."

²²⁻²⁸ "Fellow Israelites, listen carefully to these words: Jesus the Nazarene, a man thoroughly accredited by God to you—the miracles and wonders and signs that God did through him are common knowledge—this Jesus, following the deliberate and well-thought-out plan of God, was betrayed by men who took the law into their own hands, and was handed over to you. And you pinned him to a cross and killed him. But God untied the death ropes and raised him up. Death was no match for him. David said it all:

> I saw God before me for all time.
>   Nothing can shake me; he's right by my side.
> I'm glad from the inside out, ecstatic;
>   I've pitched my tent in the land of hope.
> I know you'll never dump me in Hades;
>   I'll never even smell the stench of death.
> You've got my feet on the life-path,
>   with your face shining sun-joy all around.

²⁹⁻³⁶ "Dear friends, let me be completely frank with you. Our ancestor David is dead and buried—his tomb is in plain sight today. But being also a prophet and knowing that God had solemnly sworn that a descendant of his would rule his kingdom, seeing far ahead, he talked of the resurrection of the Messiah—'no trip to Hades, no stench of death.' This Jesus, God raised up. And every one of us here is a witness to it. Then, raised to the heights at

the right hand of God and receiving the promise of the Holy Spirit from the Father, he poured out the Spirit he had just received. That is what you see and hear. For David himself did not ascend to heaven, but he did say,

> God said to my Master, "Sit at my right hand
> Until I make your enemies a stool for resting your feet."

"All Israel, then, know this: There's no longer room for doubt—God made him Master and Messiah, this Jesus whom you killed on a cross."

37 Cut to the quick, those who were there listening asked Peter and the other apostles, "Brothers! Brothers! So now what do we do?"

38-39 Peter said, "Change your life. Turn to God and be baptized, each of you, in the name of Jesus Christ, so your sins are forgiven. Receive the gift of the Holy Spirit. The promise is targeted to you and your children, but also to all who are far away—whomever, in fact, our Master God invites."

40 He went on in this vein for a long time, urging them over and over, "Get out while you can; get out of this sick and stupid culture!"

41-42 That day about three thousand took him at his word, were baptized and were signed up. They committed themselves to the teaching of the apostles, the life together, the common meal, and the prayers.

43-45 Everyone around was in awe—all those wonders and signs done through the apostles! And all the believers lived in a wonderful harmony, holding everything in common. They sold whatever they owned and pooled their resources so that each person's need was met.

46-47 They followed a daily discipline of worship in the Temple followed by meals at home, every meal a celebration, exuberant and joyful, as they praised God. People in general liked what they saw. Every day their number grew as God added those who were saved.

1-5 One day at three o'clock in the afternoon, Peter and John were on their way into the Temple for prayer meeting. At the same time there was a man crippled from birth being carried up. Every day he was set down at the Temple gate, the one named Beautiful, to beg from those going into the Temple. When he saw Peter and John about to enter the Temple, he asked for a handout. Peter, with John at his side, looked him straight in the eye and said, "Look here." He looked up, expecting to get something from them.

6-8 Peter said, "I don't have a nickel to my name, but what I do have, I give you: In the name of Jesus Christ of Nazareth, walk!" He grabbed him by the right hand and pulled him up. In an instant his feet and ankles became firm. He jumped to his feet and walked.

8-10 The man went into the Temple with them, walking back and forth, dancing and praising God. Everybody there saw him walking around and praising God. They recognized him as the one who sat begging at the Temple's Gate Beautiful and rubbed their eyes, astonished, scarcely believing what they were seeing.

11 The man threw his arms around Peter and John, ecstatic. All the people ran up to where they were at Solomon's Porch to see it for themselves.

Turn to Face God

12-16 When Peter saw he had a congregation, he addressed the people:

"Oh, Israelites, why does this take you by such complete surprise, and why stare at us as if *our* power or piety made him walk? The God of Abraham and Isaac and Jacob, the God of our ancestors, has glorified his Son Jesus. The very One that Pilate called innocent, you repudiated. You repudiated the Holy One, the Just One, and asked for a murderer in his place. You no sooner killed the Author of Life than God raised him from the dead — and we're the witnesses. Faith in Jesus' name put this man, whose condition you know so well, on his feet — yes, faith and nothing but faith put this man healed and whole right before your eyes.

17-18 "And now, friends, I know you had no idea what you were doing when you killed Jesus, and neither did your leaders. But God, who through the preaching of all the prophets had said all along that his Messiah would be killed, knew exactly what you were doing and used it to fulfill his plans.

19-23 "Now it's time to change your ways! Turn to face God so he can wipe away your sins, pour out showers of blessing to refresh you, and send you the Messiah he prepared for you, namely, Jesus. For the time being he must remain out of sight in heaven until everything is restored to order again just the way God, through the preaching of his holy prophets of old, said it would be. Moses, for instance, said, 'Your God will raise up for you a prophet just like me from your family. Listen to every word he speaks to you. Every last living soul who refuses to listen to that prophet will be wiped out from the people.'

24-26 "All the prophets from Samuel on down said the same thing, said most emphatically that these days would come. These prophets, along with the covenant God made with your ancestors, are your family tree. God's covenant-word to Abraham provides the text: 'By your offspring all the families of the earth will be blessed.' But you are first in line: God, having raised up his Son, sent him to bless you as you turn, one by one, from your evil ways."

Nothing to Hide

1-4 While Peter and John were addressing the people, the priests, the chief of the Temple police, and some Sadducees came up, indignant that these upstart apostles were instructing the people and proclaiming that the resurrection from the dead had taken place in Jesus. They arrested them and threw them in jail until morning, for by now it was late in the evening. But many of those who listened had already believed the Message — in round numbers about five thousand!

5-7 The next day a meeting was called in Jerusalem. The rulers, religious leaders, religion scholars, Annas the Chief Priest, Caiaphas, John, Alexander — everybody who was anybody was there. They stood Peter and John in the middle of the room and grilled them: "Who put you in charge here? What business do you have doing this?"

8-12 With that, Peter, full of the Holy Spirit, let loose: "Rulers and leaders of the people, if we have been brought to trial today for helping a sick man, put under investigation regarding this healing, I'll be completely frank with you — we have nothing to hide. By the name of Jesus Christ of Nazareth, the One you killed on a cross, the One God raised from the dead, by means of his name this man stands before you healthy and whole. Jesus is 'the stone you masons threw out, which is now the cornerstone.' Salvation comes no other way; no other name has been or will be given to us by which we can be saved, only this one."

13-14 They couldn't take their eyes off them — Peter and John standing there so confident, so sure of themselves! Their fascination deepened when they realized these two were laymen with no training in Scripture or formal education. They recognized them as companions of Jesus, but with the man right before them, seeing him standing there so upright — so healed! — what could they say against that?

15-17 They sent them out of the room so they could work out a plan. They talked it over: "What can we do with these men? By now it's known all over town that a miracle has occurred, and that they are behind it. There is no way we can refute that. But so that it doesn't go any further, let's silence them with threats so they won't dare to use Jesus' name ever again with anyone."

18-20 They called them back and warned them that they were on no account ever again to speak or teach in the name of Jesus. But Peter and John spoke right back, "Whether it's right in God's eyes to listen to you rather than to God, you decide. As for us, there's no question — we can't keep quiet about what we've seen and heard."

21-22 The religious leaders renewed their threats, but then released them. They couldn't come up with a charge that would stick, that would keep them in jail. The people wouldn't have stood for it — they were all praising God over what had happened. The man who had been miraculously healed was over forty years old.

ONE HEART, ONE MIND

23-26 As soon as Peter and John were let go, they went to their friends and told them what the high priests and religious leaders had said. Hearing the report, they lifted their voices in a wonderful harmony in prayer: "Strong God, you made heaven and earth and sea and everything in them. By the Holy Spirit you spoke through the mouth of your servant and our father, David:

> Why the big noise, nations?
> Why the mean plots, peoples?
> Earth's leaders push for position,
> Potentates meet for summit talks,
> The God-deniers, the Messiah-defiers!

27-28 "For in fact they did meet — Herod and Pontius Pilate with nations and peoples, even Israel itself! — met in this very city to plot against your holy Son Jesus, the One you made Messiah, to carry out the plans you long ago set in motion.

29-30 "And now they're at it again! Take care of their threats and give your servants fearless confidence in preaching your Message, as you stretch out your hand to us in healings and miracles and wonders done in the name of your holy servant Jesus."

31 While they were praying, the place where they were meeting trembled and shook. They were all filled with the Holy Spirit and continued to speak

God's Word with fearless confidence.

32-33   The whole congregation of believers was united as one — one heart, one mind! They didn't even claim ownership of their own possessions. No one said, "That's mine; you can't have it." They shared everything. The apostles gave powerful witness to the resurrection of the Master Jesus, and grace was on all of them.

34-35   And so it turned out that not a person among them was needy. Those who owned fields or houses sold them and brought the price of the sale to the apostles and made an offering of it. The apostles then distributed it according to each person's need.

36-37   Joseph, called by the apostles "Barnabas" (which means "Son of Comfort"), a Levite born in Cyprus, sold a field that he owned, brought the money, and made an offering of it to the apostles.

ANANIAS AND SAPPHIRA

1-2   **5** But a man named Ananias — his wife, Sapphira, conniving in this with him — sold a piece of land, secretly kept part of the price for himself, and then brought the rest to the apostles and made an offering of it.

3-4   Peter said, "Ananias, how did Satan get you to lie to the Holy Spirit and secretly keep back part of the price of the field? Before you sold it, it was all yours, and after you sold it, the money was yours to do with as you wished. So what got into you to pull a trick like this? You didn't lie to men but to God."

5-6   Ananias, when he heard those words, fell down dead. *That* put the fear of God into everyone who heard of it. The younger men went right to work and wrapped him up, then carried him out and buried him.

7-8   Not more than three hours later, his wife, knowing nothing of what had happened, came in. Peter said, "Tell me, were you given this price for your field?"

"Yes," she said, "that price."

9-10   Peter responded, "What's going on here that you connived to conspire against the Spirit of the Master? The men who buried your husband are at the door, and you're next." No sooner were the words out of his mouth than she also fell down, dead. When the young men returned they found her body. They carried her out and buried her beside her husband.

11   By this time the whole church and, in fact, everyone who heard of these things had a healthy respect for God. They knew God was not to be trifled with.

THEY ALL MET REGULARLY

12-16   Through the work of the apostles, many God-signs were set up among the people, many wonderful things done. They all met regularly and in remarkable harmony on the Temple porch named after Solomon. But even though people admired them a lot, outsiders were wary about joining them. On the other hand, those who put their trust in the Master were added right and left, men and women both. They even carried the sick out into the streets and laid them on stretchers and bedrolls, hoping they would be touched by Peter's shadow when he walked by. They came from the villages surrounding Jerusalem, throngs of them, bringing the sick and bedeviled. And they all were healed.

To Obey God Rather than Men

17-20   Provoked mightily by all this, the Chief Priest and those on his side, mainly the sect of Sadducees, went into action, arrested the apostles and put them in the town jail. But during the night an angel of God opened the jailhouse door and led them out. He said, "Go to the Temple and take your stand. Tell the people everything there is to say about this Life."

Promptly obedient, they entered the Temple at daybreak and went on with their teaching.

21-23   Meanwhile, the Chief Priest and his cronies convened the High Council, Israel's senate, and sent to the jail to have the prisoners brought in. When the police got there, they couldn't find them anywhere in the jail. They went back and reported, "We found the jail locked tight as a drum and the guards posted at the doors, but when we went inside we didn't find a soul."

24   The chief of the Temple police and the high priests were puzzled. "What's going on here anyway?"

25-26   Just then someone showed up and said, "Did you know that the men you put in jail are back in the Temple teaching the people?" The chief and his police went and got them, but they handled them gently, fearful that the people would riot and turn on them.

27-28   Bringing them back, they stood them before the High Council. The Chief Priest said, "Didn't we give you strict orders not to teach in Jesus' name? And here you have filled Jerusalem with your teaching and are trying your best to blame us for the death of this man."

29-32   Peter and the apostles answered, "It's necessary to obey God rather than men. The God of our ancestors raised up Jesus, the One you killed by hanging him on a cross. God set him on high at his side, Prince and Savior, to give Israel the gift of a changed life and sins forgiven. And we are witnesses to these things. The Holy Spirit, whom God gives to those who obey him, corroborates every detail."

33-37   When they heard that, they were furious and wanted to kill them on the spot. But one of the council members stood up, a Pharisee by the name of Gamaliel, a teacher of God's Law who was honored by everyone. He ordered the men taken out of the room for a short time, then said, "Fellow Israelites, be careful what you do to these men. Not long ago Theudas made something of a splash, claiming to be somebody, and got about four hundred men to join him. He was killed, his followers dispersed, and nothing came of it. A little later, at the time of the census, Judas the Galilean appeared and acquired a following. He also fizzled out and the people following him were scattered to the four winds.

38-39   "So I am telling you: Hands off these men! Let them alone. If this program or this work is merely human, it will fall apart, but if it is of God, there is nothing you can do about it — and you better not be found fighting against God!"

40-42   That convinced them. They called the apostles back in. After giving them a thorough whipping, they warned them not to speak in Jesus' name and sent them off. The apostles went out of the High Council overjoyed because they had been given the honor of being dishonored on account of the Name. Every day they were in the Temple and homes, teaching and preaching Christ Jesus, not letting up for a minute.

The Word of God Prospered

1-4 **6** During this time, as the disciples were increasing in numbers by leaps and bounds, hard feelings developed among the Greek-speaking believers — "Hellenists" — toward the Hebrew-speaking believers because their widows were being discriminated against in the daily food lines. So the Twelve called a meeting of the disciples. They said, "It wouldn't be right for us to abandon our responsibilities for preaching and teaching the Word of God to help with the care of the poor. So, friends, choose seven men from among you whom everyone trusts, men full of the Holy Spirit and good sense, and we'll assign them this task. Meanwhile, we'll stick to our assigned tasks of prayer and speaking God's Word."

5-6 The congregation thought this was a great idea. They went ahead and chose —

Stephen, a man full of faith and the Holy Spirit,
Philip,
Procorus,
Nicanor,
Timon,
Parmenas,
Nicolas, a convert from Antioch.

Then they presented them to the apostles. Praying, the apostles laid on hands and commissioned them for their task.

7 The Word of God prospered. The number of disciples in Jerusalem increased dramatically. Not least, a great many priests submitted themselves to the faith.

8-10 Stephen, brimming with God's grace and energy, was doing wonderful things among the people, unmistakable signs that God was among them. But then some men from the meeting place whose membership was made up of freed slaves, Cyrenians, Alexandrians, and some others from Cilicia and Asia, went up against him trying to argue him down. But they were no match for his wisdom and spirit when he spoke.

11 So in secret they bribed men to lie: "We heard him cursing Moses and God."

12-14 That stirred up the people, the religious leaders, and religion scholars. They grabbed Stephen and took him before the High Council. They put forward their bribed witnesses to testify: "This man talks nonstop against this Holy Place and God's Law. We even heard him say that Jesus of Nazareth would tear this place down and throw out all the customs Moses gave us."

15 As all those who sat on the High Council looked at Stephen, they found they couldn't take their eyes off him — his face was like the face of an angel!

Stephen, Full of the Holy Spirit

1 **7** Then the Chief Priest said, "What do you have to say for yourself?"

2-3 Stephen replied, "Friends, fathers, and brothers, the God of glory appeared to our father Abraham when he was still in Mesopotamia, before the move to Haran, and told him, 'Leave your country and family and go to the land I'll show you.'

4-7   "So he left the country of the Chaldees and moved to Haran. After the death of his father, he immigrated to this country where you now live, but God gave him nothing, not so much as a foothold. He did promise to give the country to him and his son later on, even though Abraham had no son at the time. God let him know that his offspring would move to an alien country where they would be enslaved and brutalized for four hundred years. 'But,' God said, 'I will step in and take care of those slaveholders and bring my people out so they can worship me in this place.'

8   "Then he made a covenant with him and signed it in Abraham's flesh by circumcision. When Abraham had his son Isaac, within eight days he reproduced the sign of circumcision in him. Isaac became father of Jacob, and Jacob father of twelve 'fathers,' each faithfully passing on the covenant sign.

9-10   "But then those 'fathers,' burning up with jealousy, sent Joseph off to Egypt as a slave. God was right there with him, though — he not only rescued him from all his troubles but brought him to the attention of Pharaoh, king of Egypt. He was so impressed with Joseph that he put him in charge of the whole country, including his own personal affairs.

11-15   "Later a famine descended on that entire region, stretching from Egypt to Canaan, bringing terrific hardship. Our hungry fathers looked high and low for food, but the cupboard was bare. Jacob heard there was food in Egypt and sent our fathers to scout it out. Having confirmed the report, they went back to Egypt a second time to get food. On that visit, Joseph revealed his true identity to his brothers and introduced the Jacob family to Pharaoh. Then Joseph sent for his father, Jacob, and everyone else in the family, seventy-five in all. That's how the Jacob family got to Egypt.

15-16   "Jacob died, and our fathers after him. They were taken to Shechem and buried in the tomb for which Abraham paid a good price to the sons of Hamor.

17-19   "When the four hundred years were nearly up, the time God promised Abraham for deliverance, the population of our people in Egypt had become very large. And there was now a king over Egypt who had never heard of Joseph. He exploited our race mercilessly. He went so far as forcing us to abandon our newborn infants, exposing them to the elements to die a cruel death.

20-22   "In just such a time Moses was born, a most beautiful baby. He was hidden at home for three months. When he could be hidden no longer, he was put outside — and immediately rescued by Pharaoh's daughter, who mothered him as her own son. Moses was educated in the best schools in Egypt. He was equally impressive as a thinker and an athlete.

23-26   "When he was forty years old, he wondered how everything was going with his Hebrew kin and went out to look things over. He saw an Egyptian abusing one of them and stepped in, avenging his underdog brother by knocking the Egyptian flat. He thought his brothers would be glad that he was on their side, and even see him as an instrument of God to deliver them. But they didn't see it that way. The next day two of them were fighting and he tried to break it up, told them to shake hands and get along with each other: 'Friends, you are brothers, why are you beating up on each other?'

27-29   "The one who had started the fight said, 'Who put you in charge of us? Are you going to kill me like you killed that Egyptian yesterday?' When

Moses heard that, realizing that the word was out, he ran for his life and lived in exile over in Midian. During the years of exile, two sons were born to him.

30-32   "Forty years later, in the wilderness of Mount Sinai, an angel appeared to him in the guise of flames of a burning bush. Moses, not believing his eyes, went up to take a closer look. He heard God's voice: 'I am the God of your fathers, the God of Abraham, Isaac, and Jacob.' Frightened nearly out of his skin, Moses shut his eyes and turned away.

33-34   "God said, 'Kneel and pray. You are in a holy place, on holy ground. I've seen the agony of my people in Egypt. I've heard their groans. I've come to help them. So get yourself ready; I'm sending you back to Egypt.'

35-39   "This is the same Moses whom they earlier rejected, saying, 'Who put you in charge of us?' This is the Moses that God, using the angel flaming in the burning bush, sent back as ruler and redeemer. He led them out of their slavery. He did wonderful things, setting up God-signs all through Egypt, down at the Red Sea, and out in the wilderness for forty years. This is the Moses who said to his congregation, 'God will raise up a prophet just like me from your descendants.' This is the Moses who stood between the angel speaking at Sinai and your fathers assembled in the wilderness and took the life-giving words given to him and handed them over to us, words our fathers would have nothing to do with.

39-41   "They craved the old Egyptian ways, whining to Aaron, 'Make us gods we can see and follow. This Moses who got us out here miles from nowhere—who knows what's happened to him!' That was the time when they made a calf-idol, brought sacrifices to it, and congratulated each other on the wonderful religious program they had put together.

42-43   "God wasn't at all pleased; but he let them do it their way, worship every new god that came down the pike—and live with the consequences, consequences described by the prophet Amos:

> Did you bring me offerings of animals and grains
>> those forty wilderness years, O Israel?
> Hardly. You were too busy building shrines
>> to war gods, to sex goddesses,
> Worshiping them with all your might.
>> That's why I put you in exile in Babylon.

44-47   "And all this time our ancestors had a tent shrine for true worship, made to the exact specifications God provided Moses. They had it with them as they followed Joshua, when God cleared the land of pagans, and still had it right down to the time of David. David asked God for a permanent place for worship. But Solomon built it.

48-50   "Yet that doesn't mean that Most High God lives in a building made by carpenters and masons. The prophet Isaiah put it well when he wrote,

> "Heaven is my throne room;
>> I rest my feet on earth.
> So what kind of house
>> will you build me?" says God.
> "Where I can get away and relax?
>> It's already built, and I built it."

51-53   "And you continue, so bullheaded! Calluses on your hearts, flaps on your ears! Deliberately ignoring the Holy Spirit, you're just like your ancestors. Was there ever a prophet who didn't get the same treatment? Your ancestors killed anyone who dared talk about the coming of the Just One. And you've kept up the family tradition — traitors and murderers, all of you. You had God's Law handed to you by angels — gift-wrapped! — and you squandered it!"

54-56   At that point they went wild, a rioting mob of catcalls and whistles and invective. But Stephen, full of the Holy Spirit, hardly noticed — he only had eyes for God, whom he saw in all his glory with Jesus standing at his side. He said, "Oh! I see heaven wide open and the Son of Man standing at God's side!"

57-58   Yelling and hissing, the mob drowned him out. Now in full stampede, they dragged him out of town and pelted him with rocks. The ringleaders took off their coats and asked a young man named Saul to watch them.

59-60   As the rocks rained down, Stephen prayed, "Master Jesus, take my life." Then he knelt down, praying loud enough for everyone to hear, "Master, don't blame them for this sin" — his last words. Then he died.

1   Saul was right there, congratulating the killers.

SIMON THE WIZARD

1-2   **8** That set off a terrific persecution of the church in Jerusalem. The believers were all scattered throughout Judea and Samaria. All, that is, but the apostles. Good and brave men buried Stephen, giving him a solemn funeral — not many dry eyes that day!

3-8   And Saul just went wild, devastating the church, entering house after house after house, dragging men and women off to jail. Forced to leave home base, the followers of Jesus all became missionaries. Wherever they were scattered, they preached the Message about Jesus. Going down to a Samaritan city, Philip proclaimed the Message of the Messiah. When the people heard what he had to say and saw the miracles, the clear signs of God's action, they hung on his every word. Many who could neither stand nor walk were healed that day. The evil spirits protested loudly as they were sent on their way. And what joy in the city!

9-11   Previous to Philip's arrival, a certain Simon had practiced magic in the city, posing as a famous man and dazzling all the Samaritans with his wizardry. He had them all, from little children to old men, eating out of his hand. They all thought he had supernatural powers, and called him "the Great Wizard." He had been around a long time and everyone was more or less in awe of him.

12-13   But when Philip came to town announcing the news of God's kingdom and proclaiming the name of Jesus Christ, they forgot Simon and were baptized, becoming believers right and left! Even Simon himself believed and was baptized. From that moment he was like Philip's shadow, so fascinated with all the God-signs and miracles that he wouldn't leave Philip's side.

14-17   When the apostles in Jerusalem received the report that Samaria had accepted God's Message, they sent Peter and John down to pray for them to receive the Holy Spirit. Up to this point they had only been baptized in the name of the Master Jesus; the Holy Spirit hadn't yet fallen on them. Then the apostles laid their hands on them and they did receive the Holy Spirit.

18-19 When Simon saw that the apostles by merely laying on hands conferred the Spirit, he pulled out his money, excited, and said, "Sell me your secret! Show me how you did that! How much do you want? Name your price!"

20-23 Peter said, "To hell with your money! And you along with it. Why, that's unthinkable — trying to buy God's gift! You'll never be part of what God is doing by striking bargains and offering bribes. Change your ways — and now! Ask the Master to forgive you for trying to use God to make money. I can see this is an old habit with you; you reek with money-lust."

24 "Oh!" said Simon, "pray for me! Pray to the Master that nothing like that will ever happen to me!"

25 And with that, the apostles were on their way, continuing to witness and spread the Message of God's salvation, preaching in every Samaritan town they passed through on their return to Jerusalem.

THE ETHIOPIAN EUNUCH

26-28 Later God's angel spoke to Philip: "At noon today I want you to walk over to that desolate road that goes from Jerusalem down to Gaza." He got up and went. He met an Ethiopian eunuch coming down the road. The eunuch had been on a pilgrimage to Jerusalem and was returning to Ethiopia, where he was minister in charge of all the finances of Candace, queen of the Ethiopians. He was riding in a chariot and reading the prophet Isaiah.

29-30 The Spirit told Philip, "Climb into the chariot." Running up alongside, Philip heard the eunuch reading Isaiah and asked, "Do you understand what you're reading?"

31-33 He answered, "How can I without some help?" and invited Philip into the chariot with him. The passage he was reading was this:

> As a sheep led to slaughter,
>   and quiet as a lamb being sheared,
> He was silent, saying nothing.
>   He was mocked and put down, never got a fair trial.
> But who now can count his kin
>   since he's been taken from the earth?

34-35 The eunuch said, "Tell me, who is the prophet talking about: himself or some other?" Philip grabbed his chance. Using this passage as his text, he preached Jesus to him.

36-39 As they continued down the road, they came to a stream of water. The eunuch said, "Here's water. Why can't I be baptized?" He ordered the chariot to stop. They both went down to the water, and Philip baptized him on the spot. When they came up out of the water, the Spirit of God suddenly took Philip off, and that was the last the eunuch saw of him. But he didn't mind. He had what he'd come for and went on down the road as happy as he could be.

40 Philip showed up in Azotus and continued north, preaching the Message in all the villages along that route until he arrived at Caesarea.

1-2 **9** All this time Saul was breathing down the necks of the Master's disciples, out for the kill. He went to the Chief Priest and got arrest warrants to take to the meeting places in Damascus so that if he found anyone there belonging to the Way, whether men or women, he could arrest them and bring them to Jerusalem.

3-4 He set off. When he got to the outskirts of Damascus, he was suddenly dazed by a blinding flash of light. As he fell to the ground, he heard a voice: "Saul, Saul, why are you out to get me?"

5-6 He said, "Who are you, Master?"

"I am Jesus, the One you're hunting down. I want you to get up and enter the city. In the city you'll be told what to do next."

7-9 His companions stood there dumbstruck — they could hear the sound, but couldn't see anyone — while Saul, picking himself up off the ground, found himself stone-blind. They had to take him by the hand and lead him into Damascus. He continued blind for three days. He ate nothing, drank nothing.

10 There was a disciple in Damascus by the name of Ananias. The Master spoke to him in a vision: "Ananias."

"Yes, Master?" he answered.

11-12 "Get up and go over to Straight Avenue. Ask at the house of Judas for a man from Tarsus. His name is Saul. He's there praying. He has just had a dream in which he saw a man named Ananias enter the house and lay hands on him so he could see again."

13-14 Ananias protested, "Master, you can't be serious. Everybody's talking about this man and the terrible things he's been doing, his reign of terror against your people in Jerusalem! And now he's shown up here with papers from the Chief Priest that give him license to do the same to us."

15-16 But the Master said, "Don't argue. Go! I have picked him as my personal representative to non-Jews and kings and Jews. And now I'm about to show him what he's in for — the hard suffering that goes with this job."

17-19 So Ananias went and found the house, placed his hands on blind Saul, and said, "Brother Saul, the Master sent me, the same Jesus you saw on your way here. He sent me so you could see again and be filled with the Holy Spirit." No sooner were the words out of his mouth than something like scales fell from Saul's eyes — he could see again! He got to his feet, was baptized, and sat down with them to a hearty meal.

PLOTS AGAINST SAUL

19-21 Saul spent a few days getting acquainted with the Damascus disciples, but then went right to work, wasting no time, preaching in the meeting places that this Jesus was the Son of God. They were caught off guard by this and, not at all sure they could trust him, they kept saying, "Isn't this the man who wreaked havoc in Jerusalem among the believers? And didn't he come here to do the same thing — arrest us and drag us off to jail in Jerusalem for sentencing by the high priests?"

22 But their suspicions didn't slow Saul down for even a minute. His momentum was up now and he plowed straight into the opposition, disarming the Damascus Jews and trying to show them that this Jesus was the Messiah.

23-25 After this had gone on quite a long time, some Jews conspired to kill him, but Saul got wind of it. They were watching the city gates around the clock so they could kill him. Then one night the disciples engineered his escape by lowering him over the wall in a basket.

26-27 Back in Jerusalem he tried to join the disciples, but they were all afraid of him. They didn't trust him one bit. Then Barnabas took him under his wing. He introduced him to the apostles and stood up for him, told them how Saul had seen and spoken to the Master on the Damascus Road and how in Damascus itself he had laid his life on the line with his bold preaching in Jesus' name.

28-30 After that he was accepted as one of them, going in and out of Jerusalem with no questions asked, uninhibited as he preached in the Master's name. But then he ran afoul of a group called Hellenists — he had been engaged in a running argument with them — who plotted his murder. When his friends learned of the plot, they got him out of town, took him to Caesarea, and then shipped him off to Tarsus.

31 Things calmed down after that and the church had smooth sailing for a while. All over the country — Judea, Samaria, Galilee — the church grew. They were permeated with a deep sense of reverence for God. The Holy Spirit was with them, strengthening them. They prospered wonderfully.

TABITHA

32-35 Peter went off on a mission to visit all the churches. In the course of his travels he arrived in Lydda and met with the believers there. He came across a man — his name was Aeneas — who had been in bed eight years paralyzed. Peter said, "Aeneas, Jesus Christ heals you. Get up and make your bed!" And he did it — jumped right out of bed. Everybody who lived in Lydda and Sharon saw him walking around and woke up to the fact that God was alive and active among them.

36-37 Down the road a way in Joppa there was a disciple named Tabitha, "Gazelle" in our language. She was well-known for doing good and helping out. During the time Peter was in the area she became sick and died. Her friends prepared her body for burial and put her in a cool room.

38-40 Some of the disciples had heard that Peter was visiting in nearby Lydda and sent two men to ask if he would be so kind as to come over. Peter got right up and went with them. They took him into the room where Tabitha's body was laid out. Her old friends, most of them widows, were in the room mourning. They showed Peter pieces of clothing the Gazelle had made while she was with them. Peter put the widows all out of the room. He knelt and prayed. Then he spoke directly to the body: "Tabitha, get up."

40-41 She opened her eyes. When she saw Peter, she sat up. He took her hand and helped her up. Then he called in the believers and widows, and presented her to them alive.

42-43 When this became known all over Joppa, many put their trust in the Master. Peter stayed on a long time in Joppa as a guest of Simon the Tanner.

PETER'S VISION

1-3 There was a man named Cornelius who lived in Caesarea, captain of the Italian Guard stationed there. He was a thoroughly good man. He had led everyone in his house to live worshipfully before God, was always helping people in need, and had the habit of prayer. One day about three o'clock in the afternoon he had a vision. An angel of God, as real as his next-door neighbor, came in and said, "Cornelius."

4-6 Cornelius stared hard, wondering if he was seeing things. Then he said, "What do you want, sir?"

The angel said, "Your prayers and neighborly acts have brought you to God's attention. Here's what you are to do. Send men to Joppa to get Simon, the one everyone calls Peter. He is staying with Simon the Tanner, whose house is down by the sea."

7-8 As soon as the angel was gone, Cornelius called two servants and one particularly devout soldier from the guard. He went over with them in great detail everything that had just happened, and then sent them off to Joppa.

9-13 The next day as the three travelers were approaching the town, Peter went out on the balcony to pray. It was about noon. Peter got hungry and started thinking about lunch. While lunch was being prepared, he fell into a trance. He saw the skies open up. Something that looked like a huge blanket lowered by ropes at its four corners settled on the ground. Every kind of animal and reptile and bird you could think of was on it. Then a voice came: "Go to it, Peter — kill and eat."

14 Peter said, "Oh, no, Lord. I've never so much as tasted food that was not kosher."

15 The voice came a second time: "If God says it's okay, it's okay."

16 This happened three times, and then the blanket was pulled back up into the skies.

17-20 As Peter, puzzled, sat there trying to figure out what it all meant, the men sent by Cornelius showed up at Simon's front door. They called in, asking if there was a Simon, also called Peter, staying there. Peter, lost in thought, didn't hear them, so the Spirit whispered to him, "Three men are knocking at the door looking for you. Get down there and go with them. Don't ask any questions. I sent them to get you."

21 Peter went down and said to the men, "I think I'm the man you're looking for. What's up?"

22-23 They said, "Captain Cornelius, a God-fearing man well-known for his fair play — ask any Jew in this part of the country — was commanded by a holy angel to get you and bring you to his house so he could hear what you had to say." Peter invited them in and made them feel at home.

GOD PLAYS NO FAVORITES

23-26 The next morning he got up and went with them. Some of his friends from Joppa went along. A day later they entered Caesarea. Cornelius was expecting them and had his relatives and close friends waiting with him. The minute Peter came through the door, Cornelius was up on his feet greeting him — and then down on his face worshiping him! Peter pulled him up and said, "None of that — I'm a man and only a man, no different from you."

27-29 Talking things over, they went on into the house, where Cornelius introduced Peter to everyone who had come. Peter addressed them, "You know, I'm sure that this is highly irregular. Jews just don't do this — visit and relax with people of another race. But God has just shown me that no race is better than any other. So the minute I was sent for, I came, no questions asked. But now I'd like to know why you sent for me."

30-32 Cornelius said, "Four days ago at about this time, midafternoon, I was home praying. Suddenly there was a man right in front of me, flooding the room with light. He said, 'Cornelius, your daily prayers and neighborly acts have brought you to God's attention. I want you to send to Joppa to get Simon, the one they call Peter. He's staying with Simon the Tanner down by the sea.'

33 "So I did it—I sent for you. And you've been good enough to come. And now we're all here in God's presence, ready to listen to whatever the Master put in your heart to tell us."

34-36 Peter fairly exploded with his good news: "It's God's own truth, nothing could be plainer: God plays no favorites! It makes no difference who you are or where you're from—if you want God and are ready to do as he says, the door is open. The Message he sent to the children of Israel—that through Jesus Christ everything is being put together again—well, he's doing it everywhere, among everyone.

37-38 "You know the story of what happened in Judea. It began in Galilee after John preached a total life-change. Then Jesus arrived from Nazareth, anointed by God with the Holy Spirit, ready for action. He went through the country helping people and healing everyone who was beaten down by the Devil. He was able to do all this because God was with him.

39-43 "And we saw it, saw it all, everything he did in the land of the Jews and in Jerusalem where they killed him, hung him from a cross. But in three days God had him up, alive, and out where he could be seen. Not everyone saw him—he wasn't put on public display. Witnesses had been carefully handpicked by God beforehand—us! We were the ones, there to eat and drink with him after he came back from the dead. He commissioned us to announce this in public, to bear solemn witness that he is in fact the One whom God destined as Judge of the living and dead. But we're not alone in this. Our witness that he is the means to forgiveness of sins is backed up by the witness of all the prophets."

44-46 No sooner were these words out of Peter's mouth than the Holy Spirit came on the listeners. The believing Jews who had come with Peter couldn't believe it, couldn't believe that the gift of the Holy Spirit was poured out on "outsider" non-Jews, but there it was—they heard them speaking in tongues, heard them praising God.

46-48 Then Peter said, "Do I hear any objections to baptizing these friends with water? They've received the Holy Spirit exactly as we did." Hearing no objections, he ordered that they be baptized in the name of Jesus Christ.

Then they asked Peter to stay on for a few days.

GOD HAS BROKEN THROUGH

1-3 **11** The news traveled fast and in no time the leaders and friends back in Jerusalem heard about it—heard that the non-Jewish "outsiders" were now "in." When Peter got back to Jerusalem, some of his old associates, concerned about circumcision, called him on the carpet: "What do you think you're doing rubbing shoulders with that crowd, eating what is prohibited and ruining our good name?"

4-6 So Peter, starting from the beginning, laid it out for them step-by-step: "Recently I was in the town of Joppa praying. I fell into a trance and saw a vision: Something like a huge blanket, lowered by ropes at its four corners, came down out of heaven and settled on the ground in front of me.

Milling around on the blanket were farm animals, wild animals, reptiles, birds — you name it, it was there. Fascinated, I took it all in.

7-10   "Then I heard a voice: 'Go to it, Peter — kill and eat.' I said, 'Oh, no, Master. I've never so much as tasted food that wasn't kosher.' The voice spoke again: 'If God says it's okay, it's okay.' This happened three times, and then the blanket was pulled back up into the sky.

11-14   "Just then three men showed up at the house where I was staying, sent from Caesarea to get me. The Spirit told me to go with them, no questions asked. So I went with them, I and six friends, to the man who had sent for me. He told us how he had seen an angel right in his own house, real as his next-door neighbor, saying, 'Send to Joppa and get Simon, the one they call Peter. He'll tell you something that will save your life — in fact, you and everyone you care for.'

15-17   "So I started in, talking. Before I'd spoken half a dozen sentences, the Holy Spirit fell on them just as he did on us the first time. I remembered Jesus' words: 'John baptized with water; you will be baptized with the Holy Spirit.' So I ask you: If God gave the same exact gift to them as to us when we believed in the Master Jesus Christ, how could I object to God?"

18   Hearing it all laid out like that, they quieted down. And then, as it sank in, they started praising God. "It's really happened! God has broken through to the other nations, opened them up to Life!"

19-21   Those who had been scattered by the persecution triggered by Stephen's death traveled as far as Phoenicia, Cyprus, and Antioch, but they were still only speaking and dealing with their fellow Jews. Then some of the men from Cyprus and Cyrene who had come to Antioch started talking to Greeks, giving them the Message of the Master Jesus. God was pleased with what they were doing and put his stamp of approval on it — quite a number of the Greeks believed and turned to the Master.

22-24   When the church in Jerusalem got wind of this, they sent Barnabas to Antioch to check on things. As soon as he arrived, he saw that God was behind and in it all. He threw himself in with them, got behind them, urging them to stay with it the rest of their lives. He was a good man that way, enthusiastic and confident in the Holy Spirit's ways. The community grew large and strong in the Master.

25-26   Then Barnabas went on to Tarsus to look for Saul. He found him and brought him back to Antioch. They were there a whole year, meeting with the church and teaching a lot of people. It was in Antioch that the disciples were for the first time called Christians.

27-30   It was about this same time that some prophets came to Antioch from Jerusalem. One of them named Agabus stood up one day and, prompted by the Spirit, warned that a severe famine was about to devastate the country. (The famine eventually came during the rule of Claudius.) So the disciples decided that each of them would send whatever they could to their fellow Christians in Judea to help out. They sent Barnabas and Saul to deliver the collection to the leaders in Jerusalem.

PETER UNDER HEAVY GUARD

1-4   **12** That's when King Herod got it into his head to go after some of the church members. He murdered James, John's brother. When he saw how much it raised his popularity ratings with the Jews, he arrested Peter — all this during Passover Week, mind you — and had him thrown in jail, putting four squads of four soldiers each to guard him. He was planning a public lynching after Passover.

5 All the time that Peter was under heavy guard in the jailhouse, the church prayed for him most strenuously.

6 Then the time came for Herod to bring him out for the kill. That night, even though shackled to two soldiers, one on either side, Peter slept like a baby. And there were guards at the door keeping their eyes on the place. Herod was taking no chances!

7-9 Suddenly there was an angel at his side and light flooding the room. The angel shook Peter and got him up: "Hurry!" The handcuffs fell off his wrists. The angel said, "Get dressed. Put on your shoes." Peter did it. Then, "Grab your coat and let's get out of here." Peter followed him, but didn't believe it was really an angel — he thought he was dreaming.

10-11 Past the first guard and then the second, they came to the iron gate that led into the city. It swung open before them on its own, and they were out on the street, free as the breeze. At the first intersection the angel left him, going his own way. That's when Peter realized it was no dream. "I can't believe it — this really happened! The Master sent his angel and rescued me from Herod's vicious little production and the spectacle the Jewish mob was looking forward to."

12-14 Still shaking his head, amazed, he went to Mary's house, the Mary who was John Mark's mother. The house was packed with praying friends. When he knocked on the door to the courtyard, a young woman named Rhoda came to see who it was. But when she recognized his voice — Peter's voice! — she was so excited and eager to tell everyone Peter was there that she forgot to open the door and left him standing in the street.

15-16 But they wouldn't believe her, dismissing her, dismissing her report. "You're crazy," they said. She stuck by her story, insisting. They still wouldn't believe her and said, "It must be his angel." All this time poor Peter was standing out in the street, knocking away.

16-17 Finally they opened up and saw him — and went wild! Peter put his hands up and calmed them down. He described how the Master had gotten him out of jail, then said, "Tell James and the brothers what's happened." He left them and went off to another place.

18-19 At daybreak the jail was in an uproar. "Where is Peter? What's happened to Peter?" When Herod sent for him and they could neither produce him nor explain why not, he ordered their execution: "Off with their heads!" Fed up with Judea and Jews, he went for a vacation to Caesarea.

THE DEATH OF HEROD

20-22 But things went from bad to worse for Herod. Now people from Tyre and Sidon put him on the warpath. But they got Blastus, King Herod's right-hand man, to put in a good word for them and got a delegation together to iron things out. Because they were dependent on Judea for food supplies, they couldn't afford to let this go on too long. On the day set for their meeting, Herod, robed in pomposity, took his place on the throne and regaled them with a lot of hot air. The people played their part to the hilt and shouted flatteries: "The voice of God! The voice of God!"

23 That was the last straw. God had had enough of Herod's arrogance and sent an angel to strike him down. Herod had given God no credit for anything. Down he went. Rotten to the core, a maggoty old man if there

ever was one, he died.

24　　Meanwhile, the ministry of God's Word grew by leaps and bounds.

25　　Barnabas and Saul, once they had delivered the relief offering to the church in Jerusalem, went back to Antioch. This time they took John with them, the one they called Mark.

BARNABAS, SAUL, AND DOCTOR KNOW-IT-ALL

1-2　**13** The congregation in Antioch was blessed with a number of prophet-preachers and teachers:

Barnabas,
Simon, nicknamed Niger,
Lucius the Cyrenian,
Manaen, an advisor to the ruler Herod,
Saul.

One day as they were worshiping God—they were also fasting as they waited for guidance—the Holy Spirit spoke: "Take Barnabas and Saul and commission them for the work I have called them to do."

3　　So they commissioned them. In that circle of intensity and obedience, of fasting and praying, they laid hands on their heads and sent them off.

4-5　　Sent off on their new assignment by the Holy Spirit, Barnabas and Saul went down to Seleucia and caught a ship for Cyprus. The first thing they did when they put in at Salamis was preach God's Word in the Jewish meeting places. They had John along to help out as needed.

6-7　　They traveled the length of the island, and at Paphos came upon a Jewish wizard who had worked himself into the confidence of the governor, Sergius Paulus, an intelligent man not easily taken in by charlatans. The wizard's name was Bar-Jesus. He was as crooked as a corkscrew.

7-11　　The governor invited Barnabas and Saul in, wanting to hear God's Word firsthand from them. But Dr. Know-It-All (that's the wizard's name in plain English) stirred up a ruckus, trying to divert the governor from becoming a believer. But Saul (or Paul), full of the Holy Spirit and looking him straight in the eye, said, "You bag of wind, you parody of a devil—why, you stay up nights inventing schemes to cheat people out of God. But now you've come up against God himself, and your game is up. You're about to go blind—no sunlight for you for a good long stretch." He was plunged immediately into a shadowy mist and stumbled around, begging people to take his hand and show him the way.

12　　When the governor saw what happened, he became a believer, full of enthusiasm over what they were saying about the Master.

DON'T TAKE THIS LIGHTLY

13-14　From Paphos, Paul and company put out to sea, sailing on to Perga in Pamphylia. That's where John called it quits and went back to Jerusalem. From Perga the rest of them traveled on to Antioch in Pisidia.

14-15　　On the Sabbath they went to the meeting place and took their places. After the reading of the Scriptures—God's Law and the Prophets—the president of the meeting asked them, "Friends, do you have anything you want to say? A word of encouragement, perhaps?"

16-20   Paul stood up, paused and took a deep breath, then said, "Fellow Israelites and friends of God, listen. God took a special interest in our ancestors, pulled our people who were beaten down in Egyptian exile to their feet, and led them out of there in grand style. He took good care of them for nearly forty years in that godforsaken wilderness and then, having wiped out seven enemies who stood in the way, gave them the land of Canaan for their very own—a span in all of about 450 years.

20-22   "Up to the time of Samuel the prophet, God provided judges to lead them. But then they asked for a king, and God gave them Saul, son of Kish, out of the tribe of Benjamin. After Saul had ruled forty years, God removed him from office and put King David in his place, with this commendation: 'I've searched the land and found this David, son of Jesse. He's a man whose heart beats to my heart, a man who will do what I tell him.'

23-25   "From out of David's descendants God produced a Savior for Israel, Jesus, exactly as he promised—but only after John had thoroughly alerted the people to his arrival by preparing them for a total life-change. As John was finishing up his work, he said, 'Did you think I was the One? No, I'm not the One. But the One you've been waiting for all these years is just around the corner, about to appear. And I'm about to disappear.'

26-29   "Dear brothers and sisters, children of Abraham, and friends of God, this message of salvation has been precisely targeted to you. The citizens and rulers in Jerusalem didn't recognize who he was and condemned him to death. They couldn't find a good reason, but demanded that Pilate execute him anyway. They did just what the prophets said they would do, but had no idea they were following to the letter the script of the prophets, even though those same prophets are read every Sabbath in their meeting places.

29-31   "After they had done everything the prophets said they would do, they took him down from the cross and buried him. And then God raised him from death. There is no disputing that—he appeared over and over again many times and places to those who had known him well in the Galilean years, and these same people continue to give witness that he is alive.

32-35   "And we're here today bringing you good news: the Message that what God promised the fathers has come true for the children—for us! He raised Jesus, exactly as described in the second Psalm:

My Son! My very own Son!
Today I celebrate you!

"When he raised him from the dead, he did it for good—no going back to that rot and decay for him. That's why Isaiah said, 'I'll give to all of you David's guaranteed blessings.' So also the psalmist's prayer: 'You'll never let your Holy One see death's rot and decay.'

36-39   "David, of course, having completed the work God set out for him, has been in the grave, dust and ashes, a long time now. But the One God raised up—no dust and ashes for him! I want you to know, my very dear friends, that it is on account of this resurrected Jesus that the forgiveness of your sins can be promised. He accomplishes, in those who believe, everything that the Law of Moses could never make good on. But everyone who believes in this raised-up Jesus is declared good and right and whole before God.

40-41   "Don't take this lightly. You don't want the prophet's sermon to describe you:

> Watch out, cynics;
> Look hard — watch your world fall to pieces.
> I'm doing something right before your eyes
> That you won't believe, though it's staring you in the face."

42-43 When the service was over, Paul and Barnabas were invited back to preach again the next Sabbath. As the meeting broke up, a good many Jews and converts to Judaism went along with Paul and Barnabas, who urged them in long conversations to stick with what they'd started, this living in and by God's grace.

44-45 When the next Sabbath came around, practically the whole city showed up to hear the Word of God. Some of the Jews, seeing the crowds, went wild with jealousy and tore into Paul, contradicting everything he was saying, making an ugly scene.

46-47 But Paul and Barnabas didn't back down. Standing their ground they said, "It was required that God's Word be spoken first of all to you, the Jews. But seeing that you want no part of it — you've made it quite clear that you have no taste or inclination for eternal life — the door is open to all the outsiders. And we're on our way through it, following orders, doing what God commanded when he said,

> I've set you up
>   as light to all nations.
> You'll proclaim salvation
>   to the four winds and seven seas!"

48-49 When the non-Jewish outsiders heard this, they could hardly believe their good fortune. All who were marked out for *real life* put their trust in God — they honored God's Word by receiving that life. And this Message of salvation spread like wildfire all through the region.

50-52 Some of the Jews convinced the most respected women and leading men of the town that their precious way of life was about to be destroyed. Alarmed, they turned on Paul and Barnabas and forced them to leave. Paul and Barnabas shrugged their shoulders and went on to the next town, Iconium, brimming with joy and the Holy Spirit, two happy disciples.

1-3 **14** When they got to Iconium they went, as they always did, to the meeting place of the Jews and gave their message. The Message convinced both Jews and non-Jews — and not just a few, either. But the unbelieving Jews worked up a whispering campaign against Paul and Barnabas, sowing mistrust and suspicion in the minds of the people in the street. The two apostles were there a long time, speaking freely, openly, and confidently as they presented the clear evidence of God's gifts, God corroborating their work with miracles and wonders.

4-7 But then there was a split in public opinion, some siding with the Jews, some with the apostles. One day, learning that both the Jews and non-Jews had been organized by their leaders to beat them up, they escaped as best they could to the next towns — Lyconia, Lystra, Derbe, and that neighborhood — but then were right back at it again, getting out the Message.

GODS OR MEN?

8-10 There was a man in Lystra who couldn't walk. He sat there, crippled since the day of his birth. He heard Paul talking, and Paul, looking him in the eye, saw that he was ripe for God's work, ready to believe. So he said, loud enough for everyone to hear, "Up on your feet!" The man was up in a flash—jumped up and walked around as if he'd been walking all his life.

11-13 When the crowd saw what Paul had done, they went wild, calling out in their Lyconian dialect, "The gods have come down! These men are gods!" They called Barnabas "Zeus" and Paul "Hermes" (since Paul did most of the speaking). The priest of the local Zeus shrine got up a parade—bulls and banners and people lined right up to the gates, ready for the ritual of sacrifice.

14-15 When Barnabas and Paul finally realized what was going on, they stopped them. Waving their arms, they interrupted the parade, calling out, "What do you think you're doing! We're not gods! We are men just like you, and we're here to bring you the Message, to persuade you to abandon these silly god-superstitions and embrace God himself, the living God. We don't make God; he makes us, and all of this—sky, earth, sea, and everything in them.

16-18 "In the generations before us, God let all the different nations go their own way. But even then he didn't leave them without a clue, for he made a good creation, poured down rain and gave bumper crops. When your bellies were full and your hearts happy, there was evidence of good beyond your doing." Talking fast and hard like this, they prevented them from carrying out the sacrifice that would have honored them as gods—but just barely.

19-20 Then some Jews from Antioch and Iconium caught up with them and turned the fickle crowd against them. They beat Paul unconscious, dragged him outside the town and left him for dead. But as the disciples gathered around him, he came to and got up. He went back into town and the next day left with Barnabas for Derbe.

PLENTY OF HARD TIMES

21-22 After proclaiming the Message in Derbe and establishing a strong core of disciples, they retraced their steps to Lystra, then Iconium, and then Antioch, putting muscle and sinew in the lives of the disciples, urging them to stick with what they had begun to believe and not quit, making it clear to them that it wouldn't be easy: "Anyone signing up for the kingdom of God has to go through plenty of hard times."

23-26 Paul and Barnabas handpicked leaders in each church. After praying—their prayers intensified by fasting—they presented these new leaders to the Master to whom they had entrusted their lives. Working their way back through Pisidia, they came to Pamphylia and preached in Perga. Finally, they made it to Attalia and caught a ship back to Antioch, where it had all started—launched by God's grace and now safely home by God's grace. A good piece of work.

27-28 On arrival, they got the church together and reported on their trip, telling in detail how God had used them to throw the door of faith wide open so people of all nations could come streaming in. Then they settled down for a long, leisurely visit with the disciples.

To Let Outsiders Inside

1-2 It wasn't long before some Jews showed up from Judea insisting that everyone be circumcised: "If you're not circumcised in the Mosaic fashion, you can't be saved." Paul and Barnabas were up on their feet at once in fierce protest. The church decided to resolve the matter by sending Paul, Barnabas, and a few others to put it before the apostles and leaders in Jerusalem.

3 After they were sent off and on their way, they told everyone they met as they traveled through Phoenicia and Samaria about the breakthrough to the non-Jewish outsiders. Everyone who heard the news cheered—it was terrific news!

4-5 When they got to Jerusalem, Paul and Barnabas were graciously received by the whole church, including the apostles and leaders. They reported on their recent journey and how God had used them to open things up to the outsiders. Some Pharisees stood up to say their piece. They had become believers, but continued to hold to the hard party line of the Pharisees. "You have to circumcise the pagan converts," they said. "You must make them keep the Law of Moses."

6-9 The apostles and leaders called a special meeting to consider the matter. The arguments went on and on, back and forth, getting more and more heated. Then Peter took the floor: "Friends, you well know that from early on God made it quite plain that he wanted the pagans to hear the Message of this good news and embrace it—and not in any secondhand or roundabout way, but firsthand, straight from my mouth. And God, who can't be fooled by any pretense on our part but always knows a person's thoughts, gave them the Holy Spirit exactly as he gave him to us. He treated the outsiders exactly as he treated us, beginning at the very center of who they were and working from that center outward, cleaning up their lives as they trusted and believed him.

10-11 "So why are you now trying to out-god God, loading these new believers down with rules that crushed our ancestors and crushed us, too? Don't we believe that we are saved because the Master Jesus amazingly and out of sheer generosity moved to save us just as he did those from beyond our nation? So what are we arguing about?"

12-13 There was dead silence. No one said a word. With the room quiet, Barnabas and Paul reported matter-of-factly on the miracles and wonders God had done among the other nations through their ministry. The silence deepened; you could hear a pin drop.

13-18 James broke the silence. "Friends, listen. Simeon has told us the story of how God at the very outset made sure that racial outsiders were included. This is in perfect agreement with the words of the prophets:

> After this, I'm coming back;
>   I'll rebuild David's ruined house;
> I'll put all the pieces together again;
>   I'll make it look like new
> So outsiders who seek will find,
>   so they'll have a place to come to,
> All the pagan peoples
>   included in what I'm doing.

"God said it and now he's doing it. It's no afterthought; he's always known he would do this.

19-21   "So here is my decision: We're not going to unnecessarily burden non-Jewish people who turn to the Master. We'll write them a letter and tell them, 'Be careful to not get involved in activities connected with idols, to guard the morality of sex and marriage, to not serve food offensive to Jewish Christians—blood, for instance.' This is basic wisdom from Moses, preached and honored for centuries now in city after city as we have met and kept the Sabbath."

22-23   Everyone agreed: apostles, leaders, all the people. They picked Judas (nicknamed Barsabbas) and Silas—they both carried considerable weight in the church—and sent them to Antioch with Paul and Barnabas with this letter:

> From the apostles and leaders, your friends, to our friends in Antioch, Syria, and Cilicia:
> Hello!

24-27   We heard that some men from our church went to you and said things that confused and upset you. Mind you, they had no authority from us; we didn't send them. We have agreed unanimously to pick representatives and send them to you with our good friends Barnabas and Paul. We picked men we knew you could trust, Judas and Silas — they've looked death in the face time and again for the sake of our Master Jesus Christ. We've sent them to confirm in a face-to-face meeting with you what we've written.

28-29   It seemed to the Holy Spirit and to us that you should not be saddled with any crushing burden, but be responsible only for these bare necessities: Be careful not to get involved in activities connected with idols; avoid serving food offensive to Jewish Christians (blood, for instance); and guard the morality of sex and marriage.

These guidelines are sufficient to keep relations congenial between us. And God be with you!

BARNABAS AND PAUL GO THEIR SEPARATE WAYS

30-33   And so off they went to Antioch. On arrival, they gathered the church and read the letter. The people were greatly relieved and pleased. Judas and Silas, good preachers both of them, strengthened their new friends with many words of courage and hope. Then it was time to go home. They were sent off by their new friends with laughter and embraces all around to report back to those who had sent them.

35   Paul and Barnabas stayed on in Antioch, teaching and preaching the Word of God. But they weren't alone. There were a number of teachers and preachers at that time in Antioch.

36   After a few days of this, Paul said to Barnabas, "Let's go back and visit all our friends in each of the towns where we preached the Word of God. Let's see how they're doing."

37-41   Barnabas wanted to take John along, the John nicknamed Mark. But Paul wouldn't have him; he wasn't about to take along a quitter who, as soon as the going got tough, had jumped ship on them in Pamphylia. Tempers flared, and they ended up going their separate ways: Barnabas took Mark and sailed for Cyprus; Paul chose Silas and, offered up by their friends to the grace of the Master, went to Syria and Cilicia to build up muscle and sinew in those congregations.

A DREAM GAVE PAUL HIS MAP

1-3   **16** Paul came first to Derbe, then Lystra. He found a disciple there by the name of Timothy, son of a devout Jewish mother and Greek father. Friends in Lystra and Iconium all said what a fine young man he was. Paul wanted to recruit him for their mission, but first took him aside and circumcised him so he wouldn't offend the Jews who lived in those parts. They all knew that his father was Greek.

4-5   As they traveled from town to town, they presented the simple guidelines the Jerusalem apostles and leaders had come up with. That turned out to be most helpful. Day after day the congregations became stronger in faith and larger in size.

6-8   They went to Phrygia, and then on through the region of Galatia. Their plan was to turn west into Asia province, but the Holy Spirit blocked that route. So they went to Mysia and tried to go north to Bithynia, but the Spirit of Jesus wouldn't let them go there either. Proceeding on through Mysia, they went down to the seaport Troas.

9-10   That night Paul had a dream: A Macedonian stood on the far shore and called across the sea, "Come over to Macedonia and help us!" The dream gave Paul his map. We went to work at once getting things ready to cross over to Macedonia. All the pieces had come together. We knew now for sure that God had called us to preach the good news to the Europeans.

11-12   Putting out from the harbor at Troas, we made a straight run for Samothrace. The next day we tied up at New City and walked from there to Philippi, the main city in that part of Macedonia and, even more importantly, a Roman colony. We lingered there several days.

13-14   On the Sabbath, we left the city and went down along the river where we had heard there was to be a prayer meeting. We took our place with the women who had gathered there and talked with them. One woman, Lydia, was from Thyatira and a dealer in expensive textiles, known to be a God-fearing woman. As she listened with intensity to what was being said, the Master gave her a trusting heart — and she believed!

15   After she was baptized, along with everyone in her household, she said in a surge of hospitality, "If you're confident that I'm in this with you and believe in the Master truly, come home with me and be my guests." We hesitated, but she wouldn't take no for an answer.

BEAT UP AND THROWN IN JAIL

16-18   One day, on our way to the place of prayer, a slave girl ran into us. She was a psychic and, with her fortunetelling, made a lot of money for the people who owned her. She started following Paul around, calling everyone's attention to us by yelling out, "These men are working for the Most High God. They're laying out the road of salvation for you!" She did this for a number of days until Paul, finally fed up with her, turned and commanded the spirit that possessed her, "Out! In the name of Jesus Christ, get out of her!" And it was gone, just like that.

19-22   When her owners saw that their lucrative little business was suddenly bankrupt, they went after Paul and Silas, roughed them up and dragged them into the market square. Then the police arrested them and pulled them into a court with the accusation, "These men are disturbing the peace — dangerous Jewish agitators subverting our Roman law and order." By this time the crowd had turned into a restless mob out for blood.

22-24 The judges went along with the mob, had Paul and Silas's clothes ripped off and ordered a public beating. After beating them black-and-blue, they threw them into jail, telling the jailkeeper to put them under heavy guard so there would be no chance of escape. He did just that — threw them into the maximum security cell in the jail and clamped leg irons on them.

25-26 Along about midnight, Paul and Silas were at prayer and singing a robust hymn to God. The other prisoners couldn't believe their ears. Then, without warning, a huge earthquake! The jailhouse tottered, every door flew open, all the prisoners were loose.

27-28 Startled from sleep, the jailer saw all the doors swinging loose on their hinges. Assuming that all the prisoners had escaped, he pulled out his sword and was about to do himself in, figuring he was as good as dead anyway, when Paul stopped him: "Don't do that! We're all still here! Nobody's run away!"

29-31 The jailer got a torch and ran inside. Badly shaken, he collapsed in front of Paul and Silas. He led them out of the jail and asked, "Sirs, what do I have to do to be saved, to really live?" They said, "Put your entire trust in the Master Jesus. Then you'll live as you were meant to live — and everyone in your house included!"

32-34 They went on to spell out in detail the story of the Master — the entire family got in on this part. They never did get to bed that night. The jailer made them feel at home, dressed their wounds, and then — he couldn't wait till morning! — was baptized, he and everyone in his family. There in his home, he had food set out for a festive meal. It was a night to remember: He and his entire family had put their trust in God; everyone in the house was in on the celebration.

35-36 At daybreak, the court judges sent officers with the instructions, "Release these men." The jailer gave Paul the message, "The judges sent word that you're free to go on your way. Congratulations! Go in peace!"

37 But Paul wouldn't budge. He told the officers, "They beat us up in public and threw us in jail, Roman citizens in good standing! And now they want to get us out of the way on the sly without anyone knowing? Nothing doing! If they want us out of here, let them come themselves and lead us out in broad daylight."

38-40 When the officers reported this, the judges panicked. They had no idea that Paul and Silas were Roman citizens. They hurried over and apologized, personally escorted them from the jail, and then asked them if they wouldn't please leave the city. Walking out of the jail, Paul and Silas went straight to Lydia's house, saw their friends again, encouraged them in the faith, and only then went on their way.

THESSALONICA

1-3 **17** They took the road south through Amphipolis and Apollonia to Thessalonica, where there was a community of Jews. Paul went to their meeting place, as he usually did when he came to a town, and for three Sabbaths running he preached to them from the Scriptures. He opened up the texts so they understood what they'd been reading all their lives: that the Messiah absolutely *had* to be put to death and raised from the dead — there were no other options — and that "this Jesus I'm introducing you to is that Messiah."

4-5   Some of them were won over and joined ranks with Paul and Silas, among them a great many God-fearing Greeks and a considerable number of women from the aristocracy. But the hard-line Jews became furious over the conversions. Mad with jealousy, they rounded up a bunch of brawlers off the streets and soon had an ugly mob terrorizing the city as they hunted down Paul and Silas.

5-7   They broke into Jason's house, thinking that Paul and Silas were there. When they couldn't find them, they collared Jason and his friends instead and dragged them before the city fathers, yelling hysterically, "These people are out to destroy the world, and now they've shown up on our doorstep, attacking everything we hold dear! And Jason is hiding them, these traitors and turncoats who say Jesus is king and Caesar is nothing!"

8-9   The city fathers and the crowd of people were totally alarmed by what they heard. They made Jason and his friends post heavy bail and let them go while they investigated the charges.

BEREA

10-12   That night, under cover of darkness, their friends got Paul and Silas out of town as fast as they could. They sent them to Berea, where they again met with the Jewish community. They were treated a lot better there than in Thessalonica. The Jews received Paul's message with enthusiasm and met with him daily, examining the Scriptures to see if they supported what he said. A lot of them became believers, including many Greeks who were prominent in the community, women and men of influence.

13-15   But it wasn't long before reports got back to the Thessalonian hard-line Jews that Paul was at it again, preaching the Word of God, this time in Berea. They lost no time responding, and created a mob scene there, too. With the help of his friends, Paul gave them the slip — caught a boat and put out to sea. Silas and Timothy stayed behind. The men who helped Paul escape got him as far as Athens and left him there. Paul sent word back with them to Silas and Timothy: "Come as quickly as you can!"

ATHENS

16   The longer Paul waited in Athens for Silas and Timothy, the angrier he got — all those idols! The city was a junkyard of idols.

17-18   He discussed it with the Jews and other like-minded people at their meeting place. And every day he went out on the streets and talked with anyone who happened along. He got to know some of the Epicurean and Stoic intellectuals pretty well through these conversations. Some of them dismissed him with sarcasm: "What an airhead!" But others, listening to him go on about Jesus and the resurrection, were intrigued: "That's a new slant on the gods. Tell us more."

19-21   These people got together and asked him to make a public presentation over at the Areopagus, where things were a little quieter. They said, "This is a new one on us. We've never heard anything quite like it. Where did you come up with this anyway? Explain it so we can understand." Downtown Athens was a great place for gossip. There were always people hanging around, natives and tourists alike, waiting for the latest tidbit on most anything.

22-23   So Paul took his stand in the open space at the Areopagus and laid it out for them. "It is plain to see that you Athenians take your religion seriously. When I arrived here the other day, I was fascinated with all the shrines I came across. And then I found one inscribed, TO THE GOD NOBODY KNOWS. I'm here to introduce you to this God so you can worship intelligently, know who you're dealing with.

24-29   "The God who made the world and everything in it, this Master of sky and land, doesn't live in custom-made shrines or need the human race to run errands for him, as if he couldn't take care of himself. He makes the creatures; the creatures don't make him. Starting from scratch, he made the entire human race and made the earth hospitable, with plenty of time and space for living so we could seek after God, and not just grope around in the dark but actually *find* him. He doesn't play hide-and-seek with us. He's not remote; he's *near*. We live and move in him, can't get away from him! One of your poets said it well: 'We're the God-created.' Well, if we are the God-created, it doesn't make a lot of sense to think we could hire a sculptor to chisel a god out of stone for *us*, does it?

30-31   "God overlooks it as long as you don't know any better—but that time is past. The unknown is now known, and he's calling for a radical life-change. He has set a day when the entire human race will be judged and everything set right. And he has already appointed the judge, confirming him before everyone by raising him from the dead."

32-34   At the phrase "raising him from the dead," the listeners split: Some laughed at him and walked off making jokes; others said, "Let's do this again. We want to hear more." But that was it for the day, and Paul left. There were still others, it turned out, who were convinced then and there, and stuck with Paul—among them Dionysius the Areopagite and a woman named Damaris.

CORINTH

1-4 **18** After Athens, Paul went to Corinth. That is where he discovered Aquila, a Jew born in Pontus, and his wife, Priscilla. They had just arrived from Italy, part of the general expulsion of Jews from Rome ordered by Claudius. Paul moved in with them, and they worked together at their common trade of tentmaking. But every Sabbath he was at the meeting place, doing his best to convince both Jews and Greeks about Jesus.

5-6   When Silas and Timothy arrived from Macedonia, Paul was able to give all his time to preaching and teaching, doing everything he could to persuade the Jews that Jesus was in fact God's Messiah. But no such luck. All they did was argue contentiously and contradict him at every turn. Totally exasperated, Paul had finally had it with them and gave it up as a bad job. "Have it your way, then," he said. "You've made your bed; now lie in it. From now on I'm spending my time with the other nations."

7-8   He walked out and went to the home of Titius Justus, a God-fearing man who lived right next to the Jews' meeting place. But Paul's efforts with the Jews weren't a total loss, for Crispus, the meeting-place president, put his trust in the Master. His entire family believed with him.

8-11   In the course of listening to Paul, a great many Corinthians believed and were baptized. One night the Master spoke to Paul in a dream: "Keep it up, and don't let anyone intimidate or silence you. No matter what happens, I'm with you and no one is going to be able to hurt you. You have no idea how many people I have on my side in this city." That was all he needed to stick it out. He stayed another year and a half, faithfully teaching the Word of God to the Corinthians.

12-13　　But when Gallio was governor of Achaia province, the Jews got up a campaign against Paul, hauled him into court, and filed charges: "This man is seducing people into acts of worship that are illegal."

14-16　　Just as Paul was about to defend himself, Gallio interrupted and said to the Jews, "If this was a matter of criminal conduct, I would gladly hear you out. But it sounds to me like one more Jewish squabble, another of your endless hairsplitting quarrels over religion. Take care of it on your own time. I can't be bothered with this nonsense," and he cleared them out of the courtroom.

17　　Now the street rabble turned on Sosthenes, the new meeting-place president, and beat him up in plain sight of the court. Gallio didn't raise a finger. He could not have cared less.

EPHESUS

18　　Paul stayed a while longer in Corinth, but then it was time to take leave of his friends. Saying his good-byes, he sailed for Syria, Priscilla and Aquila with him. Before boarding the ship in the harbor town of Cenchrea, he had his head shaved as part of a vow he had taken.

19-21　　They landed in Ephesus, where Priscilla and Aquila got off and stayed. Paul left the ship briefly to go to the meeting place and preach to the Jews. They wanted him to stay longer, but he said he couldn't. But after saying good-bye, he promised, "I'll be back, God willing."

21-22　　From Ephesus he sailed to Caesarea. He greeted the church there, and then went on to Antioch, completing the journey.

23　　After spending a considerable time with the Antioch Christians, Paul set off again for Galatia and Phrygia, retracing his old tracks, one town after another, putting fresh heart into the disciples.

24-26　　A man named Apollos came to Ephesus. He was a Jew, born in Alexandria, Egypt, and a terrific speaker, eloquent and powerful in his preaching of the Scriptures. He was well-educated in the way of the Master and fiery in his enthusiasm. Apollos was accurate in everything he taught about Jesus up to a point, but he only went as far as the baptism of John. He preached with power in the meeting place. When Priscilla and Aquila heard him, they took him aside and told him the rest of the story.

27-28　　When Apollos decided to go on to Achaia province, his Ephesian friends gave their blessing and wrote a letter of recommendation for him, urging the disciples there to welcome him with open arms. The welcome paid off: Apollos turned out to be a great help to those who had become believers through God's immense generosity. He was particularly effective in public debate with the Jews as he brought out proof after convincing proof from the Scriptures that Jesus was in fact God's Messiah.

1-2　　**19** Now, it happened that while Apollos was away in Corinth, Paul made his way down through the mountains, came to Ephesus, and happened on some disciples there. The first thing he said was, "Did you receive the Holy Spirit when you believed? Did you take God into your mind only, or did you also embrace him with your heart? Did he get inside you?"

"We've never even heard of that—a Holy Spirit? God within us?"

3   "How were you baptized, then?" asked Paul.

"In John's baptism."

4   "That explains it," said Paul. "John preached a baptism of radical life-change so that people would be ready to receive the One coming after him, who turned out to be Jesus. If you've been baptized in John's baptism, you're ready now for the real thing, for Jesus."

5-7   And they were. As soon as they heard of it, they were baptized in the name of the Master Jesus. Paul put his hands on their heads and the Holy Spirit entered them. From that moment on, they were praising God in tongues and talking about God's actions. Altogether there were about twelve people there that day.

8-10   Paul then went straight to the meeting place. He had the run of the place for three months, doing his best to make the things of the kingdom of God real and convincing to them. But then resistance began to form as some of them began spreading evil rumors through the congregation about the Christian way of life. So Paul left, taking the disciples with him, and set up shop in the school of Tyrannus, holding class there daily. He did this for two years, giving everyone in the province of Asia, Jews as well as Greeks, ample opportunity to hear the Message of the Master.

WITCHES CAME OUT OF THE WOODWORK

11-12   God did powerful things through Paul, things quite out of the ordinary. The word got around and people started taking pieces of clothing—handkerchiefs and scarves and the like—that had touched Paul's skin and then touching the sick with them. The touch did it—they were healed and whole.

13-16   Some itinerant Jewish exorcists who happened to be in town at the time tried their hand at what they assumed to be Paul's "game." They pronounced the name of the Master Jesus over victims of evil spirits, saying, "I command you by the Jesus preached by Paul!" The seven sons of a certain Sceva, a Jewish high priest, were trying to do this on a man when the evil spirit talked back: "I know Jesus and I've heard of Paul, but who are you?" Then the possessed man went berserk—jumped the exorcists, beat them up, and tore off their clothes. Naked and bloody, they got away as best they could.

17-20   It was soon news all over Ephesus among both Jews and Greeks. The realization spread that God was in and behind this. Curiosity about Paul developed into reverence for the Master Jesus. Many of those who thus believed came out of the closet and made a clean break with their secret sorceries. All kinds of witches and warlocks came out of the woodwork with their books of spells and incantations and made a huge bonfire of them. Someone estimated their worth at fifty thousand silver coins. In such ways it became evident that the Word of the Master was now sovereign and prevailed in Ephesus.

THE GODDESS ARTEMIS

21-22   After all this had come to a head, Paul decided it was time to move on to Macedonia and Achaia provinces, and from there to Jerusalem. "Then," he said, "I'm off to Rome. I've got to see Rome!" He sent two of his assistants, Timothy and Erastus, on to Macedonia and then stayed for a while and wrapped things up in Asia.

23-26   But before he got away, a huge ruckus occurred over what was now being referred to as "the Way." A certain silversmith, Demetrius, conducted a brisk trade in the manufacture of shrines to the goddess Artemis, employing a number of artisans in his business. He rounded up his workers and others similarly employed and said, "Men, you well know that we have a good thing going here—and you've seen how Paul has barged in and discredited what we're doing by telling people that there's no such thing as a god made with hands. A lot of people are going along with him, not only here in Ephesus but all through Asia province.

27   "Not only is our little business in danger of falling apart, but the temple of our famous goddess Artemis will certainly end up a pile of rubble as her glorious reputation fades to nothing. And this is no mere local matter—the whole world worships our Artemis!"

28-31   That set them off in a frenzy. They ran into the street yelling, "Great Artemis of the Ephesians! Great Artemis of the Ephesians!" They put the whole city in an uproar, stampeding into the stadium, and grabbing two of Paul's associates on the way, the Macedonians Gaius and Aristarchus. Paul wanted to go in, too, but the disciples wouldn't let him. Prominent religious leaders in the city who had become friendly to Paul concurred: "By no means go near that mob!"

32-34   Some were yelling one thing, some another. Most of them had no idea what was going on or why they were there. As the Jews pushed Alexander to the front to try to gain control, different factions clamored to get him on their side. But he brushed them off and quieted the mob with an impressive sweep of his arms. But the moment he opened his mouth and they knew he was a Jew, they shouted him down: "Great Artemis of the Ephesians! Great Artemis of the Ephesians!"—on and on and on, for over two hours.

35-37   Finally, the town clerk got the mob quieted down and said, "Fellow citizens, is there anyone anywhere who doesn't know that our dear city Ephesus is protector of glorious Artemis and her sacred stone image that fell straight out of heaven? Since this is beyond contradiction, you had better get hold of yourselves. This is conduct unworthy of Artemis. These men you've dragged in here have done nothing to harm either our temple or our goddess.

38-41   "So if Demetrius and his guild of artisans have a complaint, they can take it to court and make all the accusations they want. If anything else is bothering you, bring it to the regularly scheduled town meeting and let it be settled there. There is no excuse for what's happened today. We're putting our city in serious danger. Rome, remember, does not look kindly on rioters." With that, he sent them home.

MACEDONIA AND GREECE

1-2   **20** With things back to normal, Paul called the disciples together and encouraged them to keep up the good work in Ephesus. Then, saying his good-byes, he left for Macedonia. Traveling through the country, passing from one gathering to another, he gave constant encouragement, lifting their spirits and charging them with fresh hope.

2-4   Then he came to Greece and stayed on for three months. Just as he was about to sail for Syria, the Jews cooked up a plot against him. So he went the other way, by land back through Macedonia, and gave them the slip. His companions for the journey were Sopater, son of Pyrrhus, from Berea; Aristarchus and Secundus, both Thessalonians; Gaius from Derbe; Timothy; and the two from western Asia, Tychicus and Trophimus.

5-6 They went on ahead and waited for us in Troas. Meanwhile, we stayed in Philippi for Passover Week, and then set sail. Within five days we were again in Troas and stayed a week.

7-9 We met on Sunday to worship and celebrate the Master's Supper. Paul addressed the congregation. Our plan was to leave first thing in the morning, but Paul talked on, way past midnight. We were meeting in a well-lighted upper room. A young man named Eutychus was sitting in an open window. As Paul went on and on, Eutychus fell sound asleep and toppled out the third-story window. When they picked him up, he was dead.

10-12 Paul went down, stretched himself on him, and hugged him hard. "No more crying," he said. "There's life in him yet." Then Paul got up and served the Master's Supper. And went on telling stories of the faith until dawn! On that note, they left — Paul going one way, the congregation another, leading the boy off alive, and full of life themselves.

13-16 In the meantime, the rest of us had gone on ahead to the ship and sailed for Assos, where we planned to pick up Paul. Paul wanted to walk there, and so had made these arrangements earlier. Things went according to plan: We met him in Assos, took him on board, and sailed to Mitylene. The next day we put in opposite Chios, Samos a day later, and then Miletus. Paul had decided to bypass Ephesus so that he wouldn't be held up in Asia province. He was in a hurry to get to Jerusalem in time for the Feast of Pentecost, if at all possible.

On to Jerusalem

17-21 From Miletus he sent to Ephesus for the leaders of the congregation. When they arrived, he said, "You know that from day one of my arrival in Asia I was with you totally — laying my life on the line, serving the Master no matter what, putting up with no end of scheming by Jews who wanted to do me in. I didn't skimp or trim in any way. Every truth and encouragement that could have made a difference to you, you got. I taught you out in public and I taught you in your homes, urging Jews and Greeks alike to a radical life-change before God and an equally radical trust in our Master Jesus.

22-24 "But there is another urgency before me now. I feel compelled to go to Jerusalem. I'm completely in the dark about what will happen when I get there. I do know that it won't be any picnic, for the Holy Spirit has let me know repeatedly and clearly that there are hard times and imprisonment ahead. But that matters little. What matters most to me is to finish what God started: the job the Master Jesus gave me of letting everyone I meet know all about this incredibly extravagant generosity of God.

25-27 "And so this is good-bye. You're not going to see me again, nor I you, you whom I have gone among for so long proclaiming the news of God's inaugurated kingdom. I've done my best for you, given you my all, held back nothing of God's will for you.

28 "Now it's up to you. Be on your toes — both for yourselves and your congregation of sheep. The Holy Spirit has put you in charge of these people — God's people they are — to guard and protect them. God himself thought they were worth dying for.

29-31   "I know that as soon as I'm gone, vicious wolves are going to show up and rip into this flock, men from your very own ranks twisting words so as to seduce disciples into following them instead of Jesus. So stay awake and keep up your guard. Remember those three years I kept at it with you, never letting up, pouring my heart out with you, one after another.

32   "Now I'm turning you over to God, our marvelous God whose gracious Word can make you into what he wants you to be and give you everything you could possibly need in this community of holy friends.

33-35   "I've never, as you so well know, had any taste for wealth or fashion. With these bare hands I took care of my own basic needs and those who worked with me. In everything I've done, I have demonstrated to you how necessary it is to work on behalf of the weak and not exploit them. You'll not likely go wrong here if you keep remembering that our Master said, 'You're far happier giving than getting.'"

36-38   Then Paul went down on his knees, all of them kneeling with him, and prayed. And then a river of tears. Much clinging to Paul, not wanting to let him go. They knew they would never see him again — he had told them quite plainly. The pain cut deep. Then, bravely, they walked him down to the ship.

Tyre and Caesarea

1-4   **21** And so, with the tearful good-byes behind us, we were on our way. We made a straight run to Cos, the next day reached Rhodes, and then Patara. There we found a ship going direct to Phoenicia, got on board, and set sail. Cyprus came into view on our left, but was soon out of sight as we kept on course for Syria, and eventually docked in the port of Tyre. While the cargo was being unloaded, we looked up the local disciples and stayed with them seven days. Their message to Paul, from insight given by the Spirit, was "Don't go to Jerusalem."

5-6   When our time was up, they escorted us out of the city to the docks. Everyone came along — men, women, children. They made a farewell party of the occasion! We all kneeled together on the beach and prayed. Then, after another round of saying good-bye, we climbed on board the ship while they drifted back to their homes.

7-9   A short run from Tyre to Ptolemais completed the voyage. We greeted our Christian friends there and stayed with them a day. In the morning we went on to Caesarea and stayed with Philip the Evangelist, one of "the Seven." Philip had four virgin daughters who prophesied.

10-11   After several days of visiting, a prophet from Judea by the name of Agabus came down to see us. He went right up to Paul, took Paul's belt, and, in a dramatic gesture, tied himself up, hands and feet. He said, "This is what the Holy Spirit says: The Jews in Jerusalem are going to tie up the man who owns this belt just like this and hand him over to godless unbelievers."

12-13   When we heard that, we and everyone there that day begged Paul not to be stubborn and persist in going to Jerusalem. But Paul wouldn't budge: "Why all this hysteria? Why do you insist on making a scene and making it even harder for me? You're looking at this backward. The issue in Jerusalem is not what they do to me, whether arrest or murder, but what the Master Jesus does through my obedience. Can't you see that?"

14   We saw that we weren't making even a dent in his resolve, and gave up. "It's in God's hands now," we said. "Master, you handle it."

15-16 It wasn't long before we had our luggage together and were on our way to Jerusalem. Some of the disciples from Caesarea went with us and took us to the home of Mnason, who received us warmly as his guests. A native of Cyprus, he had been among the earliest disciples.

JERUSALEM

17-19 In Jerusalem, our friends, glad to see us, received us with open arms. The first thing next morning, we took Paul to see James. All the church leaders were there. After a time of greeting and small talk, Paul told the story, detail by detail, of what God had done among the non-Jewish people through his ministry. They listened with delight and gave God the glory.

20-21 They had a story to tell, too: "And just look at what's been happening here — thousands upon thousands of God-fearing Jews have become believers in Jesus! But there's also a problem because they are more zealous than ever in observing the laws of Moses. They've been told that you advise believing Jews who live surrounded by unbelieving outsiders to go light on Moses, telling them that they don't need to circumcise their children or keep up the old traditions. This isn't sitting at all well with them.

22-24 "We're worried about what will happen when they discover you're in town. There's bound to be trouble. So here is what we want you to do: There are four men from our company who have taken a vow involving ritual purification, but have no money to pay the expenses. Join these men in their vows and pay their expenses. Then it will become obvious to everyone that there is nothing to the rumors going around about you and that you are in fact scrupulous in your reverence for the laws of Moses.

25 "In asking you to do this, we're not going back on our agreement regarding non-Jews who have become believers. We continue to hold fast to what we wrote in that letter, namely, to be careful not to get involved in activities connected with idols; to avoid serving food offensive to Jewish Christians; to guard the morality of sex and marriage."

26 So Paul did it — took the men, joined them in their vows, and paid their way. The next day he went to the Temple to make it official and stay there until the proper sacrifices had been offered and completed for each of them.

PAUL UNDER ARREST

27-29 When the seven days of their purification were nearly up, some Jews from around Ephesus spotted him in the Temple. At once they turned the place upside-down. They grabbed Paul and started yelling at the top of their lungs, "Help! You Israelites, help! This is the man who is going all over the world telling lies against us and our religion and this place. He's even brought Greeks in here and defiled this holy place." (What had happened was that they had seen Paul and Trophimus, the Ephesian Greek, walking together in the city and had just assumed that he had also taken him to the Temple and shown him around.)

30 Soon the whole city was in an uproar, people running from everywhere to the Temple to get in on the action. They grabbed Paul, dragged him outside, and locked the Temple gates so he couldn't get back in and gain sanctuary.

31-32 As they were trying to kill him, word came to the captain of the guard, "A riot! The whole city's boiling over!" He acted swiftly. His soldiers and centurions ran to the scene at once. As soon as the mob saw the captain and his soldiers, they quit beating Paul.

33-36   The captain came up and put Paul under arrest. He first ordered him handcuffed, and then asked who he was and what he had done. All he got from the crowd were shouts, one yelling this, another that. It was impossible to tell one word from another in the mob hysteria, so the captain ordered Paul taken to the military barracks. But when they got to the Temple steps, the mob became so violent that the soldiers had to carry Paul. As they carried him away, the crowd followed, shouting, "Kill him! Kill him!"

37-38   When they got to the barracks and were about to go in, Paul said to the captain, "Can I say something to you?"

He answered, "Oh, I didn't know you spoke Greek. I thought you were the Egyptian who not long ago started a riot here, and then hid out in the desert with his four thousand thugs."

39   Paul said, "No, I'm a Jew, born in Tarsus. And I'm a citizen still of that influential city. I have a simple request: Let me speak to the crowd."

PAUL TELLS HIS STORY

40   Standing on the barracks steps, Paul turned and held his arms up. A hush fell over the crowd as Paul began to speak. He spoke in Hebrew.

1-2   **22** "My dear brothers and fathers, listen carefully to what I have to say before you jump to conclusions about me." When they heard him speaking Hebrew, they grew even quieter. No one wanted to miss a word of this.

2-3   He continued, "I am a good Jew, born in Tarsus in the province of Cilicia, but educated here in Jerusalem under the exacting eye of Rabbi Gamaliel, thoroughly instructed in our religious traditions. And I've always been passionately on God's side, just as you are right now.

4-5   "I went after anyone connected with this 'Way,' went at them hammer and tongs, ready to kill for God. I rounded up men and women right and left and had them thrown in prison. You can ask the Chief Priest or anyone in the High Council to verify this; they all knew me well. Then I went off to our brothers in Damascus, armed with official documents authorizing me to hunt down the followers of Jesus there, arrest them, and bring them back to Jerusalem for sentencing.

6-7   "As I arrived on the outskirts of Damascus about noon, a blinding light blazed out of the skies and I fell to the ground, dazed. I heard a voice: 'Saul, Saul, why are you out to get me?'

8-9   "'Who are you, Master?' I asked.

"He said, 'I am Jesus the Nazarene, the One you're hunting down.' My companions saw the light, but they didn't hear the conversation.

10-11   "Then I said, 'What do I do now, Master?'

"He said, 'Get to your feet and enter Damascus. There you'll be told everything that's been set out for you to do.' And so we entered Damascus, but nothing like the entrance I had planned—I was blind as a bat and my companions had to lead me in by the hand.

12-13   "And that's when I met Ananias, a man with a sterling reputation in observing our laws—the Jewish community in Damascus is unanimous on that score. He came and put his arm on my shoulder. 'Look up,' he said. I looked, and found myself looking right into his eyes—I could see again!

14-16　　"Then he said, 'The God of our ancestors has handpicked you to be briefed on his plan of action. You've actually seen the Righteous Innocent and heard him speak. You are to be a key witness to everyone you meet of what you've seen and heard. So what are you waiting for? Get up and get yourself baptized, scrubbed clean of those sins and personally acquainted with God.'

17-18　　"Well, it happened just as Ananias said. After I was back in Jerusalem and praying one day in the Temple, lost in the presence of God, I saw him, saw God's Righteous Innocent, and heard him say to me, 'Hurry up! Get out of here as quickly as you can. None of the Jews here in Jerusalem are going to accept what you say about me.'

19-20　　"At first I objected: 'Who has better credentials? They all know how obsessed I was with hunting out those who believed in you, beating them up in the meeting places and throwing them in jail. And when your witness Stephen was murdered, I was right there, holding the coats of the murderers and cheering them on. And now they see me totally converted. What better qualification could I have?'

21　　"But he said, 'Don't argue. Go. I'm sending you on a long journey to outsider non-Jews.'"

A ROMAN CITIZEN

22-25　　The people in the crowd had listened attentively up to this point, but now they broke loose, shouting out, "Kill him! He's an insect! Stomp on him!" They shook their fists. They filled the air with curses. That's when the captain intervened and ordered Paul taken into the barracks. By now the captain was thoroughly exasperated. He decided to interrogate Paul under torture in order to get to the bottom of this, to find out what he had done that provoked this outraged violence. As they spread-eagled him with thongs, getting him ready for the whip, Paul said to the centurion standing there, "Is this legal: torturing a Roman citizen without a fair trial?"

26　　When the centurion heard that, he went directly to the captain. "Do you realize what you've done? This man is a Roman citizen!"

27　　The captain came back and took charge. "Is what I hear right? You're a Roman citizen?"

Paul said, "I certainly am."

28　　The captain was impressed. "I paid a huge sum for my citizenship. How much did it cost you?"

"Nothing," said Paul. "It cost me nothing. I was free from the day of my birth."

29　　That put a stop to the interrogation. And it put the fear of God into the captain. He had put a Roman citizen in chains and come within a whisker of putting him under torture!

30　　The next day, determined to get to the root of the trouble and know for sure what was behind the Jewish accusation, the captain released Paul and ordered a meeting of the high priests and the High Council to see what they could make of it. Paul was led in and took his place before them.

BEFORE THE HIGH COUNCIL

1-3　　**23** Paul surveyed the members of the council with a steady gaze, and then said his piece: "Friends, I've lived with a clear conscience before God all my life, up to this very moment." That set the Chief Priest Ananias off. He ordered his aides to slap Paul in the face. Paul shot back, "God will slap you down! What a fake you are! You sit there and judge me by the Law and then break the Law by ordering me slapped around!"

4 The aides were scandalized: "How dare you talk to God's Chief Priest like that!"

5 Paul acted surprised. "How was I to know he was Chief Priest? He doesn't act like a Chief Priest. You're right, the Scripture does say, 'Don't speak abusively to a ruler of the people.' Sorry."

6 Paul, knowing some of the council was made up of Sadducees and others of Pharisees and how they hated each other, decided to exploit their antagonism: "Friends, I am a stalwart Pharisee from a long line of Pharisees. It's because of my Pharisee convictions — the hope and resurrection of the dead — that I've been hauled into this court."

7-9 The moment he said this, the council split right down the middle, Pharisees and Sadducees going at each other in heated argument. Sadducees have nothing to do with a resurrection or angels or even a spirit. If they can't see it, they don't believe it. Pharisees believe it all. And so a huge and noisy quarrel broke out. Then some of the religion scholars on the Pharisee side shouted down the others: "We don't find anything wrong with this man! And what if a spirit has spoken to him? Or maybe an angel? What if it turns out we're fighting against God?"

10 That was fuel on the fire. The quarrel flamed up and became so violent the captain was afraid they would tear Paul apart, limb from limb. He ordered the soldiers to get him out of there and escort him back to the safety of the barracks.

A Plot Against Paul

11 That night the Master appeared to Paul: "It's going to be all right. Everything is going to turn out for the best. You've been a good witness for me here in Jerusalem. Now you're going to be my witness in Rome!"

12-15 Next day the Jews worked up a plot against Paul. They took a solemn oath that they would neither eat nor drink until they had killed him. Over forty of them ritually bound themselves to this murder pact and presented themselves to the high priests and religious leaders. "We've bound ourselves by a solemn oath to eat nothing until we have killed Paul. But we need your help. Send a request from the council to the captain to bring Paul back so that you can investigate the charges in more detail. We'll do the rest. Before he gets anywhere near you, we'll have killed him. You won't be involved."

16-17 Paul's nephew, his sister's son, overheard them plotting the ambush. He went immediately to the barracks and told Paul. Paul called over one of the centurions and said, "Take this young man to the captain. He has something important to tell him."

18 The centurion brought him to the captain and said, "The prisoner Paul asked me to bring this young man to you. He said he has something urgent to tell you."

19 The captain took him by the arm and led him aside privately. "What is it? What do you have to tell me?"

20-21 Paul's nephew said, "The Jews have worked up a plot against Paul. They're going to ask you to bring Paul to the council first thing in the morning on the pretext that they want to investigate the charges against him in more detail. But it's a trick to get him out of your safekeeping so they can murder him. Right now there are more than forty men lying in ambush for him. They've all taken a vow to neither eat nor drink until they've killed him. The ambush is set — all they're waiting for is for you to send him over."

22   The captain dismissed the nephew with a warning: "Don't breathe a word of this to a soul."

23-24   The captain called up two centurions. "Get two hundred soldiers ready to go immediately to Caesarea. Also seventy cavalry and two hundred light infantry. I want them ready to march by nine o'clock tonight. And you'll need a couple of mules for Paul and his gear. We're going to present this man safe and sound to Governor Felix."

25-30   Then he wrote this letter:

> From Claudius Lysias, to the Most Honorable Governor Felix:
> Greetings!
> I rescued this man from a Jewish mob. They had seized him and were about to kill him when I learned that he was a Roman citizen. So I sent in my soldiers. Wanting to know what he had done wrong, I had him brought before their council. It turned out to be a squabble turned vicious over some of their religious differences, but nothing remotely criminal.
> The next thing I knew, they had cooked up a plot to murder him. I decided that for his own safety I'd better get him out of here in a hurry. So I'm sending him to you. I'm informing his accusers that he's now under your jurisdiction.

31-33   The soldiers, following orders, took Paul that same night to safety in Antipatris. In the morning the soldiers returned to their barracks in Jerusalem, sending Paul on to Caesarea under guard of the cavalry. The cavalry entered Caesarea and handed Paul and the letter over to the governor.

34-35   After reading the letter, the governor asked Paul what province he came from and was told "Cilicia." Then he said, "I'll take up your case when your accusers show up." He ordered him locked up for the meantime in King Herod's official quarters.

PAUL STATES HIS DEFENSE

1-4   **24** Within five days, the Chief Priest Ananias arrived with a contingent of leaders, along with Tertullus, a trial lawyer. They presented the governor with their case against Paul. When Paul was called before the court, Tertullus spoke for the prosecution: "Most Honorable Felix, we are most grateful in all times and places for your wise and gentle rule. We are much aware that it is because of you and you alone that we enjoy all this peace and gain daily profit from your reforms. I'm not going to tire you out with a long speech. I beg your kind indulgence in listening to me. I'll be quite brief.

5-8   "We've found this man time and again disturbing the peace, stirring up riots against Jews all over the world, the ringleader of a seditious sect called Nazarenes. He's a real bad apple, I must say. We caught him trying to defile our holy Temple and arrested him. You'll be able to verify all these accusations when you examine him yourself."

9   The Jews joined in: "Hear, hear! That's right!"

10-13   The governor motioned to Paul that it was now his turn. Paul said, "I count myself fortunate to be defending myself before you, Governor, knowing how fair-minded you've been in judging us all these years. I've been back in the country only twelve days—you can check out these dates easily enough. I came with the express purpose of worshiping in Jerusalem on Pentecost, and I've been minding my own business the whole time. Nobody can say they saw me arguing in the Temple or working up a crowd in the streets. Not one of their charges can be backed up with evidence or witnesses.

14-15   "But I do freely admit this: In regard to the Way, which they malign as a dead-end street, I serve and worship the very same God served and worshiped by all our ancestors and embrace everything written in all our Scriptures. And I admit to living in hopeful anticipation that God will raise the dead, both the good and the bad. If that's my crime, my accusers are just as guilty as I am.

16-19   "Believe me, I do my level best to keep a clear conscience before God and my neighbors in everything I do. I've been out of the country for a number of years and now I'm back. While I was away, I took up a collection for the poor and brought that with me, along with offerings for the Temple. It was while making those offerings that they found me quietly at my prayers in the Temple. There was no crowd, there was no disturbance. It was some Jews from around Ephesus who started all this trouble. And you'll notice they're not here today. They're cowards, too cowardly to accuse me in front of you.

20-21   "So ask these others what crime they've caught me in. Don't let them hide behind this smooth-talking Tertullus. The only thing they have on me is that one sentence I shouted out in the council: 'It's because I believe in the resurrection that I've been hauled into this court!' Does that sound to you like grounds for a criminal case?"

22-23   Felix shilly-shallied. He knew far more about the Way than he let on, and could have settled the case then and there. But uncertain of his best move politically, he played for time. "When Captain Lysias comes down, I'll decide your case." He gave orders to the centurion to keep Paul in custody, but to more or less give him the run of the place and not prevent his friends from helping him.

24-26   A few days later Felix and his wife, Drusilla, who was Jewish, sent for Paul and listened to him talk about a life of believing in Jesus Christ. As Paul continued to insist on right relations with God and his people, about a life of moral discipline and the coming Judgment, Felix felt things getting a little too close for comfort and dismissed him. "That's enough for today. I'll call you back when it's convenient." At the same time he was secretly hoping that Paul would offer him a substantial bribe. These conversations were repeated frequently.

27   After two years of this, Felix was replaced by Porcius Festus. Still playing up to the Jews and ignoring justice, Felix left Paul in prison.

AN APPEAL TO CAESAR

1-3   # 25   Three days after Festus arrived in Caesarea to take up his duties as governor, he went up to Jerusalem. The high priests and top leaders renewed their vendetta against Paul. They asked Festus if he wouldn't please do them a favor by sending Paul to Jerusalem to respond to their charges. A lie, of course—they had revived their old plot to set an ambush and kill him along the way.

4-5   Festus answered that Caesarea was the proper jurisdiction for Paul, and that he himself was going back there in a few days. "You're perfectly welcome," he said, "to go back with me then and accuse him of whatever you think he's done wrong."

6-7   About eight or ten days later, Festus returned to Caesarea. The next morning he took his place in the courtroom and had Paul brought in. The minute he walked in, the Jews who had come down from Jerusalem were all over him, hurling the most extreme accusations, none of which they could prove.

8   Then Paul took the stand and said simply, "I've done nothing wrong against the Jewish religion, or the Temple, or Caesar. Period."

9   Festus, though, wanted to get on the good side of the Jews and so said, "How would you like to go up to Jerusalem, and let me conduct your trial there?"

10-11   Paul answered, "I'm standing at this moment before Caesar's bar of justice, where I have a perfect right to stand. And I'm going to keep standing here. I've done nothing wrong to the Jews, and you know it as well as I do. If I've committed a crime and deserve death, name the day. I can face it. But if there's nothing to their accusations—and you know there isn't—nobody can force me to go along with their nonsense. We've fooled around here long enough. I appeal to Caesar."

12   Festus huddled with his advisors briefly and then gave his verdict: "You've appealed to Caesar; you'll go to Caesar!"

13-17   A few days later King Agrippa and his wife, Bernice, visited Caesarea to welcome Festus to his new post. After several days, Festus brought up Paul's case to the king. "I have a man on my hands here, a prisoner left by Felix. When I was in Jerusalem, the high priests and Jewish leaders brought a bunch of accusations against him and wanted me to sentence him to death. I told them that wasn't the way we Romans did things. Just because a man is accused, we don't throw him out to the dogs. We make sure the accused has a chance to face his accusers and defend himself of the charges. So when they came down here I got right on the case. I took my place in the courtroom and put the man on the stand.

18-21   "The accusers came at him from all sides, but their accusations turned out to be nothing more than arguments about their religion and a dead man named Jesus, who the prisoner claimed was alive. Since I'm a newcomer here and don't understand everything involved in cases like this, I asked if he'd be willing to go to Jerusalem and be tried there. Paul refused and demanded a hearing before His Majesty in our highest court. So I ordered him returned to custody until I could send him to Caesar in Rome."

22   Agrippa said, "I'd like to see this man and hear his story."

"Good," said Festus. "We'll bring him in first thing in the morning and you'll hear it for yourself."

23   The next day everybody who was anybody in Caesarea found his way to the Great Hall, along with the top military brass. Agrippa and Bernice made a flourishing grand entrance and took their places. Festus then ordered Paul brought in.

24-26   Festus said, "King Agrippa and distinguished guests, take a good look at this man. A bunch of Jews petitioned me first in Jerusalem, and later here, to do away with him. They have been most vehement in demanding his execution. I looked into it and decided that he had committed no crime. He requested a trial before Caesar and I agreed to send him to Rome. But what am I going to write to my master, Caesar? All the charges made by the Jews were fabrications, and I've uncovered nothing else.

26-27   "That's why I've brought him before this company, and especially you, King Agrippa: so we can come up with something in the nature of a charge that will hold water. For it seems to me silly to send a prisoner all that way for a trial and not be able to document what he did wrong."

"I Couldn't Just Walk Away"

1-3   **26** Agrippa spoke directly to Paul: "Go ahead — tell us about yourself."

Paul took the stand and told his story. "I can't think of any-one, King Agrippa, before whom I'd rather be answering all these Jewish accusations than you, knowing how well you are acquainted with Jewish ways and all our family quarrels.

4-8   "From the time of my youth, my life has been lived among my own people in Jerusalem. Practically every Jew in town who watched me grow up — and if they were willing to stick their necks out they'd tell you in person — knows that I lived as a strict Pharisee, the most demanding branch of our religion. It's because I believed it and took it seriously, committed myself heart and soul to what God promised my ancestors — the identical hope, mind you, that the twelve tribes have lived for night and day all these centuries — it's because I have held on to this tested and tried hope that I'm being called on the carpet by the Jews. They should be the ones standing trial here, not me! For the life of me, I can't see why it's a criminal offense to believe that God raises the dead.

9-11   "I admit that I didn't always hold to this position. For a time I thought it was my duty to oppose this Jesus of Nazareth with all my might. Backed with the full authority of the high priests, I threw these believers — I had no idea they were God's people! — into the Jerusalem jail right and left, and whenever it came to a vote, I voted for their execution. I stormed through their meeting places, bullying them into cursing Jesus, a one-man terror obsessed with obliterating these people. And then I started on the towns outside Jerusalem.

12-14   "One day on my way to Damascus, armed as always with papers from the high priests authorizing my action, right in the middle of the day a blaze of light, light outshining the sun, poured out of the sky on me and my com-panions. Oh, King, it was so bright! We fell flat on our faces. Then I heard a voice in Hebrew: 'Saul, Saul, why are you out to get me? Why do you insist on going against the grain?'

15-16   "I said, 'Who are you, Master?'

"The voice answered, 'I am Jesus, the One you're hunting down like an animal. But now, up on your feet — I have a job for you. I've handpicked you to be a servant and witness to what's happened today, and to what I am going to show you.

17-18   "'I'm sending you off to open the eyes of the outsiders so they can see the difference between dark and light, and choose light, see the difference between Satan and God, and choose God. I'm sending you off to present my offer of sins forgiven, and a place in the family, inviting them into the company of those who begin real living by believing in me.'

19-20 "What could I do, King Agrippa? I couldn't just walk away from a vision like that! I became an obedient believer on the spot. I started preaching this life-change—this radical turn to God and everything it meant in everyday life—right there in Damascus, went on to Jerusalem and the surrounding countryside, and from there to the whole world.

21-23 "It's because of this 'whole world' dimension that the Jews grabbed me in the Temple that day and tried to kill me. They want to keep God for themselves. But God has stood by me, just as he promised, and I'm standing here saying what I've been saying to anyone, whether king or child, who will listen. And everything I'm saying is completely in line with what the prophets and Moses said would happen: One, the Messiah must die; two, raised from the dead, he would be the first rays of God's daylight shining on people far and near, people both godless and God-fearing."

24 That was too much for Festus. He interrupted with a shout: "Paul, you're crazy! You've read too many books, spent too much time staring off into space! Get a grip on yourself, get back in the real world!"

25-27 But Paul stood his ground. "With all respect, Festus, Your Honor, I'm not crazy. I'm both accurate and sane in what I'm saying. The king knows what I'm talking about. I'm sure that nothing of what I've said sounds crazy to him. He's known all about it for a long time. You must realize that this wasn't done behind the scenes. You believe the prophets, don't you, King Agrippa? Don't answer that—I know you believe."

28 But Agrippa did answer: "Keep this up much longer and you'll make a Christian out of me!"

29 Paul, still in chains, said, "That's what I'm praying for, whether now or later, and not only you but everyone listening today, to become like me—except, of course, for this prison jewelry!"

30-31 The king and the governor, along with Bernice and their advisors, got up and went into the next room to talk over what they had heard. They quickly agreed on Paul's innocence, saying, "There's nothing in this man deserving prison, let alone death."

32 Agrippa told Festus, "He could be set free right now if he hadn't requested the hearing before Caesar."

A STORM AT SEA

1-2 **27** As soon as arrangements were complete for our sailing to Italy, Paul and a few other prisoners were placed under the supervision of a centurion named Julius, a member of an elite guard. We boarded a ship from Adramyttium that was bound for Ephesus and ports west. Aristarchus, a Macedonian from Thessalonica, went with us.

3 The next day we put in at Sidon. Julius treated Paul most decently—let him get off the ship and enjoy the hospitality of his friends there.

4-8 Out to sea again, we sailed north under the protection of the northeast shore of Cyprus because winds out of the west were against us, and then along the coast westward to the port of Myra. There the centurion found an Egyptian ship headed for Italy and transferred us on board. We ran into bad weather and found it impossible to stay on course. After much difficulty, we finally made it to the southern coast of the island of Crete and docked at

Good Harbor (appropriate name!).

9-10 By this time we had lost a lot of time. We had passed the autumn equinox, so it would be stormy weather from now on through the winter, too dangerous for sailing. Paul warned, "I see only disaster ahead for cargo and ship — to say nothing of our lives! — if we put out to sea now."

12,11 But it was not the best harbor for staying the winter. Phoenix, a few miles further on, was more suitable. The centurion set Paul's warning aside and let the ship captain and the shipowner talk him into trying for the next harbor.

13-15 When a gentle southerly breeze came up, they weighed anchor, thinking it would be smooth sailing. But they were no sooner out to sea than a gale-force wind, the infamous nor'easter, struck. They lost all control of the ship. It was a cork in the storm.

16-17 We came under the lee of the small island named Clauda, and managed to get a lifeboat ready and reef the sails. But rocky shoals prevented us from getting close. We only managed to avoid them by throwing out drift anchors.

18-20 Next day, out on the high seas again and badly damaged now by the storm, we dumped the cargo overboard. The third day the sailors lightened the ship further by throwing off all the tackle and provisions. It had been many days since we had seen either sun or stars. Wind and waves were battering us unmercifully, and we lost all hope of rescue.

21-22 With our appetite for both food and life long gone, Paul took his place in our midst and said, "Friends, you really should have listened to me back in Crete. We could have avoided all this trouble and trial. But there's no need to dwell on that now. From now on, things are looking up! I can assure you that there'll not be a single drowning among us, although I can't say as much for the ship — the ship itself is doomed.

23-26 "Last night God's angel stood at my side, an angel of this God I serve, saying to me, 'Don't give up, Paul. You're going to stand before Caesar yet — and everyone sailing with you is also going to make it.' So, dear friends, take heart. I believe God will do exactly what he told me. But we're going to shipwreck on some island or other."

27-29 On the fourteenth night, adrift somewhere on the Adriatic Sea, at about midnight the sailors sensed that we were approaching land. Sounding, they measured a depth of 120 feet, and shortly after that ninety feet. Afraid that we were about to run aground, they threw out four anchors and prayed for daylight.

30-32 Some of the sailors tried to jump ship. They let down the lifeboat, pretending they were going to set out more anchors from the bow. Paul saw through their guise and told the centurion and his soldiers, "If these sailors don't stay with the ship, we're all going down." So the soldiers cut the lines to the lifeboat and let it drift off.

33-34 With dawn about to break, Paul called everyone together and proposed breakfast: "This is the fourteenth day we've gone without food. None of us has felt like eating! But I urge you to eat something now. You'll need strength for the rescue ahead. You're going to come out of this without even a scratch!"

35-38 He broke the bread, gave thanks to God, passed it around, and they all ate heartily — 276 of us, all told! With the meal finished and everyone full, the ship was further lightened by dumping the grain overboard.

39-41　　At daybreak, no one recognized the land—but then they did notice a bay with a nice beach. They decided to try to run the ship up on the beach. They cut the anchors, loosed the tiller, raised the sail, and ran before the wind toward the beach. But we didn't make it. Still far from shore, we hit a reef and the ship began to break up.

42-44　　The soldiers decided to kill the prisoners so none could escape by swimming, but the centurion, determined to save Paul, stopped them. He gave orders for anyone who could swim to dive in and go for it, and for the rest to grab a plank. Everyone made it to shore safely.

1-2　　**28** Once everyone was accounted for and we realized we had all made it, we learned that we were on the island of Malta. The natives went out of their way to be friendly to us. The day was rainy and cold and we were already soaked to the bone, but they built a huge bonfire and gathered us around it.

3-6　　Paul pitched in and helped. He had gathered up a bundle of sticks, but when he put it on the fire, a venomous snake, roused from its torpor by the heat, struck his hand and held on. Seeing the snake hanging from Paul's hand like that, the natives jumped to the conclusion that he was a murderer getting his just deserts. Paul shook the snake off into the fire, none the worse for wear. They kept expecting him to drop dead, but when it was obvious he wasn't going to, they jumped to the conclusion that he was a god!

7-9　　The head man in that part of the island was Publius. He took us into his home as his guests, drying us out and putting us up in fine style for the next three days. Publius's father was sick at the time, down with a high fever and dysentery. Paul went to the old man's room, and when he laid hands on him and prayed, the man was healed. Word of the healing got around fast, and soon everyone on the island who was sick came and got healed.

ROME

10-11　　We spent a wonderful three months on Malta. They treated us royally, took care of all our needs and outfitted us for the rest of the journey. When an Egyptian ship that had wintered there in the harbor prepared to leave for Italy, we got on board. The ship had a carved Gemini for its figurehead: "the Heavenly Twins."

12-14　　We put in at Syracuse for three days and then went up the coast to Rhegium. Two days later, with the wind out of the south, we sailed into the Bay of Naples. We found Christian friends there and stayed with them for a week.

14-16　　And then we came to Rome. Friends in Rome heard we were on the way and came out to meet us. One group got as far as Appian Court; another group met us at Three Taverns—emotion-packed meetings, as you can well imagine. Paul, brimming over with praise, led us in prayers of thanksgiving. When we actually entered Rome, they let Paul live in his own private quarters with a soldier who had been assigned to guard him.

17-20　　Three days later, Paul called the Jewish leaders together for a meeting at his house. He said, "The Jews in Jerusalem arrested me on trumped-up charges, and I was taken into custody by the Romans. I assure you that I did absolutely nothing against Jewish laws or Jewish customs. After the Romans investigated the charges and found there was nothing to them, they wanted to set me free, but the Jews objected so fiercely that I was forced to appeal to Caesar. I did this not to accuse them of any wrongdoing or to get our people in trouble with Rome. We've had enough trouble through the years that way. I did it *for* Israel. I asked you to come and listen to me today to make it clear that I'm on Israel's side, not against her. I'm a hostage here for hope, not doom."

21-22 They said, "Nobody wrote warning us about you. And no one has shown up saying anything bad about you. But we would like very much to hear more. The only thing we know about this Christian sect is that nobody seems to have anything good to say about it."

23 They agreed on a time. When the day arrived, they came back to his home with a number of their friends. Paul talked to them all day, from morning to evening, explaining everything involved in the kingdom of God, and trying to persuade them all about Jesus by pointing out what Moses and the prophets had written about him.

24-27 Some of them were persuaded by what he said, but others refused to believe a word of it. When the unbelievers got cantankerous and started bickering with each other, Paul interrupted: "I have just one more thing to say to you. The Holy Spirit sure knew what he was talking about when he addressed our ancestors through Isaiah the prophet:

Go to this people and tell them this:
"You're going to listen with your ears,
    but you won't hear a word;
You're going to stare with your eyes,
    but you won't see a thing.
These people are blockheads!
They stick their fingers in their ears
    so they won't have to listen;
They screw their eyes shut
    so they won't have to look,
    so they won't have to deal with me face-to-face
    and let me heal them."

28 "You've had your chance. The non-Jewish outsiders are next on the list. And believe me, they're going to receive it with open arms!"

30-31 Paul lived for two years in his rented house. He welcomed everyone who came to visit. He urgently presented all matters of the kingdom of God. He explained everything about Jesus Christ. His door was always open.

ROMANS

The event that split history into "before" and "after" and changed the world took place about thirty years before Paul wrote this letter. The event — the life, death, and resurrection of Jesus — took place in a remote corner of the extensive Roman Empire: the province of Judea in Palestine. Hardly anyone noticed, certainly no one in busy and powerful Rome.

And when this letter arrived in Rome, hardly anyone read it, certainly no one of influence. There was much to read in Rome — imperial decrees, exquisite poetry, finely crafted moral philosophy — and much of it was world-class. And yet in no time, as such things go, this letter left all those other writings in the dust. Paul's letter to the Romans has had a far larger impact on its readers than the volumes of all those Roman writers put together.

The quick rise of this letter to a peak of influence is extraordinary, written as it was by an obscure Roman citizen without connections. But when we read it for ourselves, we begin to realize that it is the letter itself that is truly extraordinary, and that no obscurity in writer or readers could have kept it obscure for long.

The letter to the Romans is a piece of exuberant and passionate thinking. This is the glorious life of the mind enlisted in the service of God. Paul takes the well-witnessed and devoutly believed fact of the life, death, and resurrection of Jesus of Nazareth and thinks through its implications. How does it happen that in the death and resurrection of Jesus, world history took a new direction, and at the same moment the life of every man, woman, and child on the planet was eternally affected? What is God up to? What does it *mean* that Jesus "saves"? What's behind all this, and where is it going?

These are the questions that drive Paul's thinking. Paul's mind is supple and capacious. He takes logic and argument, poetry and imagination, Scripture and prayer, creation and history and experience, and weaves them into this letter that has become the premier document of Christian theology.

ROMANS

1 I, Paul, am a devoted slave of Jesus Christ on assignment, authorized as an apostle to proclaim God's words and acts. I write this letter to all the believers in Rome, God's friends.

2-7 The sacred writings contain preliminary reports by the prophets on God's Son. His descent from David roots him in history; his unique identity as Son of God was shown by the Spirit when Jesus was raised from the dead, setting him apart as the Messiah, our Master. Through him we received both the generous gift of his life and the urgent task of passing it on to others who receive it by entering into obedient trust in Jesus. You are who you are through this gift and call of Jesus Christ! And I greet you now with all the generosity of God our Father and our Master Jesus, the Messiah.

8-12 I thank God through Jesus for every one of you. That's first. People everywhere keep telling me about your lives of faith, and every time I hear them, I thank him. And God, whom I so love to worship and serve by spreading the good news of his Son — the Message! — knows that every time I think of you in my prayers, which is practically all the time, I ask him to clear the way for me to come and see you. The longer this waiting goes on, the deeper the ache. I so want to be there to deliver God's gift in person and watch you grow stronger right before my eyes! But don't think I'm not expecting to get something out of this, too! You have as much to give me as I do to you.

13-15 Please don't misinterpret my failure to visit you, friends. You have no idea how many times I've made plans for Rome. I've been determined to get some personal enjoyment out of God's work among you, as I have in so many other non-Jewish towns and communities. But something has always come up and prevented it. Everyone I meet — it matters little whether they're mannered or rude, smart or simple — deepens my sense of interdependence and obligation. And that's why I can't wait to get to you in Rome, preaching this wonderful good news of God.

16-17 It's news I'm most proud to proclaim, this extraordinary Message of God's powerful plan to rescue everyone who trusts him, starting with Jews and then right on to everyone else! God's way of putting people right shows up in the acts of faith, confirming what Scripture has said all along: "The person in right standing before God by trusting him really lives."

IGNORING GOD LEADS TO A DOWNWARD SPIRAL

18-23 But God's angry displeasure erupts as acts of human mistrust and wrongdoing and lying accumulate, as people try to put a shroud over truth. But the basic reality of God is plain enough. Open your eyes and there it is! By taking a long and thoughtful look at what God has created, people have always been able to see what their eyes as such can't see: eternal power, for instance, and the mystery of his divine being. So nobody has a good excuse. What happened was this: People knew God perfectly well, but when they didn't treat him like God, refusing to worship him, they trivialized themselves into silliness and confusion so that there was neither sense nor direction left in their lives. They pretended to know it all, but were illiterate regarding life. They traded the glory of God who holds the whole world in his hands for cheap figurines you can buy at any roadside stand.

24-25 So God said, in effect, "If that's what you want, that's what you get." It wasn't long before they were living in a pigpen, smeared with filth, filthy inside and out. And all this because they traded the true God for a fake god, and worshiped the god they made instead of the God who made them — the God we bless, the God who blesses *us*. Oh, yes!

26-27 Worse followed. Refusing to know God, they soon didn't know how to be human either — women didn't know how to be women, men didn't know how to be men. Sexually confused, they abused and defiled one another, women with women, men with men — all lust, no love. And then they paid for it, oh, how they paid for it — emptied of God and love, godless and loveless wretches.

28-32 Since they didn't bother to acknowledge God, God quit bothering them and let them run loose. And then all hell broke loose: rampant evil, grabbing and grasping, vicious backstabbing. They made life hell on earth with their envy, wanton killing, bickering, and cheating. Look at them: mean-spirited, venomous, fork-tongued God-bashers. Bullies, swaggerers, insufferable windbags! They keep inventing new ways of wrecking lives. They ditch their parents when they get in the way. Stupid, slimy, cruel, cold-blooded. And it's not as if they don't know better. They know perfectly well they're spitting in God's face. And they don't care — worse, they hand out prizes to those who do the worst things best!

GOD IS KIND, BUT NOT SOFT

1-2 2 Those people are on a dark spiral downward. But if you think that leaves you on the high ground where you can point your finger at others, think again. Every time you criticize someone, you condemn yourself. It takes one to know one. Judgmental criticism of others is a well-known way of escaping detection in your own crimes and misdemeanors. But God isn't so easily diverted. He sees right through all such smoke screens and holds you to what *you've* done.

3-4 You didn't think, did you, that just by pointing your finger at others you would distract God from seeing all your misdoings and from coming down on you hard? Or did you think that because he's such a nice God, he'd let you off the hook? Better think this one through from the beginning. God is kind, but he's not soft. In kindness he takes us firmly by the hand and leads us into a radical life-change.

5-8 You're not getting by with anything. Every refusal and avoidance of God adds fuel to the fire. The day is coming when it's going to blaze hot and high, God's fiery and righteous judgment. Make no mistake: In the end you get what's coming to you — *Real Life* for those who work on God's side, but to those who insist on getting their own way and take the path of least resistance, *Fire!*

9-11 If you go against the grain, you get splinters, regardless of which neighborhood you're from, what your parents taught you, what schools you attended. But if you embrace the way God does things, there are wonderful payoffs, again without regard to where you are from or how you were brought up. Being a Jew won't give you an automatic stamp of approval. God pays no attention to what others say (or what you think) about you. He makes up his own mind.

12-13 If you sin without knowing what you're doing, God takes that into account. But if you sin knowing full well what you're doing, that's a different story entirely. Merely hearing God's law is a waste of your time if you don't do what he commands. Doing, not hearing, is what makes the difference with God.

14-16   When outsiders who have never heard of God's law follow it more or less by instinct, they confirm its truth by their obedience. They show that God's law is not something alien, imposed on us from without, but woven into the very fabric of our creation. There is something deep within them that echoes God's yes and no, right and wrong. Their response to God's yes and no will become public knowledge on the day God makes his final decision about every man and woman. The Message from God that I proclaim through Jesus Christ takes into account all these differences.

RELIGION CAN'T SAVE YOU

17-24   If you're brought up Jewish, don't assume that you can lean back in the arms of your religion and take it easy, feeling smug because you're an insider to God's revelation, a connoisseur of the best things of God, informed on the latest doctrines! I have a special word of caution for you who are sure that you have it all together yourselves and, because you know God's revealed Word inside and out, feel qualified to guide others through their blind alleys and dark nights and confused emotions to God. While you are guiding others, who is going to guide you? I'm quite serious. While preaching "Don't steal!" are you going to rob people blind? Who would suspect you? The same with adultery. The same with idolatry. You can get by with almost anything if you front it with eloquent talk about God and his law. The line from Scripture, "It's because of you Jews that the outsiders are down on God," shows it's an old problem that isn't going to go away.

25-29   Circumcision, the surgical ritual that marks you as a Jew, is great if you live in accord with God's law. But if you don't, it's worse than not being circumcised. The reverse is also true: The uncircumcised who keep God's ways are as good as the circumcised — in fact, better. Better to keep God's law uncircumcised than break it circumcised. Don't you see: It's not the cut of a knife that makes a Jew. You become a Jew by who you *are*. It's the mark of God on your heart, not of a knife on your skin, that makes a Jew. And recognition comes from God, not legalistic critics.

1-2   **3** So what difference does it make who's a Jew and who isn't, who has been trained in God's ways and who hasn't? As it turns out, it makes a lot of difference — but not the difference so many have assumed.

2-6   First, there's the matter of being put in charge of writing down and caring for God's revelation, these Holy Scriptures. So, what if, in the course of doing that, some of those Jews abandoned their post? God didn't abandon them. Do you think their faithlessness cancels out his faithfulness? Not on your life! Depend on it: God keeps his word even when the whole world is lying through its teeth. Scripture says the same:

Your words stand fast and true;
Rejection doesn't faze you.

But if our wrongdoing only underlines and confirms God's rightdoing, shouldn't we be commended for helping out? Since our bad words don't even make a dent in his good words, isn't it wrong of God to back us to the wall and hold us to our word? These questions come up. The answer to such questions is *no*, a most emphatic *No!* How else would things ever get straightened out if *God* didn't do the straightening?

7-8   It's simply perverse to say, "If my lies serve to show off God's truth all the more gloriously, why blame me? I'm doing God a favor." Some people are actually trying to put such words in our mouths, claiming that we go around saying, "The more evil we do, the more good God does, so let's just do it!" That's pure slander, as I'm sure you'll agree.

We're All in the Same Sinking Boat

9-20   So where does that put us? Do we Jews get a better break than the others? Not really. Basically, all of us, whether insiders or outsiders, start out in identical conditions, which is to say that we all start out as sinners. Scripture leaves no doubt about it:

> There's nobody living right, not even one,
>   nobody who knows the score, nobody alert for God.
> They've all taken the wrong turn;
>   they've all wandered down blind alleys.
> No one's living right;
>   I can't find a single one.
> Their throats are gaping graves,
>   their tongues slick as mudslides.
> Every word they speak is tinged with poison.
>   They open their mouths and pollute the air.
> They race for the honor of sinner-of-the-year,
>   litter the land with heartbreak and ruin,
> Don't know the first thing about living with others.
>   They never give God the time of day.

This makes it clear, doesn't it, that whatever is written in these Scriptures is not what God says *about others* but *to us* to whom these Scriptures were addressed in the first place! And it's clear enough, isn't it, that we're sinners, every one of us, in the same sinking boat with everybody else? Our involvement with God's revelation doesn't put us right with God. What it does is force us to face our complicity in everyone else's sin.

God Has Set Things Right

21-24   But in our time something new has been added. What Moses and the prophets witnessed to all those years has happened. The God-setting-things-right that we read about has become Jesus-setting-things-right for us. And not only for us, but for everyone who believes in him. For there is no difference between us and them in this. Since we've compiled this long and sorry record as sinners (both us and them) and proved that we are utterly incapable of living the glorious lives God wills for us, God did it for us. Out of sheer generosity he put us in right standing with himself. A pure gift. He got us out of the mess we're in and restored us to where he always wanted us to be. And he did it by means of Jesus Christ.

25-26   God sacrificed Jesus on the altar of the world to clear that world of sin. Having faith in him sets us in the clear. God decided on this course of action in full view of the public — to set the world in the clear with himself through the sacrifice of Jesus, finally taking care of the sins he had so patiently endured. This is not only clear, but it's *now* — this is current history! God sets things right. He also makes it possible for us to live in his rightness.

27-28 So where does that leave our proud Jewish insider claims and counter-claims? Canceled? Yes, canceled. What we've learned is this: God does not respond to what *we* do; we respond to what *God* does. We've finally figured it out. Our lives get in step with God and all others by letting him set the pace, not by proudly or anxiously trying to run the parade.

29-30 And where does that leave our proud Jewish claim of having a corner on God? Also canceled. God is the God of outsider non-Jews as well as insider Jews. How could it be otherwise since there is only one God? God sets right all who welcome his action and enter into it, both those who follow our religious system and those who have never heard of our religion.

31 But by shifting our focus from what *we* do to what *God* does, don't we cancel out all our careful keeping of the rules and ways God commanded? Not at all. What happens, in fact, is that by putting that entire way of life in its proper place, we confirm it.

TRUSTING GOD

1-3 So how do we fit what we know of Abraham, our first father in the faith, into this new way of looking at things? If Abraham, by what he did for God, got God to approve him, he could certainly have taken credit for it. But the story we're given is a God-story, not an Abraham-story. What we read in Scripture is, "Abraham entered into what God was doing for him, and *that* was the turning point. He trusted God to set him right instead of trying to be right on his own."

4-5 If you're a hard worker and do a good job, you deserve your pay; we don't call your wages a gift. But if you see that the job is too big for you, that it's something only *God* can do, and you trust him to do it — you could never do it for yourself no matter how hard and long you worked — well, that trust-ing-him-to-do-it is what gets you set right with God, *by* God. Sheer gift.

6-9 David confirms this way of looking at it, saying that the one who trusts God to do the putting-everything-right without insisting on having a say in it is one fortunate man:

Fortunate those whose crimes are carted off,
    whose sins are wiped clean from the slate.
Fortunate the person against
    whom the Lord does not keep score.

Do you think for a minute that this blessing is only pronounced over those of us who keep our religious ways and are circumcised? Or do you think it possible that the blessing could be given to those who never even heard of our ways, who were never brought up in the disciplines of God? We all agree, don't we, that it was by embracing what God did for him that Abraham was declared fit before God?

10-11 Now *think*: Was that declaration made before or after he was marked by the covenant rite of circumcision? That's right, *before* he was marked. That means that he underwent circumcision as evidence and confirmation of what God had done long before to bring him into this acceptable standing with himself, an act of God he had embraced with his whole life.

12   And it means further that Abraham is father of *all* people who embrace what God does for them while they are still on the "outs" with God, as yet unidentified as God's, in an "uncircumcised" condition. It is precisely these people in this condition who are called "set right by God and with God"! Abraham is also, of course, father of those who have undergone the religious rite of circumcision *not* just because of the ritual but because they were willing to live in the risky faith-embrace of God's action for them, the way Abraham lived long before he was marked by circumcision.

13-15   That famous promise God gave Abraham — that he and his children would possess the earth — was not given because of something Abraham did or would do. It was based on God's decision to put everything together for him, which Abraham then entered when he believed. If those who get what God gives them only get it by doing everything they are told to do and filling out all the right forms properly signed, that eliminates personal trust completely and turns the promise into an ironclad *contract*! That's not a holy promise; that's a business deal. A contract drawn up by a hard-nosed lawyer and with plenty of fine print only makes sure that you will never be able to collect. But if there is no contract in the first place, simply a *promise* — and God's promise at that — you can't break it.

16   This is why the fulfillment of God's promise depends entirely on trusting God and his way, and then simply embracing him and what he does. God's promise arrives as pure gift. That's the only way everyone can be sure to get in on it, those who keep the religious traditions *and* those who have never heard of them. For Abraham is father of us all. He is not our racial father — that's reading the story backward. He is our *faith* father.

17-18   We call Abraham "father" not because he got God's attention by living like a saint, but because God made something out of Abraham when he was a nobody. Isn't that what we've always read in Scripture, God saying to Abraham, "I set you up as father of many peoples"? Abraham was first named "father" and then *became* a father because he dared to trust God to do what only God could do: raise the dead to life, with a word make something out of nothing. When everything was hopeless, Abraham believed anyway, deciding to live not on the basis of what he saw he *couldn't* do but on what God said he *would* do. And so he was made father of a multitude of peoples. God himself said to him, "You're going to have a big family, Abraham!"

19-25   Abraham didn't focus on his own impotence and say, "It's hopeless. This hundred-year-old body could never father a child." Nor did he survey Sarah's decades of infertility and give up. He didn't tiptoe around God's promise asking cautiously skeptical questions. He plunged into the promise and came up strong, ready for God, sure that God would make good on what he had said. That's why it is said, "Abraham was declared fit before God by trusting God to set him right." But it's not just Abraham; it's also us! The same thing gets said about us when we embrace and believe the One who brought Jesus to life when the conditions were equally hopeless. The sacrificed Jesus made us fit for God, set us *right with God*.

DEVELOPING PATIENCE

1-2   **5** By entering through faith into what God has always wanted to do for us — set us right with him, make us fit for him — we have it all together with God because of our Master Jesus. And that's not all:

We throw open our doors to God and discover at the same moment that he has already thrown open his door to us. We find ourselves standing where we always hoped we might stand—out in the wide open spaces of God's grace and glory, standing tall and shouting our praise.

3-5 There's more to come: We continue to shout our praise even when we're hemmed in with troubles, because we know how troubles can develop passionate patience in us, and how that patience in turn forges the tempered steel of virtue, keeping us alert for whatever God will do next. In alert expectancy such as this, we're never left feeling shortchanged. Quite the contrary—we can't round up enough containers to hold everything God generously pours into our lives through the Holy Spirit!

6-8 Christ arrives right on time to make this happen. He didn't, and doesn't, wait for us to get ready. He presented himself for this sacrificial death when we were far too weak and rebellious to do anything to get ourselves ready. And even if we hadn't been so weak, we wouldn't have known what to do anyway. We can understand someone dying for a person worth dying for, and we can understand how someone good and noble could inspire us to selfless sacrifice. But God put his love on the line for us by offering his Son in sacrificial death while we were of no use whatever to him.

9-11 Now that we are set right with God by means of this sacrificial death, the consummate blood sacrifice, there is no longer a question of being at odds with God in any way. If, when we were at our worst, we were put on friendly terms with God by the sacrificial death of his Son, now that we're at our best, just think of how our lives will expand and deepen by means of his resurrection life! Now that we have actually received this amazing friendship with God, we are no longer content to simply say it in plodding prose. We sing and shout our praises to God through Jesus, the Messiah!

The Death-Dealing Sin, the Life-Giving Gift

12-14 You know the story of how Adam landed us in the dilemma we're in—first sin, then death, and no one exempt from either sin or death. That sin disturbed relations with God in everything and everyone, but the extent of the disturbance was not clear until God spelled it out in detail to Moses. So death, this huge abyss separating us from God, dominated the landscape from Adam to Moses. Even those who didn't sin precisely as Adam did by disobeying a specific command of God still had to experience this termination of life, this separation from God. But Adam, who got us into this, also points ahead to the One who will get us out of it.

15-17 Yet the rescuing gift is not exactly parallel to the death-dealing sin. If one man's sin put crowds of people at the dead-end abyss of separation from God, just think what God's gift poured through one man, Jesus Christ, will do! There's no comparison between that death-dealing sin and this generous, life-giving gift. The verdict on that one sin was the death sentence; the verdict on the many sins that followed was this wonderful life sentence. If death got the upper hand through one man's wrongdoing, can you imagine the breathtaking recovery life makes, sovereign life, in those who grasp with both hands this wildly extravagant life-gift, this grand setting-everything-right, that the one man Jesus Christ provides?

18-19 Here it is in a nutshell: Just as one person did it wrong and got us in all this trouble with sin and death, another person did it right and got us out of it. But more than just getting us out of trouble, he got us into life! One man said no to God and put many people in the wrong; one man said yes to God and put many in the right.

20-21   All that passing laws against sin did was produce more lawbreakers. But sin didn't, and doesn't, have a chance in competition with the aggressive forgiveness we call *grace*. When it's sin versus grace, grace wins hands down. All sin can do is threaten us with death, and that's the end of it. Grace, because God is putting everything together again through the Messiah, invites us into life — a life that goes on and on and on, world without end.

WHEN DEATH BECOMES LIFE

1-3   **6** So what do we do? Keep on sinning so God can keep on forgiving? I should hope not! If we've left the country where sin is sovereign, how can we still live in our old house there? Or didn't you realize we packed up and left there for good? That is what happened in baptism. When we went under the water, we left the old country of sin behind; when we came up out of the water, we entered into the new country of grace — a new life in a new land!

3-5   That's what baptism into the life of Jesus means. When we are lowered into the water, it is like the burial of Jesus; when we are raised up out of the water, it is like the resurrection of Jesus. Each of us is raised into a light-filled world by our Father so that we can see where we're going in our new grace-sovereign country.

6-11   Could it be any clearer? Our old way of life was nailed to the cross with Christ, a decisive end to that sin-miserable life — no longer at sin's every beck and call! What we believe is this: If we get included in Christ's sin-conquering death, we also get included in his life-saving resurrection. We know that when Jesus was raised from the dead it was a signal of the end of death-as-the-end. Never again will death have the last word. When Jesus died, he took sin down with him, but alive he brings God down to us. From now on, think of it this way: Sin speaks a dead language that means nothing to you; God speaks your mother tongue, and you hang on every word. You are dead to sin and alive to God. That's what Jesus did.

12-14   That means you must not give sin a vote in the way you conduct your lives. Don't give it the time of day. Don't even run little errands that are connected with that old way of life. Throw yourselves wholeheartedly and full-time — remember, you've been raised from the dead! — into God's way of doing things. Sin can't tell you how to live. After all, you're not living under that old tyranny any longer. You're living in the freedom of God.

WHAT IS TRUE FREEDOM?

15-18   So, since we're out from under the old tyranny, does that mean we can live any old way we want? Since we're free in the freedom of God, can we do anything that comes to mind? Hardly. You know well enough from your own experience that there are some acts of so-called freedom that destroy freedom. Offer yourselves to sin, for instance, and it's your last free act. But offer yourselves to the ways of God and the freedom never quits. All your lives you've let sin tell you what to do. But thank God you've started listening to a new master, one whose commands set you free to live openly in *his* freedom!

19   I'm using this freedom language because it's easy to picture. You can readily recall, can't you, how at one time the more you did just what you

felt like doing—not caring about others, not caring about God—the worse your life became and the less freedom you had? And how much different is it now as you live in God's freedom, your lives healed and expansive in holiness?

20-21   As long as you did what you felt like doing, ignoring God, you didn't have to bother with right thinking or right living, or right *anything* for that matter. But do you call that a free life? What did you get out of it? Nothing you're proud of now. Where did it get you? A dead end.

22-23   But now that you've found you don't have to listen to sin tell you what to do, and have discovered the delight of listening to God telling you, what a surprise! A whole, healed, put-together life right now, with more and more of life on the way! Work hard for sin your whole life and your pension is death. But God's gift is *real life*, eternal life, delivered by Jesus, our Master.

TORN BETWEEN ONE WAY AND ANOTHER

1-3   7 You shouldn't have any trouble understanding this, friends, for you know all the ins and outs of the law—how it works and how its power touches only the living. For instance, a wife is legally tied to her husband while he lives, but if he dies, she's free. If she lives with another man while her husband is living, she's obviously an adulteress. But if he dies, she is quite free to marry another man in good conscience, with no one's disapproval.

4-6   So, my friends, this is something like what has taken place with you. When Christ died he took that entire rule-dominated way of life down with him and left it in the tomb, leaving you free to "marry" a resurrection life and bear "offspring" of faith for God. For as long as we lived that old way of life, doing whatever we felt we could get away with, sin was calling most of the shots as the old law code hemmed us in. And this made us all the more rebellious. In the end, all we had to show for it was miscarriages and stillbirths. But now that we're no longer shackled to that domineering mate of sin, and out from under all those oppressive regulations and fine print, we're free to live a new life in the freedom of God.

7   But I can hear you say, "If the law code was as bad as all that, it's no better than sin itself." That's certainly not true. The law code had a perfectly legitimate function. Without its clear guidelines for right and wrong, moral behavior would be mostly guesswork. Apart from the succinct, surgical command, "You shall not covet," I could have dressed covetousness up to look like a virtue and ruined my life with it.

8-12   Don't you remember how it was? I do, perfectly well. The law code started out as an excellent piece of work. What happened, though, was that sin found a way to pervert the command into a temptation, making a piece of "forbidden fruit" out of it. The law code, instead of being used to guide me, was used to seduce me. Without all the paraphernalia of the law code, sin looked pretty dull and lifeless, and I went along without paying much attention to it. But once sin got its hands on the law code and decked itself out in all that finery, I was fooled, and fell for it. The very command that was supposed to guide me into life was cleverly used to trip me up, throwing me headlong. So sin was plenty alive, and I was stone dead. But the law code itself is God's good and common sense, each command sane and holy counsel.

13   I can already hear your next question: "Does that mean I can't even trust what is good [that is, the law]? Is good just as dangerous as evil?" No

again! Sin simply did what sin is so famous for doing: using the good as a cover to tempt me to do what would finally destroy me. By hiding within God's good commandment, sin did far more mischief than it could ever have accomplished on its own.

14-16   I can anticipate the response that is coming: "I know that all God's commands are spiritual, but I'm not. Isn't this also your experience?" Yes. I'm full of myself—after all, I've spent a long time in sin's prison. What I don't understand about myself is that I decide one way, but then I act another, doing things I absolutely despise. So if I can't be trusted to figure out what is best for myself and then do it, it becomes obvious that God's command is necessary.

17-20   But I need something *more*! For if I know the law but still can't keep it, and if the power of sin within me keeps sabotaging my best intentions, I obviously need help! I realize that I don't have what it takes. I can will it, but I can't *do* it. I decide to do good, but I don't *really* do it; I decide not to do bad, but then I do it anyway. My decisions, such as they are, don't result in actions. Something has gone wrong deep within me and gets the better of me every time.

21-23   It happens so regularly that it's predictable. The moment I decide to do good, sin is there to trip me up. I truly delight in God's commands, but it's pretty obvious that not all of me joins in that delight. Parts of me covertly rebel, and just when I least expect it, they take charge.

24   I've tried everything and nothing helps. I'm at the end of my rope. Is there no one who can do anything for me? Isn't that the real question?

25   The answer, thank God, is that Jesus Christ can and does. He acted to set things right in this life of contradictions where I want to serve God with all my heart and mind, but am pulled by the influence of sin to do something totally different.

The Solution Is Life on God's Terms

1-2   **8** With the arrival of Jesus, the Messiah, that fateful dilemma is resolved. Those who enter into Christ's being-here-for-us no longer have to live under a continuous, low-lying black cloud. A new power is in operation. The Spirit of life in Christ, like a strong wind, has magnificently cleared the air, freeing you from a fated lifetime of brutal tyranny at the hands of sin and death.

3-4   God went for the jugular when he sent his own Son. He didn't deal with the problem as something remote and unimportant. In his Son, Jesus, he personally took on the human condition, entered the disordered mess of struggling humanity in order to set it right once and for all. The law code, weakened as it always was by fractured human nature, could never have done that.

The law always ended up being used as a Band-Aid on sin instead of a deep healing of it. And now what the law code asked for but we couldn't deliver is accomplished as we, instead of redoubling our own efforts, simply embrace what the Spirit is doing in us.

5-8   Those who think they can do it on their own end up obsessed with measuring their own moral muscle but never get around to exercising it in real life. Those who trust God's action in them find that God's Spirit is in them—living and breathing God! Obsession with self in these matters is a dead end; attention to God leads us out into the open, into a spacious, free life. Focusing on the self is the opposite of focusing on God. Anyone completely absorbed in self ignores God, ends up thinking more about self than God. That person ignores who God is and what he is doing. And God isn't pleased at being ignored.

9-11 But if God himself has taken up residence in your life, you can hardly be thinking more of yourself than of him. Anyone, of course, who has not welcomed this invisible but clearly present God, the Spirit of Christ, won't know what we're talking about. But for you who welcome him, in whom he dwells—even though you still experience all the limitations of sin—you yourself experience life on God's terms. It stands to reason, doesn't it, that if the alive-and-present God who raised Jesus from the dead moves into your life, he'll do the same thing in you that he did in Jesus, bringing you alive to himself? When God lives and breathes in you (and he does, as surely as he did in Jesus), you are delivered from that dead life. With his Spirit living in you, your body will be as alive as Christ's!

12-14 So don't you see that we don't owe this old do-it-yourself life one red cent. There's nothing in it for us, nothing at all. The best thing to do is give it a decent burial and get on with your new life. God's Spirit beckons. There are things to do and places to go!

15-17 This resurrection life you received from God is not a timid, grave-tending life. It's adventurously expectant, greeting God with a childlike "What's next, Papa?" God's Spirit touches our spirits and confirms who we really are. We know who he is, and we know who we are: Father and children. And we know we are going to get what's coming to us—an unbelievable inheritance! We go through exactly what Christ goes through. If we go through the hard times with him, then we're certainly going to go through the good times with him!

18-21 That's why I don't think there's any comparison between the present hard times and the coming good times. The created world itself can hardly wait for what's coming next. Everything in creation is being more or less held back. God reins it in until both creation and all the creatures are ready and can be released at the same moment into the glorious times ahead. Meanwhile, the joyful anticipation deepens.

22-25 All around us we observe a pregnant creation. The difficult times of pain throughout the world are simply birth pangs. But it's not only around us; it's *within* us. The Spirit of God is arousing us within. We're also feeling the birth pangs. These sterile and barren bodies of ours are yearning for full deliverance. That is why waiting does not diminish us, any more than waiting diminishes a pregnant mother. We are enlarged in the waiting. We, of course, don't see what is enlarging us. But the longer we wait, the larger we become, and the more joyful our expectancy.

26-28 Meanwhile, the moment we get tired in the waiting, God's Spirit is right alongside helping us along. If we don't know how or what to pray, it doesn't matter. He does our praying in and for us, making prayer out of our wordless sighs, our aching groans. He knows us far better than we know ourselves, knows our pregnant condition, and keeps us present before God. That's why we can be so sure that every detail in our lives of love for God is worked into something good.

29-30 God knew what he was doing from the very beginning. He decided from the outset to shape the lives of those who love him along the same lines as the life of his Son. The Son stands first in the line of humanity he restored. We see the original and intended shape of our lives there in him. After God made that decision of what his children should be like, he followed it up by calling people by name. After he called them by name, he set them on a solid basis with himself. And then, after getting them established, he stayed with them to the end, gloriously completing what he had begun.

31-39 So, what do you think? With God on our side like this, how can we lose? If God didn't hesitate to put everything on the line for us, embracing our condition and exposing himself to the worst by sending his own Son, is there anything else he wouldn't gladly and freely do for us? And who would dare tangle with God by messing with one of God's chosen? Who would dare even to point a finger? The One who died for us—who was raised to life for us!—is in the presence of God at this very moment sticking up for us. Do you think anyone is going to be able to drive a wedge between us and Christ's love for us? There is no way! Not trouble, not hard times, not hatred, not hunger, not homelessness, not bullying threats, not backstabbing, not even the worst sins listed in Scripture:

They kill us in cold blood because they hate you.
We're sitting ducks; they pick us off one by one.

None of this fazes us because Jesus loves us. I'm absolutely convinced that nothing—nothing living or dead, angelic or demonic, today or tomorrow, high or low, thinkable or unthinkable—absolutely *nothing* can get between us and God's love because of the way that Jesus our Master has embraced us.

GOD IS CALLING HIS PEOPLE

1-5 **9** At the same time, you need to know that I carry with me at all times a huge sorrow. It's an enormous pain deep within me, and I'm never free of it. I'm not exaggerating—Christ and the Holy Spirit are my witnesses. It's the Israelites . . . If there were any way I could be cursed by the Messiah so they could be blessed by him, I'd do it in a minute. They're my family. I grew up with them. They had everything going for them—family, glory, covenants, revelation, worship, promises, to say nothing of being the race that produced the Messiah, the Christ, who is God over everything, always. Oh, yes!

6-9 Don't suppose for a moment, though, that God's Word has malfunctioned in some way or other. The problem goes back a long way. From the outset, not all Israelites of the flesh were Israelites of the spirit. It wasn't Abraham's sperm that gave identity here, but God's *promise*. Remember how it was put: "Your family will be defined by Isaac"? That means that Israelite identity was never racially determined by sexual transmission, but it was *God*-determined by promise. Remember that promise, "When I come back next year at this time, Sarah will have a son"?

10-13 And that's not the only time. To Rebecca, also, a promise was made that took priority over genetics. When she became pregnant by our one-of-a-kind ancestor, Isaac, and her babies were still innocent in the womb—incapable of good or bad—she received a special assurance from God. What God did in this case made it perfectly plain that his purpose is not a hit-or-miss thing dependent on what we do or don't do, but a sure thing determined by his decision, flowing steadily from his initiative. God told Rebecca, "The firstborn of your twins will take second place." Later that was turned into a stark epigram: "I loved Jacob; I hated Esau."

14-18 Is that grounds for complaining that God is unfair? Not so fast, please. God told Moses, "*I'm* in charge of mercy. *I'm* in charge of compassion." Compassion doesn't originate in our bleeding hearts or moral sweat, but in God's mercy. The same point was made when God said to Pharaoh, "I picked you as a bit player in this drama of my salvation power." All we're saying is that God has the first word, initiating the action in which we play our part for good or ill.

19 Are you going to object, "So how can God blame us for anything since he's in charge of everything? If the big decisions are already made, what say do we have in it?"

20-33 Who in the world do you think you are to second-guess God? Do you for one moment suppose any of us knows enough to call God into question? Clay doesn't talk back to the fingers that mold it, saying, "Why did you shape me like this?" Isn't it obvious that a potter has a perfect right to shape one lump of clay into a vase for holding flowers and another into a pot for cooking beans? If God needs one style of pottery especially designed to show his angry displeasure and another style carefully crafted to show his glorious goodness, isn't that all right? Either or both happens to Jews, but it also happens to the other people. Hosea put it well:

> I'll call nobodies and make them somebodies;
> I'll call the unloved and make them beloved.
> In the place where they yelled out, "You're nobody!"
> they're calling you "God's living children."

Isaiah maintained this same emphasis:
> If each grain of sand on the seashore were numbered
> and the sum labeled "chosen of God,"
> They'd be numbers still, not names;
> salvation comes by personal selection.
> God doesn't count us; he calls us by name.
> Arithmetic is not his focus.

Isaiah had looked ahead and spoken the truth:
> If our powerful God
> had not provided us a legacy of living children,
> We would have ended up like ghost towns,
> like Sodom and Gomorrah.

How can we sum this up? All those people who didn't seem interested in what God was doing actually *embraced* what God was doing as he straightened out their lives. And Israel, who seemed so interested in reading and talking about what God was doing, missed it. How could they miss it? Because instead of trusting God, *they* took over. They were absorbed in what they themselves were doing. They were so absorbed in their "God projects" that they didn't notice God right in front of them, like a huge rock in the middle of the road. And so they stumbled into him and went sprawling.

Isaiah (again!) gives us the metaphor for pulling this together:

> Careful! I've put a huge stone on the road to Mount Zion,
>> a stone you can't get around.
> But the stone is me! If you're looking for me,
>> you'll find me on the way, not in the way.

ISRAEL REDUCED TO RELIGION

1-3 **10** Believe me, friends, all I want for Israel is what's best for Israel: salvation, nothing less. I want it with all my heart and pray to God for it all the time. I readily admit that the Jews are impressively energetic regarding God — but they are doing everything exactly backward. They don't seem to realize that this comprehensive setting-things-right that is salvation is *God's* business, and a most flourishing business it is. Right across the street they set up their own salvation shops and noisily hawk their wares. After all these years of refusing to really deal with God on his terms, insisting instead on making their own deals, they have nothing to show for it.

4-10 The earlier revelation was intended simply to get us ready for the Messiah, who then puts everything right for those who trust him to do it. Moses wrote that anyone who insists on using the law code to live right before God soon discovers it's not so easy — every detail of life regulated by fine print! But trusting God to shape the right living in us is a different story — no precarious climb up to heaven to recruit the Messiah, no dangerous descent into hell to rescue the Messiah. So what exactly was Moses saying?

> The word that saves is right here,
>> as near as the tongue in your mouth,
>> as close as the heart in your chest.

It's the word of faith that welcomes God to go to work and set things right for us. This is the core of our preaching. Say the welcoming word to God — "Jesus is my Master" — embracing, body and soul, God's work of doing in us what he did in raising Jesus from the dead. That's it. You're not "doing" anything; you're simply calling out to God, trusting him to do it for you. That's salvation. With your whole being you embrace God setting things right, and then you say it, right out loud: "God has set everything right between him and me!"

11-13 Scripture reassures us, "No one who trusts God like this — heart and soul — will ever regret it." It's exactly the same no matter what a person's religious background may be: the same God for all of us, acting the same incredibly generous way to everyone who calls out for help. "Everyone who calls, 'Help, God!' gets help."

14-17 But how can people call for help if they don't know who to trust? And how can they know who to trust if they haven't heard of the One who can be trusted? And how can they hear if nobody tells them? And how is anyone going to tell them, unless someone is sent to do it? That's why Scripture exclaims,

> A sight to take your breath away!
> Grand processions of people
>> telling all the good things of God!

But not everybody is ready for this, ready to see and hear and act. Isaiah asked what we all ask at one time or another: "Does anyone care, God? Is anyone listening and believing a word of it?" The point is: Before you trust, you have to listen. But unless Christ's Word is preached, there's nothing to listen to.

18-21   But haven't there been plenty of opportunities for Israel to listen and understand what's going on? *Plenty*, I'd say.

> Preachers' voices have gone 'round the world,
> Their message to earth's seven seas.

So the big question is, Why didn't Israel understand that she had no corner on this message? Moses had it right when he predicted,

> When you see God reach out to those
>   you consider your inferiors — outsiders! —
>   you'll become insanely jealous.
> When you see God reach out to people
>   you think are religiously stupid,
>   you'll throw temper tantrums.

Isaiah dared to speak out these words of God:
> People found and welcomed me
>   who never so much as looked for me.
> And I found and welcomed people
>   who had never even asked about me.

Then he capped it with a damning indictment:
> Day after day after day,
>   I beckoned Israel with open arms,
> And got nothing for my trouble
>   but cold shoulders and icy stares.

THE LOYAL MINORITY

1-2   **11** Does this mean, then, that God is so fed up with Israel that he'll have nothing more to do with them? Hardly. Remember that I, the one writing these things, am an Israelite, a descendant of Abraham out of the tribe of Benjamin. You can't get much more Semitic than that! So we're not talking about repudiation. God has been too long involved with Israel, has too much invested, to simply wash his hands of them.

2-6   Do you remember that time Elijah was agonizing over this same Israel and cried out in prayer?

> God, they murdered your prophets,
> They trashed your altars;
> I'm the only one left and now they're after me!

And do you remember God's answer?
> I still have seven thousand who haven't quit,
> Seven thousand who are loyal to the finish.

It's the same today. There's a fiercely loyal minority still—not many, perhaps, but probably more than you think. They're holding on, not because of what they think they're going to get out of it, but because they're convinced of God's grace and purpose in choosing them. If they were only thinking of their own immediate self-interest, they would have left long ago.

⁷⁻¹⁰ And then what happened? Well, when Israel tried to be right with God on her own, pursuing her own self-interest, she didn't succeed. The chosen ones of God were those who let God pursue his interest in them, and as a result received his stamp of legitimacy. The "self-interest Israel" became thick-skinned toward God. Moses and Isaiah both commented on this:

> Fed up with their quarrelsome, self-centered ways,
>   God blurred their eyes and dulled their ears,
> Shut them in on themselves in a hall of mirrors,
>   and they're there to this day.

David was upset about the same thing:
>   I hope they get sick eating self-serving meals,
>   break a leg walking their self-serving ways.
>   I hope they go blind staring in their mirrors,
>   get ulcers from playing at god.

PRUNING AND GRAFTING BRANCHES

¹¹⁻¹² The next question is, "Are they down for the count? Are they out of this for good?" And the answer is a clear-cut *No*. Ironically when they walked out, they left the door open and the outsiders walked in. But the next thing you know, the Jews were starting to wonder if perhaps they had walked out on a good thing. Now, if their leaving triggered this worldwide coming of non-Jewish outsiders to God's kingdom, just imagine the effect of their coming back! What a homecoming!

¹³⁻¹⁵ But I don't want to go on about them. It's you, the outsiders, that I'm concerned with now. Because my personal assignment is focused on the so-called outsiders, I make as much of this as I can when I'm among my Israelite kin, the so-called *insiders*, hoping they'll realize what they're missing and want to get in on what God is doing. If their falling out initiated this worldwide coming together, their recovery is going to set off something even better: mass homecoming! If the first thing the Jews did, even though it was wrong for them, turned out for your good, just think what's going to happen when they get it right!

¹⁶⁻¹⁸ Behind and underneath all this there is a holy, God-planted, God-tended root. If the primary root of the tree is holy, there's bound to be some holy fruit. Some of the tree's branches were pruned and you wild olive shoots were grafted in. Yet the fact that you are now fed by that rich and holy root gives you no cause to crow over the pruned branches. Remember, you aren't feeding the root; the root is feeding you.

¹⁹⁻²⁰ It's certainly possible to say, "Other branches were pruned so that *I* could be grafted in!" Well and good. But they were pruned because they were deadwood, no longer connected by belief and commitment to the root. The only reason you're on the tree is because your graft "took" when you believed, and because you're connected to that belief-nurturing root. So don't get cocky and strut your branch. Be humbly mindful of the root that

keeps you lithe and green.

21-22 　　If God didn't think twice about taking pruning shears to the natural branches, why would he hesitate over you? He wouldn't give it a second thought. Make sure you stay alert to these qualities of gentle kindness and ruthless severity that exist side by side in God—ruthless with the deadwood, gentle with the grafted shoot. But don't presume on this gentleness. The moment you become deadwood, you're out of there.

23-24 　　And don't get to feeling superior to those pruned branches down on the ground. If they don't persist in remaining deadwood, they could very well get grafted back in. God can do that. He can perform miracle grafts. Why, if he could graft *you*—branches cut from a tree out in the wild—into an orchard tree, he certainly isn't going to have any trouble grafting branches back into the tree they grew from in the first place. Just be glad you're in the tree, and hope for the best for the others.

A COMPLETE ISRAEL

25-29 　I want to lay all this out on the table as clearly as I can, friends. This is complicated. It would be easy to misinterpret what's going on and arrogantly assume that you're royalty and they're just rabble, out on their ears for good. But that's not it at all. This hardness on the part of insider Israel toward God is temporary. Its effect is to open things up to all the outsiders so that we end up with a full house. Before it's all over, there will be a complete Israel. As it is written,

> A champion will stride down from the mountain of Zion;
> 　he'll clean house in Jacob.
> And this is my commitment to my people:
> 　removal of their sins.

From your point of view as you hear and embrace the good news of the Message, it looks like the Jews are God's enemies. But looked at from the long-range perspective of God's overall purpose, they remain God's oldest friends. God's gifts and God's call are under full warranty—never canceled, never rescinded.

30-32 　　There was a time not so long ago when you were on the outs with God. But then the Jews slammed the door on him and things opened up for you. Now *they* are on the outs. But with the door held wide open for you, they have a way back in. In one way or another, God makes sure that we all experience what it means to be outside so that he can personally open the door and welcome us back in.

33-36 　　Have you ever come on anything quite like this extravagant generosity of God, this deep, deep wisdom? It's way over our heads. We'll never figure it out.

> Is there anyone around who can explain God?
> Anyone smart enough to tell him what to do?
> Anyone who has done him such a huge favor
> 　that God has to ask his advice?

> Everything comes from him;
> Everything happens through him;

Everything ends up in him.
Always glory! Always praise!
   Yes. Yes. Yes.

PLACE YOUR LIFE BEFORE GOD

1-2 **12** So here's what I want you to do, God helping you: Take your everyday, ordinary life—your sleeping, eating, going-to-work, and walking-around life—and place it before God as an offering. Embracing what God does for you is the best thing you can do for him. Don't become so well-adjusted to your culture that you fit into it without even thinking. Instead, fix your attention on God. You'll be changed from the inside out. Readily recognize what he wants from you, and quickly respond to it. Unlike the culture around you, always dragging you down to its level of immaturity, God brings the best out of you, develops well-formed maturity in you.

3   I'm speaking to you out of deep gratitude for all that God has given me, and especially as I have responsibilities in relation to you. Living then, as every one of you does, in pure grace, it's important that you not misinterpret yourselves as people who are bringing this goodness to God. No, God brings it all to you. The only accurate way to understand ourselves is by what God is and by what he does for us, not by what we are and what we do for him.

4-6   In this way we are like the various parts of a human body. Each part gets its meaning from the body as a whole, not the other way around. The body we're talking about is Christ's body of chosen people. Each of us finds our meaning and function as a part of his body. But as a chopped-off finger or cut-off toe we wouldn't amount to much, would we? So since we find ourselves fashioned into all these excellently formed and marvelously functioning parts in Christ's body, let's just go ahead and be what we were made to be, without enviously or pridefully comparing ourselves with each other, or trying to be something we aren't.

6-8   If you preach, just preach God's Message, nothing else; if you help, just help, don't take over; if you teach, stick to your teaching; if you give encouraging guidance, be careful that you don't get bossy; if you're put in charge, don't manipulate; if you're called to give aid to people in distress, keep your eyes open and be quick to respond; if you work with the disadvantaged, don't let yourself get irritated with them or depressed by them. Keep a smile on your face.

9-10   Love from the center of who you are; don't fake it. Run for dear life from evil; hold on for dear life to good. Be good friends who love deeply; practice playing second fiddle.

11-13   Don't burn out; keep yourselves fueled and aflame. Be alert servants of the Master, cheerfully expectant. Don't quit in hard times; pray all the harder. Help needy Christians; be inventive in hospitality.

14-16   Bless your enemies; no cursing under your breath. Laugh with your happy friends when they're happy; share tears when they're down. Get along with each other; don't be stuck-up. Make friends with nobodies; don't be the great somebody.

17-19   Don't hit back; discover beauty in everyone. If you've got it in you, get along with everybody. Don't insist on getting even; that's not for you to do. "I'll do the judging," says God. "I'll take care of it."

20-21   Our Scriptures tell us that if you see your enemy hungry, go buy that person lunch, or if he's thirsty, get him a drink. Your generosity will surprise him with goodness. Don't let evil get the best of you; get the best of evil by doing good.

TO BE A RESPONSIBLE CITIZEN

1-3   **13** Be a good citizen. All governments are under God. Insofar as there is peace and order, it's God's order. So live responsibly as a citizen. If you're irresponsible to the state, then you're irresponsible with God, and God will hold you responsible. Duly constituted authorities are only a threat if you're trying to get by with something. Decent citizens should have nothing to fear.

3-5   Do you want to be on good terms with the government? Be a responsible citizen and you'll get on just fine, the government working to your advantage. But if you're breaking the rules right and left, watch out. The police aren't there just to be admired in their uniforms. God also has an interest in keeping order, and he uses them to do it. That's why you must live responsibly — not just to avoid punishment but also because it's the right way to live.

6-7   That's also why you pay taxes — so that an orderly way of life can be maintained. Fulfill your obligations as a citizen. Pay your taxes, pay your bills, respect your leaders.

8-10   Don't run up debts, except for the huge debt of love you owe each other. When you love others, you complete what the law has been after all along. The law code — don't sleep with another person's spouse, don't take someone's life, don't take what isn't yours, don't always be wanting what you don't have, and any other "don't" you can think of — finally adds up to this: Love other people as well as you do yourself. You can't go wrong when you love others. When you add up everything in the law code, the sum total is *love*.

11-14   But make sure that you don't get so absorbed and exhausted in taking care of all your day-by-day obligations that you lose track of the time and doze off, oblivious to God. The night is about over, dawn is about to break. Be up and awake to what God is doing! God is putting the finishing touches on the salvation work he began when we first believed. We can't afford to waste a minute, must not squander these precious daylight hours in frivolity and indulgence, in sleeping around and dissipation, in bickering and grabbing everything in sight. Get out of bed and get dressed! Don't loiter and linger, waiting until the very last minute. Dress yourselves in Christ, and be up and about!

CULTIVATING GOOD RELATIONSHIPS

1   **14** Welcome with open arms fellow believers who don't see things the way you do. And don't jump all over them every time they do or say something you don't agree with — even when it seems that they are strong on opinions but weak in the faith department. Remember, they have their own history to deal with. Treat them gently.

2-4   For instance, a person who has been around for a while might well be convinced that he can eat anything on the table, while another, with a different background, might assume he should only be a vegetarian and eat accordingly. But since both are guests at Christ's table, wouldn't it be terribly rude if they fell to criticizing what the other ate or didn't eat? God, after all, invited them both to the table. Do you have any business crossing people off the guest list or interfering with God's welcome? If there are corrections to be made or manners to be learned, God can handle that without your help.

⁵ Or, say, one person thinks that some days should be set aside as holy and another thinks that each day is pretty much like any other. There are good reasons either way. So, each person is free to follow the convictions of conscience.

⁶⁻⁹ What's important in all this is that if you keep a holy day, keep it for *God's* sake; if you eat meat, eat it to the glory of God and thank God for prime rib; if you're a vegetarian, eat vegetables to the glory of God and thank God for broccoli. None of us are permitted to insist on our own way in these matters. It's *God* we are answerable to — all the way from life to death and everything in between — not each other. That's why Jesus lived and died and then lived again: so that he could be our Master across the entire range of life and death, and free us from the petty tyrannies of each other.

¹⁰⁻¹² So where does that leave you when you criticize a brother? And where does that leave you when you condescend to a sister? I'd say it leaves you looking pretty silly — or worse. Eventually, we're all going to end up kneeling side by side in the place of judgment, facing God. Your critical and condescending ways aren't going to improve your position there one bit. Read it for yourself in Scripture:

> "As I live and breathe," God says,
>   "every knee will bow before me;
> Every tongue will tell the honest truth
>   that I and only I am God."

So tend to your knitting. You've got your hands full just taking care of your own life before God.

¹³⁻¹⁴ Forget about deciding what's right for each other. Here's what you need to be concerned about: that you don't get in the way of someone else, making life more difficult than it already is. I'm convinced — Jesus convinced me! — that everything as it is in itself is holy. We, of course, by the way we treat it or talk about it, can contaminate it.

¹⁵⁻¹⁶ If you confuse others by making a big issue over what they eat or don't eat, you're no longer a companion with them in love, are you? These, remember, are persons for whom Christ died. Would you risk sending them to hell over an item in their diet? Don't you dare let a piece of God-blessed food become an occasion of soul-poisoning!

¹⁷⁻¹⁸ God's kingdom isn't a matter of what you put in your stomach, for goodness' sake. It's what God does with your life as he sets it right, puts it together, and completes it with joy. Your task is to single-mindedly serve Christ. Do that and you'll kill two birds with one stone: pleasing the God above you and proving your worth to the people around you.

¹⁹⁻²¹ So let's agree to use all our energy in getting along with each other. Help others with encouraging words; don't drag them down by finding fault. You're certainly not going to permit an argument over what is served or not served at supper to wreck God's work among you, are you? I said it

before and I'll say it again: All food is good, but it can turn bad if you use it badly, if you use it to trip others up and send them sprawling. When you sit down to a meal, your primary concern should not be to feed your own face but to share the life of Jesus. So be sensitive and courteous to the others who are eating. Don't eat or say or do things that might interfere with the free exchange of love.

22-23   Cultivate your own relationship with God, but don't impose it on others. You're fortunate if your behavior and your belief are coherent. But if you're not sure, if you notice that you are acting in ways inconsistent with what you believe—some days trying to impose your opinions on others, other days just trying to please them—then you know that you're out of line. If the way you live isn't consistent with what you believe, then it's wrong.

1-2   15 Those of us who are strong and able in the faith need to step in and lend a hand to those who falter, and not just do what is most convenient for us. Strength is for service, not status. Each one of us needs to look after the good of the people around us, asking ourselves, "How can I help?"

3-6   That's exactly what Jesus did. He didn't make it easy for himself by avoiding people's troubles, but waded right in and helped out. "I took on the troubles of the troubled," is the way Scripture puts it. Even if it was written in Scripture long ago, you can be sure it's written for *us*. God wants the combination of his steady, constant calling and warm, personal counsel in Scripture to come to characterize *us*, keeping us alert for whatever he will do next. May our dependably steady and warmly personal God develop maturity in you so that you get along with each other as well as Jesus gets along with us all. Then we'll be a choir—not our voices only, but our very lives singing in harmony in a stunning anthem to the God and Father of our Master Jesus!

7-13   So reach out and welcome one another to God's glory. Jesus did it; now *you* do it! Jesus, staying true to God's purposes, reached out in a special way to the Jewish insiders so that the old ancestral promises would come true for them. As a result, the non-Jewish outsiders have been able to experience mercy and to show appreciation to God. Just think of all the Scriptures that will come true in what we do! For instance:

> Then I'll join outsiders in a hymn-sing;
> I'll sing to your name!

And this one:
> Outsiders and insiders, rejoice together!

And again:
> People of all nations, celebrate God!
> All colors and races, give hearty praise!

And Isaiah's word:
> There's the root of our ancestor Jesse,
> breaking through the earth and growing tree tall,
> Tall enough for everyone everywhere to see and take hope!

Oh! May the God of green hope fill you up with joy, fill you up with peace, so that your believing lives, filled with the life-giving energy of the Holy Spirit, will brim over with hope!

14-16 Personally, I've been completely satisfied with who you are and what you are doing. You seem to me to be well-motivated and well-instructed, quite capable of guiding and advising one another. So, my dear friends, don't take my rather bold and blunt language as criticism. It's not criticism. I'm simply underlining how very much I need your help in carrying out this highly focused assignment God gave me, this priestly and gospel work of serving the spiritual needs of the non-Jewish outsiders so they can be presented as an acceptable offering to God, made whole and holy by God's Holy Spirit.

17-21 Looking back over what has been accomplished and what I have observed, I must say I am most pleased — in the context of Jesus, I'd even say *proud*, but only in that context. I have no interest in giving you a chatty account of my adventures, only the wondrously powerful and transformingly present words and deeds of Christ in me that triggered a believing response among the outsiders. In such ways I have trailblazed a preaching of the Message of Jesus all the way from Jerusalem far into northwestern Greece. This has all been pioneer work, bringing the Message only into those places where Jesus was not yet known and worshiped. My text has been,

> Those who were never told of him —
>   they'll see him!
> Those who've never heard of him —
>   they'll get the message!

22-24 And that's why it has taken me so long to finally get around to coming to you. But now that there is no more pioneering work to be done in these parts, and since I have looked forward to seeing you for many years, I'm planning my visit. I'm headed for Spain, and expect to stop off on the way to enjoy a good visit with you, and eventually have you send me off with God's blessing.

25-29 First, though, I'm going to Jerusalem to deliver a relief offering to the followers of Jesus there. The Greeks — all the way from the Macedonians in the north to the Achaians in the south — decided they wanted to take up a collection for the poor among the believers in Jerusalem. They were happy to do this, but it was also their duty. Seeing that they got in on all the spiritual gifts that flowed out of the Jerusalem community so generously, it is only right that they do what they can to relieve their poverty. As soon as I have done this — personally handed over this "fruit basket" — I'm off to Spain, with a stopover with you in Rome. My hope is that my visit with you is going to be one of Christ's more extravagant blessings.

30-33 I have one request, dear friends: Pray for me. Pray strenuously with and for me — to God the Father, through the power of our Master Jesus, through the love of the Spirit — that I will be delivered from the lions' den of unbelievers in Judea. Pray also that my relief offering to the Jerusalem believers will be accepted in the spirit in which it is given. Then, God willing, I'll be on my way to you with a light and eager heart, looking forward to being refreshed by your company. God's peace be with all of you. Oh, yes!

* * *

1-2 **16** Be sure to welcome our friend Phoebe in the way of the Master, with all the generous hospitality we Christians are famous for. I heartily endorse both her and her work. She's a key representative of the church at Cenchrea. Help her out in whatever she asks. She deserves anything you can do for her. She's helped many a person, including me.

3-5 Say hello to Priscilla and Aquila, who have worked hand in hand with me in serving Jesus. They once put their lives on the line for me. And I'm not the only one grateful to them. All the non-Jewish gatherings of believers also owe them plenty, to say nothing of the church that meets in their house.

Hello to my dear friend Epenetus. He was the very first follower of Jesus in the province of Asia.

6 Hello to Mary. What a worker she has turned out to be!

7 Hello to my cousins Andronicus and Junias. We once shared a jail cell. They were believers in Christ before I was. Both of them are outstanding leaders.

8 Hello to Ampliatus, my good friend in the family of God.

9 Hello to Urbanus, our companion in Christ's work, and my good friend Stachys.

10 Hello to Apelles, a tried-and-true veteran in following Christ.

Hello to the family of Aristobulus.

11 Hello to my cousin Herodion.

Hello to those who belong to the Lord from the family of Narcissus.

12 Hello to Tryphena and Tryphosa — such diligent women in serving the Master.

Hello to Persis, a dear friend and hard worker in Christ.

13 Hello to Rufus — a good choice by the Master! — and his mother. She has also been a dear mother to me.

14 Hello to Asyncritus, Phlegon, Hermes, Patrobas, Hermas, and also to all of their families.

15 Hello to Philologus, Julia, Nereus and his sister, and Olympas — and all the followers of Jesus who live with them.

16 Holy embraces all around! All the churches of Christ send their warmest greetings!

17-18 One final word of counsel, friends. Keep a sharp eye out for those who take bits and pieces of the teaching that you learned and then use them to make trouble. Give these people a wide berth. They have no intention of living for our Master Christ. They're only in this for what they can get out of it, and aren't above using pious sweet talk to dupe unsuspecting innocents.

19-20 And so while there has never been any question about your honesty in these matters — I couldn't be more proud of you! — I want you also to be smart, making sure every "good" thing is the *real* thing. Don't be gullible in regard to smooth-talking evil. Stay alert like this, and before you know it the God of peace will come down on Satan with both feet, stomping him into the dirt. Enjoy the best of Jesus!

21 And here are some more greetings from our end. Timothy, my partner

in this work, Lucius, and my cousins Jason and Sosipater all said to tell you hello.

22 I, Tertius, who wrote this letter at Paul's dictation, send you my personal greetings.

23 Gaius, who is host here to both me and the whole church, wants to be remembered to you.

Erastus, the city treasurer, and our good friend Quartus send their greetings.

25-26 All of our praise rises to the One who is strong enough to make *you* strong, exactly as preached in Jesus Christ, precisely as revealed in the mystery kept secret for so long but now an open book through the prophetic Scriptures. All the nations of the world can now know the truth and be brought into obedient belief, carrying out the orders of God, who got all this started, down to the very last letter.

27 All our praise is focused through Jesus on this incomparably wise God! Yes!

1 CORINTHIANS

When people become Christians, they don't at the same moment become nice. This always comes as something of a surprise. Conversion to Christ and his ways doesn't automatically furnish a person with impeccable manners and suitable morals.

The people of Corinth had a reputation in the ancient world as an unruly, hard-drinking, sexually promiscuous bunch of people. When Paul arrived with the Message and many of them became believers in Jesus, they brought their reputations with them right into the church.

Paul spent a year and a half with them as their pastor, going over the Message of the "good news" in detail, showing them how to live out this new life of salvation and holiness as a community of believers. Then he went on his way to other towns and churches.

Sometime later Paul received a report from one of the Corinthian families that in his absence things had more or less fallen apart. He also received a letter from Corinth asking for help. Factions had developed, morals were in disrepair, worship had degenerated into a selfish grabbing for the supernatural. It was the kind of thing that might have been expected from Corinthians!

Paul's first letter to the Corinthians is a classic of pastoral response: affectionate, firm, clear, and unswerving in the conviction that God among them, revealed in Jesus and present in his Holy Spirit, continued to be the central issue in their lives, regardless of how much of a mess they had made of things. Paul doesn't disown them as brother and sister Christians, doesn't throw them out because of their bad behavior, and doesn't fly into a tirade over their irresponsible ways. He takes it all more or less in stride, but also takes them by the hand and goes over all the old ground again, directing them in how to work all the glorious details of God's saving love into their love for one another.

1 CORINTHIANS

1-2 **1** I, Paul, have been called and sent by Jesus, the Messiah, according to God's plan, along with my friend Sosthenes. I send this letter to you in God's church at Corinth, believers cleaned up by Jesus and set apart for a God-filled life. I include in my greeting all who call out to Jesus, wherever they live. He's their Master as well as ours!

3 May all the gifts and benefits that come from God our Father, and the Master, Jesus Christ, be yours.

4-6 Every time I think of you—and I think of you often!—I thank God for your lives of free and open access to God, given by Jesus. There's no end to what has happened in you—it's beyond speech, beyond knowledge. The evidence of Christ has been clearly verified in your lives.

7-9 Just think—you don't need a thing, you've got it all! All God's gifts are right in front of you as you wait expectantly for our Master Jesus to arrive on the scene for the Finale. And not only that, but God himself is right alongside to keep you steady and on track until things are all wrapped up by Jesus. God, who got you started in this spiritual adventure, shares with us the life of his Son and our Master Jesus. He will never give up on you. Never forget that.

THE CROSS: THE IRONY OF GOD'S WISDOM

10 I have a serious concern to bring up with you, my friends, using the authority of Jesus, our Master. I'll put it as urgently as I can: You *must* get along with each other. You must learn to be considerate of one another, cultivating a life in common.

11-12 I bring this up because some from Chloe's family brought a most disturbing report to my attention—that you're fighting among yourselves! I'll tell you exactly what I was told: You're all picking sides, going around saying, "I'm on Paul's side," or "I'm for Apollos," or "Peter is my man," or "I'm in the Messiah group."

13-16 I ask you, "Has the Messiah been chopped up in little pieces so we can each have a relic all our own? Was Paul crucified for you? Was a single one of you baptized in Paul's name?" I was not involved with any of your baptisms—except for Crispus and Gaius—and on getting this report, I'm sure glad I wasn't. At least no one can go around saying he was baptized in my name. (Come to think of it, I also baptized Stephanas's family, but as far as I can recall, that's it.)

17 God didn't send me out to collect a following for myself, but to preach the Message of what he has done, collecting a following for him. And he didn't send me to do it with a lot of fancy rhetoric of my own, lest the powerful action at the center—Christ on the Cross—be trivialized into mere words.

18-21 The Message that points to Christ on the Cross seems like sheer silliness to those hellbent on destruction, but for those on the way of salvation it makes perfect sense. This is the way God works, and most powerfully as it turns out. It's written,

I'll turn conventional wisdom on its head,
I'll expose so-called experts as crackpots.

So where can you find someone truly wise, truly educated, truly intelligent in this day and age? Hasn't God exposed it all as pretentious nonsense? Since the world in all its fancy wisdom never had a clue when it came to knowing God, God in his wisdom took delight in using what the world considered dumb—*preaching*, of all things!—to bring those who trust him into the way of salvation.

22-25   While Jews clamor for miraculous demonstrations and Greeks go in for philosophical wisdom, we go right on proclaiming Christ, the Crucified. Jews treat this like an *anti*-miracle—and Greeks pass it off as absurd. But to us who are personally called by God himself—both Jews and Greeks—Christ is God's ultimate miracle and wisdom all wrapped up in one. Human wisdom is so tinny, so impotent, next to the seeming absurdity of God. Human strength can't begin to compete with God's "weakness."

26-31   Take a good look, friends, at who you were when you got called into this life. I don't see many of "the brightest and the best" among you, not many influential, not many from high-society families. Isn't it obvious that God deliberately chose men and women that the culture overlooks and exploits and abuses, chose these "nobodies" to expose the hollow pretensions of the "somebodies"? That makes it quite clear that none of you can get by with blowing your own horn before God. Everything that we have—right thinking and right living, a clean slate and a fresh start—comes from God by way of Jesus Christ. That's why we have the saying, "If you're going to blow a horn, blow a trumpet for God."

1-2   **2** You'll remember, friends, that when I first came to you to let you in on God's master stroke, I didn't try to impress you with polished speeches and the latest philosophy. I deliberately kept it plain and simple: first Jesus and who he is; then Jesus and what he did—Jesus crucified.

3-5   I was unsure of how to go about this, and felt totally inadequate—I was scared to death, if you want the truth of it—and so nothing I said could have impressed you or anyone else. But the Message came through anyway. God's Spirit and God's power did it, which made it clear that your life of faith is a response to God's power, not to some fancy mental or emotional footwork by me or anyone else.

6-10   We, of course, have plenty of wisdom to pass on to you once you get your feet on firm spiritual ground, but it's not popular wisdom, the fashionable wisdom of high-priced experts that will be out-of-date in a year or so. God's wisdom is something mysterious that goes deep into the interior of his purposes. You don't find it lying around on the surface. It's not the latest message, but more like the oldest—what God determined as the way to bring out his best in us, long before we ever arrived on the scene. The experts of our day haven't a clue about what this eternal plan is. If they had, they wouldn't have killed the Master of the God-designed life on a cross. That's why we have this Scripture text:

No one's ever seen or heard anything like this,
Never so much as imagined anything quite like it—
What God has arranged for those who love him.

But *you've* seen and heard it because God by his Spirit has brought it all out into the open before you.

10-13 The Spirit, not content to flit around on the surface, dives into the depths of God, and brings out what God planned all along. Who ever knows what you're thinking and planning except you yourself? The same with God — except that he not only knows what he's thinking, but he lets *us* in on it. God offers a full report on the gifts of life and salvation that he is giving us. We don't have to rely on the world's guesses and opinions. We didn't learn this by reading books or going to school; we learned it from God, who taught us person-to-person through Jesus, and we're passing it on to you in the same firsthand, personal way.

14-16 The unspiritual self, just as it is by nature, can't receive the gifts of God's Spirit. There's no capacity for them. They seem like so much silliness. Spirit can be known only by spirit — God's Spirit and our spirits in open communion. Spiritually alive, we have access to everything God's Spirit is doing, and can't be judged by unspiritual critics. Isaiah's question, "Is there anyone around who knows God's Spirit, anyone who knows what he is doing?" has been answered: Christ knows, and we have Christ's Spirit.

1-4 **3** But for right now, friends, I'm completely frustrated by your unspiritual dealings with each other and with God. You're acting like infants in relation to Christ, capable of nothing much more than nursing at the breast. Well, then, I'll nurse you since you don't seem capable of anything more. As long as you grab for what makes you feel good or makes you look important, are you really much different than a babe at the breast, content only when everything's going your way? When one of you says, "I'm on Paul's side," and another says, "I'm for Apollos," aren't you being totally infantile?

5-9 Who do you think Paul is, anyway? Or Apollos, for that matter? Servants, both of us — servants who waited on you as you gradually learned to entrust your lives to our mutual Master. We each carried out our servant assignment. I planted the seed, Apollos watered the plants, but *God* made you grow. It's not the one who plants or the one who waters who is at the center of this process but God, who makes things grow. Planting and watering are menial servant jobs at minimum wages. What makes them worth doing is the God we are serving. You happen to be God's field in which we are working.

9-15 Or, to put it another way, you are God's house. Using the gift God gave me as a good architect, I designed blueprints; Apollos is putting up the walls. Let each carpenter who comes on the job take care to build on the foundation! Remember, there is only one foundation, the one already laid: Jesus Christ. Take particular care in picking out your building materials. Eventually there is going to be an inspection. If you use cheap or inferior materials, you'll be found out. The inspection will be thorough and rigorous. You won't get by with a thing. If your work passes inspection, fine; if it doesn't, your part of the building will be torn out and started over. But *you* won't be torn out; you'll survive — but just barely.

16-17 You realize, don't you, that you are the temple of God, and God himself is present in you? No one will get by with vandalizing God's temple, you can be sure of that. God's temple is sacred — and you, remember, *are* the temple.

18-20
Don't fool yourself. Don't think that you can be wise merely by being up-to-date with the times. Be God's fool—that's the path to true wisdom. What the world calls smart, God calls stupid. It's written in Scripture,

> He exposes the chicanery of the chic.
> The Master sees through the smoke screens
>   of the know-it-alls.

21-23
I don't want to hear any of you bragging about yourself or anyone else. Everything is already yours as a gift—Paul, Apollos, Peter, the world, life, death, the present, the future—all of it is yours, and you are privileged to be in union with Christ, who is in union with God.

1-4
4 Don't imagine us leaders to be something we aren't. We are servants of Christ, not his masters. We are guides into God's most sublime secrets, not security guards posted to protect them. The requirements for a good guide are reliability and accurate knowledge. It matters very little to me what you think of me, even less where I rank in popular opinion. I don't even rank myself. Comparisons in these matters are pointless. I'm not aware of anything that would disqualify me from being a good guide for you, but that doesn't mean much. The *Master* makes that judgment.

5
So don't get ahead of the Master and jump to conclusions with your judgments before all the evidence is in. When he comes, he will bring out in the open and place in evidence all kinds of things we never even dreamed of—inner motives and purposes and prayers. Only then will any one of us get to hear the "Well done!" of God.

6
All I'm doing right now, friends, is showing how these things pertain to Apollos and me so that you will learn restraint and not rush into making judgments without knowing all the facts. It's important to look at things from God's point of view. I would rather not see you inflating or deflating reputations based on mere hearsay.

7-8
For who do you know that really knows *you*, knows your heart? And even if they did, is there anything they would discover in you that you could take credit for? Isn't everything you *have* and everything you *are* sheer gifts from God? So what's the point of all this comparing and competing? You already have all you need. You already have more access to God than you can handle. Without bringing either Apollos or me into it, you're sitting on top of the world—at least God's world—and we're right there, sitting alongside you!

9-13
It seems to me that God has put us who bear his Message on stage in a theater in which no one wants to buy a ticket. We're something everyone stands around and stares at, like an accident in the street. We're the Messiah's misfits. You might be sure of yourselves, but we live in the midst of frailties and uncertainties. You might be well-thought-of by others, but we're mostly kicked around. Much of the time we don't have enough to eat, we wear patched and threadbare clothes, we get doors slammed in our faces, and we pick up odd jobs anywhere we can to eke out a living. When they call us names, we say, "God bless you." When they spread rumors about *us*, we put in a good word for *them*. We're treated like garbage, potato peelings from the culture's kitchen. And it's not getting any better.

14-16 I'm not writing all this as a neighborhood scold just to make you feel rotten. I'm writing as a father to you, my children. I love you and want you to grow up well, not spoiled. There are a lot of people around who can't wait to tell you what you've done wrong, but there aren't many fathers willing to take the time and effort to help you grow up. It was as Jesus helped me proclaim God's Message to you that I became your father. I'm not, you know, asking you to do anything I'm not already doing myself.

17 This is why I sent Timothy to you earlier. He is also my dear son, and true to the Master. He will refresh your memory on the instructions I regularly give all the churches on the way of Christ.

18-20 I know there are some among you who are so full of themselves they never listen to anyone, let alone me. They don't think I'll ever show up in person. But I'll be there sooner than you think, God willing, and then we'll see if they're full of anything but hot air. God's Way is not a matter of mere talk; it's an empowered life.

21 So how should I prepare to come to you? As a severe disciplinarian who makes you toe the mark? Or as a good friend and counselor who wants to share heart-to-heart with you? You decide.

THE MYSTERY OF SEX

1-2 5 I also received a report of scandalous sex within your church family, a kind that wouldn't be tolerated even outside the church: One of your men is sleeping with his stepmother. And you're so above it all that it doesn't even faze you! Shouldn't this break your hearts? Shouldn't it bring you to your knees in tears? Shouldn't this person and his conduct be confronted and dealt with?

3-5 I'll tell you what I would do. Even though I'm not there in person, consider me right there with you, because I can fully see what's going on. I'm telling you that this is wrong. You must not simply look the other way and hope it goes away on its own. Bring it out in the open and deal with it in the authority of Jesus our Master. Assemble the community—I'll be present in spirit with you and our Master Jesus will be present in power. Hold this man's conduct up to public scrutiny. Let him defend it if he can! But if he can't, then out with him! It will be totally devastating to him, of course, and embarrassing to you. But better devastation and embarrassment than damnation. You want him on his feet and forgiven before the Master on the Day of Judgment.

6-8 Your flip and callous arrogance in these things bothers me. You pass it off as a small thing, but it's anything but that. Yeast, too, is a "small thing," but it works its way through a whole batch of bread dough pretty fast. So get rid of this "yeast." Our true identity is flat and plain, not puffed up with the wrong kind of ingredient. The Messiah, our Passover Lamb, has already been sacrificed for the Passover meal, and we are the Unraised Bread part of the Feast. So let's live out our part in the Feast, not as raised bread swollen with the yeast of evil, but as flat bread—simple, genuine, unpretentious.

9-13 I wrote you in my earlier letter that you shouldn't make yourselves at home among the sexually promiscuous. I didn't mean that you should have nothing at all to do with outsiders of that sort. Or with crooks, whether blue- or white-collar. Or with spiritual phonies, for that matter. You'd have to leave the world entirely to do that! But I *am* saying that you shouldn't act as if everything is just fine when a friend who claims to be a Christian is promiscuous or crooked, is flip with God or rude to friends, gets drunk or becomes greedy and predatory. You can't just go along with this, treating it as acceptable behavior. I'm not responsible for what the *outsiders* do, but don't we have some responsibility for those within our community of believers? God decides on the outsiders, but we need to decide when our brothers and sisters are out of line and, if necessary, clean house.

1-4   6And how dare you take each other to court! When you think you have been wronged, does it make any sense to go before a court that knows nothing of God's ways instead of a family of Christians? The day is coming when the world is going to stand before a jury made up of followers of Jesus. If someday you are going to rule on the world's fate, wouldn't it be a good idea to practice on some of these smaller cases? Why, we're even going to judge angels! So why not these everyday affairs? As these disagreements and wrongs surface, why would you ever entrust them to the judgment of people you don't trust in any other way?

5-6   I say this as bluntly as I can to wake you up to the stupidity of what you're doing. Is it possible that there isn't one levelheaded person among you who can make fair decisions when disagreements and disputes come up? I don't believe it. And here you are taking each other to court before people who don't even believe in God! How can they render justice if they don't believe in the *God* of justice?

7-8   These court cases are an ugly blot on your community. Wouldn't it be far better to just take it, to let yourselves be wronged and forget it? All you're doing is providing fuel for more wrong, more injustice, bringing more hurt to the people of your own spiritual family.

9-11   Don't you realize that this is not the way to live? Unjust people who don't care about God will not be joining in his kingdom. Those who use and abuse each other, use and abuse sex, use and abuse the earth and everything in it, don't qualify as citizens in God's kingdom. A number of you know from experience what I'm talking about, for not so long ago you were on that list. Since then, you've been cleaned up and given a fresh start by Jesus, our Master, our Messiah, and by our God present in us, the Spirit.

12   Just because something is technically legal doesn't mean that it's spiritually appropriate. If I went around doing whatever I thought I could get by with, I'd be a slave to my whims.

13   You know the old saying, "First you eat to live, and then you live to eat"? Well, it may be true that the body is only a temporary thing, but that's no excuse for stuffing your body with food, or indulging it with sex. Since the Master honors you with a body, honor him with your body!

14-15   God honored the Master's body by raising it from the grave. He'll treat yours with the same resurrection power. Until that time, remember that your bodies are created with the same dignity as the Master's body. You wouldn't take the Master's body off to a whorehouse, would you? I should hope not.

16-20   There's more to sex than mere skin on skin. Sex is as much spiritual mystery as physical fact. As written in Scripture, "The two become one." Since we want to become spiritually one with the Master, we must not pursue the kind of sex that avoids commitment and intimacy, leaving us more lonely than ever—the kind of sex that can never "become one." There is a sense in which sexual sins are different from all others. In sexual sin we violate the sacredness of our own bodies, these bodies that were made for God-given and God-modeled love, for "becoming one" with another. Or didn't you realize that your body is a sacred place, the place of the Holy Spirit? Don't you see that you can't live however you please, squandering what God paid such a high price for? The physical part of you is not some piece of property belonging to the spiritual part of you. God owns the whole works. So let people see God in and through your body.

To Be Married, to Be Single . . .

1 7 Now, getting down to the questions you asked in your letter to me. First, Is it a good thing to have sexual relations?

2-6 Certainly—but only within a certain context. It's good for a man to have a wife, and for a woman to have a husband. Sexual drives are strong, but marriage is strong enough to contain them and provide for a balanced and fulfilling sexual life in a world of sexual disorder. The marriage bed must be a place of mutuality—the husband seeking to satisfy his wife, the wife seeking to satisfy her husband. Marriage is not a place to "stand up for your rights." Marriage is a decision to serve the other, whether in bed or out. Abstaining from sex is permissible for a period of time if you both agree to it, and if it's for the purposes of prayer and fasting—but only for such times. Then come back together again. Satan has an ingenious way of tempting us when we least expect it. I'm not, understand, commanding these periods of abstinence—only providing my best counsel if you should choose them.

7 Sometimes I wish everyone were single like me—a simpler life in many ways! But celibacy is not for everyone any more than marriage is. God gives the gift of the single life to some, the gift of the married life to others.

8-9 I do, though, tell the unmarried and widows that singleness might well be the best thing for them, as it has been for me. But if they can't manage their desires and emotions, they should by all means go ahead and get married. The difficulties of marriage are preferable by far to a sexually tortured life as a single.

10-11 And if you are married, stay married. This is the Master's command, not mine. If a wife should leave her husband, she must either remain single or else come back and make things right with him. And a husband has no right to get rid of his wife.

12-14 For the rest of you who are in mixed marriages—Christian married to non-Christian—we have no explicit command from the Master. So this is what you must do. If you are a man with a wife who is not a believer but who still wants to live with you, hold on to her. If you are a woman with a husband who is not a believer but he wants to live with you, hold on to him. The unbelieving husband shares to an extent in the holiness of his wife, and the unbelieving wife is likewise touched by the holiness of her husband. Otherwise, your children would be left out; as it is, they also are included in the spiritual purposes of God.

15-16 On the other hand, if the unbelieving spouse walks out, you've got to let him or her go. You don't have to hold on desperately. God has called us to make the best of it, as peacefully as we can. You never know, wife: The way you handle this might bring your husband not only back to you but to God. You never know, husband: The way you handle this might bring your wife not only back to you but to God.

17 And don't be wishing you were someplace else or with someone else. Where you are right now is God's place for you. Live and obey and love and believe right there. God, not your marital status, defines your life. Don't think I'm being harder on you than on the others. I give this same counsel in all the churches.

18-19 Were you Jewish at the time God called you? Don't try to remove the evidence. Were you non-Jewish at the time of your call? Don't become a Jew. Being Jewish isn't the point. The really important thing is obeying God's call, following his commands.

20-22 Stay where you were when God called your name. Were you a slave? Slavery is no roadblock to obeying and believing. I don't mean you're stuck and can't leave. If you have a chance at freedom, go ahead and take it. I'm simply trying to point out that under your new Master you're going to experience a marvelous freedom you would never have dreamed of. On the other hand, if you were free when Christ called you, you'll experience a delightful "enslavement to God" you would never have dreamed of.

23-24 All of you, slave and free both, were once held hostage in a sinful society. Then a huge sum was paid out for your ransom. So please don't, out of old habit, slip back into being or doing what everyone else tells you. Friends, stay where you were called to be. God is there. Hold the high ground with him at your side.

25-28 The Master did not give explicit direction regarding virgins, but as one much experienced in the mercy of the Master and loyal to him all the way, you can trust my counsel. Because of the current pressures on us from all sides, I think it would probably be best to stay just as you are. Are you married? Stay married. Are you unmarried? Don't get married. But there's certainly no sin in getting married, whether you're a virgin or not. All I am saying is that when you marry, you take on additional stress in an already stressful time, and I want to spare you if possible.

29-31 I do want to point out, friends, that time is of the essence. There is no time to waste, so don't complicate your lives unnecessarily. Keep it simple — in marriage, grief, joy, whatever. Even in ordinary things — your daily routines of shopping, and so on. Deal as sparingly as possible with the things the world thrusts on you. This world as you see it is on its way out.

32-35 I want you to live as free of complications as possible. When you're unmarried, you're free to concentrate on simply pleasing the Master. Marriage involves you in all the nuts and bolts of domestic life and in wanting to please your spouse, leading to so many more demands on your attention. The time and energy that married people spend on caring for and nurturing each other, the unmarried can spend in becoming whole and holy instruments of God. I'm trying to be helpful and make it as easy as possible for you, not make things harder. All I want is for you to be able to develop a way of life in which you can spend plenty of time together with the Master without a lot of distractions.

36-38 If a man has a woman friend to whom he is loyal but never intended to marry, having decided to serve God as a "single," and then changes his mind, deciding he should marry her, he should go ahead and marry. It's no sin; it's not even a "step down" from celibacy, as some say. On the other hand, if a man is comfortable in his decision for a single life in service to God and it's entirely his own conviction and not imposed on him by others, he ought to stick with it. Marriage is spiritually and morally right and not inferior to singleness in any way, although as I indicated earlier, because of the times we live in, I do have pastoral reasons for encouraging singleness.

39-40 A wife must stay with her husband as long as he lives. If he dies, she is free to marry anyone she chooses. She will, of course, want to marry a believer and have the blessing of the Master. By now you know that I think she'll be better off staying single. The Master, in my opinion, thinks so, too.

FREEDOM WITH RESPONSIBILITY

1-3 8 The question keeps coming up regarding meat that has been offered up to an idol: Should you attend meals where such meat is served, or not? We sometimes tend to think we know all we need to know to answer these kinds of questions — but sometimes our humble hearts can help us more than our proud minds. We never really know enough until we recognize that God alone knows it all.

4-6 Some people say, quite rightly, that idols have no actual existence, that there's nothing to them, that there is no God other than our one God, that no matter how many of these so-called gods are named and worshiped they still don't add up to anything but a tall story. They say — again, quite rightly — that there is only one God the Father, that everything comes from him, and that he wants us to live for him. Also, they say that there is only one Master — Jesus the Messiah — and that everything is for his sake, including us. Yes. It's true.

7 In strict logic, then, nothing happened to the meat when it was offered up to an idol. It's just like any other meat. I know that, and you know that. But knowing isn't everything. If it becomes everything, some people end up as know-it-alls who treat others as know-nothings. Real knowledge isn't that insensitive.

We need to be sensitive to the fact that we're not all at the same level of understanding in this. Some of you have spent your entire lives eating "idol meat," and are sure that there's something bad in the meat that then becomes something bad inside of you. An imagination and conscience shaped under those conditions isn't going to change overnight.

8-9 But fortunately God doesn't grade us on our diet. We're neither commended when we clean our plate nor reprimanded when we just can't stomach it. But God *does* care when you use your freedom carelessly in a way that leads a fellow believer still vulnerable to those old associations to be thrown off track.

10 For instance, say you flaunt your freedom by going to a banquet thrown in honor of idols, where the main course is meat sacrificed to idols. Isn't there great danger if someone still struggling over this issue, someone who looks up to you as knowledgeable and mature, sees you go into that banquet? The danger is that he will become terribly confused — maybe even to the point of getting mixed up himself in what his conscience tells him is wrong.

11-13 Christ gave up his life for that person. Wouldn't you at least be willing to give up going to dinner for him — because, as you say, it doesn't really make any difference? But it *does* make a difference if you hurt your friend terribly, risking his eternal ruin! When you hurt your friend, you hurt Christ. A free meal here and there isn't worth it at the cost of even one of these "weak ones." So, never go to these idol-tainted meals if there's any chance it will trip up one of your brothers or sisters.

꧁

1-2 9 And don't tell me that I have no authority to write like this. I'm perfectly free to do this — isn't that obvious? Haven't I been given a job to do? Wasn't I commissioned to this work in a face-to-face meeting with Jesus, our Master? Aren't you yourselves proof of the good work that I've done for the Master? Even if no one else admits the authority of my commission, *you* can't deny it. Why, my work with you is living proof of my authority!

3-7 I'm not shy in standing up to my critics. We who are on missionary assignments for God have a right to decent accommodations, and we have a right to support for us and our families. You don't seem to have raised questions with the other apostles and our Master's brothers and Peter in these matters. So, why me? Is it just Barnabas and I who have to go it alone and pay our own way? Are soldiers self-employed? Are gardeners forbidden to eat vegetables from their own gardens? Don't milkmaids get to drink their fill from the pail?

8-12 I'm not just sounding off because I'm irritated. This is all written in the scriptural law. Moses wrote, "Don't muzzle an ox to keep it from eating the grain when it's threshing." Do you think Moses' primary concern was the care of farm animals? Don't you think his concern extends to us? Of course. Farmers plow and thresh expecting something when the crop comes in. So if we have planted spiritual seed among you, is it out of line to expect a meal or two from you? Others demand plenty from you in these ways. Don't we who have never demanded deserve even more?

12-14 But we're not going to start demanding now what we've always had a perfect right to. Our decision all along has been to put up with anything rather than to get in the way or detract from the Message of Christ. All I'm concerned with right now is that you not use our decision to take advantage of others, depriving them of what is rightly theirs. You know, don't you, that it's always been taken for granted that those who work in the Temple live off the proceeds of the Temple, and that those who offer sacrifices at the altar eat their meals from what has been sacrificed? Along the same lines, the Master directed that those who spread the Message be supported by those who believe the Message.

15-18 Still, I want it made clear that I've never gotten anything out of this for myself, and that I'm not writing now to get something. I'd rather die than give anyone ammunition to discredit me or impugn my motives. If I proclaim the Message, it's not to get something out of it for myself. I'm *compelled* to do it, and doomed if I don't! If this was my own idea of just another way to make a living, I'd expect some pay. But since it's *not* my idea but something solemnly entrusted to me, why would I expect to get paid? So am I getting anything out of it? Yes, as a matter of fact: the pleasure of proclaiming the Message at no cost to you. You don't even have to pay my expenses!

19-23 Even though I am free of the demands and expectations of everyone, I have voluntarily become a servant to any and all in order to reach a wide range of people: religious, nonreligious, meticulous moralists, loose-living immoralists, the defeated, the demoralized — whoever. I didn't take on their way of life. I kept my bearings in Christ — but I entered their world and tried to experience things from their point of view. I've become just about every sort of servant there is in my attempts to lead those I meet into a God-saved life. I did all this because of the Message. I didn't just want to talk about it; I wanted to be *in* on it!

24-25 You've all been to the stadium and seen the athletes race. Everyone runs; one wins. Run to win. All good athletes train hard. They do it for a gold medal that tarnishes and fades. You're after one that's gold eternally.

26-27 I don't know about you, but I'm running hard for the finish line. I'm giving it everything I've got. No sloppy living for me! I'm staying alert and in top condition. I'm not going to get caught napping, telling everyone else all about it and then missing out myself.

1-5 **10** Remember our history, friends, and be warned. All our ancestors were led by the providential Cloud and taken miraculously through the Sea. They went through the waters, in a baptism like ours, as Moses led them from enslaving death to salvation life. They all ate and drank identical food and drink, meals provided daily by God. They drank from the Rock, God's fountain for them that stayed with them wherever they were. And the Rock was Christ. But just experiencing God's wonder and grace didn't seem to mean much — most of them were defeated by temptation during the hard times in the desert, and God was not pleased.

6-10 The same thing could happen to us. We must be on guard so that we never get caught up in wanting our own way as they did. And we must not turn our religion into a circus as they did — "First the people partied, then they threw a dance." We must not be sexually promiscuous — they paid for that, remember, with 23,000 deaths in one day! We must never try to get Christ to serve us instead of us serving him; they tried it, and God launched an epidemic of poisonous snakes. We must be careful not to stir up discontent; discontent destroyed them.

11-12 These are all warning markers — DANGER! — in our history books, written down so that we don't repeat their mistakes. Our positions in the story are parallel — they at the beginning, we at the end — and we are just as capable of messing it up as they were. Don't be so naive and self-confident. You're not exempt. You could fall flat on your face as easily as anyone else. Forget about self-confidence; it's useless. Cultivate God-confidence.

13 No test or temptation that comes your way is beyond the course of what others have had to face. All you need to remember is that God will never let you down; he'll never let you be pushed past your limit; he'll always be there to help you come through it.

14 So, my very dear friends, when you see people reducing God to something they can use or control, get out of their company as fast as you can.

15-18 I assume I'm addressing believers now who are mature. Draw your own conclusions: When we drink the cup of blessing, aren't we taking into ourselves the blood, the very life, of Christ? And isn't it the same with the loaf of bread we break and eat? Don't we take into ourselves the body, the very life, of Christ? Because there is one loaf, our many-ness becomes oneness — Christ doesn't become fragmented in us. Rather, we become unified in him. We don't reduce Christ to what we are; he raises us to what he is. That's basically what happened even in old Israel — those who ate the sacrifices offered on God's altar entered into God's action at the altar.

19-22 Do you see the difference? Sacrifices offered to idols are offered to nothing, for what's the idol but a nothing? Or worse than nothing, a minus, a demon! I don't want you to become part of something that reduces you to less than yourself. And you can't have it both ways, banqueting with the Master one day and slumming with demons the next. Besides, the Master won't put up with it. He wants *us*—all or nothing. Do you think you can get off with anything less?

23-24   Looking at it one way, you could say, "Anything goes. Because of God's immense generosity and grace, we don't have to dissect and scrutinize every action to see if it will pass muster." But the point is not to just get by. We want to live well, but our foremost efforts should be to help *others* live well.

25-28   With that as a base to work from, common sense can take you the rest of the way. Eat anything sold at the butcher shop, for instance; you don't have to run an "idolatry test" on every item. "The earth," after all, "is God's, and everything in it." That "everything" certainly includes the leg of lamb in the butcher shop. If a nonbeliever invites you to dinner and you feel like going, go ahead and enjoy yourself; eat everything placed before you. It would be both bad manners and bad spirituality to cross-examine your host on the ethical purity of each course as it is served. On the other hand, if he goes out of his way to tell you that this or that was sacrificed to god or goddess so-and-so, you should pass. Even though you may be indifferent as to where it came from, he isn't, and you don't want to send mixed messages to him about who *you* are worshiping.

29-30   But, except for these special cases, I'm not going to walk around on eggshells worrying about what small-minded people might say; I'm going to stride free and easy, knowing what our large-minded Master has already said. If I eat what is served to me, grateful to God for what is on the table, how can I worry about what someone will say? I thanked God for it and he blessed it!

31-33   So eat your meals heartily, not worrying about what others say about you—you're eating to God's glory, after all, not to please them. As a matter of fact, do everything that way, heartily and freely to God's glory. At the same time, don't be callous in your exercise of freedom, thoughtlessly stepping on the toes of those who aren't as free as you are. I try my best to be considerate of everyone's feelings in all these matters; I hope you will be, too.

TO HONOR GOD

1-2   **11** It pleases me that you continue to remember and honor me by keeping up the traditions of the faith I taught you. All actual authority stems from Christ.

3-9   In a marriage relationship, there is authority from Christ to husband, and from husband to wife. The authority of Christ is the authority of God. Any man who speaks with God or about God in a way that shows a lack of respect for the authority of Christ, dishonors Christ. In the same way, a wife who speaks with God in a way that shows a lack of respect for the authority of her husband, dishonors her husband. Worse, she dishonors herself—an ugly sight, like a woman with her head shaved. This is basically the origin of these customs we have of women wearing head coverings in worship, while men take their hats off. By these symbolic acts, men and women, who far too often butt heads with each other, submit their "heads" to the Head: God.

10-12   Don't, by the way, read too much into the differences here between men and women. Neither man nor woman can go it alone or claim priority. Man was created first, as a beautiful shining reflection of God—that is true. But the head on a woman's body clearly outshines in beauty the head of her "head," her husband. The first woman came from man, true—but ever since then, every man comes from a woman! And since virtually everything comes from God anyway, let's quit going through these "who's first" routines.

13-16   Don't you agree there is something naturally powerful in the symbolism—a woman, her beautiful hair reminiscent of angels, praying in adoration; a man, his head bared in reverence, praying in submission? I hope you're not going to be argumentative about this. All God's churches see it this way; I don't want you standing out as an exception.

17-19   Regarding this next item, I'm not at all pleased. I am getting the picture that when you meet together it brings out your worst side instead of your best! First, I get this report on your divisiveness, competing with and criticizing each other. I'm reluctant to believe it, but there it is. The best that can be said for it is that the testing process will bring truth into the open and confirm it.

20-22   And then I find that you bring your divisions to worship—you come together, and instead of eating the Lord's Supper, you bring in a lot of food from the outside and make pigs of yourselves. Some are left out, and go home hungry. Others have to be carried out, too drunk to walk. I can't believe it! Don't you have your own homes to eat and drink in? Why would you stoop to desecrating God's church? Why would you actually shame God's poor? I never would have believed you would stoop to this. And I'm not going to stand by and say nothing.

23-26   Let me go over with you again exactly what goes on in the Lord's Supper and why it is so centrally important. I received my instructions from the Master himself and passed them on to you. The Master, Jesus, on the night of his betrayal, took bread. Having given thanks, he broke it and said,

> This is my body, broken for you.
> Do this to remember me.

After supper, he did the same thing with the cup:
> This cup is my blood, my new covenant with you.
> Each time you drink this cup, remember me.

What you must solemnly realize is that every time you eat this bread and every time you drink this cup, you reenact in your words and actions the death of the Master. You will be drawn back to this meal again and again until the Master returns. You must never let familiarity breed contempt.

27-28   Anyone who eats the bread or drinks the cup of the Master irreverently is like part of the crowd that jeered and spit on him at his death. Is that the kind of "remembrance" you want to be part of? Examine your motives, test your heart, come to this meal in holy awe.

29-32   If you give no thought (or worse, don't care) about the broken body of the Master when you eat and drink, you're running the risk of serious consequences. That's why so many of you even now are listless and sick, and others have gone to an early grave. If we get this straight now, we won't have to be straightened out later on. Better to be confronted by the Master now than to face a fiery confrontation later.

33-34 So, my friends, when you come together to the Lord's Table, be reverent and courteous with one another. If you're so hungry that you can't wait to be served, go home and get a sandwich. But by no means risk turning this Meal into an eating and drinking binge or a family squabble. It is a spiritual meal—a love feast.

The other things you asked about, I'll respond to in person when I make my next visit.

SPIRITUAL GIFTS

1-3 **12** What I want to talk about now is the various ways God's Spirit gets worked into our lives. This is complex and often mis-understood, but I want you to be informed and knowledgeable. Remember how you were when you didn't know God, led from one phony god to another, never knowing what you were doing, just doing it because everybody else did it? It's different in this life. God wants us to use our intelligence, to seek to understand as well as we can. For instance, by using your heads, you know perfectly well that the Spirit of God would never prompt anyone to say "Jesus be damned!" Nor would anyone be inclined to say "Jesus is Master!" without the insight of the Holy Spirit.

4-11 God's various gifts are handed out everywhere; but they all originate in God's Spirit. God's various ministries are carried out everywhere; but they all originate in God's Spirit. God's various expressions of power are in action everywhere; but God himself is behind it all. Each person is given something to do that shows who God is: Everyone gets in on it, everyone benefits. All kinds of things are handed out by the Spirit, and to all kinds of people! The variety is wonderful:

> wise counsel
> clear understanding
> simple trust
> healing the sick
> miraculous acts
> proclamation
> distinguishing between spirits
> tongues
> interpretation of tongues.

All these gifts have a common origin, but are handed out one by one by the one Spirit of God. He decides who gets what, and when.

12-13 You can easily enough see how this kind of thing works by looking no further than your own body. Your body has many parts—limbs, organs, cells—but no matter how many parts you can name, you're still one body. It's exactly the same with Christ. By means of his one Spirit, we all said good-bye to our partial and piecemeal lives. We each used to independently call our own shots, but then we entered into a large and integrated life in which *he* has the final say in everything. (This is what we proclaimed in word and action when we were baptized.) Each of us is now a part of his resurrection body, refreshed and sustained at one fountain—his Spirit—where we all come to drink. The old labels we once used to identify ourselves—labels like Jew or Greek, slave or free—are no longer useful. We need something larger, more comprehensive.

14-18   I want you to think about how all this makes you more significant, not less. A body isn't just a single part blown up into something huge. It's all the different-but-similar parts arranged and functioning together. If Foot said, "I'm not elegant like Hand, embellished with rings; I guess I don't belong to this body," would that make it so? If Ear said, "I'm not beautiful like Eye, limpid and expressive; I don't deserve a place on the head," would you want to remove it from the body? If the body was all eye, how could it hear? If all ear, how could it smell? As it is, we see that God has carefully placed each part of the body right where he wanted it.

19-24   But I also want you to think about how this keeps your significance from getting blown up into self-importance. For no matter how significant you are, it is only because of what you are a *part* of. An enormous eye or a gigantic hand wouldn't be a body, but a monster. What we have is one body with many parts, each its proper size and in its proper place. No part is important on its own. Can you imagine Eye telling Hand, "Get lost; I don't need you"? Or, Head telling Foot, "You're fired; your job has been phased out"? As a matter of fact, in practice it works the other way—the "lower" the part, the more basic, and therefore necessary. You can live without an eye, for instance, but not without a stomach. When it's a part of your own body you are concerned with, it makes *no* difference whether the part is visible or clothed, higher or lower. You give it dignity and honor just as it is, without comparisons. If anything, you have more concern for the lower parts than the higher. If you had to choose, wouldn't you prefer good digestion to full-bodied hair?

25-26   The way God designed our bodies is a model for understanding our lives together as a church: every part dependent on every other part, the parts we mention and the parts we don't, the parts we see and the parts we don't. If one part hurts, every other part is involved in the hurt, and in the healing. If one part flourishes, every other part enters into the exuberance.

27-31   You are Christ's body—that's who you are! You must never forget this. Only as you accept your part of that body does your "part" mean anything. You're familiar with some of the parts that God has formed in his church, which is his "body":

apostles
prophets
teachers
miracle workers
healers
helpers
organizers
those who pray in tongues.

But it's obvious by now, isn't it, that Christ's church is a complete Body and not a gigantic, unidimensional Part? It's not all Apostle, not all Prophet, not all Miracle Worker, not all Healer, not all Prayer in Tongues, not all Interpreter of Tongues. And yet some of you keep competing for so-called "important" parts.

But now I want to lay out a far better way for you.

1 **13** If I speak with human eloquence and angelic ecstasy but don't love, I'm nothing but the creaking of a rusty gate.

2 If I speak God's Word with power, revealing all his mysteries and making everything plain as day, and if I have faith that says to a mountain, "Jump," and it jumps, but I don't love, I'm nothing.

3-7 If I give everything I own to the poor and even go to the stake to be burned as a martyr, but I don't love, I've gotten nowhere. So, no matter what I say, what I believe, and what I do, I'm bankrupt without love.

Love never gives up.
Love cares more for others than for self.
Love doesn't want what it doesn't have.
Love doesn't strut,
Doesn't have a swelled head,
Doesn't force itself on others,
Isn't always "me first,"
Doesn't fly off the handle,
Doesn't keep score of the sins of others,
Doesn't revel when others grovel,
Takes pleasure in the flowering of truth,
Puts up with anything,
Trusts God always,
Always looks for the best,
Never looks back,
But keeps going to the end.

8-10 Love never dies. Inspired speech will be over some day; praying in tongues will end; understanding will reach its limit. We know only a portion of the truth, and what we say about God is always incomplete. But when the Complete arrives, our incompletes will be canceled.

11 When I was an infant at my mother's breast, I gurgled and cooed like any infant. When I grew up, I left those infant ways for good.

12 We don't yet see things clearly. We're squinting in a fog, peering through a mist. But it won't be long before the weather clears and the sun shines bright! We'll see it all then, see it all as clearly as God sees us, knowing him directly just as he knows us!

13 But for right now, until that completeness, we have three things to do to lead us toward that consummation: Trust steadily in God, hope unswervingly, love extravagantly. And the best of the three is love.

1-3 **14** Go after a life of love as if your life depended on it—because it does. Give yourselves to the gifts God gives you. Most of all, try to proclaim his truth. If you praise him in the private language of tongues, God understands you but no one else does, for you are sharing intimacies just between you and him. But when you proclaim his truth in everyday speech, you're letting *others* in on the truth so that they can grow and be strong and experience his presence with you.

4-5 The one who prays using a private "prayer language" certainly gets a lot out of it, but proclaiming God's truth to the church in its common language brings the whole church into growth and strength. I want all of you to develop intimacies with God in prayer, but please don't stop with that. Go on and proclaim his clear truth to others. It's more important that everyone have access to the knowledge and love of God in language everyone understands than that you go off and cultivate God's presence in a mysterious prayer language — unless, of course, there is someone who can interpret what you are saying for the benefit of all.

6-8   Think, friends: If I come to you and all I do is pray privately to God in a way only he can understand, what are you going to get out of that? If I don't address you plainly with some insight or truth or proclamation or teaching, what help am I to you? If musical instruments — flutes, say, or harps — aren't played so that each note is distinct and in tune, how will anyone be able to catch the melody and enjoy the music? If the trumpet call can't be distinguished, will anyone show up for the battle?

9-12   So if you speak in a way no one can understand, what's the point of opening your mouth? There are many languages in the world and they all mean something to someone. But if I don't understand the language, it's not going to do me much good. It's no different with you. Since you're so eager to participate in what God is doing, why don't you concentrate on doing what helps everyone in the church?

13-17   So, when you pray in your private prayer language, don't hoard the experience for yourself. Pray for the insight and ability to bring others into that intimacy. If I pray in tongues, my spirit prays but my mind lies fallow, and all that intelligence is wasted. So what's the solution? The answer is simple enough. Do both. I should be spiritually free and expressive as I pray, but I should also be thoughtful and mindful as I pray. I should sing with my spirit, and sing with my mind. If you give a blessing using your private prayer language, which no one else understands, how can some outsider who has just shown up and has no idea what's going on know when to say "Amen"? Your blessing might be beautiful, but you have very effectively cut that person out of it.

18-19   I'm grateful to God for the gift of praying in tongues that he gives us for praising him, which leads to wonderful intimacies we enjoy with him. I enter into this as much or more than any of you. But when I'm in a church assembled for worship, I'd rather say five words that everyone can understand and learn from than say ten thousand that sound to others like gibberish.

20-25   To be perfectly frank, I'm getting exasperated with your infantile thinking. How long before you grow up and use your head — your *adult* head? It's all right to have a childlike unfamiliarity with evil; a simple *no* is all that's needed there. But there's far more to saying *yes* to something. Only mature and well-exercised intelligence can save you from falling into gullibility. It's written in Scripture that God said,

> In strange tongues
> and from the mouths of strangers
> I will preach to this people,
> but they'll neither listen nor believe.

So where does it get you, all this speaking in tongues no one understands? It doesn't help believers, and it only gives unbelievers something to gawk at. Plain truth-speaking, on the other hand, goes straight to the heart of believers and doesn't get in the way of unbelievers. If you come together as a congregation and some unbelieving outsiders walk in on you as you're all praying in tongues, unintelligible to each other and to them, won't they assume you've taken leave of your senses and get out of there as fast as they can? But if some unbelieving outsiders walk in on a service where people are speaking out God's truth, the plain words will bring them up against the truth and probe their hearts. Before you know it, they're going to be on their faces before God, recognizing that God is among you.

26-33   So here's what I want you to do. When you gather for worship, each one of you be prepared with something that will be useful for all: Sing a hymn, teach a lesson, tell a story, lead a prayer, provide an insight. If prayers are offered in tongues, two or three's the limit, and then only if someone is present who can interpret what you're saying. Otherwise, keep it between God and yourself. And no more than two or three speakers at a meeting, with the rest of you listening and taking it to heart. Take your turn, no one person taking over. Then each speaker gets a chance to say something special from God, and you all learn from each other. If you choose to speak, you're also responsible for how and when you speak. When we worship the right way, God doesn't stir us up into confusion; he brings us into harmony. This goes for all the churches — no exceptions.

34-36   Wives must not disrupt worship, talking when they should be listening, asking questions that could more appropriately be asked of their husbands at home. God's Book of the law guides our manners and customs here. Wives have no license to use the time of worship for unwarranted speaking. Do you — both women *and* men — imagine that you're a sacred oracle determining what's right and wrong? Do you think everything revolves around you?

37-38   If any one of you thinks God has something for you to say or has inspired you to do something, pay close attention to what I have written. This is the way the Master wants it. If you won't play by these rules, God can't use you. Sorry.

39-40   Three things, then, to sum this up: When you speak forth God's truth, speak your heart out. Don't tell people how they should or shouldn't pray when they're praying in tongues that you don't understand. Be courteous and considerate in everything.

RESURRECTION

1-2   **15** Friends, let me go over the Message with you one final time — this Message that I proclaimed and that you made your own; this Message on which you took your stand and by which your life has been saved. (I'm assuming, now, that your belief was the real thing and not a passing fancy, that you're in this for good and holding fast.)

3-9   The first thing I did was place before you what was placed so emphatically before me: that the Messiah died for our sins, exactly as Scripture tells it; that he was buried; that he was raised from death on the third day, again exactly as Scripture says; that he presented himself alive to Peter, then to his closest followers, and later to more than five hundred of his followers all at the same time, most of them still around (although a few have since died); that he then spent time with James and the rest of those he commissioned to represent him; and that he finally presented himself alive to *me*. It was fitting that I bring up the rear. I don't deserve to be included in that inner circle, as you well know, having spent all those early years trying my best to stamp God's church right out of existence.

10-11 But because God was so gracious, so very generous, here I am. And I'm not about to let his grace go to waste. Haven't I worked hard trying to do more than any of the others? Even then, my work didn't amount to all that much. It was God giving me the work to do, God giving me the energy to do it. So whether you heard it from me or from those others, it's all the same: We spoke God's truth and you entrusted your lives.

12-15 Now, let me ask you something profound yet troubling. If you became believers because you trusted the proclamation that Christ is alive, risen from the dead, how can you let people say that there is no such thing as a resurrection? If there's no resurrection, there's no living Christ. And face it—if there's no resurrection for Christ, everything we've told you is smoke and mirrors, and everything you've staked your life on is smoke and mirrors. Not only that, but we would be guilty of telling a string of barefaced lies about God, all these affidavits we passed on to you verifying that God raised up Christ—sheer fabrications, if there's no resurrection.

16-20 If corpses can't be raised, then Christ wasn't, because he was indeed dead. And if Christ weren't raised, then all you're doing is wandering about in the dark, as lost as ever. It's even worse for those who died hoping in Christ and resurrection, because they're already in their graves. If all we get out of Christ is a little inspiration for a few short years, we're a pretty sorry lot. But the truth is that Christ *has* been raised up, the first in a long legacy of those who are going to leave the cemeteries.

21-28 There is a nice symmetry in this: Death initially came by a man, and resurrection from death came by a man. Everybody dies in Adam; everybody comes alive in Christ. But we have to wait our turn: Christ is first, then those with him at his Coming, the grand consummation when, after crushing the opposition, he hands over his kingdom to God the Father. He won't let up until the last enemy is down—and the very last enemy is death! As the psalmist said, "He laid them low, one and all; he walked all over them." When Scripture says that "he walked all over them," it's obvious that he couldn't at the same time be walked on. When everything and everyone is finally under God's rule, the Son will step down, taking his place with everyone else, showing that God's rule is absolutely comprehensive—a perfect ending!

29 Why do you think people offer themselves to be baptized for those already in the grave? If there's no chance of resurrection for a corpse, if God's power stops at the cemetery gates, why do we keep doing things that suggest he's going to clean the place out someday, pulling everyone up on their feet alive?

30-33 And why do you think I keep risking my neck in this dangerous work? I look death in the face practically every day I live. Do you think I'd do this if I wasn't convinced of your resurrection and mine as guaranteed by the resurrected Messiah Jesus? Do you think I was just trying to act heroic when I fought the wild beasts at Ephesus, hoping it wouldn't be the end of me? Not on your life! It's resurrection, resurrection, always resurrection, that undergirds what I do and say, the way I live. If there's no resurrection, "We eat, we drink, the next day we die," and that's all there is to it. But don't fool yourselves. Don't let yourselves be poisoned by this anti-resurrection loose talk. "Bad company ruins good manners."

34   Think straight. Awaken to the holiness of life. No more playing fast and loose with resurrection facts. Ignorance of God is a luxury you can't afford in times like these. Aren't you embarrassed that you've let this kind of thing go on as long as you have?

35-38   Some skeptic is sure to ask, "Show me how resurrection works. Give me a diagram; draw me a picture. What does this 'resurrection body' look like?" If you look at this question closely, you realize how absurd it is. There are no diagrams for this kind of thing. We do have a parallel experience in gardening. You plant a "dead" seed; soon there is a flourishing plant. There is no visual likeness between seed and plant. You could never guess what a tomato would look like by looking at a tomato seed. What we plant in the soil and what grows out of it don't look anything alike. The dead body that we bury in the ground and the resurrection body that comes from it will be dramatically different.

39-41   You will notice that the variety of bodies is stunning. Just as there are different kinds of seeds, there are different kinds of bodies—humans, animals, birds, fish—each unprecedented in its form. You get a hint at the diversity of resurrection glory by looking at the diversity of bodies not only on earth but in the skies—sun, moon, stars—all these varieties of beauty and brightness. And we're only looking at pre-resurrection "seeds"—who can imagine what the resurrection "plants" will be like!

42-44   This image of planting a dead seed and raising a live plant is a mere sketch at best, but perhaps it will help in approaching the mystery of the resurrection body—but only if you keep in mind that when we're raised, we're raised for *good*, alive forever! The corpse that's planted is no beauty, but when it's raised, it's glorious. Put in the ground weak, it comes up powerful. The seed sown is natural; the seed grown is supernatural—same seed, same body, but what a difference from when it goes down in physical mortality to when it is raised up in spiritual immortality!

45-49   We follow this sequence in Scripture: The First Adam received life, the Last Adam is a life-giving Spirit. Physical life comes first, then spiritual—a firm base shaped from the earth, a final completion coming out of heaven. The First Man was made out of earth, and people since then are earthy; the Second Man was made out of heaven, and people now can be heavenly. In the same way that we've worked from our earthy origins, let's embrace our heavenly ends.

50   I need to emphasize, friends, that our natural, earthy lives don't in themselves lead us by their very nature into the kingdom of God. Their very "nature" is to die, so how could they "naturally" end up in the Life kingdom?

51-57   But let me tell you something wonderful, a mystery I'll probably never fully understand. We're not all going to die—*but* we are all going to be changed. You hear a blast to end all blasts from a trumpet, and in the time that you look up and blink your eyes—it's over. On signal from that trumpet from heaven, the dead will be up and out of their graves, beyond the reach of death, never to die again. At the same moment and in the same way, we'll all be changed. In the resurrection scheme of things, this has to happen: everything perishable taken off the shelves and replaced by the imperishable, this mortal replaced by the immortal. Then the saying will come true:

Death swallowed by triumphant Life!
Who got the last word, oh, Death?
Oh, Death, who's afraid of you now?

It was sin that made death so frightening and law-code guilt that gave sin its leverage, its destructive power. But now in a single victorious stroke of Life, all three — sin, guilt, death — are gone, the gift of our Master, Jesus Christ. Thank God!

58 With all this going for us, my dear, dear friends, stand your ground. And don't hold back. Throw yourselves into the work of the Master, confident that nothing you do for him is a waste of time or effort.

COMING TO SEE YOU

1-4 **16** Regarding the relief offering for poor Christians that is being collected, you get the same instructions I gave the churches in Galatia. Every Sunday each of you make an offering and put it in safekeeping. Be as generous as you can. When I get there you'll have it ready, and I won't have to make a special appeal. Then after I arrive, I'll write letters authorizing whomever you delegate, and send them off to Jerusalem to deliver your gift. If you think it best that I go along, I'll be glad to travel with them.

5-9 I plan to visit you after passing through northern Greece. I won't be staying long there, but maybe I can stay awhile with you — maybe even spend the winter? Then you could give me a good send-off, wherever I may be headed next. I don't want to just drop by in between other "primary" destinations. I want a good, long, leisurely visit. If the Master agrees, we'll have it! For the present, I'm staying right here in Ephesus. A huge door of opportunity for good work has opened up here. (There is also mushrooming opposition.)

10-11 If Timothy shows up, take good care of him. Make him feel completely at home among you. He works so hard for the Master, just as I do. Don't let anyone disparage him. After a while, send him on to me with your blessing. Tell him I'm expecting him, and any friends he has with him.

12 About our friend Apollos, I've done my best to get him to pay you a visit, but haven't talked him into it yet. He doesn't think this is the right time. But there will be a "right time."

13-14 Keep your eyes open, hold tight to your convictions, give it all you've got, be resolute, and love without stopping.

15-16 Would you do me a favor, friends, and give special recognition to the family of Stephanas? You know, they were among the first converts in Greece, and they've put themselves out, serving Christians ever since then. I want you to honor and look up to people like that: companions and workers who show us how to do it, giving us something to aspire to.

17-18 I want you to know how delighted I am to have Stephanas, Fortunatus, and Achaicus here with me. They partially make up for your absence! They've refreshed me by keeping me in touch with you. Be proud that you have people like this among you.

19 The churches here in western Asia send greetings.

Aquila, Priscilla, and the church that meets in their house say hello.

20 All the friends here say hello.

Pass the greetings around with holy embraces!

21 And I, Paul—in my own handwriting!—send you my regards.

22 If anyone won't love the Master, throw him out. Make room for the Master!

23 Our Master Jesus has his arms wide open for you.

24 And I love all of you in the Messiah, in Jesus.

2 CORINTHIANS

The Corinthian Christians gave their founding pastor, Paul, more trouble than all his other churches put together. No sooner did Paul get one problem straightened out in Corinth than three more appeared.

For anyone operating under the naive presumption that joining a Christian church is a good way to meet all the best people and cultivate smooth social relations, a reading of Paul's Corinthian correspondence is the prescribed cure. But however much trouble the Corinthians were to each other and to Paul, they prove to be a cornucopia of blessings to us, for they triggered some of Paul's most profound and vigorous writing.

The provocation for Paul's second letter to the Christians in Corinth was an attack on his leadership. In his first letter, though he wrote most kindly and sympathetically, he didn't mince words. He wrote with the confident authority of a pastor who understands the ways God's salvation works and the kind of community that comes into being as a result. At least some of what he wrote to them was hard to hear and hard to take.

So they bucked his authority—accused him of inconsistencies, impugned his motives, questioned his credentials. They didn't argue with what he had written; they simply denied his right to tell them what to do.

And so Paul was forced to defend his leadership. After mopping up a few details left over from the first letter, he confronted the challenge, and in the process probed the very nature of leadership in a community of believers.

Because leadership is necessarily an exercise of authority, it easily shifts into an exercise of power. But the minute it does that, it begins to inflict damage on both the leader and the led. Paul, studying Jesus, had learned a kind of leadership in which he managed to stay out of the way so that the others could deal with God without having to go through him. All who are called to exercise leadership in whatever capacity—parent or coach, pastor or president, teacher or manager—can be grateful to Paul for this letter, and to the Corinthians for provoking it.

2 CORINTHIANS

1-2 1 I, Paul, have been sent on a special mission by the Messiah, Jesus, planned by God himself. I write this to God's congregation in Corinth, and to believers all over Achaia province. May all the gifts and benefits that come from God our Father and the Master, Jesus Christ, be yours! Timothy, someone you know and trust, joins me in this greeting.

THE RESCUE

3-5 All praise to the God and Father of our Master, Jesus the Messiah! Father of all mercy! God of all healing counsel! He comes alongside us when we go through hard times, and before you know it, he brings us alongside someone else who is going through hard times so that we can be there for that person just as God was there for us. We have plenty of hard times that come from following the Messiah, but no more so than the good times of his healing comfort — we get a full measure of that, too.

6-7 When we suffer for Jesus, it works out for your healing and salvation. If we are treated well, given a helping hand and encouraging word, that also works to your benefit, spurring you on, face forward, unflinching. Your hard times are also our hard times. When we see that you're just as willing to endure the hard times as to enjoy the good times, we know you're going to make it, no doubt about it.

8-11 We don't want you in the dark, friends, about how hard it was when all this came down on us in Asia province. It was so bad we didn't think we were going to make it. We felt like we'd been sent to death row, that it was all over for us. As it turned out, it was the best thing that could have happened. Instead of trusting in our own strength or wits to get out of it, we were forced to trust God totally — not a bad idea since he's the God who raises the dead! And he did it, rescued us from certain doom. *And* he'll do it again, rescuing us as many times as we need rescuing. You and your prayers are part of the rescue operation — I don't want you in the dark about that either. I can see your faces even now, lifted in praise for God's deliverance of us, a rescue in which your prayers played such a crucial part.

12-14 Now that the worst is over, we're pleased we can report that we've come out of this with conscience and faith intact, and can face the world — and even more importantly, face you with our heads held high. But it wasn't by any fancy footwork on our part. It was *God* who kept us focused on him, uncompromised. Don't try to read between the lines or look for hidden meanings in this letter. We're writing plain, unembellished truth, hoping that you'll now see the whole picture as well as you've seen some of the details. We want you to be as proud of us as we are of you when we stand together before our Master Jesus.

15-16 Confident of your welcome, I had originally planned two great visits with you — coming by on my way to Macedonia province, and then again on my return trip. Then we could have had a bon-voyage party as you sent me off to Judea. That was the plan.

17-19 Are you now going to accuse me of being flip with my promises because it didn't work out? Do you think I talk out of both sides of my mouth — a glib *yes* one moment, a glib *no* the next? Well, you're wrong. I try to be as true to my word as God is to his. Our word to you wasn't a careless yes canceled by an indifferent no. How could it be? When Silas and Timothy and I proclaimed the Son of God among you, did you pick up on any yes-and-no, on-again, off-again waffling? Wasn't it a clean, strong Yes?

20-22   Whatever God has promised gets stamped with the Yes of Jesus. In him, this is what we preach and pray, the great Amen, God's Yes and our Yes together, gloriously evident. God affirms us, making us a sure thing in Christ, putting his Yes within us. By his Spirit he has stamped us with his eternal pledge—a sure beginning of what he is destined to complete.

23   Now, are you ready for the real reason I didn't visit you in Corinth? As God is my witness, the only reason I didn't come was to spare you pain. I was being *considerate* of you, not indifferent, not manipulative.

24   We're not in charge of how you live out the faith, looking over your shoulders, suspiciously critical. We're partners, working alongside you, joyfully expectant. I know that you stand by your own faith, not by ours.

1-2   2 That's why I decided not to make another visit that could only be painful to both of us. If by merely showing up I would put you in an embarrassingly painful position, how would you then be free to cheer and refresh me?

3-4   That was my reason for writing a letter instead of coming—so I wouldn't have to spend a miserable time disappointing the very friends I had looked forward to cheering me up. I was convinced at the time I wrote it that what was best for me was also best for you. As it turned out, there was pain enough just in writing that letter, more tears than ink on the parchment. But I didn't write it to cause pain; I wrote it so you would know how much I care—oh, more than care—*love* you!

5-8   Now, regarding the one who started all this—the person in question who caused all this pain—I want you to know that I am not the one injured in this as much as, with a few exceptions, all of you. So I don't want to come down too hard. What the majority of you agreed to as punishment is punishment enough. Now is the time to forgive this man and help him back on his feet. If all you do is pour on the guilt, you could very well drown him in it. My counsel now is to pour on the love.

9-11   The focus of my letter wasn't on punishing the offender but on getting you to take responsibility for the health of the church. So if you forgive him, I forgive him. Don't think I'm carrying around a list of personal grudges. The fact is that I'm joining in with *your* forgiveness, as Christ is with us, guiding us. After all, we don't want to unwittingly give Satan an opening for yet more mischief—we're not oblivious to his sly ways!

AN OPEN DOOR

12-14   When I arrived in Troas to proclaim the Message of the Messiah, I found the place wide open: God had opened the door; all I had to do was walk through it. But when I didn't find Titus waiting for me with news of your condition, I couldn't relax. Worried about you, I left and came on to Macedonia province looking for Titus and a reassuring word on you. And I got it, thank God!

14-16   In the Messiah, in Christ, God leads us from place to place in one perpetual victory parade. Through us, he brings knowledge of Christ. Everywhere we go, people breathe in the exquisite fragrance. Because of Christ, we give off a sweet scent rising to God, which is recognized by those on the way of salvation — an aroma redolent with life. But those on the way to destruction treat us more like the stench from a rotting corpse.

16-17   This is a terrific responsibility. Is anyone competent to take it on? No — but at least we don't take God's Word, water it down, and then take it to the streets to sell it cheap. We stand in Christ's presence when we speak; God looks us in the face. We get what we say straight from God and say it as honestly as we can.

1-3   3 Does it sound like we're patting ourselves on the back, insisting on our credentials, asserting our authority? Well, we're not. Neither do we need letters of endorsement, either to you or from you. You yourselves are all the endorsement we need. Your very lives are a letter that anyone can read by just looking at you. Christ himself wrote it — not with ink, but with God's living Spirit; not chiseled into stone, but carved into human lives — and we publish it.

4-6   We couldn't be more sure of ourselves in this — that *you*, written by Christ himself for God, are our letter of recommendation. We wouldn't think of writing this kind of letter about ourselves. Only God can write such a letter. His letter authorizes us to help carry out this new plan of action. The plan wasn't written out with ink on paper, with pages and pages of legal footnotes, killing your spirit. It's written with Spirit on spirit, his life on our lives!

LIFTING THE VEIL

7-8   The Government of Death, its constitution chiseled on stone tablets, had a dazzling inaugural. Moses' face as he delivered the tablets was so bright that day (even though it would fade soon enough) that the people of Israel could no more look right at him than stare into the sun. How much more dazzling, then, the Government of Living Spirit?

9-11   If the Government of Condemnation was impressive, how about this Government of Affirmation? Bright as that old government was, it would look downright dull alongside this new one. If that makeshift arrangement impressed us, how much more this brightly shining government installed for eternity?

12-15   With that kind of hope to excite us, nothing holds us back. Unlike Moses, we have nothing to hide. Everything is out in the open with us. He wore a veil so the children of Israel wouldn't notice that the glory was fading away — and they *didn't* notice. They didn't notice it then and they don't notice it now, don't notice that there's nothing left behind that veil. Even today when the proclamations of that old, bankrupt government are read out, they can't see through it. Only Christ can get rid of the veil so they can see for themselves that there's nothing there.

16-18   Whenever, though, they turn to face God as Moses did, God removes the veil and there they are — face-to-face! They suddenly recognize that God is a living, personal presence, not a piece of chiseled stone. And when God is personally present, a living Spirit, that old, constricting legislation is recognized as obsolete. We're free of it! All of us! Nothing between us and God, our faces shining with the brightness of his face. And so we are transfigured much like the Messiah, our lives gradually becoming brighter and more beautiful as God enters our lives and we become like him.

TRIAL AND TORTURE

1-2 **4** Since God has so generously let us in on what he is doing, we're not about to throw up our hands and walk off the job just because we run into occasional hard times. We refuse to wear masks and play games. We don't maneuver and manipulate behind the scenes. And we don't twist God's Word to suit ourselves. Rather, we keep everything we do and say out in the open, the whole truth on display, so that those who want to can see and judge for themselves in the presence of God.

3-4 If our Message is obscure to anyone, it's not because we're holding back in any way. No, it's because these other people are looking or going the wrong way and refuse to give it serious attention. All they have eyes for is the fashionable god of darkness. They think he can give them what they want, and that they won't have to bother believing a Truth they can't see. They're stone-blind to the dayspring brightness of the Message that shines with Christ, who gives us the best picture of God we'll ever get.

5-6 Remember, our Message is not about ourselves; we're proclaiming Jesus Christ, the Master. All we are is messengers, errand runners from Jesus for you. It started when God said, "Light up the darkness!" and our lives filled up with light as we saw and understood God in the face of Christ, all bright and beautiful.

7-12 If you only look at *us*, you might well miss the brightness. We carry this precious Message around in the unadorned clay pots of our ordinary lives. That's to prevent anyone from confusing God's incomparable power with us. As it is, there's not much chance of that. You know for yourselves that we're not much to look at. We've been surrounded and battered by troubles, but we're not demoralized; we're not sure what to do, but we know that God knows what to do; we've been spiritually terrorized, but God hasn't left our side; we've been thrown down, but we haven't broken. What they did to Jesus, they do to us — trial and torture, mockery and murder; what Jesus did among them, he does in us — he lives! Our lives are at constant risk for Jesus' sake, which makes Jesus' life all the more evident in us. While we're going through the worst, you're getting in on the best!

13-15 We're not keeping this quiet, not on your life. Just like the psalmist who wrote, "I believed it, so I said it," we say what we believe. And what we believe is that the One who raised up the Master Jesus will just as certainly raise us up with you, alive. Every detail works to your advantage and to God's glory: more and more grace, more and more people, more and more praise!

16-18 So we're not giving up. How could we! Even though on the outside it often looks like things are falling apart on us, on the inside, where God is making new life, not a day goes by without his unfolding grace. These hard times are small potatoes compared to the coming good times, the lavish celebration prepared for us. There's far more here than meets the eye. The things we see now are here today, gone tomorrow. But the things we can't see now will last forever.

1-5 **5** For instance, we know that when these bodies of ours are taken down like tents and folded away, they will be replaced by resurrection bodies in heaven — God-made, not handmade — and we'll never have to relocate our "tents" again. Sometimes we can hardly wait to move — and so we cry out in frustration. Compared to what's coming, living conditions around here seem like a stopover in an unfurnished shack, and we're tired of it! We've been given a glimpse of the real thing, our true home, our resurrection bodies! The Spirit of God whets our appetite by giving us a taste of what's ahead. He puts a little of heaven in our hearts so that we'll never settle for less.

6-8   That's why we live with such good cheer. You won't see us drooping our heads or dragging our feet! Cramped conditions here don't get us down. They only remind us of the spacious living conditions ahead. It's what we trust in but don't yet see that keeps us going. Do you suppose a few ruts in the road or rocks in the path are going to stop us? When the time comes, we'll be plenty ready to exchange exile for homecoming.

9-10   But neither exile nor homecoming is the main thing. Cheerfully pleasing God is the main thing, and that's what we aim to do, regardless of our conditions. Sooner or later we'll all have to face God, regardless of our conditions. We will appear before Christ and take what's coming to us as a result of our actions, either good or bad.

11-14   *That* keeps us vigilant, you can be sure. It's no light thing to know that we'll all one day stand in that place of Judgment. That's why we work urgently with everyone we meet to get them ready to face God. God alone knows how well we do this, but I hope you realize how much and deeply we care. We're not saying this to make ourselves look good to you. We just thought it would make you feel good, proud even, that we're on your side and not just nice to your face as so many people are. If I acted crazy, I did it for God; if I acted overly serious, I did it for you. Christ's love has moved me to such extremes. His love has the first and last word in everything we do.

A NEW LIFE

14-15   Our firm decision is to work from this focused center: One man died for everyone. That puts everyone in the same boat. He included everyone in his death so that everyone could also be included in his life, a resurrection life, a far better life than people ever lived on their own.

16-20   Because of this decision we don't evaluate people by what they have or how they look. We looked at the Messiah that way once and got it all wrong, as you know. We certainly don't look at him that way anymore. Now we look inside, and what we see is that anyone united with the Messiah gets a fresh start, is created new. The old life is gone; a new life burgeons! Look at it! All this comes from the God who settled the relationship between us and him, and then called us to settle our relationships with each other. God put the world square with himself through the Messiah, giving the world a fresh start by offering forgiveness of sins. God has given us the task of telling everyone what he is doing. We're Christ's representatives. God uses us to persuade men and women to drop their differences and enter into God's work of making things right between them. We're speaking for Christ himself now: Become friends with God; he's already a friend with you.

21   How? you ask. In Christ. God put the wrong on him who never did anything wrong, so we could be put right with God.

STAYING AT OUR POST

1-10   6 Companions as we are in this work with you, we beg you, please don't squander one bit of this marvelous life God has given us. God reminds us,

I heard your call in the nick of time;
The day you needed me, I was there to help.

Well, now is the right time to listen, the day to be helped. Don't put it off; don't frustrate God's work by showing up late, throwing a question mark over everything we're doing. Our work as God's servants gets validated — or not — in the details. People are watching us as we stay at our post, alertly, unswervingly . . . in hard times, tough times, bad times; when we're beaten up, jailed, and mobbed; working hard, working late, working without eating; with pure heart, clear head, steady hand; in gentleness, holiness, and honest love; when we're telling the truth, and when God's showing his power; when we're doing our best setting things right; when we're praised, and when we're blamed; slandered, and honored; true to our word, though distrusted; ignored by the world, but recognized by God; terrifically alive, though rumored to be dead; beaten within an inch of our lives, but refusing to die; immersed in tears, yet always filled with deep joy; living on handouts, yet enriching many; having nothing, having it all.

11-13   Dear, dear Corinthians, I can't tell you how much I long for you to enter this wide-open, spacious life. We didn't fence you in. The smallness you feel comes from within you. Your lives aren't small, but you're living them in a small way. I'm speaking as plainly as I can and with great affection. Open up your lives. Live openly and expansively!

14-18   Don't become partners with those who reject God. How can you make a partnership out of right and wrong? That's not partnership; that's war. Is light best friends with dark? Does Christ go strolling with the Devil? Do trust and mistrust hold hands? Who would think of setting up pagan idols in God's holy Temple? But that is exactly what we are, each of us a temple in whom God lives. God himself put it this way:

"I'll live in them, move into them;
    I'll be their God and they'll be my people.
So leave the corruption and compromise;
    leave it for good," says God.
"Don't link up with those who will pollute you.
    I want you all for myself.
I'll be a Father to you;
    you'll be sons and daughters to me."
The Word of the Master, God.

1   With promises like this to pull us on, dear friends, let's make a clean break with everything that defiles or distracts us, both within and without. Let's make our entire lives fit and holy temples for the worship of God.

MORE PASSIONATE, MORE RESPONSIBLE

2-4   Trust us. We've never hurt a soul, never exploited or taken advantage of anyone. Don't think I'm finding fault with you. I told you earlier that I'm with you all the way, no matter what. I have, in fact, the greatest confidence in you. If only you knew how proud I am of you! I am overwhelmed with joy despite all our troubles.

5-7   When we arrived in Macedonia province, we couldn't settle down. The fights in the church and the fears in our hearts kept us on pins and needles. We couldn't relax because we didn't know how it would turn out. Then the God who lifts up the downcast lifted our heads and our hearts with the arrival of Titus. We were glad just to see him, but the true reassurance came in what he told us about you: how much you cared, how much you grieved, how concerned you were for me. I went from worry to tranquility in no time!

8-9   I know I distressed you greatly with my letter. Although I felt awful at the time, I don't feel at all bad now that I see how it turned out. The letter upset you, but only for a while. Now I'm glad — not that you were upset, but that you were jarred into turning things around. You let the distress bring you to God, not drive you from him. The result was all gain, no loss.

10   Distress that drives us to God does that. It turns us around. It gets us back in the way of salvation. We never regret that kind of pain. But those who let distress drive them away from God are full of regrets, end up on a deathbed of regrets.

11-13   And now, isn't it wonderful all the ways in which this distress has goaded you closer to God? You're more alive, more concerned, more sensitive, more reverent, more human, more passionate, more responsible. Looked at from any angle, you've come out of this with purity of heart. And that is what I was hoping for in the first place when I wrote the letter. My primary concern was not for the one who did the wrong or even the one wronged, but for you — that you would realize and act upon the deep, deep ties between us before God. That's what happened — and we felt just great.

13-16   And then, when we saw how Titus felt — his exuberance over your response — our joy doubled. It was wonderful to see how revived and refreshed he was by everything you did. If I went out on a limb in telling Titus how great I thought you were, you didn't cut off that limb. As it turned out, I hadn't exaggerated one bit. Titus saw for himself that everything I had said about you was true. He can't quit talking about it, going over again and again the story of your prompt obedience, and the dignity and sensitivity of your hospitality. He was quite overwhelmed by it all! And I couldn't be more pleased — I'm so confident and proud of you.

THE OFFERING

1-4   8 Now, friends, I want to report on the surprising and generous ways in which God is working in the churches in Macedonia province. Fierce troubles came down on the people of those churches, pushing them to the very limit. The trial exposed their true colors: They were incredibly happy, though desperately poor. The pressure triggered something totally unexpected: an outpouring of pure and generous gifts. I was there and saw it for myself. They gave offerings of whatever they could — far more than they could afford! — pleading for the privilege of helping out in the relief of poor Christians.

5-7   This was totally spontaneous, entirely their own idea, and caught us completely off guard. What explains it was that they had first given themselves unreservedly to God and to us. The other giving simply flowed out of the purposes of God working in their lives. That's what prompted us to ask Titus to bring the relief offering to your attention, so that what was so well begun could be finished up. You do so well in so many things — you trust God, you're articulate, you're insightful, you're passionate, you love us — now, do your best in this, too.

8-9 I'm not trying to order you around against your will. But by bringing in the Macedonians' enthusiasm as a stimulus to your love, I am hoping to bring the best out of you. You are familiar with the generosity of our Master, Jesus Christ. Rich as he was, he gave it all away for us — in one stroke he became poor and we became rich.

10-20 So here's what I think: The best thing you can do right now is to finish what you started last year and not let those good intentions grow stale. Your heart's been in the right place all along. You've got what it takes to finish it up, so go to it. Once the commitment is clear, you do what you can, not what you can't. The heart regulates the hands. This isn't so others can take it easy while you sweat it out. No, you're shoulder to shoulder with them all the way, your surplus matching their deficit, their surplus matching your deficit. In the end you come out even. As it is written,

> Nothing left over to the one with the most,
> Nothing lacking to the one with the least.

I thank God for giving Titus the same devoted concern for you that I have. He was most considerate of how we felt, but his eagerness to go to you and help out with this relief offering is his own idea. We're sending a companion along with him, someone very popular in the churches for his preaching of the Message. But there's far more to him than popularity. He's rock-solid trustworthy. The churches handpicked him to go with us as we travel about doing this work of sharing God's gifts to honor God as well as we can, taking every precaution against scandal.

20-22 We don't want anyone suspecting us of taking one penny of this money for ourselves. We're being as careful in our reputation with the public as in our reputation with God. That's why we're sending another trusted friend along. He's proved his dependability many times over, and carries on as energetically as the day he started. He's heard much about you, and liked what he's heard — so much so that he can't wait to get there.

23-24 I don't need to say anything further about Titus. We've been close associates in this work of serving you for a long time. The brothers who travel with him are delegates from churches, a real credit to Christ. Show them what you're made of, the love I've been talking up in the churches. Let them see it for themselves!

1-2 If I wrote any more on this relief offering for the poor Christians, I'd be repeating myself. I know you're on board and ready to go. I've been bragging about you all through Macedonia province, telling them, "Achaia province has been ready to go on this since last year." Your enthusiasm by now has spread to most of them.

3-5 Now I'm sending the brothers to make sure you're ready, as I said you would be, so my bragging won't turn out to be just so much hot air. If some Macedonians and I happened to drop in on you and found you weren't prepared, we'd all be pretty red-faced — you and us — for acting so sure of ourselves. So to make sure there will be no slipup, I've recruited these brothers as an advance team to get you and your promised offering all ready before I get there. I want you to have all the time you need to make this offering in your own way. I don't want anything forced or hurried at the last minute.

6-7   Remember: A stingy planter gets a stingy crop; a lavish planter gets a lavish crop. I want each of you to take plenty of time to think it over, and make up your own mind what you will give. That will protect you against sob stories and arm-twisting. God loves it when the giver delights in the giving.

8-11   God can pour on the blessings in astonishing ways so that you're ready for anything and everything, more than just ready to do what needs to be done. As one psalmist puts it,

> He throws caution to the winds,
>   giving to the needy in reckless abandon.
> His right-living, right-giving ways
>   never run out, never wear out.

This most generous God who gives seed to the farmer that becomes bread for your meals is more than extravagant with you. He gives you something you can then give away, which grows into full-formed lives, robust in God, wealthy in every way, so that you can be generous in every way, producing with us great praise to God.

12-15   Carrying out this social relief work involves far more than helping meet the bare needs of poor Christians. It also produces abundant and bountiful thanksgivings to God. This relief offering is a prod to live at your very best, showing your gratitude to God by being openly obedient to the plain meaning of the Message of Christ. You show your gratitude through your generous offerings to your needy brothers and sisters, and really toward everyone. Meanwhile, moved by the extravagance of God in your lives, they'll respond by praying for you in passionate intercession for whatever you need. Thank God for this gift, his gift. No language can praise it enough!

TEARING DOWN BARRIERS

1-2   **10** And now a personal but most urgent matter; I write in the gentle but firm spirit of Christ. I hear that I'm being painted as cringing and wishy-washy when I'm with you, but harsh and demanding when at a safe distance writing letters. Please don't force me to take a hard line when I'm present with you. Don't think that I'll hesitate a single minute to stand up to those who say I'm an unprincipled opportunist. Then they'll have to eat their words.

3-6   The world is unprincipled. It's dog-eat-dog out there! The world doesn't fight fair. But we don't live or fight our battles that way—never have and never will. The tools of our trade aren't for marketing or manipulation, but they are for demolishing that entire massively corrupt culture. We use our powerful God-tools for smashing warped philosophies, tearing down barriers erected against the truth of God, fitting every loose thought and emotion and impulse into the structure of life shaped by Christ. Our tools are ready at hand for clearing the ground of every obstruction and building lives of obedience into maturity.

7-8   You stare and stare at the obvious, but you can't see the forest for the trees. If you're looking for a clear example of someone on Christ's side, why do you so quickly cut me out? Believe me, I am quite sure of my standing with Christ. You may think I overstate the authority he gave me, but I'm not backing off. Every bit of my commitment is for the purpose of building you up, after all, not tearing you down.

9-11 And what's this talk about me bullying you with my letters? "His letters are brawny and potent, but in person he's a weakling and mumbles when he talks." Such talk won't survive scrutiny. What we write when away, we do when present. We're the exact same people, absent or present, in letter or in person.

12 We're not, understand, putting ourselves in a league with those who boast that they're our superiors. We wouldn't dare do that. But in all this comparing and grading and competing, they quite miss the point.

13-14 We aren't making outrageous claims here. We're sticking to the limits of what God has set for us. But there can be no question that those limits reach to and include you. We're not moving into someone else's "territory." We were already there with you, weren't we? We were the first ones to get there with the Message of Christ, right? So how can there be any question of overstepping our bounds by writing or visiting you?

15-18 We're not barging in on the rightful work of others, interfering with their ministries, demanding a place in the sun with them. What we're hoping for is that as your lives grow in faith, you'll play a part within our expanding work. And we'll all still be within the limits God sets as we proclaim the Message in countries beyond Corinth. But we have no intention of moving in on what others have done and taking credit for it. "If you want to claim credit, claim it for God." What you say about yourself means nothing in God's work. It's what God says about you that makes the difference.

PSEUDO-SERVANTS OF GOD

1-3 **11** Will you put up with a little foolish aside from me? Please, just for a moment. The thing that has me so upset is that I care about you so much—this is the passion of God burning inside me! I promised your hand in marriage to Christ, presented you as a pure virgin to her husband. And now I'm afraid that exactly as the Snake seduced Eve with his smooth patter, you are being lured away from the simple purity of your love for Christ.

4-6 It seems that if someone shows up preaching quite another Jesus than we preached—different spirit, different message—you put up with him quite nicely. But if you put up with these big-shot "apostles," why can't you put up with simple me? I'm as good as they are. It's true that I don't have their voice, haven't mastered that smooth eloquence that impresses you so much. But when I do open my mouth, I at least know what I'm talking about. We haven't kept anything back. We let you in on everything.

7-12 I wonder, did I make a bad mistake in proclaiming God's Message to you without asking for something in return, serving you free of charge so that you wouldn't be inconvenienced by me? It turns out that the other churches paid my way so that you could have a free ride. Not once during the time I lived among you did anyone have to lift a finger to help me out. My needs were always supplied by the believers from Macedonia province. I was careful never to be a burden to you, and I never will be, you can count on it. With Christ as my witness, it's a point of honor with me, and I'm not going to keep it quiet just to protect you from what the neighbors will think.

It's not that I don't love you; God knows I do. I'm just trying to keep things open and honest between us.

12-15   And I'm not changing my position on this. I'd die before taking your money. I'm giving nobody grounds for lumping me in with those money-grubbing "preachers," vaunting themselves as something special. They're a sorry bunch — pseudo-apostles, lying preachers, crooked workers — posing as Christ's agents but sham to the core. And no wonder! Satan does it all the time, dressing up as a beautiful angel of light. So it shouldn't surprise us when his servants masquerade as servants of God. But they're not getting by with anything. They'll pay for it in the end.

MANY A LONG AND LONELY NIGHT

16-21   Let me come back to where I started — and don't hold it against me if I continue to sound a little foolish. Or if you'd rather, just accept that I am a fool and let me rant on a little. I didn't learn this kind of talk from Christ. Oh, no, it's a bad habit I picked up from the three-ring preachers that are so popular these days. Since you sit there in the judgment seat observing all these shenanigans, you can afford to humor an occasional fool who happens along. You have such admirable tolerance for impostors who rob your freedom, rip you off, steal you blind, put you down — even slap your face! I shouldn't admit it to you, but our stomachs aren't strong enough to tolerate that kind of stuff.

21-23   Since you admire the egomaniacs of the pulpit so much (remember, this is your old friend, the fool, talking), let me try my hand at it. Do they brag of being Hebrews, Israelites, the pure race of Abraham? I'm their match. Are they servants of Christ? I can go them one better. (I can't believe I'm saying these things. It's crazy to talk this way! But I started, and I'm going to finish.)

23-27   I've worked much harder, been jailed more often, beaten up more times than I can count, and at death's door time after time. I've been flogged five times with the Jews' thirty-nine lashes, beaten by Roman rods three times, pummeled with rocks once. I've been shipwrecked three times, and immersed in the open sea for a night and a day. In hard traveling year in and year out, I've had to ford rivers, fend off robbers, struggle with friends, struggle with foes. I've been at risk in the city, at risk in the country, endangered by desert sun and sea storm, and betrayed by those I thought were my brothers. I've known drudgery and hard labor, many a long and lonely night without sleep, many a missed meal, blasted by the cold, naked to the weather.

28-29   And that's not the half of it, when you throw in the daily pressures and anxieties of all the churches. When someone gets to the end of his rope, I feel the desperation in my bones. When someone is duped into sin, an angry fire burns in my gut.

30-33   If I have to "brag" about myself, I'll brag about the humiliations that make me like Jesus. The eternal and blessed God and Father of our Master Jesus knows I'm not lying. Remember the time I was in Damascus and the governor of King Aretas posted guards at the city gates to arrest me? I crawled through a window in the wall, was let down in a basket, and had to run for my life.

STRENGTH FROM WEAKNESS

1-5 **12** You've forced me to talk this way, and I do it against my better judgment. But now that we're at it, I may as well bring up the matter of visions and revelations that God gave me. For instance, I know a man who, fourteen years ago, was seized by Christ and swept in ecstasy to the heights of heaven. I really don't know if this took place in the body or out of it; only God knows. I also know that this man was hijacked into paradise — again, whether in or out of the body, I don't know; God knows. There he heard the unspeakable spoken, but was forbidden to tell what he heard. This is the man I want to talk about. But about myself, I'm not saying another word apart from the humiliations.

6 If I had a mind to brag a little, I could probably do it without looking ridiculous, and I'd still be speaking plain truth all the way. But I'll spare you. I don't want anyone imagining me as anything other than the fool you'd encounter if you saw me on the street or heard me talk.

7-10 Because of the extravagance of those revelations, and so I wouldn't get a big head, I was given the gift of a handicap to keep me in constant touch with my limitations. Satan's angel did his best to get me down; what he in fact did was push me to my knees. No danger then of walking around high and mighty! At first I didn't think of it as a gift, and begged God to remove it. Three times I did that, and then he told me,

My grace is enough; it's all you need.
My strength comes into its own in your weakness.

Once I heard that, I was glad to let it happen. I quit focusing on the handicap and began appreciating the gift. It was a case of Christ's strength moving in on my weakness. Now I take limitations in stride, and with good cheer, these limitations that cut me down to size — abuse, accidents, opposition, bad breaks. I just let Christ take over! And so the weaker I get, the stronger I become.

11-13 Well, now I've done it! I've made a complete fool of myself by going on like this. But it's not all my fault; you put me up to it. You should have been doing this for me, sticking up for me and commending me instead of making me do it for myself. You know from personal experience that even if I'm a nobody, a nothing, I wasn't second-rate compared to those big-shot apostles you're so taken with. All the signs that mark a true apostle were in evidence while I was with you through both good times and bad: signs of portent, signs of wonder, signs of power. Did you get less of me or of God than any of the other churches? The only thing you got less of was less responsibility for my upkeep. Well, I'm sorry. Forgive me for depriving you.

14-15 Everything is in readiness now for this, my third visit to you. But don't worry about it; you won't have to put yourselves out. I'll be no more of a bother to you this time than on the other visits. I have no interest in what you have — only in you. Children shouldn't have to look out for their parents; parents look out for the children. I'd be most happy to empty my pockets, even mortgage my life, for your good. So how does it happen that the more I love you, the less I'm loved?

16-18   And why is it that I keep coming across these whiffs of gossip about how my self-support was a front behind which I worked an elaborate scam? Where's the evidence? Did I cheat or trick you through anyone I sent? I asked Titus to visit, and sent some brothers along. Did they swindle you out of anything? And haven't we always been just as aboveboard, just as honest?

19   I hope you don't think that all along we've been making our defense before you, the jury. You're not the jury; God is the jury — God revealed in Christ — and we make our case before him. And we've gone to all the trouble of supporting ourselves so that we won't be in the way or get in the way of your growing up.

20-21   I do admit that I have fears that when I come you'll disappoint me and I'll disappoint you, and in frustration with each other everything will fall to pieces — quarrels, jealousy, flaring tempers, taking sides, angry words, vicious rumors, swelled heads, and general bedlam. I don't look forward to a second humiliation by God among you, compounded by hot tears over that crowd that keeps sinning over and over in the same old ways, who refuse to turn away from the pigsty of evil, sexual disorder, and indecency in which they wallow.

HE'S ALIVE NOW!

1-4   **13** Well, this is my third visit coming up. Remember the Scripture that says, "A matter becomes clear after two or three witnesses give evidence"? On my second visit I warned that bunch that keeps sinning over and over in the same old ways that when I came back I wouldn't go easy on them. Now, preparing for the third, I'm saying it again from a distance. If you haven't changed your ways by the time I get there, look out. You who have been demanding proof that Christ speaks through me will get more than you bargained for. You'll get the full force of Christ, don't think you won't. He was sheer weakness and humiliation when he was killed on the cross, but oh, he's alive now — in the mighty power of God! We weren't much to look at, either, when we were humiliated among you, but when we deal with you this next time, we'll be alive in Christ, strengthened by God.

5-9   Test yourselves to make sure you are solid in the faith. Don't drift along taking everything for granted. Give yourselves regular checkups. You need firsthand evidence, not mere hearsay, that Jesus Christ is in you. Test it out. If you fail the test, do something about it. I hope the test won't show that we have failed. But if it comes to that, we'd rather the test showed our failure than yours. We're rooting for the truth to win out in you. We couldn't possibly do otherwise.

We don't just put up with our limitations; we celebrate them, and then go on to celebrate every strength, every triumph of the truth in you. We pray hard that it will all come together in your lives.

10   I'm writing this to you now so that when I come I won't have to say another word on the subject. The authority the Master gave me is for putting people together, not taking them apart. I want to get on with it, and not have to spend time on reprimands.

11-13 And that's about it, friends. Be cheerful. Keep things in good repair. Keep your spirits up. Think in harmony. Be agreeable. Do all that, and the God of love and peace will be with you for sure. Greet one another with a holy embrace. All the brothers and sisters here say hello.

14 The amazing grace of the Master, Jesus Christ, the extravagant love of God, the intimate friendship of the Holy Spirit, be with all of you.

GALATIANS

When men and women get their hands on religion, one of the first things they often do is turn it into an instrument for controlling others, either putting or keeping them "in their place." The history of such religious manipulation and coercion is long and tedious. It is little wonder that people who have only known religion on such terms experience release or escape from it as freedom. The problem is that the freedom turns out to be short-lived.

Paul of Tarsus was doing his diligent best to add yet another chapter to this dreary history when he was converted by Jesus to something radically and entirely different — a free life in God. Through Jesus, Paul learned that God was not an impersonal force to be used to make people behave in certain prescribed ways, but a personal Savior who set us free to live a free life. God did not coerce us from without, but set us free from within.

It was a glorious experience, and Paul set off telling others, introducing and inviting everyone he met into this free life. In his early travels he founded a series of churches in the Roman province of Galatia. A few years later Paul learned that religious leaders of the old school had come into those churches, called his views and authority into question, and were reintroducing the old ways, herding all these freedom-loving Christians back into the corral of religious rules and regulations.

Paul was, of course, furious. He was furious with the old guard for coming in with their strong-arm religious tactics and intimidating the Christians into giving up their free life in Jesus. But he was also furious with the Christians for caving in to the intimidation.

His letter to the Galatian churches helps them, and us, recover the original freedom. It also gives direction in the nature of God's gift of freedom — most necessary guidance, for freedom is a delicate and subtle gift, easily perverted and often squandered.

GALATIANS

¹⁻⁵ **1** I, Paul, and my companions in faith here, send greetings to the Galatian churches. My authority for writing to you does not come from any popular vote of the people, nor does it come through the appointment of some human higher-up. It comes directly from Jesus the Messiah and God the Father, who raised him from the dead. I'm God-commissioned. So I greet you with the great words, grace and peace! We know the meaning of those words because Jesus Christ rescued us from this evil world we're in by offering himself as a sacrifice for our sins. God's plan is that we all experience that rescue. Glory to God forever! Oh, yes!

THE MESSAGE

⁶⁻⁹ I can't believe your fickleness—how easily you have turned traitor to him who called you by the grace of Christ by embracing a variant message! It is not a minor variation, you know; it is completely other, an alien message, a no-message, a lie about God. Those who are provoking this agitation among you are turning the Message of Christ on its head. Let me be blunt: If one of us—even if an angel from heaven!—were to preach something other than what we preached originally, let him be cursed. I said it once; I'll say it again: If anyone, regardless of reputation or credentials, preaches something other than what you received originally, let him be cursed.

¹⁰⁻¹² Do you think I speak this strongly in order to manipulate crowds? Or curry favor with God? Or get popular applause? If my goal was popularity, I wouldn't bother being Christ's slave. Know this—I am most emphatic here, friends—this great Message I delivered to you is not mere human optimism. I didn't receive it through the traditions, and I wasn't taught it in some school. I got it straight from God, received the Message directly from Jesus Christ.

¹³⁻¹⁶ I'm sure that you've heard the story of my earlier life when I lived in the Jewish way. In those days I went all out in persecuting God's church. I was systematically destroying it. I was so enthusiastic about the traditions of my ancestors that I advanced head and shoulders above my peers in my career. Even then God had designs on me. Why, when I was still in my mother's womb he chose and called me out of sheer generosity! Now he has intervened and revealed his Son to me so that I might joyfully tell non-Jews about him.

¹⁶⁻²⁰ Immediately after my calling—without consulting anyone around me and without going up to Jerusalem to confer with those who were apostles long before I was—I got away to Arabia. Later I returned to Damascus, but it was three years before I went up to Jerusalem to compare stories with Peter. I was there only fifteen days—but what days they were! Except for our Master's brother James, I saw no other apostles. (I'm telling you the absolute truth in this.)

²¹⁻²⁴ Then I began my ministry in the regions of Syria and Cilicia. After all that time and activity I was still unknown by face among the Christian churches in Judea. There was only this report: "That man who once persecuted us is now preaching the very message he used to try to destroy." Their response was to recognize and worship *God* because of *me*!

WHAT IS CENTRAL?

1-5 **2** Fourteen years after that first visit, Barnabas and I went up to Jerusalem and took Titus with us. I went to clarify with them what had been revealed to me. At that time I placed before them exactly what I was preaching to the non-Jews. I did this in private with the leaders, those held in esteem by the church, so that our concern would not become a controversial public issue, marred by ethnic tensions, exposing my years of work to denigration and endangering my present ministry. Significantly, Titus, non-Jewish though he was, was not required to be circumcised. While we were in conference we were infiltrated by spies pretending to be Christians, who slipped in to find out just how free true Christians are. Their ulterior motive was to reduce us to their brand of servitude. We didn't give them the time of day. We were determined to preserve the truth of the Message for you.

6-10 As for those who were considered important in the church, their reputation doesn't concern me. God isn't impressed with mere appearances, and neither am I. And of course these leaders were able to add nothing to the message I had been preaching. It was soon evident that God had entrusted me with the same message to the non-Jews as Peter had been preaching to the Jews. Recognizing that my calling had been given by God, James, Peter, and John — the pillars of the church — shook hands with me and Barnabas, assigning us to a ministry to the non-Jews, while they continued to be responsible for reaching out to the Jews. The only additional thing they asked was that we remember the poor, and I was already eager to do that.

11-13 Later, when Peter came to Antioch, I had a face-to-face confrontation with him because he was clearly out of line. Here's the situation. Earlier, before certain persons had come from James, Peter regularly ate with the non-Jews. But when that conservative group came from Jerusalem, he cautiously pulled back and put as much distance as he could manage between himself and his non-Jewish friends. That's how fearful he was of the conservative Jewish clique that's been pushing the old system of circumcision. Unfortunately, the rest of the Jews in the Antioch church joined in that hypocrisy so that even Barnabas was swept along in the charade.

14 But when I saw that they were not maintaining a steady, straight course according to the Message, I spoke up to Peter in front of them all: "If you, a Jew, live like a non-Jew when you're not being observed by the watchdogs from Jerusalem, what right do you have to require non-Jews to conform to Jewish customs just to make a favorable impression on your old Jerusalem cronies?"

15-16 We Jews know that we have no advantage of birth over "non-Jewish sinners." We know very well that we are not set right with God by rule-keeping but only through personal faith in Jesus Christ. How do we know? We tried it — and we had the best system of rules the world has ever seen! Convinced that no human being can please God by self-improvement, we believed in Jesus as the Messiah so that we might be set right before God by trusting in the Messiah, not by trying to be good.

17-18 Have some of you noticed that we are not yet perfect? (No great surprise, right?) And are you ready to make the accusation that since people like me, who go through Christ in order to get things right with God, aren't perfectly virtuous, Christ must therefore be an accessory to sin? The accusation is frivolous. If I was "trying to be good," I would be rebuilding the same old barn that I tore down. I would be acting as a charlatan.

19-21 What actually took place is this: I tried keeping rules and working my head off to please God, and it didn't work. So I quit being a "law man" so that I could be *God's* man. Christ's life showed me how, and enabled me to do it. I identified myself completely with him. Indeed, I have been crucified with Christ. My ego is no longer central. It is no longer important that I appear righteous before you or have your good opinion, and I am no longer driven to impress God. Christ lives in me. The life you see me living is not "mine," but it is lived by faith in the Son of God, who loved me and gave himself for me. I am not going to go back on that.

21 Is it not clear to you that to go back to that old rule-keeping, peer-pleasing religion would be an abandonment of everything personal and free in my relationship with God? I refuse to do that, to repudiate God's grace. If a living relationship with God could come by rule-keeping, then Christ died unnecessarily.

TRUST IN CHRIST, NOT THE LAW

1 3 You crazy Galatians! Did someone put a hex on you? Have you taken leave of your senses? Something crazy has happened, for it's obvious that you no longer have the crucified Jesus in clear focus in your lives. His sacrifice on the cross was certainly set before you clearly enough.

2-4 Let me put this question to you: How did your new life begin? Was it by working your heads off to please God? Or was it by responding to God's Message to you? Are you going to continue this craziness? For only crazy people would think they could complete by their own efforts what was begun by God. If you weren't smart enough or strong enough to begin it, how do you suppose you could perfect it? Did you go through this whole painful learning process for nothing? It is not yet a total loss, but it certainly will be if you keep this up!

5-6 Answer this question: Does the God who lavishly provides you with his own presence, his Holy Spirit, working things in your lives you could never do for yourselves, does he do these things because of your strenuous moral striving *or* because you trust him to do them in you? Don't these things happen among you just as they happened with Abraham? He believed God, and that act of belief was turned into a life that was right with God.

7-8 Is it not obvious to you that persons who put their trust in Christ (not persons who put their trust in the law!) are like Abraham: children of faith? It was all laid out beforehand in Scripture that God would set things right with non-Jews by *faith*. Scripture anticipated this in the promise to Abraham: "All nations will be blessed in you."

9-10 So those now who live by faith are blessed along with Abraham, who lived by faith — this is no new doctrine! And that means that anyone who tries to live by his own effort, independent of God, is doomed to failure. Scripture backs this up: "Utterly cursed is every person who fails to carry out every detail written in the Book of the law."

11-12 The obvious impossibility of carrying out such a moral program should make it plain that no one can sustain a relationship with God that way. The person who lives in right relationship with God does it by embracing what God arranges for him. Doing things for God is the opposite of entering into what God does for you. Habakkuk had it right: "The person who believes God, is set right by God — and that's the real life." Rule-keeping does not naturally evolve into living by faith, but only perpetuates itself in more and more rule-keeping, a fact observed in Scripture: "The one who does these things [rule-keeping] continues to live by them."

13-14   Christ redeemed us from that self-defeating, cursed life by absorbing it completely into himself. Do you remember the Scripture that says, "Cursed is everyone who hangs on a tree"? That is what happened when Jesus was nailed to the cross: He became a curse, and at the same time dissolved the curse. And now, because of that, the air is cleared and we can see that Abraham's blessing is present and available for non-Jews, too. We are *all* able to receive God's life, his Spirit, in and with us by believing — just the way Abraham received it.

15-18   **F**riends, let me give you an example from everyday affairs of the free life I am talking about. Once a person's will has been ratified, no one else can annul it or add to it. Now, the promises were made to Abraham and to his descendant. You will observe that Scripture, in the careful language of a legal document, does not say "to descendants," referring to everybody in general, but "to your descendant" (the noun, note, is singular), referring to Christ. This is the way I interpret this: A will, earlier ratified by God, is not annulled by an addendum attached 430 years later, thereby negating the promise of the will. No, this addendum, with its instructions and regulations, has nothing to do with the promised inheritance in the will.

18-20   What is the point, then, of the law, the attached addendum? It was a thoughtful addition to the original covenant promises made to Abraham. The purpose of the law was to keep a sinful people in the way of salvation until Christ (the descendant) came, inheriting the promises and distributing them to us. Obviously this law was not a firsthand encounter with God. It was arranged by angelic messengers through a middleman, Moses. But if there is a middleman as there was at Sinai, then the people are not dealing directly with God, are they? But the original promise is the *direct* blessing of God, received by faith.

21-22   If such is the case, is the law, then, an anti-promise, a negation of God's will for us? Not at all. Its purpose was to make obvious to everyone that we are, in ourselves, out of right relationship with God, and therefore to show us the futility of devising some religious system for getting by our own efforts what we can only get by waiting in faith for God to complete his promise. For if any kind of rule-keeping had power to create life in us, we would certainly have gotten it by this time.

23-24   Until the time when we were mature enough to respond freely in faith to the living God, we were carefully surrounded and protected by the Mosaic law. The law was like those Greek tutors, with which you are familiar, who escort children to school and protect them from danger or distraction, making sure the children will really get to the place they set out for.

25-27   But now you have arrived at your destination: By faith in Christ you are in direct relationship with God. Your baptism in Christ was not just washing you up for a fresh start. It also involved dressing you in an adult faith wardrobe — Christ's life, the fulfillment of God's original promise.

In Christ's Family

28-29 In Christ's family there can be no division into Jew and non-Jew, slave and free, male and female. Among us you are all equal. That is, we are all in a common relationship with Jesus Christ. Also, since you are Christ's family, then you are Abraham's famous "descendant," heirs according to the covenant promises.

1-3 4 Let me show you the implications of this. As long as the heir is a minor, he has no advantage over the slave. Though legally he owns the entire inheritance, he is subject to tutors and administrators until whatever date the father has set for emancipation. That is the way it is with us: When we were minors, we were just like slaves ordered around by simple instructions (the tutors and administrators of this world), with no say in the conduct of our own lives.

4-7 But when the time arrived that was set by God the Father, God sent his Son, born among us of a woman, born under the conditions of the law so that he might redeem those of us who have been kidnapped by the law. Thus we have been set free to experience our rightful heritage. You can tell for sure that you are now fully adopted as his own children because God sent the Spirit of his Son into our lives crying out, "Papa! Father!" Doesn't that privilege of intimate conversation with God make it plain that you are not a slave, but a child? And if you are a child, you're also an heir, with complete access to the inheritance.

8-11 Earlier, before you knew God personally, you were enslaved to so-called gods that had nothing of the divine about them. But now that you know the real God—or rather since God knows you—how can you possibly subject yourselves again to those paper tigers? For that is exactly what you do when you are intimidated into scrupulously observing all the traditions, taboos, and superstitions associated with special days and seasons and years. I am afraid that all my hard work among you has gone up in a puff of smoke!

12-13 My dear friends, what I would really like you to do is try to put yourselves in my shoes to the same extent that I, when I was with you, put myself in yours. You were very sensitive and kind then. You did not come down on me personally. You were well aware that the reason I ended up preaching to you was that I was physically broken, and so, prevented from continuing my journey, I was forced to stop with you. That is how I came to preach to you.

14-16 And don't you remember that even though taking in a sick guest was most troublesome for you, you chose to treat me as well as you would have treated an angel of God—as well as you would have treated Jesus himself if he had visited you? What has happened to the satisfaction you felt at that time? There were some of you then who, if possible, would have given your very eyes to me—that is how deeply you cared! And now have I suddenly become your enemy simply by telling you the truth? I can't believe it.

17 Those heretical teachers go to great lengths to flatter you, but their motives are rotten. They want to shut you out of the free world of God's grace so that you will always depend on them for approval and direction, making them feel important.

18-20   It is a good thing to be ardent in doing good, but not just when I am in your presence. Can't you continue the same concern for both my person and my message when I am away from you that you had when I was with you? Do you know how I feel right now, and will feel until Christ's life becomes visible in your lives? Like a mother in the pain of childbirth. Oh, I keep wishing that I was with you. Then I wouldn't be reduced to this blunt, letter-writing language out of sheer frustration.

21-31   Tell me now, you who have become so enamored with the law: Have you paid close attention to that law? Abraham, remember, had *two* sons: one by the slave woman and one by the free woman. The son of the slave woman was born by human connivance; the son of the free woman was born by God's promise. This illustrates the very thing we are dealing with now. The two births represent two ways of being in relationship with God. One is from Mount Sinai in Arabia. It corresponds with what is now going on in Jerusalem — a slave life, producing slaves as offspring. This is the way of Hagar. In contrast to that, there is an invisible Jerusalem, a free Jerusalem, and she is our mother — this is the way of Sarah. Remember what Isaiah wrote:

> Rejoice, barren woman who bears no children,
>   shout and cry out, woman who has no birth pangs,
> Because the children of the barren woman
>   now surpass the children of the chosen woman.

Isn't it clear, friends, that you, like Isaac, are children of promise? In the days of Hagar and Sarah, the child who came from faithless connivance (Ishmael) harassed the child who came — empowered by the Spirit — from the faithful promise (Isaac). Isn't it clear that the harassment you are now experiencing from the Jerusalem heretics follows that old pattern? There is a Scripture that tells us what to do: "Expel the slave mother with her son, for the slave son will not inherit with the free son." Isn't that conclusive? We are not children of the slave woman, but of the free woman.

THE LIFE OF FREEDOM

1   **5** Christ has set us free to live a free life. So take your stand! Never again let anyone put a harness of slavery on you.

2-3   I am emphatic about this. The moment any one of you submits to circumcision or any other rule-keeping system, at that same moment Christ's hard-won gift of freedom is squandered. I repeat my warning: The person who accepts the ways of circumcision trades all the advantages of the free life in Christ for the obligations of the slave life of the law.

4-6   I suspect you would never intend this, but this is what happens. When you attempt to live by your own religious plans and projects, you are cut off from Christ, you fall out of grace. Meanwhile we expectantly wait for a satisfying relationship with the Spirit. For in Christ, neither our most conscientious religion nor disregard of religion amounts to anything. What matters is something far more interior: faith expressed in love.

7-10   You were running superbly! Who cut in on you, deflecting you from the true course of obedience? This detour doesn't come from the One who called you into the race in the first place. And please don't toss this off as insignificant. It only takes a minute amount of yeast, you know, to permeate an entire loaf of bread. Deep down, the Master has given me confidence that you will not defect. But the one who is upsetting you, whoever he is, will bear the divine judgment.

11-12 As for the rumor that I continue to preach the ways of circumcision (as I did in those pre-Damascus Road days), that is absurd. Why would I still be persecuted, then? If I were preaching that old message, no one would be offended if I mentioned the Cross now and then — it would be so watered-down it wouldn't matter one way or the other. Why don't these agitators, obsessive as they are about circumcision, go all the way and castrate themselves!

13-15 It is absolutely clear that God has called you to a free life. Just make sure that you don't use this freedom as an excuse to do whatever you want to do and destroy your freedom. Rather, use your freedom to serve one another in love; that's how freedom grows. For everything we know about God's Word is summed up in a single sentence: Love others as you love yourself. That's an act of true freedom. If you bite and ravage each other, watch out — in no time at all you will be annihilating each other, and where will your precious freedom be then?

16-18 My counsel is this: Live freely, animated and motivated by God's Spirit. Then you won't feed the compulsions of selfishness. For there is a root of sinful self-interest in us that is at odds with a free spirit, just as the free spirit is incompatible with selfishness. These two ways of life are antithetical, so that you cannot live at times one way and at times another way according to how you feel on any given day. Why don't you choose to be led by the Spirit and so escape the erratic compulsions of a law-dominated existence?

19-21 It is obvious what kind of life develops out of trying to get your own way all the time: repetitive, loveless, cheap sex; a stinking accumulation of mental and emotional garbage; frenzied and joyless grabs for happiness; trinket gods; magic-show religion; paranoid loneliness; cutthroat competition; all-consuming-yet-never-satisfied wants; a brutal temper; an impotence to love or be loved; divided homes and divided lives; small-minded and lopsided pursuits; the vicious habit of depersonalizing everyone into a rival; uncontrolled and uncontrollable addictions; ugly parodies of community. I could go on.

This isn't the first time I have warned you, you know. If you use your freedom this way, you will not inherit God's kingdom.

22-23 But what happens when we live God's way? He brings gifts into our lives, much the same way that fruit appears in an orchard — things like affection for others, exuberance about life, serenity. We develop a willingness to stick with things, a sense of compassion in the heart, and a conviction that a basic holiness permeates things and people. We find ourselves involved in loyal commitments, not needing to force our way in life, able to marshal and direct our energies wisely.

23-24 Legalism is helpless in bringing this about; it only gets in the way. Among those who belong to Christ, everything connected with getting our own way and mindlessly responding to what everyone else calls necessities is killed off for good — crucified.

25-26 Since this is the kind of life we have chosen, the life of the Spirit, let us make sure that we do not just hold it as an idea in our heads or a sentiment in our hearts, but work out its implications in every detail of our lives. That means we will not compare ourselves with each other as if one of us were better and another worse. We have far more interesting things to do with our lives. Each of us is an original.

NOTHING BUT THE CROSS

1-3 6 Live creatively, friends. If someone falls into sin, forgivingly restore him, saving your critical comments for yourself. *You* might be needing forgiveness before the day's out. Stoop down and reach out to those who are oppressed. Share their burdens, and so complete Christ's law. If you think you are too good for that, you are badly deceived.

4-5 Make a careful exploration of who you are and the work you have been given, and then sink yourself into that. Don't be impressed with yourself. Don't compare yourself with others. Each of you must take responsibility for doing the creative best you can with your own life.

6 Be very sure now, you who been trained to a self-sufficient maturity, that you enter into a generous common life with those who have trained you, sharing all the good things that you have and experience.

7-8 Don't be misled: No one makes a fool of God. What a person plants, he will harvest. The person who plants selfishness, ignoring the needs of others — ignoring God! — harvests a crop of weeds. All he'll have to show for his life is weeds! But the one who plants in response to God, letting God's Spirit do the growth work in him, harvests a crop of real life, eternal life.

9-10 So let's not allow ourselves to get fatigued doing good. At the right time we will harvest a good crop if we don't give up, or quit. Right now, therefore, every time we get the chance, let us work for the benefit of all, starting with the people closest to us in the community of faith.

11-13 Now, in these last sentences, I want to emphasize in the bold scrawls of my personal handwriting the immense importance of what I have written to you. These people who are attempting to force the ways of circumcision on you have only one motive: They want an easy way to look good before others, lacking the courage to live by a faith that shares Christ's suffering and death. All their talk about the law is gas. They *themselves* don't keep the law! And they are highly selective in the laws they *do* observe. They only want you to be circumcised so they can boast of their success in recruiting you to their side. That is contemptible!

14-16 For my part, I am going to boast about nothing but the Cross of our Master, Jesus Christ. Because of that Cross, I have been crucified in relation to the world, set free from the stifling atmosphere of pleasing others and fitting into the little patterns that they dictate. Can't you see the central issue in all this? It is not what you and I do — submit to circumcision, reject circumcision. It is what *God* is doing, and he is creating something totally new, a free life! All who walk by this standard are the true Israel of God — his chosen people. Peace and mercy on them!

17 Quite frankly, I don't want to be bothered anymore by these disputes. I have far more important things to do — the serious living of this faith. I bear in my body scars from my service to Jesus.

18 May what our Master Jesus Christ gives freely be deeply and personally yours, my friends. Oh, yes!

EPHESIANS

What we know about God and what we do for God have a way of getting broken apart in our lives. The moment the organic unity of belief and behavior is damaged in any way, we are incapable of living out the full humanity for which we were created.

Paul's letter to the Ephesians joins together what has been torn apart in our sin-wrecked world. He begins with an exuberant exploration of what Christians believe about God, and then, like a surgeon skillfully setting a compound fracture, "sets" this belief in God into our behavior before God so that the bones—belief and behavior—knit together and heal.

Once our attention is called to it, we notice these fractures all over the place. There is hardly a bone in our bodies that has escaped injury, hardly a relationship in city or job, school or church, family or country, that isn't out of joint or limping in pain. There is much work to be done.

And so Paul goes to work. He ranges widely, from heaven to earth and back again, showing how Jesus, the Messiah, is eternally and tirelessly bringing everything and everyone together. He also shows us that in addition to having this work done in and for us, we are participants in this most urgent work. Now that we know what is going on, that the energy of reconciliation is the dynamo at the heart of the universe, it is imperative that we join in vigorously and perseveringly, convinced that every detail in our lives contributes (or not) to what Paul describes as God's plan worked out by Christ, "a long-range plan in which everything would be brought together and summed up in him, everything in deepest heaven, everything on planet earth."

EPHESIANS

1-2 1 I, Paul, am under God's plan as an apostle, a special agent of Christ Jesus, writing to you faithful believers in Ephesus. I greet you with the grace and peace poured into our lives by God our Father and our Master, Jesus Christ.

THE GOD OF GLORY

3-6 How blessed is God! And what a blessing he is! He's the Father of our Master, Jesus Christ, and takes us to the high places of blessing in him. Long before he laid down earth's foundations, he had us in mind, had settled on us as the focus of his love, to be made whole and holy by his love. Long, long ago he decided to adopt us into his family through Jesus Christ. (What pleasure he took in planning this!) He wanted us to enter into the celebration of his lavish gift-giving by the hand of his beloved Son.

7-10 Because of the sacrifice of the Messiah, his blood poured out on the altar of the Cross, we're a free people — free of penalties and punishments chalked up by all our misdeeds. And not just barely free, either. *Abundantly* free! He thought of everything, provided for everything we could possibly need, letting us in on the plans he took such delight in making. He set it all out before us in Christ, a long-range plan in which everything would be brought together and summed up in him, everything in deepest heaven, everything on planet earth.

11-12 It's in Christ that we find out who we are and what we are living for. Long before we first heard of Christ and got our hopes up, he had his eye on us, had designs on us for glorious living, part of the overall purpose he is working out in everything and everyone.

13-14 It's in Christ that you, once you heard the truth and believed it (this Message of your salvation), found yourselves home free — signed, sealed, and delivered by the Holy Spirit. This signet from God is the first installment on what's coming, a reminder that we'll get everything God has planned for us, a praising and glorious life.

15-19 That's why, when I heard of the solid trust you have in the Master Jesus and your outpouring of love to all the followers of Jesus, I couldn't stop thanking God for you — every time I prayed, I'd think of you and give thanks. But I do more than thank. I ask — ask the God of our Master, Jesus Christ, the God of glory — to make you intelligent and discerning in knowing him personally, your eyes focused and clear, so that you can see exactly what it is he is calling you to do, grasp the immensity of this glorious way of life he has for his followers, oh, the utter extravagance of his work in us who trust him — endless energy, boundless strength!

20-23 All this energy issues from Christ: God raised him from death and set him on a throne in deep heaven, in charge of running the universe, everything from galaxies to governments, no name and no power exempt from his rule. And not just for the time being, but *forever*. He is in charge of it all, has the final word on everything. At the center of all this, Christ rules the church. The church, you see, is not peripheral to the world; the world is peripheral to the church. The church is Christ's body, in which he speaks and acts, by which he fills everything with his presence.

He Tore Down the Wall

1-6 2 It wasn't so long ago that you were mired in that old stagnant life of sin. You let the world, which doesn't know the first thing about living, tell you how to live. You filled your lungs with polluted unbelief, and then exhaled disobedience. We all did it, all of us doing what we felt like doing, when we felt like doing it, all of us in the same boat. It's a wonder God didn't lose his temper and do away with the whole lot of us. Instead, immense in mercy and with an incredible love, he embraced us. He took our sin-dead lives and made us alive in Christ. He did all this on his own, with no help from us! Then he picked us up and set us down in highest heaven in company with Jesus, our Messiah.

7-10 Now God has us where he wants us, with all the time in this world and the next to shower grace and kindness upon us in Christ Jesus. Saving is all his idea, and all his work. All we do is trust him enough to let him do it. It's God's gift from start to finish! We don't play the major role. If we did, we'd probably go around bragging that we'd done the whole thing! No, we neither make nor save ourselves. God does both the making and saving. He creates each of us by Christ Jesus to join him in the work he does, the good work he has gotten ready for us to do, work we had better be doing.

11-13 But don't take any of this for granted. It was only yesterday that you outsiders to God's ways had no idea of any of this, didn't know the first thing about the way God works, hadn't the faintest idea of Christ. You knew nothing of that rich history of God's covenants and promises in Israel, hadn't a clue about what God was doing in the world at large. Now because of Christ—dying that death, shedding that blood—you who were once out of it altogether are in on everything.

14-15 The Messiah has made things up between us so that we're now together on this, both non-Jewish outsiders and Jewish insiders. He tore down the wall we used to keep each other at a distance. He repealed the law code that had become so clogged with fine print and footnotes that it hindered more than it helped. Then he started over. Instead of continuing with two groups of people separated by centuries of animosity and suspicion, he created a new kind of human being, a fresh start for everybody.

16-18 Christ brought us together through his death on the cross. The Cross got us to embrace, and that was the end of the hostility. Christ came and preached peace to you outsiders and peace to us insiders. He treated us as equals, and so made us equals. Through him we both share the same Spirit and have equal access to the Father.

19-22 That's plain enough, isn't it? You're no longer wandering exiles. This kingdom of faith is now your home country. You're no longer strangers or outsiders. You *belong* here, with as much right to the name Christian as anyone. God is building a home. He's using us all—irrespective of how we got here—in what he is building. He used the apostles and prophets for the foundation. Now he's using you, fitting you in brick by brick, stone by stone, with Christ Jesus as the cornerstone that holds all the parts together. We see it taking shape day after day—a holy temple built by God, all of us built into it, a temple in which God is quite at home.

THE SECRET PLAN OF GOD

¹⁻³ **3** This is why I, Paul, am in jail for Christ, having taken up the cause of you outsiders, so-called. I take it that you're familiar with the part I was given in God's plan for including everybody. I got the inside story on this from God himself, as I just wrote you in brief.

⁴⁻⁶ As you read over what I have written to you, you'll be able to see for your-selves into the mystery of Christ. None of our ancestors understood this. Only in our time has it been made clear by God's Spirit through his holy apostles and prophets of this new order. The mystery is that people who have never heard of God and those who have heard of him all their lives (what I've been calling outsiders and insiders) stand on the same ground before God. They get the same offer, same help, same promises in Christ Jesus. The Message is accessible and welcoming to everyone, across the board.

⁷⁻⁸ This is my life work: helping people understand and respond to this Message. It came as a sheer gift to me, a real surprise, God handling all the details. When it came to presenting the Message to people who had no background in God's way, I was the least qualified of any of the available Christians. God saw to it that I was equipped, but you can be sure that it had nothing to do with my natural abilities.

⁸⁻¹⁰ And so here I am, preaching and writing about things that are way over my head, the inexhaustible riches and generosity of Christ. My task is to bring out in the open and make plain what God, who created all this in the first place, has been doing in secret and behind the scenes all along. Through followers of Jesus like yourselves gathered in churches, this extraordinary plan of God is becoming known and talked about even among the angels!

¹¹⁻¹³ All this is proceeding along lines planned all along by God and then executed in Christ Jesus. When we trust in him, we're free to say whatever needs to be said, bold to go wherever we need to go. So don't let my present trouble on your behalf get you down. Be proud!

¹⁴⁻¹⁹ My response is to get down on my knees before the Father, this mag-nificent Father who parcels out all heaven and earth. I ask him to strengthen you by his Spirit — not a brute strength but a glorious inner strength — that Christ will live in you as you open the door and invite him in. And I ask him that with both feet planted firmly on love, you'll be able to take in with all followers of Jesus the extravagant dimensions of Christ's love. Reach out and experience the breadth! Test its length! Plumb the depths! Rise to the heights! Live full lives, full in the fullness of God.

²⁰⁻²¹ God can do anything, you know—far more than you could ever imagine or guess or request in your wildest dreams! He does it not by pushing us around but by working within us, his Spirit deeply and gently within us.

Glory to God in the church!
Glory to God in the Messiah, in Jesus!
Glory down all the generations!
Glory through all millennia! Oh, yes!

To Be Mature

1-3   **4** In light of all this, here's what I want you to do. While I'm locked up here, a prisoner for the Master, I want you to get out there and walk—better yet, run!—on the road God called you to travel. I don't want any of you sitting around on your hands. I don't want anyone strolling off, down some path that goes nowhere. And mark that you do this with humility and discipline—not in fits and starts, but steadily, pouring yourselves out for each other in acts of love, alert at noticing differences and quick at mending fences.

4-6   You were all called to travel on the same road and in the same direction, so stay together, both outwardly and inwardly. You have one Master, one faith, one baptism, one God and Father of all, who rules over all, works through all, and is present in all. Everything you are and think and do is permeated with Oneness.

7-13   But that doesn't mean you should all look and speak and act the same. Out of the generosity of Christ, each of us is given his own gift. The text for this is,

> He climbed the high mountain,
> He captured the enemy and seized the booty,
> He handed it all out in gifts to the people.

Is it not true that the One who climbed up also climbed down, down to the valley of earth? And the One who climbed down is the One who climbed back up, up to highest heaven. He handed out gifts above and below, filled heaven with his gifts, filled earth with his gifts. He handed out gifts of apostle, prophet, evangelist, and pastor-teacher to train Christ's followers in skilled servant work, working within Christ's body, the church, until we're all moving rhythmically and easily with each other, efficient and graceful in response to God's Son, fully mature adults, fully developed within and without, fully alive like Christ.

14-16   No prolonged infancies among us, please. We'll not tolerate babes in the woods, small children who are an easy mark for impostors. God wants us to grow up, to know the whole truth and tell it in love—like Christ in everything. We take our lead from Christ, who is the source of everything we do. He keeps us in step with each other. His very breath and blood flow through us, nourishing us so that we will grow up healthy in God, robust in love.

The Old Way Has to Go

17-19   And so I insist—and God backs me up on this—that there be no going along with the crowd, the empty-headed, mindless crowd. They've refused for so long to deal with God that they've lost touch not only with God but with reality itself. They can't think straight anymore. Feeling no pain, they let themselves go in sexual obsession, addicted to every sort of perversion.

20-24   But that's no life for you. You learned Christ! My assumption is that you have paid careful attention to him, been well instructed in the truth precisely as we have it in Jesus. Since, then, we do not have the excuse of ignorance, everything—and I do mean everything—connected with that old way of life has to go. It's rotten through and through. Get rid of it! And then take on an entirely new way of life—a God-fashioned life, a life renewed from the inside and working itself into your conduct as God accurately reproduces his character in you.

25 What this adds up to, then, is this: no more lies, no more pretense. Tell your neighbor the truth. In Christ's body we're all connected to each other, after all. When you lie to others, you end up lying to yourself.

26-27 Go ahead and be angry. You do well to be angry—but don't use your anger as fuel for revenge. And don't stay angry. Don't go to bed angry. Don't give the Devil that kind of foothold in your life.

28 Did you use to make ends meet by stealing? Well, no more! Get an honest job so that you can help others who can't work.

29 Watch the way you talk. Let nothing foul or dirty come out of your mouth. Say only what helps, each word a gift.

30 Don't grieve God. Don't break his heart. His Holy Spirit, moving and breathing in you, is the most intimate part of your life, making you fit for himself. Don't take such a gift for granted.

31-32 Make a clean break with all cutting, backbiting, profane talk. Be gentle with one another, sensitive. Forgive one another as quickly and thoroughly as God in Christ forgave you.

WAKE UP FROM YOUR SLEEP

1-2 5 Watch what God does, and then you do it, like children who learn proper behavior from their parents. Mostly what God does is love you. Keep company with him and learn a life of love. Observe how Christ loved us. His love was not cautious but extravagant. He didn't love in order to get something from us but to give everything of himself to us. Love like that.

3-4 Don't allow love to turn into lust, setting off a downhill slide into sexual promiscuity, filthy practices, or bullying greed. Though some tongues just love the taste of gossip, those who follow Jesus have better uses for language than that. Don't talk dirty or silly. That kind of talk doesn't fit our style. Thanksgiving is our dialect.

5 You can be sure that using people or religion or things just for what you can get out of them—the usual variations on idolatry—will get you nowhere, and certainly nowhere near the kingdom of Christ, the kingdom of God.

6-7 Don't let yourselves get taken in by religious smooth talk. God gets furious with people who are full of religious sales talk but want nothing to do with him. Don't even hang around people like that.

8-10 You groped your way through that murk once, but no longer. You're out in the open now. The bright light of Christ makes your way plain. So no more stumbling around. Get on with it! The good, the right, the true—these are the actions appropriate for daylight hours. Figure out what will please Christ, and then do it.

11-16 Don't waste your time on useless work, mere busywork, the barren pursuits of darkness. Expose these things for the sham they are. It's a scandal when people waste their lives on things they must do in the darkness where no one will see. Rip the cover off those frauds and see how attractive they look in the light of Christ.

Wake up from your sleep,
Climb out of your coffins;
Christ will show you the light!

So watch your step. Use your head. Make the most of every chance you get. These are desperate times!

17 Don't live carelessly, unthinkingly. Make sure you understand what the Master wants.

18-20 Don't drink too much wine. That cheapens your life. Drink the Spirit of God, huge draughts of him. Sing hymns instead of drinking songs! Sing songs from your heart to Christ. Sing praises over everything, any excuse for a song to God the Father in the name of our Master, Jesus Christ.

R ELATIONSHIPS

21 Out of respect for Christ, be courteously reverent to one another.

22-24 Wives, understand and support your husbands in ways that show your support for Christ. The husband provides leadership to his wife the way Christ does to his church, not by domineering but by cherishing. So just as the church submits to Christ as he exercises such leadership, wives should likewise submit to their husbands.

25-28 Husbands, go all out in your love for your wives, exactly as Christ did for the church — a love marked by giving, not getting. Christ's love makes the church whole. His words evoke her beauty. Everything he does and says is designed to bring the best out of her, dressing her in dazzling white silk, radiant with holiness. And that is how husbands ought to love their wives. They're really doing themselves a favor — since they're already "one" in marriage.

29-33 No one abuses his own body, does he? No, he feeds and pampers it. That's how Christ treats us, the church, since we are part of his body. And this is why a man leaves father and mother and cherishes his wife. No longer two, they become "one flesh." This is a huge mystery, and I don't pretend to understand it all. What is clearest to me is the way Christ treats the church. And this provides a good picture of how each husband is to treat his wife, loving himself in loving her, and how each wife is to honor her husband.

1-3 6 Children, do what your parents tell you. This is only right. "Honor your father and mother" is the first commandment that has a promise attached to it, namely, "so you will live well and have a long life."

4 Fathers, don't exasperate your children by coming down hard on them. Take them by the hand and lead them in the way of the Master.

5-8 Servants, respectfully obey your earthly masters but always with an eye to obeying the *real* master, Christ. Don't just do what you have to do to get by, but work heartily, as Christ's servants doing what God wants you to do. And work with a smile on your face, always keeping in mind that no matter who happens to be giving the orders, you're really serving God. Good work will get you good pay from the Master, regardless of whether you are slave or free.

9 Masters, it's the same with you. No abuse, please, and no threats. You and your servants are both under the same Master in heaven. He makes no distinction between you and them.

A FIGHT TO THE FINISH

¹⁰⁻¹² And that about wraps it up. God is strong, and he wants you strong. So take everything the Master has set out for you, well-made weapons of the best materials. And put them to use so you will be able to stand up to everything the Devil throws your way. This is no afternoon athletic contest that we'll walk away from and forget about in a couple of hours. This is for keeps, a life-or-death fight to the finish against the Devil and all his angels.

¹³⁻¹⁸ Be prepared. You're up against far more than you can handle on your own. Take all the help you can get, every weapon God has issued, so that when it's all over but the shouting you'll still be on your feet. Truth, righteousness, peace, faith, and salvation are more than words. Learn how to apply them. You'll need them throughout your life. God's Word is an *indispensable* weapon. In the same way, prayer is essential in this ongoing warfare. Pray hard and long. Pray for your brothers and sisters. Keep your eyes open. Keep each other's spirits up so that no one falls behind or drops out.

¹⁹⁻²⁰ And don't forget to pray for me. Pray that I'll know what to say and have the courage to say it at the right time, telling the mystery to one and all, the Message that I, jailbird preacher that I am, am responsible for getting out.

²¹⁻²² Tychicus, my good friend here, will tell you what I'm doing and how things are going with me. He is certainly a dependable servant of the Master! I've sent him not only to tell you about us but to cheer you on in your faith.

²³⁻²⁴ Good-bye, friends. Love mixed with faith be yours from God the Father and from the Master, Jesus Christ. Pure grace and nothing but grace be with all who love our Master, Jesus Christ.

PHILIPPIANS

This is Paul's happiest letter. And the happiness is infectious. Before we've read a dozen lines, we begin to feel the joy ourselves — the dance of words and the exclamations of delight have a way of getting inside us.

But happiness is not a word we can understand by looking it up in the dictionary. In fact, none of the qualities of the Christian life can be learned out of a book. Something more like apprenticeship is required, being around someone who out of years of devoted discipline shows us, by his or her entire behavior, what it is. Moments of verbal instruction will certainly occur, but mostly an apprentice acquires skill by daily and intimate association with a "master," picking up subtle but absolutely essential things, such as timing and rhythm and "touch."

When we read what Paul wrote to the Christian believers in the city of Philippi, we find ourselves in the company of just such a master. Paul doesn't tell us that we can be happy, or how to be happy. He simply and unmistakably *is* happy. None of his circumstances contribute to his joy: He wrote from a jail cell, his work was under attack by competitors, and after twenty years or so of hard traveling in the service of Jesus, he was tired and would have welcomed some relief.

But circumstances are incidental compared to the life of Jesus, the Messiah, that Paul experiences from the inside. For it is a life that not only happened at a certain point in history, but continues to happen, spilling out into the lives of those who receive him, and then continues to spill out all over the place. Christ is, among much else, the revelation that God cannot be contained or hoarded. It is this "spilling out" quality of Christ's life that accounts for the happiness of Christians, for joy is life in excess, the overflow of what cannot be contained within any one person.

PHILIPPIANS

1-2 **1** Paul and Timothy, both of us committed servants of Christ Jesus, write this letter to all the followers of Jesus in Philippi, pastors and ministers included. We greet you with the grace and peace that comes from God our Father and our Master, Jesus Christ.

A LOVE THAT WILL GROW

3-6 Every time you cross my mind, I break out in exclamations of thanks to God. Each exclamation is a trigger to prayer. I find myself praying for you with a glad heart. I am so pleased that you have continued on in this with us, believing and proclaiming God's Message, from the day you heard it right up to the present. There has never been the slightest doubt in my mind that the God who started this great work in you would keep at it and bring it to a flourishing finish on the very day Christ Jesus appears.

7-8 It's not at all fanciful for me to think this way about you. My prayers and hopes have deep roots in reality. You have, after all, stuck with me all the way from the time I was thrown in jail, put on trial, and came out of it in one piece. All along you have experienced with me the most generous help from God. He knows how much I love and miss you these days. Sometimes I think I feel as strongly about you as Christ does!

9-11 So this is my prayer: that your love will flourish and that you will not only love much but well. Learn to love appropriately. You need to use your head and test your feelings so that your love is sincere and intelligent, not sentimental gush. Live a lover's life, circumspect and exemplary, a life Jesus will be proud of: bountiful in fruits from the soul, making Jesus Christ attractive to all, getting everyone involved in the glory and praise of God.

THEY CAN'T IMPRISON THE MESSAGE

12-14 I want to report to you, friends, that my imprisonment here has had the opposite of its intended effect. Instead of being squelched, the Message has actually prospered. All the soldiers here, and everyone else, too, found out that I'm in jail because of this Messiah. That piqued their curiosity, and now they've learned all about him. Not only that, but most of the followers of Jesus here have become far more sure of themselves in the faith than ever, speaking out fearlessly about God, about the Messiah.

15-17 It's true that some here preach Christ because with me out of the way, they think they'll step right into the spotlight. But the others do it with the best heart in the world. One group is motivated by pure love, knowing that I am here defending the Message, wanting to help. The others, now that I'm out of the picture, are merely greedy, hoping to get something out of it for themselves. Their motives are bad. They see me as their competition, and so the worse it goes for me, the better — they think — for them.

18-21 So how am I to respond? I've decided that I really don't care about their motives, whether mixed, bad, or indifferent. Every time one of them opens his mouth, Christ is proclaimed, so I just cheer them on!

And I'm going to keep that celebration going because I know how it's going to turn out. Through your faithful prayers and the generous response of the Spirit of Jesus Christ, everything he wants to do in and through me will be done. I can hardly wait to continue on my course. I don't expect to be embarrassed in the least. On the contrary, everything happening to me in this jail only serves to make Christ more accurately known, regardless of whether I live or die. They didn't shut me up; they gave me a pulpit! Alive, I'm Christ's messenger; dead, I'm his bounty. Life versus even more life! I can't lose.

22-26   As long as I'm alive in this body, there is good work for me to do. If I had to choose right now, I hardly know which I'd choose. Hard choice! The desire to break camp here and be with Christ is powerful. Some days I can think of nothing better. But most days, because of what you are going through, I am sure that it's better for me to stick it out here. So I plan to be around awhile, companion to you as your growth and joy in this life of trusting God continues. You can start looking forward to a great reunion when I come visit you again. We'll be praising Christ, enjoying each other.

27-30   Meanwhile, live in such a way that you are a credit to the Message of Christ. Let nothing in your conduct hang on whether I come or not. Your conduct must be the same whether I show up to see things for myself or hear of it from a distance. Stand united, singular in vision, contending for people's trust in the Message, the good news, not flinching or dodging in the slightest before the opposition. Your courage and unity will show them what they're up against: defeat for them, victory for you — and both because of God. There's far more to this life than trusting in Christ. There's also suffering for him. And the suffering is as much a gift as the trusting. You're involved in the same kind of struggle you saw me go through, on which you are now getting an updated report in this letter.

HE TOOK ON THE STATUS OF A SLAVE

1-4   2 If you've gotten anything at all out of following Christ, if his love has made any difference in your life, if being in a community of the Spirit means anything to you, if you have a heart, if you *care* — then do me a favor: Agree with each other, love each other, be deep-spirited friends. Don't push your way to the front; don't sweet-talk your way to the top. Put yourself aside, and help others get ahead. Don't be obsessed with getting your own advantage. Forget yourselves long enough to lend a helping hand.

5-8   Think of yourselves the way Christ Jesus thought of himself. He had equal status with God but didn't think so much of himself that he had to cling to the advantages of that status no matter what. Not at all. When the time came, he set aside the privileges of deity and took on the status of a slave, became *human*! Having become human, he stayed human. It was an incredibly humbling process. He didn't claim special privileges. Instead, he lived a selfless, obedient life and then died a selfless, obedient death — and the worst kind of death at that — a crucifixion.

9-11   Because of that obedience, God lifted him high and honored him far beyond anyone or anything, ever, so that all created beings in heaven and on earth — even those long ago dead and buried — will bow in worship before this Jesus Christ, and call out in praise that he is the Master of all, to the glorious honor of God the Father.

REJOICING TOGETHER

12-13   What I'm getting at, friends, is that you should simply keep on doing what you've done from the beginning. When I was living among you, you lived in responsive obedience. Now that I'm separated from you, keep it up. Better yet, redouble your efforts. Be energetic in your life of salvation, reverent and sensitive before God. That energy is *God's* energy, an energy deep within you, God himself willing and working at what will give him the most pleasure.

14-16　Do everything readily and cheerfully—no bickering, no second-guessing allowed! Go out into the world uncorrupted, a breath of fresh air in this squalid and polluted society. Provide people with a glimpse of good living and of the living God. Carry the light-giving Message into the night so I'll have good cause to be proud of you on the day that Christ returns. You'll be living proof that I didn't go to all this work for nothing.

17-18　Even if I am executed here and now, I'll rejoice in being an element in the offering of your faith that you make on Christ's altar, a part of your rejoicing. But turnabout's fair play—you must join me in *my* rejoicing. Whatever you do, don't feel sorry for me.

19-24　I plan (according to Jesus' plan) to send Timothy to you very soon so he can bring back all the news of you he can gather. Oh, how that will do my heart good! I have no one quite like Timothy. He is loyal, and genuinely concerned for you. Most people around here are looking out for themselves, with little concern for the things of Jesus. But you know yourselves that Timothy's the real thing. He's been a devoted son to me as together we've delivered the Message. As soon as I see how things are going to fall out for me here, I plan to send him off. And then I'm hoping and praying to be right on his heels.

25-27　But for right now, I'm dispatching Epaphroditus, my good friend and companion in my work. You sent him to help me out; now I'm sending him to help you out. He has been wanting in the worst way to get back with you. Especially since recovering from the illness you heard about, he's been wanting to get back and reassure you that he is just fine. He nearly died, as you know, but God had mercy on him. And not only on him—he had mercy on me, too. His death would have been one huge grief piled on top of all the others.

28-30　So you can see why I'm so delighted to send him on to you. When you see him again, hale and hearty, how you'll rejoice and how relieved I'll be. Give him a grand welcome, a joyful embrace! People like him deserve the best you can give. Remember the ministry to me that you started but weren't able to complete? Well, in the process of finishing up that work, he put his life on the line and nearly died doing it.

TO KNOW HIM PERSONALLY

1　3 And that's about it, friends. Be glad in God!

I don't mind repeating what I have written in earlier letters, and I hope you don't mind hearing it again. Better safe than sorry—so here goes.

2-6　Steer clear of the barking dogs, those religious busybodies, all bark and no bite. All they're interested in is appearances—knife-happy circum-cisers, I call them. The *real* believers are the ones the Spirit of God leads to work away at this ministry, filling the air with Christ's praise as we do it. We couldn't carry this off by our own efforts, and we know it—even though we can list what many might think are impressive credentials. You know my pedigree: a legitimate birth, circumcised on the eighth day; an

Israelite from the elite tribe of Benjamin; a strict and devout adherent to God's law; a fiery defender of the purity of my religion, even to the point of persecuting the church; a meticulous observer of everything set down in God's law Book.

7-9 The very credentials these people are waving around as something special, I'm tearing up and throwing out with the trash — along with everything else I used to take credit for. And why? Because of Christ. Yes, all the things I once thought were so important are gone from my life. Compared to the high privilege of knowing Christ Jesus as my Master, firsthand, everything I once thought I had going for me is insignificant — dog dung. I've dumped it all in the trash so that I could embrace Christ and be embraced by him. I didn't want some petty, inferior brand of righteousness that comes from keeping a list of rules when I could get the robust kind that comes from trusting Christ — *God's* righteousness.

10-11 I gave up all that inferior stuff so I could know Christ personally, experience his resurrection power, be a partner in his suffering, and go all the way with him to death itself. If there was any way to get in on the resurrection from the dead, I wanted to do it.

FOCUSED ON THE GOAL

12-14 I'm not saying that I have this all together, that I have it made. But I am well on my way, reaching out for Christ, who has so wondrously reached out for me. Friends, don't get me wrong: By no means do I count myself an expert in all of this, but I've got my eye on the goal, where God is beckoning us onward — to Jesus. I'm off and running, and I'm not turning back.

15-16 So let's keep focused on that goal, those of us who want everything God has for us. If any of you have something else in mind, something less than total commitment, God will clear your blurred vision — you'll see it yet! Now that we're on the right track, let's stay on it.

17-19 Stick with me, friends. Keep track of those you see running this same course, headed for this same goal. There are many out there taking other paths, choosing other goals, and trying to get you to go along with them. I've warned you of them many times; sadly, I'm having to do it again. All they want is easy street. They hate Christ's Cross. But easy street is a dead-end street. Those who live there make their bellies their gods; belches are their praise; all they can think of is their appetites.

20-21 But there's far more to life for us. We're citizens of high heaven! We're waiting the arrival of the Savior, the Master, Jesus Christ, who will transform our earthy bodies into glorious bodies like his own. He'll make us beautiful and whole with the same powerful skill by which he is putting everything as it should be, under and around him.

1 4 My dear, dear friends! I love you so much. I do want the very best for you. You make me feel such joy, fill me with such pride. Don't waver. Stay on track, steady in God.

PRAY ABOUT EVERYTHING

2 I urge Euodia and Syntyche to iron out their differences and make up. God doesn't want his children holding grudges.

3 And, oh, yes, Syzygus, since you're right there to help them work things out, do your best with them. These women worked for the Message

hand in hand with Clement and me, and with the other veterans — worked as hard as any of us. Remember, their names are also in the Book of Life.

4-5   Celebrate God all day, every day. I mean, *revel* in him! Make it as clear as you can to all you meet that you're on their side, working with them and not against them. Help them see that the Master is about to arrive. He could show up any minute!

6-7   Don't fret or worry. Instead of worrying, pray. Let petitions and praises shape your worries into prayers, letting God know your concerns. Before you know it, a sense of God's wholeness, everything coming together for good, will come and settle you down. It's wonderful what happens when Christ displaces worry at the center of your life.

8-9   Summing it all up, friends, I'd say you'll do best by filling your minds and meditating on things true, noble, reputable, authentic, compelling, gracious — the best, not the worst; the beautiful, not the ugly; things to praise, not things to curse. Put into practice what you learned from me, what you heard and saw and realized. Do that, and God, who makes everything work together, will work you into his most excellent harmonies.

Content Whatever the Circumstances

10-14 I'm glad in God, far happier than you would ever guess — happy that you're again showing such strong concern for me. Not that you ever quit praying and thinking about me. You just had no chance to show it. Actually, I don't have a sense of needing anything personally. I've learned by now to be quite content whatever my circumstances. I'm just as happy with little as with much, with much as with little. I've found the recipe for being happy whether full or hungry, hands full or hands empty. Whatever I have, wherever I am, I can make it through anything in the One who makes me who I am. I don't mean that your help didn't mean a lot to me — it did. It was a beautiful thing that you came alongside me in my troubles.

15-17   You Philippians well know, and you can be sure I'll never forget it, that when I first left Macedonia province, venturing out with the Message, not one church helped out in the give-and-take of this work except you. You were the only one. Even while I was in Thessalonica, you helped out — and not only once, but twice. Not that I'm looking for handouts, but I do want you to experience the blessing that issues from generosity.

18-20   And now I have it all — and keep getting more! The gifts you sent with Epaphroditus were more than enough, like a sweet-smelling sacrifice roasting on the altar, filling the air with fragrance, pleasing God no end. You can be sure that God will take care of everything you need, his generosity exceeding even yours in the glory that pours from Jesus. Our God and Father abounds in glory that just pours out into eternity. Yes.

21-22   Give our regards to every follower of Jesus you meet. Our friends here say hello. All the Christians here, especially the believers who work in the palace of Caesar, want to be remembered to you.

23   Receive and experience the amazing grace of the Master, Jesus Christ, deep, deep within yourselves.

COLOSSIANS

Hardly anyone who hears the full story of Jesus and learns the true facts of his life and teaching, crucifixion and resurrection, walks away with a shrug of the shoulders, dismissing him as unimportant. People ignorant of the story or misinformed about it, of course, regularly dismiss him. But with few exceptions, the others know instinctively that they are dealing with a most remarkable greatness.

But it is quite common for those who consider him truly important to include others who seem to be equally important in his company —Buddha, Moses, Socrates, and Muhammad for a historical start, along with some personal favorites. For these people, Jesus is important, but not central; his prestige is considerable, but he is not preeminent.

The Christians in the town of Colosse, or at least some of them, seem to have been taking this line. For them, cosmic forces of one sort or another were getting equal billing with Jesus. Paul writes to them in an attempt to restore Jesus, the Messiah, to the center of their lives.

The way he makes his argument is as significant as the argument he makes. Claims for the uniqueness of Jesus are common enough. But such claims about Jesus are frequently made with an arrogance that is completely incompatible with Jesus himself. Sometimes the claims are enforced with violence.

But Paul, although unswervingly confident in the conviction that Christ occupies the center of creation and salvation without peers, is not arrogant. And he is certainly not violent. He argues from a position of rooted humility. He writes with the energies of most considerate love. He exhibits again what Christians have come to appreciate so much in Paul—the wedding of a brilliant and uncompromising intellect with a heart that is warmly and wonderfully kind.

COLOSSIANS

1-2   I, Paul, have been sent on special assignment by Christ as part of God's master plan. Together with my friend Timothy, I greet the Christians and stalwart followers of Christ who live in Colosse. May everything good from God our Father be yours!

WORKING IN HIS ORCHARD

3-5   Our prayers for you are always spilling over into thanksgivings. We can't quit thanking God our Father and Jesus our Messiah for you! We keep getting reports on your steady faith in Christ, our Jesus, and the love you continuously extend to all Christians. The lines of purpose in your lives never grow slack, tightly tied as they are to your future in heaven, kept taut by hope.

5-8   The Message is as true among you today as when you first heard it. It doesn't diminish or weaken over time. It's the same all over the world. The Message bears fruit and gets larger and stronger, just as it has in you. From the very first day you heard and recognized the truth of what God is doing, you've been hungry for more. It's as vigorous in you now as when you learned it from our friend and close associate Epaphras. He is one reliable worker for Christ! I could always depend on him. He's the one who told us how thoroughly love had been worked into your lives by the Spirit.

9-12   Be assured that from the first day we heard of you, we haven't stopped praying for you, asking God to give you wise minds and spirits attuned to his will, and so acquire a thorough understanding of the ways in which God works. We pray that you'll live well for the Master, making him proud of you as you work hard in his orchard. As you learn more and more how God works, you will learn how to do *your* work. We pray that you'll have the strength to stick it out over the long haul—not the grim strength of gritting your teeth but the glory-strength God gives. It is strength that endures the unendurable and spills over into joy, thanking the Father who makes us strong enough to take part in everything bright and beautiful that he has for us.

13-14   God rescued us from dead-end alleys and dark dungeons. He's set us up in the kingdom of the Son he loves so much, the Son who got us out of the pit we were in, got rid of the sins we were doomed to keep repeating.

CHRIST HOLDS IT ALL TOGETHER

15-18   We look at this Son and see the God who cannot be seen. We look at this Son and see God's original purpose in everything created. For everything, absolutely everything, above and below, visible and invisible, rank after rank after rank of angels—*everything* got started in him and finds its purpose in him. He was there before any of it came into existence and holds it all together right up to this moment. And when it comes to the church, he organizes and holds it together, like a head does a body.

18-20   He was supreme in the beginning and—leading the resurrection parade—he is supreme in the end. From beginning to end he's there, towering far above everything, everyone. So spacious is he, so roomy, that everything of God finds its proper place in him without crowding. Not only that, but all the broken and dislocated pieces of the universe—people and things, animals and atoms — get properly fixed and fit together in vibrant harmonies, all because of his death, his blood that poured down from the cross.

21-23   You yourselves are a case study of what he does. At one time you all had your backs turned to God, thinking rebellious thoughts of him, giving him trouble every chance you got. But now, by giving himself completely at the Cross, actually *dying* for you, Christ brought you over to God's side and put your lives together, whole and holy in his presence. You don't walk away from a gift like that! You stay grounded and steady in that bond of trust, constantly tuned in to the Message, careful not to be distracted or diverted. There is no other Message — just this one. Every creature under heaven gets this same Message. I, Paul, am a messenger of this Message.

24-25   I want you to know how glad I am that it's me sitting here in this jail and not you. There's a lot of suffering to be entered into in this world — the kind of suffering Christ takes on. I welcome the chance to take my share in the church's part of that suffering. When I became a servant in this church, I experienced this suffering as a sheer gift, God's way of helping me serve you, laying out the whole truth.

26-29   This mystery has been kept in the dark for a long time, but now it's out in the open. God wanted everyone, not just Jews, to know this rich and glorious secret inside and out, regardless of their background, regardless of their religious standing. The mystery in a nutshell is just this: Christ is in you, so therefore you can look forward to sharing in God's glory. It's that simple. That is the substance of our Message. We preach *Christ*, warning people not to add to the Message. We teach in a spirit of profound common sense so that we can bring each person to maturity. To be mature is to be basic. Christ! No more, no less. That's what I'm working so hard at day after day, year after year, doing my best with the energy God so generously gives me.

1   2 I want you to realize that I continue to work as hard as I know how for you, and also for the Christians over at Laodicea. Not many of you have met me face-to-face, but that doesn't make any difference. Know that I'm on your side, right alongside you. You're not in this alone.

2-4   I want you woven into a tapestry of love, in touch with everything there is to know of God. Then you will have minds confident and at rest, focused on Christ, God's great mystery. All the richest treasures of wisdom and knowledge are embedded in that mystery and nowhere else. And we've been shown the mystery! I'm telling you this because I don't want anyone leading you off on some wild-goose chase, after other so-called mysteries, or "the Secret."

5   I'm a long way off, true, and you may never lay eyes on me, but believe me, I'm on your side, right beside you. I am delighted to hear of the careful and orderly ways you conduct your affairs, and impressed with the solid substance of your faith in Christ.

FROM THE SHADOWS TO THE SUBSTANCE

6-7   My counsel for you is simple and straightforward: Just go ahead with what you've been given. You received Christ Jesus, the Master; now *live* him. You're deeply rooted in him. You're well constructed upon him. You know your way around the faith. Now do what you've been taught. School's out;

quit studying the subject and start *living* it! And let your living spill over into thanksgiving.

8-10   Watch out for people who try to dazzle you with big words and intellectual double-talk. They want to drag you off into endless arguments that never amount to anything. They spread their ideas through the empty traditions of human beings and the empty superstitions of spirit beings. But that's not the way of Christ. Everything of God gets expressed in him, so you can see and hear him clearly. You don't need a telescope, a microscope, or a horoscope to realize the fullness of Christ, and the emptiness of the universe without him. When you come to him, that fullness comes together for you, too. His power extends over everything.

11-15   Entering into this fullness is not something you figure out or achieve. It's not a matter of being circumcised or keeping a long list of laws. No, you're already *in* — insiders — not through some secretive initiation rite but rather through what Christ has already gone through for you, destroying the power of sin. If it's an initiation ritual you're after, you've already been through it by submitting to baptism. Going under the water was a burial of your old life; coming up out of it was a resurrection, God raising you from the dead as he did Christ. When you were stuck in your old sin-dead life, you were incapable of responding to God. God brought you alive — right along with Christ! Think of it! All sins forgiven, the slate wiped clean, that old arrest warrant canceled and nailed to Christ's cross. He stripped all the spiritual tyrants in the universe of their sham authority at the Cross and marched them naked through the streets.

16-17   So don't put up with anyone pressuring you in details of diet, worship services, or holy days. All those things are mere shadows cast before what was to come; the substance is Christ.

18-19   Don't tolerate people who try to run your life, ordering you to bow and scrape, insisting that you join their obsession with angels and that you seek out visions. They're a lot of hot air, that's all they are. They're completely out of touch with the source of life, Christ, who puts us together in one piece, whose very breath and blood flow through us. He is the Head and we are the body. We can grow up healthy in God only as he nourishes us.

20-23   So, then, if with Christ you've put all that pretentious and infantile religion behind you, why do you let yourselves be bullied by it? "Don't touch this! Don't taste that! Don't go near this!" Do you think things that are here today and gone tomorrow are worth that kind of attention? Such things sound impressive if said in a deep enough voice. They even give the illusion of being pious and humble and ascetic. But they're just another way of showing off, making yourselves look important.

HE IS YOUR LIFE

1-2   So if you're serious about living this new resurrection life with Christ, *act* like it. Pursue the things over which Christ presides. Don't shuffle along, eyes to the ground, absorbed with the things right in front of you. Look up, and be alert to what is going on around Christ — that's where the action is. See things from *his* perspective.

3-4   Your old life is dead. Your new life, which is your *real* life — even though invisible to spectators — is with Christ in God. *He* is your life. When Christ (your real life, remember) shows up again on this earth, you'll show up, too — the real you, the glorious you. Meanwhile, be content with obscurity, like Christ.

5-8   And that means killing off everything connected with that way of death: sexual promiscuity, impurity, lust, doing whatever you feel like whenever you feel like it, and grabbing whatever attracts your fancy. That's a life shaped by things and feelings instead of by God. It's because of this kind of thing that God is about to explode in anger. It wasn't long ago that you were doing all that stuff and not knowing any better. But you know better now, so make sure it's all gone for good: bad temper, irritability, meanness, profanity, dirty talk.

9-11   Don't lie to one another. You're done with that old life. It's like a filthy set of ill-fitting clothes you've stripped off and put in the fire. Now you're dressed in a new wardrobe. Every item of your new way of life is custom-made by the Creator, with his label on it. All the old fashions are now obsolete. Words like Jewish and non-Jewish, religious and irreligious, insider and outsider, uncivilized and uncouth, slave and free, mean nothing. From now on everyone is defined by Christ, everyone is included in Christ.

12-14   So, chosen by God for this new life of love, dress in the wardrobe God picked out for you: compassion, kindness, humility, quiet strength, discipline. Be even-tempered, content with second place, quick to forgive an offense. Forgive as quickly and completely as the Master forgave you. And regardless of what else you put on, wear love. It's your basic, all-purpose garment. Never be without it.

15-17   Let the peace of Christ keep you in tune with each other, in step with each other. None of this going off and doing your own thing. And cultivate thankfulness. Let the Word of Christ — the Message — have the run of the house. Give it plenty of room in your lives. Instruct and direct one another using good common sense. And sing, sing your hearts out to God! Let every detail in your lives — words, actions, whatever — be done in the name of the Master, Jesus, thanking God the Father every step of the way.

18   Wives, understand and support your husbands by submitting to them in ways that honor the Master.

19   Husbands, go all out in love for your wives. Don't take advantage of them.

20   Children, do what your parents tell you. This delights the Master no end.

21   Parents, don't come down too hard on your children or you'll crush their spirits.

22-25   Servants, do what you're told by your earthly masters. And don't just do the minimum that will get you by. Do your best. Work from the heart for your real Master, for God, confident that you'll get paid in full when you come into your inheritance. Keep in mind always that the ultimate Master you're serving is Christ. The sullen servant who does shoddy work will be held responsible. Being a follower of Jesus doesn't cover up bad work.

1   4 And masters, treat your servants considerately. Be fair with them. Don't forget for a minute that you, too, serve a Master — God in heaven.

PRAY FOR OPEN DOORS

2-4 Pray diligently. Stay alert, with your eyes wide open in gratitude. Don't forget to pray for us, that God will open doors for telling the mystery of Christ, even while I'm locked up in this jail. Pray that every time I open my mouth I'll be able to make Christ plain as day to them.

5-6 Use your heads as you live and work among outsiders. Don't miss a trick. Make the most of every opportunity. Be gracious in your speech. The goal is to bring out the best in others in a conversation, not put them down, not cut them out.

7-9 My good friend Tychicus will tell you all about me. He's a trusted minister and companion in the service of the Master. I've sent him to you so that you would know how things are with us, and so he could encourage you in your faith. And I've sent Onesimus with him. Onesimus is one of you, and has become such a trusted and dear brother! Together they'll bring you up-to-date on everything that has been going on here.

10-11 Aristarchus, who is in jail here with me, sends greetings; also Mark, cousin of Barnabas (you received a letter regarding him; if he shows up, welcome him); and also Jesus, the one they call Justus. These are the only ones left from the old crowd who have stuck with me in working for God's kingdom. Don't think they haven't been a big help!

12-13 Epaphras, who is one of you, says hello. What a trooper he has been! He's been tireless in his prayers for you, praying that you'll stand firm, mature and confident in everything God wants you to do. I've watched him closely, and can report on how hard he has worked for you and for those in Laodicea and Hierapolis.

14 Luke, good friend and physician, and Demas both send greetings.

15 Say hello to our friends in Laodicea; also to Nympha and the church that meets in her house.

16 After this letter has been read to you, make sure it gets read also in Laodicea. And get the letter that went to Laodicea and have it read to you.

17 And, oh, yes, tell Archippus, "Do your best in the job you received from the Master. Do your very best."

18 I'm signing off in my own handwriting—Paul. Remember to pray for me in this jail. Grace be with you.

1 & 2 THESSALONIANS

The way we conceive the future sculpts the present, gives contour and tone to nearly every action and thought through the day. If our sense of future is weak, we live listlessly. Much emotional and mental illness and most suicides occur among men and women who feel that they "have no future."

The Christian faith has always been characterized by a strong and focused sense of future, with belief in the Second Coming of Jesus as the most distinctive detail. From the day Jesus ascended into heaven, his followers lived in expectancy of his return. He told them he was coming back. They believed he was coming back. They continue to believe it. For Christians, it is the most important thing to know and believe about the future.

The practical effect of this belief is to charge each moment of the present with hope. For if the future is dominated by the coming again of Jesus, there is little room left on the screen for projecting our anxieties and fantasies. It takes the clutter out of our lives. We're far more free to respond spontaneously to the freedom of God.

All the same, the belief can be misconceived so that it results in paralyzing fear for some, shiftless indolence in others. Paul's two letters to the Christians in Thessalonica, among much else, correct such debilitating misconceptions, prodding us to continue to live forward in taut and joyful expectancy for what God will do next in Jesus.

1 THESSALONIANS

1 I, Paul, together here with Silas and Timothy, send greetings to the church at Thessalonica, Christians assembled by God the Father and by the Master, Jesus Christ. God's amazing grace be with you! God's robust peace!

CONVICTIONS OF STEEL

2-5   Every time we think of you, we thank God for you. Day and night you're in our prayers as we call to mind your work of faith, your labor of love, and your patience of hope in following our Master, Jesus Christ, before God our Father. It is clear to us, friends, that God not only loves you very much but also has put his hand on you for something special. When the Message we preached came to you, it wasn't just words. Something happened in you. The Holy Spirit put steel in your convictions.

5-6   You paid careful attention to the way we lived among you, and determined to live that way yourselves. In imitating us, you imitated the Master. Although great trouble accompanied the Word, you were able to take great joy from the Holy Spirit! — taking the trouble with the joy, the joy with the trouble.

7-10   Do you know that all over the provinces of both Macedonia and Achaia believers look up to you? The word has gotten around. Your lives are echoing the Master's Word, not only in the provinces but all over the place. The news of your faith in God is out. We don't even have to say anything anymore — *you're* the message! People come up and tell us how you received us with open arms, how you deserted the dead idols of your old life so you could embrace and serve God, the true God. They marvel at how expectantly you await the arrival of his Son, whom he raised from the dead — Jesus, who rescued us from certain doom.

2 So, friends, it's obvious that our visit to you was no waste of time. We had just been given rough treatment in Philippi, as you know, but that didn't slow us down. We were sure of ourselves in God, and went right ahead and said our piece, presenting God's Message to you, defiant of the opposition.

NO HIDDEN AGENDAS

3-5   God tested us thoroughly to make sure we were qualified to be trusted with this Message. Be assured that when we speak to you we're not after crowd approval — only God approval. Since we've been put through that battery of tests, you're guaranteed that both we and the Message are free of error, mixed motives, or hidden agendas. We never used words to butter you up. No one knows that better than you. And God knows we never used words as a smoke screen to take advantage of you.

6-8   Even though we had some standing as Christ's apostles, we never threw our weight around or tried to come across as important, with you or anyone else. We weren't aloof with you. We took you just as you were. We were never patronizing, never condescending, but we cared for you the way a mother cares for her children. We loved you dearly. Not content to just pass on the Message, we wanted to give you our hearts. And we *did*.

9-12 You remember us in those days, friends, working our fingers to the bone, up half the night, moonlighting so you wouldn't have the burden of supporting us while we proclaimed God's Message to you. You saw with your own eyes how discreet and courteous we were among you, with keen sensitivity to you as fellow believers. And God knows we weren't free-loaders! You experienced it all firsthand. With each of you we were like a father with his child, holding your hand, whispering encouragement, showing you step-by-step how to live well before God, who called us into his own kingdom, into this delightful life.

13 And now we look back on all this and thank God, an artesian well of thanks! When you got the Message of God we preached, you didn't pass it off as just one more human opinion, but you took it to heart as God's true word to you, which it is, God himself at work in you believers!

14-16 Friends, do you realize that you followed in the exact footsteps of the churches of God in Judea, those who were the first to follow in the footsteps of Jesus Christ? You got the same bad treatment from your countrymen as they did from theirs, the Jews who killed the Master Jesus (to say nothing of the prophets) and followed it up by running us out of town. They make themselves offensive to God and everyone else by trying to keep us from telling people who've never heard of our God how to be saved. They've made a career of opposing God, and have gotten mighty good at it. But God is fed up, ready to put an end to it.

17-20 Do you have any idea how very homesick we became for you, dear friends? Even though it hadn't been that long and it was only our bodies that were separated from you, not our hearts, we tried our very best to get back to see you. You can't imagine how much we missed you! I, Paul, tried over and over to get back, but Satan stymied us each time. Who do you think we're going to be proud of when our Master Jesus appears if it's not you? You're our pride and joy!

1-2 **3** So when we couldn't stand being separated from you any longer and could find no way to visit you ourselves, we stayed in Athens and sent Timothy to get you up and about, cheering you on so you wouldn't be discouraged by these hard times. He's a brother and companion in the faith, God's man in spreading the Message, preaching Christ.

3-5 Not that the troubles should come as any surprise to you. You've always known that we're in for this kind of thing. It's part of our calling. When we were with you, we made it quite clear that there was trouble ahead. And now that it's happened, you know what it's like. That's why I couldn't quit worrying; I had to know for myself how you were doing in the faith. I didn't want the Tempter getting to you and tearing down everything we had built up together.

6-8 But now that Timothy is back, bringing this terrific report on your faith and love, we feel a lot better. It's especially gratifying to know that you continue to think well of us, and that you want to see us as much as we want to see you! In the middle of our trouble and hard times here, just knowing how you're doing keeps us going. Knowing that your faith is alive keeps us alive.

9-10 What would be an adequate thanksgiving to offer God for all the joy we experience before him because of you? We do what we can, praying away, night and day, asking for the bonus of seeing your faces again and doing what we can to help when your faith falters.

11-13   May God our Father himself and our Master Jesus clear the road to you! And may the Master pour on the love so it fills your lives and splashes over on everyone around you, just as it does from us to you. May you be infused with strength and purity, filled with confidence in the presence of God our Father when our Master Jesus arrives with all his followers.

You're God-Taught

1-3   One final word, friends. We ask you — *urge* is more like it — that you keep on doing what we told you to do to please God, not in a dogged religious plod, but in a living, spirited dance. You know the guidelines we laid out for you from the Master Jesus. God wants you to live a pure life.

Keep yourselves from sexual promiscuity.

4-5   Learn to appreciate and give dignity to your body, not abusing it, as is so common among those who know nothing of God.

6-7   Don't run roughshod over the concerns of your brothers and sisters. Their concerns are God's concerns, and *he* will take care of them. We've warned you about this before. God hasn't invited us into a disorderly, unkempt life but into something holy and beautiful — as beautiful on the inside as the outside.

8   If you disregard this advice, you're not offending your neighbors; you're rejecting God, who is making you a gift of his Holy Spirit.

9-10   Regarding life together and getting along with each other, you don't need me to tell you what to do. You're *God*-taught in these matters. Just love one another! You're already good at it; your friends all over the province of Macedonia are the evidence. Keep it up; get better and better at it.

11-12   Stay calm; mind your own business; do your own job. You've heard all this from us before, but a reminder never hurts. We want you living in a way that will command the respect of outsiders, not lying around sponging off your friends.

The Master's Coming

13-14   And regarding the question, friends, that has come up about what happens to those already dead and buried, we don't want you in the dark any longer. First off, you must not carry on over them like people who have nothing to look forward to, as if the grave were the last word. Since Jesus died and broke loose from the grave, God will most certainly bring back to life those who died in Jesus.

15-18   And then this: We can tell you with complete confidence — we have the Master's word on it — that when the Master comes again to get us, those of us who are still alive will not get a jump on the dead and leave them behind. In actual fact, they'll be ahead of us. The Master himself will give the command. Archangel thunder! God's trumpet blast! He'll come down from heaven and the dead in Christ will rise — they'll go first. Then the rest of us who are still alive at the time will be caught up with them into the clouds to meet the Master. Oh, we'll be walking on air! And then there will be one huge family reunion with the Master. So reassure one another with these words.

5 ¹⁻³ I don't think, friends, that I need to deal with the question of when all this is going to happen. You know as well as I that the day of the Master's coming can't be posted on our calendars. He won't call ahead and make an appointment any more than a burglar would. About the time everybody's walking around complacently, congratulating each other — "We've sure got it made! Now we can take it easy!" — suddenly everything will fall apart. It's going to come as suddenly and inescapably as birth pangs to a pregnant woman.

⁴⁻⁸ But friends, you're not in the dark, so how could you be taken off guard by any of this? You're sons of Light, daughters of Day. We live under wide open skies and know where we stand. So let's not sleepwalk through life like those others. Let's keep our eyes open and be smart. People sleep at night and get drunk at night. But not us! Since we're creatures of Day, let's act like it. Walk out into the daylight sober, dressed up in faith, love, and the hope of salvation.

⁹⁻¹¹ God didn't set us up for an angry rejection but for salvation by our Master, Jesus Christ. He died for us, a death that triggered life. Whether we're awake with the living or asleep with the dead, we're *alive* with him! So speak encouraging words to one another. Build up hope so you'll all be together in this, no one left out, no one left behind. I know you're already doing this; just keep on doing it.

The Way He Wants You to Live

¹²⁻¹³ And now, friends, we ask you to honor those leaders who work so hard for you, who have been given the responsibility of urging and guiding you along in your obedience. Overwhelm them with appreciation and love!

¹³⁻¹⁵ Get along among yourselves, each of you doing your part. Our counsel is that you warn the freeloaders to get a move on. Gently encourage the stragglers, and reach out for the exhausted, pulling them to their feet. Be patient with each person, attentive to individual needs. And be careful that when you get on each other's nerves you don't snap at each other. Look for the best in each other, and always do your best to bring it out.

¹⁶⁻¹⁸ Be cheerful no matter what; pray all the time; thank God no matter what happens. This is the way God wants you who belong to Christ Jesus to live.

¹⁹⁻²² Don't suppress the Spirit, and don't stifle those who have a word from the Master. On the other hand, don't be gullible. Check out everything, and keep only what's good. Throw out anything tainted with evil.

²³⁻²⁴ May God himself, the God who makes everything holy and whole, make you holy and whole, put you together — spirit, soul, and body — and keep you fit for the coming of our Master, Jesus Christ. The One who called you is completely dependable. If he said it, he'll do it!

²⁵⁻²⁷ Friends, keep up your prayers for us. Greet all the followers of Jesus there with a holy embrace. And make sure this letter gets read to all the brothers and sisters. Don't leave anyone out.

²⁸ The amazing grace of Jesus Christ be with you!

2 THESSALONIANS

1 1-2 I, Paul, together with Silas and Timothy, greet the church of the Thessalonian Christians in the name of God our Father and our Master, Jesus Christ. Our God gives you everything you need, makes you everything you're to be.

JUSTICE IS ON THE WAY

3-4 You need to know, friends, that thanking God over and over for you is not only a pleasure; it's a must. We *have* to do it. Your faith is growing phenomenally; your love for each other is developing wonderfully. Why, it's only right that we give thanks. We're so proud of you; you're so steady and determined in your faith despite all the hard times that have come down on you. We tell everyone we meet in the churches all about you.

5-10 All this trouble is a clear sign that God has decided to make you fit for the kingdom. You're suffering now, but justice is on the way. When the Master Jesus appears out of heaven in a blaze of fire with his strong angels, he'll even up the score by settling accounts with those who gave you such a bad time. His coming will be the break we've been waiting for. Those who refuse to know God and refuse to obey the Message will pay for what they've done. Eternal exile from the presence of the Master and his splendid power is their sentence. But on that very same day when he comes, he will be exalted by his followers and celebrated by all who believe — and all because you believed what we told you.

11-12 Because we know that this extraordinary day is just ahead, we pray for you all the time — pray that our God will make you fit for what he's called you to be, pray that he'll fill your good ideas and acts of faith with his own energy so that it all amounts to something. If your life honors the name of Jesus, he will honor you. Grace is behind and through all of this, our God giving himself freely, the Master, Jesus Christ, giving himself freely.

THE ANARCHIST

2 1-3 Now, friends, read these next words carefully. Slow down and don't go jumping to conclusions regarding the day when our Master, Jesus Christ, will come back and we assemble to welcome him. Don't let anyone shake you up or get you excited over some breathless report or rumored letter from me that the day of the Master's arrival has come and gone. Don't fall for any line like that.

3-5 Before that day comes, a couple of things have to happen. First, the Apostasy. Second, the debut of the Anarchist, a real dog of Satan. He'll defy and then take over every so-called god or altar. Having cleared away the opposition, he'll then set himself up in God's Temple as "God Almighty." Don't you remember me going over all this in detail when I was with you? Are your memories that short?

6-8 You'll also remember that I told you the Anarchist is being held back until just the right time. That doesn't mean that the spirit of anarchy is not now at work. It is, secretly and underground. But the time will come when the Anarchist will no longer be held back, but will be let loose. But don't worry. The Master Jesus will be right on his heels and blow him away. The Master appears and — puff! — the Anarchist is out of there.

9-12   The Anarchist's coming is all Satan's work. All his power and signs and miracles are fake, evil sleight of hand that plays to the gallery of those who hate the truth that could save them. And since they're so obsessed with evil, God rubs their noses in it — gives them what they want. Since they refuse to trust truth, they're banished to their chosen world of lies and illusions.

13-14   Meanwhile, we've got our hands full continually thanking God for you, our good friends — so loved by God! God picked you out as his from the very start. Think of it: included in God's original plan of salvation by the bond of faith in the living truth. This is the life of the Spirit he invited you to through the Message we delivered, in which you get in on the glory of our Master, Jesus Christ.

15-17   So, friends, take a firm stand, feet on the ground and head high. Keep a tight grip on what you were taught, whether in personal conversation or by our letter. May Jesus himself and God our Father, who reached out in love and surprised you with gifts of unending help and confidence, put a fresh heart in you, invigorate your work, enliven your speech.

THOSE WHO ARE LAZY

1-3   **3** One more thing, friends: Pray for us. Pray that the Master's Word will simply take off and race through the country to a groundswell of response, just as it did among you. And pray that we'll be rescued from these scoundrels who are trying to do us in. I'm finding that not all "believers" are believers. But the Master never lets us down. He'll stick by you and protect you from evil.

4-5   Because of the *Master*, we have great confidence in *you*. We know you're doing everything we told you and will continue doing it. May the Master take you by the hand and lead you along the path of God's love and Christ's endurance.

6-9   Our orders — backed up by the Master, Jesus — are to refuse to have anything to do with those among you who are lazy and refuse to work the way we taught you. Don't permit them to freeload on the rest. We showed you how to pull your weight when we were with you, so get on with it. We didn't sit around on our hands expecting others to take care of us. In fact, we worked our fingers to the bone, up half the night moonlighting so you wouldn't be burdened with taking care of us. And it wasn't because we didn't have a right to your support; we did. We simply wanted to provide an example of diligence, hoping it would prove contagious.

10-13   Don't you remember the rule we had when we lived with you? "If you don't work, you don't eat." And now we're getting reports that a bunch of lazy good-for-nothings are taking advantage of you. This must not be tolerated. We command them to get to work immediately — no excuses, no arguments — and earn their own keep. Friends, don't slack off in doing your duty.

14-15   If anyone refuses to obey our clear command written in this letter, don't let him get by with it. Point out such a person and refuse to subsidize his freeloading. Maybe then he'll think twice. But don't treat him as an enemy. Sit him down and talk about the problem as someone who cares.

16   May the Master of Peace himself give you the gift of getting along with each other at all times, in all ways. May the Master be truly among you!

17   I, Paul, bid you good-bye in my own handwriting. I do this in all my letters, so examine my signature as proof that the letter is genuine.

18   The incredible grace of our Master, Jesus Christ, be with all of you!

1 & 2 TIMOTHY & TITUS

Christians are quite serious in believing that when they gather together for worship and work, God is present and sovereign, really present and absolutely sovereign. God creates and guides, God saves and heals, God corrects and blesses, God calls and judges. With such comprehensive and personal leadership from God, what is the place of *human* leadership?

Quite obviously, it has to be second place. It must not elbow its way to the front, it must not bossily take over. Ego-centered, ego-prominent leadership betrays the Master. The best leadership in spiritual communities formed in the name of Jesus, the Messiah, is inconspicuous, not calling attention to itself but not sacrificing anything in the way of conviction and firmness either.

In his letters to two young associates — Timothy in Ephesus and Titus in Crete — we see Paul encouraging and guiding the development of just such leadership. What he had learned so thoroughly himself, he was now passing on, and showing them, in turn, how to develop a similar leadership in local congregations. This is essential reading because ill-directed and badly formed spiritual leadership causes much damage in souls. Paul in both his life and his letters shows us how to do it right.

1 TIMOTHY

¹⁻² **1** I, Paul, am an apostle on special assignment for Christ, our living hope. Under God our Savior's command, I'm writing this to you, Timothy, my son in the faith. All the best from our God and Christ be yours!

SELF-APPOINTED EXPERTS ON LIFE

³⁻⁴ On my way to the province of Macedonia, I advised you to stay in Ephesus. Well, I haven't changed my mind. Stay right there on top of things so that the teaching stays on track. Apparently some people have been introducing fantasy stories and fanciful family trees that digress into silliness instead of pulling the people back into the center, deepening faith and obedience.

⁵⁻⁷ The whole point of what we're urging is simply *love*—love uncontaminated by self-interest and counterfeit faith, a life open to God. Those who fail to keep to this point soon wander off into cul-de-sacs of gossip. They set themselves up as experts on religious issues, but haven't the remotest idea of what they're holding forth with such imposing eloquence.

⁸⁻¹¹ It's true that moral guidance and counsel need to be given, but the way you say it and to whom you say it are as important as what you say. It's obvious, isn't it, that the law code isn't primarily for people who live responsibly, but for the irresponsible, who defy all authority, riding roughshod over God, life, sex, truth, whatever! They are contemptuous of this great Message I've been put in charge of by this great God.

¹²⁻¹⁴ I'm so grateful to Christ Jesus for making me adequate to do this work. He went out on a limb, you know, in trusting me with this ministry. The only credentials I brought to it were invective and witch hunts and arrogance. But I was treated mercifully because I didn't know what I was doing—didn't know Who I was doing it against! Grace mixed with faith and love poured over me and into me. And all because of Jesus.

¹⁵⁻¹⁹ Here's a word you can take to heart and depend on: Jesus Christ came into the world to save sinners. I'm proof—Public Sinner Number One—of someone who could never have made it apart from sheer mercy. And now he shows me off—evidence of his endless patience—to those who are right on the edge of trusting him forever.

> Deep honor and bright glory
>   to the King of All Time—
> One God, Immortal, Invisible,
>   ever and always. Oh, yes!

I'm passing this work on to you, my son Timothy. The prophetic word that was directed to you prepared us for this. All those prayers are coming together now so you will do this well, fearless in your struggle, keeping a firm grip on your faith and on yourself. After all, this is a fight we're in.

¹⁹⁻²⁰ There are some, you know, who by relaxing their grip and thinking anything goes have made a thorough mess of their faith. Hymenaeus and

Alexander are two of them. I let them wander off to Satan to be taught a lesson or two about not blaspheming.

SIMPLE FAITH AND PLAIN TRUTH

1-3
2 The first thing I want you to do is pray. Pray every way you know how, for everyone you know. Pray especially for rulers and their governments to rule well so we can be quietly about our business of living simply, in humble contemplation. This is the way our Savior God wants us to live.

4-7
He wants not only us but *everyone* saved, you know, everyone to get to know the truth *we've* learned: that there's one God and only one, and one Priest-Mediator between God and us—Jesus, who offered himself in exchange for everyone held captive by sin, to set them all free. Eventually the news is going to get out. This and this only has been my appointed work: getting this news to those who have never heard of God, and explaining how it works by simple faith and plain truth.

8-10
Since prayer is at the bottom of all this, what I want mostly is for men to pray—not shaking angry fists at enemies but raising holy hands to God. And I want women to get in there with the men in humility before God, not primping before a mirror or chasing the latest fashions but doing something beautiful for God and becoming beautiful doing it.

11-15
I don't let women take over and tell the men what to do. They should study to be quiet and obedient along with everyone else. Adam was made first, then Eve; woman was deceived first—our pioneer in sin!—with Adam right on her heels. On the other hand, her childbearing brought about salvation, reversing Eve. But this salvation only comes to those who continue in faith, love, and holiness, gathering it all into maturity. You can depend on this.

LEADERSHIP IN THE CHURCH

1-7
3 If anyone wants to provide leadership in the church, good! But there are preconditions: A leader must be well-thought-of, committed to his wife, cool and collected, accessible, and hospitable. He must know what he's talking about, not be overfond of wine, not pushy but gentle, not thin-skinned, not money-hungry. He must handle his own affairs well, attentive to his own children and having their respect. For if someone is unable to handle his own affairs, how can he take care of God's church? He must not be a new believer, lest the position go to his head and the Devil trip him up. Outsiders must think well of him, or else the Devil will figure out a way to lure him into his trap.

8-13
The same goes for those who want to be servants in the church: serious, not deceitful, not too free with the bottle, not in it for what they can get out of it. They must be reverent before the mystery of the faith, not using their position to try to run things. Let them prove themselves first. If they show they can do it, take them on. No exceptions are to be made for women—same qualifications: serious, dependable, not sharp-tongued, not overfond of wine. Servants in the church are to be committed to their spouses, attentive to their own children, and diligent in looking after their own affairs. Those who do this servant work will come to be highly respected, a real credit to this Jesus-faith.

14-16
I hope to visit you soon, but just in case I'm delayed, I'm writing this

letter so you'll know how things ought to go in God's household, this God-alive church, bastion of truth. This Christian life is a great mystery, far exceeding our understanding, but some things are clear enough:

> He appeared in a human body,
> > was proved right by the invisible Spirit,
> > > was seen by angels.
> He was proclaimed among all kinds of peoples,
> > believed in all over the world,
> > > taken up into heavenly glory.

TEACH WITH YOUR LIFE

1-5   4 The Spirit makes it clear that as time goes on, some are going to give up on the faith and chase after demonic illusions put forth by professional liars. These liars have lied so well and for so long that they've lost their capacity for truth. They will tell you not to get married. They'll tell you not to eat this or that food—perfectly good food God created to be eaten heartily and with thanksgiving by believers who know better! Everything God created is good, and to be received with thanks. Nothing is to be sneered at and thrown out. God's Word and our prayers make every item in creation holy.

6-10   You've been raised on the Message of the faith and have followed sound teaching. Now pass on this counsel to the followers of Jesus there, and you'll be a good servant of Jesus. Stay clear of silly stories that get dressed up as religion. Exercise daily in God—no spiritual flabbiness, please! Workouts in the gymnasium are useful, but a disciplined life in God is far more so, making you fit both today and forever. You can count on this. Take it to heart. This is why we've thrown ourselves into this venture so totally. We're banking on the living God, Savior of all men and women, especially believers.

11-14   Get the word out. Teach all these things. And don't let anyone put you down because you're young. Teach believers with your life: by word, by demeanor, by love, by faith, by integrity. Stay at your post reading Scripture, giving counsel, teaching. And that special gift of ministry you were given when the leaders of the church laid hands on you and prayed—keep that dusted off and in use.

15-16   Cultivate these things. Immerse yourself in them. The people will all see you mature right before their eyes! Keep a firm grasp on both your character and your teaching. Don't be diverted. Just keep at it. Both you and those who hear you will experience salvation.

THE FAMILY OF FAITH

1-2   5 Don't be harsh or impatient with an older man. Talk to him as you would your own father, and to the younger men as your brothers. Reverently honor an older woman as you would your mother, and the younger women as sisters.

3-8   Take care of widows who are destitute. If a widow has family members to take care of her, let them learn that religion begins at their own doorstep and that they should pay back with gratitude some of what they have received. This pleases God immensely. You can tell a legitimate widow by the way she has put all her hope in God, praying to him constantly for the needs of others as well as her own. But a widow who exploits people's emotions and pocketbooks — well, there's nothing to her. Tell these things to the people so that they will do the right thing in their extended family. Anyone who neglects to care for family members in need repudiates the faith. That's worse than refusing to believe in the first place.

9-10 Sign some widows up for the special ministry of offering assistance. They will in turn receive support from the church. They must be over sixty, married only once, and have a reputation for helping out with children, strangers, tired Christians, the hurt and troubled.

11-15 Don't put young widows on this list. No sooner will they get on than they'll want to get off, obsessed with wanting to get a husband rather than serving Christ in this way. By breaking their word, they're liable to go from bad to worse, frittering away their days on empty talk, gossip, and triviali-ties. No, I'd rather the young widows go ahead and get married in the first place, have children, manage their homes, and not give critics any foothold for finding fault. Some of them have already left and gone after Satan.

16 Any Christian woman who has widows in her family is responsible for them. They shouldn't be dumped on the church. The church has its hands full already with widows who need help.

17-18 Give a bonus to leaders who do a good job, especially the ones who work hard at preaching and teaching. Scripture tells us, "Don't muzzle a working ox" and "A worker deserves his pay."

19 Don't listen to a complaint against a leader that isn't backed up by two or three responsible witnesses.

20 If anyone falls into sin, call that person on the carpet. Those who are inclined that way will know right off they can't get by with it.

21-23 God and Jesus and angels all back me up in these instructions. Carry them out without favoritism, without taking sides. Don't appoint people to church leadership positions too hastily. If a person is involved in some seri-ous sins, you don't want to become an unwitting accomplice. In any event, keep a close check on yourself. And don't worry too much about what the critics will say. Go ahead and drink a little wine, for instance; it's good for your digestion, good medicine for what ails you.

24-25 The sins of some people are blatant and march them right into court. The sins of others don't show up until much later. The same with good deeds. Some you see right off, but none are hidden forever.

1-2 Whoever is a slave must make the best of it, giving respect to his master so that outsiders don't blame God and our teaching for his behavior. Slaves with Christian masters all the more so — their masters are really their beloved brothers!

THE LUST FOR MONEY

2-5 These are the things I want you to teach and preach. If you have leaders there who teach otherwise, who refuse the solid words of our Master Jesus and this godly instruction, tag them for what they are: ignorant windbags who infect the air with germs of envy, controversy, bad-mouthing, suspi-cious rumors. Eventually there's an epidemic of backstabbing, and truth is but a distant memory. They think religion is a way to make a fast buck.

6-8   A devout life does bring wealth, but it's the rich simplicity of being yourself before God. Since we entered the world penniless and will leave it penniless, if we have bread on the table and shoes on our feet, that's enough.

9-10   But if it's only money these leaders are after, they'll self-destruct in no time. Lust for money brings trouble and nothing but trouble. Going down that path, some lose their footing in the faith completely and live to regret it bitterly ever after.

RUNNING HARD

11-12   But you, Timothy, man of God: Run for your life from all this. Pursue a righteous life — a life of wonder, faith, love, steadiness, courtesy. Run hard and fast in the faith. Seize the eternal life, the life you were called to, the life you so fervently embraced in the presence of so many witnesses.

13-16   I'm charging you before the life-giving God and before Christ, who took his stand before Pontius Pilate and didn't give an inch: Keep this command to the letter, and don't slack off. Our Master, Jesus Christ, is on his way. He'll show up right on time, his arrival guaranteed by the Blessed and Undisputed Ruler, High King, High God. He's the only one death can't touch, his light so bright no one can get close. He's never been seen by human eyes — human eyes can't take him in! Honor to him, and eternal rule! Oh, yes.

17-19   Tell those rich in this world's wealth to quit being so full of themselves and so obsessed with money, which is here today and gone tomorrow. Tell them to go after God, who piles on all the riches we could ever manage — to do good, to be rich in helping others, to be extravagantly generous. If they do that, they'll build a treasury that will last, gaining life that is truly life.

20-21   And oh, my dear Timothy, guard the treasure you were given! Guard it with your life. Avoid the talk-show religion and the practiced confusion of the so-called experts. People caught up in a lot of talk can miss the whole point of faith.

    Overwhelming grace keep you!

2 TIMOTHY

1-2 1 I, Paul, am on special assignment for Christ, carrying out God's plan laid out in the Message of Life by Jesus. I write this to you, Timothy, the son I love so much. All the best from our God and Christ be yours!

To Be Bold with God's Gifts

3-4 Every time I say your name in prayer—which is practically all the time—I thank God for you, the God I worship with my whole life in the tradition of my ancestors. I miss you a lot, especially when I remember that last tearful good-bye, and I look forward to a joy-packed reunion.

5-7 That precious memory triggers another: your honest faith—and what a rich faith it is, handed down from your grandmother Lois to your mother Eunice, and now to you! And the special gift of ministry you received when I laid hands on you and prayed—keep that ablaze! God doesn't want us to be shy with his gifts, but bold and loving and sensible.

8-10 So don't be embarrassed to speak up for our Master or for me, his prisoner. Take your share of suffering for the Message along with the rest of us. We can only keep on going, after all, by the power of God, who first saved us and then called us to this holy work. We had nothing to do with it. It was all *his* idea, a gift prepared for us in Jesus long before we knew anything about it. But we know it now. Since the appearance of our Savior, nothing could be plainer: death defeated, life vindicated in a steady blaze of light, all through the work of Jesus.

11-12 This is the Message I've been set apart to proclaim as preacher, emissary, and teacher. It's also the cause of all this trouble I'm in. But I have no regrets. I couldn't be more sure of my ground—the One I've trusted in can take care of what he's trusted me to do right to the end.

13-14 So keep at your work, this faith and love rooted in Christ, exactly as I set it out for you. It's as sound as the day you first heard it from me. Guard this precious thing placed in your custody by the Holy Spirit who works in us.

15-18 I'm sure you know by now that everyone in the province of Asia deserted me, even Phygelus and Hermogenes. But God bless Onesiphorus and his family! Many's the time I've been refreshed in that house. And he wasn't embarrassed a bit that I was in jail. The first thing he did when he got to Rome was look me up. May God on the Last Day treat him as well as he treated me. And then there was all the help he provided in Ephesus—but you know that better than I.

Doing Your Best for God

1-7 2 So, my son, throw yourself into this work for Christ. Pass on what you heard from me—the whole congregation saying Amen!— to reliable leaders who are competent to teach others. When the going gets rough, take it on the chin with the rest of us, the way Jesus did. A soldier on duty doesn't get caught up in making deals at the marketplace. He concentrates on carrying out orders. An athlete who refuses to play by the rules will never get anywhere. It's the diligent farmer who gets the produce. Think it over. God will make it all plain.

8-13 Fix this picture firmly in your mind: Jesus, descended from the line of David, raised from the dead. It's what you've heard from me all along. It's why I'm sitting in jail for right now — but God's Word isn't in jail! That's why I stick it out here — so that everyone God calls will get in on the salvation of Christ in all its glory. This is a sure thing:

> If we die with him, we'll live with him;
> If we stick it out with him, we'll rule with him;
> If we turn our backs on him, he'll turn his back on us;
> If we give up on him, he does not give up —
>   for there's no way he can be false to himself.

14-18 Repeat these basic essentials over and over to God's people. Warn them before God against pious nitpicking, which chips away at the faith. It just wears everyone out. Concentrate on doing your best for God, work you won't be ashamed of, laying out the truth plain and simple. Stay clear of pious talk that is only talk. Words are not mere words, you know. If they're not backed by a godly life, they accumulate as poison in the soul. Hymenaeus and Philetus are examples, throwing believers off stride and missing the truth by a mile by saying the resurrection is over and done with.

19 Meanwhile, God's firm foundation is as firm as ever, these sentences engraved on the stones:

GOD KNOWS WHO BELONGS TO HIM.

SPURN EVIL, ALL YOU WHO NAME GOD AS GOD.

20-21 In a well-furnished kitchen there are not only crystal goblets and silver platters, but waste cans and compost buckets — some containers used to serve fine meals, others to take out the garbage. Become the kind of container God can use to present any and every kind of gift to his guests for their blessing.

22-26 Run away from infantile indulgence. Run after mature righteousness — faith, love, peace — joining those who are in honest and serious prayer before God. Refuse to get involved in inane discussions; they always end up in fights. God's servant must not be argumentative, but a gentle listener and a teacher who keeps cool, working firmly but patiently with those who refuse to obey. You never know how or when God might sober them up with a change of heart and a turning to the truth, enabling them to escape the Devil's trap, where they are caught and held captive, forced to run his errands.

DIFFICULT TIMES AHEAD

1-5 3 Don't be naive. There are difficult times ahead. As the end approaches, people are going to be self-absorbed, money-hungry, self-promoting, stuck-up, profane, contemptuous of parents, crude, coarse, dog-eat-dog, unbending, slanderers, impulsively wild, savage, cynical, treacherous, ruthless, bloated windbags, addicted to lust, and allergic to God. They'll make a show of religion, but behind the scenes they're animals. Stay clear of these people.

6-9 These are the kind of people who smooth-talk themselves into the homes of unstable and needy women and take advantage of them; women who, depressed by their sinfulness, take up with every new religious fad that calls itself "truth." They get exploited every time and never really learn. These men are like those old Egyptian frauds Jannes and Jambres, who challenged Moses. They were rejects from the faith, twisted in their thinking, defying truth itself. But nothing will come of these latest impostors. Everyone will see through them, just as people saw through that Egyptian hoax.

KEEP THE MESSAGE ALIVE

10-13 You've been a good apprentice to me, a part of my teaching, my manner of life, direction, faith, steadiness, love, patience, troubles, sufferings — suffering along with me in all the grief I had to put up with in Antioch, Iconium, and Lystra. And you also well know that God rescued me! Anyone who wants to live all out for Christ is in for a lot of trouble; there's no getting around it. Unscrupulous con men will continue to exploit the faith. They're as deceived as the people they lead astray. As long as they are out there, things can only get worse.

14-17 But don't let it faze you. Stick with what you learned and believed, sure of the integrity of your teachers — why, you took in the sacred Scriptures with your mother's milk! There's nothing like the written Word of God for showing you the way to salvation through faith in Christ Jesus. Every part of Scripture is God-breathed and useful one way or another — showing us truth, exposing our rebellion, correcting our mistakes, training us to live God's way. Through the Word we are put together and shaped up for the tasks God has for us.

1-2 4 I can't impress this on you too strongly. God is looking over your shoulder. Christ himself is the Judge, with the final say on everyone, living and dead. He is about to break into the open with his rule, so proclaim the Message with intensity; keep on your watch. Challenge, warn, and urge your people. Don't ever quit. Just keep it simple.

3-5 You're going to find that there will be times when people will have no stomach for solid teaching, but will fill up on spiritual junk food — catchy opinions that tickle their fancy. They'll turn their backs on truth and chase mirages. But *you* — keep your eye on what you're doing; accept the hard times along with the good; keep the Message alive; do a thorough job as God's servant.

6-8 You take over. I'm about to die, my life an offering on God's altar. This is the only race worth running. I've run hard right to the finish, believed all the way. All that's left now is the shouting — God's applause! Depend on it, he's an honest judge. He'll do right not only by me, but by everyone eager for his coming.

9-13 Get here as fast as you can. Demas, chasing fads, went off to Thessalonica and left me here. Crescens is in Galatia province, Titus in Dalmatia. Luke is the only one here with me. Bring Mark with you; he'll be my right-hand man since I'm sending Tychicus to Ephesus. Bring the winter coat I left in Troas with Carpus; also the books and parchment notebooks.

14-15 Watch out for Alexander the coppersmith. Fiercely opposed to our Message, he caused no end of trouble. God will give him what he's got coming.

16-18 At my preliminary hearing no one stood by me. They all ran like scared rabbits. But it doesn't matter—the Master stood by me and helped me spread the Message loud and clear to those who had never heard it. I was snatched from the jaws of the lion! God's looking after me, keeping me safe in the kingdom of heaven. All praise to him, praise forever! Oh, yes!

19-20 Say hello to Priscilla and Aquila; also, the family of Onesiphorus. Erastus stayed behind in Corinth. I had to leave Trophimus sick in Miletus.

21 Try hard to get here before winter.

Eubulus, Pudens, Linus, Claudia, and all your friends here send greetings.

22 God be with you. Grace be with you.

TITUS

1-4 1 I, Paul, am God's slave and Christ's agent for promoting the faith among God's chosen people, getting out the accurate word on God and how to respond rightly to it. My aim is to raise hopes by pointing the way to life without end. This is the life God promised long ago — and he doesn't break promises! And then when the time was ripe, he went public with his truth. I've been entrusted to proclaim this Message by order of our Savior, God himself. Dear Titus, legitimate son in the faith: Receive everything God our Father and Jesus our Savior give you!

A GOOD GRIP ON THE MESSAGE

5-9 I left you in charge in Crete so you could complete what I left half-done. Appoint leaders in every town according to my instructions. As you select them, ask, "Is this man well-thought-of? Is he committed to his wife? Are his children believers? Do they respect him and stay out of trouble?" It's important that a church leader, responsible for the affairs in God's house, be looked up to — not pushy, not short-tempered, not a drunk, not a bully, not money-hungry. He must welcome people, be helpful, wise, fair, reverent, have a good grip on himself, and have a good grip on the Message, knowing how to use the truth to either spur people on in knowledge or stop them in their tracks if they oppose it.

10-16 For there are a lot of rebels out there, full of loose, confusing, and deceiving talk. Those who were brought up religious and ought to know better are the worst. They've got to be shut up. They're disrupting entire families with their teaching, and all for the sake of a fast buck. One of their own prophets said it best:

> The Cretans are liars from the womb,
> barking dogs, lazy bellies.

He certainly spoke the truth. Get on them right away. Stop that diseased talk of Jewish make-believe and made-up rules so they can recover a robust faith. Everything is clean to the clean-minded; nothing is clean to dirty-minded unbelievers. They leave their dirty fingerprints on every thought and act. They say they know God, but their actions speak louder than their words. They're real creeps, disobedient good-for-nothings.

A GOD-FILLED LIFE

1-6 2 Your job is to speak out on the things that make for solid doctrine. Guide older men into lives of temperance, dignity, and wisdom, into healthy faith, love, and endurance. Guide older women into lives of reverence so they end up as neither gossips nor drunks, but models of goodness. By looking at them, the younger women will know how to love their husbands and children, be virtuous and pure, keep a good house, be good wives. We don't want anyone looking down on God's Message because of their behavior. Also, guide the young men to live disciplined lives.

7-8 But mostly, show them all this by doing it yourself, incorruptible in your teaching, your words solid and sane. Then anyone who is dead set against us, when he finds nothing weird or misguided, might eventually come around.

9-10   Guide slaves into being loyal workers, a bonus to their masters — no back talk, no petty thievery. Then their good character will shine through their actions, adding luster to the teaching of our Savior God.

11-14   God's readiness to give and forgive is now public. Salvation's available for everyone! We're being shown how to turn our backs on a godless, indulgent life, and how to take on a God-filled, God-honoring life. This new life is starting right now, and is whetting our appetites for the glorious day when our great God and Savior, Jesus Christ, appears. He offered himself as a sacrifice to free us from a dark, rebellious life into this good, pure life, making us a people he can be proud of, energetic in goodness.

15   Tell them all this. Build up their courage, and discipline them if they get out of line. You're in charge. Don't let anyone put you down.

HE PUT OUR LIVES TOGETHER

1-2   **3** Remind the people to respect the government and be law-abiding, always ready to lend a helping hand. No insults, no fights. God's people should be bighearted and courteous.

3-8   It wasn't so long ago that we ourselves were stupid and stubborn, dupes of sin, ordered every which way by our glands, going around with a chip on our shoulder, hated and hating back. But when God, our kind and loving Savior God, stepped in, he saved us from all that. It was all his doing; we had nothing to do with it. He gave us a good bath, and we came out of it new people, washed inside and out by the Holy Spirit. Our Savior Jesus poured out new life so generously. God's gift has restored our relationship with him and given us back our lives. And there's more life to come — an eternity of life! You can count on this.

8-11   I want you to put your foot down. Take a firm stand on these matters so that those who have put their trust in God will concentrate on the essentials that are good for everyone. Stay away from mindless, pointless quarreling over genealogies and fine print in the law code. That gets you nowhere. Warn a quarrelsome person once or twice, but then be done with him. It's obvious that such a person is out of line, rebellious against God. By persisting in divisiveness he cuts himself off.

12-13   As soon as I send either Artemas or Tychicus to you, come immediately and meet me in Nicopolis. I've decided to spend the winter there. Give Zenas the lawyer and Apollos a hearty send-off. Take good care of them.

14   Our people have to learn to be diligent in their work so that all necessities are met (especially among the needy) and they don't end up with nothing to show for their lives.

15   All here want to be remembered to you. Say hello to our friends in the faith. Grace to all of you.

PHILEMON

Every movement we make in response to God has a ripple effect, touching family, neighbors, friends, community. Belief in God alters our language. Love of God affects daily relationships. Hope in God enters into our work. Also their opposites — unbelief, indifference, and despair. None of these movements and responses, beliefs and prayers, gestures and searches, can be confined to the soul. They spill out and make history. If they don't, they are under suspicion of being fantasies at best, hypocrisies at worst.

Christians have always insisted on the historicity of Jesus — an actual birth, a datable death, a witnessed resurrection, locatable towns. There is a parallel historicity in the followers of Jesus. As they take in everything Jesus said and did — all of it a personal revelation of God in time and place — it all gets worked into local history, eventually into world history.

Philemon and Onesimus, the slave owner and slave who figure prominently in this letter from Paul, had no idea that believing in Jesus would involve them in radical social change. But as the two of them were brought together by this letter, it did. And it still does.

PHILEMON

1-3 I, Paul, am a prisoner for the sake of Christ, here with my brother Timothy. I write this letter to you, Philemon, my good friend and companion in this work—also to our sister Apphia, to Archippus, a real trooper, and to the church that meets in your house. God's best to you! Christ's blessings on you!

4-7 Every time your name comes up in my prayers, I say, "Oh, thank you, God!" I keep hearing of the love and faith you have for the Master Jesus, which brims over to other believers. And I keep praying that this faith we hold in common keeps showing up in the good things we do, and that people recognize Christ in all of it. Friend, you have no idea how good your love makes me feel, doubly so when I see your hospitality to fellow believers.

To Call the Slave Your Friend

8-9 In line with all this I have a favor to ask of you. As Christ's ambassador and now a prisoner for him, I wouldn't hesitate to command this if I thought it necessary, but I'd rather make it a personal request.

10-14 While here in jail, I've fathered a child, so to speak. And here he is, hand-carrying this letter—Onesimus! He was useless to you before; now he's useful to both of us. I'm sending him back to you, but it feels like I'm cutting off my right arm in doing so. I wanted in the worst way to keep him here as your stand-in to help out while I'm in jail for the Message. But I didn't want to do anything behind your back, make you do a good deed that you hadn't willingly agreed to.

15-16 Maybe it's all for the best that you lost him for a while. You're getting him back now for good—and no mere slave this time, but a true Christian brother! That's what he was to me—he'll be even more than that to you.

17-20 So if you still consider me a comrade-in-arms, welcome him back as you would me. If he damaged anything or owes you anything, chalk it up to my account. This is my personal signature—Paul—and I stand behind it. (I don't need to remind you, do I, that you owe your very life to me?) Do me this big favor, friend. You'll be doing it for Christ, but it will also do my heart good.

21-22 I know you well enough to know you will. You'll probably go far beyond what I've written. And by the way, get a room ready for me. Because of your prayers, I fully expect to be your guest again.

23-25 Epaphras, my cellmate in the cause of Christ, says hello. Also my coworkers Mark, Aristarchus, Demas, and Luke. All the best to you from the Master, Jesus Christ!

HEBREWS

It seems odd to have to say so, but too much religion is a bad thing. We can't get too much of God, can't get too much faith and obedience, can't get too much love and worship. But *religion* — the well-intentioned efforts we make to "get it all together" for God — can very well get in the way of what God is doing for us. The main and central action is everywhere and always *what God has done, is doing, and will do for us.* Jesus is the revelation of that action. Our main and central task is to live in responsive obedience to God's action revealed in Jesus. Our part in the action is the act of faith.

But more often than not we become impatiently self-important along the way and decide to improve matters with our two cents' worth. We add on, we supplement, we embellish. But instead of improving on the purity and simplicity of Jesus, we dilute the purity, clutter the simplicity. We become fussily religious, or anxiously religious. We get in the way.

That's when it's time to read and pray our way through the letter to the Hebrews again, written for "too religious" Christians, for "Jesus-and" Christians. In the letter, it is Jesus-and-angels, or Jesus-and-Moses, or Jesus-and-priesthood. In our time it is more likely to be Jesus-and-politics, or Jesus-and-education, or even Jesus-and-Buddha. This letter deletes the hyphens, the add-ons. The focus becomes clear and sharp again: God's action in Jesus. And we are free once more for the act of faith, the one human action in which we don't get *in* the way but *on* the Way.

HEBREWS

1-3 Going through a long line of prophets, God has been addressing our ancestors in different ways for centuries. Recently he spoke to us directly through his Son. By his Son, God created the world in the beginning, and it will all belong to the Son at the end. This Son perfectly mirrors God, and is stamped with God's nature. He holds everything together by what he says — powerful words!

THE SON IS HIGHER THAN ANGELS

3-6 After he finished the sacrifice for sins, the Son took his honored place high in the heavens right alongside God, far higher than any angel in rank and rule. Did God ever say to an angel, "You're my Son; today I celebrate you" or "I'm his Father, he's my Son"? When he presents his honored Son to the world, he says, "All angels must worship him."

7 Regarding angels he says,

The messengers are winds,
the servants are tongues of fire.

8-9 But he says to the Son,
You're God, and on the throne for good;
your rule makes everything right.
You love it when things are right;
you hate it when things are wrong.
That is why God, your God,
poured fragrant oil on your head,
Marking you out as king,
far above your dear companions.

10-12 And again to the Son,
You, Master, started it all, laid earth's foundations,
then crafted the stars in the sky.
Earth and sky will wear out, but not you;
they become threadbare like an old coat;
You'll fold them up like a worn-out cloak,
and lay them away on the shelf.
But you'll stay the same, year after year;
you'll never fade, you'll never wear out.

13 And did he ever say anything like this to an angel?
Sit alongside me here on my throne
Until I make your enemies a stool for your feet.

14 Isn't it obvious that all angels are sent to help out with those lined up to receive salvation?

1-4 It's crucial that we keep a firm grip on what we've heard so that we don't drift off. If the old message delivered by the angels was valid and nobody got away with anything, do you think we can risk neglecting this latest message, this magnificent salvation? First of all, it was delivered in person by the Master, then accurately passed on to us by those who heard it from him. All the while God was validating it with gifts through the Holy Spirit, all sorts of signs and miracles, as he saw fit.

THE SALVATION PIONEER

5-9 God didn't put angels in charge of this business of salvation that we're dealing with here. It says in Scripture,

> What is man and woman that you bother with them;
>   why take a second look their way?
> You made them not quite as high as angels,
>   bright with Eden's dawn light;
> Then you put them in charge
>   of your entire handcrafted world.

When God put them in charge of everything, nothing was excluded. But we don't see it yet, don't see everything under human jurisdiction. What we do see is Jesus, made "not quite as high as angels," and then, through the experience of death, crowned so much higher than any angel, with a glory "bright with Eden's dawn light." In that death, by God's grace, he fully experienced death in every person's place.

10-13 It makes good sense that the God who got everything started and keeps everything going now completes the work by making the Salvation Pioneer perfect through suffering as he leads all these people to glory. Since the One who saves and those who are saved have a common origin, Jesus doesn't hesitate to treat them as family, saying,

> I'll tell my good friends, my brothers and sisters, all I know
>   about you;
> I'll join them in worship and praise to you.

Again, he puts himself in the same family circle when he says,
> Even *I* live by placing my trust in God.

And yet again,
> I'm here with the children God gave me.

14-15 Since the children are made of flesh and blood, it's logical that the Savior took on flesh and blood in order to rescue them by his death. By embracing death, taking it into himself, he destroyed the Devil's hold on death and freed all who cower through life, scared to death of death.

16-18 It's obvious, of course, that he didn't go to all this trouble for angels. It was for people like us, children of Abraham. That's why he had to enter into every detail of human life. Then, when he came before God as high priest to get rid of the people's sins, he would have already experienced it all himself — all the pain, all the testing — and would be able to help where help was needed.

THE CENTERPIECE OF ALL WE BELIEVE

1-6 **3** So, my dear Christian friends, companions in following this call to the heights, take a good hard look at Jesus. He's the centerpiece of everything we believe, faithful in everything God gave him to do. Moses was also faithful, but Jesus gets far more honor. A builder is more valuable than a building any day. Every house has a builder, but the Builder behind them all is God. Moses did a good job in God's house, but it was all servant work, getting things ready for what was to come. Christ as Son is in charge of the house.

6-11   Now, if we can only keep a firm grip on this bold confidence, we're the house! That's why the Holy Spirit says,

> Today, please listen;
>   don't turn a deaf ear as in "the bitter uprising,"
>   that time of wilderness testing!
> Even though they watched me at work for forty years,
>   your ancestors refused to let me do it my way;
>   over and over they tried my patience.
> And I was provoked, oh, so provoked!
>   I said, "They'll never keep their minds on God;
>   they refuse to walk down my road."
> Exasperated, I vowed,
>   "They'll never get where they're going,
>   never be able to sit down and rest."

12-14   So watch your step, friends. Make sure there's no evil unbelief lying around that will trip you up and throw you off course, diverting you from the living God. For as long as it's still God's Today, keep each other on your toes so sin doesn't slow down your reflexes. If we can only keep our grip on the sure thing we started out with, we're in this with Christ for the long haul.

Those words keep ringing in our ears:

> Today, please listen;
>   don't turn a deaf ear as in the bitter uprising.

15-19   For who were the people who turned a deaf ear? Weren't they the very ones Moses led out of Egypt? And who was God provoked with for forty years? Wasn't it those who turned a deaf ear and ended up corpses in the wilderness? And when he swore that they'd never get where they were going, wasn't he talking to the ones who turned a deaf ear? They never got there because they never listened, never believed.

WHEN THE PROMISES ARE MIXED WITH FAITH

1-3 **4** For as long, then, as that promise of resting in him pulls us on to God's goal for us, we need to be careful that we're not disqualified. We received the same promises as those people in the wilderness, but the promises didn't do them a bit of good because they didn't receive the promises with faith. If we believe, though, we'll experience that state of resting. But not if we don't have faith. Remember that God said,

Exasperated, I vowed,
    "They'll never get where they're going,
    never be able to sit down and rest."

3-7   God made that vow, even though he'd finished *his* part before the foundation of the world. Somewhere it's written, "God rested the seventh day, having completed his work," but in this other text he says, "They'll never be able to sit down and rest." So this promise has not yet been fulfilled. Those earlier ones never did get to the place of rest because they were disobedient. God keeps renewing the promise and setting the date as *today*, just as he did in David's psalm, centuries later than the original invitation:

Today, please listen,
    don't turn a deaf ear . . .

8-11   And so this is still a live promise. It wasn't canceled at the time of Joshua; otherwise, God wouldn't keep renewing the appointment for "today." The promise of "arrival" and "rest" is still there for God's people. God himself is at rest. And at the end of the journey we'll surely rest with God. So let's keep at it and eventually arrive at the place of rest, not drop out through some sort of disobedience.

12-13   God means what he says. What he says goes. His powerful Word is sharp as a surgeon's scalpel, cutting through everything, whether doubt or defense, laying us open to listen and obey. Nothing and no one is impervious to God's Word. We can't get away from it — no matter what.

THE HIGH PRIEST WHO CRIED OUT IN PAIN

14-16   Now that we know what we have — Jesus, this great High Priest with ready access to God — let's not let it slip through our fingers. We don't have a priest who is out of touch with our reality. He's been through weakness and testing, experienced it all — all but the sin. So let's walk right up to him and get what he is so ready to give. Take the mercy, accept the help.

1-3   **5** Every high priest selected to represent men and women before God and offer sacrifices for their sins should be able to deal gently with their failings, since he knows what it's like from his own experience. But that also means that he has to offer sacrifices for his own sins as well as the peoples'.

4-6   No one elects himself to this honored position. He's called to it by God, as Aaron was. Neither did Christ presume to set himself up as high priest, but was set apart by the One who said to him, "You're my Son; today I celebrate you!" In another place God declares, "You're a priest forever in the royal order of Melchizedek."

7-10   While he lived on earth, anticipating death, Jesus cried out in pain and wept in sorrow as he offered up priestly prayers to God. Because he honored God, God answered him. Though he was God's Son, he learned trusting-obedience by what he suffered, just as we do. Then, having arrived at the full stature of his maturity and having been announced by God as high priest in the order of Melchizedek, he became the source of eternal salvation to all who believingly obey him.

RE-CRUCIFYING JESUS

11-14 I have a lot more to say about this, but it is hard to get it across to you since you've picked up this bad habit of not listening. By this time you ought to be teachers yourselves, yet here I find you need someone to sit down with you and go over the basics on God again, starting from square one — baby's milk, when you should have been on solid food long ago! Milk is for beginners, inexperienced in God's ways; solid food is for the mature, who have some practice in telling right from wrong.

1-3 6 So come on, let's leave the preschool fingerpainting exercises on Christ and get on with the grand work of art. Grow up in Christ. The basic foundational truths are in place: turning your back on "salvation by self-help" and turning in trust toward God; baptismal instructions; laying on of hands; resurrection of the dead; eternal judgment. God helping us, we'll stay true to all that. But there's so much more. Let's get on with it!

4-8 Once people have seen the light, gotten a taste of heaven and been part of the work of the Holy Spirit, once they've personally experienced the sheer goodness of God's Word and the powers breaking in on us — if then they turn their backs on it, washing their hands of the whole thing, well, they can't start over as if nothing happened. That's impossible. Why, they've re-crucified Jesus! They've repudiated him in public! Parched ground that soaks up the rain and then produces an abundance of carrots and corn for its gardener gets God's "Well done!" But if it produces weeds and thistles, it's more likely to get cussed out. Fields like that are burned, not harvested.

9-12 I'm sure that won't happen to you, friends. I have better things in mind for you — salvation things! God doesn't miss anything. He knows perfectly well all the love you've shown him by helping needy Christians, and that you keep at it. And now I want each of you to extend that same intensity toward a full-bodied hope, and keep at it till the finish. Don't drag your feet. Be like those who stay the course with committed faith and then get everything promised to them.

GOD GAVE HIS WORD

13-18 When God made his promise to Abraham, he backed it to the hilt, putting his own reputation on the line. He said, "I promise that I'll bless you with everything I have — bless and bless and bless!" Abraham stuck it out and got everything that had been promised to him. When people make promises, they guarantee them by appeal to some authority above them so that if there is any question that they'll make good on the promise, the authority will back them up. When God wanted to guarantee his promises, he gave his word, a rock-solid guarantee — God *can't* break his word. And because his word cannot change, the promise is likewise unchangeable.

18-20 We who have run for our very lives to God have every reason to grab the promised hope with both hands and never let go. It's an unbreakable spiritual lifeline, reaching past all appearances right to the very presence of God where Jesus, running on ahead of us, has taken up his permanent post as high priest for us, in the order of Melchizedek.

MELCHIZEDEK, PRIEST OF GOD

1-3 **7** Melchizedek was king of Salem and priest of the Highest God. He met Abraham, who was returning from "the royal massacre," and gave him his blessing. Abraham in turn gave him a tenth of the spoils. "Melchizedek" means "King of Righteousness." "Salem" means "Peace." So, he is also "King of Peace." Melchizedek towers out of the past—without record of family ties, no account of beginning or end. In this way he is like the Son of God, one huge priestly presence dominating the landscape always.

4-7 You realize just how great Melchizedek is when you see that Father Abraham gave him a tenth of the captured treasure. Priests descended from Levi are commanded by law to collect tithes from the people, even though they are all more or less equals, priests and people, having a common father in Abraham. But this man, a complete outsider, collected tithes from Abraham and blessed him, the one to whom the promises had been given. In acts of blessing, the lesser is blessed by the greater.

8-10 Or look at it this way: We pay our tithes to priests who die, but Abraham paid tithes to a priest who, the Scripture says, "lives." Ultimately you could even say that since Levi descended from Abraham, who paid tithes to Melchizedek, when we pay tithes to the priestly tribe of Levi they end up with Melchizedek.

A PERMANENT PRIESTHOOD

11-14 If the priesthood of Levi and Aaron, which provided the framework for the giving of the law, could really make people perfect, there wouldn't have been need for a new priesthood like that of Melchizedek. But since it didn't get the job done, there was a change of priesthood, which brought with it a radical new kind of law. There is no way of understanding this in terms of the old Levitical priesthood, which is why there is nothing in Jesus' family tree connecting him with that priestly line.

15-19 But the Melchizedek story provides a perfect analogy: Jesus, a priest like Melchizedek, not by genealogical descent but by the sheer force of resurrection life—he lives!—"priest forever in the royal order of Melchizedek." The former way of doing things, a system of commandments that never worked out the way it was supposed to, was set aside; the law brought nothing to maturity. Another way—Jesus!—a way that *does* work, that brings us right into the presence of God, is put in its place.

20-22 The old priesthood of Aaron perpetuated itself automatically, father to son, without explicit confirmation by God. But then God intervened and called this new, permanent priesthood into being with an added promise:

> God gave his word;
>   he won't take it back:
> "You're the permanent priest."

This makes Jesus the guarantee of a far better way between us and God—one that really works! A new covenant.

23-25 Earlier there were a lot of priests, for they died and had to be replaced. But Jesus' priesthood is permanent. He's there from now to eternity to save everyone who comes to God through him, always on the job to speak up for them.

26-28 So now we have a high priest who perfectly fits our needs: completely holy, uncompromised by sin, with authority extending as high as God's presence in heaven itself. Unlike the other high priests, he doesn't have to offer sacrifices for his own sins every day before he can get around to us and our sins. He's done it, once and for all: offered up *himself* as the sacrifice. The law appoints as high priests men who are never able to get the job done right. But this intervening command of God, which came later, appoints the Son, who is absolutely, eternally perfect.

A NEW PLAN WITH ISRAEL

1-2 8 In essence, we have just such a high priest: authoritative right alongside God, conducting worship in the one true sanctuary built by God.

3-5 The assigned task of a high priest is to offer both gifts and sacrifices, and it's no different with the priesthood of Jesus. If he were limited to earth, he wouldn't even be a priest. We wouldn't need him since there are plenty of priests who offer the gifts designated in the law. These priests provide only a hint of what goes on in the true sanctuary of heaven, which Moses caught a glimpse of as he was about to set up the tent-shrine. It was then that God said, "Be careful to do it exactly as you saw it on the Mountain."

6-13 But Jesus' priestly work far surpasses what these other priests do, since he's working from a far better plan. If the first plan — the old covenant — had worked out, a second wouldn't have been needed. But we know the first was found wanting, because God said,

> Heads up! The days are coming
>   when I'll set up a new plan
>   for dealing with Israel and Judah.
> I'll throw out the old plan
>   I set up with their ancestors
>   when I led them by the hand out of Egypt.
> They didn't keep their part of the bargain,
>   so I looked away and let it go.
> This new plan I'm making with Israel
>   isn't going to be written on paper,
>   isn't going to be chiseled in stone;
> This time I'm writing out the plan *in* them,
>   carving it on the lining of their hearts.
> I'll be their God,
>   they'll be my people.
> They won't go to school to learn about me,
>   or buy a book called *God in Five Easy Lessons*.
> They'll all get to know me firsthand,
>   the little and the big, the small and the great.
> They'll get to know me by being kindly forgiven,
>   with the slate of their sins forever wiped clean.

By coming up with a new plan, a new covenant between God and his people, God put the old plan on the shelf. And there it stays, gathering dust.

1-5
9 That first plan contained directions for worship, and a specially designed place of worship. A large outer tent was set up. The lamp- stand, the table, and "the bread of presence" were placed in it. This was called "the Holy Place." Then a curtain was stretched, and behind it a smaller, inside tent set up. This was called "the Holy of Holies." In it were placed the gold incense altar and the gold-covered ark of the covenant con- taining the gold urn of manna, Aaron's rod that budded, the covenant tablets, and the angel-wing-shadowed mercy seat. But we don't have time to com- ment on these now.

6-10
After this was set up, the priests went about their duties in the large tent. Only the high priest entered the smaller, inside tent, and then only once a year, offering a blood sacrifice for his own sins and the people's accumulated sins. This was the Holy Spirit's way of showing with a visible parable that as long as the large tent stands, people can't just walk in on God. Under this system, the gifts and sacrifices can't really get to the heart of the matter, can't assuage the conscience of the people, but are limited to matters of ritual and behavior. It's essentially a temporary arrangement until a complete overhaul could be made.

POINTING TO THE REALITIES OF HEAVEN

11-15
But when the Messiah arrived, high priest of the superior things of this new covenant, he bypassed the old tent and its trappings in this created world and went straight into heaven's "tent"—the true Holy Place—once and for all. He also bypassed the sacrifices consisting of goat and calf blood, instead using his own blood as the price to set us free once and for all. If that animal blood and the other rituals of purification were effective in cleaning up certain matters of our religion and behavior, think how much more the blood of Christ cleans up our whole lives, inside and out. Through the Spirit, Christ offered himself as an unblemished sacrifice, freeing us from all those dead-end efforts to make ourselves respectable, so that we can live all out for God.

16-17
Like a will that takes effect when someone dies, the new covenant was put into action at Jesus' death. His death marked the transition from the old plan to the new one, canceling the old obligations and accompanying sins, and summoning the heirs to receive the eternal inheritance that was prom- ised them. He brought together God and his people in this new way.

18-22
Even the first plan required a death to set it in motion. After Moses had read out all the terms of the plan of the law—God's "will"—he took the blood of sacrificed animals and, in a solemn ritual, sprinkled the document and the people who were its beneficiaries. And then he attested its validity with the words, "This is the blood of the covenant commanded by God." He did the same thing with the place of worship and its furniture. Moses said to the people, "This is the blood of the covenant God has established with you." Practically everything in a will hinges on a death. That's why blood, the evidence of death, is used so much in our tradition, especially regarding forgiveness of sins.

23-26
That accounts for the prominence of blood and death in all these secondary practices that point to the realities of heaven. It also accounts for why, when the real thing takes place, these animal sacrifices aren't needed

anymore, having served their purpose. For Christ didn't enter the earthly version of the Holy Place; he entered the Place Itself, and offered himself to God as the sacrifice for our sins. He doesn't do this every year as the high priests did under the old plan with blood that was not their own; if that had been the case, he would have to sacrifice himself repeatedly throughout the course of history. But instead he sacrificed himself once and for all, summing up all the other sacrifices in this sacrifice of himself, the final solution of sin.

27-28   Everyone has to die once, then face the consequences. Christ's death was also a one-time event, but it was a sacrifice that took care of sins forever. And so, when he next appears, the outcome for those eager to greet him is, precisely, *salvation*.

The Sacrifice of Jesus

1-10   **10** The old plan was only a hint of the good things in the new plan. Since that old "law plan" wasn't complete in itself, it couldn't complete those who followed it. No matter how many sacrifices were offered year after year, they never added up to a complete solution. If they had, the worshipers would have gone merrily on their way, no longer dragged down by their sins. But instead of removing awareness of sin, when those animal sacrifices were repeated over and over they actually heightened awareness and guilt. The plain fact is that bull and goat blood can't get rid of sin. That is what is meant by this prophecy, put in the mouth of Christ:

> You don't want sacrifices and offerings year after year;
>   you've prepared a body for me for a sacrifice.
> It's not fragrance and smoke from the altar
>   that whet your appetite.
> So I said, "I'm here to do it your way, O God,
>   the way it's described in your Book."

When he said, "You don't want sacrifices and offerings," he was referring to practices according to the old plan. When he added, "I'm here to do it your way," he set aside the first in order to enact the new plan — *God's* way — by which we are made fit for God by the once-for-all sacrifice of Jesus.

11-18   Every priest goes to work at the altar each day, offers the same old sacrifices year in, year out, and never makes a dent in the sin problem. As a priest, Christ made a single sacrifice for sins, and that was it! Then he sat down right beside God and waited for his enemies to cave in. It was a perfect sacrifice by a perfect person to perfect some very imperfect people. By that single offering, he did everything that needed to be done for everyone who takes part in the purifying process. The Holy Spirit confirms this:

> This new plan I'm making with Israel
>   isn't going to be written on paper,
>   isn't going to be chiseled in stone;
> This time "I'm writing out the plan *in* them,
>   carving it on the lining of their hearts."

He concludes,
    I'll forever wipe the slate clean of their sins.

Once sins are taken care of for good, there's no longer any need to offer sacrifices for them.

DON'T THROW IT ALL AWAY

19-21   So, friends, we can now — without hesitation — walk right up to God, into "the Holy Place." Jesus has cleared the way by the blood of his sacrifice, acting as our priest before God. The "curtain" into God's presence is his body.

22-25   So let's *do* it — full of belief, confident that we're presentable inside and out. Let's keep a firm grip on the promises that keep us going. He always keeps his word. Let's see how inventive we can be in encouraging love and helping out, not avoiding worshiping together as some do but spurring each other on, especially as we see the big Day approaching.

26-31   If we give up and turn our backs on all we've learned, all we've been given, all the truth we now know, we repudiate Christ's sacrifice and are left on our own to face the Judgment — and a mighty fierce judgment it will be! If the penalty for breaking the law of Moses is physical death, what do you think will happen if you turn on God's Son, spit on the sacrifice that made you whole, and insult this most gracious Spirit? This is no light matter. God has warned us that he'll hold us to account and make us pay. He was quite explicit: "Vengeance is mine, and I won't overlook a thing" and "God will judge his people." Nobody's getting by with anything, believe me.

32-39   Remember those early days after you first saw the light? Those were the hard times! Kicked around in public, targets of every kind of abuse — some days it was you, other days your friends. If some friends went to prison, you stuck by them. If some enemies broke in and seized your goods, you let them go with a smile, knowing they couldn't touch your real treasure. Nothing they did bothered you, nothing set you back. So don't throw it all away now. You were sure of yourselves then. It's *still* a sure thing! But you need to stick it out, staying with God's plan so you'll be there for the promised completion.

It won't be long now, he's on the way;
    he'll show up most any minute.
But anyone who is right with me thrives on loyal trust;
    if he cuts and runs, I won't be very happy.

But we're not quitters who lose out. Oh, no! We'll stay with it and survive, trusting all the way.

FAITH IN WHAT WE DON'T SEE

1-2   **11** The fundamental fact of existence is that this trust in God, this faith, is the firm foundation under everything that makes life worth living. It's our handle on what we can't see. The act of faith is what distinguished our ancestors, set them above the crowd.

3   By faith, we see the world called into existence by God's word, what we see created by what we don't see.

4   By an act of faith, Abel brought a better sacrifice to God than Cain. It was what he *believed*, not what he *brought*, that made the difference. That's what God noticed and approved as righteous. After all these centuries, that belief continues to catch our notice.

5-6 By an act of faith, Enoch skipped death completely. "They looked all over and couldn't find him because God had taken him." We know on the basis of reliable testimony that before he was taken "he pleased God." It's impossible to please God apart from faith. And why? Because anyone who wants to approach God must believe both that he exists *and* that he cares enough to respond to those who seek him.

7 By faith, Noah built a ship in the middle of dry land. He was warned about something he couldn't see, and acted on what he was told. The result? His family was saved. His act of faith drew a sharp line between the evil of the unbelieving world and the rightness of the believing world. As a result, Noah became intimate with God.

8-10 By an act of faith, Abraham said yes to God's call to travel to an unknown place that would become his home. When he left he had no idea where he was going. By an act of faith he lived in the country promised him, lived as a stranger camping in tents. Isaac and Jacob did the same, living under the same promise. Abraham did it by keeping his eye on an unseen city with real, eternal foundations — the City designed and built by God.

11-12 By faith, barren Sarah was able to become pregnant, old woman as she was at the time, because she believed the One who made a promise would do what he said. That's how it happened that from one man's dead and shriveled loins there are now people numbering into the millions.

13-16 Each one of these people of faith died not yet having in hand what was promised, but still believing. How did they do it? They saw it way off in the distance, waved their greeting, and accepted the fact that they were transients in this world. People who live this way make it plain that they are looking for their true home. If they were homesick for the old country, they could have gone back any time they wanted. But they were after a far better country than that — *heaven* country. You can see why God is so proud of them, and has a City waiting for them.

17-19 By faith, Abraham, at the time of testing, offered Isaac back to God. Acting in faith, he was as ready to return the promised son, his only son, as he had been to receive him — and this after he had already been told, "Your descendants shall come from Isaac." Abraham figured that if God wanted to, he could raise the dead. In a sense, that's what happened when he received Isaac back, alive from off the altar.

20 By an act of faith, Isaac reached into the future as he blessed Jacob and Esau.

21 By an act of faith, Jacob on his deathbed blessed each of Joseph's sons in turn, blessing them with God's blessing, not his own — as he bowed worshipfully upon his staff.

22 By an act of faith, Joseph, while dying, prophesied the exodus of Israel, and made arrangements for his own burial.

23 By an act of faith, Moses' parents hid him away for three months after his birth. They saw the child's beauty, and they braved the king's decree.

24-28 By faith, Moses, when grown, refused the privileges of the Egyptian royal house. He chose a hard life with God's people rather than an opportunistic soft life of sin with the oppressors. He valued suffering in the Messiah's camp far greater than Egyptian wealth because he was looking ahead, anticipating the payoff. By an act of faith, he turned his heel on

Egypt, indifferent to the king's blind rage. He had his eye on the One no eye can see, and kept right on going. By an act of faith, he kept the Passover Feast and sprinkled Passover blood on each house so that the destroyer of the firstborn wouldn't touch them.

29 By an act of faith, Israel walked through the Red Sea on dry ground. The Egyptians tried it and drowned.

30 By faith, the Israelites marched around the walls of Jericho for seven days, and the walls fell flat.

31 By an act of faith, Rahab, the Jericho harlot, welcomed the spies and escaped the destruction that came on those who refused to trust God.

32-38 I could go on and on, but I've run out of time. There are so many more — Gideon, Barak, Samson, Jephthah, David, Samuel, the prophets. . . . Through acts of faith, they toppled kingdoms, made justice work, took the promises for themselves. They were protected from lions, fires, and sword thrusts, turned disadvantage to advantage, won battles, routed alien armies. Women received their loved ones back from the dead. There were those who, under torture, refused to give in and go free, preferring something better: resurrection. Others braved abuse and whips, and, yes, chains and dungeons. We have stories of those who were stoned, sawed in two, murdered in cold blood; stories of vagrants wandering the earth in animal skins, homeless, friendless, powerless — the world didn't deserve them! — making their way as best they could on the cruel edges of the world.

39-40 Not one of these people, even though their lives of faith were exemplary, got their hands on what was promised. God had a better plan for us: that their faith and our faith would come together to make one completed whole, their lives of faith not complete apart from ours.

DISCIPLINE IN A LONG-DISTANCE RACE

1-3 **12** Do you see what this means — all these pioneers who blazed the way, all these veterans cheering us on? It means we'd better get on with it. Strip down, start running — and never quit! No extra spiritual fat, no parasitic sins. Keep your eyes on *Jesus*, who both began and finished this race we're in. Study how he did it. Because he never lost sight of where he was headed — that exhilarating finish in and with God — he could put up with anything along the way: Cross, shame, whatever. And now he's *there*, in the place of honor, right alongside God. When you find yourselves flagging in your faith, go over that story again, item by item, that long litany of hostility he plowed through. *That* will shoot adrenaline into your souls!

4-11 In this all-out match against sin, others have suffered far worse than you, to say nothing of what Jesus went through — all that bloodshed! So don't feel sorry for yourselves. Or have you forgotten how good parents treat children, and that God regards you as *his* children?

My dear child, don't shrug off God's discipline,
    but don't be crushed by it either.
It's the child he loves that he disciplines;
    the child he embraces, he also corrects.

God is educating you; that's why you must never drop out. He's treating you as dear children. This trouble you're in isn't punishment; it's *training*, the normal experience of children. Only irresponsible parents leave children to fend for themselves. Would you prefer an irresponsible God? We respect our own parents for training and not spoiling us, so why not embrace God's training so we can truly *live*? While we were children, our parents did what *seemed* best to them. But God is doing what *is* best for us, training us to live God's holy best. At the time, discipline isn't much fun. It always feels like it's going against the grain. Later, of course, it pays off handsomely, for it's the well-trained who find themselves mature in their relationship with God.

12-13 So don't sit around on your hands! No more dragging your feet! Clear the path for long-distance runners so no one will trip and fall, so no one will step in a hole and sprain an ankle. Help each other out. And run for it!

14-17 Work at getting along with each other and with God. Otherwise you'll never get so much as a glimpse of God. Make sure no one gets left out of God's generosity. Keep a sharp eye out for weeds of bitter discontent. A thistle or two gone to seed can ruin a whole garden in no time. Watch out for the Esau syndrome: trading away God's lifelong gift in order to satisfy a short-term appetite. You well know how Esau later regretted that impulsive act and wanted God's blessing—but by then it was too late, tears or no tears.

An Unshakable Kingdom

18-21 Unlike your ancestors, you didn't come to Mount Sinai—all that volcanic blaze and earthshaking rumble—to hear God speak. The earsplitting words and soul-shaking message terrified them and they begged him to stop. When they heard the words—"If an animal touches the Mountain, it's as good as dead"—they were afraid to move. Even Moses was terrified.

22-24 No, that's not *your* experience at all. You've come to Mount Zion, the city where the living God resides. The invisible Jerusalem is populated by throngs of festive angels and Christian citizens. It is the city where God is Judge, with judgments that make us just. You've come to Jesus, who presents us with a new covenant, a fresh charter from God. He is the Mediator of this covenant. The murder of Jesus, unlike Abel's—a homicide that cried out for vengeance—became a proclamation of grace.

25-27 So don't turn a deaf ear to these gracious words. If those who ignored earthly warnings didn't get away with it, what will happen to us if we turn our backs on heavenly warnings? His voice that time shook the earth to its foundations; this time—he's told us this quite plainly—he'll also rock the heavens: "One last shaking, from top to bottom, stem to stern." The phrase "one last shaking" means a thorough housecleaning, getting rid of all the historical and religious junk so that the unshakable essentials stand clear and uncluttered.

28-29 Do you see what we've got? An unshakable kingdom! And do you see how thankful we must be? Not only thankful, but brimming with worship, deeply reverent before God. For God is not an indifferent bystander. He's actively cleaning house, torching all that needs to burn, and he won't quit until it's all cleansed. God himself is Fire!

JESUS DOESN'T CHANGE

1-4 **13** Stay on good terms with each other, held together by love. Be ready with a meal or a bed when it's needed. Why, some have extended hospitality to angels without ever knowing it! Regard prisoners as if you were in prison with them. Look on victims of abuse as if what happened to them had happened to you. Honor marriage, and guard the sacredness of sexual intimacy between wife and husband. God draws a firm line against casual and illicit sex.

5-6 Don't be obsessed with getting more material things. Be relaxed with what you have. Since God assured us, "I'll never let you down, never walk off and leave you," we can boldly quote,

God is there, ready to help;
I'm fearless no matter what.
Who or what can get to me?

7-8 Appreciate your pastoral leaders who gave you the Word of God. Take a good look at the way they live, and let their faithfulness instruct you, as well as their truthfulness. There should be a consistency that runs through us all. For Jesus doesn't change—yesterday, today, tomorrow, he's always totally himself.

9 Don't be lured away from him by the latest speculations about him. The grace of Christ is the only good ground for life. Products named after Christ don't seem to do much for those who buy them.

10-12 The altar from which God gives us the gift of himself is not for exploitation by insiders who grab and loot. In the old system, the animals are killed and the bodies disposed of outside the camp. The blood is then brought inside to the altar as a sacrifice for sin. It's the same with Jesus. He was crucified outside the city gates—*that* is where he poured out the sacrificial blood that was brought to God's altar to cleanse his people.

13-15 So let's go outside, where Jesus is, where the action is—not trying to be privileged insiders, but taking our share in the abuse of Jesus. This "insider world" is not our home. We have our eyes peeled for the City about to come. Let's take our place outside with Jesus, no longer pouring out the sacrificial blood of animals but pouring out sacrificial praises from our lips to God in Jesus' name.

16 Make sure you don't take things for granted and go slack in working for the common good; share what you have with others. God takes particular pleasure in acts of worship—a different kind of "sacrifice"—that take place in kitchen and workplace and on the streets.

17 Be responsive to your pastoral leaders. Listen to their counsel. They are alert to the condition of your lives and work under the strict supervision of God. Contribute to the joy of their leadership, not its drudgery. Why would you want to make things harder for them?

18-21 Pray for us. We have no doubts about what we're doing or why, but it's hard going and we need your prayers. All we care about is living well before God. Pray that we may be together soon.

May God, who puts all things together,
    makes all things whole,
Who made a lasting mark through the sacrifice of Jesus,
    the sacrifice of blood that sealed the eternal covenant,
Who led Jesus, our Great Shepherd,
    up and alive from the dead,
Now put you together, provide you
    with everything you need to please him,
Make us into what gives him most pleasure,
    by means of the sacrifice of Jesus, the Messiah.
All glory to Jesus forever and always!
    Oh, yes, yes, yes.

22-23   Friends, please take what I've written most seriously. I've kept this as brief as possible; I haven't piled on a lot of extras. You'll be glad to know that Timothy has been let out of prison. If he leaves soon, I'll come with him and get to see you myself.

24   Say hello to your pastoral leaders and all the congregations. Everyone here in Italy wants to be remembered to you.

25   Grace be with you, every one.

JAMES

When Christian believers gather in churches, everything that can go wrong sooner or later does. Outsiders, on observing this, conclude that there is nothing to the religion business except, perhaps, business — and dishonest business at that. Insiders see it differently. Just as a hospital collects the sick under one roof and labels them as such, the church collects sinners. Many of the people outside the hospital are every bit as sick as the ones inside, but their illnesses are either undiagnosed or disguised. It's similar with sinners outside the church.

So Christian churches are not, as a rule, model communities of good behavior. They are, rather, places where human misbehavior is brought out in the open, faced, and dealt with.

The letter of James shows one of the church's early pastors skillfully going about his work of confronting, diagnosing, and dealing with areas of misbelief and misbehavior that had turned up in congregations committed to his care. Deep and living wisdom is on display here, wisdom both rare and essential. Wisdom is not primarily knowing the truth, although it certainly includes that; it is skill in living. For, what good is a truth if we don't know how to live it? What good is an intention if we can't sustain it?

According to church traditions, James carried the nickname "Old Camel Knees" because of thick calluses built up on his knees from many years of determined prayer. The prayer is foundational to the wisdom. Prayer is *always* foundational to wisdom.

JAMES

¹ **1** I, James, am a slave of God and the Master Jesus, writing to the twelve tribes scattered to Kingdom Come: Hello!

FAITH UNDER PRESSURE

2-4 Consider it a sheer gift, friends, when tests and challenges come at you from all sides. You know that under pressure, your faith-life is forced into the open and shows its true colors. So don't try to get out of anything prematurely. Let it do its work so you become mature and well-developed, not deficient in any way.

5-8 If you don't know what you're doing, pray to the Father. He loves to help. You'll get his help, and won't be condescended to when you ask for it. Ask boldly, believingly, without a second thought. People who "worry their prayers" are like wind-whipped waves. Don't think you're going to get anything from the Master that way, adrift at sea, keeping all your options open.

9-11 When down-and-outers get a break, cheer! And when the arrogant rich are brought down to size, cheer! Prosperity is as short-lived as a wildflower, so don't ever count on it. You know that as soon as the sun rises, pouring down its scorching heat, the flower withers. Its petals wilt and, before you know it, that beautiful face is a barren stem. Well, that's a picture of the "prosperous life." At the very moment everyone is looking on in admiration, it fades away to nothing.

12 Anyone who meets a testing challenge head-on and manages to stick it out is mighty fortunate. For such persons loyally in love with God, the reward is life and more life.

13-15 Don't let anyone under pressure to give in to evil say, "God is trying to trip me up." God is impervious to evil, and puts evil in no one's way. The temptation to give in to evil comes from us and only us. We have no one to blame but the leering, seducing flare-up of our own lust. Lust gets pregnant, and has a baby: sin! Sin grows up to adulthood, and becomes a real killer.

16-18 So, my very dear friends, don't get thrown off course. Every desirable and beneficial gift comes out of heaven. The gifts are rivers of light cascading down from the Father of Light. There is nothing deceitful in God, nothing two-faced, nothing fickle. He brought us to life using the true Word, showing us off as the crown of all his creatures.

ACT ON WHAT YOU HEAR

19-21 Post this at all the intersections, dear friends: Lead with your ears, follow up with your tongue, and let anger straggle along in the rear. God's righteousness doesn't grow from human anger. So throw all spoiled virtue and cancerous evil in the garbage. In simple humility, let our gardener, God, landscape you with the Word, making a salvation-garden of your life.

22-24 Don't fool yourself into thinking that you are a listener when you are anything but, letting the Word go in one ear and out the other. *Act* on what you hear! Those who hear and don't act are like those who glance in the mirror, walk away, and two minutes later have no idea who they are, what they look like.

25 But whoever catches a glimpse of the revealed counsel of God—the free

life!—even out of the corner of his eye, and sticks with it, is no distracted scatterbrain but a man or woman of action. That person will find delight and affirmation in the action.

26-27 Anyone who sets himself up as "religious" by talking a good game is self-deceived. This kind of religion is hot air and only hot air. Real religion, the kind that passes muster before God the Father, is this: Reach out to the homeless and loveless in their plight, and guard against corruption from the godless world.

THE ROYAL RULE OF LOVE

1-4 2 My dear friends, don't let public opinion influence how you live out our glorious, Christ-originated faith. If a man enters your church wearing an expensive suit, and a street person wearing rags comes in right after him, and you say to the man in the suit, "Sit here, sir; this is the best seat in the house!" and either ignore the street person or say, "Better sit here in the back row," haven't you segregated God's children and proved that you are judges who can't be trusted?

5-7 Listen, dear friends. Isn't it clear by now that God operates quite differently? He chose the world's down-and-out as the kingdom's first citizens, with full rights and privileges. This kingdom is promised to anyone who loves God. And here you are abusing these same citizens! Isn't it the high and mighty who exploit you, who use the courts to rob you blind? Aren't they the ones who scorn the new name—"Christian"—used in your baptisms?

8-11 You do well when you complete the Royal Rule of the Scriptures: "Love others as you love yourself." But if you play up to these so-called important people, you go against the Rule and stand convicted by it. You can't pick and choose in these things, specializing in keeping one or two things in God's law and ignoring others. The same God who said, "Don't commit adultery," also said, "Don't murder." If you don't commit adultery but go ahead and murder, do you think your non-adultery will cancel out your murder? No, you're a murderer, period.

12-13 Talk and act like a person expecting to be judged by the Rule that sets us free. For if you refuse to act kindly, you can hardly expect to be treated kindly. Kind mercy wins over harsh judgment every time.

FAITH IN ACTION

14-17 Dear friends, do you think you'll get anywhere in this if you learn all the right words but never do anything? Does merely talking about faith indicate that a person really has it? For instance, you come upon an old friend dressed in rags and half-starved and say, "Good morning, friend! Be clothed in Christ! Be filled with the Holy Spirit!" and walk off without providing so much as a coat or a cup of soup—where does that get you? Isn't it obvious that God-talk without God-acts is outrageous nonsense?

18 I can already hear one of you agreeing by saying, "Sounds good. You take care of the faith department, I'll handle the works department."

Not so fast. You can no more show me your works apart from your faith than I can show you my faith apart from my works. Faith and works, works and faith, fit together hand in glove.

19-20 Do I hear you professing to believe in the one and only God, but then observe you complacently sitting back as if you had done something wonderful? That's just great. Demons do that, but what good does it do them? Use your heads! Do you suppose for a minute that you can cut faith and works in two and not end up with a corpse on your hands?

21-24 Wasn't our ancestor Abraham "made right with God by works" when he placed his son Isaac on the sacrificial altar? Isn't it obvious that faith and works are yoked partners, that faith expresses itself in works? That the works are "works of faith"? The full meaning of "believe" in the Scripture sentence, "Abraham believed God and was set right with God," includes his action. It's that mesh of believing and acting that got Abraham named "God's friend." Is it not evident that a person is made right with God not by a barren faith but by faith fruitful in works?

25-26 The same with Rahab, the Jericho harlot. Wasn't her action in hiding God's spies and helping them escape — that seamless unity of *believing* and *doing* — what counted with God? The very moment you separate body and spirit, you end up with a corpse. Separate faith and works and you get the same thing: a corpse.

WHEN YOU OPEN YOUR MOUTH

1-2 **3** Don't be in any rush to become a teacher, my friends. Teaching is highly responsible work. Teachers are held to the strictest standards. And none of us is perfectly qualified. We get it wrong nearly every time we open our mouths. If you could find someone whose speech was perfectly true, you'd have a perfect person, in perfect control of life.

3-5 A bit in the mouth of a horse controls the whole horse. A small rudder on a huge ship in the hands of a skilled captain sets a course in the face of the strongest winds. A word out of your mouth may seem of no account, but it can accomplish nearly anything — or destroy it!

5-6 It only takes a spark, remember, to set off a forest fire. A careless or wrongly placed word out of your mouth can do that. By our speech we can ruin the world, turn harmony to chaos, throw mud on a reputation, send the whole world up in smoke and go up in smoke with it, smoke right from the pit of hell.

7-10 This is scary: You can tame a tiger, but you can't tame a tongue — it's never been done. The tongue runs wild, a wanton killer. With our tongues we bless God our Father; with the same tongues we curse the very men and women he made in his image. Curses and blessings out of the same mouth!

10-12 My friends, this can't go on. A spring doesn't gush fresh water one day and brackish the next, does it? Apple trees don't bear strawberries, do they? Raspberry bushes don't bear apples, do they? You're not going to dip into a polluted mud hole and get a cup of clear, cool water, are you?

LIVE WELL, LIVE WISELY

13-16 Do you want to be counted wise, to build a reputation for wisdom? Here's what you do: Live well, live wisely, live humbly. It's the way you live, not the way you talk, that counts. Mean-spirited ambition isn't wisdom. Boasting that you are wise isn't wisdom. Twisting the truth to make yourselves sound wise isn't wisdom. It's the furthest thing from wisdom — it's animal cunning, devilish conniving. Whenever you're trying to look better than others or get the better of others, things fall apart and everyone ends up at the others' throats.

17-18 Real wisdom, God's wisdom, begins with a holy life and is characterized by getting along with others. It is gentle and reasonable, overflowing with mercy and blessings, not hot one day and cold the next, not two-faced. You can develop a healthy, robust community that lives right with God and enjoy its results *only* if you do the hard work of getting along with each other, treating each other with dignity and honor.

GET SERIOUS

1-2 4 Where do you think all these appalling wars and quarrels come from? Do you think they just happen? Think again. They come about because you want your own way, and fight for it deep inside yourselves. You lust for what you don't have and are willing to kill to get it. You want what isn't yours and will risk violence to get your hands on it.

2-3 You wouldn't think of just asking God for it, would you? And why not? Because you know you'd be asking for what you have no right to. You're spoiled children, each wanting your own way.

4-6 You're cheating on God. If all you want is your own way, flirting with the world every chance you get, you end up enemies of God and his way. And do you suppose God doesn't care? The proverb has it that "he's a fiercely jealous lover." And what he gives in love is far better than anything else you'll find. It's common knowledge that "God goes against the willful proud; God gives grace to the willing humble."

7-10 So let God work his will in you. Yell a loud *no* to the Devil and watch him scamper. Say a quiet *yes* to God and he'll be there in no time. Quit dabbling in sin. Purify your inner life. Quit playing the field. Hit bottom, and cry your eyes out. The fun and games are over. Get serious, really serious. Get down on your knees before the Master; it's the only way you'll get on your feet.

11-12 Don't bad-mouth each other, friends. It's God's Word, his Message, his Royal Rule, that takes a beating in that kind of talk. You're supposed to be honoring the Message, not writing graffiti all over it. God is in charge of deciding human destiny. Who do you think you are to meddle in the destiny of others?

NOTHING BUT A WISP OF FOG

13-15 And now I have a word for you who brashly announce, "Today—at the latest, tomorrow—we're off to such and such a city for the year. We're going to start a business and make a lot of money." You don't know the first thing about tomorrow. You're nothing but a wisp of fog, catching a brief bit of sun before disappearing. Instead, make it a habit to say, "If the Master wills it and we're still alive, we'll do this or that."

16-17 As it is, you are full of your grandiose selves. All such vaunting self-importance is evil. In fact, if you know the right thing to do and don't do it, that, for you, *is* evil.

DESTROYING YOUR LIFE FROM WITHIN

1-3 5 And a final word to you arrogant rich: Take some lessons in lament. You'll need buckets for the tears when the crash comes upon you. Your money is corrupt and your fine clothes stink. Your greedy luxuries are a cancer in your gut, destroying your life from within. You thought you were piling up wealth. What you've piled up is judgment.

4-6 All the workers you've exploited and cheated cry out for judgment.

The groans of the workers you used and abused are a roar in the ears of the Master Avenger. You've looted the earth and lived it up. But all you'll have to show for it is a fatter than usual corpse. In fact, what you've done is condemn and murder perfectly good persons, who stand there and take it.

7-8　Meanwhile, friends, wait patiently for the Master's Arrival. You see farmers do this all the time, waiting for their valuable crops to mature, patiently letting the rain do its slow but sure work. Be patient like that. Stay steady and strong. The Master could arrive at any time.

9　Friends, don't complain about each other. A far greater complaint could be lodged against you, you know. The Judge is standing just around the corner.

10-11　Take the old prophets as your mentors. They put up with anything, went through everything, and never once quit, all the time honoring God. What a gift life is to those who stay the course! You've heard, of course, of Job's staying power, and you know how God brought it all together for him at the end. That's because God cares, cares right down to the last detail.

12　And since you know that he cares, let your language show it. Don't add words like "I swear to God" to your own words. Don't show your impatience by concocting oaths to hurry up God. Just say yes or no. Just say what is true. That way, your language can't be used against you.

PRAYER TO BE RECKONED WITH

13-15　Are you hurting? Pray. Do you feel great? Sing. Are you sick? Call the church leaders together to pray and anoint you with oil in the name of the Master. Believing-prayer will heal you, and Jesus will put you on your feet. And if you've sinned, you'll be forgiven — healed inside and out.

16-18　Make this your common practice: Confess your sins to each other and pray for each other so that you can live together whole and healed. The prayer of a person living right with God is something powerful to be reckoned with. Elijah, for instance, human just like us, prayed hard that it wouldn't rain, and it didn't — not a drop for three and a half years. Then he prayed that it would rain, and it did. The showers came and everything started growing again.

19-20　My dear friends, if you know people who have wandered off from God's truth, don't write them off. Go after them. Get them back and you will have rescued precious lives from destruction and prevented an epidemic of wandering away from God.

1 & 2 PETER

Peter's concise confession — "You are the Messiah, the Christ" — focused the faith of the disciples on Jesus as God among us, in person, carrying out the eternal work of salvation. Peter seems to have been a natural leader, commanding the respect of his peers by sheer force of personality. In every listing of Jesus' disciples, Peter's name is invariably first.

In the early church, his influence was enormous and acknowledged by all. By virtue of his position, he was easily the most powerful figure in the Christian community. And his energetic preaching, ardent prayer, bold healing, and wise direction confirmed the trust placed in him.

The way Peter handled himself in that position of power is even more impressive than the power itself. He stayed out of the center, didn't "wield" power, maintained a scrupulous subordination to Jesus. Given his charismatic personality and well-deserved position at the head, he could easily have taken over, using the prominence of his association with Jesus to promote himself. That he didn't do it, given the frequency with which spiritual leaders do exactly that, is impressive. Peter is a breath of fresh air.

The two letters Peter wrote exhibit the qualities of Jesus that the Holy Spirit shaped in him: a readiness to embrace suffering rather than prestige, a wisdom developed from experience and not imposed from a book, a humility that lacked nothing in vigor or imagination. From what we know of the early stories of Peter, he had in him all the makings of a bully. That he didn't become a bully (and religious bullies are the worst kind) but rather the boldly confident and humbly self-effacing servant of Jesus Christ that we discern in these letters, is a compelling witness to what he himself describes as "a brand-new life, with everything to live for."

1 PETER

1-2 I, Peter, am an apostle on assignment by Jesus, the Messiah, writing to exiles scattered to the four winds. Not one is missing, not one forgotten. God the Father has his eye on each of you, and has determined by the work of the Spirit to keep you obedient through the sacrifice of Jesus. May everything good from God be yours!

A NEW LIFE

3-5 What a God we have! And how fortunate we are to have him, this Father of our Master Jesus! Because Jesus was raised from the dead, we've been given a brand-new life and have everything to live for, including a future in heaven—and the future starts now! God is keeping careful watch over us and the future. The Day is coming when you'll have it all—life healed and whole.

6-7 I know how great this makes you feel, even though you have to put up with every kind of aggravation in the meantime. Pure gold put in the fire comes out of it *proved* pure; genuine faith put through this suffering comes out *proved* genuine. When Jesus wraps this all up, it's your faith, not your gold, that God will have on display as evidence of his victory.

8-9 You never saw him, yet you love him. You still don't see him, yet you trust him—with laughter and singing. Because you kept on believing, you'll get what you're looking forward to: total salvation.

10-12 The prophets who told us this was coming asked a lot of questions about this gift of life God was preparing. The Messiah's Spirit let them in on some of it—that the Messiah would experience suffering, followed by glory. They clamored to know who and when. All they were told was that they were serving you, you who by orders from heaven have now heard for yourselves—through the Holy Spirit—the Message of those prophecies fulfilled. Do you realize how fortunate you are? Angels would have given anything to be in on this!

A FUTURE IN GOD

13-16 So roll up your sleeves, put your mind in gear, be totally ready to receive the gift that's coming when Jesus arrives. Don't lazily slip back into those old grooves of evil, doing just what you feel like doing. You didn't know any better then; you do now. As obedient children, let yourselves be pulled into a way of life shaped by God's life, a life energetic and blazing with holiness. God said, "I am holy; you be holy."

17 You call out to God for help and he helps—he's a good Father that way. But don't forget, he's also a responsible Father, and won't let you get by with sloppy living.

18-21 Your life is a journey you must travel with a deep consciousness of God. It cost God plenty to get you out of that dead-end, empty-headed life you grew up in. He paid with Christ's sacred blood, you know. He died like an unblemished, sacrificial lamb. And this was no afterthought. Even though it has only lately—at the end of the ages—become public knowledge, God always knew he was going to do this for you. It's because of this sacrificed Messiah, whom God then raised from the dead and glorified, that you trust God, that you know you have a future in God.

22-25 Now that you've cleaned up your lives by following the truth, love one another as if your lives depended on it. Your new life is not like your old life. Your old birth came from mortal sperm; your new birth comes from God's living Word. Just think: a life conceived by God himself! That's why the prophet said,

> The old life is a grass life,
>   its beauty as short-lived as wildflowers;
> Grass dries up, flowers droop,
>   God's Word goes on and on forever.

This is the Word that conceived the new life in you.

1-3 **2** So clean house! Make a clean sweep of malice and pretense, envy and hurtful talk. You've had a taste of God. Now, like infants at the breast, drink deep of God's pure kindness. Then you'll grow up mature and whole in God.

THE STONE

4-8 Welcome to the living Stone, the source of life. The workmen took one look and threw it out; God set it in the place of honor. Present yourselves as building stones for the construction of a sanctuary vibrant with life, in which you'll serve as holy priests offering Christ-approved lives up to God. The Scriptures provide precedent:

> Look! I'm setting a stone in Zion,
>   a cornerstone in the place of honor.
> Whoever trusts in this stone as a foundation
>   will never have cause to regret it.

To you who trust him, he's a Stone to be proud of, but to those who refuse to trust him,

> The stone the workmen threw out
>   is now the chief foundation stone.

For the untrusting it's
> . . . a stone to trip over,
>   a boulder blocking the way.

They trip and fall because they refuse to obey, just as predicted.

9-10 But you are the ones chosen by God, chosen for the high calling of priestly work, chosen to be a holy people, God's instruments to do his work and speak out for him, to tell others of the night-and-day difference he made for you — from nothing to something, from rejected to accepted.

11-12 Friends, this world is not your home, so don't make yourselves cozy in it. Don't indulge your ego at the expense of your soul. Live an exemplary life among the natives so that your actions will refute their prejudices. Then they'll be won over to God's side and be there to join in the celebration when he arrives.

13-17 Make the Master proud of you by being good citizens. Respect the authorities, whatever their level; they are God's emissaries for keeping order. It is God's will that by doing good, you might cure the ignorance of the fools who think you're a danger to society. Exercise your freedom by serving God, not by breaking the rules. Treat everyone you meet with dignity. Love your spiritual family. Revere God. Respect the government.

The Kind of Life He Lived

18-20 You who are servants, be good servants to your masters — not just to good masters, but also to bad ones. What counts is that you put up with it for God's sake when you're treated badly for no good reason. There's no particular virtue in accepting punishment that you well deserve. But if you're treated badly for good behavior and continue in spite of it to be a good servant, that is what counts with God.

21-25 This is the kind of life you've been invited into, the kind of life Christ lived. He suffered everything that came his way so you would know that it could be done, and also know how to do it, step-by-step.

> He never did one thing wrong,
> Not once said anything amiss.

They called him every name in the book and he said nothing back. He suffered in silence, content to let God set things right. He used his servant body to carry our sins to the Cross so we could be rid of sin, free to live the right way. His wounds became your healing. You were lost sheep with no idea who you were or where you were going. Now you're named and kept for good by the Shepherd of your souls.

Cultivate Inner Beauty

1-4 **3** The same goes for you wives: Be good wives to your husbands, responsive to their needs. There are husbands who, indifferent as they are to any words about God, will be captivated by your life of holy beauty. What matters is not your outer appearance — the styling of your hair, the jewelry you wear, the cut of your clothes — but your inner disposition.

4-6 Cultivate inner beauty, the gentle, gracious kind that God delights in. The holy women of old were beautiful before God that way, and were good, loyal wives to their husbands. Sarah, for instance, taking care of Abraham, would address him as "my dear husband." You'll be true daughters of Sarah if you do the same, unanxious and unintimidated.

7 The same goes for you husbands: Be good husbands to your wives. Honor them, delight in them. As women they lack some of your advantages. But in the new life of God's grace, you're equals. Treat your wives, then, as equals so your prayers don't run aground.

Suffering for Doing Good

8-12 Summing up: Be agreeable, be sympathetic, be loving, be compassionate, be humble. That goes for all of you, no exceptions. No retaliation. No sharp-tongued sarcasm. Instead, bless — that's your job, to bless. You'll be a blessing and also get a blessing.

Whoever wants to embrace life
    and see the day fill up with good,
Here's what you do:
    Say nothing evil or hurtful;
Snub evil and cultivate good;
    run after peace for all you're worth.
God looks on all this with approval,
    listening and responding well to what he's asked;
But he turns his back
    on those who do evil things.

13-18   If with heart and soul you're doing good, do you think you can be stopped? Even if you suffer for it, you're still better off. Don't give the opposition a second thought. Through thick and thin, keep your hearts at attention, in adoration before Christ, your Master. Be ready to speak up and tell anyone who asks why you're living the way you are, and always with the utmost courtesy. Keep a clear conscience before God so that when people throw mud at you, none of it will stick. They'll end up realizing that *they're* the ones who need a bath. It's better to suffer for doing good, if that's what God wants, than to be punished for doing bad. That's what Christ did definitively: suffered because of others' sins, the Righteous One for the unrighteous ones. He went through it all — was put to death and then made alive — to bring us to God.

19-22   He went and proclaimed God's salvation to earlier generations who ended up in the prison of judgment because they wouldn't listen. You know, even though God waited patiently all the days that Noah built his ship, only a few were saved then, eight to be exact — saved *from* the water *by* the water. The waters of baptism do that for you, not by washing away dirt from your skin but by presenting you through Jesus' resurrection before God with a clear conscience. Jesus has the last word on everything and everyone, from angels to armies. He's standing right alongside God, and what he says goes.

LEARN TO THINK LIKE HIM

1-2   4 Since Jesus went through everything you're going through and more, learn to think like him. Think of your sufferings as a weaning from that old sinful habit of always expecting to get your own way. Then you'll be able to live out your days free to pursue what God wants instead of being tyrannized by what you want.

3-5   You've already put in your time in that God-ignorant way of life, partying night after night, a drunken and profligate life. Now it's time to be done with it for good. Of course, your old friends don't understand why you don't join in with the old gang anymore. But you don't have to give an account to them. They're the ones who will be called on the carpet — and before God himself.

6   Listen to the Message. It was preached to those believers who are now dead, and yet even though they died (just as all people must), they will still get in on the *life* that God has given in Jesus.

7-11   Everything in the world is about to be wrapped up, so take nothing for granted. Stay wide-awake in prayer. Most of all, love each other as if your life depended on it. Love makes up for practically anything. Be quick to give a meal to the hungry, a bed to the homeless — cheerfully. Be generous with the different things God gave you, passing them around so all get in on it: if words, let it be God's words; if help, let it be God's hearty help. That way, God's bright presence will be evident in everything through Jesus, and *he'll* get all the credit as the One mighty in everything—encores to the end of time. Oh, yes!

GLORY JUST AROUND THE CORNER

12-13   Friends, when life gets really difficult, don't jump to the conclusion that God isn't on the job. Instead, be glad that you are in the very thick of what Christ experienced. This is a spiritual refining process, with glory just around the corner.

14-16   If you're abused because of Christ, count yourself fortunate. It's the Spirit of God and his glory in you that brought you to the notice of others. If they're on you because you broke the law or disturbed the peace, that's a different matter. But if it's because you're a Christian, don't give it a second thought. Be proud of the distinguished status reflected in that name!

17-19   It's judgment time for God's own family. We're first in line. If it starts with us, think what it's going to be like for those who refuse God's Message!

If good people barely make it,
What's in store for the bad?

So if you find life difficult because you're doing what God said, take it in stride. Trust him. He knows what he's doing, and he'll keep on doing it.

HE'LL PROMOTE YOU AT THE RIGHT TIME

1-3   5 I have a special concern for you church leaders. I know what it's like to be a leader, in on Christ's sufferings as well as the coming glory. Here's my concern: that you care for God's flock with all the diligence of a shepherd. Not because you have to, but because you want to please God. Not calculating what you can get out of it, but acting spontaneously. Not bossily telling others what to do, but tenderly showing them the way.

4-5   When God, who is the best shepherd of all, comes out in the open with his rule, he'll see that you've done it right and commend you lavishly. And you who are younger must follow your leaders. But all of you, leaders and followers alike, are to be down to earth with each other, for—

God has had it with the proud,
But takes delight in just plain people.

6-7   So be content with who you are, and don't put on airs. God's strong hand is on you; he'll promote you at the right time. Live carefree before God; he is most careful with you.

HE GETS THE LAST WORD

8-11   Keep a cool head. Stay alert. The Devil is poised to pounce, and would like nothing better than to catch you napping. Keep your guard up. You're not the only ones plunged into these hard times. It's the same with Christians all over the world. So keep a firm grip on the faith. The suffering won't last forever. It won't be long before this generous God who has great plans for us in Christ — eternal and glorious plans they are! — will have you put together and on your feet for good. He gets the last word; yes, he does.

12 I'm sending this brief letter to you by Silas, a most dependable brother. I have the highest regard for him.

I've written as urgently and accurately as I know how. This is God's generous truth; embrace it with both arms!

13-14 The church in exile here with me — but not for a moment forgotten by God — wants to be remembered to you. Mark, who is like a son to me, says hello. Give holy embraces all around! Peace to you — to all who walk in Christ's ways.

2 PETER

1-2 **1** I, Simon Peter, am a servant and apostle of Jesus Christ. I write this to you whose experience with God is as life-changing as ours, all due to our God's straight dealing and the intervention of our God and Savior, Jesus Christ. Grace and peace to you many times over as you deepen in your experience with God and Jesus, our Master.

DON'T PUT IT OFF

3-4 Everything that goes into a life of pleasing God has been miraculously given to us by getting to know, personally and intimately, the One who invited us to God. The best invitation we ever received! We were also given absolutely terrific promises to pass on to you — your tickets to participation in the life of God after you turned your back on a world corrupted by lust.

5-9 So don't lose a minute in building on what you've been given, complementing your basic faith with good character, spiritual understanding, alert discipline, passionate patience, reverent wonder, warm friendliness, and generous love, each dimension fitting into and developing the others. With these qualities active and growing in your lives, no grass will grow under your feet, no day will pass without its reward as you mature in your experience of our Master Jesus. Without these qualities you can't see what's right before you, oblivious that your old sinful life has been wiped off the books.

10-11 So, friends, confirm God's invitation to you, his choice of you. Don't put it off; do it now. Do this, and you'll have your life on a firm footing, the streets paved and the way wide open into the eternal kingdom of our Master and Savior, Jesus Christ.

THE ONE LIGHT IN A DARK TIME

12-15 Because the stakes are so high, even though you're up-to-date on all this truth and practice it inside and out, I'm not going to let up for a minute in calling you to attention before it. This is the post to which I've been assigned — keeping you alert with frequent reminders — and I'm sticking to it as long as I live. I know that I'm to die soon; the Master has made that quite clear to me. And so I am especially eager that you have all this down in black and white so that after I die, you'll have it for ready reference.

16-18 We weren't, you know, just wishing on a star when we laid the facts out before you regarding the powerful return of our Master, Jesus Christ. We were there for the preview! We saw it with our own eyes: Jesus resplendent with light from God the Father as the voice of Majestic Glory spoke: "This is my Son, marked by my love, focus of all my delight." We were there on the holy mountain with him. We heard the voice out of heaven with our very own ears.

19-21 We couldn't be more sure of what we saw and heard — *God's* glory, *God's* voice. The prophetic Word was confirmed to us. You'll do well to keep focusing on it. It's the one light you have in a dark time as you wait for daybreak and the rising of the Morning Star in your hearts. The main thing to keep in mind here is that no prophecy of Scripture is a matter of private opinion. And why? Because it's not something concocted in the human heart. Prophecy resulted when the Holy Spirit prompted men and women to speak God's Word.

LYING RELIGIOUS LEADERS

1-2 **2**But there were also *lying* prophets among the people then, just as there will be lying religious teachers among you. They'll smuggle in destructive divisions, pitting you against each other—biting the hand of the One who gave them a chance to have their lives back! They've put themselves on a fast downhill slide to destruction, but not before they recruit a crowd of mixed-up followers who can't tell right from wrong.

2-3 They give the way of truth a bad name. They're only out for themselves. They'll say anything, *anything*, that sounds good to exploit you. They won't, of course, get by with it. They'll come to a bad end, for God has never just stood by and let that kind of thing go on.

4-5 God didn't let the rebel angels off the hook, but jailed them in hell till Judgment Day. Neither did he let the ancient ungodly world off. He wiped it out with a flood, rescuing only eight people—Noah, the sole voice of righteousness, was one of them.

6-8 God decreed destruction for the cities of Sodom and Gomorrah. A mound of ashes was all that was left—grim warning to anyone bent on an ungodly life. But that good man Lot, driven nearly out of his mind by the sexual filth and perversity, was rescued. Surrounded by moral rot day after day after day, that righteous man was in constant torment.

9 So God knows how to rescue the godly from evil trials. And he knows how to hold the feet of the wicked to the fire until Judgment Day.

PREDATORS ON THE PROWL

10-11 God is especially incensed against these "teachers" who live by lust, addicted to a filthy existence. They despise interference from true authority, preferring to indulge in self-rule. Insolent egotists, they don't hesitate to speak evil against the most splendid of creatures. Even angels, their superiors in every way, wouldn't think of throwing their weight around like that, trying to slander others before God.

12-14 These people are nothing but brute beasts, born in the wild, predators on the prowl. In the very act of bringing down others with their ignorant blasphemies, they themselves will be brought down, losers in the end. Their evil will boomerang on them. They're so despicable and addicted to pleasure that they indulge in wild parties, carousing in broad daylight. They're obsessed with adultery, compulsive in sin, seducing every vulnerable soul they come upon. Their specialty is greed, and they're experts at it. Dead souls!

15-16 They've left the main road and are directionless, having taken the way of Balaam, son of Beor, the prophet who turned profiteer, a connoisseur of evil. But Balaam was stopped in his wayward tracks: A dumb animal spoke in a human voice and prevented the prophet's craziness.

17-19 There's nothing to these people—they're dried-up fountains, storm-scattered clouds, headed for a black hole in hell. They are loudmouths, full of hot air, but still they're dangerous. Men and women who have recently escaped from a deviant life are most susceptible to their brand of seduction. They promise these newcomers freedom, but they themselves are slaves of corruption, for if they're addicted to corruption—and they are—they're *enslaved*.

20-22 If they've escaped from the slum of sin by experiencing our Master and Savior, Jesus Christ, and then slid back into that same old life again, they're worse than if they had never left. Better not to have started out on the straight road to God than to start out and then turn back, repudiating the experience and the holy command. They prove the point of the proverbs, "A dog goes back to its own vomit" and "A scrubbed-up pig heads for the mud."

In the Last Days

1-2 3 My dear friends, this is now the second time I've written to you, both letters reminders to hold your minds in a state of undistracted attention. Keep in mind what the holy prophets said, and the command of our Master and Savior that was passed on by your apostles.

3-4   First off, you need to know that in the last days, mockers are going to have a heyday. Reducing everything to the level of their puny feelings, they'll mock, "So what's happened to the promise of his Coming? Our ancestors are dead and buried, and everything's going on just as it has from the first day of creation. Nothing's changed."

5-7   They conveniently forget that long ago all the galaxies and this very planet were brought into existence out of watery chaos by God's word. Then God's word brought the chaos back in a flood that destroyed the world. The current galaxies and earth are fuel for the final fire. God is poised, ready to speak his word again, ready to give the signal for the judgment and destruction of the desecrating skeptics.

The Day the Sky Will Collapse

8-9   Don't overlook the obvious here, friends. With God, one day is as good as a thousand years, a thousand years as a day. God isn't late with his promise as some measure lateness. He is restraining himself on account of you, holding back the End because he doesn't want anyone lost. He's giving everyone space and time to change.

10   But when the Day of God's Judgment does come, it will be unannounced, like a thief. The sky will collapse with a thunderous bang, everything disintegrating in a huge conflagration, earth and all its works exposed to the scrutiny of Judgment.

11-13   Since everything here today might well be gone tomorrow, do you see how essential it is to live a holy life? Daily expect the Day of God, eager for its arrival. The galaxies will burn up and the elements melt down that day — but *we'll* hardly notice. We'll be looking the other way, ready for the promised new heavens and the promised new earth, all landscaped with righteousness.

14-16   So, my dear friends, since this is what you have to look forward to, do your very best to be found living at your best, in purity and peace. Interpret our Master's patient restraint for what it is: salvation. Our good brother Paul, who was given much wisdom in these matters, refers to this in all his letters, and has written you essentially the same thing. Some things Paul writes are difficult to understand. Irresponsible people who don't know what they are talking about twist them every which way. They do it to the rest of the Scriptures, too, destroying themselves as they do it.

17-18   But you, friends, are well-warned. Be on guard lest you lose your footing and get swept off your feet by these lawless and loose-talking teachers. Grow in grace and understanding of our Master and Savior, Jesus Christ.

Glory to the Master, now and forever! Yes!

1, 2, & 3 JOHN

The two most difficult things to get straight in life are love and God. More often than not, the mess people make of their lives can be traced to failure or stupidity or meanness in one or both of these areas.

The basic and biblical Christian conviction is that the two subjects are intricately related. If we want to deal with God the right way, we have to learn to love the right way. If we want to love the right way, we have to deal with God the right way. God and love can't be separated.

John's three letters provide wonderfully explicit direction in how this works. Jesus, the Messiah, is the focus: Jesus provides the full and true understanding of God; Jesus shows us the mature working-out of love. In Jesus, God and love are linked accurately, intricately, and indissolubly.

But there are always people around who don't want to be pinned down to the God Jesus reveals, to the love Jesus reveals. They want to make up their own idea of God, make up their own style of love. John was pastor to a church (or churches) disrupted by some of these people. In his letters we see him reestablishing the original and organic unity of God and love that comes to focus and becomes available to us in Jesus Christ.

1 JOHN

¹⁻² **1** From the very first day, we were there, taking it all in—we heard it with our own ears, saw it with our own eyes, verified it with our own hands. The Word of Life appeared right before our eyes; we saw it happen! And now we're telling you in most sober prose that what we witnessed was, incredibly, this: The infinite Life of God himself took shape before us.

³⁻⁴ We saw it, we heard it, and now we're telling you so you can experience it along with us, this experience of communion with the Father and his Son, Jesus Christ. Our motive for writing is simply this: We want you to enjoy this, too. Your joy will double our joy!

WALK IN THE LIGHT

⁵ This, in essence, is the message we heard from Christ and are passing on to you: God is light, pure light; there's not a trace of darkness in him.

⁶⁻⁷ If we claim that we experience a shared life with him and continue to stumble around in the dark, we're obviously lying through our teeth—we're not *living* what we claim. But if we walk in the light, God himself being the light, we also experience a shared life with one another, as the sacrificed blood of Jesus, God's Son, purges all our sin.

⁸⁻¹⁰ If we claim that we're free of sin, we're only fooling ourselves. A claim like that is errant nonsense. On the other hand, if we admit our sins—make a clean breast of them—he won't let us down; he'll be true to himself. He'll forgive our sins and purge us of all wrongdoing. If we claim that we've never sinned, we out-and-out contradict God—make a liar out of him. A claim like that only shows off our ignorance of God.

¹⁻² **2** I write this, dear children, to guide you out of sin. But if anyone does sin, we have a Priest-Friend in the presence of the Father: Jesus Christ, righteous Jesus. When he served as a sacrifice for our sins, he solved the sin problem for good—not only ours, but the whole world's.

THE ONLY WAY TO KNOW WE'RE IN HIM

²⁻³ Here's how we can be sure that we know God in the right way: Keep his commandments.

⁴⁻⁶ If someone claims, "I know him well!" but doesn't keep his commandments, he's obviously a liar. His life doesn't match his words. But the one who keeps God's word is the person in whom we see God's mature love. This is the only way to be sure we're in God. Anyone who claims to be intimate with God ought to live the same kind of life Jesus lived.

⁷⁻⁸ My dear friends, I'm not writing anything new here. This is the oldest commandment in the book, and you've known it from day one. It's always been implicit in the Message you've heard. On the other hand, perhaps it is new, freshly minted as it is in both Christ and you—the darkness on its way out and the True Light already blazing!

⁹⁻¹¹ Anyone who claims to live in God's light and hates a brother or sister is still in the dark. It's the person who loves brother and sister who dwells in God's light and doesn't block the light from others. But whoever hates is still in the dark, stumbles around in the dark, doesn't know which end is up, blinded by the darkness.

LOVING THE WORLD

12-13   I remind you, my dear children: Your sins are forgiven in Jesus' name. You veterans were in on the ground floor, and know the One who started all this; you newcomers have won a big victory over the Evil One.

13-14   And a second reminder, dear children: You know the Father from personal experience. You veterans know the One who started it all; and you newcomers—such vitality and strength! God's word is so steady in you. Your fellowship with God enables you to gain a victory over the Evil One.

15-17   Don't love the world's ways. Don't love the world's goods. Love of the world squeezes out love for the Father. Practically everything that goes on in the world—wanting your own way, wanting everything for yourself, wanting to appear important—has nothing to do with the Father. It just isolates you from him. The world and all its wanting, wanting, wanting is on the way out—but whoever does what God wants is set for eternity.

ANTICHRISTS EVERYWHERE YOU LOOK

18   Children, time is just about up. You heard that Antichrist is coming. Well, they're all over the place, antichrists everywhere you look. That's how we know that we're close to the end.

19   They left us, but they were never really with us. If they had been, they would have stuck it out with us, loyal to the end. In leaving, they showed their true colors, showed they never did belong.

20-21   But you belong. The Holy One anointed you, and you all know it. I haven't been writing this to tell you something you don't know, but to confirm the truth you do know, and to remind you that the truth doesn't breed lies.

22-23   So who is lying here? It's the person who denies that Jesus is the Divine Christ, that's who. This is what makes an antichrist: denying the Father, denying the Son. No one who denies the Son has any part with the Father, but affirming the Son is an embrace of the Father as well.

24-25   Stay with what you heard from the beginning, the original message. Let it sink into your life. If what you heard from the beginning lives deeply in you, you will live deeply in both Son and Father. This is exactly what Christ promised: eternal life, real life!

26-27   I've written to warn you about those who are trying to deceive you. But they're no match for what is embedded deeply within you—Christ's anointing, no less! You don't need any of their so-called teaching. Christ's anointing teaches you the truth on everything you need to know about yourself and him, uncontaminated by a single lie. Live deeply in what you were taught.

LIVE DEEPLY IN CHRIST

28   And now, children, stay with Christ. Live deeply in Christ. Then we'll be ready for him when he appears, ready to receive him with open arms, with no cause for red-faced guilt or lame excuses when he arrives.

29   Once you're convinced that he is right and righteous, you'll recognize that all who practice righteousness are God's true children.

1   **3** What marvelous love the Father has extended to us! Just look at it—we're called children of God! That's who we really are. But that's also why the world doesn't recognize us or take us seriously, because

it has no idea who he is or what he's up to.

2-3 But friends, that's exactly who we are: children of God. And that's only the beginning. Who knows how we'll end up! What we know is that when Christ is openly revealed, we'll see him — and in seeing him, become like him. All of us who look forward to his Coming stay ready, with the glistening purity of Jesus' life as a model for our own.

4-6 All who indulge in a sinful life are dangerously lawless, for sin is a major disruption of God's order. Surely you know that Christ showed up in order to get rid of sin. There is no sin in him, and sin is not part of his program. No one who lives deeply in Christ makes a practice of sin. None of those who do practice sin have taken a good look at Christ. They've got him all backward.

7-8 So, my dear children, don't let anyone divert you from the truth. It's the person who *acts* right who *is* right, just as we see it lived out in our righteous Messiah. Those who make a practice of sin are straight from the Devil, the pioneer in the practice of sin. The Son of God entered the scene to abolish the Devil's ways.

9-10 People conceived and brought into life by God don't make a practice of sin. How could they? God's seed is deep within them, making them who they are. It's not in the nature of the God-begotten to practice and parade sin. Here's how you tell the difference between God's children and the Devil's children: The one who won't practice righteous ways isn't from God, nor is the one who won't love brother or sister. A simple test.

11 For this is the original message we heard: We should love each other.

12-13 We must not be like Cain, who joined the Evil One and then killed his brother. And why did he kill him? Because he was deep in the practice of evil, while the acts of his brother were righteous. So don't be surprised, friends, when the world hates you. This has been going on a long time.

14-15 The way we know we've been transferred from death to life is that we love our brothers and sisters. Anyone who doesn't love is as good as dead. Anyone who hates a brother or sister is a murderer, and you know very well that eternal life and murder don't go together.

16-17 This is how we've come to understand and experience love: Christ sacrificed his life for us. This is why we ought to live sacrificially for our fellow believers, and not just be out for ourselves. If you see some brother or sister in need and have the means to do something about it but turn a cold shoulder and do nothing, what happens to God's love? It disappears. And you made it disappear.

WHEN WE PRACTICE REAL LOVE

18-20 My dear children, let's not just talk about love; let's practice real love. This is the only way we'll know we're living truly, living in God's reality. It's also the way to shut down debilitating self-criticism, even when there is something to it. For God is greater than our worried hearts and knows more about us than we do ourselves.

21-24 And friends, once that's taken care of and we're no longer accusing or condemning ourselves, we're bold and free before God! We're able to stretch our hands out and receive what we asked for because we're doing what he said, doing what pleases him. Again, this is God's command: to believe in his personally named Son, Jesus Christ. He told us to love each other, in line with the original command. As we keep his commands, we live deeply and surely in him, and he lives in us. And this is how we experience his deep and abiding presence in us: by the Spirit he gave us.

Don't Believe Everything You Hear

1   **4** My dear friends, don't believe everything you hear. Carefully weigh and examine what people tell you. Not everyone who talks about God comes from God. There are a lot of lying preachers loose in the world.

2-3   Here's how you test for the genuine Spirit of God. Everyone who confesses openly his faith in Jesus Christ — the Son of God, who came as an actual flesh-and-blood person — comes from God and belongs to God. And everyone who refuses to confess faith in Jesus has nothing in common with God. This is the spirit of antichrist that you heard was coming. Well, here it is, sooner than we thought!

4-6   My dear children, you come from God and belong to God. You have already won a big victory over those false teachers, for the Spirit in you is far stronger than anything in the world. These people belong to the Christ-denying world. They talk the world's language and the world eats it up. But we come from God and belong to God. Anyone who knows God understands us and listens. The person who has nothing to do with God will, of course, not listen to us. This is another test for telling the Spirit of Truth from the spirit of deception.

God Is Love

7-10   My beloved friends, let us continue to love each other since love comes from God. Everyone who loves is born of God and experiences a relationship with God. The person who refuses to love doesn't know the first thing about God, because God *is* love — so you can't know him if you don't love. This is how God showed his love for us: God sent his only Son into the world so we might live through him. This is the kind of love we are talking about — not that we once upon a time loved God, but that he loved us and sent his Son as a sacrifice to clear away our sins and the damage they've done to our relationship with God.

11-12   My dear, dear friends, if God loved us like this, we certainly ought to love each other. No one has seen God, ever. But if we love one another, God dwells deeply within us, and his love becomes complete in us — perfect love!

13-16   This is how we know we're living steadily and deeply in him, and he in us: He's given us life from his life, from his very own Spirit. Also, we've seen for ourselves and continue to state openly that the Father sent his Son as Savior of the world. Everyone who confesses that Jesus is God's Son participates continuously in an intimate relationship with God. We know it so well, we've embraced it heart and soul, this love that comes from God.

To Love, to Be Loved

17-18   God is love. When we take up permanent residence in a life of love, we live in God and God lives in us. This way, love has the run of the house, becomes at home and mature in us, so that we're free of worry on Judgment Day — our standing in the world is identical with Christ's. There is no room in love for fear. Well-formed love banishes fear. Since fear is crippling, a fearful life — fear of death, fear of judgment — is one not yet fully formed in love.

19   We, though, are going to love — love and be loved. First we were loved, now we love. He loved us first.

20-21   If anyone boasts, "I love God," and goes right on hating his brother or sister, thinking nothing of it, he is a liar. If he won't love the person he can see, how can he love the God he can't see? The command we have from Christ is blunt: Loving God includes loving people. You've got to love both.

1-3   **5** Every person who believes that Jesus is, in fact, the Messiah, is God-begotten. If we love the One who conceives the child, we'll surely love the child who was conceived. The reality test on whether or not we love God's children is this: Do we love God? Do we keep his commands? The proof that we love God comes when we keep his commandments and they are not at all troublesome.

THE POWER THAT BRINGS THE WORLD TO ITS KNEES

4-5   Every God-begotten person conquers the world's ways. The conquering power that brings the world to its knees is our faith. The person who wins out over the world's ways is simply the one who believes Jesus is the Son of God.

6-8   Jesus — the Divine Christ! He experienced a life-giving birth and a death-killing death. Not only birth from the womb, but baptismal birth of his ministry and sacrificial death. And all the while the Spirit is confirming the truth, the reality of God's presence at Jesus' baptism and crucifixion, bringing those occasions alive for us. A triple testimony: the Spirit, the Baptism, the Crucifixion. And the three in perfect agreement.

9-10   If we take human testimony at face value, how much more should we be reassured when God gives testimony as he does here, testifying concerning his Son. Whoever believes in the Son of God inwardly confirms God's testimony. Whoever refuses to believe in effect calls God a liar, refusing to believe God's own testimony regarding his Son.

11-12   This is the testimony in essence: God gave us eternal life; the life is in his Son. So, whoever has the Son, has life; whoever rejects the Son, rejects life.

THE REALITY, NOT THE ILLUSION

13-15   My purpose in writing is simply this: that you who believe in God's Son will know beyond the shadow of a doubt that you have eternal life, the reality and not the illusion. And how bold and free we then become in his presence, freely asking according to his will, sure that he's listening. And if we're confident that he's listening, we know that what we've asked for is as good as ours.

16-17   For instance, if we see a Christian believer sinning (clearly I'm not talking about those who make a practice of sin in a way that is "fatal," leading to eternal death), we ask for God's help and he gladly gives it, gives life to the sinner whose sin is not fatal. There is such a thing as a fatal sin, and I'm not urging you to pray about that. Everything we do wrong is sin, but not all sin is fatal.

18-21   We know that none of the God-begotten makes a practice of sin — fatal sin. The God-begotten are also the God-protected. The Evil One can't lay a hand on them. We know that we are held firm by God; it's only the people of the world who continue in the grip of the Evil One. And we know that the Son of God came so we could recognize and understand the truth of God—what a gift!—and we are living in the Truth itself, in God's Son, Jesus Christ. This Jesus is both True God and Real Life. Dear children, be on guard against all clever facsimiles.

2 JOHN

1-2 My dear congregation, I, your pastor, love you in very truth. And I'm not alone—everyone who knows the Truth that has taken up permanent residence in us loves you.

3 Let grace, mercy, and peace be with us in truth and love from God the Father and from Jesus Christ, Son of the Father!

4-6 I can't tell you how happy I am to learn that many members of your congregation are diligent in living out the Truth, exactly as commanded by the Father. But permit me a reminder, friends, and this is not a new commandment but simply a repetition of our original and basic charter: that we love each other. Love means following his commandments, and his unifying commandment is that you conduct your lives in love. This is the first thing you heard, and nothing has changed.

DON'T WALK OUT ON GOD

7 There are a lot of smooth-talking charlatans loose in the world who refuse to believe that Jesus Christ was truly human, a flesh-and-blood human being. Give them their true title: Deceiver! Antichrist!

8-9 And be very careful around them so you don't lose out on what we've worked so diligently in together; I want you to get every reward you have coming to you. Anyone who gets so progressive in his thinking that he walks out on the teaching of Christ, walks out on God. But whoever stays with the teaching, stays faithful to both the Father and the Son.

10-11 If anyone shows up who doesn't hold to this teaching, don't invite him in and give him the run of the place. That would just give him a platform to perpetuate his evil ways, making you his partner.

12-13 I have a lot more things to tell you, but I'd rather not use paper and ink. I hope to be there soon in person and have a heart-to-heart talk. That will be far more satisfying to both you and me. Everyone here in your sister congregation sends greetings.

3 JOHN

1-4 The Pastor, to my good friend Gaius: How truly I love you! We're the best of friends, and I pray for good fortune in everything you do, and for your good health—that your everyday affairs prosper, as well as your soul! I was most happy when some friends arrived and brought the news that you persist in following the way of Truth. Nothing could make me happier than getting reports that my children continue diligently in the way of Truth!

MODEL THE GOOD

5-8 Dear friend, when you extend hospitality to Christian brothers and sisters, even when they are strangers, you make the faith visible. They've made a full report back to the church here, a message about your love. It's good work you're doing, helping these travelers on their way, hospitality worthy of God himself! They set out under the banner of the Name, and get no help from unbelievers. So they deserve any support we can give them. In providing meals and a bed, we become their companions in spreading the Truth.

9-10 Earlier I wrote something along this line to the church, but Diotrephes, who loves being in charge, denigrates my counsel. If I come, you can be sure I'll hold him to account for spreading vicious rumors about us.

As if that weren't bad enough, he not only refuses hospitality to traveling Christians but tries to stop others from welcoming them. Worse yet, instead of inviting them in he throws them out.

11 Friend, don't go along with evil. Model the good. The person who does good does God's work. The person who does evil falsifies God, doesn't know the first thing about God.

12 Everyone has a good word for Demetrius—the Truth itself stands up for Demetrius! We concur, and you know we don't hand out endorsements lightly.

13-14 I have a lot more things to tell you, but I'd rather not use pen and ink. I hope to be there soon in person and have a heart-to-heart talk.

Peace to you. The friends here say hello. Greet our friends there by name.

JUDE

Our spiritual communities are as susceptible to disease as our physical bodies. But it is easier to detect whatever is wrong in our stomachs and lungs than in our worship and witness. When our physical bodies are sick or damaged, the pain calls our attention to it, and we do something quick. But a dangerous, even deadly, virus in our spiritual communities can go undetected for a long time. As much as we need physicians for our bodies, we have even greater need for diagnosticians and healers of the spirit.

Jude's letter to an early community of Christians is just such diagnosis. It is all the more necessary in that those believers apparently didn't know anything was wrong, or at least not as desperately wrong as Jude points out.

There is far more, of course, to living in Christian community than protecting the faith against assault or subversion. Paranoia is as unhealthy spiritually as it is mentally. The primary Christian posture is, in Jude's words, "keeping your arms open and outstretched, ready for the mercy of our Master, Jesus Christ." All the same, energetic watchfulness is required. Jude's whistle-blowing has prevented many a disaster.

JUDE

1-2   I, Jude, am a slave to Jesus Christ and brother to James, writing to those loved by God the Father, called and kept safe by Jesus Christ. Relax, everything's going to be all right; rest, everything's coming together; open your hearts, love is on the way!

FIGHT WITH ALL YOU HAVE IN YOU

3-4   Dear friends, I've dropped everything to write you about this life of salvation that we have in common. I have to write insisting — begging! — that you fight with everything you have in you for this faith entrusted to us as a gift to guard and cherish. What has happened is that some people have infiltrated our ranks (our Scriptures warned us this would happen), who beneath their pious skin are shameless scoundrels. Their design is to replace the sheer grace of our God with sheer license — which means doing away with Jesus Christ, our one and only Master.

LOST STARS IN OUTER SPACE

5-7   I'm laying this out as clearly as I can, even though you once knew all this well enough and shouldn't need reminding. Here it is in brief: The Master saved a people out of the land of Egypt. Later he destroyed those who defected. And you know the story of the angels who didn't stick to their post, abandoning it for other, darker missions. But they are now chained and jailed in a black hole until the great Judgment Day. Sodom and Gomorrah, which went to sexual rack and ruin along with the surrounding cities that acted just like them, are another example. Burning and burning and never burning up, they serve still as a stock warning.

8   This is exactly the same program of these latest infiltrators: dirty sex, rule and rulers thrown out, glory dragged in the mud.

9-11   The Archangel Michael, who went to the mat with the Devil as they fought over the body of Moses, wouldn't have dared level him with a blasphemous curse, but said simply, "No you don't. *God* will take care of you!" But these people sneer at anything they can't understand, and by doing whatever they feel like doing — living by animal instinct only — they participate in their own destruction. I'm fed up with them! They've gone down Cain's road; they've been sucked into Balaam's error by greed; they're canceled out in Korah's rebellion.

12-13   These people are warts on your love feasts as you worship and eat together. They're giving you a black eye — carousing shamelessly, grabbing anything that isn't nailed down. They're —

> Puffs of smoke pushed by gusts of wind;
>   late autumn trees stripped clean of leaf and fruit,
> Doubly dead, pulled up by the roots;
>   wild ocean waves leaving nothing on the beach
>   but the foam of their shame;
> Lost stars in outer space
>   on their way to the black hole.

14-16　　Enoch, the seventh after Adam, prophesied of them: "Look! The Master comes with thousands of holy angels to bring judgment against them all, convicting each person of every defiling act of shameless sacrilege, of every dirty word they have spewed of their pious filth." These are the "grumpers," the bellyachers, grabbing for the biggest piece of the pie, talking big, saying anything they think will get them ahead.

17-19　　But remember, dear friends, that the apostles of our Master, Jesus Christ, told us this would happen: "In the last days there will be people who don't take these things seriously anymore. They'll treat them like a joke, and make a religion of their own whims and lusts." These are the ones who split churches, thinking only of themselves. There's nothing to them, no sign of the Spirit!

20-21　　But you, dear friends, carefully build yourselves up in this most holy faith by praying in the Holy Spirit, staying right at the center of God's love, keeping your arms open and outstretched, ready for the mercy of our Master, Jesus Christ. This is the unending life, the *real* life!

22-23　　Go easy on those who hesitate in the faith. Go after those who take the wrong way. Be tender with sinners, but not soft on sin. The sin itself stinks to high heaven.

24-25　　And now to him who can keep you on your feet, standing tall in his bright presence, fresh and celebrating — to our one God, our only Savior, through Jesus Christ, our Master, be glory, majesty, strength, and rule before all time, and now, and to the end of all time. Yes.

REVELATION

The Bible ends with a flourish: vision and song, doom and deliverance, terror and triumph. The rush of color and sound, image and energy, leaves us reeling. But if we persist through the initial confusion and read on, we begin to pick up the rhythms, realize the connections, and find ourselves enlisted as participants in a multidimensional act of Christian worship.

John of Patmos, a pastor of the late first century, has worship on his mind, is preeminently concerned with worship. The vision, which is The Revelation, comes to him while he is at worship on a certain Sunday on the Mediterranean island of Patmos. He is responsible for a circuit of churches on the mainland whose primary task is worship. Worship shapes the human community in response to the living God. If worship is neglected or perverted, our communities fall into chaos or under tyranny.

Our times are not propitious for worship. The times never are. The world is hostile to worship. The Devil hates worship. As The Revelation makes clear, worship must be carried out under conditions decidedly uncongenial to it. Some Christians even get killed because they worship.

John's Revelation is not easy reading. Besides being a pastor, John is a poet, fond of metaphor and symbol, image and allusion, passionate in his desire to bring us into the presence of Jesus believing and adoring. But the demands he makes on our intelligence and imagination are well rewarded, for in keeping company with John, our worship of God will almost certainly deepen in urgency and joy.

REVELATION

1-2 **1** A revealing of Jesus, the Messiah. God gave it to make plain to his servants what is about to happen. He published and delivered it by Angel to his servant John. And John told everything he saw: God's Word— the witness of Jesus Christ!

3 How blessed the reader! How blessed the hearers and keepers of these oracle words, all the words written in this book!

Time is just about up.

HIS EYES POURING FIRE-BLAZE

4-7 I, John, am writing this to the seven churches in Asia province: All the best to you from THE GOD WHO IS, THE GOD WHO WAS, AND THE GOD ABOUT TO ARRIVE, and from the Seven Spirits assembled before his throne, and from Jesus Christ—Loyal Witness, Firstborn from the dead, Ruler of all earthly kings.

> Glory and strength to Christ, who loves us,
>   who blood-washed our sins from our lives,
> Who made us a Kingdom, Priests for his Father,
>   forever—and yes, he's on his way!
> Riding the clouds, he'll be seen by every eye,
>   those who mocked and killed him will see him,
> People from all nations and all times
>   will tear their clothes in lament.
>   Oh, Yes.

8 The Master declares, "I'm A to Z. I'm THE GOD WHO IS, THE GOD WHO WAS, AND THE GOD ABOUT TO ARRIVE. I'm the Sovereign-Strong."

9-17 I, John, with you all the way in the trial and the Kingdom and the passion of patience in Jesus, was on the island called Patmos because of God's Word, the witness of Jesus. It was Sunday and I was in the Spirit, praying. I heard a loud voice behind me, trumpet-clear and piercing: "Write what you see into a book. Send it to the seven churches: to Ephesus, Smyrna, Pergamum, Thyatira, Sardis, Philadelphia, Laodicea." I turned and saw the voice.

> I saw a gold menorah
>   with seven branches,
> And in the center, the Son of Man,
>   in a robe and gold breastplate,
>   hair a blizzard of white,
> Eyes pouring fire-blaze,
>   both feet furnace-fired bronze,
> His voice a cataract,
>   right hand holding the Seven Stars,
> His mouth a sharp-biting sword,
>   his face a perigee sun.

I saw this and fainted dead at his feet. His right hand pulled me upright, his voice reassured me:

17-20   "Don't fear: I am First, I am Last, I'm Alive. I died, but I came to life, and my life is now forever. See these keys in my hand? They open and lock Death's doors, they open and lock Hell's gates. Now write down everything you see: things that are, things about to be. The Seven Stars you saw in my right hand and the seven-branched gold menorah—do you want to know what's behind them? The Seven Stars are the Angels of the seven churches; the menorah's seven branches are the seven churches."

To Ephesus

1   **W**rite this to Ephesus, to the Angel of the church. The One with Seven Stars in his right-fist grip, striding through the golden seven-lights' circle, speaks:

2-3   "I see what you've done, your hard, hard work, your refusal to quit. I know you can't stomach evil, that you weed out apostolic pretenders. I know your persistence, your courage in my cause, that you never wear out.

4-5   "But you walked away from your first love—why? What's going on with you, anyway? Do you have any idea how far you've fallen? A Lucifer fall!

"Turn back! Recover your dear early love. No time to waste, for I'm well on my way to removing your light from the golden circle.

6   "You do have this to your credit: You hate the Nicolaitan business. I hate it, too.

7   "Are your ears awake? Listen. Listen to the Wind Words, the Spirit blowing through the churches. I'm about to call each conqueror to dinner. I'm spreading a banquet of Tree-of-Life fruit, a supper plucked from God's orchard."

To Smyrna

8   **W**rite this to Smyrna, to the Angel of the church. The Beginning and Ending, the First and Final One, the Once Dead and Then Come Alive, speaks:

9   "I can see your pain and poverty—constant pain, dire poverty—but I also see your wealth. And I hear the lie in the claims of those who pretend to be good Jews, who in fact belong to Satan's crowd.

10   "Fear nothing in the things you're about to suffer—but stay on guard! Fear nothing! The Devil is about to throw you in jail for a time of testing—ten days. It won't last forever.

"Don't quit, even if it costs you your life. Stay there believing. I have a Life-Crown sized and ready for you.

11   "Are your ears awake? Listen. Listen to the Wind Words, the Spirit blowing through the churches. Christ-conquerors are safe from Devil-death."

To Pergamum

12   **W**rite this to Pergamum, to the Angel of the church. The One with the sharp-biting sword draws from the sheath of his mouth—out come the sword words:

13   "I see where you live, right under the shadow of Satan's throne. But you continue boldly in my Name; you never once denied my Name, even when

the pressure was worst, when they martyred Antipas, my witness who stayed faithful to me on Satan's turf.

14-15 "But why do you indulge that Balaam crowd? Don't you remember that Balaam was an enemy agent, seducing Balak and sabotaging Israel's holy pilgrimage by throwing unholy parties? And why do you put up with the Nicolaitans, who do the same thing?

16 "Enough! Don't give in to them; I'll be with you soon. I'm fed up and about to cut them to pieces with my sword-sharp words.

17 "Are your ears awake? Listen. Listen to the Wind Words, the Spirit blowing through the churches. I'll give the sacred manna to every conqueror; I'll also give a clear, smooth stone inscribed with your new name, your secret new name."

To Thyatira

18 Write this to Thyatira, to the Angel of the church. God's Son, eyes pouring fire-blaze, standing on feet of furnace-fired bronze, says this:

19 "I see everything you're doing for me. Impressive! The love and the faith, the service and persistence. Yes, very impressive! You get better at it every day.

20-23 "But why do you let that Jezebel who calls herself a prophet mislead my dear servants into Cross-denying, self-indulging religion? I gave her a chance to change her ways, but she has no intention of giving up a career in the god-business. I'm about to lay her low, along with her partners, as they play their sex-and-religion games. The bastard offspring of their idol-whoring I'll kill. Then every church will know that appearances don't impress me. I x-ray every motive and make sure you get what's coming to you.

24-25 "The rest of you Thyatirans, who have nothing to do with this outrage, who scorn this playing around with the Devil that gets paraded as profundity, be assured I'll not make life any harder for you than it already is. Hold on to the truth you have until I get there.

26-28 "Here's the reward I have for every conqueror, everyone who keeps at it, refusing to give up: You'll rule the nations, your Shepherd-King rule as firm as an iron staff, their resistance fragile as clay pots. This was the gift my Father gave me; I pass it along to you—and with it, the Morning Star!

29 "Are your ears awake? Listen. Listen to the Wind Words, the Spirit blowing through the churches."

To Sardis

1 **3** Write this to Sardis, to the Angel of the church. The One holding the Seven Spirits of God in one hand, a firm grip on the Seven Stars with the other, speaks:

"I see right through your work. You have a reputation for vigor and zest, but you're dead, stone-dead.

2-3 "Up on your feet! Take a deep breath! Maybe there's life in you yet. But I wouldn't know it by looking at your busywork; nothing of *God's* work has been completed. Your condition is desperate. Think of the gift you once had in your hands, the Message you heard with your ears—grasp it again and turn back to God.

"If you pull the covers back over your head and sleep on, oblivious to God, I'll return when you least expect it, break into your life like a thief in the night.

4 "You still have a few followers of Jesus in Sardis who haven't ruined themselves wallowing in the muck of the world's ways. They'll walk with me on parade! They've proved their worth!

5 "Conquerors will march in the victory parade, their names indelible in the Book of Life. I'll lead them up and present them by name to my Father and his Angels.

6 "Are your ears awake? Listen. Listen to the Wind Words, the Spirit blowing through the churches."

TO PHILADELPHIA

7 Write this to Philadelphia, to the Angel of the church. The Holy, the True — David's key in his hand, opening doors no one can lock, locking doors no one can open — speaks:

8 "I see what you've done. Now see what *I've* done. I've opened a door before you that no one can slam shut. You don't have much strength, I know that; you used what you had to keep my Word. You didn't deny me when times were rough.

9 "And watch as I take those who call themselves true believers but are nothing of the kind, pretenders whose true membership is in the club of Satan — watch as I strip off their pretensions and they're forced to acknowledge it's you that I've loved.

10 "Because you kept my Word in passionate patience, I'll keep you safe in the time of testing that will be here soon, and all over the earth, every man, woman, and child put to the test.

11 "I'm on my way; I'll be there soon. Keep a tight grip on what you have so no one distracts you and steals your crown.

12 "I'll make each conqueror a pillar in the sanctuary of my God, a permanent position of honor. Then I'll write names on you, the pillars: the Name of my God, the Name of God's City — the new Jerusalem coming down out of Heaven — and my new Name.

13 "Are your ears awake? Listen. Listen to the Wind Words, the Spirit blowing through the churches."

TO LAODICEA

14 Write to Laodicea, to the Angel of the church. God's Yes, the Faithful and Accurate Witness, the First of God's creation, says:

15-17 "I know you inside and out, and find little to my liking. You're not cold, you're not hot — far better to be either cold or hot! You're stale. You're stagnant. You make me want to vomit. You brag, 'I'm rich, I've got it made, I need nothing from anyone,' oblivious that in fact you're a pitiful, blind beggar, threadbare and homeless.

18 "Here's what I want you to do: Buy your gold from me, gold that's been through the refiner's fire. Then you'll be rich. Buy your clothes from me, clothes designed in Heaven. You've gone around half-naked long enough. And buy medicine for your eyes from me so you can see, *really* see.

19 "The people I love, I call to account — prod and correct and guide so that they'll live at their best. Up on your feet, then! About face! Run after God!

20-21 "Look at me. I stand at the door. I knock. If you hear me call and open the door, I'll come right in and sit down to supper with you. Conquerors will sit alongside me at the head table, just as I, having conquered, took the place of honor at the side of my Father. That's my gift to the conquerors!

22 "Are your ears awake? Listen. Listen to the Wind Words, the Spirit blowing through the churches."

A Door into Heaven

1 **4** Then I looked, and, oh!—a door open into Heaven. The trumpet-voice, the first voice in my vision, called out, "Ascend and enter. I'll show you what happens next."

2-6 I was caught up at once in deep worship and, oh!—a Throne set in Heaven with One Seated on the Throne, suffused in gem hues of amber and flame with a nimbus of emerald. Twenty-four thrones circled the Throne, with Twenty-four Elders seated, white-robed, gold-crowned. Lightning flash and thunder crash pulsed from the Throne. Seven fire-blazing torches fronted the Throne (these are the Sevenfold Spirit of God). Before the Throne it was like a clear crystal sea.

6-8 Prowling around the Throne were Four Animals, all eyes. Eyes to look ahead, eyes to look behind. The first Animal like a lion, the second like an ox, the third with a human face, the fourth like an eagle in flight. The Four Animals were winged, each with six wings. They were all eyes, seeing around and within. And they chanted night and day, never taking a break:

> Holy, holy, holy
> Is God our Master, Sovereign-Strong,
> THE WAS, THE IS, THE COMING.

9-11 Every time the Animals gave glory and honor and thanks to the One Seated on the Throne—the age-after-age Living One—the Twenty-four Elders would fall prostrate before the One Seated on the Throne. They worshiped the age-after-age Living One. They threw their crowns at the foot of the Throne, chanting,

> Worthy, O Master! Yes, our God!
> Take the glory! the honor! the power!
> You created it all;
> It was created because you wanted it.

The Lion Is a Lamb

1-2 **5** I saw a scroll in the right hand of the One Seated on the Throne. It was written on both sides, fastened with seven seals. I also saw a powerful Angel, calling out in a voice like thunder, "Is there anyone who can open the scroll, who can break its seals?"

3 There was no one—no one in Heaven, no one on earth, no one from the underworld—able to break open the scroll and read it.

4-5 I wept and wept and wept that no one was found able to open the scroll, able to read it. One of the Elders said, "Don't weep. Look—the Lion from Tribe Judah, the Root of David's Tree, has conquered. He can open the scroll, can rip through the seven seals."

6-10 So I looked, and there, surrounded by Throne, Animals, and Elders, was a Lamb, slaughtered but standing tall. Seven horns he had, and seven eyes, the Seven Spirits of God sent into all the earth. He came to the One Seated on the Throne and took the scroll from his right hand. The moment he took the scroll, the Four Animals and Twenty-four Elders fell down and worshiped the Lamb. Each had a harp and each had a bowl, a gold bowl filled with incense, the prayers of God's holy people. And they sang a new song:

> Worthy! Take the scroll, open its seals.
> Slain! Paying in blood, you bought men and women,
> Bought them back from all over the earth,
> Bought them back for God.
> Then you made them a Kingdom, Priests for our God,
> Priest-kings to rule over the earth.

11-14   I looked again. I heard a company of Angels around the Throne, the Animals, and the Elders — ten thousand times ten thousand their number, thousand after thousand after thousand in full song:

> The slain Lamb is worthy!
> Take the power, the wealth, the wisdom, the strength!
> Take the honor, the glory, the blessing!

Then I heard every creature in Heaven and earth, in underworld and sea, join in, all voices in all places, singing:

> To the One on the Throne! To the Lamb!
> The blessing, the honor, the glory, the strength,
> For age after age after age.

The Four Animals called out, "Oh, Yes!" The Elders fell to their knees and worshiped.

UNSEALING THE SCROLL

1-2   **6** I watched while the Lamb ripped off the first of the seven seals. I heard one of the Animals roar, "Come out!" I looked — I saw a white horse. Its rider carried a bow and was given a victory garland. He rode off victorious, conquering right and left.

3-4   When the Lamb ripped off the second seal, I heard the second Animal cry, "Come out!" Another horse appeared, this one red. Its rider was off to take peace from the earth, setting people at each other's throats, killing one another. He was given a huge sword.

5-6   When he ripped off the third seal, I heard the third Animal cry, "Come out!" I looked. A black horse this time. Its rider carried a set of scales in his hand. I heard a message (it seemed to issue from the Four Animals): "A quart of wheat for a day's wages, or three quarts of barley, but all the oil and wine you want."

7-8   When he ripped off the fourth seal, I heard the fourth Animal cry, "Come out!" I looked. A colorless horse, sickly pale. Its rider was Death, and Hell was close on its heels. They were given power to destroy a fourth of the earth by war, famine, disease, and wild beasts.

9-11   When he ripped off the fifth seal, I saw the souls of those killed because they had held firm in their witness to the Word of God. They were gathered under the Altar, and cried out in loud prayers, "How long, Strong

God, Holy and True? How long before you step in and avenge our murders?" Then each martyr was given a white robe and told to sit back and wait until the full number of martyrs was filled from among their servant companions and friends in the faith.

12-17   I watched while he ripped off the sixth seal: a bone-jarring earthquake, sun turned black as ink, moon all bloody, stars falling out of the sky like figs shaken from a tree in a high wind, sky snapped shut like a book, islands and mountains sliding this way and that. And then pandemonium, everyone and his dog running for cover — kings, princes, generals, rich and strong, along with every commoner, slave or free. They hid in mountain caves and rocky dens, calling out to mountains and rocks, "Refuge! Hide us from the One Seated on the Throne and the wrath of the Lamb! The great Day of their wrath has come — who can stand it?"

THE SERVANTS OF GOD

1   7 Immediately I saw Four Angels standing at the four corners of earth, standing steady with a firm grip on the four winds so no wind would blow on earth or sea, not even rustle a tree.

2-3   Then I saw another Angel rising from where the sun rose, carrying the seal of the Living God. He thundered to the Four Angels assigned the task of hurting earth and sea, "Don't hurt the earth! Don't hurt the sea! Don't so much as hurt a tree until I've sealed the servants of our God on their foreheads!"

4-8   I heard the count of those who were sealed: 144,000! They were sealed out of every Tribe of Israel: 12,000 sealed from Judah, 12,000 from Reuben, 12,000 from Gad, 12,000 from Asher, 12,000 from Naphtali, 12,000 from Manasseh, 12,000 from Simeon, 12,000 from Levi, 12,000 from Issachar, 12,000 from Zebulun, 12,000 from Joseph, 12,000 sealed from Benjamin.

9-12   I looked again. I saw a huge crowd, too huge to count. Everyone was there — all nations and tribes, all races and languages. And they were *standing*, dressed in white robes and waving palm branches, standing before the Throne and the Lamb and heartily singing:

> Salvation to our God on his Throne!
> Salvation to the Lamb!

All who were standing around the Throne — Angels, Elders, Animals — fell on their faces before the Throne and worshiped God, singing:

> Oh, Yes!
> The blessing and glory and wisdom and thanksgiving,
> The honor and power and strength,
> To our God forever and ever and ever!
> Oh, Yes!

13-14   Just then one of the Elders addressed me: "Who are these dressed in white robes, and where did they come from?" Taken aback, I said, "O Sir, I have no idea — but you must know."

14-17   Then he told me, "These are those who come from the great tribulation, and they've washed their robes, scrubbed them clean in the blood of the Lamb. That's why they're standing before God's Throne. They serve him day and night in his Temple. The One on the Throne will pitch his tent there for them: no more hunger, no more thirst, no more scorching heat. The Lamb on the Throne will shepherd them, will lead them to spring waters of Life. And God will wipe every last tear from their eyes."

1   When the Lamb ripped off the seventh seal, Heaven fell quiet — complete silence for about half an hour.

BLOWING THE TRUMPETS

2-4   I saw the Seven Angels who are always in readiness before God handed seven trumpets. Then another Angel, carrying a gold censer, came and stood at the Altar. He was given a great quantity of incense so that he could offer up the prayers of all the holy people of God on the Golden Altar before the Throne. Smoke billowed up from the incense-laced prayers of the holy ones, rose before God from the hand of the Angel.

5   Then the Angel filled the censer with fire from the Altar and heaved it to earth. It set off thunders, voices, lightnings, and an earthquake.

6-7   The Seven Angels with the trumpets got ready to blow them. At the first trumpet blast, hail and fire mixed with blood were dumped on earth. A third of the earth was scorched, a third of the trees, and every blade of green grass — burned to a crisp.

8-9   The second Angel trumpeted. Something like a huge mountain blazing with fire was flung into the sea. A third of the sea turned to blood, a third of the living sea creatures died, and a third of the ships sank.

10-11   The third Angel trumpeted. A huge Star, blazing like a torch, fell from Heaven, wiping out a third of the rivers and a third of the springs. The Star's name was Wormwood. A third of the water turned bitter, and many people died from the poisoned water.

12   The fourth Angel trumpeted. A third of the sun, a third of the moon, and a third of the stars were hit, blacked out by a third, both day and night in one-third blackout.

13   I looked hard; I heard a lone eagle, flying through Middle-Heaven, crying out ominously, "Doom! Doom! Doom to everyone left on earth! There are three more Angels about to blow their trumpets. Doom is on its way!"

1-2   The fifth Angel trumpeted. I saw a Star plummet from Heaven to earth. The Star was handed a key to the Well of the Abyss. He unlocked the Well of the Abyss — smoke poured out of the Well, billows and billows of smoke, sun and air in blackout from smoke pouring out of the Well.

3-6   Then out of the smoke crawled locusts with the venom of scorpions. They were given their orders: "Don't hurt the grass, don't hurt anything green, don't hurt a single tree — only men and women, and then only those who lack the seal of God on their foreheads." They were ordered to torture but not kill, torture them for five months, the pain like a scorpion sting. When this happens, people are going to prefer death to torture, look for ways to kill themselves. But they won't find a way — death will have gone into hiding.

7-11   The locusts looked like horses ready for war. They had gold crowns, human faces, women's hair, the teeth of lions, and iron breastplates. The sound of their wings was the sound of horse-drawn chariots charging into battle. Their tails were equipped with stings, like scorpion tails. With those tails they were ordered to torture the human race for five months. They had a king over them, the Angel of the Abyss. His name in Hebrew is *Abaddon*, in Greek, *Apollyon* — "Destroyer."

12   The first doom is past. Two dooms yet to come.

13-14   The sixth Angel trumpeted. I heard a voice speaking to the sixth Angel from the horns of the Golden Altar before God: "Let the Four Angels loose, the Angels confined at the great River Euphrates."

15-19   The Four Angels were untied and let loose, Four Angels all prepared for the exact year, month, day, and even hour when they were to kill a third of the human race. The number of the army of horsemen was twice ten thousand times ten thousand. I heard the count and saw both horses and riders in my vision: fiery breastplates on the riders, lion heads on the horses breathing out fire and smoke and brimstone. With these three weapons — fire and smoke and brimstone — they killed a third of the human race. The horses killed with their mouths and tails; their serpentlike tails also had heads that wreaked havoc.

20-21   The remaining men and women who weren't killed by these weapons went on their merry way — didn't change their way of life, didn't quit worshiping demons, didn't quit centering their lives around lumps of gold and silver and brass, hunks of stone and wood that couldn't see or hear or move. There wasn't a sign of a change of heart. They plunged right on in their murderous, occult, promiscuous, and thieving ways.

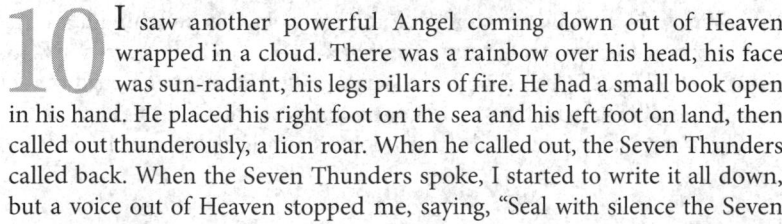

1-4   **10** I saw another powerful Angel coming down out of Heaven wrapped in a cloud. There was a rainbow over his head, his face was sun-radiant, his legs pillars of fire. He had a small book open in his hand. He placed his right foot on the sea and his left foot on land, then called out thunderously, a lion roar. When he called out, the Seven Thunders called back. When the Seven Thunders spoke, I started to write it all down, but a voice out of Heaven stopped me, saying, "Seal with silence the Seven Thunders; don't write a word."

5-7   Then the Angel I saw astride sea and land lifted his right hand to Heaven and swore by the One Living Forever and Ever, who created Heaven and everything in it, earth and everything in it, sea and everything in it, that time was up — that when the seventh Angel blew his trumpet, which he was about to do, the Mystery of God, all the plans he had revealed to his servants, the prophets, would be completed.

8-11   The voice out of Heaven spoke to me again: "Go, take the book held open in the hand of the Angel astride sea and earth." I went up to the Angel and said, "Give me the little book." He said, "Take it, then eat it. It will taste sweet like honey, but turn sour in your stomach." I took the little book from the Angel's hand and it was sweet honey in my mouth, but when I swallowed, my stomach curdled. Then I was told, "You must go back and prophesy again over many peoples and nations and languages and kings."

THE TWO WITNESSES

1-2 **11** I was given a stick for a measuring rod and told, "Get up and measure God's Temple and Altar and everyone worshiping in it. Exclude the outside court; don't measure it. It's been handed over to non-Jewish outsiders. They'll desecrate the Holy City for forty-two months.

3-6 "Meanwhile, I'll provide my two Witnesses. Dressed in sackcloth, they'll prophesy for 1,260 days. These are the two Olive Trees, the two Lampstands, standing at attention before God on earth. If anyone tries to hurt them, a blast of fire from their mouths will incinerate them — burn them to a crisp just like that. They'll have power to seal the sky so that it doesn't rain for the time of their prophesying, power to turn rivers and springs to blood, power to hit earth with any and every disaster as often as they want.

7-10 "When they've completed their witness, the Beast from the Abyss will emerge and fight them, conquer and kill them, leaving their corpses exposed on the street of the Great City spiritually called Sodom and Egypt, the same City where their Master was crucified. For three and a half days they'll be there — exposed, prevented from getting a decent burial, stared at by the curious from all over the world. Those people will cheer at the spectacle, shouting 'Good riddance!' and calling for a celebration, for these two prophets pricked the conscience of all the people on earth, made it impossible for them to enjoy their sins.

11 "Then, after three and a half days, the Living Spirit of God will enter them — they're on their feet! — and all those gloating spectators will be scared to death."

12-13 I heard a strong voice out of Heaven calling, "Come up here!" and up they went to Heaven, wrapped in a cloud, their enemies watching it all. At that moment there was a gigantic earthquake — a tenth of the city fell to ruin, seven thousand perished in the earthquake, the rest frightened to the core of their being, frightened into giving honor to the God-of-Heaven.

14 The second doom is past, the third doom coming right on its heels.

THE LAST TRUMPET SOUNDS

15-18 The seventh Angel trumpeted. A crescendo of voices in Heaven sang out,

> The kingdom of the world is now
>   the Kingdom of our God and his Messiah!
> He will rule forever and ever!

The Twenty-four Elders seated before God on their thrones fell to their knees, worshiped, and sang,

> We thank you, O God, Sovereign-Strong,
>   WHO IS AND WHO WAS.
> You took your great power
>   and took over — reigned!
> The angry nations now
>   get a taste of *your* anger.

The time has come to judge the dead,
  to reward your servants, all prophets and saints,
Reward small and great who fear your Name,
  and destroy the destroyers of earth.

19 The doors of God's Temple in Heaven flew open, and the Ark of his Covenant was clearly seen surrounded by flashes of lightning, loud shouts, peals of thunder, an earthquake, and a fierce hailstorm.

THE WOMAN, HER SON, AND THE DRAGON

1-2 **12** A great Sign appeared in Heaven: a Woman dressed all in sunlight, standing on the moon, and crowned with Twelve Stars. She was giving birth to a Child and cried out in the pain of childbirth.

3-4 And then another Sign alongside the first: a huge and fiery Dragon! It had seven heads and ten horns, a crown on each of the seven heads. With one flick of its tail it knocked a third of the Stars from the sky and dumped them on earth. The Dragon crouched before the Woman in childbirth, poised to eat up the Child when it came.

5-6 The Woman gave birth to a Son who will shepherd all nations with an iron rod. Her Son was seized and placed safely before God on his Throne. The Woman herself escaped to the desert to a place of safety prepared by God, all comforts provided her for 1,260 days.

7-12 War broke out in Heaven. Michael and his Angels fought the Dragon. The Dragon and his Angels fought back, but were no match for Michael. They were cleared out of Heaven, not a sign of them left. The great Dragon — ancient Serpent, the one called Devil and Satan, the one who led the whole earth astray — thrown out, and all his Angels thrown out with him, thrown down to earth. Then I heard a strong voice out of Heaven saying,

Salvation and power are established!
  Kingdom of our God, authority of his Messiah!
The Accuser of our brothers and sisters thrown out,
  who accused them day and night before God.
They defeated him through the blood of the Lamb
  and the bold word of their witness.
They weren't in love with themselves;
  they were willing to die for Christ.
So rejoice, O Heavens, and all who live there,
  but doom to earth and sea,
For the Devil's come down on you with both feet;
  he's had a great fall;
He's wild and raging with anger;
  he hasn't much time and he knows it.

13-17 When the Dragon saw he'd been thrown to earth, he went after the Woman who had given birth to the Man-Child. The Woman was given wings of a great eagle to fly to a place in the desert to be kept in safety and comfort for a time and times and half a time, safe and sound from the Serpent. The Serpent vomited a river of water to swamp and drown her, but earth came to her help, swallowing the water the Dragon spewed from its mouth. Helpless with rage, the Dragon raged at the Woman, then went off to make war with the rest of her children, the children who keep God's commands and hold firm to the witness of Jesus.

THE BEAST FROM THE SEA

1-2
13 And the Dragon stood on the shore of the sea. I saw a Beast rising from the sea. It had ten horns and seven heads — on each horn a crown, and each head inscribed with a blasphemous name. The Beast I saw looked like a leopard with bear paws and a lion's mouth. The Dragon turned over its power to it, its throne and great authority.

3-4
One of the Beast's heads looked as if it had been struck a deathblow, and then healed. The whole earth was agog, gaping at the Beast. They worshiped the Dragon who gave the Beast authority, and they worshiped the Beast, exclaiming, "There's never been anything like the Beast! No one would dare go to war with the Beast!"

5-8
The Beast had a loud mouth, boastful and blasphemous. It could do anything it wanted for forty-two months. It yelled blasphemies against God, blasphemed his Name, blasphemed his Church, especially those already dwelling with God in Heaven. It was permitted to make war on God's holy people and conquer them. It held absolute sway over all tribes and peoples, tongues and races. Everyone on earth whose name was not written from the world's foundation in the slaughtered Lamb's Book of Life will worship the Beast.

9-10
Are you listening to this? They've made their bed; now they must lie in it. Anyone marked for prison goes straight to prison; anyone pulling a sword goes down by the sword. Meanwhile, God's holy people passionately and faithfully stand their ground.

THE BEAST FROM UNDER THE GROUND

11-12
I saw another Beast rising out of the ground. It had two horns like a lamb but sounded like a dragon when it spoke. It was a puppet of the first Beast, made earth and everyone in it worship the first Beast, which had been healed of its deathblow.

13-17
This second Beast worked magical signs, dazzling people by making fire come down from Heaven. It used the magic it got from the Beast to dupe earth dwellers, getting them to make an image of the Beast that received the deathblow and lived. It was able to animate the image of the Beast so that it talked, and then arrange that anyone not worshiping the Beast would be killed. It forced all people, small and great, rich and poor, free and slave, to have a mark on the right hand or forehead. Without the mark of the name of the Beast or the number of its name, it was impossible to buy or sell anything.

18
Solve a riddle: Put your heads together and figure out the meaning of the number of the Beast. It's a human number: 666.

A PERFECT OFFERING

1-2
14 I saw — it took my breath away! — the Lamb standing on Mount Zion, 144,000 standing there with him, his Name and the Name of his Father inscribed on their foreheads. And I heard a voice out of Heaven, the sound like a cataract, like the crash of thunder.

2-5   And then I heard music, harp music and the harpists singing a new song before the Throne and the Four Animals and the Elders. Only the 144,000 could learn to sing the song. They were bought from earth, lived without compromise, virgin-fresh before God. Wherever the Lamb went, they followed. They were bought from humankind, firstfruits of the harvest for God and the Lamb. Not a false word in their mouths. A perfect offering.

VOICES FROM HEAVEN

6-7   I saw another Angel soaring in Middle-Heaven. He had an Eternal Message to preach to all who were still on earth, every nation and tribe, every tongue and people. He preached in a loud voice, "Fear God and give him glory! His hour of judgment has come! Worship the Maker of Heaven and earth, salt sea and fresh water!"

8   A second Angel followed, calling out, "Ruined, ruined, Great Babylon ruined! She made all the nations drunk on the wine of her whoring!"

9-11   A third Angel followed, shouting, warning, "If anyone worships the Beast and its image and takes the mark on forehead or hand, that person will drink the wine of God's wrath, prepared unmixed in his chalice of anger, and suffer torment from fire and brimstone in the presence of Holy Angels, in the presence of the Lamb. Smoke from their torment will rise age after age. No respite for those who worship the Beast and its image, who take the mark of its name."

12   Meanwhile, the saints stand passionately patient, keeping God's commands, staying faithful to Jesus.

13   I heard a voice out of Heaven, "Write this: Blessed are those who die in the Master from now on; how blessed to die that way!"

    "Yes," says the Spirit, "and blessed rest from their hard, hard work. None of what they've done is wasted; God blesses them for it all in the end."

HARVEST TIME

14-16   I looked up, I caught my breath!—a white cloud and one like the Son of Man sitting on it. He wore a gold crown and held a sharp sickle. Another Angel came out of the Temple, shouting to the Cloud-Enthroned, "Swing your sickle and reap. It's harvest time. Earth's harvest is ripe for reaping." The Cloud-Enthroned gave a mighty sweep of his sickle, began harvesting earth in a stroke.

17-18   Then another Angel came out of the Temple in Heaven. He also had a sharp sickle. Yet another Angel, the one in charge of tending the fire, came from the Altar. He thundered to the Angel who held the sharp sickle, "Swing your sharp sickle. Harvest earth's vineyard. The grapes are bursting with ripeness."

19-20   The Angel swung his sickle, harvested earth's vintage, and heaved it into the winepress, the giant winepress of God's wrath. The winepress was outside the City. As the vintage was trodden, blood poured from the winepress as high as a horse's bridle, a river of blood for two hundred miles.

THE SONG OF MOSES, THE SONG OF THE LAMB

1   **15** I saw another Sign in Heaven, huge and breathtaking: seven Angels with seven disasters. These are the final disasters, the wrap-up of God's wrath.

2-4 I saw something like a sea made of glass, the glass all shot through with fire. Carrying harps of God, triumphant over the Beast, its image, and the number of its name, the saved ones stood on the sea of glass. They sang the Song of Moses, servant of God; they sang the Song of the Lamb:

> Mighty your acts and marvelous,
>> O God, the Sovereign-Strong!
> Righteous your ways and true,
>> King of the nations!
> Who can fail to fear you, God,
>> give glory to your Name?
> Because you and you only are holy,
>> all nations will come and worship you,
>> because they see your judgments are right.

5-8 Then I saw the doors of the Temple, the Tent of Witness in Heaven, open wide. The Seven Angels carrying the seven disasters came out of the Temple. They were dressed in clean, bright linen and wore gold vests. One of the Four Animals handed the Seven Angels seven gold bowls, brimming with the wrath of God, who lives forever and ever. Smoke from God's glory and power poured out of the Temple. No one was permitted to enter the Temple until the seven disasters of the Seven Angels were finished.

POURING OUT THE SEVEN DISASTERS

1 **16** I heard a shout of command from the Temple to the Seven Angels: "Begin! Pour out the seven bowls of God's wrath on earth!"

2 The first Angel stepped up and poured his bowl out on earth: Loathsome, stinking sores erupted on all who had taken the mark of the Beast and worshiped its image.

3 The second Angel poured his bowl on the sea: The sea coagulated into blood, and everything in it died.

4-7 The third Angel poured his bowl on rivers and springs: The waters turned to blood. I heard the Angel of Waters say,

> Righteous you are, and your judgments are righteous,
>> THE IS, THE WAS, THE HOLY.
> They poured out the blood of saints and prophets
>> so you've given them blood to drink—
>> they've gotten what they deserve!

Just then I heard the Altar chime in,

> Yes, O God, the Sovereign-Strong!
> Your judgments are true and just!

8-9 The fourth Angel poured his bowl on the sun: Fire blazed from the sun and scorched men and women. Burned and blistered, they cursed God's Name, the God behind these disasters. They refused to repent, refused to honor God.

10-11 The fifth Angel poured his bowl on the throne of the Beast: Its kingdom fell into sudden eclipse. Mad with pain, men and women bit and chewed their tongues, cursed the God-of-Heaven for their torment and sores, and refused to repent and change their ways.

12-14   The sixth Angel poured his bowl on the great Euphrates River: It dried up to nothing. The dry riverbed became a fine roadbed for the kings from the East. From the mouths of the Dragon, the Beast, and the False Prophet I saw three foul demons crawl out — they looked like frogs. These are demon spirits performing signs. They're after the kings of the whole world to get them gathered for battle on the Great Day of God, the Sovereign-Strong.

15   "Keep watch! I come unannounced, like a thief. You're blessed if, awake and dressed, you're ready for me. Too bad if you're found running through the streets, naked and ashamed."

16   The frog-demons gathered the kings together at the place called in Hebrew *Armageddon*.

17-21   The seventh Angel poured his bowl into the air: From the Throne in the Temple came a shout, "Done!" followed by lightning flashes and shouts, thunder crashes and a colossal earthquake — a huge and devastating earthquake, never an earthquake like it since time began. The Great City split three ways, the cities of the nations toppled to ruin. Great Babylon had to drink the wine of God's raging anger — God remembered to give her the cup! Every island fled and not a mountain was to be found. Hailstones weighing a ton plummeted, crushing and smashing men and women as they cursed God for the hail, the epic disaster of hail.

GREAT BABYLON, MOTHER OF WHORES

1-2   **17** One of the Seven Angels who carried the seven bowls came and invited me, "Come, I'll show you the judgment of the great Whore who sits enthroned over many waters, the Whore with whom the kings of the earth have gone whoring, show you the judgment on earth dwellers drunk on her whorish lust."

3-6   In the Spirit he carried me out in the desert. I saw a woman mounted on a Scarlet Beast. Stuffed with blasphemies, the Beast had seven heads and ten horns. The woman was dressed in purple and scarlet, festooned with gold and gems and pearls. She held a gold chalice in her hand, brimming with defiling obscenities, her foul fornications. A riddle-name was branded on her forehead: GREAT BABYLON, MOTHER OF WHORES AND ABOMINATIONS OF THE EARTH. I could see that the woman was drunk, drunk on the blood of God's holy people, drunk on the blood of the martyrs of Jesus.

6-8   Astonished, I rubbed my eyes. I shook my head in wonder. The Angel said, "Does this surprise you? Let me tell you the riddle of the woman and the Beast she rides, the Beast with seven heads and ten horns. The Beast you saw once was, is no longer, and is about to ascend from the Abyss and head straight for Hell. Earth dwellers whose names weren't written in the Book of Life from the foundation of the world will be dazzled when they see the Beast that once was, is no longer, and is to come.

9-11   "But don't drop your guard. Use your head. The seven heads are seven hills; they are where the woman sits. They are also seven kings: five dead, one living, the other not yet here — and when he does come his time will be brief. The Beast that once was and is no longer is both an eighth and one of the seven — and headed for Hell.

12-14   "The ten horns you saw are ten kings, but they're not yet in power. They will come to power with the Scarlet Beast, but won't last long—a *very* brief reign. These kings will agree to turn over their power and authority to the Beast. They will go to war against the Lamb but the Lamb will defeat them, proof that he is Lord over all lords, King over all kings, and those with him will be the called, chosen, and faithful."

15-18 The Angel continued, "The waters you saw on which the Whore was enthroned are peoples and crowds, nations and languages. And the ten horns you saw, together with the Beast, will turn on the Whore—they'll hate her, violate her, strip her naked, rip her apart with their teeth, then set fire to her. It was God who put the idea in their heads to turn over their rule to the Beast until the words of God are completed. The woman you saw is the great city, tyrannizing the kings of the earth."

Doom to the City of Darkness

1-8 **18** Following this I saw another Angel descend from Heaven. His authority was immense, his glory flooded earth with brightness, his voice thunderous:
Ruined, ruined, Great Babylon, ruined!
    A ghost town for demons is all that's left!
A garrison of carrion spirits,
    garrison of loathsome, carrion birds.
All nations drank the wild wine of her whoring;
    kings of the earth went whoring with her;
    entrepreneurs made millions exploiting her.

Just then I heard another shout out of Heaven:

Get out, my people, as fast as you can,
    so you don't get mixed up in her sins,
    so you don't get caught in her doom.
Her sins stink to high Heaven;
    God has remembered every evil she's done.
Give her back what she's given,
    double what she's doubled in her works,
    double the recipe in the cup she mixed;
Bring her flaunting and wild ways
    to torment and tears.
Because she gloated, "I'm queen over all,
    and no widow, never a tear on my face,"
In one day, disasters will crush her—
    death, heartbreak, and famine—
Then she'll be burned by fire, because God,
    the Strong God who judges her,
    has had enough.

9-10 "The kings of the earth will see the smoke of her burning, and they'll cry and carry on, the kings who went night after night to her brothel. They'll keep their distance for fear they'll get burned, and they'll cry their lament:

Doom, doom, the great city doomed!

City of Babylon, strong city!
In one hour it's over, your judgment come!

11-17 "The traders will cry and carry on because the bottom dropped out of business, no more market for their goods: gold, silver, precious gems, pearls; fabrics of fine linen, purple, silk, scarlet; perfumed wood and vessels of ivory, precious woods, bronze, iron, and marble; cinnamon and spice, incense, myrrh, and frankincense; wine and oil, flour and wheat; cattle, sheep, horses, and chariots. And slaves — their terrible traffic in human lives.

Everything you've lived for, gone!
All delicate and delectable luxury, lost!
Not a scrap, not a thread to be found!

"The traders who made millions off her kept their distance for fear of getting burned, and cried and carried on all the more:

Doom, doom, the great city doomed!
Dressed in the latest fashions,
adorned with the finest jewels,
in one hour such wealth wiped out!

17-19 "All the ship captains and travelers by sea, sailors and toilers of the sea, stood off at a distance and cried their lament when they saw the smoke from her burning: 'Oh, what a city! There was never a city like her!' They threw dust on their heads and cried as if the world had come to an end:

Doom, doom, the great city doomed!
All who owned ships or did business by sea
Got rich on her getting and spending.
And now it's over — wiped out in one hour!

20 "O Heaven, celebrate! And join in, saints, apostles, and prophets! God has judged her; every wrong you suffered from her has been judged."

21-24 A strong Angel reached for a boulder — huge, like a millstone — and heaved it into the sea, saying,

Heaved and sunk, the great city Babylon,
sunk in the sea, not a sign of her ever again.
Silent the music of harpists and singers —
you'll never hear flutes and trumpets again.
Artisans of every kind — gone;
you'll never see their likes again.
The voice of a millstone grinding falls dumb;
you'll never hear that sound again.
The light from lamps, never again;
never again laughter of bride and groom.
Her traders robbed the whole earth blind,
and by black-magic arts deceived the nations.
The only thing left of Babylon is blood —

the blood of saints and prophets,
the murdered and the martyred.

THE SOUND OF HALLELUJAHS

1-3 **19** I heard a sound like massed choirs in Heaven singing,

Hallelujah!
The salvation and glory and power are God's —
    his judgments true, his judgments just.
He judged the great Whore
    who corrupted the earth with her lust.
He avenged on her the blood of his servants.

Then, more singing:
Hallelujah!
The smoke from her burning billows up
    to high Heaven forever and ever and ever.

4 The Twenty-four Elders and the Four Animals fell to their knees and worshiped God on his Throne, praising,

Amen! Yes! Hallelujah!

5 From the Throne came a shout, a command:

Praise our God, all you his servants,
All you who fear him, small and great!

6-8 Then I heard the sound of massed choirs, the sound of a mighty cataract, the sound of strong thunder:

Hallelujah!
The Master reigns,
    our God, the Sovereign-Strong!
Let us celebrate, let us rejoice,
    let us give him the glory!
The Marriage of the Lamb has come;
    his Wife has made herself ready.
She was given a bridal gown
    of bright and shining linen.
The linen is the righteousness of the saints.

9 The Angel said to me, "Write this: 'Blessed are those invited to the Wedding Supper of the Lamb.'" He added, "These are the true words of God!"

10 I fell at his feet to worship him, but he wouldn't let me. "Don't do that," he said. "I'm a servant just like you, and like your brothers and sisters who hold to the witness of Jesus. The witness of Jesus is the spirit of prophecy."

A White Horse and Its Rider

11-16 Then I saw Heaven open wide—and oh! a white horse and its Rider. The Rider, named Faithful and True, judges and makes war in pure righteousness. His eyes are a blaze of fire, on his head many crowns. He has a Name inscribed that's known only to himself. He is dressed in a robe soaked with blood, and he is addressed as "Word of God." The armies of Heaven, mounted on white horses and dressed in dazzling white linen, follow him. A sharp sword comes out of his mouth so he can subdue the nations, then rule them with a rod of iron. He treads the winepress of the raging wrath of God, the Sovereign-Strong. On his robe and thigh is written, KING OF KINGS, LORD OF LORDS.

17-18 I saw an Angel standing in the sun, shouting to all flying birds in Middle-Heaven, "Come to the Great Supper of God! Feast on the flesh of kings and captains and champions, horses and their riders. Eat your fill of them all—free and slave, small and great!"

19-21 I saw the Beast and, assembled with him, earth's kings and their armies, ready to make war against the One on the horse and his army. The Beast was taken, and with him, his puppet, the False Prophet, who used signs to dazzle and deceive those who had taken the mark of the Beast and worshiped his image. They were thrown alive, those two, into Lake Fire and Brimstone. The rest were killed by the sword of the One on the horse, the sword that comes from his mouth. All the birds held a feast on their flesh.

A Thousand Years

1-3 **20** I saw an Angel descending out of Heaven. He carried the key to the Abyss and a chain—a huge chain. He grabbed the Dragon, that old Snake—the very Devil, Satan himself!—chained him up for a thousand years, dumped him into the Abyss, slammed it shut and sealed it tight. No more trouble out of him, deceiving the nations—until the thousand years are up. After that he has to be let loose briefly.

4-6 I saw thrones. Those put in charge of judgment sat on the thrones. I also saw the souls of those beheaded because of their witness to Jesus and the Word of God, who refused to worship either the Beast or his image, refused to take his mark on forehead or hand—they lived and reigned with Christ for a thousand years! The rest of the dead did not live until the thousand years were up. This is the first resurrection—and those involved most blessed, most holy. No second death for them! They're priests of God and Christ; they'll reign with him a thousand years.

7-10 When the thousand years are up, Satan will be let loose from his cell, and will launch again his old work of deceiving the nations, searching out victims in every nook and cranny of earth, even Gog and Magog! He'll talk them into going to war and will gather a huge army, millions strong. They'll stream across the earth, surround and lay siege to the camp of God's holy people, the Beloved City. They'll no sooner get there than fire will pour out of Heaven and burn them up. The Devil who deceived them will be hurled into Lake Fire and Brimstone, joining the Beast and False Prophet, the three in torment around the clock for ages without end.

Judgment

11-15 I saw a Great White Throne and the One Enthroned. Nothing could stand before or against the Presence, nothing in Heaven, nothing on earth.

And then I saw all the dead, great and small, standing there—before the Throne! And books were opened. Then another book was opened: the Book of Life. The dead were judged by what was written in the books, by the way they had lived. Sea released its dead, Death and Hell turned in their dead. Each man and woman was judged by the way he or she had lived. Then Death and Hell were hurled into Lake Fire. This is the second death—Lake Fire. Anyone whose name was not found inscribed in the Book of Life was hurled into Lake Fire.

EVERYTHING NEW

1   **21** I saw Heaven and earth new-created. Gone the first Heaven, gone the first earth, gone the sea.

2   I saw Holy Jerusalem, new-created, descending resplendent out of Heaven, as ready for God as a bride for her husband.

3-5   I heard a voice thunder from the Throne: "Look! Look! God has moved into the neighborhood, making his home with men and women! They're his people, he's their God. He'll wipe every tear from their eyes. Death is gone for good—tears gone, crying gone, pain gone—all the first order of things gone." The Enthroned continued, "Look! I'm making everything new. Write it all down—each word dependable and accurate."

6-8   Then he said, "It's happened. I'm A to Z. I'm the Beginning, I'm the Conclusion. From Water-of-Life Well I give freely to the thirsty. Conquerors inherit all this. I'll be God to them, they'll be sons and daughters to me. But for the rest—the feckless and faithless, degenerates and murderers, sex peddlers and sorcerers, idolaters and all liars—for them it's Lake Fire and Brimstone. Second death!"

THE CITY OF LIGHT

9-12   One of the Seven Angels who had carried the bowls filled with the seven final disasters spoke to me: "Come here. I'll show you the Bride, the Wife of the Lamb." He took me away in the Spirit to an enormous, high mountain and showed me Holy Jerusalem descending out of Heaven from God, resplendent in the bright glory of God.

12-14   The City shimmered like a precious gem, light-filled, pulsing light. She had a wall majestic and high with twelve gates. At each gate stood an Angel, and on the gates were inscribed the names of the Twelve Tribes of the sons of Israel: three gates on the east, three gates on the north, three gates on the south, three gates on the west. The wall was set on twelve foundations, the names of the Twelve Apostles of the Lamb inscribed on them.

15-21   The Angel speaking with me had a gold measuring stick to measure the City, its gates, and its wall. The City was laid out in a perfect square. He measured the City with the measuring stick: twelve thousand stadia, its length, width, and height all equal. Using the standard measure, the Angel measured the thickness of its wall: 144 cubits. The wall was jasper, the color of Glory, and the City was pure gold, translucent as glass. The foundations of the City walls were garnished with every precious gem imaginable: the first foundation jasper, the second sapphire, the third agate, the fourth emerald, the fifth onyx, the sixth carnelian, the seventh chrysolite, the eighth beryl, the ninth topaz, the tenth chrysoprase, the eleventh jacinth, the twelfth amethyst. The twelve gates were twelve pearls, each gate a single pearl.

21-27   The main street of the City was pure gold, translucent as glass. But there was no sign of a Temple, for the Lord God — the Sovereign-Strong — and the Lamb are the Temple. The City doesn't need sun or moon for light. God's Glory is its light, the Lamb its lamp! The nations will walk in its light and earth's kings bring in their splendor. Its gates will never be shut by day, and there won't be any night. They'll bring the glory and honor of the nations into the City. Nothing dirty or defiled will get into the City, and no one who defiles or deceives. Only those whose names are written in the Lamb's Book of Life will get in.

1-5   **22** Then the Angel showed me Water-of-Life River, crystal bright. It flowed from the Throne of God and the Lamb, right down the middle of the street. The Tree of Life was planted on each side of the River, producing twelve kinds of fruit, a ripe fruit each month. The leaves of the Tree are for healing the nations. Never again will anything be cursed. The Throne of God and of the Lamb is at the center. His servants will offer God service — worshiping, they'll look on his face, their foreheads mirroring God. Never again will there be any night. No one will need lamplight or sunlight. The shining of God, the Master, is all the light anyone needs. And they will rule with him age after age after age.

DON'T PUT IT AWAY ON THE SHELF

6-7   The Angel said to me, "These are dependable and accurate words, every one. The God and Master of the spirits of the prophets sent his Angel to show his servants what must take place, and soon. And tell them, 'Yes, I'm on my way!' Blessed be the one who keeps the words of the prophecy of this book."

8-9   I, John, saw all these things with my own eyes, heard them with my ears. Immediately when I heard and saw, I fell on my face to worship at the feet of the Angel who laid it all out before me. He objected, "No you don't! I'm a servant just like you and your companions, the prophets, and all who keep the words of this book. Worship God!"

10-11   The Angel continued, "Don't seal the words of the prophecy of this book; don't put it away on the shelf. Time is just about up. Let evildoers do their worst and the dirty-minded go all out in pollution, but let the righteous maintain a straight course and the holy continue on in holiness."

12-13   "Yes, I'm on my way! I'll be there soon! I'm bringing my payroll with me. I'll pay all people in full for their life's work. I'm A to Z, the First and the Final, Beginning and Conclusion.

14-15   "How blessed are those who wash their robes! The Tree of Life is theirs for good, and they'll walk through the gates to the City. But outside for good are the filthy curs: sorcerers, fornicators, murderers, idolaters — all who love and live lies.

16   "I, Jesus, sent my Angel to testify to these things for the churches. I'm the Root and Branch of David, the Bright Morning Star."

17   "Come!" say the Spirit and the Bride.
     Whoever hears, echo, "Come!"

Is anyone thirsty? Come!
All who will, come and drink,
Drink freely of the Water of Life!

18-19   I give fair warning to all who hear the words of the prophecy of this book: If you add to the words of this prophecy, God will add to your life the disasters written in this book; if you subtract from the words of the book of this prophecy, God will subtract your part from the Tree of Life and the Holy City that are written in this book.

20   He who testifies to all these things says it again: "I'm on my way! I'll be there soon!"

Yes! Come, Master Jesus!

21   The grace of the Master Jesus be with all of you. Oh, Yes!

THE STORY OF THE BIBLE
IN FIVE ACTS

The heart and soul of the Bible is its story. It is the real saga of a particular people, how God called them and intended for them to bring blessing to all people.

Story is also the word that best describes our own lives. While we may or may not follow the right rules, investigate certain facts, and attempt to live wisely, none of these activities provides the central way we make sense of our lives. Stories give context and provide meaning.

All the different parts of the Bible come together as one narrative.

To understand the Bible you must get to know its characters, understand its setting, and follow its plot.

The climax and ultimate resolution will make sense only if you've followed the earlier parts as a story. Learn to feel the tension and wrestle with its major conflict. Lose yourself in this story the way you do with a good novel.

We present here an abbreviated version of the story of the Bible as a drama in five acts.

ACT | I   Creation

The drama begins with God already on the stage. He is creating the world. He makes a man, Adam, and places him in the Garden of Eden to work in it and take care of it. God's intention is for humanity to be in close relationship with him and in harmony with the rest of creation around them. God is described in these early chapters of the Bible as dwelling in the garden together with the first human beings, Adam and Eve. At the end of the first chapter of Genesis, God gives his own assessment of his work:

> *God looked over everything he had made;*
> *it was so good, so very good! (verse 31)*

Act I reveals God's desire for people and provides the setting for all the action that follows.

Tension is introduced in the story when Adam and Eve decide to go their own way and seek their own wisdom. They listen to the deceptive voice of God's enemy, Satan, and doubt God's trustworthiness.

As a result of this rebellion:

> *God expelled them from the Garden of Eden and sent them to work the ground, the same dirt out of which they'd been made. He threw them out of the garden and stationed angel-cherubim and a revolving sword of fire east of it, guarding the path to the Tree-of-Life.* (Genesis 3:23–24)

God's intention in creation is known, but part of his own creation has put his plan off course. Can God regain his relationship with humanity and remove the curse from creation? Or did God's enemy effectively end the plan and subvert the story?

Acts I and II take only the first few pages in the Bible to be completed. Yet they introduce the struggle that dominates the rest of the story.

ACT | III Israel

> GOD told Abram: "Leave your country, your family, and your father's home for a land that I will show you.
> > *I'll make you a great nation*
> > > *and bless you.*
> > *I'll make you famous;*
> > > *you'll be a blessing.*
> > *I'll bless those who bless you;*
> > > *those who curse you I'll curse.*
> > *All the families of the Earth*
> > > *will be blessed through you."*
> (Genesis 12:1–3)

In calling Abram (God later renamed him Abraham) and promising to make him into a great nation, God is narrowing his focus and concentrating on one group of people for a period of time. But the ultimate goal remains the same: to bless all the peoples on earth, remove the curse from creation, and restore the original relationship that existed in the garden.

When Abraham's descendants are later enslaved in Egypt, a central pattern in the story is set: God returns to his people, frees them, and restores them to the land promised to them. God makes a covenant with this new nation of Israel at Mt. Sinai. He appoints Moses to be their leader during their liberation from Egypt—the Exodus. As part of the covenant, God makes it clear that if his people remain true to him and faithfully follow his ways, he will bless them in their new land and make it like the original Garden of Eden.

However, if Israel is not faithful to the covenant, God warns them that he will send them out of the land, just as he did with Adam and Eve. Sadly, and in spite of God's repeated warnings and pleadings, they are determined to go their own way. They break the covenant, follow the false gods of the nations that surround them and bring the judgment of God down upon themselves.

Abraham's descendants, chosen to reverse the failure of Adam, have now apparently failed themselves. Along the way, however, God has planted the seeds of a different outcome. One of Israel's kings, David, is noted for being "*a man after God's own heart.*" So God promises to send another king to Israel, a son of David, who will lead Israel wisely, bring the nation back to God and be the agent of blessing to the peoples of the world.

So while Act III ends tragically, with God apparently absent, the hope of a promise remains.

ACT IV Jesus

Four centuries later, the people of Israel are suffering under Roman occupation and waiting for God to return. An angel of God comes to a young woman named Mary and announces,

> *You will become pregnant and give birth to a son and call his name Jesus.*
> > *He will be great,*
> > > *be called "Son of the Highest."*
> > *The Lord God will give him*
> > > *the throne of his father David;*
> > *He will rule Jacob's house forever —*
> > > *no end, ever, to his kingdom.*
> (Luke 1:31–33)

Jesus' arrival is introduced with the claim that God is keeping his promise.

So Jesus begins his mission. He heals sickness and disease among the people. He confronts God's enemies in the spiritual realm, the demons, and forcefully orders them to leave the people whom they torment. Jesus forgives the sins of those who humbly come to him. He proclaims the gospel, or good news, that:

> *"Time's up! God's kingdom is here. Change your life and believe the Message."* (Mark 1:15)

The very heart of Jesus' Message is the good news of the coming of God's reign. God is coming back to dwell with his people. This is why Jesus is called Immanuel, which means "God with us."

But Jesus' message receives mixed responses. Some people believe, but most people simply watch him with amazement, never knowing quite what to make of him. The established religious leaders quickly become hostile toward him. Eventually this conflict escalates to the breaking point and the religious leaders conspire to have Jesus arrested and killed on a cross.

But this defeat is actually God's greatest victory. Jesus' death turns the tables on God's enemy and turns the world upside down. By willingly giving up his life as a sacrifice, Jesus takes onto himself God's judgment for our wrongdoing. He gives up his own life as a sacrifice for his people as Israel's true priest. He leads his people to a new Exodus, through death to a new life. In all of this Jesus shows himself to be the promised child of Abraham who reconciles humanity with God. It is through Jesus that Israel can finally fulfill its role, the purpose for which God called Abraham.

This account of Jesus is the focal point of the Bible's entire story. The key struggle with God's enemy, the desperate attempts to correct what has gone wrong at the very heart of things, comes to a head in the life of Jesus. He is the one and only hero of the story.

ACT | V The New People of God

If the key victory has already been secured, why is there an Act V? God wants the victory of Jesus to spread to all the nations of the world. Those who follow Jesus are being built into God's new temple, the place where God's Spirit lives. God is gathering these people from all around the world and forming them into his church. When this is complete, Jesus will return and the reign of God will become a reality throughout God's creation (1 Corinthians 15:24–25). The curse imposed during Act II will be removed (Revelation 22:3).

The task of bringing blessing to the peoples of the world has been given again to the descendants of Abraham. According to the New Testament, all those who belong to Christ are true children of Abraham (Galatians 3:29). Act V emphasizes the mission of Christ-followers: to proclaim and live out the liberating message of the good news of Christ's kingdom.

Act V moves through history to our own time, enveloping us in its drama. The Message of Christ and his kingdom has now come to us. The challenge of a decision now confronts us too. What will we do? How will we fit into this story?

The story of the Bible is the true account of the central conflict winding its way through the history of the world. Will we be a part of God's mission of re-creation — of restoring the world around us — and making the world (including ourselves) new?

WHAT NOW?

The most important thing you can do is to read these Scriptures carefully. God's Spirit uses them actively and powerfully to accomplish his purposes — in you and through you to impact the world.

The Bible is not necessarily an easy book to read. Some passages are difficult for everyone to understand. But if you stick with it, if you are committed to learning more about God and the story he's given us in the Bible, it will guide you, change you and keep you close to God.

A special thanks to the International Bible Society for permission to include an edited version of the Bible notes, The Drama of the Bible® 2002 by International Bible Society®. Used by permission. All rights reserved worldwide.

THE DRAMA OF THE BIBLE

A Visual Chronology

World Events

Pyramids built 2500s B.C.
Hinduism gains influence in India 1100s B.C.
Buddhism founded in India 500s B.C.
Alexander the Great begins rule 336 B.C.
China begins construction on The Great Wall 214 B.C.
Rise of the Roman Empire 28 B.C.

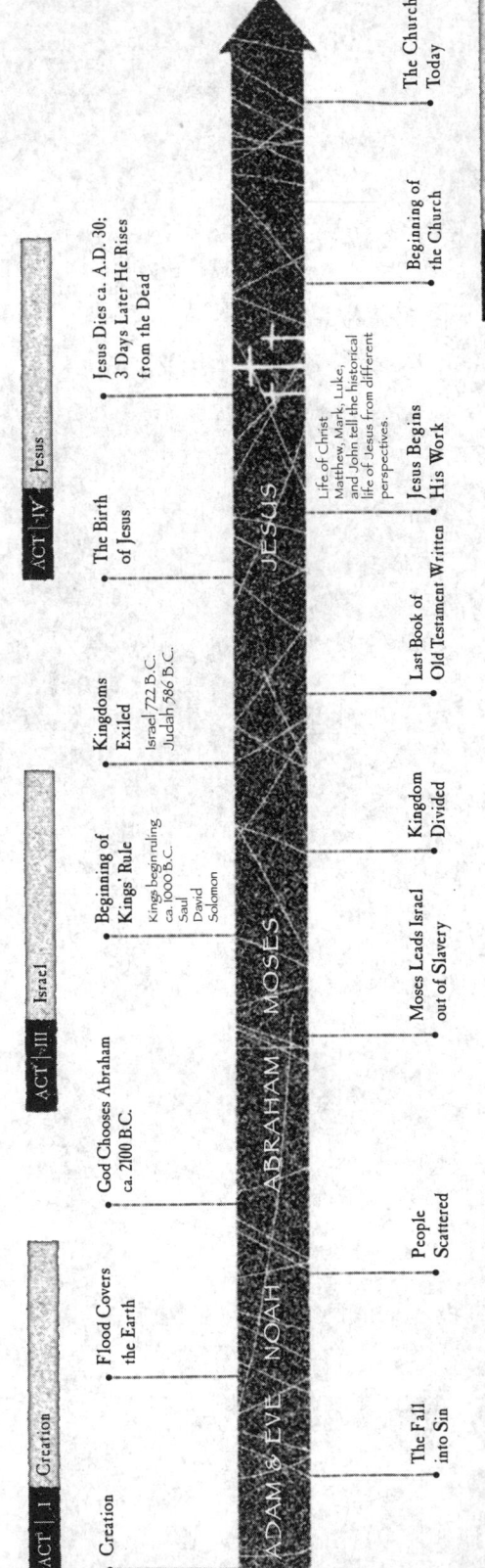

ACT I Creation

Creation

Flood Covers the Earth

God Chooses Abraham ca. 2100 B.C.

Beginning of Kings' Rule

kings begin ruling ca. 1000 B.C.
Saul
David
Solomon

Kingdoms Exiled

Israel 722 B.C.
Judah 586 B.C.

ACT III Israel

ACT IV Jesus

The Birth of Jesus

Jesus Dies ca. A.D. 30; 3 Days Later He Rises from the Dead

ACT V The New People of God

The Church Today

Beginning of the Church

Life of Christ
Matthew, Mark, Luke, and John tell the historical life of Jesus from different perspectives.

Jesus Begins His Work

Last Book of Old Testament Written

Kingdom Divided

Moses Leads Israel out of Slavery

JESUS

MOSES

ABRAHAM

NOAH

ADAM & EVE

ACT II The Fall

The Fall into Sin

People Scattered